THE NCV

Daily Bible

To Barbara
our dear and much loved
friend
on your 75th birthday

May The Lord Richly Bless you today
& all ways
all our love
Linda Peggy & Anddrene.
Xx.

Prov. 3 v 5-6.

THE NCV
Daily Bible

NCV
NEW CENTURY VERSION®
www.myfaithandlife.com

NELSON BIBLES
A Division of Thomas Nelson Publishers
Since 1798

www.thomasnelson.com

TABLE OF CONTENTS

BOOKS OF THE BIBLE

THE OLD TESTAMENT

Genesis	1	Ecclesiastes	784
Exodus	83	Song of Songs	800
Leviticus	152	Isaiah	810
Numbers	201	Jeremiah	918
Deuteronomy	260	Lamentations	1013
Joshua	315	Ezekiel	1021
Judges	354	Daniel	1099
Ruth	389	Hosea	1122
1 Samuel	395	Joel	1139
2 Samuel	443	Amos	1145
1 Kings	484	Obadiah	1157
2 Kings	528	Jonah	1160
1 Chronicles	574	Micah	1163
2 Chronicles	621	Nahum	1173
Ezra	675	Habakkuk	1177
Nehemiah	691	Zephaniah	1181
Esther	714	Haggai	1185
Job	728	Zechariah	1188
Psalms	2	Malachi	1203
Proverbs	3		

THE NEW TESTAMENT

Matthew	3	1 Timothy	969
Mark	163	2 Timothy	989
Luke	267	Titus	1006
John	431	Philemon	1020
Acts	561	Hebrews	1023
Romans	713	James	1071
1 Corinthians	766	1 Peter	1088
2 Corinthians	827	2 Peter	1107
Galatians	869	1 John	1118
Ephesians	892	2 John	1131
Philippians	913	3 John	1134
Colossians	930	Jude	1136
1 Thessalonians	944	Revelation	1139
2 Thessalonians	960		

HOW TO USE YOUR NCV DAILY BIBLE

For each day of the year, there are four portions to read: a portion from the Old Testament, from Psalms, from Proverbs, and from the New Testament. By following this plan, at the end of one year you will have read through the entire Bible in consecutive daily installments.

If you aren't ready for the entire Bible in a year, an alternative two-year plan would be to read the portions from Psalms, Proverbs, and the New Testament the first year, and then the portions from the Old Testament the second year.

Either way, you will develop a habit of thorough, daily Bible reading that will bless you in life.

INTRODUCTION

The story is told that many years ago, Art Linkletter saw a small boy scrawling wildly on a sheet of paper. "What are you drawing?" Linkletter asked.

"I'm drawing a picture of God."

"You can't do that, because nobody knows what God looks like."

"They will when I'm finished," the boy confidently replied.

As senseless as this story is, many of us have based our life beliefs on foundations no more solid than the young boy's drawing. It is no surprise that life's difficulties expose the lack of meaning in our lives and the inadequacy of our sources for answers to the questions of our hearts.

Let's face it, we all have questions in life. When you lay your head down on the pillow at night, what are the questions that you ask? When you're alone in the dark, do you find life's really hard questions running through your mind? *How can I find peace and true contentment? What is the purpose of life? Why am I here? Where have I come from, and where am I going? Is there a God, and if so, what is he like? Can I know God personally? Is there a source of ultimate truth for me to live by?*

Many of those questions relate to our faith and our own search for truth. For instance, who has not asked the question, "Why does God allow unthinkable acts of terrorism?" Or, "When my world seems to be falling apart around me, who can I trust?" Or, "What do I do with my fears?" So where do we find the answers? Must we end our days with the same questions staring us in the face? Can our questions be answered, and can we find the peace we are seeking?

We answer that with a resounding "Yes!" In your hands you hold what reveals the *real answers*—God's Word. The Bible is *the* most important book and the single most popular book ever written. Within its pages God speaks with divine instruction to multiple generations of people who faced the same life issues and questions that you face today. He reveals himself through his Word and presents the absolute truth that provides the only reliable answers to all of life's ultimate questions. It dares tackle those questions honestly and openly and offers counsel for our problems, comfort for our sorrows, guidance for our confusion, inspiration for our needs, and hope for our despair.

WHAT IS THE BIBLE ABOUT?

The Bible cannot be considered just a "crutch" that you can turn to when the pressures of life overwhelm you. It is a supernatural book that has survived and thrived through centuries of being scoffed at, ridiculed, and banned. Kings have branded it as illegal, and countless lives have been martyred because they had the courage to stand by its truths. For the millions and millions of people who have tested its answers to life's questions and found them true, there is only one conclusion—the Bible is God's book. Every word is inspired by him and reveals something very important about him. From these pages we hear the voice of God.

In reality, the Bible is a library of books. It contains sixty-six different books, which together tell the story of God's wonderful love for people. It teaches us how to live the way God wants us to live. The Bible reveals the truth about God, explains the origin of humankind, offers the only way to salvation and eternal life in Jesus Christ, and does not sidestep the ancient problem of sin and suffering. It's a book you'll want to read and study over and over again.

Who is the Bible for? Most of the books in the Old Testament were written for the Jewish people (also called Israelites). They were the nation God chose to be a part of bringing his Son into the world. Books in the New Testament were written to many others. Sometimes the names of the books give you a clue. For instance, Paul wrote Romans to the Christians who live in Rome. Other New

Testament books were addressed to all of Christ's followers. These books were passed around from church to church for everyone to read and hear.

But wait! The Bible was written for you, too. Just as it told the Christians in the first century how to live for God, it tells the same to you, too. God's Word, the Bible, is a personal guide for everyone who wants to follow God. It's God's love letter just for you.

SO WHY THE NCV?

The New Century Version is one of the easiest translations of the Bible to understand. It accurately communicates the messages found in the original languages of biblical manuscripts, using the kind of terms you use every day. It uses contemporary phrases, word pictures, and expressions, and replaces vague and overly religious language with down-to-earth vocabulary. The end result is a fresh, straightforward, and strong translation of God's truth; and it is something you can connect with in your daily life. You'll find it easier to experience God's Word as it truly is—absolutely clear, powerfully alive, and completely life-changing.

This may be the greatest opportunity you will ever find to read and understand the Bible and to come to a personal understanding of God's plan for your life. The Bible, it should be remembered, is not an end in itself, but it is a means to the end of knowing God and doing his will on earth. Through his Word we hear his voice and come to understand his mind.

So we challenge you to read the NCV. Anyone who will take the time can see and understand what God has given us in his Word and how it applies to us today. It may be the most important and life-changing step you will ever take.

PREFACE

God intended for everyone to be able to read and understand his Word. The Old Testament is written in Hebrew, the language of the people of Israel. Through the use of vivid stories based on real events and beautiful poetry, it appeals to the minds and hearts of the educated and the uneducated. The New Testament was first written in the simple Greek of everyday life, not in the Latin of Roman courts or the classical Greek of the academies. Even Jesus, the Master Teacher, taught spiritual principles by comparing them to such familiar terms as pearls, seeds, rocks, trees, and sheep. Likewise, the New Century Version translates the Scriptures in familiar, everyday words of our times.

The New Century Version is a translation of God's Word from the original Hebrew and Greek languages. A previous edition of the complete New Century Version, the International Children's Bible, was published in 1986.

A TRUSTWORTHY TRANSLATION

Two basic premises guided the translation process of the New Century Version. The first concern was that the translation be faithful to the manuscripts in the original languages. A team composed of the World Bible Translation Center and fifty additional, highly qualified and experienced Bible scholars and translators was assembled. The team included people with translation experience on such accepted versions as the New International Version, the New American Standard Bible, and the New King James Version. The most recent scholarship and the best available Hebrew and Greek texts were used, principally the third edition of the United Bible Societies' Greek text and the latest edition of the *Biblia Hebraica,* along with the Septuagint.

A CLEAR TRANSLATION

The second concern was to make the language clear enough for anyone to read the Bible and understand it. In maintaining clear language, several guidelines were followed. Vocabulary choice has been based upon *The Living Word Vocabulary* by Dr. Edgar Dale and Dr. Joseph O'Rourke (Worldbook-Childcraft International, 1981), which is the standard used by the editors of *The World Book Encyclopedia* to determine appropriate vocabulary. For difficult words that have no simpler synonyms, footnotes and references are provided. Footnotes appear at the bottom of the page and are indicated in the text by an n (for "note").

The New Century Version aids understanding by putting concepts into natural terms. Modern measurements and geographical locations have been used as much as possible. For instance, terms such as "shekels," "cubits," "omer," and "hin" have been converted to modern equivalents of weights and measures. Where geographical references are identical, the modern name has been used, such as the "Mediterranean Sea" instead of "Great Sea" or "Western Sea." Also, to minimize confusion, the most familiar name for a place is used consistently instead of using variant names for the same place. "Lake Galilee" is used throughout the text rather than its variant forms, "Sea of Kinnereth," "Lake Gennesaret," and "Sea of Tiberias."

Ancient customs are often unfamiliar to modern readers. Customs such as shaving a man's beard to shame him or walking between the halves of a dead animal to seal an agreement are meaningless to most people today. So these are clarified either in the text or in a footnote.

Since *meanings* of words change with time, care has been taken to avoid potential misunderstandings. Frequently in the Old Testament God tells his people to "devote" something to him, as when he tells the Israelites to devote Jericho and everything in it to him. While we might understand this to mean he is telling them to keep it safe and holy, the exact opposite is true. He is telling them to destroy it totally as an offering to him. The New Century Version communicates the idea clearly by translating "devoted" in these situations as "destroyed as an offering to the LORD."

Rhetorical questions in many instances have been stated according to their implied answer. The psalmist's question "What god is so great as our God?" has been stated more directly as "No god is as great as our God."

Figures of speech have been translated according to their meanings. For instance, the expression "the Virgin Daughter of Zion," which is frequently used in the Old Testament, is simply translated "the people of Jerusalem."

Idiomatic expressions of the biblical languages are translated to communicate the same meaning to today's reader that would have been understood by the original audience. For example, the Hebrew idiom "he rested with his fathers" is translated by its meaning—"he died."

Obscure terms have been clarified. In the Old Testament God frequently condemns the people for their "high places" and "Asherah poles." The New Century Version translates these according to their meanings, which would have been understood by the Hebrews. "High places" is translated "places where gods were worshiped," and "Asherah poles" is translated "Asherah idols."

Gender language has been rendered in keeping with the principles of meaning-based translation. In the interest of providing the best rendering of the original Hebrew and Greek texts in contemporary English, appropriate gender terms are used whenever it is possible to do so without hindering clarity or accuracy. Masculine terms are used when the meaning of the original

has to do with males, including references to deity and to male cultural situations such as the military and the priesthood. Feminine terms are used when the meaning of the original has to do with females. When the meaning of the original has to do with both males and females, nongendered terms are used. (In such cases, the masculine resumptive pronoun has sometimes been preferred to changing person or number.)

The divine name YHWH, *the tetragrammaton,* has been indicated in the New Century Version by putting "LORD," and sometimes "GOD," in capital letters, following the tradition of other English versions. This is to distinguish it from *Adonai,* another Hebrew word that is translated "Lord."

Proper English style has been maintained while clarifying concepts and communication. The beauty of the Hebrew parallelism in poetry and the wordplays have been retained, and the images of the ancient languages have been captured in equivalent English images wherever possible.

STUDY AIDS

Other features to enhance understanding of the text include subject headings throughout the text to identify speakers and topics and footnotes offering additional information on selected verses.

OUR PRAYER

It is with great humility and prayerfulness that this Bible is presented. We acknowledge the infallibility of God's Word, as well as our own human frailty. We pray that God has worked through us as his vessels so that we all might better learn his truth for ourselves and that it might richly grow in our lives. It is to his glory that this Bible is given.

THE PUBLISHER

JANUARY 1

GENESIS 1:1—2:25

The Beginning of the World

1 In the beginning God created the sky and the earth. ²The earth was empty and had no form. Darkness covered the ocean, and God's Spirit was moving over the water.

³Then God said, "Let there be light," and there was light. ⁴God saw that the light was good, so he divided the light from the darkness. ⁵God named the light "day" and the darkness "night." Evening passed, and morning came. This was the first day.

⁶Then God said, "Let there be something to divide the water in two." ⁷So God made the air and placed some of the water above the air and some below it. ⁸God named the air "sky." Evening passed, and morning came. This was the second day.

⁹Then God said, "Let the water under the sky be gathered together so the dry land will appear." And it happened. ¹⁰God named the dry land "earth" and the water that was gathered together "seas." God saw that this was good.

¹¹Then God said, "Let the earth produce plants—some to make grain for seeds and others to make fruits with seeds in them. Every seed will produce more of its own kind of plant." And it happened. ¹²The earth produced plants with grain for seeds and trees that made fruits with seeds in them. Each seed grew its own kind of plant. God saw that all this was good. ¹³Evening passed, and morning came. This was the third day.

¹⁴Then God said, "Let there be lights in the sky to separate day from night. These lights will be used for signs, seasons, days, and years. ¹⁵They will be in the sky to give light to the earth." And it happened.

¹⁶So God made the two large lights. He made the brighter light to rule the day and made the smaller light to rule the night. He also made the stars. ¹⁷God put all these in the sky to shine on the earth, ¹⁸to rule over the day and over the night, and to separate the light from the darkness. God saw that all these things were good. ¹⁹Evening passed, and morning came. This was the fourth day.

²⁰Then God said, "Let the water be filled with living things, and let birds fly in the air above the earth."

²¹So God created the large sea animals and every living thing that moves in the sea. The sea is filled with these living things, with each one producing more of its own kind. He also made every bird that flies, and each bird produced more of its own kind. God saw that this was good. ²²God blessed them and said, "Have many young ones so that you may grow in number. Fill the water of the seas, and let the birds grow in number on the earth." ²³Evening passed, and morning came. This was the fifth day.

²⁴Then God said, "Let the earth be filled with animals, each producing more of its own kind. Let there be tame animals and small crawling animals and wild animals, and let each produce more of its kind." And it happened.

²⁵So God made the wild animals, the tame animals, and all the small crawling animals to produce more of their own kind. God saw that this was good.

²⁶Then God said, "Let us make human beings in our image and likeness. And let them rule over the fish in the sea and the birds in the sky, over the tame animals, over all the earth, and over all the small crawling animals on the earth."

²⁷So God created human beings in his image. In the image of God he created them. He created them male and female. ²⁸God blessed them and said, "Have many children and grow in number. Fill the earth and be its master. Rule over the fish in the sea and over the birds in the sky and over every living thing that moves on the earth."

²⁹God said, "Look, I have given you all the plants that have grain for seeds and all the trees whose fruits have seeds in them. They will be food for you. ³⁰I have given all the green plants as food for every wild animal, every bird of the air, and every small crawling animal." And it happened. ³¹God looked

at everything he had made, and it was very good. Evening passed, and morning came. This was the sixth day.

The Seventh Day—Rest

2 So the sky, the earth, and all that filled them were finished. [2]By the seventh day God finished the work he had been doing, so he rested from all his work. [3]God blessed the seventh day and made it a holy day, because on that day he rested from all the work he had done in creating the world.

The First People

[4]This is the story of the creation of the sky and the earth. When the LORD God first made the earth and the sky, [5]there were still no plants on the earth. Nothing was growing in the fields because the LORD God had not yet made it rain on the land. And there was no person to care for the ground, [6]but a mist would rise up from the earth and water all the ground.

[7]Then the LORD God took dust from the ground and formed a man from it. He breathed the breath of life into the man's nose, and the man became a living person. [8]Then the LORD God planted a garden in the east, in a place called Eden, and put the man he had formed into it. [9]The LORD God caused every beautiful tree and every tree that was good for food to grow out of the ground. In the middle of the garden, God put the tree that gives life and also the tree that gives knowledge of good and evil.

[10]A river flowed through Eden and watered the garden. From there the river branched out to become four rivers. [11]The first river, named Pishon, flows around the whole land of Havilah, where there is gold. [12]The gold of that land is excellent. Bdellium and onyx[n] are also found there. [13]The second river, named Gihon, flows around the whole land of Cush. [14]The third river, named Tigris, flows out of Assyria toward the east. The fourth river is the Euphrates.

[15]The LORD God put the man in the garden of Eden to care for it and work it. [16]The LORD God commanded him, "You may eat the fruit from any tree in the garden, [17]but you must not eat the fruit from the tree which gives the knowledge of good and evil. If you ever eat fruit from that tree, you will die!"

The First Woman

[18]Then the LORD God said, "It is not good for the man to be alone. I will make a helper who is right for him."

[19]From the ground God formed every wild animal and every bird in the sky, and he brought them to the man so the man could name them. Whatever the man called each living thing, that became its name. [20]The man gave names to all the tame animals, to the birds in the sky, and to all the wild animals. But Adam[n] did not find a helper that was right for him. [21]So the LORD God caused the man to sleep very deeply, and while he was asleep, God removed one of the man's ribs. Then God closed up the man's skin at the place where he took the rib. [22]The LORD God used the rib from the man to make a woman, and then he brought the woman to the man.

[23]And the man said,

"Now, this is someone whose bones
        came from my bones,
    whose body came from my body.
I will call her 'woman,'
    because she was taken out of man."

[24]So a man will leave his father and mother and be united with his wife, and the two will become one body. [25]The man and his wife were naked, but they were not ashamed.

PSALM 1:1–6

Two Ways to Live

1 Happy are those who don't listen to the wicked,
    who don't go where sinners go,
    who don't do what evil people do.
[2]They love the LORD's teachings,
    and they think about those teachings day and night.
[3]They are strong, like a tree planted by a river.

2:12 bdellium and onyx Bdellium is an expensive, sweet-smelling resin like myrrh, and onyx is a gem. **2:20 Adam** This is the name of the first man. It also means "humans," including men and women.

The tree produces fruit in season,
and its leaves don't die.
Everything they do will succeed.

[4]But wicked people are not like that.
They are like chaff that the wind blows
away.
[5]So the wicked will not escape God's
punishment.
Sinners will not worship with God's
people.
[6]This is because the LORD takes care of his
people,
but the wicked will be destroyed.

PROVERBS 1:1–7

The Importance of Proverbs

1 These are the wise words of Solomon son
of David, king of Israel.
[2]They teach wisdom and self-control;
they will help you understand wise
words.
[3]They will teach you how to be wise and
self-controlled
and will teach you to do what is honest
and fair and right.
[4]They make the uneducated wise
and give knowledge and sense to the
young.
[5]Wise people can also listen and learn;
even they can find good advice in these
words.
[6]Then anyone can understand wise words
and stories,
the words of the wise and their riddles.

[7]Knowledge begins with respect for the
LORD,
but fools hate wisdom and discipline.

MATTHEW 1:1–25

The Family History of Jesus

1 This is the family history of Jesus Christ.
He came from the family of David, and
David came from the family of Abraham.
[2]Abraham was the father[n] of Isaac.
Isaac was the father of Jacob.
Jacob was the father of Judah and his
brothers.
[3]Judah was the father of Perez and Zerah.
(Their mother was Tamar.)
Perez was the father of Hezron.
Hezron was the father of Ram.
[4]Ram was the father of Amminadab.
Amminadab was the father of Nahshon.
Nahshon was the father of Salmon.
[5]Salmon was the father of Boaz.
(Boaz's mother was Rahab.)
Boaz was the father of Obed.
(Obed's mother was Ruth.)
Obed was the father of Jesse.
[6]Jesse was the father of King David.
David was the father of Solomon.
(Solomon's mother had been Uriah's
wife.)
[7]Solomon was the father of Rehoboam.
Rehoboam was the father of Abijah.
Abijah was the father of Asa.[n]
[8]Asa was the father of Jehoshaphat.
Jehoshaphat was the father of Jehoram.
Jehoram was the ancestor of Uzziah.
[9]Uzziah was the father of Jotham.
Jotham was the father of Ahaz.
Ahaz was the father of Hezekiah.
[10]Hezekiah was the father of Manasseh.
Manasseh was the father of Amon.
Amon was the father of Josiah.
[11]Josiah was the grandfather of Jehoiachin[n]
and his brothers.
(This was at the time that the people
were taken to Babylon.)
[12]After they were taken to Babylon:
Jehoiachin was the father of Shealtiel.
Shealtiel was the grandfather of
Zerubbabel.
[13]Zerubbabel was the father of Abiud.
Abiud was the father of Eliakim.
Eliakim was the father of Azor.
[14]Azor was the father of Zadok.
Zadok was the father of Akim.
Akim was the father of Eliud.
[15]Eliud was the father of Eleazar.
Eleazar was the father of Matthan.
Matthan was the father of Jacob.

1:2 father "Father" in Jewish lists of ancestors can sometimes mean grandfather or more distant relative.   **1:7 Asa** Some
Greek copies read "Asaph," another name for Asa (see 1 Chronicles 3:10).   **1:11 Jehoiachin** The Greek reads "Jeconiah,"
another name for Jehoiachin (see 2 Kings 24:6 and 1 Chronicles 3:16).

[16]Jacob was the father of Joseph.
Joseph was the husband of Mary,
and Mary was the mother of Jesus.
Jesus is called the Christ.

[17]So there were fourteen generations from Abraham to David. And there were fourteen generations from David until the people were taken to Babylon. And there were fourteen generations from the time when the people were taken to Babylon until Christ was born.

The Birth of Jesus Christ

[18]This is how the birth of Jesus Christ came about. His mother Mary was engaged[n] to marry Joseph, but before they married, she learned she was pregnant by the power of the Holy Spirit. [19]Because Mary's husband, Joseph, was a good man, he did not want to disgrace her in public, so he planned to divorce her secretly.

[20]While Joseph thought about these things, an angel of the Lord came to him in a dream. The angel said, "Joseph, descendant of David, don't be afraid to take Mary as your wife, because the baby in her is from the Holy Spirit. [21]She will give birth to a son, and you will name him Jesus,[n] because he will save his people from their sins."

[22]All this happened to bring about what the Lord had said through the prophet: [23]"The virgin will be pregnant. She will have a son, and they will name him Immanuel,"[n] which means "God is with us."

[24]When Joseph woke up, he did what the Lord's angel had told him to do. Joseph took Mary as his wife, [25]but he did not have sexual relations with her until she gave birth to the son. And Joseph named him Jesus.

JANUARY 2

GENESIS 3:1—4:26

The Beginning of Sin

3 Now the snake was the most clever of all the wild animals the LORD God had made. One day the snake said to the woman, "Did God really say that you must not eat fruit from any tree in the garden?"

[2]The woman answered the snake, "We may eat fruit from the trees in the garden. [3]But God told us, 'You must not eat fruit from the tree that is in the middle of the garden. You must not even touch it, or you will die.'"

[4]But the snake said to the woman, "You will not die. [5]God knows that if you eat the fruit from that tree, you will learn about good and evil and you will be like God!"

[6]The woman saw that the tree was beautiful, that its fruit was good to eat, and that it would make her wise. So she took some of its fruit and ate it. She also gave some of the fruit to her husband who was with her, and he ate it.

[7]Then, it was as if their eyes were opened. They realized they were naked, so they sewed fig leaves together and made something to cover themselves.

[8]Then they heard the LORD God walking in the garden during the cool part of the day, and the man and his wife hid from the LORD God among the trees in the garden. [9]But the LORD God called to the man and said, "Where are you?"

[10]The man answered, "I heard you walking in the garden, and I was afraid because I was naked, so I hid."

[11]God asked, "Who told you that you were naked? Did you eat fruit from the tree from which I commanded you not to eat?"

[12]The man said, "You gave this woman to me and she gave me fruit from the tree, so I ate it."

1:18 engaged For the Jewish people an engagement was a lasting agreement, which could only be broken by a divorce. If a bride-to-be was unfaithful, it was considered adultery, and she could be put to death. **1:21 Jesus** The name "Jesus" means "salvation." **1:23 "The virgin . . . Immanuel"** Quotation from Isaiah 7:14.

[13]Then the LORD God said to the woman, "How could you have done such a thing?"

She answered, "The snake tricked me, so I ate the fruit."

[14]The LORD God said to the snake,

"Because you did this,
  a curse will be put on you.
You will be cursed as no other animal,
  tame or wild, will ever be.
You will crawl on your stomach,
  and you will eat dust all the days of
    your life.
[15]I will make you and the woman
  enemies to each other.
Your descendants and her descendants
  will be enemies.
One of her descendants will crush your
    head,
  and you will bite his heel."

[16]Then God said to the woman,

"I will cause you to have much trouble
  when you are pregnant,
and when you give birth to children,
  you will have great pain.
You will greatly desire your husband,
  but he will rule over you."

[17]Then God said to the man, "You listened to what your wife said, and you ate fruit from the tree from which I commanded you not to eat.

"So I will put a curse on the ground,
  and you will have to work very hard for
    your food.
In pain you will eat its food
  all the days of your life.
[18]The ground will produce thorns and
    weeds for you,
  and you will eat the plants of the field.
[19]You will sweat and work hard for your
    food.
Later you will return to the ground,
  because you were taken from it.
You are dust,
  and when you die, you will return to
    the dust."

[20]The man named his wife Eve,[n] because she was the mother of all the living.

[21]The LORD God made clothes from animal skins for the man and his wife and dressed them. [22]Then the LORD God said, "Humans have become like one of us; they know good and evil. We must keep them from eating some of the fruit from the tree of life, or they will live forever." [23]So the LORD God forced Adam out of the garden of Eden to work the ground from which he was taken. [24]After God forced humans out of the garden, he placed angels and a sword of fire that flashed around in every direction on its eastern border. This kept people from getting to the tree of life.

The First Family

4 Adam had sexual relations with his wife Eve, and she became pregnant and gave birth to Cain.[n] Eve said, "With the LORD's help, I have given birth to a man." [2]After that, Eve gave birth to Cain's brother Abel. Abel took care of flocks, and Cain became a farmer.

[3]Later, Cain brought some food from the ground as a gift to God. [4]Abel brought the best parts from some of the firstborn of his flock. The LORD accepted Abel and his gift, [5]but he did not accept Cain and his gift. So Cain became very angry and felt rejected.

[6]The LORD asked Cain, "Why are you angry? Why do you look so unhappy? [7]If you do things well, I will accept you, but if you do not do them well, sin is ready to attack you. Sin wants you, but you must rule over it."

[8]Cain said to his brother Abel, "Let's go out into the field." While they were out in the field, Cain attacked his brother Abel and killed him.

[9]Later, the LORD said to Cain, "Where is your brother Abel?"

Cain answered, "I don't know. Is it my job to take care of my brother?"

[10]Then the LORD said, "What have you done? Your brother's blood is crying out to me from the ground. [11]And now you will be cursed in your work with the ground, the same ground where your brother's blood fell and where your hands killed him. [12]You will work the ground, but it will not grow good

---

3:20 Eve This name sounds like the Hebrew word meaning "alive." **4:1 Cain** This name sounds like the Hebrew word for "I have given birth."

crops for you anymore, and you will wander around on the earth."

¹³Then Cain said to the LORD, "This punishment is more than I can stand! ¹⁴Today you have forced me to stop working the ground, and now I must hide from you. I must wander around on the earth, and anyone who meets me can kill me."

¹⁵The LORD said to Cain, "No! If anyone kills you, I will punish that person seven times more." Then the LORD put a mark on Cain warning anyone who met him not to kill him.

Cain's Family

¹⁶So Cain went away from the LORD and lived in the land of Nod,ⁿ east of Eden. ¹⁷He had sexual relations with his wife, and she became pregnant and gave birth to Enoch. At that time Cain was building a city, which he named after his son Enoch. ¹⁸Enoch had a son named Irad, Irad had a son named Mehujael, Mehujael had a son named Methushael, and Methushael had a son named Lamech.

¹⁹Lamech married two women, Adah and Zillah. ²⁰Adah gave birth to Jabal, who became the first person to live in tents and raise cattle. ²¹Jabal's brother was Jubal, the first person to play the harp and flute. ²²Zillah gave birth to Tubal-Cain, who made tools out of bronze and iron. The sister of Tubal-Cain was Naamah.

²³Lamech said to his wives:
"Adah and Zillah, hear my voice!
  You wives of Lamech, listen to what I say.
I killed a man for wounding me,
  a young man for hitting me.
²⁴If Cain's killer is punished seven times,
  then Lamech's killer will be punished seventy-seven times."

Adam and Eve Have a New Son

²⁵Adam had sexual relations with his wife Eve again, and she gave birth to a son. She named him Sethⁿ and said, "God has given me another child. He will take the place of Abel, who was killed by Cain." ²⁶Seth also had a son, and they named him Enosh. At that time people began to pray to the LORD.

PSALM 2:1–6

The Lord's Chosen King

2 Why are the nations so angry?
  Why are the people making useless plans?
²The kings of the earth prepare to fight,
  and their leaders make plans together against the LORD
  and his appointed one.
³They say, "Let's break the chains that hold us back
  and throw off the ropes that tie us down."

⁴But the one who sits in heaven laughs;
  the Lord makes fun of them.
⁵Then the LORD warns them
  and frightens them with his anger.
⁶He says, "I have appointed my own king
  to rule in Jerusalem on my holy mountain, Zion."

PROVERBS 1:8–9

Warnings Against Evil

⁸My child, listen to your father's teaching
  and do not forget your mother's advice.
⁹Their teaching will be like flowers in your hair
  or a necklace around your neck.

MATTHEW 2:1–23

Wise Men Come to Visit Jesus

2 Jesus was born in the town of Bethlehem in Judea during the time when Herod was king. When Jesus was born, some wise men from the east came to Jerusalem. ²They asked, "Where is the baby who was born to be the king of the Jews? We saw his star in the east and have come to worship him."

³When King Herod heard this, he was troubled, as were all the people in Jerusalem. ⁴Herod called a meeting of all the leading priests and teachers of the law and asked them where the Christ would be born. ⁵They answered, "In the town of Bethlehem in

4:16 Nod This name sounds like the Hebrew word for "wander." **4:25 Seth** This name sounds like the Hebrew word for "to give."

Judea. The prophet wrote about this in the Scriptures:

⁶"But you, Bethlehem, in the land of Judah,
   are not just an insignificant village in
   Judah.
A ruler will come from you
   who will be like a shepherd for my
   people Israel.'"   *Micah 5:2*

⁷Then Herod had a secret meeting with the wise men and learned from them the exact time they first saw the star. ⁸He sent the wise men to Bethlehem, saying, "Look carefully for the child. When you find him, come tell me so I can worship him too."

⁹After the wise men heard the king, they left. The star that they had seen in the east went before them until it stopped above the place where the child was. ¹⁰When the wise men saw the star, they were filled with joy. ¹¹They came to the house where the child was and saw him with his mother, Mary, and they bowed down and worshiped him. They opened their gifts and gave him treasures of gold, frankincense, and myrrh. ¹²But God warned the wise men in a dream not to go back to Herod, so they returned to their own country by a different way.

Jesus' Parents Take Him to Egypt

¹³After they left, an angel of the Lord came to Joseph in a dream and said, "Get up! Take the child and his mother and escape to Egypt, because Herod is starting to look for the child so he can kill him. Stay in Egypt until I tell you to return."

¹⁴So Joseph got up and left for Egypt during the night with the child and his mother.

¹⁵And Joseph stayed in Egypt until Herod died. This happened to bring about what the Lord had said through the prophet: "I called my son out of Egypt."ⁿ

Herod Kills the Baby Boys

¹⁶When Herod saw that the wise men had tricked him, he was furious. So he gave an order to kill all the baby boys in Bethlehem and in the surrounding area who were two years old or younger. This was in keeping with the time he learned from the wise men. ¹⁷So what God had said through the prophet Jeremiah came true:

¹⁸"A voice was heard in Ramah
   of painful crying and deep sadness:
   Rachel crying for her children.
She refused to be comforted,
   because her children are dead."

                              Jeremiah 31:15

Joseph and Mary Return

¹⁹After Herod died, an angel of the Lord spoke to Joseph in a dream while he was in Egypt. ²⁰The angel said, "Get up! Take the child and his mother and go to the land of Israel, because the people who were trying to kill the child are now dead."

²¹So Joseph took the child and his mother and went to Israel. ²²But he heard that Archelaus was now king in Judea since his father Herod had died. So Joseph was afraid to go there. After being warned in a dream, he went to the area of Galilee, ²³to a town called Nazareth, and lived there. And so what God had said through the prophets came true: "He will be called a Nazarene."ⁿ

JANUARY 3

GENESIS 5:1—6:22

Adam's Family History

5 This is the family history of Adam. When God created human beings, he made them in his own likeness. ²He created them male and female, and on that day he blessed them and named them human beings.

³When Adam was 130 years old, he became the father of another son in his like-

---

2:15 **"I called . . . Egypt."** Quotation from Hosea 11:1.   2:23 **Nazarene** A person from the town of Nazareth. Matthew may be referring to Isaiah 11:1, where the Hebrew word translated "branch" sounds like "Nazarene."

ness and image, and Adam named him Seth. [4]After Seth was born, Adam lived 800 years and had other sons and daughters. [5]So Adam lived a total of 930 years, and then he died.

[6]When Seth was 105 years old, he had a son named Enosh. [7]After Enosh was born, Seth lived 807 years and had other sons and daughters. [8]So Seth lived a total of 912 years, and then he died.

[9]When Enosh was 90 years old, he had a son named Kenan. [10]After Kenan was born, Enosh lived 815 years and had other sons and daughters. [11]So Enosh lived a total of 905 years, and then he died.

[12]When Kenan was 70 years old, he had a son named Mahalalel. [13]After Mahalalel was born, Kenan lived 840 years and had other sons and daughters. [14]So Kenan lived a total of 910 years, and then he died.

[15]When Mahalalel was 65 years old, he had a son named Jared. [16]After Jared was born, Mahalalel lived 830 years and had other sons and daughters. [17]So Mahalalel lived a total of 895 years, and then he died.

[18]When Jared was 162 years old, he had a son named Enoch. [19]After Enoch was born, Jared lived 800 years and had other sons and daughters. [20]So Jared lived a total of 962 years, and then he died.

[21]When Enoch was 65 years old, he had a son named Methuselah. [22]After Methuselah was born, Enoch walked with God 300 years more and had other sons and daughters. [23]So Enoch lived a total of 365 years. [24]Enoch walked with God; one day Enoch could not be found, because God took him.

[25]When Methuselah was 187 years old, he had a son named Lamech. [26]After Lamech was born, Methuselah lived 782 years and had other sons and daughters. [27]So Methuselah lived a total of 969 years, and then he died.

[28]When Lamech was 182, he had a son. [29]Lamech named his son Noah[n] and said, "He will comfort us in our work, which comes from the ground the LORD has cursed." [30]After Noah was born, Lamech lived 595 years and had other sons and daughters. [31]So Lamech lived a total of 777 years, and then he died.

[32]After Noah was 500 years old, he became the father of Shem, Ham, and Japheth.

The Human Race Becomes Evil

6The number of people on earth began to grow, and daughters were born to them. [2]When the sons of God saw that these girls were beautiful, they married any of them they chose. [3]The LORD said, "My Spirit will not remain in human beings forever, because they are flesh. They will live only 120 years."

[4]The Nephilim were on the earth in those days and also later. That was when the sons of God had sexual relations with the daughters of human beings. These women gave birth to children, who became famous and were the mighty warriors of long ago.

[5]The LORD saw that the human beings on the earth were very wicked and that everything they thought about was evil. [6]He was sorry he had made human beings on the earth, and his heart was filled with pain. [7]So the LORD said, "I will destroy all human beings that I made on the earth. And I will destroy every animal and everything that crawls on the earth and the birds of the air, because I am sorry I have made them." [8]But Noah pleased the LORD.

Noah and the Great Flood

[9]This is the family history of Noah. Noah was a good man, the most innocent man of his time, and he walked with God. [10]He had three sons: Shem, Ham, and Japheth.

[11]People on earth did what God said was evil, and violence was everywhere. [12]When God saw that everyone on the earth did only evil, [13]he said to Noah, "Because people have made the earth full of violence, I will destroy all of them from the earth. [14]Build a boat of cypress wood for yourself. Make rooms in it and cover it inside and outside with tar. [15]This is how big I want you to build the boat: four hundred fifty feet long, seventy-five feet wide, and forty-five feet high. [16]Make an opening around the top of the boat that is eighteen inches high from the edge of the roof down. Put a door in the side of the boat. Make an up-

5:29 Noah This name sounds like the Hebrew word for "rest."

per, middle, and lower deck in it. ¹⁷I will bring a flood of water on the earth to destroy all living things that live under the sky, including everything that has the breath of life. Everything on the earth will die. ¹⁸But I will make an agreement with you—you, your sons, your wife, and your sons' wives will all go into the boat. ¹⁹Also, you must bring into the boat two of every living thing, male and female. Keep them alive with you. ²⁰Two of every kind of bird, animal, and crawling thing will come to you to be kept alive. ²¹Also gather some of every kind of food and store it on the boat as food for you and the animals."

²²Noah did everything that God commanded him.

PSALM 2:7–12

⁷Now I will tell you what the LORD has declared:
He said to me, "You are my son.
Today I have become your father.
⁸If you ask me, I will give you the nations;
all the people on earth will be yours.
⁹You will rule over them with an iron rod.
You will break them into pieces like pottery."
¹⁰So, kings, be wise;
rulers, learn this lesson.
¹¹Obey the LORD with great fear.
Be happy, but tremble.
¹²Show that you are loyal to his son,
or you will be destroyed by his anger,
because he can quickly become angry.
But happy are those who trust him for protection.

PROVERBS 1:10–19

¹⁰My child, if sinners try to lead you into sin,
do not follow them.
¹¹They will say, "Come with us.
Let's ambush and kill someone;
let's attack some innocent people just for fun.
¹²Let's swallow them alive, as death does;
let's swallow them whole, as the grave does.

¹³We will take all kinds of valuable things
and fill our houses with stolen goods.
¹⁴Come join us,
and we will share with you stolen goods."
¹⁵My child, do not go along with them;
do not do what they do.
¹⁶They are eager to do evil
and are quick to kill.
¹⁷It is useless to spread out a net
right where the birds can see it.
¹⁸But sinners will fall into their own traps;
they will only catch themselves!
¹⁹All greedy people end up this way;
greed kills selfish people.

MATTHEW 3:1–17

The Work of John the Baptist

3 About that time John the Baptist began preaching in the desert area of Judea. ²John said, "Change your hearts and lives because the kingdom of heaven is near." ³John the Baptist is the one Isaiah the prophet was talking about when he said:
"This is a voice of one
who calls out in the desert:
'Prepare the way for the Lord.
Make the road straight for him.'"

Isaiah 40:3

⁴John's clothes were made from camel's hair, and he wore a leather belt around his waist. For food, he ate locusts and wild honey. ⁵Many people came from Jerusalem and Judea and all the area around the Jordan River to hear John. ⁶They confessed their sins, and he baptized them in the Jordan River.

⁷Many of the Pharisees and Sadducees came to the place where John was baptizing people. When John saw them, he said, "You are snakes! Who warned you to run away from God's coming punishment? ⁸Do the things that show you really have changed your hearts and lives. ⁹And don't think you can say to yourselves, 'Abraham is our father.' I tell you that God could make children for Abraham from these rocks. ¹⁰The ax is now ready to cut down the trees, and every tree that does not produce good fruit will be cut down and thrown into the fire.ⁿ

3:10 The ax . . . fire. This means that God is ready to punish his people who do not obey him.

11"I baptize you with water to show that your hearts and lives have changed. But there is one coming after me who is greater than I am, whose sandals I am not good enough to carry. He will baptize you with the Holy Spirit and fire. 12He will come ready to clean the grain, separating the good grain from the chaff. He will put the good part of the grain into his barn, but he will burn the chaff with a fire that cannot be put out."*n*

Jesus Is Baptized by John

13At that time Jesus came from Galilee to the Jordan River and wanted John to baptize him. 14But John tried to stop him, saying, "Why do you come to me to be baptized? I need to be baptized by you!"

15Jesus answered, "Let it be this way for now. We should do all things that are God's will." So John agreed to baptize Jesus.

16As soon as Jesus was baptized, he came up out of the water. Then heaven opened, and he saw God's Spirit coming down on him like a dove. 17And a voice from heaven said, "This is my Son, whom I love, and I am very pleased with him."

JANUARY 4

GENESIS 7:1—8:22

The Flood Begins

7Then the LORD said to Noah, "I have seen that you are the best person among the people of this time, so you and your family can go into the boat. 2Take with you seven pairs, each male with its female, of every kind of clean animal, and take one pair, each male with its female, of every kind of unclean animal. 3Take seven pairs of all the birds of the sky, each male with its female. This will allow all these animals to continue living on the earth after the flood. 4Seven days from now I will send rain on the earth. It will rain forty days and forty nights, and I will wipe off from the earth every living thing that I have made."

5Noah did everything the LORD commanded him.

6Noah was six hundred years old when the flood came. 7He and his wife and his sons and their wives went into the boat to escape the waters of the flood. 8The clean animals, the unclean animals, the birds, and everything that crawls on the ground 9came to Noah. They went into the boat in groups of two, male and female, just as God had commanded Noah. 10Seven days later the flood started. 11When Noah was six hundred years old,

the flood started. On the seventeenth day of the second month of that year the underground springs split open, and the clouds in the sky poured out rain. 12The rain fell on the earth for forty days and forty nights.

13On that same day Noah and his wife, his sons Shem, Ham, and Japheth, and their wives went into the boat. 14They had every kind of wild and tame animal, every kind of animal that crawls on the earth, and every kind of bird. 15Every creature that had the breath of life came to Noah in the boat in groups of two. 16One male and one female of every living thing came, just as God had commanded Noah. Then the LORD closed the door behind them.

17Water flooded the earth for forty days, and as it rose it lifted the boat off the ground. 18The water continued to rise, and the boat floated on it above the earth. 19The water rose so much that even the highest mountains under the sky were covered by it. 20It continued to rise until it was more than twenty feet above the mountains.

21All living things that moved on the earth died. This included all the birds, tame animals, wild animals, and creatures that swarm on the earth, as well as all human beings. 22So everything on dry land that had

---

3:12 He will . . . out. This means that Jesus will come to separate good people from bad people, saving the good and punishing the bad.

the breath of life in it died. [23]God destroyed from the earth every living thing that was on the land—every man, animal, crawling thing, and bird of the sky. All that was left was Noah and what was with him in the boat. [24]And the waters continued to cover the earth for one hundred fifty days.

The Flood Ends

8 But God remembered Noah and all the wild and tame animals with him in the boat. He made a wind blow over the earth, and the water went down. [2]The underground springs stopped flowing, and the clouds in the sky stopped pouring down rain. [3-4]The water that covered the earth began to go down. After one hundred fifty days it had gone down so much that the boat touched land again. It came to rest on one of the mountains of Ararat[n] on the seventeenth day of the seventh month. [5]The water continued to go down so that by the first day of the tenth month the tops of the mountains could be seen.

[6]Forty days later Noah opened the window he had made in the boat, and [7]he sent out a raven. It flew here and there until the water had dried up from the earth. [8]Then Noah sent out a dove to find out if the water had dried up from the ground. [9]The dove could not find a place to land because water still covered the earth, so it came back to the boat. Noah reached out his hand and took the bird and brought it back into the boat. [10]After seven days Noah again sent out the dove from the boat, [11]and that evening it came back to him with a fresh olive leaf in its mouth. Then Noah knew that the ground was almost dry. [12]Seven days later he sent the dove out again, but this time it did not come back.

[13]When Noah was six hundred and one years old, in the first day of the first month of that year, the water was dried up from the land. Noah removed the covering of the boat and saw that the land was dry. [14]By the twenty-seventh day of the second month the land was completely dry.

[15]Then God said to Noah, [16]"You and your wife, your sons, and their wives should go out of the boat. [17]Bring every animal out of the boat with you—the birds, animals, and everything that crawls on the earth. Let them have many young ones so that they might grow in number."

[18]So Noah went out with his sons, his wife, and his sons' wives. [19]Every animal, everything that crawls on the earth, and every bird went out of the boat by families.

[20]Then Noah built an altar to the LORD. He took some of all the clean birds and animals, and he burned them on the altar as offerings to God. [21]The LORD was pleased with these sacrifices and said to himself, "I will never again curse the ground because of human beings. Their thoughts are evil even when they are young, but I will never again destroy every living thing on the earth as I did this time.
[22]"As long as the earth continues,
   planting and harvest,
   cold and hot,
   summer and winter,
   day and night
   will not stop."

PSALM 3:1–4

A Morning Prayer

David sang this when he ran away from his son Absalom.

3 LORD, I have many enemies!
   Many people have turned against me.
[2]Many are saying about me,
   "God won't rescue him."   *Selah*

[3]But, LORD, you are my shield,
   my wonderful God who gives me
      courage.
[4]I will pray to the LORD,
   and he will answer me from his holy
      mountain.   *Selah*

PROVERBS 1:20–23

Wisdom Speaks

[20]Wisdom is like a woman shouting in the
      street;
   she raises her voice in the city squares.
[21]She cries out in the noisy street
   and shouts at the city gates:

8:3–4 Ararat The ancient land of Urartu, an area in Eastern Turkey.

22"You fools, how long will you be foolish?
How long will you make fun of wisdom
and hate knowledge?
23If only you had listened when I corrected
you,
I would have told you what's in my heart;
I would have told you what I am
thinking.

MATTHEW 4:1–25

The Temptation of Jesus

4 Then the Spirit led Jesus into the desert to
be tempted by the devil. 2Jesus fasted for
forty days and nights. After this, he was very
hungry. 3The devil came to Jesus to tempt
him, saying, "If you are the Son of God, tell
these rocks to become bread."

4Jesus answered, "It is written in the
Scriptures, 'A person lives not on bread
alone, but by everything God says.'"[n]

5Then the devil led Jesus to the holy city
of Jerusalem and put him on a high place of
the Temple. 6The devil said, "If you are the
Son of God, jump down, because it is written
in the Scriptures:

'He has put his angels in charge of you.
They will catch you in their hands
so that you will not hit your foot on a
rock.'" *Psalm 91:11–12*

7Jesus answered him, "It also says in the
Scriptures, 'Do not test the Lord your God.'"[n]

8Then the devil led Jesus to the top of a
very high mountain and showed him all the
kingdoms of the world and all their splendor.
9The devil said, "If you will bow down and
worship me, I will give you all these things."

10Jesus said to the devil, "Go away from
me, Satan! It is written in the Scriptures, 'You
must worship the Lord your God and serve
only him.'"[n]

11So the devil left Jesus, and angels came
and took care of him.

Jesus Begins Work in Galilee

12When Jesus heard that John had been
put in prison, he went back to Galilee. 13He
left Nazareth and went to live in Capernaum,
a town near Lake Galilee, in the area near
Zebulun and Naphtali. 14Jesus did this to
bring about what the prophet Isaiah had said:
15"Land of Zebulun and land of Naphtali
along the sea,
beyond the Jordan River.
This is Galilee where the non-Jewish
people live.
16These people who live in darkness
will see a great light.
They live in a place covered with the
shadows of death,
but a light will shine on them."
Isaiah 9:1–2

Jesus Chooses Some Followers

17From that time Jesus began to preach,
saying, "Change your hearts and lives, because the kingdom of heaven is near."

18As Jesus was walking by Lake Galilee, he
saw two brothers, Simon (called Peter) and
his brother Andrew. They were throwing a net
into the lake because they were fishermen.
19Jesus said, "Come follow me, and I will make
you fish for people." 20So Simon and Andrew
immediately left their nets and followed him.

21As Jesus continued walking by Lake
Galilee, he saw two other brothers, James
and John, the sons of Zebedee. They were in
a boat with their father Zebedee, mending
their nets. Jesus told them to come with him.
22Immediately they left the boat and their father, and they followed Jesus.

Jesus Teaches and Heals People

23Jesus went everywhere in Galilee, teaching in the synagogues, preaching the Good
News about the kingdom of heaven, and
healing all the people's diseases and sicknesses. 24The news about Jesus spread all
over Syria, and people brought all the sick to
him. They were suffering from different
kinds of diseases. Some were in great pain,
some had demons, some were epileptics,[n]
and some were paralyzed. Jesus healed all of
them. 25Many people from Galilee, the Ten
Towns,[n] Jerusalem, Judea, and the land
across the Jordan River followed him.

4:4 'A person . . . says.' Quotation from Deuteronomy 8:3.   **4:7 'Do . . . God.'** Quotation from Deuteronomy 6:16.
4:10 'You . . . him.' Quotation from Deuteronomy 6:13.   **4:24 epileptics** People with a disease that causes them sometimes
to lose control of their bodies and maybe faint, shake strongly, or not be able to move.   **4:25 Ten Towns** In Greek, called
"Decapolis." It was an area east of Lake Galilee that once had ten main towns.

JANUARY 5

GENESIS 9:1—10:32

The New Beginning

9 Then God blessed Noah and his sons and said to them, "Have many children; grow in number and fill the earth. ²Every animal on earth, every bird in the sky, every animal that crawls on the ground, and every fish in the sea will respect and fear you. I have given them to you.

³"Everything that moves, everything that is alive, is yours for food. Earlier I gave you the green plants, but now I give you everything for food. ⁴But you must not eat meat that still has blood in it, because blood gives life. ⁵I will demand blood for life. I will demand the life of any animal that kills a person, and I will demand the life of anyone who takes another person's life.

⁶"Whoever kills a human being
    will be killed by a human being,
because God made humans
    in his own image.

⁷"As for you, Noah, I want you and your family to have many children, to grow in number on the earth, and to become many."

⁸Then God said to Noah and his sons, ⁹"Now I am making my agreement with you and your people who will live after you, ¹⁰and with every living thing that is with you—the birds, the tame and the wild animals, and with everything that came out of the boat with you—with every living thing on earth. ¹¹I make this agreement with you: I will never again destroy all living things by a flood. A flood will never again destroy the earth."

¹²And God said, "This is the sign of the agreement between me and you and every living creature that is with you. ¹³I am putting my rainbow in the clouds as the sign of the agreement between me and the earth. ¹⁴When I bring clouds over the earth and a rainbow appears in them, ¹⁵I will remember my agreement between me and you and every living thing. Floods will never again destroy all life on the earth. ¹⁶When the rainbow appears in the clouds, I will see it and I will remember the agreement that continues forever between me and every living thing on the earth."

¹⁷So God said to Noah, "The rainbow is a sign of the agreement that I made with all living things on earth."

Noah and His Sons

¹⁸The sons of Noah who came out of the boat with him were Shem, Ham, and Japheth. (Ham was the father of Canaan.) ¹⁹These three men were Noah's sons, and all the people on earth came from these three sons.

²⁰Noah became a farmer and planted a vineyard. ²¹When he drank wine made from his grapes, he became drunk and lay naked in his tent. ²²Ham, the father of Canaan, looked at his naked father and told his brothers outside. ²³Then Shem and Japheth got a coat and, carrying it on both their shoulders, they walked backwards into the tent and covered their father. They turned their faces away so that they did not see their father's nakedness.

²⁴Noah was sleeping because of the wine. When he woke up and learned what his youngest son, Ham, had done to him, ²⁵he said,

"May there be a curse on Canaan!
May he be the lowest slave to his
    brothers."

²⁶Noah also said,

"May the LORD, the God of Shem, be
    praised!
May Canaan be Shem's slave.

²⁷May God give more land to Japheth.
May Japheth live in Shem's tents,
    and may Canaan be their slave."

²⁸After the flood Noah lived 350 years. ²⁹He lived a total of 950 years, and then he died.

Nations Grow and Spread

10 This is the family history of Shem, Ham, and Japheth, the sons of Noah. After the flood these three men had sons.

Japheth's Sons

[2]The sons of Japheth were Gomer, Magog, Madai, Javan, Tubal, Meshech, and Tiras.

[3]The sons of Gomer were Ashkenaz, Riphath, and Togarmah.

[4]The sons of Javan were Elishah, Tarshish, Kittim,[n] and Rodanim. [5]Those who lived in the lands around the Mediterranean Sea came from these sons of Japheth. All the families grew and became different nations, each nation with its own land and its own language.

Ham's Sons

[6]The sons of Ham were Cush, Mizraim,[n] Put, and Canaan.

[7]The sons of Cush were Seba, Havilah, Sabtah, Raamah, and Sabteca.

The sons of Raamah were Sheba and Dedan.

[8]Cush also had a descendant named Nimrod, who became a very powerful man on earth. [9]He was a great hunter before the LORD, which is why people say someone is "like Nimrod, a great hunter before the LORD." [10]At first Nimrod's kingdom covered Babylon, Erech, Akkad, and Calneh in the land of Babylonia. [11]From there he went to Assyria, where he built the cities of Nineveh, Rehoboth Ir, and Calah. [12]He also built Resen, the great city between Nineveh and Calah.

[13]Mizraim was the father of the Ludites, Anamites, Lehabites, Naphtuhites, [14]Pathrusites, Casluhites, and the people of Crete. (The Philistines came from the Casluhites.)

[15]Canaan was the father of Sidon, his first son, and of Heth. [16]He was also the father of the Jebusites, Amorites, Girgashites, [17]Hivites, Arkites, Sinites, [18]Arvadites, Zemarites, and Hamathites. The families of the Canaanites scattered. [19]Their land reached from Sidon to Gerar as far as Gaza, and then to Sodom, Gomorrah, Admah, and Zeboiim, as far as Lasha.

[20]All these people were the sons of Ham, and all these families had their own languages, their own lands, and their own nations.

Shem's Sons

[21]Shem, Japheth's older brother, also had sons. One of his descendants was the father of all the sons of Eber.

[22]The sons of Shem were Elam, Asshur, Arphaxad, Lud, and Aram.

[23]The sons of Aram were Uz, Hul, Gether, and Meshech.

[24]Arphaxad was the father of Shelah, who was the father of Eber. [25]Eber was the father of two sons—one named Peleg,[n] because the earth was divided during his life, and the other was named Joktan.

[26]Joktan was the father of Almodad, Sheleph, Hazarmaveth, Jerah, [27]Hadoram, Uzal, Diklah, [28]Obal, Abimael, Sheba, [29]Ophir, Havilah, and Jobab. All these people were the sons of Joktan. [30]They lived in the area between Mesha and Sephar in the hill country in the East.

[31]These are the people from the family of Shem, arranged by families, languages, countries, and nations.

[32]This is the list of the families from the sons of Noah, arranged according to their nations. From these families came all the nations who spread across the earth after the flood.

PSALM 3:5–8

[5]I can lie down and go to sleep,
    and I will wake up again,
    because the LORD gives me strength.
[6]Thousands of troops may surround me,
    but I am not afraid.

[7]LORD, rise up!
    My God, come save me!
    You have struck my enemies on the cheek;
    you have broken the teeth of the
        wicked.
[8]The LORD can save his people.
    LORD, bless your people.   *Selah*

PROVERBS 1:24–27

[24]I called, but you refused to listen;
    I held out my hand, but you paid no
        attention.

10:4 **Kittim** His descendants were the people of Cyprus. 10:6 **Mizraim** This is another name for Egypt. 10:25 **Peleg** This name sounds like the Hebrew word for "divided."

²⁵You did not follow my advice
  and did not listen when I corrected
    you.
²⁶So I will laugh when you are in trouble.
  I will make fun when disaster strikes
    you,
²⁷when disaster comes over you like a
    storm,
  when trouble strikes you like a
    whirlwind,
  when pain and trouble overwhelm you.

MATTHEW 5:1–26

Jesus Teaches the People

5 When Jesus saw the crowds, he went up on a hill and sat down. His followers came to him, ²and he began to teach them, saying:
³"They are blessed who realize their
    spiritual poverty,
  for the kingdom of heaven belongs to
    them.
⁴They are blessed who grieve,
  for God will comfort them.
⁵They are blessed who are humble,
  for the whole earth will be theirs.
⁶They are blessed who hunger and thirst
    after justice,
  for they will be satisfied.
⁷They are blessed who show mercy to
    others,
  for God will show mercy to them.
⁸They are blessed whose thoughts are
    pure,
  for they will see God.
⁹They are blessed who work for peace,
  for they will be called God's children.
¹⁰They are blessed who are persecuted for
    doing good,
  for the kingdom of heaven belongs to
    them.
¹¹"People will insult you and hurt you. They will lie and say all kinds of evil things about you because you follow me. But when they do, you will be blessed. ¹²Rejoice and be glad, because you have a great reward waiting for you in heaven. People did the same evil things to the prophets who lived before you.

You Are Like Salt and Light

¹³"You are the salt of the earth. But if the salt loses its salty taste, it cannot be made salty again. It is good for nothing, except to be thrown out and walked on.

¹⁴"You are the light that gives light to the world. A city that is built on a hill cannot be hidden. ¹⁵And people don't hide a light under a bowl. They put it on a lampstand so the light shines for all the people in the house. ¹⁶In the same way, you should be a light for other people. Live so that they will see the good things you do and will praise your Father in heaven.

The Importance of the Law

¹⁷"Don't think that I have come to destroy the law of Moses or the teaching of the prophets. I have not come to destroy them but to bring about what they said. ¹⁸I tell you the truth, nothing will disappear from the law until heaven and earth are gone. Not even the smallest letter or the smallest part of a letter will be lost until everything has happened. ¹⁹Whoever refuses to obey any command and teaches other people not to obey that command will be the least important in the kingdom of heaven. But whoever obeys the commands and teaches other people to obey them will be great in the kingdom of heaven. ²⁰I tell you that if you are no more obedient than the teachers of the law and the Pharisees, you will never enter the kingdom of heaven.

Jesus Teaches About Anger

²¹"You have heard that it was said to our people long ago, 'You must not murder anyone.'ⁿ Anyone who murders another will be judged.' ²²But I tell you, if you are angry with a brother or sister,ⁿ you will be judged. If you say bad things to a brother or sister, you will be judged by the council. And if you call someone a fool, you will be in danger of the fire of hell.

²³"So when you offer your gift to God at the altar, and you remember that your brother or sister has something against you,

---

5:21 'You . . . anyone.' Quotation from Exodus 20:13; Deuteronomy 5:17. **5:22 sister** Some Greek copies continue, "without a reason."

²⁴leave your gift there at the altar. Go and make peace with that person, and then come and offer your gift.

²⁵"If your enemy is taking you to court, become friends quickly, before you go to court. Otherwise, your enemy might turn you over to the judge, and the judge might give you to a guard to put you in jail. ²⁶I tell you the truth, you will not leave there until you have paid everything you owe.

JANUARY 6

GENESIS 11:1—12:20

The Languages Confused

11 At this time the whole world spoke one language, and everyone used the same words. ²As people moved from the east, they found a plain in the land of Babylonia and settled there.

³They said to each other, "Let's make bricks and bake them to make them hard." So they used bricks instead of stones, and tar instead of mortar. ⁴Then they said to each other, "Let's build a city and a tower for ourselves, whose top will reach high into the sky. We will become famous. Then we will not be scattered over all the earth."

⁵The LORD came down to see the city and the tower that the people had built. ⁶The LORD said, "Now, these people are united, all speaking the same language. This is only the beginning of what they will do. They will be able to do anything they want. ⁷Come, let us go down and confuse their language so they will not be able to understand each other."

⁸So the LORD scattered them from there over all the earth, and they stopped building the city. ⁹The place is called Babelⁿ since that is where the LORD confused the language of the whole world. So the LORD caused them to spread out from there over the whole world.

The Story of Shem's Family

¹⁰This is the family history of Shem. Two years after the flood, when Shem was 100 years old, his son Arphaxad was born. ¹¹After that, Shem lived 500 years and had other sons and daughters.

¹²When Arphaxad was 35 years old, his son Shelah was born. ¹³After that, Arphaxad lived 403 years and had other sons and daughters.

¹⁴When Shelah was 30 years old, his son Eber was born. ¹⁵After that, Shelah lived 403 years and had other sons and daughters.

¹⁶When Eber was 34 years old, his son Peleg was born. ¹⁷After that, Eber lived 430 years and had other sons and daughters.

¹⁸When Peleg was 30 years old, his son Reu was born. ¹⁹After that, Peleg lived 209 years and had other sons and daughters.

²⁰When Reu was 32 years old, his son Serug was born. ²¹After that, Reu lived 207 years and had other sons and daughters.

²²When Serug was 30 years old, his son Nahor was born. ²³After that, Serug lived 200 years and had other sons and daughters.

²⁴When Nahor was 29 years old, his son Terah was born. ²⁵After that, Nahor lived 119 years and had other sons and daughters.

²⁶After Terah was 70 years old, his sons Abram, Nahor, and Haran were born.

The Story of Terah's Family

²⁷This is the family history of Terah. Terah was the father of Abram, Nahor, and Haran. Haran was the father of Lot. ²⁸While his father, Terah, was still alive, Haran died in Ur in Babylonia, where he was born. ²⁹Abram and Nahor both married. Abram's wife was named Sarai, and Nahor's wife was named Milcah. She was the daughter of Haran, who was the father of both Milcah and Iscah. ³⁰Sarai was not able to have children.

³¹Terah took his son Abram, his grandson

11:9 Babel This name sounds like the Hebrew word for "confused."

Lot (Haran's son), and his daughter-in-law Sarai (Abram's wife) and moved out of Ur of Babylonia. They had planned to go to the land of Canaan, but when they reached the city of Haran, they settled there.

³²Terah lived to be 205 years old, and then he died in Haran.

God Calls Abram

12 The LORD said to Abram, "Leave your country, your relatives, and your father's family, and go to the land I will show you.

²I will make you a great nation,
  and I will bless you.
I will make you famous,
  and you will be a blessing to others.
³I will bless those who bless you,
  and I will place a curse on those who
    harm you.
And all the people on earth
  will be blessed through you."

⁴So Abram left Haran as the LORD had told him, and Lot went with him. At this time Abram was 75 years old. ⁵He took his wife Sarai, his nephew Lot, and everything they owned, as well as all the servants they had gotten in Haran. They set out from Haran, planning to go to the land of Canaan, and in time they arrived there.

⁶Abram traveled through that land as far as the great tree of Moreh at Shechem. The Canaanites were living in the land at that time. ⁷The LORD appeared to Abram and said, "I will give this land to your descendants." So Abram built an altar there to the LORD, who had appeared to him. ⁸Then he traveled from Shechem to the mountain east of Bethel and set up his tent there. Bethel was to the west, and Ai was to the east. There Abram built another altar to the LORD and worshiped him. ⁹After this, he traveled on toward southern Canaan.

Abram Goes to Egypt

¹⁰At this time there was not much food in the land, so Abram went down to Egypt to live because there was so little food. ¹¹Just before they arrived in Egypt, he said to his wife Sarai, "I know you are a very beautiful woman. ¹²When the Egyptians see you, they will say, 'This woman is his wife.' Then they will kill me but let you live. ¹³Tell them you are my sister so

that things will go well with me and I may be allowed to live because of you."

¹⁴When Abram came to Egypt, the Egyptians saw that Sarai was very beautiful. ¹⁵The Egyptian officers saw her and told the king of Egypt how beautiful she was. They took her to the king's palace, and ¹⁶the king was kind to Abram because he thought Abram was her brother. He gave Abram sheep, cattle, male and female donkeys, male and female servants, and camels.

¹⁷But the LORD sent terrible diseases on the king and all the people in his house because of Abram's wife Sarai. ¹⁸So the king sent for Abram and said, "What have you done to me? Why didn't you tell me Sarai was your wife? ¹⁹Why did you say, 'She is my sister' so that I made her my wife? Now, here is your wife. Take her and leave!" ²⁰Then the king commanded his men to make Abram leave Egypt; so Abram and his wife left with everything they owned.

PSALM 4:1–5

An Evening Prayer

For the director of music. With stringed instruments. A psalm of David.

4 Answer me when I pray to you,
  my God who does what is right.
  Make things easier for me when I am in
    trouble.
  Have mercy on me and hear my
    prayer.

²People, how long will you turn my honor
    into shame?
  How long will you love what is false and
    look for new lies?   *Selah*
³You know that the LORD has chosen for
    himself those who are loyal to him.
  The LORD listens when I pray to him.
⁴When you are angry, do not sin.
  Think about these things quietly
    as you go to bed.   *Selah*
⁵Do what is right as a sacrifice to the LORD
  and trust the LORD.

PROVERBS 1:28–33

²⁸"Then you will call to me,
  but I will not answer.

You will look for me,
    but you will not find me.
[29]It is because you rejected knowledge
    and did not choose to respect the
    LORD.
[30]You did not accept my advice,
    and you rejected my correction.
[31]So you will get what you deserve;
    you will get what you planned for
    others.
[32]Fools will die because they refuse to
    listen;
    they will be destroyed because they do
    not care.
[33]But those who listen to me will live in
    safety
    and be at peace, without fear of injury."

MATTHEW 5:27–48

Jesus Teaches About Sexual Sin

[27]"You have heard that it was said, 'You
must not be guilty of adultery.'[n] [28]But I tell
you that if anyone looks at a woman and
wants to sin sexually with her, in his mind he
has already done that sin with the woman.
[29]If your right eye causes you to sin, take it
out and throw it away. It is better to lose one
part of your body than to have your whole
body thrown into hell. [30]If your right hand
causes you to sin, cut it off and throw it away.
It is better to lose one part of your body than
for your whole body to go into hell.

Jesus Teaches About Divorce

[31]"It was also said, 'Anyone who divorces
his wife must give her a written divorce paper.'[n] [32]But I tell you that anyone who divorces his wife forces her to be guilty of
adultery. The only reason for a man to divorce his wife is if she has sexual relations
with another man. And anyone who marries
that divorced woman is guilty of adultery.

Make Promises Carefully

[33]"You have heard that it was said to our
people long ago, 'Don't break your promises,
but keep the promises you make to the
Lord.'[n] [34]But I tell you, never swear an oath.
Don't swear an oath using the name of
heaven, because heaven is God's throne.
[35]Don't swear an oath using the name of the
earth, because the earth belongs to God.
Don't swear an oath using the name of
Jerusalem, because that is the city of the
great King. [36]Don't even swear by your own
head, because you cannot make one hair on
your head become white or black. [37]Say only
yes if you mean yes, and no if you mean no.
If you say more than yes or no, it is from the
Evil One.

Don't Fight Back

[38]"You have heard that it was said, 'An eye
for an eye, and a tooth for a tooth.'[n] [39]But I
tell you, don't stand up against an evil person. If someone slaps you on the right cheek,
turn to him the other cheek also. [40]If someone wants to sue you in court and take your
shirt, let him have your coat also. [41]If someone forces you to go with him one mile, go
with him two miles. [42]If a person asks you
for something, give it to him. Don't refuse to
give to someone who wants to borrow from
you.

Love All People

[43]"You have heard that it was said, 'Love
your neighbor[n] and hate your enemies.'
[44]But I say to you, love your enemies. Pray
for those who hurt you.[n] [45]If you do this,
you will be true children of your Father in
heaven. He causes the sun to rise on good
people and on evil people, and he sends
rain to those who do right and to those who
do wrong. [46]If you love only the people who
love you, you will get no reward. Even the
tax collectors do that. [47]And if you are nice
only to your friends, you are no better than
other people. Even those who don't know
God are nice to their friends. [48]So you must
be perfect, just as your Father in heaven is
perfect.

5:27 'You . . . adultery.' Quotation from Exodus 20:14; Deuteronomy 5:18.   **5:31 'Anyone . . . divorce paper.'** Quotation from
Deuteronomy 24:1.   **5:33 'Don't . . . Lord.'** This refers to Leviticus 19:12; Numbers 30:2; Deuteronomy 23:21.   **5:38 'An eye . . .
tooth.'** Quotation from Exodus 21:24; Leviticus 24:20; Deuteronomy 19:21.   **5:43 'Love your neighbor'** Quotation from
Leviticus 19:18.   **5:44 you** Some Greek copies continue, "Bless those who curse you, do good to those who hate you." Compare Luke 6:28.

JANUARY 7

GENESIS 13:1—14:24

Abram and Lot Separate

13 So Abram, his wife, and Lot left Egypt, taking everything they owned, and traveled to southern Canaan. ²Abram was very rich in cattle, silver, and gold.

³He left southern Canaan and went back to Bethel where he had camped before, between Bethel and Ai, ⁴and where he had built an altar. So he worshiped the LORD there.

⁵During this time Lot was traveling with Abram, and Lot also had flocks, herds, and tents. ⁶Abram and Lot had so many animals that the land could not support both of them together, ⁷so Abram's herdsmen and Lot's herdsmen began to argue. The Canaanites and the Perizzites were living in the land at this time.

⁸Abram said to Lot, "There should be no arguing between you and me, or between your herdsmen and mine, because we are brothers. ⁹We should separate. The whole land is there in front of you. If you go to the left, I will go to the right. If you go to the right, I will go to the left."

¹⁰Lot looked all around and saw the whole Jordan Valley and that there was much water there. It was like the LORD's garden, like the land of Egypt in the direction of Zoar. (This was before the LORD destroyed Sodom and Gomorrah.) ¹¹So Lot chose to move east and live in the Jordan Valley. In this way Abram and Lot separated. ¹²Abram lived in the land of Canaan, but Lot lived among the cities in the Jordan Valley, very near to Sodom. ¹³Now the people of Sodom were very evil and were always sinning against the LORD.

¹⁴After Lot left, the LORD said to Abram, "Look all around you—to the north and south and east and west. ¹⁵All this land that you see I will give to you and your descendants forever. ¹⁶I will make your descendants as many as the dust of the earth. If anyone could count the dust on the earth, he could count your people. ¹⁷Get up! Walk

through all this land because I am now giving it to you."

¹⁸So Abram moved his tents and went to live near the great trees of Mamre at the city of Hebron. There he built an altar to the LORD.

Lot Is Captured

14 Now Amraphel was king of Babylonia, Arioch was king of Ellasar, Kedorlaomer was king of Elam, and Tidal was king of Goiim. ²All these kings went to war against several other kings: Bera king of Sodom, Birsha king of Gomorrah, Shinab king of Admah, Shemeber king of Zeboiim, and the king of Bela. (Bela is also called Zoar.)

³These kings who were attacked united their armies in the Valley of Siddim (now the Dead Sea). ⁴They had served Kedorlaomer for twelve years, but in the thirteenth year, they all turned against him. ⁵Then in the fourteenth year, Kedorlaomer and the kings with him came and defeated the Rephaites in Ashteroth Karnaim, the Zuzites in Ham, and the Emites in Shaveh Kiriathaim. ⁶They also defeated the Horites in the mountains of Edom to El Paran (near the desert). ⁷Then they turned back and went to En Mishpat (that is, Kadesh). They defeated all the Amalekites, as well as the Amorites who lived in Hazazon Tamar.

⁸At that time the kings of Sodom, Gomorrah, Admah, Zeboiim, and Bela went out to fight in the Valley of Siddim. (Bela is called Zoar.) ⁹They fought against Kedorlaomer king of Elam, Tidal king of Goiim, Amraphel king of Babylonia, and Arioch king of Ellasar—four kings fighting against five. ¹⁰There were many tar pits in the Valley of Siddim. When the kings of Sodom and Gomorrah and their armies ran away, some of the soldiers fell into the tar pits, but the others ran away to the mountains.

¹¹Now Kedorlaomer and his armies took everything the people of Sodom and Gomorrah owned, including their food. ¹²They took Lot, Abram's nephew who was living in Sodom, and everything he owned. Then they left. ¹³One of the men who was not captured

went to Abram, the Hebrew, and told him what had happened. At that time Abram was camped near the great trees of Mamre the Amorite. Mamre was a brother of Eshcol and Aner, and they had all made an agreement to help Abram.

Abram Rescues Lot

¹⁴When Abram learned that Lot had been captured, he called out his 318 trained men who had been born in his camp. He led the men and chased the enemy all the way to the town of Dan. ¹⁵That night he divided his men into groups, and they made a surprise attack against the enemy. They chased them all the way to Hobah, north of Damascus. ¹⁶Then Abram brought back everything the enemy had stolen, the women and the other people, and Lot, and everything Lot owned.

¹⁷After defeating Kedorlaomer and the kings who were with him, Abram went home. As he was returning, the king of Sodom came out to meet him in the Valley of Shaveh (now called King's Valley).

¹⁸Melchizedek king of Salem brought out bread and wine. He was a priest for God Most High ¹⁹and blessed Abram, saying,

"Abram, may you be blessed by God
  Most High,
  the God who made heaven and earth.
²⁰And we praise God Most High,
  who has helped you to defeat your
  enemies."

Then Abram gave Melchizedek a tenth of everything he had brought back from the battle.

²¹The king of Sodom said to Abram, "You may keep all these things for yourself. Just give me my people who were captured."

²²But Abram said to the king of Sodom, "I make a promise to the LORD, the God Most High, who made heaven and earth. ²³I promise that I will not keep anything that is yours. I will not keep even a thread or a sandal strap so that you cannot say, 'I made Abram rich.' ²⁴I will keep nothing but the food my young men have eaten. But give Aner, Eshcol, and Mamre their share of what we won, because they went with me into battle."

PSALM 4:6–8

⁶Many people ask,
  "Who will give us anything good?"
LORD, be kind to us.
⁷But you have made me very happy,
  happier than they are,
  even with all their grain and new
  wine.
⁸I go to bed and sleep in peace,
  because, LORD, only you keep me safe.

PROVERBS 2:1–5

Rewards of Wisdom

2 My child, listen to what I say
  and remember what I command
    you.
²Listen carefully to wisdom;
  set your mind on understanding.
³Cry out for wisdom,
  and beg for understanding.
⁴Search for it like silver,
  and hunt for it like hidden treasure.
⁵Then you will understand respect for the
  LORD,
  and you will find that you know God.

MATTHEW 6:1–18

Jesus Teaches About Giving

6 "Be careful! When you do good things, don't do them in front of people to be seen by them. If you do that, you will have no reward from your Father in heaven.

²"When you give to the poor, don't be like the hypocrites. They blow trumpets in the synagogues and on the streets so that people will see them and honor them. I tell you the truth, those hypocrites already have their full reward. ³So when you give to the poor, don't let anyone know what you are doing. ⁴Your giving should be done in secret. Your Father can see what is done in secret, and he will reward you.

Jesus Teaches About Prayer

⁵"When you pray, don't be like the hypocrites. They love to stand in the synagogues and on the street corners and pray so people will see them. I tell you the truth, they already have their full reward. ⁶When you pray,

you should go into your room and close the door and pray to your Father who cannot be seen. Your Father can see what is done in secret, and he will reward you.

7"And when you pray, don't be like those people who don't know God. They continue saying things that mean nothing, thinking that God will hear them because of their many words. 8Don't be like them, because your Father knows the things you need before you ask him. 9So when you pray, you should pray like this:

'Our Father in heaven,
  may your name always be kept holy.
10May your kingdom come
  and what you want to be done,
  here on earth as it is in heaven.
11Give us the food we need for each day.
12Forgive us for our sins,
  just as we have forgiven those who
    sinned against us.
13And do not cause us to be tempted,
  but save us from the Evil One.' [The
    kingdom, the power, and the glory
    are yours forever. Amen.]*n*

14Yes, if you forgive others for their sins, your Father in heaven will also forgive you for your sins. 15But if you don't forgive others, your Father in heaven will not forgive your sins.

Jesus Teaches About Worship

16"When you fast,*n* don't put on a sad face like the hypocrites. They make their faces look sad to show people they are fasting. I tell you the truth, those hypocrites already have their full reward. 17So when you fast, comb your hair and wash your face. 18Then people will not know that you are fasting, but your Father, whom you cannot see, will see you. Your Father sees what is done in secret, and he will reward you.

JANUARY 8

GENESIS 15:1—16:16

God's Agreement with Abram

15After these things happened, the LORD spoke his word to Abram in a vision: "Abram, don't be afraid. I will defend you, and I will give you a great reward."

2But Abram said, "Lord GOD, what can you give me? I have no son, so my slave Eliezer from Damascus will get everything I own after I die." 3Abram said, "Look, you have given me no son, so a slave born in my house will inherit everything I have."

4Then the LORD spoke his word to Abram: "He will not be the one to inherit what you have. You will have a son of your own who will inherit what you have."

5Then God led Abram outside and said, "Look at the sky. There are so many stars you cannot count them. Your descendants also will be too many to count."

6Abram believed the LORD. And the LORD accepted Abram's faith, and that faith made him right with God.

7God said to Abram, "I am the LORD who led you out of Ur of Babylonia so that I could give you this land to own."

8But Abram said, "Lord GOD, how can I be sure that I will own this land?"

9The LORD said to Abram, "Bring me a three-year-old cow, a three-year-old goat, a three-year-old male sheep, a dove, and a young pigeon."

10Abram brought them all to God. Then Abram killed the animals and cut each of them into two pieces, laying each half opposite the other half. But he did not cut the birds in half. 11Later, large birds flew down to eat the animals, but Abram chased them away.

12As the sun was going down, Abram fell into a deep sleep. While he was asleep, a very terrible darkness came. 13Then the LORD said

6:13 The . . . Amen. Some Greek copies do not contain the bracketed text.   **6:16 fast** The people would give up eating for a special time of prayer and worship to God. It was also done to show sadness and disappointment.

to Abram, "You can be sure that your descendants will be strangers and travel in a land they don't own. The people there will make them slaves and be cruel to them for four hundred years. [14]But I will punish the nation where they are slaves. Then your descendants will leave that land, taking great wealth with them. [15]And you, Abram, will die in peace and will be buried at an old age. [16]After your great-great-grandchildren are born, your people will come to this land again. It will take that long, because I am not yet going to punish the Amorites for their evil behavior."

[17]After the sun went down, it was very dark. Suddenly a smoking firepot and a blazing torch passed between the halves of the dead animals.[n] [18]So on that day the LORD made an agreement with Abram and said, "I will give to your descendants the land between the river of Egypt and the great river Euphrates. [19]This is the land of the Kenites, Kenizzites, Kadmonites, [20]Hittites, Perizzites, Rephaites, [21]Amorites, Canaanites, Girgashites, and Jebusites."

Ishmael Is Born

16Sarai, Abram's wife, had no children, but she had a slave girl from Egypt named Hagar. [2]Sarai said to Abram, "Look, the LORD has not allowed me to have children, so have sexual relations with my slave girl. If she has a child, maybe I can have my own family through her."

Abram did what Sarai said. [3]It was after he had lived ten years in Canaan that Sarai gave Hagar to her husband Abram. (Hagar was her slave girl from Egypt.)

[4]Abram had sexual relations with Hagar, and she became pregnant. When Hagar learned she was pregnant, she began to treat her mistress Sarai badly. [5]Then Sarai said to Abram, "This is your fault. I gave my slave girl to you, and when she became pregnant, she began to treat me badly. Let the LORD decide who is right—you or me."

[6]But Abram said to Sarai, "You are Hagar's mistress. Do anything you want to her." Then

Sarai was hard on Hagar, and Hagar ran away.

[7]The angel of the LORD found Hagar beside a spring of water in the desert, by the road to Shur. [8]The angel said, "Hagar, Sarai's slave girl, where have you come from? Where are you going?"

Hagar answered, "I am running away from my mistress Sarai."

[9]The angel of the LORD said to her, "Go home to your mistress and obey her." [10]The angel also said, "I will give you so many descendants they cannot be counted."

[11]The angel added,

"You are now pregnant,
  and you will have a son.
You will name him Ishmael,[n]
  because the LORD has heard your cries.
[12]Ishmael will be like a wild donkey.
  He will be against everyone,
  and everyone will be against him.
He will attack all his brothers."

[13]The slave girl gave a name to the LORD who spoke to her: "You are 'God who sees me,'" because she said to herself, "Have I really seen God who sees me?" [14]So the well there, between Kadesh and Bered, was called Beer Lahai Roi.[n]

[15]Hagar gave birth to a son for Abram, and Abram named him Ishmael. [16]Abram was eighty-six years old when Hagar gave birth to Ishmael.

PSALM 5:1-6

A Morning Prayer for Protection

For the director of music. For flutes. A psalm of David.

5LORD, listen to my words.
  Understand my sadness.
[2]Listen to my cry for help, my King and
    my God,
  because I pray to you.
[3]LORD, every morning you hear my voice.
  Every morning, I tell you what I need,
  and I wait for your answer.

[4]You are not a God who is pleased with
    the wicked;

15:17 passed . . . animals This showed that God sealed the agreement between himself and Abram. **16:11 Ishmael** The Hebrew words for "Ishmael" and "has heard" sound similar. **16:14 Beer Lahai Roi** This means "the well of the Living One who sees me."

you do not live with those who do evil.
⁵Those people who make fun of you
    cannot stand before you.
You hate all those who do evil.
⁶You destroy liars;
    the LORD hates those who kill and trick
        others.

PROVERBS 2:6-8

⁶Only the LORD gives wisdom;
    he gives knowledge and understanding.
⁷He stores up wisdom for those who are
        honest.
Like a shield he protects the innocent.
⁸He makes sure that justice is done,
    and he protects those who are loyal to
        him.

MATTHEW 6:19-34

God Is More Important than Money

¹⁹"Don't store treasures for yourselves here on earth where moths and rust will destroy them and thieves can break in and steal them. ²⁰But store your treasures in heaven where they cannot be destroyed by moths or rust and where thieves cannot break in and steal them. ²¹Your heart will be where your treasure is.

²²"The eye is a light for the body. If your eyes are good, your whole body will be full of light. ²³But if your eyes are evil, your whole body will be full of darkness. And if the only light you have is really darkness, then you have the worst darkness.

²⁴"No one can serve two masters. The person will hate one master and love the other, or will follow one master and refuse to follow the other. You cannot serve both God and worldly riches.

Don't Worry

²⁵"So I tell you, don't worry about the food or drink you need to live, or about the clothes you need for your body. Life is more than food, and the body is more than clothes. ²⁶Look at the birds in the air. They don't plant or harvest or store food in barns, but your heavenly Father feeds them. And you know that you are worth much more than the birds. ²⁷You cannot add any time to your life by worrying about it.

²⁸"And why do you worry about clothes? Look at how the lilies in the field grow. They don't work or make clothes for themselves. ²⁹But I tell you that even Solomon with his riches was not dressed as beautifully as one of these flowers. ³⁰God clothes the grass in the field, which is alive today but tomorrow is thrown into the fire. So you can be even more sure that God will clothe you. Don't have so little faith! ³¹Don't worry and say, 'What will we eat?' or 'What will we drink?' or 'What will we wear?' ³²The people who don't know God keep trying to get these things, and your Father in heaven knows you need them. ³³Seek first God's kingdom and what God wants. Then all your other needs will be met as well. ³⁴So don't worry about tomorrow, because tomorrow will have its own worries. Each day has enough trouble of its own.

JANUARY 9

GENESIS 17:1—18:33

Proof of the Agreement

17 When Abram was ninety-nine years old, the LORD appeared to him and said, "I am God Almighty. Obey me and do what is right. ²I will make an agreement between us, and I will make you the ancestor of many people."

³Then Abram bowed facedown on the ground. God said to him, ⁴"I am making my agreement with you: I will make you the father of many nations. ⁵I am changing your name from Abram[n] to Abraham[n] because I

17:5 Abram This name means "honored father."   **17:5 Abraham** The end of the Hebrew word for "Abraham" sounds like the beginning of the Hebrew word for "many."

am making you a father of many nations. [6]I will give you many descendants. New nations will be born from you, and kings will come from you. [7]And I will make an agreement between me and you and all your descendants from now on: I will be your God and the God of all your descendants. [8]You live in the land of Canaan now as a stranger, but I will give you and your descendants all this land forever. And I will be the God of your descendants."

[9]Then God said to Abraham, "You and your descendants must keep this agreement from now on. [10]This is my agreement with you and all your descendants, which you must obey: Every male among you must be circumcised. [11]Cut away your foreskin to show that you are prepared to follow the agreement between me and you. [12]From now on when a baby boy is eight days old, you will circumcise him. This includes any boy born among your people or any who is your slave, who is not one of your descendants. [13]Circumcise every baby boy whether he is born in your family or bought as a slave. Your bodies will be marked to show that you are part of my agreement that lasts forever. [14]Any male who is not circumcised will be cut off from his people, because he has broken my agreement."

Isaac—the Promised Son

[15]God said to Abraham, "I will change the name of Sarai,[n] your wife, to Sarah.[n] [16]I will bless her and give her a son, and you will be the father. She will be the mother of many nations. Kings of nations will come from her."

[17]Abraham bowed facedown on the ground and laughed. He said to himself, "Can a man have a child when he is a hundred years old? Can Sarah give birth to a child when she is ninety?" [18]Then Abraham said to God, "Please let Ishmael be the son you promised."

[19]God said, "No, Sarah your wife will have a son, and you will name him Isaac.[n] I will make my agreement with him to be an agreement that continues forever with all his descendants.

[20]"As for Ishmael, I have heard you. I will bless him and give him many descendants. And I will cause their numbers to grow greatly. He will be the father of twelve great leaders, and I will make him into a great nation. [21]But I will make my agreement with Isaac, the son whom Sarah will have at this same time next year." [22]After God finished talking with Abraham, God rose and left him.

[23]Then Abraham gathered Ishmael, all the males born in his camp, and the slaves he had bought. So that day Abraham circumcised every man and boy in his camp as God had told him to do. [24]Abraham was ninety-nine years old when he was circumcised. [25]And Ishmael, his son, was thirteen years old when he was circumcised. [26]Abraham and his son were circumcised on the same day. [27]Also on that day all the men in Abraham's camp were circumcised, including all those born in his camp and all the slaves he had bought from other nations.

The Three Visitors

18Later, the LORD again appeared to Abraham near the great trees of Mamre. Abraham was sitting at the entrance of his tent during the hottest part of the day. [2]He looked up and saw three men standing near him. When Abraham saw them, he ran from his tent to meet them. He bowed facedown on the ground before them [3]and said, "Sir, if you think well of me, please stay awhile with me, your servant. [4]I will bring some water so all of you can wash your feet. You may rest under the tree, [5]and I will get some bread for you so you can regain your strength. Then you may continue your journey."

The three men said, "That is fine. Do as you said."

[6]Abraham hurried to the tent where Sarah was and said to her, "Hurry, prepare twenty quarts of fine flour, and make it into loaves of bread." [7]Then Abraham ran to his herd and took one of his best calves. He gave it to a servant, who hurried to kill it and to prepare it for food. [8]Abraham gave the three men the calf that had been cooked and milk

---

17:15 Sarai An Aramaic name meaning "princess." **17:15 Sarah** A Hebrew name meaning "princess." **17:19 Isaac** The Hebrew words for "he laughed" (v. 17) and "Isaac" sound the same.

curds and milk. While they ate, he stood under the tree near them.

⁹The men asked Abraham, "Where is your wife Sarah?"

"There, in the tent," said Abraham.

¹⁰Then the LORD said, "I will certainly return to you about this time a year from now. At that time your wife Sarah will have a son."

Sarah was listening at the entrance of the tent which was behind him. ¹¹Abraham and Sarah were very old. Since Sarah was past the age when women normally have children, ¹²she laughed to herself, "My husband and I are too old to have a baby."

¹³Then the LORD said to Abraham, "Why did Sarah laugh? Why did she say, 'I am too old to have a baby'? ¹⁴Is anything too hard for the LORD? No! I will return to you at the right time a year from now, and Sarah will have a son."

¹⁵Sarah was afraid, so she lied and said, "I didn't laugh."

But the LORD said, "No. You did laugh."

¹⁶Then the men got up to leave and started out toward Sodom. Abraham walked along with them a short time to send them on their way.

Abraham's Bargain with God

¹⁷The LORD said, "Should I tell Abraham what I am going to do now? ¹⁸Abraham's children will certainly become a great and powerful nation, and all nations on earth will be blessed through him. ¹⁹I have chosen him so he would command his children and his descendants to live the way the LORD wants them to, to live right and be fair. Then I, the LORD, will give Abraham what I promised him."

²⁰Then the LORD said, "I have heard many complaints against the people of Sodom and Gomorrah. They are very evil. ²¹I will go down and see if they are as bad as I have heard. If not, I will know."

²²So the men turned and went toward Sodom, but Abraham stood there before the LORD. ²³Then Abraham approached him and asked, "Do you plan to destroy the good people along with the evil ones? ²⁴What if there are fifty good people in that city? Will you still destroy it? Surely you will save the city for the fifty good people living there. ²⁵Surely you will not destroy the good people along with the evil ones; then they would be treated the same. You are the judge of all the earth. Won't you do what is right?"

²⁶The LORD said, "If I find fifty good people in the city of Sodom, I will save the whole city because of them."

²⁷Then Abraham said, "Though I am only dust and ashes, I have been brave to speak to the Lord. ²⁸What if there are only forty-five good people in the city? Will you destroy the whole city for the lack of five good people?"

The LORD said, "If I find forty-five there, I will not destroy the city."

²⁹Again Abraham said to him, "If you find only forty good people there, will you destroy the city?"

The LORD said, "If I find forty, I will not destroy it."

³⁰Then Abraham said, "Lord, please don't be angry with me, but let me ask you this. If you find only thirty good people in the city, will you destroy it?"

He said, "If I find thirty good people there, I will not destroy the city."

³¹Then Abraham said, "I have been brave to speak to the Lord. But what if there are twenty good people in the city?"

He answered, "If I find twenty there, I will not destroy the city."

³²Then Abraham said, "Lord, please don't be angry with me, but let me bother you this one last time. What if you find ten there?"

He said, "If I find ten there, I will not destroy it."

³³When the LORD finished speaking to Abraham, he left, and Abraham returned home.

PSALM 5:7–12

⁷Because of your great love,
  I can come into your Temple.
Because I fear and respect you,
  I can worship in your holy Temple.

⁸LORD, since I have many enemies,
  show me the right thing to do.
  Show me clearly how you want me to
    live.

⁹My enemies' mouths do not tell the truth;
  in their hearts they want to destroy
    others.

Their throats are like open graves;
　they use their tongues for telling lies.
[10]God, declare them guilty!
　Let them fall into their own traps.
Send them away because their sins are
　many;
　they have turned against you.

[11]But let everyone who trusts you be
　happy;
　let them sing glad songs forever.
Protect those who love you
　and who are happy because of you.
[12]LORD, you bless who do what is
　right;
　you protect them like a soldier's shield.

PROVERBS 2:9–22

[9]Then you will understand what is honest
　and fair
　and what is the good and right thing to
　do.
[10]Wisdom will come into your mind,
　and knowledge will be pleasing to you.
[11]Good sense will protect you;
　understanding will guard you.
[12]It will keep you from the wicked,
　from those whose words are bad,
[13]who don't do what is right
　but what is evil.
[14]They enjoy doing wrong
　and are happy to do what is crooked
　and evil.
[15]What they do is wrong,
　and their ways are dishonest.

[16]It will save you from the unfaithful wife
　who tries to lead you into adultery with
　pleasing words.
[17]She leaves the husband she married
　when she was young.
　She ignores the promise she made
　before God.
[18]Her house is on the way to death;
　those who took that path are now all
　dead.
[19]No one who goes to her comes back
　or walks the path of life again.

[20]But wisdom will help you be good
　and do what is right.

[21]Those who are honest will live in the land,
　and those who are innocent will remain
　in it.
[22]But the wicked will be removed from the
　land,
　and the unfaithful will be thrown out of
　it.

MATTHEW 7:1–29

Be Careful About Judging Others

7 [1]"Don't judge others, or you will be judged.
[2]You will be judged in the same way that
you judge others, and the amount you give to
others will be given to you.

[3]"Why do you notice the little piece of
dust in your friend's eye, but you don't notice
the big piece of wood in your own eye? [4]How
can you say to your friend, 'Let me take that
little piece of dust out of your eye'? Look at
yourself! You still have that big piece of wood
in your own eye. [5]You hypocrite! First, take
the wood out of your own eye. Then you will
see clearly to take the dust out of your
friend's eye.

[6]"Don't give holy things to dogs, and don't
throw your pearls before pigs. Pigs will only
trample on them, and dogs will turn to attack you.

Ask God for What You Need

[7]"Ask, and God will give to you. Search,
and you will find. Knock, and the door will
open for you. [8]Yes, everyone who asks will
receive. Everyone who searches will find.
And everyone who knocks will have the door
opened.

[9]"If your children ask for bread, which of
you would give them a stone? [10]Or if your
children ask for a fish, would you give them
a snake? [11]Even though you are bad, you
know how to give good gifts to your children. How much more your heavenly Father
will give good things to those who ask him!

The Most Important Rule

[12]"Do to others what you want them to do
to you. This is the meaning of the law of
Moses and the teaching of the prophets.

The Way to Heaven Is Hard

[13]"Enter through the narrow gate. The
gate is wide and the road is wide that leads

to hell, and many people enter through that gate. [14]But the gate is small and the road is narrow that leads to true life. Only a few people find that road.

People Know You by Your Actions

[15]"Be careful of false prophets. They come to you looking gentle like sheep, but they are really dangerous like wolves. [16]You will know these people by what they do. Grapes don't come from thornbushes, and figs don't come from thorny weeds. [17]In the same way, every good tree produces good fruit, but a bad tree produces bad fruit. [18]A good tree cannot produce bad fruit, and a bad tree cannot produce good fruit. [19]Every tree that does not produce good fruit is cut down and thrown into the fire. [20]In the same way, you will know these false prophets by what they do.

[21]"Not all those who say 'You are our Lord' will enter the kingdom of heaven. The only people who will enter the kingdom of heaven are those who do what my Father in heaven wants. [22]On the last day many people will say to me, 'Lord, Lord, we spoke for you, and through you we forced out demons and did many miracles.' [23]Then I will tell them clearly, 'Get away from me, you who do evil. I never knew you.'

Two Kinds of People

[24]"Everyone who hears my words and obeys them is like a wise man who built his house on rock. [25]It rained hard, the floods came, and the winds blew and hit that house. But it did not fall, because it was built on rock. [26]Everyone who hears my words and does not obey them is like a foolish man who built his house on sand. [27]It rained hard, the floods came, and the winds blew and hit that house, and it fell with a big crash."

[28]When Jesus finished saying these things, the people were amazed at his teaching, [29]because he did not teach like their teachers of the law. He taught like a person who had authority.

JANUARY 10

GENESIS 19:1—20:18

Lot Leaves Sodom

19 The two angels came to Sodom in the evening as Lot was sitting near the city gate. When he saw them, he got up and went to them and bowed facedown on the ground. [2]Lot said, "Sirs, please come to my house and spend the night. There you can wash your feet, and then tomorrow you may continue your journey."

The angels answered, "No, we will spend the night in the city's public square."

[3]But Lot begged them to come, so they agreed and went to his house. Then Lot prepared a meal for them. He baked bread without yeast, and they ate it.

[4]Before bedtime, men both young and old and from every part of Sodom surrounded Lot's house. [5]They called to Lot, "Where are the two men who came to you tonight? Bring them out to us so we can have sexual relations with them."

[6]Lot went outside to them, closing the door behind him. [7]He said, "No, my brothers! Do not do this evil thing. [8]Look! I have two daughters who have never slept with a man. I will give them to you, and you may do anything you want with them. But please don't do anything to these men. They have come to my house, and I must protect them."

[9]The men around the house answered, "Move out of the way!" Then they said to each other, "This man Lot came to our city as a stranger, and now he wants to tell us what to do!" They said to Lot, "We will do worse things to you than to them." They started pushing him back and were ready to break down the door.

[10]But the two men staying with Lot opened the door, pulled him back inside the house, and then closed the door. [11]They struck those outside the door with blindness, so the men, both young and old, could not find the door.

¹²The two men said to Lot, "Do you have any other relatives in this city? Do you have any sons-in-law, sons, daughters, or any other relatives? If you do, tell them to leave now, ¹³because we are about to destroy this city. The LORD has heard of all the evil that is here, so he has sent us to destroy it."

¹⁴So Lot went out and said to his future sons-in-law who were pledged to marry his daughters, "Hurry and leave this city! The LORD is about to destroy it!" But they thought Lot was joking.

¹⁵At dawn the next morning, the angels begged Lot to hurry. They said, "Go! Take your wife and your two daughters with you so you will not be destroyed when the city is punished."

¹⁶But Lot delayed. So the two men took the hands of Lot, his wife, and his two daughters and led them safely out of the city. So the LORD was merciful to Lot and his family. ¹⁷After they brought them out of the city, one of the men said, "Run for your lives! Don't look back or stop anywhere in the valley. Run to the mountains, or you will be destroyed."

¹⁸But Lot said to one of them, "Sir, please don't force me to go so far! ¹⁹You have been merciful and kind to me and have saved my life. But I can't run to the mountains. The disaster will catch me, and I will die. ²⁰Look, that little town over there is not too far away. Let me run there. It's really just a little town, and I'll be safe there."

²¹The angel said to Lot, "Very well, I will allow you to do this also. I will not destroy that town. ²²But run there fast, because I cannot destroy Sodom until you are safely in that town." (That town is named Zoar,ⁿ because it is little.)

Sodom and Gomorrah Are Destroyed

²³The sun had already come up when Lot entered Zoar. ²⁴The LORD sent a rain of burning sulfur down from the sky on Sodom and Gomorrah ²⁵and destroyed those cities. He also destroyed the whole Jordan Valley, everyone living in the cities, and even all the plants.

²⁶At that point Lot's wife looked back. When she did, she became a pillar of salt.

²⁷Early the next morning, Abraham got up and went to the place where he had stood before the LORD. ²⁸He looked down toward Sodom and Gomorrah and all the Jordan Valley and saw smoke rising from the land, like smoke from a furnace.

²⁹God destroyed the cities in the valley, but he remembered what Abraham had asked. So God saved Lot's life, but he destroyed the city where Lot had lived.

Lot and His Daughters

³⁰Lot was afraid to continue living in Zoar, so he and his two daughters went to live in the mountains in a cave. ³¹One day the older daughter said to the younger, "Our father is old. Everywhere on the earth women and men marry, but there are no men around here for us to marry. ³²Let's get our father drunk and have sexual relations with him. We can use him to have children and continue our family."

³³That night the two girls got their father drunk, and the older daughter went and had sexual relations with him. But Lot did not know when she lay down or when she got up. ³⁴The next day the older daughter said to the younger, "Last night I had sexual relations with my father. Let's get him drunk again tonight so you can go and have sexual relations with him, too. In this way we can use our father to have children to continue our family." ³⁵So that night they got their father drunk again, and the younger daughter went and had sexual relations with him. Again, Lot did not know when she lay down or when she got up.

³⁶So both of Lot's daughters became pregnant by their father. ³⁷The older daughter gave birth to a son and named him Moab. He is the ancestor of all the Moabite people who are still living today. ³⁸The younger daughter also gave birth to a son and named him Ben-Ammi. He is the father of all the Ammonite people who are still living today.

Abraham Tricks Abimelech

20Abraham left Hebron and traveled to southern Canaan where he stayed awhile between Kadesh and Shur. When he moved to Gerar, [2]he told people that his wife Sarah was his sister. Abimelech king of Gerar heard this, so he sent some servants to take her. [3]But one night God spoke to Abimelech in a dream and said, "You will die. The woman you took is married."

[4]But Abimelech had not gone near Sarah, so he said, "Lord, would you destroy an innocent nation? [5]Abraham himself told me, 'This woman is my sister,' and she also said, 'He is my brother.' I am innocent. I did not know I was doing anything wrong."

[6]Then God said to Abimelech in the dream, "Yes, I know you did not realize what you were doing. So I did not allow you to sin against me and touch her. [7]Give Abraham his wife back. He is a prophet. He will pray for you, and you will not die. But if you do not give Sarah back, you and all your family will surely die."

[8]So early the next morning, Abimelech called all his officers and told them everything that had happened in the dream. They were very afraid. [9]Then Abimelech called Abraham to him and said, "What have you done to us? What wrong did I do against you? Why did you bring this trouble to my kingdom? You should not have done these things to me. [10]What were you thinking that caused you to do this?"

[11]Then Abraham answered, "I thought no one in this place respected God and that someone would kill me to get Sarah. [12]And it is true that she is my sister. She is the daughter of my father, but she is not the daughter of my mother. [13]When God told me to leave my father's house and wander in many different places, I told Sarah, 'You must do a special favor for me. Everywhere we go tell people I am your brother.'"

[14]Then Abimelech gave Abraham some sheep, cattle, and male and female slaves. He also gave Sarah, Abraham's wife, back to him [15]and said, "Look around you at my land. You may live anywhere you want."

[16]Abimelech said to Sarah, "I gave your brother Abraham twenty-five pounds of silver to make up for any wrong that people may think about you. I want everyone to know that you are innocent."

[17]Then Abraham prayed to God, and God healed Abimelech, his wife, and his servant girls so they could have children. [18]The LORD had kept all the women in Abimelech's house from having children as a punishment on Abimelech for taking Abraham's wife Sarah.

PSALM 6:1–5

A Prayer for Mercy in Troubled Times

For the director of music. With stringed instruments. Upon the sheminith. A psalm of David.

6 LORD, don't correct me when you are angry;
   don't punish me when you are very angry.
[2]LORD, have mercy on me because I am weak.
   Heal me, LORD, because my bones ache.
[3]I am very upset.
   LORD, how long will it be?

[4]LORD, return and save me;
   save me because of your kindness.
[5]Dead people don't remember you;
   those in the grave don't praise you.

PROVERBS 3:1–4

Advice to Children

3 My child, do not forget my teaching,
   but keep my commands in mind.
[2]Then you will live a long time,
   and your life will be successful.

[3]Don't ever forget kindness and truth.
   Wear them like a necklace.
   Write them on your heart as if on a tablet.
[4]Then you will be respected
   and will please both God and people.

MATTHEW 8:1–17

Jesus Heals a Sick Man

8 When Jesus came down from the hill, great crowds followed him. [2]Then a man with a skin disease came to Jesus. The man bowed down before him and said, "Lord, you can heal me if you will."

[3]Jesus reached out his hand and touched the man and said, "I will. Be healed!" And

immediately the man was healed from his disease. [4]Then Jesus said to him, "Don't tell anyone about this. But go and show yourself to the priest[n] and offer the gift Moses commanded[n] for people who are made well. This will show the people what I have done."

Jesus Heals a Soldier's Servant

[5]When Jesus entered the city of Capernaum, an army officer came to him, begging for help. [6]The officer said, "Lord, my servant is at home in bed. He can't move his body and is in much pain."

[7]Jesus said to the officer, "I will go and heal him."

[8]The officer answered, "Lord, I am not worthy for you to come into my house. You only need to command it, and my servant will be healed. [9]I, too, am a man under the authority of others, and I have soldiers under my command. I tell one soldier, 'Go,' and he goes. I tell another soldier, 'Come,' and he comes. I say to my servant, 'Do this,' and my servant does it."

[10]When Jesus heard this, he was amazed. He said to those who were following him, "I tell you the truth, this is the greatest faith I have found, even in Israel. [11]Many people will come from the east and from the west and will sit and eat with Abraham, Isaac, and Jacob in the kingdom of heaven. [12]But those people who should be in the kingdom will be thrown outside into the darkness, where people will cry and grind their teeth with pain."

[13]Then Jesus said to the officer, "Go home. Your servant will be healed just as you believed he would." And his servant was healed that same hour.

Jesus Heals Many People

[14]When Jesus went to Peter's house, he saw that Peter's mother-in-law was sick in bed with a fever. [15]Jesus touched her hand, and the fever left her. Then she stood up and began to serve Jesus.

[16]That evening people brought to Jesus many who had demons. Jesus spoke and the demons left them, and he healed all the sick. [17]He did these things to bring about what Isaiah the prophet had said:

"He took our suffering on him
  and carried our diseases."   *Isaiah 53:4*

JANUARY 11

GENESIS 21:1—22:24

A Baby for Sarah

21 The LORD cared for Sarah as he had said and did for her what he had promised. [2]Sarah became pregnant and gave birth to a son for Abraham in his old age. Everything happened at the time God had said it would. [3]Abraham named his son Isaac, the son Sarah gave birth to. [4]He circumcised Isaac when he was eight days old as God had commanded.

[5]Abraham was one hundred years old when his son Isaac was born. [6]And Sarah said, "God has made me laugh.[n] Everyone who hears about this will laugh with me. [7]No one thought that I would be able to have Abraham's child, but even though Abraham is old I have given him a son."

Hagar and Ishmael Leave

[8]Isaac grew, and when he became old enough to eat food, Abraham gave a great feast. [9]But Sarah saw Ishmael making fun of Isaac. (Ishmael was the son of Abraham by Hagar, Sarah's Egyptian slave.) [10]So Sarah said to Abraham, "Throw out this slave woman and her son. Her son should not inherit anything; my son Isaac should receive it all."

8:4 show . . . priest The Law of Moses said a priest must say when a Jewish person with a skin disease was well.
8:4 Moses commanded Read about this in Leviticus 14:1–32. • **21:6 laugh** The Hebrew words for "he laughed" and "Isaac" sound the same.

[11]This troubled Abraham very much because Ishmael was also his son. [12]But God said to Abraham, "Don't be troubled about the boy and the slave woman. Do whatever Sarah tells you. The descendants I promised you will be from Isaac. [13]I will also make the descendants of Ishmael into a great nation because he is your son, too."

[14]Early the next morning Abraham took some food and a leather bag full of water. He gave them to Hagar and sent her away. Carrying these things and her son, Hagar went and wandered in the desert of Beersheba.

[15]Later, when all the water was gone from the bag, Hagar put her son under a bush. [16]Then she went away a short distance and sat down. She thought, "My son will die, and I cannot watch this happen." She sat there and began to cry.

[17]God heard the boy crying, and God's angel called to Hagar from heaven. He said, "What is wrong, Hagar? Don't be afraid! God has heard the boy crying there. [18]Help him up and take him by the hand. I will make his descendants into a great nation."

[19]Then God showed Hagar a well of water. So she went to the well and filled her bag with water and gave the boy a drink.

[20]God was with the boy as he grew up. Ishmael lived in the desert and became an archer. [21]He lived in the Desert of Paran, and his mother found a wife for him in Egypt.

Abraham's Bargain with Abimelech

[22]Then Abimelech came with Phicol, the commander of his army, and said to Abraham, "God is with you in everything you do. [23]So make a promise to me here before God that you will be fair with me and my children and my descendants. Be kind to me and to this land where you have lived as a stranger—as kind as I have been to you."

[24]And Abraham said, "I promise." [25]Then Abraham complained to Abimelech about Abimelech's servants who had seized a well of water.

[26]But Abimelech said, "I don't know who did this. You never told me about this before today."

[27]Then Abraham gave Abimelech some sheep and cattle, and they made an agreement. [28]Abraham also put seven female lambs in front of Abimelech.

[29]Abimelech asked Abraham, "Why did you put these seven female lambs by themselves?"

[30]Abraham answered, "Accept these lambs from me to prove that you believe I dug this well."

[31]So that place was called Beersheba[n] because they made a promise to each other there.

[32]After Abraham and Abimelech made the agreement at Beersheba, Abimelech and Phicol, the commander of his army, went back to the land of the Philistines.

[33]Abraham planted a tamarisk tree at Beersheba and prayed to the LORD, the God who lives forever. [34]And Abraham lived as a stranger in the land of the Philistines for a long time.

God Tests Abraham

22 After these things God tested Abraham's faith. God said to him, "Abraham!"

And he answered, "Here I am."

[2]Then God said, "Take your only son, Isaac, the son you love, and go to the land of Moriah. Kill him there and offer him as a whole burnt offering on one of the mountains I will tell you about."

[3]Abraham got up early in the morning and saddled his donkey. He took Isaac and two servants with him. After he cut the wood for the sacrifice, they went to the place God had told them to go. [4]On the third day Abraham looked up and saw the place in the distance. [5]He said to his servants, "Stay here with the donkey. My son and I will go over there and worship, and then we will come back to you."

[6]Abraham took the wood for the sacrifice and gave it to his son to carry, but he himself took the knife and the fire. So he and his son went on together.

[7]Isaac said to his father Abraham, "Father!"

Abraham answered, "Yes, my son."

Isaac said, "We have the fire and the

21:31 **Beersheba** This name means "well of the promise" or "well of seven."

wood, but where is the lamb we will burn as a sacrifice?"

⁸Abraham answered, "God will give us the lamb for the sacrifice, my son."

So Abraham and his son went on together ⁹and came to the place God had told him about. Abraham built an altar there. He laid the wood on it and then tied up his son Isaac and laid him on the wood on the altar. ¹⁰Then Abraham took his knife and was about to kill his son.

¹¹But the angel of the LORD called to him from heaven and said, "Abraham! Abraham!"

Abraham answered, "Yes."

¹²The angel said, "Don't kill your son or hurt him in any way. Now I can see that you trust God and that you have not kept your son, your only son, from me."

¹³Then Abraham looked up and saw a male sheep caught in a bush by its horns. So Abraham went and took the sheep and killed it. He offered it as a whole burnt offering to God, and his son was saved. ¹⁴So Abraham named that place The LORD Provides. Even today people say, "On the mountain of the LORD it will be provided."

¹⁵The angel of the LORD called to Abraham from heaven a second time ¹⁶and said, "The LORD says, 'Because you did not keep back your son, your only son, from me, I make you this promise by my own name: ¹⁷I will surely bless you and give you many descendants. They will be as many as the stars in the sky and the sand on the seashore, and they will capture the cities of their enemies. ¹⁸Through your descendants all the nations on the earth will be blessed, because you obeyed me.'"

¹⁹Then Abraham returned to his servants. They all traveled back to Beersheba, and Abraham stayed there.

²⁰After these things happened, someone told Abraham: "Your brother Nahor and his wife Milcah have children now. ²¹The first son is Uz, and the second is Buz. The third son is Kemuel (the father of Aram). ²²Then there are Kesed, Hazo, Pildash, Jidlaph, and Bethuel." ²³Bethuel became the father of Rebekah. Milcah was the mother of these eight sons, and Nahor, Abraham's brother, was the father. ²⁴Also Nahor had four other sons by his slave woman Reumah. Their names were Tebah, Gaham, Tahash, and Maacah.

PSALM 6:6–10

⁶I am tired of crying to you.
　Every night my bed is wet with tears;
　my bed is soaked from my crying.
⁷My eyes are weak from so much crying;
　they are weak from crying about my
　　enemies.

⁸Get away from me, all you who do evil,
　because the LORD has heard my crying.
⁹The LORD has heard my cry for help;
　the LORD will answer my prayer.
¹⁰All my enemies will be ashamed and
　troubled.
　They will turn and suddenly leave in
　shame.

PROVERBS 3:5–6

⁵Trust the LORD with all your heart,
　and don't depend on your own
　understanding.
⁶Remember the LORD in all you do,
　and he will give you success.

MATTHEW 8:18–34

People Want to Follow Jesus

¹⁸When Jesus saw the crowd around him, he told his followers to go to the other side of the lake. ¹⁹Then a teacher of the law came to Jesus and said, "Teacher, I will follow you any place you go."

²⁰Jesus said to him, "The foxes have holes to live in, and the birds have nests, but the Son of Man has no place to rest his head."

²¹Another man, one of Jesus' followers, said to him, "Lord, first let me go and bury my father."

²²But Jesus told him, "Follow me, and let the people who are dead bury their own dead."

Jesus Calms a Storm

²³Jesus got into a boat, and his followers went with him. ²⁴A great storm arose on the lake so that waves covered the boat, but Jesus was sleeping. ²⁵His followers went to him

and woke him, saying, "Lord, save us! We will drown!"

²⁶Jesus answered, "Why are you afraid? You don't have enough faith." Then Jesus got up and gave a command to the wind and the waves, and it became completely calm.

²⁷The men were amazed and said, "What kind of man is this? Even the wind and the waves obey him!"

Jesus Heals Two Men with Demons

²⁸When Jesus arrived at the other side of the lake in the area of the Gadarene[n] people, two men who had demons in them met him. These men lived in the burial caves and were so dangerous that people could not use the road by those caves. ²⁹They shouted, "What

do you want with us, Son of God? Did you come here to torture us before the right time?"

³⁰Near that place there was a large herd of pigs feeding. ³¹The demons begged Jesus, "If you make us leave these men, please send us into that herd of pigs."

³²Jesus said to them, "Go!" So the demons left the men and went into the pigs. Then the whole herd rushed down the hill into the lake and were drowned. ³³The herdsmen ran away and went into town, where they told about all of this and what had happened to the men who had demons. ³⁴Then the whole town went out to see Jesus. When they saw him, they begged him to leave their area.

JANUARY 12

GENESIS 23:1—24:67

Sarah Dies

23 Sarah lived to be one hundred twenty-seven years old. ²She died in Kiriath Arba (that is, Hebron) in the land of Canaan. Abraham was very sad and cried because of her. ³After a while he got up from the side of his wife's body and went to talk to the Hittites. He said, ⁴"I am only a stranger and a foreigner here. Sell me some of your land so that I can bury my dead wife."

⁵The Hittites answered Abraham, ⁶"Sir, you are a great leader among us. You may have the best place we have to bury your dead. You may have any of our burying places that you want, and none of us will stop you from burying your dead wife."

⁷Abraham rose and bowed to the people of the land, the Hittites. ⁸He said to them, "If you truly want to help me bury my dead wife here, speak to Ephron, the son of Zohar for me. ⁹Ask him to sell me the cave of Machpelah at the edge of his field. I will pay him the full price. You can be the witnesses that I am buying it as a burial place."

¹⁰Ephron was sitting among the Hittites at the city gate. He answered Abraham, ¹¹"No, sir. I will give you the land and the cave that is in it, with these people as witnesses. Bury your dead wife."

¹²Then Abraham bowed down before the Hittites. ¹³He said to Ephron before all the people, "Please let me pay you the full price for the field. Accept my money, and I will bury my dead there."

¹⁴Ephron answered Abraham, ¹⁵"Sir, the land is worth ten pounds of silver, but I won't argue with you over the price. Take the land, and bury your dead wife."

¹⁶Abraham agreed and paid Ephron in front of the Hittite witnesses. He weighed out the full price, ten pounds of silver, and they counted the weight as the traders normally did.

¹⁷⁻¹⁸So Ephron's field in Machpelah, east of Mamre, was sold. Abraham became the owner of the field, the cave in it, and all the trees that were in the field. The sale was made at the city gate, with the Hittites as witnesses. ¹⁹After this, Abraham buried his

---

8:28 Gadarene From Gadara, an area southeast of Lake Galilee. The exact location is uncertain and some Greek copies read "Gergesene"; others read "Gerasene."

wife Sarah in the cave in the field of Mach-pelah, near Mamre. (Mamre was later called Hebron in the land of Canaan.) [20]So Abraham bought the field and the cave in it from the Hittites to use as a burying place.

A Wife for Isaac

24 Abraham was now very old, and the LORD had blessed him in every way. [2]Abraham said to his oldest servant, who was in charge of everything he owned, "Put your hand under my leg.[n] [3]Make a promise to me before the LORD, the God of heaven and earth. Don't get a wife for my son from the Canaanite girls who live around here. [4]Instead, go back to my country, to the land of my relatives, and get a wife for my son Isaac."

[5]The servant said to him, "What if this woman does not want to return with me to this land? Then, should I take your son with me back to your homeland?"

[6]Abraham said to him, "No! Don't take my son back there. [7]The LORD, the God of heaven, brought me from the home of my father and the land of my relatives. And he promised me, 'I will give this land to your descendants.' The LORD will send his angel before you to help you get a wife for my son there. [8]If the girl won't come back with you, you will be free from this promise. But you must not take my son back there." [9]So the servant put his hand under his master's leg and made a promise to Abraham about this.

[10]The servant took ten of Abraham's camels and left, carrying with him many different kinds of beautiful gifts. He went to Northwest Mesopotamia to Nahor's city. [11]In the evening, when the women come out to get water, he made the camels kneel down at the well outside the city.

[12]The servant said, "LORD, God of my master Abraham, allow me to find a wife for his son today. Please show this kindness to my master Abraham. [13]Here I am, standing by the spring, and the girls from the city are coming out to get water. [14]I will say to one of them, 'Please put your jar down so I can drink.' Then let her say, 'Drink, and I will also give water to your camels.' If that happens, I will know she is the right one for your servant Isaac and that you have shown kindness to my master."

[15]Before the servant had finished praying, Rebekah, the daughter of Bethuel, came out of the city. (Bethuel was the son of Milcah and Nahor, Abraham's brother.) Rebekah was carrying her water jar on her shoulder. [16]She was very pretty, a virgin; she had never had sexual relations with a man. She went down to the spring and filled her jar, then came back up. [17]The servant ran to her and said, "Please give me a little water from your jar."

[18]Rebekah said, "Drink, sir." She quickly lowered the jar from her shoulder and gave him a drink. [19]After he finished drinking, Rebekah said, "I will also pour some water for your camels." [20]So she quickly poured all the water from her jar into the drinking trough for the camels. Then she kept running to the well until she had given all the camels enough to drink.

[21]The servant quietly watched her. He wanted to be sure the LORD had made his trip successful. [22]After the camels had finished drinking, he gave Rebekah a gold ring weighing one-fifth of an ounce and two gold arm bracelets weighing about four ounces each. [23]He asked, "Who is your father? Is there a place in his house for me and my men to spend the night?"

[24]Rebekah answered, "My father is Bethuel, the son of Milcah and Nahor." [25]Then she said, "And, yes, we have straw for your camels and a place for you to spend the night."

[26]The servant bowed and worshiped the LORD [27]and said, "Blessed is the LORD, the God of my master Abraham. The LORD has been kind and truthful to him and has led me to my master's relatives."

[28]Then Rebekah ran and told her mother's family about all these things. [29]She had a brother named Laban, who ran out to Abraham's servant, who was still at the spring. [30]Laban had heard what she had said and had seen the ring and the bracelets on his sister's arms. So he ran out to the well,

---

24:2 Put . . . leg This showed that a person would keep the promise.

and there was the man standing by the camels at the spring. ³¹Laban said, "Sir, you are welcome to come in; you don't have to stand outside. I have prepared the house for you and also a place for your camels."

³²So Abraham's servant went into the house. After Laban unloaded the camels and gave them straw and food, he gave water to Abraham's servant so he and the men with him could wash their feet. ³³Then Laban gave the servant food, but the servant said, "I will not eat until I have told you why I came."

So Laban said, "Then tell us."

³⁴He said, "I am Abraham's servant. ³⁵The LORD has greatly blessed my master in everything, and he has become a rich man. The LORD has given him many flocks of sheep, herds of cattle, silver and gold, male and female servants, camels, and horses. ³⁶Sarah, my master's wife, gave birth to a son when she was old, and my master has given everything he owns to that son. ³⁷My master had me make a promise to him and said, 'Don't get a wife for my son from the Canaanite girls who live around here. ³⁸Instead, you must go to my father's people and to my family. There you must get a wife for my son.' ³⁹I said to my master, 'What if the woman will not come back with me?' ⁴⁰But he said, 'I serve the LORD, who will send his angel with you and will help you. You will get a wife for my son from my family and my father's people. ⁴¹Then you will be free from the promise. But if they will not give you a wife for my son, you will be free from this promise.'

⁴²"Today I came to this spring. I said, 'LORD, God of my master Abraham, please make my trip successful. ⁴³I am standing by this spring. I will wait for a young woman to come out to get water, and I will say, "Please give me water from your jar to drink." ⁴⁴Then let her say, "Drink this water, and I will also get water for your camels." By this I will know the LORD has chosen her for my master's son.'

⁴⁵"Before I finished my silent prayer, Rebekah came out of the city with her water jar on her shoulder. She went down to the spring and got water. I said to her, 'Please give me a drink.' ⁴⁶She quickly lowered the jar from her shoulder and said, 'Drink this. I will also get water for your camels.' So I drank, and she gave water to my camels too. ⁴⁷When I asked her, 'Who is your father?' she answered, 'My father is Bethuel son of Milcah and Nahor.' Then I put the ring in her nose and the bracelets on her arms, ⁴⁸and I bowed my head and thanked the LORD. I praised the LORD, the God of my master Abraham, because he led me on the right road to get the granddaughter of my master's brother for his son. ⁴⁹Now, tell me, will you be kind and truthful to my master? And if not, tell me so. Then I will know what I should do."

⁵⁰Laban and Bethuel answered, "This is clearly from the LORD, and we cannot change what must happen. ⁵¹Rebekah is yours. Take her and go. Let her marry your master's son as the LORD has commanded."

⁵²When Abraham's servant heard these words, he bowed facedown on the ground before the LORD. ⁵³Then he gave Rebekah gold and silver jewelry and clothes. He also gave expensive gifts to her brother and mother. ⁵⁴The servant and the men with him ate and drank and spent the night there. When they got up the next morning, the servant said, "Now let me go back to my master."

⁵⁵Rebekah's mother and her brother said, "Let Rebekah stay with us at least ten days. After that she may go."

⁵⁶But the servant said to them, "Do not make me wait, because the LORD has made my trip successful. Now let me go back to my master."

⁵⁷Rebekah's brother and mother said, "We will call Rebekah and ask her what she wants to do." ⁵⁸They called her and asked her, "Do you want to go with this man now?"

She said, "Yes, I do."

⁵⁹So they allowed Rebekah and her nurse to go with Abraham's servant and his men. ⁶⁰They blessed Rebekah and said,

"Our sister, may you be the mother of
    thousands of people,
and may your descendants capture the
    cities of their enemies."

⁶¹Then Rebekah and her servant girls got on the camels and followed the servant and his men. So the servant took Rebekah and left. ⁶²At this time Isaac had left Beer Lahai

Roi and was living in southern Canaan. [63]One evening when he went out to the field to think, he looked up and saw camels coming. [64]Rebekah also looked and saw Isaac. Then she jumped down from the camel [65]and asked the servant, "Who is that man walking in the field to meet us?"

The servant answered, "That is my master." So Rebekah covered her face with her veil.

[66]The servant told Isaac everything that had happened. [67]Then Isaac brought Rebekah into the tent of Sarah, his mother, and she became his wife. Isaac loved her very much, and so he was comforted after his mother's death.

PSALM 7:1–5

A Prayer for Fairness

A shiggaion of David which he sang to the LORD about Cush, from the tribe of Benjamin.

7LORD my God, I trust in you for
protection.
  Save me and rescue me
    from those who are chasing me.
[2]Otherwise, like a lion they will tear me
    apart.
  They will rip me to pieces, and no one
    can save me.

[3]LORD my God, what have I done?
  Have my hands done something
    wrong?
[4]Have I done wrong to my friend
  or stolen without reason from my
    enemy?
[5]If I have, let my enemy chase me and
    capture me.
  Let him trample me into the dust
    and bury me in the ground.   Selah

PROVERBS 3:7–8

[7]Don't depend on your own wisdom.
  Respect the LORD and refuse to do
    wrong.
[8]Then your body will be healthy,
  and your bones will be strong.

MATTHEW 9:1–17

Jesus Heals a Paralyzed Man

9Jesus got into a boat and went back across the lake to his own town. [2]Some people brought to Jesus a man who was paralyzed and lying on a mat. When Jesus saw the faith of these people, he said to the paralyzed man, "Be encouraged, young man. Your sins are forgiven."

[3]Some of the teachers of the law said to themselves, "This man speaks as if he were God. That is blasphemy!"[n]

[4]Knowing their thoughts, Jesus said, "Why are you thinking evil thoughts? [5]Which is easier: to say, 'Your sins are forgiven,' or to tell him, 'Stand up and walk'? [6]But I will prove to you that the Son of Man has authority on earth to forgive sins." Then Jesus said to the paralyzed man, "Stand up, take your mat, and go home." [7]And the man stood up and went home. [8]When the people saw this, they were amazed and praised God for giving power like this to human beings.

Jesus Chooses Matthew

[9]When Jesus was leaving, he saw a man named Matthew sitting in the tax collector's booth. Jesus said to him, "Follow me," and he stood up and followed Jesus.

[10]As Jesus was having dinner at Matthew's house, many tax collectors and "sinners" came and ate with Jesus and his followers. [11]When the Pharisees saw this, they asked Jesus' followers, "Why does your teacher eat with tax collectors and sinners?"

[12]When Jesus heard them, he said, "It is not the healthy people who need a doctor, but the sick. [13]Go and learn what this means: 'I want kindness more than I want animal sacrifices.'[n] I did not come to invite good people but to invite sinners."

Jesus' Followers Are Criticized

[14]Then the followers of John[n] came to Jesus and said, "Why do we and the Pharisees often fast[n] for a certain time, but your followers don't?"

[15]Jesus answered, "The friends of the

9:3 blasphemy Saying things against God or not showing respect for God.   **9:13 'I want . . . sacrifices.'** Quotation from Hosea 6:6.   **9:14 John** John the Baptist, who preached to people about Christ's coming (Matthew 3, Luke 3).   **9:14 fast** The people would give up eating for a special time of prayer and worship to God. It was also done to show sadness and disappointment.

bridegroom are not sad while he is with them. But the time will come when the bridegroom will be taken from them, and then they will fast.

[16]"No one sews a patch of unshrunk cloth over a hole in an old coat. If he does, the patch will shrink and pull away from the coat, making the hole worse. [17]Also, people never pour new wine into old leather bags. Otherwise, the bags will break, the wine will spill, and the wine bags will be ruined. But people always pour new wine into new wine bags. Then both will continue to be good."

JANUARY 13

GENESIS 25:1—26:35

Abraham's Family

25 Abraham married again, and his new wife was Keturah. [2]She gave birth to Zimran, Jokshan, Medan, Midian, Ishbak, and Shuah. [3]Jokshan was the father of Sheba and Dedan. Dedan's descendants were the people of Assyria, Letush, and Leum. [4]The sons of Midian were Ephah, Epher, Hanoch, Abida, and Eldaah. All these were descendants of Keturah. [5]Abraham left everything he owned to Isaac. [6]But before Abraham died, he did give gifts to the sons of his other wives, then sent them to the East to be away from Isaac.

[7]Abraham lived to be one hundred seventy-five years old. [8]He breathed his last breath and died at an old age, after a long and satisfying life. [9]His sons Isaac and Ishmael buried him in the cave of Machpelah in the field of Ephron east of Mamre. (Ephron was the son of Zohar the Hittite.) [10]So Abraham was buried with his wife Sarah in the same field that he had bought from the Hittites. [11]After Abraham died, God blessed his son Isaac. Isaac was now living at Beer Lahai Roi.

[12]This is the family history of Ishmael, Abraham's son. (Hagar, Sarah's Egyptian servant, was Ishmael's mother.) [13]These are the names of Ishmael's sons in the order they were born: Nebaioth, the first son, then Kedar, Adbeel, Mibsam, [14]Mishma, Dumah, Massa, [15]Hadad, Tema, Jetur, Naphish, and Kedemah. [16]These were Ishmael's sons, and these are the names of the tribal leaders listed according to their settlements and camps. [17]Ishmael lived one hundred thirty-seven years and then breathed his last breath and died. [18]His descendants lived from Havilah to Shur, which is east of Egypt stretching toward Assyria. They often attacked the descendants of his brothers.

Isaac's Family

[19]This is the family history of Isaac. Abraham had a son named Isaac. [20]When Isaac was forty years old, he married Rebekah, who came from Northwest Mesopotamia. She was Bethuel's daughter and the sister of Laban the Aramean. [21]Isaac's wife could not have children, so Isaac prayed to the LORD for her. The LORD heard Isaac's prayer, and Rebekah became pregnant.

[22]While she was pregnant, the babies struggled inside her. She asked, "Why is this happening to me?" Then she went to get an answer from the LORD.

[23]The LORD said to her,

"Two nations are in your body,
    and two groups of people will be taken
        from you.
One group will be stronger than the other,
    and the older will serve the younger."

[24]When the time came, Rebekah gave birth to twins. [25]The first baby was born red. Since his skin was like a hairy robe, he was named Esau.[n] [26]When the second baby was born, he was holding on to Esau's heel, so that baby was named Jacob.[n] Isaac was sixty years old when they were born.

[27]When the boys grew up, Esau became a

skilled hunter. He loved to be out in the fields. But Jacob was a quiet man and stayed among the tents. [28]Isaac loved Esau because he hunted the wild animals that Isaac enjoyed eating. But Rebekah loved Jacob.

[29]One day Jacob was boiling a pot of vegetable soup. Esau came in from hunting in the fields, weak from hunger. [30]So Esau said to Jacob, "Let me eat some of that red soup, because I am weak with hunger." (That is why people call him Edom.[n])

[31]But Jacob said, "You must sell me your rights as the firstborn son."[n]

[32]Esau said, "I am almost dead from hunger. If I die, all of my father's wealth will not help me."

[33]But Jacob said, "First, promise me that you will give it to me." So Esau made a promise to Jacob and sold his part of their father's wealth to Jacob. [34]Then Jacob gave Esau bread and vegetable soup, and he ate and drank, and then left. So Esau showed how little he cared about his rights as the firstborn son.

Isaac Lies to Abimelech

26 Now there was a time of hunger in the land, besides the time of hunger that happened during Abraham's life. So Isaac went to the town of Gerar to see Abimelech king of the Philistines. [2]The LORD appeared to Isaac and said, "Don't go down to Egypt, but live in the land where I tell you to live. [3]Stay in this land, and I will be with you and bless you. I will give you and your descendants all these lands, and I will keep the oath I made to Abraham your father. [4]I will give you many descendants, as hard to count as the stars in the sky, and I will give them all these lands. Through your descendants all the nations on the earth will be blessed. [5]I will do this because your father Abraham obeyed me. He did what I said and obeyed my commands, my teachings, and my rules."

[6]So Isaac stayed in Gerar. [7]His wife Rebekah was very beautiful, and the men of that place asked Isaac about her. Isaac said, "She is my sister," because he was afraid to tell them she was his wife. He thought they might kill him so they could have her.

[8]Isaac lived there a long time. One day as Abimelech king of the Philistines looked out his window, he saw Isaac holding his wife Rebekah tenderly. [9]Abimelech called for Isaac and said, "This woman is your wife. Why did you say she was your sister?"

Isaac said to him, "I was afraid you would kill me so you could have her."

[10]Abimelech said, "What have you done to us? One of our men might have had sexual relations with your wife. Then we would have been guilty of a great sin."

[11]So Abimelech warned everyone, "Anyone who touches this man or his wife will be put to death."

Isaac Becomes Rich

[12]Isaac planted seed in that land, and that year he gathered a great harvest. The LORD blessed him very much, [13]and he became rich. He gathered more wealth until he became a very rich man. [14]He had so many slaves and flocks and herds that the Philistines envied him. [15]So they stopped up all the wells the servants of Isaac's father Abraham had dug. (They had dug them when Abraham was alive.) The Philistines filled those wells with dirt. [16]And Abimelech said to Isaac, "Leave our country because you have become much more powerful than we are."

[17]So Isaac left that place and camped in the Valley of Gerar and lived there. [18]Long before this time Abraham had dug many wells, but after he died, the Philistines filled them with dirt. So Isaac dug those wells again and gave them the same names his father had given them. [19]Isaac's servants dug a well in the valley, from which a spring of water flowed. [20]But the herdsmen of Gerar argued with them and said, "This water is ours." So Isaac named that well Argue because they argued with him. [21]Then his servants dug another well. When the people also argued about it, Isaac named that well Fight. [22]He moved from there and dug another well. No one argued about this one, so he named it Room Enough. Isaac said, "Now the LORD has made room for us, and we will be successful in this land."

25:30 Edom This name sounds like the Hebrew word for "red." **25:31 rights . . . son** Usually the firstborn son had a high rank in the family. The firstborn son usually became the new head of the family.

[23]From there Isaac went to Beersheba. [24]The LORD appeared to him that night and said, "I am the God of your father Abraham. Don't be afraid, because I am with you. I will bless you and give you many descendants because of my servant Abraham." [25]So Isaac built an altar and worshiped the LORD there. He also made a camp there, and his servants dug a well.

[26]Abimelech came from Gerar to see Isaac. He brought with him Ahuzzath, who advised him, and Phicol, the commander of his army. [27]Isaac asked them, "Why have you come to see me? You were my enemy and forced me to leave your country."

[28]They answered, "Now we know that the LORD is with you. Let us swear an oath to each other. Let us make an agreement with you [29]that since we did not hurt you, you will not hurt us. We were good to you and sent you away in peace. Now the LORD has blessed you."

[30]So Isaac prepared food for them, and they all ate and drank. [31]Early the next morning the men swore an oath to each other. Then Isaac sent them away, and they left in peace.

[32]That day Isaac's servants came and told him about the well they had dug, saying, "We found water in that well." [33]So Isaac named it Shibah[n] and that city is called Beersheba even now.

[34]When Esau was forty years old, he married two Hittite women—Judith daughter of Beeri and Basemath daughter of Elon. [35]These women brought much sorrow to Isaac and Rebekah.

PSALM 7:6–9

[6]LORD, rise up in your anger;
    stand up against my enemies' anger.
    Get up and demand fairness.
[7]Gather the nations around you
    and rule them from above.
[8]LORD, judge the people.
    LORD, defend me because I am
    right,
    because I have done no wrong, God
    Most High.

[9]God, you do what is right.
    You know our thoughts and feelings.
    Stop those wicked actions done by evil
    people,
    and help those who do what is right.

PROVERBS 3:9–10

[9]Honor the LORD with your wealth
    and the firstfruits from all your crops.
[10]Then your barns will be full,
    and your wine barrels will overflow
    with new wine.

MATTHEW 9:18–38

Jesus Gives Life to a Dead Girl and Heals a Sick Woman

[18]While Jesus was saying these things, a leader of the synagogue came to him. He bowed down before Jesus and said, "My daughter has just died. But if you come and lay your hand on her, she will live again." [19]So Jesus and his followers stood up and went with the leader.

[20]Then a woman who had been bleeding for twelve years came behind Jesus and touched the edge of his coat. [21]She was thinking, "If I can just touch his clothes, I will be healed."

[22]Jesus turned and saw the woman and said, "Be encouraged, dear woman. You are made well because you believed." And the woman was healed from that moment on.

[23]Jesus continued along with the leader and went into his house. There he saw the funeral musicians and many people crying. [24]Jesus said, "Go away. The girl is not dead, only asleep." But the people laughed at him. [25]After the crowd had been thrown out of the house, Jesus went into the girl's room and took hold of her hand, and she stood up. [26]The news about this spread all around the area.

Jesus Heals More People

[27]When Jesus was leaving there, two blind men followed him. They cried out, "Have mercy on us, Son of David!"

[28]After Jesus went inside, the blind men went with him. He asked the men, "Do you believe that I can make you see again?"

They answered, "Yes, Lord."

²⁹Then Jesus touched their eyes and said, "Because you believe I can make you see again, it will happen." ³⁰Then the men were able to see. But Jesus warned them strongly, saying, "Don't tell anyone about this." ³¹But the blind men left and spread the news about Jesus all around that area.

³²When the two men were leaving, some people brought another man to Jesus. This man could not talk because he had a demon in him. ³³After Jesus forced the demon to leave the man, he was able to speak. The crowd was amazed and said, "We have never seen anything like this in Israel."

³⁴But the Pharisees said, "The prince of demons is the one that gives him power to force demons out."

³⁵Jesus traveled through all the towns and villages, teaching in their synagogues, preaching the Good News about the kingdom, and healing all kinds of diseases and sicknesses. ³⁶When he saw the crowds, he felt sorry for them because they were hurting and helpless, like sheep without a shepherd. ³⁷Jesus said to his followers, "There are many people to harvest but only a few workers to help harvest them. ³⁸Pray to the Lord, who owns the harvest, that he will send more workers to gather his harvest."[n]

JANUARY 14

GENESIS 27:1—28:22

Jacob Tricks Isaac

27 When Isaac was old, his eyesight was poor, so he could not see clearly. One day he called his older son Esau to him and said, "Son."

Esau answered, "Here I am."

²Isaac said, "I am old and don't know when I might die. ³So take your bow and arrows and go hunting in the field for an animal for me to eat. ⁴When you prepare the tasty food that I love, bring it to me, and I will eat. Then I will bless you before I die."

⁵So Esau went out in the field to hunt.

Rebekah was listening as Isaac said this to his son Esau. ⁶She said to her son Jacob, "Listen, I heard your father saying to your brother Esau, ⁷'Kill an animal and prepare some tasty food for me to eat. Then I will bless you in the presence of the LORD before I die.' ⁸So obey me, my son, and do what I tell you. ⁹Go out to our goats and bring me two of the best young ones. I will prepare them just the way your father likes them. ¹⁰Then you will take the food to your father, and he will bless you before he dies."

¹¹But Jacob said to his mother Rebekah, "My brother Esau is a hairy man, and I am smooth! ¹²If my father touches me, he will know I am not Esau. Then he will not bless me but will place a curse on me because I tried to trick him."

¹³So Rebekah said to him, "If your father puts a curse on you, I will accept the blame. Just do what I said. Go get the goats for me."

¹⁴So Jacob went out and got two goats and brought them to his mother, and she cooked them in the special way Isaac enjoyed. ¹⁵She took the best clothes of her older son Esau that were in the house and put them on the younger son Jacob. ¹⁶She also took the skins of the goats and put them on Jacob's hands and neck. ¹⁷Then she gave Jacob the tasty food and the bread she had made.

¹⁸Jacob went in to his father and said, "Father."

And his father said, "Yes, my son. Who are you?"

¹⁹Jacob said to him, "I am Esau, your first son. I have done what you told me. Now sit up and eat some meat of the animal I hunted for you. Then bless me."

9:37-38 "There are . . . harvest." As a farmer sends workers to harvest the grain, Jesus sends his followers to bring people to God.

[20]But Isaac asked his son, "How did you find and kill the animal so quickly?"

Jacob answered, "Because the LORD your God helped me to find it."

[21]Then Isaac said to Jacob, "Come near so I can touch you, my son. Then I will know if you are really my son Esau."

[22]So Jacob came near to Isaac his father. Isaac touched him and said, "Your voice sounds like Jacob's voice, but your hands are hairy like the hands of Esau." [23]Isaac did not know it was Jacob, because his hands were hairy like Esau's hands, so Isaac blessed him. [24]Isaac asked, "Are you really my son Esau?"

Jacob answered, "Yes, I am."

[25]Then Isaac said, "Bring me the food, and I will eat it and bless you." So Jacob gave him the food, and he ate. Jacob gave him wine, and he drank. [26]Then Isaac said to him, "My son, come near and kiss me." [27]So Jacob went to his father and kissed him. When Isaac smelled Esau's clothes, he blessed him and said,

"The smell of my son
    is like the smell of the field
    that the LORD has blessed.
[28]May God give you plenty of rain
    and good soil
    so that you will have plenty of grain
        and new wine.
[29]May nations serve you
    and peoples bow down to you.
May you be master over your brothers,
    and may your mother's sons bow down
        to you.
May everyone who curses you be cursed,
    and may everyone who blesses you be
        blessed."

[30]Isaac finished blessing Jacob. Then, just as Jacob left his father Isaac, Esau came in from hunting. [31]He also prepared some tasty food and brought it to his father. He said, "Father, rise and eat the food that your son killed for you and then bless me."

[32]Isaac asked, "Who are you?"

He answered, "I am your son—your first-born son—Esau."

[33]Then Isaac trembled greatly and said, "Then who was it that hunted the animals and brought me food before you came? I ate it, and I blessed him, and it is too late now to take back my blessing."

[34]When Esau heard the words of his father, he let out a loud and bitter cry. He said to his father, "Bless me—me, too, my father!"

[35]But Isaac said, "Your brother came and tricked me. He has taken your blessing."

[36]Esau said, "Jacob[n] is the right name for him. He has tricked me these two times. He took away my share of everything you own, and now he has taken away my blessing." Then Esau asked, "Haven't you saved a blessing for me?"

[37]Isaac answered, "I gave Jacob the power to be master over you, and all his brothers will be his servants. And I kept him strong with grain and new wine. There is nothing left to give you, my son."

[38]But Esau continued, "Do you have only one blessing, Father? Bless me, too, Father!" Then Esau began to cry out loud.

[39]Isaac said to him,

"You will live far away from the best
    land,
    far from the rain.
[40]You will live by using your sword,
    and you will be a slave to your brother.
But when you struggle,
    you will break free from him."

[41]After that Esau hated Jacob because of the blessing from Isaac. He thought to himself, "My father will soon die, and I will be sad for him. Then I will kill Jacob."

[42]Rebekah heard about Esau's plan to kill Jacob. So she sent for Jacob and said to him, "Listen, your brother Esau is comforting himself by planning to kill you. [43]So, my son, do what I say. My brother Laban is living in Haran. Go to him at once! [44]Stay with him for a while, until your brother is not so angry. [45]In time, your brother will not be angry, and he will forget what you did to him. Then I will send a servant to bring you back. I don't want to lose both of my sons on the same day."

27:36 Jacob This name sounds like the Hebrew word for "heel." "Grabbing someone's heel" is a Hebrew saying for tricking someone.

[46]Then Rebekah said to Isaac, "I am tired of Hittite women. If Jacob marries one of these Hittite women here in this land, I want to die."

Jacob Searches for a Wife

28 Isaac called Jacob and blessed him and commanded him, "You must not marry a Canaanite woman. [2]Go to the house of Bethuel, your mother's father, in Northwest Mesopotamia. Laban, your mother's brother, lives there. Marry one of his daughters. [3]May God Almighty bless you and give you many children, and may you become a group of many peoples. [4]May he give you and your descendants the blessing of Abraham so that you may own the land where you are now living as a stranger, the land God gave to Abraham." [5]So Isaac sent Jacob to Northwest Mesopotamia, to Laban the brother of Rebekah. Bethuel the Aramean was the father of Laban and Rebekah, and Rebekah was the mother of Jacob and Esau.

[6]Esau learned that Isaac had blessed Jacob and sent him to Northwest Mesopotamia to find a wife there. He also learned that Isaac had commanded Jacob not to marry a Canaanite woman [7]and that Jacob had obeyed his father and mother and had gone to Northwest Mesopotamia. [8]So Esau saw that his father Isaac did not want his sons to marry Canaanite women. [9]Now Esau already had wives, but he went to Ishmael son of Abraham, and he married Mahalath, Ishmael's daughter. Mahalath was the sister of Nebaioth.

Jacob's Dream at Bethel

[10]Jacob left Beersheba and set out for Haran. [11]When he came to a place, he spent the night there because the sun had set. He found a stone and laid his head on it to go to sleep. [12]Jacob dreamed that there was a ladder resting on the earth and reaching up into heaven, and he saw angels of God going up and coming down the ladder. [13]Then Jacob saw the LORD standing above the ladder, and he said, "I am the LORD, the God of Abraham your grandfather, and the God of Isaac. I will give you and your descendants the land on which you are now sleeping. [14]Your descendants will be as many as the dust of the earth. They will spread west and east, north and south, and all the families of the earth will be blessed through you and your descendants. [15]I am with you and will protect you everywhere you go and will bring you back to this land. I will not leave you until I have done what I have promised you."

[16]Then Jacob woke from his sleep and said, "Surely the LORD is in this place, but I did not know it." [17]He was afraid and said, "This place frightens me! It is surely the house of God and the gate of heaven."

[18]Jacob rose early in the morning and took the stone he had slept on and set it up on its end. Then he poured olive oil on the top of it. [19]At first, the name of that city was Luz, but Jacob named it Bethel.[n]

[20]Then Jacob made a promise. He said, "I want God to be with me and to protect me on this journey. I want him to give me food to eat and clothes to wear [21]so I will be able to return in peace to my father's house. If the LORD does these things, he will be my God. [22]This stone which I have set up on its end will be the house of God. And I will give God one-tenth of all he gives me."

PSALM 7:10–17

[10]God protects me like a shield;
he saves those whose hearts are right.
[11]God judges by what is right,
and God is always ready to punish the
wicked.
[12]If they do not change their lives,
God will sharpen his sword;
he will string his bow and take aim.
[13]He has prepared his deadly weapons;
he has made his flaming arrows.

[14]There are people who think up evil
and plan trouble and tell lies.
[15]They dig a hole to trap others,
but they will fall into it themselves.
[16]They will get themselves into trouble;
the violence they cause will hurt only
themselves.

[17]I praise the LORD because he does what is
right.
I sing praises to the LORD Most High.

28:19 Bethel This name means "house of God."

PROVERBS 3:11–12

[11]My child, do not reject the LORD's discipline,
and don't get angry when he corrects you.
[12]The LORD corrects those he loves,
just as parents correct the child they delight in.

MATTHEW 10:1–15

Jesus Sends Out His Apostles

10 Jesus called his twelve followers together and gave them authority to drive out evil spirits and to heal every kind of disease and sickness. [2]These are the names of the twelve apostles: Simon (also called Peter) and his brother Andrew; James son of Zebedee, and his brother John; [3]Philip and Bartholomew; Thomas and Matthew, the tax collector; James son of Alphaeus, and Thaddaeus; [4]Simon the Zealot and Judas Iscariot, who turned against Jesus.

[5]Jesus sent out these twelve men with the following order: "Don't go to the non-Jewish people or to any town where the Samaritans live. [6]But go to the people of Israel, who are like lost sheep. [7]When you go, preach this: 'The kingdom of heaven is near.' [8]Heal the sick, raise the dead to life again, heal those who have skin diseases, and force demons out of people. I give you these powers freely, so help other people freely. [9]Don't carry any money with you— gold or silver or copper. [10]Don't carry a bag or extra clothes or sandals or a walking stick. Workers should be given what they need.

[11]"When you enter a city or town, find some worthy person there and stay in that home until you leave. [12]When you enter that home, say, 'Peace be with you.' [13]If the people there welcome you, let your peace stay there. But if they don't welcome you, take back the peace you wished for them. [14]And if a home or town refuses to welcome you or listen to you, leave that place and shake its dust off your feet.[n] [15]I tell you the truth, on the Judgment Day it will be better for the towns of Sodom and Gomorrah[n] than for the people of that town.

JANUARY 15

GENESIS 29:1–30:43

Jacob Arrives in Northwest Mesopotamia

29 Then Jacob continued his journey and came to the land of the people of the East. [2]He looked and saw a well in the field and three flocks of sheep lying nearby, because they drank water from this well. A large stone covered the mouth of the well. [3]When all the flocks would gather there, the shepherds would roll the stone away from the well and water the sheep. Then they would put the stone back in its place.

[4]Jacob said to the shepherds there, "My brothers, where are you from?"

They answered, "We are from Haran."

[5]Then Jacob asked, "Do you know Laban, grandson of Nahor?"

They answered, "We know him."

[6]Then Jacob asked, "How is he?"

They answered, "He is well. Look, his daughter Rachel is coming now with his sheep."

[7]Jacob said, "But look, it is still the middle of the day. It is not time for the sheep to be gathered for the night, so give them water and let them go back into the pasture."

[8]But they said, "We cannot do that until all the flocks are gathered. Then we will roll away the stone from the mouth of the well and water the sheep."

[9]While Jacob was talking with the shep-

herds, Rachel came with her father's sheep, because it was her job to care for the sheep. [10]When Jacob saw Laban's daughter Rachel and Laban's sheep, he went to the well and rolled the stone from its mouth and watered Laban's sheep. Now Laban was the brother of Rebekah, Jacob's mother. [11]Then Jacob kissed Rachel and cried. [12]He told her that he was from her father's family and that he was the son of Rebekah. So Rachel ran home and told her father.

[13]When Laban heard the news about his sister's son Jacob, he ran to meet him. Laban hugged him and kissed him and brought him to his house, where Jacob told Laban everything that had happened.

[14]Then Laban said, "You are my own flesh and blood."

Jacob Is Tricked

Jacob stayed there a month. [15]Then Laban said to Jacob, "You are my relative, but it is not right for you to work for me without pay. What would you like me to pay you?"

[16]Now Laban had two daughters. The older was Leah, and the younger was Rachel. [17]Leah had weak eyes, but Rachel was very beautiful. [18]Jacob loved Rachel, so he said to Laban, "Let me marry your younger daughter Rachel. If you will, I will work seven years for you."

[19]Laban said, "It would be better for her to marry you than someone else, so stay here with me." [20]So Jacob worked for Laban seven years so he could marry Rachel. But they seemed like just a few days to him because he loved Rachel very much.

[21]After seven years Jacob said to Laban, "Give me Rachel so that I may marry her. The time I promised to work for you is over."

[22]So Laban gave a feast for all the people there. [23]That evening he brought his daughter Leah to Jacob, and they had sexual relations. [24](Laban gave his slave girl Zilpah to his daughter to be her servant.) [25]In the morning when Jacob saw that he had had sexual relations with Leah, he said to Laban, "What have you done to me? I worked hard for you so that I could marry Rachel! Why did you trick me?"

[26]Laban said, "In our country we do not allow the younger daughter to marry before the older daughter. [27]But complete the full week of the marriage ceremony with Leah, and I will give you Rachel to marry also. But you must serve me another seven years."

[28]So Jacob did this, and when he had completed the week with Leah, Laban gave him his daughter Rachel as a wife. [29](Laban gave his slave girl Bilhah to his daughter Rachel to be her servant.) [30]So Jacob had sexual relations with Rachel also, and Jacob loved Rachel more than Leah. Jacob worked for Laban for another seven years.

Jacob's Family Grows

[31]When the LORD saw that Jacob loved Rachel more than Leah, he made it possible for Leah to have children, but not Rachel. [32]Leah became pregnant and gave birth to a son. She named him Reuben,[n] because she said, "The LORD has seen my troubles. Surely now my husband will love me."

[33]Leah became pregnant again and gave birth to another son. She named him Simeon[n] and said, "The LORD has heard that I am not loved, so he has given me this son."

[34]Leah became pregnant again and gave birth to another son. She named him Levi[n] and said, "Now, surely my husband will be close to me, because I have given him three sons."

[35]Then Leah gave birth to another son. She named him Judah,[n] because she said, "Now I will praise the LORD." Then Leah stopped having children.

30 When Rachel saw that she was not having children for Jacob, she envied her sister Leah. She said to Jacob, "Give me children, or I'll die!" [2]Jacob became angry with her and said, "Can I do what only God can do? He is the one who has kept you from having children."

[3]Then Rachel said, "Here is my slave girl Bilhah. Have sexual relations with her so she can give birth to a child for me. Then I can have my own family through her."

29:32 Reuben This name sounds like the Hebrew word for "he has seen my troubles." **29:33 Simeon** This name sounds like the Hebrew word for "has heard." **29:34 Levi** This name sounds like the Hebrew word for "be close to." **29:35 Judah** This name sounds like the Hebrew word for "praise."

[4]So Rachel gave Bilhah, her slave girl, to Jacob as a wife, and he had sexual relations with her. [5]She became pregnant and gave Jacob a son. [6]Rachel said, "God has judged me innocent. He has listened to my prayer and has given me a son," so she named him Dan.[n]

[7]Bilhah became pregnant again and gave Jacob a second son. [8]Rachel said, "I have struggled hard with my sister, and I have won." So she named that son Naphtali.[n]

[9]Leah saw that she had stopped having children, so she gave her slave girl Zilpah to Jacob as a wife. [10]When Zilpah had a son, [11]Leah said, "I am lucky," so she named him Gad.[n] [12]Zilpah gave birth to another son, [13]and Leah said, "I am very happy! Now women will call me happy," so she named him Asher.[n]

[14]During the wheat harvest Reuben went into the field and found some mandrake[n] plants and brought them to his mother Leah. But Rachel said to Leah, "Please give me some of your son's mandrakes."

[15]Leah answered, "You have already taken away my husband, and now you are trying to take away my son's mandrakes."

But Rachel answered, "If you will give me your son's mandrakes, you may sleep with Jacob tonight."

[16]When Jacob came in from the field that night, Leah went out to meet him. She said, "You will have sexual relations with me tonight because I have paid for you with my son's mandrakes." So Jacob slept with her that night.

[17]Then God answered Leah's prayer, and she became pregnant again. She gave birth to a fifth son [18]and said, "God has given me what I paid for, because I gave my slave girl to my husband." So Leah named her son Issachar.[n]

[19]Leah became pregnant again and gave birth to a sixth son. [20]She said, "God has given me a fine gift. Now surely Jacob will honor me, because I have given him six sons," so she named him Zebulun.[n] [21]Later Leah gave birth to a daughter and named her Dinah.

[22]Then God remembered Rachel and answered her prayer, making it possible for her to have children. [23]When she became pregnant and gave birth to a son, she said, "God has taken away my shame," [24]and she named him Joseph.[n] Rachel said, "I wish the LORD would give me another son."

Jacob Tricks Laban

[25]After the birth of Joseph, Jacob said to Laban, "Now let me go to my own home and country. [26]Give me my wives and my children and let me go. I have earned them by working for you, and you know that I have served you well."

[27]Laban said to him, "If I have pleased you, please stay. I know the LORD has blessed me because of you. [28]Tell me what I should pay you, and I will give it to you."

[29]Jacob answered, "You know that I have worked hard for you, and your flocks have grown while I cared for them. [30]When I came, you had little, but now you have much. Every time I did something for you, the LORD blessed you. But when will I be able to do something for my own family?"

[31]Laban asked, "Then what should I give you?"

Jacob answered, "I don't want you to give me anything. Just do this one thing, and I will come back and take care of your flocks. [32]Today let me go through all your flocks. I will take every speckled or spotted sheep, every black lamb, and every spotted or speckled goat. That will be my pay. [33]In the future you can easily see if I am honest. When you come to look at my flocks, if I have any goat that isn't speckled or spotted or any lamb that isn't black, you will know I stole it."

[34]Laban answered, "Agreed! We will do what you ask." [35]But that day Laban took away all the male goats that had streaks or spots, all the speckled and spotted female goats (all those that had white on them), and all the

---

30:6 Dan This name means "he has judged." **30:8 Naphtali** This name sounds like the Hebrew word for "my struggle." **30:11 Gad** This name may mean "lucky." **30:13 Asher** This name may mean "happy." **30:14 mandrake** A plant which was believed to cause a woman to become pregnant. **30:18 Issachar** This name sounds like the Hebrew word for "paid for." **30:20 Zebulun** This name sounds like the Hebrew word for "honor." **30:24 Joseph** This name sounds like the Hebrew word for "he adds."

black sheep. He told his sons to watch over them. [36]Then he took these animals to a place that was three days' journey away from Jacob. Jacob took care of all the flocks that were left.

[37]So Jacob cut green branches from poplar, almond, and plane trees and peeled off some of the bark so that the branches had white stripes on them. [38]He put the branches in front of the flocks at the watering places. When the animals came to drink, they also mated there, [39]so the flocks mated in front of the branches. Then the young that were born were streaked, speckled, or spotted. [40]Jacob separated the young animals from the others, and he made them face the streaked and dark animals in Laban's flock. Jacob kept his animals separate from Laban's. [41]When the stronger animals in the flock were mating, Jacob put the branches before their eyes so they would mate near the branches. [42]But when the weaker animals mated, Jacob did not put the branches there. So the animals born from the weaker animals were Laban's, and those born from the stronger animals were Jacob's. [43]In this way Jacob became very rich. He had large flocks, many male and female servants, camels, and donkeys.

PSALM 8:1–2

The Lord's Greatness

For the director of music. On the gittith. A psalm of David.

8 LORD our Lord,
 your name is the most wonderful
 name in all the earth!
 It brings you praise in heaven above.
 [2]You have taught children and babies
 to sing praises to you
 because of your enemies.
 And so you silence your enemies
 and destroy those who try to get even.

PROVERBS 3:13–18

[13]Happy is the person who finds wisdom,
 the one who gets understanding.
[14]Wisdom is worth more than silver;
 it brings more profit than gold.
[15]Wisdom is more precious than rubies;
 nothing you could want is equal to it.

[16]With her right hand wisdom offers you a
 long life,
 and with her left hand she gives you
 riches and honor.
[17]Wisdom will make your life pleasant
 and will bring you peace.
[18]As a tree produces fruit, wisdom gives
 life to those who use it,
 and everyone who uses it will be
 happy.

MATTHEW 10:16–42

Jesus Warns His Apostles

[16]"Listen, I am sending you out like sheep among wolves. So be as clever as snakes and as innocent as doves. [17]Be careful of people, because they will arrest you and take you to court and whip you in their synagogues. [18]Because of me you will be taken to stand before governors and kings, and you will tell them and the non-Jewish people about me. [19]When you are arrested, don't worry about what to say or how to say it. At that time you will be given the things to say. [20]It will not really be you speaking but the Spirit of your Father speaking through you.

[21]"Brothers will give their own brothers to be killed, and fathers will give their own children to be killed. Children will fight against their own parents and have them put to death. [22]All people will hate you because you follow me, but those people who keep their faith until the end will be saved. [23]When you are treated badly in one city, run to another city. I tell you the truth, you will not finish going through all the cities of Israel before the Son of Man comes.

[24]"A student is not better than his teacher, and a servant is not better than his master. [25]A student should be satisfied to become like his teacher; a servant should be satisfied to become like his master. If the head of the family is called Beelzebul, then the other members of the family will be called worse names!

Fear God, Not People

[26]"So don't be afraid of those people, because everything that is hidden will be shown. Everything that is secret will be made known. [27]I tell you these things in the

dark, but I want you to tell them in the light. What you hear whispered in your ear you should shout from the housetops. ²⁸Don't be afraid of people, who can kill the body but cannot kill the soul. The only one you should fear is the one who can destroy the soul and the body in hell. ²⁹Two sparrows cost only a penny, but not even one of them can die without your Father's knowing it. ³⁰God even knows how many hairs are on your head. ³¹So don't be afraid. You are worth much more than many sparrows.

Tell People About Your Faith

³²"All those who stand before others and say they believe in me, I will say before my Father in heaven that they belong to me. ³³But all who stand before others and say they do not believe in me, I will say before my Father in heaven that they do not belong to me.

³⁴"Don't think that I came to bring peace to the earth. I did not come to bring peace, but a sword. ³⁵I have come so that

'a son will be against his father,
   a daughter will be against her mother,
a daughter-in-law will be against her
   mother-in-law.
³⁶   A person's enemies will be members of
      his own family.'   *Micah 7:6*

³⁷"Those who love their father or mother more than they love me are not worthy to be my followers. Those who love their son or daughter more than they love me are not worthy to be my followers. ³⁸Whoever is not willing to carry the cross and follow me is not worthy of me. ³⁹Those who try to hold on to their lives will give up true life. Those who give up their lives for me will hold on to true life. ⁴⁰Whoever accepts you also accepts me, and whoever accepts me also accepts the One who sent me. ⁴¹Whoever meets a prophet and accepts him will receive the reward of a prophet. And whoever accepts a good person because that person is good will receive the reward of a good person. ⁴²Those who give one of these little ones a cup of cold water because they are my followers will truly get their reward."

JANUARY 16

GENESIS 31:1—32:32

Jacob Runs Away

31 One day Jacob heard Laban's sons talking. They said, "Jacob has taken everything our father owned, and in this way he has become rich." ²Then Jacob noticed that Laban was not as friendly as he had been before. ³The LORD said to Jacob, "Go back to the land where your ancestors lived, and I will be with you."

⁴So Jacob told Rachel and Leah to meet him in the field where he kept his flocks. ⁵He said to them, "I have seen that your father is not as friendly with me as he used to be, but the God of my father has been with me. ⁶You both know that I have worked as hard as I could for your father, ⁷but he cheated me and changed my pay ten times. But God has not allowed your father to harm me. ⁸When

Laban said, 'You can have all the speckled animals as your pay,' all the animals gave birth to speckled young ones. But when he said, 'You can have all the streaked animals as your pay,' all the flocks gave birth to streaked babies. ⁹So God has taken the animals away from your father and has given them to me.

¹⁰"I had a dream during the season when the flocks were mating. I saw that the only male goats who were mating were streaked, speckled, or spotted. ¹¹The angel of God spoke to me in that dream and said, 'Jacob!' I answered, 'Yes!' ¹²The angel said, 'Look! Only the streaked, speckled, or spotted male goats are mating. I have seen all the wrong things Laban has been doing to you. ¹³I am the God who appeared to you at Bethel, where you poured olive oil on the stone you set up on end and where you

made a promise to me. Now I want you to leave here and go back to the land where you were born.'"

¹⁴Rachel and Leah answered Jacob, "Our father has nothing to give us when he dies. ¹⁵He has treated us like strangers. He sold us to you, and then he spent all of the money you paid for us. ¹⁶God took all this wealth from our father, and now it belongs to us and our children. So do whatever God has told you to do."

¹⁷So Jacob put his children and his wives on camels, ¹⁸and they began their journey back to Isaac, his father, in the land of Canaan. All the flocks of animals that Jacob owned walked ahead of them. He carried everything with him that he had gotten while he lived in Northwest Mesopotamia.

¹⁹While Laban was gone to cut the wool from his sheep, Rachel stole the idols that belonged to him. ²⁰And Jacob tricked Laban the Aramean by not telling him he was leaving. ²¹Jacob and his family left quickly, crossed the Euphrates River, and traveled toward the mountains of Gilead.

²²Three days later Laban learned that Jacob had run away, ²³so he gathered his relatives and began to chase him. After seven days Laban found him in the mountains of Gilead. ²⁴That night God came to Laban the Aramean in a dream and said, "Be careful! Do not say anything to Jacob, good or bad."

The Search for the Stolen Idols

²⁵So Laban caught up with Jacob. Now Jacob had made his camp in the mountains, so Laban and his relatives set up their camp in the mountains of Gilead. ²⁶Laban said to Jacob, "What have you done? You cheated me and took my daughters as if you had captured them in a war. ²⁷Why did you run away secretly and trick me? Why didn't you tell me? Then I could have sent you away with joy and singing and with the music of tambourines and harps. ²⁸You did not even let me kiss my grandchildren and my daughters good-bye. You were very foolish to do this! ²⁹I have the power to harm you, but last night the God of your father spoke to me and warned me not to say anything to you, good or bad. ³⁰I know you want to go

back to your home, but why did you steal my idols?"

³¹Jacob answered Laban, "I left without telling you, because I was afraid you would take your daughters away from me. ³²If you find anyone here who has taken your idols, that person will be killed! Your relatives will be my witnesses. You may look for anything that belongs to you and take anything that is yours." (Now Jacob did not know that Rachel had stolen Laban's idols.)

³³So Laban looked in Jacob's tent, in Leah's tent, and in the tent where the two slave women stayed, but he did not find his idols. When he left Leah's tent, he went into Rachel's tent. ³⁴Rachel had hidden the idols inside her camel's saddle and was sitting on them. Although Laban looked through the whole tent, he did not find them.

³⁵Rachel said to her father, "Father, don't be angry with me. I am not able to stand up before you because I am having my monthly period." So Laban looked through the camp, but he did not find his idols.

³⁶Then Jacob became very angry and said, "What wrong have I done? What law have I broken to cause you to chase me? ³⁷You have looked through everything I own, but you have found nothing that belongs to you. If you have found anything, show it to everyone. Put it in front of your relatives and my relatives, and let them decide which one of us is right. ³⁸I have worked for you now for twenty years. During all that time none of the lambs and kids died during birth, and I have not eaten any of the male sheep from your flocks. ³⁹Any time an animal was killed by wild beasts, I did not bring it to you, but made up for the loss myself. You made me pay for any animal that was stolen during the day or night. ⁴⁰In the daytime the sun took away my strength, and at night I was cold and could not sleep. ⁴¹I worked like a slave for you for twenty years—the first fourteen to get your two daughters and the last six to earn your flocks. During that time you changed my pay ten times. ⁴²But the God of my father, the God of Abraham and the God of Isaac, was with me. Otherwise, you would have sent me away with nothing. But he saw the

trouble I had and the hard work I did, and last night he corrected you."

Jacob and Laban's Agreement

[43]Laban said to Jacob, "These girls are my daughters. Their children belong to me, and these flocks are mine. Everything you see here belongs to me, but I can do nothing to keep my daughters and their children. [44]Let us make an agreement, and let us set up a pile of stones to remind us of it."

[45]So Jacob took a large rock and set it up on its end. [46]He told his relatives to gather rocks, so they took the rocks and piled them up; then they ate beside the pile. [47]Laban named that place in his language A Pile to Remind Us, and Jacob gave the place the same name in Hebrew.

[48]Laban said to Jacob, "This pile of rocks will remind us of the agreement between us." That is why the place was called A Pile to Remind Us. [49]It was also called Mizpah,[n] because Laban said, "Let the LORD watch over us while we are separated from each other. [50]Remember that God is our witness even if no one else is around us. He will know if you harm my daughters or marry other women. [51]Here is the pile of rocks that I have put between us and here is the rock I set up on end. [52]This pile of rocks and this rock set on end will remind us of our agreement. I will never go past this pile to hurt you, and you must never come to my side of them to hurt me. [53]Let the God of Abraham, who is the God of Nahor and the God of their ancestors, punish either of us if we break this agreement."

So Jacob made a promise in the name of the God whom his father Isaac worshiped. [54]Then Jacob killed an animal and offered it as a sacrifice on the mountain, and he invited his relatives to share in the meal. After they finished eating, they spent the night on the mountain. [55]Early the next morning Laban kissed his grandchildren and his daughters and blessed them, and then he left to return home.

Jacob Meets Esau

32 When Jacob also went his way, the angels of God met him. [2]When he saw them, he said, "This is the camp of God!" So he named that place Mahanaim.[n]

[3]Jacob's brother Esau was living in the area called Seir in the country of Edom. Jacob sent messengers to Esau, [4]telling them, "Give this message to my master Esau: 'This is what Jacob, your servant, says: I have lived with Laban and have remained there until now. [5]I have cattle, donkeys, flocks, and male and female servants. I send this message to you and ask you to accept us.'"

[6]The messengers returned to Jacob and said, "We went to your brother Esau. He is coming to meet you and has four hundred men with him."

[7]Then Jacob was very afraid and worried. He divided the people who were with him and all the flocks, herds, and camels into two camps. [8]Jacob thought, "Esau might come and destroy one camp, but the other camp can run away and be saved."

[9]Then Jacob said, "God of my father Abraham! God of my father Isaac! LORD, you told me to return to my country and my family. You said that you would treat me well. [10]I am not worthy of the kindness and continual goodness you have shown me. The first time I traveled across the Jordan River, I had only my walking stick, but now I own enough to have two camps. [11]Please save me from my brother Esau. I am afraid he will come and kill all of us, even the mothers with the children. [12]You said to me, 'I will treat you well and will make your children as many as the sand of the seashore. There will be too many to count.'"

[13]Jacob stayed there for the night and prepared a gift for Esau from what he had with him: [14]two hundred female goats and twenty male goats, two hundred female sheep and twenty male sheep, [15]thirty female camels and their young, forty cows and ten bulls, twenty female donkeys, and ten male donkeys. [16]Jacob gave each separate flock of animals to one of his servants and said to them, "Go ahead of me and keep some space between each herd." [17]Jacob gave them their orders. To the servant with the first group of animals he said, "My brother Esau will come

to you and ask, 'Whose servant are you? Where are you going and whose animals are these?' [18]Then you will answer, 'They belong to your servant Jacob. He sent them as a gift to you, my master Esau, and he also is coming behind us.'"

[19]Jacob ordered the second servant, the third servant, and all the other servants to do the same thing. He said, "Say the same thing to Esau when you meet him. [20]Say, 'Your servant Jacob is coming behind us.'" Jacob thought, "If I send these gifts ahead of me, maybe Esau will forgive me. Then when I see him, perhaps he will accept me." [21]So Jacob sent the gifts to Esau, but he himself stayed that night in the camp.

Jacob Wrestles with God

[22]During the night Jacob rose and crossed the Jabbok River at the crossing, taking with him his two wives, his two slave girls, and his eleven sons. [23]He sent his family and everything he had across the river. [24]So Jacob was alone, and a man came and wrestled with him until the sun came up. [25]When the man saw he could not defeat Jacob, he struck Jacob's hip and put it out of joint. [26]Then he said to Jacob, "Let me go. The sun is coming up."

But Jacob said, "I will let you go if you will bless me."

[27]The man said to him, "What is your name?"

And he answered, "Jacob."

[28]Then the man said, "Your name will no longer be Jacob. Your name will now be Israel,[n] because you have wrestled with God and with people, and you have won."

[29]Then Jacob asked him, "Please tell me your name."

But the man said, "Why do you ask my name?" Then he blessed Jacob there.

[30]So Jacob named that place Peniel,[n] saying, "I have seen God face to face, but my life was saved." [31]Then the sun rose as he was leaving that place, and Jacob was limping because of his leg. [32]So even today the people of Israel do not eat the muscle that is on the hip joint of animals, because Jacob was touched there.

PSALM 8:3–9

[3]I look at your heavens,
  which you made with your fingers.
I see the moon and stars,
  which you created.
[4]But why are people even important to
    you?
Why do you take care of human
    beings?
[5]You made them a little lower than the
    angels
and crowned them with glory and
    honor.

[6]You put them in charge of everything
    you made.
You put all things under their
    control:
[7]all the sheep, the cattle,
  and the wild animals,
[8]the birds in the sky,
  the fish in the sea,
  and everything that lives under water.

[9]LORD our Lord,
  your name is the most wonderful
    name in all the earth!

PROVERBS 3:19–20

[19]The LORD made the earth, using his
    wisdom.
He set the sky in place, using his
    understanding.
[20]With his knowledge, he made springs
    flow into rivers
and the clouds drop rain on the
    earth.

MATTHEW 11:1–30

Jesus and John the Baptist

11 After Jesus finished telling these things to his twelve followers, he left there and went to the towns in Galilee to teach and preach.

[2]John the Baptist was in prison, but he heard about what the Christ was doing. So John sent some of his followers to Jesus. [3]They asked him, "Are you the One who is to come, or should we wait for someone else?"

32:28 Israel This name means "he wrestles with God." **32:30 Peniel** This name means "the face of God."

[4]Jesus answered them, "Go tell John what you hear and see: [5]The blind can see, the crippled can walk, and people with skin diseases are healed. The deaf can hear, the dead are raised to life, and the Good News is preached to the poor. [6]Those who do not stumble in their faith because of me are blessed."

[7]As John's followers were leaving, Jesus began talking to the people about John. Jesus said, "What did you go out into the desert to see? A reed[n] blown by the wind? [8]What did you go out to see? A man dressed in fine clothes? No, those who wear fine clothes live in kings' palaces. [9]So why did you go out? To see a prophet? Yes, and I tell you, John is more than a prophet. [10]This was written about him:

'I will send my messenger ahead of you, who will prepare the way for you.'

Malachi 3:1

[11]I tell you the truth, John the Baptist is greater than any other person ever born, but even the least important person in the kingdom of heaven is greater than John. [12]Since the time John the Baptist came until now, the kingdom of heaven has been going forward in strength, and people have been trying to take it by force. [13]All the prophets and the law of Moses told about what would happen until the time John came. [14]And if you will believe what they said, you will believe that John is Elijah, whom they said would come. [15]Let those with ears use them and listen!

[16]"What can I say about the people of this time? What are they like? They are like children sitting in the marketplace, who call out to each other,

[17]"We played music for you, but you did not dance;

we sang a sad song, but you did not cry.'

[18]John came and did not eat or drink like other people. So people say, 'He has a demon.' [19]The Son of Man came, eating and drinking, and people say, 'Look at him! He eats too much and drinks too much wine, and he is a friend of tax collectors and sinners.' But wisdom is proved to be right by what she does."

Jesus Warns Unbelievers

[20]Then Jesus criticized the cities where he did most of his miracles, because the people did not change their lives and stop sinning. [21]He said, "How terrible for you, Korazin! How terrible for you, Bethsaida! If the same miracles I did in you had happened in Tyre and Sidon,[n] those people would have changed their lives a long time ago. They would have worn rough cloth and put ashes on themselves to show they had changed. [22]But I tell you, on the Judgment Day it will be better for Tyre and Sidon than for you. [23]And you, Capernaum,[n] will you be lifted up to heaven? No, you will be thrown down to the depths. If the miracles I did in you had happened in Sodom,[n] its people would have stopped sinning, and it would still be a city today. [24]But I tell you, on the Judgment Day it will be better for Sodom than for you."

Jesus Offers Rest to People

[25]At that time Jesus said, "I praise you, Father, Lord of heaven and earth, because you have hidden these things from the people who are wise and smart. But you have shown them to those who are like little children. [26]Yes, Father, this is what you really wanted.

[27]"My Father has given me all things. No one knows the Son, except the Father. And no one knows the Father, except the Son and those whom the Son chooses to tell.

[28]"Come to me, all of you who are tired and have heavy loads, and I will give you rest. [29]Accept my teachings and learn from me, because I am gentle and humble in spirit, and you will find rest for your lives. [30]The burden that I ask you to accept is easy; the load I give you to carry is light."

11:7 reed It means that John was not ordinary or weak like grass blown by the wind. **11:21 Tyre and Sidon** Towns where wicked people lived. **11:21, 23 Korazin . . . Bethsaida . . . Capernaum** Towns by Lake Galilee where Jesus preached to the people. **11:23 Sodom** A city that God destroyed because the people were so evil.

JANUARY 17

GENESIS 33:1—34:31

Jacob Shows His Bravery

33 Jacob looked up and saw Esau coming, and with him were four hundred men. So Jacob divided his children among Leah, Rachel, and the two slave girls. ²Jacob put the slave girls with their children first, then Leah and her children behind them, and Rachel and Joseph last. ³Jacob himself went out in front of them and bowed down flat on the ground seven times as he was walking toward his brother.

⁴But Esau ran to meet Jacob and put his arms around him and hugged him. Then Esau kissed him, and they both cried. ⁵When Esau looked up and saw the women and children, he asked, "Who are these people with you?"

Jacob answered, "These are the children God has given me. God has been good to me, your servant."

⁶Then the two slave girls and their children came up to Esau and bowed down flat on the earth before him. ⁷Leah and her children also came up to Esau and also bowed down flat on the earth. Last of all, Joseph and Rachel came up to Esau, and they, too, bowed down flat before him.

⁸Esau said, "I saw many herds as I was coming here. Why did you bring them?"

Jacob answered, "They were to please you, my master."

⁹But Esau said, "I already have enough, my brother. Keep what you have."

¹⁰Jacob said, "No! Please! If I have pleased you, then accept the gift I give you. I am very happy to see your face again. It is like seeing the face of God, because you have accepted me. ¹¹So I beg you to accept the gift I give you. God has been very good to me, and I have more than I need." And because Jacob begged, Esau accepted the gift.

¹²Then Esau said, "Let us be going. I will travel with you."

¹³But Jacob said to him, "My master, you know that the children are weak. And I must be careful with my flocks and their young ones. If I force them to go too far in one day, all the animals will die. ¹⁴So, my master, you go on ahead of me, your servant. I will follow you slowly and let the animals and the children set the speed at which we travel. I will meet you, my master, in Edom."

¹⁵So Esau said, "Then let me leave some of my people with you."

"No, thank you," said Jacob. "I only want to please you, my master." ¹⁶So that day Esau started back to Edom. ¹⁷But Jacob went to Succoth, where he built a house for himself and shelters for his animals. That is why the place was named Succoth.ⁿ

¹⁸Jacob left Northwest Mesopotamia and arrived safely at the city of Shechem in the land of Canaan. There he camped east of the city. ¹⁹He bought a part of the field where he had camped from the sons of Hamor father of Shechem for one hundred pieces of silver. ²⁰He built an altar there and named it after God, the God of Israel.

Dinah Is Attacked

34 At this time Dinah, the daughter of Leah and Jacob, went out to visit the women of the land. ²When Shechem son of Hamor the Hivite, the ruler of the land, saw her, he took her and forced her to have sexual relations with him. ³Shechem fell in love with Dinah, and he spoke kindly to her. ⁴He told his father, Hamor, "Please get this girl for me so I can marry her."

⁵Jacob learned how Shechem had disgraced his daughter, but since his sons were out in the field with the cattle, Jacob said nothing until they came home. ⁶While he waited, Hamor father of Shechem went to talk with Jacob.

⁷When Jacob's sons heard what had happened, they came in from the field. They were very angry that Shechem had done such a wicked thing to Israel. It was wrong for him to have sexual relations with Jacob's daughter; a thing like this should not be done.

33:17 Succoth This name means "shelters."

⁸But Hamor talked to Dinah's brothers and said, "My son Shechem is deeply in love with Dinah. Please let him marry her. ⁹Marry our people. Give your women to our men as wives and take our women for your men as wives. ¹⁰You can live in the same land with us. You will be free to own land and to trade here."

¹¹Shechem also talked to Jacob and to Dinah's brothers and said, "Please accept my offer. I will give anything you ask. ¹²Ask as much as you want for the payment for the bride, and I will give it to you. Just let me marry Dinah."

¹³Jacob's sons answered Shechem and his father with lies, because Shechem had disgraced their sister Dinah. ¹⁴The brothers said to them, "We cannot allow you to marry our sister, because you are not circumcised. That would be a disgrace to us. ¹⁵But we will allow you to marry her if you do this one thing: Every man in your town must be circumcised like us. ¹⁶Then your men can marry our women, and our men can marry your women, and we will live in your land and become one people. ¹⁷If you refuse to be circumcised, we will take Dinah and leave."

¹⁸What they asked seemed fair to Hamor and Shechem. ¹⁹So Shechem quickly went to be circumcised because he loved Jacob's daughter.

Now Shechem was the most respected man in his family. ²⁰So Hamor and Shechem went to the gate of their city and spoke to the men of their city, saying, ²¹"These people want to be friends with us. So let them live in our land and trade here. There is enough land for all of us. Let us marry their women, and we can let them marry our women. ²²But we must agree to one thing: All our men must be circumcised as they are. Then they will agree to live in our land, and we will be one people. ²³If we do this, their cattle and their animals will belong to us. Let us do what they say, and they will stay in our land." ²⁴All the people who had come to the city gate heard this. They agreed with Hamor and Shechem, and every man was circumcised.

²⁵Three days later the men who were circumcised were still in pain. Two of Jacob's sons, Simeon and Levi (Dinah's brothers), took their swords and made a surprise attack on the city, killing all the men there. ²⁶They killed Hamor and his son Shechem and then took Dinah out of Shechem's house and left. ²⁷Jacob's sons came upon the dead bodies and stole everything that was in the city, to pay them back for what Shechem had done to their sister. ²⁸So the brothers took the flocks, herds, and donkeys, and everything in the city and in the fields. ²⁹They took every valuable thing the people owned, even their wives and children and everything in the houses.

³⁰Then Jacob said to Simeon and Levi, "You have caused me a lot of trouble. Now the Canaanites and the Perizzites who live in the land will hate me. Since there are only a few of us, if they join together to attack us, my people and I will be destroyed." ³¹But the brothers said, "We will not allow our sister to be treated like a prostitute."

PSALM 9:1–6

Thanksgiving for Victory

For the director of music. To the tune of "The Death of the Son." A psalm of David.

9 I will praise you, LORD, with all my heart.
I will tell all the miracles you have done.
²I will be happy because of you;
God Most High, I will sing praises to your name.

³My enemies turn back;
they are overwhelmed and die because of you.
⁴You have heard my complaint;
you sat on your throne and judged by what was right.
⁵You spoke strongly against the foreign nations and destroyed the wicked;
you wiped out their names forever and ever.
⁶The enemy is gone forever.
You destroyed their cities;
no one even remembers them.

PROVERBS 3:21–26

²¹My child, hold on to wisdom and good sense.
Don't let them out of your sight.
²²They will give you life

and beauty like a necklace around your neck.

²³Then you will go your way in safety,
and you will not get hurt.

²⁴When you lie down, you won't be afraid;
when you lie down, you will sleep in peace.

²⁵You won't be afraid of sudden trouble;
you won't fear the ruin that comes to the wicked,

²⁶because the LORD will keep you safe.
He will keep you from being trapped.

MATTHEW 12:1–21

Jesus Is Lord of the Sabbath

12At that time Jesus was walking through some fields of grain on a Sabbath day. His followers were hungry, so they began to pick the grain and eat it. ²When the Pharisees saw this, they said to Jesus, "Look! Your followers are doing what is unlawful to do on the Sabbath day."

³Jesus answered, "Have you not read what David did when he and the people with him were hungry? ⁴He went into God's house, and he and those with him ate the holy bread, which was lawful only for priests to eat. ⁵And have you not read in the law of Moses that on every Sabbath day the priests in the Temple break this law about the Sabbath day? But the priests are not wrong for doing that. ⁶I tell you that there is something here that is greater than the Temple. ⁷The Scripture says, 'I want kindness more than I want animal sacrifices.'ⁿ You don't really know what those words mean. If you understood them, you would not judge those who have done nothing wrong.

⁸"So the Son of Man is Lord of the Sabbath day."

Jesus Heals a Man's Hand

⁹Jesus left there and went into their synagogue, ¹⁰where there was a man with a crippled hand. They were looking for a reason to accuse Jesus, so they asked him, "Is it right to heal on the Sabbath day?"ⁿ

¹¹Jesus answered, "If any of you has a sheep, and it falls into a ditch on the Sabbath day, you will help it out of the ditch. ¹²Surely a human being is more important than a sheep. So it is lawful to do good things on the Sabbath day."

¹³Then Jesus said to the man with the crippled hand, "Hold out your hand." The man held out his hand, and it became well again, like the other hand. ¹⁴But the Pharisees left and made plans to kill Jesus.

Jesus Is God's Chosen Servant

¹⁵Jesus knew what the Pharisees were doing, so he left that place. Many people followed him, and he healed all who were sick. ¹⁶But Jesus warned the people not to tell who he was. ¹⁷He did these things to bring about what Isaiah the prophet had said:

¹⁸"Here is my servant whom I have chosen.
I love him, and I am pleased with him.
I will put my Spirit upon him,
and he will tell of my justice to all people.

¹⁹He will not argue or cry out;
no one will hear his voice in the streets.

²⁰He will not break a crushed blade of grass
or put out even a weak flame
until he makes justice win the victory.

²¹ In him will the non-Jewish people find hope."   *Isaiah 42:1–4*

JANUARY 18

GENESIS 35:1—36:43

Jacob in Bethel

35God said to Jacob, "Go to the city of Bethel and live there. Make an altar to the God who appeared to you there when you were running away from your brother Esau."

²So Jacob said to his family and to all who were with him, "Put away the foreign gods

---

12:7 'I . . . sacrifices.' Quotation from Hosea 6:6.   **12:10 Is it right . . . day?** It was against Jewish Law to work on the Sabbath day.

you have, and make yourselves clean, and change your clothes. [3]We will leave here and go to Bethel. There I will build an altar to God, who has helped me during my time of trouble. He has been with me everywhere I have gone." [4]So they gave Jacob all the foreign gods they had, and the earrings they were wearing, and he hid them under the great tree near the town of Shechem. [5]Then Jacob and his sons left there. But God caused the people in the nearby cities to be afraid, so they did not follow them. [6]And Jacob and all the people who were with him went to Luz, which is now called Bethel, in the land of Canaan. [7]There Jacob built an altar and named the place Bethel, after God, because God had appeared to him there when he was running from his brother.

[8]Deborah, Rebekah's nurse, died and was buried under the oak tree at Bethel, so they named that place Oak of Crying.

Jacob's New Name

[9]When Jacob came back from Northwest Mesopotamia, God appeared to him again and blessed him. [10]God said to him, "Your name is Jacob, but you will not be called Jacob any longer. Your new name will be Israel." So he called him Israel. [11]God said to him, "I am God Almighty. Have many children and grow in number as a nation. You will be the ancestor of many nations and kings. [12]The same land I gave to Abraham and Isaac I will give to you and your descendants." [13]Then God left him. [14]Jacob set up a stone on edge in that place where God had talked to him, and he poured a drink offering and olive oil on it to make it special for God. [15]And Jacob named the place Bethel.

Rachel Dies Giving Birth

[16]Jacob and his group left Bethel. Before they came to Ephrath, Rachel began giving birth to her baby, [17]but she was having much trouble. When Rachel's nurse saw this, she said, "Don't be afraid, Rachel. You are giving birth to another son." [18]Rachel gave birth to the son, but she herself died. As she lay dying, she named the boy Son of My Suffering, but Jacob called him Benjamin.[n]

[19]Rachel was buried on the road to Ephrath, a district of Bethlehem, [20]and Jacob set up a rock on her grave to honor her. That rock is still there. [21]Then Israel[n] continued his journey and camped just south of Migdal Eder.

[22]While Israel was there, Reuben had sexual relations with Israel's slave woman Bilhah, and Israel heard about it.

The Family of Israel

Jacob had twelve sons. [23]He had six sons by his wife Leah: Reuben, his first son, then Simeon, Levi, Judah, Issachar, and Zebulun. [24]He had two sons by his wife Rachel: Joseph and Benjamin. [25]He had two sons by Rachel's slave girl Bilhah: Dan and Naphtali. [26]And he had two sons by Leah's slave girl Zilpah: Gad and Asher.

These are Jacob's sons who were born in Northwest Mesopotamia.

[27]Jacob went to his father Isaac at Mamre near Hebron, where Abraham and Isaac had lived. [28]Isaac lived one hundred eighty years. [29]So Isaac breathed his last breath and died when he was very old, and his sons Esau and Jacob buried him.

Esau's Family

36 This is the family history of Esau (also called Edom). [2]Esau married women from the land of Canaan: Adah daughter of Elon the Hittite; and Oholibamah daughter of Anah, the son of Zibeon the Hivite; [3]and Basemath, Ishmael's daughter, the sister of Nebaioth.

[4]Adah gave birth to Eliphaz for Esau. Basemath gave him Reuel, [5]and Oholibamah gave him Jeush, Jalam, and Korah. These were Esau's sons who were born in the land of Canaan.

[6]Esau took his wives, his sons, his daughters, and all the people who lived with him, his herds and other animals, and all the belongings he had gotten in Canaan, and he went to a land away from his brother Jacob. [7]Esau and Jacob's belongings were becoming too many for them to live in the same land. The land where they had lived could not

support both of them, because they had too many herds. [8]So Esau lived in the mountains of Edom. (Esau is also named Edom.)

[9]This is the family history of Esau. He is the ancestor of the Edomites, who live in the mountains of Edom.

[10]Esau's sons were Eliphaz, son of Adah and Esau, and Reuel, son of Basemath and Esau.

[11]Eliphaz had five sons: Teman, Omar, Zepho, Gatam, and Kenaz. [12]Eliphaz also had a slave woman named Timna, and Timna and Eliphaz gave birth to Amalek. These were Esau's grandsons by his wife Adah.

[13]Reuel had four sons: Nahath, Zerah, Shammah, and Mizzah. These were Esau's grandsons by his wife Basemath.

[14]Esau's third wife was Oholibamah the daughter of Anah. (Anah was the son of Zibeon.) Esau and Oholibamah gave birth to Jeush, Jalam, and Korah.

[15]These were the leaders that came from Esau: Esau's first son was Eliphaz. From him came these leaders: Teman, Omar, Zepho, Kenaz, [16]Korah, Gatam, and Amalek. These were the leaders that came from Eliphaz in the land of Edom. They were the grandsons of Adah.

[17]Esau's son Reuel was the father of these leaders: Nahath, Zerah, Shammah, and Mizzah. These were the leaders that came from Reuel in the land of Edom. They were the grandsons of Esau's wife Basemath.

[18]Esau's wife Oholibamah gave birth to these leaders: Jeush, Jalam, and Korah. These are the leaders that came from Esau's wife Oholibamah the daughter of Anah. [19]These were the sons of Esau (also called Edom), and these were their leaders.

[20]These were the sons of Seir the Horite, who were living in the land: Lotan, Shobal, Zibeon, Anah, [21]Dishon, Ezer, and Dishan. These sons of Seir were the leaders of the Horites in Edom.

[22]The sons of Lotan were Hori and Homam. (Timna was Lotan's sister.)

[23]The sons of Shobal were Alvan, Manahath, Ebal, Shepho, and Onam.

[24]The sons of Zibeon were Aiah and Anah. Anah is the man who found the hot springs in the desert while he was caring for his father's donkeys.

[25]The children of Anah were Dishon and Oholibamah daughter of Anah.

[26]The sons of Dishon were Hemdan, Eshban, Ithran, and Keran.

[27]The sons of Ezer were Bilhan, Zaavan, and Akan.

[28]The sons of Dishan were Uz and Aran.

[29]These were the names of the Horite leaders: Lotan, Shobal, Zibeon, Anah, [30]Dishon, Ezer, and Dishan.

These men were the leaders of the Horite families who lived in the land of Edom.

[31]These are the kings who ruled in the land of Edom before the Israelites ever had a king:

[32]Bela son of Beor was the king of Edom. He came from the city of Dinhabah.

[33]When Bela died, Jobab son of Zerah became king. Jobab was from Bozrah.

[34]When Jobab died, Husham became king. He was from the land of the Temanites.

[35]When Husham died, Hadad son of Bedad, who had defeated Midian in the country of Moab, became king. Hadad was from the city of Avith.

[36]When Hadad died, Samlah became king. He was from Masrekah.

[37]When Samlah died, Shaul became king. He was from Rehoboth on the Euphrates River.

[38]When Shaul died, Baal-Hanan son of Acbor became king.

[39]When Baal-Hanan son of Acbor died, Hadad became king. He was from the city of Pau. His wife's name was Mehetabel daughter of Matred, who was the daughter of Me-Zahab.

[40]These Edomite leaders, listed by their families and regions, came from Esau. Their names were Timna, Alvah, Jetheth, [41]Oholibamah, Elah, Pinon, [42]Kenaz, Teman, Mibzar, [43]Magdiel, and Iram. They were the leaders of Edom. (Esau was the father of the Edomites.) The area where each of these families lived was named after that family.

PSALM 9:7–10

[7]But the LORD rules forever.
He sits on his throne to judge,

8and he will judge the world in fairness;
he will decide what is fair for the
nations.
9The Lord defends those who suffer;
he defends them in times of trouble.
10Those who know the Lord trust him,
because he will not leave those who
come to him.

PROVERBS 3:27–30

27Whenever you are able,
do good to people who need help.
28If you have what your neighbor asks
for,
don't say, "Come back later.
I will give it to you tomorrow."
29Don't make plans to hurt your
neighbor
who lives nearby and trusts you.
30Don't accuse a person for no good
reason;
don't accuse someone who has not
harmed you.

MATTHEW 12:22–50

Jesus' Power Is from God

22Then some people brought to Jesus a
man who was blind and could not talk, because he had a demon. Jesus healed the man
so that he could talk and see. 23All the people
were amazed and said, "Perhaps this man is
the Son of David!"

24When the Pharisees heard this, they
said, "Jesus uses the power of Beelzebul, the
ruler of demons, to force demons out of people."

25Jesus knew what the Pharisees were
thinking, so he said to them, "Every kingdom that is divided against itself will be destroyed. And any city or family that is
divided against itself will not continue.
26And if Satan forces out himself, then Satan
is divided against himself, and his kingdom
will not continue. 27You say that I use the
power of Beelzebul to force out demons. If
that is true, then what power do your people
use to force out demons? So they will be your
judges. 28But if I use the power of God's

Spirit to force out demons, then the kingdom
of God has come to you.

29"If anyone wants to enter a strong person's house and steal his things, he must first
tie up the strong person. Then he can steal
the things from the house.

30"Whoever is not with me is against me.
Whoever does not work with me is working
against me. 31So I tell you, people can be forgiven for every sin and everything they say
against God. But whoever speaks against the
Holy Spirit will not be forgiven. 32Anyone
who speaks against the Son of Man can be
forgiven, but anyone who speaks against the
Holy Spirit will not be forgiven, now or in the
future.

People Know You by Your Words

33"If you want good fruit, you must make
the tree good. If your tree is not good, it will
have bad fruit. A tree is known by the kind of
fruit it produces. 34You snakes! You are evil
people, so how can you say anything good?
The mouth speaks the things that are in the
heart. 35Good people have good things in
their hearts, and so they say good things. But
evil people have evil in their hearts, so they
say evil things. 36And I tell you that on the
Judgment Day people will be responsible for
every careless thing they have said. 37The
words you have said will be used to judge
you. Some of your words will prove you
right, but some of your words will prove you
guilty."

The People Ask for a Miracle

38Then some of the Pharisees and teachers of the law answered Jesus, saying,
"Teacher, we want to see you work a miracle
as a sign."

39Jesus answered, "Evil and sinful people
are the ones who want to see a miracle for a
sign. But no sign will be given to them, except the sign of the prophet Jonah. 40Jonah
was in the stomach of the big fish for three
days and three nights. In the same way, the
Son of Man will be in the grave three days
and three nights. 41On the Judgment Day the
people from Nineveh*n* will stand up with you
people who live now, and they will show that

12:41 **Nineveh** The city where Jonah preached to warn the people. Read Jonah 3.

you are guilty. When Jonah preached to them, they were sorry and changed their lives. And I tell you that someone greater than Jonah is here. [42]On the Judgment Day, the Queen of the South[n] will stand up with you people who live today. She will show that you are guilty, because she came from far away to listen to Solomon's wise teaching. And I tell you that someone greater than Solomon is here.

People Today Are Full of Evil

[43]"When an evil spirit comes out of a person, it travels through dry places, looking for a place to rest, but it doesn't find it. [44]So the spirit says, 'I will go back to the house I left.' When the spirit comes back, it finds the house still empty, swept clean, and made neat. [45]Then the evil spirit goes out and brings seven other spirits even more evil than it is, and they go in and live there. So the person has even more trouble than before. It is the same way with the evil people who live today."

Jesus' True Family

[46]While Jesus was talking to the people, his mother and brothers stood outside, trying to find a way to talk to him. [47]Someone told Jesus, "Your mother and brothers are standing outside, and they want to talk to you."[n]

[48]He answered, "Who is my mother? Who are my brothers?" [49]Then he pointed to his followers and said, "Here are my mother and my brothers. [50]My true brother and sister and mother are those who do what my Father in heaven wants."

JANUARY 19

GENESIS 37:1—38:30

Joseph the Dreamer

37 Jacob lived in the land of Canaan, where his father had lived. [2]This is the family history of Jacob:

Joseph was a young man, seventeen years old. He and his brothers, the sons of Bilhah and Zilpah, his father's wives, cared for the flocks. Joseph gave his father bad reports about his brothers. [3]Since Joseph was born when his father Israel[n] was old, Israel loved him more than his other sons. He made Joseph a special robe with long sleeves. [4]When Joseph's brothers saw that their father loved him more than he loved them, they hated their brother and could not speak to him politely.

[5]One time Joseph had a dream, and when he told his brothers about it, they hated him even more. [6]Joseph said, "Listen to the dream I had. [7]We were in the field tying bundles of wheat together. My bundle stood up, and your bundles of wheat gathered around it and bowed down to it."

[8]His brothers said, "Do you really think you will be king over us? Do you truly think you will rule over us?" His brothers hated him even more because of his dreams and what he had said.

[9]Then Joseph had another dream, and he told his brothers about it also. He said, "Listen, I had another dream. I saw the sun, moon, and eleven stars bowing down to me."

[10]Joseph also told his father about this dream, but his father scolded him, saying, "What kind of dream is this? Do you really believe that your mother, your brothers, and I will bow down to you?" [11]Joseph's brothers were jealous of him, but his father thought about what all these things could mean.

[12]One day Joseph's brothers went to Shechem to graze their father's flocks. [13]Israel said to Joseph, "Go to Shechem where your brothers are grazing the flocks."

Joseph answered, "I will go."

[14]His father said, "Go and see if your brothers and the flocks are all right. Then

come back and tell me." So Joseph's father sent him from the Valley of Hebron.

When Joseph came to Shechem, [15]a man found him wandering in the field and asked him, "What are you looking for?"

[16]Joseph answered, "I am looking for my brothers. Can you tell me where they are grazing the flocks?"

[17]The man said, "They have already gone. I heard them say they were going to Dothan." So Joseph went to look for his brothers and found them in Dothan.

Joseph Sold into Slavery

[18]Joseph's brothers saw him coming from far away. Before he reached them, they made a plan to kill him. [19]They said to each other, "Here comes that dreamer. [20]Let's kill him and throw his body into one of the wells. We can tell our father that a wild animal killed him. Then we will see what will become of his dreams."

[21]But Reuben heard their plan and saved Joseph, saying, "Let's not kill him. [22]Don't spill any blood. Throw him into this well here in the desert, but don't hurt him!" Reuben planned to save Joseph later and send him back to his father. [23]So when Joseph came to his brothers, they pulled off his robe with long sleeves [24]and threw him into the well. It was empty, and there was no water in it.

[25]While Joseph was in the well, the brothers sat down to eat. When they looked up, they saw a group of Ishmaelites traveling from Gilead to Egypt. Their camels were carrying spices, balm, and myrrh.

[26]Then Judah said to his brothers, "What will we gain if we kill our brother and hide his death? [27]Let's sell him to these Ishmaelites. Then we will not be guilty of killing our own brother. After all, he is our brother, our own flesh and blood." And the other brothers agreed. [28]So when the Midianite traders came by, the brothers took Joseph out of the well and sold him to the Ishmaelites for eight ounces of silver. And the Ishmaelites took him to Egypt.

[29]When Reuben came back to the well and Joseph was not there, he tore his clothes

to show he was upset. [30]Then he went back to his brothers and said, "The boy is not there! What shall I do?" [31]The brothers killed a goat and dipped Joseph's robe in its blood. [32]Then they brought the long-sleeved robe to their father and said, "We found this robe. Look it over carefully and see if it is your son's robe."

[33]Jacob looked it over and said, "It is my son's robe! Some savage animal has eaten him. My son Joseph has been torn to pieces!" [34]Then Jacob tore his clothes and put on rough cloth to show that he was upset, and he continued to be sad about his son for a long time. [35]All of his sons and daughters tried to comfort him, but he could not be comforted. He said, "I will be sad about my son until the day I die." So Jacob cried for his son Joseph.

[36]Meanwhile the Midianites who had bought Joseph had taken him to Egypt. There they sold him to Potiphar, an officer to the king of Egypt and captain of the palace guard.

Judah and Tamar

38 About that time, Judah left his brothers and went to stay with a man named Hirah in the town of Adullam. [2]There Judah met a Canaanite girl, the daughter of a man named Shua, and married her. Judah had sexual relations with her, [3]and she became pregnant and gave birth to a son, whom Judah named Er. [4]Later she gave birth to another son and named him Onan. [5]Still later she had another son and named him Shelah. She was at Kezib when this third son was born.

[6]Judah chose a girl named Tamar to be the wife of his first son Er. [7]But Er, Judah's oldest son, did what the LORD said was evil, so the LORD killed him. [8]Then Judah said to Er's brother Onan, "Go and have sexual relations with your dead brother's wife.[n] It is your duty to provide children for your brother in this way."

[9]But Onan knew that the children would not belong to him, so when he was supposed to have sexual relations with Tamar he did not complete the sex act. This made it impossible for Tamar to become pregnant and for Er to have descendants. [10]The LORD was displeased by this wicked thing Onan had done, so the

---

38:8 Go . . . wife It was a custom in Israel that if a man died without children, one of his brothers would marry the widow. If a child was born, it would be considered the dead man's child.

LORD killed Onan also. [11]Then Judah said to his daughter-in-law Tamar, "Go back to live in your father's house, and don't marry until my young son Shelah grows up." Judah was afraid that Shelah also would die like his brothers. So Tamar returned to her father's home.

[12]After a long time Judah's wife, the daughter of Shua, died. After Judah had gotten over his sorrow, he went to Timnah to his men who were cutting the wool from his sheep. His friend Hirah from Adullam went with him. [13]Tamar learned that Judah, her father-in-law, was going to Timnah to cut the wool from his sheep. [14]So she took off the clothes that showed she was a widow and covered her face with a veil to hide who she was. Then she sat down by the gate of Enaim on the road to Timnah. She did this because Judah's younger son Shelah had grown up, but Judah had not made plans for her to marry him.

[15]When Judah saw her, he thought she was a prostitute, because she had covered her face with a veil. [16]So Judah went to her and said, "Let me have sexual relations with you." He did not know that she was Tamar, his daughter-in-law.

She asked, "What will you give me if I let you have sexual relations with me?"

[17]Judah answered, "I will send you a young goat from my flock."

She answered, "First give me something to keep as a deposit until you send the goat."

[18]Judah asked, "What do you want me to give you as a deposit?"

Tamar answered, "Give me your seal and its cord,[n] and give me your walking stick." So Judah gave these things to her. Then Judah and Tamar had sexual relations, and Tamar became pregnant. [19]When Tamar went home, she took off the veil that covered her face and put on the clothes that showed she was a widow.

[20]Judah sent his friend Hirah with the young goat to find the woman and get back his seal and the walking stick he had given her, but Hirah could not find her. [21]He asked some of the people at the town of Enaim, "Where is the prostitute who was here by the road?"

They answered, "There has never been a prostitute here."

[22]So he went back to Judah and said, "I could not find the woman, and the people who lived there said, 'There has never been a prostitute here.'"

[23]Judah said, "Let her keep the things. I don't want people to laugh at us. I sent her the goat as I promised, but you could not find her."

[24]About three months later someone told Judah, "Tamar, your daughter-in-law, is guilty of acting like a prostitute, and now she is pregnant."

Then Judah said, "Bring her out and let her be burned to death."

[25]When the people went to bring Tamar out, she sent a message to her father-in-law that said, "The man who owns these things has made me pregnant. Look at this seal and its cord and this walking stick, and tell me whose they are."

[26]Judah recognized them and said, "She is more in the right than I. She did this because I did not give her to my son Shelah as I promised." And Judah did not have sexual relations with her again.

[27]When the time came for Tamar to give birth, there were twins in her body. [28]While she was giving birth, one baby put his hand out. The nurse tied a red string on his hand and said, "This baby came out first." [29]But he pulled his hand back in, so the other baby was born first. The nurse said, "So you are able to break out first," and they named him Perez.[n] [30]After this, the baby with the red string on his hand was born, and they named him Zerah.

PSALM 9:11–20

[11]Sing praises to the LORD who is king on
  Mount Zion.
Tell the nations what he has done.
[12]He remembers who the murderers are;
  he will not forget the cries of those who
  suffer.

38:18 seal . . . cord A seal was used like a rubber stamp, and people ran a string through it to tie around the neck. They wrote a contract, folded it, put wax or clay on the contract, and pressed the seal onto it as a signature. **38:29 Perez** This name means "breaking out."

[13]LORD, have mercy on me.
See how my enemies hurt me.
Do not let me go through the gates of
death.
[14]Then, at the gates of Jerusalem, I will
praise you;
I will rejoice because you saved me.

[15]The nations have fallen into the pit they
dug.
Their feet are caught in the nets they
laid.
[16]The LORD has made himself known by
his fair decisions;
the wicked get trapped by what they do.
Higgaion. Selah

[17]Wicked people will go to the grave,
and so will all those who forget God.
[18]But those who have troubles will not be
forgotten.
The hopes of the poor will never die.

[19]LORD, rise up and judge the nations.
Don't let people think they are strong.
[20]Teach them to fear you, LORD.
The nations must learn that they are
only human. *Selah*

PROVERBS 3:31–35

[31]Don't be jealous of those who use
violence,
and don't choose to be like them.
[32]The LORD hates those who do wrong,
but he is a friend to those who are
honest.
[33]The LORD will curse the evil person's
house,
but he will bless the home of those who
do right.
[34]The LORD laughs at those who laugh at
him,
but he gives grace to those who are not
proud.
[35]Wise people will receive honor,
but fools will be disgraced.

MATTHEW 13:1–30

A Story About Planting Seed

13 That same day Jesus went out of the
house and sat by the lake. [2]Large
crowds gathered around him, so he got into
a boat and sat down, while the people stood
on the shore. [3]Then Jesus used stories to
teach them many things. He said: "A farmer
went out to plant his seed. [4]While he was
planting, some seed fell by the road, and the
birds came and ate it all up. [5]Some seed fell
on rocky ground, where there wasn't much
dirt. That seed grew very fast, because the
ground was not deep. [6]But when the sun
rose, the plants dried up, because they did
not have deep roots. [7]Some other seed fell
among thorny weeds, which grew and
choked the good plants. [8]Some other seed
fell on good ground where it grew and produced a crop. Some plants made a hundred
times more, some made sixty times more,
and some made thirty times more. [9]Let
those with ears use them and listen."

Why Jesus Used Stories to Teach

[10]The followers came to Jesus and asked,
"Why do you use stories to teach the people?"

[11]Jesus answered, "You have been chosen
to know the secrets about the kingdom of
heaven, but others cannot know these secrets. [12]Those who have understanding will
be given more, and they will have all they
need. But those who do not have understanding, even what they have will be taken
away from them. [13]This is why I use stories
to teach the people: They see, but they don't
really see. They hear, but they don't really
hear or understand. [14]So they show that the
things Isaiah said about them are true:
'You will listen and listen, but you will
not understand.
You will look and look, but you will not
learn.
[15]For the minds of these people have
become stubborn.
They do not hear with their ears,
and they have closed their eyes.
Otherwise they might really understand
what they see with their eyes
and hear with their ears.
They might really understand in their
minds
and come back to me and be healed.'
Isaiah 6:9–10

¹⁶But you are blessed, because you see with your eyes and hear with your ears. ¹⁷I tell you the truth, many prophets and good people wanted to see the things that you now see, but they did not see them. And they wanted to hear the things that you now hear, but they did not hear them.

Jesus Explains the Seed Story

¹⁸"So listen to the meaning of that story about the farmer. ¹⁹What is the seed that fell by the road? That seed is like the person who hears the message about the kingdom but does not understand it. The Evil One comes and takes away what was planted in that person's heart. ²⁰And what is the seed that fell on rocky ground? That seed is like the person who hears the teaching and quickly accepts it with joy. ²¹But he does not let the teaching go deep into his life, so he keeps it only a short time. When trouble or persecution comes because of the teaching he accepted, he quickly gives up. ²²And what is the seed that fell among the thorny weeds? That seed is like the person who hears the teaching but lets worries about this life and the temptation of wealth stop that teaching from growing. So the teaching does not produce fruit*ⁿ* in that person's life. ²³But what is the seed that fell on the good ground? That seed is like the person who hears the teaching and understands it. That person grows and produces fruit, sometimes a hundred times more, sometimes sixty times more, and sometimes thirty times more."

A Story About Wheat and Weeds

²⁴Then Jesus told them another story: "The kingdom of heaven is like a man who planted good seed in his field. ²⁵That night, when everyone was asleep, his enemy came and planted weeds among the wheat and then left. ²⁶Later, the wheat sprouted and the heads of grain grew, but the weeds also grew. ²⁷Then the man's servants came to him and said, 'You planted good seed in your field. Where did the weeds come from?' ²⁸The man answered, 'An enemy planted weeds.' The servants asked, 'Do you want us to pull up the weeds?' ²⁹The man answered, 'No, because when you pull up the weeds, you might also pull up the wheat. ³⁰Let the weeds and the wheat grow together until the harvest time. At harvest time I will tell the workers, "First gather the weeds and tie them together to be burned. Then gather the wheat and bring it to my barn."'"

JANUARY 20

GENESIS 39:1—40:23

Joseph Is Sold to Potiphar

39 Now Joseph had been taken down to Egypt. An Egyptian named Potiphar was an officer to the king of Egypt and the captain of the palace guard. He bought Joseph from the Ishmaelites who had brought him down there. ²The LORD was with Joseph, and he became a successful man. He lived in the house of his master, Potiphar the Egyptian.

³Potiphar saw that the LORD was with Joseph and that the LORD made Joseph successful in everything he did. ⁴So Potiphar was very happy with Joseph and allowed him to be his personal servant. He put Joseph in charge of the house, trusting him with everything he owned. ⁵When Joseph was put in charge of the house and everything Potiphar owned, the LORD blessed the people in Potiphar's house because of Joseph. And the LORD blessed everything that belonged to Potiphar, both in the house and in the field. ⁶So Potiphar left Joseph in charge of everything he owned and was not concerned about anything except the food he ate.

13:22 produce fruit To produce fruit means to have in your life the good things God wants.

Joseph Is Put into Prison

Now Joseph was well built and handsome. [7]After some time the wife of Joseph's master began to desire Joseph, and one day she said to him, "Have sexual relations with me."

[8]But Joseph refused and said to her, "My master trusts me with everything in his house. He has put me in charge of everything he owns. [9]There is no one in his house greater than I. He has not kept anything from me except you, because you are his wife. How can I do such an evil thing? It is a sin against God."

[10]The woman talked to Joseph every day, but he refused to have sexual relations with her or even spend time with her.

[11]One day Joseph went into the house to do his work as usual and was the only man in the house at that time. [12]His master's wife grabbed his coat and said to him, "Come and have sexual relations with me." But Joseph left his coat in her hand and ran out of the house.

[13]When she saw that Joseph had left his coat in her hands and had run outside, [14]she called to the servants in her house and said, "Look! This Hebrew slave was brought here to shame us. He came in and tried to have sexual relations with me, but I screamed. [15]My scream scared him and he ran away, but he left his coat with me." [16]She kept his coat until her husband came home, [17]and she told him the same story. She said, "This Hebrew slave you brought here came in to shame me! [18]When he came near me, I screamed. He ran away, but he left his coat."

[19]When Joseph's master heard what his wife said Joseph had done, he became very angry. [20]So Potiphar arrested Joseph and put him into the prison where the king's prisoners were put. And Joseph stayed there in the prison.

[21]But the LORD was with Joseph and showed him kindness and caused the prison warden to like Joseph. [22]The prison warden chose Joseph to take care of all the prisoners, and he was responsible for whatever was done in the prison. [23]The warden paid no attention to anything that was in Joseph's care because the LORD was with Joseph and made him successful in everything he did.

Joseph Interprets Two Dreams

40 After these things happened, two of the king's officers displeased the king—the man who served wine to the king and the king's baker. [2]The king became angry with his officer who served him wine and his baker, [3]so he put them in the prison of the captain of the guard, the same prison where Joseph was kept. [4]The captain of the guard put the two prisoners in Joseph's care, and they stayed in prison for some time.

[5]One night both the king's officer who served him wine and the baker had a dream. Each had his own dream with its own meaning. [6]When Joseph came to them the next morning, he saw they were worried. [7]He asked the king's officers who were with him, "Why do you look so unhappy today?"

[8]The two men answered, "We both had dreams last night, but no one can explain their meaning to us."

Joseph said to them, "God is the only One who can explain the meaning of dreams. Tell me your dreams."

[9]So the man who served wine to the king told Joseph his dream. He said, "I dreamed I saw a vine, and [10]on the vine were three branches. I watched the branches bud and blossom, and then the grapes ripened. [11]I was holding the king's cup, so I took the grapes and squeezed the juice into the cup. Then I gave it to the king."

[12]Then Joseph said, "I will explain the dream to you. The three branches stand for three days. [13]Before the end of three days the king will free you, and he will allow you to return to your work. You will serve the king his wine just as you did before. [14]But when you are free, remember me. Be kind to me, and tell the king about me so I can get out of this prison. [15]I was taken by force from the land of the Hebrews, and I have done nothing here to deserve being put in prison."

[16]The baker saw that Joseph's explanation of the dream was good, so he said to him, "I also had a dream. I dreamed there were three bread baskets on my head. [17]In the top basket were all kinds of baked food for the king, but the birds were eating this food out of the basket on my head."

[18]Joseph answered, "I will tell you what

the dream means. The three baskets stand for three days. ¹⁹Before the end of three days, the king will cut off your head! He will hang your body on a pole, and the birds will eat your flesh."

²⁰Three days later, on his birthday, the king gave a feast for all his officers. In front of his officers, he released from prison the chief officer who served his wine and the chief baker. ²¹The king gave his chief officer who served wine his old position, and once again he put the king's cup of wine into the king's hand. ²²But the king hanged the baker on a pole. Everything happened just as Joseph had said it would, ²³but the officer who served wine did not remember Joseph. He forgot all about him.

PSALM 10:1–11

A Complaint About Evil People

10 LORD, why are you so far away?
Why do you hide when there is trouble?
²Proudly the wicked chase down those who suffer.
Let them be caught in their own traps.
³They brag about the things they want.
They bless the greedy but hate the LORD.
⁴The wicked people are too proud.
They do not look for God;
there is no room for God in their thoughts.
⁵They always succeed.
They are far from keeping your laws;
they make fun of their enemies.
⁶They say to themselves, "Nothing bad will ever happen to me;
I will never be ruined."
⁷Their mouths are full of curses, lies, and threats;
they use their tongues for sin and evil.
⁸They hide near the villages.
They look for innocent people to kill;
they watch in secret for the helpless.
⁹They wait in hiding like a lion.
They wait to catch poor people;
they catch the poor in nets.
¹⁰The poor are thrown down and crushed;
they are defeated because the others are stronger.

¹¹The wicked think, "God has forgotten us.
He doesn't see what is happening."

PROVERBS 4:1–6

Wisdom Is Important

4 My children, listen to your father's teaching;
pay attention so you will understand.
²What I am telling you is good,
so do not forget what I teach you.
³When I was a young boy in my father's house
and like an only child to my mother,
⁴my father taught me and said,
"Hold on to my words with all your heart.
Keep my commands and you will live.
⁵Get wisdom and understanding.
Don't forget or ignore my words.
⁶Hold on to wisdom, and it will take care of you.
Love it, and it will keep you safe.

MATTHEW 13:31–58

Stories of Mustard Seed and Yeast

³¹Then Jesus told another story: "The kingdom of heaven is like a mustard seed that a man planted in his field. ³²That seed is the smallest of all seeds, but when it grows, it is one of the largest garden plants. It becomes big enough for the wild birds to come and build nests in its branches."

³³Then Jesus told another story: "The kingdom of heaven is like yeast that a woman took and hid in a large tub of flour until it made all the dough rise."

³⁴Jesus used stories to tell all these things to the people; he always used stories to teach them. ³⁵This is as the prophet said:

"I will speak using stories;
I will tell things that have been secret since the world was made."

Psalm 78:2

Jesus Explains About the Weeds

³⁶Then Jesus left the crowd and went into the house. His followers came to him and said, "Explain to us the meaning of the story about the weeds in the field."

³⁷Jesus answered, "The man who planted

the good seed in the field is the Son of Man. [38]The field is the world, and the good seed are all of God's children who belong to the kingdom. The weeds are those people who belong to the Evil One. [39]And the enemy who planted the bad seed is the devil. The harvest time is the end of the age, and the workers who gather are God's angels.

[40]"Just as the weeds are pulled up and burned in the fire, so it will be at the end of the age. [41]The Son of Man will send out his angels, and they will gather out of his kingdom all who cause sin and all who do evil. [42]The angels will throw them into the blazing furnace, where the people will cry and grind their teeth with pain. [43]Then the good people will shine like the sun in the kingdom of their Father. Let those with ears use them and listen.

Stories of a Treasure and a Pearl

[44]"The kingdom of heaven is like a treasure hidden in a field. One day a man found the treasure, and then he hid it in the field again. He was so happy that he went and sold everything he owned to buy that field.

[45]"Also, the kingdom of heaven is like a man looking for fine pearls. [46]When he found a very valuable pearl, he went and sold everything he had and bought it.

A Story of a Fishing Net

[47]"Also, the kingdom of heaven is like a net that was put into the lake and caught many different kinds of fish. [48]When it was full, the fishermen pulled the net to the shore. They sat down and put all the good fish in baskets and threw away the bad fish. [49]It will be this way at the end of the age. The angels will come and separate the evil people from the good people. [50]The angels will throw the evil people into the blazing furnace, where people will cry and grind their teeth with pain."

[51]Jesus asked his followers, "Do you understand all these things?"

They answered, "Yes, we understand."

[52]Then Jesus said to them, "So every teacher of the law who has been taught about the kingdom of heaven is like the owner of a house. He brings out both new things and old things he has saved."

Jesus Goes to His Hometown

[53]When Jesus finished teaching with these stories, he left there. [54]He went to his hometown and taught the people in the synagogue, and they were amazed. They said, "Where did this man get this wisdom and this power to do miracles? [55]He is just the son of a carpenter. His mother is Mary, and his brothers are James, Joseph, Simon, and Judas. [56]And all his sisters are here with us. Where then does this man get all these things?" [57]So the people were upset with Jesus.

But Jesus said to them, "A prophet is honored everywhere except in his hometown and in his own home."

[58]So he did not do many miracles there because they had no faith.

JANUARY 21

GENESIS 41:1—42:38

The King's Dreams

41 Two years later the king dreamed he was standing on the bank of the Nile River. [2]He saw seven fat and beautiful cows come up out of the river, and they stood there, eating the grass. [3]Then seven more cows came up out of the river, but they were thin and ugly. They stood beside the seven beautiful cows on the bank of the Nile. [4]The seven thin and ugly cows ate the seven beautiful fat cows. Then the king woke up. [5]The king slept again and dreamed a second time. In his dream he saw seven full and good heads of grain growing on one stalk. [6]After that, seven more heads of grain sprang up, but they were thin and burned by the hot east wind. [7]The thin heads of grain ate the seven full and good heads. Then the king

woke up again, and he realized it was only a dream. [8]The next morning the king was troubled about these dreams, so he sent for all the magicians and wise men of Egypt. The king told them his dreams, but no one could explain their meaning to him.

[9]Then the chief officer who served wine to the king said to him, "Now I remember something I promised to do, but I forgot about it. [10]There was a time when you were angry with the baker and me, and you put us in prison in the house of the captain of the guard. [11]In prison we each had a dream on the same night, and each dream had a different meaning. [12]A young Hebrew man, a servant of the captain of the guard, was in the prison with us. When we told him our dreams, he explained their meanings to us. He told each man the meaning of his dream, and [13]things happened exactly as he said they would: I was given back my old position, and the baker was hanged."

[14]So the king called for Joseph. The guards quickly brought him out of the prison, and he shaved, put on clean clothes, and went before the king.

[15]The king said to Joseph, "I have had a dream, but no one can explain its meaning to me. I have heard that you can explain a dream when someone tells it to you."

[16]Joseph answered the king, "I am not able to explain the meaning of dreams, but God will do this for the king."

[17]Then the king said to Joseph, "In my dream I was standing on the bank of the Nile River. [18]I saw seven fat and beautiful cows that came up out of the river and ate the grass. [19]Then I saw seven more cows come out of the river that were thin and lean and ugly—the worst looking cows I have seen in all the land of Egypt. [20]And these thin and ugly cows ate the first seven fat cows, [21]but after they had eaten the seven cows, no one could tell they had eaten them. They looked just as thin and ugly as they did in the beginning. Then I woke up.

[22]"I had another dream. I saw seven full and good heads of grain growing on one stalk. [23]Then seven more heads of grain sprang up after them, but these heads were thin and ugly and were burned by the hot east wind. [24]Then the thin heads ate the seven good heads. I told this dream to the magicians, but no one could explain its meaning to me."

Joseph Tells the Dreams' Meaning

[25]Then Joseph said to the king, "Both of these dreams mean the same thing. God is telling you what he is about to do. [26]The seven good cows stand for seven years, and the seven good heads of grain stand for seven years. Both dreams mean the same thing. [27]The seven thin and ugly cows stand for seven years, and the seven thin heads of grain burned by the hot east wind stand for seven years of hunger. [28]This will happen as I told you. God is showing the king what he is about to do. [29]You will have seven years of good crops and plenty to eat in all the land of Egypt. [30]But after those seven years, there will come seven years of hunger, and all the food that grew in the land of Egypt will be forgotten. The time of hunger will eat up the land. [31]People will forget what it was like to have plenty of food, because the hunger that follows will be so great. [32]You had two dreams which mean the same thing. This shows that God has firmly decided that this will happen, and he will make it happen soon.

[33]"So let the king choose a man who is very wise and understanding and set him over the land of Egypt. [34]And let the king also appoint officers over the land, who should take one-fifth of all the food that is grown during the seven good years. [35]They should gather all the food that is produced during the good years that are coming, and under the king's authority they should store the grain in the cities and guard it. [36]That food should be saved to use during the seven years of hunger that will come on the land of Egypt. Then the people in Egypt will not die during the seven years of hunger."

Joseph Is Made Ruler over Egypt

[37]This seemed like a very good idea to the king, and all his officers agreed. [38]And the king asked them, "Can we find a better man than Joseph to take this job? God's spirit is truly in him!"

[39]So the king said to Joseph, "God has

shown you all this. There is no one as wise and understanding as you are, so [40]I will put you in charge of my palace. All the people will obey your orders, and only I will be greater than you."

[41]Then the king said to Joseph, "Look! I have put you in charge of all the land of Egypt." [42]Then the king took off from his own finger his ring with the royal seal on it, and he put it on Joseph's finger. He gave Joseph fine linen clothes to wear, and he put a gold chain around Joseph's neck. [43]The king had Joseph ride in the second royal chariot, and people walked ahead of his chariot calling, "Bow down!" By doing these things, the king put Joseph in charge of all of Egypt.

[44]The king said to him, "I am the king, and I say that no one in all the land of Egypt may lift a hand or a foot without your permission." [45]The king gave Joseph the name Zaphenath-Paneah. He also gave Joseph a wife named Asenath, who was the daughter of Potiphar, priest of On. So Joseph traveled through all the land of Egypt.

[46]Joseph was thirty years old when he began serving the king of Egypt. And he left the king's court and traveled through all the land of Egypt. [47]During the seven good years, the crops in the land grew well. [48]And Joseph gathered all the food produced in Egypt during those seven years of good crops and stored the food in the cities. In every city he stored grain that had been grown in the fields around that city. [49]Joseph stored much grain, as much as the sand of the seashore—so much that he could not measure it.

[50]Joseph's wife was Asenath daughter of Potiphera, the priest of On. Before the years of hunger came, Joseph and Asenath had two sons. [51]Joseph named the first son Manasseh[n] and said, "God has made me forget all the troubles I have had and all my father's family." [52]Joseph named the second son Ephraim[n] and said, "God has given me children in the land of my troubles."

[53]The seven years of good crops came to an end in the land of Egypt. [54]Then the seven years of hunger began, just as Joseph had said. In all the lands people had nothing to eat, but in Egypt there was food. [55]The time of hunger became terrible in all of Egypt, and the people cried to the king for food. He said to all the Egyptians, "Go to Joseph and do whatever he tells you."

[56]The hunger was everywhere in that part of the world. And Joseph opened the storehouses and sold grain to the people of Egypt, because the time of hunger became terrible in Egypt. [57]And all the people in that part of the world came to Joseph in Egypt to buy grain because the hunger was terrible everywhere in that part of the world.

The Dreams Come True

42 Jacob learned that there was grain in Egypt, so he said to his sons, "Why are you just sitting here looking at one another? [2]I have heard that there is grain in Egypt. Go down there and buy grain for us to eat, so that we will live and not die."

[3]So ten of Joseph's brothers went down to buy grain from Egypt. [4]But Jacob did not send Benjamin, Joseph's brother, with them, because he was afraid that something terrible might happen to him. [5]Along with many other people, the sons of Israel[n] went to Egypt to buy grain, because the people in the land of Canaan were also hungry.

[6]Now Joseph was governor over Egypt. He was the one who sold the grain to people who came to buy it. So Joseph's brothers came to him and bowed facedown on the ground before him. [7]When Joseph saw his brothers, he knew who they were, but he acted as if he didn't know them. He asked unkindly, "Where do you come from?"

They answered, "We have come from the land of Canaan to buy food."

[8]Joseph knew they were his brothers, but they did not know who he was. [9]And Joseph remembered his dreams about his brothers bowing to him. He said to them, "You are spies! You came to learn where the nation is weak!"

[10]But his brothers said to him, "No, my

41:51 Manasseh This name sounds like the Hebrew word for "made me forget." **41:52 Ephraim** This name sounds like the Hebrew word for "given me children." **42:5 Israel** Also called Jacob.

master. We come as your servants just to buy food. [11]We are all sons of the same father. We are honest men, not spies."

[12]Then Joseph said to them, "No! You have come to learn where this nation is weak!"

[13]And they said, "We are ten of twelve brothers, sons of the same father, and we live in the land of Canaan. Our youngest brother is there with our father right now, and our other brother is gone."

[14]But Joseph said to them, "I can see I was right! You are spies! [15]But I will give you a way to prove you are telling the truth. As surely as the king lives, you will not leave this place until your youngest brother comes here. [16]One of you must go and get your brother. The rest of you will stay here in prison. We will see if you are telling the truth. If not, as surely as the king lives, you are spies." [17]Then Joseph put them all in prison for three days.

[18]On the third day Joseph said to them, "I am a God-fearing man. Do this and I will let you live: [19]If you are honest men, let one of your brothers stay here in prison while the rest of you go and carry grain back to feed your hungry families. [20]Then bring your youngest brother back here to me. If you do this, I will know you are telling the truth, and you will not die."

The brothers agreed to this. [21]They said to each other, "We are being punished for what we did to our brother. We saw his trouble, and he begged us to save him, but we refused to listen. That is why we are in this trouble now."

[22]Then Reuben said to them, "I told you not to harm the boy, but you refused to listen to me. So now we are being punished for what we did to him."

[23]When Joseph talked to his brothers, he used an interpreter, so they did not know that Joseph understood what they were saying. [24]Then Joseph left them and cried. After a short time he went back and spoke to them. He took Simeon and tied him up while the other brothers watched. [25]Joseph told his servants to fill his brothers' bags with grain and to put the money the brothers had paid for the grain back in their bags. The servants were also to give them what they would need

for their trip back home. And the servants did this.

[26]So the brothers put the grain on their donkeys and left. [27]When they stopped for the night, one of the brothers opened his sack to get food for his donkey. Then he saw his money in the top of the sack. [28]He said to the other brothers, "The money I paid for the grain has been put back. Here it is in my sack!"

The brothers were very frightened. They said to each other, "What has God done to us?"

The Brothers Return to Jacob

[29]The brothers went to their father Jacob in the land of Canaan and told him everything that had happened. [30]They said, "The master of that land spoke unkindly to us. He accused us of spying on his country, [31]but we told him that we were honest men, not spies. [32]We told him that we were ten of twelve brothers—sons of one father. We said that one of our brothers was gone and that our youngest brother was with our father in Canaan.

[33]"Then the master of the land said to us, 'Here is a way I can know you are honest men: Leave one of your brothers with me, and take grain to feed your hungry families, and go. [34]And bring your youngest brother to me so I will know you are not spies but honest men. Then I will give you back your brother whom you leave with me, and you can move about freely in our land.'"

[35]As the brothers emptied their sacks, each of them found his money in his sack. When they and their father saw it, they were afraid.

[36]Their father Jacob said to them, "You are robbing me of all my children. Joseph is gone, Simeon is gone, and now you want to take Benjamin away, too. Everything is against me."

[37]Then Reuben said to his father, "You may put my two sons to death if I don't bring Benjamin back to you. Trust him to my care, and I will bring him back to you."

[38]But Jacob said, "I will not allow Benjamin to go with you. His brother is dead, and he is the only son left from my wife

(continued)

Rachel. I am afraid something terrible might happen to him during the trip to Egypt. Then I would be sad until the day I die."

PSALM 10:12–18

[12]LORD, rise up and punish the wicked.
    Don't forget those who need help.
[13]Why do wicked people hate God?
    They say to themselves, "God won't
        punish us."
[14]LORD, surely you see these cruel and evil
        things;
    look at them and do something.
    People in trouble look to you for help.
    You are the one who helps the orphans.
[15]Break the power of wicked people.
    Punish them for the evil they have done.

[16]The LORD is King forever and ever.
    Destroy from your land those nations
        that do not worship you.
[17]LORD, you have heard what the poor
        people want.
    Do what they ask, and listen to them.
[18]Protect the orphans and put an end to
        suffering
    so they will no longer be afraid of evil
        people.

PROVERBS 4:7–9

[7]Wisdom is the most important thing; so
    get wisdom.
    If it costs everything you have, get
        understanding.
[8]Treasure wisdom, and it will make you
        great;
    hold on to it, and it will bring you
        honor.
[9]It will be like flowers in your hair
    and like a beautiful crown on your head."

MATTHEW 14:1–21

How John the Baptist Was Killed

14 At that time Herod, the ruler of Galilee, heard the reports about Jesus. [2]So he said to his servants, "Jesus is John the Baptist, who has risen from the dead. That is why he can work these miracles."

[3]Sometime before this, Herod had arrested John, tied him up, and put him into prison. Herod did this because of Herodias, who had been the wife of Philip, Herod's brother. [4]John had been telling Herod, "It is not lawful for you to be married to Herodias." [5]Herod wanted to kill John, but he was afraid of the people, because they believed John was a prophet.

[6]On Herod's birthday, the daughter of Herodias danced for Herod and his guests, and she pleased him. [7]So he promised with an oath to give her anything she wanted. [8]Herodias told her daughter what to ask for, so she said to Herod, "Give me the head of John the Baptist here on a platter." [9]Although King Herod was very sad, he had made a promise, and his dinner guests had heard him. So Herod ordered that what she asked for be done. [10]He sent soldiers to the prison to cut off John's head. [11]And they brought it on a platter and gave it to the girl, and she took it to her mother. [12]John's followers came and got his body and buried it. Then they went and told Jesus.

More than Five Thousand Fed

[13]When Jesus heard what had happened to John, he left in a boat and went to a lonely place by himself. But the crowds heard about it and followed him on foot from the towns. [14]When he arrived, he saw a great crowd waiting. He felt sorry for them and healed those who were sick.

[15]When it was evening, his followers came to him and said, "No one lives in this place, and it is already late. Send the people away so they can go to the towns and buy food for themselves."

[16]But Jesus answered, "They don't need to go away. You give them something to eat."

[17]They said to him, "But we have only five loaves of bread and two fish."

[18]Jesus said, "Bring the bread and the fish to me." [19]Then he told the people to sit down on the grass. He took the five loaves and the two fish and, looking to heaven, he thanked God for the food. Jesus divided the bread and gave it to his followers, who gave it to the people. [20]All the people ate and were satisfied. Then the followers filled twelve baskets with the leftover pieces of food. [21]There were about five thousand men there who ate, not counting women and children.

JANUARY 22

GENESIS 43:1—44:34

The Brothers Go Back to Egypt

43 Still no food grew in the land of Canaan. ²When Jacob's family had eaten all the grain they had brought from Egypt, Jacob said to them, "Go to Egypt again and buy a little more grain for us to eat."

³But Judah said to Jacob, "The governor of that country strongly warned us, 'If you don't bring your brother back with you, you will not be allowed to see me.' ⁴If you will send Benjamin with us, we will go down and buy food for you. ⁵But if you refuse to send Benjamin, we will not go. The governor of that country warned us that we would not see him if we didn't bring Benjamin with us."

⁶Israel[n] said, "Why did you tell the man you had another brother? You have caused me a lot of trouble."

⁷The brothers answered, "He questioned us carefully about ourselves and our family. He asked us, 'Is your father still alive? Do you have another brother?' We just answered his questions. How could we know he would ask us to bring our other brother to him?"

⁸Then Judah said to his father Jacob, "Send Benjamin with me, and we will go at once so that we, you, and our children may live and not die. ⁹I will guarantee you that he will be safe, and I will be personally responsible for him. If I don't bring him back to you, you can blame me all my life. ¹⁰If we had not wasted all this time, we could have already made two trips."

¹¹Then their father Jacob said to them, "If it has to be that way, then do this: Take some of the best foods in our land in your packs. Give them to the man as a gift: some balm, some honey, spices, myrrh, pistachio nuts, and almonds. ¹²Take twice as much money with you this time, and take back the money that was returned to you in your sacks last time. Maybe it was a mistake. ¹³And take Benjamin with you. Now leave and go to the man. ¹⁴I pray that God Almighty will cause the governor to be merciful to you and that he will allow Simeon and Benjamin to come back with you. If I am robbed of my children, then I am robbed of them!"

¹⁵So the brothers took the gifts. They also took twice as much money as they had taken the first time, and they took Benjamin. They hurried down to Egypt and stood before Joseph.

¹⁶When Joseph saw Benjamin with them, he said to the servant in charge of his house, "Bring those men into my house. Kill an animal and prepare a meal. Those men will eat with me today at noon." ¹⁷The servant did as Joseph told him and brought the men to Joseph's house.

¹⁸The brothers were afraid when they were brought to Joseph's house and thought, "We were brought here because of the money that was put in our sacks on the first trip. He wants to attack us, make us slaves, and take our donkeys." ¹⁹So the brothers went to the servant in charge of Joseph's house and spoke to him at the door of the house. ²⁰They said, "Master, we came here once before to buy food. ²¹While we were going home, we stopped for the night and when we opened our sacks each of us found all his money in his sack. We brought that money with us to give it back to you. ²²And we have brought more money to pay for the food we want to buy this time. We don't know who put that money in our sacks."

²³But the servant answered, "It's all right. Don't be afraid. Your God, the God of your father, must have put the money in your sacks. I got the money you paid me for the grain last time." Then the servant brought Simeon out to them.

²⁴The servant led the men into Joseph's house and gave them water, and they washed their feet. Then he gave their donkeys food to eat. ²⁵The men prepared their gift to give to Joseph when he arrived at noon, because they had heard they were going to eat with him there.

43:6 Israel Also called Jacob.

26When Joseph came home, the brothers gave him the gift they had brought into the house and bowed down to the ground in front of him. 27Joseph asked them how they were doing. He said, "How is your aged father you told me about? Is he still alive?"

28The brothers answered, "Your servant, our father, is well. He is still alive." And they bowed low before Joseph to show him respect.

29When Joseph saw his brother Benjamin, who had the same mother as he, Joseph asked, "Is this your youngest brother you told me about?" Then he said to Benjamin, "God be good to you, my son!" 30Then Joseph hurried off because he had to hold back the tears when he saw his brother Benjamin. So Joseph went into his room and cried there. 31Then he washed his face and came out. He controlled himself and said, "Serve the meal."

32So they served Joseph at one table, his brothers at another table, and the Egyptians who ate with him at another table. This was because Egyptians did not like Hebrews and never ate with them. 33Joseph's brothers were seated in front of him in order of their ages, from oldest to youngest. They looked at each other because they were so amazed. 34Food from Joseph's table was taken to them, but Benjamin was given five times more food than the others. Joseph's brothers ate and drank freely with him.

Joseph Sets a Trap

44 Then Joseph gave a command to the servant in charge of his house. He said, "Fill the men's sacks with as much grain as they can carry, and put each man's money into his sack with the grain. 2Put my silver cup in the sack of the youngest brother, along with his money for the grain." The servant did what Joseph told him.

3At dawn the brothers were sent away with their donkeys. 4They were not far from the city when Joseph said to the servant in charge of his house, "Go after the men. When you catch up with them, say, 'Why have you paid back evil for good? 5The cup you have stolen is the one my master uses for drinking and for explaining dreams. You have done a very wicked thing!'"

6So the servant caught up with the brothers and said to them what Joseph had told him to say.

7But the brothers said to the servant, "Why do you say these things? We would not do anything like that! 8We brought back to you from the land of Canaan the money we found in our sacks. So surely we would not steal silver or gold from your master's house. 9If you find that silver cup in the sack of one of us, then let him die, and we will be your slaves."

10The servant said, "We will do as you say, but only the man who has taken the cup will become my slave. The rest of you may go free."

11Then every brother quickly lowered his sack to the ground and opened it. 12The servant searched the sacks, going from the oldest brother to the youngest, and found the cup in Benjamin's sack. 13The brothers tore their clothes to show they were afraid. Then they put their sacks back on the donkeys and returned to the city.

14When Judah and his brothers went back to Joseph's house, Joseph was still there, so the brothers bowed facedown on the ground before him. 15Joseph said to them, "What have you done? Didn't you know that a man like me can learn things by signs and dreams?"

16Judah said, "Master, what can we say? And how can we show we are not guilty? God has uncovered our guilt, so all of us will be your slaves, not just Benjamin."

17But Joseph said, "I will not make you all slaves! Only the man who stole the cup will be my slave. The rest of you may go back safely to your father."

18Then Judah went to Joseph and said, "Master, please let me speak plainly to you, and please don't be angry with me. I know that you are as powerful as the king of Egypt himself. 19When we were here before, you asked us, 'Do you have a father or a brother?' 20And we answered you, 'We have an old father. And we have a younger brother, who was born when our father was old. This youngest son's brother is dead, so he is the only one of his mother's children left alive, and our father loves him very much.' 21Then you said to us, 'Bring that brother to me. I want to see him.' ²²And we said to you, 'That young boy cannot leave his father, because if he leaves him, his father would die.' ²³But you said to us, 'If you don't bring your youngest brother, you will not be allowed to see me again.' ²⁴So we went back to our father and told him what you had said.

²⁵"Later, our father said, 'Go again and buy us a little more food.' ²⁶We said to our father, 'We cannot go without our youngest brother. Without our youngest brother, we will not be allowed to see the governor.' ²⁷Then my father said to us, 'You know that my wife Rachel gave me two sons. ²⁸When one son left me, I thought, "Surely he has been torn apart by a wild animal," and I haven't seen him since. ²⁹Now you want to take this son away from me also. But something terrible might happen to him, and I would be miserable until the day I die.' ³⁰Now what will happen if we go home to our father without our youngest brother? He is so important in our father's life that ³¹when our father sees the young boy is not with us, he will die. And it will be our fault. We will cause the great sorrow that kills our father.

³²"I gave my father a guarantee that the young boy would be safe. I said to my father, 'If I don't bring him back to you, you can blame me all my life.' ³³So now, please allow me to stay here and be your slave, and let the young boy go back home with his brothers. ³⁴I cannot go back to my father if the boy is not with me. I couldn't stand to see my father that sad."

PSALM 11:1–7

Trust in the Lord

For the director of music. Of David.

11 I trust in the LORD for protection.
So why do you say to me,
"Fly like a bird to your mountain.
²Like hunters, the wicked string their
bows;
they set their arrows on the bowstrings.
They shoot from dark places
at those who are honest.

³When the foundations for good collapse,
what can good people do?"

⁴The LORD is in his holy temple;
the LORD sits on his throne in heaven.
He sees what people do;
he keeps his eye on them.
⁵The LORD tests those who do right,
but he hates the wicked and those who
love to hurt others.
⁶He will send hot coals and burning sulfur
on the wicked.
A whirlwind is what they will get.
⁷The LORD does what is right, and he loves
justice,
so honest people will see his face.

PROVERBS 4:10–13

¹⁰My child, listen and accept what I say.
Then you will have a long life.
¹¹I am guiding you in the way of wisdom,
and I am leading you on the right path.
¹²Nothing will hold you back;
you will not be overwhelmed.
¹³Always remember what you have been
taught,
and don't let go of it.
Keep all that you have learned;
it is the most important thing in life.

MATTHEW 14:22–36

Jesus Walks on the Water

²²Immediately Jesus told his followers to get into the boat and go ahead of him across the lake. He stayed there to send the people home. ²³After he had sent them away, he went by himself up into the hills to pray. It was late, and Jesus was there alone. ²⁴By this time, the boat was already far away from land. It was being hit by waves, because the wind was blowing against it.

²⁵Between three and six o'clock in the morning, Jesus came to them, walking on the water. ²⁶When his followers saw him walking on the water, they were afraid. They said, "It's a ghost!" and cried out in fear.

²⁷But Jesus quickly spoke to them, "Have courage! It is I. Do not be afraid."

²⁸Peter said, "Lord, if it is really you, then command me to come to you on the water."

²⁹Jesus said, "Come."

And Peter left the boat and walked on the water to Jesus. ³⁰But when Peter saw the wind and the waves, he became afraid and began to sink. He shouted, "Lord, save me!"

³¹Immediately Jesus reached out his hand and caught Peter. Jesus said, "Your faith is small. Why did you doubt?"

³²After they got into the boat, the wind became calm. ³³Then those who were in the boat worshiped Jesus and said, "Truly you are the Son of God!"

³⁴When they had crossed the lake, they came to shore at Gennesaret. ³⁵When the people there recognized Jesus, they told people all around there that Jesus had come, and they brought all their sick to him. ³⁶They begged Jesus to let them touch just the edge of his coat, and all who touched it were healed.

JANUARY 23

GENESIS 45:1—46:34

Joseph Reveals Who He Is

45 Joseph could not control himself in front of his servants any longer, so he cried out, "Have everyone leave me." When only the brothers were left with Joseph, he told them who he was. ²Joseph cried so loudly that the Egyptians heard him, and the people in the king's palace heard about it. ³He said to his brothers, "I am Joseph. Is my father still alive?" But the brothers could not answer him, because they were very afraid of him.

⁴So Joseph said to them, "Come close to me." When the brothers came close to him, he said to them, "I am your brother Joseph, whom you sold as a slave to go to Egypt. ⁵Now don't be worried or angry with yourselves because you sold me here. God sent me here ahead of you to save people's lives. ⁶No food has grown on the land for two years now, and there will be five more years without planting or harvest. ⁷So God sent me here ahead of you to make sure you have some descendants left on earth and to keep you alive in an amazing way. ⁸So it was not you who sent me here, but God. God has made me the highest officer of the king of Egypt. I am in charge of his palace, and I am the master of all the land of Egypt.

⁹"So leave quickly and go to my father. Tell him, 'Your son Joseph says: God has made me master over all Egypt. Come down to me quickly. ¹⁰Live in the land of Goshen where you will be near me. Your children,

your grandchildren, your flocks and herds, and all that you have will also be near me. ¹¹I will care for you during the next five years of hunger so that you and your family and all that you have will not starve.'

¹²"Now you can see for yourselves, and so can my brother Benjamin, that the one speaking to you is really Joseph. ¹³So tell my father about how powerful I have become in Egypt. Tell him about everything you have seen. Now hurry and bring him back to me." ¹⁴Then Joseph hugged his brother Benjamin and cried, and Benjamin cried also. ¹⁵And Joseph kissed all his brothers and cried as he hugged them. After this, his brothers talked with him.

¹⁶When the king of Egypt and his officers learned that Joseph's brothers had come, they were very happy. ¹⁷So the king said to Joseph, "Tell your brothers to load their animals and go back to the land of Canaan ¹⁸and bring their father and their families back here to me. I will give them the best land in Egypt, and they will eat the best food we have here. ¹⁹Tell them to take some wagons from Egypt for their children and their wives and to bring their father back also. ²⁰Tell them not to worry about bringing any of their things with them, because we will give them the best of what we have in Egypt."

²¹So the sons of Israel did this. Joseph gave them wagons as the king had ordered and food for their trip. ²²He gave each brother a change of clothes, but he gave Benjamin five changes of clothes and about seven and one-half pounds of silver.

[23]Joseph also sent his father ten donkeys loaded with the best things from Egypt and ten female donkeys loaded with grain, bread, and other food for his father on his trip back. [24]Then Joseph told his brothers to go. As they were leaving, he said to them, "Don't quarrel on the way home."

[25]So the brothers left Egypt and went to their father Jacob in the land of Canaan. [26]They told him, "Joseph is still alive and is the ruler over all the land of Egypt." Their father was shocked and did not believe them. [27]But when the brothers told him everything Joseph had said, and when Jacob saw the wagons Joseph had sent to carry him back to Egypt, he felt better. [28]Israel[n] said, "Now I believe you. My son Joseph is still alive, and I will go and see him before I die."

Jacob Goes to Egypt

46 So Israel[n] took all he had and started his trip. He went to Beersheba, where he offered sacrifices to the God of his father Isaac. [2]During the night God spoke to Israel in a vision and said, "Jacob, Jacob."

And Jacob answered, "Here I am."

[3]Then God said, "I am God, the God of your father. Don't be afraid to go to Egypt, because I will make your descendants a great nation there. [4]I will go to Egypt with you, and I will bring you out of Egypt again. Joseph's own hands will close your eyes when you die."

[5]Then Jacob left Beersheba. The sons of Israel loaded their father, their children, and their wives in the wagons the king of Egypt had sent. [6]They also took their farm animals and everything they had gotten in Canaan. So Jacob went to Egypt with all his descendants— [7]his sons and grandsons, his daughters and granddaughters. He took all his family to Egypt with him.

Jacob's Family

[8]Now these are the names of the children of Israel who went into Egypt (Jacob and his descendants).

Reuben was Jacob's first son. [9]Reuben's sons were Hanoch, Pallu, Hezron, and Carmi. [10]Simeon's sons were Jemuel, Jamin, Ohad, Jakin, Zohar, and Shaul (Simeon's son by a Canaanite woman).

[11]Levi's sons were Gershon, Kohath, and Merari.

[12]Judah's sons were Er, Onan, Shelah, Perez, and Zerah (but Er and Onan had died in the land of Canaan). Perez's sons were Hezron and Hamul.

[13]Issachar's sons were Tola, Puah, Jashub, and Shimron.

[14]Zebulun's sons were Sered, Elon, and Jahleel.

[15]These are the sons of Leah and Jacob born in Northwest Mesopotamia, in addition to his daughter Dinah. There were thirty-three persons in this part of Jacob's family.

[16]Gad's sons were Zephon, Haggi, Shuni, Ezbon, Eri, Arodi, and Areli.

[17]Asher's sons were Imnah, Ishvah, Ishvi, and Beriah, and their sister was Serah. Beriah's sons were Heber and Malkiel.

[18]These are Jacob's sons by Zilpah, the slave girl whom Laban gave to his daughter Leah. There were sixteen persons in this part of Jacob's family.

[19]The sons of Jacob's wife Rachel were Joseph and Benjamin. [20]In Egypt, Joseph became the father of Manasseh and Ephraim by his wife Asenath, the daughter of Potiphera, priest of On.

[21]Benjamin's sons were Bela, Beker, Ashbel, Gera, Naaman, Ehi, Rosh, Muppim, Huppim, and Ard.

[22]These are the sons of Jacob by his wife Rachel. There were fourteen persons in this part of Jacob's family.

[23]Dan's son was Hushim.

[24]Naphtali's sons were Jahziel, Guni, Jezer, and Shillem.

[25]These are Jacob's sons by Bilhah, the slave girl whom Laban gave to his daughter Rachel. There were seven persons in this part of Jacob's family.

[26]So the total number of Jacob's direct descendants who went to Egypt was sixty-six, not counting the wives of Jacob's sons. [27]Joseph had two sons born in Egypt, so the total number in the family of Jacob in Egypt was seventy.

Jacob Arrives in Egypt

²⁸Jacob sent Judah ahead of him to see Joseph in Goshen. When Jacob and his people came into the land of Goshen, ²⁹Joseph prepared his chariot and went to meet his father Israel in Goshen. As soon as Joseph saw his father, he hugged him, and cried there for a long time.

³⁰Then Israel said to Joseph, "Now I am ready to die, because I have seen your face and I know you are still alive."

³¹Joseph said to his brothers and his father's family, "I will go and tell the king you are here. I will say, 'My brothers and my father's family have left the land of Canaan and have come here to me. ³²They are shepherds and take care of farm animals, and they have brought their flocks and their herds and everything they own with them.' ³³When the king calls you, he will ask, 'What work do you do?' ³⁴This is what you should tell him: 'We, your servants, have taken care of farm animals all our lives. Our ancestors did the same thing.' Then the king will allow you to settle in the land of Goshen, away from the Egyptians, because they don't like to be near shepherds."

PSALM 12:1–8

A Prayer Against Liars

For the director of music. Upon the sheminith. A psalm of David.

12 Save me, LORD, because the good
     people are all gone;
   no true believers are left on earth.
²Everyone lies to his neighbors;
   they say one thing and mean another.

³The LORD will stop those flattering lips
   and cut off those bragging tongues.
⁴They say, "Our tongues will help us win.
   We can say what we wish; no one is our
     master."

⁵But the LORD says,
   "I will now rise up,
   because the poor are being hurt.
Because of the moans of the helpless,
   I will give them the help they want."

⁶The LORD's words are pure,
   like silver purified by fire,
   like silver purified seven times over.

⁷LORD, you will keep us safe;
   you will always protect us from such
     people.
⁸But the wicked are all around us;
   everyone loves what is wrong.

PROVERBS 4:14–17

¹⁴Don't follow the ways of the wicked;
   don't do what evil people do.
¹⁵Avoid their ways, and don't follow them.
   Stay away from them and keep on
     going,
¹⁶because they cannot sleep until they do
     evil.
   They cannot rest until they harm
     someone.
¹⁷They feast on wickedness and cruelty
   as if they were eating bread and
     drinking wine.

MATTHEW 15:1–20

Obey God's Law

15 Then some Pharisees and teachers of the law came to Jesus from Jerusalem. They asked him, ²"Why don't your followers obey the unwritten laws which have been handed down to us? They don't wash their hands before they eat."

³Jesus answered, "And why do you refuse to obey God's command so that you can follow your own teachings? ⁴God said, 'Honor your father and your mother,'[n] and 'Anyone who says cruel things to his father or mother must be put to death.'[n] ⁵But you say a person can tell his father or mother, 'I have something I could use to help you, but I have given it to God already.' ⁶You teach that person not to honor his father or his mother. You rejected what God said for the sake of your own rules. ⁷You are hypocrites! Isaiah was right when he said about you:

⁸"These people show honor to me with
     words,
   but their hearts are far from me.

15:4 'Honor . . . mother.' Quotation from Exodus 20:12; Deuteronomy 5:16.   15:4 'Anyone . . . death.' Quotation from Exodus 21:17.

⁹Their worship of me is worthless.
The things they teach are nothing but
human rules.'"   *Isaiah 29:13*

¹⁰After Jesus called the crowd to him, he said, "Listen and understand what I am saying. ¹¹It is not what people put into their mouths that makes them unclean. It is what comes out of their mouths that makes them unclean."

¹²Then his followers came to him and asked, "Do you know that the Pharisees are angry because of what you said?"

¹³Jesus answered, "Every plant that my Father in heaven has not planted himself will be pulled up by the roots. ¹⁴Stay away from the Pharisees; they are blind leaders.ⁿ And if a blind person leads a blind person, both will fall into a ditch."

¹⁵Peter said, "Explain the example to us."

¹⁶Jesus said, "Do you still not understand? ¹⁷Surely you know that all the food that enters the mouth goes into the stomach and then goes out of the body. ¹⁸But what people say with their mouths comes from the way they think; these are the things that make people unclean. ¹⁹Out of the mind come evil thoughts, murder, adultery, sexual sins, stealing, lying, and speaking evil of others. ²⁰These things make people unclean; eating with unwashed hands does not make them unclean."

JANUARY 24

GENESIS 47:1—48:22

Jacob Settles in Goshen

47 Joseph went in to the king and said, "My father and my brothers have arrived from Canaan with their flocks and herds and everything they own. They are now in the land of Goshen." ²Joseph chose five of his brothers to introduce to the king.

³The king said to the brothers, "What work do you do?"

And they said to him, "We, your servants, are shepherds, just as our ancestors were." ⁴They said to the king, "We have come to live in this land, because there is no grass in the land of Canaan for our animals to eat, and the hunger is terrible there. So please allow us to live in the land of Goshen."

⁵Then the king said to Joseph, "Your father and your brothers have come to you, ⁶and you may choose any place in Egypt for them to live. Give your father and your brothers the best land; let them live in the land of Goshen. And if any of them are skilled shepherds, put them in charge of my sheep and cattle."

⁷Then Joseph brought in his father Jacob and introduced him to the king, and Jacob blessed the king.

⁸Then the king said to Jacob, "How old are you?"

⁹Jacob said to him, "My life has been spent wandering from place to place. It has been short and filled with trouble—only one hundred thirty years. My ancestors lived much longer than I." ¹⁰Then Jacob blessed the king and left.

¹¹Joseph obeyed the king and gave his father and brothers the best land in Egypt, near the city of Rameses. ¹²And Joseph gave his father, his brothers, and everyone who lived with them the food they needed.

Joseph Buys Land for the King

¹³The hunger became worse, and since there was no food anywhere in the land, Egypt and Canaan became very poor. ¹⁴Joseph collected all the money that was to be found in Egypt and Canaan. People paid for the grain they were buying, and he brought that money to the king's palace. ¹⁵After some time, when the people in Egypt and Canaan had no money left, they went to Joseph and said, "Please give us food. Our

15:14 leaders Some Greek copies continue, "of blind people."

money is gone, and if we don't eat, we will die here in front of you."

[16]Joseph answered, "Since you have no money, give me your farm animals, and I will give you food in return." [17]So people brought their farm animals to Joseph, and he gave them food in exchange for their horses, sheep, goats, cattle, and donkeys. And he kept them alive by trading food for their farm animals that year.

[18]The next year the people came to Joseph and said, "You know we have no money left, and all our animals belong to you. We have nothing left except our bodies and our land. [19]Surely both we and our land will die here in front of you. Buy us and our land in exchange for food, and we will be slaves to the king, together with our land. Give us seed to plant so that we will live and not die, and the land will not become a desert."

[20]So Joseph bought all the land in Egypt for the king. Every Egyptian sold Joseph his field, because the hunger was very great. So the land became the king's, [21]and Joseph made the people slaves from one end of Egypt to the other. [22]The only land he did not buy was the land the priests owned. They did not need to sell their land because the king paid them for their work. So they had money to buy food.

[23]Joseph said to the people, "Now I have bought you and your land for the king, so I will give you seed and you can plant your fields. [24]At harvest time you must give one-fifth to the king. You may keep four-fifths for yourselves to use as seed for the field and as food for yourselves, your families, and your children."

[25]The people said, "You have saved our lives. If you like, we will become slaves of the king."

[26]So Joseph made a law in Egypt, which continues today: One-fifth of everything from the land belongs to the king. The only land the king did not get was the priests' land.

"Don't Bury Me in Egypt"

[27]The Israelites continued to live in the land of Goshen in Egypt. There they got pos-

sessions and had many children and grew in number.

[28]Jacob[n] lived in Egypt seventeen years, so he lived to be one hundred forty-seven years old. [29]When Israel knew he soon would die, he called his son Joseph to him and said to him, "If you love me, put your hand under my leg.[n] Promise me you will not bury me in Egypt. [30]When I die, carry me out of Egypt, and bury me where my ancestors are buried."

Joseph answered, "I will do as you say."

[31]Then Jacob said, "Promise me." And Joseph promised him that he would do this. Then Israel worshiped as he leaned on the top of his walking stick.

Blessings for Manasseh and Ephraim

48 Some time later Joseph learned that his father was very sick, so he took his two sons Manasseh and Ephraim and went to his father. [2]When Joseph arrived, someone told Jacob,[n] "Your son Joseph has come to see you." Jacob was weak, so he used all his strength and sat up on his bed.

[3]Then Jacob said to Joseph, "God Almighty appeared to me at Luz in the land of Canaan and blessed me there. [4]He said to me, 'I will give you many children. I will make you the father of many peoples, and I will give your descendants this land forever.' [5]Your two sons, who were born here in Egypt before I came, will be counted as my own sons. Ephraim and Manasseh will be my sons just as Reuben and Simeon are my sons. [6]But if you have other children, they will be your own, and their land will be part of the land given to Ephraim and Manasseh. [7]When I came from Northwest Mesopotamia, Rachel died in the land of Canaan, as we were traveling toward Ephrath. This made me very sad, and I buried her there beside the road to Ephrath." (Today Ephrath is Bethlehem.)

[8]Then Israel saw Joseph's sons and said, "Who are these boys?"

[9]Joseph said to his father, "They are my sons that God has given me here in Egypt."

Israel said, "Bring your sons to me so I may bless them."

47:28; 48:2 Jacob Also called Israel.   47:29 put . . . leg This showed that a person would keep a promise.

[10]At this time Israel's eyesight was bad because he was old. So Joseph brought the boys close to him, and Israel kissed the boys and put his arms around them. [11]He said to Joseph, "I thought I would never see you alive again, and now God has let me see you and also your children." [12]Then Joseph moved his sons off Israel's lap and bowed facedown to the ground. [13]He put Ephraim on his right side and Manasseh on his left. (So Ephraim was near Israel's left hand, and Manasseh was near Israel's right hand.) Joseph brought the boys close to Israel. [14]But Israel crossed his arms and put his right hand on the head of Ephraim, who was younger. He put his left hand on the head of Manasseh, the firstborn son. [15]And Israel blessed Joseph and said,

"My ancestors Abraham and Isaac
    served our God,
and like a shepherd God has led me all
    my life.
[16]He was the Angel who saved me from all
    my troubles.
Now I pray that he will bless these
    boys.
May my name be known through these
    boys,
and may the names of my ancestors
    Abraham and Isaac be known
    through them.
May they have many descendants
    on the earth."

[17]When Joseph saw that his father put his right hand on Ephraim's head, he didn't like it. So he took hold of his father's hand, wanting to move it from Ephraim's head to Manasseh's head. [18]Joseph said to his father, "You are doing it wrong, Father. Manasseh is the firstborn son. Put your right hand on his head."

[19]But his father refused and said, "I know, my son, I know. Manasseh will be great and have many descendants. But his younger brother will be greater, and his descendants will be enough to make a nation."

[20]So Israel blessed them that day and said,

"When a blessing is given in Israel, they
    will say:
'May God make you like Ephraim and
    Manasseh.'"

In this way he made Ephraim greater than Manasseh.

[21]Then Israel said to Joseph, "Look at me; I am about to die. But God will be with you and will take you back to the land of your fathers. [22]I have given you something that I did not give your brothers—the land of Shechem that I took from the Amorite people with my sword and my bow."

PSALM 13:1-6

A Prayer for God to Be Near

For the director of music. A psalm of David.

13 How long will you forget me,
    LORD? Forever?
How long will you hide from me?
[2]How long must I worry
    and feel sad in my heart all day?
How long will my enemy win over me?

[3]LORD, look at me.
    Answer me, my God;
    tell me, or I will die.
[4]Otherwise my enemy will say, "I have
    won!"
Those against me will rejoice that I've
    been defeated.

[5]I trust in your love.
My heart is happy because you saved
    me.
[6]I sing to the LORD
because he has taken care of me.

PROVERBS 4:18-19

[18]The way of the good person is like the
    light of dawn,
growing brighter and brighter until full
    daylight.
[19]But the wicked walk around in the dark;
they can't even see what makes them
    stumble.

MATTHEW 15:21-39

Jesus Helps a Non-Jewish Woman

[21]Jesus left that place and went to the area of Tyre and Sidon. [22]A Canaanite woman from that area came to Jesus and cried out, "Lord, Son of David, have mercy on me! My

daughter has a demon, and she is suffering very much."

[23]But Jesus did not answer the woman. So his followers came to Jesus and begged him, "Tell the woman to go away. She is following us and shouting."

[24]Jesus answered, "God sent me only to the lost sheep, the people of Israel."

[25]Then the woman came to Jesus again and bowed before him and said, "Lord, help me!"

[26]Jesus answered, "It is not right to take the children's bread and give it to the dogs."

[27]The woman said, "Yes, Lord, but even the dogs eat the crumbs that fall from their masters' table."

[28]Then Jesus answered, "Woman, you have great faith! I will do what you asked." And at that moment the woman's daughter was healed.

Jesus Heals Many People

[29]After leaving there, Jesus went along the shore of Lake Galilee. He went up on a hill and sat there.

[30]Great crowds came to Jesus, bringing with them the lame, the blind, the crippled, those who could not speak, and many others. They put them at Jesus' feet, and he healed them. [31]The crowd was amazed when they saw that people who could not speak before were now able to speak. The crippled were made strong. The lame could walk, and the blind could see. And they praised the God of Israel for this.

More than Four Thousand Fed

[32]Jesus called his followers to him and said, "I feel sorry for these people, because they have already been with me three days, and they have nothing to eat. I don't want to send them away hungry. They might faint while going home."

[33]His followers asked him, "How can we get enough bread to feed all these people? We are far away from any town."

[34]Jesus asked, "How many loaves of bread do you have?"

They answered, "Seven, and a few small fish."

[35]Jesus told the people to sit on the ground. [36]He took the seven loaves of bread and the fish and gave thanks to God. Then he divided the food and gave it to his followers, and they gave it to the people. [37]All the people ate and were satisfied. Then his followers filled seven baskets with the leftover pieces of food. [38]There were about four thousand men there who ate, besides women and children. [39]After sending the people home, Jesus got into the boat and went to the area of Magadan.

JANUARY 25

GENESIS 49:1—50:26

Jacob Blesses His Sons

49 Then Jacob called his sons to him. He said, "Come here to me, and I will tell you what will happen to you in the future.

[2]"Come together and listen, sons of Jacob. Listen to Israel, your father."

[3]"Reuben, my first son, you are my strength.
Your birth showed I could be a father.
You have the highest position among my sons,
and you are the most powerful.

[4]But you are uncontrolled like water,
so you will no longer lead your brothers.
This is because you got into your father's bed
and shamed me by having sexual relations with my slave girl.

[5]"Simeon and Levi are brothers
who used their swords to do violence.
[6]I will not join their secret talks,
and I will not meet with them to plan evil.
They killed men because they were angry,
and they crippled oxen just for fun.

[7]May their anger be cursed, because it is
  too violent.
May their violence be cursed, because it
  is too cruel.
I will divide them up among the tribes of
  Jacob
and scatter them through all the tribes
  of Israel.

[8]"Judah, your brothers will praise you.
You will grab your enemies by the neck,
and your brothers will bow down to
  you.
[9]Judah is like a young lion.
You have returned from killing, my son.
Like a lion, he stretches out and lies
  down to rest,
and no one is brave enough to wake him.
[10]Kings will come from Judah's family;
someone from Judah will always be on
  the throne.
Judah will rule until Shiloh comes,
and the nations will obey him.
[11]He ties his donkey to a grapevine,
his young donkey to the best branch.
He can afford to use wine to wash his
  clothes
and the best wine to wash his robes.
[12]His eyes are dark like the color of wine,
and his teeth are as white as the color
  of milk.

[13]"Zebulun will live near the sea.
His shore will be a safe place for ships,
and his land will reach as far as Sidon.

[14]"Issachar is like a strong donkey
who lies down while carrying his load.
[15]When he sees his resting place is good
and how pleasant his land is,
he will put his back to the load
and become a slave.

[16]"Dan will rule his own people
like the other tribes in Israel.
[17]Dan will be like a snake by the side of the
  road,
a dangerous snake lying near the path.
That snake bites a horse's leg,
and the rider is thrown off backward.

[18]"LORD, I wait for your salvation.

[19]"Robbers will attack Gad,

but he will defeat them and drive them
  away.

[20]"Asher's land will grow much good food;
he will grow food fit for a king.

[21]"Naphtali is like a female deer that runs
  free,
that has beautiful fawns.

[22]"Joseph is like a grapevine that produces
  much fruit,
a healthy vine watered by a spring,
whose branches grow over the wall.
[23]Archers attack him violently
and shoot at him angrily,
[24]but he aims his bow well.
His arms are made strong.
He gets his power from the Mighty God
  of Jacob
and his strength from the Shepherd, the
  Rock of Israel.
[25]Your father's God helps you.
God Almighty blesses you.
He blesses you with rain from above,
with water from springs below,
with many babies born to your wives,
and many young ones born to your
  animals.
[26]The blessings of your father are greater
than the blessings of the oldest
  mountains,
greater than the good things of the
  long-lasting hills.
May these blessings rest on the head of
  Joseph,
on the forehead of the one who was
  separated from his brothers.

[27]"Benjamin is like a hungry wolf.
In the morning he eats what he has
  caught,
and in the evening he divides what he
  has taken."

[28]These are the twelve tribes of Israel,
and this is what their father said to them.
He gave each son the blessing that was right
for him. [29]Then Israel gave them a command and said, "I am about to die. Bury me
with my ancestors in the cave in the field of
Ephron the Hittite. [30]That cave is in the field
of Machpelah east of Mamre in the land of
Canaan. Abraham bought the field and cave

from Ephron the Hittite for a burying place. [31]Abraham and Sarah his wife are buried there. Isaac and Rebekah his wife are buried there, and I buried my wife Leah there. [32]The field and the cave in it were bought from the Hittite people." [33]After Jacob finished talking to his sons, he lay down. He put his feet back on the bed, took his last breath, and died.

Jacob's Burial

50 When Jacob died, Joseph hugged his father and cried over him and kissed him. [2]He commanded the doctors who served him to prepare his father's body, so the doctors prepared Jacob's body to be buried. [3]It took the doctors forty days to prepare his body (the usual time it took). And the Egyptians had a time of sorrow for Jacob that lasted seventy days.

[4]When this time of sorrow had ended, Joseph spoke to the king's officers and said, "If you think well of me, please tell this to the king: [5]'When my father was near death, I made a promise to him that I would bury him in a cave in the land of Canaan, in a burial place that he cut out for himself. So please let me go and bury my father, and then I will return.'"

[6]The king answered, "Keep your promise. Go and bury your father."

[7]So Joseph went to bury his father. All the king's officers, the elders of his court, and all the elders of Egypt went with Joseph. [8]Everyone who lived with Joseph and his brothers went with him, as well as everyone who lived with his father. They left only their children, their flocks, and their herds in the land of Goshen. [9]They went with Joseph in chariots and on horses. It was a very large group.

[10]When they came to the threshing floor of Atad, near the Jordan River, they cried loudly and bitterly for his father. Joseph's time of sorrow continued for seven days. [11]The people that lived in Canaan saw the sadness at the threshing floor of Atad and said, "Those Egyptians are showing great sorrow!" So now that place is named Sorrow of the Egyptians.

[12]So Jacob's sons did as their father commanded. [13]They carried his body to the land of Canaan and buried it in the cave in the field of Machpelah near Mamre. Abraham had bought this cave and field from Ephron the Hittite to use as a burial place. [14]After Joseph buried his father, he returned to Egypt, along with his brothers and everyone who had gone with him to bury his father.

The Brothers Fear Joseph

[15]After Jacob died, Joseph's brothers said, "What if Joseph is still angry with us? We did many wrong things to him. What if he plans to pay us back?" [16]So they sent a message to Joseph that said, "Your father gave this command before he died. [17]He said to us, 'You have done wrong and have sinned and done evil to Joseph. Tell Joseph to forgive you, his brothers.' So now, Joseph, we beg you to forgive our wrong. We are the servants of the God of your father." When Joseph received the message, he cried.

[18]And his brothers went to him and bowed low before him and said, "We are your slaves."

[19]Then Joseph said to them, "Don't be afraid. Can I do what only God can do? [20]You meant to hurt me, but God turned your evil into good to save the lives of many people, which is being done. [21]So don't be afraid. I will take care of you and your children." So Joseph comforted his brothers and spoke kind words to them.

[22]Joseph continued to live in Egypt with all his father's family. He died when he was one hundred ten years old. [23]During Joseph's life Ephraim had children and grandchildren, and Joseph's son Manasseh had a son named Makir. Joseph accepted Makir's children as his own.

The Death of Joseph

[24]Joseph said to his brothers, "I am about to die, but God will take care of you. He will lead you out of this land to the land he promised to Abraham, Isaac, and Jacob." [25]Then Joseph had the sons of Israel make a promise. He said, "Promise me that you will carry my bones with you out of Egypt."

[26]Joseph died when he was one hundred ten years old. Doctors prepared his body for burial, and then they put him in a coffin in Egypt.

PSALM 14:1–7

The Unbelieving Fool

For the director of music. Of David.

14 Fools say to themselves,
    "There is no God."
  Fools are evil and do terrible things;
    there is no one who does anything
    good.

²The LORD looked down from heaven on
    all people
  to see if anyone understood,
    if anyone was looking to God for help.
³But all have turned away.
  Together, everyone has become evil.
  There is no one who does anything
    good,
    not even one.

⁴Don't the wicked understand?
  They destroy my people as if they were
    eating bread.
  They do not ask the LORD for help.
⁵But the wicked are filled with terror,
    because God is with those who do what
    is right.
⁶The wicked upset the plans of the poor,
    but the LORD will protect them.

⁷I pray that victory will come to Israel
    from Mount Zion!
  May the LORD bring them back.
  Then the people of Jacob will rejoice,
    and the people of Israel will be glad.

PROVERBS 4:20–24

²⁰My child, pay attention to my words;
    listen closely to what I say.
²¹Don't ever forget my words;
    keep them always in mind.
²²They are the key to life for those who
    find them;
    they bring health to the whole body.
²³Be careful what you think,
    because your thoughts run your life.
²⁴Don't use your mouth to tell lies;
    don't ever say things that are not true.

MATTHEW 16:1–28

The Leaders Ask for a Miracle

16 The Pharisees and Sadducees came to
  Jesus, wanting to trick him. So they
asked him to show them a miracle from
God.

²Jesus answered,ⁿ "At sunset you say we
will have good weather, because the sky is
red. ³And in the morning you say that it will
be a rainy day, because the sky is dark and
red. You see these signs in the sky and know
what they mean. In the same way, you see the
things that I am doing now, but you don't
know their meaning. ⁴Evil and sinful people
ask for a miracle as a sign, but they will not
be given any sign, except the sign of Jonah."ⁿ
Then Jesus left them and went away.

Guard Against Wrong Teachings

⁵Jesus' followers went across the lake, but
they had forgotten to bring bread. ⁶Jesus said
to them, "Be careful! Beware of the yeast of
the Pharisees and the Sadducees."

⁷His followers discussed the meaning of
this, saying, "He said this because we forgot
to bring bread."

⁸Knowing what they were talking about,
Jesus asked them, "Why are you talking
about not having bread? Your faith is small.
⁹Do you still not understand? Remember the
five loaves of bread that fed the five thousand? And remember that you filled many
baskets with the leftovers? ¹⁰Or the seven
loaves of bread that fed the four thousand
and the many baskets you filled then also?
¹¹I was not talking to you about bread. Why
don't you understand that? I am telling you
to beware of the yeast of the Pharisees and
the Sadducees." ¹²Then the followers understood that Jesus was not telling them to beware of the yeast used in bread but to beware
of the teaching of the Pharisees and the Sadducees.

Peter Says Jesus Is the Christ

¹³When Jesus came to the area of Caesarea Philippi, he asked his followers, "Who
do people say the Son of Man is?"

¹⁴They answered, "Some say you are John

16:2–3 answered Some Greek copies do not have the rest of verse 2 and verse 3. **16:4 sign of Jonah** Jonah's three days in the fish are like Jesus' three days in the tomb. The story about Jonah is in the Book of Jonah.

the Baptist. Others say you are Elijah, and still others say you are Jeremiah or one of the prophets."

[15]Then Jesus asked them, "And who do you say I am?"

[16]Simon Peter answered, "You are the Christ, the Son of the living God."

[17]Jesus answered, "You are blessed, Simon son of Jonah, because no person taught you that. My Father in heaven showed you who I am. [18]So I tell you, you are Peter.[n] On this rock I will build my church, and the power of death will not be able to defeat it. [19]I will give you the keys of the kingdom of heaven; the things you don't allow on earth will be the things that God does not allow, and the things you allow on earth will be the things that God allows." [20]Then Jesus warned his followers not to tell anyone he was the Christ.

Jesus Says that He Must Die

[21]From that time on Jesus began telling his followers that he must go to Jerusalem, where the Jewish elders, the leading priests, and the teachers of the law would make him suffer many things. He told them he must be killed and then be raised from the dead on the third day.

[22]Peter took Jesus aside and told him not to talk like that. He said, "God save you from those things, Lord! Those things will never happen to you!"

[23]Then Jesus said to Peter, "Go away from me, Satan![n] You are not helping me! You don't care about the things of God, but only about the things people think are important."

[24]Then Jesus said to his followers, "If people want to follow me, they must give up the things they want. They must be willing even to give up their lives to follow me. [25]Those who want to save their lives will give up true life, and those who give up their lives for me will have true life. [26]It is worthless to have the whole world if they lose their souls. They could never pay enough to buy back their souls. [27]The Son of Man will come again with his Father's glory and with his angels. At that time, he will reward them for what they have done. [28]I tell you the truth, some people standing here will see the Son of Man coming with his kingdom before they die."

JANUARY 26

EXODUS 1:1—2:25

Jacob's Family Grows Strong

1 When Jacob[n] went to Egypt, he took his sons, and each son took his own family with him. These are the names of the sons of Israel: [2]Reuben, Simeon, Levi, Judah, [3]Issachar, Zebulun, Benjamin, [4]Dan, Naphtali, Gad, and Asher. [5]There was a total of seventy people who were descendants of Jacob. Jacob's son Joseph was already in Egypt.

[6]Some time later, Joseph and his brothers died, along with all the people who had lived at that same time. [7]But the people of Israel had many children, and their number grew greatly. They became very strong, and the country of Egypt was filled with them.

Trouble for the People of Israel

[8]Then a new king began to rule Egypt, who did not know who Joseph was. [9]This king said to his people, "Look! The people of Israel are too many and too strong for us to handle! [10]If we don't make plans against them, the number of their people will grow even more. Then if there is a war, they might join our enemies and fight us and escape from the country!"

[11]So the Egyptians made life hard for the Israelites. They put slave masters over them, who forced the Israelites to build the cities

---

16:18 Peter The Greek name "Peter," like the Aramaic name "Cephas," means "rock." **16:23 Satan** Name for the devil, meaning "the enemy." Jesus means that Peter was talking like Satan. • **1:1 Jacob** Also called Israel.

Pithom and Rameses as supply centers for the king. [12]But the harder the Egyptians forced the Israelites to work, the more the Israelites grew in number and spread out. So the Egyptians became very afraid of them [13]and demanded even more of them. [14]They made their lives bitter. They forced the Israelites to work hard to make bricks and mortar and to do all kinds of work in the fields. The Egyptians were not merciful to them in all their painful work.

[15]Two Hebrew nurses, named Shiphrah and Puah, helped the Israelite women give birth to their babies. The king of Egypt said to the nurses, [16]"When you are helping the Hebrew women give birth to their babies, watch! If the baby is a girl, let her live, but if it is a boy, kill him!" [17]But the nurses feared God, so they did not do as the king told them; they let all the boy babies live. [18]Then the king of Egypt sent for the nurses and said, "Why did you do this? Why did you let the boys live?"

[19]The nurses said to him, "The Hebrew women are much stronger than the Egyptian women. They give birth to their babies before we can get there." [20]God was good to the nurses. And the Hebrew people continued to grow in number, so they became even stronger. [21]Because the nurses feared God, he gave them families of their own.

[22]So the king commanded all his people, "Every time a boy is born to the Hebrews, you must throw him into the Nile River, but let all the girl babies live."

Baby Moses

2 Now a man from the family of Levi married a woman who was also from the family of Levi. [2]She became pregnant and gave birth to a son. When she saw how wonderful the baby was, she hid him for three months. [3]But after three months she was not able to hide the baby any longer, so she got a basket made of reeds and covered it with tar so that it would float. She put the baby in the basket. Then she put the basket among the tall stalks of grass at the edge of the Nile River. [4]The baby's sister stood a short distance away to see what would happen to him.

[5]Then the daughter of the king of Egypt came to the river to take a bath, and her servant girls were walking beside the river. When she saw the basket in the tall grass, she sent her slave girl to get it. [6]The king's daughter opened the basket and saw the baby boy. He was crying, so she felt sorry for him and said, "This is one of the Hebrew babies."

[7]Then the baby's sister asked the king's daughter, "Would you like me to go and find a Hebrew woman to nurse the baby for you?"

[8]The king's daughter said, "Go!" So the girl went and got the baby's own mother.

[9]The king's daughter said to the woman, "Take this baby and nurse him for me, and I will pay you." So the woman took her baby and nursed him. [10]When the child grew older, the woman took him to the king's daughter, and she adopted the baby as her own son. The king's daughter named him Moses,[n] because she had pulled him out of the water.

Moses Tries to Help

[11]Moses grew and became a man. One day he visited his people and saw that they were forced to work very hard. He saw an Egyptian beating a Hebrew man, one of Moses' own people. [12]Moses looked all around and saw that no one was watching, so he killed the Egyptian and hid his body in the sand. [13]The next day Moses returned and saw two Hebrew men fighting each other. He said to the one that was in the wrong, "Why are you hitting one of your own people?"

[14]The man answered, "Who made you our ruler and judge? Are you going to kill me as you killed the Egyptian?"

Moses was afraid and thought, "Now everyone knows what I did." [15]When the king heard what Moses had done, he tried to kill him. But Moses ran away from the king and went to live in the land of Midian. There he sat down near a well.

Moses in Midian

[16]There was a priest in Midian who had seven daughters. His daughters went to that

---

2:10 Moses The name "Moses" sounds like the Hebrew word for "to pull out."

well to get water to fill the water troughs for their father's flock. [17]Some shepherds came and chased the girls away, but Moses defended the girls and watered their flock.

[18]When they went back to their father Reuel,[n] he asked them, "Why have you come home early today?"

[19]The girls answered, "The shepherds chased us away, but an Egyptian defended us. He got water for us and watered our flock."

[20]He asked his daughters, "Where is this man? Why did you leave him? Invite him to eat with us."

[21]Moses agreed to stay with Jethro, and he gave his daughter Zipporah to Moses to be his wife. [22]Zipporah gave birth to a son. Moses named him Gershom,[n] because Moses was a stranger in a land that was not his own.

[23]After a long time, the king of Egypt died. The people of Israel groaned, because they were forced to work very hard. When they cried for help, God heard them. [24]God heard their cries, and he remembered the agreement he had made with Abraham, Isaac, and Jacob. [25]He saw the troubles of the people of Israel, and he was concerned about them.

PSALM 15:1–5

What the Lord Demands

A psalm of David.

15 LORD, who may enter your Holy Tent?
  Who may live on your holy mountain?

[2]Only those who are innocent
  and who do what is right.
  Such people speak the truth from their hearts
[3] and do not tell lies about others.
  They do no wrong to their neighbors
  and do not gossip.
[4]They do not respect hateful people
  but honor those who honor the LORD.
  They keep their promises to their neighbors,

even when it hurts.
[5]They do not charge interest on money they lend
  and do not take money to hurt innocent people.

Whoever does all these things will never be destroyed.

PROVERBS 4:25–27

[25]Keep your eyes focused on what is right,
  and look straight ahead to what is good.
[26]Be careful what you do,
  and always do what is right.
[27]Don't turn off the road of goodness;
  keep away from evil paths.

MATTHEW 17:1–27

Jesus Talks with Moses and Elijah

17 Six days later, Jesus took Peter, James, and John, the brother of James, up on a high mountain by themselves. [2]While they watched, Jesus' appearance was changed; his face became bright like the sun, and his clothes became white as light. [3]Then Moses and Elijah[n] appeared to them, talking with Jesus.

[4]Peter said to Jesus, "Lord, it is good that we are here. If you want, I will put up three tents here—one for you, one for Moses, and one for Elijah."

[5]While Peter was talking, a bright cloud covered them. A voice came from the cloud and said, "This is my Son, whom I love, and I am very pleased with him. Listen to him!"

[6]When his followers heard the voice, they were so frightened they fell to the ground. [7]But Jesus went to them and touched them and said, "Stand up. Don't be afraid." [8]When they looked up, they saw Jesus was now alone.

[9]As they were coming down the mountain, Jesus commanded them not to tell anyone about what they had seen until the Son of Man had risen from the dead. [10]Then his followers asked him, "Why do the teachers of the law say that Elijah must come first?"

2:18 Reuel He was also called Jethro. **2:22 Gershom** This name sounds like the Hebrew word meaning "a stranger there." • **17:3 Moses and Elijah** Two of the most important Jewish leaders in the past. God had given Moses the Law, and Elijah was an important prophet.

[11]Jesus answered, "They are right to say that Elijah is coming and that he will make everything the way it should be. [12]But I tell you that Elijah has already come, and they did not recognize him. They did to him whatever they wanted to do. It will be the same with the Son of Man; those same people will make the Son of Man suffer." [13]Then the followers understood that Jesus was talking about John the Baptist.

Jesus Heals a Sick Boy

[14]When Jesus and his followers came back to the crowd, a man came to Jesus and bowed before him. [15]The man said, "Lord, have mercy on my son. He has epilepsy[n] and is suffering very much, because he often falls into the fire or into the water. [16]I brought him to your followers, but they could not cure him."

[17]Jesus answered, "You people have no faith, and your lives are all wrong. How long must I put up with you? How long must I continue to be patient with you? Bring the boy here." [18]Jesus commanded the demon inside the boy. Then the demon came out, and the boy was healed from that time on.

[19]The followers came to Jesus when he was alone and asked, "Why couldn't we force the demon out?"

[20]Jesus answered, "Because your faith is too small. I tell you the truth, if your faith is as big as a mustard seed, you can say to this mountain, 'Move from here to there,' and it will move. All things will be possible for you. [[21]That kind of spirit comes out only if you use prayer and fasting.]"[n]

Jesus Talks About His Death

[22]While Jesus' followers were gathering in Galilee, he said to them, "The Son of Man will be handed over to people, [23]and they will kill him. But on the third day he will be raised from the dead." And the followers were filled with sadness.

Jesus Talks About Paying Taxes

[24]When Jesus and his followers came to Capernaum, the men who collected the Temple tax came to Peter. They asked, "Does your teacher pay the Temple tax?"

[25]Peter answered, "Yes, Jesus pays the tax."

Peter went into the house, but before he could speak, Jesus said to him, "What do you think? The kings of the earth collect different kinds of taxes. But who pays the taxes—the king's children or others?"

[26]Peter answered, "Other people pay the taxes."

Jesus said to Peter, "Then the children of the king don't have to pay taxes. [27]But we don't want to upset these tax collectors. So go to the lake and fish. After you catch the first fish, open its mouth and you will find a coin. Take that coin and give it to the tax collectors for you and me."

JANUARY 27

EXODUS 3:1—4:31

The Burning Bush

3 One day Moses was taking care of Jethro's flock. (Jethro was the priest of Midian and also Moses' father-in-law.) When Moses led the flock to the west side of the desert, he came to Sinai, the mountain of God. [2]There the angel of the LORD appeared to him in flames of fire coming out of a bush. Moses saw that the bush was on fire, but it was not burning up. [3]So he said, "I will go closer to this strange thing. How can a bush continue burning without burning up?"

[4]When the LORD saw Moses was coming to look at the bush, God called to him from the bush, "Moses, Moses!"

And Moses said, "Here I am."

[5]Then God said, "Do not come any closer. Take off your sandals, because you are

---

17:15 epilepsy A disease that causes a person sometimes to lose control of his body and maybe faint, shake strongly, or not be able to move. **17:21 That . . . fasting.** Some Greek copies do not contain the bracketed text.

standing on holy ground. [6]I am the God of your ancestors—the God of Abraham, the God of Isaac, and the God of Jacob." Moses covered his face because he was afraid to look at God.

[7]The LORD said, "I have seen the troubles my people have suffered in Egypt, and I have heard their cries when the Egyptian slave masters hurt them. I am concerned about their pain, [8]and I have come down to save them from the Egyptians. I will bring them out of that land and lead them to a good land with lots of room—a fertile land. It is the land of the Canaanites, Hittites, Amorites, Perizzites, Hivites, and Jebusites. [9]I have heard the cries of the people of Israel, and I have seen the way the Egyptians have made life hard for them. [10]So now I am sending you to the king of Egypt. Go! Bring my people, the Israelites, out of Egypt!"

[11]But Moses said to God, "I am not a great man! How can I go to the king and lead the Israelites out of Egypt?"

[12]God said, "I will be with you. This will be the proof that I am sending you: After you lead the people out of Egypt, all of you will worship me on this mountain."

[13]Moses said to God, "When I go to the Israelites, I will say to them, 'The God of your ancestors sent me to you.' What if the people say, 'What is his name?' What should I tell them?"

[14]Then God said to Moses, "I AM WHO I AM.[n] When you go to the people of Israel, tell them, 'I AM sent me to you.'"

[15]God also said to Moses, "This is what you should tell the people: 'The LORD is the God of your ancestors—the God of Abraham, the God of Isaac, and the God of Jacob. He sent me to you.' This will always be my name, by which people from now on will know me.

[16]"Go and gather the elders and tell them this: 'The LORD, the God of your ancestors Abraham, Isaac, and Jacob, has appeared to me. He said, I care about you, and I have seen what has happened to you in Egypt. [17]I promised I would take you out of your trou-

bles in Egypt. I will lead you to the land of the Canaanites, Hittites, Amorites, Perizzites, Hivites, and Jebusites—a fertile land.'

[18]"The elders will listen to you. And then you and the elders of Israel will go to the king of Egypt and tell him, 'The LORD, the God of the Hebrews, appeared to us. Let us travel three days into the desert to offer sacrifices to the LORD our God.'

[19]"But I know that the king of Egypt will not let you go. Only a great power will force him to let you go, [20]so I will use my great power against Egypt. I will strike Egypt with all the miracles that will happen in that land. After I do that, he will let you go. [21]I will cause the Egyptians to think well of the Israelites. So when you leave, they will give gifts to your people. [22]Each woman should ask her Egyptian neighbor and any Egyptian woman living in her house for gifts—silver, gold, and clothing. You should put those gifts on your children when you leave Egypt. In this way you will take with you the riches of the Egyptians."

Proof for Moses

4 Then Moses answered, "What if the people of Israel do not believe me or listen to me? What if they say, 'The LORD did not appear to you'?"

[2]The LORD said to him, "What is that in your hand?"

Moses answered, "It is my walking stick."

[3]The LORD said, "Throw it on the ground."

So Moses threw it on the ground, and it became a snake. Moses ran from the snake, [4]but the LORD said to him, "Reach out and grab the snake by its tail." When Moses reached out and took hold of the snake, it again became a stick in his hand. [5]The LORD said, "This is so that the Israelites will believe that the LORD appeared to you. I am the God of their ancestors, the God of Abraham, the God of Isaac, and the God of Jacob."

[6]Then the LORD said to Moses, "Put your hand inside your coat." So Moses put his hand inside his coat. When he took it out, it was white with a skin disease.

[7]Then he said, "Now put your hand inside

3:14 I . . . I AM The Hebrew words are like the name "Yahweh." This Hebrew name for God, usually called "LORD," shows that God always lives and is always with his people.

your coat again." So Moses put his hand inside his coat again. When he took it out, his hand was healthy again, like the rest of his skin.

[8]Then the LORD said, "If the people do not believe you or pay attention to the first miracle, they may believe you when you show them this second miracle. [9]After these two miracles, if they still do not believe or listen to you, take some water from the Nile River and pour it on the dry ground. The water will become blood when it touches the ground."

[10]But Moses said to the LORD, "Please, Lord, I have never been a skilled speaker. Even now, after talking to you, I cannot speak well. I speak slowly and can't find the best words."

[11]Then the LORD said to him, "Who made a person's mouth? And who makes someone deaf or not able to speak? Or who gives a person sight or blindness? It is I, the LORD. [12]Now go! I will help you speak, and I will teach you what to say."

[13]But Moses said, "Please, Lord, send someone else."

[14]The LORD became angry with Moses and said, "Your brother Aaron, from the family of Levi, is a skilled speaker. He is already coming to meet you, and he will be happy when he sees you. [15]You will speak to Aaron and tell him what to say. I will help both of you to speak and will teach you what to do. [16]Aaron will speak to the people for you. You will tell him what God says, and he will speak for you. [17]Take your walking stick with you, and use it to do the miracles."

Moses Returns to Egypt

[18]Moses went back to Jethro, his father-in-law, and said to him, "Let me go back to my people in Egypt. I want to see if they are still alive."

Jethro said to Moses, "Go! I wish you well."

[19]While Moses was still in Midian, the LORD said to him, "Go back to Egypt, because the men who wanted to kill you are dead now."

[20]So Moses took his wife and his sons, put them on a donkey, and started back to Egypt. He took with him the walking stick of God.

[21]The LORD said to Moses, "When you get back to Egypt, do all the miracles I have given you the power to do. Show them to the king of Egypt. But I will make the king very stubborn, and he will not let the people go. [22]Then say to the king, 'This is what the LORD says: Israel is my firstborn son. [23]I told you to let my son go so he may worship me. But you refused to let Israel go, so I will kill your firstborn son.'"

[24]As Moses was on his way to Egypt, he stopped at a resting place for the night. The LORD met him there and tried to kill him. [25]But Zipporah took a flint knife and circumcised her son. Taking the skin, she touched Moses' feet with it and said to him, "You are a bridegroom of blood to me." [26]She said, "You are a bridegroom of blood," because she had to circumcise her son. So the LORD let Moses alone.

[27]Meanwhile the LORD said to Aaron, "Go out into the desert to meet Moses." When Aaron went, he met Moses at Sinai, the mountain of God, and kissed him. [28]Moses told Aaron everything the LORD had said to him when he sent him to Egypt. He also told him about the miracles which the LORD had commanded him to do.

[29]Moses and Aaron gathered all the elders of the Israelites, [30]and Aaron told them everything that the LORD had told Moses. Then Moses did the miracles for all the people to see, [31]and the Israelites believed. When they heard that the LORD was concerned about them and had seen their troubles, they bowed down and worshiped him.

PSALM 16:1–6

The Lord Takes Care of His People

A miktam of David.

16 Protect me, God,
because I trust in you.
[2]I said to the LORD, "You are my Lord.
Every good thing I have comes from
you."
[3]As for the godly people in the world,
they are the wonderful ones I enjoy.

4But those who turn to idols
will have much pain.
I will not offer blood to those idols
or even speak their names.

5No, the LORD is all I need.
He takes care of me.
6My share in life has been pleasant;
my part has been beautiful.

PROVERBS 5:1–6

Warning About Adultery

5 My son, pay attention to my wisdom;
listen to my words of understanding.
2Be careful to use good sense,
and watch what you say.
3The words of another man's wife may
seem sweet as honey;
they may be as smooth as olive oil.
4But in the end she will bring you
sorrow,
causing you pain like a two-edged
sword.
5She is on the way to death;
her steps are headed straight to the
grave.
6She gives little thought to life.
She doesn't even know that her ways
are wrong.

MATTHEW 18:1–20

Who Is the Greatest?

18 At that time the followers came to Jesus and asked, "Who is greatest in the
kingdom of heaven?"
2Jesus called a little child to him and
stood the child before his followers. 3Then he
said, "I tell you the truth, you must change
and become like little children. Otherwise,
you will never enter the kingdom of heaven.
4The greatest person in the kingdom of
heaven is the one who makes himself humble like this child.
5"Whoever accepts a child in my name
accepts me. 6If one of these little children believes in me, and someone causes that child
to sin, it would be better for that person to

have a large stone tied around the neck and
be drowned in the sea. 7How terrible for the
people of the world because of the things
that cause them to sin. Such things will happen, but how terrible for the one who causes
them to happen! 8If your hand or your foot
causes you to sin, cut it off and throw it away.
It is better for you to lose part of your body
and live forever than to have two hands and
two feet and be thrown into the fire that
burns forever. 9If your eye causes you to sin,
take it out and throw it away. It is better for
you to have only one eye and live forever
than to have two eyes and be thrown into the
fire of hell.

A Lost Sheep

10"Be careful. Don't think these little children are worth nothing. I tell you that they
have angels in heaven who are always with
my Father in heaven. [11The Son of Man
came to save lost people.]n
12"If a man has a hundred sheep but one
of the sheep gets lost, he will leave the other
ninety-nine on the hill and go to look for the
lost sheep. 13I tell you the truth, if he finds it
he is happier about that one sheep than
about the ninety-nine that were never lost.
14In the same way, your Father in heaven
does not want any of these little children to
be lost.

When a Person Sins Against You

15"If your fellow believer sins against
you,n go and tell him in private what he did
wrong. If he listens to you, you have helped
that person to be your brother or sister
again. 16But if he refuses to listen, go to him
again and take one or two other people with
you. 'Every case may be proved by two or
three witnesses.'n 17If he refuses to listen to
them, tell the church. If he refuses to listen to
the church, then treat him like a person who
does not believe in God or like a tax collector.
18"I tell you the truth, the things you don't
allow on earth will be the things God does
not allow. And the things you allow on earth
will be the things that God allows.

18:11 The . . . people. Some Greek copies do not contain the bracketed text. **18:15 against you** Some Greek copies do not have "against you." **18:16 'Every . . . witnesses.'** Quotation from Deuteronomy 19:15.

¹⁹"Also, I tell you that if two of you on earth agree about something and pray for it, it will be done for you by my Father in heaven. ²⁰This is true because if two or three people come together in my name, I am there with them."

JANUARY 28

EXODUS 5:1—6:30

Moses and Aaron Before the King

5 After Moses and Aaron talked to the people, they went to the king of Egypt and said, "This is what the LORD, the God of Israel, says: 'Let my people go so they may hold a feast for me in the desert.'"

²But the king of Egypt said, "Who is the LORD? Why should I obey him and let Israel go? I do not know the LORD, and I will not let Israel go."

³Then Aaron and Moses said, "The God of the Hebrews has met with us. Now let us travel three days into the desert to offer sacrifices to the LORD our God. If we don't do this, he may kill us with a disease or in war."

⁴But the king said to them, "Moses and Aaron, why are you taking the people away from their work? Go back to your jobs! ⁵There are very many Hebrews, and now you want them to quit working!"

⁶That same day the king gave a command to the slave masters and foremen. ⁷He said, "Don't give the people straw to make bricks as you used to do. Let them gather their own straw. ⁸But they must still make the same number of bricks as they did before. Do not accept fewer. They have become lazy, and that is why they are asking me, 'Let us go to offer sacrifices to our God.' ⁹Make these people work harder and keep them busy; then they will not have time to listen to the lies of Moses."

¹⁰So the slave masters and foremen went to the Israelites and said, "This is what the king says: I will no longer give you straw. ¹¹Go and get your own straw wherever you can find it. But you must make as many bricks as you made before." ¹²So the people went everywhere in Egypt looking for dry stalks to use for straw. ¹³The slave masters kept forcing the people to work harder. They said, "You must make just as many bricks as you did when you were given straw." ¹⁴The king's slave masters had made the Israelite foremen responsible for the work the people did. The Egyptian slave masters beat these men and asked them, "Why aren't you making as many bricks as you made in the past?"

¹⁵Then the Israelite foremen went to the king and complained, "Why are you treating us, your servants, this way? ¹⁶You give us no straw, but we are commanded to make bricks. Our slave masters beat us, but it is your own people's fault."

¹⁷The king answered, "You are lazy! You don't want to work! That is why you ask to leave here and make sacrifices to the LORD. ¹⁸Now, go back to work! We will not give you any straw, but you must make just as many bricks as you did before."

¹⁹The Israelite foremen knew they were in trouble, because the king had told them, "You must make just as many bricks each day as you did before." ²⁰As they were leaving the meeting with the king, they met Moses and Aaron, who were waiting for them. ²¹So they said to Moses and Aaron, "May the LORD punish you. You caused the king and his officers to hate us. You have given them an excuse to kill us."

Moses Complains to God

²²Then Moses returned to the LORD and said, "Lord, why have you brought this trouble on your people? Is this why you sent me here? ²³I went to the king and said what you told me to say, but ever since that time he has made the people suffer. And you have done nothing to save them."

6 Then the LORD said to Moses, "Now you will see what I will do to the king of Egypt. I will use my great power against

him, and he will let my people go. Because of my power, he will force them out of his country."

²Then God said to Moses, "I am the LORD. ³I appeared to Abraham, Isaac, and Jacob by the name God Almighty, but they did not know me by my name, the LORD. ⁴I also made my agreement with them to give them the land of Canaan. They lived in that land, but it was not their own. ⁵Now I have heard the cries of the Israelites, whom the Egyptians are treating as slaves, and I remember my agreement. ⁶So tell the people of Israel that I say to them, 'I am the LORD. I will save you from the hard work the Egyptians force you to do. I will make you free, so you will not be slaves to the Egyptians. I will free you by my great power, and I will punish the Egyptians terribly. ⁷I will make you my own people, and I will be your God. You will know that I am the LORD your God, the One who saves you from the hard work the Egyptians force you to do. ⁸I will lead you to the land that I promised to Abraham, Isaac, and Jacob, and I will give you that land to own. I am the LORD.'"

⁹So Moses told this to the Israelites, but they would not listen to him. They were discouraged, and their slavery was hard.

¹⁰Then the LORD said to Moses, ¹¹"Go tell the king of Egypt that he must let the Israelites leave his land."

¹²But Moses answered, "The Israelites will not listen to me, so surely the king will not listen to me either. I am not a good speaker."

¹³But the LORD spoke to Moses and Aaron and gave them orders about the Israelites and the king of Egypt. He commanded them to lead the Israelites out of Egypt.

Families of Israel

¹⁴These are the leaders of the families of Israel:

Israel's first son, Reuben, had four sons: Hanoch, Pallu, Hezron, and Carmi. These are the family groups of Reuben. ¹⁵Simeon's sons were Jemuel, Jamin, Ohad, Jakin, Zohar, and Shaul, the son of a Canaanite woman. These are the family groups of Simeon. ¹⁶Levi lived one hundred thirty-seven years. These are the names of his sons according to their family history: Gershon, Kohath, and Merari.

¹⁷Gershon had two sons, Libni and Shimei, with their families.

¹⁸Kohath lived one hundred thirty-three years. The sons of Kohath were Amram, Izhar, Hebron, and Uzziel.

¹⁹The sons of Merari were Mahli and Mushi.

These are the family groups of Levi, according to their family history.

²⁰Amram married his father's sister Jochebed, who gave birth to Aaron and Moses. Amram lived one hundred thirty-seven years.

²¹Izhar's sons were Korah, Nepheg, and Zicri.

²²Uzziel's sons were Mishael, Elzaphan, and Sithri.

²³Aaron married Elisheba, the daughter of Amminadab and the sister of Nahshon. Elisheba gave birth to Nadab, Abihu, Eleazar, and Ithamar.

²⁴The sons of Korah were Assir, Elkanah, and Abiasaph. These are the family groups of the Korahites.

²⁵Eleazar son of Aaron married a daughter of Putiel, and she gave birth to Phinehas.

These are the leaders of the family groups of the Levites.

²⁶This was the Aaron and Moses to whom the LORD said, "Lead the people of Israel out of Egypt by their divisions." ²⁷Aaron and Moses are the ones who talked to the king of Egypt and told him to let the Israelites leave Egypt.

God Repeats His Call to Moses

²⁸The LORD spoke to Moses in the land of Egypt ²⁹and said, "I am the LORD. Tell the king of Egypt everything I tell you."

³⁰But Moses answered, "I am not a good speaker. The king will not listen to me."

PSALM 16:7–11

⁷I praise the LORD because he advises me.
  Even at night, I feel his leading.
⁸I keep the LORD before me always.
  Because he is close by my side,
  I will not be hurt.

⁹So I rejoice and am glad.
  Even my body has hope,
¹⁰because you will not leave me in the grave.
  You will not let your holy one rot.
¹¹You will teach me how to live a holy life.
  Being with you will fill me with joy;
  at your right hand I will find pleasure
  forever.

PROVERBS 5:7—14

⁷Now, my sons, listen to me,
  and don't ignore what I say.
⁸Stay away from such a woman.
  Don't even go near the door of her house,
⁹or you will give your riches to others,
  and the best years of your life will be
  given to someone cruel.
¹⁰Strangers will enjoy your wealth,
  and what you worked so hard for will
  go to someone else.
¹¹You will groan at the end of your life
  when your health is gone.
¹²Then you will say, "I hated being told
  what to do!
  I would not listen to correction!
¹³I would not listen to my teachers
  or pay attention to my instructors.
¹⁴I came close to being completely ruined
  in front of a whole group of people."

MATTHEW 18:21—35

An Unforgiving Servant

²¹Then Peter came to Jesus and asked, "Lord, when my fellow believer sins against me, how many times must I forgive him? Should I forgive him as many as seven times?"
²²Jesus answered, "I tell you, you must forgive him more than seven times. You must forgive him even if he wrongs you seventy times seven.

²³"The kingdom of heaven is like a king who decided to collect the money his servants owed him. ²⁴When the king began to collect his money, a servant who owed him several million dollars was brought to him. ²⁵But the servant did not have enough money to pay his master, the king. So the master ordered that everything the servant owned should be sold, even the servant's wife and children. Then the money would be used to pay the king what the servant owed.

²⁶"But the servant fell on his knees and begged, 'Be patient with me, and I will pay you everything I owe.' ²⁷The master felt sorry for his servant and told him he did not have to pay it back. Then he let the servant go free.

²⁸"Later, that same servant found another servant who owed him a few dollars. The servant grabbed him around the neck and said, 'Pay me the money you owe me!'

²⁹"The other servant fell on his knees and begged him, 'Be patient with me, and I will pay you everything I owe.'

³⁰"But the first servant refused to be patient. He threw the other servant into prison until he could pay everything he owed. ³¹When the other servants saw what had happened, they were very sorry. So they went and told their master all that had happened.

³²"Then the master called his servant in and said, 'You evil servant! Because you begged me to forget what you owed, I told you that you did not have to pay anything. ³³You should have showed mercy to that other servant, just as I showed mercy to you.' ³⁴The master was very angry and put the servant in prison to be punished until he could pay everything he owed.

³⁵"This king did what my heavenly Father will do to you if you do not forgive your brother or sister from your heart."

JANUARY 29

EXODUS 7:1—8:32

7 The LORD said to Moses, "I have made you like God to the king of Egypt, and your

brother Aaron will be like a prophet for you. ²Tell Aaron your brother everything that I command you, and let him tell the king of Egypt to let the Israelites leave his country.

3But I will make the king stubborn. I will do many miracles in Egypt, 4but he will still refuse to listen. So then I will punish Egypt terribly, and I will lead my divisions, my people the Israelites, out of that land. 5I will punish Egypt with my power, and I will bring the Israelites out of that land. Then they will know I am the LORD."

6Moses and Aaron did just as the LORD had commanded them. 7Moses was eighty years old and Aaron was eighty-three when they spoke to the king.

Aaron's Walking Stick Becomes a Snake

8The LORD said to Moses and Aaron, 9"Moses, when the king asks you to do a miracle, tell Aaron to throw his walking stick down in front of the king, and it will become a snake."

10So Moses and Aaron went to the king as the LORD had commanded. Aaron threw his walking stick down in front of the king and his officers, and it became a snake. 11So the king called in his wise men and his magicians, and with their tricks the Egyptian magicians were able to do the same thing. 12They threw their walking sticks on the ground, and their sticks became snakes. But Aaron's stick swallowed theirs. 13Still the king was stubborn and refused to listen to Moses and Aaron, just as the LORD had said.

The Water Becomes Blood

14Then the LORD said to Moses, "The king is being stubborn and refuses to let the people go. 15In the morning the king will go out to the Nile River. Go meet him by the edge of the river, and take with you the walking stick that became a snake. 16Tell him: The LORD, the God of the Hebrews, sent me to you. He said, 'Let my people go worship me in the desert.' Until now you have not listened. 17This is what the LORD says: 'This is how you will know that I am the LORD. I will strike the water of the Nile River with this stick in my hand, and the water will change into blood. 18Then the fish in the Nile will die, and the river will begin to stink. The Egyptians will not be able to drink the water from the Nile.'"

19The LORD said to Moses, "Tell Aaron: 'Take the walking stick in your hand and stretch your hand over the rivers, canals, ponds, and pools in Egypt.' The water will become blood everywhere in Egypt, both in wooden buckets and in stone jars."

20So Moses and Aaron did just as the LORD had commanded. In front of the king and his officers, Aaron raised his walking stick and struck the water in the Nile River. So all the water in the Nile changed into blood. 21The fish in the Nile died, and the river began to stink, so the Egyptians could not drink water from it. Blood was everywhere in the land of Egypt.

22Using their tricks, the magicians of Egypt did the same thing. So the king was stubborn and refused to listen to Moses and Aaron, just as the LORD had said. 23The king turned and went into his palace and ignored what Moses and Aaron had done. 24The Egyptians could not drink the water from the Nile, so all of them dug along the bank of the river, looking for water to drink.

The Frogs

25Seven days passed after the LORD changed the Nile River.

8 Then the LORD told Moses, "Go to the king of Egypt and tell him, 'This is what the LORD says: Let my people go to worship me. 2If you refuse, I will punish Egypt with frogs. 3The Nile River will be filled with frogs. They will come up into your palace, into your bedroom, on your bed, into the houses of your officers, and onto your people. They will come into your ovens and into your baking pans. 4The frogs will jump all over you, your people, and your officers.'"

5Then the LORD said to Moses, "Tell Aaron to hold his walking stick in his hand over the rivers, canals, and ponds. Make frogs come up out of the water onto the land of Egypt."

6So Aaron held his hand over all the waters of Egypt, and the frogs came up out of the water and covered the land of Egypt. 7The magicians used their tricks to do the same thing, so even more frogs came up onto the land of Egypt.

8The king called for Moses and Aaron and said, "Pray to the LORD to take the frogs away from me and my people. I will let your people go to offer sacrifices to the LORD."

⁹Moses said to the king, "Please set the time when I should pray for you, your people, and your officers. Then the frogs will leave you and your houses and will remain only in the Nile."

¹⁰The king answered, "Tomorrow."

Moses said, "What you want will happen. By this you will know that there is no one like the LORD our God. ¹¹The frogs will leave you, your houses, your officers, and your people. They will remain only in the Nile."

¹²After Moses and Aaron left the king, Moses asked the LORD about the frogs he had sent to the king. ¹³And the LORD did as Moses asked. The frogs died in the houses, in the yards, and in the fields. ¹⁴The Egyptians put them in piles, and the whole country began to stink. ¹⁵But when the king saw that they were free of the frogs, he became stubborn again. He did not listen to Moses and Aaron, just as the LORD had said.

The Gnats

¹⁶Then the LORD said to Moses, "Tell Aaron to raise his walking stick and strike the dust on the ground. Then everywhere in Egypt the dust will change into gnats." ¹⁷They did this, and when Aaron raised the walking stick that was in his hand and struck the dust on the ground, everywhere in Egypt the dust changed into gnats. The gnats got on the people and animals. ¹⁸Using their tricks, the magicians tried to do the same thing, but they could not make the dust change into gnats. The gnats remained on the people and animals. ¹⁹So the magicians told the king that the power of God had done this. But the king was stubborn and refused to listen to them, just as the LORD had said.

The Flies

²⁰The LORD told Moses, "Get up early in the morning, and meet the king of Egypt as he goes out to the river. Tell him, 'This is what the LORD says: Let my people go so they can worship me. ²¹If you don't let them go, I will send swarms of flies into your houses. The flies will be on you, your officers, and your people. The houses of Egypt will be full of flies, and they will be all over the ground, too. ²²But I will not treat the Israelites the same as the Egyptian people. There will not

be any flies in the land of Goshen, where my people live. By this you will know that I, the LORD, am in this land. ²³I will treat my people differently from your people. This miracle will happen tomorrow.'"

²⁴So the LORD did as he had said, and great swarms of flies came into the king's palace and his officers' houses. All over Egypt flies were ruining the land. ²⁵The king called for Moses and Aaron and told them, "Offer sacrifices to your God here in this country."

²⁶But Moses said, "It wouldn't be right to do that, because the Egyptians hate the sacrifices we offer to the LORD our God. If they see us offering sacrifices they hate, they will throw stones at us and kill us. ²⁷Let us make a three-day journey into the desert. We must offer sacrifices to the LORD our God there, as the LORD told us to do."

²⁸The king said, "I will let you go so that you may offer sacrifices to the LORD your God in the desert, but you must not go very far away. Now go and pray for me."

²⁹Moses said, "I will leave and pray to the LORD, and he will take the flies away from you, your officers, and your people tomorrow. But do not try to trick us again. Do not stop the people from going to offer sacrifices to the LORD."

³⁰So Moses left the king and prayed to the LORD, ³¹and the LORD did as he asked. He removed the flies from the king, his officers, and his people so that not one fly was left. ³²But the king became stubborn again and did not let the people go.

PSALM 17:1–5

A Prayer for Protection

A prayer of David.

17LORD, hear me begging for fairness;
  listen to my cry for help.
Pay attention to my prayer,
  because I speak the truth.
²You will judge that I am right;
  your eyes can see what is true.
³You have examined my heart;
  you have tested me all night.
You questioned me without finding
    anything wrong;
  I have not sinned with my mouth.

⁴I have obeyed your commands,
  so I have not done what evil people do.
⁵I have done what you told me;
  I have not failed.

PROVERBS 5:15–20

¹⁵Be faithful to your own wife,
  just as you drink water from your own
    well.
¹⁶Don't pour your water in the streets;
  don't give your love to just any woman.
¹⁷These things are yours alone
  and shouldn't be shared with strangers.
¹⁸Be happy with the wife you married
  when you were young.
  She gives you joy, as your fountain gives
    you water.
¹⁹She is as lovely and graceful as a deer.
  Let her love always make you happy;
  let her love always hold you captive.
²⁰My son, don't be held captive by a
  woman who takes part in adultery.
  Don't fondle a woman who is not your
    wife.

MATTHEW 19:1–30

Jesus Teaches About Divorce

19 After Jesus said all these things, he left Galilee and went into the area of Judea on the other side of the Jordan River. ²Large crowds followed him, and he healed them there.

³Some Pharisees came to Jesus and tried to trick him. They asked, "Is it right for a man to divorce his wife for any reason he chooses?"

⁴Jesus answered, "Surely you have read in the Scriptures: When God made the world, 'he made them male and female.'ⁿ ⁵And God said, 'So a man will leave his father and mother and be united with his wife, and the two will become one body.'ⁿ ⁶So there are not two, but one. God has joined the two together, so no one should separate them."

⁷The Pharisees asked, "Why then did Moses give a command for a man to divorce his wife by giving her divorce papers?"

⁸Jesus answered, "Moses allowed you to divorce your wives because you refused to accept God's teaching, but divorce was not allowed in the beginning. ⁹I tell you that anyone who divorces his wife and marries another woman is guilty of adultery.ⁿ The only reason for a man to divorce his wife is if his wife has sexual relations with another man."

¹⁰The followers said to him, "If that is the only reason a man can divorce his wife, it is better not to marry."

¹¹Jesus answered, "Not everyone can accept this teaching, but God has made some able to accept it. ¹²There are different reasons why some men cannot marry. Some men were born without the ability to become fathers. Others were made that way later in life by other people. And some men have given up marriage because of the kingdom of heaven. But the person who can marry should accept this teaching about marriage."ⁿ

Jesus Welcomes Children

¹³Then the people brought their little children to Jesus so he could put his hands on themⁿ and pray for them. His followers told them to stop, ¹⁴but Jesus said, "Let the little children come to me. Don't stop them, because the kingdom of heaven belongs to people who are like these children." ¹⁵After Jesus put his hands on the children, he left there.

A Rich Young Man's Question

¹⁶A man came to Jesus and asked, "Teacher, what good thing must I do to have life forever?"

¹⁷Jesus answered, "Why do you ask me about what is good? Only God is good. But if you want to have life forever, obey the commands."

¹⁸The man asked, "Which commands?"

Jesus answered, " 'You must not murder anyone; you must not be guilty of adultery; you must not steal; you must not tell lies

---

19:4 'he made . . . female' Quotation from Genesis 1:27 or 5:2.   **19:5 'So . . . body.'** Quotation from Genesis 2:24.
19:9 adultery Some Greek copies continue, "And anyone who marries a divorced woman is guilty of adultery." Compare Matthew 5:32.   **19:12 But . . . marriage.** This may also mean, "The person who can accept this teaching about not marrying should accept it."   **19:13 put his hands on them** Showing that Jesus gave special blessings to these children.

about your neighbor; [19]honor your father and mother;[n] and love your neighbor as you love yourself.' "[n]

[20]The young man said, "I have obeyed all these things. What else do I need to do?"

[21]Jesus answered, "If you want to be perfect, then go and sell your possessions and give the money to the poor. If you do this, you will have treasure in heaven. Then come and follow me."

[22]But when the young man heard this, he left sorrowfully, because he was rich.

[23]Then Jesus said to his followers, "I tell you the truth, it will be hard for a rich person to enter the kingdom of heaven. [24]Yes, I tell you that it is easier for a camel to go through the eye of a needle than for a rich person to enter the kingdom of God."

[25]When Jesus' followers heard this, they were very surprised and asked, "Then who can be saved?"

[26]Jesus looked at them and said, "For people this is impossible, but for God all things are possible."

[27]Peter said to Jesus, "Look, we have left everything and followed you. So what will we have?"

[28]Jesus said to them, "I tell you the truth, when the age to come has arrived, the Son of Man will sit on his great throne. All of you who followed me will also sit on twelve thrones, judging the twelve tribes of Israel. [29]And all those who have left houses, brothers, sisters, father, mother,[n] children, or farms to follow me will get much more than they left, and they will have life forever. [30]Many who are first now will be last in the future. And many who are last now will be first in the future.

JANUARY 30

EXODUS 9:1—10:29

The Disease on the Farm Animals

9Then the LORD told Moses, "Go to the king of Egypt and tell him, 'This is what the LORD, the God of the Hebrews, says: Let my people go to worship me. [2]If you refuse to let them go and continue to hold them, [3]the LORD will punish you. He will send a terrible disease on your farm animals that are in the fields. He will cause your horses, donkeys, camels, cattle, goats, and sheep to become sick. [4]But the LORD will treat Israel's animals differently from the animals of Egypt. None of the animals that belong to the Israelites will die. [5]The LORD has set tomorrow as the time he will do this in the land.' " [6]The next day the LORD did as he promised. All the farm animals in Egypt died, but none of the animals belonging to Israelites died. [7]The king sent people to see what had happened to the animals of Israel, and they found that not one of them had died. But the king was still stubborn and did not let the people go.

The Boils

[8]The LORD said to Moses and Aaron, "Fill your hands with ashes from a furnace. Moses, throw the ashes into the air in front of the king of Egypt. [9]The ashes will spread like dust through all the land of Egypt. They will cause boils to break out and become sores on the skin of people and animals everywhere in the land."

[10]So Moses and Aaron took ashes from a furnace and went and stood before the king. Moses threw ashes into the air, which caused boils to break out and become sores on people and animals. [11]The magicians could not stand before Moses, because all the Egyptians had boils, even the magicians. [12]But the LORD made the king stubborn, so he refused to listen to Moses and Aaron, just as the LORD had said.

The Hail

[13]Then the LORD said to Moses, "Get up early in the morning and go to the king of Egypt. Tell him, 'This is what the LORD, the

---

19:19 'You . . . mother' Quotation from Exodus 20:12–16; Deuteronomy 5:16–20. **19:19 'love . . . yourself'** Quotation from Leviticus 19:18. **19:29 mother** Some Greek copies continue, "or wife."

God of the Hebrews, says: Let my people go to worship me. [14]If you don't, this time I will punish you, your officers, and your people, with all my power. Then you will know there is no one in the whole land like me. [15]By now I could have used my power and caused a terrible disease that would have destroyed you and your people from the earth. [16]But I have let you live for this reason: to show you my power so that my name will be talked about in all the earth. [17]You are still against my people and do not want to let them go. [18]So at this time tomorrow, I will send a terrible hailstorm, the worst in Egypt since it became a nation. [19]Now send for your animals and whatever you have in the fields, and bring them into a safe place. The hail will fall on every person or animal that is still in the fields. If they have not been brought in, they will die.' " [20]Some of the king's officers respected the word of the LORD and hurried to bring their slaves and animals inside. [21]But others ignored the LORD's message and left their slaves and animals in the fields.

[22]The LORD told Moses, "Raise your hand toward the sky. Then the hail will start falling in all the land of Egypt. It will fall on people, animals, and on everything that grows in the fields of Egypt." [23]When Moses raised his walking stick toward the sky, the LORD sent thunder and hail, and lightning flashed down to the earth. So he caused hail to fall upon the land of Egypt. [24]There was hail, and lightning flashed as it hailed—the worst hailstorm in Egypt since it had become a nation. [25]The hail destroyed all the people and animals that were in the fields in all the land of Egypt. It also destroyed everything that grew in the fields and broke all the trees in the fields. [26]The only place it did not hail was in the land of Goshen, where the Israelites lived.

[27]The king sent for Moses and Aaron and told them, "This time I have sinned. The LORD is in the right, and I and my people are in the wrong. [28]Pray to the LORD. We have had enough of God's thunder and hail. I will let you go; you do not have to stay here any longer."

[29]Moses told the king, "When I leave the city, I will raise my hands to the LORD in prayer, and the thunder and hail will stop.

Then you will know that the earth belongs to the LORD. [30]But I know that you and your officers do not yet fear the LORD God."

[31]The flax was in bloom, and the barley had ripened, so these crops were destroyed. [32]But both wheat crops ripen later, so they were not destroyed.

[33]Moses left the king and went outside the city. He raised his hands to the LORD, and the thunder and hail stopped. The rain also stopped falling to the ground. [34]When the king saw that the rain, hail, and thunder had stopped, he sinned again, and he and his officers became stubborn. [35]So the king became stubborn and refused to let the Israelites go, just as the LORD had said through Moses.

The Locusts

10 The LORD said to Moses, "Go to the king of Egypt. I have made him and his officers stubborn so I could show them my powerful miracles. [2]I also did this so you could tell your children and your grandchildren how I was hard on the Egyptians. Tell them about the miracles I did among them so that all of you will know that I am the LORD."

[3]So Moses and Aaron went to the king and told him, "This is what the LORD, the God of the Hebrews, says: 'How long will you refuse to be sorry for what you have done? Let my people go to worship me. [4]If you refuse to let my people go, tomorrow I will bring locusts into your country. [5]They will cover the land so that no one will be able to see the ground. They will eat anything that was left from the hailstorm and the leaves from every tree growing in the field. [6]They will fill your palaces and all your officers' houses, as well as the houses of all the Egyptians. There will be more locusts than your fathers or ancestors have ever seen—more than there have been since people began living in Egypt.' " Then Moses turned and walked away from the king.

[7]The king's officers asked him, "How long will this man make trouble for us? Let the Israelites go to worship the LORD their God. Don't you know that Egypt is ruined?"

[8]So Moses and Aaron were brought back to the king. He said to them, "Go and worship the LORD your God. But tell me, just who is going?"

⁹Moses answered, "We will go with our young and old people, our sons and daughters, and our flocks and herds, because we are going to have a feast to honor the LORD."

¹⁰The king said to them, "The LORD will really have to be with you if ever I let you and all of your children leave Egypt. See, you are planning something evil! ¹¹No! Only the men may go and worship the LORD, which is what you have been asking for." Then the king forced Moses and Aaron out of his palace.

¹²The LORD told Moses, "Raise your hand over the land of Egypt, and the locusts will come. They will spread all over the land of Egypt and will eat all the plants the hail did not destroy."

¹³So Moses raised his walking stick over the land of Egypt, and the LORD caused a strong wind to blow from the east. It blew across the land all that day and night, and when morning came, the east wind had brought the locusts. ¹⁴Swarms of locusts covered all the land of Egypt and settled everywhere. There were more locusts than ever before or after, ¹⁵and they covered the whole land so that it was black. They ate everything that was left after the hail—every plant in the field and all the fruit on the trees. Nothing green was left on any tree or plant anywhere in Egypt.

¹⁶The king quickly called for Moses and Aaron. He said, "I have sinned against the LORD your God and against you. ¹⁷Now forgive my sin this time. Pray to the LORD your God, and ask him to stop this punishment that kills."

¹⁸Moses left the king and prayed to the LORD. ¹⁹So the LORD changed the wind. He made a very strong wind blow from the west, and it blew the locusts away into the Red Sea. Not one locust was left anywhere in Egypt. ²⁰But the LORD caused the king to be stubborn again, and he did not let the Israelites go.

The Darkness

²¹Then the LORD told Moses, "Raise your hand toward the sky, and darkness will cover the land of Egypt. It will be so dark you will be able to feel it." ²²Moses raised his hand toward the sky, and total darkness was everywhere in Egypt for three days. ²³No one could see anyone else, and no one could go anywhere for three days. But the Israelites had light where they lived.

²⁴Again the king of Egypt called for Moses. He said, "All of you may go and worship the LORD. You may take your women and children with you, but you must leave your flocks and herds here."

²⁵Moses said, "You must let us have animals to use as sacrifices and burnt offerings, because we have to offer them to the LORD our God. ²⁶So we must take our animals with us; not a hoof will be left behind. We have to use some of the animals to worship the LORD our God. We won't know exactly what we will need to worship the LORD until we get there."

²⁷But the LORD made the king stubborn again, so he refused to let them go. ²⁸Then he told Moses, "Get out of here, and don't come again! The next time you see me, you will die."

²⁹Then Moses told the king, "I'll do what you say. I will not come to see you again."

PSALM 17:6–15

⁶I call to you, God,
  and you answer me.
 Listen to me now,
  and hear what I say.
⁷Your love is wonderful.
  By your power you save those who trust
    you
  from their enemies.
⁸Protect me as you would protect your own
    eye.
  Hide me under the shadow of your
    wings.
⁹Keep me from the wicked who attack me,
  from my enemies who surround me.
¹⁰They are selfish
  and brag about themselves.
¹¹They have chased me until they have
    surrounded me.
  They plan to throw me to the ground.
¹²They are like lions ready to kill;
  like lions, they sit in hiding.
¹³LORD, rise up, face the enemy, and throw
    them down.
  Save me from the wicked with your
    sword.

[14]LORD, save me by your power
from those whose reward is in this life.
They have plenty of food.
They have many sons
and leave much money to their children.

[15]Because I have lived right, I will see your
face.
When I wake up, I will see your likeness
and be satisfied.

PROVERBS 5:21–23

[21]The LORD sees everything you do,
and he watches where you go.
[22]An evil man will be caught in his wicked
ways;
the ropes of his sins will tie him up.
[23]He will die because he does not control
himself,
and he will be held captive by his
foolishness.

MATTHEW 20:1–16

A Story About Workers

20 "The kingdom of heaven is like a person who owned some land. One morning, he went out very early to hire some people to work in his vineyard. [2]The man agreed to pay the workers one coin[n] for working that day. Then he sent them into the vineyard to work. [3]About nine o'clock the man went to the marketplace and saw some other people standing there, doing nothing. [4]So he said to them, 'If you go and work in my vineyard, I will pay you what your work is worth.' [5]So they went to work in the vineyard. The man went out again about twelve o'clock and three o'clock and did the same thing. [6]About five o'clock the man went to the marketplace again and saw others standing there. He asked them, 'Why did you stand here all day doing nothing?' [7]They answered, 'No one gave us a job.' The man said to them, 'Then you can go and work in my vineyard.'

[8]"At the end of the day, the owner of the vineyard said to the boss of all the workers, 'Call the workers and pay them. Start with the last people I hired and end with those I hired first.'

[9]"When the workers who were hired at five o'clock came to get their pay, each received one coin. [10]When the workers who were hired first came to get their pay, they thought they would be paid more than the others. But each one of them also received one coin. [11]When they got their coin, they complained to the man who owned the land. [12]They said, 'Those people were hired last and worked only one hour. But you paid them the same as you paid us who worked hard all day in the hot sun.' [13]But the man who owned the vineyard said to one of those workers, 'Friend, I am being fair to you. You agreed to work for one coin. [14]So take your pay and go. I want to give the man who was hired last the same pay that I gave you. [15]I can do what I want with my own money. Are you jealous because I am good to those people?'

[16]"So those who are last now will someday be first, and those who are first now will someday be last."

JANUARY 31

EXODUS 11:1–12:51

The Death of the Firstborn

11 Now the LORD had told Moses, "I have one more way to punish the king and the people of Egypt. After this, the king will send all of you away from Egypt. When he does, he will force you to leave completely. [2]Tell the men and women of Israel to ask their neighbors for things made of silver and gold." [3]The LORD had caused the Egyptians to respect the Israelites, and both the king's

20:2 coin A Roman denarius. One coin was the average pay for one day's work.

officers and the Egyptian people considered Moses to be a great man.

⁴So Moses said to the king, "This is what the LORD says: 'About midnight tonight I will go through all Egypt. ⁵Every firstborn son in the land of Egypt will die—from the firstborn son of the king, who sits on his throne, to the firstborn of the slave girl grinding grain. Also the firstborn farm animals will die. ⁶There will be loud outcries everywhere in Egypt, worse than any time before or after this. ⁷But not even a dog will bark at the Israelites or their animals.' Then you will know that the LORD treats Israel differently from Egypt. ⁸All your officers will come to me. They will bow facedown to the ground before me and say, 'Leave and take all your people with you.' After that, I will leave." Then Moses very angrily left the king.

⁹The LORD had told Moses, "The king will not listen to you and Aaron so that I may do many miracles in the land of Egypt." ¹⁰Moses and Aaron did all these great miracles in front of the king. But the LORD made him stubborn, and the king would not let the Israelites leave his country.

The First Passover

12 The LORD spoke to Moses and Aaron in the land of Egypt: ²"This month will be the beginning of months, the first month of the year for you. ³Tell the whole community of Israel that on the tenth day of this month each man must get one lamb for the people in his house. ⁴If there are not enough people in his house to eat a whole lamb, he must share it with his closest neighbor, considering the number of people. There must be enough lamb for everyone to eat. ⁵The lamb must be a one-year-old male that has nothing wrong with it. This animal can be either a young sheep or a young goat. ⁶Take care of the animals until the fourteenth day of the month. On that day all the people of the community of Israel will kill them in the evening before dark. ⁷The people must take some of the blood and put it on the sides and tops of the doorframes of the houses where they eat the lambs. ⁸On this night they must roast the lamb over a fire. They must eat it with bitter herbs and bread made without yeast. ⁹Do not eat the lamb raw or boiled in water. Roast the whole lamb over a fire—with its head, legs, and inner organs. ¹⁰You must not leave any of it until morning, but if any of it is left over until morning, you must burn it with fire.

¹¹"This is the way you must eat it: You must be fully dressed as if you were going on a trip. You must have your sandals on and your walking stick in your hand. You must eat it in a hurry; this is the LORD's Passover.

¹²"That night I will go through the land of Egypt and kill all the firstborn animals and people in the land of Egypt. I will also punish all the gods of Egypt. I am the LORD. ¹³But the blood will be a sign on the houses where you are. When I see the blood, I will pass over you. Nothing terrible will hurt you when I punish the land of Egypt.

¹⁴"You are always to remember this day and celebrate it with a feast to the LORD. Your descendants are to honor the LORD with this feast from now on. ¹⁵For this feast you must eat bread made without yeast for seven days. On the first day, you are to remove all the yeast from your houses. No one should eat any yeast for the full seven days of the feast, or that person will be cut off from Israel. ¹⁶You are to have holy meetings on the first and last days of the feast. You must not do any work on these days; the only work you may do is to prepare your meals. ¹⁷You must celebrate the Feast of Unleavened Bread, because on this very day I brought your divisions of people out of Egypt. So all of your descendants must celebrate this day. This is a law that will last from now on. ¹⁸In the first month of the year you are to eat bread made without yeast, from the evening of the fourteenth day until the evening of the twenty-first day. ¹⁹For seven days there must not be any yeast in your houses. Anybody who eats yeast during this time, either an Israelite or non-Israelite, must be cut off from the community of Israel. ²⁰During this feast you must not eat anything made with yeast. You must eat only bread made without yeast wherever you live."

²¹Then Moses called all the elders of Israel together and told them, "Get the animals for your families and kill the lamb for the Passover. ²²Take a branch of the hyssop plant, dip it into the bowl filled with blood, and then wipe the blood on the sides and tops of the doorframes. No one may leave that house until morning. ²³When the Lord goes through Egypt to kill the Egyptians, he will see the blood on the sides and tops of the doorframes, and he will pass over that house. He will not let the one who brings death come into your houses and kill you.

²⁴"You must keep this command as a law for you and your descendants from now on. ²⁵Do this when you go to the land the Lord has promised to give you. ²⁶When your children ask you, 'Why are we doing these things?' ²⁷you will say, 'This is the Passover sacrifice to honor the Lord. When we were in Egypt, the Lord passed over the houses of Israel, and when he killed the Egyptians, he saved our homes.'" Then the people bowed down and worshiped the Lord. ²⁸They did just as the Lord commanded Moses and Aaron.

²⁹At midnight the Lord killed all the firstborn sons in the land of Egypt—from the firstborn of the king who sat on the throne to the firstborn of the prisoner in jail. Also, all the firstborn farm animals died. ³⁰The king, his officers, and all the Egyptians got up during the night because someone had died in every house. So there was a loud outcry everywhere in Egypt.

Israel Leaves Egypt

³¹During the night the king called for Moses and Aaron and said, "Get up and leave my people. You and your people may do as you have asked; go and worship the Lord. ³²Take all of your flocks and herds as you have asked, and go. And also bless me." ³³The Egyptians also asked the Israelites to hurry and leave, saying, "If you don't leave, we will all die!"

³⁴So the people took their dough before the yeast was added. They wrapped the bowls for making dough in clothing and carried them on their shoulders. ³⁵The Is-raelites did what Moses told them to do and asked their Egyptian neighbors for things made of silver and gold and for clothing. ³⁶The Lord caused the Egyptians to think well of them, and the Egyptians gave the people everything they asked for. So the Israelites took rich gifts from them.

³⁷The Israelites traveled from Rameses to Succoth. There were about six hundred thousand men walking, not including the women and children. ³⁸Many other people who were not Israelites went with them, as well as a large number of sheep, goats, and cattle. ³⁹The Israelites used the dough they had brought out of Egypt to bake loaves of bread without yeast. The dough had no yeast in it, because they had been rushed out of Egypt and had no time to get food ready for their trip.

⁴⁰The people of Israel had lived in Egypt for four hundred thirty years; ⁴¹on the very day the four hundred thirty years ended, the Lord's divisions of people left Egypt. ⁴²That night the Lord kept watch to bring them out of Egypt, and so on this same night the Israelites are to keep watch to honor the Lord from now on.

⁴³The Lord told Moses and Aaron, "Here are the rules for Passover: No foreigner is to eat the Passover. ⁴⁴If someone buys a slave and circumcises him, the slave may eat the Passover. ⁴⁵But neither a person who lives for a short time in your country nor a hired worker may eat it.

⁴⁶"The meal must be eaten inside a house; take none of the meat outside the house. Don't break any of the bones. ⁴⁷The whole community of Israel must take part in this feast. ⁴⁸A foreigner who lives with you may share in the Lord's Passover if all the males in his house become circumcised. Then, since he will be like a citizen of Israel, he may share in the meal. But a man who is not circumcised may not eat the Passover meal. ⁴⁹The same rules apply to an Israelite born in the country or to a foreigner living there."

⁵⁰So all the Israelites did just as the Lord had commanded Moses and Aaron. ⁵¹On

that same day the LORD led the Israelites out of Egypt by their divisions.

PSALM 18:1–6

A Song of Victory

For the director of music. By the LORD's servant, David. David sang this song to the LORD when the LORD had saved him from Saul and all his other enemies.

18 I love you, LORD. You are my strength.

²The LORD is my rock, my protection, my Savior.
My God is my rock.
I can run to him for safety.
He is my shield and my saving strength, my defender.
³I will call to the LORD, who is worthy of praise,
and I will be saved from my enemies.
⁴The ropes of death came around me;
the deadly rivers overwhelmed me.
⁵The ropes of death wrapped around me.
The traps of death were before me.
⁶In my trouble I called to the LORD.
I cried out to my God for help.
From his temple he heard my voice;
my call for help reached his ears.

PROVERBS 6:1–5

Dangers of Being Foolish

6 My child, be careful about giving a guarantee for somebody else's loan, about promising to pay what someone else owes.
²You might get trapped by what you say;
you might be caught by your own words.
³My child, if you have done this and are under your neighbor's control,
here is how to get free.
Don't be proud. Go to your neighbor and beg to be free from your promise.
⁴Don't go to sleep
or even rest your eyes,
⁵but free yourself like a deer running from a hunter,
like a bird flying away from a trapper.

MATTHEW 20:17–34

Jesus Talks About His Own Death

¹⁷While Jesus was going to Jerusalem, he took his twelve followers aside privately and said to them, ¹⁸"Look, we are going to Jerusalem. The Son of Man will be turned over to the leading priests and the teachers of the law, and they will say that he must die. ¹⁹They will give the Son of Man to the non-Jewish people to laugh at him and beat him with whips and crucify him. But on the third day, he will be raised to life again."

A Mother Asks Jesus a Favor

²⁰Then the wife of Zebedee came to Jesus with her sons. She bowed before him and asked him to do something for her.

²¹Jesus asked, "What do you want?"

She said, "Promise that one of my sons will sit at your right side and the other will sit at your left side in your kingdom."

²²But Jesus said, "You don't understand what you are asking. Can you drink the cup that I am about to drink?"ⁿ

The sons answered, "Yes, we can."

²³Jesus said to them, "You will drink from my cup. But I cannot choose who will sit at my right or my left; those places belong to those for whom my Father has prepared them."

²⁴When the other ten followers heard this, they were angry with the two brothers. ²⁵Jesus called all the followers together and said, "You know that the rulers of the non-Jewish people love to show their power over the people. And their important leaders love to use all their authority. ²⁶But it should not be that way among you. Whoever wants to become great among you must serve the rest of you like a servant. ²⁷Whoever wants to become first among you must serve the rest of you like a slave. ²⁸In the same way, the Son of Man did not come to be served. He came to serve others and to give his life as a ransom for many people."

Jesus Heals Two Blind Men

²⁹When Jesus and his followers were leaving Jericho, a great many people followed him.

20:22 drink . . . drink Jesus used the idea of drinking from a cup to ask if they could accept the same terrible things that would happen to him.

[30]Two blind men sitting by the road heard that Jesus was going by, so they shouted, "Lord, Son of David, have mercy on us!"

[31]The people warned the blind men to be quiet, but they shouted even more, "Lord, Son of David, have mercy on us!"

[32]Jesus stopped and said to the blind men, "What do you want me to do for you?"

[33]They answered, "Lord, we want to see."

[34]Jesus felt sorry for the blind men and touched their eyes, and at once they could see. Then they followed Jesus.

FEBRUARY 1

EXODUS 13:1—14:31

The Law of the Firstborn

13 Then the LORD said to Moses, [2]"Give every firstborn male to me. Every firstborn male among the Israelites belongs to me, whether human or animal."

[3]Moses said to the people, "Remember this day, the day you left Egypt. You were slaves in that land, but the LORD with his great power brought you out of it. You must not eat bread made with yeast. [4]Today, in the month of Abib, you are leaving Egypt. [5]The LORD will lead you to the land of the Canaanites, Hittites, Amorites, Hivites, and Jebusites. This is the land he promised your ancestors he would give you, a fertile land. There you must celebrate this feast during the first month of every year. [6]For seven days you must eat bread made without yeast, and on the seventh day there will be a feast to honor the LORD. [7]So for seven days you must not eat any bread made with yeast. There must be no bread made with yeast anywhere in your land. [8]On that day you should tell your son: 'We are having this feast because of what the LORD did for me when I came out of Egypt.' [9]This feast will help you remember, like a mark on your hand or a reminder on your forehead. This feast will remind you to speak the LORD's teachings, because the LORD used his great power to bring you out of Egypt. [10]So celebrate this feast every year at the right time.

[11]"And when the LORD takes you into the land of the Canaanites, the land he promised to give you and your ancestors, [12]you must give him every firstborn male. Also every firstborn male animal must be given to the LORD. [13]Buy back every firstborn donkey by offering a lamb. But if you don't want to buy the donkey back, then break its neck. You must buy back from the LORD every firstborn of your sons.

[14]"From now on when your son asks you, 'What does this mean?' you will answer, 'With his great power, the LORD brought us out from Egypt, the land where we were slaves. [15]The king of Egypt was stubborn and re-

fused to let us leave. But the LORD killed every firstborn male in Egypt, both human and animal. That is why I sacrifice every firstborn male animal to the LORD, and that is why I buy back each of my firstborn sons from the LORD.' [16]This feast is like a mark on your hand and a reminder on your forehead to help you remember that the LORD brought us out of Egypt with his great power."

The Way Out of Egypt

[17]When the king sent the people out of Egypt, God did not lead them on the road through the Philistine country, though that was the shortest way. God said, "If they have to fight, they might change their minds and go back to Egypt." [18]So God led them through the desert toward the Red Sea. The Israelites were dressed for fighting when they left the land of Egypt.

[19]Moses carried the bones of Joseph with him, because before Joseph died, he had made the Israelites promise to do this. He had said, "When God saves you, remember to carry my bones with you out of Egypt."

[20]The Israelites left Succoth and camped at Etham, on the edge of the desert. [21]The LORD showed them the way; during the day he went ahead of them in a pillar of cloud, and during the night he was in a pillar of fire to give them light. In this way they could travel during the day or night. [22]The pillar of cloud was always with them during the day, and the pillar of fire was always with them at night.

14 Then the LORD said to Moses, [2]"Tell the Israelites to turn back to Pi Hahiroth and to camp between Migdol and the Red Sea. Camp across from Baal Zephon, on the shore of the sea. [3]The king will think, 'The Israelites are lost, trapped by the desert.' [4]I will make the king stubborn again so he will chase after them, but I will defeat the king and his army. This will bring honor to me, and the Egyptians will know that I am the LORD." The Israelites did just as they were told.

The King Chases the Israelites

[5]When the king of Egypt was told that the Israelites had left, he and his officers

changed their minds about them. They said, "What have we done? We have let the Israelites leave. We have lost our slaves!" 6So the king prepared his war chariot and took his army with him. 7He took six hundred of his best chariots, together with all the other chariots of Egypt, each with an officer in it. 8The LORD made the king of Egypt stubborn, so he chased the Israelites, who were leaving victoriously. 9The Egyptians—with all the king's horses, chariot drivers, and army—chased the Israelites. They caught up with them while they were camped by the Red Sea, near Pi Hahiroth and Baal Zephon.

10When the Israelites saw the king and his army coming after them, they were very frightened and cried to the LORD for help. 11They said to Moses, "What have you done to us? Why did you bring us out of Egypt to die in the desert? There were plenty of graves for us in Egypt. 12We told you in Egypt, 'Let us alone; we will stay and serve the Egyptians.' Now we will die in the desert."

13But Moses answered, "Don't be afraid! Stand still and you will see the LORD save you today. You will never see these Egyptians again after today. 14You only need to remain calm; the LORD will fight for you."

15Then the LORD said to Moses, "Why are you crying out to me? Command the Israelites to start moving. 16Raise your walking stick and hold it over the sea so that the sea will split and the people can cross it on dry land. 17I will make the Egyptians stubborn so they will chase the Israelites, but I will be honored when I defeat the king and all of his chariot drivers and chariots. 18When I defeat the king, his chariot drivers, and chariots, the Egyptians will know that I am the LORD."

19Now the angel of God that usually traveled in front of Israel's army moved behind them. Also, the pillar of cloud moved from in front of the people and stood behind them. 20So the cloud came between the Egyptians and the Israelites. This made it dark for the Egyptians but gave light to the Israelites. So the cloud kept the two armies apart all night. 21Then Moses held his hand over the sea. All that night the LORD drove back the sea with a strong east wind, making the sea be-

come dry ground. The water was split, 22and the Israelites went through the sea on dry land, with a wall of water on their right and on their left.

23Then all the king's horses, chariots, and chariot drivers followed them into the sea. 24When morning came, the LORD looked down from the pillar of cloud and fire at the Egyptian army and made them panic. 25He kept the wheels of the chariots from turning, making it hard to drive the chariots. The Egyptians shouted, "Let's get away from the Israelites! The LORD is fighting for them and against Egypt."

26Then the LORD told Moses, "Hold your hand over the sea so that the water will come back over the Egyptians, their chariots, and chariot drivers." 27So Moses raised his hand over the sea, and at dawn the sea returned to its place. The Egyptians tried to run from it, but the LORD swept them away into the sea. 28The water returned, covering the chariots, chariot drivers, and all the king's army that had followed the Israelites into the sea. Not one of them survived.

29But the Israelites crossed the sea on dry land, with a wall of water on their right and on their left. 30So that day the LORD saved the Israelites from the Egyptians, and the Israelites saw the Egyptians lying dead on the seashore. 31When the Israelites saw the great power the LORD had used against the Egyptians, they feared the LORD, and they trusted him and his servant Moses.

PSALM 18:7–19

7The earth trembled and shook.
The foundations of the mountains
  began to shake.
They trembled because the LORD was
  angry.
8Smoke came out of his nose,
  and burning fire came out of his mouth.
  Burning coals went before him.
9He tore open the sky and came down
  with dark clouds under his feet.
10He rode a creature with wings and flew.
  He raced on the wings of the wind.
11He made darkness his covering, his
  shelter around him,
  surrounded by fog and clouds.

¹²Out of the brightness of his presence
came clouds
with hail and lightning.
¹³The LORD thundered from heaven;
the Most High raised his voice,
and there was hail and lightning.
¹⁴He shot his arrows and scattered his
enemies.
His many bolts of lightning confused
them with fear.
¹⁵LORD, you spoke strongly.
The wind blew from your nose.
Then the valleys of the sea appeared,
and the foundations of the earth were
seen.
¹⁶The LORD reached down from above and
took me;
he pulled me from the deep water.
¹⁷He saved me from my powerful enemies,
from those who hated me, because they
were too strong for me.
¹⁸They attacked me at my time of trouble,
but the LORD supported me.
¹⁹He took me to a safe place.
Because he delights in me, he saved me.

PROVERBS 6:6–11

⁶Go watch the ants, you lazy person.
Watch what they do and be wise.
⁷Ants have no commander,
no leader or ruler,
⁸but they store up food in the summer
and gather their supplies at harvest.
⁹How long will you lie there, you lazy
person?
When will you get up from sleeping?
¹⁰You sleep a little; you take a nap.
You fold your hands and lie down to rest.
¹¹So you will be as poor as if you had been
robbed;
you will have as little as if you had been
held up.

MATTHEW 21:1–22

Jesus Enters Jerusalem as a King

21 As Jesus and his followers were coming closer to Jerusalem, they stopped
at Bethphage at the hill called the Mount of
Olives. From there Jesus sent two of his followers ²and said to them, "Go to the town
you can see there. When you enter it, you will
quickly find a donkey tied there with its colt.
Untie them and bring them to me. ³If anyone
asks you why you are taking the donkeys, say
that the Master needs them, and he will send
them at once."

⁴This was to bring about what the prophet
had said:

⁵"Tell the people of Jerusalem,
'Your king is coming to you.
He is gentle and riding on a donkey,
on the colt of a donkey.'"

Isaiah 62:11; Zechariah 9:9

⁶The followers went and did what Jesus
told them to do. ⁷They brought the donkey
and the colt to Jesus and laid their coats on
them, and Jesus sat on them. ⁸Many people
spread their coats on the road. Others cut
branches from the trees and spread them on
the road. ⁹The people were walking ahead of
Jesus and behind him, shouting,

"Praiseⁿ to the Son of David!
God bless the One who comes in the
name of the Lord! *Psalm 118:26*
Praise to God in heaven!"

¹⁰When Jesus entered Jerusalem, all the
city was filled with excitement. The people
asked, "Who is this man?"

¹¹The crowd said, "This man is Jesus, the
prophet from the town of Nazareth in Galilee."

Jesus Goes to the Temple

¹²Jesus went into the Temple and threw out
all the people who were buying and selling
there. He turned over the tables of those who
were exchanging different kinds of money,
and he upset the benches of those who were
selling doves. ¹³Jesus said to all the people
there, "It is written in the Scriptures, 'My Temple will be called a house for prayer.'ⁿ But you
are changing it into a 'hideout for robbers.'"ⁿ

¹⁴The blind and crippled people came to
Jesus in the Temple, and he healed them.
¹⁵The leading priests and the teachers of the
law saw that Jesus was doing wonderful
things and that the children were praising

him in the Temple, saying, "Praise[n] to the Son of David." All these things made the priests and the teachers of the law very angry.

[16]They asked Jesus, "Do you hear the things these children are saying?"

Jesus answered, "Yes. Haven't you read in the Scriptures, 'You have taught children and babies to sing praises'?"[n]

[17]Then Jesus left and went out of the city to Bethany, where he spent the night.

The Power of Faith

[18]Early the next morning, as Jesus was going back to the city, he became hungry. [19]Seeing a fig tree beside the road, Jesus went to it, but there were no figs on the tree, only leaves. So Jesus said to the tree, "You will never again have fruit." The tree immediately dried up.

[20]When his followers saw this, they were amazed. They asked, "How did the fig tree dry up so quickly?"

[21]Jesus answered, "I tell you the truth, if you have faith and do not doubt, you will be able to do what I did to this tree and even more. You will be able to say to this mountain, 'Go, fall into the sea.' And if you have faith, it will happen. [22]If you believe, you will get anything you ask for in prayer."

FEBRUARY 2

EXODUS 15:1—16:36

The Song of Moses

15 Then Moses and the Israelites sang this song to the LORD:

"I will sing to the LORD,
  because he is worthy of great honor.
He has thrown the horse and its rider
  into the sea.
[2]The LORD gives me strength and makes
  me sing;
  he has saved me.
He is my God,
  and I will praise him.
He is the God of my ancestors,
  and I will honor him.
[3]The LORD is a warrior;
  the LORD is his name.
[4]The chariots and soldiers of the king of
  Egypt
  he has thrown into the sea.
The king's best officers
  are drowned in the Red Sea.
[5]The deep waters covered them,
  and they sank to the bottom like a
  rock.
[6]Your right hand, LORD,
  is amazingly strong.

LORD, your right hand
  broke the enemy to pieces.
[7]In your great victory
  you destroyed those who were against
  you.
Your anger destroyed them,
  like fire burning straw.
[8]Just a blast of your breath,
  and the waters piled up.
The moving water stood like a wall;
  the deep waters became solid in the
  middle of the sea.

[9]"The enemy bragged,
  'I'll chase them and catch them.
I'll take all their riches;
  I'll take all I want.
I'll pull out my sword,
  and my hand will destroy them.'
[10]But you blew on them with your breath
  and covered them with the sea.
They sank like lead
  in the raging water.

[11]"Are there any gods like you, LORD?
  There are no gods like you.
You are wonderfully holy,
  amazingly powerful,

21:9; 15 Praise Literally, "Hosanna," a Hebrew word used at first in praying to God for help. At this time it was probably a shout of joy used in praising God or his Messiah. **21:16 'You . . . praises.'** Quotation from the Septuagint (Greek) version of Psalm 8:2.

a worker of miracles.
¹²You reached out with your right hand,
and the earth swallowed our enemies.
¹³You keep your loving promise
and lead the people you have saved.
With your strength you will guide them
to your holy place.

¹⁴"The other nations will hear this and
tremble with fear;
terror will take hold of the Philistines.
¹⁵The leaders of the tribes of Edom will be
very frightened;
the powerful men of Moab will shake
with fear;
the people of Canaan will lose all their
courage.
¹⁶Terror and horror will fall on them.
When they see your strength,
they will be as still as a rock.
They will be still until your people pass
by, LORD.
They will be still until the people you
have taken as your own pass by.
¹⁷You will lead your people and place them
on your very own mountain,
the place that you, LORD, made for
yourself to live,
the temple, Lord, that your hands have
made.
¹⁸The LORD will be king forever!"

¹⁹The horses, chariot drivers, and chariots
of the king of Egypt went into the sea, and
the LORD covered them with water from the
sea. But the Israelites walked through the sea
on dry land. ²⁰Then Aaron's sister Miriam, a
prophetess, took a tambourine in her hand.
All the women followed her, playing tambourines and dancing. ²¹Miriam told them:
"Sing to the LORD,
because he is worthy of great honor;
he has thrown the horse and its rider
into the sea."

Bitter Water Becomes Good

²²Moses led the Israelites away from the
Red Sea into the Desert of Shur. They traveled
for three days in the desert but found no water. ²³Then they came to Marah, where there
was water, but they could not drink it because

it was too bitter. (That is why the place was
named Marah.ⁿ) ²⁴The people grumbled to
Moses and asked, "What will we drink?"

²⁵So Moses cried out to the LORD, and the
LORD showed him a tree. When Moses threw
the tree into the water, the water became
good to drink.

There the LORD gave the people a rule and
a law to live by, and there he tested their loyalty to him. ²⁶He said, "You must obey the
LORD your God and do what he says is right.
If you obey all his commands and keep his
rules, I will not bring on you any of the sicknesses I brought on the Egyptians. I am the
LORD who heals you."

²⁷Then the people traveled to Elim, where
there were twelve springs of water and seventy palm trees. So the people camped there
near the water.

The People Demand Food

16 The whole Israelite community left
Elim and came to the Desert of Sin,
which was between Elim and Sinai; they arrived there on the fifteenth day of the second
month after they had left Egypt. ²Then the
whole Israelite community grumbled to
Moses and Aaron in the desert. ³They said to
them, "It would have been better if the LORD
had killed us in the land of Egypt. There we
had meat to eat and all the food we wanted.
But you have brought us into this desert to
starve us to death."

⁴Then the LORD said to Moses, "I will
cause food to fall like rain from the sky for
all of you. Every day the people must go out
and gather what they need for that day. I
want to see if the people will do what I teach
them. ⁵On the sixth day of each week, they
are to gather twice as much as they gather on
other days. Then they are to prepare it."

⁶So Moses and Aaron said to all the Israelites: "This evening you will know that
the LORD is the one who brought you out of
Egypt. ⁷Tomorrow morning you will see the
glory of the LORD, because he has heard you
grumble against him. We are nothing, so you
are not grumbling against us, but against the
LORD." ⁸And Moses said, "Each evening the
LORD will give you meat to eat, and every

15:23 Marah This name means "bitter."

morning he will give you all the bread you want, because he has heard you grumble against him. You are not grumbling against Aaron and me, because we are nothing; you are grumbling against the LORD."

⁹Then Moses said to Aaron, "Speak to the whole community of the Israelites, and say to them, 'Meet together in the presence of the LORD, because he has heard your grumblings.'"

¹⁰While Aaron was speaking to the whole community of the Israelites, they looked toward the desert. There the glory of the LORD appeared in a cloud.

¹¹The LORD said to Moses, ¹²"I have heard the grumblings of the people of Israel. So tell them, 'At twilight you will eat meat, and every morning you will eat all the bread you want. Then you will know I am the LORD your God.'"

¹³That evening quail came and covered the camp, and in the morning dew lay around the camp. ¹⁴When the dew was gone, thin flakes like frost were on the desert ground. ¹⁵When the Israelites saw it, they asked each other, "What is it?" because they did not know what it was.

So Moses told them, "This is the bread the LORD has given you to eat. ¹⁶The LORD has commanded, 'Each one of you must gather what he needs, about two quarts for every person in your family.'"

¹⁷So the people of Israel did this; some people gathered much, and some gathered little. ¹⁸Then they measured it. The person who gathered more did not have too much, nor did the person who gathered less have too little. Each person gathered just as much as he needed.

¹⁹Moses said to them, "Don't keep any of it to eat the next day." ²⁰But some of the people did not listen to Moses and kept part of it to eat the next morning. It became full of worms and began to stink, so Moses was angry with those people.

²¹Every morning each person gathered as much food as he needed, but when the sun became hot, it melted away.

²²On the sixth day the people gathered twice as much food—four quarts for every person. When all the leaders of the community came and told this to Moses, ²³he said to them, "This is what the LORD commanded, because tomorrow is the Sabbath, the LORD's holy day of rest. Bake what you want to bake, and boil what you want to boil today. Save the rest of the food until tomorrow morning."

²⁴So the people saved it until the next morning, as Moses had commanded, and none of it began to stink or have worms in it. ²⁵Moses told the people, "Eat the food you gathered yesterday. Today is a Sabbath, the LORD's day of rest; you will not find any out in the field today. ²⁶You should gather the food for six days, but the seventh day is a Sabbath day. On that day there will not be any food on the ground."

²⁷On the seventh day some of the people went out to gather food, but they couldn't find any. ²⁸Then the LORD said to Moses, "How long will you people refuse to obey my commands and teachings? ²⁹Look, the LORD has made the Sabbath a day of rest for you. So on the sixth day he will give you enough food for two days, but on the seventh day each of you must stay where you are. Do not go anywhere." ³⁰So the people rested on the seventh day.

³¹The people of Israel called the food manna. It was like small white seeds and tasted like wafers made with honey.

³²Then Moses said, "The LORD said, 'Save two quarts of this food for your descendants. Then they can see the food I gave you to eat in the desert when I brought you out of Egypt.'"

³³Moses told Aaron, "Take a jar and fill it with two quarts of manna. Then place it before the LORD, and save it for your descendants." ³⁴So Aaron did what the LORD had commanded Moses. He put the jar of manna in front of the Agreement to keep it safe. ³⁵The Israelites ate manna for forty years, until they came to the land where they settled—the edge of the land of Canaan. ³⁶The measure they used for the manna was two quarts, or one-tenth of an ephah."ⁿ

16:36 ephah An ephah was a measure that equaled twenty quarts.

PSALM 18:20–29

²⁰The LORD spared me because I did what
was right.
Because I have not done evil, he has
rewarded me.
²¹I have followed the ways of the LORD;
I have not done evil by turning away
from my God.
²²I remember all his laws
and have not broken his rules.
²³I am innocent before him;
I have kept myself from doing evil.
²⁴The LORD rewarded me because I did
what was right,
because I did what the LORD said was
right.
²⁵LORD, you are loyal to those who are loyal,
and you are good to those who are
good.
²⁶You are pure to those who are pure,
but you are against those who are bad.
²⁷You save the humble,
but you bring down those who are
proud.
²⁸LORD, you give light to my lamp.
My God brightens the darkness around
me.
²⁹With your help I can attack an army.
With God's help I can jump over a wall.

PROVERBS 6:12–15

¹²Some people are wicked and no good.
They go around telling lies,
¹³winking with their eyes, tapping with
their feet,
and making signs with their fingers.
¹⁴They make evil plans in their hearts
and are always starting arguments.
¹⁵So trouble will strike them in an instant;
suddenly they will be so hurt no one
can help them.

MATTHEW 21:23–46

Leaders Doubt Jesus' Authority

²³Jesus went to the Temple, and while he
was teaching there, the leading priests and
the elders of the people came to him. They
said, "What authority do you have to do
these things? Who gave you this authority?"

²⁴Jesus answered, "I also will ask you a
question. If you answer me, then I will tell you
what authority I have to do these things. ²⁵Tell
me: When John baptized people, did that
come from God or just from other people?"

They argued about Jesus' question, saying,
"If we answer, 'John's baptism was from God,'
Jesus will say, 'Then why didn't you believe
him?' ²⁶But if we say, 'It was from people,' we
are afraid of what the crowd will do because
they all believe that John was a prophet."

²⁷So they answered Jesus, "We don't
know."

Jesus said to them, "Then I won't tell you
what authority I have to do these things.

A Story About Two Sons

²⁸"Tell me what you think about this: A
man had two sons. He went to the first son
and said, 'Son, go and work today in my
vineyard.' ²⁹The son answered, 'I will not go.'
But later the son changed his mind and
went. ³⁰Then the father went to the other son
and said, 'Son, go and work today in my
vineyard.' The son answered, 'Yes, sir, I will
go and work,' but he did not go. ³¹Which of
the two sons obeyed his father?"

The priests and leaders answered, "The
first son."

Jesus said to them, "I tell you the truth,
the tax collectors and the prostitutes will enter the kingdom of God before you do. ³²John
came to show you the right way to live. You
did not believe him, but the tax collectors
and prostitutes believed him. Even after seeing this, you still refused to change your
ways and believe him.

A Story About God's Son

³³"Listen to this story: There was a man
who owned a vineyard. He put a wall around
it and dug a hole for a winepress and built a
tower. Then he leased the land to some farmers and left for a trip. ³⁴When it was time for
the grapes to be picked, he sent his servants
to the farmers to get his share of the grapes.
³⁵But the farmers grabbed the servants, beat
one, killed another, and then killed a third
servant with stones. ³⁶So the man sent some
other servants to the farmers, even more than
he sent the first time. But the farmers did the
same thing to the servants that they had done

before. [37]So the man decided to send his son to the farmers. He said, 'They will respect my son.' [38]But when the farmers saw the son, they said to each other, 'This son will inherit the vineyard. If we kill him, it will be ours!' [39]Then the farmers grabbed the son, threw him out of the vineyard, and killed him. [40]So what will the owner of the vineyard do to these farmers when he comes?"

[41]The priests and leaders said, "He will surely kill those evil men. Then he will lease the vineyard to some other farmers who will give him his share of the crop at harvest time."

[42]Jesus said to them, "Surely you have read this in the Scriptures:

'The stone that the builders rejected
   became the cornerstone.
The Lord did this,
   and it is wonderful to us.' *Psalm 118:22–23*

[43]"So I tell you that the kingdom of God will be taken away from you and given to people who do the things God wants in his kingdom. [44]The person who falls on this stone will be broken, and on whomever that stone falls, that person will be crushed."[n]

[45]When the leading priests and the Pharisees heard these stories, they knew Jesus was talking about them. [46]They wanted to arrest him, but they were afraid of the people, because the people believed that Jesus was a prophet.

FEBRUARY 3

EXODUS 17:1—18:27

Water from a Rock

17 The whole Israelite community left the Desert of Sin and traveled from place to place, as the LORD commanded. They camped at Rephidim, but there was no water there for the people to drink. [2]So they quarreled with Moses and said, "Give us water to drink."

Moses said to them, "Why do you quarrel with me? Why are you testing the LORD?"

[3]But the people were very thirsty for water, so they grumbled against Moses. They said, "Why did you bring us out of Egypt? Was it to kill us, our children, and our farm animals with thirst?"

[4]So Moses cried to the LORD, "What can I do with these people? They are almost ready to stone me to death."

[5]The LORD said to Moses, "Go ahead of the people, and take some of the elders of Israel with you. Carry with you the walking stick that you used to strike the Nile River. Now go! [6]I will stand in front of you on a rock at Mount Sinai. Hit that rock with the stick, and water will come out of it so that the people

can drink." Moses did these things as the elders of Israel watched. [7]He named that place Massah,[n] because the Israelites tested the LORD when they asked, "Is the LORD with us or not?" He also named it Meribah,[n] because they quarreled.

The Amalekites Fight Israel

[8]At Rephidim the Amalekites came and fought the Israelites. [9]So Moses said to Joshua, "Choose some men and go and fight the Amalekites. Tomorrow I will stand on the top of the hill, holding the walking stick of God in my hands."

[10]Joshua obeyed Moses and went to fight the Amalekites, while Moses, Aaron, and Hur went to the top of the hill. [11]As long as Moses held his hands up, the Israelites would win the fight, but when Moses put his hands down, the Amalekites would win. [12]Later, when Moses' arms became tired, the men put a large rock under him, and he sat on it. Then Aaron and Hur held up Moses' hands—Aaron on one side and Hur on the other. They kept his hands steady until the sun went down. [13]So Joshua defeated the Amalekites in this battle.

21:44 The . . . crushed. Some Greek copies do not have verse 44.   •   **17:7 Massah** This name is the Hebrew word for "testing."   **17:7 Meribah** This name is the Hebrew word for "quarrel."

[14]Then the LORD said to Moses, "Write about this battle in a book so people will remember. And be sure to tell Joshua, because I will completely destroy the Amalekites from the earth."

[15]Then Moses built an altar and named it The LORD Is My Banner. [16]Moses said, "I lifted my hands toward the LORD's throne. The LORD will fight against the Amalekites forever."

Jethro Visits Moses

18 Jethro, Moses' father-in-law, was the priest of Midian. He heard about everything that God had done for Moses and his people, the Israelites, and how the LORD had led the Israelites out of Egypt. [2]Now Moses had sent his wife Zipporah to Jethro, his father-in-law, [3]along with his two sons. The first son was named Gershom,[n] because when he was born, Moses said, "I am a stranger in a foreign country." [4]The other son was named Eliezer,[n] because when he was born, Moses said, "The God of my father is my help. He saved me from the king of Egypt."

[5]So Jethro, Moses' father-in-law, took Moses' wife and his two sons and went to Moses. He was camped in the desert near the mountain of God. [6]Jethro had sent a message ahead to Moses that said, "I, Jethro, your father-in-law, am coming to you with your wife and her two sons."

[7]So Moses went out to meet his father-in-law and bowed down and kissed him. After the two men asked about each other's health, they went into Moses' tent. [8]Moses told his father-in-law everything the LORD had done to the king and the Egyptians to help Israel. He told about all the problems they had faced along the way and how the LORD had saved them.

[9]Jethro was very happy to hear all the good things the LORD had done for Israel when he had saved them from the Egyptians. [10]He said, "Praise the LORD. He has saved you from the Egyptians and their king, and he has saved the people from the power of the Egyptians. [11]Now I know the LORD is greater than all gods, because he did this to those who looked down on Israel." [12]Then Jethro, Moses' father-in-law, gave a whole burnt offering and other sacrifices to God. Aaron and all the elders of Israel came to Moses' father-in-law to eat the holy meal together before God.

[13]The next day Moses solved disagreements among the people, and the people stood around him from morning until night. [14]When Moses' father-in-law saw all that Moses was doing for the people, he asked, "What is all this you are doing for the people? Why are you the only one to solve disagreements? All the people are standing around you from morning until night!"

[15]Then Moses said to his father-in-law, "It is because the people come to me for God's help in solving their disagreements. [16]When people have a disagreement, they come to me, and I decide who is right. I tell them God's laws and teachings."

[17]Moses' father-in-law said to him, "You are not doing this right. [18]You and the people who come to you will get too tired. This is too much work for you; you can't do it by yourself. [19]Now listen to me, and I will give you some advice. I want God to be with you. You must speak to God for the people and tell him about their disagreements. [20]Warn them about the laws and teachings, and teach them the right way to live and what they should do. [21]But choose some capable men from among the people—men who respect God, who can be trusted, and who will not change their decisions for money. Make these men officers over the people, to rule over groups of thousands, hundreds, fifties, and tens. [22]Let these officers solve the disagreements among the people all the time. They can bring the hard cases to you, but they can decide the simple cases themselves. That will make it easier for you, because they will share the work with you. [23]If you do this as God commands you, then you will be able to do your job, and all the people will go home with their disagreements solved."

[24]So Moses listened to his father-in-law and did everything he said. [25]He chose capa-

---

18:3 Gershom This name sounds like the Hebrew word for "a stranger there." **18:4 Eliezer** This name sounds like the Hebrew words "My God is my help."

ble men from all the Israelites and made them leaders over the people; they were officers over groups of thousands, hundreds, fifties, and tens. ²⁶These officers solved disagreements among the people all the time. They brought the hard cases to Moses, but they decided the simple cases themselves.

²⁷So Moses sent his father-in-law on his way, and Jethro went back to his own home.

PSALM 18:30–42

³⁰The ways of God are without fault.
  The LORD's words are pure.
He is a shield to those who trust him.
³¹Who is God? Only the LORD.
  Who is the Rock? Only our God.
³²God is my protection.
  He makes my way free from fault.
³³He makes me like a deer that does not stumble;
  he helps me stand on the steep mountains.
³⁴He trains my hands for battle
  so my arms can bend a bronze bow.
³⁵You protect me with your saving shield.
  You support me with your right hand.
  You have stooped to make me great.
³⁶You give me a better way to live,
  so I live as you want me to.
³⁷I chased my enemies and caught them.
  I did not quit until they were destroyed.
³⁸I crushed them so they couldn't rise up again.
  They fell beneath my feet.
³⁹You gave me strength in battle.
  You made my enemies bow before me.
⁴⁰You made my enemies turn back,
  and I destroyed those who hated me.
⁴¹They called for help,
  but no one came to save them.
  They called to the LORD,
  but he did not answer them.
⁴²I beat my enemies into pieces, like dust in the wind.
  I poured them out like mud in the streets.

PROVERBS 6:16–19

¹⁶There are six things the LORD hates.
  There are seven things he cannot stand:

¹⁷ a proud look,
  a lying tongue,
  hands that kill innocent people,
¹⁸ a mind that thinks up evil plans,
  feet that are quick to do evil,
¹⁹ a witness who lies,
  and someone who starts arguments among families.

MATTHEW 22:1–22

A Story About a Wedding Feast

22 Jesus again used stories to teach them. He said, ²"The kingdom of heaven is like a king who prepared a wedding feast for his son. ³The king invited some people to the feast. When the feast was ready, the king sent his servants to tell the people, but they refused to come.

⁴"Then the king sent other servants, saying, 'Tell those who have been invited that my feast is ready. I have killed my best bulls and calves for the dinner, and everything is ready. Come to the wedding feast.'

⁵"But the people refused to listen to the servants and left to do other things. One went to work in his field, and another went to his business. ⁶Some of the other people grabbed the servants, beat them, and killed them. ⁷The king was furious and sent his army to kill the murderers and burn their city.

⁸"After that, the king said to his servants, 'The wedding feast is ready. I invited those people, but they were not worthy to come. ⁹So go to the street corners and invite everyone you find to come to my feast.' ¹⁰So the servants went into the streets and gathered all the people they could find, both good and bad. And the wedding hall was filled with guests.

¹¹"When the king came in to see the guests, he saw a man who was not dressed for a wedding. ¹²The king said, 'Friend, how were you allowed to come in here? You are not dressed for a wedding.' But the man said nothing. ¹³So the king told some servants, 'Tie this man's hands and feet. Throw him out into the darkness, where people will cry and grind their teeth with pain.'

¹⁴"Yes, many are invited, but only a few are chosen."

Is It Right to Pay Taxes or Not?

¹⁵Then the Pharisees left that place and made plans to trap Jesus in saying something wrong. ¹⁶They sent some of their own followers and some people from the group called Herodians.ⁿ They said, "Teacher, we know that you are an honest man and that you teach the truth about God's way. You are not afraid of what other people think about you, because you pay no attention to who they are. ¹⁷So tell us what you think. Is it right to pay taxes to Caesar or not?"

¹⁸But knowing that these leaders were trying to trick him, Jesus said, "You hypocrites! Why are you trying to trap me? ¹⁹Show me a coin used for paying the tax." So the men showed him a coin.ⁿ ²⁰Then Jesus asked, "Whose image and name are on the coin?"

²¹The men answered, "Caesar's."

Then Jesus said to them, "Give to Caesar the things that are Caesar's, and give to God the things that are God's."

²²When the men heard what Jesus said, they were amazed and left him and went away.

FEBRUARY 4

EXODUS 19:1—20:26

Israel Camps at Sinai

19 Exactly three months after the Israelites had left Egypt, they reached the Desert of Sinai. ²When they left Rephidim, they came to the Desert of Sinai and camped in the desert in front of the mountain. ³Then Moses went up on the mountain to God. The LORD called to him from the mountain and said, "Say this to the family of Jacob, and tell the people of Israel: ⁴'Every one of you has seen what I did to the people of Egypt. You saw how I carried you out of Egypt, as if on eagle's wings. And I brought you here to me. ⁵So now if you obey me and keep my agreement, you will be my own possession, chosen from all nations. Even though the whole earth is mine, ⁶you will be my kingdom of priests and a holy nation.' You must tell the Israelites these words."

⁷So Moses went down and called the elders of the people together. He told them all the words the LORD had commanded him to say. ⁸All the people answered together, "We will do everything he has said." Then Moses took their answer back to the LORD.

⁹And the LORD said to Moses, "I will come to you in a thick cloud and speak to you. The people will hear me speaking with you and will always trust you." Then Moses told the LORD what the people had said.

¹⁰The LORD said to Moses, "Go to the people and have them spend today and tomorrow preparing themselves. They must wash their clothes ¹¹and be ready by the day after tomorrow. On that day I, the LORD, will come down on Mount Sinai, and all the people will see me. ¹²But you must set a limit around the mountain that the people are not to cross. Tell them not to go up on the mountain and not to touch the foot of it. Anyone who touches the mountain must be put to death ¹³with stones or shot with arrows. No one is allowed to touch him. Whether it is a person or an animal, he will not live. But the trumpet will make a long blast, and only then may the people go up on the mountain."

¹⁴After Moses went down from the mountain to the people, he made them prepare themselves for service to God, and they washed their clothes. ¹⁵Then Moses said to the people, "Be ready in three days. Do not have sexual relations during this time."

¹⁶On the morning of the third day, there was thunder and lightning with a thick cloud on the mountain. There was a very loud blast from a trumpet, and all the people in the camp trembled. ¹⁷Then Moses led the

---

22:16 Herodians A political group that followed Herod and his family.   **22:19 coin** A Roman denarius. One coin was the average pay for one day's work.

people out of the camp to meet God, and they stood at the foot of the mountain. [18]Mount Sinai was covered with smoke, because the LORD came down on it in fire. The smoke rose from the mountain like smoke from a furnace, and the whole mountain shook wildly. [19]The sound from the trumpet became louder. Then Moses spoke, and the voice of God answered him.

[20]When the LORD came down on top of Mount Sinai, he called Moses to come up to the top of the mountain, and Moses went up. [21]The LORD said to Moses, "Go down and warn the people that they must not force their way through to see me. If they do, many of them will die. [22]Even the priests, who may come near me, must first prepare themselves. If they don't, I, the LORD, will punish them."

[23]Moses told the LORD, "The people cannot come up on Mount Sinai, because you yourself told us, 'Set a limit around the mountain, and set it apart as holy.'"

[24]The LORD said to him, "Go down and bring Aaron up with you, but don't allow the priests or the people to force their way through. They must not come up to the LORD, or I will punish them."

[25]So Moses went down to the people and told them these things.

The Ten Commandments

20 Then God spoke all these words: [2]"I am the LORD your God, who brought you out of the land of Egypt where you were slaves.

[3]"You must not have any other gods except me.

[4]"You must not make for yourselves an idol that looks like anything in the sky above or on the earth below or in the water below the land. [5]You must not worship or serve any idol, because I, the LORD your God, am a jealous God. If you hate me, I will punish your children, and even your grandchildren and great-grandchildren. [6]But I show kindness to thousands who love me and obey my commands.

[7]"You must not use the name of the LORD your God thoughtlessly; the LORD will punish anyone who misuses his name.

[8]"Remember to keep the Sabbath holy. [9]Work and get everything done during six days each week, [10]but the seventh day is a day of rest to honor the LORD your God. On that day no one may do any work: not you, your son or daughter, your male or female slaves, your animals, or the foreigners living in your cities. [11]The reason is that in six days the LORD made everything—the sky, the earth, the sea, and everything in them. On the seventh day he rested. So the LORD blessed the Sabbath day and made it holy.

[12]"Honor your father and your mother so that you will live a long time in the land that the LORD your God is going to give you.

[13]"You must not murder anyone.

[14]"You must not be guilty of adultery.

[15]"You must not steal.

[16]"You must not tell lies about your neighbor.

[17]"You must not want to take your neighbor's house. You must not want his wife or his male or female slaves, or his ox or his donkey, or anything that belongs to your neighbor."

[18]When the people heard the thunder and the trumpet, and when they saw the lightning and the smoke rising from the mountain, they shook with fear and stood far away from the mountain. [19]Then they said to Moses, "Speak to us yourself, and we will listen. But don't let God speak to us, or we will die."

[20]Then Moses said to the people, "Don't be afraid, because God has come to test you. He wants you to respect him so you will not sin."

[21]The people stood far away from the mountain while Moses went near the dark cloud where God was. [22]Then the LORD told Moses to say these things to the Israelites: "You yourselves have seen that I talked with you from heaven. [23]You must not use gold or silver to make idols for yourselves; do not worship these gods in addition to me.

[24]"Make an altar of dirt for me, and sacrifice on it your whole burnt offerings and fellowship offerings, your sheep and your cattle. Worship me in every place that I choose, and I will come and bless you. [25]If you use stones to make an altar for me, don't use stones that you have shaped with tools. When you use any tools on them, you make them unsuitable for use in worship. [26]And you must not go up to my altar on steps, or people will be able to see under your clothes."

PSALM 18:43-45

⁴³You saved me when the people attacked
  me.
  You made me the leader of nations.
  People I never knew serve me.
⁴⁴As soon as they hear me, they obey me.
  Foreigners obey me.
⁴⁵They all become afraid
  and tremble in their hiding places.

PROVERBS 6:20-25

Warning About Adultery

²⁰My son, keep your father's commands,
  and don't forget your mother's teaching.
²¹Keep their words in mind forever
  as though you had them tied around
  your neck.
²²They will guide you when you walk.
  They will guard you when you sleep.
  They will speak to you when you are
  awake.
²³These commands are like a lamp;
  this teaching is like a light.
  And the correction that comes from them
  will help you have life.
²⁴They will keep you from sinful women
  and from the pleasing words of another
  man's unfaithful wife.
²⁵Don't desire her because she is beautiful.
  Don't let her capture you by the way she
  looks at you.

MATTHEW 22:23-46

Some Sadducees Try to Trick Jesus

²³That same day some Sadducees came to
Jesus and asked him a question. (Sadducees
believed that people would not rise from the
dead.) ²⁴They said, "Teacher, Moses said if a
married man dies without having children,
his brother must marry the widow and have
children for him. ²⁵Once there were seven
brothers among us. The first one married
and died. Since he had no children, his
brother married the widow. ²⁶Then the second brother also died. The same thing happened to the third brother and all the other
brothers. ²⁷Finally, the woman died. ²⁸Since

all seven men had married her, when people
rise from the dead, whose wife will she be?"

²⁹Jesus answered, "You don't understand,
because you don't know what the Scriptures
say, and you don't know about the power of
God. ³⁰When people rise from the dead, they
will not marry, nor will they be given to
someone to marry. They will be like the angels in heaven. ³¹Surely you have read what
God said to you about rising from the dead.
³²God said, 'I am the God of Abraham, the
God of Isaac, and the God of Jacob.'ⁿ God is
the God of the living, not the dead."

³³When the people heard this, they were
amazed at Jesus' teaching.

The Most Important Command

³⁴When the Pharisees learned that the
Sadducees could not argue with Jesus' answers to them, the Pharisees met together.
³⁵One Pharisee, who was an expert on the
law of Moses, asked Jesus this question to
test him: ³⁶"Teacher, which command in the
law is the most important?"

³⁷Jesus answered, "'Love the Lord your God
with all your heart, all your soul, and all your
mind.'ⁿ ³⁸This is the first and most important
command. ³⁹And the second command is like
the first: 'Love your neighbor as you love yourself.'ⁿ ⁴⁰All the law and the writings of the
prophets depend on these two commands."

Jesus Questions the Pharisees

⁴¹While the Pharisees were together, Jesus
asked them, ⁴²"What do you think about the
Christ? Whose son is he?"

They answered, "The Christ is the Son of
David."

⁴³Then Jesus said to them, "Then why did
David call him 'Lord'? David, speaking by the
power of the Holy Spirit, said,

⁴⁴'The Lord said to my Lord,
  "Sit by me at my right side,
  until I put your enemies under your
    control." '   *Psalm 110:1*
⁴⁵David calls the Christ 'Lord,' so how can the
Christ be his son?"

⁴⁶None of the Pharisees could answer Jesus' question, and after that day no one was
brave enough to ask him any more questions.

22:32 'I am . . . Jacob.' Quotation from Exodus 3:6.   **22:37 'Love . . . mind.'** Quotation from Deuteronomy 6:5.
22:39 'Love . . . yourself.' Quotation from Leviticus 19:18.

FEBRUARY 5

EXODUS 21:1—22:31

Laws for Living

21 Then God said to Moses, "These are the laws for living that you will give to the Israelites:

²"If you buy a Hebrew slave, he will serve you for six years. In the seventh year you are to set him free, and he will have to pay nothing. ³If he is not married when he becomes your slave, he must leave without a wife. But if he is married when he becomes your slave, he may take his wife with him. ⁴If the slave's master gives him a wife, and she gives birth to sons or daughters, the woman and her children will belong to the master. When the slave is set free, only he may leave.

⁵"But if the slave says, 'I love my master, my wife and my children, and I don't want to go free,' ⁶then the slave's master must take him to God. The master is to take him to a door or doorframe and punch a hole through the slave's ear using a sharp tool. Then the slave will serve that master all his life.

⁷"If a man sells his daughter as a slave, the rules for setting her free are different from the rules for setting the male slaves free. ⁸If the master wanted to marry her but then decided he was not pleased with her, he must let one of her close relatives buy her back. He has no right to sell her to foreigners, because he has treated her unfairly. ⁹If the man who bought her promises to let the woman marry his son, he must treat her as a daughter. ¹⁰If the man who bought her marries another woman, he must not keep his first wife from having food or clothing or sexual relations. ¹¹If he does not give her these three things, she may go free, and she owes him no money.

Laws About Injuries

¹²"Anyone who hits a person and kills him must be put to death. ¹³But if a person kills someone accidentally, God allowed that to happen, so the person must go to a place I will choose. ¹⁴But if someone plans and murders another person on purpose, put

him to death, even if he has run to my altar for safety.

¹⁵"Anyone who hits his father or his mother must be put to death.

¹⁶"Anyone who kidnaps someone and either sells him as a slave or still has him when he is caught must be put to death.

¹⁷"Anyone who says cruel things to his father or mother must be put to death.

¹⁸"If two men argue, and one hits the other with a rock or with his fist, the one who is hurt but not killed might have to stay in bed. ¹⁹Later if he is able to get up and walk around outside with his walking stick, the one who hit him is not to be punished. But he must pay the injured man for the loss of his time, and he must support the injured man until he is completely healed.

²⁰"If a man beats his male or female slave with a stick, and the slave dies on the spot, the owner must be punished. ²¹But if the slave gets well after a day or two, the owner will not be punished since the slave belongs to him.

²²"Suppose two men are fighting and hit a pregnant woman, causing the baby to come out. If there is no further injury, the man who caused the accident must pay money—whatever amount the woman's husband says and the court allows. ²³But if there is further injury, then the punishment that must be paid is life for life, ²⁴eye for eye, tooth for tooth, hand for hand, foot for foot, ²⁵burn for burn, wound for wound, and bruise for bruise.

²⁶"If a man hits his male or female slave in the eye, and the eye is blinded, the man is to free the slave to pay for the eye. ²⁷If a master knocks out a tooth of his male or female slave, the man is to free the slave to pay for the tooth.

²⁸"If a man's bull kills a man or woman, you must kill that bull by throwing stones at it, and you should not eat the bull. But the owner of the bull is not guilty. ²⁹However, suppose the bull has hurt people in the past and the owner, though warned, did not keep it in a pen. Then if it kills a man or woman,

the bull must be stoned to death, and the owner must also be put to death. ³⁰But if the family of the dead person accepts money, the one who owned the bull may buy back his life, but he must pay whatever is demanded. ³¹Use this same law if the bull kills a person's son or daughter. ³²If the bull kills a male or female slave, the owner must pay the master the price for a new slave, or twelve ounces of silver, and the bull must also be stoned to death.

³³"If a man takes the cover off a pit, or digs a pit and does not cover it, and another man's ox or donkey comes and falls into it, ³⁴the owner of the pit must pay the owner of the animal for the loss. The dead animal will belong to the one who pays.

³⁵"If a man's bull kills another man's bull, they must sell the bull that is alive. Both men will get half of the money and half of the bull that was killed. ³⁶But if a person's bull has hurt other animals in the past and the owner did not keep it in a pen, that owner must pay bull for bull, and the dead animal is his.

Property Laws

22 "If a man steals a bull or a sheep and kills or sells it, he must pay back five bulls for the one bull he stole and four sheep for the one sheep he stole.

²⁻⁴"The robber who is caught must pay back what he stole. If he owns nothing, he must be sold as a slave to pay for what he stole. If the stolen animal is found alive with the robber, he must give the owner two animals for every animal he stole, whether it was a bull, donkey, or sheep.

"If a thief is killed while breaking into a house at night, the one who killed him is not guilty of murder. But if this happens during the day, he is guilty of murder.

⁵"If a man lets his farm animal graze in his field or vineyard, and it wanders into another man's field or vineyard, the owner of the animal must pay back the loss from the best of his crop.

⁶"Suppose a man starts a fire that spreads through the thornbushes to his neighbor's field. If the fire burns his neighbor's growing grain or grain that has been stacked, or if it burns his whole field, the person who started the fire must pay for what was burned.

⁷"Suppose a man gives his neighbor money or other things to keep for him and those things are stolen from the neighbor's house. If the thief is caught, he must pay back twice as much as he stole. ⁸But if the thief is never found, the owner of the house must make a promise before God that he has not stolen his neighbor's things.

⁹"Suppose two men disagree about who owns something—whether ox, donkey, sheep, clothing, or something else that is lost. If each says, 'This is mine,' each man must bring his case to God. God's judges will decide who is guilty, and that person must pay the other man twice as much as the object is worth.

¹⁰"Suppose a man asks his neighbor to keep his donkey, ox, sheep, or some other animal for him, and that animal dies, gets hurt, or is taken away, without anyone seeing what happened. ¹¹That neighbor must promise before the LORD that he did not harm or kill the other man's animal, and the owner of the animal must accept his promise made before God. The neighbor does not have to pay the owner for the animal. ¹²But if the animal was stolen from the neighbor, he must pay the owner for it. ¹³If wild animals killed it, the neighbor must bring the body as proof, and he will not have to pay for the animal that was killed.

¹⁴"If a man borrows an animal from his neighbor, and it gets hurt or dies while the owner is not there, the one who borrowed it must pay the owner for the animal. ¹⁵But if the owner is with the animal, the one who borrowed it does not have to pay. If the animal was rented, the rental price covers the loss.

Laws and Relationships

¹⁶"Suppose a man finds a woman who is not pledged to be married and has never had sexual relations with a man. If he tricks her into having sexual relations with him, he must give her family the payment to marry her, and she will become his wife. ¹⁷But if her father refuses to allow his daughter to marry him, the man must still give the usual pay-

ment for a bride who has never had sexual relations.

¹⁸"Put to death any woman who does evil magic.

¹⁹"Put to death anyone who has sexual relations with an animal.

²⁰"Destroy completely any person who makes a sacrifice to any god except the LORD.

²¹"Do not cheat or hurt a foreigner, because you were foreigners in the land of Egypt.

²²"Do not cheat a widow or an orphan. ²³If you do, and they cry out to me for help, I certainly will hear their cry. ²⁴And I will be very angry and kill you in war. Then your wives will become widows, and your children will become orphans.

²⁵"If you lend money to one of my people who is poor, do not treat him as a moneylender would. Charge him nothing for using your money. ²⁶If your neighbor gives you his coat as a promise for the money he owes you, you must give it back to him by sunset, ²⁷because it is the only cover to keep his body warm. He has nothing else to sleep in. If he cries out to me for help, I will listen, because I am merciful.

²⁸"You must not speak against God or curse a leader of your people.

²⁹"Do not hold back your offering from the first of your harvest and the first wine that you make. Also, you must give me your firstborn sons. ³⁰You must do the same with your bulls and your sheep. Let the firstborn males stay with their mothers for seven days, and on the eighth day you must give them to me.

³¹"You are to be my holy people. You must not eat the meat of any animal that has been killed by wild animals. Instead, give it to the dogs.

PSALM 18:46-50

⁴⁶The LORD lives!
  May my Rock be praised.
  Praise the God who saves me!
⁴⁷God gives me victory over my enemies
  and brings people under my rule.
⁴⁸He saves me from my enemies.

You set me over those who hate me.
  You saved me from violent people.
⁴⁹So I will praise you, LORD, among the
    nations.
  I will sing praises to your name.
⁵⁰The LORD gives great victories to his
    king.
  He is loyal to his appointed king,
  to David and his descendants forever.

PROVERBS 6:26-29

²⁶A prostitute will treat you like a loaf of
    bread,
  and a woman who takes part in
    adultery may cost you your life.
²⁷You cannot carry hot coals against your
    chest
  without burning your clothes,
²⁸and you cannot walk on hot coals
  without burning your feet.
²⁹The same is true if you have sexual
    relations with another man's wife.
  Anyone who does so will be punished.

MATTHEW 23:1-22

Jesus Accuses Some Leaders

23 Then Jesus said to the crowds and to his followers, ²"The teachers of the law and the Pharisees have the authority to tell you what the law of Moses says. ³So you should obey and follow whatever they tell you, but their lives are not good examples for you to follow. They tell you to do things, but they themselves don't do them. ⁴They make strict rules and try to force people to obey them, but they are unwilling to help those who struggle under the weight of their rules.

⁵"They do good things so that other people will see them. They enlarge the little boxes[n] holding Scriptures that they wear, and they make their special prayer clothes very long. ⁶Those Pharisees and teachers of the law love to have the most important seats at feasts and in the synagogues. ⁷They love people to greet them with respect in the marketplaces, and they love to have people call them 'Teacher.'

23:5 boxes Small leather boxes containing four important Scriptures. Some Jews tied these to their foreheads and left arms, probably to show they were very religious.

⁸"But you must not be called 'Teacher,' because you have only one Teacher, and you are all brothers and sisters together. ⁹And don't call any person on earth 'Father,' because you have one Father, who is in heaven. ¹⁰And you should not be called 'Master,' because you have only one Master, the Christ. ¹¹Whoever is your servant is the greatest among you. ¹²Whoever makes himself great will be made humble. Whoever makes himself humble will be made great.

¹³"How terrible for you, teachers of the law and Pharisees! You are hypocrites! You close the door for people to enter the kingdom of heaven. You yourselves don't enter, and you stop others who are trying to enter. [¹⁴How terrible for you, teachers of the law and Pharisees. You are hypocrites. You take away widows' houses, and you say long prayers so that people will notice you. So you will have a worse punishment.]ⁿ

¹⁵"How terrible for you, teachers of the law and Pharisees! You are hypocrites! You travel across land and sea to find one person who will change to your ways. When you find that person, you make him more fit for hell than you are.

¹⁶"How terrible for you! You guide the people, but you are blind. You say, 'If people swear by the Temple when they make a promise, that means nothing. But if they swear by the gold that is in the Temple, they must keep that promise.' ¹⁷You are blind fools! Which is greater: the gold or the Temple that makes that gold holy? ¹⁸And you say, 'If people swear by the altar when they make a promise, that means nothing. But if they swear by the gift on the altar, they must keep that promise.' ¹⁹You are blind! Which is greater: the gift or the altar that makes the gift holy? ²⁰The person who swears by the altar is really using the altar and also everything on the altar. ²¹And the person who swears by the Temple is really using the Temple and also everything in the Temple. ²²The person who swears by heaven is also using God's throne and the One who sits on that throne.

FEBRUARY 6

EXODUS 23:1—24:18

Laws About Fairness

23 "You must not tell lies. If you are a witness in court, don't help a wicked person by telling lies.

²"You must not do wrong just because everyone else is doing it. If you are a witness in court, you must not ruin a fair trial. You must not tell lies just because everyone else is. ³If a poor person is in court, you must not take his side just because he is poor.

⁴"If you see your enemy's ox or donkey wandering away, you must return it to him. ⁵If you see that your enemy's donkey has fallen because its load is too heavy, do not leave it there. You must help your enemy get the donkey back on its feet.

⁶"You must not be unfair to a poor person when he is in court. ⁷You must not lie when you accuse someone in court. Never allow an innocent or honest person to be put to death as punishment, because I will not treat guilty people as if they were innocent.

⁸"You must not accept money from a person who wants you to lie in court, because such money will not let you see what is right. Such money makes good people tell lies.

⁹"You must not mistreat a foreigner. You know how it feels to be a foreigner, because you were foreigners in Egypt.

Laws for the Sabbath

¹⁰"For six years you are to plant and harvest crops on your land. ¹¹Then during the seventh year, do not plow or plant your land. If any food grows there, allow the poor people to have it, and let the wild animals eat

what is left. You should do the same with your vineyards and your orchards of olive trees.

¹²"You should work six days a week, but on the seventh day you must rest. This lets your ox and your donkey rest, and it also lets the slave born in your house and the foreigner be refreshed.

¹³"Be sure to do all that I have said to you. You must not even say the names of other gods; those names must not come out of your mouth.

Three Yearly Feasts

¹⁴"Three times each year you must hold a feast to honor me. ¹⁵You must celebrate the Feast of Unleavened Bread in the way I commanded you. For seven days you must eat bread that is made without yeast at the set time during the month of Abib, the month when you came out of Egypt. No one is to come to worship me without bringing an offering.

¹⁶"You must celebrate the Feast of Weeks. Offer to God the first things you harvest from the crops you planted in your fields.

"You must celebrate the Feast of Shelters in the fall, when you gather all the crops from your fields.

¹⁷"So three times during every year all your males must come to worship the LORD God.

¹⁸"You must not offer animal blood along with anything that has yeast in it.

"You must not save any of the fat from the sacrifice for the next day.

¹⁹"You must bring the best of the first-fruits of your land to the Holy Tent[n] of the LORD your God.

"You must not cook a young goat in its mother's milk.

God Will Help Israel

²⁰"I am sending an angel ahead of you, who will protect you as you travel. He will lead you to the place I have prepared. ²¹Pay attention to the angel and obey him. Do not turn against him; he will not forgive such turning against him because my power is in him. ²²If you listen carefully to all he says

and do everything that I tell you, I will be an enemy to your enemies. I will fight all who fight against you. ²³My angel will go ahead of you and take you into the land of the Amorites, Hittites, Perizzites, Canaanites, Hivites, and Jebusites, and I will destroy them.

²⁴"You must not bow down to their gods or worship them. You must not live the way those people live. You must destroy their idols, breaking into pieces the stone pillars they use in worship. ²⁵If you worship the LORD your God, I will bless your bread and your water. I will take away sickness from you. ²⁶None of your women will have her baby die before it is born, and all women will have children. I will allow you to live long lives.

²⁷"I will make your enemies afraid of me. I will confuse any people you fight against, and I will make all your enemies run away from you. ²⁸I will send terror ahead of you that will force the Hivites, Canaanites, and Hittites out of your way. ²⁹But I will not force all those people out in only one year. If I did, the land would become a desert and the wild animals would become too many for you. ³⁰Instead, I will force those people out slowly, until there are enough of you to take over the land.

³¹"I will give you the land from the Red Sea to the Mediterranean Sea, and from the desert to the Euphrates River. I will give you power over the people who now live in the land, and you will force them out ahead of you. ³²You must not make an agreement with those people or with their gods. ³³You must not let them live in your land, or they will make you sin against me. If you worship their gods, you will be caught in a trap."

God and Israel Make Their Agreement

24 The LORD told Moses, "You, Aaron, Nadab, Abihu, and seventy of the elders of Israel must come up to me and worship me from a distance. ²Then Moses alone must come near me; the others must not come near. The rest of the people must not come up the mountain with Moses."

³Moses told the people all the LORD's words and laws for living. Then all of the

23:19 **Holy Tent** Literally, "house of the LORD your God." See Exodus 25:9.

people answered out loud together, "We will do all the things the LORD has said." ⁴So Moses wrote down all the words of the LORD. And he got up early the next morning and built an altar near the bottom of the mountain. He set up twelve stones, one stone for each of the twelve tribes of Israel. ⁵Then Moses sent young Israelite men to offer whole burnt offerings and to sacrifice young bulls as fellowship offerings to the LORD. ⁶Moses put half of the blood of these animals in bowls, and he sprinkled the other half of the blood on the altar. ⁷Then he took the Book of the Agreement and read it so the people could hear him. And they said, "We will do everything that the LORD has said; we will obey."

⁸Then Moses took the blood from the bowls and sprinkled it on the people, saying, "This is the blood that begins the Agreement, the Agreement which the LORD has made with you about all these words."

⁹Moses, Aaron, Nadab, Abihu, and seventy of the elders of Israel went up the mountain ¹⁰and saw the God of Israel. Under his feet was a surface that looked as if it were paved with blue sapphire stones, and it was as clear as the sky! ¹¹These leaders of the Israelites saw God, but God did not destroy them. Then they ate and drank together.

God Promises Moses the Stone Tablets

¹²The LORD said to Moses, "Come up the mountain to me. Wait there, and I will give you two stone tablets. On these are the teachings and the commands I have written to instruct the people."

¹³So Moses and his helper Joshua set out, and Moses went up to Sinai, the mountain of God. ¹⁴Moses said to the elders, "Wait here for us until we come back to you. Aaron and Hur are with you, and anyone who has a disagreement with others can take it to them."

Moses Meets with God

¹⁵When Moses went up on the mountain, the cloud covered it. ¹⁶The glory of the LORD came down on Mount Sinai, and the cloud covered it for six days. On the seventh day

the LORD called to Moses from inside the cloud. ¹⁷To the Israelites the glory of the LORD looked like a fire burning on top of the mountain. ¹⁸Then Moses went into the cloud and went higher up the mountain. He was on the mountain for forty days and forty nights.

PSALM 19:1-6

God's Works and Word

For the director of music. A psalm of David.

19 The heavens declare the glory of God,
  and the skies announce what his hands
    have made.
²Day after day they tell the story;
  night after night they tell it again.
³They have no speech or words;
  they have no voice to be heard.
⁴But their message goes out through all
    the world;
  their words go everywhere on earth.
  The sky is like a home for the sun.
⁵ The sun comes out like a bridegroom
    from his bedroom.
  It rejoices like an athlete eager to run a
    race.
⁶The sun rises at one end of the sky
  and follows its path to the other end.
  Nothing hides from its heat.

PROVERBS 6:30-31

³⁰People don't hate a thief
  when he steals because he is hungry.
³¹But if he is caught, he must pay back
    seven times what he stole,
  and it may cost him everything he owns.

MATTHEW 23:23-39

²³"How terrible for you, teachers of the law and Pharisees! You are hypocrites! You give to God one-tenth of everything you earn—even your mint, dill, and cumin.ⁿ But you don't obey the really important teachings of the law—justice, mercy, and being loyal. These are the things you should do, as

---

23:23 mint, dill, and cumin Small plants grown in gardens and used for spices. Only very religious people would be careful enough to give a tenth of these plants.

well as those other things. [24]You guide the people, but you are blind! You are like a person who picks a fly out of a drink and then swallows a camel![n]

[25]"How terrible for you, teachers of the law and Pharisees! You are hypocrites! You wash the outside of your cups and dishes, but inside they are full of things you got by cheating others and by pleasing only yourselves. [26]Pharisees, you are blind! First make the inside of the cup clean, and then the outside of the cup can be truly clean.

[27]"How terrible for you, teachers of the law and Pharisees! You are hypocrites! You are like tombs that are painted white. Outside, those tombs look fine, but inside, they are full of the bones of dead people and all kinds of unclean things. [28]It is the same with you. People look at you and think you are good, but on the inside you are full of hypocrisy and evil.

[29]"How terrible for you, teachers of the law and Pharisees! You are hypocrites! You build tombs for the prophets, and you show honor to the graves of those who lived good lives. [30]You say, 'If we had lived during the time of our ancestors, we would not have helped them kill the prophets.' [31]But you give proof that you are descendants of those who murdered the prophets. [32]And you will complete the sin that your ancestors started.

[33]"You are snakes! A family of poisonous snakes! How are you going to escape God's judgment? [34]So I tell you this: I am sending to you prophets and wise men and teachers. Some of them you will kill and crucify. Some of them you will beat in your synagogues and chase from town to town. [35]So you will be guilty for the death of all the good people who have been killed on earth—from the murder of that good man Abel to the murder of Zechariah[n] son of Berakiah, whom you murdered between the Temple and the altar. [36]I tell you the truth, all of these things will happen to you people who are living now.

Jesus Feels Sorry for Jerusalem

[37]"Jerusalem, Jerusalem! You kill the prophets and stone to death those who are sent to you. Many times I wanted to gather your people as a hen gathers her chicks under her wings, but you did not let me.[38]Now your house will be left completely empty. [39]I tell you, you will not see me again until that time when you will say, 'God bless the One who comes in the name of the Lord.'"[n]

FEBRUARY 7

EXODUS 25:1—26:37

Gifts for the Lord

25 The LORD said to Moses, [2]"Tell the Israelites to bring me gifts. Receive for me the gifts each person wants to give. [3]These are the gifts that you should receive from them: gold, silver, bronze; [4]blue, purple, and red thread; fine linen, goat hair, [5]sheepskins that are dyed red; fine leather; acacia wood; [6]olive oil to burn in the lamps; spices for sweet-smelling incense, and the special olive oil poured on a person's head to make him a priest; [7]onyx stones, and other jewels to be put on the holy vest and the chest covering.

[8]"The people must build a holy place for me so that I can live among them. [9]Build this Holy Tent and everything in it by the plan I will show you.

The Ark of the Agreement

[10]"Use acacia wood and build an Ark forty-five inches long, twenty-seven inches wide, and twenty-seven inches high. [11]Cover the Ark inside and out with pure gold, and put a gold strip all around it. [12]Make four gold rings for the Ark and attach them to its

four feet, two rings on each side. ¹³Then make poles from acacia wood and cover them with gold. ¹⁴Put the poles through the rings on the sides of the Ark, and use these poles to carry it. ¹⁵These poles must always stay in the rings of the Ark. Do not take them out. ¹⁶Then put in the Ark the Agreement which I will make with you.

¹⁷"Then make a lid of pure gold for the Ark; this is the mercy seat. Make it forty-five inches long and twenty-seven inches wide. ¹⁸Then hammer gold to make two creatures with wings, and put one on each end of the lid. ¹⁹Attach one creature on one end of the lid and the other creature on the other end. Make them to be one piece with the lid at the ends. ²⁰The creatures' wings should be spread upward, covering the lid, and the creatures are to face each other across the lid. ²¹Put this lid on top of the Ark, and put in the Ark the Agreement which I will make with you. ²²I will meet with you there, above the lid between the two winged creatures on the Ark of the Agreement. There I will give you all my commands for the Israelites.

The Table

²³"Make a table out of acacia wood, thirty-six inches long, eighteen inches wide, and twenty-seven inches high. ²⁴Cover it with pure gold, and put a gold strip around it. ²⁵Make a frame three inches high that stands up all around the edge, and put a gold strip around it. ²⁶Then make four gold rings. Attach them to the four corners of the table where the four legs are. ²⁷Put the rings close to the frame around the top of the table, because they will hold the poles for carrying it. ²⁸Make the poles out of acacia wood, cover them with gold, and carry the table with these poles. ²⁹Make the plates and bowls for the table, as well as the jars and cups, out of pure gold. They will be used for pouring out the drink offerings. ³⁰On this table put the bread that shows you are in my presence so that it is always there in front of me.

The Lampstand

³¹"Hammer pure gold to make a lampstand. Its base, stand, flower-like cups, buds, and petals must all be joined together in one piece. ³²The lampstand must have six

branches going out from its sides—three on one side and three on the other. ³³Each branch must have three cups shaped like almond flowers on it. Each cup must have a bud and a petal. Each of the six branches going out from the lampstand must be the same. ³⁴And there must be four more cups made like almond flowers on the lampstand itself. These cups must also have buds and petals. ³⁵Put a bud under each pair of branches that goes out from the lampstand. Each of the six branches going out from the lampstand must be the same. ³⁶The branches, buds, and lampstand must be made of one piece, hammered out of pure gold.

³⁷"Then make seven small oil lamps and put them on the lampstand so that they give light to the area in front of it. ³⁸The wick trimmers and trays must be made of pure gold. ³⁹Use seventy-five pounds of pure gold to make the lampstand and everything with it. ⁴⁰Be very careful to make them by the plan I showed you on the mountain.

The Holy Tent

26 "Make for the Holy Tent ten curtains of fine linen and blue, purple, and red thread. Have a skilled craftsman sew designs of creatures with wings on the pieces of cloth. ²Make each curtain the same size— forty-two feet long and six feet wide. ³Sew five curtains together for one set, and sew the other curtains together for the second set. ⁴Make loops of blue cloth on the edge of the end curtain of one set, and do the same for the end curtain of the other set. ⁵Make fifty loops on the end curtain of the first set and fifty loops on the end curtain of the second set. These loops must be opposite each other. ⁶And make fifty gold hooks to join the two sets of curtains so that the Holy Tent is one piece.

⁷"Then make another tent that will cover the Holy Tent, using eleven curtains made from goat hair. ⁸All these curtains must be the same size—forty-five feet long and six feet wide. ⁹Sew five of the curtains together into one set. Then sew the other six curtains together into the second set. Fold the sixth curtain double over the front of the Tent.

[10]Make fifty loops down the edge of the end curtain of one set, and do the same for the end curtain of the other set. [11]Then make fifty bronze hooks and put them in the loops to join the tent together so that the covering is one piece. [12]Let the extra half piece of cloth hang over the back of the Holy Tent. [13]There will be eighteen inches hanging over the sides of the Holy Tent, to protect it. [14]Make a covering for the Holy Tent from sheepskins colored red, and over that make a covering from fine leather.

[15]"Use acacia wood to make upright frames for the Holy Tent. [16]Each frame must be fifteen feet long and twenty-seven inches wide, [17]with two pegs side by side. Every frame must be made the same way. [18]Make twenty frames for the south side of the Holy Tent. [19]Each frame must have two silver bases to go under it, a peg fitting into each base. You must make forty silver bases for the frames. [20]Make twenty more frames for the north side of the Holy Tent [21]and forty silver bases for them—two bases for each frame. [22]You must make six frames for the rear or west end of the Holy Tent [23]and two frames for each corner at the rear. [24]The two frames are to be doubled at the bottom and joined at the top with a metal ring. Both corner frames must be made this way. [25]So there will be a total of eight frames at the rear of the Tent, and there will be sixteen silver bases—two bases under each frame.

[26]"Make crossbars of acacia wood to connect the upright frames of the Holy Tent. Make five crossbars to hold the frames together on one side [27]and five to hold the frames together on the other side. Also make five crossbars to hold the frames together on the west end, at the rear. [28]The middle crossbar is to be set halfway up the frames, and it is to run along the entire length of each side and rear. [29]Make gold rings on the sides of the frames to hold the crossbars, and cover the frames and the crossbars with gold. [30]Set up the Holy Tent by the plan shown to you on the mountain.

[31]"Make a curtain of fine linen and blue, purple, and red thread, and have a skilled craftsman sew designs of creatures with wings on it. [32]Hang the curtain by gold hooks on four posts of acacia wood that are covered with gold, and set them in four silver bases. [33]Hang the curtain from the hooks in the roof, and put the Ark of the Agreement containing the two stone tablets behind it. This curtain will separate the Holy Place from the Most Holy Place. [34]Put the lid on the Ark of the Agreement in the Most Holy Place.

[35]"Outside the curtain, put the table on the north side of the Holy Tent. Put the lampstand on the south side of the Holy Tent across from the table.

The Entrance of the Holy Tent

[36]"Then, for the entrance of the Tent, make a curtain with fine linen and blue, purple, and red thread. Someone who can sew well is to sew designs on it. [37]Make five posts of acacia wood covered with gold. Make gold hooks for them on which to hang the curtain, and make five bronze bases for them.

PSALM 19:7–14

[7]The teachings of the LORD are perfect;
  they give new strength.
The rules of the LORD can be trusted;
  they make plain people wise.
[8]The orders of the LORD are right;
  they make people happy.
The commands of the LORD are pure;
  they light up the way.
[9]Respect for the LORD is good;
  it will last forever.
The judgments of the LORD are true;
  they are completely right.
[10]They are worth more than gold,
  even the purest gold.
They are sweeter than honey,
  even the finest honey.
[11]By them your servant is warned.
  Keeping them brings great reward.

[12]People cannot see their own mistakes.
  Forgive me for my secret sins.
[13]Keep me from the sins of pride;
  don't let them rule me.
Then I can be pure
  and innocent of the greatest of sins.

[14]I hope my words and thoughts please
  you.

Lord, you are my Rock, the one who saves me.

PROVERBS 6:32–35

32 A man who takes part in adultery has no sense;
    he will destroy himself.
33 He will be beaten up and disgraced,
    and his shame will never go away.
34 Jealousy makes a husband very angry,
    and he will have no pity when he gets revenge.
35 He will accept no payment for the wrong;
    he will take no amount of money.

MATTHEW 24:1–35

The Temple Will Be Destroyed

24 As Jesus left the Temple and was walking away, his followers came up to show him the Temple's buildings. 2 Jesus asked, "Do you see all these buildings? I tell you the truth, not one stone will be left on another. Every stone will be thrown down to the ground."

3 Later, as Jesus was sitting on the Mount of Olives, his followers came to be alone with him. They said, "Tell us, when will these things happen? And what will be the sign that it is time for you to come again and for this age to end?"

4 Jesus answered, "Be careful that no one fools you. 5 Many will come in my name, saying, 'I am the Christ,' and they will fool many people. 6 You will hear about wars and stories of wars that are coming, but don't be afraid. These things must happen before the end comes. 7 Nations will fight against other nations; kingdoms will fight against other kingdoms. There will be times when there is no food for people to eat, and there will be earthquakes in different places. 8 These things are like the first pains when something new is about to be born.

9 "Then people will arrest you, hand you over to be hurt, and kill you. They will hate you because you believe in me. 10 At that time, many will lose their faith, and they will turn against each other and hate each other. 11 Many false prophets will come and cause many people to believe lies. 12 There will be more and more evil in the world, so most people will stop showing their love for each other. 13 But those people who keep their faith until the end will be saved. 14 The Good News about God's kingdom will be preached in all the world, to every nation. Then the end will come.

15 "Daniel the prophet spoke about 'a blasphemous object that brings destruction.'[n] You will see this standing in the holy place." (You who read this should understand what it means.) 16 "At that time, the people in Judea should run away to the mountains. 17 If people are on the roofs[n] of their houses, they must not go down to get anything out of their houses. 18 If people are in the fields, they must not go back to get their coats. 19 At that time, how terrible it will be for women who are pregnant or have nursing babies! 20 Pray that it will not be winter or a Sabbath day when these things happen and you have to run away, 21 because at that time there will be much trouble. There will be more trouble than there has ever been since the beginning of the world until now, and nothing as bad will ever happen again. 22 God has decided to make that terrible time short. Otherwise, no one would go on living. But God will make that time short to help the people he has chosen. 23 At that time, someone might say to you, 'Look, there is the Christ!' Or another person might say, 'There he is!' But don't believe them. 24 False Christs and false prophets will come and perform great wonders and miracles. They will try to fool even the people God has chosen, if that is possible. 25 Now I have warned you about this before it happens.

26 "If people tell you, 'The Christ is in the desert,' don't go there. If they say, 'The Christ is in the inner room,' don't believe it. 27 When the Son of Man comes, he will be seen by everyone, like lightning flashing from the east to the west. 28 Wherever the dead body is, there the vultures will gather.

24:15 'a blasphemous object that brings destruction' Mentioned in Daniel 9:27; 12:11 (see also Daniel 11:31). 24:17 roofs In Bible times houses were built with flat roofs. The roof was used for drying things such as flax and fruit. And it was used as an extra room, as a place for worship, and as a cool place to sleep in the summer.

[29]"Soon after the trouble of those days,
'the sun will grow dark,
and the moon will not give its light.
The stars will fall from the sky.
And the powers of the heavens will be
shaken.'   *Isaiah 13:10; 34:4*
[30]"At that time, the sign of the Son of Man will appear in the sky. Then all the peoples of the world will cry. They will see the Son of Man coming on clouds in the sky with great power and glory. [31]He will use a loud trumpet to send his angels all around the earth, and they will gather his chosen people from every part of the world.

[32]"Learn a lesson from the fig tree: When its branches become green and soft and new leaves appear, you know summer is near. [33]In the same way, when you see all these things happening, you will know that the time is near, ready to come. [34]I tell you the truth, all these things will happen while the people of this time are still living. [35]Earth and sky will be destroyed, but the words I have said will never be destroyed.

FEBRUARY 8

EXODUS 27:1—28:43

The Altar for Burnt Offerings

27 "Make an altar of acacia wood, four and one-half feet high. It should be square—seven and one-half feet long and seven and one-half feet wide. [2]Make each of the four corners of the altar stick out like a horn, in such a way that the corners with their horns are all one piece. Then cover the whole altar with bronze.

[3]"Use bronze to make all the tools and dishes that will be used on the altar: the pots to remove the ashes, the shovels, the bowls for sprinkling blood, the meat forks, and the pans for carrying the burning wood.

[4]"Make a large bronze screen to hold the burning wood, and put a bronze ring at each of the four corners of it. [5]Put the screen inside the altar, under its rim, halfway up from the bottom.

[6]"Make poles of acacia wood for the altar, and cover them with bronze. [7]Put the poles through the rings on both sides of the altar to carry it. [8]Make the altar out of boards and leave the inside hollow. Make it as you were shown on the mountain.

The Courtyard of the Holy Tent

[9]"Make a wall of curtains to form a courtyard around the Holy Tent. The south side should have a wall of fine linen curtains one hundred fifty feet long. [10]Hang the curtains with silver hooks and bands on twenty bronze posts with twenty bronze bases. [11]The north side must also be one hundred fifty feet long. Hang its curtains on silver hooks and bands on twenty bronze posts with twenty bronze bases.

[12]"The west end of the courtyard must have a wall of curtains seventy-five feet long, with ten posts and ten bases on that wall. [13]The east end of the courtyard must also be seventy-five feet long. [14]On one side of the entry, there is to be a wall of curtains twenty-two and one-half feet long, held up by three posts on three bases. [15]On the other side of the entry, there is also to be a wall of curtains twenty-two and one-half feet long, held up by three posts on three bases.

[16]"The entry to the courtyard is to be a curtain thirty feet wide, made of fine linen with blue, purple, and red thread. Someone who can sew well is to sew designs on it. It is to be held up by four posts on four bases. [17]All the posts around the courtyard must have silver bands and hooks and bronze bases. [18]The courtyard must be one hundred fifty feet long and seventy-five feet wide, with a wall of curtains around it seven and one-half feet high, made of fine linen. The bases in which the posts are set must be bronze. [19]All the things used in the Holy Tent and all the tent pegs for the Holy Tent and the wall around the courtyard must be made of bronze.

Oil for the Lamp

²⁰"Command the people of Israel to bring you pure olive oil, made from pressed olives, to keep the lamps on the lampstand burning. ²¹Aaron and his sons must keep the lamps burning before the LORD from evening till morning. This will be in the Meeting Tent, outside the curtain which is in front of the Ark. The Israelites and their descendants must obey this rule from now on.

Clothes for the Priests

28 "Tell your brother Aaron to come to you, along with his sons Nadab, Abihu, Eleazar, and Ithamar. Separate them from the other Israelites to serve me as priests. ²Make holy clothes for your brother Aaron to give him honor and beauty. ³Tell all the skilled craftsmen to whom I have given wisdom to make special clothes for Aaron—clothes to show that he belongs to me so that he may serve me as a priest. ⁴These are the clothes they must make: a chest covering, a holy vest, an outer robe, a woven inner robe, a turban, and a cloth belt. The craftsmen must make these holy clothes for your brother Aaron and his sons. Then they may serve me as priests. ⁵The craftsmen must use gold and blue, purple and red thread, and fine linen.

The Holy Vest

⁶"Use gold and blue, purple and red thread, and fine linen to make the holy vest; skilled craftsmen are to make it. ⁷At each top corner of this holy vest there will be a pair of shoulder straps tied together over each shoulder.

⁸"The craftsmen will very carefully weave a belt on the holy vest that is made with the same materials—gold and blue, purple and red thread, and fine linen.

⁹"Take two onyx stones and write the names of the twelve sons of Israel on them, ¹⁰six on one stone and six on the other. Write the names in order, from the oldest son to the youngest. ¹¹Carve the names of the sons of Israel on these stones in the same way a person carves words and designs on a seal. Put gold around the stones to hold them on the holy vest. ¹²Then put the two stones on the two straps of the holy vest as reminders of the twelve sons of Israel. Aaron is to wear their names on his shoulders in the presence

of the LORD as reminders of the sons of Israel. ¹³Make two gold pieces to hold the stones ¹⁴and two chains of pure gold, twisted together like a rope. Attach the chains to the two gold pieces that hold the stones.

The Chest Covering

¹⁵"Make a chest covering to help in making decisions. The craftsmen should make it as they made the holy vest, using gold and blue, purple and red thread, and fine linen. ¹⁶The chest covering must be square—nine inches long and nine inches wide—and folded double to make a pocket. ¹⁷Put four rows of beautiful gems on the chest covering: The first row must have a ruby, topaz, and yellow quartz; ¹⁸the second must have turquoise, a sapphire, and an emerald; ¹⁹the third must have a jacinth, an agate, and an amethyst; ²⁰the fourth must have a chrysolite, an onyx, and a jasper. Put gold around these jewels to attach them to the chest covering. ²¹There must be twelve jewels on the chest covering—one jewel for each of the names of the sons of Israel. Carve the name of one of the twelve tribes on each of the stones as you would carve a seal.

²²"Make chains of pure gold, twisted together like rope, for the chest covering. ²³Make two gold rings and put them on the two upper corners of the chest covering. ²⁴Attach the two gold chains to the two rings at the upper corners of the chest covering. ²⁵Attach the other ends of the two chains to the two gold pieces on the shoulder straps in the front of the holy vest.

²⁶"Make two gold rings and put them at the two lower corners of the chest covering, on the inside edge next to the holy vest. ²⁷Make two more gold rings and attach them to the bottom of the shoulder straps in the front of the holy vest. Put them close to the seam above the woven belt of the holy vest. ²⁸Join the rings of the chest covering to the rings of the holy vest with blue ribbon, connecting it to the woven belt so the chest covering will not swing out from the holy vest.

²⁹"When Aaron enters the Holy Place, he will wear the names of the sons of Israel over his heart, on the chest covering that helps in making decisions. This will be a continual

reminder before the LORD. [30]And put the Urim and Thummim inside the chest covering so that they will be on Aaron's heart when he goes before the LORD. They will help in making decisions for the Israelites. So Aaron will always carry them with him when he is before the LORD.

[31]"Make the outer robe to be worn under the holy vest, using only blue cloth. [32]Make a hole in the center for Aaron's head, with a woven collar around the hole so it will not tear. [33]Make balls like pomegranates of blue, purple, and red thread, and hang them around the bottom of the outer robe with gold bells between them. [34]All around the bottom of the outer robe there should be a gold bell and a pomegranate ball, a gold bell and a pomegranate ball. [35]Aaron must wear this robe when he serves as priest. The ringing of the bells will be heard when he enters and leaves the Holy Place before the LORD so that Aaron will not die.

[36]"Make a strip of pure gold and carve these words on it as you would carve a seal: 'Holy to the LORD.' [37]Use blue ribbon to tie it to the turban; put it on the front of the turban. [38]Aaron must wear this on his forehead. In this way, he will be blamed if anything is wrong with the gifts of the Israelites. Aaron must always wear this on his head so the LORD will accept the gifts of the people.

[39]"Make the woven inner robe of fine linen, and make the turban of fine linen also. Make the cloth belt with designs sewn on it. [40]Also make woven inner robes, cloth belts, and headbands for Aaron's sons, to give them honor and beauty. [41]Put these clothes on your brother Aaron and his sons, and pour olive oil on their heads to appoint them as priests. Make them belong to me so they may serve me as priests.

[42]"Make for them linen underclothes to cover them from the waist to the upper parts of the legs. [43]Aaron and his sons must wear these underclothes when they enter the Meeting Tent and anytime they come near the altar to serve as priests in the Holy Place. If they do not wear these clothes, they will be guilty of wrong, and they will die. This will be a law that will last from now on for Aaron and all his descendants.

PSALM 20:1–5

A Prayer for the King

For the director of music. A psalm of David.

20 May the LORD answer you in times of trouble.
  May the God of Jacob protect you.
[2]May he send you help from his Temple
  and support you from Mount Zion.
[3]May he remember all your offerings
  and accept all your sacrifices. *Selah*
[4]May he give you what you want
  and make all your plans succeed,
[5]and we will shout for joy when you succeed,
  and we will raise a flag in the name of our God.
  May the LORD give you all that you ask for.

PROVERBS 7:1–5

The Woman of Adultery

7 My son, remember what I say, and treasure my commands.
[2]Obey my commands, and you will live.
  Guard my teachings as you would your own eyes.
[3]Remind yourself of them;
  write them on your heart as if on a tablet.
[4]Treat wisdom as a sister,
  and make understanding your closest friend.
[5]Wisdom and understanding will keep you away from adultery,
  away from the unfaithful wife and her pleasing words.

MATTHEW 24:36–51

When Will Jesus Come Again?

[36]"No one knows when that day or time will be, not the angels in heaven, not even the Son."[n] Only the Father knows. [37]When the Son of Man comes, it will be like what happened during Noah's time. [38]In those days before the flood, people were eating and drinking, marrying and giving their chil-

---

24:36 not even the Son Some Greek copies do not have this phrase.

dren to be married, until the day Noah entered the boat. [39]They knew nothing about what was happening until the flood came and destroyed them. It will be the same when the Son of Man comes. [40]Two men will be in the field. One will be taken, and the other will be left. [41]Two women will be grinding grain with a mill.[n] One will be taken, and the other will be left.

[42]"So always be ready, because you don't know the day your Lord will come. [43]Remember this: If the owner of the house knew what time of night a thief was coming, the owner would watch and not let the thief break in. [44]So you also must be ready, because the Son of Man will come at a time you don't expect him.

[45]"Who is the wise and loyal servant that the master trusts to give the other servants their food at the right time? [46]When the master comes and finds the servant doing his work, the servant will be blessed. [47]I tell you the truth, the master will choose that servant to take care of everything he owns. [48]But suppose that evil servant thinks to himself, 'My master will not come back soon,' [49]and he begins to beat the other servants and eat and get drunk with others like him? [50]The master will come when that servant is not ready and is not expecting him. [51]Then the master will cut him in pieces and send him away to be with the hypocrites, where people will cry and grind their teeth with pain.

FEBRUARY 9

EXODUS 29:1—30:38

Appointing the Priests

29 [1]"This is what you must do to appoint Aaron and his sons to serve me as priests. Take one young bull and two male sheep that have nothing wrong with them. [2]Use fine wheat flour without yeast to make bread, cakes mixed with olive oil, and wafers brushed with olive oil. [3]Put these in one basket, and bring them along with the bull and two male sheep. [4]Bring Aaron and his sons to the entrance of the Meeting Tent and wash them with water. [5]Take the clothes and dress Aaron in the inner robe and the outer robe of the holy vest. Then put on him the holy vest and the chest covering, and tie the holy vest on him with its skillfully woven belt. [6]Put the turban on his head, and put the holy crown on the turban. [7]Take the special olive oil and pour it on his head to make him a priest.

[8]"Then bring his sons and put the inner robes on them. [9]Put the headbands on their heads, and tie cloth belts around their waists. Aaron and his descendants will be priests in Israel, according to a rule that will continue from now on. This is how you will appoint Aaron and his sons as priests.

[10]"Bring the bull to the front of the Meeting Tent, and Aaron and his sons must put their hands on the bull's head. [11]Then kill the bull before the LORD at the entrance to the Meeting Tent. [12]Use your finger to put some of the bull's blood on the corners of the altar, and then pour the blood that is left at the bottom of the altar. [13]Take all the fat that covers the inner organs, as well as the best part of the liver, both kidneys, and the fat around them, and burn them on the altar. [14]Take the bull's meat, skin, and intestines, and burn them outside the camp. This is an offering to take away sin.

[15]"Take one of the male sheep, and have Aaron and his sons put their hands on its head. [16]Kill it, and take its blood and sprinkle it on all four sides of the altar. [17]Then cut it into pieces and wash its inner organs and its legs, putting them with its head and its other pieces. [18]Burn the whole sheep on the altar; it is a burnt offering made by fire to the LORD. Its smell is pleasing to the LORD.

[19]"Take the other male sheep, and have Aaron and his sons put their hands on its

24:41 mill Two large, round, flat rocks used for grinding grain to make flour.

head. [20]Kill it and take some of its blood. Put the blood on the bottom of the right ears of Aaron and his sons and on the thumbs of their right hands and on the big toes of their right feet. Then sprinkle the rest of the blood against all four sides of the altar. [21]Take some of the blood from the altar, and mix it with the special oil used in appointing priests. Sprinkle this on Aaron and his clothes and on his sons and their clothes. This will show that Aaron and his sons and their clothes are given to my service.

[22]"Then take the fat from the male sheep, the fat tail, and the fat that covers the inner organs. In addition, take the best part of the liver, both kidneys, and the fat around them, and the right thigh. (This is the male sheep to be used in appointing priests.)

[23]"Then take the basket of bread that you made without yeast, which you put before the LORD. From it take a loaf of bread, a cake made with olive oil, and a wafer. [24]Put all of these in the hands of Aaron and his sons, and tell them to present them as an offering to the LORD. [25]Then take them from their hands and burn them on the altar with the whole burnt offering. This is an offering made by fire to the LORD; its smell is pleasing to the LORD. [26]Then take the breast of the male sheep used to appoint Aaron as priest, and present it before the LORD as an offering. This part of the animal will be your share. [27]Set aside the breast and the thigh of the sheep that were used to appoint Aaron and his sons as priests. These parts belong to them. [28]They are to be the regular share which the Israelites will always give to Aaron and his sons. It is the gift the Israelites must give to the LORD from their fellowship offerings.

[29]"The holy clothes made for Aaron will belong to his descendants so that they can wear these clothes when they are appointed as priests. [30]Aaron's son, who will become high priest after Aaron, will come to the Meeting Tent to serve in the Holy Place. He is to wear these clothes for seven days.

[31]"Take the male sheep used to appoint priests and boil its meat in a place that is holy. [32]Then at the entrance of the Meeting Tent, Aaron and his sons must eat the meat of the sheep and the bread that is in the basket. [33]They should eat these offerings that were used to remove their sins and to make them holy when they were made priests. But no one else is to eat them, because they are holy things. [34]If any of the meat from that sheep or any of the bread is left the next morning, it must be burned. It must not be eaten, because it is holy.

[35]"Do all these things that I commanded you to do to Aaron and his sons, and spend seven days appointing them. [36]Each day you are to offer a bull to remove the sins of Aaron and his sons so they will be given for service to the LORD. Make the altar ready for service to the LORD, and pour oil on it to make it holy. [37]Spend seven days making the altar ready for service to God and making it holy. Then the altar will become very holy, and anything that touches it must be holy.

The Daily Sacrifices

[38]"Every day from now on, offer on the altar two lambs that are one year old. [39]Offer one lamb in the morning and the other in the evening before dark. [40]In the morning, when you offer the first lamb, offer also two quarts of fine flour mixed with one quart of oil from pressed olives. Pour out a quart of wine as a drink offering. [41]Offer the second lamb in the evening with the same grain offering and drink offering as you did in the morning. This is an offering made by fire to the LORD, and its smell is pleasing to him.

[42]"You must burn these things as an offering to the LORD every day, from now on, at the entrance of the Meeting Tent before the LORD. When you make the offering, I, the LORD, will meet you there and speak to you. [43]I will meet with the people of Israel there, and that place will be holy because of my glory.

[44]"So I will make the Meeting Tent and the altar holy; I will also make Aaron and his sons holy so they may serve me as priests. [45]I will live with the people of Israel and be their God. [46]And they will know that I am the LORD their God who led them out of Egypt so that I could live with them. I am the LORD their God.

The Altar for Burning Incense

30 "Make an altar out of acacia wood for burning incense. ²Make it square— eighteen inches long and eighteen inches wide—and make it thirty-six inches high. The corners that stick out like horns must be one piece with the altar. ³Cover its top, its sides, and its corners with pure gold, and put a gold strip all around the altar. ⁴Make two gold rings beneath the gold strip on opposite sides of the altar, and slide poles through them to carry the altar. ⁵Make the poles from acacia wood and cover them with gold. ⁶Put the altar of incense in front of the curtain that is near the Ark of the Agreement, in front of the lid that covers that Ark. There I will meet with you.

⁷"Aaron must burn sweet-smelling incense on the altar every morning when he comes to take care of the oil lamps. ⁸He must burn incense again in the evening when he lights the lamps, so incense will burn before the LORD every day from now on. ⁹Do not use this altar for offering any other incense, or burnt offering, or any kind of grain offering, or drink offering. ¹⁰Once a year Aaron must make the altar ready for service to God by putting blood on its corners—the blood of the animal offered to remove sins. He is to do this once a year from now on. This altar belongs completely to the LORD's service."

The Tax for the Meeting Tent

¹¹The LORD said to Moses, ¹²"When you count the people of Israel, every person must buy back his life from the LORD so that no terrible things will happen to the people when you number them. ¹³Every person who is counted must pay one-fifth of an ounce of silver. (This is set by using one-half of the Holy Place measure, which weighs two-fifths of an ounce.) This amount is a gift to the LORD. ¹⁴Every person who is counted and is twenty years old or older must give this amount to the LORD. ¹⁵A rich person must not give more than one-fifth of an ounce, and a poor person must not give less. You are paying this to the LORD to buy back your lives. ¹⁶Gather from the people of Israel this money paid to buy back their lives, and spend it on things for the service in the Meeting Tent. This payment will remind the LORD that the Israelites' lives have been bought back."

The Bronze Bowl

¹⁷The LORD said to Moses, ¹⁸"Make a bronze bowl, on a bronze stand, for washing. Put the bowl and stand between the Meeting Tent and the altar, and put water in the bowl. ¹⁹Aaron and his sons must wash their hands and feet with the water from this bowl. ²⁰Each time they enter the Meeting Tent they must wash with water so they will not die. Whenever they approach the altar to serve as priests and offer a sacrifice to the LORD by fire, ²¹they must wash their hands and their feet so they will not die. This is a rule which Aaron and his descendants are to keep from now on."

Oil for Appointing

²²Then the LORD said to Moses, ²³"Take the finest spices: twelve pounds of liquid myrrh, half that amount (that is, six pounds) of sweet-smelling cinnamon, six pounds of sweet-smelling cane, ²⁴and twelve pounds of cassia. Weigh all these by the Holy Place measure. Also take four quarts of olive oil, ²⁵and mix all these things like a perfume to make a holy olive oil. This special oil must be put on people and things to make them ready for service to God. ²⁶Put this oil on the Meeting Tent and the Ark of the Agreement, ²⁷on the table and all its dishes, on the lampstand and all its tools, and on the incense altar. ²⁸Also, put the oil on the altar for burnt offerings and on all its tools, as well as on the bowl and the stand under the bowl. ²⁹You will prepare all these things for service to God, and they will be very holy. Anything that touches these things must be holy.

³⁰"Put the oil on Aaron and his sons to give them for service to me, that they may serve me as priests. ³¹Tell the Israelites, 'This is to be my holy olive oil from now on. It is to be put on people and things to make them ready for service to God. ³²Do not pour it on the bodies of ordinary people, and do not make perfume the same way you make this oil. It is holy, and you must treat it as holy. ³³If anyone makes perfume like it or puts it on someone who is not a priest, that person must be cut off from his people.'"

Incense

³⁴Then the LORD said to Moses, "Take these sweet-smelling spices: resin, onycha, galbanum, and pure frankincense. Be sure that you have equal amounts of each. ³⁵Make incense as a person who makes perfume would do. Add salt to it to keep it pure and holy. ³⁶Beat some of the incense into a fine powder, and put it in front of the Ark of the Agreement in the Meeting Tent, where I will meet with you. You must use this incense powder only for its very special purpose. ³⁷Do not make incense for yourselves the same way you make this incense. Treat it as holy to the LORD. ³⁸Whoever makes incense like this to use as perfume must be cut off from his people."

PSALM 20:6–9

⁶Now I know the LORD helps his appointed king.
He answers him from his holy heaven and saves him with his strong right hand.
⁷Some trust in chariots, others in horses, but we trust the LORD our God.
⁸They are overwhelmed and defeated, but we march forward and win.
⁹LORD, save the king!
Answer us when we call for help.

PROVERBS 7:6–23

⁶Once while I was at the window of my house
I looked out through the shutters
⁷and saw some foolish, young men.
I noticed one of them had no wisdom.
⁸He was walking down the street near the corner
on the road leading to her house.
⁹It was the twilight of the evening;
the darkness of the night was just beginning.
¹⁰Then the woman approached him, dressed like a prostitute
and planning to trick him.
¹¹She was loud and stubborn
and never stayed at home.
¹²She was always out in the streets or in the city squares,

waiting around on the corners of the streets.
¹³She grabbed him and kissed him.
Without shame she said to him,
¹⁴"I made my fellowship offering and took some of the meat home.
Today I have kept my special promises.
¹⁵So I have come out to meet you;
I have been looking for you and have found you.
¹⁶I have covered my bed
with colored sheets from Egypt.
¹⁷I have made my bed smell sweet
with myrrh, aloes, and cinnamon.
¹⁸Come, let's make love until morning.
Let's enjoy each other's love.
¹⁹My husband is not home;
he has gone on a long trip.
²⁰He took a lot of money with him
and won't be home for weeks."
²¹By her clever words she made him give in;
by her pleasing words she led him into doing wrong.
²²All at once he followed her,
like an ox led to the butcher,
like a deer caught in a trap,
²³ and shot through the liver with an arrow.
Like a bird caught in a trap,
he didn't know what he did would kill him.

MATTHEW 25:1–30

A Story About Ten Bridesmaids

25 "At that time the kingdom of heaven will be like ten bridesmaids who took their lamps and went to wait for the bridegroom. ²Five of them were foolish and five were wise. ³The five foolish bridesmaids took their lamps, but they did not take more oil for the lamps to burn. ⁴The wise bridesmaids took their lamps and more oil in jars. ⁵Because the bridegroom was late, they became sleepy and went to sleep.

⁶"At midnight someone cried out, 'The bridegroom is coming! Come and meet him!' ⁷Then all the bridesmaids woke up and got their lamps ready. ⁸But the foolish ones said to the wise, 'Give us some of your oil,

because our lamps are going out.' ⁹The wise bridesmaids answered, 'No, the oil we have might not be enough for all of us. Go to the people who sell oil and buy some for yourselves.'

¹⁰"So while the five foolish bridesmaids went to buy oil, the bridegroom came. The bridesmaids who were ready went in with the bridegroom to the wedding feast. Then the door was closed and locked.

¹¹"Later the others came back and said, 'Sir, sir, open the door to let us in.' ¹²But the bridegroom answered, 'I tell you the truth, I don't want to know you.'

¹³"So always be ready, because you don't know the day or the hour the Son of Man will come.

A Story About Three Servants

¹⁴"The kingdom of heaven is like a man who was going to another place for a visit. Before he left, he called for his servants and told them to take care of his things while he was gone. ¹⁵He gave one servant five bags of gold, another servant two bags of gold, and a third servant one bag of gold, to each one as much as he could handle. Then he left. ¹⁶The servant who got five bags went quickly to invest the money and earned five more bags. ¹⁷In the same way, the servant who had two bags invested them and earned two more. ¹⁸But the servant who got one bag went out and dug a hole in the ground and hid the master's money.

¹⁹"After a long time the master came home and asked the servants what they did with his money. ²⁰The servant who was given five bags of gold brought five more bags to the master and said, 'Master, you trusted me to care for five bags of gold, so I used your five bags to earn five more.' ²¹The master answered, 'You did well. You are a good and loyal servant. Because you were loyal with small things, I will let you care for much greater things. Come and share my joy with me.'

²²"Then the servant who had been given two bags of gold came to the master and said, 'Master, you gave me two bags of gold to care for, so I used your two bags to earn two more.' ²³The master answered, 'You did well. You are a good and loyal servant. Because you were loyal with small things, I will let you care for much greater things. Come and share my joy with me.'

²⁴"Then the servant who had been given one bag of gold came to the master and said, 'Master, I knew that you were a hard man. You harvest things you did not plant. You gather crops where you did not sow any seed. ²⁵So I was afraid and went and hid your money in the ground. Here is your bag of gold.' ²⁶The master answered, 'You are a wicked and lazy servant! You say you knew that I harvest things I did not plant and that I gather crops where I did not sow any seed. ²⁷So you should have put my gold in the bank. Then, when I came home, I would have received my gold back with interest.'

²⁸"So the master told his other servants, 'Take the bag of gold from that servant and give it to the servant who has ten bags of gold. ²⁹Those who have much will get more, and they will have much more than they need. But those who do not have much will have everything taken away from them.' ³⁰Then the master said, 'Throw that useless servant outside, into the darkness where people will cry and grind their teeth with pain.'

FEBRUARY 10

EXODUS 31:1—32:35

Bezalel and Oholiab Help

31 Then the LORD said to Moses, ²"See, I have chosen Bezalel son of Uri from the tribe of Judah. (Uri was the son of Hur.) ³I have filled Bezalel with the Spirit of God and have given him the skill, ability, and knowledge to do all kinds of work. ⁴He is able to design pieces to be made from gold, silver, and bronze, ⁵to cut jewels and put them in metal, to carve wood, and to do all kinds of work. ⁶I have also chosen Oholiab son of Ahisamach from the tribe of Dan to work with Bezalel. I have given skills to all the craftsmen, and they will be able to make all these things I have commanded you: ⁷the Meeting Tent, the Ark of the Agreement, the lid that covers the Ark, and everything in the Tent. ⁸This includes the table and everything on it, the pure gold lampstand and everything with it, the altar of incense, ⁹the altar for burnt offerings and everything used with it, and the bowl and the stand under it. ¹⁰They will make the woven clothes and the holy clothes for Aaron and the clothes for his sons to wear when they serve as priests. ¹¹They will also make the special olive oil used in appointing people and things to the service of the LORD, and the sweet-smelling incense for the Holy Place.

"These workers will make all these things just as I have commanded you."

The Day of Rest

¹²Then the LORD said to Moses, ¹³"Tell the Israelites, 'You must keep the rules about my Sabbaths, because they will be a sign between you and me from now on. In this way you will know that I, the LORD, make you holy.

¹⁴"'Make the Sabbath a holy day. If anyone treats the Sabbath like any other day, that person must be put to death; anyone who works on the Sabbath day must be cut off from his people. ¹⁵There are six days for working, but the seventh day is a day of rest, a day holy for the LORD. Anyone who works during the Sabbath day must be put to death. ¹⁶The Israelites must remember the Sabbath day as an agreement between them and me that will continue from now on. ¹⁷The Sabbath day will be a sign between me and the Israelites forever, because in six days I, the LORD, made the sky and the earth. On the seventh day I did not work; I rested.'"

¹⁸When the LORD finished speaking to Moses on Mount Sinai, he gave him the two stone tablets with the Agreement written on them, written by the finger of God.

The People Make a Gold Calf

32 The people saw that a long time had passed and Moses had not come down from the mountain. So they gathered around Aaron and said, "Moses led us out of Egypt, but we don't know what has happened to him. Make us gods who will lead us."

²Aaron said to the people, "Take off the gold earrings that your wives, sons, and daughters are wearing, and bring them to me." ³So all the people took their gold earrings and brought them to Aaron. ⁴He took the gold from the people and formed it with a tool and made a statue of a calf. Then the people said, "Israel, these are your gods who brought you out of the land of Egypt!"

⁵When Aaron saw all this, he built an altar before the calf and announced, "Tomorrow there will be a special feast to honor the LORD." ⁶The people got up early the next morning and offered whole burnt offerings and fellowship offerings. They sat down to eat and drink, and then they got up and sinned sexually.

⁷Then the LORD said to Moses, "Go down from this mountain, because your people, the people you brought out of the land of Egypt, have ruined themselves. ⁸They have quickly turned away from the things I commanded them to do. They have made for themselves a calf covered with gold, and they have worshiped it and offered sacrifices to it. They have said, 'Israel, these are your gods who brought you out of Egypt.'"

⁹The LORD said to Moses, "I have seen these people, and I know that they are very stubborn. ¹⁰So now do not stop me. I am so angry with them that I am going to destroy them. Then I will make you and your descendants a great nation."

¹¹But Moses begged the LORD his God and said, "LORD, don't let your anger destroy your people, whom you brought out of Egypt with your great power and strength. ¹²Don't let the people of Egypt say, 'The LORD brought the Israelites out of Egypt for an evil purpose. He planned to kill them in the mountains and destroy them from the earth.' So stop being angry, and don't destroy your people. ¹³Remember the men who served you— Abraham, Isaac, and Israel. You promised

with an oath to them and said, 'I will make your descendants as many as the stars in the sky. I will give your descendants all this land that I have promised them, and it will be theirs forever.' " [14]So the LORD changed his mind and did not destroy the people as he had said he might.

[15]Then Moses went down the mountain, and in his hands he had the two stone tablets with the Agreement on them. The commands were written on both sides of each stone, front and back. [16]God himself had made the tablets, and God himself had written the commands on the tablets.

[17]When Joshua heard the sound of the people shouting, he said to Moses, "It sounds like war down in the camp."

[18]Moses answered:

"It is not a shout of victory;
    it is not a cry of defeat.
It is the sound of singing that I hear."

[19]When Moses came close to the camp, he saw the gold calf and the dancing, and he became very angry. He threw down the stone tablets that he was carrying and broke them at the bottom of the mountain. [20]Then he took the calf that the people had made and melted it in the fire. He ground it into powder. Then he threw the powder into the water and forced the Israelites to drink it.

[21]Moses said to Aaron, "What did these people do to you? Why did you cause them to do such a terrible sin?"

[22]Aaron answered, "Don't be angry, master. You know that these people are always ready to do wrong. [23]The people said to me, 'Moses led us out of Egypt, but we don't know what has happened to him. Make us gods who will lead us.' [24]So I told the people, 'Take off your gold jewelry.' When they gave me the gold, I threw it into the fire and out came this calf!"

[25]Moses saw that the people were acting wildly. Aaron had let them get out of control and become fools in front of their enemies. [26]So Moses stood at the entrance to the camp and said, "Let anyone who wants to follow the LORD come to me." And all the people from the family of Levi gathered around Moses.

[27]Then Moses said to them, "The LORD, the God of Israel, says this: 'Every man must put on his sword and go through the camp from one end to the other. Each man must kill his brother, his friend, and his neighbor.' "

[28]The people from the family of Levi obeyed Moses, and that day about three thousand of the Israelites died. [29]Then Moses said, "Today you have been given for service to the LORD. You were willing to kill your own sons and brothers, and God has blessed you for this."

[30]The next day Moses told the people, "You have done a terrible sin. But now I will go up to the LORD. Maybe I can do something so your sins will be removed." [31]So Moses went back to the LORD and said, "How terribly these people have sinned! They have made for themselves gods from gold. [32]Now, please forgive them of this sin. If you will not, then erase my name from the book in which you have written the names of your people."

[33]But the LORD told Moses, "I will erase from my book the names of the people who sin against me. [34]So now, go. Lead the people where I have told you, and my angel will lead you. When the time comes to punish, I will punish them for their sin."

[35]So the LORD caused terrible things to happen to the people because of what they did with the calf Aaron had made.

PSALM 21:1–7

Thanksgiving for the King

For the director of music. A psalm of David.

21 LORD, the king rejoices because of your strength;
    he is so happy when you save him!
[2]You gave the king what he wanted
    and did not refuse what he asked for.

Selah

[3]You put good things before him
    and placed a gold crown on his head.
[4]He asked you for life,
    and you gave it to him,
    so his years go on and on.
[5]He has great glory because you gave him
victories;
    you gave him honor and praise.

⁶You always gave him blessings;
   you made him glad because you were
      with him.
⁷The king truly trusts the LORD.
   Because God Most High always loves
      him,
   he will not be overwhelmed.

PROVERBS 7:24–27

²⁴Now, my sons, listen to me;
   pay attention to what I say.
²⁵Don't let yourself be tricked by such a
      woman;
   don't go where she leads you.
²⁶She has ruined many good men,
   and many have died because of her.
²⁷Her house is on the road to death,
   the road that leads down to the grave.

MATTHEW 25:31–46

The King Will Judge All People

³¹"The Son of Man will come again in his great glory, with all his angels. He will be King and sit on his great throne. ³²All the nations of the world will be gathered before him, and he will separate them into two groups as a shepherd separates the sheep from the goats. ³³The Son of Man will put the sheep on his right and the goats on his left.

³⁴"Then the King will say to the people on his right, 'Come, my Father has given you his blessing. Receive the kingdom God has prepared for you since the world was made. ³⁵I was hungry, and you gave me food. I was thirsty, and you gave me something to drink. I was alone and away from home, and you invited me into your house. ³⁶I was without clothes, and you gave me something to wear. I was sick, and you cared for me. I was in prison, and you visited me.'

³⁷"Then the good people will answer, 'Lord, when did we see you hungry and give you food, or thirsty and give you something to drink? ³⁸When did we see you alone and away from home and invite you into our house? When did we see you without clothes and give you something to wear? ³⁹When did we see you sick or in prison and care for you?'

⁴⁰"Then the King will answer, 'I tell you the truth, anything you did for even the least of my people here, you also did for me.'

⁴¹"Then the King will say to those on his left, 'Go away from me. You will be punished. Go into the fire that burns forever that was prepared for the devil and his angels. ⁴²I was hungry, and you gave me nothing to eat. I was thirsty, and you gave me nothing to drink. ⁴³I was alone and away from home, and you did not invite me into your house. I was without clothes, and you gave me nothing to wear. I was sick and in prison, and you did not care for me.'

⁴⁴"Then those people will answer, 'Lord, when did we see you hungry or thirsty or alone and away from home or without clothes or sick or in prison? When did we see these things and not help you?'

⁴⁵"Then the King will answer, 'I tell you the truth, anything you refused to do for even the least of my people here, you refused to do for me.'

⁴⁶"These people will go off to be punished forever, but the good people will go to live forever."

FEBRUARY 11

EXODUS 33:1–34:35

33 Then the LORD said to Moses, "You and the people you brought out of Egypt must leave this place. Go to the land that I promised with an oath to give to Abraham, Isaac, and Jacob when I said, 'I will give that land to your descendants.' ²I will send an angel to lead you, and I will force these people out of the land: the Canaanites, Amorites, Hittites, Perizzites, Hivites, and Jebusites. ³Go up to a fertile land. But I will not go with you, because I might destroy you on the way, since you are such a stubborn people."

⁴When the people heard this bad news, they became very sad, and none of them put on jewelry. ⁵This was because the LORD had said to Moses, "Tell the Israelites, 'You are a stubborn people. If I were to go with you even for a moment, I would destroy you. So take off all your jewelry, and I will decide what to do with you.'" ⁶So the people of Israel took off their jewelry at Mount Sinai.

The Meeting Tent

⁷Moses used to take a tent and set it up a long way outside the camp; he called it the "Meeting Tent." Anyone who wanted to ask the LORD about something would go to the Meeting Tent outside the camp. ⁸Whenever Moses went out to the Tent, all the people would rise and stand at the entrances of their tents, watching him until he entered the Meeting Tent. ⁹When Moses went into the Tent, the pillar of cloud would always come down and stay at the entrance of the Tent while the LORD spoke with Moses. ¹⁰Whenever the people saw the pillar of cloud at the entrance of the Tent, they stood and worshiped, each person at the entrance of his own tent.

¹¹The LORD spoke to Moses face to face as a man speaks with his friend. Then Moses would return to the camp, but Moses' young helper, Joshua son of Nun, did not leave the Tent.

¹²Moses said to the LORD, "You have told me to lead these people, but you did not say whom you would send with me. You have said to me, 'I know you very well, and I am pleased with you.' ¹³If I have truly pleased you, show me your plans so that I may know you and continue to please you. Remember that this nation is your people."

¹⁴The LORD answered, "I myself will go with you, and I will give you victory."

¹⁵Then Moses said to him, "If you yourself don't go with us, then don't send us away from this place. ¹⁶If you don't go with us, no one will know that you are pleased with me and with your people. These people and I will be no different from any other people on earth."

¹⁷Then the LORD said to Moses, "I will do what you ask, because I know you very well, and I am pleased with you."

Moses Sees God's Glory

¹⁸Then Moses said, "Now, please show me your glory."

¹⁹The LORD answered, "I will cause all my goodness to pass in front of you, and I will announce my name, the LORD, so you can hear it. I will show kindness to anyone to whom I want to show kindness, and I will show mercy to anyone to whom I want to show mercy. ²⁰But you cannot see my face, because no one can see me and live.

²¹"There is a place near me where you may stand on a rock. ²²When my glory passes that place, I will put you in a large crack in the rock and cover you with my hand until I have passed by. ²³Then I will take away my hand, and you will see my back. But my face must not be seen."

Moses Gets New Stone Tablets

34 The LORD said to Moses, "Cut two more stone tablets like the first two, and I will write the same words on them that were on the first two stones which you broke. ²Be ready tomorrow morning, and then come up on Mount Sinai. Stand before me there on the top of the mountain. ³No one may come with you or even be seen any place on the mountain. Not even the flocks or herds may eat grass near that mountain."

⁴So Moses cut two stone tablets like the first ones. Then early the next morning he went up Mount Sinai, just as the LORD had commanded him, carrying the two stone tablets with him. ⁵Then the LORD came down in the cloud and stood there with Moses, and the LORD called out his name: the LORD.

⁶The LORD passed in front of Moses and said, "I am the LORD. The LORD is a God who shows mercy, who is kind, who doesn't become angry quickly, who has great love and faithfulness ⁷and is kind to thousands of people. The LORD forgives people for evil, for sin, and for turning against him, but he does not forget to punish guilty people. He will punish not only the guilty people, but also their children, their grandchildren, their great-grandchildren, and their great-great-grandchildren."

[8]Then Moses quickly bowed to the ground and worshiped. [9]He said, "Lord, if you are pleased with me, please go with us. I know that these are stubborn people, but forgive our evil and our sin. Take us as your own people."

[10]Then the LORD said, "I am making this agreement with you. I will do miracles in front of all your people—things that have never before been done for any other nation on earth—and the people with you will see my work. I, the LORD, will do wonderful things for you. [11]Obey the things I command you today, and I will force out the Amorites, Canaanites, Hittites, Perizzites, Hivites, and Jebusites ahead of you. [12]Be careful that you don't make an agreement with the people who live in the land where you are going, because it will bring you trouble. [13]Destroy their altars, break their stone pillars, and cut down their Asherah idols. [14]Don't worship any other god, because I, the LORD, the Jealous One, am a jealous God.

[15]"Be careful that you don't make an agreement with the people who live in that land. When they worship their gods, they will invite you to join them. Then you will eat their sacrifices. [16]If you choose some of their daughters as wives for your sons and those daughters worship gods, they will lead your sons to do the same thing.

[17]"Do not make gods of melted metal.

[18]"Celebrate the Feast of Unleavened Bread. For seven days you must eat bread made without yeast as I commanded you. Do this during the month I have chosen, the month of Abib, because in that month you came out of Egypt.

[19]"The firstborn of every mother belongs to me, including every firstborn male animal that is born in your flocks and herds. [20]You may buy back a donkey by paying for it with a lamb, but if you don't want to buy back a donkey, you must break its neck. You must buy back all your firstborn sons.

"No one is to come before me without a gift.

[21]"You must work for six days, but on the seventh day you must rest—even during the planting season and the harvest season.

[22]"Celebrate the Feast of Weeks when you gather the first grain of the wheat harvest. And celebrate the Feast of Shelters in the fall.

[23]"Three times each year all your males must come before the Lord GOD, the God of Israel. [24]I will force out nations ahead of you and expand the borders of your land. You will go before the LORD your God three times each year, and at that time no one will try to take your land from you.

[25]"Do not offer the blood of a sacrifice to me with anything containing yeast, and do not leave any of the sacrifice of the Feast of Passover until the next morning.

[26]"Bring the best first crops that you harvest from your ground to the Tent of the LORD your God.

"You must not cook a young goat in its mother's milk."

[27]Then the LORD said to Moses, "Write down these words, because with these words I have made an agreement with you and Israel."

[28]Moses stayed there with the LORD forty days and forty nights, and during that time he did not eat food or drink water. And Moses wrote the words of the Agreement—the Ten Commandments—on the stone tablets.

The Face of Moses Shines

[29]Then Moses came down from Mount Sinai, carrying the two stone tablets of the Agreement in his hands. But he did not know that his face was shining because he had talked with the LORD. [30]When Aaron and all the people of Israel saw that Moses' face was shining, they were afraid to go near him. [31]But Moses called to them, so Aaron and all the leaders of the people returned to Moses, and he talked with them. [32]After that, all the people of Israel came near him, and he gave them all the commands that the LORD had given him on Mount Sinai.

[33]When Moses finished speaking to the people, he put a covering over his face. [34]Anytime Moses went before the LORD to speak with him, Moses took off the covering until he came out. Then Moses would come out and tell the Israelites what the LORD had commanded. [35]They would see that Moses' face was shining. So he would cover his face

again until the next time he went in to speak with the LORD.

PSALM 21:8–13

8Your hand is against all your enemies;
 those who hate you will feel your
  power.
9When you appear,
 you will burn them as in a furnace.
 In your anger you will swallow them up,
  and fire will burn them up.
10You will destroy their families from the
  earth;
 their children will not live.
11They made evil plans against you,
 but their traps won't work.
12You will make them turn their backs
 when you aim your arrows at them.
13Be supreme, LORD, in your power.
 We sing and praise your greatness.

PROVERBS 8:1–5

Listen to Wisdom

8 Wisdom calls to you like someone
  shouting;
 understanding raises her voice.
2On the hilltops along the road
 and at the crossroads, she stands
  calling.
3Beside the city gates,
 at the entrances into the city, she calls
  out:
4"Listen, everyone, I'm calling out to you;
 I am shouting to all people.
5You who are uneducated, seek wisdom.
 You who are foolish, get understanding.

MATTHEW 26:1–25

The Plan to Kill Jesus

26 After Jesus finished saying all these things, he told his followers, 2"You know that the day after tomorrow is the day of the Passover Feast. On that day the Son of Man will be given to his enemies to be crucified."

3Then the leading priests and the elders had a meeting at the palace of the high priest, named Caiaphas. 4At the meeting, they planned to set a trap to arrest Jesus and kill him. 5But they said, "We must not do it during the feast, because the people might cause a riot."

Perfume for Jesus' Burial

6Jesus was in Bethany at the house of Simon, who had a skin disease. 7While Jesus was there, a woman approached him with an alabaster jar filled with expensive perfume. She poured this perfume on Jesus' head while he was eating.

8His followers were upset when they saw the woman do this. They asked, "Why waste that perfume? 9It could have been sold for a great deal of money and the money given to the poor."

10Knowing what had happened, Jesus said, "Why are you troubling this woman? She did an excellent thing for me. 11You will always have the poor with you, but you will not always have me. 12This woman poured perfume on my body to prepare me for burial. 13I tell you the truth, wherever the Good News is preached in all the world, what this woman has done will be told, and people will remember her."

Judas Becomes an Enemy of Jesus

14Then one of the twelve apostles, Judas Iscariot, went to talk to the leading priests. 15He said, "What will you pay me for giving Jesus to you?" And they gave him thirty silver coins. 16After that, Judas watched for the best time to turn Jesus in.

Jesus Eats the Passover Meal

17On the first day of the Feast of Unleavened Bread, the followers came to Jesus. They said, "Where do you want us to prepare for you to eat the Passover meal?"

18Jesus answered, "Go into the city to a certain man and tell him, 'The Teacher says: "The chosen time is near. I will have the Passover with my followers at your house." ' "
19The followers did what Jesus told them to do, and they prepared the Passover meal.

20In the evening Jesus was sitting at the table with his twelve followers. 21As they were eating, Jesus said, "I tell you the truth, one of you will turn against me."

22This made the followers very sad. Each

one began to say to Jesus, "Surely, Lord, I am not the one who will turn against you, am I?" [23]Jesus answered, "The man who has dipped his hand with me into the bowl is the one who will turn against me. [24]The Son of Man will die, just as the Scriptures say. But how terrible it will be for the person who

hands the Son of Man over to be killed. It would be better for him if he had never been born." [25]Then Judas, who would give Jesus to his enemies, said to Jesus, "Teacher, surely I am not the one, am I?"

Jesus answered, "Yes, it is you."

FEBRUARY 12

EXODUS 35:1—36:38

Rules About the Sabbath

35 Moses gathered all the Israelite community together and said to them, "These are the things the LORD has commanded you to do. [2]You are to work for six days, but the seventh day will be a holy day, a Sabbath of rest to honor the LORD. Anyone who works on that day must be put to death. [3]On the Sabbath day you must not light a fire in any of your houses."

[4]Moses said to all the Israelites, "This is what the LORD has commanded: [5]From what you have, take an offering for the LORD. Let everyone who is willing bring this offering to the LORD: gold, silver, bronze, [6]blue, purple, and red thread, and fine linen, goat hair [7]and male sheepskins that are colored red. They may also bring fine leather, acacia wood, [8]olive oil for the lamps, spices for the special olive oil used for appointing priests and for the sweet-smelling incense, [9]onyx stones, and other jewels to be put on the holy vest and chest covering of the priests.

[10]"Let all the skilled workers come and make everything the LORD commanded: [11]the Holy Tent, its outer tent and its covering, the hooks, frames, crossbars, posts, and bases; [12]the Ark of the Agreement, its poles, lid, and the curtain in front of it; [13]the table, and its poles, all the things that go with the table, and the bread that shows we are in God's presence; [14]the lampstand for the light and all the things that go with it, the lamps, and olive oil for the light; [15]the altar of incense and its poles, the special oil and the sweet-smelling incense, the curtain for the

entrance of the Meeting Tent; [16]the altar of burnt offering and its bronze screen, its poles and all its tools, the bronze bowl and its base; [17]the curtains around the courtyard, their posts and bases, and the curtain at the entry to the courtyard; [18]the pegs of the Holy Tent and of the courtyard and their ropes; [19]the special clothes that the priest will wear in the Holy Place. These are the holy clothes for Aaron the priest and his sons to wear when they serve as priests."

[20]Then all the people of Israel went away from Moses. [21]Everyone who wanted to give came and brought a gift to the LORD for making the Meeting Tent, all the things in the Tent, and the special clothes. [22]All the men and women who wanted to give brought gold jewelry of all kinds—pins, earrings, rings, and bracelets. They all presented their gold to the LORD. [23]Everyone who had blue, purple, and red thread, and fine linen, and anyone who had goat hair or male sheepskins colored red or fine leather brought them to the LORD. [24]Everyone who could give silver or bronze brought that as a gift to the LORD, and everyone who had acacia wood to be used in the work brought it. [25]Every skilled woman used her hands to make the blue, purple, and red thread, and fine linen, and they brought what they had made. [26]All the women who were skilled and wanted to help made thread of the goat hair. [27]The leaders brought onyx stones and other jewels to put on the holy vest and chest covering for the priest. [28]They also brought spices and olive oil for the sweet-smelling incense, the special oil, and the oil to burn in the lamps. [29]All the men and women of Israel who wanted to help brought gifts to

the LORD for all the work the LORD had commanded Moses and the people to do.

[30]Then Moses said to the Israelites, "Look, the LORD has chosen Bezalel son of Uri the son of Hur, from the tribe of Judah. [31]The LORD has filled Bezalel with the Spirit of God and has given him the skill, ability, and knowledge to do all kinds of work. [32]He is able to design pieces to be made of gold, silver, and bronze, [33]to cut stones and jewels and put them in metal, to carve wood, and to do all kinds of work. [34]Also, the LORD has given Bezalel and Oholiab, the son of Ahisamach from the tribe of Dan, the ability to teach others. [35]The LORD has given them the skill to do all kinds of work. They are able to cut designs in metal and stone. They can plan and sew designs in the fine linen with the blue, purple, and red thread. And they are also able to weave things.

36[1]So Bezalel, Oholiab, and every skilled person will do the work the LORD has commanded, because he gave them the wisdom and understanding to do all the skilled work needed to build the Holy Tent."

[2]Then Moses called Bezalel, Oholiab, and all the other skilled people to whom the LORD had given skills, and they came because they wanted to help with the work. [3]They received from Moses everything the people of Israel had brought as gifts to build the Holy Tent. The people continued to bring gifts each morning because they wanted to. [4]So all the skilled workers left the work they were doing on the Holy Tent, [5]and they said to Moses, "The people are bringing more than we need to do the work the LORD commanded."

[6]Then Moses sent this command throughout the camp: "No man or woman should make anything else as a gift for the Holy Tent." So the people were kept from giving more, [7]because what they had was already more than enough to do all the work.

The Holy Tent

[8]Then the skilled workers made the Holy Tent. They made the ten curtains of blue, purple, and red cloth, and they sewed designs of creatures with wings on the curtains. [9]Each curtain was the same size—forty-two feet long and six feet wide. [10]Five of the curtains were fastened together to make one set, and the other five were fastened together to make another set. [11]Then they made loops of blue cloth along the edge of the end curtain on the first set of five, and they did the same thing with the other set of five. [12]There were fifty loops on one curtain and fifty loops on the other curtain, with the loops opposite each other. [13]They made fifty gold hooks to join the two curtains together so that the Holy Tent was joined together as one piece.

[14]Then the workers made another tent of eleven curtains made of goat hair, to put over the Holy Tent. [15]All eleven curtains were the same size—forty-five feet long and six feet wide. [16]The workers sewed five curtains together into one set and six together into another set. [17]They made fifty loops along the edge of the outside curtain of one set and fifty loops along the edge of the outside curtain of the other set. [18]Then they made fifty bronze rings to join the two sets of cloth together and make the tent one piece. [19]They made two more coverings for the outer tent—one made of male sheepskins colored red and the other made of fine leather.

[20]Then they made upright frames of acacia wood for the Holy Tent. [21]Each frame was fifteen feet tall and twenty-seven inches wide, [22]and there were two pegs side by side on each one. Every frame of the Holy Tent was made this same way. [23]They made twenty frames for the south side of the Tent, [24]and they made forty silver bases that went under the twenty frames. There were two bases for every frame—one for each peg of each frame. [25]They also made twenty frames for the north side of the Holy Tent [26]and forty silver bases—two to go under each frame. [27]They made six frames for the rear or west end of the Holy Tent [28]and two frames for the corners at the rear of the Holy Tent. [29]These two frames were doubled at the bottom and joined at the top with a metal ring. They did this for each of these corners. [30]So there were eight frames and sixteen silver bases—two bases under each frame.

[31]Then they made crossbars of acacia wood to connect the upright frames of the Holy Tent. Five crossbars held the frames together on one side of the Tent, [32]and five held the frames together on the other side. Also, five crossbars held the frames together on

the west end, at the rear of the Tent. ³³They made the middle crossbar run along the entire length of each side and rear of the Tent. It was set halfway up the frames. ³⁴They made gold rings on the sides of the frames to hold the crossbars, and they covered the frames and the crossbars with gold.

³⁵Then they made the curtain of blue, purple, and red thread, and fine linen. A skilled craftsman sewed designs of creatures with wings on it. ³⁶They made four posts of acacia wood for it and covered them with gold. Then they made gold hooks for the posts, as well as four silver bases in which to set the posts. ³⁷For the entrance to the Tent, they made a curtain of blue, purple, and red thread, and fine linen. A person who sewed well sewed designs on it. ³⁸Then they made five posts and hooks for it. They covered the tops of the posts and their bands with gold, and they made five bronze bases for the posts.

PSALM 22:1–8

The Prayer of a Suffering Man

For the director of music. To the tune of "The Doe of Dawn." A psalm of David.

22 My God, my God, why have you abandoned me?
You seem far from saving me,
  far away from my groans.
²My God, I call to you during the day,
  but you do not answer.
I call at night;
  I am not silent.

³You sit as the Holy One.
  The praises of Israel are your throne.
⁴Our ancestors trusted you;
  they trusted, and you saved them.
⁵They called to you for help
  and were rescued.
They trusted you
  and were not disappointed.

⁶But I am like a worm instead of a man.
  People make fun of me and hate me.
⁷Those who look at me laugh.
  They stick out their tongues and shake
    their heads.

⁸They say, "Turn to the LORD for help.
  Maybe he will save you.
If he likes you,
  maybe he will rescue you."

PROVERBS 8:6–11

⁶Listen, because I have important things
    to say,
  and what I tell you is right.
⁷What I say is true,
  I refuse to speak evil.
⁸Everything I say is honest;
  nothing I say is crooked or false.
⁹People with good sense know what I say
    is true;
  and those with knowledge know my
    words are right.
¹⁰Choose my teachings instead of silver,
  and knowledge rather than the finest
    gold.
¹¹Wisdom is more precious than rubies.
  Nothing you could want is equal to it.

MATTHEW 26:26–56

The Lord's Supper

²⁶While they were eating, Jesus took some bread and thanked God for it and broke it. Then he gave it to his followers and said, "Take this bread and eat it; this is my body." ²⁷Then Jesus took a cup and thanked God for it and gave it to the followers. He said, "Every one of you drink this. ²⁸This is my blood which is the new[n] agreement that God makes with his people. This blood is poured out for many to forgive their sins. ²⁹I tell you this: I will not drink of this fruit of the vine[n] again until that day when I drink it new with you in my Father's kingdom."

³⁰After singing a hymn, they went out to the Mount of Olives.

Jesus' Followers Will Leave Him

³¹Jesus told his followers, "Tonight you will all stumble in your faith on account of me, because it is written in the Scriptures:
'I will kill the shepherd,
  and the sheep will scatter.'   *Zechariah 13:7*
³²But after I rise from the dead, I will go ahead of you into Galilee."

26:28 new Some Greek copies do not have this word. Compare Luke 22:20. **26:29 fruit of the vine** Product of the grapevine; this may also be translated "wine."

[33]Peter said, "Everyone else may stumble in their faith because of you, but I will not."

[34]Jesus said, "I tell you the truth, tonight before the rooster crows you will say three times that you don't know me."

[35]But Peter said, "I will never say that I don't know you! I will even die with you!" And all the other followers said the same thing.

Jesus Prays Alone

[36]Then Jesus went with his followers to a place called Gethsemane. He said to them, "Sit here while I go over there and pray." [37]He took Peter and the two sons of Zebedee with him, and he began to be very sad and troubled. [38]He said to them, "My heart is full of sorrow, to the point of death. Stay here and watch with me."

[39]After walking a little farther away from them, Jesus fell to the ground and prayed, "My Father, if it is possible, do not give me this cup[n] of suffering. But do what you want, not what I want." [40]Then Jesus went back to his followers and found them asleep. He said to Peter, "You men could not stay awake with me for one hour? [41]Stay awake and pray for strength against temptation. The spirit wants to do what is right, but the body is weak."

[42]Then Jesus went away a second time and prayed, "My Father, if it is not possible for this painful thing to be taken from me, and if I must do it, I pray that what you want will be done."

[43]Then he went back to his followers, and again he found them asleep, because their eyes were heavy. [44]So Jesus left them and went away and prayed a third time, saying the same thing.

[45]Then Jesus went back to his followers and said, "Are you still sleeping and resting? The time has come for the Son of Man to be handed over to sinful people. [46]Get up, we must go. Look, here comes the man who has turned against me."

Jesus Is Arrested

[47]While Jesus was still speaking, Judas, one of the twelve apostles, came up. With him were many people carrying swords and clubs who had been sent from the leading priests and the Jewish elders of the people. [48]Judas had planned to give them a signal, saying, "The man I kiss is Jesus. Arrest him." [49]At once Judas went to Jesus and said, "Greetings, Teacher!" and kissed him.

[50]Jesus answered, "Friend, do what you came to do."

Then the people came and grabbed Jesus and arrested him. [51]When that happened, one of Jesus' followers reached for his sword and pulled it out. He struck the servant of the high priest and cut off his ear.

[52]Jesus said to the man, "Put your sword back in its place. All who use swords will be killed with swords. [53]Surely you know I could ask my Father, and he would give me more than twelve armies of angels. [54]But it must happen this way to bring about what the Scriptures say."

[55]Then Jesus said to the crowd, "You came to get me with swords and clubs as if I were a criminal. Every day I sat in the Temple teaching, and you did not arrest me there. [56]But all these things have happened so that it will come about as the prophets wrote." Then all of Jesus' followers left him and ran away.

FEBRUARY 13

EXODUS 37:1—38:31

The Ark of the Agreement

37 [1]Bezalel made the Ark of acacia wood; it was forty-five inches long, twenty-seven inches wide, and twenty-seven inches high. [2]He covered it, both inside and out, with pure gold, and he put a gold strip around it. [3]He made four gold rings for it and attached them to its four feet, with two rings

---

26:39 cup Jesus is talking about the terrible things that will happen to him. Accepting these things will be very hard, like drinking a cup of something bitter.

on each side. ⁴Then he made poles of acacia wood and covered them with gold. ⁵He put the poles through the rings on each side of the Ark to carry it. ⁶Then he made a lid of pure gold that was forty-five inches long and twenty-seven inches wide. ⁷Then Bezalel hammered gold to make two creatures with wings and attached them to each end of the lid. ⁸He made one creature on one end of the lid and the other creature on the other end. He attached them to the lid so that it would be one piece. ⁹The creatures' wings were spread upward, covering the lid, and the creatures faced each other across the lid.

The Table

¹⁰Then he made the table of acacia wood; it was thirty-six inches long, eighteen inches wide, and twenty-seven inches high. ¹¹He covered it with pure gold and put a gold strip around it. ¹²He made a frame three inches high that stood up all around the edge, and he put a gold strip around it. ¹³Then he made four gold rings for the table and attached them to the four corners of the table where the four legs were. ¹⁴The rings were put close to the frame around the top of the table, because they held the poles for carrying it. ¹⁵The poles for carrying the table were made of acacia wood and were covered with gold. ¹⁶He made of pure gold all the things that were used on the table: the plates, bowls, cups, and jars used for pouring the drink offerings.

The Lampstand

¹⁷Then he made the lampstand of pure gold, hammering out its base and stand. Its flower-like cups, buds, and petals were joined together in one piece with the base and stand. ¹⁸Six branches went out from the sides of the lampstand—three on one side and three on the other. ¹⁹Each branch had three cups shaped like almond flowers, and each cup had a bud and a petal. Each of the six branches going out from the lampstand was the same. ²⁰There were four more cups shaped like almond flowers on the lampstand itself, each with its buds and petals. ²¹Three pairs of branches went out from the lampstand. A bud was under the place where each pair was attached to the lampstand.

Each of the six branches going out from the lampstand was the same. ²²The buds, branches, and lampstand were all one piece of pure, hammered gold. ²³He made seven pure gold lamps for this lampstand, and he made pure gold wick trimmers and trays. ²⁴He used about seventy-five pounds of pure gold to make the lampstand and all the things that go with it.

The Altar for Burning Incense

²⁵Then he made the altar of incense out of acacia wood. It was square—eighteen inches long and eighteen inches wide—and it was thirty-six inches high. Each corner that stuck out like a horn was joined into one piece with the altar. ²⁶He covered the top and all the sides and the corners with pure gold, and he put gold trim around the altar. ²⁷He made two gold rings and put them below the trim on opposite sides of the altar; these rings held the poles for carrying it. ²⁸He made the poles of acacia wood and covered them with gold.

²⁹Then he made the holy olive oil for appointing the priests and the pure, sweet-smelling incense. He made them like a person who mixes perfumes.

The Altar for Burnt Offerings

38 Then he built the altar for burnt offerings out of acacia wood. The altar was square—seven and one-half feet long and seven and one-half feet wide—and it was four and one-half feet high. ²He made each corner stick out like a horn so that the horns and the altar were joined together in one piece. Then he covered the altar with bronze. ³He made all the tools of bronze to use on the altar: the pots, shovels, bowls for sprinkling blood, meat forks, and pans for carrying the fire. ⁴He made a large bronze screen to hold the burning wood for the altar and put it inside the altar, under its rim, halfway up from the bottom. ⁵He made bronze rings to hold the poles for carrying the altar, and he put them at the four corners of the screen. ⁶Then he made poles of acacia wood and covered them with bronze. ⁷He put the poles through the rings on both sides of the altar, to carry it. He made the altar of boards and left the inside hollow.

The Bronze Bowl

[8]He made the bronze bowl for washing, and he built it on a bronze stand. He used the bronze from mirrors that belonged to the women who served at the entrance to the Meeting Tent.

The Courtyard of the Holy Tent

[9]Then he made a wall of curtains to form a courtyard around the Holy Tent. On the south side the curtains were one hundred fifty feet long and were made of fine linen. [10]The curtains hung on silver hooks and bands, placed on twenty bronze posts with twenty bronze bases. [11]On the north side the wall of curtains was also one hundred fifty feet long, and it hung on silver hooks and bands on twenty posts with twenty bronze bases.

[12]On the west side of the courtyard, the wall of curtains was seventy-five feet long. It was held up by silver hooks and bands on ten posts with ten bases. [13]The east side was also seventy-five feet long. [14]On one side of the entry there was a wall of curtains twenty-two and one-half feet long, held up by three posts and three bases. [15]On the other side of the entry there was also a wall of curtains twenty-two and one-half feet long, held up by three posts and three bases. [16]All the curtains around the courtyard were made of fine linen. [17]The bases for the posts were made of bronze. The hooks and the bands on the posts were made of silver, and the tops of the posts were covered with silver also. All the posts in the courtyard had silver bands.

[18]The curtain for the entry of the courtyard was made of blue, purple, and red thread, and fine linen, sewn by a person who could sew well. The curtain was thirty feet long and seven and one-half feet high, the same height as the curtains around the courtyard. [19]It was held up by four posts and four bronze bases. The hooks and bands on the posts were made of silver, and the tops on the posts were covered with silver. [20]All the tent pegs for the Holy Tent and for the curtains around the courtyard were made of bronze.

[21]This is a list of the materials used to make the Holy Tent, where the Agreement was kept. Moses ordered the Levites to make this list, and Ithamar son of Aaron was in charge of keeping it. [22]Bezalel son of Uri, the son of Hur of the tribe of Judah, made everything the LORD commanded Moses. [23]Oholiab son of Ahisamach of the tribe of Dan helped him. He could cut designs into metal and stone; he was a designer and also skilled at sewing the blue, purple, and red thread, and fine linen.

[24]The total amount of gold used to build the Holy Tent was presented to the LORD. It weighed over 2,000 pounds, as set by the Holy Place measure.

[25]The silver was given by the members of the community who were counted. It weighed 7,550 pounds, as set by the Holy Place measure. [26]All the men twenty years old or older were counted. There were 603,550 men, and each man had to pay one-fifth of an ounce of silver, as set by the Holy Place measure. [27]Of this silver, 7,500 pounds were used to make the one hundred bases for the Holy Tent and for the curtain—75 pounds of silver in each base. [28]They used 50 pounds of silver to make the hooks for the posts and to cover the tops of the posts and to make the bands on them.

[29]The bronze which was presented to the LORD weighed about 5,000 pounds. [30]They used the bronze to make the bases at the entrance of the Meeting Tent, to make the altar and the bronze screen, and to make all the tools for the altar. [31]This bronze was also used to make bases for the wall of curtains around the courtyard and bases for curtains at the entry to the courtyard, as well as to make the tent pegs for the Holy Tent and the curtains that surrounded the courtyard.

PSALM 22:9–18

[9]You had my mother give birth to me.
   You made me trust you
      while I was just a baby.
[10]I have leaned on you since the day I was
      born;
   you have been my God since my
      mother gave me birth.
[11]So don't be far away from me.

Now trouble is near,
and there is no one to help.
[12]People have surrounded me like angry
bulls.
Like the strong bulls of Bashan, they
are on every side.
[13]Like hungry, roaring lions
they open their mouths at me.
[14]My strength is gone,
like water poured out onto the ground,
and my bones are out of joint.
My heart is like wax;
it has melted inside me.
[15]My strength has dried up like a clay pot,
and my tongue sticks to the top of my
mouth.
You laid me in the dust of death.
[16]Evil people have surrounded me;
like dogs they have trapped me.
They have bitten my arms and legs.
[17]I can count all my bones;
people look and stare at me.
[18]They divided my clothes among them,
and they threw lots for my clothing.

PROVERBS 8:12–21

[12]"I am wisdom, and I have good
judgment.
I also have knowledge and good sense.
[13]If you respect the LORD, you will also hate
evil.
I hate pride and bragging,
evil ways and lies.
[14]I have good sense and advice,
and I have understanding and power.
[15]I help kings to govern
and rulers to make fair laws.
[16]Princes use me to lead,
and so do all important people who
judge fairly.
[17]I love those who love me,
and those who seek me find me.
[18]Riches and honor are mine to give.
So are wealth and lasting success.
[19]What I give is better than the finest gold,
better than the purest silver.
[20]I do what is right
and follow the path of justice.
[21]I give wealth to those who love me,
filling their houses with treasures.

MATTHEW 26:57–75

Jesus Before the Leaders

[57]Those people who arrested Jesus led him to the house of Caiaphas, the high priest, where the teachers of the law and the elders were gathered. [58]Peter followed far behind to the courtyard of the high priest's house, and he sat down with the guards to see what would happen to Jesus.

[59]The leading priests and the whole Jewish council tried to find something false against Jesus so they could kill him. [60]Many people came and told lies about him, but the council could find no real reason to kill him. Then two people came and said, [61]"This man said, 'I can destroy the Temple of God and build it again in three days.'"

[62]Then the high priest stood up and said to Jesus, "Aren't you going to answer? Don't you have something to say about their charges against you?" [63]But Jesus said nothing.

Again the high priest said to Jesus, "I command you by the power of the living God: Tell us if you are the Christ, the Son of God."

[64]Jesus answered, "Those are your words. But I tell you, in the future you will see the Son of Man sitting at the right hand of God, the Powerful One, and coming on clouds in the sky."

[65]When the high priest heard this, he tore his clothes and said, "This man has said things that are against God! We don't need any more witnesses; you all heard him say these things against God. [66]What do you think?"

The people answered, "He should die."

[67]Then the people there spat in Jesus' face and beat him with their fists. Others slapped him. [68]They said, "Prove to us that you are a prophet, you Christ! Tell us who hit you!"

Peter Says He Doesn't Know Jesus

[69]At that time, as Peter was sitting in the courtyard, a servant girl came to him and said, "You also were with Jesus of Galilee."

[70]But Peter said to all the people there that he was never with Jesus. He said, "I don't know what you are talking about."

[71]When he left the courtyard and was at the gate, another girl saw him. She said to the people there, "This man was with Jesus of Nazareth."

[72]Again, Peter said he was never with him, saying, "I swear I don't know this man Jesus!"

[73]A short time later, some people standing there went to Peter and said, "Surely you are one of those who followed Jesus. The way you talk shows it."

[74]Then Peter began to place a curse on himself and swear, "I don't know the man." At once, a rooster crowed. [75]And Peter remembered what Jesus had told him: "Before the rooster crows, you will say three times that you don't know me." Then Peter went outside and cried painfully.

FEBRUARY 14

EXODUS 39:1—40:38

Clothes for the Priests

39 They used blue, purple, and red thread to make woven clothes for the priests to wear when they served in the Holy Place. They made the holy clothes for Aaron as the LORD had commanded Moses.

[2]They made the holy vest of gold, and blue, purple, and red thread, and fine linen. [3]They hammered the gold into sheets and then cut it into long, thin strips. They worked the gold into the blue, purple, and red thread, and fine linen. This was done by skilled craftsmen. [4]They made the shoulder straps for the holy vest, which were attached to the top corners of the vest and tied together over each shoulder. [5]The skillfully woven belt was made in the same way; it was joined to the holy vest as one piece. It was made of gold, and blue, purple, and red thread, and fine linen, the way the LORD commanded Moses.

[6]They put gold around the onyx stones and then wrote the names of the sons of Israel on these gems, as a person carves words and designs on a seal. [7]Then they attached the gems on the shoulder straps of the holy vest, as reminders of the twelve sons of Israel. This was done just as the LORD had commanded Moses.

[8]The skilled craftsmen made the chest covering like the holy vest; it was made of gold, and blue, purple, and red thread, and fine linen. [9]The chest covering was square—nine inches long and nine inches wide—and it was folded double to make a pocket. [10]Then they put four rows of beautiful jewels on it: In the first row there was a ruby, a topaz, and a yellow quartz; [11]in the second there was a turquoise, a sapphire, and an emerald; [12]in the third there was a jacinth, an agate, and an amethyst; [13]in the fourth there was a chrysolite, an onyx, and a jasper. Gold was put around these jewels to attach them to the chest covering, [14]and the names of the sons of Israel were carved on these twelve jewels as a person carves a seal. Each jewel had the name of one of the twelve tribes of Israel.

[15]They made chains of pure gold, twisted together like a rope, for the chest covering. [16]The workers made two gold pieces and two gold rings. They put the two gold rings on the two upper corners of the chest covering. [17]Then they put two gold chains in the two rings at the ends of the chest covering, [18]and they fastened the other two ends of the chains to the two gold pieces. They attached these gold pieces to the two shoulder straps in the front of the holy vest. [19]They made two gold rings and put them at the lower corners of the chest covering on the inside edge next to the holy vest. [20]They made two more gold rings on the bottom of the shoulder straps in front of the holy vest, near the seam, just above the woven belt of the holy vest. [21]They used a blue ribbon and tied the rings of the chest covering to the rings of the holy vest, connecting it to the woven belt. In this way the chest covering would not swing out from

the holy vest. They did all these things the way the LORD commanded.

²²Then they made the outer robe to be worn under the holy vest. It was woven only of blue cloth. ²³They made a hole in the center of the outer robe, with a woven collar sewn around it so it would not tear. ²⁴Then they made balls like pomegranates of blue, purple, and red thread, and fine linen and hung them around the bottom of the outer robe. ²⁵They also made bells of pure gold and hung these around the bottom of the outer robe between the balls. ²⁶So around the bottom of the outer robe there was a bell and a pomegranate ball, a bell and a pomegranate ball. The priest wore this outer robe when he served as priest, just as the LORD had commanded Moses.

²⁷They wove inner robes of fine linen for Aaron and his sons, ²⁸and they made turbans, headbands, and underclothes of fine linen. ²⁹Then they made the cloth belt of fine linen, and blue, purple, and red thread, and designs were sewn onto it, just as the LORD had commanded Moses.

³⁰They made a strip of pure gold, which is the holy crown, and carved these words in the gold, as one might carve on a seal: "Holy to the LORD." ³¹Then they tied this flat piece to the turban with a blue ribbon, as the LORD had commanded Moses.

³²So all the work on the Meeting Tent was finished. The Israelites did everything just as the LORD had commanded Moses. ³³Then they brought the Holy Tent to Moses: the Tent and all its furniture, hooks, frames, crossbars, posts, and bases; ³⁴the covering made of male sheepskins colored red, the covering made of fine leather, and the curtain that covered the entrance to the Most Holy Place; ³⁵the Ark of the Agreement, its poles and lid; ³⁶the table, all its containers, and the bread that showed they were in God's presence; ³⁷the pure gold lampstand with its lamps in a row, all its tools, and the olive oil for the light; ³⁸the gold altar, the special olive oil used for appointing priests, the sweet-smelling incense, and the curtain that covered the entrance to the Tent; ³⁹the bronze altar and its screen, its poles and all its tools, the bowl and its stand; ⁴⁰the cur-

tains for the courtyard with their posts and bases, the curtain that covered the entry to the courtyard, the cords, pegs, and all the things in the Meeting Tent. ⁴¹They brought the clothes for the priests to wear when they served in the Holy Tent—the holy clothes for Aaron the priest and the clothes for his sons, which they wore when they served as priests.

⁴²The Israelites had done all this work just as the LORD had commanded Moses. ⁴³Moses looked closely at all the work and saw they had done it just as the LORD had commanded. So Moses blessed them.

Setting Up the Holy Tent

40Then the LORD said to Moses: ²"On the first day of the first month, set up the Holy Tent, which is the Meeting Tent. ³Put the Ark of the Agreement in it and hang the curtain in front of the Ark. ⁴Bring in the table and arrange everything on the table that should be there. Then bring in the lampstand and set up its lamps. ⁵Put the gold altar for burning incense in front of the Ark of the Agreement, and put the curtain at the entrance to the Holy Tent.

⁶"Put the altar of burnt offerings in front of the entrance of the Holy Tent, the Meeting Tent. ⁷Put the bowl between the Meeting Tent and the altar, and put water in it. ⁸Set up the courtyard around the Holy Tent, and put the curtain at the entry to the courtyard.

⁹"Use the special olive oil and pour it on the Holy Tent and everything in it, in order to give the Tent and all that is in it for service to the LORD. They will be holy. ¹⁰Pour the special oil on the altar for burnt offerings and on all its tools. Give the altar for service to God, and it will be very holy. ¹¹Then pour the special olive oil on the bowl and the base under it so that they will be given for service to God.

¹²"Bring Aaron and his sons to the entrance of the Meeting Tent, and wash them with water. ¹³Then put the holy clothes on Aaron. Pour the special oil on him, and give him for service to God so that he may serve me as a priest. ¹⁴Bring Aaron's sons and put the inner robes on them. ¹⁵Pour the special

oil on them in the same way that you appointed their father as priest so that they
may also serve me as priests. Pouring oil on
them will make them a family of priests,
they and their descendants from now on."
[16]Moses did everything that the LORD commanded him.

[17]So the Holy Tent was set up on the first
day of the first month during the second
year after they left Egypt. [18]When Moses set
up the Holy Tent, he put the bases in place,
and he put the frames on the bases. Next he
put the crossbars through the rings of the
frames and set up the posts. [19]After that,
Moses spread the cloth over the Holy Tent
and put the covering over it, just as the
LORD commanded.

[20]Moses put the stone tablets that had
the Agreement written on them into the
Ark. He put the poles through the rings of
the Ark and put the lid on it. [21]Next he
brought the Ark into the Tent and hung the
curtain to cover the Ark, just as the LORD
commanded him.

[22]Moses put the table in the Meeting Tent
on the north side of the Holy Tent in front of
the curtain. [23]Then he put the bread on the
table before the LORD, just as the LORD commanded him. [24]Moses put the lampstand in
the Meeting Tent on the south side of the
Holy Tent across from the table. [25]Then he
put the lamps on the lampstand before the
LORD, just as the LORD commanded him.

[26]Moses put the gold altar for burning
incense in the Meeting Tent in front of the
curtain. [27]Then he burned sweet-smelling
incense on it, just as the LORD commanded
him. [28]Then he hung the curtain at the entrance to the Holy Tent.

[29]He put the altar for burnt offerings at
the entrance to the Holy Tent, the Meeting
Tent, and offered a whole burnt offering
and grain offerings on it, just as the LORD
commanded him. [30]Moses put the bowl between the Meeting Tent and the altar for
burnt offerings, and he put water in it for
washing. [31]Moses, Aaron, and Aaron's sons
used this water to wash their hands and
feet. [32]They washed themselves every time
they entered the Meeting Tent and every
time they went near the altar for burnt

offerings, just as the LORD commanded
Moses.

[33]Then Moses set up the courtyard
around the Holy Tent and the altar, and he
put up the curtain at the entry to the courtyard. So Moses finished the work.

The Cloud over the Holy Tent

[34]Then the cloud covered the Meeting
Tent, and the glory of the LORD filled the Holy
Tent. [35]Moses could not enter the Meeting
Tent, because the cloud had settled on it, and
the glory of the LORD filled the Holy Tent.

[36]When the cloud rose from the Holy Tent,
the Israelites would begin to travel, [37]but as
long as the cloud stayed on the Holy Tent,
they did not travel. They stayed in that place
until the cloud rose. [38]So the cloud of the
LORD was over the Holy Tent during the day,
and there was a fire in the cloud at night. So
all the Israelites could see the cloud while
they traveled.

PSALM 22:19–21

[19]But, LORD, don't be far away.
   You are my strength; hurry to help me.
[20]Save me from the sword;
   save my life from the dogs.
[21]Rescue me from the lion's mouth;
   save me from the horns of the bulls.

PROVERBS 8:22–31

[22]"I, wisdom, was with the LORD when he
      began his work,
   long before he made anything else.
[23]I was created in the very beginning,
   even before the world began.
[24]I was born before there were oceans,
   or springs overflowing with water,
[25]before the hills were there,
   before the mountains were put in place.
[26]God had not made the earth or fields,
   not even the first dust of the earth.
[27]I was there when God put the skies in
      place,
   when he stretched the horizon over the
      oceans,
[28]when he made the clouds above
   and put the deep underground springs
      in place.

[29]I was there when he ordered the sea
  not to go beyond the borders he had
  set.
I was there when he laid the earth's
  foundation.
[30] I was like a child by his side.
I was delighted every day,
  enjoying his presence all the time,
[31]enjoying the whole world,
  and delighted with all its people.

MATTHEW 27:1–31

Jesus Is Taken to Pilate

27 Early the next morning, all the leading priests and elders of the people decided that Jesus should die. [2]They tied him, led him away, and turned him over to Pilate, the governor.

Judas Kills Himself

[3]Judas, the one who had given Jesus to his enemies, saw that they had decided to kill Jesus. Then he was very sorry for what he had done. So he took the thirty silver coins back to the priests and the leaders, [4]saying, "I sinned; I handed over to you an innocent man."

The leaders answered, "What is that to us? That's your problem, not ours."

[5]So Judas threw the money into the Temple. Then he went off and hanged himself.

[6]The leading priests picked up the silver coins in the Temple and said, "Our law does not allow us to keep this money with the Temple money, because it has paid for a man's death." [7]So they decided to use the coins to buy Potter's Field as a place to bury strangers who died in Jerusalem. [8]That is why that field is still called the Field of Blood. [9]So what Jeremiah the prophet had said came true: "They took thirty silver coins. That is how little the Israelites thought he was worth. [10]They used those thirty silver coins to buy the potter's field, as the Lord commanded me."[n]

Pilate Questions Jesus

[11]Jesus stood before Pilate the governor, and Pilate asked him, "Are you the king of the Jews?"

Jesus answered, "Those are your words."

[12]When the leading priests and the elders accused Jesus, he said nothing.

[13]So Pilate said to Jesus, "Don't you hear them accusing you of all these things?"

[14]But Jesus said nothing in answer to Pilate, and Pilate was very surprised at this.

Pilate Tries to Free Jesus

[15]Every year at the time of Passover the governor would free one prisoner whom the people chose. [16]At that time there was a man in prison, named Barabbas,[n] who was known to be very bad. [17]When the people gathered at Pilate's house, Pilate said, "Whom do you want me to set free: Barabbas[n] or Jesus who is called the Christ?" [18]Pilate knew that they turned Jesus in to him because they were jealous.

[19]While Pilate was sitting there on the judge's seat, his wife sent this message to him: "Don't do anything to that man, because he is innocent. Today I had a dream about him, and it troubled me very much."

[20]But the leading priests and elders convinced the crowd to ask for Barabbas to be freed and for Jesus to be killed.

[21]Pilate said, "I have Barabbas and Jesus. Which do you want me to set free for you?"

The people answered, "Barabbas."

[22]Pilate asked, "So what should I do with Jesus, the one called the Christ?"

They all answered, "Crucify him!"

[23]Pilate asked, "Why? What wrong has he done?"

But they shouted louder, "Crucify him!"

[24]When Pilate saw that he could do nothing about this and that a riot was starting, he took some water and washed his hands[n] in front of the crowd. Then he said, "I am not guilty of this man's death. You are the ones who are causing it!"

[25]All the people answered, "We and our children will be responsible for his death."

[26]Then he set Barabbas free. But Jesus was beaten with whips and handed over to the soldiers to be crucified.

[27]The governor's soldiers took Jesus into

27:9–10 "They . . . commanded me." See Zechariah 11:12–13 and Jeremiah 32:6–9.   **27:16–17 Barabbas** Some Greek copies read "Jesus Barabbas."   **27:24 washed his hands** He did this as a sign to show that he wanted no part in what the people did.

the governor's palace, and they all gathered around him. [28]They took off his clothes and put a red robe on him. [29]Using thorny branches, they made a crown, put it on his head, and put a stick in his right hand. Then the soldiers bowed before Jesus and made fun of him, saying, "Hail, King of the Jews!" [30]They spat on Jesus. Then they took his stick and began to beat him on the head. [31]After they finished, the soldiers took off the robe and put his own clothes on him again. Then they led him away to be crucified.

FEBRUARY 15

LEVITICUS 1:1—2:16

The Burnt Offering

1 The LORD called to Moses and spoke to him from the Meeting Tent, saying, [2]"Tell the people of Israel: 'When you bring an offering to the LORD, bring as your offering an animal from the herd or flock.

[3]" 'If the offering is a whole burnt offering from the herd, it must be a male that has nothing wrong with it. The person must take the animal to the entrance of the Meeting Tent so that the LORD will accept the offering. [4]He must put his hand on the animal's head, and the LORD will accept it to remove the person's sin so he will belong to God. [5]He must kill the young bull before the LORD, and Aaron's sons, the priests, must bring its blood and sprinkle it on all sides of the altar at the entrance to the Meeting Tent. [6]After that he will skin the animal and cut it into pieces. [7]The priests, when they have put wood and fire on the altar, [8]are to lay the head, the fat, and other pieces on the wood that is on the fire of the altar. [9]The animal's inner organs and legs must be washed with water. Then the priest must burn all the animal's parts on the altar. It is a whole burnt offering, an offering made by fire, and its smell is pleasing to the LORD.

[10]" 'If the burnt offering is a sheep or a goat from the flock, it must be a male that has nothing wrong with it. [11]The person must kill the animal on the north side of the altar before the LORD, and Aaron's sons, the priests, must sprinkle its blood on all sides of the altar. [12]The person must cut the animal into pieces, and the priest must lay them, with the head and fat, on the wood that is on the fire of the altar. [13]The person must wash the animal's inner organs and legs with water, and then the priest must burn all its parts on the altar. It is a whole burnt offering, an offering made by fire, and its smell is pleasing to the LORD.

[14]" 'If the whole burnt offering for the LORD is a bird, it must be a dove or a young pigeon. [15]The priest will bring it to the altar and pull off its head, which he will burn on the altar; the bird's blood must be drained out on the side of the altar. [16]The priest must remove the bird's crop[n] and its contents and throw them on the east side of the altar, where the ashes are. [17]Then he must tear the bird open by its wings without dividing it into two parts. He must burn the bird on the altar, on the wood which is on the fire. It is a whole burnt offering, an offering made by fire, and its smell is pleasing to the LORD.

The Grain Offering

2 " 'When anyone offers a grain offering to the LORD, it must be made from fine flour. The person must pour oil on it, put incense on it, [2]and then take it to Aaron's sons, the priests. The priest must take a handful of the fine flour and oil and all the incense, and burn it on the altar as a memorial portion. It is an offering made by fire, and its smell is pleasing to the LORD. [3]The rest of the grain offering will belong to Aaron and the priests;

1:16 crop A small bag inside a bird's throat. When a bird eats, its food goes into this part first. There, the food is made soft before it goes into the stomach.

it is a most holy part of the offerings made by fire to the LORD.

4" 'If you bring a grain offering that was baked in the oven, it must be made from fine flour. It may be loaves made without yeast and mixed with oil, or it may be wafers made without yeast that have oil poured over them. ⁵If your grain offering is cooked on a griddle, it must be made, without yeast, of fine flour mixed with oil. ⁶Crumble it and pour oil over it; it is a grain offering. ⁷If your grain offering is cooked in a pan, it must be made from fine flour and oil. ⁸Bring the grain offering made of these things to the LORD. Give it to the priest, and he will take it to the altar. ⁹He will take out the memorial portion from the grain offering and burn it on the altar, as an offering made by fire. Its smell is pleasing to the LORD. ¹⁰The rest of the grain offering belongs to Aaron and the priests. It is a most holy part of the offerings made to the LORD by fire.

11" 'Every grain offering you bring to the LORD must be made without yeast, because you must not burn any yeast or honey in an offering made by fire to the LORD. ¹²You may bring yeast and honey to the LORD as an offering from the first harvest, but they must not be burned on the altar as a pleasing smell. ¹³You must also put salt on all your grain offerings. Salt stands for your agreement with God that will last forever; do not leave it out of your grain offering. You must add salt to all your offerings.

14" 'If you bring a grain offering from the first harvest to the LORD, bring crushed heads of new grain roasted in the fire. ¹⁵Put oil and incense on it; it is a grain offering. ¹⁶The priest will burn the memorial portion of the crushed grain and oil, with the incense on it. It is an offering by fire to the LORD.

PSALM 22:22–31

²²Then I will tell my brothers and sisters
    about you;
  I will praise you in the public meeting.
²³Praise the LORD, all you who respect him.
  All you descendants of Jacob, honor him;
    fear him, all you Israelites.
²⁴He does not ignore those in trouble.
  He doesn't hide from them

but listens when they call out to him.
²⁵LORD, I praise you in the great meeting of
    your people;
  these worshipers will see me do what I
    promised.
²⁶Poor people will eat until they are full;
  those who look to the LORD will praise
    him.
  May your hearts live forever!
²⁷People everywhere will remember
  and will turn to the LORD.
  All the families of the nations
    will worship him
²⁸because the LORD is King,
  and he rules the nations.

²⁹All the powerful people on earth will eat
    and worship.
  Everyone will bow down to him,
    all who will one day die.
³⁰The people in the future will serve him;
  they will always be told about the Lord.
³¹They will tell that he does what is right.
  People who are not yet born
  will hear what God has done.

PROVERBS 8:32–36

³²"Now, my children, listen to me,
  because those who follow my ways are
    happy.
³³Listen to my teaching, and you will be
    wise;
  do not ignore it.
³⁴Happy are those who listen to me,
  watching at my door every day,
  waiting at my open doorway.
³⁵Those who find me find life,
  and the LORD will be pleased with
    them.
³⁶Those who do not find me hurt
    themselves.
  Those who hate me love death."

MATTHEW 27:32–56

Jesus Is Crucified

³²As the soldiers were going out of the city with Jesus, they forced a man from Cyrene, named Simon, to carry the cross for Jesus. ³³They all came to the place called Golgotha, which means the Place of the Skull. ³⁴The

soldiers gave Jesus wine mixed with gall[n] to drink. He tasted the wine but refused to drink it. [35]When the soldiers had crucified him, they threw lots to decide who would get his clothes.[n] [36]The soldiers sat there and continued watching him. [37]They put a sign above Jesus' head with a charge against him. It said: THIS IS JESUS, THE KING OF THE JEWS. [38]Two robbers were crucified beside Jesus, one on the right and the other on the left. [39]People walked by and insulted Jesus and shook their heads, [40]saying, "You said you could destroy the Temple and build it again in three days. So save yourself! Come down from that cross if you are really the Son of God!"

[41]The leading priests, the teachers of the law, and the Jewish elders were also making fun of Jesus. [42]They said, "He saved others, but he can't save himself! He says he is the king of Israel! If he is the king, let him come down now from the cross. Then we will believe in him. [43]He trusts in God, so let God save him now, if God really wants him. He himself said, 'I am the Son of God.'" [44]And in the same way, the robbers who were being crucified beside Jesus also insulted him.

Jesus Dies

[45]At noon the whole country became dark, and the darkness lasted for three hours. [46]About three o'clock Jesus cried out in a loud voice, "Eli, Eli, lama sabachthani?" This means, "My God, my God, why have you abandoned me?"

[47]Some of the people standing there who heard this said, "He is calling Elijah."

[48]Quickly one of them ran and got a sponge and filled it with vinegar and tied it to a stick and gave it to Jesus to drink. [49]But the others said, "Don't bother him. We want to see if Elijah will come to save him."

[50]But Jesus cried out again in a loud voice and died.

[51]Then the curtain in the Temple[n] was torn into two pieces, from the top to the bottom. Also, the earth shook and rocks broke apart. [52]The graves opened, and many of God's people who had died were raised from the dead. [53]They came out of the graves after Jesus was raised from the dead and went into the holy city, where they appeared to many people.

[54]When the army officer and the soldiers guarding Jesus saw this earthquake and everything else that happened, they were very frightened and said, "He really was the Son of God!"

[55]Many women who had followed Jesus from Galilee to help him were standing at a distance from the cross, watching. [56]Mary Magdalene, and Mary the mother of James and Joseph, and the mother of James and John were there.

FEBRUARY 16

LEVITICUS 3:1—4:35

The Fellowship Offering

3 " 'If a person's fellowship offering to the LORD is from the herd, it may be a male or female, but it must have nothing wrong with it. [2]The person must put his hand on the animal's head and kill it at the entrance to the Meeting Tent. Then Aaron's sons, the priests, must sprinkle the blood on all sides of the altar. [3]From the fellowship offering he must make a sacrifice by fire to the LORD. He must offer the fat of the animal's inner organs (both the fat that is in them and that covers them), [4]both kidneys with the fat that is on them near the lower back muscle, and the best part of the liver, which he will remove with the kidneys. [5]Then the priests

---

27:34 gall Probably a drink of wine mixed with drugs to help a person feel less pain.   **27:35 clothes** Some Greek copies continue, "So what God said through the prophet came true, 'They divided my clothes among them, and they threw lots for my clothing.' " See Psalm 22:18.   **27:51 curtain in the Temple** A curtain divided the Most Holy Place from the other part of the Temple. That was the special building in Jerusalem where God commanded the Jewish people to worship him.

will burn these parts on the altar, on the whole burnt offering that is on the wood of the fire. It is an offering made by fire, and its smell is pleasing to the LORD.

⁶" 'If a person's fellowship offering to the LORD is a lamb or a goat, it may be a male or female, but it must have nothing wrong with it. ⁷If he offers a lamb, he must bring it before the LORD ⁸and put his hand on its head. Then he must kill the animal in front of the Meeting Tent, and the priests must sprinkle its blood on all sides of the altar. ⁹From the fellowship offering the person must make a sacrifice by fire to the LORD. He must bring the fat, the whole fat tail cut off close to the backbone, the fat of the inner organs (both the fat that is in them and that covers them), ¹⁰both kidneys with the fat that is on them, near the lower back muscle, and the best part of the liver, which he will remove with the kidneys. ¹¹Then the priest will burn these parts on the altar as food; it will be an offering made by fire to the LORD.

¹²" 'If a person's offering is a goat, he must offer it before the LORD ¹³and put his hand on its head. Then he must kill it in front of the Meeting Tent, and the priests must sprinkle its blood on all sides of the altar. ¹⁴From this offering the person must make a sacrifice by fire to the LORD. He must offer all the fat of the goat's inner organs (both the fat that is in them and that covers them), ¹⁵both kidneys with the fat that is on them near the lower back muscle, and the best part of the liver, which he will remove with the kidneys. ¹⁶The priest will burn these parts on the altar as food. It is an offering made by fire, and its smell is pleasing to the LORD. All the fat belongs to the LORD.

¹⁷" 'This law will continue for people from now on, wherever you live: You must not eat any fat or blood.' "

The Sin Offering

4 The LORD said to Moses, ²"Tell the people of Israel this: 'When a person sins by accident and does some things the LORD has commanded not to be done, that person must do these things:

³" 'If the appointed priest sins so that he brings guilt on the people, then he must offer a young bull to the LORD, one that has nothing wrong with it, as a sin offering for the sin he has done. ⁴He will bring the bull to the entrance of the Meeting Tent in front of the LORD, put his hand on its head, and kill it before the LORD. ⁵Then the appointed priest must bring some of the bull's blood into the Meeting Tent. ⁶The priest is to dip his finger into the blood and sprinkle it seven times before the LORD in front of the curtain of the Most Holy Place. ⁷The priest must also put some of the blood on the corners of the altar of incense that stands before the LORD in the Meeting Tent. The rest of the blood he must pour out at the bottom of the altar of burnt offering, which is at the entrance of the Meeting Tent. ⁸He must remove all the fat from the bull of the sin offering—the fat on and around the inner organs, ⁹both kidneys with the fat that is on them near the lower back muscle, and the best part of the liver which he will remove with the kidneys. ¹⁰(He must do this in the same way the fat is removed from the bull of the fellowship offering.) Then the priest must burn the animal parts on the altar of burnt offering. ¹¹But the priest must carry off the skin of the bull and all its meat, along with the rest of the bull—its head, legs, intestines, and other inner organs. ¹²He must take it outside the camp to the special clean place where the ashes are poured out. He must burn it on a wood fire on the pile of ashes.

¹³" 'If the whole nation of Israel sins accidentally without knowing it and does something the LORD has commanded not to be done, they are guilty. ¹⁴When they learn about the sin they have done, they must offer a young bull as a sin offering and bring it before the Meeting Tent. ¹⁵The elders of the group of people must put their hands on the bull's head before the LORD, and it must be killed before the LORD. ¹⁶Then the appointed priest must bring some of the bull's blood into the Meeting Tent. ¹⁷Dipping his finger in the blood, he must sprinkle it seven times before the LORD in front of the curtain. ¹⁸Then he must put some of the

blood on the corners of the altar that is before the LORD in the Meeting Tent. The priest must pour out the rest of the blood at the bottom of the altar of burnt offering, which is at the entrance to the Meeting Tent. ¹⁹He must remove all the fat from the animal and burn it on the altar; ²⁰he will do the same thing with this bull that he did with the first bull of the sin offering. In this way the priest removes the sins of the people so they will belong to the LORD and be forgiven. ²¹Then the priest must carry the bull outside the camp and burn it, just as he did with the first bull. This is the sin offering for the whole community.

²²" 'If a ruler sins by accident and does something the LORD his God has commanded must not be done, he is guilty. ²³When he learns about his sin, he must bring a male goat that has nothing wrong with it as his offering. ²⁴The ruler must put his hand on the goat's head and kill it in the place where they kill the whole burnt offering before the LORD; it is a sin offering. ²⁵The priest must take some of the blood of the sin offering on his finger and put it on the corners of the altar of burnt offering. He must pour out the rest of the blood at the bottom of the altar of burnt offering. ²⁶He must burn all the goat's fat on the altar in the same way he burns the fat of the fellowship offerings. In this way the priest removes the ruler's sin so he belongs to the LORD, and the LORD will forgive him.

²⁷" 'If any person in the community sins by accident and does something which the LORD has commanded must not be done, he is guilty. ²⁸When the person learns about his sin, he must bring a female goat that has nothing wrong with it as an offering for his sin. ²⁹He must put his hand on the animal's head and kill it at the place of the whole burnt offering. ³⁰Then the priest must take some of the goat's blood on his finger and put it on the corners of the altar of burnt offering. He must pour out the rest of the goat's blood at the bottom of the altar. ³¹Then the priest must remove all the goat's fat in the same way the fat is removed from

the fellowship offerings. He must burn it on the altar as a smell pleasing to the LORD. In this way the priest will remove that person's sin so he will belong to the LORD, and the LORD will forgive him.

³²" 'If this person brings a lamb as his offering for sin, he must bring a female that has nothing wrong with it. ³³He must put his hand on the animal's head and kill it as a sin offering in the place where the whole burnt offering is killed. ³⁴The priest must take some of the blood from the sin offering on his finger and put it on the corners of the altar of burnt offering. He must pour out the rest of the lamb's blood at the bottom of the altar. ³⁵Then the priest must remove all the lamb's fat in the same way that the lamb's fat is removed from the fellowship offerings. He must burn the pieces on the altar on top of the offerings made by fire for the LORD. In this way the priest will remove that person's sins so he will belong to the LORD, and the LORD will forgive him.

PSALM 23:1–6

The Lord the Shepherd

A psalm of David.

23 The LORD is my shepherd;
I have everything I need.
²He lets me rest in green pastures.
He leads me to calm water.
³He gives me new strength.
He leads me on paths that are right
for the good of his name.
⁴Even if I walk through a very dark
valley,
I will not be afraid,
because you are with me.
Your rod and your shepherd's staff
comfort me.

⁵You prepare a meal for me
in front of my enemies.
You pour oil of blessing on my head;ⁿ
you fill my cup to overflowing.
⁶Surely your goodness and love will be
with me

23:5 pour oil . . . head This can mean that God gave him great wealth and blessed him.

all my life,
and I will live in the house of the LORD
forever.

PROVERBS 9:1–6

Being Wise or Foolish

9 Wisdom has built her house;
she has made its seven columns.
[2]She has prepared her food and wine;
she has set her table.
[3]She has sent out her servant girls,
and she calls out from the highest
place in the city.
[4]She says to those who are uneducated,
"Come in here, you foolish people!
[5]Come and eat my food
and drink the wine I have prepared.
[6]Stop your foolish ways, and you will live;
take the road of understanding.

MATTHEW 27:57–66

Jesus Is Buried

[57]That evening a rich man named Joseph, a follower of Jesus from the town of Arimathea, came to Jerusalem. [58]Joseph went to Pilate and asked to have Jesus' body.

So Pilate gave orders for the soldiers to give it to Joseph. [59]Then Joseph took the body and wrapped it in a clean linen cloth. [60]He put Jesus' body in a new tomb that he had cut out of a wall of rock, and he rolled a very large stone to block the entrance of the tomb. Then Joseph went away. [61]Mary Magdalene and the other woman named Mary were sitting near the tomb.

The Tomb of Jesus Is Guarded

[62]The next day, the day after Preparation Day, the leading priests and the Pharisees went to Pilate. [63]They said, "Sir, we remember that while that liar was still alive he said, 'After three days I will rise from the dead.' [64]So give the order for the tomb to be guarded closely till the third day. Otherwise, his followers might come and steal the body and tell people that he has risen from the dead. That lie would be even worse than the first one."

[65]Pilate said, "Take some soldiers and go guard the tomb the best way you know." [66]So they all went to the tomb and made it safe from thieves by sealing the stone in the entrance and putting soldiers there to guard it.

FEBRUARY 17

LEVITICUS 5:1—6:30

Special Types of Accidental Sins

5 " 'If a person is ordered to tell in court what he has seen or what he knows and he does not tell the court, he is guilty of sin.
[2]" 'Or someone might touch something unclean, such as the dead body of an unclean wild animal or an unclean farm animal or an unclean crawling animal. Even if he does not know that he touched it, he will still be unclean and guilty of sin.
[3]" 'Someone might touch human uncleanness—anything that makes someone unclean—and not know it. But when he learns about it, he will be guilty.

[4]" 'Or someone might make a promise before the LORD without thinking. It might be a promise to do something bad or something good; it might be about anything. Even if he forgets about it, when he remembers, he will be guilty.
[5]" 'When anyone is guilty of any of these things, he must tell how he sinned. [6]He must bring an offering to the LORD as a penalty for sin; it must be a female lamb or goat from the flock. The priest will perform the acts to remove that person's sin so he will belong to the LORD.
[7]" 'But if the person cannot afford a lamb, he must bring two doves or two young pigeons to the LORD as the penalty for his sin. One bird must be for a sin offering, and the

other must be for a whole burnt offering. [8]He must bring them to the priest, who will first offer the one for the sin offering. He will pull the bird's head from its neck, but he will not pull it completely off. [9]He must sprinkle the blood from the sin offering on the side of the altar, and then he must pour the rest of the blood at the bottom of the altar; it is a sin offering. [10]Then the priest must offer the second bird as a whole burnt offering, as the law says. In this way the priest will remove the person's sin so he will belong to the LORD, and the LORD will forgive him.

[11]" 'If the person cannot afford two doves or two pigeons, he must bring about two quarts of fine flour as an offering for sin. He must not put oil or incense on the flour, because it is a sin offering. [12]He must bring the flour to the priest. The priest will take a handful of the flour as a memorial offering and burn it on the altar on top of the offerings made by fire to the LORD; it is a sin offering. [13]In this way the priest will remove the person's sins so he will belong to the LORD, and the LORD will forgive him. What is left of the sin offering belongs to the priest, like the grain offering.' "

The Penalty Offering

[14]The LORD said to Moses, [15]"If a person accidentally sins and does something against the holy things of the LORD, he must bring from the flock a male sheep that has nothing wrong with it. This will be his penalty offering to the LORD. Its value in silver must be correct as set by the Holy Place measure. It is a penalty offering. [16]That person must pay for the sin he did against the holy thing, adding one-fifth to its value. Then he must give it all to the priest. In this way the priest will remove the person's sin so he will belong to the LORD, by using the male sheep as the penalty offering. And the LORD will forgive the person.

[17]"If a person sins and does something the LORD has commanded not to be done, even if he does not know it, he is still guilty. He is responsible for his sin. [18]He must bring the priest a male sheep from the flock, one that has nothing wrong with it and that is worth the correct amount. It will be a

penalty offering. Though the person sinned without knowing it, with this offering the priest will remove the sin so the person will belong to the LORD, and the LORD will forgive him. [19]The person is guilty of doing wrong, so he must give the penalty offering to the LORD."

6 The LORD said to Moses, [2]"A person might sin against the LORD by doing one of these sins: He might lie about what happened to something he was taking care of for someone else, or he might lie about a promise he made. He might steal something or cheat someone. [3]He might find something that had been lost and then lie about it. He might make a promise before the LORD about something and not mean it, or he might do some other sin. [4]If he does any of these things, he is guilty of sin. He must bring back whatever he stole or whatever he took by cheating. He must bring back the thing he took care of for someone else. He must bring back what he found and lied about [5]or what he made a false promise about. He must pay the full price plus an extra one-fifth of the value of what he took. He must give the money to the true owner on the day he brings his penalty offering. [6]He must bring his penalty to the priest—a male sheep from the flock, one that does not have anything wrong with it and that is worth the correct amount. It will be a penalty offering to the LORD. [7]Then the priest will perform the acts to remove that person's sin so he will belong to the LORD, and the LORD will forgive him for the sins that made him guilty."

The Whole Burnt Offering

[8]The LORD said to Moses, [9]"Give this command to Aaron and the priests: 'These are the teachings about the whole burnt offering: The burnt offering must stay on the altar all night until morning, and the altar's fire must be kept burning. [10]The priest must put on his linen robe and linen underclothes next to his body. Then he will remove the ashes from the burnt offering on the altar and put them beside the altar. [11]Then he must take off those clothes and put on others and carry the ashes outside the camp to

a special clean place. [12]But the fire must be kept burning on the altar; it must not be allowed to go out. The priest must put more firewood on the altar every morning, place the whole burnt offering on the fire, and burn the fat of the fellowship offerings. [13]The fire must be kept burning on the altar all the time; it must not go out.

The Grain Offering

[14]" 'These are the teachings about the grain offering: The priests must bring it to the LORD in front of the altar. [15]The priest must take a handful of fine flour, with the oil and all of the incense on it, and burn the grain offering on the altar as a memorial offering to the LORD. Its smell is pleasing to him. [16]Aaron and the priests may eat what is left, but it must be eaten without yeast in a holy place. They must eat it in the courtyard of the Meeting Tent. [17]It must not be cooked with yeast. I have given it as their share of the offerings made to me by fire; it is most holy, like the sin offering and the penalty offering. [18]Any male descendant of Aaron may eat it as his share of the offerings made to the LORD by fire, and this will continue from now on. Whatever touches these offerings shall become holy.' "

[19]The LORD said to Moses, [20]"This is the offering Aaron and the priests must bring to the LORD on the day they appoint Aaron as high priest: They must bring two quarts of fine flour for a continual grain offering, half of it in the morning and half in the evening. [21]The fine flour must be mixed with oil and cooked on a griddle. Bring it when it is well mixed. Present the grain offering that is broken into pieces, and it will be a smell that is pleasing to the LORD. [22]One of the priests appointed to take Aaron's place as high priest must make the grain offering. It is a rule forever that the grain offering must be completely burned to the LORD. [23]Every grain offering made by a priest must be completely burned; it must not be eaten."

The Sin Offering

[24]The LORD said to Moses, [25]"Tell Aaron and the priests: 'These are the teachings about the sin offering: The sin offering must be killed in front of the LORD in the same place the whole burnt offering is killed; it is most holy. [26]The priest who offers the sin offering must eat it in a holy place, in the courtyard of the Meeting Tent. [27]Whatever touches the meat of the sin offering must be holy, and if the blood is sprinkled on any clothes, you must wash them in a holy place. [28]The clay pot the meat is cooked in must be broken, or if a bronze pot is used, it must be scrubbed and rinsed with water. [29]Any male in a priest's family may eat the offering; it is most holy. [30]But if the blood of the sin offering is taken into the Meeting Tent and used to remove sin in the Holy Place, that sin offering must be burned with fire. It must not be eaten.

PSALM 24:1–6

A Welcome for God into the Temple

A psalm of David.

24 The earth belongs to the LORD, and everything in it—
  the world and all its people.
[2]He built it on the waters
  and set it on the rivers.

[3]Who may go up on the mountain of the LORD?
  Who may stand in his holy Temple?
[4]Only those with clean hands and pure hearts,
  who have not worshiped idols,
  who have not made promises in the name of a false god.
[5]They will receive a blessing from the LORD;
  the God who saves them will declare them right.
[6]They try to follow God;
  they look to the God of Jacob for help.
                                    Selah

PROVERBS 9:7–9

[7]"If you correct someone who makes fun of wisdom, you will be insulted.
  If you correct an evil person, you will get hurt.
[8]Do not correct those who make fun of wisdom, or they will hate you.

But correct the wise, and they will love you.

⁹Teach the wise, and they will become even wiser;

teach good people, and they will learn even more.

MATTHEW 28:1–20

Jesus Rises from the Dead

28 The day after the Sabbath day was the first day of the week. At dawn on the first day, Mary Magdalene and another woman named Mary went to look at the tomb.

²At that time there was a strong earthquake. An angel of the Lord came down from heaven, went to the tomb, and rolled the stone away from the entrance. Then he sat on the stone. ³He was shining as bright as lightning, and his clothes were white as snow. ⁴The soldiers guarding the tomb shook with fear because of the angel, and they became like dead men.

⁵The angel said to the women, "Don't be afraid. I know that you are looking for Jesus, who has been crucified. ⁶He is not here. He has risen from the dead as he said he would. Come and see the place where his body was. ⁷And go quickly and tell his followers, 'Jesus has risen from the dead. He is going into Galilee ahead of you, and you will see him there.'" Then the angel said, "Now I have told you."

⁸The women left the tomb quickly. They were afraid, but they were also very happy. They ran to tell Jesus' followers what had happened. ⁹Suddenly, Jesus met them and said, "Greetings." The women came up to him, took hold of his feet, and worshiped him. ¹⁰Then Jesus said to them, "Don't be afraid. Go and tell my followers to go on to Galilee, and they will see me there."

The Soldiers Report to the Leaders

¹¹While the women went to tell Jesus' followers, some of the soldiers who had been guarding the tomb went into the city to tell the leading priests everything that had happened. ¹²Then the priests met with the elders and made a plan. They paid the soldiers a large amount of money ¹³and said to them, "Tell the people that Jesus' followers came during the night and stole the body while you were asleep. ¹⁴If the governor hears about this, we will satisfy him and save you from trouble." ¹⁵So the soldiers kept the money and did as they were told. And that story is still spread among the people even today.

Jesus Talks to His Followers

¹⁶The eleven followers went to Galilee to the mountain where Jesus had told them to go. ¹⁷On the mountain they saw Jesus and worshiped him, but some of them did not believe it was really Jesus. ¹⁸Then Jesus came to them and said, "All power in heaven and on earth is given to me. ¹⁹So go and make followers of all people in the world. Baptize them in the name of the Father and the Son and the Holy Spirit. ²⁰Teach them to obey everything that I have taught you, and I will be with you always, even until the end of this age."

FEBRUARY 18

LEVITICUS 7:1–8:36

The Penalty Offering

7 " 'These are the teachings about the penalty offering, which is most holy: ²The penalty offering must be killed where the whole burnt offering is killed. Then the priest must sprinkle its blood on all sides of the altar. ³He must offer all the fat from the penalty offering—the fat tail, the fat that covers the inner organs, ⁴both kidneys with the fat that is on them near the lower back muscle, and the best part of the liver, which is to be removed with the kidneys. ⁵The priest must burn all these things on the altar as an offering made by fire to the LORD. It is

a penalty offering. [6]Any male in a priest's family may eat it. It is most holy, so it must be eaten in a holy place.

[7]"'The penalty offering is like the sin offering in that the teachings are the same for both. The priest who offers the sacrifice to remove sins will get the meat for food. [8]The priest who offers the burnt offering may also have the skin from it. [9]Every grain offering that is baked in an oven, cooked on a griddle, or baked in a dish belongs to the priest who offers it. [10]Every grain offering, either dry or mixed with oil, belongs to the priests, and all priests will share alike.

The Fellowship Offering

[11]"'These are the teachings about the fellowship offering a person may offer to the LORD: [12]If he brings the fellowship offering to show his thanks, he should also bring loaves of bread made without yeast that are mixed with oil, wafers made without yeast that have oil poured over them, and loaves of fine flour that are mixed with oil. [13]He must also offer loaves of bread made with yeast along with his fellowship offering, which he gives to show thanks. [14]One of each kind of offering will be for the LORD; it will be given to the priest who sprinkles the blood of the fellowship offering. [15]When the fellowship offering is given to thank the LORD, the meat from it must be eaten the same day it is offered; none of it must be left until morning.

[16]"'If a person brings a fellowship offering just to give a gift to God or because of a special promise to him, the sacrifice should be eaten the same day he offers it. If there is any left, it may be eaten the next day. [17]If any meat from this sacrifice is left on the third day, it must be burned up. [18]Any meat of the fellowship offering eaten on the third day will not be accepted, nor will the sacrifice count for the person who offered it. It will become unclean, and anyone who eats the meat will be guilty of sin.

[19]"'People must not eat meat that touches anything unclean; they must burn this meat with fire. Anyone who is clean may eat other meat. [20]But if anyone is unclean and eats the meat from the fellowship offering that belongs to the LORD, he must be cut off from his people.

[21]"'If anyone touches something unclean—uncleanness that comes from people, from an animal, or from some hated thing—touching it will make him unclean. If he then eats meat from the fellowship offering that belongs to the LORD, he must be cut off from his people.'"

[22]The LORD said to Moses, [23]"Tell the people of Israel: 'You must not eat any of the fat from cattle, sheep, or goats. [24]If an animal is found dead or torn by wild animals, you may use its fat for other things, but you must not eat it. [25]If someone eats fat from an animal offering made by fire to the LORD, he must be cut off from his people. [26]No matter where you live, you must not eat blood from any bird or animal. [27]Anyone who eats blood must be cut off from his people.'"

The Priests' Share

[28]The LORD said to Moses, [29]"Tell the people of Israel: 'If someone brings a fellowship offering to the LORD, he must give part of it as his sacrifice to the LORD. [30]He must carry that part of the gift in his own hands as an offering made by fire to the LORD. He must bring the fat and the breast of the animal to the priest, to be presented to the LORD as the priests' share. [31]Then the priest must burn the fat on the altar, but the breast of the animal will belong to Aaron and the priests. [32]You must also give the right thigh from the fellowship offering to the priest as a gift; [33]it will belong to the priest who offers the blood and fat of the fellowship offering. [34]I have taken the breast and the thigh from the fellowship offerings of the Israelites, and I have given these parts to Aaron and the priests as their share for all time from the Israelites.'"

[35]This is the portion that belongs to Aaron and his sons from the offerings made by fire to the LORD. They were given this share on the day they were presented to the LORD as priests. [36]On the day the LORD appointed the priests, he commanded Israel to give this share to them, and it is to be given to the priests as their share from now on.

³⁷These are the teachings about the whole burnt offering, the grain offering, the sin offering, the penalty offering, the offering for the appointment of priests, and the fellowship offering. ³⁸The LORD gave these teachings to Moses on Mount Sinai on the day he commanded the Israelites to bring their offerings to the LORD in the Sinai Desert.

Aaron and His Sons Appointed

8 The LORD said to Moses, ²"Bring Aaron and his sons and their clothes, the special olive oil used in appointing people and things to the service of the LORD, the bull of the sin offering and the two male sheep, and the basket of bread made without yeast. ³Then gather the people together at the entrance to the Meeting Tent." ⁴Moses did as the LORD commanded him, and the people met together at the entrance to the Meeting Tent.

⁵Then Moses spoke to the people and said, "This is what the LORD has commanded to be done." ⁶Bringing Aaron and his sons forward, Moses washed them with water. ⁷He put the inner robe on Aaron and tied the cloth belt around him. Then Moses put the outer robe on him and placed the holy vest on him. He tied the skillfully woven belt around him so that the holy vest was tied to Aaron. ⁸Then Moses put the chest covering on him and put the Urim and the Thummim in the chest covering. ⁹He also put the turban on Aaron's head. He put the strip of gold, the holy crown, on the front of the turban, as the LORD commanded him to do.

¹⁰Then Moses put the special oil on the Holy Tent and everything in it, making them holy for the LORD. ¹¹He sprinkled some oil on the altar seven times, sprinkling the altar and all its tools and the large bowl and its base. In this way he made them holy for the LORD. ¹²He poured some of the special oil on Aaron's head to make Aaron holy for the LORD. ¹³Then Moses brought Aaron's sons forward. He put the inner robes on them, tied cloth belts around them, and put headbands on them, as the LORD had commanded him.

¹⁴Then Moses brought the bull for the sin offering, and Aaron and his sons put their hands on its head. ¹⁵Moses killed the bull, took the blood, and with his finger put some of it on all the corners of the altar, to make it pure. Then he poured out the rest of the blood at the bottom of the altar. In this way he made it holy and ready for service to God. ¹⁶Moses took all the fat from the inner organs of the bull, the best part of the liver, and both kidneys with the fat that is on them, and he burned them on the altar. ¹⁷But he took the bull's skin, its meat, and its intestines and burned them in a fire outside the camp, as the LORD had commanded him.

¹⁸Next Moses brought the male sheep of the burnt offering, and Aaron and his sons put their hands on its head. ¹⁹Then Moses killed it and sprinkled the blood on all sides of the altar. ²⁰He cut the male sheep into pieces and burned the head, the pieces, and the fat. ²¹He washed the inner organs and legs with water and burned the whole sheep on the altar as a burnt offering made by fire to the LORD; its smell was pleasing to the LORD. Moses did these things as the LORD had commanded him.

²²Then Moses brought the other male sheep, the one used in appointing Aaron and his sons as priests, and Aaron and his sons put their hands on its head. ²³Then Moses killed the sheep and put some of its blood on the bottom of Aaron's right ear, some on the thumb of Aaron's right hand, and some on the big toe of his right foot. ²⁴Then Moses brought Aaron's sons close to the altar. He put some of the blood on the bottom of their right ears, some on the thumbs of their right hands, and some on the big toes of their right feet. Then he sprinkled blood on all sides of the altar. ²⁵He took the fat, the fat tail, all the fat on the inner organs, the best part of the liver, both kidneys with their fat, and the right thigh. ²⁶From the basket of bread made without yeast that is put before the LORD each day, Moses took a loaf of bread, a loaf made with oil, and a wafer. He put these pieces of bread on the fat and right thigh of the male sheep. ²⁷All these things he put in the hands of Aaron and his sons and presented them as an offering before the LORD. ²⁸Then Moses took them from their hands and burned

them on the altar on top of the burnt offering. So this was the offering for appointing Aaron and his sons as priests. It was an offering made by fire to the LORD, and its smell was pleasing to him. ²⁹Moses also took the breast and presented it as an offering before the LORD. It was Moses' share of the male sheep used in appointing the priests, as the LORD had commanded him.

³⁰Moses took some of the special oil and some of the blood which was on the altar, and he sprinkled them on Aaron and Aaron's clothes and on Aaron's sons and their clothes. In this way Moses made Aaron, his clothes, his sons, and their clothes holy for the LORD.

³¹Then Moses said to Aaron and his sons, "I gave you a command, saying, 'Aaron and his sons will eat these things.' So take the meat and basket of bread from the offering for appointing priests. Boil the meat at the door of the Meeting Tent, and eat it there with the bread. ³²If any of the meat or bread is left, burn it. ³³The time of appointing will last seven days; you must not go outside the entrance of the Meeting Tent until that time is up. Stay there until the time of your appointing is finished. ³⁴The LORD commanded the things that were done today to remove your sins so you will belong to him. ³⁵You must stay at the entrance of the Meeting Tent day and night for seven days. If you don't obey the LORD's commands, you will die. The LORD has given me these commands."

³⁶So Aaron and his sons did everything the LORD had commanded through Moses.

PSALM 24:7–10

⁷Open up, you gates.
   Open wide, you aged doors
   and the glorious King will come in.
⁸Who is this glorious King?
   The LORD, strong and mighty.
   The LORD, the powerful warrior.
⁹Open up, you gates.
   Open wide, you aged doors
   and the glorious King will come in.
¹⁰Who is this glorious King?

The LORD All-Powerful—
   he is the glorious King.   *Selah*

PROVERBS 9:10–12

¹⁰"Wisdom begins with respect for the
      LORD,
   and understanding begins with
      knowing the Holy One.
¹¹If you live wisely, you will live a long
      time;
   wisdom will add years to your life.
¹²The wise person is rewarded by
      wisdom,
   but whoever makes fun of wisdom will
      suffer for it."

MARK 1:1–20

John Prepares for Jesus

1 This is the beginning of the Good News about Jesus Christ, the Son of God,ⁿ ²as the prophet Isaiah wrote:
   "I will send my messenger ahead of you,
      who will prepare your way."   *Malachi 3:1*
³"This is a voice of one
      who calls out in the desert:
   'Prepare the way for the Lord.
   Make the road straight for him.'"

                                 Isaiah 40:3
⁴John was baptizing people in the desert and preaching a baptism of changed hearts and lives for the forgiveness of sins. ⁵All the people from Judea and Jerusalem were going out to him. They confessed their sins and were baptized by him in the Jordan River. ⁶John wore clothes made from camel's hair, had a leather belt around his waist, and ate locusts and wild honey. ⁷This is what John preached to the people: "There is one coming after me who is greater than I; I am not good enough even to kneel down and untie his sandals. ⁸I baptize you with water, but he will baptize you with the Holy Spirit."

Jesus Is Baptized

⁹At that time Jesus came from the town of Nazareth in Galilee and was baptized by John in the Jordan River. ¹⁰Immediately, as Jesus was coming up out of the water, he saw

---

1:1 **the Son of God** Some Greek copies do not have this phrase.

heaven open. The Holy Spirit came down on him like a dove, [11]and a voice came from heaven: "You are my Son, whom I love, and I am very pleased with you."

[12]Then the Spirit sent Jesus into the desert. [13]He was in the desert forty days and was tempted by Satan. He was with the wild animals, and the angels came and took care of him.

Jesus Chooses Some Followers

[14]After John was put in prison, Jesus went into Galilee, preaching the Good News from God. [15]He said, "The right time has come. The kingdom of God is near. Change your hearts and lives and believe the Good News!"

[16]When Jesus was walking by Lake Galilee, he saw Simon[n] and his brother Andrew throwing a net into the lake because they were fishermen. [17]Jesus said to them, "Come follow me, and I will make you fish for people." [18]So Simon and Andrew immediately left their nets and followed him.

[19]Going a little farther, Jesus saw two more brothers, James and John, the sons of Zebedee. They were in a boat, mending their nets. [20]Jesus immediately called them, and they left their father in the boat with the hired workers and followed Jesus.

FEBRUARY 19

LEVITICUS 9:1—10:20

Aaron and His Sons Offer Sacrifices

9 On the eighth day after the time of appointing, Moses called for Aaron and his sons and for the elders of Israel. [2]He said to Aaron, "Take a bull calf and a male sheep that have nothing wrong with them, and offer them to the LORD. The calf will be a sin offering, and the male sheep will be a whole burnt offering. [3]Tell the people of Israel, 'Take a male goat for a sin offering and a calf and a lamb for a whole burnt offering; each must be one year old, and it must have nothing wrong with it. [4]Also take a bull and a male sheep for fellowship offerings, along with a grain offering mixed with oil. Offer all these things to the LORD, because the LORD will appear to you today.'"

[5]So all the people came to the front of the Meeting Tent, bringing the things Moses had commanded them to bring, and they stood before the LORD. [6]Moses said, "You have done what the LORD commanded, so you will see the LORD's glory."

[7]Then Moses told Aaron, "Go to the altar and offer sin offerings and whole burnt offerings. Do this to remove your sins and the people's sins so you will belong to God. Offer the sacrifices for the people and perform the acts to remove their sins for them so they will belong to the LORD, as the LORD has commanded."

[8]So Aaron went to the altar and killed the bull calf as a sin offering for himself. [9]Then his sons brought the blood to him, and he dipped his finger in the blood and put it on the corners of the altar. He poured out the rest of the blood at the bottom of the altar. [10]Aaron took the fat, the kidneys, and the best part of the liver from the sin offering and burned them on the altar, in the way the LORD had commanded Moses. [11]The meat and skin he burned outside the camp.

[12]Then Aaron killed the animal for the whole burnt offering. His sons brought the blood to him, and he sprinkled it on all sides of the altar. [13]As they gave him the pieces and head of the burnt offering, Aaron burned them on the altar. [14]He also washed the inner organs and the legs of the burnt offering and burned them on top of the burnt offering on the altar.

[15]Then Aaron brought the offering that was for the people. He took the goat of the people's sin offering and killed it and offered

---

1:16 Simon Simon's other name was Peter.

it for the sin offering, just as he had done the first sin offering.

¹⁶Then Aaron brought the whole burnt offering and offered it in the way that the LORD had commanded. ¹⁷He also brought the grain offering to the altar. He took a handful of the grain and burned it on the altar, in addition to the morning's burnt offering.

¹⁸Aaron also killed the bull and the male sheep as the fellowship offerings for the people. His sons brought him the blood, and he sprinkled it on all sides of the altar. ¹⁹Aaron's sons also brought to Aaron the fat of the bull and the male sheep—the fat tail, the fat covering the inner organs, the kidneys, and the best part of the liver. ²⁰Aaron's sons put them on the breasts of the bull and the sheep. Then Aaron burned these fat parts on the altar. ²¹He presented the breasts and the right thigh before the LORD as the priests' share of the offering, as Moses had commanded.

²²Then Aaron lifted his hands toward the people and blessed them. When he had finished offering the sin offering, the burnt offering, and the fellowship offering, he stepped down from the altar.

²³Moses and Aaron went into the Meeting Tent. Then they came out and blessed the people, and the LORD's glory came to all the people. ²⁴Fire came out from the LORD and burned up the burnt offering and fat on the altar. When the people saw this, they shouted with joy and bowed facedown on the ground.

God Destroys Nadab and Abihu

10 Aaron's sons Nadab and Abihu took their pans for burning incense, put fire in them, and added incense; but they did not use the special fire Moses had commanded them to use in the presence of the LORD. ²So fire came down from the LORD and destroyed Nadab and Abihu, and they died in front of the LORD. ³Then Moses said to Aaron, "This is what the LORD was speaking about when he said,

'I must be respected as holy
   by those who come near me;
before all the people
   I must be given honor.'"

So Aaron did not say anything about the death of his sons.

⁴Aaron's uncle Uzziel had two sons named Mishael and Elzaphan. Moses said to them, "Come here and pick up your cousins' bodies. Carry them outside the camp away from the front of the Holy Place." ⁵So Mishael and Elzaphan obeyed Moses and carried the bodies of Nadab and Abihu, still clothed in the special priest's inner robes, outside the camp.

⁶Then Moses said to Aaron and his other sons, Eleazar and Ithamar, "Don't show sadness by tearing your clothes or leaving your hair uncombed. If you do, you will die, and the LORD will be angry with all the people. All the people of Israel, your relatives, may cry loudly about the LORD burning Nadab and Abihu, ⁷but you must not even leave the Meeting Tent. If you go out of the entrance, you will die, because the LORD has appointed you to his service." So Aaron, Eleazar, and Ithamar obeyed Moses.

⁸Then the LORD said to Aaron, ⁹"You and your sons must not drink wine or beer when you go into the Meeting Tent. If you do, you will die. This law will continue from now on. ¹⁰You must keep what is holy separate from what is not holy; you must keep what is clean separate from what is unclean. ¹¹You must teach the people all the laws that the LORD gave to them through Moses."

¹²Moses said to Aaron and his remaining sons, Eleazar and Ithamar, "Eat the part of the grain offering that is left from the sacrifices offered by fire to the LORD, but do not add yeast to it. Eat it near the altar because it is most holy. ¹³You must eat it in a holy place, because this part of the offerings made by fire to the LORD belongs to you and your sons. I have been commanded to tell you this.

¹⁴"Also, you and your sons and daughters may eat the breast and thigh of the fellowship offering that was presented to the LORD. You must eat them in a clean place; they are your share of the fellowship offerings given by the Israelites. ¹⁵The people must bring the fat from their animals that was part of the offering made by fire, and they must present it to the LORD along with the thigh and the breast of the fellowship offering. They will be the regular share of

the offerings for you and your children, as the LORD has commanded."

¹⁶Moses looked for the goat of the sin offering, but it had already been burned up. So he became very angry with Eleazar and Ithamar, Aaron's remaining sons. He said, ¹⁷"Why didn't you eat that goat in a holy place? It is most holy, and the LORD gave it to you to take away the guilt of the people, to remove their sins so they will belong to the LORD. ¹⁸You didn't bring the goat's blood inside the Holy Place. You were supposed to eat the goat in a holy place, as I commanded!"

¹⁹But Aaron said to Moses, "Today they brought their sin offering and burnt offering before the LORD, but these terrible things have still happened to me! Do you think the LORD would be any happier if I ate the sin offering today?" ²⁰When Moses heard this, he was satisfied.

PSALM 25:1–7

A Prayer for God to Guide

Of David.

25 LORD, I give myself to you;
2 my God, I trust you.
Do not let me be disgraced;
do not let my enemies laugh at me.
³No one who trusts you will be disgraced,
but those who sin without excuse will
be disgraced.

⁴LORD, tell me your ways.
Show me how to live.
⁵Guide me in your truth,
and teach me, my God, my Savior.
I trust you all day long.
⁶LORD, remember your mercy and love
that you have shown since long ago.
⁷Do not remember the sins
and wrong things I did when I was
young.
But remember to love me always
because you are good, LORD.

PROVERBS 9:13–18

¹³Foolishness is like a loud woman;
she does not have wisdom or knowledge.

¹⁴She sits at the door of her house
at the highest place in the city.
¹⁵She calls out to those who are passing
by,
who are going along, minding their
own business.
¹⁶She says to those who are uneducated,
"Come in here, you foolish people!"
¹⁷Stolen water is sweeter,
and food eaten in secret tastes
better."
¹⁸But these people don't know that
everyone who goes there dies,
that her guests end up deep in the
grave.

MARK 1:21–45

Jesus Forces Out an Evil Spirit

²¹Jesus and his followers went to Capernaum. On the Sabbath day He went to the synagogue and began to teach. ²²The people were amazed at his teaching, because he taught like a person who had authority, not like their teachers of the law. ²³Just then, a man was there in the synagogue who had an evil spirit in him. He shouted, ²⁴"Jesus of Nazareth! What do you want with us? Did you come to destroy us? I know who you are—God's Holy One!"

²⁵Jesus commanded the evil spirit, "Be quiet! Come out of the man!" ²⁶The evil spirit shook the man violently, gave a loud cry, and then came out of him.

²⁷The people were so amazed they asked each other, "What is happening here? This man is teaching something new, and with authority. He even gives commands to evil spirits, and they obey him." ²⁸And the news about Jesus spread quickly everywhere in the area of Galilee.

Jesus Heals Many People

²⁹As soon as Jesus and his followers left the synagogue, they went with James and John to the home of Simonⁿ and Andrew. ³⁰Simon's mother-in-law was sick in bed with a fever, and the people told Jesus about her. ³¹So Jesus went to her bed, took her

1:29 Simon Simon's other name was Peter.

hand, and helped her up. The fever left her, and she began serving them.

³²That evening, after the sun went down, the people brought to Jesus all who were sick and had demons in them. ³³The whole town gathered at the door. ³⁴Jesus healed many who had different kinds of sicknesses, and he forced many demons to leave people. But he would not allow the demons to speak, because they knew who he was.

³⁵Early the next morning, while it was still dark, Jesus woke and left the house. He went to a lonely place, where he prayed. ³⁶Simon and his friends went to look for Jesus. ³⁷When they found him, they said, "Everyone is looking for you!"

³⁸Jesus answered, "We should go to other towns around here so I can preach there too. That is the reason I came." ³⁹So he went everywhere in Galilee, preaching in the synagogues and forcing out demons.

Jesus Heals a Sick Man

⁴⁰A man with a skin disease came to Jesus. He fell to his knees and begged Jesus, "You can heal me if you will."

⁴¹Jesus felt sorry for the man, so he reached out his hand and touched him and said, "I will. Be healed!" ⁴²Immediately the disease left the man, and he was healed.

⁴³Jesus told the man to go away at once, but he warned him strongly, ⁴⁴"Don't tell anyone about this. But go and show yourself to the priest. And offer the gift Moses commanded for people who are made well.ⁿ This will show the people what I have done." ⁴⁵The man left there, but he began to tell everyone that Jesus had healed him, and so he spread the news about Jesus. As a result, Jesus could not enter a town if people saw him. He stayed in places where nobody lived, but people came to him from everywhere.

FEBRUARY 20

LEVITICUS 11:1—12:8

Rules About What May Be Eaten

11 The LORD said to Moses and Aaron, ²"Tell the Israelites this: 'These are the land animals you may eat: ³You may eat any animal that has split hoofs completely divided and that chews the cud.

⁴"'Some animals only chew the cud or only have split hoofs, and you must not eat them. The camel chews the cud but does not have a split hoof; it is unclean for you. ⁵The rock badger chews the cud but does not have a split hoof; it is unclean for you. ⁶The rabbit chews the cud but does not have a split hoof; it is unclean for you. ⁷Now the pig has a split hoof that is completely divided, but it does not chew the cud; it is unclean for you. ⁸You must not eat the meat from these animals or even touch their dead bodies; they are unclean for you.

⁹"'Of the animals that live in the sea or in a river, if the animal has fins and scales, you may eat it. ¹⁰But whatever lives in the sea or in a river and does not have fins and scales—including the things that fill the water and all other things that live in it—you should hate. ¹¹You must not eat any meat from them or even touch their dead bodies, because you should hate them. ¹²You must hate any animal in the water that does not have fins and scales.

¹³"'Also, these are the birds you are to hate. They are hateful and should not be eaten. You must not eat eagles, vultures, black vultures, ¹⁴kites, any kind of falcon, ¹⁵any kind of raven, ¹⁶horned owls, screech owls, sea gulls, any kind of hawk, ¹⁷little owls, cormorants, great owls, ¹⁸white owls, desert owls, ospreys, ¹⁹storks, any kind of heron, hoopoes, or bats.

²⁰"'Don't eat insects that have wings and walk on all four feet; they also are to be hated.

1:44 Moses . . . well Read about this in Leviticus 14:1–32.

21" 'But you may eat certain insects that have wings and walk on four feet. You may eat those that have legs with joints above their feet so they can jump. 22These are the insects you may eat: all kinds of locusts, winged locusts, crickets, and grasshoppers. 23But all other insects that have wings and walk on four feet you are to hate. 24Those insects will make you unclean, and anyone who touches the dead body of one of these insects will become unclean until evening. 25Anyone who picks up one of these dead insects must wash his clothes and be unclean until evening.

26" 'Some animals have split hoofs, but the hoofs are not completely divided; others do not chew the cud. They are unclean for you, and anyone who touches the dead body of one of these animals will become unclean. 27Of all the animals that walk on four feet, the animals that walk on their paws are unclean for you. Anyone who touches the dead body of one of these animals will become unclean until evening. 28Anyone who picks up their dead bodies must wash his clothes and be unclean until evening; these animals are unclean for you.

29" 'These crawling animals are unclean for you: moles, rats, all kinds of great lizards, 30geckos, crocodiles, lizards, sand reptiles, and chameleons. 31These crawling animals are unclean for you; anyone who touches their dead bodies will be unclean until evening.

32" 'If an unclean animal dies and falls on something, that item will also become unclean. This includes anything made from wood, cloth, leather, or rough cloth, regardless of its use. Whatever the animal falls on must be washed with water and be unclean until evening; then it will become clean again. 33If the dead, unclean animal falls into a clay bowl, anything in the bowl will become unclean, and you must break the bowl. 34If water from the unclean clay bowl gets on any food, that food will become unclean. 35If any dead, unclean animal falls on something, it becomes unclean. If it is a clay oven or a clay baking pan, it must be broken into pieces. These things will be unclean; they are unclean for you.

36" 'A spring or well that collects water will stay clean, but anyone who touches the dead body of any unclean animal will become unclean. 37If a dead, unclean animal falls on a seed to be planted, that seed is still clean. 38But if you put water on some seeds and a dead, unclean animal falls on them, they are unclean for you.

39" 'Also, if an animal which you use for food dies, anyone who touches its body will be unclean until evening. 40Anyone who eats meat from this animal's dead body must wash his clothes and be unclean until evening. Anyone who picks up the animal's dead body must wash his clothes and be unclean until evening.

41" 'Every animal that crawls on the ground is to be hated; it must not be eaten. 42You must not eat any of the animals that crawl on the ground, including those that crawl on their stomachs, that walk on all four feet, or on many feet. They are to be hated. 43Do not make yourself unclean by these animals; you must not become unclean by them. 44I am the LORD your God. Keep yourselves holy for me because I am holy. Don't make yourselves unclean with any of these crawling animals. 45I am the LORD who brought you out of Egypt to be your God; you must be holy because I am holy.

46" 'These are the teachings about all of the cattle, birds, and other animals on earth, as well as the animals in the sea and those that crawl on the ground. 47These teachings help people know the difference between unclean animals and clean animals; they help people know which animals may be eaten and which ones must not be eaten.' "

Rules for New Mothers

12 The LORD said to Moses, 2"Tell the people of Israel this: 'If a woman gives birth to a son, she will become unclean for seven days, as she is unclean during her monthly period. 3On the eighth day the boy must be circumcised. 4Then it will be thirty-three days before she becomes clean from her loss of blood. She must not touch anything that is holy or enter the Holy Tent until her time of cleansing is finished. 5But if she

gives birth to a daughter, the mother will be unclean for two weeks, as she is unclean during her monthly period. It will be sixty-six days before she becomes clean from her loss of blood.

⁶"After she has a son or daughter and her days of cleansing are over, the new mother must bring certain sacrifices to the Meeting Tent. She must give the priest at the entrance a year-old lamb for a burnt offering and a dove or young pigeon for a sin offering. ⁷He will offer them before the LORD to make her clean so she will belong to the LORD again; then she will be clean from her loss of blood. These are the teachings for a woman who gives birth to a boy or girl.

⁸"'If she cannot afford a lamb, she is to bring two doves or two young pigeons, one for a burnt offering and one for a sin offering. In this way the priest will make her clean so she will belong to the LORD again, and she will be clean.'"

PSALM 25:8-15

⁸The LORD is good and right;
  he points sinners to the right way.
⁹He shows those who are humble how to do right,
  and he teaches them his ways.
¹⁰All the LORD's ways are loving and true
  for those who follow the demands of his agreement.
¹¹For the sake of your name, LORD,
  forgive my many sins.
¹²Are there those who respect the LORD?
  He will point them to the best way.
¹³They will enjoy a good life,
  and their children will inherit the land.
¹⁴The LORD tells his secrets to those who respect him;
  he tells them about his agreement.
¹⁵My eyes are always looking to the LORD for help.
  He will keep me from any traps.

PROVERBS 10:1-3

The Wise Words of Solomon

10 These are the wise words of Solomon:
Wise children make their father happy,

but foolish children make their mother sad.
²Riches gotten by doing wrong have no value,
  but right living will save you from death.
³The LORD does not let good people go hungry,
  but he keeps evil people from getting what they want.

MARK 2:1-28

Jesus Heals a Paralyzed Man

2 A few days later, when Jesus came back to Capernaum, the news spread that he was at home. ²Many people gathered together so that there was no room in the house, not even outside the door. And Jesus was teaching them God's message. ³Four people came, carrying a paralyzed man. ⁴Since they could not get to Jesus because of the crowd, they dug a hole in the roof right above where he was speaking. When they got through, they lowered the mat with the paralyzed man on it. ⁵When Jesus saw the faith of these people, he said to the paralyzed man, "Young man, your sins are forgiven."

⁶Some of the teachers of the law were sitting there, thinking to themselves, ⁷"Why does this man say things like that? He is speaking as if he were God. Only God can forgive sins."

⁸Jesus knew immediately what these teachers of the law were thinking. So he said to them, "Why are you thinking these things? ⁹Which is easier: to tell this paralyzed man, 'Your sins are forgiven,' or to tell him, 'Stand up. Take your mat and walk'? ¹⁰But I will prove to you that the Son of Man has authority on earth to forgive sins." So Jesus said to the paralyzed man, ¹¹"I tell you, stand up, take your mat, and go home." ¹²Immediately the paralyzed man stood up, took his mat, and walked out while everyone was watching him.

The people were amazed and praised God. They said, "We have never seen anything like this!"

¹³Jesus went to the lake again. The whole crowd followed him there, and he taught

them. [14]While he was walking along, he saw a man named Levi son of Alphaeus, sitting in the tax collector's booth. Jesus said to him, "Follow me," and he stood up and followed Jesus.

[15]Later, as Jesus was having dinner at Levi's house, many tax collectors and "sinners" were eating there with Jesus and his followers. Many people like this followed Jesus. [16]When the teachers of the law who were Pharisees saw Jesus eating with the tax collectors and "sinners," they asked his followers, "Why does he eat with tax collectors and sinners?"

[17]Jesus heard this and said to them, "It is not the healthy people who need a doctor, but the sick. I did not come to invite good people but to invite sinners."

Jesus' Followers Are Criticized

[18]Now the followers of John[n] and the Pharisees often fasted[n] for a certain time. Some people came to Jesus and said, "Why do John's followers and the followers of the Pharisees often fast, but your followers don't?"

[19]Jesus answered, "The friends of the bridegroom do not fast while the bridegroom is still with them. As long as the bridegroom is with them, they cannot fast. [20]But the time will come when the bridegroom will be taken from them, and then they will fast.

[21]"No one sews a patch of unshrunk cloth over a hole in an old coat. Otherwise, the patch will shrink and pull away—the new patch will pull away from the old coat. Then the hole will be worse. [22]Also, no one ever pours new wine into old leather bags. Otherwise, the new wine will break the bags, and the wine will be ruined along with the bags. But new wine should be put into new leather bags."

Jesus Is Lord of the Sabbath

[23]One Sabbath day, as Jesus was walking through some fields of grain, his followers began to pick some grain to eat. [24]The Pharisees said to Jesus, "Why are your followers doing what is not lawful on the Sabbath day?"

[25]Jesus answered, "Have you never read what David did when he and those with him were hungry and needed food? [26]During the time of Abiathar the high priest, David went into God's house and ate the holy bread, which is lawful only for priests to eat. And David also gave some of the bread to those who were with him."

[27]Then Jesus said to the Pharisees, "The Sabbath day was made to help people; they were not made to be ruled by the Sabbath day. [28]So then, the Son of Man is Lord even of the Sabbath day."

FEBRUARY 21

LEVITICUS 13:1–59

Rules About Skin Diseases

13 The LORD said to Moses and Aaron, [2]"Someone might have on his skin a swelling or a rash or a bright spot. If the sore looks like a harmful skin disease, the person must be brought to Aaron the priest or to one of Aaron's sons, the priests. [3]The priest must look at the sore on the person's skin. If the hair in the sore has become white, and the sore seems deeper than the person's skin, it is a harmful skin disease. When he has finished looking at the person, the priest must announce that the person is unclean.

[4]"If there is a white spot on a person's skin, but the spot does not seem deeper than the skin, and if the hair from the spot has not turned white, the priest must separate that person from other people for seven

---

2:18 John John the Baptist, who preached to the Jewish people about Christ's coming (Mark 1:4–8). **2:18 fasted** The people would give up eating for a special time of prayer and worship to God. It was also done to show sadness and disappointment.

days. [5]On the seventh day the priest must look at the person again. If he sees that the sore has not changed and it has not spread on the skin, the priest must keep the person separated for seven more days. [6]On the seventh day the priest must look at the person again. If the sore has faded and has not spread on the skin, the priest must announce that the person is clean. The sore is only a rash. The person must wash his clothes, and he will become clean again.

[7]"But if the rash spreads again after the priest has announced him clean, the person must come again to the priest. [8]The priest must look at him, and if the rash has spread on the skin, the priest must announce that the person is unclean; it is a harmful skin disease.

[9]"If a person has a harmful skin disease, he must be brought to the priest, [10]and the priest must look at him. If there is a white swelling in the skin, and the hair has become white, and the skin looks raw in the swelling, [11]it is a harmful skin disease. It is one he has had for a long time. The priest must announce that the person is unclean. He will not need to separate that person from other people, because everyone already knows that the person is unclean.

[12]"If the skin disease spreads all over a person's body, covering his skin from his head to his feet, as far as the priest can see, the priest must look at the person's whole body. [13]If the priest sees that the disease covers the whole body and has turned all of the person's skin white, he must announce that the person is clean.

[14]"But when the person has an open sore, he is unclean. [15]When the priest sees the open sore, he must announce that the person is unclean. The open sore is not clean; it is a harmful skin disease. [16]If the open sore becomes white again, the person must come to the priest. [17]The priest must look at him, and if the sores have become white, the priest must announce that the person with the sores is clean. Then he will be clean.

[18]"Someone may have a boil on his skin that is healed. [19]If in the place where the boil was, there is a white swelling or a bright red spot, this place on the skin must be shown to the priest. [20]And the priest must look at it. If the spot seems deeper than the skin and the hair on it has become white, the priest must announce that the person is unclean. The spot is a harmful skin disease that has broken out from inside the boil. [21]But if the priest looks at the spot and there are no white hairs in it and the spot is not deeper than the skin and it has faded, the priest must separate the person from other people for seven days. [22]If the spot spreads on the skin, the priest must announce that the person is unclean; it is a disease that will spread. [23]But if the bright spot does not spread or change, it is only the scar from the old boil. Then the priest must announce that the person is clean.

[24]"When a person gets a burn on his skin, if the open sore becomes white or red, [25]the priest must look at it. If the white spot seems deeper than the skin and the hair at that spot has become white, it is a harmful skin disease. The disease has broken out in the burn, and the priest must announce that the person is unclean. It is a harmful skin disease. [26]But if the priest looks at the spot and there is no white hair in the bright spot, and the spot is no deeper than the skin and has faded, the priest must separate the person from other people for seven days. [27]On the seventh day the priest must look at him again. If the spot has spread on the skin, the priest must announce that the person is unclean. It is a harmful skin disease. [28]But if the bright spot has not spread on the skin but has faded, it is the swelling from the burn. The priest must announce that the person is clean, because the spot is only a scar from the burn.

[29]"When a man or a woman gets a sore on the scalp or on the chin, [30]a priest must look at the sore. If it seems deeper than the skin and the hair around it is thin and yellow, the priest must announce that the person is unclean. It is an itch, a harmful skin disease of the head or chin. [31]But if the priest looks at it and it does not seem deeper than the skin and there is no black hair in it, the priest must separate the person from other people for seven days. [32]On the seventh day the priest must look at the sore. If it has not

spread, and there are no yellow hairs growing in it, and the sore does not seem deeper than the skin, [33]the person must shave himself, but he must not shave the sore place. The priest must separate that person from other people for seven more days. [34]On the seventh day the priest must look at the sore. If it has not spread on the skin and it does not seem deeper than the skin, the priest must announce that the person is clean. So the person must wash his clothes and become clean. [35]But if the sore spreads on the skin after the person has become clean, [36]the priest must look at him again. If the sore has spread on the skin, the priest doesn't need to look for the yellowish hair; the person is unclean. [37]But if the priest thinks the sore has stopped spreading, and black hair is growing in it, the sore has healed. The person is clean, and the priest must announce that he is clean.

[38]"When a man or a woman has white spots on the skin, [39]a priest must look at them. If the spots on the skin are dull white, the disease is only a harmless rash. That person is clean.

[40]"When anyone loses hair from his head and is bald, he is clean. [41]If he loses hair from the front of his head and has a bald forehead, he is clean. [42]But if there is a red-white sore on his bald head or forehead, it is a skin disease breaking out in those places. [43]A priest must look at that person. If the swelling of the sore on his bald head or forehead is red-white, like a skin disease that spreads, [44]that person has a skin disease. He is unclean. The priest must announce that the person is unclean because of the sore on his head.

[45]"If a person has a skin disease that spreads, he must warn other people by shouting, 'Unclean, unclean!' His clothes must be torn at the seams, he must let his hair stay uncombed, and he must cover his mouth. [46]That person will be unclean the whole time he has the disease; he is unclean. He must live alone outside the camp.

Rules About Mildew

[47]"Clothing might have mildew on it. It might be clothing made of linen or wool [48](either woven or knitted), or of leather, or something made from leather. [49]If the mildew in the clothing, leather, or woven or knitted material is green or red, it is a spreading mildew. It must be shown to the priest. [50]The priest must look at the mildew, and he must put that piece of clothing in a separate place for seven days. [51]On the seventh day he must look at the mildew again. If the mildew has spread on the cloth (either woven or knitted) or the leather, no matter what the leather was used for, it is a mildew that destroys; it is unclean. [52]The priest must burn the clothing. It does not matter if it is woven or knitted, wool or linen, or made of leather, because the mildew is spreading. It must be burned.

[53]"If the priest sees that the mildew has not spread in the cloth (either knitted or woven) or leather, [54]he must order the people to wash that piece of leather or cloth. Then he must separate the clothing for seven more days. [55]After the piece with the mildew has been washed, the priest must look at it again. If the mildew still looks the same, the piece is unclean, even if the mildew has not spread. You must burn it in fire; it does not matter if the mildew is on one side or the other.

[56]"But when the priest looks at that piece of leather or cloth, the mildew might have faded after the piece has been washed. Then the priest must tear the mildew out of the piece of leather or cloth (either woven or knitted). [57]But if the mildew comes back to that piece of leather or cloth (either woven or knitted), the mildew is spreading. And whatever has the mildew must be burned with fire. [58]When the cloth (either woven or knitted) or the leather is washed and the mildew is gone, it must be washed again; then it will be clean.

[59]"These are the teachings about mildew on pieces of cloth (either woven or knitted) or leather, to decide if they are clean or unclean."

PSALM 25:16–22

[16]Turn to me and have mercy on me,
  because I am lonely and hurting.
[17]My troubles have grown larger;
  free me from my problems.

¹⁸Look at my suffering and troubles,
and take away all my sins.
¹⁹Look at how many enemies I have!
See how much they hate me!
²⁰Protect me and save me.
I trust you, so do not let me be
disgraced.
²¹My hope is in you,
so may goodness and honesty guard me.
²²God, save Israel from all their troubles!

PROVERBS 10:4

⁴A lazy person will end up poor,
but a hard worker will become rich.

MARK 3:1–19

Jesus Heals a Man's Hand

3 Another time when Jesus went into a synagogue, a man with a crippled hand was there. ²Some people watched Jesus closely to see if he would heal the man on the Sabbath day so they could accuse him.

³Jesus said to the man with the crippled hand, "Stand up here in the middle of everyone."

⁴Then Jesus asked the people, "Which is lawful on the Sabbath day: to do good or to do evil, to save a life or to kill?" But they said nothing to answer him.

⁵Jesus was angry as he looked at the people, and he felt very sad because they were stubborn. Then he said to the man, "Hold out your hand." The man held out his hand

and it was healed. ⁶Then the Pharisees left and began making plans with the Herodians[n] about a way to kill Jesus.

Many People Follow Jesus

⁷Jesus left with his followers for the lake, and a large crowd from Galilee followed him. ⁸Also many people came from Judea, from Jerusalem, from Idumea, from the lands across the Jordan River, and from the area of Tyre and Sidon. When they heard what Jesus was doing, many people came to him. ⁹When Jesus saw the crowds, he told his followers to get a boat ready for him to keep people from crowding against him. ¹⁰He had healed many people, so all the sick were pushing toward him to touch him. ¹¹When evil spirits saw Jesus, they fell down before him and shouted, "You are the Son of God!" ¹²But Jesus strongly warned them not to tell who he was.

Jesus Chooses His Twelve Apostles

¹³Then Jesus went up on a mountain and called to him those he wanted, and they came to him. ¹⁴Jesus chose twelve and called them apostles.[n] He wanted them to be with him, and he wanted to send them out to preach ¹⁵and to have the authority to force demons out of people. ¹⁶These are the twelve men he chose: Simon (Jesus named him Peter), ¹⁷James and John, the sons of Zebedee (Jesus named them Boanerges, which means "Sons of Thunder"), ¹⁸Andrew, Philip, Bartholomew, Matthew, Thomas, James the son of Alphaeus, Thaddaeus, Simon the Zealot, ¹⁹and Judas Iscariot, who later turned against Jesus.

FEBRUARY 22

LEVITICUS 14:1–57

Rules for Cleansing from Skin Diseases

14 The LORD said to Moses, ²"These are the teachings for the time at which people who had a harmful skin disease are made clean.

"The person shall be brought to the priest, ³and the priest must go outside the camp and look at the one who had the skin disease. If the skin disease is healed, ⁴the priest will command that two living, clean birds, a piece of cedar wood, a piece of red string, and a hyssop plant be brought

3:6 Herodians A political group that followed Herod and his family.   **3:14 and called them apostles** Some Greek copies do not have this phrase.

for cleansing the person with the skin disease.

5"The priest must order one bird to be killed in a clay bowl containing fresh water. 6Then he will take the living bird, the piece of cedar wood, the red string, and the hyssop; all these he will dip into the blood of the bird that was killed over the fresh water. 7The priest will sprinkle the blood seven times on the person being cleansed from the skin disease. He must announce that the person is clean and then go to an open field and let the living bird go free.

8"The person to be cleansed must wash his clothes, shave off all his hair, and bathe in water. Then he will be clean and may go into the camp, though he must stay outside his tent for the first seven days. 9On the seventh day he must shave off all his hair—the hair from his head, his beard, his eyebrows, and the rest of his hair. He must wash his clothes and bathe his body in water, and he will be clean.

10"On the eighth day the person who had the skin disease must take two male lambs that have nothing wrong with them and a year-old female lamb that has nothing wrong with it. He must also take six quarts of fine flour mixed with oil for a grain offering and two-thirds of a pint of olive oil. 11The priest who is to announce that the person is clean must bring him and his sacrifices before the LORD at the entrance of the Meeting Tent. 12The priest will take one of the male lambs and offer it with the olive oil as a penalty offering; he will present them before the LORD as an offering. 13Then he will kill the male lamb in the holy place, where the sin offering and the whole burnt offering are killed. The penalty offering is like the sin offering—it belongs to the priest and it is most holy.

14"The priest will take some of the blood of the penalty offering and put it on the bottom of the right ear of the person to be made clean. He will also put some of it on the thumb of the person's right hand and on the big toe of the person's right foot. 15Then the priest will take some of the oil and pour it into his own left hand. 16He will dip a finger of his right hand into the oil that is in his left hand, and with his finger he will sprinkle some of the oil seven times before the LORD. 17The priest will put some oil from his hand on the bottom of the right ear of the person to be made clean, some on the thumb of the person's right hand, and some on the big toe of the person's right foot. The oil will go on these places on top of the blood for the penalty offering. 18He will put the rest of the oil that is in his left hand on the head of the person to be made clean. In this way the priest will make that person clean so he can belong to the LORD again.

19"Next the priest will offer the sin offering to make that person clean so he can belong to the LORD again. After this the priest will kill the animal for the whole burnt offering, 20and he will offer the burnt offering and grain offering on the altar. In this way he will make that person clean so he can belong to the LORD again.

21"But if the person is poor and unable to afford these offerings, he must take one male lamb for a penalty offering. It will be presented to the LORD to make him clean so he can belong to the LORD again. The person must also take two quarts of fine flour mixed with oil for a grain offering. He must also take two-thirds of a pint of olive oil 22and two doves or two young pigeons, which he can afford. One bird is for a sin offering and the other for a whole burnt offering. 23On the eighth day the person will bring them for his cleansing to the priest at the entrance of the Meeting Tent, before the LORD. 24The priest will take the lamb for the penalty offering and the oil, and he will present them as an offering before the LORD. 25Then he will kill the lamb of the penalty offering, take some of its blood, and put it on the bottom of the right ear of the person to be made clean. The priest will put some of this blood on the thumb of the person's right hand and some on the big toe of the person's right foot. 26He will also pour some of the oil into his own left hand. 27Then with a finger of his right hand, he will sprinkle some of the oil from his left hand seven times before the LORD. 28The priest will take some of the oil from his hand and put it on the bottom of the right ear of the person to be made clean. He will also put some of it on the thumb of the person's right hand and some on the big toe of the person's right foot. The oil will go on these places on top of the blood from the penalty offering. [29]The priest must put the rest of the oil that is in his hand on the head of the person to be made clean, to make him clean so he can belong to the LORD again. [30]Then the priest will offer one of the doves or young pigeons, which the person can afford. [31]He must offer one of the birds for a sin offering and the other for a whole burnt offering, along with the grain offering. In this way the priest will make the person clean so he can belong to the LORD again; he will become clean.

[32]"These are the teachings for making a person clean after he has had a skin disease, if he cannot afford the regular sacrifices for becoming clean."

Rules for Cleaning Mildew

[33]The LORD also said to Moses and Aaron, [34]"I am giving the land of Canaan to your people. When they enter that land, if I cause mildew to grow in someone's house in that land, [35]the owner of that house must come and tell the priest. He should say, 'I have seen something like mildew in my house.' [36]Then the priest must order the people to empty the house before he goes in to look at the mildew. This is so he will not have to say that everything in the house is unclean. After this, the priest will go in to look at it. [37]He will look at the mildew, and if the mildew on the walls of the house is green or red and goes into the wall's surface, [38]he must go out and close up the house for seven days. [39]On the seventh day the priest must come back and check the house. If the mildew has spread on the walls of the house, [40]the priest must order the people to tear out the stones with the mildew on them. They should throw them away, at a certain unclean place outside the city. [41]Then the priest must have all the inside of the house scraped. The people must throw away the plaster they scraped off the walls, at a certain unclean place outside the city. [42]Then the owner must put new stones in the walls, and he must cover the walls with new clay plaster.

[43]"Suppose a person has taken away the old stones and plaster and put in new stones and plaster. If mildew again appears in his house, [44]the priest must come back and check the house again. If the mildew has spread in the house, it is a mildew that destroys things; the house is unclean. [45]Then the owner must tear down the house, remove all its stones, plaster, and wood, and take them to the unclean place outside the city. [46]Anyone who goes into that house while it is closed up will be unclean until evening. [47]Anyone who eats in that house or lies down there must wash his clothes.

[48]"Suppose after new stones and plaster have been put in a house, the priest checks it again and the mildew has not spread. Then the priest will announce that the house is clean, because the mildew is gone.

[49]"Then, to make the house clean, the priest must take two birds, a piece of cedar wood, a piece of red string, and a hyssop plant. [50]He will kill one bird in a clay bowl containing fresh water. [51]Then he will take the bird that is still alive, the cedar wood, the hyssop, and the red string, and he will dip them into the blood of the bird that was killed over the fresh water. The priest will sprinkle the blood on the house seven times. [52]He will use the bird's blood, the fresh water, the live bird, the cedar wood, the hyssop, and the red string to make the house clean. [53]He will then go to an open field outside the city and let the living bird go free. This is how the priest makes the house clean and ready for service to the LORD."

[54]These are the teachings about any kind of skin disease, [55]mildew on pieces of cloth or in a house, [56]swellings, rashes, or bright spots on the skin; [57]they help people decide when things are unclean and when they are clean. These are the teachings about all these kinds of diseases.

PSALM 26:1–5

The Prayer of an Innocent Believer

Of David.

26 LORD, defend me because I have lived an innocent life.
I have trusted the LORD and never doubted.
[2]LORD, try me and test me;
look closely into my heart and mind.

³I see your love,
and I live by your truth.
⁴I do not spend time with liars,
nor do I make friends with those who
hide their sin.
⁵I hate the company of evil people,
and I won't sit with the wicked.

PROVERBS 10:5–7

⁵Those who gather crops on time are wise,
but those who sleep through the
harvest are a disgrace.

⁶Good people will have rich blessings,
but the wicked will be overwhelmed by
violence.

⁷Good people will be remembered as a
blessing,
but evil people will soon be forgotten.

MARK 3:20–35

Some People Say Jesus Has a Devil

²⁰Then Jesus went home, but again a crowd gathered. There were so many people that Jesus and his followers could not eat. ²¹When his family heard this, they went to get him because they thought he was out of his mind. ²²But the teachers of the law from Jerusalem were saying, "Beelzebul is living inside him! He uses power from the ruler of demons to force demons out of people."

²³So Jesus called the people together and taught them with stories. He said, "Satan will not force himself out of people. ²⁴A kingdom that is divided cannot continue, ²⁵and a family that is divided cannot continue. ²⁶And if Satan is against himself and fights against his own people, he cannot continue; that is the end of Satan. ²⁷No one can enter a strong person's house and steal his things unless he first ties up the strong person. Then he can steal things from the house. ²⁸I tell you the truth, all sins that people do and all the things people say against God can be forgiven. ²⁹But anyone who speaks against the Holy Spirit will never be forgiven; he is guilty of a sin that continues forever."

³⁰Jesus said this because the teachers of the law said that he had an evil spirit inside him.

Jesus' True Family

³¹Then Jesus' mother and brothers arrived. Standing outside, they sent someone in to tell him to come out. ³²Many people were sitting around Jesus, and they said to him, "Your mother and brothers" are waiting for you outside."

³³Jesus asked, "Who are my mother and my brothers?" ³⁴Then he looked at those sitting around him and said, "Here are my mother and my brothers! ³⁵My true brother and sister and mother are those who do what God wants."

FEBRUARY 23

LEVITICUS 15:1—16:34

Rules About a Person's Body

15 The LORD also said to Moses and Aaron, ²"Say to the people of Israel: 'When a fluid comes from a person's body, the fluid is unclean. ³It doesn't matter if the fluid flows freely or if it is blocked from flowing; the fluid will make him unclean. This is the way the fluid makes him unclean:

⁴"If the person who discharges the body fluid lies on a bed, that bed becomes unclean, and everything he sits on becomes unclean. ⁵Anyone who touches his bed must wash his clothes and bathe in water, and the person will be unclean until evening. ⁶Whoever sits on something that the person who discharges the fluid sat on must wash his clothes and bathe in water; he will be unclean until evening. ⁷Anyone who touches

3:32 brothers Some Greek copies continue, "and sisters."

the person who discharges the body fluid must wash his clothes and bathe in water; he will be unclean until evening.

8" 'If the person who discharges the body fluid spits on someone who is clean, that person must wash his clothes and bathe in water; he will be unclean until evening. 9Everything on which the person who is unclean sits when riding will become unclean. 10Anyone who touches something that was under him will be unclean until evening. And anyone who carries these things must wash his clothes and bathe in water; he will be unclean until evening.

11" 'If the person who discharges a body fluid has not washed his hands in water and touches another person, that person must wash his clothes and bathe in water; he will be unclean until evening.

12" 'If a person who discharges a body fluid touches a clay bowl, that bowl must be broken. If he touches a wooden bowl, that bowl must be washed in water.

13" 'When a person who discharges a body fluid is made clean, he must count seven days for himself for his cleansing. He must wash his clothes and bathe his body in fresh water, and he will be clean. 14On the eighth day he must take two doves or two young pigeons before the LORD at the entrance of the Meeting Tent. He will give the two birds to the priest. 15The priest will offer the birds, one for a sin offering and the other for a burnt offering. And the priest will make that person clean so he can belong to the LORD again.

16" 'If semen[n] goes out from a man, he must bathe in water; he will be unclean until evening. 17If the fluid gets on any clothing or leather, it must be washed with water; it will be unclean until evening.

18" 'If a man has sexual relations with a woman and semen comes out, both people must bathe in water; they will be unclean until evening.

Rules About a Woman's Body

19" 'When a woman has her monthly period, she is unclean for seven days; anyone who touches her will be unclean until evening. 20Anything she lies on during this time will be unclean, and everything she sits on during this time will be unclean. 21Anyone who touches her bed must wash his clothes and bathe in water; that person will be unclean until evening. 22Anyone who touches something she has sat on must wash his clothes and bathe in water; that person will be unclean until evening. 23It does not matter if the person touched the woman's bed or something she sat on; he will be unclean until evening.

24" 'If a man has sexual relations with a woman and her monthly period touches him, he will be unclean for seven days; every bed he lies on will be unclean.

25" 'If a woman has a loss of blood for many days and it is not during her regular monthly period, or if she continues to have a loss of blood after her regular period, she will be unclean, as she is during her monthly period. She will be unclean for as long as she continues to bleed. 26Any bed she lies on during all the time of her bleeding will be like her bed during her regular monthly period. Everything she sits on will be unclean, as during her regular monthly period.

27" 'Whoever touches those things will be unclean and must wash his clothes and bathe in water; he will be unclean until evening. 28When the woman becomes clean from her bleeding, she must wait seven days, and after this she will be clean. 29Then on the eighth day she must take two doves or two young pigeons and bring them to the priest at the entrance of the Meeting Tent. 30The priest must offer one bird for a sin offering and the other for a whole burnt offering. In this way the priest will make her clean so she can belong to the LORD again.

31" 'So you must warn the people of Israel to stay separated from things that make them unclean. If you don't warn the people, they might make my Holy Tent unclean, and then they would have to die!'"

32These are the teachings for the person who discharges a body fluid and for the man who becomes unclean from semen[n] coming out of his body. 33These are the teachings for

---

15:16; 32 semen A man's body fluid by which he can make a woman pregnant.

the woman who becomes unclean from her monthly period, for a man or woman who has a discharge, and for a man who becomes unclean by having sexual relations with a woman who is unclean.

The Day of Cleansing

16 Now two of Aaron's sons had died while offering incense to the LORD, and after that time the LORD spoke to Moses. ²The LORD said to him, "Tell your brother Aaron that there are times when he cannot go behind the curtain into the Most Holy Place where the Ark is. If he goes in when I appear in a cloud over the lid on the Ark, he will die.

³"This is how Aaron may enter the Most Holy Place: Before he enters, he must offer a bull for a sin offering and a male sheep for a whole burnt offering. ⁴He must put on the holy linen inner robe, with the linen underclothes next to his body. His belt will be the cloth belt, and he will wear the linen turban. These are holy clothes, so he must bathe his body in water before he puts them on.

⁵"Aaron must take from the people of Israel two male goats for a sin offering and one male sheep for a burnt offering. ⁶Then he will offer the bull for the sin offering for himself to remove sins from him and his family so they will belong to the LORD.

⁷"Next Aaron will take the two goats and bring them before the LORD at the entrance to the Meeting Tent. ⁸He will throw lots for the two goats—one will be for the LORD and the other for the goat that removes sin. ⁹Then Aaron will take the goat that was chosen for the LORD by throwing the lot, and he will offer it as a sin offering. ¹⁰The other goat, which was chosen by lot to remove the sin, must be brought alive before the LORD. The priest will use it to perform the acts that remove Israel's sin so they will belong to the LORD. Then this goat will be sent out into the desert as a goat that removes sin.

¹¹"Then Aaron will offer the bull as a sin offering for himself, to remove the sins from him and his family so they will belong to the LORD; he will kill the bull for the sin offering for himself. ¹²Then he must take a pan full of burning coals from the altar before the LORD and two handfuls of sweet incense that has been ground into powder. He must bring it into the room behind the curtain. ¹³He must put the incense on the fire before the LORD so that the cloud of incense will cover the lid on the Ark. Then when Aaron comes in, he will not die. ¹⁴Also, he must take some of the blood from the bull and sprinkle it with his finger on the front of the lid; with his finger he will sprinkle the blood seven times in front of the lid.

¹⁵"Then Aaron must kill the goat of the sin offering for the people and bring its blood into the room behind the curtain. He must do with the goat's blood as he did with the bull's blood, sprinkling it on the lid and in front of the lid. ¹⁶Because the people of Israel have been unclean, Aaron will perform the acts to make the Most Holy Place ready for service to the LORD. Then it will be clean from the sins and crimes of the Israelites. He must also do this for the Meeting Tent, because it stays in the middle of unclean people. ¹⁷When Aaron makes the Most Holy Place ready for service to the LORD, no one is allowed in the Meeting Tent until he comes out. So Aaron will perform the acts to remove sins from himself, his family, and all the people of Israel, so they will belong to the LORD. ¹⁸Afterward he will go out to the altar that is before the LORD and will make it ready for service to the LORD. Aaron will take some of the bull's blood and some of the goat's blood and put it on the corners of the altar on all sides. ¹⁹Then, with his finger, he will sprinkle some of the blood on the altar seven times to make the altar holy for the LORD and clean from all the sins of the Israelites.

²⁰"When Aaron has finished making the Most Holy Place, the Meeting Tent, and the altar ready for service to the LORD, he will offer the living goat. ²¹He will put both his hands on the head of the living goat, and he will confess over it all the sins and crimes of Israel. In this way Aaron will put the people's sins on the goat's head. Then he will send the goat away into the desert, and a man who has been appointed will lead the goat away. ²²So the goat will carry on itself all the people's sins to a lonely place in the desert. The man who leads the goat will let it loose there. ²³"Then Aaron will enter the Meeting Tent

and take off the linen clothes he had put on before he went into the Most Holy Place; he must leave these clothes there. ²⁴He will bathe his body in water in a holy place and put on his regular clothes. Then he will come out and offer the whole burnt offering for himself and for the people, to remove sins from himself and the people so they will belong to the LORD. ²⁵Then he will burn the fat of the sin offering on the altar.

²⁶"The person who led the goat, the goat to remove sins, into the desert must wash his clothes and bathe his body in water. After that, he may come back into the camp.

²⁷"The bull and the goat for the sin offerings, whose blood was brought into the Most Holy Place to make it ready for service to the LORD, must be taken outside the camp; the animals' skins, bodies, and intestines will be burned in the fire. ²⁸Then the one who burns them must wash his clothes and bathe his body in water. After that, he may come back into the camp.

²⁹"This law will always continue for you: On the tenth day of the seventh month, you must deny yourself and you must not do any work. The travelers or foreigners living with you must not work either. ³⁰It is on this day that the priests will make you clean so you will belong to the LORD again. All your sins will be removed. ³¹This is a very important day of rest for you, and you must deny yourselves. This law will continue forever.

³²"The priest appointed to take his father's place, on whom the oil was poured, will perform the acts for making things ready for service to the LORD. He must put on the holy linen clothes ³³and make the Most Holy Place, the Meeting Tent, and the altar ready for service to the LORD. He must also remove the sins of the priests and all the people of Israel so they will belong to the LORD. ³⁴That law for removing the sins of the Israelites so they will belong to the LORD will continue forever. You will do these things once a year."

So they did the things the LORD had commanded Moses.

PSALM 26:6–12

⁶I wash my hands to show I am innocent,
  and I come to your altar, LORD.
⁷I raise my voice in praise
  and tell of all the miracles you have
    done.
⁸LORD, I love the Temple where you live,
  where your glory is.
⁹Do not kill me with those sinners
  or take my life with those murderers.
¹⁰Evil is in their hands,
  and they do wrong for money.
¹¹But I have lived an innocent life,
  so save me and have mercy on me.
¹²I stand in a safe place.
  LORD, I praise you in the great meeting.

PROVERBS 10:8

⁸The wise do what they are told,
  but a talkative fool will be ruined.

MARK 4:1–20

A Story About Planting Seed

4 Again Jesus began teaching by the lake. A great crowd gathered around him, so he sat down in a boat near the shore. All the people stayed on the shore close to the water. ²Jesus taught them many things, using stories. He said, ³"Listen! A farmer went out to plant his seed. ⁴While he was planting, some seed fell by the road, and the birds came and ate it up. ⁵Some seed fell on rocky ground where there wasn't much dirt. That seed grew very fast, because the ground was not deep. ⁶But when the sun rose, the plants dried up because they did not have deep roots. ⁷Some other seed fell among thorny weeds, which grew and choked the good plants. So those plants did not produce a crop. ⁸Some other seed fell on good ground and began to grow. It got taller and produced a crop. Some plants made thirty times more, some made sixty times more, and some made a hundred times more."

⁹Then Jesus said, "Let those with ears use them and listen!"

Jesus Tells Why He Used Stories

¹⁰Later, when Jesus was alone, the twelve apostles and others around him asked him about the stories. ¹¹Jesus said, "You can know the secret about the kingdom of God. But to other

people I tell everything by using stories [12]so that:

'They will look and look, but they will not learn.

They will listen and listen, but they will not understand.

If they did learn and understand,
they would come back to me and be forgiven.'"
Isaiah 6:9–10

Jesus Explains the Seed Story

[13]Then Jesus said to his followers, "Don't you understand this story? If you don't, how will you understand any story? [14]The farmer is like a person who plants God's message in people. [15]Sometimes the teaching falls on the road. This is like the people who hear the teaching of God, but Satan quickly comes and takes away the teaching that was planted in them. [16]Others are like the seed planted on rocky ground. They hear the teaching and quickly accept it with joy. [17]But since they don't allow the teaching to go deep into their lives, they keep it only a short time. When trouble or persecution comes because of the teaching they accepted, they quickly give up. [18]Others are like the seed planted among the thorny weeds. They hear the teaching, [19]but the worries of this life, the temptation of wealth, and many other evil desires keep the teaching from growing and producing fruit[n] in their lives. [20]Others are like the seed planted in the good ground. They hear the teaching and accept it. Then they grow and produce fruit—sometimes thirty times more, sometimes sixty times more, and sometimes a hundred times more."

FEBRUARY 24

LEVITICUS 17:1—18:30

Offering Sacrifices

17 The LORD said to Moses, [2]"Speak to Aaron, his sons, and all the people of Israel. Tell them: 'This is what the LORD has commanded. [3]If an Israelite kills an ox, a lamb, or a goat either inside the camp or outside it, [4]when he should have brought the animal to the entrance of the Meeting Tent as a gift to the LORD in front of the LORD's Holy Tent, he is guilty of killing. He has killed, and he must be cut off from the people. [5]This rule is so people will bring their sacrifices, which they have been sacrificing in the open fields, to the LORD. They must bring those animals to the LORD at the entrance of the Meeting Tent; they must bring them to the priest and offer them as fellowship offerings. [6]Then the priest will sprinkle the blood from those animals on the LORD's altar near the entrance of the Meeting Tent. And he will burn the fat from those animals on the al-tar, as a smell pleasing to the LORD. [7]They must not offer any more sacrifices to their goat idols, which they have chased like prostitutes. These rules will continue for people from now on.'

[8]"Tell the people this: 'If any citizen of Israel or foreigner living with you offers a burnt offering or sacrifice, [9]that person must take his sacrifice to the entrance of the Meeting Tent to offer it to the LORD. If he does not do this, he must be cut off from the people.

[10]" 'I will be against any citizen of Israel or foreigner living with you who eats blood. I will cut off that person from the people. [11]This is because the life of the body is in the blood, and I have given you rules for pouring that blood on the altar to remove your sins so you will belong to the LORD. It is the blood that removes the sins, because it is life. [12]So I tell the people of Israel this: "None of you may eat blood, and no foreigner living among you may eat blood."

4:19 producing fruit To produce fruit means to have in your life the good things God wants.

¹³" 'If any citizen of Israel or foreigner living among you catches a wild animal or bird that can be eaten, that person must pour the blood on the ground and cover it with dirt. ¹⁴If blood is still in the meat, the animal's life is still in it. So I give this command to the people of Israel: "Don't eat meat that still has blood in it, because the animal's life is in its blood. Anyone who eats blood must be cut off."

¹⁵" 'If a person, either a citizen or a foreigner, eats an animal that died by itself or was killed by another animal, he must wash his clothes and bathe in water. He will be unclean until evening; then he will be clean. ¹⁶If he does not wash his clothes and bathe his body, he will be guilty of sin.' "

Rules About Sexual Relations

18 The LORD said to Moses, ²"Tell the people of Israel: 'I am the LORD your God. ³In the past you lived in Egypt, but you must not do what was done in that country. And you must not do as they do in the land of Canaan, where I am bringing you. Do not follow their customs. ⁴You must obey my rules and follow them. I am the LORD your God. ⁵Obey my laws and rules; a person who obeys them will live because of them. I am the LORD.

⁶" 'You must never have sexual relations with your close relatives. I am the LORD.

⁷" 'You must not shame your father by having sexual relations with your mother. She is your mother; do not have sexual relations with her. ⁸You must not have sexual relations with your father's wife; that would shame your father.

⁹" 'You must not have sexual relations with your sister, either the daughter of your father or your mother. It doesn't matter if she was born in your house or somewhere else.

¹⁰" 'You must not have sexual relations with your son's daughter or your daughter's daughter; that would bring shame on you.

¹¹" 'If your father and his wife have a daughter, she is your sister. You must not have sexual relations with her.

¹²" 'You must not have sexual relations with your father's sister; she is your father's close relative. ¹³You must not have sexual relations with your mother's sister; she is your mother's close relative. ¹⁴You must not have sexual relations with the wife of your father's brother, because this would shame him. She is your aunt.

¹⁵" 'You must not have sexual relations with your daughter-in-law; she is your son's wife. Do not have sexual relations with her.

¹⁶" 'You must not have sexual relations with your brother's wife. That would shame your brother.

¹⁷" 'You must not have sexual relations with both a woman and her daughter. And do not have sexual relations with this woman's granddaughter, either the daughter of her son or her daughter; they are her close relatives. It is evil to do this.

¹⁸" 'While your wife is still living, you must not take her sister as another wife. Do not have sexual relations with her.

¹⁹" 'You must not go near a woman to have sexual relations with her during her monthly period, when she is unclean.

²⁰" 'You must not have sexual relations with your neighbor's wife and make yourself unclean with her.

²¹" 'You must not give any of your children to be sacrificed to Molech, because this would show that you do not respect your God. I am the LORD.

²²" 'You must not have sexual relations with a man as you would a woman. That is a hateful sin.

²³" 'You must not have sexual relations with an animal and make yourself unclean with it. Also a woman must not have sexual relations with an animal; it is not natural.

²⁴" 'Don't make yourself unclean by any of these wrong things. I am forcing nations out of their countries because they did these sins, and I am giving their land to you. ²⁵The land has become unclean, and I punished it for its sins, so the land is throwing out those people who live there. ²⁶You must obey my laws and rules, and you must not do any of these hateful sins. These rules are for the citizens of Israel and for the people who live with you. ²⁷The people who lived in the land before you did all

these hateful things and made the land unclean. [28]If you do these things, you will also make the land unclean, and it will throw you out as it threw out the nations before you. [29]Anyone who does these hateful sins must be cut off from the people. [30]Keep my command not to do these hateful sins that were done by the people who lived in the land before you. Don't make yourself unclean by doing them. I am the LORD your God.'"

PSALM 27:1–3

A Song of Trust in God

Of David.

27 The LORD is my light and the one who saves me.
So why should I fear anyone?
The LORD protects my life.
So why should I be afraid?
[2]Evil people may try to destroy my body.
My enemies and those who hate me attack me,
but they are overwhelmed and defeated.
[3]If an army surrounds me,
I will not be afraid.
If war breaks out,
I will trust the LORD.

PROVERBS 10:9

[9]The honest person will live in safety,
but the dishonest will be caught.

MARK 4:21–41

Use What You Have

[21]Then Jesus said to them, "Do you hide a lamp under a bowl or under a bed? No! You put the lamp on a lampstand. [22]Everything that is hidden will be made clear and every secret thing will be made known. [23]Let those with ears use them and listen!

[24]"Think carefully about what you hear. The way you give to others is the way God will give to you, but God will give you even more. [25]Those who have understanding will be given more. But those who do not have understanding, even what they have will be taken away from them."

Jesus Uses a Story About Seed

[26]Then Jesus said, "The kingdom of God is like someone who plants seed in the ground. [27]Night and day, whether the person is asleep or awake, the seed still grows, but the person does not know how it grows. [28]By itself the earth produces grain. First the plant grows, then the head, and then all the grain in the head. [29]When the grain is ready, the farmer cuts it, because this is the harvest time."

A Story About Mustard Seed

[30]Then Jesus said, "How can I show you what the kingdom of God is like? What story can I use to explain it? [31]The kingdom of God is like a mustard seed, the smallest seed you plant in the ground. [32]But when planted, this seed grows and becomes the largest of all garden plants. It produces large branches, and the wild birds can make nests in its shade."

[33]Jesus used many stories like these to teach the crowd God's message—as much as they could understand. [34]He always used stories to teach them. But when he and his followers were alone, Jesus explained everything to them.

Jesus Calms a Storm

[35]That evening, Jesus said to his followers, "Let's go across the lake." [36]Leaving the crowd behind, they took him in the boat just as he was. There were also other boats with them. [37]A very strong wind came up on the lake. The waves came over the sides and into the boat so that it was already full of water. [38]Jesus was at the back of the boat, sleeping with his head on a cushion. His followers woke him and said, "Teacher, don't you care that we are drowning!"

[39]Jesus stood up and commanded the wind and said to the waves, "Quiet! Be still!" Then the wind stopped, and it became completely calm.

[40]Jesus said to his followers, "Why are you afraid? Do you still have no faith?"

[41]The followers were very afraid and asked each other, "Who is this? Even the wind and the waves obey him!"

FEBRUARY 25

LEVITICUS 19:1—20:27

Other Laws

19 The LORD said to Moses, [2]"Tell all the people of Israel: 'I am the LORD your God. You must be holy because I am holy.

[3]" 'You must respect your mother and father, and you must keep my Sabbaths. I am the LORD your God.

[4]" 'Do not worship idols or make statues or gods for yourselves. I am the LORD your God.

[5]" 'When you sacrifice a fellowship offering to the LORD, offer it in such a way that will be accepted. [6]You may eat it the same day you offer it or on the next day. But if any is left on the third day, you must burn it up. [7]If any of it is eaten on the third day, it is unclean, and it will not be accepted. [8]Anyone who eats it then will be guilty of sin, because he did not respect the holy things that belong to the LORD. He must be cut off from the people.

[9]" 'When you harvest your crops on your land, do not harvest all the way to the corners of your fields. If grain falls onto the ground, don't gather it up. [10]Don't pick all the grapes in your vineyards, and don't pick up the grapes that fall to the ground. You must leave those things for poor people and for people traveling through your country. I am the LORD your God.

[11]" 'You must not steal. You must not cheat people, and you must not lie to each other. [12]You must not make a false promise by my name, or you will show that you don't respect your God. I am the LORD.

[13]" 'You must not cheat your neighbor or rob him. You must not keep a hired worker's salary all night until morning. [14]You must not curse a deaf person or put something in front of a blind person to make him fall. But you must respect your God. I am the LORD.

[15]" 'Be fair in your judging. You must not show special favor to poor people or great people, but be fair when you judge your neighbor. [16]You must not spread false stories against other people, and you must not do anything that would put your neighbor's life in danger. I am the LORD.

[17]" 'You must not hate your fellow citizen in your heart. If your neighbor does something wrong, tell him about it, or you will be partly to blame. [18]Forget about the wrong things people do to you, and do not try to get even. Love your neighbor as you love yourself. I am the LORD.

[19]" 'Obey my laws. You must not mate two different kinds of cattle or sow your field with two different kinds of seed. You must not wear clothing made from two different kinds of material mixed together.

[20]" 'If a man has sexual relations with a slave girl of another man, but this slave girl has not been bought or given her freedom, there must be punishment. But they are not to be put to death, because the woman was not free. [21]The man must bring a male sheep as his penalty offering to the LORD at the entrance to the Meeting Tent. [22]The priest will offer the sheep as a penalty offering before the LORD for the man's sin, to remove the sins of the man so he will belong to the LORD. Then he will be forgiven for his sin.

[23]" 'In the future, when you enter your country, you will plant many kinds of trees for food. After planting a tree, wait three years before using its fruit. [24]In the fourth year the fruit from the tree will be the LORD's, a holy offering of praise to him. [25]Then in the fifth year, you may eat the fruit from the tree. The tree will then produce more fruit for you. I am the LORD your God.

[26]" 'You must not eat anything with the blood in it.

" 'You must not try to tell the future by signs or black magic.

[27]" 'You must not cut the hair on the sides of your heads or cut the edges of your beard. [28]You must not cut your body to show sadness for someone who died or put tattoo marks on yourselves. I am the LORD.

[29]" 'Do not dishonor your daughter by making her become a prostitute. If you do this, the country will be filled with all kinds of sin.

³⁰" 'Obey the laws about Sabbaths, and respect my Most Holy Place. I am the LORD.

³¹" 'Do not go to mediums or fortune-tellers for advice, or you will become unclean. I am the LORD your God.

³²" 'Show respect to old people; stand up in their presence. Show respect also to your God. I am the LORD.

³³" 'Do not mistreat foreigners living in your country, ³⁴but treat them just as you treat your own citizens. Love foreigners as you love yourselves, because you were foreigners one time in Egypt. I am the LORD your God.

³⁵" 'Do not cheat when you measure the length or weight or amount of something. ³⁶Your weights and balances should weigh correctly, with your weighing baskets the right size and your jars holding the right amount of liquid. I am the LORD your God. I brought you out of the land of Egypt.

³⁷" 'Remember all my laws and rules, and obey them. I am the LORD.' "

Warnings About Various Sins

20 The LORD said to Moses, ²"You must also tell the people of Israel these things: 'If a person in your country gives one of his children to Molech, that person must be killed. It doesn't matter if he is a citizen or a foreigner living in Israel; you must throw stones at him and kill him. ³I will be against him and cut him off from his people, because he gave his children to Molech. He showed that he did not respect my holy name, and he made my Holy Place unclean. ⁴The people of the community might ignore that person and not kill the one who gave his children to Molech. ⁵But I will be against him and his family, and I will cut him off from his people. I will do this to anyone who follows him in being unfaithful to me by worshiping Molech.

⁶" 'I will be against anyone who goes to mediums and fortune-tellers for advice, because that person is being unfaithful to me. So I will cut him off from his people.

⁷" 'Be my holy people. Be holy because I am the LORD your God. ⁸Remember and obey my laws. I am the LORD, and I have made you holy.

⁹" 'Anyone who curses his father or mother must be put to death. He has cursed his father or mother, so he has brought his own death on himself.

Punishments for Sexual Sins

¹⁰" 'If a man has sexual relations with his neighbor's wife, both the man and the woman are guilty of adultery and must be put to death. ¹¹If a man has sexual relations with his father's wife, he has shamed his father, and both the man and his father's wife must be put to death. They have brought it on themselves.

¹²" 'If a man has sexual relations with his daughter-in-law, both of them must be put to death. What they have done is not natural. They have brought their own deaths on themselves.

¹³" 'If a man has sexual relations with another man as a man does with a woman, these two men have done a hateful sin. They must be put to death. They have brought it on themselves.

¹⁴" 'If a man has sexual relations with both a woman and her mother, this is evil. The people must burn that man and the two women in fire so that your people will not be evil.

¹⁵" 'If a man has sexual relations with an animal, he must be put to death. You must also kill the animal. ¹⁶If a woman approaches an animal and has sexual relations with it, you must kill the woman and the animal. They must be put to death. They have brought it on themselves.

¹⁷" 'It is shameful for a brother to marry his sister, the daughter of either his father or his mother, and to have sexual relations with her. In front of everyone they must both be cut off from their people. The man has shamed his sister, and he is guilty of sin.

¹⁸" 'If a man has sexual relations with a woman during her monthly period, both the woman and the man must be cut off from their people. They sinned because they showed the source of her blood.

¹⁹" 'Do not have sexual relations with your mother's sister or your father's sister, because that would shame a close relative. Both of you are guilty of this sin.

²⁰" 'If a man has sexual relations with his uncle's wife, he has shamed his uncle. That

man and his uncle's wife will die without children; they are guilty of sin.

21" 'It is unclean for a man to marry his brother's wife. That man has shamed his brother, and they will have no children.

22" 'Remember all my laws and rules, and obey them. I am leading you to your own land, and if you obey my laws and rules, that land will not throw you out. 23I am forcing out ahead of you the people who live there. Because they did all these sins, I have hated them. Do not live the way those people lived.

24" 'I have told you that you will get their land, which I will give to you as your very own; it is a fertile land. I am the LORD your God, and I have set you apart from other people and made you my own. 25So you must treat clean animals and birds differently from unclean animals and birds. Do not make yourselves unclean by any of these unclean birds or animals or things that crawl on the ground, which I have made unclean for you. 26So you must be holy to me because I, the LORD, am holy, and I have set you apart from other people to be my own.

27" 'A man or woman who is a medium or a fortune-teller must be put to death. You must stone them to death; they have brought it on themselves.' "

PSALM 27:4–6

4I ask only one thing from the LORD.
  This is what I want:
Let me live in the LORD's house
  all my life.
Let me see the LORD's beauty
  and look with my own eyes at his
  Temple.
5During danger he will keep me safe in
  his shelter.
He will hide me in his Holy Tent,
  or he will keep me safe on a high
  mountain.
6My head is higher than my enemies
  around me.
I will offer joyful sacrifices in his Holy
  Tent.
I will sing and praise the LORD.

PROVERBS 10:10–12

10A wink may get you into trouble,
  and foolish talk will lead to your
  ruin.

11The words of a good person give life, like
  a fountain of water,
  but the words of the wicked contain
  nothing but violence.

12Hatred stirs up trouble,
  but love forgives all wrongs.

MARK 5:1–20

A Man with Demons Inside Him

5 Jesus and his followers went to the other side of the lake to the area of the Gerasene[n] people. 2When Jesus got out of the boat, instantly a man with an evil spirit came to him from the burial caves. 3This man lived in the caves, and no one could tie him up, not even with a chain. 4Many times people had used chains to tie the man's hands and feet, but he always broke them off. No one was strong enough to control him. 5Day and night he would wander around the burial caves and on the hills, screaming and cutting himself with stones. 6While Jesus was still far away, the man saw him, ran to him, and fell down before him.

7The man shouted in a loud voice, "What do you want with me, Jesus, Son of the Most High God? I command you in God's name not to torture me!" 8He said this because Jesus was saying to him, "You evil spirit, come out of the man."

9Then Jesus asked him, "What is your name?"

He answered, "My name is Legion,[n] because we are many spirits." 10He begged Jesus again and again not to send them out of that area.

11A large herd of pigs was feeding on a hill near there. 12The demons begged Jesus, "Send us into the pigs; let us go into them." 13So Jesus allowed them to do this. The evil

5:1 Gerasene From Gerasa, an area southeast of Lake Galilee. The exact location is uncertain and some Greek copies read "Gergesene"; others read "Gadarene." **5:9 Legion** Means very many. A legion was about five thousand men in the Roman army.

spirits left the man and went into the pigs. Then the herd of pigs—about two thousand of them—rushed down the hill into the lake and were drowned.

[14]The herdsmen ran away and went to the town and to the countryside, telling everyone about this. So people went out to see what had happened. [15]They came to Jesus and saw the man who used to have the many evil spirits, sitting, clothed, and in his right mind. And they were frightened. [16]The people who saw this told the others what had happened to the man who had the demons living in him, and they told about the pigs. [17]Then the people began to beg Jesus to leave their area.

[18]As Jesus was getting back into the boat, the man who was freed from the demons begged to go with him. [19]But Jesus would not let him. He said, "Go home to your family and tell them how much the Lord has done for you and how he has had mercy on you." [20]So the man left and began to tell the people in the Ten Towns[n] about what Jesus had done for him. And everyone was amazed.

FEBRUARY 26

LEVITICUS 21:1—22:33

How Priests Must Behave

21 The LORD said to Moses, "Tell these things to Aaron's sons, the priests: 'A priest must not make himself unclean by touching a dead person. [2]But if the dead person was one of his close relatives, he may touch him. The priest may make himself unclean if the dead person is his mother or father, son or daughter, brother or [3]unmarried sister who is close to him because she has no husband. The priest may make himself unclean for her if she dies. [4]But a priest must not make himself unclean if the dead person was only related to him by marriage.

[5]"'Priests must not shave their heads, or shave off the edges of their beards, or cut their bodies. [6]They must be holy to their God and show respect for God's name, because they present the offerings made by fire to the LORD, which is the food of their God. So they must be holy.

[7]"'A priest must not marry an unclean prostitute or a divorced woman, because he is holy to his God. [8]Treat him as holy, because he offers up the food of your God. Think of him as holy; I am the LORD who makes you holy, and I am holy.

[9]"'If a priest's daughter makes herself unclean by becoming a prostitute, she shames her father. She must be burned with fire.

[10]"'The high priest, who was chosen from among his brothers, had the special olive oil poured on his head. He was also appointed to wear the priestly clothes. So he must not show his sadness by letting his hair go uncombed or tearing his clothes. [11]He must not go into a house where there is a dead body. He must not make himself unclean, even if it is for his own father or mother. [12]The high priest must not go out of the Holy Place, because if he does and becomes unclean, he will make God's Holy Place unclean. The special oil used in appointing priests was poured on his head to separate him from the rest of the people. I am the LORD.

[13]"'The high priest must marry a woman who is a virgin. [14]He must not marry a widow, a divorced woman, or a prostitute. He must marry a virgin from his own people [15]so the people will respect his children as his own. I am the LORD. I have set the high priest apart for his special job.'"

[16]The LORD said to Moses, [17]"Tell Aaron: 'If any of your descendants have something wrong with them, they must never come near to offer the special food of their God. [18]Anyone who has something wrong with

---

5:20 Ten Towns In Greek, called "Decapolis." It was an area east of Lake Galilee that once had ten main towns.

him must not come near: blind men, crippled men, men with damaged faces, deformed men, [19]men with a crippled foot or hand, [20]hunchbacks, dwarfs, men who have something wrong with their eyes, men who have an itching disease or a skin disease, or men who have damaged sex glands.

[21]" 'If one of Aaron's descendants has something wrong with him, he cannot come near to make the offerings made by fire to the LORD. He has something wrong with him; he cannot offer the food of his God. [22]He may eat the most holy food and also the holy food. [23]But he may not go through the curtain into the Most Holy Place, and he may not go near the altar, because he has something wrong with him. He must not make my Holy Place unfit. I am the LORD who makes these places holy.'"

[24]So Moses told these things to Aaron, Aaron's sons, and all the people of Israel.

22 The LORD said to Moses, [2]"Tell Aaron and his sons: 'The people of Israel will give offerings to me. These offerings are holy, and they are mine, so you must respect them to show that you respect my holy name. I am the LORD.' [3]Say to them: 'If any one of your descendants from now on is unclean and comes near the offerings that the Israelites made holy for me, that person must be cut off from appearing before me. I am the LORD.

[4]" 'If one of Aaron's descendants has a harmful skin disease, or if he discharges a body fluid, he cannot eat the holy offerings until he becomes clean. He could also become unclean from touching a dead body, from his own semen,[n] [5]from touching any unclean crawling animal, or from touching an unclean person (no matter what made the person unclean). [6]Anyone who touches those things will become unclean until evening. That person must not eat the holy offerings unless he washes with water. [7]He will be clean only after the sun goes down. Then he may eat the holy offerings; the offerings are his food.

[8]" 'If a priest finds an animal that died by itself or that was killed by some other animal, he must not eat it. If he does, he will become unclean. I am the LORD.

[9]" 'If the priests keep all the rules I have given, they will not become guilty; if they are careful, they will not die. I am the LORD who has made them holy. [10]Only people in a priest's family may eat the holy offering. A visitor staying with the priest or a hired worker must not eat it. [11]But if the priest buys a slave with his own money, that slave may eat the holy offerings; slaves who were born in his house may also eat his food. [12]If a priest's daughter marries a person who is not a priest, she must not eat any of the holy offerings. [13]But if the priest's daughter becomes widowed or divorced, with no children to support her, and if she goes back to her father's house where she lived as a child, she may eat some of her father's food. But only people from a priest's family may eat this food.

[14]" 'If someone eats some of the holy offering by mistake, that person must pay back the priest for that holy food, adding another one-fifth of the price of that food.

[15]" 'When the Israelites give their holy offerings to the LORD, the priest must not treat these holy things as though they were not holy. [16]The priests must not allow those who are not priests to eat the holy offerings. If they do, they cause the ones who eat the holy offerings to become guilty, and they will have to pay for it. I am the LORD, who makes them holy.'"

[17]The LORD said to Moses, [18]"Tell Aaron and his sons and all the people of Israel: 'A citizen of Israel or a foreigner living in Israel might want to bring a whole burnt offering, either for some special promise he has made or for a special gift he wants to give to the LORD. [19]If he does, he must bring a male animal that has nothing wrong with it—a bull, a sheep, or a goat—so it might be accepted for him. [20]He must not bring an animal that has something wrong with it, or it will not be accepted for him.

[21]" 'If someone brings a fellowship offering to the LORD, either as payment for a special promise the person has made or as a

---

22:4 semen A man's body fluid by which he can make a woman pregnant.

special gift the person wants to give the LORD, it might be from the herd or from the flock. But it must be healthy, with nothing wrong with it, so that it will be accepted. 22You must not offer to the LORD any animal that is blind, that has broken bones or is crippled, that has running sores or any sort of skin disease. You must not offer any animals like these on the altar as an offering by fire to the LORD.

23" 'If an ox or lamb is smaller than normal or is not perfectly formed, you may give it as a special gift to the LORD; it will be accepted. But it will not be accepted as payment for a special promise you have made.

24" 'If an animal has bruised, crushed, torn, or cut sex glands, you must not offer it to the LORD. You must not do this in your own land, 25and you must not take such animals from foreigners as sacrifices to the LORD. Because the animals have been hurt in some way and have something wrong with them, they will not be accepted for you.' "

26The LORD said to Moses, 27"When an ox, a sheep, or a goat is born, it must stay seven days with its mother. But from the eighth day on, this animal will be accepted as a sacrifice by fire to the LORD. 28But you must not kill the animal and its mother on the same day, either an ox or a sheep.

29"If you want to offer some special offering of thanks to the LORD, you must do it in a way that pleases him. 30You must eat the whole animal that same day and not leave any of the meat for the next morning. I am the LORD.

31"Remember my commands and obey them; I am the LORD. 32Show respect for my holy name. You Israelites must remember that I am holy; I am the LORD, who has made you holy. 33I brought you out of Egypt to be your God. I am the LORD."

PSALM 27:7–14

7LORD, hear me when I call;
   have mercy and answer me.
8My heart said of you, "Go, worship him."
   So I come to worship you, LORD.
9Do not turn away from me.
   Do not turn your servant away in anger;
   you have helped me.

Do not push me away or leave me alone,
   God, my Savior.
10If my father and mother leave me,
   the LORD will take me in.
11LORD, teach me your ways,
   and guide me to do what is right
   because I have enemies.
12Do not hand me over to my enemies,
   because they tell lies about me
   and say they will hurt me.
13I truly believe
   I will live to see the LORD's goodness.
14Wait for the LORD's help.
   Be strong and brave,
   and wait for the LORD's help.

PROVERBS 10:13–16

13Wise people speak with understanding,
   but people without wisdom should be
   punished.

14The wise don't tell everything they know,
   but the foolish talk too much and are
   ruined.

15Having lots of money protects the rich,
   but having no money destroys the poor.

16Good people are rewarded with life,
   but evil people are paid with
   punishment.

MARK 5:21–43

Jesus Gives Life to a Dead Girl and Heals a Sick Woman

21When Jesus went in the boat back to the other side of the lake, a large crowd gathered around him there. 22A leader of the synagogue, named Jairus, came there, saw Jesus, and fell at his feet. 23He begged Jesus, saying again and again, "My daughter is dying. Please come and put your hands on her so she will be healed and will live." 24So Jesus went with him.

A large crowd followed Jesus and pushed very close around him. 25Among them was a woman who had been bleeding for twelve years. 26She had suffered very much from many doctors and had spent all the money she had, but instead of improving, she was getting worse. [27]When the woman heard about Jesus, she came up behind him in the crowd and touched his coat. [28]She thought, "If I can just touch his clothes, I will be healed." [29]Instantly her bleeding stopped, and she felt in her body that she was healed from her disease.

[30]At once Jesus felt power go out from him. So he turned around in the crowd and asked, "Who touched my clothes?"

[31]His followers said, "Look at how many people are pushing against you! And you ask, 'Who touched me?'"

[32]But Jesus continued looking around to see who had touched him. [33]The woman, knowing that she was healed, came and fell at Jesus' feet. Shaking with fear, she told him the whole truth. [34]Jesus said to her, "Dear woman, you are made well because you believed. Go in peace; be healed of your disease."

[35]While Jesus was still speaking, some people came from the house of the synagogue leader. They said, "Your daughter is dead. There is no need to bother the teacher anymore."

[36]But Jesus paid no attention to what they said. He told the synagogue leader, "Don't be afraid; just believe."

[37]Jesus let only Peter, James, and John the brother of James go with him. [38]When they came to the house of the synagogue leader, Jesus found many people there making lots of noise and crying loudly. [39]Jesus entered the house and said to them, "Why are you crying and making so much noise? The child is not dead, only asleep." [40]But they laughed at him. So, after throwing them out of the house, Jesus took the child's father and mother and his three followers into the room where the child was. [41]Taking hold of the girl's hand, he said to her, "Talitha, koum!" (This means, "Young girl, I tell you to stand up!") [42]At once the girl stood right up and began walking. (She was twelve years old.) Everyone was completely amazed. [43]Jesus gave them strict orders not to tell people about this. Then he told them to give the girl something to eat.

FEBRUARY 27

LEVITICUS 23:1—24:23

Special Holidays

23 The LORD said to Moses, [2]"Tell the people of Israel: 'You will announce the LORD's appointed feasts as holy meetings. These are my special feasts.

The Sabbath

[3]" 'There are six days for you to work, but the seventh day will be a special day of rest. It is a day for a holy meeting; you must not do any work. It is a Sabbath to the LORD in all your homes.

The Passover and Unleavened Bread

[4]" 'These are the LORD's appointed feasts, the holy meetings, which you will announce at the times set for them. [5]The LORD's Passover is on the fourteenth day of the first month, beginning at twilight. [6]The Feast of Unleavened Bread begins on the fifteenth day of the same month. You will eat bread made without yeast for seven days. [7]On the first day of this feast you will have a holy meeting, and you must not do any work. [8]For seven days you will bring an offering made by fire to the LORD. There will be a holy meeting on the seventh day, and on that day you must not do any regular work.' "

The First of the Harvest

[9]The LORD said to Moses, [10]"Tell the people of Israel: 'You will enter the land I will give you and gather its harvest. At that time you must bring the first bundle of grain from your harvest to the priest. [11]The priest will present the bundle before the LORD, and it will be accepted for you; he will present the bundle on the day after the Sabbath. [12]" 'On the day when you present the bundle of grain, offer a male lamb, one year old, that has nothing wrong with it, as a burnt

offering to the LORD. [13]You must also offer a grain offering—four quarts of fine flour mixed with olive oil as an offering made by fire to the LORD; its smell will be pleasing to him. You must also offer a quart of wine as a drink offering. [14]Until the day you bring your offering to your God, do not eat any new grain, roasted grain, or bread made from new grain. This law will always continue for people from now on, wherever you live.

The Feast of Weeks

[15]" 'Count seven full weeks from the morning after the Sabbath. (This is the Sabbath that you bring the bundle of grain to present as an offering.) [16]On the fiftieth day, the first day after the seventh week, you will bring a new grain offering to the LORD. [17]On that day bring two loaves of bread from your homes to be presented as an offering. Use yeast and four quarts of flour to make those loaves of bread; they will be your gift to the LORD from the first wheat of your harvest.

[18]" 'Offer with the bread one young bull, two male sheep, and seven male lambs that are one year old and have nothing wrong with them. Offer them with their grain offerings and drink offerings, as a burnt offering to the LORD. They will be an offering made by fire, and the smell will be pleasing to the LORD. [19]You must also offer one male goat for a sin offering and two male, one-year-old lambs as a fellowship offering.

[20]" 'The priest will present the two lambs as an offering before the LORD, along with the bread from the first wheat of the harvest. They are holy to the LORD, and they will belong to the priest. [21]On that same day you will call a holy meeting; you must not do any work that day. This law will continue for you from now on, wherever you live.

[22]" 'When you harvest your crops on your land, do not harvest all the way to the corners of your field. If grain falls onto the ground, don't gather it up. Leave it for poor people and foreigners in your country. I am the LORD your God.' "

The Feast of Trumpets

[23]Again the LORD said to Moses, [24]"Tell the people of Israel: 'On the first day of the seventh month you must have a special day of rest, a holy meeting, when you blow the trumpet for a special time of remembering. [25]Do not do any work, and bring an offering made by fire to the LORD.' "

The Day of Cleansing

[26]The LORD said to Moses, [27]"The Day of Cleansing will be on the tenth day of the seventh month. There will be a holy meeting, and you will deny yourselves and bring an offering made by fire to the LORD. [28]Do not do any work on that day, because it is the Day of Cleansing. On that day the priests will go before the LORD and perform the acts to make you clean from sin so you will belong to the LORD.

[29]"Anyone who refuses to give up food on this day must be cut off from the people. [30]If anyone works on this day, I will destroy that person from among the people. [31]You must not do any work at all; this law will continue for people from now on wherever you live. [32]It will be a special day of rest for you, and you must deny yourselves. You will start this special day of rest on the evening after the ninth day of the month, and it will continue from that evening until the next evening."

The Feast of Shelters

[33]Again the LORD said to Moses, [34]"Tell the people of Israel: 'On the fifteenth day of the seventh month is the Feast of Shelters. This feast to the LORD will continue for seven days. [35]There will be a holy meeting on the first day; do not do any work. [36]You will bring an offering made by fire to the LORD each day for seven days. On the eighth day you will have another holy meeting, and you will bring an offering made by fire to the LORD. This will be a holy meeting; do not do any work.

[37](" 'These are the LORD's special feasts, when there will be holy meetings and when you bring offerings made by fire to the LORD. You will bring whole burnt offerings, grain offerings, sacrifices, and drink offerings— each at the right time. [38]These offerings are in addition to those for the LORD's Sabbath days, in addition to offerings you give as payment for special promises, and in addition to special offerings you want to give to the LORD.)

[39] "So on the fifteenth day of the seventh month, after you have gathered in the crops of the land, celebrate the LORD's festival for seven days. You must rest on the first day and the eighth day. [40]On the first day you will take good fruit from the fruit trees, as well as branches from palm trees, poplars, and other leafy trees. You will celebrate before the LORD your God for seven days. [41]Celebrate this festival to the LORD for seven days each year. This law will continue from now on; you will celebrate it in the seventh month. [42]Live in shelters for seven days. All the people born in Israel must live in shelters [43]so that all your descendants will know I made Israel live in shelters during the time I brought them out of Egypt. I am the LORD your God.'"

[44]So Moses told the people of Israel about all of the LORD's appointed feast days.

The Lampstand and the Holy Bread

24 The LORD said to Moses, [2]"Command the people of Israel to bring you pure oil from crushed olives. That oil is for the lamps so that these lamps may never go out. [3]Aaron will keep the lamps burning in the Meeting Tent from evening until morning before the LORD; this is in front of the curtain of the Ark of the Agreement. This law will continue from now on. [4]Aaron must always keep the lamps burning on the lampstands of pure gold before the LORD.

[5]"Take fine flour and bake twelve loaves of bread with it, using four quarts of flour for each loaf. [6]Put them in two rows on the golden table before the LORD, six loaves in each row. [7]Put pure incense on each row as the memorial portion to take the place of the bread. It is an offering made by fire to the LORD. [8]Every Sabbath day Aaron will put the bread in order before the LORD, as an agreement with the people of Israel that will continue forever. [9]That bread will belong to Aaron and his sons. They will eat it in a holy place, because it is a most holy part of the offerings made by fire to the LORD. That bread is their share forever."

The Man Who Cursed God

[10]Now there was a son of an Israelite woman and an Egyptian father who was walking among the Israelites. A fight broke out in the camp between him and an Israelite. [11]The son of the Israelite woman began cursing and speaking against the LORD, so the people took him to Moses. (The mother's name was Shelomith, the daughter of Dibri from the family of Dan.) [12]The people held him as a prisoner while they waited for the LORD's command to be made clear to them.

[13]Then the LORD said to Moses, [14]"Take the one who spoke against me outside the camp. Then all the people who heard him must put their hands on his head, and all the people must throw stones at him and kill him. [15]Tell the people of Israel this: 'If anyone curses his God, he is guilty of sin. [16]Anyone who speaks against the LORD must be put to death; all the people must kill him by throwing stones at him. Foreigners must be punished just like the people born in Israel; if they speak against the LORD, they must be put to death.

[17]"'Whoever kills another person must be put to death. [18]Whoever kills an animal that belongs to another person must give that person another animal to take its place. [19]And whoever causes an injury to a neighbor must receive the same kind of injury in return: [20]Broken bone for broken bone, eye for eye, tooth for tooth. Anyone who injures another person must be injured in the same way in return. [21]Whoever kills another person's animal must give that person another animal to take its place. But whoever kills another person must be put to death.

[22]"'The law will be the same for the foreigner as for those from your own country. I am the LORD your God.'"

[23]Then Moses spoke to the people of Israel, and they took the person who had cursed outside the camp and killed him by throwing stones at him. So the people of Israel did as the LORD had commanded Moses.

PSALM 28:1–5

A Prayer in Troubled Times

Of David.

28 LORD, my Rock, I call out to you for help.
Do not be deaf to me.

If you are silent,
    I will be like those in the grave.
[2]Hear the sound of my prayer,
    when I cry out to you for help.
I raise my hands
    toward your Most Holy Place.
[3]Don't drag me away with the wicked,
    with those who do evil.
They say "Peace" to their neighbors,
    but evil is in their hearts.
[4]Pay them back for what they have done,
    for their evil deeds.
Pay them back for what they have done;
    give them their reward.
[5]They don't understand what the LORD has done
    or what he has made.
So he will knock them down
    and not lift them up.

PROVERBS 10:17–18

[17]Whoever accepts correction is on the way to life,
    but whoever ignores correction will
    lead others away from life.
[18]Whoever hides hate is a liar.
    Whoever tells lies is a fool.

MARK 6:1–29

Jesus Goes to His Hometown

6 Jesus left there and went to his hometown, and his followers went with him. [2]On the Sabbath day he taught in the synagogue. Many people heard him and were amazed, saying, "Where did this man get these teachings? What is this wisdom that has been given to him? And where did he get the power to do miracles? [3]He is just the carpenter, the son of Mary and the brother of James, Joseph, Judas, and Simon. And his sisters are here with us." So the people were upset with Jesus.

[4]Jesus said to them, "A prophet is honored everywhere except in his hometown and with his own people and in his own home."

[5]So Jesus was not able to work any miracles there except to heal a few sick people by putting his hands on them. [6]He was amazed at how many people had no faith.

Then Jesus went to other villages in that area and taught. [7]He called his twelve followers together and got ready to send them out two by two and gave them authority over evil spirits. [8]This is what Jesus commanded them: "Take nothing for your trip except a walking stick. Take no bread, no bag, and no money in your pockets. [9]Wear sandals, but take only the clothes you are wearing. [10]When you enter a house, stay there until you leave that town. [11]If the people in a certain place refuse to welcome you or listen to you, leave that place. Shake its dust off your feet[n] as a warning to them."[n]

[12]So the followers went out and preached that people should change their hearts and lives. [13]They forced many demons out and put olive oil on many sick people and healed them.

How John the Baptist Was Killed

[14]King Herod heard about Jesus, because he was now well known. Some people said,[n] "He is John the Baptist, who has risen from the dead. That is why he can work these miracles."

[15]Others said, "He is Elijah."[n]

Other people said, "Jesus is a prophet, like the prophets who lived long ago."

[16]When Herod heard this, he said, "I killed John by cutting off his head. Now he has risen from the dead!"

[17]Herod himself had ordered his soldiers to arrest John and put him in prison in order to please his wife, Herodias. She had been the wife of Philip, Herod's brother, but then Herod had married her. [18]John had been telling Herod, "It is not lawful for you to be married to your brother's wife." [19]So Herodias hated John and wanted to kill him. But she couldn't, [20]because Herod was afraid of John and protected him. He knew John was a good and holy man. Also, though John's

6:11 **Shake . . . feet** A warning. It showed that they were rejecting these people. 6:11 **them** Some Greek copies continue, "I tell you the truth, on the Judgment Day it will be better for the towns of Sodom and Gomorrah than for the people of that town." See Matthew 10:15. 6:14 **Some people said** Some Greek copies read "He said." 6:15 **Elijah** A great prophet who spoke for God and who lived hundreds of years before Christ. See 1 Kings 17.

preaching always bothered him, he enjoyed listening to John.

²¹Then the perfect time came for Herodias to cause John's death. On Herod's birthday, he gave a dinner party for the most important government leaders, the commanders of his army, and the most important people in Galilee. ²²When the daughter of Herodias^n came in and danced, she pleased Herod and the people eating with him.

So King Herod said to the girl, "Ask me for anything you want, and I will give it to you." ²³He promised her, "Anything you ask for I will give to you—up to half of my kingdom."

²⁴The girl went to her mother and asked, "What should I ask for?"

Her mother answered, "Ask for the head of John the Baptist."

²⁵At once the girl went back to the king and said to him, "I want the head of John the Baptist right now on a platter."

²⁶Although the king was very sad, he had made a promise, and his dinner guests had heard it. So he did not want to refuse what she asked. ²⁷Immediately the king sent a soldier to bring John's head. The soldier went and cut off John's head in the prison ²⁸and brought it back on a platter. He gave it to the girl, and the girl gave it to her mother. ²⁹When John's followers heard this, they came and got John's body and put it in a tomb.

FEBRUARY 28

LEVITICUS 25:1–55

The Time of Rest for the Land

25 The LORD said to Moses at Mount Sinai, ²"Tell the people of Israel this: 'When you enter the land I will give you, let it have a special time of rest, to honor the LORD. ³You may plant seed in your field for six years, and you may trim your vineyards for six years and bring in their fruits. ⁴But during the seventh year, you must let the land rest. This will be a special time to honor the LORD. You must not plant seed in your field or trim your vineyards. ⁵You must not cut the crops that grow by themselves after harvest, or gather the grapes from your vines that are not trimmed. The land will have a year of rest.

⁶" 'You may eat whatever the land produces during that year of rest. It will be food for your men and women servants, for your hired workers, and for the foreigners living in your country. ⁷It will also be food for your cattle and the wild animals of your land. Whatever the land produces may be eaten.

The Year of Jubilee

⁸" 'Count off seven groups of seven years, or forty-nine years. During that time there will be seven years of rest for the land. ⁹On the Day of Cleansing, you must blow the horn of a male sheep; this will be on the tenth day of the seventh month. You must blow the horn through the whole country. ¹⁰Make the fiftieth year a special year, and announce freedom for all the people living in your country. This time will be called Jubilee.^{n} You will each go back to your own property, each to your own family and family group. ¹¹The fiftieth year will be a special time for you to celebrate. Don't plant seeds, or harvest the crops that grow by themselves, or gather grapes from the vines that are not trimmed. ¹²That year is Jubilee; it will be a holy time for you. You may eat only the crops that come from the field. ¹³In the year of Jubilee you each must go back to your own property.

¹⁴" 'If you sell your land to your neighbor, or if you buy land from your neighbor, don't cheat each other. ¹⁵If you want to buy your neighbor's land, count the number of years

6:22 When . . . Herodias Some Greek copies read "When his daughter Herodias." • **25:10 Jubilee** This word comes from the Hebrew word for a horn of a male sheep.

since the last Jubilee, and use that number to decide the right price. If your neighbor sells the land to you, count the number of years left for harvesting crops, and use that number to decide the right price. ¹⁶If there are many years, the price will be high. But if there are only a few years, lower the price, because your neighbor is really selling only a few crops to you. ¹⁷You must not cheat each other, but you must respect your God. I am the LORD your God.

¹⁸" 'Remember my laws and rules, and obey them so that you will live safely in the land. ¹⁹The land will give good crops to you, and you will eat as much as you want and live safely in the land.

²⁰" 'But you might ask, "If we don't plant seeds or gather crops, what will we eat the seventh year?" ²¹I will send you such a great blessing during the sixth year that the land will produce enough crops for three years. ²²When you plant in the eighth year, you will still be eating from the old crop; you will eat the old crop until the harvest of the ninth year.

Property Laws

²³" 'The land really belongs to me, so you can't sell it for all time. You are only foreigners and travelers living for a while on my land. ²⁴People might sell their land, but it must always be possible for the family to get its land back. ²⁵If a person in your country becomes very poor and sells some land, then close relatives must come and buy it back. ²⁶If there is not a close relative to buy the land back, but if the person makes enough money to be able to buy it back, ²⁷the years must be counted since the land was sold. That number must be used to decide how much the first owner should pay back the one who bought it. Then the land will belong to the first owner again. ²⁸But if there is not enough money to buy it back, the one who bought it will keep it until the year of Jubilee. During that celebration, the land will go back to the first owner's family.

²⁹" 'If someone sells a home in a walled city, for a full year after it is sold, the person has the right to buy it back. ³⁰But if the owner does not buy back the house before a full year is over, it will belong to the one who bought it and to his future sons. The house will not go back to the first owner at Jubilee. ³¹But houses in small towns without walls are like open country; they can be bought back, and they must be returned to their first owner at Jubilee.

³²" 'The Levites may always buy back their houses in the cities that belong to them. ³³If someone buys a house from a Levite, that house in the Levites' city will again belong to the Levites in the Jubilee. This is because houses in Levite cities belong to the people of Levi; the Israelites gave these cities to them. ³⁴Also the fields and pastures around the Levites' cities cannot be sold, because those fields belong to the Levites forever.

Rules for Slave Owners

³⁵" 'If anyone from your country becomes too poor to support himself, help him to live among you as you would a stranger or foreigner. ³⁶Do not charge him any interest on money you loan to him, but respect your God; let the poor live among you. ³⁷Don't lend him money for interest, and don't try to make a profit from the food he buys. ³⁸I am the LORD your God, who brought you out of the land of Egypt to give the land of Canaan to you and to become your God.

³⁹" 'If anyone from your country becomes very poor and sells himself as a slave to you, you must not make him work like a slave. ⁴⁰He will be like a hired worker and a visitor with you until the year of Jubilee. ⁴¹Then he may leave you, take his children, and go back to his family and the land of his ancestors. ⁴²This is because the Israelites are my servants, and I brought them out of slavery in Egypt. They must not become slaves again. ⁴³You must not rule this person cruelly, but you must respect your God.

⁴⁴" 'Your men and women slaves must come from other nations around you; from them you may buy slaves. ⁴⁵Also you may buy as slaves children from the families of foreigners living in your land. These child slaves will belong to you, ⁴⁶and you may even pass them on to your children after you die; you can make them slaves forever. But you must not rule cruelly over your own people, the Israelites.

⁴⁷" 'Suppose a foreigner or visitor among you becomes rich. If someone in your country becomes so poor that he has to sell himself as a slave to the foreigner living among you or to a member of the foreigner's family, ⁴⁸the poor person has the right to be bought back and become free. One of his relatives may buy him back: ⁴⁹His uncle, his uncle's son, or any one of his close relatives may buy him back. Or, if he gets enough money, he may pay the money to free himself.

⁵⁰" 'He and the one who bought him must count the time from when he sold himself up to the next year of Jubilee. Use that number to decide the price, because the person really only hired himself out for a certain number of years. ⁵¹If there are still many years before the year of Jubilee, the person must pay back a large part of the price. ⁵²If there are only a few years left until Jubilee, the person must pay a small part of the first price. ⁵³But he will live like a hired person with the foreigner every year; don't let the foreigner rule cruelly over him.

⁵⁴" 'Even if no one buys him back, at the year of Jubilee, he and his children will become free. ⁵⁵This is because the people of Israel are servants to me. They are my servants, whom I brought out of Egypt. I am the LORD your God.

PSALM 28:6–9

⁶Praise the LORD,
  because he heard my prayer for help.
⁷The LORD is my strength and shield.
  I trust him, and he helps me.
I am very happy,
  and I praise him with my song.
⁸The LORD is powerful;
  he gives victory to his chosen one.
⁹Save your people
  and bless those who are your own.
  Be their shepherd and carry them
    forever.

PROVERBS 10:19–21

¹⁹If you talk a lot, you are sure to sin;
  if you are wise, you will keep quiet.

²⁰The words of a good person are like pure silver,
  but an evil person's thoughts are worth very little.
²¹Good people's words will help many others,
  but fools will die because they don't have wisdom.

MARK 6:30–56

More than Five Thousand Fed

³⁰The apostles gathered around Jesus and told him about all the things they had done and taught. ³¹Crowds of people were coming and going so that Jesus and his followers did not even have time to eat. He said to them, "Come away by yourselves, and we will go to a lonely place to get some rest."

³²So they went in a boat by themselves to a lonely place. ³³But many people saw them leave and recognized them. So from all the towns they ran to the place where Jesus was going, and they got there before him. ³⁴When he arrived, he saw a great crowd waiting. He felt sorry for them, because they were like sheep without a shepherd. So he began to teach them many things.

³⁵When it was late in the day, his followers came to him and said, "No one lives in this place, and it is already very late. ³⁶Send the people away so they can go to the countryside and towns around here to buy themselves something to eat."

³⁷But Jesus answered, "You give them something to eat."

They said to him, "We would all have to work a month to earn enough money to buy that much bread!"

³⁸Jesus asked them, "How many loaves of bread do you have? Go and see."

When they found out, they said, "Five loaves and two fish."

³⁹Then Jesus told his followers to have the people sit in groups on the green grass. ⁴⁰So they sat in groups of fifty or a hundred. ⁴¹Jesus took the five loaves and two fish and, looking up to heaven, he thanked God for the food. He divided the bread and gave it to his followers for them to give to the people. Then he divided the two fish among them

all. [42]All the people ate and were satisfied. [43]The followers filled twelve baskets with the leftover pieces of bread and fish. [44]There were five thousand men who ate.

Jesus Walks on the Water

[45]Immediately Jesus told his followers to get into the boat and go ahead of him to Bethsaida across the lake. He stayed there to send the people home. [46]After sending them away, he went into the hills to pray.

[47]That night, the boat was in the middle of the lake, and Jesus was alone on the land. [48]He saw his followers struggling hard to row the boat, because the wind was blowing against them. Between three and six o'clock in the morning, Jesus came to them, walking on the water, and he wanted to walk past the boat. [49]But when they saw him walking on the water, they thought he was a ghost and cried out. [50]They all saw him and were afraid. But quickly Jesus spoke to them and said, "Have courage! It is I. Do not be afraid." [51]Then he got into the boat with them, and the wind became calm. The followers were greatly amazed. [52]They did not understand about the miracle of the five loaves, because their minds were closed.

[53]When they had crossed the lake, they came to shore at Gennesaret and tied the boat there. [54]When they got out of the boat, people immediately recognized Jesus. [55]They ran everywhere in that area and began to bring sick people on mats wherever they heard he was. [56]And everywhere he went—into towns, cities, or countryside—the people brought the sick to the marketplaces. They begged him to let them touch just the edge of his coat, and all who touched it were healed.

MARCH 1

Rewards for Obeying God

26 " 'Don't make idols for yourselves or set up statues or memorials. Don't put stone statues in your land to bow down to, because I am the LORD your God.

²" 'Remember my Sabbaths, and respect my Holy Place. I am the LORD.

³" 'If you remember my laws and commands and obey them, ⁴I will give you rains at the right season; the land will produce crops, and the trees of the field will produce their fruit. ⁵Your threshing will continue until the grape harvest, and your grape harvest will continue until it is time to plant. Then you will have plenty to eat and live safely in your land. ⁶I will give peace to your country; you will lie down in peace, and no one will make you afraid. I will keep harmful animals out of your country, and armies will not pass through it.

⁷" 'You will chase your enemies and defeat them, killing them with your sword. ⁸Five of you will chase a hundred men; a hundred of you will chase ten thousand men. You will defeat your enemies and kill them with your sword.

⁹" 'Then I will show kindness to you and let you have many children; I will keep my agreement with you. ¹⁰You will have enough crops to last for more than a year. When you harvest the new crops, you will have to throw out the old ones to make room for them. ¹¹Also I will place my Holy Tent among you, and I will not turn away from you. ¹²I will walk with you and be your God, and you will be my people. ¹³I am the LORD your God, who brought you out of Egypt, where you were slaves. I broke the heavy weights that were on your shoulders and let you walk proudly again.

Punishment for Not Obeying God

¹⁴" 'But if you do not obey me and keep all my commands, ¹⁵and if you turn away from my rules and hate my laws, refusing to obey

all my commands, you have broken our agreement. ¹⁶As a result, I will do this to you: I will cause terrible things to happen to you. I will cause you to have disease and fever that will destroy your eyes and slowly kill you. You will not have success when you plant your seed, and your enemy will eat your crops. ¹⁷I will be against you, and your enemies will defeat you. These people who hate you will rule over you, and you will run away even when no one is chasing you.

¹⁸" 'If after all this you still do not obey me, I will punish you seven times more for your sins. ¹⁹I will break your great pride, and I will make the sky like iron and the earth like bronze.ⁿ ²⁰You will work hard, but it will not help. Your land will not grow any crops, and your trees will not give their fruit.

²¹" 'If you still turn against me and refuse to obey me, I will beat you seven times harder. The more you sin, the more you will be punished. ²²I will send wild animals to attack you, and they will take your children away from you and destroy your cattle. They will make you so few in number the roads will be empty.

²³" 'If you don't learn your lesson after all these things, and if you still turn against me, ²⁴I will also turn against you. I will punish you seven more times for your sins. ²⁵You broke my agreement, and I will punish you. I will bring armies against you, and if you go into your cities for safety, I will cause diseases to spread among you so that your enemy will defeat you. ²⁶There will be very little bread to eat; ten women will be able to cook all your bread in one oven. They will measure each piece of bread, and you will eat, but you will still be hungry.

²⁷" 'If you still refuse to listen to me and still turn against me, ²⁸I will show my great anger; I will punish you seven more times for your sins. ²⁹You will eat the bodies of your sons and daughters. ³⁰I will destroy your places where gods are worshiped and cut down your incense altars. I will pile your

26:19 **sky . . . bronze** This means the sky will give no rain and the earth will produce no crops.

dead bodies on the lifeless forms of your idols. I will hate you. [31]I will destroy your cities and make your holy places empty, and I will not smell the pleasing smell of your offerings. [32]I will make the land empty so that your enemies who come to live in it will be shocked at it. [33]I will scatter you among the nations, and I will pull out my sword and destroy you. Your land will become empty, your cities a waste. [34]When you are taken to your enemy's country, your land will finally get its rest. It will enjoy its time of rest all the time it lies empty. [35]During the time the land is empty, it will have the rest you should have given it while you lived in it.

[36] 'Those of you who are left alive will lose their courage in the land of their enemies. They will be frightened by the sound of a leaf being blown by the wind. They will run as if someone were chasing them with a sword, and they will fall even when no one is chasing them. [37]They will fall over each other, as if someone were chasing them with a sword, even though no one is chasing them. You will not be strong enough to stand up against your enemies. [38]You will die among other nations and disappear in your enemies' countries. [39]So those who are left alive will rot away in their enemies' countries because of their sins. They will also rot away because of their ancestors' sins.

There Is Always Hope

[40] 'But maybe the people will confess their sins and the sins of their ancestors; maybe they will admit they turned against me and sinned against me, [41]which made me turn against them and send them into the land of their enemies. If these disobedient people are sorry for what they did and accept punishment for their sin, [42]I will remember my agreement with Jacob, my agreement with Isaac, and my agreement with Abraham, and I will remember the land. [43]The land will be left empty by its people, and it will enjoy its time of rest as it lies bare without them. Then those who are left alive will accept the punishment for their sins. They will learn that they were punished because they hated my laws and refused to obey my rules. [44]But even though this is true,

I will not turn away from them when they are in the land of their enemies. I will not hate them so much that I completely destroy them and break my agreement with them, because I am the LORD their God. [45]For their good I will remember the agreement with their ancestors, whom I brought out of the land of Egypt so I could become their God; the other nations saw these things. I am the LORD.' "

[46]These are the laws, rules, and teachings the LORD made between himself and the Israelites through Moses at Mount Sinai.

Promises Are Important

27 The LORD said to Moses, [2]"Speak to the people of Israel and tell them: 'If someone makes a special promise to give a person as a servant to the LORD by paying a price that is the same value as that person, [3]the price for a man twenty to sixty years old is about one and one-fourth pounds of silver. (You must use the measure as set by the Holy Place.) [4]The price for a woman twenty to sixty years old is about twelve ounces of silver. [5]The price for a man five to twenty years old is about eight ounces of silver; for a woman it is about four ounces of silver. [6]The price for a baby boy one month to five years old is about two ounces of silver; for a baby girl the price is about one and one-half ounces of silver. [7]The price for a man sixty years old or older is about six ounces of silver; for a woman it is about four ounces of silver.

[8] 'If anyone is too poor to pay the price, bring him to the priest, and the priest will set the price. The priest will decide how much money the person making the vow can afford to pay.

Gifts to the Lord

[9] 'Some animals may be used as sacrifices to the LORD. If someone promises to bring one of these to the LORD, it will become holy. [10]That person must not try to put another animal in its place or exchange it, a good animal for a bad one, or a bad animal for a good one. If this happens, both animals will become holy.

[11] 'Unclean animals cannot be offered as sacrifices to the LORD, and if someone brings one of them to the LORD, that animal must be

brought to the priest. ¹²The priest will decide a price for the animal, according to whether it is good or bad; as the priest decides, that is the price for the animal. ¹³If the person wants to buy back the animal, an additional one-fifth must be added to the price.

Value of a House

¹⁴"If a person gives a house as holy to the LORD, the priest must decide its value, according to whether the house is good or bad; as the priest decides, that is the price for the house. ¹⁵But if the person who gives the house wants to buy it back, an additional one-fifth must be added to the price. Then the house will belong to that person again.

Value of Land

¹⁶"If a person gives some family property to the LORD, the value of the fields will depend on how much seed is needed to plant them. It will cost about one and one-fourth pounds of silver for each six bushels of barley seed needed. ¹⁷If the person gives a field at the year of Jubilee, its value will stay at what the priest has decided. ¹⁸But if the person gives the field after the Jubilee, the priest must decide the exact price by counting the number of years to the next year of Jubilee. Then he will subtract that number from its value. ¹⁹If the person who gave the field wants to buy it back, one-fifth must be added to that price, and the field will belong to the first owner again.

²⁰"If the person does not buy back the field, or if it is sold to someone else, the first person cannot ever buy it back. ²¹When the land is released at the year of Jubilee, it will become holy to the LORD, like land specially given to him. It will become the property of the priests.

²²"If someone gives to the LORD a field he has bought, which is not a part of his family land, ²³the priest must count the years to the next Jubilee. He must decide the price for the land, and the price must be paid on that day. Then that land will be holy to the LORD. ²⁴At the year of Jubilee, the land will go back to its first owner, to the family who sold the land.

²⁵"You must use the measure as set by the Holy Place in paying these prices; it weighs two-fifths of an ounce.

Value of Animals

²⁶"If an animal is the first one born to its parent, it already belongs to the LORD, so people may not give it again. If it is a cow or a sheep, it is the LORD's. ²⁷If the animal is unclean, the person must buy it back for the price set by the priest, and the person must add one-fifth to that price. If it is not bought back, the priest must sell it for the price he had decided.

²⁸"There is a special kind of gift that people set apart to give to the LORD; it may be a person, animal, or field from the family property. That gift cannot be bought back or sold. Every special kind of gift is most holy to the LORD.

²⁹"If anyone is given for the purpose of being destroyed, he cannot be bought back; he must be put to death.

³⁰"One-tenth of all crops belongs to the LORD, including the crops from fields and the fruit from trees. That one-tenth is holy to the LORD. ³¹If a person wants to get back that tenth, one-fifth must be added to its price.

³²"The priest will take every tenth animal from a person's herd or flock, and it will be holy to the LORD. ³³The owner should not pick out the good animals from the bad or exchange one animal for another. If that happens, both animals will become holy; they cannot be bought back.'"

³⁴These are the commands the LORD gave to Moses at Mount Sinai for the people of Israel.

PSALM 29:1–9

God in the Thunderstorm

A psalm of David.

29 Praise the LORD, you angels;
 praise the LORD's glory and
 power.
²Praise the LORD for the glory of his name;
 worship the LORD because he is holy.

³The LORD's voice is heard over the sea.
 The glorious God thunders;
 the LORD thunders over the ocean.
⁴The LORD's voice is powerful;
 the LORD's voice is majestic.

⁵The LORD's voice breaks the trees;
  the LORD breaks the cedars of Lebanon.
⁶He makes the land of Lebanon dance like a
    calf
  and Mount Hermon jump like a baby
    bull.
⁷The LORD's voice makes the lightning
    flash.
⁸The LORD's voice shakes the desert;
  the LORD shakes the Desert of Kadesh.
⁹The LORD's voice shakes the oaks
  and strips the leaves off the trees.
  In his Temple everyone says, "Glory to
    God!"

PROVERBS 10:22–25

²²The LORD's blessing brings wealth,
  and no sorrow comes with it.

²³A foolish person enjoys doing wrong,
  but a person with understanding enjoys
    doing what is wise.

²⁴Evil people will get what they fear most,
  but good people will get what they want
    most.

²⁵A storm will blow the evil person away,
  but a good person will always be safe.

MARK 7:1–23

Obey God's Law

7 When some Pharisees and some teachers
of the law came from Jerusalem, they
gathered around Jesus. ²They saw that some
of Jesus' followers ate food with hands that
were not clean, that is, they hadn't washed
them. ³(The Pharisees and all the Jews never
eat before washing their hands in the way required by their unwritten laws. ⁴And when
they buy something in the market, they
never eat it until they wash themselves in a
special way. They also follow many other unwritten laws, such as the washing of cups,
pitchers, and pots.ⁿ)
  ⁵The Pharisees and the teachers of the law
said to Jesus, "Why don't your followers obey

the unwritten laws which have been handed
down to us? Why do your followers eat their
food with hands that are not clean?"
  ⁶Jesus answered, "Isaiah was right when
he spoke about you hypocrites. He wrote,
'These people show honor to me with
    words,
  but their hearts are far from me.
⁷Their worship of me is worthless.
  The things they teach are nothing but
    human rules.'   *Isaiah 29:13*
⁸You have stopped following the commands
of God, and you follow only human teachings."ⁿ
  ⁹Then Jesus said to them, "You cleverly ignore the commands of God so you can follow your own teachings. ¹⁰Moses said,
'Honor your father and your mother,'ⁿ and
'Anyone who says cruel things to his father
or mother must be put to death.'ⁿ ¹¹But you
say a person can tell his father or mother, 'I
have something I could use to help you, but
it is Corban—a gift to God.' ¹²You no longer
let that person use that money for his father
or his mother. ¹³By your own rules, which
you teach people, you are rejecting what God
said. And you do many things like that."
  ¹⁴After Jesus called the crowd to him
again, he said, "Every person should listen to
me and understand what I am saying.
¹⁵There is nothing people put into their bodies that makes them unclean. People are
made unclean by the things that come out of
them. [¹⁶Let those with ears use them and
listen.]"ⁿ
  ¹⁷When Jesus left the people and went
into the house, his followers asked him
about this story. ¹⁸Jesus said, "Do you still
not understand? Surely you know that nothing that enters someone from the outside
can make that person unclean. ¹⁹It does not
go into the mind, but into the stomach. Then
it goes out of the body." (When Jesus said
this, he meant that no longer was any food
unclean for people to eat.)
  ²⁰And Jesus said, "The things that come

7:4 pots Some Greek copies continue, "and dining couches." **7:8 teachings** Some Greek copies continue, "You wash pitchers and jugs and do many other such things." **7:10 'Honor . . . mother.'** Quotation from Exodus 20:12; Deuteronomy 5:16.
7:10 'Anyone . . . death.' Quotation from Exodus 21:17. **7:16 Let . . . listen.** Some Greek copies do not contain the bracketed text.

out of people are the things that make them unclean. [21]All these evil things begin inside people, in the mind: evil thoughts, sexual sins, stealing, murder, adultery, [22]greed, evil

actions, lying, doing sinful things, jealousy, speaking evil of others, pride, and foolish living. [23]All these evil things come from inside and make people unclean."

MARCH 2

NUMBERS 1:1—2:34

The People of Israel Are Counted

1 The LORD spoke to Moses in the Meeting Tent in the Desert of Sinai. This was on the first day of the second month in the second year after the Israelites left Egypt. He said to Moses: [2]"You and Aaron must count all the people of Israel by families and family groups, listing the name of each man. [3]You and Aaron must count every man twenty years old or older who will serve in the army of Israel, and list them by their divisions. [4]One man from each tribe, the leader of his family, will help you. [5]These are the names of the men who will help you:

from the tribe of Reuben—Elizur son of Shedeur;
[6]from the tribe of Simeon—Shelumiel son of Zurishaddai;
[7]from the tribe of Judah—Nahshon son of Amminadab;
[8]from the tribe of Issachar—Nethanel son of Zuar;
[9]from the tribe of Zebulun—Eliab son of Helon;
[10]from the tribe of Ephraim son of Joseph—Elishama son of Ammihud;
from the tribe of Manasseh son of Joseph—Gamaliel son of Pedahzur;
[11]from the tribe of Benjamin—Abidan son of Gideoni;
[12]from the tribe of Dan—Ahiezer son of Ammishaddai;
[13]from the tribe of Asher—Pagiel son of Ocran;
[14]from the tribe of Gad—Eliasaph son of Deuel;
[15]from the tribe of Naphtali—Ahira son of Enan."

[16]These were the men chosen from the people to be leaders of their tribes, the heads of Israel's family groups.

[17]Moses and Aaron took these men who had been picked [18]and called all the people of Israel together on the first day of the second month. Then the people were listed by their families and family groups, and all the men who were twenty years old or older were listed by name. [19]Moses did exactly what the LORD had commanded and listed the people while they were in the Desert of Sinai.

[20]The tribe of Reuben, the first son born to Israel, was counted; all the men twenty years old or older who were able to serve in the army were listed by name with their families and family groups. [21]The tribe of Reuben totaled 46,500 men.

[22]The tribe of Simeon was counted; all the men twenty years old or older who were able to serve in the army were listed by name with their families and family groups. [23]The tribe of Simeon totaled 59,300 men.

[24]The tribe of Gad was counted; all the men twenty years old or older who were able to serve in the army were listed by name with their families and family groups. [25]The tribe of Gad totaled 45,650 men.

[26]The tribe of Judah was counted; all the men twenty years old or older who were able to serve in the army were listed by name with their families and family groups. [27]The tribe of Judah totaled 74,600 men.

[28]The tribe of Issachar was counted; all the men twenty years old or older who were able to serve in the army were listed by name with their families and family groups. [29]The tribe of Issachar totaled 54,400 men.

[30]The tribe of Zebulun was counted; all

the men twenty years old or older who were able to serve in the army were listed by name with their families and family groups. [31]The tribe of Zebulun totaled 57,400 men.

[32]The tribe of Ephraim, a son of Joseph, was counted; all the men twenty years old or older who were able to serve in the army were listed by name with their families and family groups. [33]The tribe of Ephraim totaled 40,500 men.

[34]The tribe of Manasseh, also a son of Joseph, was counted; all the men twenty years old or older who were able to serve in the army were listed by name with their families and family groups. [35]The tribe of Manasseh totaled 32,200 men.

[36]The tribe of Benjamin was counted; all the men twenty years old or older who were able to serve in the army were listed by name with their families and family groups. [37]The tribe of Benjamin totaled 35,400 men.

[38]The tribe of Dan was counted; all the men twenty years old or older who were able to serve in the army were listed by name with their families and family groups. [39]The tribe of Dan totaled 62,700 men.

[40]The tribe of Asher was counted; all the men twenty years old or older who were able to serve in the army were listed by name with their families and family groups. [41]The tribe of Asher totaled 41,500 men.

[42]The tribe of Naphtali was counted; all the men twenty years old or older who were able to serve in the army were listed by name with their families and family groups. [43]The tribe of Naphtali totaled 53,400 men.

[44]Moses, Aaron, and the twelve leaders of Israel, one from each of the families, counted these men. [45]Every man of Israel twenty years old or older who was able to serve in the army was counted and listed with his family. [46]The total number of men was 603,550.

[47]The families from the tribe of Levi were not listed with the others, because [48]the LORD had told Moses: [49]"Do not count the tribe of Levi or include them with the other Israelites. [50]Instead put the Levites in charge of the Holy Tent of the Agreement and everything that is with it. They must carry the Holy Tent and everything in it, and they must take care of it and make their camp

around it. [51]Any time the Holy Tent is moved, the Levites must take it down, and any time it is set up, the Levites must do it. Anyone else who goes near the Holy Tent will be put to death. [52]The Israelites will make their camps in separate divisions, each family near its flag. [53]But the Levites must make their camp around the Holy Tent of the Agreement so that I will not be angry with the Israelites. The Levites will take care of the Holy Tent of the Agreement."

[54]So the Israelites did everything just as the LORD commanded Moses.

The Camp Arrangement

2 The LORD said to Moses and Aaron: [2]"The Israelites should make their camps around the Meeting Tent, but they should not camp too close to it. They should camp under their family flag and banners."

[3]The camp of Judah will be on the east side, where the sun rises, and they will camp by divisions there under their flag. The leader of the people of Judah is Nahshon son of Amminadab. [4]There are 74,600 men in his division.

[5]Next to them the tribe of Issachar will camp. The leader of the people of Issachar is Nethanel son of Zuar. [6]There are 54,400 men in his division.

[7]Next is the tribe of Zebulun. The leader of the people of Zebulun is Eliab son of Helon. [8]There are 57,400 men in his division.

[9]There are a total of 186,400 men in the camps of Judah and its neighbors, in all their divisions. They will be the first to march out of camp.

[10]The divisions of the camp of Reuben will be on the south side, where they will camp under their flag. The leader of the people of Reuben is Elizur son of Shedeur. [11]There are 46,500 men in his division.

[12]Next to them the tribe of Simeon will camp. The leader of the people of Simeon is Shelumiel son of Zurishaddai. [13]There are 59,300 men in his division.

[14]Next is the tribe of Gad. The leader of the people of Gad is Eliasaph son of Deuel. [15]There are 45,650 men in his division.

[16]There are a total of 151,450 men in the camps of Reuben and its neighbors, in all

their divisions. They will be the second group to march out of camp.

[17]When the Levites march out with the Meeting Tent, they will be in the middle of the other camps. The tribes will march out in the same order as they camp, each in its place under its flag.

[18]The divisions of the camp of Ephraim will be on the west side, where they will camp under their flag. The leader of the people of Ephraim is Elishama son of Ammihud. [19]There are 40,500 men in his division.

[20]Next to them the tribe of Manasseh will camp. The leader of the people of Manasseh is Gamaliel son of Pedahzur. [21]There are 32,200 men in his division.

[22]Next is the tribe of Benjamin. The leader of the people of Benjamin is Abidan son of Gideoni. [23]There are 35,400 men in his division.

[24]There are a total of 108,100 men in the camps of Ephraim and its neighbors, in all their divisions. They will be the third group to march out of camp.

[25]The divisions of the camp of Dan will be on the north side, where they will camp under their flag. The leader of the people of Dan is Ahiezer son of Ammishaddai. [26]There are 62,700 men in his division.

[27]Next to them the tribe of Asher will camp. The leader of the people of Asher is Pagiel son of Ocran. [28]There are 41,500 men in his division.

[29]Next is the tribe of Naphtali. The leader of the people of Naphtali is Ahira son of Enan. [30]There are 53,400 men in his division.

[31]There are 157,600 men in the camps of Dan and its neighbors. They will be the last to march out of camp, and they will travel under their own flag.

[32]These are the Israelites who were counted by families. The total number of Israelites in the camps, counted by divisions, is 603,550. [33]Moses obeyed the LORD and did not count the Levites among the other people of Israel.

[34]So the Israelites obeyed everything the LORD commanded Moses. They camped under their flags and marched out by families and family groups.

PSALM 29:10–11

[10]The LORD controls the flood.
　　The LORD will be King forever.
[11]The LORD gives strength to his people;
　　the LORD blesses his people with peace.

PROVERBS 10:26–29

[26]A lazy person affects the one he works for
　　like vinegar on the teeth or smoke in the eyes.

[27]Whoever respects the LORD will have a long life,
　　but the life of an evil person will be cut short.

[28]A good person can look forward to happiness,
　　but an evil person can expect nothing.

[29]The LORD will protect good people
　　but will ruin those who do evil.

MARK 7:24–37

Jesus Helps a Non-Jewish Woman

[24]Jesus left that place and went to the area around Tyre.[n] When he went into a house, he did not want anyone to know he was there, but he could not stay hidden. [25]A woman whose daughter had an evil spirit in her heard that he was there. So she quickly came to Jesus and fell at his feet. [26]She was Greek, born in Phoenicia, in Syria. She begged Jesus to force the demon out of her daughter.

[27]Jesus told the woman, "It is not right to take the children's bread and give it to the dogs. First let the children eat all they want."

[28]But she answered, "Yes, Lord, but even the dogs under the table can eat the children's crumbs."

[29]Then Jesus said, "Because of your answer, you may go. The demon has left your daughter."

[30]The woman went home and found her daughter lying in bed; the demon was gone.

7:24 Tyre Some Greek copies continue, "and Sidon."

Jesus Heals a Deaf Man

[31]Then Jesus left the area around Tyre and went through Sidon to Lake Galilee, to the area of the Ten Towns.[n] [32]While he was there, some people brought a man to him who was deaf and could not talk plainly. The people begged Jesus to put his hand on the man to heal him. [33]Jesus led the man away from the crowd, by himself. He put his fingers in the man's ears and then spit and touched the man's tongue. [34]Looking up to heaven, he sighed and said to the man, "Ephphatha!" (This means, "Be opened.") [35]Instantly the man was able to hear and to use his tongue so that he spoke clearly.

[36]Jesus commanded the people not to tell anyone about what happened. But the more he commanded them, the more they told about it. [37]They were completely amazed and said, "Jesus does everything well. He makes the deaf hear! And those who can't talk he makes able to speak."

MARCH 3

NUMBERS 3:1—4:49

Aaron's Family, the Priests

3 This is the family history of Aaron and Moses at the time the LORD talked to Moses on Mount Sinai.

[2]Aaron had four sons: Nadab, the oldest, Abihu, Eleazar, and Ithamar. [3]These were the names of Aaron's sons, who were appointed to serve as priests. [4]But Nadab and Abihu died in the presence of the LORD when they offered the wrong kind of fire before the LORD in the Desert of Sinai. They had no sons. So Eleazar and Ithamar served as priests during the lifetime of their father Aaron.

[5]The LORD said to Moses, [6]"Bring the tribe of Levi and present them to Aaron the priest to help him. [7]They will help him and all the Israelites at the Meeting Tent, doing the work in the Holy Tent. [8]The Levites must take care of everything in the Meeting Tent and serve the people of Israel by doing the work in the Holy Tent. [9]Give the Levites to Aaron and his sons; of all the Israelites, the Levites are given completely to him. [10]Appoint Aaron and his sons to serve as priests, but anyone else who comes near the holy things must be put to death."

[11]The LORD also said to Moses, [12]"I am choosing the Levites from all the Israelites to take the place of all the firstborn children of Israel. The Levites will be mine, [13]because the firstborn are mine. When you were in Egypt, I killed all the firstborn children of the Egyptians and took all the firstborn of Israel to be mine, both animals and children. They are mine. I am the LORD."

[14]The LORD again said to Moses in the Desert of Sinai, [15]"Count the Levites by families and family groups. Count every male one month old or older." [16]So Moses obeyed the LORD and counted them all.

[17]Levi had three sons, whose names were Gershon, Kohath, and Merari.

[18]The Gershonite family groups were Libni and Shimei.

[19]The Kohathite family groups were Amram, Izhar, Hebron, and Uzziel.

[20]The Merarite family groups were Mahli and Mushi.

These were the family groups of the Levites.

[21]The family groups of Libni and Shimei belonged to Gershon; they were the Gershonite family groups. [22]The number that was counted was 7,500 males one month old or older. [23]The Gershonite family groups camped on the west side, behind the Holy Tent. [24]The leader of the families of Gershon was Eliasaph son of Lael. [25]In the Meeting Tent the Gershonites were in charge of the Holy Tent, its covering, the curtain at the entrance to the Meeting Tent, [26]the curtains in

---

the courtyard, the curtain at the entry to the courtyard around the Holy Tent and the altar, the ropes, and all the work connected with these items.

²⁷The family groups of Amram, Izhar, Hebron, and Uzziel belonged to Kohath; they were the Kohathite family groups. ²⁸They had 8,600 males one month old or older, and they were responsible for taking care of the Holy Place. ²⁹The Kohathite family groups camped south of the Holy Tent. ³⁰The leader of the Kohathite families was Elizaphan son of Uzziel. ³¹They were responsible for the Ark, the table, the lampstand, the altars, the tools of the Holy Place which they were to use, the curtain, and all the work connected with these items. ³²The main leader of the Levites was Eleazar son of Aaron, the priest, who was in charge of all those responsible for the Holy Place.

³³The family groups of Mahli and Mushi belonged to Merari; they were the Merarite family groups. ³⁴The number that was counted was 6,200 males one month old or older. ³⁵The leader of the Merari families was Zuriel son of Abihail, and they were to camp north of the Holy Tent. ³⁶The Merarites were responsible for the frames of the Holy Tent, the braces, the posts, the bases, and all the work connected with these items. ³⁷They were also responsible for the posts in the courtyard around the Holy Tent and their bases, tent pegs, and ropes.

³⁸Moses, Aaron, and his sons camped east of the Holy Tent, toward the sunrise, in front of the Meeting Tent. They were responsible for the Holy Place for the Israelites. Anyone else who came near the Holy Place was to be put to death.

³⁹Moses and Aaron counted the Levite men by their families, as the LORD commanded, and there were 22,000 males one month old or older.

Levites Take the Place of the Firstborn Sons

⁴⁰The LORD said to Moses, "Count all the firstborn sons in Israel one month old or older, and list their names. ⁴¹Take the Levites for me instead of the firstborn sons of Israel; take the animals of the Levites instead of the

firstborn animals from the rest of Israel. I am the LORD."

⁴²So Moses did what the LORD commanded and counted all the firstborn sons of the Israelites. ⁴³When he listed all the firstborn sons one month old or older, there were 22,273 names.

⁴⁴The LORD also said to Moses, ⁴⁵"Take the Levites instead of all the firstborn sons of the Israelites, and take the animals of the Levites instead of the animals of the other people. The Levites are mine. I am the LORD. ⁴⁶Since there are 273 more firstborn sons than Levites, ⁴⁷collect two ounces of silver for each of the 273 sons. Use the measure as set by the Holy Place, which is two-fifths of an ounce. ⁴⁸Give the silver to Aaron and his sons as the payment for the 273 Israelites."

⁴⁹So Moses collected the money for the people the Levites could not replace. ⁵⁰From the firstborn of the Israelites, he collected thirty-five pounds of silver, using the measure set by the Holy Place. ⁵¹Moses obeyed the command of the LORD and gave the silver to Aaron and his sons.

The Jobs of the Kohath Family

4 The LORD said to Moses and Aaron, ²"Count the Kohathites among the Levites by family groups and families. ³Count the men from thirty to fifty years old, all who come to serve in the Meeting Tent.

⁴"The Kohathites are responsible for the most holy things in the Meeting Tent. ⁵When the Israelites are ready to move, Aaron and his sons must go into the Holy Tent, take down the curtain, and cover the Ark of the Agreement with it. ⁶Over this they must put a covering made from fine leather, then spread the solid blue cloth over that, and put the poles in place.

⁷"Then they must spread a blue cloth over the table for the bread that shows a person is in God's presence. They must put the plates, pans, bowls, and the jars for drink offerings on the table; they must leave the bread that is always there on the table. ⁸Then they must put a red cloth over all of these things, cover everything with fine leather, and put the poles in place.

⁹"With a blue cloth they must cover the

lampstand, its lamps, its wick trimmers, its trays, and all the jars for the oil used in the lamps. [10]Then they must wrap everything in fine leather and put all these things on a frame for carrying them.

[11]"They must spread a blue cloth over the gold altar, cover it with fine leather, and put the poles in place.

[12]"They must gather all the things used for serving in the Holy Place and wrap them in a blue cloth. Then they must cover that with fine leather and put these things on a frame for carrying them.

[13]"They must clean the ashes off the bronze altar and spread a purple cloth over it. [14]They must gather all the things used for serving at the altar—the pans for carrying the fire, the meat forks, the shovels, and the bowls—and put them on the bronze altar. Then they must spread a covering of fine leather over it and put the poles in place.

[15]"When the Israelites are ready to move, and when Aaron and his sons have covered the holy furniture and all the holy things, the Kohathites may go in and carry them away. In this way they won't touch the holy things and die. It is the Kohathites' job to carry the things that are in the Meeting Tent.

[16]"Eleazar son of Aaron, the priest, will be responsible for the Holy Tent and for everything in it, for all the holy things it has: the oil for the lamp, the sweet-smelling incense, the continual grain offering, and the oil used to appoint priests and things to the LORD's service."

[17]The LORD said to Moses and Aaron, [18]"Don't let the Kohathites be cut off from the Levites. [19]Do this for the Kohathites so that they may go near the Most Holy Place and not die: Aaron and his sons must go in and show each Kohathite what to do and what to carry. [20]The Kohathites must not enter and look at the holy things, even for a second, or they will die."

The Jobs of the Gershon Family

[21]The LORD said to Moses, [22]"Count the Gershonites by families and family groups. [23]Count the men from thirty to fifty years old, all who have a job to do in the Meeting Tent.

[24]"This is what the Gershonite family groups must do and what they must carry. [25]They must carry the curtains of the Holy Tent, the Meeting Tent, its covering, and its outer covering made from fine leather. They must also carry the curtains for the entrance to the Meeting Tent, [26]the curtains of the courtyard that go around the Holy Tent and the altar, the curtain for the entry to the courtyard, the ropes, and all the things used with the curtains. They must do everything connected with these things. [27]Aaron and his sons are in charge of what the Gershonites do or carry; you tell them what they are responsible for carrying. [28]This is the work of the Gershonite family group at the Meeting Tent. Ithamar son of Aaron, the priest, will direct their work.

The Jobs of the Merari Family

[29]"Count the Merarite families and family groups. [30]Count the men from thirty to fifty years old, all who work at the Meeting Tent. [31]It is their job to carry the following as they serve in the Meeting Tent: the frames of the Holy Tent, the crossbars, the posts, and bases, [32]in addition to the posts that go around the courtyard, their bases, tent pegs, ropes, and everything that is used with the poles around the courtyard. Tell each man exactly what to carry. [33]This is the work the Merarite family group will do for the Meeting Tent. Ithamar son of Aaron, the priest, will direct their work."

The Levite Families

[34]Moses, Aaron, and the leaders of Israel counted the Kohathites by families and family groups, [35]the men from thirty to fifty years old who were to work at the Meeting Tent. [36]There were 2,750 men in the family groups. [37]This was the total of the Kohath family groups who worked at the Meeting Tent, whom Moses and Aaron counted as the LORD had commanded Moses.

[38]Also, the Gershonites were counted by families and family groups, [39]the men from thirty to fifty years old who were given work at the Meeting Tent. [40]The families and family groups had 2,630 men. [41]This was the to-

tal of the Gershon family groups who worked at the Meeting Tent, whom Moses and Aaron counted as the LORD had commanded. ⁴²Also, the men in the families and family groups of the Merari family were counted, ⁴³the men from thirty to fifty years old who were to work at the Meeting Tent. ⁴⁴The family groups had 3,200 men. ⁴⁵This was the total of the Merari family groups, whom Moses and Aaron counted as the LORD had commanded Moses.

⁴⁶So Moses, Aaron, and the leaders of Israel counted all the Levites by families and family groups. ⁴⁷They counted the men from thirty to fifty who were given work at the Meeting Tent and who carried the Tent. ⁴⁸The total number of these men was 8,580. ⁴⁹Each man was counted as the LORD had commanded Moses; each man was given his work and told what to carry as the LORD had commanded Moses.

PSALM 30:1–7

Thanksgiving for Escaping Death

A psalm of David. A song for giving the Temple to the LORD.

30 ¹I will praise you, LORD,
   because you rescued me.
   You did not let my enemies laugh at
      me.
²LORD, my God, I prayed to you,
   and you healed me.
³You lifted me out of the grave;
   you spared me from going down to the
      place of the dead.

⁴Sing praises to the LORD, you who belong
      to him;
   praise his holy name.
⁵His anger lasts only a moment,
   but his kindness lasts for a lifetime.
   Crying may last for a night,
   but joy comes in the morning.

⁶When I felt safe, I said,
   "I will never fear."
⁷LORD, in your kindness you made my
      mountain safe.
   But when you turned away, I was
      frightened.

PROVERBS 10:30–32

³⁰Good people will always be safe,
   but evil people will not remain in the
      land.

³¹A good person says wise things,
   but a liar's tongue will be stopped.

³²Good people know the right thing to
      say,
   but evil people only tell lies.

MARK 8:1–21

More than Four Thousand People Fed

8 Another time there was a great crowd with Jesus that had nothing to eat. So Jesus called his followers and said, ²"I feel sorry for these people, because they have already been with me for three days, and they have nothing to eat. ³If I send them home hungry, they will faint on the way. Some of them live a long way from here."

⁴Jesus' followers answered, "How can we get enough bread to feed all these people? We are far away from any town."

⁵Jesus asked, "How many loaves of bread do you have?"

They answered, "Seven."

⁶Jesus told the people to sit on the ground. Then he took the seven loaves, gave thanks to God, and divided the bread. He gave the pieces to his followers to give to the people, and they did so. ⁷The followers also had a few small fish. After Jesus gave thanks for the fish, he told his followers to give them to the people also. ⁸All the people ate and were satisfied. Then his followers filled seven baskets with the leftover pieces of food. ⁹There were about four thousand people who ate. After they had eaten, Jesus sent them home. ¹⁰Then right away he got into a boat with his followers and went to the area of Dalmanutha.

The Leaders Ask for a Miracle

¹¹The Pharisees came to Jesus and began to ask him questions. Hoping to trap him, they asked Jesus for a miracle from God. ¹²Jesus sighed deeply and said, "Why do you people ask for a miracle as a sign? I tell you the truth, no sign will be given to you."

¹³Then Jesus left the Pharisees and went in the boat to the other side of the lake.

Guard Against Wrong Teachings

¹⁴His followers had only one loaf of bread with them in the boat; they had forgotten to bring more. ¹⁵Jesus warned them, "Be careful! Beware of the yeast of the Pharisees and the yeast of Herod."

¹⁶His followers discussed the meaning of this, saying, "He said this because we have no bread."

¹⁷Knowing what they were talking about, Jesus asked them, "Why are you talking about not having bread? Do you still not see or understand? Are your minds closed? ¹⁸You have eyes, but you don't really see. You have ears, but you don't really listen. Remember when ¹⁹I divided five loaves of bread for the five thousand? How many baskets did you fill with leftover pieces of food?"

They answered, "Twelve."

²⁰"And when I divided seven loaves of bread for the four thousand, how many baskets did you fill with leftover pieces of food?"

They answered, "Seven."

²¹Then Jesus said to them, "Don't you understand yet?"

MARCH 4

NUMBERS 5:1—6:27

Rules About Cleanliness

5 The LORD said to Moses, ²"Command the Israelites to send away from camp anyone with a harmful skin disease. Send away anyone who gives off body fluid or who has become unclean by touching a dead body. ³Send both men and women outside the camp so that they won't spread the disease there, where I am living among you." ⁴So Israel obeyed the LORD's command and sent those people outside the camp. They did just as the LORD had told Moses.

Paying for Doing Wrong

⁵The LORD said to Moses, ⁶"Tell the Israelites: 'When a man or woman does something wrong to another person, that is really sinning against the LORD. That person is guilty ⁷and must admit the wrong that has been done. The person must fully pay for the wrong that has been done, adding one-fifth to it, and giving it to the person who was wronged. ⁸But if that person is dead and does not have any close relatives to receive the payment, the one who did wrong owes the LORD and must pay the priest. In addition, the priest must sacrifice a male sheep to remove the wrong so that the person will belong to the LORD. ⁹When an Israelite brings a holy gift, it should be given to the priest. ¹⁰No one has to give these holy gifts, but if someone does give them, they belong to the priest.'"

Suspicious Husbands

¹¹Then the LORD said to Moses, ¹²"Tell the Israelites: 'A man's wife might be unfaithful to him ¹³and have sexual relations with another man. Her sin might be kept hidden from her husband so that he does not know about the wrong she did. Perhaps no one saw it, and she wasn't caught. ¹⁴But if her husband has feelings of jealousy and suspects she has sinned—whether she has or not— ¹⁵he should take her to the priest. The husband must also take an offering for her of two quarts of barley flour. He must not pour oil or incense on it, because this is a grain offering for jealousy, an offering of remembrance. It is to find out if she is guilty.

¹⁶"'The priest will bring in the woman and make her stand before the LORD. ¹⁷He will take some holy water in a clay jar, and he will put some dirt from the floor of the Holy Tent into the water. ¹⁸The priest will make the woman stand before the LORD, and he will loosen her hair. He will hand her the offering of remembrance, the grain offering for jealousy; he will hold the bitter water that brings a curse. ¹⁹The priest will make her take an oath and ask her, "Has another man

had sexual relations with you? Have you been unfaithful to your husband? If you haven't, this bitter water that brings a curse won't hurt you. 20But if you have been unfaithful to your husband and have had sexual relations with a man besides him"— 21the priest will then put on her the curse that the oath will bring—"the LORD will make the people curse and reject you. He will make your stomach get big, and he will make your body unable to give birth to another baby. 22This water that brings a curse will go inside you and make your body unable to give birth to another baby."

" 'The woman must say, "I agree."

23" 'The priest should write these curses on a scroll, wash the words off into the bitter water, 24and make the woman drink the bitter water that brings a curse. If she is guilty, the water will make her sick. 25Then the priest will take the grain offering for jealousy from her. He will present it before the LORD and bring it to the altar. 26He will take a handful of the grain, which is a memorial offering, and burn it on the altar. After that he will make the woman drink the water 27to see if she is not pure and if she has sinned against her husband. When it goes into her, if her stomach gets big and she is not able to have another baby, her people will reject her. 28But if the woman has not sinned, she is pure. She is not guilty, and she will be able to have babies.

29" 'So this is the teaching about jealousy. This is what to do when a woman does wrong and is unfaithful while she is married to her husband. 30It also should be done if the man gets jealous because he suspects his wife. The priest will have her stand before the LORD, and he will do all these things, just as the teaching commands. 31In this way the husband can be proven correct, and the woman will suffer if she has done wrong.' "

Rules for the Nazirites

6 The LORD said to Moses, 2"Tell the Israelites: 'If men or women want to promise to belong to the LORD in a special way, they will be called Nazirites. 3During this time, they must not drink wine or beer, or vinegar made from wine or beer. They must not even drink grape juice or eat grapes or raisins. 4While they are Nazirites, they must not eat anything that comes from the grapevine, even the seeds or the skin.

5" 'During the time they have promised to belong to the LORD, they must not cut their hair. They must be holy until this special time is over. They must let their hair grow long. 6During their special time of belonging to the LORD, Nazirites must not go near a dead body. 7Even if their own father, mother, brother, or sister dies, they must not touch them, or they will become unclean. They must still keep their promise to belong to God in a special way. 8While they are Nazirites, they belong to the LORD in a special way.

9" 'If they are next to someone who dies suddenly, their hair, which was part of their promise, has been made unclean. So they must shave their head seven days later to be clean. 10Then on the eighth day, they must bring two doves or two young pigeons to the priest at the entrance to the Meeting Tent. 11The priest will offer one as a sin offering and the other as a burnt offering. This removes sin so they will belong to the LORD. (They had sinned because they were near a dead body.) That same day they will again promise to let their hair grow 12and give themselves to the LORD for another special time. They must bring a male lamb a year old as a penalty offering. The days of the special time before don't count, because they became unclean during their first special time.

13" 'This is the teaching for the Nazirites. When the promised time is over, they must go to the entrance of the Meeting Tent 14and give their offerings to the LORD. They must offer a year-old male lamb that has nothing wrong with it, as a burnt offering, a year-old female lamb that has nothing wrong with it, as a sin offering, and a male sheep that has nothing wrong with it, for a fellowship offering. 15They must also bring the grain offerings and drink offerings that go with them. And they must bring a basket of bread made without yeast, loaves made with fine flour mixed with oil, and wafers made without yeast spread with oil.

16" 'The priest will give these offerings to the LORD and make the sin offering and the burnt offering. 17Then he will kill the male sheep as a fellowship offering to the LORD; along with it, he will present the basket of bread made without yeast, the grain offering, and the drink offering.

18" 'The Nazirites must go to the entrance of the Meeting Tent and shave off their hair that they grew for their promise. The hair will be put in the fire that is under the sacrifice of the fellowship offering.

19" 'After the Nazirites cut off their hair, the priest will give them a boiled shoulder from the male sheep. From the basket he will also give a loaf and a wafer, both made without yeast. 20Then the priest will present them to the LORD. They are holy and belong to the priest. Also, he is to present the breast and the thigh from the male sheep. After that, the Nazirites may drink wine.

21" 'This is the teaching for the Nazirites who make a promise. Everyone who makes the Nazirite promise must give all of these gifts to the LORD. If they promised to do more, they must keep their promise, according to the teaching of the Nazirites.'"

The Priests' Blessings

22The LORD said to Moses, 23"Tell Aaron and his sons, 'This is how you should bless the Israelites. Say to them:

24"May the LORD bless you and keep you.
25May the LORD show you his kindness
    and have mercy on you.
26May the LORD watch over you
    and give you peace."'

27"So Aaron and his sons will bless the Israelites with my name, and I will bless them."

PSALM 30:8–12

8I called to you, LORD,
    and asked you to have mercy on me.
9I said, "What good will it do if I die
    or if I go down to the grave?
Dust cannot praise you;
    it cannot speak about your truth.

10LORD, hear me and have mercy on me.
    LORD, help me."

11You changed my sorrow into dancing.
    You took away my clothes of sadness,
    and clothed me in happiness.
12I will sing to you and not be silent.
    LORD, my God, I will praise you forever.

PROVERBS 11:1–3

11 The LORD hates dishonest scales,
    but he is pleased with honest
        weights.

2Pride leads only to shame;
    it is wise to be humble.

3Good people will be guided by honesty;
    dishonesty will destroy those who are
        not trustworthy.

MARK 8:22—9:1

Jesus Heals a Blind Man

22Jesus and his followers came to Bethsaida. There some people brought a blind man to Jesus and begged him to touch the man. 23So Jesus took the blind man's hand and led him out of the village. Then he spit on the man's eyes and put his hands on the man and asked, "Can you see now?"

24The man looked up and said, "Yes, I see people, but they look like trees walking around."

25Again Jesus put his hands on the man's eyes. Then the man opened his eyes wide and they were healed, and he was able to see everything clearly. 26Jesus told him to go home, saying, "Don't go into the town."[n]

Peter Says Jesus Is the Christ

27Jesus and his followers went to the towns around Caesarea Philippi. While they were traveling, Jesus asked them, "Who do people say I am?"

28They answered, "Some say you are John the Baptist. Others say you are Elijah,[n] and others say you are one of the prophets."

29Then Jesus asked, "But who do you say I am?"

8:26 town Some Greek copies continue, "Don't even go and tell anyone in the town." **8:28 Elijah** A man who spoke for God and who lived hundreds of years before Christ. See 1 Kings 17.

Peter answered, "You are the Christ."
[30]Jesus warned his followers not to tell anyone who he was.

[31]Then Jesus began to teach them that the Son of Man must suffer many things and that he would be rejected by the Jewish elders, the leading priests, and the teachers of the law. He told them that the Son of Man must be killed and then rise from the dead after three days. [32]Jesus told them plainly what would happen. Then Peter took Jesus aside and began to tell him not to talk like that. [33]But Jesus turned and looked at his followers. Then he told Peter not to talk that way. He said, "Go away from me, Satan![n] You don't care about the things of God, but only about things people think are important."

[34]Then Jesus called the crowd to him, along with his followers. He said, "If people want to follow me, they must give up the things they want. They must be willing even to give up their lives to follow me. [35]Those who want to save their lives will give up true life. But those who give up their lives for me and for the Good News will have true life. [36]It is worthless to have the whole world if they lose their souls. [37]They could never pay enough to buy back their souls. [38]The people who live now are living in a sinful and evil time. If people are ashamed of me and my teaching, the Son of Man will be ashamed of them when he comes with his Father's glory and with the holy angels."

9 Then Jesus said to the people, "I tell you the truth, some people standing here will see the kingdom of God come with power before they die."

MARCH 5

NUMBERS 7:1—8:26

The Holy Tent

7 When Moses finished setting up the Holy Tent, he gave it for service to the Lord by pouring olive oil on the Tent and on everything used in it. He also poured oil on the altar and all its tools to prepare them for service to the Lord. [2]Then the leaders of Israel made offerings. These were the heads of the families, the leaders of each tribe who counted the people. [3]They brought to the Lord six covered carts and twelve oxen—each leader giving an ox, and every two leaders giving a cart. They brought these to the Holy Tent.

[4]The Lord said to Moses, [5]"Accept these gifts from the leaders and use them in the work of the Meeting Tent. Give them to the Levites as they need them."

[6]So Moses accepted the carts and the oxen and gave them to the Levites. [7]He gave two carts and four oxen to the Gershonites, which they needed for their work. [8]Then Moses gave four carts and eight oxen to the Merarites, which they needed for their work. Ithamar son of Aaron, the priest, directed the work of all of them. [9]Moses did not give any oxen or carts to the Kohathites, because their job was to carry the holy things on their shoulders.

[10]When the oil was poured on the altar, the leaders brought their offerings to it to give it to the Lord's service; they presented them in front of the altar. [11]The Lord told Moses, "Each day one leader must bring his gift to make the altar ready for service to me."

[12-83]Each of the twelve leaders brought these gifts. Each leader brought one silver plate that weighed about three and one-fourth pounds, and one silver bowl that weighed about one and three-fourths pounds. These weights were set by the Holy Place measure. The bowl and the plate were filled with fine flour mixed with oil for a grain offering. Each leader also brought a large gold dish that weighed about four ounces and was filled with incense.

8:33 Satan Name for the devil meaning "the enemy." Jesus means that Peter was talking like Satan.

In addition, each of the leaders brought one young bull, one male sheep, and one male lamb a year old for a burnt offering; one male goat for a sin offering; and two oxen, five male sheep, five male goats, and five male lambs a year old for a fellowship offering.

On the first day Nahshon son of Amminadab brought his gifts. He was the leader of the tribe of Judah.

On the second day Nethanel son of Zuar brought his gifts. He was the leader of the tribe of Issachar.

On the third day Eliab son of Helon brought his gifts. He was the leader of the tribe of Zebulun.

On the fourth day Elizur son of Shedeur brought his gifts. He was the leader of the tribe of Reuben.

On the fifth day Shelumiel son of Zurishaddai brought his gifts. He was the leader of the tribe of Simeon.

On the sixth day Eliasaph son of Deuel brought his gifts. He was the leader of the tribe of Gad.

On the seventh day Elishama son of Ammihud brought his gifts. He was the leader of the tribe of Ephraim.

On the eighth day Gamaliel son of Pedahzur brought his gifts. He was the leader of the tribe of Manasseh.

On the ninth day Abidan son of Gideoni brought his gifts. He was the leader of the tribe of Benjamin.

On the tenth day Ahiezer son of Ammishaddai brought his gifts. He was the leader of the tribe of Dan.

On the eleventh day Pagiel son of Ocran brought his gifts. He was the leader of the tribe of Asher.

On the twelfth day Ahira son of Enan brought his gifts. He was the leader of the tribe of Naphtali.

[84]So these were the gifts from the Israelite leaders when oil was poured on the altar and it was given for service to the LORD: twelve silver plates, twelve silver bowls, and twelve gold dishes. [85]Each silver plate weighed about three and one-fourth pounds, and each bowl weighed about one and three-fourths pounds. All the silver plates and silver bowls together weighed about sixty pounds according to a weight set by the Holy Place measure. [86]The twelve gold dishes filled with incense weighed four ounces each, according to the weight set by the Holy Place measure. Together the gold dishes weighed about three pounds. [87]The total number of animals for the burnt offering was twelve bulls, twelve male sheep, and twelve male lambs a year old. There was also a grain offering, and there were twelve male goats for a sin offering. [88]The total number of animals for the fellowship offering was twenty-four bulls, sixty male sheep, sixty male goats, and sixty male lambs a year old. All these offerings were for giving the altar to the service of the LORD after the oil had been poured on it.

[89]When Moses went into the Meeting Tent to speak with the LORD, he heard the LORD speaking to him. The voice was coming from between the two gold creatures with wings that were above the lid of the Ark of the Agreement. In this way the LORD spoke with him.

The Lampstand

8The LORD said to Moses, [2]"Speak to Aaron and tell him, 'Put the seven lamps where they can light the area in front of the lampstand.'"

[3]Aaron did this, putting the lamps so they lighted the area in front of the lampstand; he obeyed the command the LORD gave Moses. [4]The lampstand was made from hammered gold, from its base to the flowers. It was made exactly the way the LORD had showed Moses.

The Levites Are Given to God

[5]The LORD said to Moses, [6]"Take the Levites away from the other Israelites and make them clean. [7]This is what you should do to make them clean: Sprinkle the cleansing water on them, and have them shave their bodies and wash their clothes so they will be clean. [8]They must take a young bull and the grain offering of flour mixed with oil that goes with it. Then take a second young bull for a sin offering. [9]Bring the Levites to the front of the Meeting Tent, and gather all the Israelites around. [10]When you bring the Levites before the LORD, the Is-

raelites should put their hands on them.[n] [11]Aaron will present the Levites before the LORD as an offering presented from the Israelites. Then the Levites will be ready to do the work of the LORD.

[12]"The Levites will put their hands on the bulls' heads—one bull will be a sin offering to the LORD, and the other will be a burnt offering, to remove the sins of the Levites so they will belong to the LORD. [13]Make the Levites stand in front of Aaron and his sons and present the Levites as an offering to the LORD. [14]In this way you must set apart the Levites from the other Israelites; the Levites will be mine.

[15]"Make the Levites pure, and present them as an offering so that they may come to work at the Meeting Tent. [16]They will be given completely to me from the Israelites; I have taken them for myself instead of the firstborn of every Israelite woman. [17]All the firstborn in Israel—people or animals—are mine. When I killed all the firstborn in Egypt, I set the firstborn in Israel aside for myself. [18]But I have taken the Levites instead of all the firstborn in Israel. [19]From all the Israelites I have given the Levites to Aaron and his sons so that they may serve the Israelites at the Meeting Tent. They will help remove the Israelites' sins so they will belong to the LORD and so that no disaster will strike the Israelites when they approach the Holy Place."

[20]So Moses, Aaron, and all the Israelites obeyed and did with the Levites what the LORD commanded Moses. [21]The Levites made themselves clean and washed their clothes. Then Aaron presented them as an offering to the LORD. He also removed their sins so they would be pure. [22]After that, the Levites came to the Meeting Tent to work, and Aaron and his sons told them what to do. They did with the Levites what the LORD commanded Moses.

[23]The LORD said to Moses, [24]"This command is for the Levites. Everyone twenty-five years old or older must come to the Meeting Tent, because they all have jobs to do there. [25]At the age of fifty, they must re-tire from their jobs and not work again. [26]They may help their fellow Levites with their work at the Meeting Tent, but they must not do the work themselves. This is the way you are to give the Levites their jobs."

PSALM 31:1–5

A Prayer of Faith in Troubled Times

For the director of music. A psalm of David.

31 LORD, I trust in you;
   let me never be disgraced.
   Save me because you do what is
      right.
[2]Listen to me
   and save me quickly.
   Be my rock of protection,
      a strong city to save me.
[3]You are my rock and my protection.
   For the good of your name, lead me
      and guide me.
[4]Set me free from the trap they set for
      me,
   because you are my protection.
[5]I give you my life.
   Save me, LORD, God of truth.

PROVERBS 11:4–6

[4]Riches will not help when it's time to
      die,
   but right living will save you from
      death.

[5]The goodness of the innocent makes
      life easier,
   but the wicked will be destroyed by
      their wickedness.

[6]Doing right brings freedom to honest
      people,
   but those who are not trustworthy will
      be caught by their own desires.

MARK 9:2–29

Jesus Talks with Moses and Elijah

[2]Six days later, Jesus took Peter, James, and John up on a high mountain by themselves. While they watched, Jesus' appear-

8:10 put . . . them This showed that the people had a part in giving the Levites their special work.

ance was changed. [3]His clothes became shining white, whiter than any person could make them. [4]Then Elijah and Moses[n] appeared to them, talking with Jesus.

[5]Peter said to Jesus, "Teacher, it is good that we are here. Let us make three tents—one for you, one for Moses, and one for Elijah." [6]Peter did not know what to say, because he and the others were so frightened.

[7]Then a cloud came and covered them, and a voice came from the cloud, saying, "This is my Son, whom I love. Listen to him!"

[8]Suddenly Peter, James, and John looked around, but they saw only Jesus there alone with them.

[9]As they were coming down the mountain, Jesus commanded them not to tell anyone about what they had seen until the Son of Man had risen from the dead. [10]So the followers obeyed Jesus, but they discussed what he meant about rising from the dead.

[11]Then they asked Jesus, "Why do the teachers of the law say that Elijah must come first?"

[12]Jesus answered, "They are right to say that Elijah must come first and make everything the way it should be. But why does the Scripture say that the Son of Man will suffer much and that people will treat him as if he were nothing? [13]I tell you that Elijah has already come. And people did to him whatever they wanted to do, just as the Scriptures said it would happen."

Jesus Heals a Sick Boy

[14]When Jesus, Peter, James, and John came back to the other followers, they saw a great crowd around them and the teachers of the law arguing with them. [15]But as soon as the crowd saw Jesus, the people were surprised and ran to welcome him.

[16]Jesus asked, "What are you arguing about?"

[17]A man answered, "Teacher, I brought my son to you. He has an evil spirit in him that stops him from talking. [18]When the spirit attacks him, it throws him on the ground. Then my son foams at the mouth, grinds his teeth, and becomes very stiff. I asked your followers to force the evil spirit out, but they couldn't."

[19]Jesus answered, "You people have no faith. How long must I stay with you? How long must I put up with you? Bring the boy to me."

[20]So the followers brought him to Jesus. As soon as the evil spirit saw Jesus, it made the boy lose control of himself, and he fell down and rolled on the ground, foaming at the mouth.

[21]Jesus asked the boy's father, "How long has this been happening?"

The father answered, "Since he was very young. [22]The spirit often throws him into a fire or into water to kill him. If you can do anything for him, please have pity on us and help us."

[23]Jesus said to the father, "You said, 'If you can!' All things are possible for the one who believes."

[24]Immediately the father cried out, "I do believe! Help me to believe more!"

[25]When Jesus saw that a crowd was quickly gathering, he ordered the evil spirit, saying, "You spirit that makes people unable to hear or speak, I command you to come out of this boy and never enter him again!"

[26]The evil spirit screamed and caused the boy to fall on the ground again. Then the spirit came out. The boy looked as if he were dead, and many people said, "He is dead!" [27]But Jesus took hold of the boy's hand and helped him to stand up.

[28]When Jesus went into the house, his followers began asking him privately, "Why couldn't we force that evil spirit out?"

[29]Jesus answered, "That kind of spirit can only be forced out by prayer."[n]

9:4 Elijah and Moses Two of the most important Jewish leaders in the past. God had given Moses the Law, and Elijah was an important prophet. **9:29 prayer** Some Greek copies continue, "and fasting."

MARCH 6

NUMBERS 9:1—10:36

The Passover Is Celebrated

9 The LORD spoke to Moses in the Desert of Sinai in the first month of the second year after the Israelites left Egypt. He said, ²"Tell the Israelites to celebrate the Passover at the appointed time. ³That appointed time is the fourteenth day of this month at twilight; they must obey all the rules about it."

⁴So Moses told the Israelites to celebrate the Passover, ⁵and they did; it was in the Desert of Sinai at twilight on the fourteenth day of the first month. The Israelites did everything just as the LORD commanded Moses.

⁶But some of the people could not celebrate the Passover on that day because they were unclean from touching a dead body. So they went to Moses and Aaron that day and ⁷said to Moses, "We are unclean because of touching a dead body. But why should we be kept from offering gifts to the LORD at this appointed time? Why can't we join the other Israelites?"

⁸Moses said to them, "Wait, and I will find out what the LORD says about you."

⁹Then the LORD said to Moses, ¹⁰"Tell the Israelites this: 'If you or your descendants become unclean because of a dead body, or if you are away on a trip during the Passover, you must still celebrate the LORD's Passover. ¹¹But celebrate it at twilight on the fourteenth day of the second month. Eat the lamb with bitter herbs and bread made without yeast. ¹²Don't leave any of it until the next morning or break any of its bones. When you celebrate the Passover, follow all the rules. ¹³Anyone who is clean and is not away on a trip but does not eat the Passover must be cut off from the people. That person did not give an offering to the LORD at the appointed time and must be punished for the sin.

¹⁴" 'Foreigners among you may celebrate the LORD's Passover, but they must follow all the rules. You must have the same rules for foreigners as you have for yourselves.' "

The Cloud Above the Tent

¹⁵On the day the Holy Tent, the Tent of the Agreement, was set up, a cloud covered it. From dusk until dawn the cloud above the Tent looked like fire. ¹⁶The cloud stayed above the Tent, and at night it looked like fire. ¹⁷When the cloud moved from its place over the Tent, the Israelites moved, and wherever the cloud stopped, the Israelites camped. ¹⁸So the Israelites moved at the LORD's command, and they camped at his command. While the cloud stayed over the Tent, they remained camped. ¹⁹Sometimes the cloud stayed over the Tent for a long time, but the Israelites obeyed the LORD and did not move. ²⁰Sometimes the cloud was over it only a few days. At the LORD's command the people camped, and at his command they moved. ²¹Sometimes the cloud stayed only from dusk until dawn; when the cloud lifted the next morning, the people moved. When the cloud lifted, day or night, the people moved. ²²The cloud might stay over the Tent for two days, a month, or a year. As long as it stayed, the people camped, but when it lifted, they moved. ²³At the LORD's command the people camped, and at his command they moved. They obeyed the LORD's order that he commanded through Moses.

The Silver Trumpets

10 The LORD said to Moses, ²"Make two trumpets of hammered silver, and use them to call the people together and to march out of camp. ³When both trumpets are blown, the people should gather before you at the entrance to the Meeting Tent. ⁴If you blow only one trumpet, the leaders, the heads of the family groups of Israel, should meet before you. ⁵When you loudly blow the trumpets, the tribes camping on the east should move. ⁶When you loudly blow them again, the tribes camping on the south should move; the loud sound will tell them to move. ⁷When you want to gather the people, blow the trumpets, but don't blow them as loudly.

[8]"Aaron's sons, the priests, should blow the trumpets. This is a law for you and your descendants from now on. [9]When you are fighting an enemy who attacks you in your own land, blow the trumpets loudly. The LORD your God will take notice of you and will save you from your enemies. [10]Also blow your trumpets at happy times and during your feasts and at New Moon festivals. Blow them over your burnt offerings and fellowship offerings, because they will help you remember your God. I am the LORD your God."

The Israelites Move Camp

[11]The cloud lifted from the Tent of the Agreement on the twentieth day of the second month of the second year. [12]So the Israelites moved from the Desert of Sinai and continued until the cloud stopped in the Desert of Paran. [13]This was their first time to move, and they did it as the LORD had commanded Moses.

[14]The divisions from the camp of Judah moved first under their flag. Nahshon son of Amminadab was the commander. [15]Nethanel son of Zuar was over the division of the tribe of Issachar. [16]Eliab son of Helon was over the division of the tribe of Zebulun. [17]Then the Holy Tent was taken down, and the Gershonites and Merarites, who carried it, moved next.

[18]Then came the divisions from the camp of Reuben under their flag, and Elizur son of Shedeur was the commander. [19]Shelumiel son of Zurishaddai was over the division of the tribe of Simeon. [20]Eliasaph son of Deuel was over the division of the tribe of Gad. [21]Then came the Kohathites, who carried the holy things; the Holy Tent was to be set up before they arrived.

[22]Next came the divisions from the camp of Ephraim under their flag, and Elishama son of Ammihud was the commander. [23]Gamaliel son of Pedahzur was over the division of the tribe of Manasseh, [24]and Abidan son of Gideoni was over the division of the tribe of Benjamin.

[25]The last ones were the rear guard for all the tribes. These were the divisions from the camp of Dan under their flag, and Ahiezer son of Ammishaddai was the commander. [26]Pagiel son of Ocran was over the division of the tribe of Asher; [27]Ahira son of Enan was over the division of the tribe of Naphtali. [28]This was the order the Israelite divisions marched in when they moved.

[29]Hobab was the son of Reuel the Midianite,[n] who was Moses' father-in-law. Moses said to Hobab, "We are moving to the land the LORD promised to give us. Come with us and we will be good to you, because the LORD has promised good things to Israel."

[30]But Hobab answered, "No, I will not go. I will go back to my own land where I was born."

[31]But Moses said, "Please don't leave us. You know where we can camp in the desert, and you can be our guide. [32]Come with us. We will share with you all the good things the LORD gives us." [33]So they left the mountain of the LORD and traveled for three days. The Ark of the LORD's Agreement went in front of the people for those three days, as they looked for a place to camp. [34]The LORD's cloud was over them during the day when they left their camp.

[35]When the Ark left the camp, Moses said, "Rise up, LORD!

Scatter your enemies:
make those who hate you run from
   you."

[36]And when the Ark was set down, Moses said,

"Return, LORD,
to the thousands of people of Israel."

PSALM 31:6–13

[6]I hate those who worship false gods.
   I trust only in the LORD.
[7]I will be glad and rejoice in your love,
   because you saw my suffering;
   you knew my troubles.
[8]You have not handed me over to my
      enemies
   but have set me in a safe place.

[9]LORD, have mercy, because I am in
   misery.

10:29 Reuel the Midianite Also called Jethro.

My eyes are weak from so much crying,
and my whole being is tired from grief.
[10]My life is ending in sadness,
and my years are spent in crying.
My troubles are using up my strength,
and my bones are getting weaker.
[11]Because of all my troubles, my enemies
hate me,
and even my neighbors look down on
me.
When my friends see me,
they are afraid and run.
[12]I am like a piece of a broken pot.
I am forgotten as if I were dead.
[13]I have heard many insults.
Terror is all around me.
They make plans against me
and want to kill me.

PROVERBS 11:7–11

[7]When the wicked die, hope dies with
them;
their hope in riches will come to
nothing.

[8]The good person is saved from trouble;
it comes to the wicked instead.

[9]With words an evil person can destroy a
neighbor,
but a good person will escape by being
resourceful.

[10]When good people succeed, the city is
happy.
When evil people die, there are shouts
of joy.

[11]Good people bless and build up their
city,
but the wicked can destroy it with their
words.

MARK 9:30–50

Jesus Talks About His Death

[30]Then Jesus and his followers left that
place and went through Galilee. He didn't
want anyone to know where he was, [31]be-
cause he was teaching his followers. He said
to them, "The Son of Man will be handed

over to people, and they will kill him. After
three days, he will rise from the dead." [32]But
the followers did not understand what Jesus
meant, and they were afraid to ask him.

Who Is the Greatest?

[33]Jesus and his followers went to Capernaum. When they went into a house there, he
asked them, "What were you arguing about
on the road?" [34]But the followers did not answer, because their argument on the road
was about which one of them was the greatest.

[35]Jesus sat down and called the twelve
apostles to him. He said, "Whoever wants to
be the most important must be last of all and
servant of all."

[36]Then Jesus took a small child and had
him stand among them. Taking the child in
his arms, he said, [37]"Whoever accepts a child
like this in my name accepts me. And whoever accepts me accepts the One who sent
me."

Anyone Not Against Us Is for Us

[38]Then John said, "Teacher, we saw someone using your name to force demons out of
a person. We told him to stop, because he
does not belong to our group."

[39]But Jesus said, "Don't stop him, because
anyone who uses my name to do powerful
things will not easily say evil things about
me. [40]Whoever is not against us is with us.
[41]I tell you the truth, whoever gives you a
drink of water because you belong to the
Christ will truly get his reward.

[42]"If one of these little children believes in
me, and someone causes that child to sin, it
would be better for that person to have a
large stone tied around his neck and be
drowned in the sea. [43]If your hand causes
you to sin, cut it off. It is better for you to lose
part of your body and live forever than to
have two hands and go to hell, where the fire
never goes out. [[44]In hell the worm does not
die; the fire is never put out.][n] [45]If your foot
causes you to sin, cut it off. It is better for you
to lose part of your body and to live forever
than to have two feet and be thrown into
hell. [[46]In hell the worm does not die; the fire

9:44 In . . . out. Some Greek copies do not contain the bracketed text.

is never put out.]*n* *47*If your eye causes you to sin, take it out. It is better for you to enter the kingdom of God with only one eye than to have two eyes and be thrown into hell. *48*In hell the worm does not die; the fire is never put out. *49*Every person will be salted with fire.

50"Salt is good, but if the salt loses its salty taste, you cannot make it salty again. So, be full of salt, and have peace with each other."

MARCH 7

NUMBERS 11:1—12:16

Fire from the Lord

11 Now the people complained to the LORD about their troubles, and when he heard them, he became angry. Then fire from the LORD burned among the people at the edge of the camp. *2*The people cried out to Moses, and when he prayed to the LORD, the fire stopped burning. *3*So that place was called Taberah,*n* because the LORD's fire had burned among them.

Seventy Elders Help Moses

*4*Some troublemakers among them wanted better food, and soon all the Israelites began complaining. They said, "We want meat! *5*We remember the fish we ate for free in Egypt. We also had cucumbers, melons, leeks, onions, and garlic. *6*But now we have lost our appetite; we never see anything but this manna!"

*7*The manna was like small white seeds. *8*The people would go to gather it, and then grind it in handmills, or crush it between stones. After they cooked it in a pot or made cakes with it, it tasted like bread baked with olive oil. *9*When the dew fell on the camp each night, so did the manna.

*10*Moses heard every family crying as they stood in the entrances of their tents. Then the LORD became very angry, and Moses got upset. *11*He asked the LORD, "Why have you brought me, your servant, this trouble? What have I done wrong that you made me responsible for all these people? *12*I am not the father of all these people, and I didn't give birth to them. So why do you make me carry them to the land you promised to our ancestors? Must

I carry them in my arms as a nurse carries a baby? *13*Where can I get meat for all these people? They keep crying to me, 'We want meat!' *14*I can't take care of all these people alone. It is too much for me. *15*If you are going to continue doing this to me, then kill me now. If you care about me, put me to death, and then I won't have any more troubles."

*16*The LORD said to Moses, "Bring me seventy of Israel's elders, men that you know are leaders among the people. Bring them to the Meeting Tent, and have them stand there with you. *17*I will come down and speak with you there. I will take some of the Spirit that is in you, and I will give it to them. They will help you care for the people so that you will not have to care for them alone.

18"Tell the people this: 'Make yourselves holy for tomorrow, and you will eat meat. You cried to the LORD, "We want meat! We were better off in Egypt!" So now the LORD will give you meat to eat. *19*You will eat it not for just one, two, five, ten, or even twenty days, *20*but you will eat that meat for a whole month. You will eat it until it comes out your nose, and you will grow to hate it. This is because you have rejected the LORD, who is with you. You have cried to him, saying, "Why did we ever leave Egypt?" ' "

*21*Moses said, "LORD, here are six hundred thousand people standing around me, and you say, 'I will give them enough meat to eat for a month!' *22*If we killed all the flocks and herds, that would not be enough. If we caught all the fish in the sea, that would not be enough."

*23*But the LORD said to Moses, "Do you

think I'm weak? Now you will see if I can do what I say."

²⁴So Moses went out to the people and told them what the LORD had said. He gathered seventy of the elders together and had them stand around the Tent. ²⁵Then the LORD came down in the cloud and spoke to Moses. The LORD took some of the Spirit Moses had, and he gave it to the seventy leaders. With the Spirit in them, they prophesied, but just that one time.

²⁶Two men named Eldad and Medad were also listed as leaders, but they did not go to the Tent. They stayed in the camp, but the Spirit was also given to them, and they prophesied in the camp. ²⁷A young man ran to Moses and said, "Eldad and Medad are prophesying in the camp."

²⁸Joshua son of Nun said, "Moses, my master, stop them!" (Ever since he was a young boy, Joshua had been Moses' assistant.)

²⁹But Moses answered, "Are you jealous for me? I wish all the LORD's people could prophesy. I wish the LORD would give his Spirit to all of them!" ³⁰Then Moses and the leaders of Israel went back to the camp.

The Lord Sends Quail

³¹The LORD sent a strong wind from the sea, and it blew quail into the area all around the camp. The quail were about three feet deep on the ground, and there were quail a day's walk in any direction. ³²The people went out and gathered quail all that day, that night, and the next day. Everyone gathered at least sixty bushels, and they spread them around the camp. ³³But the LORD became very angry, and he gave the people a terrible sickness that came while the meat was still in their mouths. ³⁴So the people named that place Kibroth Hattaavah,ⁿ because there they buried those who wanted other food.

³⁵From Kibroth Hattaavah the people went to stay at Hazeroth.

Miriam and Aaron Speak Against Moses

12Miriam and Aaron began to talk against Moses because of his Cushite wife (he had married a Cushite). ²They said, "Is Moses the only one the LORD speaks through? Doesn't he also speak through us?" And the LORD heard this.

³(Now Moses was very humble. He was the least proud person on earth.)

⁴So the LORD suddenly spoke to Moses, Aaron, and Miriam and said, "All three of you come to the Meeting Tent." So they went. ⁵The LORD came down in a pillar of cloud and stood at the entrance to the Tent. He called to Aaron and Miriam, and they both came near. ⁶He said, "Listen to my words:

When prophets are among you,
  I, the LORD, will show myself to them
    in visions;
  I will speak to them in dreams.
⁷But this is not true with my servant
    Moses.
  I trust him to lead all my people.
⁸I speak face to face with him—
  clearly, not with hidden meanings.
  He has even seen the form of the LORD.
You should be afraid
  to speak against my servant Moses."

⁹The LORD was very angry with them, and he left.

¹⁰When the cloud lifted from the Tent and Aaron turned toward Miriam, she was as white as snow; she had a skin disease. ¹¹Aaron said to Moses, "Please, my master, forgive us for our foolish sin. ¹²Don't let her be like a baby who is born dead. (Sometimes a baby is born with half of its flesh eaten away.)"

¹³So Moses cried out to the LORD, "God, please heal her!"

¹⁴The LORD answered Moses, "If her father had spit in her face, she would have been shamed for seven days, so put her outside the camp for seven days. After that, she may come back." ¹⁵So Miriam was put outside of the camp for seven days, and the people did not move on until she came back.

¹⁶After that, the people left Hazeroth and camped in the Desert of Paran.

PSALM 31:14-18

¹⁴LORD, I trust you.
  I have said, "You are my God."
¹⁵My life is in your hands.

11:34 Kibroth Hattaavah This name in Hebrew means "graves of wanting."

Save me from my enemies
and from those who are chasing me.
[16]Show your kindness to me, your servant.
Save me because of your love.
[17]LORD, I called to you,
so do not let me be disgraced.
Let the wicked be disgraced
and lie silent in the grave.
[18]With pride and hatred
they speak against those who do right.
So silence their lying lips.

PROVERBS 11:12-14

[12]People without good sense find fault with
their neighbors,
but those with understanding keep quiet.

[13]Gossips can't keep secrets,
but a trustworthy person can.

[14]Without leadership a nation falls,
but lots of good advice will save it.

MARK 10:1-31

Jesus Teaches About Divorce

10 Then Jesus left that place and went into the area of Judea and across the Jordan River. Again, crowds came to him, and he taught them as he usually did.

[2]Some Pharisees came to Jesus and tried to trick him. They asked, "Is it right for a man to divorce his wife?"

[3]Jesus answered, "What did Moses command you to do?"

[4]They said, "Moses allowed a man to write out divorce papers and send her away."[n]

[5]Jesus said, "Moses wrote that command for you because you were stubborn. [6]But when God made the world, 'he made them male and female.'[n] [7]So a man will leave his father and mother and be united with his wife,[n] [8]and the two will become one body.'[n] So there are not two, but one. [9]God has joined these two together, so no one should separate them."

[10]Later, in the house, his followers asked Jesus again about the question of divorce.

[11]He answered, "Anyone who divorces his wife and marries another woman is guilty of adultery against her. [12]And the woman who divorces her husband and marries another man is also guilty of adultery."

Jesus Accepts Children

[13]Some people brought their little children to Jesus so he could touch them, but his followers told them to stop. [14]When Jesus saw this, he was upset and said to them, "Let the little children come to me. Don't stop them, because the kingdom of God belongs to people who are like these children. [15]I tell you the truth, you must accept the kingdom of God as if you were a little child, or you will never enter it." [16]Then Jesus took the children in his arms, put his hands on them, and blessed them.

A Rich Young Man's Question

[17]As Jesus started to leave, a man ran to him and fell on his knees before Jesus. The man asked, "Good teacher, what must I do to have life forever?"

[18]Jesus answered, "Why do you call me good? Only God is good. [19]You know the commands: 'You must not murder anyone. You must not be guilty of adultery. You must not steal. You must not tell lies about your neighbor. You must not cheat. Honor your father and mother.'"[n]

[20]The man said, "Teacher, I have obeyed all these things since I was a boy."

[21]Jesus, looking at the man, loved him and said, "There is one more thing you need to do. Go and sell everything you have, and give the money to the poor, and you will have treasure in heaven. Then come and follow me."

[22]He was very sad to hear Jesus say this, and he left sorrowfully, because he was rich.

[23]Then Jesus looked at his followers and said, "How hard it will be for the rich to enter the kingdom of God!"

[24]The followers were amazed at what Jesus said. But he said again, "My children, it is very hard[n] to enter the kingdom of God! [25]It

---

10:4 "Moses . . . away." Quotation from Deuteronomy 24:1.   10:6 'he made . . . female' Quotation from Genesis 1:27.
10:7 and . . . wife Some Greek copies do not have this phrase.   10:7-8 'So . . . body.' Quotation from Genesis 2:24.
10:19 'You . . . mother.' Quotation from Exodus 20:12-16; Deuteronomy 5:16-20.   10:24 hard Some Greek copies continue,
"for those who trust in riches."

is easier for a camel to go through the eye of a needle than for a rich person to enter the kingdom of God."

²⁶The followers were even more surprised and said to each other, "Then who can be saved?"

²⁷Jesus looked at them and said, "For people this is impossible, but for God all things are possible."

²⁸Peter said to Jesus, "Look, we have left everything and followed you."

²⁹Jesus said, "I tell you the truth, all those who have left houses, brothers, sisters, mother, father, children, or farms for me and for the Good News ³⁰will get more than they left. Here in this world they will have a hundred times more homes, brothers, sisters, mothers, children, and fields. And with those things, they will also suffer for their belief. But in this age they will have life forever. ³¹Many who are first now will be last in the future. And many who are last now will be first in the future."

MARCH 8

NUMBERS 13:1—14:45

The Spies Explore Canaan

13 The LORD said to Moses, ²"Send men to explore the land of Canaan, which I will give to the Israelites. Send one leader from each tribe."

³So Moses obeyed the LORD's command and sent the Israelite leaders out from the Desert of Paran. ⁴These are their names: from the tribe of Reuben, Shammua son of Zaccur; ⁵from the tribe of Simeon, Shaphat son of Hori; ⁶from the tribe of Judah, Caleb son of Jephunneh; ⁷from the tribe of Issachar, Igal son of Joseph; ⁸from the tribe of Ephraim, Hoshea son of Nun; ⁹from the tribe of Benjamin, Palti son of Raphu; ¹⁰from the tribe of Zebulun, Gaddiel son of Sodi; ¹¹from the tribe of Manasseh (a tribe of Joseph), Gaddi son of Susi; ¹²from the tribe of Dan, Ammiel son of Gemalli; ¹³from the tribe of Asher, Sethur son of Michael; ¹⁴from the tribe of Naphtali, Nahbi son of Vophsi; ¹⁵from the tribe of Gad, Geuel son of Maki.

¹⁶These are the names of the men Moses sent to explore the land. (Moses gave Hoshea son of Nun the new name Joshua.)

¹⁷Moses sent them to explore Canaan and said, "Go through southern Canaan and then into the mountains. ¹⁸See what the land looks like. Are the people who live there strong or weak? Are there a few or many? ¹⁹What kind of land do they live in? Is it good or bad? What about the towns they live in—are they open like camps, or do they have walls? ²⁰What about the soil? Is it fertile or poor? Are there trees there? Try to bring back some of the fruit from that land." (It was the season for the first grapes.)

²¹So they went up and explored the land, from the Desert of Zin all the way to Rehob by Lebo Hamath. ²²They went through the southern area to Hebron, where Ahiman, Sheshai, and Talmai, the descendants of Anak lived. (The city of Hebron had been built seven years before Zoan in Egypt.) ²³In the Valley of Eshcol, they cut off a branch of a grapevine that had one bunch of grapes on it and carried that branch on a pole between two of them. They also got some pomegranates and figs. ²⁴That place was called the Valley of Eshcol,ⁿ because the Israelites cut off the bunch of grapes there. ²⁵After forty days of exploring the land, the men returned to the camp.

²⁶They came back to Moses and Aaron and all the Israelites at Kadesh, in the Desert of Paran. The men reported to them and showed everybody the fruit from the land. ²⁷They told Moses, "We went to the land where you sent us, and it is a fertile land! Here is some of its fruit. ²⁸But the people

13:24 Eshcol This name in Hebrew means "bunch."

who live there are strong. Their cities are walled and very large. We even saw some Anakites there. ²⁹The Amalekites live in the southern area; the Hittites, Jebusites, and Amorites live in the mountains; and the Canaanites live near the sea and along the Jordan River."

³⁰Then Caleb told the people near Moses to be quiet, and he said, "We should certainly go up and take the land for ourselves. We can certainly do it."

³¹But the men who had gone with him said, "We can't attack those people; they are stronger than we are." ³²And those men gave the Israelites a bad report about the land they explored, saying, "The land that we explored is too large to conquer. All the people we saw are very tall. ³³We saw the Nephilim people there. (The Anakites come from the Nephilim people.) We felt like grasshoppers, and we looked like grasshoppers to them."

The People Complain Again

14 That night all the people in the camp began crying loudly. ²All the Israelites complained against Moses and Aaron, and all the people said to them, "We wish we had died in Egypt or in this desert. ³Why is the LORD bringing us to this land to be killed with swords? Our wives and children will be taken away. We would be better off going back to Egypt." ⁴They said to each other, "Let's choose a leader and go back to Egypt."

⁵Then Moses and Aaron bowed facedown in front of all the Israelites gathered there. ⁶Joshua son of Nun and Caleb son of Jephunneh, who had explored the land, tore their clothes. ⁷They said to all of the Israelites, "The land we explored is very good. ⁸If the LORD is pleased with us, he will lead us into that land and give us that fertile land. ⁹Don't turn against the LORD! Don't be afraid of the people in that land! We will chew them up. They have no protection, but the LORD is with us. So don't be afraid of them."

¹⁰Then all the people talked about killing them with stones. But the glory of the LORD appeared at the Meeting Tent to all the Israelites. ¹¹The LORD said to Moses, "How long will these people ignore me? How long will they not believe me in spite of the miracles I

have done among them? ¹²I will give them a terrible sickness and get rid of them. But I will make you into a great nation that will be stronger than they are."

¹³Then Moses said to the LORD, "The Egyptians will hear about it! You brought these people from there by your great power, ¹⁴and the Egyptians will tell this to those who live in this land. They have already heard about you, LORD. They know that you are with your people and that you were seen face to face. They know that your cloud stays over your people and that you lead your people with that cloud during the day and with fire at night. ¹⁵If you put these people to death all at once, the nations who have heard about your power will say, ¹⁶'The LORD was not able to bring them into the land he promised them. So he killed them in the desert.'

¹⁷"So show your strength now, Lord. Do what you said: ¹⁸'The LORD doesn't become angry quickly, but he has great love. He forgives sin and law breaking. But the LORD never forgets to punish guilty people. When parents sin, he will also punish their children, their grandchildren, their great-grandchildren, and their great-great-grandchildren.' ¹⁹By your great love, forgive these people's sin, just as you have forgiven them from the time they left Egypt until now."

²⁰The LORD answered, "I have forgiven them as you asked. ²¹But, as surely as I live and as surely as my glory fills the whole earth, I make this promise: ²²All these people saw my glory and the miracles I did in Egypt and in the desert, but they disobeyed me and tested me ten times. ²³So not one of them will see the land I promised to their ancestors. No one who rejected me will see that land. ²⁴But my servant Caleb thinks differently and follows me completely. So I will bring him into the land he has already seen, and his children will own that land. ²⁵Since the Amalekites and the Canaanites are living in the valleys, leave tomorrow and follow the desert road toward the Red Sea."

The Lord Punishes the People

²⁶The LORD said to Moses and Aaron, ²⁷"How long will these evil people complain

about me? I have heard the grumbling and complaining of these Israelites. ²⁸So tell them, 'This is what the LORD says. I heard what you said, and as surely as I live, I will do those very things to you: ²⁹You will die in this desert. Every one of you who is twenty years old or older and who was counted with the people—all of you who complained against me—will die. ³⁰Not one of you will enter the land where I promised you would live; only Caleb son of Jephunneh and Joshua son of Nun will go in. ³¹You said that your children would be taken away, but I will bring them into the land to enjoy what you refused. ³²As for you, you will die in this desert. ³³Your children will be shepherds here for forty years. Because you were not loyal, they will suffer until you lie dead in the desert. ³⁴For forty years you will suffer for your sins—a year for each of the forty days you explored the land. You will know me as your enemy.' ³⁵I, the LORD, have spoken, and I will certainly do these things to all these evil people who have come together against me. So they will all die here in this desert.' "

³⁶The men Moses had sent to explore the land had returned and spread complaints among all the people. They had given a bad report about the land. ³⁷The men who gave a very bad report died; the LORD killed them with a terrible sickness. ³⁸Only two of the men who explored the land did not die— Joshua son of Nun and Caleb son of Jephunneh.

³⁹When Moses told these things to all the Israelites, they were very sad. ⁴⁰Early the next morning they started to go toward the top of the mountains, saying, "We have sinned. We will go where the LORD told us."

⁴¹But Moses said, "Why are you disobeying the LORD's command? You will not win! ⁴²Don't go, because the LORD is not with you and you will be beaten by your enemies. ⁴³You will run into the Amalekites and Canaanites, who will kill you with swords. You have turned away from the LORD, so the LORD will not be with you."

⁴⁴But they were proud. They went toward the top of the mountains, but Moses and the Ark of the Agreement with the LORD did not leave the camp. ⁴⁵The Amalekites and the

Canaanites who lived in those mountains came down and attacked the Israelites and beat them back all the way to Hormah.

PSALM 31:19-24

¹⁹How great is your goodness
    that you have stored up for those who
        fear you,
    that you have given to those who trust
        you.
    You do this for all to see.
²⁰You protect them by your presence
    from what people plan against them.
    You shelter them from evil words.
²¹Praise the LORD.
    His love to me was wonderful
        when my city was attacked.
²²In my distress, I said,
    "God cannot see me!"
    But you heard my prayer
        when I cried out to you for help.
²³Love the LORD, all you who belong to him.
    The LORD protects those who truly
        believe,
    but he punishes the proud as much as
        they have sinned.
²⁴All you who put your hope in the LORD
    be strong and brave.

PROVERBS 11:15

¹⁵Whoever guarantees to pay somebody
    else's loan will suffer.
    It is safer to avoid such promises.

MARK 10:32-52

Jesus Talks About His Death

³²As Jesus and the people with him were on the road to Jerusalem, he was leading the way. His followers were amazed, but others in the crowd who followed were afraid. Again Jesus took the twelve apostles aside and began to tell them what was about to happen in Jerusalem. ³³He said, "Look, we are going to Jerusalem. The Son of Man will be turned over to the leading priests and the teachers of the law. They will say that he must die, and they will turn him over to the non-Jewish people, ³⁴who will laugh at him and spit on him. They will beat him with whips and

crucify him. But on the third day, he will rise to life again."

Two Followers Ask Jesus a Favor

[35]Then James and John, sons of Zebedee, came to Jesus and said, "Teacher, we want to ask you to do something for us."

[36]Jesus asked, "What do you want me to do for you?"

[37]They answered, "Let one of us sit at your right side and one of us sit at your left side in your glory in your kingdom."

[38]Jesus said, "You don't understand what you are asking. Can you drink the cup that I must drink? And can you be baptized with the same kind of baptism that I must go through?"[n]

[39]They answered, "Yes, we can."

Jesus said to them, "You will drink the same cup that I will drink, and you will be baptized with the same baptism that I must go through. [40]But I cannot choose who will sit at my right or my left; those places belong to those for whom they have been prepared."

[41]When the other ten followers heard this, they began to be angry with James and John.

[42]Jesus called them together and said, "The other nations have rulers. You know that those rulers love to show their power over the people, and their important leaders love to use all their authority. [43]But it should not be that way among you. Whoever wants to become great among you must serve the rest of you like a servant. [44]Whoever wants to become the first among you must serve all of you like a slave. [45]In the same way, the Son of Man did not come to be served. He came to serve others and to give his life as a ransom for many people."

Jesus Heals a Blind Man

[46]Then they came to the town of Jericho. As Jesus was leaving there with his followers and a great many people, a blind beggar named Bartimaeus son of Timaeus was sitting by the road. [47]When he heard that Jesus from Nazareth was walking by, he began to shout, "Jesus, Son of David, have mercy on me!"

[48]Many people warned the blind man to be quiet, but he shouted even more, "Son of David, have mercy on me!"

[49]Jesus stopped and said, "Tell the man to come here."

So they called the blind man, saying, "Cheer up! Get to your feet. Jesus is calling you." [50]The blind man jumped up, left his coat there, and went to Jesus.

[51]Jesus asked him, "What do you want me to do for you?"

The blind man answered, "Teacher, I want to see."

[52]Jesus said, "Go, you are healed because you believed." At once the man could see, and he followed Jesus on the road.

MARCH 9

NUMBERS 15:1—16:50

Rules About Sacrifices

15 The LORD said to Moses, [2]"Speak to the Israelites and say to them, 'When you enter the land that I am giving you as a home, [3]give the LORD offerings made by fire. These may be from your herds or flocks, as a smell pleasing to the LORD. These may be burnt offerings or sacrifices for special promises, or as gifts to him, or as festival offerings. [4]The one who brings the offering shall also give the LORD a grain offering. It should be two quarts of fine flour mixed with one quart of olive oil. [5]Each time you offer a lamb as a burnt offering or sacrifice, also prepare a quart of wine as a drink offering.

[6]"'If you are giving a male sheep, also prepare a grain offering of four quarts of fine

flour mixed with one and one-fourth quarts of olive oil. [7]Also prepare one and one-fourth quarts of wine as a drink offering. Its smell will be pleasing to the LORD.

[8] 'If you prepare a young bull as a burnt offering or sacrifice, whether it is for a special promise or a fellowship offering to the LORD, [9]bring a grain offering with the bull. It should be six quarts of fine flour mixed with two quarts of olive oil. [10]Also bring two quarts of wine as a drink offering. This offering is made by fire, and its smell will be pleasing to the LORD. [11]Prepare each bull or male sheep, lamb or young goat this way. [12]Do this for every one of the animals you bring.

[13] 'All citizens must do these things in this way, and the smell of their offerings by fire will be pleasing to the LORD. [14]From now on if foreigners who live among you want to make offerings by fire so the smell will be pleasing to the LORD, they must offer them the same way you do. [15]The law is the same for you and for foreigners, and it will be from now on; you and the foreigners are alike before the LORD. [16]The teachings and rules are the same for you and for the foreigners among you.'"

[17]The LORD said to Moses, [18]"Tell the Israelites: 'You are going to another land, where I am taking you. [19]When you eat the food there, offer part of it to the LORD. [20]Offer a loaf of bread from the first of your grain, which will be your offering from the threshing floor. [21]From now on offer to the LORD the first part of your grain.

[22] 'Now what if you forget to obey any of these commands the LORD gave Moses? [23]These are the LORD's commands given to you through Moses, which began the day the LORD gave them to you and will continue from now on. [24]If the people forget to obey one of these commands, all the people must offer a young bull as a burnt offering, a smell pleasing to the LORD. By law you must also give the grain offering and the drink offering with it, and you must bring a male goat as a sin offering. [25]The priest will remove that sin for all the Israelites so they will belong to the LORD. They are forgiven, because they didn't know

they were sinning. For the wrong they did they brought offerings to the LORD, an offering by fire and a sin offering. [26]So all of the people of Israel and the foreigners living among them will be forgiven. No one meant to do wrong.

[27] 'If just one person sins without meaning to, a year-old female goat must be brought for a sin offering. [28]The priest will remove the sin of the person who sinned accidentally. He will remove it before the LORD, and the person will be forgiven. [29]The same teaching is for everyone who sins accidentally—for those born Israelites and for foreigners living among you.

[30] 'But anyone who sins on purpose is against the LORD and must be cut off from the people, whether it is someone born among you or a foreigner. [31]That person has turned against the LORD's word and has not obeyed his commands. Such a person must surely be cut off from the others. He is guilty.'"

A Man Worked on the Sabbath

[32]When the Israelites were still in the desert, they found a man gathering wood on the Sabbath day. [33]Those who found him gathering wood brought him to Moses and Aaron and all the people. [34]They held the man under guard, because they did not know what to do with him. [35]Then the LORD said to Moses, "The man must surely die. All the people must kill him by throwing stones at him outside the camp." [36]So all the people took him outside the camp and stoned him to death, as the LORD commanded Moses.

The Tassels

[37]The LORD said to Moses, [38]"Speak to the Israelites and tell them this: 'Tie several pieces of thread together and attach them to the corners of your clothes. Put a blue thread in each one of these tassels. Wear them from now on. [39]You will have these tassels to look at to remind you of all the LORD's commands. Then you will obey them and not be disloyal by following what your bodies and eyes want. [40]Then you will remember to obey all my commands, and you will be God's holy people. [41]I am the LORD your God, who brought you out of Egypt to be your God. I am the LORD your God.'"

Korah, Dathan, Abiram, and On

16 Korah, Dathan, Abiram, and On turned against Moses. (Korah was the son of Izhar, the son of Kohath, the son of Levi; Dathan and Abiram were brothers, the sons of Eliab; and On was the son of Peleth; Dathan, Abiram, and On were from the tribe of Reuben.) ²These men gathered two hundred fifty other Israelite men, well-known leaders chosen by the community, and challenged Moses. ³They came as a group to speak to Moses and Aaron and said, "You have gone too far. All the people are holy, every one of them, and the LORD is among them. So why do you put yourselves above all the people of the LORD?"

⁴When Moses heard this, he bowed facedown. ⁵Then he said to Korah and all his followers: "Tomorrow morning the LORD will show who belongs to him. He will bring the one who is holy near to him; he will bring to himself the person he chooses. ⁶So Korah, you and all your followers do this: Get some pans for burning incense. ⁷Tomorrow put fire and incense in them and take them before the LORD. He will choose the man who is holy. You Levites have gone too far."

⁸Moses also said to Korah, "Listen, you Levites. ⁹The God of Israel has separated you from the rest of the Israelites. He brought you near to himself to do the work in the LORD's Holy Tent and to stand before all the Israelites and serve them. Isn't that enough? ¹⁰He has brought you and all your fellow Levites near to himself, yet now you want to be priests. ¹¹You and your followers have joined together against the LORD. Your complaint is not against Aaron."

¹²Then Moses called Dathan and Abiram, the sons of Eliab, but they said, "We will not come! ¹³You have brought us out of a fertile land to this desert to kill us, and now you want to order us around. ¹⁴You haven't brought us into a fertile land; you haven't given us any land with fields and vineyards. Will you put out the eyes of these men? No! We will not come!"

¹⁵Then Moses became very angry and said to the LORD, "Don't accept their gifts. I have not taken anything from them, not even a donkey, and I have not done wrong to any of them."

¹⁶Then Moses said to Korah, "You and all your followers must stand before the LORD tomorrow. And Aaron will stand there with you and them. ¹⁷Each of you must take your pan and put incense in it; present these two hundred fifty pans before the LORD. You and Aaron must also present your pans." ¹⁸So each man got his pan and put burning incense in it and stood with Moses and Aaron at the entrance to the Meeting Tent. ¹⁹Korah gathered all his followers who were against Moses and Aaron, and they stood at the entrance to the Meeting Tent. Then the glory of the LORD appeared to everyone.

²⁰The LORD said to Moses and Aaron, ²¹"Move away from these men so I can destroy them quickly."

²²But Moses and Aaron bowed facedown and cried out, "God, you are the God over the spirits of all people. Please don't be angry with this whole group. Only one man has really sinned."

²³Then the LORD said to Moses, ²⁴"Tell everyone to move away from the tents of Korah, Dathan, and Abiram."

²⁵Moses stood and went to Dathan and Abiram; the elders of Israel followed him. ²⁶Moses warned the people, "Move away from the tents of these evil men! Don't touch anything of theirs, or you will be destroyed because of their sins." ²⁷So they moved away from the tents of Korah, Dathan, and Abiram. Dathan and Abiram were standing outside their tents with their wives, children, and little babies.

²⁸Then Moses said, "Now you will know that the LORD has sent me to do all these things; it was not my idea. ²⁹If these men die a normal death—the way men usually die—then the LORD did not really send me. ³⁰But if the LORD does something new, you will know they have insulted the LORD. The ground will open and swallow them. They will be buried alive and will go to the place of the dead, and everything that belongs to them will go with them."

³¹When Moses finished saying these things, the ground under the men split open. ³²The earth opened and swallowed them and all their families. All Korah's men and everything they owned went down. ³³They were

buried alive, going to the place of the dead, and everything they owned went with them. Then the earth covered them. They died and were gone from the community. [34]The people of Israel around them heard their screams and ran away, saying, "The earth will swallow us, too!"

[35]Then a fire came down from the LORD and destroyed the two hundred fifty men who had presented the incense.

[36]The LORD said to Moses, [37]"Tell Eleazar son of Aaron, the priest, to take all the incense pans out of the fire. Have him scatter the coals a long distance away. But the incense pans are still holy. [38]Take the pans of these men who sinned and lost their lives, and hammer them into flat sheets that will be used to cover the altar. They are holy, because they were presented to the LORD, and they will be a sign to the Israelites."

[39]So Eleazar the priest gathered all the bronze pans that had been brought by the men who were burned up. He had the pans hammered into flat sheets to put on the altar, [40]as the LORD had commanded him through Moses. These sheets were to remind the Israelites that only descendants of Aaron should burn incense before the LORD. Anyone else would die like Korah and his followers.

Aaron Saves the People

[41]The next day all the Israelites complained against Moses and Aaron and said, "You have killed the LORD's people."

[42]When the people gathered to complain against Moses and Aaron, they turned toward the Meeting Tent, and the cloud covered it. The glory of the LORD appeared. [43]Then Moses and Aaron went in front of the Meeting Tent.

[44]The LORD said to Moses, [45]"Move away from these people so I can destroy them quickly." So Moses and Aaron bowed facedown.

[46]Then Moses said to Aaron, "Get your pan, and put fire from the altar and incense in it. Hurry to the people and remove their sin. The LORD is angry with them; the sickness has already started." [47]So Aaron did as Moses said. He ran to the middle of the people, where the sickness had already started among them. So

Aaron offered the incense to remove their sin. [48]He stood between the dead and the living, and the sickness stopped there. [49]But 14,700 people died from that sickness, in addition to those who died because of Korah. [50]Then Aaron went back to Moses at the entrance to the Meeting Tent. The terrible sickness had been stopped.

PSALM 32:1–5

It Is Better to Confess Sin

A maskil of David.

32 Happy is the person
whose sins are forgiven,
whose wrongs are pardoned.
[2]Happy is the person
whom the LORD does not consider guilty
and in whom there is nothing false.

[3]When I kept things to myself,
I felt weak deep inside me.
I moaned all day long.
[4]Day and night you punished me.
My strength was gone as in the
summer heat.   *Selah*
[5]Then I confessed my sins to you
and didn't hide my guilt.
I said, "I will confess my sins to the LORD,"
and you forgave my guilt.   *Selah*

PROVERBS 11:16–18

[16]A kind woman gets respect,
but cruel men get only wealth.

[17]Kind people do themselves a favor,
but cruel people bring trouble on
themselves.

[18]An evil person really earns nothing,
but a good person will surely be
rewarded.

MARK 11:1–19

Jesus Enters Jerusalem as a King

11 As Jesus and his followers were coming closer to Jerusalem, they came to the towns of Bethphage and Bethany near the Mount of Olives. From there Jesus sent two of his followers [2]and said to them, "Go to

the town you can see there. When you enter it, you will quickly find a colt tied, which no one has ever ridden. Untie it and bring it here to me. [3]If anyone asks you why you are doing this, tell him its Master needs the colt, and he will send it at once."

[4]The followers went into the town, found a colt tied in the street near the door of a house, and untied it. [5]Some people were standing there and asked, "What are you doing? Why are you untying that colt?" [6]The followers answered the way Jesus told them to answer, and the people let them take the colt.

[7]They brought the colt to Jesus and put their coats on it, and Jesus sat on it. [8]Many people spread their coats on the road. Others cut branches in the fields and spread them on the road. [9]The people were walking ahead of Jesus and behind him, shouting,

"Praise God!
God bless the One who comes in the
    name of the Lord!   *Psalm 118:26*
[10]God bless the kingdom of our father
    David!
That kingdom is coming!
Praise[n] to God in heaven!"

[11]Jesus entered Jerusalem and went into the Temple. After he had looked at everything, since it was already late, he went out to Bethany with the twelve apostles.

[12]The next day as Jesus was leaving Bethany, he became hungry. [13]Seeing a fig tree in leaf from far away, he went to see if it had any figs on it. But he found no figs, only leaves, because it was not the right season for figs. [14]So Jesus said to the tree, "May no one ever eat fruit from you again." And Jesus' followers heard him say this.

Jesus Goes to the Temple

[15]When Jesus returned to Jerusalem, he went into the Temple and began to throw out those who were buying and selling there. He turned over the tables of those who were exchanging different kinds of money, and he upset the benches of those who were selling doves. [16]Jesus refused to allow anyone to carry goods through the Temple courts. [17]Then he taught the people, saying, "It is written in the Scriptures, 'My Temple will be called a house for prayer for people from all nations.'[n] But you are changing God's house into a 'hide-out for robbers.'"[n]

[18]The leading priests and the teachers of the law heard all this and began trying to find a way to kill Jesus. They were afraid of him, because all the people were amazed at his teaching. [19]That evening, Jesus and his followers[n] left the city.

MARCH 10

NUMBERS 17:1—18:32

Aaron's Walking Stick Buds

17 The LORD said to Moses, [2]"Speak to the people of Israel and get twelve walking sticks from them—one from the leader of each tribe. Write the name of each man on his stick, and [3]on the stick from Levi, write Aaron's name. There must be one stick for the head of each tribe. [4]Put them in the Meeting Tent in front of the Ark of the Agreement, where I meet with you. [5]I will choose one man whose walking stick will begin to grow leaves; in this way I will stop the Israelites from always complaining against you."

[6]So Moses spoke to the Israelites. Each of the twelve leaders gave him a walking stick—one from each tribe—and Aaron's walking stick was among them. [7]Moses put them before the LORD in the Tent of the Agreement.

11:10 Praise Literally, "Hosanna," a Hebrew word used at first in praying to God for help, but at this time it was probably a shout of joy used in praising God or his Messiah.   **11:17 'My Temple . . . nations.'** Quotation from Isaiah 56:7.   **11:17 'hide-out for robbers'** Quotation from Jeremiah 7:11.   **11:19 his followers** Some Greek copies mention only Jesus here.

[8]The next day, when Moses entered the Tent, he saw that Aaron's stick (which stood for the family of Levi) had grown leaves. It had even budded, blossomed, and produced almonds. [9]So Moses brought out to the Israelites all the walking sticks from the LORD's presence. They all looked, and each man took back his stick.

[10]Then the LORD said to Moses, "Put Aaron's walking stick back in front of the Ark of the Agreement. It will remind these people who are always turning against me to stop their complaining against me so they won't die." [11]So Moses obeyed what the LORD commanded him.

[12]The people of Israel said to Moses, "We are going to die! We are destroyed. We are all destroyed! [13]Anyone who even comes near the Holy Tent of the LORD will die. Will we all die?"

The Work of the Priests and Levites

18 The LORD said to Aaron, "You, your sons, and your family are now responsible for any wrongs done against the Holy Place; you and your sons are responsible for any wrongs done against the priests. [2]Bring with you your fellow Levites from your tribe, and they will help you and your sons serve in the Tent of the Agreement. [3]They are under your control, to do all the work that needs to be done in the Tent. But they must not go near the things in the Holy Place or near the altar. If they do, both you and they will die. [4]They will join you in taking care of the Meeting Tent. They must do the work at the Tent, and no one else may come near you.

[5]"You must take care of the Holy Place and the altar so that I won't become angry with the Israelites again. [6]I myself chose your fellow Levites from among the Israelites as a gift given for you to the LORD, to work at the Meeting Tent. [7]But only you and your sons may serve as priests. Only you may serve at the altar or go behind the curtain. I am giving you this gift of serving as a priest, and anyone else who comes near the Holy Place will be put to death."

[8]Then the LORD said to Aaron, "I myself make you responsible for the offerings given to me. All the holy offerings that the Israelites give to me, I give to you and your sons as your share, your continual portion. [9]Your share of the holy offerings is that part which is not burned. When the people bring me gifts as most holy offerings, whether they are grain or sin or penalty offerings, they will be set apart for you and your sons. [10]You must eat the offering in a most holy place. Any male may eat it, but you must respect it as holy.

[11]"I also give you the offerings the Israelites present to me. I give these to you and your sons and daughters as your continual share. Anyone in your family who is clean may eat it.

[12]"And I give you all the best olive oil and all the best new wine and grain. This is what the Israelites give to me, the LORD, from the first crops they harvest. [13]When they bring to the LORD all the first things they harvest, they will be yours. Anyone in your family who is clean may eat these things.

[14]"Everything in Israel that is given to the LORD is yours. [15]The first one born to any family, whether people or animals, will be offered to the LORD. And that will be yours. But you must make a payment for every firstborn child and every firstborn animal that is unclean. [16]When they are one month old, you must make a payment for them of two ounces of silver, as set by the Holy Place measure.

[17]"But you must not make a payment for the firstborn ox or sheep or goat. Those animals are holy. Sprinkle their blood on the altar and burn their fat as an offering made by fire. The smell is pleasing to the LORD. [18]But the meat will be yours, just as the breast that is presented and the right thigh will be yours. [19]Anything the Israelites present as holy gifts I, the LORD, give to you, your sons and daughters as your continual portion. This is a lasting agreement of salt[n] before the LORD for you and your children forever."

[20]The LORD also said to Aaron, "You will not inherit any of the land, and you will not

---

18:19 agreement of salt The meaning is not clear, but Leviticus 2:13 says, "Salt stands for your agreement with God that will last forever."

own any land among the other people. I will be yours. Out of all the Israelites, only you will inherit me.

²¹"When the people of Israel give me a tenth of what they make, I will give that tenth to the Levites. This is their payment for the work they do serving at the Meeting Tent. ²²But the other Israelites must never go near the Meeting Tent, or they will die for their sin. ²³Only the Levites should work in the Meeting Tent and be responsible for any sins against it. This is a rule from now on. The Levites will not inherit any land among the other Israelites, ²⁴but when the Israelites give a tenth of everything they make to me, I will give that tenth to the Levites as a reward. That is why I said about the Levites: 'They will not inherit any land among the Israelites.'"

²⁵The LORD said to Moses, ²⁶"Speak to the Levites and tell them: 'You will receive a tenth of everything the Israelites make, which I will give to you. But you must give a tenth of that back to the LORD. ²⁷I will accept your offering just as much as I accept the offerings from others, who give new grain or new wine. ²⁸In this way you will present an offering to the LORD as the other Israelites do. When you receive a tenth from the Israelites, you will give a tenth of that to Aaron, the priest, as the LORD's share. ²⁹Choose the best and holiest part from what you are given as the portion you must give to the LORD.'

³⁰"Say to the Levites: 'When you present the best, it will be accepted as much as the grain and wine from the other people. ³¹You and your families may eat all that is left anywhere, because it is your pay for your work in the Meeting Tent. ³²And if you always give the best part to the LORD, you will never be guilty. If you do not sin against the holy offerings of the Israelites, you will not die.'"

PSALM 32:6–11

⁶For this reason, all who obey you
    should pray to you while they still can.
  When troubles rise like a flood,
    they will not reach them.
⁷You are my hiding place.

You protect me from my troubles
    and fill me with songs of salvation.   *Selah*

⁸The LORD says, "I will make you wise and
    show you where to go.
  I will guide you and watch over you.
⁹So don't be like a horse or donkey,
    that doesn't understand.
  They must be led with bits and reins,
    or they will not come near you."

¹⁰Wicked people have many troubles,
    but the LORD's love surrounds those
      who trust him.
¹¹Good people, rejoice and be happy in the
    LORD.
  Sing all you whose hearts are right.

PROVERBS 11:19–21

¹⁹Those who are truly good will live,
    but those who chase after evil will die.

²⁰The LORD hates those with evil hearts
    but is pleased with those who are
      innocent.

²¹Evil people will certainly be punished,
    but those who do right will be set free.

MARK 11:20–33

The Power of Faith

²⁰The next morning as Jesus was passing by with his followers, they saw the fig tree dry and dead, even to the roots. ²¹Peter remembered the tree and said to Jesus, "Teacher, look! The fig tree you cursed is dry and dead!"

²²Jesus answered, "Have faith in God. ²³I tell you the truth, you can say to this mountain, 'Go, fall into the sea.' And if you have no doubts in your mind and believe that what you say will happen, God will do it for you. ²⁴So I tell you to believe that you have received the things you ask for in prayer, and God will give them to you. ²⁵When you are praying, if you are angry with someone, forgive him so that your Father in heaven will also forgive your sins. [²⁶But if you don't forgive other people, then your Father in heaven will not forgive your sins.]" [n]

11:26 But . . . sins. Some Greek copies do not contain the bracketed text.

Leaders Doubt Jesus' Authority

²⁷Jesus and his followers went again to Jerusalem. As Jesus was walking in the Temple, the leading priests, the teachers of the law, and the elders came to him. ²⁸They said to him, "What authority do you have to do these things? Who gave you this authority?"

²⁹Jesus answered, "I will ask you one question. If you answer me, I will tell you what authority I have to do these things. ³⁰Tell me: When John baptized people, was that authority from God or just from other people?"

³¹They argued about Jesus' question, saying, "If we answer, 'John's baptism was from God,' Jesus will say, 'Then why didn't you believe him?' ³²But if we say, 'It was from other people,' the crowd will be against us." (These leaders were afraid of the people, because all the people believed that John was a prophet.)

³³So they answered Jesus, "We don't know."

Jesus said to them, "Then I won't tell you what authority I have to do these things."

MARCH 11

NUMBERS 19:1—20:29

The Offering for Cleansing

19The LORD said to Moses and Aaron, ²"These are the teachings that the LORD commanded. Tell the Israelites to get a young red cow that does not have anything wrong with it and that has never been worked. ³Give the cow to Eleazar the priest; he will take it outside the camp and kill it. ⁴Then Eleazar the priest must put some of its blood on his finger and sprinkle it seven times toward the front of the Meeting Tent. ⁵The whole cow must be burned while he watches; the skin, the meat, the blood, and the intestines must all be burned. ⁶Then the priest must take a cedar stick, a hyssop branch, and a red string and throw them onto the burning cow. ⁷After the priest has washed himself and his clothes with water, he may come back into the camp, but he will be unclean until evening. ⁸The man who burns the cow must wash himself and his clothes in water; he will be unclean until evening.

⁹"Then someone who is clean will collect the ashes from the cow and put them in a clean place outside the camp. The Israelites will keep these ashes to use in the cleansing water, in a special ceremony to cleanse away sin. ¹⁰The man who collected the cow's ashes must wash his clothes and be unclean until evening. This is a lasting rule for the Israelites and for the foreigners among them.

¹¹"Those who touch a dead person's body will be unclean for seven days. ¹²They must wash themselves with the cleansing water on the third day and on the seventh day; then they will be clean. But if they do not wash themselves on the third day and the seventh day, they cannot be clean. ¹³If those who touch a dead person's body stay unclean and go to the LORD's Holy Tent, it becomes unclean; they must be cut off from Israel. If the cleansing water is not sprinkled on them, they are unclean and will stay unclean.

¹⁴"This is the teaching about someone who dies in a tent: Anyone in the tent or anyone who enters it will be unclean for seven days. ¹⁵And every open jar or pot without a cover becomes unclean. ¹⁶If anyone is outside and touches someone who was killed by a sword or who died a natural death, or if anyone touches a human bone or a grave, that person will be unclean for seven days.

¹⁷"So you must use the ashes from the burnt offering to make that person clean again. Pour fresh water over the ashes into a jar. ¹⁸A clean person must take a hyssop branch and dip it into the water, and then he must sprinkle it over the tent and all its objects. He must also sprinkle the people who were there, as well as anyone who touched a bone, or the body of someone who was killed, or a dead person, or a grave. ¹⁹The person who is clean must sprinkle this water

on the unclean people on the third day and on the seventh day. On the seventh day they will become clean. They must wash their clothes and take a bath, and they will be clean that evening. ²⁰If any who are unclean do not become clean, they must be cut off from the community. Since they were not sprinkled with the cleansing water, they stay unclean, and they could make the LORD's Holy Tent unclean. ²¹This is a lasting rule. Those who sprinkle the cleansing water must also wash their clothes, and anyone who touches the water will be unclean until evening. ²²Anything an unclean person touches becomes unclean, and whoever touches it will be unclean until evening."

Moses Disobeys God

20 In the first month all the people of Israel arrived at the Desert of Zin, and they stayed at Kadesh. There Miriam died and was buried. ²There was no water for the people, so they came together against Moses and Aaron. ³They argued with Moses and said, "We should have died in front of the LORD as our brothers did. ⁴Why did you bring the LORD's people into this desert? Are we and our animals to die here? ⁵Why did you bring us from Egypt to this terrible place? It has no grain, figs, grapevines, or pomegranates, and there's no water to drink!"

⁶So Moses and Aaron left the people and went to the entrance of the Meeting Tent. There they bowed facedown, and the glory of the LORD appeared to them. ⁷The LORD said to Moses, ⁸"Take your walking stick, and you and your brother Aaron should gather the people. Speak to that rock in front of them so that its water will flow from it. When you bring the water out from that rock, give it to the people and their animals."

⁹So Moses took the stick from in front of the LORD, as he had said. ¹⁰Moses and Aaron gathered the people in front of the rock, and Moses said, "Now listen to me, you who turn against God! Do you want us to bring water out of this rock?" ¹¹Then Moses lifted his hand and hit the rock twice with his stick. Water began pouring out, and the people and their animals drank it.

¹²But the LORD said to Moses and Aaron, "Because you did not believe me, and because you did not honor me as holy before the people, you will not lead them into the land I will give them."

¹³These are the waters of Meribah,ⁿ where the Israelites argued with the LORD and where he showed them he was holy.

Edom Will Not Let Israel Pass

¹⁴From Kadesh, Moses sent messengers to the king of Edom. He said, "Your brothers, the Israelites, say to you: You know about all the troubles we have had, ¹⁵how our ancestors went down into Egypt and we lived there for many years. The people of Egypt were cruel to us and our ancestors, ¹⁶but when we cried out to the LORD, he heard us and sent us an angel to bring us out of Egypt.

"Now we are here at Kadesh, a town on the edge of your land. ¹⁷Please let us pass through your country. We will not touch any fields of grain or vineyards, and will not drink water from the wells. We will travel only along the king's road, not turning right or left until we have passed through your country."

¹⁸But the king of Edom answered: "You may not pass through here. If you try, I will come and meet you with swords."

¹⁹The Israelites answered: "We will go along the main road, and if we or our animals drink any of your water, we will pay for it. We only want to walk through. That's all."

²⁰But he answered: "You may not pass through here."

Then the Edomites went out to meet the Israelites with a large and powerful army. ²¹The Edomites refused to let them pass through their country, so the Israelites turned back.

Aaron Dies

²²All the Israelites moved from Kadesh to Mount Hor, ²³near the border of Edom. There the LORD said to Moses and Aaron, ²⁴"Aaron will die. He will not enter the land that I'm giving to the Israelites, because you both acted against my command at the waters of Meribah. ²⁵Take Aaron and his son Eleazar up on Mount Hor, ²⁶and take off

20:13 Meribah This name in Hebrew means "argument."

Aaron's special clothes and put them on his son Eleazar. Aaron will die there; he will join his ancestors."

²⁷Moses obeyed the LORD's command. They climbed up Mount Hor, and all the people saw them go. ²⁸Moses took off Aaron's clothes and put them on Aaron's son Eleazar. Then Aaron died there on top of the mountain. Moses and Eleazar came back down the mountain, ²⁹and when all the people learned that Aaron was dead, everyone in Israel cried for him for thirty days.

PSALM 33:1–5

Praise God Who Creates and Saves

33 Sing to the LORD, you who do what is right;
   honest people should praise him.
²Praise the LORD on the harp;
   make music for him on a ten-stringed lyre.
³Sing a new song to him;
   play well and joyfully.

⁴God's word is true,
   and everything he does is right.
⁵He loves what is right and fair;
   the LORD's love fills the earth.

PROVERBS 11:22–23

²²A beautiful woman without good sense
   is like a gold ring in a pig's snout.

²³Those who do right only wish for good,
   but the wicked can expect to be
   defeated by God's anger.

MARK 12:1–27

A Story About God's Son

12 Jesus began to use stories to teach the people. He said, "A man planted a vineyard. He put a wall around it and dug a hole for a winepress and built a tower. Then he leased the land to some farmers and left for a trip. ²When it was time for the grapes to be picked, he sent a servant to the farmers to get his share of the grapes. ³But the farmers grabbed the servant and beat him and sent

him away empty-handed. ⁴Then the man sent another servant. They hit him on the head and showed no respect for him. ⁵So the man sent another servant, whom they killed. The man sent many other servants; the farmers beat some of them and killed others.

⁶"The man had one person left to send, his son whom he loved. He sent him last of all, saying, 'They will respect my son.'

⁷"But the farmers said to each other, 'This son will inherit the vineyard. If we kill him, it will be ours.' ⁸So they took the son, killed him, and threw him out of the vineyard.

⁹"So what will the owner of the vineyard do? He will come and kill those farmers and will give the vineyard to other farmers. ¹⁰Surely you have read this Scripture:

'The stone that the builders rejected
   became the cornerstone.
¹¹The Lord did this,
   and it is wonderful to us.'" *Psalm 118:22–23*

¹²The Jewish leaders knew that the story was about them. So they wanted to find a way to arrest Jesus, but they were afraid of the people. So the leaders left him and went away.

Is It Right to Pay Taxes or Not?

¹³Later, the Jewish leaders sent some Pharisees and Herodians*ⁿ* to Jesus to trap him in saying something wrong. ¹⁴They came to him and said, "Teacher, we know that you are an honest man. You are not afraid of what other people think about you, because you pay no attention to who they are. And you teach the truth about God's way. Tell us: Is it right to pay taxes to Caesar or not? ¹⁵Should we pay them, or not?"

But knowing what these men were really trying to do, Jesus said to them, "Why are you trying to trap me? Bring me a coin to look at." ¹⁶They gave Jesus a coin, and he asked, "Whose image and name are on the coin?"

They answered, "Caesar's."

¹⁷Then Jesus said to them, "Give to Caesar the things that are Caesar's, and give to God the things that are God's." The men were amazed at what Jesus said.

12:13 Herodians A political group that followed Herod and his family.

Some Sadducees Try to Trick Jesus

[18]Then some Sadducees came to Jesus and asked him a question. (Sadducees believed that people would not rise from the dead.) [19]They said, "Teacher, Moses wrote that if a man's brother dies, leaving a wife but no children, then that man must marry the widow and have children for his brother. [20]Once there were seven brothers. The first brother married and died, leaving no children. [21]So the second brother married the widow, but he also died and had no children. The same thing happened with the third brother. [22]All seven brothers married her and died, and none of the brothers had any children. Finally the woman died too. [23]Since all seven brothers had married her, when people rise from the dead, whose wife will she be?"

[24]Jesus answered, "Why don't you understand? Don't you know what the Scriptures say, and don't you know about the power of God? [25]When people rise from the dead, they will not marry, nor will they be given to someone to marry. They will be like the angels in heaven. [26]Surely you have read what God said about people rising from the dead. In the book in which Moses wrote about the burning bush,[n] it says that God told Moses, 'I am the God of Abraham, the God of Isaac, and the God of Jacob.'[n] [27]God is the God of the living, not the dead. You Sadducees are wrong!"

MARCH 12

NUMBERS 21:1—22:41

War with the Canaanites

21 The Canaanite king of Arad lived in the southern area. When he heard that the Israelites were coming on the road to Atharim, he attacked them and captured some of them. [2]Then the Israelites made this promise to the LORD: "If you will help us defeat these people, we will completely destroy their cities." [3]The LORD listened to the Israelites, and he let them defeat the Canaanites. The Israelites completely destroyed the Canaanites and their cities, so the place was named Hormah.[n]

The Bronze Snake

[4]The Israelites left Mount Hor and went on the road toward the Red Sea, in order to go around the country of Edom. But the people became impatient on the way [5]and grumbled at God and Moses. They said, "Why did you bring us out of Egypt to die in this desert? There is no bread and no water, and we hate this terrible food!"

[6]So the LORD sent them poisonous snakes; they bit the people, and many of the Is-raelites died. [7]The people came to Moses and said, "We sinned when we grumbled at you and the LORD. Pray that the LORD will take away these snakes." So Moses prayed for the people.

[8]The LORD said to Moses, "Make a bronze snake, and put it on a pole. When anyone who is bitten looks at it, that person will live." [9]So Moses made a bronze snake and put it on a pole. Then when a snake bit anyone, that person looked at the bronze snake and lived.

The Journey to Moab

[10]The Israelites went and camped at Oboth. [11]They went from Oboth to Iye Abarim, in the desert east of Moab. [12]From there they went and camped in the Zered Valley. [13]From there they went and camped across the Arnon, in the desert just inside the Amorite country. The Arnon is the border between the Moabites and the Amorites. [14]That is why the Book of the Wars of the LORD says:

"...and Waheb in Suphah, and the
    ravines,

---

the Arnon, [15]and the slopes of the ravines
that lead to the settlement of Ar.
These places are at the border of Moab."

[16]The Israelites went from there to Beer; a well is there where the LORD said to Moses, "Gather the people and I will give them water."

[17]Then the Israelites sang this song:
"Pour out water, well!
Sing about it.
[18]Princes dug this well.
Important men made it.
With their scepters and poles, they dug it."

The people went from the desert to Mattanah. [19]From Mattanah they went to Nahaliel and on to Bamoth. [20]From Bamoth they went to the valley of Moab where the top of Mount Pisgah looks over the desert.

Israel Kills Sihon and Og

[21]The Israelites sent messengers to Sihon, king of the Amorites, saying, [22]"Let us pass through your country. We will not go through any fields of grain or vineyards, or drink water from the wells. We will travel only along the king's road until we have passed through your country."

[23]But King Sihon would not let the Israelites pass through his country. He gathered his whole army together, and they marched out to meet Israel in the desert. At Jahaz they fought the Israelites. [24]Israel killed the king and captured his land from the Arnon River to the Jabbok River. They took the land as far as the Ammonite border, which was strongly defended. [25]Israel captured all the Amorite cities and lived in them, taking Heshbon and all the towns around it. [26]Heshbon was the city where Sihon, the Amorite king, lived. In the past he had fought with the king of Moab and had taken all the land as far as the Arnon.

[27]That is why the poets say:
"Come to Heshbon
and rebuild it;
rebuild Sihon's city.
[28]A fire began in Heshbon;
flames came from Sihon's city.

It destroyed Ar in Moab,
and it burned the Arnon highlands.
[29]How terrible for you, Moab!
The people of Chemosh are ruined.
His sons ran away
and his daughters were captured
by Sihon, king of the Amorites.
[30]But we defeated those Amorites.
We ruined their towns from Heshbon
to Dibon,
and we destroyed them as far as
Nophah, near Medeba."

[31]So Israel lived in the land of the Amorites. [32]After Moses sent spies to the town of Jazer, they captured the towns around it, forcing out the Amorites who lived there.

[33]Then the Israelites went up the road toward Bashan. Og king of Bashan and his whole army marched out to meet the Israelites, and they fought at Edrei.

[34]The LORD said to Moses, "Don't be afraid of him. I will hand him, his whole army, and his land over to you. Do to him what you did to Sihon, the Amorite king who lived in Heshbon."

[35]So the Israelites killed Og and his sons and all his army; no one was left alive. And they took his land.

Balak Sends for Balaam

22 Then the people of Israel went to the plains of Moab, and they camped near the Jordan River across from Jericho.

[2]Balak son of Zippor saw everything the Israelites had done to the Amorites. [3]And Moab was scared of so many Israelites; truly, Moab was terrified by them.

[4]The Moabites said to the elders of Midian, "These people will take everything around us like an ox eating grass."

Balak son of Zippor was the king of Moab at this time. [5]He sent messengers to Balaam son of Beor at Pethor, near the Euphrates River in his native land. Balak said, "A nation has come out of Egypt that covers the land. They have camped next to me, [6]and they are too powerful for me. So come and put a curse on them. Maybe then I can defeat them and make them leave the area. I know that if you bless someone, the blessings happen, and if you put a curse on someone, it happens."

[7]The elders of Moab and Midian went with payment in their hands. When they found Balaam, they told him what Balak had said.

[8]Balaam said to them, "Stay here for the night, and I will tell you what the LORD tells me." So the Moabite leaders stayed with him.

[9]God came to Balaam and asked, "Who are these men with you?"

[10]Balaam said to God, "The king of Moab, Balak son of Zippor, sent them to me with this message: [11]'A nation has come out of Egypt that covers the land. So come and put a curse on them, and maybe I can fight them and force them out of my land.'"

[12]But God said to Balaam, "Do not go with them. Don't put a curse on those people, because I have blessed them."

[13]The next morning Balaam awoke and said to Balak's leaders, "Go back to your own country; the LORD has refused to let me go with you."

[14]So the Moabite leaders went back to Balak and said, "Balaam refused to come with us."

[15]So Balak sent other leaders—this time there were more of them, and they were more important. [16]They went to Balaam and said, "Balak son of Zippor says this: Please don't let anything stop you from coming to me. [17]I will pay you very well, and I will do what you say. Come and put a curse on these people for me."

[18]But Balaam answered Balak's servants, "King Balak could give me his palace full of silver and gold, but I cannot disobey the LORD my God in anything, great or small. [19]You stay here tonight as the other men did, and I will find out what more the LORD tells me."

[20]That night God came to Balaam and said, "These men have come to ask you to go with them. Go, but only do what I tell you."

Balaam's Donkey Speaks

[21]Balaam got up the next morning and put a saddle on his donkey. Then he went with the Moabite leaders. [22]But God became angry because Balaam went, so the angel of the LORD stood in the road to stop Balaam.

Balaam was riding his donkey, and he had two servants with him. [23]When the donkey saw the angel of the LORD standing in the road with a sword in his hand, the donkey left the road and went into the field. Balaam hit the donkey to force her back on the road.

[24]Later, the angel of the LORD stood on a narrow path between two vineyards, with walls on both sides. [25]Again the donkey saw the angel of the LORD, and she walked close to one wall, crushing Balaam's foot against it. So he hit her again.

[26]The angel of the LORD went ahead again and stood at a narrow place, too narrow to turn left or right. [27]When the donkey saw the angel of the LORD, she lay down under Balaam. This made him so angry that he hit her with his stick. [28]Then the LORD made the donkey talk, and she said to Balaam, "What have I done to make you hit me three times?"

[29]Balaam answered the donkey, "You have made me look foolish! I wish I had a sword in my hand! I would kill you right now!"

[30]But the donkey said to Balaam, "I am your very own donkey, which you have ridden for years. Have I ever done this to you before?"

"No," Balaam said.

[31]Then the LORD let Balaam see the angel of the LORD, who was standing in the road with his sword drawn. Then Balaam bowed facedown on the ground.

[32]The angel of the LORD asked Balaam, "Why have you hit your donkey three times? I have stood here to stop you, because what you are doing is wrong. [33]The donkey saw me and turned away from me three times. If she had not turned away, I would have killed you by now, but I would have let her live."

[34]Then Balaam said to the angel of the LORD, "I have sinned; I did not know you were standing in the road to stop me. If I am wrong, I will go back."

[35]The angel of the LORD said to Balaam, "Go with these men, but say only what I tell you." So Balaam went with Balak's leaders.

[36]When Balak heard that Balaam was coming, he went out to meet him at Ar in Moab, which was beside the Arnon, at the edge of his country. [37]Balak said to Balaam, "I had asked you before to come quickly.

Why didn't you come to me? I am able to reward you well."

[38]But Balaam answered, "I have come to you now, but I can't say just anything. I can only say what God tells me to say."

[39]Then Balaam went with Balak to Kiriath Huzoth. [40]Balak offered cattle and sheep as a sacrifice and gave some meat to Balaam and the leaders with him.

[41]The next morning Balak took Balaam to Bamoth Baal; from there he could see the edge of the Israelite camp.

PSALM 33:6−15

[6]The sky was made at the LORD's
command.
By the breath from his mouth, he made
all the stars.
[7]He gathered the water of the sea into a
heap.
He made the great ocean stay in its
place.
[8]All the earth should worship the LORD;
the whole world should fear him.
[9]He spoke, and it happened.
He commanded, and it appeared.
[10]The LORD upsets the plans of nations;
he ruins all their plans.
[11]But the LORD's plans will stand forever;
his ideas will last from now on.
[12]Happy is the nation whose God is the
LORD,
the people he chose for his very own.
[13]The LORD looks down from heaven
and sees every person.
[14]From his throne he watches
all who live on earth.
[15]He made their hearts
and understands everything they do.

PROVERBS 11:24−26

[24]Some people give much but get back
even more.
Others don't give what they should and
end up poor.
[25]Whoever gives to others will get richer;
those who help others will themselves
be helped.

[26]People curse those who keep all the grain,
but they bless the one who is willing to
sell it.

MARK 12:28−44

The Most Important Command

[28]One of the teachers of the law came and heard Jesus arguing with the Sadducees. Seeing that Jesus gave good answers to their questions, he asked Jesus, "Which of the commands is most important?"

[29]Jesus answered, "The most important command is this:'Listen, people of Israel! The Lord our God is the only Lord.[30]Love the Lord your God with all your heart, all your soul, all your mind, and all your strength.'[n] [31]The second command is this:'Love your neighbor as you love yourself.'[n] There are no commands more important than these."

[32]The man answered, "That was a good answer, Teacher. You were right when you said God is the only Lord and there is no other God besides him. [33]One must love God with all his heart, all his mind, and all his strength. And one must love his neighbor as he loves himself. These commands are more important than all the animals and sacrifices we offer to God."

[34]When Jesus saw that the man answered him wisely, Jesus said to him, "You are close to the kingdom of God." And after that, no one was brave enough to ask Jesus any more questions.

[35]As Jesus was teaching in the Temple, he asked, "Why do the teachers of the law say that the Christ is the son of David? [36]David himself, speaking by the Holy Spirit, said:
'The Lord said to my Lord,
"Sit by me at my right side,
until I put your enemies under your
control."'   *Psalm 110:1*
[37]David himself calls the Christ 'Lord,' so how can the Christ be his son?" The large crowd listened to Jesus with pleasure.

[38]Jesus continued teaching and said, "Beware of the teachers of the law. They like to walk around wearing fancy clothes, and they love for people to greet them with respect in

the marketplaces. [39]They love to have the most important seats in the synagogues and at feasts. [40]But they cheat widows and steal their houses and then try to make themselves look good by saying long prayers. They will receive a greater punishment."

True Giving

[41]Jesus sat near the Temple money box and watched the people put in their money. Many rich people gave large sums of money. [42]Then a poor widow came and put in two small copper coins, which were only worth a few cents. [43]Calling his followers to him, Jesus said, "I tell you the truth, this poor widow gave more than all those rich people. [44]They gave only what they did not need. This woman is very poor, but she gave all she had; she gave all she had to live on."

MARCH 13

NUMBERS 23:1—24:25

Balaam's First Message

23 Balaam said to Balak, "Build me seven altars here, and prepare seven bulls and seven male sheep for me." [2]Balak did what Balaam asked, and they offered a bull and a male sheep on each of the altars.

[3]Then Balaam said to Balak, "Stay here beside your burnt offering and I will go. If the LORD comes to me, I will tell you whatever he shows me." Then Balaam went to a higher place.

[4]God came to Balaam there, and Balaam said to him, "I have prepared seven altars, and I have offered a bull and a male sheep on each altar."

[5]The LORD told Balaam what he should say. Then the LORD said, "Go back to Balak and give him this message."

[6]So Balaam went back to Balak. Balak and all the leaders of Moab were still standing beside his burnt offering [7]when Balaam gave them this message:

"Balak brought me here from Aram;
    the king of Moab brought me from the
        eastern mountains.
Balak said, 'Come, put a curse on the
        people of Jacob for me.
Come, call down evil on the people of
        Israel.'
[8]But God has not cursed them,
    so I cannot curse them.
The LORD has not called down evil on
        them,

so I cannot call down evil on them.
[9]I see them from the top of the mountains;
    I see them from the hills.
I see a people who live alone,
    who think they are different from other
        nations.
[10]No one can number the many people of
        Jacob,
    and no one can count a fourth of Israel.
Let me die like good men,
    and let me end up like them!"

[11]Balak said to Balaam, "What have you done to me? I brought you here to curse my enemies, but you have only blessed them!"

[12]But Balaam answered, "I must say what the LORD tells me to say."

Balaam's Second Message

[13]Then Balak said to him, "Come with me to another place, where you can also see the people. But you can only see part of them, not all of them. Curse them for me from there." [14]So Balak took Balaam to the field of Zophim, on top of Mount Pisgah. There Balak built seven altars and offered a bull and a male sheep on each altar.

[15]So Balaam said to Balak, "Stay here by your burnt offering, and I will meet with God over there."

[16]So the LORD came to Balaam and told him what to say. Then he said, "Go back to Balak and say such and such."

[17]So Balaam went to Balak, where he and the leaders of Moab were standing beside his burnt offering. Balak asked him, "What did the LORD say?"

18Then Balaam gave this message:
"Stand up, Balak, and listen.
Hear me, son of Zippor.
19God is not a human being, and he will not
lie.
He is not a human, and he does not
change his mind.
What he says he will do, he does.
What he promises, he makes come
true.
20He told me to bless them,
so I cannot change the blessing.
21He has found no wrong in the people of
Jacob;
he saw no fault in Israel.
The LORD their God is with them,
and they praise their King.
22God brought them out of Egypt;
they are as strong as a wild ox.
23No tricks will work on the people of Jacob,
and no magic will work against Israel.
People now say about them,
'Look what God has done for Israel!'
24The people rise up like a lioness;
they get up like a lion.
Lions don't rest until they have eaten,
until they have drunk their enemies'
blood."

25Then Balak said to Balaam, "You haven't
cursed these people, so at least don't bless
them!"

26Balaam answered Balak, "I told you before that I can only do what the LORD tells me."

Balaam's Third Message

27Then Balak said to Balaam, "Come, I will
take you to another place. Maybe God will be
pleased to let you curse them from there."
28So Balak took Balaam to the top of Peor,
the mountain that looks over the desert.

29Balaam told Balak, "Build me seven altars here and prepare for me seven bulls and
seven male sheep." 30Balak did what Balaam
asked, and he offered a bull and a male sheep
on each altar.

24 Balaam saw that the LORD wanted to
bless Israel, so he did not try to use any
magic but looked toward the desert. 2When
Balaam saw the Israelites camped in their
tribes, the Spirit of God took control of him,
3and he gave this message:

"This is the message of Balaam son of
Beor,
the message of a man who sees
clearly;
4this is the message of a man who hears the
words of God.
I see a vision from the Almighty,
and my eyes are open as I fall before
him.
5Your tents are beautiful, people of Jacob!
So are your homes, Israel!
6Your tents spread out like valleys,
like gardens beside a river.
They are like spices planted by the
LORD,
like cedar trees growing by the water.
7Israel's water buckets will always be
full,
and their crops will have plenty of
water.
Their king will be greater than Agag;
their kingdom will be very great.
8God brought them out of Egypt;
they are as strong as a wild ox.
They will defeat their enemies
and break their enemies' bones;
they will shoot them with arrows.
9Like a lion, they lie waiting to attack;
like a lioness, no one would be brave
enough to wake them.
Anyone who blesses you will be
blessed,
and anyone who curses you will be
cursed."

10Then Balak was angry with Balaam, and
he pounded his fist. He said to Balaam, "I
called you here to curse my enemies, but you
have continued to bless them three times.
11Now go home! I said I would pay you well,
but the LORD has made you lose your reward."

12Balaam said to Balak, "When you sent
messengers to me, I told them, 13'Balak
could give me his palace filled with silver
and gold, but I still cannot go against the
LORD's commands. I could not do anything,
good or bad, on my own, but I must say
what the LORD says.' 14Now I am going back
to my own people, but I will tell you what
these people will do to your people in the
future."

Balaam's Final Message

15Then Balaam gave this message:
"This is the message of Balaam son of Beor,
the message of a man who sees clearly;
16this is the message of a man who hears the words of God.
I know well the Most High God.
I see a vision from the Almighty,
and my eyes are open as I fall before him.
17I see someone who will come someday,
someone who will come, but not soon.
A star will come from Jacob;
a ruler will rise from Israel.
He will crush the heads of the Moabites
and smash the skulls of the sons of Sheth.
18Edom will be conquered;
his enemy Edom will be conquered,
but Israel will grow wealthy.
19A ruler will come from the descendants of Jacob
and will destroy those left in the city."
20Then Balaam saw Amalek and gave this message:
"Amalek was the most important nation,
but Amalek will be destroyed at last."
21Then Balaam saw the Kenites and gave this message:
"Your home is safe,
like a nest on a cliff.
22But you Kenites will be burned up;
Assyria will keep you captive."
23Then Balaam gave this message:
"No one can live when God does this.
24 Ships will sail from the shores of Cyprus
and defeat Assyria and Eber,
but they will also be destroyed."
25Then Balaam got up and returned home, and Balak also went on his way.

PSALM 33:16–22

16No king is saved by his great army.
No warrior escapes by his great strength.
17Horses can't bring victory;
they can't save by their strength.
18But the LORD looks after those who fear him,
those who put their hope in his love.
19He saves them from death
and spares their lives in times of hunger.
20So our hope is in the LORD.
He is our help, our shield to protect us.
21We rejoice in him,
because we trust his holy name.
22LORD, show your love to us
as we put our hope in you.

PROVERBS 11:27

27Whoever looks for good will find kindness,
but whoever looks for evil will find trouble.

MARK 13:1–27

The Temple Will Be Destroyed

13As Jesus was leaving the Temple, one of his followers said to him, "Look, Teacher! How beautiful the buildings are! How big the stones are!"

2Jesus said, "Do you see all these great buildings? Not one stone will be left on another. Every stone will be thrown down to the ground."

3Later, as Jesus was sitting on the Mount of Olives, opposite the Temple, he was alone with Peter, James, John, and Andrew. They asked Jesus, 4"Tell us, when will these things happen? And what will be the sign that they are going to happen?"

5Jesus began to answer them, "Be careful that no one fools you. 6Many people will come in my name, saying, 'I am the One,' and they will fool many people. 7When you hear about wars and stories of wars that are coming, don't be afraid. These things must happen before the end comes. 8Nations will fight against other nations, and kingdoms against other kingdoms. There will be earthquakes in different places, and there will be times when there is no food for people to eat. These things are like the first pains when something new is about to be born.

9"You must be careful. People will arrest you and take you to court and beat you in their synagogues. You will be forced to stand before kings and governors, to tell them about me. This will happen to you because you follow me. [10]But before these things happen, the Good News must be told to all people. [11]When you are arrested and judged, don't worry ahead of time about what you should say. Say whatever is given you to say at that time, because it will not really be you speaking; it will be the Holy Spirit.

[12]"Brothers will give their own brothers to be killed, and fathers will give their own children to be killed. Children will fight against their own parents and cause them to be put to death. [13]All people will hate you because you follow me, but those people who keep their faith until the end will be saved.

[14]"You will see 'a blasphemous object that brings destruction'[n] standing where it should not be." (You who read this should understand what it means.) "At that time, the people in Judea should run away to the mountains. [15]If people are on the roofs[n] of their houses, they must not go down or go inside to get anything out of their houses. [16]If people are in the fields, they must not go back to get their coats. [17]At that time, how terrible it will be for women who are pregnant or have nursing babies! [18]Pray that these things will not happen in winter, [19]because those days will be full of trouble. There will

be more trouble than there has ever been since the beginning, when God made the world, until now, and nothing as bad will ever happen again. [20]God has decided to make that terrible time short. Otherwise, no one would go on living. But God will make that time short to help the people he has chosen. [21]At that time, someone might say to you, 'Look, there is the Christ!' Or another person might say, 'There he is!' But don't believe them. [22]False Christs and false prophets will come and perform great wonders and miracles. They will try to fool even the people God has chosen, if that is possible. [23]So be careful. I have warned you about all this before it happens.

[24]"During the days after this trouble comes,
'the sun will grow dark,
and the moon will not give its light.
[25]The stars will fall from the sky.
And the powers of the heavens will be
shaken.'   *Isaiah 13:10; 34:4*
[26]"Then people will see the Son of Man coming in clouds with great power and glory. [27]Then he will send his angels all around the earth to gather his chosen people from every part of the earth and from every part of heaven.

MARCH 14

NUMBERS 25:1—26:65

Israel Worships Baal at Peor

25 While the people of Israel were still camped at Acacia, the men began sinning sexually with Moabite women. [2]The women invited them to their sacrifices to their gods, and the Israelites ate food there and worshiped these gods. [3]So the Israelites began to worship Baal of Peor, and the LORD was very angry with them.

[4]The LORD said to Moses, "Get all the leaders of the people and kill them in open day-

light in the presence of the LORD. Then the LORD will not be angry with the people of Israel."

[5]So Moses said to Israel's judges, "Each of you must put to death your people who have become worshipers of Baal of Peor."

[6]Moses and the Israelites were gathered at the entrance to the Meeting Tent, crying there. Then an Israelite man brought a Midianite woman to his brothers in plain sight of Moses and all the people. [7]Phinehas son of Eleazar, the son of Aaron, the priest, saw this, so he left the meeting and got his spear. [8]He

---

13:14 'a blasphemous object that brings destruction' Mentioned in Daniel 9:27; 12:11 (cf. Daniel 11:31). **13:15 roofs** In Bible times houses were built with flat roofs. The roof was used for drying things such as flax and fruit. And it was used as an extra room, as a place for worship, and as a cool place to sleep in the summer.

followed the Israelite into his tent and drove his spear through both the Israelite man and the Midianite woman. Then the terrible sickness among the Israelites stopped.

[9]This sickness had killed twenty-four thousand people.

[10]The LORD said to Moses, [11]"Phinehas son of Eleazar, the son of Aaron, the priest, has saved the Israelites from my anger. He hates sin as much as I do. Since he tried to save my honor among them, I will not kill them. [12]So tell Phinehas that I am making my peace agreement with him. [13]He and his descendants will always be priests, because he had great concern for the honor of his God. He removed the sins of the Israelites so they would belong to God."

[14]The Israelite man who was killed with the Midianite woman was named Zimri son of Salu. He was the leader of a family in the tribe of Simeon. [15]And the name of the Midianite woman who was put to death was Cozbi daughter of Zur, who was the chief of a Midianite family.

[16]The LORD said to Moses, [17]"The Midianites are your enemies, and you should kill them. [18]They have already made you their enemies, because they tricked you at Peor and because of their sister Cozbi, the daughter of a Midianite leader. She was the woman who was killed when the sickness came because the people sinned at Peor."

The People Are Counted

26After the great sickness, the LORD said to Moses and Eleazar son of Aaron, the priest, [2]"Count all the people of Israel by families. Count all the men who are twenty years old or older who will serve in the army of Israel." [3]Moses and Eleazar the priest spoke to the people on the plains of Moab near the Jordan River, across from Jericho. They said, [4]"Count the men twenty years old or older, as the LORD commanded Moses."

Here are the Israelites who came out of Egypt:

[5]The tribe of Reuben, the first son born to Israel, was counted. From Hanoch came the Hanochite family group; from Pallu came the Palluite family group; [6]from Hezron came the Hezronite family group; from Carmi came the Carmite family group. [7]These were the family groups of Reuben, and the total number of men was 43,730.

[8]The son of Pallu was Eliab, [9]and Eliab's sons were Nemuel, Dathan, and Abiram. Dathan and Abiram were the leaders who turned against Moses and Aaron and followed Korah when he turned against the LORD. [10]The earth opened up and swallowed them and Korah; they died at the same time the fire burned up the 250 men. This was a warning, [11]but the children of Korah did not die.

[12]These were the family groups in the tribe of Simeon: From Nemuel came the Nemuelite family group; from Jamin came the Jaminite family group; from Jakin came the Jakinite family group; [13]from Zerah came the Zerahite family group; from Shaul came the Shaulite family group. [14]These were the family groups of Simeon, and the total number of men was 22,200.

[15]These were the family groups in the tribe of Gad: From Zephon came the Zephonite family group; from Haggi came the Haggite family group; from Shuni came the Shunite family group; [16]from Ozni came the Oznite family group; from Eri came the Erite family group; [17]from Arodi came the Arodite family group; from Areli came the Arelite family group. [18]These were the family groups of Gad, and the total number of men was 40,500.

[19]Two of Judah's sons, Er and Onan, died in Canaan.

[20]These were the family groups in the tribe of Judah: From Shelah came the Shelanite family group; from Perez came the Perezite family group; from Zerah came the Zerahite family group. [21]These were the family groups from Perez: From Hezron came the Hezronite family group; from Hamul came the Hamulite family group. [22]These were the family groups of Judah, and the total number of men was 76,500.

[23]These were the family groups in the tribe of Issachar: From Tola came the Tolaite family group; from Puah came the Puite family group; [24]from Jashub came the Jashubite family group; from Shimron came the Shimronite family group. [25]These were the family groups of Issachar, and the total number of men was 64,300.

[26]These were the family groups in the tribe of Zebulun: From Sered came the Seredite family group; from Elon came the Elonite family group; from Jahleel came the Jahleelite family group. [27]These were the family groups of Zebulun, and the total number of men was 60,500.

[28]These were the family groups of Joseph through Manasseh and Ephraim.

[29]These were the family groups of Manasseh: From Makir came the Makirite family group (Makir was the father of Gilead); from Gilead came the Gileadite family group. [30]These were the family groups that came from Gilead: From Iezer came the Iezerite family group; from Helek came the Helekite family group; [31]from Asriel came the Asrielite family group; from Shechem came the Shechemite family group; [32]from Shemida came the Shemidaite family group; from Hepher came the Hepherite family group. [33](Zelophehad son of Hepher had no sons; he had only daughters, and their names were Mahlah, Noah, Hoglah, Milcah, and Tirzah.) [34]These were the family groups of Manasseh, and the total number of men was 52,700.

[35]These were the family groups in the tribe of Ephraim: From Shuthelah came the Shuthelahite family group; from Beker came the Bekerite family group; from Tahan came the Tahanite family group. [36]This was the family group from Shuthelah: From Eran came the Eranite family group. [37]These were the family groups of Ephraim, and the total number of men was 32,500. These are the family groups that came from Joseph.

[38]These were the family groups in the tribe of Benjamin: From Bela came the Belaite family group; from Ashbel came the Ashbelite family group; from Ahiram came the Ahiramite family group; [39]from Shupham came the Shuphamite family group; from Hupham came the Huphamite family group. [40]These were the family groups from Bela through Ard and Naaman: From Ard came the Ardite family group; from Naaman came the Naamite family group. [41]These were the family groups of Benjamin, and the total number of men was 45,600.

[42]This was the family group in the tribe of Dan: From Shuham came the Shuhamite family group. That was the family of Dan, [43]and the total number of men in the Shuhamite family group of Dan was 64,400.

[44]These were the family groups in the tribe of Asher: From Imnah came the Imnite family group; from Ishvi came the Ishvite family group; from Beriah came the Beriite family group. [45]These were the family groups that came from Beriah: From Heber came the Heberite family group; from Malkiel came the Malkielite family group. [46](Asher also had a daughter named Serah.) [47]These were the family groups of Asher, and the total number of men was 53,400.

[48]These were the family groups in the tribe of Naphtali: From Jahzeel came the Jahzeelite family group; from Guni came the Gunite family group; [49]from Jezer came the Jezerite family group; from Shillem came the Shillemite family group. [50]These were the family groups of Naphtali, and the total number of men was 45,400.

[51]So the total number of the men of Israel was 601,730.

[52]The LORD said to Moses, [53]"Divide the land among these people by the number of names. [54]A large tribe will get more land, and a small tribe will get less land; the amount of land each tribe gets will depend on the number of its people. [55]Divide the land by drawing lots, and the land each tribe gets will be named for that tribe. [56]Divide the land between large and small groups by drawing lots."

[57]The tribe of Levi was also counted. These were the family groups of Levi: From Gershon came the Gershonite family group; from Kohath came the Kohathite family group; from Merari came the Merarite family group. [58]These also were Levite family groups: the Libnite family group, the Hebronite family group, the Mahlite family group, the Mushite family group, and the Korahite family group. (Kohath was the ancestor of Amram, [59]whose wife was named Jochebed. She was from the tribe of Levi and she was born in Egypt. She and Amram had two sons, Aaron and Moses, and their sister Miriam. [60]Aaron was the father of Nadab, Abihu, Eleazar, and Ithamar. [61]But Nadab and Abihu died because they made an offering before the LORD with the wrong kind of fire.)

[62]The total number of male Levites one month old or older was 23,000. But these

men were not counted with the other Israelites, because they were not given any of the land among the other Israelites.

⁶³Moses and Eleazar the priest counted all these people. They counted the Israelites on the plains of Moab across the Jordan River from Jericho. ⁶⁴Moses and Aaron the priest had counted the Israelites in the Desert of Sinai, but no one Moses counted on the plains of Moab was in the first counting. ⁶⁵The LORD had told the Israelites they would all die in the desert, and the only two left were Caleb son of Jephunneh and Joshua son of Nun.

PSALM 34:1–7

Praise God Who Judges and Saves

David's song from the time he acted crazy so Abimelech would send him away, and David did leave.

34 I will praise the LORD at all times;
his praise is always on my lips.
²My whole being praises the LORD.
The poor will hear and be glad.
³Glorify the LORD with me,
and let us praise his name together.

⁴I asked the LORD for help, and he
answered me.
He saved me from all that I feared.
⁵Those who go to him for help are happy,
and they are never disgraced.
⁶This poor man called, and the LORD heard
him
and saved him from all his troubles.
⁷The angel of the LORD camps around those
who fear God,
and he saves them.

NUMBERS 27:1—28:31

Zelophehad's Daughters

27 Then the daughters of Zelophehad came near. Zelophehad was the son of Hepher, the son of Gilead, the son of Makir, the son of Manasseh. Zelophehad's daugh-

PROVERBS 11:28

²⁸Those who trust in riches will be
ruined,
but a good person will be healthy like a
green leaf.

MARK 13:28–37

²⁸"Learn a lesson from the fig tree: When its branches become green and soft and new leaves appear, you know summer is near. ²⁹In the same way, when you see these things happening, you will know that the time is near, ready to come. ³⁰I tell you the truth, all these things will happen while the people of this time are still living. ³¹Earth and sky will be destroyed, but the words I have said will never be destroyed.

³²"No one knows when that day or time will be, not the angels in heaven, not even the Son. Only the Father knows. ³³Be careful! Always be ready,ⁿ because you don't know when that time will be. ³⁴It is like a man who goes on a trip. He leaves his house and lets his servants take care of it, giving each one a special job to do. The man tells the servant guarding the door always to be watchful. ³⁵So always be ready, because you don't know when the owner of the house will come back. It might be in the evening, or at midnight, or in the morning while it is still dark, or when the sun rises. ³⁶Always be ready. Otherwise he might come back suddenly and find you sleeping. ³⁷I tell you this, and I say this to everyone: 'Be ready!'"

MARCH 15

ters belonged to the family groups of Manasseh son of Joseph. The daughters' names were Mahlah, Noah, Hoglah, Milcah, and Tirzah. ²They went to the entrance of the Meeting Tent and stood before Moses, Eleazar the priest, the leaders, and all the people. They said, ³"Our father died in the

13:33 ready Some Greek copies continue, "and pray."

desert. He was not one of Korah's followers who came together against the LORD, but he died because of his own sin, and he had no sons. ⁴Our father's name will die out because he had no sons. Give us property among our father's relatives."

⁵So Moses brought their case to the LORD, ⁶and the LORD said to him, ⁷"The daughters of Zelophehad are right; they should certainly get what their father owned. Give them property among their father's relatives.

⁸"Tell the Israelites, 'If a man dies and has no son, then everything he owned should go to his daughter. ⁹If he has no daughter, then everything he owned should go to his brothers. ¹⁰If he has no brothers, then everything he owned should go to his father's brothers. ¹¹And if his father had no brothers, then everything he owned should go to the nearest relative in his family group. This should be a rule among the people of Israel, as the LORD has given this command to Moses.'"

Joshua Is the New Leader

¹²Then the LORD said to Moses, "Climb this mountain in the Abarim Mountains, and look at the land I have given to the Israelites. ¹³After you have seen it, you will die and join your ancestors as your brother Aaron did, ¹⁴because you both acted against my command in the Desert of Zin. You did not honor me as holy before the people at the waters of Meribah." (This was at Meribah in Kadesh in the Desert of Zin.)

¹⁵Moses said to the LORD, ¹⁶"The LORD is the God of the spirits of all people. May he choose a leader for these people, ¹⁷who will go in and out before them. He must lead them out like sheep and bring them in; the LORD's people must not be like sheep without a shepherd."

¹⁸So the LORD said to Moses, "Take Joshua son of Nun, because my Spirit is in him. Put your hand on him, ¹⁹and have him stand before Eleazar the priest and all the people. Then give him his orders as they watch. ²⁰Let him share your honor so that all the Israelites will obey him. ²¹He must stand before Eleazar the priest, and Eleazar will get advice from the LORD by using the Urim. At his command all the Israelites will

go out, and at his command they will all come in."

²²Moses did what the LORD told him. He took Joshua and had him stand before Eleazar the priest and all the people, ²³and he put his hands on him and gave him orders, just as the LORD had told him.

Daily Offerings

28 The LORD said to Moses, ²"Give this command to the Israelites. Tell them: 'Bring me food offerings made by fire, for a smell that is pleasing to me, and be sure to bring them at the right time.' ³Say to them, 'These are the offerings you must bring to the LORD: two male lambs, a year old, as a burnt offering each day. They must have nothing wrong with them. ⁴Offer one lamb in the morning and the other lamb at twilight. ⁵Also bring a grain offering of two quarts of fine flour, mixed with one quart of oil from pressed olives. ⁶This is the daily burnt offering which began at Mount Sinai; its smell is pleasing to the LORD. ⁷Offer one quart of wine with each lamb as a drink offering; pour it out to the LORD at the Holy Place. ⁸Offer the second lamb at twilight. As in the morning, also give a grain offering and a drink offering. This offering is made by fire, and its smell is pleasing to the LORD.

Sabbath Offerings

⁹"'On the Sabbath day you must give two male lambs, a year old, that have nothing wrong with them. Also give a drink offering and a grain offering; the grain offering must be four quarts of fine flour mixed with olive oil. ¹⁰This is the burnt offering for every Sabbath, in addition to the daily burnt offering and drink offering.

Monthly Offerings

¹¹"'On the first day of each month bring a burnt offering to the LORD. This will be two young bulls, one male sheep, and seven male lambs a year old, and they must have nothing wrong with them. ¹²Give a grain offering with each bull of six quarts of fine flour mixed with olive oil. Also give a grain offering with the male sheep. It must be four quarts of fine flour mixed with olive oil. ¹³And give a grain offering with each lamb of

two quarts of fine flour mixed with olive oil. This is a burnt offering, and its smell is pleasing to the LORD. [14]The drink offering with each bull will be two quarts of wine, with the male sheep it will be one and one-third quarts, and with each lamb it will be one quart of wine. This is the burnt offering that must be offered each month of the year. [15]Besides the daily burnt offerings and drink offerings, bring a sin offering of one goat to the LORD.

The Passover

[16]" 'The LORD's Passover will be on the fourteenth day of the first month. [17]The Feast of Unleavened Bread begins on the fifteenth day of that month. For seven days, you may eat only bread made without yeast. [18]Have a holy meeting on the first day of the festival, and don't work that day. [19]Bring to the LORD an offering made by fire, a burnt offering of two young bulls, one male sheep, and seven male lambs a year old. They must have nothing wrong with them. [20]With each bull give a grain offering of six quarts of fine flour mixed with olive oil. With the male sheep it must be four quarts of fine flour mixed with oil. [21]With each of the seven lambs, it must be two quarts of fine flour mixed with oil. [22]Bring one goat as a sin offering, to remove your sins so you will belong to God. [23]Bring these offerings in addition to the burnt offerings you give every morning. [24]So bring food for the offering made by fire each day for seven days, for a smell that is pleasing to the LORD. Do it in addition to the daily burnt offering and its drink offering. [25]On the seventh day have a holy meeting, and don't work that day.

The Feast of Weeks

[26]" 'On the day of firstfruits when you bring new grain to the LORD during the Feast of Weeks, have a holy meeting. Don't work that day. [27]Bring this burnt offering to the LORD: two young bulls, one male sheep, and seven male lambs a year old. This smell is pleasing to the LORD. [28]Also, with each bull give a grain offering of six quarts of fine flour mixed with oil. With the male sheep, it must be four quarts of flour, [29]and with each of the seven lambs offer two quarts of flour.

[30]Offer one male goat to remove your sins so you will belong to God. [31]Bring these offerings and their drink offerings in addition to the daily burnt offering and its grain offering. The animals must have nothing wrong with them.

PSALM 34:8–14

[8]Examine and see how good the LORD is.
 Happy is the person who trusts him.
[9]You who belong to the LORD, fear him!
 Those who fear him will have
  everything they need.
[10]Even lions may get weak and hungry,
 but those who look to the LORD will
  have every good thing.
[11]Children, come and listen to me.
 I will teach you to worship the LORD.
[12]You must do these things
 to enjoy life and have many happy days.
[13]You must not say evil things,
 and you must not tell lies.
[14]Stop doing evil and do good.
 Look for peace and work for it.

PROVERBS 11:29

[29]Whoever brings trouble to his family
 will be left with nothing but the wind.
 A fool will be a servant to the wise.

MARK 14:1–26

The Plan to Kill Jesus

14 It was now only two days before the Passover and the Feast of Unleavened Bread. The leading priests and teachers of the law were trying to find a trick to arrest Jesus and kill him. [2]But they said, "We must not do it during the feast, because the people might cause a riot."

A Woman with Perfume for Jesus

[3]Jesus was in Bethany at the house of Simon, who had a skin disease. While Jesus was eating there, a woman approached him with an alabaster jar filled with very expensive perfume, made of pure nard. She opened the jar and poured the perfume on Jesus' head. [4]Some who were there became upset and said to each other, "Why waste that perfume?

[5]It was worth a full year's work. It could have been sold and the money given to the poor." And they got very angry with the woman.

[6]Jesus said, "Leave her alone. Why are you troubling her? She did an excellent thing for me. [7]You will always have the poor with you, and you can help them anytime you want. But you will not always have me. [8]This woman did the only thing she could do for me; she poured perfume on my body to prepare me for burial. [9]I tell you the truth, wherever the Good News is preached in all the world, what this woman has done will be told, and people will remember her."

Judas Becomes an Enemy of Jesus

[10]One of the twelve apostles, Judas Iscariot, went to talk to the leading priests to offer to hand Jesus over to them. [11]These priests were pleased about this and promised to pay Judas money. So he watched for the best time to turn Jesus in.

Jesus Eats the Passover Meal

[12]It was now the first day of the Feast of Unleavened Bread when the Passover lamb was sacrificed. Jesus' followers said to him, "Where do you want us to go and prepare for you to eat the Passover meal?"

[13]Jesus sent two of his followers and said to them, "Go into the city and a man carrying a jar of water will meet you. Follow him. [14]When he goes into a house, tell the owner of the house, 'The Teacher says: "Where is my guest room in which I can eat the Passover meal with my followers?" ' [15]The owner will show you a large room upstairs that is furnished and ready. Prepare the food for us there."

[16]So the followers left and went into the city. Everything happened as Jesus had said, so they prepared the Passover meal.

[17]In the evening, Jesus went to that house with the twelve. [18]While they were all eating, Jesus said, "I tell you the truth, one of you will turn against me—one of you eating with me now."

[19]The followers were very sad to hear this. Each one began to say to Jesus, "I am not the one, am I?"

[20]Jesus answered, "It is one of the twelve—the one who dips his bread into the bowl with me. [21]The Son of Man will die, just as the Scriptures say. But how terrible it will be for the person who hands the Son of Man over to be killed. It would be better for him if he had never been born."

The Lord's Supper

[22]While they were eating, Jesus took some bread and thanked God for it and broke it. Then he gave it to his followers and said, "Take it; this is my body."

[23]Then Jesus took a cup and thanked God for it and gave it to the followers, and they all drank from the cup.

[24]Then Jesus said, "This is my blood which is the new[n] agreement that God makes with his people. This blood is poured out for many. [25]I tell you the truth, I will not drink of this fruit of the vine[n] again until that day when I drink it new in the kingdom of God."

[26]After singing a hymn, they went out to the Mount of Olives.

MARCH 16

NUMBERS 29:1—30:16

The Feast of Trumpets

29 " 'Have a holy meeting on the first day of the seventh month, and don't work on that day. That is the day you blow the trumpets. [2]Bring these burnt offerings as a smell pleasing to the LORD: one young bull, one male sheep, and seven male lambs a year old. They must have nothing wrong with

---

14:24 new Some Greek copies do not have this word. Compare Luke 22:20. **14:25 fruit of the vine** Product of the grapevine; this may also be translated "wine."

them. [3]With the bull give a grain offering of six quarts of fine flour mixed with oil. With the male sheep offer four quarts, [4]and with each of the seven lambs offer two quarts. [5]Offer one male goat for a sin offering to remove your sins so you will belong to God. [6]These offerings are in addition to the monthly and daily burnt offerings. Their grain offerings and drink offerings must be done as you have been told. These offerings are made by fire to the LORD, and their smell is pleasing to him.

The Day of Cleansing

[7]" 'Have a holy meeting on the tenth day of the seventh month. On that day do not eat and do not work. [8]Bring these burnt offerings as a smell pleasing to the LORD: one young bull, one male sheep, and seven male lambs a year old. They must have nothing wrong with them. [9]With the bull give a grain offering of six quarts of fine flour mixed with oil. With the male sheep it must be four quarts, [10]and with each of the seven lambs it must be two quarts. [11]Offer one male goat as a sin offering. This will be in addition to the sin offering which removes your sins, the daily burnt offering with its grain offering, and the drink offerings.

The Feast of Shelters

[12]" 'Have a holy meeting on the fifteenth day of the seventh month, and do not work on that day. Celebrate a festival to the LORD for seven days. [13]Bring these burnt offerings, made by fire, as a smell pleasing to the LORD: thirteen young bulls, two male sheep, and fourteen male lambs a year old. They must have nothing wrong with them. [14]With each of the thirteen bulls offer a grain offering of six quarts of fine flour mixed with oil. With each of the two male sheep it must be four quarts, [15]and with each of the fourteen lambs it must be two quarts. [16]Offer one male goat as a sin offering in addition to the daily burnt offering with its grain and drink offerings.

[17]" 'On the second day of this festival give an offering of twelve bulls, two male sheep, and fourteen male lambs a year old. They must have nothing wrong with them. [18]Bring the grain and drink offerings for the bulls, sheep, and lambs, according to the number required. [19]Offer one male goat as a sin offer-

ing, in addition to the daily burnt offering with its grain and drink offerings.

[20]" 'On the third day offer eleven bulls, two male sheep, and fourteen male lambs a year old. They must have nothing wrong with them. [21]Bring the grain and drink offerings for the bulls, sheep, and lambs, according to the number required. [22]Offer one male goat as a sin offering, in addition to the daily burnt offering with its grain and drink offerings.

[23]" 'On the fourth day offer ten bulls, two male sheep, and fourteen male lambs a year old. They must have nothing wrong with them. [24]Bring the grain and drink offerings for the bulls, sheep, and lambs, according to the number required. [25]Offer one male goat as a sin offering, in addition to the daily burnt offering with its grain and drink offerings.

[26]" 'On the fifth day offer nine bulls, two male sheep, and fourteen male lambs a year old. They must have nothing wrong with them. [27]Bring the grain and drink offerings for the bulls, sheep, and lambs, according to the number required. [28]Offer one male goat as a sin offering, in addition to the daily burnt offering with its grain and drink offerings.

[29]" 'On the sixth day offer eight bulls, two male sheep, and fourteen male lambs a year old. They must have nothing wrong with them. [30]Bring the grain and drink offerings for the bulls, sheep, and lambs, according to the number required. [31]Offer one male goat as a sin offering, in addition to the daily burnt offering with its grain and drink offerings.

[32]" 'On the seventh day offer seven bulls, two male sheep, and fourteen male lambs a year old. They must have nothing wrong with them. [33]Bring the grain and drink offerings for the bulls, sheep, and lambs, according to the number required. [34]Offer one male goat as a sin offering, in addition to the daily burnt offering with its grain and drink offerings.

[35]" 'On the eighth day have a closing meeting, and do not work on that day. [36]Bring an offering made by fire, a burnt offering, as a smell pleasing to the LORD. Offer one bull, one male sheep, and seven male lambs a year old. They must have nothing wrong with them. [37]Bring the grain and drink offerings for the bull, the male sheep, and the lambs, according to the number required. [38]Offer one male goat

as a sin offering, in addition to the daily burnt offering with its grain and drink offerings.

³⁹"At your festivals you should bring these to the LORD: your burnt offerings, grain offerings, drink offerings and fellowship offerings. These are in addition to other promised offerings and special gifts you want to give to the LORD.'"

⁴⁰Moses told the Israelites everything the LORD had commanded him.

Rules About Special Promises

30Moses spoke with the leaders of the Israelite tribes. He told them these commands from the LORD.

²"If a man makes a promise to the LORD or says he will do something special, he must keep his promise. He must do what he said. ³If a young woman still living at home makes a promise to the LORD or pledges to do something special, ⁴and if her father hears about the promise or pledge and says nothing, she must do what she promised. She must keep her pledge. ⁵But if her father hears about the promise or pledge and does not allow it, then the promise or pledge does not have to be kept. Her father would not allow it, so the LORD will free her from her promise.

⁶"If a woman makes a pledge or a careless promise and then gets married, ⁷and if her husband hears about it and says nothing, she must keep her promise or the pledge she made. ⁸But if her husband hears about it and does not allow it, he cancels her pledge or the careless promise she made. The LORD will free her from keeping it.

⁹"If a widow or divorced woman makes a promise, she must do whatever she promised.

¹⁰"If a woman makes a promise or pledge while she is married, ¹¹and if her husband hears about it but says nothing and does not stop her, she must keep her promise or pledge. ¹²But if her husband hears about it and cancels it, she does not have to do what she said. Her husband has canceled it, so the LORD will free her from it. ¹³A woman's husband may make her keep or cancel any promise or pledge she has made. ¹⁴If he says nothing to her about it for several days, she must keep her promises. If he hears about them and says nothing, she must keep her

promises. ¹⁵But if he cancels them long after he heard about them, he is responsible if she breaks her promise."

¹⁶These are commands that the LORD gave to Moses for husbands and wives, and for fathers with daughters living at home.

PSALM 34:15–22

¹⁵The LORD sees the good people
    and listens to their prayers.
¹⁶But the LORD is against those who do evil;
    he makes the world forget them.
¹⁷The LORD hears good people when they
        cry out to him,
    and he saves them from all their
        troubles.
¹⁸The LORD is close to the brokenhearted,
    and he saves those whose spirits have
        been crushed.
¹⁹People who do what is right may have
        many problems,
    but the LORD will solve them all.
²⁰He will protect their very bones;
    not one of them will be broken.
²¹Evil will kill the wicked;
    those who hate good people will be
        judged guilty.
²²But the LORD saves his servants' lives;
    no one who trusts him will be judged
        guilty.

PROVERBS 11:30–31

³⁰A good person gives life to others;
    the wise person teaches others how to
        live.
³¹Good people will be rewarded on earth,
    and the wicked and the sinners will be
        punished.

MARK 14:27–52

Jesus' Followers Will Leave Him

²⁷Then Jesus told the followers, "You will all stumble in your faith, because it is written in the Scriptures:

'I will kill the shepherd,
    and the sheep will scatter.'   *Zechariah 13:7*
²⁸But after I rise from the dead, I will go ahead of you into Galilee."

²⁹Peter said, "Everyone else may stumble in their faith, but I will not."

³⁰Jesus answered, "I tell you the truth, tonight before the rooster crows twice you will say three times you don't know me."

³¹But Peter insisted, "I will never say that I don't know you! I will even die with you!" And all the other followers said the same thing.

Jesus Prays Alone

³²Jesus and his followers went to a place called Gethsemane. He said to them, "Sit here while I pray." ³³Jesus took Peter, James, and John with him, and he began to be very sad and troubled. ³⁴He said to them, "My heart is full of sorrow, to the point of death. Stay here and watch."

³⁵After walking a little farther away from them, Jesus fell to the ground and prayed that, if possible, he would not have this time of suffering. ³⁶He prayed, "Abba,ⁿ Father! You can do all things. Take away this cupⁿ of suffering. But do what you want, not what I want."

³⁷Then Jesus went back to his followers and found them asleep. He said to Peter, "Simon, are you sleeping? Couldn't you stay awake with me for one hour? ³⁸Stay awake and pray for strength against temptation. The spirit wants to do what is right, but the body is weak."

³⁹Again Jesus went away and prayed the same thing. ⁴⁰Then he went back to his followers, and again he found them asleep, because their eyes were very heavy. And they did not know what to say to him.

⁴¹After Jesus prayed a third time, he went back to his followers and said to them, "Are you still sleeping and resting? That's enough. The time has come for the Son of Man to be handed over to sinful people. ⁴²Get up, we must go. Look, here comes the man who has turned against me."

Jesus Is Arrested

⁴³At once, while Jesus was still speaking, Judas, one of the twelve apostles, came up. With him were many people carrying swords and clubs who had been sent from the leading priests, the teachers of the law, and the Jewish elders.

⁴⁴Judas had planned a signal for them, saying, "The man I kiss is Jesus. Arrest him and guard him while you lead him away." ⁴⁵So Judas went straight to Jesus and said, "Teacher!" and kissed him. ⁴⁶Then the people grabbed Jesus and arrested him. ⁴⁷One of his followers standing nearby pulled out his sword and struck the servant of the high priest and cut off his ear.

⁴⁸Then Jesus said, "You came to get me with swords and clubs as if I were a criminal. ⁴⁹Every day I was with you teaching in the Temple, and you did not arrest me there. But all these things have happened to make the Scriptures come true." ⁵⁰Then all of Jesus' followers left him and ran away.

⁵¹A young man, wearing only a linen cloth, was following Jesus, and the people also grabbed him. ⁵²But the cloth he was wearing came off, and he ran away naked.

MARCH 17

NUMBERS 31:1—32:42

Israel Attacks the Midianites

31 The LORD spoke to Moses and said, ²"Pay back the Midianites for what they did to the Israelites; after that you will die."

³So Moses said to the people, "Get some men ready for war. The LORD will use them to pay back the Midianites. ⁴Send to war a thousand men from each of the tribes of Israel." ⁵So twelve thousand men got ready for war, a thousand men from each tribe. ⁶Moses sent those men to war; Phinehas son of Eleazar the priest was with them. He took with him the holy things and the trumpets

---

14:36 Abba Name that a Jewish child called his father.   **14:36 cup** Jesus is talking about the terrible things that will happen to him. Accepting these things will be very hard, like drinking a cup of something bitter.

for giving the alarm. [7]They fought the Midianites as the LORD had commanded Moses, and they killed every Midianite man. [8]Among those they killed were Evi, Rekem, Zur, Hur, and Reba, who were the five kings of Midian. They also killed Balaam son of Beor with a sword.

[9]The Israelites captured the Midianite women and children, and they took all their flocks, herds, and goods. [10]They burned all the Midianite towns where they had settled and all their camps, [11]but they took all the people and animals and goods. [12]Then they brought the captives, the animals, and the goods back to Moses and Eleazar the priest and all the Israelites. Their camp was on the plains of Moab near the Jordan River, across from Jericho.

[13]Moses, Eleazar the priest, and all the leaders of the people went outside the camp to meet them. [14]Moses was angry with the army officers, the commanders over a thousand men, and those over a hundred men, who returned from war.

[15]He asked them, "Why did you let the women live? [16]They were the ones who followed Balaam's advice and turned the Israelites from the LORD at Peor. Then a terrible sickness struck the LORD's people. [17]Kill all the Midianite boys, and kill all the Midianite women who have had sexual relations. [18]But save for yourselves the girls who have not had sexual relations with a man.

[19]"All you men who killed anyone or touched a dead body must stay outside the camp for seven days. On the third and seventh days you and your captives must make yourselves clean. [20]You must clean all your clothes and anything made of leather, goat hair, or wood."

[21]Then Eleazar the priest said to the soldiers who had gone to war, "These are the teachings that the LORD gave to Moses: [22]Put any gold, silver, bronze, iron, tin, or lead— [23]anything that will not burn—into the fire, and then it will be clean. But also purify those things with the cleansing water. Then they will be clean. If something cannot stand the fire, wash it with the water. [24]On the seventh day wash your clothes, and you will be clean. After that you may come into the camp."

Dividing the Goods

[25]The LORD said to Moses, [26]"You, Eleazar the priest, and the leaders of the family groups should take a count of the goods, the men, and the animals that were taken. [27]Then divide those possessions between the soldiers who went to war and the rest of the people. [28]From the soldiers who went to war, take a tax for the LORD of one item out of every five hundred. This includes people, cattle, donkeys, or sheep. [29]Take it from the soldiers' half, and give it to Eleazar the priest as the LORD's share. [30]And from the people's half, take one item out of every fifty. This includes people, cattle, donkeys, sheep, or other animals. Give that to the Levites, who take care of the LORD's Holy Tent." [31]So Moses and Eleazar did as the LORD commanded Moses.

[32]There remained from what the soldiers had taken 675,000 sheep, [33]72,000 cattle, [34]61,000 donkeys, [35]and 32,000 women who had not had sexual relations with a man. [36]The soldiers who went to war got 337,000 sheep, [37]and they gave 675 of them to the LORD. [38]They got 36,000 cattle, and they gave 72 of them to the LORD. [39]They got 30,500 donkeys, and they gave 61 of them to the LORD. [40]They got 16,000 people, and they gave 32 of them to the LORD. [41]Moses gave the LORD's share to Eleazar the priest, as the LORD had commanded him.

[42]Moses separated the people's half from the soldiers' half. [43]The people got 337,500 sheep, [44]36,000 cattle, [45]30,500 donkeys, [46]and 16,000 people. [47]From the people's half Moses took one item out of every fifty for the LORD. This included the animals and the people. Then he gave them to the Levites, who took care of the LORD's Holy Tent. This was what the LORD had commanded Moses.

[48]Then the officers of the army, the commanders of a thousand men and commanders of a hundred men, came to Moses. [49]They told Moses, "We, your servants, have counted our soldiers under our command, and not one of them is missing. [50]So we have brought the LORD a gift of the gold things that each of us found: arm bands, bracelets, signet rings, earrings, and necklaces. These are to remove our sins so we will belong to the LORD."

⁵¹So Moses and Eleazar the priest took the gold from them, which had been made into all kinds of objects. ⁵²The commanders of a thousand men and the commanders of a hundred men gave the LORD the gold, and all of it together weighed about 420 pounds; ⁵³each soldier had taken something for himself. ⁵⁴Moses and Eleazar the priest took the gold from the commanders of a thousand men and the commanders of a hundred men. Then they put it in the Meeting Tent as a memorial before the LORD for the people of Israel.

The Tribes East of the Jordan

32 The people of Reuben and Gad had large flocks and herds. When they saw that the lands of Jazer and Gilead were good for the animals, ²they came to Moses, Eleazar the priest, and the leaders of the people. ³⁻⁴They said, "We, your servants, have flocks and herds. The LORD has captured for the Israelites a land that is good for animals—the land around Ataroth, Dibon, Jazer, Nimrah, Heshbon, Elealeh, Sebam, Nebo, and Beon. ⁵If it pleases you, we would like this land to be given to us. Don't make us cross the Jordan River."

⁶Moses told the people of Gad and Reuben, "Shall your brothers go to war while you stay behind? ⁷You will discourage the Israelites from going over to the land the LORD has given them. ⁸Your ancestors did the same thing. I sent them from Kadesh Barnea to look at the land. ⁹They went as far as the Valley of Eshcol, and when they saw the land, they discouraged the Israelites from going into the land the LORD had given them. ¹⁰The LORD became very angry that day and made this promise: ¹¹'None of the people who came from Egypt and who are twenty years old or older will see the land that I promised to Abraham, Isaac, and Jacob. These people have not followed me completely. ¹²Only Caleb son of Jephunneh the Kenizzite and Joshua son of Nun followed the LORD completely.'

¹³"The LORD was angry with Israel, so he made them wander in the desert for forty years. Finally all the people who had sinned against the LORD died, ¹⁴and now you are act-ing just like your ancestors! You sinful people are making the LORD even more angry with Israel. ¹⁵If you quit following him, it will add to their stay in the desert, and you will destroy all these people."

¹⁶Then the Reubenites and Gadites came up to Moses and said, "We will build pens for our animals and cities for our children here. ¹⁷Then our children will be in strong, walled cities, safe from the people who live in this land. Then we will prepare for war. We will help the other Israelites get their land, ¹⁸and we will not return home until every Israelite has received his land. ¹⁹We won't take any of the land west of the Jordan River; our part of the land is east of the Jordan."

²⁰So Moses told them, "You must do these things. You must go before the LORD into battle ²¹and cross the Jordan River armed, until the LORD forces out the enemy. ²²After the LORD helps us take the land, you may return home. You will have done your duty to the LORD and Israel, and you may have this land as your own.

²³"But if you don't do these things, you will be sinning against the LORD; know for sure that you will be punished for your sin. ²⁴Build cities for your children and pens for your animals, but then you must do what you promised."

²⁵The Gadites and Reubenites said to Moses, "We are your servants, and we will do what you, our master, command. ²⁶Our children, wives, and all our cattle will stay in the cities of Gilead, ²⁷but we, your servants, will prepare for battle. We will go over and fight for the LORD, as you, our master, have said."

²⁸So Moses gave orders about them to Eleazar the priest, to Joshua son of Nun, and to the leaders of the tribes of Israel. ²⁹Moses said to them, "If the Gadites and Reubenites prepare for battle and cross the Jordan River with you, to go before the LORD and help you take the land, give them the land of Gilead for their own. ³⁰But if they do not go over armed, they will not receive it; their land will be in Canaan with you."

³¹The Gadites and Reubenites answered, "We are your servants, and we will do as the LORD said. ³²We will cross over into Canaan

and go before the LORD ready for battle. But our land will be east of the Jordan River."

³³So Moses gave that land to the tribes of Gad, Reuben, and East Manasseh. (Manasseh was Joseph's son.) That land had been the kingdom of Sihon, king of the Amorites, and the kingdom of Og, king of Bashan, as well as all the cities and the land around them.

³⁴The Gadites rebuilt the cities of Dibon, Ataroth, Aroer, ³⁵Atroth Shophan, Jazer, Jogbehah, ³⁶Beth Nimrah, and Beth Haran. These were strong, walled cities. And they built sheep pens.

³⁷The Reubenites rebuilt Heshbon, Elealeh, Kiriathaim, ³⁸Nebo, Baal Meon, and Sibmah. They renamed Nebo and Baal Meon when they rebuilt them.

³⁹The descendants of Makir son of Manasseh went and captured Gilead and forced out the Amorites who were there. ⁴⁰So Moses gave Gilead to the family of Makir son of Manasseh, and they settled there. ⁴¹Jair son of Manasseh went out and captured the small towns there, and he called them the Towns of Jair. ⁴²Nobah went and captured Kenath and the small towns around it; then he named it Nobah after himself.

PSALM 35:1–10

A Prayer for Help

Of David.

35 LORD, battle with those who battle with me.
Fight against those who fight against me.
²Pick up the shield and armor.
Rise up and help me.
³Lift up your spears, both large and small, against those who chase me.
Tell me, "I will save you."

⁴Make those who want to kill me be ashamed and disgraced.
Make those who plan to harm me turn back and run away.
⁵Make them like chaff blown by the wind as the angel of the LORD forces them away.
⁶Let their road be dark and slippery as the angel of the LORD chases them.

⁷For no reason they spread out their net to trap me;
for no reason they dug a pit for me.
⁸So let ruin strike them suddenly.
Let them be caught in their own nets;
let them fall into the pit and die.
⁹Then I will rejoice in the LORD;
I will be happy when he saves me.
¹⁰Even my bones will say,
"LORD, who is like you?
You save the weak from the strong,
the weak and poor from robbers."

PROVERBS 12:1

12 Anyone who loves learning accepts correction,
but a person who hates being corrected is stupid.

MARK 14:53–72

Jesus Before the Leaders

⁵³The people who arrested Jesus led him to the house of the high priest, where all the leading priests, the elders, and the teachers of the law were gathered. ⁵⁴Peter followed far behind and entered the courtyard of the high priest's house. There he sat with the guards, warming himself by the fire.

⁵⁵The leading priests and the whole Jewish council tried to find something that Jesus had done wrong so they could kill him. But the council could find no proof of anything. ⁵⁶Many people came and told false things about him, but all said different things— none of them agreed.

⁵⁷Then some people stood up and lied about Jesus, saying, ⁵⁸"We heard this man say, 'I will destroy this Temple that people made. And three days later, I will build another Temple not made by people.' " ⁵⁹But even the things these people said did not agree.

⁶⁰Then the high priest stood before them and asked Jesus, "Aren't you going to answer? Don't you have something to say about their charges against you?" ⁶¹But Jesus said nothing; he did not answer.

The high priest asked Jesus another question: "Are you the Christ, the Son of the blessed God?"

[62]Jesus answered, "I am. And in the future you will see the Son of Man sitting at the right hand of God, the Powerful One, and coming on clouds in the sky."

[63]When the high priest heard this, he tore his clothes and said, "We don't need any more witnesses! [64]You all heard him say these things against God. What do you think?"

They all said that Jesus was guilty and should die. [65]Some of the people there began to spit at Jesus. They blindfolded him and beat him with their fists and said, "Prove you are a prophet!" Then the guards led Jesus away and beat him.

Peter Says He Doesn't Know Jesus

[66]While Peter was in the courtyard, a servant girl of the high priest came there. [67]She saw Peter warming himself at the fire and looked closely at him.

Then she said, "You also were with Jesus, that man from Nazareth."

[68]But Peter said that he was never with Jesus. He said, "I don't know or understand what you are talking about." Then Peter left and went toward the entrance of the courtyard. And the rooster crowed.[n]

[69]The servant girl saw Peter there, and again she said to the people who were standing nearby, "This man is one of those who followed Jesus." [70]Again Peter said that it was not true.

A short time later, some people were standing near Peter saying, "Surely you are one of those who followed Jesus, because you are from Galilee, too."

[71]Then Peter began to place a curse on himself and swear, "I don't know this man you're talking about!"

[72]At once, the rooster crowed the second time. Then Peter remembered what Jesus had told him: "Before the rooster crows twice, you will say three times that you don't know me." Then Peter lost control of himself and began to cry.

MARCH 18

NUMBERS 33:1—34:29

Israel's Journey from Egypt

33 These are the places the Israelites went as Moses and Aaron led them out of Egypt in divisions. [2]At the LORD's command Moses recorded the places they went, and these are the places they went.

[3]On the fifteenth day of the first month, the day after the Passover, the Israelites left Rameses and marched out boldly in front of all the Egyptians. [4]The Egyptians were burying their firstborn sons, whom the LORD had killed; the LORD showed that the gods of Egypt were false.

[5]The Israelites left Rameses and camped at Succoth.

[6]They left Succoth and camped at Etham, at the edge of the desert.

[7]They left Etham and went back to Pi Hahiroth, to the east of Baal Zephon, and camped near Migdol.

[8]They left Pi Hahiroth and walked through the sea into the desert. After going three days through the Desert of Etham, they camped at Marah.

[9]They left Marah and went to Elim; there were twelve springs of water and seventy palm trees where they camped.

[10]They left Elim and camped near the Red Sea.

[11]They left the Red Sea and camped in the Desert of Sin.

[12]They left the Desert of Sin and camped at Dophkah.

[13]They left Dophkah and camped at Alush.

[14]They left Alush and camped at Rephidim, where the people had no water to drink.

14:68 And the rooster crowed. Some Greek copies do not have this phrase.

¹⁵They left Rephidim and camped in the Desert of Sinai.

¹⁶They left the Desert of Sinai and camped at Kibroth Hattaavah.

¹⁷They left Kibroth Hattaavah and camped at Hazeroth.

¹⁸They left Hazeroth and camped at Rithmah.

¹⁹They left Rithmah and camped at Rimmon Perez.

²⁰They left Rimmon Perez and camped at Libnah.

²¹They left Libnah and camped at Rissah.

²²They left Rissah and camped at Kehelathah.

²³They left Kehelathah and camped at Mount Shepher.

²⁴They left Mount Shepher and camped at Haradah.

²⁵They left Haradah and camped at Makheloth.

²⁶They left Makheloth and camped at Tahath.

²⁷They left Tahath and camped at Terah.

²⁸They left Terah and camped at Mithcah.

²⁹They left Mithcah and camped at Hashmonah.

³⁰They left Hashmonah and camped at Moseroth.

³¹They left Moseroth and camped at Bene Jaakan.

³²They left Bene Jaakan and camped at Hor Haggidgad.

³³They left Hor Haggidgad and camped at Jotbathah.

³⁴They left Jotbathah and camped at Abronah.

³⁵They left Abronah and camped at Ezion Geber.

³⁶They left Ezion Geber and camped at Kadesh in the Desert of Zin.

³⁷They left Kadesh and camped at Mount Hor, on the border of Edom. ³⁸Aaron the priest obeyed the LORD and went up Mount Hor. There he died on the first day of the fifth month in the fortieth year after the Israelites left Egypt. ³⁹Aaron was 123 years old when he died on Mount Hor.

⁴⁰The Canaanite king of Arad, who lived in the southern area of Canaan, heard that the Israelites were coming.

⁴¹The people left Mount Hor and camped at Zalmonah.

⁴²They left Zalmonah and camped at Punon.

⁴³They left Punon and camped at Oboth.

⁴⁴They left Oboth and camped at Iye Abarim, on the border of Moab.

⁴⁵They left Iye Abarim and camped at Dibon Gad.

⁴⁶They left Dibon Gad and camped at Almon Diblathaim.

⁴⁷They left Almon Diblathaim and camped in the mountains of Abarim, near Nebo.

⁴⁸They left the mountains of Abarim and camped on the plains of Moab near the Jordan River across from Jericho. ⁴⁹They camped along the Jordan on the plains of Moab, and their camp went from Beth Jeshimoth to Abel Acacia.

⁵⁰On the plains of Moab by the Jordan River across from Jericho, the LORD spoke to Moses. He said, ⁵¹"Speak to the Israelites and tell them, 'When you cross the Jordan River and go into Canaan, ⁵²force out all the people who live there. Destroy all of their carved statues and metal idols. Wreck all of their places of worship. ⁵³Take over the land and settle there, because I have given this land to you to own. ⁵⁴Throw lots to divide up the land by family groups, giving larger portions to larger family groups and smaller portions to smaller family groups. The land will be given as the lots decide; each tribe will get its own land.

⁵⁵"'But if you don't force those people out of the land, they will bring you trouble. They will be like sharp hooks in your eyes and thorns in your sides. They will bring trouble to the land where you live. ⁵⁶Then I will punish you as I had planned to punish them.'"

The Borders of Canaan

34The LORD said to Moses, ²"Give this command to the people of Israel: 'You will soon enter Canaan and it will be yours. These shall be the borders: ³On the south you will get part of the Desert of Zin near the border of Edom. On the east side your southern border will start at the south end of the Dead Sea, ⁴cross south of Scorpion Pass, and go through the Desert of Zin and south of Kadesh Barnea. Then it will go to Hazar Addar and over to Azmon. [5]From Azmon it will go to the brook of Egypt, and it will end at the Mediterranean Sea.

[6]" 'Your western border will be the Mediterranean Sea.

[7]" 'Your northern border will begin at the Mediterranean Sea and go to Mount Hor. [8]From Mount Hor it will go to Lebo Hamath, and on to Zedad. [9]Then the border will go to Ziphron, and it will end at Hazar Enan. This will be your northern border.

[10]" 'Your eastern border will begin at Hazar Enan and go to Shepham. [11]From Shepham the border will go east of Ain to Riblah and along the hills east of Lake Galilee. [12]Then the border will go down along the Jordan River and end at the Dead Sea.

" 'These are the borders around your country.'"

[13]So Moses gave this command to the Israelites: "This is the land you will receive. Throw lots to divide it among the nine and one-half tribes, because the LORD commanded that it should be theirs. [14]The tribes of Reuben, Gad, and East Manasseh have already received their land. [15]These two and one-half tribes received land east of the Jordan River, across from Jericho."

[16]Then the LORD said to Moses, [17]"These are the men who will divide the land: Eleazar the priest and Joshua son of Nun. [18]Also take one leader from each tribe to help divide the land. [19]These are the names of the leaders: from the tribe of Judah, Caleb son of Jephunneh; [20]from the tribe of Simeon, Shemuel son of Ammihud; [21]from the tribe of Benjamin, Elidad son of Kislon; [22]from the tribe of Dan, Bukki son of Jogli; [23]from the tribe of Manasseh son of Joseph, Hanniel son of Ephod; [24]from the tribe of Ephraim son of Joseph, Kemuel son of Shiphtan; [25]from the tribe of Zebulun, Elizaphan son of Parnach; [26]from the tribe of Issachar, Paltiel son of Azzan; [27]from the tribe of Asher, Ahihud son of Shelomi; [28]from the tribe of Naphtali, Pedahel son of Ammihud."

[29]The LORD commanded these men to divide the land of Canaan among the Israelites.

PSALM 35:11-16

[11]Men without mercy stand up to testify.
  They ask me things I do not know.
[12]They repay me with evil for the good I
    have done,
  and they make me very sad.
[13]Yet when they were sick, I put on clothes of
    sadness
  and showed my sorrow by fasting.
  But my prayers were not answered.
[14] I acted as if they were my friends or
    brothers.
  I bowed in sadness as if I were crying for
    my mother.
[15]But when I was in trouble, they gathered
    and laughed;
  they gathered to attack before I knew it.
  They insulted me without stopping.
[16]They made fun of me and were cruel to
    me
  and ground their teeth at me in anger.

PROVERBS 12:2

[2]The LORD is pleased with a good person,
  but he will punish anyone who plans
    evil.

MARK 15:1-20

Pilate Questions Jesus

15 Very early in the morning, the leading priests, the elders, the teachers of the law, and all the Jewish council decided what to do with Jesus. They tied him, led him away, and turned him over to Pilate, the governor.

[2]Pilate asked Jesus, "Are you the king of the Jews?"

Jesus answered, "Those are your words."

[3]The leading priests accused Jesus of many things. [4]So Pilate asked Jesus another question, "You can see that they are accusing you of many things. Aren't you going to answer?"

[5]But Jesus still said nothing, so Pilate was very surprised.

Pilate Tries to Free Jesus

[6]Every year at the time of the Passover the governor would free one prisoner whom the people chose. [7]At that time, there was a man

named Barabbas in prison who was a rebel and had committed murder during a riot. ⁸The crowd came to Pilate and began to ask him to free a prisoner as he always did.

⁹So Pilate asked them, "Do you want me to free the king of the Jews?" ¹⁰Pilate knew that the leading priests had turned Jesus in to him because they were jealous. ¹¹But the leading priests had persuaded the people to ask Pilate to free Barabbas, not Jesus.

¹²Then Pilate asked the crowd again, "So what should I do with this man you call the king of the Jews?"

¹³They shouted, "Crucify him!"

¹⁴Pilate asked, "Why? What wrong has he done?"

But they shouted even louder, "Crucify him!"

¹⁵Pilate wanted to please the crowd, so he freed Barabbas for them. After having Jesus beaten with whips, he handed Jesus over to the soldiers to be crucified.

¹⁶The soldiers took Jesus into the governor's palace (called the Praetorium) and called all the other soldiers together. ¹⁷They put a purple robe on Jesus and used thorny branches to make a crown for his head. ¹⁸They began to call out to him, "Hail, King of the Jews!" ¹⁹The soldiers beat Jesus on the head many times with a stick. They spit on him and made fun of him by bowing on their knees and worshiping him. ²⁰After they finished, the soldiers took off the purple robe and put his own clothes on him again. Then they led him out of the palace to be crucified.

MARCH 19

NUMBERS 35:1—36:13

The Levites' Towns

35 The LORD spoke to Moses on the plains of Moab across from Jericho by the Jordan River. He said, ²"Command the Israelites to give the Levites cities to live in from the land they receive. Also give the Levites the pastureland around these cities. ³Then the Levites will have cities where they may live and pastureland for their cattle, flocks, and other animals. ⁴The pastureland you give the Levites will extend fifteen hundred feet from the city wall. ⁵Also measure three thousand feet in each direction outside the city wall—three thousand feet east of the city, three thousand feet south of the city, three thousand feet west of the city, and three thousand feet north of the city, with the city in the center. This will be pastureland for the Levites' cities.

Cities of Safety

⁶"Six of the cities you give the Levites will be cities of safety. A person who accidentally kills someone may run to one of those cities for safety. You must also give forty-two other cities to the Levites; ⁷give the Levites a total

of forty-eight cities and their pastures. ⁸The larger tribes of Israel must give more cities, and the smaller tribes must give fewer cities. Each tribe must give some of its cities to the Levites, but the number of cities they give will depend on the size of their land."

⁹Then the LORD said to Moses, ¹⁰"Tell the Israelites these things: 'When you cross the Jordan River and go into Canaan, ¹¹you must choose cities to be cities of safety, so that a person who accidentally kills someone may run to them for safety. ¹²There the person will be safe from the dead person's relative who has the duty of punishing the killer. He will not die before he receives a fair trial in court. ¹³The six cities you give will be cities of safety. ¹⁴Give three cities east of the Jordan River and three cities in Canaan as cities of safety. ¹⁵These six cities will be places of safety for citizens of Israel, as well as for foreigners and other people living with you. Any of these people who accidentally kills someone may run to one of these cities.

¹⁶"'Anyone who uses an iron weapon to kill someone is a murderer. He must be put to death. ¹⁷Anyone who takes a rock and kills a person with it is a murderer. He must be put

to death. [18]Anyone who picks up a piece of wood and kills someone with it is a murderer. He must be put to death. [19]A relative of the dead person must put the murderer to death; when they meet, the relative must kill the murderer. [20]A person might shove someone or throw something at someone and cause death. [21]Or a person might hit someone with his hand and cause death. If it were done from hate, the person is a murderer and must be put to death. A relative of the dead person must kill the murderer when they meet.

[22]" 'But a person might suddenly shove someone, and not from hatred. Or a person might accidentally throw something and hit someone. [23]Or a person might drop a rock on someone he couldn't see and kill that person. There was no plan to hurt anyone and no hatred for the one who was killed. [24]If that happens, the community must judge between the relative of the dead person and the killer, according to these rules. [25]They must protect the killer from the dead person's relative, sending the killer back to the original city of safety, to stay there until the high priest dies (the high priest had the holy oil poured on him).

[26]"Such a person must never go outside the limits of the city of safety. [27]If a relative of the dead person finds the killer outside the city, the relative may kill that person and not be guilty of murder. [28]The killer must stay in the city of safety until the high priest dies. After the high priest dies, the killer may go home.

[29]" 'These laws are for you from now on, wherever you live.

[30]" 'If anyone kills a person, the murderer may be put to death only if there are witnesses. No one may be put to death with only one witness.

[31]" 'Don't take money to spare the life of a murderer who should be put to death. A murderer must be put to death.

[32]" 'If someone has run to a city of safety, don't take money to let the person go back home before the high priest dies.

[33]" 'Don't let murder spoil your land. The only way to remove the sin of killing an innocent person is for the murderer to be put to death. [34]I am the LORD, and I live among the Israelites. I live in that land with you, so do not spoil it with murder.' "

Land for Zelophehad's Daughters

36The leaders of Gilead's family group went to talk to Moses and the leaders of the families of Israel. (Gilead was the son of Makir, the son of Manasseh, the son of Joseph.) [2]They said, "The LORD commanded you, our master, to give the land to the Israelites by throwing lots, and the LORD commanded you to give the land of Zelophehad, our brother, to his daughters. [3]But if his daughters marry men from other tribes of Israel, then that land will leave our family, and the people of the other tribes will get that land. So we will lose some of our land. [4]When the time of Jubilee comes for the Israelites, their land will go to the tribes of the people they marry; their land will be taken away from us, the land we received from our fathers."

[5]Then Moses gave the Israelites this command from the LORD: "These men from the tribe of Joseph are right. [6]This is the LORD's command to Zelophehad's daughters: You may marry anyone you wish, as long as the person is from your own tribe. [7]In this way the Israelites' land will not pass from tribe to tribe, and each Israelite will keep the land in the tribe that belonged to his ancestors. [8]A woman who inherits her father's land may marry, but she must marry someone from her own tribe. In this way every Israelite will keep the land that belonged to his ancestors. [9]The land must not pass from tribe to tribe, and each Israelite tribe will keep the land it received from its ancestors."

[10]Zelophehad's daughters obeyed the LORD's command to Moses.

[11]So Zelophehad's daughters—Mahlah, Tirzah, Hoglah, Milcah, and Noah—married their cousins, their father's relatives. [12]Their husbands were from the tribe of Manasseh son of Joseph, so their land stayed in their father's family group and tribe.

[13]These were the laws and commands that the LORD gave to the Israelites through Moses on the plains of Moab by the Jordan River, across from Jericho.

PSALM 35:17−28

[17]Lord, how long will you watch this happen?

Save my life from their attacks;
save me from these people who are like
lions.
¹⁸I will praise you in the great meeting.
I will praise you among crowds of
people.
¹⁹Do not let my enemies laugh at me;
they hate me for no reason.
Do not let them make fun of me;
they have no cause to hate me.
²⁰Their words are not friendly
but are lies about peace-loving
people.
²¹They speak against me
and say, "Aha! We saw what you did!"

²²LORD, you have been watching. Do not
keep quiet.
Lord, do not leave me alone.
²³Wake up! Come and defend me!
My God and Lord, fight for me!
²⁴LORD my God, defend me with your justice.
Don't let them laugh at me.
²⁵Don't let them think, "Aha! We got what we
wanted!"
Don't let them say, "We destroyed
him."
²⁶Let them be ashamed and embarrassed,
because they were happy when I hurt.
Cover them with shame and disgrace,
because they thought they were better
than I was.
²⁷May my friends sing and shout for joy.
May they always say, "Praise the
greatness of the LORD,
who loves to see his servants do well."
²⁸I will tell of your goodness
and will praise you every day.

PROVERBS 12:3

³Doing evil brings no safety at all,
but a good person has safety and
security.

MARK 15:21–47

Jesus Is Crucified

²¹A man named Simon from Cyrene, the
father of Alexander and Rufus, was coming
from the fields to the city. The soldiers forced
Simon to carry the cross for Jesus. ²²They led
Jesus to the place called Golgotha, which
means the Place of the Skull. ²³The soldiers
tried to give Jesus wine mixed with myrrh to
drink, but he refused. ²⁴The soldiers crucified Jesus and divided his clothes among
themselves, throwing lots to decide what
each soldier would get.

²⁵It was nine o'clock in the morning
when they crucified Jesus. ²⁶There was a
sign with this charge against Jesus written
on it: THE KING OF THE JEWS. ²⁷They also put
two robbers on crosses beside Jesus, one on
the right, and the other on the left. [²⁸And
the Scripture came true that says, "They
put him with criminals."]ⁿ ²⁹People walked
by and insulted Jesus and shook their
heads, saying, "You said you could destroy
the Temple and build it again in three days.
³⁰So save yourself! Come down from that
cross!"

³¹The leading priests and the teachers of
the law were also making fun of Jesus. They
said to each other, "He saved other people,
but he can't save himself. ³²If he is really the
Christ, the king of Israel, let him come down
now from the cross. When we see this, we
will believe in him." The robbers who were
being crucified beside Jesus also insulted
him.

Jesus Dies

³³At noon the whole country became
dark, and the darkness lasted for three
hours. ³⁴At three o'clock Jesus cried in a loud
voice, "Eloi, Eloi, lama sabachthani." This
means, "My God, my God, why have you
abandoned me?"

³⁵When some of the people standing
there heard this, they said, "Listen! He is calling Elijah."

³⁶Someone there ran and got a sponge,
filled it with vinegar, tied it to a stick, and
gave it to Jesus to drink. He said, "We want to
see if Elijah will come to take him down
from the cross."

³⁷Then Jesus cried in a loud voice and
died.

15:28 And . . . criminals." Some Greek copies do not contain the bracketed text, which quotes from Isaiah 53:12.

[38]The curtain in the Temple[n] was torn into two pieces, from the top to the bottom. [39]When the army officer who was standing in front of the cross saw what happened when Jesus died,[n] he said, "This man really was the Son of God!"

[40]Some women were standing at a distance from the cross, watching; among them were Mary Magdalene, Salome, and Mary the mother of James and Joseph. (James was her youngest son.) [41]These women had followed Jesus in Galilee and helped him. Many other women were also there who had come with Jesus to Jerusalem.

Jesus Is Buried

[42]This was Preparation Day. (That means the day before the Sabbath day.) That evening, [43]Joseph from Arimathea was brave enough to go to Pilate and ask for Jesus' body. Joseph, an important member of the Jewish council, was one of the people who was waiting for the kingdom of God to come. [44]Pilate was amazed that Jesus would have already died, so he called the army officer who had guarded Jesus and asked him if Jesus had already died. [45]The officer told Pilate that he was dead, so Pilate told Joseph he could have the body. [46]Joseph bought some linen cloth, took the body down from the cross, and wrapped it in the linen. He put the body in a tomb that was cut out of a wall of rock. Then he rolled a very large stone to block the entrance of the tomb. [47]And Mary Magdalene and Mary the mother of Joseph saw the place where Jesus was laid.

MARCH 20

DEUTERONOMY 1:1—2:37

Moses Talks to the Israelites

1 This is the message Moses gave to all the people of Israel in the desert east of the Jordan River. They were in the desert area near Suph, between Paran and the towns of Tophel, Laban, Hazeroth, and Dizahab. [2](The trip from Mount Sinai to Kadesh Barnea on the Mount Seir road takes eleven days.) [3]Forty years after the Israelites had left Egypt, on the first day of the eleventh month, Moses told the people of Israel everything the LORD had commanded him to tell them. [4]This was after the LORD had defeated Sihon and Og. Sihon was king of the Amorite people and lived in Heshbon. Og was king of Bashan and lived in Ashteroth and Edrei.

[5]Now the Israelites were east of the Jordan River in the land of Moab, and there Moses began to explain what God had commanded. He said:

[6]The LORD our God spoke to us at Mount Sinai and said, "You have stayed long enough at this mountain. [7]Get ready, and go to the mountain country of the Amorites, and to all the places around there—the Jordan Valley, the mountains, the western hills, the southern area, the seacoast, the land of Canaan, and Lebanon. Go as far as the great river, the Euphrates. [8]See, I have given you this land, so go in and take it for yourselves. The LORD promised it to your ancestors—Abraham, Isaac, and Jacob and their descendants."

Moses Appoints Leaders

[9]At that time I said, "I am not able to take care of you by myself. [10]The LORD your God has made you grow in number so that there are as many of you as there are stars in the sky. [11]I pray that the LORD, the God of your ancestors, will give you a thousand times more people and do all the wonderful things he promised. [12]But I cannot take care of your problems, your troubles, and your arguments by myself. [13]So choose some men from each tribe—wise men who have un-

---

15:38 curtain in the Temple A curtain divided the Most Holy Place from the other part of the Temple. That was the special building in Jerusalem where God commanded the Jewish people to worship him. **15:39 when Jesus died** Some Greek copies read "when Jesus cried out and died."

derstanding and experience—and I will make them leaders over you."

[14]And you said, "That's a good thing to do."

[15]So I took the wise and experienced leaders of your tribes, and I made them your leaders. I appointed commanders over a thousand people, over a hundred people, over fifty people, and over ten people and made them officers over your tribes. [16]Then I told your leaders, "Listen to the arguments between your people. Judge fairly between two Israelites or between an Israelite and a foreigner. [17]When you judge, be fair to everyone; don't act as if one person is more important than another, and don't be afraid of anyone, because your decision comes from God. Bring the hard cases to me, and I will judge them." [18]At that time I told you everything you must do.

Spies Enter the Land

[19]Then, as the LORD our God commanded us, we left Mount Sinai and went toward the mountain country of the Amorite people. We went through that large and terrible desert you saw, and then we came to Kadesh Barnea. [20]I said to you, "You have now come to the mountain country of the Amorites, to the land the LORD our God will give us. [21]Look, here it is! Go up and take it. The LORD, the God of your ancestors, told you to do this, so don't be afraid and don't worry."

[22]Then all of you came to me and said, "Let's send men before us to spy out the land. They can come back and tell us about the way we should go and the cities we will find."

[23]I thought that was a good idea, so I chose twelve of your men, one for each tribe. [24]They left and went up to the mountains, and when they came to the Valley of Eshcol they explored it. [25]They took some of the fruit from that land and brought it down to us, saying, "It is a good land that the LORD our God is giving us."

Israel Refuses to Enter

[26]But you refused to go. You would not obey the command of the LORD your God, [27]but grumbled in your tents, saying, "The LORD hates us. He brought us out of Egypt just to give us to the Amorites, who will de-

stroy us. [28]Where can we go now? The spies we sent have made us afraid, because they said, 'The people there are stronger and taller than we are. The cities are big, with walls up to the sky. And we saw the Anakites there!'"

[29]Then I said to you, "Don't be frightened; don't be afraid of those people. [30]The LORD your God will go ahead of you and fight for you as he did in Egypt; you saw him do it. [31]And in the desert you saw how the LORD your God carried you, like one carries a child. And he has brought you safely all the way to this place."

[32]But you still did not trust the LORD your God, even though [33]he had always gone before you to find places for you to camp. In a fire at night and in a cloud during the day, he showed you which way to go.

[34]When the LORD heard what you said, he was angry and made an oath, saying, [35]"I promised a good land to your ancestors, but none of you evil people will see it. [36]Only Caleb son of Jephunneh will see it. I will give him and his descendants the land he walked on, because he followed the LORD completely."

[37]Because of you, the LORD was also angry with me and said, "You won't enter the land either, [38]but your assistant, Joshua son of Nun, will enter it. Encourage him, because he will lead Israel to take the land for their own.

[39]"Your little children that you said would be captured, who do not know right from wrong at this time, will go into the land. I will give the land to them, and they will take it for their own. [40]But you must turn around and follow the desert road toward the Red Sea."

[41]Then you said to me, "We have sinned against the LORD, but now we will go up and fight, as the LORD our God commanded us." Then all of you put on weapons, thinking it would be easy to go into the mountains.

[42]But the LORD said to me, "Tell the people, 'You must not go up there and fight. I will not be with you, and your enemies will defeat you.'"

[43]So I told you, but you would not listen. You would not obey the LORD's command.

You were proud, so you went on up into the mountains, ⁴⁴and the Amorites who lived in those mountains came out and fought you. They chased you like bees and defeated you from Edom to Hormah. ⁴⁵So you came back and cried before the LORD, but the LORD did not listen to you; he refused to pay attention to you. ⁴⁶So you stayed in Kadesh a long time.

Israel Wanders in the Desert

2 Then we turned around, and we traveled on the desert road toward the Red Sea, as the LORD had told me to do. We traveled through the mountains of Edom for many days.

²Then the LORD said to me, ³"You have traveled through these mountains long enough. Turn north ⁴and give the people this command: 'You will soon go through the land that belongs to your relatives, the descendants of Esau who live in Edom. They will be afraid of you, but be very careful. ⁵Do not go to war against them. I will not give you any of their land—not even a foot of it, because I have given the mountains of Edom to Esau as his own. ⁶You must pay them in silver for any food you eat or water you drink.'"

⁷The LORD your God has blessed everything you have done; he has protected you while you traveled through this great desert. The LORD your God has been with you for the past forty years, and you have had everything you needed.

⁸So we passed by our relatives, the descendants of Esau who lived in Edom. We turned off the Jordan Valley road that comes from the towns of Elath and Ezion Geber and traveled along the desert road to Moab.

The Land of Ar

⁹Then the LORD said to me, "Don't bother the people of Moab. Don't go to war against them, because I will not give you any of their land as your own; I have given Ar to the descendants of Lot as their own." ¹⁰(The Emites, who lived in Ar before, were strong people, and there were many of them. They were very tall, like the Anakites. ¹¹The Emites were thought to be Rephaites, like the Anakites, but the Moabite people called

them Emites. ¹²The Horites also lived in Edom before, but the descendants of Esau forced them out and destroyed them, taking their place as Israel did in the land the LORD gave them as their own.)

¹³And the LORD said to me, "Now get up and cross the Zered Valley." So we crossed the valley. ¹⁴It had been thirty-eight years from the time we left Kadesh Barnea until we crossed the Zered Valley. By then, all the fighting men from that time had died, as the LORD had promised would happen. ¹⁵The LORD continued to work against them to remove them from the camp until they were all dead.

¹⁶When the last of those fighting men had died, ¹⁷the LORD said to me, ¹⁸"Today you will pass by Ar, on the border of Moab. ¹⁹When you come near the people of Ammon, don't bother them or go to war against them, because I will not give you any of their land as your own. I have given it to the descendants of Lot for their own."

²⁰(That land was also thought to be a land of the Rephaites, because those people used to live there, but the Ammonites called them Zamzummites. ²¹They were strong people, and there were many of them; they were very tall, like the Anakites. The LORD destroyed the Zamzummites, and the Ammonites forced them out of the land and took their place. ²²The LORD did the same thing for the descendants of Esau, who lived in Edom, when he destroyed the Horites. The Edomites forced them out of the land and took their place, and they live there to this day. ²³The Cretan people came from Crete and destroyed the Avvites, who lived in towns all the way to Gaza; the Cretans destroyed them and took their place.)

Fighting the Amorites

²⁴The LORD said, "Get up and cross the Arnon Ravine. See, I am giving you the power to defeat Sihon the Amorite, king of Heshbon, and I am giving you his land. So fight against him and begin taking his land. ²⁵Today I will begin to make all the people in the world afraid of you. When they hear reports about you, they will shake with fear, and they will be terrified of you."

26I sent messengers from the desert of Kedemoth to Sihon king of Heshbon. They offered him peace, saying, 27"If you let us pass through your country, we will stay on the road and not turn right or left. 28We will pay you in silver for any food we eat or water we drink. We only want to walk through your country. 29The descendants of Esau in Edom let us go through their land, and so did the Moabites in Ar. We want to cross the Jordan River into the land the LORD our God has given us." 30But Sihon king of Heshbon would not let us pass, because the LORD your God had made him stubborn. The LORD wanted you to defeat Sihon, and now this has happened.

31The LORD said to me, "See, I have begun to give Sihon and his country to you. Begin taking the land as your own."

32Then Sihon and all his army came out and fought us at Jahaz, 33but the LORD our God gave Sihon to us. We defeated him, his sons, and all his army. 34We captured all his cities at that time and completely destroyed them, as well as the men, women, and children. We left no one alive. 35But we kept the cattle and valuable things from the cities for ourselves. 36We defeated Aroer on the edge of the Arnon Ravine, and we defeated the town in the ravine, and even as far as Gilead. No town was too strong for us; the LORD our God gave us all of them. 37But you did not go near the land of the Ammonites, on the shores of the Jabbok River, or the towns in the mountains, as the LORD our God had commanded.

PSALM 36:1–4

Wicked People and a Good God

For the director of music. Of David, the servant of the LORD.

36 Sin speaks to the wicked in their hearts.
> They have no fear of God.
2They think too much of themselves
> so they don't see their sin and hate it.
3Their words are wicked lies;
> they are no longer wise or good.
4At night they make evil plans;
> what they do leads to nothing good.
> They don't refuse things that are evil.

PROVERBS 12:4–6

4A good wife is like a crown for her husband,
> but a disgraceful wife is like a disease in his bones.

5The plans that good people make are fair,
> but the advice of the wicked will trick you.

6The wicked talk about killing people,
> but the words of good people will save them.

MARK 16:1–20

Jesus Rises from the Dead

16 The day after the Sabbath day, Mary Magdalene, Mary the mother of James, and Salome bought some sweet-smelling spices to put on Jesus' body. 2Very early on that day, the first day of the week, soon after sunrise, the women were on their way to the tomb. 3They said to each other, "Who will roll away for us the stone that covers the entrance of the tomb?"

4Then the women looked and saw that the stone had already been rolled away, even though it was very large. 5The women entered the tomb and saw a young man wearing a white robe and sitting on the right side, and they were afraid.

6But the man said, "Don't be afraid. You are looking for Jesus from Nazareth, who has been crucified. He has risen from the dead; he is not here. Look, here is the place they laid him. 7Now go and tell his followers and Peter, 'Jesus is going into Galilee ahead of you, and you will see him there as he told you before.'"

8The women were confused and shaking with fear, so they left the tomb and ran away. They did not tell anyone about what happened, because they were afraid.

Verses 9–20 are not included in some of the earliest surviving Greek copies of Mark.

Some Followers See Jesus

[9After Jesus rose from the dead early on the first day of the week, he showed himself first to Mary Magdalene. One time in the past, he had forced seven demons out of her. [10]After Mary saw Jesus, she went and told his followers, who were very sad and were crying. [11]But Mary told them that Jesus was alive. She said that she had seen him, but the followers did not believe her.

[12]Later, Jesus showed himself to two of his followers while they were walking in the country, but he did not look the same as before. [13]These followers went back to the others and told them what had happened, but again, the followers did not believe them.

Jesus Talks to the Apostles

[14]Later Jesus showed himself to the eleven apostles while they were eating, and he criticized them because they had no faith. They were stubborn and refused to believe those who had seen him after he had risen from the dead.

[15]Jesus said to his followers, "Go everywhere in the world, and tell the Good News to everyone. [16]Anyone who believes and is baptized will be saved, but anyone who does not believe will be punished. [17]And those who believe will be able to do these things as proof: They will use my name to force out demons. They will speak in new languages.[n] [18]They will pick up snakes and drink poison without being hurt. They will touch the sick, and the sick will be healed."

[19]After the Lord Jesus said these things to his followers, he was carried up into heaven, and he sat at the right side of God. [20]The followers went everywhere in the world and told the Good News to people, and the Lord helped them. The Lord proved that the Good News they told was true by giving them power to work miracles.]

MARCH 21

DEUTERONOMY 3:1—4:49

The Battle at Bashan

3 When we turned and went up the road toward Bashan, Og king of Bashan and all his army came out to fight us at Edrei. [2]The LORD said to me, "Don't be afraid of Og, because I will hand him, his whole army, and his land over to you. Do to him what you did to Sihon king of the Amorites, who ruled in Heshbon."

[3]So the LORD our God gave us Og king of Bashan and all his army; we defeated them and left no one alive. [4]Then we captured all of Og's cities, all sixty of them, and took the whole area of Argob, Og's kingdom in Bashan. [5]All these were strong cities, with high walls and gates with bars. And there were also many small towns with no walls. [6]We completely destroyed them, just like the cities of Sihon king of Heshbon. We killed all the men, women, and children, [7]but we kept all the cattle and valuable things from the cities for ourselves.

[8]So at that time we took the land east of the Jordan River, from the Arnon Ravine to Mount Hermon, from these two Amorite kings. [9](Hermon is called Sirion by the Sidonian people, but the Amorites call it Senir.) [10]We captured all the cities on the high plain and all of Gilead, and we took all of Bashan as far as Salecah and Edrei, towns in Og's kingdom of Bashan. [11](Only Og king of Bashan was left of the few Rephaites. His bed was made of iron, and it was more than thirteen feet long and six feet wide! It is still in the Ammonite city of Rabbah.)

The Land Is Divided

[12]At that time we took this land to be our own. I gave the people of Reuben and Gad the land from Aroer by the Arnon Ravine, as well as half of the mountain country of Gilead and the cities in it. [13]To the people of

---

16:17 languages This can also be translated "tongues."

East Manasseh I gave the rest of Gilead and all of Bashan, the kingdom of Og. (The area of Argob in Bashan was called the land of the Rephaites. [14]Jair, a descendant of Manasseh, took the whole area of Argob, all the way to the border of the Geshurites and Maacathites. So that land was named for Jair, and even today Bashan is called the Towns of Jair.) [15]I gave Gilead to Makir. [16]I gave the Reubenites and the Gadites the land that begins at Gilead and goes from the Arnon Ravine (the middle of the Arnon is the border) to the Jabbok River, which is the Ammonite border. [17]The border on the west was the Jordan River in the Jordan Valley, and it goes from Lake Galilee to the Dead Sea west of Mount Pisgah.

[18]At that time I gave you this command: "The LORD your God has given you this land as your own. Now your fighting men must take their weapons, and you must lead the other Israelites across the river. [19]Your wives, your young children, and your cattle may stay here. I know you have many cattle, and they may stay here in the cities I have given you, [20]until the LORD also gives your Israelite relatives a place to rest. They will receive the land the LORD your God has given them on the other side of the Jordan River. After that, you may each return to the land I have given you."

[21]Then I gave this command to Joshua: "You have seen for yourself all that the LORD your God has done to these two kings. The LORD will do the same thing to all the kingdoms where you are going. [22]Don't be afraid of them, because the LORD your God will fight for you."

Moses Cannot Enter the Land

[23]Then I begged the LORD: [24]"Lord GOD, you have begun to show me, your servant, how great you are. You have great strength, and no other god in heaven or on earth can do the powerful things you do. There is no other god like you. [25]Please let me cross the Jordan River so that I may see the good land by the Jordan. I want to see the beautiful mountains and Lebanon."

[26]But the LORD was angry with me because of you, and he would not listen to me.

The LORD said to me, "That's enough. Don't talk to me anymore about it. [27]Climb to the top of Mount Pisgah and look west, north, south, and east. You can look at the land, but you will not cross the Jordan River. [28]Appoint Joshua and help him be brave and strong. He will lead the people across the river and give them the land that they are to inherit, but you can only look at it." [29]So we stayed in the valley opposite Beth Peor.

Moses Tells Israel to Obey

4 Now, Israel, listen to the laws and commands I will teach you. Obey them so that you will live and so that you will go over and take the land the LORD, the God of your ancestors, is giving to you. [2]Don't add to these commands, and don't leave anything out, but obey the commands of the LORD your God that I give you.

[3]You have seen for yourselves what the LORD did at Baal Peor, how the LORD your God destroyed everyone among you who followed Baal in Peor. [4]But all of you who continued following the LORD your God are still alive today.

[5]Look, I have taught you the laws and rules the LORD my God commanded me. Now you can obey the laws in the land you are entering, in the land you will take. [6]Obey these laws carefully, in order to show the other nations that you have wisdom and understanding. When they hear about these laws, they will say, "This great nation of Israel is wise and understanding." [7]No other nation is as great as we are. Their gods do not come near them, but the LORD our God comes near when we pray to him. [8]And no other nation has such good teachings and commands as those I am giving to you today.

[9]But be careful! Watch out and don't forget the things you have seen. Don't forget them as long as you live, but teach them to your children and grandchildren. [10]Remember the day you stood before the LORD your God at Mount Sinai. He said to me, "Bring the people together so I can tell them what I have to say. Then they will respect me as long as they live in the land, and they will teach these things to their children." [11]When you

came and stood at the bottom of the mountain, it blazed with fire that reached to the sky, and black clouds made it very dark. [12]The LORD spoke to you from the fire. You heard the sound of words, but you did not see him; there was only a voice. [13]The LORD told you about his Agreement, the Ten Commandments. He told you to obey them, and he wrote them on two stone tablets. [14]Then the LORD commanded me to teach you the laws and rules that you must obey in the land you will take when you cross the Jordan River.

Laws About Idols

[15]Since the LORD spoke to you from the fire at Mount Sinai, but you did not see him, watch yourselves carefully! [16]Don't sin by making idols of any kind, and don't make statues—of men or women, [17]of animals on earth or birds that fly in the air, [18]of anything that crawls on the ground, or of fish in the water below. [19]When you look up at the sky, you see the sun, moon, and stars, and everything in the sky. But don't bow down and worship them, because the LORD your God has made these things for all people everywhere. [20]But the LORD brought you out of Egypt, which tested you like a furnace for melting iron, and he made you his very own people, as you are now.

[21]The LORD was angry with me because of you, and he swore that I would not cross the Jordan River to go into the good land the LORD your God is giving you as your own. [22]I will die here in this land and not cross the Jordan, but you will soon go across and take that good land. [23]Be careful. Don't forget the Agreement of the LORD your God that he made with you, and don't make any idols for yourselves, as the LORD your God has commanded you not to do. [24]The LORD your God is a jealous God, like a fire that burns things up.

[25]Even after you have lived in the land a long time and have had children and grandchildren, don't do evil things. Don't make any kind of idol, and don't do what the LORD your God says is evil, because that will make him angry. [26]If you do, I ask heaven and earth to speak against you this day that you will quickly be removed from this land that you are crossing the Jordan River to take. You will not live there long after that, but you will be completely destroyed. [27]The LORD will scatter you among the other nations. Only a few of you will be left alive, and those few will be in other nations where the LORD will send you. [28]There you will worship gods made by people, gods made of wood and stone, that cannot see, hear, eat, or smell. [29]But even there you can look for the LORD your God, and you will find him if you look for him with your whole being. [30]It will be hard when all these things happen to you. But after that you will come back to the LORD your God and obey him, [31]because the LORD your God is a merciful God. He will not leave you or destroy you. He will not forget the Agreement with your ancestors, which he swore to them.

The Lord Is Great

[32]Nothing like this has ever happened before! Look at the past, long before you were even born. Go all the way back to when God made humans on the earth, and look from one end of heaven to the other. Nothing like this has ever been heard of! [33]No other people have ever heard God speak from a fire and have still lived. But you have. [34]No other god has ever taken for himself one nation out of another. But the LORD your God did this for you in Egypt, right before your own eyes. He did it with tests, signs, miracles, war, and great sights, by his great power and strength.

[35]He showed you things so you would know that the LORD is God, and there is no other God besides him. [36]He spoke to you from heaven to teach you. He showed you his great fire on earth, and you heard him speak from the fire. [37]Because the LORD loved your ancestors, he chose you, their descendants, and he brought you out of Egypt himself by his great strength. [38]He forced nations out of their land ahead of you, nations that were bigger and stronger than you were. The LORD did this so he could bring you into their land and give it to you as your own, and this land is yours today.

[39]Know and believe today that the LORD is God. He is God in heaven above and on the

earth below. There is no other god! [40]Obey his laws and commands that I am giving you today so that things will go well for you and your children. Then you will live a long time in the land that the LORD your God is giving to you forever.

Cities of Safety

[41]Moses chose three cities east of the Jordan River, [42]where a person who accidentally killed someone could go. If the person was not killed because of hatred, the murderer's life could be saved by running to one of these cities. [43]These were the cities: Bezer in the desert high plain was for the Reubenites; Ramoth in Gilead was for the Gadites; and Golan in Bashan was for the Manassites.

The Laws Moses Gave

[44]These are the teachings Moses gave to the people of Israel. [45]They are the rules, commands, and laws he gave them when they came out of Egypt. [46]They were in the valley near Beth Peor, east of the Jordan River, in the land of Sihon. Sihon king of the Amorites ruled in Heshbon and was defeated by Moses and the Israelites as they came out of Egypt. [47]The Israelites took his land and the land of Og king of Bashan, the two Amorite kings east of the Jordan River. [48]This land went from Aroer, on the edge of the Arnon Ravine, to Mount Hermon. [49]It included all the Jordan Valley east of the Jordan River, and it went as far as the Dead Sea below Mount Pisgah.

PSALM 36:5–12

[5]LORD, your love reaches to the heavens,
  your loyalty to the skies.
[6]Your goodness is as high as the
    mountains.
  Your justice is as deep as the great
    ocean.
  LORD, you protect both people and
    animals.
[7]God, your love is so precious!
  You protect people in the shadow of
    your wings.

[8]They eat the rich food in your house,
  and you let them drink from your river
    of pleasure.
[9]You are the giver of life.
  Your light lets us enjoy life.
[10]Continue to love those who know you
  and to do good to those who are good.
[11]Don't let proud people attack me
  and the wicked force me away.
[12]Those who do evil have been defeated.
  They are overwhelmed;
  they cannot do evil any longer.

PROVERBS 12:7

[7]Wicked people die and they are no more,
  but a good person's family continues.

LUKE 1:1–25

Luke Writes About Jesus' Life

[1]Many have tried to report on the things that happened among us. [2]They have written the same things that we learned from others—the people who saw those things from the beginning and served God by telling people his message. [3]Since I myself have studied everything carefully from the beginning, most excellent[n] Theophilus, it seemed good for me to write it out for you. I arranged it in order, [4]to help you know that what you have been taught is true.

Zechariah and Elizabeth

[5]During the time Herod ruled Judea, there was a priest named Zechariah who belonged to Abijah's group.[n] Zechariah's wife, Elizabeth, came from the family of Aaron. [6]Zechariah and Elizabeth truly did what God said was good. They did everything the Lord commanded and were without fault in keeping his law. [7]But they had no children, because Elizabeth could not have a baby, and both of them were very old.

[8]One day Zechariah was serving as a priest before God, because his group was on duty. [9]According to the custom of the priests, he was chosen by lot to go into the Temple of the Lord and burn incense.

1:3 excellent This word was used to show respect to an important person like a king or ruler. **1:5 Abijah's group** The Jewish priests were divided into twenty-four groups. See 1 Chronicles 24.

¹⁰There were a great many people outside praying at the time the incense was offered. ¹¹Then an angel of the Lord appeared to Zechariah, standing on the right side of the incense table. ¹²When he saw the angel, Zechariah was startled and frightened. ¹³But the angel said to him, "Zechariah, don't be afraid. God has heard your prayer. Your wife, Elizabeth, will give birth to a son, and you will name him John. ¹⁴He will bring you joy and gladness, and many people will be happy because of his birth. ¹⁵John will be a great man for the Lord. He will never drink wine or beer, and even from birth, he will be filled with the Holy Spirit. ¹⁶He will help many people of Israel return to the Lord their God. ¹⁷He will go before the Lord in spirit and power like Elijah. He will make peace between parents and their children and will bring those who are not obeying God back to the right way of thinking, to make a people ready for the coming of the Lord."

¹⁸Zechariah said to the angel, "How can I know that what you say is true? I am an old man, and my wife is old, too."

¹⁹The angel answered him, "I am Gabriel. I stand before God, who sent me to talk to you and to tell you this good news. ²⁰Now, listen! You will not be able to speak until the day these things happen, because you did not believe what I told you. But they will really happen."

²¹Outside, the people were still waiting for Zechariah and were surprised that he was staying so long in the Temple. ²²When Zechariah came outside, he could not speak to them, and they knew he had seen a vision in the Temple. He could only make signs to them and remained unable to speak. ²³When his time of service at the Temple was finished, he went home.

²⁴Later, Zechariah's wife, Elizabeth, became pregnant and did not go out of her house for five months. Elizabeth said, ²⁵"Look what the Lord has done for me! My people were ashamed[n] of me, but now the Lord has taken away that shame."

MARCH 22

DEUTERONOMY 5:1—6:25

The Ten Commandments

5 Moses called all the people of Israel together and said: Listen, Israel, to the commands and laws I am giving you today. Learn them and obey them carefully. ²The LORD our God made an Agreement with us at Mount Sinai. ³He did not make this Agreement with our ancestors, but he made it with us, with all of us who are alive here today. ⁴The LORD spoke to you face to face from the fire on the mountain. ⁵(At that time I stood between you and the LORD in order to tell you what the LORD said; you were afraid of the fire, so you would not go up on the mountain.) The LORD said:

⁶"I am the LORD your God; I brought you out of the land of Egypt where you were slaves.

⁷"You must not have any other gods except me.

⁸"You must not make for yourselves any idols or anything to worship that looks like something in the sky above or on the earth below or in the water below the land. ⁹You must not worship or serve any idol, because I, the LORD your God, am a jealous God. If people sin against me and hate me, I will punish their children, even their grandchildren and great-grandchildren. ¹⁰But I will be very kind for a thousand lifetimes to those who love me and obey my commands.

¹¹"You must not use the name of the LORD your God thoughtlessly, because the LORD will punish anyone who uses his name in this way.

¹²"Keep the Sabbath as a holy day, as the

1:25 ashamed The Jewish people thought it was a disgrace for women not to have children.

LORD your God has commanded you. [13]You may work and get everything done during six days each week, [14]but the seventh day is a day of rest to honor the LORD your God. On that day no one may do any work: not you, your son or daughter, your male or female slaves, your ox, your donkey, or any of your animals, or the foreigners living in your cities. That way your servants may rest as you do. [15]Remember that you were slaves in Egypt and that the LORD your God brought you out of there by his great power and strength. So the LORD your God has commanded you to rest on the Sabbath day.

[16]"Honor your father and your mother as the LORD your God has commanded you. Then you will live a long time, and things will go well for you in the land that the LORD your God is going to give you.

[17]"You must not murder anyone.

[18]"You must not be guilty of adultery.

[19]"You must not steal.

[20]"You must not tell lies about your neighbor.

[21]"You must not want to take your neighbor's wife. You must not want to take your neighbor's house or land, his male or female slaves, his ox or his donkey, or anything that belongs to your neighbor."

[22]The LORD spoke these commands to all of you on the mountain in a loud voice out of the fire, the cloud, and the deep darkness; he did not say anything else. Then he wrote them on two stone tablets, and he gave them to me.

[23]When you heard the voice from the darkness, as the mountain was blazing with fire, all the leaders of your tribes and your elders came to me. [24]And you said, "The LORD our God has shown us his glory and majesty, and we have heard his voice from the fire. Today we have seen that a person can live even if God speaks to him. [25]But now, we will die! This great fire will burn us up, and we will die if we hear the LORD our God speak anymore. [26]No human being has ever heard the living God speaking from a fire and still lived, but we have. [27]Moses, you go near and listen to everything the LORD our God says. Then you tell us what the LORD

our God tells you, and we will listen and obey."

[28]The LORD heard what you said to me, and he said to me, "I have heard what the people said to you. Everything they said was good. [29]I wish their hearts would always respect me and that they would always obey my commands so that things would go well for them and their children forever!

[30]"Go and tell the people to return to their tents, [31]but you stay here with me so that I may give you all the commands, rules, and laws that you must teach the people to obey in the land I am giving them as their own."

[32]So be careful to do what the LORD your God has commanded you, and follow the commands exactly. [33]Live the way the LORD your God has commanded you so that you may live and have what is good and have a long life in the land you will take.

The Command to Love God

6 These are the commands, rules, and laws that the LORD your God told me to teach you to obey in the land you are crossing the Jordan River to take. [2]You, your children, and your grandchildren must respect the LORD your God as long as you live. Obey all his rules and commands I give you so that you will live a long time. [3]Listen, Israel, and carefully obey these laws. Then all will go well for you, and you will become a great nation in a fertile land, just as the LORD, the God of your ancestors, has promised you.

[4]Listen, people of Israel! The LORD our God is the only LORD. [5]Love the LORD your God with all your heart, all your soul, and all your strength. [6]Always remember these commands I give you today. [7]Teach them to your children, and talk about them when you sit at home and walk along the road, when you lie down and when you get up. [8]Write them down and tie them to your hands as a sign. Tie them on your forehead to remind you, [9]and write them on your doors and gates.

[10]The LORD your God will bring you into the land he promised to your ancestors, to Abraham, Isaac, and Jacob, and he will give it to you. The land has large, growing cities you

did not build, [11]houses full of good things you did not buy, wells you did not dig, and vineyards and olive trees you did not plant. You will eat as much as you want. [12]But be careful! Do not forget the LORD, who brought you out of the land of Egypt where you were slaves.

[13]Respect the LORD your God. You must worship him and make your promises only in his name. [14]Do not worship other gods as the people around you do, [15]because the LORD your God is a jealous God. He is present with you, and if you worship other gods, he will become angry with you and destroy you from the earth. [16]Do not test the LORD your God as you did at Massah. [17]Be sure to obey the commands of the LORD your God and the rules and laws he has given you. [18]Do what the LORD says is good and right so that things will go well for you. Then you may go in and take the good land the LORD promised to your ancestors. [19]He will force all your enemies out as you go in, as the LORD has said.

[20]In the future when your children ask you, "What is the meaning of the laws, commands, and rules the LORD our God gave us?" [21]tell them, "We were slaves to the king of Egypt, but the LORD brought us out of Egypt by his great power. [22]The LORD showed us great and terrible signs and miracles, which he did to Egypt, the king, and his whole family. [23]The LORD brought us out of Egypt to lead us here and to give us the land he promised our ancestors. [24]The LORD ordered us to obey all these commands and to respect the LORD our God so that we will always do well and stay alive, as we are today. [25]The right thing for us to do is this: Obey all these rules in the presence of the LORD our God, as he has commanded."

PSALM 37:1-6

God Will Reward Fairly

Of David.

37 Don't be upset because of evil people.
  Don't be jealous of those who do wrong,
[2]because like the grass, they will soon dry up.
  Like green plants, they will soon die away.

[3]Trust the LORD and do good.
  Live in the land and feed on truth.
[4]Enjoy serving the LORD,
  and he will give you what you want.
[5]Depend on the LORD;
  trust him, and he will take care of you.
[6]Then your goodness will shine like the sun,
  and your fairness like the noonday sun.

PROVERBS 12:8

[8]The wisdom of the wise wins praise,
  but there is no respect for the stupid.

LUKE 1:26-38

An Angel Appears to Mary

[26]During Elizabeth's sixth month of pregnancy, God sent the angel Gabriel to Nazareth, a town in Galilee, [27]to a virgin. She was engaged to marry a man named Joseph from the family of David. Her name was Mary. [28]The angel came to her and said, "Greetings! The Lord has blessed you and is with you."

[29]But Mary was very startled by what the angel said and wondered what this greeting might mean.

[30]The angel said to her, "Don't be afraid, Mary; God has shown you his grace. [31]Listen! You will become pregnant and give birth to a son, and you will name him Jesus. [32]He will be great and will be called the Son of the Most High. The Lord God will give him the throne of King David, his ancestor. [33]He will rule over the people of Jacob forever, and his kingdom will never end."

[34]Mary said to the angel, "How will this happen since I am a virgin?"

[35]The angel said to Mary, "The Holy Spirit will come upon you, and the power of the Most High will cover you. For this reason the baby will be holy and will be called the Son of God. [36]Now Elizabeth, your relative, is also pregnant with a son though she is very old. Everyone thought she could not have a baby, but she has been pregnant for six months. [37]God can do anything!"

[38]Mary said, "I am the servant of the Lord. Let this happen to me as you say!" Then the angel went away.

MARCH 23

DEUTERONOMY 7:1—8:20

You Are God's People

7 The LORD your God will bring you into the land that you are entering and that you will have as your own. As you go in, he will force out these nations: the Hittites, Girgashites, Amorites, Canaanites, Perizzites, Hivites, and Jebusites—seven nations that are stronger than you. ²The LORD your God will hand these nations over to you, and when you defeat them, you must destroy them completely. Do not make a peace treaty with them or show them any mercy. ³Do not marry any of them, or let your daughters marry their sons, or let your sons marry their daughters. ⁴If you do, those people will turn your children away from me, to begin serving other gods. Then the LORD will be very angry with you, and he will quickly destroy you. ⁵This is what you must do to those people: Tear down their altars, smash their holy stone pillars, cut down their Asherah idols, and burn their idols in the fire. ⁶You are holy people who belong to the LORD your God. He has chosen you from all the people on earth to be his very own.

⁷The LORD did not care for you and choose you because there were many of you—you are the smallest nation of all. ⁸But the LORD chose you because he loved you, and he kept his promise to your ancestors. So he brought you out of Egypt by his great power and freed you from the land of slavery, from the power of the king of Egypt. ⁹So know that the LORD your God is God, the faithful God. He will keep his agreement of love for a thousand lifetimes for people who love him and obey his commands. ¹⁰But he will pay back those people who hate him. He will destroy them, and he will not be slow to pay back those who hate him. ¹¹So be careful to obey the commands, rules, and laws I give you today.

¹²If you pay attention to these laws and obey them carefully, the LORD your God will keep his agreement and show his love to you, as he promised your ancestors. ¹³He will love

and bless you. He will make the number of your people grow; he will bless you with children. He will bless your fields with good crops and will give you grain, new wine, and oil. He will bless your herds with calves and your flocks with lambs in the land he promised your ancestors he would give you. ¹⁴You will be blessed more than any other people. Every husband and wife will have children, and all your cattle will have calves. ¹⁵The LORD will take away all disease from you; you will not have the terrible diseases that were in Egypt, but he will give them to all the people who hate you. ¹⁶You must destroy all the people the LORD your God hands over to you. Do not feel sorry for them, and do not worship their gods, or they will trap you.

¹⁷You might say to yourselves, "Because these nations are stronger than we are, we can't force them out." ¹⁸But don't be afraid of them. Remember what the LORD your God did to all of Egypt and its king. ¹⁹You saw for yourselves the troubles, signs, and miracles he did, how the LORD's great power and strength brought you out of Egypt. The LORD your God will do the same thing to all the nations you now fear. ²⁰The LORD your God will also send terror among them so that even those who are alive and hiding from you will die. ²¹Don't be afraid of them, because the LORD your God is with you; he is a great God and people are afraid of him. ²²When the LORD your God forces those nations out of the land, he will do it little by little ahead of you. You won't be able to destroy them all at once; otherwise, the wild animals will grow too many in number. ²³But the LORD your God will hand those nations over to you, confusing them until they are destroyed. ²⁴The LORD will help you defeat their kings, and the world will forget who they were. No one will be able to stop you; you will destroy them all. ²⁵Burn up their idols in the fire. Do not wish for the silver and gold they have, and don't take it for yourselves, or you will be trapped by it. The LORD your God hates it. ²⁶Do not bring one of those hateful things into your house, or you will be com-

pletely destroyed along with it. Hate and reject those things; they must be completely destroyed.

Remember the Lord

8 Carefully obey every command I give you today. Then you will live and grow in number, and you will enter and take the land the LORD promised your ancestors. ²Remember how the LORD your God has led you in the desert for these forty years, taking away your pride and testing you, because he wanted to know what was in your heart. He wanted to know if you would obey his commands. ³He took away your pride when he let you get hungry, and then he fed you with manna, which neither you nor your ancestors had ever seen. This was to teach you that a person does not live on bread alone, but by everything the LORD says. ⁴During these forty years, your clothes did not wear out, and your feet did not swell. ⁵Know in your heart that the LORD your God corrects you as a parent corrects a child.

⁶Obey the commands of the LORD your God, living as he has commanded you and respecting him. ⁷The LORD your God is bringing you into a good land, a land with rivers and pools of water, with springs that flow in the valleys and hills, ⁸a land that has wheat and barley, vines, fig trees, pomegranates, olive oil, and honey. ⁹It is a land where you will have plenty of food, where you will have everything you need, where the rocks are iron, and where you can dig copper out of the hills.

¹⁰When you have all you want to eat, then praise the LORD your God for giving you a good land. ¹¹Be careful not to forget the LORD your God so that you fail to obey his commands, laws, and rules that I am giving to you today. ¹²When you eat all you want and build nice houses and live in them, ¹³when your herds and flocks grow large and your silver and gold increase, when you have more of everything, ¹⁴then your heart will become proud. You will forget the LORD your God, who brought you out of the land of Egypt, where you were slaves. ¹⁵He led you through the large and terrible desert that was dry and had no water, and that had poisonous snakes

and stinging insects. He gave you water from a solid rock ¹⁶and manna to eat in the desert. Manna was something your ancestors had never seen. He did this to take away your pride and to test you, so things would go well for you in the end. ¹⁷You might say to yourself, "I am rich because of my own power and strength," ¹⁸but remember the LORD your God! It is he who gives you the power to become rich, keeping the agreement he promised to your ancestors, as it is today.

¹⁹If you ever forget the LORD your God and follow other gods and worship them and bow down to them, I warn you today that you will be destroyed. ²⁰Just as the LORD destroyed the other nations for you, you can be destroyed if you do not obey the LORD your God.

PSALM 37:7–11

⁷Wait and trust the LORD.
　　Don't be upset when others get rich
　　or when someone else's plans succeed.
⁸Don't get angry.
　　Don't be upset; it only leads to trouble.
⁹Evil people will be sent away,
　　but those who trust the LORD will
　　　inherit the land.
¹⁰In a little while the wicked will be no
　　more.
　　You may look for them, but they will be
　　　gone.
¹¹People who are not proud will inherit the
　　land
　　and will enjoy complete peace.

PROVERBS 12:9–10

⁹A person who is not important but has a
　　servant is better off
　　than someone who acts important but
　　has no food.

¹⁰Good people take care of their animals,
　　but even the kindest acts of the wicked
　　are cruel.

LUKE 1:39–56

Mary Visits Elizabeth

³⁹Mary got up and went quickly to a town in the hills of Judea. ⁴⁰She came to Zechariah's

house and greeted Elizabeth. ⁴¹When Elizabeth heard Mary's greeting, the unborn baby inside her jumped, and Elizabeth was filled with the Holy Spirit. ⁴²She cried out in a loud voice, "God has blessed you more than any other woman, and he has blessed the baby to which you will give birth. ⁴³Why has this good thing happened to me, that the mother of my Lord comes to me? ⁴⁴When I heard your voice, the baby inside me jumped with joy. ⁴⁵You are blessed because you believed that what the Lord said to you would really happen."

Mary Praises God

⁴⁶Then Mary said,
"My soul praises the Lord;
⁴⁷ my heart rejoices in God my Savior,
⁴⁸because he has shown his concern for his
    humble servant girl.
From now on, all people will say that I
    am blessed,
⁴⁹ because the Powerful One has done great
    things for me.

His name is holy.
⁵⁰God will show his mercy forever and ever
    to those who worship and serve him.
⁵¹He has done mighty deeds by his
    power.
He has scattered the people who are
    proud
and think great things about
    themselves.
⁵²He has brought down rulers from their
    thrones
and raised up the humble.
⁵³He has filled the hungry with good things
    and sent the rich away with nothing.
⁵⁴He has helped his servant, the people of
    Israel,
    remembering to show them mercy
⁵⁵as he promised to our ancestors,
    to Abraham and to his children
    forever."

⁵⁶Mary stayed with Elizabeth for about three months and then returned home.

MARCH 24

DEUTERONOMY 9:1—10:22

The Lord Will Be with Israel

9 Listen, Israel. You will soon cross the Jordan River to go in and force out nations that are bigger and stronger than you. They have large cities with walls up to the sky. ²The people there are Anakites, who are strong and tall. You know about them, and you have heard it said: "No one can stop the Anakites." ³But today remember that the LORD your God goes in before you to destroy them like a fire that burns things up. He will defeat them ahead of you, and you will force them out and destroy them quickly, just as the LORD has said.

⁴After the LORD your God has forced those nations out ahead of you, don't say to yourself, "The LORD brought me here to take this land because I am so good." No! It is because these nations are evil that the LORD will force them out ahead of you. ⁵You are

going in to take the land, not because you are good and honest, but because these nations are evil. That is why the LORD your God will force them out ahead of you, to keep his promise to your ancestors, to Abraham, Isaac, and Jacob. ⁶The LORD your God is giving you this good land to take as your own. But know this: It is not because you are good; you are a stubborn people.

Remember the Lord's Anger

⁷Remember this and do not forget it: You made the LORD your God angry in the desert. You would not obey the LORD from the day you left Egypt until you arrived here. ⁸At Mount Sinai you made the LORD angry—angry enough to destroy you. ⁹When I went up on the mountain to receive the stone tablets, the tablets with the Agreement the LORD had made with you, I stayed on the mountain for forty days and forty nights; I did not eat bread or drink

water. [10]The LORD gave me two stone tablets, which God had written on with his own finger. On them were all the commands that the LORD gave to you on the mountain out of the fire, on the day you were gathered there.

[11]When the forty days and forty nights were over, the LORD gave me the two stone tablets, the tablets with the Agreement on them. [12]Then the LORD told me, "Get up and go down quickly from here, because the people you brought out from Egypt are ruining themselves. They have quickly turned away from what I commanded and have made an idol for themselves."

[13]The LORD said to me, "I have watched these people, and they are very stubborn! [14]Get away so that I may destroy them and make the whole world forget who they are. Then I will make another nation from you that will be bigger and stronger than they are."

[15]So I turned and came down the mountain that was burning with fire, and the two stone tablets with the Agreement were in my hands. [16]When I looked, I saw you had sinned against the LORD your God and had made an idol in the shape of a calf. You had quickly turned away from what the LORD had told you to do. [17]So I took the two tablets and threw them down, breaking them into pieces right in front of you.

[18]Then I again bowed facedown on the ground before the LORD for forty days and forty nights; I did not eat bread or drink water. You had sinned by doing what the LORD said was evil, and you made him angry. [19]I was afraid of the LORD's anger and rage, because he was angry enough with you to destroy you, but the LORD listened to me again. [20]And the LORD was angry enough with Aaron to destroy him, but then I prayed for Aaron, too. [21]I took that sinful calf idol you had made and burned it in the fire. I crushed it into a powder like dust and threw the dust into a stream that flowed down the mountain.

[22]You also made the LORD angry at Taberah, Massah, and Kibroth Hattaavah. [23]Then the LORD sent you away from Kadesh Barnea and said, "Go up and take the land I have given you." But you rejected the command of the LORD your God. You did not trust him or obey him. [24]You have refused to obey the LORD as long as I have known you.

[25]The LORD had said he would destroy you, so I threw myself down in front of him for those forty days and forty nights. [26]I prayed to the LORD and said, "Lord GOD, do not destroy your people, your own people, whom you freed and brought out of Egypt by your great power and strength. [27]Remember your servants Abraham, Isaac, and Jacob. Don't look at how stubborn these people are, and don't look at their sin and evil. [28]Otherwise, Egypt will say, 'It was because the LORD was not able to take his people into the land he promised them, and it was because he hated them that he took them into the desert to kill them.' [29]But they are your people, LORD, your own people, whom you brought out of Egypt with your great power and strength."

New Stone Tablets

10 At that time the LORD said to me, "Cut two stone tablets like the first ones and come up to me on the mountain. Also make a wooden Ark. [2]I will write on the tablets the same words that were on the first tablets, which you broke, and you will put the new tablets in the Ark."

[3]So I made the Ark out of acacia wood, and I cut out two stone tablets like the first ones. Then I went up on the mountain with the two tablets in my hands. [4]The LORD wrote the same things on these tablets he had written before—the Ten Commandments that he had told you on the mountain from the fire, on the day you were gathered there. And the LORD gave them to me. [5]Then I turned and came down the mountain; I put the tablets in the Ark I had made, as the LORD had commanded, and they are still there.

[6](The people of Israel went from the wells of the Jaakanites to Moserah. Aaron died there and was buried; his son Eleazar became priest in his place. [7]From Moserah

they went to Gudgodah, and from Gudgodah they went to Jotbathah, a place with streams of water. [8]At that time the LORD chose the tribe of Levi to carry the Ark of the Agreement with the LORD. They were to serve the LORD and to bless the people in his name, which they still do today. [9]That is why the Levites did not receive any land of their own; instead, they received the LORD himself as their gift, as the LORD your God told them.)

[10]I stayed on the mountain forty days and forty nights just like the first time, and the LORD listened to me this time also. He did not want to destroy you. [11]The LORD said to me, "Go and lead the people so that they will go in and take the land I promised their ancestors."

What the Lord Wants You to Do

[12]Now, Israel, this is what the LORD your God wants you to do: Respect the LORD your God, and do what he has told you to do. Love him. Serve the LORD your God with your whole being, [13]and obey the LORD's commands and laws that I am giving you today for your own good.

[14]The LORD owns the world and everything in it—the heavens, even the highest heavens, are his. [15]But the LORD cared for and loved your ancestors, and he chose you, their descendants, over all the other nations, just as it is today. [16]Give yourselves completely to serving him, and do not be stubborn any longer. [17]The LORD your God is God of all gods and Lord of all lords. He is the great God, who is strong and wonderful. He does not take sides, and he will not be talked into doing evil. [18]He helps orphans and widows, and he loves foreigners and gives them food and clothes. [19]You also must love foreigners, because you were foreigners in Egypt. [20]Respect the LORD your God and serve him. Be loyal to him and make your promises in his name. [21]He is the one you should praise; he is your God, who has done great and wonderful things for you, which you have seen with your own eyes. [22]There were only seventy of your ancestors when they went down to Egypt, and

now the LORD your God has made you as many as the stars in the sky.

PSALM 37:12–15

[12]The wicked make evil plans against
good people.
They grind their teeth at them in anger.
[13]But the Lord laughs at the wicked,
because he sees that their day is
coming.
[14]The wicked draw their swords
and bend their bows
to kill the poor and helpless,
to kill those who are honest.
[15]But their swords will stab their own
hearts,
and their bows will break.

PROVERBS 12:11

[11]Those who work their land will have
plenty of food,
but the one who chases empty dreams
is not wise.

LUKE 1:57–80

The Birth of John

[57]When it was time for Elizabeth to give birth, she had a boy. [58]Her neighbors and relatives heard how good the Lord was to her, and they rejoiced with her.

[59]When the baby was eight days old, they came to circumcise him. They wanted to name him Zechariah because this was his father's name, [60]but his mother said, "No! He will be named John."

[61]The people said to Elizabeth, "But no one in your family has this name." [62]Then they made signs to his father to find out what he would like to name him.

[63]Zechariah asked for a writing tablet and wrote, "His name is John," and everyone was surprised. [64]Immediately Zechariah could talk again, and he began praising God. [65]All their neighbors became alarmed, and in all the mountains of Judea people continued talking about all these things. [66]The people who heard about them wondered, saying, "What will this child be?" because the Lord was with him.

Zechariah Praises God

⁶⁷Then Zechariah, John's father, was filled with the Holy Spirit and prophesied:
⁶⁸"Let us praise the Lord, the God of Israel,
because he has come to help his people
and has given them freedom.
⁶⁹He has given us a powerful Savior
from the family of God's servant David.
⁷⁰He said that he would do this
through his holy prophets who lived long ago:
⁷¹He promised he would save us from our enemies
and from the power of all those who hate us.
⁷²He said he would give mercy to our ancestors
and that he would remember his holy promise.
⁷³God promised Abraham, our father,
⁷⁴   that he would save us from the power of our enemies

so we could serve him without fear,
⁷⁵being holy and good before God as long as we live.

⁷⁶"Now you, child, will be called a prophet
of the Most High God.
You will go before the Lord to prepare his way.
⁷⁷You will make his people know that they will be saved
by having their sins forgiven.
⁷⁸With the loving mercy of our God,
a new day from heaven will dawn upon us.
⁷⁹It will shine on those who live in darkness,
in the shadow of death.
It will guide us into the path of peace."

⁸⁰And so the child grew up and became strong in spirit. John lived in the desert until the time when he came out to preach to Israel.

MARCH 25

DEUTERONOMY 11:1—12:32

Great Things Israel Saw

11 Love the LORD your God and always obey his orders, rules, laws, and commands. ²Remember today it was not your children who saw and felt the correction of the LORD your God. They did not see his majesty, his power, his strength, ³or his signs and the things he did in Egypt to the king and his whole country. ⁴They did not see what he did to the Egyptian army, its horses and chariots, when he drowned them in the Red Sea as they were chasing you. The LORD ruined them forever. ⁵They did not see what he did for you in the desert until you arrived here. ⁶They did not see what he did to Dathan and Abiram, the sons of Eliab the Reubenite, when the ground opened up and swallowed them, their families, their tents, and everyone who stood with them in Israel. ⁷It was you who saw all these great things the LORD has done.

⁸So obey all the commands I am giving you today so that you will be strong and can go in and take the land you are going to take as your own. ⁹Then you will live a long time in the land that the LORD promised to give to your ancestors and their descendants, a fertile land. ¹⁰The land you are going to take is not like Egypt, where you were. There you had to plant your seed and water it, like a vegetable garden, by using your feet. ¹¹But the land that you will soon cross the Jordan River to take is a land of hills and valleys, a land that drinks rain from heaven. ¹²It is a land the LORD your God cares for. His eyes are on it continually, and he watches it from the beginning of the year to the end.

¹³If you carefully obey the commands I am giving you today and love the LORD your

God and serve him with your whole being, [14]then he will send rain on your land at the right time, in the fall and spring, and you will be able to gather your grain, new wine, and oil. [15]He will put grass in the fields for your cattle, and you will have plenty to eat.

[16]Be careful, or you will be fooled and will turn away to serve and worship other gods. [17]If you do, the LORD will become angry with you and will shut the heavens so it will not rain. Then the land will not grow crops, and you will soon die in the good land the LORD is giving you. [18]Remember my words with your whole being. Write them down and tie them to your hands as a sign; tie them on your foreheads to remind you. [19]Teach them well to your children, talking about them when you sit at home and walk along the road, when you lie down and when you get up. [20]Write them on your doors and gates [21]so that both you and your children will live a long time in the land the LORD promised your ancestors, as long as the skies are above the earth.

[22]If you are careful to obey every command I am giving you to follow, and love the LORD your God, and do what he has told you to do, and are loyal to him, [23]then the LORD will force all those nations out of the land ahead of you, and you will take the land from nations that are bigger and stronger than you. [24]Everywhere you step will be yours. Your land will go from the desert to Lebanon and from the Euphrates River to the Mediterranean Sea. [25]No one will be able to stop you. The LORD your God will do what he promised and will make the people afraid everywhere you go.

[26]See, today I am letting you choose a blessing or a curse. [27]You will be blessed if you obey the commands of the LORD your God that I am giving you today. [28]But you will be cursed if you disobey the commands of the LORD your God. So do not disobey the commands I am giving you today, and do not worship other gods you do not know. [29]When the LORD your God brings you into the land you will take as your own, you are to announce the blessings from Mount Gerizim and the curses from Mount Ebal. [30](These mountains are on the other side of the Jordan River, to the west, toward the sunset. They are near the great trees of Moreh in the land of the Canaanites who live in the Jordan Valley opposite Gilgal.) [31]You will soon cross the Jordan River to enter and take the land the LORD your God is giving you. When you take it over and live there, [32]be careful to obey all the commands and laws I am giving you today.

The Place for Worship

12 These are the commands and laws you must carefully obey in the land the LORD, the God of your ancestors, is giving you. Obey them as long as you live in the land. [2]When you inherit the lands of these nations, you must completely destroy all the places where they serve their gods, on high mountains and hills and under every green tree. [3]Tear down their altars, smash their holy stone pillars, and burn their Asherah idols in the fire. Cut down their idols and destroy their names from those places.

[4]Don't worship the LORD your God that way, [5]but look for the place the LORD your God will choose—a place among your tribes where he is to be worshiped. Go there, [6]and bring to that place your burnt offerings and sacrifices; bring a tenth of what you gain and your special gifts; bring what you have promised and the special gifts you want to give the LORD, and bring the first animals born to your herds and flocks.

[7]There you will be together with the LORD your God. There you and your families will eat, and you will enjoy all the good things for which you have worked, because the LORD your God has blessed you.

[8]Do not worship the way we have been doing today, each person doing what he thinks is right. [9]You have not yet come to a resting place, to the land the LORD your God will give you as your own. [10]But soon you will cross the Jordan River to live in the land the LORD your God is giving you as your own, where he will give you rest from all your enemies and you will live in safety.

[11]Then the LORD your God will choose a place where he is to be worshiped. To that place you must bring everything I tell you: your burnt offerings and sacrifices, your offerings of a tenth of what you gain, your special gifts, and all your best things you promised to the LORD. [12]There rejoice before the LORD your God. Everyone should rejoice: you, your sons and daughters, your male and female servants, and the Levites from your towns who have no land of their own. [13]Be careful that you don't sacrifice your burnt offerings just anywhere you please. [14]Offer them only in the place the LORD will choose. He will choose a place in one of your tribes, and there you must do everything I am commanding you.

[15]But you may kill your animals in any of your towns and eat as much of the meat as you want, as if it were a deer or a gazelle; this is the blessing the LORD your God is giving you. Anyone, clean or unclean, may eat this meat, [16]but do not eat the blood. Pour it out on the ground like water. [17]Do not eat in your own towns what belongs to the LORD: one-tenth of your grain, new wine, or oil; the first animals born to your herds or flocks; whatever you have promised to give; the special gifts you want to give to the LORD, or any other gifts. [18]Eat these things when you are together with the LORD your God, in the place the LORD your God chooses to be worshiped. Everyone must do this: you, your sons and daughters, your male and female servants, and the Levites from your towns. Rejoice in the LORD your God's presence about the things you have worked for. [19]Be careful not to forget the Levites as long as you live in the land.

[20]When the LORD your God enlarges your country as he has promised, and you want some meat so you say, "I want some meat," you may eat as much meat as you want. [21]If the LORD your God chooses a place where he is to be worshiped that is too far away from you, you may kill animals from your herds and flocks, which the LORD has given to you. I have commanded that you may do this. You may eat as much of them as you want in your own towns, [22]as you would eat gazelle or deer meat. Both clean and unclean people may eat this meat, [23]but be sure you don't eat the blood, because the life is in the blood. Don't eat the life with the meat. [24]Don't eat the blood, but pour it out on the ground like water. [25]If you don't eat it, things will go well for you and your children, because you will be doing what the LORD says is right.

[26]Take your holy things and the things you have promised to give, and go to the place the LORD will choose. [27]Present your burnt offerings on the altar of the LORD your God, both the meat and the blood. The blood of your sacrifices should be poured beside the altar of the LORD your God, but you may eat the meat. [28]Be careful to obey all the rules I am giving you so that things will always go well for you and your children, and you will be doing what the LORD your God says is good and right.

[29]You will enter the land and take it away from the nations that the LORD your God will destroy ahead of you. When you force them out and live in their land, [30]they will be destroyed for you, but be careful not to be trapped by asking about their gods. Don't say, "How do these nations worship? I will do the same." [31]Don't worship the LORD your God that way, because the LORD hates the evil ways they worship their gods. They even burn their sons and daughters as sacrifices to their gods!

[32]Be sure to do everything I have commanded you. Do not add anything to it, and do not take anything away from it.

PSALM 37:16–22

[16]It is better to have little and be right
    than to have much and be wrong.
[17]The power of the wicked will be broken,
    but the LORD supports those who do
        right.
[18]The LORD watches over the lives of the
        innocent,
    and their reward will last forever.
[19]They will not be ashamed when trouble
        comes.

They will be full in times of hunger.
20But the wicked will die.
The LORD's enemies will be like the
flowers of the fields;
they will disappear like smoke.
21The wicked borrow and don't pay back,
but those who do right give freely to
others.
22Those whom the LORD blesses will
inherit the land,
but those he curses will be sent away.

PROVERBS 12:12–14

12The wicked want what other evil people
have stolen,
but good people want to give what
they have to others.

13Evil people are trapped by their evil talk,
but good people stay out of trouble.

14People will be rewarded for what they
say,
and they will also be rewarded for
what they do.

LUKE 2:1–24

The Birth of Jesus

2 At that time, Augustus Caesar sent an order that all people in the countries under
Roman rule must list their names in a register. 2This was the first registration;[n] it was
taken while Quirinius was governor of
Syria. 3And all went to their own towns to
be registered.
4So Joseph left Nazareth, a town in Galilee, and went to the town of Bethlehem in
Judea, known as the town of David. Joseph
went there because he was from the family
of David. 5Joseph registered with Mary, to
whom he was engaged[n] and who was now
pregnant. 6While they were in Bethlehem,
the time came for Mary to have the baby,
7and she gave birth to her first son. Because
there were no rooms left in the inn, she
wrapped the baby with pieces of cloth and
laid him in a feeding trough.

Shepherds Hear About Jesus

8That night, some shepherds were in the
fields nearby watching their sheep. 9Then
an angel of the Lord stood before them. The
glory of the Lord was shining around them,
and they became very frightened. 10The angel said to them, "Do not be afraid. I am
bringing you good news that will be a great
joy to all the people. 11Today your Savior
was born in the town of David. He is Christ,
the Lord. 12This is how you will know him:
You will find a baby wrapped in pieces of
cloth and lying in a feeding box."
13Then a very large group of angels from
heaven joined the first angel, praising God
and saying:
14"Give glory to God in heaven,
and on earth let there be peace among
the people who please God."[n]
15When the angels left them and went
back to heaven, the shepherds said to each
other, "Let's go to Bethlehem. Let's see this
thing that has happened which the Lord
has told us about."
16So the shepherds went quickly and
found Mary and Joseph and the baby, who
was lying in a feeding trough. 17When they
had seen him, they told what the angels had
said about this child. 18Everyone was
amazed at what the shepherds said to them.
19But Mary treasured these things and continued to think about them. 20Then the
shepherds went back to their sheep, praising God and thanking him for everything
they had seen and heard. It had been just as
the angel had told them.
21When the baby was eight days old, he
was circumcised and was named Jesus, the
name given by the angel before the baby began to grow inside Mary.

Jesus Is Presented in the Temple

22When the time came for Mary and
Joseph to do what the law of Moses taught
about being made pure,[n] they took Jesus
to Jerusalem to present him to the Lord.

2:2 registration Census. A counting of all the people and the things they own.   **2:5 engaged** For the Jewish people, an engagement was a lasting agreement. It could only be broken by divorce.   **2:14 and . . . God** Some Greek copies read "and on
earth let there be peace and goodwill among people."   **2:22 pure** The Law of Moses said that forty days after a Jewish
woman gave birth to a son, she must be cleansed by a ceremony at the Temple. Read Leviticus 12:2–8.

²³(It is written in the law of the Lord: "Every firstborn male shall be given to the Lord.")ⁿ ²⁴Mary and Joseph also went to offer a sacrifice, as the law of the Lord says: "You must sacrifice two doves or two young pigeons."ⁿ

MARCH 26

DEUTERONOMY 13:1—14:29

False Prophets

13 Prophets or those who tell the future with dreams might come to you and say they will show you a miracle or a sign. ²The miracle or sign might even happen, and then they might say, "Let's serve other gods" (gods you have not known) "and let's worship them." ³But you must not listen to those prophets or dreamers. The LORD your God is testing you, to find out if you love him with your whole being. ⁴Serve only the LORD your God. Respect him, keep his commands, and obey him. Serve him and be loyal to him. ⁵The prophets or dreamers must be killed, because they said you should turn against the LORD your God, who brought you out of Egypt and saved you from the land where you were slaves. They tried to turn you from doing what the LORD your God commanded you to do. You must get rid of the evil among you.

⁶Someone might try to lead you to serve other gods—it might be your brother, your son or daughter, the wife you love, or a close friend. The person might say, "Let's go and worship other gods." (These are gods that neither you nor your ancestors have known, ⁷gods of the people who live around you, either nearby or far away, from one end of the land to the other.) ⁸Do not give in to such people. Do not listen or feel sorry for them, and do not let them go free or protect them. ⁹You must put them to death. You must be the first one to start to kill them, and then everyone else must join in. ¹⁰You must throw stones at them until they die, because they tried to turn you away from the LORD your God, who brought you out of the land of Egypt, where you were slaves. ¹¹Then every-one in Israel will hear about this and be afraid, and no one among you will ever do such an evil thing again.

Cities to Destroy

¹²The LORD your God is giving you cities in which to live, and you might hear something about one of them. Someone might say ¹³that evil people have moved in among you. And they might lead the people of that city away from God, saying, "Let's go and worship other gods." (These are gods you have not known.) ¹⁴Then you must ask about it, looking into the matter and checking carefully whether it is true. If it is proved that a hateful thing has happened among you, ¹⁵you must kill with a sword everyone who lives in that city. Destroy the city completely and kill everyone in it, as well as the animals, with a sword. ¹⁶Gather up everything those people owned, and put it in the middle of the city square. Then completely burn the city and everything they owned as a burnt offering to the LORD your God. That city should never be rebuilt; let it be ruined forever. ¹⁷Don't keep for yourselves any of the things found in that city, so the LORD will not be angry anymore. He will give you mercy and feel sorry for you, and he will make your nation grow larger, as he promised to your ancestors. ¹⁸You will have obeyed the LORD your God by keeping all his commands that I am giving to you today, and you will be doing what the LORD says is right.

God's Special People

14 You are the children of the LORD your God. When someone dies, do not cut yourselves or shave your heads to show your sadness. ²You are holy people, who belong to the LORD your God. He has chosen you from all the people on earth to be his very own.

2:23 "Every . . . Lord." Quotation from Exodus 13:2. **2:24 "You . . . pigeons."** Quotation from Leviticus 12:8.

[3]Do not eat anything the LORD hates. [4]These are the animals you may eat: oxen, sheep, goats, [5]deer, gazelle, roe deer, wild goats, ibex, antelope, and mountain sheep. [6]You may eat any animal that has a split hoof and chews the cud, [7]but you may not eat camels, rabbits, or rock badgers. These animals chew the cud, but they do not have split hoofs, so they are unclean for you. [8]Pigs are also unclean for you; they have split hoofs, but they do not chew the cud. Do not eat their meat or touch their dead bodies.

[9]There are many things that live in the water. You may eat anything that has fins and scales, [10]but do not eat anything that does not have fins and scales. It is unclean for you.

[11]You may eat any clean bird. [12]But do not eat these birds: eagles, vultures, black vultures, [13]red kites, falcons, any kind of kite, [14]any kind of raven, [15]horned owls, screech owls, sea gulls, any kind of hawk, [16]little owls, great owls, white owls, [17]desert owls, ospreys, cormorants, [18]storks, any kind of heron, the hoopoes, or bats.

[19]All insects with wings are unclean for you; do not eat them. [20]Other things with wings are clean, and you may eat them.

[21]Do not eat anything you find that is already dead. You may give it to a foreigner living in your town, and he may eat it, or you may sell it to a foreigner. But you are holy people, who belong to the LORD your God.

Do not cook a baby goat in its mother's milk.

Giving One-Tenth

[22]Be sure to save one-tenth of all your crops each year. [23]Take it to the place the LORD your God will choose where he is to be worshiped. There, where you will be together with the LORD, eat the tenth of your grain, new wine, and oil, and eat the animals born first to your herds and flocks. Do this so that you will learn to respect the LORD your God always. [24]But if the place the LORD will choose to be worshiped is too far away and he has blessed you so much you cannot carry a tenth, [25]exchange your one-tenth for silver. Then take the silver with you to the place the LORD your God shall choose. [26]Use the silver to buy anything you

wish—cattle, sheep, wine, beer, or anything you wish. Then you and your family will eat and celebrate there before the LORD your God. [27]Do not forget the Levites in your town, because they have no land of their own among you.

[28]At the end of every third year, everyone should bring one-tenth of that year's crop and store it in your towns. [29]This is for the Levites so they may eat and be full. (They have no land of their own among you.) It is also for strangers, orphans, and widows who live in your towns so that all of them may eat and be full. Then the LORD your God will bless you and all the work you do.

PSALM 37:23–29

[23]When people's steps follow the LORD,
    God is pleased with their ways.
[24]If they stumble, they will not fall,
    because the LORD holds their hand.

[25]I was young, and now I am old,
    but I have never seen good people left
      helpless
    or their children begging for food.
[26]Good people always lend freely to others,
    and their children are a blessing.

[27]Stop doing evil and do good,
    so you will live forever.
[28]The LORD loves justice
    and will not leave those who worship
      him.
He will always protect them,
    but the children of the wicked will die.
[29]Good people will inherit the land
    and will live in it forever.

PROVERBS 12:15–16

[15]Fools think they are doing right,
    but the wise listen to advice.

[16]Fools quickly show that they are upset,
    but the wise ignore insults.

LUKE 2:25–52

Simeon Sees Jesus

[25]In Jerusalem lived a man named Simeon who was a good man and godly. He was wait-

ing for the time when God would take away Israel's sorrow, and the Holy Spirit was in him. [26]Simeon had been told by the Holy Spirit that he would not die before he saw the Christ promised by the Lord. [27]The Spirit led Simeon to the Temple. When Mary and Joseph brought the baby Jesus to the Temple to do what the law said they must do, [28]Simeon took the baby in his arms and thanked God:

[29]"Now, Lord, you can let me, your servant,
  die in peace as you said.
[30]With my own eyes I have seen your
  salvation,
[31] which you prepared before all people.
[32]It is a light for the non-Jewish people to
  see
  and an honor for your people, the
  Israelites."

[33]Jesus' father and mother were amazed at what Simeon had said about him. [34]Then Simeon blessed them and said to Mary, "God has chosen this child to cause the fall and rise of many in Israel. He will be a sign from God that many people will not accept [35]so that the thoughts of many will be made known. And the things that will happen will make your heart sad, too."

Anna Sees Jesus

[36]There was a prophetess, Anna, from the family of Phanuel in the tribe of Asher. Anna was very old. She had once been married for seven years. [37]Then her husband died, and she was a widow for eighty-four years. Anna never left the Temple but worshiped God, going without food and praying day and night. [38]Standing there at that time, she thanked God and spoke about Jesus to all who were waiting for God to free Jerusalem.

Joseph and Mary Return Home

[39]When Joseph and Mary had done everything the law of the Lord commanded, they went home to Nazareth, their own town in Galilee. [40]The little child grew and became strong. He was filled with wisdom, and God's goodness was upon him.

Jesus As a Boy

[41]Every year Jesus' parents went to Jerusalem for the Passover Feast. [42]When he was twelve years old, they went to the feast as they always did. [43]After the feast days were over, they started home. The boy Jesus stayed behind in Jerusalem, but his parents did not know it. [44]Thinking that Jesus was with them in the group, they traveled for a whole day. Then they began to look for him among their family and friends. [45]When they did not find him, they went back to Jerusalem to look for him there. [46]After three days they found Jesus sitting in the Temple with the teachers, listening to them and asking them questions. [47]All who heard him were amazed at his understanding and answers. [48]When Jesus' parents saw him, they were astonished. His mother said to him, "Son, why did you do this to us? Your father and I were very worried about you and have been looking for you."

[49]Jesus said to them, "Why were you looking for me? Didn't you know that I must be in my Father's house?" [50]But they did not understand the meaning of what he said.

[51]Jesus went with them to Nazareth and was obedient to them. But his mother kept in her mind all that had happened. [52]Jesus became wiser and grew physically. People liked him, and he pleased God.

MARCH 27

DEUTERONOMY 15:1—17:7

The Special Seventh Year

15 At the end of every seven years, you must tell those who owe you anything that they do not have to pay you back. [2]This is how you must do it: Everyone who has loaned money must cancel the loan and not make a neighbor or relative pay it back. This is the LORD's time for canceling what

people owe. ³You may make a foreigner pay what is owed to you, but you must not collect what another Israelite owes you. ⁴But there should be no poor people among you, because the LORD your God will richly bless you in the land he is giving you as your own. ⁵He will bless you if you obey the LORD your God completely, but you must be careful to obey all the commands I am giving you today. ⁶The LORD your God will bless you as he promised, and you will lend to other nations, but you will not need to borrow from them. You will rule over many nations, but none will rule over you.

⁷If there are poor among you, in one of the towns of the land the LORD your God is giving you, do not be selfish or greedy toward them. ⁸But give freely to them, and freely lend them whatever they need. ⁹Beware of evil thoughts. Don't think, "The seventh year is near, the year to cancel what people owe." You might be mean to the needy and not give them anything. Then they will complain to the LORD about you, and he will find you guilty of sin. ¹⁰Give freely to the poor person, and do not wish that you didn't have to give. The LORD your God will bless your work and everything you touch. ¹¹There will always be poor people in the land, so I command you to give freely to your neighbors and to the poor and needy in your land.

Letting Slaves Go Free

¹²If one of your own people sells himself to you as a slave, whether it is a Hebrew man or woman, that person will serve you for six years. But in the seventh year you must let the slave go free. ¹³When you let slaves go, don't send them away without anything. ¹⁴Give them some of your flock, your grain, and your wine, giving to them as the LORD has given to you. ¹⁵Remember that you were slaves in Egypt, and the LORD your God saved you. That is why I am commanding this to you today.

¹⁶But if your slave says to you, "I don't want to leave you," because he loves you and your family and has a good life with you,

¹⁷stick an awl[n] through his ear into the door; he will be your slave for life. Also do this to a female slave.

¹⁸Do not think of it as a hard thing when you let your slaves go free. After all, they served you six years and did twice the work of a hired person. The LORD your God will bless you in everything you do.

Rules About Firstborn Animals

¹⁹Save all the first male animals born to your herds and flocks. They are for the LORD your God. Do not work the first calf born to your oxen, and do not cut off the wool from the first lamb born to your sheep. ²⁰Each year you and your family are to eat these animals in the presence of the LORD your God, in the place he will choose to be worshiped. ²¹If an animal is crippled or blind or has something else wrong, do not sacrifice it to the LORD your God. ²²But you may eat that animal in your own town. Both clean and unclean people may eat it, as they would eat a gazelle or a deer. ²³But don't eat its blood; pour it out on the ground like water.

The Passover

16Celebrate the Passover of the LORD your God during the month of Abib, because it was during Abib that he brought you out of Egypt at night. ²As the sacrifice for the Passover to the LORD your God, offer an animal from your flock or herd at the place the LORD will choose to be worshiped. ³Do not eat it with bread made with yeast. But for seven days eat bread made without yeast, the bread of suffering, because you left Egypt in a hurry. So all your life you will remember the time you left Egypt. ⁴There must be no yeast anywhere in your land for seven days. Offer the sacrifice on the evening of the first day, and eat all the meat before morning; do not leave it overnight.

⁵Do not offer the Passover sacrifice in just any town the LORD your God gives you, ⁶but offer it in the place he will choose to be worshiped. Offer it in the evening as the sun goes down, which is when you left Egypt. ⁷Roast the meat and eat it at the place the

15:17 awl A tool like a big needle with a handle at one end.

LORD your God will choose. The next morning go back to your tents. [8]Eat bread made without yeast for six days. On the seventh day have a special meeting for the LORD your God, and do not work that day.

The Feast of Weeks

[9]Count seven weeks from the time you begin to harvest the grain, [10]and then celebrate the Feast of Weeks for the LORD your God. Bring an offering as a special gift to him, giving to him just as he has blessed you. [11]Rejoice before the LORD your God at the place he will choose to be worshiped. Everybody should rejoice: you, your sons and daughters, your male and female servants, the Levites in your town, the strangers, orphans, and widows living among you. [12]Remember that you were slaves in Egypt, and carefully obey all these laws.

The Feast of Shelters

[13]Celebrate the Feast of Shelters for seven days, after you have gathered your harvest from the threshing floor and winepress. [14]Everybody should rejoice at your Feast: you, your sons and daughters, your male and female servants, the Levites, strangers, orphans, and widows who live in your towns. [15]Celebrate the Feast to the LORD your God for seven days at the place he will choose, because the LORD your God will bless all your harvest and all the work you do, and you will be completely happy.

[16]All your men must come before the LORD three times a year to the place he will choose. They must come at these times: the Feast of Unleavened Bread, the Feast of Weeks, and the Feast of Shelters. No man should come before the LORD without a gift. [17]Each of you must bring a gift that will show how much the LORD your God has blessed you.

Judges for the People

[18]Appoint judges and officers for your tribes in every town the LORD your God is giving you; they must judge the people fairly. [19]Do not judge unfairly or take sides. Do not let people pay you to make wrong decisions, because that kind of payment

makes wise people seem blind, and it changes the words of good people. [20]Always do what is right so that you will live and always have the land the LORD your God is giving you.

God Hates Idols

[21]Do not set up a wooden Asherah idol next to the altar you build for the LORD your God, [22]and do not set up holy stone pillars. The LORD your God hates them.

17If an ox or sheep has something wrong with it, do not offer it as a sacrifice to the LORD your God. He would hate that.

[2]A man or woman in one of the towns the LORD gave you might be found doing something evil and breaking the Agreement. [3]That person may have served other gods and bowed down to them or to the sun or moon or stars of the sky, which I have commanded should not be done. [4]If someone has told you about it, you must look into the matter carefully. If it is true that such a hateful thing has happened in Israel, [5]take the man or woman who has done the evil thing to the city gates and throw stones at that person until he dies. [6]There must be two or three witnesses that it is true before the person is put to death; if there is only one witness, the person should not be put to death. [7]The witnesses must be the first to throw stones at the person, and then everyone else will follow. You must get rid of the evil among you.

PSALM 37:30–36

[30]Good people speak with wisdom,
and they say what is fair.
[31]The teachings of their God are in their
heart,
so they do not fail to keep them.
[32]The wicked watch for good people
so that they may kill them.
[33]But the LORD will not take away his
protection
or let good people be judged guilty.

[34]Wait for the LORD's help
and follow him.

He will honor you and give you the land,
and you will see the wicked sent away.

[35]I saw a wicked and cruel man
who looked strong like a healthy tree
in good soil.
[36]But he died and was gone;
I looked for him, but he couldn't be
found.

PROVERBS 12:17–19

[17]An honest witness tells the truth,
but a dishonest witness tells lies.

[18]Careless words stab like a sword,
but wise words bring healing.

[19]Truth will continue forever,
but lies are only for a moment.

LUKE 3:1–38

The Preaching of John

3 It was the fifteenth year of the rule of
Tiberius Caesar. These men were under
Caesar: Pontius Pilate, the ruler of Judea;
Herod, the ruler of Galilee; Philip, Herod's
brother, the ruler of Iturea and Traconitis;
and Lysanias, the ruler of Abilene. [2]Annas
and Caiaphas were the high priests. At this
time, the word of God came to John son of
Zechariah in the desert. [3]He went all over
the area around the Jordan River preaching
a baptism of changed hearts and lives for
the forgiveness of sins. [4]As it is written in
the book of Isaiah the prophet:
"This is a voice of one
who calls out in the desert:
'Prepare the way for the Lord.
Make the road straight for him.
[5]Every valley should be filled in,
and every mountain and hill should be
made flat.
Roads with turns should be made
straight,
and rough roads should be made
smooth.
[6]And all people will know about the
salvation of God!'"   *Isaiah 40:3–5*

[7]To the crowds of people who came to be
baptized by John, he said, "You are all
snakes! Who warned you to run away from
God's coming punishment? [8]Do the things
that show you really have changed your
hearts and lives. Don't begin to say to yourselves, 'Abraham is our father.' I tell you that
God could make children for Abraham
from these rocks. [9]The ax is now ready to
cut down the trees, and every tree that does
not produce good fruit will be cut down
and thrown into the fire."[n]
[10]The people asked John, "Then what
should we do?"
[11]John answered, "If you have two shirts,
share with the person who does not have
one. If you have food, share that also."
[12]Even tax collectors came to John to be
baptized. They said to him, "Teacher, what
should we do?"
[13]John said to them, "Don't take more
taxes from people than you have been ordered to take."
[14]The soldiers asked John, "What about
us? What should we do?"
John said to them, "Don't force people to
give you money, and don't lie about them.
Be satisfied with the pay you get."
[15]Since the people were hoping for the
Christ to come, they wondered if John
might be the one.
[16]John answered everyone, "I baptize you
with water, but there is one coming who is
greater than I am. I am not good enough to
untie his sandals. He will baptize you with
the Holy Spirit and fire. [17]He will come
ready to clean the grain, separating the
good grain from the chaff. He will put the
good part of the grain into his barn, but he
will burn the chaff with a fire that cannot
be put out."[n] [18]And John continued to
preach the Good News, saying many other
things to encourage the people.
[19]But John spoke against Herod, the governor, because of his sin with Herodias, the
wife of Herod's brother, and because of the
many other evil things Herod did. [20]So

3:9 The ax . . . fire. This means that God is ready to punish his people who do not obey him.   **3:17 He will . . . out.** This
means that Jesus will come to separate good people from bad people, saving the good and punishing the bad.

Herod did something even worse: He put John in prison.

Jesus Is Baptized by John

[21]When all the people were being baptized by John, Jesus also was baptized. While Jesus was praying, heaven opened [22]and the Holy Spirit came down on him in the form of a dove. Then a voice came from heaven, saying, "You are my Son, whom I love, and I am very pleased with you."

The Family History of Jesus

[23]When Jesus began his ministry, he was about thirty years old. People thought that Jesus was Joseph's son.

Joseph was the son[n] of Heli.
[24]Heli was the son of Matthat.
Matthat was the son of Levi.
Levi was the son of Melki.
Melki was the son of Jannai.
Jannai was the son of Joseph.
[25]Joseph was the son of Mattathias.
Mattathias was the son of Amos.
Amos was the son of Nahum.
Nahum was the son of Esli.
Esli was the son of Naggai.
[26]Naggai was the son of Maath.
Maath was the son of Mattathias.
Mattathias was the son of Semein.
Semein was the son of Josech.
Josech was the son of Joda.
[27]Joda was the son of Joanan.
Joanan was the son of Rhesa.
Rhesa was the son of Zerubbabel.
Zerubbabel was the grandson of Shealtiel.
Shealtiel was the son of Neri.
[28]Neri was the son of Melki.
Melki was the son of Addi.
Addi was the son of Cosam.
Cosam was the son of Elmadam.
Elmadam was the son of Er.
[29]Er was the son of Joshua.
Joshua was the son of Eliezer.
Eliezer was the son of Jorim.
Jorim was the son of Matthat.

Matthat was the son of Levi.
[30]Levi was the son of Simeon.
Simeon was the son of Judah.
Judah was the son of Joseph.
Joseph was the son of Jonam.
Jonam was the son of Eliakim.
[31]Eliakim was the son of Melea.
Melea was the son of Menna.
Menna was the son of Mattatha.
Mattatha was the son of Nathan.
Nathan was the son of David.
[32]David was the son of Jesse.
Jesse was the son of Obed.
Obed was the son of Boaz.
Boaz was the son of Salmon.[n]
Salmon was the son of Nahshon.
[33]Nahshon was the son of Amminadab.
Amminadab was the son of Admin.
Admin was the son of Arni.
Arni was the son of Hezron.
Hezron was the son of Perez.
Perez was the son of Judah.
[34]Judah was the son of Jacob.
Jacob was the son of Isaac.
Isaac was the son of Abraham.
Abraham was the son of Terah.
Terah was the son of Nahor.
[35]Nahor was the son of Serug.
Serug was the son of Reu.
Reu was the son of Peleg.
Peleg was the son of Eber.
Eber was the son of Shelah.
[36]Shelah was the son of Cainan.
Cainan was the son of Arphaxad.
Arphaxad was the son of Shem.
Shem was the son of Noah.
Noah was the son of Lamech.
[37]Lamech was the son of Methuselah.
Methuselah was the son of Enoch.
Enoch was the son of Jared.
Jared was the son of Mahalalel.
Mahalalel was the son of Kenan.
[38]Kenan was the son of Enosh.
Enosh was the son of Seth.
Seth was the son of Adam.
Adam was the son of God.

3:23 son "Son" in Jewish lists of ancestors can sometimes mean grandson or more distant relative. **3:32 Salmon** Some Greek copies read "Sala."

MARCH 28

DEUTERONOMY 17:8—18:22

Courts of Law

⁸Some cases that come before you, such as murder, quarreling, or attack, may be too difficult to judge. Take these cases to the place the LORD your God will choose. ⁹Go to the priests who are Levites and to the judge who is on duty at that time. Ask them about the case, and they will decide. ¹⁰You must follow the decision they give you at the place the LORD your God will choose. Be careful to do everything they tell you. ¹¹Follow the teachings they give you, and do whatever they decide, exactly as they tell you. ¹²The person who does not show respect for the judge or priest who is there serving the LORD your God must be put to death. You must get rid of that evil from Israel. ¹³Then everyone will hear about this and will be afraid, and they will not show disrespect anymore.

Choosing a King

¹⁴When you enter the land the LORD your God is giving you, taking it as your own and living in it, you will say, "Let's appoint a king over us like the nations all around us." ¹⁵Be sure to appoint over you the king the LORD your God chooses. He must be one of your own people. Do not appoint as your king a foreigner who is not a fellow Israelite. ¹⁶The king must not have too many horses for himself, and he must not send people to Egypt to get more horses, because the LORD has told you, "Don't return that way again." ¹⁷The king must not have many wives, or his heart will be led away from God. He must not have too much silver and gold.

¹⁸When he becomes king, he should write a copy of the teachings on a scroll for himself, a copy taken from the priests and Levites. ¹⁹He should keep it with him all the time and read from it every day of his life. Then he will learn to respect the LORD his God, and he will obey all the teachings and commands. ²⁰He should not think he is better than his fellow Israelites, and he must not stop obeying the law in any way so that he and his descendants may rule the kingdom for a long time.

Shares for Priests and Levites

18 The priests are from the tribe of Levi, and that tribe will not receive a share of the land with the Israelites. They will eat the offerings made to the LORD by fire, which is their share. ²They will not inherit any of the land like their brothers, but they will inherit the LORD himself, as he has promised them.

³When you offer a bull or sheep as a sacrifice, you must share with the priests, giving them the shoulder, the cheeks, and the inner organs. ⁴Give them the first of your grain, new wine, and oil, as well as the first wool you cut from your sheep. ⁵The LORD your God has chosen the priests and their descendants out of all your tribes to stand and serve the LORD always.

⁶If a Levite moves from one of your towns anywhere in Israel where he lives and comes to the place the LORD will choose, because he wants to serve the LORD there, ⁷he may serve the LORD his God. He will be like his fellow Levites who serve there before the LORD. ⁸They all will have an equal share of the food. That is separate from what he has received from the sale of family possessions.

Do Not Follow Other Nations

⁹When you enter the land the LORD your God is giving you, don't learn to do the hateful things the other nations do. ¹⁰Don't let anyone among you offer a son or daughter as a sacrifice in the fire. Don't let anyone use magic or witchcraft, or try to explain the meaning of signs. ¹¹Don't let anyone try to control others with magic, and don't let them be mediums or try to talk with the spirits of dead people. ¹²The LORD hates anyone who does these things. Because the other nations do these things, the LORD your God will force them out of the land ahead of you. ¹³But you must be innocent in the presence of the LORD your God.

The Lord's Special Prophet

¹⁴The nations you will force out listen to people who use magic and witchcraft, but the LORD your God will not let you do those things. ¹⁵The LORD your God will give you a prophet like me, who is one of your own

people. Listen to him. [16]This is what you asked the LORD your God to do when you were gathered at Mount Sinai. You said, "Don't make us listen to the voice of the LORD our God again, and don't make us look at this terrible fire anymore, or we will die."

[17]So the LORD said to me, "What they have said is good. [18]So I will give them a prophet like you, who is one of their own people. I will tell him what to say, and he will tell them everything I command. [19]This prophet will speak for me; anyone who does not listen when he speaks will answer to me. [20]But if a prophet says something I did not tell him to say as though he were speaking for me, or if a prophet speaks in the name of other gods, that prophet must be killed."

[21]You might be thinking, "How can we know if a message is not from the LORD?" [22]If what a prophet says in the name of the LORD does not happen, it is not the LORD's message. That prophet was speaking his own ideas. Don't be afraid of him.

PSALM 37:37–40

[37]Think of the innocent person,
  and watch the honest one.
The man who has peace
  will have children to live after him.
[38]But sinners will be destroyed;
  in the end the wicked will die.

[39]The LORD saves good people;
  he is their strength in times of trouble.
[40]The LORD helps them and saves them;
  he saves them from the wicked,
  because they trust in him for protection.

PROVERBS 12:20–22

[20]Those who plan evil are full of lies,
  but those who plan peace are happy.

[21]No harm comes to a good person,
  but an evil person's life is full of trouble.

[22]The LORD hates those who tell lies
  but is pleased with those who keep their
  promises.

LUKE 4:1–30

Jesus Is Tempted by the Devil

4 Jesus, filled with the Holy Spirit, returned from the Jordan River. The Spirit led Jesus into the desert [2]where the devil tempted Jesus for forty days. Jesus ate nothing during that time, and when those days were ended, he was very hungry.

[3]The devil said to Jesus, "If you are the Son of God, tell this rock to become bread."

[4]Jesus answered, "It is written in the Scriptures: 'A person does not live on bread alone.'"[n]

[5]Then the devil took Jesus and showed him all the kingdoms of the world in an instant. [6]The devil said to Jesus, "I will give you all these kingdoms and all their power and glory. It has all been given to me, and I can give it to anyone I wish. [7]If you worship me, then it will all be yours."

[8]Jesus answered, "It is written in the Scriptures: 'You must worship the Lord your God and serve only him.'"[n]

[9]Then the devil led Jesus to Jerusalem and put him on a high place of the Temple. He said to Jesus, "If you are the Son of God, jump down. [10]It is written in the Scriptures:
  'He has put his angels in charge of you
    to watch over you.' *Psalm 91:11*
[11]It is also written:
  'They will catch you in their hands
    so that you will not hit your foot on a
    rock.'" *Psalm 91:12*
[12]Jesus answered, "But it also says in the Scriptures: 'Do not test the Lord your God.'"[n]

[13]After the devil had tempted Jesus in every way, he left him to wait until a better time.

Jesus Teaches the People

[14]Jesus returned to Galilee in the power of the Holy Spirit, and stories about him spread all through the area. [15]He began to teach in their synagogues, and everyone praised him.

[16]Jesus traveled to Nazareth, where he had grown up. On the Sabbath day he went to the synagogue, as he always did, and stood up to read. [17]The book of Isaiah the prophet was given to him. He opened the book and found the place where this is written:

4:4 'A person . . . alone.' Quotation from Deuteronomy 8:3. 4:8 'You . . . him.' Quotation from Deuteronomy 6:13.
4:12 'Do . . . God.' Quotation from Deuteronomy 6:16.

[18]"The Lord has put his Spirit in me,
   because he appointed me to tell the
   Good News to the poor.
He has sent me to tell the captives they
      are free
   and to tell the blind that they can see
      again.   *Isaiah 61:1*
God sent me to free those who have been
   treated unfairly   *Isaiah 58:6*
[19] and to announce the time when the
   Lord will show his kindness."

                              Isaiah 61:2

[20]Jesus closed the book, gave it back to the
assistant, and sat down. Everyone in the synagogue was watching Jesus closely. [21]He began
to say to them, "While you heard these words
just now, they were coming true!"

[22]All the people spoke well of Jesus and
were amazed at the words of grace he spoke.
They asked, "Isn't this Joseph's son?"

[23]Jesus said to them, "I know that you will
tell me the old saying: 'Doctor, heal yourself.'

You want to say, 'We heard about the things
you did in Capernaum. Do those things here
in your own town!' " [24]Then Jesus said, "I tell
you the truth, a prophet is not accepted in his
hometown. [25]But I tell you the truth, there
were many widows in Israel during the time
of Elijah. It did not rain in Israel for three and
one-half years, and there was no food anywhere in the whole country. [26]But Elijah was
sent to none of those widows, only to a widow
in Zarephath, a town in Sidon. [27]And there
were many with skin diseases living in Israel
during the time of the prophet Elisha. But
none of them were healed, only Naaman, who
was from the country of Syria."

[28]When all the people in the synagogue
heard these things, they became very angry.
[29]They got up, forced Jesus out of town, and
took him to the edge of the cliff on which the
town was built. They planned to throw him
off the edge, [30]but Jesus walked through the
crowd and went on his way.

MARCH 29

DEUTERONOMY 19:1—20:20

Cities of Safety

19 When the LORD your God gives you
land that belongs to the other nations,
nations that he will destroy, you will force
them out and live in their cities and houses.
[2]Then choose three cities in the middle of
the land the LORD your God is giving you as
your own. [3]Build roads to these cities, and
divide the land the LORD is giving you into
three parts so that someone who kills another person may run to these cities.

[4]This is the rule for someone who kills
another person and runs to one of these
cities in order to save his life. But the person
must have killed a neighbor without meaning to, not out of hatred. [5]For example, suppose someone goes into the forest with a
neighbor to cut wood and swings an ax to
cut down a tree. If the ax head flies off the
handle, hitting and killing the neighbor, the

one who killed him may run to one of these
cities to save his life. [6]Otherwise, the dead
person's relative who has the duty of punishing a murderer might be angry and chase
him. If the city is far away, the relative might
catch and kill the person, even though he
should not be killed because there was no
intent to kill his neighbor. [7]This is why I
command you to choose these three cities.

[8-9]Carefully obey all these laws I'm giving
you today. Love the LORD your God, and always
do what he wants you to do. Then the LORD
your God will enlarge your land as he promised your ancestors, giving you the whole land
he promised to them. After that, choose three
more cities of safety [10]so that innocent people
will not be killed in your land, the land that
the LORD your God is giving you as your own.
By doing this you will not be guilty of allowing
the death of innocent people.

[11]But if a person hates his neighbor and,
after hiding and waiting, attacks and kills

him and then runs to one of these cities for safety, [12]the elders of his own city should send for the murderer. They should bring the person back from the city of safety and hand him over to the relative who has the duty of punishing the murderer. [13]Show no mercy. You must remove from Israel the guilt of murdering innocent people so that things will go well for you.

[14]Do not move the stone that marks the border of your neighbor's land, which people long ago set in place. It marks what you inherit in the land the LORD your God is giving you as your own.

Rules About Witnesses

[15]One witness is not enough to accuse a person of a crime or sin. A case must be proved by two or three witnesses.

[16]If a witness lies and accuses a person of a crime, [17]the two people who are arguing must stand in the presence of the LORD before the priests and judges who are on duty. [18]The judges must check the matter carefully. The witness who is a liar, lying about a fellow Israelite, [19]must be punished. He must be punished in the same way the other person would have been punished. You must get rid of the evil among you. [20]The rest of the people will hear about this and be afraid, and no one among you will ever do such an evil thing again. [21]Show no mercy. A life must be paid for a life, an eye for an eye, a tooth for a tooth, a hand for a hand, a foot for a foot.

Laws for War

20 When you go to war against your enemies and you see horses and chariots and an army that is bigger than yours, don't be afraid of them. The LORD your God, who brought you out of Egypt, will be with you. [2]The priest must come and speak to the army before you go into battle. [3]He will say, "Listen, Israel! Today you are going into battle against your enemies. Don't lose your courage or be afraid. Don't panic or be frightened, [4]because the LORD your God goes with you, to fight for you against your enemies and to save you."

[5]The officers should say to the army, "Has anyone built a new house but not given it to God? He may go home, because he might die in battle and someone else would get to give his house to God. [6]Has anyone planted a vine-yard and not begun to enjoy it? He may go home, because he might die in battle and someone else would enjoy his vineyard. [7]Is any man engaged to a woman and not yet married to her? He may go home, because he might die in battle and someone else would marry her." [8]Then the officers should also say, "Is anyone here afraid? Has anyone lost his courage? He may go home so that he will not cause others to lose their courage, too." [9]When the officers finish speaking to the army, they should appoint commanders to lead it.

[10]When you march up to attack a city, first make them an offer of peace. [11]If they accept your offer and open their gates to you, all the people of that city will become your slaves and work for you. [12]But if they do not make peace with you and fight you in battle, you should surround that city. [13]The LORD your God will give it to you. Then kill all the men with your swords, [14]and you may take everything else in the city for yourselves. Take the women, children, and animals, and you may use these things the LORD your God gives you from your enemies. [15]Do this to all the cities that are far away, that do not belong to the nations nearby.

[16]But leave nothing alive in the cities of the land the LORD your God is giving you. [17]Completely destroy these people: the Hittites, Amorites, Canaanites, Perizzites, Hivites, and Jebusites, as the LORD your God has commanded. [18]Otherwise, they will teach you what they do for their gods, and if you do these hateful things, you will sin against the LORD your God.

[19]If you surround and attack a city for a long time, trying to capture it, do not destroy its trees with an ax. You can eat the fruit from the trees, but do not cut them down. These trees are not the enemy, so don't make war against them. [20]But you may cut down trees that you know are not fruit trees and use them to build devices to attack the city walls, until the city is captured.

PSALM 38:1–8

A Prayer in Time of Sickness

A psalm of David to remember.

38 LORD, don't correct me when you are angry.

Don't punish me when you are furious.
2Your arrows have wounded me,
and your hand has come down on me.
3My body is sick from your punishment.
Even my bones are not healthy because
of my sin.
4My guilt has overwhelmed me;
like a load it weighs me down.

5My sores stink and become infected
because I was foolish.
6I am bent over and bowed down;
I am sad all day long.
7I am burning with fever,
and my whole body is sore.
8I am weak and faint.
I moan from the pain I feel.

PROVERBS 12:23–25

23Wise people keep what they know to
themselves,
but fools can't keep from showing how
foolish they are.

24Hard workers will become leaders,
but those who are lazy will be slaves.

25Worry is a heavy load,
but a kind word cheers you up.

LUKE 4:31–44

Jesus Forces Out an Evil Spirit

31Jesus went to Capernaum, a city in
Galilee, and on the Sabbath day, he taught
the people. 32They were amazed at his teaching, because he spoke with authority. 33In the
synagogue a man who had within him an
evil spirit shouted in a loud voice, 34"Jesus of
Nazareth! What do you want with us? Did
you come to destroy us? I know who you
are—God's Holy One!"

35Jesus commanded the evil spirit, "Be
quiet! Come out of the man!" The evil spirit
threw the man down to the ground before all
the people and then left the man without
hurting him.

36The people were amazed and said to
each other, "What does this mean? With authority and power he commands evil spirits,
and they come out." 37And so the news about
Jesus spread to every place in the whole area.

Jesus Heals Many People

38Jesus left the synagogue and went to the
home of Simon.[n] Simon's mother-in-law was
sick with a high fever, and they asked Jesus
to help her. 39He came to her side and
commanded the fever to leave. It left her, and
immediately she got up and began serving
them.

40When the sun went down, the people
brought those who were sick to Jesus.
Putting his hands on each sick person, he
healed every one of them. 41Demons came
out of many people, shouting, "You are the
Son of God." But Jesus commanded the
demons and would not allow them to speak,
because they knew Jesus was the Christ.

42At daybreak, Jesus went to a lonely
place, but the people looked for him. When
they found him, they tried to keep him from
leaving. 43But Jesus said to them, "I must
preach about God's kingdom to other towns,
too. This is why I was sent."

44Then he kept on preaching in the synagogues of Judea.[n]

MARCH 30

DEUTERONOMY 21:1—22:30

A Person Found Murdered

21 Suppose someone is found murdered,
lying in a field in the land the LORD
your God is giving you as your own, and no
one knows who killed the person. 2Your elders and judges should go to where the body
was found, and they should measure how far
it is to the nearby cities. 3The elders of the

4:38 Simon Simon's other name was Peter. **4:44 Judea** Some Greek copies read "Galilee."

city nearest the body must take a young cow that has never worked or worn a yoke, [4]and they must lead her down to a valley that has never been plowed or planted, with a stream flowing through it. There they must break the young cow's neck. [5]The priests, the sons of Levi, should come forward, because they have been chosen by the LORD your God to serve him and to give blessings in the LORD's name. They are the ones who decide cases of quarreling and attacks. [6]Then all the elders of the city nearest the murdered person should wash their hands over the young cow whose neck was broken in the valley. [7]They should declare: "We did not kill this person, and we did not see it happen. [8]LORD, remove this sin from your people Israel, whom you have saved. Don't blame your people, the Israelites, for the murder of this innocent person." And so the murder will be paid for. [9]Then you will have removed from yourselves the guilt of murdering an innocent person, because you will be doing what the LORD says is right.

Captive Women as Wives

[10]When you go to war against your enemies, the LORD will help you defeat them so that you will take them captive. [11]If you see a beautiful woman among the captives and are attracted to her, you may take her as your wife. [12]Bring her into your home, where she must shave her head and cut her nails [13]and change the clothes she was wearing when you captured her. After she has lived in your house and cried for her parents for a month, you may marry her. You will be her husband, and she will be your wife. [14]But if you are not pleased with her, you must let her go anywhere she wants. You must not sell her for money or make her a slave, because you have taken away her honor.

The Oldest Son

[15]A man might have two wives, one he loves and one he doesn't. Both wives might have sons by him. If the older son belongs to the wife he does not love, [16]when that man wills his property to his sons he must not give the son of the wife he loves what belongs to the older son, the son of the wife he does not love. [17]He must agree to give the older son two shares of everything he owns,

even though the older son is from the wife he does not love. That son was the first to prove his father could have children, so he has the rights that belong to the older son.

Sons Who Refuse to Obey

[18]If someone has a son who is stubborn, who turns against his father and mother and doesn't obey them or listen when they correct him, [19]his parents must take him to the elders at the city gate. [20]They will say to the elders, "Our son is stubborn and turns against us. He will not obey us. He eats too much, and he is always drunk." [21]Then all the men in his town must throw stones at him until he dies. Get rid of the evil among you, because then all the people of Israel will hear about this and be afraid.

Other Laws

[22]If someone is guilty of a sin worthy of death, he must be put to death and his body displayed on a tree. [23]But don't leave his body hanging on the tree overnight; be sure to bury him that same day, because anyone whose body is displayed on a tree is cursed by God. You must not ruin the land the LORD your God is giving you as your own.

22 If you see your fellow Israelite's ox or sheep wandering away, don't ignore it. Take it back to its owner. [2]If the owner does not live close to you, or if you do not know who the owner is, take the animal home with you. Keep it until the owner comes looking for it; then give it back. [3]Do the same thing if you find a donkey or coat or anything someone lost. Don't just ignore it.

[4]If you see your fellow Israelite's donkey or ox fallen on the road, don't ignore it. Help the owner get it up.

[5]A woman must not wear men's clothes, and a man must not wear women's clothes. The LORD your God hates anyone who does that.

[6]If you find a bird's nest by the road, either in a tree or on the ground, and the mother bird is sitting on the young birds or eggs, do not take the mother bird with the young birds. [7]You may take the young birds, but you must let the mother bird go free. Then things will go well for you, and you will live a long time.

[8]When you build a new house, build a low wall around the edge of the roof[n] so you will not be guilty if someone falls off the roof.

[9]Don't plant two different kinds of seeds in your vineyard. Otherwise, both crops will be ruined.

[10]Don't plow with an ox and a donkey tied together.

[11]Don't wear clothes made of wool and linen woven together.

[12]Tie several pieces of thread together; then put these tassels on the four corners of your coat.

Marriage Laws

[13]If a man marries a girl and has sexual relations with her but then decides he does not like her, [14]he might talk badly about her and give her a bad name. He might say, "I married this woman, but when I had sexual relations with her, I did not find that she was a virgin." [15]Then the girl's parents must bring proof that she was a virgin to the elders at the city gate. [16]The girl's father will say to the elders, "I gave my daughter to this man to be his wife, but now he does not want her. [17]This man has told lies about my daughter. He has said, 'I did not find your daughter to be a virgin,' but here is the proof that my daughter was a virgin." Then her parents are to show the sheet to the elders of the city, [18]and the elders must take the man and punish him. [19]They must make him pay about two and one-half pounds of silver to the girl's father, because the man has given an Israelite virgin a bad name. The girl will continue to be the man's wife, and he may not divorce her as long as he lives.

[20]But if the things the husband said about his wife are true, and there is no proof that she was a virgin, [21]the girl must be brought to the door of her father's house. Then the men of the town must put her to death by throwing stones at her. She has done a disgraceful thing in Israel by having sexual relations before she was married. You must get rid of the evil among you.

[22]If a man is found having sexual relations with another man's wife, both the woman and the man who had sexual relations with her must die. Get rid of this evil from Israel.

[23]If a man meets a virgin in a city and has sexual relations with her, but she is engaged to another man, [24]you must take both of them to the city gate and put them to death by throwing stones at them. Kill the girl, because she was in a city and did not scream for help. And kill the man for having sexual relations with another man's wife. You must get rid of the evil among you.

[25]But if a man meets an engaged girl out in the country and forces her to have sexual relations with him, only the man who had sexual relations with her must be put to death. [26]Don't do anything to the girl, because she has not done a sin worthy of death. This is like the person who attacks and murders a neighbor; [27]the man found the engaged girl in the country and she screamed, but no one was there to save her.

[28]If a man meets a virgin who is not engaged to be married and forces her to have sexual relations with him and people find out about it, [29]the man must pay the girl's father about one and one-fourth pounds of silver. He must also marry the girl, because he has dishonored her, and he may never divorce her for as long as he lives.

[30]A man must not marry his father's wife; he must not dishonor his father in this way.

PSALM 38:9–22

[9]Lord, you know everything I want;
  my cries are not hidden from you.
[10]My heart pounds, and my strength is gone.
  I am losing my sight.
[11]Because of my wounds, my friends and
    neighbors avoid me,
  and my relatives stay far away.
[12]Some people set traps to kill me.
  Those who want to hurt me plan
    trouble;
  all day long they think up lies.

[13]I am like the deaf; I cannot hear.
  Like the mute, I cannot speak.

22:8 roof In Bible times houses were built with flat roofs. The roof was used for drying things such as flax and fruit. And it was used as an extra room, as a place for worship, and as a cool place to sleep in the summer.

¹⁴I am like those who do not hear,
  who have no answer to give.
¹⁵I trust you, LORD.
  You will answer, my Lord and God.
¹⁶I said, "Don't let them laugh at me
  or brag when I am defeated."
¹⁷I am about to die,
  and I cannot forget my pain.
¹⁸I confess my guilt;
  I am troubled by my sin.
¹⁹My enemies are strong and healthy,
  and many hate me for no reason.
²⁰They repay me with evil for the good I did.
  They lie about me because I try to do
  good.

²¹LORD, don't leave me;
  my God, don't go away.
²²Quickly come and help me,
  my Lord and Savior.

PROVERBS 12:26-28

²⁶Good people take advice from their
  friends,
  but an evil person is easily led to do
  wrong.
²⁷The lazy catch no food to cook,
  but a hard worker will have great
  wealth.
²⁸Doing what is right is the way to life,
  but there is another way that leads to
  death.

LUKE 5:1-16

Jesus' First Followers

5 One day while Jesus was standing beside Lake Galilee, many people were pressing all around him to hear the word of God. ²Jesus saw two boats at the shore of the lake. The fishermen had left them and were washing their nets. ³Jesus got into one of the boats, the one that belonged to Simon,ⁿ and asked him to push off a little from the land. Then Jesus sat down and continued to teach the people from the boat.

⁴When Jesus had finished speaking, he said to Simon, "Take the boat into deep water, and put your nets in the water to catch some fish."

⁵Simon answered, "Master, we worked hard all night trying to catch fish, and we caught nothing. But you say to put the nets in the water, so I will." ⁶When the fishermen did as Jesus told them, they caught so many fish that the nets began to break. ⁷They called to their partners in the other boat to come and help them. They came and filled both boats so full that they were almost sinking.

⁸When Simon Peter saw what had happened, he bowed down before Jesus and said, "Go away from me, Lord. I am a sinful man!" ⁹He and the other fishermen were amazed at the many fish they caught, as were ¹⁰James and John, the sons of Zebedee, Simon's partners.

Jesus said to Simon, "Don't be afraid. From now on you will fish for people." ¹¹When the men brought their boats to the shore, they left everything and followed Jesus.

Jesus Heals a Sick Man

¹²When Jesus was in one of the towns, there was a man covered with a skin disease. When he saw Jesus, he bowed before him and begged him, "Lord, you can heal me if you will."

¹³Jesus reached out his hand and touched the man and said, "I will. Be healed!" Immediately the disease disappeared. ¹⁴Then Jesus said, "Don't tell anyone about this, but go and show yourself to the priestⁿ and offer a gift for your healing, as Moses commanded.ⁿ This will show the people what I have done."

¹⁵But the news about Jesus spread even more. Many people came to hear Jesus and to be healed of their sicknesses, ¹⁶but Jesus often slipped away to be alone so he could pray.

5:3 Simon Simon's other name was Peter. **5:14 show . . . priest** The Law of Moses said a priest must say when a Jewish person with a skin disease was well. **5:14 Moses commanded** Read about this in Leviticus 14:1-32.

MARCH 31

DEUTERONOMY 23:1—24:22

The Lord's People

23 No man who has had part of his sex organ cut off may come into the meeting to worship the LORD.

²No one born to parents who were forbidden by law to marry may come into the meeting to worship the LORD. The descendants for ten generations may not come in either.

³No Ammonite or Moabite may come into the meeting to worship the LORD, and none of their descendants for ten generations may come in. ⁴This is because the Ammonites and Moabites did not give you bread and water when you came out of Egypt. And they hired Balaam son of Beor, from Pethor in Northwest Mesopotamia, to put a curse on you. ⁵But the LORD your God would not listen to Balaam. He turned the curse into a blessing for you, because the LORD your God loves you. ⁶Don't wish for their peace or success as long as you live.

⁷Don't hate Edomites; they are your close relatives. Don't hate Egyptians, because you were foreigners in their country. ⁸The great-grandchildren of these two peoples may come into the meeting to worship the LORD.

Keeping the Camp Clean

⁹When you are camped in time of war, keep away from unclean things. ¹⁰If a man becomes unclean during the night, he must go outside the camp and not come back. ¹¹But when evening comes, he must wash himself, and at sunset he may come back into the camp. ¹²Choose a place outside the camp where people may go to relieve themselves. ¹³Carry a tent peg with you, and when you relieve yourself, dig a hole and cover up your dung. ¹⁴The LORD your God moves around through your camp to protect you and to defeat your enemies for you, so the camp must be holy. He must not see anything unclean among you so that he will not leave you.

Other Laws

¹⁵If an escaped slave comes to you, do not hand over the slave to his master. ¹⁶Let the slave live with you anywhere he likes, in any town he chooses. Do not mistreat him.

¹⁷No Israelite man or woman must ever become a temple prostitute. ¹⁸Do not bring a male or female prostitute's pay to the Temple of the LORD your God to pay what you have promised to the LORD, because the LORD your God hates prostitution.

¹⁹If you loan your fellow Israelites money or food or anything else, don't make them pay back more than you loaned them. ²⁰You may charge foreigners, but not fellow Israelites. Then the LORD your God will bless everything you do in the land you are entering to take as your own.

²¹If you make a promise to give something to the LORD your God, do not be slow to pay it, because the LORD your God demands it from you. Do not be guilty of sin. ²²But if you do not make the promise, you will not be guilty. ²³You must do whatever you say you will do, because you chose to make the promise to the LORD your God.

²⁴If you go into your neighbor's vineyard, you may eat as many grapes as you wish, but do not put any grapes into your basket. ²⁵If you go into your neighbor's grainfield, you may pick grain with your hands, but you must not cut down your neighbor's grain with your sickle.

24 A man might marry a woman but later decide she doesn't please him because he has found something bad about her. He writes out divorce papers for her, gives them to her, and sends her away from his house. ²After she leaves his house, she goes and marries another man, ³but her second husband does not like her either. So he writes out divorce papers for her, gives them to her, and sends her away from his house. Or the second husband might die. ⁴In either case, her first husband who divorced her must not marry her again, because she has become unclean. The LORD would hate this. Don't bring this sin into the land the LORD your God is giving you as your own.

⁵A man who has just married must not be sent to war or be given any other duty. He

should be free to stay home for a year to make his new wife happy.

⁶If someone owes you something, do not take his two stones for grinding grain—not even the upper one—in place of what he owes, because this is how the person makes a living.

⁷If someone kidnaps a fellow Israelite, either to make him a slave or sell him, the kidnapper must be killed. You must get rid of the evil among you.

⁸Be careful when someone has a skin disease. Do exactly what the priests, the Levites, teach you, being careful to do what I have commanded them. ⁹Remember what the LORD your God did to Miriam on your way out of Egypt.

¹⁰When you make a loan to your neighbors, don't go into their homes to get something in place of it. ¹¹Stay outside and let them go in and get what they promised you. ¹²If a poor person gives you a coat to show he will pay the loan back, don't keep it overnight. ¹³Give the coat back at sunset, because your neighbor needs that coat to sleep in, and he will be grateful to you. And the LORD your God will see that you have done a good thing.

¹⁴Don't cheat hired servants who are poor and needy, whether they are fellow Israelites or foreigners living in one of your towns. ¹⁵Pay them each day before sunset, because they are poor and need the money. Otherwise, they may complain to the LORD about you, and you will be guilty of sin.

¹⁶Parents must not be put to death if their children do wrong, and children must not be put to death if their parents do wrong. Each person must die for his own sin.

¹⁷Do not be unfair to a foreigner or an orphan. Don't take a widow's coat to make sure she pays you back. ¹⁸Remember that you were slaves in Egypt, and the LORD your God saved you from there. That is why I am commanding you to do this.

¹⁹When you are gathering your harvest in the field and leave behind a bundle of grain, don't go back and get it. Leave it there for foreigners, orphans, and widows so that the LORD your God can bless everything you do. ²⁰When you beat your olive trees to knock the olives off, don't beat the trees a second time. Leave what is left for foreigners, orphans, and widows. ²¹When you harvest the grapes in your vineyard, don't pick the vines a second time. Leave what is left for foreigners, orphans, and widows. ²²Remember that you were slaves in Egypt; that is why I am commanding you to do this.

PSALM 39:1–6

Life Is Short

For the director of music. For Jeduthun. A psalm of David.

39 I said, "I will be careful how I act
and will not sin by what I say.
I will be careful what I say
around wicked people."
²So I kept very quiet.
I didn't even say anything good,
but I became even more upset.
³I became very angry inside,
and as I thought about it, my anger burned.
So I spoke:
⁴"LORD, tell me when the end will come
and how long I will live.
Let me know how long I have.
⁵You have given me only a short life;
my lifetime is like nothing to you.
Everyone's life is only a breath.   *Selah*
⁶People are like shadows moving about.
All their work is for nothing;
they collect things but don't know who will get them.

PROVERBS 13:1–3

13 Wise children take their parents'
advice,
but whoever makes fun of wisdom
won't listen to correction.

²People will be rewarded for what they say,
but those who can't be trusted want only violence.

³Those who are careful about what they say protect their lives,
but whoever speaks without thinking will be ruined.

LUKE 5:17–39

Jesus Heals a Paralyzed Man

[17]One day as Jesus was teaching the people, the Pharisees and teachers of the law from every town in Galilee and Judea and from Jerusalem were there. The Lord was giving Jesus the power to heal people. [18]Just then, some men were carrying on a mat a man who was paralyzed. They tried to bring him in and put him down before Jesus. [19]But because there were so many people there, they could not find a way in. So they went up on the roof and lowered the man on his mat through the ceiling into the middle of the crowd right before Jesus. [20]Seeing their faith, Jesus said, "Friend, your sins are forgiven."

[21]The Jewish teachers of the law and the Pharisees thought to themselves, "Who is this man who is speaking as if he were God? Only God can forgive sins."

[22]But Jesus knew what they were thinking and said, "Why are you thinking these things? [23]Which is easier: to say, 'Your sins are forgiven,' or to say, 'Stand up and walk'? [24]But I will prove to you that the Son of Man has authority on earth to forgive sins." So Jesus said to the paralyzed man, "I tell you, stand up, take your mat, and go home."

[25]At once the man stood up before them, picked up his mat, and went home, praising God. [26]All the people were fully amazed and began to praise God. They were filled with much respect and said, "Today we have seen amazing things!"

Levi Follows Jesus

[27]After this, Jesus went out and saw a tax collector named Levi sitting in the tax collector's booth. Jesus said to him, "Follow me!" [28]So Levi got up, left everything, and followed him.

[29]Then Levi gave a big dinner for Jesus at his house. Many tax collectors and other people were eating there, too. [30]But the Pharisees and the men who taught the law for the Pharisees began to complain to Jesus' followers, "Why do you eat and drink with tax collectors and sinners?"

[31]Jesus answered them, "It is not the healthy people who need a doctor, but the sick. [32]I have not come to invite good people but sinners to change their hearts and lives."

Jesus Answers a Question

[33]They said to Jesus, "John's followers often fast[n] for a certain time and pray, just as the Pharisees do. But your followers eat and drink all the time."

[34]Jesus said to them, "You cannot make the friends of the bridegroom fast while he is still with them. [35]But the time will come when the bridegroom will be taken away from them, and then they will fast."

[36]Jesus told them this story: "No one takes cloth off a new coat to cover a hole in an old coat. Otherwise, he ruins the new coat, and the cloth from the new coat will not be the same as the old cloth. [37]Also, no one ever pours new wine into old leather bags. Otherwise, the new wine will break the bags, the wine will spill out, and the leather bags will be ruined. [38]New wine must be put into new leather bags. [39]No one after drinking old wine wants new wine, because he says, 'The old wine is better.'"

5:33 fast The people would give up eating for a special time of prayer and worship to God. It was also done to show sadness and disappointment.

APRIL 1

DEUTERONOMY 25:1—26:19

25 If two people have an argument and go to court, the judges will decide the case. They will declare one person right and the other guilty. ²If the guilty person has to be punished with a beating, the judge will make that person lie down and be beaten in front of him. The number of lashes should match the crime. ³But don't hit a person more than forty times, because more than that would disgrace him before others.

⁴When an ox is working in the grain, do not cover its mouth to keep it from eating.

⁵If two brothers are living together, and one of them dies without having a son, his widow must not marry someone outside her husband's family. Her husband's brother must marry her, which is his duty to her as a brother-in-law. ⁶The first son she has counts as the son of the dead brother so that his name will not be forgotten in Israel.

⁷But if a man does not want to marry his brother's widow, she should go to the elders at the town gate. She should say, "My brother-in-law will not carry on his brother's name in Israel. He refuses to do his duty for me."

⁸Then the elders of the town must call for the man and talk to him. But if he is stubborn and says, "I don't want to marry her," ⁹the woman must go up to him in front of the elders. She must take off one of his sandals and spit in his face and say, "This is for the man who won't continue his brother's family!" ¹⁰Then that man's family shall be known in Israel as the Family of the Unsandaled.

¹¹If two men are fighting and one man's wife comes to save her husband from his attacker, grabbing the attacker by his sex organs, ¹²you must cut off her hand. Show her no mercy.

¹³Don't carry two sets of weights with you, one heavy and one light. ¹⁴Don't have two different sets of measures in your house, one large and one small. ¹⁵You must have true and honest weights and measures so that you will live a long time in the land the Lord your God is giving you. ¹⁶The Lord your God hates anyone who is dishonest and uses dishonest measures.

¹⁷Remember what the Amalekites did to you when you came out of Egypt. ¹⁸When you were tired and worn out, they met you on the road and attacked all those lagging behind. They were not afraid of God. ¹⁹When the Lord your God gives you rest from all the enemies around you in the land he is giving you as your own, you shall destroy any memory of the Amalekites on the earth. Do not forget!

The First Harvest

26 When you go into the land the Lord your God is giving you as your own, to take it over and live in it, ²you must take some of the first harvest of crops that grow from the land the Lord your God is giving you. Put the food in a basket and go to the place where the Lord your God will choose to be worshiped. ³Say to the priest on duty at that time, "Today I declare before the Lord your God that I have come into the land the Lord promised our ancestors that he would give us." ⁴The priest will take your basket and set it down in front of the altar of the Lord your God. ⁵Then you shall announce before the Lord your God: "My father was a wandering Aramean. He went down to Egypt with only a few people, but they became a great, powerful, and large nation there. ⁶But the Egyptians were cruel to us, making us suffer and work very hard. ⁷So we prayed to the Lord, the God of our ancestors, and he heard us. When he saw our trouble, hard work, and suffering, ⁸the Lord brought us out of Egypt with his great power and strength, using great terrors, signs, and miracles. ⁹Then he brought us to this place and gave us this fertile land. ¹⁰Now I bring part of the first harvest from this land that you, Lord, have given me." Place the basket before the Lord your God and bow down before him. ¹¹Then you and the Levites and foreigners among you should rejoice, because the Lord your God has given good things to you and your family.

¹²Bring a tenth of all your harvest the third year (the year to give a tenth of your harvest). Give it to the Levites, foreigners, orphans, and widows so that they may eat in your towns and be full. ¹³Then say to the LORD your God, "I have taken out of my house the part of my harvest that belongs to God, and I have given it to the Levites, foreigners, orphans, and widows. I have done everything you commanded me; I have not broken your commands, and I have not forgotten any of them. ¹⁴I have not eaten any of the holy part while I was in sorrow. I have not removed any of it while I was unclean, and I have not offered it for dead people. I have obeyed you, the LORD my God, and have done everything you commanded me. ¹⁵So look down from heaven, your holy home. Bless your people Israel and bless the land you have given us, which you promised to our ancestors—a fertile land."

Obey the Lord's Commands

¹⁶Today the LORD your God commands you to obey all these rules and laws; be careful to obey them with your whole being. ¹⁷Today you have said that the LORD is your God, and you have promised to do what he wants you to do—to keep his rules, commands, and laws. You have said you will obey him. ¹⁸And today the LORD has said that you are his very own people, as he has promised you. But you must obey his commands. ¹⁹He will make you greater than all the other nations he made. He will give you praise, fame, and honor, and you will be a holy people to the LORD your God, as he has said.

PSALM 39:7–11

⁷"So, Lord, what hope do I have?
    You are my hope.
⁸Save me from all my sins.
    Don't let wicked fools make fun of me.
⁹I am quiet; I do not open my mouth,
    because you are the one who has done this.
¹⁰Quit punishing me;
    your beating is about to kill me.
¹¹You correct and punish people for their sins;

like a moth, you destroy what they love.
Everyone's life is only a breath. *Selah*

PROVERBS 13:4–6

⁴The lazy will not get what they want,
    but those who work hard will.

⁵Good people hate what is false,
    but the wicked do shameful and
        disgraceful things.

⁶Doing what is right protects the honest person,
    but doing evil ruins the sinner.

LUKE 6:1–26

Jesus Is Lord over the Sabbath

6 One Sabbath day Jesus was walking through some fields of grain. His followers picked the heads of grain, rubbed them in their hands, and ate them. ²Some Pharisees said, "Why do you do what is not lawful on the Sabbath day?"

³Jesus answered, "Have you not read what David did when he and those with him were hungry? ⁴He went into God's house and took and ate the holy bread, which is lawful only for priests to eat. And he gave some to the people who were with him." ⁵Then Jesus said to the Pharisees, "The Son of Man is Lord of the Sabbath day."

Jesus Heals a Man's Hand

⁶On another Sabbath day Jesus went into the synagogue and was teaching, and a man with a crippled right hand was there. ⁷The teachers of the law and the Pharisees were watching closely to see if Jesus would heal on the Sabbath day so they could accuse him. ⁸But he knew what they were thinking, and he said to the man with the crippled hand, "Stand up here in the middle of everyone." The man got up and stood there. ⁹Then Jesus said to them, "I ask you, which is lawful on the Sabbath day: to do good or to do evil, to save a life or to destroy it?" ¹⁰Jesus looked around at all of them and said to the man, "Hold out your hand." The man held out his hand, and it was healed.

¹¹But the Pharisees and the teachers of the law were very angry and discussed with each other what they could do to Jesus.

Jesus Chooses His Apostles

¹²At that time Jesus went off to a mountain to pray, and he spent the night praying to God. ¹³The next morning, Jesus called his followers to him and chose twelve of them, whom he named apostles: ¹⁴Simon (Jesus named him Peter), his brother Andrew, James, John, Philip, Bartholomew, ¹⁵Matthew, Thomas, James son of Alphaeus, Simon (called the Zealot), ¹⁶Judas son of James, and Judas Iscariot, who later turned Jesus over to his enemies.

Jesus Teaches and Heals

¹⁷Jesus and the apostles came down from the mountain, and he stood on level ground. A large group of his followers was there, as well as many people from all around Judea, Jerusalem, and the seacoast cities of Tyre and Sidon. ¹⁸They all came to hear Jesus teach and to be healed of their sicknesses, and he healed those who were troubled by evil spirits. ¹⁹All the people were trying to touch Jesus, because power was coming from him and healing them all.

²⁰Jesus looked at his followers and said,
"You people who are poor are blessed,

because the kingdom of God belongs to you.
²¹You people who are now hungry are blessed,
because you will be satisfied.
You people who are now crying are blessed,
because you will laugh with joy.

²²"People will hate you, shut you out, insult you, and say you are evil because you follow the Son of Man. But when they do, you will be blessed. ²³Be full of joy at that time, because you have a great reward in heaven. Their ancestors did the same things to the prophets.

²⁴"But how terrible it will be for you who are rich,
because you have had your easy life.
²⁵How terrible it will be for you who are full now,
because you will be hungry.
How terrible it will be for you who are laughing now,
because you will be sad and cry.

²⁶"How terrible when everyone says only good things about you, because their ancestors said the same things about the false prophets.

APRIL 2

DEUTERONOMY 27:1—28:68

The Law Written on Stones

27 Then Moses, along with the elders of Israel, commanded the people, saying, "Keep all the commands I have given you today. ²Soon you will cross the Jordan River to go into the land the LORD your God is giving you. On that day set up some large stones and cover them with plaster. ³When you cross over, write all the words of these teachings on them. Then you may enter the land the LORD your God is giving you, a fertile land, just as the LORD, the God of your ancestors, promised. ⁴After you have crossed the Jordan River, set up these stones on Mount Ebal, as I command you today, and cover them with plaster. ⁵Build an altar of stones

there to the LORD your God, but don't use any iron tool to cut the stones; ⁶build the altar of the LORD your God with stones from the field. Offer burnt offerings on it to the LORD your God, ⁷and offer fellowship offerings there, and eat them and rejoice before the LORD your God. ⁸Then write clearly all the words of these teachings on the stones."

Curses of the Law

⁹Then Moses and the Levites who were priests spoke to all Israel and said, "Be quiet, Israel. Listen! Today you have become the people of the LORD your God. ¹⁰Obey the LORD your God, and keep his commands and laws that I give you today."

¹¹That day Moses also gave the people this command:

[12]When you cross the Jordan River, these tribes must stand on Mount Gerizim to bless the people: Simeon, Levi, Judah, Issachar, Joseph and Benjamin. [13]And these tribes must stand on Mount Ebal to announce the curses: Reuben, Gad, Asher, Zebulun, Dan, and Naphtali.

[14]The Levites will say to all the people of Israel in a loud voice:

[15]"Anyone will be cursed who makes an idol or statue and secretly sets it up, because the LORD hates the idols people make."

Then all the people will say, "Amen!"

[16]"Anyone will be cursed who dishonors his father or mother."

Then all the people will say, "Amen!"

[17]"Anyone will be cursed who moves the stone that marks a neighbor's border."

Then all the people will say, "Amen!"

[18]"Anyone will be cursed who sends a blind person down the wrong road."

Then all the people will say, "Amen!"

[19]"Anyone will be cursed who is unfair to foreigners, orphans, or widows."

Then all the people will say, "Amen!"

[20]"A man will be cursed who has sexual relations with his father's wife, because it is a dishonor to his father."

Then all the people will say, "Amen!"

[21]"Anyone will be cursed who has sexual relations with an animal."

Then all the people will say, "Amen!"

[22]"A man will be cursed who has sexual relations with his sister, whether she is his father's daughter or his mother's daughter."

Then all the people will say, "Amen!"

[23]"A man will be cursed who has sexual relations with his mother-in-law."

Then all the people will say, "Amen!"

[24]"Anyone will be cursed who kills a neighbor secretly."

Then all the people will say, "Amen!"

[25]"Anyone will be cursed who takes money to murder an innocent person."

Then all the people will say, "Amen!"

[26]"Anyone will be cursed who does not agree with the words of these teachings and does not obey them."

Then all the people will say, "Amen!"

Blessings for Obeying

28You must completely obey the LORD your God, and you must carefully follow all his commands I am giving you today. Then the LORD your God will make you greater than any other nation on earth. [2]Obey the LORD your God so that all these blessings will come and stay with you:

[3]You will be blessed in the city and blessed in the country.

[4]Your children will be blessed, as well as your crops; your herds will be blessed with calves and your flocks with lambs.

[5]Your basket and your kitchen will be blessed.

[6]You will be blessed when you come in and when you go out.

[7]The LORD will help you defeat the enemies that come to fight you. They will attack you from one direction, but they will run from you in seven directions.

[8]The LORD your God will bless you with full barns, and he will bless everything you do. He will bless the land he is giving you.

[9]The LORD will make you his holy people, as he promised. But you must obey his commands and do what he wants you to do. [10]Then everyone on earth will see that you are the LORD's people, and they will be afraid of you. [11]The LORD will make you rich: You will have many children, your animals will have many young, and your land will give good crops. It is the land that the LORD promised your ancestors he would give to you.

[12]The LORD will open up his heavenly storehouse so that the skies send rain on your land at the right time, and he will bless everything you do. You will lend to other nations, but you will not need to borrow from them. [13]The LORD will make you like the head and not like the tail; you will be on top and not on bottom. But you must obey the commands of the LORD your God that I am giving you today, being careful to keep them. [14]Do not disobey anything I command you today. Do exactly as I command, and do not follow other gods or serve them.

Curses for Disobeying

[15]But if you do not obey the LORD your God and carefully follow all his commands

and laws I am giving you today, all these curses will come upon you and stay: [16]You will be cursed in the city and cursed in the country.

[17]Your basket and your kitchen will be cursed.

[18]Your children will be cursed, as well as your crops; the calves of your herds and the lambs of your flocks will be cursed.

[19]You will be cursed when you go in and when you go out.

[20]The LORD will send you curses, confusion, and punishment in everything you do. You will be destroyed and suddenly ruined because you did wrong when you left him. [21]The LORD will give you terrible diseases and destroy you from the land you are going to take. [22]The LORD will punish you with disease, fever, swelling, heat, lack of rain, plant diseases, and mildew until you die. [23]The sky above will be like bronze, and the ground below will be like iron.[n] [24]The LORD will turn the rain into dust and sand, which will fall from the skies until you are destroyed.

[25]The LORD will help your enemies defeat you. You will attack them from one direction, but you will run from them in seven directions. And you will become a thing of horror among all the kingdoms on earth. [26]Your dead bodies will be food for all the birds and wild animals, and there will be no one to scare them away. [27]The LORD will punish you with boils like those the Egyptians had. You will have bad growths, sores, and itches that can't be cured. [28]The LORD will give you madness, blindness, and a confused mind. [29]You will have to feel around in the daylight like a blind person. You will fail in everything you do. People will hurt you and steal from you every day, and no one will save you.

[30]You will be engaged to a woman, but another man will force her to have sexual relations with him. You will build a house, but you will not live in it. You will plant a vineyard, but you will not get its grapes. [31]Your ox will be killed before your eyes, but you will not eat any of it. Your donkey will be taken away from you, and it will not be brought back. Your sheep will be given to your ene-

mies, and no one will save you. [32]Your sons and daughters will be given to another nation, and you will grow tired looking for them every day, but there will be nothing you can do. [33]People you don't know will eat the crops your land and hard work have produced. You will be mistreated and abused all your life. [34]The things you see will cause you to go mad. [35]The LORD will give you sore boils on your knees and legs that cannot be cured, and they will go from the soles of your feet to the tops of your heads.

[36]The LORD will send you and your king away to a nation neither you nor your ancestors know, where you will serve other gods made of wood and stone. [37]You will become a hated thing to the nations where the LORD sends you; they will laugh at you and make fun of you.

[38]You will plant much seed in your field, but your harvest will be small, because locusts will eat the crop. [39]You will plant vineyards and work hard in them, but you will not pick the grapes or drink the wine, because the worms will eat them. [40]You will have olive trees in all your land, but you will not get any olive oil, because the olives will drop off the trees. [41]You will have sons and daughters, but you will not be able to keep them, because they will be taken captive. [42]Locusts will destroy all your trees and crops.

[43]The foreigners who live among you will get stronger and stronger, and you will get weaker and weaker. [44]Foreigners will lend money to you, but you will not be able to lend to them. They will be like the head, and you will be like the tail.

[45]All these curses will come upon you. They will chase you and catch you and destroy you, because you did not obey the LORD your God and keep the commands and laws he gave you. [46]The curses will be signs and miracles to you and your descendants forever. [47]You had plenty of everything, but you did not serve the LORD your God with joy and a pure heart, [48]so you will serve the enemies the LORD sends against you. You will be hungry, thirsty, naked, and poor, and the

---

28:23 sky . . . iron This means the sky will give no rain and the earth will produce no crops.

LORD will put a load on you until he has destroyed you.

The Curse of an Enemy Nation

49The LORD will bring a nation against you from far away, from the end of the world, and it will swoop down like an eagle. You won't understand their language, 50and they will look mean. They will not respect old people or feel sorry for the young. 51They will eat the calves from your herds and the harvest of your field, and you will be destroyed. They will not leave you any grain, new wine or oil, or any calves from your herds or lambs from your flocks. You will be ruined. 52That nation will surround and attack all your cities. You trust in your high, strong walls, but they will fall down. That nation will surround all your cities everywhere in the land the LORD your God is giving you.

53Your enemy will surround you. Those people will make you starve so that you will eat your own babies, the bodies of the sons and daughters the LORD your God gave you. 54Even the most gentle and kind man among you will become cruel to his brother, his wife whom he loves, and his children who are still alive. 55He will not even give them any of the flesh of his children he is eating, because it will be all he has left. Your enemy will surround you and make you starve in all your cities. 56The most gentle and kind woman among you, so gentle and kind she would hardly even walk on the ground, will be cruel to her husband whom she loves and to her son and daughter. 57She will give birth to a baby, but she will plan to eat the baby and what comes after the birth itself. She will eat them secretly while the enemy surrounds the city. Those people will make you starve in all your cities.

58Be careful to obey everything in these teachings that are written in this book. You must respect the glorious and wonderful name of the LORD your God, 59or the LORD will give terrible diseases to you and your descendants. You will have long and serious diseases, and long and miserable sicknesses. 60He will give you all the diseases of Egypt that you dread, and the diseases will stay with you. 61The LORD will also give you every disease and sickness not written in this Book of the Teachings, until you are destroyed. 62You people may have outnumbered the stars, but only a few of you will be left, because you did not obey the LORD your God. 63Just as the LORD was once happy with you and gave you good things and made you grow in number, so then the LORD will be happy to ruin and destroy you, and you will be removed from the land you are entering to take as your own.

64Then the LORD will scatter you among the nations—from one end of the earth to the other. There you will serve other gods of wood and stone, gods that neither you nor your ancestors have known. 65You will have no rest among those nations and no place that is yours. The LORD will make your mind worried, your sight weak, and your soul sad. 66You will live with danger and be afraid night and day. You will not be sure that you will live. 67In the morning you will say, "I wish it were evening," and in the evening you will say, "I wish it were morning." Terror will be in your heart, and the things you have seen will scare you. 68The LORD will send you back to Egypt in ships, even though I, Moses, said you would never go back to Egypt. And there you will try to sell yourselves as slaves to your enemies, but no one will buy you.

PSALM 39:12–13

12"LORD, hear my prayer,
    and listen to my cry.
Do not ignore my tears.
    I am like a visitor with you.
    Like my ancestors, I'm only here a short time.
13Leave me alone so I can be happy
    before I leave and am no more."

PROVERBS 13:7–8

7Some people pretend to be rich but really
    have nothing.
    Others pretend to be poor but really are
    wealthy.
8The rich may have to pay a ransom for
    their lives,
    but the poor will face no such danger.

LUKE 6:27—49

Love Your Enemies

[27]"But I say to you who are listening, love your enemies. Do good to those who hate you, [28]bless those who curse you, pray for those who are cruel to you. [29]If anyone slaps you on one cheek, offer him the other cheek, too. If someone takes your coat, do not stop him from taking your shirt. [30]Give to everyone who asks you, and when someone takes something that is yours, don't ask for it back. [31]Do to others what you would want them to do to you. [32]If you love only the people who love you, what praise should you get? Even sinners love the people who love them. [33]If you do good only to those who do good to you, what praise should you get? Even sinners do that! [34]If you lend things to people, always hoping to get something back, what praise should you get? Even sinners lend to other sinners so that they can get back the same amount! [35]But love your enemies, do good to them, and lend to them without hoping to get anything back. Then you will have a great reward, and you will be children of the Most High God, because he is kind even to people who are ungrateful and full of sin. [36]Show mercy, just as your Father shows mercy.

Look at Yourselves

[37]"Don't judge others, and you will not be judged. Don't accuse others of being guilty, and you will not be accused of being guilty. Forgive, and you will be forgiven. [38]Give, and you will receive. You will be given much. Pressed down, shaken together, and running over, it will spill into your lap. The way you give to others is the way God will give to you."

[39]Jesus told them this story: "Can a blind person lead another blind person? No! Both of them will fall into a ditch. [40]A student is not better than the teacher, but the student who has been fully trained will be like the teacher.

[41]"Why do you notice the little piece of dust in your friend's eye, but you don't notice the big piece of wood in your own eye? [42]How can you say to your friend, 'Friend, let me take that little piece of dust out of your eye' when you cannot see that big piece of wood in your own eye! You hypocrite! First, take the wood out of your own eye. Then you will see clearly to take the dust out of your friend's eye.

Two Kinds of Fruit

[43]"A good tree does not produce bad fruit, nor does a bad tree produce good fruit. [44]Each tree is known by its own fruit. People don't gather figs from thornbushes, and they don't get grapes from bushes. [45]Good people bring good things out of the good they stored in their hearts. But evil people bring evil things out of the evil they stored in their hearts. People speak the things that are in their hearts.

Two Kinds of People

[46]"Why do you call me, 'Lord, Lord,' but do not do what I say? [47]I will show you what everyone is like who comes to me and hears my words and obeys. [48]That person is like a man building a house who dug deep and laid the foundation on rock. When the floods came, the water tried to wash the house away, but it could not shake it, because the house was built well. [49]But the one who hears my words and does not obey is like a man who built his house on the ground without a foundation. When the floods came, the house quickly fell and was completely destroyed."

APRIL 3

DEUTERONOMY 29:1—30:20

The Agreement in Moab

29 The LORD commanded Moses to make an agreement with the Israelites in Moab in addition to the agreement he had made with them at Mount Sinai. These are the words of that agreement.

[2]Moses called all the Israelites together and said to them:

You have seen everything the LORD did before your own eyes to the king of Egypt and to the king's leaders and to the whole country. ³With your own eyes you saw the great troubles, signs, and miracles. ⁴But to this day the LORD has not given you a mind that understands; you don't really understand what you see with your eyes or hear with your ears. ⁵I led you through the desert for forty years, and during that time neither your clothes nor sandals wore out. ⁶You ate no bread and drank no wine or beer. This was so you would understand that I am the LORD your God.

⁷When you came to this place, Sihon king of Heshbon and Og king of Bashan came out to fight us, but we defeated them. ⁸We captured their land and gave it to the tribes of Reuben, Gad, and East Manasseh to be their own.

⁹You must carefully obey everything in this agreement so that you will succeed in everything you do. ¹⁰Today you are all standing here before the LORD your God—your leaders and important men, your elders, officers, and all the other men of Israel, ¹¹your wives and children and the foreigners who live among you, who chop your wood and carry your water. ¹²You are all here to enter into an agreement and a promise with the LORD your God, an agreement the LORD your God is making with you today. ¹³This will make you today his own people. He will be your God, as he told you and as he promised your ancestors Abraham, Isaac, and Jacob. ¹⁴But I am not just making this agreement and its promises with you ¹⁵who are standing here before the LORD your God today, but also with those who are not here today.

¹⁶You know how we lived in Egypt and how we passed through the countries when we came here. ¹⁷You saw their hateful idols made of wood, stone, silver, and gold. ¹⁸Make sure no man, woman, family group, or tribe among you leaves the LORD our God to go and serve the gods of those nations. They would be to you like a plant that grows bitter, poisonous fruit.

¹⁹These are the kind of people who hear these curses but bless themselves, thinking, "We will be safe even though we continue doing what we want to do." Those people may destroy all of your land, both wet and dry. ²⁰The LORD will not forgive them. His anger will be like a burning fire against those people, and all the curses written in this book will come on them. The LORD will destroy any memory of them on the earth. ²¹He will separate them from all the tribes of Israel for punishment. All the curses of the Agreement that are written in this Book of the Teachings will happen to them.

²²Your children who will come after you, as well as foreigners from faraway lands, will see the disasters that come to this land and the diseases the LORD will send on it. They will say, ²³"The land is nothing but burning cinders and salt. Nothing is planted, nothing grows, and nothing blooms. It is like Sodom and Gomorrah, and Admah and Zeboiim, which the LORD destroyed because he was very angry." ²⁴All the other nations will ask, "Why has the LORD done this to the land? Why is he so angry?"

²⁵And the answer will be, "It is because the people broke the Agreement of the LORD, the God of their ancestors, which he made with them when he brought them out of Egypt. ²⁶They went and served other gods and bowed down to gods they did not even know. The LORD did not allow that, ²⁷so he became very angry at the land and brought all the curses on it that are written in this book. ²⁸Since the LORD became angry and furious with them, he took them out of their land and put them in another land where they are today."

²⁹There are some things the LORD our God has kept secret, but there are some things he has let us know. These things belong to us and our children forever so that we will do everything in these teachings.

The Israelites Will Return

30When all these blessings and curses I have described happen to you, and the LORD your God has sent you away to other nations, think about these things. ²Then you and your children will return to the LORD your God, and you will obey him with your whole being in everything I am commanding you today. ³Then the LORD your God will give you back your freedom. He will feel sorry for you, and he will bring you back again from the nations where he scattered you. [4]He may send you to the ends of the earth, but he will gather you and bring you back from there, [5]back to the land that belonged to your ancestors. It will be yours. He will give you success, and there will be more of you than there were of your ancestors. [6]The LORD your God will prepare you and your descendants to love him with your whole being so that you will live. [7]The LORD your God will put all these curses on your enemies, who hate you and are cruel to you. [8]And you will again obey the LORD, keeping all his commands that I give you today. [9]The LORD your God will make you successful in everything you do. You will have many children, your cattle will have many calves, and your fields will produce good crops, because the LORD will again be happy with you, just as he was with your ancestors. [10]But you must obey the LORD your God by keeping all his commands and rules that are written in this Book of the Teachings. You must return to the LORD your God with your whole being.

Choose Life or Death

[11]This command I give you today is not too hard for you; it is not beyond what you can do. [12]It is not up in heaven. You do not have to ask, "Who will go up to heaven and get it for us so we can obey it and keep it?" [13]It is not on the other side of the sea. You do not have to ask, "Who will go across the sea and get it? Who will tell it to us so we can keep it?" [14]No, the word is very near you. It is in your mouth and in your heart so you may obey it.

[15]Look, today I offer you life and success, death and destruction. [16]I command you today to love the LORD your God, to do what he wants you to do, and to keep his commands, his rules, and his laws. Then you will live and grow in number, and the LORD your God will bless you in the land you are entering to take as your own.

[17]But if you turn away from the LORD and do not obey him, if you are led to bow and serve other gods, [18]I tell you today that you will surely be destroyed. And you will not live long in the land you are crossing the Jordan River to enter and take as your own.

[19]Today I ask heaven and earth to be witnesses. I am offering you life or death, blessings or curses. Now, choose life! Then you and your children may live. [20]To choose life is to love the LORD your God, obey him, and stay close to him. He is your life, and he will let you live many years in the land, the land he promised to give your ancestors Abraham, Isaac, and Jacob.

PSALM 40:1–5

Praise and Prayer for Help

For the director of music. A psalm of David.

40 I waited patiently for the LORD.
He turned to me and heard my cry.
[2]He lifted me out of the pit of destruction,
out of the sticky mud.
He stood me on a rock
and made my feet steady.
[3]He put a new song in my mouth,
a song of praise to our God.
Many people will see this and worship
him.
Then they will trust the LORD.

[4]Happy is the person
who trusts the LORD,
who doesn't turn to those who are proud
or to those who worship false gods.
[5]LORD my God, you have done many
miracles.
Your plans for us are many.
If I tried to tell them all,
there would be too many to count.

PROVERBS 13:9–10

[9]Good people can look forward to a bright
future,
but the future of the wicked is like a
flame going out.

[10]Pride only leads to arguments,
but those who take advice are wise.

LUKE 7:1–35

Jesus Heals a Soldier's Servant

7 When Jesus finished saying all these things to the people, he went to Capernaum. [2]There was an army officer who had a servant who was very important to him. The servant was so sick he was nearly dead. [3]When the officer heard about Jesus, he sent some Jewish elders to him to ask Jesus to come and heal his servant. [4]The men went to Jesus and begged him, saying, "This officer is worthy of your help. [5]He loves our people, and he built us a synagogue."

[6]So Jesus went with the men. He was getting near the officer's house when the officer sent friends to say, "Lord, don't trouble yourself, because I am not worthy to have you come into my house. [7]That is why I did not come to you myself. But you only need to command it, and my servant will be healed. [8]I, too, am a man under the authority of others, and I have soldiers under my command. I tell one soldier, 'Go,' and he goes. I tell another soldier, 'Come,' and he comes. I say to my servant, 'Do this,' and my servant does it."

[9]When Jesus heard this, he was amazed. Turning to the crowd that was following him, he said, "I tell you, this is the greatest faith I have found anywhere, even in Israel." [10]Those who had been sent to Jesus went back to the house where they found the servant in good health.

Jesus Brings a Man Back to Life

[11]Soon afterwards Jesus went to a town called Nain, and his followers and a large crowd traveled with him. [12]When he came near the town gate, he saw a funeral. A mother, who was a widow, had lost her only son. A large crowd from the town was with the mother while her son was being carried out. [13]When the Lord saw her, he felt very sorry for her and said, "Don't cry." [14]He went up and touched the coffin, and the people who were carrying it stopped. Jesus said, "Young man, I tell you, get up!" [15]And the son sat up and began to talk. Then Jesus gave him back to his mother.

[16]All the people were amazed and began praising God, saying, "A great prophet has come to us! God has come to help his people."

[17]This news about Jesus spread through all Judea and into all the places around there.

John Asks a Question

[18]John's followers told him about all these things. He called for two of his followers [19]and sent them to the Lord to ask, "Are you the One who is to come, or should we wait for someone else?"

[20]When the men came to Jesus, they said, "John the Baptist sent us to you with this question: 'Are you the One who is to come, or should we wait for someone else?'"

[21]At that time, Jesus healed many people of their sicknesses, diseases, and evil spirits, and he gave sight to many blind people. [22]Then Jesus answered John's followers, "Go tell John what you saw and heard here. The blind can see, the crippled can walk, and people with skin diseases are healed. The deaf can hear, the dead are raised to life, and the Good News is preached to the poor. [23]Those who do not stumble in their faith because of me are blessed!"

[24]When John's followers left, Jesus began talking to the people about John: "What did you go out into the desert to see? A reed[n] blown by the wind? [25]What did you go out to see? A man dressed in fine clothes? No, people who have fine clothes and much wealth live in kings' palaces. [26]But what did you go out to see? A prophet? Yes, and I tell you, John is more than a prophet. [27]This was written about him:

'I will send my messenger ahead of you,
who will prepare the way for you.'

Malachi 3:1

[28]I tell you, John is greater than any other person ever born, but even the least important person in the kingdom of God is greater than John."

[29](When the people, including the tax collectors, heard this, they all agreed that God's teaching was good, because they had been baptized by John. [30]But the Pharisees and experts on the law refused to accept God's plan for themselves; they did not let John baptize them.)

[31]Then Jesus said, "What shall I say about

7:24 reed It means that John was not ordinary or weak like grass blown by the wind.

the people of this time? What are they like? ³²They are like children sitting in the marketplace, calling to one another and saying,

'We played music for you, but you did
        not dance;
    we sang a sad song, but you did not cry.'

³³John the Baptist came and did not eat bread or drink wine, and you say, 'He has a demon in him.' ³⁴The Son of Man came eating and drinking, and you say, 'Look at him! He eats too much and drinks too much wine, and he is a friend of tax collectors and sinners!' ³⁵But wisdom is proved to be right by what it does."

APRIL 4

DEUTERONOMY 31:1—32:52

Joshua Takes Moses' Place

31 Then Moses went and spoke these words to all the Israelites: ²"I am now one hundred twenty years old, and I cannot lead you anymore. The LORD told me I would not cross the Jordan River; ³the LORD your God will lead you across himself. He will destroy those nations for you, and you will take over their land. Joshua will also lead you across, as the LORD has said. ⁴The LORD will do to those nations what he did to Sihon and Og, the kings of the Amorites, when he destroyed them and their land. ⁵The LORD will give those nations to you; do to them everything I told you. ⁶Be strong and brave. Don't be afraid of them and don't be frightened, because the LORD your God will go with you. He will not leave you or forget you."

⁷Then Moses called Joshua and said to him in front of the people, "Be strong and brave, because you will lead these people into the land the LORD promised to give their ancestors, and help them take it as their own. ⁸The LORD himself will go before you. He will be with you; he will not leave you or forget you. Don't be afraid and don't worry."

Moses Writes the Teachings

⁹So Moses wrote down these teachings and gave them to the priests and all the elders of Israel. (The priests are the sons of Levi, who carry the Ark of the Agreement with the LORD.) ¹⁰⁻¹¹Then Moses commanded them: "Read these teachings for all Israel to hear at the end of every seven years, which is the year to cancel what people owe. Do it during the Feast of Shelters, when all the Israelites will come to appear before the LORD your God and stand at the place he will choose. ¹²Gather all the people: the men, women, children, and foreigners living in your towns so that they can listen and learn to respect the LORD your God and carefully obey everything in this law. ¹³Since their children do not know this law, they must hear it. They must learn to respect the LORD your God for as long as they live in the land you are crossing the Jordan River to take for your own."

The Lord Calls Moses and Joshua

¹⁴The LORD said to Moses, "Soon you will die. Get Joshua and come to the Meeting Tent so that I may command him." So Moses and Joshua went to the Meeting Tent.

¹⁵The LORD appeared at the Meeting Tent in a cloud; the cloud stood over the entrance of the Tent. ¹⁶And the LORD said to Moses, "You will soon die. Then these people will not be loyal to me but will worship the foreign gods of the land they are entering. They will leave me, breaking the Agreement I made with them. ¹⁷Then I will become very angry at them, and I will leave them. I will turn away from them, and they will be destroyed. Many terrible things will happen to them. Then they will say, 'It is because God is not with us that these terrible things are happening.' ¹⁸I will surely turn away from them then, because they have done wrong and have turned to other gods.

¹⁹"Now write down this song and teach it to the Israelites. Then have them sing it, because it will be my witness against them. ²⁰When I bring them into the land I prom-

ised to their ancestors, a fertile land, they will eat as much as they want and get fat. Then they will turn to other gods and serve them. They will reject me and break my Agreement. ²¹Then when many troubles and terrible things happen to them, this song will testify against them, because the song will not be forgotten by their descendants. I know what they plan to do, even before I take them into the land I promised them." ²²So Moses wrote down the song that day, and he taught it to the Israelites.

²³Then the LORD gave this command to Joshua son of Nun: "Be strong and brave, because you will lead the people of Israel to the land I promised them, and I will be with you."

²⁴After Moses finished writing all the words of the teachings in a book, ²⁵he gave a command to the Levites, who carried the Ark of the Agreement with the LORD. ²⁶He said, "Take this Book of the Teachings and put it beside the Ark of the Agreement with the LORD your God. It must stay there as a witness against you. ²⁷I know how stubborn and disobedient you are. You have disobeyed the LORD while I am alive and with you, and you will disobey even more after I die! ²⁸Gather all the elders of your tribes and all your officers to me so that I may say these things for them to hear, and so that I may ask heaven and earth to testify against them. ²⁹I know that after I die you will become completely evil. You will turn away from the commands I have given you. Terrible things will happen to you in the future when you do what the LORD says is evil, and you will make him angry with the idols you have made."

Moses' Song

³⁰And Moses spoke this whole song for all the people of Israel to hear:

32 Hear, heavens, and I will speak.
Listen, earth, to what I say.
²My teaching will drop like rain;
  my words will fall like dew.
They will be like showers on the grass;
  they will pour down like rain on young plants.
³I will announce the name of the LORD.
  Praise God because he is great!

⁴He is like a rock; what he does is perfect,
  and he is always fair.
He is a faithful God who does no wrong,
  who is right and fair.

⁵They have done evil against him.
  To their shame they are no longer his children;
  they are an evil and lying people.
⁶This is not the way to repay the LORD,
  you foolish and unwise people.
He is your Father and Maker,
  who made you and formed you.

⁷Remember the old days.
  Think of the years already passed.
Ask your father and he will tell you;
  ask your elders and they will inform you.
⁸God Most High gave the nations their lands,
  dividing up the human race.
He set up borders for the people
  and even numbered the Israelites.
⁹The LORD took his people as his share,
  the people of Jacob as his very own.

¹⁰He found them in a desert,
  a windy, empty land.
He surrounded them and brought them up,
  guarding them as those he loved very much.
¹¹He was like an eagle building its nest
  that flutters over its young.
It spreads its wings to catch them
  and carries them on its feathers.
¹²The LORD alone led them,
  and there was no foreign god helping him.

¹³The LORD brought them to the heights of the land
  and fed them the fruit of the fields.
He gave them honey from the rocks,
  bringing oil from the solid rock.
¹⁴There were milk curds from the cows
  and milk from the flock;
  there were fat sheep and goats.
There were sheep and goats from Bashan
  and the best of the wheat.
You drank the juice of grapes.

15Israel grew fat and kicked;
   they were fat and full and firm.
They left the God who made them
   and rejected the Rock who saved them.
16They made God jealous with foreign
      gods
   and angry with hateful idols.
17They made sacrifices to demons, not
      God,
   to gods they had never known,
   new gods from nearby,
   gods your ancestors did not fear.
18You left God who is the Rock, your
      Father,
   and you forgot the God who gave you
      birth.

19The LORD saw this and rejected them;
   his sons and daughters had made him
      angry.
20He said, "I will turn away from them
   and see what will happen to them.
They are evil people,
   unfaithful children.
21They used things that are not gods to
      make me jealous
   and worthless idols to make me angry.
So I will use those who are not a nation
      to make them jealous;
   I will use a nation that does not
      understand to make them angry.
22My anger has started a fire
   that burns down to the place of the
      dead.
It will burn up the ground and its crops,
   and it will set fire to the base of the
      mountains.

23"I will pile troubles upon them
   and shoot my arrows at them.
24They will be starved and sick,
   destroyed by terrible diseases.
I will send them vicious animals
   and gliding, poisonous snakes.
25In the streets the sword will kill;
   in their homes there will be terror.
Young men and women will die,
   and so will babies and gray-haired
      men.
26I will scatter them as I said,
   and no one will remember them.

27But I didn't want their enemy to brag;
   their enemy might misunderstand
and say, 'We have won!
   The LORD has done none of this.'"

28Israel has no sense;
   they do not understand.
29I wish they were wise and understood
      this;
   I wish they could see what will happen
      to them.
30One person cannot chase a thousand
      people,
   and two people cannot fight ten
      thousand
unless their Rock has sold them,
   unless the LORD has given them up.
31The rock of these people is not like our
      Rock;
   our enemies agree to that.
32Their vine comes from Sodom,
   and their fields are like Gomorrah.
Their grapes are full of poison;
   their bunches of grapes are bitter.
33Their wine is like snake poison,
   like the deadly poison of cobras.

34"I have been saving this,
   and I have it locked in my storehouses.
35I will punish those who do wrong; I will
      repay them.
Soon their foot will slip,
because their day of trouble is near,
   and their punishment will come quickly."

36The LORD will defend his people
   and have mercy on his servants.
He will see that their strength is gone,
   that nobody is left, slaves or free.
37Then he will say, "Where are their gods?
   Where is the rock they trusted?
38Who ate the fat from their sacrifices,
   and who drank the wine of their drink
      offerings?
Let those gods come to help you!
   Let them protect you!

39"Now you will see that I am the one God!
   There is no god but me.
I send life and death;
   I can hurt, and I can heal.

No one can escape from me.
[40]I raise my hand toward heaven and make
this promise:
As surely as I live forever,
[41]I will sharpen my flashing sword,
and I will take it in my hand to judge.
I will punish my enemies
and pay back those who hate me.
[42]My arrows will be covered with their
blood;
my sword will eat their flesh.
The blood will flow from those who are
killed and the captives.
The heads of the enemy leaders will be
cut off."

[43]Be happy, nations, with his people,
because he will repay you for the blood
of his servants.
He will punish his enemies,
and he will remove the sin of his land
and people.

[44]Moses came with Joshua son of Nun,
and they spoke all the words of this song for
the people to hear. [45]When Moses finished
speaking these words to all Israel, [46]he said
to them: "Pay careful attention to all the
words I have said to you today, and command your children to obey carefully everything in these teachings. [47]These should not
be unimportant words for you, but rather
they mean life for you! By these words you
will live a long time in the land you are
crossing the Jordan River to take as your
own."

Moses Goes Up to Mount Nebo

[48]The LORD spoke to Moses again that
same day and said, [49]"Go up the Abarim
Mountains, to Mount Nebo in the country of
Moab, across from Jericho. Look at the land
of Canaan that I am giving to the Israelites
as their own. [50]On that mountain that you
climb, you will die and join your ancestors,
just as your brother Aaron died on Mount
Hor and joined his ancestors. [51]You both
sinned against me at the waters of Meribah
Kadesh in the Desert of Zin, and you did not
honor me as holy there among the Israelites.
[52]So now you will only look at the land from
far away. You will not enter the land I am giving the people of Israel."

PSALM 40:6–10

[6]You do not want sacrifices and offerings.
But you have made a hole in my ear
to show that my body and life are
yours.
You do not ask for burnt offerings
and sacrifices to take away sins.
[7]Then I said, "Look, I have come.
It is written about me in the book.
[8]My God, I want to do what you want.
Your teachings are in my heart."

[9]I will tell about your goodness in the
great meeting of your people.
LORD, you know my lips are not silent.
[10]I do not hide your goodness in my heart;
I speak about your loyalty and
salvation.
I do not hide your love and truth
from the people in the great meeting.

PROVERBS 13:11–12

[11]Money that comes easily disappears
quickly,
but money that is gathered little by
little will grow.

[12]It is sad not to get what you hoped for.
But wishes that come true are like
eating fruit from the tree of life.

LUKE 7:36–50

A Woman Washes Jesus' Feet

[36]One of the Pharisees asked Jesus to eat
with him, so Jesus went into the Pharisee's
house and sat at the table. [37]A sinful woman
in the town learned that Jesus was eating at
the Pharisee's house. So she brought an alabaster jar of perfume [38]and stood behind
Jesus at his feet, crying. She began to wash
his feet with her tears, and she dried them
with her hair, kissing them many times and
rubbing them with the perfume. [39]When the
Pharisee who asked Jesus to come to his
house saw this, he thought to himself, "If Jesus were a prophet, he would know that the
woman touching him is a sinner!"
[40]Jesus said to the Pharisee, "Simon, I
have something to say to you."
Simon said, "Teacher, tell me."

[41]Jesus said, "Two people owed money to the same banker. One owed five hundred coins[n] and the other owed fifty. [42]They had no money to pay what they owed, but the banker told both of them they did not have to pay him. Which person will love the banker more?"

[43]Simon, the Pharisee, answered, "I think it would be the one who owed him the most money."

Jesus said to Simon, "You are right." [44]Then Jesus turned toward the woman and said to Simon, "Do you see this woman? When I came into your house, you gave me no water for my feet, but she washed my feet with her tears and dried them with her hair. [45]You gave me no kiss of greeting, but she has been kissing my feet since I came in. [46]You did not put oil on my head, but she poured perfume on my feet. [47]I tell you that her many sins are forgiven, so she showed great love. But the person who is forgiven only a little will love only a little."

[48]Then Jesus said to her, "Your sins are forgiven."

[49]The people sitting at the table began to say among themselves, "Who is this who even forgives sins?"

[50]Jesus said to the woman, "Because you believed, you are saved from your sins. Go in peace."

APRIL 5

DEUTERONOMY 33:1—34:12

Moses Blesses the People

33 Moses, the man of God, gave this blessing to the Israelites before he died. [2]He said:

"The LORD came from Mount Sinai
and rose like the sun from Edom;
he showed his greatness from Mount
Paran.
He came with thousands of angels
from the southern mountains.
[3]The LORD surely loves his people
and takes care of all those who belong
to him.
They bow down at his feet,
and they are taught by him.
[4]Moses gave us the teachings
that belong to the people of Jacob.
[5]The LORD became king of Israel
when the leaders of the people
gathered,
when the tribes of Israel came together.

[6]"Let the people of Reuben live and not
die,
but let the people be few."

[7]Moses said this about the people of
Judah:
"LORD, listen to Judah's prayer;
bring them back to their people.
They defend themselves with their
hands.
Help them fight their enemies!"

[8]Moses said this about the people of Levi:
"LORD, your Thummim and Urim belong
to Levi, whom you love.
LORD, you tested him at Massah
and argued with him at the waters of
Meribah.
[9]He said about his father and mother,
'I don't care about them.'
He did not treat his brothers as favorites
or give special favors to his children,
but he protected your word
and guarded your agreement.
[10]He teaches your laws to the people of
Jacob
and your teachings to the people of
Israel.
He burns incense before you
and makes whole burnt offerings on
your altar.

¹¹LORD, make them strong;
   be pleased with the work they do.
Defeat those who attack them,
   and don't let their enemies rise up
      again."

¹²Moses said this about the people of Benjamin:
   "The LORD's loved ones will lie down in
      safety,
   because he protects them all day long.
   The ones he loves rest with him."

¹³Moses said this about the people of Joseph:
   "May the LORD bless their land with
      wonderful dew from heaven,
   with water from the springs below,
¹⁴with the best fruits that the sun brings,
   and with the best fruits that the moon
      brings.
¹⁵Let the old mountains give the finest
      crops,
   and let the everlasting hills give the
      best fruits.
¹⁶Let the full earth give the best fruits,
   and let the LORD who lived in the
      burning bush be pleased.
May these blessings rest on the head of
      Joseph,
   on the forehead of the one who was
      blessed among his brothers.
¹⁷Joseph has the majesty of a firstborn
      bull;
   he is as strong as a wild ox.
He will stab other nations,
   even those nations far away.
These are the ten thousands of Ephraim,
   and these are the thousands of
      Manasseh."

¹⁸Moses said this about the people of Zebulun:
   "Be happy when you go out, Zebulun,
   and be happy in your tents, Issachar.
¹⁹They will call the people to the mountain,
   and there they will offer the right
      sacrifices.
They will do well from all that is in the
      sea,
   and they will do well from the treasures
      hidden in the sand on the shore."

²⁰Moses said this about the people of Gad:
   "Praise God who gives Gad more land!
Gad lives there like a lion,
   who tears off arms and heads.
²¹They chose the best land for themselves.
   They received a large share, like that
      given to an officer.
When the leaders of the people gathered,
   the people of Gad did what the LORD
      said was right,
   and they judged Israel fairly."

²²Moses said this about the people of Dan:
   "Dan is like a lion's cub,
   who jumps out of Bashan."

²³Moses said this about the people of Naphtali:
   "Naphtali enjoys special kindnesses,
   and they are full of the LORD's blessings.
Take as your own the west and south."

²⁴Moses said this about the people of
Asher:
   "Asher is the most blessed of the sons;
   let him be his brothers' favorite.
   Let him bathe his feet in olive oil.
²⁵Your gates will have locks of iron and
      bronze,
   and you will be strong as long as you
      live.

²⁶"There is no one like the God of Israel,
   who rides through the skies to help you,
   who rides on the clouds in his majesty.
²⁷The everlasting God is your place of
      safety,
   and his arms will hold you up forever.
He will force your enemy out ahead of
      you,
   saying, 'Destroy the enemy!'
²⁸The people of Israel will lie down in
      safety.
   Jacob's spring is theirs alone.
Theirs is a land full of grain and new
      wine,
   where the skies drop their dew.
²⁹Israel, you are blessed!
   No one else is like you,
   because you are a people saved by the
      LORD.
He is your shield and helper,
   your glorious sword."

Your enemies will be afraid of you,
  and you will walk all over their holy
    places."

Moses Dies

34 Then Moses climbed Mount Nebo from the plains of Moab to the top of Mount Pisgah, across from Jericho. From there the LORD showed him all the land from Gilead to Dan, ²all of Naphtali and the lands of Ephraim and Manasseh, all the land of Judah as far as the Mediterranean Sea, ³as well as the southern desert and the whole Valley of Jericho up to Zoar. (Jericho is called the city of palm trees.) ⁴Then the LORD said to Moses, "This is the land I promised to Abraham, Isaac, and Jacob when I said to them, 'I will give this land to your descendants.' I have let you look at it, Moses, but you will not cross over there."

⁵Then Moses, the servant of the LORD, died there in Moab, as the LORD had said. ⁶He buried Moses in Moab in the valley opposite Beth Peor, but even today no one knows where his grave is. ⁷Moses was one hundred twenty years old when he died. His eyes were not weak, and he was still strong. ⁸The Israelites cried for Moses for thirty days, staying in the plains of Moab until the time of sadness was over.

⁹Joshua son of Nun was then filled with wisdom, because Moses had put his hands on him. So the Israelites listened to Joshua, and they did what the LORD had commanded Moses.

¹⁰There has never been another prophet in Israel like Moses. The LORD knew Moses face to face ¹¹and sent him to do signs and miracles in Egypt—to the king, to all his officers, and to the whole land of Egypt. ¹²Moses had great power, and he did great and wonderful things for all the Israelites to see.

PSALM 40:11–17

¹¹LORD, do not hold back your mercy from
    me;
  let your love and truth always protect
    me.
¹²Troubles have surrounded me;
  there are too many to count.
My sins have caught me
  so that I cannot see a way to escape.
I have more sins than hairs on my head,
  and I have lost my courage.
¹³Please, LORD, save me.
  Hurry, LORD, to help me.
¹⁴People are trying to kill me.
  Shame them and disgrace them.
People want to hurt me.
  Let them run away in disgrace.
¹⁵People are making fun of me.
  Let them be shamed into silence.
¹⁶But let those who follow you
  be happy and glad.
They love you for saving them.
  May they always say, "Praise the LORD!"

¹⁷Lord, because I am poor and helpless,
    please remember me.
You are my helper and savior.
  My God, do not wait.

PROVERBS 13:13–14

¹³Those who reject what they are taught
    will pay for it,
  but those who obey what they are told
    will be rewarded.
¹⁴The teaching of a wise person gives life.
  It is like a fountain that can save people
    from death.

LUKE 8:1–25

The Group with Jesus

8 After this, while Jesus was traveling through some cities and small towns, he preached and told the Good News about God's kingdom. The twelve apostles were with him, ²and also some women who had been healed of sicknesses and evil spirits: Mary, called Magdalene, from whom seven demons had gone out; ³Joanna, the wife of Cuza (the manager of Herod's house); Susanna; and many others. These women used their own money to help Jesus and his apostles.

A Story About Planting Seed

⁴When a great crowd was gathered, and people were coming to Jesus from every town, he told them this story:

⁵"A farmer went out to plant his seed. While he was planting, some seed fell by the road. People walked on the seed, and the

birds ate it up. [6]Some seed fell on rock, and when it began to grow, it died because it had no water. [7]Some seed fell among thorny weeds, but the weeds grew up with it and choked the good plants. [8]And some seed fell on good ground and grew and made a hundred times more."

As Jesus finished the story, he called out, "Let those with ears use them and listen!"

[9]Jesus' followers asked him what this story meant.

[10]Jesus said, "You have been chosen to know the secrets about the kingdom of God. But I use stories to speak to other people so that:

'They will look, but they may not see.
They will listen, but they may not
understand.'   *Isaiah 6:9*

[11]"This is what the story means: The seed is God's message. [12]The seed that fell beside the road is like the people who hear God's teaching, but the devil comes and takes it away from them so they cannot believe it and be saved. [13]The seed that fell on rock is like those who hear God's teaching and accept it gladly, but they don't allow the teaching to go deep into their lives. They believe for a while, but when trouble comes, they give up. [14]The seed that fell among the thorny weeds is like those who hear God's teaching, but they let the worries, riches, and pleasures of this life keep them from growing and producing good fruit. [15]And the seed that fell on the good ground is like those who hear God's teaching with good, honest hearts and obey it and patiently produce good fruit.

Use What You Have

[16]"No one after lighting a lamp covers it with a bowl or hides it under a bed. Instead, the person puts it on a lampstand so those who come in will see the light. [17]Everything that is hidden will become clear, and every secret thing will be made known. [18]So be careful how you listen. Those who have understanding will be given more. But those who do not have understanding, even what they think they have will be taken away from them."

Jesus' True Family

[19]Jesus' mother and brothers came to see him, but there was such a crowd they could not get to him. [20]Someone said to Jesus, "Your mother and your brothers are standing outside, wanting to see you."

[21]Jesus answered them, "My mother and my brothers are those who listen to God's teaching and obey it!"

Jesus Calms a Storm

[22]One day Jesus and his followers got into a boat, and he said to them, "Let's go across the lake." And so they started across. [23]While they were sailing, Jesus fell asleep. A very strong wind blew up on the lake, causing the boat to fill with water, and they were in danger.

[24]The followers went to Jesus and woke him, saying, "Master! Master! We will drown!"

Jesus got up and gave a command to the wind and the waves. They stopped, and it became calm. [25]Jesus said to his followers, "Where is your faith?"

The followers were afraid and amazed and said to each other, "Who is this that commands even the wind and the water, and they obey him?"

APRIL 6

JOSHUA 1:1—2:24

God's Command to Joshua

1 After Moses, the servant of the LORD, died, the LORD spoke to Joshua son of Nun, Moses' assistant. [2]The LORD said, "My servant Moses is dead. Now you and all these people go across the Jordan River into the land I am giving to the Israelites. [3]I promised Moses I would give you this land, so I will give you every place you go in the land. [4]All the land from the desert in the south to

Lebanon in the north will be yours. All the land from the great river, the Euphrates, in the east, to the Mediterranean Sea in the west will be yours, too, including the land of the Hittites. ⁵No one will be able to defeat you all your life. Just as I was with Moses, so I will be with you. I will not leave you or forget you.

⁶"Joshua, be strong and brave! You must lead these people so they can take the land that I promised their fathers I would give them. ⁷Be strong and brave. Be sure to obey all the teachings my servant Moses gave you. If you follow them exactly, you will be successful in everything you do. ⁸Always remember what is written in the Book of the Teachings. Study it day and night to be sure to obey everything that is written there. If you do this, you will be wise and successful in everything. ⁹Remember that I commanded you to be strong and brave. Don't be afraid, because the LORD your God will be with you everywhere you go."

Joshua's Orders to the People

¹⁰Then Joshua gave orders to the officers of the people: ¹¹"Go through the camp and tell the people, 'Get your supplies ready. Three days from now you will cross the Jordan River and take the land the LORD your God is giving you.'"

¹²Then Joshua said to the people of Reuben, Gad, and East Manasseh, ¹³"Remember what Moses, the servant of the LORD, told you. He said the LORD your God would give you rest and would give you this land. ¹⁴Now the LORD has given you this land east of the Jordan River. Your wives, children, and animals may stay here, but your fighting men must dress for war and cross the Jordan River ahead of your brothers to help them. ¹⁵The LORD has given you a place to rest and will do the same for your brothers. But you must help them until they take the land the LORD their God is giving them. Then you may return to your own land east of the Jordan River, the land that Moses, the servant of the LORD, gave you."

¹⁶Then the people answered Joshua, "Any-thing you command us to do, we will do. Any place you send us, we will go. ¹⁷Just as we fully obeyed Moses, we will obey you. We ask only that the LORD your God be with you just as he was with Moses. ¹⁸Whoever refuses to obey your commands or turns against you will be put to death. Just be strong and brave!"

Spies Sent to Jericho

2 Joshua son of Nun secretly sent out two spies from Acacia and said to them, "Go and look at the land, particularly at the city of Jericho."

So the men went to Jericho and stayed at the house of a prostitute named Rahab.

²Someone told the king of Jericho, "Some men from Israel have come here tonight to spy out the land."

³So the king of Jericho sent this message to Rahab: "Bring out the men who came to you and entered your house. They have come to spy out our whole land."

⁴But the woman had hidden the two men. She said, "They did come here, but I didn't know where they came from. ⁵In the evening, when it was time to close the city gate, they left. I don't know where they went, but if you go quickly, maybe you can catch them." ⁶(The woman had taken the men up to the roof*ⁿ* and had hidden them there under stalks of flax that she had spread out.) ⁷So the king's men went out looking for the spies on the road that leads to the crossings of the Jordan River. The city gate was closed just after the king's men left the city.

⁸Before the spies went to sleep for the night, Rahab went up to the roof. ⁹She said to them, "I know the LORD has given this land to your people. You frighten us very much. Everyone living in this land is terribly afraid of you ¹⁰because we have heard how the LORD dried up the Red Sea when you came out of Egypt. We have heard how you destroyed Sihon and Og, two Amorite kings who lived east of the Jordan. ¹¹When we heard this, we were very frightened. Now our men are afraid to fight you because the LORD your God rules the heavens above and the earth below! ¹²So now, promise me before

2:6 roof In Bible times houses were built with flat roofs. The roof was used for drying things such as flax and fruit. And it was used as an extra room, as a place for worship, and as a cool place to sleep in the summer.

the LORD that you will show kindness to my family just as I showed kindness to you. Give me some proof that you will do this. [13]Allow my father, mother, brothers, sisters, and all of their families to live. Save us from death."

[14]The men agreed and said, "It will be our lives for your lives if you don't tell anyone what we are doing. When the LORD gives us the land, we will be kind and true to you."

[15]The house Rahab lived in was built on the city wall, so she used a rope to let the men down through a window. [16]She said to them, "Go into the hills so the king's men will not find you. Hide there for three days. After the king's men return, you may go on your way."

[17]The men said to her, "You must do as we say. If not, we cannot be responsible for keeping this oath you have made us swear. [18]When we return to this land, you must tie this red rope in the window through which you let us down. Bring your father, mother, brothers, and all your family into your house. [19]If anyone leaves your house and is killed, it is his own fault. We cannot be responsible for him. If anyone in your house is hurt, we will be responsible. [20]But if you tell anyone about this, we will be free from the oath you made us swear."

[21]Rahab answered, "I agree to this." So she sent them away, and they left. Then she tied the red rope in the window.

[22]The men left and went into the hills where they stayed for three days. The king's men looked for them all along the road, but after three days, they returned to the city without finding them. [23]Then the two men started back. They left the hills and crossed the river and came to Joshua son of Nun and told him everything that had happened to them. [24]They said, "The LORD surely has given us all of the land. All the people in that land are terribly afraid of us."

PSALM 41:1–13

A Prayer in Time of Sickness

For the director of music. A psalm of David.

41 Happy are those who think about the poor.
When trouble comes, the LORD will save them.
[2]The LORD will protect them and spare their life
and will bless them in the land.
He will not let their enemies take them.
[3]The LORD will give them strength when they are sick,
and he will make them well again.

[4]I said, "LORD, have mercy on me.
Heal me, because I have sinned against you."
[5]My enemies are saying evil things about me.
They say, "When will he die and be forgotten?"
[6]Some people come to see me,
but they lie.
They just come to get bad news.
Then they go and gossip.
[7]All my enemies whisper about me
and think the worst about me.
[8]They say, "He has a terrible disease.
He will never get out of bed again."
[9]My best and truest friend, who ate at my table,
has even turned against me.

[10]LORD, have mercy on me.
Give me strength so I can pay them back.
[11]Because my enemies do not defeat me,
I know you are pleased with me.
[12]Because I am innocent, you support me
and will let me be with you forever.

[13]Praise the LORD, the God of Israel.
He has always been,
and he will always be.
Amen and amen.

PROVERBS 13:15–16

[15]People with good understanding will be well liked,
but the lives of those who are not trustworthy are hard.

[16]Every wise person acts with good sense,
but fools show how foolish they are.

LUKE 8:26–56

A Man with Demons Inside Him

[26]Jesus and his followers sailed across the lake from Galilee to the area of the Gerasene[n] people. [27]When Jesus got out on the land, a man from the town who had demons inside him came to Jesus. For a long time he had worn no clothes and had lived in the burial caves, not in a house. [28]When he saw Jesus, he cried out and fell down before him. He said with a loud voice, "What do you want with me, Jesus, Son of the Most High God? I beg you, don't torture me!" [29]He said this because Jesus was commanding the evil spirit to come out of the man. Many times it had taken hold of him. Though he had been kept under guard and chained hand and foot, he had broken his chains and had been forced by the demon out into a lonely place.

[30]Jesus asked him, "What is your name?"

He answered, "Legion,"[n] because many demons were in him. [31]The demons begged Jesus not to send them into eternal darkness.[n] [32]A large herd of pigs was feeding on a hill, and the demons begged Jesus to allow them to go into the pigs. So Jesus allowed them to do this. [33]When the demons came out of the man, they went into the pigs, and the herd ran down the hill into the lake and was drowned.

[34]When the herdsmen saw what had happened, they ran away and told about this in the town and the countryside. [35]And people went to see what had happened. When they came to Jesus, they found the man sitting at Jesus' feet, clothed and in his right mind, because the demons were gone. But the people were frightened. [36]The people who saw this happen told the others how Jesus had made the man well. [37]All the people of the Gerasene country asked Jesus to leave, because they were all very afraid. So Jesus got into the boat and went back to Galilee.

[38]The man whom Jesus had healed begged to go with him, but Jesus sent him away, saying, [39]"Go back home and tell people how much God has done for you." So the man went all over town telling how much Jesus had done for him.

Jesus Gives Life to a Dead Girl and Heals a Sick Woman

[40]When Jesus got back to Galilee, a crowd welcomed him, because everyone was waiting for him. [41]A man named Jairus, a leader of the synagogue, came to Jesus and fell at his feet, begging him to come to his house. [42]Jairus' only daughter, about twelve years old, was dying.

While Jesus was on his way to Jairus' house, the people were crowding all around him. [43]A woman was in the crowd who had been bleeding for twelve years,[n] but no one was able to heal her. [44]She came up behind Jesus and touched the edge of his coat, and instantly her bleeding stopped. [45]Then Jesus said, "Who touched me?"

When all the people said they had not touched him, Peter said, "Master, the people are all around you and are pushing against you."

[46]But Jesus said, "Someone did touch me, because I felt power go out from me." [47]When the woman saw she could not hide, she came forward, shaking, and fell down before Jesus. While all the people listened, she told why she had touched him and how she had been instantly healed. [48]Jesus said to her, "Dear woman, you are made well because you believed. Go in peace."

[49]While Jesus was still speaking, someone came from the house of the synagogue leader and said to him, "Your daughter is dead. Don't bother the teacher anymore." [50]When Jesus heard this, he said to Jairus, "Don't be afraid. Just believe, and your daughter will be well."

[51]When Jesus went to the house, he let only Peter, John, James, and the girl's father and mother go inside with him. [52]All the people were crying and feeling sad because the girl was dead, but Jesus said, "Stop crying. She is not dead, only asleep."

8:26 Gerasene From Gerasa, an area southeast of Lake Galilee. The exact location is uncertain and some Greek copies read "Gadarene"; others read "Gergesene." **8:30 Legion** Means very many. A legion was about five thousand men in the Roman army. **8:31 eternal darkness** Literally, "the abyss," something like a pit or a hole that has no end. **8:43 years** Some Greek copies continue, "and she had spent all the money she had on doctors."

⁵³The people laughed at Jesus because they knew the girl was dead. ⁵⁴But Jesus took hold of her hand and called to her, "My child, stand up!" ⁵⁵Her spirit came back into her, and she stood up at once. Then Jesus ordered that she be given something to eat. ⁵⁶The girl's parents were amazed, but Jesus told them not to tell anyone what had happened.

APRIL 7

JOSHUA 3:1—5:1

Crossing the Jordan

3 Early the next morning Joshua and all the Israelites left Acacia. They traveled to the Jordan River and camped there before crossing it. ²After three days the officers went through the camp ³and gave orders to the people: "When you see the priests and Levites carrying the Ark of the Agreement with the Lord your God, leave where you are and follow it. ⁴That way you will know which way to go since you have never been here before. But do not follow too closely. Stay about a thousand yards behind the Ark."

⁵Then Joshua told the people, "Make yourselves holy, because tomorrow the Lord will do amazing things among you."

⁶Joshua said to the priests, "Take the Ark of the Agreement and go ahead of the people." So the priests lifted the Ark and carried it ahead of the people.

⁷Then the Lord said to Joshua, "Today I will begin to make you great in the opinion of all the Israelites so the people will know I am with you just as I was with Moses. ⁸Tell the priests who carry the Ark of the Agreement to go to the edge of the Jordan River and stand in the water."

⁹Then Joshua said to the Israelites, "Come here and listen to the words of the Lord your God. ¹⁰Here is proof that the living God is with you and that he will force out the Canaanites, Hittites, Hivites, Perizzites, Girgashites, Amorites, and Jebusites. ¹¹The Ark of the Agreement with the Lord of the whole world will go ahead of you into the Jordan River. ¹²Now choose twelve men from among you, one from each of the twelve tribes of Israel. ¹³The priests will carry the Ark of the Lord, the Master of the whole world, into the Jordan ahead of you. When they step into the water, it will stop. The river will stop flowing and will stand up in a heap."

¹⁴So the people left the place where they had camped, and they followed the priests who carried the Ark of the Agreement across the Jordan River. ¹⁵During harvest the Jordan overflows its banks. When the priests carrying the Ark came to the edge of the river and stepped into the water, ¹⁶the water upstream stopped flowing. It stood up in a heap a great distance away at Adam, a town near Zarethan. The water flowing down to the Sea of Arabah (the Dead Sea) was completely cut off. So the people crossed the river near Jericho. ¹⁷The priests carried the Ark of the Agreement with the Lord to the middle of the river and stood there on dry ground. They waited there while all the people of Israel walked across the Jordan River on dry land.

Rocks to Remind the People

4 After all the people had finished crossing the Jordan, the Lord said to Joshua, ²"Choose twelve men from among the people, one from each tribe. ³Tell them to get twelve rocks from the middle of the river, from where the priests stood. Carry the rocks and put them down where you stay tonight."

⁴So Joshua chose one man from each tribe. Then he called the twelve men together ⁵and said to them, "Go out into the river where the Ark of the Lord your God is. Each of you bring back one rock, one for each tribe of Israel, and carry it on your shoulder. ⁶They will be a sign among you. In the future your children will ask you, 'What do these rocks mean?' ⁷Tell them the water stopped flowing in the Jordan when the Ark

of the Agreement with the LORD crossed the river. These rocks will always remind the Israelites of this."

⁸So the Israelites obeyed Joshua and carried twelve rocks from the middle of the Jordan River, one rock for each of the twelve tribes of Israel, just as the LORD had commanded Joshua. They carried the rocks with them and put them down where they made their camp. ⁹Joshua also put twelve rocks in the middle of the Jordan River where the priests had stood while carrying the Ark of the Agreement. These rocks are still there today.

¹⁰The priests carrying the Ark continued standing in the middle of the river until everything was done that the LORD had commanded Joshua to tell the people, just as Moses had told Joshua. The people hurried across the river. ¹¹After they finished crossing the river, the priests carried the Ark of the LORD to the other side as the people watched. ¹²The men from the tribes of Reuben, Gad, and East Manasseh obeyed what Moses had told them. They were dressed for war, and they crossed the river ahead of the other people. ¹³About forty thousand soldiers prepared for war passed before the LORD as they marched across the river, going toward the plains of Jericho.

¹⁴That day the LORD made Joshua great in the opinion of all the Israelites. They respected Joshua all his life, just as they had respected Moses.

¹⁵Then the LORD said to Joshua, ¹⁶"Command the priests to bring the Ark of the Agreement out of the river."

¹⁷So Joshua commanded the priests, "Come up out of the Jordan."

¹⁸Then the priests carried the Ark of the Agreement with the LORD out of the river. As soon as their feet touched dry land, the water began flowing again. The river again overflowed its banks, just as it had before they crossed.

¹⁹The people crossed the Jordan on the tenth day of the first month and camped at Gilgal, east of Jericho. ²⁰They carried with them the twelve rocks taken from the Jordan, and Joshua set them up at Gilgal. ²¹Then he spoke to the Israelites: "In the future your

children will ask you, 'What do these rocks mean?' ²²Tell them, 'Israel crossed the Jordan River on dry land. ²³The LORD your God caused the water to stop flowing until you finished crossing it, just as the LORD did to the Red Sea. He stopped the water until we crossed it. ²⁴The LORD did this so all people would know he has great power and so you would always respect the LORD your God.'"

5 All the kings of the Amorites west of the Jordan and the Canaanite kings living by the Mediterranean Sea heard that the LORD dried up the Jordan River until the Israelites had crossed it. After that they were scared and too afraid to face the Israelites.

PSALM 42:1–4

Wishing to Be Near God

For the director of music. A maskil of the sons of Korah.

42 As a deer thirsts for streams of water,
so I thirst for you, God.
²I thirst for the living God.
When can I go to meet with him?
³Day and night, my tears have been my food.
People are always saying,
"Where is your God?"
⁴When I remember these things,
I speak with a broken heart.
I used to walk with the crowd
and lead them to God's Temple
with songs of praise.

PROVERBS 13:17–18

¹⁷A wicked messenger brings nothing but trouble,
but a trustworthy one makes everything right.

¹⁸A person who refuses correction will end up poor and disgraced,
but the one who accepts correction will be honored.

LUKE 9:1–17

Jesus Sends Out the Apostles

9 Jesus called the twelve apostles together and gave them power and authority over all demons and the ability to heal sicknesses.

²He sent the apostles out to tell about God's kingdom and to heal the sick. ³He said to them, "Take nothing for your trip, neither a walking stick, bag, bread, money, or extra clothes. ⁴When you enter a house, stay there until it is time to leave. ⁵If people do not welcome you, shake the dust off of your feet^n as you leave the town, as a warning to them."

⁶So the apostles went out and traveled through all the towns, preaching the Good News and healing people everywhere.

Herod Is Confused About Jesus

⁷Herod, the governor, heard about all the things that were happening and was confused, because some people said, "John the Baptist has risen from the dead." ⁸Others said, "Elijah has come to us." And still others said, "One of the prophets who lived long ago has risen from the dead." ⁹Herod said, "I cut off John's head, so who is this man I hear such things about?" And Herod kept trying to see Jesus.

More than Five Thousand Fed

¹⁰When the apostles returned, they told Jesus everything they had done. Then Jesus took them with him to a town called Beth-saida where they could be alone together. ¹¹But the people learned where Jesus went and followed him. He welcomed them and talked with them about God's kingdom and healed those who needed to be healed.

¹²Late in the afternoon, the twelve apostles came to Jesus and said, "Send the people away. They need to go to the towns and countryside around here and find places to sleep and something to eat, because no one lives in this place."

¹³But Jesus said to them, "You give them something to eat."

They said, "We have only five loaves of bread and two fish, unless we go buy food for all these people." ¹⁴(There were about five thousand men there.)

Jesus said to his followers, "Tell the people to sit in groups of about fifty people."

¹⁵So the followers did this, and all the people sat down. ¹⁶Then Jesus took the five loaves of bread and two fish, and looking up to heaven, he thanked God for the food. Then he divided the food and gave it to the followers to give to the people. ¹⁷They all ate and were satisfied, and what was left over was gathered up, filling twelve baskets.

APRIL 8

JOSHUA 5:2—6:27

The Israelites Are Circumcised

²At that time the LORD said to Joshua, "Make knives from flint stones and circumcise the Israelites." ³So Joshua made knives from flint stones and circumcised the Israelites at Gibeath Haaraloth.

⁴This is why Joshua circumcised the men: After the Israelites left Egypt, all the men old enough to serve in the army died in the desert on the way out of Egypt. ⁵The men who had come out of Egypt had been circumcised, but none of those who were born in the desert on the trip from Egypt had been circumcised.

⁶The Israelites had moved about in the desert for forty years. During that time all the fighting men who had left Egypt had died because they had not obeyed the LORD. So the LORD swore they would not see the land he had promised their ancestors to give them, a fertile land. ⁷Their sons took their places. But none of the sons born on the trip from Egypt had been circumcised, so Joshua circumcised them. ⁸After all the Israelites had been circumcised, they stayed in camp until they were healed.

⁹Then the LORD said to Joshua, "As slaves in Egypt you were ashamed, but today I have removed that shame." So Joshua named that place Gilgal, which it is still named today.

¹⁰The people of Israel were camped at Gilgal on the plains of Jericho. It was there, on the evening of the fourteenth day of the month, they celebrated the Passover Feast. ¹¹The day after the Passover, the people ate food grown on that land: bread made without yeast and roasted grain. ¹²The day they ate this food, the manna stopped coming. The Israelites no longer got the manna from heaven. They ate the food grown in the land of Canaan that year.

¹³Joshua was near Jericho when he looked up and saw a man standing in front of him with a sword in his hand. Joshua went to him and asked, "Are you a friend or an enemy?"

¹⁴The man answered, "I am neither. I have come as the commander of the LORD's army."

Then Joshua bowed facedown on the ground and asked, "Does my master have a command for me, his servant?"

¹⁵The commander of the LORD's army answered, "Take off your sandals, because the place where you are standing is holy." So Joshua did.

The Fall of Jericho

6 The people of Jericho were afraid because the Israelites were near. They closed the city gates and guarded them. No one went into the city, and no one came out.

²Then the LORD said to Joshua, "Look, I have given you Jericho, its king, and all its fighting men. ³March around the city with your army once a day for six days. ⁴Have seven priests carry trumpets made from horns of male sheep and have them march in front of the Ark. On the seventh day march around the city seven times and have the priests blow the trumpets as they march. ⁵They will make one long blast on the trumpets. When you hear that sound, have all the people give a loud shout. Then the walls of the city will fall so the people can go straight into the city."

⁶So Joshua son of Nun called the priests together and said to them, "Carry the Ark of the Agreement. Tell seven priests to carry trumpets and march in front of it." ⁷Then Joshua ordered the people, "Now go! March around the city. The soldiers with weapons should march in front of the Ark of the Agreement with the LORD."

⁸When Joshua finished speaking to the people, the seven priests began marching before the LORD. They carried the seven trumpets and blew them as they marched. The priests carrying the Ark of the Agreement with the LORD followed them. ⁹Soldiers with weapons marched in front of the priests, and armed men walked behind the Ark. The priests were blowing their trumpets. ¹⁰But Joshua had told the people not to give a war cry. He said, "Don't shout. Don't say a word until the day I tell you. Then shout." ¹¹So Joshua had the Ark of the LORD carried around the city one time. Then they went back to camp for the night.

¹²Early the next morning Joshua got up, and the priests carried the Ark of the LORD again. ¹³The seven priests carried the seven trumpets and marched in front of the Ark of the LORD, blowing their trumpets. Soldiers with weapons marched in front of them, and other soldiers walked behind the Ark of the LORD. All this time the priests were blowing their trumpets. ¹⁴So on the second day they marched around the city one time and then went back to camp. They did this every day for six days.

¹⁵On the seventh day they got up at dawn and marched around the city, just as they had on the days before. But on that day they marched around the city seven times. ¹⁶The seventh time around the priests blew their trumpets. Then Joshua gave the command: "Now, shout! The LORD has given you this city! ¹⁷The city and everything in it are to be destroyed as an offering to the LORD. Only Rahab the prostitute and everyone in her house should remain alive. They must not be killed, because Rahab hid the two spies we sent out. ¹⁸Don't take any of the things that are to be destroyed as an offering to the LORD. If you take them and bring them into our camp, you yourselves will be destroyed, and you will bring trouble to all of Israel. ¹⁹All the silver and gold and things made from bronze and iron belong to the LORD and must be saved for him."

²⁰When the priests blew the trumpets, the people shouted. At the sound of the trumpets and the people's shout, the walls fell, and everyone ran straight into the city. So

the Israelites defeated that city. ²¹They completely destroyed with the sword every living thing in the city—men and women, young and old, cattle, sheep, and donkeys.

²²Joshua said to the two men who had spied out the land, "Go into the prostitute's house. Bring her out and bring out those who are with her, because of the promise you made to her." ²³So the two men went into the house and brought out Rahab, her father, mother, brothers, and all those with her. They put all of her family in a safe place outside the camp of Israel.

²⁴Then Israel burned the whole city and everything in it, but they did not burn the things made from silver, gold, bronze, and iron. These were saved for the LORD. ²⁵Joshua saved Rahab the prostitute, her family, and all who were with her, because Rahab had helped the men he had sent to spy out Jericho. Rahab still lives among the Israelites today.

²⁶Then Joshua made this oath:
"Anyone who tries to rebuild this city of Jericho
    will be cursed by the LORD.
The one who lays the foundation of this city
    will lose his oldest son,
and the one who sets up the gates
    will lose his youngest son."

²⁷So the LORD was with Joshua, and Joshua became famous through all the land.

PSALM 42:5–11

⁵Why am I so sad?
    Why am I so upset?
I should put my hope in God
    and keep praising him,
    my Savior and ⁶my God.

I am very sad.
    So I remember you where the Jordan River begins,
    near the peaks of Hermon and Mount Mizar.
⁷Troubles have come again and again,
    sounding like waterfalls.
    Your waves are crashing all around me.
⁸The LORD shows his true love every day.

At night I have a song,
    and I pray to my living God.
⁹I say to God, my Rock,
    "Why have you forgotten me?
Why am I sad
    and troubled by my enemies?"
¹⁰My enemies' insults make me feel
    as if my bones were broken.
They are always saying,
    "Where is your God?"

¹¹Why am I so sad?
    Why am I so upset?
I should put my hope in God
    and keep praising him,
    my Savior and my God.

PROVERBS 13:19–21

¹⁹It is so good when wishes come true,
    but fools hate to stop doing evil.

²⁰Spend time with the wise and you will become wise,
    but the friends of fools will suffer.

²¹Trouble always comes to sinners,
    but good people enjoy success.

LUKE 9:18–36

Jesus Is the Christ

¹⁸One time when Jesus was praying alone, his followers were with him, and he asked them, "Who do the people say I am?"

¹⁹They answered, "Some say you are John the Baptist. Others say you are Elijah." And others say you are one of the prophets from long ago who has come back to life."

²⁰Then Jesus asked, "But who do you say I am?"

Peter answered, "You are the Christ from God."

²¹Jesus warned them not to tell anyone, saying, ²²"The Son of Man must suffer many things. He will be rejected by the Jewish elders, the leading priests, and the teachers of the law. He will be killed and after three days will be raised from the dead."

²³Jesus said to all of them, "If people want to follow me, they must give up the

9:19 Elijah A man who spoke for God and who lived hundreds of years before Christ. See 1 Kings 17.

things they want. They must be willing to give up their lives daily to follow me. [24]Those who want to save their lives will give up true life. But those who give up their lives for me will have true life. [25]It is worthless to have the whole world if they themselves are destroyed or lost. [26]If people are ashamed of me and my teaching, then the Son of Man will be ashamed of them when he comes in his glory and with the glory of the Father and the holy angels. [27]I tell you the truth, some people standing here will see the kingdom of God before they die."

Jesus Talks with Moses and Elijah

[28]About eight days after Jesus said these things, he took Peter, John, and James and went up on a mountain to pray. [29]While Jesus was praying, the appearance of his face changed, and his clothes became shining white. [30]Then two men, Moses and Elijah,[n]

were talking with Jesus. [31]They appeared in heavenly glory, talking about his departure which he would soon bring about in Jerusalem. [32]Peter and the others were very sleepy, but when they awoke fully, they saw the glory of Jesus and the two men standing with him. [33]When Moses and Elijah were about to leave, Peter said to Jesus, "Master, it is good that we are here. Let us make three tents—one for you, one for Moses, and one for Elijah." (Peter did not know what he was talking about.)

[34]While he was saying these things, a cloud came and covered them, and they became afraid as the cloud covered them. [35]A voice came from the cloud, saying, "This is my Son, whom I have chosen. Listen to him!"

[36]When the voice finished speaking, only Jesus was there. Peter, John, and James said nothing and told no one at that time what they had seen.

APRIL 9

JOSHUA 7:1—8:35

The Sin of Achan

7 But the Israelites did not obey the LORD. There was a man from the tribe of Judah named Achan. (He was the son of Carmi and grandson of Zabdi, who was the son of Zerah.) Because Achan kept some of the things that were to be given to the LORD, the LORD became very angry at the Israelites.

[2]Joshua sent some men from Jericho to Ai, which was near Beth Aven, east of Bethel. He told them, "Go to Ai and spy out the area." So the men went to spy on Ai.

[3]Later they came back to Joshua and said, "There are only a few people in Ai, so we will not need all our people to defeat them. Send only two or three thousand men to fight. There is no need to send all of our people." [4]So about three thousand men went up to Ai,

but the people of Ai beat them badly. [5]The people of Ai killed about thirty-six Israelites and then chased the rest from the city gate all the way down to the canyon, killing them as they went down the hill. When the Israelites saw this, they lost their courage.

[6]Then Joshua tore his clothes in sorrow. He bowed facedown on the ground before the Ark of the LORD and stayed there until evening. The leaders of Israel did the same thing. They also threw dirt on their heads to show their sorrow. [7]Then Joshua said, "Lord GOD, you brought our people across the Jordan River. Why did you bring us this far and then let the Amorites destroy us? We would have been happy to stay on the other side of the Jordan. [8]Lord, there is nothing I can say now. Israel has been beaten by the enemy. [9]The Canaanites and all the other people in this country will hear about this and will

---

9:30 Moses and Elijah Two of the most important Jewish leaders in the past. God had given Moses the Law, and Elijah was an important prophet.

surround and kill us all! Then what will you do for your own great name?"

¹⁰The LORD said to Joshua, "Stand up! Why are you down on your face? ¹¹The Israelites have sinned; they have broken the agreement I commanded them to obey. They took some of the things I commanded them to destroy. They have stolen and lied and have taken those things for themselves. ¹²That is why the Israelites cannot face their enemies. They turn away from the fight and run, because I have commanded that they be destroyed. I will not help you anymore unless you destroy everything as I commanded you.

¹³"Now go! Make the people holy. Tell them, 'Set yourselves apart to the LORD for tomorrow. The LORD, the God of Israel, says some of you are keeping things he commanded you to destroy. You will never defeat your enemies until you throw away those things.

¹⁴"'Tomorrow morning you must be present with your tribes. The LORD will choose one tribe to stand alone before him. Then the LORD will choose one family group from that tribe to stand before him. Then the LORD will choose one family from that family group to stand before him, person by person. ¹⁵The one who is keeping what should have been destroyed will himself be destroyed by fire. Everything he owns will be destroyed with him. He has broken the agreement with the LORD and has done a disgraceful thing among the people of Israel!'"

¹⁶Early the next morning Joshua led all of Israel to present themselves in their tribes, and the LORD chose the tribe of Judah. ¹⁷So the family groups of Judah presented themselves, and the LORD then chose the family group of Zerah. When all the families of Zerah presented themselves, the family of Zabdi was chosen. ¹⁸And Joshua told all the men in that family to present themselves. The LORD chose Achan son of Carmi. (Carmi was the son of Zabdi, who was the son of Zerah.)

¹⁹Then Joshua said to Achan, "My son, tell the truth. Confess to the LORD, the God of Israel. Tell me what you did, and don't try to hide anything from me."

²⁰Achan answered, "It is true! I have sinned against the LORD, the God of Israel. This is what I did: ²¹Among the things I saw was a beautiful coat from Babylonia and about five pounds of silver and more than one and one-fourth pounds of gold. I wanted these things very much for myself, so I took them. You will find them buried in the ground under my tent, with the silver underneath."

²²So Joshua sent men who ran to the tent and found the things hidden there, with the silver. ²³The men brought them out of the tent, took them to Joshua and all the Israelites, and spread them out on the ground before the LORD. ²⁴Then Joshua and all the people led Achan son of Zerah to the Valley of Trouble. They also took the silver, the coat, the gold, Achan's sons, daughters, cattle, donkeys, sheep, tent, and everything he owned. ²⁵Joshua said, "I don't know why you caused so much trouble for us, but now the LORD will bring trouble to you." Then all the people threw stones at Achan and his family until they died. Then the people burned them. ²⁶They piled rocks over Achan's body, and they are still there today. That is why it is called the Valley of Trouble. After this the LORD was no longer angry.

Ai Is Destroyed

8 Then the LORD said to Joshua, "Don't be afraid or give up. Lead all your fighting men to Ai. I will help you defeat the king of Ai, his people, his city, and his land. ²You will do to Ai and its king what you did to Jericho and its king. Only this time you may take all the wealth and keep it for yourselves. Now tell some of your soldiers to set up an ambush behind the city."

³So Joshua led his whole army toward Ai. Then he chose thirty thousand of his best fighting men and sent them out at night. ⁴Joshua gave them these orders: "Listen carefully. You must set up an ambush behind the city. Don't go far from it, but continue to watch and be ready. ⁵I and the men who are with me will march toward the city, and the men in the city will come out to fight us, just as they did before. Then we will turn and run away from them. ⁶They will chase us away

from the city, thinking we are running away from them as we did before. When we run away, [7]come out from your ambush and take the city. The LORD your God will give you the power to win. [8]After you take the city, burn it. See to it! You have your orders."

[9]Then Joshua sent them to wait in ambush between Bethel and Ai, to the west of Ai. But Joshua stayed the night with his people.

[10]Early the next morning Joshua gathered his men together. He and the older leaders of Israel led them up to Ai. [11]All of the soldiers who were with Joshua marched up to Ai and stopped in front of the city and made camp north of it. There was a valley between them and the city. [12]Then Joshua chose about five thousand men and set them in ambush in the area west of the city between Bethel and Ai. [13]So the people took their positions; the main camp was north of the city, and the other men were hiding to the west. That night Joshua went down into the valley.

[14]Now when the king of Ai saw the army of Israel, he and his people got up early the next morning and hurried out to fight them. They went out to a place east of the city, but the king did not know soldiers were waiting in ambush behind the city. [15]Joshua and all the men of Israel let the army of Ai push them back. Then they ran toward the desert. [16]The men in Ai were called to chase Joshua and his men, so they left the city and went after them. [17]All the men of Ai and Bethel chased the army of Israel. The city was left open; not a man stayed to protect it.

[18]Then the LORD said to Joshua, "Hold your spear toward Ai, because I will give you that city." So Joshua held his spear toward the city of Ai. [19]When the Israelites who were in ambush saw this, they quickly came out of their hiding place and hurried toward the city. They entered the city, took control of it, and quickly set it on fire.

[20]When the men of Ai looked back, they saw smoke rising from their city. At the same time the Israelites stopped running and turned against the men of Ai, who could not escape in any direction. [21]When Joshua and all his men saw that the army had taken control of the city and saw the smoke rising from

it, they stopped running and turned to fight the men of Ai. [22]The men who were in ambush also came out of the city to help with the fight. So the men of Ai were caught between the armies of Israel. None of the enemy escaped. The Israelites fought until not one of the men of Ai was left alive, except [23]the king of Ai, and they brought him to Joshua.

A Review of the Fighting

[24]During the fighting the army of Israel chased the men of Ai into the fields and desert and killed all of them. Then they went back to Ai and killed everyone there. [25]All the people of Ai died that day, twelve thousand men and women. [26]Joshua had held his spear toward Ai, as a sign to destroy the city, and did not draw it back until all the people of Ai were destroyed. [27]The people of Israel kept for themselves the animals and the other things the people of Ai had owned, as the LORD had commanded Joshua to do.

[28]Then Joshua burned the city of Ai and made it a pile of ruins. And it is still like that today. [29]Joshua hanged the king of Ai on a tree and left him there until evening. At sunset Joshua told his men to take the king's body down from the tree and to throw it down at the city gate. Then they covered it with a pile of rocks, which is still there today.

[30]Joshua built an altar for the LORD, the God of Israel, on Mount Ebal, as [31]Moses, the LORD's servant, had commanded. Joshua built the altar as it was explained in the Book of the Teachings of Moses. It was made from uncut stones; no tool was ever used on them. On that altar the Israelites offered burnt offerings to the LORD and fellowship offerings. [32]There Joshua wrote the teachings of Moses on stones for all the people of Israel to see. [33]The elders, officers, judges, and all the Israelites were there; Israelites and non-Israelites were all standing around the Ark of the Agreement with the LORD in front of the priests, the Levites who had carried the Ark. Half of the people stood in front of Mount Ebal, and half stood in front of Mount Gerizim. This was the way the LORD's servant Moses had earlier commanded the people to be blessed.

[34]Then Joshua read all the words of the teachings, the blessings and the curses, ex-

actly as they were written in the Book of the Teachings. 35All the Israelites were gathered together—men, women, and children—along with the non-Israelites who lived among them. Joshua read every command that Moses had given.

PSALM 43:1–5

A Prayer for Protection

43 God, defend me.
Argue my case against those who don't follow you.
Save me from liars and those who do evil.
2God, you are my strength.
Why have you rejected me?
Why am I sad
and troubled by my enemies?
3Send me your light and truth
to guide me.
Let them lead me to your holy mountain,
to where you live.
4Then I will go to the altar of God,
to God who is my joy and happiness.
I will praise you with a harp,
God, my God.

5Why am I so sad?
Why am I so upset?
I should put my hope in God
and keep praising him,
my Savior and my God.

PROVERBS 13:22–23

22Good people leave their wealth to their grandchildren,
but a sinner's wealth is stored up for good people.

23A poor person's field might produce plenty of food,
but others often steal it away.

LUKE 9:37–62

Jesus Heals a Sick Boy

37The next day, when they came down from the mountain, a large crowd met Jesus. 38A man in the crowd shouted to him, "Teacher, please come and look at my son, because he is my only child. 39An evil spirit seizes my son, and suddenly he screams. It causes him to lose control of himself and foam at the mouth. The evil spirit keeps on hurting him and almost never leaves him. 40I begged your followers to force the evil spirit out, but they could not do it."

41Jesus answered, "You people have no faith, and your lives are all wrong. How long must I stay with you and put up with you? Bring your son here."

42While the boy was coming, the demon threw him on the ground and made him lose control of himself. But Jesus gave a strong command to the evil spirit and healed the boy and gave him back to his father. 43All the people were amazed at the great power of God.

Jesus Talks About His Death

While everyone was wondering about all that Jesus did, he said to his followers, 44"Don't forget what I tell you now: The Son of Man will be handed over to people." 45But the followers did not understand what this meant; the meaning was hidden from them so they could not understand. But they were afraid to ask Jesus about it.

Who Is the Greatest?

46Jesus' followers began to have an argument about which one of them was the greatest. 47Jesus knew what they were thinking, so he took a little child and stood the child beside him. 48Then Jesus said, "Whoever accepts this little child in my name accepts me. And whoever accepts me accepts the One who sent me, because whoever is least among you all is really the greatest."

Anyone Not Against Us Is for Us

49John answered, "Master, we saw someone using your name to force demons out of people. We told him to stop, because he does not belong to our group."

50But Jesus said to him, "Don't stop him, because whoever is not against you is for you."

A Town Rejects Jesus

51When the time was coming near for Jesus to depart, he was determined to go to Jerusalem. 52He sent some messengers ahead of him, who went into a town in Samaria to make everything ready for him.

[53]But the people there would not welcome him, because he was set on going to Jerusalem. [54]When James and John, followers of Jesus, saw this, they said, "Lord, do you want us to call fire down from heaven and destroy those people?"[n]

[55]But Jesus turned and scolded them. [And Jesus said, "You don't know what kind of spirit you belong to. [56]The Son of Man did not come to destroy the souls of people but to save them."][n] Then they went to another town.

Following Jesus

[57]As they were going along the road, someone said to Jesus, "I will follow you any place you go."

[58]Jesus said to them, "The foxes have holes to live in, and the birds have nests, but the Son of Man has no place to rest his head."

[59]Jesus said to another man, "Follow me!"

But he said, "Lord, first let me go and bury my father."

[60]But Jesus said to him, "Let the people who are dead bury their own dead. You must go and tell about the kingdom of God."

[61]Another man said, "I will follow you, Lord, but first let me go and say good-bye to my family."

[62]Jesus said, "Anyone who begins to plow a field but keeps looking back is of no use in the kingdom of God."

APRIL 10

JOSHUA 9:1—10:43

The Gibeonite Trickery

9 All the kings west of the Jordan River heard about these things: the kings of the Hittites, Amorites, Canaanites, Perizzites, Hivites, and Jebusites. They lived in the mountains and on the western hills and along the whole Mediterranean Sea coast. [2]So all these kings gathered to fight Joshua and the Israelites.

[3]When the people of Gibeon heard how Joshua had defeated Jericho and Ai, [4]they decided to trick the Israelites. They gathered old sacks and old leather wine bags that were cracked and mended, and they put them on the backs of their donkeys. [5]They put old sandals on their feet and wore old clothes, and they took some dry, moldy bread. [6]Then they went to Joshua in the camp near Gilgal.

The men said to Joshua and the Israelites, "We have traveled from a faraway country. Make a peace agreement with us."

[7]The Israelites said to these Hivites, "Maybe you live near us. How can we make a peace agreement with you?"

[8]The Hivites said to Joshua, "We are your servants."

But Joshua asked, "Who are you? Where do you come from?"

[9]The men answered, "We are your servants who have come from a far country, because we heard of the fame of the LORD your God. We heard about what he has done and everything he did in Egypt. [10]We heard that he defeated the two kings of the Amorites from the east side of the Jordan River—Sihon king of Heshbon and Og king of Bashan who ruled in Ashtaroth. [11]So our elders and our people said to us, 'Take food for your journey and go and meet the Israelites. Tell them, "We are your servants. Make a peace agreement with us."'

[12]"Look at our bread. On the day we left home to come to you it was warm and fresh, but now it is dry and moldy. [13]Look at our leather wine bags. They were new and filled with wine, but now they are cracked and old. Our clothes and sandals are worn out from the long journey."

[14]The men of Israel tasted the bread, but they did not ask the LORD what to do. [15]So

---

9:54 people Some Greek copies continue "as Elijah did." **9:55–56 And . . . them."** Some Greek copies do not contain the bracketed text.

Joshua agreed to make peace with the Gibeonites and to let them live. And the leaders of the Israelites swore an oath to keep the agreement.

[16]Three days after they had made the agreement, the Israelites learned that the Gibeonites lived nearby. [17]So the Israelites went to where they lived and on the third day came to their cities: Gibeon, Kephirah, Beeroth, and Kiriath Jearim. [18]But the Israelites did not attack those cities, because they had made a promise to them before the LORD, the God of Israel.

All the Israelites grumbled against the leaders. [19]But the leaders answered, "We have given our promise before the LORD, the God of Israel, so we cannot attack them now. [20]This is what we must do. We must let them live. Otherwise, God's anger will be against us for breaking the oath we swore to them. [21]So let them live, but they will cut wood and carry water for our people." So the leaders kept their promise to them.

[22]Joshua called for the Gibeonites and asked, "Why did you lie to us? Your land was near our camp, but you told us you were from a far country. [23]Now, you will be placed under a curse to be our slaves. You will have to cut wood and carry water for the house of my God."

[24]The Gibeonites answered Joshua, "We lied to you because we were afraid you would kill us. We heard that the LORD your God commanded his servant Moses to give you all of this land and to kill all the people who lived in it. That is why we did this. [25]Now you can decide what to do with us, whatever you think is right."

[26]So Joshua saved their lives by not allowing the Israelites to kill them, [27]but he made the Gibeonites slaves. They cut wood and carried water for the Israelites, and they did it for the altar of the LORD—wherever he chose it to be. They are still doing this today.

The Sun Stands Still

10 At this time Adoni-Zedek king of Jerusalem heard that Joshua had defeated Ai and completely destroyed it, as he had also done to Jericho and its king. The king also learned that the Gibeonites had made a peace agreement with Israel and that they lived nearby. [2]Adoni-Zedek and his people were very afraid because of this. Gibeon was not a little town like Ai; it was a large city, as big as a city that had a king, and all its men were good fighters. [3]So Adoni-Zedek king of Jerusalem sent a message to Hoham king of Hebron, Piram king of Jarmuth, Japhia king of Lachish, and Debir king of Eglon. He begged them, [4]"Come with me and help me attack Gibeon, which has made a peace agreement with Joshua and the Israelites."

[5]Then these five Amorite kings—the kings of Jerusalem, Hebron, Jarmuth, Lachish, and Eglon—gathered their armies, went to Gibeon, surrounded it, and attacked it.

[6]The Gibeonites sent this message to Joshua in his camp at Gilgal: "Don't let us, your servants, be destroyed. Come quickly and help us! Save us! All the Amorite kings from the mountains have joined their armies and are fighting against us."

[7]So Joshua marched out of Gilgal with his whole army, including his best fighting men. [8]The LORD said to Joshua, "Don't be afraid of those armies, because I will hand them over to you. None of them will be able to stand against you."

[9]Joshua and his army marched all night from Gilgal for a surprise attack. [10]The LORD confused those armies when Israel attacked, so Israel defeated them in a great victory at Gibeon. They chased them along the road going up to Beth Horon and killed men all the way to Azekah and Makkedah. [11]As they chased the enemy down the Beth Horon Pass to Azekah, the LORD threw large hailstones on them from the sky and killed them. More people were killed by the hailstones than by the Israelites' swords.

[12]On the day that the LORD gave up the Amorites to the Israelites, Joshua stood before all the people of Israel and said to the LORD:

"Sun, stand still over Gibeon.
    Moon, stand still over the Valley of
        Aijalon."
[13]So the sun stood still,
    and the moon stopped
        until the people defeated their enemies.

These words are written in the Book of Jashar.

The sun stopped in the middle of the sky and waited to go down for a full day. [14]That has never happened at any time before that day or since. That was the day the LORD listened to a human being. Truly the LORD was fighting for Israel!

[15]After this, Joshua and his army went back to the camp at Gilgal.

[16]During the fight the five kings ran away and hid in a cave near Makkedah, [17]but someone found them hiding in the cave at Makkedah and told Joshua. [18]So he said, "Cover the opening of the cave with large rocks. Put some men there to guard it, [19]but don't stay there yourselves. Continue chasing the enemy and attacking them from behind. Don't let them get to their cities, because the LORD your God will hand them over to you."

[20]So Joshua and the Israelites killed the enemy, but a few were able to get back to their strong, walled cities. [21]After the fighting, Joshua's men came back safely to him at Makkedah. No one was brave enough to say a word against the Israelites.

[22]Joshua said, "Move the rocks that are covering the opening of the cave and bring those five kings out to me." [23]So Joshua's men brought the five kings out of the cave—the kings of Jerusalem, Hebron, Jarmuth, Lachish, and Eglon. [24]When they brought the five kings out to Joshua, he called for all his men. He said to the commanders of his army, "Come here! Put your feet on the necks of these kings." So they came close and put their feet on their necks.

[25]Joshua said to his men, "Be strong and brave! Don't be afraid, because I will show you what the LORD will do to the enemies you will fight in the future." [26]Then Joshua killed the five kings and hung their bodies on five trees, where he left them until evening.

[27]At sunset Joshua told his men to take the bodies down from the trees. Then they threw them into the same cave where they had been hiding and covered the opening of the cave with large rocks, which are still there today.

[28]That day Joshua defeated Makkedah. He killed the king and completely destroyed all the people in that city as an offering to the LORD; no one was left alive. He did the same thing to the king of Makkedah that he had done to the king of Jericho.

Defeating Southern Cities

[29]Joshua and all the Israelites traveled from Makkedah to Libnah and attacked it. [30]The LORD handed over the city and its king. They killed every person in the city; no one was left alive. And they did the same thing to that king that they had done to the king of Jericho.

[31]Then Joshua and all the Israelites left Libnah and went to Lachish, which they surrounded and attacked. [32]The LORD handed over Lachish on the second day. The Israelites killed everyone in that city just as they had done to Libnah. [33]During this same time Horam king of Gezer came to help Lachish, but Joshua also defeated him and his army; no one was left alive.

[34]Then Joshua and all the Israelites went from Lachish to Eglon. They surrounded Eglon, attacked it, and [35]captured it the same day. They killed all its people and completely destroyed everything in it as an offering to the LORD, just as they had done to Lachish.

[36]Then Joshua and the Israelites went from Eglon to Hebron and attacked it, [37]capturing it and all the little towns near it. The Israelites killed everyone in Hebron; no one was left alive there. Just as they had done to Eglon, they completely destroyed the city and all its people as an offering to the LORD.

[38]Then Joshua and the Israelites went back to Debir and attacked it. [39]They captured that city, its king, and all the little towns near it, completely destroying everyone in Debir as an offering to the LORD; no one was left alive there. Israel did to Debir and its king just as they had done to Libnah and its king, just as they had done to Hebron.

[40]So Joshua defeated all the kings of the cities of these areas: the mountains, southern Canaan, the western hills, and the slopes. The LORD, the God of Israel, had told Joshua to completely destroy all the people as an offering to the LORD, so he left no one alive in those places. [41]Joshua captured all the cities

from Kadesh Barnea to Gaza, and from Goshen to Gibeon. [42]He captured all these cities and their kings on one trip, because the LORD, the God of Israel, was fighting for Israel.

[43]Then Joshua and all the Israelites returned to their camp at Gilgal.

PSALM 44:1–3

A Prayer for Help

For the director of music. A maskil of the sons of Korah.

44 God, we have heard about you.
Our ancestors told us
what you did in their days,
in days long ago.
[2]With your power you forced the nations
out of the land
and placed our ancestors here.
You destroyed those other nations,
but you made our ancestors grow
strong.
[3]It wasn't their swords that took the land.
It wasn't their power that gave them
victory.
But it was your great power and
strength.
You were with them because you loved
them.

PROVERBS 13:24–25

[24]If you do not punish your children, you
don't love them,
but if you love your children, you will
correct them.

[25]Good people have enough to eat,
but the wicked will go hungry.

LUKE 10:1–24

Jesus Sends Out the Seventy-Two

10 After this, the Lord chose seventy-two[n] others and sent them out in pairs ahead of him into every town and place where he planned to go. [2]He said to them, "There are a great many people to harvest, but there are only a few workers. So pray to God, who owns the harvest, that he will send more workers to help gather his harvest. [3]Go now, but listen! I am sending you out like sheep among wolves. [4]Don't carry a purse, a bag, or sandals, and don't waste time talking with people on the road. [5]Before you go into a house, say, 'Peace be with this house.' [6]If peace-loving people live there, your blessing of peace will stay with them, but if not, then your blessing will come back to you. [7]Stay in the same house, eating and drinking what the people there give you. A worker should be given his pay. Don't move from house to house. [8]If you go into a town and the people welcome you, eat what they give you. [9]Heal the sick who live there, and tell them, 'The kingdom of God is near you.' [10]But if you go into a town, and the people don't welcome you, then go into the streets and say, [11]'Even the dirt from your town that sticks to our feet we wipe off against you.[n] But remember that the kingdom of God is near.' [12]I tell you, on the Judgment Day it will be better for the people of Sodom[n] than for the people of that town.

Jesus Warns Unbelievers

[13]"How terrible for you, Korazin! How terrible for you, Bethsaida! If the miracles I did in you had happened in Tyre and Sidon,[n] those people would have changed their lives long ago. They would have worn rough cloth and put ashes on themselves to show they had changed. [14]But on the Judgment Day it will be better for Tyre and Sidon than for you. [15]And you, Capernaum,[n] will you be lifted up to heaven? No! You will be thrown down to the depths!

[16]"Whoever listens to you listens to me, and whoever refuses to accept you refuses to accept me. And whoever refuses to accept me refuses to accept the One who sent me."

Satan Falls

[17]When the seventy-two[n] came back, they were very happy and said, "Lord, even the

---

10:1 seventy-two Some Greek copies read "seventy." **10:11 dirt . . . you** A warning. It showed that they had rejected these people. **10:12 Sodom** City that God destroyed because the people were so evil. **10:13 Tyre and Sidon** Towns where wicked people lived. **10:13, 15 Korazin, Bethsaida, Capernaum** Towns by Lake Galilee where Jesus preached to the people. **10:17 seventy-two** Some Greek copies read "seventy."

demons obeyed us when we used your name!"

[18]Jesus said, "I saw Satan fall like lightning from heaven. [19]Listen, I have given you power to walk on snakes and scorpions, power that is greater than the enemy has. So nothing will hurt you. [20]But you should not be happy because the spirits obey you but because your names are written in heaven."

Jesus Prays to the Father

[21]Then Jesus rejoiced in the Holy Spirit and said, "I praise you, Father, Lord of heaven and earth, because you have hidden these things from the people who are wise and smart. But you have shown them to those who are like little children. Yes, Father, this is what you really wanted.

[22]"My Father has given me all things. No one knows who the Son is, except the Father. And no one knows who the Father is, except the Son and those whom the Son chooses to tell."

[23]Then Jesus turned to his followers and said privately, "You are blessed to see what you now see. [24]I tell you, many prophets and kings wanted to see what you now see, but they did not, and they wanted to hear what you now hear, but they did not."

APRIL 11

Defeating Northern Kings

11 When Jabin king of Hazor heard about all that had happened, he sent messages to Jobab king of Madon, to the king of Shimron, and to the king of Acshaph. [2]He sent messages to the kings in the northern mountains and also to the kings in the Jordan Valley south of Lake Galilee and in the western hills. He sent a message to the king of Naphoth Dor in the west [3]and to the kings of the Canaanites in the east and in the west. He sent messages to the Amorites, Hittites, Perizzites, and Jebusites in the mountains. Jabin also sent one to the Hivites, who lived below Mount Hermon in the area of Mizpah. [4]So the armies of all these kings came together with their horses and chariots. There were as many soldiers as grains of sand on the seashore.

[5]All of these kings met together at the waters of Merom, joined their armies together into one camp, and made plans to fight against the Israelites.

[6]Then the LORD said to Joshua, "Don't be afraid of them, because at this time tomorrow I will give them to you. You will cripple their horses and burn all their chariots."

[7]So Joshua and his whole army surprised the enemy by attacking them at the waters of Merom. [8]The LORD handed them over to Israel. They chased them to Greater Sidon, Misrephoth Maim, and the Valley of Mizpah in the east. Israel fought until none of the enemy was left alive. [9]Joshua did what the LORD said to do; he crippled their horses and burned their chariots.

[10]Then Joshua went back and captured the city of Hazor and killed its king. (Hazor had been the leader of all the kingdoms that fought against Israel.) [11]Israel killed everyone in Hazor, completely destroying them; no one was left alive. Then they burned Hazor itself.

[12]Joshua captured all of these cities, killed all of their kings, and completely destroyed everything in these cities. He did this just as Moses, the servant of the LORD, had commanded. [13]But the Israelites did not burn any cities that were built on their mounds, except Hazor; only that city was burned by Joshua. [14]The people of Israel kept for themselves everything they found in the cities, including all the animals. But they killed all the people there; they left no one alive. [15]Long ago the LORD had commanded his servant Moses to do this, and then Moses had commanded Joshua to do it. Joshua did everything the LORD had commanded Moses.

[16]So Joshua defeated all the people in the land. He had control of the mountains and the area of southern Canaan, all the areas of Goshen, the western hills, and the Jordan Valley. He controlled the mountains of Israel and all the hills near them. [17]Joshua controlled all the land from Mount Halak near Edom to Baal Gad in the Valley of Lebanon, below Mount Hermon. Joshua also captured all the kings in the land and killed them. [18]He fought against them for many years. [19]The people of only one city in all the land had made a peace agreement with Israel— the Hivites living in Gibeon. All the other cities were defeated in war. [20]The LORD made those people stubborn so they would fight against Israel and he could completely destroy them without mercy. This is what the LORD had commanded Moses to do.

[21]Now Joshua fought the Anakites who lived in the mountains of Hebron, Debir, Anab, Judah, and Israel, and he completely destroyed them and their towns. [22]There were no Anakites left living in the land of the Israelites and only a few were left in Gaza, Gath, and Ashdod. [23]Joshua took control of all the land of Israel as the LORD had told Moses to do long ago. He gave the land to Israel, because he had promised it to them. Then Joshua divided the land among the tribes of Israel, and there was peace in the land.

Kings Defeated by Israel

12 The Israelites took control of the land east of the Jordan River from the Arnon Ravine to Mount Hermon and all the land along the eastern side of the Jordan Valley. These lands belonged to the kings whom the Israelites defeated.

[2]Sihon king of the Amorites lived in the city of Heshbon and ruled the land from Aroer at the Arnon Ravine to the Jabbok River. His land started in the middle of the ravine, which was their border with the Ammonites. Sihon ruled over half the land of Gilead [3]and over the eastern side of the Jordan Valley from Lake Galilee to the Dead Sea. And he ruled from Beth Jeshimoth south to the slopes of Pisgah.

[4]Og king of Bashan was one of the last of the Rephaites. He ruled the land in Ashtaroth and Edrei. [5]He ruled over Mount Hermon, Salecah, and all the area of Bashan up to where the people of Geshur and Maacah lived. Og also ruled half the land of Gilead up to the border of Sihon king of Heshbon.

[6]The LORD's servant Moses and the Israelites defeated all these kings, and Moses gave that land to the tribes of Reuben and Gad and to East Manasseh as their own.

[7]Joshua and the Israelites also defeated kings in the land west of the Jordan River. He gave the people the land and divided it among the twelve tribes to be their own. It was between Baal Gad in the Valley of Lebanon and Mount Halak near Edom. [8]This included the mountains, the western hills, the Jordan Valley, the slopes, the desert, and southern Canaan. This was the land where the Hittites, Amorites, Canaanites, Perizzites, Hivites, and Jebusites had lived. The Israelites defeated the king of each of the following cities: [9]Jericho, Ai (near Bethel), [10]Jerusalem, Hebron, [11]Jarmuth, Lachish, [12]Eglon, Gezer, [13]Debir, Geder, [14]Hormah, Arad, [15]Libnah, Adullam, [16]Makkedah, Bethel, [17]Tappuah, Hepher, [18]Aphek, Lasharon, [19]Madon, Hazor, [20]Shimron Meron, Acshaph, [21]Taanach, Megiddo, [22]Kedesh, Jokneam in Carmel, [23]Dor (in Naphoth Dor), Goyim in Gilgal, and [24]Tirzah.

The total number of kings was thirty-one.

PSALM 44:4–19

[4]My God, you are my King.
Your commands led Jacob's people to victory.
[5]With your help we pushed back our enemies.
In your name we trampled those who came against us.
[6]I don't trust my bow to help me,
and my sword can't save me.
[7]You saved us from our foes,
and you made our enemies ashamed.
[8]We will praise God every day;
we will praise your name forever.   Selah

[9]But you have rejected us and shamed us.
You don't march with our armies anymore.

[10]You let our enemies push us back,
and those who hate us have taken our
wealth.
[11]You gave us away like sheep to be eaten
and have scattered us among the
nations.
[12]You sold your people for nothing
and made no profit on the sale.

[13]You made us a joke to our neighbors;
those around us laugh and make fun of
us.
[14]You made us a joke to the other nations;
people shake their heads.
[15]I am always in disgrace,
and I am covered with shame.
[16]My enemy is getting even
with insults and curses.

[17]All these things have happened to us,
but we have not forgotten you
or failed to keep our agreement with
you.
[18]Our hearts haven't turned away from
you,
and we haven't stopped following you.
[19]But you crushed us in this place where
wild dogs live,
and you covered us with deep
darkness.

PROVERBS 14:1–2

14 A wise woman strengthens her
family,
but a foolish woman destroys hers by
what she does.

[2]People who live good lives respect the
LORD,
but those who live evil lives don't.

LUKE 10:25–42

The Good Samaritan

[25]Then an expert on the law stood up to
test Jesus, saying, "Teacher, what must I do to
get life forever?"

[26]Jesus said, "What is written in the law?
What do you read there?"

[27]The man answered, "Love the Lord your
God with all your heart, all your soul, all your
strength, and all your mind."[n] Also, "Love
your neighbor as you love yourself."[n]

[28]Jesus said to him, "Your answer is right.
Do this and you will live."

[29]But the man, wanting to show the importance of his question, said to Jesus, "And
who is my neighbor?"

[30]Jesus answered, "As a man was going
down from Jerusalem to Jericho, some robbers attacked him. They tore off his clothes,
beat him, and left him lying there, almost
dead. [31]It happened that a priest was going
down that road. When he saw the man, he
walked by on the other side. [32]Next, a Levite[n]
came there, and after he went over and
looked at the man, he walked by on the other
side of the road. [33]Then a Samaritan[n] traveling down the road came to where the hurt
man was. When he saw the man, he felt very
sorry for him. [34]The Samaritan went to him,
poured olive oil and wine[n] on his wounds,
and bandaged them. Then he put the hurt
man on his own donkey and took him to an
inn where he cared for him. [35]The next day,
the Samaritan brought out two coins,[n] gave
them to the innkeeper, and said, 'Take care of
this man. If you spend more money on him,
I will pay it back to you when I come again.'"

[36]Then Jesus said, "Which one of these
three men do you think was a neighbor to
the man who was attacked by the robbers?"

[37]The expert on the law answered, "The
one who showed him mercy."

Jesus said to him, "Then go and do what
he did."

Mary and Martha

[38]While Jesus and his followers were traveling, Jesus went into a town. A woman
named Martha let Jesus stay at her house.
[39]Martha had a sister named Mary, who was

10:27 "Love . . . mind." Quotation from Deuteronomy 6:5.   **10:27 "Love . . . yourself."** Quotation from Leviticus 19:18.
10:32 Levite Levites were members of the tribe of Levi who helped the Jewish priests with their work in the Temple. Read
1 Chronicles 23:24–32.   **10:33 Samaritan** Samaritans were people from Samaria. These people were part Jewish, but the
Jews did not accept them as true Jews. Samaritans and Jews disliked each other.   **10:34 olive oil and wine** Oil and wine
were used like medicine to soften and clean wounds.   **10:35 coins** Roman denarii. One coin was the average pay for one
day's work.

sitting at Jesus' feet and listening to him teach. ⁴⁰But Martha was busy with all the work to be done. She went in and said, "Lord, don't you care that my sister has left me alone to do all the work? Tell her to help me."

⁴¹But the Lord answered her, "Martha, Martha, you are worried and upset about many things. ⁴²Only one thing is important. Mary has chosen the better thing, and it will never be taken away from her."

APRIL 12

JOSHUA 13:1—14:15

Land Still to Be Taken

13 When Joshua was very old, the LORD said to him, "Joshua, you have grown old, but there is still much land for you to take. ²This is what is left: the regions of Geshur and of the Philistines; ³the area from the Shihor River at the border of Egypt to Ekron in the north, which belongs to the Canaanites; the five Philistine leaders at Gaza, Ashdod, Ashkelon, Gath, and Ekron; the Avvites, ⁴who live south of the Canaanite land; ⁵the Gebalites, and the area of Lebanon east of Baal Gad below Mount Hermon to Lebo Hamath.

⁶"The Sidonians are living in the hill country from Lebanon to Misrephoth Maim, but I will force all of them out ahead of the Israelites. Be sure to remember this land when you divide the land among the Israelites, as I told you.

⁷"Now divide the land among the nine tribes and West Manasseh."

Dividing the Land

⁸East Manasseh and the tribes of Reuben and Gad had received their land. The LORD's servant Moses had given them the land east of the Jordan River. ⁹Their land started at Aroer at the Arnon Ravine and continued to the town in the middle of the ravine, and it included the whole plain from Medeba to Dibon. ¹⁰All the towns ruled by Sihon king of the Amorites, who ruled in the city of Heshbon, were in that land. The land continued to the area where the Ammonites lived. ¹¹Gilead was also there, as well as the area where the people of Geshur and Maacah lived, and all of Mount Hermon and Bashan

as far as Salecah. ¹²All the kingdom of Og king of Bashan was in the land. Og was one of the last of the Rephaites, and in the past he ruled in Ashtaroth and Edrei. Moses had defeated them and had taken their land. ¹³Because the Israelites did not force out the people of Geshur and Maacah, they still live among the Israelites today.

¹⁴The tribe of Levi was the only one that did not get any land. Instead, they were given all the burned sacrifices made to the LORD, the God of Israel, as he had promised them.

¹⁵Moses had given each family group from the tribe of Reuben some land: ¹⁶Theirs was the land from Aroer near the Arnon Ravine to the town of Medeba, including the whole plain and the town in the middle of the ravine; ¹⁷Heshbon and all the towns on the plain: Dibon, Bamoth Baal, and Beth Baal Meon, ¹⁸Jahaz, Kedemoth, Mephaath, ¹⁹Kiriathaim, Sibmah, Zereth Shahar on the hill in the valley, ²⁰Beth Peor, the hills of Pisgah, and Beth Jeshimoth. ²¹So that land included all the towns on the plain and all the area that Sihon king of the Amorites had ruled from the town of Heshbon. Moses had defeated him along with the leaders of the Midianites, including Evi, Rekem, Zur, Hur, and Reba. All these leaders fought together with Sihon and lived in that country. ²²The Israelites killed many people during the fighting, including Balaam of Beor, who tried to use magic to tell the future. ²³The land given to Reuben stopped at the shore of the Jordan River. So the land given to the family groups of Reuben included all these towns and their villages that were listed.

²⁴This is the land Moses gave to the tribe of Gad, to all its family groups: ²⁵the land of

Jazer and all the towns of Gilead; half the land of the Ammonites that went as far as Aroer near Rabbah; ²⁶the area from Heshbon to Ramath Mizpah and Betonim; the area from Mahanaim to the land of Debir; ²⁷in the valley, Beth Haram, Beth Nimrah, Succoth, and Zaphon, the other land Sihon king of Heshbon had ruled east of the Jordan River and continuing to the end of Lake Galilee. ²⁸All this land went to the family groups of Gad, including all these towns and their villages.

²⁹This is the land Moses had given to East Manasseh. Half of all the family groups in the tribe of Manasseh were given this land: ³⁰The land started at Mahanaim and included all of Bashan and the land ruled by Og king of Bashan; all the towns of Jair in Bashan, sixty cities in all; ³¹half of Gilead, Ashtaroth, and Edrei, the cities where Og king of Bashan had ruled. All this went to the family of Makir son of Manasseh, and half of all his sons were given this land.

³²Moses had given this land to these tribes on the plains of Moab across the Jordan River east of Jericho. ³³But Moses had given no land to the tribe of Levi because the LORD, the God of Israel, promised that he himself would be the gift for the Levites.

14 Eleazar the priest, Joshua son of Nun, and the leaders of all the tribes of Israel decided what land to give to the people in the land of Canaan. ²The LORD had commanded Moses long ago how he wanted the people to choose their land. The people of the nine-and-a-half tribes threw lots to decide which land they would receive. ³Moses had already given the two-and-a-half tribes their land east of the Jordan River. But the tribe of Levi was not given any land like the others. ⁴The sons of Joseph had divided into two tribes—Manasseh and Ephraim. The tribe of Levi was not given any land. It was given only some towns in which to live and pastures for its animals. ⁵The LORD had told Moses how to give the land to the tribes of Israel, and the Israelites divided the land.

Caleb's Land

⁶One day some men from the tribe of Judah went to Joshua at Gilgal. Among them was Caleb son of Jephunneh the Kenizzite.

He said to Joshua, "You remember what the LORD said at Kadesh Barnea when he was speaking to the prophet Moses about you and me. ⁷Moses, the LORD's servant, sent me to look at the land where we were going. I was forty years old then. When I came back, I told Moses what I thought about the land. ⁸The other men who went with me frightened the people, but I fully believed the LORD would allow us to take the land. ⁹So that day Moses promised me, 'The land where you went will become your land, and your children will own it forever. I will give you that land because you fully believed in the LORD, my God.'

¹⁰"Now then, the LORD has kept his promise. He has kept me alive for forty-five years from the time he said this to Moses during the time we all wandered in the desert. Now here I am, eighty-five years old. ¹¹I am still as strong today as I was the day Moses sent me out, and I am just as ready to fight now as I was then. ¹²So give me the mountain country the LORD promised me that day long ago. Back then you heard that the Anakite people lived there and the cities were large and well protected. But now with the LORD helping me, I will force them out, just as the LORD said."

¹³Joshua blessed Caleb son of Jephunneh and gave him the city of Hebron as his own. ¹⁴Hebron still belongs to the family of Caleb son of Jephunneh the Kenizzite because he had faith and obeyed the LORD, the God of Israel. ¹⁵(In the past it was called Kiriath Arba, named for Arba, the greatest man among the Anakites.)

After this there was peace in the land.

PSALM 44:20–26

²⁰If we had forgotten our God
    or lifted our hands in prayer to foreign
        gods,
²¹God would have known,
    because he knows what is in our
        hearts.
²²But for you we are in danger of death all
        the time.
    People think we are worth no more
        than sheep to be killed.

23Wake up, Lord! Why are you sleeping?
  Get up! Don't reject us forever.
24Why do you hide from us?
  Have you forgotten our pain and
    troubles?

25We have been pushed down into the dirt;
  we are flat on the ground.
26Get up and help us.
  Because of your love, save us.

PROVERBS 14:3

3Fools will be punished for their proud
    words,
  but the words of the wise will protect
    them.

LUKE 11:1–28

Jesus Teaches About Prayer

11 One time Jesus was praying in a certain place. When he finished, one of his
followers said to him, "Lord, teach us to pray
as John taught his followers."
  2Jesus said to them, "When you pray, say:
  'Father, may your name always be kept
    holy.
  May your kingdom come.
  3Give us the food we need for each day.
  4Forgive us for our sins,
    because we forgive everyone who has
      done wrong to us.
  And do not cause us to be tempted.' "[n]

Continue to Ask

5Then Jesus said to them, "Suppose one of
you went to your friend's house at midnight
and said to him, 'Friend, loan me three loaves
of bread. 6A friend of mine has come into
town to visit me, but I have nothing for him to
eat.' 7Your friend inside the house answers,
'Don't bother me! The door is already locked,
and my children and I are in bed. I cannot get
up and give you anything.' 8I tell you, if friendship is not enough to make him get up to give
you the bread, your boldness will make him
get up and give you whatever you need. 9So I
tell you, ask, and God will give to you. Search,
and you will find. Knock, and the door will

open for you. 10Yes, everyone who asks will receive. The one who searches will find. And
everyone who knocks will have the door
opened. 11If your children ask for[n] a fish,
which of you would give them a snake instead? 12Or, if your children ask for an egg,
would you give them a scorpion? 13Even
though you are bad, you know how to give
good things to your children. How much
more your heavenly Father will give the Holy
Spirit to those who ask him!"

Jesus' Power Is from God

14One time Jesus was sending out a demon who could not talk. When the demon
came out, the man who had been unable to
speak, then spoke. The people were amazed.
15But some of them said, "Jesus uses the
power of Beelzebul, the ruler of demons, to
force demons out of people."
  16Other people, wanting to test Jesus,
asked him to give them a sign from heaven.
17But knowing their thoughts, he said to
them, "Every kingdom that is divided
against itself will be destroyed. And a family
that is divided against itself will not continue. 18So if Satan is divided against himself, his kingdom will not continue. You say
that I use the power of Beelzebul to force out
demons. 19But if I use the power of Beelzebul
to force out demons, what power do your
people use to force demons out? So they will
be your judges. 20But if I use the power of
God to force out demons, then the kingdom
of God has come to you.
  21"When a strong person with many
weapons guards his own house, his possessions are safe. 22But when someone stronger
comes and defeats him, the stronger one will
take away the weapons the first man trusted
and will give away the possessions.
  23"Anyone who is not with me is against
me, and anyone who does not work with me
is working against me.

The Empty Person

24"When an evil spirit comes out of a person, it travels through dry places, looking for
a place to rest. But when it finds no place, it

11:2-4 'Father . . . tempted.' Some Greek copies include phrases from Matthew's version of this prayer (Matthew 6:9–13).
11:11 for Some Greek copies include the phrase "for bread, which of you would give them a stone, or if they ask for . . ."

says, 'I will go back to the house I left.' ²⁵And when it comes back, it finds that house swept clean and made neat. ²⁶Then the evil spirit goes out and brings seven other spirits more evil than it is, and they go in and live there. So the person has even more trouble than before."

People Who Are Truly Blessed

²⁷As Jesus was saying these things, a woman in the crowd called out to Jesus, "Blessed is the mother who gave birth to you and nursed you."

²⁸But Jesus said, "No, blessed are those who hear the teaching of God and obey it."

APRIL 13

JOSHUA 15:1—16:10

Land for Judah

15 The land that was given to the tribe of Judah was divided among all the family groups. It went all the way to the Desert of Zin in the far south, at the border of Edom.

²The southern border of Judah's land started at the south end of the Dead Sea ³and went south of Scorpion Pass to Zin. From there it passed to the south of Kadesh Barnea and continued past Hezron to Addar. From Addar it turned and went to Karka. ⁴It continued to Azmon, the brook of Egypt, and then to the Mediterranean Sea. This was the southern border.

⁵The eastern border was the shore of the Dead Sea, as far as the mouth of the Jordan River.

The northern border started at the bay of the sea at the mouth of the Jordan River. ⁶Then it went to Beth Hoglah and continued north of Beth Arabah to the stone of Bohan son of Reuben. ⁷Then the northern border went through the Valley of Achor to Debir where it turned toward the north and went to Gilgal. Gilgal is across from the road that goes through Adummim Pass, on the south side of the ravine. The border continued to the waters of En Shemesh and stopped at En Rogel. ⁸Then it went through the Valley of Ben Hinnom, next to the southern side of the Jebusite city (which is called Jerusalem). There the border went to the top of the hill on the west side of Hinnom Valley, at the northern end of the Valley of Giants. ⁹From there it went to the spring of the waters of Nephtoah and then it went to the cities near

Mount Ephron. There it turned and went toward Baalah, which is called Kiriath Jearim. ¹⁰At Baalah the border turned west and went toward Mount Seir. It continued along the north side of Mount Jearim (also called Kesalon) and came to Beth Shemesh. From there it went past Timnah ¹¹to the hill north of Ekron. Then it turned toward Shikkeron and went past Mount Baalah and continued on to Jabneel, ending at the sea.

¹²The Mediterranean Sea was the western border. Inside these borders lived the family groups of Judah.

¹³The LORD had commanded Joshua to give Caleb son of Jephunneh part of the land in Judah, so he gave Caleb the town of Kiriath Arba, also called Hebron. (Arba was the father of Anak.) ¹⁴Caleb forced out the three Anakite families living in Hebron: Sheshai, Ahiman, and Talmai, the descendants of Anak. ¹⁵Then he left there and went to fight against the people living in Debir. (In the past Debir had been called Kiriath Sepher.) ¹⁶Caleb said, "I will give Acsah, my daughter, as a wife to the man who attacks and captures the city of Kiriath Sepher." ¹⁷Othniel son of Kenaz, Caleb's brother, captured the city, so Caleb gave his daughter Acsah to Othniel to be his wife. ¹⁸When Acsah came to Othniel, she told him to ask her father for a field.

So Acsah went to her father. When she got down from her donkey, Caleb asked her, "What do you want?"

¹⁹Acsah answered, "Do me a special favor. Since you have given me land in southern Canaan, also give me springs of water." So Caleb gave her the upper and lower springs.

20The tribe of Judah got the land God had promised them. Each family group got part of the land.

21The tribe of Judah got all these towns in the southern part of Canaan near the border of Edom: Kabzeel, Eder, Jagur, 22Kinah, Dimonah, Adadah, 23Kedesh, Hazor, Ithnan, 24Ziph, Telem, Bealoth, 25Hazor Hadattah, Kerioth Hezron (also called Hazor), 26Amam, Shema, Moladah, 27Hazar Gaddah, Heshmon, Beth Pelet, 28Hazar Shual, Beersheba, Biziothiah, 29Baalah, Iim, Ezem, 30Eltolad, Kesil, Hormah, 31Ziklag, Madmannah, Sansannah, 32Lebaoth, Shilhim, Ain, and Rimmon. There were twenty-nine towns and their villages.

33The tribe of Judah got these towns in the western hills: Eshtaol, Zorah, Ashnah, 34Zanoah, En Gannim, Tappuah, Enam, 35Jarmuth, Adullam, Socoh, Azekah, 36Shaaraim, Adithaim, and Gederah (also called Gederothaim). There were fourteen towns and their villages.

37Judah was also given these towns in the western hills: Zenan, Hadashah, Migdal Gad, 38Dilean, Mizpah, Joktheel, 39Lachish, Bozkath, Eglon, 40Cabbon, Lahmas, Kitlish, 41Gederoth, Beth Dagon, Naamah, and Makkedah. There were sixteen towns and their villages.

42Judah was also given these towns in the western hills: Libnah, Ether, Ashan, 43Iphtah, Ashnah, Nezib, 44Keilah, Aczib, and Mareshah. There were nine towns and their villages.

45The tribe of Judah was also given these towns: Ekron and all the small towns and villages near it; 46the area west of Ekron and all the villages and small towns near Ashdod; 47Ashdod and the small towns and villages around it; the villages and small towns around Gaza as far as the brook of Egypt and along the coast of the Mediterranean Sea.

48The tribe of Judah was also given these towns in the mountains: Shamir, Jattir, Socoh, 49Dannah, Kiriath Sannah (also called Debir), 50Anab, Eshtemoh, Anim, 51Goshen, Holon, and Giloh. There were eleven towns and their villages.

52They were also given these towns in the mountains: Arab, Dumah, Eshan, 53Janim, Beth Tappuah, Aphekah, 54Humtah, Kiriath Arba (also called Hebron), and Zior. There were nine towns and their villages.

55Judah was also given these towns in the mountains: Maon, Carmel, Ziph, Juttah, 56Jezreel, Jokdeam, Zanoah, 57Kain, Gibeah, and Timnah. There were ten towns and their villages.

58They were also given these towns in the mountains: Halhul, Beth Zur, Gedor, 59Maarath, Beth Anoth, and Eltekon. There were six towns and their villages.

60The people of Judah were also given the two towns of Rabbah and Kiriath Baal (also called Kiriath Jearim) and their villages.

61Judah was given these towns in the desert: Beth Arabah, Middin, Secacah, 62Nibshan, the City of Salt, and En Gedi. There were six towns and all their villages.

63The army of Judah was not able to force out the Jebusites living in Jerusalem, so the Jebusites still live among the people of Judah to this day.

Land for Ephraim and Manasseh

16 This is the land the tribe of Joseph received. It started at the Jordan River near Jericho and continued to the waters of Jericho, just east of the city. The border went up from Jericho to the mountains of Bethel. 2Then it continued from Bethel (also called Luz) to the Arkite border at Ataroth. 3From there it went west to the border of the Japhletites and continued to the area of the Lower Beth Horon. Then it went to Gezer and ended at the sea.

4So Manasseh and Ephraim, sons of Joseph, received their land.

5This is the land that was given to the family groups of Ephraim: Their border started at Ataroth Addar in the east, went to Upper Beth Horon, 6and then to the sea. From Micmethath it turned eastward toward Taanath Shiloh and continued eastward to Janoah. 7Then it went down from Janoah to Ataroth and to Naarah. It continued until it touched Jericho and stopped at the Jordan River. 8The border went from Tappuah west to Kanah Ravine and ended at the sea. This is all the land that was given to each family group in the tribe of the

Ephraimites. [9]Many of the towns were actually within Manasseh's borders, but the people of Ephraim got those towns and their villages. [10]The Ephraimites could not force the Canaanites to leave Gezer, so the Canaanites still live among the Ephraimites today, but they became slaves of the Ephraimites.

PSALM 45:1–9

A Song for the King's Wedding

For the director of music. To the tune of "Lilies." A maskil. A love song of the sons of Korah.

45 Beautiful words fill my mind.
I am speaking of royal things.
My tongue is like the pen of a skilled writer.

[2]You are more handsome than anyone,
and you are an excellent speaker,
so God has blessed you forever.
[3]Put on your sword, powerful warrior.
Show your glory and majesty.
[4]In your majesty win the victory
for what is true and right.
Your power will do amazing things.
[5]Your sharp arrows will enter
the hearts of the king's enemies.
Nations will be defeated before you.
[6]God, your throne will last forever and ever.
You will rule your kingdom with fairness.
[7]You love right and hate evil,
so God has chosen you from among your friends;
he has set you apart with much joy.
[8]Your clothes smell like myrrh, aloes, and cassia.
From palaces of ivory
music comes to make you happy.
[9]Kings' daughters are among your honored women.
Your bride stands at your right side
wearing gold from Ophir.

PROVERBS 14:4–5

[4]When there are no oxen, no food is in the barn.

But with a strong ox, much grain can be grown.

[5]A truthful witness does not lie,
but a false witness tells nothing but lies.

LUKE 11:29–54

The People Want a Miracle

[29]As the crowd grew larger, Jesus said, "The people who live today are evil. They want to see a miracle for a sign, but no sign will be given them, except the sign of Jonah.[n] [30]As Jonah was a sign for those people who lived in Nineveh, the Son of Man will be a sign for the people of this time. [31]On the Judgment Day the Queen of the South[n] will stand up with the people who live now. She will show they are guilty, because she came from far away to listen to Solomon's wise teaching. And I tell you that someone greater than Solomon is here. [32]On the Judgment Day the people of Nineveh will stand up with the people who live now, and they will show that you are guilty. When Jonah preached to them, they were sorry and changed their lives. And I tell you that someone greater than Jonah is here.

Be a Light for the World

[33]"No one lights a lamp and puts it in a secret place or under a bowl, but on a lampstand so the people who come in can see. [34]Your eye is a light for the body. When your eyes are good, your whole body will be full of light. But when your eyes are evil, your whole body will be full of darkness. [35]So be careful not to let the light in you become darkness. [36]If your whole body is full of light, and none of it is dark, then you will shine bright, as when a lamp shines on you."

Jesus Accuses the Pharisees

[37]After Jesus had finished speaking, a Pharisee asked Jesus to eat with him. So Jesus went in and sat at the table. [38]But the Pharisee was surprised when he saw that Jesus did not wash his hands[n] before the meal.

11:29 sign of Jonah Jonah's three days in the fish are like Jesus' three days in the tomb. See Matthew 12:40. **11:31 Queen of the South** The Queen of Sheba. She traveled a thousand miles to learn God's wisdom from Solomon. Read 1 Kings 10:1–3. **11:38 wash his hands** This was a Jewish religious custom that the Pharisees thought was very important.

[39]The Lord said to him, "You Pharisees clean the outside of the cup and the dish, but inside you are full of greed and evil. [40]You foolish people! The same one who made what is outside also made what is inside. [41]So give what is in your dishes to the poor, and then you will be fully clean. [42]How terrible for you Pharisees! You give God one-tenth of even your mint, your rue, and every other plant in your garden. But you fail to be fair to others and to love God. These are the things you should do while continuing to do those other things. [43]How terrible for you Pharisees, because you love to have the most important seats in the synagogues, and you love to be greeted with respect in the marketplaces. [44]How terrible for you, because you are like hidden graves, which people walk on without knowing."

Jesus Talks to Experts on the Law

[45]One of the experts on the law said to Jesus, "Teacher, when you say these things, you are insulting us, too."

[46]Jesus answered, "How terrible for you, you experts on the law! You make strict rules that are very hard for people to obey, but you

yourselves don't even try to follow those rules. [47]How terrible for you, because you build tombs for the prophets whom your ancestors killed! [48]And now you show that you approve of what your ancestors did. They killed the prophets, and you build tombs for them! [49]This is why in his wisdom God said, 'I will send prophets and apostles to them. They will kill some, and they will treat others cruelly.' [50]So you who live now will be punished for the deaths of all the prophets who were killed since the beginning of the world— [51]from the killing of Abel to the killing of Zechariah,[n] who died between the altar and the Temple. Yes, I tell you that you who are alive now will be punished for them all.

[52]"How terrible for you, you experts on the law. You have taken away the key to learning about God. You yourselves would not learn, and you stopped others from learning, too."

[53]When Jesus left, the teachers of the law and the Pharisees began to give him trouble, asking him questions about many things, [54]trying to catch him saying something wrong.

APRIL 14

JOSHUA 17:1—18:28

17 Then land was given to the tribe of Manasseh, Joseph's first son. Manasseh's first son was Makir, the father of Gilead. Makir was a great soldier, so the lands of Gilead and Bashan were given to his family. [2]Land was also given to the other family groups of Manasseh—Abiezer, Helek, Asriel, Shechem, Hepher, and Shemida. These were all the other sons of Manasseh son of Joseph.

[3]Zelophehad was the son of Hepher, who was the son of Gilead, who was the son of Makir, who was the son of Manasseh. Zelophehad had no sons, but he had five daughters, named Mahlah, Noah, Hoglah,

Milcah, and Tirzah. [4]They went to Eleazar the priest and to Joshua son of Nun and all the leaders. They said, "The LORD told Moses to give us land like the men received." So Eleazar obeyed the LORD and gave the daughters some land, just like the brothers of their father. [5]So the tribe of Manasseh had ten sections of land west of the Jordan River and two more sections, Gilead and Bashan, on the east side of the Jordan River. [6]The daughters of Manasseh received land just as the sons did. Gilead was given to the rest of the families of Manasseh.

[7]The lands of Manasseh were in the area between Asher and Micmethath, near Shechem. The border went south to the En

11:51 Abel . . . Zechariah In the Hebrew Old Testament, the first and last men to be murdered.

Tappuah area, [8]which belonged to Manasseh, except for the town of Tappuah. It was along the border of Manasseh's land and belonged to the sons of Ephraim. [9]The border of Manasseh continued south to Kanah Ravine. The cities in this area of Manasseh belonged to Ephraim. Manasseh's border was on the north side of the ravine and went to the sea. [10]The land to the south belonged to Ephraim, and the land to the north belonged to Manasseh. The Mediterranean Sea was the western border. The border touched Asher's land on the north and Issachar's land on the east.

[11]In the areas of Issachar and Asher, the people of Manasseh owned these towns: Beth Shan and its small towns; Ibleam and its small towns; the people who lived in Dor and its small towns; the people in Naphoth Dor and its small towns; the people who lived in Taanach and its small towns; the people in Megiddo and its small towns. [12]Manasseh was not able to defeat those cities, so the Canaanites continued to live there. [13]When the Israelites grew strong, they forced the Canaanites to work for them, although they did not force them to leave the land.

[14]The people from the tribes of Joseph said to Joshua, "You gave us only one area of land, but we are many people. Why did you give us only one part of all the land the LORD gave his people?"

[15]And Joshua answered them, "If you have too many people, go up to the forest and make a place for yourselves to live there in the land of the Perizzites and the Rephaites. The mountain country of Ephraim is too small for you."

[16]The people of Joseph said, "It is true. The mountain country of Ephraim is not enough for us, but the land where the Canaanites live is dangerous. They are skilled fighters. They have powerful weapons in Beth Shan and all the small towns in that area, and they are also in the Valley of Jezreel."

[17]Then Joshua said to the people of Joseph—to Ephraim and Manasseh, "There are many of you, and you have great power. You should be given more than one share of land. [18]You also will have the mountain country. It is a forest, but you can cut down the trees and make it a good place to live. You will own all of it because you will force the Canaanites to leave the land even though they have powerful weapons and are strong."

The Rest of the Land Divided

18 All of the Israelites gathered together at Shiloh where they set up the Meeting Tent. The land was now under their control. [2]But there were still seven tribes of Israel that had not yet received their land.

[3]So Joshua said to the Israelites: "Why do you wait so long to take your land? The LORD, the God of your ancestors, has given this land to you. [4]Choose three men from each tribe, and I will send them out to study the land. They will describe in writing the land their tribe wants as its share, and then they will come back to me. [5]They will divide the land into seven parts. The people of Judah will keep their land in the south, and the people of Joseph will keep their land in the north. [6]You should describe the seven parts of land in writing and bring what you have written to me. Then I will throw lots in the presence of the LORD our God. [7]But the Levites do not get any part of these lands, because they are priests, and their work is to serve the LORD. Gad, Reuben, and East Manasseh have received the land promised to them, which is east of the Jordan River. Moses, the servant of the LORD, gave it to them."

[8]So the men who were chosen to map the land started out. Joshua told them, "Go and study the land and describe it in writing. Then come back to me, and I will throw lots in the presence of the LORD here in Shiloh." [9]So the men left and went into the land. They described in a scroll each town in the seven parts of the land. Then they came back to Joshua, who was still at the camp at Shiloh. [10]There Joshua threw lots in the presence of the LORD to choose the lands that should be given to each tribe.

Land for Benjamin

[11]The first part of the land was given to the tribe of Benjamin. Each family group received some land between the land of Judah and the land of Joseph. This is the land chosen for Benjamin: [12]The northern border started at the Jordan River and went along the northern

edge of Jericho, and then it went west into the mountains. That boundary continued until it was just east of Beth Aven. [13]From there it went south to Luz (also called Bethel) and then down to Ataroth Addar, which is on the hill south of Lower Beth Horon.

[14]At the hill to the south of Beth Horon, the border turned and went south near the western side of the hill. It went to Kiriath Baal (also called Kiriath Jearim), a town where people of Judah lived. This was the western border.

[15]The southern border started near Kiriath Jearim and went west to the waters of Nephtoah. [16]Then it went down to the bottom of the hill, which was near the Valley of Ben Hinnom, on the north side of the Valley of Rephaim. The border continued down the Hinnom Valley just south of the Jebusite city to En Rogel. [17]There it turned north and went to En Shemesh. It continued to Geliloth near the Adummim Pass. Then it went down to the great Stone of Bohan son of Reuben. [18]The border continued to the northern part of Beth Arabah and went down into the Jordan Valley. [19]From there it went to the northern part of Beth Hoglah and ended at the north shore of the Dead Sea, where the Jordan River flows into the sea. This was the southern border.

[20]The Jordan River was the border on the eastern side. So this was the land given to the family groups of Benjamin with the borders on all sides.

[21]The family groups of Benjamin received these cities: Jericho, Beth Hoglah, Emek Keziz, [22]Beth Arabah, Zemaraim, Bethel, [23]Avvim, Parah, Ophrah, [24]Kephar Ammoni, Ophni, and Geba. There were twelve towns and all their villages.

[25]The tribe of Benjamin also received Gibeon, Ramah, Beeroth, [26]Mizpah, Kephirah, Mozah, [27]Rekem, Irpeel, Taralah, [28]Zelah, Haeleph, the Jebusite city (Jerusalem), Gibeah, and Kiriath. There were fourteen towns and their villages. All these areas are the lands the family groups of Benjamin were given.

PSALM 45:10–17

[10]Listen to me, daughter; look and pay attention.

Forget your people and your father's family.
[11]The king loves your beauty.
Because he is your master, you should obey him.
[12]People from the city of Tyre have brought a gift.
Wealthy people will want to meet you.

[13]The princess is very beautiful.
Her gown is woven with gold.
[14]In her beautiful clothes she is brought to the king.
Her bridesmaids follow behind her, and they are also brought to him.
[15]They come with happiness and joy; they enter the king's palace.

[16]You will have sons to replace your fathers.
You will make them rulers through all the land.
[17]I will make your name famous from now on,
so people will praise you forever and ever.

PROVERBS 14:6

[6]Those who make fun of wisdom look for it and do not find it,
but knowledge comes easily to those with understanding.

LUKE 12:1–31

Don't Be Like the Pharisees

12 So many thousands of people had gathered that they were stepping on each other. Jesus spoke first to his followers, saying, "Beware of the yeast of the Pharisees, because they are hypocrites. [2]Everything that is hidden will be shown, and everything that is secret will be made known. [3]What you have said in the dark will be heard in the light, and what you have whispered in an inner room will be shouted from the housetops.

[4]"I tell you, my friends, don't be afraid of people who can kill the body but after that can do nothing more to hurt you. [5]I will show

you the one to fear. Fear the one who has the power to kill you and also to throw you into hell. Yes, this is the one you should fear.

⁶"Five sparrows are sold for only two pennies, and God does not forget any of them. ⁷But God even knows how many hairs you have on your head. Don't be afraid. You are worth much more than many sparrows.

Don't Be Ashamed of Jesus

⁸"I tell you, all those who stand before others and say they believe in me, I, the Son of Man, will say before the angels of God that they belong to me. ⁹But all who stand before others and say they do not believe in me, I will say before the angels of God that they do not belong to me.

¹⁰"Anyone who speaks against the Son of Man can be forgiven, but anyone who speaks against the Holy Spirit will not be forgiven.

¹¹"When you are brought into the synagogues before the leaders and other powerful people, don't worry about how to defend yourself or what to say. ¹²At that time the Holy Spirit will teach you what you must say."

Jesus Warns Against Selfishness

¹³Someone in the crowd said to Jesus, "Teacher, tell my brother to divide with me the property our father left us."

¹⁴But Jesus said to him, "Who said I should judge or decide between you?" ¹⁵Then Jesus said to them, "Be careful and guard against all kinds of greed. Life is not measured by how much one owns."

¹⁶Then Jesus told this story: "There was a rich man who had some land, which grew a good crop. ¹⁷He thought to himself, 'What will I do? I have no place to keep all my crops.' ¹⁸Then he said, 'This is what I will do: I will

tear down my barns and build bigger ones, and there I will store all my grain and other goods. ¹⁹Then I can say to myself, "I have enough good things stored to last for many years. Rest, eat, drink, and enjoy life!"'

²⁰"But God said to him, 'Foolish man! Tonight your life will be taken from you. So who will get those things you have prepared for yourself?'

²¹"This is how it will be for those who store up things for themselves and are not rich toward God."

Don't Worry

²²Jesus said to his followers, "So I tell you, don't worry about the food you need to live, or about the clothes you need for your body. ²³Life is more than food, and the body is more than clothes. ²⁴Look at the birds. They don't plant or harvest, they don't have storerooms or barns, but God feeds them. And you are worth much more than birds. ²⁵You cannot add any time to your life by worrying about it. ²⁶If you cannot do even the little things, then why worry about the big things? ²⁷Consider how the lilies grow; they don't work or make clothes for themselves. But I tell you that even Solomon with his riches was not dressed as beautifully as one of these flowers. ²⁸God clothes the grass in the field, which is alive today but tomorrow is thrown into the fire. So how much more will God clothe you? Don't have so little faith! ²⁹Don't always think about what you will eat or what you will drink, and don't keep worrying. ³⁰All the people in the world are trying to get these things, and your Father knows you need them. ³¹But seek God's kingdom, and all your other needs will be met as well.

APRIL 15

JOSHUA 19:1—20:9

Land for Simeon

19The second part of the land was given to the tribe of Simeon. Each family group received some of the land inside the

area of Judah. ²They received Beersheba (also called Sheba), Moladah, ³Hazar Shual, Balah, Ezem, ⁴Eltolad, Bethul, Hormah, ⁵Ziklag, Beth Marcaboth, Hazar Susah, ⁶Beth Lebaoth, and Sharuhen. There were thirteen towns and their villages.

[7]They received the towns of Ain, Rimmon, Ether, and Ashan, four towns and their villages. [8]They also received all the very small areas with people living in them as far as Baalath Beer (this is the same as Ramah in southern Canaan). So these were the lands given to the family groups in the tribe of Simeon. [9]The land of the Simeonites was taken from part of the land of Judah. Since Judah had much more land than they needed, the Simeonites received part of their land.

Land for Zebulun

[10]The third part of the land was given to the tribe of Zebulun. Each family group of Zebulun received some of the land. The border of Zebulun went as far as Sarid. [11]Then it went west to Maralah and came near Dabbesheth and then near Jokneam. [12]Then it turned to the east. It went from Sarid to the area of Kisloth Tabor and on to Daberath and to Japhia. [13]It continued eastward to Gath Hepher and Eth Kazin, ending at Rimmon. There the border turned and went toward Neah. [14]At Neah it turned again and went to the north to Hannathon and continued to the Valley of Iphtah El. [15]Inside this border were the cities of Kattath, Nahalal, Shimron, Idalah, and Bethlehem. There were twelve towns and their villages. [16]So these are the towns and the villages that were given to the family groups of Zebulun.

Land for Issachar

[17]The fourth part of the land was given to the tribe of Issachar. Each family group of Issachar received some of the land. [18]Their land included Jezreel, Kesulloth, Shunem, [19]Hapharaim, Shion, Anaharath, [20]Rabbith, Kishion, Ebez, [21]Remeth, En Gannim, En Haddah, and Beth Pazzez. [22]The border of their land touched the area called Tabor, Shahazumah, and Beth Shemesh and stopped at the Jordan River. There were sixteen towns and their villages. [23]These cities and towns were part of the land that was given to the family groups of Issachar.

Land for Asher

[24]The fifth part of the land was given to the tribe of Asher. Each family group of Asher received some of the land. [25]Their land included Helkath, Hali, Beten, Acshaph, [26]Allammelech, Amad, and Mishal.

The western border touched Mount Carmel and Shihor Libnath. [27]Then it turned east and went to Beth Dagon, touching Zebulun and the Valley of Iphtah El. Then it went north of Beth Emek and Neiel and passed north to Cabul. [28]From there it went to Abdon, Rehob, Hammon, and Kanah and continued to Greater Sidon. [29]Then the border went back south toward Ramah and continued to the strong, walled city of Tyre. There it turned and went toward Hosah, ending at the sea. This was in the area of Aczib, [30]Ummah, Aphek, and Rehob. There were twenty-two towns and their villages. [31]These cities and their villages were part of the land that was given to the family groups of Asher.

Land for Naphtali

[32]The sixth part of the land was given to the tribe of Naphtali. Each family group of Naphtali received some of the land. [33]The border of their land started at the large tree in Zaanannim, which is near Heleph. Then it went through Adami Nekeb and Jabneel, as far as Lakkum, and ended at the Jordan River. [34]Then it went to the west through Aznoth Tabor and stopped at Hukkok. It went to the area of Zebulun on the south, Asher on the west, and Judah, at the Jordan River, on the east. [35]The strong, walled cities inside these borders were called Ziddim, Zer, Hammath, Rakkath, Kinnereth, [36]Adamah, Ramah, Hazor, [37]Kedesh, Edrei, En Hazor, [38]Iron, Migdal El, Horem, Beth Anath, and Beth Shemesh. There were nineteen towns and all their villages. [39]The towns and the villages around them were in the land that was given to the family groups of Naphtali.

Land for Dan

[40]The seventh part of the land was given to the tribe of Dan. Each family group of Dan received some of the land. [41]Their land included Zorah, Eshtaol, Ir Shemesh, [42]Shaalabbin, Aijalon, Ithlah, [43]Elon, Timnah, Ekron, [44]Eltekeh, Gibbethon, Baalath, [45]Jehud, Bene Berak, Gath Rimmon, [46]Me Jarkon, Rakkon, and the area near Joppa.

⁴⁷(But the Danites had trouble taking their land. They went and fought against Leshem, defeated it, and killed the people who lived there. So the Danites moved into the town of Leshem and changed its name to Dan, because he was the father of their tribe.) ⁴⁸All of these towns and villages were given to the family groups of Dan.

Land for Joshua

⁴⁹After the leaders finished dividing the land and giving it to the different tribes, the Israelites gave Joshua son of Nun his land also. ⁵⁰They gave Joshua the town he asked for, Timnath Serah in the mountains of Ephraim, just as the LORD commanded. He built up the town and lived there.

⁵¹So these lands were given to the different tribes of Israel. Eleazar the priest, Joshua son of Nun, and the leaders of each tribe divided up the land by lots at Shiloh. They met in the presence of the LORD at the entrance to the Meeting Tent. Now they were finished dividing the land.

Cities of Safety

20 Then the LORD said to Joshua: ²"Tell the Israelites to choose the special cities of safety, as I had Moses command you to do. ³If a person kills someone accidentally and without meaning to kill him, that person may go to a city of safety to hide. There the killer will be safe from the relative who has the duty of punishing a murderer.

⁴"When the killer runs to one of those cities, he must stop at the entrance gate, stand there, and tell the leaders of the people what happened. Then that person will be allowed to enter the city and will be given a place to live among them. ⁵But if the one who is chasing him follows him to that city, the leaders of the city must not hand over the killer. It was an accident. He did not hate him beforehand or kill him on purpose. ⁶The killer must stay in the city until a court comes to a decision and until the high priest dies. Then he may go back home to the town from which he ran away."

⁷So the Israelites chose these cities to be cities of safety: Kedesh in Galilee in the mountains of Naphtali; Shechem in the mountains of Ephraim; Kiriath Arba (also called Hebron) in the mountains of Judah; ⁸Bezer on the east side of the Jordan River near Jericho in the desert in the land of Reuben; Ramoth in Gilead in the land of Gad; and Golan in Bashan in the land of Manasseh. ⁹Any Israelite or anyone living among them who killed someone accidentally was to be allowed to run to one of these cities of safety. There he would not be killed, before he was judged, by the relative who had the duty of punishing a murderer.

PSALM 46:1-6

God Protects His People

For the director of music. By alamoth. A psalm of the sons of Korah.

46 God is our protection and our
      strength.
   He always helps in times of trouble.
²So we will not be afraid even if the earth
      shakes,
   or the mountains fall into the sea,
³even if the oceans roar and foam,
   or the mountains shake at the raging
      sea.   *Selah*

⁴There is a river that brings joy to the city
      of God,
   the holy place where God Most High
      lives.
⁵God is in that city, and so it will not be
      shaken.
   God will help her at dawn.
⁶Nations tremble and kingdoms shake.
   God shouts and the earth crumbles.

PROVERBS 14:7-11

⁷Stay away from fools,
   because they can't teach you anything.

⁸A wise person will understand what to
      do,
   but a foolish person is dishonest.

⁹Fools don't care if they sin,
   but honest people work at being right.

¹⁰No one else can know your sadness,
   and strangers cannot share your joy.

¹¹The wicked person's house will be
      destroyed,

but a good person's tent will still be standing.

LUKE 12:32–59

Don't Trust in Money

[32]"Don't fear, little flock, because your Father wants to give you the kingdom. [33]Sell your possessions and give to the poor. Get for yourselves purses that will not wear out, the treasure in heaven that never runs out, where thieves can't steal and moths can't destroy. [34]Your heart will be where your treasure is.

Always Be Ready

[35]"Be dressed, ready for service, and have your lamps shining. [36]Be like servants who are waiting for their master to come home from a wedding party. When he comes and knocks, the servants immediately open the door for him. [37]They will be blessed when their master comes home, because he sees that they were watching for him. I tell you the truth, the master will dress himself to serve and tell the servants to sit at the table, and he will serve them. [38]Those servants will be blessed when he comes in and finds them still waiting, even if it is midnight or later. [39]"Remember this: If the owner of the house knew what time a thief was coming, he would not allow the thief to enter his house. [40]So you also must be ready, because the Son of Man will come at a time when you don't expect him!"

Who Is the Trusted Servant?

[41]Peter said, "Lord, did you tell this story to us or to all people?"

[42]The Lord said, "Who is the wise and trusted servant that the master trusts to give the other servants their food at the right time? [43]When the master comes and finds the servant doing his work, the servant will be blessed. [44]I tell you the truth, the master will choose that servant to take care of everything he owns. [45]But suppose the servant thinks to himself, 'My master will not come back soon,' and he begins to beat the other servants, men and women, and to eat and drink and get drunk. [46]The master will

come when that servant is not ready and is not expecting him. Then the master will cut him in pieces and send him away to be with the others who don't obey.

[47]"The servant who knows what his master wants but is not ready, or who does not do what the master wants, will be beaten with many blows! [48]But the servant who does not know what his master wants and does things that should be punished will be beaten with few blows. From everyone who has been given much, much will be demanded. And from the one trusted with much, much more will be expected.

Jesus Causes Division

[49]"I came to set fire to the world, and I wish it were already burning! [50]I have a baptism[n] to suffer through, and I feel very troubled until it is over. [51]Do you think I came to give peace to the earth? No, I tell you, I came to divide it. [52]From now on, a family with five people will be divided, three against two, and two against three. [53]They will be divided: father against son and son against father, mother against daughter and daughter against mother, mother-in-law against daughter-in-law and daughter-in-law against mother-in-law."

Understanding the Times

[54]Then Jesus said to the people, "When you see clouds coming up in the west, you say, 'It's going to rain,' and it happens. [55]When you feel the wind begin to blow from the south, you say, 'It will be a hot day,' and it happens. [56]Hypocrites! You know how to understand the appearance of the earth and sky. Why don't you understand what is happening now?

Settle Your Problems

[57]"Why can't you decide for yourselves what is right? [58]If your enemy is taking you to court, try hard to settle it on the way. If you don't, your enemy might take you to the judge, and the judge might turn you over to the officer, and the officer might throw you into jail. [59]I tell you, you will not get out of there until you have paid everything you owe."

12:50 I . . . baptism Jesus was talking about the suffering he would soon go through.

APRIL 16

Towns for the Levites

21 The heads of the Levite families went to talk to Eleazar the priest, to Joshua son of Nun, and to the heads of the families of all the tribes of Israel. 2At Shiloh in the land of Canaan, the heads of the Levite families said to them, "The LORD commanded Moses that you give us towns where we may live and pastures for our animals." 3So the Israelites obeyed this command of the LORD and gave the Levite people these towns and pastures for their own land: 4The Kohath family groups are part of the tribe of Levi. Some of the Levites in the Kohath family groups were from the family of Aaron the priest. To these Levites were given thirteen towns in the areas of Judah, Simeon, and Benjamin. 5The other family groups of Kohath were given ten towns in the areas of Ephraim, Dan, and West Manasseh.

6The people from the Gershon family groups were given thirteen towns in the land of Issachar, Asher, Naphtali, and the East Manasseh in Bashan.

7The family groups of Merari were given twelve towns in the areas of Reuben, Gad, and Zebulun.

8So the Israelites gave the Levites these towns and the pastures around them, just as the LORD had commanded Moses.

9These are the names of the towns that came from the lands of Judah and Simeon. 10The first choice of towns was given to the Kohath family groups of the Levites. 11They gave them Kiriath Arba, also called Hebron, and all its pastures in the mountains of Judah. (Arba was the father of Anak.) 12But the fields and the villages around Kiriath Arba had been given to Caleb son of Jephunneh.

13So they gave the city of Hebron to the descendants of Aaron (Hebron was a city of safety). They also gave them the towns of Libnah, 14Jattir, Eshtemoa, 15Holon, Debir, 16Ain, Juttah, and Beth Shemesh, and all the pastures around them. Nine towns were given from these two tribes.

17They also gave the people of Aaron these cities that belonged to the tribe of Benjamin: Gibeon, Geba, 18Anathoth, and Almon. They gave them these four towns and the pastures around them.

19So these thirteen towns with their pastures were given to the priests, who were from the family of Aaron.

20The other Kohathite family groups of the Levites were given these towns from the tribe of Ephraim: 21Shechem in the mountains of Ephraim (which was a city of safety), Gezer, 22Kibzaim, and Beth Horon. There were four towns and their pastures.

23The tribe of Dan gave them Eltekeh, Gibbethon, 24Aijalon, and Gath Rimmon. There were four towns and their pastures.

25West Manasseh gave them Taanach and Gath Rimmon and the pastures around these two towns.

26So these ten towns and the pastures around them were given to the rest of the Kohathite family groups.

27The Gershonite family groups of the Levite tribe were given these towns: East Manasseh gave them Golan in Bashan, which was a city of safety, and Be Eshtarah, and the pastures around these two towns.

28The tribe of Issachar gave them Kishion, Daberath, 29Jarmuth, and En Gannim, and the pastures around these four towns.

30The tribe of Asher gave them Mishal, Abdon, 31Helkath, and Rehob, and the pastures around these four towns.

32The tribe of Naphtali gave them Kedesh in Galilee (a city of safety), Hammoth Dor, and Kartan, and the pastures around these three towns.

33So the Gershonite family groups received thirteen towns and the pastures around them.

34The Merarite family groups (the rest of the Levites) were given these towns: The tribe of Zebulun gave them Jokneam, Kartah, 35Dimnah, and Nahalal, and the pastures around these four towns.

36The tribe of Reuben gave them Bezer, Jahaz, 37Kedemoth, and Mephaath, along with the pastures around these four towns.

[38]The tribe of Gad gave them Ramoth in Gilead (a city of safety), Mahanaim, [39]Heshbon, and Jazer, and the pastures around these four towns.

[40]So the total number of towns given to the Merarite family groups was twelve.

[41]A total of forty-eight towns with their pastures in the land of Israel were given to the Levites. [42]Each town had pastures around it.

[43]So the LORD gave the people all the land he had promised their ancestors. The people took the land and lived there. [44]The LORD gave them peace on all sides, as he had promised their ancestors. None of their enemies defeated them; the LORD handed all their enemies over to them. [45]He kept every promise he had made to the Israelites; each one came true.

Three Tribes Go Home

22 Then Joshua called a meeting of all the people from the tribes of Reuben, Gad, and East Manasseh. [2]He said to them, "You have done everything Moses, the LORD's servant, told you to do. You have also obeyed all my commands. [3]For a long time you have supported the other Israelites. You have been careful to obey the commands the LORD your God gave you. [4]The LORD your God promised to give the Israelites peace, and he has kept his promise. Now you may go back to your homes, to the land that Moses, the LORD's servant, gave you, on the east side of the Jordan River. [5]But be careful to obey the teachings and laws Moses, the LORD's servant, gave you: to love the LORD your God and obey his commands, to continue to follow him and serve him the very best you can."

[6]Then Joshua said good-bye to them, and they left and went away to their homes. [7]Moses had given the land of Bashan to East Manasseh. Joshua gave land on the west side of the Jordan River to West Manasseh. And he sent them to their homes and he blessed them. [8]He said, "Go back to your homes and your riches. You have many animals, silver, gold, bronze, and iron, and many beautiful clothes. Also, you have taken many things from your enemies that you should divide among yourselves."

[9]So the people from the tribes of Reuben, Gad, and East Manasseh left the other Israelites at Shiloh in Canaan and went back to Gilead. It was their own land, given to them by Moses as the LORD had commanded.

[10]The people of Reuben, Gad, and East Manasseh went to Geliloth, near the Jordan River in the land of Canaan. There they built a beautiful altar. [11]The other Israelites still at Shiloh heard about the altar these three tribes built at the border of Canaan at Geliloth, near the Jordan River on Israel's side. [12]All the Israelites became very angry at these three tribes, so they met together and decided to fight them.

[13]The Israelites sent Phinehas son of Eleazar the priest to Gilead to talk to the people of Reuben, Gad, and East Manasseh. [14]They also sent one leader from each of the ten tribes at Shiloh. Each of them was a leader of his family group of Israelites.

[15]These leaders went to Gilead to talk to the people of Reuben, Gad, and East Manasseh. They said: [16]"All the Israelites ask you: 'Why did you turn against the God of Israel by building an altar for yourselves? You know that this is against God's law. [17]Remember what happened at Peor? We still suffer today because of that sin, for which God made many Israelites very sick. [18]And now are you turning against the LORD and refusing to follow him?

" 'If you don't stop what you're doing today, the LORD will be angry with everyone in Israel tomorrow. [19]If your land is unclean, come over into our land where the LORD's Tent is. Share it with us. But don't turn against the LORD and us by building another altar for the LORD our God. [20]Remember how Achan son of Zerah refused to obey the command about what must be completely destroyed. That one man broke God's law, but all the Israelites were punished. Achan died because of his sin, but others also died.' "

[21]The people from Reuben, Gad, and East Manasseh answered, [22]"The LORD is God of gods! The LORD is God of gods! God knows, and we want you to know also. If we have done something wrong, you may kill us. [23]If we broke God's law, we ask the LORD himself

to punish us. We did not build this altar to offer burnt offerings or grain and fellowship offerings.

²⁴"We did not build it for that reason. We feared that someday your people would not accept us as part of your nation. Then they might say, 'You cannot worship the LORD, the God of Israel. ²⁵The LORD made the Jordan River a border between us and you people of Reuben and Gad. You cannot worship the LORD.' So we feared that your children might make our children stop worshiping the LORD.

²⁶"That is why we decided to build this altar. But it is not for burnt offerings and sacrifices. ²⁷This altar is proof to you and us and to all our children who will come after us that we worship the LORD with our whole burnt offerings, grain, and fellowship offerings. This was so your children would not say to our children, 'You are not the LORD's.'

²⁸"In the future if your children say that, our children can say, 'See the altar made by our ancestors. It is exactly like the LORD's altar, but we do not use it for sacrifices. It shows that we are part of Israel.'

²⁹"Truly, we don't want to be against the LORD or to stop following him by building an altar for burnt offerings, grain offerings, or sacrifices. We know the only true altar to the LORD our God is in front of the Holy Tent."

³⁰When Phinehas the priest and the ten leaders heard the people of Reuben, Gad, and East Manasseh, they were pleased. ³¹So Phinehas, son of Eleazar the priest, said, "Now we know the LORD is with us and that you didn't turn against him. Now the Israelites will not be punished by the LORD."

³²Then Phinehas and the leaders left the people of Reuben and Gad in Gilead and went back to Canaan where they told the Israelites what had happened. ³³They were pleased and thanked God. So they decided not to fight the people of Reuben and Gad and destroy those lands.

³⁴And the people of Reuben and Gad named the altar Proof That We Believe the LORD Is God.

PSALM 46:7–11

⁷The LORD All-Powerful is with us;
   the God of Jacob is our defender.   *Selah*

⁸Come and see what the LORD has done,
   the amazing things he has done on the earth.
⁹He stops wars everywhere on the earth.
   He breaks all bows and spears
   and burns up the chariots with fire.
¹⁰God says, "Be still and know that I am God.
   I will be praised in all the nations;
   I will be praised throughout the earth."

¹¹The LORD All-Powerful is with us;
   the God of Jacob is our defender.   *Selah*

PROVERBS 14:12–13

¹²Some people think they are doing right,
   but in the end it leads to death.

¹³Someone who is laughing may be sad inside,
   and joy may end in sadness.

LUKE 13:1–21

Change Your Hearts

13 At that time some people were there who told Jesus that Pilate[n] had killed some people from Galilee while they were worshiping. He mixed their blood with the blood of the animals they were sacrificing to God. ²Jesus answered, "Do you think this happened to them because they were more sinful than all others from Galilee? ³No, I tell you. But unless you change your hearts and lives, you will be destroyed as they were! ⁴What about those eighteen people who died when the tower of Siloam fell on them? Do you think they were more sinful than all the others who live in Jerusalem? ⁵No, I tell you. But unless you change your hearts and lives, you will all be destroyed too!"

The Useless Tree

⁶Jesus told this story: "A man had a fig tree planted in his vineyard. He came looking for some fruit on the tree, but he found

---

13:1 Pilate Pontius Pilate was the Roman governor of Judea from A.D. 26 to A.D. 36.

none. ⁷So the man said to his gardener, 'I have been looking for fruit on this tree for three years, but I never find any. Cut it down. Why should it waste the ground?' ⁸But the servant answered, 'Master, let the tree have one more year to produce fruit. Let me dig up the dirt around it and put on some fertilizer. ⁹If the tree produces fruit next year, good. But if not, you can cut it down.'"

Jesus Heals on the Sabbath

¹⁰Jesus was teaching in one of the synagogues on the Sabbath day. ¹¹A woman was there who, for eighteen years, had an evil spirit in her that made her crippled. Her back was always bent; she could not stand up straight. ¹²When Jesus saw her, he called her over and said, "Woman, you are free from your sickness." ¹³Jesus put his hands on her, and immediately she was able to stand up straight and began praising God.

¹⁴The synagogue leader was angry because Jesus healed on the Sabbath day. He said to the people, "There are six days when one has to work. So come to be healed on one of those days, and not on the Sabbath day."

¹⁵The Lord answered, "You hypocrites! Doesn't each of you untie your work animals and lead them to drink water every day—even on the Sabbath day? ¹⁶This woman that I healed, a daughter of Abraham, has been held by Satan for eighteen years. Surely it is not wrong for her to be freed from her sickness on a Sabbath day!" ¹⁷When Jesus said this, all of those who were criticizing him were ashamed, but the entire crowd rejoiced at all the wonderful things Jesus was doing.

Stories of Mustard Seed and Yeast

¹⁸Then Jesus said, "What is God's kingdom like? What can I compare it with? ¹⁹It is like a mustard seed that a man plants in his garden. The seed grows and becomes a tree, and the wild birds build nests in its branches."

²⁰Jesus said again, "What can I compare God's kingdom with? ²¹It is like yeast that a woman took and hid in a large tub of flour until it made all the dough rise."

APRIL 17

JOSHUA 23:1—24:33

The Last Words of Joshua

23 The LORD gave Israel peace from their enemies around them. Many years passed, and Joshua grew very old. ²He called a meeting of all the elders, heads of families, judges, and officers of Israel. He said, "I am now very old. ³You have seen what the LORD has done to our enemies to help us. The LORD your God fought for you. ⁴Remember that your people have been given their land between the Jordan River and the Mediterranean Sea in the west, the land I promised to give you. ⁵The LORD your God will force out the people living there. The LORD will push them out ahead of you. And you will own the land, as he has promised you.

⁶"Be strong. You must be careful to obey everything commanded in the Book of the Teachings of Moses. Do not stray from it either from the left or the right. ⁷Don't become friends with the people living among us who are not Israelites. Don't say the names of their gods or make anyone swear by them. Don't serve or worship them. ⁸You must continue to follow the LORD your God, as you have done in the past.

⁹"The LORD has forced many great and powerful nations to leave ahead of you. No nation has been able to defeat you. ¹⁰With his help, one Israelite could defeat a thousand, because the LORD your God fights for you, as he promised to do. ¹¹So you must be careful to love the LORD your God.

¹²"If you turn away from the way of the LORD and become friends with these people who are not part of Israel and marry them, ¹³the LORD your God will not help you defeat your enemies. They will be like traps for you,

like whips on your back and thorns in your eyes, and none of you will be left in this good land the LORD your God has given you.

¹⁴"It's almost time for me to die. You know and fully believe that the LORD has done great things for you. You know that he has not failed to keep any of his promises. ¹⁵Every good promise that the LORD your God made has come true, and in the same way, his other promises will come true. He promised that evil will come to you and that he will destroy you from this good land that he gave you. ¹⁶This will happen if you don't keep your agreement with the LORD your God. If you go and serve other gods and worship them, the LORD will become very angry with you. Then none of you will be left in this good land he has given you."

24 Joshua gathered all the tribes of Israel together at Shechem. He called the elders, heads of families, judges, and officers of Israel to stand before God.

²Then Joshua said to all the people, "Here's what the LORD, the God of Israel, says to you: 'A long time ago your ancestors lived on the other side of the Euphrates River. Terah, the father of Abraham and Nahor, worshiped other gods. ³But I, the LORD, took your ancestor Abraham from the other side of the river and led him through the land of Canaan. And I gave him many children, including his son Isaac. ⁴I gave Isaac two sons named Jacob and Esau. I gave the land around the mountains of Edom to Esau, but Jacob and his sons went down to Egypt. ⁵Then I sent Moses and Aaron to Egypt, where I brought many disasters on the Egyptians. Afterwards I brought you out. ⁶When I brought your ancestors out of Egypt, they came to the Red Sea, and the Egyptians chased them with chariots and men on horses. ⁷So the people called out to the LORD. And I brought darkness between you and the Egyptians and made the sea to cover them. You yourselves saw what I did to the army of Egypt. After that, you lived in the desert for a long time.

⁸" 'Then I brought you to the land of the Amorites, east of the Jordan River. They fought against you, but I handed them over to you. I destroyed them before you, and you

took control of that land. ⁹But the king of Moab, Balak son of Zippor, prepared to fight against the Israelites. The king sent for Balaam son of Beor to curse you, ¹⁰but I refused to listen to Balaam. So he asked for good things to happen to you! I saved you and brought you out of his power.

¹¹" 'Then you crossed the Jordan River and came to Jericho, where the people of Jericho fought against you. Also, the Amorites, Perizzites, Canaanites, Hittites, Girgashites, Hivites, and Jebusites fought against you. But I handed them over to you. ¹²I sent terror ahead of you to force out two Amorite kings. You took the land without using swords and bows. ¹³I gave you that land where you did not have to work. I gave you cities that you did not have to build. And now you live in that land and in those cities, and you eat from vineyards and olive trees that you did not plant.' "

¹⁴Then Joshua said to the people, "Now respect the LORD and serve him fully and sincerely. Throw away the gods that your ancestors worshiped on the other side of the Euphrates River and in Egypt. Serve the LORD. ¹⁵But if you don't want to serve the LORD, you must choose for yourselves today whom you will serve. You may serve the gods that your ancestors worshiped when they lived on the other side of the Euphrates River, or you may serve the gods of the Amorites who lived in this land. As for me and my family, we will serve the LORD."

¹⁶Then the people answered, "We will never stop following the LORD to serve other gods! ¹⁷It was the LORD our God who brought our ancestors out of Egypt. We were slaves in that land, but the LORD did great things for us there. He brought us out and protected us while we traveled through other lands. ¹⁸Then he forced out all the people living in these lands, even the Amorites. So we will serve the LORD, because he is our God."

¹⁹Then Joshua said, "You are not able to serve the LORD, because he is a holy God and a jealous God. If you turn against him and sin, he will not forgive you. ²⁰If you leave the LORD and serve other gods, he will send you great trouble. The LORD may have been good

to you, but if you turn against him, he will destroy you."

²¹But the people said to Joshua, "No! We will serve the LORD."

²²Then Joshua said, "You are your own witnesses that you have chosen to serve the LORD."

The people said, "Yes, we are."

²³Then Joshua said, "Now throw away the gods that you have. Love the LORD, the God of Israel, with all your heart."

²⁴Then the people said to Joshua, "We will serve the LORD our God, and we will obey him."

²⁵On that day at Shechem Joshua made an agreement for the people. He made rules and laws for them to follow. ²⁶Joshua wrote these things in the Book of the Teachings of God. Then he took a large stone and set it up under the oak tree near the LORD's Holy Tent.

²⁷Joshua said to all the people, "See this stone! It will remind you of what we did today. It was here the LORD spoke to us today. It will remind you of what happened so you will not turn against your God."

Joshua Dies

²⁸Then Joshua sent the people back to their land.

²⁹After that, Joshua son of Nun died at the age of one hundred ten. ³⁰They buried him in his own land at Timnath Serah, in the mountains of Ephraim, north of Mount Gaash.

³¹The Israelites served the LORD during the lifetime of Joshua and during the lifetimes of the elders who lived after Joshua who had seen what the LORD had done for Israel.

Joseph Comes Home

³²When the Israelites left Egypt, they carried the bones of Joseph with them. They buried them at Shechem, in the land Jacob had bought for a hundred pieces of silver from the sons of Hamor (Hamor was the father of Shechem). This land now belonged to Joseph's children.

³³And Eleazar son of Aaron died and was buried at Gibeah in the mountains of Ephraim, which had been given to Eleazar's son Phinehas.

PSALM 47:1–9

God, the King of the World

For the director of music. A psalm of the sons of Korah.

47 Clap your hands, all you people. Shout to God with joy.
²The LORD Most High is wonderful.
He is the great King over all the earth!
³He defeated nations for us
and put them under our control.
⁴He chose the land we would inherit.
We are the children of Jacob, whom he loved. *Selah*

⁵God has risen with a shout of joy;
the LORD has risen as the trumpets sounded.
⁶Sing praises to God. Sing praises.
Sing praises to our King. Sing praises.
⁷God is King of all the earth,
so sing a song of praise to him.
⁸God is King over the nations.
God sits on his holy throne.
⁹The leaders of the nations meet
with the people of the God of Abraham,
because the leaders of the earth belong to God.
He is supreme.

PROVERBS 14:14

¹⁴Evil people will be paid back for their evil ways,
and good people will be rewarded for their good ones.

LUKE 13:22–35

The Narrow Door

²²Jesus was teaching in every town and village as he traveled toward Jerusalem. ²³Someone said to Jesus, "Lord, will only a few people be saved?"

Jesus said, ²⁴"Try hard to enter through the narrow door, because many people will try to enter there, but they will not be able. ²⁵When the owner of the house gets up and closes the door, you can stand outside and knock on the door and say, 'Sir, open the door for us.' But he will answer, 'I don't know you or where you come from.' ²⁶Then you will say, 'We ate and drank with you, and you taught in the streets of our town.' ²⁷But he will say to you, 'I don't know you or where you come from. Go away from me, all you who do evil!' ²⁸You will cry and grind your teeth with pain when you see Abraham, Isaac, Jacob, and all the prophets in God's kingdom, but you yourselves thrown outside. ²⁹People will come from the east, west, north, and south and will sit down at the table in the kingdom of God. ³⁰There are those who are last now who will be first in the future. And there are those who are first now who will be last in the future."

Jesus Will Die in Jerusalem

³¹At that time some Pharisees came to Jesus and said, "Go away from here! Herod wants to kill you!"

³²Jesus said to them, "Go tell that fox Herod, 'Today and tomorrow I am forcing demons out and healing people. Then, on the third day, I will reach my goal.' ³³Yet I must be on my way today and tomorrow and the next day. Surely it cannot be right for a prophet to be killed anywhere except in Jerusalem.

³⁴"Jerusalem, Jerusalem! You kill the prophets and stone to death those who are sent to you. Many times I wanted to gather your people as a hen gathers her chicks under her wings, but you would not let me. ³⁵Now your house is left completely empty. I tell you, you will not see me until that time when you will say, 'God bless the One who comes in the name of the Lord.'"[n]

APRIL 18

JUDGES 1:1—3:6

Judah Fights the Canaanites

1 After Joshua died, the Israelites asked the LORD, "Who will be first to go and fight for us against the Canaanites?"

²The LORD said to them, "The tribe of Judah will go. I have handed the land over to them."

³The men of Judah said to the men of Simeon, their relatives, "Come and help us fight the Canaanites for our land. If you do, we will go and help you fight for your land." So the men of Simeon went with them.

⁴When Judah attacked, the LORD handed over the Canaanites and the Perizzites to them, and they defeated ten thousand men at the city of Bezek. ⁵There they found Adoni-Bezek, the ruler of the city, and fought him. The men of Judah defeated the Canaanites and the Perizzites, ⁶but Adoni-Bezek ran away. The men of Judah chased him, and when they caught him, they cut off his thumbs and big toes.

⁷Adoni-Bezek said, "Seventy kings whose thumbs and big toes had been cut off used to eat scraps that fell from my table. Now God

has paid me back for what I did to them." The men of Judah took Adoni-Bezek to Jerusalem, and he died there.

⁸Then the men of Judah fought against Jerusalem and captured it. They attacked with their swords and burned the city.

⁹Later, they went down to fight the Canaanites who lived in the mountains, in the dry country to the south, and in the western hills. ¹⁰The men of Judah went to fight against the Canaanites in the city of Hebron (which used to be called Kiriath Arba). And they defeated Sheshai, Ahiman, and Talmai.

Caleb and His Daughter

¹¹Then they left there and went to fight against the people living in Debir. (In the past Debir had been called Kiriath Sepher.) ¹²Before attacking the city, Caleb said, "I will give Acsah, my daughter, as a wife to the man who attacks and captures the city of Kiriath Sepher." ¹³Othniel son of Kenaz, Caleb's younger brother, captured the city, so Caleb gave his daughter Acsah to Othniel to be his wife. ¹⁴When Acsah came to Othniel, she told him to ask her father for a field.

When she got down from her donkey, Caleb asked her, "What do you want?"

¹⁵Acsah answered him, "Do me a special favor. Since you have given me land in southern Canaan, also give me springs of water." So Caleb gave her the upper and lower springs.

Fights with the Canaanites

¹⁶The Kenite people, who were from the family of Moses' father-in-law, left Jericho, the city of palm trees. They went with the men of Judah to the Desert of Judah to live with them there in southern Judah near the city of Arad.

¹⁷The men of Judah and the men of Simeon, their relatives, defeated the Canaanites who lived in Zephath. They completely destroyed the city, so they called it Hormah.ⁿ ¹⁸The men of Judah captured Gaza, Ashkelon, Ekron, and the lands around them.

¹⁹The LORD was with the men of Judah. They took the land in the mountains, but they could not force out the people living on the plain, because they had iron chariots. ²⁰As Moses had promised, Hebron was given to Caleb, and Caleb forced out the three sons of Anak. ²¹But the people of Benjamin could not make the Jebusite people leave Jerusalem. Since that time the Jebusites have lived with the Benjaminites in Jerusalem.

²²The men of Joseph went to fight against the city of Bethel, and the LORD was with them. ²³They sent some spies to Bethel (which used to be called Luz). ²⁴The spies saw a man coming out of the city and said to him, "Show us a way into the city, and we will be kind to you." ²⁵So the man showed them the way into the city. The men of Joseph attacked with swords the people in Bethel, but they let the man and his family go free. ²⁶He went to the land where the Hittites lived and built a city. He named it Luz, which it is called even today.

²⁷There were Canaanites living in the cities of Beth Shan, Taanach, Dor, Ibleam, Megiddo, and the small towns around them. The people of Manasseh did not force those people out of their towns, because the Canaanites were determined to stay there. ²⁸Later, the Israelites grew strong and forced

the Canaanites to work as slaves, but they did not make all the Canaanites leave their land. ²⁹The people of Ephraim did not force out all of the Canaanites living in Gezer. So the Canaanites continued to live in Gezer with the people of Ephraim. ³⁰The people of Zebulun did not force out the Canaanites living in the cities of Kitron and Nahalol. They stayed and lived with the people of Zebulun, but Zebulun made them work as slaves.

³¹The people of Asher did not force the Canaanites from the cities of Acco, Sidon, Ahlab, Aczib, Helbah, Aphek, and Rehob. ³²Since the people of Asher did not force them out, the Canaanites continued to live with them. ³³The people of Naphtali did not force out the people of the cities of Beth Shemesh and Beth Anath. So they continued to live with the Canaanites in those cities, and the Canaanites worked as slaves. ³⁴The Amorites forced the Danites back into the mountains and would not let them come down to live in the plain. ³⁵The Amorites were determined to stay in Mount Heres, Aijalon, and Shaalbim. But when the Israelites grew stronger, they made the Amorites work as slaves. ³⁶The land of the Amorites was from Scorpion Pass to Sela and beyond.

The Angel of the Lord at Bokim

2 The angel of the LORD went up from Gilgal to Bokim and said, "I brought you up from Egypt and led you to the land I promised to give your ancestors. I said, 'I will never break my agreement with you. ²But you must not make an agreement with the people who live in this land. You must destroy their altars.' But you did not obey me. How could you do this? ³Now I tell you, 'I will not force out the people in this land. They will be your enemies, and their gods will be a trap for you.'"

⁴After the angel gave Israel this message from the LORD, they cried loudly. ⁵So they named the place Bokim.ⁿ There they offered sacrifices to the LORD.

Joshua Dies

⁶Then Joshua sent the people back to their land. ⁷The people served the LORD during the

lifetime of Joshua and during the lifetimes of the elders who lived after Joshua and who had seen what great things the LORD had done for Israel. [8]Joshua son of Nun, the servant of the LORD, died at the age of one hundred ten. [9]They buried him in his own land at Timnath Serah in the mountains of Ephraim, north of Mount Gaash.

The People Disobey

[10]After those people had died, their children grew up and did not know the LORD or what he had done for Israel. [11]So they did what the LORD said was wrong, and they worshiped the Baal idols. [12]They quit following the LORD, the God of their ancestors who had brought them out of Egypt. They began to worship the gods of the people who lived around them, and that made the LORD angry. [13]The Israelites quit following the LORD and worshiped Baal and Ashtoreth. [14]The LORD was angry with the people of Israel, so he handed them over to robbers who took their possessions. He let their enemies who lived around them defeat them; they could not protect themselves. [15]When the Israelites went out to fight, they always lost, because the LORD was not with them. The LORD had sworn to them this would happen. So the Israelites suffered very much.

God Chooses Judges

[16]Then the LORD chose leaders called judges,[n] who saved the Israelites from the robbers. [17]But the Israelites did not listen to their judges. They were not faithful to God but worshiped other gods instead. Their ancestors had obeyed the LORD's commands, but they quickly turned away and did not obey. [18]When their enemies hurt them, the Israelites cried for help. So the LORD felt sorry for them and sent judges to save them from their enemies. The LORD was with those judges all their lives. [19]But when the judges died, the Israelites again sinned and worshiped other gods. They became worse than their ancestors. The Israelites were very stubborn and refused to change their evil ways.

[20]So the LORD became angry with the Is-

raelites. He said, "These people have broken the agreement I made with their ancestors. They have not listened to me. [21]I will no longer defeat the nations who were left when Joshua died. [22]I will use them to test Israel, to see if Israel will keep the LORD's commands as their ancestors did." [23]In the past the LORD had permitted those nations to stay in the land. He did not quickly force them out or help Joshua's army defeat them.

3These are the nations the LORD did not force to leave. He wanted to test the Israelites who had not fought in the wars of Canaan. [2](The only reason the LORD left those nations in the land was to teach the descendants of the Israelites who had not fought in those wars how to fight.) [3]These are the nations: the five rulers of the Philistines, all the Canaanites, the people of Sidon, and the Hivites who lived in the Lebanon mountains from Mount Baal Hermon to Lebo Hamath. [4]Those nations were in the land to test the Israelites—to see if they would obey the commands the LORD had given to their ancestors by Moses.

[5]The people of Israel lived with the Canaanites, Hittites, Amorites, Perizzites, Hivites, and Jebusites. [6]The Israelites began to marry the daughters of those people, and they allowed their daughters to marry the sons of those people. Israel also served their gods.

PSALM 48:1–7

Jerusalem, the City of God

A psalm of the sons of Korah.

48The LORD is great; he should be praised in the city of our God, on his holy mountain.
[2]It is high and beautiful
and brings joy to the whole world.
Mount Zion is like the high mountains of the north;
it is the city of the Great King.
[3]God is within its palaces;
he is known as its defender.
[4]Kings joined together
and came to attack the city.

[5]But when they saw it, they were amazed.
They ran away in fear.
[6]Fear took hold of them;
they hurt like a woman having a baby.
[7]You destroyed the large trading ships
with an east wind.

PROVERBS 14:15–17

[15]Fools will believe anything,
but the wise think about what they do.

[16]Wise people are careful and stay out of
trouble,
but fools are careless and quick to act.

[17]Someone with a quick temper does
foolish things,
but someone with understanding
remains calm.

LUKE 14:1–24

Healing on the Sabbath

14 On a Sabbath day, when Jesus went to
eat at the home of a leading Pharisee,
the people were watching Jesus very closely.
[2]And in front of him was a man with
dropsy.[n] [3]Jesus said to the Pharisees and experts on the law, "Is it right or wrong to heal
on the Sabbath day?" [4]But they would not
answer his question. So Jesus took the man,
healed him, and sent him away. [5]Jesus said to
the Pharisees and teachers of the law, "If
your child[n] or ox falls into a well on the Sabbath day, will you not pull him out quickly?"
[6]And they could not answer him.

Don't Make Yourself Important

[7]When Jesus noticed that some of the
guests were choosing the best places to sit,
he told this story: [8]"When someone invites
you to a wedding feast, don't take the most
important seat, because someone more important than you may have been invited.
[9]The host, who invited both of you, will come
to you and say, 'Give this person your seat.'
Then you will be embarrassed and will have
to move to the last place. [10]So when you are
invited, go sit in a seat that is not important.
When the host comes to you, he may say,

'Friend, move up here to a more important
place.' Then all the other guests will respect
you. [11]All who make themselves great will be
made humble, but those who make themselves humble will be made great."

You Will Be Rewarded

[12]Then Jesus said to the man who had invited him, "When you give a lunch or a dinner, don't invite only your friends, your
family, your other relatives, and your rich
neighbors. At another time they will invite
you to eat with them, and you will be repaid.
[13]Instead, when you give a feast, invite the
poor, the crippled, the lame, and the blind.
[14]Then you will be blessed, because they
have nothing and cannot pay you back. But
you will be repaid when the good people rise
from the dead."

A Story About a Big Banquet

[15]One of those at the table with Jesus
heard these things and said to him, "Blessed
are the people who will share in the meal in
God's kingdom."

[16]Jesus said to him, "A man gave a big
banquet and invited many people. [17]When
it was time to eat, the man sent his servant
to tell the guests, 'Come. Everything is
ready.'

[18]"But all the guests made excuses. The
first one said, 'I have just bought a field, and
I must go look at it. Please excuse me.' [19]An-
other said, 'I have just bought five pairs of
oxen; I must go and try them. Please excuse
me.' [20]A third person said, 'I just got married; I can't come.' [21]So the servant returned
and told his master what had happened.
Then the master became angry and said,
'Go at once into the streets and alleys of the
town, and bring in the poor, the crippled,
the blind, and the lame.' [22]Later the servant
said to him, 'Master, I did what you commanded, but we still have room.' [23]The master said to the servant, 'Go out to the roads
and country lanes, and urge the people
there to come so my house will be full. [24]I
tell you, none of those whom I invited first
will eat with me.'"

14:2 dropsy A sickness that causes the body to swell larger and larger. **14:5 child** Some Greek copies read "donkey."

APRIL 19

JUDGES 3:7—4:24

Othniel, the First Judge

[7]The Israelites did what the LORD said was wrong. They forgot about the LORD their God and served the idols of Baal and Asherah. [8]So the LORD was angry with Israel and allowed Cushan-Rishathaim king of Northwest Mesopotamia to rule over the Israelites for eight years. [9]When Israel cried to the LORD, the LORD sent someone to save them. Othniel son of Kenaz, Caleb's younger brother, saved the Israelites. [10]The Spirit of the LORD entered Othniel, and he became Israel's judge. When he went to war, the LORD handed over to him Cushan-Rishathaim king of Northwest Mesopotamia. [11]So the land was at peace for forty years. Then Othniel son of Kenaz died.

Ehud, the Judge

[12]Again the people of Israel did what the LORD said was wrong. So the LORD gave Eglon king of Moab power to defeat Israel because of the evil Israel did. [13]Eglon got the Ammonites and the Amalekites to join him. Then he attacked Israel and took Jericho, the city of palm trees. [14]So the people of Israel were ruled by Eglon king of Moab for eighteen years.

[15]When the people cried to the LORD, he sent someone to save them. He was Ehud, son of Gera from the people of Benjamin, who was left-handed. Israel sent Ehud to give Eglon king of Moab the payment he demanded. [16]Ehud made himself a sword with two edges, about eighteen inches long, and he tied it to his right hip under his clothes. [17]Ehud gave Eglon king of Moab the payment he demanded. Now Eglon was a very fat man. [18]After he had given Eglon the payment, Ehud sent away the people who had carried it. [19]When he passed the statues near Gilgal, he turned around and said to Eglon, "I have a secret message for you, King Eglon."

The king said, "Be quiet!" Then he sent all of his servants out of the room. [20]Ehud went to King Eglon, as he was sitting alone in the room above his summer palace.

Ehud said, "I have a message from God for you." As the king stood up from his chair, [21]Ehud reached with his left hand and took out the sword that was tied to his right hip. Then he stabbed the sword deep into the king's belly! [22]Even the handle sank in, and the blade came out his back. The king's fat covered the whole sword, so Ehud left the sword in Eglon. [23]Then he went out of the room and closed and locked the doors behind him.

[24]When the servants returned just after Ehud left, they found the doors to the room locked. So they thought the king was relieving himself. [25]They waited for a long time. Finally they became worried because he still had not opened the doors. So they got the key and unlocked them and saw their king lying dead on the floor!

[26]While the servants were waiting, Ehud had escaped. He passed by the statues and went to Seirah. [27]When he reached the mountains of Ephraim he blew the trumpet. The people of Israel heard it and went down from the hills with Ehud leading them.

[28]He said to them, "Follow me! The LORD has helped you to defeat your enemies, the Moabites." So Israel followed Ehud and captured the crossings of the Jordan River. They did not allow the Moabites to cross the Jordan River. [29]Israel killed about ten thousand strong and able men from Moab; not one escaped. [30]So that day Moab was forced to be under the rule of Israel, and there was peace in the land for eighty years.

Shamgar, the Judge

[31]After Ehud, Shamgar son of Anath saved Israel. Shamgar killed six hundred Philistines with a sharp stick used to guide oxen.

Deborah, the Woman Judge

4 After Ehud died, the Israelites again did what the LORD said was wrong. [2]So he let Jabin, a king of Canaan who ruled in the city of Hazor, defeat Israel. Sisera, who lived in Harosheth Haggoyim, was the commander

of Jabin's army. ³Because he had nine hundred iron chariots and was very cruel to the people of Israel for twenty years, they cried to the LORD for help.

⁴A prophetess named Deborah, the wife of Lappidoth, was judge of Israel at that time. ⁵Deborah would sit under the Palm Tree of Deborah, which was between the cities of Ramah and Bethel, in the mountains of Ephraim. And the people of Israel would come to her to settle their arguments.

⁶Deborah sent a message to Barak son of Abinoam. Barak lived in the city of Kedesh, which is in the area of Naphtali. Deborah said to Barak, "The LORD, the God of Israel, commands you: 'Go and gather ten thousand men of Naphtali and Zebulun and lead them to Mount Tabor. ⁷I will make Sisera, the commander of Jabin's army, and his chariots, and his army meet you at the Kishon River. I will hand Sisera over to you.'"

⁸Then Barak said to Deborah, "I will go if you will go with me, but if you won't go with me, I won't go."

⁹"Of course I will go with you," Deborah answered, "but you will not get credit for the victory. The LORD will let a woman defeat Sisera." So Deborah went with Barak to Kedesh. ¹⁰At Kedesh, Barak called the people of Zebulun and Naphtali together. From them, he gathered ten thousand men to follow him, and Deborah went with him also.

¹¹Now Heber the Kenite had left the other Kenites, the descendants of Hobab, Moses' brother-in-law. Heber had put up his tent by the great tree in Zaanannim, near Kedesh.

¹²When Sisera was told that Barak son of Abinoam had gone to Mount Tabor, ¹³Sisera gathered his nine hundred iron chariots and all the men with him, from Harosheth Haggoyim to the Kishon River.

¹⁴Then Deborah said to Barak, "Get up! Today is the day the LORD will hand over Sisera. The LORD has already cleared the way for you." So Barak led ten thousand men down Mount Tabor. ¹⁵As Barak approached, the LORD confused Sisera and his army and chariots. The LORD defeated them with the sword, but Sisera left his chariot and ran away on foot. ¹⁶Barak and his men chased Sisera's chariots

and army to Harosheth Haggoyim. With their swords they killed all of Sisera's men; not one of them was left alive.

¹⁷But Sisera himself ran away to the tent where Jael lived. She was the wife of Heber, one of the Kenite family groups. Heber's family was at peace with Jabin king of Hazor. ¹⁸Jael went out to meet Sisera and said to him, "Come into my tent, master! Come in. Don't be afraid." So Sisera went into Jael's tent, and she covered him with a rug.

¹⁹Sisera said to Jael, "I am thirsty. Please give me some water to drink." So she opened a leather bag of milk and gave him a drink. Then she covered him up.

²⁰He said to her, "Go stand at the entrance to the tent. If anyone comes and asks you, 'Is anyone here?' say, 'No.'"

²¹But Jael, the wife of Heber, took a tent peg and a hammer and quietly went to Sisera. Since he was very tired, he was in a deep sleep. She hammered the tent peg through the side of Sisera's head and into the ground. And so Sisera died.

²²At that very moment Barak came by Jael's tent, chasing Sisera. Jael went out to meet him and said, "Come. I will show you the man you are looking for." So Barak entered her tent, and there Sisera lay dead, with the tent peg in his head.

²³On that day God defeated Jabin king of Canaan in the sight of Israel. ²⁴Israel became stronger and stronger against Jabin king of Canaan until finally they destroyed him.

PSALM 48:8–14

⁸First we heard
  and now we have seen
  that God will always keep his city safe.
  It is the city of the LORD All-Powerful,
    the city of our God.   *Selah*

⁹God, we come into your Temple
  to think about your love.
¹⁰God, your name is known everywhere;
  all over the earth people praise you.
  Your right hand is full of goodness.
¹¹Mount Zion is happy
  and all the towns of Judah rejoice,
  because your decisions are fair.

[12]Walk around Jerusalem
and count its towers.
[13]Notice how strong they are.
Look at the palaces.
Then you can tell your children about
them.
[14]This God is our God forever and ever.
He will guide us from now on.

PROVERBS 14:18–19

[18]Fools are rewarded with nothing but
more foolishness,
but the wise are rewarded with
knowledge.
[19]Evil people will bow down to those who
are good;
the wicked will bow down at the door
of those who do right.

LUKE 14:25–35

The Cost of Being Jesus' Follower

[25]Large crowds were traveling with Jesus,
and he turned and said to them, [26]"If anyone
comes to me but loves his father, mother,
wife, children, brothers, or sisters—or even
life—more than me, he cannot be my follower. [27]Whoever is not willing to carry his
cross and follow me cannot be my follower.
[28]If you want to build a tower, you first sit
down and decide how much it will cost, to
see if you have enough money to finish the
job. [29]If you don't, you might lay the foundation, but you would not be able to finish.
Then all who would see it would make fun of
you, [30]saying, 'This person began to build
but was not able to finish.'
[31]"If a king is going to fight another king,
first he will sit down and plan. He will decide
if he and his ten thousand soldiers can defeat the other king who has twenty thousand
soldiers. [32]If he can't, then while the other
king is still far away, he will send some people to speak to him and ask for peace. [33]In
the same way, you must give up everything
you have to be my follower.

Don't Lose Your Influence

[34]"Salt is good, but if it loses its salty taste,
you cannot make it salty again. [35]It is no
good for the soil or for manure; it is thrown
away.
"Let those with ears use them and listen."

APRIL 20

JUDGES 5:1—6:32

The Song of Deborah

5 On that day Deborah and Barak son of
Abinoam sang this song:
[2]"The leaders led Israel.
The people volunteered to go to battle.
Praise the LORD!
[3]Listen, kings.
Pay attention, rulers!
I myself will sing to the LORD.
I will make music to the LORD, the God
of Israel.

[4]"LORD, when you came from Edom,
when you marched from the land of
Edom,
the earth shook,
the skies rained,

and the clouds dropped water.
[5]The mountains shook before the LORD,
the God of Mount Sinai,
before the LORD, the God of Israel!

[6]"In the days of Shamgar son of Anath,
in the days of Jael, the main roads were
empty.
Travelers went on the back roads.
[7]There were no warriors in Israel
until I, Deborah, arose,
until I arose to be a mother to Israel.
[8]At that time they chose to follow new
gods.
Because of this, enemies fought us at
our city gates.
No one could find a shield or a spear
among the forty thousand people of
Israel.

⁹My heart is with the commanders of
Israel.
They volunteered freely from among
the people.
Praise the LORD!

¹⁰"You who ride on white donkeys
and sit on saddle blankets,
and you who walk along the road,
listen!
¹¹Listen to the sound of the singers
at the watering holes.
There they tell about the victories of the
LORD,
the victories of the LORD's warriors in
Israel.
Then the LORD's people went down to the
city gates.

¹²"Wake up, wake up, Deborah!
Wake up, wake up, sing a song!
Get up, Barak!
Go capture your enemies, son of
Abinoam!

¹³"Then those who were left came down to
the important leaders.
The LORD's people came down to me
with strong men.
¹⁴They came from Ephraim in the
mountains of Amalek.
Benjamin was among the people who
followed you.
From the family group of Makir, the
commanders came down.
And from Zebulun came those who lead.
¹⁵The princes of Issachar were with
Deborah.
The people of Issachar were loyal to
Barak
and followed him into the valley.
The Reubenites thought hard
about what they would do.
¹⁶Why did you stay by the sheepfold?
Was it to hear the music played for your
sheep?
The Reubenites thought hard
about what they would do.
¹⁷The people of Gilead stayed east of the
Jordan River.
People of Dan, why did you stay by the
ships?

The people of Asher stayed at the
seashore,
at their safe harbors.
¹⁸But the people of Zebulun risked their
lives,
as did the people of Naphtali on the
battlefield.

¹⁹"The kings came, and they fought.
At that time the kings of Canaan fought
at Taanach, by the waters of Megiddo.
But they took away no silver or
possessions of Israel.
²⁰The stars fought from heaven;
from their paths, they fought Sisera.
²¹The Kishon River swept Sisera's men away,
that old river, the Kishon River.
March on, my soul, with strength!
²²Then the horses' hoofs beat the ground.
Galloping, galloping go Sisera's mighty
horses.
²³'May the town of Meroz be cursed,' said
the angel of the LORD.
'Bitterly curse its people,
because they did not come to help the
LORD.
They did not fight the strong enemy.'

²⁴"May Jael, the wife of Heber the Kenite,
be blessed above all women who live in
tents.
²⁵Sisera asked for water,
but Jael gave him milk.
In a bowl fit for a ruler,
she brought him cream.
²⁶Jael reached out and took the tent peg.
Her right hand reached for the
workman's hammer.
She hit Sisera! She smashed his head!
She crushed and pierced the side of his
head!
²⁷At Jael's feet he sank.
He fell, and he lay there.
At her feet he sank. He fell.
Where Sisera sank, there he fell, dead!

²⁸"Sisera's mother looked out through the
window.
She looked through the curtains and
cried out,
'Why is Sisera's chariot so late in
coming?

Why are sounds of his chariots' horses
delayed?'
²⁹The wisest of her servant ladies answer
her,
and Sisera's mother says to herself,
³⁰'Surely they are robbing the people they
defeated!
Surely they are dividing those things
among themselves!
Each soldier is given a girl or two.
Maybe Sisera is taking pieces of dyed
cloth.
Maybe they are even taking
pieces of dyed, embroidered cloth for
the necks of the victors!'

³¹"Let all your enemies die this way, LORD!
But let all the people who love you
be as strong as the rising sun!"

Then there was peace in the land for forty
years.

The Midianites Attack Israel

6 Again the Israelites did what the LORD
said was wrong. So for seven years the
LORD handed them over to Midian. ²Because
the Midianites were very powerful and were
cruel to Israel, the Israelites made hiding
places in the mountains, in caves, and in safe
places. ³Whenever the Israelites planted
crops, the Midianites, Amalekites, and other
peoples from the east would come and at-
tack them. ⁴They camped in the land and destroyed the crops that the Israelites had
planted as far away as Gaza. They left nothing for Israel to eat, and no sheep, cattle, or
donkeys. ⁵The Midianites came with their
tents and their animals like swarms of locusts to ruin the land. There were so many
people and camels they could not be
counted. ⁶Israel became very poor because
of the Midianites, so they cried out to the
LORD.

⁷When the Israelites cried out to the LORD
against the Midianites, ⁸the LORD sent a
prophet to them. He said, "This is what the
LORD, the God of Israel, says: I brought you
out of Egypt, the land of slavery. ⁹I saved you
from the Egyptians and from all those who
were against you. I forced the Canaanites out
of their land and gave it to you. ¹⁰Then I said
to you, 'I am the LORD your God. Live in the
land of the Amorites, but do not worship
their gods.' But you did not obey me."

The Angel of the Lord Visits Gideon

¹¹The angel of the LORD came and sat
down under the oak tree at Ophrah that belonged to Joash, one of the Abiezrite people.
Gideon, Joash's son, was separating some
wheat from the chaff in a winepress to keep
the wheat from the Midianites. ¹²The angel
of the LORD appeared to Gideon and said,
"The LORD is with you, mighty warrior!"

¹³Then Gideon said, "Sir, if the LORD is
with us, why are we having so much trouble?
Where are the miracles our ancestors told us
he did when the LORD brought them out of
Egypt? But now he has left us and has
handed us over to the Midianites."

¹⁴The LORD turned to Gideon and said,
"Go with your strength and save Israel from
the Midianites. I am the one who is sending
you."

¹⁵But Gideon answered, "Lord, how can I
save Israel? My family group is the weakest
in Manasseh, and I am the least important
member of my family."

¹⁶The LORD answered him, "I will be with
you. It will seem as if the Midianites you are
fighting are only one man."

¹⁷Then Gideon said to the LORD, "If you
are pleased with me, give me proof that it is
really you talking with me. ¹⁸Please wait here
until I come back to you. Let me bring my offering and set it in front of you."

And the LORD said, "I will wait until you
return."

¹⁹So Gideon went in and cooked a young
goat, and with twenty quarts of flour, made
bread without yeast. Then he put the meat
into a basket and the broth into a pot. He
brought them out and gave them to the angel
under the oak tree.

²⁰The angel of God said to Gideon, "Put
the meat and the bread without yeast on that
rock over there. Then pour the broth on
them." And Gideon did as he was told. ²¹The
angel of the LORD touched the meat and the
bread with the end of the stick that was in
his hand. Then fire jumped up from the rock
and completely burned up the meat and the
bread! And the angel of the LORD disap-

peared! ²²Then Gideon understood he had been talking to the angel of the Lᴏʀᴅ. So Gideon cried out, "Lord Gᴏᴅ! I have seen the angel of the Lᴏʀᴅ face to face!"

²³But the Lᴏʀᴅ said to Gideon, "Calm down! Don't be afraid! You will not die!"

²⁴So Gideon built an altar there to worship the Lᴏʀᴅ and named it The Lᴏʀᴅ Is Peace. It still stands at Ophrah, where the Abiezrites live.

Gideon Tears Down the Altar of Baal

²⁵That same night the Lᴏʀᴅ said to Gideon, "Take the bull that belongs to your father and a second bull seven years old. Pull down your father's altar to Baal, and cut down the Asherah idol beside it. ²⁶Then build an altar to the Lᴏʀᴅ your God with its stones in the right order on this high ground. Kill and burn a second bull on this altar, using the wood from the Asherah idol."

²⁷So Gideon got ten of his servants and did what the Lᴏʀᴅ had told him to do. But Gideon was afraid that his family and the men of the city might see him, so he did it at night, not in the daytime.

²⁸When the men of the city got up the next morning, they saw that the altar for Baal had been destroyed and that the Asherah idol beside it had been cut down! They also saw the altar Gideon had built and the second bull that had been sacrificed on it. ²⁹The men of the city asked each other, "Who did this?"

After they asked many questions, someone told them, "Gideon son of Joash did this."

³⁰So they said to Joash, "Bring your son out. He has pulled down the altar of Baal and cut down the Asherah idol beside it. He must die!"

³¹But Joash said to the angry crowd around him, "Are you going to take Baal's side? Are you going to defend him? Anyone who takes Baal's side will be killed by morning! If Baal is a god, let him fight for himself. It's his altar that has been pulled down." ³²So on that day Gideon got the name Jerub-Baal, which means "let Baal fight against him," because Gideon pulled down Baal's altar.

PSALM 49:1-9

Trusting Money Is Foolish

For the director of music. A psalm of the sons of Korah.

49 Listen to this, all you nations;
   listen, all you who live on earth.
²Listen, both great and small,
   rich and poor together.
³What I say is wise,
   and my heart speaks with
      understanding.
⁴I will pay attention to a wise saying;
   I will explain my riddle on the harp.

⁵Why should I be afraid of bad days?
   Why should I fear when evil people
      surround me?
⁶They trust in their money
   and brag about their riches.
⁷No one can buy back the life of another.
   No one can pay God for his own life,
⁸because the price of a life is high.
   No payment is ever enough.
⁹Do people live forever?
   Don't they all face death?

PROVERBS 14:20-21

²⁰The poor are rejected, even by their
      neighbors,
   but the rich have many friends.

²¹It is a sin to hate your neighbor,
   but being kind to the needy brings
      happiness.

LUKE 15:1-10

A Lost Sheep, a Lost Coin

15 The tax collectors and sinners all came to listen to Jesus. ²But the Pharisees and the teachers of the law began to complain: "Look, this man welcomes sinners and even eats with them."

³Then Jesus told them this story: ⁴"Suppose one of you has a hundred sheep but loses one of them. Then he will leave the other ninety-nine sheep in the open field and go out and look for the lost sheep until he finds it. ⁵And when he finds it, he happily puts it on his shoulders ⁶and goes home. He calls to his friends and neighbors

and says, 'Be happy with me because I found my lost sheep.' [7]In the same way, I tell you there is more joy in heaven over one sinner who changes his heart and life, than over ninety-nine good people who don't need to change.

[8]"Suppose a woman has ten silver coins,[n] but loses one. She will light a lamp, sweep the house, and look carefully for the coin until she finds it. [9]And when she finds it, she will call her friends and neighbors and say, 'Be happy with me because I have found the coin that I lost.' [10]In the same way, there is joy in the presence of the angels of God when one sinner changes his heart and life."

APRIL 21

JUDGES 6:33—8:35

Gideon Defeats Midian

[33]All the Midianites, the Amalekites, and other peoples from the east joined together and came across the Jordan River and camped in the Valley of Jezreel. [34]But the Spirit of the LORD entered Gideon, and he blew a trumpet to call the Abiezrites to follow him. [35]He sent messengers to all of Manasseh, calling them to follow him. He also sent messengers to the people of Asher, Zebulun, and Naphtali. So they also went up to meet Gideon and his men.

[36]Then Gideon said to God, "You said you would help me save Israel. [37]I will put some wool on the threshing floor. If there is dew only on the wool but all of the ground is dry, then I will know that you will use me to save Israel, as you said." [38]And that is just what happened. When Gideon got up early the next morning and squeezed the wool, he got a full bowl of water from it.

[39]Then Gideon said to God, "Don't be angry with me if I ask just one more thing. Please let me make one more test. Let only the wool be dry while the ground around it gets wet with dew." [40]That night God did that very thing. Just the wool was dry, but the ground around it was wet with dew.

7 Early in the morning Jerub-Baal (also called Gideon) and all his men set up their camp at the spring of Harod. The Midianites were camped north of them in the valley at the bottom of the hill called Moreh.

[2]Then the LORD said to Gideon, "You have too many men to defeat the Midianites. I don't want the Israelites to brag that they saved themselves. [3]So now, announce to the people, 'Anyone who is afraid may leave Mount Gilead and go back home.' " So twenty-two thousand men returned home, but ten thousand remained.

[4]Then the LORD said to Gideon, "There are still too many men. Take the men down to the water, and I will test them for you there. If I say, 'This man will go with you, he will go. But if I say, 'That one will not go with you,' he will not go."

[5]So Gideon led the men down to the water. There the LORD said to him, "Separate them into those who drink water by lapping it up like a dog and those who bend down to drink." [6]There were three hundred men who used their hands to bring water to their mouths, lapping it as a dog does. All the rest got down on their knees to drink.

[7]Then the LORD said to Gideon, "Using the three hundred men who lapped the water, I will save you and hand Midian over to you. Let all the others go home." [8]So Gideon sent the rest of Israel to their homes. But he kept three hundred men and took the jars and the trumpets of those who left.

Now the camp of Midian was in the valley below Gideon. [9]That night the LORD said to Gideon, "Get up. Go down and attack the camp of the Midianites, because I will give them to you. [10]But if you are afraid to go down, take your servant Purah with you.

15:8 silver coins Roman denarii. One coin was the average pay for one day's work.

[11]When you come to the camp of Midian, you will hear what they are saying. Then you will not be afraid to attack the camp."

Gideon Is Encouraged

So Gideon and his servant Purah went down to the edge of the enemy camp. [12]The Midianites, the Amalekites, and all the peoples from the east were camped in that valley. There were so many of them they seemed like locusts. Their camels could not be counted because they were as many as the grains of sand on the seashore!

[13]When Gideon came to the enemy camp, he heard a man telling his friend about a dream. He was saying, "I dreamed that a loaf of barley bread rolled into the camp of Midian. It hit the tent so hard that the tent turned over and fell flat!"

[14]The man's friend said, "Your dream is about the sword of Gideon son of Joash, a man of Israel. God will hand Midian and the whole army over to him!"

[15]When Gideon heard about the dream and what it meant, he worshiped God. Then Gideon went back to the camp of Israel and called out to them, "Get up! The LORD has handed the army of Midian over to you!" [16]Gideon divided the three hundred men into three groups. He gave each man a trumpet and an empty jar with a burning torch inside.

[17]Gideon told the men, "Watch me and do what I do. When I get to the edge of the camp, do what I do. [18]Surround the enemy camp. When I and everyone with me blow our trumpets, you blow your trumpets, too. Then shout, 'For the LORD and for Gideon!'"

Midian Is Defeated

[19]So Gideon and the one hundred men with him came to the edge of the enemy camp just after they had changed guards. It was during the middle watch of the night. Then Gideon and his men blew their trumpets and smashed their jars. [20]All three groups of Gideon's men blew their trumpets and smashed their jars. They held the torches in their left hands and the trumpets in their right hands. Then they shouted, "A sword for the LORD and for Gideon!" [21]Each of Gideon's men stayed in his place around

the camp, but the Midianites began shouting and running to escape.

[22]When Gideon's three hundred men blew their trumpets, the LORD made all the Midianites fight each other with their swords! The enemy army ran away to the city of Beth Shittah toward Zererah. They ran as far as the border of Abel Meholah, near the city of Tabbath. [23]Then men of Israel from Naphtali, Asher, and all of Manasseh were called out to chase the Midianites. [24]Gideon sent messengers through all the mountains of Ephraim, saying, "Come down and attack the Midianites. Take control of the Jordan River as far as Beth Barah before the Midianites can get to it."

So they called out all the men of Ephraim, who took control of the Jordan River as far as Beth Barah. [25]The men of Ephraim captured two princes of Midian named Oreb and Zeeb. They killed Oreb at the rock of Oreb and Zeeb at the winepress of Zeeb, and they continued chasing the Midianites. They brought the heads of Oreb and Zeeb to Gideon, who was east of the Jordan River.

8 The men of Ephraim asked Gideon, "Why did you treat us this way? Why didn't you call us when you went to fight against Midian?" They argued angrily with Gideon.

[2]But he answered them, "I have not done as well as you! The small part you did was better than all that my people of Abiezer did. [3]God let you capture Oreb and Zeeb, the princes of Midian. How can I compare what I did with what you did?" When the men of Ephraim heard Gideon's answer, they were not as angry anymore.

Gideon Captures Two Kings

[4]When Gideon and his three hundred men came to the Jordan River, they were tired, but they chased the enemy across to the other side. [5]Gideon said to the men of Succoth, "Please give my soldiers some bread because they are very tired. I am chasing Zebah and Zalmunna, the kings of Midian."

[6]But the leaders of Succoth said, "Why should we give your soldiers bread? You haven't caught Zebah and Zalmunna yet."

[7]Then Gideon said, "The LORD will sur-

render Zebah and Zalmunna to me. After that, I will whip your skin with thorns and briers from the desert."

[8]Gideon left Succoth and went to the city of Peniel and asked them for food. But the people of Peniel gave him the same answer as the people of Succoth. [9]So Gideon said to the men of Peniel, "After I win the victory, I will return and pull down this tower."

[10]Zebah and Zalmunna and their army were in the city of Karkor. About fifteen thousand men were left of the armies of the peoples of the east. Already one hundred twenty thousand soldiers had been killed. [11]Gideon went up the road of those who live in tents east of Nobah and Jogbehah, and he attacked the enemy army when they did not expect it. [12]Zebah and Zalmunna, the kings of Midian, ran away, but Gideon chased and captured them and frightened away their army.

[13]Then Gideon son of Joash returned from the battle by the Pass of Heres. [14]Gideon captured a young man from Succoth and asked him some questions. So the young man wrote down for Gideon the names of seventy-seven officers and elders of Succoth.

Gideon Punishes Succoth

[15]When Gideon came to Succoth, he said to the people of that city, "Here are Zebah and Zalmunna. You made fun of me by saying, 'Why should we give bread to your tired men? You have not caught Zebah and Zalmunna yet.'" [16]So Gideon took the elders of the city and punished them with thorns and briers from the desert. [17]He also pulled down the tower of Peniel and killed the people in that city.

[18]Gideon asked Zebah and Zalmunna, "What were the men like that you killed on Mount Tabor?"

They answered, "They were like you. Each one of them looked like a prince."

[19]Gideon said, "Those were my brothers, my mother's sons. As surely as the LORD lives, I would not kill you if you had spared them." [20]Then Gideon said to Jether, his oldest son, "Kill them." But Jether was only a boy

and was afraid, so he did not take out his sword.

[21]Then Zebah and Zalmunna said to Gideon, "Come on. Kill us yourself. As the saying goes, 'It takes a man to do a man's job.'" So Gideon got up and killed Zebah and Zalmunna and took the decorations off their camels' necks.

Gideon Makes an Idol

[22]The people of Israel said to Gideon, "You saved us from the Midianites. Now, we want you and your son and your grandson to rule over us."

[23]But Gideon told them, "The LORD will be your ruler. I will not rule over you, nor will my son rule over you." [24]He said, "I want you to do this one thing for me. I want each of you to give me a gold earring from the things you took in the fighting." (The Ishmaelites[n] wore gold earrings.)

[25]They said, "We will gladly give you what you want." So they spread out a coat, and everyone threw down an earring from what he had taken. [26]The gold earrings weighed about forty-three pounds. This did not count the decorations, necklaces, and purple robes worn by the kings of Midian, nor the chains from the camels' necks. [27]Gideon used the gold to make a holy vest, which he put in his hometown of Ophrah. But all the Israelites were unfaithful to God and worshiped it, so it became a trap for Gideon and his family.

The Death of Gideon

[28]So Midian was under the rule of Israel; they did not cause trouble anymore. And the land had peace for forty years, as long as Gideon was alive.

[29]Gideon[n] son of Joash went to his home to live. [30]He had seventy sons of his own, because he had many wives. [31]He had a slave woman who lived in Shechem, and he had a son by her, whom he named Abimelech. [32]So Gideon son of Joash died at a good old age. He was buried in the tomb of Joash, his father, in Ophrah, where the Abiezrites live.

[33]As soon as Gideon died, the people of

8:24 Ishmaelites Another name for the Midianites. See Genesis 37:25-28.
8:29 Gideon Also called Jerub-Baal.

Israel were again unfaithful to God and followed the Baals. They made Baal-Berith
their god. [34]The Israelites did not remember
the LORD their God, who had saved them
from all their enemies living all around
them. [35]And they were not kind to the family
of Jerub-Baal, also called Gideon, for all the
good he had done for Israel.

PSALM 49:10–20

[10]See, even wise people die.
  Fools and stupid people also die
  and leave their wealth to others.
[11]Their graves will always be their homes.
  They will live there from now on,
  even though they named places after
    themselves.
[12]Even rich people do not live forever;
  like the animals, people die.
[13]This is what will happen to those who
    trust in themselves
  and to their followers who believe
    them.   *Selah*
[14]Like sheep, they must die,
  and death will be their shepherd.
  Honest people will rule over them in the
    morning,
  and their bodies will rot in a grave far
    from home.
[15]But God will save my life
  and will take me from the grave.   *Selah*

[16]Don't be afraid of rich people
  because their houses are more beautiful.
[17]They don't take anything to the grave;
  their wealth won't go down with them.
[18]Even though they were praised when
    they were alive—
  and people may praise you when you
    succeed—
[19]they will go to where their ancestors are.
  They will never see light again.
[20]Rich people with no understanding
  are just like animals that die.

PROVERBS 14:22–24

[22]Those who make evil plans will be
    ruined,

but those who plan to do good will be
  loved and trusted.

[23]Those who work hard make a profit,
  but those who only talk will be poor.

[24]Wise people are rewarded with wealth,
  but fools only get more foolishness.

LUKE 15:11–32

The Son Who Left Home
[11]Then Jesus said, "A man had two sons.
[12]The younger son said to his father, 'Give me
my share of the property.' So the father divided the property between his two sons.
[13]Then the younger son gathered up all that
was his and traveled far away to another
country. There he wasted his money in foolish living. [14]After he had spent everything, a
time came when there was no food anywhere in the country, and the son was poor
and hungry. [15]So he got a job with one of the
citizens there who sent the son into the fields
to feed pigs. [16]The son was so hungry that he
wanted to eat the pods the pigs were eating,
but no one gave him anything. [17]When he realized what he was doing, he thought, 'All of
my father's servants have plenty of food. But
I am here, almost dying with hunger. [18]I will
leave and return to my father and say to him,
"Father, I have sinned against God and
against you. [19]I am no longer worthy to be
called your son, but let me be like one of
your servants."' [20]So the son left and went to
his father.

"While the son was still a long way off, his
father saw him and felt sorry for his son. So
the father ran to him and hugged and kissed
him. [21]The son said, 'Father, I have sinned
against God and against you. I am no longer
worthy to be called your son.'[n] [22]But the father
said to his servants, 'Hurry! Bring the best
clothes and put them on him. Also, put a ring
on his finger and sandals on his feet. [23]And
get our fat calf and kill it so we can have a
feast and celebrate. [24]My son was dead, but
now he is alive again! He was lost, but now he
is found!' So they began to celebrate.

[25]"The older son was in the field, and as
he came closer to the house, he heard the

15:21 son Some Greek copies continue, "but let me be like one of your servants" (see verse 19).

sound of music and dancing. [26]So he called to one of the servants and asked what all this meant. [27]The servant said, 'Your brother has come back, and your father killed the fat calf, because your brother came home safely.' [28]The older son was angry and would not go in to the feast. So his father went out and begged him to come in. [29]But the older son said to his father, 'I have served you like a slave for many years and have always obeyed your commands. But you never gave me even a young goat to have at a feast with my friends. [30]But your other son, who wasted all your money on prostitutes, comes home, and you kill the fat calf for him!' [31]The father said to him, 'Son, you are always with me, and all that I have is yours. [32]We had to celebrate and be happy because your brother was dead, but now he is alive. He was lost, but now he is found.'"

APRIL 22

JUDGES 9:1—10:18

Abimelech Becomes King

9Abimelech son of Gideon went to his uncles in the city of Shechem. He said to his uncles and all of his mother's family group, [2]"Ask the leaders of Shechem, 'Is it better for the seventy sons of Gideon to rule over you or for one man to rule?' Remember, I am your relative."

[3]Abimelech's uncles spoke to all the leaders of Shechem about this. And they decided to follow Abimelech, because they said, "He is our relative." [4]So the leaders of Shechem gave Abimelech about one and three-quarter pounds of silver from the temple of the god Baal-Berith. Abimelech used the silver to hire some worthless, reckless men, who followed him wherever he went. [5]He went to Ophrah, the hometown of his father, and murdered his seventy brothers, the sons of Gideon. He killed them all on one stone. But Gideon's youngest son, Jotham, hid from Abimelech and escaped. [6]Then all of the leaders of Shechem and Beth Millo gathered beside the great tree standing in Shechem. There they made Abimelech their king.

Jotham's Story

[7]When Jotham heard this, he went and stood on the top of Mount Gerizim. He shouted to the people: "Listen to me, you leaders of Shechem, so that God will listen to you! [8]One day the trees decided to appoint a king to rule over them. They said to the olive tree, 'You be king over us!'

[9]"But the olive tree said, 'Men and gods are honored by my oil. Should I stop making it and go and sway over the other trees?'

[10]"Then the trees said to the fig tree, 'Come and be king over us!'

[11]"But the fig tree answered, 'Should I stop making my sweet and good fruit and go and sway over the other trees?'

[12]"Then the trees said to the vine, 'Come and be king over us!'

[13]"But the vine answered, 'My new wine makes men and gods happy. Should I stop making it and go and sway over the trees?'

[14]"Then all the trees said to the thornbush, 'Come and be king over us.'

[15]"But the thornbush said to the trees, 'If you really want to appoint me king over you, come and find shelter in my shade! But if not, let fire come out of the thornbush and burn up the cedars of Lebanon!'

[16]"Now, were you completely honest and sincere when you made Abimelech king? Have you been fair to Gideon[n] and his family? Have you treated Gideon as you should? [17]Remember, my father fought for you and risked his life to save you from the power of the Midianites. [18]But now you have turned against my father's family and have killed his seventy sons on one stone. You have made Abimelech, the son of my father's slave girl, king over the leaders of Shechem just

9:16 Gideon Also called Jerub-Baal.

because he is your relative! [19]So then, if you have been honest and sincere to Gideon and his family today, be happy with Abimelech as your king. And may he be happy with you! [20]But if not, may fire come out of Abimelech and completely burn you leaders of Shechem and Beth Millo! Also may fire come out of the leaders of Shechem and Beth Millo and burn up Abimelech!"

[21]Then Jotham ran away and escaped to the city of Beer. He lived there because he was afraid of his brother Abimelech.

Abimelech Fights Against Shechem

[22]Abimelech ruled Israel for three years. [23]Then God sent an evil spirit to make trouble between Abimelech and the leaders of Shechem so that the leaders of Shechem turned against him. [24]Abimelech had killed Gideon's[n] seventy sons, his own brothers, and the leaders of Shechem had helped him. So God sent the evil spirit to punish them. [25]The leaders of Shechem were against Abimelech then. They put men on the hilltops in ambush who robbed everyone going by. And Abimelech was told.

[26]A man named Gaal son of Ebed and his brothers moved into Shechem, and the leaders of Shechem trusted him. [27]They went out to the vineyards to pick grapes, and they squeezed the grapes. Then they had a feast in the temple of their god, where they ate and drank and cursed Abimelech. [28]Gaal son of Ebed said, "We are the men of Shechem. Who is Abimelech that we should serve him? Isn't he one of Gideon's sons, and isn't Zebul his officer? We should serve the men of Hamor, Shechem's father. Why should we serve Abimelech? [29]If you made me commander of these people, I would get rid of Abimelech. I would say to him, 'Get your army ready and come out to battle.'"

[30]Now when Zebul, the ruler of Shechem, heard what Gaal son of Ebed said, he was very angry. [31]He sent secret messengers to Abimelech, saying, "Gaal son of Ebed and Gaal's brothers have come to Shechem, and they are turning the city against you! [32]You and your men should get up during the night and hide in the fields outside the city. [33]As soon as the sun comes up in the morning, attack the city. When Gaal and his men come out to fight you, do what you can to them."

[34]So Abimelech and all his soldiers got up during the night and hid near Shechem in four groups. [35]Gaal son of Ebed went out and was standing at the entrance to the city gate. As he was standing there, Abimelech and his soldiers came out of their hiding places. [36]When Gaal saw the soldiers, he said to Zebul, "Look! There are people coming down from the mountains!"

But Zebul said, "You are seeing the shadows of the mountains. The shadows just look like people."

[37]But again Gaal said, "Look, there are people coming down from the center of the land, and there is a group coming from the fortune-tellers' tree!"

[38]Zebul said to Gaal, "Where is your bragging now? You said, 'Who is Abimelech that we should serve him?' You made fun of these men. Now go out and fight them."

[39]So Gaal led the men of Shechem out to fight Abimelech. [40]Abimelech and his men chased them, and many of Gaal's men were killed before they could get back to the city gate. [41]While Abimelech stayed at Arumah, Zebul forced Gaal and his brothers to leave Shechem.

[42]The next day the people of Shechem went out to the fields. When Abimelech was told about it, [43]he separated his men into three groups and hid them in the fields. When he saw the people coming out of the city, he jumped up and attacked them. [44]Abimelech and his group ran to the entrance gate to the city. The other two groups ran out to the people in the fields and struck them down. [45]Abimelech and his men fought the city of Shechem all day until they captured it and killed its people. Then he tore it down and threw salt[n] over the ruins.

The Tower of Shechem Burns

[46]When the leaders who were in the Tower of Shechem heard what had happened to Shechem, they gathered in the safest room of

---

9:24 Gideon Also called Jerub-Baal.   **9:45 salt** The salt would keep crops from growing there.

the temple of El Berith. [47]Abimelech heard that all the leaders of the Tower of Shechem had gathered there. [48]So he and all his men went up Mount Zalmon, near Shechem. Abimelech took an ax and cut some branches and put them on his shoulders. He said to all those with him, "Hurry! Do what I have done!" [49]So all those men cut branches and followed Abimelech and piled them against the safest room of the temple. Then they set them on fire and burned the people inside. So all the people who were at the Tower of Shechem also died—about a thousand men and women.

Abimelech's Death

[50]Then Abimelech went to the city of Thebez. He surrounded the city, attacked it, and captured it. [51]But inside the city was a strong tower, so all the men, women, and leaders of that city ran to the tower. When they got inside, they locked the door behind them. Then they climbed up to the roof of the tower. [52]Abimelech came to the tower to attack it. He approached the door of the tower to set it on fire, [53]but as he came near, a woman dropped a grinding stone on his head, crushing his skull.

[54]He quickly called to the officer who carried his armor and said, "Take out your sword and kill me. I don't want people to say, 'A woman killed Abimelech.'" So the officer stabbed Abimelech, and he died. [55]When the people of Israel saw Abimelech was dead, they all returned home.

[56]In that way God punished Abimelech for all the evil he had done to his father by killing his seventy brothers. [57]God also punished the men of Shechem for the evil they had done. So the curse spoken by Jotham, the youngest son of Gideon,[n] came true.

Tola, the Judge

10 After Abimelech died, another judge came to save Israel. He was Tola son of Puah, the son of Dodo. Tola was from the people of Issachar and lived in the city of Shamir in the mountains of Ephraim. [2]Tola was a judge for Israel for twenty-three years. Then he died and was buried in Shamir.

Jair, the Judge

[3]After Tola died, Jair from the region of Gilead became judge. He was a judge for Israel for twenty-two years. [4]Jair had thirty sons, who rode thirty donkeys. These thirty sons controlled thirty towns in Gilead, which are called the Towns of Jair to this day. [5]Jair died and was buried in the city of Kamon.

The Ammonites Trouble Israel

[6]Again the Israelites did what the LORD said was wrong. They worshiped Baal and Ashtoreth, the gods of Aram, Sidon, Moab, and Ammon, and the gods of the Philistines. The Israelites left the LORD and stopped serving him. [7]So the LORD was angry with them and handed them over to the Philistines and the Ammonites. [8]In the same year those people destroyed the Israelites who lived east of the Jordan River in the region of Gilead, where the Amorites lived. So the Israelites suffered for eighteen years. [9]The Ammonites then crossed the Jordan River to fight the people of Judah, Benjamin, and Ephraim, causing much trouble to the people of Israel. [10]So the Israelites cried out to the LORD, "We have sinned against you. We left our God and worshiped the Baal idols."

[11]The LORD answered the Israelites, "When the Egyptians, Amorites, Ammonites, Philistines, [12]Sidonians, Amalekites, and Maonites were cruel to you, you cried out to me, and I saved you. [13]But now you have left me again and have worshiped other gods. So I refuse to save you again. [14]You have chosen those gods. So go call to them for help. Let them save you when you are in trouble."

[15]But the people of Israel said to the LORD, "We have sinned. Do to us whatever you want, but please save us today!" [16]Then the Israelites threw away the foreign gods among them, and they worshiped the LORD again. So he felt sorry for them when he saw their suffering.

[17]The Ammonites gathered for war and camped in Gilead. The Israelites gathered and camped at Mizpah. [18]The leaders of the people of Gilead said, "Who will lead us to

attack the Ammonites? He will become the head of all those who live in Gilead."

PSALM 50:1–6

God Wants True Worship

A psalm of Asaph.

50 The God of gods, the LORD, speaks.
He calls the earth from the
rising to the setting sun.
[2] God shines from Jerusalem,
whose beauty is perfect.
[3] Our God comes, and he will not be silent.
A fire burns in front of him,
and a powerful storm surrounds him.
[4] He calls to the sky above and to the earth
that he might judge his people.
[5] He says, "Gather around, you who
worship me,
who have made an agreement with me,
using a sacrifice."
[6] God is the judge,
and even the skies say he is right.   *Selah*

PROVERBS 14:25–27

[25] A truthful witness saves lives,
but a false witness is a traitor.

[26] Those who respect the LORD will have
security,
and their children will be protected.

[27] Respect for the LORD gives life.
It is like a fountain that can save people
from death.

LUKE 16:1–31

True Wealth

16 Jesus also said to his followers, "Once
there was a rich man who had a manager to take care of his business. This manager was accused of cheating him. [2] So he called the manager in and said to him, 'What is this I hear about you? Give me a report of what you have done with my money, because you can't be my manager any longer.' [3] The manager thought to himself, 'What will I do since my master is taking my job away from me? I am not strong enough to dig ditches,

and I am ashamed to beg. [4] I know what I'll do so that when I lose my job people will welcome me into their homes.'

[5] "So the manager called in everyone who owed the master any money. He asked the first one, 'How much do you owe?' [6] He answered, 'Eight hundred gallons of olive oil.' The manager said to him, 'Take your bill, sit down quickly, and write four hundred gallons.' [7] Then the manager asked another one, 'How much do you owe?' He answered, 'One thousand bushels of wheat.' Then the manager said to him, 'Take your bill and write eight hundred bushels.' [8] So, the master praised the dishonest manager for being clever. Yes, worldly people are more clever with their own kind than spiritual people are.

[9] "I tell you, make friends for yourselves using worldly riches so that when those riches are gone, you will be welcomed in those homes that continue forever. [10] Whoever can be trusted with a little can also be trusted with a lot, and whoever is dishonest with a little is dishonest with a lot. [11] If you cannot be trusted with worldly riches, then who will trust you with true riches? [12] And if you cannot be trusted with things that belong to someone else, who will give you things of your own?

[13] "No servant can serve two masters. The servant will hate one master and love the other, or will follow one master and refuse to follow the other. You cannot serve both God and worldly riches."

God's Law Cannot Be Changed

[14] The Pharisees, who loved money, were listening to all these things and made fun of Jesus. [15] He said to them, "You make yourselves look good in front of people, but God knows what is really in your hearts. What is important to people is hateful in God's sight.

[16] "The law of Moses and the writings of the prophets were preached until John[n] came. Since then the Good News about the kingdom of God is being told, and everyone tries to enter it by force. [17] It would be easier for heaven and earth to pass away than for

16:16 John John the Baptist, who preached to people about Christ's coming (Matthew 3, Luke 3).

the smallest part of a letter in the law to be changed.

Divorce and Remarriage

¹⁸"If a man divorces his wife and marries another woman, he is guilty of adultery, and the man who marries a divorced woman is also guilty of adultery."

The Rich Man and Lazarus

¹⁹Jesus said, "There was a rich man who always dressed in the finest clothes and lived in luxury every day. ²⁰And a very poor man named Lazarus, whose body was covered with sores, was laid at the rich man's gate. ²¹He wanted to eat only the small pieces of food that fell from the rich man's table. And the dogs would come and lick his sores. ²²Later, Lazarus died, and the angels carried him to the arms of Abraham. The rich man died, too, and was buried. ²³In the place of the dead, he was in much pain. The rich man saw Abraham far away with Lazarus at his side. ²⁴He called, 'Father Abraham, have mercy on me! Send Lazarus to dip his finger in water and cool my tongue, because I am suffering in this fire!' ²⁵But Abraham said, 'Child, remember when you were alive you had the good things in life, but bad things happened to Lazarus. Now he is comforted here, and you are suffering. ²⁶Besides, there is a big pit between you and us, so no one can cross over to you, and no one can leave there and come here.' ²⁷The rich man said, 'Father, then please send Lazarus to my father's house. ²⁸I have five brothers, and Lazarus could warn them so that they will not come to this place of pain.' ²⁹But Abraham said, 'They have the law of Moses and the writings of the prophets; let them learn from them.' ³⁰The rich man said, 'No, father Abraham! If someone goes to them from the dead, they would believe and change their hearts and lives.' ³¹But Abraham said to him, 'If they will not listen to Moses and the prophets, they will not listen to someone who comes back from the dead.'"

APRIL 23

JUDGES 11:1—12:15

Jephthah Is Chosen as Leader

11 Jephthah was a strong soldier from Gilead. His father was named Gilead, and his mother was a prostitute. ²Gilead's wife had several sons. When they grew up, they forced Jephthah to leave his home, saying to him, "You will not get any of our father's property, because you are the son of another woman." ³So Jephthah ran away from his brothers and lived in the land of Tob. There some worthless men began to follow him.

⁴After a time the Ammonites fought against Israel. ⁵When the Ammonites made war against Israel, the elders of Gilead went to Jephthah to bring him back from Tob. ⁶They said to him, "Come and lead our army so we can fight the Ammonites."

⁷But Jephthah said to them, "Didn't you hate me? You forced me to leave my father's house. Why are you coming to me now that you are in trouble?"

⁸The elders of Gilead said to Jephthah, "It is because of those troubles that we come to you now. Please come with us and fight against the Ammonites. You will be the ruler over everyone who lives in Gilead."

⁹Then Jephthah answered, "If you take me back to Gilead to fight the Ammonites and the LORD helps me win, I will be your ruler."

¹⁰The elders of Gilead said to him, "The LORD is listening to everything we are saying. We promise to do all that you tell us to do." ¹¹So Jephthah went with the elders of Gilead, and the people made him their leader and commander of their army. Jephthah repeated all of his words in front of the LORD at Mizpah.

Jephthah Sends Messengers to the Ammonite King

¹²Jephthah sent messengers to the king of the Ammonites, asking, "What have you got

against Israel? Why have you come to attack our land?"

¹³The king of the Ammonites answered the messengers of Jephthah, "We are fighting Israel because you took our land when you came up from Egypt. You took our land from the Arnon River to the Jabbok River to the Jordan River. Now give our land back to us peacefully."

¹⁴Jephthah sent the messengers to the Ammonite king again. ¹⁵They said:

"This is what Jephthah says: Israel did not take the land of the people of Moab or Ammon. ¹⁶When the Israelites came out of Egypt, they went into the desert to the Red Sea and then to Kadesh. ¹⁷Israel sent messengers to the king of Edom, saying, 'Let the people of Israel go across your land.' But the king of Edom refused. We sent the same message to the king of Moab, but he also refused. So the Israelites stayed at Kadesh.

¹⁸"Then the Israelites went into the desert around the borders of the lands of Edom and Moab. Israel went east of the land of Moab and camped on the other side of the Arnon River, the border of Moab. They did not cross it to go into the land of Moab.

¹⁹"Then Israel sent messengers to Sihon king of the Amorites, king of the city of Heshbon, asking, 'Let the people of Israel pass through your land to go to our land.' ²⁰But Sihon did not trust the Israelites to cross his land. So he gathered all of his people and camped at Jahaz and fought with Israel.

²¹"But the LORD, the God of Israel, handed Sihon and his army over to Israel. All the land of the Amorites became the property of Israel. ²²So Israel took all the land of the Amorites from the Arnon River to the Jabbok River, from the desert to the Jordan River.

²³"It was the LORD, the God of Israel, who forced out the Amorites ahead of the people of Israel. So do you think you can make them leave? ²⁴Take the land that your god Chemosh has given you. We will live in the land the LORD our God has given us!

²⁵"Are you any better than Balak son of Zippor, king of Moab? Did he ever quarrel or fight with the people of Israel? ²⁶For three hundred years the Israelites have lived in Heshbon and Aroer and the towns around them and in all the cities along the Arnon River. Why have you not taken these cities back in all that time? ²⁷I have not sinned against you, but you are sinning against me by making war on me. May the LORD, the Judge, decide whether the Israelites or the Ammonites are right."

²⁸But the king of the Ammonites ignored this message from Jephthah.

Jephthah's Promise

²⁹Then the Spirit of the LORD entered Jephthah. Jephthah passed through Gilead and Manasseh and the city of Mizpah in Gilead to the land of the Ammonites. ³⁰Jephthah made a promise to the LORD, saying, "If you will hand over the Ammonites to me, ³¹I will give you as a burnt offering the first thing that comes out of my house to meet me when I return from the victory. It will be the LORD's."

³²Then Jephthah went over to fight the Ammonites, and the LORD handed them over to him. ³³In a great defeat Jephthah struck them down from the city of Aroer to the area of Minnith, and twenty cities as far as the city of Abel Keramim. So the Ammonites were defeated by the Israelites.

³⁴When Jephthah returned to his home in Mizpah, his daughter was the first one to come out to meet him, playing a tambourine and dancing. She was his only child; he had no other sons or daughters. ³⁵When Jephthah saw his daughter, he tore his clothes to show his sorrow. He said, "My daughter! You have made me so sad because I made a promise to the LORD, and I cannot break it!"

³⁶Then his daughter said, "Father, you made a promise to the LORD. So do to me just what you promised, because the LORD helped you defeat your enemies, the Ammonites." ³⁷She also said, "But let me do one thing. Let me be alone for two months to go to the mountains. Since I will never marry, let me and my friends go and cry together."

³⁸Jephthah said, "Go." So he sent her away for two months. She and her friends stayed in the mountains and cried for her because she would never marry. ³⁹After two months she returned to her father, and Jephthah did

to her what he had promised. Jephthah's daughter never had a husband.

From this came a custom in Israel that ⁴⁰every year the young women of Israel would go out for four days to remember the daughter of Jephthah from Gilead.

Jephthah and Ephraim

12 The men of Ephraim called all their soldiers together and crossed the river to the town of Zaphon. They said to Jephthah, "Why didn't you call us to help you fight the Ammonites? We will burn your house down with you in it."

²Jephthah answered them, "My people and I fought a great battle against the Ammonites. I called you, but you didn't come to help me. ³When I saw that you would not help me, I risked my own life and went against the Ammonites. The LORD handed them over to me. So why have you come to fight against me today?"

⁴Then Jephthah called the men of Gilead together and fought the men of Ephraim. The men of Gilead struck them down because the Ephraimites had said, "You men of Gilead are nothing but deserters from Ephraim—living between Ephraim and Manasseh." ⁵The men of Gilead captured the crossings of the Jordan River that led to the country of Ephraim. A person from Ephraim trying to escape would say, "Let me cross the river." Then the men of Gilead would ask him, "Are you from Ephraim?" If he replied no, ⁶they would say to him, "Say the word 'Shibboleth.'" The men of Ephraim could not say that word correctly. So if the person from Ephraim said, "Sibboleth," the men of Gilead would kill him at the crossing. So forty-two thousand people from Ephraim were killed at that time.

⁷Jephthah was a judge for Israel for six years. Then Jephthah, the man from Gilead, died and was buried in a town in Gilead.

Ibzan, the Judge

⁸After Jephthah died, Ibzan from Bethlehem was a judge for Israel. ⁹He had thirty sons and thirty daughters. He let his daughters marry men who were not in his family group, and he brought thirty women who were not in his tribe to be wives for his sons. Ibzan judged Israel for seven years. ¹⁰Then he died and was buried in Bethlehem.

Elon, the Judge

¹¹After Ibzan died, Elon from the tribe of Zebulun was a judge for Israel. He judged Israel for ten years. ¹²Then Elon, the man of Zebulun, died and was buried in the city of Aijalon in the land of Zebulun.

Abdon, the Judge

¹³After Elon died, Abdon son of Hillel from the city of Pirathon was a judge for Israel. ¹⁴He had forty sons and thirty grandsons, who rode on seventy donkeys. He judged Israel for eight years. ¹⁵Then Abdon son of Hillel died and was buried in Pirathon in the land of Ephraim, in the mountains where the Amalekites lived.

PSALM 50:7–15

⁷God says, "My people, listen to me;
Israel, I will testify against you.
I am God, your God.
⁸I do not scold you for your sacrifices.
You always bring me your burnt offerings.
⁹But I do not need bulls from your stalls
or goats from your pens,
¹⁰because every animal of the forest is already mine.
The cattle on a thousand hills are mine.
¹¹I know every bird on the mountains,
and every living thing in the fields is mine.
¹²If I were hungry, I would not tell you,
because the earth and everything in it are mine.
¹³I don't eat the meat of bulls
or drink the blood of goats.
¹⁴Give an offering to show thanks to God.
Give God Most High what you have promised.
¹⁵Call to me in times of trouble.
I will save you, and you will honor me."

PROVERBS 14:28

²⁸A king is honored when he has many people to rule,
but a prince is ruined if he has none.

LUKE 17:1–19

Sin and Forgiveness

17 Jesus said to his followers, "Things that cause people to sin will happen, but how terrible for the person who causes them to happen! [2]It would be better for you to be thrown into the sea with a large stone around your neck than to cause one of these little ones to sin. [3]So be careful!

"If another follower sins, warn him, and if he is sorry and stops sinning, forgive him. [4]If he sins against you seven times in one day and says that he is sorry each time, forgive him."

How Big Is Your Faith?

[5]The apostles said to the Lord, "Give us more faith!"

[6]The Lord said, "If your faith were the size of a mustard seed, you could say to this mulberry tree, 'Dig yourself up and plant yourself in the sea,' and it would obey you.

Be Good Servants

[7]"Suppose one of you has a servant who has been plowing the ground or caring for the sheep. When the servant comes in from working in the field, would you say, 'Come in and sit down to eat'? [8]No, you would say to him, 'Prepare something for me to eat. Then get yourself ready and serve me. After I finish eating and drinking, you can eat.' [9]The servant does not get any special thanks for doing what his master commanded. [10]It is the same with you. When you have done everything you are told to do, you should say, 'We are unworthy servants; we have only done the work we should do.'"

Be Thankful

[11]While Jesus was on his way to Jerusalem, he was going through the area between Samaria and Galilee. [12]As he came into a small town, ten men who had a skin disease met him there. They did not come close to Jesus [13]but called to him, "Jesus! Master! Have mercy on us!"

[14]When Jesus saw the men, he said, "Go and show yourselves to the priests."[n]

As the ten men were going, they were healed. [15]When one of them saw that he was healed, he went back to Jesus, praising God in a loud voice. [16]Then he bowed down at Jesus' feet and thanked him. (And this man was a Samaritan.) [17]Jesus said, "Weren't ten men healed? Where are the other nine? [18]Is this Samaritan the only one who came back to thank God?" [19]Then Jesus said to him, "Stand up and go on your way. You were healed because you believed."

APRIL 24

JUDGES 13:1—14:20

The Birth of Samson

13 Again the people of Israel did what the LORD said was wrong. So he handed them over to the Philistines for forty years.

[2]There was a man named Manoah from the tribe of Dan, who lived in the city of Zorah. He had a wife, but she could not have children. [3]The angel of the LORD appeared to Manoah's wife and said, "You have not been able to have children, but you will become pregnant and give birth to a son. [4]Be careful not to drink wine or beer or eat anything that is unclean, [5]because you will become pregnant and have a son. You must never cut his hair, because he will be a Nazirite, given to God from birth. He will begin to save Israel from the power of the Philistines."

[6]Then Manoah's wife went to him and told him what had happened. She said, "A man from God came to me. He looked like an angel from God; his appearance was frightening. I didn't ask him where he was from, and he didn't tell me his name. [7]But he said to me, 'You will become pregnant and

---

17:14 show . . . priests The Law of Moses said a priest must say when a person with a skin disease became well.

will have a son. Don't drink wine or beer or eat anything that is unclean, because the boy will be a Nazirite to God from his birth until the day of his death.'"

⁸Then Manoah prayed to the LORD: "Lord, I beg you to let the man of God come to us again. Let him teach us what we should do for the boy who will be born to us."

⁹God heard Manoah's prayer, and the angel of God came to Manoah's wife again while she was sitting in the field. But her husband Manoah was not with her. ¹⁰So she ran to tell him, "He is here! The man who appeared to me the other day is here!"

¹¹Manoah got up and followed his wife. When he came to the man, he said, "Are you the man who spoke to my wife?"

The man said, "I am."

¹²So Manoah asked, "When what you say happens, what kind of life should the boy live? What should he do?"

¹³The angel of the LORD said, "Your wife must be careful to do everything I told her to do. ¹⁴She must not eat anything that grows on a grapevine, or drink any wine or beer, or eat anything that is unclean. She must do everything I have commanded her."

¹⁵Manoah said to the angel of the LORD, "We would like you to stay awhile so we can cook a young goat for you."

¹⁶The angel of the LORD answered, "Even if I stay awhile, I would not eat your food. But if you want to prepare something, offer a burnt offering to the LORD." (Manoah did not understand that the man was really the angel of the LORD.)

¹⁷Then Manoah asked the angel of the LORD, "What is your name? Then we will honor you when what you have said really happens."

¹⁸The angel of the LORD said, "Why do you ask my name? It is too amazing for you to understand." ¹⁹So Manoah sacrificed a young goat on a rock and offered some grain as a gift to the LORD. Then an amazing thing happened as Manoah and his wife watched. ²⁰The flames went up to the sky from the altar. As the fire burned, the angel of the LORD went up to heaven in the flame. When Manoah and his wife saw that, they bowed facedown on the ground. ²¹The angel of the LORD did not appear to them again. Then

Manoah understood that the man was really the angel of the LORD. ²²Manoah said, "We have seen God, so we will surely die."

²³But his wife said to him, "If the LORD wanted to kill us, he would not have accepted our burnt offering or grain offering. He would not have shown us all these things or told us all this."

²⁴So the woman gave birth to a boy and named him Samson. He grew, and the LORD blessed him. ²⁵The Spirit of the LORD began to work in Samson while he was in the city of Mahaneh Dan, between the cities of Zorah and Eshtaol.

Samson's First Marriage

14 Samson went down to the city of Timnah where he saw a Philistine woman. ²When he returned home, he said to his father and mother, "I saw a Philistine woman in Timnah. I want you to get her for me so I can marry her."

³His father and mother answered, "Surely there is a woman from Israel you can marry. Do you have to marry a woman from the Philistines, who are not circumcised?"

But Samson said, "Get that woman for me! She is the one I want!" ⁴(Samson's parents did not know that the LORD wanted this to happen because he was looking for a way to challenge the Philistines, who were ruling over Israel at this time.) ⁵Samson went down with his father and mother to Timnah, as far as the vineyard near there. Suddenly, a young lion came roaring toward Samson! ⁶The Spirit of the LORD entered Samson with great power, and he tore the lion apart with his bare hands. For him it was as easy as tearing apart a young goat. But Samson did not tell his father or mother what he had done. ⁷Then he went down to the city and talked to the Philistine woman, and he liked her.

⁸Several days later Samson went back to marry her. On his way he went over to look at the body of the dead lion and found a swarm of bees and honey in it. ⁹Samson got some of the honey with his hands and walked along eating it. When he came to his parents, he gave some to them. They ate it, too, but Samson did not tell them he had taken the honey from the body of the dead lion.

[10]Samson's father went down to see the Philistine woman. And Samson gave a feast, as was the custom for the bridegroom. [11]When the people saw him, they sent thirty friends to be with him.

Samson's Riddle

[12]Samson said to them, "Let me tell you a riddle. Try to find the answer during the seven days of the feast. If you can, I will give you thirty linen shirts and thirty changes of clothes. [13]But if you can't, you must give me thirty linen shirts and thirty changes of clothes."

So they said, "Tell us your riddle so we can hear it."

[14]Samson said,

"Out of the eater comes something to eat.
    Out of the strong comes something sweet."

After three days, they had not found the answer.

[15]On the fourth[n] day they said to Samson's wife, "Did you invite us here to make us poor? Trick your husband into telling us the answer to the riddle. If you don't, we will burn you and everyone in your father's house."

[16]So Samson's wife went to him, crying, and said, "You hate me! You don't really love me! You told my people a riddle, but you won't tell me the answer."

Samson said, "I haven't even told my father or mother. Why should I tell you?"

[17]Samson's wife cried for the rest of the seven days of the feast. So he finally gave her the answer on the seventh day, because she kept bothering him. Then she told her people the answer to the riddle.

[18]Before sunset on the seventh day of the feast, the Philistine men had the answer. They came to Samson and said,

"What is sweeter than honey?
    What is stronger than a lion?"

Then Samson said to them,

"If you had not plowed with my young cow,
    you would not have solved my riddle!"

[19]Then the Spirit of the LORD entered Samson and gave him great power. Samson went down to the city of Ashkelon and killed thirty of its men and took all that they had and gave the clothes to the men who had answered his riddle. Then he went to his father's house very angry. [20]And Samson's wife was given to his best man.

PSALM 50:16–23

[16]But God says to the wicked,
    "Why do you talk about my laws?
    Why do you mention my agreement?
[17]You hate my teachings
    and turn your back on what I say.
[18]When you see a thief, you join him.
    You take part in adultery.
[19]You don't stop your mouth from speaking evil,
    and your tongue makes up lies.
[20]You speak against your brother
    and lie about your mother's son.
[21]I have kept quiet while you did these things,
    so you thought I was just like you.
But I will scold you
    and accuse you to your face.
[22]"Think about this, you who forget God.
    Otherwise, I will tear you apart,
    and no one will save you.
[23]Those people honor me
    who bring me offerings to show thanks.
And I, God, will save those who do that."

PROVERBS 14:29–30

[29]Patient people have great understanding,
    but people with quick tempers show their foolishness.

[30]Peace of mind means a healthy body,
    but jealousy will rot your bones.

LUKE 17:20–37

God's Kingdom Is Within You

[20]Some of the Pharisees asked Jesus, "When will the kingdom of God come?"

Jesus answered, "God's kingdom is com-

14:15 fourth The Hebrew word is "seventh." Some old translations say "fourth," which fits the order of events better.

ing, but not in a way that you will be able to see with your eyes. [21]People will not say, 'Look, here it is!' or, 'There it is!' because God's kingdom is within[n] you."

[22]Then Jesus said to his followers, "The time will come when you will want very much to see one of the days of the Son of Man. But you will not see it. [23]People will say to you, 'Look, there he is!' or, 'Look, here he is!' Stay where you are; don't go away and search.

When Jesus Comes Again

[24]"When the Son of Man comes again, he will shine like lightning, which flashes across the sky and lights it up from one side to the other. [25]But first he must suffer many things and be rejected by the people of this time. [26]When the Son of Man comes again, it will be as it was when Noah lived. [27]People were eating, drinking, marrying, and giving their children to be married until the day Noah entered the boat. Then the flood came and killed them all. [28]It will be the same as

during the time of Lot. People were eating, drinking, buying, selling, planting, and building. [29]But the day Lot left Sodom,[n] fire and sulfur rained down from the sky and killed them all. [30]This is how it will be when the Son of Man comes again.

[31]"On that day, a person who is on the roof and whose belongings are in the house should not go inside to get them. A person who is in the field should not go back home. [32]Remember Lot's wife.[n] [33]Those who try to keep their lives will lose them. But those who give up their lives will save them. [34]I tell you, on that night two people will be sleeping in one bed; one will be taken and the other will be left. [35]There will be two women grinding grain together; one will be taken, and the other will be left. [[36]Two people will be in the field. One will be taken, and the other will be left.]"[n]

[37]The followers asked Jesus, "Where will this be, Lord?"

Jesus answered, "Where there is a dead body, there the vultures will gather."

APRIL 25

JUDGES 15:1—16:31

Samson Troubles the Philistines

15 At the time of the wheat harvest, Samson went to visit his wife, taking a young goat with him. He said, "I'm going to my wife's room," but her father would not let him go in.

[2]He said to Samson, "I thought you really hated your wife, so I gave her to your best man. Her younger sister is more beautiful. Take her instead."

[3]But Samson said to them, "This time no one will blame me for hurting you Philistines!" [4]So Samson went out and caught three hundred foxes. He took two foxes at a time, tied their tails together, and then tied a

torch to the tails of each pair of foxes. [5]After he lit the torches, he let the foxes loose in the grainfields of the Philistines so that he burned up their standing grain, the piles of grain, their vineyards, and their olive trees.

[6]The Philistines asked, "Who did this?"

Someone told them, "Samson, the son-in-law of the man from Timnah, did because his father-in-law gave his wife to his best man."

So the Philistines burned Samson's wife and her father to death. [7]Then Samson said to the Philistines, "Since you did this, I won't stop until I pay you back!" [8]Samson attacked the Philistines and killed many of them. Then he went down and stayed in a cave in the rock of Etam.

9The Philistines went up and camped in the land of Judah, near a place named Lehi. 10The men of Judah asked them, "Why have you come here to fight us?"

They answered, "We have come to make Samson our prisoner, to pay him back for what he did to our people."

11Then three thousand men of Judah went to the cave in the rock of Etam and said to Samson, "What have you done to us? Don't you know that the Philistines rule over us?"

Samson answered, "I only paid them back for what they did to me."

12Then they said to him, "We have come to tie you up and to hand you over to the Philistines."

Samson said to them, "Promise me you will not hurt me yourselves."

13The men from Judah said, "We agree. We will just tie you up and give you to the Philistines. We will not kill you." So they tied Samson with two new ropes and led him up from the cave in the rock. 14When Samson came to the place named Lehi, the Philistines came to meet him, shouting for joy. Then the Spirit of the LORD entered Samson and gave him great power. The ropes on him weakened like burned strings and fell off his hands! 15Samson found the jawbone of a dead donkey, took it, and killed a thousand men with it!

16Then Samson said,

"With a donkey's jawbone
I made donkeys out of them.
With a donkey's jawbone
I killed a thousand men!"

17When he finished speaking, he threw away the jawbone. So that place was named Ramath Lehi.ⁿ

18Samson was very thirsty, so he cried out to the LORD, "You gave me, your servant, this great victory. Do I have to die of thirst now? Do I have to be captured by people who are not circumcised?" 19Then God opened up a hole in the ground at Lehi, and water came out. When Samson drank, he felt better; he felt strong again. So he named that spring Caller's Spring, which is still in Lehi.

20Samson judged Israel for twenty years in the days of the Philistines.

Samson Goes to the City of Gaza

16 One day Samson went to Gaza and saw a prostitute there. He went in to spend the night with her. 2When the people of Gaza heard, "Samson has come here!" they surrounded the place and waited for him near the city gate all night. They whispered to each other, "When dawn comes, we will kill Samson!"

3But Samson only stayed with the prostitute until midnight. Then he got up and took hold of the doors and the two posts of the city gate and tore them loose, along with the bar. He put them on his shoulders and carried them to the top of the hill that faces the city of Hebron.

Samson and Delilah

4After this, Samson fell in love with a woman named Delilah, who lived in the Valley of Sorek. 5The Philistine rulers went to Delilah and said, "Find out what makes Samson so strong. Trick him into telling you how we can overpower him and capture him and tie him up. If you do this, each one of us will give you twenty-eight pounds of silver."

6So Delilah said to Samson, "Tell me why you are so strong. How can someone tie you up and capture you?"

7Samson answered, "Someone would have to tie me up with seven new bowstrings that have not been dried. Then I would be as weak as any other man."

8The Philistine rulers brought Delilah seven new bowstrings that had not been dried, and she tied Samson with them. 9Some men were hiding in another room. Delilah said to him, "Samson, the Philistines are here!" But Samson broke the bowstrings like pieces of burned string. So the Philistines did not find out the secret of Samson's strength.

10Then Delilah said to Samson, "You made a fool of me. You lied to me. Now tell me how someone can tie you up."

11Samson said, "They would have to tie me with new ropes that have not been used before. Then I would become as weak as any other man."

15:17 **Ramath Lehi** This name means "Jawbone Hill."

¹²So Delilah took new ropes and tied Samson. Some men were hiding in another room. She called out to him, "Samson, the Philistines are here!" But he broke the ropes as easily as if they were threads.

¹³Then Delilah said to Samson, "Again you have made a fool of me. You lied to me. Tell me how someone can tie you up."

He said, "Using the loom,^{n} weave the seven braids of my hair into the cloth, and tighten it with a pin. Then I will be as weak as any other man."

While Samson slept, Delilah wove the seven braids of his hair into the cloth. ¹⁴Then she fastened it with a pin.

Again she said to him, "Samson, the Philistines are here!" Samson woke up and pulled out the pin and the loom with the cloth.

¹⁵Then Delilah said to him, "How can you say, 'I love you,' when you don't even trust me? This is the third time you have made a fool of me. You haven't told me the secret of your great strength." ¹⁶She kept bothering Samson about his secret day after day until he felt he was going to die!

¹⁷So he told her everything. He said, "I have never had my hair cut, because I have been set apart to God as a Nazirite since I was born. If someone shaved my head, I would lose my strength and be as weak as any other man."

¹⁸When Delilah saw that he had told her everything sincerely, she sent a message to the Philistine rulers. She said, "Come back one more time, because he has told me everything." So the Philistine rulers came back to Delilah and brought the silver with them. ¹⁹Delilah got Samson to sleep, lying in her lap. Then she called in a man to shave off the seven braids of Samson's hair. In this way she began to make him weak, and his strength left him.

²⁰Then she said, "Samson, the Philistines are here!"

He woke up and thought, "I'll leave as I did before and shake myself free." But he did not know that the LORD had left him.

²¹Then the Philistines captured Samson and tore out his eyes. They took him down to Gaza, where they put bronze chains on him and made him grind grain in the prison. ²²But his hair began to grow again.

Samson Dies

²³The Philistine rulers gathered to celebrate and to offer a great sacrifice to their god Dagon. They said, "Our god has handed Samson our enemy over to us." ²⁴When the people saw him, they praised their god, saying,

"This man destroyed our country.
He killed many of us!
But our god handed over
    our enemy to us."

²⁵While the people were enjoying the celebration, they said, "Bring Samson out to perform for us." So they brought Samson from the prison, and he performed for them. They made him stand between the pillars. ²⁶Samson said to the servant holding his hand, "Let me feel the pillars that hold up the temple so I can lean against them." ²⁷Now the temple was full of men and women. All the Philistine rulers were there, and about three thousand men and women were on the roof^n watching Samson perform. ²⁸Then Samson prayed to the LORD, "Lord GOD, remember me. God, please give me strength one more time so I can pay these Philistines back for putting out my two eyes!" ²⁹Then Samson turned to the two center pillars that supported the whole temple. He braced himself between the two pillars, with his right hand on one and his left hand on the other. ³⁰Samson said, "Let me die with these Philistines!" Then he pushed as hard as he could, causing the temple to fall on the rulers and all the people in it. So Samson killed more of the Philistines when he died than when he was alive.

³¹Samson's brothers and his whole family went down to get his body. They brought him back and buried him in the tomb of Manoah, his father, between the cities of Zorah and Eshtaol. Samson was a judge for the people of Israel for twenty years.

16:13 loom A machine for making cloth from thread.   **16:27 roof** In Bible times houses were built with flat roofs. The roof was used for drying things such as flax and fruit. And it was used as an extra room, as a place for worship, and as a cool place to sleep in the summer.

PSALM 51:1–5

A Prayer for Forgiveness

For the director of music. A psalm of David when the prophet Nathan came to David after David's sin with Bathsheba.

51 God, be merciful to me
because you are loving.
Because you are always ready to be
merciful,
wipe out all my wrongs.
²Wash away all my guilt
and make me clean again.

³I know about my wrongs,
and I can't forget my sin.
⁴You are the only one I have sinned against;
I have done what you say is wrong.
You are right when you speak
and fair when you judge.
⁵I was brought into this world in sin.
In sin my mother gave birth to me.

PROVERBS 14:31–32

³¹Whoever mistreats the poor insults their
Maker,
but whoever is kind to the needy
honors God.

³²The wicked are ruined by their own evil,
but those who do right are protected
even in death.

LUKE 18:1–25

God Will Answer His People

18 Then Jesus used this story to teach his
followers that they should always pray
and never lose hope. ²"In a certain town there
was a judge who did not respect God or care
about people. ³In that same town there was a
widow who kept coming to this judge, saying,
'Give me my rights against my enemy.' ⁴For a
while the judge refused to help her. But afterwards, he thought to himself, 'Even though I
don't respect God or care about people, ⁵I will
see that she gets her rights. Otherwise she will
continue to bother me until I am worn out.'"

⁶The Lord said, "Listen to what the unfair
judge said. ⁷God will always give what is

right to his people who cry to him night and
day, and he will not be slow to answer them.
⁸I tell you, God will help his people quickly.
But when the Son of Man comes again, will
he find those on earth who believe in him?"

Being Right with God

⁹Jesus told this story to some people who
thought they were very good and looked down
on everyone else: ¹⁰"A Pharisee and a tax collector both went to the Temple to pray. ¹¹The
Pharisee stood alone and prayed, 'God, I thank
you that I am not like other people who steal,
cheat, or take part in adultery, or even like this
tax collector. ¹²I fast[n] twice a week, and I give
one-tenth of everything I get!'

¹³"The tax collector, standing at a distance, would not even look up to heaven. But
he beat on his chest because he was so sad.
He said, 'God, have mercy on me, a sinner.' ¹⁴I
tell you, when this man went home, he was
right with God, but the Pharisee was not. All
who make themselves great will be made
humble, but all who make themselves humble will be made great."

Who Will Enter God's Kingdom?

¹⁵Some people brought even their babies
to Jesus so he could touch them. When the
followers saw this, they told them to stop.
¹⁶But Jesus called for the children, saying,
"Let the little children come to me. Don't
stop them, because the kingdom of God belongs to people who are like these children.
¹⁷I tell you the truth, you must accept the
kingdom of God as if you were a child, or you
will never enter it."

A Rich Man's Question

¹⁸A certain leader asked Jesus, "Good
Teacher, what must I do to have life forever?"
¹⁹Jesus said to him, "Why do you call me
good? Only God is good. ²⁰You know the
commands: 'You must not be guilty of adultery. You must not murder anyone. You must
not steal. You must not tell lies about your
neighbor. Honor your father and mother.'"[n]
²¹But the leader said, "I have obeyed all
these commands since I was a boy."
²²When Jesus heard this, he said to him,
"There is still one more thing you need to do.

18:12 fast The people would give up eating for a special time of prayer and worship to God. It was also done to show sadness and disappointment. **18:20 'You . . . mother.'** Quotation from Exodus 20:12–16; Deuteronomy 5:16–20.

Sell everything you have and give it to the poor, and you will have treasure in heaven. Then come and follow me." ²³But when the man heard this, he became very sad, because he was very rich.

²⁴Jesus looked at him and said, "It is very hard for rich people to enter the kingdom of God. ²⁵It is easier for a camel to go through the eye of a needle than for a rich person to enter the kingdom of God."

APRIL 26

JUDGES 17:1—19:30

Micah's Idols

17 There was a man named Micah who lived in the mountains of Ephraim. ²He said to his mother, "I heard you speak a curse about the twenty-eight pounds of silver that were taken from you. I have the silver with me; I took it."

His mother said, "The LORD bless you, my son!"

³Micah gave the twenty-eight pounds of silver to his mother. Then she said, "I will give this silver to the LORD. I will have my son make an idol and a statue. So I will give the silver back to you."

⁴When he gave the silver back to his mother, she took about five pounds and gave it to a silversmith. With it he made an idol and a statue, which stood in Micah's house. ⁵Micah had a special holy place, and he made a holy vest and some household idols. Then Micah chose one of his sons to be his priest. ⁶At that time Israel did not have a king, so everyone did what seemed right.

⁷There was a young man who was a Levite[n] from the city of Bethlehem in Judah who was from the people of Judah. ⁸He left Bethlehem to look for another place to live, and on his way he came to Micah's house in the mountains of Ephraim. ⁹Micah asked him, "Where are you from?"

He answered, "I'm a Levite from Bethlehem in Judah. I'm looking for a place to live."

¹⁰Micah said to him, "Live with me and be my father and my priest. I will give you four ounces of silver each year and clothes and food." So the Levite went in. ¹¹He agreed to live with Micah and became like one of Micah's own sons. ¹²Micah made him a priest, and he lived in Micah's house. ¹³Then Micah said, "Now I know the LORD will be good to me, because I have a Levite as my priest."

Dan's Family Captures Laish

18 At that time Israel did not have a king. And at that time the tribe of Dan was still looking for a land where they could live, a land of their own. The Danites had not yet been given their own land among the tribes of Israel. ²So, from their family groups, they chose five soldiers from the cities of Zorah and Eshtaol to spy out and explore the land. They were told, "Go, explore the land."

They came to the mountains of Ephraim, to Micah's house, where they spent the night. ³When they came near Micah's house, they recognized the voice of the young Levite.[n] So they stopped there and asked him, "Who brought you here? What are you doing here? Why are you here?"

⁴He told them what Micah had done for him, saying, "He hired me. I am his priest."

⁵They said to him, "Please ask God if our journey will be successful."

⁶The priest said to them, "Go in peace. The LORD is pleased with your journey."

⁷So the five men left. When they came to the city of Laish, they saw that the people there lived in safety, like the people of Sidon. They thought they were safe and had plenty of everything. They lived a long way from the Sidonians and had no dealings with anyone else. ⁸When the five men returned to Zorah

---

17:7; 18:3 **Levite** The Levites were the only ones God had appointed as priests.

and Eshtaol, their relatives asked them, "What did you find?"

⁹They answered, "We have seen the land, and it is very good. We should attack them. Aren't you going to do something? Don't wait! Let's go and take that land! ¹⁰When you go, you will see there is plenty of land— plenty of everything! The people are not expecting an attack. Surely God has handed that land over to us!"

¹¹So six hundred Danites left Zorah and Eshtaol ready for war. ¹²On their way they set up camp near the city of Kiriath Jearim in Judah. That is why the place west of Kiriath Jearim is named Mahaneh Dan*ⁿ* to this day. ¹³From there they traveled on to the mountains of Ephraim. Then they came to Micah's house.

¹⁴The five men who had explored the land around Laish said to their relatives, "Do you know in one of these houses there are a holy vest, household gods, an idol, and a statue? You know what to do." ¹⁵So they stopped at the Levite's house, which was also Micah's house, and greeted the Levite. ¹⁶The six hundred Danites stood at the entrance gate, wearing their weapons of war. ¹⁷The five spies went into the house and took the idol, the holy vest, the household idols, and the statue. The priest and the six hundred men armed for war stood by the entrance gate.

¹⁸When the spies went into Micah's house and took the image, the holy vest, the household idols, and the statue, the priest asked them, "What are you doing?"

¹⁹They answered, "Be quiet! Don't say a word. Come with us and be our father and priest. Is it better for you to be a priest for one man's house or for a tribe and family group in Israel?" ²⁰This made the priest happy. So he took the holy vest, the household idols, and the idol and went with the Danites. ²¹They left Micah's house, putting their little children, their animals, and everything they owned in front of them.

²²When they had gone a little way from Micah's house, the men who lived near Micah were called out and caught up with them. ²³The men with Micah shouted at the Danites, who turned around and said to Micah, "What's the matter with you? Why have you been called out to fight?"

²⁴Micah answered, "You took my gods that I made and my priest. What do I have left? How can you ask me, 'What's the matter?'"

²⁵The Danites answered, "You should not argue with us. Some of our angry men might attack you, killing you and your family." ²⁶Then the Danites went on their way. Micah knew they were too strong for him, so he turned and went back home.

²⁷Then the Danites took what Micah had made and his priest and went on to Laish. They attacked those peaceful people and killed them with their swords and then burned the city. ²⁸There was no one to save the people of Laish. They lived too far from Sidon, and they had no dealings with anyone else. Laish was in a valley near Beth Rehob.

The people of Dan rebuilt the city and lived there. ²⁹They changed the name of Laish to Dan, naming it for their ancestor Dan, one of the sons of Israel.

³⁰The people of Dan set up the idols in the city of Dan. Jonathan son of Gershom, Moses' son, and his sons served as priests for the tribe of Dan until the land was captured. ³¹The people of Dan set up the idols Micah had made as long as the Holy Tent of God was in Shiloh.

A Levite and His Servant

19At that time Israel did not have a king.

There was a Levite who lived in the far-away mountains of Ephraim. He had taken a slave woman from the city of Bethlehem in the land of Judah to live with him, ²but she was unfaithful to him. She left him and went back to her father's house in Bethlehem in Judah and stayed there for four months. ³Then her husband went to ask her to come back to him, taking with him his servant and two donkeys. When the Levite came to her father's house, she invited him to come in, and her father was happy to see him. ⁴The father-in-law, the young woman's father, asked him to stay. So he stayed for three days and ate, drank, and slept there.

18:12 Mahaneh Dan This name means "the camp of Dan."

[5]On the fourth day they got up early in the morning. The Levite was getting ready to leave, but the woman's father said to his son-in-law, "Refresh yourself by eating something. Then go." [6]So the two men sat down to eat and drink together. After that, the father said to him, "Please stay tonight. Relax and enjoy yourself." [7]When the man got up to go, his father-in-law asked him to stay. So he stayed again that night. [8]On the fifth day the man got up early in the morning to leave. The woman's father said, "Refresh yourself. Wait until this afternoon." So the two men ate together.

[9]When the Levite, his slave woman, and his servant got up to leave, the father-in-law, the young woman's father, said, "It's almost night. The day is almost gone. Spend the night here and enjoy yourself. Tomorrow morning you can get up early and go home." [10]But the Levite did not want to stay another night. So he took his two saddled donkeys and his slave woman and traveled toward the city of Jebus (also called Jerusalem).

[11]As the day was almost over, they came near Jebus. So the servant said to his master, "Let's stop at this city of the Jebusites, and spend the night here."

[12]But his master said, "No. We won't go inside a foreign city. Those people are not Israelites. We will go on to the city of Gibeah." [13]He said, "Come on. Let's try to make it to Gibeah or Ramah so we can spend the night in one of those cities." [14]So they went on. The sun went down as they came near Gibeah, which belongs to the tribe of Benjamin. [15]They stopped there to spend the night. They came to the public square of the city and sat down, but no one invited them home to spend the night.

[16]Finally, in the evening an old man came in from his work in the fields. His home was in the mountains of Ephraim, but now he was living in Gibeah. (The people of Gibeah were from the tribe of Benjamin.) [17]He saw the traveler in the public square and asked, "Where are you going? Where did you come from?"

[18]The Levite answered, "We are traveling from Bethlehem in Judah to my home in the mountains of Ephraim. I have been to Bethlehem in Judah, but now I am going to the Holy Tent of the LORD. No one has invited me to stay in his house. [19]We already have straw and food for our donkeys and bread and wine for me, the young woman, and my servant. We don't need anything."

[20]The old man said, "You are welcome to stay at my house. Let me give you anything you need, but don't spend the night in the public square." [21]So the old man took the Levite into his house, and he fed their donkeys. They washed their feet and had something to eat and drink.

[22]While they were enjoying themselves, some wicked men of the city surrounded the house and beat on the door. They shouted to the old man who owned the house, "Bring out the man who came to your house. We want to have sexual relations with him."

[23]The owner of the house went outside and said to them, "No, my friends. Don't be so evil. This man is a guest in my house. Don't do this terrible thing! [24]Look, here are my daughter, who has never had sexual relations before, and the man's slave woman. I will bring them out to you now. Do anything you want with them, but don't do such a terrible thing to this man."

[25]But the men would not listen to him. So the Levite took his slave woman and sent her outside to them. They forced her to have sexual relations with them, and they abused her all night long. Then, at dawn, they let her go. [26]She came back to the house where her master was staying and fell down at the door and lay there until daylight.

[27]In the morning when the Levite got up, he opened the door of the house and went outside to go on his way. But his slave woman was lying at the doorway of the house, with her hands on the doorsill. [28]The Levite said to her, "Get up; let's go." But she did not answer. So he put her on his donkey and went home.

[29]When the Levite got home, he took a knife and cut his slave woman into twelve parts, limb by limb. Then he sent a part to each area of Israel. [30]Everyone who saw this said, "Nothing like this has ever happened before, not since the people of Israel came

out of Egypt. Think about it. Tell us what to do."

PSALM 51:6–9

⁶You want me to be completely truthful,
so teach me wisdom.
⁷Take away my sin, and I will be clean.
Wash me, and I will be whiter than snow.
⁸Make me hear sounds of joy and gladness;
let the bones you crushed be happy
again.
⁹Turn your face from my sins
and wipe out all my guilt.

PROVERBS 14:33–35

³³Wisdom lives in those with understanding,
and even fools recognize it.

³⁴Doing what is right makes a nation great,
but sin will bring disgrace to any people.

³⁵A king is pleased with a wise servant,
but he will become angry with one who
causes him shame.

LUKE 18:26–43

Who Can Be Saved?

²⁶When the people heard this, they asked, "Then who can be saved?"

²⁷Jesus answered, "The things impossible for people are possible for God."

²⁸Peter said, "Look, we have left everything and followed you."

²⁹Jesus said, "I tell you the truth, all those who have left houses, wives, brothers, parents, or children for the kingdom of God ³⁰will get much more in this life. And in the age that is coming, they will have life forever."

Jesus Will Rise from the Dead

³¹Then Jesus took the twelve apostles aside and said to them, "We are going to Jerusalem. Everything the prophets wrote about the Son of Man will happen. ³²He will be turned over to those who are evil. They will laugh at him, insult him, spit on him, ³³beat him with whips, and kill him. But on the third day, he will rise to life again." ³⁴The apostles did not understand this; the meaning was hidden from them, and they did not realize what was said.

Jesus Heals a Blind Man

³⁵As Jesus came near the city of Jericho, a blind man was sitting beside the road, begging. ³⁶When he heard the people coming down the road, he asked, "What is happening?"

³⁷They told him, "Jesus, from Nazareth, is going by."

³⁸The blind man cried out, "Jesus, Son of David, have mercy on me!"

³⁹The people leading the group warned the blind man to be quiet. But the blind man shouted even more, "Son of David, have mercy on me!"

⁴⁰Jesus stopped and ordered the blind man to be brought to him. When he came near, Jesus asked him, ⁴¹"What do you want me to do for you?"

He said, "Lord, I want to see."

⁴²Jesus said to him, "Then see. You are healed because you believed."

⁴³At once the man was able to see, and he followed Jesus, thanking God. All the people who saw this praised God.

APRIL 27

JUDGES 20:1–21:25

The War Between Israel and Benjamin

20 So all the Israelites from Dan to Beersheba,ⁿ including the land of Gilead, joined together before the LORD in the city of Mizpah. ²The leaders of all the tribes of Israel took their places in the meeting of the people of God. There were 400,000 soldiers with swords. ³(The people of Benjamin

20:1 Dan . . . Beersheba Dan was the city farthest north in Israel. Beersheba was the city farthest south. So this means all the people of Israel.

heard that the Israelites had gone up to Mizpah.) Then the Israelites said to the Levite, "Tell us how this evil thing happened."

⁴So the husband of the murdered woman answered, "My slave woman and I came to Gibeah in Benjamin to spend the night. ⁵During the night the men of Gibeah came after me. They surrounded the house and wanted to kill me. They forced my slave woman to have sexual relations and she died. ⁶I took her and cut her into parts and sent one part to each area of Israel because the people of Benjamin did this wicked and terrible thing in Israel. ⁷Now, all you Israelites, speak up. What is your decision?"

⁸Then all the people stood up at the same time, saying, "None of us will go home. Not one of us will go back to his house! ⁹Now this is what we will do to Gibeah. We will throw lots. ¹⁰That way we will choose ten men from every hundred men from all the tribes of Israel, and we will choose a hundred men from every thousand, and a thousand men from every ten thousand. These will find supplies for the army. Then the army will go to the city of Gibeah of Benjamin to repay them for the terrible thing they have done in Israel." ¹¹So all the men of Israel were united and gathered against the city.

¹²The tribes of Israel sent men throughout the tribe of Benjamin demanding, "What is this evil thing some of your men have done? ¹³Hand over the wicked men in Gibeah so that we can put them to death. We must remove this evil from Israel."

But the Benjaminites would not listen to their fellow Israelites. ¹⁴The Benjaminites left their own cities and met at Gibeah to fight the Israelites. ¹⁵In only one day the Benjaminites got 26,000 soldiers together who were trained with swords. They also had 700 chosen men from Gibeah. ¹⁶Seven hundred of these trained soldiers were left-handed, each of whom could sling a stone at a hair and not miss!

¹⁷The Israelites, except for the Benjaminites, gathered 400,000 soldiers with swords.

¹⁸The Israelites went up to the city of Bethel and asked God, "Which tribe shall be first to attack the Benjaminites?"

The LORD answered, "Judah shall go first."

¹⁹The next morning the Israelites got up and made a camp near Gibeah. ²⁰The men of Israel went out to fight the Benjaminites and took their battle position at Gibeah. ²¹Then the Benjaminites came out of Gibeah and killed 22,000 Israelites during the battle that day. ²²⁻²³The Israelites went before the LORD and cried until evening. They asked the LORD, "Shall we go to fight our relatives, the Benjaminites, again?"

The LORD answered, "Go up and fight them." The men of Israel encouraged each other. So they took the same battle positions they had taken the first day.

²⁴The Israelites came to fight the Benjaminites the second day. ²⁵The Benjaminites came out of Gibeah to attack the Israelites. This time, the Benjaminites killed 18,000 Israelites, all of whom carried swords.

²⁶Then the Israelites went up to Bethel. There they sat down and cried to the LORD and fasted all day until evening. They also brought burnt offerings and fellowship offerings to the LORD. ²⁷The Israelites asked the LORD a question. (In those days the Ark of the Agreement with God was there at Bethel. ²⁸A priest named Phinehas son of Eleazar, the son of Aaron, served before the Ark of the Agreement.) They asked, "Shall we go to fight our relatives, the Benjaminites, again, or shall we stop fighting?"

The LORD answered, "Go, because tomorrow I will hand them over to you."

²⁹Then the Israelites set up ambushes all around Gibeah. ³⁰They went to fight against the Benjaminites at Gibeah on the third day, getting into position for battle as they had done before. ³¹When the Benjaminites came out to fight them, the Israelites backed up and led the Benjaminites away from the city. The Benjaminites began to kill some of the Israelites as they had done before. About thirty Israelites were killed—some in the fields and some on the roads leading to Bethel and to Gibeah.

³²The Benjaminites said, "We are winning as before!"

But the Israelites said, "Let's run. Let's trick them into going farther away from their city and onto the roads."

[33]All the Israelites moved from their places and got into battle positions at a place named Baal Tamar. Then the Israelites ran out from their hiding places west of Gibeah. [34]Ten thousand of the best trained soldiers from all of Israel attacked Gibeah. The battle was very hard. The Benjaminites did not know disaster was about to come to them. [35]The LORD used the Israelites to defeat the Benjaminites. On that day the Israelites killed 25,100 Benjaminites, all armed with swords. [36]Then the Benjaminites saw that they were defeated.

The Israelites had moved back because they were depending on the surprise attack they had set up near Gibeah. [37]The men in hiding rushed into Gibeah, spread out, and killed everyone in the city with their swords. [38]Now the Israelites had set up a signal with the men in hiding. The men in the surprise attack were to send up a cloud of smoke from the city. [39]Then the army of Israel turned around in the battle.

The Benjaminites had killed about thirty Israelites. They were saying, "We are winning, as in the first battle!" [40]But then a cloud of smoke began to rise from the city. The Benjaminites turned around and saw that the whole city was going up in smoke. [41]Then the Israelites turned and began to fight. The Benjaminites were terrified because they knew that disaster was coming to them. [42]So the Benjaminites ran away from the Israelites toward the desert, but they could not escape the battle. And the Israelites who came out of the cities killed them. [43]They surrounded the Benjaminites and chased them and caught them in the area east of Gibeah. [44]So 18,000 brave Benjaminite fighters were killed. [45]The Benjaminites ran toward the desert to the rock of Rimmon, but the Israelites killed 5,000 Benjaminites along the roads. They chased them as far as Gidom and killed 2,000 more Benjaminites there.

[46]On that day 25,000 Benjaminites were killed, all of whom had fought bravely with swords. [47]But 600 Benjaminites ran to the rock of Rimmon in the desert, where they stayed for four months. [48]Then the Israelites went back to the land of Benjamin and killed the people in every city and also the animals and everything they could find. And they burned every city they found.

Wives for the Men of Benjamin

21 At Mizpah the men of Israel had sworn, "Not one of us will let his daughter marry a man from the tribe of Benjamin."

[2]The people went to the city of Bethel and sat before God until evening, crying loudly. [3]They said, "LORD, God of Israel, why has this terrible thing happened to us so that one tribe of Israel is missing today?"

[4]Early the next day the people built an altar and put burnt offerings and fellowship offerings to God on it.

[5]Then the Israelites asked, "Did any tribe of Israel not come here to meet with us in the presence of the LORD?" They asked this question because they had sworn that anyone who did not meet with them at Mizpah would be killed.

[6]The Israelites felt sorry for their relatives, the Benjaminites. They said, "Today one tribe has been cut off from Israel. [7]We swore before the LORD that we would not allow our daughters to marry a Benjaminite. How can we make sure that the remaining men of Benjamin will have wives?" [8]Then they asked, "Which one of the tribes of Israel did not come here to Mizpah?" They found that no one from the city of Jabesh Gilead had come. [9]The people of Israel counted everyone, but there was no one from Jabesh Gilead.

[10]So the whole group of Israelites sent twelve thousand soldiers to Jabesh Gilead to kill the people with their swords, even the women and children. [11]"This is what you must do: Kill every man in Jabesh Gilead and every married woman." [12]The soldiers found four hundred young unmarried women in Jabesh Gilead, so they brought them to the camp at Shiloh in Canaan.

[13]Then the whole group of Israelites sent a message to the men of Benjamin, who were at the rock of Rimmon, offering to make peace with them. [14]So the men of Benjamin came back at that time. The Israelites gave them the women from Jabesh Gilead who had not been killed, but there were not enough women.

[15]The people of Israel felt sorry for the Benjaminites because the LORD had separated the tribes of Israel. [16]The elders of the Israelites said, "The women of Benjamin have been killed. Where can we get wives for the men of Benjamin who are still alive? [17]These men must have children to continue their families so a tribe in Israel will not die out. [18]But we cannot allow our daughters to marry them, because we swore, 'Anyone who gives a wife to a man of Benjamin is cursed.' [19]We have an idea! There is a yearly festival of the LORD at Shiloh, which is north of the city of Bethel, east of the road that goes from Bethel to Shechem, and south of the city of Lebonah."

[20]So the elders told the men of Benjamin, "Go and hide in the vineyards. [21]Watch for the young women from Shiloh to come out to join the dancing. Then run out from the vineyards and take one of the young Shiloh women and return to the land of Benjamin. [22]If their fathers or brothers come to us and complain, we will say: 'Be kind to the men of Benjamin. We did not get wives for Benjamin during the war, and you did not give the women to the men from Benjamin. So you are not guilty.'"

[23]So that is what the Benjaminites did. While the young women were dancing, each man caught one of them, took her away, and married her. Then they went back to the land God had given them and rebuilt their cities and lived there.

[24]Then the Israelites went home to their own tribes and family groups, to their own land that God had given them.

[25]In those days Israel did not have a king. All the people did whatever seemed right in their own eyes.

PSALM 51:10-19

[10]Create in me a pure heart, God,
  and make my spirit right again.
[11]Do not send me away from you
  or take your Holy Spirit away from me.
[12]Give me back the joy of your salvation.
  Keep me strong by giving me a willing
    spirit.
[13]Then I will teach your ways to those who
    do wrong,
  and sinners will turn back to you.

[14]God, save me from the guilt of murder,
  God of my salvation,
  and I will sing about your goodness.
[15]Lord, let me speak
  so I may praise you.
[16]You are not pleased by sacrifices, or I
    would give them.
  You don't want burnt offerings.
[17]The sacrifice God wants is a broken
    spirit.
  God, you will not reject a heart that is
    broken and sorry for sin.

[18]Do whatever good you wish for
    Jerusalem.
  Rebuild the walls of Jerusalem.
[19]Then you will be pleased with right
    sacrifices and whole burnt offerings,
  and bulls will be offered on your altar.

PROVERBS 15:1-3

15 A gentle answer will calm a
  person's anger,
  but an unkind answer will cause more
    anger.

[2]Wise people use knowledge when they
    speak,
  but fools pour out foolishness.

[3]The LORD's eyes see everything;
  he watches both evil and good people.

LUKE 19:1-27

Zacchaeus Meets Jesus

19 Jesus was going through the city of
  Jericho. [2]A man was there named Zacchaeus, who was a very important tax collector, and he was wealthy. [3]He wanted to see who Jesus was, but he was not able because he was too short to see above the crowd. [4]He ran ahead to a place where Jesus would come, and he climbed a sycamore tree so he could see him. [5]When Jesus came to that place, he looked up and said to him, "Zacchaeus, hurry and come down! I must stay at your house today."

[6]Zacchaeus came down quickly and welcomed him gladly. [7]All the people saw this and began to complain, "Jesus is staying with a sinner!"

[8]But Zacchaeus stood and said to the Lord, "I will give half of my possessions to the poor. And if I have cheated anyone, I will pay back four times more."

[9]Jesus said to him, "Salvation has come to this house today, because this man also belongs to the family of Abraham. [10]The Son of Man came to find lost people and save them."

A Story About Three Servants

[11]As the people were listening to this, Jesus told them a story because he was near Jerusalem and they thought God's kingdom would appear immediately. [12]He said: "A very important man went to a country far away to be made a king and then to return home. [13]So he called ten of his servants and gave a coin[n] to each servant. He said, 'Do business with this money until I get back.' [14]But the people in the kingdom hated the man. So they sent a group to follow him and say, 'We don't want this man to be our king.'

[15]"But the man became king. When he returned home, he said, 'Call those servants who have my money so I can know how much they earned with it.'

[16]"The first servant came and said, 'Sir, I earned ten coins with the one you gave me.' [17]The king said to the servant, 'Excellent! You

are a good servant. Since I can trust you with small things, I will let you rule over ten of my cities.'

[18]"The second servant said, 'Sir, I earned five coins with your one.' [19]The king said to this servant, 'You can rule over five cities.'

[20]"Then another servant came in and said to the king, 'Sir, here is your coin which I wrapped in a piece of cloth and hid. [21]I was afraid of you, because you are a hard man. You even take money that you didn't earn and gather food that you didn't plant.' [22]Then the king said to the servant, 'I will condemn you by your own words, you evil servant. You knew that I am a hard man, taking money that I didn't earn and gathering food that I didn't plant. [23]Why then didn't you put my money in the bank? Then when I came back, my money would have earned some interest.'

[24]"The king said to the men who were standing by, 'Take the coin away from this servant and give it to the servant who earned ten coins.' [25]They said, 'But sir, that servant already has ten coins.' [26]The king said, 'Those who have will be given more, but those who do not have anything will have everything taken away from them. [27]Now where are my enemies who didn't want me to be king? Bring them here and kill them before me.'"

APRIL 28

RUTH 1:1—2:23

1 Long ago when the judges[n] ruled Israel, there was a shortage of food in the land. [2]So a man named Elimelech left the town of Bethlehem in Judah to live in the country of Moab with his wife and his two sons. His wife was named Naomi, and his two sons were named Mahlon and Kilion. They were Ephrathahites from Bethlehem in Judah. When they came to Moab, they settled there.

[3]Then Naomi's husband, Elimelech, died, and she was left with her two sons. [4]These

sons married women from Moab. One was named Orpah, and the other was named Ruth. Naomi and her sons had lived in Moab about ten years [5]when Mahlon and Kilion also died. So Naomi was left alone without her husband or her two sons.

[6]While Naomi was in Moab, she heard that the LORD had come to help his people and had given them food again. So she and her daughters-in-law got ready to leave Moab and return home. [7]Naomi and her daughters-in-law left the place where they had lived and started back to the land of

19:13 coin A Greek "mina." One mina was enough money to pay a person for working three months. • **1:1 judges** They were not judges in courts of law, but leaders of the people in times of emergency.

Judah. [8]But Naomi said to her two daughters-in-law, "Go back home, each of you to your own mother's house. May the LORD be as kind to you as you have been to me and my sons who are now dead. [9]May the LORD give you another happy home and a new husband."

When Naomi kissed the women goodbye, they began to cry out loud. [10]They said to her, "No, we want to go with you to your people."

[11]But Naomi said, "My daughters, return to your own homes. Why do you want to go with me? I cannot give birth to more sons to give you new husbands; [12]go back, my daughters, to your own homes. I am too old to have another husband. Even if I told myself, 'I still have hope' and had another husband tonight, and even if I had more sons, [13]should you wait until they were grown into men? Should you live for so many years without husbands? Don't do that, my daughters. My life is much too sad for you to share, because the LORD has been against me!"

[14]The women cried together out loud again. Then Orpah kissed her mother-in-law Naomi good-bye, but Ruth held on to her tightly.

[15]Naomi said to Ruth, "Look, your sister-in-law is going back to her own people and her own gods. Go back with her."

Ruth Stays with Naomi

[16]But Ruth said, "Don't beg me to leave you or to stop following you. Where you go, I will go. Where you live, I will live. Your people will be my people, and your God will be my God. [17]And where you die, I will die, and there I will be buried. I ask the LORD to punish me terribly if I do not keep this promise: Not even death will separate us."

[18]When Naomi saw that Ruth had firmly made up her mind to go with her, she stopped arguing with her. [19]So Naomi and Ruth went on until they came to the town of Bethlehem. When they entered Bethlehem, all the people became very excited. The women of the town said, "Is this really Naomi?"

[20]Naomi answered the people, "Don't call me Naomi.[n] Call me Mara,[n] because the Almighty has made my life very sad. [21]When I left, I had all I wanted, but now, the LORD has brought me home with nothing. Why should you call me Naomi when the LORD has spoken against me and the Almighty has given me so much trouble?"

[22]So Naomi and her daughter-in-law Ruth, the Moabite, returned from Moab and arrived at Bethlehem at the beginning of the barley harvest.

Ruth Meets Boaz

2 Now Naomi had a rich relative named Boaz, from Elimelech's family.

[2]One day Ruth, the Moabite, said to Naomi, "I am going to the fields. Maybe someone will be kind enough to let me gather the grain he leaves behind."

Naomi said, "Go, my daughter."

[3]So Ruth went to the fields and gathered the grain that the workers cutting the grain had left behind. It just so happened that the field belonged to Boaz, from Elimelech's family.

[4]Soon Boaz came from Bethlehem and greeted his workers, "The LORD be with you!"

And the workers answered, "May the LORD bless you!"

[5]Then Boaz asked his servant in charge of the workers, "Whose girl is that?"

[6]The servant answered, "She is the young Moabite woman who came back with Naomi from the country of Moab. [7]She said, 'Please let me follow the workers cutting grain and gather what they leave behind.' She came and has remained here, from morning until just now. She has stopped only a few moments to rest in the shelter."

[8]Then Boaz said to Ruth, "Listen, my daughter. Don't go to gather grain for yourself in another field. Don't even leave this field at all, but continue following closely behind my women workers. [9]Watch to see into which fields they go to cut grain and follow them. I have warned the young men not to bother you. When you are thirsty, you may go and drink from the water jugs that the young men have filled."

[10]Then Ruth bowed low with her face to the

ground and said to him, "I am not an Israelite. Why have you been so kind to notice me?"

[11]Boaz answered her, "I know about all the help you have given your mother-in-law after your husband died. You left your father and mother and your own country to come to a nation where you did not know anyone. [12]May the LORD reward you for all you have done. May your wages be paid in full by the LORD, the God of Israel, under whose wings you have come for shelter."

[13]Then Ruth said, "I hope I can continue to please you, sir. You have said kind and encouraging words to me, your servant, though I am not one of your servants."

[14]At mealtime Boaz told Ruth, "Come here. Eat some of our bread and dip it in our sauce."

So Ruth sat down beside the workers. Boaz handed her some roasted grain, and she ate until she was full; she even had some food left over. [15]When Ruth rose and went back to work, Boaz commanded his workers, "Let her gather even around the piles of cut grain. Don't tell her to go away. [16]In fact, drop some full heads of grain for her from what you have in your hands, and let her gather them. Don't tell her to stop."

[17]So Ruth gathered grain in the field until evening. Then she separated the grain from the chaff, and there was about one-half bushel of barley. [18]Ruth carried the grain into town, and her mother-in-law saw how much she had gathered. Ruth also took out the food that was left over from lunch and gave it to Naomi.

[19]Naomi asked her, "Where did you gather all this grain today? Where did you work? Blessed be whoever noticed you!"

Ruth told her mother-in-law whose field she had worked in. She said, "The man I worked with today is named Boaz."

[20]Naomi told her daughter-in-law, "The LORD bless him! He continues to be kind to us—both the living and the dead!" Then Naomi told Ruth, "Boaz is one of our close relatives,[n] one who should take care of us."

[21]Then Ruth, the Moabite, said, "Boaz also told me, 'Keep close to my workers until they have finished my whole harvest.'"

[22]But Naomi said to her daughter-in-law Ruth, "It is better for you to continue working with his women workers. If you work in another field, someone might hurt you." [23]So Ruth continued working closely with the workers of Boaz, gathering grain until the barley harvest and the wheat harvest were finished. And she continued to live with Naomi, her mother-in-law.

PSALM 52:1–7

God Will Punish the Proud

For the director of music. A maskil of David. When Doeg the Edomite came to Saul and said to him, "David is in Ahimelech's house."

52 Mighty warrior, why do you brag about the evil you do?
  God's love will continue forever.
[2]You think up evil plans.
  Your tongue is like a sharp razor,
  making up lies.
[3]You love wrong more than right
  and lies more than truth.   *Selah*
[4]You love words that bite
  and tongues that lie.

[5]But God will ruin you forever.
  He will grab you and throw you out of your tent;
  he will tear you away from the land of the living.   *Selah*
[6]Those who do right will see this and fear God.
  They will laugh at you and say,
[7]"Look what happened to the man
  who did not depend on God
  but depended on his money.
  He grew strong by his evil plans."

PROVERBS 15:4–5

[4]As a tree gives fruit, healing words give life,
  but dishonest words crush the spirit.

[5]Fools reject their parents' correction,
  but anyone who accepts correction is wise.

2:20 close relatives In Bible times the closest relative could marry a widow without children so she could have children. He would care for this family, but they and their property would not belong to him. They would belong to the dead husband.

LUKE 19:28–48

Jesus Enters Jerusalem as a King

28After Jesus said this, he went on toward Jerusalem. 29As Jesus came near Bethphage and Bethany, towns near the hill called the Mount of Olives, he sent out two of his followers. 30He said, "Go to the town you can see there. When you enter it, you will find a colt tied there, which no one has ever ridden. Untie it and bring it here to me. 31If anyone asks you why you are untying it, say that the Master needs it."

32The two followers went into town and found the colt just as Jesus had told them. 33As they were untying it, its owners came out and asked the followers, "Why are you untying our colt?"

34The followers answered, "The Master needs it." 35So they brought it to Jesus, threw their coats on the colt's back, and put Jesus on it. 36As Jesus rode toward Jerusalem, others spread their coats on the road before him.

37As he was coming close to Jerusalem, on the way down the Mount of Olives, the whole crowd of followers began joyfully shouting praise to God for all the miracles they had seen. 38They said,

"God bless the king who comes in the
    name of the Lord! *Psalm 118:26*
There is peace in heaven and glory to God!"

39Some of the Pharisees in the crowd said to Jesus, "Teacher, tell your followers not to say these things."

40But Jesus answered, "I tell you, if my followers didn't say these things, then the stones would cry out."

Jesus Cries for Jerusalem

41As Jesus came near Jerusalem, he saw the city and cried for it, 42saying, "I wish you knew today what would bring you peace. But now it is hidden from you. 43The time is coming when your enemies will build a wall around you and will hold you in on all sides. 44They will destroy you and all your people, and not one stone will be left on another. All this will happen because you did not recognize the time when God came to save you."

Jesus Goes to the Temple

45Jesus went into the Temple and began to throw out the people who were selling things there. 46He said, "It is written in the Scriptures, 'My Temple will be a house for prayer.'*n* But you have changed it into a 'hideout for robbers'!"*n*

47Jesus taught in the Temple every day. The leading priests, the experts on the law, and some of the leaders of the people wanted to kill Jesus. 48But they did not know how they could do it, because all the people were listening closely to him.

APRIL 29

RUTH 3:1—4:22

Naomi's Plan

3 Then Naomi, Ruth's mother-in-law, said to her, "My daughter, I must find a suitable home for you, one that will be good for you. 2Now Boaz, whose young women you worked with, is our close relative.*n* Tonight he will be working at the threshing floor. 3Wash yourself, put on perfume, change your clothes, and go down to the threshing floor. But don't let him know you're there until he has finished his dinner. 4Watch him so you will know where he lies down to sleep. When he lies down, go and lift the cover off his feet*n* and lie down. He will tell you what you should do."

5Then Ruth answered, "I will do everything you say."

19:46 'My Temple . . . prayer.' Quotation from Isaiah 56:7. **19:46 'hideout for robbers'** Quotation from Jeremiah 7:11.
• **3:2 close relative** In Bible times the closest relative could marry a widow without children so she could have children. He would care for this family, but they and their property would not belong to him. They would belong to the dead husband. **3:4 lift . . . feet** This showed Ruth was asking him to be her husband.

[6]So Ruth went down to the threshing floor and did all her mother-in-law told her to do. [7]After his evening meal, Boaz felt good and went to sleep lying beside the pile of grain. Ruth went to him quietly and lifted the cover from his feet and lay down.

[8]About midnight Boaz was startled and rolled over. There was a woman lying near his feet! [9]Boaz asked, "Who are you?"

She said, "I am Ruth, your servant girl. Spread your cover over me, because you are a relative who is supposed to take care of me."[n]

[10]Then Boaz said, "The LORD bless you, my daughter. This act of kindness is greater than the kindness you showed to Naomi in the beginning. You didn't look for a young man to marry, either rich or poor. [11]Now, my daughter, don't be afraid. I will do everything you ask, because all the people in our town know you are a good woman. [12]It is true that I am a relative who is to take care of you, but you have a closer relative than I. [13]Stay here tonight, and in the morning we will see if he will take care of you. If he decides to take care of you, that is fine. But if he refuses, I will take care of you myself, as surely as the LORD lives. So stay here until morning."

[14]So Ruth stayed near his feet until morning but got up while it was still too dark to recognize anyone. Boaz thought, "People in town must not know that the woman came here to the threshing floor." [15]So Boaz said to Ruth, "Bring me your shawl and hold it open."

So Ruth held her shawl open, and Boaz poured six portions of barley into it. Boaz then put it on her head and went back to the city.

[16]When Ruth went back to her mother-in-law, Naomi asked, "How did you do, my daughter?"

Ruth told Naomi everything that Boaz did for her. [17]She said, "Boaz gave me these six portions of barley, saying, 'You must not go home without a gift for your mother-in-law.'"

[18]Naomi answered, "Ruth, my daughter, wait here until you see what happens. Boaz will not rest until he has finished doing what he should do today."

Boaz Marries Ruth

4 Boaz went to the city gate and sat there until the close relative he had mentioned passed by. Boaz called to him, "Come here, friend, and sit down." So the man came over and sat down. [2]Boaz gathered ten of the elders of the city and told them, "Sit down here!" So they sat down.

[3]Then Boaz said to the close relative, "Naomi, who has come back from the country of Moab, wants to sell the piece of land that belonged to our relative Elimelech. [4]So I decided to tell you about it: If you want to buy back the land, then buy it in front of the people who are sitting here and in front of the elders of my people. But if you don't want to buy it, tell me, because you are the only one who can buy it, and I am next after you."

The close relative answered, "I will buy back the land."

[5]Then Boaz explained, "When you buy the land from Naomi, you must also marry Ruth, the Moabite, the dead man's wife. That way, the land will stay in the dead man's name."

[6]The close relative answered, "I can't buy back the land. If I did, I might harm what I can pass on to my own sons. I cannot buy the land back, so buy it yourself."

[7]Long ago in Israel when people traded or bought back something, one person took off his sandal and gave it to the other person. This was the proof of ownership in Israel.

[8]So the close relative said to Boaz, "Buy the land yourself," and he took off his sandal.

[9]Then Boaz said to the elders and to all the people, "You are witnesses today. I am buying from Naomi everything that belonged to Elimelech and Kilion and Mahlon. [10]I am also taking Ruth, the Moabite who was the wife of Mahlon, as my wife. I am doing this so her dead husband's property will stay in his name and his name will not be separated from his family and his hometown. You are witnesses today."

[11]So all the people and elders who were at the city gate said, "We are witnesses. May

---

3:9 Spread . . . me By this, Ruth was asking Boaz to marry her.

the LORD make this woman, who is coming into your home, like Rachel and Leah, who had many children and built up the people of Israel. May you become powerful in the district of Ephrathah and famous in Bethlehem. [12]As Tamar gave birth to Judah's son Perez,[n] may the LORD give you many children through Ruth. May your family be great like his."

[13]So Boaz took Ruth home as his wife and had sexual relations with her. The LORD let her become pregnant, and she gave birth to a son. [14]The women told Naomi, "Praise the LORD who gave you this grandson. May he become famous in Israel. [15]He will give you new life and will take care of you in your old age because of your daughter-in-law who loves you. She is better for you than seven sons, because she has given birth to your grandson."

[16]Naomi took the boy, held him in her arms, and cared for him. [17]The neighbors gave the boy his name, saying, "This boy was born for Naomi." They named him Obed. Obed was the father of Jesse, and Jesse was the father of David.

[18]This is the family history of Perez, the father of Hezron. [19]Hezron was the father of Ram, who was the father of Amminadab. [20]Amminadab was the father of Nahshon, who was the father of Salmon. [21]Salmon was the father of Boaz, who was the father of Obed. [22]Obed was the father of Jesse, and Jesse was the father of David.

PSALM 52:8–9

[8]But I am like an olive tree
    growing in God's Temple.
I trust God's love
    forever and ever.
[9]God, I will thank you forever for what
    you have done.
With those who worship you, I will
    trust you because you are good.

PROVERBS 15:6–7

[6]Much wealth is in the houses of good
    people,
but evil people get nothing but trouble.

[7]Wise people use their words to spread
    knowledge,
but there is no knowledge in the
    thoughts of fools.

LUKE 20:1–26

Jewish Leaders Question Jesus

20 One day Jesus was in the Temple, teaching the people and telling them the Good News. The leading priests, teachers of the law, and elders came up to talk with him, [2]saying, "Tell us what authority you have to do these things? Who gave you this authority?"

[3]Jesus answered, "I will also ask you a question. Tell me: [4]When John baptized people, was that authority from God or just from other people?"

[5]They argued about this, saying, "If we answer, 'John's baptism was from God,' Jesus will say, 'Then why did you not believe him?' [6]But if we say, 'It was from other people,' all the people will stone us to death, because they believe John was a prophet." [7]So they answered that they didn't know where it came from.

[8]Jesus said to them, "Then I won't tell you what authority I have to do these things."

A Story About God's Son

[9]Then Jesus told the people this story: "A man planted a vineyard and leased it to some farmers. Then he went away for a long time. [10]When it was time for the grapes to be picked, he sent a servant to the farmers to get some of the grapes. But they beat the servant and sent him away empty-handed. [11]Then he sent another servant. They beat this servant also, and showed no respect for him, and sent him away empty-handed. [12]So the man sent a third servant. The farmers wounded him and threw him out. [13]The owner of the vineyard said, 'What will I do now? I will send my son whom I love. Maybe they will respect him.' [14]But when the farmers saw the son, they said to each other, 'This son will inherit the vineyard. If we kill him, it will be ours.' [15]So the farmers threw the son out of the vineyard and killed him.

"What will the owner of this vineyard do to them? [16]He will come and kill those farmers and will give the vineyard to other farmers."

4:12 Perez One of Boaz's ancestors.

When the people heard this story, they said, "Let this never happen!"

[17]But Jesus looked at them and said, "Then what does this verse mean:

'The stone that the builders rejected became the cornerstone'? *Psalm 118:22*

[18]Everyone who falls on that stone will be broken, and the person on whom it falls, that person will be crushed!"

[19]The teachers of the law and the leading priests wanted to arrest Jesus at once, because they knew the story was about them. But they were afraid of what the people would do.

Is It Right to Pay Taxes or Not?

[20]So they watched Jesus and sent some spies who acted as if they were sincere. They wanted to trap Jesus in saying something wrong so they could hand him over to the authority and power of the governor. [21]So the spies asked Jesus, "Teacher, we know that what you say and teach is true. You pay no attention to who people are, and you always teach the truth about God's way. [22]Tell us, is it right for us to pay taxes to Caesar or not?"

[23]But Jesus, knowing they were trying to trick him, said, [24]"Show me a coin. Whose image and name are on it?"

They said, "Caesar's."

[25]Jesus said to them, "Then give to Caesar the things that are Caesar's, and give to God the things that are God's."

[26]So they were not able to trap Jesus in anything he said in the presence of the people. And being amazed at his answer, they became silent.

APRIL 30

1 SAMUEL 1:1—4:1a

Samuel's Birth

1 There was a man named Elkanah son of Jeroham from Ramathaim in the mountains of Ephraim. Elkanah was from the family of Zuph. (Jeroham was Elihu's son. Elihu was Tohu's son, and Tohu was the son of Zuph from the family group of Ephraim.) [2]Elkanah had two wives named Hannah and Peninnah. Peninnah had children, but Hannah had none.

[3]Every year Elkanah left his town of Ramah and went up to Shiloh to worship the Lord All-Powerful and to offer sacrifices to him. Shiloh was where Hophni and Phinehas, the sons of Eli, served as priests of the Lord. [4]When Elkanah offered sacrifices, he always gave a share of the meat to his wife Peninnah and to her sons and daughters. [5]But Elkanah always gave a special share of the meat to Hannah, because he loved Hannah and because the Lord had kept her from having children. [6]Peninnah would tease Hannah and upset her, because the Lord had made her unable to have children. [7]This happened every year when they went up to the house of the Lord at Shiloh. Peninnah would upset Hannah until Hannah would cry and not eat anything. [8]Her husband Elkanah would say to her, "Hannah, why are you crying and why won't you eat? Why are you sad? Don't I mean more to you than ten sons?"

[9]Once, after they had eaten their meal in Shiloh, Hannah got up. Now Eli the priest was sitting on a chair near the entrance to the Lord's house. [10]Hannah was so sad that she cried and prayed to the Lord. [11]She made a promise, saying, "Lord All-Powerful, see how sad I am. Remember me and don't forget me. If you will give me a son, I will give him back to you all his life, and no one will ever cut his hair with a razor."[n]

[12]While Hannah kept praying, Eli watched her mouth. [13]She was praying in her heart so her lips moved, but her voice was not heard. Eli thought she was drunk [14]and

---

1:11 cut . . . razor People who made special promises not to cut their hair or to drink wine or beer were called Nazirites. These people gave a specific time in their lives, or sometimes their entire lives, to the Lord. See Numbers 6:1–5.

said to her, "Stop getting drunk! Throw away your wine!"

[15]Hannah answered, "No, sir, I have not drunk any wine or beer. I am a deeply troubled woman, and I was telling the LORD about all my problems. [16]Don't think I am an evil woman. I have been praying because I have many troubles and am very sad."

[17]Eli answered, "Go! I wish you well. May the God of Israel give you what you asked of him."

[18]Hannah said, "May I always please you." When she left and ate something, she was not sad anymore.

[19]Early the next morning Elkanah's family got up and worshiped the LORD. Then they went back home to Ramah. Elkanah had sexual relations with his wife Hannah, and the LORD remembered her. [20]So Hannah became pregnant, and in time she gave birth to a son. She named him Samuel,[n] saying, "His name is Samuel because I asked the LORD for him."

Hannah Gives Samuel to God

[21]Every year Elkanah went with his whole family to Shiloh to offer sacrifices and to keep the promise he had made to God. [22]But one time Hannah did not go with him. She told him, "When the boy is old enough to eat solid food, I will take him to Shiloh. Then I will give him to the LORD, and he will always live there."

[23]Elkanah, Hannah's husband, said to her, "Do what you think is best. You may stay home until the boy is old enough to eat. May the LORD do what you have said." So Hannah stayed at home to nurse her son until he was old enough to eat.

[24]When Samuel was old enough to eat, Hannah took him to the house of the LORD at Shiloh, along with a three-year-old bull, one-half bushel of flour, and a leather bag filled with wine. [25]After they had killed the bull for the sacrifice, Hannah brought Samuel to Eli. [26]She said to Eli, "As surely as you live, sir, I am the same woman who stood near you praying to the LORD. [27]I prayed for this child, and the LORD answered my prayer and gave him to me. [28]Now I give him back to the

LORD. He will belong to the LORD all his life." And he worshiped the LORD there.

Hannah Gives Thanks

2 Hannah prayed:
"The LORD has filled my heart with joy;
    I feel very strong in the LORD.
I can laugh at my enemies;
    I am glad because you have helped me!

[2]"There is no one holy like the LORD.
    There is no God but you;
    there is no Rock like our God.

[3]"Don't continue bragging,
    don't speak proud words.
The LORD is a God who knows
        everything,
    and he judges what people do.

[4]"The bows of warriors break,
    but weak people become strong.
[5]Those who once had plenty of food now
        must work for food,
    but people who were hungry are
        hungry no more.
The woman who could not have children
        now has seven,
    but the woman who had many children
        now is sad.

[6]"The LORD sends death,
    and he brings to life.
He sends people to the grave,
    and he raises them to life again.
[7]The LORD makes some people poor,
    and others he makes rich.
He makes some people humble,
    and others he makes great.
[8]The LORD raises the poor up from the
        dust,
    and he lifts the needy from the ashes.
He lets the poor sit with princes
    and receive a throne of honor.

"The foundations of the earth belong to
        the LORD,
    and the LORD set the world upon them.
[9]He protects those who are loyal to him,
    but evil people will be silenced in
        darkness.
Power is not the key to success.

1:20 Samuel This name sounds like the Hebrew word for "God heard."

[10]The LORD destroys his enemies;
he will thunder in heaven against them.
The LORD will judge all the earth.
He will give power to his king
and make his appointed king strong."

Eli's Evil Sons

[11]Then Elkanah went home to Ramah, but the boy continued to serve the LORD under Eli the priest.

[12]Now Eli's sons were evil men; they did not care about the LORD. [13]This is what the priests would normally do to the people: Every time someone brought a sacrifice, the meat would be cooked in a pot. The priest's servant would then come carrying a fork that had three prongs. [14]He would plunge the fork into the pot or the kettle. Whatever the fork brought out of the pot belonged to the priest. But this is how they treated all the Israelites who came to Shiloh to offer sacrifices. [15]Even before the fat was burned, the priest's servant would come to the person offering sacrifices and say, "Give the priest some meat to roast. He won't accept boiled meat from you, only raw meat."

[16]If the one who offered the sacrifice said, "Let the fat be burned up first as usual, and then take anything you want," the priest's servant would answer, "No, give me the meat now. If you don't, I'll take it by force."

[17]The LORD saw that the sin of the servants was very great because they did not show respect for the offerings made to the LORD.

Samuel Grows Up

[18]But Samuel obeyed the LORD. As a boy he wore a linen holy vest. [19]Every year Samuel's mother made a little coat for him and took it to him when she went with her husband to Shiloh for the sacrifice. [20]When Eli blessed Elkanah and his wife, he would say, "May the LORD repay you with children through Hannah to take the place of the boy Hannah prayed for and gave back to the LORD." Then Elkanah and Hannah would go home. [21]The LORD was kind to Hannah, so she became the mother of three sons and two daughters. And the boy Samuel grew up serving the LORD.

[22]Now Eli was very old. He heard about everything his sons were doing to all the Israelites and how his sons had sexual relations with the women who served at the entrance to the Meeting Tent. [23]Eli said to his sons, "Why do you do these evil things that the people tell me about? [24]No, my sons. The LORD's people are spreading a bad report about you. [25]If you sin against someone, God can help you. But if you sin against the LORD himself, no one can help you!" But Eli's sons would not listen to him, because the LORD had decided to put them to death.

[26]The boy Samuel grew physically. He pleased the LORD and the people.

[27]A man of God came to Eli and said, "This is what the LORD says: 'I clearly showed myself to the family of your ancestor Aaron when they were slaves to the king of Egypt. [28]I chose them from all the tribes of Israel to be my priests. I wanted them to go up to my altar, to burn incense, and to wear the holy vest. I also let the family of your ancestor have part of all the offerings sacrificed by the Israelites. [29]So why don't you respect the sacrifices and gifts? You honor your sons more than me. You grow fat on the best parts of the meat the Israelites bring to me.'

[30]"So the LORD, the God of Israel, says: 'I promised that your family and your ancestor's family would serve me always.' But now the LORD says: 'This must stop! I will honor those who honor me, but I will dishonor those who ignore me. [31]The time is coming when I will destroy the descendants of both you and your ancestors. No man will grow old in your family. [32]You will see trouble in my house. No matter what good things happen to Israel, there will never be an old man in your family. [33]I will not totally cut off your family from my altar. But your eyes will cry and your heart be sad, because all your descendants will die.

[34]" 'I will give you a sign. Both your sons, Hophni and Phinehas, will die on the same day. [35]I will choose a loyal priest for myself who will listen to me and do what I want. I will make his family continue, and he will always serve before my appointed king. [36]Then everyone left in your family will come and bow down before him. They will beg for a little money or a little food and say, "Please

give me a job as priest so I can have food to eat.'"'

God Calls Samuel

3 The boy Samuel served the LORD under Eli. In those days the LORD did not speak directly to people very often; there were very few visions.

²Eli's eyes were so weak he was almost blind. One night he was lying in bed. ³Samuel was also in bed in the LORD's house, where the Ark of the Agreement was. God's lamp was still burning.

⁴Then the LORD called Samuel, and Samuel answered, "I am here!" ⁵He ran to Eli and said, "I am here. You called me."

But Eli said, "I didn't call you. Go back to bed." So Samuel went back to bed.

⁶The LORD called again, "Samuel!"

Samuel again went to Eli and said, "I am here. You called me."

Again Eli said, "I didn't call you. Go back to bed."

⁷Samuel did not yet know the LORD, and the LORD had not spoken directly to him yet.

⁸The LORD called Samuel for the third time. Samuel got up and went to Eli and said, "I am here. You called me."

Then Eli realized the LORD was calling the boy. ⁹So he told Samuel, "Go to bed. If he calls you again, say, 'Speak, LORD. I am your servant and I am listening.'" So Samuel went and lay down in bed.

¹⁰The LORD came and stood there and called as he had before, "Samuel, Samuel!"

Samuel said, "Speak, LORD. I am your servant and I am listening."

¹¹The LORD said to Samuel, "Watch, I am going to do something in Israel that will shock those who hear about it. ¹²At that time I will do to Eli and his family everything I promised, from beginning to end. ¹³I told Eli I would punish his family always, because he knew his sons were evil. They acted without honor, but he did not stop them. ¹⁴So I swore to Eli's family, 'Your guilt will never be removed by sacrifice or offering.'"

¹⁵Samuel lay down until morning. Then he opened the doors of the house of the LORD. He was afraid to tell Eli about the vision, ¹⁶but Eli called to him, "Samuel, my son!"

Samuel answered, "I am here."

¹⁷Eli asked, "What did the LORD say to you? Don't hide it from me. May God punish you terribly if you hide from me anything he said to you." ¹⁸So Samuel told Eli everything and did not hide anything from him. Then Eli said, "He is the LORD. Let him do what he thinks is best."

¹⁹The LORD was with Samuel as he grew up; he did not let any of Samuel's messages fail to come true. ²⁰Then all Israel, from Dan to Beersheba,ⁿ knew Samuel was a true prophet of the LORD. ²¹And the LORD continued to show himself at Shiloh, and he showed himself to Samuel through his word.

4 So, news about Samuel spread through all of Israel.

PSALM 53:1-6

The Unbelieving Fool

For the director of music. By mahalath. A maskil of David.

53 Fools say to themselves,
    "There is no God."
  Fools are evil and do terrible things;
    none of them does anything good.

²God looked down from heaven on all people
    to see if anyone was wise,
    if anyone was looking to God for help.
³But all have turned away.
    Together, everyone has become evil;
    none of them does anything good.
    Not a single person.

⁴Don't the wicked understand?
    They destroy my people as if they were
      eating bread.
    They do not ask God for help.
⁵The wicked are filled with terror
    where there had been nothing to fear.
    God will scatter the bones of your
      enemies.
  You will defeat them,
    because God has rejected them.

3:20 Dan to Beersheba Dan was the city farthest north in Israel, and Beersheba was the city farthest south. So this means all the people of Israel.

⁶I pray that victory will come to Israel
from Mount Zion!
May God bring them back.
Then the people of Jacob will rejoice,
and the people of Israel will be glad.

PROVERBS 15:8–11

⁸The LORD hates the sacrifice that the
wicked offer,
but he likes the prayers of honest people.

⁹The LORD hates what evil people do,
but he loves those who do what is right.

¹⁰The person who quits doing what is right
will be punished,
and the one who hates to be corrected
will die.

¹¹The LORD knows what is happening in
the world of the dead,
so he surely knows the thoughts of the
living.

LUKE 20:27–47

Some Sadducees Try to Trick Jesus

²⁷Some Sadducees, who believed people
would not rise from the dead, came to Jesus.
²⁸They asked, "Teacher, Moses wrote that if a
man's brother dies and leaves a wife but no
children, then that man must marry the
widow and have children for his brother.
²⁹Once there were seven brothers. The first
brother married and died, but had no children. ³⁰Then the second brother married the
widow, and he died. ³¹And the third brother
married the widow, and he died. The same
thing happened with all seven brothers; they
died and had no children. ³²Finally, the
woman died also. ³³Since all seven brothers
had married her, whose wife will she be
when people rise from the dead?"

³⁴Jesus said to them, "On earth, people
marry and are given to someone to marry.
³⁵But those who will be worthy to be raised
from the dead and live again will not marry,
nor will they be given to someone to marry.
³⁶In that life they are like angels and cannot
die. They are children of God, because they
have been raised from the dead. ³⁷Even
Moses clearly showed that the dead are
raised to life. When he wrote about the burning bush,ⁿ he said that the Lord is 'the God of
Abraham, the God of Isaac, and the God of
Jacob.'ⁿ ³⁸God is the God of the living, not the
dead, because all people are alive to him."

³⁹Some of the teachers of the law said,
"Teacher, your answer was good." ⁴⁰No one
was brave enough to ask him another question.

Is the Christ the Son of David?

⁴¹Then Jesus said, "Why do people say
that the Christ is the Son of David? ⁴²In the
book of Psalms, David himself says:
'The Lord said to my Lord,
"Sit by me at my right side,
⁴³   until I put your enemies under your
control." 'ⁿ   *Psalm 110:1*
⁴⁴David calls the Christ 'Lord,' so how can the
Christ be his son?"

Jesus Accuses Some Leaders

⁴⁵While all the people were listening, Jesus said to his followers, ⁴⁶"Beware of the
teachers of the law. They like to walk around
wearing fancy clothes, and they love for people to greet them with respect in the marketplaces. They love to have the most important
seats in the synagogues and at feasts. ⁴⁷But
they cheat widows and steal their houses
and then try to make themselves look good
by saying long prayers. They will receive a
greater punishment."

20:37 *burning bush* Read Exodus 3:1–12 in the Old Testament.   20:37 *'the God of . . . Jacob'* These words are taken from Exodus 3:6.   20:43 *until . . . control* Literally, "until I make your enemies a footstool for your feet."

MAY 1

1 SAMUEL 4:1b—5:12

The Philistines Capture the Ark of the Agreement

At that time the Israelites went out to fight the Philistines. The Israelites camped at Ebenezer and the Philistines at Aphek. ²The Philistines went to meet the Israelites in battle. And as the battle spread, they defeated the Israelites, killing about four thousand soldiers on the battlefield. ³When some Israelite soldiers went back to their camp, the elders of Israel asked, "Why did the LORD let the Philistines defeat us? Let's bring the Ark of the Agreement with the LORD here from Shiloh and take it with us into battle. Then God will save us from our enemies."

⁴So the people sent men to Shiloh. They brought back the Ark of the Agreement with the LORD All-Powerful, who sits between the gold creatures with wings. Eli's two sons, Hophni and Phinehas, were there with the Ark.

⁵When the Ark of the Agreement with the LORD came into the camp, all the Israelites gave a great shout of joy that made the ground shake. ⁶When the Philistines heard Israel's shout, they asked, "What's all this shouting in the Hebrew camp?"

Then the Philistines found out that the Ark of the LORD had come into the Hebrew camp. ⁷They were afraid and said, "A god has come into the Hebrew camp! We're in trouble! This has never happened before! ⁸How terrible it will be for us! Who can save us from these powerful gods? They are the ones who struck the Egyptians with all kinds of disasters in the desert. ⁹Be brave, Philistines! Fight like men! In the past they were our slaves. So fight like men, or we will become their slaves."

¹⁰So the Philistines fought hard and defeated the Israelites, and every Israelite soldier ran away to his own home. It was a great defeat for Israel, because thirty thousand Israelite soldiers were killed. ¹¹The Ark of God was taken by the Philistines, and Eli's two sons, Hophni and Phinehas, died.

¹²That same day a man from the tribe of Benjamin ran from the battle. He tore his clothes and put dust on his head to show his great sadness. ¹³When he arrived in Shiloh, Eli was by the side of the road. He was sitting there in a chair, watching, because he was worried about the Ark of God. When the Benjaminite entered Shiloh, he told the bad news. Then all the people in town cried loudly. ¹⁴Eli heard the crying and asked, "What's all this noise?"

The Benjaminite ran to Eli and told him what had happened. ¹⁵Eli was now ninety-eight years old, and he was blind. ¹⁶The Benjaminite told him, "I have come from the battle. I ran all the way here today."

Eli asked, "What happened, my son?"

¹⁷The Benjaminite answered, "Israel ran away from the Philistines, and the Israelite army has lost many soldiers. Your two sons are both dead, and the Philistines have taken the Ark of God."

¹⁸When he mentioned the Ark of God, Eli fell backward off his chair. He fell beside the gate, broke his neck, and died, because he was old and fat. He had led Israel for forty years.

The Glory Is Gone

¹⁹Eli's daughter-in-law, the wife of Phinehas, was pregnant and was about to give birth. When she heard the news that the Ark of God had been taken and that Eli, her father-in-law, and Phinehas, her husband, were both dead, she began to give birth to her child. The child was born, but the mother had much trouble in giving birth. ²⁰As she was dying, the women who helped her said, "Don't worry! You've given birth to a son!" But she did not answer or pay attention. ²¹She named the baby Ichabod,ⁿ saying, "Israel's glory is gone." She said this because the Ark of God had been taken and her father-in-law and husband were dead. ²²She said, "Israel's glory is gone, because the Ark of God has been taken away."

4:21 Ichabod This name means "no glory."

Trouble for the Philistines

5 After the Philistines had captured the Ark of God, they took it from Ebenezer to Ashdod. [2]They carried it into Dagon's temple and put it next to Dagon. [3]When the people of Ashdod rose early the next morning, they found that Dagon had fallen on his face on the ground before the Ark of the LORD. So they put Dagon back in his place. [4]The next morning when they rose, they again found Dagon fallen on the ground before the Ark of the LORD. His head and hands had broken off and were lying in the doorway. Only his body was still in one piece. [5]So, even today, Dagon's priests and others who enter his temple at Ashdod refuse to step on the doorsill.

[6]The LORD was hard on the people of Ashdod and their neighbors. He caused them to suffer and gave them growths on their skin. [7]When the people of Ashdod saw what was happening, they said, "The Ark of the God of Israel can't stay with us. God is punishing us and Dagon our god." [8]The people of Ashdod called all five Philistine kings together and asked them, "What should we do with the Ark of the God of Israel?"

The rulers answered, "Move the Ark of the God of Israel to Gath." So the Philistines moved it to Gath.

[9]But after they moved it to Gath, there was a great panic. The LORD was hard on that city also, and he gave both old and young people in Gath growths on their skin. [10]Then the Philistines sent the Ark of God to Ekron.

But when it came into Ekron, the people of Ekron yelled, "Why are you bringing the Ark of the God of Israel to our city? Do you want to kill us and our people?" [11]So they called all the kings of the Philistines together and said, "Send the Ark of the God of Israel back to its place before it kills us and our people!" All the people in the city were struck with terror because God was so hard on them there. [12]The people who did not die were troubled with growths on their skin. So the people of Ekron cried loudly to heaven.

PSALM 54:1–7

A Prayer for Help

For the director of music. With stringed instruments. A maskil of David when the Ziphites went to Saul and said, "We think David is hiding among our people."

54 God, save me because of who you are.
By your strength show that I am innocent.
[2]Hear my prayer, God;
listen to what I say.
[3]Strangers turn against me,
and cruel people want to kill me.
They do not care about God.   *Selah*

[4]See, God will help me;
the Lord will support me.
[5]Let my enemies be punished with their own evil.
Destroy them because you are loyal to me.
[6]I will offer a sacrifice as a special gift to you.
I will thank you, LORD, because you are good.
[7]You have saved me from all my troubles,
and I have seen my enemies defeated.

PROVERBS 15:12–13

[12]Those who make fun of wisdom don't like to be corrected;
they will not ask the wise for advice.

[13]Happiness makes a person smile,
but sadness can break a person's spirit.

LUKE 21:1–19

True Giving

21 As Jesus looked up, he saw some rich people putting their gifts into the Temple money box.[n] [2]Then he saw a poor widow putting two small copper coins into the box. [3]He said, "I tell you the truth, this poor widow gave more than all those rich people. [4]They gave only what they did not need. This woman is very poor, but she gave all she had to live on."

21:1 **money box** A special box in the Jewish place of worship where people put their gifts to God.

The Temple Will Be Destroyed

⁵Some people were talking about the Temple and how it was decorated with beautiful stones and gifts offered to God.

But Jesus said, ⁶"As for these things you are looking at, the time will come when not one stone will be left on another. Every stone will be thrown down."

⁷They asked Jesus, "Teacher, when will these things happen? What will be the sign that they are about to take place?"

⁸Jesus said, "Be careful so you are not fooled. Many people will come in my name, saying, 'I am the One' and, 'The time has come!' But don't follow them. ⁹When you hear about wars and riots, don't be afraid, because these things must happen first, but the end will come later."

¹⁰Then he said to them, "Nations will fight against other nations, and kingdoms against other kingdoms. ¹¹In various places there will be great earthquakes, sicknesses, and a lack of food. Fearful events and great signs will come from heaven.

¹²"But before all these things happen, people will arrest you and treat you cruelly. They will judge you in their synagogues and put you in jail and force you to stand before kings and governors, because you follow me. ¹³But this will give you an opportunity to tell about me. ¹⁴Make up your minds not to worry ahead of time about what you will say. ¹⁵I will give you the wisdom to say things that none of your enemies will be able to stand against or prove wrong. ¹⁶Even your parents, brothers, relatives, and friends will turn against you, and they will kill some of you. ¹⁷All people will hate you because you follow me. ¹⁸But none of these things can really harm you. ¹⁹By continuing to have faith you will save your lives.

MAY 2

1 SAMUEL 6:1—7:17

The Ark of God Is Sent Home

6 The Philistines kept the Ark of God in their land seven months. ²Then they called for their priests and magicians and said, "What should we do with the Ark of the LORD? Tell us how to send it back home!"

³The priests and magicians answered, "If you send back the Ark of the God of Israel, don't send it back empty. You must give a penalty offering. If you are then healed, you will know that it was because of the Ark that you had such trouble."

⁴The Philistines asked, "What kind of penalty offering should we send to Israel's God?"

They answered, "Make five gold models of the growths on your skin and five gold models of rats. The number of models must match the number of Philistine kings, because the same sickness has come on you and your kings. ⁵Make models of the growths and the rats that are ruining the country, and give honor to Israel's God. Then maybe he will stop being so hard on you, your gods, and your land. ⁶Don't be stubborn like the king of Egypt and the Egyptians. After God punished them terribly, they let the Israelites leave Egypt.

⁷"You must build a new cart and get two cows that have just had calves. These must be cows that have never had yokes on their necks. Hitch the cows to the cart, and take the calves home, away from their mothers. ⁸Put the Ark of the LORD on the cart and the gold models for the penalty offering in a box beside the Ark. Then send the cart straight on its way. ⁹Watch the cart. If it goes toward Beth Shemesh in Israel's own land, the LORD has given us this great sickness. But if it doesn't, we will know that Israel's God has not punished us. Our sickness just happened by chance."

¹⁰The Philistines did what the priests and magicians said. They took two cows that had just had calves and hitched them to the cart, but they kept their calves at home. ¹¹They

put the Ark of the LORD and the box with the gold rats and models of growths on the cart. [12]Then the cows went straight toward Beth Shemesh. They stayed on the road, mooing all the way, and did not turn right or left. The Philistine kings followed the cows as far as the border of Beth Shemesh.

[13]Now the people of Beth Shemesh were harvesting their wheat in the valley. When they looked up and saw the Ark of the LORD, they were very happy. [14]The cart came to the field belonging to Joshua of Beth Shemesh and stopped near a large rock. The people of Beth Shemesh chopped up the wood of the cart. Then they sacrificed the cows as burnt offerings to the LORD. [15]The Levites took down the Ark of the LORD and the box that had the gold models, and they put both on the large rock. That day the people of Beth Shemesh offered whole burnt offerings and made sacrifices to the LORD. [16]After the five Philistine kings saw this, they went back to Ekron the same day.

[17]The Philistines had sent these gold models of the growths as penalty offerings to the LORD. They sent one model for each Philistine town: Ashdod, Gaza, Ashkelon, Gath, and Ekron. [18]And the Philistines also sent gold models of rats. The number of rats matched the number of towns belonging to the Philistine kings, including both strong, walled cities and country villages. The large rock on which they put the Ark of the LORD is still there in the field of Joshua of Beth Shemesh.

[19]But some of the men of Beth Shemesh looked into the Ark of the LORD. So God killed seventy of them. The people of Beth Shemesh cried because the LORD had struck them down. [20]They said, "Who can stand before the LORD, this holy God? Whom will he strike next?"

[21]Then they sent messengers to the people of Kiriath Jearim, saying, "The Philistines have brought back the Ark of the LORD. Come down and take it to your city."

7 The men of Kiriath Jearim came and took the Ark of the LORD to Abinadab's house on a hill. There they made Abinadab's son

Eleazar holy for the LORD so he could guard the Ark of the LORD.

The Lord Saves the Israelites

[2]The Ark stayed at Kiriath Jearim a long time—twenty years in all. And the people of Israel began to follow the LORD again. [3]Samuel spoke to the whole group of Israel, saying, "If you're turning back to the LORD with all your hearts, you must remove your foreign gods and your idols of Ashtoreth. You must give yourselves fully to the LORD and serve only him. Then he will save you from the Philistines."

[4]So the Israelites put away their idols of Baal and Ashtoreth, and they served only the LORD.

[5]Samuel said, "All Israel must meet at Mizpah, and I will pray to the LORD for you." [6]So the Israelites met together at Mizpah. They drew water from the ground and poured it out before the LORD and fasted that day. They confessed, "We have sinned against the LORD." And Samuel served as judge of Israel at Mizpah.

[7]The Philistines heard the Israelites were meeting at Mizpah, so the Philistine kings came up to attack them. When the Israelites heard they were coming, they were afraid. [8]They said to Samuel, "Don't stop praying to the LORD our God for us! Ask him to save us from the Philistines!" [9]Then Samuel took a baby lamb and offered it to the LORD as a whole burnt offering. He called to the LORD for Israel's sake, and the LORD answered him.

[10]While Samuel was burning the offering, the Philistines came near to attack Israel. But the LORD thundered against them with loud thunder. They were so frightened they became confused. So the Israelites defeated the Philistines in battle. [11]The men of Israel ran out of Mizpah and chased the Philistines almost to Beth Car, killing the Philistines along the way.

Peace Comes to Israel

[12]After this happened Samuel took a stone and set it up between Mizpah and Shen. He named the stone Ebenezer,[n] saying, "The LORD has helped us to this point." [13]So

---

7:12 Ebenezer This name means "stone of help."

the Philistines were defeated and did not enter the Israelites' land again.

The LORD was against the Philistines all Samuel's life. [14]Earlier the Philistines had taken towns from the Israelites, but the Israelites won them back, from Ekron to Gath. They also took back from the Philistines the lands near these towns. There was peace also between Israel and the Amorites.

[15]Samuel continued as judge of Israel all his life. [16]Every year he went from Bethel to Gilgal to Mizpah and judged the Israelites in all these towns. [17]But Samuel always went back to Ramah, where his home was. There he judged Israel and built an altar to the LORD.

PSALM 55:1-8

A Prayer About a False Friend

For the director of music. With stringed instruments. A maskil of David.

55 God, listen to my prayer
and do not ignore my cry for help.
[2]Pay attention to me and answer me.
I am troubled and upset
[3]by what the enemy says
and how the wicked look at me.
They bring troubles down on me,
and in anger they attack me.

[4]I am frightened inside;
the terror of death has attacked me.
[5]I am scared and shaking,
and terror grips me.
[6]I said, "I wish I had wings like a dove.
Then I would fly away and rest.
[7]I would wander far away
and stay in the desert.   *Selah*
[8]I would hurry to my place of escape,
far away from the wind and storm."

PROVERBS 15:14

[14]People with understanding want more
knowledge,
but fools just want more foolishness.

LUKE 21:20-38

Jerusalem Will Be Destroyed

[20]"When you see armies all around Jerusalem, you will know it will soon be de-stroyed. [21]At that time, the people in Judea should run away to the mountains. The people in Jerusalem must get out, and those who are near the city should not go in. [22]These are the days of punishment to bring about all that is written in the Scriptures. [23]How terrible it will be for women who are pregnant or have nursing babies! Great trouble will come upon this land, and God will be angry with these people. [24]They will be killed by the sword and taken as prisoners to all nations. Jerusalem will be crushed by non-Jewish people until their time is over.

Don't Fear

[25]"There will be signs in the sun, moon, and stars. On earth, nations will be afraid and confused because of the roar and fury of the sea. [26]People will be so afraid they will faint, wondering what is happening to the world, because the powers of the heavens will be shaken. [27]Then people will see the Son of Man coming in a cloud with power and great glory. [28]When these things begin to happen, look up and hold your heads high, because the time when God will free you is near!"

Jesus' Words Will Live Forever

[29]Then Jesus told this story: "Look at the fig tree and all the other trees. [30]When their leaves appear, you know that summer is near. [31]In the same way, when you see these things happening, you will know that God's kingdom is near.

[32]"I tell you the truth, all these things will happen while the people of this time are still living. [33]Earth and sky will be destroyed, but the words I have spoken will never be destroyed.

Be Ready All the Time

[34]"Be careful not to spend your time feasting, drinking, or worrying about worldly things. If you do, that day might come on you suddenly, [35]like a trap on all people on earth. [36]So be ready all the time. Pray that you will be strong enough to escape all these things that will happen and that you will be able to stand before the Son of Man."

³⁷During the day, Jesus taught the people in the Temple, and at night he went out of the city and stayed on the Mount of Olives. ³⁸Every morning all the people got up early to go to the Temple to listen to him.

MAY 3

1 SAMUEL 8:1—9:27

Israel Asks for a King

8 When Samuel was old, he made his sons judges for Israel. ²His first son was named Joel, and his second son was named Abijah. Joel and Abijah were judges in Beersheba. ³But Samuel's sons did not live as he did. They tried to get money dishonestly, and they accepted money secretly to make wrong judgments.

⁴So all the elders came together and met Samuel at Ramah. ⁵They said to him, "You're old, and your sons don't live as you do. Give us a king to rule over us like all the other nations."

⁶When the elders said that, Samuel was not pleased. He prayed to the LORD, ⁷and the LORD told Samuel, "Listen to whatever the people say to you. They have not rejected you. They have rejected me from being their king. ⁸They are doing as they have always done. When I took them out of Egypt, they left me and served other gods. They are doing the same to you. ⁹Now listen to the people, but warn them what the king who rules over them will do."

¹⁰So Samuel told those who had asked him for a king what the LORD had said. ¹¹Samuel said, "If you have a king ruling over you, this is what he will do: He will take your sons and make them serve with his chariots and his horses, and they will run in front of the king's chariot. ¹²The king will make some of your sons commanders over thousands or over fifties. He will make some of your other sons plow his ground and reap his harvest. He will take others to make weapons of war and equipment for his chariots. ¹³He will take your daughters to make perfume and cook and bake for him. ¹⁴He will take your best fields, vineyards, and olive groves and give them to his servants.

¹⁵He will take one-tenth of your grain and grapes and give it to his officers and servants. ¹⁶He will take your male and female servants, your best cattle, and your donkeys and use them all for his own work. ¹⁷He will take one-tenth of your flocks, and you yourselves will become his slaves. ¹⁸When that time comes, you will cry out because of the king you chose. But the LORD will not answer you then."

¹⁹But the people would not listen to Samuel. They said, "No! We want a king to rule over us. ²⁰Then we will be the same as all the other nations. Our king will judge for us and go with us and fight our battles."

²¹After Samuel heard all that the people said, he repeated their words to the LORD. ²²The LORD answered, "You must listen to them. Give them a king."

Then Samuel told the people of Israel, "Go back to your towns."

Saul Looks for His Father's Donkeys

9 Kish, son of Abiel from the tribe of Benjamin, was an important man. (Abiel was the son of Zeror, who was the son of Becorath, who was the son of Aphiah of Benjamin.) ²Kish had a son named Saul, who was a fine young man. There was no Israelite better than he. Saul stood a head taller than any other man in Israel.

³Now the donkeys of Saul's father, Kish, were lost. So Kish said to Saul, his son, "Take one of the servants, and go and look for the donkeys." ⁴Saul went through the mountains of Ephraim and the land of Shalisha, but he and the servant could not find the donkeys. They went into the land of Shaalim, but the donkeys were not there. They went through the land of Benjamin, but they still did not find them. ⁵When they arrived in the area of Zuph, Saul said to his servant, "Let's go back

or my father will stop thinking about the donkeys and will start worrying about us."

⁶But the servant answered, "A man of God is in this town. People respect him because everything he says comes true. Let's go into the town now. Maybe he can tell us something about the journey we have taken."

⁷Saul said to his servant, "If we go into the town, what can we give him? The food in our bags is gone. We have no gift to give him. Do we have anything?"

⁸Again the servant answered Saul. "Look, I have one-tenth of an ounce of silver. Give it to the man of God. Then he will tell us about our journey." ⁹(In the past, if someone in Israel wanted to ask something from God, he would say, "Let's go to the seer." We call the person a prophet today, but in the past he was called a seer.)

¹⁰Saul said to his servant, "That's a good idea. Come, let's go." So they went toward the town where the man of God was.

¹¹As Saul and the servant were going up the hill to the town, they met some young women coming out to get water. Saul and the servant asked them, "Is the seer here?"

¹²The young women answered, "Yes, he's here. He's ahead of you. Hurry now. He has just come to our town today, because the people will offer a sacrifice at the place of worship. ¹³As soon as you enter the town, you will find him before he goes up to the place of worship to eat. The people will not begin eating until the seer comes, because he must bless the sacrifice. After that, the guests will eat. Go now, and you should find him."

Saul Meets Samuel

¹⁴Saul and the servant went up to the town. Just as they entered it, they saw Samuel coming toward them on his way up to the place of worship.

¹⁵The day before Saul came, the LORD had told Samuel: ¹⁶"About this time tomorrow I will send you a man from the land of Benjamin. Appoint him to lead my people Israel. He will save my people from the Philistines. I have seen the suffering of my people, and I have listened to their cry."

¹⁷When Samuel first saw Saul, the LORD said to Samuel, "This is the man I told you about. He will organize my people."

¹⁸Saul approached Samuel at the gate and said, "Please tell me where the seer's house is."

¹⁹Samuel answered, "I am the seer. Go with me to the place of worship. Today you and your servant are to eat with me. Tomorrow morning I will answer all your questions and send you home. ²⁰Don't worry about the donkeys you lost three days ago, because they have been found. Soon all the wealth of Israel will belong to you and your family."

²¹Saul answered, "But I am from the tribe of Benjamin, the smallest tribe in Israel. And my family group is the smallest in the tribe of Benjamin. Why are you saying such things?"

²²Then Samuel took Saul and his servant into a large room and gave them a choice place at the table. About thirty guests were there. ²³Samuel said to the cook, "Bring the meat I gave you, the portion I told you to set aside."

²⁴So the cook took the thigh and put it on the table in front of Saul. Samuel said, "This is the meat saved for you. Eat it, because it was set aside for you for this special time. As I said, 'I had invited the people.'" So Saul ate with Samuel that day.

²⁵After they finished eating, they came down from the place of worship and went to the town. Then Samuel talked with Saul on the roof[n] of his house. ²⁶At dawn they got up, and Samuel called to Saul on the roof. He said, "Get up, and I will send you on your way." So Saul got up and went out of the house with Samuel. ²⁷As Saul, his servant, and Samuel were getting near the edge of the city, Samuel said to Saul, "Tell the servant to go on ahead of us, but you stay, because I have a message from God for you."

PSALM 55:9–14

⁹Lord, destroy and confuse their words,
    because I see violence and fighting in
        the city.
¹⁰Day and night they are all around its walls,

9:25 roof In Bible times houses were built with flat roofs. The roof was used for drying things such as flax and fruit. And it was used as an extra room, as a place for worship, and as a cool place to sleep in the summer. See Deuteronomy 22:8.

and evil and trouble are everywhere
inside.
[11]Destruction is everywhere in the city;
trouble and lying never leave its streets.

[12]It was not an enemy insulting me.
I could stand that.
It was not someone who hated me.
I could hide from him.
[13]But it is you, a person like me,
my companion and good friend.
[14]We had a good friendship
and walked together to God's Temple.

PROVERBS 15:15–17

[15]Every day is hard for those who suffer,
but a happy heart is like a continual
feast.

[16]It is better to be poor and respect the
LORD
than to be wealthy and have much
trouble.

[17]It is better to eat vegetables with those
who love you
than to eat meat with those who hate
you.

LUKE 22:1–23

Judas Becomes an Enemy of Jesus

22 It was almost time for the Feast of Unleavened Bread, called the Passover
Feast. [2]The leading priests and teachers of
the law were trying to find a way to kill Jesus,
because they were afraid of the people.
[3]Satan entered Judas Iscariot, one of Jesus' twelve apostles. [4]Judas went to the leading priests and some of the soldiers who
guarded the Temple and talked to them
about a way to hand Jesus over to them.
[5]They were pleased and agreed to give Judas
money. [6]He agreed and watched for the best
time to hand Jesus over to them when he was
away from the crowd.

Jesus Eats the Passover Meal

[7]The Day of Unleavened Bread came
when the Passover lambs had to be sacrificed. [8]Jesus said to Peter and John, "Go and
prepare the Passover meal for us to eat."
[9]They asked, "Where do you want us to
prepare it?" [10]Jesus said to them, "After you
go into the city, a man carrying a jar of water
will meet you. Follow him into the house that
he enters, [11]and tell the owner of the house,
'The Teacher says: "Where is the guest room
in which I may eat the Passover meal with
my followers?" ' [12]Then he will show you a
large, furnished room upstairs. Prepare the
Passover meal there."
[13]So Peter and John left and found everything as Jesus had said. And they prepared
the Passover meal.

The Lord's Supper

[14]When the time came, Jesus and the
apostles were sitting at the table. [15]He said to
them, "I wanted very much to eat this
Passover meal with you before I suffer. [16]I
will not eat another Passover meal until it is
given its true meaning in the kingdom of
God."
[17]Then Jesus took a cup, gave thanks,
and said, "Take this cup and share it among
yourselves. [18]I will not drink again from
the fruit of the vine[n] until God's kingdom
comes."
[19]Then Jesus took some bread, gave
thanks, broke it, and gave it to the apostles,
saying, "This is my body,[n] which I am giving
for you. Do this to remember me." [20]In the
same way, after supper, Jesus took the cup
and said, "This cup is the new agreement
that God makes with his people. This new
agreement begins with my blood which is
poured out for you.

Who Will Turn Against Jesus?

[21]"But one of you will turn against me,
and his hand is with mine on the table.
[22]What God has planned for the Son of
Man will happen, but how terrible it will be
for that one who turns against the Son of
Man."
[23]Then the apostles asked each other
which one of them would do that.

22:18 fruit of the vine Product of the grapevine; this may also be translated "wine." **22:19b–20 body** Some Greek copies
do not have the rest of verse 19 or verse 20.

MAY 4

1 SAMUEL 10:1—11:15

Samuel Appoints Saul

10 Samuel took a jar of olive oil and poured it on Saul's head. He kissed Saul and said, "The LORD has appointed you to lead his people. ²After you leave me today, you will meet two men near Rachel's tomb on the border of Benjamin at Zelzah. They will say to you, 'The donkeys you were looking for have been found. But now your father has stopped thinking about his donkeys and is worrying about you. He is asking, "What will I do about my son?" '

³"Then you will go on until you reach the big tree at Tabor. Three men on their way to worship God at Bethel will meet you there. One man will be carrying three goats. Another will be carrying three loaves of bread. And the third will have a leather bag full of wine. ⁴They will greet you and offer you two loaves of bread, which you must accept. ⁵Then you will go to Gibeah of God, where a Philistine camp is. When you approach this town, a group of prophets will come down from the place of worship. They will be playing harps, tambourines, flutes, and lyres, and they will be prophesying. ⁶Then the Spirit of the LORD will rush upon you with power. You will prophesy with these prophets, and you will be changed into a different man. ⁷After these signs happen, do whatever you find to do, because God will help you.

⁸"Go ahead of me to Gilgal. I will come down to you to offer whole burnt offerings and fellowship offerings. But you must wait seven days. Then I will come and tell you what to do."

Saul Made King

⁹When Saul turned to leave Samuel, God changed Saul's heart. All these signs came true that day. ¹⁰When Saul and his servant arrived at Gibeah, Saul met a group of prophets. The Spirit of God rushed upon him, and he prophesied with the prophets. ¹¹When people who had known Saul before saw him prophesying with the prophets,

they asked each other, "What has happened to Kish's son? Is even Saul one of the prophets?"

¹²A man who lived there said, "Who is the father of these prophets?" So this became a famous saying: "Is even Saul one of the prophets?" ¹³When Saul finished prophesying, he entered the place of worship.

¹⁴Saul's uncle asked him and his servant, "Where have you been?"

Saul said, "We were looking for the donkeys. When we couldn't find them, we went to talk to Samuel."

¹⁵Saul's uncle asked, "Please tell me. What did Samuel say to you?"

¹⁶Saul answered, "He told us the donkeys had already been found." But Saul did not tell his uncle what Samuel had said about his becoming king.

¹⁷Samuel called all the people of Israel to meet with the LORD at Mizpah. ¹⁸He said, "This is what the LORD, the God of Israel, says: 'I led Israel out of Egypt. I saved you from Egypt's control and from other kingdoms that were troubling you.' ¹⁹But now you have rejected your God. He saves you from all your troubles and problems, but you said, 'No! We want a king to rule over us.' Now come, stand before the LORD in your tribes and family groups."

²⁰When Samuel gathered all the tribes of Israel, the tribe of Benjamin was picked. ²¹Samuel had them pass by in family groups, and Matri's family was picked. Then he had each man of Matri's family pass by, and Saul son of Kish was picked. But when they looked for Saul, they could not find him. ²²They asked the LORD, "Has Saul come here yet?"

The LORD said, "Yes. He's hiding behind the baggage."

²³So they ran and brought him out. When Saul stood among the people, he was a head taller than anyone else. ²⁴Then Samuel said to the people, "See the man the LORD has chosen. There is no one like him among all the people."

Then the people shouted, "Long live the king!"

²⁵Samuel explained the rights and duties of the king and then wrote them in a book and put it before the LORD. Then he told the people to go to their homes.

²⁶Saul also went to his home in Gibeah. God touched the hearts of certain brave men who went along with him. ²⁷But some troublemakers said, "How can this man save us?" They disapproved of Saul and refused to bring gifts to him. But Saul kept quiet.

Nahash Troubles Jabesh Gilead

11 About a month later Nahash the Ammonite and his army surrounded the city of Jabesh in Gilead. All the people of Jabesh said to Nahash, "Make a treaty with us, and we will serve you."

²But he answered, "I will make a treaty with you only if I'm allowed to poke out the right eye of each of you. Then all Israel will be ashamed!"

³The elders of Jabesh said to Nahash, "Give us seven days to send messengers through all Israel. If no one comes to help us, we will give ourselves up to you."

⁴When the messengers came to Gibeah where Saul lived and told the people the news, they cried loudly. ⁵Saul was coming home from plowing the fields with his oxen when he heard the people crying. He asked, "What's wrong with the people that they are crying?" Then they told Saul what the messengers from Jabesh had said. ⁶When Saul heard their words, God's Spirit rushed upon him with power, and he became very angry. ⁷So he took a pair of oxen and cut them into pieces. Then he gave the pieces of the oxen to messengers and ordered them to carry them through all the land of Israel.

The messengers said, "This is what will happen to the oxen of anyone who does not follow Saul and Samuel." So the people became very afraid of the LORD. They all came together as if they were one person. ⁸Saul gathered the people together at Bezek. There were three hundred thousand men from Israel and thirty thousand men from Judah.

⁹They said to the messengers who had come, "Tell the people at Jabesh Gilead this: 'Before the day warms up tomorrow, you will be saved.'" So the messengers went and reported this to the people at Jabesh, and they were very happy. ¹⁰The people said to Nahash the Ammonite, "Tomorrow we will come out to meet you. Then you can do anything you want to us."

¹¹The next morning Saul divided his soldiers into three groups. At dawn they entered the Ammonite camp and defeated them before the heat of the day. The Ammonites who escaped were scattered; no two of them were still together.

¹²Then the people said to Samuel, "Who didn't want Saul as king? Bring them here and we will kill them!"

¹³But Saul said, "No! No one will be put to death today. Today the LORD has saved Israel!"

¹⁴Then Samuel said to the people, "Come, let's go to Gilgal. There we will again promise to obey the king." ¹⁵So all the people went to Gilgal, and there, before the LORD, the people made Saul king. They offered fellowship offerings to the LORD, and Saul and all the Israelites had a great celebration.

PSALM 55:15–23

¹⁵Let death take away my enemies.
    Let them die while they are still young
    because evil lives with them.
¹⁶But I will call to God for help,
    and the LORD will save me.
¹⁷Morning, noon, and night I am troubled
        and upset,
    but he will listen to me.
¹⁸Many are against me,
    but he keeps me safe in battle.
¹⁹God who lives forever
    will hear me and punish them.   *Selah*
    But they will not change;
        they do not fear God.

²⁰The one who was my friend attacks his
        friends
    and breaks his promises.

²¹His words are slippery like butter,
but war is in his heart.
His words are smoother than oil,
but they cut like knives.

²²Give your worries to the LORD,
and he will take care of you.
He will never let good people down.
²³But, God, you will bring down
the wicked to the grave.
Murderers and liars will live
only half a lifetime.
But I will trust in you.

PROVERBS 15:18–20

¹⁸People with quick tempers cause trouble,
but those who control their tempers
stop a quarrel.

¹⁹A lazy person's life is like a patch of thorns,
but an honest person's life is like a
smooth highway.

²⁰Wise children make their father happy,
but foolish children disrespect their
mother.

LUKE 22:24–46

Be Like a Servant

²⁴The apostles also began to argue about which one of them was the most important. ²⁵But Jesus said to them, "The kings of the non-Jewish people rule over them, and those who have authority over others like to be called 'friends of the people.' ²⁶But you must not be like that. Instead, the greatest among you should be like the youngest, and the leader should be like the servant. ²⁷Who is more important: the one sitting at the table or the one serving? You think the one at the table is more important, but I am like a servant among you. ²⁸"You have stayed with me through my struggles. ²⁹Just as my Father has given me a kingdom, I also give you a kingdom ³⁰so you may eat and drink at my table in my kingdom. And you will sit on thrones, judging the twelve tribes of Israel.

Don't Lose Your Faith!

³¹"Simon, Simon, Satan has asked to test all of you as a farmer sifts his wheat. ³²I have prayed that you will not lose your faith! Help your brothers be stronger when you come back to me."

³³But Peter said to Jesus, "Lord, I am ready to go with you to prison and even to die with you!"

³⁴But Jesus said, "Peter, before the rooster crows this day, you will say three times that you don't know me."

Be Ready for Trouble

³⁵Then Jesus said to the apostles, "When I sent you out without a purse, a bag, or sandals, did you need anything?"

They said, "No."

³⁶He said to them, "But now if you have a purse or a bag, carry that with you. If you don't have a sword, sell your coat and buy one. ³⁷The Scripture says, 'He was treated like a criminal,'[n] and I tell you this scripture must have its full meaning. It was written about me, and it is happening now."

³⁸His followers said, "Look, Lord, here are two swords."

He said to them, "That is enough."

Jesus Prays Alone

³⁹Jesus left the city and went to the Mount of Olives, as he often did, and his followers went with him. ⁴⁰When he reached the place, he said to them, "Pray for strength against temptation."

⁴¹Then Jesus went about a stone's throw away from them. He kneeled down and prayed, ⁴²"Father, if you are willing, take away this cup[n] of suffering. But do what you want, not what I want." ⁴³Then an angel from heaven appeared to him to strengthen him. ⁴⁴Being full of pain, Jesus prayed even harder. His sweat was like drops of blood falling to the ground. ⁴⁵When he finished praying, he went to his followers and found them asleep because of their sadness. ⁴⁶Jesus said to them, "Why are you sleeping? Get up and pray for strength against temptation."

22:37 'He . . . criminal.' Quotation from Isaiah 53:12.   **22:42 cup** Jesus is talking about the painful things that will happen to him. Accepting these things will be hard, like drinking a cup of something bitter.

MAY 5

1 SAMUEL 12:1—13:22

Samuel's Farewell Speech

12Samuel said to all Israel, "I have done everything you wanted me to do and have put a king over you. ²Now you have a king to lead you. I am old and gray, and my sons are here with you. I have been your leader since I was young. ³Here I am. If I have done anything wrong, you must testify against me before the LORD and his appointed king. Did I steal anyone's ox or donkey? Did I hurt or cheat anyone? Did I ever secretly accept money to pretend not to see something wrong? If I did any of these things, I will make it right."

⁴The Israelites answered, "You have not cheated us, or hurt us, or taken anything unfairly from anyone."

⁵Samuel said to them, "The LORD is a witness to what you have said. His appointed king is also a witness today that you did not find anything wrong in me."

"He is our witness," they said.

⁶Then Samuel said to the people, "It is the LORD who chose Moses and Aaron and brought your ancestors out of Egypt. ⁷Now, stand there, and I will remind you of all the good things the LORD did for you and your ancestors.

⁸"After Jacob entered Egypt, his descendants cried to the LORD for help. So the LORD sent Moses and Aaron, who took your ancestors out of Egypt and brought them to live in this place.

⁹"But they forgot the LORD their God. So he handed them over as slaves to Sisera, the commander of the army of Hazor, and as slaves to the Philistines and the king of Moab. They all fought against your ancestors. ¹⁰Then your ancestors cried to the LORD and said, 'We have sinned. We have left the LORD and served the Baals and the Ashtoreths. But now save us from our enemies, and we will serve you.' ¹¹So the LORD sent Gideon,ⁿ Barak, Jephthah, and Samuel. He

saved you from your enemies around you, and you lived in safety. ¹²But when you saw Nahash king of the Ammonites coming against you, you said, 'No! We want a king to rule over us!'—even though the LORD your God was your king. ¹³Now here is the king you chose, the one you asked for. The LORD has put him over you. ¹⁴You must honor the LORD and serve him. You must obey his word and not turn against his commands. Both you and the king ruling over you must follow the LORD your God. If you do, it will be well with you. ¹⁵But if you don't obey the LORD, and if you turn against his commands, he will be against you. He will do to you what he did to your ancestors.

¹⁶"Now stand still and see the great thing the LORD will do before your eyes. ¹⁷It is now the time of the wheat harvest.ⁿ I will pray for the LORD to send thunder and rain. Then you will know what an evil thing you did against the LORD when you asked for a king."

¹⁸Then Samuel prayed to the LORD, and that same day the LORD sent thunder and rain. So the people were very afraid of the LORD and Samuel. ¹⁹They said to Samuel, "Pray to the LORD your God for us, your servants! Don't let us die! We've added to all our sins the evil of asking for a king."

²⁰Samuel answered, "Don't be afraid. It's true that you did wrong, but don't turn away from the LORD. Serve the LORD with all your heart. ²¹Idols are of no use, so don't worship them. They can't help you or save you. They are useless! ²²For his own sake, the LORD won't leave his people. Instead, he was pleased to make you his own people. ²³I will surely not stop praying for you, because that would be sinning against the LORD. I will teach you what is good and right. ²⁴You must honor the LORD and truly serve him with all your heart. Remember the wonderful things he did for you! ²⁵But if you are stubborn and do evil, he will sweep you and your king away."

12:11 Gideon Also called Jerub-Baal. **12:17 time . . . harvest** This was a dry time in the summer when no rains fell.

13 Saul was thirty years old when he became king, and he was king over Israel forty-two years.[n] [2]Saul chose three thousand men from Israel. Two thousand men stayed with him at Micmash in the mountains of Bethel, and one thousand men stayed with Jonathan at Gibeah in Benjamin. Saul sent the other men in the army back home.

[3]Jonathan attacked the Philistine camp in Geba, and the other Philistines heard about it. Saul said, "Let the Hebrews hear what happened." So he told the men to blow trumpets through all the land of Israel. [4]All the Israelites heard the news. The men said, "Saul has defeated the Philistine camp. Now the Philistines will really hate us!" Then the Israelites were called to join Saul at Gilgal.

[5]The Philistines gathered to fight Israel with three thousand[n] chariots and six thousand men to ride in them. Their soldiers were as many as the grains of sand on the seashore. The Philistines went and camped at Micmash, which is east of Beth Aven. [6]When the Israelites saw that they were in trouble, they went to hide in caves and bushes, among the rocks, and in pits and wells. [7]Some Hebrews even went across the Jordan River to the land of Gad and Gilead.

But Saul stayed at Gilgal, and all the men in his army were shaking with fear. [8]Saul waited seven days, because Samuel had said he would meet him then. But Samuel did not come to Gilgal, and the soldiers began to leave.

[9]So Saul said, "Bring me the whole burnt offering and the fellowship offerings." Then Saul offered the whole burnt offering. [10]Just as he finished, Samuel arrived, and Saul went to greet him.

[11]Samuel asked, "What have you done?"

Saul answered, "I saw the soldiers leaving me, and you were not here when you said you would be. The Philistines were gathering at Micmash. [12]Then I thought, 'The Philistines will come against me at Gilgal, and I haven't asked for the LORD's approval.' So I forced myself to offer the whole burnt offering."

[13]Samuel said, "You acted foolishly! You haven't obeyed the command of the LORD your God. If you had obeyed him, the LORD would have made your kingdom continue in Israel always, [14]but now your kingdom will not continue. The LORD has looked for the kind of man he wants. He has appointed him to rule his people, because you haven't obeyed his command."

[15]Then Samuel left Gilgal and went to Gibeah in Benjamin. Saul counted the men who were still with him, and there were about six hundred.

Hard Times for Israel

[16]Saul and his son Jonathan and the soldiers with him stayed in Gibeah in the land of Benjamin. The Philistines made their camp at Micmash. [17]Three groups went out from the Philistine camp to make raids. One group went on the Ophrah road in the land of Shual. [18]The second group went on the Beth Horon road. The third group went on the border road that overlooks the Valley of Zeboim toward the desert.

[19]The whole land of Israel had no blacksmith because the Philistines had said, "The Hebrews might make swords and spears." [20]So all the Israelites had to go down to the Philistines to have their plows, hoes, axes, and sickles sharpened. [21]The Philistine blacksmiths charged about one-fourth of an ounce of silver for sharpening plows and hoes. And they charged one-eighth of an ounce of silver for sharpening picks, axes, and the sticks used to guide oxen.

[22]So when the battle came, the soldiers with Saul and Jonathan had no swords or spears. Only Saul and his son Jonathan had them.

PSALM 56:1–13

Trusting God for Help

For the director of music. To the tune of "The Dove in the Distant Oak." A miktam of David when the Philistines captured him in Gath.

56 God, be merciful to me because
    people are chasing me;
  the battle has pressed me all day long.
  [2]My enemies have chased me all day;
  there are many proud people fighting
      me.

13:1 Saul . . . years This is how the verse is worded in some early Greek copies. The Hebrew is not clear here.   **13:5 three thousand** Some Greek copies say three thousand. The Hebrew copies say thirty thousand.

³When I am afraid,
I will trust you.
⁴I praise God for his word.
I trust God, so I am not afraid.
What can human beings do to me?

⁵All day long they twist my words;
all their evil plans are against me.
⁶They wait. They hide.
They watch my steps,
hoping to kill me.
⁷God, do not let them escape;
punish the foreign nations in your anger.
⁸You have recorded my troubles.
You have kept a list of my tears.
Aren't they in your records?
⁹On the day I call for help, my enemies
will be defeated.
I know that God is on my side.
¹⁰I praise God for his word to me;
I praise the LORD for his word.
¹¹I trust in God. I will not be afraid.
What can people do to me?

¹²God, I must keep my promises to you.
I will give you my offerings to thank you,
¹³because you have saved me from death.
You have kept me from being defeated.
So I will walk with God
in light among the living.

PROVERBS 15:21–23

²¹A person without wisdom enjoys being
foolish,
but someone with understanding does
what is right.
²²Plans fail without good advice,
but they succeed with the advice of
many others.
²³People enjoy giving good advice.
Saying the right word at the right time
is so pleasing.

LUKE 22:47–71

Jesus Is Arrested

⁴⁷While Jesus was speaking, a crowd came
up, and Judas, one of the twelve apostles, was
leading them. He came close to Jesus so he
could kiss him. ⁴⁸But Jesus said to him, "Judas, are you us-

ing the kiss to give the Son of Man to his enemies?"

⁴⁹When those who were standing around
him saw what was happening, they said,
"Lord, should we strike them with our
swords?" ⁵⁰And one of them struck the servant of the high priest and cut off his right
ear.

⁵¹Jesus said, "Stop! No more of this." Then
he touched the servant's ear and healed him.

⁵²Those who came to arrest Jesus were the
leading priests, the soldiers who guarded the
Temple, and the elders. Jesus said to them,
"You came out here with swords and clubs as
though I were a criminal. ⁵³I was with you
every day in the Temple, and you didn't arrest me there. But this is your time—the
time when darkness rules."

Peter Says He Doesn't Know Jesus

⁵⁴They arrested Jesus, and led him away,
and brought him into the house of the high
priest. Peter followed far behind them. ⁵⁵Af-
ter the soldiers started a fire in the middle of
the courtyard and sat together, Peter sat with
them. ⁵⁶A servant girl saw Peter sitting there
in the firelight, and looking closely at him,
she said, "This man was also with him."

⁵⁷But Peter said this was not true; he said,
"Woman, I don't know him."

⁵⁸A short time later, another person saw
Peter and said, "You are also one of them."

But Peter said, "Man, I am not!"

⁵⁹About an hour later, another man insisted, "Certainly this man was with him, because he is from Galilee, too."

⁶⁰But Peter said, "Man, I don't know what
you are talking about!"

At once, while Peter was still speaking, a
rooster crowed. ⁶¹Then the Lord turned and
looked straight at Peter. And Peter remembered what the Lord had said: "Before the
rooster crows this day, you will say three
times that you don't know me." ⁶²Then Peter
went outside and cried painfully.

The People Make Fun of Jesus

⁶³The men who were guarding Jesus began making fun of him and beating him.
⁶⁴They blindfolded him and said, "Prove
that you are a prophet, and tell us who hit
you." ⁶⁵They said many cruel things to Jesus.

Jesus Before the Leaders

⁶⁶When day came, the council of the elders of the people, both the leading priests and the teachers of the law, came together and led Jesus to their highest court. ⁶⁷They said, "If you are the Christ, tell us."

Jesus said to them, "If I tell you, you will not believe me. ⁶⁸And if I ask you, you will not answer. ⁶⁹But from now on, the Son of Man will sit at the right hand of the powerful God."

⁷⁰They all said, "Then are you the Son of God?"

Jesus said to them, "You say that I am."

⁷¹They said, "Why do we need witnesses now? We ourselves heard him say this."

MAY 6

1 SAMUEL 13:23—15:35

Israel Defeats the Philistines

²³A group from the Philistine army had gone out to the pass at Micmash.

14One day Jonathan, Saul's son, said to the officer who carried his armor, "Come, let's go over to the Philistine camp on the other side." But Jonathan did not tell his father.

²Saul was sitting under a pomegranate tree at the threshing floor near Gibeah. He had about six hundred men with him. ³One man was Ahijah who was wearing the holy vest. (Ahijah was a son of Ichabod's brother Ahitub. Ichabod was the son of Phinehas, the son of Eli, the LORD's priest in Shiloh.) No one knew Jonathan had left.

⁴There was a steep slope on each side of the pass that Jonathan planned to go through to reach the Philistine camp. The cliff on one side was named Bozez, and the cliff on the other side was named Seneh. ⁵One cliff faced north toward Micmash. The other faced south toward Geba.

⁶Jonathan said to his officer who carried his armor, "Come. Let's go to the camp of those men who are not circumcised. Maybe the LORD will help us. The LORD can give us victory if we have many people, or just a few."

⁷The officer who carried Jonathan's armor said to him, "Do whatever you think is best. Go ahead. I'm with you."

⁸Jonathan said, "Then come. We will cross over to the Philistines and let them see us. ⁹If they say to us, 'Stay there until we come to you,' we will stay where we are. We won't go up to them. ¹⁰But if they say, 'Come up to us,' we will climb up, and the LORD will let us defeat them. This will be the sign for us."

¹¹When both Jonathan and his officer let the Philistines see them, the Philistines said, "Look! The Hebrews are crawling out of the holes they were hiding in!" ¹²The Philistines in the camp shouted to Jonathan and his officer, "Come up to us. We'll teach you a lesson!"

Jonathan said to his officer, "Climb up behind me, because the LORD has given the Philistines to Israel!" ¹³So Jonathan climbed up, using his hands and feet, and his officer climbed just behind him. Jonathan struck down the Philistines as he went, and his officer killed them as he followed behind him. ¹⁴In that first fight Jonathan and his officer killed about twenty Philistines over a half acre of ground.

¹⁵All the Philistine soldiers panicked— those in the camp and those in the raiding party. The ground itself shook! God had caused the panic.

¹⁶Saul's guards were at Gibeah in the land of Benjamin when they saw the Philistine soldiers running in every direction. ¹⁷Saul said to his army, "Check to see who has left our camp." When they checked, they learned that Jonathan and his officer were gone.

¹⁸So Saul said to Ahijah the priest, "Bring the Ark of God." (At that time it was with the Israelites.) ¹⁹While Saul was talking to the priest, the confusion in the Philistine camp was growing. Then Saul said to Ahijah, "Put your hand down!"

²⁰Then Saul gathered his army and en-

tered the battle. They found the Philistines confused, striking each other with their swords! [21]Earlier, there were Hebrews who had served the Philistines and had stayed in their camp, but now they joined the Israelites with Saul and Jonathan. [22]When all the Israelites hidden in the mountains of Ephraim heard that the Philistine soldiers were running away, they also joined the battle and chased the Philistines. [23]So the LORD saved the Israelites that day, and the battle moved on past Beth Aven.

Saul Makes Another Mistake

[24]The men of Israel were miserable that day because Saul had made an oath for all of them. He had said, "No one should eat food before evening and before I finish defeating my enemies. If he does, he will be cursed!" So no Israelite soldier ate food.

[25]Now the army went into the woods, where there was some honey on the ground. [26]They came upon some honey, but no one took any because they were afraid of the oath. [27]Jonathan had not heard the oath Saul had put on the army, so he dipped the end of his stick into the honey and lifted some out and ate it. Then he felt better. [28]Then one of the soldiers told Jonathan, "Your father made an oath for all the soldiers. He said any man who eats today will be cursed! That's why they are so weak."

[29]Jonathan said, "My father has made trouble for the land! See how much better I feel after just tasting a little of this honey! [30]It would have been much better for the men to eat the food they took from their enemies today. We could have killed many more Philistines!"

[31]That day the Israelites defeated the Philistines from Micmash to Aijalon. After that, they were very tired. [32]They had taken sheep, cattle, and calves from the Philistines. Now they were so hungry they killed the animals on the ground and ate them, without draining the blood from them! [33]Someone said to Saul, "Look! The men are sinning against the LORD. They're eating meat without draining the blood from it!"

Saul said, "You have sinned! Roll a large stone over here now!" [34]Then he said, "Go to the men and tell them that each person must bring his ox and sheep to me and kill it here and eat it. Don't sin against the LORD by eating meat without draining the blood from it."

That night everyone brought his animals and killed them there. [35]Then Saul built an altar to the LORD. It was the first altar he had built to the LORD.

[36]Saul said, "Let's go after the Philistines tonight and rob them. We won't let any of them live!"

The men answered, "Do whatever you think is best."

But the priest said, "Let's ask God."

[37]So Saul asked God, "Should I chase the Philistines? Will you let us defeat them?" But God did not answer Saul at that time. [38]Then Saul said to all the leaders of his army, "Come here. Let's find out what sin has been done today. [39]As surely as the LORD lives who has saved Israel, even if my son Jonathan did the sin, he must die." But no one in the army spoke.

[40]Then Saul said to all the Israelites, "You stand on this side. I and my son Jonathan will stand on the other side."

The men answered, "Do whatever you think is best."

[41]Then Saul prayed to the LORD, the God of Israel, "Give me the right answer."

And Saul and Jonathan were picked; the other men went free. [42]Saul said, "Now let us discover if it is I or Jonathan my son who is guilty." And Jonathan was picked.

[43]Saul said to Jonathan, "Tell me what you have done."

So Jonathan told Saul, "I only tasted a little honey from the end of my stick. And must I die now?"

[44]Saul said, "Jonathan, if you don't die, may God punish me terribly."

[45]But the soldiers said to Saul, "Must Jonathan die? Never! He is responsible for saving Israel today! As surely as the LORD lives, not even a hair of his head will fall to the ground! Today Jonathan fought against the Philistines with God's help!" So the army saved Jonathan, and he did not die.

[46]Then Saul stopped chasing the Philistines, and they went back to their own land.

Saul Fights Israel's Enemies

⁴⁷When Saul became king over Israel, he fought against Israel's enemies all around. He fought Moab, the Ammonites, Edom, the king of Zobah, and the Philistines. Everywhere Saul went he defeated Israel's enemies. ⁴⁸He fought bravely and defeated the Amalekites. He saved the Israelites from their enemies who had robbed them.

⁴⁹Saul's sons were Jonathan, Ishvi, and Malki-Shua. His older daughter was named Merab, and his younger daughter was named Michal. ⁵⁰Saul's wife was Ahinoam daughter of Ahimaaz. The commander of his army was Abner son of Ner, Saul's uncle. ⁵¹Saul's father Kish and Abner's father Ner were sons of Abiel.

⁵²All Saul's life he fought hard against the Philistines. When he saw strong or brave men, he took them into his army.

Saul Rejected as King

15 Samuel said to Saul, "The LORD sent me to appoint you king over Israel. Now listen to his message. ²This is what the LORD All-Powerful says: 'When the Israelites came out of Egypt, the Amalekites tried to stop them from going to Canaan. So I will punish them. ³Now go, attack the Amalekites and destroy everything they own as an offering to the LORD. Don't let anything live. Put to death men and women, children and small babies, cattle and sheep, camels and donkeys.'"

⁴So Saul called the army together at Telaim. There were two hundred thousand foot soldiers and ten thousand men from Judah. ⁵Then Saul went to the city of Amalek and set up an ambush in the ravine. ⁶He said to the Kenites, "Go away. Leave the Amalekites so that I won't destroy you with them, because you showed kindness to the Israelites when they came out of Egypt." So the Kenites moved away from the Amalekites.

⁷Then Saul defeated the Amalekites. He fought them all the way from Havilah to Shur, at the border of Egypt. ⁸He took King Agag of the Amalekites alive, but he killed all of Agag's army with the sword. ⁹Saul and the army let Agag live, along with the best sheep, fat cattle, and lambs. They let every good animal live, because they did not want to destroy them. But when they found an animal that was weak or useless, they killed it.

¹⁰Then the LORD spoke his word to Samuel: ¹¹"I am sorry I made Saul king, because he has stopped following me and has not obeyed my commands." Samuel was upset, and he cried out to the LORD all night long.

¹²Early the next morning Samuel got up and went to meet Saul. But the people told Samuel, "Saul has gone to Carmel, where he has put up a monument in his own honor. Now he has gone down to Gilgal."

¹³When Samuel came to Saul, Saul said, "May the LORD bless you! I have obeyed the LORD's commands."

¹⁴But Samuel said, "Then why do I hear cattle mooing and sheep bleating?"

¹⁵Saul answered, "The soldiers took them from the Amalekites. They saved the best sheep and cattle to offer as sacrifices to the LORD your God, but we destroyed all the other animals."

¹⁶Samuel said to Saul, "Stop! Let me tell you what the LORD said to me last night."

Saul answered, "Tell me."

¹⁷Samuel said, "Once you didn't think much of yourself, but now you have become the leader of the tribes of Israel. The LORD appointed you to be king over Israel. ¹⁸And he sent you on a mission. He said, 'Go and destroy those evil people, the Amalekites. Make war on them until all of them are dead.' ¹⁹Why didn't you obey the LORD? Why did you take the best things? Why did you do what the LORD said was wrong?"

²⁰Saul said, "But I did obey the LORD. I did what the LORD told me to do. I destroyed all the Amalekites, and I brought back Agag their king. ²¹The soldiers took the best sheep and cattle to sacrifice to the LORD your God at Gilgal."

²²But Samuel answered,

"What pleases the LORD more:
    burnt offerings and sacrifices
    or obedience to his voice?
It is better to obey than to sacrifice.
    It is better to listen to God than to offer
        the fat of sheep.
²³Disobedience is as bad as the sin of
        sorcery.
    Pride is as bad as the sin of worshiping
        idols.

You have rejected the LORD's command.
Now he rejects you as king."

²⁴Then Saul said to Samuel, "I have sinned. I didn't obey the LORD's commands and your words. I was afraid of the people, and I did what they said. ²⁵Now, I beg you, forgive my sin. Come back with me so I may worship the LORD."

²⁶But Samuel said to Saul, "I won't go back with you. You rejected the LORD's command, and now he rejects you as king of Israel."

²⁷As Samuel turned to leave, Saul caught his robe, and it tore. ²⁸Samuel said to him, "The LORD has torn the kingdom of Israel from you today and has given it to one of your neighbors who is better than you. ²⁹The LORD is the Eternal One of Israel. He does not lie or change his mind. He is not a human being, so he does not change his mind."

³⁰Saul answered, "I have sinned. But please honor me in front of the elders of my people and in front of the Israelites. Come back with me so that I can worship the LORD your God." ³¹So Samuel went back with Saul, and Saul worshiped the LORD.

³²Then Samuel said, "Bring me King Agag of the Amalekites."

Agag came to Samuel in chains, but Agag thought, "Surely the threat of death has passed."

³³Samuel said to him, "Your sword made other mothers lose their children. Now your mother will have no children." And Samuel cut Agag to pieces before the LORD at Gilgal.

³⁴Then Samuel left and went to Ramah, but Saul went up to his home in Gibeah. ³⁵And Samuel never saw Saul again the rest of his life, but he was sad for Saul. And the LORD was very sorry he had made Saul king of Israel.

PSALM 57:1–3

A Prayer in Troubled Times

For the director of music. To the tune of "Do Not Destroy." A miktam of David when he escaped from Saul in the cave.

57 Be merciful to me, God; be merciful to me
because I come to you for protection.

Let me hide under the shadow of your wings
until the trouble has passed.

²I cry out to God Most High,
to the God who does everything for me.
³He sends help from heaven and saves me.
He punishes those who chase me.   *Selah*
God sends me his love and truth.

PROVERBS 15:24–25

²⁴Wise people's lives get better and better.
They avoid what would cause their death.

²⁵The LORD will tear down the proud person's house,
but he will protect the widow's property.

LUKE 23:1–25

Pilate Questions Jesus

23 Then the whole group stood up and led Jesus to Pilate.ⁿ ²They began to accuse Jesus, saying, "We caught this man telling things that mislead our people. He says that we should not pay taxes to Caesar, and he calls himself the Christ, a king."

³Pilate asked Jesus, "Are you the king of the Jews?"

Jesus answered, "Those are your words."

⁴Pilate said to the leading priests and the people, "I find nothing against this man."

⁵They were insisting, saying, "But Jesus makes trouble with the people, teaching all around Judea. He began in Galilee, and now he is here."

Pilate Sends Jesus to Herod

⁶Pilate heard this and asked if Jesus was from Galilee. ⁷Since Jesus was under Herod's authority, Pilate sent Jesus to Herod, who was in Jerusalem at that time. ⁸When Herod saw Jesus, he was very glad, because he had heard about Jesus and had wanted to meet him for a long time. He was hoping to see Jesus work a miracle. ⁹Herod asked Jesus many questions, but Jesus said nothing. ¹⁰The leading priests and teachers of the law were standing there, strongly accusing Jesus.

23:1 Pilate Pontius Pilate was the Roman governor of Judea from A.D. 26 to A.D. 36.

[11]After Herod and his soldiers had made fun of Jesus, they dressed him in a kingly robe and sent him back to Pilate. [12]In the past, Pilate and Herod had always been enemies, but on that day they became friends.

Jesus Must Die

[13]Pilate called the people together with the leading priests and the rulers. [14]He said to them, "You brought this man to me, saying he makes trouble among the people. But I have questioned him before you all, and I have not found him guilty of what you say. [15]Also, Herod found nothing wrong with him; he sent him back to us. Look, he has done nothing for which he should die. [16]So, after I punish him, I will let him go free." [[17]Every year at the Passover Feast, Pilate had to release one prisoner to the people.][n]

[18]But the people shouted together, "Take this man away! Let Barabbas go free!" [19](Barabbas was a man who was in prison for his part in a riot in the city and for murder.)

[20]Pilate wanted to let Jesus go free and told this to the crowd. [21]But they shouted again, "Crucify him! Crucify him!"

[22]A third time Pilate said to them, "Why? What wrong has he done? I can find no reason to kill him. So I will have him punished and set him free."

[23]But they continued to shout, demanding that Jesus be crucified. Their yelling became so loud that [24]Pilate decided to give them what they wanted. [25]He set free the man who was in jail for rioting and murder, and he handed Jesus over to them to do with him as they wished.

MAY 7

1 SAMUEL 16:1—17:58

Samuel Goes to Bethlehem

16 The LORD said to Samuel, "How long will you continue to feel sorry for Saul? I have rejected him as king of Israel. Fill your container with olive oil and go. I am sending you to Jesse who lives in Bethlehem, because I have chosen one of his sons to be king."

[2]But Samuel said, "If I go, Saul will hear the news and will try to kill me."

The LORD said, "Take a young calf with you. Say, 'I have come to offer a sacrifice to the LORD.' [3]Invite Jesse to the sacrifice. Then I will tell you what to do. You must appoint the one I show you."

[4]Samuel did what the LORD told him to do. When he arrived at Bethlehem, the elders of Bethlehem shook with fear. They met him and asked, "Are you coming in peace?"

[5]Samuel answered, "Yes, I come in peace. I have come to make a sacrifice to the LORD. Set yourselves apart to the LORD and come to the sacrifice with me." Then he set Jesse and his sons apart to the LORD, and he invited them to come to the sacrifice.

[6]When they arrived, Samuel saw Eliab, and he thought, "Surely the LORD has appointed this person standing here before him."

[7]But the LORD said to Samuel, "Don't look at how handsome Eliab is or how tall he is, because I have not chosen him. God does not see the same way people see. People look at the outside of a person, but the LORD looks at the heart."

[8]Then Jesse called Abinadab and told him to pass by Samuel. But Samuel said, "The LORD has not chosen this man either." [9]Then Jesse had Shammah pass by. But Samuel said, "No, the LORD has not chosen this one." [10]Jesse had seven of his sons pass by Samuel. But Samuel said to him, "The LORD has not chosen any of these."

[11]Then he asked Jesse, "Are these all the sons you have?"

Jesse answered, "I still have the youngest son. He is out taking care of the sheep."

Samuel said, "Send for him. We will not sit down to eat until he arrives."

¹²So Jesse sent and had his youngest son brought in. He was a fine boy, tanned, and handsome.

The LORD said to Samuel, "Go, appoint him, because he is the one."

¹³So Samuel took the container of olive oil and poured it on Jesse's youngest son to appoint him in front of his brothers. From that day on, the LORD's Spirit worked in David. Samuel then went back to Ramah.

David Serves Saul

¹⁴But the LORD's Spirit had left Saul, and an evil spirit from the LORD troubled him.

¹⁵Saul's servants said to him, "See, an evil spirit from God is troubling you. ¹⁶Give us the command to look for someone who can play the harp. When the evil spirit from God troubles you, he will play, and you will feel better."

¹⁷So Saul said to his servants, "Find someone who can play well and bring him to me."

¹⁸One of the servants said, "I have seen a son of Jesse of Bethlehem play the harp. He is brave and courageous. He is a good speaker and handsome, and the LORD is with him."

¹⁹Then Saul sent messengers to Jesse, saying, "Send me your son David, who is with the sheep." ²⁰So Jesse loaded a donkey with bread, a leather bag full of wine, and a young goat, and he sent them with his son David to Saul.

²¹When David came to Saul, he began to serve him. Saul liked David and made him the officer who carried his armor. ²²Saul sent a message to Jesse, saying, "Let David stay and serve me because I like him."

²³When the evil spirit from God troubled Saul, David would take his harp and play. Then the evil spirit would leave him, and Saul would feel better.

David and Goliath

17 The Philistines gathered their armies for war. They met at Socoh in Judah and camped at Ephes Dammim between Socoh and Azekah. ²Saul and the Israelites gathered in the Valley of Elah and camped there and took their positions to fight the Philistines. ³The Philistines controlled one hill while the Israelites controlled another. The valley was between them.

⁴The Philistines had a champion fighter from Gath named Goliath. He was about nine feet, four inches tall. He came out of the Philistine camp ⁵with a bronze helmet on his head and a coat of bronze armor that weighed about one hundred twenty-five pounds. ⁶He wore bronze protectors on his legs, and he had a bronze spear on his back. ⁷The wooden part of his larger spear was like a weaver's rod, and its blade weighed about fifteen pounds. The officer who carried his shield walked in front of him.

⁸Goliath stood and shouted to the Israelite soldiers, "Why have you taken positions for battle? I am a Philistine, and you are Saul's servants! Choose a man and send him to fight me. ⁹If he can fight and kill me, we will be your servants. But if I can kill him, you will be our servants." ¹⁰Then he said, "Today I stand and dare the army of Israel! Send one of your men to fight me!" ¹¹When Saul and the Israelites heard the Philistine's words, they were very scared.

¹²Now David was the son of Jesse, an Ephrathite from Bethlehem in Judah. Jesse had eight sons. In Saul's time Jesse was an old man. ¹³His three oldest sons followed Saul to the war. The first son was Eliab, the second was Abinadab, and the third was Shammah. ¹⁴David was the youngest. Jesse's three oldest sons followed Saul, ¹⁵but David went back and forth from Saul to Bethlehem, where he took care of his father's sheep.

¹⁶For forty days the Philistine came out every morning and evening and stood before the Israelite army.

¹⁷Jesse said to his son David, "Take this half bushel of cooked grain and ten loaves of bread to your brothers in the camp. ¹⁸Also take ten pieces of cheese to the commander and to your brothers. See how your brothers are and bring back some proof to show me that they are all right. ¹⁹Your brothers are with Saul and the army in the Valley of Elah, fighting against the Philistines."

²⁰Early in the morning David left the sheep with another shepherd. He took the food and left as Jesse had told him. When

David arrived at the camp, the army was going out to their battle positions, shouting their war cry. ²¹The Israelites and Philistines were lining up their men to face each other in battle.

²²David left the food with the man who kept the supplies and ran to the battle line to talk to his brothers. ²³While he was talking with them, Goliath, the Philistine champion from Gath, came out. He shouted things against Israel as usual, and David heard him. ²⁴When the Israelites saw Goliath, they were very much afraid and ran away.

²⁵They said, "Look at this man! He keeps coming out to challenge Israel. The king will give much money to whoever kills him. He will also let whoever kills him marry his daughter. And his father's family will not have to pay taxes in Israel."

²⁶David asked the men who stood near him, "What will be done to reward the man who kills this Philistine and takes away the shame from Israel? Who does this uncircumcised Philistine think he is? Does he think he can speak against the armies of the living God?"

²⁷The Israelites told David what would be done for the man who would kill Goliath.

²⁸When David's oldest brother Eliab heard David talking with the soldiers, he was angry with David. He asked David, "Why did you come here? Who's taking care of those few sheep of yours in the desert? I know you are proud and wicked at heart. You came down here just to watch the battle."

²⁹David asked, "Now what have I done wrong? Can't I even talk?" ³⁰When he turned to other people and asked the same questions, they gave him the same answer as before. ³¹Yet what David said was told to Saul, and he sent for David.

³²David said to Saul, "Don't let anyone be discouraged. I, your servant, will go and fight this Philistine!"

³³Saul answered, "You can't go out against this Philistine and fight him. You're only a boy. Goliath has been a warrior since he was a young man."

³⁴But David said to Saul, "I, your servant, have been keeping my father's sheep. When a lion or bear came and took a sheep from the flock, ³⁵I would chase it. I would attack it and save the sheep from its mouth. When it attacked me, I caught it by its fur and hit it and killed it. ³⁶I, your servant, have killed both a lion and a bear! This uncircumcised Philistine will be like them, because he has spoken against the armies of the living God. ³⁷The LORD who saved me from a lion and a bear will save me from this Philistine."

Saul said to David, "Go, and may the LORD be with you." ³⁸Saul put his own clothes on David. He put a bronze helmet on his head and dressed him in armor. ³⁹David put on Saul's sword and tried to walk around, but he was not used to all the armor Saul had put on him.

He said to Saul, "I can't go in this, because I'm not used to it." Then David took it all off. ⁴⁰He took his stick in his hand and chose five smooth stones from a stream. He put them in his shepherd's bag and grabbed his sling. Then he went to meet the Philistine.

⁴¹At the same time, the Philistine was coming closer to David. The man who held his shield walked in front of him. ⁴²When Goliath looked at David and saw that he was only a boy, tanned and handsome, he looked down on David with disgust. ⁴³He said, "Do you think I am a dog, that you come at me with a stick?" He used his gods' names to curse David. ⁴⁴He said to David, "Come here. I'll feed your body to the birds of the air and the wild animals!"

⁴⁵But David said to him, "You come to me using a sword and two spears. But I come to you in the name of the LORD All-Powerful, the God of the armies of Israel! You have spoken against him. ⁴⁶Today the LORD will hand you over to me, and I'll kill you and cut off your head. Today I'll feed the bodies of the Philistine soldiers to the birds of the air and the wild animals. Then all the world will know there is a God in Israel! ⁴⁷Everyone gathered here will know the LORD does not need swords or spears to save people. The battle belongs to him, and he will hand you over to us."

⁴⁸As Goliath came near to attack him, David ran quickly to meet him. ⁴⁹He took a stone from his bag, put it into his sling, and slung it. The stone hit the Philistine and

went deep into his forehead, and Goliath fell facedown on the ground.

⁵⁰So David defeated the Philistine with only a sling and a stone. He hit him and killed him. He did not even have a sword in his hand. ⁵¹Then David ran and stood beside him. He took Goliath's sword out of its holder and killed him by cutting off his head.

When the Philistines saw that their champion was dead, they turned and ran. ⁵²The men of Israel and Judah shouted and chased the Philistines all the way to the entrance of the city of Gath and to the gates of Ekron. The Philistines' bodies lay on the Shaaraim road as far as Gath and Ekron. ⁵³The Israelites returned after chasing the Philistines and robbed their camp. ⁵⁴David took Goliath's head to Jerusalem and put Goliath's weapons in his own tent.

⁵⁵When Saul saw David go out to meet Goliath, Saul asked Abner, commander of the army, "Abner, who is that young man's father?"

Abner answered, "As surely as you live, my king, I don't know."

⁵⁶The king said, "Find out whose son he is."

⁵⁷When David came back from killing Goliath, Abner brought him to Saul. David was still holding Goliath's head.

⁵⁸Saul asked him, "Young man, who is your father?"

David answered, "I am the son of your servant Jesse of Bethlehem."

PSALM 57:4–11

⁴Enemies, like lions, are all around me;
 I must lie down among them.
 Their teeth are like spears and arrows,
 their tongues as sharp as swords.

⁵God is supreme over the skies;
 his majesty covers the earth.

⁶They set a trap for me.
 I am very worried.
 They dug a pit in my path,
 but they fell into it themselves.   *Selah*

⁷My heart is steady, God; my heart is
  steady.
 I will sing and praise you.
⁸Wake up, my soul.
 Wake up, harp and lyre!
 I will wake up the dawn.
⁹Lord, I will praise you among the
  nations;
 I will sing songs of praise about you to
  all the nations.
¹⁰Your great love reaches to the skies,
 your truth to the clouds.
¹¹God, you are supreme above the skies.
 Let your glory be over all the earth.

PROVERBS 15:26

²⁶The LORD hates evil thoughts
 but is pleased with kind words.

LUKE 23:26–56

Jesus Is Crucified

²⁶As they led Jesus away, Simon, a man from Cyrene, was coming in from the fields. They forced him to carry Jesus' cross and to walk behind him.

²⁷A large crowd of people was following Jesus, including some women who were sad and crying for him. ²⁸But Jesus turned and said to them, "Women of Jerusalem, don't cry for me. Cry for yourselves and for your children. ²⁹The time is coming when people will say, 'Blessed are the women who cannot have children and who have no babies to nurse.' ³⁰Then people will say to the mountains, 'Fall on us!' And they will say to the hills, 'Cover us!' ³¹If they act like this now when life is good, what will happen when bad times come?"[n]

³²There were also two criminals led out with Jesus to be put to death. ³³When they came to a place called the Skull, the soldiers crucified Jesus and the criminals—one on his right and the other on his left. ³⁴Jesus said, "Father, forgive them, because they don't know what they are doing."[n]

The soldiers threw lots to decide who would get his clothes. ³⁵The people stood

23:31 If . . . come? Literally, "If they do these things in the green tree, what will happen in the dry?" **23:34 Jesus . . . doing."** Some Greek copies do not have this first part of verse 34.

there watching. And the leaders made fun of Jesus, saying, "He saved others. Let him save himself if he is God's Chosen One, the Christ."

[36]The soldiers also made fun of him, coming to Jesus and offering him some vinegar. [37]They said, "If you are the king of the Jews, save yourself!" [38]At the top of the cross these words were written: THIS IS THE KING OF THE JEWS.

[39]One of the criminals on a cross began to shout insults at Jesus: "Aren't you the Christ? Then save yourself and us."

[40]But the other criminal stopped him and said, "You should fear God! You are getting the same punishment he is. [41]We are punished justly, getting what we deserve for what we did. But this man has done nothing wrong." [42]Then he said, "Jesus, remember me when you come into your kingdom."

[43]Jesus said to him, "I tell you the truth, today you will be with me in paradise."[n]

Jesus Dies

[44]It was about noon, and the whole land became dark until three o'clock in the afternoon, [45]because the sun did not shine. The curtain in the Temple[n] was torn in two. [46]Jesus cried out in a loud voice, "Father, I give you my life." After Jesus said this, he died.

[47]When the army officer there saw what happened, he praised God, saying, "Surely this was a good man!"

[48]When all the people who had gathered there to watch saw what happened, they returned home, beating their chests because they were so sad. [49]But those who were close friends of Jesus, including the women who had followed him from Galilee, stood at a distance and watched.

Joseph Takes Jesus' Body

[50]There was a good and religious man named Joseph who was a member of the council. [51]But he had not agreed to the other leaders' plans and actions against Jesus. He was from the town of Arimathea and was waiting for the kingdom of God to come. [52]Joseph went to Pilate to ask for the body of Jesus. [53]He took the body down from the cross, wrapped it in cloth, and put it in a tomb that was cut out of a wall of rock. This tomb had never been used before. [54]This was late on Preparation Day, and when the sun went down, the Sabbath day would begin.

[55]The women who had come from Galilee with Jesus followed Joseph and saw the tomb and how Jesus' body was laid. [56]Then the women left to prepare spices and perfumes.

On the Sabbath day they rested, as the law of Moses commanded.

MAY 8

1 SAMUEL 18:1—19:24

Saul Fears David

18 When David finished talking with Saul, Jonathan felt very close to David. He loved David as much as he loved himself. [2]Saul kept David with him from that day on and did not let him go home to his father's house. [3]Jonathan made an agreement with David, because he loved David as much as himself. [4]He took off his coat and gave it to David, along with his armor, including his sword, bow, and belt.

[5]Saul sent David to fight in different battles, and David was very successful. Then Saul put David over the soldiers, which pleased Saul's officers and all the other people.

[6]After David had killed the Philistine, he and the men returned home. Women came out from all the towns of Israel to meet King Saul. They sang songs of joy, danced, and

---

23:43 paradise Another word for heaven.   **23:45 curtain in the Temple** A curtain divided the Most Holy Place from the other part of the Temple, the special building in Jerusalem where God commanded the Jewish people to worship him.

played tambourines and stringed instruments. [7]As they played, they sang,

"Saul has killed thousands of his
enemies,
but David has killed tens of thousands."

[8]The women's song upset Saul, and he became very angry. He thought, "The women say David has killed tens of thousands, but they say I have killed only thousands. The only thing left for him to have is the kingdom!" [9]So Saul watched David closely from then on, because he was jealous.

[10]The next day an evil spirit from God rushed upon Saul, and he prophesied in his house. David was playing the harp as he usually did, but Saul had a spear in his hand. [11]He threw the spear, thinking, "I'll pin David to the wall." But David escaped from him twice.

[12]The LORD was with David but had left Saul. So Saul was afraid of David. [13]He sent David away and made him commander of a thousand soldiers. So David led them in battle. [14]He had great success in everything he did because the LORD was with him. [15]When Saul saw that David was very successful, he feared David even more. [16]But all the people of Israel and Judah loved David because he led them well in battle.

Saul's Daughter Marries David

[17]Saul said to David, "Here is my older daughter Merab. I will let you marry her. All I ask is that you remain brave and fight the LORD's battles." Saul thought, "I won't have to kill David. The Philistines will do that."

[18]But David answered Saul, saying, "Who am I? My family is not important enough for me to become the king's son-in-law." [19]So, when the time came for Saul's daughter Merab to marry David, Saul gave her instead to Adriel of Meholah.

[20]Now Saul's other daughter, Michal, loved David. When they told Saul, he was pleased. [21]He thought, "I will let her marry David. Then she will be a trap for him, and the Philistines will defeat him." So Saul said to David a second time, "You may become my son-in-law."

[22]And Saul ordered his servants to talk with David in private and say, "Look, the king likes you. His servants love you. You should be his son-in-law."

[23]Saul's servants said these words to David, but David answered, "Do you think it is easy to become the king's son-in-law? I am poor and unimportant."

[24]When Saul's servants told him what David had said, [25]Saul said, "Tell David, 'The king doesn't want money for the bride. All he wants is a hundred Philistine foreskins to get even with his enemies.'" Saul planned to let the Philistines kill David.

[26]When Saul's servants told this to David, he was pleased to become the king's son-in-law. [27]So he and his men went out and killed two hundred Philistines. David brought all their foreskins to Saul so he could be the king's son-in-law. Then Saul gave him his daughter Michal for his wife. [28]Saul saw that the LORD was with David and that his daughter Michal loved David. [29]So he grew even more afraid of David, and he was David's enemy all his life.

[30]The Philistine commanders continued to go out to fight the Israelites, but every time, David was more skillful than Saul's officers. So he became famous.

Saul Tries to Kill David

19Saul told his son Jonathan and all his servants to kill David, but Jonathan liked David very much. [2]So he warned David, "My father Saul is looking for a chance to kill you. Watch out in the morning. Hide in a secret place. [3]I will go out and stand with my father in the field where you are hiding, and I'll talk to him about you. Then I'll let you know what I find out."

[4]When Jonathan talked to Saul his father, he said good things about David. Jonathan said, "The king should do no wrong to your servant David since he has done nothing wrong to you. What he has done has helped you greatly. [5]David risked his life when he killed Goliath the Philistine, and the LORD won a great victory for all Israel. You saw it and were happy. Why would you do wrong against David? He's innocent. There's no reason to kill him!"

[6]Saul listened to Jonathan and then made this promise: "As surely as the LORD lives, David won't be put to death."

[7]So Jonathan called to David and told him

everything that had been said. He brought David to Saul, and David was with Saul as before.

⁸When war broke out again, David went out to fight the Philistines. He defeated them, and they ran away from him.

⁹But once again an evil spirit from the LORD rushed upon Saul as he was sitting in his house with his spear in his hand. David was playing the harp. ¹⁰Saul tried to pin David to the wall with his spear, but David jumped out of the way. So Saul's spear went into the wall, and David ran away that night.

¹¹Saul sent messengers to David's house to watch it and to kill him in the morning. But Michal, David's wife, warned him, saying, "Tonight you must run for your life. If you don't, you will be dead in the morning." ¹²So she let David down out of a window, and he ran away and escaped. ¹³Then Michal took an idol, laid it on the bed, covered it with clothes, and put goats' hair at its head.

¹⁴Saul sent messengers to take David prisoner, but Michal said, "He is sick."

¹⁵Saul sent them back to see David, saying, "Bring him to me on his bed so I can kill him."

¹⁶When the messengers entered David's house, they found just an idol on the bed with goats' hair on its head.

¹⁷Saul said to Michal, "Why did you trick me this way? You let my enemy go so he could run away!"

Michal answered Saul, "David told me if I did not help him escape, he would kill me."

¹⁸After David had escaped from Saul, he went to Samuel at Ramah and told him everything Saul had done to him. Then David and Samuel went to Naioth and stayed there. ¹⁹Saul heard that David was in Naioth at Ramah. ²⁰So he sent messengers to capture him. But they met a group of prophets prophesying, with Samuel standing there leading them. So the Spirit of God entered Saul's men, and they also prophesied. ²¹When Saul heard the news, he sent more messengers, but they also prophesied. Then he sent messengers a third time, but they also prophesied. ²²Finally, Saul himself went to Ramah, to the well at Secu. He asked, "Where are Samuel and David?"

The people answered, "In Naioth at Ramah."

²³When Saul went to Naioth at Ramah, the Spirit of God also rushed upon him. And he walked on, prophesying until he came to Naioth at Ramah. ²⁴He took off his robes and prophesied in front of Samuel. He lay that way all day and all night. That is why people ask, "Is even Saul one of the prophets?"

PSALM 58:1–11

Unfair Judges

For the director of music. To the tune of "Do Not Destroy." A miktam of David.

58 Do you rulers really say what is right?
Do you judge people fairly?
²No, in your heart you plan evil;
you think up violent crimes in the land.
³From birth, evil people turn away from God;
they wander off and tell lies as soon as they are born.
⁴They are like poisonous snakes,
like deaf cobras that stop up their ears
⁵so they cannot hear the music of the snake charmer
no matter how well he plays.

⁶God, break the teeth in their mouths!
Tear out the fangs of those lions, LORD!
⁷Let them disappear like water that flows away.
Let them be cut short like a broken arrow.
⁸Let them be like snails that melt as they move.
Let them be like a child born dead who never saw the sun.
⁹His anger will blow them away alive
faster than burning thorns can heat a pot.
¹⁰Good people will be glad when they see him get even.
They will wash their feet in the blood of the wicked.
¹¹Then people will say,
"There really are rewards for doing what is right.
There really is a God who judges the world."

PROVERBS 15:27–30

²⁷Greedy people bring trouble to their
   families,
   but the person who can't be paid to do
      wrong will live.

²⁸Good people think before they answer,
   but the wicked simply pour out evil.

²⁹The LORD does not listen to the wicked,
   but he hears the prayers of those who
      do right.

³⁰Good news makes you feel better.
   Your happiness will show in your eyes.

LUKE 24:1–35

Jesus Rises from the Dead

24 Very early on the first day of the week,
at dawn, the women came to the tomb,
bringing the spices they had prepared. ²They
found the stone rolled away from the entrance of the tomb, ³but when they went in,
they did not find the body of the Lord Jesus.
⁴While they were wondering about this, two
men in shining clothes suddenly stood beside them. ⁵The women were very afraid and
bowed their heads to the ground. The men
said to them, "Why are you looking for a living person in this place for the dead? ⁶He is
not here; he has risen from the dead. Do you
remember what he told you in Galilee? ⁷He
said the Son of Man must be handed over to
sinful people, be crucified, and rise from the
dead on the third day." ⁸Then the women remembered what Jesus had said.

⁹The women left the tomb and told all
these things to the eleven apostles and the
other followers. ¹⁰It was Mary Magdalene,
Joanna, Mary the mother of James, and some
other women who told the apostles everything that had happened at the tomb. ¹¹But
they did not believe the women, because it
sounded like nonsense. ¹²But Peter got up and
ran to the tomb. Bending down and looking
in, he saw only the cloth that Jesus' body had
been wrapped in. Peter went away to his
home, wondering about what had happened.

Jesus on the Road to Emmaus

¹³That same day two of Jesus' followers
were going to a town named Emmaus, about

seven miles from Jerusalem. ¹⁴They were talking about everything that had happened.
¹⁵While they were talking and discussing, Jesus himself came near and began walking
with them, ¹⁶but they were kept from recognizing him. ¹⁷Then he said, "What are these
things you are talking about while you walk?"

The two followers stopped, looking very
sad. ¹⁸The one named Cleopas answered,
"Are you the only visitor in Jerusalem who
does not know what just happened there?"

¹⁹Jesus said to them, "What are you talking about?"

They said, "About Jesus of Nazareth. He
was a prophet who said and did many powerful things before God and all the people.
²⁰Our leaders and the leading priests handed
him over to be sentenced to death, and they
crucified him. ²¹But we were hoping that he
would free Israel. Besides this, it is now the
third day since this happened. ²²And today
some women among us amazed us. Early
this morning they went to the tomb, ²³but
they did not find his body there. They came
and told us that they had seen a vision of angels who said that Jesus was alive! ²⁴So some
of our group went to the tomb, too. They
found it just as the women said, but they did
not see Jesus."

²⁵Then Jesus said to them, "You are foolish
and slow to believe everything the prophets
said. ²⁶They said that the Christ must suffer
these things before he enters his glory."
²⁷Then starting with what Moses and all the
prophets had said about him, Jesus began to
explain everything that had been written
about himself in the Scriptures.

²⁸They came near the town of Emmaus,
and Jesus acted as if he were going farther.
²⁹But they begged him, "Stay with us, because it is late; it is almost night." So he went
in to stay with them.

³⁰When Jesus was at the table with them,
he took some bread, gave thanks, divided it,
and gave it to them. ³¹And then, they were allowed to recognize Jesus. But when they saw
who he was, he disappeared. ³²They said to
each other, "It felt like a fire burning in us
when Jesus talked to us on the road and explained the Scriptures to us."

³³So the two followers got up at once and

went back to Jerusalem. There they found the eleven apostles and others gathered. ³⁴They were saying, "The Lord really has risen from the dead! He showed himself to Simon."

³⁵Then the two followers told what had happened on the road and how they recognized Jesus when he divided the bread.

MAY 9

1 SAMUEL 20:1—21:15

Jonathan Helps David

20 Then David ran away from Naioth in Ramah. He went to Jonathan and asked, "What have I done? What is my crime? How did I sin against your father? Why is he trying to kill me?"

²Jonathan answered, "No! You won't die! See, my father doesn't do anything great or small without first telling me. Why would he keep this from me? It's not true!"

³But David took an oath, saying, "Your father knows very well that you like me. He says to himself, 'Jonathan must not know about it, or he will tell David.' As surely as the LORD lives and as you live, I am only a step away from death!"

⁴Jonathan said to David, "I'll do anything you want me to do."

⁵So David said, "Look, tomorrow is the New Moon festival. I am supposed to eat with the king, but let me hide in the field until the third evening. ⁶If your father notices I am gone, tell him, 'David begged me to let him go to his hometown of Bethlehem. Every year at this time his family group offers a sacrifice.' ⁷If your father says, 'Fine,' I am safe. But if he becomes angry, you will know that he wants to hurt me. ⁸Jonathan, be loyal to me, your servant. You have made an agreement with me before the LORD. If I am guilty, you may kill me yourself! Why hand me over to your father?"

⁹Jonathan answered, "No, never! If I learn that my father plans to hurt you, I will warn you!"

¹⁰David asked, "Who will let me know if your father answers you unkindly?"

¹¹Then Jonathan said, "Come, let's go out into the field." So the two of them went out into the field.

¹²Jonathan said to David, "I promise this before the LORD, the God of Israel: At this same time the day after tomorrow, I will find out how my father feels. If he feels good toward you, I will send word to you and let you know. ¹³But if my father plans to hurt you, I will let you know and send you away safely. May the LORD punish me terribly if I don't do this. And may the LORD be with you as he has been with my father. ¹⁴But show me the kindness of the LORD as long as I live so that I may not die. ¹⁵You must never stop showing your kindness to my family, even when the LORD has destroyed all your enemies from the earth."

¹⁶So Jonathan made an agreement with David. He said, "May the LORD hold David's enemies responsible." ¹⁷And Jonathan asked David to repeat his promise of love for him, because he loved David as much as he loved himself.

¹⁸Jonathan said to David, "Tomorrow is the New Moon festival. Your seat will be empty, so my father will miss you. ¹⁹On the third day go to the place where you hid when this trouble began. Wait by the rock Ezel. ²⁰On the third day I will shoot three arrows to the side of the rock as if I am shooting at a target. ²¹Then I will send a boy to find the arrows. If I say to him, 'The arrows are near you; bring them here,' you may come out of hiding. You are safe. As the LORD lives, there is no danger. ²²But if I say to the boy, 'Look, the arrows are beyond you,' you must go, because the LORD is sending you away. ²³Remember what we talked about. The LORD is a witness between you and me forever."

²⁴So David hid in the field. When the New Moon festival came, the king sat down to eat. ²⁵He sat where he always sat, near the wall. Jonathan sat across from him, and Ab-

ner sat next to Saul, but David's place was empty. ²⁶That day Saul said nothing. He thought, "Maybe something has happened to David so that he is unclean." ²⁷But the next day was the second day of the month, and David's place was still empty. So Saul said to Jonathan, "Why hasn't the son of Jesse come to the feast yesterday or today?"

²⁸Jonathan answered, "David begged me to let him go to Bethlehem. ²⁹He said, 'Let me go, because our family has a sacrifice in the town, and my brother has ordered me to be there. Now if I am your friend, please let me go to see my brothers.' That is why he has not come to the king's table."

³⁰Then Saul became very angry with Jonathan. He said, "You son of a wicked, worthless woman! I know you are on the side of David son of Jesse! You bring shame on yourself and on your mother who gave birth to you. ³¹As long as Jesse's son lives, you will never be king or have a kingdom. Now send for David and bring him to me. He must die!"

³²Jonathan asked his father, "Why should David be killed? What wrong has he done?" ³³Then Saul threw his spear at Jonathan, trying to kill him. So Jonathan knew that his father really wanted to kill David. ³⁴Jonathan was very angry and left the table. That second day of the month he refused to eat. He was ashamed of his father and upset over David.

³⁵The next morning Jonathan went out to the field to meet David as they had agreed. He had a young boy with him. ³⁶Jonathan said to the boy, "Run and find the arrows I shoot." When he ran, Jonathan shot an arrow beyond him. ³⁷The boy ran to the place where Jonathan's arrow fell, but Jonathan called, "The arrow is beyond you!" ³⁸Then he shouted, "Hurry! Go quickly! Don't stop!" The boy picked up the arrow and brought it back to his master. ³⁹(The boy knew nothing about what this meant; only Jonathan and David knew.) ⁴⁰Then Jonathan gave his weapons to the boy and told him, "Go back to town."

⁴¹When the boy left, David came out from the south side of the rock. He bowed face-down on the ground before Jonathan three times. Then David and Jonathan kissed each other and cried together, but David cried the most.

⁴²Jonathan said to David, "Go in peace. We have promised by the LORD that we will be friends. We said, 'The LORD will be a witness between you and me, and between our descendants always.' " Then David left, and Jonathan went back to town.

David Goes to See Ahimelech

21 David went to Nob to see Ahimelech the priest. Ahimelech shook with fear when he saw David, and he asked, "Why are you alone? Why is no one with you?"

²David answered him, "The king gave me a special order. He told me, 'No one must know what I am sending you to do or what I told you to do.' I told my men where to meet me. ³Now, what food do you have with you? Give me five loaves of bread or anything you find."

⁴The priest said to David, "I don't have any plain bread here, but I do have some holy bread.ⁿ You may eat it if your men have kept themselves from women."

⁵David answered, "No women have been near us for days. My men always keep themselves holy, even when we do ordinary work. And this is especially true when the work is holy."

⁶So the priest gave David the holy bread from the presence of God because there was no other. Each day the holy bread was replaced with hot bread.

⁷One of Saul's servants happened to be there that day. He had been held there before the LORD. He was Doeg the Edomite, the chief of Saul's shepherds.

⁸David asked Ahimelech, "Do you have a spear or sword here? The king's business was very important, so I left without my sword or any other weapon."

⁹The priest answered, "The sword of Goliath the Philistine, the one you killed in the Valley of Elah, is here. It is wrapped in a cloth

21:4 holy bread This was the bread that showed the people were in the presence of God. Normally only the priests ate this bread.

behind the holy vest. If you want it, you may take it. There's no other sword here but that one."

David said, "There is no other sword like it. Give it to me."

David Goes to Gath

¹⁰That day David ran away from Saul and went to Achish king of Gath. ¹¹But the servants of Achish said to him, "This is David, the king of the Israelites. He's the man they dance and sing about, saying:

'Saul has killed thousands of his enemies,
but David has killed tens of thousands.'"

¹²David paid attention to these words and was very much afraid of Achish king of Gath. ¹³So he pretended to be crazy in front of Achish and his servants. While he was with them, he acted like a madman and clawed on the doors of the gate and let spit run down his beard.

¹⁴Achish said to his servants, "Look at the man! He's crazy! Why do you bring him to me? ¹⁵I have enough madmen. I don't need you to bring him here to act like this in front of me! Don't let him in my house!"

PSALM 59:1–5

A Prayer for Protection

For the director of music. To the tune of "Do Not Destroy." A miktam of David when Saul sent men to watch David's house to kill him.

59 God, save me from my enemies.
Protect me from those who come against me.
²Save me from those who do evil
and from murderers.

³Look, they are waiting to ambush me.
Cruel people attack me,
but I have not sinned or done wrong,
LORD.
⁴I have done nothing wrong, but they are ready to attack me.
Wake up to help me, and look.
⁵You are the LORD God All-Powerful, the God of Israel.
Arise and punish those people.
Do not give those traitors any mercy.
Selah

PROVERBS 15:31–33

³¹If you listen to correction to improve your life,
you will live among the wise.

³²Those who refuse correction hate themselves,
but those who accept correction gain understanding.

³³Respect for the LORD will teach you wisdom.
If you want to be honored, you must be humble.

LUKE 24:36–53

Jesus Appears to His Followers

³⁶While the two followers were telling this, Jesus himself stood right in the middle of them and said, "Peace be with you."

³⁷They were fearful and terrified and thought they were seeing a ghost. ³⁸But Jesus said, "Why are you troubled? Why do you doubt what you see? ³⁹Look at my hands and my feet. It is myself! Touch me and see, because a ghost does not have a living body as you see I have."

⁴⁰After Jesus said this, he showed them his hands and feet. ⁴¹While they still could not believe it because they were amazed and happy, Jesus said to them, "Do you have any food here?" ⁴²They gave him a piece of broiled fish. ⁴³While the followers watched, Jesus took the fish and ate it.

⁴⁴He said to them, "Remember when I was with you before? I said that everything written about me must happen—everything in the law of Moses, the books of the prophets, and the Psalms."

⁴⁵Then Jesus opened their minds so they could understand the Scriptures. ⁴⁶He said to them, "It is written that the Christ would suffer and rise from the dead on the third day ⁴⁷and that a change of hearts and lives and forgiveness of sins would be preached in his name to all nations, starting at Jerusalem. ⁴⁸You are witnesses of these things. ⁴⁹I will send you what my Father has promised, but you must stay in Jerusalem until you have received that power from heaven."

Jesus Goes Back to Heaven

⁵⁰Jesus led his followers as far as Bethany, and he raised his hands and blessed them. ⁵¹While he was blessing them, he was separated from them and carried into heaven. ⁵²They worshiped him and returned to Jerusalem very happy. ⁵³They stayed in the Temple all the time, praising God.

MAY 10

1 SAMUEL 22:1—23:29

David at Adullam and Mizpah

22David left Gath and escaped to the cave of Adullam. When his brothers and other relatives heard that he was there, they went to see him. ²Everyone who was in trouble, or who owed money, or who was unsatisfied gathered around David, and he became their leader. About four hundred men were with him.

³From there David went to Mizpah in Moab and spoke to the king of Moab. He said, "Please let my father and mother come and stay with you until I learn what God is going to do for me." ⁴So he left them with the king of Moab, and they stayed with him as long as David was hiding in the stronghold.

⁵But the prophet Gad said to David, "Don't stay in the stronghold. Go to the land of Judah." So David left and went to the forest of Hereth.

Saul Destroys Ahimelech's Family

⁶Saul heard that David and his men had been seen. Saul was sitting under the tamarisk tree on the hill at Gibeah, and all his officers were standing around him. He had a spear in his hand. ⁷Saul said to them, "Listen, men of Benjamin! Do you think the son of Jesse will give all of you fields and vineyards? Will David make you commanders over thousands of men or hundreds of men? ⁸You have all made plans against me! No one tells me when my son makes an agreement with the son of Jesse! No one cares about me! No one tells me when my son has encouraged my servant to ambush me this very day!"

⁹Doeg the Edomite, who was standing there with Saul's officers, said, "I saw the son of Jesse. He came to see Ahimelech son of Ahitub at Nob. ¹⁰Ahimelech prayed to the LORD for David and gave him food and gave him the sword of Goliath the Philistine."

¹¹Then the king sent for the priest Ahimelech son of Ahitub and for all of Ahimelech's relatives who were priests at Nob. And they all came to the king. ¹²Saul said to Ahimelech, "Listen now, son of Ahitub."

Ahimelech answered, "Yes, master."

¹³Saul said, "Why are you and Jesse's son against me? You gave him bread and a sword! You prayed to God for him. David has turned against me and is waiting to attack me even now!"

¹⁴Ahimelech answered, "You have no other servant who is as loyal as David, your own son-in-law and captain of your bodyguards. Everyone in your house respects him. ¹⁵That was not the first time I prayed to God for David. Don't blame me or any of my relatives. I, your servant, know nothing about what is going on."

¹⁶But the king said, "Ahimelech, you and all your relatives must die!" ¹⁷Then he told the guards at his side, "Go and kill the priests of the LORD, because they are on David's side. They knew he was running away, but they didn't tell me."

But the king's officers refused to kill the priests of the LORD.

¹⁸Then the king ordered Doeg, "Go and kill the priests." So Doeg the Edomite went and killed the priests. That day he killed eighty-five men who wore the linen holy vest. ¹⁹He also killed the people of Nob, the city of the priests. With the sword he killed men, women, children, babies, cattle, donkeys, and sheep.

²⁰But Abiathar, a son of Ahimelech, who was the son of Ahitub, escaped. He ran away and joined David. ²¹He told David that

Saul had killed the LORD's priests. ²²Then David told him, "Doeg the Edomite was there at Nob that day. I knew he would surely tell Saul. So I am responsible for the death of all your father's family. ²³Stay with me. Don't be afraid. The man who wants to kill you also wants to kill me. You will be safe with me."

David Saves the People of Keilah

23 Someone told David, "Look, the Philistines are fighting against Keilah and stealing grain from the threshing floors."

²David asked the LORD, "Should I go and fight these Philistines?"

The LORD answered him, "Go. Attack them, and save Keilah."

³But David's men said to him, "We're afraid here in Judah. We will be more afraid if we go to Keilah where the Philistine army is."

⁴David again asked the LORD, and the LORD answered, "Go down to Keilah. I will help you defeat the Philistines." ⁵So David and his men went to Keilah and fought the Philistines and took their cattle. David killed many Philistines and saved the people of Keilah. ⁶(Now Abiathar son of Ahimelech had brought the holy vest with him when he came to David at Keilah.)

Saul Chases David

⁷Someone told Saul that David was now at Keilah. Saul said, "God has handed David over to me! He has trapped himself, because he has entered a town with gates and bars." ⁸Saul called all his army together for battle, and they prepared to go down to Keilah to attack David and his men.

⁹David learned Saul was making evil plans against him. So he said to Abiathar the priest, "Bring the holy vest." ¹⁰David prayed, "LORD, God of Israel, I have heard that Saul plans to come to Keilah to destroy the town because of me. ¹¹Will the leaders of Keilah hand me over to Saul? Will Saul come down to Keilah, as I heard? LORD, God of Israel, tell me, your servant!"

The LORD answered, "Saul will come down."

¹²Again David asked, "Will the leaders of Keilah hand me and my men over to Saul?"

The LORD answered, "They will."

¹³So David and his six hundred men left Keilah and kept moving from place to place. When Saul found out that David had escaped from Keilah, he did not go there.

¹⁴David stayed in the desert hideouts and in the hills of the Desert of Ziph. Every day Saul looked for David, but the LORD did not surrender David to him.

¹⁵While David was at Horesh in the Desert of Ziph, he learned that Saul was coming to kill him. ¹⁶But Saul's son Jonathan went to David at Horesh and strengthened his faith in God. ¹⁷Jonathan told him, "Don't be afraid, because my father won't touch you. You will be king of Israel, and I will be second to you. Even my father Saul knows this." ¹⁸The two of them made an agreement before the LORD. Then Jonathan went home, but David stayed at Horesh.

¹⁹The people from Ziph went to Saul at Gibeah and told him, "David is hiding in our land. He's at the hideouts of Horesh, on the hill of Hakilah, south of Jeshimon. ²⁰Now, our king, come down anytime you want. It's our duty to hand David over to you."

²¹Saul answered, "The LORD bless you for helping me. ²²Go and learn more about him. Find out where he is staying and who has seen him there. I have heard that he is clever. ²³Find all the hiding places he uses, and come back and tell me everything. Then I'll go with you. If David is in the area, I will track him down among all the families in Judah."

²⁴So they went back to Ziph ahead of Saul. Now David and his men were in the Desert of Maon[n] in the desert area south of Jeshimon. ²⁵Saul and his men went to look for David, but David heard about it and went down to a rock and stayed in the Desert of Maon. When Saul heard that, he followed David into the Desert of Maon.

²⁶Saul was going along one side of the mountain, and David and his men were on the other side. They were hurrying to get away from Saul, because Saul and his men were closing in on them. ²⁷But a messenger

---

23:24 Maon Some early Greek copies say "Maon." The Hebrew copies say "Paran."

came to Saul, saying, "Come quickly! The Philistines are attacking our land!" [28] So Saul stopped chasing David and went to challenge the Philistines. That is why people call this place Rock of Parting. [29] David also left the Desert of Maon and stayed in the hideouts of En Gedi.

PSALM 59:6–17

[6] They come back at night.
  Like dogs they growl and roam around the city.
[7] Notice what comes from their mouths.
  Insults come from their lips,
  because they say, "Who's listening?"
[8] But, LORD, you laugh at them;
  you make fun of all of them.

[9] God, my strength, I am looking to you,
  because God is my defender.
[10] My God loves me, and he goes in front of me.
  He will help me defeat my enemies.
[11] Lord, our protector, do not kill them, or my people will forget.
  With your power scatter them and defeat them.
[12] They sin by what they say;
  they sin with their words.
  They curse and tell lies,
  so let their pride trap them.
[13] Destroy them in your anger;
  destroy them completely!
  Then they will know
  that God rules over Israel
  and to the ends of the earth.   *Selah*

[14] They come back at night.
  Like dogs they growl
  and roam around the city.
[15] They wander about looking for food,
  and they howl if they do not find enough.
[16] But I will sing about your strength.
  In the morning I will sing about your love.
  You are my defender,
  my place of safety in times of trouble.

[17] God, my strength, I will sing praises to you.
  God, my defender, you are the God who loves me.

PROVERBS 16:1–2

16 People may make plans in their minds,
  but only the LORD can make them come true.

[2] You may believe you are doing right,
  but the LORD will judge your reasons.

JOHN 1:1–34

Christ Comes to the World

1 In the beginning there was the Word.[n] The Word was with God, and the Word was God. [2] He was with God in the beginning. [3] All things were made by him, and nothing was made without him. [4] In him there was life, and that life was the light of all people. [5] The Light shines in the darkness, and the darkness has not overpowered[n] it.

[6] There was a man named John[n] who was sent by God. [7] He came to tell people the truth about the Light so that through him all people could hear about the Light and believe. [8] John was not the Light, but he came to tell people the truth about the Light. [9] The true Light that gives light to all was coming into the world!

[10] The Word was in the world, and the world was made by him, but the world did not know him. [11] He came to the world that was his own, but his own people did not accept him. [12] But to all who did accept him and believe in him he gave the right to become children of God. [13] They did not become his children in any human way—by any human parents or human desire. They were born of God.

[14] The Word became a human and lived among us. We saw his glory—the glory that belongs to the only Son of the Father—and he was full of grace and truth. [15] John tells the truth about him and cries out, saying, "This is the One I told you about: 'The One who

---

1:1 Word The Greek word is "logos," meaning any kind of communication; it could be translated "message." Here, it means Christ, because Christ was the way God told people about himself. **1:5 overpowered** This can also be translated, "understood." **1:6 John** John the Baptist, who preached to people about Christ's coming (Matthew 3, Luke 3).

comes after me is greater than I am, because he was living before me.'"

[16]Because he was full of grace and truth, from him we all received one gift after another. [17]The law was given through Moses, but grace and truth came through Jesus Christ. [18]No one has ever seen God. But God the only Son is very close to the Father,[n] and he has shown us what God is like.

John Tells People About Jesus

[19]Here is the truth John[n] told when the leaders in Jerusalem sent priests and Levites to ask him, "Who are you?"

[20]John spoke freely and did not refuse to answer. He said, "I am not the Christ."

[21]So they asked him, "Then who are you? Are you Elijah?"[n]

He answered, "No, I am not."

"Are you the Prophet?"[n] they asked.

He answered, "No."

[22]Then they said, "Who are you? Give us an answer to tell those who sent us. What do you say about yourself?"

[23]John told them in the words of the prophet Isaiah:

"I am the voice of one
    calling out in the desert:
'Make the road straight for the Lord.'"

Isaiah 40:3

[24]Some Pharisees who had been sent asked John: [25]"If you are not the Christ or Elijah or the Prophet, why do you baptize people?"

[26]John answered, "I baptize with water, but there is one here with you that you don't know about. [27]He is the One who comes after me. I am not good enough to untie the strings of his sandals."

[28]This all happened at Bethany on the other side of the Jordan River, where John was baptizing people.

[29]The next day John saw Jesus coming toward him. John said, "Look, the Lamb of God,[n] who takes away the sin of the world! [30]This is the One I was talking about when I said, 'A man will come after me, but he is greater than I am, because he was living before me.' [31]Even I did not know who he was, although I came baptizing with water so that the people of Israel would know who he is."

[32-33]Then John said, "I saw the Spirit come down from heaven in the form of a dove and rest on him. Until then I did not know who the Christ was. But the God who sent me to baptize with water told me, 'You will see the Spirit come down and rest on a man; he is the One who will baptize with the Holy Spirit.' [34]I have seen this happen, and I tell you the truth: This man is the Son of God."[n]

MAY 11

1 SAMUEL 24:1—25:44

David Shames Saul

24 After Saul returned from chasing the Philistines, he was told, "David is in the Desert of En Gedi." [2]So he took three thousand chosen men from all Israel and began looking for David and his men near the Rocks of the Wild Goats.

[3]Saul came to the sheep pens beside the road. A cave was there, and he went in to relieve himself. Now David and his men were hiding far back in the cave. [4]The men said to David, "Today is the day the LORD spoke of when he said, 'I will give your enemy over to you. Do anything you want with him.'"

Then David crept up to Saul and quietly cut off a corner of Saul's robe. [5]Later David

---

1:18 But . . . Father This could be translated, "But the only God is very close to the Father." Also, some Greek copies read "But the only Son is very close to the Father." **1:19 John** John the Baptist, who preached to people about Christ's coming (Matthew 3, Luke 3). **1:21 Elijah** A prophet who spoke for God. He lived hundreds of years before Christ and was expected to return before Christ (Malachi 4:5–6). **1:21 Prophet** They probably meant the prophet that God told Moses he would send (Deuteronomy 18:15–19). **1:29 Lamb of God** Name for Jesus. Jesus is like the lambs that were offered for a sacrifice to God. **1:34 the Son of God** Some Greek copies read "God's Chosen One."

felt guilty because he had cut off a corner of Saul's robe. [6]He said to his men, "May the LORD keep me from doing such a thing to my master! Saul is the LORD's appointed king. I should not do anything against him, because he is the LORD's appointed king!" [7]David used these words to stop his men; he did not let them attack Saul. Then Saul left the cave and went his way.

[8]When David came out of the cave, he shouted to Saul, "My master and king!" Saul looked back, and David bowed facedown on the ground. [9]He said to Saul, "Why do you listen when people say, 'David wants to harm you'? [10]You have seen something with your own eyes today. The LORD put you in my power in the cave. They said I should kill you, but I was merciful. I said, 'I won't harm my master, because he is the LORD's appointed king.' [11]My father, look at this piece of your robe in my hand! I cut off the corner of your robe, but I didn't kill you. Now understand and know I am not planning any evil against you. I did nothing wrong to you, but you are hunting me to kill me. [12]May the LORD judge between us, and may he punish you for the wrong you have done to me! But I am not against you. [13]There is an old saying: 'Evil things come from evil people.' But I am not against you. [14]Whom is the king of Israel coming out against? Whom are you chasing? It's as if you are chasing a dead dog or a flea. [15]May the LORD be our judge and decide between you and me. May he support me and show that I am right. May he save me from you!"

[16]When David finished saying these words, Saul asked, "Is that your voice, David my son?" And he cried loudly. [17]He said, "You are a better man than I am. You have been good to me, but I have done wrong to you. [18]You told me what good things you did. The LORD handed me over to you, but you did not kill me. [19]People don't normally let an enemy get away like this, do they? May the LORD reward you because you were good to me today. [20]I know you will surely be king, and you will rule the kingdom of Israel. [21]Now swear to me by the LORD that you will not kill my

descendants and that you won't wipe out my name from my father's family."

[22]So David made the promise to Saul. Then Saul went back home, and David and his men went up to their hideout.

Nabal Insults David

25 Now Samuel died, and all the Israelites met and had a time of sadness for him. Then they buried him at his home in Ramah.

David moved to the Desert of Maon.[n] [2]A man in Maon who had land at Carmel was very rich. He had three thousand sheep and a thousand goats. He was cutting the wool off his sheep at Carmel. [3]His name was Nabal, and he was a descendant of Caleb. His wife was named Abigail. She was wise and beautiful, but Nabal was cruel and mean.

[4]While David was in the desert, he heard that Nabal was cutting the wool from his sheep. [5]So he sent ten young men and told them, "Go to Nabal at Carmel, and greet him for me. [6]Say to Nabal, 'May you and your family and all who belong to you have good health! [7]I have heard that you are cutting the wool from your sheep. When your shepherds were with us, we did not harm them. All the time your shepherds were at Carmel, we stole nothing from them. [8]Ask your servants, and they will tell you. We come at a happy time, so be kind to my young men. Please give anything you can find for them and for your son David.'"

[9]When David's men arrived, they gave the message to Nabal, but Nabal insulted them. [10]He answered them, "Who is David? Who is this son of Jesse? Many slaves are running away from their masters today! [11]I have bread and water, and I have meat that I killed for my servants who cut the wool. But I won't give it to men I don't know."

[12]David's men went back and told him all Nabal had said. [13]Then David said to them, "Put on your swords!" So they put on their swords, and David put on his also. About four hundred men went with David, but two hundred men stayed with the supplies.

25:1 **Maon** Some early Greek copies say "Maon." The Hebrew copies say "Paran."

¹⁴One of Nabal's servants said to Abigail, Nabal's wife, "David sent messengers from the desert to greet our master, but Nabal insulted them. ¹⁵These men were very good to us. They did not harm us. They stole nothing from us during all the time we were out in the field with them. ¹⁶Night and day they protected us. They were like a wall around us while we were with them caring for the sheep. ¹⁷Now think about it, and decide what you can do. Terrible trouble is coming to our master and all his family. Nabal is such a wicked man that no one can even talk to him."

¹⁸Abigail hurried. She took two hundred loaves of bread, two leather bags full of wine, five cooked sheep, a bushel of cooked grain, a hundred cakes of raisins, and two hundred cakes of pressed figs and put all these on donkeys. ¹⁹Then she told her servants, "Go on. I'll follow you." But she did not tell her husband.

²⁰Abigail rode her donkey and came down toward the mountain hideout. There she met David and his men coming down toward her.

²¹David had just said, "It's been useless! I watched over Nabal's property in the desert. I made sure none of his sheep was missing. I did good to him, but he has paid me back with evil. ²²May God punish my enemies even more. I will not leave one of Nabal's men alive until morning."

²³When Abigail saw David, she quickly got off her donkey and bowed facedown on the ground before him. ²⁴She fell at David's feet and said, "My master, let the blame be on me! Please let me talk to you. Listen to what I say. ²⁵My master, don't pay attention to this worthless man Nabal. He is like his name. His name means 'fool,' and he is truly a fool. But I, your servant, didn't see the men you sent. ²⁶The LORD has kept you from killing and punishing anyone. As surely as the LORD lives and as surely as you live, may your enemies become like Nabal! ²⁷I have brought a gift to you for the men who follow you.²⁸Please forgive my wrong. The LORD will certainly let your family have many kings, because you fight his battles. As long as you live, may you do nothing

bad. ²⁹Someone might chase you to kill you, but the LORD your God will keep you alive. He will throw away your enemies' lives as he would throw a stone from a sling. ³⁰The LORD will keep all his promises of good things for you. He will make you leader over Israel. ³¹Then you won't feel guilty or troubled because you killed innocent people and punished them. Please remember me when the LORD brings you success."

³²David answered Abigail, "Praise the LORD, the God of Israel, who sent you to meet me. ³³May you be blessed for your wisdom. You have kept me from killing or punishing people today. ³⁴As surely as the LORD, the God of Israel, lives, he has kept me from hurting you. If you hadn't come quickly to meet me, not one of Nabal's men would have lived until morning."

³⁵Then David accepted Abigail's gifts. He told her, "Go home in peace. I have heard your words, and I will do what you have asked."

Nabal's Death

³⁶When Abigail went back to Nabal, he was in the house, eating like a king. He was very drunk and in a good mood. So she told him nothing until the next morning. ³⁷In the morning when he was not drunk, his wife told him everything. His heart stopped, and he became like stone. ³⁸About ten days later the LORD struck Nabal and he died.

³⁹When David heard that Nabal was dead, he said, "Praise the LORD! Nabal insulted me, but the LORD has supported me! He has kept me from doing wrong. The LORD has punished Nabal for his wrong."

Then David sent a message to Abigail, asking her to be his wife. ⁴⁰His servants went to Carmel and said to Abigail, "David sent us to take you so you can become his wife."

⁴¹Abigail bowed facedown on the ground and said, "I am your servant. I'm ready to serve you and to wash the feet of my master's servants." ⁴²Abigail quickly got on a donkey and went with David's messengers, with her five maids following her. And she became David's wife.

[43]David also had married Ahinoam of Jezreel. So they were both David's wives. [44]Saul's daughter Michal was also David's wife, but Saul had given her to Paltiel son of Laish, who was from Gallim.

PSALM 60:1–5

A Prayer After a Defeat

For the director of music. To the tune of "Lily of the Agreement." A miktam of David. For teaching. When David fought the Arameans of Northwest Mesopotamia and Zobah, and when Joab returned and defeated twelve thousand Edomites at the Valley of Salt.

60 God, you have rejected us and
　　scattered us.
You have been angry, but please come
　　back to us.
[2]You made the earth shake and crack.
　　Heal its breaks because it is shaking.
[3]You have given your people trouble.
　　You made us unable to walk straight,
　　like people drunk with wine.
[4]You have raised a banner to gather those
　　who fear you.
　　Now they can stand up against the
　　enemy.　　　　　　　　　*Selah*

[5]Answer us and save us by your power
　　so the people you love will be rescued.

PROVERBS 16:3

[3]Depend on the LORD in whatever you do,
　　and your plans will succeed.

JOHN 1:35–51

The First Followers of Jesus

[35]The next day John[n] was there again with two of his followers. [36]When he saw Jesus walking by, he said, "Look, the Lamb of God!"[n]

[37]The two followers heard John say this, so they followed Jesus. [38]When Jesus turned and saw them following him, he asked, "What are you looking for?"

They said, "Rabbi, where are you staying?" ("Rabbi" means "Teacher.")

[39]He answered, "Come and see." So the two men went with Jesus and saw where he was staying and stayed there with him that day. It was about four o'clock in the afternoon.

[40]One of the two men who followed Jesus after they heard John speak about him was Andrew, Simon Peter's brother. [41]The first thing Andrew did was to find his brother Simon and say to him, "We have found the Messiah." ("Messiah" means "Christ.")

[42]Then Andrew took Simon to Jesus. Jesus looked at him and said, "You are Simon son of John. You will be called Cephas." ("Cephas" means "Peter."[n])

[43]The next day Jesus decided to go to Galilee. He found Philip and said to him, "Follow me."

[44]Philip was from the town of Bethsaida, where Andrew and Peter lived. [45]Philip found Nathanael and told him, "We have found the man that Moses wrote about in the law, and the prophets also wrote about him. He is Jesus, the son of Joseph, from Nazareth."

[46]But Nathanael said to Philip, "Can anything good come from Nazareth?"

Philip answered, "Come and see."

[47]As Jesus saw Nathanael coming toward him, he said, "Here is truly an Israelite. There is nothing false in him."

[48]Nathanael asked, "How do you know me?"

Jesus answered, "I saw you when you were under the fig tree, before Philip told you about me."

[49]Then Nathanael said to Jesus, "Teacher, you are the Son of God; you are the King of Israel."

[50]Jesus said to Nathanael, "Do you believe simply because I told you I saw you under the fig tree? You will see greater things than that." [51]And Jesus said to them, "I tell you the truth, you will all see heaven open and 'angels of God going up and coming down'[n] on the Son of Man."

1:35 John John the Baptist, who preached to people about Christ's coming (Matthew 3, Luke 3). **1:36 Lamb of God** Name for Jesus. Jesus is like the lambs that were offered for a sacrifice to God. **1:42 Peter** The Greek name "Peter," like the Aramaic name "Cephas," means "rock." **1:51 'angels . . . down'** These words are from Genesis 28:12.

MAY 12

1 SAMUEL 26:1—27:12

David Shames Saul Again

26 The people of Ziph went to Saul at Gibeah and said to him, "David is hiding on the hill of Hakilah opposite Jeshimon."

²So Saul went down to the Desert of Ziph with three thousand chosen men of Israel to look for David there. ³Saul made his camp beside the road on the hill of Hakilah opposite Jeshimon, but David stayed in the desert. When he heard Saul had followed him, ⁴he sent out spies and learned for certain that Saul had come to Hakilah.

⁵Then David went to the place where Saul had camped. He saw where Saul and Abner son of Ner, the commander of Saul's army, were sleeping. Saul was sleeping in the middle of the camp with all the army around him.

⁶David asked Ahimelech the Hittite and Abishai son of Zeruiah, Joab's brother, "Who will go down into Saul's camp with me?"

Abishai answered, "I'll go with you."

⁷So that night David and Abishai went into Saul's camp. Saul was asleep in the middle of the camp with his spear stuck in the ground near his head. Abner and the army were sleeping around Saul. ⁸Abishai said to David, "Today God has handed your enemy over to you. Let me pin Saul to the ground with my spear. I'll only have to do it once. I won't need to hit him twice."

⁹But David said to Abishai, "Don't kill Saul! No one can harm the LORD's appointed king and still be innocent! ¹⁰As surely as the LORD lives, the LORD himself will punish Saul. Maybe Saul will die naturally, or maybe he will go into battle and be killed. ¹¹But may the LORD keep me from harming his appointed king! Take the spear and water jug that are near Saul's head. Then let's go."

¹²So David took the spear and water jug that were near Saul's head, and they left. No one saw them or knew about it or woke up, because the LORD had put them sound asleep.

¹³David crossed over to the other side of the hill and stood on top of the mountain far from Saul's camp. They were a long way away from each other. ¹⁴David shouted to the army and to Abner son of Ner, "Won't you answer me, Abner?"

Abner answered, "Who is calling for the king? Who are you?"

¹⁵David said, "You're the greatest man in Israel. Isn't that true? Why didn't you guard your master the king? Someone came into your camp to kill your master the king! ¹⁶You have not done well. As surely as the LORD lives, you and your men should die. You haven't guarded your master, the LORD's appointed king. Look! Where are the king's spear and water jug that were near his head?"

¹⁷Saul knew David's voice. He said, "Is that your voice, David my son?"

David answered, "Yes, it is, my master and king." ¹⁸David also said, "Why are you chasing me, my master? What wrong have I done? What evil am I guilty of? ¹⁹My master and king, listen to me. If the LORD made you angry with me, let him accept an offering. But if people did it, may the LORD curse them! They have made me leave the land the LORD gave me. They have told me, 'Go and serve other gods.' ²⁰Now don't let me die far away from the LORD's presence. The king of Israel has come out looking for a flea! You're just hunting a bird in the mountains!"

²¹Then Saul said, "I have sinned. Come back, David my son. Today you respected my life, so I will not try to hurt you. I have been very stupid and foolish."

²²David answered, "Here is your spear. Let one of your young men come here and get it. ²³The LORD rewards us for the things we do right and for our loyalty to him. The LORD handed you over to me today, but I wouldn't harm the LORD's appointed king. ²⁴As I respected your life today, may the LORD also respect my life and save me from all trouble."

²⁵Then Saul said to David, "You are blessed, my son David. You will do great things and succeed."

So David went on his way, and Saul went back home.

David Lives with the Philistines

27 But David thought to himself, "Saul will catch me someday. The best thing I can do is escape to the land of the Philistines. Then he will give up looking for me in Israel, and I can get away from him."

[2]So David and his six hundred men left Israel and went to Achish son of Maoch, king of Gath. [3]David, his men, and their families made their home in Gath with Achish. David had his two wives with him—Ahinoam of Jezreel and Abigail of Carmel, the widow of Nabal. [4]When Saul heard that David had run away to Gath, he stopped looking for him.

[5]Then David said to Achish, "If you are pleased with me, give me a place in one of the country towns where I can live. I don't need to live in the royal city with you."

[6]That day Achish gave David the town of Ziklag, and Ziklag has belonged to the kings of Judah ever since. [7]David lived in the Philistine land a year and four months.

[8]David and his men raided the people of Geshur, Girzi, and Amalek. (These people had lived for a long time in the land that reached to Shur and Egypt.) [9]When David fought them, he killed all the men and women and took their sheep, cattle, donkeys, camels, and clothes. Then he returned to Achish.

[10]Achish would ask David, "Where did you go raiding today?" And David would tell him that he had gone to the southern part of Judah, or Jerahmeel, or to the land of the Kenites. [11]David never brought a man or woman alive to Gath. He thought, "If we bring people alive, they may tell Achish, 'This is what David really did.'" David did this all the time he lived in the Philistine land. [12]So Achish trusted David and said to himself, "David's own people, the Israelites, now hate him very much. He will serve me forever."

PSALM 60:6-12

[6]God has said from his Temple,
  "When I win, I will divide Shechem
  and measure off the Valley of Succoth.

[7]Gilead and Manasseh are mine.
  Ephraim is like my helmet.
  Judah holds my royal scepter.
[8]Moab is like my washbowl.
  I throw my sandals at Edom.
  I shout at Philistia."

[9]Who will bring me to the strong, walled city?
  Who will lead me to Edom?
[10]God, surely you have rejected us;
  you do not go out with our armies.
[11]Help us fight the enemy.
  Human help is useless,
[12]but we can win with God's help.
  He will defeat our enemies.

PROVERBS 16:4-5

[4]The LORD makes everything go as he pleases.
  He has even prepared a day of disaster for evil people.

[5]The LORD hates those who are proud.
  They will surely be punished.

JOHN 2:1-25

The Wedding at Cana

2 Two days later there was a wedding in the town of Cana in Galilee. Jesus' mother was there, [2]and Jesus and his followers were also invited to the wedding. [3]When all the wine was gone, Jesus' mother said to him, "They have no more wine."

[4]Jesus answered, "Dear woman, why come to me? My time has not yet come."

[5]His mother said to the servants, "Do whatever he tells you to do."

[6]In that place there were six stone water jars that the Jews used in their washing ceremony.[n] Each jar held about twenty or thirty gallons.

[7]Jesus said to the servants, "Fill the jars with water." So they filled the jars to the top.

[8]Then he said to them, "Now take some out and give it to the master of the feast."

So they took the water to the master. [9]When he tasted it, the water had become wine. He did not know where the wine came

---

2:6 washing ceremony The Jewish people washed themselves in special ways before eating, before worshiping in the Temple, and at other special times.

from, but the servants who had brought the water knew. The master of the wedding called the bridegroom [10]and said to him, "People always serve the best wine first. Later, after the guests have been drinking awhile, they serve the cheaper wine. But you have saved the best wine till now."

[11]So in Cana of Galilee Jesus did his first miracle. There he showed his glory, and his followers believed in him.

Jesus in the Temple

[12]After this, Jesus went to the town of Capernaum with his mother, brothers, and followers. They stayed there for just a few days. [13]When it was almost time for the Jewish Passover Feast, Jesus went to Jerusalem. [14]In the Temple he found people selling cattle, sheep, and doves. He saw others sitting at tables, exchanging different kinds of money. [15]Jesus made a whip out of cords and forced all of them, both the sheep and cattle, to leave the Temple. He turned over the tables and scattered the money of those who were exchanging it. [16]Then he said to those who were selling pigeons, "Take these things out of here! Don't make my Father's house a place for buying and selling!"

[17]When this happened, the followers remembered what was written in the Scriptures: "My strong love for your Temple completely controls me."[n]

[18]Some of his people said to Jesus, "Show us a miracle to prove you have the right to do these things."

[19]Jesus answered them, "Destroy this temple, and I will build it again in three days."

[20]They answered, "It took forty-six years to build this Temple! Do you really believe you can build it again in three days?"

[21](But the temple Jesus meant was his own body. [22]After Jesus was raised from the dead, his followers remembered that Jesus had said this. Then they believed the Scripture and the words Jesus had said.)

[23]When Jesus was in Jerusalem for the Passover Feast, many people believed in him because they saw the miracles he did. [24]But Jesus did not believe in them because he knew them all. [25]He did not need anyone to tell him about people, because he knew what was in people's minds.

MAY 13

1 SAMUEL 28:1–25

Saul and the Medium of Endor

28 Later, the Philistines gathered their armies to fight against Israel. Achish said to David, "You understand that you and your men must join my army."

[2]David answered, "You will see for yourself what I, your servant, can do!"

Achish said, "Fine, I'll make you my permanent bodyguard."

[3]Now Samuel was dead, and all the Israelites had shown their sadness for him. They had buried Samuel in his hometown of Ramah.

And Saul had forced out the mediums and fortune-tellers from the land.

[4]The Philistines came together and made camp at Shunem. Saul gathered all the Israelites and made camp at Gilboa. [5]When he saw the Philistine army, he was afraid, and his heart pounded with fear. [6]He prayed to the LORD, but the LORD did not answer him through dreams, Urim, or prophets. [7]Then Saul said to his servants, "Find me a woman who is a medium so I may go and ask her what will happen."

His servants answered, "There is a medium in Endor."

[8]Then Saul put on other clothes to disguise himself, and at night he and two of his men went to see the woman. Saul said to her, "Talk to a spirit for me. Bring up the person I name."

2:17 "My . . . me." Quotation from Psalm 69:9.

[9]But the woman said to him, "Surely you know what Saul has done. He has forced the mediums and fortune-tellers from the land. You are trying to trap me and get me killed."

[10]Saul made a promise to the woman in the name of the LORD. He said, "As surely as the LORD lives, you won't be punished for this."

[11]The woman asked, "Whom do you want me to bring up?"

He answered, "Bring up Samuel."

[12]When the woman saw Samuel, she screamed. She said, "Why have you tricked me? You are Saul!"

[13]The king said to the woman, "Don't be afraid! What do you see?"

The woman said, "I see a spirit coming up out of the ground."

[14]Saul asked, "What does he look like?"

The woman answered, "An old man wearing a coat is coming up."

Then Saul knew it was Samuel, and he bowed facedown on the ground.

[15]Samuel asked Saul, "Why have you disturbed me by bringing me up?"

Saul said, "I am greatly troubled. The Philistines are fighting against me, and God has left me. He won't answer me anymore, either by prophets or in dreams. That's why I called for you. Tell me what to do."

[16]Samuel said, "The LORD has left you and has become your enemy. So why do you call on me? [17]He has done what he said he would do—the things he said through me. He has torn the kingdom out of your hands and given it to one of your neighbors, David. [18]You did not obey the LORD; you did not show the Amalekites how angry he was with them. That's why he has done this to you today. [19]The LORD will hand over both Israel and you to the Philistines. Tomorrow you and your sons will be with me. The LORD will hand over the army of Israel to the Philistines."

[20]Saul quickly fell flat on the ground and was afraid of what Samuel had said. He was also very weak because he had eaten nothing all that day and night.

[21]Then the woman came to Saul and saw that he was really frightened. She said, "Look, I, your servant, have obeyed you. I have risked my life and done what you told me to do. [22]Now please listen to me. Let me give you some food so you may eat and have enough strength to go on your way."

[23]But Saul refused, saying, "I won't eat."

His servants joined the woman in asking him to eat, and he listened to them. So he got up from the ground and sat on the bed.

[24]At the house the woman had a fat calf, which she quickly killed. She took some flour and mixed dough with her hands. Then she baked some bread without yeast. [25]She put the food before them, and they ate. That same night they got up and left.

PSALM 61:1–3

A Prayer for Protection

For the director of music. With stringed instruments. Of David.

61 God, hear my cry;
     listen to my prayer.
[2]I call to you from the ends of the earth
     when I am afraid.
     Carry me away to a high mountain.
[3]You have been my protection,
     like a strong tower against my enemies.

PROVERBS 16:6

[6]Love and truth bring forgiveness of sin.
     By respecting the LORD you will avoid
        evil.

JOHN 3:1–21

Nicodemus Comes to Jesus

3 There was a man named Nicodemus who was one of the Pharisees and an important Jewish leader. [2]One night Nicodemus came to Jesus and said, "Teacher, we know you are a teacher sent from God, because no one can do the miracles you do unless God is with him."

[3]Jesus answered, "I tell you the truth, unless you are born again, you cannot be in God's kingdom."

[4]Nicodemus said, "But if a person is already old, how can he be born again? He cannot enter his mother's womb again. So how can a person be born a second time?"

[5]But Jesus answered, "I tell you the truth,

unless you are born from water and the Spirit, you cannot enter God's kingdom. [6]Human life comes from human parents, but spiritual life comes from the Spirit. [7]Don't be surprised when I tell you, 'You must all be born again.' [8]The wind blows where it wants to and you hear the sound of it, but you don't know where the wind comes from or where it is going. It is the same with every person who is born from the Spirit."

[9]Nicodemus asked, "How can this happen?"

[10]Jesus said, "You are an important teacher in Israel, and you don't understand these things? [11]I tell you the truth, we talk about what we know, and we tell about what we have seen, but you don't accept what we tell you. [12]I have told you about things here on earth, and you do not believe me. So you will not believe me if I tell you about things of heaven. [13]The only one who has ever gone up to heaven is the One who came down from heaven—the Son of Man.[n]

[14]"Just as Moses lifted up the snake in the desert,[n] the Son of Man must also be lifted up. [15]So that everyone who believes can have eternal life in him.

[16]"God loved the world so much that he gave his one and only Son so that whoever believes in him may not be lost, but have eternal life. [17]God did not send his Son into the world to judge the world guilty, but to save the world through him. [18]People who believe in God's Son are not judged guilty. Those who do not believe have already been judged guilty, because they have not believed in God's one and only Son. [19]They are judged by this fact: The Light has come into the world, but they did not want light. They wanted darkness, because they were doing evil things. [20]All who do evil hate the light and will not come to the light, because it will show all the evil things they do. [21]But those who follow the true way come to the light, and it shows that the things they do were done through God."

MAY 14

1 SAMUEL 29:1—31:13

David Goes Back to Ziklag

29 The Philistines gathered all their soldiers at Aphek. Israel camped by the spring at Jezreel. [2]The Philistine kings were marching with their groups of a hundred and a thousand men. David and his men were marching behind Achish. [3]The Philistine commanders asked, "What are these Hebrews doing here?"

Achish told them, "This is David. He served Saul king of Israel, but he has been with me for over a year now. I have found nothing wrong in David since the time he left Saul."

[4]But the Philistine commanders were angry with Achish and said, "Send David back to the city you gave him. He cannot go with

us into battle. If he does, we'll have an enemy in our own camp. He could please his king by killing our own men. [5]David is the one the Israelites dance and sing about, saying:

'Saul has killed thousands of his
        enemies,
    but David has killed tens of thousands.'"

[6]So Achish called David and said to him, "As surely as the LORD lives, you are loyal. I would be pleased to have you serve in my army. Since the day you came to me, I have found no wrong in you. But the other kings don't trust you. [7]Go back in peace. Don't do anything to displease the Philistine kings."

[8]David asked, "What wrong have I done? What evil have you found in me from the day I came to you until now? Why can't I go fight your enemies, my lord and king?"

3:13 the Son of Man Some Greek copies continue, "who is in heaven."   **3:14 Moses . . . desert** When the Israelites were dying from snakebites, God told Moses to put a bronze snake on a pole. The people who looked at the snake were healed (Numbers 21:4–9).

⁹Achish answered, "I know you are as good as an angel from God. But the Philistine commanders have said, 'David must not go with us into battle.' ¹⁰Early in the morning you and your master's servants should leave. Get up as soon as it is light and go."

¹¹So David and his men got up early in the morning and went back to the country of the Philistines. And the Philistines went up to Jezreel.

David's War with the Amalekites

30 On the third day, when David and his men arrived at Ziklag, he found that the Amalekites had raided southern Judah and Ziklag, attacking Ziklag and burning it. ²They captured the women and everyone, young and old, but they had not killed anyone. They had only taken them away.

³When David and his men came to Ziklag, they found the town had been burned and their wives, sons, and daughters had been taken as prisoners. ⁴Then David and his army cried loudly until they were too weak to cry anymore. ⁵David's two wives had also been taken—Ahinoam of Jezreel and Abigail the widow of Nabal from Carmel. ⁶The men in the army were threatening to kill David with stones, which greatly upset David. Each man was sad and angry because his sons and daughters had been captured, but David found strength in the LORD his God. ⁷David said to Abiathar the priest, "Bring me the holy vest."

⁸Then David asked the LORD, "Should I chase the people who took our families? Will I catch them?"

The LORD answered, "Chase them. You will catch them, and you will succeed in saving your families."

⁹David and the six hundred men with him came to the Besor Ravine, where some of the men stayed. ¹⁰David and four hundred men kept up the chase. The other two hundred men stayed behind because they were too tired to cross the ravine.

¹¹They found an Egyptian in a field and brought him to David. They gave the Egyptian some water to drink and some food to eat. ¹²And they gave him a piece of a fig cake and two clusters of raisins. Then he felt better, because he had not eaten any food or drunk any water for three days and nights.

¹³David asked him, "Who is your master? Where do you come from?"

He answered, "I'm an Egyptian, the slave of an Amalekite. Three days ago my master left me, because I was sick. ¹⁴We had raided the southern area of the Kerethites, the land of Judah, and the southern area of Caleb. We burned Ziklag, as well."

¹⁵David asked him, "Can you lead me to the people who took our families?"

He answered, "Yes, if you promise me before God that you won't kill me or give me back to my master. Then I will take you to them."

¹⁶So the Egyptian led David to the Amalekites. They were lying around on the ground, eating and drinking and celebrating with the things they had taken from the land of the Philistines and from Judah. ¹⁷David fought them from sunset until the evening of the next day. None of them escaped, except four hundred young men who rode off on their camels. ¹⁸David got his two wives back and everything the Amalekites had taken. ¹⁹Nothing was missing. David brought back everyone, young and old, sons and daughters. He recovered the valuable things and everything the Amalekites had taken. ²⁰David took all the sheep and cattle, and his men made these animals go in front, saying, "They are David's prize."

²¹Then David came to the two hundred men who had been too tired to follow him, who had stayed at the Besor Ravine. They came out to meet David and the people with him. When he came near, David greeted the men at the ravine.

²²But the evil men and troublemakers among those who followed David said, "Since these two hundred men didn't go with us, we shouldn't give them any of the things we recovered. Just let each man take his wife and children and go."

²³David answered, "No, my brothers. Don't do that after what the LORD has given us. He has protected us and given us the enemy who attacked us. ²⁴Who will listen to what you say? The share will be the same for the one who stayed with the supplies as for the one who went into battle. All will share

alike." 25David made this an order and rule for Israel, which continues even today.

26When David arrived in Ziklag, he sent some of the things he had taken from the Amalekites to his friends, the leaders of Judah. He said, "Here is a present for you from the things we took from the LORD's enemies."

27David also sent some things to the leaders in Bethel, Ramoth in the southern part of Judah, Jattir, 28Aroer, Siphmoth, Eshtemoa, 29Racal, the cities of the Jerahmeelites and the Kenites, 30Hormah, Bor Ashan, Athach, 31Hebron, and to the people in all the other places where he and his men had been.

The Death of Saul

31 The Philistines fought against Israel, and the Israelites ran away from them. Many Israelites were killed on Mount Gilboa. 2The Philistines fought hard against Saul and his sons, killing his sons Jonathan, Abinadab, and Malki-Shua. 3The fighting was heavy around Saul. The archers shot him, and he was badly wounded. 4He said to the officer who carried his armor, "Pull out your sword and kill me. Then those uncircumcised men won't make fun of me and kill me." But Saul's officer refused, because he was afraid. So Saul took his own sword and threw himself on it. 5When the officer saw that Saul was dead, he threw himself on his own sword, and he died with Saul. 6So Saul, his three sons, and the officer who carried his armor died together that day.

7When the Israelites who lived across the Jezreel Valley and those who lived across the Jordan River saw how the Israelite army had run away, and that Saul and his sons were dead, they left their cities and ran away. Then the Philistines came and lived there.

8The next day when the Philistines came to take all the valuable things from the dead soldiers, they found Saul and his three sons dead on Mount Gilboa. 9They cut off Saul's head and took off his armor. Then they sent messengers through all the land of the Philistines to tell the news in the temple of their idols and to their people. 10They put Saul's armor in the temple of the Ashtoreths and hung his body on the wall of Beth Shan.

11When the people living in Jabesh Gilead heard what the Philistines had done to Saul, 12the brave men of Jabesh marched all night and came to Beth Shan. They removed the bodies of Saul and his sons from the wall of Beth Shan and brought them to Jabesh. There they burned the bodies. 13They took their bones and buried them under the tamarisk tree in Jabesh. Then the people of Jabesh fasted for seven days.

PSALM 61:4–8

4Let me live in your Holy Tent forever.
　Let me find safety in the shelter of your
　　wings.   *Selah*

5God, you have heard my promises.
　You have given me what belongs to
　　those who fear you.

6Give the king a long life;
　let him live many years.
7Let him rule in the presence of God
　forever.
　Protect him with your love and truth.
8Then I will praise your name forever,
　and every day I will keep my promises.

PROVERBS 16:7–9

7When people live so that they please the
　LORD,
　even their enemies will make peace
　　with them.

8It is better to be poor and right
　than to be wealthy and dishonest.

9People may make plans in their minds,
　but the LORD decides what they will
　　do.

JOHN 3:22–36

Jesus and John the Baptist

22After this, Jesus and his followers went into the area of Judea, where he stayed with his followers and baptized people. 23John was also baptizing in Aenon, near Salim, because there was plenty of water there. People were going there to be baptized. 24(This was before John was put into prison.) 25Some of John's followers had an argument with a Jew about religious washing.[n] [26]So they came to John and said, "Teacher, remember the man who was with you on the other side of the Jordan River, the one you spoke about so much? He is baptizing, and everyone is going to him."

[27]John answered, "A man can get only what God gives him. [28]You yourselves heard me say, 'I am not the Christ, but I am the one sent to prepare the way for him.' [29]The bride belongs only to the bridegroom. But the friend who helps the bridegroom stands by and listens to him. He is thrilled that he gets to hear the bridegroom's voice. In the same way, I am really happy. [30]He must become greater, and I must become less important.

The One Who Comes from Heaven

[31]"The One who comes from above is greater than all. The one who is from the earth belongs to the earth and talks about things on the earth. But the One who comes from heaven is greater than all. [32]He tells what he has seen and heard, but no one accepts what he says. [33]Whoever accepts what he says has proven that God is true. [34]The One whom God sent speaks the words of God, because God gives him the Spirit fully. [35]The Father loves the Son and has given him power over everything. [36]Those who believe in the Son have eternal life, but those who do not obey the Son will never have life. God's anger stays on them."

MAY 15

2 SAMUEL 1:1—3:1

David Learns About Saul's Death

1 Now Saul was dead. After David had defeated the Amalekites, he returned to Ziklag and stayed there two days. [2]On the third day a young man from Saul's camp came to Ziklag. To show his sadness, his clothes were torn and he had dirt on his head. He came and bowed facedown on the ground before David.

[3]David asked him, "Where did you come from?"

The man answered, "I escaped from the Israelite camp."

[4]David asked him, "What happened? Please tell me!"

The man answered, "The people have run away from the battle, and many of them have fallen and are dead. Saul and his son Jonathan are dead also."

[5]David asked him, "How do you know Saul and his son Jonathan are dead?"

[6]The young man answered, "I happened to be on Mount Gilboa. There I saw Saul leaning on his spear. The Philistine chariots and the men riding in them were coming closer to Saul. [7]When he looked back and saw me, he called to me. I answered him, 'Here I am!'

[8]"Then Saul asked me, 'Who are you?'

"I told him, 'I am an Amalekite.'

[9]"Then Saul said to me, 'Please come here and kill me. I am badly hurt and am almost dead already.'

[10]"So I went over and killed him. He had been hurt so badly I knew he couldn't live. Then I took the crown from his head and the bracelet from his arm, and I have brought them here to you, my master."

[11]Then David tore his clothes to show his sorrow, and all the men with him did also. [12]They were very sad and cried and fasted until evening. They cried for Saul and his son Jonathan and for all the people of the LORD and for all the Israelites who had died in the battle.

David Orders the Amalekite Killed

[13]David asked the young man who brought the report, "Where are you from?"

3:25 religious washing The Jewish people washed themselves in special ways before eating, before worshiping in the Temple, and at other special times.

The young man answered, "I am the son of a foreigner, an Amalekite."

[14]David asked him, "Why were you not afraid to kill the LORD's appointed king?" [15]Then David called one of his men and told him, "Go! Kill the Amalekite!" So the Israelite killed him. [16]David had said to the Amalekite, "You are responsible for your own death. You confessed by saying, 'I have killed the LORD's appointed king.'"

David's Song About Saul and Jonathan

[17]David sang a funeral song about Saul and his son Jonathan, [18]and he ordered that the people of Judah be taught this song. It is called "The Bow," and it is written in the Book of Jashar:

[19]"Israel, your leaders have been killed on
     the hills.
 How the mighty have fallen in battle!
[20]Don't tell it in Gath.
 Don't announce it in the streets of
     Ashkelon.
 If you do, the Philistine women will be
     happy.
 The daughters of the Philistines will
     rejoice.
[21]"May there be no dew or rain on the
     mountains of Gilboa,
 and may their fields produce no grain,
 because there the mighty warrior's shield
     was dishonored.
 Saul's shield will no longer be rubbed
     with oil.
[22]Jonathan's bow did not fail
     to kill many soldiers.
 Saul's sword did not fail
     to wound many strong men.
[23]"We loved Saul and Jonathan
     and enjoyed them while they lived.
 They are together even in death.
 They were faster than eagles.
 They were stronger than lions.
[24]"You daughters of Israel, cry for Saul.
 Saul clothed you with red dresses
     and put gold decorations on them.
[25]"How the mighty have fallen in battle!
 Jonathan is dead on Gilboa's hills.

[26]I cry for you, my brother Jonathan.
 I enjoyed your friendship so much.
 Your love to me was wonderful,
     better than the love of women.
[27]"How the mighty have fallen!
 The weapons of war are gone."

David Is Made King of Judah

2 Later, David prayed to the LORD, saying, "Should I go up to any of the cities of Judah?"

The LORD said to David, "Go."

David asked, "Where should I go?"

The LORD answered, "To Hebron."

[2]So David went up to Hebron with his two wives: Ahinoam from Jezreel and Abigail, the widow of Nabal from Carmel. [3]David also brought his men and their families, and they all made their homes in the cities of Hebron. [4]Then the men of Judah came to Hebron and appointed David king over Judah.

They told David that the men of Jabesh Gilead had buried Saul. [5]So David sent messengers to the men of Jabesh Gilead and said to them, "The LORD bless you. You have shown loyalty to your master Saul by burying him. [6]May the LORD now be loyal and true to you. I will also treat you well because you have done this. [7]Now be strong and brave. Saul your master is dead, and the people of Judah have appointed me their king."

War Between Judah and Israel

[8]Abner son of Ner was the commander of Saul's army. Abner took Saul's son Ish-Bosheth to Mahanaim [9]and made him king of Gilead, Ashuri, Jezreel, Ephraim, Benjamin, and all Israel. [10]Saul's son Ish-Bosheth was forty years old when he became king over Israel, and he ruled two years. But the people of Judah followed David. [11]David was king in Hebron for seven years and six months.

[12]Abner son of Ner and the servants of Ish-Bosheth son of Saul left Mahanaim and went to Gibeon. [13]Joab son of Zeruiah and David's men also went there and met Abner and Ish-Bosheth's men at the pool of Gibeon. Abner's group sat on one side of the pool; Joab's group sat on the other.

[14]Abner said to Joab, "Let the young men have a contest here."

Joab said, "Yes, let them have a contest."

¹⁵Then the men got up and were counted —twelve from the people of Benjamin for Ish-Bosheth son of Saul, and twelve from David's men. ¹⁶Each man grabbed the one opposite him by the head and stabbed him in the side with a knife. So the men fell down together. For that reason, that place in Gibeon is called the Field of Knives. ¹⁷That day there was a terrible battle, and David's men defeated Abner and the Israelites.

Abner Kills Asahel

¹⁸Zeruiah's three sons, Joab, Abishai, and Asahel, were there. Now Asahel was a fast runner, as fast as a deer in the field. ¹⁹Asahel chased Abner, going straight toward him. ²⁰Abner looked back and asked, "Is that you, Asahel?"

Asahel said, "Yes, it is."

²¹Then Abner said to Asahel, "Turn to your right or left and catch one of the young men and take his armor." But Asahel refused to stop chasing him.

²²Abner again said to Asahel, "Stop chasing me! If you don't stop, I'll have to kill you! Then I won't be able to face your brother Joab again!"

²³But Asahel refused to stop chasing Abner. So using the back end of his spear, Abner stabbed Asahel in the stomach, and the spear came out of his back. Asahel died right there, and everyone stopped when they came to the place where Asahel's body lay.

²⁴But Joab and Abishai continued chasing Abner. As the sun was going down, they arrived at the hill of Ammah, near Giah on the way to the desert near Gibeon. ²⁵The men of Benjamin came to Abner, and all stood together at the top of the hill.

²⁶Abner shouted to Joab, "Must the sword kill forever? Surely you must know this will only end in sadness! Tell the people to stop chasing their own brothers!"

²⁷Then Joab said, "As surely as God lives, if you had not said anything, the people would have chased their brothers until morning." ²⁸Then Joab blew a trumpet, and his people stopped chasing the Israelites. They did not fight them anymore.

²⁹Abner and his men marched all night through the Jordan Valley. They crossed the Jordan River, and after marching all day, arrived at Mahanaim.

³⁰After he had stopped chasing Abner, Joab came back and gathered the people together. Asahel and nineteen of David's men were missing. ³¹But David's men had killed three hundred sixty Benjaminites who had followed Abner. ³²David's men took Asahel and buried him in the tomb of his father at Bethlehem. Then Joab and his men marched all night. The sun came up as they reached Hebron.

3 There was a long war between the people who supported Saul's family and those who supported David's family. The supporters of David's family became stronger and stronger, but the supporters of Saul's family became weaker and weaker.

PSALM 62:1–4

Trust Only in God

For the director of music. For Jeduthun. A psalm of David.

62 I find rest in God;
only he can save me.
²He is my rock and my salvation.
He is my defender;
I will not be defeated.

³How long will you attack someone?
Will all of you kill that person?
Who is like a leaning wall, like a fence ready to fall?
⁴They are planning to make that person fall.
They enjoy telling lies.
With their mouths they bless,
but in their hearts they curse. *Selah*

PROVERBS 16:10–12

¹⁰The words of a king are like a message from God,
so his decisions should be fair.

¹¹The LORD wants honest balances and scales;
all the weights are his work.

¹²Kings hate those who do wrong,
because governments only continue if they are fair.

JOHN 4:1–42

Jesus and a Samaritan Woman

4 The Pharisees heard that Jesus was making and baptizing more followers than John, [2]although Jesus himself did not baptize people, but his followers did. [3]Jesus knew that the Pharisees had heard about him, so he left Judea and went back to Galilee. [4]But on the way he had to go through the country of Samaria.

[5]In Samaria Jesus came to the town called Sychar, which is near the field Jacob gave to his son Joseph. [6]Jacob's well was there. Jesus was tired from his long trip, so he sat down beside the well. It was about twelve o'clock noon. [7]When a Samaritan woman came to the well to get some water, Jesus said to her, "Please give me a drink." [8](This happened while Jesus' followers were in town buying some food.)

[9]The woman said, "I am surprised that you ask me for a drink, since you are a Jewish man and I am a Samaritan woman." (Jewish people are not friends with Samaritans.[n])

[10]Jesus said, "If you only knew the free gift of God and who it is that is asking you for water, you would have asked him, and he would have given you living water."

[11]The woman said, "Sir, where will you get this living water? The well is very deep, and you have nothing to get water with. [12]Are you greater than Jacob, our father, who gave us this well and drank from it himself along with his sons and flocks?"

[13]Jesus answered, "Everyone who drinks this water will be thirsty again, [14]but whoever drinks the water I give will never be thirsty. The water I give will become a spring of water gushing up inside that person, giving eternal life."

[15]The woman said to him, "Sir, give me this water so I will never be thirsty again and will not have to come back here to get more water."

[16]Jesus told her, "Go get your husband and come back here."

[17]The woman answered, "I have no husband."

Jesus said to her, "You are right to say you have no husband. [18]Really you have had five husbands, and the man you live with now is not your husband. You told the truth."

[19]The woman said, "Sir, I can see that you are a prophet. [20]Our ancestors worshiped on this mountain, but you say that Jerusalem is the place where people must worship."

[21]Jesus said, "Believe me, woman. The time is coming when neither in Jerusalem nor on this mountain will you actually worship the Father. [22]You Samaritans worship something you don't understand. We understand what we worship, because salvation comes from the Jews. [23]The time is coming when the true worshipers will worship the Father in spirit and truth, and that time is here already. You see, the Father too is actively seeking such people to worship him. [24]God is spirit, and those who worship him must worship in spirit and truth."

[25]The woman said, "I know that the Messiah is coming." (Messiah is the One called Christ.) "When the Messiah comes, he will explain everything to us."

[26]Then Jesus said, "I am he—I, the one talking to you."

[27]Just then his followers came back from town and were surprised to see him talking with a woman. But none of them asked, "What do you want?" or "Why are you talking with her?"

[28]Then the woman left her water jar and went back to town. She said to the people, [29]"Come and see a man who told me everything I ever did. Do you think he might be the Christ?" [30]So the people left the town and went to see Jesus.

[31]Meanwhile, his followers were begging him, "Teacher, eat something."

[32]But Jesus answered, "I have food to eat that you know nothing about."

[33]So the followers asked themselves, "Did somebody already bring him food?"

[34]Jesus said, "My food is to do what the One who sent me wants me to do and to finish his work. [35]You have a saying, 'Four more months till harvest.' But I tell you, open your eyes and look at the fields ready for harvest

---

4:9 Jewish people . . . Samaritans. This can also be translated "Jewish people don't use things that Samaritans have used."

now. [36]Already, the one who harvests is being paid and is gathering crops for eternal life. So the one who plants and the one who harvests celebrate at the same time. [37]Here the saying is true, 'One person plants, and another harvests.' [38]I sent you to harvest a crop that you did not work on. Others did the work, and you get to finish up their work."[n]

[39]Many of the Samaritans in that town believed in Jesus because of what the woman said: "He told me everything I ever did." [40]When the Samaritans came to Jesus, they begged him to stay with them, so he stayed there two more days. [41]And many more believed because of the things he said.

[42]They said to the woman, "First we believed in Jesus because of what you said, but now we believe because we heard him ourselves. We know that this man really is the Savior of the world."

MAY 16

2 SAMUEL 3:2—4:12

David's Sons

[2]Sons were born to David at Hebron. The first was Amnon, whose mother was Ahinoam from Jezreel. [3]The second son was Kileab, whose mother was Abigail, the widow of Nabal from Carmel. The third son was Absalom, whose mother was Maacah daughter of Talmai, the king of Geshur. [4]The fourth son was Adonijah, whose mother was Haggith. The fifth son was Shephatiah, whose mother was Abital. [5]The sixth son was Ithream, whose mother was Eglah, David's wife. These sons were born to David at Hebron.

Abner Joins David

[6]During the war between the supporters of Saul's family and the supporters of David's family, Abner made himself a main leader among the supporters of Saul.

[7]Saul once had a slave woman named Rizpah, who was the daughter of Aiah. Ish-Bosheth said to Abner, "Why did you have sexual relations with my father's slave woman?"

[8]Abner was very angry because of what Ish-Bosheth said, and he replied, "I have been loyal to Saul and his family and friends! I didn't hand you over to David. I am not a traitor working for Judah! But now you are saying I did something wrong with this woman! [9]May God help me if I don't join David! I will make sure that what the LORD promised does happen! [10]I will take the kingdom from the family of Saul and make David king of Israel and Judah, from Dan to Beersheba!"[n]

[11]Ish-Bosheth couldn't say anything to Abner, because he was afraid of him.

[12]Then Abner sent messengers to ask David, "Who is going to rule the land? Make an agreement with me, and I will help you unite all Israel."

[13]David answered, "Good! I will make an agreement with you, but I ask you one thing. I will not meet with you unless you bring Saul's daughter Michal to me." [14]Then David sent messengers to Saul's son Ish-Bosheth, saying, "Give me my wife Michal. She was promised to me, and I killed a hundred Philistines to get her."

[15]So Ish-Bosheth sent men to take Michal from her husband Paltiel son of Laish. [16]Michal's husband went with her, crying as he followed her to Bahurim. But Abner said to Paltiel, "Go back home." So he went home.

[17]Abner sent this message to the elders of Israel: "You have been wanting to make David your king. [18]Now do it! The LORD said of David, 'Through my servant David, I will save my people Israel from the Philistines and all their enemies.'"

[19]Abner also said these things to the people of Benjamin. He then went to Hebron to tell David what the Benjaminites and Israel

---

4:38 I . . . their work. As a farmer sends workers to harvest grain, Jesus sends his followers out to bring people to God.
• 3:10 Dan to Beersheba Dan was the city farthest north in Israel, and Beersheba was the city farthest south. So this means all the people of Israel.

wanted to do. ²⁰Abner came with twenty men to David at Hebron. There David prepared a feast for them. ²¹Abner said to David, "My master and king, I will go and bring all the Israelites to you. Then they will make an agreement with you so you will rule over all Israel as you wanted." So David let Abner go, and he left in peace.

Abner's Death

²²Just then Joab and David's men came from a battle, bringing many valuable things they had taken from the enemy. David had let Abner leave in peace, so he was not with David at Hebron. ²³When Joab and all his army arrived at Hebron, the army said to Joab, "Abner son of Ner came to King David, and David let him leave in peace."

²⁴Joab came to the king and said, "What have you done? Abner came to you. Why did you let him go? Now he's gone. ²⁵You know Abner son of Ner! He came to trick you! He came to learn about everything you are doing!"

²⁶After Joab left David, he sent messengers after Abner, and they brought him back from the well of Sirah. But David did not know this. ²⁷When Abner arrived at Hebron, Joab took him aside into the gateway. He acted as though he wanted to talk with Abner in private, but Joab stabbed him in the stomach, and Abner died. Abner had killed Joab's brother Asahel, so Joab killed Abner to pay him back.

²⁸Later when David heard the news, he said, "My kingdom and I are innocent forever of the death of Abner son of Ner. The LORD knows this. ²⁹Joab and his family are responsible for this. May his family always have someone with sores or with a skin disease. May they always have someone who must lean on a crutch. May some of his family be killed in war. May they always have someone without food to eat."

³⁰(Joab and his brother Abishai killed Abner, because he had killed their brother Asahel in the battle at Gibeon.)

³¹Then David said to Joab and to all the people with Joab, "Tear your clothes and put on rough cloth to show how sad you are. Cry for Abner." King David himself followed the body of Abner. ³²They buried Abner in Hebron, and David and all the people cried at Abner's grave.

³³King David sang this funeral song for Abner.

"Did Abner die like a fool?
³⁴ His hands were not tied.
His feet were not in chains.
He fell at the hands of evil men."

Then all the people cried again for Abner. ³⁵They came to encourage David to eat while it was still day. But he made a promise, saying, "May God punish me terribly if I eat bread or anything else before the sun sets!" ³⁶All the people saw what happened, and they agreed with what the king was doing, just as they agreed with everything he did. ³⁷That day all the people of Judah and Israel understood that David did not order the killing of Abner son of Ner. ³⁸David said to his officers, "You know that a great man died today in Israel. ³⁹Even though I am the appointed king, I feel empty. These sons of Zeruiah are too much for me. May the LORD give them the punishment they should have."

Ish-Bosheth's Death

4 When Ish-Bosheth son of Saul heard that Abner had died at Hebron, he was shocked and all Israel became frightened. ²Two men who were captains in Saul's army came to Ish-Bosheth. One was named Baanah, and the other was named Recab. They were the sons of Rimmon of Beeroth, who was a Benjaminite. (The town Beeroth belonged to the tribe of Benjamin. ³The people of Beeroth ran away to Gittaim, and they still live there as foreigners today.)

⁴(Saul's son Jonathan had a son named Mephibosheth, who was crippled in both feet. He was five years old when the news came from Jezreel that Saul and Jonathan were dead. Mephibosheth's nurse had picked him up and run away. But as she hurried to leave, she dropped him, and now he was lame.)

⁵Recab and Baanah, sons of Rimmon from Beeroth, went to Ish-Bosheth's house in the afternoon while he was taking a nap. ⁶⁻⁷They went into the middle of the house as if to get some wheat. Ish-Bosheth was lying on his bed in his bedroom. Then Recab and

Baanah stabbed him in the stomach, killed him, cut off his head, and took it with them. They escaped and traveled all night through the Jordan Valley. [8]When they arrived at Hebron, they gave his head to David and said to the king, "Here is the head of Ish-Bosheth son of Saul, your enemy. He tried to kill you! Today the LORD has paid back Saul and his family for what they did to you!"

[9]David answered Recab and his brother Baanah, the sons of Rimmon of Beeroth, "As surely as the LORD lives, he has saved me from all trouble! [10]Once a man thought he was bringing me good news. When he told me, 'Saul is dead!' I seized him and killed him at Ziklag. That was the reward I gave him for his news! [11]So even more I must put you evil men to death because you have killed an innocent man on his own bed in his own house!"

[12]So David commanded his men to kill Recab and Baanah. They cut off the hands and feet of Recab and Baanah and hung them over the pool of Hebron. Then they took Ish-Bosheth's head and buried it in Abner's tomb at Hebron.

PSALM 62:5-12

[5]I find rest in God;
  only he gives me hope.
[6]He is my rock and my salvation.
  He is my defender;
  I will not be defeated.
[7]My honor and salvation come from God.
  He is my mighty rock and my protection.

[8]People, trust God all the time.
  Tell him all your problems,
  because God is our protection.   *Selah*

[9]The least of people are only a breath,
  and even the greatest are just a lie.
  On the scales, they weigh nothing;
  together they are only a breath.
[10]Do not trust in force.
  Stealing is of no use.
  Even if you gain more riches,
  don't put your trust in them.

[11]God has said this,
  and I have heard it over and over:
  God is strong.
[12]The Lord is loving.

You reward people for what they have done.

PROVERBS 16:13-15

[13]Kings like honest people;
  they value someone who speaks the truth.

[14]An angry king can put someone to death,
  so a wise person will try to make him happy.

[15]A smiling king can give people life;
  his kindness is like a spring shower.

JOHN 4:43-54

Jesus Heals an Officer's Son

[43]Two days later, Jesus left and went to Galilee. [44](Jesus had said before that a prophet is not respected in his own country.) [45]When Jesus arrived in Galilee, the people there welcomed him. They had seen all the things he did at the Passover Feast in Jerusalem, because they had been there, too.

[46]Jesus went again to visit Cana in Galilee where he had changed the water into wine. One of the king's important officers lived in the city of Capernaum, and his son was sick. [47]When he heard that Jesus had come from Judea to Galilee, he went to Jesus and begged him to come to Capernaum and heal his son, because his son was almost dead. [48]Jesus said to him, "You people must see signs and miracles before you will believe in me."

[49]The officer said, "Sir, come before my child dies."

[50]Jesus answered, "Go. Your son will live."

The man believed what Jesus told him and went home. [51]On the way the man's servants came and met him and told him, "Your son is alive."

[52]The man asked, "What time did my son begin to get well?"

They answered, "Yesterday at one o'clock the fever left him."

[53]The father knew that one o'clock was the exact time that Jesus had said, "Your son will live." So the man and all the people who lived in his house believed in Jesus.

[54]That was the second miracle Jesus did after coming from Judea to Galilee.

MAY 17

2 SAMUEL 5:1—6:23

David Is Made King of Israel

5 Then all the tribes of Israel came to David at Hebron and said to him, "Look, we are your own family. [2] Even when Saul was king, you were the one who led Israel in battle. The LORD said to you, 'You will be a shepherd for my people Israel. You will be their leader.'"

[3] So all the elders of Israel came to King David at Hebron, and he made an agreement with them in Hebron in the presence of the LORD. Then they poured oil on David to make him king over Israel.

[4] David was thirty years old when he became king, and he ruled forty years. [5] He was king over Judah in Hebron for seven years and six months, and he was king over all Israel and Judah in Jerusalem for thirty-three years.

[6] When the king and his men went to Jerusalem to attack the Jebusites who lived there, the Jebusites said to David, "You can't get inside our city. Even the blind and the crippled can stop you." They thought David could not enter their city. [7] But David did take the city of Jerusalem with its strong walls, and it became the City of David.

[8] That day David said to his men, "To defeat the Jebusites you must go through the water tunnel. Then you can reach those 'crippled' and 'blind' enemies. This is why people say, 'The blind and the crippled may not enter the palace.'"

[9] So David lived in the strong, walled city and called it the City of David. David built more buildings around it, beginning where the land was filled in. He also built more buildings inside the city. [10] He became stronger and stronger, because the LORD God All-Powerful was with him.

[11] Hiram king of the city of Tyre sent messengers to David, along with cedar logs, carpenters, and stonecutters. They built a palace for David. [12] Then David knew that the LORD really had made him king of Israel and that the LORD had made his kingdom great because the LORD loved his people Israel.

[13] After he came from Hebron, David took for himself more slave women and wives in Jerusalem. More sons and daughters were born to David. [14] These are the names of the sons born to David in Jerusalem: Shammua, Shobab, Nathan, Solomon, [15] Ibhar, Elishua, Nepheg, Japhia, [16] Elishama, Eliada, and Eliphelet.

David Defeats the Philistines

[17] When the Philistines heard that David had been made king over Israel, all the Philistines went to look for him. But when David heard the news, he went down to the stronghold. [18] The Philistines came and camped in the Valley of Rephaim. [19] David asked the LORD, "Should I attack the Philistines? Will you hand them over to me?"

The LORD said to David, "Go! I will certainly hand them over to you."

[20] So David went to Baal Perazim and defeated the Philistines there. David said, "Like a flood of water, the LORD has broken through my enemies in front of me." So David named the place Baal Perazim.[n] [21] The Philistines left their idols behind at Baal Perazim, so David and his men carried them away.

[22] Once again the Philistines came and camped at the Valley of Rephaim. [23] When David prayed to the LORD, he answered, "Don't attack the Philistines from the front. Instead, go around and attack them in front of the balsam trees. [24] When you hear the sound of marching in the tops of the balsam trees, act quickly. I, the LORD, will have gone ahead of you to defeat the Philistine army." [25] So David did what the LORD commanded. He defeated the Philistines and chased them all the way from Gibeon to Gezer.

The Ark Is Brought to Jerusalem

6 David again gathered all the chosen men of Israel—thirty thousand of them. [2] Then he and all his people went to Baalah in Judah[n] to bring back the Ark of God. The Ark is called by the Name, the name of the LORD All-Powerful, whose throne is between the gold

---

5:20 Baal Perazim This name means "the Lord breaks through."   **6:2 Baalah in Judah** Another name for Kiriath Jearim.

creatures with wings. ³They put the Ark of God on a new cart and brought it out of Abinadab's house on the hill. Uzzah and Ahio, sons of Abinadab, led the new cart ⁴which had the Ark of God on it. Ahio was walking in front of it. ⁵David and all the Israelites were celebrating in the presence of the LORD. They were playing wooden instruments: lyres, harps, tambourines, rattles, and cymbals.

⁶When David's men came to the threshing floor of Nacon, the oxen stumbled. So Uzzah reached out to steady the Ark of God. ⁷The LORD was angry with Uzzah and killed him because of what he did. So Uzzah died there beside the Ark of God. ⁸David was angry because the LORD had killed Uzzah. Now that place is called the Punishment of Uzzah.

⁹David was afraid of the LORD that day, and he said, "How can the Ark of the LORD come to me now?" ¹⁰So David would not move the Ark of the LORD to be with him in Jerusalem. Instead, he took it to the house of Obed-Edom, a man from Gath. ¹¹The Ark of the LORD stayed in Obed-Edom's house for three months, and the LORD blessed Obed-Edom and all his family.

¹²The people told David, "The LORD has blessed the family of Obed-Edom and all that belongs to him, because the Ark of God is there." So David went and brought it up from Obed-Edom's house to Jerusalem with joy. ¹³When the men carrying the Ark of the LORD had walked six steps, David sacrificed a bull and a fat calf. ¹⁴Then David danced with all his might before the LORD. He had on a holy linen vest. ¹⁵David and all the Israelites shouted with joy and blew the trumpets as they brought the Ark of the LORD to the city.

¹⁶As the Ark of the LORD came into the city, Saul's daughter Michal looked out the window. When she saw David jumping and dancing in the presence of the LORD, she hated him.

¹⁷David put up a tent for the Ark of the LORD, and then the Israelites put it in its place inside the tent. David offered whole burnt offerings and fellowship offerings before the LORD. ¹⁸When David finished offering the whole burnt offerings and the fellowship offerings, he blessed the people in the name of the LORD All-Powerful. ¹⁹David

gave a loaf of bread, a cake of dates, and a cake of raisins to every Israelite, both men and women. Then all the people went home.

²⁰David went back to bless the people in his home, but Saul's daughter Michal came out to meet him. She said, "With what honor the king of Israel acted today! You took off your clothes in front of the servant girls of your officers like one who takes off his clothes without shame!"

²¹Then David said to Michal, "I did it in the presence of the LORD. The LORD chose me, not your father or anyone from Saul's family. The LORD appointed me to be over Israel. So I will celebrate in the presence of the LORD. ²²Maybe I will lose even more honor, and maybe I will be brought down in my own opinion, but the girls you talk about will honor me!"

²³And Saul's daughter Michal had no children to the day she died.

PSALM 63:1–11

Wishing to Be Near God

A psalm of David when he was in the desert of Judah.

63 God, you are my God.
    I search for you.
  I thirst for you
    like someone in a dry, empty land
    where there is no water.
²I have seen you in the Temple
    and have seen your strength and glory.
³Because your love is better than life,
    I will praise you.
⁴I will praise you as long as I live.
    I will lift up my hands in prayer to your
      name.
⁵I will be content as if I had eaten the best
    foods.
  My lips will sing, and my mouth will
    praise you.

⁶I remember you while I'm lying in bed;
    I think about you through the night.
⁷You are my help.
  Because of your protection, I sing.
⁸I stay close to you;
    you support me with your right hand.

⁹Some people are trying to kill me,
    but they will go down to the grave.

[10]They will be killed with swords
  and eaten by wild dogs.
[11]But the king will rejoice in his God.
  All who make promises in his name
    will praise him,
  but the mouths of liars will be shut.

PROVERBS 16:16–17

[16]It is better to get wisdom than gold,
  and to choose understanding rather
    than silver!

[17]Good people stay away from evil.
  By watching what they do, they protect
    their lives.

JOHN 5:1–18

Jesus Heals a Man at a Pool

5 Later Jesus went to Jerusalem for a special feast. [2]In Jerusalem there is a pool with five covered porches, which is called Bethesda[n] in the Hebrew language.[n] This pool is near the Sheep Gate. [3]Many sick people were lying on the porches beside the pool. Some were blind, some were crippled, and some were paralyzed [, and they waited for the water to move. [4]Sometimes an angel of the Lord came down to the pool and stirred up the water. After the angel did this, the first person to go into the pool was healed from any sickness he had].[n] [5]A man was lying there who had been sick for thirty-eight years. [6]When Jesus saw the man and knew that he had been sick for such a long time, Jesus asked him, "Do you want to be well?"

[7]The sick man answered, "Sir, there is no one to help me get into the pool when the water starts moving. While I am coming to the water, someone else always gets in before me."

[8]Then Jesus said, "Stand up. Pick up your mat and walk." [9]And immediately the man was well; he picked up his mat and began to walk.

The day this happened was a Sabbath day. [10]So the Jews said to the man who had been healed, "Today is the Sabbath. It is against our law for you to carry your mat on the Sabbath day."

[11]But he answered, "The man who made me well told me, 'Pick up your mat and walk.'"

[12]Then they asked him, "Who is the man who told you to pick up your mat and walk?"

[13]But the man who had been healed did not know who it was, because there were many people in that place, and Jesus had left.

[14]Later, Jesus found the man at the Temple and said to him, "See, you are well now. Stop sinning so that something worse does not happen to you."

[15]Then the man left and told his people that Jesus was the one who had made him well.

[16]Because Jesus was doing this on the Sabbath day, some evil people began to persecute him. [17]But Jesus said to them, "My Father never stops working, and so I keep working, too."

[18]This made them try still harder to kill him. They said, "First Jesus was breaking the law about the Sabbath day. Now he says that God is his own Father, making himself equal with God!"

MAY 18

2 SAMUEL 7:1–8:18

David Wants to Build a Temple

7 King David was living in his palace, and the LORD had given him peace from all his enemies around him. [2]Then David said to Nathan the prophet, "Look, I am living in a palace made of cedar wood, but the Ark of God is in a tent!"

[3]Nathan said to the king, "Go and do what

you really want to do, because the LORD is with you."

⁴But that night the LORD spoke his word to Nathan, ⁵"Go and tell my servant David, 'This is what the LORD says: Will you build a house for me to live in? ⁶From the time I brought the Israelites out of Egypt until now I have not lived in a house. I have been moving around all this time with a tent as my home. ⁷As I have moved with the Israelites, I have never said to the tribes, whom I commanded to take care of my people Israel, "Why haven't you built me a house of cedar?"'

⁸"You must tell my servant David, 'This is what the LORD All-Powerful says: I took you from the pasture and from tending the sheep and made you leader of my people Israel. ⁹I have been with you everywhere you have gone and have defeated your enemies for you. I will make you as famous as any of the great people on the earth. ¹⁰Also I will choose a place for my people Israel, and I will plant them so they can live in their own homes. They will not be bothered anymore. Wicked people will no longer bother them as they have in the past ¹¹when I chose judges for my people Israel. But I will give you peace from all your enemies. I also tell you that I will make your descendants kings of Israel after you.

¹²"'When you die and join your ancestors, I will make one of your sons the next king, and I will set up his kingdom. ¹³He will build a house for me, and I will let his kingdom rule always. ¹⁴I will be his father, and he will be my son. When he sins, I will use other people to punish him. They will be my whips. ¹⁵I took away my love from Saul, whom I removed before you, but I will never stop loving your son. ¹⁶But your family and your kingdom will continue always before me. Your throne will last forever.'"

¹⁷Nathan told David everything God had said in this vision.

David Prays to God

¹⁸Then King David went in and sat in front of the LORD. David said, "Lord GOD, who am I? What is my family? Why did you bring me to this point? ¹⁹But even this is not enough for you, Lord GOD. You have also made promises about my future family. This is extraordinary, Lord GOD.

²⁰"What more can I say to you, Lord GOD, since you know me, your servant, so well! ²¹You have done this great thing because you said you would and because you wanted to, and you have let me know about it. ²²This is why you are great, Lord GOD! There is no one like you. There is no God except you. We have heard all this ourselves! ²³There is no nation like your people Israel. They are the only people on earth that God chose to be his own. You made your name well known. You did great and wonderful miracles for them. You went ahead of them and forced other nations and their gods out of the land. You freed your people from slavery in Egypt. ²⁴You made the people of Israel your very own people forever, and, LORD, you are their God.

²⁵"Now, LORD God, keep the promise forever that you made about my family and me, your servant. Do what you have said. ²⁶Then you will be honored always, and people will say, 'The LORD All-Powerful is God over Israel!' And the family of your servant David will continue before you.

²⁷"LORD All-Powerful, the God of Israel, you have said to me, 'I will make your family great.' So I, your servant, am brave enough to pray to you. ²⁸Lord GOD, you are God, and your words are true. And you have promised these good things to me, your servant. ²⁹Please, bless my family. Let it continue before you always. Lord GOD, you have said so. With your blessing let my family always be blessed."

David Wins Many Wars

8 Later, David defeated the Philistines, conquered them, and took the city of Metheg Ammah.

²He also defeated the people of Moab. He made them lie on the ground, and then he used a rope to measure them. Those who were measured within two rope lengths were killed, but those who were within the next rope length were allowed to live. So the people of Moab became servants of David and gave him the payment he demanded.

³David also defeated Hadadezer son of Rehob, king of Zobah, as he went to take control again at the Euphrates River. ⁴David captured one thousand chariots, seven thousand men who rode in chariots, and twenty thousand foot soldiers. He crippled all but a hundred of the chariot horses.

⁵Arameans from Damascus came to help Hadadezer king of Zobah, but David killed twenty-two thousand of them. ⁶Then David put groups of soldiers in Damascus in Aram. The Arameans became David's servants and gave him the payment he demanded. The LORD gave David victory everywhere he went.

⁷David took the shields of gold that had belonged to Hadadezer's officers and brought them to Jerusalem. ⁸David also took many things made of bronze from Tebah and Berothai, which had been cities under Hadadezer's control.

⁹Toi king of Hamath heard that David had defeated all the army of Hadadezer. ¹⁰So Toi sent his son Joram to greet and congratulate King David for defeating Hadadezer. (Hadadezer had been at war with Toi.) Joram brought items made of silver, gold, and bronze. ¹¹King David gave them to the LORD, along with the silver and gold he had taken from the other nations he had defeated. ¹²These nations were Edom, Moab, Ammon, Philistia, and Amalek. David also gave the LORD what he had taken from Hadadezer son of Rehob, king of Zobah.

¹³David was famous after he returned from defeating eighteen thousand Arameans in the Valley of Salt. ¹⁴He put groups of soldiers all over Edom, and all the Edomites became his servants. The LORD gave David victory everywhere he went.

¹⁵David was king over all Israel, and he did what was fair and right for all his people. ¹⁶Joab son of Zeruiah was commander over the army. Jehoshaphat son of Ahilud was the recorder. ¹⁷Zadok son of Ahitub and Abiathar son of Ahimelech were priests. Seraiah was the royal secretary. ¹⁸Benaiah son of Jehoiada was over the Kerethites and Pelethites.ⁿ And David's sons were priests.

PSALM 64:1–10

A Prayer Against Enemies

For the director of music. A psalm of David.

64 God, listen to my complaint.
I am afraid of my enemies;
protect my life from them.
²Hide me from those who plan wicked things,
from that gang who does evil.
³They sharpen their tongues like swords
and shoot bitter words like arrows.
⁴From their hiding places they shoot at innocent people;
they shoot suddenly and are not afraid.
⁵They encourage each other to do wrong.
They talk about setting traps,
thinking no one will see them.
⁶They plan wicked things and say,
"We have a perfect plan."
The mind of human beings is hard to understand.

⁷But God will shoot them with arrows;
they will suddenly be struck down.
⁸Their own words will be used against them.
All who see them will shake their heads.
⁹Then everyone will fear God.
They will tell what God has done,
and they will learn from what he has done.
¹⁰Good people will be happy in the LORD
and will find protection in him.
Let everyone who is honest praise the LORD.

PROVERBS 16:18–19

¹⁸Pride leads to destruction;
a proud attitude brings ruin.

¹⁹It is better to be humble and be with those who suffer
than to share stolen property with the proud.

8:18 Kerethites and Pelethites These were probably special units of the army that were responsible for the king's safety, a kind of palace guard.

JOHN 5:19–47

Jesus Has God's Authority

¹⁹But Jesus said, "I tell you the truth, the Son can do nothing alone. The Son does only what he sees the Father doing, because the Son does whatever the Father does. ²⁰The Father loves the Son and shows the Son all the things he himself does. But the Father will show the Son even greater things than this so that you can all be amazed. ²¹Just as the Father raises the dead and gives them life, so also the Son gives life to those he wants to. ²²In fact, the Father judges no one, but he has given the Son power to do all the judging ²³so that all people will honor the Son as much as they honor the Father. Anyone who does not honor the Son does not honor the Father who sent him.

²⁴"I tell you the truth, whoever hears what I say and believes in the One who sent me has eternal life. That person will not be judged guilty but has already left death and entered life. ²⁵I tell you the truth, the time is coming and is already here when the dead will hear the voice of the Son of God, and those who hear will have life. ²⁶Life comes from the Father himself, and he has allowed the Son to have life in himself as well. ²⁷And the Father has given the Son the approval to judge, because he is the Son of Man. ²⁸Don't be surprised at this: A time is coming when all who are dead and in their graves will hear his voice. ²⁹Then they will come out of their graves. Those who did good will rise and have life forever, but those who did evil will rise to be judged guilty.

Jesus Is God's Son

³⁰"I can do nothing alone. I judge only the way I am told, so my judgment is fair. I don't try to please myself, but I try to please the One who sent me.

³¹"If only I tell people about myself, what I say is not true. ³²But there is another who tells about me, and I know that the things he says about me are true.

³³"You have sent people to John, and he has told you the truth. ³⁴It is not that I need what humans say; I tell you this so you can be saved. ³⁵John was like a burning and shining lamp, and you were happy to enjoy his light for a while.

³⁶"But I have a proof about myself that is greater than that of John. The things I do, which are the things my Father gave me to do, prove that the Father sent me. ³⁷And the Father himself who sent me has given proof about me. You have never heard his voice or seen what he looks like. ³⁸His teaching does not live in you, because you don't believe in the One the Father sent. ³⁹You carefully study the Scriptures because you think they give you eternal life. They do in fact tell about me, ⁴⁰but you refuse to come to me to have that life.

⁴¹"I don't need praise from people. ⁴²But I know you—I know that you don't have God's love in you. ⁴³I have come from my Father and speak for him, but you don't accept me. But when another person comes, speaking only for himself, you will accept him. ⁴⁴You try to get praise from each other, but you do not try to get the praise that comes from the only God. So how can you believe? ⁴⁵Don't think that I will stand before the Father and say you are wrong. The one who says you are wrong is Moses, the one you hoped would save you. ⁴⁶If you really believed Moses, you would believe me, because Moses wrote about me. ⁴⁷But if you don't believe what Moses wrote, how can you believe what I say?"

MAY 19

2 SAMUEL 9:1—10:19

David Helps Saul's Family

9David asked, "Is anyone still left in Saul's family? I want to show kindness to that person for Jonathan's sake!"

²Now there was a servant named Ziba from Saul's family. So David's servants called Ziba to him. King David said to him, "Are you Ziba?"

He answered, "Yes, I am your servant."

³The king asked, "Is anyone left in Saul's

family? I want to show God's kindness to that person."

Ziba answered the king, "Jonathan has a son still living who is crippled in both feet."

[4]The king asked Ziba, "Where is this son?"

Ziba answered, "He is at the house of Makir son of Ammiel in Lo Debar."

[5]Then King David had servants bring Jonathan's son from the house of Makir son of Ammiel in Lo Debar. [6]Mephibosheth, Jonathan's son, came before David and bowed facedown on the floor.

David said, "Mephibosheth!"

Mephibosheth said, "I am your servant."

[7]David said to him, "Don't be afraid. I will be kind to you for your father Jonathan's sake. I will give you back all the land of your grandfather Saul, and you will always eat at my table."

[8]Mephibosheth bowed to David again and said, "You are being very kind to me, your servant! And I am no better than a dead dog!"

[9]Then King David called Saul's servant Ziba. David said to him, "I have given your master's grandson everything that belonged to Saul and his family. [10]You, your sons, and your servants will farm the land and harvest the crops. Then your family will have food to eat. But Mephibosheth, your master's grandson, will always eat at my table."

(Now Ziba had fifteen sons and twenty servants.) [11]Ziba said to King David, "I, your servant, will do everything my master, the king, commands me."

So Mephibosheth ate at David's table as if he were one of the king's sons. [12]Mephibosheth had a young son named Mica. Everyone in Ziba's family became Mephibosheth's servants. [13]Mephibosheth lived in Jerusalem, because he always ate at the king's table. And he was crippled in both feet.

War with the Ammonites and Arameans

10 When Nahash king of the Ammonites died, his son Hanun became king after him. [2]David said, "Nahash was loyal to me, so I will be loyal to his son Hanun." So David sent his messengers to comfort Hanun about his father's death.

David's officers went to the land of the Ammonites. [3]But the Ammonite leaders said to Hanun, their master, "Do you think David wants to honor your father by sending men to comfort you? No! David sent them to study the city and spy it out and capture it!" [4]So Hanun arrested David's officers. To shame them he shaved off half their beards and cut off their clothes at the hips. Then he sent them away.

[5]When the people told David, he sent messengers to meet his officers because they were very ashamed. King David said, "Stay in Jericho until your beards have grown back. Then come home."

[6]The Ammonites knew that they had insulted David. So they hired twenty thousand Aramean foot soldiers from Beth Rehob and Zobah. They also hired the king of Maacah with a thousand men and twelve thousand men from Tob.

[7]When David heard about this, he sent Joab with the whole army. [8]The Ammonites came out and prepared for battle at the city gate. The Arameans from Zobah and Rehob and the men from Tob and Maacah were out in the field by themselves.

[9]Joab saw that there were enemies both in front of him and behind him. So he chose some of the best soldiers of Israel and sent them out to fight the Arameans. [10]Joab put the rest of the army under the command of Abishai, his brother. Then he sent them out to fight the Ammonites. [11]Joab said to Abishai, "If the Arameans are too strong for me, you must help me. Or, if the Ammonites are too strong for you, I will help you. [12]Be strong. We must fight bravely for our people and the cities of our God. The LORD will do what he thinks is right."

[13]Then Joab and the army with him went to attack the Arameans, and the Arameans ran away. [14]When the Ammonites saw that the Arameans were running away, they also ran away from Abishai and went back to their city. So Joab returned from the battle with the Ammonites and came to Jerusalem. [15]When the Arameans saw that Israel had

defeated them, they came together into one big army. [16]Hadadezer sent messengers to bring the Arameans from east of the Euphrates River, and they went to Helam. Their leader was Shobach, the commander of Hadadezer's army.

[17]When David heard about this, he gathered all the Israelites together. They crossed over the Jordan River and went to Helam. There the Arameans prepared for battle and attacked him. [18]But the Arameans ran away from the Israelites. David killed seven hundred Aramean chariot drivers and forty thousand Aramean horsemen. He also killed Shobach, the commander of the Aramean army.

[19]When the kings who served Hadadezer saw that the Israelites had defeated them, they made peace with the Israelites and served them. And the Arameans were afraid to help the Ammonites again.

PSALM 65:1–8

A Hymn of Thanksgiving

For the director of music. A psalm of David. A song.

65 God, you will be praised in Jerusalem. We will keep our promises to you.
[2]You hear our prayers.
  All people will come to you.
[3]Our guilt overwhelms us,
  but you forgive our sins.
[4]Happy are the people you choose
  and invite to stay in your court.
  We are filled with good things in your house,
  your holy Temple.

[5]You answer us in amazing ways,
  God our Savior.
  People everywhere on the earth
  and beyond the sea trust you.
[6]You made the mountains by your strength;
  you are dressed in power.
[7]You stopped the roaring seas,
  the roaring waves,
  and the uproar of the nations.
[8]Even those people at the ends of the earth fear your miracles.

You are praised from where the sun rises to where it sets.

PROVERBS 16:20–21

[20]Whoever listens to what is taught will succeed,
  and whoever trusts the LORD will be happy.

[21]The wise are known for their understanding.
  Their pleasant words make them better teachers.

JOHN 6:1–21

More than Five Thousand Fed

6 After this, Jesus went across Lake Galilee (or, Lake Tiberias). [2]Many people followed him because they saw the miracles he did to heal the sick. [3]Jesus went up on a hill and sat down there with his followers. [4]It was almost the time for the Jewish Passover Feast.

[5]When Jesus looked up and saw a large crowd coming toward him, he said to Philip, "Where can we buy enough bread for all these people to eat?" [6](Jesus asked Philip this question to test him, because Jesus already knew what he planned to do.)

[7]Philip answered, "Someone would have to work almost a year to buy enough bread for each person to have only a little piece."

[8]Another one of his followers, Andrew, Simon Peter's brother, said, [9]"Here is a boy with five loaves of barley bread and two little fish, but that is not enough for so many people."

[10]Jesus said, "Tell the people to sit down." There was plenty of grass there, and about five thousand men sat down there. [11]Then Jesus took the loaves of bread, thanked God for them, and gave them to the people who were sitting there. He did the same with the fish, giving as much as the people wanted.

[12]When they had all had enough to eat, Jesus said to his followers, "Gather the leftover pieces of fish and bread so that nothing is wasted." [13]So they gathered up the pieces and filled twelve baskets with the pieces left from the five barley loaves.

¹⁴When the people saw this miracle that Jesus did, they said, "He must truly be the Prophet[n] who is coming into the world."

¹⁵Jesus knew that the people planned to come and take him by force and make him their king, so he left and went into the hills alone.

Jesus Walks on the Water

¹⁶That evening Jesus' followers went down to Lake Galilee. ¹⁷It was dark now, and Jesus had not yet come to them. The followers got into a boat and started across the lake to Capernaum. ¹⁸By now a strong wind was blowing, and the waves on the lake were getting bigger. ¹⁹When they had rowed the boat about three or four miles, they saw Jesus walking on the water, coming toward the boat. The followers were afraid, ²⁰but Jesus said to them, "It is I. Do not be afraid." ²¹Then they were glad to take him into the boat. At once the boat came to land at the place where they wanted to go.

MAY 20

2 SAMUEL 11:1—12:31

David Sins with Bathsheba

11 In the spring, when the kings normally went out to war, David sent out Joab, his servants, and all the Israelites. They destroyed the Ammonites and attacked the city of Rabbah. But David stayed in Jerusalem. ²One evening David got up from his bed and walked around on the roof[n] of his palace. While he was on the roof, he saw a woman bathing. She was very beautiful. ³So David sent his servants to find out who she was. A servant answered, "That woman is Bathsheba daughter of Eliam. She is the wife of Uriah the Hittite." ⁴So David sent messengers to bring Bathsheba to him. When she came to him, he had sexual relations with her. (Now Bathsheba had purified herself from her monthly period.) Then she went back to her house. ⁵But Bathsheba became pregnant and sent word to David, saying, "I am pregnant."

⁶So David sent a message to Joab: "Send Uriah the Hittite to me." And Joab sent Uriah to David. ⁷When Uriah came to him, David asked him how Joab was, how the soldiers were, and how the war was going. ⁸Then David said to Uriah, "Go home and rest."

So Uriah left the palace, and the king sent a gift to him. ⁹But Uriah did not go home. Instead, he slept outside the door of the palace as all the king's officers did.

¹⁰The officers told David, "Uriah did not go home."

Then David said to Uriah, "You came from a long trip. Why didn't you go home?"

¹¹Uriah said to him, "The Ark and the soldiers of Israel and Judah are staying in tents. My master Joab and his officers are camping out in the fields. It isn't right for me to go home to eat and drink and have sexual relations with my wife!"

¹²David said to Uriah, "Stay here today. Tomorrow I'll send you back to the battle." So Uriah stayed in Jerusalem that day and the next. ¹³Then David called Uriah to come to see him, so Uriah ate and drank with David. David made Uriah drunk, but he still did not go home. That evening Uriah again slept with the king's officers.

¹⁴The next morning David wrote a letter to Joab and sent it by Uriah. ¹⁵In the letter David wrote, "Put Uriah on the front lines where the fighting is worst and leave him there alone. Let him be killed in battle."

¹⁶Joab watched the city and saw where its strongest defenders were and put Uriah there. ¹⁷When the men of the city came out to fight

6:14 Prophet They probably meant the prophet that God told Moses he would send (Deuteronomy 18:15–19). • **11:2 roof** In Bible times houses were built with flat roofs. The roof was used for drying things such as flax and fruit. And it was used as an extra room, as a place for worship, and as a cool place to sleep in the summer.

against Joab, some of David's men were killed. And Uriah the Hittite was one of them.

¹⁸Then Joab sent David a complete account of the war. ¹⁹Joab told the messenger, "Tell King David what happened in the war. ²⁰After you finish, the king may be angry and ask, 'Why did you go so near the city to fight? Didn't you know they would shoot arrows from the city wall? ²¹Do you remember who killed Abimelech son of Jerub-Besheth?ⁿ It was a woman on the city wall. She threw a large stone for grinding grain on Abimelech and killed him there in Thebez. Why did you go so near the wall?' If King David asks that, tell him, 'Your servant Uriah the Hittite also died.'"

²²The messenger left and went to David and told him everything Joab had told him to say. ²³The messenger told David, "The men of Ammon were winning. They came out and attacked us in the field, but we fought them back to the city gate. ²⁴The archers on the city wall shot at your servants, and some of your men were killed. Your servant Uriah the Hittite also died."

²⁵David said to the messenger, "Say this to Joab: 'Don't be upset about this. The sword kills everyone the same. Make a stronger attack against the city and capture it.' Encourage Joab with these words."

²⁶When Bathsheba heard that her husband was dead, she cried for him. ²⁷After she finished her time of sadness, David sent servants to bring her to his house. She became David's wife and gave birth to his son, but the LORD did not like what David had done.

David's Son Dies

12 The LORD sent Nathan to David. When he came to David, he said, "There were two men in a city. One was rich, but the other was poor. ²The rich man had many sheep and cattle. ³But the poor man had nothing except one little female lamb he had bought. The poor man fed the lamb, and it grew up with him and his children. It shared his food and drank from his cup and slept in his arms. The lamb was like a daughter to him. ⁴Then a traveler stopped to visit the rich man. The rich man wanted to feed the traveler, but he didn't want to take one of his own sheep or cattle. Instead, he took the lamb from the poor man and cooked it for his visitor."

⁵David became very angry at the rich man. He said to Nathan, "As surely as the LORD lives, the man who did this should die! ⁶He must pay for the lamb four times for doing such a thing. He had no mercy!"

⁷Then Nathan said to David, "You are the man! This is what the LORD, the God of Israel, says: 'I appointed you king of Israel and saved you from Saul. ⁸I gave you his kingdom and his wives. And I made you king of Israel and Judah. And if that had not been enough, I would have given you even more. ⁹So why did you ignore the LORD's command? Why did you do what he says is wrong? You killed Uriah the Hittite with the sword of the Ammonites and took his wife to be your wife! ¹⁰Now there will always be people in your family who will die by a sword, because you did not respect me; you took the wife of Uriah the Hittite for yourself.'

¹¹"This is what the LORD says: 'I am bringing trouble to you from your own family. While you watch, I will take your wives from you and give them to someone who is very close to you. He will have sexual relations with your wives, and everyone will know it. ¹²You had sexual relations with Bathsheba in secret, but I will do this so all the people of Israel can see it.'"

¹³Then David said to Nathan, "I have sinned against the LORD."

Nathan answered, "The LORD has taken away your sin. You will not die. ¹⁴But what you did caused the LORD's enemies to lose all respect for him. For this reason the son who was born to you will die."

¹⁵Then Nathan went home. And the LORD caused the son of David and Bathsheba, Uriah's widow, to be very sick. ¹⁶David prayed to God for the baby. David fasted and went into his house and stayed there, lying on the ground all night. ¹⁷The elders of David's family came to him and tried to pull him up from the ground, but he refused to get up or to eat food with them.

11:21 Jerub-Besheth Another name for Gideon.

[18]On the seventh day the baby died. David's servants were afraid to tell him that the baby was dead. They said, "Look, we tried to talk to David while the baby was alive, but he refused to listen to us. If we tell him the baby is dead, he may do something awful."

[19]When David saw his servants whispering, he knew that the baby was dead. So he asked them, "Is the baby dead?"

They answered, "Yes, he is dead."

[20]Then David got up from the floor, washed himself, put lotions on, and changed his clothes. Then he went into the LORD's house to worship. After that, he went home and asked for something to eat. His servants gave him some food, and he ate.

[21]David's servants said to him, "Why are you doing this? When the baby was still alive, you fasted and you cried. Now that the baby is dead, you get up and eat food."

[22]David said, "While the baby was still alive, I fasted, and I cried. I thought, 'Who knows? Maybe the LORD will feel sorry for me and let the baby live.' [23]But now that the baby is dead, why should I fast? I can't bring him back to life. Someday I will go to him, but he cannot come back to me."

[24]Then David comforted Bathsheba his wife. He slept with her and had sexual relations with her. She became pregnant again and had another son, whom David named Solomon. The LORD loved Solomon. [25]The LORD sent word through Nathan the prophet to name the baby Jedidiah,[n] because the LORD loved the child.

David Captures Rabbah

[26]Joab fought against Rabbah, a royal city of the Ammonites, and he was about to capture it. [27]Joab sent messengers to David and said, "I have fought against Rabbah and have captured its water supply. [28]Now bring the other soldiers together and attack this city. Capture it before I capture it myself and it is called by my name!"

[29]So David gathered all the army and went to Rabbah and fought against it and captured it. [30]David took the crown off their king's head and had it placed on his own head. That gold crown weighed about sev-enty-five pounds, and it had valuable gems in it. And David took many valuable things from the city. [31]He also brought out the people of the city and forced them to work with saws, iron picks, and axes. He also made them build with bricks. David did this to all the Ammonite cities. Then David and all his army returned to Jerusalem.

PSALM 65:9–13

[9]You take care of the land and water it;
  you make it very fertile.
The rivers of God are full of water.
  Grain grows because you make it grow.
[10]You send rain to the plowed fields;
  you fill the rows with water.
You soften the ground with rain,
  and then you bless it with crops.
[11]You give the year a good harvest,
  and you load the wagons with many
    crops.
[12]The desert is covered with grass
  and the hills with happiness.
[13]The pastures are full of flocks,
  and the valleys are covered with grain.
Everything shouts and sings for joy.

PROVERBS 16:22–24

[22]Understanding is like a fountain which
    gives life to those who use it,
  but foolishness brings punishment to
    fools.

[23]Wise people's minds tell them what to
    say,
  and that helps them be better
    teachers.

[24]Pleasant words are like a honeycomb,
  making people happy and healthy.

JOHN 6:22–59

The People Seek Jesus

[22]The next day the people who had stayed on the other side of the lake knew that Jesus had not gone in the boat with his followers but that they had left without him. And they knew that only one boat had been there. [23]But then some boats came from Tiberias and landed

near the place where the people had eaten the bread after the Lord had given thanks. [24]When the people saw that Jesus and his followers were not there now, they got into boats and went to Capernaum to find Jesus.

Jesus, the Bread of Life

[25]When the people found Jesus on the other side of the lake, they asked him, "Teacher, when did you come here?"

[26]Jesus answered, "I tell you the truth, you aren't looking for me because you saw me do miracles. You are looking for me because you ate the bread and were satisfied. [27]Don't work for the food that spoils. Work for the food that stays good always and gives eternal life. The Son of Man will give you this food, because on him God the Father has put his power."

[28]The people asked Jesus, "What are the things God wants us to do?"

[29]Jesus answered, "The work God wants you to do is this: Believe the One he sent."

[30]So the people asked, "What miracle will you do? If we see a miracle, we will believe you. What will you do? [31]Our ancestors ate the manna in the desert. This is written in the Scriptures: 'He gave them bread from heaven to eat.'"[n]

[32]Jesus said, "I tell you the truth, it was not Moses who gave you bread from heaven; it is my Father who is giving you the true bread from heaven. [33]God's bread is the One who comes down from heaven and gives life to the world."

[34]The people said, "Sir, give us this bread always."

[35]Then Jesus said, "I am the bread that gives life. Whoever comes to me will never be hungry, and whoever believes in me will never be thirsty. [36]But as I told you before, you have seen me and still don't believe. [37]The Father gives me the people who are mine. Every one of them will come to me, and I will always accept them. [38]I came down from heaven to do what God wants me to do, not what I want to do. [39]Here is what the One who sent me wants me to do: I must not lose even one whom God gave me, but I must raise them all on the last day. [40]Those who

see the Son and believe in him have eternal life, and I will raise them on the last day. This is what my Father wants."

[41]Some people began to complain about Jesus because he said, "I am the bread that comes down from heaven." [42]They said, "This is Jesus, the son of Joseph. We know his father and mother. How can he say, 'I came down from heaven'?"

[43]But Jesus answered, "Stop complaining to each other. [44]The Father is the One who sent me. No one can come to me unless the Father draws him to me, and I will raise that person up on the last day. [45]It is written in the prophets, 'They will all be taught by God.'[n] Everyone who listens to the Father and learns from him comes to me. [46]No one has seen the Father except the One who is from God; only he has seen the Father. [47]I tell you the truth, whoever believes has eternal life. [48]I am the bread that gives life. [49]Your ancestors ate the manna in the desert, but still they died. [50]Here is the bread that comes down from heaven. Anyone who eats this bread will never die. [51]I am the living bread that came down from heaven. Anyone who eats this bread will live forever. This bread is my flesh, which I will give up so that the world may have life."

[52]Then the evil people began to argue among themselves, saying, "How can this man give us his flesh to eat?"

[53]Jesus said, "I tell you the truth, you must eat the flesh of the Son of Man and drink his blood. Otherwise, you won't have real life in you. [54]Those who eat my flesh and drink my blood have eternal life, and I will raise them up on the last day. [55]My flesh is true food, and my blood is true drink. [56]Those who eat my flesh and drink my blood live in me, and I live in them. [57]The living Father sent me, and I live because of the Father. So whoever eats me will live because of me. [58]I am not like the bread your ancestors ate. They ate that bread and still died. I am the bread that came down from heaven, and whoever eats this bread will live forever." [59]Jesus said all these things while he was teaching in the synagogue in Capernaum.

6:31 'He gave . . . eat.' Quotation from Psalm 78:24. **6:45 'They . . . God.'** Quotation from Isaiah 54:13.

MAY 21

Amnon and Tamar

13 David had a son named Absalom and a son named Amnon. Absalom had a beautiful sister named Tamar, and Amnon loved her. ²Tamar was a virgin. Amnon made himself sick just thinking about her, because he could not find any chance to be alone with her.

³Amnon had a friend named Jonadab son of Shimeah, David's brother. Jonadab was a very clever man. ⁴He asked Amnon, "Son of the king, why do you look so sad day after day? Tell me what's wrong!"

Amnon told him, "I love Tamar, the sister of my half-brother Absalom."

⁵Jonadab said to Amnon, "Go to bed and act as if you are sick. Then your father will come to see you. Tell him, 'Please let my sister Tamar come in and give me food to eat. Let her make the food in front of me so I can watch and eat it from her hand.'"

⁶So Amnon went to bed and acted sick. When King David came in to see him, Amnon said to him, "Please let my sister Tamar come in. Let her make two of her special cakes for me while I watch. Then I will eat them from her hands."

⁷David sent for Tamar in the palace, saying, "Go to your brother Amnon's house and make some food for him." ⁸So Tamar went to her brother Amnon's house, and he was in bed. Tamar took some dough and pressed it together with her hands. She made some special cakes while Amnon watched. Then she baked them. ⁹Next she took the pan and served him, but he refused to eat.

He said to his servants, "All of you, leave me alone!" So they all left him alone. ¹⁰Amnon said to Tamar, "Bring the food into the bedroom so I may eat from your hand."

Tamar took the cakes she had made and brought them to her brother Amnon in the bedroom. ¹¹She went to him so he could eat from her hands, but Amnon grabbed her. He said, "Sister, come and have sexual relations with me."

¹²Tamar said to him, "No, brother! Don't force me! This should never be done in Israel! Don't do this shameful thing! ¹³I could never get rid of my shame! And you will be like the shameful fools in Israel! Please talk with the king, and he will let you marry me."

¹⁴But Amnon refused to listen to her. He was stronger than she was, so he forced her to have sexual relations with him. ¹⁵After that, Amnon hated Tamar. He hated her more than he had loved her before. Amnon said to her, "Get up and leave!"

¹⁶Tamar said to him, "No! Sending me away would be worse than what you've already done!"

But he refused to listen to her. ¹⁷He called his young servant back in and said, "Get this woman out of here and away from me! Lock the door after her." ¹⁸So his servant led her out of the room and bolted the door after her.

Tamar was wearing a special robe with long sleeves, because the king's virgin daughters wore this kind of robe. ¹⁹To show how upset she was, Tamar put ashes on her head and tore her special robe and put her hand on her head. Then she went away, crying loudly.

²⁰Absalom, Tamar's brother, said to her, "Has Amnon, your brother, forced you to have sexual relations with him? For now, sister, be quiet. He is your half-brother. Don't let this upset you so much!" So Tamar lived in her brother Absalom's house and was sad and lonely.

²¹When King David heard the news, he was very angry. ²²Absalom did not say a word, good or bad, to Amnon. But he hated Amnon for disgracing his sister Tamar.

Absalom's Revenge

²³Two years later Absalom had some men come to Baal Hazor, near Ephraim, to cut the wool from his sheep. Absalom invited all the king's sons to come also. ²⁴Absalom went to the king and said, "I have men coming to cut the wool. Please come with your officers and join me."

²⁵King David said to Absalom, "No, my

son. We won't all go, because it would be too much trouble for you." Although Absalom begged David, he would not go, but he did give his blessing.

²⁶Absalom said, "If you don't want to come, then please let my brother Amnon come with us."

King David asked, "Why should he go with you?"

²⁷Absalom kept begging David until he let Amnon and all the king's sons go with Absalom.

²⁸Then Absalom instructed his servants, "Watch Amnon. When he is drunk, I will tell you, 'Kill Amnon.' Right then, kill him! Don't be afraid, because I have commanded you! Be strong and brave!" ²⁹So Absalom's young men killed Amnon as Absalom commanded, but all of David's other sons got on their mules and escaped.

³⁰While the king's sons were on their way, the news came to David, "Absalom has killed all of the king's sons! Not one of them is left alive!" ³¹King David tore his clothes and lay on the ground to show his sadness. All his servants standing nearby tore their clothes also.

³²Jonadab son of Shimeah, David's brother, said to David, "Don't think all the young men, your sons, are killed. No, only Amnon is dead! Absalom has planned this ever since Amnon forced his sister Tamar to have sexual relations with him. ³³My master and king, don't think that all of the king's sons are dead. Only Amnon is dead!"

³⁴In the meantime Absalom had run away.

A guard standing on the city wall saw many people coming from the other side of the hill. ³⁵So Jonadab said to King David, "Look, I was right! The king's sons are coming!"

³⁶As soon as Jonadab had said this, the king's sons arrived, crying loudly. David and all his servants began crying also. ³⁷David cried for his son every day.

But Absalom ran away to Talmai[n] son of Ammihud, the king of Geshur. ³⁸After Absalom ran away to Geshur, he stayed there for three years. ³⁹When King David got over Amnon's death, he missed Absalom greatly.

Joab Sends a Wise Woman to David

14 Joab son of Zeruiah knew that King David missed Absalom very much. ²So Joab sent messengers to Tekoa to bring a wise woman from there. He said to her, "Pretend to be very sad. Put on funeral clothes and don't put lotion on yourself. Act like a woman who has been crying many days for someone who died. ³Then go to the king and say these words." Then Joab told her what to say.

⁴So the woman from Tekoa spoke to the king. She bowed facedown on the ground to show respect and said, "My king, help me!"

⁵King David asked her, "What is the matter?"

The woman said, "I am a widow; my husband is dead. ⁶I had two sons. They were out in the field fighting, and no one was there to stop them. So one son killed the other son. ⁷Now all the family group is against me. They said to me, 'Bring the son who killed his brother so we may kill him for killing his brother.' That way we will also get rid of the one who would receive what belonged to his father.' My son is like the last spark of a fire. He is all I have left. If they kill him, my husband's name and property will be gone from the earth."

⁸Then the king said to the woman, "Go home. I will take care of this for you."

⁹The woman of Tekoa said to him, "Let the blame be on me and my father's family. My master and king, you and your throne are innocent."

¹⁰King David said, "Bring me anyone who says anything bad to you. Then he won't bother you again."

¹¹The woman said, "Please promise in the name of the LORD your God. Then my relative who has the duty of punishing a murderer won't add to the destruction by killing my son."

David said, "As surely as the LORD lives, no one will hurt your son. Not one hair from his head will fall to the ground."

13:37 Talmai He was Absalom's grandfather.

¹²The woman said, "Let me say something to you, my master and king."

The king said, "Speak."

¹³Then the woman said, "Why have you decided this way against the people of God? When you judge this way, you show that you are guilty for not bringing back your son who was forced to leave home. ¹⁴We will all die someday. We're like water spilled on the ground; no one can gather it back. But God doesn't take away life. Instead, he plans ways that those who have been sent away will not have to stay away from him! ¹⁵My master and king, I came to say this to you because the people have made me afraid! I thought, 'Let me talk to the king. Maybe he will do what I ask. ¹⁶Maybe he will listen. Perhaps he will save me from those who want to keep both me and my son from getting what God gave us.'

¹⁷"Now I say, 'May the words of my master the king give me rest. Like an angel of God, you know what is good and what is bad. May the LORD your God be with you!' "

¹⁸Then King David said, "Do not hide the truth. Answer me one question."

The woman said, "My master the king, please ask your question."

¹⁹The king said, "Did Joab tell you to say all these things?"

The woman answered, "As you live, my master the king, no one could avoid that question. You are right. Your servant Joab did tell me to say these things. ²⁰Joab did it so you would see things differently. My master, you are wise like an angel of God who knows everything that happens on earth."

Absalom Returns to Jerusalem

²¹The king said to Joab, "Look, I will do what I promised. Bring back the young man Absalom."

²²Joab bowed facedown on the ground and blessed the king. Then he said, "Today I know you are pleased with me, because you have done what I asked."

²³Then Joab got up and went to Geshur and brought Absalom back to Jerusalem. ²⁴But King David said, "Absalom must go to his own house. He may not come to see me." So Absalom went to his own house and did not go to see the king.

²⁵Absalom was greatly praised for his handsome appearance. No man in Israel was as handsome as he. No blemish was on him from his head to his foot. ²⁶At the end of every year, Absalom would cut his hair, because it became too heavy. When he weighed it, it would weigh about five pounds by the royal measure.

²⁷Absalom had three sons and one daughter. His daughter's name was also Tamar, and she was a beautiful woman.

²⁸Absalom lived in Jerusalem for two full years without seeing King David. ²⁹Then Absalom sent for Joab so he could send him to the king, but Joab would not come. Absalom sent a message a second time, but Joab still refused to come. ³⁰Then Absalom said to his servants, "Look, Joab's field is next to mine, and he has barley growing there. Go burn it." So Absalom's servants set fire to Joab's field.

³¹Then Joab went to Absalom's house and said to him, "Why did your servants burn my field?"

³²Absalom said to Joab, "I sent a message to you, asking you to come here. I wanted to send you to the king to ask him why he brought me home from Geshur. It would have been better for me to stay there! Now let me see the king. If I have sinned, he can put me to death!"

³³So Joab went to the king and told him Absalom's words. Then the king called for Absalom. Absalom came and bowed facedown on the ground before the king, and the king kissed him.

PSALM 66:1-7

Praise God for What He Has Done

For the director of music. A song. A psalm.

66 Everything on earth, shout with joy to God!
²Sing about his glory!
Make his praise glorious!
³Say to God, "Your works are amazing!
Because your power is great,
your enemies fall before you.
⁴All the earth worships you
and sings praises to you.
They sing praises to your name." *Selah*

⁵Come and see what God has done,
the amazing things he has done for
people.
⁶He turned the sea into dry land.
The people crossed the river on foot.
So let us rejoice because of what he
did.
⁷He rules forever with his power.
He keeps his eye on the nations,
so people should not turn against him.

Selah

PROVERBS 16:25–26

²⁵Some people think they are doing right,
but in the end it leads to death.

²⁶The workers' hunger helps them,
because their desire to eat makes them
work.

JOHN 6:60–71

The Words of Eternal Life

⁶⁰When the followers of Jesus heard this,
many of them said, "This teaching is hard.
Who can accept it?"

⁶¹Knowing that his followers were complaining about this, Jesus said, "Does this
teaching bother you? ⁶²Then will it also
bother you to see the Son of Man going back
to the place where he came from? ⁶³It is the
Spirit that gives life. The flesh doesn't give
life. The words I told you are spirit, and they
give life. ⁶⁴But some of you don't believe." (Jesus knew from the beginning who did not
believe and who would turn against him.)
⁶⁵Jesus said, "That is the reason I said, 'If the
Father does not bring a person to me, that
one cannot come.'"

⁶⁶After Jesus said this, many of his followers left him and stopped following him.

⁶⁷Jesus asked the twelve followers, "Do
you want to leave, too?"

⁶⁸Simon Peter answered him, "Lord, who
would we go to? You have the words that give
eternal life. ⁶⁹We believe and know that you
are the Holy One from God."

⁷⁰Then Jesus answered, "I chose all twelve
of you, but one of you is a devil."

⁷¹Jesus was talking about Judas, the son of
Simon Iscariot. Judas was one of the twelve,
but later he was going to turn against Jesus.

MAY 22

2 SAMUEL 15:1—16:19

Absalom Plans to Take David's Kingdom

15After this, Absalom got a chariot and
horses for himself and fifty men to run
before him. ²Absalom would get up early
and stand near the city gate.ⁿ Anyone who
had a problem for the king to settle would
come here. When someone came, Absalom
would call out and say, "What city are you
from?"

The person would answer, "I'm from one
of the tribes of Israel."

³Then Absalom would say, "Look, your
claims are right, but the king has no one to
listen to you." ⁴Absalom would also say, "I
wish someone would make me judge in this
land! Then people with problems could
come to me, and I could help them get justice."

⁵People would come near Absalom to bow
to him. When they did, Absalom would reach
out his hand and take hold of them and kiss
them. ⁶Absalom did that to all the Israelites
who came to King David for decisions. In this
way, Absalom stole the hearts of all Israel.

⁷After four years Absalom said to King
David, "Please let me go to Hebron. I want to
carry out my promise that I made to the
LORD ⁸while I was living in Geshur in Aram.
I said, 'If the LORD takes me back to Jerusa-
lem, I will worship him in Hebron.'"

⁹The king said, "Go in peace."

So Absalom went to Hebron. ¹⁰But he sent

15:2 city gate People came here to conduct business. Public meetings and court cases were also held here.

secret messengers through all the tribes of Israel. They told the people, "When you hear the trumpets, say this: 'Absalom is the king at Hebron!'"

¹¹Absalom had invited two hundred men to go with him. So they went from Jerusalem with him, but they didn't know what he was planning. ¹²While Absalom was offering sacrifices, he sent for Ahithophel, one of the people who advised David, to come from his hometown of Giloh. So Absalom's plans were working very well. More and more people began to support him.

¹³A messenger came to David, saying, "The Israelites are giving their loyalty to Absalom."

¹⁴Then David said to all his officers who were with him in Jerusalem, "We must leave quickly! If we don't, we won't be able to get away from Absalom. We must hurry before he catches us and destroys us and kills the people of Jerusalem."

¹⁵The king's officers said to him, "We will do anything you say."

¹⁶The king set out with everyone in his house, but he left ten slave women to take care of the palace. ¹⁷The king left with all his people following him, and they stopped at a house far away. ¹⁸All the king's servants passed by him—the Kerethites and Pelethites,ⁿ all those from Gath, and the six hundred men who had followed him.

¹⁹The king said to Ittai, a man from Gath, "Why are you also going with us? Turn back and stay with King Absalom because you are a foreigner. This is not your homeland. ²⁰You joined me only a short time ago. Should I make you wander with us when I don't even know where I'm going? Turn back and take your brothers with you. May kindness and loyalty be shown to you."

²¹But Ittai said to the king, "As surely as the LORD lives and as you live, I will stay with you, whether it means life or death."

²²David said to Ittai, "Go, march on." So Ittai from Gath and all his people with their children marched on. ²³All the people cried loudly as everyone passed by. King David

crossed the Kidron Valley, and then all the people went on to the desert. ²⁴Zadok and all the Levites with him carried the Ark of the Agreement with God. They set it down, and Abiathar offered sacrifices until all the people had left the city.

²⁵The king said to Zadok, "Take the Ark of God back into the city. If the LORD is pleased with me, he will bring me back and will let me see both it and Jerusalem again. ²⁶But if the LORD says he is not pleased with me, I am ready. He can do what he wants with me."

²⁷The king also said to Zadok the priest, "Aren't you a seer? Go back to the city in peace and take your son Ahimaaz and Abiathar's son Jonathan with you. ²⁸I will wait near the crossings into the desert until I hear from you." ²⁹So Zadok and Abiathar took the Ark of God back to Jerusalem and stayed there.

³⁰David went up the Mount of Olives, crying as he went. He covered his head and went barefoot. All the people with David covered their heads also and cried as they went. ³¹Someone told David, "Ahithophel is one of the people with Absalom who made secret plans against you."

So David prayed, "LORD, please make Ahithophel's advice foolish."

³²When David reached the top of the mountain where people used to worship God, Hushai the Arkite came to meet him. Hushai's coat was torn, and there was dirt on his head to show how sad he was. ³³David said to Hushai, "If you go with me, you will be just one more person for me to take care of. ³⁴But if you return to the city, you can make Ahithophel's advice useless. Tell Absalom, 'I am your servant, my king. In the past I served your father, but now I will serve you.' ³⁵The priests Zadok and Abiathar will be with you. Tell them everything you hear in the royal palace. ³⁶Zadok's son Ahimaaz and Abiathar's son Jonathan are with them. Send them to tell me everything you hear." ³⁷So David's friend Hushai entered Jerusalem just as Absalom arrived.

15:18 Kerethites and Pelethites These were probably special units of the army that were responsible for the king's safety, a kind of palace guard.

Ziba Meets David

16 When David had passed a short way over the top of the Mount of Olives, Ziba, Mephibosheth's servant, met him. Ziba had a row of donkeys loaded with two hundred loaves of bread, one hundred cakes of raisins, one hundred cakes of figs, and leather bags full of wine. ²The king asked Ziba, "What are these things for?"

Ziba answered, "The donkeys are for your family to ride. The bread and cakes of figs are for the servants to eat. And the wine is for anyone to drink who might become weak in the desert."

³The king asked, "Where is Mephibosheth?"

Ziba answered him, "Mephibosheth is staying in Jerusalem because he thinks, 'Today the Israelites will give my father's kingdom back to me!'"

⁴Then the king said to Ziba, "All right. Everything that belonged to Mephibosheth, I now give to you!"

Ziba said, "I bow to you. I hope I will always be able to please you."

Shimei Curses David

⁵As King David came to Bahurim, a man came out and cursed him. He was from Saul's family group, and his name was Shimei son of Gera. ⁶He threw stones at David and his officers, but the people and soldiers gathered all around David. ⁷Shimei cursed David, saying, "Get out, get out, you murderer, you troublemaker. ⁸The LORD is punishing you for the people in Saul's family you killed! You took Saul's place as king, but now the LORD has given the kingdom to your son Absalom! Now you are ruined because you are a murderer!"

⁹Abishai son of Zeruiah said to the king, "Why should this dead dog curse you, the king? Let me go over and cut off his head!"

¹⁰But the king answered, "This does not concern you, sons of Zeruiah! If he is cursing me because the LORD told him to, who can question him?"

¹¹David also said to Abishai and all his officers, "My own son is trying to kill me! This man is a Benjaminite and has more right to kill me! Leave him alone, and let him curse me because the LORD told him to do this. ¹²Maybe the LORD will see my misery and repay me with something good for Shimei's curses today!"

¹³So David and his men went on down the road, but Shimei followed on the nearby hillside. He kept cursing David and throwing stones and dirt at him. ¹⁴When the king and all his people arrived at the Jordan, they were very tired, so they rested there.

¹⁵Meanwhile, Absalom, Ahithophel, and all the Israelites arrived at Jerusalem. ¹⁶David's friend Hushai the Arkite came to Absalom and said to him, "Long live the king! Long live the king!"

¹⁷Absalom asked, "Why are you not loyal to your friend David? Why didn't you leave Jerusalem with your friend?"

¹⁸Hushai said, "I belong to the one chosen by the LORD and by these people and everyone in Israel. I will stay with you. ¹⁹In the past I served your father. So whom should I serve now? David's son! I will serve you as I served him."

PSALM 66:8–15

⁸You people, praise our God;
    loudly sing his praise.
⁹He protects our lives
    and does not let us be defeated.
¹⁰God, you have tested us;
    you have purified us like silver.
¹¹You let us be trapped
    and put a heavy load on us.
¹²You let our enemies walk on our heads.
    We went through fire and flood,
        but you brought us to a place with good
            things.

¹³I will come to your Temple with burnt
    offerings.
    I will give you what I promised,
¹⁴   things I promised when I was in trouble.
¹⁵I will bring you offerings of fat animals,
    and I will offer sheep, bulls, and goats.
                         Selah

PROVERBS 16:27–30

²⁷Useless people make evil plans,
    and their words are like a burning fire.

²⁸A useless person causes trouble,
and a gossip ruins friendships.

²⁹Cruel people trick their neighbors
and lead them to do wrong.

³⁰Someone who winks is planning evil,
and the one who grins is planning
something wrong.

JOHN 7:1–24

Jesus' Brothers Don't Believe

7 After this, Jesus traveled around Galilee.
He did not want to travel in Judea, because some evil people there wanted to kill
him. ²It was time for the Feast of Shelters.
³So Jesus' brothers said to him, "You should
leave here and go to Judea so your followers
there can see the miracles you do. ⁴Anyone
who wants to be well known does not hide
what he does. If you are doing these things,
show yourself to the world." ⁵(Even Jesus'
brothers did not believe in him.)

⁶Jesus said to his brothers, "The right time
for me has not yet come, but any time is right
for you. ⁷The world cannot hate you, but it
hates me, because I tell it the evil things it
does. ⁸So you go to the feast. I will not go yet[n]
to this feast, because the right time for me
has not yet come." ⁹After saying this, Jesus
stayed in Galilee.

¹⁰But after Jesus' brothers had gone to the
feast, Jesus went also. But he did not let people
see him. ¹¹At the feast some people were looking for him and saying, "Where is that man?"

¹²Within the large crowd there, many people were whispering to each other about Jesus. Some said, "He is a good man."

Others said, "No, he fools the people."
¹³But no one was brave enough to talk about
Jesus openly, because they were afraid of the
elders.

Jesus Teaches at the Feast

¹⁴When the feast was about half over, Jesus went to the Temple and began to teach.
¹⁵The people were amazed and said, "This
man has never studied in school. How did he
learn so much?"

¹⁶Jesus answered, "The things I teach are
not my own, but they come from him who
sent me. ¹⁷If people choose to do what God
wants, they will know that my teaching
comes from God and not from me. ¹⁸Those
who teach their own ideas are trying to get
honor for themselves. But those who try to
bring honor to the one who sent them speak
the truth, and there is nothing false in them.
¹⁹Moses gave you the law,[n] but none of you
obeys that law. Why are you trying to kill
me?"

²⁰The people answered, "A demon has
come into you. We are not trying to kill
you."

²¹Jesus said to them, "I did one miracle,
and you are all amazed. ²²Moses gave you the
law about circumcision. (But really Moses
did not give you circumcision; it came from
our ancestors.) And yet you circumcise a
baby boy on a Sabbath day. ²³If a baby boy
can be circumcised on a Sabbath day to obey
the law of Moses, why are you angry at me
for healing a person's whole body on the
Sabbath day? ²⁴Stop judging by the way
things look, but judge by what is really
right."

MAY 23

2 SAMUEL 16:20—18:33

Ahithophel's Advice

²⁰Absalom said to Ahithophel, "Tell us
what we should do."

²¹Ahithophel said, "Your father left behind some of his slave women to take care of
the palace. Have sexual relations with them.
Then all Israel will hear that your father is
your enemy, and all your people will be en-

7:8 yet Some Greek copies do not have this word.   **7:19 law** Moses gave God's people the Law that God gave him on Mount
Sinai (Exodus 34:29–32).

couraged to give you more support." [22]So they put up a tent for Absalom on the roof[n] of the palace where everyone in Israel could see it. And Absalom had sexual relations with his father's slave women.

[23]At that time people thought Ahithophel's advice was as reliable as God's own word. Both David and Absalom thought it was that reliable.

17 Ahithophel said to Absalom, "Let me choose twelve thousand men and chase David tonight. [2]I'll catch him while he is tired and weak, and I'll frighten him so all his people will run away. But I'll kill only King David. [3]Then I'll bring everyone back to you. If the man you are looking for is dead, everyone else will return safely." [4]This plan seemed good to Absalom and to all the leaders of Israel.

[5]But Absalom said, "Now call Hushai the Arkite, so I can hear what he says." [6]When Hushai came to Absalom, Absalom said to him, "This is the plan Ahithophel gave. Should we follow it? If not, tell us."

[7]Hushai said to Absalom, "Ahithophel's advice is not good this time." [8]Hushai added, "You know your father and his men are strong. They are as angry as a bear that is robbed of its cubs. Your father is a skilled fighter. He won't stay all night with the army. [9]He is probably already hiding in a cave or some other place. If the first attack fails, people will hear the news and think, 'Absalom's followers are losing!' [10]Then even the men who are as brave as lions will be frightened, because all the Israelites know your father is a fighter. They know his men are brave!

[11]"This is what I suggest: Gather all the Israelites from Dan to Beersheba.[n] There will be as many people as grains of sand by the sea. Then you yourself must go into the battle. [12]We will go to David wherever he is hiding. We will fall on him as dew falls on the ground. We will kill him and all of his men so that no one will be left alive. [13]If David escapes into a city, all the Israelites will bring ropes to that city and pull it into the valley. Not a stone will be left!"

[14]Absalom and all the Israelites said, "The advice of Hushai the Arkite is better than that of Ahithophel." (The LORD had planned to destroy the good advice of Ahithophel so the LORD could bring disaster on Absalom.)

[15]Hushai told Zadok and Abiathar, the priests, what Ahithophel had suggested to Absalom and the elders of Israel. He also reported to them what he himself had suggested. Hushai said, [16]"Quickly! Send a message to David. Tell him not to stay tonight at the crossings into the desert but to cross over the Jordan River at once. If he crosses the river, he and all his people won't be destroyed."

[17]Jonathan and Ahimaaz were waiting at En Rogel. They did not want to be seen going into the city, so a servant girl would go out to them and give them messages. Then Jonathan and Ahimaaz would go and tell King David. [18]But a boy saw Jonathan and Ahimaaz and told Absalom. So Jonathan and Ahimaaz left quickly and went to a man's house in Bahurim. He had a well in his courtyard, and they climbed down into it. [19]The man's wife spread a sheet over the opening of the well and covered it with grain. No one could tell that anyone was hiding there.

[20]Absalom's servants came to the woman at the house and asked, "Where are Ahimaaz and Jonathan?"

She said to them, "They have already crossed the brook."

Absalom's servants then went to look for Jonathan and Ahimaaz, but they could not find them. So they went back to Jerusalem.

[21]After Absalom's servants left, Jonathan and Ahimaaz climbed out of the well and went to tell King David. They said, "Hurry, cross over the river! Ahithophel has said these things against you!" [22]So David and all his people crossed the Jordan River. By dawn, everyone had crossed the Jordan.

[23]When Ahithophel saw that the Israelites did not accept his advice, he saddled his donkey and went to his hometown. He left orders for his family and property, and then he hanged himself. He died and was buried in his father's tomb.

16:22 roof In Bible times houses were built with flat roofs. The roof was used for drying things such as flax and fruit. And it was used as an extra room, as a place for worship, and as a cool place to sleep in the summer. **17:11 Dan to Beersheba** Dan was the city farthest north in Israel, and Beersheba was the city farthest south. So this means all the people of Israel.

War Between David and Absalom

²⁴David arrived at Mahanaim. And Absalom and all his Israelites crossed over the Jordan River. ²⁵Absalom had made Amasa captain of the army instead of Joab. Amasa was the son of a man named Jether the Ishmaelite. Amasa's mother was Abigail daughter of Nahash and sister of Zeruiah, Joab's mother. ²⁶Absalom and the Israelites camped in the land of Gilead.

²⁷Shobi, Makir, and Barzillai were at Mahanaim when David arrived. Shobi son of Nahash was from the Ammonite town of Rabbah. Makir son of Ammiel was from Lo Debar, and Barzillai was from Rogelim in Gilead. ²⁸They brought beds, bowls, clay pots, wheat, barley, flour, roasted grain, beans, small peas, ²⁹honey, milk curds, sheep, and cheese made from cows' milk for David and his people. They said, "The people are hungry and tired and thirsty in the desert."

18 David counted his men and placed over them commanders of thousands and commanders of hundreds. ²He sent the troops out in three groups. Joab commanded one-third of the men. Joab's brother Abishai son of Zeruiah commanded another third. And Ittai from Gath commanded the last third. King David said to them, "I will also go with you."

³But the men said, "You must not go with us! If we run away in the battle, Absalom's men won't care. Even if half of us are killed, Absalom's men won't care. But you're worth ten thousand of us! You can help us most by staying in the city."

⁴The king said to his people, "I will do what you think is best." So the king stood at the side of the gate as the army went out in groups of a hundred and a thousand.

⁵The king commanded Joab, Abishai, and Ittai, "Be gentle with young Absalom for my sake." Everyone heard the king's orders to the commanders about Absalom.

⁶David's army went out into the field against Absalom's Israelites, and they fought in the forest of Ephraim. ⁷There David's army defeated the Israelites. Many died that day— twenty thousand men. ⁸The battle spread through all the country, but that day more men died in the forest than in the fighting.

Absalom Dies

⁹Then Absalom happened to meet David's troops. As Absalom was riding his mule, it went under the thick branches of a large oak tree. Absalom's head got caught in the tree, and his mule ran out from under him. So Absalom was left hanging above the ground.

¹⁰When one of the men saw it happen, he told Joab, "I saw Absalom hanging in an oak tree!"

¹¹Joab said to him, "You saw him? Why didn't you kill him and let him fall to the ground? I would have given you a belt and four ounces of silver!"

¹²The man answered, "I wouldn't touch the king's son even if you gave me twenty-five pounds of silver. We heard the king command you, Abishai, and Ittai, 'Be careful not to hurt young Absalom.' ¹³If I had killed him, the king would have found out, and you would not have protected me!"

¹⁴Joab said, "I won't waste time here with you!" Absalom was still alive in the oak tree, so Joab took three spears and stabbed him in the heart. ¹⁵Ten young men who carried Joab's armor also gathered around Absalom and struck him and killed him.

¹⁶Then Joab blew the trumpet, so the troops stopped chasing the Israelites. ¹⁷Then Joab's men took Absalom's body and threw it into a large pit in the forest and filled the pit with many stones. All the Israelites ran away to their homes.

¹⁸When Absalom was alive, he had set up a pillar for himself in the King's Valley. He said, "I have no son to keep my name alive." So he named the pillar after himself, and it is called Absalom's Monument even today.

¹⁹Ahimaaz son of Zadok said to Joab, "Let me run and take the news to King David. I'll tell him the LORD has saved him from his enemies."

²⁰Joab answered Ahimaaz, "No, you are not the one to take the news today. You may do it another time, but do not take it today, because the king's son is dead."

²¹Then Joab said to a man from Cush, "Go, tell the king what you have seen." The Cushite bowed to Joab and ran to tell David. ²²But Ahimaaz son of Zadok begged Joab

again, "No matter what happens, please let me go along with the Cushite!"

Joab said, "Son, why do you want to carry the news? You won't get any reward."

23Ahimaaz answered, "No matter what happens, I will run."

So Joab said to Ahimaaz, "Run!" Then Ahimaaz ran by way of the Jordan Valley and passed the Cushite.

24David was sitting between the inner and outer gates of the city. The watchman went up to the roof of the gate by the walls, and as he looked up, he saw a man running alone. 25He shouted the news to the king.

The king said, "If he is alone, he is bringing good news!"

The man came nearer and nearer to the city. 26Then the watchman saw another man running, and he called to the gatekeeper, "Look! Another man is running alone!"

The king said, "He is also bringing good news!"

27The watchman said, "I think the first man runs like Ahimaaz son of Zadok."

The king said, "Ahimaaz is a good man. He must be bringing good news!"

28Then Ahimaaz called a greeting to the king. He bowed facedown on the ground before the king and said, "Praise the LORD your God! The LORD has defeated those who were against you, my king."

29The king asked, "Is young Absalom all right?"

Ahimaaz answered, "When Joab sent me, I saw some great excitement, but I don't know what it was."

30The king said, "Step over here and wait." So Ahimaaz stepped aside and stood there.

31Then the Cushite arrived. He said, "Master and king, hear the good news! Today the LORD has punished those who were against you!"

32The king asked the Cushite, "Is young Absalom all right?"

The Cushite answered, "May your enemies and all who come to hurt you be like that young man!"

33Then the king was very upset, and he went to the room over the city gate and cried. As he went, he cried out, "My son Absalom, my son Absalom! I wish I had died and not you. Absalom, my son, my son!"

PSALM 66:16–20

16All of you who fear God, come and listen,
   and I will tell you what he has done for
      me.
17I cried out to him with my mouth
   and praised him with my tongue.
18If I had known of any sin in my heart,
   the Lord would not have listened to me.
19But God has listened;
   he has heard my prayer.
20Praise God,
   who did not ignore my prayer
   or hold back his love from me.

PROVERBS 16:31–32

31Gray hair is like a crown of honor;
   it is earned by living a good life.

32Patience is better than strength.
   Controlling your temper is better than
      capturing a city.

JOHN 7:25–52

Is Jesus the Christ?

25Then some of the people who lived in Jerusalem said, "This is the man they are trying to kill. 26But he is teaching where everyone can see and hear him, and no one is trying to stop him. Maybe the leaders have decided he really is the Christ. 27But we know where this man is from. Yet when the real Christ comes, no one will know where he comes from."

28Jesus, teaching in the Temple, cried out, "Yes, you know me, and you know where I am from. But I have not come by my own authority. I was sent by the One who is true, whom you don't know. 29But I know him, because I am from him, and he sent me."

30When Jesus said this, they tried to seize him. But no one was able to touch him, because it was not yet the right time. 31But many of the people believed in Jesus. They said, "When the Christ comes, will he do more miracles than this man has done?"

The Leaders Try to Arrest Jesus

32The Pharisees heard the crowd whispering these things about Jesus. So the leading priests and the Pharisees sent some Temple guards to arrest him. 33Jesus said, "I will be with you a little while longer. Then I will go back to the One who sent me. [34]You will look for me, but you will not find me. And you cannot come where I am."

[35]Some people said to each other, "Where will this man go so we cannot find him? Will he go to the Greek cities where our people live and teach the Greek people there? [36]What did he mean when he said, 'You will look for me, but you will not find me,' and 'You cannot come where I am'?"

Jesus Talks About the Spirit

[37]On the last and most important day of the feast Jesus stood up and said in a loud voice, "Let anyone who is thirsty come to me and drink. [38]If anyone believes in me, rivers of living water will flow out from that person's heart, as the Scripture says." [39]Jesus was talking about the Holy Spirit. The Spirit had not yet been given, because Jesus had not yet been raised to glory. But later, those who believed in Jesus would receive the Spirit.

The People Argue About Jesus

[40]When the people heard Jesus' words, some of them said, "This man really is the Prophet."[n]
[41]Others said, "He is the Christ."

Still others said, "The Christ will not come from Galilee. [42]The Scripture says that the Christ will come from David's family and from Bethlehem, the town where David lived." [43]So the people did not agree with each other about Jesus. [44]Some of them wanted to arrest him, but no one was able to touch him.

Some Leaders Won't Believe

[45]The Temple guards went back to the leading priests and the Pharisees, who asked, "Why didn't you bring Jesus?"

[46]The guards answered, "The words he says are greater than the words of any other person who has ever spoken!"

[47]The Pharisees answered, "So Jesus has fooled you also! [48]Have any of the leaders or the Pharisees believed in him? No! [49]But these people, who know nothing about the law, are under God's curse."

[50]Nicodemus, who had gone to see Jesus before, was in that group.[n] He said, [51]"Our law does not judge a person without hearing him and knowing what he has done."

[52]They answered, "Are you from Galilee, too? Study the Scriptures, and you will learn that no prophet comes from Galilee."

MAY 24

2 SAMUEL 19:1—20:26

Joab Scolds David

19People told Joab, "Look, the king is sad and crying because of Absalom." [2]David's army had won the battle that day. But it became a very sad day for all the people, because they heard that the king was very sad for his son. [3]The people came into the city quietly that day. They were like an army that had been defeated in battle and had run away. [4]The king covered his face and cried loudly, "My son Absalom! Absalom, my son, my son!"

[5]Joab went into the king's house and

said, "Today you have shamed all your men. They saved your life and the lives of your sons, daughters, wives, and slave women. [6]You have shamed them because you love those who hate you, and you hate those who love you. Today you have made it clear that your commanders and men mean nothing to you. What if Absalom had lived and all of us were dead? I can see you would be pleased. [7]Now go out and encourage your servants. I swear by the LORD that if you don't go out, no man will be left with you by tonight! That will be worse than all the troubles you have had from your youth until today."

7:40 Prophet They probably meant the prophet God told Moses he would send (Deuteronomy 18:15–19). **7:50 Nicodemus . . . group.** The story about Nicodemus going and talking to Jesus is in John 3:1–21.

[8]So the king went to the city gate.[n] When the news spread that the king was at the gate, everyone came to see him.

David Goes Back to Jerusalem

All the Israelites who had followed Absalom had run away to their homes. [9]People in all the tribes of Israel began to argue, saying, "The king saved us from the Philistines and our other enemies, but he left the country because of Absalom. [10]We appointed Absalom to rule us, but now he has died in battle. We should make David the king again."

[11]King David sent a message to Zadok and Abiathar, the priests, that said, "Speak to the elders of Judah. Say, 'Even in my house I have heard what all the Israelites are saying. So why are you the last tribe to bring the king back to his palace? [12]You are my brothers, my own family. Why are you the last tribe to bring back the king?' [13]And say to Amasa, 'You are part of my own family. May God punish me terribly if I don't make you commander of the army in Joab's place!'"

[14]David touched the hearts of all the people of Judah at once. They sent a message to the king that said, "Return with all your men." [15]Then the king returned as far as the Jordan River. The men of Judah came to Gilgal to meet him and to bring him across the Jordan.

[16]Shimei son of Gera, a Benjaminite who lived in Bahurim, hurried down with the men of Judah to meet King David. [17]With Shimei came a thousand Benjaminites. Ziba, the servant from Saul's family, also came, bringing his fifteen sons and twenty servants with him. They all hurried to the Jordan River to meet the king. [18]The people went across the Jordan to help bring the king's family back to Judah and to do whatever the king wanted. As the king was crossing the river, Shimei son of Gera came to him and bowed facedown on the ground in front of the king. [19]He said to the king, "My master, don't hold me guilty. Don't remember the wrong I did when you left Jerusalem! Don't hold it against me. [20]I know I have sinned. That is why I am the first person

from Joseph's family to come down and meet you today, my master and king!"

[21]But Abishai son of Zeruiah said, "Shimei should die because he cursed you, the LORD's appointed king!"

[22]David said, "This does not concern you, sons of Zeruiah! Today you're against me! No one will be put to death in Israel today. Today I know I am king over Israel!" [23]Then the king promised Shimei, "You won't die."

[24]Mephibosheth, Saul's grandson, also went down to meet King David. Mephibosheth had not cared for his feet, cut his beard, or washed his clothes from the time the king had left Jerusalem until he returned safely. [25]When Mephibosheth came from Jerusalem to meet the king, the king asked him, "Mephibosheth, why didn't you go with me?"

[26]He answered, "My master, my servant Ziba tricked me! I said to Ziba, 'I am crippled, so saddle a donkey. Then I will ride it so I can go with the king.' [27]But he lied about me to you. You, my master and king, are like an angel from God. Do what you think is good. [28]You could have killed all my grandfather's family. Instead, you put me with those people who eat at your own table. So I don't have a right to ask anything more from the king!"

[29]The king said to him, "Don't say anything more. I have decided that you and Ziba will divide the land."

[30]Mephibosheth said to the king, "Let Ziba take all the land now that my master the king has arrived safely home."

[31]Barzillai of Gilead came down from Rogelim to cross the Jordan River with the king. [32]Barzillai was a very old man, eighty years old. He had taken care of the king when David was staying at Mahanaim, because Barzillai was a very rich man. [33]David said to Barzillai, "Cross the river with me. Come with me to Jerusalem, and I will take care of you."

[34]But Barzillai answered the king, "Do you know how old I am? Do you think I can go with you to Jerusalem? [35]I am eighty years old! I am too old to taste what I eat or drink. I am too old to hear the voices of men and

19:8 city gate People came here to conduct business. Public meetings and court cases were also held here.

women singers. Why should you be bothered with me? ³⁶I am not worthy of a reward from you, but I will cross the Jordan River with you. ³⁷Then let me go back so I may die in my own city near the grave of my father and mother. But here is Kimham, your servant. Let him go with you, my master and king. Do with him whatever you want."

³⁸The king answered, "Kimham will go with me. I will do for him anything you wish, and I will do anything for you that you wish." ³⁹The king kissed Barzillai and blessed him. Then Barzillai returned home, and the king and all the people crossed the Jordan.

⁴⁰When the king crossed over to Gilgal, Kimham went with him. All the troops of Judah and half the troops of Israel led David across the river.

⁴¹Soon all the Israelites came to the king and said to him, "Why did our relatives, the people of Judah, steal you away? Why did they bring you and your family across the Jordan River with your men?"

⁴²All the people of Judah answered the Israelites, "We did this because the king is our close relative. Why are you angry about it? We have not eaten food at the king's expense or taken anything for ourselves!"

⁴³The Israelites answered the people of Judah, "We have ten tribes in the kingdom, so we have more right to David than you do! But you ignored us! We were the first ones to talk about bringing our king back!"

But the people of Judah spoke even more unkindly than the people of Israel.

Sheba Leads Israel Away from David

20 It happened that a troublemaker named Sheba son of Bicri from the tribe of Benjamin was there. He blew the trumpet and said:

"We have no share in David!
    We have no part in the son of Jesse!
People of Israel, let's go home!"

²So all the Israelites left David and followed Sheba son of Bicri. But the people of Judah stayed with their king all the way from the Jordan River to Jerusalem.

³David came back to his palace in Jerusalem. He had left ten of his slave women there to take care of the palace. Now he put them in a locked house. He gave them food, but he did not have sexual relations with them. So they lived like widows until they died.

⁴The king said to Amasa, "Tell the men of Judah to meet with me in three days, and you must also be here." ⁵So Amasa went to call the men of Judah together, but he took more time than the king had said.

⁶David said to Abishai, "Sheba son of Bicri is more dangerous to us than Absalom was. Take my men and chase him before he finds walled cities and escapes from us." ⁷So Joab's men, the Kerethites and the Pelethites,ⁿ and all the soldiers went with Abishai. They went out from Jerusalem to chase Sheba son of Bicri.

⁸When Joab and the army came to the great rock at Gibeon, Amasa came out to meet them. Joab was wearing his uniform, and at his waist he wore a belt that held his sword in its case. As Joab stepped forward, his sword fell out of its case. ⁹Joab asked Amasa, "Brother, is everything all right with you?" Then with his right hand he took Amasa by the beard to kiss him. ¹⁰Amasa was not watching the sword in Joab's hand. So Joab pushed the sword into Amasa's stomach, causing Amasa's insides to spill onto the ground. Joab did not have to stab Amasa again; he was already dead. Then Joab and his brother Abishai continued to chase Sheba son of Bicri.

¹¹One of Joab's young men stood by Amasa's body and said, "Everyone who is for Joab and David should follow Joab!" ¹²Amasa lay in the middle of the road, covered with his own blood. When the young man saw that everyone was stopping to look at the body, he dragged it from the road, laid it in a field, and put a cloth over it. ¹³After Amasa's body was taken off the road, all the men followed Joab to chase Sheba son of Bicri.

¹⁴Sheba went through all the tribes of Israel to Abel Beth Maacah. All the Berites also came together and followed him. ¹⁵So Joab and his men came to Abel Beth Maacah and

---

20:7 Kerethites and Pelethites These were probably special units of the army that were responsible for the king's safety, a kind of palace guard.

surrounded it. They piled dirt up against the city wall, and they began hacking at the walls to bring them down.

[16]But a wise woman shouted out from the city, "Listen! Listen! Tell Joab to come here. I want to talk to him!"

[17]So Joab came near her. She asked him, "Are you Joab?"

He answered, "Yes, I am."

Then she said, "Listen to what I say."

Joab said, "I'm listening."

[18]Then the woman said, "In the past people would say, 'Ask for advice at Abel,' and the problem would be solved. [19]I am one of the peaceful, loyal people of Israel. You are trying to destroy an important city of Israel. Why must you destroy what belongs to the LORD?"

[20]Joab answered, "I would prefer not to destroy or ruin anything! [21]That is not what I want. But there is a man here from the mountains of Ephraim, who is named Sheba son of Bicri. He has turned against King David. If you bring him to me, I will leave the city alone."

The woman said to Joab, "His head will be thrown over the wall to you."

[22]Then the woman spoke very wisely to all the people of the city. They cut off the head of Sheba son of Bicri and threw it over the wall to Joab. So he blew the trumpet, and the army left the city. Every man returned home, and Joab went back to the king in Jerusalem.

[23]Joab was commander of all the army of Israel. Benaiah son of Jehoiada led the Kerethites and Pelethites. [24]Adoniram was in charge of the men who were forced to do hard work. Jehoshaphat son of Ahilud was the recorder. [25]Sheba was the royal secretary. Zadok and Abiathar were the priests, [26]and Ira the Jairite was David's priest.

PSALM 67:1–7

Everyone Should Praise God

For the director of music. With stringed instruments. A psalm. A song.

67 God, have mercy on us and bless us
and show us your kindness   *Selah*
[2]so the world will learn your ways,

and all nations will learn that you can save.

[3]God, the people should praise you;
all people should praise you.
[4]The nations should be glad and sing
because you judge people fairly.
You guide all the nations on earth. *Selah*
[5]God, the people should praise you;
all people should praise you.

[6]The land has given its crops.
God, our God, blesses us.
[7]God blesses us
so people all over the earth will fear him.

PROVERBS 16:33–17:1

[33]People throw lots to make a decision,
but the answer comes from the LORD.

17 It is better to eat a dry crust of bread in peace
than to have a feast where there is quarreling.

JOHN 7:53—8:20

Some of the earliest surviving Greek copies do not contain 7:53—8:11.

[[53]And everyone left and went home.

The Woman Caught in Adultery

8 Jesus went to the Mount of Olives. [2]But early in the morning he went back to the Temple, and all the people came to him, and he sat and taught them. [3]The teachers of the law and the Pharisees brought a woman who had been caught in adultery. They forced her to stand before the people. [4]They said to Jesus, "Teacher, this woman was caught having sexual relations with a man who is not her husband. [5]The law of Moses commands that we stone to death every woman who does this. What do you say we should do?" [6]They were asking this to trick Jesus so that they could have some charge against him.

But Jesus bent over and started writing on the ground with his finger. [7]When they continued to ask Jesus their question, he raised up and said, "Anyone here who has never sinned can throw the first stone at her." [8]Then Jesus bent over again and wrote on the ground.

⁹Those who heard Jesus began to leave one by one, first the older men and then the others. Jesus was left there alone with the woman standing before him. ¹⁰Jesus raised up again and asked her, "Woman, where are they? Has no one judged you guilty?"

¹¹She answered, "No one, sir."

Then Jesus said, "I also don't judge you guilty. You may go now, but don't sin anymore."]

Jesus Is the Light of the World

¹²Later, Jesus talked to the people again, saying, "I am the light of the world. The person who follows me will never live in darkness but will have the light that gives life."

¹³The Pharisees said to Jesus, "When you talk about yourself, you are the only one to say these things are true. We cannot accept what you say."

¹⁴Jesus answered, "Yes, I am saying these things about myself, but they are true. I know where I came from and where I am going. But you don't know where I came from or where I am going. ¹⁵You judge by human standards. I am not judging anyone. ¹⁶But when I do judge, I judge truthfully, because I am not alone. The Father who sent me is with me. ¹⁷Your own law says that when two witnesses say the same thing, you must accept what they say. ¹⁸I am one of the witnesses who speaks about myself, and the Father who sent me is the other witness."

¹⁹They asked, "Where is your father?"

Jesus answered, "You don't know me or my Father. If you knew me, you would know my Father, too." ²⁰Jesus said these things while he was teaching in the Temple, near where the money is kept. But no one arrested him, because the right time for him had not yet come.

MAY 25

2 SAMUEL 21:1—22:51

The Gibeonites Punish Saul's Family

21 During the time David was king, there was a shortage of food that lasted for three years. So David prayed to the LORD.

The LORD answered, "Saul and his family of murderers are the reason for this shortage, because he killed the Gibeonites." ²(Now the Gibeonites were not Israelites; they were a group of Amorites who were left alive. The Israelites had promised not to hurt the Gibeonites, but Saul had tried to kill them, because he was eager to help the people of Israel and Judah.)

King David called the Gibeonites together and spoke to them. ³He asked, "What can I do for you? How can I make up for the harm done so you can bless the LORD's people?"

⁴The Gibeonites said to David, "We cannot demand silver or gold from Saul or his family. And we don't have the right to kill anyone in Israel."

Then David asked, "What do you want me to do for you?"

⁵The Gibeonites said, "Saul made plans against us and tried to destroy all our people who are left in the land of Israel. ⁶So bring seven of his sons to us. Then we will kill them and hang them on stakes in the presence of the LORD at Gibeah, the hometown of Saul, the LORD's chosen king."

The king said, "I will give them to you." ⁷But the king protected Mephibosheth, the son of Jonathan, the son of Saul, because of the promise he had made to Jonathan in the LORD's name. ⁸The king did take Armoni and Mephibosheth,ⁿ sons of Rizpah and Saul. (Rizpah was the daughter of Aiah.) And the king took the five sons of Saul's daughter Merab. (Adriel son of Barzillai the Meholathite was the father of Merab's five sons.)

21:8 Mephibosheth This is not Jonathan's son but another man with the same name.

⁹David gave these seven sons to the Gibeonites. Then the Gibeonites killed them and hung them on stakes on a hill in the presence of the LORD. All seven sons died together. They were put to death during the first days of the harvest season at the beginning of barley harvest.

¹⁰Aiah's daughter Rizpah took the rough cloth that was worn to show sadness and put it on a rock for herself. She stayed there from the beginning of the harvest until the rain fell on her sons' bodies. During the day she did not let the birds of the sky touch her sons' bodies, and during the night she did not let the wild animals touch them.

¹¹People told David what Aiah's daughter Rizpah, Saul's slave woman, was doing. ¹²Then David took the bones of Saul and Jonathan from the men of Jabesh Gilead. (The Philistines had hung the bodies of Saul and Jonathan in the public square of Beth Shan after they had killed Saul at Gilboa. Later the men of Jabesh Gilead had secretly taken them from there.) ¹³David brought the bones of Saul and his son Jonathan from Gilead. Then the people gathered the bodies of Saul's seven sons who were hanged on stakes. ¹⁴The people buried the bones of Saul and his son Jonathan at Zela in Benjamin in the tomb of Saul's father Kish. The people did everything the king commanded.

Then God answered the prayers for the land.

Wars with the Philistines

¹⁵Again there was war between the Philistines and Israel. David and his men went out to fight the Philistines, but David became tired. ¹⁶Ishbi-Benob, one of the sons of Rapha, had a bronze spearhead weighing about seven and one-half pounds and a new sword. He planned to kill David, ¹⁷but Abishai son of Zeruiah killed the Philistine and saved David's life.

Then David's men made a promise to him, saying, "Never again will you go out with us to battle. If you were killed, Israel would lose its greatest leader."

¹⁸Later, at Gob, there was another battle with the Philistines. Sibbecai the Hushathite killed Saph, another one of the sons of Rapha. ¹⁹Later, there was another battle at Gob with the Philistines. Elhanan son of Jaare-Oregim from Bethlehem killed Goliath[n] from Gath. His spear was as large as a weaver's rod. ²⁰At Gath another battle took place. A huge man was there; he had six fingers on each hand and six toes on each foot—twenty-four fingers and toes in all. This man also was one of the sons of Rapha. ²¹When he challenged Israel, Jonathan son of Shimeah, David's brother, killed him.

²²These four sons of Rapha from Gath were killed by David and his men.

David's Song of Praise

22 David sang this song to the LORD when the LORD saved him from Saul and all his other enemies. ²He said:

"The LORD is my rock, my fortress, my
   Savior.
³My God is my rock.
   I can run to him for safety.
He is my shield and my saving
   strength,
   my defender and my place of safety.
The LORD saves me from those who
   want to harm me.
⁴I will call to the LORD, who is worthy of
   praise,
and I will be saved from my enemies.

⁵"The waves of death came around me;
   the deadly rivers overwhelmed me.
⁶The ropes of death wrapped around
   me.
The traps of death were before me.
⁷In my trouble I called to the LORD;
   I cried out to my God.
From his temple he heard my voice;
   my call for help reached his ears.

⁸"The earth trembled and shook.
   The foundations of heaven began to
     shake.
They trembled because the LORD was
   angry.

21:19 Goliath In 1 Chronicles 20:5 he is called Lahmi, brother of Goliath.

9Smoke came out of his nose,
  and burning fire came out of his
    mouth.
  Burning coals went before him.
10He tore open the sky and came down
    with dark clouds under his feet.
11He rode a creature with wings and
    flew.
  He raced on the wings of the wind.
12He made darkness his shelter,
    surrounded by fog and clouds.
13Out of the brightness of his presence
    came flashes of lightning.
14The LORD thundered from heaven;
    the Most High raised his voice.
15He shot his arrows and scattered his
    enemies.
  His bolts of lightning confused them
    with fear.
16The LORD spoke strongly.
  The wind blew from his nose.
  Then the valleys of the sea appeared,
    and the foundations of the earth were
      seen.

17"The LORD reached down from above
    and took me;
  he pulled me from the deep water.
18He saved me from my powerful
    enemies,
  from those who hated me, because
    they were too strong for me.
19They attacked me at my time of
    trouble,
  but the LORD supported me.
20He took me to a safe place.
  Because he delights in me, he saved
    me.
21"The LORD spared me because I did
    what was right.
  Because I have not done evil, he has
    rewarded me.
22I have followed the ways of the LORD;
  I have not done evil by turning from
    my God.
23I remember all his laws
    and have not broken his rules.
24I am innocent before him;
  I have kept myself from doing evil.
25The LORD rewarded me because I did
    what was right,

because I did what the LORD said was
    right.
26"LORD, you are loyal to those who are
    loyal,
  and you are good to those who are
    good.
27You are pure to those who are pure,
  but you are against those who are
    evil.
28You save the humble,
  but you bring down those who are
    proud.
29LORD, you give light to my lamp.
  The LORD brightens the darkness
    around me.
30With your help I can attack an army.
  With God's help I can jump over a
    wall.

31"The ways of God are without fault;
  the LORD's words are pure.
  He is a shield to those who trust him.
32Who is God? Only the LORD.
  Who is the Rock? Only our God.
33God is my protection.
  He makes my way free from fault.
34He makes me like a deer that does not
    stumble;
  he helps me stand on the steep
    mountains.
35He trains my hands for battle
  so my arms can bend a bronze bow.
36You protect me with your saving
    shield.
  You have stooped to make me great.
37You give me a better way to live,
  so I live as you want me to.
38I chased my enemies and destroyed
    them.
  I did not quit till they were destroyed.
39I destroyed and crushed them
  so they couldn't rise up again.
  They fell beneath my feet.
40You gave me strength in battle.
  You made my enemies bow before me.
41You made my enemies turn back,
  and I destroyed those who hated me.
42They called for help,
  but no one came to save them.
  They called to the LORD,
  but he did not answer them.

⁴³I beat my enemies into pieces,
  like dust on the ground.
 I poured them out and walked on
    them
  like mud in the streets.

⁴⁴"You saved me when my people
    attacked me.
  You kept me as the leader of nations.
 People I never knew serve me.
⁴⁵Foreigners obey me.
  As soon as they hear me, they obey
    me.
⁴⁶They all become afraid
  and tremble in their hiding places.

⁴⁷"The LORD lives!
  May my Rock be praised!
  Praise God, the Rock, who saves me!
⁴⁸God gives me victory over my
    enemies
  and brings people under my rule.
⁴⁹He frees me from my enemies.
  "You set me over those who hate me.
  You saved me from violent people.
⁵⁰So I will praise you, LORD, among the
    nations.
  I will sing praises to your name.
⁵¹The LORD gives great victories to his
    king.
  He is loyal to his appointed king,
  to David and his descendants
    forever."

PSALM 68:1–6

Praise God Who Saved the Nation

For the director of music. A psalm of David. A song.

68 Let God rise up and scatter his
    enemies;
  let those who hate him run away
    from him.
²Blow them away as smoke
  is driven away by the wind.
 As wax melts before a fire,
  let the wicked be destroyed before
    God.
³But those who do right should be
    glad
  and should rejoice before God;
  they should be happy and glad.

⁴Sing to God; sing praises to his name.
 Prepare the way for him
  who rides through the desert,
  whose name is the LORD.
  Rejoice before him.
⁵God is in his holy Temple.
  He is a father to orphans,
  and he defends the widows.
⁶God gives the lonely a home.
  He leads prisoners out with joy,
  but those who turn against God will
    live in a dry land.

PROVERBS 17:2–4

²A wise servant will rule over the
    master's disgraceful child
  and will even inherit a share of what
    the master leaves his children.

³A hot furnace tests silver and gold,
  but the LORD tests hearts.

⁴Evil people listen to evil words.
 Liars pay attention to cruel words.

JOHN 8:21–59

The People Misunderstand Jesus

²¹Again, Jesus said to the people, "I will leave you, and you will look for me, but you will die in your sins. You cannot come where I am going."

²²So the Jews asked, "Will he kill himself? Is that why he said, 'You cannot come where I am going'?"

²³Jesus said, "You people are from here below, but I am from above. You belong to this world, but I don't belong to this world. ²⁴So I told you that you would die in your sins. Yes, you will die in your sins if you don't believe that I am he."

²⁵They asked, "Then who are you?"

Jesus answered, "I am what I have told you from the beginning. ²⁶I have many things to say and decide about you. But I tell people only the things I have heard from the One who sent me, and he speaks the truth."

²⁷The people did not understand that he was talking to them about the Father. ²⁸So Jesus said to them, "When you lift up the

Son of Man, you will know that I am he. You will know that these things I do are not by my own authority but that I say only what the Father has taught me. [29]The One who sent me is with me. I always do what is pleasing to him, so he has not left me alone." [30]While Jesus was saying these things, many people believed in him.

Freedom from Sin

[31]So Jesus said to the Jews who believed in him, "If you continue to obey my teaching, you are truly my followers. [32]Then you will know the truth, and the truth will make you free."

[33]They answered, "We are Abraham's children, and we have never been anyone's slaves. So why do you say we will be free?"

[34]Jesus answered, "I tell you the truth, everyone who lives in sin is a slave to sin. [35]A slave does not stay with a family forever, but a son belongs to the family forever. [36]So if the Son makes you free, you will be truly free. [37]I know you are Abraham's children, but you want to kill me because you don't accept my teaching. [38]I am telling you what my Father has shown me, but you do what your father has told you."

[39]They answered, "Our father is Abraham."

Jesus said, "If you were really Abraham's children, you would do[n] the things Abraham did. [40]I am a man who has told you the truth which I heard from God, but you are trying to kill me. Abraham did nothing like that. [41]So you are doing the things your own father did."

But they said, "We are not like children who never knew who their father was. God is our Father; he is the only Father we have."

[42]Jesus said to them, "If God were really your Father, you would love me, because I came from God and now I am here. I did not come by my own authority; God sent me. [43]You don't understand what I say, because you cannot accept my teaching. [44]You belong to your father the devil, and you want to do what he wants. He was a murderer from the beginning and was against the truth, because there is no truth in him. When he tells a lie, he shows what he is really like, because he is a liar and the father of lies. [45]But because I speak the truth, you don't believe me. [46]Can any of you prove that I am guilty of sin? If I am telling the truth, why don't you believe me? [47]The person who belongs to God accepts what God says. But you don't accept what God says, because you don't belong to God."

Jesus Is Greater than Abraham

[48]They answered, "We say you are a Samaritan and have a demon in you. Are we not right?"

[49]Jesus answered, "I have no demon in me. I give honor to my Father, but you dishonor me. [50]I am not trying to get honor for myself. There is One who wants this honor for me, and he is the judge. [51]I tell you the truth, whoever obeys my teaching will never die."

[52]They said to Jesus, "Now we know that you have a demon in you! Even Abraham and the prophets died. But you say, 'Whoever obeys my teaching will never die.' [53]Do you think you are greater than our father Abraham, who died? And the prophets died, too. Who do you think you are?"

[54]Jesus answered, "If I give honor to myself, that honor is worth nothing. The One who gives me honor is my Father, and you say he is your God. [55]You don't really know him, but I know him. If I said I did not know him, I would be a liar like you. But I do know him, and I obey what he says. [56]Your father Abraham was very happy that he would see my day. He saw that day and was glad."

[57]They said to him, "You have never seen Abraham! You are not even fifty years old."

[58]Jesus answered, "I tell you the truth, before Abraham was even born, I am!" [59]When Jesus said this, the people picked up stones to throw at him. But Jesus hid himself, and then he left the Temple.

8:39 If . . . do Some Greek copies read "If you are really Abraham's children, you will do."

MAY 26

2 SAMUEL 23:1—24:25

David's Last Words

23 These are the last words of David.
This is the message of David son of
Jesse.
The man made great by the Most High
God speaks.
He is the appointed king of the God of
Jacob;
he is the sweet singer of Israel:

2"The LORD's Spirit spoke through me,
and his word was on my tongue.
3The God of Israel spoke;
the Rock of Israel said to me:
'Whoever rules fairly over people,
who rules with respect for God,
4is like the morning light at dawn,
like a morning without clouds.
He is like sunshine after a rain
that makes the grass sprout from the
ground.'

5"This is how God has cared for my
family.
God made a lasting agreement with
me,
right and sure in every way.
He will accomplish my salvation
and satisfy all my desires.

6"But all evil people will be thrown away
like thorns
that cannot be held in a hand.
7No one can touch them
except with a tool of iron or wood.
They will be thrown in the fire and
burned where they lie."

David's Army

8These are the names of David's warriors:
Josheb-Basshebeth, the Tahkemonite, was
head of the Three.[n] He killed eight hundred
men at one time.

9Next was Eleazar son of Dodai the Ahohite. Eleazar was one of the three soldiers
who were with David when they challenged
the Philistines. The Philistines were gathered for battle, and the Israelites drew back.
10But Eleazar stayed where he was and
fought the Philistines until he was so tired
his hand stuck to his sword. The LORD gave a
great victory for the Israelites that day. The
troops came back after Eleazar had won the
battle, but only to take weapons and armor
from the enemy.

11Next there was Shammah son of Agee
the Hararite. The Philistines came together
to fight in a vegetable field. Israel's troops
ran away from the Philistines, 12but Shammah stood in the middle of the field and
fought for it and killed the Philistines. And
the LORD gave a great victory.

13Once, three of the Thirty, David's chief
soldiers, came down to him at the cave of
Adullam during harvest. The Philistine
army had camped in the Valley of Rephaim.
14At that time David was in the stronghold,
and some of the Philistines were in Bethlehem.

15David had a strong desire for some water. He said, "Oh, I wish someone would get
me water from the well near the city gate of
Bethlehem!" 16So the three warriors broke
through the Philistine army and took water
from the well near the city gate of Bethlehem. Then they brought it to David, but he
refused to drink it. He poured it out before
the LORD, 17saying, "May the LORD keep me
from drinking this water! It would be like
drinking the blood of the men who risked
their lives!" So David refused to drink it.
These were the brave things that the three
warriors did.

18Abishai, brother of Joab son of Zeruiah,
was captain of the Three. Abishai fought three
hundred soldiers with his spear and killed
them. He became as famous as the Three
19and was more honored than the Three. He
became their commander even though he
was not one of them.

20Benaiah son of Jehoiada was a brave
fighter from Kabzeel who did mighty things.

23:8 Three These were David's most powerful soldiers. See 1 Chronicles 11:11.

He killed two of the best warriors from Moab. He also went down into a pit and killed a lion on a snowy day. [21]Benaiah killed a large Egyptian who had a spear in his hand. Benaiah had a club, but he grabbed the spear from the Egyptian's hand and killed him with his own spear. [22]These were the things Benaiah son of Jehoiada did. He was as famous as the Three. [23]He received more honor than the Thirty, but he did not become a member of the Three. David made him leader of his bodyguards.

The Thirty Chief Soldiers

[24]The following men were among the Thirty:

Asahel brother of Joab;
Elhanan son of Dodo from Bethlehem;
[25]Shammah the Harodite;
Elika the Harodite;
[26]Helez the Paltite;
Ira son of Ikkesh from Tekoa;
[27]Abiezer the Anathothite;
Mebunnai the Hushathite;
[28]Zalmon the Ahohite;
Maharai the Netophathite;
[29]Heled son of Baanah the Netophathite;
Ithai son of Ribai from Gibeah in Benjamin;
[30]Benaiah the Pirathonite;
Hiddai from the ravines of Gaash;
[31]Abi-Albon the Arbathite;
Azmaveth the Barhumite;
[32]Eliahba the Shaalbonite;
the sons of Jashen;
Jonathan [33]son of Shammah the Hararite;
Ahiam son of Sharar the Hararite;
[34]Eliphelet son of Ahasbai the Maacathite;
Eliam son of Ahithophel the Gilonite;
[35]Hezro the Carmelite;
Paarai the Arbite;
[36]Igal son of Nathan of Zobah;
the son of Hagri;
[37]Zelek the Ammonite;
Naharai the Beerothite, who carried the armor of Joab son of Zeruiah;
[38]Ira the Ithrite;
Gareb the Ithrite,

[39]and Uriah the Hittite.
There were thirty-seven in all.

David Counts His Army

24 The LORD was angry with Israel again, and he caused David to turn against the Israelites. He said, "Go, count the people of Israel and Judah."

[2]So King David said to Joab, the commander of the army, "Go through all the tribes of Israel, from Dan to Beersheba,[n] and count the people. Then I will know how many there are."

[3]But Joab said to the king, "May the LORD your God give you a hundred times more people, and may my master the king live to see this happen. Why do you want to do this?"

[4]But the king commanded Joab and the commanders of the army, so they left the king to count the Israelites.

[5]After crossing the Jordan River, they camped near Aroer on the south side of the city in the ravine. They went through Gad and on to Jazer. [6]Then they went to Gilead and the land of Tahtim Hodshi and to Dan Jaan and around to Sidon. [7]They went to the strong, walled city of Tyre and to all the cities of the Hivites and Canaanites. Finally, they went to southern Judah, to Beersheba. [8]After nine months and twenty days, they had gone through all the land. Then they came back to Jerusalem.

[9]Joab gave the list of the people to the king. There were eight hundred thousand men in Israel who could use the sword and five hundred thousand men in Judah.

[10]David felt ashamed after he had counted the people. He said to the LORD, "I have sinned greatly by what I have done. LORD, I beg you to forgive me, your servant, because I have been very foolish."

[11]When David got up in the morning, the LORD spoke his word to Gad, who was a prophet and David's seer. [12]The LORD told Gad, "Go and tell David, 'This is what the LORD says: I offer you three choices. Choose one of them and I will do it to you.'"

24:2 *Dan to Beersheba* Dan was the city farthest north in Israel, and Beersheba was the city farthest south. So this means all the people of Israel.

¹³So Gad went to David and said to him, "Should three years of hunger come to you and your land? Or should your enemies chase you for three months? Or should there be three days of disease in your land? Think about it. Then decide which of these things I should tell the LORD who sent me."

¹⁴David said to Gad, "I am in great trouble. Let the LORD punish us, because the LORD is very merciful. Don't let my punishment come from human beings!"

¹⁵So the LORD sent a terrible disease on Israel. It began in the morning and continued until the chosen time to stop. From Dan to Beersheba seventy thousand people died. ¹⁶When the angel raised his arm toward Jerusalem to destroy it, the LORD felt very sorry about the terrible things that had happened. He said to the angel who was destroying the people, "That is enough! Put down your arm!" The angel of the LORD was then by the threshing floor of Araunah the Jebusite.

¹⁷When David saw the angel that killed the people, he said to the LORD, "I am the one who sinned and did wrong. These people only followed me like sheep. They did nothing wrong. Please punish me and my family."

¹⁸That day Gad came to David and said, "Go and build an altar to the LORD on the threshing floor of Araunah the Jebusite." ¹⁹So David did what Gad told him to do, just as the LORD commanded.

²⁰Araunah looked and saw the king and his servants coming to him. So he went out and bowed facedown on the ground before the king. ²¹He said, "Why has my master the king come to me?"

David answered, "To buy the threshing floor from you so I can build an altar to the LORD. Then the terrible disease will stop."

²²Araunah said to David, "My master and king, you may take anything you want for a sacrifice. Here are some oxen for the whole burnt offering and the threshing boards and the yokes for the wood. ²³My king, I give everything to you." Araunah also said to the king, "May the LORD your God be pleased with you."

²⁴But the king answered Araunah, "No, I will pay you for the land. I won't offer to the LORD my God burnt offerings that cost me nothing."

So David bought the threshing floor and the oxen for one and one-fourth pounds of silver. ²⁵He built an altar to the LORD there and offered whole burnt offerings and fellowship offerings. Then the LORD answered his prayer for the country, and the disease in Israel stopped.

PSALM 68:7–10

⁷God, you led your people out
when you marched through the
desert.   *Selah*

⁸The ground shook
and the sky poured down rain
before God, the God of Mount Sinai,
before God, the God of Israel.
⁹God, you sent much rain;
you refreshed your tired land.
¹⁰Your people settled there.
God, in your goodness
you took care of the poor.

PROVERBS 17:5–6

⁵Whoever mistreats the poor insults their
Maker;
whoever enjoys someone's trouble will
be punished.

⁶Old people are proud of their
grandchildren,
and children are proud of their parents.

JOHN 9:1–23

Jesus Heals a Man Born Blind

9 As Jesus was walking along, he saw a man who had been born blind. ²His followers asked him, "Teacher, whose sin caused this man to be born blind—his own sin or his parents' sin?"

³Jesus answered, "It is not this man's sin or his parents' sin that made him blind. This man was born blind so that God's power could be shown in him. ⁴While it is daytime, we must continue doing the work of the One who sent me. Night is coming, when no one can work. ⁵While I am in the world, I am the light of the world."

⁶After Jesus said this, he spit on the ground and made some mud with it and put the mud on the man's eyes. ⁷Then he told the man, "Go and wash in the Pool of Siloam." (Siloam means Sent.) So the man went, washed, and came back seeing.

⁸The neighbors and some people who had earlier seen this man begging said, "Isn't this the same man who used to sit and beg?"

⁹Some said, "He is the one," but others said, "No, he only looks like him."

The man himself said, "I am the man."

¹⁰They asked, "How did you get your sight?"

¹¹He answered, "The man named Jesus made some mud and put it on my eyes. Then he told me to go to Siloam and wash. So I went and washed, and then I could see."

¹²They asked him, "Where is this man?"

"I don't know," he answered.

Pharisees Question the Healing

¹³Then the people took to the Pharisees the man who had been blind. ¹⁴The day Jesus had made mud and healed his eyes was a Sabbath day. ¹⁵So now the Pharisees asked the man, "How did you get your sight?"

He answered, "He put mud on my eyes, I washed, and now I see."

¹⁶So some of the Pharisees were saying, "This man does not keep the Sabbath day, so he is not from God."

But others said, "A man who is a sinner can't do miracles like these." So they could not agree with each other.

¹⁷They asked the man again, "What do you say about him since it was your eyes he opened?"

The man answered, "He is a prophet."

¹⁸These leaders did not believe that he had been blind and could now see again. So they sent for the man's parents ¹⁹and asked them, "Is this your son who you say was born blind? Then how does he now see?"

²⁰His parents answered, "We know that this is our son and that he was born blind. ²¹But we don't know how he can now see. We don't know who opened his eyes. Ask him. He is old enough to speak for himself." ²²His parents said this because they were afraid of the elders, who had already decided that anyone who said Jesus was the Christ would be avoided. ²³That is why his parents said, "He is old enough. Ask him."

MAY 27

1 KINGS 1:1—2:46

Adonijah Tries to Become King

1 At this time King David was very old, and although his servants covered him with blankets, he could not keep warm. ²They said to him, "We will look for a young woman to care for you. She will lie close to you and keep you warm." ³After searching everywhere in Israel for a beautiful young woman, they found a girl named Abishag from Shunam and brought her to the king. ⁴The girl was very beautiful, and she cared for the king and served him. But the king did not have sexual relations with her.

⁵Adonijah was the son of King David and Haggith, and he was very proud. "I will be the king," he said. So he got chariots and horses for himself and fifty men for his personal bodyguard. ⁶Now David had never interfered with Adonijah by questioning what he did. Born next after Absalom, Adonijah was a very handsome man.

⁷Adonijah spoke with Joab son of Zeruiah and Abiathar the priest, and they agreed to help him. ⁸But Zadok the priest, Benaiah son of Jehoiada, Nathan the prophet, Shimei, Rei, and King David's special guard did not join Adonijah.

⁹Then Adonijah killed some sheep, cows, and fat calves for sacrifices at the Stone of Zoheleth near the spring of Rogel. He invited all his brothers, the other sons of King David, to come, as well as all the men of Judah. ¹⁰But Adonijah did not invite Nathan

the prophet, Benaiah, his father's special guard, or his brother Solomon.

[11]When Nathan heard about this, he went to Bathsheba, Solomon's mother. "Have you heard that Adonijah, Haggith's son, has made himself king?" Nathan asked. "Our real king, David, does not know it. [12]I strongly advise you to save yourself and your sons. [13]Go to King David and tell him, 'My master and king, you promised that my son Solomon would be king and would rule on your throne after you. Why then has Adonijah become king?' [14]While you are still talking to the king, I will come in and tell him that what you have said about Adonijah is true."

[15]So Bathsheba went in to see the aged king in his bedroom, where Abishag, the girl from Shunam, was caring for him. [16]Bathsheba bowed and knelt before the king. He asked, "What do you want?"

[17]She answered, "My master, you made a promise to me in the name of the LORD your God. You said, 'Your son Solomon will become king after me, and he will rule on my throne.' [18]But now, unknown to you, Adonijah has become king. [19]He has killed many cows, fat calves, and sheep for sacrifices. And he has invited all your sons, as well as Abiathar the priest and Joab the commander of the army, but he did not invite Solomon, who serves you. [20]My master and king, all the Israelites are watching you, waiting for you to decide who will be king after you. [21]As soon as you die, Solomon and I will be treated as criminals."

[22]While Bathsheba was still talking with the king, Nathan the prophet arrived. [23]The servants told the king, "Nathan the prophet is here." So Nathan went to the king and bowed facedown on the ground before him.

[24]Nathan said, "My master and king, have you said that Adonijah will be the king after you and that he will rule on your throne? [25]Today he has sacrificed many cows, fat calves, and sheep, and he has invited all your other sons, the commanders of the army, and Abiathar the priest. Right now they are eating and drinking with him. They are saying, 'Long live King Adonijah!' [26]But he did not invite me, your own servant, or Zadok the priest, or Benaiah son of Jehoiada, or your son Solomon. [27]Did you do this? Since we are your servants, why didn't you tell us who should be king after you?'"

David Makes Solomon King

[28]Then the king said, "Tell Bathsheba to come in!" So she came in and stood before the king.

[29]Then the king made this promise, "The LORD has saved me from all trouble. As surely as he lives, [30]I will do today what I have promised you in the name of the LORD, the God of Israel. I promised that your son Solomon would be king after me and rule on my throne in my place."

[31]Then Bathsheba bowed facedown on the ground and knelt before the king and said, "Long live my master King David!"

[32]Then King David said, "Tell Zadok the priest, Nathan the prophet, and Benaiah son of Jehoiada to come in." When they came before the king, [33]he said to them, "Take my servants with you and put my son Solomon on my own mule. Take him down to the spring called Gihon. [34]There Zadok the priest and Nathan the prophet should pour olive oil on him and make him king over Israel. Blow the trumpet and shout, 'Long live King Solomon!' [35]Then come back up here with him. He will sit on my throne and rule in my place, because he is the one I have chosen to be the ruler over Israel and Judah."

[36]Benaiah son of Jehoiada answered the king, "Amen! This is what the LORD, the God of my master, has declared! [37]The LORD has always helped you, our king. May he also help Solomon and make King Solomon's throne an even greater throne than yours."

[38]So Zadok the priest, Nathan the prophet, and Benaiah son of Jehoiada left with the Kerethites and Pelethites.[n] They put Solomon on King David's mule and took him to the spring called Gihon. [39]Zadok the priest took the container of olive oil from the Holy Tent and poured the oil on Solomon's head to

1:38 Kerethites and Pelethites These were probably special units of the army that were responsible for the king's safety, a kind of palace guard.

show he was the king. Then they blew the trumpet, and all the people shouted, "Long live King Solomon!" [40]All the people followed Solomon into the city. Playing flutes and shouting for joy, they made so much noise the ground shook.

[41]At this time Adonijah and all the guests with him were finishing their meal. When he heard the sound from the trumpet, Joab asked, "What does all that noise from the city mean?"

[42]While Joab was speaking, Jonathan son of Abiathar the priest arrived. Adonijah said, "Come in! You are an important man, so you must be bringing good news."

[43]But Jonathan answered, "No! Our master King David has made Solomon the new king. [44]King David sent Zadok the priest, Nathan the prophet, Benaiah son of Jehoiada, and all the king's bodyguards with him, and they have put Solomon on the king's own mule. [45]Then Zadok the priest and Nathan the prophet poured olive oil on Solomon at Gihon to make him king. After that they went into the city, shouting with joy. Now the whole city is excited, and that is the noise you hear. [46]Solomon has now become the king. [47]All the king's officers have come to tell King David that he has done a good thing. They are saying, 'May your God make Solomon even more famous than you and an even greater king than you.'" Jonathan continued, "And King David bowed down on his bed to worship God, [48]saying, 'Bless the LORD, the God of Israel. Today he has made one of my sons the king and allowed me to see it.'"

[49]Then all of Adonijah's guests were afraid, and they left quickly and scattered. [50]Adonijah was also afraid of Solomon, so he went and took hold of the corners of the altar.[n] [51]Then someone told Solomon, "Adonijah is afraid of you, so he is at the altar, holding on to its corners. He says, 'Tell King Solomon to promise me today that he will not kill me.'"

[52]So Solomon answered, "Adonijah must show that he is a man of honor. If he does

that, I promise he will not lose even a single hair from his head. But if he does anything wrong, he will die." [53]Then King Solomon sent some men to get Adonijah. When he was brought from the altar, he came before King Solomon and bowed down. Solomon told him, "Go home."

The Death of David

2 Since it was almost time for David to die, he gave his son Solomon his last commands. [2]David said, "My time to die is near. Be a good and strong leader. [3]Obey the LORD your God. Follow him by obeying his demands, his commands, his laws, and his rules that are written in the teachings of Moses. If you do these things, you will be successful in all you do and wherever you go. [4]And if you obey the LORD, he will keep the promise he made to me. He said: 'If your descendants live as I tell them and have complete faith in me, a man from your family will always be king over the people of Israel.'

[5]"Also, you remember what Joab son of Zeruiah did to me. He killed the two commanders of Israel's armies: Abner son of Ner and Amasa son of Jether. He did this as if he and they were at war, although it was a time of peace. He put their blood on the belt around his waist and on his sandals on his feet. [6]Punish him in the way you think is wisest, but do not let him die peacefully of old age.

[7]"Be kind to the children of Barzillai of Gilead, and allow them to eat at your table. They welcomed me when I ran away from your brother Absalom.

[8]"And remember, Shimei son of Gera, the Benjaminite, is here with you. He cursed me the day I went to Mahanaim. But when he came down to meet me at the Jordan River, I promised him before the Lord, 'Shimei, I will not kill you.' [9]But you should not leave him unpunished. You are a wise man, and you will know what to do to him, but you must be sure he is killed."

[10]Then David died and was buried with his ancestors in Jerusalem. [11]He had ruled over Israel forty years—seven years in Hebron and thirty-three years in Jerusalem.

1:50 corners of the altar If a person were innocent of a crime, he could run into the Holy Place where the altar was. If he held on to the corners of the altar, which looked like horns, he would be safe.

Solomon Takes Control as King

[12]Solomon became king after David, his father, and he was in firm control of his kingdom.

[13]At this time Adonijah son of Haggith went to Bathsheba, Solomon's mother. "Do you come in peace?" Bathsheba asked.

"Yes. This is a peaceful visit," Adonijah answered. [14]"I have something to say to you."

"You may speak," she said.

[15]"You remember that at one time the kingdom was mine," Adonijah said. "All the people of Israel recognized me as their king, but things have changed. Now my brother is the king, because the LORD chose him. [16]Now I have one thing to ask you; please do not refuse me."

Bathsheba answered, "What do you want?"

[17]"I know King Solomon will do anything you ask him," Adonijah continued. "Please ask him to give me Abishag the Shunammite to be my wife."

[18]"Very well," she answered. "I will speak to the king for you."

[19]So Bathsheba went to King Solomon to speak to him for Adonijah. When Solomon saw her, he stood up to meet her, then bowed down, and sat on the throne. He told some servants to bring another throne for his mother. Then she sat down at his right side.

[20]Bathsheba said, "I have one small thing to ask you. Please do not refuse me."

"Ask, mother," the king answered. "I will not refuse you."

[21]So she said, "Allow Abishag the Shunammite to marry your brother Adonijah."

[22]King Solomon answered his mother, "Why do you ask me to give him Abishag? Why don't you also ask for him to become the king since he is my older brother? Abiathar the priest and Joab son of Zeruiah would support him!"

[23]Then King Solomon swore by the name of the LORD, saying, "May God punish me terribly if this doesn't cost Adonijah his life! [24]By the LORD who has given me the throne that belonged to my father David and who has kept his promise and given the kingdom to me and my people, Adonijah will die today!" [25]Then King Solomon gave orders to Benaiah son of Jehoiada, and he went and killed Adonijah.

[26]King Solomon said to Abiathar the priest, "I should kill you too, but I will allow you to go back to your fields in Anathoth. I will not kill you at this time, because you helped carry the Ark of the Lord GOD while marching with my father David. And I know you shared in all the hard times with him." [27]Then Solomon removed Abiathar from being the LORD's priest. This happened as the LORD had said it would, when he was speaking in Shiloh about the priest Eli and his descendants.

[28]When Joab heard about what had happened, he was afraid. He had supported Adonijah but not Absalom. So Joab ran to the Tent of the LORD and took hold of the corners of the altar.[n] [29]Someone told King Solomon that Joab had run to the Tent of the LORD and was beside the altar. Then Solomon ordered Benaiah to go and kill him.

[30]Benaiah went into the Tent of the LORD and said to Joab, "The king says, 'Come out!'"

But Joab answered, "No, I will die here."

So Benaiah went back to the king and told him what Joab had said. [31]Then the king ordered Benaiah, "Do as he says! Kill him there and bury him. Then my family and I will be free of the guilt of Joab, who has killed innocent people. [32]Without my father knowing it, he killed two men who were much better than he was—Abner son of Ner, the commander of Israel's army, and Amasa son of Jether, the commander of Judah's army. So the LORD will pay him back for those deaths. [33]Joab and his family will be forever guilty for their deaths, but there will be peace from the LORD for David, his descendants, his family, and his throne forever."

[34]So Benaiah son of Jehoiada killed Joab, and he was buried near his home in the desert. [35]The king then made Benaiah son of Jehoiada commander of the army in Joab's place. He also made Zadok the new high priest in Abiathar's place.

2:28 corners of the altar If a person were innocent of a crime, he could run into the Holy Place where the altar was. If he held on to the corners of the altar, which looked like horns, he would be safe.

36Next the king sent for Shimei. Solomon said to him, "Build a house for yourself in Jerusalem and live there. Don't leave the city. 37The very day you leave and cross the Kidron Valley, someone will kill you, and it will be your own fault."

38So Shimei answered the king, "I agree with what you say. I will do what you say, my master and king." So Shimei lived in Jerusalem for a long time.

39But three years later two of Shimei's slaves ran away to Achish king of Gath, who was the son of Maacah. Shimei heard that his slaves were in Gath, 40so he put his saddle on his donkey and went to Achish at Gath to find them. Then he brought them back from Gath.

41Someone told Solomon that Shimei had gone from Jerusalem to Gath and had returned. 42So Solomon sent for Shimei and said, "I made you promise in the name of the LORD not to leave Jerusalem. I warned you if you went out anywhere you would die, and you agreed to what I said. 43Why did you break your promise to the LORD and disobey my command?" 44The king also said, "You know the many wrong things you did to my father David, so now the LORD will punish you for those wrongs. 45But the LORD will bless me and make the rule of David safe before the LORD forever."

46Then the king ordered Benaiah to kill Shimei, and he did. Now Solomon was in full control of his kingdom.

PSALM 68:11–14

11The Lord gave the command,
    and a great army told the news:
12"Kings and their armies run away.
    In camp they divide the wealth taken in war.
13Those who stayed by the campfires
    will share the riches taken in battle."
14The Almighty scattered kings
    like snow on Mount Zalmon.

PROVERBS 17:7–9

7Fools should not be proud,
    and rulers should not be liars.

8Some people think they can pay others to
    do anything they ask.
    They think it will work every time.

9Whoever forgives someone's sin makes a friend,
    but gossiping about the sin breaks up friendships.

JOHN 9:24–41

24So for the second time, they called the man who had been blind. They said, "You should give God the glory by telling the truth. We know that this man is a sinner."

25He answered, "I don't know if he is a sinner. One thing I do know: I was blind, and now I see."

26They asked, "What did he do to you? How did he make you see again?"

27He answered, "I already told you, and you didn't listen. Why do you want to hear it again? Do you want to become his followers, too?"

28Then they insulted him and said, "You are his follower, but we are followers of Moses. 29We know that God spoke to Moses, but we don't even know where this man comes from."

30The man answered, "This is a very strange thing. You don't know where he comes from, and yet he opened my eyes. 31We all know that God does not listen to sinners, but he listens to anyone who worships and obeys him. 32Nobody has ever heard of anyone giving sight to a man born blind. 33If this man were not from God, he could do nothing."

34They answered, "You were born full of sin! Are you trying to teach us?" And they threw him out.

Spiritual Blindness

35When Jesus heard that they had thrown him out, Jesus found him and said, "Do you believe in the Son of Man?"

36He asked, "Who is the Son of Man, sir, so that I can believe in him?"

37Jesus said to him, "You have seen him. The Son of Man is the one talking with you."

38He said, "Lord, I believe!" Then the man worshiped Jesus.

[39]Jesus said, "I came into this world so that the world could be judged. I came so that the blind[n] would see and so that those who see will become blind."

[40]Some of the Pharisees who were nearby heard Jesus say this and asked, "Are you saying we are blind, too?"

[41]Jesus said, "If you were blind, you would not be guilty of sin. But since you keep saying you see, your guilt remains."

MAY 28

1 KINGS 3:1—4:34

Solomon Asks for Wisdom

3 Solomon made an agreement with the king of Egypt by marrying his daughter and bringing her to Jerusalem. At this time Solomon was still building his palace and the Temple of the LORD, as well as a wall around Jerusalem. [2]The Temple for the worship of the LORD had not yet been finished, so people were still sacrificing at altars in many places of worship. [3]Solomon showed he loved the LORD by following the commands his father David had given him, except many other places of worship were still used to offer sacrifices and to burn incense.

[4]King Solomon went to Gibeon to offer a sacrifice, because it was the most important place of worship. He offered a thousand burnt offerings on that altar. [5]While he was at Gibeon, the LORD appeared to him in a dream during the night. God said, "Ask for whatever you want me to give you."

[6]Solomon answered, "You were very kind to your servant, my father David. He obeyed you, and he was honest and lived right. You showed great kindness to him when you allowed his son to be king after him. [7]LORD my God, now you have made me, your servant, king in my father's place. But I am like a little child; I don't know how to do what must be done. [8]I, your servant, am here among your chosen people, and there are too many of them to count. [9]I ask that you give me a heart that understands, so I can rule the people in the right way and will know the difference between right and wrong. Otherwise, it is impossible to rule this great people of yours."

[10]The Lord was pleased that Solomon had asked this. [11]So God said to him, "You did not ask for a long life, or riches for yourself, or the death of your enemies. Since you asked for wisdom to make the right decisions, [12]I will do what you asked. I will give you wisdom and understanding that is greater than anyone has had in the past or will have in the future. [13]I will also give you what you did not ask for: riches and honor. During your life no other king will be as great as you. [14]If you follow me and obey my laws and commands, as your father David did, I will also give you a long life."

[15]After Solomon woke up from the dream, he went to Jerusalem. He stood before the Ark of the Agreement with the LORD, where he made burnt offerings and fellowship offerings. After that, he gave a feast for all his leaders and officers.

Solomon Makes a Wise Decision

[16]One day two women who were prostitutes came to Solomon. As they stood before him, [17]one of the women said, "My master, this woman and I live in the same house. I gave birth to a baby while she was there with me. [18]Three days later this woman also gave birth to a baby. No one else was in the house with us; it was just the two of us. [19]One night this woman rolled over on her baby, and he died. [20]So she took my son from my bed during the night while I was asleep, and she carried him to her bed. Then she put the dead baby in my bed. [21]The next morning when I got up to feed my baby, I saw that he was dead! When I looked at him more closely, I realized he was not my son."

9:39 blind Jesus is talking about people who are spiritually blind, not physically blind.

²²"No!" the other woman cried. "The living baby is my son, and the dead baby is yours!"

But the first woman said, "No! The dead baby is yours, and the living one is mine!" So the two women argued before the king.

²³Then King Solomon said, "One of you says, 'My son is alive and your son is dead.' Then the other one says, 'No! Your son is dead and my son is alive.'"

²⁴The king sent his servants to get a sword. When they brought it to him, ²⁵he said, "Cut the living baby into two pieces, and give each woman half."

²⁶The real mother of the living child was full of love for her son. So she said to the king, "Please, my master, don't kill him! Give the baby to her!"

But the other woman said, "Neither of us will have him. Cut him into two pieces!"

²⁷Then King Solomon said, "Don't kill him. Give the baby to the first woman, because she is the real mother."

²⁸When the people of Israel heard about King Solomon's decision, they respected him very much. They saw he had wisdom from God to make the right decisions.

Solomon's Officers

4 King Solomon ruled over all Israel. ²These are the names of his leading officers:

Azariah son of Zadok was the priest;

³Elihoreph and Ahijah, sons of Shisha, recorded what happened in the courts;

Jehoshaphat son of Ahilud recorded the history of the people;

⁴Benaiah son of Jehoiada was commander of the army;

Zadok and Abiathar were priests;

⁵Azariah son of Nathan was in charge of the district governors;

Zabud son of Nathan was a priest and adviser to the king;

⁶Ahishar was responsible for everything in the palace;

Adoniram son of Abda was in charge of the labor force.

⁷Solomon placed twelve governors over the districts of Israel, who gathered food from their districts for the king and his family. Each governor was responsible for bringing food to the king one month of each year. ⁸These are the names of the twelve governors:

Ben-Hur was governor of the mountain country of Ephraim.

⁹Ben-Deker was governor of Makaz, Shaalbim, Beth Shemesh, and Elon Bethhanan.

¹⁰Ben-Hesed was governor of Arubboth, Socoh, and all the land of Hepher.

¹¹Ben-Abinadab was governor of Naphoth Dor. (He was married to Taphath, Solomon's daughter.)

¹²Baana son of Ahilud was governor of Taanach, Megiddo, and all of Beth Shan next to Zarethan. This was below Jezreel from Beth Shan to Abel Meholah across from Jokmeam.

¹³Ben-Geber was governor of Ramoth in Gilead. (He was governor of all the towns of Jair in Gilead. Jair was the son of Manasseh. Ben-Geber was also over the district of Argob in Bashan, which had sixty large, walled cities with bronze bars on their gates.)

¹⁴Ahinadab son of Iddo was governor of Mahanaim.

¹⁵Ahimaaz was governor of Naphtali. (He was married to Basemath, Solomon's daughter.)

¹⁶Baana son of Hushai was governor of Asher and Aloth.

¹⁷Jehoshaphat son of Paruah was governor of Issachar.

¹⁸Shimei son of Ela was governor of Benjamin.

¹⁹Geber son of Uri was governor of Gilead. Gilead had been the country of Sihon king of the Amorites and Og king of Bashan. But Geber was the only governor over this district.

Solomon's Kingdom

²⁰There were as many people in Judah and Israel as grains of sand on the seashore. The people ate, drank, and were happy. ²¹Solomon ruled over all the kingdoms from the Euphrates River to the land of the Philistines, as far as the border of Egypt. These countries brought Solomon the payments he demanded, and they were under his control all his life.

²²Solomon needed much food each day to feed himself and all the people who ate at his table: one hundred ninety-five bushels of fine flour, three hundred ninety bushels of grain, ²³ten cows that were fed on good grain, twenty cows that were raised in the fields, one hundred sheep, three kinds of deer, and fattened birds.

²⁴Solomon controlled all the countries west of the Euphrates River—the land from Tiphsah to Gaza. And he had peace on all sides of his kingdom. ²⁵During Solomon's life Judah and Israel, from Dan to Beersheba,ⁿ also lived in peace; all of his people were able to sit under their own fig trees and grapevines.

²⁶Solomon had four thousand stalls for his chariot horses and twelve thousand horses. ²⁷Each month one of the district governors gave King Solomon all the food he needed—enough for every person who ate at the king's table. The governors made sure he had everything he needed. ²⁸They also brought enough barley and straw for Solomon's chariot and work horses; each person brought this grain to the right place.

Solomon's Wisdom

²⁹God gave Solomon great wisdom so he could understand many things. His wisdom was as hard to measure as the grains of sand on the seashore. ³⁰His wisdom was greater than any wisdom of the East, or any wisdom in Egypt. ³¹He was wiser than anyone on earth. He was even wiser than Ethan the Ezrahite, as well as Heman, Calcol, and Darda—the three sons of Mahol. King Solomon became famous in all the surrounding countries. ³²During his life he spoke three thousand wise sayings and also wrote one thousand five songs. ³³He taught about many kinds of plants—everything from the great cedar trees of Lebanon to the weeds that grow out of the walls. He also taught about animals, birds, crawling things, and fish. ³⁴People from all nations came to listen to King Solomon's wisdom. The kings of all nations sent them to him, because they had heard of Solomon's wisdom.

PSALM 68:15–20

¹⁵The mountains of Bashan are high;
 the mountains of Bashan have many
  peaks.
¹⁶Why do you mountains with many peaks
 look with envy
 on the mountain that God chose for his
  home?
 The LORD will live there forever.
¹⁷God comes with millions of chariots;
 the Lord comes from Mount Sinai to
  his holy place.
¹⁸When you went up to the heights,
 you led a parade of captives.
 You received gifts from the people,
 even from those who turned against you.
 And the LORD God will live there.

¹⁹Praise the Lord, God our Savior,
 who helps us every day.   *Selah*
²⁰Our God is a God who saves us;
 the LORD God saves us from death.

PROVERBS 17:10–12

¹⁰A wise person will learn more from a
  warning
 than a fool will learn from a hundred
  lashings.

¹¹Disobedient people look only for trouble,
 so a cruel messenger will be sent
  against them.

¹²It is better to meet a bear robbed of her
  cubs
 than to meet a fool doing foolish things.

JOHN 10:1–21

The Shepherd and His Sheep

10 Jesus said, "I tell you the truth, the person who does not enter the sheepfold by the door, but climbs in some other way, is a thief and a robber. ²The one who enters by the door is the shepherd of the sheep. ³The one who guards the door opens it for him. And the sheep listen to the voice of the shepherd. He calls his own sheep by name and leads them out. ⁴When he brings all his

---

4:25 Dan to Beersheba Dan was the city farthest north in Israel, and Beersheba was the city farthest south. So this means all the people of Israel.

sheep out, he goes ahead of them, and they follow him because they know his voice. [5]But they will never follow a stranger. They will run away from him because they don't know his voice." [6]Jesus told the people this story, but they did not understand what it meant.

Jesus Is the Good Shepherd

[7]So Jesus said again, "I tell you the truth, I am the door for the sheep. [8]All the people who came before me were thieves and robbers. The sheep did not listen to them. [9]I am the door, and the person who enters through me will be saved and will be able to come in and go out and find pasture. [10]A thief comes to steal and kill and destroy, but I came to give life—life in all its fullness.

[11]"I am the good shepherd. The good shepherd gives his life for the sheep. [12]The worker who is paid to keep the sheep is different from the shepherd who owns them. When the worker sees a wolf coming, he runs away and leaves the sheep alone. Then the wolf attacks the sheep and scatters them.

[13]The man runs away because he is only a paid worker and does not really care about the sheep.

[14]"I am the good shepherd. I know my sheep, and my sheep know me, [15]just as the Father knows me, and I know the Father. I give my life for the sheep. [16]I have other sheep that are not in this flock, and I must bring them also. They will listen to my voice, and there will be one flock and one shepherd. [17]The Father loves me because I give my life so that I can take it back again. [18]No one takes it away from me; I give my own life freely. I have the right to give my life, and I have the right to take it back. This is what my Father commanded me to do."

[19]Again the leaders did not agree with each other because of these words of Jesus. [20]Many of them said, "A demon has come into him and made him crazy. Why listen to him?"

[21]But others said, "A man who is crazy with a demon does not say things like this. Can a demon open the eyes of the blind?"

MAY 29

1 KINGS 5:1—6:38

Preparing to Build the Temple

5 Hiram, the king of Tyre, had always been David's friend. When Hiram heard that Solomon had been made king in David's place, he sent his messengers to Solomon. [2]Solomon sent this message back to King Hiram: [3]"You remember my father David had to fight many wars with the countries around him, so he was never able to build a temple for worshiping the LORD his God. David was waiting until the LORD allowed him to defeat all his enemies. [4]But now the LORD my God has given me peace on all sides of my country. I have no enemies now, and no danger threatens my people. [5]"The LORD promised my father David, 'I will make your son king after you, and he will build a temple for worshiping me.' Now, I plan to build that temple for worshiping

the LORD my God. [6]So send your men to cut down cedar trees for me from Lebanon. My servants will work with yours, and I will pay them whatever wages you decide. We don't have anyone who can cut down trees as well as the people of Sidon."

[7]When Hiram heard what Solomon asked, he was very happy. He said, "Praise the LORD today! He has given David a wise son to rule over this great nation!" [8]Then Hiram sent back this message to Solomon: "I received the message you sent, and I will give you all the cedar and pine trees you want. [9]My servants will bring them down from Lebanon to the sea. There I will tie them together and float them along the shore to the place you choose. Then I will separate the logs there, and you can take them away. In return it is my wish that you give food to all those who live with me." [10]So Hiram gave Solomon as much cedar and

pine as he wanted. [11]And Solomon gave Hiram about one hundred twenty-five thousand bushels of wheat each year to feed the people who lived with him. Solomon also gave him about one hundred fifteen thousand gallons of pure olive oil every year.

[12]The LORD gave Solomon wisdom as he had promised. And there was peace between Hiram and Solomon; these two kings made a treaty between themselves.

[13]King Solomon forced thirty thousand men of Israel to help in this work. [14]He sent a group of ten thousand men each month to Lebanon. Each group worked in Lebanon one month, then went home for two months. A man named Adoniram was in charge. [15]Solomon forced eighty thousand men to work in the hill country, cutting stone, and he had seventy thousand men to carry the stones. [16]There were also thirty-three hundred men who directed the workers. [17]King Solomon commanded them to cut large blocks of fine stone to be used for the foundation of the Temple. [18]Solomon's and Hiram's builders and the men from Byblos carved the stones and prepared the stones and the logs for building the Temple.

Solomon Builds the Temple

6Solomon began to build the Temple four hundred eighty years after the people of Israel had left Egypt. This was during the fourth year of King Solomon's rule over Israel. It was the second month, the month of Ziv.

[2]The Temple was ninety feet long, thirty feet wide, and forty-five feet high. [3]The porch in front of the main room of the Temple was fifteen feet deep and thirty feet wide. This room ran along the front of the Temple itself. Its width was equal to that of the Temple. [4]The Temple also had windows that opened and closed. [5]Solomon also built some side rooms against the walls of the main room and the inner room of the Temple. He built rooms all around. [6]The rooms on the bottom floor were seven and one-half feet wide. Those on the middle floor were nine feet wide, and the rooms above them were ten and one-half feet wide. The Temple wall that formed the side of each room was

thinner than the wall in the room below. These rooms were pushed against the Temple wall, but they did not have their main beams built into this wall.

[7]The stones were prepared at the same place where they were cut from the ground. Since these stones were the only ones used to build the Temple, there was no noise of hammers, axes, or any other iron tools at the Temple.

[8]The entrance to the lower rooms beside the Temple was on the south side. From there, stairs went up to the second-floor rooms. And from there, stairs went on to the third-floor rooms. [9]Solomon put a roof made from beams and cedar boards on the Temple. So he finished building the Temple [10]as well as the bottom floor that was beside the Temple. This bottom floor was seven and one-half feet high and was attached to the Temple by cedar beams.

[11]The LORD said to Solomon: [12]"If you obey all my laws and commands, I will do for you what I promised your father David. [13]I will live among the Israelites in this Temple, and I will never leave my people Israel."

[14]So Solomon finished building the Temple. [15]The inside walls were covered from floor to ceiling with cedar boards. The floor was made from pine boards. [16]A room thirty feet long was built in the back part of the Temple. This room, called the Most Holy Place, was separated from the rest of Temple by cedar boards which reached from floor to ceiling. [17]The main room, the one in front of the Most Holy Place, was sixty feet long. [18]Everything inside the Temple was covered with cedar, which was carved with pictures of flowers and plants. A person could not see the stones of the wall, only the cedar.

[19]Solomon prepared the inner room at the back of the Temple to keep the Ark of the Agreement with the LORD. [20]This inner room was thirty feet long, thirty feet wide, and thirty feet high. He covered this room with pure gold, and he also covered the altar of cedar. [21]He covered the inside of the Temple with pure gold, placing gold chains across the front of the inner room, which was also covered with gold. [22]So all the inside of the

Temple, as well as the altar of the Most Holy Place, was covered with gold.

²³Solomon made two creatures from olive wood and placed them in the Most Holy Place. Each creature was fifteen feet tall ²⁴and had two wings. Each wing was seven and one-half feet long, so it was fifteen feet from the end of one wing to the end of the other. ²⁵The creatures were the same size and shape; ²⁶each was fifteen feet tall. ²⁷These creatures were put beside each other in the Most Holy Place with their wings spread out. One creature's wing touched one wall, and the other creature's wing touched the other wall with their wings touching each other in the middle of the room. ²⁸These two creatures were covered with gold.

²⁹All the walls around the Temple were carved with pictures of creatures with wings, as well as palm trees and flowers. This was true for both the main room and the inner room. ³⁰The floors of both rooms were covered with gold.

³¹Doors made from olive wood were placed at the entrance to the Most Holy Place. These doors had five-sided frames. ³²Creatures with wings, as well as palm trees and flowers, were also carved on the two olive wood doors that were covered with gold. The creatures and the palm trees on the doors were covered with gold as well. ³³At the entrance to the main room there was a square door frame made of olive wood. ³⁴Two doors were made from pine. Each door had two parts so the doors folded. ³⁵The doors were covered with pictures of creatures with wings, as well as palm trees and flowers. All of the carvings were covered with gold, which was evenly spread over them.

³⁶The inner courtyard was enclosed by walls, which were made of three rows of cut stones and one row of cedar boards.

³⁷Work began on the Temple in Ziv, the second month, during the fourth year Solomon was king over Israel. ³⁸The Temple was finished during the eleventh year he was king, in the eighth month, the month of Bul. It was built exactly as it was planned. Solomon had spent seven years building it.

PSALM 68:21–27

²¹God will crush his enemies' heads,
  the hairy skulls of those who continue to sin.
²²The Lord said, "I will bring the enemy back from Bashan;
  I will bring them back from the depths of the sea.
²³Then you can stick your feet in their blood,
  and your dogs can lick their share."

²⁴God, people have seen your victory march;
  God my King marched into the holy place.
²⁵The singers are in front and the instruments are behind.
  In the middle are the girls with the tambourines.
²⁶Praise God in the meeting place;
  praise the LORD in the gathering of Israel.
²⁷There is the smallest tribe, Benjamin, leading them.
  And there are the leaders of Judah with their group.
  There also are the leaders of Zebulun and of Naphtali.

PROVERBS 17:13–15

¹³Whoever gives evil in return for good will always have trouble at home.

¹⁴Starting a quarrel is like a leak in a dam, so stop it before a fight breaks out.

¹⁵The LORD hates both of these things: freeing the guilty and punishing the innocent.

JOHN 10:22–42

Jesus Is Rejected

²²The time came for the Feast of Dedication at Jerusalem. It was winter, ²³and Jesus was walking in the Temple in Solomon's Porch. ²⁴Some people gathered around him and said, "How long will you make us wonder about you? If you are the Christ, tell us plainly."

²⁵Jesus answered, "I told you already, but

you did not believe. The miracles I do in my Father's name show who I am. [26]But you don't believe, because you are not my sheep. [27]My sheep listen to my voice; I know them, and they follow me. [28]I give them eternal life, and they will never die, and no one can steal them out of my hand. [29]My Father gave my sheep to me. He is greater than all, and no person can steal my sheep out of my Father's hand. [30]The Father and I are one."

[31]Again some of the people picked up stones to kill Jesus. [32]But he said to them, "I have done many good works from the Father. Which of these good works are you killing me for?"

[33]They answered, "We are not killing you because of any good work you did, but because you speak against God. You are only a human, but you say you are the same as God!"

[34]Jesus answered, "It is written in your law that God said, 'I said, you are gods.'[n] [35]This Scripture called those people gods who received God's message, and Scripture is always true. [36]So why do you say that I speak against God because I said, 'I am God's Son'? I am the one God chose and sent into the world. [37]If I don't do what my Father does, then don't believe me. [38]But if I do what my Father does, even though you don't believe in me, believe what I do. Then you will know and understand that the Father is in me and I am in the Father."

[39]They tried to take Jesus again, but he escaped from them.

[40]Then he went back across the Jordan River to the place where John had first baptized. Jesus stayed there, [41]and many people came to him and said, "John never did a miracle, but everything John said about this man is true." [42]And in that place many believed in Jesus.

MAY 30

1 KINGS 7:1—8:66

Solomon's Palace

7 King Solomon also built a palace for himself; it took him thirteen years to finish it. [2]Built of cedars from the Forest of Lebanon, it was one hundred fifty feet long, seventy-five feet wide, and forty-five feet high. It had four rows of cedar columns which supported the cedar beams. [3]There were forty-five beams on the roof, with fifteen beams in each row, and the ceiling was covered with cedar above the beams. [4]Windows were placed in three rows facing each other. [5]All the doors were square, and the three doors at each end faced each other.

[6]Solomon also built the porch that had pillars. This porch was seventy-five feet long and forty-five feet wide. Along the front of the porch was a roof supported by pillars.

[7]Solomon also built a throne room where he judged people, called the Hall of Justice. This room was covered with cedar from the floor to the ceiling. [8]The palace where Solomon lived was built like the Hall of Justice, and it was behind this hall. Solomon also built the same kind of palace for his wife, who was the daughter of the king of Egypt.

[9]All these buildings were made with blocks of fine stone. First they were carefully cut. Then they were trimmed with a saw in the front and back. These fine stones went from the foundations of the buildings to the top of the walls. Even the courtyard was made with blocks of stone. [10]The foundations were made with large blocks of fine stone, some as long as fifteen feet. Others were twelve feet long. [11]On top of these foundation stones were other blocks of fine stone and cedar beams. [12]The palace courtyard, the courtyard inside the Temple, and the porch of the Temple were surrounded by walls. All of these walls had three rows of stone blocks and one row of cedar beams.

10:34 'I . . . gods.' Quotation from Psalm 82:6.

The Temple Is Completed Inside

¹³King Solomon sent to Tyre and had Huram brought to him. ¹⁴Huram's mother was a widow from the tribe of Naphtali. His father was from Tyre and had been skilled in making things from bronze. Huram was also very skilled and experienced in bronze work. So he came to King Solomon and did all the bronze work.

¹⁵He made two bronze pillars, each one twenty-seven feet tall and eighteen feet around. ¹⁶He also made two bronze capitals that were seven and one-half feet tall, and he put them on top of the pillars. ¹⁷Then he made a net of seven chains for each capital, which covered the capitals on top of the two pillars. ¹⁸He made two rows of bronze pomegranates to go on the nets. These covered the capitals at the top of the pillars. ¹⁹The capitals on top of the pillars in the porch were shaped like lilies, and they were six feet tall. ²⁰The capitals were on top of both pillars, above the bowl-shaped section and next to the nets. At that place there were two hundred pomegranates in rows all around the capitals. ²¹Huram put these two bronze pillars at the porch of the Temple. He named the south pillar He Establishes and the north pillar In Him Is Strength. ²²The capitals on top of the pillars were shaped like lilies. So the work on the pillars was finished.

²³Then Huram made from bronze a large round bowl, which was called the Sea. It was forty-five feet around, fifteen feet across, and seven and one-half feet deep. ²⁴Around the outer edge of the bowl was a rim. Under this rim were two rows of bronze plants which surrounded the bowl. There were ten plants every eighteen inches, and these plants were made in one piece with the bowl. ²⁵The bowl rested on the backs of twelve bronze bulls that faced outward from the center of the bowl. Three bulls faced north, three faced west, three faced south, and three faced east. ²⁶The sides of the bowl were four inches thick, and it held about eleven thousand gallons. The rim of the bowl was like the rim of a cup or like a lily blossom.

²⁷Then Huram made ten bronze stands, each one six feet long, six feet wide, and four and one-half feet high. ²⁸The stands were made from square sides, which were put on frames. ²⁹On the sides were bronze lions, bulls, and creatures with wings. On the frames above and below the lions and bulls were designs of flowers hammered into the bronze. ³⁰Each stand had four bronze wheels with bronze axles. At the corners there were bronze supports for a large bowl, and the supports had designs of flowers. ³¹There was a frame on top of the bowls, eighteen inches high above the bowls. The opening of the bowl was round, twenty-seven inches deep. Designs were carved into the bronze on the frame, which was square, not round. ³²The four wheels, placed under the frame, were twenty-seven inches high. The axles between the wheels were made as one piece with the stand. ³³The wheels were like a chariot's wheels. Everything on the wheels—the axles, rims, spokes, and hubs—were made of bronze.

³⁴The four supports were on the four corners of each stand. They were made as one piece with the stand. ³⁵A strip of bronze around the top of each stand was nine inches deep. It was also made as one piece with the stand. ³⁶The sides of the stand and the frames were covered with carvings of creatures with wings, as well as lions, palm trees, and flowers. ³⁷This is the way Huram made the ten stands. The bronze for each stand was melted and poured into a mold, so all the stands were the same size and shape.

³⁸Huram also made ten bronze bowls, one bowl for each of the ten stands. Each bowl was six feet across and could hold about two hundred thirty gallons. ³⁹Huram put five stands on the south side of the Temple and five on the north side. He put the large bowl in the southeast corner of the Temple. ⁴⁰Huram also made bowls, shovels, and small bowls.

So Huram finished all his work for King Solomon on the Temple of the LORD:

⁴¹two pillars;
two large bowls for the capitals on top of the pillars;
two nets to cover the two large bowls for the capitals on top of the pillars;
⁴²four hundred pomegranates for the two nets (there were two rows of pomegranates for each net covering the bowls for the capitals on top of the pillars);

⁴³ten stands with a bowl on each stand; ⁴⁴the large bowl with twelve bulls under it; ⁴⁵the pots, shovels, small bowls, and all the utensils for the Temple of the LORD.

Huram made everything King Solomon wanted from polished bronze. ⁴⁶The king had these things poured into clay molds that were made in the plain of the Jordan River between Succoth and Zarethan. ⁴⁷Solomon never weighed the bronze used to make these things, because there was too much to weigh. So the total weight of all the bronze was never known.

⁴⁸Solomon also made all the items for the Temple of the LORD:

the golden altar;

the golden table which held the bread that shows God's people are in his presence;

⁴⁹the lampstands of pure gold (five on the right side and five on the left side in front of the Most Holy Place);

the flowers, lamps, and tongs of gold;

⁵⁰the pure gold bowls, wick trimmers, small bowls, pans, and dishes used to carry coals;

the gold hinges for the doors of the Most Holy Place and the main room of the Temple.

⁵¹Finally the work King Solomon did for the Temple of the LORD was finished. Solomon brought in everything his father David had set apart for the Temple—silver, gold, and other articles. He put everything in the treasuries of the Temple of the LORD.

The Ark Is Brought into the Temple

8 King Solomon called for the elders of Israel, the heads of the tribes, and the leaders of the families to come to him in Jerusalem. He wanted them to bring the Ark of the Agreement with the LORD from the older part of the city. ²So all the Israelites came together with King Solomon during the festival in the month of Ethanim, the seventh month.

³When all the elders of Israel arrived, the priests lifted up the Ark. ⁴They carried the Ark of the LORD, the Meeting Tent, and the holy utensils; the priests and the Levites

brought them up. ⁵King Solomon and all the Israelites gathered before the Ark and sacrificed so many sheep and cattle no one could count them all. ⁶Then the priests put the Ark of the Agreement with the LORD in its place inside the Most Holy Place in the Temple, under the wings of the golden creatures. ⁷The wings of these creatures were spread out over the place for the Ark, covering it and its carrying poles. ⁸The carrying poles were so long that anyone standing in the Holy Place in front of the Most Holy Place could see the ends of the poles, but no one could see them from outside the Holy Place. The poles are still there today. ⁹The only things inside the Ark were two stone tablets[n] that Moses had put in the Ark at Mount Sinai. That was where the LORD made his agreement with the Israelites after they came out of Egypt.

¹⁰When the priests left the Holy Place, a cloud filled the Temple of the LORD. ¹¹The priests could not continue their work, because the Temple was filled with the glory of the LORD.

Solomon Speaks to the People

¹²Then Solomon said, "The LORD said he would live in a dark cloud. ¹³LORD, I have truly built a wonderful Temple for you—a place for you to live forever."

¹⁴While all the Israelites were standing there, King Solomon turned to them and blessed them.

¹⁵Then he said, "Praise the LORD, the God of Israel. He has done what he promised to my father David. The LORD said, ¹⁶'Since the time I brought my people Israel out of Egypt, I have not chosen a city in any tribe of Israel where a temple will be built for me. But I have chosen David to lead my people Israel.'

¹⁷"My father David wanted to build a temple for the LORD, the God of Israel. ¹⁸But the LORD said to my father David, 'It was good that you wanted to build a temple for me. ¹⁹But you are not the one to build it. Your son, who comes from your own body, is the one who will build my temple.'

²⁰"Now the LORD has kept his promise. I am the king now in place of David my father.

8:9 stone tablets They were the two tablets on which God wrote the Ten Commandments.

Now I rule Israel as the LORD promised, and I have built the Temple for the LORD, the God of Israel. [21]I have made a place there for the Ark, in which is the Agreement the LORD made with our ancestors when he brought them out of Egypt."

Solomon's Prayer

[22]Then Solomon stood facing the LORD's altar, and all the Israelites were standing behind him. He spread out his hands toward the sky [23]and said:

"LORD, God of Israel, there is no god like you in heaven above or on earth below. You keep your agreement of love with your servants who truly follow you. [24]You have kept the promise you made to your servant David, my father. You spoke it with your own mouth and finished it with your hands today. [25]Now LORD, God of Israel, keep the promise you made to your servant David, my father. You said, 'If your sons are careful to obey me as you have obeyed me, there will always be someone from your family ruling Israel.' [26]Now, God of Israel, please continue to keep that promise you made to your servant David, my father.

[27]"But, God, can you really live here on the earth? The sky and the highest place in heaven cannot contain you. Surely this house which I have built cannot contain you. [28]But please listen to my prayer and my request, because I am your servant. LORD my God, hear this prayer your servant prays to you today. [29]Night and day please watch over this Temple where you have said, 'I will be worshiped there.' Hear the prayer I pray facing this Temple. [30]Hear my prayers and the prayers of your people Israel when we pray facing this place. Hear from your home in heaven, and when you hear, forgive us.

[31]"If someone wrongs another person, he will be brought to the altar in this Temple. If he swears an oath that he is not guilty, [32]then hear in heaven. Judge the case, punish the guilty, but declare that the innocent person is not guilty.

[33]"When your people, the Israelites, sin against you, their enemies will defeat them. But if they come back to you and praise you and pray to you in this Temple, [34]then hear them in heaven. Forgive the sins of your people Israel, and bring them back to the land you gave to their ancestors.

[35]"When they sin against you, you will stop the rain from falling on their land. Then they will pray, facing this place and praising you; they will stop sinning when you make them suffer. [36]When this happens, please hear their prayer in heaven, and forgive the sins of your servants, the Israelites. Teach them to do what is right. Then please send rain to this land you have given particularly to them.

[37]"At times the land will become so dry that no food will grow, or a great sickness will spread among the people. Sometimes all the crops will be destroyed by locusts or grasshoppers. Your people will be attacked in their cities by their enemy or will become sick. [38]When any of these things happen, the people will become truly sorry. If your people spread their hands in prayer toward this Temple, [39]then hear their prayers from your home in heaven. Forgive and treat each person as he should be treated because you know what is in a person's heart. Only you know what is in everyone's heart. [40]Then your people will respect you as long as they live in this land you gave to our ancestors.

[41-42]"People who are not Israelites, foreigners from other lands, will hear about your greatness and power. They will come from far away to pray at this Temple. [43]Then hear from your home in heaven, and do whatever they ask you. Then people everywhere will know you and respect you, just as your people in Israel do. Then everyone will know I built this Temple as a place to worship you.

[44]"When your people go out to fight their enemies along some road on which you send them, your people will pray to you, facing the city which you have chosen and the Temple I have built for you. [45]Then hear in heaven their prayers, and do what is right.

[46]"Everyone sins, so your people will also sin against you. You will become angry with them and hand them over to their enemies. Their enemies will capture them and take them away to their countries far or near. [47]Your people will be sorry for their sins when they are held as prisoners in another country. They will be sorry and pray to you in the land where they are held as prisoners, saying, 'We

have sinned. We have done wrong and acted wickedly." [48]They will truly turn back to you in the land of their enemies. They will pray to you, facing this land you gave their ancestors, this city you have chosen, and the Temple I have built for you. [49]Then hear their prayers from your home in heaven, and do what is right. [50]Forgive your people of all their sins and for turning against you. Make those who have captured them show them mercy. [51]Remember, they are your special people. You brought them out of Egypt, as if you were pulling them out of a blazing furnace.

[52]"Give your attention to my prayers and the prayers of your people Israel. Listen to them anytime they ask you for help. [53]You chose them from all the nations on earth to be your very own people. This is what you promised through Moses your servant when you brought our ancestors out of Egypt, Lord GOD."

[54]Solomon prayed this prayer to the LORD, kneeling in front of the altar with his arms raised toward heaven. When he finished praying, he got up. [55]Then, in a loud voice, he stood and blessed all the people of Israel, saying: [56]"Praise the LORD! He promised he would give rest to his people Israel, and he has given us rest. The LORD has kept all the good promises he gave through his servant Moses. [57]May the LORD our God be with us as he was with our ancestors. May he never leave us, [58]and may he turn us to himself so we will follow him. Let us obey all the laws and commands he gave our ancestors. [59]May the LORD our God remember this prayer day and night and do what is right for his servant and his people Israel day by day. [60]Then all the people of the world will know the LORD is the only true God. [61]You must fully obey the LORD our God and follow all his laws and commands. Continue to obey in the future as you do now."

Sacrifices Are Offered

[62]Then King Solomon and all Israel with him offered sacrifices to the LORD. [63]Solomon killed twenty-two thousand cattle and one hundred twenty thousand sheep as fellowship offerings. So the king and all the people gave the Temple to the LORD.

[64]On that day King Solomon made holy the middle part of the courtyard which is in front of the Temple of the LORD. There he offered whole burnt offerings, grain offerings, and the fat of the fellowship offerings. He offered them in the courtyard, because the bronze altar before the LORD was too small to hold all the burnt offerings, the grain offerings, and the fat of the fellowship offerings.

[65]Solomon and all the Israelites celebrated the other festival that came at that time. People came from as far away as Lebo Hamath and the brook of Egypt. A great many people celebrated before the LORD for seven days, then seven more days, for a total of fourteen days. [66]On the following day Solomon sent the people home. They blessed the king as they went, happy because of all the good things the LORD had done for his servant David and his people Israel.

PSALM 68:28-35

[28]God, order up your power;
     show the mighty power you have used
       for us before.
[29]Kings will bring their wealth to you,
     to your Temple in Jerusalem.
[30]Punish Egypt, the beast in the tall grass
       along the river.
   Punish the leaders of nations, those
     bulls among the cows.
   Defeated, they will bring you their silver.
   Scatter those nations that love war.
[31]Messengers will come from Egypt;
     the people of Cush will pray to God.

[32]Kingdoms of the earth, sing to God;
     sing praises to the Lord.   *Selah*
[33]Sing to the one who rides through the
       skies, which are from long ago.
   He speaks with a thundering voice.
[34]Announce that God is powerful.
   He rules over Israel,
     and his power is in the skies.
[35]God, you are wonderful in your Temple.
   The God of Israel gives his people
     strength and power.

   Praise God!

PROVERBS 17:16-17

[16]It won't do a fool any good to try to buy
     wisdom,

because he doesn't have the ability to be wise.

[17]A friend loves you all the time,
  and a brother helps in time of trouble.

JOHN 11:1–27

The Death of Lazarus

11 A man named Lazarus was sick. He lived in the town of Bethany, where Mary and her sister Martha lived. [2]Mary was the woman who later put perfume on the Lord and wiped his feet with her hair. Mary's brother was Lazarus, the man who was now sick. [3]So Mary and Martha sent someone to tell Jesus, "Lord, the one you love is sick."

[4]When Jesus heard this, he said, "This sickness will not end in death. It is for the glory of God, to bring glory to the Son of God." [5]Jesus loved Martha and her sister and Lazarus. [6]But when he heard that Lazarus was sick, he stayed where he was for two more days. [7]Then Jesus said to his followers, "Let's go back to Judea."

[8]The followers said, "But Teacher, some people there tried to stone you to death only a short time ago. Now you want to go back there?"

[9]Jesus answered, "Are there not twelve hours in the day? If anyone walks in the daylight, he will not stumble, because he can see by this world's light. [10]But if anyone walks at night, he stumbles because there is no light to help him see."

[11]After Jesus said this, he added, "Our friend Lazarus has fallen asleep, but I am going there to wake him."

[12]The followers said, "But Lord, if he is only asleep, he will be all right."

[13]Jesus meant that Lazarus was dead, but his followers thought he meant Lazarus was really sleeping. [14]So then Jesus said plainly, "Lazarus is dead. [15]And I am glad for your sakes I was not there so that you may believe. But let's go to him now."

[16]Then Thomas (the one called Didymus) said to the other followers, "Let us also go so that we can die with him."

Jesus in Bethany

[17]When Jesus arrived, he learned that Lazarus had already been dead and in the tomb for four days. [18]Bethany was about two miles from Jerusalem. [19]Many of the Jews had come there to comfort Martha and Mary about their brother.

[20]When Martha heard that Jesus was coming, she went out to meet him, but Mary stayed home. [21]Martha said to Jesus, "Lord, if you had been here, my brother would not have died. [22]But I know that even now God will give you anything you ask."

[23]Jesus said, "Your brother will rise and live again."

[24]Martha answered, "I know that he will rise and live again in the resurrection[n] on the last day."

[25]Jesus said to her, "I am the resurrection and the life. Those who believe in me will have life even if they die. [26]And everyone who lives and believes in me will never die. Martha, do you believe this?"

[27]Martha answered, "Yes, Lord. I believe that you are the Christ, the Son of God, the One coming to the world."

MAY 31

1 KINGS 9:1—10:29

The Lord Appears to Solomon Again

9 Solomon finished building the Temple of the LORD and his royal palace and every-

thing he wanted to build. [2]Then the LORD appeared to him again just as he had done before, in Gibeon. [3]The LORD said to him: "I have heard your prayer and what you have asked me to do. You built this Temple, and I

11:24 resurrection Being raised from the dead to live again.

have made it a holy place. I will be worshiped there forever and will watch over it and protect it always.

⁴"But you must serve me as your father David did; he was fair and sincere. You must obey all I have commanded and keep my laws and rules. ⁵If you do, I will make your kingdom strong. This is the promise I made to your father David—that someone from his family would always rule Israel.

⁶"But you and your children must follow me and obey the laws and commands I have given you. You must not serve or worship other gods. ⁷If you do, I will force Israel to leave the land I have given them, and I will leave this Temple that I have made holy. All the nations will make fun of Israel and speak evil about them. ⁸If the Temple is destroyed, everyone who passes by will be shocked. They will make fun of you and ask, 'Why did the LORD do this terrible thing to this land and this Temple?' ⁹People will answer, 'This happened because they left the LORD their God. This was the God who brought their ancestors out of Egypt, but they decided to follow other gods. They worshiped and served those gods, so the LORD brought all this disaster on them.'"

Solomon's Other Achievements

¹⁰By the end of twenty years, King Solomon had built two buildings—the Temple of the LORD and the royal palace. ¹¹At that time King Solomon gave twenty towns in Galilee to Hiram king of Tyre, because Hiram had helped with the buildings. Hiram had given Solomon all the cedar, pine, and gold he wanted. ¹²So Hiram traveled from Tyre to see the towns Solomon had given him, but when he saw them, he was not pleased. ¹³He asked, "What good are these towns you have given me, my brother?" So he named them the Land of Cabul,ⁿ and they are still called that today. ¹⁴Hiram had sent Solomon about nine thousand pounds of gold.

¹⁵This is the account of the forced labor Solomon used to build the Temple and the palace. He had them fill in the land and build the wall around Jerusalem. He also had them

rebuild the cities of Hazor, Megiddo, and Gezer. ¹⁶(In the past the king of Egypt had attacked and captured Gezer. After burning it, he killed the Canaanites who lived there. Then he gave it as a wedding present to his daughter, who married Solomon. ¹⁷So Solomon rebuilt it.) He also built the cities of Lower Beth Horon ¹⁸and Baalath, as well as Tadmor, which is in the desert. ¹⁹King Solomon also built cities for storing grain and supplies and cities for his chariots and horses. He built whatever he wanted in Jerusalem, Lebanon, and everywhere he ruled.

²⁰There were other people in the land who were not Israelites—Amorites, Hittites, Perizzites, Hivites, and Jebusites. ²¹They were descendants of people that the Israelites had not destroyed. Solomon forced them to work for him as slaves, as is still true today. ²²But Solomon did not make slaves of the Israelites. They were his soldiers, government leaders, officers, captains, chariot commanders, and drivers.

²³These were his most important officers over the work. There were five hundred fifty supervisors over the people who did the work on Solomon's projects.

²⁴The daughter of the king of Egypt moved from the old part of Jerusalem to the palace that Solomon had built for her. Then Solomon filled in the surrounding land.

²⁵Three times each year Solomon offered whole burnt offerings and fellowship offerings on the altar he had built for the LORD. He also burned incense before the LORD. So he finished the work on the Temple.

²⁶King Solomon also built ships at Ezion Geber, a town near Elath on the shore of the Red Sea, in the land of Edom. ²⁷Hiram had skilled sailors, so he sent them to serve in these ships with Solomon's men. ²⁸The ships sailed to Ophir and brought back about thirty-two thousand pounds of gold to King Solomon.

The Queen of Sheba Visits Solomon

10 When the queen of Sheba heard about Solomon, she came to test him with

9:13 Cabul This name sounds like the Hebrew word for "worthless."

hard questions. [2]She traveled to Jerusalem with a large group of servants and camels carrying spices, jewels, and much gold. When she came to Solomon, she talked with him about all she had in mind, [3]and Solomon answered all her questions. Nothing was too hard for him to explain to her. [4]The queen of Sheba learned that Solomon was very wise. She saw the palace he had built, [5]the food on his table, his many officers, the palace servants, and their good clothes. She saw the servants who served him at feasts and the whole burnt offerings he made in the Temple of the Lord. All these things amazed her.

[6]So she said to King Solomon, "What I heard in my own country about your achievements and wisdom is true. [7]I could not believe it then, but now I have come and seen it with my own eyes. I was not told even half of it! Your wisdom and wealth are much greater than I had heard. [8]Your men and officers are very lucky, because in always serving you, they are able to hear your wisdom. [9]Praise the Lord your God, who was pleased to make you king of Israel. The Lord has constant love for Israel, so he made you king to keep justice and to rule fairly."

[10]Then she gave the king about nine thousand pounds of gold and many spices and jewels. No one since that time has brought more spices than the queen of Sheba gave to King Solomon.

[11](Hiram's ships brought gold from Ophir, as well as much juniper wood and jewels. [12]Solomon used the juniper wood to build supports for the Temple of the Lord and the palace, and to make harps and lyres for the musicians. Such fine juniper wood has not been brought in or been seen since that time.)

[13]King Solomon gave the queen of Sheba everything she wanted and asked for, in addition to what he had already given her of his wealth. Then she and her servants returned to her own country.

Solomon's Wealth

[14]Every year King Solomon received about fifty thousand pounds of gold. [15]Be-

sides that, he also received gold from the traders and merchants, as well as from the kings of Arabia and governors of the land.

[16]King Solomon made two hundred large shields of hammered gold, each of which contained about seven and one-half pounds of gold. [17]He also made three hundred smaller shields of hammered gold, each of which contained about four pounds of gold. The king put them in the Palace of the Forest of Lebanon.

[18]The king built a large throne of ivory and covered it with fine gold. [19]The throne had six steps on it, and its back was round at the top. There were armrests on both sides of the chair, and each armrest had a lion beside it. [20]Twelve lions stood on the six steps, one lion at each end of each step. Nothing like this had ever been made for any other kingdom. [21]All of Solomon's drinking cups, as well as the dishes in the Palace of the Forest of Lebanon, were made of pure gold. Nothing was made from silver, because silver was not valuable in Solomon's time.

[22]King Solomon also had many trading ships at sea, along with Hiram's ships. Every three years the ships returned, bringing back gold, silver, ivory, apes, and baboons.

[23]So Solomon had more riches and wisdom than all the other kings on earth. [24]People everywhere wanted to see King Solomon and listen to the wisdom God had given him. [25]Every year those who came brought gifts of silver and gold, clothes, weapons, spices, horses, and mules.

[26]Solomon had fourteen hundred chariots and twelve thousand horses. He kept some in special cities for the chariots, and others he kept with him in Jerusalem. [27]In Jerusalem Solomon made silver as common as stones and cedar trees as common as the fig trees on the western hills. [28]He imported horses from Egypt and Kue. His traders bought them in Kue. [29]A chariot from Egypt cost about fifteen pounds of silver, and a horse cost nearly four pounds of silver. Solomon's traders also sold horses and chariots to all the kings of the Hittites and the Arameans.

PSALM 69:1–4

A Cry for Help

For the director of music. To the tune of "Lilies." A psalm of David.

69 God, save me,
because the water has risen to my neck.
²I'm sinking down into the mud,
and there is nothing to stand on.
I am in deep water,
and the flood covers me.
³I am tired from calling for help;
my throat is sore.
My eyes are tired from waiting
for God to help me.
⁴There are more people who hate me for
no reason than hairs on my head;
powerful enemies want to destroy me
for no reason.
They make me pay back
what I did not steal.

PROVERBS 17:18–19

¹⁸It is not wise to promise
to pay what your neighbor owes.

¹⁹Whoever loves to argue loves to sin.
Whoever brags a lot is asking for trouble.

JOHN 11:28–57

Jesus Cries

²⁸After Martha said this, she went back and talked to her sister Mary alone. Martha said, "The Teacher is here and he is asking for you." ²⁹When Mary heard this, she got up quickly and went to Jesus. ³⁰Jesus had not yet come into the town but was still at the place where Martha had met him. ³¹The Jews were with Mary in the house, comforting her. When they saw her stand and leave quickly, they followed her, thinking she was going to the tomb to cry there.

³²But Mary went to the place where Jesus was. When she saw him, she fell at his feet and said, "Lord, if you had been here, my brother would not have died."

³³When Jesus saw Mary crying and the Jews who came with her also crying, he was upset and was deeply troubled. ³⁴He asked, "Where did you bury him?"

"Come and see, Lord," they said.

³⁵Jesus cried.

³⁶So the Jews said, "See how much he loved him."

³⁷But some of them said, "If Jesus opened the eyes of the blind man, why couldn't he keep Lazarus from dying?"

Jesus Raises Lazarus

³⁸Again feeling very upset, Jesus came to the tomb. It was a cave with a large stone covering the entrance. ³⁹Jesus said, "Move the stone away."

Martha, the sister of the dead man, said, "But, Lord, it has been four days since he died. There will be a bad smell."

⁴⁰Then Jesus said to her, "Didn't I tell you that if you believed you would see the glory of God?"

⁴¹So they moved the stone away from the entrance. Then Jesus looked up and said, "Father, I thank you that you heard me. ⁴²I know that you always hear me, but I said these things because of the people here around me. I want them to believe that you sent me." ⁴³After Jesus said this, he cried out in a loud voice, "Lazarus, come out!" ⁴⁴The dead man came out, his hands and feet wrapped with pieces of cloth, and a cloth around his face.

Jesus said to them, "Take the cloth off of him and let him go."

The Plan to Kill Jesus

⁴⁵Many of the people, who had come to visit Mary and saw what Jesus did, believed in him. ⁴⁶But some of them went to the Pharisees and told them what Jesus had done. ⁴⁷Then the leading priests and Pharisees called a meeting of the council. They asked, "What should we do? This man is doing many miracles. ⁴⁸If we let him continue doing these things, everyone will believe in him. Then the Romans will come and take away our Temple and our nation."

⁴⁹One of the men there was Caiaphas, the high priest that year. He said, "You people know nothing! ⁵⁰You don't realize that it is better for one man to die for the people than for the whole nation to be destroyed." ⁵¹Caiaphas did not think of this himself.

As high priest that year, he was really prophesying that Jesus would die for their nation 52and for God's scattered children to bring them all together and make them one.

53That day they started planning to kill Jesus. 54So Jesus no longer traveled openly among the people. He left there and went to a place near the desert, to a town called Ephraim and stayed there with his followers.

55It was almost time for the Passover Feast. Many from the country went up to Jerusalem before the Passover to do the special things to make themselves pure. 56The people looked for Jesus and stood in the Temple asking each other, "Is he coming to the Feast? What do you think?" 57But the leading priests and the Pharisees had given orders that if anyone knew where Jesus was, he must tell them. Then they could arrest him.

JUNE 1

1 KINGS 11:1—12:33

Solomon's Many Wives

11 King Solomon loved many women who were not from Israel. He loved the daughter of the king of Egypt, as well as women of the Moabites, Ammonites, Edomites, Sidonians, and Hittites. ²The LORD had told the Israelites, "You must not marry people of other nations. If you do, they will cause you to follow their gods." But Solomon fell in love with these women. ³He had seven hundred wives who were from royal families and three hundred slave women who gave birth to his children. His wives caused him to turn away from God. ⁴As Solomon grew old, his wives caused him to follow other gods. He did not follow the LORD completely as his father David had done. ⁵Solomon worshiped Ashtoreth, the goddess of the people of Sidon, and Molech, the hated god of the Ammonites. ⁶So Solomon did what the LORD said was wrong and did not follow the LORD completely as his father David had done.

⁷On a hill east of Jerusalem, Solomon built two places for worship. One was a place to worship Chemosh, the hated god of the Moabites, and the other was a place to worship Molech, the hated god of the Ammonites. ⁸Solomon did the same thing for all his foreign wives so they could burn incense and offer sacrifices to their gods.

⁹The LORD had appeared to Solomon twice, but the king turned away from following the LORD, the God of Israel. The LORD was angry with Solomon, ¹⁰because he had commanded Solomon not to follow other gods. But Solomon did not obey the LORD's command. ¹¹So the LORD said to Solomon, "Because you have chosen to break your agreement with me and have not obeyed my commands, I will tear your kingdom away from you and give it to one of your officers. ¹²But I will not take it away while you are alive because of my love for your father David. I will tear it away from your son when he becomes king. ¹³I will not tear away all the kingdom from him, but I will leave him one tribe to rule. I will do this be-cause of David, my servant, and because of Jerusalem, the city I have chosen."

Solomon's Enemies

¹⁴The LORD caused Hadad the Edomite, a member of the family of the king of Edom, to become Solomon's enemy. ¹⁵Earlier, David had defeated Edom. When Joab, the commander of David's army, went into Edom to bury the dead, he killed all the males. ¹⁶Joab and all the Israelites stayed in Edom for six months and killed every male in Edom. ¹⁷At that time Hadad was only a young boy, so he ran away to Egypt with some of his father's officers. ¹⁸They left Midian and went to Paran, where they were joined by other men. Then they all went to Egypt to see the king, who gave Hadad a house, some food, and some land.

¹⁹The king liked Hadad so much he gave Hadad a wife—the sister of Tahpenes, the king's wife. ²⁰They had a son named Genubath. Queen Tahpenes brought him up in the royal palace with the king's own children.

²¹While he was in Egypt, Hadad heard that David had died and that Joab, the commander of the army, was dead also. So Hadad said to the king, "Let me go; I will return to my own country."

²²"Why do you want to go back to your own country?" the king asked. "What haven't I given you here?"

"Nothing," Hadad answered, "but please, let me go."

²³God also caused another man to be Solomon's enemy—Rezon son of Eliada. Rezon had run away from his master, Hadadezer king of Zobah. ²⁴After David defeated the army of Zobah, Rezon gathered some men and became the leader of a small army. They went to Damascus and settled there, and Rezon became king of Damascus. ²⁵Rezon ruled Aram, and he hated Israel. So he was an enemy of Israel all the time Solomon was alive. Both Rezon and Hadad made trouble for Israel.

²⁶Jeroboam son of Nebat was one of Solomon's officers. He was an Ephraimite

from the town of Zeredah, and he was the son of a widow named Zeruah. Jeroboam turned against the king.

²⁷This is the story of how Jeroboam turned against the king. Solomon was filling in the land and repairing the wall of Jerusalem, the city of David, his father. ²⁸Jeroboam was a capable man, and Solomon saw that this young man was a good worker. So Solomon put him over all the workers from the tribes of Ephraim and Manasseh.

²⁹One day as Jeroboam was leaving Jerusalem, Ahijah, the prophet from Shiloh, who was wearing a new coat, met him on the road. The two men were alone out in the country. ³⁰Ahijah took his new coat and tore it into twelve pieces. ³¹Then he said to Jeroboam, "Take ten pieces of this coat for yourself. The LORD, the God of Israel, says: 'I will tear the kingdom away from Solomon and give you ten tribes. ³²But I will allow him to control one tribe. I will do this for the sake of my servant David and for Jerusalem, the city I have chosen from all the tribes of Israel. ³³I will do this because Solomon has stopped following me and has worshiped the Sidonian god Ashtoreth, the Moabite god Chemosh, and the Ammonite god Molech. Solomon has not obeyed me by doing what I said is right and obeying my laws and commands, as his father David did.

³⁴" 'But I will not take all the kingdom away from Solomon. I will let him rule all his life because of my servant David, whom I chose, who obeyed all my commands and laws. ³⁵But I will take the kingdom away from his son, and I will allow you to rule over the ten tribes. ³⁶I will allow Solomon's son to continue to rule over one tribe so that there will always be a descendant of David, my servant, in Jerusalem, the city where I chose to be worshiped. ³⁷But I will make you rule over everything you want. You will rule over all of Israel, ³⁸and I will always be with you if you do what I say is right. You must obey all my commands. If you obey my laws and commands as David did, I will be with you. I will make your family a lasting family of kings, as I did for David, and give Israel to you. ³⁹I will punish David's children because of this, but I will not punish them forever.' "

Solomon's Death

⁴⁰Solomon tried to kill Jeroboam, but he ran away to Egypt, to Shishak king of Egypt, where he stayed until Solomon died.

⁴¹Everything else King Solomon did, and the wisdom he showed, is written in the book of the history of Solomon. ⁴²Solomon ruled in Jerusalem over all Israel for forty years. ⁴³Then he died and was buried in Jerusalem, the city of David, his father. And his son Rehoboam became king in his place.

Israel Turns Against Rehoboam

12 Rehoboam went to Shechem, where all the Israelites had gone to make him king. ²Jeroboam son of Nebat was still in Egypt, where he had gone to escape from Solomon. When Jeroboam heard about Rehoboam being made king, he was living in Egypt. ³After the people sent for him, he and the people went to Rehoboam and said to him, ⁴"Your father forced us to work very hard. Now, make it easier for us, and don't make us work as hard as he did. Then we will serve you."

⁵Rehoboam answered, "Go away for three days, and then come back to me." So the people left.

⁶King Rehoboam asked the elders who had advised Solomon during his lifetime, "How do you think I should answer these people?"

⁷They said, "You should be like a servant to them today. If you serve them and give them a kind answer, they will serve you always."

⁸But Rehoboam rejected this advice. Instead, he asked the young men who had grown up with him and who served as his advisers. ⁹Rehoboam asked them, "What is your advice? How should we answer these people who said, 'Don't make us work as hard as your father did'?"

¹⁰The young men who had grown up with him answered, "Those people said to you, 'Your father forced us to work very hard. Now make our work easier.' You should tell them, 'My little finger is bigger than my father's legs. ¹¹He forced you to work hard, but I will make you work even harder. My father beat you with whips, but I will beat you with whips that have sharp points.' "

¹²Rehoboam had told the people, "Come back to me in three days." So after three days Jeroboam and all the people returned to Rehoboam. ¹³King Rehoboam spoke cruel words to them, because he had rejected the advice the elders had given him. ¹⁴He followed the advice of the young men and said to the people, "My father forced you to work hard, but I will make you work even harder. My father beat you with whips, but I will beat you with whips that have sharp points." ¹⁵So the king did not listen to the people. The LORD caused this to happen to keep the promise he had made to Jeroboam son of Nebat through Ahijah, a prophet from Shiloh.

¹⁶When all the Israelites saw that the new king refused to listen to them, they said to the king,

"We have no share in David!
We have no part in the son of Jesse!
People of Israel, let's go to our own
   homes!
Let David's son rule his own people!"

So the Israelites went home. ¹⁷But Rehoboam still ruled over the Israelites who lived in the towns of Judah.

¹⁸Adoniram was in charge of the forced labor. When Rehoboam sent him to the people of Israel, they threw stones at him until he died. But King Rehoboam ran to his chariot and escaped to Jerusalem. ¹⁹Since then, Israel has been against the family of David.

²⁰When all the Israelites heard that Jeroboam had returned, they called him to a meeting and made him king over all Israel. Only the tribe of Judah continued to follow the family of David.

²¹When Rehoboam arrived in Jerusalem, he gathered one hundred eighty thousand of the best soldiers from the tribes of Judah and Benjamin. As son of Solomon, Rehoboam wanted to fight the people of Israel to take back his kingdom.

²²But God spoke his word to Shemaiah, a man of God, saying, ²³"Speak to Solomon's son Rehoboam, the king of Judah, and to all the people of Judah and Benjamin and the rest of the people. Say to them, ²⁴'The LORD says you must not go to war against your brothers, the Israelites. Every one of you should go home, because I made all these

things happen.'" So they obeyed the LORD's command and went home as the LORD had commanded.

²⁵Then Jeroboam made Shechem in the mountains of Ephraim a very strong city, and he lived there. He also went to the city of Peniel and made it stronger.

Jeroboam Builds Golden Calves

²⁶Jeroboam said to himself, "The kingdom will probably go back to David's family. ²⁷If the people continue going to the Temple of the LORD in Jerusalem to offer sacrifices, they will want to be ruled again by Rehoboam. Then they will kill me and follow Rehoboam king of Judah."

²⁸King Jeroboam asked for advice. Then he made two golden calves. "It is too long a journey for you to go to Jerusalem to worship," he said to the people. "Israel, here are your gods who brought you out of Egypt." ²⁹Jeroboam put one golden calf in the city of Bethel and the other in the city of Dan. ³⁰This became a very great sin, because the people traveled as far as Dan to worship the calf there.

³¹Jeroboam built temples on the places of worship. He also chose priests from all the people, not just from the tribe of Levi. ³²And he started a new festival on the fifteenth day of the eighth month, just like the festival in Judah. During that time the king offered sacrifices on the altar, along with sacrifices to the calves in Bethel he had made. He also chose priests in Bethel to serve at the places of worship he had made. ³³So Jeroboam chose his own time for a festival for the Israelites—the fifteenth day of the eighth month. During that time he offered sacrifices on the altar he had built in Bethel. He set up a festival for the Israelites and offered sacrifices on the altar.

PSALM 69:5–12

⁵God, you know what I have done wrong;
   I cannot hide my guilt from you.
⁶Lord GOD All-Powerful,
   do not let those who hope in you be
      ashamed because of me.
God of Israel,
   do not let your worshipers be disgraced
      because of me.

⁷For you, I carry this shame,
and my face is covered with disgrace.
⁸I am like a stranger to my closest relatives
and a foreigner to my mother's children.
⁹My strong love for your Temple
completely controls me.
When people insult you, it hurts me.
¹⁰When I cry and fast,
they make fun of me.
¹¹When I wear clothes of sadness,
they joke about me.
¹²They make fun of me in public places,
and the drunkards make up songs
about me.

PROVERBS 17:20–22

²⁰A person with an evil heart will find no
success,
and the person whose words are evil
will get into trouble.

²¹It is sad to have a foolish child;
there is no joy in being the parent of a
fool.

²²A happy heart is like good medicine,
but a broken spirit drains your strength.

JOHN 12:1–19

Jesus with Friends in Bethany

12 Six days before the Passover Feast, Jesus went to Bethany, where Lazarus
lived. (Lazarus is the man Jesus raised from
the dead.) ²There they had a dinner for Jesus.
Martha served the food, and Lazarus was one
of the people eating with Jesus. ³Mary
brought in a pint of very expensive perfume
made from pure nard. She poured the perfume on Jesus' feet, and then she wiped his
feet with her hair. And the sweet smell from
the perfume filled the whole house.
⁴Judas Iscariot, one of Jesus' followers who
would later turn against him, was there. Judas said, ⁵"This perfume was worth an entire
year's wages. Why wasn't it sold and the
money given to the poor?" ⁶But Judas did not
really care about the poor; he said this because he was a thief. He was the one who kept
the money box, and he often stole from it.

⁷Jesus answered, "Leave her alone. It was
right for her to save this perfume for today,
the day for me to be prepared for burial. ⁸You
will always have the poor with you, but you
will not always have me."

The Plot Against Lazarus

⁹A large crowd of people heard that Jesus
was in Bethany. So they went there to see not
only Jesus but Lazarus, whom Jesus raised
from the dead. ¹⁰So the leading priests made
plans to kill Lazarus, too. ¹¹Because of Lazarus many of the Jews were leaving them and
believing in Jesus.

Jesus Enters Jerusalem

¹²The next day a great crowd who had
come to Jerusalem for the Passover Feast
heard that Jesus was coming there. ¹³So they
took branches of palm trees and went out to
meet Jesus, shouting,
"Praiseⁿ God!
God bless the One who comes in the
name of the Lord!
God bless the King of Israel!"

Psalm 118:25–26

¹⁴Jesus found a colt and sat on it. This was
as the Scripture says,
¹⁵"Don't be afraid, people of Jerusalem!
Your king is coming,
sitting on the colt of a donkey."

Zechariah 9:9

¹⁶The followers of Jesus did not understand this at first. But after Jesus was raised to
glory, they remembered that this had been
written about him and that they had done
these things to him.

People Tell About Jesus

¹⁷There had been many people with Jesus
when he raised Lazarus from the dead and
told him to come out of the tomb. Now they
were telling others about what Jesus did.
¹⁸Many people went out to meet Jesus, because they had heard about this miracle. ¹⁹So
the Pharisees said to each other, "You can see
that nothing is going right for us. Look! The
whole world is following him."

12:13 Praise Literally, "Hosanna," a Hebrew word used at first in praying to God for help, but at this time it was probably a
shout of joy used in praising God or his Messiah.

JUNE 2

The Man of God Speaks Against Bethel

13 The LORD commanded a man of God from Judah to go to Bethel. When he arrived, Jeroboam was standing by the altar to offer a sacrifice. ²The LORD had commanded the man of God to speak against the altar. The man said, "Altar, altar, the LORD says to you: 'David's family will have a son named Josiah. The priests for the places of worship now make their sacrifices on you, but Josiah will sacrifice those priests on you. Human bones will be burned on you.'" ³That same day the man of God gave proof that these things would happen. "This is the LORD's sign that this will happen," he said. "This altar will break apart, and the ashes on it will fall to the ground."

⁴When King Jeroboam heard what the man of God said about the altar in Bethel, the king raised his hand from the altar and pointed at the man. "Take him!" he said. But when the king said this, his arm was paralyzed, and he could not move it. ⁵The altar also broke into pieces, and its ashes fell to the ground. This was the sign the LORD had told the man of God to give.

⁶Then the king said to the man of God, "Please pray to the LORD your God for me, and ask him to heal my arm."

So the man of God prayed to the LORD, and the king's arm was healed, becoming as it was before.

⁷Then the king said to the man of God, "Please come home and eat with me, and I will give you a gift."

⁸But the man of God answered the king, "Even if you gave me half of your kingdom, I would not go with you. I will not eat or drink anything in this place. ⁹The LORD commanded me not to eat or drink anything nor to return on the same road by which I came."

¹⁰So he took a different road and did not return on the same road by which he had come to Bethel.

¹¹Now an old prophet was living in Bethel. His sons came and told him what the man of God had done there that day. They also told their father what he had said to King Jeroboam. ¹²The father asked, "Which road did he use when he left?" So his sons showed him the road the man of God from Judah had taken. ¹³Then the prophet told his sons to put a saddle on his donkey. So they saddled the donkey, and he left.

¹⁴He went after the man of God and found him sitting under an oak tree. The prophet asked, "Are you the man of God who came from Judah?"

The man answered, "Yes, I am."

¹⁵The prophet said, "Please come home and eat with me."

¹⁶"I can't go home with you," the man of God answered. "I can't eat or drink with you in this place. ¹⁷The LORD said to me, 'Don't eat or drink anything there or return on the same road by which you came.'"

¹⁸Then the old prophet said, "But I also am a prophet like you." Then he told a lie. He said, "An angel from the LORD came to me and told me to bring you to my home. He said you should eat and drink with me."

¹⁹So the man of God went to the old prophet's house, and he ate and drank with him there.

²⁰While they were sitting at the table, the LORD spoke his word to the old prophet. ²¹The old prophet cried out to the man of God from Judah, "The LORD said you did not obey him! He said you did not do what the LORD your God commanded you. ²²The LORD commanded you not to eat or drink anything in this place, but you came back and ate and drank. So your body will not be buried in your family grave."

²³After the man of God finished eating and drinking, the prophet put a saddle on his donkey for him, and the man left. ²⁴As he was traveling home, a lion attacked and killed him. His body lay on the road, with the donkey and the lion standing nearby. ²⁵Some men who were traveling on that

road saw the body and the lion standing nearby. So they went to the city where the old prophet lived and told what they had seen.

²⁶The old prophet who had brought back the man of God heard what had happened. "It is the man of God who did not obey the LORD's command," he said. "So the LORD sent a lion to kill him, just as he said he would."

²⁷Then the prophet said to his sons, "Put a saddle on my donkey," which they did. ²⁸The old prophet went out and found the body lying on the road, with the donkey and the lion still standing nearby. The lion had not eaten the body or hurt the donkey. ²⁹The prophet put the body on his donkey and carried it back to the city to have a time of sadness for him and to bury him. ³⁰The prophet buried the body in his own family grave, and they were sad for the man of God and said, "Oh, my brother."

³¹After the prophet buried the body, he said to his sons, "When I die, bury me in this same grave. Put my bones next to his. ³²Through him the LORD spoke against the altar at Bethel and against the places of worship in the towns of Samaria. What the LORD spoke through him will certainly come true."

³³After this incident King Jeroboam did not stop doing evil. He continued to choose priests for the places of worship from among all the people. Anyone who wanted to be a priest for the places of worship was allowed to be one. ³⁴In this way the family of Jeroboam sinned, and this sin caused its ruin and destruction from the earth.

Jeroboam's Son Dies

14 At that time Jeroboam's son Abijah became very sick. ²So Jeroboam said to his wife, "Go to Shiloh to see the prophet Ahijah. He is the one who said I would become king of Israel. But dress yourself so people won't know you are my wife. ³Take the prophet ten loaves of bread, some cakes, and a jar of honey. Then ask him what will happen to our son, and he will tell you." ⁴So the king's wife did as he said and went to Ahijah's home in Shiloh.

Now Ahijah was very old and blind. ⁵The LORD said to him, "Jeroboam's son is sick, and Jeroboam's wife is coming to ask you about him. When she arrives, she will pretend to be someone else." Then the LORD told Ahijah what to say.

⁶When Ahijah heard her walking to the door, he said, "Come in, wife of Jeroboam. Why are you pretending to be someone else? I have bad news for you. ⁷Go back and tell Jeroboam that this is what the LORD, the God of Israel, says: 'Jeroboam, I chose you from among all the people and made you the leader of my people Israel. ⁸I tore the kingdom away from David's family, and I gave it to you. But you are not like my servant David, who always obeyed my commands and followed me with all his heart. He did only what I said was right. ⁹But you have done more evil than anyone who ruled before you. You have quit following me and have made other gods and idols of metal. This has made me very angry, ¹⁰so I will soon bring disaster to your family. I will kill all the men in your family, both slaves and free men. I will destroy your family as completely as fire burns up manure. ¹¹Anyone from your family who dies in the city will be eaten by dogs, and those who die in the fields will be eaten by the birds. The LORD has spoken.'"

¹²Then Ahijah said to Jeroboam's wife, "Go home now. As soon as you enter your city, your son will die, ¹³and all Israel will be sad for him and bury him. He is the only one of Jeroboam's family who will be buried, because he is the only one in the king's family who pleased the LORD, the God of Israel.

¹⁴"The LORD will put a new king over Israel, who will destroy Jeroboam's family, and this will happen soon. ¹⁵Then the LORD will punish Israel, which will be like reeds swaying in the water. The LORD will pull up Israel from this good land, the land he gave their ancestors. He will scatter Israel beyond the Euphrates River, because he is angry with the people. They made the LORD angry when they set up idols to worship Asherah. ¹⁶Jeroboam sinned, and then he made the people

of Israel sin. So the LORD will let the people of Israel be defeated."

[17]Then Jeroboam's wife left and returned to Tirzah. As soon as she entered her home, the boy died. [18]After they buried him, all Israel had a time of sadness for him, just as the LORD had said through his servant, the prophet Ahijah.

[19]Everything else Jeroboam did is written in the book of the history of the kings of Israel. He fought wars and continued to rule the people, [20]serving as king for twenty-two years. Then he died, and his son Nadab became king in his place.

The Death of Rehoboam

[21]Solomon's son Rehoboam was forty-one years old when he became king of Judah. His mother was Naamah from Ammon. Rehoboam ruled in Jerusalem for seventeen years. (The LORD had chosen that city from all the land of Israel as the place where he would be worshiped.)

[22]The people of Judah did what the LORD said was wrong. Their sins made the LORD very angry, even more angry than he had been at their ancestors. [23]The people built stone pillars and places to worship gods and Asherah idols on every high hill and under every green tree. [24]There were even male prostitutes in the land. They acted like the people who had lived in the land before the Israelites. They had done many evil things, and God had taken the land away from them.

[25]During the fifth year Rehoboam was king, Shishak king of Egypt attacked Jerusalem. [26]He took the treasures from the Temple of the LORD and the king's palace. He took everything, even the gold shields Solomon had made. [27]So King Rehoboam made bronze shields to put in their place and gave them to the commanders of the guards for the palace gates. [28]Whenever the king went to the Temple of the LORD, the guards carried the shields. Later, they would put them back in the guardroom.

[29]Everything else King Rehoboam did is written in the book of the history of the kings of Judah. [30]There was war between Rehoboam and Jeroboam the whole time. [31]Rehoboam, son of Naamah from Ammon, died and was buried with his ancestors in Jerusalem, and his son Abijam[n] became king in his place.

PSALM 69:13–21

[13]But I pray to you, LORD, for favor.
 God, because of your great love, answer me.
 You are truly able to save.
[14]Pull me from the mud,
 and do not let me sink.
 Save me from those who hate me
 and from the deep water.
[15]Do not let the flood drown me
 or the deep water swallow me
 or the grave close its mouth over me.
[16]LORD, answer me because your love is so good.
 Because of your great kindness, turn to me.
[17]Do not hide from me, your servant.
 I am in trouble. Hurry to help me!
[18]Come near and save me;
 rescue me from my enemies.

[19]You see my shame and disgrace.
 You know all my enemies and what they have said.
[20]Insults have broken my heart
 and left me weak.
 I looked for sympathy, but there was none;
 I found no one to comfort me.
[21]They put poison in my food
 and gave me vinegar to drink.

PROVERBS 17:23–24

[23]When the wicked accept money to do wrong
 there can be no justice.

[24]The person with understanding is always looking for wisdom,

14:31 **Abijam** A negative name for Abijah. See 2 Chronicles 13.

but the mind of a fool wanders everywhere.

JOHN 12:20–50

Jesus Talks About His Death

20There were some Greek people, too, who came to Jerusalem to worship at the Passover Feast. 21They went to Philip, who was from Bethsaida in Galilee, and said, "Sir, we would like to see Jesus." 22Philip told Andrew, and then Andrew and Philip told Jesus.

23Jesus said to them, "The time has come for the Son of Man to receive his glory. 24I tell you the truth, a grain of wheat must fall to the ground and die to make many seeds. But if it never dies, it remains only a single seed. 25Those who love their lives will lose them, but those who hate their lives in this world will keep true life forever. 26Whoever serves me must follow me. Then my servant will be with me everywhere I am. My Father will honor anyone who serves me.

27"Now I am very troubled. Should I say, 'Father, save me from this time'? No, I came to this time so I could suffer. 28Father, bring glory to your name!"

Then a voice came from heaven, "I have brought glory to it, and I will do it again."

29The crowd standing there, who heard the voice, said it was thunder.

But others said, "An angel has spoken to him."

30Jesus said, "That voice was for your sake, not mine. 31Now is the time for the world to be judged; now the ruler of this world will be thrown down. 32If I am lifted up from the earth, I will draw all people toward me." 33Jesus said this to show how he would die.

34The crowd said, "We have heard from the law that the Christ will live forever. So why do you say, 'The Son of Man must be lifted up'? Who is this 'Son of Man'?"

35Then Jesus said, "The light will be with you for a little longer, so walk while you have the light. Then the darkness will not catch you. If you walk in the darkness, you will not know where you are going. 36Believe in the light while you still have it so that you will become children of light." When Jesus had said this, he left and hid himself from them.

Some People Won't Believe in Jesus

37Though Jesus had done many miracles in front of the people, they still did not believe in him. 38This was to bring about what Isaiah the prophet had said:

"Lord, who believed what we told them?
Who saw the Lord's power in this?"
Isaiah 53:1

39This is why the people could not believe: Isaiah also had said,

40"He has blinded their eyes,
and he has closed their minds.
Otherwise they would see with their eyes
and understand in their minds
and come back to me and be healed."
Isaiah 6:10

41Isaiah said this because he saw Jesus' glory and spoke about him.

42But many believed in Jesus, even many of the leaders. But because of the Pharisees, they did not say they believed in him for fear they would be put out of the synagogue. 43They loved praise from people more than praise from God.

44Then Jesus cried out, "Whoever believes in me is really believing in the One who sent me. 45Whoever sees me sees the One who sent me. 46I have come as light into the world so that whoever believes in me would not stay in darkness.

47"Anyone who hears my words and does not obey them, I do not judge, because I did not come to judge the world, but to save the world. 48There is a judge for those who refuse to believe in me and do not accept my words. The word I have taught will be their judge on the last day. 49The things I taught were not from myself. The Father who sent me told me what to say and what to teach. 50And I know that eternal life comes from what the Father commands. So whatever I say is what the Father told me to say."

JUNE 3

1 KINGS 15:1—16:34

Abijam King of Judah

15 Abijam became king of Judah during the eighteenth year Jeroboam son of Nebat was king of Israel. ²Abijam ruled in Jerusalem for three years. His mother was Maacah daughter of Abishalom. ³He did all the same sins his father before him had done. Abijam was not faithful to the LORD his God as David, his great-grandfather, had been. ⁴Because the LORD loved David, the LORD gave him a kingdom in Jerusalem and allowed him to have a son to be king after him. The LORD also kept Jerusalem safe. ⁵David always did what the LORD said was right and obeyed his commands all his life, except the one time when David sinned against Uriah the Hittite.

⁶There was war between Abijam and Jeroboam during Abijam's lifetime. ⁷Everything else Abijam did is written in the book of the history of the kings of Judah. During the time Abijam ruled, there was war between Abijam and Jeroboam. ⁸Abijam died and was buried in Jerusalem, and his son Asa became king in his place.

Asa King of Judah

⁹During the twentieth year Jeroboam was king of Israel, Asa became king of Judah. ¹⁰His grandmother's name was Maacah, the daughter of Abishalom. Asa ruled in Jerusalem for forty-one years.

¹¹Asa did what the LORD said was right, as his ancestor David had done. ¹²He forced the male prostitutes at the worship places to leave the country. He also took away the idols that his ancestors had made. ¹³His grandmother Maacah had made a terrible Asherah idol, so Asa removed her from being queen mother. He cut down that idol and burned it in the Kidron Valley. ¹⁴The places of worship to gods were not removed. Even so, Asa was faithful to the LORD all his life. ¹⁵Asa brought into the Temple of the LORD the gifts he and his father had given: gold, silver, and utensils.

¹⁶There was war between Asa and Baasha king of Israel all the time they were kings. ¹⁷Baasha attacked Judah, and he made the town of Ramah strong so he could keep people from leaving or entering Judah, Asa's country.

¹⁸Asa took the rest of the silver and gold from the treasuries of the Temple of the LORD and his own palace and gave it to his officers. Then he sent them to Ben-Hadad son of Tabrimmon, who was the son of Hezion. Ben-Hadad was the king of Aram and ruled in the city of Damascus. Asa said, ¹⁹"Let there be a treaty between you and me as there was between my father and your father. I am sending you a gift of silver and gold. Break your treaty with Baasha king of Israel so he will leave my land."

²⁰Ben-Hadad agreed with King Asa, so he sent the commanders of his armies to attack the towns of Israel. They defeated the towns of Ijon, Dan, and Abel Beth Maacah, as well as all Galilee and the area of Naphtali. ²¹When Baasha heard about these attacks, he stopped building up Ramah and returned to Tirzah. ²²Then King Asa gave an order to all the people of Judah; everyone had to help. They carried away all the stones and wood Baasha had been using in Ramah, and they used them to build up Geba and Mizpah in the land of Benjamin.

²³Everything else Asa did—his victories and the cities he built—is written in the book of the history of the kings of Judah. When he became old, he got a disease in his feet. ²⁴After Asa died, he was buried with his ancestors in Jerusalem, the city of David, his ancestor. Then Jehoshaphat, Asa's son, became king in his place.

Nadab King of Israel

²⁵Nadab son of Jeroboam became king of Israel during the second year Asa was king of Judah. Nadab was king of Israel for two years, ²⁶and he did what the LORD said was wrong. Jeroboam had led the people of Israel to sin, and Nadab sinned in the same way as his father Jeroboam.

²⁷Baasha son of Ahijah, from the tribe of Issachar, made plans to kill Nadab. Nadab and all Israel were attacking the Philistine town of Gibbethon, so Baasha killed Nadab there. ²⁸This happened during Asa's third year as king of Judah, and Baasha became the next king of Israel.

Baasha King of Israel

²⁹As soon as Baasha became king, he killed all of Jeroboam's family, leaving no one in Jeroboam's family alive. He destroyed them all as the LORD had said would happen through his servant Ahijah from Shiloh. ³⁰King Jeroboam had sinned very much and had led the people of Israel to sin, so he made the LORD, the God of Israel, very angry.

³¹Everything else Nadab did is written in the book of the history of the kings of Israel. ³²There was war between Asa king of Judah and Baasha king of Israel all the time they ruled.

³³Baasha son of Ahijah became king of Israel during Asa's third year as king of Judah. Baasha ruled in Tirzah for twenty-four years, ³⁴and he did what the LORD said was wrong. Jeroboam had led the people of Israel to sin, and Baasha sinned in the same way as Jeroboam.

16 Jehu son of Hanani spoke the word of the LORD against King Baasha. ²The LORD said, "You were nothing, but I took you and made you a leader over my people Israel. But you have followed the ways of Jeroboam and have led my people Israel to sin. Their sins have made me angry, ³so, Baasha, I will soon destroy you and your family. I will do to you what I did to the family of Jeroboam son of Nebat. ⁴Anyone from your family who dies in the city will be eaten by dogs, and anyone from your family who dies in the fields will be eaten by birds."

⁵Everything else Baasha did and all his victories are written down in the book of the history of the kings of Israel. ⁶So Baasha died and was buried in Tirzah, and his son Elah became king in his place.

⁷The LORD spoke his word against Baasha and his family through the prophet Jehu son of Hanani. Baasha had done many things the LORD said were wrong, which made the LORD very angry. He did the same evil deeds that Jeroboam's family had done before him. The LORD also spoke against Baasha because he killed all of Jeroboam's family.

Elah King of Israel

⁸Elah son of Baasha became king of Israel during Asa's twenty-sixth year as king of Judah, and Elah ruled in Tirzah for two years.

⁹Zimri, one of Elah's officers, commanded half of Elah's chariots. Zimri made plans against Elah while the king was in Tirzah, getting drunk at Arza's home. (Arza was in charge of the palace at Tirzah.) ¹⁰Zimri went into Arza's house and killed Elah during Asa's twenty-seventh year as king of Judah. Then Zimri became king of Israel in Elah's place.

Zimri King of Israel

¹¹As soon as Zimri became king, he killed all of Baasha's family, not allowing any of Baasha's family or friends to live. ¹²So Zimri destroyed all of Baasha's family just as the LORD had said it would happen through the prophet Jehu. ¹³Baasha and his son Elah sinned and led the people of Israel to sin, and they made the LORD, the God of Israel, angry because of their worthless idols.

¹⁴Everything else Elah did is written in the book of the history of the kings of Israel.

¹⁵So during Asa's twenty-seventh year as king of Judah, Zimri became king of Israel and ruled in Tirzah seven days.

The army of Israel was camped near Gibbethon, a Philistine town. ¹⁶The men in the camp heard that Zimri had made secret plans against King Elah and had killed him. So that day in the camp they made Omri, the commander of the army, king over Israel. ¹⁷So Omri and all the Israelite army left Gibbethon and attacked Tirzah. ¹⁸When Zimri saw that the city had been captured, he went into the palace and set it on fire, burning the palace and himself with it. ¹⁹So Zimri died because he had sinned by doing what the LORD said was wrong. Jeroboam had led the people of Israel to sin, and Zimri sinned in the same way as Jeroboam.

²⁰Everything else Zimri did and the story

of how he turned against King Elah are written down in the book of the history of the kings of Israel.

Omri King of Israel

²¹The people of Israel were divided into two groups. Half of the people wanted Tibni son of Ginath to be king, while the other half wanted Omri. ²²Omri's followers were stronger than the followers of Tibni son of Ginath, so Tibni died, and Omri became king.

²³Omri became king of Israel during the thirty-first year Asa was king of Judah. Omri ruled Israel for twelve years, six of those years in the city of Tirzah. ²⁴He bought the hill of Samaria from Shemer for about one hundred fifty pounds of silver. Omri built a city on that hill and called it Samaria after the name of its earlier owner, Shemer.

²⁵But Omri did what the Lord said was wrong; he did more evil than all the kings who came before him. ²⁶Jeroboam son of Nebat had led the people of Israel to sin, and Omri sinned in the same way as Jeroboam. The Israelites made the Lord, the God of Israel, very angry because they worshiped worthless idols.

²⁷Everything else Omri did and all his successes are written in the book of the history of the kings of Israel. ²⁸So Omri died and was buried in Samaria, and his son Ahab became king in his place.

Ahab King of Israel

²⁹Ahab son of Omri became king of Israel during Asa's thirty-eighth year as king of Judah, and Ahab ruled Israel in the city of Samaria for twenty-two years. ³⁰More than any king before him, Ahab son of Omri did many things the Lord said were wrong. ³¹He sinned in the same ways as Jeroboam son of Nebat, but he did even worse things. He married Jezebel daughter of Ethbaal, the king of Sidon. Then Ahab began to serve Baal and worship him. ³²He built a temple in Samaria for worshiping Baal and put an altar there for Baal. ³³Ahab also made an idol for worshiping Asherah. He did more things to make the Lord, the God of Israel, angry than all the other kings before him.

³⁴During the time of Ahab, Hiel from Bethel rebuilt the city of Jericho. It cost Hiel the life of Abiram, his oldest son, to begin work on the city, and it cost the life of Segub, his youngest son, to build the city gates. This happened just as the Lord, speaking through Joshua son of Nun, said it would happen.ⁿ

PSALM 69:22–28

²²Let their own feasts cause their ruin;
   let their feasts trap them and pay them back.
²³Let their eyes be closed so they cannot see
   and their backs be forever weak from troubles.
²⁴Pour your anger out on them;
   let your anger catch up with them.
²⁵May their place be empty;
   leave no one to live in their tents.
²⁶They chase after those you have hurt,
   and they talk about the pain of those you have wounded.
²⁷Charge them with crime after crime,
   and do not let them have anything good.
²⁸Wipe their names from the book of life,
   and do not list them with those who do what is right.

PROVERBS 17:25–26

²⁵Foolish children make their father sad
   and cause their mother great sorrow.

²⁶It is not good to punish the innocent
   or to beat leaders for being honest.

JOHN 13:1–20

Jesus Washes His Followers' Feet

13 It was almost time for the Passover Feast. Jesus knew that it was time for him to leave this world and go back to the Father. He had always loved those who were

---

16:34 the Lord . . . happen When Joshua destroyed Jericho, he said whoever rebuilt the city would lose his oldest and youngest sons. See Joshua 6:26.

his own in the world, and he loved them all the way to the end.

[2]Jesus and his followers were at the evening meal. The devil had already persuaded Judas Iscariot, the son of Simon, to turn against Jesus. [3]Jesus knew that the Father had given him power over everything and that he had come from God and was going back to God. [4]So during the meal Jesus stood up and took off his outer clothing. Taking a towel, he wrapped it around his waist. [5]Then he poured water into a bowl and began to wash the followers' feet, drying them with the towel that was wrapped around him.

[6]Jesus came to Simon Peter, who said to him, "Lord, are you going to wash my feet?"

[7]Jesus answered, "You don't understand now what I am doing, but you will understand later."

[8]Peter said, "No, you will never wash my feet."

Jesus answered, "If I don't wash your feet, you are not one of my people."

[9]Simon Peter answered, "Lord, then wash not only my feet, but wash my hands and my head, too!"

[10]Jesus said, "After a person has had a bath, his whole body is clean. He needs only to wash his feet. And you men are clean, but not all of you." [11]Jesus knew who would turn against him, and that is why he said, "Not all of you are clean."

[12]When he had finished washing their feet, he put on his clothes and sat down again. He asked, "Do you understand what I have just done for you? [13]You call me 'Teacher' and 'Lord,' and you are right, because that is what I am. [14]If I, your Lord and Teacher, have washed your feet, you also should wash each other's feet. [15]I did this as an example so that you should do as I have done for you. [16]I tell you the truth, a servant is not greater than his master. A messenger is not greater than the one who sent him. [17]If you know these things, you will be blessed if you do them.

[18]"I am not talking about all of you. I know those I have chosen. But this is to bring about what the Scripture said: 'The man who ate at my table has turned against me.'[n] [19]I am telling you this now before it happens so that when it happens, you will believe that I am he. [20]I tell you the truth, whoever accepts anyone I send also accepts me. And whoever accepts me also accepts the One who sent me."

JUNE 4

1 KINGS 17:1—18:46

Elijah Stops the Rain

17Now Elijah the Tishbite was a prophet from the settlers in Gilead. "I serve the LORD, the God of Israel," Elijah said to Ahab. "As surely as the LORD lives, no rain or dew will fall during the next few years unless I command it."

[2]Then the LORD spoke his word to Elijah: [3]"Leave this place and go east and hide near Kerith Ravine east of the Jordan River. [4]You may drink from the stream, and I have commanded ravens to bring you food there." [5]So

Elijah did what the LORD said; he went to Kerith Ravine, east of the Jordan, and lived there. [6]The birds brought Elijah bread and meat every morning and evening, and he drank water from the stream.

[7]After a while the stream dried up because there was no rain. [8]Then the LORD spoke his word to Elijah, [9]"Go to Zarephath in Sidon and live there. I have commanded a widow there to take care of you."

[10]So Elijah went to Zarephath. When he reached the town gate, he saw a widow gathering wood for a fire. Elijah asked her, "Would you bring me a little water in a cup

13:18 'The man . . . me.' Quotation from Psalm 41:9.

so I may have a drink?" ¹¹As she was going to get his water, Elijah said, "Please bring me a piece of bread, too."

¹²The woman answered, "As surely as the Lord your God lives, I have no bread. I have only a handful of flour in a jar and only a little olive oil in a jug. I came here to gather some wood so I could go home and cook our last meal. My son and I will eat it and then die from hunger."

¹³"Don't worry," Elijah said to her. "Go home and cook your food as you have said. But first make a small loaf of bread from the flour you have, and bring it to me. Then cook something for yourself and your son. ¹⁴The Lord, the God of Israel, says, 'That jar of flour will never be empty, and the jug will always have oil in it, until the day the Lord sends rain to the land.'"

¹⁵So the woman went home and did what Elijah told her to do. And the woman and her son and Elijah had enough food every day. ¹⁶The jar of flour and the jug of oil were never empty, just as the Lord, through Elijah, had promised.

Elijah Brings a Boy Back to Life

¹⁷Some time later the son of the woman who owned the house became sick. He grew worse and worse and finally stopped breathing. ¹⁸The woman said to Elijah, "Man of God, what have you done to me? Did you come here to remind me of my sin and to kill my son?"

¹⁹Elijah said to her, "Give me your son." Elijah took the boy from her, carried him upstairs, and laid him on the bed in the room where he was staying. ²⁰Then he prayed to the Lord: "Lord my God, this widow is letting me stay in her house. Why have you done this terrible thing to her and caused her son to die?" ²¹Then Elijah lay on top of the boy three times. He prayed to the Lord, "Lord my God, let this boy live again!"

²²The Lord answered Elijah's prayer; the boy began breathing again and was alive. ²³Elijah carried the boy downstairs and gave him to his mother and said, "See! Your son is alive!"

²⁴"Now I know you really are a man from God," the woman said to Elijah. "I know that the Lord truly speaks through you!"

Elijah Kills the Prophets of Baal

18 During the third year without rain, the Lord spoke his word to Elijah: "Go and meet King Ahab, and I will soon send rain." ²So Elijah went to meet Ahab.

By this time there was no food in Samaria. ³King Ahab sent for Obadiah, who was in charge of the king's palace. (Obadiah was a true follower of the Lord. ⁴When Jezebel was killing all the Lord's prophets, Obadiah hid a hundred of them in two caves, fifty in one cave and fifty in another. He also brought them food and water.) ⁵Ahab said to Obadiah, "Let's check every spring and valley in the land. Maybe we can find enough grass to keep our horses and mules alive and not have to kill our animals." ⁶So each one chose a part of the country to search; Ahab went in one direction and Obadiah in another.

⁷While Obadiah was on his way, Elijah met him. Obadiah recognized Elijah, so he bowed down to the ground and said, "Elijah? Is it really you, master?"

⁸"Yes," Elijah answered. "Go tell your master that I am here."

⁹Then Obadiah said, "What wrong have I done for you to hand me over to Ahab like this? He will put me to death. ¹⁰As surely as the Lord your God lives, the king has sent people to every country to search for you. If the ruler said you were not there, Ahab forced the ruler to swear you could not be found in his country. ¹¹Now you want me to go to my master and tell him, 'Elijah is here'? ¹²The Spirit of the Lord may carry you to some other place after I leave. If I go tell King Ahab you are here, and he comes and doesn't find you, he will kill me! I have followed the Lord since I was a boy. ¹³Haven't you been told what I did? When Jezebel was killing the Lord's prophets, I hid a hundred of them, fifty in one cave and fifty in another. I brought them food and water. ¹⁴Now you want me to go and tell my master you are here? He will kill me!"

¹⁵Elijah answered, "As surely as the Lord All-Powerful lives, whom I serve, I will be seen by Ahab today."

¹⁶So Obadiah went to Ahab and told him where Elijah was. Then Ahab went to meet Elijah.

¹⁷When he saw Elijah, he asked, "Is it you—the biggest troublemaker in Israel?"

¹⁸Elijah answered, "I have not made trouble in Israel. You and your father's family have made all this trouble by not obeying the LORD's commands. You have gone after the Baals. ¹⁹Now tell all Israel to meet me at Mount Carmel. Also bring the four hundred fifty prophets of Baal and the four hundred prophets of Asherah, who eat at Jezebel's table."

²⁰So Ahab called all the Israelites and those prophets to Mount Carmel. ²¹Elijah approached the people and said, "How long will you not decide between two choices? If the LORD is the true God, follow him, but if Baal is the true God, follow him!" But the people said nothing.

²²Elijah said, "I am the only prophet of the LORD here, but there are four hundred fifty prophets of Baal. ²³Bring two bulls. Let the prophets of Baal choose one bull and kill it and cut it into pieces. Then let them put the meat on the wood, but they are not to set fire to it. I will prepare the other bull, putting the meat on the wood but not setting fire to it. ²⁴You prophets of Baal, pray to your god, and I will pray to the LORD. The god who answers by setting fire to his wood is the true God."

All the people agreed that this was a good idea.

²⁵Then Elijah said to the prophets of Baal, "There are many of you, so you go first. Choose a bull and prepare it. Pray to your god, but don't start the fire."

²⁶So they took the bull that was given to them and prepared it. They prayed to Baal from morning until noon, shouting "Baal, answer us!" But there was no sound, and no one answered. They danced around the altar they had built.

²⁷At noon Elijah began to make fun of them. "Pray louder!" he said. "If Baal really is a god, maybe he is thinking, or busy, or traveling! Maybe he is sleeping so you will have to wake him!" ²⁸The prophets prayed louder, cutting themselves with swords and spears until their blood flowed, which was the way they worshiped. ²⁹The afternoon passed, and the prophets continued to act like this until it was time for the evening sacrifice. But no voice was heard; Baal did not answer, and no one paid attention.

³⁰Then Elijah said to all the people, "Now come to me." So they gathered around him, and Elijah rebuilt the altar of the LORD, which had been torn down. ³¹He took twelve stones, one stone for each of the twelve tribes, the number of Jacob's sons. (The LORD changed Jacob's name to Israel.) ³²Elijah used these stones to rebuild the altar in honor of the LORD. Then he dug a ditch around the altar that was big enough to hold about thirteen quarts of seed. ³³Elijah put the wood on the altar, cut the bull into pieces, and laid the pieces on the wood. ³⁴Then he said, "Fill four jars with water, and pour it on the meat and on the wood." Then Elijah said, "Do it again," and they did it again. Then he said, "Do it a third time," and they did it the third time. ³⁵So the water ran off the altar and filled the ditch.

³⁶At the time for the evening sacrifice, the prophet Elijah went near the altar. "LORD, you are the God of Abraham, Isaac, and Israel," he prayed. "Prove that you are the God of Israel and that I am your servant. Show these people that you commanded me to do all these things. ³⁷LORD, answer my prayer so these people will know that you, LORD, are God and that you will change their minds."

³⁸Then fire from the LORD came down and burned the sacrifice, the wood, the stones, and the ground around the altar. It also dried up the water in the ditch. ³⁹When all the people saw this, they fell down to the ground, crying, "The LORD is God! The LORD is God!"

⁴⁰Then Elijah said, "Capture the prophets of Baal! Don't let any of them run away!" The people captured all the prophets. Then Elijah led them down to the Kishon Valley, where he killed them.

The Rain Comes Again

⁴¹Then Elijah said to Ahab, "Now, go, eat, and drink, because a heavy rain is coming." ⁴²So King Ahab went to eat and drink. At the same time Elijah climbed to the top of Mount Carmel, where he bent down to the ground with his head between his knees.

⁴³Then Elijah said to his servant, "Go and look toward the sea."

The servant went and looked. "I see nothing," he said.

Elijah told him to go and look again. This happened seven times. ⁴⁴The seventh time, the servant said, "I see a small cloud, the size of a human fist, coming from the sea."

Elijah told the servant, "Go to Ahab and tell him to get his chariot ready and go home now. Otherwise, the rain will stop him."

⁴⁵After a short time the sky was covered with dark clouds. The wind began to blow, and soon a heavy rain began to fall. Ahab got in his chariot and started back to Jezreel. ⁴⁶The LORD gave his power to Elijah, who tightened his clothes around him and ran ahead of King Ahab all the way to Jezreel.

PSALM 69:29–36

²⁹I am sad and hurting.
   God, save me and protect me.

³⁰I will praise God in a song
   and will honor him by giving thanks.
³¹That will please the LORD more than
      offering him cattle,
   more than sacrificing a bull with horns
      and hoofs.
³²Poor people will see this and be glad.
   Be encouraged, you who worship God.
³³The LORD listens to those in need
   and does not look down on captives.

³⁴Heaven and earth should praise him,
   the seas and everything in them.
³⁵God will save Jerusalem
   and rebuild the cities of Judah.
   Then people will live there and own the
      land.
³⁶   The descendants of his servants will
         inherit that land,
      and those who love him will live
         there.

PROVERBS 17:27–28

²⁷The wise say very little,
   and those with understanding stay
      calm.

²⁸Even fools seem to be wise if they keep
      quiet;
   if they don't speak, they appear to
      understand.

JOHN 13:21–38

Jesus Talks About His Death

²¹After Jesus said this, he was very troubled. He said openly, "I tell you the truth, one of you will turn against me."

²²The followers all looked at each other, because they did not know whom Jesus was talking about. ²³One of the followers sitting[n] next to Jesus was the follower Jesus loved. ²⁴Simon Peter motioned to him to ask Jesus whom he was talking about.

²⁵That follower leaned closer to Jesus and asked, "Lord, who is it?"

²⁶Jesus answered, "I will dip this bread into the dish. The man I give it to is the man who will turn against me." So Jesus took a piece of bread, dipped it, and gave it to Judas Iscariot, the son of Simon. ²⁷As soon as Judas took the bread, Satan entered him. Jesus said to him, "The thing that you will do—do it quickly." ²⁸No one at the table understood why Jesus said this to Judas. ²⁹Since he was the one who kept the money box, some of the followers thought Jesus was telling him to buy what was needed for the feast or to give something to the poor.

³⁰Judas took the bread Jesus gave him and immediately went out. It was night.

³¹When Judas was gone, Jesus said, "Now the Son of Man receives his glory, and God receives glory through him. ³²If God receives glory through him,[n] then God will give glory to the Son through himself. And God will give him glory quickly."

³³Jesus said, "My children, I will be with you only a little longer. You will look for me, and what I told the Jews, I tell you now: Where I am going you cannot come. ³⁴"I give you a new command: Love each other. You must love each other as I have loved you. ³⁵All people will know that you are my followers if you love each other."

13:23 sitting Literally, "lying." The people of that time ate lying down and leaning on one arm. **13:32 If . . . him** Some Greek copies do not have this phrase.

Peter Will Say He Doesn't Know Jesus

³⁶Simon Peter asked Jesus, "Lord, where are you going?"

Jesus answered, "Where I am going you cannot follow now, but you will follow later."

³⁷Peter asked, "Lord, why can't I follow you now? I am ready to die for you!"

³⁸Jesus answered, "Are you ready to die for me? I tell you the truth, before the rooster crows, you will say three times that you don't know me."

JUNE 5

1 KINGS 19:1—20:43

Elijah Runs Away

19 King Ahab told Jezebel every thing Elijah had done and how Elijah had killed all the prophets with a sword. ²So Jezebel sent a messenger to Elijah, saying, "May the gods punish me terribly if by this time tomorrow I don't kill you just as you killed those prophets."

³When Elijah heard this, he was afraid and ran for his life, taking his servant with him. When they came to Beersheba in Judah, Elijah left his servant there. ⁴Then Elijah walked for a whole day into the desert. He sat down under a bush and asked to die. "I have had enough, LORD," he prayed. "Let me die. I am no better than my ancestors." ⁵Then he lay down under the tree and slept.

Suddenly an angel came to him and touched him. "Get up and eat," the angel said. ⁶Elijah saw near his head a loaf baked over coals and a jar of water, so he ate and drank. Then he went back to sleep.

⁷Later the LORD's angel came to him a second time. The angel touched him and said, "Get up and eat. If you don't, the journey will be too hard for you." ⁸So Elijah got up and ate and drank. The food made him strong enough to walk for forty days and nights to Mount Sinai, the mountain of God. ⁹There Elijah went into a cave and stayed all night.

Then the LORD spoke his word to him: "Elijah! Why are you here?"

¹⁰He answered, "LORD God All-Powerful, I have always served you as well as I could. But the people of Israel have broken their agreement with you, destroyed your altars, and killed your prophets with swords. I am the only prophet left, and now they are trying to kill me, too."

¹¹The LORD said to Elijah, "Go, stand in front of me on the mountain, and I will pass by you." Then a very strong wind blew until it caused the mountains to fall apart and large rocks to break in front of the LORD. But the LORD was not in the wind. After the wind, there was an earthquake, but the LORD was not in the earthquake. ¹²After the earthquake, there was a fire, but the LORD was not in the fire. After the fire, there was a quiet, gentle sound. ¹³When Elijah heard it, he covered his face with his coat and went out and stood at the entrance to the cave.

Then a voice said to him, "Elijah! Why are you here?"

¹⁴He answered, "LORD God All-Powerful, I have always served you as well as I could. But the people of Israel have broken their agreement with you, destroyed your altars, and killed your prophets with swords. I am the only prophet left, and now they are trying to kill me, too."

¹⁵The LORD said to him, "Go back on the road that leads to the desert around Damascus. Enter that city, and pour olive oil on Hazael to make him king over Aram. ¹⁶Then pour oil on Jehu son of Nimshi to make him king over Israel. Next, pour oil on Elisha son of Shaphat from Abel Meholah to make him a prophet in your place. ¹⁷Jehu will kill anyone who escapes from Hazael's sword, and Elisha will kill anyone who escapes from Jehu's sword. ¹⁸I have seven thousand people left in Israel who have never bowed down before Baal and whose mouths have never kissed his idol."

Elisha Becomes a Prophet

[19]So Elijah left that place and found Elisha son of Shaphat plowing a field with a team of oxen. He owned twelve teams of oxen and was plowing with the twelfth team. Elijah came up to Elisha, took off his coat, and put it on Elisha. [20]Then Elisha left his oxen and ran to follow Elijah. "Let me kiss my father and my mother good-bye," Elisha said. "Then I will go with you."

Elijah answered, "Go back. It does not matter to me."

[21]So Elisha went back and took his pair of oxen and killed them. He used their wooden yoke for a fire. Then he cooked the meat and gave it to the people. After they ate it, Elisha left and followed Elijah and became his helper.

Ben-Hadad and Ahab Go to War

20 Ben-Hadad king of Aram gathered together all his army. There were thirty-two kings with their horses and chariots who went with him and surrounded Samaria and attacked it. [2]The king sent messengers into the city to Ahab king of Israel.

This was his message: "Ben-Hadad says, [3]'Your silver and gold belong to me, as well as the best of your wives and children.'"

[4]Ahab king of Israel answered, "My master and king, I agree to what you say. I and everything I have belong to you."

[5]Then the messengers came to Ahab again. They said, "Ben-Hadad says, 'I told you before that you must give me your silver and gold, your wives and your children. [6]About this time tomorrow I will send my men, who will search everywhere in your palace and in the homes of your officers. Whatever they want they will take and carry off.'"

[7]Then Ahab called a meeting of all the elders of his country. He said, "Ben-Hadad is looking for trouble. First he said I had to give him my wives, my children, my silver, and my gold, and I have not refused him."

[8]The elders and all the people said, "Don't listen to him or agree to this."

[9]So Ahab said to Ben-Hadad's messengers, "Tell my master the king: 'I will do what you said at first, but I cannot allow this sec-

ond command.'" And King Ben-Hadad's men carried the message back to him.

[10]Then Ben-Hadad sent another message to Ahab: "May the gods punish me terribly if I don't completely destroy Samaria. There won't be enough left for each of my men to get a handful of dust!"

[11]Ahab answered, "Tell Ben-Hadad, 'The man who puts on his armor should not brag. It's the man who lives to take it off who has the right to brag.'"

[12]Ben-Hadad was drinking in his tent with the other rulers when the message came from Ahab. Ben-Hadad commanded his men to prepare to attack the city, and they moved into place for battle.

[13]At the same time a prophet came to Ahab king of Israel. The prophet said, "Ahab, the LORD says to you, 'Do you see that big army? I will hand it over to you today so you will know I am the LORD.'"

[14]Ahab asked, "Who will you use to defeat them?"

The prophet answered, "The LORD says, 'The young officers of the district governors will defeat them.'"

Then the king asked, "Who will command the main army?"

The prophet answered, "You will."

[15]So Ahab gathered the young officers of the district governors, two hundred thirty-two of them. Then he called together the army of Israel, about seven thousand people in all.

[16]They marched out at noon, while Ben-Hadad and the thirty-two rulers helping him were getting drunk in their tents. [17]The young officers of the district governors attacked first. Ben-Hadad sent out scouts who told him that soldiers were coming from Samaria. [18]Ben-Hadad said, "They may be coming to fight, or they may be coming to ask for peace. In either case capture them alive."

[19]The young officers of the district governors led the attack, followed by the army of Israel. [20]Each officer of Israel killed the man who came against him. The men from Aram ran away as Israel chased them, but Ben-Hadad king of Aram escaped on a horse with some of his horsemen. [21]Ahab king of Israel

led the army and destroyed the Arameans' horses and chariots. King Ahab thoroughly defeated the Aramean army.

²²Then the prophet went to Ahab king of Israel and said, "The king of Aram will attack you again next spring. So go home now and strengthen your army and see what you need to do."

²³Meanwhile the officers of Ben-Hadad king of Aram said to him, "The gods of Israel are mountain gods. Since we fought in a mountain area, Israel won. Let's fight them on the flat land, and then we will win. ²⁴This is what you should do. Don't allow the thirty-two rulers to command the armies, but put other commanders in their places. ²⁵Gather an army like the one that was destroyed and as many horses and chariots as before. We will fight the Israelites on flat land, and then we will win." Ben-Hadad agreed with their advice and did what they said.

²⁶The next spring Ben-Hadad gathered the army of Aram and went up to Aphek to fight against Israel.

²⁷The Israelites also had prepared for war. They marched out to meet the Arameans and camped opposite them. The Israelites looked like two small flocks of goats, but the Arameans covered the area.

²⁸A man of God came to the king of Israel with this message: "The LORD says, 'The people of Aram say that I, the LORD, am a god of the mountains, not a god of the valleys. So I will allow you to defeat this huge army, and then you will know I am the LORD.' "

²⁹The armies were camped across from each other for seven days. On the seventh day the battle began. The Israelites killed one hundred thousand Aramean soldiers in one day. ³⁰The rest of them ran away to the city of Aphek, where a city wall fell on twenty-seven thousand of them. Ben-Hadad also ran away to the city and hid in a room.

³¹His officers said to him, "We have heard that the kings of Israel are trustworthy. Let's dress in rough cloth to show our sadness, and wear ropes on our heads. Then we will go to the king of Israel, and perhaps he will let you live."

³²So they dressed in rough cloth and wore ropes on their heads and went to the king of Israel. They said, "Your servant Ben-Hadad says, 'Please let me live.' "

Ahab answered, "Is he still alive? He is my brother."

³³Ben-Hadad's men had wanted a sign from Ahab. So when Ahab called Ben-Hadad his brother, they quickly said, "Yes! Ben-Hadad is your brother."

Ahab said, "Bring him to me." When Ben-Hadad came, Ahab asked him to join him in the chariot.

³⁴Ben-Hadad said to him, "Ahab, I will give you back the cities my father took from your father. And you may put shops in Damascus, as my father did in Samaria."

Ahab said, "If you agree to this, I will allow you to go free." So the two kings made a peace agreement. Then Ahab let Ben-Hadad go free.

A Prophet Speaks Against Ahab

³⁵One prophet from one of the groups of prophets told another, "Hit me!" He said this because the LORD had commanded it, but the other man refused. ³⁶The prophet said, "You did not obey the LORD's command, so a lion will kill you as soon as you leave me." When the man left, a lion found him and killed him.

³⁷The prophet went to another man and said, "Hit me, please!" So the man hit him and hurt him. ³⁸The prophet wrapped his face in a cloth so no one could tell who he was. Then he went and waited by the road for the king. ³⁹As Ahab king of Israel passed by, the prophet called out to him. "I went to fight in the battle," the prophet said. "One of our men brought an enemy soldier to me. Our man said, 'Guard this man. If he runs away, you will have to give your life in his place. Or, you will have to pay a fine of seventy-five pounds of silver.' ⁴⁰But I was busy doing other things, so the man ran away."

The king of Israel answered, "You have already said what the punishment is. You must do what the man said."

⁴¹Then the prophet quickly took the cloth from his face. When the king of Israel saw him, he knew he was one of the prophets. ⁴²The prophet said to the king, "This is what the LORD says: 'You freed the man I said

should die, so your life will be taken instead of his. The lives of your people will also be taken instead of the lives of his people.'"

[43]Then King Ahab went back to his palace in Samaria, angry and upset.

PSALM 70:1–5

A Cry for God to Help Quickly

For the director of music. A psalm of David. To help people remember.

70 God, come quickly and save me.
LORD, hurry to help me.
[2]Let those who are trying to kill me
be ashamed and disgraced.
Let those who want to hurt me
run away in disgrace.
[3]Let those who make fun of me
stop because of their shame.
[4]But let all those who worship you
rejoice and be glad.
Let those who love your salvation
always say, "Praise the greatness of
God."
[5]I am poor and helpless;
God, hurry to me.
You help me and save me.
LORD, do not wait.

PROVERBS 18:1–2

18 Unfriendly people are selfish
and hate all good sense.

[2]Fools do not want to understand
anything.
They only want to tell others what they
think.

JOHN 14:1–31

Jesus Comforts His Followers

14 Jesus said, "Don't let your hearts be troubled. Trust in God, and trust in me. [2]There are many rooms in my Father's house; I would not tell you this if it were not true. I am going there to prepare a place for you. [3]After I go and prepare a place for you, I will come back and take you to be with me so that you may be where I am. [4]You know the way to the place where I am going."[n]

[5]Thomas said to Jesus, "Lord, we don't know where you are going. So how can we know the way?"

[6]Jesus answered, "I am the way, and the truth, and the life. The only way to the Father is through me. [7]If you really knew me, you would know my Father, too. But now you do know him, and you have seen him."

[8]Philip said to him, "Lord, show us the Father. That is all we need."

[9]Jesus answered, "I have been with you a long time now. Do you still not know me, Philip? Whoever has seen me has seen the Father. So why do you say, 'Show us the Father'? [10]Don't you believe that I am in the Father and the Father is in me? The words I say to you don't come from me, but the Father lives in me and does his own work. [11]Believe me when I say that I am in the Father and the Father is in me. Or believe because of the miracles I have done. [12]I tell you the truth, whoever believes in me will do the same things that I do. Those who believe will do even greater things than these, because I am going to the Father. [13]And if you ask for anything in my name, I will do it for you so that the Father's glory will be shown through the Son. [14]If you ask me for anything in my name, I will do it.

The Promise of the Holy Spirit

[15]"If you love me, you will obey my commands. [16]I will ask the Father, and he will give you another Helper[n] to be with you forever— [17]the Spirit of truth. The world cannot accept him, because it does not see him or know him. But you know him, because he lives with you and he will be in you. [18]"I will not leave you all alone like orphans; I will come back to you. [19]In a little while the world will not see me anymore, but you will see me. Because I live, you will live, too. [20]On that day you will know that I am in my Father, and that you are in me and I am in you. [21]Those who know my commands and obey them are the ones who love me, and my Father will love those who love me. I will love them and will show myself to them."

14:4 You . . . going. Some Greek copies read "You know where I am going and the way to the place I am going."
14:16 Helper "Counselor" or "Comforter." Jesus is talking about the Holy Spirit.

²²Then Judas (not Judas Iscariot) said, "But, Lord, why do you plan to show yourself to us and not to the rest of the world?"

²³Jesus answered, "If people love me, they will obey my teaching. My Father will love them, and we will come to them and make our home with them. ²⁴Those who do not love me do not obey my teaching. This teaching that you hear is not really mine; it is from my Father, who sent me.

²⁵"I have told you all these things while I am with you. ²⁶But the Helper will teach you everything and will cause you to remember all that I told you. This Helper is the Holy Spirit whom the Father will send in my name.

²⁷"I leave you peace; my peace I give you. I do not give it to you as the world does. So don't let your hearts be troubled or afraid. ²⁸You heard me say to you, 'I am going, but I am coming back to you.' If you loved me, you should be happy that I am going back to the Father, because he is greater than I am. ²⁹I have told you this now, before it happens, so that when it happens, you will believe. ³⁰I will not talk with you much longer, because the ruler of this world is coming. He has no power over me, ³¹but the world must know that I love the Father, so I do exactly what the Father told me to do.

"Come now, let us go.

JUNE 6

1 KINGS 21:1—22:53

Ahab Takes Naboth's Vineyard

21 After these things had happened, this is what followed. A man named Naboth owned a vineyard in Jezreel, near the palace of Ahab king of Israel. ²One day Ahab said to Naboth, "Give me your vineyard. It is near my palace, and I want to make it into a vegetable garden. I will give you a better vineyard in its place, or, if you prefer, I will pay you what it is worth."

³Naboth answered, "May the Lord keep me from ever giving my land to you. It belongs to my family."

⁴Ahab went home angry and upset, because he did not like what Naboth from Jezreel had said. (Naboth had said, "I will not give you my family's land.") Ahab lay down on his bed, turned his face to the wall, and refused to eat.

⁵His wife, Jezebel, came in and asked him, "Why are you so upset that you refuse to eat?"

⁶Ahab answered, "I talked to Naboth, the man from Jezreel. I said, 'Sell me your vineyard, or, if you prefer, I will give you another vineyard for it.' But Naboth refused."

⁷Jezebel answered, "Is this how you rule as king over Israel? Get up, eat something, and cheer up. I will get Naboth's vineyard for you."

⁸So Jezebel wrote some letters, signed Ahab's name to them, and used his own seal to seal them. Then she sent them to the elders and important men who lived in Naboth's town. ⁹The letter she wrote said: "Declare a day during which the people are to fast. Call the people together, and give Naboth a place of honor among them. ¹⁰Seat two troublemakers across from him, and have them say they heard Naboth speak against God and the king. Then take Naboth out of the city and kill him with stones."

¹¹The elders and important men of Jezreel obeyed Jezebel's command, just as she wrote in the letters. ¹²They declared a special day on which the people were to fast. And they put Naboth in a place of honor before the people. ¹³Two troublemakers sat across from Naboth and said in front of everybody that they had heard him speak against God and the king. So the people carried Naboth out of the city and killed him with stones. ¹⁴Then the leaders sent a message to Jezebel, saying, "Naboth has been killed."

¹⁵When Jezebel heard that Naboth had been killed, she told Ahab, "Naboth of Jezreel is dead. Now you may go and take for yourself the vineyard he would not sell to you."

16When Ahab heard that Naboth of Jezreel was dead, he got up and went to the vineyard to take it for his own.

17At this time the LORD spoke his word to the prophet Elijah the Tishbite. The LORD said, 18"Go to Ahab king of Israel in Samaria. He is at Naboth's vineyard, where he has gone to take it as his own. 19Tell Ahab that I, the LORD, say to him, 'You have murdered Naboth and taken his land. So I tell you this: In the same place the dogs licked up Naboth's blood, they will also lick up your blood!'"

20When Ahab saw Elijah, he said, "So you have found me, my enemy!"

Elijah answered, "Yes, I have found you. You have always chosen to do what the LORD says is wrong. 21So the LORD says to you, 'I will soon destroy you. I will kill you and every male in your family, both slave and free. 22Your family will be like the family of King Jeroboam son of Nebat and like the family of King Baasha son of Ahijah. I will destroy you, because you have made me angry and have led the people of Israel to sin.'

23"And the LORD also says, 'Dogs will eat the body of Jezebel in the city of Jezreel.'

24"Anyone in your family who dies in the city will be eaten by dogs, and anyone who dies in the fields will be eaten by birds."

25There was no one like Ahab who had chosen so often to do what the LORD said was wrong, because his wife Jezebel influenced him to do evil. 26Ahab sinned terribly by worshiping idols, just as the Amorite people did. And the LORD had taken away their land and given it to the people of Israel.

27After Elijah finished speaking, Ahab tore his clothes. He put on rough cloth, fasted, and even slept in the rough cloth to show how sad and upset he was.

28The LORD spoke his word to Elijah the Tishbite: 29"I see that Ahab is now sorry for what he has done. So I will not cause the trouble to come to him during his life, but I will wait until his son is king. Then I will bring this trouble to Ahab's family."

The Death of Ahab

22 For three years there was peace between Israel and Aram. 2During the third year Jehoshaphat king of Judah went to visit Ahab king of Israel.

3At that time Ahab asked his officers, "Do you remember that the king of Aram took Ramoth in Gilead from us? Why have we done nothing to get it back?" 4So Ahab asked King Jehoshaphat, "Will you go with me to fight at Ramoth in Gilead?"

"I will go with you," Jehoshaphat answered. "My soldiers are yours, and my horses are yours." 5Jehoshaphat also said to Ahab, "But first we should ask if this is the LORD's will."

6Ahab called about four hundred prophets together and asked them, "Should I go to war against Ramoth in Gilead or not?"

They answered, "Go, because the Lord will hand them over to you."

7But Jehoshaphat asked, "Isn't there a prophet of the LORD here? Let's ask him what we should do."

8Then King Ahab said to Jehoshaphat, "There is one other prophet. We could ask the LORD through him, but I hate him. He never prophesies anything good about me, but something bad. He is Micaiah son of Imlah."

Jehoshaphat said, "King Ahab, you shouldn't say that!"

9So Ahab king of Israel told one of his officers to bring Micaiah to him at once.

10Ahab king of Israel and Jehoshaphat king of Judah had on their royal robes and were sitting on their thrones at the threshing floor, near the entrance to the gate of Samaria. All the prophets were standing before them, speaking their messages. 11Zedekiah son of Kenaanah had made some iron horns. He said to Ahab, "This is what the LORD says, 'You will use these horns to fight the Arameans until they are destroyed.'"

12All the other prophets said the same thing. "Attack Ramoth in Gilead and win, because the LORD will hand the Arameans over to you."

13The messenger who had gone to get Micaiah said to him, "All the other prophets are saying King Ahab will succeed. You should agree with them and give the king a good answer."

14But Micaiah answered, "As surely as

the LORD lives, I can tell him only what the LORD tells me."

¹⁵When Micaiah came to Ahab, the king asked him, "Micaiah, should we attack Ramoth in Gilead or not?"

Micaiah answered, "Attack and win! The LORD will hand them over to you."

¹⁶But Ahab said to Micaiah, "How many times do I have to tell you to speak only the truth to me in the name of the LORD?"

¹⁷So Micaiah answered, "I saw the army of Israel scattered over the hills like sheep without a shepherd. The LORD said, 'They have no leaders. They should go home and not fight.'"

¹⁸Then Ahab king of Israel said to Jehoshaphat, "I told you! He never prophesies anything good about me, but only bad."

¹⁹But Micaiah said, "Hear the message from the LORD: I saw the LORD sitting on his throne with his heavenly army standing near him on his right and on his left. ²⁰The LORD said, 'Who will trick Ahab into attacking Ramoth in Gilead where he will be killed?'

"Some said one thing; some said another. ²¹Then one spirit came and stood before the LORD and said, 'I will trick him.'

²²"The LORD asked, 'How will you do it?'

"The spirit answered, 'I will go to Ahab's prophets and make them tell lies.'

"So the LORD said, 'You will succeed in tricking him. Go and do it.'"

²³Micaiah said, "Ahab, the LORD has made your prophets lie to you, and the LORD has decided that disaster should come to you."

²⁴Then Zedekiah son of Kenaanah went up to Micaiah and slapped him in the face. Zedekiah said, "Has the LORD's spirit left me to speak through you?"

²⁵Micaiah answered, "You will find out on the day you go to hide in an inside room."

²⁶Then Ahab king of Israel ordered, "Take Micaiah and send him to Amon, the governor of the city, and to Joash, the king's son. ²⁷Tell them I said to put this man in prison and give him only bread and water until I return safely from the battle."

²⁸Micaiah said, "Ahab, if you come back safely from battle, the LORD has not spoken through me. Remember my words, all you people!"

²⁹So Ahab king of Israel and Jehoshaphat king of Judah went to Ramoth in Gilead. ³⁰King Ahab said to Jehoshaphat, "I will go into battle, but I will wear other clothes so no one will recognize me. But you wear your royal clothes." So Ahab wore other clothes and went into battle.

³¹The king of Aram had ordered his thirty-two chariot commanders, "Don't fight with anyone—important or unimportant—except the king of Israel." ³²When these commanders saw Jehoshaphat, they thought he was certainly the king of Israel, so they turned to attack him. But Jehoshaphat began shouting. ³³When they saw he was not King Ahab, they stopped chasing him.

³⁴By chance, a soldier shot an arrow, but he hit Ahab king of Israel between the pieces of his armor. King Ahab said to his chariot driver, "Turn around and get me out of the battle, because I am hurt!" ³⁵The battle continued all day. King Ahab was held up in his chariot and faced the Arameans. His blood flowed down to the bottom of the chariot. That evening he died. ³⁶Near sunset a cry went out through the army of Israel: "Each man go back to his own city and land."

³⁷In that way King Ahab died. His body was carried to Samaria and buried there. ³⁸The men cleaned Ahab's chariot at a pool in Samaria where prostitutes bathed, and the dogs licked his blood from the chariot. These things happened as the LORD had said they would.

³⁹Everything else Ahab did is written in the book of the history of the kings of Israel. It tells about the palace Ahab built and decorated with ivory and the cities he built. ⁴⁰So Ahab died, and his son Ahaziah became king in his place.

Jehoshaphat King of Judah

⁴¹Jehoshaphat son of Asa became king of Judah during Ahab's fourth year as king of Israel. ⁴²Jehoshaphat was thirty-five years old when he became king, and he ruled in Jerusalem for twenty-five years. His mother's name was Azubah daughter of Shilhi. ⁴³Jehoshaphat was good, like his father Asa, and he did what the LORD said was right. But Jehoshaphat did not destroy the places where

gods were worshiped, so the people continued offering sacrifices and burning incense there. ⁴⁴Jehoshaphat was at peace with the king of Israel. ⁴⁵Jehoshaphat fought many wars, and these wars and his successes are written in the book of the history of the kings of Judah. ⁴⁶There were male prostitutes still in the places of worship from the days of his father, Asa. So Jehoshaphat forced them to leave.

⁴⁷During this time the land of Edom had no king; it was ruled by a governor.

⁴⁸King Jehoshaphat built trading ships to sail to Ophir for gold. But the ships were wrecked at Ezion Geber, so they never set sail. ⁴⁹Ahaziah son of Ahab went to help Jehoshaphat, offering to give Jehoshaphat some men to sail with his men, but Jehoshaphat refused.

⁵⁰Jehoshaphat died and was buried with his ancestors in Jerusalem, the city of David, his ancestor. Then his son Jehoram became king in his place.

Ahaziah King of Israel

⁵¹Ahaziah son of Ahab became king of Israel in Samaria during Jehoshaphat's seventeenth year as king over Judah. Ahaziah ruled Israel for two years, ⁵²and he did what the LORD said was wrong. He did the same evil his father Ahab, his mother Jezebel, and Jeroboam son of Nebat had done. All these rulers led the people of Israel into more sin. ⁵³Ahaziah worshiped and served the god Baal, and this made the LORD, the God of Israel, very angry. In these ways Ahaziah did what his father had done.

PSALM 71:1-6

An Old Person's Prayer

71 In you, LORD, is my protection.
  Never let me be ashamed.
²Because you do what is right, save and rescue me;
  listen to me and save me.
³Be my place of safety
  where I can always come.
Give the command to save me,
  because you are my rock and my strong, walled city.
⁴My God, save me from the power of the wicked

and from the hold of evil and cruel people.
⁵LORD, you are my hope.
  LORD, I have trusted you since I was young.
⁶I have depended on you since I was born;
  you helped me even on the day of my birth.
I will always praise you.

PROVERBS 18:3-5

³Do something evil, and people won't like you.
  Do something shameful, and they will make fun of you.

⁴Spoken words can be like deep water,
  but wisdom is like a flowing stream.

⁵It is not good to honor the wicked
  or to be unfair to the innocent.

JOHN 15:1—16:4a

Jesus Is Like a Vine

15 "I am the true vine; my Father is the gardener. ²He cuts off every branch of mine that does not produce fruit. And he trims and cleans every branch that produces fruit so that it will produce even more fruit. ³You are already clean because of the words I have spoken to you. ⁴Remain in me, and I will remain in you. A branch cannot produce fruit alone but must remain in the vine. In the same way, you cannot produce fruit alone but must remain in me.

⁵"I am the vine, and you are the branches. If any remain in me and I remain in them, they produce much fruit. But without me they can do nothing. ⁶If any do not remain in me, they are like a branch that is thrown away and then dies. People pick up dead branches, throw them into the fire, and burn them. ⁷If you remain in me and follow my teachings, you can ask anything you want, and it will be given to you. ⁸You should produce much fruit and show that you are my followers, which brings glory to my Father. ⁹I loved you as the Father loved me. Now remain in my love. ¹⁰I have obeyed my Father's commands, and I remain in his love. In the same way, if you obey my commands, you

will remain in my love. [11]I have told you these things so that you can have the same joy I have and so that your joy will be the fullest possible joy.

[12]"This is my command: Love each other as I have loved you. [13]The greatest love a person can show is to die for his friends. [14]You are my friends if you do what I command you. [15]I no longer call you servants, because a servant does not know what his master is doing. But I call you friends, because I have made known to you everything I heard from my Father. [16]You did not choose me; I chose you. And I gave you this work: to go and produce fruit, fruit that will last. Then the Father will give you anything you ask for in my name. [17]This is my command: Love each other.

Jesus Warns His Followers

[18]"If the world hates you, remember that it hated me first. [19]If you belonged to the world, it would love you as it loves its own. But I have chosen you out of the world, so you don't belong to it. That is why the world hates you. [20]Remember what I told you: A servant is not greater than his master. If people did wrong to me, they will do wrong to you, too. And if they obeyed my teaching, they will obey yours, too. [21]They will do all

this to you on account of me, because they do not know the One who sent me. [22]If I had not come and spoken to them, they would not be guilty of sin, but now they have no excuse for their sin. [23]Whoever hates me also hates my Father. [24]I did works among them that no one else has ever done. If I had not done these works, they would not be guilty of sin. But now they have seen what I have done, and yet they have hated both me and my Father. [25]But this happened so that what is written in their law would be true: 'They hated me for no reason.'[n]

[26]"I will send you the Helper[n] from the Father; he is the Spirit of truth who comes from the Father. When he comes, he will tell about me, [27]and you also must tell people about me, because you have been with me from the beginning.

16 "I have told you these things to keep you from giving up. [2]People will put you out of their synagogues. Yes, the time is coming when those who kill you will think they are offering service to God. [3]They will do this because they have not known the Father and they have not known me. [4]I have told you these things now so that when the time comes you will remember that I warned you.

JUNE 7

2 KINGS 1:1—2:25

Elijah and King Ahaziah

1 After Ahab died, Moab broke away from Israel's rule. [2]Ahaziah fell down through the wooden bars in his upstairs room in Samaria and was badly hurt. He sent messengers and told them, "Go, ask Baal-Zebub, god of Ekron, if I will recover from my injuries."

[3]But the LORD's angel said to Elijah the Tishbite, "Go up and meet the messengers sent by the king of Samaria. Ask them, 'Why

are you going to ask questions of Baal-Zebub, god of Ekron? Is it because you think there is no God in Israel?' [4]This is what the LORD says: 'You will never get up from the bed you are lying on; you will die.'" Then Elijah left.

[5]When the messengers returned to Ahaziah, he asked them, "Why have you returned?"

[6]They said, "A man came to meet us. He said, 'Go back to the king who sent you and tell him what the LORD says: "Why do you send messengers to ask questions of Baal-

---

15:25 'They . . . reason.' These words could be from Psalm 35:19 or Psalm 69:4. **15:26 Helper** "Counselor" or "Comforter." Jesus is talking about the Holy Spirit.

Zebub, god of Ekron? Is it because you think there is no God in Israel? You will never get up from the bed you are lying on; you will die.'"

⁷Ahaziah asked them, "What did the man look like who met you and told you this?"

⁸They answered, "He was a hairy man and wore a leather belt around his waist."

Ahaziah said, "It was Elijah the Tishbite."

⁹Then he sent a captain with his fifty men to Elijah. The captain went to Elijah, who was sitting on top of the hill, and said to him, "Man of God, the king says, 'Come down!'"

¹⁰Elijah answered the captain, "If I am a man of God, let fire come down from heaven and burn up you and your fifty men." Then fire came down from heaven and burned up the captain and his fifty men.

¹¹Ahaziah sent another captain and fifty men to Elijah. The captain said to him, "Man of God, this is what the king says: 'Come down quickly!'"

¹²Elijah answered, "If I am a man of God, let fire come down from heaven and burn up you and your fifty men!" Then fire came down from heaven and burned up the captain and his fifty men.

¹³Ahaziah then sent a third captain with his fifty men. The third captain came and fell down on his knees before Elijah and begged, "Man of God, please respect my life and the lives of your fifty servants. ¹⁴See, fire came down from heaven and burned up the first two captains of fifty with all their men. But now, respect my life."

¹⁵The LORD's angel said to Elijah, "Go down with him and don't be afraid of him." So Elijah got up and went down with him to see the king.

¹⁶Elijah told Ahaziah, "This is what the LORD says: 'You have sent messengers to ask questions of Baal-Zebub, god of Ekron. Is it because you think there is no God in Israel to ask? Because of this, you will never get up from your bed; you will die.'" ¹⁷So

Ahaziah died, just as the LORD, through Elijah, had said he would.

Joram became king in Ahaziah's place during the second year Jehoram son of Jehoshaphat was king of Judah. Joram ruled because Ahaziah had no son to take his place. ¹⁸The other things Ahaziah did are written in the book of the history of the kings of Israel.

Elijah Is Taken to Heaven

2 It was almost time for the LORD to take Elijah by a whirlwind up into heaven. While Elijah and Elisha were leaving Gilgal, ²Elijah said to Elisha, "Please stay here. The LORD has told me to go to Bethel."

But Elisha said, "As the LORD lives, and as you live, I won't leave you." So they went down to Bethel. ³The groups of prophets at Bethel came out to Elisha and said to him, "Do you know the LORD will take your master away from you today?"

Elisha said, "Yes, I know, but don't talk about it."

⁴Elijah said to him, "Stay here, Elisha, because the LORD has sent me to Jericho."

But Elisha said, "As the LORD lives, and as you live, I won't leave you."

So they went to Jericho. ⁵The groups of prophets at Jericho came to Elisha and said, "Do you know that the LORD will take your master away from you today?"

Elisha answered, "Yes, I know, but don't talk about it."

⁶Elijah said to Elisha, "Stay here. The LORD has sent me to the Jordan River."

Elisha answered, "As the LORD lives, and as you live, I won't leave you."

So the two of them went on. ⁷Fifty men of the groups of prophets came and stood far from where Elijah and Elisha were by the Jordan. ⁸Elijah took off his coat, rolled it up, and hit the water. The water divided to the right and to the left, and Elijah and Elisha crossed over on dry ground.

⁹After they had crossed over, Elijah said to Elisha, "What can I do for you before I am taken from you?"

Elisha said, "Leave me a double share of your spirit."ⁿ

2:9 Leave . . . spirit By law, the first son in a family would inherit a double share of his father's possessions. Elisha is asking to inherit a share of his master's power as his follower. He is not asking for twice as much power as Elijah had.

¹⁰Elijah said, "You have asked a hard thing. But if you see me when I am taken from you, it will be yours. If you don't, it won't happen."

¹¹As they were walking and talking, a chariot and horses of fire appeared and separated Elijah from Elisha. Then Elijah went up to heaven in a whirlwind. ¹²Elisha saw it and shouted, "My father! My father! The chariots of Israel and their horsemen!" And Elisha did not see him anymore. Then Elisha grabbed his own clothes and tore them to show how sad he was.

¹³He picked up Elijah's coat that had fallen from him. Then he returned and stood on the bank of the Jordan. ¹⁴Elisha hit the water with Elijah's coat and said, "Where is the LORD, the God of Elijah?" When he hit the water, it divided to the right and to the left, and Elisha crossed over.

¹⁵The groups of prophets at Jericho were watching and said, "Elisha now has the spirit Elijah had." And they came to meet him, bowing down to the ground before him. ¹⁶They said to him, "There are fifty strong men with us. Please let them go and look for your master. Maybe the Spirit of the LORD has taken Elijah up and set him down on some mountain or in some valley."

But Elisha answered, "No, don't send them."

¹⁷When the groups of prophets had begged Elisha until he couldn't refuse them anymore, he said, "Send them." So they sent fifty men who looked for three days, but they could not find him. ¹⁸Then they came back to Elisha at Jericho where he was staying. He said to them, "I told you not to go, didn't I?"

Elisha Makes the Water Pure

¹⁹The people of the city said to Elisha, "Look, master, this city is a nice place to live as you can see. But the water is so bad the land cannot grow crops."

²⁰Elisha said, "Bring me a new bowl and put salt in it." So they brought it to him. ²¹Then he went out to the spring and threw the salt in it. He said, "This is what the LORD says: 'I have healed this water. From now on it won't cause death, and it won't keep the land from growing crops.'" ²²So the water has been healed to this day just as Elisha had said.

Boys Make Fun of Elisha

²³From there Elisha went up to Bethel. On the way some boys came out of the city and made fun of him. They said to him, "Go up too, you baldhead! Go up too, you baldhead!" ²⁴Elisha turned around, looked at them, and put a curse on them in the name of the LORD. Then two mother bears came out of the woods and tore forty-two of the boys to pieces. ²⁵Elisha went to Mount Carmel and from there he returned to Samaria.

PSALM 71:7–16

⁷I am an example to many people,
   because you are my strong protection.
⁸I am always praising you;
   all day long I honor you.
⁹Do not reject me when I am old;
   do not leave me when my strength is
      gone.
¹⁰My enemies make plans against me,
   and they meet together to kill me.
¹¹They say, "God has left him.
   Go after him and take him,
   because no one will save him."

¹²God, don't be far off.
   My God, hurry to help me.
¹³Let those who accuse me
   be ashamed and destroyed.
   Let those who are trying to hurt me
   be covered with shame and disgrace.
¹⁴But I will always have hope
   and will praise you more and more.
¹⁵I will tell how you do what is right.
   I will tell about your salvation all day
      long,
   even though it is more than I can tell.
¹⁶I will come and tell about your powerful
      works, Lord GOD.
   I will remind people that only you do
      what is right.

PROVERBS 18:6–8

⁶The words of fools start quarrels.
   They make people want to beat them.

⁷The words of fools will ruin them;
   their own words will trap them.

[8]The words of a gossip are like tasty bits of
food.
People like to gobble them up.

JOHN 16:4b–33

The Work of the Holy Spirit

"I did not tell you these things at the beginning, because I was with you then. [5]Now I
am going back to the One who sent me. But
none of you asks me, 'Where are you going?'
[6]Your hearts are filled with sadness because I
have told you these things. [7]But I tell you the
truth, it is better for you that I go away. When
I go away, I will send the Helper[n] to you. If I do
not go away, the Helper will not come. [8]When
the Helper comes, he will prove to the people
of the world the truth about sin, about being
right with God, and about judgment. [9]He will
prove to them that sin is not believing in me.
[10]He will prove to them that being right with
God comes from my going to the Father and
not being seen anymore. [11]And the Helper
will prove to them that judgment happened
when the ruler of this world was judged.

[12]"I have many more things to say to you,
but they are too much for you now. [13]But
when the Spirit of truth comes, he will lead
you into all truth. He will not speak his own
words, but he will speak only what he hears,
and he will tell you what is to come. [14]The
Spirit of truth will bring glory to me, because
he will take what I have to say and tell it to
you. [15]All that the Father has is mine. That is
why I said that the Spirit will take what I have
to say and tell it to you.

Sadness Will Become Happiness

[16]"After a little while you will not see me,
and then after a little while you will see me
again."

[17]Some of the followers said to each other,
"What does Jesus mean when he says, 'After a
little while you will not see me, and then after
a little while you will see me again'? And what
does he mean when he says, 'Because I am going to the Father'?" [18]They also asked, "What
does he mean by 'a little while'? We don't understand what he is saying."

[19]Jesus saw that the followers wanted to
ask him about this, so he said to them, "Are
you asking each other what I meant when I
said, 'After a little while you will not see me,
and then after a little while you will see me
again'? [20]I tell you the truth, you will cry and
be sad, but the world will be happy. You will be
sad, but your sadness will become joy. [21]When
a woman gives birth to a baby, she has pain,
because her time has come. But when her
baby is born, she forgets the pain, because she
is so happy that a child has been born into the
world. [22]It is the same with you. Now you are
sad, but I will see you again and you will be
happy, and no one will take away your joy. [23]In
that day you will not ask me for anything. I
tell you the truth, my Father will give you anything you ask for in my name. [24]Until now you
have not asked for anything in my name. Ask
and you will receive, so that your joy will be
the fullest possible joy.

Victory over the World

[25]"I have told you these things indirectly in
stories. But the time will come when I will not
use stories like that to tell you things; I will
speak to you in plain words about the Father.
[26]In that day you will ask the Father for things
in my name. I mean, I will not need to ask the
Father for you. [27]The Father himself loves you.
He loves you because you loved me and believed that I came from God. [28]I came from
the Father into the world. Now I am leaving
the world and going back to the Father."

[29]Then the followers of Jesus said, "You are
speaking clearly to us now and are not using
stories that are hard to understand. [30]We can
see now that you know all things. You can answer a person's question even before it is
asked. This makes us believe you came from
God."

[31]Jesus answered, "So now you believe?
[32]Listen to me; a time is coming when you
will be scattered, each to your own home.
That time is now here. You will leave me
alone, but I am never really alone, because the
Father is with me.

[33]"I told you these things so that you can
have peace in me. In this world you will have
trouble, but be brave! I have defeated the
world."

16:7 Helper "Counselor" or "Comforter." Jesus is talking about the Holy Spirit.

JUNE 8

2 KINGS 3:1—4:44

War Between Israel and Moab

3 Joram son of Ahab became king over Israel at Samaria in Jehoshaphat's eighteenth year as king of Judah. And Joram ruled twelve years. ²He did what the LORD said was wrong, but he was not like his father and mother; he removed the stone pillars his father had made for Baal. ³But he continued to sin like Jeroboam son of Nebat who had led Israel to sin. Joram did not stop doing these same sins.

⁴Mesha king of Moab raised sheep. He paid the king of Israel one hundred thousand lambs and the wool of one hundred thousand sheep. ⁵But when Ahab died, the king of Moab turned against the king of Israel. ⁶So King Joram went out from Samaria and gathered Israel's army. ⁷He also sent messengers to Jehoshaphat king of Judah. "The king of Moab has turned against me," he said. "Will you go with me to fight Moab?"

Jehoshaphat replied, "I will go with you. My soldiers and my horses are yours."

⁸Jehoshaphat asked, "Which way should we attack?"

Joram answered, "Through the Desert of Edom."

⁹So the king of Israel went with the king of Judah and the king of Edom. After they had marched seven days, there was no more water for the army or for their animals that were with them. ¹⁰The king of Israel said, "This is terrible! The LORD has called us three kings together to hand us over to the Moabites!"

¹¹But Jehoshaphat asked, "Is there a prophet of the LORD here? We can ask the LORD through him."

An officer of the king of Israel answered, "Elisha son of Shaphat is here. He was Elijah's servant."

¹²Jehoshaphat said, "He speaks the LORD's truth." So the king of Israel and Jehoshaphat and the king of Edom went down to see Elisha.

¹³Elisha said to the king of Israel, "I have nothing to do with you. Go to the prophets of your father and to the prophets of your mother!"

The king of Israel said to Elisha, "No, the LORD has called us three kings together to hand us over to the Moabites."

¹⁴Elisha said, "As surely as the LORD All-Powerful lives, whom I serve, I tell you the truth. I wouldn't even look at you or notice you if Jehoshaphat king of Judah were not here. I respect him. ¹⁵Now bring me someone who plays the harp."

While the harp was being played, the LORD gave Elisha power. ¹⁶Then Elisha said, "The LORD says to dig holes in the valley. ¹⁷The LORD says you won't see wind or rain, but the valley will be filled with water. Then you, your cattle, and your other animals can drink. ¹⁸This is easy for the LORD to do; he will also hand Moab over to you. ¹⁹You will destroy every strong, walled city and every important town. You will cut down every good tree and stop up all springs. You will ruin every good field with rocks."

²⁰The next morning, about the time the sacrifice was offered, water came from the direction of Edom and filled the valley.

²¹All the Moabites heard that the kings had come up to fight against them. So they gathered everyone old enough to put on armor and waited at the border. ²²But when the Moabites got up early in the morning, the sun was shining on the water. They saw the water across from them, and it looked as red as blood. ²³Then they said, "This is blood! The kings must have fought and killed each other! Come, Moabites, let's take the valuables from the dead bodies!"

²⁴When the Moabites came to the camp of Israel, the Israelites came out and fought them until they ran away. Then the Israelites went on into the land, killing the Moabites. ²⁵They tore down the cities and threw rocks all over every good field. They stopped up all the springs and cut down all the good trees. Kir Hareseth was the only city with its stones still in place, but the

men with slingshots surrounded it and conquered it, too.

[26]When the king of Moab saw that the battle was too much for him, he took seven hundred men with swords to try to break through to the king of Edom. But they could not break through. [27]Then the king of Moab took his oldest son, who would have been king after him, and offered him as a burnt offering on the wall. So there was great anger against the Israelites, who left and went back to their own land.

A Widow Asks Elisha for Help

4 The wife of a man from the groups of prophets said to Elisha, "Your servant, my husband, is dead. You know he honored the LORD. But now the man he owes money to is coming to take my two boys as his slaves!"

[2]Elisha answered, "How can I help you? Tell me, what do you have in your house?"

The woman said, "I don't have anything there except a pot of oil."

[3]Then Elisha said, "Go and get empty jars from all your neighbors. Don't ask for just a few. [4]Then go into your house and shut the door behind you and your sons. Pour oil into all the jars, and set the full ones aside."

[5]So she left Elisha and shut the door behind her and her sons. As they brought the jars to her, she poured out the oil. [6]When the jars were all full, she said to her son, "Bring me another jar."

But he said, "There are no more jars." Then the oil stopped flowing.

[7]She went and told Elisha. And the prophet said to her, "Go, sell the oil and pay what you owe. You and your sons can live on what is left."

The Shunammite Woman

[8]One day Elisha went to Shunem, where an important woman lived. She begged Elisha to stay and eat. So every time Elisha passed by, he stopped there to eat. [9]The woman said to her husband, "I know that this is a holy man of God who passes by our house all the time. [10]Let's make a small room on the roof[n] and put a bed in the

room for him. We can put a table, a chair, and a lampstand there. Then when he comes by, he can stay there."

[11]One day Elisha came to the woman's house. After he went to his room and rested, [12]he said to his servant Gehazi, "Call the Shunammite woman."

When the servant had called her, she stood in front of him. [13]Elisha had told his servant, "Now say to her, 'You have gone to all this trouble for us. What can I do for you? Do you want me to speak to the king or the commander of the army for you?'"

She answered, "I live among my own people."

[14]Elisha said to Gehazi, "But what can we do for her?"

He answered, "She has no son, and her husband is old."

[15]Then Elisha said to Gehazi, "Call her." When he called her, she stood in the doorway. [16]Then Elisha said, "About this time next year, you will hold a son in your arms."

The woman said, "No, master, man of God, don't lie to me, your servant!"

[17]But the woman became pregnant and gave birth to a son at that time the next year, just as Elisha had told her.

[18]The boy grew up and one day went out to his father, who was with the grain harvesters. [19]The boy said to his father, "My head! My head!"

The father said to his servant, "Take him to his mother!" [20]The servant took him to his mother, and he lay on his mother's lap until noon. Then he died. [21]So she took him up and laid him on Elisha's bed. Then she shut the door and left.

[22]She called to her husband, "Send me one of the servants and one of the donkeys. Then I can go quickly to the man of God and return."

[23]The husband said, "Why do you want to go to him today? It isn't the New Moon or the Sabbath day."

She said, "It will be all right."

[24]Then she saddled the donkey and said to her servant, "Lead on. Don't slow down

---

4:10 roof In Bible times houses were built with flat roofs. The roof was used for drying things such as flax and fruit. And it was used as an extra room, as a place for worship, and as a cool place to sleep in the summer.

for me unless I tell you." ²⁵So she went to Elisha, the man of God, at Mount Carmel.

When he saw her coming from far away, he said to his servant Gehazi, "Look, there's the Shunammite woman! ²⁶Run to meet her and ask, 'Are you all right? Is your husband all right? Is the boy all right?'"

She answered, "Everything is all right."

²⁷Then she came to Elisha at the hill and grabbed his feet. Gehazi came near to pull her away, but Elisha said to him, "Leave her alone. She's very upset, and the LORD has not told me about it. He has hidden it from me."

²⁸She said, "Master, did I ask you for a son? Didn't I tell you not to lie to me?"

²⁹Then Elisha said to Gehazi, "Get ready. Take my walking stick in your hand and go quickly. If you meet anyone, don't say hello. If anyone greets you, don't respond. Lay my walking stick on the boy's face."

³⁰The boy's mother said, "As surely as the LORD lives and as you live, I won't leave you!" So Elisha got up and followed her.

³¹Gehazi went on ahead and laid the walking stick on the boy's face, but the boy did not talk or move. Then Gehazi went back to meet Elisha. "The boy has not awakened," he said.

³²When Elisha came into the house, the boy was lying dead on his bed. ³³Elisha entered the room and shut the door, so only he and the boy were in the room. Then he prayed to the LORD. ³⁴He went to the bed and lay on the boy, putting his mouth on the boy's mouth, his eyes on the boy's eyes, and his hands on the boy's hands. He stretched himself out on top of the boy. Soon the boy's skin became warm. ³⁵Elisha turned away and walked around the room. Then he went back and put himself on the boy again. The boy sneezed seven times and opened his eyes.

³⁶Elisha called Gehazi and said, "Call the Shunammite!" So he did. When she came, Elisha said, "Pick up your son." ³⁷She came in and fell at Elisha's feet, bowing facedown to the floor. Then she picked up her son and went out.

Elisha and the Stew

³⁸When Elisha returned to Gilgal, there was a shortage of food in the land. While the groups of prophets were sitting in front of him, he said to his servant, "Put the large pot on the fire, and boil some stew for these men."

³⁹One of them went out into the field to gather plants. Finding a wild vine, he picked fruit from the vine and filled his robe with it. Then he came and cut up the fruit into the pot. But they didn't know what kind of fruit it was. ⁴⁰They poured out the stew for the others to eat. When they began to eat it, they shouted, "Man of God, there's death in the pot!" And they could not eat it.

⁴¹Elisha told them to bring some flour. He threw it into the pot and said, "Pour it out for the people to eat." Then there was nothing harmful in the pot.

Elisha Feeds the People

⁴²A man from Baal Shalishah came to Elisha, bringing him twenty loaves of barley bread from the first harvest. He also brought fresh grain in his sack. Elisha said, "Give it to the people to eat."

⁴³Elisha's servant asked, "How can I feed a hundred people with so little?"

"Give the bread to the people to eat," Elisha said. "This is what the LORD says: 'They will eat and will have food left over.'" ⁴⁴After he gave it to them, the people ate and had food left over, as the LORD had said.

PSALM 71:17–24

¹⁷God, you have taught me since I was
    young.
  To this day I tell about the miracles you
    do.
¹⁸Even though I am old and gray,
    do not leave me, God.
  I will tell the children about your power;
  I will tell those who live after me about
    your might.

¹⁹God, your justice reaches to the skies.
  You have done great things;
  God, there is no one like you.
²⁰You have given me many troubles and
    bad times,
  but you will give me life again.
  When I am almost dead,
    you will keep me alive.

²¹You will make me greater than ever,
  and you will comfort me again.

²²I will praise you with the harp.
  I trust you, my God.
  I will sing to you with the lyre,
  Holy One of Israel.
²³I will shout for joy when I sing praises to
  you.
  You have saved me.
²⁴I will tell about your justice all day long.
  And those who want to hurt me
  will be ashamed and disgraced.

PROVERBS 18:9

⁹A person who doesn't work hard
  is just like someone who destroys
    things.

JOHN 17:1–26

Jesus Prays for His Followers

17After Jesus said these things, he
looked toward heaven and prayed,
"Father, the time has come. Give glory to
your Son so that the Son can give glory to
you. ²You gave the Son power over all people
so that the Son could give eternal life to all
those you gave him. ³And this is eternal life:
that people know you, the only true God,
and that they know Jesus Christ, the One
you sent. ⁴Having finished the work you
gave me to do, I brought you glory on earth.
⁵And now, Father, give me glory with you;
give me the glory I had with you before the
world was made.
⁶"I showed what you are like to those you
gave me from the world. They belonged to
you, and you gave them to me, and they
have obeyed your teaching. ⁷Now they know
that everything you gave me comes from
you. ⁸I gave them the teachings you gave
me, and they accepted them. They knew
that I truly came from you, and they believed that you sent me. ⁹I am praying for
them. I am not praying for people in the
world but for those you gave me, because
they are yours. ¹⁰All I have is yours, and all
you have is mine. And my glory is shown
through them. ¹¹I am coming to you; I will
not stay in the world any longer. But they
are still in the world. Holy Father, keep
them safe by the power of your name, the
name you gave me, so that they will be one,
just as you and I are one. ¹²While I was with
them, I kept them safe by the power of your
name, the name you gave me. I protected
them, and only one of them, the one worthy
of destruction, was lost so that the Scripture would come true.
¹³"I am coming to you now. But I pray
these things while I am still in the world so
that these followers can have all of my joy in
them. ¹⁴I have given them your teaching.
And the world has hated them, because
they don't belong to the world, just as I don't
belong to the world. ¹⁵I am not asking you
to take them out of the world but to keep
them safe from the Evil One. ¹⁶They don't
belong to the world, just as I don't belong to
the world. ¹⁷Make them ready for your service through your truth; your teaching is
truth. ¹⁸I have sent them into the world, just
as you sent me into the world. ¹⁹For their
sake, I am making myself ready to serve so
that they can be ready for their service of
the truth.
²⁰"I pray for these followers, but I am also
praying for all those who will believe in me
because of their teaching. ²¹Father, I pray
that they can be one. As you are in me and I
am in you, I pray that they can also be one in
us. Then the world will believe that you sent
me. ²²I have given these people the glory
that you gave me so that they can be one,
just as you and I are one. ²³I will be in them
and you will be in me so that they will be
completely one. Then the world will know
that you sent me and that you loved them
just as much as you loved me.
²⁴"Father, I want these people that you
gave me to be with me where I am. I want
them to see my glory, which you gave me because you loved me before the world was
made. ²⁵Father, you are the One who is good.
The world does not know you, but I know
you, and these people know you sent me. ²⁶I
showed them what you are like, and I will
show them again. Then they will have the
same love that you have for me, and I will
live in them."

JUNE 9

2 KINGS 5:1—6:23

Naaman Is Healed

5 Naaman was commander of the army of the king of Aram. He was honored by his master, and he had much respect because the LORD used him to give victory to Aram. He was a mighty and brave man, but he had a skin disease.

²The Arameans had gone out to raid the Israelites and had taken a little girl as a captive. This little girl served Naaman's wife. ³She said to her mistress, "I wish my master would meet the prophet who lives in Samaria. He would cure him of his disease."

⁴Naaman went to the king and told him what the girl from Israel had said. ⁵The king of Aram said, "Go ahead, and I will send a letter to the king of Israel." So Naaman left and took with him about seven hundred fifty pounds of silver, as well as one hundred fifty pounds of gold and ten changes of clothes. ⁶He brought the letter to the king of Israel, which read, "I am sending my servant Naaman to you so you can heal him of his skin disease."

⁷When the king of Israel read the letter, he tore his clothes to show how upset he was. He said, "I'm not God! I can't kill and make alive again! Why does this man send someone with a skin disease for me to heal? You can see that the king of Aram is trying to start trouble with me."

⁸When Elisha, the man of God, heard that the king of Israel had torn his clothes, he sent the king this message: "Why have you torn your clothes? Let Naaman come to me. Then he will know there is a prophet in Israel." ⁹So Naaman went with his horses and chariots to Elisha's house and stood outside the door.

¹⁰Elisha sent Naaman a messenger who said, "Go and wash in the Jordan River seven times. Then your skin will be healed, and you will be clean."

¹¹Naaman became angry and left. He said,

"I thought Elisha would surely come out and stand before me and call on the name of the LORD his God. I thought he would wave his hand over the place and heal the disease. ¹²The Abana and the Pharpar, the rivers of Damascus, are better than all the waters of Israel. Why can't I wash in them and become clean?" So Naaman went away very angry.

¹³Naaman's servants came near and said to him, "My father, if the prophet had told you to do some great thing, wouldn't you have done it? Doesn't it make more sense just to do it? After all, he only told you, 'Wash, and you will be clean.'" ¹⁴So Naaman went down and dipped in the Jordan seven times, just as Elisha had said. Then his skin became new again, like the skin of a child. And he was clean.

¹⁵Naaman and all his group returned to Elisha. He stood before Elisha and said, "Look, I now know there is no God in all the earth except in Israel. Now please accept a gift from me."

¹⁶But Elisha said, "As surely as the LORD lives whom I serve, I won't accept anything." Naaman urged him to take the gift, but he refused.

¹⁷Then Naaman said, "If you won't take the gift, then please give me some soil—as much as two of my mules can carry. From now on I'll not offer any burnt offering or sacrifice to any other gods but the LORD. ¹⁸But let the LORD pardon me for this: When my master goes into the temple of Rimmon" to worship, he leans on my arm. Then I must bow in that temple. May the LORD pardon me when I do that."

¹⁹Elisha said to him, "Go in peace."

Naaman left Elisha and went a short way. ²⁰Gehazi, the servant of Elisha the man of God, thought, "My master has not accepted what Naaman the Aramean brought. As surely as the LORD lives, I'll run after him and get something from him." ²¹So Gehazi went after Naaman.

When Naaman saw someone running af-

5:18 temple of Rimmon The place where the Aramean people worshiped the god Rimmon.

ter him, he got off the chariot to meet Gehazi. He asked, "Is everything all right?"

22Gehazi said, "Everything is all right. My master has sent me. He said, 'Two young men from the groups of prophets in the mountains of Ephraim just came to me. Please give them seventy-five pounds of silver and two changes of clothes.'"

23Naaman said, "Please take one hundred fifty pounds," and he urged Gehazi to take it. He tied one hundred fifty pounds of silver in two bags with two changes of clothes. Then he gave them to two of his servants to carry for Gehazi. 24When they came to the hill, Gehazi took these things from Naaman's servants and put them in the house. Then he let Naaman's servants go, and they left.

25When he came in and stood before his master, Elisha said to him, "Where have you been, Gehazi?"

"I didn't go anywhere," he answered.

26But Elisha said to him, "My spirit was with you. I knew when the man turned from his chariot to meet you. This isn't a time to take money, clothes, olives, grapes, sheep, oxen, male servants, or female servants. 27So Naaman's skin disease will come on you and your children forever." When Gehazi left Elisha, he had the disease and was as white as snow.

An Axhead Floats

6 The groups of prophets said to Elisha, "The place where we meet with you is too small for us. 2Let's go to the Jordan River. There everyone can get a log, and let's build a place there to live."

Elisha said, "Go."

3One of them said, "Please go with us."

Elisha answered, "I will go," 4so he went with them. When they arrived at the Jordan, they cut down some trees. 5As one man was cutting down a tree, the head of his ax fell into the water. He yelled, "Oh, my master! I borrowed that ax!"

6Elisha asked, "Where did it fall?" The man showed him the place. Then Elisha cut down a stick and threw it into the water, and it made the iron head float. 7Elisha said, "Pick up the axhead." Then the man reached out and took it.

Elisha and the Blinded Arameans

8The king of Aram was at war with Israel. He had a council meeting with his officers and said, "I will set up my camp in this place."

9Elisha, the man of God, sent a message to the king of Israel, saying, "Be careful! Don't pass that place, because the Arameans are going down there!"

10The king of Israel checked the place about which Elisha had warned him. Elisha warned him several times, so the king protected himself there.

11The king of Aram was angry about this. He called his officers together and demanded, "Tell me who of us is working for the king of Israel."

12One of the officers said, "None, my master and king. It's Elisha, the prophet from Israel. He can tell you what you speak in your bedroom."

13The king said, "Go and find him so I can send men and catch him."

The servants came back and reported, "He is in Dothan."

14Then the king sent horses, chariots, and many troops to Dothan. They arrived at night and surrounded the city.

15Elisha's servant got up early, and when he went out, he saw an army with horses and chariots all around the city. The servant said to Elisha, "Oh, my master, what can we do?"

16Elisha said, "Don't be afraid. The army that fights for us is larger than the one against us."

17Then Elisha prayed, "LORD, open my servant's eyes, and let him see."

The LORD opened the eyes of the young man, and he saw that the mountain was full of horses and chariots of fire all around Elisha.

18As the enemy came down toward Elisha, he prayed to the LORD, "Make these people blind." So he made the Aramean army blind, as Elisha had asked.

19Elisha said to them, "This is not the right road or the right city. Follow me and I'll take you to the man you are looking for." Then Elisha led them to Samaria.

20After they entered Samaria, Elisha said, "LORD, open these men's eyes so they can see." So the LORD opened their eyes, and the

Aramean army saw that they were inside the city of Samaria!

²¹When the king of Israel saw the Aramean army, he said to Elisha, "My father, should I kill them? Should I kill them?"

²²Elisha answered, "Don't kill them. You wouldn't kill people whom you captured with your sword and bow. Give them food and water, and let them eat and drink and then go home to their master." ²³So he prepared a great feast for the Aramean army. After they ate and drank, the king sent them away, and they went home to their master. The soldiers of Aram did not come anymore into the land of Israel.

PSALM 72:1–7

A Prayer for the King

Of Solomon.

72 God, give the king your good
judgment
and the king's son your goodness.
²Help him judge your people fairly
and decide what is right for the poor.
³Let there be peace on the mountains
and goodness on the hills for the
people.
⁴Help him be fair to the poor
and save the needy
and punish those who hurt them.

⁵May they respect you as long as the sun
shines
and as long as the moon glows.
⁶Let him be like rain on the grass,
like showers that water the earth.
⁷Let goodness be plentiful while he lives.
Let peace continue as long as there is a
moon.

PROVERBS 18:10–11

¹⁰The LORD is like a strong tower;
those who do right can run to him for
safety.

¹¹Rich people trust their wealth to protect
them.

They think it is like the high walls of a city.

JOHN 18:1–18

Jesus Is Arrested

18 When Jesus finished praying, he went with his followers across the Kidron Valley. On the other side there was a garden, and Jesus and his followers went into it.

²Judas knew where this place was, because Jesus met there often with his followers. Judas was the one who turned against Jesus. ³So Judas came there with a group of soldiers and some guards from the leading priests and the Pharisees. They were carrying torches, lanterns, and weapons.

⁴Knowing everything that would happen to him, Jesus went out and asked, "Who is it you are looking for?"

⁵They answered, "Jesus from Nazareth."

"I am he," Jesus said. (Judas, the one who turned against Jesus, was standing there with them.) ⁶When Jesus said, "I am he," they moved back and fell to the ground.

⁷Jesus asked them again, "Who is it you are looking for?"

They said, "Jesus of Nazareth."

⁸"I told you that I am he," Jesus said. "So if you are looking for me, let the others go." ⁹This happened so that the words Jesus said before would come true: "I have not lost any of the ones you gave me."

¹⁰Simon Peter, who had a sword, pulled it out and struck the servant of the high priest, cutting off his right ear. (The servant's name was Malchus.) ¹¹Jesus said to Peter, "Put your sword back. Shouldn't I drink the cup[n] the Father gave me?"

Jesus Is Brought Before Annas

¹²Then the soldiers with their commander and the guards arrested Jesus. They tied him ¹³and led him first to Annas, the father-in-law of Caiaphas, the high priest that year. ¹⁴Caiaphas was the one who told the Jews that it would be better if one man died for all the people.

18:11 cup Jesus is talking about the painful things that will happen to him. Accepting these things will be very hard, like drinking a cup of something bitter.

Peter Says He Doesn't Know Jesus

¹⁵Simon Peter and another one of Jesus' followers went along after Jesus. This follower knew the high priest, so he went with Jesus into the high priest's courtyard. ¹⁶But Peter waited outside near the door. The follower who knew the high priest came back outside, spoke to the girl at the door, and brought Peter inside. ¹⁷The girl at the door said to Peter, "Aren't you also one of that man's followers?"

Peter answered, "No, I am not!"

¹⁸It was cold, so the servants and guards had built a fire and were standing around it, warming themselves. Peter also was standing with them, warming himself.

JUNE 10

2 KINGS 6:24—8:29

A Shortage of Food

²⁴Later, Ben-Hadad king of Aram gathered his whole army and surrounded and attacked Samaria. ²⁵There was a shortage of food in Samaria. It was so bad that a donkey's head sold for about two pounds of silver, and half of a pint of dove's dung sold for about two ounces of silver.

²⁶As the king of Israel was passing by on the wall, a woman yelled out to him, "Help me, my master and king!"

²⁷The king said, "If the LORD doesn't help you, how can I? Can I get help from the threshing floor or from the winepress?" ²⁸Then the king said to her, "What is your trouble?"

She answered, "This woman said to me, 'Give up your son so we can eat him today. Then we will eat my son tomorrow.' ²⁹So we boiled my son and ate him. Then the next day I said to her, 'Give up your son so we can eat him.' But she had hidden him."

³⁰When the king heard the woman's words, he tore his clothes in grief. As he walked along the wall, the people looked and saw he had on rough cloth under his clothes to show his sadness. ³¹He said, "May God punish me terribly if the head of Elisha son of Shaphat isn't cut off from his body today!"

³²The king sent a messenger to Elisha, who was sitting in his house with the elders. But before the messenger arrived, Elisha said to them, "See, this murderer is sending men to cut off my head. When the messenger arrives, shut the door and hold it; don't let him in. The sound of his master's feet is behind him."

³³Elisha was still talking with the leaders when the messenger arrived. The king said, "This trouble has come from the LORD. Why should I wait for the LORD any longer?"

7 Elisha said, "Listen to the LORD's word. This is what the LORD says: 'About this time tomorrow seven quarts of fine flour will be sold for two-fifths of an ounce of silver, and thirteen quarts of barley will be sold for two-fifths of an ounce of silver. This will happen at the gate of Samaria.'"

²Then the officer who was close to the king answered Elisha, "Even if the LORD opened windows in the sky, that couldn't happen."

Elisha said, "You will see it with your eyes, but you will not eat any of it."

³There were four men with a skin disease at the entrance to the city gate. They said to each other, "Why do we sit here until we die? ⁴There is no food in the city. So if we go into the city, we will die there. If we stay here, we will die. So let's go to the Aramean camp. If they let us live, we will live. If they kill us, we die."

⁵So they got up at twilight and went to the Aramean camp, but when they arrived, no one was there. ⁶The Lord had caused the Aramean army to hear the sound of chariots, horses, and a large army. They had said to each other, "The king of Israel has hired the Hittite and Egyptian kings to attack us!" ⁷So they got up and ran away in the twilight, leaving their tents, horses, and donkeys. They left the camp standing and ran for their lives.

8When the men with the skin disease came to the edge of the camp, they went into one of the tents and ate and drank. They carried silver, gold, and clothes out of the camp and hid them. Then they came back and entered another tent. They carried things from this tent and hid them, also. 9Then they said to each other, "We're doing wrong. Today we have good news, but we are silent. If we wait until the sun comes up, we'll be discovered. Let's go right now and tell the people in the king's palace."

10So they went and called to the gatekeepers of the city. They said, "We went to the Aramean camp, but no one is there; we didn't hear anyone. The horses and donkeys were still tied up, and the tents were still standing." 11Then the gatekeepers shouted out and told the people in the palace.

12The king got up in the night and said to his officers, "I'll tell you what the Arameans are doing to us. They know we are starving. They have gone out of the camp to hide in the field. They're saying, 'When the Israelites come out of the city, we'll capture them alive. Then we'll enter the city.'"

13One of his officers answered, "Let some men take five of the horses that are still left in the city. These men are like all the Israelites who are left; they are also about to die. Let's send them to see what has happened."

14So the men took two chariots with horses. The king sent them after the Aramean army, saying, "Go and see what has happened." 15The men followed the Aramean army as far as the Jordan River. The road was full of clothes and equipment that the Arameans had thrown away as they had hurriedly left. So the messengers returned and told the king. 16Then the people went out and took valuables from the Aramean camp. So seven quarts of fine flour were sold for two-fifths of an ounce of silver, and thirteen quarts of barley were sold for two-fifths of an ounce of silver, just as the LORD had said.

17The king chose the officer who was close to him to guard the gate, but the people trampled the officer to death. This happened just as Elisha had told the king when the king came to his house. 18He had said, "Thir-teen quarts of barley and seven quarts of fine flour will each sell for two-fifths of an ounce of silver about this time tomorrow at the gate of Samaria."

19But the officer had answered, "Even if the LORD opened windows in the sky, that couldn't happen." And Elisha had told him, "You will see it with your eyes, but you won't eat any of it." 20It happened to the officer just that way. The people trampled him in the gateway, and he died.

The Shunammite Regains Her Land

8Elisha spoke to the woman whose son he had brought back to life. He said, "Get up and go with your family. Stay any place you can, because the LORD has called for a time without food that will last seven years." 2So the woman got up and did as the man of God had said. She left with her family, and they stayed in the land of the Philistines for seven years. 3After seven years she returned from the land of the Philistines and went to beg the king for her house and land. 4The king was talking with Gehazi, the servant of the man of God. The king had said, "Please tell me all the great things Elisha has done." 5Gehazi was telling the king how Elisha had brought a dead boy back to life. Just then the woman whose son Elisha had brought back to life came and begged the king for her house and land.

Gehazi said, "My master and king, this is the woman, and this is the son Elisha brought back to life."

6The king asked the woman, and she told him about it. Then the king chose an officer to help her. "Give the woman everything that is hers," the king said. "Give her all the money made from her land from the day she left until now."

Ben-Hadad Is Killed

7Then Elisha went to Damascus, where Ben-Hadad king of Aram was sick. Someone told him, "The man of God has arrived."

8The king said to Hazael, "Take a gift in your hand and go meet him. Ask the LORD through him if I will recover from my sickness."

9So Hazael went to meet Elisha, taking with him a gift of forty camels loaded with every good thing in Damascus. He came and stood before Elisha and said, "Your son Ben-Hadad king of Aram sent me to you. He asks if he will recover from his sickness."

¹⁰Elisha said to Hazael, "Go and tell Ben-Hadad, 'You will surely recover,' but the LORD has told me he will really die." ¹¹Hazael stared at Elisha until he felt ashamed. Then Elisha cried.

¹²Hazael asked, "Why are you crying, master?"

Elisha answered, "Because I know what evil you will do to the Israelites. You will burn their strong, walled cities with fire and kill their young men with swords. You will throw their babies to the ground and split open their pregnant women."

¹³Hazael said, "Am I a dog? How could I do such things?"

Elisha answered, "The LORD has shown me that you will be king over Aram."

¹⁴Then Hazael left Elisha and came to his master. Ben-Hadad said to him, "What did Elisha say to you?"

Hazael answered, "He told me that you will surely recover." ¹⁵But the next day Hazael took a blanket and dipped it in water. Then he put it over Ben-Hadad's face, and he died. So Hazael became king in Ben-Hadad's place.

Jehoram King of Judah

¹⁶While Jehoshaphat was king in Judah, Jehoram son of Jehoshaphat became king of Judah. This was during the fifth year Joram son of Ahab was king of Israel. ¹⁷Jehoram was thirty-two years old when he began to rule, and he ruled eight years in Jerusalem. ¹⁸He followed the ways of the kings of Israel, just as the family of Ahab had done, because he married Ahab's daughter. Jehoram did what the LORD said was wrong. ¹⁹But the LORD would not destroy Judah because of his servant David. The LORD had promised that one of David's descendants would always rule.

²⁰In Jehoram's time Edom broke away from Judah's rule and chose their own king. ²¹So Jehoram and all his chariots went to Zair. The Edomites surrounded him and his chariot commanders. Jehoram got up and attacked the Edomites at night, but his army ran away to their tents. ²²From then until now the country of Edom has fought against the rule of Judah. At the same time Libnah also broke away from Judah's rule.

²³The other acts of Jehoram and all the things he did are written in the book of the history of the kings of Judah. ²⁴Jehoram died and was buried with his ancestors in Jerusalem, and Jehoram's son Ahaziah ruled in his place.

²⁵Ahaziah son of Jehoram became king of Judah during the twelfth year Joram son of Ahab was king of Israel. ²⁶Ahaziah was twenty-two years old when he became king, and he ruled one year in Jerusalem. His mother's name was Athaliah, a granddaughter of Omri king of Israel. ²⁷Ahaziah followed the ways of Ahab's family. He did what the LORD said was wrong, as Ahab's family had done, because he was a son-in-law to Ahab.

²⁸Ahaziah went with Joram son of Ahab to Ramoth in Gilead, where they fought against Hazael king of Aram. The Arameans wounded Joram. ²⁹So King Joram returned to Jezreel to heal from the wound he had received from the Arameans at Ramoth when he fought Hazael king of Aram. Ahaziah son of Jehoram king of Judah went down to visit Joram son of Ahab at Jezreel, because he had been wounded.

PSALM 72:8–14

⁸Let his kingdom go from sea to sea,
  and from the Euphrates River to the
    ends of the earth.
⁹Let the people of the desert bow down to
  him,
  and make his enemies lick the dust.
¹⁰Let the kings of Tarshish and the faraway
  lands
    bring him gifts.
  Let the kings of Sheba and Seba
    bring their presents to him.
¹¹Let all kings bow down to him
  and all nations serve him.

¹²He will help the poor when they cry out
  and will save the needy when no one
    else will help.

[13] He will be kind to the weak and poor,
and he will save their lives.
[14] He will save them from cruel people who
try to hurt them,
because their lives are precious to
him.

PROVERBS 18:12–13

[12] Proud people will be ruined,
but the humble will be honored.

[13] Anyone who answers without listening
is foolish and confused.

JOHN 18:19–40

The High Priest Questions Jesus

[19] The high priest asked Jesus questions about his followers and his teaching. [20] Jesus answered, "I have spoken openly to everyone. I have always taught in synagogues and in the Temple, where all the Jews come together. I never said anything in secret. [21] So why do you question me? Ask the people who heard my teaching. They know what I said."

[22] When Jesus said this, one of the guards standing there hit him. The guard said, "Is that the way you answer the high priest?"

[23] Jesus answered him, "If I said something wrong, then show what it was. But if what I said is true, why do you hit me?"

[24] Then Annas sent Jesus, who was still tied, to Caiaphas the high priest.

Peter Says Again He Doesn't Know Jesus

[25] As Simon Peter was standing and warming himself, they said to him, "Aren't you one of that man's followers?"

Peter said it was not true; he said, "No, I am not."

[26] One of the servants of the high priest was there. This servant was a relative of the man whose ear Peter had cut off. The servant said, "Didn't I see you with him in the garden?"

[27] Again Peter said it wasn't true. At once a rooster crowed.

Jesus Is Brought Before Pilate

[28] Early in the morning they led Jesus from Caiaphas's house to the Roman governor's palace. They would not go inside the palace, because they did not want to make themselves unclean;[n] they wanted to eat the Passover meal. [29] So Pilate went outside to them and asked, "What charges do you bring against this man?"

[30] They answered, "If he were not a criminal, we wouldn't have brought him to you."

[31] Pilate said to them, "Take him yourselves and judge him by your own law."

"But we are not allowed to put anyone to death," the Jews answered. [32] (This happened so that what Jesus said about how he would die would come true.)

[33] Then Pilate went back inside the palace and called Jesus to him and asked, "Are you the king of the Jews?"

[34] Jesus said, "Is that your own question, or did others tell you about me?"

[35] Pilate answered, "I am not one of you. It was your own people and their leading priests who handed you over to me. What have you done wrong?"

[36] Jesus answered, "My kingdom does not belong to this world. If it belonged to this world, my servants would have fought to keep me from being given over to the Jewish leaders. But my kingdom is from another place."

[37] Pilate said, "So you are a king!"

Jesus answered, "You are the one saying I am a king. This is why I was born and came into the world: to tell people the truth. And everyone who belongs to the truth listens to me."

[38] Pilate said, "What is truth?" After he said this, he went out to the crowd again and said to them, "I find nothing against this man. [39] But it is your custom that I free one prisoner to you at Passover time. Do you want me to free the 'king of the Jews'?"

[40] They shouted back, "No, not him! Let Barabbas go free!" (Barabbas was a robber.)

18:28 unclean Going into the Roman palace would make them unfit to eat the Passover Feast, according to their Law.

JUNE 11

2 KINGS 9:1—10:36

Jehu Is Chosen King

9 At the same time, Elisha the prophet called a man from the groups of prophets. Elisha said, "Get ready, and take this small bottle of olive oil in your hand. Go to Ramoth in Gilead. ²When you arrive, find Jehu son of Jehoshaphat, the son of Nimshi. Go in and make Jehu get up from among his brothers, and take him to an inner room. ³Then take the bottle and pour the oil on Jehu's head and say, 'This is what the LORD says: I have appointed you king over Israel.' Then open the door and run away. Don't wait!"

⁴So the young man, the prophet, went to Ramoth in Gilead. ⁵When he arrived, he saw the officers of the army sitting together. He said, "Commander, I have a message for you."

Jehu asked, "For which one of us?"

The young man said, "For you, commander."

⁶Jehu got up and went into the house. Then the young prophet poured the olive oil on Jehu's head and said to him, "This is what the LORD, the God of Israel says: 'I have appointed you king over the LORD's people Israel. ⁷You must destroy the family of Ahab your master. I will punish Jezebel for the deaths of my servants the prophets and for all the LORD's servants who were murdered. ⁸All of Ahab's family must die. I will not let any male child in Ahab's family live in Israel, whether slave or free. ⁹I will make Ahab's family like the family of Jeroboam son of Nebat and like the family of Baasha son of Ahijah. ¹⁰The dogs will eat Jezebel at Jezreel, and no one will bury her.'"

Then the young prophet opened the door and ran away.

¹¹When Jehu went back to his master's officers, one of them said to Jehu, "Is everything all right? Why did this crazy man come to you?"

Jehu answered, "You know the man and how he talks."

¹²They answered, "That's not true. Tell us."

Jehu said, "He said to me, 'This is what the LORD says: I have appointed you to be king over Israel.'"

¹³Then the officers hurried, and each man took off his own coat and put it on the stairs for Jehu. They blew the trumpet and shouted, "Jehu is king!"

Joram and Ahaziah Are Killed

¹⁴So Jehu son of Jehoshaphat, the son of Nimshi, made plans against Joram. Now Joram and all Israel had been defending Ramoth in Gilead from Hazael king of Aram. ¹⁵But King Joram had to return to Jezreel to heal from the injuries the Arameans had given him when he fought against Hazael king of Aram.

Jehu said, "If you agree with this, don't let anyone leave the city. They might tell the news in Jezreel." ¹⁶Then he got into his chariot and set out for Jezreel, where Joram was resting. Ahaziah king of Judah had gone down to see him.

¹⁷The lookout was standing on the watchtower in Jezreel when he saw Jehu's troops coming. He said, "I see some soldiers!"

Joram said, "Take a horseman and send him to meet them. Tell him to ask, 'Is all in order?'"

¹⁸The horseman rode out to meet Jehu, and he said, "This is what the king says: 'Is all in order?'"

Jehu said, "Why bother yourself with order? Come along behind me."

The lookout reported, "The messenger reached them, but he is not coming back."

¹⁹Then Joram sent out a second horseman. This rider came to Jehu's group and said, "This is what the king says: 'Is all in order?'"

Jehu answered, "Why bother yourself with order? Come along behind me."

²⁰The lookout reported, "The second man reached them, but he is not coming back. The man in the chariot is driving like Jehu son of Nimshi. He drives as if he were crazy!"

²¹Joram said, "Get my chariot ready." Then

the servant got Joram's chariot ready. Joram king of Israel and Ahaziah king of Judah went out, each in his own chariot, to meet Jehu at the property of Naboth the Jezreelite. [22]When Joram saw Jehu, he said, "Is all in order, Jehu?"

Jehu answered, "There will never be any order as long as your mother Jezebel worships idols and uses witchcraft."

[23]Joram turned the horses to run away and yelled to Ahaziah, "It's a trick, Ahaziah!" [24]Then Jehu drew his bow and shot Joram between his shoulders. The arrow went through Joram's heart, and he fell down in his chariot.

[25]Jehu ordered Bidkar, his chariot officer, "Pick up Joram's body, and throw it into the field of Naboth the Jezreelite. Remember when you and I rode together with Joram's father Ahab. The LORD made this prophecy against him: [26]'Yesterday I saw the blood of Naboth and his sons, says the LORD, so I will punish Ahab in his field, says the LORD.' Take Joram's body and throw it into the field, as the LORD has said."

[27]When Ahaziah king of Judah saw this, he ran away toward Beth Haggan. Jehu chased him, saying, "Shoot Ahaziah, too!" Ahaziah was wounded in his chariot on the way up to Gur near Ibleam. He got as far as Megiddo but died there. [28]Ahaziah's servants carried his body in a chariot to Jerusalem and buried him with his ancestors in his tomb in Jerusalem. [29](Ahaziah had become king over Judah in the eleventh year Joram son of Ahab was king.)

Death of Jezebel

[30]When Jehu came to Jezreel, Jezebel heard about it. She put on her eye makeup and fixed her hair. Then she looked out the window. [31]When Jehu entered the city gate, Jezebel said, "Have you come in peace, you Zimri,[n] you who killed your master?"

[32]Jehu looked up at the window and said, "Who is on my side? Who?" Two or three servants looked out the window at Jehu. [33]He said to them, "Throw her down." So they threw Jezebel down, and the horses ran over

her. Some of her blood splashed on the wall and on the horses.

[34]Jehu went into the house and ate and drank. Then he said, "Now see about this cursed woman. Bury her, because she is a king's daughter."

[35]The men went to bury Jezebel, but they could not find her. They found only her skull, feet, and the palms of her hands. [36]When they came back and told Jehu, he said, "The LORD said this through his servant Elijah the Tishbite: 'The dogs will eat Jezebel at Jezreel. [37]Her body will be like manure on the field in the land at Jezreel. No one will be able to say that this is Jezebel.'"

Families of Ahab and Ahaziah Killed

10 Ahab had seventy sons in Samaria. Jehu wrote letters and sent them to Samaria to the officers and elders of Jezreel and to the guardians of the sons of Ahab. Jehu said, [2]"You have your master's sons with you, and you have chariots, horses, a city with strong walls, and weapons. When you get this letter, [3]choose the best and most worthy person among your master's sons, and make him king. Then fight for your master's family."

[4]But the officers and leaders of Jezreel were frightened. They said, "Two kings could not stand up to Jehu, so how can we?"

[5]The palace manager, the city governor, the leaders, and the guardians sent a message to Jehu. "We are your servants," they said. "We will do everything you tell us to do. We won't make any man king, so do whatever you think is best."

[6]Then Jehu wrote a second letter, saying, "If you are on my side and will obey me, cut off the heads of your master's sons and come to me at Jezreel tomorrow about this time."

Now the seventy sons of the king's family were with the leading men of the city who were their guardians. [7]When the leaders received the letter, they took the king's sons and killed all seventy of them. They put their heads in baskets and sent them to Jehu at Jezreel. [8]The messenger came to Jehu and told him, "They have brought the heads of the king's sons."

9:31 Zimri He was the man who killed Elah and the family of Baasha. Read 1 Kings 16:8–12.

Then Jehu said, "Lay the heads in two piles at the city gate until morning."

⁹In the morning, Jehu went out and stood before the people and said to them, "You are innocent. Look, I made plans against my master and killed him. But who killed all these? ¹⁰You should know that everything the LORD said about Ahab's family will come true. The LORD has spoken through his servant Elijah, and the LORD has done what he said." ¹¹So Jehu killed everyone of Ahab's family in Jezreel who was still alive. He also killed all Ahab's leading men, close friends, and priests. No one who had helped Ahab was left alive.

¹²Then Jehu left and went to Samaria by way of the road to Beth Eked of the Shepherds. ¹³There Jehu met some relatives of Ahaziah king of Judah. Jehu asked, "Who are you?"

They answered, "We are relatives of Ahaziah. We have come down to get revenge for the families of the king and the king's mother."

¹⁴Then Jehu said, "Take them alive!" So they captured Ahaziah's relatives alive and killed them at the well near Beth Eked—forty-two of them. Jehu did not leave anyone alive.

¹⁵After Jehu left there, he met Jehonadab son of Recab, who was also on his way to meet Jehu. Jehu greeted him and said, "Are you as good a friend to me as I am to you?"

Jehonadab answered, "Yes, I am."

Jehu said, "If you are, then give me your hand." So Jehonadab gave him his hand, and Jehu pulled him into the chariot. ¹⁶"Come with me," Jehu said. "You can see how strong my feelings are for the LORD." So Jehu had Jehonadab ride in his chariot.

¹⁷When Jehu came to Samaria, he killed all of Ahab's family in Samaria. He destroyed all those who were left, just as the LORD had told Elijah it would happen.

Baal Worshipers Killed

¹⁸Then Jehu gathered all the people together and said to them, "Ahab served Baal a little, but Jehu will serve Baal much. ¹⁹Now call for me all Baal's prophets and priests and all the people who worship Baal. Don't let anyone miss this meeting, because I have a great sacrifice for Baal. Anyone who is not there will not live." But Jehu was tricking them so he could destroy the worshipers of Baal. ²⁰He said, "Prepare a holy meeting for Baal." So they announced the meeting. ²¹Then Jehu sent word through all Israel, and all the worshipers of Baal came; not one stayed home. They came into the temple of Baal, and the temple was filled from one side to the other.

²²Jehu said to the man who kept the robes, "Bring out robes for all the worshipers of Baal." After he brought out robes for them, ²³Jehu and Jehonadab son of Recab went into the temple of Baal. Jehu said to the worshipers of Baal, "Look around, and make sure there are no servants of the LORD with you. Be sure there are only worshipers of Baal." ²⁴Then the worshipers of Baal went in to offer sacrifices and burnt offerings.

Jehu had eighty men waiting outside. He had told them, "Don't let anyone escape. If you do, you must pay with your own life."

²⁵As soon as Jehu finished offering the burnt offering, he ordered the guards and the captains, "Go in and kill the worshipers of Baal. Don't let anyone come out." So the guards and captains killed the worshipers of Baal with the sword and threw their bodies out. Then they went to the inner rooms of the temple ²⁶and brought out the pillars of the temple of Baal and burned them. ²⁷They tore down the stone pillar of Baal, as well as the temple of Baal. And they made it into a sewage pit, as it is today.

²⁸So Jehu destroyed Baal worship in Israel, ²⁹but he did not stop doing the sins Jeroboam son of Nebat had done. Jeroboam had led Israel to sin by worshiping the golden calves in Bethel and Dan.

³⁰The LORD said to Jehu, "You have done well in obeying what I said was right. You have done to the family of Ahab as I wanted. Because of this, your descendants as far as your great-great-grandchildren will be kings of Israel." ³¹But Jehu was not careful to follow the teachings of the LORD, the God of Israel, with all his heart. He did not stop doing the same sins Jeroboam had done, by which he had led Israel to sin.

³²At that time the LORD began to make Israel smaller. Hazael defeated the Israelites in all the land of Israel, ³³taking all the land of the Jordan known as the land of Gilead. (It

was the region of Gad, Reuben, and Manasseh.) He took land from Aroer by the Arnon Ravine through Gilead to Bashan.

³⁴The other things Jehu did—everything he did and all his victories—are recorded in the book of the history of the kings of Israel. ³⁵Jehu died and was buried in Samaria, and his son Jehoahaz became king in his place. ³⁶Jehu was king over Israel in Samaria for twenty-eight years.

PSALM 72:15–20

¹⁵Long live the king!
  Let him receive gold from Sheba.
  Let people always pray for him
    and bless him all day long.
¹⁶Let the fields grow plenty of grain
    and the hills be covered with crops.
  Let the land be as fertile as Lebanon,
    and let the cities grow like the grass in
      a field.
¹⁷Let the king be famous forever;
    let him be remembered as long as the
      sun shines.
  Let the nations be blessed because of him,
    and may they all bless him.

¹⁸Praise the LORD God, the God of Israel,
    who alone does such miracles.
¹⁹Praise his glorious name forever.
  Let his glory fill the whole world.
      Amen and amen.

²⁰This ends the prayers of David son of Jesse.

PROVERBS 18:14–15

¹⁴The will to live can get you through
    sickness,
  but no one can live with a broken spirit.

¹⁵The mind of a person with
    understanding gets knowledge;
  the wise person listens to learn more.

JOHN 19:1–16a

19 Then Pilate ordered that Jesus be taken away and whipped. ²The soldiers made a crown from some thorny branches and put it on Jesus' head and put a purple robe around him. ³Then they came to him many times and said, "Hail, King of the Jews!" and hit him in the face.

⁴Again Pilate came out and said to them, "Look, I am bringing Jesus out to you. I want you to know that I find nothing against him." ⁵So Jesus came out, wearing the crown of thorns and the purple robe. Pilate said to them, "Here is the man!"

⁶When the leading priests and the guards saw Jesus, they shouted, "Crucify him! Crucify him!"

But Pilate answered, "Crucify him yourselves, because I find nothing against him."

⁷The leaders answered, "We have a law that says he should die, because he said he is the Son of God."

⁸When Pilate heard this, he was even more afraid. ⁹He went back inside the palace and asked Jesus, "Where do you come from?" But Jesus did not answer him. ¹⁰Pilate said, "You refuse to speak to me? Don't you know I have power to set you free and power to have you crucified?"

¹¹Jesus answered, "The only power you have over me is the power given to you by God. The man who turned me in to you is guilty of a greater sin."

¹²After this, Pilate tried to let Jesus go. But some in the crowd cried out, "Anyone who makes himself king is against Caesar. If you let this man go, you are no friend of Caesar."

¹³When Pilate heard what they were saying, he brought Jesus out and sat down on the judge's seat at the place called The Stone Pavement. (In the Hebrew language[n] the name is Gabbatha.) ¹⁴It was about noon on Preparation Day of Passover week. Pilate said to the crowd, "Here is your king!"

¹⁵They shouted, "Take him away! Take him away! Crucify him!"

Pilate asked them, "Do you want me to crucify your king?"

The leading priests answered, "The only king we have is Caesar."

¹⁶So Pilate handed Jesus over to them to be crucified.

19:13 Hebrew language Or Aramaic, the languages of many people in this region in the first century.

JUNE 12

2 KINGS 11:1—13:25

Athaliah and Joash

11 When Ahaziah's mother, Athaliah, saw that her son was dead, she killed all the royal family. ²But Jehosheba, King Jehoram's daughter and Ahaziah's sister, took Joash, Ahaziah's son. She stole him from among the other sons of the king who were about to be murdered. She put Joash and his nurse in a bedroom to hide him from Athaliah, so he was not killed. ³He hid with her in the Temple of the LORD for six years. During that time Athaliah ruled the land.

⁴In the seventh year Jehoiada sent for the commanders of groups of a hundred men, as well as the Carites.ⁿ He brought them together in the Temple of the LORD and made an agreement with them. There, in the Temple of the LORD, he made them promise loyalty, and then he showed them the king's son. ⁵He commanded them, "This is what you must do. A third of you who go on duty on the Sabbath will guard the king's palace. ⁶A third of you will be at the Sur Gate, and another third will be at the gate behind the guard. This way you will guard the Temple. ⁷The two groups who go off duty on the Sabbath must protect the Temple of the LORD for the king. ⁸All of you must stand around the king, with weapons in hand. Kill anyone who comes near. Stay close to the king when he goes out and when he comes in."

⁹The commanders over a hundred men obeyed everything Jehoiada the priest had commanded. Each one took his men who came on duty on the Sabbath and those who went off duty on the Sabbath, and they came to Jehoiada the priest. ¹⁰He gave the commanders the spears and shields that had belonged to King David and that were kept in the Temple of the LORD.

Joash Becomes King

¹¹Then each guard took his place with his weapons in his hand. There were guards from the south side of the Temple to the north side. They stood by the altar and the Temple and around the king. ¹²Jehoiada brought out the king's son and put the crown on him and gave him a copy of the agreement. They appointed him king and poured olive oil on him. Then they clapped their hands and said, "Long live the king!"

¹³When Athaliah heard the noise of the guards and the people, she went to them at the Temple of the LORD. ¹⁴She looked, and there was the king, standing by the pillar, as the custom was. The officers and trumpeters were standing beside him, and all the people of the land were very happy and were blowing trumpets. Then Athaliah tore her clothes and screamed, "Traitors! Traitors!"

¹⁵Jehoiada the priest gave orders to the commanders of a hundred men, who led the army. He said, "Surround her with soldiers and kill with a sword anyone who follows her." He commanded this because he had said, "Don't put Athaliah to death in the Temple of the LORD." ¹⁶So they caught her when she came to the horses' entrance near the palace. There she was put to death.

¹⁷Then Jehoiada made an agreement between the LORD and the king and the people that they would be the LORD's special people. He also made an agreement between the king and the people. ¹⁸All the people of the land went to the temple of Baal and tore it down, smashing the altars and idols. They also killed Mattan, the priest of Baal, in front of the altars.

Then Jehoiada the priest placed guards at the Temple of the LORD. ¹⁹He took with him the commanders of a hundred men and the Carites, the royal bodyguards, as well as the guards and all the people of the land. Together they took the king out of the Temple of the LORD and went into the palace through the gate of the guards. Then the king sat on the royal throne. ²⁰So all the people of the

---

11:4 Carites This was probably a special unit of the army that was responsible for the king's safety, a kind of palace guard similar to the Kerethites and the Pelethites.

land were very happy, and Jerusalem had peace, because Athaliah had been put to death with the sword at the palace.

²¹Joash was seven years old when he became king.

12 Joash became king of Judah in Jehu's seventh year as king of Israel, and he ruled for forty years in Jerusalem. His mother's name was Zibiah, and she was from Beersheba. ²Joash did what the LORD said was right as long as Jehoiada the priest taught him. ³But the places where gods were worshiped were not removed; the people still made sacrifices and burned incense there.

Joash Repairs the Temple

⁴Joash said to the priests, "Take all the money brought as offerings to the Temple of the LORD. This includes the money each person owes in taxes and the money each person promises or brings freely to the LORD. ⁵Each priest will take the money from the people he serves. Then the priests must repair any damage they find in the Temple."

⁶But by the twenty-third year Joash was king, the priests still had not repaired the Temple. ⁷So King Joash called for Jehoiada the priest and the other priests and said to them, "Why aren't you repairing the damage of the Temple? Don't take any more money from the people you serve, but hand over the money for the repair of the Temple." ⁸The priests agreed not to take any more money from the people and not to repair the Temple themselves.

⁹Jehoiada the priest took a box and made a hole in the top of it. Then he put it by the altar, on the right side as the people came into the Temple of the LORD. The priests guarding the doorway put all the money brought to the Temple of the LORD into the box.

¹⁰Each time the priests saw that the box was full of money, the king's royal secretary and the high priest came. They counted the money that had been brought to the Temple of the LORD, and they put it into bags. ¹¹Next they weighed the money and gave it to the people in charge of the work on the Temple.

With it they paid the carpenters and the builders who worked on the Temple of the LORD, ¹²as well as the bricklayers and stonecutters. They also used the money to buy timber and cut stone to repair the damage of the Temple of the LORD. It paid for everything.

¹³The money brought into the Temple of the LORD was not used to make silver cups, wick trimmers, bowls, trumpets, or gold or silver vessels. ¹⁴They paid the money to the workers, who used it to repair the Temple of the LORD. ¹⁵They did not demand to know how the money was spent, because the workers were honest. ¹⁶The money from the penalty offerings and sin offerings was not brought into the Temple of the LORD, because it belonged to the priests.

Joash Saves Jerusalem

¹⁷About this time Hazael king of Aram attacked Gath and captured it. Then he went to attack Jerusalem. ¹⁸Joash king of Judah took all the holy things given by his ancestors, the kings of Judah—Jehoshaphat, Jehoram, and Ahaziah. He also took his own holy things as well as the gold that was found in the treasuries of the Temple of the LORD and the gold from the palace. Joash sent all this treasure to Hazael king of Aram, who turned away from Jerusalem.

¹⁹Everything else Joash did is written in the book of the history of the kings of Judah. ²⁰His officers made plans against him and killed him at Beth Millo on the road down to Silla. ²¹The officers who killed him were Jozabad son of Shimeath and Jehozabad son of Shomer. Joash was buried with his ancestors in Jerusalem, and Amaziah, his son, became king in his place.

Jehoahaz King of Israel

13 Jehoahaz son of Jehu became king over Israel in Samaria during the twenty-third year Joash son of Ahaziah was king of Judah. Jehoahaz ruled seventeen years, ²and he did what the LORD said was wrong. Jehoahaz did the same sins Jeroboam son of Nebat had done. Jeroboam had led Israel to sin, and Jehoahaz did not stop doing these same sins. ³So the LORD was angry with Israel and

handed them over to Hazael king of Aram and his son Ben-Hadad for a long time. ⁴Then Jehoahaz begged the LORD, and the LORD listened to him. The LORD had seen the troubles of Israel; he saw how terribly the king of Aram was treating them. ⁵He gave Israel a man to save them, and they escaped from the Arameans. The Israelites then lived in their own homes as they had before, ⁶but they still did not stop doing the same sins that the family of Jeroboam had done. He had led Israel to sin, and they continued doing those sins. The Asherah idol also was left standing in Samaria.

⁷Nothing was left of Jehoahaz's army except fifty horsemen, ten chariots, and ten thousand foot soldiers. The king of Aram had destroyed them and made them like chaff.

⁸Everything else Jehoahaz did and all his victories are written in the book of the history of the kings of Israel. ⁹Jehoahaz died and was buried in Samaria, and his son Jehoash became king in his place.

Jehoash King of Israel

¹⁰Jehoash son of Jehoahaz became king of Israel in Samaria during Joash's thirty-seventh year as king of Judah. Jehoash ruled sixteen years, ¹¹and he did what the LORD said was wrong. He did not stop doing the same sins Jeroboam son of Nebat had done. Jeroboam had led Israel to sin, and Jehoash continued to do the same thing. ¹²Everything else he did and all his victories, including his war against Amaziah king of Judah, are written in the book of the history of the kings of Israel. ¹³Jehoash died, and Jeroboam took his place on the throne. Jehoash was buried in Samaria with the kings of Israel.

The Death of Elisha

¹⁴At this time Elisha became sick. Before he died, Jehoash king of Israel went to Elisha and cried for him. Jehoash said, "My father, my father! The chariots of Israel and their horsemen!"

¹⁵Elisha said to Jehoash, "Take a bow and arrows." So he took a bow and arrows. ¹⁶Then Elisha said to him, "Put your hand on the bow." So Jehoash put his hand on the bow. Then Elisha put his hands on the king's hands. ¹⁷Elisha said, "Open the east window." So Jehoash opened the window. Then Elisha said, "Shoot," and Jehoash shot. Elisha said, "The LORD's arrow of victory over Aram! You will defeat the Arameans at Aphek until you destroy them."

¹⁸Elisha said, "Take the arrows." So Jehoash took them. Then Elisha said to him, "Strike the ground." So Jehoash struck the ground three times and stopped. ¹⁹The man of God was angry with him. "You should have struck five or six times!" Elisha said. "Then you would have struck Aram until you had completely destroyed it. But now you will defeat it only three times."

²⁰Then Elisha died and was buried.

At that time groups of Moabites would rob the land in the springtime. ²¹Once as some Israelites were burying a man, suddenly they saw a group of Moabites coming. The Israelites threw the dead man into Elisha's grave. When the man touched Elisha's bones, the man came back to life and stood on his feet.

War with Aram

²²During all the days Jehoahaz was king, Hazael king of Aram troubled Israel. ²³But the LORD was kind to the Israelites; he had mercy on them and helped them because of his agreement with Abraham, Isaac, and Jacob. To this day he has never wanted to destroy them or reject them.

²⁴When Hazael king of Aram died, his son Ben-Hadad became king in his place. ²⁵During a war Hazael had taken some cities from Jehoahaz, Jehoash's father. Now Jehoash took back those cities from Hazael's son Ben-Hadad. He defeated Ben-Hadad three times and took back the cities of Israel.

PSALM 73:1–14

Should the Wicked Be Rich?

A psalm of Asaph.

73 God is truly good to Israel,
to those who have pure hearts.

[2]But I had almost stopped believing;
  I had almost lost my faith
[3]because I was jealous of proud people.
  I saw wicked people doing well.

[4]They are not suffering;
  they are healthy and strong.
[5]They don't have troubles like the rest of
  us;
  they don't have problems like other
  people.
[6]They wear pride like a necklace
  and put on violence as their clothing.
[7]They are looking for profits
  and do not control their selfish
  desires.
[8]They make fun of others and speak
  evil;
  proudly they speak of hurting others.
[9]They brag to the sky.
  They say that they own the earth.
[10]So their people turn to them
  and give them whatever they want.
[11]They say, "How can God know?
  What does God Most High know?"
[12]These people are wicked,
  always at ease, and getting richer.
[13]So why have I kept my heart pure?
  Why have I kept my hands from doing
  wrong?
[14]I have suffered all day long;
  I have been punished every morning.

PROVERBS 18:16–17

[16]Taking gifts to important people
  will help get you in to see them.

[17]The person who tells one side of a story
  seems right,
  until someone else comes and asks
  questions.

JOHN 19:16b–42

Jesus Is Crucified

The soldiers took charge of Jesus. [17]Carrying his own cross, Jesus went out to a place called The Place of the Skull, which in the Hebrew language[n] is called Golgotha. [18]There they crucified Jesus. They also crucified two other men, one on each side, with Jesus in the middle. [19]Pilate wrote a sign and put it on the cross. It read: JESUS OF NAZARETH, THE KING OF THE JEWS. [20]The sign was written in Hebrew, in Latin, and in Greek. Many of the people read the sign, because the place where Jesus was crucified was near the city. [21]The leading priests said to Pilate, "Don't write, 'The King of the Jews.' But write, 'This man said, "I am the King of the Jews."'"

[22]Pilate answered, "What I have written, I have written."

[23]After the soldiers crucified Jesus, they took his clothes and divided them into four parts, with each soldier getting one part. They also took his long shirt, which was all one piece of cloth, woven from top to bottom. [24]So the soldiers said to each other, "We should not tear this into parts. Let's throw lots to see who will get it." This happened so that this Scripture would come true:

  "They divided my clothes among them,
    and they threw lots for my clothing."

Psalm 22:18

So the soldiers did this.

[25]Standing near his cross were Jesus' mother, his mother's sister, Mary the wife of Clopas, and Mary Magdalene. [26]When Jesus saw his mother and the follower he loved standing nearby, he said to his mother, "Dear woman, here is your son." [27]Then he said to the follower, "Here is your mother." From that time on, the follower took her to live in his home.

Jesus Dies

[28]After this, Jesus knew that everything had been done. So that the Scripture would come true, he said, "I am thirsty."[n] [29]There was a jar full of vinegar there, so the soldiers soaked a sponge in it, put the sponge on a branch of a hyssop plant, and lifted it to Jesus' mouth. [30]When Jesus tasted the vinegar, he said, "It is finished." Then he bowed his head and died.

19:17 Hebrew language Or Aramaic, the languages of many people in this region in the first century.   **19:28 "I am thirsty."** Read Psalms 22:15; 69:21.

[31]This day was Preparation Day, and the next day was a special Sabbath day. Since the religious leaders did not want the bodies to stay on the cross on the Sabbath day, they asked Pilate to order that the legs of the men be broken[n] and the bodies be taken away. [32]So the soldiers came and broke the legs of the first man on the cross beside Jesus. Then they broke the legs of the man on the other cross beside Jesus. [33]But when the soldiers came to Jesus and saw that he was already dead, they did not break his legs. [34]But one of the soldiers stuck his spear into Jesus' side, and at once blood and water came out. [35](The one who saw this happen is the one who told us this, and whatever he says is true. And he knows that he tells the truth, and he tells it so that you might believe.) [36]These things happened to make the Scripture come true: "Not one of his bones will be broken."[n] [37]And another Scripture says, "They will look at the one they stabbed."[n]

Jesus Is Buried

[38]Later, Joseph from Arimathea asked Pilate if he could take the body of Jesus. (Joseph was a secret follower of Jesus, because he was afraid of some of the leaders.) Pilate gave his permission, so Joseph came and took Jesus' body away. [39]Nicodemus, who earlier had come to Jesus at night, went with Joseph. He brought about seventy-five pounds of myrrh and aloes. [40]These two men took Jesus' body and wrapped it with the spices in pieces of linen cloth, which is how they bury the dead. [41]In the place where Jesus was crucified, there was a garden. In the garden was a new tomb that had never been used before. [42]The men laid Jesus in that tomb because it was nearby, and they were preparing to start their Sabbath day.

JUNE 13

2 KINGS 14:1–29

Amaziah King of Judah

14 Amaziah son of Joash became king of Judah during the second year Jehoash son of Jehoahaz was king of Israel. [2]Amaziah was twenty-five years old when he became king, and he ruled twenty-nine years in Jerusalem. His mother was named Jehoaddin, and she was from Jerusalem. [3]Amaziah did what the LORD said was right. He did everything his father Joash had done, but he did not do as his ancestor David had done. [4]The places where gods were worshiped were not removed, so the people still sacrificed and burned incense there.

[5]As soon as Amaziah took control of the kingdom, he executed the officers who had murdered his father the king. [6]But he did not put to death the children of the murderers because of the rule written in the Book of the Teachings of Moses. The LORD had commanded: "Parents must not be put to death when their children do wrong, and children must not be put to death when their parents do wrong. Each must die for his own sins."[n]

[7]In battle Amaziah killed ten thousand Edomites in the Valley of Salt. He also took the city of Sela. He called it Joktheel, as it is still called today.

[8]Amaziah sent messengers to Jehoash son of Jehoahaz, the son of Jehu, king of Israel. They said, "Come, let's meet face to face."

[9]Then Jehoash king of Israel answered Amaziah king of Judah, "A thornbush in Lebanon sent a message to a cedar tree in Lebanon. It said, 'Let your daughter marry my son.' But then a wild animal from

---

19:31 broken The breaking of their bones would make them die sooner. **19:36 "Not one . . . broken."** Quotation from Psalm 34:20. The idea is from Exodus 12:46; Numbers 9:12. **19:37 "They . . . stabbed."** Quotation from Zechariah 12:10.
• **14:6 "Parents . . . sins."** See Deuteronomy 24:16.

Lebanon came by, walking on and crushing the thornbush. [10]You have defeated Edom, but you have become proud. Stay at home and brag. Don't ask for trouble, or you and Judah will be defeated."

[11]But Amaziah would not listen, so Jehoash king of Israel went to attack. He and Amaziah king of Judah faced each other in battle at Beth Shemesh in Judah. [12]Israel defeated Judah, and every man of Judah ran away to his home. [13]At Beth Shemesh Jehoash king of Israel captured Amaziah king of Judah. (Amaziah was the son of Joash, who was the son of Ahaziah.) Jehoash went up to Jerusalem and broke down the wall of Jerusalem from the Gate of Ephraim to the Corner Gate, which was about six hundred feet. [14]He took all the gold and silver and all the utensils in the Temple of the LORD, and he took the treasuries of the palace and some hostages. Then he returned to Samaria.

[15]The other acts of Jehoash and his victories, including his war against Amaziah king of Judah, are written in the book of the history of the kings of Israel. [16]Jehoash died and was buried in Samaria with the kings of Israel, and his son Jeroboam became king in his place.

[17]Amaziah son of Joash, the king of Judah, lived fifteen years after the death of Jehoash son of Jehoahaz, the king of Israel. [18]The other things Amaziah did are written in the book of the history of the kings of Judah. [19]The people in Jerusalem made plans against him. So he ran away to the town of Lachish, but they sent men after him to Lachish and killed him. [20]They brought his body back on horses, and he was buried with his ancestors in Jerusalem, in the city of David.

[21]Then all the people of Judah made Uzziah[n] king in place of his father Amaziah. Uzziah was sixteen years old. [22]He rebuilt the town of Elath and made it part of Judah again after Amaziah died.

Jeroboam King of Israel

[23]Jeroboam son of Jehoash became king of Israel in Samaria during the fifteenth year Amaziah was king of Judah. (Amaziah was the son of Joash.) Jeroboam ruled forty-one years, [24]and he did what the LORD said was wrong. Jeroboam son of Nebat had led Israel to sin, and Jeroboam son of Jehoash did not stop doing the same sins. [25]Jeroboam won back Israel's border from Lebo Hamath to the Dead Sea. This happened as the LORD, the God of Israel, had said through his servant Jonah son of Amittai, the prophet from Gath Hepher. [26]The LORD had seen how the Israelites, both slave and free, were suffering terribly. No one was left who could help Israel. [27]The LORD had not said he would completely destroy Israel from the world, so he saved the Israelites through Jeroboam son of Jehoash.

[28]Everything else Jeroboam did is written down—all his victories and how he won back from Judah the towns of Damascus and Hamath for Israel. All this is written in the book of the history of the kings of Israel. [29]Jeroboam died and was buried with his ancestors, the kings of Israel. Jeroboam's son Zechariah became king in his place.

PSALM 73:15–20

[15]God, if I had decided to talk like this,
    I would have let your people down.
[16]I tried to understand all this,
    but it was too hard for me to see
[17]until I went to the Temple of God.
    Then I understood what will happen to
      them.
[18]You have put them in danger;
    you cause them to be destroyed.
[19]They are destroyed in a moment;
    they are swept away by terrors.
[20]It will be like waking from a dream.
    Lord, when you rise up, they will
      disappear.

PROVERBS 18:18–19

[18]Throwing lots can settle arguments
    and keep the two sides from fighting.

[19]A brother who has been insulted is
    harder to win back than a walled city,

14:21 **Uzziah** Also called Azariah.

and arguments separate people like the barred gates of a palace.

JOHN 20:1–31

Jesus' Tomb Is Empty

20 Early on the first day of the week, Mary Magdalene went to the tomb while it was still dark. When she saw that the large stone had been moved away from the tomb, [2]she ran to Simon Peter and the follower whom Jesus loved. Mary said, "They have taken the Lord out of the tomb, and we don't know where they have put him."

[3]So Peter and the other follower started for the tomb. [4]They were both running, but the other follower ran faster than Peter and reached the tomb first. [5]He bent down and looked in and saw the strips of linen cloth lying there, but he did not go in. [6]Then following him, Simon Peter arrived and went into the tomb and saw the strips of linen lying there. [7]He also saw the cloth that had been around Jesus' head, which was folded up and laid in a different place from the strips of linen. [8]Then the other follower, who had reached the tomb first, also went in. He saw and believed. [9](They did not yet understand from the Scriptures that Jesus must rise from the dead.)

Jesus Appears to Mary Magdalene

[10]Then the followers went back home. [11]But Mary stood outside the tomb, crying. As she was crying, she bent down and looked inside the tomb. [12]She saw two angels dressed in white, sitting where Jesus' body had been, one at the head and one at the feet.

[13]They asked her, "Woman, why are you crying?"

She answered, "They have taken away my Lord, and I don't know where they have put him." [14]When Mary said this, she turned around and saw Jesus standing there, but she did not know it was Jesus.

[15]Jesus asked her, "Woman, why are you crying? Whom are you looking for?"

Thinking he was the gardener, she said to him, "Did you take him away, sir? Tell me where you put him, and I will get him."

[16]Jesus said to her, "Mary."

Mary turned toward Jesus and said in the Hebrew language,[n] "Rabboni." (This means "Teacher.")

[17]Jesus said to her, "Don't hold on to me, because I have not yet gone up to the Father. But go to my brothers and tell them, 'I am going back to my Father and your Father, to my God and your God.'"

[18]Mary Magdalene went and said to the followers, "I saw the Lord!" And she told them what Jesus had said to her.

Jesus Appears to His Followers

[19]When it was evening on the first day of the week, Jesus' followers were together. The doors were locked, because they were afraid of the elders. Then Jesus came and stood right in the middle of them and said, "Peace be with you." [20]After he said this, he showed them his hands and his side. His followers were thrilled when they saw the Lord.

[21]Then Jesus said again, "Peace be with you. As the Father sent me, I now send you." [22]After he said this, he breathed on them and said, "Receive the Holy Spirit. [23]If you forgive anyone his sins, they are forgiven. If you don't forgive them, they are not forgiven."

Jesus Appears to Thomas

[24]Thomas (called Didymus), who was one of the twelve, was not with them when Jesus came. [25]The other followers kept telling Thomas, "We saw the Lord."

But Thomas said, "I will not believe it until I see the nail marks in his hands and put my finger where the nails were and put my hand into his side."

[26]A week later the followers were in the house again, and Thomas was with them. The doors were locked, but Jesus came in and stood right in the middle of them. He said, "Peace be with you." [27]Then he said to Thomas, "Put your finger here, and look at my hands. Put your hand here in

20:16 Hebrew language Or Aramaic, the languages of many people in this region in the first century.

my side. Stop being an unbeliever and believe."

²⁸Thomas said to him, "My Lord and my God!"

²⁹Then Jesus told him, "You believe because you see me. Those who believe without seeing me will be truly blessed."

Why John Wrote This Book
³⁰Jesus did many other miracles in the presence of his followers that are not written in this book. ³¹But these are written so that you may believe that Jesus is the Christ, the Son of God. Then, by believing, you may have life through his name.

JUNE 14

2 KINGS 15:1—16:20

Uzziah King of Judah

15Uzziah son of Amaziah became king of Judah during Jeroboam's twenty-seventh year as king of Israel. ²Uzziah was sixteen years old when he became king, and he ruled fifty-two years in Jerusalem. His mother was named Jecoliah, and she was from Jerusalem. ³He did what the LORD said was right, just as his father Amaziah had done. ⁴But the places where gods were worshiped were not removed, so the people still made sacrifices and burned incense there.

⁵The LORD struck Uzziah with a skin disease, which he had until the day he died. So he had to live in a separate house. Jotham, the king's son, was in charge of the palace, and he governed the people of the land.

⁶All the other things Uzziah did are written in the book of the history of the kings of Judah. ⁷Uzziah died and was buried near his ancestors in Jerusalem, and his son Jotham became king in his place.

Zechariah King of Israel

⁸Zechariah son of Jeroboam was king over Israel in Samaria. He ruled for six months during Uzziah's[n] thirty-eighth year as king of Judah. ⁹Zechariah did what the LORD said was wrong, just as his ancestors had done. Jeroboam son of Nebat had led the people of Israel to sin, and Zechariah did not stop doing the same sins.

¹⁰Shallum son of Jabesh made plans against Zechariah and killed him in front of the people. Then Shallum became king in his place. ¹¹The other acts of Zechariah are written in the book of the history of the kings of Israel. ¹²The LORD had told Jehu: "Your sons down to your great-great-grandchildren will be kings of Israel," and the LORD's word came true.

Shallum King of Israel

¹³Shallum son of Jabesh became king during Uzziah's thirty-ninth year as king of Judah. Shallum ruled for a month in Samaria. ¹⁴Then Menahem son of Gadi came up from Tirzah to Samaria and attacked Shallum son of Jabesh in Samaria. He killed him and became king in Shallum's place.

¹⁵The other acts of Shallum and his secret plans are written in the book of the history of the kings of Israel.

Menahem King of Israel

¹⁶Menahem started out from Tirzah and attacked Tiphsah, destroying the city and the area nearby. This was because the people had refused to open the city gate for him. He defeated them and ripped open all their pregnant women.

¹⁷Menahem son of Gadi became king over Israel during Uzziah's thirty-ninth year as king of Judah. Menahem ruled ten years in Samaria, ¹⁸and he did what the LORD said was wrong. Jeroboam son of Nebat had led Israel to sin, and all the time Menahem was king, he did not stop doing the same sins.

¹⁹Pul king of Assyria came to attack the land. Menahem gave him about seventy-four thousand pounds of silver so Pul would support him and make his hold on the kingdom

---

15:8 Uzziah Also called Azariah.

stronger. [20]Menahem taxed Israel to pay about one and one-fourth pounds of silver to each soldier of the king of Assyria. So the king left and did not stay in the land.

[21]Everything else Menahem did is written in the book of the history of the kings of Israel. [22]Then Menahem died, and his son Pekahiah became king in his place.

Pekahiah King of Israel

[23]Pekahiah son of Menahem became king over Israel in Samaria during Uzziah's[n] fiftieth year as king of Judah. Pekahiah ruled two years, [24]and he did what the LORD said was wrong. Jeroboam son of Nebat had led Israel to sin, and Pekahiah did not stop doing the same sins.

[25]Pekah son of Remaliah was one of Pekahiah's captains, and he made plans against Pekahiah. He took fifty men of Gilead with him and killed Pekahiah, as well as Argob and Arieh, in the palace at Samaria. Then Pekah became king in Pekahiah's place.

[26]Everything else Pekahiah did is written in the book of the history of the kings of Israel.

Pekah King of Israel

[27]Pekah son of Remaliah became king over Israel in Samaria during Uzziah's[n] fifty-second year as king of Judah. Pekah ruled twenty years, [28]and he did what the LORD said was wrong. Jeroboam son of Nebat had led Israel to sin, and Pekah did not stop doing the same sins.

[29]Tiglath-Pileser[n] was king of Assyria. He attacked while Pekah was king of Israel, capturing the cities of Ijon, Abel Beth Maacah, Janoah, Kedesh, and Hazor. He also captured Gilead and Galilee and all the land of Naphtali and carried the people away to Assyria. [30]Then Hoshea son of Elah made plans against Pekah son of Remaliah and attacked and killed him. Then Hoshea became king in Pekah's place during the twentieth year Jotham son of Uzziah was king.

[31]Everything else Pekah did is written in the book of the history of the kings of Israel.

Jotham King of Judah

[32]Jotham son of Uzziah became king of Judah during the second year Pekah son of Remaliah was king of Israel. [33]Jotham was twenty-five years old when he became king, and he ruled sixteen years in Jerusalem. His mother's name was Jerusha daughter of Zadok. [34]Jotham did what the LORD said was right, just as his father Uzziah had done. [35]But the places where gods were worshiped were not removed, and the people still made sacrifices and burned incense there. Jotham rebuilt the Upper Gate of the Temple of the LORD.

[36]The other things Jotham did while he was king are written in the book of the history of the kings of Judah. [37]At that time the LORD began to send Rezin king of Aram and Pekah son of Remaliah against Judah. [38]Jotham died and was buried with his ancestors in Jerusalem, the city of David, his ancestor. Then Jotham's son Ahaz became king in his place.

Ahaz King of Judah

16 Ahaz was the son of Jotham king of Judah. Ahaz became king of Judah in the seventeenth year Pekah son of Remaliah was king of Israel. [2]Ahaz was twenty years old when he became king, and he ruled sixteen years in Jerusalem. Unlike his ancestor David, he did not do what the LORD his God said was right. [3]Ahaz did the same things the kings of Israel had done. He even made his son pass through fire. He did the same hateful sins as the nations had done whom the LORD had forced out of the land ahead of the Israelites. [4]Ahaz offered sacrifices and burned incense at the places where gods were worshiped, on the hills, and under every green tree.

[5]Rezin king of Aram and Pekah son of Remaliah, the king of Israel, came up to attack Jerusalem. They surrounded Ahaz but could not defeat him. [6]At that time Rezin king of Aram took back the city of Elath for Aram, and he forced out all the people of Judah. Then Edomites moved into Elath, and they still live there today.

[7]Ahaz sent messengers to Tiglath-Pileser king of Assyria, saying, "I am your servant and your friend. Come and save me from the

king of Aram and the king of Israel, who are attacking me." ⁸Ahaz took the silver and gold that was in the Temple of the LORD and in the treasuries of the palace, and he sent these as a gift to the king of Assyria. ⁹So the king of Assyria listened to Ahaz. He attacked Damascus and captured it and sent all its people away to Kir. And he killed Rezin.

¹⁰Then King Ahaz went to Damascus to meet Tiglath-Pileser king of Assyria. Ahaz saw an altar at Damascus, and he sent plans and a pattern of this altar to Uriah the priest. ¹¹So Uriah the priest built an altar, just like the plans King Ahaz had sent him from Damascus. Uriah finished the altar before King Ahaz came back from Damascus. ¹²When the king arrived from Damascus, he saw the altar and went near and offered sacrifices on it. ¹³He burned his burnt offerings and grain offerings and poured out his drink offering. He also sprinkled the blood of his fellowship offerings on the altar.

¹⁴Ahaz moved the bronze altar that was before the LORD at the front of the Temple. It was between Ahaz's altar and the Temple of the LORD, but he put it on the north side of his altar. ¹⁵King Ahaz commanded Uriah the priest, "On the large altar burn the morning burnt offering, the evening grain offering, the king's burnt offering and grain offering, and the whole burnt offering, the grain offering, and the drink offering for all the people of the land. Sprinkle on the altar all the blood of the burnt offering and of the sacrifice. But I will use the bronze altar to ask questions of God." ¹⁶So Uriah the priest did everything as King Ahaz commanded him.

¹⁷Then King Ahaz took off the side panels from the bases and removed the washing bowls from the top of the bases. He also took the large bowl, which was called the Sea, off the bronze bulls that held it up, and he put it on a stone base. ¹⁸Ahaz took away the platform for the royal throne, which had been built at the Temple of the LORD. He also took away the outside entrance for the king. He did these things because of the king of Assyria.

¹⁹The other things Ahaz did as king are written in the book of the history of the kings of Judah. ²⁰Ahaz died and was buried with his ancestors in Jerusalem, and Ahaz's son Hezekiah became king in his place.

PSALM 73:21–28

²¹When my heart was sad
   and I was angry,
²²I was senseless and stupid.
   I acted like an animal toward you.
²³But I am always with you;
   you have held my hand.
²⁴You guide me with your advice,
   and later you will receive me in honor.
²⁵I have no one in heaven but you;
   I want nothing on earth besides you.
²⁶My body and my mind may become weak,
   but God is my strength.
   He is mine forever.

²⁷Those who are far from God will die;
   you destroy those who are unfaithful.
²⁸But I am close to God, and that is good.
   The Lord GOD is my protection.
   I will tell all that you have done.

PROVERBS 18:20–21

²⁰People will be rewarded for what they say;
   they will be rewarded by how they speak.
²¹What you say can mean life or death.
   Those who speak with care will be
   rewarded.

JOHN 21:1–25

Jesus Appears to Seven Followers

21 Later, Jesus showed himself to his followers again—this time at Lake Galilee.ⁿ This is how he showed himself: ²Some of the followers were together: Simon Peter, Thomas (called Didymus), Nathanael from Cana in Galilee, the two sons of Zebedee, and two other followers. ³Simon Peter said, "I am going out to fish."

The others said, "We will go with you." So they went out and got into the boat. They fished that night but caught nothing.

⁴Early the next morning Jesus stood on the shore, but the followers did not know it was Jesus. ⁵Then he said to them, "Friends, did you catch any fish?"

They answered, "No."

⁶He said, "Throw your net on the right side

of the boat, and you will find some." So they did, and they caught so many fish they could not pull the net back into the boat.

[7]The follower whom Jesus loved said to Peter, "It is the Lord!" When Peter heard him say this, he wrapped his coat around himself. (Peter had taken his clothes off.) Then he jumped into the water. [8]The other followers went to shore in the boat, dragging the net full of fish. They were not very far from shore, only about a hundred yards. [9]When the followers stepped out of the boat and onto the shore, they saw a fire of hot coals. There were fish on the fire, and there was bread.

[10]Then Jesus said, "Bring some of the fish you just caught."

[11]Simon Peter went into the boat and pulled the net to the shore. It was full of big fish, one hundred fifty-three in all, but even though there were so many, the net did not tear. [12]Jesus said to them, "Come and eat." None of the followers dared ask him, "Who are you?" because they knew it was the Lord. [13]Jesus came and took the bread and gave it to them, along with the fish.

[14]This was now the third time Jesus showed himself to his followers after he was raised from the dead.

Jesus Talks to Peter

[15]When they finished eating, Jesus said to Simon Peter, "Simon son of John, do you love me more than these?"

He answered, "Yes, Lord, you know that I love you."

Jesus said, "Feed my lambs."

[16]Again Jesus said, "Simon son of John, do you love me?"

He answered, "Yes, Lord, you know that I love you."

Jesus said, "Take care of my sheep."

[17]A third time he said, "Simon son of John, do you love me?"

Peter was hurt because Jesus asked him the third time, "Do you love me?" Peter said, "Lord, you know everything; you know that I love you!"

He said to him, "Feed my sheep. [18]I tell you the truth, when you were younger, you tied your own belt and went where you wanted. But when you are old, you will put out your hands and someone else will tie you and take you where you don't want to go." [19](Jesus said this to show how Peter would die to give glory to God.) Then Jesus said to Peter, "Follow me!"

[20]Peter turned and saw that the follower Jesus loved was walking behind them. (This was the follower who had leaned against Jesus at the supper and had said, "Lord, who will turn against you?") [21]When Peter saw him behind them, he asked Jesus, "Lord, what about him?"

[22]Jesus answered, "If I want him to live until I come back, that is not your business. You follow me."

[23]So a story spread among the followers that this one would not die. But Jesus did not say he would not die. He only said, "If I want him to live until I come back, that is not your business."

[24]That follower is the one who is telling these things and who has now written them down. We know that what he says is true.

[25]There are many other things Jesus did. If every one of them were written down, I suppose the whole world would not be big enough for all the books that would be written.

JUNE 15

2 KINGS 17:1—18:37

Hoshea, Last King of Israel

17 Hoshea son of Elah became king over Israel during Ahaz's twelfth year as king of Judah. Hoshea ruled in Samaria nine years. [2]He did what the LORD said was wrong, but he was not as bad as the kings of Israel who had ruled before him.

[3]Shalmaneser king of Assyria came to

attack Hoshea. Hoshea had been Shalmaneser's servant and had made the payments to Shalmaneser that he had demanded. [4]But the king of Assyria found out that Hoshea had made plans against him by sending messengers to So, the king of Egypt. Hoshea had also stopped giving Shalmaneser the payments, which he had paid every year in the past. For that, the king put Hoshea in prison. [5]Then the king of Assyria came and attacked all the land of Israel. He surrounded Samaria and attacked it for three years. [6]He defeated Samaria in the ninth year Hoshea was king, and he took the Israelites away to Assyria. He settled them in Halah, in Gozan on the Habor River, and in the cities of the Medes.

Israelites Punished for Sin

[7]All these things happened because the Israelites had sinned against the LORD their God. He had brought them out of Egypt and had rescued them from the power of the king of Egypt, but the Israelites had honored other gods. [8]They lived like the nations the LORD had forced out of the land ahead of them. They lived as their evil kings had shown them, [9]secretly sinning against the LORD their God. They built places to worship gods in all their cities, from the watchtower to the strong, walled city. [10]They put up stone pillars to gods and Asherah idols on every high hill and under every green tree. [11]The Israelites burned incense everywhere gods were worshiped, just as the nations who lived there before them had done, whom the LORD had forced out of the land. The Israelites did wicked things that made the LORD angry. [12]They served idols when the LORD had said, "You must not do this." [13]The LORD used every prophet and seer to warn Israel and Judah. He said, "Stop your evil ways and obey my commands and laws. Follow all the teachings that I commanded your ancestors, the teachings that I gave you through my servants the prophets."

[14]But the people would not listen. They were stubborn, just as their ancestors had been who did not believe in the LORD their God. [15]They rejected the LORD's laws and the agreement he had made with their ancestors. And they refused to listen to his warnings. They worshiped useless idols and

became useless themselves. They did what the nations around them did, which the LORD had warned them not to do.

[16]The people rejected all the commands of the LORD their God. They molded statues of two calves, and they made an Asherah idol. They worshiped all the stars of the sky and served Baal. [17]They made their sons and daughters pass through fire and tried to find out the future by magic and witchcraft. They always chose to do what the LORD said was wrong, which made him angry. [18]Because he was very angry with the people of Israel, he removed them from his presence. Only the tribe of Judah was left.

Judah Is Also Guilty

[19]But even Judah did not obey the commands of the LORD their God. They did what the Israelites had done, [20]so the LORD rejected all the people of Israel. He punished them and let others destroy them; he threw them out of his presence. [21]When the LORD separated them from the family of David, the Israelites made Jeroboam son of Nebat their king. Jeroboam led the Israelites away from the LORD and led them to sin greatly. [22]So they continued to do all the sins Jeroboam did. They did not stop doing these sins [23]until the LORD removed the Israelites from his presence, just as he had said through all his servants the prophets. So the Israelites were taken out of their land to Assyria, and they have been there to this day.

The Beginning of the Samaritan People

[24]The king of Assyria brought people from Babylon, Cuthah, Avva, Hamath, and Sepharvaim and put them in the cities of Samaria to replace the Israelites. These people took over Samaria and lived in the cities. [25]At first they did not worship the LORD, so he sent lions among them which killed some of them. [26]The king of Assyria was told, "You sent foreigners into the cities of Samaria who do not know the law of the god of the land. This is why he has sent lions among them. The lions are killing them because they don't know what the god wants."

[27]Then the king of Assyria commanded, "Send back one of the priests you took away. Let him live there and teach the peo-

ple what the god wants." [28]So one of the priests who had been carried away from Samaria returned to live in Bethel. And he taught the people how to honor the LORD.

[29]But each nation made gods of its own and put them in the cities where they lived and in the temples where gods were worshiped. These temples had been built by the Samaritans. [30]The people from Babylon made Succoth Benoth their god. The people from Cuthah worshiped Nergal. The people of Hamath worshiped Ashima. [31]The Avvites worshiped Nibhaz and Tartak. The Sepharvites burned their children in the fire, sacrificing them to Adrammelech and Anammelech, the gods of Sepharvaim. [32]They also honored the LORD, but they chose priests for the places where gods were worshiped. The priests were chosen from among themselves, and they made sacrifices for the people. [33]The people honored the LORD but also served their own gods, just as the nations did from which they had been brought. [34]Even today they do as they did in the past. They do not worship the LORD nor obey his rules and commands. They do not obey the teachings or the commands of the LORD, which he gave to the children of Jacob, whom he had named Israel. [35]The LORD had made an agreement with them and had commanded them, "Do not honor other gods. Do not bow down to them or worship them or offer sacrifices to them. [36]Worship the LORD who brought you up out of the land of Egypt with great power and strength. Bow down to him and offer sacrifices to him. [37]Always obey the rules, orders, teachings, and commands he wrote for you. Do not honor other gods. [38]Do not forget the agreement I made with you, and do not honor other gods. [39]Instead worship the LORD your God, who will save you from all your enemies."

[40]But the Israelites did not listen. They kept on doing the same things they had done before. [41]So these nations honored the LORD but also worshiped their idols, and their children and grandchildren still do as their ancestors did.

Hezekiah King of Judah

18 Hezekiah son of Ahaz king of Judah became king during the third year Hoshea son of Elah was king of Israel. [2]Hezekiah was twenty-five years old when he became king, and he ruled twenty-nine years in Jerusalem. His mother's name was Abijah daughter of Zechariah. [3]Hezekiah did what the LORD said was right, just as his ancestor David had done. [4]He removed the places where gods were worshiped. He smashed the stone pillars and cut down the Asherah idols. Also the Israelites had been burning incense to Nehushtan, the bronze snake Moses had made. But Hezekiah broke it into pieces.

[5]Hezekiah trusted in the LORD, the God of Israel. There was no one like him among all the kings of Judah, either before him or after him. [6]Hezekiah was loyal to the LORD and did not stop following him; he obeyed the commands the LORD had given Moses. [7]And the LORD was with Hezekiah, so he had success in everything he did. He turned against the king of Assyria and stopped serving him. [8]Hezekiah defeated the Philistines all the way to Gaza and its borders, including the watchtowers and the strong, walled cities.

The Assyrians Capture Samaria

[9]Shalmaneser king of Assyria surrounded Samaria and attacked it in the fourth year Hezekiah was king. This was the seventh year Hoshea son of Elah was king of Israel. [10]After three years the Assyrians captured Samaria. This was in the sixth year Hezekiah was king, which was Hoshea's ninth year as king of Israel. [11]The king of Assyria took the Israelites away to Assyria and settled them in Halah, in Gozan on the Habor River, and in the cities of the Medes. [12]This happened because they did not obey the LORD their God. They broke his agreement and did not obey all that Moses, the LORD's servant, had commanded. They would not listen to the commands or do them.

Assyria Attacks Judah

[13]During Hezekiah's fourteenth year as king, Sennacherib king of Assyria attacked all the strong, walled cities of Judah and captured them. [14]Then Hezekiah king of Judah sent a message to the king of Assyria at Lachish. He said, "I have done wrong. Leave me alone, and I will pay anything you ask."

So the king of Assyria made Hezekiah pay about twenty-two thousand pounds of silver and two thousand pounds of gold. [15]Hezekiah gave him all the silver that was in the Temple of the LORD and in the palace treasuries. [16]Hezekiah stripped all the gold that covered the doors and doorposts of the Temple of the LORD. Hezekiah had put gold on these doors himself, but he gave it all to the king of Assyria.

[17]The king of Assyria sent out his supreme commander, his chief officer, and his field commander. They went with a large army from Lachish to King Hezekiah in Jerusalem. When they came near the waterway from the upper pool on the road where people do their laundry, they stopped. [18]They called for the king, so the king sent Eliakim, Shebna, and Joah out to meet them. Eliakim son of Hilkiah was the palace manager, Shebna was the royal secretary, and Joah son of Asaph was the recorder.

[19]The field commander said to them, "Tell Hezekiah this:

" 'The great king, the king of Assyria, says: What can you trust in now? [20]You say you have battle plans and power for war, but your words mean nothing. Whom are you trusting for help so that you turn against me? [21]Look, you are depending on Egypt to help you, but Egypt is like a splintered walking stick. If you lean on it for help, it will stab your hand and hurt you. The king of Egypt will hurt all those who depend on him. [22]You might say, "We are depending on the LORD our God," but Hezekiah destroyed the LORD's altars and the places of worship. Hezekiah told Judah and Jerusalem, "You must worship only at this one altar in Jerusalem."

[23]" 'Now make an agreement with my master, the king of Assyria: I will give you two thousand horses if you can find enough men to ride them. [24]You cannot defeat one of my master's least important officers, so why do you depend on Egypt to give you chariots and horsemen? [25]I have not come to attack and destroy this place without an order from the LORD. The LORD himself told me to come to this country and destroy it.' "

[26]Then Eliakim son of Hilkiah, Shebna, and Joah said to the field commander, "Please speak to us in the Aramaic language. We understand it. Don't speak to us in Hebrew, because the people on the city wall can hear you."

[27]"No," the commander said, "my master did not send me to tell these things only to you and your king. He sent me to speak also to those people sitting on the wall who will have to eat their own dung and drink their own urine like you."

[28]Then the commander stood and shouted loudly in the Hebrew language, "Listen to what the great king, the king of Assyria, says! [29]The king says you should not let Hezekiah fool you, because he can't save you from my power. [30]Don't let Hezekiah talk you into trusting the LORD by saying, 'The LORD will surely save us. This city won't be handed over to the king of Assyria.'

[31]"Don't listen to Hezekiah. The king of Assyria says, 'Make peace with me, and come out of the city to me. Then everyone will be free to eat the fruit from his own grapevine and fig tree and to drink water from his own well. [32]After that I will come and take you to a land like your own—a land with grain and new wine, bread and vineyards, olives, and honey. Choose to live and not to die!'

"Don't listen to Hezekiah. He is fooling you when he says, 'The LORD will save us.' [33]Has a god of any other nation saved his people from the power of the king of Assyria? [34]Where are the gods of Hamath and Arpad? Where are the gods of Sepharvaim, Hena, and Ivvah? They did not save Samaria from my power. [35]Not one of all the gods of these countries has saved his people from me. Neither can the LORD save Jerusalem from my power."

[36]The people were silent. They didn't answer the commander at all, because King Hezekiah had ordered, "Don't answer him."

[37]Then Eliakim, Shebna, and Joah tore their clothes to show how upset they were. (Eliakim son of Hilkiah was the palace manager, Shebna was the royal secretary, and Joah son of Asaph was the recorder.) The three men went to Hezekiah and told him what the field commander had said.

PSALM 74:1–11

A Nation in Trouble Prays

A maskil of Asaph.

74 God, why have you rejected us for so long?
Why are you angry with us, the sheep of your pasture?
²Remember the people you bought long ago.
You saved us, and we are your very own.
After all, you live on Mount Zion.
³Make your way through these old ruins;
the enemy wrecked everything in the Temple.
⁴Those who were against you shouted in your meeting place
and raised their flags there.
⁵They came with axes raised
as if to cut down a forest of trees.
⁶They smashed the carved panels
with their axes and hatchets.
⁷They burned your Temple to the ground;
they have made the place where you live unclean.
⁸They thought, "We will completely crush them!"
They burned every place where God was worshiped in the land.
⁹We do not see any signs.
There are no more prophets,
and no one knows how long this will last.
¹⁰God, how much longer will the enemy make fun of you?
Will they insult you forever?
¹¹Why do you hold back your power?
Bring your power out in the open and destroy them!

PROVERBS 18:22–24

²²When a man finds a wife, he finds something good.
It shows that the LORD is pleased with him.
²³The poor beg for mercy,
but the rich give rude answers.

²⁴Some friends may ruin you,
but a real friend will be more loyal than a brother.

ACTS 1:1–26

Luke Writes Another Book

1 To Theophilus.
The first book I wrote was about everything Jesus began to do and teach ²until the day he was taken up into heaven. Before this, with the help of the Holy Spirit, Jesus told the apostles he had chosen what they should do. ³After his death, he showed himself to them and proved in many ways that he was alive. The apostles saw Jesus during the forty days after he was raised from the dead, and he spoke to them about the kingdom of God. ⁴Once when he was eating with them, he told them not to leave Jerusalem. He said, "Wait here to receive the promise from the Father which I told you about. ⁵John baptized people with water, but in a few days you will be baptized with the Holy Spirit."

Jesus Is Taken Up into Heaven

⁶When the apostles were all together, they asked Jesus, "Lord, are you now going to give the kingdom back to Israel?"
⁷Jesus said to them, "The Father is the only One who has the authority to decide dates and times. These things are not for you to know. ⁸But when the Holy Spirit comes to you, you will receive power. You will be my witnesses—in Jerusalem, in all of Judea, in Samaria, and in every part of the world."
⁹After he said this, as they were watching, he was lifted up, and a cloud hid him from their sight. ¹⁰As he was going, they were looking into the sky. Suddenly, two men wearing white clothes stood beside them. ¹¹They said, "Men of Galilee, why are you standing here looking into the sky? Jesus, whom you saw taken up from you into heaven, will come back in the same way you saw him go."

A New Apostle Is Chosen

¹²Then they went back to Jerusalem from the Mount of Olives. (This mountain is about half a mile from Jerusalem.) ¹³When they entered the city, they went to

the upstairs room where they were staying. Peter, John, James, Andrew, Philip, Thomas, Bartholomew, Matthew, James son of Alphaeus, Simon (known as the Zealot), and Judas son of James were there. ¹⁴They all continued praying together with some women, including Mary the mother of Jesus, and Jesus' brothers.

¹⁵During this time there was a meeting of the believers (about one hundred twenty of them). Peter stood up and said, ¹⁶⁻¹⁷"Brothers and sisters, in the Scriptures the Holy Spirit said through David something that must happen involving Judas. He was one of our own group and served together with us. He led those who arrested Jesus." ¹⁸(Judas bought a field with the money he got for his evil act. But he fell to his death, his body burst open, and all his intestines poured out. ¹⁹Everyone in Jerusalem learned about this so they named this place Akeldama. In their language Akeldama means "Field of Blood.") ²⁰"In the Book of Psalms," Peter said, "this is written:

'May his place be empty; leave no one to live in it.' *Psalm 69:25*

And it is also written:

'Let another man replace him as leader.' *Psalm 109:8*

²¹⁻²²"So now a man must become a witness with us of Jesus' being raised from the dead. He must be one of the men who were part of our group during all the time the Lord Jesus was among us—from the time John was baptizing people until the day Jesus was taken up from us to heaven."

²³They put the names of two men before the group. One was Joseph Barsabbas, who was also called Justus. The other was Matthias. ²⁴⁻²⁵The apostles prayed, "Lord, you know the thoughts of everyone. Show us which one of these two you have chosen to do this work. Show us who should be an apostle in place of Judas, who turned away and went where he belongs." ²⁶Then they used lots to choose between them, and the lots showed that Matthias was the one. So he became an apostle with the other eleven.

JUNE 16

2 KINGS 19:1—21:26

Jerusalem Will Be Saved

19 When King Hezekiah heard the message, he tore his clothes and put on rough cloth to show how sad he was. Then he went into the Temple of the LORD. ²Hezekiah sent Eliakim, the palace manager, and Shebna, the royal secretary, and the older priests to Isaiah. They were all wearing rough cloth when they came to Isaiah the prophet, the son of Amoz. ³They told Isaiah, "This is what Hezekiah says: Today is a day of sorrow and punishment and disgrace, as when a child should be born, but the mother is not strong enough to give birth to it. ⁴The king of Assyria sent his field commander to make fun of the living God. Maybe the LORD your God will hear what the commander said and will punish him for it. So pray for the few of us who are left alive."

⁵When Hezekiah's officers came to Isaiah, ⁶he said to them, "Tell your master this: The LORD says, 'Don't be afraid of what you have heard. Don't be frightened by the words the servants of the king of Assyria have spoken against me. ⁷Listen! I am going to put a spirit in the king of Assyria. He will hear a report that will make him return to his own country, and I will cause him to die by the sword there.'"

⁸The field commander heard that the king of Assyria had left Lachish. When he went back, he found the king fighting against the city of Libnah.

⁹The king received a report that Tirhakah, the Cushite king of Egypt, was coming to attack him. When the king of Assyria heard this, he sent messengers to Hezekiah, saying, ¹⁰"Tell Hezekiah king of Judah: Don't be fooled by the god you trust. Don't believe him when he says Jerusalem will not be handed

over to the king of Assyria. ¹¹You have heard what the kings of Assyria have done. They have completely defeated every country, so do not think you will be saved. ¹²Did the gods of those people save them? My ancestors destroyed them, defeating the cities of Gozan, Haran, and Rezeph, and the people of Eden living in Tel Assar. ¹³Where are the kings of Hamath and Arpad? Where are the kings of Sepharvaim, Hena, and Ivvah?"

Hezekiah Prays to the Lord

¹⁴When Hezekiah received the letter from the messengers and read it, he went up to the Temple of the LORD. He spread the letter out before the LORD ¹⁵and prayed to the LORD: "LORD, God of Israel, whose throne is between the gold creatures with wings, only you are God of all the kingdoms of the earth. You made the heavens and the earth. ¹⁶Hear, LORD, and listen. Open your eyes, LORD, and see. Listen to the words Sennacherib has said to insult the living God. ¹⁷It is true, LORD, that the kings of Assyria have destroyed these countries and their lands. ¹⁸They have thrown the gods of these nations into the fire, but they were only wood and rock statues that people made. So the kings have destroyed them. ¹⁹Now, LORD our God, save us from the king's power so that all the kingdoms of the earth will know that you, LORD, are the only God."

God Answers Hezekiah

²⁰Then Isaiah son of Amoz sent a message to Hezekiah that said, "This is what the LORD, the God of Israel, says: I have heard your prayer to me about Sennacherib king of Assyria. ²¹This is what the LORD has said against Sennacherib:

'The people of Jerusalem
  hate you and make fun of you.
The people of Jerusalem
  laugh at you as you run away.
²²You have insulted me and spoken against me;
  you have raised your voice against me.
You have a proud look on your face,
  which is against me, the Holy One of Israel.
²³You have sent your messengers to insult the Lord.

You have said, "With my many chariots
I have gone to the tops of the mountains,
  to the highest mountains of Lebanon.
I have cut down its tallest cedars
  and its best pine trees.
I have gone to its farthest places
  and to its best forests.
²⁴I have dug wells in foreign countries
  and drunk water there.
By the soles of my feet,
  I have dried up all the rivers of Egypt."

²⁵" 'King of Assyria, surely you have heard.
  Long ago I, the LORD, planned these things.
Long ago I designed them,
  and now I have made them happen.
I allowed you to turn those strong,
    walled cities
  into piles of rocks.
²⁶The people in those cities were weak;
  they were frightened and put to shame.
They were like grass in the field,
  like tender, young grass,
like grass on the housetop
  that is burned by the wind before it can grow.

²⁷" 'I know when you rest,
  when you come and go,
  and how you rage against me.
²⁸Because you rage against me,
  and because I have heard your proud words,
I will put my hook in your nose
  and my bit in your mouth.
Then I will force you to leave my country
  the same way you came.'

²⁹"Then the LORD said, 'Hezekiah, I will give you this sign:
This year you will eat the grain that grows wild,
  and the second year you will eat what grows wild from that.
But in the third year, plant grain and harvest it.
Plant vineyards and eat their fruit.
³⁰Some of the people in the family of Judah
  will escape.

Like plants that take root,
    they will grow strong and have many
    children.
31A few people will come out of Jerusalem
    alive;
    a few from Mount Zion will live.
The strong love of the LORD All-Powerful
    will make this happen.'
32"So this is what the LORD says about the
king of Assyria:
'He will not enter this city
    or even shoot an arrow here.
He will not fight against it with shields
    or build a ramp to attack the city walls.
33He will return to his country the same
    way he came,
    and he will not enter this city,'
    says the LORD.
34'I will defend and save this city
    for my sake and for the sake of David,
    my servant.'"

35That night the angel of the LORD went out and killed one hundred eighty-five thousand men in the Assyrian camp. When the people got up early the next morning, they saw all the dead bodies. 36So Sennacherib king of Assyria left and went back to Nineveh and stayed there.

37One day as Sennacherib was worshiping in the temple of his god Nisroch, his sons Adrammelech and Sharezer killed him with a sword. Then they escaped to the land of Ararat. So Sennacherib's son Esarhaddon became king of Assyria.

Hezekiah's Illness

20At that time Hezekiah became so sick he almost died. The prophet Isaiah son of Amoz went to see him and told him, "This is what the LORD says: Make arrangements because you are not going to live, but die."

2Hezekiah turned toward the wall and prayed to the LORD, 3"LORD, please remember that I have always obeyed you. I have given myself completely to you and have done what you said was right." Then Hezekiah cried loudly.

4Before Isaiah had left the middle courtyard, the LORD spoke his word to Isaiah: 5"Go back and tell Hezekiah, the leader of my people: 'This is what the LORD, the God of your ancestor David, says: I have heard your prayer and seen your tears, so I will heal you. Three days from now you will go up to the Temple of the LORD. 6I will add fifteen years to your life. I will save you and this city from the king of Assyria; I will protect the city for my sake and for the sake of my servant David.'"

7Then Isaiah said, "Make a paste from figs." So they made it and put it on Hezekiah's boil, and he got well.

8Hezekiah had asked Isaiah, "What will be the sign that the LORD will heal me and that I will go up to the Temple of the LORD on the third day?"

9Isaiah said, "The LORD will do what he says. This is the sign from the LORD to show you: Do you want the shadow to go forward ten steps or back ten steps?"

10Hezekiah answered, "It's easy for the shadow to go forward ten steps. Instead, let it go back ten steps."

11Then Isaiah the prophet called to the LORD, and the LORD brought the shadow ten steps back up the stairway of Ahaz that it had gone down.

Messengers from Babylon

12At that time Merodach-Baladan son of Baladan was king of Babylon. He sent letters and a gift to Hezekiah, because he had heard that Hezekiah was sick. 13Hezekiah listened to the messengers, so he showed them what was in his storehouses: the silver, gold, spices, expensive perfumes, his swords and shields, and all his wealth. He showed them everything in his palace and his kingdom.

14Then Isaiah the prophet went to King Hezekiah and asked him, "What did these men say? Where did they come from?"

Hezekiah said, "They came from a faraway country—from Babylon."

15So Isaiah asked him, "What did they see in your palace?"

Hezekiah said, "They saw everything in my palace. I showed them all my wealth."

16Then Isaiah said to Hezekiah, "Listen to the words of the LORD: 17'In the future everything in your palace and everything your ancestors have stored up until this day will be taken away to Babylon. Nothing will be left,' says the Lord. [18]"Some of your own children, those who will be born to you, will be taken away. And they will become servants in the palace of the king of Babylon.' "

[19]Hezekiah told Isaiah, "These words from the Lord are good." He said this because he thought, "There will be peace and security in my lifetime."

[20]Everything else Hezekiah did—all his victories, his work on the pool, his work on the tunnel to bring water into the city—is written in the book of the history of the kings of Judah. [21]Then Hezekiah died, and his son Manasseh became king in his place.

Manasseh King of Judah

21 Manasseh was twelve years old when he became king, and he was king fifty-five years in Jerusalem. His mother's name was Hephzibah. [2]He did what the Lord said was wrong. He did the hateful things the other nations had done—the nations that the Lord had forced out of the land ahead of the Israelites. [3]Manasseh's father, Hezekiah, had destroyed the places where gods were worshiped, but Manasseh rebuilt them. He built altars for Baal, and he made an Asherah idol as Ahab king of Israel had done. Manasseh also worshiped all the stars of the sky and served them. [4]The Lord had said about the Temple, "I will be worshiped in Jerusalem," but Manasseh built altars in the Temple of the Lord. [5]He built altars to worship the stars in the two courtyards of the Temple of the Lord. [6]He made his own son pass through fire. He practiced magic and told the future by explaining signs and dreams, and he got advice from mediums and fortune-tellers. He did many things the Lord said were wrong, which made the Lord angry.

[7]Manasseh carved an Asherah idol and put it in the Temple. The Lord had said to David and his son Solomon about the Temple, "I will be worshiped forever in this Temple and in Jerusalem, which I have chosen from all the tribes of Israel. [8]I will never again make the Israelites wander out of the land I gave their ancestors. But they must obey everything I have commanded them

and all the teachings my servant Moses gave them." [9]But the people did not listen. Manasseh led them to do more evil than the nations the Lord had destroyed ahead of the Israelites.

[10]The Lord said through his servants the prophets, [11]"Manasseh king of Judah has done these hateful things. He has done more evil than the Amorites before him. He also has led Judah to sin with his idols. [12]So this is what the Lord, the God of Israel, says: 'I will bring so much trouble on Jerusalem and Judah that anyone who hears about it will be shocked. [13]I will stretch the measuring line of Samaria over Jerusalem, and the plumb line used against Ahab's family will be used on Jerusalem. I will wipe out Jerusalem as a person wipes a dish and turns it upside down. [14]I will throw away the rest of my people who are left. I will give them to their enemies, and they will be robbed by all their enemies, [15]because my people did what I said was wrong. They have made me angry from the day their ancestors left Egypt until now.' "

[16]Manasseh also killed many innocent people, filling Jerusalem from one end to the other with their blood. This was besides the sin he led Judah to do; he led Judah to do what the Lord said was wrong.

[17]The other things Manasseh did as king, even the sin he did, are written in the book of the history of the kings of Judah. [18]Manasseh died and was buried in the garden of his own palace, the garden of Uzza. Then Manasseh's son Amon became king in his place.

Amon King of Judah

[19]Amon was twenty-two years old when he became king, and he was king for two years in Jerusalem. His mother's name was Meshullemeth daughter of Haruz, who was from Jotbah. [20]Amon did what the Lord said was wrong, as his father Manasseh had done. [21]He lived in the same way his father had lived: he worshiped the idols his father had worshiped, and he bowed down before them. [22]Amon rejected the Lord, the God of his ancestors, and did not follow the ways of the Lord.

[23]Amon's officers made plans against him

and killed him in his palace. [24]Then the people of the land killed all those who had made plans to kill King Amon, and they made his son Josiah king in his place.

[25]Everything else Amon did is written in the book of the history of the kings of Judah. [26]He was buried in his grave in the garden of Uzza, and his son Josiah became king in his place.

PSALM 74:12–17

[12]God, you have been our king for a long
  time.
  You bring salvation to the earth.
[13]You split open the sea by your power
  and broke the heads of the sea monster.
[14]You smashed the heads of the monster
  Leviathan
  and gave it to the desert creatures as
  food.
[15]You opened up the springs and streams
  and made the flowing rivers run dry.
[16]Both the day and the night are yours;
  you made the sun and the moon.
[17]You set all the limits on the earth;
  you created summer and winter.

PROVERBS 19:1–2

19 It is better to be poor and honest
  than to be foolish and tell lies.

[2]Enthusiasm without knowledge is not
  good.
  If you act too quickly, you might make a
  mistake.

ACTS 2:1–21

The Coming of the Holy Spirit

2 When the day of Pentecost came, they were all together in one place. [2]Suddenly a noise like a strong, blowing wind came from heaven and filled the whole house where they were sitting. [3]They saw something like flames of fire that were separated and stood over each person there. [4]They were all filled with the Holy Spirit, and they began to speak different languages[n] by the power the Holy Spirit was giving them.

[5]There were some religious Jews staying in Jerusalem who were from every country in the world. [6]When they heard this noise, a crowd came together. They were all surprised, because each one heard them speaking in his own language. [7]They were completely amazed at this. They said, "Look! Aren't all these people that we hear speaking from Galilee? [8]Then how is it possible that we each hear them in our own languages? We are from different places: [9]Parthia, Media, Elam, Mesopotamia, Judea, Cappadocia, Pontus, Asia, [10]Phrygia, Pamphylia, Egypt, the areas of Libya near Cyrene, Rome [11](both Jews and those who had become Jews), Crete, and Arabia. But we hear them telling in our own languages about the great things God has done!" [12]They were all amazed and confused, asking each other, "What does this mean?"

[13]But others were making fun of them, saying, "They have had too much wine."

Peter Speaks to the People

[14]But Peter stood up with the eleven apostles, and in a loud voice he spoke to the crowd: "My fellow Jews, and all of you who are in Jerusalem, listen to me. Pay attention to what I have to say. [15]These people are not drunk, as you think; it is only nine o'clock in the morning! [16]But Joel the prophet wrote about what is happening here today:

[17]'God says: In the last days
  I will pour out my Spirit on all kinds of
  people.
  Your sons and daughters will prophesy.
  Your young men will see visions,
  and your old men will dream dreams.
[18]At that time I will pour out my Spirit
  also on my male slaves and female
  slaves,
  and they will prophesy.
[19]I will show miracles
  in the sky and on the earth:
  blood, fire, and thick smoke.
[20]The sun will become dark,
  the moon red as blood,
  before the overwhelming and glorious
  day of the Lord will come.
[21]Then anyone who calls on the Lord will
  be saved.'
  Joel 2:28–32

2:4 languages This can also be translated "tongues."

JUNE 17

2 KINGS 22:1—24:20a

Josiah King of Judah

22 Josiah was eight years old when he became king, and he ruled thirty-one years in Jerusalem. His mother's name was Jedidah daughter of Adaiah, who was from Bozkath. ²Josiah did what the LORD said was right. He lived as his ancestor David had lived, and he did not stop doing what was right.

³In Josiah's eighteenth year as king, he sent Shaphan to the Temple of the LORD. Shaphan son of Azaliah, the son of Meshullam, was the royal secretary. Josiah said, ⁴"Go up to Hilkiah the high priest, and have him empty out the money the gatekeepers have gathered from the people. This is the money they have brought into the Temple of the LORD. ⁵Have him give the money to the supervisors of the work on the Temple of the LORD. They must pay the workers who repair the Temple of the LORD— ⁶the carpenters, builders, and bricklayers. Also use the money to buy timber and cut stone to repair the Temple. ⁷They do not need to report how they use the money given to them, because they are working honestly."

The Book of the Teachings Is Found

⁸Hilkiah the high priest said to Shaphan the royal secretary, "I've found the Book of the Teachings in the Temple of the LORD." He gave it to Shaphan, who read it.

⁹Then Shaphan the royal secretary went to the king and reported to Josiah, "Your officers have paid out the money that was in the Temple of the LORD. They have given it to the workers and supervisors at the Temple." ¹⁰Then Shaphan the royal secretary told the king, "Hilkiah the priest has given me a book." And Shaphan read from the book to the king.

¹¹When the king heard the words of the Book of the Teachings, he tore his clothes to show how upset he was. ¹²He gave orders to Hilkiah the priest, Ahikam son of Shaphan, Acbor son of Micaiah, Shaphan the royal secretary, and Asaiah the king's servant. These were the orders: ¹³"Go and ask the LORD about the words in the book that was found. Ask for me, for all the people, and for all Judah. The LORD's anger is burning against us, because our ancestors did not obey the words of this book; they did not do all the things written for us to do."

¹⁴So Hilkiah the priest, Ahikam, Acbor, Shaphan, and Asaiah went to talk to Huldah the prophetess. She was the wife of Shallum son of Tikvah, the son of Harhas, who took care of the king's clothes. Huldah lived in Jerusalem, in the new area of the city.

¹⁵She said to them, "This is what the LORD, the God of Israel, says: Tell the man who sent you to me, ¹⁶'This is what the LORD says: I will bring trouble to this place and to the people living here, as it is written in the book which the king of Judah has read. ¹⁷The people of Judah have left me and have burned incense to other gods. They have made me angry by all that they have done. My anger burns against this place like a fire, and it will not be put out.' ¹⁸Tell the king of Judah, who sent you to ask the LORD, 'This is what the LORD, the God of Israel, says about the words you heard: ¹⁹When you heard my words against this place and its people, you became sorry for what you had done and humbled yourself before me. I said they would be cursed and would be destroyed. You tore your clothes to show how upset you were, and you cried in my presence. This is why I have heard you, says the LORD. ²⁰So I will let you die, and you will be buried in peace. You won't see all the trouble I will bring to this place.'"

So they took her message back to the king.

The People Hear the Agreement

23 Then the king gathered all the elders of Judah and Jerusalem together. ²He went up to the Temple of the LORD, and all the people from Judah and Jerusalem went with him. The priests, prophets, and all the people—from the least important to the most important—went with him. He read to them all the words of the Book of the Agreement that was found in the Temple of the LORD. [3]The king stood by the pillar and made an agreement in the presence of the LORD to follow the LORD and obey his commands, rules, and laws with his whole being, and to obey the words of the agreement written in this book. Then all the people promised to obey the agreement.

Josiah Destroys the Places for Idol Worship

[4]The king commanded Hilkiah the high priest and the priests of the next rank and the gatekeepers to bring out of the Temple of the LORD everything made for Baal, Asherah, and all the stars of the sky. Then Josiah burned them outside Jerusalem in the open country of the Kidron Valley and carried their ashes to Bethel. [5]The kings of Judah had chosen priests for these gods. These priests burned incense in the places where gods were worshiped in the cities of Judah and the towns around Jerusalem. They burned incense to Baal, the sun, the moon, the planets, and all the stars of the sky. But Josiah took those priests away. [6]He removed the Asherah idol from the Temple of the LORD and took it outside Jerusalem to the Kidron Valley, where he burned it and beat it into dust. Then he threw the dust on the graves of the common people. [7]He also tore down the houses of the male prostitutes who were in the Temple of the LORD, where the women did weaving for Asherah.

[8]King Josiah brought all the false priests from the cities of Judah. He ruined the places where gods were worshiped, where the priests had burned incense, from Geba to Beersheba. He destroyed the places of worship at the entrance to the Gate of Joshua, the ruler of the city, on the left side of the city gate. [9]The priests at the places where gods were worshiped were not allowed to serve at the LORD's altar in Jerusa-lem. But they could eat bread made without yeast with their brothers.

[10]Josiah ruined Topheth, in the Valley of Ben Hinnom, so no one could sacrifice his son or daughter to Molech. [11]Judah's kings had placed horses at the front door of the Temple of the LORD in the courtyard near the room of Nathan-Melech, an officer. These horses were for the worship of the sun. So Josiah removed them and burned the chariots that were for sun worship also.

[12]The kings of Judah had built altars on the roof[n] of the upstairs room of Ahaz. Josiah broke down these altars and the altars Manasseh had made in the two courtyards of the Temple of the LORD. Josiah smashed them to pieces and threw their dust into the Kidron Valley. [13]King Josiah ruined the places where gods were worshiped east of Jerusalem, south of the Mount of Olives.[n] Solomon king of Israel had built these places. One was for Ashtoreth, the hated goddess of the Sidonians. One was for Chemosh, the hated god of Moab. And one was for Molech, the hated god of the Ammonites. [14]Josiah smashed to pieces the stone pillars they worshiped, and he cut down the Asherah idols. Then he covered the places with human bones.

[15]Josiah also broke down the altar at Bethel—the place of worship made by Jeroboam son of Nebat, who had led Israel to sin. Josiah burned that place, broke the stones of the altar into pieces, then beat them into dust. He also burned the Asherah idol. [16]When he turned around, he saw the graves on the mountain. He had the bones taken from the graves, and he burned them on the altar to ruin it. This happened as the LORD had said it would through the man of God.

[17]Josiah asked, "What is that monument I see?"

The people of the city answered, "It's the grave of the man of God who came from Judah. This prophet announced the things you have done against the altar of Bethel."

23:12 roof In Bible times houses were built with flat roofs. The roof was used for drying things such as flax and fruit. And it was used as an extra room, as a place for worship, and as a cool place to sleep in the summer. **23:13 Mount of Olives** Literally, "The Mountain of Ruin."

[18]Josiah said, "Leave the grave alone. No one may move this man's bones." So they left his bones and the bones of the prophet who had come from Samaria.

[19]The kings of Israel had built temples for worshiping gods in the cities of Samaria, which had caused the LORD to be angry. Josiah removed all those temples and did the same things as he had done at Bethel. [20]He killed all the priests of those places of worship; he killed them on the altars and burned human bones on the altars. Then he went back to Jerusalem.

Josiah Celebrates the Passover

[21]The king commanded all the people, "Celebrate the Passover to the LORD your God as it is written in this Book of the Agreement." [22]The Passover had not been celebrated like this since the judges led Israel. Nor had one like it happened while there were kings of Israel and kings of Judah. [23]This Passover was celebrated to the LORD in Jerusalem in the eighteenth year of King Josiah's rule.

[24]Josiah destroyed the mediums, fortunetellers, house gods, and idols. He also destroyed all the hated gods seen in the land of Judah and Jerusalem. This was to obey the words of the teachings written in the book Hilkiah the priest had found in the Temple of the LORD.

[25]There was no king like Josiah before or after him. He obeyed the LORD with all his heart, soul, and strength, following all the Teachings of Moses.

[26]Even so, the LORD did not stop his strong and terrible anger. His anger burned against Judah because of all Manasseh had done to make him angry. [27]The LORD said, "I will send Judah out of my sight, as I have sent Israel away. I will reject Jerusalem, which I chose. And I will take away the Temple about which I said, 'I will be worshiped there.'"

[28]Everything else Josiah did is written in the book of the history of the kings of Judah.

[29]While Josiah was king, Neco king of Egypt went to help the king of Assyria at the Euphrates River. King Josiah marched out to fight against Neco, but at Megiddo, Neco faced him and killed him. [30]Josiah's servants carried his body in a chariot from Megiddo to Jerusalem and buried him in his own grave. Then the people of Judah chose Josiah's son Jehoahaz and poured olive oil on him to make him king in his father's place.

Jehoahaz King of Judah

[31]Jehoahaz was twenty-three years old when he became king, and he was king in Jerusalem for three months. His mother's name was Hamutal, who was the daughter of Jeremiah from Libnah. [32]Jehoahaz did what the LORD said was wrong, just as his ancestors had done.

[33]King Neco took Jehoahaz prisoner at Riblah in the land of Hamath so that Jehoahaz could not rule in Jerusalem. Neco made the people of Judah pay about seventy-five hundred pounds of silver and about seventy-five pounds of gold.

[34]King Neco made Josiah's son Eliakim the king in place of Josiah his father. Then Neco changed Eliakim's name to Jehoiakim. But Neco took Jehoahaz to Egypt, where he died. [35]Jehoiakim gave King Neco the silver and gold he demanded. Jehoiakim taxed the land and took silver and gold from the people of the land to give to King Neco. Each person had to pay his share.

Jehoiakim King of Judah

[36]Jehoiakim was twenty-five years old when he became king, and he was king in Jerusalem for eleven years. His mother's name was Zebidah daughter of Pedaiah, who was from Rumah. [37]Jehoiakim did what the LORD said was wrong, just as his ancestors had done.

24 While Jehoiakim was king, Nebuchadnezzar king of Babylon attacked the land of Judah. So Jehoiakim became Nebuchadnezzar's servant for three years. Then he turned against Nebuchadnezzar and broke away from his rule. [2]The LORD sent raiding parties from Babylon, Aram, Moab, and Ammon against Jehoiakim to destroy Judah. This happened as the LORD had said it would through his servants the prophets.

³The LORD commanded this to happen to the people of Judah, to remove them from his presence, because of all the sins of Manasseh. ⁴He had killed many innocent people and had filled Jerusalem with their blood. And the LORD would not forgive these sins.

⁵The other things that happened while Jehoiakim was king and all he did are written in the book of the history of the kings of Judah. ⁶Jehoiakim died, and his son Jehoiachin became king in his place.

⁷The king of Egypt did not leave his land again, because the king of Babylon had captured all that belonged to the king of Egypt, from the brook of Egypt to the Euphrates River.

Jehoiachin King of Judah

⁸Jehoiachin was eighteen years old when he became king, and he was king three months in Jerusalem. His mother's name was Nehushta daughter of Elnathan from Jerusalem. ⁹Jehoiachin did what the LORD said was wrong, just as his father had done.

¹⁰At that time the officers of Nebuchadnezzar king of Babylon came up to Jerusalem. When they reached the city, they attacked it. ¹¹Nebuchadnezzar himself came to the city while his officers were attacking it. ¹²Jehoiachin king of Judah surrendered to the king of Babylon, along with Jehoiachin's mother, servants, nobles, and officers. So Nebuchadnezzar made Jehoiachin a prisoner in the eighth year he was king of Babylon. ¹³Nebuchadnezzar took all the treasures from the Temple of the LORD and from the palace. He cut up all the gold objects Solomon king of Israel had made for the Temple of the LORD. This happened as the LORD had said it would. ¹⁴Nebuchadnezzar took away all the people of Jerusalem, including all the leaders, all the wealthy people, and all the craftsmen and metal workers. There were ten thousand prisoners in all. Only the poorest people in the land were left. ¹⁵Nebuchadnezzar carried away Jehoiachin to Babylon, as well as the king's mother and his wives, the officers, and

the leading men of the land. They were taken captive from Jerusalem to Babylon. ¹⁶The king of Babylon also took all seven thousand soldiers, who were strong and able to fight in war, and about a thousand craftsmen and metal workers. Nebuchadnezzar took them as prisoners to Babylon. ¹⁷Then he made Mattaniah, Jehoiachin's uncle, king in Jehoiachin's place. He also changed Mattaniah's name to Zedekiah.

Zedekiah King of Judah

¹⁸Zedekiah was twenty-one years old when he became king, and he was king in Jerusalem for eleven years. His mother's name was Hamutal daughter of Jeremiah^n from Libnah. ¹⁹Zedekiah did what the LORD said was wrong, just as Jehoiakim had done. ²⁰All this happened in Jerusalem and Judah because the LORD was angry with them. Finally, he threw them out of his presence.

PSALM 74:18–23

¹⁸LORD, remember how the enemy insulted
    you.
  Remember how those foolish people
    made fun of you.
¹⁹Do not give us, your doves, to those wild
    animals.
  Never forget your poor people.
²⁰Remember the agreement you made
    with us,
  because violence fills every dark
    corner of this land.
²¹Do not let your suffering people be
    disgraced.
  Let the poor and helpless praise you.

²²God, arise and defend yourself.
  Remember the insults that come from
    those foolish people all day long.
²³Don't forget what your enemies said;
  don't forget their roar as they rise
    against you always.

PROVERBS 19:3

³People's own foolishness ruins their
    lives,

24:18 Jeremiah This is not the prophet Jeremiah, but a different man with the same name.

but in their minds they blame the LORD.

ACTS 2:22–47

[22]"People of Israel, listen to these words: Jesus from Nazareth was a very special man. God clearly showed this to you by the miracles, wonders, and signs he did through Jesus. You all know this, because it happened right here among you. [23]Jesus was given to you, and with the help of those who don't know the law, you put him to death by nailing him to a cross. But this was God's plan which he had made long ago; he knew all this would happen. [24]God raised Jesus from the dead and set him free from the pain of death, because death could not hold him. [25]For David said this about him:

'I keep the Lord before me always.
　Because he is close by my side,
　I will not be hurt.
[26]So I am glad, and I rejoice.
　Even my body has hope,
[27]because you will not leave me in the grave.
　You will not let your Holy One rot.
[28]You will teach me how to live a holy life.
　Being with you will fill me with joy.'

Psalm 16:8–11

[29]"Brothers and sisters, I can tell you truly that David, our ancestor, died and was buried. His grave is still here with us today. [30]He was a prophet and knew God had promised him that he would make a person from David's family a king just as he was.[n] [31]Knowing this before it happened, David talked about the Christ rising from the dead. He said:

'He was not left in the grave.
　His body did not rot.'

[32]So Jesus is the One whom God raised from the dead. And we are all witnesses to this. [33]Jesus was lifted up to heaven and is now at God's right side. The Father has given the Holy Spirit to Jesus as he promised. So Jesus has poured out that Spirit, and this is what you now see and hear. [34]David was not the one who was lifted up to heaven, but he said:

'The Lord said to my Lord,
　"Sit by me at my right side,
[35] until I put your enemies under your control."'[n]

Psalm 110:1

[36]"So, all the people of Israel should know this truly: God has made Jesus—the man you nailed to the cross—both Lord and Christ."

[37]When the people heard this, they felt guilty and asked Peter and the other apostles, "What shall we do?"

[38]Peter said to them, "Change your hearts and lives and be baptized, each one of you, in the name of Jesus Christ for the forgiveness of your sins. And you will receive the gift of the Holy Spirit. [39]This promise is for you, for your children, and for all who are far away. It is for everyone the Lord our God calls to himself."

[40]Peter warned them with many other words. He begged them, "Save yourselves from the evil of today's people!" [41]Then those people who accepted what Peter said were baptized. About three thousand people were added to the number of believers that day. [42]They spent their time learning the apostles' teaching, sharing, breaking bread,[n] and praying together.

The Believers Share

[43]The apostles were doing many miracles and signs, and everyone felt great respect for God. [44]All the believers were together and shared everything. [45]They would sell their land and the things they owned and then divide the money and give it to anyone who needed it. [46]The believers met together in the Temple every day. They ate together in their homes, happy to share their food with joyful hearts. [47]They praised God and were liked by all the people. Every day the Lord added those who were being saved to the group of believers.

2:30 God . . . was See 2 Samuel 7:13; Psalm 132:11. **2:35 until . . . control** Literally, "until I make your enemies a footstool for your feet." **2:42 breaking bread** This may mean a meal as in verse 46, or the Lord's Supper, the special meal Jesus told his followers to eat to remember him (Luke 22:14–20).

JUNE 18

2 KINGS 24:20b—25:30

The Fall of Jerusalem

Zedekiah turned against the king of Babylon.

25Nebuchadnezzar king of Babylon marched against Jerusalem with his whole army during Zedekiah's ninth year as king, on the tenth day of the tenth month. He made a camp around the city and piled dirt against the city walls to attack it. ²The city was under attack until Zedekiah's eleventh year as king. ³By the ninth day of the fourth month, the hunger was terrible in the city. There was no food for the people to eat. ⁴Then the city was broken into, and the whole army ran away at night through the gate between the two walls by the king's garden. While the Babylonians were still surrounding the city, Zedekiah and his men ran away toward the Jordan Valley. ⁵But the Babylonian army chased King Zedekiah and caught up with him in the plains of Jericho. All of his army was scattered from him, ⁶so they captured Zedekiah and took him to the king of Babylon at Riblah. There he passed sentence on Zedekiah. ⁷They killed Zedekiah's sons as he watched. Then they put out his eyes and put bronze chains on him and took him to Babylon.

⁸Nebuzaradan was the commander of the king's special guards. This officer of the king of Babylon came to Jerusalem on the seventh day of the fifth month, in Nebuchadnezzar's nineteenth year as king of Babylon. ⁹Nebuzaradan set fire to the Temple of the LORD and the palace and all the houses of Jerusalem. Every important building was burned.

¹⁰The whole Babylonian army, led by the commander of the king's special guards, broke down the walls around Jerusalem. ¹¹Nebuzaradan, the commander of the guards, captured the people left in Jerusalem, those who had surrendered to the king of Babylon, and the rest of the people. ¹²But the commander left behind some of the poorest people of the land to take care of the vineyards and fields.

¹³The Babylonians broke up the bronze pillars, the bronze stands, and the large bronze bowl, which was called the Sea, in the Temple of the LORD. Then they carried the bronze to Babylon. ¹⁴They also took the pots, shovels, wick trimmers, dishes, and all the bronze objects used to serve in the Temple. ¹⁵The commander of the king's special guards took away the pans for carrying hot coals, the bowls, and everything made of pure gold or silver. ¹⁶There were two pillars and the large bronze bowl and the movable stands which Solomon had made for the Temple of the LORD. There was so much bronze that it could not be weighed. ¹⁷Each pillar was about twenty-seven feet high. The bronze capital on top of the pillar was about four and one-half feet high. It was decorated with a net design and bronze pomegranates all around it. The other pillar also had a net design and was like the first pillar.

Judah Is Taken Prisoner

¹⁸The commander of the guards took some prisoners—Seraiah the chief priest, Zephaniah the priest next in rank, and the three doorkeepers. ¹⁹Of the people who were still in the city, he took the officer in charge of the fighting men, as well as five people who advised the king. He took the royal secretary who selected people for the army and sixty other men who were in the city. ²⁰Nebuzaradan, the commander, took all these people and brought them to the king of Babylon at Riblah. ²¹There at Riblah, in the land of Hamath, the king had them killed. So the people of Judah were led away from their country as captives.

Gedaliah Becomes Governor

²²Nebuchadnezzar king of Babylon left some people in the land of Judah. He appointed Gedaliah son of Ahikam, the son of Shaphan, as governor.

²³The army captains and their men heard that the king of Babylon had made Gedaliah

governor, so they came to Gedaliah at Mizpah. They were Ishmael son of Nethaniah, Johanan son of Kareah, Seraiah son of Tanhumeth the Netophathite, Jaazaniah son of the Maacathite, and their men. ²⁴Then Gedaliah promised these army captains and their men, "Don't be afraid of the Babylonian officers. Live in the land and serve the king of Babylon, and everything will go well for you."

²⁵In the seventh month Ishmael son of Nethaniah, son of Elishama from the king's family, came with ten men and killed Gedaliah. They also killed the men of Judah and Babylon who were with Gedaliah at Mizpah. ²⁶Then all the people, from the least important to the most important, along with the army leaders, ran away to Egypt, because they were afraid of the Babylonians.

Jehoiachin Is Set Free

²⁷Jehoiachin king of Judah was held in Babylon for thirty-seven years. In the thirty-seventh year Evil-Merodach became king of Babylon, and he let Jehoiachin out of prison on the twenty-seventh day of the twelfth month. ²⁸Evil-Merodach spoke kindly to Jehoiachin and gave him a seat of honor above the seats of the other kings who were with him in Babylon. ²⁹So Jehoiachin put away his prison clothes. For the rest of his life, he ate at the king's table. ³⁰Every day, for as long as Jehoiachin lived, the king gave him an allowance.

PSALM 75:1-10

God the Judge

For the director of music. To the tune of "Do Not Destroy." A psalm of Asaph. A song.

75 God, we thank you;
    we thank you because you are near.
    We tell about the miracles you do.

²You say, "I set the time for trial,
    and I will judge fairly.
³The earth with all its people may shake,
    but I am the one who holds it steady.

Selah

⁴I say to those who are proud, 'Don't brag,'

and to the wicked, 'Don't show your
    power.
⁵Don't try to use your power against
    heaven.
Don't be stubborn.'"

⁶No one from the east or the west
    or the desert can judge you.
⁷God is the judge;
    he judges one person as guilty and
        another as innocent.
⁸The LORD holds a cup of anger in his
        hand;
    it is full of wine mixed with spices.
He pours it out even to the last drop,
    and the wicked drink it all.
⁹I will tell about this forever;
    I will sing praise to the God of Jacob.
¹⁰He will take all power away from the
        wicked,
    but the power of good people will grow.

PROVERBS 19:4-5

⁴Wealthy people are always finding more
        friends,
    but the poor lose all theirs.

⁵A witness who lies will not go free;
    liars will never escape.

ACTS 3:1-26

Peter Heals a Crippled Man

3 One day Peter and John went to the Temple at three o'clock, the time set each day for the afternoon prayer service. ²There, at the Temple gate called Beautiful Gate, was a man who had been crippled all his life. Every day he was carried to this gate to beg for money from the people going into the Temple. ³The man saw Peter and John going into the Temple and asked them for money. ⁴Peter and John looked straight at him and said, "Look at us!" ⁵The man looked at them, thinking they were going to give him some money. ⁶But Peter said, "I don't have any silver or gold, but I do have something else I can give you. By the power of Jesus Christ from Nazareth, stand up and walk!" ⁷Then Peter took the man's right hand and lifted him up. Immediately the man's feet and

ankles became strong. [8]He jumped up, stood on his feet, and began to walk. He went into the Temple with them, walking and jumping and praising God. [9-10]All the people recognized him as the crippled man who always sat by the Beautiful Gate begging for money. Now they saw this same man walking and praising God, and they were amazed. They wondered how this could happen.

Peter Speaks to the People

[11]While the man was holding on to Peter and John, all the people were amazed and ran to them at Solomon's Porch. [12]When Peter saw this, he said to them, "People of Israel, why are you surprised? You are looking at us as if it were our own power or goodness that made this man walk. [13]The God of Abraham, Isaac, and Jacob, the God of our ancestors, gave glory to Jesus, his servant. But you handed him over to be killed. Pilate decided to let him go free, but you told Pilate you did not want Jesus. [14]You did not want the One who is holy and good but asked Pilate to give you a murderer[n] instead. [15]And so you killed the One who gives life, but God raised him from the dead. We are witnesses to this. [16]It was faith in Jesus that made this crippled man well. You can see this man, and you know him. He was made completely well because of trust in Jesus, and you all saw it happen!

[17]"Brothers and sisters, I know you did those things to Jesus because neither you nor your leaders understood what you were doing. [18]God said through the prophets that his Christ would suffer and die. And now God has made these things come true in this way. [19]So you must change your hearts and lives! Come back to God, and he will forgive your sins. Then the Lord will send the time of rest. [20]And he will send Jesus, the One he chose to be the Christ. [21]But Jesus must stay in heaven until the time comes when all things will be made right again. God told about this time long ago when he spoke through his holy prophets. [22]Moses said, 'The Lord your God will give you a prophet like me, who is one of your own people. You must listen to everything he tells you. [23]Anyone who does not listen to that prophet will die, cut off from God's people.'[n] [24]Samuel, and all the other prophets who spoke for God after Samuel, told about this time now. [25]You are descendants of the prophets. You have received the agreement God made with your ancestors. He said to your father Abraham, 'Through your descendants all the nations on the earth will be blessed.'[n] [26]God has raised up his servant Jesus and sent him to you first to bless you by turning each of you away from doing evil."

JUNE 19

1 CHRONICLES 1:1—2:55

From Adam to Abraham

1 Adam was the father of Seth. Seth was the father of Enosh. Enosh was the father of Kenan. [2]Kenan was the father of Mahalalel. Mahalalel was the father of Jared. Jared was the father of Enoch. [3]Enoch was the father of Methuselah. Methuselah was the father of Lamech, and Lamech was the father of Noah.

[4]The sons of Noah were Shem, Ham, and Japheth.

[5]Japheth's sons were Gomer, Magog, Madai, Javan, Tubal, Meshech, and Tiras.

[6]Gomer's sons were Ashkenaz, Riphath, and Togarmah.

[7]Javan's sons were Elishah, Tarshish, Kittim,[n] and Rodanim.

[8]Ham's sons were Cush, Mizraim,[n] Put, and Canaan.

3:14 murderer Barabbas, the man the crowd asked Pilate to set free instead of Jesus (Luke 23:18). **3:22-23 'The Lord . . . people.'** Quotation from Deuteronomy 18:15, 19. **3:25 'Through . . . blessed.'** Quotation from Genesis 22:18; 26:4.
• **1:7 Kittim** His descendants were the people of Cyprus. **1:8 Mizraim** This is another name for Egypt.

[9]Cush's sons were Seba, Havilah, Sabta, Raamah, and Sabteca.

Raamah's sons were Sheba and Dedan.

[10]Cush was the father of Nimrod, who grew up to become a mighty warrior on the earth.

[11]Mizraim was the father of the Ludites, Anamites, Lehabites, and Naphtuhites, [12]Pathrusites, Casluhites, and Caphtorites. (The Philistines came from the Casluhites.)

[13]Canaan's first child was Sidon. He was also the father of the Hittites, [14]Jebusites, Amorites, Girgashites, [15]Hivites, Arkites, Sinites, [16]Arvadites, Zemarites, and Hamathites.

[17]Shem's sons were Elam, Asshur, Arphaxad, Lud, and Aram.

Aram's sons were Uz, Hul, Gether, and Meshech.

[18]Arphaxad was the father of Shelah, who was the father of Eber.

[19]Eber had two sons. One son was named Peleg,[n] because the people on the earth were divided into different languages during his life. Peleg's brother was named Joktan.

[20]Joktan was the father of Almodad, Sheleph, Hazarmaveth, Jerah, [21]Hadoram, Uzal, Diklah, [22]Obal, Abimael, Sheba, [23]Ophir, Havilah, and Jobab. All these were Joktan's sons. [24]The family line included Shem, Arphaxad, Shelah, [25]Eber, Peleg, Reu, [26]Serug, Nahor, Terah, [27]and Abram, who was called Abraham.

Abraham's Family

[28]Abraham's sons were Isaac and Ishmael.

[29]These were the sons of Isaac and Ishmael. Ishmael's first son was Nebaioth. His other sons were Kedar, Adbeel, Mibsam, [30]Mishma, Dumah, Massa, Hadad, Tema, [31]Jetur, Naphish, and Kedemah. These were Ishmael's sons. [32]Keturah, Abraham's slave woman, gave birth to Zimran, Jokshan, Medan, Midian, Ishbak, and Shuah.

Jokshan's sons were Sheba and Dedan.

[33]Midian's sons were Ephah, Epher, Hanoch, Abida, and Eldaah. All these were descendants of Keturah.

[34]Abraham was the father of Isaac, and Isaac's sons were Esau and Israel.

[35]Esau's sons were Eliphaz, Reuel, Jeush, Jalam, and Korah.

[36]Eliphaz's sons were Teman, Omar, Zepho, Gatam, Kenaz, Timna, and Amalek.

[37]Reuel's sons were Nahath, Zerah, Shammah, and Mizzah.

The Edomites from Seir

[38]Seir's sons were Lotan, Shobal, Zibeon, Anah, Dishon, Ezer, and Dishan.

[39]Lotan's sons were Hori and Homam, and his sister was Timna.

[40]Shobal's sons were Alvan, Manahath, Ebal, Shepho, and Onam.

Zibeon's sons were Aiah and Anah.

[41]Anah's son was Dishon.

Dishon's sons were Hemdan, Eshban, Ithran, and Keran.

[42]Ezer's sons were Bilhan, Zaavan, and Akan.

Dishan's sons were Uz and Aran.

The Kings of Edom

[43]These kings ruled in Edom before there were kings in Israel. Bela son of Beor was king of Edom, and his city was named Dinhabah.

[44]When Bela died, Jobab son of Zerah became king. He was from Bozrah.

[45]When Jobab died, Husham became king. He was from the land of the Temanites.

[46]When Husham died, Hadad son of Bedad became king, and his city was named Avith. Hadad defeated Midian in the country of Moab.

[47]When Hadad died, Samlah became king. He was from Masrekah.

[48]When Samlah died, Shaul became king. He was from Rehoboth by the river.

[49]When Shaul died, Baal-Hanan son of Acbor became king.

[50]When Baal-Hanan died, Hadad became king, and his city was named Pau. Hadad's wife was named Mehetabel, and she was the daughter of Matred, who was the daughter of Me-Zahab. [51]Then Hadad died.

The leaders of the family groups of Edom

1:19 Peleg This name sounds like the Hebrew word for "divided."

were Timna, Alvah, Jetheth, [52]Oholibamah, Elah, Pinon, [53]Kenaz, Teman, Mibzar, [54]Magdiel, and Iram. These were the leaders of Edom.

Israel's Family

2 The sons of Israel[n] were Reuben, Simeon, Levi, Judah, Issachar, Zebulun, [2]Dan, Joseph, Benjamin, Naphtali, Gad, and Asher.

Judah's Family

[3]Judah's sons were Er, Onan, and Shelah. A Canaanite woman, the daughter of Shua, was their mother. Judah's first son, Er, did what the LORD said was wicked, so the LORD put him to death. [4]Judah's daughter-in-law Tamar gave birth to Perez and Zerah. Judah was the father, so Judah had five sons.

[5]Perez's sons were Hezron and Hamul.

[6]Zerah had five sons: Zimri, Ethan, Heman, Calcol, and Darda.

[7]Carmi's son was Achan, who caused trouble for Israel because he took things that had been given to the LORD to be destroyed.

[8]Ethan's son was Azariah.

[9]Hezron's sons were Jerahmeel, Ram, and Caleb.

[10]Ram was Amminadab's father, and Amminadab was Nahshon's father. Nahshon was the leader of the people of Judah. [11]Nahshon was the father of Salmon, who was the father of Boaz. [12]Boaz was the father of Obed, and Obed was the father of Jesse.

[13]Jesse's first son was Eliab. His second son was Abinadab, his third was Shimea, [14]his fourth was Nethanel, his fifth was Raddai, [15]his sixth was Ozem, and his seventh son was David. [16]Their sisters were Zeruiah and Abigail. Zeruiah's three sons were Abishai, Joab, and Asahel. [17]Abigail was the mother of Amasa, and his father was Jether, an Ishmaelite.

Caleb's Family

[18]Caleb son of Hezron had children by his wife Azubah and by Jerioth. Caleb and Azubah's sons were Jesher, Shobab, and Ardon. [19]When Azubah died, Caleb married Ephrath. They had a son named Hur, [20]who was the father of Uri, who was the father of Bezalel.

[21]Later, when Hezron was sixty years old, he married the daughter of Makir, Gilead's father. Hezron had sexual relations with Makir's daughter, and she had a son named Segub. [22]Segub was the father of Jair. Jair controlled twenty-three cities in the country of Gilead. [23](But Geshur and Aram captured the Towns of Jair, as well as Kenath and the small towns around it— sixty towns in all.) All these were descendants of Makir, the father of Gilead.

[24]After Hezron died in Caleb Ephrathah, his wife Abijah had his son, named Ashhur. Ashhur became the father of Tekoa.

Jerahmeel's Family

[25]Hezron's first son was Jerahmeel. Jerahmeel's sons were Ram, Bunah, Oren, Ozem, and Ahijah. Ram was Jerahmeel's first son. [26]Jerahmeel had another wife, named Atarah. She was the mother of Onam.

[27]Jerahmeel's first son, Ram, had sons. They were Maaz, Jamin, and Eker.

[28]Onam's sons were Shammai and Jada.

Shammai's sons were Nadab and Abishur. [29]Abishur's wife was named Abihail, and their sons were Ahban and Molid.

[30]Nadab's sons were Seled and Appaim. Seled died without having children.

[31]Appaim's son was Ishi, who became the father of Sheshan.

Sheshan was the father of Ahlai.

[32]Jada was Shammai's brother, and Jada's sons were Jether and Jonathan. Jether died without having children.

[33]Jonathan's sons were Peleth and Zaza.

These were Jerahmeel's descendants.

[34]Sheshan did not have any sons, only daughters. He had a servant from Egypt named Jarha. [35]Sheshan let his daughter marry his servant Jarha, and she had a son named Attai.

[36]Attai was the father of Nathan. Nathan was the father of Zabad. [37]Zabad was the father of Ephlal. Ephlal was the father of Obed. [38]Obed was the father of Jehu. Jehu was the

---

2:1 Israel Another name for Jacob.

father of Azariah. ³⁹Azariah was the father of Helez. Helez was the father of Eleasah. ⁴⁰Eleasah was the father of Sismai. Sismai was the father of Shallum. ⁴¹Shallum was the father of Jekamiah, and Jekamiah was the father of Elishama.

Caleb's Family

⁴²Caleb was Jerahmeel's brother. Caleb's first son was Mesha. Mesha was the father of Ziph, and his son Mareshah was the father of Hebron.

⁴³Hebron's sons were Korah, Tappuah, Rekem, and Shema. ⁴⁴Shema was the father of Raham, who was the father of Jorkeam. Rekem was the father of Shammai. ⁴⁵Shammai was the father of Maon, and Maon was the father of Beth Zur.

⁴⁶Caleb's slave woman was named Ephah, and she was the mother of Haran, Moza, and Gazez. Haran was the father of Gazez.

⁴⁷Jahdai's sons were Regem, Jotham, Geshan, Pelet, Ephah, and Shaaph.

⁴⁸Caleb had another slave woman named Maacah. She was the mother of Sheber, Tirhanah, ⁴⁹Shaaph, and Sheva. Shaaph was the father of Madmannah. Sheva was the father of Macbenah and Gibea. Caleb's daughter was Acsah.

⁵⁰⁻⁵¹These were Caleb's descendants: Caleb's son Hur was the first son of his mother Ephrathah. Hur's sons were Shobal, Salma, and Hareph. Shobal was the father of Kiriath Jearim. Salma was the father of Bethlehem. And Hareph was the father of Beth Gader.

⁵²Shobal was the father of Kiriath Jearim. Shobal's descendants were Haroeh, half the Manahathites, ⁵³and the family groups of Kiriath Jearim: the Ithrites, Puthites, Shumathites, and Mishraites. The Zorathites and the Eshtaolites came from the Mishraite people.

⁵⁴Salma's descendants were Bethlehem, the Netophathites, Atroth Beth Joab, half the Manahathites, and the Zorites. ⁵⁵His descendants included the families who lived at Jabez, who wrote and copied important papers. They were called the Tirathites, Shimeathites, and Sucathites and were from the Kenite family group who came from Hammath. He was the father of the people living in Recab.

PSALM 76:1–10

The God Who Always Wins

For the director of music. With stringed instruments. A psalm of Asaph. A song.

76 People in Judah know God; is fame is great in Israel.
²His Tent is in Jerusalem; his home is on Mount Zion.
³There God broke the flaming arrows, the shields, the swords, and the weapons of war.　　　Selah

⁴God, how wonderful you are! You are more splendid than the hills full of animals.
⁵The brave soldiers were stripped as they lay asleep in death. Not one warrior had the strength to stop it.
⁶God of Jacob, when you spoke strongly, horses and riders fell dead.
⁷You are feared; no one can stand against you when you are angry.
⁸From heaven you gave the decision, and the earth was afraid and silent.
⁹God, you stood up to judge and to save the needy people of the earth.　　　Selah
¹⁰People praise you for your anger against evil. Those who live through your anger are stopped from doing more evil.

PROVERBS 19:6–7

⁶Many people want to please a leader, and everyone is friends with those who give gifts.

⁷Poor people's relatives avoid them; even their friends stay far away. They run after them, begging, but they are gone.

ACTS 4:1–22

Peter and John at the Council

4 While Peter and John were speaking to the people, priests, the captain of the soldiers that guarded the Temple, and Sadducees came up to them. ²They were upset because the two apostles were teaching the people and were preaching that people will rise from the dead through the power of Jesus. ³The older leaders grabbed Peter and John and put them in jail. Since it was already night, they kept them in jail until the next day. ⁴But many of those who had heard Peter and John preach believed the things they said. There were now about five thousand in the group of believers.

⁵The next day the rulers, the elders, and the teachers of the law met in Jerusalem. ⁶Annas the high priest, Caiaphas, John, and Alexander were there, as well as everyone from the high priest's family. ⁷They made Peter and John stand before them and then asked them, "By what power or authority did you do this?"

⁸Then Peter, filled with the Holy Spirit, said to them, "Rulers of the people and you elders, ⁹are you questioning us about a good thing that was done to a crippled man? Are you asking us who made him well? ¹⁰We want all of you and all the people to know that this man was made well by the power of Jesus Christ from Nazareth. You crucified him, but God raised him from the dead. This man was crippled, but he is now well and able to stand here before you because of the power of Jesus. ¹¹Jesus is

'the stoneⁿ that you builders rejected,

which has become the cornerstone.'
Psalm 118:22
¹²Jesus is the only One who can save people. No one else in the world is able to save us."

¹³The leaders saw that Peter and John were not afraid to speak, and they understood that these men had no special training or education. So they were amazed. Then they realized that Peter and John had been with Jesus. ¹⁴Because they saw the healed man standing there beside the two apostles, they could say nothing against them. ¹⁵After the leaders ordered them to leave the meeting, they began to talk to each other. ¹⁶They said, "What shall we do with these men? Everyone in Jerusalem knows they have done a great miracle, and we cannot say it is not true. ¹⁷But to keep it from spreading among the people, we must warn them not to talk to people anymore using that name."

¹⁸So they called Peter and John in again and told them not to speak or to teach at all in the name of Jesus. ¹⁹But Peter and John answered them, "You decide what God would want. Should we obey you or God? ²⁰We cannot keep quiet. We must speak about what we have seen and heard." ²¹The leaders warned the apostles again and let them go free. They could not find a way to punish them, because all the people were praising God for what had been done. ²²The man who received the miracle of healing was more than forty years old.

JUNE 20

1 CHRONICLES 3:1—4:43

David's Family

3 These are David's sons who were born in Hebron. The first was Amnon, whose mother was Ahinoam from Jezreel. The second son was Daniel, whose mother was Abigail from Carmel. ²The third son was Absalom, whose mother was Maacah daughter of Talmai, the king of Geshur. The

fourth son was Adonijah, whose mother was Haggith. ³The fifth son was Shephatiah, whose mother was Abital. The sixth son was Ithream, whose mother was Eglah. ⁴These six sons of David were born to him in Hebron, where David ruled for seven and one-half years.

David ruled in Jerusalem thirty-three years. ⁵These were his children who were born in Jerusalem: Shammua, Shobab,

4:11 stone A symbol meaning Jesus.

Nathan, and Solomon—the four children of David and Bathsheba, Ammiel's daughter. ⁶⁻⁸David's other nine children were Ibhar, Elishua, Eliphelet, Nogah, Nepheg, Japhia, Elishama, Eliada, and Eliphelet. ⁹These were all of David's sons, except for those born to his slave women. David also had a daughter named Tamar.

The Kings of Judah

¹⁰Solomon's son was Rehoboam. Rehoboam's son was Abijah. Abijah's son was Asa. Asa's son was Jehoshaphat. ¹¹Jehoshaphat's son was Jehoram. Jehoram's son was Ahaziah. Ahaziah's son was Joash. ¹²Joash's son was Amaziah. Amaziah's son was Azariah. Azariah's son was Jotham. ¹³Jotham's son was Ahaz. Ahaz's son was Hezekiah. Hezekiah's son was Manasseh. ¹⁴Manasseh's son was Amon, and Amon's son was Josiah.

¹⁵These were Josiah's sons: His first son was Johanan, his second was Jehoiakim, his third was Zedekiah, and his fourth was Shallum. ¹⁶Jehoiakim was followed by Jehoiachin, and he was followed by Zedekiah.

David's Descendants After the Babylonian Captivity

¹⁷Jehoiachin was taken as a prisoner. His sons were Shealtiel, ¹⁸Malkiram, Pedaiah, Shenazzar, Jekamiah, Hoshama, and Nedabiah.

¹⁹Pedaiah's sons were Zerubbabel and Shimei.

Zerubbabel's sons were Meshullam and Hananiah, and their sister was Shelomith. ²⁰Zerubbabel also had five other sons: Hashubah, Ohel, Berekiah, Hasadiah, and Jushab-Hesed.

²¹Hananiah's descendants were Pelatiah and Jeshaiah, and the sons of Rephaiah, Arnan, Obadiah, and Shecaniah.

²²Shecaniah's son was Shemaiah. Shemaiah's sons were Hattush, Igal, Bariah, Neariah, and Shaphat. There were six in all.

²³Neariah had three sons: Elioenai, Hizkiah, and Azrikam.

²⁴Elioenai had seven sons: Hodaviah, Eliashib, Pelaiah, Akkub, Johanan, Delaiah, and Anani.

Other Family Groups of Judah

4 Judah's descendants were Perez, Hezron, Carmi, Hur, and Shobal.

²Reaiah was Shobal's son. Reaiah was the father of Jahath, and Jahath was the father of Ahumai and Lahad. They were the family groups of the Zorathite people.

³⁻⁴Hur was the oldest son of Caleb and his wife Ephrathah. Hur was the leader of Bethlehem. His three sons were Etam, Penuel, and Ezer. Etam's sons were Jezreel, Ishma, and Idbash. They had a sister named Hazzelelponi. Penuel was the father of Gedor, and Ezer was the father of Hushah.

⁵Tekoa's father was Ashhur. Ashhur had two wives named Helah and Naarah.

⁶The sons of Ashhur and Naarah were Ahuzzam, Hepher, Temeni, and Haahashtari. These were the descendants of Naarah.

⁷Helah's sons were Zereth, Zohar, Ethnan, ⁸and Koz. Koz was the father of Anub, Hazzobebah, and the Aharhel family group. Aharhel was the son of Harum.

⁹There was a man named Jabez, who was respected more than his brothers. His mother named him Jabez[n] because she said, "I was in much pain when I gave birth to him." ¹⁰Jabez prayed to the God of Israel, "Please do good things for me and give me more land. Stay with me, and don't let anyone hurt me. Then I won't have any pain." And God did what Jabez had asked.

¹¹Kelub, Shuhah's brother, was the father of Mehir. Mehir was the father of Eshton. ¹²Eshton was the father of Beth Rapha, Paseah, and Tehinnah. Tehinnah was the father of the people from the town of Nahash. These people were from Recah.

¹³The sons of Kenaz were Othniel and Seraiah.

Othniel's sons were Hathath and Meonothai. ¹⁴Meonothai was the father of Ophrah.

Seraiah was the father of Joab. Joab was the ancestor of the people from Craftsmen's

---

4:9 Jabez This name in Hebrew sounds like the word for "pain."

Valley, named that because the people living there were craftsmen.

[15]Caleb was Jephunneh's son. Caleb's sons were Iru, Elah, and Naam. Elah's son was Kenaz.

[16]Jehallelel's sons were Ziph, Ziphah, Tiria, and Asarel.

[17-18]Ezrah's sons were Jether, Mered, Epher, and Jalon. Mered married Bithiah, the daughter of the king of Egypt. The children of Mered and Bithiah were Miriam, Shammai, and Ishbah. Ishbah was the father of Eshtemoa. Mered also had a wife from Judah, who gave birth to Jered, Heber, and Jekuthiel. Jered became the father of Gedor. Heber became the father of Soco. And Jekuthiel became the father of Zanoah.

[19]Hodiah's wife was Naham's sister. The sons of Hodiah's wife were Eshtemoa and the father of Keilah. Keilah was from the Garmite people, and Eshtemoa was from the Maacathite people.

[20]Shimon's sons were Amnon, Rinnah, Ben-Hanan, and Tilon.

Ishi's sons were Zoheth and Ben-Zoheth.

[21-22]Shelah was Judah's son. Shelah's sons were Er, Laadah, Jokim, the men from Cozeba, Joash, and Saraph. Er was the father of Lecah. Laadah was the father of Mareshah and the family groups of linen workers at Beth Ashbea. Joash and Saraph ruled in Moab and Jashubi Lehem. The writings about this family are very old. [23]These sons of Shelah were potters. They lived in Netaim and Gederah and worked for the king.

Simeon's Children

[24]Simeon's sons were Nemuel, Jamin, Jarib, Zerah, and Shaul. [25]Shaul's son was Shallum. Shallum's son was Mibsam. Mibsam's son was Mishma.

[26]Mishma's son was Hammuel. Hammuel's son was Zaccur. Zaccur's son was Shimei. [27]Shimei had sixteen sons and six daughters, but his brothers did not have many children, so there were not as many people in their family group as there were in Judah.

[28]Shimei's children lived in Beersheba, Moladah, Hazar Shual, [29]Bilhah, Ezem, Tolad, [30]Bethuel, Hormah, Ziklag, [31]Beth Marcaboth, Hazar Susim, Beth Biri, and Shaaraim. They lived in these cities until David became king. [32]The five villages near these cities were Etam, Ain, Rimmon, Token, and Ashan. [33]There were also other villages as far away as Baalath. This is where they lived. And they wrote the history of their family.

[34-38]The men in this list were leaders of their family groups: Meshobab, Jamlech, Joshah son of Amaziah, Joel, Jehu son of Joshibiah (Joshibiah was the son of Seraiah, who was the son of Asiel), Elioenai, Jaakobah, Jeshohaiah, Asaiah, Adiel, Jesimiel, Benaiah, and Ziza. (Ziza was the son of Shiphi, who was the son of Allon. Allon was the son of Jedaiah, who was the son of Shimri. And Shimri was the son of Shemaiah.)

These families grew very large. [39]They went outside the city of Gedor to the east side of the valley to look for pasture for their flocks. [40]They found good pastures with plenty of grass, and the land was open country and peaceful and quiet. Ham's descendants had lived there in the past.

[41]These men who were listed came to Gedor while Hezekiah was king of Judah. They fought against the Hamites, destroying their tents, and also against the Meunites who lived there, and completely destroyed them. So there are no Meunites there even today. Then these men began to live there, because there was pasture for their flocks. [42]Ishi's sons, Pelatiah, Neariah, Rephaiah, and Uzziel, led five hundred of the Simeonites and attacked the people living in the mountains of Edom. [43]They killed the few Amalekites who were still alive. From that time until now these Simeonites have lived in Edom.

PSALM 76:11–12

[11]Make and keep your promises to the
   LORD your God.
   From all around, gifts should come to
      the God we worship.
[12]God breaks the spirits of great leaders;
   the kings on earth fear him.

PROVERBS 19:8–9

⁸Those who get wisdom do themselves a
favor,
and those who love learning will
succeed.

⁹A witness who lies will not go free,
liars will die.

ACTS 4:23–37

The Believers Pray

²³After Peter and John left the meeting of
leaders, they went to their own group and
told them everything the leading priests and
the elders had said to them. ²⁴When the believers heard this, they prayed to God together, "Lord, you are the One who made the
sky, the earth, the sea, and everything in
them. ²⁵By the Holy Spirit, through our father David your servant, you said:

'Why are the nations so angry?
Why are the people making useless
plans?
²⁶The kings of the earth prepare to fight,
and their leaders make plans together
against the Lord
and his Christ.'   *Psalm 2:1–2*
²⁷These things really happened when Herod,
Pontius Pilate, and some Jews and non-Jews
all came together against Jesus here in
Jerusalem. Jesus is your holy servant, the

One you made to be the Christ. ²⁸These people made your plan happen because of your
power and your will. ²⁹And now, Lord, listen
to their threats. Lord, help us, your servants,
to speak your word without fear. ³⁰Show us
your power to heal. Give proofs and make
miracles happen by the power of Jesus, your
holy servant."

³¹After they had prayed, the place where
they were meeting was shaken. They were all
filled with the Holy Spirit, and they spoke
God's word without fear.

The Believers Share

³²The group of believers were united in
their hearts and spirit. All those in the group
acted as though their private property belonged to everyone in the group. In fact, they
shared everything. ³³With great power the
apostles were telling people that the Lord Jesus was truly raised from the dead. And God
blessed all the believers very much. ³⁴There
were no needy people among them. From
time to time those who owned fields or
houses sold them, brought the money, ³⁵and
gave it to the apostles. Then the money was
given to anyone who needed it.

³⁶One of the believers was named Joseph, a
Levite born in Cyprus. The apostles called him
Barnabas (which means "one who encourages"). ³⁷Joseph owned a field, sold it, brought
the money, and gave it to the apostles.

JUNE 21

1 CHRONICLES 5:1—6:81

Reuben's Children

5 Reuben was Israel's first son. Reuben
should have received the special privileges of the oldest son, but he had sexual relations with his father's slave woman. So
those special privileges were given to
Joseph's sons. (Joseph was a son of Israel.) In
the family history Reuben's name is not
listed as the first son. ²Judah became
stronger than his brothers, and a leader
came from his family. But Joseph's family re-

ceived the privileges that belonged to the
oldest son. ³Reuben was Israel's first son.
Reuben's sons were Hanoch, Pallu, Hezron,
and Carmi.

⁴These were the children of Joel: Shemaiah was Joel's son. Gog was Shemaiah's
son. Shimei was Gog's son. ⁵Micah was
Shimei's son. Reaiah was Micah's son. Baal
was Reaiah's son. ⁶Beerah was Baal's son.
Beerah was a leader of the tribe of Reuben.
Tiglath-Pileser king of Assyria captured him
and took him away.

⁷Joel's brothers and all his family groups

are listed just as they are written in their family histories: Jeiel was the first, then Zechariah, ⁸and Bela. (Bela was the son of Azaz. Azaz was the son of Shema, and Shema was the son of Joel.) They lived in the area of Aroer all the way to Nebo and Baal Meon. ⁹Bela's people lived to the east—as far as the edge of the desert, which is beside the Euphrates River—because they had too many cattle for the land of Gilead.

¹⁰When Saul was king, Bela's people fought a war against the Hagrite people and defeated them. Then Bela's people lived in the tents that had belonged to the Hagrites in all the area east of Gilead.

Gad's Children

¹¹The people from the tribe of Gad lived near the Reubenites. The Gadites lived in the area of Bashan all the way to Salecah. ¹²Joel was the main leader, Shapham was second, and then Janai and Shaphat were leaders in Bashan.

¹³The seven relatives in their families were Michael, Meshullam, Sheba, Jorai, Jacan, Zia, and Eber. ¹⁴They were the descendants of Abihail. Abihail was Huri's son. Huri was Jaroah's son. Jaroah was Gilead's son. Gilead was Michael's son. Michael was Jeshishai's son. Jeshishai was Jahdo's son, and Jahdo was the son of Buz. ¹⁵Ahi was Abdiel's son, and Abdiel was Guni's son. Ahi was the leader of their family.

¹⁶The Gadites lived in Gilead, Bashan and the small towns around it, and on all the pasturelands in the Plain of Sharon all the way to the borders.

¹⁷All these names were written in the family history of Gad during the time Jotham was king of Judah and Jeroboam was king of Israel.

Soldiers Skilled in War

¹⁸There were forty-four thousand seven hundred sixty soldiers from the tribes of Reuben and Gad and East Manasseh who carried shields and swords and bows. They were skilled in war. ¹⁹They started a war against the Hagrites and the people of Jetur, Naphish, and Nodab. ²⁰The men from the tribes of Manasseh, Reuben, and Gad prayed to God during the war, asking him to help them. So he helped them because they trusted him. He handed over to them the Hagrites and all those who were with them. ²¹They took the animals that belonged to the Hagrites: fifty thousand camels, two hundred fifty thousand sheep, and two thousand donkeys. They also captured one hundred thousand people. ²²Many Hagrites were killed because God helped the people of Reuben, Gad, and Manasseh. Then they lived there until Babylon captured them and took them away.

East Manasseh

²³There were many people in East Manasseh, and they lived in the area of Bashan all the way to Baal Hermon, Senir, and Mount Hermon.

²⁴These were the family leaders: Epher, Ishi, Eliel, Azriel, Jeremiah, Hodaviah, and Jahdiel. They were all strong, brave, and famous men, and leaders in their families. ²⁵But they sinned against the God that their ancestors had worshiped. They began worshiping the gods of the people in that land, and those were the people God was destroying. ²⁶So the God of Israel made Pul king of Assyria want to go to war. (Pul was also called Tiglath-Pileser.) He captured the people of Reuben, Gad, and East Manasseh, and he took them away to Halah, Habor, Hara, and near the Gozan River. They have lived there from that time until this day.

Levi's Children

6Levi's sons were Gershon, Kohath, and Merari.

²Kohath's sons were Amram, Izhar, Hebron, and Uzziel.

³Amram's children were Aaron, Moses, and Miriam.

Aaron's sons were Nadab, Abihu, Eleazar, and Ithamar. ⁴Eleazar was the father of Phinehas. Phinehas was the father of Abishua. ⁵Abishua was the father of Bukki. Bukki was the father of Uzzi. ⁶Uzzi was the father of Zerahiah. Zerahiah was the father of Meraioth. ⁷Meraioth was the father of Amariah. Amariah was the father of Ahitub. ⁸Ahitub was the father of Zadok. Zadok was the father of Ahimaaz. ⁹Ahimaaz was the father of Azariah. Azariah was the father of Johanan. ¹⁰Johanan was the father of Azariah. (Azariah was a priest in the Temple Solomon built in Jerusalem.) ¹¹Azariah was the father of Amariah. Amariah was the father of Ahitub. ¹²Ahitub was the father of Zadok. Zadok was the father of Shallum. ¹³Shallum was the father of Hilkiah. Hilkiah was the father of Azariah. ¹⁴Azariah was the father of Seraiah, and Seraiah was the father of Jehozadak.

¹⁵Jehozadak was forced to leave his home when the LORD sent Judah and Jerusalem into captivity under the control of Nebuchadnezzar.

¹⁶Levi's sons were Gershon, Kohath, and Merari.

¹⁷The names of Gershon's sons were Libni and Shimei.

¹⁸Kohath's sons were Amram, Izhar, Hebron, and Uzziel.

¹⁹Merari's sons were Mahli and Mushi.

This is a list of the family groups of Levi, listed by the name of the father of each group. ²⁰Gershon's son was Libni. Libni's son was Jehath. Jehath's son was Zimmah. ²¹Zimmah's son was Joah. Joah's son was Iddo. Iddo's son was Zerah. And Zerah's son was Jeatherai.

²²Kohath's son was Amminadab. Amminadab's son was Korah. Korah's son was Assir. ²³Assir's son was Elkanah. Elkanah's son was Ebiasaph. Ebiasaph's son was Assir. ²⁴Assir's son was Tahath. Tahath's son was Uriel. Uriel's son was Uzziah, and Uzziah's son was Shaul.

²⁵Elkanah's sons were Amasai and Ahimoth. ²⁶Ahimoth's son was Elkanah. Elkanah's son was Zophai. Zophai's son was Nahath. ²⁷Nahath's son was Eliab. Eliab's son was Jeroham. Jeroham's son was Elkanah, and Elkanah's son was Samuel.

²⁸Samuel's sons were Joel, the first son, and Abijah, the second son.

²⁹Merari's son was Mahli. Mahli's son was Libni. Libni's son was Shimei. Shimei's son was Uzzah. ³⁰Uzzah's son was Shimea. Shimea's son was Haggiah, and Haggiah's son was Asaiah.

The Temple Musicians

³¹David chose some people to be in charge of the music in the house of the LORD.

They began their work after the Ark of the Agreement was put there. ³²They served by making music at the Holy Tent (also called the Meeting Tent), and they served until Solomon built the Temple of the LORD in Jerusalem. They followed the rules for their work.

³³These are the musicians and their sons:

From Kohath's family there was Heman the singer. Heman was Joel's son. Joel was Samuel's son. ³⁴Samuel was Elkanah's son. Elkanah was Jeroham's son. Jeroham was Eliel's son. Eliel was Toah's son. ³⁵Toah was Zuph's son. Zuph was Elkanah's son. Elkanah was Mahath's son. Mahath was Amasai's son. ³⁶Amasai was Elkanah's son. Elkanah was Joel's son. Joel was Azariah's son. Azariah was Zephaniah's son. ³⁷Zephaniah was Tahath's son. Tahath was Assir's son. Assir was Ebiasaph's son. Ebiasaph was Korah's son. ³⁸Korah was Izhar's son. Izhar was Kohath's son. Kohath was Levi's son. Levi was Israel's son.

³⁹There was Heman's helper Asaph, whose group stood by Heman's right side. Asaph was Berekiah's son. Berekiah was Shimea's son. ⁴⁰Shimea was Michael's son. Michael was Baaseiah's son. Baaseiah was Malkijah's son. ⁴¹Malkijah was Ethni's son. Ethni was Zerah's son. Zerah was Adaiah's son. ⁴²Adaiah was Ethan's son. Ethan was Zimmah's son. Zimmah was Shimei's son. ⁴³Shimei was Jahath's son. Jahath was Gershon's son, and Gershon was Levi's son.

⁴⁴Merari's family were the helpers of Heman and Asaph, and they stood by Heman's left side. In this group was Ethan son of Kishi. Kishi was Abdi's son. Abdi was Malluch's son. ⁴⁵Malluch was Hashabiah's son. Hashabiah was Amaziah's son. Amaziah was Hilkiah's son. ⁴⁶Hilkiah was Amzi's son. Amzi was Bani's son. Bani was Shemer's son. ⁴⁷Shemer was Mahli's son. Mahli was Mushi's son. Mushi was Merari's son, and Merari was Levi's son.

⁴⁸The other Levites served by doing their own special work in the Holy Tent, the house of God. ⁴⁹Aaron and his descendants offered the sacrifices on the altar of burnt offering and burned the incense on the altar of incense. They offered the sacrifices that

removed the Israelites' sins so they could belong to God. They did all the work in the Most Holy Place and followed all the laws that Moses, God's servant, had commanded.

[50]These were Aaron's sons: Eleazar was Aaron's son. Phinehas was Eleazar's son. Abishua was Phinehas' son. [51]Bukki was Abishua's son. Uzzi was Bukki's son. Zerahiah was Uzzi's son. [52]Meraioth was Zerahiah's son. Amariah was Meraioth's son. Ahitub was Amariah's son. [53]Zadok was Ahitub's son, and Ahimaaz was Zadok's son.

Land for the Levites

[54]These are the places where Aaron's descendants lived. His descendants from the Kohath family group received the first share of the land.

[55]They were given the city of Hebron in Judah and the pastures around it, [56]but the fields farther from the city and the villages near Hebron were given to Caleb son of Jephunneh. [57]So the descendants of Aaron were given Hebron, one of the cities of safety. They also received the towns and pastures of Libnah, Jattir, Eshtemoa, [58]Hilen, Debir, [59]Ashan, Juttah, and Beth Shemesh. [60]They also received these towns and pastures from the tribe of Benjamin: Gibeon, Geba, Alemeth, and Anathoth.

The Kohath family groups received a total of thirteen towns.

[61]The rest of the Kohath family group was given ten towns from the family groups of West Manasseh. The towns were chosen by throwing lots.

[62]The Gershon family group received thirteen towns from the tribes of Issachar, Asher, Naphtali, and the part of Manasseh living in Bashan.

[63]The Merari family group received twelve towns from the tribes of Reuben, Gad, and Zebulun. Those towns were chosen by throwing lots.

[64]So the Israelites gave these towns and their pastures to the Levites. [65]The towns from the tribes of Judah, Simeon, and Benjamin, which were named, were chosen by throwing lots.

[66]Some of the Kohath family groups received towns and pastures from the tribe of Ephraim. [67]They received Shechem, one of the cities of safety,[n] with its pastures in the mountains of Ephraim. They also received the towns and pastures of Gezer, [68]Jokmeam, Beth Horon, [69]Aijalon, and Gath Rimmon.

[70]The rest of the people in the Kohath family group received the towns of Aner and Bileam and their pastures from West Manasseh.

[71]From East Manasseh, the Gershon family received the towns and pastures of Golan in Bashan and Ashtaroth.

[72-73]From the tribe of Issachar, the Gershon family received the towns and pastures of Kedesh, Daberath, Ramoth, and Anem.

[74-75]From the tribe of Asher, the Gershon family received the towns and pastures of Mashal, Abdon, Hukok, and Rehob.

[76]From the tribe of Naphtali, the Gershon family received the towns and pastures of Kedesh in Galilee, Hammon, and Kiriathaim.

[77]The rest of the Levites, the people from the Merari family, received from the tribe of Zebulun the towns and pastures of Jokneam, Kartah, Rimmono, and Tabor.

[78-79]From the tribe of Reuben, the Merari family received the towns and pastures of Bezer in the desert, Jahzah, Kedemoth, and Mephaath. (The tribe of Reuben lived east of the Jordan River, across from Jericho.)

[80-81]From the tribe of Gad, the Merari family received the towns and pastures of Ramoth in Gilead, Mahanaim, Heshbon, and Jazer.

PSALM 77:1–3

Remembering God's Help

For the director of music. For Jeduthun. A psalm of Asaph.

77 I cry out to God;
I call to God, and he will hear me.
[2]I look for the Lord on the day of trouble.
All night long I reach out my hands,
but I cannot be comforted.
[3]When I remember God, I become upset;
when I think, I become afraid. *Selah*

6:67 cities of safety A person who had accidentally killed someone could go to one of the six cities of safety to receive protection and a fair trial.

PROVERBS 19:10–12

¹⁰A fool should not live in luxury.
   A slave should not rule over princes.

¹¹The wise are patient;
   they will be honored if they ignore
   insults.

¹²An angry king is like a roaring lion,
   but his kindness is like the dew on the
   grass.

ACTS 5:1–16

Ananias and Sapphira Die

5 But a man named Ananias and his wife Sapphira sold some land. ²He kept back part of the money for himself; his wife knew about this and agreed to it. But he brought the rest of the money and gave it to the apostles. ³Peter said, "Ananias, why did you let Satan rule your thoughts to lie to the Holy Spirit and to keep for yourself part of the money you received for the land? ⁴Before you sold the land, it belonged to you. And even after you sold it, you could have used the money any way you wanted. Why did you think of doing this? You lied to God, not to us!" ⁵⁻⁶When Ananias heard this, he fell down and died. Some young men came in, wrapped up his body, carried it out, and buried it. And everyone who heard about this was filled with fear.

⁷About three hours later his wife came in, but she did not know what had happened. ⁸Peter said to her, "Tell me, was the money you got for your field this much?"

Sapphira answered, "Yes, that was the price."

⁹Peter said to her, "Why did you and your husband agree to test the Spirit of the Lord? Look! The men who buried your husband are at the door, and they will carry you out." ¹⁰At that moment Sapphira fell down by his feet and died. When the young men came in and saw that she was dead, they carried her out and buried her beside her husband. ¹¹The whole church and all the others who heard about these things were filled with fear.

The Apostles Heal Many

¹²The apostles did many signs and miracles among the people. And they would all meet together on Solomon's Porch. ¹³None of the others dared to join them, but all the people respected them. ¹⁴More and more men and women believed in the Lord and were added to the group of believers. ¹⁵The people placed their sick on beds and mats in the streets, hoping that when Peter passed by at least his shadow might fall on them. ¹⁶Crowds came from all the towns around Jerusalem, bringing their sick and those who were bothered by evil spirits, and all of them were healed.

JUNE 22

1 CHRONICLES 7:1—9:1a

Issachar's Children

7 Issachar had four sons: Tola, Puah, Jashub, and Shimron.
   ²Tola's sons were Uzzi, Rephaiah, Jeriel, Jahmai, Ibsam, and Samuel, and they were leaders of their families. In the family history of Tola's descendants, twenty-two thousand six hundred men were listed as fighting men during the time David was king.
   ³Uzzi's son was Izrahiah.
   Izrahiah's sons were Michael, Obadiah,

Joel, and Isshiah. All five of them were leaders. ⁴Their family history shows they had thirty-six thousand men ready to serve in the army, because they had many wives and children.
   ⁵The records of the family groups of Issachar show there were eighty-seven thousand fighting men.

Benjamin's Children

⁶Benjamin had three sons: Bela, Beker, and Jediael.
   ⁷Bela had five sons: Ezbon, Uzzi, Uzziel,

Jerimoth, and Iri, and they were leaders of their families. Their family history shows they had twenty-two thousand thirty-four fighting men.

[8]Beker's sons were Zemirah, Joash, Eliezer, Elioenai, Omri, Jeremoth, Abijah, Anathoth, and Alemeth. They all were Beker's sons. [9]Their family history listed the family leaders and twenty thousand two hundred fighting men.

[10]Jediael's son was Bilhan.

Bilhan's sons were Jeush, Benjamin, Ehud, Kenaanah, Zethan, Tarshish, and Ahishahar. [11]All these sons of Jediael were leaders of their families. They had seventeen thousand two hundred fighting men ready to serve in the army.

[12]The Shuppites and Huppites were descendants of Ir, and the Hushites were descendants of Aher.

Naphtali's Children

[13]Naphtali's sons were Jahziel, Guni, Jezer, and Shillem. They were Bilhah's grandsons.

Manasseh's Children

[14]These are Manasseh's descendants. Manasseh had an Aramean slave woman, who was the mother of Asriel and Makir. Makir was Gilead's father. [15]Makir took a wife from the Huppites and Shuppites. His sister was named Maacah. His second son was named Zelophehad, and he had only daughters. [16]Makir's wife Maacah had a son whom she named Peresh. Peresh's brother was named Sheresh. Sheresh's sons were Ulam and Rakem.

[17]Ulam's son was Bedan.

These were the sons of Gilead, who was the son of Makir. Makir was Manasseh's son. [18]Makir's sister Hammoleketh gave birth to Ishhod, Abiezer, and Mahlah.

[19]The sons of Shemida were Ahian, Shechem, Likhi, and Aniam.

Ephraim's Children

[20]These are the names of Ephraim's descendants. Ephraim's son was Shuthelah. Shuthelah's son was Bered. Bered's son was Tahath. Tahath's son was Eleadah. Eleadah's

son was Tahath. [21]Tahath's son was Zabad. Zabad's son was Shuthelah.

Ezer and Elead went to Gath to steal cows and sheep and were killed by some men who grew up in that city. [22]Their father Ephraim cried for them many days, and his family came to comfort him. [23]Then he had sexual relations with his wife again. She became pregnant and gave birth to a son whom Ephraim named Beriah[n] because of the trouble that had happened to his family. [24]Ephraim's daughter was Sheerah. She built Lower Beth Horon, Upper Beth Horon, and Uzzen Sheerah.

[25]Rephah was Ephraim's son. Resheph was Rephah's son. Telah was Resheph's son. Tahan was Telah's son. [26]Ladan was Tahan's son. Ammihud was Ladan's son. Elishama was Ammihud's son. [27]Nun was Elishama's son, and Joshua was the son of Nun.

[28]Ephraim's descendants lived in these lands and towns: Bethel and the villages near it, Naaran on the east, Gezer and the villages near it on the west, and Shechem and the villages near it. These villages went all the way to Ayyah and its villages. [29]Along the borders of Manasseh's land were the towns of Beth Shan, Taanach, Megiddo, and Dor, and the villages near them. The descendants of Joseph son of Israel lived in these towns.

Asher's Children

[30]Asher's sons were Imnah, Ishvah, Ishvi, and Beriah. Their sister was Serah.

[31]Beriah's sons were Heber and Malkiel. Malkiel was Birzaith's father.

[32]Heber was the father of Japhlet, Shomer, Hotham, and their sister Shua.

[33]Japhlet's sons were Pasach, Bimhal, and Ashvath. They were Japhlet's children.

[34]Japhlet's brother was Shomer. Shomer's sons were Rohgah, Hubbah, and Aram.

[35]Shomer's brother was Hotham. Hotham's sons were Zophah, Imna, Shelesh, and Amal.

[36]Zophah's sons were Suah, Harnepher, Shual, Beri, Imrah, [37]Bezer, Hod, Shamma, Shilshah, Ithran, and Beera.

[38]Jether's sons were Jephunneh, Pispah, and Ara.

7:23 Beriah This name sounds like the Hebrew word for "trouble."

[39]Ulla's sons were Arah, Hanniel, and Rizia. [40]All these men were descendants of Asher and leaders of their families. They were powerful warriors and outstanding leaders. Their family history lists that they had twenty-six thousand soldiers ready to serve in the army.

The Family History of King Saul

8 Benjamin was the father of Bela, his first son. Ashbel was his second son, Aharah was his third, [2]Nohah was his fourth, and Rapha was his fifth son.

[3]Bela's sons were Addar, Gera, Abihud, [4]Abishua, Naaman, Ahoah, [5]Gera, Shephuphan, and Huram.

[6]These were the descendants of Ehud and leaders of their families in Geba. They were forced to move to Manahath. [7]Ehud's descendants were Naaman, Ahijah, and Gera. Gera forced them to leave. He was the father of Uzza and Ahihud.

[8-11]Shaharaim and his wife Hushim had sons named Abitub and Elpaal. In Moab, Shaharaim divorced his wives Hushim and Baara. Shaharaim and his wife Hodesh had these sons: Jobab, Zibia, Mesha, Malcam, Jeuz, Sakia, and Mirmah. They were leaders of their families.

[12-13]Elpaal's sons were Eber, Misham, Shemed, Beriah, and Shema. Shemed built the towns of Ono and Lod and the villages around them. Beriah and Shema were leaders of the families living in Aijalon, and they forced out the people who lived in Gath.

[14]Beriah's sons were Ahio, Shashak, Jeremoth, [15]Zebadiah, Arad, Eder, [16]Michael, Ishpah, and Joha.

[17]Elpaal's sons were Zebadiah, Meshullam, Hizki, Heber, [18]Ishmerai, Izliah, and Jobab.

[19]Shimei's sons were Jakim, Zicri, Zabdi, [20]Elienai, Zillethai, Eliel, [21]Adaiah, Beraiah, and Shimrath.

[22]Shashak's sons were Ishpan, Eber, Eliel, [23]Abdon, Zicri, Hanan, [24]Hananiah, Elam, Anthothijah, [25]Iphdeiah, and Penuel.

[26]Jeroham's sons were Shamsherai, Shehariah, Athaliah, [27]Jaareshiah, Elijah, and Zicri.

[28]The family histories show that all these men were leaders of their families and lived in Jerusalem.

[29]Jeiel lived in the town of Gibeon, where he was the leader. His wife was named Maacah. [30]Jeiel's first son was Abdon. His other sons were Zur, Kish, Baal, Ner, Nadab, [31]Gedor, Ahio, Zeker, [32]and Mikloth. Mikloth was the father of Shimeah. These sons also lived near their relatives in Jerusalem.

[33]Ner was the father of Kish. Kish was the father of Saul, and Saul was the father of Jonathan, Malki-Shua, Abinadab, and Esh-Baal.

[34]Jonathan's son was Merib-Baal, who was the father of Micah.

[35]Micah's sons were Pithon, Melech, Tarea, and Ahaz. [36]Ahaz was the father of Jehoaddah. Jehoaddah was the father of Alemeth, Azmaveth, and Zimri. Zimri was the father of Moza. [37]Moza was the father of Binea. Raphah was Binea's son. Eleasah was Raphah's son, and Azel was Eleasah's son.

[38]Azel had six sons: Azrikam, Bokeru, Ishmael, Sheariah, Obadiah, and Hanan. All these were Azel's sons.

[39]Azel's brother was Eshek. Eshek's first son was Ulam, his second was Jeush, and Eliphelet was his third. [40]Ulam's sons were mighty warriors and good archers. They had many sons and grandsons—one hundred fifty of them in all.

All these men were Benjamin's descendants.

9 The names of all the people of Israel were listed in their family histories, and those family histories were put in the book of the kings of Israel.

PSALM 77:4–10

[4]You keep my eyes from closing.
   I am too upset to say anything.
[5]I keep thinking about the old days,
   the years of long ago.
[6]At night I remember my songs.
   I think and I ask myself:
[7]"Will the Lord reject us forever?
   Will he never be kind to us again?
[8]Is his love gone forever?
   Has he stopped speaking for all time?
[9]Has God forgotten mercy?
   Is he too angry to pity us?"   *Selah*

¹⁰Then I say, "This is what makes me sad:
For years the power of God Most High
was with us."

PROVERBS 19:13–14

¹³A foolish child brings disaster to a father,
and a quarreling wife is like dripping
water.

¹⁴Houses and wealth are inherited from
parents,
but a wise wife is a gift from the LORD.

ACTS 5:17–42

Leaders Try to Stop the Apostles

¹⁷The high priest and all his friends (a
group called the Sadducees) became very
jealous. ¹⁸They took the apostles and put
them in jail. ¹⁹But during the night, an angel
of the Lord opened the doors of the jail and
led the apostles outside. The angel said,
²⁰"Go stand in the Temple and tell the people
everything about this new life." ²¹When the
apostles heard this, they obeyed and went
into the Temple early in the morning and
continued teaching.

When the high priest and his friends arrived, they called a meeting of the leaders
and all the important elders. They sent some
men to the jail to bring the apostles to them.
²²But, upon arriving, the officers could not
find the apostles. So they went back and reported to the leaders. ²³They said, "The jail
was closed and locked, and the guards were
standing at the doors. But when we opened
the doors, the jail was empty!" ²⁴Hearing
this, the captain of the Temple guards and
the leading priests were confused and wondered what was happening.

²⁵Then someone came and told them,
"Listen! The men you put in jail are standing
in the Temple teaching the people." ²⁶Then
the captain and his men went out and
brought the apostles back. But the soldiers
did not use force, because they were afraid
the people would stone them to death.

²⁷The soldiers brought the apostles to the
meeting and made them stand before the
leaders. The high priest questioned them,

²⁸saying, "We gave you strict orders not to
continue teaching in that name. But look,
you have filled Jerusalem with your teaching
and are trying to make us responsible for
this man's death."

²⁹Peter and the other apostles answered,
"We must obey God, not human authority!
³⁰You killed Jesus by hanging him on a cross.
But God, the God of our ancestors, raised Jesus up from the dead! ³¹Jesus is the One
whom God raised to be on his right side, as
Leader and Savior. Through him, all people
could change their hearts and lives and have
their sins forgiven. ³²We saw all these things
happen. The Holy Spirit, whom God has
given to all who obey him, also proves these
things are true."

³³When the leaders heard this, they became angry and wanted to kill them. ³⁴But a
Pharisee named Gamaliel stood up in the
meeting. He was a teacher of the law, and all
the people respected him. He ordered the
apostles to leave the meeting for a little
while. ³⁵Then he said, "People of Israel, be
careful what you are planning to do to these
men. ³⁶Remember when Theudas appeared?
He said he was a great man, and about four
hundred men joined him. But he was killed,
and all his followers were scattered; they
were able to do nothing. ³⁷Later, a man
named Judas came from Galilee at the time
of the registration.[n] He also led a group of
followers and was killed, and all his followers were scattered. ³⁸And so now I tell you:
Stay away from these men, and leave them
alone. If their plan comes from human authority, it will fail. ³⁹But if it is from God, you
will not be able to stop them. You might even
be fighting against God himself!"

The leaders agreed with what Gamaliel
said. ⁴⁰They called the apostles in, beat them,
and told them not to speak in the name of
Jesus again. Then they let them go free. ⁴¹The
apostles left the meeting full of joy because
they were given the honor of suffering disgrace for Jesus. ⁴²Every day in the Temple
and in people's homes they continued teaching the people and telling the Good News—
that Jesus is the Christ.

5:37 registration Census. A counting of all the people and the things they own.

JUNE 23

1 CHRONICLES 9:1b—10:14

The People in Jerusalem

The people of Judah were captured and forced to go to Babylon, because they were not faithful to God. ²The first people to come back and live in their own lands and towns were some Israelites, priests, Levites, and Temple servants.

³People from the tribes of Judah, Benjamin, Ephraim, and Manasseh lived in Jerusalem. This is a list of those people.

⁴There was Uthai son of Ammihud. (Ammihud was Omri's son. Omri was Imri's son. Imri was Bani's son. Bani was a descendant of Perez, and Perez was Judah's son.)

⁵Of the Shilonite people there were Asaiah and his sons. Asaiah was the oldest son in his family.

⁶Of the Zerahite people there were Jeuel and other relatives of Zerah. There were six hundred ninety of them in all.

⁷From the tribe of Benjamin there was Sallu son of Meshullam. (Meshullam was Hodaviah's son, and Hodaviah was Hassenuah's son.) ⁸There was also Ibneiah son of Jeroham and Elah son of Uzzi. (Uzzi was Micri's son.) And there was Meshullam son of Shephatiah. (Shephatiah was Reuel's son, and Reuel was Ibnijah's son.) ⁹The family history of Benjamin lists nine hundred fifty-six people living in Jerusalem, and all these were leaders of their families.

¹⁰Of the priests there were Jedaiah, Jehoiarib, Jakin, and ¹¹Azariah son of Hilkiah. (Hilkiah was Meshullam's son. Meshullam was Zadok's son. Zadok was Meraioth's son. Meraioth was Ahitub's son. Ahitub was the officer responsible for the Temple of God.) ¹²Also there was Adaiah son of Jeroham. (Jeroham was Pashhur's son, and Pashhur was Malkijah's son.) And there was Maasai son of Adiel. (Adiel was Jahzerah's son. Jahzerah was Meshullam's son. Meshullam was Meshillemith's son, and Meshillemith was Immer's son.) ¹³There were one thousand seven hundred sixty priests. They were leaders of their families, and they were responsible for serving in the Temple of God.

¹⁴Of the Levites there was Shemaiah son of Hasshub. (Hasshub was Azrikam's son, and Azrikam was Hashabiah's son. Hashabiah was from the family of Merari.) ¹⁵There were also Bakbakkar, Heresh, Galal, and Mattaniah son of Mica. (Mica was Zicri's son, and Zicri was Asaph's son.) ¹⁶There was also Obadiah son of Shemaiah. (Shemaiah was Galal's son, and Galal was Jeduthun's son.) And there was Berekiah son of Asa. (Asa was the son of Elkanah, who lived in the villages of the Netophathites.)

¹⁷Of the gatekeepers there were Shallum, Akkub, Talmon, Ahiman, and their relatives. Shallum was their leader. ¹⁸These gatekeepers from the tribe of Levi still stand next to the King's Gate on the east side of the city. ¹⁹Shallum was Kore's son. Kore was Ebiasaph's son, and Ebiasaph was Korah's son. Shallum and his relatives from the family of Korah were gatekeepers and were responsible for guarding the gates of the Temple. Their ancestors had also been responsible for guarding the entrance to the Temple of the LORD. ²⁰In the past Phinehas, Eleazar's son, was in charge of the gatekeepers, and the LORD was with Phinehas. ²¹Zechariah son of Meshelemiah was the gatekeeper at the entrance to the Temple.

²²In all, two hundred twelve men were chosen to guard the gates, and their names were written in their family histories in their villages. David and Samuel the seer chose these men because they were dependable. ²³The gatekeepers and their descendants had to guard the gates of the Temple of the LORD. (The Temple took the place of the Holy Tent.) ²⁴There were gatekeepers on all four sides of the Temple: east, west, north, and south. ²⁵The gatekeepers' relatives who lived in the villages had to come and help them at times. Each time they came they helped the gatekeepers

for seven days. ²⁶Because they were dependable, four gatekeepers were made the leaders of all the gatekeepers. They were Levites, and they were responsible for the rooms and treasures in the Temple of God. ²⁷They stayed up all night guarding the Temple of God, and they opened it every morning.

²⁸Some of the gatekeepers were responsible for the utensils used in the Temple services. They counted these utensils when people took them out and when they brought them back. ²⁹Other gatekeepers were chosen to take care of the furniture and utensils in the Holy Place. They also took care of the flour, wine, oil, incense, and spices, ³⁰but some of the priests took care of mixing the spices. ³¹There was a Levite named Mattithiah who was dependable and had the job of baking the bread used for the offerings. He was the first son of Shallum, who was from the family of Korah. ³²Some of the gatekeepers from the Kohath family had the job of preparing the special bread that was put on the table every Sabbath day.

³³Some of the Levites were musicians in the Temple. The leaders of these families stayed in the rooms of the Temple. Since they were on duty day and night, they did not do other work in the Temple.

³⁴These are the leaders of the Levite families. Their names were listed in their family histories, and they lived in Jerusalem.

The Family History of King Saul

³⁵Jeiel lived in the town of Gibeon, where he was the leader. His wife was named Maacah. ³⁶Jeiel's first son was Abdon. His other sons were Zur, Kish, Baal, Ner, Nadab, ³⁷Gedor, Ahio, Zechariah, and Mikloth. ³⁸Mikloth was Shimeam's father. Jeiel's family lived near their relatives in Jerusalem.

³⁹Ner was Kish's father. Kish was Saul's father. Saul was the father of Jonathan, Malki-Shua, Abinadab, and Esh-Baal.

⁴⁰Jonathan's son was Merib-Baal, who was the father of Micah.

⁴¹Micah's sons were Pithon, Melech, Tahrea, and Ahaz. ⁴²Ahaz was Jadah's father. Jadah was the father of Alemeth, Azmaveth, and Zimri. Zimri was Moza's father. ⁴³Moza was Binea's father. Rephaiah was Binea's son. Eleasah was Rephaiah's son, and Azel was Eleasah's son.

⁴⁴Azel had six sons: Azrikam, Bokeru, Ishmael, Sheariah, Obadiah, and Hanan. They were Azel's sons.

The Death of King Saul

10The Philistines fought against Israel, and the Israelites ran away from them. Many Israelites were killed on Mount Gilboa. ²The Philistines fought hard against Saul and his sons, killing his sons Jonathan, Abinadab, and Malki-Shua. ³The fighting was heavy around Saul, and the archers shot him with their arrows and wounded him.

⁴Then Saul said to the officer who carried his armor, "Pull out your sword and stab me. If you don't, these Philistines who are not circumcised will come and hurt me." But Saul's officer refused, because he was afraid. So Saul took his own sword and threw himself on it. ⁵When the officer saw that Saul was dead, he threw himself on his own sword and died. ⁶So Saul and three of his sons died; all his family died together.

⁷When the Israelites living in the valley saw that their army had run away and that Saul and his sons were dead, they left their towns and ran away. Then the Philistines came and settled in them.

⁸The next day when the Philistines came to strip the dead soldiers, they found Saul and his sons dead on Mount Gilboa. ⁹The Philistines stripped Saul's body and took his head and his armor. Then they sent messengers through all their country to tell the news to their idols and to their people. ¹⁰The Philistines put Saul's armor in the temple of their idols and hung his head in the temple of Dagon.

¹¹All the people in Jabesh Gilead heard what the Philistines had done to Saul. ¹²So the brave men of Jabesh went and got the bodies of Saul and his sons and brought

them to Jabesh. They buried their bones under the large tree in Jabesh. Then the people of Jabesh fasted for seven days.

¹³Saul died because he was not faithful to the LORD and did not obey the LORD. He even went to a medium and asked her for advice ¹⁴instead of asking the LORD. This is why the LORD put Saul to death and gave the kingdom to Jesse's son David.

PSALM 77:11–15

¹¹I remember what the LORD did;
 I remember the miracles you did long
 ago.
¹²I think about all the things you did
 and consider your deeds.

¹³God, your ways are holy.
 No god is as great as our God.
¹⁴You are the God who does miracles;
 you have shown people your power.
¹⁵By your power you have saved your
 people,
 the descendants of Jacob and Joseph.

Selah

PROVERBS 19:15–16

¹⁵Lazy people sleep a lot,
 and idle people will go hungry.

¹⁶Those who obey the commands protect
 themselves,
 but those who are careless will die.

ACTS 6:1–15

Seven Leaders Are Chosen

6 The number of followers was growing. But during this same time, the Greek-speaking followers had an argument with the other followers. The Greek-speaking widows were not getting their share of the food that was given out every day. ²The twelve apostles called the whole group of followers together and said, "It is not right for us to stop our work of teaching God's word in order to serve tables. ³So, brothers and sisters, choose seven of your own men who are good, full of the Spirit and full of wisdom. We will put them in charge of this work. ⁴Then we can continue to pray and to teach the word of God."

⁵The whole group liked the idea, so they chose these seven men: Stephen (a man with great faith and full of the Holy Spirit), Philip,ⁿ Procorus, Nicanor, Timon, Parmenas, and Nicolas (a man from Antioch who had become a follower of the Jewish religion). ⁶Then they put these men before the apostles, who prayed and laid their handsⁿ on them.

⁷The word of God was continuing to spread. The group of followers in Jerusalem increased, and a great number of the Jewish priests believed and obeyed.

Stephen Is Accused

⁸Stephen was richly blessed by God who gave him the power to do great miracles and signs among the people. ⁹But some people were against him. They belonged to the synagogue of Free Menⁿ (as it was called), which included people from Cyrene, Alexandria, Cilicia, and Asia. They all came and argued with Stephen.

¹⁰But the Spirit was helping him to speak with wisdom, and his words were so strong that they could not argue with him. ¹¹So they secretly urged some men to say, "We heard Stephen speak against Moses and against God."

¹²This upset the people, the elders, and the teachers of the law. They came and grabbed Stephen and brought him to a meeting of the leaders. ¹³They brought in some people to tell lies about Stephen, saying, "This man is always speaking against this holy place and the law of Moses. ¹⁴We heard him say that Jesus from Nazareth will destroy this place and that Jesus will change the customs Moses gave us." ¹⁵All the people in the meeting were watching Stephen closely and saw that his face looked like the face of an angel.

6:5 Philip Not the apostle named Philip. **6:6 laid their hands** The laying on of hands had many purposes, including the giving of a blessing, power, or authority. **6:9 Free Men** Jewish people who had been slaves or whose fathers had been slaves, but were now free.

JUNE 24

1 CHRONICLES 11:1—12:40

David Becomes King

11 Then the people of Israel came to David at the town of Hebron and said, "Look, we are your own family. ²Even when Saul was king, you were the one who led Israel in battle. The LORD your God said to you, 'You will be the shepherd for my people Israel. You will be their leader.'"

³So all the elders of Israel came to King David at Hebron. He made an agreement with them in Hebron in the presence of the LORD. Then they poured oil on David to make him king over Israel. The LORD had promised through Samuel that this would happen.

David Captures Jerusalem

⁴David and all the Israelites went to the city of Jerusalem. At that time Jerusalem was called Jebus, and the people living there were named Jebusites. ⁵They said to David, "You can't get inside our city." But David did take the city of Jerusalem with its strong walls, and it became the City of David.

⁶David had said, "The person who leads the attack against the Jebusites will become the commander over all my army." Joab son of Zeruiah led the attack, so he became the commander of the army.

⁷Then David made his home in the strong, walled city, which is why it was named the City of David. ⁸David rebuilt the city, beginning where the land was filled in and going to the wall that was around the city. Joab repaired the other parts of the city. ⁹David became stronger and stronger, and the LORD All-Powerful was with him.

David's Mighty Warriors

¹⁰This is a list of the leaders over David's warriors who helped make David's kingdom strong. All the people of Israel also supported David's kingdom. These heroes and all the people of Israel made David king, just as the LORD had promised.

¹¹This is a list of David's warriors:

Jashobeam was from the Hacmonite people. He was the head of the Three,[n] David's most powerful soldiers. He used his spear to fight three hundred men at one time, and he killed them all.

¹²Next was Eleazar, one of the Three. Eleazar was Dodai's son from the Ahohite people. ¹³Eleazar was with David at Pas Dammim when the Philistines came there to fight. There was a field of barley at that place. The Israelites ran away from the Philistines, ¹⁴but they stopped in the middle of that field and fought for it and killed the Philistines. The LORD gave them a great victory.

¹⁵Once, three of the Thirty, David's chief soldiers, came down to him at the rock by the cave near Adullam. At the same time the Philistine army had camped in the Valley of Rephaim.

¹⁶At that time David was in a stronghold, and some of the Philistines were in Bethlehem. ¹⁷David had a strong desire for some water. He said, "Oh, I wish someone would get me water from the well near the city gate of Bethlehem!" ¹⁸So the Three broke through the Philistine army and took water from the well near the city gate in Bethlehem. Then they brought it to David, but he refused to drink it. He poured it out before the LORD, ¹⁹saying, "May God keep me from drinking this water! It would be like drinking the blood of the men who risked their lives to bring it to me!" So David refused to drink it.

These were the brave things that the three warriors did.

²⁰Abishai brother of Joab was the captain of the Three. Abishai fought three hundred soldiers with his spear and killed them. He became as famous as the Three ²¹and was more honored than the Three. He became their commander even though he was not one of them.

²²Benaiah son of Jehoiada was a brave fighter from Kabzeel who did mighty things.

11:11 Three Or maybe "Thirty." These were David's most powerful soldiers. See 2 Samuel 23:8.

He killed two of the best warriors from Moab. He also went down into a pit and killed a lion on a snowy day. ²³Benaiah killed an Egyptian who was about seven and one-half feet tall and had a spear as large as a weaver's rod. Benaiah had a club, but he grabbed the spear from the Egyptian's hand and killed him with his own spear. ²⁴These were the things Benaiah son of Jehoiada did. He was as famous as the Three. ²⁵He received more honor than the Thirty, but he did not become a member of the Three. David made him leader of his bodyguards.

The Thirty Chief Soldiers

²⁶These were also mighty warriors:
Asahel brother of Joab;
Elhanan son of Dodo from Bethlehem;
²⁷Shammoth the Harorite;
Helez the Pelonite;
²⁸Ira son of Ikkesh from Tekoa;
Abiezer the Anathothite;
²⁹Sibbecai the Hushathite;
Ilai the Ahohite;
³⁰Maharai the Netophathite;
Heled son of Baanah the Netophathite;
³¹Ithai son of Ribai from Gibeah in Benjamin;
Benaiah the Pirathonite;
³²Hurai from the ravines of Gaash;
Abiel the Arbathite;
³³Azmaveth the Baharumite;
Eliahba the Shaalbonite;
³⁴the sons of Hashem the Gizonite;
Jonathan son of Shagee the Hararite;
³⁵Ahiam son of Sacar the Hararite;
Eliphal son of Ur;
³⁶Hepher the Mekerathite;
Ahijah the Pelonite;
³⁷Hezro the Carmelite;
Naarai son of Ezbai;
³⁸Joel brother of Nathan;
Mibhar son of Hagri;
³⁹Zelek the Ammonite;
Naharai the Berothite, the officer who carried the armor for Joab son of Zeruiah;
⁴⁰Ira the Ithrite;
Gareb the Ithrite;

⁴¹Uriah the Hittite;
Zabad son of Ahlai;
⁴²Adina son of Shiza the Reubenite, who was the leader of the Reubenites, and his thirty soldiers;
⁴³Hanan son of Maacah;
Joshaphat the Mithnite;
⁴⁴Uzzia the Ashterathite;
Shama and Jeiel sons of Hotham the Aroerite;
⁴⁵Jediael son of Shimri;
Joha, Jediael's brother, the Tizite;
⁴⁶Eliel the Mahavite;
Jeribai and Joshaviah, Elnaam's sons;
Ithmah the Moabite;
⁴⁷Eliel, Obed, and Jaasiel the Mezobaites.

Warriors Join David

12These were the men who came to David at Ziklag when David was hiding from Saul son of Kish. They were among the warriors who helped David in battle. ²They came with bows for weapons and could use either their right or left hands to shoot arrows or to sling rocks. They were Saul's relatives from the tribe of Benjamin. ³Ahiezer was their leader, and there was Joash. (Ahiezer and Joash were sons of Shemaah, who was from the town of Gibeah.) There were also Jeziel and Pelet, the sons of Azmaveth. There were Beracah and Jehu from the town of Anathoth. ⁴And there was Ishmaiah from the town of Gibeon; he was one of the Thirty. In fact, he was the leader of the Thirty. There were Jeremiah, Jahaziel, Johanan, and Jozabad from Gederah. ⁵There were Eluzai, Jerimoth, Bealiah, and Shemariah. There was Shephatiah from Haruph. ⁶There were Elkanah, Isshiah, Azarel, Joezer, and Jashobeam from the family group of Korah. ⁷And there were Joelah and Zebadiah, the sons of Jeroham, from the town of Gedor.

⁸Part of the people of Gad joined David at his stronghold in the desert. They were brave warriors trained for war and skilled with shields and spears. They were as fierce as lions and as fast as gazelles over the hills.

⁹Ezer was the leader of Gad's army, and Obadiah was second in command. Eliab was third, ¹⁰Mishmannah was fourth, Jeremiah was fifth, ¹¹Attai was sixth, Eliel was seventh,

JUNE 24 · 594

[12]Johanan was eighth, Elzabad was ninth, [13]Jeremiah was tenth, and Macbannai was eleventh in command.

[14]They were the commanders of the army from Gad. The least of these leaders was in charge of a hundred soldiers, and the greatest was in charge of a thousand. [15]They crossed the Jordan River and chased away the people living in the valleys, to the east and to the west. This happened in the first month of the year when the Jordan floods the valley.

[16]Other people from the tribes of Benjamin and Judah also came to David at his stronghold. [17]David went out to meet them and said to them, "If you have come peacefully to help me, I welcome you. Join me. But if you have come to turn me over to my enemies, even though I have done nothing wrong, the God of our ancestors will see this and punish you."

[18]Then the Spirit entered Amasai, the leader of the Thirty, and he said:

"We belong to you, David.
We are with you, son of Jesse.
Success, success to you.
Success to those who help you,
because your God helps you."

So David welcomed these men and made them leaders of his army.

[19]Some of the men from Manasseh also joined David when he went with the Philistines to fight Saul. But David and his men did not really help the Philistines. After talking about it, the Philistine leaders decided to send David away. They said, "If David goes back to his master Saul, we will be killed." [20]These are the men from Manasseh who joined David when he went to Ziklag: Adnah, Jozabad, Jediael, Michael, Jozabad, Elihu, and Zillethai. Each of them was a leader of a thousand men from Manasseh. [21]All these men of Manasseh were brave soldiers, and they helped David fight against groups of men who went around the country robbing people. These soldiers became commanders in David's army. [22]Every day more men joined David, and his army became large, like the army of God.

Others Join David at Hebron

[23]These are the numbers of the soldiers ready for battle who joined David at Hebron. They came to help turn the kingdom of Saul over to David, just as the LORD had said.

[24]There were sixty-eight hundred men with their weapons from Judah. They carried shields and spears.

[25]There were seventy-one hundred men from Simeon. They were warriors ready for war.

[26]There were forty-six hundred men from Levi. [27]Jehoiada, a leader from Aaron's family, was in that group. There were thirty-seven hundred with him. [28]Zadok was also in that group. He was a strong young warrior, and with him came twenty-two leaders from his family.

[29]There were three thousand men from Benjamin, who were Saul's relatives. Most of them had remained loyal to Saul's family until then.

[30]There were twenty thousand eight hundred men from Ephraim. They were brave warriors and were famous men in their own family groups.

[31]There were eighteen thousand men from West Manasseh. Each one was especially chosen to make David king.

[32]There were two hundred leaders from Issachar. They knew what Israel should do, and they knew the right time to do it. Their relatives were with them and under their command.

[33]There were fifty thousand men from Zebulun. They were trained soldiers and knew how to use every kind of weapon of war. They followed David completely.

[34]There were one thousand officers from Naphtali. They had thirty-seven thousand soldiers with them who carried shields and spears.

[35]There were twenty-eight thousand six hundred men from Dan, who were ready for war.

[36]There were forty thousand trained soldiers from Asher, who were ready for war.

[37]There were one hundred twenty thousand soldiers from the east side of the Jordan River from the people of Reuben, Gad, and East Manasseh. They had every kind of weapon.

[38]All these fighting men were ready to go to war. They came to Hebron fully agreed to

make David king of all Israel. All the other Israelites also agreed to make David king. [39]They spent three days there with David, eating and drinking, because their relatives had prepared food for them. [40]Also, their neighbors came from as far away as Issachar, Zebulun, and Naphtali, bringing food on donkeys, camels, mules, and oxen. They brought much flour, fig cakes, raisins, wine, oil, cows, and sheep, because the people of Israel were very happy.

PSALM 77:16–20

[16]God, the waters saw you;
   they saw you and became afraid;
   the deep waters shook with fear.
[17]The clouds poured down their rain.
   The sky thundered.
   Your lightning flashed back and forth
      like arrows.
[18]Your thunder sounded in the whirlwind.
   Lightning lit up the world.
   The earth trembled and shook.
[19]You made a way through the sea
   and paths through the deep waters,
   but your footprints were not seen.
[20]You led your people like a flock
   by using Moses and Aaron.

PROVERBS 19:17–19

[17]Being kind to the poor is like lending to
      the Lord;
   he will reward you for what you have
      done.
[18]Correct your children while there is still
      hope;
   do not let them destroy themselves.
[19]People with quick tempers will have to
      pay for it.
   If you help them out once, you will have
      to do it again.

ACTS 7:1–22

Stephen's Speech

7 The high priest said to Stephen, "Are these things true?"

[2]Stephen answered, "Brothers and fathers, listen to me. Our glorious God appeared to Abraham, our ancestor, in Mesopotamia before he lived in Haran. [3]God said to Abraham, 'Leave your country and your relatives, and go to the land I will show you.'[n] [4]So Abraham left the country of Chaldea and went to live in Haran. After Abraham's father died, God sent him to this place where you now live. [5]God did not give Abraham any of this land, not even a foot of it. But God promised that he would give this land to him and his descendants, even before Abraham had a child. [6]This is what God said to him: 'Your descendants will be strangers in a land they don't own. The people there will make them slaves and will mistreat them for four hundred years. [7]But I will punish the nation where they are slaves. Then your descendants will leave that land and will worship me in this place.'[n] [8]God made an agreement with Abraham, the sign of which was circumcision. And so when Abraham had his son Isaac, Abraham circumcised him when he was eight days old. Isaac also circumcised his son Jacob, and Jacob did the same for his sons, the twelve ancestors[n] of our people.

[9]"Jacob's sons became jealous of Joseph and sold him to be a slave in Egypt. But God was with him [10]and saved him from all his troubles. The king of Egypt liked Joseph and respected him because of the wisdom God gave him. The king made him governor of Egypt and put him in charge of all the people in his palace.

[11]"Then all the land of Egypt and Canaan became so dry that nothing would grow, and the people suffered very much. Jacob's sons, our ancestors, could not find anything to eat. [12]But when Jacob heard there was grain in Egypt, he sent his sons there. This was their first trip to Egypt. [13]When they went there a second time, Joseph told his brothers who he was, and the king learned about Joseph's family. [14]Then Joseph sent messengers to invite Jacob, his father, to come to Egypt along with all his relatives (seventy-five persons altogether). [15]So Jacob went down to Egypt,

---

7:3 'Leave . . . you.' Quotation from Genesis 12:1. **7:6–7 'Your descendants . . . place.'** Quotation from Genesis 15:13–14 and Exodus 3:12. **7:8 twelve ancestors** Important ancestors of the people of Israel; the leaders of the twelve tribes of Israel.

where he and his sons died. ¹⁶Later their bodies were moved to Shechem and put in a grave there. (It was the same grave Abraham had bought for a sum of money from the sons of Hamor in Shechem.)

¹⁷"The promise God made to Abraham was soon to come true, and the number of people in Egypt grew large. ¹⁸Then a new king, who did not know who Joseph was, began to rule Egypt. ¹⁹This king tricked our people and was cruel to our ancestors, forcing them to leave their babies outside to die. ²⁰At this time Moses was born, and he was very beautiful. For three months Moses was cared for in his father's house. ²¹When they put Moses outside, the king's daughter adopted him and raised him as if he were her own son. ²²The Egyptians taught Moses everything they knew, and he was a powerful man in what he said and did.

JUNE 25

1 CHRONICLES 13:1—14:17

Bringing Back the Ark

13 David talked with all the officers of his army, the commanders of a hundred men and the commanders of a thousand men. ²Then David called the people of Israel together and said, "If you think it is a good idea, and if it is what the LORD our God wants, let's send a message. Let's tell our fellow Israelites in all the areas of Israel and the priests and Levites living with them in their towns and pastures to come and join us. ³Let's bring the Ark of our God back to us. We did not use it to ask God for help while Saul was king." ⁴All the people agreed with David, because they all thought it was the right thing to do.

⁵So David gathered all the Israelites, from the Shihor River in Egypt to Lebo Hamath, to bring the Ark of God back from the town of Kiriath Jearim. ⁶David and all the Israelites with him went to Baalah of Judah, which is Kiriath Jearim, to get the Ark of God the LORD. God's throne is between the golden, winged creatures on the Ark, and the Ark is called by his name.

⁷The people carried the Ark of God from Abinadab's house on a new cart, and Uzzah and Ahio guided it. ⁸David and all the Israelites were celebrating in the presence of God. With all their strength they were singing and playing lyres, harps, tambourines, cymbals, and trumpets.

⁹When David's men came to the threshing floor of Kidon, the oxen stumbled, and Uzzah reached out his hand to steady the Ark. ¹⁰The LORD was angry with Uzzah and killed him, because he had touched the Ark. So Uzzah died there in the presence of God.

¹¹David was angry because the LORD had punished Uzzah in his anger. Now that place is called The Punishment of Uzzah.

¹²David was afraid of God that day and asked, "How can I bring the Ark of God home to me?" ¹³So David did not take the Ark with him to Jerusalem. Instead, he took it to the house of Obed-Edom who was from Gath. ¹⁴The Ark of God stayed with Obed-Edom's family in his house for three months, and the LORD blessed Obed-Edom's family and everything he owned.

David's Kingdom Grows

14 Hiram king of the city of Tyre sent messengers to David. He also sent cedar logs, bricklayers, and carpenters to build a palace for David. ²Then David knew that the LORD really had made him king of Israel and that he had made his kingdom great. The LORD did this because he loved his people Israel.

³David married more women in Jerusalem and had more sons and daughters. ⁴These are the names of David's children born in Jerusalem: Shammua, Shobab, Nathan, Solomon, ⁵Ibhar, Elishua, Elpelet, ⁶Nogah, Nepheg, Japhia, ⁷Elishama, Beeliada, and Eliphelet.

David Defeats the Philistines

[8]When the Philistines heard that David had been made king of all Israel, they went to look for him. But David heard about it and went out to fight them. [9]The Philistines had attacked and robbed the people in the Valley of Rephaim. [10]David asked God, "Should I go and attack the Philistines? Will you hand them over to me?"

The LORD answered him, "Go, I will hand them over to you."

[11]So David and his men went up to the town of Baal Perazim and defeated the Philistines. David said, "Like a flood of water, God has broken through my enemies by using me." So that place was named Baal Perazim.[n] [12]The Philistines had left their idols there, so David ordered his men to burn them.

[13]Soon the Philistines attacked the people in the valley again. [14]David prayed to God again, and God answered him, saying, "Don't attack the Philistines from the front. Instead, go around them and attack them in front of the balsam trees. [15]When you hear the sound of marching in the tops of the balsam trees, then attack. I, God, will have gone out before you to defeat the Philistine army." [16]David did as God commanded, and he and his men defeated the Philistine army all the way from Gibeon to Gezer.

[17]So David became famous in all the countries, and the LORD made all nations afraid of him.

PSALM 78:1-8

God Saved Israel from Egypt

A maskil of Asaph.

78 My people, listen to my teaching;
listen to what I say.
[2]I will speak using stories;
I will tell secret things from long ago.
[3]We have heard them and known them
by what our ancestors have told us.
[4]We will not keep them from our children;
we will tell those who come later
about the praises of the LORD.

We will tell about his power
and the miracles he has done.

[5]The LORD made an agreement with Jacob
and gave the teachings to Israel,
which he commanded our ancestors
to teach to their children.
[6]Then their children would know them,
even their children not yet born.
And they would tell their children.
[7]So they would all trust God
and would not forget what he had done
but would obey his commands.
[8]They would not be like their ancestors
who were stubborn and disobedient.
Their hearts were not loyal to God,
and they were not true to him.

PROVERBS 19:20-21

[20]Listen to advice and accept correction,
and in the end you will be wise.

[21]People can make all kinds of plans,
but only the LORD's plan will happen.

ACTS 7:23-43

[23]"When Moses was about forty years old, he thought it would be good to visit his own people, the people of Israel. [24]Moses saw an Egyptian mistreating one of his people, so he defended the Israelite and punished the Egyptian by killing him. [25]Moses thought his own people would understand that God was using him to save them, but they did not. [26]The next day when Moses saw two men of Israel fighting, he tried to make peace between them. He said, 'Men, you are brothers. Why are you hurting each other?' [27]The man who was hurting the other pushed Moses away and said, 'Who made you our ruler and judge? [28]Are you going to kill me as you killed the Egyptian yesterday?'[n] [29]When Moses heard him say this, he left Egypt and went to live in the land of Midian where he was a stranger. While Moses lived in Midian, he had two sons.

[30]"Forty years later an angel appeared to Moses in the flames of a burning bush as he was in the desert near Mount Sinai. [31]When

---

14:11 Baal Perazim This name means "the Lord breaks through." • **7:27-28 'Who . . . yesterday?'** Quotation from Exodus 2:14.

Moses saw this, he was amazed and went near to look closer. Moses heard the Lord's voice say, [32]'I am the God of your ancestors, the God of Abraham, Isaac, and Jacob.'[n] Moses began to shake with fear and was afraid to look. [33]The Lord said to him, 'Take off your sandals, because you are standing on holy ground. [34]I have seen the troubles my people have suffered in Egypt. I have heard their cries and have come down to save them. And now, Moses, I am sending you back to Egypt.'[n]

[35]'This Moses was the same man the two men of Israel rejected, saying, 'Who made you a ruler and judge?'[n] Moses is the same man God sent to be a ruler and savior, with the help of the angel that Moses saw in the burning bush. [36]So Moses led the people out of Egypt. He worked miracles and signs in Egypt, at the Red Sea, and then in the desert for forty years. [37]This is the same Moses that said to the people of Israel, 'God will give you a prophet like me, who is one of your own people.'[n] [38]This is the Moses who was with the gathering of the Israelites in the desert. He was with the angel that spoke to him at

Mount Sinai, and he was with our ancestors. He received commands from God that give life, and he gave those commands to us.

[39]'But our ancestors did not want to obey Moses. They rejected him and wanted to go back to Egypt. [40]They said to Aaron, 'Make us gods who will lead us. Moses led us out of Egypt, but we don't know what has happened to him.'[n] [41]So the people made an idol that looked like a calf. Then they brought sacrifices to it and were proud of what they had made with their own hands. [42]But God turned against them and did not try to stop them from worshiping the sun, moon, and stars. This is what is written in the book of the prophets: God says,

'People of Israel, you did not bring me
    sacrifices and offerings
while you traveled in the desert for
    forty years.
[43]You have carried with you
    the tent to worship Molech
and the idols of the star god Rephan
    that you made to worship.
So I will send you away beyond Babylon.'

Amos 5:25–27

JUNE 26

1 CHRONICLES 15:1—16:43

The Ark Is Brought to Jerusalem

15 David built houses for himself in Jerusalem. Then he prepared a place for the Ark of God, and he set up a tent for it. [2]David said, "Only the Levites may carry the Ark of God. The LORD chose them to carry the Ark of the LORD and to serve him forever."

[3]David called all the people of Israel to come to Jerusalem. He wanted to bring the Ark of the LORD to the place he had made for it. [4]David called together the descendants of Aaron and the Levites. [5]There were one hundred twenty people from Kohath's

family group, with Uriel as their leader. [6]There were two hundred twenty people from Merari's family group, with Asaiah as their leader. [7]There were one hundred thirty people from Gershon's family group, with Joel as their leader. [8]There were two hundred people from Elizaphan's family group, with Shemaiah as their leader. [9]There were eighty people from Hebron's family group, with Eliel as their leader. [10]And there were one hundred twelve people from Uzziel's family group, with Amminadab as their leader.

[11]Then David asked the priests Zadok and Abiathar and these Levites to come to him: Uriel, Asaiah, Joel, Shemaiah, Eliel,

7:32 'I am . . . Jacob.' Quotation from Exodus 3:6.   **7:33–34 'Take . . . Egypt.'** Quotation from Exodus 3:5–10.
7:35 'Who . . . judge?' Quotation from Exodus 2:14.   **7:37 'God . . . people.'** Quotation from Deuteronomy 18:15.
7:40 'Make . . . him.' Quotation from Exodus 32:1.

and Amminadab. [12]David said to them, "You are the leaders of the families of Levi. You and the other Levites must give yourselves for service to the LORD. Bring up the Ark of the LORD, the God of Israel, to the place I have made for it. [13]The last time we did not ask the LORD how to carry it. You Levites didn't carry it, so the LORD our God punished us."

[14]Then the priests and Levites prepared themselves for service to the LORD so they could carry the Ark of the LORD, the God of Israel. [15]The Levites used special poles to carry the Ark of God on their shoulders, as Moses had commanded, just as the LORD had said they should.

[16]David told the leaders of the Levites to appoint their brothers as singers to play their lyres, harps, and cymbals and to sing happy songs.

[17]So the Levites appointed Heman and his relatives Asaph and Ethan. Heman was Joel's son. Asaph was Berekiah's son. And Ethan, from the Merari family group, was Kushaiah's son. [18]There was also a second group of Levites: Zechariah, Jaaziel, Shemiramoth, Jehiel, Unni, Eliab, Benaiah, Maaseiah, Mattithiah, Eliphelehu, Mikneiah, Obed-Edom, and Jeiel. They were the Levite guards.

[19]The singers Heman, Asaph, and Ethan played bronze cymbals. [20]Zechariah, Jaaziel, Shemiramoth, Jehiel, Unni, Eliab, Maaseiah, and Benaiah played the lyres. [21]Mattithiah, Eliphelehu, Mikneiah, Obed-Edom, Jeiel, and Azaziah played the harps. [22]The Levite leader Kenaniah was in charge of the singing, because he was very good at it.

[23]Berekiah and Elkanah were two of the guards for the Ark of the Agreement. [24]The priests Shebaniah, Joshaphat, Nethanel, Amasai, Zechariah, Benaiah, and Eliezer had the job of blowing trumpets in front of the Ark of God. Obed-Edom and Jehiah were also guards for the Ark.

[25]David, the leaders of Israel, and the commanders of a thousand soldiers went to get the Ark of the Agreement with the LORD. They all went to bring the Ark from Obed-Edom's house with great joy. [26]Because God helped the Levites who carried the Ark of the Agreement with the LORD, they sacrificed seven bulls and seven male sheep. [27]All the Levites who carried the Ark, and Kenaniah, the man in charge of the singing, and all the singers wore robes of fine linen. David also wore a robe of fine linen and a holy vest of fine linen. [28]So all the people of Israel brought up the Ark of the Agreement with the LORD. They shouted, blew horns and trumpets, and played cymbals, lyres, and harps.

[29]As the Ark of the Agreement with the LORD entered Jerusalem, Saul's daughter Michal watched from a window. When she saw King David dancing and celebrating, she hated him.

16 They brought the Ark of God and put it inside the tent that David had set up for it. Then they offered burnt offerings and fellowship offerings to God. [2]When David had finished giving the burnt offerings and fellowship offerings, he blessed the people in the name of the LORD. [3]He gave a loaf of bread, some dates, and raisins to every Israelite man and woman.

[4]Then David appointed some of the Levites to serve before the Ark of the LORD. They had the job of leading the worship and giving thanks and praising the LORD, the God of Israel. [5]Asaph, who played the cymbals, was the leader. Zechariah was second to him. The other Levites were Jaaziel, Shemiramoth, Jehiel, Mattithiah, Eliab, Benaiah, Obed-Edom, and Jeiel. They played the lyres and harps. [6]Benaiah and Jahaziel were priests who blew the trumpets regularly before the Ark of the Agreement with God. [7]That day David first gave Asaph and his relatives the job of singing praises to the LORD.

David's Song of Thanks

[8]Give thanks to the LORD and pray to
  him.
  Tell the nations what he has done.
[9]Sing to him; sing praises to him.
  Tell about all his miracles.
[10]Be glad that you are his;
  let those who seek the LORD be happy.
[11]Depend on the LORD and his strength;
  always go to him for help.

¹²Remember the miracles he has done,
his wonders, and his decisions.
¹³You are the descendants of his servant,
Israel;
you are the children of Jacob, his
chosen people.

¹⁴He is the LORD our God.
His laws are for all the world.
¹⁵He will keep his agreement forever;
he will keep his promises always.
¹⁶He will keep the agreement he made
with Abraham
and the promise he made to Isaac.
¹⁷He made it a law for the people of Jacob;
he made it an agreement with Israel to
last forever.
¹⁸He said, "I will give the land of Canaan
to you,
to belong to you."

¹⁹Then God's people were few in number,
and they were strangers in the land.
²⁰They went from one nation to another,
from one kingdom to another.
²¹But he did not let anyone hurt them;
he warned kings not to harm them.
²²He said, "Don't touch my chosen people,
and don't harm my prophets."

²³Sing to the LORD, all the earth.
Every day tell how he saves us.
²⁴Tell the nations about his glory;
tell all peoples the miracles he does.
²⁵The LORD is great; he should be praised.
He should be respected more than all
the gods.
²⁶All the gods of the nations are only
idols,
but the LORD made the skies.
²⁷He has glory and majesty;
he has power and joy in his Temple.

²⁸Praise the LORD, all nations on earth.
Praise the LORD's glory and power;
²⁹   praise the glory of the LORD's name.
Bring an offering and come to him.
Worship the LORD because he is holy.
³⁰Tremble before him, everyone on earth.
The earth is set, and it cannot be
moved.
³¹Let the skies rejoice and the earth be
glad.

Let people everywhere say, "The LORD
is king!"
³²Let the sea and everything in it shout;
let the fields and everything in them
rejoice.
³³Then the trees of the forest will sing
for joy before the LORD.
They will sing because he is coming to
judge the world.

³⁴Thank the LORD because he is good.
His love continues forever.
³⁵Say to him, "Save us, God our Savior,
and bring us back and save us from
other nations.
Then we will thank you
and will gladly praise you."
³⁶Praise the LORD, the God of Israel.
He always was and always will be.
All the people said "Amen" and praised the
LORD.

³⁷Then David left Asaph and the other
Levites there in front of the Ark of the
Agreement with the LORD. They were to
serve there every day. ³⁸David also left
Obed-Edom and sixty-eight other Levites
to serve with them. Hosah and Obed-Edom
son of Jeduthun were guards.

³⁹David left Zadok the priest and the
other priests who served with him in front
of the Tent of the LORD at the place of worship in Gibeon. ⁴⁰Every morning and
evening they offered burnt offerings on the
altar of burnt offerings, following the rules
written in the Teachings of the LORD, which
he had given Israel. ⁴¹With them were Heman and Jeduthun and other Levites. They
were chosen by name to sing praises to the
LORD because his love continues forever.
⁴²Heman and Jeduthun also had the job of
playing the trumpets and cymbals and
other musical instruments when songs
were sung to God. Jeduthun's sons guarded
the gates.

⁴³Then all the people left. Each person
went home, and David also went home to
bless the people in his home.

PSALM 78:9–16

⁹The men of Ephraim had bows for
weapons,

but they ran away on the day of battle.
¹⁰They didn't keep their agreement with
God
and refused to live by his teachings.
¹¹They forgot what he had done
and the miracles he had shown them.
¹²He did miracles while their ancestors
watched,
in the fields of Zoan in Egypt.
¹³He divided the Red Sea and led them
through.
He made the water stand up like a wall.
¹⁴He led them with a cloud by day
and by the light of a fire by night.
¹⁵He split the rocks in the desert
and gave them more than enough
water, as if from the deep ocean.
¹⁶He brought streams out of the rock
and caused water to flow down like
rivers.

PROVERBS 19:22–24

²²People want others to be loyal,
so it is better to be poor than to be a
liar.
²³Those who respect the LORD will live
and be satisfied, unbothered by
trouble.
²⁴Though the lazy person puts his hand in
the dish,
he won't lift the food to his mouth.

ACTS 7:44—8:1a

⁴⁴"The Holy Tent where God spoke to our ancestors was with them in the desert. God told Moses how to make this Tent, and he made it like the plan God showed him. ⁴⁵Later, Joshua led our ancestors to capture the lands of the other nations. Our people went in, and God forced the other people out. When our people went into this new land, they took with them this same Tent they had received from their ancestors. They kept it until the time of David, ⁴⁶who pleased God and asked God to let him build a house for him, the God of Jacob.ⁿ

⁴⁷But Solomon was the one who built the Temple.
⁴⁸"But the Most High does not live in houses that people build with their hands. As the prophet says:
⁴⁹'Heaven is my throne,
and the earth is my footstool.
So do you think you can build a house
for me? says the Lord.
Do I need a place to rest?
⁵⁰Remember, my hand made all these
things!'" *Isaiah 66:1–2*

⁵¹Stephen continued speaking: "You stubborn people! You have not given your hearts to God, nor will you listen to him! You are always against what the Holy Spirit is trying to tell you, just as your ancestors were. ⁵²Your ancestors tried to hurt every prophet who ever lived. Those prophets said long ago that the One who is good would come, but your ancestors killed them. And now you have turned against and killed the One who is good. ⁵³You received the law of Moses, which God gave you through his angels, but you haven't obeyed it."

Stephen Is Killed

⁵⁴When the leaders heard this, they became furious. They were so mad they were grinding their teeth at Stephen. ⁵⁵But Stephen was full of the Holy Spirit. He looked up to heaven and saw the glory of God and Jesus standing at God's right side. ⁵⁶He said, "Look! I see heaven open and the Son of Man standing at God's right side."

⁵⁷Then they shouted loudly and covered their ears and all ran at Stephen. ⁵⁸They took him out of the city and began to throw stones at him to kill him. And those who told lies against Stephen left their coats with a young man named Saul. ⁵⁹While they were throwing stones, Stephen prayed, "Lord Jesus, receive my spirit." ⁶⁰He fell on his knees and cried in a loud voice, "Lord, do not hold this sin against them." After Stephen said this, he died.

8 Saul agreed that the killing of Stephen was good.

JUNE 27

1 CHRONICLES 17:1—18:17

God's Promise to David

17 When David moved into his palace, he said to Nathan the prophet, "Look, I am living in a palace made of cedar, but the Ark of the Agreement with the LORD sits in a tent."

²Nathan said to David, "Do what you want to do, because God is with you."

³But that night God spoke his word to Nathan, saying, ⁴"Go and tell David my servant, 'This is what the LORD says: You are not the person to build a house for me to live in. ⁵From the time I brought Israel out of Egypt until now I have not lived in a house. I have moved from one tent site to another and from one place to another. ⁶As I have moved with the Israelites to different places, I have never said to the leaders, whom I commanded to take care of my people, "Why haven't you built me a house of cedar?" '

⁷"Now, tell my servant David: 'This is what the LORD All-Powerful says: I took you from the pasture and from tending the sheep and made you king of my people Israel. ⁸I have been with you everywhere you have gone. I have defeated your enemies for you. I will make you as famous as any of the great people on the earth. ⁹I will choose a place for my people Israel, and I will plant them so they can live in their own homes. They will not be bothered anymore. Wicked people will no longer hurt them as they have in the past ¹⁰when I chose judges for my people Israel. I will defeat all your enemies.

" 'I tell you that the LORD will make your descendants kings of Israel after you. ¹¹When you die and join your ancestors, I will make one of your sons the new king, and I will set up his kingdom. ¹²He will build a house for me, and I will let his kingdom rule always. ¹³I will be his father, and he will be my son. I took away my love from Saul, who ruled before you, but I will never stop loving your son. ¹⁴I will put him in charge of my house and kingdom forever. His family will rule forever.' "

¹⁵Nathan told David everything God had said in this vision.

David Prays to God

¹⁶Then King David went in and sat in front of the LORD. David said, "LORD God, who am I? What is my family? Why did you bring me to this point? ¹⁷But that was not enough for you, God. You have also made promises about my future family. LORD God, you have treated me like a very important person.

¹⁸"What more can I say to you for honoring me, your servant? You know me so well. ¹⁹LORD, you have done this wonderful thing for my sake and because you wanted to. You have made known all these great things.

²⁰"There is no one like you, LORD. There is no God except you. We have heard all this ourselves! ²¹There is no nation like your people Israel. They are the only people on earth that God chose to be his own. You made your name well known by the great and wonderful things you did for them. You went ahead of them and forced other nations out of the land. You freed your people from slavery in Egypt. ²²You made the people of Israel your very own people forever, and, LORD, you are their God.

²³"LORD, keep the promise forever that you made about my family and me, your servant. Do what you have said. ²⁴Then you will be honored always, and people will say, 'The LORD All-Powerful, the God over Israel, is Israel's God!' And the family of your servant David will continue before you.

²⁵"My God, you have told me that you would make my family great. So I, your servant, am brave enough to pray to you. ²⁶LORD, you are God, and you have promised these good things to me, your servant. ²⁷You have chosen to bless my family. Let it continue before you always. LORD, you have blessed my family, so it will always be blessed."

David Defeats Nations

18 Later, David defeated the Philistines, conquered them, and took the city of Gath and the small towns around it.

²He also defeated the people of Moab. So the people of Moab became servants of David and gave him the payment he demanded.

³David also defeated Hadadezer king of Zobah all the way to the town of Hamath as he tried to spread his kingdom to the Euphrates River. ⁴David captured one thousand of his chariots, seven thousand men who rode in chariots, and twenty thousand foot soldiers. He crippled all but a hundred of the chariot horses.

⁵Arameans from Damascus came to help Hadadezer king of Zobah, but David killed twenty-two thousand of them. ⁶Then David put groups of soldiers in Damascus in Aram. The Arameans became David's servants and gave him the payments he demanded. So the LORD gave David victory everywhere he went.

⁷David took the shields of gold that had belonged to Hadadezer's officers and brought them to Jerusalem. ⁸David also took many things made of bronze from Tebah and Cun, which had been cities under Hadadezer's control. Later, Solomon used this bronze to make things for the Temple: the large bronze bowl, which was called the Sea, the pillars, and other bronze utensils.

⁹Toi king of Hamath heard that David had defeated all the army of Hadadezer king of Zobah. ¹⁰So Toi sent his son Hadoram to greet and congratulate King David for defeating Hadadezer. (Hadadezer had been at war with Toi.) Hadoram brought items made of gold, silver, and bronze. ¹¹King David gave them to the LORD, along with the silver and gold he had taken from these nations: Edom, Moab, the Ammonites, the Philistines, and Amalek.

¹²Abishai son of Zeruiah killed eighteen thousand Edomites in the Valley of Salt. ¹³David put groups of soldiers in Edom, and all the Edomites became his servants. The LORD gave David victory everywhere he went.

David's Important Officers
¹⁴David was king over all of Israel, and he did what was fair and right for all his people. ¹⁵Joab son of Zeruiah was commander over the army. Jehoshaphat son of Ahilud was the recorder. ¹⁶Zadok son of Ahitub and Abiathar son of Ahimelech were priests. Shavsha was the royal secretary. ¹⁷Benaiah son of Jehoiada was over the Kerethites and Pelethites.ⁿ And David's sons were important officers who served at his side.

PSALM 78:17-25

¹⁷But the people continued to sin against him;
in the desert they turned against God Most High.
¹⁸They decided to test God
by asking for the food they wanted.
¹⁹Then they spoke against God,
saying, "Can God prepare food in the desert?
²⁰When he hit the rock, water poured out and rivers flowed down.
But can he give us bread also?
Will he provide his people with meat?"
²¹When the LORD heard them, he was very angry.
His anger was like fire to the people of Jacob;
his anger grew against the people of Israel.
²²They had not believed God
and had not trusted him to save them.
²³But he gave a command to the clouds above
and opened the doors of heaven.
²⁴He rained manna down on them to eat;
he gave them grain from heaven.
²⁵So they ate the bread of angels.
He sent them all the food they could eat.

PROVERBS 19:25-26

²⁵Whip those who make fun of wisdom,
and perhaps foolish people will gain some wisdom.
Correct those with understanding, and they will gain knowledge.

²⁶A child who robs his father and sends away his mother
brings shame and disgrace on himself.

ACTS 8:1b-25

Troubles for the Believers
On that day the church of Jerusalem began to be persecuted, and all the believers, except

---

18:17 Kerethites and Pelethites These were probably special units of the army that were responsible for the king's safety, a kind of palace guard.

the apostles, were scattered throughout Judea and Samaria.

[2]And some religious people buried Stephen and cried loudly for him. [3]Saul was also trying to destroy the church, going from house to house, dragging out men and women and putting them in jail. [4]And wherever they were scattered, they told people the Good News.

Philip Preaches in Samaria

[5]Philip went to the city of Samaria and preached about the Christ. [6]When the people there heard Philip and saw the miracles he was doing, they all listened carefully to what he said. [7]Many of these people had evil spirits in them, but Philip made the evil spirits leave. The spirits made a loud noise when they came out. Philip also healed many weak and crippled people there. [8]So the people in that city were very happy.

[9]But there was a man named Simon in that city. Before Philip came there, Simon had practiced magic and amazed all the people of Samaria. He bragged and called himself a great man. [10]All the people—the least important and the most important—paid attention to Simon, saying, "This man has the power of God, called 'the Great Power'!" [11]Simon had amazed them with his magic so long that the people became his followers. [12]But when Philip told them the Good News about the kingdom of God and the power of Jesus Christ, men and women believed Philip and were baptized. [13]Simon himself believed, and after he was baptized, he stayed very close to Philip. When he saw the miracles and the powerful things Philip did, Simon was amazed.

[14]When the apostles who were still in Jerusalem heard that the people of Samaria had accepted the word of God, they sent Peter and John to them. [15]When Peter and John arrived, they prayed that the Samaritan believers might receive the Holy Spirit. [16]These people had been baptized in the name of the Lord Jesus, but the Holy Spirit had not yet come upon any of them. [17]Then, when the two apostles began laying their hands on the people, they received the Holy Spirit.

[18]Simon saw that the Spirit was given to people when the apostles laid their hands on them. So he offered the apostles money, [19]saying, "Give me also this power so that anyone on whom I lay my hands will receive the Holy Spirit."

[20]Peter said to him, "You and your money should both be destroyed, because you thought you could buy God's gift with money. [21]You cannot share with us in this work since your heart is not right before God. [22]Change your heart! Turn away from this evil thing you have done, and pray to the Lord. Maybe he will forgive you for thinking this. [23]I see that you are full of bitter jealousy and ruled by sin."

[24]Simon answered, "Both of you pray for me to the Lord so the things you have said will not happen to me."

[25]After Peter and John told the people what they had seen Jesus do and after they had spoken the message of the Lord, they went back to Jerusalem. On the way, they went through many Samaritan towns and preached the Good News to the people.

JUNE 28

1 CHRONICLES 19:1—20:8

War with the Ammonites and Arameans

19 When Nahash king of the Ammonites died, his son became king after him. [2]David said, "Nahash was loyal to me, so I will be loyal to his son Hanun." So David sent

messengers to comfort Hanun about his father's death.

David's officers went to the land of the Ammonites to comfort Hanun. [3]But the Ammonite leaders said to Hanun, "Do you think David wants to honor your father by sending men to comfort you? No! David sent them to study the land and capture it and spy it out." [4]So Hanun arrested David's officers. To shame them he shaved their beards and cut off their clothes at the hips. Then he sent them away.

[5]When the people told David what had happened to his officers, he sent messengers to meet them, because they were very ashamed. King David said, "Stay in Jericho until your beards have grown back. Then come home."

[6]The Ammonites knew that they had insulted David. So Hanun and the Ammonites sent about seventy-four thousand pounds of silver to hire chariots and chariot drivers from Northwest Mesopotamia, Aram Maacah, and Zobah. [7]The Ammonites hired thirty-two thousand chariots and the king of Maacah and his army. So they came and set up camp near the town of Medeba. The Ammonites themselves came out of their towns and got ready for battle.

[8]When David heard about this, he sent Joab with the whole army. [9]The Ammonites came out and prepared for battle at the city gate. The kings who had come to help were out in the field by themselves.

[10]Joab saw that there were enemies both in front of him and behind him. So he chose some of the best soldiers of Israel and sent them out to fight the Arameans. [11]Joab put the rest of the army under the command of Abishai, his brother. Then they went out to fight the Ammonites. [12]Joab said to Abishai, "If the Arameans are too strong for me, you must help me. Or, if the Ammonites are too strong for you, I will help you. [13]Be strong. We must fight bravely for our people and the cities of our God. The LORD will do what he thinks is right."

[14]Then Joab and the army with him went to attack the Arameans, and the Arameans ran away. [15]When the Ammonites saw that the Arameans were running away, they also ran away from Joab's brother Abishai and went back to their city. So Joab went back to Jerusalem.

[16]When the Arameans saw that Israel had defeated them, they sent messengers to bring other Arameans from east of the Euphrates River. Their leader was Shophach, the commander of Hadadezer's army.

[17]When David heard about this, he gathered all the Israelites, and they crossed over the Jordan River. He prepared them for battle, facing the Arameans. The Arameans fought with him, [18]but they ran away from the Israelites. David killed seven thousand Aramean chariot drivers and forty thousand Aramean foot soldiers. He also killed Shophach, the commander of the Aramean army.

[19]When those who served Hadadezer saw that the Israelites had defeated them, they made peace with David and served him. So the Arameans refused to help the Ammonites again.

Joab Destroys the Ammonites

20 In the spring, the time of year when kings normally went out to battle, Joab led out the army of Israel. But David stayed in Jerusalem. The army of Israel destroyed the land of Ammon and went to the city of Rabbah and attacked it. [2]David took the crown off the head of their king,[n] and had it placed on his own head. That gold crown weighed about seventy-five pounds, and it had valuable gems in it. And David took many valuable things from the city. [3]He also brought out the people of the city and forced them to work with saws, iron picks, and axes. David did this to all the Ammonite cities. Then David and all his army returned to Jerusalem.

Philistine Giants Are Killed

[4]Later, at Gezer, war broke out with the Philistines. Sibbecai the Hushathite killed Sippai, who was one of the descendants of the Rephaites. So those Philistines were defeated.

[5]Later, there was another battle with the Philistines. Elhanan son of Jair killed Lahmi, the brother of Goliath, who was from the town of Gath. His spear was as large as a weaver's rod.

[6]At Gath another battle took place. A huge man was there; he had six fingers on each

---

20:2 their king Or, "Milcom," the god of the Ammonite people.

hand and six toes on each foot—twenty-four fingers and toes in all. This man also was one of the sons of Rapha. [7]When he spoke against Israel, Jonathan son of Shimea, David's brother, killed him.

[8]These descendants of Rapha from Gath were killed by David and his men.

PSALM 78:26–33

[26]He sent the east wind from heaven
    and led the south wind by his power.
[27]He rained meat on them like dust.
    The birds were as many as the sand of
        the sea.
[28]He made the birds fall inside the camp,
    all around the tents.
[29]So the people ate and became very full.
    God had given them what they wanted.
[30]While they were still eating,
    and while the food was still in their
        mouths,
[31]God became angry with them.
    He killed some of the healthiest of them;
    he struck down the best young men of
        Israel.

[32]But they kept on sinning;
    they did not believe even with the
        miracles.
[33]So he ended their days without meaning
    and their years in terror.

PROVERBS 19:27–29

[27]Don't stop listening to correction, my child,
    or you will forget what you have already
        learned.

[28]An evil witness makes fun of fairness,
    and wicked people love what is evil.

[29]People who make fun of wisdom will be
        punished,
    and the backs of foolish people will be
        beaten.

ACTS 8:26–40

Philip Teaches an Ethiopian

[26]An angel of the Lord said to Philip, "Get ready and go south to the road that leads down to Gaza from Jerusalem—the desert road." [27]So Philip got ready and went. On the road he saw a man from Ethiopia, a eunuch. He was an important officer in the service of Candace, the queen of the Ethiopians; he was responsible for taking care of all her money. He had gone to Jerusalem to worship. [28]Now, as he was on his way home, he was sitting in his chariot reading from the Book of Isaiah, the prophet. [29]The Spirit said to Philip, "Go to that chariot and stay near it."

[30]So when Philip ran toward the chariot, he heard the man reading from Isaiah the prophet. Philip asked, "Do you understand what you are reading?"

[31]He answered, "How can I understand unless someone explains it to me?" Then he invited Philip to climb in and sit with him. [32]The portion of Scripture he was reading was this:

"He was like a sheep being led to be
        killed.
    He was quiet, as a lamb is quiet while
        its wool is being cut;
    he never opened his mouth.
[33]   He was shamed and was treated
        unfairly.
    He died without children to continue his
        family.
    His life on earth has ended."   *Isaiah 53:7–8*

[34]The officer said to Philip, "Please tell me, who is the prophet talking about—himself or someone else?" [35]Philip began to speak, and starting with this same Scripture, he told the man the Good News about Jesus.

[36]While they were traveling down the road, they came to some water. The officer said, "Look, here is water. What is stopping me from being baptized?" [[37]Philip answered, "If you believe with all your heart, you can." The officer said, "I believe that Jesus Christ is the Son of God."][n] [38]Then the officer commanded the chariot to stop. Both Philip and the officer went down into the water, and Philip baptized him. [39]When they came up out of the water, the Spirit of the Lord took Philip away; the officer never saw him again. And the officer continued on his way home, full of joy. [40]But Philip appeared in a city called Azotus and preached the Good News in all the towns on the way from Azotus to Caesarea.

8:37 **Philip . . . God."** Some Greek copies do not contain the bracketed text.

JUNE 29

1 CHRONICLES 21:1—22:19

David Counts the Israelites

21 Satan was against Israel, and he caused David to count the people of Israel. ²So David said to Joab and the commanders of the troops, "Go and count all the Israelites from Beersheba to Dan.ⁿ Then tell me so I will know how many there are."

³But Joab said, "May the LORD give the nation a hundred times more people. My master the king, all the Israelites are your servants. Why do you want to do this, my master? You will make Israel guilty of sin."

⁴But the king commanded Joab, so Joab left and went through all Israel. Then he returned to Jerusalem. ⁵Joab gave the list of the people to David. There were one million one hundred thousand men in all of Israel who could use the sword, and there were four hundred seventy thousand men in Judah who could use the sword. ⁶But Joab did not count the tribes of Levi and Benjamin, because he didn't like King David's order. ⁷David had done something God had said was wrong, so God punished Israel.

⁸Then David said to God, "I have sinned greatly by what I have done! Now, I beg you to forgive me, your servant, because I have been very foolish."

⁹The LORD said to Gad, who was David's seer, ¹⁰"Go and tell David, 'This is what the LORD says: I offer you three choices. Choose one of them and I will do it.'"

¹¹So Gad went to David and said to him, "This is what the LORD says: 'Choose for yourself ¹²three years of hunger. Or choose three months of running from your enemies as they chase you with their swords. Or choose three days of punishment from the LORD, in which a terrible disease will spread through the country. The angel of the LORD will go through Israel destroying the people.' Now, David, decide which of these things I should tell the LORD who sent me."

¹³David said to Gad, "I am in great trou-ble. Let the LORD punish me, because the LORD is very merciful. Don't let my punishment come from human beings."

¹⁴So the LORD sent a terrible disease on Israel, and seventy thousand people died. ¹⁵God sent an angel to destroy Jerusalem, but when the angel started to destroy it, the LORD saw it and felt very sorry about the terrible things that had happened. So he said to the angel who was destroying, "That is enough! Put down your arm!" The angel of the LORD was then standing at the threshing floor of Araunah the Jebusite.

¹⁶David looked up and saw the angel of the LORD in the sky, holding his sword drawn and pointed at Jerusalem. Then David and the elders bowed facedown on the ground. They were wearing rough cloth to show their grief. ¹⁷David said to God, "I am the one who sinned and did wrong. I gave the order for the people to be counted. These people only followed me like sheep. They did nothing wrong. LORD my God, please punish me and my family, but stop the terrible disease that is killing your people."

¹⁸Then the angel of the LORD told Gad to tell David that he should build an altar to the LORD on the threshing floor of Araunah the Jebusite. ¹⁹So David did what Gad told him to do, in the name of the LORD.

²⁰Araunah was separating the wheat from the straw. When he turned around, he saw the angel. Araunah's four sons who were with him hid. ²¹David came to Araunah, and when Araunah saw him, he left the threshing floor and bowed facedown on the ground before David.

²²David said to him, "Sell me your threshing floor so I can build an altar to the LORD here. Then the terrible disease will stop. Sell it to me for the full price."

²³Araunah said to David, "Take this threshing floor. My master the king, do anything you want. Look, I will also give you oxen for the whole burnt offerings, the threshing

---

21:2 Beersheba to Dan Beersheba was the city farthest south in Israel. Dan was the city farthest north. So this means all the people of Israel.

boards for the wood, and wheat for the grain offering. I give everything to you."

²⁴But King David answered Araunah, "No, I will pay the full price for the land. I won't take anything that is yours and give it to the LORD. I won't offer a burnt offering that costs me nothing."

²⁵So David paid Araunah about fifteen pounds of gold for the place. ²⁶David built an altar to the LORD there and offered whole burnt offerings and fellowship offerings. David prayed to the LORD, and he answered him by sending down fire from heaven on the altar of burnt offering. ²⁷Then the LORD commanded the angel to put his sword back into its holder.

²⁸When David saw that the LORD had answered him on the threshing floor of Araunah, he offered sacrifices there. ²⁹The Holy Tent that Moses made while the Israelites were in the desert and the altar of burnt offerings were in Gibeon at the place of worship. ³⁰But David could not go to the Holy Tent to speak with God, because he was afraid of the angel of the LORD and his sword.

22 David said, "The Temple of the LORD God and the altar for Israel's burnt offerings will be built here."

David Makes Plans for the Temple

²So David ordered all foreigners living in Israel to gather together. From that group David chose stonecutters to cut stones to be used in building the Temple of God. ³David supplied a large amount of iron to be used for making nails and hinges for the gate doors. He also supplied more bronze than could be weighed, ⁴and he supplied more cedar logs than could be counted. Much of the cedar had been brought to David by the people from Sidon and Tyre.

⁵David said, "We should build a great Temple for the LORD, which will be famous everywhere for its greatness and beauty. But my son Solomon is young. He hasn't yet learned what he needs to know, so I will prepare for the building of it." So David got many of the materials ready before he died.

⁶Then David called for his son Solomon and told him to build the Temple for the LORD, the God of Israel. ⁷David said to him, "My son, I wanted to build a temple for worshiping the LORD my God. ⁸But the LORD spoke his word to me, 'David, you have killed many people. You have fought many wars. You cannot build a temple for worship to me, because you have killed many people. ⁹But, you will have a son, a man of peace and rest. I will give him rest from all his enemies around him. His name will be Solomon,ⁿ and I will give Israel peace and quiet while he is king. ¹⁰Solomon will build a temple for worship to me. He will be my son, and I will be his father. I will make his kingdom strong; someone from his family will rule Israel forever.'"

¹¹David said, "Now, my son, may the LORD be with you. May you build a temple for the LORD your God, as he said you would. ¹²He will make you the king of Israel. May the LORD give you wisdom and understanding so you will be able to obey the teachings of the LORD your God. ¹³Be careful to obey the rules and laws the LORD gave Moses for Israel. If you obey them, you will have success. Be strong and brave. Don't be afraid or discouraged.

¹⁴"Solomon, I have worked hard getting many of the materials for building the Temple of the LORD. I have supplied about seven and one-half million pounds of gold, about seventy-five million pounds of silver, so much bronze and iron it cannot be weighed, and wood and stone. You may add to them. ¹⁵You have many workmen—stonecutters, bricklayers, carpenters, and people skilled in every kind of work. ¹⁶They are skilled in working with gold, silver, bronze, and iron. You have more craftsmen than can be counted. Now begin the work, and may the LORD be with you."

¹⁷Then David ordered all the leaders of Israel to help his son Solomon. ¹⁸David said to them, "The LORD your God is with you. He has given you rest from our enemies. He has handed over to me the people living around us. The LORD and his people are in control of this land. ¹⁹Now give yourselves completely to obeying the LORD your God. Build the holy

---

22:9 Solomon This name sounds like the Hebrew word for "peace."

place of the LORD God; build the Temple for worship to the LORD. Then bring the Ark of the Agreement with the LORD and the holy items that belong to God into the Temple."

PSALM 78:34–39

34Anytime he killed them, they would look
  to him for help;
  they would come back to God and
  follow him.
35They would remember that God was
  their Rock,
  that God Most High had saved them.
36But their words were false,
  and their tongues lied to him.
37Their hearts were not really loyal to God;
  they did not keep his agreement.
38Still God was merciful.
  He forgave their sins
  and did not destroy them.
  Many times he held back his anger
  and did not stir up all his anger.
39He remembered that they were only
  human,
  like a wind that blows and does not
  come back.

PROVERBS 20:1–2

20 Wine and beer make people loud and
  uncontrolled;
  it is not wise to get drunk on them.

2An angry king is like a roaring lion.
  Making him angry may cost you your
  life.

ACTS 9:1–19a

Saul Is Converted

9 In Jerusalem Saul was still threatening the followers of the Lord by saying he would kill them. So he went to the high priest 2and asked him to write letters to the synagogues in the city of Damascus. Then if Saul found any followers of Christ's Way, men or women, he would arrest them and bring them back to Jerusalem.

3So Saul headed toward Damascus. As he came near the city, a bright light from heaven suddenly flashed around him. 4Saul fell to the ground and heard a voice saying to him, "Saul, Saul! Why are you persecuting me?"

5Saul said, "Who are you, Lord?"

The voice answered, "I am Jesus, whom you are persecuting. 6Get up now and go into the city. Someone there will tell you what you must do."

7The people traveling with Saul stood there but said nothing. They heard the voice, but they saw no one. 8Saul got up from the ground and opened his eyes, but he could not see. So those with Saul took his hand and led him into Damascus. 9For three days Saul could not see and did not eat or drink.

10There was a follower of Jesus in Damascus named Ananias. The Lord spoke to Ananias in a vision, "Ananias!"

Ananias answered, "Here I am, Lord."

11The Lord said to him, "Get up and go to Straight Street. Find the house of Judas,n and ask for a man named Saul from the city of Tarsus. He is there now, praying. 12Saul has seen a vision in which a man named Ananias comes to him and lays his hands on him. Then he is able to see again."

13But Ananias answered, "Lord, many people have told me about this man and the terrible things he did to your holy people in Jerusalem. 14Now he has come here to Damascus, and the leading priests have given him the power to arrest everyone who worships you."

15But the Lord said to Ananias, "Go! I have chosen Saul for an important work. He must tell about me to those who are not Jews, to kings, and to the people of Israel. 16I will show him how much he must suffer for my name."

17So Ananias went to the house of Judas. He laid his hands on Saul and said, "Brother Saul, the Lord Jesus sent me. He is the one you saw on the road on your way here. He sent me so that you can see again and be filled with the Holy Spirit." 18Immediately, something that looked like fish scales fell from Saul's eyes, and he was able to see again! Then Saul got up and was baptized. 19After he ate some food, his strength returned.

9:11 Judas This is not either of the apostles named Judas.

JUNE 30

1 CHRONICLES 23:1—25:31

The Levites

23 After David had lived long and was old, he made his son Solomon the new king of Israel. ²David gathered all the leaders of Israel, along with the priests and Levites. ³He counted the Levites who were thirty years old and older. In all, there were thirty-eight thousand Levites. ⁴David said, "Of these, twenty-four thousand Levites will direct the work of the Temple of the LORD, six thousand Levites will be officers and judges, ⁵four thousand Levites will be gatekeepers, and four thousand Levites will praise the LORD with musical instruments I made for giving praise."

⁶David separated the Levites into three groups that were led by Levi's three sons: Gershon, Kohath, and Merari.

The People of Gershon

⁷From the people of Gershon, there were Ladan and Shimei.

⁸Ladan had three sons. His first son was Jehiel, and his other sons were Zetham and Joel.

⁹Shimei's sons were Shelomoth, Haziel, and Haran. These three sons were leaders of Ladan's families. ¹⁰Shimei had four sons: Jahath, Ziza, Jeush, and Beriah. ¹¹Jahath was the first son, and Ziza was the second son. But Jeush and Beriah did not have many children, so they were counted as if they were one family.

The People of Kohath

¹²Kohath had four sons: Amram, Izhar, Hebron, and Uzziel.

¹³Amram's sons were Aaron and Moses. Aaron and his descendants were chosen to be special forever. They were chosen to prepare the holy things for the LORD's service, to offer sacrifices before the LORD, and to serve him as priests. They were to give blessings in his name forever.

¹⁴Moses was the man of God, and his sons were counted as part of the tribe of Levi. ¹⁵Moses' sons were Gershom and Eliezer. ¹⁶Gershom's first son was Shubael. ¹⁷Eliezer's first son was Rehabiah. Eliezer had no other sons, but Rehabiah had many sons.

¹⁸Izhar's first son was Shelomith.

¹⁹Hebron's first son was Jeriah, his second was Amariah, his third was Jahaziel, and his fourth was Jekameam.

²⁰Uzziel's first son was Micah and his second was Isshiah.

The People of Merari

²¹Merari's sons were Mahli and Mushi. Mahli's sons were Eleazar and Kish. ²²Eleazar died without sons; he had only daughters. Eleazar's daughters married their cousins, the sons of Kish. ²³Mushi's three sons were Mahli, Eder, and Jerimoth.

The Levites' Work

²⁴These were Levi's descendants listed by their families. They were the leaders of families. Each person who was twenty years old or older was listed. They served in the LORD's Temple.

²⁵David had said, "The LORD, the God of Israel, has given rest to his people. He has come to live in Jerusalem forever. ²⁶So the Levites don't need to carry the Holy Tent or any of the things used in its services anymore." ²⁷David's last instructions were to count the Levites who were twenty years old and older.

²⁸The Levites had the job of helping Aaron's descendants in the service of the Temple of the LORD. They cared for the Temple courtyard and side rooms, and they made all the holy things pure. Their job was to serve in the Temple of God. ²⁹They were responsible for putting the holy bread on the table, for the flour in the grain offerings, for the bread made without yeast, for the baking and mixing, and for the measuring. ³⁰The Levites also stood every morning and gave thanks and praise to the LORD. They also did this every evening. ³¹The Levites offered all the burnt offerings to the LORD on the special days of rest, at the New Moon festivals, and at all appointed feasts. They served before the LORD every day. They were to follow the rules for how many Levites should serve each time. ³²So the Levites took care of the

Meeting Tent and the Holy Place. And they helped their relatives, Aaron's descendants, with the services at the Temple of the LORD.

The Groups of the Priests

24 These were the groups of Aaron's sons: Aaron's sons were Nadab, Abihu, Eleazar, and Ithamar. ²But Nadab and Abihu died before their father did, and they had no sons. So Eleazar and Ithamar served as the priests. ³David, with the help of Zadok, a descendant of Eleazar, and Ahimelech, a descendant of Ithamar, separated their family groups into two different groups. Each group had certain duties. ⁴There were more leaders from Eleazar's family than from Ithamar's—sixteen leaders from Eleazar's family and eight leaders from Ithamar's family. ⁵Men were chosen from Eleazar's and Ithamar's families by throwing lots. Some men from each family were chosen to be in charge of the Holy Place, and some were chosen to serve as priests.

⁶Shemaiah son of Nethanel, from the tribe of Levi, was the secretary. He recorded the names of those descendants in front of King David, the officers, Zadok the priest, Ahimelech son of Abiathar, and the leaders of the families of the priests and Levites. The work was divided by lots among the families of Eleazar and Ithamar. The following men with their groups were chosen.

⁷The first one chosen was Jehoiarib. The second was Jedaiah. ⁸The third was Harim. The fourth was Seorim. ⁹The fifth was Malkijah. The sixth was Mijamin. ¹⁰The seventh was Hakkoz. The eighth was Abijah. ¹¹The ninth was Jeshua. The tenth was Shecaniah. ¹²The eleventh was Eliashib. The twelfth was Jakim. ¹³The thirteenth was Huppah. The fourteenth was Jeshebeab. ¹⁴The fifteenth was Bilgah. The sixteenth was Immer. ¹⁵The seventeenth was Hezir. The eighteenth was Happizzez. ¹⁶The nineteenth was Pethahiah. The twentieth was Jehezkel. ¹⁷The twenty-first was Jakin. The twenty-second was Gamul. ¹⁸The twenty-third was Delaiah. The twenty-fourth was Maaziah.

¹⁹These were the groups chosen to serve in the Temple of the LORD. They obeyed the rules given them by Aaron, just as the LORD, the God of Israel, had commanded him.

The Other Levites

²⁰These are the names of the rest of Levi's descendants:

Shubael was a descendant of Amram, and Jehdeiah was a descendant of Shubael.

²¹Isshiah was the first son of Rehabiah.

²²From the Izhar family group, there was Shelomoth, and Jahath was a descendant of Shelomoth.

²³Hebron's first son was Jeriah, Amariah was his second, Jahaziel was his third, and Jekameam was his fourth.

²⁴Uzziel's son was Micah. Micah's son was Shamir. ²⁵Micah's brother was Isshiah, and Isshiah's son was Zechariah.

²⁶Merari's descendants were Mahli and Mushi. Merari's son was Jaaziah. ²⁷Jaaziah son of Merari had sons named Shoham, Zaccur, and Ibri. ²⁸Mahli's son was Eleazar, but Eleazar did not have any sons.

²⁹Kish's son was Jerahmeel.

³⁰Mushi's sons were Mahli, Eder, and Jerimoth.

These are the Levites, listed by their families. ³¹They were chosen for special jobs by throwing lots in front of King David, Zadok, Ahimelech, the leaders of the families of the priests, and the Levites. They did this just as their relatives, the priests, Aaron's descendants, had done. The families of the oldest brother and the youngest brother were treated the same.

The Music Groups

25 David and the commanders of the army chose some of the sons of Asaph, Heman, and Jeduthun to preach and play harps, lyres, and cymbals. Here is a list of the men who served in this way:

²Asaph's sons who served were Zaccur, Joseph, Nethaniah, and Asarelah. King David chose Asaph to preach, and Asaph directed his sons.

³Jeduthun's sons who served were Gedaliah, Zeri, Jeshaiah, Shimei, Hashabiah, and Mattithiah. There were six of them, and Jeduthun directed them. He preached and used a harp to give thanks and praise to the LORD.

⁴Heman's sons who served were Bukkiah, Mattaniah, Uzziel, Shubael, Jerimoth, Hananiah, Hanani, Eliathah, Giddalti, Romamti-

Ezer, Joshbekashah, Mallothi, Hothir, and Mahazioth. ⁵All these were sons of Heman, David's seer. God promised to make Heman strong, so Heman had many sons. God gave him fourteen sons and three daughters. ⁶Heman directed all his sons in making music for the Temple of the LORD with cymbals, lyres, and harps; that was their way of serving in the Temple of God. King David was in charge of Asaph, Jeduthun, and Heman. ⁷These men and their relatives were trained and skilled in making music for the LORD. There were two hundred eighty-eight of them. ⁸Everyone threw lots to choose the time his family was to serve at the Temple. The young and the old, the teacher and the student, had to throw lots.

⁹First, the lot fell to Joseph, from the family of Asaph.

Second, twelve men were chosen from Gedaliah, his sons and relatives.

¹⁰Third, twelve men were chosen from Zaccur, his sons and relatives.

¹¹Fourth, twelve men were chosen from Izri, his sons and relatives.

¹²Fifth, twelve men were chosen from Nethaniah, his sons and relatives.

¹³Sixth, twelve men were chosen from Bukkiah, his sons and relatives.

¹⁴Seventh, twelve men were chosen from Jesarelah, his sons and relatives.

¹⁵Eighth, twelve men were chosen from Jeshaiah, his sons and relatives.

¹⁶Ninth, twelve men were chosen from Mattaniah, his sons and relatives.

¹⁷Tenth, twelve men were chosen from Shimei, his sons and relatives.

¹⁸Eleventh, twelve men were chosen from Azarel, his sons and relatives.

¹⁹Twelfth, twelve men were chosen from Hashabiah, his sons and relatives.

²⁰Thirteenth, twelve men were chosen from Shubael, his sons and relatives.

²¹Fourteenth, twelve men were chosen from Mattithiah, his sons and relatives.

²²Fifteenth, twelve men were chosen from Jerimoth, his sons and relatives.

²³Sixteenth, twelve men were chosen from Hananiah, his sons and relatives.

²⁴Seventeenth, twelve men were chosen from Joshbekashah, his sons and relatives.

²⁵Eighteenth, twelve men were chosen from Hanani, his sons and relatives.

²⁶Nineteenth, twelve men were chosen from Mallothi, his sons and relatives.

²⁷Twentieth, twelve men were chosen from Eliathah, his sons and relatives.

²⁸Twenty-first, twelve men were chosen from Hothir, his sons and relatives.

²⁹Twenty-second, twelve men were chosen from Giddalti, his sons and relatives.

³⁰Twenty-third, twelve men were chosen from Mahazioth, his sons and relatives.

³¹Twenty-fourth, twelve men were chosen from Romamti-Ezer, his sons and relatives.

PSALM 78:40–55

⁴⁰They turned against God so often in the desert
    and grieved him there.
⁴¹Again and again they tested God
    and brought pain to the Holy One of Israel.
⁴²They did not remember his power
    or the time he saved them from the enemy.
⁴³They forgot the signs he did in Egypt
    and his wonders in the fields of Zoan.
⁴⁴He turned their rivers to blood
    so no one could drink the water.
⁴⁵He sent flies that bit the people.
    He sent frogs that destroyed them.
⁴⁶He gave their crops to grasshoppers
    and what they worked for to locusts.
⁴⁷He destroyed their vines with hail
    and their sycamore trees with sleet.
⁴⁸He killed their animals with hail
    and their cattle with lightning.
⁴⁹He showed them his hot anger.
    He sent his strong anger against them,
    his destroying angels.
⁵⁰He found a way to show his anger.
    He did not keep them from dying
    but let them die by a terrible disease.
⁵¹God killed all the firstborn sons in Egypt,
    the oldest son of each family of Ham.ⁿ
⁵²But God led his people out like sheep

78:51 Ham The people in Egypt were descendants of Ham, one of Noah's sons. See Genesis 10:6.

and he guided them like a flock
through the desert.
[53]He led them to safety so they had
nothing to fear,
but their enemies drowned in the sea.
[54]So God brought them to his holy land,
to the mountain country he took with
his own power.
[55]He forced out the other nations,
and he had his people inherit the land.
He let the tribes of Israel settle there in
tents.

PROVERBS 20:3

[3]Foolish people are always fighting,
but avoiding quarrels will bring you
honor.

ACTS 9:19b–43

Saul Preaches in Damascus

Saul stayed with the followers of Jesus in
Damascus for a few days. [20]Soon he began to
preach about Jesus in the synagogues, saying, "Jesus is the Son of God."
[21]All the people who heard him were
amazed. They said, "This is the man who
was in Jerusalem trying to destroy those
who trust in this name! He came here to arrest the followers of Jesus and take them
back to the leading priests."
[22]But Saul grew more powerful. His proofs
that Jesus is the Christ were so strong that
his own people in Damascus could not argue
with him.
[23]After many days, they made plans to kill
Saul. [24]They were watching the city gates day
and night, but Saul learned about their plan.
[25]One night some followers of Saul helped
him leave the city by lowering him in a basket through an opening in the city wall.

Saul Preaches in Jerusalem

[26]When Saul went to Jerusalem, he tried
to join the group of followers, but they were
all afraid of him. They did not believe he was
really a follower. [27]But Barnabas accepted
Saul and took him to the apostles. Barnabas
explained to them that Saul had seen the
Lord on the road and the Lord had spoken to
Saul. Then he told them how boldly Saul had
preached in the name of Jesus in Damascus.

[28]And so Saul stayed with the followers,
going everywhere in Jerusalem, preaching
boldly in the name of the Lord. [29]He would
often talk and argue with the Jewish people
who spoke Greek, but they were trying to kill
him. [30]When the followers learned about
this, they took Saul to Caesarea and from
there sent him to Tarsus.
[31]The church everywhere in Judea, Galilee,
and Samaria had a time of peace and became
stronger. Respecting the Lord by the way they
lived, and being encouraged by the Holy Spirit,
the group of believers continued to grow.

Peter Heals Aeneas

[32]As Peter was traveling through all the
area, he visited God's people who lived in
Lydda. [33]There he met a man named Aeneas,
who was paralyzed and had not been able to
leave his bed for the past eight years. [34]Peter
said to him, "Aeneas, Jesus Christ heals you.
Stand up and make your bed." Aeneas stood
up immediately. [35]All the people living in
Lydda and on the Plain of Sharon saw him
and turned to the Lord.

Peter Heals Tabitha

[36]In the city of Joppa there was a follower
named Tabitha (whose Greek name was Dor-
cas). She was always doing good deeds and
kind acts. [37]While Peter was in Lydda, Tabitha
became sick and died. Her body was washed
and put in a room upstairs. [38]Since Lydda is
near Joppa and the followers in Joppa heard
that Peter was in Lydda, they sent two messengers to Peter. They begged him, "Hurry,
please come to us!" [39]So Peter got ready and
went with them. When he arrived, they took
him to the upstairs room where all the widows stood around Peter, crying. They showed
him the shirts and coats Tabitha had made
when she was still alive. [40]Peter sent everyone
out of the room and kneeled and prayed.
Then he turned to the body and said,
"Tabitha, stand up." She opened her eyes, and
when she saw Peter, she sat up. [41]He gave her
his hand and helped her up. Then he called
the saints and the widows into the room and
showed them that Tabitha was alive. [42]People
everywhere in Joppa learned about this, and
many believed in the Lord. [43]Peter stayed in
Joppa for many days with a man named Simon who was a tanner.

JULY 1

1 CHRONICLES 26:1—27:34

The Gatekeepers

26 These are the groups of the gatekeepers. From the family of Korah, there was Meshelemiah son of Kore, who was from Asaph's family. ²Meshelemiah had sons. Zechariah was his first son, Jediael was second, Zebadiah was third, Jathniel was fourth, ³Elam was fifth, Jehohanan was sixth, and Eliehoenai was seventh.

⁴Obed-Edom had sons. Shemaiah was his first son, Jehozabad was second, Joah was third, Sacar was fourth, Nethanel was fifth, ⁵Ammiel was sixth, Issachar was seventh, and Peullethai was eighth. God blessed Obed-Edom with children.

⁶Obed-Edom's son Shemaiah also had sons. They were leaders in their father's family because they were capable men. ⁷Shemaiah's sons were Othni, Rephael, Obed, Elzabad, Elihu, and Semakiah. Elihu, and Semakiah were skilled workers. ⁸All these were Obed-Edom's descendants. They and their sons and relatives were capable men and strong workers. Obed-Edom had sixty-two descendants in all.

⁹Meshelemiah had sons and relatives who were skilled workers. In all, there were eighteen.

¹⁰From the Merari family, Hosah had sons. Shimri was chosen to be in charge. Although he was not the oldest son, his father chose him to be in charge. ¹¹Hilkiah was his second son, Tabaliah was third, and Zechariah was fourth. In all, Hosah had thirteen sons and relatives.

¹²These were the leaders of the groups of gatekeepers, and they served in the Temple of the LORD. Their relatives also worked in the Temple. ¹³By throwing lots, each family chose a gate to guard. Young and old threw lots.

¹⁴Meshelemiah was chosen by lot to guard the East Gate. Then lots were thrown for Meshelemiah's son Zechariah. He was a wise counselor and was chosen for the North Gate. ¹⁵Obed-Edom was chosen for the South Gate, and Obed-Edom's sons were chosen to guard the storehouse. ¹⁶Shuppim and Hosah were chosen for the West Gate and the Shalleketh Gate on the upper road.

Guards stood side by side with guards. ¹⁷Six Levites stood guard every day at the East Gate; four Levites stood guard every day at the North Gate; four Levites stood guard every day at the South Gate; and two Levites at a time guarded the storehouse. ¹⁸There were two guards at the western court and four guards on the road to the court.

¹⁹These were the groups of the gatekeepers from the families of Korah and Merari.

Other Leaders

²⁰Other Levites were responsible for guarding the treasuries of the Temple of God and for the places where the holy items were kept.

²¹Ladan was Gershon's son and the ancestor of several family groups. Jehiel was a leader of one of the family groups. ²²His sons were Zetham and Joel his brother, and they were responsible for the treasuries of the Temple of the LORD.

²³Other leaders were chosen from the family groups of Amram, Izhar, Hebron, and Uzziel. ²⁴Shubael, the descendant of Gershom, who was Moses' son, was the leader responsible for the treasuries. ²⁵These were Shubael's relatives from Eliezer: Eliezer's son Rehabiah, Rehabiah's son Jeshaiah, Jeshaiah's son Joram, Joram's son Zicri, and Zicri's son Shelomith. ²⁶Shelomith and his relatives were responsible for everything that had been collected for the Temple by King David, by the heads of families, by the commanders of a thousand men and of a hundred men, and by other army commanders. ²⁷They also gave some of the things they had taken in wars to be used in repairing the Temple of the LORD. ²⁸Shelomith and his relatives took care of all the holy items. Some had been given by Samuel the seer, Saul son of Kish, Abner son of Ner, and Joab son of Zeruiah.

²⁹Kenaniah was from the Izhar family. He and his sons worked outside the Temple as

officers and judges in different places in Israel.

³⁰Hashabiah was from the Hebron family. He and his relatives were responsible for the LORD's work and the king's business in Israel west of the Jordan River. There were seventeen hundred skilled men in Hashabiah's group. ³¹The history of the Hebron family shows that Jeriah was their leader. In David's fortieth year as king, the records were searched, and some capable men of the Hebron family were found living at Jazer in Gilead. ³²Jeriah had twenty-seven hundred relatives who were skilled men and leaders of families. King David gave them the responsibility of directing the tribes of Reuben, Gad, and East Manasseh in God's work and the king's business.

Army Divisions

27 This is the list of the Israelites who served the king in the army. Each division was on duty one month each year. There were leaders of families, commanders of a hundred men, commanders of a thousand men, and other officers. Each division had twenty-four thousand men.

²Jashobeam son of Zabdiel was in charge of the first division for the first month. There were twenty-four thousand men in his division. ³Jashobeam, one of the descendants of Perez, was leader of all the army officers for the first month.

⁴Dodai, from the Ahohites, was in charge of the division for the second month. Mikloth was a leader in the division. There were twenty-four thousand men in Dodai's division.

⁵The third commander, for the third month, was Benaiah son of Jehoiada the priest. There were twenty-four thousand men in his division. ⁶He was the Benaiah who was one of the Thirty[n] soldiers. Benaiah was a brave warrior who led those men. Benaiah's son Ammizabad was in charge of Benaiah's division.

⁷The fourth commander, for the fourth month, was Asahel, the brother of Joab. Later, Asahel's son Zebadiah took his place

as commander. There were twenty-four thousand men in his division.

⁸The fifth commander, for the fifth month, was Shamhuth, from Izrah's family. There were twenty-four thousand men in his division.

⁹The sixth commander, for the sixth month, was Ira son of Ikkesh from the town of Tekoa. There were twenty-four thousand men in his division.

¹⁰The seventh commander, for the seventh month, was Helez. He was from the Pelonites and a descendant of Ephraim. There were twenty-four thousand men in his division.

¹¹The eighth commander, for the eighth month, was Sibbecai. He was from Hushah and was from Zerah's family. There were twenty-four thousand men in his division.

¹²The ninth commander, for the ninth month, was Abiezer. He was from Anathoth in Benjamin. There were twenty-four thousand men in his division.

¹³The tenth commander, for the tenth month, was Maharai. He was from Netophah and was from Zerah's family. There were twenty-four thousand men in his division.

¹⁴The eleventh commander, for the eleventh month, was Benaiah. He was from Pirathon in Ephraim. There were twenty-four thousand men in his division.

¹⁵The twelfth commander, for the twelfth month, was Heldai. He was from Netophah and was from Othniel's family. There were twenty-four thousand men in his division.

Leaders of the Tribes

¹⁶These were the leaders of the tribes of Israel. Eliezer son of Zicri was over the tribe of Reuben. Shephatiah son of Maacah was over the tribe of Simeon. ¹⁷Hashabiah son of Kemuel was over the tribe of Levi. Zadok was over the people of Aaron. ¹⁸Elihu, one of David's brothers, was over the tribe of Judah. Omri son of Michael was over the tribe of Issachar. ¹⁹Ishmaiah son of Obadiah was over the tribe of Zebulun. Jerimoth son of Azriel was over the tribe of Naphtali. ²⁰Hoshea son of Azaziah was over the tribe of Ephraim.

27:6 Thirty These were David's most powerful soldiers. See 2 Samuel 23:24.

Joel son of Pedaiah was over West Manasseh. [21]Iddo son of Zechariah was over East Manasseh. Jaasiel son of Abner was over the tribe of Benjamin. [22]Azarel son of Jeroham was over the tribe of Dan.

These were the leaders of the tribes of Israel.

[23]The LORD had promised to make the Israelites as many as the stars in the sky. So David only counted the men who were twenty years old and older. [24]Joab son of Zeruiah began to count the people, but he did not finish. God became angry with Israel for counting the people, so the number of the people was not put in the history book about King David's rule.

The King's Directors

[25]Azmaveth son of Adiel was in charge of the royal storehouses.

Jonathan son of Uzziah was in charge of the storehouses in the country, towns, villages, and towers.

[26]Ezri son of Kelub was in charge of the field workers who farmed the land.

[27]Shimei, from the town of Ramah, was in charge of the vineyards.

Zabdi, from Shapham, was in charge of storing the wine that came from the vineyards.

[28]Baal-Hanan, from Geder, was in charge of the olive trees and sycamore trees in the western hills.

Joash was in charge of storing the olive oil.

[29]Shitrai, from Sharon, was in charge of the herds that fed in the Plain of Sharon.

Shaphat son of Adlai was in charge of the herds in the valleys.

[30]Obil, an Ishmaelite, was in charge of the camels.

Jehdeiah, from Meronoth, was in charge of the donkeys.

[31]Jaziz, from the Hagrites, was in charge of the flocks.

All these men were the officers who took care of King David's property.

[32]Jonathan was David's uncle, and he advised David. Jonathan was a wise man and a teacher of the law. Jehiel son of Hacmoni took care of the king's sons. [33]Ahithophel advised the king. Hushai, from the Arkite people, was the king's friend. [34]Jehoiada and Abiathar later took Ahithophel's place in advising the king. Jehoiada was Benaiah's son. Joab was the commander of the king's army.

PSALM 78:56–64

[56]But they tested God
  and turned against God Most High;
  they did not keep his rules.
[57]They turned away and were disloyal just
    like their ancestors.
  They were like a crooked bow that does
    not shoot straight.
[58]They made God angry by building places
    to worship gods;
  they made him jealous with their idols.
[59]When God heard them, he became very
    angry
  and rejected the people of Israel
    completely.
[60]He left his dwelling at Shiloh,
  the Tent where he lived among the
    people.
[61]He let the Ark, his power, be captured;
  he let the Ark, his glory, be taken by
    enemies.
[62]He let his people be killed;
  he was very angry with his children.
[63]The young men died by fire,
  and the young women had no one to
    marry.
[64]Their priests fell by the sword,
  but their widows were not allowed to
    cry.

PROVERBS 20:4–5

[4]Lazy farmers don't plow when they
    should;
  they expect a harvest, but there is none.

[5]People's thoughts can be like a deep well,
  but someone with understanding can
    find the wisdom there.

ACTS 10:1–23a

Peter Teaches Cornelius

10At Caesarea there was a man named Cornelius, an officer in the Italian group of the Roman army. [2]Cornelius was a religious man. He and all the other people who lived in his house worshiped the true God. He gave much of his money to the poor and prayed to God often. ³One afternoon about three o'clock, Cornelius clearly saw a vision. An angel of God came to him and said, "Cornelius!"

⁴Cornelius stared at the angel. He became afraid and said, "What do you want, Lord?"

The angel said, "God has heard your prayers. He has seen that you give to the poor, and he remembers you. ⁵Send some men now to Joppa to bring back a man named Simon who is also called Peter. ⁶He is staying with a man, also named Simon, who is a tanner and has a house beside the sea." ⁷When the angel who spoke to Cornelius left, Cornelius called two of his servants and a soldier, a religious man who worked for him. ⁸Cornelius explained everything to them and sent them to Joppa.

⁹About noon the next day as they came near Joppa, Peter was going up to the roof[n] to pray. ¹⁰He was hungry and wanted to eat, but while the food was being prepared, he had a vision. ¹¹He saw heaven opened and something coming down that looked like a big sheet being lowered to earth by its four corners. ¹²In it were all kinds of animals, rep-

tiles, and birds. ¹³Then a voice said to Peter, "Get up, Peter; kill and eat."

¹⁴But Peter said, "No, Lord! I have never eaten food that is unholy or unclean."

¹⁵But the voice said to him again, "God has made these things clean, so don't call them 'unholy'!" ¹⁶This happened three times, and at once the sheet was taken back to heaven.

¹⁷While Peter was wondering what this vision meant, the men Cornelius sent had found Simon's house and were standing at the gate. ¹⁸They asked, "Is Simon Peter staying here?"

¹⁹While Peter was still thinking about the vision, the Spirit said to him, "Listen, three men are looking for you. ²⁰Get up and go downstairs. Go with them without doubting, because I have sent them to you."

²¹So Peter went down to the men and said, "I am the one you are looking for. Why did you come here?"

²²They said, "A holy angel spoke to Cornelius, an army officer and a good man; he worships God. All the people respect him. The angel told Cornelius to ask you to come to his house so that he can hear what you have to say." ²³So Peter asked the men to come in and spend the night.

JULY 2

1 CHRONICLES 28:1—29:30

David's Plans for the Temple

28 David commanded all the leaders of Israel to come to Jerusalem. There were the leaders of the tribes, commanders of the divisions serving the king, commanders of a thousand men and of a hundred men, leaders who took care of the property and animals that belonged to the king and his sons, men over the palace, the powerful men, and all the brave warriors.

²King David stood up and said, "Listen to

me, my relatives and my people. I wanted to build a place to keep the Ark of the Agreement with the LORD. I wanted it to be God's footstool. So I made plans to build a temple. ³But God said to me, 'You must not build a temple for worshiping me, because you are a soldier and have killed many people.'

⁴"But the LORD, the God of Israel, chose me from my whole family to be king of Israel forever. He chose the tribe of Judah to lead, and from the people of Judah, he chose my father's family. From that family God was pleased to make me king of Israel. ⁵The LORD

10:9 roof In Bible times houses were built with flat roofs. The roof was used for drying things such as flax and fruit. And it was used as an extra room, as a place for worship, and as a cool place to sleep in the summer.

has given me many sons, and from those sons he has chosen Solomon to be the new king of Israel. Israel is the Lord's kingdom. [6]The Lord said to me, 'Your son Solomon will build my Temple and its courtyards. I have chosen Solomon to be my son, and I will be his father. [7]He is obeying my laws and commands now. If he continues to obey them, I will make his kingdom strong forever.'"

[8]David said, "Now, in front of all Israel, the assembly of the Lord, and in the hearing of God, I tell you these things: Be careful to obey all the commands of the Lord your God. Then you will keep this good land and pass it on to your descendants forever.

[9]"And you, my son Solomon, accept the God of your father. Serve him completely and willingly, because the Lord knows what is in everyone's mind. He understands everything you think. If you go to him for help, you will get an answer. But if you turn away from him, he will leave you forever. [10]Solomon, you must understand this. The Lord has chosen you to build the Temple as his holy place. Be strong and finish the job."

[11]Then David gave his son Solomon the plans for building the Temple and the courtyard around the Temple. They included its buildings, its storerooms, its upper rooms, its inside rooms, and the place where the people's sins were removed. [12]David gave him plans for everything he had in mind: the courtyards around the Lord's Temple and all the rooms around it, the Temple treasuries, and the treasuries of the holy items used in the Temple. [13]David gave Solomon directions for the groups of the priests and Levites. David told him about all the work of serving in the Temple of the Lord and about the items to be used in the Temple service [14]that were made of gold or silver. David told Solomon how much gold or silver should be used to make each thing. [15]David told him how much gold to use for each gold lampstand and its lamps and how much silver to use for each silver lampstand and its lamps. The different lampstands were to be used where needed. [16]David told how much gold should be used for each table that held the holy bread and how much silver should be used for the silver tables. [17]He told how

much pure gold should be used to make the forks, bowls, and pitchers and how much gold should be used to make each gold dish. He told how much silver should be used to make each silver dish [18]and how much pure gold should be used for the altar of incense. He also gave Solomon the plans for the chariot of the golden creatures that spread their wings over the Ark of the Agreement with the Lord.

[19]David said, "All these plans were written with the Lord guiding me. He helped me understand everything in the plans."

[20]David also said to his son Solomon, "Be strong and brave, and do the work. Don't be afraid or discouraged, because the Lord God, my God, is with you. He will not fail you or leave you until all the work for the Temple of the Lord is finished. [21]The groups of the priests and Levites are ready for all the work on the Temple of God. Every skilled worker is ready to help you with all the work. The leaders and all the people will obey every command you give."

Gifts for Building the Temple

29King David said to all the Israelites who were gathered, "God chose my son Solomon, who is young and hasn't yet learned what he needs to know, but the work is important. This palace is not for people; it is for the Lord God. [2]I have done my best to prepare for building the Temple of God. I have given gold for the things made of gold and silver for the things made of silver. I have given bronze for the things made of bronze and iron for the things made of iron. I have given wood for the things made of wood and onyx for the settings. I have given turquoise gems of many different colors, valuable stones, and white marble. I have given much of all these things. [3]I have already given this for the Temple, but now I am also giving my own treasures of gold and silver, because I really want the Temple of my God to be built. [4]I have given about two hundred twenty thousand pounds of pure gold from Ophir and about five hundred twenty thousand pounds of pure silver. They will be used to cover the walls of the buildings [5]and for all the gold and silver work. Skilled men may use the gold and silver to make things for the Temple. Now, who is ready to give himself to the service of the LORD today?"

⁶The family leaders and the leaders of the tribes of Israel, the commanders of a thousand men and of a hundred men, and the leaders responsible for the king's work gave their valuable things. ⁷They donated about three hundred eighty thousand pounds of gold, about seven hundred fifty thousand pounds of silver, about one million three hundred fifty thousand pounds of bronze, and about seven million five hundred thousand pounds of iron to the Temple of God. ⁸People who had valuable gems gave them to the treasury of the Temple of the LORD, and Jehiel, from the Gershon family, took care of the valuable gems. ⁹The leaders gave willingly and completely to the LORD. The people rejoiced to see their leaders give so gladly, and King David was also very happy.

David's Prayer

¹⁰David praised the LORD in front of all the people who were gathered. He said:
"We praise you, LORD,
   God of our father Israel.
We praise you forever and ever.
¹¹LORD, you are great and powerful.
   You have glory, victory, and honor.
   Everything in heaven and on earth
      belongs to you.
   The kingdom belongs to you, LORD;
      you are the ruler over everything.
¹²Riches and honor come from you.
   You rule everything.
   You have the power and strength
      to make anyone great and strong.
¹³Now, our God, we thank you
   and praise your glorious name.

¹⁴"These things did not really come from
      me and my people.
   Everything comes from you;
   we have given you back what you gave
      us.
¹⁵We are like foreigners and strangers,
      as our ancestors were.
   Our time on earth is like a shadow.
   There is no hope.
¹⁶LORD our God, we have gathered all this
   to build your Temple for worship to you.

But everything has come from you;
   everything belongs to you.
¹⁷I know, my God, that you test people's
      hearts.
   You are happy when people do what is
      right.
   I was happy to give all these things,
   and I gave with an honest heart.
   Your people gathered here are happy to
      give to you,
   and I rejoice to see their giving.
¹⁸LORD, you are the God of our ancestors,
   the God of Abraham, Isaac, and Jacob.
   Make your people want to serve you
      always,
   and make them want to obey you.
¹⁹Give my son Solomon a desire to serve
      you.
   Help him always obey your commands,
      laws, and rules.
   Help him build the Temple
   for which I have prepared."

²⁰Then David said to all the people who were gathered, "Praise the LORD your God." So they all praised the LORD, the God of their ancestors, and they bowed to the ground to give honor to the LORD and the king.

Solomon Becomes King

²¹The next day the people sacrificed to the LORD. They offered burnt offerings to him of a thousand bulls, a thousand male sheep, and a thousand male lambs. They also brought drink offerings. Many sacrifices were made for all the people of Israel. ²²That day the people ate and drank with much joy, and the LORD was with them.

And they made David's son Solomon king for the second time. They poured olive oil on Solomon to appoint him king in the presence of the LORD. And they poured oil on Zadok to appoint him as priest. ²³Then Solomon sat on the LORD's throne as king and took his father David's place. Solomon was very successful, and all the people of Israel obeyed him. ²⁴All the leaders and soldiers and King David's sons accepted Solomon as king and promised to obey him. ²⁵The LORD made Solomon great before all the Israelites and gave Solomon much honor. No king of Israel before Solomon had such honor.

David's Death

[26]David son of Jesse was king over all Israel. [27]He had ruled over Israel forty years—seven years in Hebron and thirty-three years in Jerusalem. [28]David died when he was old. He had lived a good, long life and had received many riches and honors. His son Solomon became king after him.

[29]Everything David did as king, from beginning to end, is recorded in the records of Samuel the seer, the records of Nathan the prophet, and the records of Gad the seer. [30]Those writings tell what David did as king of Israel. They tell about his power and what happened to him and to Israel and to all the kingdoms around them.

PSALM 78:65–72

[65]Then the Lord got up as if he had been
asleep;
he awoke like a man who had been
drunk with wine.
[66]He struck down his enemies
and disgraced them forever.
[67]But God rejected the family of Joseph;
he did not choose the tribe of Ephraim.
[68]Instead, he chose the tribe of Judah
and Mount Zion, which he loves.
[69]And he built his Temple high like the
mountains.
Like the earth, he built it to last forever.
[70]He chose David to be his servant
and took him from the sheep pens.
[71]He brought him from tending the sheep
so he could lead the flock, the people of
Jacob,
his own people, the people of Israel.
[72]And David led them with an innocent
heart
and guided them with skillful hands.

PROVERBS 20:6–7

[6]Many people claim to be loyal,
but it is hard to find a trustworthy
person.

[7]The good people who live honest lives
will be a blessing to their children.

ACTS 10:23b–48

The next day Peter got ready and went with them, and some of the followers from Joppa joined him. [24]On the following day they came to Caesarea. Cornelius was waiting for them and had called together his relatives and close friends. [25]When Peter entered, Cornelius met him, fell at his feet, and worshiped him. [26]But Peter helped him up, saying, "Stand up. I too am only a human." [27]As he talked with Cornelius, Peter went inside where he saw many people gathered. [28]He said, "You people understand that it is against our law for Jewish people to associate with or visit anyone who is not Jewish. But God has shown me that I should not call any person 'unholy' or 'unclean.' [29]That is why I did not argue when I was asked to come here. Now, please tell me why you sent for me."

[30]Cornelius said, "Four days ago, I was praying in my house at this same time—three o'clock in the afternoon. Suddenly, there was a man standing before me wearing shining clothes. [31]He said, 'Cornelius, God has heard your prayer and has seen that you give to the poor and remembers you. [32]So send some men to Joppa and ask Simon Peter to come. Peter is staying in the house of a man, also named Simon, who is a tanner and has a house beside the sea.' [33]So I sent for you immediately, and it was very good of you to come. Now we are all here before God to hear everything the Lord has commanded you to tell us."

[34]Peter began to speak: "I really understand now that to God every person is the same. [35]In every country God accepts anyone who worships him and does what is right. [36]You know the message that God has sent to the people of Israel is the Good News that peace has come through Jesus Christ. Jesus is the Lord of all people! [37]You know what has happened all over Judea, beginning in Galilee after John[n] preached to the people about baptism. [38]You know about Jesus from Nazareth, that God gave him the Holy Spirit and power. You know how Jesus went everywhere doing good and healing those who were ruled by the devil, because God was

---

10:37 John John the Baptist, who preached to people about Christ's coming (Luke 3).

with him. [39]We saw what Jesus did in Judea and in Jerusalem, but the Jews in Jerusalem killed him by hanging him on a cross. [40]Yet, on the third day, God raised Jesus to life and caused him to be seen, [41]not by all the people, but only by the witnesses God had already chosen. And we are those witnesses who ate and drank with him after he was raised from the dead. [42]He told us to preach to the people and to tell them that he is the one whom God chose to be the judge of the living and the dead. [43]All the prophets say it is true that all who believe in Jesus will be forgiven of their sins through Jesus' name."

[44]While Peter was still saying this, the Holy Spirit came down on all those who were listening. [45]The Jewish believers who came with Peter were amazed that the gift of the Holy Spirit had been given even to the nations. [46]These believers heard them speaking in different languages[n] and praising God. Then Peter said, [47]"Can anyone keep these people from being baptized with water? They have received the Holy Spirit just as we did!" [48]So Peter ordered that they be baptized in the name of Jesus Christ. Then they asked Peter to stay with them for a few days.

JULY 3

2 CHRONICLES 1:1—2:18

Solomon Asks for Wisdom

1 Solomon, David's son, became a powerful king, because the LORD his God was with him and made him very great.

[2]Solomon spoke to all the people of Israel—the commanders of a hundred men and of a thousand men, the judges, every leader in all Israel, and the leaders of the families. [3]Then Solomon and all the people with him went to the place of worship at the town of Gibeon. God's Meeting Tent, which Moses the LORD's servant had made in the desert, was there. [4]David had brought the Ark of God from Kiriath Jearim to Jerusalem, where he had made a place for it and had set up a tent for it. [5]The bronze altar that Bezalel son of Uri, who was the son of Hur, had made was in Gibeon in front of the Holy Tent. So Solomon and the people worshiped there. [6]Solomon went up to the bronze altar in the presence of the LORD at the Meeting Tent and offered a thousand burnt offerings on it.

[7]That night God appeared to Solomon and said to him, "Ask for whatever you want me to give you."

[8]Solomon answered, "You have been very kind to my father David, and you have made

me king in his place. [9]Now, LORD God, may your promise to my father David come true. You have made me king of a people who are as many as the dust of the earth. [10]Now give me wisdom and knowledge so I can lead these people in the right way, because no one can rule them without your help."

[11]God said to Solomon, "You have not asked for wealth or riches or honor, or for the death of your enemies, or for a long life. But since you have asked for wisdom and knowledge to lead my people, over whom I have made you king, [12]I will give you wisdom and knowledge. I will also give you more wealth, riches, and honor than any king who has lived before you or any who will live after you."

[13]Then Solomon left the place of worship, the Meeting Tent, at Gibeon and went back to Jerusalem. There King Solomon ruled over Israel.

Solomon's Wealth

[14]Solomon had fourteen hundred chariots and twelve thousand horses. He kept some in special cities for the chariots, and others he kept with him in Jerusalem. [15]In Jerusalem Solomon made silver and gold as plentiful as stones and cedar trees as

10:46 languages This can also be translated "tongues."

plentiful as the fig trees on the western hills. [16]He imported horses from Egypt and Kue; his traders bought them in Kue. [17]They imported chariots from Egypt for about fifteen pounds of silver apiece, and horses cost nearly four pounds of silver apiece. Then they sold the horses and chariots to all the kings of the Hittites and the Arameans.

Solomon Prepares for the Temple

2 Solomon decided to build a temple as a place to worship the LORD and also a palace for himself. [2]He chose seventy thousand men to carry loads, eighty thousand men to cut stone in the hill country, and thirty-six hundred men to direct the workers.

[3]Solomon sent this message to Hiram king of the city of Tyre: "Help me as you helped my father David by sending him cedar logs so he could build himself a palace to live in. [4]I will build a temple for worshiping the LORD my God, and I will give this temple to him. There we will burn sweet-smelling spices in his presence. We will continually set out the holy bread in God's presence. And we will burn sacrifices every morning and evening, on Sabbath days and New Moons, and on the other feast days commanded by the LORD our God. This is a rule for Israel to obey forever.

[5]"The temple I build will be great, because our God is greater than all gods. [6]But no one can really build a house for our God. Not even the highest of heavens can hold him. How then can I build a temple for him except as a place to burn sacrifices to him?

[7]"Now send me a man skilled in working with gold, silver, bronze, and iron, and with purple, red, and blue thread. He must also know how to make engravings. He will work with my skilled craftsmen in Judah and Jerusalem, whom my father David chose.

[8]"Also send me cedar, pine, and juniper logs from Lebanon. I know your servants are experienced at cutting down the trees in Lebanon, and my servants will help them. [9]Send me a lot of wood, because the temple I am going to build will be large and wonderful. [10]I will give your servants who cut the wood one hundred twenty-five thousand bushels of wheat, one hundred twenty-five thousand bushels of barley, one hundred fifteen thousand gallons of wine, and one hundred fifteen thousand gallons of oil."

[11]Then Hiram king of Tyre answered Solomon with this letter: "Solomon, because the LORD loves his people, he chose you to be their king." [12]Hiram also said: "Praise the LORD, the God of Israel, who made heaven and earth! He has given King David a wise son, one with wisdom and understanding, who will build a temple for the LORD and a palace for himself.

[13]"I will send you a skilled and wise man named Huram-Abi. [14]His mother was from the people of Dan, and his father was from Tyre. Huram-Abi is skilled in working with gold, silver, bronze, iron, stone, and wood, and with purple, blue, and red thread, and expensive linen. He is skilled in making engravings and can make any design you show him. He will help your craftsmen and the craftsmen of your father David.

[15]"Now send my servants the wheat, barley, oil, and wine you promised. [16]We will cut as much wood from Lebanon as you need and will bring it on rafts by sea to Joppa. Then you may carry it to Jerusalem."

[17]Solomon counted all the foreigners living in Israel. (This was after the time his father David had counted the people.) There were one hundred fifty-three thousand six hundred foreigners in the country. [18]Solomon chose seventy thousand of them to carry loads, eighty thousand of them to cut stone in the mountains, and thirty-six hundred of them to direct the workers and to keep the people working.

PSALM 79:1–4

The Nation Cries for Jerusalem

A psalm of Asaph.

79 God, nations have come against your
        chosen people.
    They have ruined your holy Temple.
    They have turned Jerusalem into ruins.
  [2]They have given the bodies of your
        servants as food to the wild birds.
    They have given the bodies of those who
        worship you to the wild animals.

[3]They have spilled blood like water all
around Jerusalem.
No one was left to bury the dead.
[4]We are a joke to the other nations;
they laugh and make fun of us.

PROVERBS 20:8–9

[8]When a king sits on his throne to judge,
he knows evil when he sees it.

[9]No one can say, "I am innocent;
I have never done anything wrong."

ACTS 11:1–30

Peter Returns to Jerusalem

11 The apostles and the believers in Judea
heard that some who were not Jewish
had accepted God's teaching too. [2]But when
Peter came to Jerusalem, some people argued with him. [3]They said, "You went into
the homes of people who are not circumcised and ate with them!"

[4]So Peter explained the whole story to
them. [5]He said, "I was in the city of Joppa,
and while I was praying, I had a vision. I saw
something that looked like a big sheet being
lowered from heaven by its four corners. It
came very close to me. [6]I looked inside it and
saw animals, wild beasts, reptiles, and birds.
[7]I heard a voice say to me, 'Get up, Peter. Kill
and eat.' [8]But I said, 'No, Lord! I have never
eaten anything that is unholy or unclean.'
[9]But the voice from heaven spoke again, 'God
has made these things clean, so don't call
them unholy.' [10]This happened three times.
Then the whole thing was taken back to
heaven. [11]Right then three men who were
sent to me from Caesarea came to the house
where I was staying. [12]The Spirit told me to
go with them without doubting. These six
believers here also went with me, and we entered the house of Cornelius. [13]He told us
about the angel he saw standing in his
house. The angel said to him, 'Send some
men to Joppa and invite Simon Peter to
come. [14]By the words he will say to you, you
and all your family will be saved.' [15]When I
began my speech, the Holy Spirit came on
them just as he came on us at the beginning.

[16]Then I remembered the words of the Lord.
He said, 'John baptized with water, but you
will be baptized with the Holy Spirit.' [17]Since
God gave them the same gift he gave us who
believed in the Lord Jesus Christ, how could
I stop the work of God?"

[18]When the believers heard this, they
stopped arguing. They praised God and said,
"So God is allowing even other nations to
turn to him and live."

The Good News Comes to Antioch

[19]Many of the believers were scattered
when they were persecuted after Stephen
was killed. Some of them went as far as
Phoenicia, Cyprus, and Antioch telling the
message to others, but only to Jews. [20]Some
of these believers were people from Cyprus
and Cyrene. When they came to Antioch,
they spoke also to Greeks,[n] telling them the
Good News about the Lord Jesus. [21]The Lord
was helping the believers, and a large group
of people believed and turned to the Lord.

[22]The church in Jerusalem heard about
all of this, so they sent Barnabas to Antioch. [23-24]Barnabas was a good man, full of
the Holy Spirit and full of faith. When he
reached Antioch and saw how God had
blessed the people, he was glad. He encouraged all the believers in Antioch always to
obey the Lord with all their hearts, and
many people became followers of the Lord.

[25]Then Barnabas went to the city of Tarsus to look for Saul, [26]and when he found
Saul, he brought him to Antioch. For a whole
year Saul and Barnabas met with the church
and taught many people there. In Antioch
the followers were called Christians for the
first time.

[27]About that time some prophets came
from Jerusalem to Antioch. [28]One of them,
named Agabus, stood up and spoke with the
help of the Holy Spirit. He said, "A very hard
time is coming to the whole world. There will
be no food to eat." (This happened when
Claudius ruled.) [29]The followers all decided
to help the believers who lived in Judea, as
much as each one could. [30]They gathered the
money and gave it to Barnabas and Saul, who
brought it to the elders in Judea.

11:20 Greeks Some Greek copies read "Hellenists," non-Greeks who spoke Greek.

JULY 4

2 CHRONICLES 3:1—5:1

Solomon Builds the Temple

3 Then Solomon began to build the Temple of the LORD in Jerusalem on Mount Moriah. This was where the LORD had appeared to David, Solomon's father. Solomon built the Temple on the place David had prepared on the threshing floor of Araunah the Jebusite. ²Solomon began building in the second month of the fourth year he ruled Israel.

³Solomon used these measurements for building the Temple of God. It was ninety feet long and thirty feet wide, using the old measurement. ⁴The porch in front of the main room of the Temple was thirty feet long and thirty feet high.

He covered the inside of the porch with pure gold. ⁵He put panels of pine on the walls of the main room and covered them with pure gold. Then he put designs of palm trees and chains in the gold. ⁶He decorated the Temple with gems and gold from Parvaim.ⁿ ⁷He put gold on the Temple's ceiling beams, doorposts, walls, and doors, and he carved creatures with wings on the walls.

⁸Then he made the Most Holy Place. It was thirty feet long and thirty feet wide, as wide as the Temple. He covered its walls with about forty-six thousand pounds of pure gold. ⁹The gold nails weighed over a pound. He also covered the upper rooms with gold.

¹⁰He made two creatures with wings for the Most Holy Place and covered them with gold. ¹¹The wings of the gold creatures were thirty feet across. One wing of one creature was seven and one-half feet long and touched the Temple wall. The creature's other wing was also seven and one-half feet long, and it touched a wing of the second creature. ¹²One wing of the second creature touched the other side of the room and was also seven and one-half feet long. The second creature's other wing touched the first creature's wing, and it was also seven and one-half feet long. ¹³Together, the creatures' wings were thirty feet across. The creatures stood on their feet, facing the main room.

¹⁴He made the curtain of blue, purple, and red thread, and expensive linen, and he put designs of creatures with wings in it.

¹⁵He made two pillars to stand in front of the Temple. They were about fifty-two feet tall, and the capital of each pillar was over seven feet tall. ¹⁶He made a net of chains and put them on the tops of the pillars. He made a hundred pomegranates and put them on the chains. ¹⁷Then he put the pillars up in front of the Temple. One pillar stood on the south side, the other on the north. He named the south pillar He Establishes and the north pillar In Him Is Strength.

Things for the Temple

4 He made a bronze altar thirty feet long, thirty feet wide, and fifteen feet tall. ²Then he made from bronze a large round bowl, which was called the Sea. It was forty-five feet around, fifteen feet across, and seven and one-half feet deep. ³There were carvings of bulls under the rim of the bowl—ten bulls every eighteen inches. They were in two rows and were made in one piece with the bowl.

⁴The bowl rested on the backs of twelve bronze bulls that faced outward from the center of the bowl. Three bulls faced north, three faced west, three faced south, and three faced east. ⁵The sides of the bowl were four inches thick, and it held about seventeen thousand five hundred gallons. The rim of the bowl was like the rim of a cup or like a lily blossom.

⁶He made ten smaller bowls and put five on the south side and five on the north. They were for washing the animals for the burnt offerings, but the large bowl was for the priests to wash in.

⁷He made ten lampstands of gold, following the plans. He put them in the Temple, five on the south side and five on the north.

⁸He made ten tables and put them in the Temple, five on the south side and five on the

north. And he used gold to make a hundred other bowls.

⁹He also made the priests' courtyard and the large courtyard. He made the doors that opened to the courtyard and covered them with bronze. ¹⁰Then he put the large bowl in the southeast corner of the Temple.

¹¹Huram also made bowls, shovels, and small bowls. So he finished his work for King Solomon on the Temple of God:

¹²two pillars;

two large bowls for the capitals on top of the pillars;

two nets to cover the two large bowls for the capitals on top of the pillars;

¹³four hundred pomegranates for the two nets (there were two rows of pomegranates for each net covering the bowls for the capitals on top of the pillars);

¹⁴the stands with a bowl on each stand;

¹⁵the large bowl with twelve bulls under it;

¹⁶the pots, shovels, forks, and all the things to go with them.

All the things that Huram-Abi made for King Solomon for the Temple of the LORD were made of polished bronze. ¹⁷The king had these things poured into clay molds that were made in the plain of the Jordan River between Succoth and Zarethan. ¹⁸Solomon had so many things made that the total weight of all the bronze was never known.

¹⁹Solomon also made all the things for God's Temple: the golden altar; tables which held the bread that shows God's people are in his presence; ²⁰the lampstands and their lamps of pure gold, to burn in front of the Most Holy Place as planned; ²¹the flowers, lamps, and tongs of pure gold; ²²the pure gold wick trimmers, small bowls, pans, and dishes used to carry coals, the gold doors for the Temple, and the inside doors of the Most Holy Place and of the main room.

5 Finally all the work Solomon did for the Temple of the LORD was finished. He brought in everything his father David had set apart for the Temple—all the silver and gold and other articles. And he put everything in the treasuries of God's Temple.

PSALM 79:5–11

⁵LORD, how long will this last?
Will you be angry forever?
How long will your jealousy burn like a fire?
⁶Be angry with the nations that do not know you
and with the kingdoms that do not honor you.
⁷They have gobbled up the people of Jacob and destroyed their land.
⁸Don't punish us for our past sins.
Show your mercy to us soon,
because we are helpless!
⁹God our Savior, help us
so people will praise you.
Save us and forgive our sins
so people will honor you.
¹⁰Why should the nations say,
"Where is their God?"
Tell the other nations in our presence that you punish those who kill your servants.
¹¹Hear the moans of the prisoners.
Use your great power
to save those sentenced to die.

PROVERBS 20:10–12

¹⁰The LORD hates both these things:
dishonest weights and dishonest measures.

¹¹Even children are known by their behavior;
their actions show if they are innocent and good.

¹²The LORD has made both these things:
ears to hear and eyes to see.

ACTS 12:1–25

Herod Agrippa Hurts the Church

12 During that same time King Herod began to mistreat some who belonged to the church. ²He ordered James, the brother of John, to be killed by the sword. ³Herod saw that some of the people liked this, so he decided to arrest Peter, too. (This happened during the time of the Feast of Unleavened Bread.) ⁴After Herod arrested Peter, he put him in

jail and handed him over to be guarded by sixteen soldiers. Herod planned to bring Peter before the people for trial after the Passover Feast. [5]So Peter was kept in jail, but the church prayed earnestly to God for him.

Peter Leaves the Jail

[6]The night before Herod was to bring him to trial, Peter was sleeping between two soldiers, bound with two chains. Other soldiers were guarding the door of the jail. [7]Suddenly, an angel of the Lord stood there, and a light shined in the cell. The angel struck Peter on the side and woke him up. "Hurry! Get up!" the angel said. And the chains fell off Peter's hands. [8]Then the angel told him, "Get dressed and put on your sandals." And Peter did. Then the angel said, "Put on your coat and follow me." [9]So Peter followed him out, but he did not know if what the angel was doing was real; he thought he might be seeing a vision. [10]They went past the first and second guards and came to the iron gate that separated them from the city. The gate opened by itself for them, and they went through it. When they had walked down one street, the angel suddenly left him.

[11]Then Peter realized what had happened. He thought, "Now I know that the Lord really sent his angel to me. He rescued me from Herod and from all the things the people thought would happen."

[12]When he considered this, he went to the home of Mary, the mother of John Mark. Many people were gathered there, praying. [13]Peter knocked on the outside door, and a servant girl named Rhoda came to answer it. [14]When she recognized Peter's voice, she was so happy she forgot to open the door. Instead, she ran inside and told the group, "Peter is at the door!"

[15]They said to her, "You are crazy!" But she kept on saying it was true, so they said, "It must be Peter's angel."

[16]Peter continued to knock, and when they opened the door, they saw him and were amazed. [17]Peter made a sign with his hand to tell them to be quiet. He explained how the Lord led him out of the jail, and he said, "Tell James and the other believers what happened." Then he left to go to another place.

[18]The next day the soldiers were very upset and wondered what had happened to Peter. [19]Herod looked everywhere for him but could not find him. So he questioned the guards and ordered that they be killed.

The Death of Herod Agrippa

Later Herod moved from Judea and went to the city of Caesarea, where he stayed. [20]Herod was very angry with the people of Tyre and Sidon, but the people of those cities all came in a group to him. After convincing Blastus, the king's personal servant, to be on their side, they asked Herod for peace, because their country got its food from his country.

[21]On a chosen day Herod put on his royal robes, sat on his throne, and made a speech to the people. [22]They shouted, "This is the voice of a god, not a human!" [23]Because Herod did not give the glory to God, an angel of the Lord immediately caused him to become sick, and he was eaten by worms and died.

[24]God's message continued to spread and reach people.

[25]After Barnabas and Saul finished their task in Jerusalem, they returned to Antioch, taking John Mark with them.

JULY 5

2 CHRONICLES 5:2—6:42

The Ark Is Brought into the Temple

[2]Solomon called for the elders of Israel, the heads of the tribes, and the leaders of the families to come to him in Jerusalem. He wanted them to bring the Ark of the Agreement with the LORD from the older part of the city. [3]So all the Israelites came together with the king during the festival in the seventh month.

[4]When all the elders of Israel arrived, the Levites lifted up the Ark. [5]They carried the Ark of the Agreement, the Meeting Tent, and the holy utensils in it; the priests and the Levites brought them up. [6]King Solomon and all the Israelites gathered before the Ark of the Agreement and sacrificed so many sheep and bulls no one could count them.

[7]Then the priests put the Ark of the Agreement with the LORD in its place inside the Most Holy Place in the Temple, under the wings of the golden creatures. [8]The wings of these creatures were spread out over the place for the Ark, covering it and its carrying poles. [9]The carrying poles were so long that anyone standing in the Holy Place in front of the Most Holy Place could see the ends of the poles. But no one could see them from outside the Holy Place. The poles are still there today. [10]The only things inside the Ark were two stone tablets[n] that Moses had put in the Ark at Mount Sinai. That was where the LORD made his agreement with the Israelites after they came out of Egypt.

[11]Then all the priests left the Holy Place. (All the priests from each group had made themselves ready to serve the LORD.) [12]All the Levite musicians—Asaph, Heman, Jeduthun, and all their sons and relatives—stood on the east side of the altar. They were dressed in white linen and played cymbals, harps, and lyres. With them were one hundred twenty priests who blew trumpets. [13]Those who blew the trumpets and those who sang together sounded like one person as they praised and thanked the LORD. They sang as others played their trumpets, cymbals, and other instruments. They praised the LORD with this song:

"He is good;
   his love continues forever."

Then the Temple of the LORD was filled with a cloud. [14]The priests could not continue their work because of the cloud, because the LORD's glory filled the Temple of God.

Solomon Speaks to the People

6 Then Solomon said, "The LORD said he would live in the dark cloud. [2]LORD, I have built a wonderful Temple for you—a place for you to live forever."

[3]While all the Israelites were standing there, King Solomon turned to them and blessed them. [4]Then he said, "Praise the LORD, the God of Israel. He has done what he promised to my father David. The LORD said, [5]'Since the time I brought my people out of Egypt, I have not chosen a city in any tribe of Israel where a temple will be built for me. I did not choose a man to lead my people Israel. [6]But now I have chosen Jerusalem as the place I am to be worshiped, and I have chosen David to lead my people Israel.'

[7]"My father David wanted to build a temple for the LORD, the God of Israel. [8]But the LORD said to my father David, 'It was good that you wanted to build a temple for me. [9]But you are not the one to build it. Your son, who comes from your own body, is the one who will build my temple.'

[10]"Now the LORD has kept his promise. I am the king now in place of David my father. Now I rule Israel as the LORD promised, and I have built the Temple for the LORD, the God of Israel. [11]There I have put the Ark, in which is the Agreement the LORD made with the Israelites."

Solomon's Prayer

[12]Then Solomon stood facing the LORD's altar, and all the Israelites were standing behind him. He spread out his hands. [13]He had made a bronze platform seven and one-half feet long, seven and one-half feet wide, and seven and one-half feet high, and he had placed it in the middle of the outer courtyard. Solomon stood on the platform. Then he kneeled in front of all the people of Israel gathered there, and he spread out his hands toward the sky. [14]He said, "LORD, God of Israel, there is no god like you in heaven or on earth. You keep your agreement of love with your servants who truly follow you. [15]You have kept the promise you made to your servant David, my father. You spoke it with your own mouth and finished it with your hands today.

[16]"Now, LORD, God of Israel, keep the

5:10 stone tablets They were the two stone tablets on which God wrote the Ten Commandments.

promise you made to your servant David, my father. You said, 'If your sons are careful to obey my teachings as you have obeyed, there will always be someone from your family ruling Israel.' [17]Now, LORD, God of Israel, please continue to keep that promise you made to your servant.

[18]"But, God, can you really live here on the earth with people? The sky and the highest place in heaven cannot contain you. Surely this house which I have built cannot contain you. [19]But please listen to my prayer and my request, because I am your servant. LORD my God, hear this prayer your servant prays to you. [20]Day and night please watch over this Temple where you have said you would be worshiped. Hear the prayer I pray facing this Temple. [21]Hear my prayers and the prayers of your people Israel when we pray facing this place. Hear from your home in heaven, and when you hear, forgive us.

[22]"If someone wrongs another person, he will be brought to the altar in this Temple. If he swears an oath that he is not guilty, [23]then hear in heaven. Judge the case, punish the guilty, but declare that the innocent person is not guilty.

[24]"When your people, the Israelites, sin against you, their enemies will defeat them. But if they come back to you and praise you and pray to you in this Temple, [25]then listen from heaven. Forgive the sin of your people Israel, and bring them back to the land you gave to them and their ancestors.

[26]"When they sin against you, you will stop the rain from falling on their land. Then they will pray, facing this place and praising you; they will stop sinning when you make them suffer. [27]When this happens, hear their prayer in heaven, and forgive the sins of your servants, the Israelites. Teach them to do what is right. Then please send rain to this land you have given particularly to them.

[28]"At times the land will get so dry that no food will grow, or a great sickness will spread among the people. Sometimes the crops will be destroyed by locusts or grasshoppers. Your people will be attacked in their cities by their enemies, or will become sick. [29]When any of these things happens, the people will become truly sorry. If your people spread their hands in prayer toward this Temple, [30]then hear their prayers from your home in heaven. Forgive and treat each person as he should be treated because you know what is in a person's heart. Only you know what is in people's hearts. [31]Then the people will respect and obey you as long as they live in this land you gave our ancestors.

[32]"People who are not Israelites, foreigners from other lands, will hear about your greatness and power. They will come from far away to pray at this Temple. [33]Then hear from your home in heaven, and do whatever they ask you. Then people everywhere will know you and respect you, just as your people Israel do. Then everyone will know that I built this Temple as a place to worship you.

[34]"When your people go out to fight their enemies along some road on which you send them, your people will pray to you, facing this city which you have chosen and the Temple I have built for you. [35]Then hear in heaven their prayers, and do what is right.

[36]"Everyone sins, so your people will also sin against you. You will become angry with them and will hand them over to their enemies. Their enemies will capture them and take them away to a country far or near. [37]Your people will be sorry for their sins when they are held as prisoners in another country. They will be sorry and pray to you in the land where they are held as prisoners, saying, 'We have sinned. We have done wrong and acted wickedly.' [38]They will truly turn back to you in the land where they are captives. They will pray, facing this land you gave their ancestors, this city you have chosen, and the Temple I have built for you. [39]Then hear their prayers from your home in heaven and do what is right. Forgive your people who have sinned against you.

[40]"Now, my God, look at us. Listen to the prayers we pray in this place.
[41]Now, rise, LORD God, and come to your
        resting place.
    Come with the Ark of the Agreement
        that shows your strength.
    Let your priests receive your salvation,
        LORD God,
    and may your holy people be happy
        because of your goodness.

[42]LORD God, do not reject your appointed
one.
Remember your love for your servant
David."

PSALM 79:12–13

[12]Repay those around us seven times over
for their insults to you, Lord.
[13]We are your people, the sheep of your
flock.
We will thank you always;
forever and ever we will praise you.

PROVERBS 20:13–14

[13]If you love to sleep, you will be poor.
If you stay awake, you will have plenty
of food.
[14]Buyers say, "This is bad. It's no good."
Then they go away and brag about what
they bought.

ACTS 13:1–25

Barnabas and Saul Are Chosen

13 In the church at Antioch there were
these prophets and teachers: Barnabas, Simeon (also called Niger), Lucius
(from the city of Cyrene), Manaen (who had
grown up with Herod, the ruler), and Saul.
[2]They were all worshiping the Lord and fasting[n] for a certain time. During this time the
Holy Spirit said to them, "Set apart for me
Barnabas and Saul to do a special work for
which I have chosen them."

[3]So after they fasted and prayed, they laid
their hands on[n] Barnabas and Saul and sent
them out.

Barnabas and Saul in Cyprus

[4]Barnabas and Saul, sent out by the Holy
Spirit, went to the city of Seleucia. From
there they sailed to the island of Cyprus.
[5]When they came to Salamis, they preached
the Good News of God in the synagogues.
John Mark was with them to help.

[6]They went across the whole island to Pa-
phos where they met a magician named Bar-

Jesus. He was a false prophet [7]who always
stayed close to Sergius Paulus, the governor
and a smart man. He asked Barnabas and
Saul to come to him, because he wanted to
hear the message of God. [8]But Elymas, the
magician, was against them. (Elymas is the
name for Bar-Jesus in the Greek language.)
He tried to stop the governor from believing
in Jesus. [9]But Saul, who was also called Paul,
was filled with the Holy Spirit. He looked
straight at Elymas [10]and said, "You son of the
devil! You are an enemy of everything that is
right! You are full of evil tricks and lies, always trying to change the Lord's truths into
lies. [11]Now the Lord will touch you, and you
will be blind. For a time you will not be able
to see anything—not even the light from the
sun."

Then everything became dark for Elymas, and he walked around, trying to find
someone to lead him by the hand. [12]When
the governor saw this, he believed because
he was amazed at the teaching about the
Lord.

Paul and Barnabas Leave Cyprus

[13]Paul and those with him sailed from Pa-
phos and came to Perga, in Pamphylia. There
John Mark left them to return to Jerusalem.
[14]They continued their trip from Perga and
went to Antioch, a city in Pisidia. On the Sabbath day they went into the synagogue and
sat down. [15]After the law of Moses and the
writings of the prophets were read, the leaders of the synagogue sent a message to Paul
and Barnabas: "Brothers, if you have any
message that will encourage the people,
please speak."

[16]Paul stood up, raised his hand, and said,
"You Israelites and you who worship God,
please listen! [17]The God of the Israelites
chose our ancestors. He made the people
great during the time they lived in Egypt,
and he brought them out of that country
with great power. [18]And he was patient with
them[n] for forty years in the desert. [19]God destroyed seven nations in the land of Canaan

---

13:2 fasting The people would give up eating for a special time of prayer and worship to God. It was also done sometimes
to show sadness and disappointment. **13:3 laid their hands on** The laying on of hands had many purposes, including the
giving of a blessing, power, or authority. **13:18 And . . . them** Some Greek copies read "And he cared for them."

and gave the land to his people. [20]All this happened in about four hundred fifty years.

"After this, God gave them judges until the time of Samuel the prophet. [21]Then the people asked for a king, so God gave them Saul son of Kish. Saul was from the tribe of Benjamin and was king for forty years. [22]After God took him away, God made David their king. God said about him: 'I have found in David son of Jesse the kind of man I want. He will do all I want him to do.' [23]So God has brought Jesus, one of David's descendants, to Israel to be its Savior, as he promised. [24]Before Jesus came, John[n] preached to all the people of Israel about a baptism of changed hearts and lives. [25]When he was finishing his work, he said, 'Who do you think I am? I am not the Christ. He is coming later, and I am not worthy to untie his sandals.'

JULY 6

2 CHRONICLES 7:1—8:18

The Temple Is Given to the Lord

7 When Solomon finished praying, fire came down from the sky and burned up the burnt offering and the sacrifices. The LORD's glory filled the Temple. [2]The priests could not enter the Temple of the LORD, because the LORD's glory filled it. [3]When all the people of Israel saw the fire come down from heaven and the LORD's glory on the Temple, they bowed down on the pavement with their faces to the ground. They worshiped and thanked the LORD, saying,

"He is good;
    his love continues forever."

[4]Then King Solomon and all the people offered sacrifices to the LORD. [5]King Solomon offered a sacrifice of twenty-two thousand cattle and one hundred twenty thousand sheep. So the king and all the people gave the Temple to God. [6]The priests stood ready to do their work. The Levites also stood with the instruments of the LORD's music that King David had made for praising the LORD. The priests and Levites were saying, "His love continues forever." The priests, who stood across from the Levites, blew their trumpets, and all the Israelites were standing.

[7]Solomon made holy the middle part of the courtyard, which is in front of the Temple of the LORD. There he offered whole burnt offerings and the fat of the fellowship offerings. He offered them in the courtyard, because the bronze altar he had made could not hold the burnt offerings, grain offerings, and fat.

[8]Solomon and all the Israelites celebrated the festival for seven days. There were many people, and they came from as far away as Lebo Hamath and the brook of Egypt. [9]For seven days they celebrated giving the altar for the worship of God. Then they celebrated the festival for seven days. On the eighth day they had a meeting. [10]On the twenty-third day of the seventh month Solomon sent the people home, full of joy. They were happy because the LORD had been so good to David, Solomon, and his people Israel.

The Lord Appears to Solomon

[11]Solomon finished the Temple of the LORD and his royal palace. He had success in doing everything he planned in the Temple of the LORD and his own palace. [12]Then the LORD appeared to Solomon at night and said to him, "I have heard your prayer and have chosen this place for myself to be a Temple for sacrifices.

[13]"I may stop the sky from sending rain. I may command the locusts to destroy the land. I may send sicknesses to my people. [14]Then if my people, who are called by my name, will humble themselves, if they will pray and seek me and stop their evil ways, I will hear them from heaven. I will forgive their sin, and I will heal their land. [15]Now I will see them, and I will listen to the prayers

---

13:24 John John the Baptist, who preached to people about Christ's coming (Luke 3).

prayed in this place. [16]I have chosen this Temple and made it holy. So I will be worshiped there forever. Yes, I will always watch over it and love it.

[17]"But you must serve me as your father David did. You must obey all I have commanded and keep my laws and rules. [18]If you do, I will make your kingdom strong. This is the agreement I made with your father David, saying, 'Someone from your family will always rule in Israel.'

[19]"But you must follow me and obey the laws and commands I have given you. You must not serve or worship other gods. [20]If you do, I will take the Israelites out of my land, the land I have given them, and I will leave this Temple that I have made holy. All the nations will make fun of it and speak evil about it. [21]This Temple is honored now, but then, everyone who passes by will be shocked. They will ask, 'Why did the LORD do this terrible thing to this land and this Temple?' [22]People will answer, 'This happened because they left the LORD, the God of their ancestors, the God who brought them out of Egypt. They decided to follow other gods and worshiped and served them, so he brought all this disaster on them.'"

Solomon's Other Achievements

8By the end of twenty years, Solomon had built the Temple of the LORD and the royal palace. [2]Solomon rebuilt the towns that Hiram had given him, and Solomon sent Israelites to live in them. [3]Then he went to Hamath Zobah and captured it. [4]Solomon also built the town of Tadmor in the desert, and he built all the towns in Hamath as towns for storing grain and supplies. [5]He rebuilt the towns of Upper Beth Horon and Lower Beth Horon, protecting them with strong walls, gates, and bars in the gates. [6]He also rebuilt the town of Baalath. And he built all the other towns for storage and all the cities for his chariots and horses. He built all he wanted in Jerusalem, Lebanon, and everywhere he ruled.

[7]There were other people in the land who were not Israelites—the Hittites, Amorites, Perizzites, Hivites, and Jebusites. [8]They were descendants of the people that the Israelites had not destroyed. Solomon forced them to be slave workers, as is still true today. [9]But Solomon did not make slaves of the Israelites. They were his soldiers, chief captains, commanders of his chariots, and his chariot drivers. [10]These were his most important officers. There were two hundred fifty of them to direct the people.

[11]Solomon brought the daughter of the king of Egypt from the older part of Jerusalem to the palace he had built for her. Solomon said, "My wife must not live in King David's palace, because the places where the Ark of the Agreement has been are holy."

[12]Then Solomon offered burnt offerings to the LORD on the altar he had built for the LORD in front of the Temple porch. [13]He offered sacrifices every day as Moses had commanded. They were offered on the Sabbath days, New Moons, and the three yearly feasts—the Feast of Unleavened Bread, the Feast of Weeks, and the Feast of Shelters. [14]Solomon followed his father David's instructions and chose the groups of priests for their service and the Levites to lead the praise and to help the priests do their daily work. And he chose the gatekeepers by their groups to serve at each gate, as David, the man of God, had commanded. [15]They obeyed all of Solomon's commands to the priests and Levites, as well as his commands about the treasuries.

[16]All Solomon's work was done as he had said from the day the foundation of the Temple of the LORD was begun, until it was finished. So the Temple was finished.

[17]Then Solomon went to the towns of Ezion Geber and Elath near the Red Sea in the land of Edom. [18]Hiram sent ships to Solomon that were commanded by his own men, who were skilled sailors. Hiram's men went with Solomon's men to Ophir and brought back about thirty-four thousand pounds of gold to King Solomon.

PSALM 80:1–6

A Prayer to Bring Israel Back

For the director of music. To the tune of "Lilies of the Agreement." A psalm of Asaph.

80 Shepherd of Israel, listen to us. You lead the people of Joseph like a flock.

You sit on your throne between the gold
creatures with wings.
Show your greatness ²to the people of
Ephraim, Benjamin, and Manasseh.
Use your strength,
and come to save us.

³God, take us back.
Show us your kindness so we can be
saved.

⁴LORD God All-Powerful,
how long will you be angry
at the prayers of your people?
⁵You have fed your people with tears;
you have made them drink many tears.
⁶You made those around us fight over us,
and our enemies make fun of us.

PROVERBS 20:15

¹⁵There is gold and plenty of rubies,
but only a few people speak with
knowledge.

ACTS 13:26–52

²⁶"Brothers, sons of the family of Abraham, and others who worship God, listen!
The news about this salvation has been sent
to us. ²⁷Those who live in Jerusalem and their
leaders did not realize that Jesus was the Savior. They did not understand the words that
the prophets wrote, which are read every
Sabbath day. But they made them come true
when they said Jesus was guilty. ²⁸They could
not find any real reason for Jesus to be put to
death, but they asked Pilate to have him
killed. ²⁹When they had done to him all that
the Scriptures had said, they took him down
from the cross and laid him in a tomb. ³⁰But
God raised him up from the dead! ³¹After
this, for many days, those who had gone with
Jesus from Galilee to Jerusalem saw him.
They are now his witnesses to the people.
³²We tell you the Good News about the promise God made to our ancestors. ³³God has
made this promise come true for us, his children, by raising Jesus from the dead. We read
about this also in Psalm 2:

'You are my Son.
Today I have become your Father.'
Psalm 2:7

³⁴God raised Jesus from the dead, and he will
never go back to the grave and become dust.
So God said:

'I will give you the holy and sure
blessings
that I promised to David.'   *Isaiah 55:3*

³⁵But in another place God says:

'You will not let your Holy One rot.'
Psalm 16:10

³⁶David did God's will during his lifetime.
Then he died and was buried beside his ancestors, and his body did rot in the grave.
³⁷But the One God raised from the dead did
not rot in the grave. ³⁸⁻³⁹Brothers, understand what we are telling you: You can have
forgiveness of your sins through Jesus. The
law of Moses could not free you from your
sins. But through Jesus everyone who believes is free from all sins. ⁴⁰Be careful! Don't
let what the prophets said happen to you:

⁴¹'Listen, you people who doubt!
You can wonder, and then die.
I will do something in your lifetime
that you won't believe even when you
are told about it!'"   *Habakkuk 1:5*

⁴²While Paul and Barnabas were leaving
the synagogue, the people asked them to tell
them more about these things on the next
Sabbath. ⁴³When the meeting was over,
many people with those who had changed to
worship God followed Paul and Barnabas
from that place. Paul and Barnabas were
persuading them to continue trusting in
God's grace.

⁴⁴On the next Sabbath day, almost everyone in the city came to hear the word of the
Lord. ⁴⁵Seeing the crowd, the Jewish people
became very jealous and said insulting
things and argued against what Paul said.
⁴⁶But Paul and Barnabas spoke very boldly,
saying, "We must speak the message of God
to you first. But you refuse to listen. You are
judging yourselves not worthy of having
eternal life! So we will now go to the people
of other nations. ⁴⁷This is what the Lord told
us to do, saying:

'I have made you a light for the nations;
you will show people all over the world
the way to be saved.'"   *Isaiah 49:6*

⁴⁸When those who were not Jewish heard
Paul say this, they were happy and gave

honor to the message of the Lord. And the people who were chosen to have life forever believed the message.

[49]So the message of the Lord was spreading through the whole country. [50]But the Jewish people stirred up some of the important religious women and the leaders of the city. They started trouble against Paul and Barnabas and forced them out of their area. [51]So Paul and Barnabas shook the dust off their feet[n] and went to Iconium. [52]But the followers were filled with joy and the Holy Spirit.

JULY 7

2 CHRONICLES 9:1—11:4

The Queen of Sheba Visits

9 When the queen of Sheba heard about Solomon's fame, she came to Jerusalem to test him with hard questions. She had a large group of servants with her and camels carrying spices, jewels, and much gold. When she came to Solomon, she talked with him about all she had in mind, [2]and Solomon answered all her questions. Nothing was too hard for him to explain to her. [3]The queen of Sheba saw that Solomon was very wise. She saw the palace he had built, [4]the food on his table, his many officers, the palace servants and their good clothes, the servants who served Solomon his wine and their good clothes. She saw the whole burnt offerings he made in the Temple of the LORD. All these things amazed her.

[5]So she said to King Solomon, "What I heard in my own country about your achievements and wisdom is true. [6]I did not believe it then, but now I have come and seen it with my own eyes. I was not told even half of your great wisdom! You are much greater than I had heard. [7]Your people and officials are very lucky, because in always serving you, they are able to hear your wisdom. [8]Praise the LORD your God who was pleased to make you king. He has put you on his throne to rule for the LORD your God, because your God loves the people of Israel and supports them forever. He has made you king over them to keep justice and to rule fairly."

[9]Then she gave the king about nine thousand pounds of gold and many spices and jewels. No one had ever given such spices as the queen of Sheba gave to King Solomon.

[10]Hiram's men and Solomon's men brought gold from Ophir, juniper wood, and jewels. [11]King Solomon used the juniper wood to build steps for the Temple of the LORD and the palace and to make lyres and harps for the musicians. No one in Judah had ever seen such beautiful things as these.

[12]King Solomon gave the queen of Sheba everything she wanted and asked for, even more than she had brought to him. Then she and her servants returned to her own country.

Solomon's Wealth

[13]Every year King Solomon received about fifty thousand pounds of gold. [14]Besides that, he also received gold from traders and merchants. All the kings of Arabia and the governors of the land also brought gold and silver.

[15]King Solomon made two hundred large shields of hammered gold, each of which contained about seven and one-half pounds of hammered gold. [16]He also made three hundred smaller shields of hammered gold, each of which contained about four pounds of gold. The king put them in the Palace of the Forest of Lebanon.

[17]The king built a large throne of ivory and covered it with pure gold. [18]The throne had six steps on it and a gold footstool. There were armrests on both sides of the chair, and each armrest had a lion beside it. [19]Twelve lions stood on the six steps, one lion at each end of each step. Nothing like this had ever been made for any other kingdom. [20]All of Solomon's drinking cups, as well as

---

13:51 shook . . . feet A warning. It showed that they had rejected these people.

the dishes in the Palace of the Forest of Lebanon, were made of pure gold. In Solomon's time people did not think silver was valuable.

²¹King Solomon had many ships that he sent out to trade, with Hiram's men as the crews. Every three years the ships returned, bringing back gold, silver, ivory, apes, and baboons.

²²King Solomon had more riches and wisdom than all the other kings on earth. ²³All the kings of the earth wanted to see Solomon and listen to the wisdom God had given him. ²⁴Year after year everyone who came brought gifts of silver and gold, clothes, weapons, spices, horses, and mules.

²⁵Solomon had four thousand stalls for horses and chariots, and he had twelve thousand horses. He kept some in special cities for the chariots, and others he kept with him in Jerusalem. ²⁶Solomon ruled over all the kingdoms from the Euphrates River to the land of the Philistines, as far as the border of Egypt. ²⁷In Jerusalem the king made silver as common as stones and cedar trees as plentiful as the fig trees on the western hills. ²⁸Solomon imported horses from Egypt and all other countries.

Solomon's Death

²⁹Everything else Solomon did, from the beginning to the end, is written in the records of Nathan the prophet, and in the prophecy of Ahijah the Shilonite, and in the visions of Iddo the seer, who wrote about Jeroboam, Nebat's son. ³⁰Solomon ruled in Jerusalem over all Israel for forty years. ³¹Then Solomon died and was buried in Jerusalem, the city of David, his father. And Solomon's son Rehoboam became king in his place.

Israel Turns Against Rehoboam

10 Rehoboam went to Shechem, where all the Israelites had gone to make him king. ²Jeroboam son of Nebat was in Egypt, where he had gone to escape from King Solomon. When Jeroboam heard about Rehoboam being made king, he returned from Egypt. ³After the people sent for him, he and the people went to Rehoboam and said to him, ⁴"Your father forced us to work very

hard. Now, make it easier for us, and don't make us work as he did. Then we will serve you."

⁵Rehoboam answered, "Come back to me in three days." So the people left.

⁶King Rehoboam asked the elders who had advised Solomon during his lifetime, "How do you think I should answer these people?"

⁷They answered, "Be kind to these people. If you please them and give them a kind answer, they will serve you always."

⁸But Rehoboam rejected this advice. Instead, he asked the young men who had grown up with him and who served as his advisers. ⁹Rehoboam asked them, "What is your advice? How should we answer these people who said, 'Don't make us work as hard as your father did'?"

¹⁰The young men who had grown up with him answered, "The people said to you, 'Your father forced us to work very hard. Now make our work easier.' You should tell them, 'My little finger is bigger than my father's legs. ¹¹He forced you to work hard, but I will make you work even harder. My father beat you with whips, but I will beat you with whips that have sharp points.'"

¹²Rehoboam had told the people, "Come back to me in three days." So after three days Jeroboam and all the people returned to Rehoboam. ¹³King Rehoboam spoke cruel words to them, because he had rejected the advice of the elders. ¹⁴He followed the advice of the young men and said, "My father forced you to work hard, but I will make you work even harder. My father beat you with whips, but I will beat you with whips that have sharp points." ¹⁵So the king did not listen to the people. God caused this to happen so that the LORD could keep the promise he had made to Jeroboam son of Nebat through Ahijah, a prophet from Shiloh.

¹⁶When all the Israelites saw that the king refused to listen to them, they said to the king,

"We have no share in David!
We have no part in the son of Jesse!
People of Israel, let's go to our own
    homes!
Let David's son rule his own people."

So all the Israelites went home. [17]But Rehoboam still ruled over the Israelites who lived in the towns of Judah.

[18]Adoniram was in charge of the forced labor. When Rehoboam sent him to the people, they threw stones at him until he died. But King Rehoboam ran to his chariot and escaped to Jerusalem. [19]Since then, Israel has been against the family of David.

11 When Rehoboam arrived in Jerusalem, he gathered one hundred eighty thousand of the best soldiers from Judah and Benjamin. He wanted to fight Israel to take back his kingdom. [2]But the LORD spoke his word to Shemaiah, a man of God, saying, [3]"Speak to Solomon's son Rehoboam, the king of Judah, and to all the Israelites living in Judah and Benjamin. Say to them, [4]'The LORD says you must not go to war against your brothers. Every one of you should go home, because I made all these things happen.'" So they obeyed the LORD's command and turned back and did not attack Jeroboam.

PSALM 80:7–13

[7]God All-Powerful, take us back.
　　Show us your kindness so we can be
　　　saved.

[8]You brought us out of Egypt as if we were
　　a vine.
　　You forced out other nations and
　　　planted us in the land.
[9]You cleared the ground for us.
　　Like a vine, we took root and filled the
　　　land.
[10]We covered the mountains with our
　　shade.
　　We had limbs like the mighty cedar
　　　tree.
[11]Our branches reached the Mediterranean
　　Sea,
　　and our shoots went to the Euphrates
　　　River.

[12]So why did you pull down our walls?
　　Now everyone who passes by steals
　　　from us.
[13]Like wild pigs they walk over us;
　　like wild animals they feed on us.

PROVERBS 20:16–18

[16]Take the coat of someone who promises
　　to pay a stranger's debts,
　　and keep it until he pays what the
　　　stranger owes.

[17]Stolen food may taste sweet at first,
　　but later it will feel like a mouth full of
　　　gravel.

[18]Get advice if you want your plans to
　　work.
　　If you go to war, get the advice of
　　　others.

ACTS 14:1–28

Paul and Barnabas in Iconium

14 In Iconium, Paul and Barnabas went as usual to the synagogue. They spoke so well that a great many Jews and Greeks believed. [2]But some people who did not believe excited the others and turned them against the believers. [3]Paul and Barnabas stayed in Iconium a long time and spoke bravely for the Lord. He showed that their message about his grace was true by giving them the power to work miracles and signs. [4]But the city was divided. Some of the people agreed with the Jews, and others believed the apostles.

[5]Some who were not Jews, some Jews, and some of their rulers wanted to mistreat Paul and Barnabas and to stone them to death. [6]When Paul and Barnabas learned about this, they ran away to Lystra and Derbe, cities in Lycaonia, and to the areas around those cities. [7]They announced the Good News there, too.

Paul in Lystra and Derbe

[8]In Lystra there sat a man who had been born crippled; he had never walked. [9]As this man was listening to Paul speak, Paul looked straight at him and saw that he believed God could heal him. [10]So he cried out, "Stand up on your feet!" The man jumped up and began walking around. [11]When the crowds saw what Paul did, they shouted in the Lycaonian language, "The gods have become like humans and have come down to us!" [12]Then the

people began to call Barnabas "Zeus"[n] and Paul "Hermes,"[n] because he was the main speaker. [13]The priest in the temple of Zeus, which was near the city, brought some bulls and flowers to the city gates. He and the people wanted to offer a sacrifice to Paul and Barnabas. [14]But when the apostles, Barnabas and Paul, heard about it, they tore their clothes. They ran in among the people, shouting, [15]"Friends, why are you doing these things? We are only human beings like you. We are bringing you the Good News and are telling you to turn away from these worthless things and turn to the living God. He is the One who made the sky, the earth, the sea, and everything in them. [16]In the past, God let all the nations do what they wanted. [17]Yet he proved he is real by showing kindness, by giving you rain from heaven and crops at the right times, by giving you food and filling your hearts with joy." [18]Even with these words, they were barely able to keep the crowd from offering sacrifices to them.

[19]Then some evil people came from Antioch and Iconium and persuaded the people to turn against Paul. So they threw stones at him and dragged him out of town, thinking they had killed him. [20]But the followers gathered around him, and he got up and went back into the town. The next day he and Barnabas left and went to the city of Derbe.

The Return to Antioch in Syria

[21]Paul and Barnabas told the Good News in Derbe, and many became followers. Paul and Barnabas returned to Lystra, Iconium, and Antioch, [22]making the followers of Jesus stronger and helping them stay in the faith. They said, "We must suffer many things to enter God's kingdom." [23]They chose elders for each church, by praying and fasting[n] for a certain time. These elders had trusted the Lord, so Paul and Barnabas put them in the Lord's care.

[24]Then they went through Pisidia and came to Pamphylia. [25]When they had preached the message in Perga, they went down to Attalia. [26]And from there they sailed away to Antioch where the believers had put them into God's care and had sent them out to do this work. Now they had finished.

[27]When they arrived in Antioch, Paul and Barnabas gathered the church together. They told the church all about what God had done with them and how God had made it possible for those who were not Jewish to believe. [28]And they stayed there a long time with the followers.

JULY 8

2 CHRONICLES 11:5—12:16

Rehoboam Makes Judah Strong

[5]Rehoboam lived in Jerusalem and built strong cities in Judah to defend it. [6]He built up the cities of Bethlehem, Etam, Tekoa, [7]Beth Zur, Soco, Adullam, [8]Gath, Mareshah, Ziph, [9]Adoraim, Lachish, Azekah, [10]Zorah, Aijalon, and Hebron. These were strong, walled cities in Judah and Benjamin. [11]When Rehoboam made those cities strong, he put commanders and supplies of food, oil, and wine in them. [12]Also, Rehoboam put shields and spears in all the cities and made them very strong. Rehoboam kept the people of Judah and Benjamin under his control.

[13]The priests and the Levites from all over Israel joined Rehoboam. [14]The Levites even left their pasturelands and property and came to Judah and Jerusalem, because Jeroboam and his sons refused to let them serve as priests to the LORD. [15]Jeroboam

---

14:12 "Zeus" The Greeks believed in many false gods, of whom Zeus was most important. **14:12 "Hermes"** The Greeks believed he was a messenger for the other gods. **14:23 fasting** The people would give up eating for a special time of prayer and worship to God. It was also done sometimes to show sadness and disappointment.

chose his own priests for the places of worship and for the goat and calf idols he had made. ¹⁶There were people from all the tribes of Israel who wanted to obey the LORD, the God of Israel. So they went to Jerusalem with the Levites to sacrifice to the LORD, the God of their ancestors. ¹⁷These people made the kingdom of Judah strong, and they supported Solomon's son Rehoboam for three years. During this time they lived the way David and Solomon had lived.

Rehoboam's Family

¹⁸Rehoboam married Mahalath, the daughter of Jerimoth and Abihail. Jerimoth was David's son, and Abihail was the daughter of Eliab, Jesse's son. ¹⁹Mahalath gave Rehoboam these sons: Jeush, Shemariah, and Zaham. ²⁰Then Rehoboam married Absalom's daughter Maacah, and she gave Rehoboam these children: Abijah, Attai, Ziza, and Shelomith. ²¹Rehoboam loved Maacah more than his other wives and slave women. Rehoboam had eighteen wives and sixty slave women and was the father of twenty-eight sons and sixty daughters.

²²Rehoboam chose Abijah son of Maacah to be the leader of his own brothers, because he planned to make Abijah king. ²³Rehoboam acted wisely. He spread his sons through all the areas of Judah and Benjamin, sending them to every strong, walled city. He gave plenty of supplies to his sons, and he also found wives for them.

Shishak Attacks Jerusalem

12 After Rehoboam's kingdom was set up and he became strong, he and the people of Judah stopped obeying the teachings of the LORD. ²During the fifth year Rehoboam was king, Shishak king of Egypt attacked Jerusalem, because Rehoboam and the people were unfaithful to the LORD. ³Shishak had twelve hundred chariots and sixty thousand horsemen. He brought troops of Libyans, Sukkites, and Cushites from Egypt with him, so many they couldn't be counted. ⁴Shishak captured the strong, walled cities of Judah and came as far as Jerusalem.

⁵Then Shemaiah the prophet came to Rehoboam and the leaders of Judah who had gathered in Jerusalem because they were afraid of Shishak. Shemaiah said to them, "This is what the LORD says: 'You have left me, so now I will leave you to face Shishak alone.'"

⁶Then the leaders of Judah and King Rehoboam were sorry for what they had done. They said, "The LORD does what is right."

⁷When the LORD saw they were sorry for what they had done, the LORD spoke his word to Shemaiah, saying, "The king and the leaders are sorry. So I will not destroy them but will save them soon. I will not use Shishak to punish Jerusalem in my anger. ⁸But the people of Jerusalem will become Shishak's servants so they may learn that serving me is different than serving the kings of other nations."

⁹Shishak king of Egypt attacked Jerusalem and took the treasures from the Temple of the LORD and the king's palace. He took everything, even the gold shields Solomon had made. ¹⁰So King Rehoboam made bronze shields to take their place and gave them to the commanders of the guards for the palace gates. ¹¹Whenever the king went to the Temple of the LORD, the guards went with him, carrying the shields. Later, they would put them back in the guardroom.

¹²When Rehoboam was sorry for what he had done, the LORD held his anger back and did not fully destroy Rehoboam. There was some good in Judah.

¹³King Rehoboam made himself a strong king in Jerusalem. He was forty-one years old when he became king, and he was king in Jerusalem for seventeen years. Jerusalem is the city that the LORD chose from all the tribes of Israel in which he was to be worshiped. Rehoboam's mother was Naamah from the country of Ammon. ¹⁴Rehoboam did evil because he did not want to obey the LORD.

¹⁵The things Rehoboam did as king, from the beginning to the end, are written in the records of Shemaiah the prophet and Iddo the seer, in the family histories. There were wars between Rehoboam and Jeroboam all the time they ruled. ¹⁶Rehoboam died and was buried in Jerusalem, and his son Abijah became king in his place.

PSALM 80:14–19

14God All-Powerful, come back.
  Look down from heaven and see.
  Take care of us, your vine.
15 You planted this shoot with your own
      hands
    and strengthened this child.
16Now it is cut down and burned with fire;
    you destroyed us by your angry looks.
17With your hand,
    strengthen the one you have chosen for
      yourself.
18Then we will not turn away from you.
    Give us life again, and we will call to
      you for help.
19LORD God All-Powerful, take us back.
    Show us your kindness so we can be
      saved.

PROVERBS 20:19–21

19Gossips can't keep secrets,
    so avoid people who talk too much.

20Those who curse their father or mother
    will be like a light going out in
      darkness.

21Wealth inherited quickly in the
      beginning
    will do you no good in the end.

ACTS 15:1–21

The Meeting at Jerusalem

15 Then some people came to Antioch
from Judea and began teaching the
non-Jewish believers: "You cannot be saved
if you are not circumcised as Moses taught
us." 2Paul and Barnabas were against this
teaching and argued with them about it. So
the church decided to send Paul, Barnabas,
and some others to Jerusalem where they
could talk more about this with the apostles
and elders.
  3The church helped them leave on the
trip, and they went through the countries of
Phoenicia and Samaria, telling all about
how the other nations had turned to God.
This made all the believers very happy.
4When they arrived in Jerusalem, they were
welcomed by the apostles, the elders, and

the church. Paul, Barnabas, and the others
told about everything God had done with
them. 5But some of the believers who belonged to the Pharisee group came forward
and said, "The non-Jewish believers must be
circumcised. They must be told to obey the
law of Moses."
  6The apostles and the elders gathered to
consider this problem. 7After a long debate,
Peter stood up and said to them, "Brothers,
you know that in the early days God chose me
from among you to preach the Good News to
the nations. They heard the Good News from
me, and they believed. 8God, who knows the
thoughts of everyone, accepted them. He
showed this to us by giving them the Holy
Spirit, just as he did to us. 9To God, those people are not different from us. When they believed, he made their hearts pure. 10So now
why are you testing God by putting a heavy
load around the necks of the non-Jewish believers? It is a load that neither we nor our ancestors were able to carry. 11But we believe
that we and they too will be saved by the
grace of the Lord Jesus."
  12Then the whole group became quiet.
They listened to Paul and Barnabas tell
about all the miracles and signs that God did
through them among the people. 13After
they finished speaking, James said, "Brothers, listen to me. 14Simon has told us how
God showed his love for those people. For
the first time he is accepting from among
them a people to be his own. 15The words of
the prophets agree with this too:
16'After these things I will return.
    The kingdom of David is like a fallen
      tent.
    But I will rebuild its ruins,
      and I will set it up.
17Then those people who are left alive may
      ask the Lord for help,
    and the other nations that belong to
      me,
  says the Lord,
    who will make it happen.
18And these things have been known for a
      long time.'   *Amos 9:11–12*
19"So I think we should not bother the
other people who are turning to God. 20In-
stead, we should write a letter to them telling

them these things: Stay away from food that has been offered to idols (which makes it unclean), any kind of sexual sin, eating animals that have been strangled, and blood.

[21]They should do these things, because for a long time in every city the law of Moses has been taught. And it is still read in the synagogue every Sabbath day."

JULY 9

2 CHRONICLES 13:1—14:15

Abijah King of Judah

13 Abijah became the king of Judah during the eighteenth year Jeroboam was king of Israel. [2]Abijah ruled in Jerusalem for three years. His mother was Maacah daughter of Uriel from the town of Gibeah.

And there was war between Abijah and Jeroboam. [3]Abijah led an army of four hundred thousand capable soldiers into battle, and Jeroboam prepared to fight him with eight hundred thousand capable soldiers.

[4]Abijah stood on Mount Zemaraim in the mountains of Ephraim and said, "Jeroboam and all Israel, listen to me! [5]You should know that the Lord, the God of Israel, gave David and his sons the right to rule Israel forever by an agreement of salt. [6]But Jeroboam son of Nebat, one of the officers of Solomon, David's son, turned against his master. [7]Then worthless, evil men joined Jeroboam against Rehoboam, Solomon's son. He was young and didn't know what to do, so he could not stop them.

[8]"Now you people are making plans against the Lord's kingdom, which belongs to David's sons. There are many of you, and you have the gold calves Jeroboam made for you as gods. [9]You have thrown out the Levites and the Lord's priests, Aaron's sons. You have chosen your own priests as people in other countries do. Anyone who comes with a young bull and seven male sheep can become a priest of idols that are not gods.

[10]"But as for us, the Lord is our God; we have not left him. The priests who serve the Lord are Aaron's sons, and the Levites help them. [11]They offer burnt offerings and sweet-smelling incense to the Lord every morning and evening. They put the bread on the special table in the Temple. And they light the lamps on the gold lampstand every evening. We obey the command of the Lord our God, but you have left him. [12]God himself is with us as our ruler. His priests blow the trumpet to call us to war against you. Men of Israel, don't fight against the Lord, the God of your ancestors, because you won't succeed."

[13]But Jeroboam had sent some troops to sneak behind Judah's army. So while Jeroboam was in front of Judah's army, Jeroboam's soldiers were behind them. [14]When the soldiers of Judah turned around, they saw Jeroboam's army attacking both in front and back. So they cried out to the Lord, and the priests blew the trumpets. [15]Then the men of Judah gave a battle cry. When they shouted, God caused Jeroboam and the army of Israel to run away from Abijah and the army of Judah. [16]When the army of Israel ran away from the men of Judah, God handed them over to Judah. [17]Abijah's army struck Israel so that five hundred thousand of Israel's best men were killed. [18]So at that time the people of Israel were defeated. And the people of Judah won, because they depended on the Lord, the God of their ancestors.

[19]Abijah's army chased Jeroboam's army and captured from him the towns of Bethel, Jeshanah, and Ephron, and the small villages near them. [20]Jeroboam never became strong again while Abijah was alive. The Lord struck Jeroboam, and he died.

[21]But Abijah became strong. He married fourteen women and was the father of twenty-two sons and sixteen daughters. [22]Everything else Abijah did—what he said and what he did—is recorded in the writings of the prophet Iddo.

14 Abijah died and was buried in Jerusalem. His son Asa became king in his place, and there was peace in the country for ten years during Asa's time.

Asa King of Judah

²Asa did what the LORD his God said was good and right. ³He removed the foreign altars and the places where gods were worshiped. He smashed the stone pillars that honored other gods, and he tore down the Asherah idols. ⁴Asa commanded the people of Judah to follow the LORD, the God of their ancestors, and to obey his teachings and commandments. ⁵He also removed the places where gods were worshiped and the incense altars from every town in Judah. So the kingdom had peace while Asa was king. ⁶Asa built strong, walled cities in Judah during the time of peace. He had no war in these years, because the LORD gave him peace.

⁷Asa said to the people of Judah, "Let's build up these towns and put walls around them. Let's make towers, gates, and bars in the gates. This country is ours, because we have obeyed the LORD our God. We have followed him, and he has given us peace all around." So they built and had success.

⁸Asa had an army of three hundred thousand men from Judah and two hundred eighty thousand men from Benjamin. The men from Judah carried large shields and spears. The men from Benjamin carried small shields and bows and arrows. All of them were brave fighting men.

⁹Then Zerah from Cush came out to fight them with an enormous army and three hundred chariots. They came as far as the town of Mareshah. ¹⁰So Asa went out to fight Zerah and prepared for battle in the Valley of Zephathah at Mareshah. ¹¹Asa called out to the LORD his God, saying, "LORD, only you can help weak people against the strong. Help us, LORD our God, because we depend on you. We fight against this enormous army in your name. LORD, you are our God. Don't let anyone win against you."

¹²So the LORD defeated the Cushites when Asa's army from Judah attacked them, and the Cushites ran away. ¹³Asa's army chased them as far as the town of Gerar. So many Cushites were killed that the army could not fight again; they were crushed by the LORD and his army. Asa and his army carried many valuable things away from the enemy. ¹⁴They destroyed all the towns near Gerar, because the people living in these towns were afraid of the LORD. Since these towns had many valuable things, Asa's army took them away. ¹⁵Asa's army also attacked the camps where the shepherds lived and took many sheep and camels. Then they returned to Jerusalem.

PSALM 81:1–5a

A Song for a Holiday

For the director of music. By the gittith. A psalm of Asaph.

81 Sing for joy to God, our strength;
shout out loud to the God of Jacob.
²Begin the music. Play the tambourines.
Play pleasant music on the harps and lyres.
³Blow the trumpet at the time of the New Moon,
when the moon is full, when our feast begins.
⁴This is the law for Israel;
it is the command of the God of Jacob.
⁵He gave this rule to the people of Joseph
when they went out of the land of Egypt.

PROVERBS 20:22–23

²²Don't say, "I'll pay you back for the wrong you did."
Wait for the LORD, and he will make things right.

²³The LORD hates dishonest weights,
and dishonest scales do not please him.

ACTS 15:22–41

Letter to Non-Jewish Believers

²²The apostles, the elders, and the whole church decided to send some of their men with Paul and Barnabas to Antioch. They chose Judas Barsabbas and Silas, who were

respected by the believers. ²³They sent the following letter with them:

> From the apostles and elders, your brothers.
>
> To all the non-Jewish believers in Antioch, Syria, and Cilicia:
>
> Greetings!
>
> ²⁴We have heard that some of our group have come to you and said things that trouble and upset you. But we did not tell them to do this. ²⁵We have all agreed to choose some messengers and send them to you with our dear friends Barnabas and Paul— ²⁶people who have given their lives to serve our Lord Jesus Christ. ²⁷So we are sending Judas and Silas, who will tell you the same things. ²⁸It has pleased the Holy Spirit that you should not have a heavy load to carry, and we agree. You need to do only these things: ²⁹Stay away from any food that has been offered to idols, eating any animals that have been strangled, and blood, and any kind of sexual sin. If you stay away from these things, you will do well.
>
> Good-bye.

³⁰So they left Jerusalem and went to Antioch where they gathered the church and gave them the letter. ³¹When they read it, they were very happy because of the encouraging message. ³²Judas and Silas, who were also prophets, said many things to encourage the believers and make them stronger. ³³After some time Judas and Silas were sent off in peace by the believers, and they went back to those who had sent them [, ³⁴but Silas decided to remain there].*ⁿ*

³⁵But Paul and Barnabas stayed in Antioch and, along with many others, preached the Good News and taught the people the message of the Lord.

Paul and Barnabas Separate

³⁶After some time, Paul said to Barnabas, "We should go back to all those towns where we preached the message of the Lord. Let's visit the believers and see how they are doing."

³⁷Barnabas wanted to take John Mark with them, ³⁸but he had left them at Pamphylia; he did not continue with them in the work. So Paul did not think it was a good idea to take him. ³⁹Paul and Barnabas had such a serious argument about this that they separated and went different ways. Barnabas took Mark and sailed to Cyprus, ⁴⁰but Paul chose Silas and left. The believers in Antioch put Paul into the Lord's care, ⁴¹and he went through Syria and Cilicia, giving strength to the churches.

JULY 10

2 CHRONICLES 15:1—16:14

Asa's Changes

15 The Spirit of God entered Azariah son of Oded. ²Azariah went to meet Asa and said, "Listen to me, Asa and all you people of Judah and Benjamin. The LORD is with you when you are with him. If you obey him, you will find him, but if you leave him, he will leave you. ³For a long time Israel was without the true God and without a priest to teach them and without the teachings. ⁴But when they were in trouble, they turned to the LORD, the God of Israel. They looked for him and found him. ⁵In those days no one could travel safely. There was much trouble in all the nations. ⁶One nation would destroy another nation, and one city would destroy another city, because God troubled them with all kinds of distress. ⁷But you should be strong. Don't give up, because you will get a reward for your good work."

15:34 but . . . there Some Greek copies do not contain the bracketed text.

⁸Asa felt brave when he heard these words and the message from Azariah son of Oded the prophet. So he removed the hateful idols from all of Judah and Benjamin and from the towns he had captured in the hills of Ephraim. He repaired the LORD's altar that was in front of the porch of the Temple of the LORD.

⁹Then Asa gathered all the people from Judah and Benjamin and from the tribes of Ephraim, Manasseh, and Simeon who were living in Judah. Many people came to Asa even from Israel, because they saw that the LORD, Asa's God, was with him.

¹⁰Asa and these people gathered in Jerusalem in the third month of the fifteenth year of Asa's rule. ¹¹At that time they sacrificed to the LORD seven hundred bulls and seven thousand sheep and goats from the valuable things Asa's army had taken from their enemies. ¹²Then they made an agreement to obey the LORD, the God of their ancestors, with their whole being. ¹³Anyone who refused to obey the LORD, the God of Israel, was to be killed. It did not matter if that person was important or unimportant, a man or woman. ¹⁴Then Asa and the people made a promise before the LORD, shouting with a loud voice and blowing trumpets and sheep's horns. ¹⁵All the people of Judah were happy about the promise, because they had promised with all their heart. They looked for God and found him. So the LORD gave them peace in all the country.

¹⁶King Asa also removed Maacah, his grandmother, from being queen mother, because she had made a terrible Asherah idol. Asa cut down that idol, smashed it into pieces, and burned it in the Kidron Valley. ¹⁷But the places of worship to gods were not removed from Judah. Even so, Asa was faithful all his life. ¹⁸Asa brought into the Temple of God the gifts he and his father had given: silver, gold, and utensils.

¹⁹There was no more war until the thirty-fifth year of Asa's rule.

Asa's Last Years

16 In the thirty-sixth year of Asa's rule, Baasha king of Israel attacked Judah. He made the town of Ramah strong so he could keep people from leaving or entering Judah, Asa's country.

²Asa took silver and gold from the treasuries of the Temple of the LORD and out of his own palace. Then he sent it with messengers to Ben-Hadad king of Aram, who lived in Damascus. Asa said, ³"Let there be a treaty between you and me as there was between my father and your father. I am sending you silver and gold. Break your treaty with Baasha king of Israel so he will leave my land."

⁴Ben-Hadad agreed with King Asa and sent the commanders of his armies to attack the towns of Israel. They defeated the towns of Ijon, Dan, and Abel Beth Maacah, and all the towns in Naphtali where treasures were stored. ⁵When Baasha heard about this, he stopped building up Ramah and left his work. ⁶Then King Asa brought all the people of Judah to Ramah, and they carried away the rocks and wood that Baasha had used. And they used them to build up Geba and Mizpah.

⁷At that time Hanani the seer came to Asa king of Judah and said to him, "You depended on the king of Aram to help you and not on the LORD your God. So the king of Aram's army escaped from you. ⁸The Cushites and Libyans had a large and powerful army and many chariots and horsemen. But you depended on the LORD to help you, so he handed them over to you. ⁹The LORD searches all the earth for people who have given themselves completely to him. He wants to make them strong. Asa, you did a foolish thing, so from now on you will have wars."

¹⁰Asa was angry with Hanani the seer because of what he had said; he was so angry that he put Hanani in prison. And Asa was cruel to some of the people at the same time.

¹¹Everything Asa did as king, from the beginning to the end, is written in the book of the kings of Judah and Israel. ¹²In the thirty-ninth year of his rule, Asa got a disease in his feet. Though his disease was very bad, he did not ask for help from the LORD, but only from the doctors. ¹³Then Asa

died in the forty-first year of his rule. ¹⁴The people buried Asa in the tomb he had made for himself in Jerusalem. They laid him on a bed filled with spices and different kinds of mixed perfumes, and they made a large fire to honor him.

PSALM 81:5b–10

I heard a language I did not know,
saying:
⁶"I took the load off their shoulders;
I let them put down their baskets.
⁷When you were in trouble, you called,
and I saved you.
I answered you with thunder.
I tested you at the waters of Meribah.
Selah
⁸My people, listen. I am warning you.
Israel, please listen to me!
⁹You must not have foreign gods;
you must not worship any false god.
¹⁰I, the LORD, am your God,
who brought you out of Egypt.
Open your mouth and I will feed
you.

PROVERBS 20:24–25

²⁴The LORD decides what a person will do;
no one understands what his life is all
about.

²⁵It's dangerous to promise something to
God too quickly.
After you've thought about it, it may be
too late.

ACTS 16:1–15

Timothy Goes with Paul

16 Paul came to Derbe and Lystra, where a follower named Timothy lived. Timothy's mother was Jewish and a believer, but his father was a Greek. ²The believers in Lystra and Iconium respected Timothy and said good things about him. ³Paul wanted Timothy to travel

with him, but all the people living in that area knew that Timothy's father was Greek. So Paul circumcised Timothy to please his mother's people. ⁴Paul and those with him traveled from town to town and gave the decisions made by the apostles and elders in Jerusalem for the people to obey. ⁵So the churches became stronger in the faith and grew larger every day.

Paul Is Called Out of Asia

⁶Paul and those with him went through the areas of Phrygia and Galatia since the Holy Spirit did not let them preach the Good News in Asia. ⁷When they came near the country of Mysia, they tried to go into Bithynia, but the Spirit of Jesus did not let them. ⁸So they passed by Mysia and went to Troas. ⁹That night Paul saw in a vision a man from Macedonia. The man stood and begged, "Come over to Macedonia and help us." ¹⁰After Paul had seen the vision, we immediately prepared to leave for Macedonia, understanding that God had called us to tell the Good News to those people.

Lydia Becomes a Christian

¹¹We left Troas and sailed straight to the island of Samothrace. The next day we sailed to Neapolis.ⁿ ¹²Then we went by land to Philippi, a Roman colonyⁿ and the leading city in that part of Macedonia. We stayed there for several days. ¹³On the Sabbath day we went outside the city gate to the river where we thought we would find a special place for prayer. Some women had gathered there, so we sat down and talked with them. ¹⁴One of the listeners was a woman named Lydia from the city of Thyatira whose job was selling purple cloth. She worshiped God, and he opened her mind to pay attention to what Paul was saying. ¹⁵She and all the people in her house were baptized. Then she invited us to her home, saying, "If you think I am truly a believer in the Lord, then come stay in my house." And she persuaded us to stay with her.

16:11 Neapolis City in Macedonia. It was the first city Paul visited on the continent of Europe. **16:12 Roman colony** A town begun by Romans with Roman laws, customs, and privileges.

JULY 11

2 CHRONICLES 17:1—19:3

Jehoshaphat King of Judah

17 Jehoshaphat, Asa's son, became king of Judah in his place. Jehoshaphat made Judah strong so they could fight against Israel. ²He put troops in all the strong, walled cities of Judah, in the land of Judah, and in the towns of Ephraim that his father Asa had captured.

³The LORD was with Jehoshaphat, because he lived as his ancestor David had lived when he first became king. Jehoshaphat did not ask for help from the Baal idols, ⁴but from the God of his father. He obeyed God's commands and did not live as the people of Israel lived. ⁵The LORD made Jehoshaphat a strong king over Judah. All the people of Judah brought gifts to Jehoshaphat, so he had much wealth and honor. ⁶He wanted very much to obey the LORD. He also removed the places for worshiping gods and the Asherah idols from Judah.

⁷During the third year of his rule, Jehoshaphat sent his officers to teach in the towns of Judah. These officers were Ben-Hail, Obadiah, Zechariah, Nethanel, and Micaiah. ⁸Jehoshaphat sent with them these Levites: Shemaiah, Nethaniah, Zebadiah, Asahel, Shemiramoth, Jehonathan, Adonijah, Tobijah, and Tob-Adonijah. He also sent the priests Elishama and Jehoram. ⁹These leaders, Levites, and priests taught the people in Judah. They took the Book of the Teachings of the LORD and went through all the towns of Judah and taught the people.

¹⁰The nations near Judah were afraid of the LORD, so they did not start a war against Jehoshaphat. ¹¹Some of the Philistines brought gifts and silver to Jehoshaphat as he demanded. Some Arabs brought him flocks: seventy-seven hundred sheep and seventy-seven hundred goats.

¹²Jehoshaphat grew more and more powerful. He built strong, walled cities and towns for storing supplies in Judah. ¹³He kept many supplies in the towns of Judah, and he kept trained soldiers in Jerusalem. ¹⁴These soldiers were listed by families. From the families of Judah, these were the commanders of groups of a thousand men: Adnah was the commander of three hundred thousand soldiers; ¹⁵Jehohanan was the commander of two hundred eighty thousand soldiers; ¹⁶Amasiah was the commander of two hundred thousand soldiers. Amasiah son of Zicri had volunteered to serve the LORD.

¹⁷These were the commanders from the families of Benjamin: Eliada, a brave soldier, had two hundred thousand soldiers who used bows and shields. ¹⁸And Jehozabad had one hundred eighty thousand men armed for war.

¹⁹All these soldiers served King Jehoshaphat. The king also put other men in the strong, walled cities through all of Judah.

Micaiah Warns King Ahab

18 Jehoshaphat had much wealth and honor, and he made an agreement with King Ahab through marriage.ⁿ ²A few years later Jehoshaphat went to visit Ahab in Samaria. Ahab sacrificed many sheep and cattle as a great feast to honor Jehoshaphat and the people with him. He encouraged Jehoshaphat to attack Ramoth in Gilead. ³Ahab king of Israel asked Jehoshaphat king of Judah, "Will you go with me to attack Ramoth in Gilead?"

Jehoshaphat answered, "I will go with you, and my soldiers are yours. We will join you in the battle." ⁴Jehoshaphat also said to Ahab, "But first we should ask if this is the LORD's will."

⁵So King Ahab called four hundred prophets together and asked them, "Should we go to war against Ramoth in Gilead or not?"

They answered, "Go, because God will hand them over to you."

⁶But Jehoshaphat asked, "Isn't there a prophet of the LORD here? Let's ask him what we should do."

18:1 agreement . . . through marriage Jehoshaphat's son Jehoram married Athaliah, Ahab's daughter. See 2 Chronicles 21:6.

[7]Then King Ahab said to Jehoshaphat, "There is one other prophet. We could ask the LORD through him, but I hate him. He never prophesies anything good about me, but always something bad. He is Micaiah son of Imlah."

Jehoshaphat said, "King Ahab, you shouldn't say that!"

[8]So Ahab king of Israel told one of his officers to bring Micaiah to him at once.

[9]Ahab king of Israel and Jehoshaphat king of Judah had on their royal robes and were sitting on their thrones at the threshing floor, near the entrance to the gate of Samaria. All the prophets were standing before them speaking their messages. [10]Zedekiah son of Kenaanah had made some iron horns. He said to Ahab, "This is what the LORD says: 'You will use these horns to fight the Arameans until they are destroyed.'"

[11]All the other prophets said the same thing, "Attack Ramoth in Gilead and win, because the LORD will hand the Arameans over to you."

[12]The messenger who had gone to get Micaiah said to him, "All the other prophets are saying King Ahab will win. You should agree with them and give the king a good answer."

[13]But Micaiah answered, "As surely as the LORD lives, I can tell him only what my God says."

[14]When Micaiah came to Ahab, the king asked him, "Micaiah, should we attack Ramoth in Gilead or not?"

Micaiah answered, "Attack and win! They will be handed over to you."

[15]But Ahab said to Micaiah, "How many times do I have to tell you to speak only the truth to me in the name of the LORD?"

[16]So Micaiah answered, "I saw the army of Israel scattered over the hills like sheep without a shepherd. The LORD said, 'They have no leaders. They should go home and not fight.'"

[17]Then Ahab king of Israel said to Jehoshaphat, "I told you! He never prophesies anything good about me, but only bad."

[18]But Micaiah said, "Hear the message from the LORD: I saw the LORD sitting on his throne with his heavenly army standing on his right and on his left. [19]The LORD said, 'Who

will trick King Ahab of Israel into attacking Ramoth in Gilead where he will be killed?'

"Some said one thing; some said another. [20]Then one spirit came and stood before the LORD and said, 'I will trick him.'

"The LORD asked, 'How will you do it?'

[21]"The spirit answered, 'I will go to Ahab's prophets and make them tell lies.'

"So the LORD said, 'You will succeed in tricking him. Go and do it.'"

[22]Micaiah said, "Ahab, the LORD has made your prophets lie to you, and the LORD has decided that disaster should come to you."

[23]Then Zedekiah son of Kenaanah went up to Micaiah and slapped him in the face. Zedekiah said, "Has the LORD's Spirit left me to speak through you?"

[24]Micaiah answered, "You will find out on the day you go to hide in an inside room."

[25]Then Ahab king of Israel ordered, "Take Micaiah and send him to Amon, the governor of the city, and to Joash, the king's son. [26]Tell them I said to put this man in prison and give him only bread and water until I return safely from the battle."

[27]Micaiah said, "Ahab, if you come back safely from the battle, the LORD has not spoken through me. Remember my words, all you people!"

Ahab Is Killed

[28]So Ahab king of Israel and Jehoshaphat king of Judah went to Ramoth in Gilead. [29]King Ahab said to Jehoshaphat, "I will go into battle, but I will wear other clothes so no one will recognize me. But you wear your royal clothes." So Ahab wore other clothes, and they went into battle.

[30]The king of Aram ordered his chariot commanders, "Don't fight with anyone—important or unimportant—except the king of Israel." [31]When these commanders saw Jehoshaphat, they thought he was the king of Israel, so they turned to attack him. But Jehoshaphat began shouting, and the LORD helped him. God made the chariot commanders turn away from Jehoshaphat. [32]When they saw he was not King Ahab, they stopped chasing him.

[33]By chance, a soldier shot an arrow which hit Ahab king of Israel between the

pieces of his armor. King Ahab said to his chariot driver, "Turn around and get me out of the battle, because I am hurt!" [34]The battle continued all day. King Ahab held himself up in his chariot and faced the Arameans until evening. Then he died at sunset.

19 Jehoshaphat king of Judah came back safely to his palace in Jerusalem. [2]Jehu son of Hanani, a seer, went out to meet him and said to the king, "Why did you help evil people? Why do you love those who hate the LORD? That is the reason the LORD is angry with you. [3]But there is some good in you. You took the Asherah idols out of this country, and you have tried to obey God."

PSALM 81:11–16

[11]"But my people did not listen to me;
    Israel did not want me.
[12]So I let them go their stubborn way
    and follow their own advice.
[13]I wish my people would listen to me;
    I wish Israel would live my way.
[14]Then I would quickly defeat their
        enemies
    and turn my hand against their foes.
[15]Those who hate the LORD would bow
        before him.
    Their punishment would continue
        forever.
[16]But I would give you the finest wheat
    and fill you with honey from the rocks."

PROVERBS 20:26–28

[26]A wise king sorts out the evil people,
    and he punishes them as they deserve.

[27]The LORD looks deep inside people
    and searches through their thoughts.

[28]Loyalty and truth keep a king in power;
    he continues to rule if he is loyal.

ACTS 16:16–40

Paul and Silas in Jail

[16]Once, while we were going to the place for prayer, a servant girl met us. She had a special spirit[n] in her, and she earned a lot of money for her owners by telling fortunes. [17]This girl followed Paul and us, shouting, "These men are servants of the Most High God. They are telling you how you can be saved."

[18]She kept this up for many days. This bothered Paul, so he turned and said to the spirit, "By the power of Jesus Christ, I command you to come out of her!" Immediately, the spirit came out.

[19]When the owners of the servant girl saw this, they knew that now they could not use her to make money. So they grabbed Paul and Silas and dragged them before the city rulers in the marketplace. [20]They brought Paul and Silas to the Roman rulers and said, "These men are Jews and are making trouble in our city. [21]They are teaching things that are not right for us as Romans to do."

[22]The crowd joined the attack against them. The Roman officers tore the clothes of Paul and Silas and had them beaten with rods. [23]Then Paul and Silas were thrown into jail, and the jailer was ordered to guard them carefully. [24]When he heard this order, he put them far inside the jail and pinned their feet down between large blocks of wood.

[25]About midnight Paul and Silas were praying and singing songs to God as the other prisoners listened. [26]Suddenly, there was a strong earthquake that shook the foundation of the jail. Then all the doors of the jail broke open, and all the prisoners were freed from their chains. [27]The jailer woke up and saw that the jail doors were open. Thinking that the prisoners had already escaped, he got his sword and was about to kill himself.[n] [28]But Paul shouted, "Don't hurt yourself! We are all here."

[29]The jailer told someone to bring a light. Then he ran inside and, shaking with fear, fell down before Paul and Silas. [30]He brought them outside and said, "Men, what must I do to be saved?"

[31]They said to him, "Believe in the Lord Jesus and you will be saved—you and all the people in your house." [32]So Paul and Silas

---

16:16 spirit This was a spirit from the devil, which caused her to say she had special knowledge. **16:27 kill himself** He thought the leaders would kill him for letting the prisoners escape.

told the message of the Lord to the jailer and all the people in his house. ³³At that hour of the night the jailer took Paul and Silas and washed their wounds. Then he and all his people were baptized immediately. ³⁴After this the jailer took Paul and Silas home and gave them food. He and his family were very happy because they now believed in God.

³⁵The next morning, the Roman officers sent the police to tell the jailer, "Let these men go free."

³⁶The jailer said to Paul, "The officers have sent an order to let you go free. You can leave now. Go in peace."

³⁷But Paul said to the police, "They beat us in public without a trial, even though we are Roman citizens.ⁿ And they threw us in jail. Now they want to make us go away quietly. No! Let them come themselves and bring us out."

³⁸The police told the Roman officers what Paul said. When the officers heard that Paul and Silas were Roman citizens, they were afraid. ³⁹So they came and told Paul and Silas they were sorry and took them out of jail and asked them to leave the city. ⁴⁰So when they came out of the jail, they went to Lydia's house where they saw some of the believers and encouraged them. Then they left.

JULY 12

2 CHRONICLES 19:4—21:3

Jehoshaphat Chooses Judges

⁴Jehoshaphat lived in Jerusalem. He went out again to be with the people, from Beersheba to the mountains of Ephraim, and he turned them back to the LORD, the God of their ancestors. ⁵Jehoshaphat appointed judges in all the land, in each of the strong, walled cities of Judah. ⁶Jehoshaphat said to them, "Watch what you do, because you are not judging for people but for the LORD. He will be with you when you make a decision. ⁷Now let each of you fear the LORD. Watch what you do, because the LORD our God wants people to be fair. He wants all people to be treated the same, and he doesn't want decisions influenced by money."

⁸And in Jerusalem Jehoshaphat appointed some of the Levites, priests, and leaders of Israelite families to be judges. They were to decide cases about the law of the LORD and settle problems between the people who lived in Jerusalem. ⁹Jehoshaphat commanded them, "You must always serve the LORD completely, and you must fear him. ¹⁰Your people living in the cities will bring you cases about killing, about the teachings, commands, rules, or some other law. In all these cases you must warn the people not to

sin against the LORD. If you don't, he will be angry with you and your people. But if you warn them, you won't be guilty.

¹¹"Amariah, the leading priest, will be over you in all cases about the LORD. Zebadiah son of Ishmael, a leader in the tribe of Judah, will be over you in all cases about the king. Also, the Levites will serve as officers for you. Have courage. May the LORD be with those who do what is right."

Jehoshaphat Faces War

20 Later the Moabites, Ammonites, and some Meunites came to start a war with Jehoshaphat. ²Messengers came and told Jehoshaphat, "A large army is coming against you from Edom, from the other side of the Dead Sea. They are already in Hazazon Tamar!" (Hazazon Tamar is also called En Gedi.) ³Jehoshaphat was afraid, so he decided to ask the LORD what to do. He announced that everyone in Judah should fast during this special time of prayer to God. ⁴The people of Judah came together to ask the LORD for help; they came from every town in Judah.

⁵The people of Judah and Jerusalem met in front of the new courtyard in the Temple of the LORD. Then Jehoshaphat stood up, ⁶and he said, "LORD, God of our ancestors,

---

16:37 Roman citizens Roman law said that Roman citizens must not be beaten before they had a trial.

you are the God in heaven. You rule over all the kingdoms of the nations. You have power and strength, so no one can stand against you. ⁷Our God, you forced out the people who lived in this land as your people Israel moved in. And you gave this land forever to the descendants of your friend Abraham. ⁸They lived in this land and built a Temple for you. They said, ⁹'If trouble comes upon us, or war, punishment, sickness, or hunger, we will stand before you and before this Temple where you have chosen to be worshiped. We will cry out to you when we are in trouble. Then you will hear and save us.'

¹⁰"But now here are men from Ammon, Moab, and Edom. You wouldn't let the Israelites enter their lands when the Israelites came from Egypt. So the Israelites turned away and did not destroy them. ¹¹But see how they repay us for not destroying them! They have come to force us out of your land, which you gave us as our own. ¹²Our God, punish those people. We have no power against this large army that is attacking us. We don't know what to do, so we look to you for help."

¹³All the men of Judah stood before the LORD with their babies, wives, and children. ¹⁴Then the Spirit of the LORD entered Jahaziel. (Jahaziel was Zechariah's son. Zechariah was Benaiah's son. Benaiah was Jeiel's son, and Jeiel was Mattaniah's son.) Jahaziel, a Levite and a descendant of Asaph, stood up in the meeting. ¹⁵He said, "Listen to me, King Jehoshaphat and all you people living in Judah and Jerusalem. The LORD says this to you: 'Don't be afraid or discouraged because of this large army. The battle is not your battle, it is God's. ¹⁶Tomorrow go down there and fight those people. They will come up through the Pass of Ziz. You will find them at the end of the ravine that leads to the Desert of Jeruel. ¹⁷You won't need to fight in this battle. Just stand strong in your places, and you will see the LORD save you. Judah and Jerusalem, don't be afraid or discouraged, because the LORD is with you. So go out against those people tomorrow.'"

¹⁸Jehoshaphat bowed facedown on the ground. All the people of Judah and Jerusa-

lem bowed down before the LORD and worshiped him. ¹⁹Then some Levites from the Kohathite and Korahite people stood up and praised the LORD, the God of Israel, with very loud voices.

²⁰Jehoshaphat's army went out into the Desert of Tekoa early in the morning. As they were starting out, Jehoshaphat stood and said, "Listen to me, people of Judah and Jerusalem. Have faith in the LORD your God, and you will stand strong. Have faith in his prophets, and you will succeed." ²¹Jehoshaphat listened to the people's advice. Then he chose men to be singers to the LORD, to praise him because he is holy and wonderful. As they marched in front of the army, they said,

"Thank the LORD,
    because his love continues forever."

²²As they began to sing and praise God, the LORD set ambushes for the people of Ammon, Moab, and Edom who had come to attack Judah. And they were defeated. ²³The Ammonites and Moabites attacked the Edomites, destroying them completely. After they had killed the Edomites, they killed each other.

²⁴When the men from Judah came to a place where they could see the desert, they looked at the enemy's large army. But they only saw dead bodies lying on the ground; no one had escaped. ²⁵When Jehoshaphat and his army came to take their valuables, they found many supplies, much clothing, and other valuable things. There was more than they could carry away; there was so much it took three days to gather it all. ²⁶On the fourth day Jehoshaphat and his army met in the Valley of Beracah and praised the LORD. That is why that place has been called the Valley of Beracahⁿ to this day.

²⁷Then Jehoshaphat led all the men from Judah and Jerusalem back to Jerusalem. The LORD had made them happy because their enemies were defeated. ²⁸They entered Jerusalem with harps, lyres, and trumpets and went to the Temple of the LORD.

²⁹When all the kingdoms of the lands around them heard how the LORD had fought Israel's enemies, they feared God. ³⁰So Je-

hoshaphat's kingdom was not at war. His God gave him peace from all the countries around him.

Jehoshaphat's Rule Ends

31 Jehoshaphat ruled over the country of Judah. He was thirty-five years old when he became king, and he ruled in Jerusalem for twenty-five years. His mother's name was Azubah daughter of Shilhi. 32 Jehoshaphat was good like his father Asa, and he did what the LORD said was right. 33 But the places where gods were worshiped were not removed, and the people did not really want to follow the God of their ancestors.

34 The other things Jehoshaphat did as king, from the beginning to the end, are written in the records of Jehu son of Hanani, which are in the book of the kings of Israel.

35 Later, Jehoshaphat king of Judah made a treaty with Ahaziah king of Israel, which was a wrong thing to do. 36 Jehoshaphat agreed with Ahaziah to build trading ships, which they built in the town of Ezion Geber. 37 Then Eliezer son of Dodavahu from the town of Mareshah spoke against Jehoshaphat. He said, "Jehoshaphat, because you joined with Ahaziah, the LORD will destroy what you have made." The ships were wrecked so they could not sail out to trade.

21 Jehoshaphat died and was buried with his ancestors in Jerusalem, the city of David. Then his son Jehoram became king in his place. 2 Jehoram's brothers were Azariah, Jehiel, Zechariah, Azariahu, Michael, and Shephatiah. They were the sons of Jehoshaphat king of Judah. 3 Jehoshaphat gave his sons many gifts of silver, gold, and valuable things, and he gave them strong, walled cities in Judah. But Jehoshaphat gave the kingdom to Jehoram, because he was the first son.

PSALM 82:1–8

A Cry for Justice

A psalm of Asaph.

82 God is in charge of the great meeting; he judges among the "gods."
2 He says, "How long will you defend evil people?

How long will you show greater kindness to the wicked? *Selah*
3 Defend the weak and the orphans; defend the rights of the poor and suffering.
4 Save the weak and helpless; free them from the power of the wicked.

5 "You know nothing. You don't understand.
You walk in the dark, while the world is falling apart.
6 I said, 'You are "gods."
You are all sons of God Most High.'
7 But you will die like any other person; you will fall like all the leaders."

8 God, come and judge the earth, because you own all the nations.

PROVERBS 20:29–30

29 The young glory in their strength, and the old are honored for their gray hair.

30 Hard punishment will get rid of evil, and whippings can change an evil heart.

ACTS 17:1–15

Paul and Silas in Thessalonica

17 Paul and Silas traveled through Amphipolis and Apollonia and came to Thessalonica where there was a synagogue. 2 Paul went into the synagogue as he always did, and on each Sabbath day for three weeks, he talked with his fellow Jews about the Scriptures. 3 He explained and proved that the Christ must die and then rise from the dead. He said, "This Jesus I am telling you about is the Christ." 4 Some of them were convinced and joined Paul and Silas, along with many of the Greeks who worshiped God and many of the important women.

5 But some others became jealous. So they got some evil men from the marketplace, formed a mob, and started a riot. They ran to Jason's house, looking for Paul and Silas, wanting to bring them out to the people. 6 But

when they did not find them, they dragged Jason and some other believers to the leaders of the city. The people were yelling, "These people have made trouble everywhere in the world, and now they have come here too! [7]Jason is keeping them in his house. All of them do things against the laws of Caesar, saying there is another king, called Jesus."

[8]When the people and the leaders of the city heard these things, they became very upset. [9]They made Jason and the others put up a sum of money. Then they let the believers go free.

Paul and Silas Go to Berea

[10]That same night the believers sent Paul and Silas to Berea where they went to the synagogue. [11]These people were more willing to listen than the people in Thessalonica. The Bereans were eager to hear what Paul and Silas said and studied the Scriptures every day to find out if these things were true. [12]So, many of them believed, as well as many important Greek women and men. [13]But the people in Thessalonica learned that Paul was preaching the word of God in Berea, too. So they came there, upsetting the people and making trouble. [14]The believers quickly sent Paul away to the coast, but Silas and Timothy stayed in Berea. [15]The people leading Paul went with him to Athens. Then they carried a message from Paul back to Silas and Timothy for them to come to him as soon as they could.

JULY 13

2 CHRONICLES 21:4—23:7

Jehoram King of Judah

[4]When Jehoram took control of his father's kingdom, he killed all his brothers with a sword and also killed some of the leaders of Judah. [5]He was thirty-two years old when he began to rule, and he ruled eight years in Jerusalem. [6]He followed in the ways of the kings of Israel, just as the family of Ahab had done, because he married Ahab's daughter. Jehoram did what the LORD said was wrong. [7]But the LORD would not destroy David's family because of the agreement he had made with David. He had promised that one of David's descendants would always rule.

[8]In Jehoram's time, Edom broke away from Judah's rule and chose their own king. [9]So Jehoram went to Edom with all his commanders and chariots. The Edomites surrounded him and his chariot commanders, but Jehoram got up and attacked the Edomites at night. [10]From then until now the country of Edom has fought against the rule of Judah. At the same time the people of Libnah also broke away from Jehoram because Jehoram left the LORD, the God of his ancestors.

[11]Jehoram also built places to worship gods on the hills in Judah. He led the people of Jerusalem to sin, and he led the people of Judah away from the LORD. [12]Then Jehoram received this letter from Elijah the prophet:

This is what the LORD, the God of your ancestor David, says, "Jehoram, you have not lived as your father Jehoshaphat lived and as Asa king of Judah lived. [13]But you have lived as the kings of Israel lived, leading the people of Judah and Jerusalem to sin against God, as Ahab and his family did. You have killed your brothers, and they were better than you. [14]So now the LORD is about to punish your people, your children, wives, and everything you own. [15]You will have a terrible disease in your intestines that will become worse every day. Finally it will cause your intestines to come out."

[16]The LORD caused the Philistines and the Arabs who lived near the Cushites to be angry with Jehoram. [17]So the Philistines and Arabs attacked Judah and carried away all the wealth of Jehoram's palace, as well as his

sons and wives. Only Jehoram's youngest son, Ahaziah, was left.

¹⁸After these things happened, the LORD gave Jehoram a disease in his intestines that could not be cured. ¹⁹After he was sick for two years, Jehoram's intestines came out because of the disease, and he died in terrible pain. The people did not make a fire to honor Jehoram as they had done for his ancestors.

²⁰Jehoram was thirty-two years old when he became king, and he ruled eight years in Jerusalem. No one was sad when he died. He was buried in Jerusalem, but not in the graves for the kings.

Ahaziah King of Judah

22 The people of Jerusalem chose Ahaziah, Jehoram's youngest son, to be king in his place. The robbers who had come with the Arabs to attack Jehoram's camp had killed all of Jehoram's older sons. So Ahaziah began to rule Judah. ²Ahaziah was twenty-two years old when he became king, and he ruled one year in Jerusalem. His mother's name was Athaliah, a granddaughter of Omri. ³Ahaziah followed the ways of Ahab's family, because his mother encouraged him to do wrong. ⁴Ahaziah did what the LORD said was wrong, as Ahab's family had done. They gave advice to Ahaziah after his father died, and their bad advice led to his death. ⁵Following their advice, Ahaziah went with Joram son of Ahab to Ramoth in Gilead, where they fought against Hazael king of Aram. The Arameans wounded Joram. ⁶So Joram returned to Jezreel to heal from the wounds he received at Ramoth when he fought Hazael king of Aram.

Ahaziah son of Jehoram and king of Judah went down to visit Joram son of Ahab at Jezreel because he had been wounded. ⁷God caused Ahaziah's death when he went to visit Joram. Ahaziah arrived and went out with Joram to meet Jehu son of Nimshi, whom the LORD had appointed to destroy Ahab's family. ⁸While Jehu was punishing Ahab's family, he found the leaders of Judah and the sons of Ahaziah's relatives who served Ahaziah, and Jehu killed them all. ⁹Then Jehu looked for Ahaziah. Jehu's

men caught him hiding in Samaria, so they brought him to Jehu. Then they killed and buried him. They said, "Ahaziah is a descendant of Jehoshaphat, and Jehoshaphat obeyed the LORD with all his heart." No one in Ahaziah's family had the power to take control of the kingdom of Judah.

Athaliah and Joash

¹⁰When Ahaziah's mother, Athaliah, saw that her son was dead, she killed all the royal family in Judah. ¹¹But Jehosheba, King Jehoram's daughter, took Joash, Ahaziah's son. She stole him from among the other sons of the king who were going to be murdered and put him and his nurse in a bedroom. So Jehosheba, who was King Jehoram's daughter and Ahaziah's sister and the wife of Jehoiada the priest, hid Joash so Athaliah could not kill him. ¹²He hid with them in the Temple of God for six years. During that time Athaliah ruled the land.

23 In the seventh year Jehoiada decided to do something. He made an agreement with the commanders of the groups of a hundred men: Azariah son of Jeroham, Ishmael son of Jehohanan, Azariah son of Obed, Maaseiah son of Adaiah, and Elishaphat son of Zicri. ²They went around in Judah and gathered the Levites from all the towns, and they gathered the leaders of the families of Judah. Then they went to Jerusalem. ³All the people together made an agreement with the king in the Temple of God.

Jehoiada said to them, "The king's son will rule, as the LORD promised about David's descendants. ⁴Now this is what you must do: You priests and Levites go on duty on the Sabbath. A third of you will guard the doors. ⁵A third of you will be at the king's palace, and a third of you will be at the Foundation Gate. All the other people will stay in the courtyards of the Temple of the LORD. ⁶Don't let anyone come into the Temple of the LORD except the priests and Levites who serve. They may come because they have been made ready to serve the LORD, but all the others must do the job the LORD has given them. ⁷The Levites must stay near the king, each man with his weapon in his hand. If anyone tries to enter the Temple, kill him. Stay close to the king when he goes in and when he goes out."

PSALM 83:1–8

A Prayer Against the Enemies

A song. A psalm of Asaph.

83 God, do not keep quiet;
God, do not be silent or still.

²Your enemies are making noises;
those who hate you are getting ready to attack.

³They are making secret plans against your people;
they plot against those you love.

⁴They say, "Come, let's destroy them as a nation.
Then no one will ever remember the name 'Israel.'"

⁵They are united in their plan.
These have made an agreement against you:

⁶the families of Edom and the Ishmaelites,
Moab and the Hagrites,

⁷the people of Byblos, Ammon, Amalek, Philistia, and Tyre.

⁸Even Assyria has joined them
to help Ammon and Moab, the descendants of Lot.   *Selah*

PROVERBS 21:1

21 The LORD can control a king's mind as he controls a river;
he can direct it as he pleases.

ACTS 17:16–34

Paul Preaches in Athens

¹⁶While Paul was waiting for Silas and Timothy in Athens, he was troubled because he saw that the city was full of idols. ¹⁷In the synagogue, he talked with the Jews and the Greeks who worshiped God. He also talked every day with people in the marketplace.

¹⁸Some of the Epicurean and Stoic philosophers[n] argued with him, saying, "This man doesn't know what he is talking about. What is he trying to say?" Others said, "He seems to be telling us about some other gods," because Paul was telling them about Jesus and his rising from the dead. ¹⁹They got Paul and took him to a meeting of the Areopagus,[n] where they said, "Please explain to us this new idea you have been teaching. ²⁰The things you are saying are new to us, and we want to know what this teaching means." ²¹(All the people of Athens and those from other countries who lived there always used their time to talk about the newest ideas.)

²²Then Paul stood before the meeting of the Areopagus and said, "People of Athens, I can see you are very religious in all things. ²³As I was going through your city, I saw the objects you worship. I found an altar that had these words written on it: TO A GOD WHO IS NOT KNOWN. You worship a god that you don't know, and this is the God I am telling you about! ²⁴The God who made the whole world and everything in it is the Lord of the land and the sky. He does not live in temples built by human hands. ²⁵This God is the One who gives life, breath, and everything else to people. He does not need any help from them; he has everything he needs. ²⁶God began by making one person, and from him came all the different people who live everywhere in the world. God decided exactly when and where they must live. ²⁷God wanted them to look for him and perhaps search all around for him and find him, though he is not far from any of us: ²⁸'By his power we live and move and exist.' Some of your own poets have said: 'For we are his children.' ²⁹Since we are God's children, you must not think that God is like something that people imagine or make from gold, silver, or rock. ³⁰In the past, people did not understand God, and he ignored this. But now, God tells all people in the world to change their hearts and lives. ³¹God has set a day that he will judge all the world

---

17:18 Epicurean and Stoic philosophers Philosophers were those who searched for truth. Epicureans believed that pleasures, especially pleasures of the mind, were the goal of life. Stoics believed that life should be without feelings of joy or grief.
17:19 Areopagus A council or group of important leaders in Athens. They were like judges.

with fairness, by the man he chose long ago. And God has proved this to everyone by raising that man from the dead!"

³²When the people heard about Jesus being raised from the dead, some of them laughed. But others said, "We will hear more about this from you later." ³³So Paul went away from them. ³⁴But some of the people believed Paul and joined him. Among those who believed was Dionysius, a member of the Areopagus, a woman named Damaris, and some others.

JULY 14

2 CHRONICLES 23:8—24:27

Joash Becomes King

⁸The Levites and all the people of Judah obeyed everything Jehoiada the priest had commanded. He did not excuse anyone from the groups of the priests. So each commander took his men who came on duty on the Sabbath with those who went off duty on the Sabbath. ⁹Jehoiada gave the commanders of a hundred men the spears and the large and small shields that had belonged to King David and that were kept in the Temple of God. ¹⁰Then Jehoiada told the soldiers where to stand with weapon in hand. There were guards from the south side of the Temple to the north side. They stood by the altar and the Temple and around the king.

¹¹Jehoiada and his sons brought out the king's son and put the crown on him and gave him a copy of the agreement. Then they appointed him king and poured olive oil on him and shouted, "Long live the king!"

¹²When Athaliah heard the noise of the people running and praising the king, she went to them at the Temple of the LORD. ¹³She looked, and there was the king standing by his pillar at the entrance. The officers and the trumpeters were standing beside him, and all the people of the land were happy and blowing trumpets. The singers were playing musical instruments and leading praises. Then Athaliah tore her clothes and screamed, "Traitors! Traitors!"

¹⁴Jehoiada the priest sent out the commanders of a hundred men, who led the army. He said, "Surround her with soldiers and take her out of the Temple area. Kill with a sword anyone who follows her." He had said, "Don't put Athaliah to death in the Temple of the LORD." ¹⁵So they caught her when she came to the entrance of the Horse Gate near the palace. There they put her to death.

¹⁶Then Jehoiada made an agreement with the people and the king that they would be the LORD's special people. ¹⁷All the people went to the temple of Baal and tore it down, smashing the altars and idols. They killed Mattan, the priest of Baal, in front of the altars.

¹⁸Then Jehoiada chose the priests, who were Levites, to be responsible for the Temple of the LORD. David had given them duties in the Temple of the LORD. They were to offer the burnt offerings to the LORD as the Teachings of Moses commanded, and they were to offer them with much joy and singing as David had commanded. ¹⁹Jehoiada put guards at the gates of the Temple of the LORD so that anyone who was unclean in any way could not enter.

²⁰Jehoiada took with him the commanders of a hundred men, the important men, the rulers of the people, and all the people of the land to take the king out of the Temple of the LORD. They went through the Upper Gate into the palace, and then they seated the king on the throne. ²¹So all the people of the land were very happy, and Jerusalem had peace, because Athaliah had been put to death with the sword.

Joash Repairs the Temple

24 Joash was seven years old when he became king, and he ruled forty years in Jerusalem. His mother's name was Zibiah, and she was from Beersheba. ²Joash did

what the LORD said was right as long as Jehoiada the priest was alive. ³Jehoiada chose two wives for Joash, and Joash had sons and daughters.

⁴Later, Joash decided to repair the Temple of the LORD. ⁵He called the priests and the Levites together and said to them, "Go to the towns of Judah and gather the money all the Israelites have to pay every year. Use it to repair the Temple of your God. Do this now." But the Levites did not hurry.

⁶So King Joash called for Jehoiada the leading priest and said to him, "Why haven't you made the Levites bring in from Judah and Jerusalem the tax money that Moses, the LORD's servant, and the people of Israel used for the Holy Tent?"

⁷In the past the sons of wicked Athaliah had broken into the Temple of God and used its holy things for worshiping the Baal idols.

⁸King Joash commanded that a box for contributions be made. They put it outside, at the gate of the Temple of the LORD. ⁹Then the Levites made an announcement in Judah and Jerusalem, telling people to bring to the LORD the tax money Moses, the servant of God, had made the Israelites give while they were in the desert. ¹⁰All the officers and people were happy to bring their money, and they put it in the box until the box was full. ¹¹When the Levites would take the box to the king's officers, they would see that it was full of money. Then the king's royal secretary and the leading priest's officer would come and take out the money and return the box to its place. They did this often and gathered much money. ¹²King Joash and Jehoiada gave the money to the people who worked on the Temple of the LORD. And they hired stoneworkers and carpenters to repair the Temple of the LORD. They also hired people to work with iron and bronze to repair the Temple.

¹³The people worked hard, and the work to repair the Temple went well. They rebuilt the Temple of God to be as it was before, but even stronger. ¹⁴When the workers finished, they brought the money that was left to King Joash and Jehoiada. They used that money to make utensils for the Temple of the LORD, utensils for the service in the Temple and for the burnt offerings, and bowls and other utensils from gold and silver. Burnt offerings were given every day in the Temple of the LORD while Jehoiada was alive.

¹⁵Jehoiada grew old and lived many years. Then he died when he was one hundred thirty years old. ¹⁶Jehoiada was buried in Jerusalem with the kings, because he had done much good in Judah for God and his Temple.

Joash Does Evil

¹⁷After Jehoiada died, the officers of Judah came and bowed down to King Joash, and he listened to them. ¹⁸The king and these leaders stopped worshiping in the Temple of the LORD, the God of their ancestors. Instead, they began to worship the Asherah idols and other idols. Because they did wrong, God was angry with the people of Judah and Jerusalem. ¹⁹Even though the LORD sent prophets to the people to turn them back to him and even though the prophets warned them, they refused to listen.

²⁰Then the Spirit of God entered Zechariah son of Jehoiada the priest. Zechariah stood before the people and said, "This is what God says: 'Why do you disobey the LORD's commands? You will not be successful. Because you have left the LORD, he has also left you.'"

²¹But the king and his officers made plans against Zechariah. At the king's command they threw stones at him in the courtyard of the Temple of the LORD until he died. ²²King Joash did not remember Jehoiada's kindness to him, so Joash killed Zechariah, Jehoiada's son. Before Zechariah died, he said, "May the LORD see what you are doing and punish you."

²³At the end of the year, the Aramean army came against Joash. They attacked Judah and Jerusalem, killed all the leaders of the people, and sent all the valuable things to their king in Damascus. ²⁴The Aramean army came with only a small group of men, but the LORD handed over to them a very large army from Judah, because the people of Judah had left the LORD, the God of their ancestors. So Joash was punished. ²⁵When the Arameans left, Joash was badly wounded. His own officers made plans against him because he had killed Zechariah son of Je-

hoiada the priest. So they killed Joash in his own bed. He died and was buried in Jerusalem but not in the graves of the kings. ²⁶The officers who made plans against Joash were Jozabad and Jehozabad. Jozabad was the son of Shimeath, a woman from Ammon. And Jehozabad was the son of Shimrith, a woman from Moab. ²⁷The story of Joash's sons, the great prophecies against him, and how he repaired the Temple of God are written in the book of the kings. Joash's son Amaziah became king in his place.

PSALM 83:9–18

⁹God, do to them what you did to Midian,
  what you did to Sisera and Jabin at the
    Kishon River.
¹⁰They died at Endor,
  and their bodies rotted on the ground.
¹¹Do to their important leaders what you
    did to Oreb and Zeeb.
  Do to their princes what you did to
    Zebah and Zalmunna.
¹²They said, "Let's take for ourselves
  the pasturelands that belong to God."
¹³My God, make them like tumbleweed,
  like chaff blown away by the wind.
¹⁴Be like a fire that burns a forest
  or like flames that blaze through the
    hills.
¹⁵Chase them with your storm,
  and frighten them with your wind.
¹⁶Cover them with shame.
  Then people will look for you, LORD.
¹⁷Make them afraid and ashamed forever.
  Disgrace them and destroy them.
¹⁸Then they will know that you are the
    LORD,
  that only you are God Most High over
    all the earth.

PROVERBS 21:2–3

²You may believe you are doing right,
  but the LORD judges your reasons.

³Doing what is right and fair
  is more important to the LORD than
    sacrifices.

ACTS 18:1–28

Paul in Corinth

18 Later Paul left Athens and went to Corinth. ²Here he met a Jew named Aquila who had been born in the country of Pontus. But Aquila and his wife, Priscilla, had recently moved to Corinth from Italy, because Claudius*ⁿ* commanded that all Jews must leave Rome. Paul went to visit Aquila and Priscilla. ³Because they were tentmakers, just as he was, he stayed with them and worked with them. ⁴Every Sabbath day he talked with the Jews and Greeks in the synagogue, trying to persuade them to believe in Jesus.

⁵Silas and Timothy came from Macedonia and joined Paul in Corinth. After this, Paul spent all his time telling people the Good News, showing them that Jesus is the Christ. ⁶But they would not accept Paul's teaching and said some evil things. So he shook off the dust from his clothes*ⁿ* and said to them, "If you are not saved, it will be your own fault! I have done all I can do! After this, I will go to other nations." ⁷Paul left the synagogue and moved into the home of Titius Justus, next to the synagogue. This man worshiped God. ⁸Crispus was the leader of that synagogue, and he and all the people living in his house believed in the Lord. Many others in Corinth also listened to Paul and believed and were baptized.

⁹During the night, the Lord told Paul in a vision: "Don't be afraid. Continue talking to people and don't be quiet. ¹⁰I am with you, and no one will hurt you because many of my people are in this city." ¹¹Paul stayed there for a year and a half, teaching God's word to the people.

Paul Is Brought Before Gallio

¹²When Gallio was the governor of the country of Southern Greece, some people came together against Paul and took him to the court. ¹³They said, "This man is teaching people to worship God in a way that is against our law."

¹⁴Paul was about to say something, but

18:2 Claudius The emperor (ruler) of Rome, A.D. 41–54.   **18:6 shook . . . clothes** This was a warning to show that Paul was finished talking to the people in that city.

Gallio spoke, saying, "I would listen to you if you were complaining about a crime or some wrong. [15]But the things you are saying are only questions about words and names—arguments about your own law. So you must solve this problem yourselves. I don't want to be a judge of these things." [16]And Gallio made them leave the court.

[17]Then they all grabbed Sosthenes, the leader of the synagogue, and beat him there before the court. But this did not bother Gallio.

Paul Returns to Antioch

[18]Paul stayed with the believers for many more days. Then he left and sailed for Syria, with Priscilla and Aquila. At Cenchrea Paul cut off his hair,[n] because he had made a promise to God. [19]Then they went to Ephesus, where Paul left Priscilla and Aquila. While Paul was there, he went into the synagogue and talked with the people. [20]When they asked him to stay with them longer, he refused. [21]But as he left, he said, "I will come back to you again if God wants me to." And so he sailed away from Ephesus.

[22]When Paul landed at Caesarea, he went and gave greetings to the church in Jerusalem.

After that, Paul went to Antioch. [23]He stayed there for a while and then left and went through the regions of Galatia and Phrygia. He traveled from town to town in these regions, giving strength to all the followers.

Apollos in Ephesus and Corinth

[24]A Jew named Apollos came to Ephesus. He was born in the city of Alexandria and was a good speaker who knew the Scriptures well. [25]He had been taught about the way of the Lord and was always very excited when he spoke and taught the truth about Jesus. But the only baptism Apollos knew about was the baptism that John[n] taught. [26]Apollos began to speak very boldly in the synagogue, and when Priscilla and Aquila heard him, they took him to their home and helped him better understand the way of God. [27]Now Apollos wanted to go to the country of Southern Greece. So the believers helped him and wrote a letter to the followers there, asking them to accept him. These followers had believed in Jesus because of God's grace, and when Apollos arrived, he helped them very much. [28]He argued very strongly with the Jews before all the people, clearly proving with the Scriptures that Jesus is the Christ.

JULY 15

2 CHRONICLES 25:1—27:9

Amaziah King of Judah

25 Amaziah was twenty-five years old when he became king, and he ruled for twenty-nine years in Jerusalem. His mother's name was Jehoaddin, and she was from Jerusalem. [2]Amaziah did what the LORD said was right, but he did not really want to obey him. [3]As soon as Amaziah took strong control of the kingdom, he executed the officers who had murdered his father the king. [4]But Amaziah did not put to death their children. He obeyed what was written in the Book of Moses, where the LORD commanded, "Parents must not be put to death when their children do wrong, and children must not be put to death when their parents do wrong. Each must die for his own sins."[n]

[5]Amaziah gathered the people of Judah together. He grouped all the people of Judah and Benjamin by families, and he put commanders over groups of a thousand and over groups of a hundred. He counted the men who were twenty years old and older. In all there were three hundred thousand soldiers ready to fight and skilled with spears and shields. [6]Amaziah also hired one hundred thousand soldiers from Israel for about seventy-five hundred pounds of silver. [7]But a

man of God came to Amaziah and said, "My king, don't let the army of Israel go with you. The LORD is not with Israel or the people from the tribe of Ephraim. [8]You can make yourself strong for war, but God will defeat you. He has the power to help you or to defeat you."

[9]Amaziah said to the man of God, "But what about the seventy-five hundred pounds of silver I paid to the Israelite army?"

The man of God answered, "The LORD can give you much more than that."

[10]So Amaziah sent the Israelite army back home to Ephraim. They were very angry with the people of Judah and went home angry.

[11]Then Amaziah became very brave and led his army to the Valley of Salt in the country of Edom. There Amaziah's army killed ten thousand Edomites. [12]The army of Judah also captured ten thousand and took them to the top of a cliff and threw them off so that they split open.

[13]At the same time the Israelite troops that Amaziah had not let fight in the war were robbing towns in Judah. From Samaria to Beth Horon they killed three thousand people and took many valuable things.

[14]When Amaziah came home after defeating the Edomites, he brought back the idols they worshiped and started to worship them himself. He bowed down to them and offered sacrifices to them. [15]The LORD was very angry with Amaziah, so he sent a prophet to him who said, "Why have you asked their gods for help? They could not even save their own people from you!"

[16]As the prophet spoke, Amaziah said to him, "We never gave you the job of advising the king. Stop, or you will be killed."

The prophet stopped speaking except to say, "I know that God has decided to destroy you because you have done this. You did not listen to my advice."

[17]Amaziah king of Judah talked with those who advised him. Then he sent a message to Jehoash son of Jehoahaz, who was the son of Jehu king of Israel. Amaziah said to Jehoash, "Come, let's meet face to face."

[18]Then Jehoash king of Israel answered Amaziah king of Judah, "A thornbush in Lebanon sent a message to a cedar tree in Lebanon. It said, 'Let your daughter marry my son.' But then a wild animal from Lebanon came by, walking on and crushing the thornbush. [19]You say to yourself that you have defeated Edom, but you have become proud, and you brag. But you stay at home! Don't ask for trouble, or you and Judah will be defeated."

[20]But Amaziah would not listen. God caused this to happen so that Jehoash would defeat Judah, because Judah asked for help from the gods of Edom. [21]So Jehoash king of Israel went to attack. He and Amaziah king of Judah faced each other in battle at Beth Shemesh in Judah. [22]Israel defeated Judah, and every man of Judah ran away to his home. [23]At Beth Shemesh Jehoash king of Israel captured Amaziah king of Judah. (Amaziah was the son of Joash, who was the son of Ahaziah.) Then Jehoash brought him to Jerusalem. Jehoash broke down the wall of Jerusalem, from the Gate of Ephraim to the Corner Gate, about six hundred feet. [24]He took all the gold and silver and all the utensils from the Temple of God that Obed-Edom had taken care of. He also took the treasures from the palace and some hostages. Then he returned to Samaria.

[25]Amaziah son of Joash, the king of Judah, lived fifteen years after the death of Jehoash son of Jehoahaz, the king of Israel. [26]The other things Amaziah did as king, from the beginning to the end, are written in the book of the kings of Judah and Israel. [27]When Amaziah stopped obeying the LORD, the people in Jerusalem made plans against him. So he ran away to the town of Lachish, but they sent men after him to Lachish and killed him. [28]They brought his body back on horses, and he was buried with his ancestors in Jerusalem, the city of David.

Uzziah King of Judah

26 Then all the people of Judah made Uzziah[n] king in place of his father Amaziah. Uzziah was sixteen years old. [2]He

---

26:1 Uzziah Also called Azariah.

rebuilt the town of Elath and made it part of Judah again after Amaziah died.

[3]Uzziah was sixteen years old when he became king, and he ruled fifty-two years in Jerusalem. His mother's name was Jecoliah, and she was from Jerusalem. [4]He did what the LORD said was right, just as his father Amaziah had done. [5]Uzziah obeyed God while Zechariah was alive, because he taught Uzziah how to respect and obey God. And as long as Uzziah obeyed the LORD, God gave him success.

[6]Uzziah fought a war against the Philistines. He tore down the walls around their towns of Gath, Jabneh, and Ashdod and built new towns near Ashdod and in other places among the Philistines. [7]God helped Uzziah fight the Philistines, the Arabs living in Gur Baal, and the Meunites. [8]Also, the Ammonites made the payments Uzziah demanded. He was very powerful, so his name became famous all the way to the border of Egypt.

[9]Uzziah built towers in Jerusalem at the Corner Gate, the Valley Gate, and where the wall turned, and he made them strong. [10]He also built towers in the desert and dug many wells, because he had many cattle on the western hills and in the plains. He had people who worked his fields and vineyards in the hills and in the fertile lands, because he loved the land.

[11]Uzziah had an army of trained soldiers. They were counted and put in groups by Jeiel the royal secretary and Maaseiah the officer. Hananiah, one of the king's commanders, was their leader. [12]There were twenty-six hundred leaders over the soldiers. [13]They were in charge of an army of three hundred seven thousand five hundred men who fought with great power to help the king against the enemy. [14]Uzziah gave his army shields, spears, helmets, armor, bows, and stones for their slings. [15]In Jerusalem Uzziah made cleverly designed devices. These devices on the towers and corners of the city walls were used to shoot arrows and large rocks. So Uzziah became famous in faraway places, because he had much help until he became powerful.

[16]But when Uzziah became powerful, his pride led to his ruin. He was unfaithful to the LORD his God; he went into the Temple of the LORD to burn incense on the altar for incense. [17]Azariah and eighty other brave priests who served the LORD followed Uzziah into the Temple. [18]They told him he was wrong and said to him, "You don't have the right to burn incense to the LORD. Only the priests, Aaron's descendants, should burn the incense, because they have been made holy. Leave this holy place. You have been unfaithful, and the LORD God will not honor you for this."

[19]Uzziah was standing beside the altar for incense in the Temple of the LORD, and in his hand was a pan for burning incense. He was very angry with the priests. As he was standing in front of the priests, a skin disease broke out on his forehead. [20]Azariah, the leading priest, and all the other priests looked at him and saw the skin disease on his forehead. So they hurried him out of the Temple. Uzziah also rushed out, because the LORD was punishing him. [21]So King Uzziah had the skin disease until the day he died. He had to live in a separate house and could not enter the Temple of the LORD. His son Jotham was in charge of the palace, and he governed the people of the land.

[22]The other things Uzziah did as king, from beginning to end, were written down by the prophet Isaiah son of Amoz. [23]Uzziah died and was buried near his ancestors in a graveyard that belonged to the kings. This was because people said, "He had a skin disease." And his son Jotham became king in his place.

Jotham King of Judah

27 Jotham was twenty-five years old when he became king, and he ruled sixteen years in Jerusalem. His mother's name was Jerusha daughter of Zadok. [2]Jotham did what the LORD said was right, just as his father Uzziah had done. But Jotham did not enter the Temple of the LORD to burn incense as his father had. But the people continued doing wrong. [3]Jotham rebuilt the Upper Gate of the Temple of the LORD, and he added greatly to the wall at Ophel. [4]He also built towns in the hill coun-

try of Judah, as well as walled cities and towers in the forests.

⁵Jotham also fought the king of the Ammonites and defeated them. So each year for three years they gave Jotham about seventy-five hundred pounds of silver, about sixty-two thousand bushels of wheat, and about sixty-two thousand bushels of barley. ⁶Jotham became powerful, because he always obeyed the LORD his God.

⁷The other things Jotham did while he was king and all his wars are written in the book of the kings of Israel and Judah. ⁸Jotham was twenty-five years old when he became king, and he ruled sixteen years in Jerusalem. ⁹Jotham died and was buried in Jerusalem, the city of David. Then Jotham's son Ahaz became king in his place.

PSALM 84:1–7

Wishing to Be in the Temple

For the director of music. On the gittith. A psalm of the sons of Korah.

84 LORD All-Powerful,
how lovely is your Temple!
²I want more than anything
to be in the courtyards of the LORD's Temple.
My whole being wants
to be with the living God.
³The sparrows have found a home,
and the swallows have nests.
They raise their young near your altars,
LORD All-Powerful, my King and my God.
⁴Happy are the people who live at your Temple;
they are always praising you.   *Selah*

⁵Happy are those whose strength comes from you,
who want to travel to Jerusalem.
⁶As they pass through the Valley of Baca,
they make it like a spring.
The autumn rains fill it with pools of water.
⁷The people get stronger as they go,
and everyone meets with God in Jerusalem.

PROVERBS 21:4–5

⁴Proud looks, proud thoughts,
and evil actions are sin.

⁵The plans of hard-working people earn a profit,
but those who act too quickly become poor.

ACTS 19:1–22

Paul in Ephesus

19 While Apollos was in Corinth, Paul was visiting some places on the way to Ephesus. There he found some followers ²and asked them, "Did you receive the Holy Spirit when you believed?"

They said, "We have never even heard of a Holy Spirit."

³So he asked, "What kind of baptism did you have?"

They said, "It was the baptism that John taught."

⁴Paul said, "John's baptism was a baptism of changed hearts and lives. He told people to believe in the one who would come after him, and that one is Jesus."

⁵When they heard this, they were baptized in the name of the Lord Jesus. ⁶Then Paul laid his hands on them,ⁿ and the Holy Spirit came upon them. They began speaking different languagesⁿ and prophesying. ⁷There were about twelve people in this group.

⁸Paul went into the synagogue and spoke out boldly for three months. He talked with the people and persuaded them to accept the things he said about the kingdom of God. ⁹But some of them became stubborn. They refused to believe and said evil things about the Way of Jesus before all the people. So Paul left them, and taking the followers with him, he went to the school of a man named Tyrannus. There Paul talked with people every day ¹⁰for two years. Because of his work, every Jew and Greek in Asia heard the word of the Lord.

The Sons of Sceva

¹¹God used Paul to do some very special miracles. ¹²Some people took handkerchiefs and clothes that Paul had used and put them

---

19:6 laid his hands on them The laying on of hands had many purposes, including the giving of a blessing, power, or authority.   **19:6 languages** This can also be translated "tongues."

on the sick. When they did this, the sick were healed and evil spirits left them.

[13]But some people also were traveling around and making evil spirits go out of people. They tried to use the name of the Lord Jesus to force the evil spirits out. They would say, "By the same Jesus that Paul talks about, I order you to come out!" [14]Seven sons of Sceva, a leading priest, were doing this.

[15]But one time an evil spirit said to them, "I know Jesus, and I know about Paul, but who are you?"

[16]Then the man who had the evil spirit jumped on them. Because he was so much stronger than all of them, they ran away from the house naked and hurt. [17]All the people in Ephesus—Jews and Greeks—learned about this and were filled with fear and gave great honor to the Lord Jesus. [18]Many of the believers began to confess openly and tell all the evil things they had done. [19]Some of them who had used magic brought their magic books and burned them before everyone. Those books were worth about fifty thousand silver coins.[n]

[20]So in a powerful way the word of the Lord kept spreading and growing.

[21]After these things, Paul decided to go to Jerusalem, planning to go through the countries of Macedonia and Southern Greece and then on to Jerusalem. He said, "After I have been to Jerusalem, I must also visit Rome." [22]Paul sent Timothy and Erastus, two of his helpers, ahead to Macedonia, but he himself stayed in Asia for a while.

JULY 16

2 CHRONICLES 28:1—29:36

Ahaz King of Judah

28 Ahaz was twenty years old when he became king, and he ruled sixteen years in Jerusalem. Unlike his ancestor David, he did not do what the LORD said was right. [2]Ahaz did the same things the kings of Israel had done. He made metal idols to worship Baal. [3]He burned incense in the Valley of Ben Hinnom and made his children pass through the fire. He did the same hateful sins as the nations had done whom the LORD had forced out of the land ahead of the Israelites. [4]Ahaz offered sacrifices and burned incense at the places where gods were worshiped, and on the hills, and under every green tree.

[5]So the LORD his God handed over Ahaz to the king of Aram. The Arameans defeated Ahaz and took many people of Judah as prisoners to Damascus.

He also handed over Ahaz to Pekah king of Israel, and Pekah's army killed many soldiers of Ahaz. [6]The army of Pekah son of Remaliah killed one hundred twenty thousand brave soldiers from Judah in one day. Pekah defeated them because they had left the LORD, the God of their ancestors. [7]Zicri, a warrior from Ephraim, killed King Ahaz's son Maaseiah. He also killed Azrikam, the officer in charge of the palace, and Elkanah, who was second in command to the king. [8]The Israelite army captured two hundred thousand of their own relatives. They took women, sons and daughters, and many valuable things from Judah and carried them back to Samaria. [9]But a prophet of the LORD named Oded was there. He met the Israelite army when it returned to Samaria and said to them, "The LORD, the God of your ancestors, handed Judah over to you, because he was angry with those people. But God has seen the cruel way you killed them. [10]Now you plan to make the people of Judah and Jerusalem your slaves, but you also have

---

19:19 fifty thousand silver coins Probably drachmas. One coin was enough to pay a worker for one day's labor.

sinned against the LORD your God. [11]Now listen to me. Send back your brothers and sisters whom you captured, because the LORD is very angry with you."

[12]Then some of the leaders in Ephraim— Azariah son of Jehohanan, Berekiah son of Meshillemoth, Jehizkiah son of Shallum, and Amasa son of Hadlai—met the Israelite soldiers coming home from war. [13]They warned the soldiers, "Don't bring the prisoners from Judah here. If you do, we will be guilty of sin against the LORD, and that will make our sin and guilt even worse. Our guilt is already so great that he is angry with Israel."

[14]So the soldiers left the prisoners and valuable things in front of the officers and people there. [15]The leaders who were named took the prisoners and gave those who were naked the clothes that the Israelite army had taken. They gave the prisoners clothes, sandals, food, drink, and medicine. They put the weak prisoners on donkeys and took them back to their families in Jericho, the city of palm trees. Then they returned home to Samaria.

[16-17]At that time the Edomites came again and attacked Judah and carried away prisoners. So King Ahaz sent to the king of Assyria for help. [18]The Philistines also robbed the towns in the western hills and in southern Judah. They captured the towns of Beth Shemesh, Aijalon, Gederoth, Soco, Timnah, and Gimzo, and the villages around them. Then the Philistines lived in those towns. [19]The LORD brought trouble on Judah because Ahaz their king led the people of Judah to sin, and he was unfaithful to the LORD. [20]Tiglath-Pileser king of Assyria came to Ahaz, but he gave Ahaz trouble instead of help. [21]Ahaz took some valuable things from the Temple of the LORD, from the palace, and from the princes, and he gave them to the king of Assyria, but it did not help.

[22]During Ahaz's troubles he was even more unfaithful to the LORD. [23]He offered sacrifices to the gods of the people of Damascus, who had defeated him. He thought, "The gods of the kings of Aram helped them. If I offer sacrifices to them, they will help me also." But this brought ruin to Ahaz and all Israel.

[24]Ahaz gathered the things from the Temple of God and broke them into pieces. Then he closed the doors of the Temple of the LORD. He made altars and put them on every street corner in Jerusalem. [25]In every town in Judah, Ahaz made places for burning sacrifices to worship other gods. So he made the LORD, the God of his ancestors, very angry.

[26]The other things Ahaz did as king, from beginning to end, are written in the book of the kings of Judah and Israel. [27]Ahaz died and was buried in the city of Jerusalem, but not in the graves of the kings of Israel. Ahaz's son Hezekiah became king in his place.

Hezekiah Purifies the Temple

29 Hezekiah was twenty-five years old when he became king, and he ruled twenty-nine years in Jerusalem. His mother's name was Abijah daughter of Zechariah. [2]Hezekiah did what the LORD said was right, just as his ancestor David had done.

[3]Hezekiah opened the doors of the Temple of the LORD and repaired them in the first month of the first year he was king. [4]Hezekiah brought in the priests and Levites and gathered them in the courtyard on the east side of the Temple. [5]Hezekiah said, "Listen to me, Levites. Make yourselves ready for the LORD's service, and make holy the Temple of the LORD, the God of your ancestors. Remove from the Temple everything that makes it impure. [6]Our ancestors were unfaithful to God and did what the LORD said was wrong. They left the LORD and stopped worshiping at the Temple where he lives. They rejected him. [7]They shut the doors of the porch of the Temple, and they let the fire go out in the lamps. They stopped burning incense and offering burnt offerings in the holy place to the God of Israel. [8]So the LORD became very angry with the people of Judah and Jerusalem, and he punished them. Other people are frightened and shocked by what he did to them. So they insult the people of Judah. You know these things are true. [9]That is why our ancestors were killed in battle and our sons, daughters, and wives were taken captive. [10]Now I, Hezekiah, have decided to make an agreement with the LORD, the God of Israel, so he

will not be angry with us anymore. [11]My sons, don't waste any more time. The LORD chose you to stand before him, to serve him, to be his servants, and to burn incense to him."

[12]These are the Levites who started to work. From the Kohathite family there were Mahath son of Amasai and Joel son of Azariah. From the Merarite family there were Kish son of Abdi and Azariah son of Jehallelel. From the Gershonite family there were Joah son of Zimmah and Eden son of Joah. [13]From Elizaphan's family there were Shimri and Jeiel. From Asaph's family there were Zechariah and Mattaniah. [14]From Heman's family there were Jehiel and Shimei. From Jeduthun's family there were Shemaiah and Uzziel.

[15]These Levites gathered their brothers together and made themselves holy for service in the Temple. Then they went into the Temple of the LORD to purify it. They obeyed the king's command that had come from the LORD. [16]When the priests went into the Temple of the LORD to purify it, they took out all the unclean things they found in the Temple of the LORD and put them in the Temple courtyard. Then the Levites took these things out to the Kidron Valley. [17]Beginning on the first day of the first month, they made the Temple holy for the LORD's service. On the eighth day of the month, they came to the porch of the Temple, and for eight more days they made the Temple of the LORD holy. So they finished on the sixteenth day of the first month.

[18]Then they went to King Hezekiah and said, "We have purified the entire Temple of the LORD, the altar for burnt offerings and its utensils, and the table for the holy bread and all its utensils. [19]When Ahaz was king, he was unfaithful to God and removed some things from the Temple. But we have put them back and made them holy for the LORD. They are now in front of the LORD's altar."

[20]Early the next morning King Hezekiah gathered the leaders of the city and went up to the Temple of the LORD. [21]They brought seven bulls, seven male sheep, seven lambs, and seven male goats. These animals were an offering to remove the sin of the people and the kingdom of Judah and to make the Temple ready for service to God. King Hezekiah commanded the priests, the descendants of Aaron, to offer these animals on the LORD's altar. [22]So the priests killed the bulls and sprinkled their blood on the altar. They killed the sheep and sprinkled their blood on the altar. Then they killed the lambs and sprinkled their blood on the altar. [23]Then the priests brought the male goats for the sin offering before the king and the people there. After the king and the people put their hands on the goats, [24]the priests killed them. With the goats' blood they made an offering on the altar to remove the sins of the Israelites so they would belong to God. The king had said that the burnt offering and sin offering should be made for all Israel.

[25]King Hezekiah put the Levites in the Temple of the LORD with cymbals, harps, and lyres, as David, Gad, and Nathan had commanded. (Gad was the king's seer, and Nathan was a prophet.) This command came from the LORD through his prophets. [26]So the Levites stood ready with David's instruments of music, and the priests stood ready with their trumpets.

[27]Then Hezekiah gave the order to sacrifice the burnt offering on the altar. When the burnt offering began, the singing to the LORD also began. The trumpets were blown, and the musical instruments of David king of Israel were played. [28]All the people worshiped, the singers sang, and the trumpeters blew their trumpets until the burnt offering was finished.

[29]When the sacrifices were completed, King Hezekiah and everyone with him bowed down and worshiped. [30]King Hezekiah and his officers ordered the Levites to praise the LORD, using the words David and Asaph the seer had used. So they praised God with joy and bowed down and worshiped.

[31]Then Hezekiah said, "Now that you people of Judah have given yourselves to the LORD, come near to the Temple of the LORD. Bring sacrifices and offerings, to show thanks to him." So the people brought sacrifices and thank offerings, and anyone who was willing also brought burnt offerings.

[32]For burnt offerings they brought a total of seventy bulls, one hundred male sheep, and two hundred lambs; all these animals were sacrificed as burnt offerings to the LORD. [33]The holy offerings totaled six hundred bulls and three thousand sheep and goats. [34]There were not enough priests to skin all the animals for the burnt offerings. So their relatives the Levites helped them until the work was finished and other priests could be made holy. The Levites had been more careful to make themselves holy for the LORD's service than the priests. [35]There were many burnt offerings along with the fat of fellowship offerings and drink offerings. So the service in the Temple of the LORD began again. [36]And Hezekiah and the people were very happy that God had made it happen so quickly for his people.

PSALM 84:8–12

[8]LORD God All-Powerful, hear my prayer;
God of Jacob, listen to me.   *Selah*

[9]God, look at our shield;
be kind to your appointed king.

[10]One day in the courtyards of your Temple
is better
than a thousand days anywhere else.
I would rather be a doorkeeper in the
Temple of my God
than live in the homes of the wicked.

[11]The LORD God is like a sun and shield;
the LORD gives us kindness and honor.
He does not hold back anything good
from those whose lives are innocent.

[12]LORD All-Powerful,
happy are the people who trust you!

PROVERBS 21:6–8

[6]Wealth that comes from telling lies
vanishes like a mist and leads to death.

[7]The violence of the wicked will destroy
them,
because they refuse to do what is right.

[8]Guilty people live dishonest lives,
but honest people do right.

ACTS 19:23–41

Trouble in Ephesus

[23]And during that time, there was some serious trouble in Ephesus about the Way of Jesus. [24]A man named Demetrius, who worked with silver, made little silver models that looked like the temple of the goddess Artemis.[n] Those who did this work made much money. [25]Demetrius had a meeting with them and some others who did the same kind of work. He told them, "Men, you know that we make a lot of money from our business. [26]But look at what this man Paul is doing. He has convinced and turned away many people in Ephesus and in almost all of Asia! He says the gods made by human hands are not real. [27]There is a danger that our business will lose its good name, but there is also another danger: People will begin to think that the temple of the great goddess Artemis is not important. Her greatness will be destroyed, and Artemis is the goddess that everyone in Asia and the whole world worships."

[28]When the others heard this, they became very angry and shouted, "Artemis, the goddess of Ephesus, is great!" [29]The whole city became confused. The people grabbed Gaius and Aristarchus, who were from Macedonia and were traveling with Paul, and ran to the theater. [30]Paul wanted to go in and talk to the crowd, but the followers did not let him. [31]Also, some leaders of Asia who were friends of Paul sent him a message, begging him not to go into the theater. [32]Some people were shouting one thing, and some were shouting another. The meeting was completely confused; most of them did not know why they had come together. [33]They put a man named Alexander in front of the people, and some of them told him what to do. Alexander waved his hand so he could explain things to the people. [34]But when they saw that Alexander was a Jew, they all shouted the same thing for two hours: "Great is Artemis of Ephesus!"

[35]Then the city clerk made the crowd be quiet. He said, "People of Ephesus, everyone knows that Ephesus is the city that keeps the

---

19:24 Artemis A Greek goddess that the people of Asia Minor worshiped.

temple of the great goddess Artemis and her holy stone[n] that fell from heaven. [36]Since no one can say this is not true, you should be quiet. Stop and think before you do anything. [37]You brought these men here, but they have not said anything evil against our goddess or stolen anything from her temple. [38]If Demetrius and those who work with him have a charge against anyone they should go to the courts and judges where they can argue with each other. [39]If there is something else you want to talk about, it can be decided at the regular town meeting of the people. [40]I say this because some people might see this trouble today and say that we are rioting. We could not explain this, because there is no real reason for this meeting." [41]After the city clerk said these things, he told the people to go home.

JULY 17

2 CHRONICLES 30:1—31:21

The Passover Celebration

30 King Hezekiah sent messages to all the people of Israel and Judah, and he wrote letters to the people of Ephraim and Manasseh. Hezekiah invited all these people to come to the Temple of the LORD in Jerusalem to celebrate the Passover for the LORD, the God of Israel. [2]King Hezekiah, his officers, and all the people in Jerusalem agreed to celebrate the Passover in the second month. [3]They could not celebrate it at the normal time, because not enough priests had made themselves ready to serve the LORD, and the people had not yet gathered in Jerusalem. [4]This plan satisfied King Hezekiah and all the people. [5]So they made an announcement everywhere in Israel, from Beersheba to Dan,[n] telling the people to come to Jerusalem to celebrate the Passover for the LORD, the God of Israel. For a long time most of the people had not celebrated the Passover as the law commanded. [6]At the king's command, the messengers took letters from him and his officers all through Israel and Judah. This is what the letters said:

People of Israel, return to the LORD, the God of Abraham, Isaac, and Israel. Then God will return to you who are still alive, who have escaped from the kings of Assyria. [7]Don't be like your an-cestors or your relatives. They turned against the LORD, the God of their ancestors, so he caused other people to be disgusted with them. You know this is true. [8]Don't be stubborn as your ancestors were, but obey the LORD willingly. Come to the Temple, which he has made holy forever. Serve the LORD your God so he will not be angry with you. [9]Come back to the LORD. Then the people who captured your relatives and children will be kind to them and will let them return to this land. The LORD your God is kind and merciful. He will not turn away from you if you return to him.

[10]The messengers went to every town in Ephraim and Manasseh, and all the way to Zebulun, but the people laughed at them and made fun of them. [11]But some men from Asher, Manasseh, and Zebulun were sorry for what they had done and went to Jerusalem. [12]And God united all the people of Judah in obeying King Hezekiah and his officers, because their command had come from the LORD.

[13]In the second month a large crowd came together in Jerusalem to celebrate the Feast of Unleavened Bread. [14]The people removed the altars and incense altars to gods in Jerusalem and threw them into the Kidron Valley.

[15]They killed the Passover lamb on the

19:35 holy stone Probably a meteorite or stone that the people thought looked like Artemis. • **30:5 Beersheba to Dan** Dan was the city farthest north in Israel, and Beersheba was the city farthest south. So this means all the people of Israel.

fourteenth day of the second month. The priests and the Levites were ashamed, so they made themselves holy and brought burnt offerings into the Temple of the LORD. ¹⁶They took their regular places in the Temple as the Teachings of Moses, the man of God, commanded. The Levites gave the blood of the sacrifices to the priests, who sprinkled it on the altar. ¹⁷Since many people in the crowd had not made themselves holy, the Levites killed the Passover lambs for everyone who was not clean. The Levites made each lamb holy for the LORD. ¹⁸⁻¹⁹Although many people from Ephraim, Manasseh, Issachar, and Zebulun had not purified themselves for the feast, they ate the Passover even though it was against the law. So Hezekiah prayed for them, saying, "LORD, you are good. You are the LORD, the God of our ancestors. Please forgive all those who try to obey you even if they did not make themselves clean as the rules of the Temple command." ²⁰The LORD listened to Hezekiah's prayer, and he healed the people. ²¹The Israelites in Jerusalem celebrated the Feast of Unleavened Bread for seven days with great joy to the LORD. The Levites and priests praised the LORD every day with loud music. ²²Hezekiah encouraged all the Levites who showed they understood well how to do their service for the LORD. The people ate the feast for seven days, offered fellowship offerings, and praised the LORD, the God of their ancestors.

²³Then all the people agreed to stay seven more days, so they celebrated with joy for seven more days. ²⁴Hezekiah king of Judah gave one thousand bulls and seven thousand sheep to the people. The officers gave one thousand bulls and ten thousand sheep to the people. Many priests made themselves holy. ²⁵All the people of Judah, the priests, the Levites, those who came from Israel, the foreigners from Israel, and the foreigners living in Judah were very happy. ²⁶There was much joy in Jerusalem, because there had not been a celebration like this since the time of Solomon son of David and king of Israel. ²⁷The priests and Levites stood up and blessed the people, and God heard them because their prayer reached heaven, his holy home.

The Collection for the Priests

31 When the Passover celebration was finished, all the Israelites in Jerusalem went out to the towns of Judah. There they smashed the stone pillars used to worship gods. They cut down the Asherah idols and destroyed the altars and places for worshiping gods in all of Judah, Benjamin, Ephraim, and Manasseh. After they had destroyed all of them, the Israelites returned to their own towns and homes.

²King Hezekiah appointed groups of priests and Levites for their special duties. They were to offer burnt offerings and fellowship offerings, to worship, and to give thanks and praise at the gates of the LORD's house. ³Hezekiah gave some of his own animals for the burnt offerings, which were given every morning and evening, on Sabbath days, during New Moons, and at other feasts commanded in the LORD's Teachings.

⁴Hezekiah commanded the people living in Jerusalem to give the priests and Levites the portion that belonged to them. Then the priests and Levites could give all their time to the LORD's Teachings. ⁵As soon as the king's command went out to the Israelites, they gave freely of the first portion of their grain, new wine, oil, honey, and everything they grew in their fields. They brought a large amount, one-tenth of everything. ⁶The people of Israel and Judah who lived in Judah also brought one-tenth of their cattle and sheep and one-tenth of the holy things that were given to the LORD their God, and they put all of them in piles. ⁷The people began the piles in the third month and finished in the seventh month. ⁸When Hezekiah and his officers came and saw the piles, they praised the LORD and his people, the people of Israel. ⁹Hezekiah asked the priests and Levites about the piles. ¹⁰Azariah, the leading priest from Zadok's family, answered Hezekiah, "Since the people began to bring their offerings to the Temple of the LORD, we have had plenty to eat and plenty left over, because the LORD has blessed his people. So we have all this left over."

¹¹Then Hezekiah commanded the priests to prepare the storerooms in the Temple of the LORD. So this was done. ¹²Then the

priests brought in the offerings and the things given to the LORD and one-tenth of everything the people had given. Conaniah the Levite was in charge of these things, and his brother Shimei was second to him. [13]Conaniah and his brother Shimei were over these supervisors: Jehiel, Azaziah, Nahath, Asahel, Jerimoth, Jozabad, Eliel, Ismakiah, Mahath, and Benaiah. King Hezekiah and Azariah the officer in charge of the Temple of God had chosen them.

[14]Kore son of Imnah the Levite was in charge of the special gifts the people wanted to give to God. He was responsible for giving out the contributions made to the LORD and the holy gifts. Kore was the guard at the East Gate. [15]Eden, Miniamin, Jeshua, Shemaiah, Amariah, and Shecaniah helped Kore in the towns where the priests lived. They gave from what was collected to the other groups of priests, both young and old.

[16]From what was collected, these men also gave to the males three years old and older who had their names in the Levite family histories. They were to enter the Temple of the LORD for their daily service, each group having its own responsibilities. [17]The priests were given their part of the collection, by families, as listed in the family histories. The Levites twenty years old and older were given their part of the collection, based on their responsibilities and their groups. [18]The Levites' babies, wives, sons, and daughters also got part of the collection. This was done for all the Levites who were listed in the family histories, because they always kept themselves ready to serve the LORD.

[19]Some of Aaron's descendants, the priests, lived on the farmlands near the towns or in the towns. Men were chosen by name to give part of the collection to these priests. All the males and those named in the family histories of the Levites received part of the collection.

[20]This is what King Hezekiah did in Judah. He did what was good and right and obedient before the LORD his God. [21]Hezekiah tried to obey God in his service of the Temple of God, and he tried to obey God's teachings and commands. He gave himself fully to his work for God. So he had success.

PSALM 85:1–7

A Prayer for the Nation

For the director of music. A psalm of the sons of Korah.

85 LORD, you have been kind to your land;
　　you brought back the people of Jacob.
[2]You forgave the guilt of the people
　　and covered all their sins.　　　*Selah*
[3]You stopped all your anger;
　　you turned back from your strong anger.

[4]God our Savior, bring us back again.
　　Stop being angry with us.
[5]Will you be angry with us forever?
　　Will you stay angry from now on?
[6]Won't you give us life again?
　　Your people would rejoice in you.
[7]LORD, show us your love,
　　and save us.

PROVERBS 21:9–11

[9]It is better to live in a corner on the roof[n]
　　than inside the house with a quarreling wife.

[10]Evil people only want to harm others.
　　Their neighbors get no mercy from them.

[11]If you punish those who make fun of wisdom, a foolish person may gain some wisdom.
　　But if you teach the wise, they will get knowledge.

ACTS 20:1–16

Paul in Macedonia and Greece

20 When the trouble stopped, Paul sent for the followers to come to him. After he encouraged them and then told them goodbye, he left and went to the country of Macedonia. [2]He said many things to strengthen the

---

21:9 roof In Bible times houses were built with flat roofs. The roof was used for drying things such as flax and fruit. And it was used as an extra room, as a place for worship, and as a cool place to sleep in the summer.

followers in the different places on his way through Macedonia. Then he went to Greece, [3]where he stayed for three months. He was ready to sail for Syria, but some evil people were planning something against him. So Paul decided to go back through Macedonia to Syria. [4]The men who went with him were Sopater son of Pyrrhus, from the city of Berea; Aristarchus and Secundus, from the city of Thessalonica; Gaius, from Derbe; Timothy; and Tychicus and Trophimus, two men from Asia. [5]These men went on ahead and waited for us at Troas. [6]We sailed from Philippi after the Feast of Unleavened Bread. Five days later we met them in Troas, where we stayed for seven days.

Paul's Last Visit to Troas

[7]On the first day of the week,[n] we all met together to break bread,[n] and Paul spoke to the group. Because he was planning to leave the next day, he kept on talking until midnight. [8]We were all together in a room upstairs, and there were many lamps in the room. [9]A young man named Eutychus was sitting in the window. As Paul continued talking, Eutychus was falling into a deep sleep. Finally, he went sound asleep and fell to the ground from the third floor. When they picked him up, he was dead. [10]Paul went down to Eutychus, knelt down, and put his arms around him. He said, "Don't worry. He is alive now." [11]Then Paul went upstairs again, broke bread, and ate. He spoke to them a long time, until it was early morning, and then he left. [12]They took the young man home alive and were greatly comforted.

The Trip from Troas to Miletus

[13]We went on ahead of Paul and sailed for the city of Assos, where he wanted to join us on the ship. Paul planned it this way because he wanted to go to Assos by land. [14]When he met us there, we took him aboard and went to Mitylene. [15]We sailed from Mitylene and the next day came to a place near Kios. The following day we sailed to Samos, and the next day we reached Miletus. [16]Paul had already decided not to stop at Ephesus, because he did not want to stay too long in Asia. He was hurrying to be in Jerusalem on the day of Pentecost, if that were possible.

JULY 18

2 CHRONICLES 32:1—33:25

Assyria Attacks Judah

32 After Hezekiah did all these things to serve the LORD, Sennacherib king of Assyria came and attacked Judah. He and his army surrounded and attacked the strong, walled cities, hoping to take them for himself. [2]Hezekiah knew that Sennacherib had come to Jerusalem to attack it. [3]So Hezekiah and his officers and army commanders decided to cut off the water from the springs outside the city. So the officers and commanders helped Hezekiah. [4]Many people came and cut off all the springs and the stream that flowed through the land. They said, "The king of Assyria will not find much water when he comes here." [5]Then Hezekiah made Jerusalem stronger. He rebuilt all the broken parts of the wall and put towers on it. He also built another wall outside the first one and strengthened the area that was filled in on the east side of the old part of Jerusalem. He also made many weapons and shields.

[6]Hezekiah put army commanders over the people and met with them at the open place near the city gate. Hezekiah encouraged them, saying, [7]"Be strong and brave. Don't be afraid or worried because of the king of Assyria or his large army. There is a greater power with us than with him. [8]He

---

20:7 first day of the week Sunday, which for Jews began at sunset on our Saturday. But if in this part of Asia a different system of time was used, then the meeting was on our Sunday night.   **20:7 break bread** Probably the Lord's Supper, the special meal that Jesus told his followers to eat to remember him (Luke 22:14–20).

only has men, but we have the LORD our God to help us and to fight our battles." The people were encouraged by the words of Hezekiah king of Judah.

[9]After this King Sennacherib of Assyria and all his army surrounded and attacked Lachish. Then he sent his officers to Jerusalem with this message for King Hezekiah of Judah and all the people of Judah in Jerusalem:

[10]Sennacherib king of Assyria says this: "You have nothing to trust in to help you. It is no use for you to stay in Jerusalem under attack. [11]Hezekiah says to you, 'The LORD our God will save us from the king of Assyria,' but he is fooling you. If you stay in Jerusalem, you will die from hunger and thirst. [12]Hezekiah himself removed your LORD's places of worship and altars. He told you people of Judah and Jerusalem that you must worship and burn incense on only one altar.

[13]"You know what my ancestors and I have done to all the people in other nations. The gods of those nations could not save their people from my power. [14]My ancestors destroyed those nations; none of their gods could save them from me. So your god cannot save you from my power. [15]Do not let Hezekiah fool you or trick you, and do not believe him. No god of any nation or kingdom has been able to save his people from me or my ancestors. Your god is even less able to save you from me."

[16]Sennacherib's officers said worse things against the LORD God and his servant Hezekiah. [17]King Sennacherib also wrote letters insulting the LORD, the God of Israel. They spoke against him, saying, "The gods of the other nations could not save their people from me. In the same way Hezekiah's god won't be able to save his people from me." [18]Then the king's officers shouted in Hebrew, calling out to the people of Jerusalem who were on the city wall. The officers wanted to scare the people away so they could capture Jerusalem. [19]They spoke about the God of Jerusalem as though he were like the gods the people of the world worshiped, which are made by human hands.

[20]King Hezekiah and the prophet Isaiah son of Amoz prayed to heaven about this. [21]Then the LORD sent an angel who killed all the soldiers, leaders, and officers in the camp of the king of Assyria. So the king went back to his own country in disgrace. When he went into the temple of his god, some of his own sons killed him with a sword.

[22]So the LORD saved Hezekiah and the people in Jerusalem from Sennacherib king of Assyria and from all other people. He took care of them on every side. [23]Many people brought gifts for the LORD to Jerusalem, and they also brought valuable gifts to King Hezekiah of Judah. From then on all the nations respected Hezekiah.

Hezekiah Dies

[24]At that time Hezekiah became so sick he almost died. When he prayed to the LORD, the LORD spoke to him and gave him a sign.[n] [25]But Hezekiah did not thank God for his kindness, because he was so proud. So the LORD was angry with him and the people of Judah and Jerusalem. [26]But later Hezekiah and the people of Jerusalem were sorry and stopped being proud, so the LORD did not punish them while Hezekiah was alive.

[27]Hezekiah had many riches and much honor. He made treasuries for his silver, gold, gems, spices, shields, and other valuable things. [28]He built storage buildings for grain, new wine, and oil and stalls for all the cattle and pens for the sheep. [29]He also built many towns. He had many flocks and herds, because God had given Hezekiah much wealth.

[30]It was Hezekiah who cut off the upper pool of the Gihon spring and made those waters flow straight down to the west side of the older part of Jerusalem. And Hezekiah was successful in everything he did. [31]But one time the leaders of Babylon sent messengers to Hezekiah, asking him about a strange sign that had happened in the land. When they came, God left Hezekiah alone to

32:24 sign See Isaiah 38:1–8. It tells the story about the sign and how the Lord gave Hezekiah fifteen more years to live.

test him so he could know everything that was in Hezekiah's heart.[n]

[32]Hezekiah's love for God and the other things he did as king are written in the vision of the prophet Isaiah son of Amoz. This is in the book of the kings of Judah and Israel. [33]Hezekiah died and was buried on a hill, where the graves of David's ancestors are. All the people of Judah and Jerusalem honored Hezekiah when he died, and his son Manasseh became king in his place.

Manasseh King of Judah

33 Manasseh was twelve years old when he became king, and he was king for fifty-five years in Jerusalem. [2]He did what the LORD said was wrong. He did the hateful things the nations had done—the nations that the LORD had forced out of the land ahead of the Israelites. [3]Manasseh's father, Hezekiah, had torn down the places where gods were worshiped, but Manasseh rebuilt them. He also built altars for the Baal gods, and he made Asherah idols and worshiped all the stars of the sky and served them. [4]The LORD had said about the Temple, "I will be worshiped in Jerusalem forever," but Manasseh built altars in the Temple of the LORD. [5]He built altars to worship the stars in the two courtyards of the Temple of the LORD. [6]He made his children pass through fire in the Valley of Ben Hinnom. He practiced magic and witchcraft and told the future by explaining signs and dreams. He got advice from mediums and fortune-tellers. He did many things the LORD said were wrong, which made the LORD angry.

[7]Manasseh carved an idol and put it in the Temple of God. God had said to David and his son Solomon about the Temple, "I will be worshiped forever in this Temple and in Jerusalem, which I have chosen from all the tribes of Israel. [8]I will never again make the Israelites leave the land I gave to their ancestors. But they must obey everything I have commanded them in all the teachings, rules, and commands I gave them through Moses." [9]But Manasseh led the people of Judah and Jerusalem to do wrong. They did more evil than the nations the LORD had destroyed ahead of the Israelites.

[10]The LORD spoke to Manasseh and his people, but they did not listen. [11]So the LORD brought the king of Assyria's army commanders to attack Judah. They captured Manasseh, put hooks in him, placed bronze chains on his hands, and took him to Babylon. [12]As Manasseh suffered, he begged the LORD his God for help and humbled himself before the God of his ancestors. [13]When Manasseh prayed, the LORD heard him and had pity on him. So the LORD let him return to Jerusalem and to his kingdom. Then Manasseh knew that the LORD is the true God.

[14]After that happened, Manasseh rebuilt the outer wall of Jerusalem and made it higher. It was in the valley on the west side of the Gihon spring and went to the entrance of the Fish Gate and around the hill of Ophel. Then he put commanders in all the strong, walled cities in Judah.

[15]Manasseh removed the idols of other nations, including the idol in the Temple of the LORD. He removed all the altars he had built on the Temple hill and in Jerusalem and threw them out of the city. [16]Then he set up the LORD's altar and sacrificed on it fellowship offerings and offerings to show thanks to God. Manasseh commanded all the people of Judah to serve the LORD, the God of Israel. [17]The people continued to offer sacrifices at the places of worship, but their sacrifices were only to the LORD their God. [18]The other things Manasseh did as king, his prayer to his God, and what the seers said to him in the name of the LORD, the God of Israel—all are recorded in the book of the history of the kings of Israel. [19]Manasseh's prayer and God's pity for him, his sins, his unfaithfulness, the places he built for worshiping gods and the Asherah idols before he humbled himself—all are written in the book of the seers. [20]Manasseh died and was buried in his palace. Then Manasseh's son Amon became king in his place.

Amon King of Judah

[21]Amon was twenty-two years old when he became king, and he was king for two years in Jerusalem. [22]He did what the LORD said was wrong, as his father Manasseh had

32:31 God . . . heart See 2 Kings 20:12–19.

done. Amon worshiped and offered sacrifices to all the carved idols Manasseh had made. ²³Amon did not humble himself before the LORD as his father Manasseh had done. Instead, Amon sinned even more.

²⁴King Amon's officers made plans against him and killed him in his palace. ²⁵Then the people of the land killed all those who had made plans to kill King Amon, and they made his son Josiah king in his place.

PSALM 85:8–13

⁸I will listen to God the LORD.
  He has ordered peace for those who
    worship him.
  Don't let them go back to foolishness.
⁹God will soon save those who respect
    him,
  and his glory will be seen in our land.
¹⁰Love and truth belong to God's people;
  goodness and peace will be theirs.
¹¹On earth people will be loyal to God,
  and God's goodness will shine down
    from heaven.
¹²The LORD will give his goodness,
  and the land will give its crops.
¹³Goodness will go before God
  and prepare the way for him.

PROVERBS 21:12

¹²God, who is always right, watches the
    house of the wicked
  and brings ruin on every evil person.

ACTS 20:17–38

The Elders from Ephesus

¹⁷Now from Miletus Paul sent to Ephesus and called for the elders of the church. ¹⁸When they came to him, he said, "You know about my life from the first day I came to Asia. You know the way I lived all the time I was with you. ¹⁹The evil people made plans against me, which troubled me very much. But you know I always served the Lord unselfishly, and I often cried. ²⁰You know I preached to you and did not hold back anything that would help you. You know that I taught you in public and in your homes. ²¹I warned both Jews and Greeks to change their lives and turn to God and believe in our Lord Jesus. ²²But now I must obey the Holy Spirit and go to Jerusalem. I don't know what will happen to me there. ²³I know only that in every city the Holy Spirit tells me that troubles and even jail wait for me. ²⁴I don't care about my own life. The most important thing is that I complete my mission, the work that the Lord Jesus gave me—to tell people the Good News about God's grace.

²⁵"And now, I know that none of you among whom I was preaching the kingdom of God will ever see me again. ²⁶So today I tell you that if any of you should be lost, I am not responsible, ²⁷because I have told you everything God wants you to know. ²⁸Be careful for yourselves and for all the people the Holy Spirit has given to you to oversee. You must be like shepherds to the church of God,ⁿ which he bought with the death of his own son. ²⁹I know that after I leave, some people will come like wild wolves and try to destroy the flock. ³⁰Also, some from your own group will rise up and twist the truth and will lead away followers after them. ³¹So be careful! Always remember that for three years, day and night, I never stopped warning each of you, and I often cried over you.

³²"Now I am putting you in the care of God and the message about his grace. It is able to give you strength, and it will give you the blessings God has for all his holy people. ³³When I was with you, I never wanted anyone's money or fine clothes. ³⁴You know I always worked to take care of my own needs and the needs of those who were with me. ³⁵I showed you in all things that you should work as I did and help the weak. I taught you to remember the words Jesus said: 'It is more blessed to give than to receive.'"

³⁶When Paul had said this, he knelt down with all of them and prayed. ³⁷⁻³⁸And they all cried because Paul had said they would never see him again. They put their arms around him and kissed him. Then they went with him to the ship.

20:28 of God Some Greek copies read "of the Lord."

JULY 19

2 CHRONICLES 34:1—36:23

Josiah King of Judah

34 Josiah was eight years old when he became king, and he ruled thirty-one years in Jerusalem. [2]He did what the LORD said was right. He lived as his ancestor David had lived, and he did not stop doing what was right.

[3]In his eighth year as king while he was still young, Josiah began to obey the God of his ancestor David. In his twelfth year as king, Josiah began to remove from Judah and Jerusalem the gods, the places for worshiping gods, the Asherah idols, and the wooden and metal idols. [4]The people tore down the altars for the Baal gods as Josiah directed. Then Josiah cut down the incense altars that were above them. He broke up the Asherah idols and the wooden and metal idols and beat them into powder. Then he sprinkled the powder on the graves of the people who had offered sacrifices to these gods. [5]He burned the bones of their priests on their own altars. So Josiah removed idol worship from Judah and Jerusalem, [6]and from the towns in the areas of Manasseh, Ephraim, and Simeon all the way to Naphtali, and in the ruins near these towns. [7]Josiah broke down the altars and Asherah idols and beat the idols into powder. He cut down all the incense altars in all of Israel. Then he went back to Jerusalem.

[8]In Josiah's eighteenth year as king, he made Judah and the Temple pure again. He sent Shaphan son of Azaliah, Maaseiah the city leader, and Joah son of Joahaz the recorder to repair the Temple of the LORD, the God of Josiah. [9]These men went to Hilkiah the high priest and gave him the money the Levite gatekeepers had gathered from the people of Manasseh, Ephraim, and all the Israelites who were left alive, and also from all the people of Judah, Benjamin, and Jerusalem. This is the money they had brought into the Temple of God. [10]Then the Levites gave it to the supervisors of the work on the Temple of the LORD, and they paid the workers who rebuilt and repaired the Temple. [11]They gave money to carpenters and builders to buy cut stone and wood. The wood was used to rebuild the buildings and to make beams for them, because the kings of Judah had let the buildings fall into ruin. [12]The men did their work well. Their supervisors were Jahath and Obadiah, who were Levites from the family of Merari, and Zechariah and Meshullam, who were from the family of Kohath. These Levites were all skilled musicians. [13]They were also in charge of the workers who carried loads and all the other workers. Some Levites worked as secretaries, officers, and gatekeepers.

The Book of the Teachings Is Found

[14]The Levites brought out the money that was in the Temple of the LORD. As they were doing this, Hilkiah the priest found the Book of the LORD's Teachings that had been given through Moses. [15]Hilkiah said to Shaphan the royal secretary, "I've found the Book of the Teachings in the Temple of the LORD!" Then he gave it to Shaphan.

[16]Shaphan took the book to the king and reported to Josiah, "Your officers are doing everything you told them to do. [17]They have paid out the money that was in the Temple of the LORD and have given it to the supervisors and the workers." [18]Then Shaphan the royal secretary told the king, "Hilkiah the priest has given me a book." And Shaphan read from the book to the king.

[19]When the king heard the words of the Teachings, he tore his clothes to show how upset he was. [20]He gave orders to Hilkiah, Ahikam son of Shaphan, Acbor son of Micaiah, Shaphan the royal secretary, and Asaiah, the king's servant. These were the orders: [21]"Go and ask the LORD about the words in the book that was found. Ask for me and for the people who are left alive in Israel and Judah. The LORD is very angry with us, because our ancestors did not obey the LORD's word; they did not do everything this book says to do."

[22]So Hilkiah and those the king sent with

him went to talk to Huldah the prophetess. She was the wife of Shallum son of Tikvah, the son of Harhas, who took care of the king's clothes. Huldah lived in Jerusalem, in the new area of the city.

²³She said to them, "This is what the LORD, the God of Israel, says: Tell the man who sent you to me, ²⁴'This is what the LORD says: I will bring trouble to this place and to the people living here. I will bring all the curses that are written in the book that was read to the king of Judah. ²⁵The people of Judah have left me and have burned incense to other gods. They have made me angry by all the evil things they have made. So I will punish them in my anger, which will not be put out.' ²⁶Tell the king of Judah, who sent you to ask the LORD, 'This is what the LORD, the God of Israel, says about the words you heard: ²⁷When you heard my words against this place and its people, you became sorry for what you had done and you humbled yourself before me. You tore your clothes to show how upset you were, and you cried in my presence. This is why I have heard you, says the LORD. ²⁸So I will let you die and be buried in peace. You won't see all the trouble I will bring to this place and the people living here.'"

So they took her message back to the king.

²⁹Then the king gathered all the elders of Judah and Jerusalem together. ³⁰He went up to the Temple of the LORD, and all the people from Judah and from Jerusalem went with him. The priests, the Levites, and all the people—from the most important to the least important—went with him. He read to them all the words in the Book of the Agreement that was found in the Temple of the LORD. ³¹The king stood by his pillar and made an agreement in the presence of the LORD to follow the LORD and obey his commands, rules, and laws with his whole being and to obey the words of the agreement written in this book. ³²Then Josiah made all the people in Jerusalem and Benjamin promise to accept the agreement. So the people of Jerusalem obeyed the agreement of God, the God of their ancestors.

³³And Josiah threw out the hateful idols

from all the land that belonged to the Israelites. He led everyone in Israel to serve the LORD their God. While Josiah lived, the people obeyed the LORD, the God of their ancestors.

Josiah Celebrates the Passover

35 King Josiah celebrated the Passover to the LORD in Jerusalem. The Passover lamb was killed on the fourteenth day of the first month. ²Josiah chose the priests to do their duties, and he encouraged them as they served in the Temple of the LORD. ³The Levites taught the Israelites and were made holy for service to the LORD. Josiah said to them, "Put the Holy Ark in the Temple that David's son Solomon, the king of Israel, built. Do not carry it from place to place on your shoulders anymore. Now serve the LORD your God and his people Israel. ⁴Prepare yourselves by your family groups for service, and do the jobs that King David and his son Solomon gave you to do.

⁵"Stand in the holy place with a group of the Levites for each family group of the people. ⁶Kill the Passover lambs, and make yourselves holy to the LORD. Prepare the lambs for your relatives, the people of Israel, as the LORD through Moses commanded us to do."

⁷Josiah gave the Israelites thirty thousand sheep and goats to kill for the Passover sacrifices, and he gave them three thousand cattle. They were all his own animals.

⁸Josiah's officers also gave willingly to the people, the priests, and the Levites. Hilkiah, Zechariah, and Jehiel, the officers in charge of the Temple, gave the priests twenty-six hundred lambs and goats and three hundred cattle for Passover sacrifices. ⁹Conaniah, his brothers Shemaiah and Nethanel, and Hashabiah, Jeiel, and Jozabad gave the Levites five thousand sheep and goats and five hundred cattle for Passover sacrifices. These men were leaders of the Levites.

¹⁰When everything was ready for the Passover service, the priests and Levites went to their places, as the king had commanded. ¹¹The Passover lambs were killed. Then the Levites skinned the animals and gave the blood to the priests, who sprinkled it on the altar. ¹²Then they gave the animals

for the burnt offerings to the different family groups so the burnt offerings could be offered to the LORD as was written in the book of Moses. They also did this with the cattle. [13]The Levites roasted the Passover sacrifices over the fire as they were commanded, and they boiled the holy offerings in pots, kettles, and pans. Then they quickly gave the meat to the people. [14]After this was finished, the Levites prepared meat for themselves and for the priests, the descendants of Aaron. The priests worked until night, offering the burnt offerings and burning the fat of the sacrifices.

[15]The Levite singers from Asaph's family stood in the places chosen for them by King David, Asaph, Heman, and Jeduthun, the king's seer. The gatekeepers at each gate did not have to leave their places, because their fellow Levites had prepared everything for them for the Passover.

[16]So everything was done that day for the worship of the LORD, as King Josiah commanded. The Passover was celebrated, and the burnt offerings were offered on the LORD's altar. [17]The Israelites who were there celebrated the Passover and the Feast of Unleavened Bread for seven days. [18]The Passover had not been celebrated like this in Israel since the prophet Samuel was alive. None of the kings of Israel had ever celebrated a Passover like it was celebrated by King Josiah, the priests, the Levites, the people of Judah and Israel who were there, and the people of Jerusalem. [19]This Passover was celebrated in the eighteenth year Josiah was king.

The Death of Josiah

[20]After Josiah did all this for the Temple, Neco king of Egypt led an army to attack Carchemish, a town on the Euphrates River. And Josiah marched out to fight against Neco. [21]But Neco sent messengers to Josiah, saying, "King Josiah, there should not be war between us. I did not come to fight you, but my enemies. God told me to hurry, and he is on my side. So don't fight God, or he will destroy you."

[22]But Josiah did not go away. He wore different clothes so no one would know who he was. Refusing to listen to what Neco said at God's command, Josiah went to fight on the plain of Megiddo. [23]In the battle King Josiah was shot by archers. He told his servants, "Take me away because I am badly wounded." [24]So they took him out of his chariot and put him in another chariot and carried him to Jerusalem. There he died and was buried in the graves where his ancestors were buried. All the people of Judah and Jerusalem were very sad because he was dead.

[25]Jeremiah wrote some sad songs about Josiah. Even to this day all the men and women singers remember and honor Josiah with these songs. It became a custom in Israel to sing these songs that are written in the collection of sad songs.

[26-27]The other things Josiah did as king, from beginning to end, are written in the book of the kings of Israel and Judah. It tells how he loved what was written in the LORD's teachings.

Jehoahaz King of Judah

36The people of Judah chose Josiah's son Jehoahaz and made him king in Jerusalem in his father's place.

[2]Jehoahaz was twenty-three years old when he became king, and he was king in Jerusalem for three months. [3]Then King Neco of Egypt removed Jehoahaz from being king in Jerusalem. Neco made the people of Judah pay about seventy-five hundred pounds of silver and about seventy-five pounds of gold. [4]The king of Egypt made Jehoahaz's brother Eliakim the king of Judah and Jerusalem and changed his name to Jehoiakim. But Neco took his brother Jehoahaz to Egypt.

Jehoiakim King of Judah

[5]Jehoiakim was twenty-five years old when he became king, and he was king in Jerusalem for eleven years. He did what the LORD his God said was wrong. [6]King Nebuchadnezzar of Babylon attacked Judah, captured Jehoiakim, put bronze chains on him, and took him to Babylon. [7]Nebuchadnezzar removed some of the things from the Temple of the LORD, took them to Babylon, and put them in his own palace.

[8]The other things Jehoiakim did as king, the hateful things he did, and everything he was guilty of doing, are written in the book of the kings of Israel and Judah. And Jehoiakim's son Jehoiachin became king in his place.

Jehoiachin King of Judah

[9]Jehoiachin was eighteen years old when he became king of Judah, and he was king in Jerusalem for three months and ten days. He did what the LORD said was wrong. [10]In the spring King Nebuchadnezzar sent for Jehoiachin and brought him and some valuable treasures from the Temple of the LORD to Babylon. Then Nebuchadnezzar made Jehoiachin's uncle Zedekiah the king of Judah and Jerusalem.

Zedekiah King of Judah

[11]Zedekiah was twenty-one years old when he became king of Judah, and he was king in Jerusalem for eleven years. [12]Zedekiah did what the LORD his God said was wrong. The prophet Jeremiah spoke messages from the LORD, but Zedekiah did not obey. [13]Zedekiah turned against King Nebuchadnezzar, who had forced him to swear in God's name to be loyal to him. But Zedekiah became stubborn and refused to obey the LORD, the God of Israel. [14]Also, all the leaders of the priests and the people of Judah became more wicked, following the evil example of the other nations. The LORD had made the Temple in Jerusalem holy, but the leaders made it unholy.

The Fall of Jerusalem

[15]The LORD, the God of their ancestors, sent prophets again and again to warn his people, because he had pity on them and on his Temple. [16]But they made fun of God's prophets and hated God's messages. They refused to listen to the prophets until, finally, the LORD became so angry with his people that he could not be stopped. [17]So God brought the king of Babylon to attack them. The king killed the young men even when they were in the Temple. He had no mercy on the young men or women, the old men or those who were sick. God handed all of them over to Nebuchadnezzar. [18]Nebuchadnezzar

carried away to Babylon all the things from the Temple of God, both large and small, and all the treasures from the Temple of the LORD and from the king and his officers. [19]Nebuchadnezzar and his army set fire to God's Temple and broke down Jerusalem's wall and burned all the palaces. They took or destroyed every valuable thing in Jerusalem.

[20]Nebuchadnezzar took captive to Babylon the people who were left alive, and he forced them to be slaves for him and his descendants. They remained there as slaves until the Persian kingdom defeated Babylon. [21]And so what the LORD had told Israel through the prophet Jeremiah happened: The country was an empty wasteland for seventy years to make up for the years of Sabbath rest[n] that the people had not kept.

[22]In the first year Cyrus was king of Persia, the LORD had Cyrus send an announcement to his whole kingdom. This happened so the LORD's message spoken by Jeremiah would come true. He wrote:

[23]This is what Cyrus king of Persia says:

The LORD, the God of heaven, has given me all the kingdoms of the earth, and he has appointed me to build a Temple for him at Jerusalem in Judah. Now may the LORD your God be with all of you who are his people. You are free to go to Jerusalem.

PSALM 86:1–7

A Cry for Help

A prayer of David.

86 LORD, listen to me and answer me. I am poor and helpless.
[2]Protect me, because I worship you.
My God, save me, your servant who trusts in you.
[3]Lord, have mercy on me,
because I have called to you all day.
[4]Give happiness to me, your servant,
because I give my life to you, Lord.
[5]Lord, you are kind and forgiving
and have great love for those who call
to you.

36:21 Sabbath rest The law said that every seventh year the land was not to be farmed. See Leviticus 25:1–7.

[6]LORD, hear my prayer,
and listen when I ask for mercy.
[7]I call to you in times of trouble,
because you will answer me.

PROVERBS 21:13–14

[13]Whoever ignores the poor when they cry
for help
will also cry for help and not be
answered.

[14]A secret gift will calm an angry person;
a present given in secrecy will quiet
great anger.

ACTS 21:1–16

Paul Goes to Jerusalem

21 After we all said good-bye to them, we sailed straight to the island of Cos. The next day we reached Rhodes, and from there we went to Patara. [2]There we found a ship going to Phoenicia, so we went aboard and sailed away. [3]We sailed near the island of Cyprus, seeing it to the north, but we sailed on to Syria. We stopped at Tyre because the ship needed to unload its cargo there. [4]We found some followers in Tyre and stayed with them for seven days. Through the Holy Spirit they warned Paul not to go to Jerusalem. [5]When we finished our visit, we left and continued our trip. All the followers, even the women and children, came outside the city with us. After we all knelt on the beach and prayed, [6]we said good-bye and got

on the ship, and the followers went back home.

[7]We continued our trip from Tyre and arrived at Ptolemais, where we greeted the believers and stayed with them for a day. [8]The next day we left Ptolemais and went to the city of Caesarea. There we went into the home of Philip the preacher, one of the seven helpers,[n] and stayed with him. [9]He had four unmarried daughters who had the gift of prophesying. [10]After we had been there for some time, a prophet named Agabus arrived from Judea. [11]He came to us and borrowed Paul's belt and used it to tie his own hands and feet. He said, "The Holy Spirit says, 'This is how evil people in Jerusalem will tie up the man who wears this belt. Then they will give him to the older leaders.'"

[12]When we all heard this, we and the people there begged Paul not to go to Jerusalem. [13]But he said, "Why are you crying and making me so sad? I am not only ready to be tied up in Jerusalem, I am ready to die for the Lord Jesus!"

[14]We could not persuade him to stay away from Jerusalem. So we stopped begging him and said, "We pray that what the Lord wants will be done."

[15]After this, we got ready and started on our way to Jerusalem. [16]Some of the followers from Caesarea went with us and took us to the home of Mnason, where we would stay. He was from Cyprus and was one of the first followers.

JULY 20

EZRA 1:1–2:70

Cyrus Helps the Captives Return

1 In the first year Cyrus was king of Persia, the LORD caused Cyrus to send an announcement to his whole kingdom and to put it in writing. This happened so the LORD's message spoken by Jeremiah would come true. He wrote:

[2]This is what Cyrus king of Persia says:
The LORD, the God of heaven, has given all the kingdoms of the earth to me, and he has appointed me to build a Temple for him at Jerusalem in Judah. [3]May God be with all of you who are his people. You are free to go to Jerusalem in Judah and build the Temple of the LORD, the God of Israel, who is in

21:8 helpers The seven men chosen for a special work described in Acts 6:1–6. Sometimes they are called "deacons."

Jerusalem. [4]Those who stay behind, wherever they live, should support those who want to go. Give them silver and gold, supplies and cattle, and special gifts for the Temple of God in Jerusalem.

[5]Then the family leaders of Judah and Benjamin and the priests and Levites got ready to go to Jerusalem—everyone God had caused to want to go to Jerusalem to build the Temple of the LORD. [6]All their neighbors helped them, giving them things made of silver and gold, along with supplies, cattle, valuable gifts, and special gifts for the Temple. [7]Also, King Cyrus brought out the bowls and pans that belonged in the Temple of the LORD, which Nebuchadnezzar had taken from Jerusalem and put in the temple of his own god. [8]Cyrus king of Persia had Mithredath the treasurer bring them and count them out for Sheshbazzar, the prince of Judah.

[9]He listed thirty gold dishes, one thousand silver dishes, twenty-nine pans, [10]thirty gold bowls, four hundred ten matching silver bowls, and one thousand other pieces.

[11]There was a total of fifty-four hundred pieces of gold and silver. Sheshbazzar brought all these things along when the captives went from Babylon to Jerusalem.

The Captives Who Returned

2 These are the people of the area who returned from captivity, whom Nebuchadnezzar king of Babylon had taken away to Babylon. They returned to Jerusalem and Judah, each going back to his own town. [2]These people returned with Zerubbabel, Jeshua, Nehemiah, Seraiah, Reelaiah, Mordecai, Bilshan, Mispar, Bigvai, Rehum, and Baanah.

These are the people from Israel: [3]the descendants of Parosh—2,172; [4]the descendants of Shephatiah—372; [5]the descendants of Arah—775; [6]the descendants of Pahath-Moab (through the family of Jeshua and Joab)—2,812; [7]the descendants of Elam—1,254; [8]the descendants of Zattu—945; [9]the descendants of Zaccai—760; [10]the descendants of Bani—642; [11]the descendants of Bebai—623; [12]the descendants of Azgad—1,222; [13]the descendants of Adonikam—666; [14]the descendants of Bigvai—2,056; [15]the descendants of Adin—454; [16]the descendants of Ater (through the family of Hezekiah)—98; [17]the descendants of Bezai—323; [18]the descendants of Jorah—112; [19]the descendants of Hashum—223; [20]the descendants of Gibbar—95.

[21]These are the people from the towns: of Bethlehem—123; [22]of Netophah—56; [23]of Anathoth—128; [24]of Azmaveth—42; [25]of Kiriath Jearim, Kephirah, and Beeroth—743; [26]of Ramah and Geba—621; [27]of Micmash—122; [28]of Bethel and Ai—223; [29]of Nebo—52; [30]of Magbish—156; [31]of the other town of Elam—1,254; [32]of Harim—320; [33]of Lod, Hadid and Ono—725; [34]of Jericho—345; [35]of Senaah—3,630.

[36]These are the priests: the descendants of Jedaiah (through the family of Jeshua)—973; [37]the descendants of Immer—1,052; [38]the descendants of Pashhur—1,247; [39]the descendants of Harim—1,017.

[40]These are the Levites: the descendants of Jeshua and Kadmiel (through the family of Hodaviah)—74.

[41]These are the singers: the descendants of Asaph—128.

[42]These are the gatekeepers of the Temple: the descendants of Shallum, Ater, Talmon, Akkub, Hatita, and Shobai—139.

[43]These are the Temple servants: the descendants of Ziha, Hasupha, Tabbaoth, [44]Keros, Siaha, Padon, [45]Lebanah, Hagabah, Akkub, [46]Hagab, Shalmai, Hanan, [47]Giddel, Gahar, Reaiah, [48]Rezin, Nekoda, Gazzam, [49]Uzza, Paseah, Besai, [50]Asnah, Meunim, Nephussim, [51]Bakbuk, Hakupha, Harhur, [52]Bazluth, Mehida, Harsha, [53]Barkos, Sisera, Temah, [54]Neziah, and Hatipha.

[55]These are the descendants of the servants of Solomon: the descendants of Sotai, Hassophereth, Peruda, [56]Jaala, Darkon, Giddel, [57]Shephatiah, Hattil, Pokereth-Hazzebaim, and Ami.

[58]The Temple servants and the descendants of the servants of Solomon numbered 392.

[59]Some people came to Jerusalem from the towns of Tel Melah, Tel Harsha, Kerub, Addon, and Immer, but they could not prove

that their ancestors came from Israel. ⁶⁰They were the descendants of Delaiah, Tobiah, and Nekoda—652.

⁶¹Also these priests: the descendants of Hobaiah, Hakkoz, and Barzillai, who had married a daughter of Barzillai from Gilead and was called by her family name.

⁶²These people searched for their family records but could not find them. So they could not be priests, because they were thought to be unclean. ⁶³The governor ordered them not to eat any of the food offered to God until a priest had settled this matter by using the Urim and Thummim.

⁶⁴The total number of those who returned was 42,360. ⁶⁵This is not counting their 7,337 male and female servants and the 200 male and female singers they had with them. ⁶⁶They had 736 horses, 245 mules, ⁶⁷435 camels, and 6,720 donkeys.

⁶⁸When they arrived at the Temple of the LORD in Jerusalem, some of the leaders of families gave offerings to rebuild the Temple of God on the same site as before. ⁶⁹They gave as much as they could to the treasury to rebuild the Temple—about 1,100 pounds of gold, about 6,000 pounds of silver, and 100 pieces of clothing for the priests.

⁷⁰All the Israelites settled in their hometowns. The priests, Levites, singers, gatekeepers, and Temple servants, along with some of the other people, settled in their own towns as well.

PSALM 86:8-13

⁸Lord, there is no god like you
 and no works like yours.
⁹Lord, all the nations you have made
 will come and worship you.
 They will honor you.
¹⁰You are great and you do miracles.
 Only you are God.
¹¹LORD, teach me what you want me to do,
 and I will live by your truth.
 Teach me to respect you completely.
¹²Lord, my God, I will praise you with all
 my heart,
 and I will honor your name forever.

¹³You have great love for me.
 You have saved me from death.

PROVERBS 21:15-16

¹⁵When justice is done, good people are
 happy,
 but evil people are ruined.

¹⁶Whoever does not use good sense
 will end up among the dead.

ACTS 21:17-40

Paul Visits James

¹⁷In Jerusalem the believers were glad to see us. ¹⁸The next day Paul went with us to visit James, and all the elders were there. ¹⁹Paul greeted them and told them everything God had done among the other nations through him. ²⁰When they heard this, they praised God. Then they said to Paul, "Brother, you can see that many thousands of our people have become believers. And they think it is very important to obey the law of Moses. ²¹They have heard about your teaching, that you tell our people who live among the nations to leave the law of Moses. They have heard that you tell them not to circumcise their children and not to obey customs. ²²What should we do? They will learn that you have come. ²³So we will tell you what to do: Four of our men have made a promise to God. ²⁴Take these men with you and share in their cleansing ceremony.ⁿ Pay their expenses so they can shave their heads.ⁿ Then it will prove to everyone that what they have heard about you is not true and that you follow the law of Moses in your own life. ²⁵We have already sent a letter to the non-Jewish believers. The letter said: 'Do not eat food that has been offered to idols, or blood, or animals that have been strangled. Do not take part in sexual sin.'"

²⁶The next day Paul took the four men and shared in the cleansing ceremony with them. Then he went to the Temple and announced the time when the days of the cleansing ceremony would be finished. On the last day an offering would be given for each of the men.

21:24 cleansing ceremony The special things Jews did to end the Nazirite promise. **21:24 shave their heads** Jews did this to show that their promise was finished.

²⁷When the seven days were almost over, some of his people from Asia saw Paul at the Temple. They caused all the people to be upset and grabbed Paul. ²⁸They shouted, "People of Israel, help us! This is the man who goes everywhere teaching against the law of Moses, against our people, and against this Temple. Now he has brought some Greeks into the Temple and has made this holy place unclean!" ²⁹(They said this because they had seen Trophimus, a man from Ephesus, with Paul in Jerusalem. They thought that Paul had brought him into the Temple.)

³⁰All the people in Jerusalem became upset. Together they ran, took Paul, and dragged him out of the Temple. The Temple doors were closed immediately. ³¹While they were trying to kill Paul, the commander of the Roman army in Jerusalem learned that there was trouble in the whole city. ³²Immediately he took some officers and soldiers and ran to the place where the crowd was gathered. When the people saw them, they stopped beating Paul. ³³The commander went to Paul and arrested him. He told his soldiers to tie Paul with two chains. Then he asked who he

was and what he had done wrong. ³⁴Some in the crowd were yelling one thing, and some were yelling another. Because of all this confusion and shouting, the commander could not learn what had happened. So he ordered the soldiers to take Paul to the army building. ³⁵When Paul came to the steps, the soldiers had to carry him because the people were ready to hurt him. ³⁶The whole mob was following them, shouting, "Kill him!"

³⁷As the soldiers were about to take Paul into the army building, he spoke to the commander, "May I say something to you?"

The commander said, "Do you speak Greek? ³⁸I thought you were the Egyptian who started some trouble against the government not long ago and led four thousand killers out to the desert."

³⁹Paul said, "No, I am a Jew from Tarsus in the country of Cilicia. I am a citizen of that important city. Please, let me speak to the people."

⁴⁰The commander gave permission, so Paul stood on the steps and waved his hand to quiet the people. When there was silence, he spoke to them in the Hebrew language.

JULY 21

EZRA 3:1—4:24

Rebuilding the Altar

3 In the seventh month, after the Israelites were settled in their hometowns, they met together in Jerusalem. ²Then Jeshua son of Jozadak and his fellow priests joined Zerubbabel son of Shealtiel and began to build the altar of the God of Israel where they could offer burnt offerings, just as it is written in the Teachings of Moses, the man of God. ³Even though they were afraid of the people living around them, they built the altar where it had been before. And they offered burnt offerings on it to the LORD morning and evening. ⁴Then, to obey what was written, they celebrated the Feast of Shelters. They offered the right number of sacrifices for each day of the festival. ⁵After

the Feast of Shelters, they had regular sacrifices every day, as well as sacrifices for the New Moon and all the festivals commanded by the LORD. Also there were special offerings brought as gifts to the LORD. ⁶On the first day of the seventh month they began to bring burnt offerings to the LORD, but the foundation of the LORD's Temple had not yet been laid.

Rebuilding the Temple

⁷Then they gave money to the bricklayers and carpenters. They also gave food, wine, and oil to the cities of Sidon and Tyre so they would float cedar logs from Lebanon to the seacoast town of Joppa. Cyrus king of Persia had given permission for this.

⁸In the second month of the second year after their arrival at the Temple of God in

Jerusalem, Zerubbabel son of Shealtiel, Jeshua son of Jozadak, their fellow priests and Levites, and all who had returned from captivity to Jerusalem began to work. They chose Levites twenty years old and older to be in charge of the building of the Temple of the LORD. ⁹These men were in charge of the work of building the Temple of God: Jeshua and his sons and brothers; Kadmiel and his sons who were the descendants of Hodaviah; and the sons of Henadad and their sons and brothers. They were all Levites.

¹⁰The builders finished laying the foundation of the Temple of the LORD. Then the priests, dressed in their robes, stood with their trumpets, and the Levites, the sons of Asaph, stood with their cymbals. They all took their places and praised the LORD just as David king of Israel had said to do. ¹¹With praise and thanksgiving, they sang to the LORD:

"He is good;
     his love for Israel continues forever."

And then all the people shouted loudly, "Praise the LORD! The foundation of his Temple has been laid." ¹²But many of the older priests, Levites, and family leaders who had seen the first Temple cried when they saw the foundation of this Temple. Most of the other people were shouting with joy. ¹³The people made so much noise it could be heard far away, and no one could tell the difference between the joyful shouting and the sad crying.

Enemies of the Rebuilding

4 When the enemies of the people of Judah and Benjamin heard that the returned captives were building a Temple for the LORD, the God of Israel, ²they came to Zerubbabel and the leaders of the families. The enemies said, "Let us help you build, because we are like you and want to worship your God. We have been offering sacrifices to him since the time of Esarhaddon king of Assyria, who brought us here."

³But Zerubbabel, Jeshua, and the leaders of Israel answered, "You will not help us build a Temple to our God. We will build it ourselves for the LORD, the God of Israel, as King Cyrus, the king of Persia, commanded us to do."

⁴Then the people around them tried to discourage the people of Judah by making them afraid to build. ⁵Their enemies hired others to delay the building plans during the time Cyrus was king of Persia. And it continued to the time Darius was king of Persia.

More Problems for the Builders

⁶When Xerxes first became king, those enemies wrote a letter against the people of Judah and Jerusalem.

⁷When Artaxerxes became king of Persia, Bishlam, Mithredath, Tabeel, and those with them wrote a letter to Artaxerxes. It was written in the Aramaic language and translated.

⁸Rehum the governor and Shimshai the governor's secretary wrote a letter against Jerusalem to Artaxerxes the king. It said:

⁹This letter is from Rehum the governor, Shimshai the secretary, and their fellow workers—the judges and important officers over the men who came from Tripolis, Persia, Erech, and Babylon, the Elamite people of Susa, ¹⁰and those whom the great and honorable Ashurbanipal forced out of their countries and settled in the city of Samaria and in other places of the Trans-Euphrates.

¹¹(This is a copy of the letter they sent to Artaxerxes.)

To King Artaxerxes.
From your servants who live in Trans-Euphrates.

¹²King Artaxerxes, you should know that the Jewish people who came to us from you have gone to Jerusalem to rebuild that evil city that refuses to obey. They are fixing the walls and repairing the foundations of the buildings.

¹³Now, King Artaxerxes, you should know that if Jerusalem is built and its walls are fixed, Jerusalem will not pay taxes of any kind. Then the amount of money your government collects will be less. ¹⁴Since we must be loyal to the government, we don't want to see the king dishonored. So we are writing to

let the king know. [15]We suggest you search the records of the kings who ruled before you. You will find out that the city of Jerusalem refuses to obey and makes trouble for kings and areas controlled by Persia. Since long ago it has been a place where disobedience has started. That is why it was destroyed. [16]We want you to know, King Artaxerxes, that if this city is rebuilt and its walls fixed, you will be left with nothing in Trans-Euphrates.

[17]King Artaxerxes sent this answer:

To Rehum the governor and Shimshai the secretary, to all their fellow workers living in Samaria, and to those in other places in Trans-Euphrates.

Greetings.

[18]The letter you sent to us has been translated and read to me. [19]I ordered the records to be searched, and it was done. We found that Jerusalem has a history of disobedience to kings and has been a place of problems and trouble. [20]Jerusalem has had powerful kings who have ruled over the whole area of Trans-Euphrates, and taxes of all kinds have been paid to them. [21]Now, give an order for those men to stop work. The city of Jerusalem will not be rebuilt until I say so. [22]Make sure you do this, because if they continue, it will hurt the government.

[23]A copy of the letter that King Artaxerxes sent was read to Rehum and Shimshai the secretary and the others. Then they quickly went to the Jewish people in Jerusalem and forced them to stop building. [24]So the work on the Temple of God in Jerusalem stopped until the second year Darius was king of Persia.

PSALM 86:14–17

[14]God, proud people are attacking me;
   a gang of cruel people is trying to kill
   me.
   They do not respect you.
[15]But, Lord, you are a God who shows
   mercy and is kind.
   You don't become angry quickly.
   You have great love and faithfulness.
[16]Turn to me and have mercy.
   Give me, your servant, strength.
   Save me, the son of your female
   servant.
[17]Show me a sign of your goodness.
   When my enemies look, they will be
   ashamed.
   You, LORD, have helped me and
   comforted me.

PROVERBS 21:17–18

[17]Whoever loves pleasure will become
   poor;
   whoever loves wine and perfume will
   never be rich.

[18]Wicked people will suffer instead of good
   people,
   and those who cannot be trusted will
   suffer instead of those who do right.

ACTS 22:1–29

Paul Speaks to the People

22 Paul said, "Brothers and fathers, listen to my defense to you." [2]When they heard him speaking the Hebrew language,[n] they became very quiet. Paul said, [3]"I am a Jew, born in Tarsus in the country of Cilicia, but I grew up in this city. I was a student of Gamaliel,[n] who carefully taught me everything about the law of our ancestors. I was very serious about serving God, just as are all of you here today. [4]I persecuted the people who followed the Way of Jesus, and some of them were even killed. I arrested men and women and put them in jail. [5]The high priest and the whole council of elders can tell you this is true. They gave me letters to the brothers in Damascus. So I was going there to arrest these people and bring them back to Jerusalem to be punished.

[6]"About noon when I came near Damascus, a bright light from heaven suddenly

---

22:2 Hebrew language Or Aramaic, the languages of many people in this region in the first century. **22:3 Gamaliel** A very important teacher of the Pharisees, a Jewish religious group (Acts 5:34).

flashed all around me. [7]I fell to the ground and heard a voice saying, 'Saul, Saul, why are you persecuting me?' [8]I asked, 'Who are you, Lord?' The voice said, 'I am Jesus from Nazareth whom you are persecuting.' [9]Those who were with me did not understand the voice, but they saw the light. [10]I said, 'What shall I do, Lord?' The Lord answered, 'Get up and go to Damascus. There you will be told about all the things I have planned for you to do.' [11]I could not see, because the bright light had made me blind. So my companions led me into Damascus.

[12]"There a man named Ananias came to me. He was a religious man; he obeyed the law of Moses, and all the Jews who lived there respected him. [13]He stood by me and said, 'Brother Saul, see again!' Immediately I was able to see him. [14]He said, 'The God of our ancestors chose you long ago to know his plan, to see the Righteous One, and to hear words from him. [15]You will be his witness to all people, telling them about what you have seen and heard. [16]Now, why wait any longer? Get up, be baptized, and wash your sins away, trusting in him to save you.'

[17]"Later, when I returned to Jerusalem, I was praying in the Temple, and I saw a vision. [18]I saw the Lord saying to me, 'Hurry! Leave Jerusalem now! The people here will not accept the truth about me.' [19]But I said, 'Lord, they know that in every synagogue I put the believers in jail and beat them. [20]They also know I was there when Stephen, your witness, was killed. I stood there agreeing and holding the coats of those who were killing him!' [21]But the Lord said to me, 'Leave now. I will send you far away to the other nations.'"

[22]The crowd listened to Paul until he said this. Then they began shouting, "Get rid of him! He doesn't deserve to live!" [23]They shouted, threw off their coats,[n] and threw dust into the air.[n]

[24]Then the commander ordered the soldiers to take Paul into the army building and beat him. He wanted to make Paul tell why the people were shouting against him like this. [25]But as the soldiers were tying him up, preparing to beat him, Paul said to an officer nearby, "Do you have the right to beat a Roman citizen[n] who has not been proven guilty?"

[26]When the officer heard this, he went to the commander and reported it. The officer said, "Do you know what you are doing? This man is a Roman citizen."

[27]The commander came to Paul and said, "Tell me, are you really a Roman citizen?"

He answered, "Yes."

[28]The commander said, "I paid a lot of money to become a Roman citizen."

But Paul said, "I was born a citizen."

[29]The men who were preparing to question Paul moved away from him immediately. The commander was frightened because he had already tied Paul, and Paul was a Roman citizen.

JULY 22

EZRA 5:1—6:22

Tattenai's Letter to Darius

5 The prophets Haggai and Zechariah, a descendant of Iddo, prophesied to the Jewish people in Judah and Jerusalem in the name of the God of Israel, who was over them. [2]Then Zerubbabel son of Shealtiel and Jeshua son of Jozadak started working again to rebuild the Temple of God in Jerusalem. And the prophets of God were there, helping them.

[3]At that time Tattenai, the governor of Trans-Euphrates, and Shethar-Bozenai, and their fellow workers went to the Jewish people and asked, "Who gave you permission to

---

22:23 threw off their coats This showed that the people were very angry with Paul. **22:23 threw dust into the air** This showed even greater anger. **22:25 Roman citizen** Roman law said that Roman citizens must not be beaten before they had a trial.

rebuild this Temple and fix these walls?" [4]They also asked, "What are the names of the men working on this building?" [5]But their God was watching over the elders of the Jewish people. The builders were not stopped until a report could go to King Darius and his written answer could be received.

[6]This is a copy of the letter that was sent to King Darius by Tattenai, the governor of Trans-Euphrates, Shethar-Bozenai, and the other important officers of Trans-Euphrates. [7]This is what was said in the report they sent to him:

To King Darius.

Greetings. May you have peace.

[8]King Darius, you should know that we went to the district of Judah where the Temple of the great God is. The people are building that Temple with large stones, and they are putting timbers in the walls. They are working very hard and are building very fast.

[9]We asked their elders, "Who gave you permission to rebuild this Temple and these walls?" [10]We also asked for their names, and we wrote down the names of their leaders so you would know who they are.

[11]This is the answer they gave to us: "We are the servants of the God of heaven and earth. We are rebuilding the Temple that a great king of Israel built and finished many years ago. [12]But our ancestors made the God of heaven angry, so he handed them over to Nebuchadnezzar king of Babylon, who destroyed this Temple and took the people to Babylon as captives.

[13]"Later, in the first year Cyrus was king of Babylon, he gave a special order for this Temple to be rebuilt. [14]Cyrus brought out from the temple in Babylon the gold and silver bowls and pans that came from the Temple of God. Nebuchadnezzar had taken them from the Temple in Jerusalem and had put them in the temple in Babylon.

"Then King Cyrus gave them to Sheshbazzar, his appointed governor.

[15]Cyrus said to him, 'Take these gold and silver bowls and pans, and put them back in the Temple in Jerusalem and rebuild the Temple of God where it was.' [16]So Sheshbazzar came and laid the foundations of the Temple of God in Jerusalem. From that day until now the work has been going on, but it is not yet finished."

[17]Now, if the king wishes, let a search be made in the royal records of Babylon. See if King Cyrus gave an order to rebuild this Temple in Jerusalem. Then let the king write us and tell us what he has decided.

The Order of Darius

6 So King Darius gave an order to search the records kept in the treasury in Babylon. [2]A scroll was found in Ecbatana, the capital city of Media. This is what was written on it:

Note:

[3]King Cyrus gave an order about the Temple of God in Jerusalem in the first year he was king. This was the order:

"Let the Temple be rebuilt as a place to present sacrifices. Let its foundations be laid; it should be ninety feet high and ninety feet wide. [4]It must have three layers of large stones and then one layer of timbers. The costs should be paid from the king's treasury. [5]The gold and silver utensils from the Temple of God should be put back in their places. Nebuchadnezzar took them from the Temple in Jerusalem and brought them to Babylon, but they are to be put back in the Temple of God in Jerusalem."

[6]Now then, Tattenai, governor of Trans-Euphrates, Shethar-Bozenai, and all the officers of that area, stay away from there. [7]Do not bother the work on that Temple of God. Let the governor of the Jewish people and the Jewish elders rebuild this Temple where it was before.

[8]Also, I order you to do this for those elders of the Jewish people who are building this Temple: The cost of the

building is to be fully paid from the royal treasury, from taxes collected from Trans-Euphrates. Do this so the work will not stop. ⁹Give those people anything they need—young bulls, male sheep, or lambs for burnt offerings to the God of heaven, or wheat, salt, wine, or olive oil. Give the priests in Jerusalem anything they ask for every day without fail. ¹⁰Then they may offer sacrifices pleasing to the God of heaven, and they may pray for the life of the king and his sons.

¹¹Also, I give this order: If anyone changes this order, a wood beam is to be pulled from his house and driven through his body. Because of his crime, make his house a pile of ruins. ¹²God has chosen Jerusalem as the place he is to be worshiped. May he punish any king or person who tries to change this order and destroy this Temple.

I, Darius, have given this order. Let it be obeyed quickly and carefully.

Completion of the Temple

¹³So, Tattenai, the governor of Trans-Euphrates, Shethar-Bozenai, and their fellow workers carried out King Darius' order quickly and carefully. ¹⁴The Jewish elders continued to build and were successful because of the preaching of Haggai the prophet and Zechariah, a descendant of Iddo. They finished building the Temple as the God of Israel had commanded and as kings Cyrus, Darius, and Artaxerxes of Persia had ordered. ¹⁵The Temple was finished on the third day of the month of Adar in the sixth year Darius was king.

¹⁶Then the people of Israel celebrated and gave the Temple to God to honor him. Everybody was happy: the priests, the Levites, and the rest of the Jewish people who had returned from captivity. ¹⁷They gave the Temple to God by offering a hundred bulls, two hundred male sheep, and four hundred lambs as sacrifices. And as an offering to forgive the sins of all Israel, they offered twelve male goats, one goat for each tribe in Israel. ¹⁸Then they put the priests and the Levites into their separate groups.

Each group had a certain time to serve God in the Temple at Jerusalem as it is written in the Book of Moses.

The Passover Is Celebrated

¹⁹The Jewish people who returned from captivity celebrated the Passover on the fourteenth day of the first month. ²⁰The priests and Levites had made themselves clean. Then the Levites killed the Passover lambs for all the people who had returned from captivity, for their relatives the priests, and for themselves. ²¹So all the people of Israel who returned from captivity ate the Passover lamb. So did the people who had given up the unclean ways of their non-Jewish neighbors in order to worship the LORD, the God of Israel. ²²For seven days they celebrated the Feast of Unleavened Bread in a very joyful way. The LORD had made them happy by changing the mind of the king of Assyria so that he helped them in the work on the Temple of the God of Israel.

PSALM 87:1–7

God Loves Jerusalem

A song. A psalm of the sons of Korah.

87 The LORD built Jerusalem on the holy mountain.
² He loves its gates more than any other place in Israel.
³City of God,
    wonderful things are said about you.
                                          Selah
⁴God says, "I will put Egypt and Babylonia on the list of nations that know me.
    People from Philistia, Tyre, and Cush will be born there."

⁵They will say about Jerusalem,
    "This one and that one were born there.
    God Most High will strengthen her."
⁶The LORD will keep a list of the nations.
    He will note, "This person was born there."
                                          Selah

⁷They will dance and sing,
    "All good things come from Jerusalem."

PROVERBS 21:19–20

[19]It is better to live alone in the desert
    than with a quarreling and
    complaining wife.

[20]Wise people's houses are full of the best
    foods and olive oil,
    but fools waste everything they have.

ACTS 22:30–23:22

Paul Speaks to Leaders

[30]The next day the commander decided to learn why the Jews were accusing Paul. So he ordered the leading priests and the council to meet. The commander took Paul's chains off. Then he brought Paul out and stood him before their meeting.

23 Paul looked at the council and said, "Brothers, I have lived my life without guilt feelings before God up to this day."[2]Ananias,[n] the high priest, heard this and told the men who were standing near Paul to hit him on the mouth. [3]Paul said to Ananias, "God will hit you, too! You are like a wall that has been painted white. You sit there and judge me, using the law of Moses, but you are telling them to hit me, and that is against the law."

[4]The men standing near Paul said to him, "You cannot insult God's high priest like that!"

[5]Paul said, "Brothers, I did not know this man was the high priest. It is written in the Scriptures, 'You must not curse a leader of your people.'"[n]

[6]Some of the men in the meeting were Sadducees, and others were Pharisees. Knowing this, Paul shouted to them, "My brothers, I am a Pharisee, and my father was a Pharisee. I am on trial here because I believe that people will rise from the dead."

[7]When Paul said this, there was an argument between the Pharisees and the Sadducees, and the group was divided. [8](The Sadducees do not believe in angels or spirits or that people will rise from the dead. But the Pharisees believe in them all.) [9]So there was a great uproar. Some of the teachers of the law, who were Pharisees, stood up and argued, "We find nothing wrong with this man. Maybe an angel or a spirit did speak to him."

[10]The argument was beginning to turn into such a fight that the commander was afraid some evil people would tear Paul to pieces. So he told the soldiers to go down and take Paul away and put him in the army building.

[11]The next night the Lord came and stood by Paul. He said, "Be brave! You have told people in Jerusalem about me. You must do the same in Rome."

[12]In the morning some evil people made a plan to kill Paul, and they took an oath not to eat or drink anything until they had killed him. [13]There were more than forty men who made this plan. [14]They went to the leading priests and the elders and said, "We have taken an oath not to eat or drink until we have killed Paul. [15]So this is what we want you to do: Send a message to the commander to bring Paul out to you as though you want to ask him more questions. We will be waiting to kill him while he is on the way here."

[16]But Paul's nephew heard about this plan and went to the army building and told Paul. [17]Then Paul called one of the officers and said, "Take this young man to the commander. He has a message for him." [18]So the officer brought Paul's nephew to the commander and said, "The prisoner, Paul, asked me to bring this young man to you. He wants to tell you something." [19]The commander took the young man's hand and led him to a place where they could be alone. He asked, "What do you want to tell me?"

[20]The young man said, "The Jews have decided to ask you to bring Paul down to their council meeting tomorrow. They want you to think they are going to ask him more questions. [21]But don't believe them! More than forty men are hiding and waiting to kill Paul. They have all taken an oath not to eat or drink until they have killed him. Now they are waiting for you to agree."

[22]The commander sent the young man away, ordering him, "Don't tell anyone that you have told me about their plan."

23:2 Ananias This is not the same man named Ananias in Acts 22:12.   **23:5 'You . . . people.'** Quotation from Exodus 22:28.

JULY 23

EZRA 7:1—8:36

Ezra Comes to Jerusalem

7After these things[n] during the rule of Artaxerxes king of Persia, Ezra came up from Babylon. Ezra was the son of Seraiah, the son of Azariah, the son of Hilkiah, [2]the son of Shallum, the son of Zadok, the son of Ahitub, [3]the son of Amariah, the son of Azariah, the son of Meraioth, [4]the son of Zerahiah, the son of Uzzi, the son of Bukki, [5]the son of Abishua, the son of Phinehas, the son of Eleazar, the son of Aaron the high priest. [6]This Ezra came to Jerusalem from Babylon. He was a teacher and knew well the Teachings of Moses that had been given by the LORD, the God of Israel. Ezra received everything he asked for from the king, because the LORD his God was helping him. [7]In the seventh year of King Artaxerxes more Israelites came to Jerusalem. Among them were priests, Levites, singers, gatekeepers, and Temple servants.

[8]Ezra arrived in Jerusalem in the fifth month of Artaxerxes' seventh year as king. [9]Ezra had left Babylon on the first day of the first month, and he arrived in Jerusalem on the first day of the fifth month, because God was helping him. [10]Ezra had worked hard to know and obey the Teachings of the LORD and to teach his rules and commands to the Israelites.

Artaxerxes' Letter to Ezra

[11]King Artaxerxes had given a letter to Ezra, a priest and teacher who taught about the commands and laws the LORD gave Israel. This is a copy of the letter:

[12]From Artaxerxes, king of kings, to Ezra the priest, a teacher of the Law of the God of heaven.

Greetings.

[13]Now I give this order: Any Israelite in my kingdom who wishes may go with you to Jerusalem, including priests and Levites. [14]Ezra, you are sent by the king and the seven people who advise him to ask how Judah and Jerusalem are obeying the Law of your God, which you are carrying with you. [15]Also take with you the silver and gold that the king and those who advise him have given freely to the God of Israel, whose Temple is in Jerusalem. [16]Also take the silver and gold you receive from the area of Babylon. Take the offerings the Israelites and their priests have given as gifts for the Temple of your God in Jerusalem. [17]With this money buy bulls, male sheep, and lambs, and the grain offerings and drink offerings that go with those sacrifices. Then sacrifice them on the altar in the Temple of your God in Jerusalem.

[18]You and your fellow Jews may spend the silver and gold left over as you want and as God wishes. [19]Take to the God of Jerusalem all the utensils for worship in the Temple of your God, [20]which we have given you. Use the royal treasury to pay for anything else you need for the Temple of your God.

[21]Now I, King Artaxerxes, give this order to all the men in charge of the treasury of Trans-Euphrates: Give Ezra, a priest and a teacher of the Law of the God of heaven, whatever he asks for. [22]Give him up to seventy-five hundred pounds of silver, six hundred bushels of wheat, six hundred gallons of wine, and six hundred gallons of olive oil. And give him as much salt as he wants. [23]Carefully give him whatever the God of heaven wants for the Temple of the God of heaven. We do not want God to be angry with the king and his sons. [24]Remember, you must not make these people pay taxes of any kind: priests, Levites, singers, gatekeepers, Temple servants, and other workers in this Temple of God.

[25]And you, Ezra, use the wisdom you have from your God to choose judges and lawmakers to rule the Jewish

---

7:1 After these things There is a time period of about sixty years between chapters six and seven.

people of Trans-Euphrates. They know the laws of your God, and you may teach anyone who does not know them. ²⁶Whoever does not obey the law of your God or of the king must be punished. He will be killed, or sent away, or have his property taken away, or be put in jail.

²⁷Praise the LORD, the God of our ancestors. He caused the king to want to honor the Temple of the LORD in Jerusalem. ²⁸The LORD has shown me, Ezra, his love in the presence of the king, those who advise the king, and the royal officers. Because the LORD my God was helping me, I had courage, and I gathered the leaders of Israel to return with me.

Leaders Who Returned with Ezra

8 These are the leaders of the family groups and those who were listed with them who came back with me from Babylon during the rule of King Artaxerxes.

²From the descendants of Phinehas: Gershom.

From the descendants of Ithamar: Daniel.

From the descendants of David: Hattush ³of the descendants of Shecaniah.

From the descendants of Parosh: Zechariah, with one hundred fifty men.

⁴From the descendants of Pahath-Moab: Eliehoenai son of Zerahiah, with two hundred men.

⁵From the descendants of Zattu: Shecaniah son of Jahaziel, with three hundred men.

⁶From the descendants of Adin: Ebed son of Jonathan, with fifty men.

⁷From the descendants of Elam: Jeshaiah son of Athaliah, with seventy men.

⁸From the descendants of Shephatiah: Zebadiah son of Michael, with eighty men.

⁹From the descendants of Joab: Obadiah son of Jehiel, with two hundred eighteen men.

¹⁰From the descendants of Bani: Shelomith son of Josiphiah, with one hundred sixty men.

¹¹From the descendants of Bebai: Zechariah son of Bebai, with twenty-eight men.

¹²From the descendants of Azgad: Johanan son of Hakkatan, with one hundred ten men.

¹³From the descendants of Adonikam, these were the last ones: Eliphelet, Jeuel, and Shemaiah, with sixty men.

¹⁴From the descendants of Bigvai: Uthai and Zaccur, with seventy men.

The Return to Jerusalem

¹⁵I called all those people together at the canal that flows toward Ahava, where we camped for three days. I checked all the people and the priests, but I did not find any Levites. ¹⁶So I called these leaders: Eliezer, Ariel, Shemaiah, Elnathan, Jarib, Elnathan, Nathan, Zechariah, and Meshullam. And I called Joiarib and Elnathan, who were teachers. ¹⁷I sent these men to Iddo, the leader at Casiphia, and told them what to say to Iddo and his relatives, who are the Temple servants in Casiphia. I sent them to bring servants to us for the Temple of our God. ¹⁸Our God was helping us, so Iddo's relatives gave us Sherebiah, a wise man from the descendants of Mahli son of Levi, who was the son of Israel. And they brought Sherebiah's sons and brothers, for a total of eighteen men. ¹⁹And they brought to us Hashabiah and Jeshaiah from the descendants of Merari, and his brothers and nephews. In all there were twenty men. ²⁰They also brought two hundred twenty of the Temple servants, a group David and the officers had set up to help the Levites. All of those men were listed by name.

²¹There by the Ahava Canal, I announced we would all fast and deny ourselves before our God. We would ask God for a safe trip for ourselves, our children, and all our possessions. ²²I was ashamed to ask the king for soldiers and horsemen to protect us from enemies on the road. We had said to the king, "Our God helps everyone who obeys him, but he is very angry with all who reject him." ²³So we fasted and prayed to our God about our trip, and he answered our prayers.

²⁴Then I chose twelve of the priests who were leaders, Sherebiah, Hashabiah, and ten of their relatives. ²⁵I weighed the offering of

silver and gold and the utensils given for the Temple of our God, and I gave them to the twelve priests I had chosen. The king, the people who advised him, his officers, and all the Israelites there with us had given these things for the Temple. ²⁶I weighed out and gave them about fifty thousand pounds of silver, about seventy-five hundred pounds of silver objects, and about seventy-five hundred pounds of gold. ²⁷I gave them twenty gold bowls that weighed about nineteen pounds and two fine pieces of polished bronze that were as valuable as gold.

²⁸Then I said to the priests, "You and these utensils belong to the LORD for his service. The silver and gold are gifts to the LORD, the God of your ancestors. ²⁹Guard these things carefully. In Jerusalem, weigh them in front of the leading priests, Levites, and the leaders of the family groups of Israel in the rooms of the Temple of the LORD." ³⁰So the priests and Levites accepted the silver, the gold, and the utensils that had been weighed to take them to the Temple of our God in Jerusalem.

³¹On the twelfth day of the first month we left the Ahava Canal and started toward Jerusalem. Our God helped us and protected us from enemies and robbers along the way. ³²Finally we arrived in Jerusalem where we rested three days.

³³On the fourth day we weighed out the silver, the gold, and the utensils in the Temple of our God. We handed them to the priest Meremoth son of Uriah. Eleazar son of Phinehas was with him, as were the Levites Jozabad son of Jeshua and Noadiah son of Binnui. ³⁴We checked everything by number and by weight, and the total weight was written down.

³⁵Then the captives who returned made burnt offerings to the God of Israel. They sacrificed twelve bulls for all Israel, ninety-six male sheep, and seventy-seven lambs. For a sin offering there were twelve male goats. All this was a burnt offering to the LORD. ³⁶They took King Artaxerxes' orders to the royal officers and to the governors of Trans-Euphrates. Then these men gave help to the people and the Temple of God.

PSALM 88:1–2

A Sad Complaint

A song. A psalm of the sons of Korah. For the director of music. By the mahalath leannoth. A maskil of Heman the Ezrahite.

88 LORD, you are the God who saves me. I cry out to you day and night. ²Receive my prayer, and listen to my cry.

PROVERBS 21:21–22

²¹Whoever tries to live right and be loyal finds life, success, and honor.

²²A wise person can defeat a city full of warriors and tear down the defenses they trust in.

ACTS 23:23–35

Paul Is Sent to Caesarea

²³Then the commander called two officers and said, "I need some men to go to Caesarea. Get two hundred soldiers, seventy horsemen, and two hundred men with spears ready to leave at nine o'clock tonight. ²⁴Get some horses for Paul to ride so he can be taken to Governor Felix safely." ²⁵And he wrote a letter that said:

²⁶From Claudius Lysias.
To the Most Excellent Governor Felix:
Greetings.

²⁷Some of the Jews had taken this man and planned to kill him. But I learned that he is a Roman citizen, so I went with my soldiers and saved him. ²⁸I wanted to know why they were accusing him, so I brought him before their council meeting. ²⁹I learned that these people said Paul did some things that were wrong by their own laws, but no charge was worthy of jail or death. ³⁰When I was told that some of them were planning to kill Paul, I sent him to you at once. I also told them to tell you what they have against him.

³¹So the soldiers did what they were told and took Paul and brought him to the city of

Antipatris that night. ³²The next day the horsemen went with Paul to Caesarea, but the other soldiers went back to the army building in Jerusalem. ³³When the horsemen came to Caesarea and gave the letter to the governor, they turned Paul over to him. ³⁴The governor read the letter and asked Paul, "What area are you from?" When he learned that Paul was from Cilicia, ³⁵he said, "I will hear your case when those who are against you come here, too." Then the governor gave orders for Paul to be kept under guard in Herod's palace.

JULY 24

EZRA 9:1—10:44

Ezra's Prayer

9 After these things had been done, the leaders came to me and said, "Ezra, the Israelites, including the priests and Levites, have not kept themselves separate from the people around us. Those neighbors do evil things, as the Canaanites, Hittites, Perizzites, Jebusites, Ammonites, Moabites, Egyptians, and Amorites did. ²The Israelite men and their sons have married these women. They have mixed the people who belong to God with the people around them. The leaders and officers of Israel have led the rest of the Israelites to do this unfaithful thing."

³When I heard this, I angrily tore my robe and coat, pulled hair from my head and beard, and sat down in shock. ⁴Everyone who trembled in fear at the word of the God of Israel gathered around me because of the unfaithfulness of the captives who had returned. I sat there in shock until the evening sacrifice.

⁵At the evening sacrifice I got up from where I had shown my shame. My robe and coat were torn, and I fell on my knees with my hands spread out to the LORD my God. ⁶I prayed,

"My God, I am too ashamed and embarrassed to lift up my face to you, my God, because our sins are so many. They are higher than our heads. Our guilt even reaches up to the sky. ⁷From the days of our ancestors until now, our guilt has been great. Because of our sins, we, our kings, and our priests have been punished by the sword and captivity. Foreign kings have taken away our things and shamed us, even as it is today.

⁸"But now, for a short time, the LORD our God has been kind to us. He has let some of us come back from captivity and has let us live in safety in his holy place. And so our God gives us hope and a little relief from our slavery. ⁹Even though we are slaves, our God has not left us. He caused the kings of Persia to be kind to us and has given us new life. We can rebuild the Temple and repair its ruins. And he has given us a wall to protect us in Judah and Jerusalem.

¹⁰"But now, our God, what can we say after you have done all this? We have disobeyed your commands ¹¹that you gave through your servants the prophets. You said, 'The land you are entering to own is ruined; the people living there have spoiled it by the evil they do. Their evil filled the land with uncleanness from one end to the other. ¹²So do not let your daughters marry their sons, and do not let their daughters marry your sons. Do not wish for their peace or success. Then you will be strong and eat the good things of the land. Then you can leave this land to your descendants forever.'

¹³"What has happened to us is our own fault. We have done evil things, and our guilt is great. But you, our God, have punished us less than we deserve; you have left a few of us alive. ¹⁴We should not again break your commands by allowing marriages with these wicked people. If we did, you would get angry enough to destroy us, and none of us would be left alive. ¹⁵LORD, God of Israel, by your goodness a few of us are left alive today. We admit that we are guilty and none of us should be allowed to stand before you."

The People Confess Sin

10 As Ezra was praying and confessing and crying and throwing himself down in front of the Temple, a large group of Israelite men, women, and children gathered around him who were also crying loudly. [2]Then Shecaniah son of Jehiel the Elamite said to Ezra, "We have been unfaithful to our God by marrying women from the peoples around us. But even so, there is still hope for Israel. [3]Now let us make an agreement before our God. We will send away all these women and their children as you and those who respect the commands of our God advise. Let it be done to obey God's Teachings. [4]Get up, Ezra. You are in charge, and we will support you. Have courage and do it."

[5]So Ezra got up and made the priests, Levites, and all the people of Israel promise to do what was suggested; and they promised. [6]Then Ezra left the Temple and went to the room of Jehohanan son of Eliashib. While Ezra was there, he did not eat or drink, because he was still sad about the unfaithfulness of the captives who had returned.

[7]They sent an order in Judah and Jerusalem for all the captives who had returned to meet together in Jerusalem. [8]Whoever did not come to Jerusalem within three days would lose his property and would no longer be a member of the community of the returned captives. That was the decision of the officers and elders.

[9]So within three days all the men of Judah and Benjamin gathered in Jerusalem. It was the twentieth day of the ninth month. All the men were sitting in the open place in front of the Temple and were upset because of the meeting and because it was raining. [10]Ezra the priest stood up and said to them, "You have been unfaithful and have married non-Jewish women. You have made Israel more guilty. [11]Now, confess it to the LORD, the God of your ancestors. Do his will and separate yourselves from the people living around you and from your non-Jewish wives."

[12]Then the whole group answered Ezra with a loud voice, "Ezra, you're right! We must do what you say. [13]But there are many people here, and it's the rainy season. We can't stand outside, and this problem can't be solved in a day or two, because we have sinned badly. [14]Let our officers make a decision for the whole group. Then let everyone in our towns who has married a non-Jewish woman meet with the elders and judges of each town at a planned time, until the hot anger of our God turns away from us." [15]Only Jonathan son of Asahel, Jahzeiah son of Tikvah, Meshullam, and Shabbethai the Levite were against the plan.

[16]So the returned captives did what was suggested. Ezra the priest chose men who were leaders of the family groups and named one from each family division. On the first day of the tenth month they sat down to study each case. [17]By the first day of the first month, they had finished with all the men who had married non-Jewish women.

Those Guilty of Marrying Non-Jewish Women

[18]These are the descendants of the priests who had married foreign women:

From the descendants of Jeshua son of Jozadak and Jeshua's brothers: Maaseiah, Eliezer, Jarib, and Gedaliah. [19](They all promised to divorce their wives, and each one brought a male sheep from the flock as a penalty offering.)

[20]From the descendants of Immer: Hanani and Zebadiah.

[21]From the descendants of Harim: Maaseiah, Elijah, Shemaiah, Jehiel, and Uzziah.

[22]From the descendants of Pashhur: Elioenai, Maaseiah, Ishmael, Nethanel, Jozabad, and Elasah.

[23]Among the Levites: Jozabad, Shimei, Kelaiah (also called Kelita), Pethahiah, Judah, and Eliezer.

[24]Among the singers: Eliashib.

Among the gatekeepers: Shallum, Telem, and Uri.

[25]And among the other Israelites, these married non-Jewish women:

From the descendants of Parosh: Ramiah, Izziah, Malkijah, Mijamin, Eleazar, Malkijah, and Benaiah.

[26]From the descendants of Elam: Mattaniah, Zechariah, Jehiel, Abdi, Jeremoth, and Elijah.

27From the descendants of Zattu: Elioenai, Eliashib, Mattaniah, Jeremoth, Zabad, and Aziza.

28From the descendants of Bebai: Jehohanan, Hananiah, Zabbai, and Athlai.

29From the descendants of Bani: Meshullam, Malluch, Adaiah, Jashub, Sheal, and Jeremoth.

30From the descendants of Pahath-Moab: Adna, Kelal, Benaiah, Maaseiah, Mattaniah, Bezalel, Binnui, and Manasseh.

31From the descendants of Harim: Eliezer, Ishijah, Malkijah, Shemaiah, Shimeon, 32Benjamin, Malluch, and Shemariah.

33From the descendants of Hashum: Mattenai, Mattattah, Zabad, Eliphelet, Jeremai, Manasseh, and Shimei.

34From the descendants of Bani: Maadai, Amram, Uel, 35Benaiah, Bedeiah, Keluhi, 36Vaniah, Meremoth, Eliashib, 37Mattaniah, Mattenai, and Jaasu.

38From the descendants of Binnui: Shimei, 39Shelemiah, Nathan, Adaiah, 40Macnadebai, Shashai, Sharai, 41Azarel, Shelemiah, Shemariah, 42Shallum, Amariah, and Joseph.

43From the descendants of Nebo: Jeiel, Mattithiah, Zabad, Zebina, Jaddai, Joel, and Benaiah.

44All these men had married non-Jewish women, and some of them had children by these wives.

PSALM 88:3–10

3My life is full of troubles,
  and I am nearly dead.
4They think I am on the way to my grave.
  I am like a man with no strength.
5I have been left as dead,
  like a body lying in a grave
whom you don't remember anymore,
  cut off from your care.
6You have brought me close to death;
  I am almost in the dark place of the
  dead.
7You have been very angry with me;
  all your waves crush me.   *Selah*
8You have taken my friends away from me
  and have made them hate me.

I am trapped and cannot escape.
9 My eyes are weak from crying.
LORD, I have prayed to you every day;
  I have lifted my hands in prayer to you.

10Do you show your miracles for the dead?
  Do their spirits rise up and praise you?
                                    Selah

PROVERBS 21:23–24

23Those who are careful about what they
  say
  keep themselves out of trouble.

24People who act with stubborn pride
  are called "proud," "bragger," and
  "mocker."

ACTS 24:1–27

Paul Is Accused

24 Five days later Ananias, the high priest, went to the city of Caesarea with some of the elders and a lawyer named Tertullus. They had come to make charges against Paul before the governor. 2Paul was called into the meeting, and Tertullus began to accuse him, saying, "Most Excellent Felix! Our people enjoy much peace because of you, and many wrong things in our country are being made right through your wise help. 3We accept these things always and in every place, and we are thankful for them. 4But not wanting to take any more of your time, I beg you to be kind and listen to our few words. 5We have found this man to be a troublemaker, stirring up his people everywhere in the world. He is a leader of the Nazarene group. 6Also, he was trying to make the Temple unclean, but we stopped him. [And we wanted to judge him by our own law. 7But the officer Lysias came and used much force to take him from us. 8And Lysias commanded those who wanted to accuse Paul to come to you.]*n* By asking him questions yourself, you can decide if all these things are true." 9The others agreed and said that all of this was true.

10When the governor made a sign for Paul to speak, Paul said, "Governor Felix, I know you have been a judge over this nation for a long time. So I am happy to defend myself before you. [11]You can learn for yourself that I went to worship in Jerusalem only twelve days ago. [12]Those who are accusing me did not find me arguing with anyone in the Temple or stirring up the people in the synagogues or in the city. [13]They cannot prove the things they are saying against me now. [14]But I will tell you this: I worship the God of our ancestors as a follower of the Way of Jesus. The others say that the Way of Jesus is not the right way. But I believe everything that is taught in the law of Moses and that is written in the books of the Prophets. [15]I have the same hope in God that they have—the hope that all people, good and bad, will surely be raised from the dead. [16]This is why I always try to do what I believe is right before God and people.

[17]"After being away from Jerusalem for several years, I went back to bring money to my people and to offer sacrifices. [18]I was doing this when they found me in the Temple. I had finished the cleansing ceremony and had not made any trouble; no people were gathering around me. [19]But there were some people from Asia who should be here, standing before you. If I have really done anything wrong, they are the ones who should accuse me. [20]Or ask these people here if they found any wrong in me when I stood before the council in Jerusalem. [21]But I did shout one thing when I stood before them: 'You are judging me today because I believe that people will rise from the dead!'"

[22]Felix already understood much about the Way of Jesus. He stopped the trial and said, "When commander Lysias comes here, I will decide your case." [23]Felix told the officer to keep Paul guarded but to give him some freedom and to let his friends bring what he needed.

Paul Speaks to Felix and His Wife

[24]After some days Felix came with his wife, Drusilla, who was Jewish, and asked for Paul to be brought to him. He listened to Paul talk about believing in Christ Jesus. [25]But Felix became afraid when Paul spoke about living right, self-control, and the time when God will judge the world. He said, "Go away now. When I have more time, I will call for you." [26]At the same time Felix hoped that Paul would give him some money, so he often sent for Paul and talked with him.

[27]But after two years, Felix was replaced by Porcius Festus as governor. But Felix had left Paul in prison to please the Jews.

JULY 25

NEHEMIAH 1:1—2:20

Nehemiah's Prayer

1 These are the words of Nehemiah son of Hacaliah.

In the month of Kislev in the twentieth year,[n] I, Nehemiah, was in the capital city of Susa. [2]One of my brothers named Hanani came with some other men from Judah. I asked them about Jerusalem and the Jewish people who lived through the captivity.

[3]They answered me, "Those who are left from the captivity are back in Judah, but they are in much trouble and are full of shame. The wall around Jerusalem is broken down, and its gates have been burned."

[4]When I heard these things, I sat down and cried for several days. I was sad and fasted. I prayed to the God of heaven, [5]"LORD, God of heaven, you are the great God who is to be respected. You are loyal, and you keep your agreement with those who love you and obey your commands. [6]Look and listen carefully. Hear the prayer that I, your servant, am praying to you day and night for your servants, the Israelites. I confess the sins we

---

1:1 twentieth year This is probably referring to the twentieth year King Artaxerxes I ruled Persia.

Israelites have done against you. My father's family and I have sinned against you. [7]We have been wicked toward you and have not obeyed the commands, rules, and laws you gave your servant Moses.

[8]"Remember what you taught your servant Moses, saying, 'If you are unfaithful, I will scatter you among the nations. [9]But if you return to me and obey my commands, I will gather your people from the far ends of the earth. And I will bring them from captivity to where I have chosen to be worshiped.'

[10]"They are your servants and your people, whom you have saved with your great strength and power. [11]Lord, listen carefully to the prayer of your servant and the prayers of your servants who love to honor you. Give me, your servant, success today; allow this king to show kindness to me."

I was the one who served wine to the king.

Nehemiah Is Sent to Jerusalem

2 It was the month of Nisan in the twentieth year Artaxerxes was king. He wanted some wine, so I took some and gave it to the king. I had not been sad in his presence before. [2]So the king said, "Why does your face look sad even though you are not sick? Your heart must be sad."

Then I was very afraid. [3]I said to the king, "May the king live forever! My face is sad because the city where my ancestors are buried lies in ruins, and its gates have been destroyed by fire."

[4]Then the king said to me, "What do you want?"

First I prayed to the God of heaven. [5]Then I answered the king, "If you are willing and if I have pleased you, send me to the city in Judah where my ancestors are buried so I can rebuild it."

[6]The queen was sitting next to the king. He asked me, "How long will your trip take, and when will you get back?" It pleased the king to send me, so I set a time.

[7]I also said to him, "If you are willing, give me letters for the governors of Trans-Euphrates. Tell them to let me pass safely through their lands on my way to Judah. [8]And may I have a letter for Asaph, the keeper of the king's forest, telling him to give me timber? I will need it to make boards for the gates of the palace, which is by the Temple, and for the city wall, and for the house in which I will live." So the king gave me the letters, because God was showing kindness to me. [9]Then I went to the governors of Trans-Euphrates and gave them the king's letters. The king had also sent army officers and soldiers on horses with me.

[10]When Sanballat the Horonite and Tobiah the Ammonite officer heard about this, they were upset that someone had come to help the Israelites.

Nehemiah Inspects Jerusalem

[11]I went to Jerusalem and stayed there three days. [12]Then at night I started out with a few men. I had not told anyone what God had caused me to do for Jerusalem. There were no animals with me except the one I was riding.

[13]I went out at night through the Valley Gate. I rode toward the Dragon Well and the Trash Gate, inspecting the walls of Jerusalem that had been broken down and the gates that had been destroyed by fire. [14]Then I rode on toward the Fountain Gate and the King's Pool, but there was not enough room for the animal I was riding to pass through. [15]So I went up the valley at night, inspecting the wall. Finally, I turned and went back in through the Valley Gate. [16]The guards did not know where I had gone or what I was doing. I had not yet said anything to the Jewish people, the priests, the important men, the officers, or any of the others who would do the work.

[17]Then I said to them, "You can see the trouble we have here. Jerusalem is a pile of ruins, and its gates have been burned. Come, let's rebuild the wall of Jerusalem so we won't be full of shame any longer." [18]I also told them how God had been kind to me and what the king had said to me.

Then they answered, "Let's start rebuilding." So they began to work hard.

[19]But when Sanballat the Horonite, Tobiah the Ammonite officer, and Geshem the Arab heard about it, they made fun of us and laughed at us. They said, "What are you doing? Are you turning against the king?"

²⁰But I answered them, "The God of heaven will give us success. We, his servants, will start rebuilding, but you have no share, claim, or memorial in Jerusalem."

PSALM 88:11–18

¹¹Will your love be told in the grave?
Will your loyalty be told in the place of death?
¹²Will your miracles be known in the dark grave?
Will your goodness be known in the land of forgetfulness?
¹³But, LORD, I have called out to you for help;
every morning I pray to you.
¹⁴LORD, why do you reject me?
Why do you hide from me?
¹⁵I have been weak and dying since I was young.
I suffer from your terrors, and I am helpless.
¹⁶You have been angry with me,
and your terrors have destroyed me.
¹⁷They surround me daily like a flood;
they are all around me.
¹⁸You have taken away my loved ones and friends.
Darkness is my only friend.

PROVERBS 21:25–26

²⁵Lazy people's desire for sleep will kill them,
because they refuse to work.
²⁶All day long they wish for more,
but good people give without holding back.

ACTS 25:1–27

Paul Asks to See Caesar

25 Three days after Festus became governor, he went from Caesarea to Jerusalem. ²There the leading priests and the important leaders made charges against Paul before Festus. ³They asked Festus to do them a favor. They wanted him to send Paul back to Jerusalem, because they had a plan to kill him on the way. ⁴But Festus answered that Paul would be kept in Caesarea and that he

himself was returning there soon. ⁵He said, "Some of your leaders should go with me. They can accuse the man there in Caesarea, if he has really done something wrong."

⁶Festus stayed in Jerusalem another eight or ten days and then went back to Caesarea. The next day he told the soldiers to bring Paul before him. Festus was seated on the judge's seat ⁷when Paul came into the room. The people who had come from Jerusalem stood around him, making serious charges against him, which they could not prove. ⁸This is what Paul said to defend himself: "I have done nothing wrong against the law, against the Temple, or against Caesar."

⁹But Festus wanted to please the people. So he asked Paul, "Do you want to go to Jerusalem for me to judge you there on these charges?"

¹⁰Paul said, "I am standing at Caesar's judgment seat now, where I should be judged. I have done nothing wrong to them; you know this is true. ¹¹If I have done something wrong and the law says I must die, I do not ask to be saved from death. But if these charges are not true, then no one can give me to them. I want Caesar to hear my case!"

¹²Festus talked about this with his advisers. Then he said, "You have asked to see Caesar, so you will go to Caesar!"

Paul Before King Agrippa

¹³A few days later King Agrippa and Bernice came to Caesarea to visit Festus. ¹⁴They stayed there for some time, and Festus told the king about Paul's case. Festus said, "There is a man that Felix left in prison. ¹⁵When I went to Jerusalem, the leading priests and the elders there made charges against him, asking me to sentence him to death. ¹⁶But I answered, 'When a man is accused of a crime, Romans do not hand him over until he has been allowed to face his accusers and defend himself against their charges.' ¹⁷So when these people came here to Caesarea for the trial, I did not waste time. The next day I sat on the judge's seat and commanded that the man be brought in. ¹⁸They stood up and accused him, but not of any serious crime as I thought they would. ¹⁹The things they said were about their own

religion and about a man named Jesus who died. But Paul said that he is still alive. [20]Not knowing how to find out about these questions, I asked Paul, 'Do you want to go to Jerusalem and be judged there?' [21]But he asked to be kept in Caesarea. He wants a decision from the emperor.[n] So I ordered that he be held until I could send him to Caesar."

[22]Agrippa said to Festus, "I would also like to hear this man myself."

Festus said, "Tomorrow you will hear him."

[23]The next day Agrippa and Bernice appeared with great show, acting like very important people. They went into the judgment room with the army leaders and the important men of Caesarea. Then Festus ordered the soldiers to bring Paul in. [24]Festus said, "King Agrippa and all who are gathered here with us, you see this man. All the people, here and in Jerusalem, have complained to me about him, shouting that he should not live any longer. [25]When I judged him, I found no reason to order his death. But since he asked to be judged by Caesar, I decided to send him. [26]But I have nothing definite to write the emperor about him. So I have brought him before all of you—especially you, King Agrippa. I hope you can question him and give me something to write. [27]I think it is foolish to send a prisoner to Caesar without telling what charges are against him."

JULY 26

NEHEMIAH 3:1—5:19

Builders of the Wall

3 Eliashib the high priest and his fellow priests went to work and rebuilt the Sheep Gate. They gave it to the Lord's service and set its doors in place. They worked as far as the Tower of the Hundred and gave it to the Lord's service. Then they went on to the Tower of Hananel. [2]Next to them, the people of Jericho built part of the wall, and Zaccur son of Imri built next to them.

[3]The sons of Hassenaah rebuilt the Fish Gate, laying its boards and setting its doors, bolts, and bars in place. [4]Meremoth son of Uriah, the son of Hakkoz, made repairs next to them. Meshullam son of Berekiah, the son of Meshezabel, made repairs next to Meremoth. And Zadok son of Baana made repairs next to Meshullam. [5]The people from Tekoa made repairs next to them, but the leading men of Tekoa would not work under their supervisors.

[6]Joiada son of Paseah and Meshullam son of Besodeiah repaired the Old Gate. They laid its boards and set its doors, bolts, and bars in place. [7]Next to them, Melatiah from Gibeon, other men from Gibeon and Mizpah, and Jadon from Meronoth made repairs. These places were ruled by the governor of Trans-Euphrates. [8]Next to them, Uzziel son of Harhaiah, a goldsmith, made repairs. And next to him, Hananiah, a perfume maker, made repairs. These men rebuilt Jerusalem as far as the Broad Wall. [9]The next part of the wall was repaired by Rephaiah son of Hur, the ruler of half of the district of Jerusalem. [10]Next to him, Jedaiah son of Harumaph made repairs opposite his own house. And next to him, Hattush son of Hashabneiah made repairs. [11]Malkijah son of Harim and Hasshub son of Pahath-Moab repaired another part of the wall and the Tower of the Ovens. [12]Next to them Shallum son of Hallohesh, the ruler of half of the district of Jerusalem, and his daughters made repairs.

[13]Hanun and the people of Zanoah repaired the Valley Gate, rebuilding it and setting its doors, bolts, and bars in place. They also repaired the five hundred yards of the wall to the Trash Gate.

[14]Malkijah son of Recab, the ruler of the district of Beth Hakkerem, repaired the

Trash Gate. He rebuilt that gate and set its doors, bolts, and bars in place.

[15]Shallun son of Col-Hozeh, the ruler of the district of Mizpah, repaired the Fountain Gate. He rebuilt it, put a roof over it, and set its doors, bolts, and bars in place. He also repaired the wall of the Pool of Siloam next to the King's Garden all the way to the steps that went down from the older part of the city. [16]Next to Shallun was Nehemiah[n] son of Azbuk, the ruler of half of the district of Beth Zur. He made repairs opposite the tombs of David and as far as the man-made pool and the House of the Heroes.

[17]Next to him, the Levites made repairs, working under Rehum son of Bani. Next to him, Hashabiah, the ruler of half of the district of Keilah, for his district. [18]Next to him, Binnui son of Henadad and his relatives made repairs. Binnui was the ruler of the other half of the district of Keilah. [19]Next to them, Ezer son of Jeshua, the ruler of Mizpah, repaired another part of the wall. He worked across from the way up to the armory, as far as the bend. [20]Next to him, Baruch son of Zabbai worked hard on the wall that went from the bend to the entrance to the house of Eliashib, the high priest. [21]Next to him, Meremoth son of Uriah, the son of Hakkoz, repaired the wall that went from the entrance to Eliashib's house to the far end of it.

[22]Next to him worked the priests from the surrounding area. [23]Next to them, Benjamin and Hasshub made repairs in front of their own house. Next to them, Azariah son of Maaseiah, the son of Ananiah, made repairs beside his own house. [24]Next to him, Binnui son of Henadad repaired the wall that went from Azariah's house to the bend and on to the corner. [25]Palal son of Uzai worked across from the bend and by the tower on the upper palace, which is near the courtyard of the king's guard. Next to Palal, Pedaiah son of Parosh made repairs. [26]The Temple servants who lived on the hill of Ophel made repairs as far as a point opposite the Water Gate. They worked toward the east and the tower that extends from the palace. [27]Next to them,

the people of Tekoa repaired the wall from the great tower that extends from the palace to the wall of Ophel.

[28]The priests made repairs above the Horse Gate, each working in front of his own house. [29]Next to them, Zadok son of Immer made repairs across from his own house. Next to him, Shemaiah son of Shecaniah, the guard of the East Gate, made repairs. [30]Next to him, Hananiah son of Shelemiah, and Hanun, the sixth son of Zalaph, made repairs on another part of the wall. Next to them, Meshullam son of Berekiah made repairs across from where he lived. [31]Next to him, Malkijah, one of the goldsmiths, made repairs. He worked as far as the house of the Temple servants and the traders, which is across from the Inspection Gate, and as far as the room above the corner of the wall. [32]The goldsmiths and the traders made repairs between the room above the corner of the wall and the Sheep Gate.

Those Against the Rebuilding

4 When Sanballat heard we were rebuilding the wall, he was very angry, even furious. He made fun of the Jewish people. [2]He said to his friends and those with power in Samaria, "What are these weak Jews doing? Will they rebuild the wall? Will they offer sacrifices? Can they finish it in one day? Can they bring stones back to life from piles of trash and ashes?"

[3]Tobiah the Ammonite, who was next to Sanballat, said, "If a fox climbed up on the stone wall they are building, it would break it down."

[4]I prayed, "Hear us, our God. We are hated. Turn the insults of Sanballat and Tobiah back on their own heads. Let them be captured and stolen like valuables. [5]Do not hide their guilt or take away their sins so that you can't see them, because they have insulted the builders."

[6]So we rebuilt the wall to half its height, because the people were willing to work.

[7]But Sanballat, Tobiah, the Arabs, the Ammonites, and the people from Ashdod were very angry when they heard that the repairs

---

to Jerusalem's walls were continuing and that the holes in the wall were being closed. [8]So they all made plans to come to Jerusalem and fight and stir up trouble. [9]But we prayed to our God and appointed guards to watch for them day and night.

[10]The people of Judah said, "The workers are getting tired. There is so much trash we cannot rebuild the wall."

[11]And our enemies said, "The Jews won't know or see anything until we come among them and kill them and stop the work."

[12]Then the Jewish people who lived near our enemies came and told us ten times, "Everywhere you turn, the enemy will attack us." [13]So I put people behind the lowest places along the wall—the open places—and I put families together with their swords, spears, and bows. [14]Then I looked around and stood up and said to the important men, the leaders, and the rest of the people: "Don't be afraid of them. Remember the Lord, who is great and powerful. Fight for your brothers, your sons and daughters, your wives, and your homes."

[15]Then our enemies heard that we knew about their plans and that God had ruined their plans. So we all went back to the wall, each to his own work.

[16]From that day on, half my people worked on the wall. The other half was ready with spears, shields, bows, and armor. The officers stood in back of the people of Judah [17]who were building the wall. Those who carried materials did their work with one hand and carried a weapon with the other. [18]Each builder wore his sword at his side as he worked. The man who blew the trumpet to warn the people stayed next to me.

[19]Then I said to the important people, the leaders, and everyone else, "This is a very big job. We are spreading out along the wall so that we are far apart. [20]Wherever you hear the sound of the trumpet, assemble there. Our God will fight for us."

[21]So we continued to work with half the men holding spears from sunrise till the stars came out. [22]At that time I also said to the people, "Let every man and his helper stay inside Jerusalem at night. They can be our guards at night and workmen during the

day." [23]Neither I, my brothers, my workers, nor the guards with me ever took off our clothes. Each person carried his weapon even when he went for water.

Nehemiah Helps Poor People

5 The men and their wives complained loudly against their fellow Jews. [2]Some of them were saying, "We have many sons and daughters in our families. To eat and stay alive, we need grain."

[3]Others were saying, "We are borrowing money against our fields, vineyards, and homes to get grain because there is not much food."

[4]And still others were saying, "We are borrowing money to pay the king's tax on our fields and vineyards. [5]We are just like our fellow Jews, and our sons are like their sons. But we have to sell our sons and daughters as slaves. Some of our daughters have already been sold. But there is nothing we can do, because our fields and vineyards already belong to other people."

[6]When I heard their complaints about these things, I was very angry. [7]After I thought about it, I accused the important people and the leaders, "You are charging your own brothers too much interest." So I called a large meeting to deal with them. [8]I said to them, "As much as possible, we have bought freedom for our fellow Jews who had been sold to foreigners. Now you are selling your fellow Jews to us!" The leaders were quiet and had nothing to say.

[9]Then I said, "What you are doing is not right. Don't you fear God? Don't let our foreign enemies shame us. [10]I, my brothers, and my men are also lending money and grain to the people. But stop charging them so much for this. [11]Give back their fields, vineyards, olive trees, and houses right now. Also give back the extra amount you charged—the hundredth part of the money, grain, new wine, and oil."

[12]They said, "We will give it back and not demand anything more from them. We will do as you say."

Then I called for the priests, and I made the important people and leaders take an oath to do what they had said. [13]Also I shook out the folds of my robe and said, "In this way may God shake out everyone who does not keep his promise. May God shake him out of his house and out of the things that are his. Let that person be shaken out and emptied!"

Then the whole group said, "Amen," and they praised the LORD. So the people did what they had promised.

¹⁴I was appointed governor in the land of Judah in the twentieth year of King Artaxerxes' rule. I was governor of Judah for twelve years, until his thirty-second year. During that time neither my brothers nor I ate the food that was allowed for a governor. ¹⁵But the governors before me had placed a heavy load on the people. They took about one pound of silver from each person, along with food and wine. The governors' helpers before me also controlled the people, but I did not do that, because I feared God. ¹⁶I worked on the wall, as did all my men who were gathered there. We did not buy any fields.

¹⁷Also, I fed one hundred fifty Jewish people and officers at my table, as well as those who came from the nations around us. ¹⁸This is what was prepared every day: one ox, six good sheep, and birds. And every ten days there were all kinds of wine. But I never demanded the food that was due a governor, because the people were already working very hard.

¹⁹Remember to be kind to me, my God, for all the good I have done for these people.

PSALM 89:1–4

A Song About God's Loyalty

A maskil of Ethan the Ezrahite.

89 I will always sing about the LORD's love;
I will tell of his loyalty from now on.
²I will say, "Your love continues forever;
your loyalty goes on and on like the sky."
³You said, "I made an agreement with the man of my choice;
I made a promise to my servant David.

⁴I told him, 'I will make your family continue forever.
Your kingdom will go on and on.'" *Selah*

PROVERBS 21:27

²⁷The LORD hates sacrifices brought by evil people,
particularly when they offer them for the wrong reasons.

ACTS 26:1–32

Paul Defends Himself

26 Agrippa said to Paul, "You may now speak to defend yourself."

Then Paul raised his hand and began to speak. ²He said, "King Agrippa, I am very blessed to stand before you and will answer all the charges the evil people make against me. ³You know so much about all the customs and the things they argue about, so please listen to me patiently.

⁴"All my people know about my whole life, how I lived from the beginning in my own country and later in Jerusalem. ⁵They have known me for a long time. If they want to, they can tell you that I was a good Pharisee. And the Pharisees obey the laws of my tradition more carefully than any other group. ⁶Now I am on trial because I hope for the promise that God made to our ancestors. ⁷This is the promise that the twelve tribes of our people hope to receive as they serve God day and night. My king, they have accused me because I hope for this same promise! ⁸Why do any of you people think it is impossible for God to raise people from the dead?

⁹"I, too, thought I ought to do many things against Jesus from Nazareth. ¹⁰And that is what I did in Jerusalem. The leading priests gave me the power to put many of God's people in jail, and when they were being killed, I agreed it was a good thing. ¹¹In every synagogue, I often punished them and tried to make them speak against Jesus. I was so angry against them I even went to other cities to find them and punish them.

¹²"One time the leading priests gave me permission and the power to go to Damascus. ¹³On the way there, at noon, I saw a light from heaven. It was brighter than the sun and

flashed all around me and those who were traveling with me. [14]We all fell to the ground. Then I heard a voice speaking to me in the Hebrew language,[n] saying, 'Saul, Saul, why are you persecuting me? You are only hurting yourself by fighting me.' [15]I said, 'Who are you, Lord?' The Lord said, 'I am Jesus, the one you are persecuting. [16]Stand up! I have chosen you to be my servant and my witness—you will tell people the things that you have seen and the things that I will show you. This is why I have come to you today. [17]I will keep you safe from your own people and also from the others. I am sending you to them [18]to open their eyes so that they may turn away from darkness to the light, away from the power of Satan and to God. Then their sins can be forgiven, and they can have a place with those people who have been made holy by believing in me.'

[19]"King Agrippa, after I had this vision from heaven, I obeyed it. [20]I began telling people that they should change their hearts and lives and turn to God and do things to show they really had changed. I told this first to those in Damascus, then in Jerusalem, and in every part of Judea, and also to the other people. [21]This is why the Jews took me and were trying to kill me in the Temple. [22]But God has helped me, and so I stand here today, telling all people, small and great, what I have seen. But I am saying only what Moses and the prophets said would happen— [23]that the Christ would die, and as the first to rise from the dead, he would bring light to all people."

Paul Tries to Persuade Agrippa

[24]While Paul was saying these things to defend himself, Festus said loudly, "Paul, you are out of your mind! Too much study has driven you crazy!"

[25]Paul said, "Most excellent Festus, I am not crazy. My words are true and sensible. [26]King Agrippa knows about these things, and I can speak freely to him. I know he has heard about all of these things, because they did not happen off in a corner. [27]King Agrippa, do you believe what the prophets wrote? I know you believe."

[28]King Agrippa said to Paul, "Do you think you can persuade me to become a Christian in such a short time?"

[29]Paul said, "Whether it is a short or a long time, I pray to God that not only you but every person listening to me today would be saved and be like me—except for these chains I have."

[30]Then King Agrippa, Governor Festus, Bernice, and all the people sitting with them stood up [31]and left the room. Talking to each other, they said, "There is no reason why this man should die or be put in jail." [32]And Agrippa said to Festus, "We could let this man go free, but he has asked Caesar to hear his case."

JULY 27

NEHEMIAH 6:1—7:73a

More Problems for Nehemiah

6 Then Sanballat, Tobiah, Geshem the Arab, and our other enemies heard that I had rebuilt the wall and that there was not one gap in it. But I had not yet set the doors in the gates. [2]So Sanballat and Geshem sent me this message: "Come, Nehemiah, let's meet together in Kephirim on the plain of Ono."

But they were planning to harm me. [3]So I sent messengers to them with this answer: "I am doing a great work, and I can't come down. I don't want the work to stop while I leave to meet you." [4]Sanballat and Geshem sent the same message to me four times, and each time I sent back the same answer.

[5]The fifth time Sanballat sent his helper to me with the message, and in his hand was an unsealed letter. [6]This is what was written:

A report is going around to all the nations, and Geshem says it is true, that you and the Jewish people are planning to turn against the king and that you are rebuilding the wall. They say you are going to be their king ⁷and that you have appointed prophets to announce in Jerusalem: "There is a king of Judah!" The king will hear about this. So come, let's discuss this together.

⁸So I sent him back this answer: "Nothing you are saying is really happening. You are just making it up in your own mind."

⁹Our enemies were trying to scare us, thinking, "They will get too weak to work. Then the wall will not be finished."

But I prayed, "God, make me strong."

¹⁰One day I went to the house of Shemaiah son of Delaiah, the son of Mehetabel. Shemaiah had to stay at home. He said, "Nehemiah, let's meet in the Temple of God. Let's go inside the Temple and close the doors, because men are coming at night to kill you."

¹¹But I said, "Should a man like me run away? Should I run for my life into the Temple? I will not go." ¹²I knew that God had not sent him but that Tobiah and Sanballat had paid him to prophesy against me. ¹³They paid him to frighten me so I would do this and sin. Then they could give me a bad name to shame me.

¹⁴I prayed, "My God, remember Tobiah and Sanballat and what they have done. Also remember the prophetess Noadiah and the other prophets who have been trying to frighten me."

The Wall Is Finished

¹⁵The wall of Jerusalem was completed on the twenty-fifth day of the month of Elul. It took fifty-two days to rebuild. ¹⁶When all our enemies heard about it and all the nations around us saw it, they were shamed. They then understood that the work had been done with the help of our God.

¹⁷Also in those days the important people of Judah sent many letters to Tobiah, and he answered them. ¹⁸Many Jewish people had promised to be faithful to Tobiah, because he was the son-in-law of Shecaniah son of Arah. And Tobiah's son Jehohanan had married the daughter of Meshullam son of Berekiah. ¹⁹These important people kept telling me about the good things Tobiah was doing, and then they would tell Tobiah what I said about him. So Tobiah sent letters to frighten me.

7 After the wall had been rebuilt and I had set the doors in place, the gatekeepers, singers, and Levites were chosen. ²I put my brother Hanani, along with Hananiah, the commander of the palace, in charge of Jerusalem. Hananiah was honest and feared God more than most people. ³I said to them, "The gates of Jerusalem should not be opened until the sun is hot. While the gatekeepers are still on duty, have them shut and bolt the doors. Appoint people who live in Jerusalem as guards, and put some at guard posts and some near their own houses."

The Captives Who Returned

⁴The city was large and roomy, but there were few people in it, and the houses had not yet been rebuilt. ⁵Then my God caused me to gather the important people, the leaders, and the common people so I could register them by families. I found the family history of those who had returned first. This is what I found written there:

⁶These are the people of the area who returned from captivity, whom Nebuchadnezzar king of Babylon had taken away. They returned to Jerusalem and Judah, each going back to his own town. ⁷These people returned with Zerubbabel, Jeshua, Nehemiah, Azariah, Raamiah, Nahamani, Mordecai, Bilshan, Mispereth, Bigvai, Nehum, and Baanah.

These are the people from Israel: ⁸the descendants of Parosh—2,172; ⁹the descendants of Shephatiah—372; ¹⁰the descendants of Arah—652; ¹¹the descendants of Pahath-Moab (through the family of Jeshua and Joab)—2,818; ¹²the descendants of Elam—1,254; ¹³the descendants of Zattu—845; ¹⁴the descendants of Zaccai—760; ¹⁵the descendants of Binnui—648; ¹⁶the descendants of Bebai—628; ¹⁷the descendants of Azgad—2,322; ¹⁸the descendants of Adonikam—667; ¹⁹the descendants of Bigvai—2,067; ²⁰the descendants of

Adin—655; [21]the descendants of Ater (through Hezekiah)—98; [22]the descendants of Hashum—328; [23]the descendants of Bezai—324; [24]the descendants of Hariph—112; [25]the descendants of Gibeon—95.

[26]These are the people from the towns of Bethlehem and Netophah—188; [27]of Anathoth—128; [28]of Beth Azmaveth—42; [29]of Kiriath Jearim, Kephirah, and Beeroth—743; [30]of Ramah and Geba—621; [31]of Micmash—122; [32]of Bethel and Ai—123; [33]of the other Nebo—52; [34]of the other Elam—1,254; [35]of Harim—320; [36]of Jericho—345; [37]of Lod, Hadid, and Ono—721; [38]of Senaah—3,930.

[39]These are the priests: the descendants of Jedaiah (through the family of Jeshua)—973; [40]the descendants of Immer—1,052; [41]the descendants of Pashhur—1,247; [42]the descendants of Harim—1,017.

[43]These are the Levites: the descendants of Jeshua (through Kadmiel through the family of Hodaviah)—74.

[44]These are the singers: the descendants of Asaph—148.

[45]These are the gatekeepers: the descendants of Shallum, Ater, Talmon, Akkub, Hatita, and Shobai—138.

[46]These are the Temple servants: the descendants of Ziha, Hasupha, Tabbaoth, [47]Keros, Sia, Padon, [48]Lebana, Hagaba, Shalmai, [49]Hanan, Giddel, Gahar, [50]Reaiah, Rezin, Nekoda, [51]Gazzam, Uzza, Paseah, [52]Besai, Meunim, Nephussim, [53]Bakbuk, Hakupha, Harhur, [54]Bazluth, Mehida, Harsha, [55]Barkos, Sisera, Temah, [56]Neziah, and Hatipha.

[57]These are the descendants of the servants of Solomon: the descendants of Sotai, Sophereth, Perida, [58]Jaala, Darkon, Giddel, [59]Shephatiah, Hattil, Pokereth-Hazzebaim, and Amon.

[60]The Temple servants and the descendants of the servants of Solomon totaled 392 people.

[61]Some people came to Jerusalem from the towns of Tel Melah, Tel Harsha, Kerub, Addon, and Immer, but they could not prove that their ancestors came from Israel. Here are their names and their number: [62]the descendants of Delaiah, Tobiah, and Nekoda—642.

[63]And these priests could not prove that their ancestors came from Israel: the descendants of Hobaiah, Hakkoz, and Barzillai. (He had married a daughter of Barzillai from Gilead and was called by her family name.)

[64]These people searched for their family records, but they could not find them. So they could not be priests, because they were thought to be unclean. [65]The governor ordered them not to eat any of the holy food until a priest settled this matter by using the Urim and Thummim.

[66]The total number of those who returned was 42,360. [67]This is not counting their 7,337 male and female servants and the 245 male and female singers with them. [68]They had 736 horses, 245 mules, [69]435 camels, and 6,720 donkeys.

[70]Some of the family leaders gave to the work. The governor gave to the treasury about 19 pounds of gold, 50 bowls, and 530 pieces of clothing for the priests. [71]Some of the family leaders gave about 375 pounds of gold and about 2,660 pounds of silver to the treasury for the work. [72]The total of what the other people gave was about 375 pounds of gold, about 2,250 pounds of silver, and 67 pieces of clothing for the priests. [73]So these people all settled in their own towns: the priests, the Levites, the gatekeepers, the singers, the Temple servants, and all the other people of Israel.

PSALM 89:5–10

[5]LORD, the heavens praise you for your miracles
and for your loyalty in the meeting of your holy ones.
[6]Who in heaven is equal to the LORD?
None of the angels is like the LORD.
[7]When the holy ones meet, it is God they fear.
He is more frightening than all who surround him.
[8]LORD God All-Powerful, who is like you?
LORD, you are powerful and completely trustworthy.
[9]You rule the mighty sea
and calm the stormy waves.

[10]You crushed the sea monster Rahab;
by your power you scattered your
enemies.

PROVERBS 21:28

[28]A lying witness will be forgotten,
but a truthful witness will speak on.

ACTS 27:1–26

Paul Sails for Rome

27 It was decided that we would sail for Italy. An officer named Julius, who served in the emperor's[n] army, guarded Paul and some other prisoners. [2]We got on a ship that was from the city of Adramyttium and was about to sail to different ports in Asia. Aristarchus, a man from the city of Thessalonica in Macedonia, went with us. [3]The next day we came to Sidon. Julius was very good to Paul and gave him freedom to go visit his friends, who took care of his needs. [4]We left Sidon and sailed close to the island of Cyprus, because the wind was blowing against us. [5]We went across the sea by Cilicia and Pamphylia and landed at the city of Myra, in Lycia. [6]There the officer found a ship from Alexandria that was going to Italy, so he put us on it.

[7]We sailed slowly for many days. We had a hard time reaching Cnidus because the wind was blowing against us, and we could not go any farther. So we sailed by the south side of the island of Crete near Salmone. [8]Sailing past it was hard. Then we came to a place called Fair Havens, near the city of Lasea.

[9]We had lost much time, and it was now dangerous to sail, because it was already after the Day of Cleansing.[n] So Paul warned them, [10]"Men, I can see there will be a lot of trouble on this trip. The ship, the cargo, and even our lives may be lost." [11]But the captain and the owner of the ship did not agree with Paul, and the officer believed what the captain and owner of the ship said. [12]Since that harbor was not a good place for the ship to stay for the winter, most of the men decided that the ship should leave. They hoped we could go to Phoenix and stay there for the winter. Phoenix, a city on the island of Crete, had a harbor which faced southwest and northwest.

The Storm

[13]When a good wind began to blow from the south, the men on the ship thought, "This is the wind we wanted, and now we have it." So they pulled up the anchor, and we sailed very close to the island of Crete. [14]But then a very strong wind named the "northeaster" came from the island. [15]The ship was caught in it and could not sail against it. So we stopped trying and let the wind carry us. [16]When we went below a small island named Cauda, we were barely able to bring in the lifeboat. [17]After the men took the lifeboat in, they tied ropes around the ship to hold it together. The men were afraid that the ship would hit the sandbanks of Syrtis,[n] so they lowered the sail and let the wind carry the ship. [18]The next day the storm was blowing us so hard that the men threw out some of the cargo. [19]A day later with their own hands they threw out the ship's equipment. [20]When we could not see the sun or the stars for many days, and the storm was very bad, we lost all hope of being saved.

[21]After the men had gone without food for a long time, Paul stood up before them and said, "Men, you should have listened to me. You should not have sailed from Crete. Then you would not have all this trouble and loss. [22]But now I tell you to cheer up because none of you will die. Only the ship will be lost. [23]Last night an angel came to me from the God I belong to and worship. [24]The angel said, 'Paul, do not be afraid. You must stand before Caesar. And God has promised you that he will save the lives of everyone sailing with you.' [25]So men, have courage. I trust in God that everything will happen as his angel told me. [26]But we will crash on an island."

27:1 emperor The ruler of the Roman Empire, which was almost all the known world. **27:9 Day of Cleansing** An important Jewish holy day in the fall of the year. This was the time of year that bad storms arose on the sea. **27:17 Syrtis** Shallow area in the sea near the Libyan coast.

JULY 28

NEHEMIAH 7:73b—9:37

Ezra Reads the Teachings

By the seventh month the Israelites were settled in their own towns.

8 All the people of Israel gathered together in the square by the Water Gate. They asked Ezra the teacher to bring out the Book of the Teachings of Moses, which the LORD had given to Israel.

²So on the first day of the seventh month, Ezra the priest brought out the Teachings for the crowd. Men, women, and all who could listen and understand had gathered. ³At the square by the Water Gate Ezra read the Teachings out loud from early morning until noon to the men, women, and everyone who could listen and understand. All the people listened carefully to the Book of the Teachings.

⁴Ezra the teacher stood on a high wooden platform that had been built just for this time. On his right were Mattithiah, Shema, Anaiah, Uriah, Hilkiah, and Maaseiah. And on his left were Pedaiah, Mishael, Malkijah, Hashum, Hashbaddanah, Zechariah, and Meshullam.

⁵Ezra opened the book in full view of everyone, because he was above them. As he opened it, all the people stood up. ⁶Ezra praised the LORD, the great God, and all the people held up their hands and said, "Amen! Amen!" Then they bowed down and worshiped the LORD with their faces to the ground.

⁷These Levites explained the Teachings to the people as they stood there: Jeshua, Bani, Sherebiah, Jamin, Akkub, Shabbethai, Hodiah, Maaseiah, Kelita, Azariah, Jozabad, Hanan, and Pelaiah. ⁸They read from the Book of the Teachings of God and explained what it meant so the people understood what was being read.

⁹Then Nehemiah the governor, Ezra the priest and teacher, and the Levites who were teaching said to all the people, "This is a holy day to the LORD your God. Don't be sad or cry." All the people had been crying as they listened to the words of the Teachings.

¹⁰Nehemiah said, "Go and enjoy good food and sweet drinks. Send some to people who have none, because today is a holy day to the Lord. Don't be sad, because the joy of the LORD will make you strong."

¹¹The Levites helped calm the people, saying, "Be quiet, because this is a holy day. Don't be sad."

¹²Then all the people went away to eat and drink, to send some of their food to others, and to celebrate with great joy. They finally understood what they had been taught.

¹³On the second day of the month, the leaders of all the families, the priests, and the Levites met with Ezra the teacher. They gathered to study the words of the Teachings. ¹⁴This is what they found written in the Teachings: The LORD commanded through Moses that the people of Israel were to live in shelters during the feast of the seventh month. ¹⁵The people were supposed to preach this message and spread it through all their towns and in Jerusalem: "Go out into the mountains, and bring back branches from olive and wild olive trees, myrtle trees, palms, and shade trees. Make shelters with them, as it is written."

¹⁶So the people went out and got tree branches. They built shelters on their roofs,[n] in their courtyards, in the courtyards of the Temple, in the square by the Water Gate, and in the square next to the Gate of Ephraim. ¹⁷The whole group that had come back from captivity built shelters and lived in them. The Israelites had not done this since the time of Joshua son of Nun. And they were very happy.

¹⁸Ezra read to them every day from the Book of the Teachings, from the first day to the last. The people of Israel celebrated the feast for seven days, and then on the eighth day the people gathered as the law said.

8:16 roofs In Bible times houses were built with flat roofs. The roof was used for drying things such as flax and fruit. And it was used as an extra room, as a place for worship, and as a cool place to sleep in the summer.

Israel Confesses Sins

9On the twenty-fourth day of that same month, the people of Israel gathered. They fasted, and they wore rough cloth and put dust on their heads to show their sadness. ²Those people whose ancestors were from Israel had separated themselves from all foreigners. They stood and confessed their sins and their ancestors' sins. ³For a fourth of the day they stood where they were and read from the Book of the Teachings of the LORD their God. For another fourth of the day they confessed their sins and worshiped the LORD their God. ⁴These Levites were standing on the stairs: Jeshua, Bani, Kadmiel, Shebaniah, Bunni, Sherebiah, Bani, and Kenani. They called out to the LORD their God with loud voices. ⁵Then these Levites spoke: Jeshua, Kadmiel, Bani, Hashabneiah, Sherebiah, Hodiah, Shebaniah, and Pethahiah. They said, "Stand up and praise the LORD your God, who lives forever and ever."

The People's Prayer

"Blessed be your wonderful name.
It is more wonderful than all blessing
and praise.
⁶You are the only LORD.
You made the heavens, even the highest
heavens,
with all the stars.
You made the earth and everything on it,
the seas and everything in them;
you give life to everything.
The heavenly army worships you.

⁷"You are the LORD,
the God who chose Abram
and brought him out of Ur in Babylonia
and named him Abraham.
⁸You found him faithful to you,
so you made an agreement with him
to give his descendants the land of the
Canaanites,
Hittites, Amorites,
Perizzites, Jebusites, and Girgashites.
You have kept your promise,
because you do what is right.

⁹"You saw our ancestors suffering in
Egypt
and heard them cry out at the Red Sea.

¹⁰You did signs and miracles against the
king of Egypt,
and against all his officers and all his
people,
because you knew how proud they
were.
You became as famous as you are today.
¹¹You divided the sea in front of our
ancestors;
they walked through on dry ground.
But you threw the people chasing them
into the deep water,
like a stone thrown into mighty waters.
¹²You led our ancestors with a pillar of
cloud by day
and with a pillar of fire at night.
It lit the way
they were supposed to go.
¹³You came down to Mount Sinai
and spoke from heaven to our
ancestors.
You gave them fair rules and true
teachings,
good orders and commands.
¹⁴You told them about your holy Sabbath
and gave them commands, orders, and
teachings
through your servant Moses.
¹⁵When they were hungry, you gave them
bread from heaven.
When they were thirsty, you brought
them water from the rock.
You told them to enter and take over
the land you had promised to give
them.

¹⁶"But our ancestors were proud and
stubborn
and did not obey your commands.
¹⁷They refused to listen;
they forgot the miracles you did for
them.
So they became stubborn and turned
against you,
choosing a leader to take them back to
slavery.
But you are a forgiving God.
You are kind and full of mercy.
You do not become angry quickly, and
you have great love.
So you did not leave them.

¹⁸Our ancestors even made an idol of a calf
  for themselves.
  They said, 'This is your god, Israel,
  who brought you up out of Egypt.'
  They spoke against you.

¹⁹"You have great mercy,
  so you did not leave them in the desert.
  The pillar of cloud guided them by day,
  and the pillar of fire led them at night,
  lighting the way they were to go.

²⁰You gave your good Spirit to teach them.
  You gave them manna to eat
  and water when they were thirsty.

²¹You took care of them for forty years in
    the desert;
  they needed nothing.
  Their clothes did not wear out,
  and their feet did not swell.

²²"You gave them kingdoms and nations;
  you gave them more land.
  They took over the country of Sihon king
    of Heshbon
  and the country of Og king of Bashan.

²³You made their children as many as the
    stars in the sky,
  and you brought them into the land
  that you told their ancestors to enter
  and take over.

²⁴So their children went into the land and
    took over.
  The Canaanites lived there, but you
    defeated them for our ancestors.
  You handed over to them the Canaanites,
    their kings, and the people of the
    land.
  Our ancestors could do what they
    wanted with them.

²⁵They captured strong, walled cities and
    fertile land.
  They took over houses full of good
    things,
  wells that were already dug,
  vineyards, olive trees, and many fruit
    trees.
  They ate until they were full and grew
    fat;
  they enjoyed your great goodness.

²⁶"But they were disobedient and turned
    against you

and ignored your teachings.
  Your prophets warned them to come
    back to you,
  but they killed those prophets
  and spoke against you.

²⁷So you handed them over to their
    enemies,
  and their enemies treated them badly.
  But in this time of trouble our ancestors
    cried out to you,
  and you heard from heaven.
  You had great mercy
  and gave them saviors who saved them
    from the power of their enemies.

²⁸But as soon as they had rest,
  they again did what was evil.
  So you left them to their enemies
  who ruled over them.
  When they cried out to you again,
  you heard from heaven.
  Because of your mercy, you saved them
    again and again.

²⁹You warned them to return to your
    teachings,
  but they were proud and did not obey
    your commands.
  If someone obeys your laws, he will live,
  but they sinned against your laws.
  They were stubborn, unwilling, and
    disobedient.

³⁰You were patient with them for many years
  and warned them by your Spirit
    through the prophets,
  but they did not pay attention.
  So you handed them over to other
    countries.

³¹But because your mercy is great, you did
    not kill them all or leave them.
  You are a kind and merciful God.

³²"And so, our God, you are the great and
    mighty and wonderful God.
  You keep your agreement of love.
  Do not let all our trouble seem
    unimportant to you.
  This trouble has come to us, to our kings
    and our leaders,
  to our priests and prophets,
  to our ancestors and all your people
  from the days of the kings of Assyria
    until today.

[33]You have been fair in everything that has happened to us;
you have been loyal, but we have been wicked.
[34]Our kings, leaders, priests, and ancestors did not obey your teachings;
they did not pay attention to the commands and warnings you gave them.
[35]Even when our ancestors were living in their kingdom,
enjoying all the good things you had given them,
enjoying the land that was fertile and full of room,
they did not stop their evil ways.
[36]"Look, we are slaves today
in the land you gave our ancestors.
They were to enjoy its fruit and its good things,
but look, we are slaves here.
[37]The land's great harvest belongs to the kings you have put over us
because of our sins.
Those kings rule over us and our cattle as they please,
so we are in much trouble.

PSALM 89:11–18

[11]The skies and the earth belong to you.
You made the world and everything in it.
[12]You created the north and the south.
Mount Tabor and Mount Hermon sing for joy at your name.
[13]Your arm has great power.
Your hand is strong; your right hand is lifted up.
[14]Your kingdom is built on what is right and fair.
Love and truth are in all you do.
[15]Happy are the people who know how to praise you.
LORD, let them live in the light of your presence.
[16]In your name they rejoice
and continually praise your goodness.

[17]You are their glorious strength,
and in your kindness you honor our king.
[18]Our king, our shield, belongs to the LORD,
to the Holy One of Israel.

PROVERBS 21:29–31

[29]Wicked people are stubborn,
but good people think carefully about what they do.
[30]There is no wisdom, understanding, or advice
that can succeed against the LORD.
[31]You can get the horses ready for battle,
but it is the LORD who gives the victory.

ACTS 27:27–44

[27]On the fourteenth night we were still being carried around in the Adriatic Sea.[n] About midnight the sailors thought we were close to land, [28]so they lowered a rope with a weight on the end of it into the water. They found that the water was one hundred twenty feet deep. They went a little farther and lowered the rope again. It was ninety feet deep. [29]The sailors were afraid that we would hit the rocks, so they threw four anchors into the water and prayed for daylight to come. [30]Some of the sailors wanted to leave the ship, and they lowered the lifeboat, pretending they were throwing more anchors from the front of the ship. [31]But Paul told the officer and the other soldiers, "If these men do not stay in the ship, your lives cannot be saved." [32]So the soldiers cut the ropes and let the lifeboat fall into the water.

[33]Just before dawn Paul began persuading all the people to eat something. He said, "For the past fourteen days you have been waiting and watching and not eating. [34]Now I beg you to eat something. You need it to stay alive. None of you will lose even one hair off your heads." [35]After he said this, Paul took some bread and thanked God for it before all of them. He broke off a piece and began eating. [36]They all felt better and started eating, too. [37]There were two hundred seventy-six people on the ship. [38]When they had eaten all

27:27 Adriatic Sea The sea between Greece and Italy, including the central Mediterranean.

they wanted, they began making the ship lighter by throwing the grain into the sea.

The Ship Is Destroyed

³⁹When daylight came, the sailors saw land. They did not know what land it was, but they saw a bay with a beach and wanted to sail the ship to the beach if they could. ⁴⁰So they cut the ropes to the anchors and left the anchors in the sea. At the same time, they untied the ropes that were holding the rudders. Then they raised the front sail into the wind and sailed toward the beach. ⁴¹But the ship hit a sandbank. The front of the ship stuck there and could not move, but the back of the ship began to break up from the big waves.

⁴²The soldiers decided to kill the prisoners so none of them could swim away and escape. ⁴³But Julius, the officer, wanted to let Paul live and did not allow the soldiers to kill the prisoners. Instead he ordered everyone who could swim to jump into the water first and swim to land. ⁴⁴The rest were to follow using wooden boards or pieces of the ship. And this is how all the people made it safely to land.

JULY 29

NEHEMIAH 9:38—11:36

The People's Agreement

³⁸"Because of all this, we are making an agreement in writing, and our leaders, Levites, and priests are putting their seals on it."

10 These are the men who sealed the agreement:

Nehemiah the governor, son of Hacaliah.

Zedekiah, ²Seraiah, Azariah, Jeremiah, ³Pashhur, Amariah, Malkijah, ⁴Hattush, Shebaniah, Malluch, ⁵Harim, Meremoth, Obadiah, ⁶Daniel, Ginnethon, Baruch, ⁷Meshullam, Abijah, Mijamin, ⁸Maaziah, Bilgai, and Shemaiah. These are the priests.

⁹These are the Levites who sealed it: Jeshua son of Azaniah, Binnui of the sons of Henadad, Kadmiel, ¹⁰and their fellow Levites: Shebaniah, Hodiah, Kelita, Pelaiah, Hanan, ¹¹Mica, Rehob, Hashabiah, ¹²Zaccur, Sherebiah, Shebaniah, ¹³Hodiah, Bani, and Beninu.

¹⁴These are the leaders of the people who sealed the agreement: Parosh, Pahath-Moab, Elam, Zattu, Bani, ¹⁵Bunni, Azgad, Bebai, ¹⁶Adonijah, Bigvai, Adin, ¹⁷Ater, Hezekiah, Azzur, ¹⁸Hodiah, Hashum, Bezai, ¹⁹Hariph, Anathoth, Nebai, ²⁰Magpiash, Meshullam, Hezir, ²¹Meshezabel, Zadok, Jaddua, ²²Pelatiah, Hanan, Anaiah, ²³Hoshea, Hananiah, Hasshub, ²⁴Hallohesh, Pilha, Shobek, ²⁵Rehum, Hashabnah, Maaseiah, ²⁶Ahiah, Hanan, Anan, ²⁷Malluch, Harim, and Baanah.

²⁸The rest of the people took an oath. They were the priests, Levites, gatekeepers, singers, Temple servants, all those who separated themselves from foreigners to keep the Teachings of God, and also their wives and their sons and daughters who could understand. ²⁹They joined their fellow Israelites and their leading men in taking an oath, which was tied to a curse in case they broke the oath. They promised to follow the Teachings of God, which they had been given through Moses the servant of God, and to obey all the commands, rules, and laws of the LORD our God.

³⁰They said:

We promise not to let our daughters marry foreigners nor to let our sons marry their daughters. ³¹Foreigners may bring goods or grain to sell on the Sabbath, but we will not buy on the Sabbath or any holy day. Every seventh year we will not plant, and that year we will forget all that people owe us.

³²We will be responsible for the commands to pay for the service of the Temple of our God. We will give an eighth of an ounce of silver each year. ³³It is for the bread that is set out on the table; the regular grain offerings and

burnt offerings; the offerings on the Sabbaths, New Moon festivals, and special feasts; the holy offerings; the offerings to remove the sins of the Israelites so they will belong to God; and for the work of the Temple of our God.

³⁴We, the priests, the Levites, and the people, have thrown lots to decide at what time of year each family must bring wood to the Temple. The wood is for burning on the altar of the LORD our God, and we will do this as it is written in the Teachings.

³⁵We also will bring the firstfruits from our crops and the firstfruits of every tree to the Temple each year.

³⁶We will bring to the Temple our firstborn sons and cattle and the firstborn of our herds and flocks, as it is written in the Teachings. We will bring them to the priests who are serving in the Temple.

³⁷We will bring to the priests at the storerooms of the Temple the first of our ground meal, our offerings, the fruit from all our trees, and our new wine and oil. And we will bring a tenth of our crops to the Levites, who will collect these things in all the towns where we work. ³⁸A priest of Aaron's family must be with the Levites when they receive the tenth of the people's crops. The Levites must bring a tenth of all they receive to the Temple of our God to put in the storerooms of the treasury. ³⁹The people of Israel and the Levites are to bring to the storerooms the gifts of grain, new wine, and oil. That is where the utensils for the Temple are kept and where the priests who are serving, the gatekeepers, and singers stay.

We will not ignore the Temple of our God.

New People Move into Jerusalem

11 The leaders of Israel lived in Jerusalem. But the rest of the people threw lots to choose one person out of every ten to come and live in Jerusalem, the holy city. The other nine could stay in their own cities. ²The people blessed those who volunteered to live in Jerusalem.

³These are the area leaders who lived in Jerusalem. (Some people lived on their own land in the cities of Judah. These included Israelites, priests, Levites, Temple servants, and descendants of Solomon's servants. ⁴Others from the families of Judah and Benjamin lived in Jerusalem.)

These are the descendants of Judah who moved into Jerusalem. There was Athaiah son of Uzziah. (Uzziah was the son of Zechariah, the son of Amariah. Amariah was the son of Shephatiah, the son of Mahalalel. Mahalalel was a descendant of Perez.) ⁵There was also Masseiah son of Baruch. (Baruch was the son of Col-Hozeh, the son of Hazaiah. Hazaiah was the son of Adaiah, the son of Joiarib. Joiarib was the son of Zechariah, a descendant of Shelah.) ⁶All the descendants of Perez who lived in Jerusalem totaled 468 men. They were soldiers.

⁷These are descendants of Benjamin who moved into Jerusalem. There was Sallu son of Meshullam. (Meshullam was the son of Joed, the son of Pedaiah. Pedaiah was the son of Kolaiah, the son of Maaseiah. Maaseiah was the son of Ithiel, the son of Jeshaiah.) ⁸Following him were Gabbai and Sallai, for a total of 928 men. ⁹Joel son of Zicri was appointed over them, and Judah son of Hassenuah was second in charge of the new area of the city.

¹⁰These are the priests who moved into Jerusalem. There was Jedaiah son of Joiarib, Jakin, ¹¹and Seraiah son of Hilkiah, the supervisor in the Temple. (Hilkiah was the son of Meshullam, the son of Zadok. Zadok was the son of Meraioth, the son of Ahitub.) ¹²And there were others with them who did the work for the Temple. All together there were 822 men. Also there was Adaiah son of Jeroham. (Jeroham was the son of Pelaliah, the son of Amzi. Amzi was the son of Zechariah, the son of Pashhur. Pashhur was the son of Malkijah.) ¹³And there were family heads with him. All together there were 242 men. Also there was Amashsai son of Azarel. (Azarel was the son of Ahzai, the son of Meshillemoth. Meshillemoth was the son of Immer.) ¹⁴And there were brave men with Amashsai. All together there were 128 men. Zabdiel son of Haggedolim was appointed over them.

¹⁵These are the Levites who moved into Jerusalem. There was Shemaiah son of Hasshub. (Hasshub was the son of Azrikam, the son of Hashabiah. Hashabiah was the son of Bunni.) ¹⁶And there were Shabbethai and Jozabad, two of the leaders of the Levites who were in charge of the work outside the Temple. ¹⁷There was Mattaniah son of Mica. (Mica was the son of Zabdi, the son of Asaph.) Mattaniah was the director who led the people in thanksgiving and prayer. There was Bakbukiah, who was second in charge over his fellow Levites. And there was Abda son of Shammua. (Shammua was the son of Galal, the son of Jeduthun.) ¹⁸All together 284 Levites lived in the holy city of Jerusalem.

¹⁹The gatekeepers who moved into Jerusalem were Akkub, Talmon, and others with them. There was a total of 172 men who guarded the city gates.

²⁰The other Israelites, priests, and Levites lived on their own land in all the cities of Judah.

²¹The Temple servants lived on the hill of Ophel, and Ziha and Gishpa were in charge of them.

²²Uzzi son of Bani was appointed over the Levites in Jerusalem. (Bani was the son of Hashabiah, the son of Mattaniah. Mattaniah was the son of Mica.) Uzzi was one of Asaph's descendants, who were the singers responsible for the service of the Temple. ²³The singers were under the king's orders, which regulated them day by day.

²⁴Pethahiah son of Meshezabel was the king's spokesman. (Meshezabel was a descendant of Zerah, the son of Judah.)

²⁵Some of the people of Judah lived in villages with their surrounding fields. They lived in Kiriath Arba and its surroundings, in Dibon and its surroundings, in Jekabzeel and its surroundings, ²⁶in Jeshua, Moladah, Beth Pelet, ²⁷Hazar Shual, Beersheba and its surroundings, ²⁸in Ziklag and Meconah and its surroundings, ²⁹in En Rimmon, Zorah, Jarmuth, ³⁰Zanoah, Adullam and their villages, in Lachish and the fields around it, and in Azekah and its surroundings. So they settled from Beersheba all the way to the Valley of Hinnom.

³¹The descendants of the Benjaminites from Geba lived in Micmash, Aija, Bethel and its surroundings, ³²in Anathoth, Nob, Ananiah, ³³Hazor, Ramah, Gittaim, ³⁴Hadid, Zeboim, Neballat, ³⁵Lod, Ono, and in the Valley of the Craftsmen.

³⁶Some groups of the Levites from Judah settled in the land of Benjamin.

PSALM 89:19–29

¹⁹Once, in a vision, you spoke
    to those who worship you.
You said, "I have given strength to a
    warrior;
  I have raised up a young man from my
    people.
²⁰I have found my servant David;
  I appointed him by pouring holy oil on
    him.
²¹I will steady him with my hand
  and strengthen him with my arm.
²²No enemy will make him give forced
    payments,
  and wicked people will not defeat
    him.
²³I will crush his enemies in front of him;
  I will defeat those who hate him.
²⁴My loyalty and love will be with him.
  Through me he will be strong.
²⁵I will give him power over the sea
  and control over the rivers.
²⁶He will say to me, 'You are my father,
  my God, the Rock, my Savior.'
²⁷I will make him my firstborn son,
  the greatest king on earth.
²⁸My love will watch over him forever,
  and my agreement with him will never
    end.
²⁹I will make his family continue,
  and his kingdom will last as long as the
    skies.

PROVERBS 22:1–2

22 Being respected is more important
    than having great riches.
To be well thought of is better than
    silver or gold.

²The rich and the poor are alike
  in that the LORD made them all.

ACTS 28:1–31

Paul on the Island of Malta

28 When we were safe on land, we learned that the island was called Malta. [2]The people who lived there were very good to us. Because it was raining and very cold, they made a fire and welcomed all of us. [3]Paul gathered a pile of sticks and was putting them on the fire when a poisonous snake came out because of the heat and bit him on the hand. [4]The people living on the island saw the snake hanging from Paul's hand and said to each other, "This man must be a murderer! He did not die in the sea, but Justice[n] does not want him to live." [5]But Paul shook the snake off into the fire and was not hurt. [6]The people thought that Paul would swell up or fall down dead. They waited and watched him for a long time, but nothing bad happened to him. So they changed their minds and said, "He is a god!"

[7]There were some fields around there owned by Publius, an important man on the island. He welcomed us into his home and was very good to us for three days. [8]Publius' father was sick with a fever and dysentery.[n] Paul went to him, prayed, and put his hands on the man and healed him. [9]After this, all the other sick people on the island came to Paul, and he healed them, too. [10-11]The people on the island gave us many honors. When we were ready to leave, three months later, they gave us the things we needed.

Paul Goes to Rome

We got on a ship from Alexandria that had stayed on the island during the winter. On the front of the ship was the sign of the twin gods.[n] [12]We stopped at Syracuse for three days. [13]From there we sailed to Rhegium. The next day a wind began to blow from the south, and a day later we came to Puteoli. [14]We found some believers there who asked us to stay with them for a week. Finally, we came to Rome. [15]The believers in Rome heard that we were there and came out as far as the Market of Appius[n] and the Three Inns[n] to meet us. When Paul saw them, he was encouraged and thanked God.

Paul in Rome

[16]When we arrived at Rome, Paul was allowed to live alone, with the soldier who guarded him.

[17]Three days later Paul sent for the leaders there. When they came together, he said, "Brothers, I have done nothing against our people or the customs of our ancestors. But I was arrested in Jerusalem and given to the Romans. [18]After they asked me many questions, they could find no reason why I should be killed. They wanted to let me go free, [19]but the evil people there argued against that. So I had to ask to come to Rome to have my trial before Caesar. But I have no charge to bring against my own people. [20]That is why I wanted to see you and talk with you. I am bound with this chain because I believe in the hope of Israel."

[21]They answered Paul, "We have received no letters from Judea about you. None of our Jewish brothers who have come from there brought news or told us anything bad about you. [22]But we want to hear your ideas, because we know that people everywhere are speaking against this religious group."

[23]Paul and the people chose a day for a meeting and on that day many more of the Jews met with Paul at the place he was staying. He spoke to them all day long. Using the law of Moses and the prophets' writings, he explained the kingdom of God, and he tried to persuade them to believe these things about Jesus. [24]Some believed what Paul said, but others did not. [25]So they argued and began leaving after Paul said one more thing to them: "The Holy Spirit spoke the truth to your ancestors through Isaiah the prophet, saying,
[26]'Go to this people and say:
You will listen and listen, but you will not understand.
You will look and look, but you will not learn,
[27]because these people have become stubborn.

28:4 Justice The people thought there was a god named Justice who would punish bad people. **28:8 dysentery** A sickness like diarrhea. **28:10-11 twin gods** Statues of Castor and Pollux, gods in old Greek tales. **28:15 Market of Appius** A town about twenty-seven miles from Rome. **28:15 Three Inns** A town about thirty miles from Rome.

They don't hear with their ears,
and they have closed their eyes.
Otherwise, they might really understand
what they see with their eyes
and hear with their ears.
They might really understand in their
minds
and come back to me and be healed.'

Isaiah 6:9–10

28"I want you to know that God has also sent his salvation to all nations, and they will listen!" [29After Paul said this, the Jews left. They were arguing very much with each other.]*n*

30Paul stayed two full years in his own rented house and welcomed all people who came to visit him. 31He boldly preached about the kingdom of God and taught about the Lord Jesus Christ, and no one stopped him.

JULY 30

NEHEMIAH 12:1—13:31

Priests and Levites

12 These are the priests and Levites who returned with Zerubbabel son of Shealtiel and with Jeshua. There were Seraiah, Jeremiah, Ezra, 2Amariah, Malluch, Hattush, 3Shecaniah, Rehum, Meremoth, 4Iddo, Ginnethon, Abijah, 5Mijamin, Moadiah, Bilgah, 6Shemaiah, Joiarib, Jedaiah, 7Sallu, Amok, Hilkiah, and Jedaiah. They were the leaders of the priests and their relatives in the days of Jeshua.

8The Levites were Jeshua, Binnui, Kadmiel, Sherebiah, Judah, and Mattaniah. Mattaniah and his relatives were in charge of the songs of thanksgiving. 9Bakbukiah and Unni, their relatives, stood across from them in the services.

10Jeshua was the father of Joiakim. Joiakim was the father of Eliashib. Eliashib was the father of Joiada. 11Joiada was the father of Jonathan, and Jonathan was the father of Jaddua.

12In the days of Joiakim, these priests were the leaders of the families of priests: Meraiah, from Seraiah's family; Hananiah, from Jeremiah's family; 13Meshullam, from Ezra's family; Jehohanan, from Amariah's family; 14Jonathan, from Malluch's family; Joseph, from Shecaniah's family; 15Adna, from Harim's family; Helkai, from Meremoth's family; 16Zechariah, from Iddo's fam-ily; Meshullam, from Ginnethon's family; 17Zicri, from Abijah's family; Piltai, from Miniamin's and Moadiah's families; 18Shammua, from Bilgah's family; Jehonathan, from Shemaiah's family; 19Mattenai, from Joiarib's family; Uzzi, from Jedaiah's family; 20Kallai, from Sallu's family; Eber, from Amok's family; 21Hashabiah, from Hilkiah's family; and Nethanel, from Jedaiah's family.

22The leaders of the families of the Levites and the priests were written down in the days of Eliashib, Joiada, Johanan, and Jaddua, while Darius the Persian was king. 23The family leaders among the Levites were written down in the history book, but only up to the time of Johanan son of Eliashib. 24The leaders of the Levites were Hashabiah, Sherebiah, Jeshua son of Kadmiel, and their relatives. Their relatives stood across from them and gave praise and thanksgiving to God. One group answered the other group, as David, the man of God, had commanded.

25These were the gatekeepers who guarded the storerooms next to the gates: Mattaniah, Bakbukiah, Obadiah, Meshullam, Talmon, and Akkub. 26They served in the days of Joiakim son of Jeshua, the son of Jozadak. They also served in the days of Nehemiah the governor and Ezra the priest and teacher.

The Wall of Jerusalem

27When the wall of Jerusalem was offered as a gift to God, they asked the Levites to

---

28:29 After . . . other. Some Greek copies do not contain the bracketed text.

come from wherever they lived to Jerusalem to celebrate with joy the gift of the wall. They were to celebrate with songs of thanksgiving and with the music of cymbals, harps, and lyres. [28]They also brought together singers from all around Jerusalem, from the Netophathite villages, [29]from Beth Gilgal, and from the areas of Geba and Azmaveth. The singers had built villages for themselves around Jerusalem. [30]The priests and Levites made themselves pure, and they also made the people, the gates, and the wall of Jerusalem pure.

[31]I had the leaders of Judah go up on top of the wall, and I appointed two large choruses to give thanks. One chorus went to the right on top of the wall, toward the Trash Gate. [32]Behind them went Hoshaiah and half the leaders of Judah. [33]Azariah, Ezra, Meshullam, [34]Judah, Benjamin, Shemaiah, and Jeremiah also went. [35]Some priests with trumpets also went, along with Zechariah son of Jonathan. (Jonathan was the son of Shemaiah, the son of Mattaniah. Mattaniah was the son of Micaiah, the son of Zaccur. Zaccur was the son of Asaph.) [36]Zechariah's relatives also went. They were Shemaiah, Azarel, Milalai, Gilalai, Maai, Nethanel, Judah, and Hanani. These men played the musical instruments of David, the man of God, and Ezra the teacher walked in front of them. [37]They went from the Fountain Gate straight up the steps to the highest part of the wall by the older part of the city. They went on above the house of David to the Water Gate on the east.

[38]The second chorus went to the left, while I followed them on top of the wall with half the people. We went from the Tower of the Ovens to the Broad Wall, [39]over the Gate of Ephraim to the Old Gate and the Fish Gate, to the Tower of Hananel and the Tower of the Hundred. We went as far as the Sheep Gate and stopped at the Gate of the Guard.

[40]The two choruses took their places at the Temple. Half of the leaders and I did also. [41]These priests were there with their trumpets: Eliakim, Maaseiah, Miniamin, Micaiah, Elioenai, Zechariah, and Hananiah. [42]These people were also there: Maaseiah, Shemaiah, Eleazar, Uzzi, Jehohanan, Malki-

jah, Elam, and Ezer. The choruses sang, led by Jezrahiah. [43]The people offered many sacrifices that day and were happy because God had given them great joy. The women and children were happy. The sound of happiness in Jerusalem could be heard far away.

[44]At that time the leaders appointed men to be in charge of the storerooms. These rooms were for the gifts, the firstfruits, and the ten percent that the people brought. The Teachings said they should bring a share for the priests and Levites from the fields around the towns. The people of Judah were happy to do this for the priests and Levites who served. [45]They performed the service of their God in making things pure. The singers and gatekeepers also did their jobs, as David had commanded his son Solomon. [46]Earlier, in the time of David and Asaph, there was a leader of the singers and of the songs of praise and thanksgiving to God. [47]So it was in the days of Zerubbabel and Nehemiah. All the people of Israel gave something to the singers and gatekeepers, and they also set aside part for the Levites. Then the Levites set aside part for the descendants of Aaron.

Foreign People Are Sent Away

13 On that day they read the Book of Moses to the people, and they found that it said no Ammonite or Moabite should ever be allowed in the meeting to worship. [2]The Ammonites and Moabites had not welcomed the Israelites with food and water. Instead, they had hired Balaam to put a curse on Israel. (But our God turned the curse into a blessing.) [3]When the people heard this teaching, they separated all foreigners from Israel.

Nehemiah Returns to Jerusalem

[4]Before that happened, Eliashib the priest, who was in charge of the Temple storerooms, was friendly with Tobiah. [5]Eliashib let Tobiah use one of the large storerooms. Earlier it had been used for grain offerings, incense, the utensils, and the tenth offerings of grain, new wine, and olive oil that belonged to the Levites, singers, and gatekeepers. It had also been used for gifts for the priests.

[6]I was not in Jerusalem when this hap-

pened. I had gone back to Artaxerxes king of Babylon in the thirty-second year he was king. Finally I asked the king to let me leave. [7]When I returned to Jerusalem, I found out the evil Eliashib had done by letting Tobiah have a room in the Temple courtyard. [8]I was very upset at this, so I threw all of Tobiah's goods out of the room. [9]I ordered the rooms to be purified, and I brought back the utensils for God's Temple, the grain offerings, and the incense.

[10]Then I found out the people were not giving the Levites their shares. So the Levites and singers who served had gone back to their own farms. [11]I argued with the officers, saying, "Why haven't you taken care of the Temple?" Then I gathered the Levites and singers and put them back at their places.

[12]All the people of Judah then brought to the storerooms a tenth of their crops, new wine, and olive oil. [13]I put these men in charge of the storerooms: Shelemiah the priest, Zadok the teacher, and Pedaiah a Levite. I made Hanan son of Zaccur, the son of Mattaniah, their helper. Everyone knew they were honest. They gave out the portions that went to their relatives.

[14]Remember me, my God, for this. Do not ignore my love for the Temple and its service.

[15]In those days I saw people in Judah working in the winepresses on the Sabbath day. They were bringing in grain and loading it on donkeys. And they were bringing loads of wine, grapes, and figs into Jerusalem on the Sabbath day. So I warned them about selling food on that day. [16]People from the city of Tyre who were living in Jerusalem brought in fish and other things and sold them there on the Sabbath day to the people of Judah. [17]I argued with the important men of Judah and said to them, "What is this evil thing you are doing? You are ruining the Sabbath day. [18]This is just what your ancestors did. So our God did terrible things to us and this city. Now you are making him even more angry at Israel by ruining the Sabbath day."

[19]So I ordered that the doors be shut at sunset before the Sabbath and not be opened until the Sabbath was over. I put my servants at the gates so no load could come in on the Sabbath. [20]Once or twice traders and sellers of all kinds of goods spent the night outside Jerusalem. [21]So I warned them, "Why are you spending the night by the wall? If you do it again, I will force you away." After that, they did not come back on the Sabbath. [22]Then I ordered the Levites to purify themselves and to guard the city gates to make sure the Sabbath remained holy.

Remember me, my God, for this. Have mercy on me because of your great love.

[23]In those days I saw men of Judah who had married women from Ashdod, Ammon, and Moab. [24]Half their children were speaking the language of Ashdod or some other place, and they couldn't speak the language of Judah. [25]I argued with those people, put curses on them, hit some of them, and pulled out their hair. I forced them to make a promise to God, saying, "Do not let your daughters marry the sons of foreigners, and do not take the daughters of foreigners as wives for your sons or yourselves. [26]Foreign women made King Solomon of Israel sin. There was never a king like him in any of the nations. God loved Solomon and made him king over all Israel, but foreign women made him sin. [27]And now you are not obedient when you do this evil thing. You are unfaithful to our God when you marry foreign wives."

[28]Joiada was the son of Eliashib the high priest. One of Joiada's sons married a daughter of Sanballat the Horonite, so I sent him away from me.

[29]Remember them, my God, because they made the priesthood unclean and the agreement of the priests and Levites unclean.

[30]So I purified them of everything that was foreign. I appointed duties for the priests and Levites, giving each man his own job. [31]I also made sure wood was brought for the altar at regular times and that the firstfruits were brought.

Remember me, my God; be kind to me.

PSALM 89:30–37

[30]"If his descendants reject my teachings
  and do not follow my laws,
[31]if they ignore my demands
  and disobey my commands,

[32]then I will punish their sins with a rod
  and their wrongs with a whip.
[33]But I will not hold back my love from
    David,
  nor will I stop being loyal.
[34]I will not break my agreement
  nor change what I have said.
[35]I have promised by my holiness,
  I will not lie to David.
[36]His family will go on forever.
  His kingdom will last before me like the
    sun.
[37]It will continue forever, like the moon,
  like a dependable witness in the sky."
                                        Selah

PROVERBS 22:3–4

[3]The wise see danger ahead and avoid it,
  but fools keep going and get into
    trouble.

[4]Respecting the LORD and not being proud
  will bring you wealth, honor, and life.

ROMANS 1:1–32

1 From Paul, a servant of Christ Jesus. God
  called me to be an apostle and chose me
to tell the Good News. [2]God promised this Good News long ago
through his prophets, as it is written in the
Holy Scriptures. [3-4]The Good News is about
God's Son, Jesus Christ our Lord. As a man,
he was born from the family of David. But
through the Spirit of holiness he was declared to be God's Son with great power by
rising from the dead. [5]Through Christ, God
gave me the special work of an apostle,
which was to lead people of all nations to believe and obey. I do this work for him. [6]And
you who are in Rome are also called to belong to Jesus Christ.

[7]To all of you in Rome whom God loves
and has called to be his holy people:

  Grace and peace to you from God our Father and the Lord Jesus Christ.

A Prayer of Thanks

[8]First I want to say that I thank my God
through Jesus Christ for all of you, because
people everywhere in the world are talking
about your faith. [9]God, whom I serve with
my whole heart by telling the Good News
about his Son, knows that I always mention
you [10]every time I pray. I pray that I will be
allowed to come to you, and this will happen
if God wants it. [11]I want very much to see
you, to give you some spiritual gift to make
you strong. [12]I mean that I want us to help
each other with the faith we have. Your faith
will help me, and my faith will help you.
[13]Brothers and sisters, I want you to know
that I planned many times to come to you,
but this has not been possible. I wanted to
come so that I could help you grow spiritually as I have helped the other non-Jewish
people.

[14]I have a duty to all people—Greeks and
those who are not Greeks, the wise and the
foolish. [15]That is why I want so much to
preach the Good News to you in Rome.

[16]I am not ashamed of the Good News,
because it is the power God uses to save
everyone who believes—to save the Jews
first, and then to save non-Jews. [17]The Good
News shows how God makes people right
with himself—that it begins and ends with
faith. As the Scripture says, "But those who
are right with God will live by faith."[n]

All People Have Done Wrong

[18]God's anger is shown from heaven
against all the evil and wrong things people
do. By their own evil lives they hide the
truth. [19]God shows his anger because some
knowledge of him has been made clear to
them. Yes, God has shown himself to them.
[20]There are things about him that people
cannot see—his eternal power and all the
things that make him God. But since the beginning of the world those things have been
easy to understand by what God has made.
So people have no excuse for the bad things
they do. [21]They knew God, but they did not
give glory to God or thank him. Their thinking became useless. Their foolish minds
were filled with darkness. [22]They said they
were wise, but they became fools. [23]They
traded the glory of God who lives forever for

1:17 "But those . . . faith." Quotation from Habakkuk 2:4.

the worship of idols made to look like earthly people, birds, animals, and snakes.

[24]Because they did these things, God left them and let them go their sinful way, wanting only to do evil. As a result, they became full of sexual sin, using their bodies wrongly with each other. [25]They traded the truth of God for a lie. They worshiped and served what had been created instead of the God who created those things, who should be praised forever. Amen.

[26]Because people did those things, God left them and let them do the shameful things they wanted to do. Women stopped having natural sex and started having sex with other women. [27]In the same way, men stopped having natural sex and began wanting each other. Men did shameful things with other men, and in their bodies they received the punishment for those wrongs.

[28]People did not think it was important to have a true knowledge of God. So God left them and allowed them to have their own worthless thinking and to do things they should not do. [29]They are filled with every kind of sin, evil, selfishness, and hatred. They are full of jealousy, murder, fighting, lying, and thinking the worst about each other. They gossip [30]and say evil things about each other. They hate God. They are rude and conceited and brag about themselves. They invent ways of doing evil. They do not obey their parents. [31]They are foolish, they do not keep their promises, and they show no kindness or mercy to others. [32]They know God's law says that those who live like this should die. But they themselves not only continue to do these evil things, they applaud others who do them.

JULY 31

ESTHER 1:1—2:23

Queen Vashti Disobeys the King

1 This is what happened during the time of King Xerxes, the king who ruled the one hundred twenty-seven states from India to Cush. [2]In those days King Xerxes ruled from his capital city of Susa. [3]In the third year of his rule, he gave a banquet for all his important men and royal officers. The army leaders from the countries of Persia and Media and the important men from all Xerxes' empire were there.

[4]The banquet lasted one hundred eighty days. All during that time King Xerxes was showing off the great wealth of his kingdom and his own great riches and glory. [5]When the one hundred eighty days were over, the king gave another banquet. It was held in the courtyard of the palace garden for seven days, and it was for everybody in the palace at Susa, from the greatest to the least. [6]The courtyard had fine white curtains and purple drapes that were tied to silver rings on marble pillars by white and purple cords.

And there were gold and silver couches on a floor set with tiles of white marble, shells, and gems. [7]Wine was served in gold cups of various kinds. And there was plenty of the king's wine, because he was very generous. [8]The king commanded that the guests be permitted to drink as much as they wished. He told the wine servers to serve each man what he wanted.

[9]Queen Vashti also gave a banquet for the women in the royal palace of King Xerxes.

[10]On the seventh day of the banquet, King Xerxes was very happy, because he had been drinking much wine. He gave a command to the seven eunuchs who served him—Mehuman, Biztha, Harbona, Bigtha, Abagtha, Zethar, and Carcas. [11]He commanded them to bring him Queen Vashti, wearing her royal crown. She was to come to show her beauty to the people and important men, because she was very beautiful. [12]The eunuchs told Queen Vashti about the king's command, but she refused to come. Then the king became very angry; his anger was like a burning fire. [13]It was a custom for the king to ask ad-

vice from experts about law and order. So King Xerxes spoke with the wise men who would know the right thing to do. 14The wise men the king usually talked to were Carshena, Shethar, Admatha, Tarshish, Meres, Marsena, and Memucan, seven of the important men of Persia and Media. These seven had special privileges to see the king and had the highest rank in the kingdom. 15The king asked them, "What does the law say must be done to Queen Vashti? She has not obeyed the command of King Xerxes, which the eunuchs took to her."

16Then Memucan said to the king and the other important men, "Queen Vashti has not done wrong to the king alone. She has also done wrong to all the important men and all the people in all the empire of King Xerxes. 17All the wives of the important men of Persia and Media will hear about the queen's actions. Then they will no longer honor their husbands. They will say, 'King Xerxes commanded Queen Vashti to be brought to him, but she refused to come.' 18Today the wives of the important men of Persia and Media have heard about the queen's actions. So they will speak in the same way to their husbands, and there will be no end to disrespect and anger.

19"So, our king, if it pleases you, give a royal order, and let it be written in the laws of Persia and Media, which cannot be changed. The law should say Vashti is never again to enter the presence of King Xerxes. Also let the king give her place as queen to someone who is better than she is. 20And let the king's order be announced everywhere in his enormous kingdom. Then all the women will respect their husbands, from the greatest to the least."

21The king and his important men were happy with this advice, so King Xerxes did as Memucan suggested. 22He sent letters to all the states of the kingdom in the writing of each state and in the language of each group of people. These letters announced that each man was to be the ruler of his own family.

Esther Is Made Queen

2 Later, when King Xerxes was not so angry, he remembered Vashti and what she had done and his order about her. 2Then the king's personal servants suggested, "Let a search be made for beautiful young girls for the king. 3Let the king choose supervisors in every state of his kingdom to bring every beautiful young girl to the palace at Susa. They should be taken to the women's quarters and put under the care of Hegai, the king's eunuch in charge of the women. And let beauty treatments be given to them. 4Then let the girl who most pleases the king become queen in place of Vashti." The king liked this idea, so he did as they said.

5Now there was a Jewish man in the palace of Susa whose name was Mordecai son of Jair. Jair was the son of Shimei, the son of Kish. Mordecai was from the tribe of Benjamin, 6which had been taken captive from Jerusalem by Nebuchadnezzar king of Babylon. They were part of the group taken into captivity with Jehoiachin king of Judah. 7Mordecai had a cousin named Hadassah, who had no father or mother, so Mordecai took care of her. Hadassah was also called Esther, and she had a very pretty figure and face. Mordecai had adopted her as his own daughter when her father and mother died.

8When the king's command and order had been heard, many girls had been brought to the palace in Susa and put under the care of Hegai. Esther was also taken to the king's palace and put under the care of Hegai, who was in charge of the women. 9Esther pleased Hegai, and he liked her. So Hegai quickly began giving Esther her beauty treatments and special food. He gave her seven servant girls chosen from the king's palace. Then he moved her and her seven servant girls to the best part of the women's quarters.

10Esther did not tell anyone about her family or who her people were, because Mordecai had told her not to. 11Every day Mordecai walked back and forth near the courtyard where the king's women lived to find out how Esther was and what was happening to her.

12Before a girl could take her turn with King Xerxes, she had to complete twelve months of beauty treatments that were ordered for the women. For six months she was treated with oil and myrrh and for six months with perfumes and cosmetics. [13]Then she was ready to go to the king. Anything she asked for was given to her to take with her from the women's quarters to the king's palace. [14]In the evening she would go to the king's palace, and in the morning she would return to another part of the women's quarters. There she would be placed under the care of Shaashgaz, the king's eunuch in charge of the slave women. The girl would not go back to the king again unless he was pleased with her and asked for her by name.

[15]The time came for Esther daughter of Abihail, Mordecai's uncle, who had been adopted by Mordecai, to go to the king. She asked for only what Hegai suggested she should take. (Hegai was the king's eunuch who was in charge of the women.) Everyone who saw Esther liked her. [16]So Esther was taken to King Xerxes in the royal palace in the tenth month, the month of Tebeth, during Xerxes' seventh year as king.

[17]And the king was pleased with Esther more than with any of the other virgins. He liked her more than any of the others, so he put a royal crown on her head and made her queen in place of Vashti. [18]Then the king gave a great banquet for Esther and invited all his important men and royal officers. He announced a holiday for all the empire and had the government give away gifts.

Mordecai Discovers an Evil Plan

[19]Now Mordecai was sitting at the king's gate when the girls were gathered the second time. [20]Esther still had not told anyone about her family or who her people were, just as Mordecai had commanded her. She obeyed Mordecai just as she had done when she was under his care.

[21]Now Bigthana and Teresh were two of the king's eunuchs who guarded the doorway. While Mordecai was sitting at the king's gate, they became angry and began to make plans to kill King Xerxes. [22]But Mordecai found out about their plans and told Queen Esther. Then Esther told the king how Mordecai had discovered the evil plan. [23]When the report was investigated, it was found to be true, and the two officers who

had planned to kill the king were hanged. All this was written down in the daily court record in the king's presence.

PSALM 89:38–45

[38]But now you have refused and rejected
your appointed king.
You have been angry with him.
[39]You have abandoned the agreement with
your servant
and thrown his crown to the ground.
[40]You have torn down all his city walls;
you have turned his strong cities into
ruins.
[41]Everyone who passes by steals from him.
His neighbors insult him.
[42]You have given strength to his enemies
and have made them all happy.
[43]You have made his sword useless;
you did not help him stand in battle.
[44]You have kept him from winning
and have thrown his throne to the
ground.
[45]You have cut his life short
and covered him with shame.   *Selah*

PROVERBS 22:5–6

[5]Evil people's lives are like paths covered
with thorns and traps.
People who guard themselves don't
have such problems.

[6]Train children to live the right way,
and when they are old, they will not
stray from it.

ROMANS 2:1–29

You People Also Are Sinful

2 If you think you can judge others, you are wrong. When you judge them, you are really judging yourself guilty, because you do the same things they do. [2]God judges those who do wrong things, and we know that his judging is right. [3]You judge those who do wrong, but you do wrong yourselves. Do you think you will be able to escape the judgment of God? [4]He has been very kind and patient, waiting for you to change, but you think nothing of his kindness. Perhaps you

do not understand that God is kind to you so you will change your hearts and lives. ⁵But you are stubborn and refuse to change, so you are making your own punishment even greater on the day he shows his anger. On that day everyone will see God's right judgments. ⁶God will reward or punish every person for what that person has done. ⁷Some people, by always continuing to do good, live for God's glory, for honor, and for life that has no end. God will give them life forever. ⁸But other people are selfish. They refuse to follow truth and, instead, follow evil. God will give them his punishment and anger. ⁹He will give trouble and suffering to everyone who does evil—to the Jews first and also to those who are not Jews. ¹⁰But he will give glory, honor, and peace to everyone who does good—to the Jews first and also to those who are not Jews. ¹¹For God judges all people in the same way.

¹²People who do not have the law and who are sinners will be lost, although they do not have the law. And, in the same way, those who have the law and are sinners will be judged by the law. ¹³Hearing the law does not make people right with God. It is those who obey the law who will be right with him. ¹⁴(Those who are not Jews do not have the law, but when they freely do what the law commands, they are the law for themselves. This is true even though they do not have the law. ¹⁵They show that in their hearts they know what is right and wrong, just as the law commands. And they show this by their consciences. Sometimes their thoughts tell them they did wrong, and sometimes their thoughts tell them they did right.) ¹⁶All these things will happen on the day when God, through Christ

Jesus, will judge people's secret thoughts. The Good News that I preach says this.

The Jews and the Law

¹⁷What about you? You call yourself a Jew. You trust in the law of Moses and brag that you are close to God. ¹⁸You know what he wants you to do and what is important, because you have learned the law. ¹⁹You think you are a guide for the blind and a light for those who are in darkness. ²⁰You think you can show foolish people what is right and teach those who know nothing. You have the law; so you think you know everything and have all truth. ²¹You teach others, so why don't you teach yourself? You tell others not to steal, but you steal. ²²You say that others must not take part in adultery, but you are guilty of that sin. You hate idols, but you steal from temples. ²³You brag about having God's law, but you bring shame to God by breaking his law, ²⁴just as the Scriptures say: "Those who are not Jews speak against God's name because of you."ⁿ

²⁵If you follow the law, your circumcision has meaning. But if you break the law, it is as if you were never circumcised. ²⁶People who are not Jews are not circumcised, but if they do what the law says, it is as if they were circumcised. ²⁷You Jews have the written law and circumcision, but you break the law. So those who are not circumcised in their bodies, but still obey the law, will show that you are guilty. ²⁸They can do this because a person is not a true Jew if he is only a Jew in his physical body; true circumcision is not only on the outside of the body. ²⁹A person is a Jew only if he is a Jew inside; true circumcision is done in the heart by the Spirit, not by the written law. Such a person gets praise from God rather than from people.

2:24 "Those . . . you." Quotation from Isaiah 52:5; Ezekiel 36:20.

AUGUST 1

ESTHER 3:1—4:17

Haman Plans to Destroy the Jewish People

3 After these things happened, King Xerxes honored Haman son of Hammedatha the Agagite. He gave him a new rank that was higher than all the important men. ²All the royal officers at the king's gate would bow down and kneel before Haman, as the king had ordered. But Mordecai would not bow down or show him honor.

³Then the royal officers at the king's gate asked Mordecai, "Why don't you obey the king's command?" ⁴And they said this to him every day. When he did not listen to them, they told Haman about it. They wanted to see if Haman would accept Mordecai's behavior because Mordecai had told them he was Jewish.

⁵When Haman saw that Mordecai would not bow down to him or honor him, he became very angry. ⁶He thought of himself as too important to try to kill only Mordecai. He had been told who the people of Mordecai were, so he looked for a way to destroy all of Mordecai's people, the Jews, in all of Xerxes' kingdom.

⁷It was in the first month of the twelfth year of King Xerxes' rule—the month of Nisan. Pur (that is, the lot) was thrown before Haman to choose a day and a month. So the twelfth month, the month of Adar, was chosen.

⁸Then Haman said to King Xerxes, "There is a certain group of people scattered among the other people in all the states of your kingdom. Their customs are different from those of all the other people, and they do not obey the king's laws. It is not right for you to allow them to continue living in your kingdom. ⁹If it pleases the king, let an order be given to destroy those people. Then I will pay seven hundred fifty thousand pounds of silver to those who do the king's business, and they will put it into the royal treasury."

¹⁰So the king took his signet ring off and gave it to Haman son of Hammedatha, the Agagite, the enemy of the Jewish people.

¹¹Then the king said to Haman, "The money and the people are yours. Do with them as you please."

¹²On the thirteenth day of the first month, the royal secretaries were called, and they wrote out all of Haman's orders. They wrote to the king's governors and to the captains of the soldiers in each state and to the important men of each group of people. The orders were written in the writing of each state and in the language of each people. They were written in the name of King Xerxes and sealed with his signet ring. ¹³Letters were sent by messengers to all the king's empire ordering them to destroy, kill, and completely wipe out all the Jewish people. That meant young and old, women and little children, too. It was to happen on a single day—the thirteenth day of the twelfth month, which was Adar. And they could take everything the Jewish people owned. ¹⁴A copy of the order was given out as a law in every state so all the people would be ready for that day.

¹⁵The messengers set out, hurried by the king's command, as soon as the order was given in the palace at Susa. The king and Haman sat down to drink, but the city of Susa was in confusion.

Mordecai Asks Esther to Help

4 When Mordecai heard about all that had been done, he tore his clothes, put on rough cloth and ashes, and went out into the city crying loudly and painfully. ²But Mordecai went only as far as the king's gate, because no one was allowed to enter that gate dressed in rough cloth. ³As the king's order reached every area, there was great sadness and loud crying among the Jewish people. They fasted and cried out loud, and many of them lay down on rough cloth and ashes to show how sad they were.

⁴When Esther's servant girls and eunuchs came to her and told her about Mordecai, she was very upset and afraid. She sent clothes for Mordecai to put on instead of the rough cloth, but he would not wear them. ⁵Then Esther called for Hathach, one of the

king's eunuchs chosen by the king to serve her. Esther ordered him to find out what was bothering Mordecai and why.

⁶So Hathach went to Mordecai, who was in the city square in front of the king's gate. ⁷Mordecai told Hathach everything that had happened to him, and he told Hathach about the amount of money Haman had promised to pay into the king's treasury for the killing of the Jewish people. ⁸Mordecai also gave him a copy of the order to kill the Jewish people, which had been given in Susa. He wanted Hathach to show it to Esther and to tell her about it. And Mordecai told him to order Esther to go into the king's presence to beg for mercy and to plead with him for her people.

⁹Hathach went back and reported to Esther everything Mordecai had said. ¹⁰Then Esther told Hathach to tell Mordecai, ¹¹"All the royal officers and people of the royal states know that no man or woman may go to the king in the inner courtyard without being called. There is only one law about this: Anyone who enters must be put to death unless the king holds out his gold scepter. Then that person may live. And I have not been called to go to the king for thirty days."

¹²Esther's message was given to Mordecai. ¹³Then Mordecai sent back word to Esther: "Just because you live in the king's palace, don't think that out of all the Jewish people you alone will escape. ¹⁴If you keep quiet at this time, someone else will help and save the Jewish people, but you and your father's family will all die. And who knows, you may have been chosen queen for just such a time as this."

¹⁵Then Esther sent this answer to Mordecai: ¹⁶"Go and get all the Jewish people in Susa together. For my sake, fast; do not eat or drink for three days, night and day. I and my servant girls will also fast. Then I will go to the king, even though it is against the law, and if I die, I die."

¹⁷So Mordecai went away and did everything Esther had told him to do.

PSALM 89:46–52

⁴⁶Lord, how long will this go on?
    Will you ignore us forever?

How long will your anger burn like a fire?
⁴⁷Remember how short my life is.
    Why did you create us? For nothing?
⁴⁸What person alive will not die?
    Who can escape the grave?   *Selah*

⁴⁹Lord, where is your love from times past,
    which in your loyalty you promised to David?
⁵⁰Lord, remember how they insulted your servant;
    remember how I have suffered the insults of the nations.
⁵¹Lord, remember how your enemies insulted you
    and how they insulted your appointed king wherever he went.

⁵²Praise the Lord forever!
    Amen and amen.

PROVERBS 22:7–8

⁷The rich rule over the poor,
    and borrowers are servants to lenders.

⁸Those who plan evil will receive trouble.
    Their cruel anger will come to an end.

ROMANS 3:1–31

3 So, do Jews have anything that other people do not have? Is there anything special about being circumcised? ²Yes, of course, there is in every way. The most important thing is this: God trusted the Jews with his teachings. ³If some Jews were not faithful to him, will that stop God from doing what he promised? ⁴No! God will continue to be true even when every person is false. As the Scriptures say:

"So you will be shown to be right when you speak,
    and you will win your case."   *Psalm 51:4*

⁵When we do wrong, that shows more clearly that God is right. So can we say that God is wrong to punish us? (I am talking as people might talk.) ⁶No! If God could not punish us, he could not judge the world.

⁷A person might say, "When I lie, it really gives him glory, because my lie shows God's truth. So why am I judged a sinner?" ⁸It would be the same to say, "We should do evil so that good will come." Some people find fault with

us and say we teach this, but they are wrong and deserve the punishment they will receive.

All People Are Guilty

⁹So are we Jews better than others? No! We have already said that Jews and those who are not Jews are all guilty of sin. ¹⁰As the Scriptures say:

"There is no one who always does what
is right,
not even one.
¹¹There is no one who understands.
There is no one who looks to God for
help.
¹²All have turned away.
Together, everyone has become useless.
There is no one who does anything good;
there is not even one."
Psalm 14:1–3
¹³"Their throats are like open graves;
they use their tongues for telling lies."
Psalm 5:9
"Their words are like snake poison."
Psalm 140:3
¹⁴ "Their mouths are full of cursing and
hate."
Psalm 10:7
¹⁵"They are always ready to kill people.
¹⁶ Everywhere they go they cause ruin and
misery.
¹⁷They don't know how to live in peace."
Isaiah 59:7–8
¹⁸ "They have no fear of God."
Psalm 36:1

¹⁹We know that the law's commands are for those who have the law. This stops all excuses and brings the whole world under God's judgment, ²⁰because no one can be made right with God by following the law. The law only shows us our sin.

How God Makes People Right

²¹But God has a way to make people right with him without the law, and he has now shown us that way which the law and the prophets told us about. ²²God makes people right with himself through their faith in Jesus Christ. This is true for all who believe in Christ, because all people are the same: ²³Everyone has sinned and fallen short of God's glorious standard, ²⁴and all need to be made right with God by his grace, which is a free gift. They need to be made free from sin through Jesus Christ. ²⁵God sent him to die in our place to take away our sins. We receive forgiveness through faith in the blood of Jesus' death. This showed that God always does what is right and fair, as in the past when he was patient and did not punish people for their sins. ²⁶And God gave Jesus to show today that he does what is right. God did this so he could judge rightly and so he could make right any person who has faith in Jesus.

²⁷So do we have a reason to brag about ourselves? No! And why not? It is the way of faith that stops all bragging, not the way of trying to obey the law. ²⁸A person is made right with God through faith, not through obeying the law. ²⁹Is God only the God of the Jews? Is he not also the God of those who are not Jews? ³⁰Of course he is, because there is only one God. He will make Jews right with him by their faith, and he will also make those who are not Jews right with him through their faith. ³¹So do we destroy the law by following the way of faith? No! Faith causes us to be what the law truly wants.

AUGUST 2

ESTHER 5:1—6:14

Esther Speaks to the King

5 On the third day Esther put on her royal robes and stood in the inner courtyard of the king's palace, facing the king's hall. The king was sitting on his royal throne in the hall, facing the doorway. ²When the king saw Queen Esther standing in the courtyard, he was pleased. He held out to her the gold scepter that was in his hand, so Esther went forward and touched the end of it.

³The king asked, "What is it, Queen Esther? What do you want to ask me? I will give you as much as half of my kingdom."

⁴Esther answered, "My king, if it pleases

you, come today with Haman to a banquet that I have prepared for you."

⁵Then the king said, "Bring Haman quickly so we may do what Esther asks."

So the king and Haman went to the banquet Esther had prepared for them. ⁶As they were drinking wine, the king said to Esther, "Now, what are you asking for? I will give it to you. What is it you want? I will give you as much as half of my kingdom."

⁷Esther answered, "This is what I want and what I ask for. ⁸My king, if you are pleased with me and if it pleases you, give me what I ask for and do what I want. Come with Haman tomorrow to the banquet I will prepare for you. Then I will answer your question about what I want."

Haman's Plans Against Mordecai

⁹Haman left the king's palace that day happy and content. But when he saw Mordecai at the king's gate and saw that Mordecai did not stand up or tremble with fear before him, Haman became very angry with Mordecai. ¹⁰But he controlled his anger and went home.

Then Haman called together his friends and his wife, Zeresh. ¹¹He told them how wealthy he was and how many sons he had. He also told them all the ways the king had honored him and how the king had placed him higher than his important men and his royal officers. ¹²He also said, "I'm the only person Queen Esther invited to come with the king to the banquet she gave. And tomorrow also the queen has asked me to be her guest with the king. ¹³But all this does not really make me happy when I see that Jew Mordecai sitting at the king's gate."

¹⁴Then Haman's wife, Zeresh, and all his friends said, "Have a seventy-five foot platform built, and in the morning ask the king to have Mordecai hanged on it. Then go to the banquet with the king and be happy." Haman liked this suggestion, so he ordered the platform to be built.

Mordecai Is Honored

6That same night the king could not sleep. So he gave an order for the daily court record to be brought in and read to him. ²It was found recorded that Mordecai had

warned the king about Bigthana and Teresh, two of the king's officers who guarded the doorway and who had planned to kill the king.

³The king asked, "What honor and reward have been given to Mordecai for this?"

The king's personal servants answered, "Nothing has been done for Mordecai."

⁴The king said, "Who is in the courtyard?" Now Haman had just entered the outer court of the king's palace. He had come to ask the king about hanging Mordecai on the platform he had prepared.

⁵The king's personal servants said, "Haman is standing in the courtyard."

The king said, "Bring him in."

⁶So Haman came in. And the king asked him, "What should be done for a man whom the king wants very much to honor?"

And Haman thought to himself, "Whom would the king want to honor more than me?" ⁷So he answered the king, "This is what you could do for the man you want very much to honor. ⁸Have the servants bring a royal robe that the king himself has worn. And also bring a horse with a royal crown on its head, a horse that the king himself has ridden. ⁹Let the robe and the horse be given to one of the king's most important men. Let the servants put the robe on the man the king wants to honor, and let them lead him on the horse through the city streets. As they are leading him, let them announce: 'This is what is done for the man whom the king wants to honor!'"

¹⁰The king commanded Haman, "Go quickly. Take the robe and the horse just as you have said, and do all this for Mordecai the Jew who sits at the king's gate. Do not leave out anything you have suggested."

¹¹So Haman took the robe and the horse, and he put the robe on Mordecai. Then he led him on horseback through the city streets, announcing before Mordecai: "This is what is done for the man whom the king wants to honor!"

¹²Then Mordecai returned to the king's gate, but Haman hurried home with his head covered, because he was embarrassed and ashamed. ¹³He told his wife, Zeresh, and all his friends everything that had happened to him.

Haman's wife and the men who gave him advice said, "You are starting to lose power to Mordecai. Since he is a Jew, you cannot win against him. You will surely be ruined." [14]While they were still talking, the king's eunuchs came to Haman's house and made him hurry to the banquet Esther had prepared.

PSALM 90:1–6

God Is Eternal, and We Are Not

A prayer of Moses, the man of God.

90 Lord, you have been our home
    since the beginning.
[2]Before the mountains were born
    and before you created the earth and
        the world,
    you are God.
    You have always been, and you will
        always be.

[3]You turn people back into dust.
    You say, "Go back into dust, human
        beings."
[4]To you, a thousand years
    is like the passing of a day,
    or like a few hours in the night.
[5]While people sleep, you take their lives.
    They are like grass that grows up in the
        morning.
[6]In the morning they are fresh and new,
    but by evening they dry up and die.

PROVERBS 22:9

[9]Generous people will be blessed,
    because they share their food with the
        poor.

ROMANS 4:1–25

The Example of Abraham

4 So what can we say that Abraham,[n] the father of our people, learned about faith? [2]If Abraham was made right by the things he did, he had a reason to brag. But this is not God's view, [3]because the Scripture says, "Abraham believed God, and God accepted Abraham's faith, and that faith made him right with God."[n]

[4]When people work, their pay is not given as a gift, but as something earned. [5]But people cannot do any work that will make them right with God. So they must trust in him, who makes even evil people right in his sight. Then God accepts their faith, and that makes them right with him. [6]David said the same thing. He said that people are truly blessed when God, without paying attention to their deeds, makes people right with himself.

[7]"Blessed are they
    whose sins are forgiven,
    whose wrongs are pardoned.
[8]Blessed is the person
    whom the Lord does not consider
        guilty."   *Psalm 32:1–2*

[9]Is this blessing only for those who are circumcised or also for those who are not circumcised? We have already said that God accepted Abraham's faith and that faith made him right with God. [10]So how did this happen? Did God accept Abraham before or after he was circumcised? It was before his circumcision. [11]Abraham was circumcised to show that he was right with God through faith before he was circumcised. So Abraham is the father of all those who believe but are not circumcised; he is the father of all believers who are accepted as being right with God. [12]And Abraham is also the father of those who have been circumcised and who live following the faith that our father Abraham had before he was circumcised.

God Keeps His Promise

[13]Abraham[n] and his descendants received the promise that they would get the whole world. He did not receive that promise through the law, but through being right with God by his faith. [14]If people could receive what God promised by following the law, then faith is worthless. And God's promise to Abraham is worthless, [15]because the law can only bring God's anger. But if there is no law, there is nothing to disobey. [16]So people receive God's promise by hav-

---

4:1 Abraham Most respected ancestor of the Jews. Every Jew hoped to see Abraham.   **4:3 "Abraham . . . God."** Quotation from Genesis 15:6.   **4:13 Abraham** Most respected ancestor of the Jews. Every Jew hoped to see Abraham.

ing faith. This happens so the promise can be a free gift. Then all of Abraham's children can have that promise. It is not only for those who live under the law of Moses but for anyone who lives with faith like that of Abraham, who is the father of us all. [17]As it is written in the Scriptures: "I am making you a father of many nations."[n] This is true before God, the God Abraham believed, the God who gives life to the dead and who creates something out of nothing.

[18]There was no hope that Abraham would have children. But Abraham believed God and continued hoping, and so he became the father of many nations. As God told him, "Your descendants also will be too many to count."[n] [19]Abraham was almost a hundred years old,

much past the age for having children, and Sarah could not have children. Abraham thought about all this, but his faith in God did not become weak. [20]He never doubted that God would keep his promise, and he never stopped believing. He grew stronger in his faith and gave praise to God. [21]Abraham felt sure that God was able to do what he had promised. [22]So, "God accepted Abraham's faith, and that faith made him right with God."[n] [23]Those words ("God accepted Abraham's faith") were written not only for Abraham [24]but also for us. God will accept us also because we believe in the One who raised Jesus our Lord from the dead. [25]Jesus was given to die for our sins, and he was raised from the dead to make us right with God.

AUGUST 3

ESTHER 7:1—8:17

Haman Is Hanged

7 So the king and Haman went in to eat with Queen Esther. [2]As they were drinking wine on the second day, the king asked Esther again, "What are you asking for? I will give it to you. What is it you want? I will give you as much as half of my kingdom."

[3]Then Queen Esther answered, "My king, if you are pleased with me, and if it pleases you, let me live. This is what I ask. And let my people live, too. This is what I want. [4]My people and I have been sold to be destroyed, to be killed and completely wiped out. If we had been sold as male and female slaves, I would have kept quiet, because that would not be enough of a problem to bother the king."

[5]Then King Xerxes asked Queen Esther, "Who is he, and where is he? Who has done such a thing?"

[6]Esther said, "Our enemy and foe is this wicked Haman!"

Then Haman was filled with terror before the king and queen. [7]The king was very angry, so he got up, left his wine, and went out

into the palace garden. But Haman stayed inside to beg Queen Esther to save his life. He could see that the king had already decided to kill him.

[8]When the king returned from the palace garden to the banquet hall, he saw Haman falling on the couch where Esther was lying. The king said, "Will he even attack the queen while I am in the house?"

As soon as the king said that, servants came in and covered Haman's face. [9]Harbona, one of the eunuchs there serving the king, said, "Look, a seventy-five foot platform stands near Haman's house. This is the one Haman had prepared for Mordecai, who gave the warning that saved the king."

The king said, "Hang Haman on it!" [10]So they hanged Haman on the platform he had prepared for Mordecai. Then the king was not so angry anymore.

The King Helps the Jewish People

8 That same day King Xerxes gave Queen Esther everything Haman, the enemy of the Jewish people, had left when he died. And Mordecai came in to see the king,

---

4:17 "I . . . nations." Quotation from Genesis 17:5.   **4:18 "Your . . . count."** Quotation from Genesis 15:5.   **4:22 "God . . . God."** Quotation from Genesis 15:6.

because Esther had told the king how he was related to her. ²Then the king took off his signet ring that he had taken back from Haman, and he gave it to Mordecai. Esther put Mordecai in charge of everything Haman left when he died.

³Once again Esther spoke to the king. She fell at the king's feet and cried and begged him to stop the evil plan that Haman the Agagite had planned against the Jews. ⁴The king held out the gold scepter to Esther. So Esther got up and stood in front of him.

⁵She said, "My king, if you are pleased with me, and if it pleases you to do this, if you think it is the right thing to do, and if you are happy with me, let an order be written to cancel the letters Haman wrote. Haman the Agagite sent messages to destroy all the Jewish people in all of your kingdom. ⁶I could not stand to see that terrible thing happen to my people. I could not stand to see my family killed."

⁷King Xerxes answered Queen Esther and Mordecai the Jew, "Because Haman was against the Jewish people, I have given his things to Esther, and my soldiers have hanged him. ⁸Now, in the king's name, write another order to the Jewish people as it seems best to you. Then seal the order with the king's signet ring, because no letter written in the king's name and sealed with his signet ring can be canceled."

⁹At that time the king's secretaries were called. This was the twenty-third day of the third month, which is Sivan. The secretaries wrote out all of Mordecai's orders to the Jews, to the governors, to the captains of the soldiers in each state, and to the important men of the one hundred twenty-seven states that reached from India to Cush. They wrote in the writing of each state and in the language of each people. They also wrote to the Jewish people in their own writing and language. ¹⁰Mordecai wrote orders in the name of King Xerxes and sealed the letters with the king's signet ring. Then he sent the king's orders by messengers on fast horses, horses that were raised just for the king.

¹¹These were the king's orders: The Jewish people in every city have the right to gather together to protect themselves. They may destroy, kill, and completely wipe out the army of any state or people who attack them. And they are to do the same to the women and children of that army. They may also take by force the property of their enemies. ¹²The one day set for the Jewish people to do this in all the empire of King Xerxes was the thirteenth day of the twelfth month, the month of Adar. ¹³A copy of the king's order was to be sent out as a law in every state. It was to be made known to the people of every nation living in the kingdom so the Jewish people would be ready on that set day to strike back at their enemies.

¹⁴The messengers hurried out, riding on the royal horses, because the king commanded those messengers to hurry. And the order was also given in the palace at Susa.

¹⁵Mordecai left the king's presence wearing royal clothes of blue and white and a large gold crown. He also had a purple robe made of the best linen. And the people of Susa shouted for joy. ¹⁶It was a time of happiness, joy, gladness, and honor for the Jewish people. ¹⁷As the king's order went to every state and city, there was joy and gladness among the Jewish people. In every state and city to which the king's order went, they were having feasts and celebrating. And many people through all the empire became Jews, because they were afraid of the Jewish people.

PSALM 90:7–17

⁷We are destroyed by your anger;
    we are terrified by your hot anger.
⁸You have put the evil we have done right
    in front of you;
    you clearly see our secret sins.
⁹All our days pass while you are angry.
    Our years end with a moan.
¹⁰Our lifetime is seventy years
    or, if we are strong, eighty years.
But the years are full of hard work and
    pain.
They pass quickly, and then we are
    gone.
¹¹Who knows the full power of your anger?
    Your anger is as great as our fear of you
    should be.

¹²Teach us how short our lives really are
  so that we may be wise.

¹³LORD, how long before you return
  and show kindness to your servants?
¹⁴Fill us with your love every morning.
  Then we will sing and rejoice all our
  lives.
¹⁵We have seen years of trouble.
  Now give us as much joy as you gave us
  sorrow.
¹⁶Show your servants the wonderful things
  you do;
  show your greatness to their children.
¹⁷Lord our God, treat us well.
  Give us success in what we do;
  yes, give us success in what we do.

PROVERBS 22:10-11

¹⁰Get rid of the one who makes fun of
  wisdom.
  Then fighting, quarrels, and insults will
  stop.
¹¹Whoever loves pure thoughts and kind
  words
  will have even the king as a friend.

ROMANS 5:1-21

Right with God

5 Since we have been made right with God
  by our faith, we have[n] peace with God.
This happened through our Lord Jesus
Christ, ²who through our faith[n] has brought
us into that blessing of God's grace that we
now enjoy. And we are happy because of the
hope we have of sharing God's glory. ³We
also have joy with our troubles, because we
know that these troubles produce patience.
⁴And patience produces character, and character produces hope. ⁵And this hope will
never disappoint us, because God has
poured out his love to fill our hearts. He gave
us his love through the Holy Spirit, whom
God has given to us.

⁶When we were unable to help ourselves,
at the right time, Christ died for us, although
we were living against God. ⁷Very few people
will die to save the life of someone else. Although perhaps for a good person someone
might possibly die. ⁸But God shows his great
love for us in this way: Christ died for us
while we were still sinners.

⁹So through Christ we will surely be saved
from God's anger, because we have been
made right with God by the blood of Christ's
death. ¹⁰While we were God's enemies, he
made us his friends through the death of his
Son. Surely, now that we are his friends, he
will save us through his Son's life. ¹¹And not
only that, but now we are also very happy in
God through our Lord Jesus Christ. Through
him we are now God's friends again.

Adam and Christ Compared

¹²Sin came into the world because of what
one man did, and with sin came death. This
is why everyone must die—because everyone sinned. ¹³Sin was in the world before the
law of Moses, but sin is not counted against
us as breaking a command when there is no
law. ¹⁴But from the time of Adam to the time
of Moses, everyone had to die, even those
who had not sinned by breaking a command, as Adam had.

Adam was like the One who was coming
in the future. ¹⁵But God's free gift is not like
Adam's sin. Many people died because of the
sin of that one man. But the grace from God
was much greater; many people received
God's gift of life by the grace of the one man,
Jesus Christ. ¹⁶After Adam sinned once, he
was judged guilty. But the gift of God is different. God's free gift came after many sins,
and it makes people right with God. ¹⁷One
man sinned, and so death ruled all people
because of that one man. But now those people who accept God's full grace and the great
gift of being made right with him will surely
have true life and rule through the one man,
Jesus Christ.

¹⁸So as one sin of Adam brought the punishment of death to all people, one good act
that Christ did makes all people right with
God. And that brings true life for all. ¹⁹One
man disobeyed God, and many became sinners. In the same way, one man obeyed God,
and many will be made right. ²⁰The law came

5:1 we have Some Greek copies read "let us have." **5:2 through our faith** Some Greek copies do not have this phrase.

to make sin worse. But when sin grew worse, God's grace increased. [21]Sin once used death to rule us, but God gave people more of his grace so that grace could rule by making people right with him. And this brings life forever through Jesus Christ our Lord.

AUGUST 4

ESTHER 9:1—10:3

Victory for the Jewish People

9 The order the king had commanded was to be done on the thirteenth day of the twelfth month, the month of Adar. That was the day the enemies of the Jewish people had hoped to defeat them, but that was changed. So the Jewish people themselves defeated those who hated them. [2]The Jews met in their cities in all the empire of King Xerxes in order to attack those who wanted to harm them. No one was strong enough to fight against them, because all the other people living in the empire were afraid of them. [3]All the important men of the states, the governors, captains of the soldiers, and the king's officers helped the Jewish people, because they were afraid of Mordecai. [4]Mordecai was very important in the king's palace. He was famous in all the empire, because he was becoming a leader of more and more people.

[5]And, with their swords, the Jewish people defeated all their enemies, killing and destroying them. And they did what they wanted with those people who hated them. [6]In the palace at Susa, they killed and destroyed five hundred men. [7]They also killed: Parshandatha, Dalphon, Aspatha, [8]Poratha, Adalia, Aridatha, [9]Parmashta, Arisai, Aridai, and Vaizatha, [10]the ten sons of Haman, son of Hammedatha, the enemy of the Jewish people. But the Jewish people did not take their belongings.

[11]On that day the number killed in the palace at Susa was reported to the king. [12]The king said to Queen Esther, "The Jewish people have killed and destroyed five hundred people in the palace at Susa, and they have also killed Haman's ten sons. What have they done in the rest of the king's empire!

Now what else are you asking? I will do it! What else do you want? It will be done!"

[13]Esther answered, "If it pleases the king, give the Jewish people who are in Susa permission to do again tomorrow what the king ordered for today. And let the bodies of Haman's ten sons be hanged on the platform."

[14]So the king ordered that it be done. A law was given in Susa, and the bodies of the ten sons of Haman were hanged. [15]The Jewish people in Susa came together on the fourteenth day of the month of Adar. They killed three hundred people in Susa, but they did not take their belongings.

[16]At that same time, all the Jewish people in the king's empire also met to protect themselves and get rid of their enemies. They killed seventy-five thousand of those who hated them, but they did not take their belongings. [17]This happened on the thirteenth day of the month of Adar. On the fourteenth day they rested and made it a day of joyful feasting.

The Feast of Purim

[18]But the Jewish people in Susa met on the thirteenth and fourteenth days of the month of Adar. Then they rested on the fifteenth day and made it a day of joyful feasting.

[19]This is why the Jewish people who live in the country and small villages celebrate on the fourteenth day of the month of Adar. It is a day of joyful feasting and a day for exchanging gifts.

[20]Mordecai wrote down everything that had happened. Then he sent letters to all the Jewish people in all the empire of King Xerxes, far and near. [21]He told them to celebrate every year on the fourteenth and fifteenth days of the month of Adar, [22]because

that was when the Jewish people got rid of their enemies. They were also to celebrate it as the month their sadness was turned to joy and their crying for the dead was turned into celebration. He told them to celebrate those days as days of joyful feasting and as a time for giving food to each other and presents to the poor.

²³So the Jewish people agreed to do what Mordecai had written to them, and they agreed to hold the celebration every year. ²⁴Haman son of Hammedatha, the Agagite, was the enemy of all the Jewish people. He had made an evil plan against the Jewish people to destroy them, and he had thrown the Pur (that is, the lot) to choose a day to ruin and destroy them. ²⁵But when the king learned of the evil plan, he sent out written orders that the evil plans Haman had made against the Jewish people would be used against him. And those orders said that Haman and his sons should be hanged on the platform. ²⁶So these days were called Purim, which comes from the word "Pur" (the lot). Because of everything written in this letter and what they had seen and what happened to them, ²⁷the Jewish people set up this custom. They and their descendants and all those who join them are always to celebrate these two days every year. They should do it in the right way and at the time Mordecai had ordered them in the letter. ²⁸These two days should be remembered and celebrated from now on in every family, in every state, and in every city. These days of Purim should always be celebrated by the Jewish people, and their descendants should always remember to celebrate them, too.

²⁹So Queen Esther daughter of Abihail, along with Mordecai the Jew, wrote this second letter about Purim. Using the power they had, they wrote to prove the first letter was true. ³⁰And Mordecai sent letters to all the Jewish people in the one hundred twenty-seven states of the kingdom of Xerxes, writing them a message of peace and truth. ³¹He wrote to set up these days of Purim at the chosen times. Mordecai the Jew and Queen Esther had sent out the order for the Jewish people, just as they had set up things for themselves and their descendants:

On these two days the people should fast and cry loudly. ³²Esther's letter set up the rules for Purim, and they were written down in the records.

The Greatness of Mordecai

10 King Xerxes demanded taxes everywhere, even from the cities on the seacoast. ²And all the great things Xerxes did by his power and strength are written in the record books of the kings of Media and Persia. Also written in those record books are all the things done by Mordecai, whom the king made great. ³Mordecai the Jew was second in importance to King Xerxes, and he was the most important man among the Jewish people. His fellow Jews respected him very much, because he worked for the good of his people and spoke up for the safety of all the Jewish people.

PSALM 91:1–8

Safe in the Lord

91 Those who go to God Most High for safety
will be protected by the Almighty.
²I will say to the LORD, "You are my place of safety and protection.
You are my God and I trust you."

³God will save you from hidden traps
and from deadly diseases.
⁴He will cover you with his feathers,
and under his wings you can hide.
His truth will be your shield and protection.
⁵You will not fear any danger by night
or an arrow during the day.
⁶You will not be afraid of diseases that come in the dark
or sickness that strikes at noon.
⁷At your side one thousand people may die,
or even ten thousand right beside you,
but you will not be hurt.
⁸You will only watch
and see the wicked punished.

PROVERBS 22:12

¹²The LORD guards knowledge,
but he destroys false words.

ROMANS 6:1—23

Dead to Sin but Alive in Christ

6 So do you think we should continue sinning so that God will give us even more grace? ²No! We died to our old sinful lives, so how can we continue living with sin? ³Did you forget that all of us became part of Christ when we were baptized? We shared his death in our baptism. ⁴When we were baptized, we were buried with Christ and shared his death. So, just as Christ was raised from the dead by the wonderful power of the Father, we also can live a new life.

⁵Christ died, and we have been joined with him by dying too. So we will also be joined with him by rising from the dead as he did. ⁶We know that our old life died with Christ on the cross so that our sinful selves would have no power over us and we would not be slaves to sin. ⁷Anyone who has died is made free from sin's control.

⁸If we died with Christ, we know we will also live with him. ⁹Christ was raised from the dead, and we know that he cannot die again. Death has no power over him now. ¹⁰Yes, when Christ died, he died to defeat the power of sin one time—enough for all time. He now has a new life, and his new life is with God. ¹¹In the same way, you should see yourselves as being dead to the power of sin and alive with God through Christ Jesus.

¹²So, do not let sin control your life here on earth so that you do what your sinful self wants to do. ¹³Do not offer the parts of your body to serve sin, as things to be used in doing evil. Instead, offer yourselves to God as people who have died and now live. Offer the parts of your body to God to be used in doing good. ¹⁴Sin will not be your master, because you are not under law but under God's grace.

Be Slaves of Righteousness

¹⁵So what should we do? Should we sin because we are under grace and not under law? No! ¹⁶Surely you know that when you give yourselves like slaves to obey someone, then you are really slaves of that person. The person you obey is your master. You can follow sin, which brings spiritual death, or you can obey God, which makes you right with him. ¹⁷In the past you were slaves to sin— sin controlled you. But thank God, you fully obeyed the things that you were taught. ¹⁸You were made free from sin, and now you are slaves to goodness. ¹⁹I use this example because this is hard for you to understand. In the past you offered the parts of your body to be slaves to sin and evil; you lived only for evil. In the same way now you must give yourselves to be slaves of goodness. Then you will live only for God.

²⁰In the past you were slaves to sin, and goodness did not control you. ²¹You did evil things, and now you are ashamed of them. Those things only bring death. ²²But now you are free from sin and have become slaves of God. This brings you a life that is only for God, and this gives you life forever. ²³The payment for sin is death. But God gives us the free gift of life forever in Christ Jesus our Lord.

AUGUST 5

JOB 1:1—2:13

Job, the Good Man

1 A man named Job lived in the land of Uz. He was an honest and innocent man; he honored God and stayed away from evil. ²Job had seven sons and three daughters. ³He owned seven thousand sheep, three thousand camels, five hundred teams of oxen, and five hundred female donkeys. He also had a large number of servants. He was the greatest man among all the people of the East.

⁴Job's sons took turns holding feasts in their homes and invited their sisters to eat and drink with them. ⁵After a feast was over, Job would send and have them made clean. Early in the morning Job would offer a burnt

offering for each of them, because he thought, "My children may have sinned and cursed God in their hearts." Job did this every time.

Satan Appears Before the Lord

⁶One day the angels came to show themselves before the LORD, and Satan*ⁿ* was with them. ⁷The LORD said to Satan, "Where have you come from?"

Satan answered the LORD, "I have been wandering around the earth, going back and forth in it."

⁸Then the LORD said to Satan, "Have you noticed my servant Job? No one else on earth is like him. He is an honest and innocent man, honoring God and staying away from evil."

⁹But Satan answered the LORD, "Job honors God for a good reason. ¹⁰You have put a wall around him, his family, and everything he owns. You have blessed the things he has done. His flocks and herds are so large they almost cover the land. ¹¹But reach out your hand and destroy everything he has, and he will curse you to your face."

¹²The LORD said to Satan, "All right, then. Everything Job has is in your power, but you must not touch Job himself." Then Satan left the LORD's presence.

¹³One day Job's sons and daughters were eating and drinking wine together at the oldest brother's house. ¹⁴A messenger came to Job and said, "The oxen were plowing and the donkeys were eating grass nearby, ¹⁵when the Sabeans attacked and carried them away. They killed the servants with swords, and I am the only one who escaped to tell you!"

¹⁶The messenger was still speaking when another messenger arrived and said, "Lightning from God fell from the sky. It burned up the sheep and the servants, and I am the only one who escaped to tell you!"

¹⁷The second messenger was still speaking when another messenger arrived and said, "The Babylonians sent three groups of attackers that swept down and stole your camels and killed the servants. I am the only one who escaped to tell you!"

¹⁸The third messenger was still speaking when another messenger arrived and said, "Your sons and daughters were eating and drinking wine together at the oldest brother's house. ¹⁹Suddenly a great wind came from the desert, hitting all four corners of the house at once. The house fell in on the young people, and they are all dead. I am the only one who escaped to tell you!"

²⁰When Job heard this, he got up and tore his robe and shaved his head to show how sad he was. Then he bowed down to the ground to worship God. ²¹He said:

"I was naked when I was born,
    and I will be naked when I die.
The LORD gave these things to me,
    and he has taken them away.
    Praise the name of the LORD."

²²In all this Job did not sin or blame God.

Satan Appears Before the Lord Again

2 On another day the angels came to show themselves before the LORD, and Satan was with them again. ²The LORD said to Satan, "Where have you come from?"

Satan answered the LORD, "I have been wandering around the earth, going back and forth in it."

³Then the LORD said to Satan, "Have you noticed my servant Job? No one else on earth is like him. He is an honest and innocent man, honoring God and staying away from evil. You caused me to ruin him for no good reason, but he continues to be without blame."

⁴"One skin for another!" Satan answered. "A man will give all he has to save his own life. ⁵But reach out your hand and destroy his flesh and bones, and he will curse you to your face."

⁶The LORD said to Satan, "All right, then. Job is in your power, but you may not take his life."

⁷So Satan left the LORD's presence. He put painful sores on Job's body, from the top of his head to the soles of his feet. ⁸Job took a piece of broken pottery to scrape himself, and he sat in ashes in misery.

⁹Job's wife said to him, "Why are you trying to stay innocent? Curse God and die!"

1:6 Satan Or "the accuser."

[10]Job answered, "You are talking like a foolish woman. Should we take only good things from God and not trouble?" In spite of all this Job did not sin in what he said.

Job's Three Friends Come to Help

[11]Now Job had three friends: Eliphaz the Temanite, Bildad the Shuhite, and Zophar the Naamathite. When these friends heard about Job's troubles, they agreed to meet and visit him. They wanted to show their concern and to comfort him. [12]They saw Job from far away, but he looked so different they almost didn't recognize him. They began to cry loudly and tore their robes and put dirt on their heads to show how sad they were. [13]Then they sat on the ground with Job seven days and seven nights. No one said a word to him because they saw how much he was suffering.

PSALM 91:9–13

[9]The LORD is your protection;
   you have made God Most High your
      place of safety.
[10]Nothing bad will happen to you;
   no disaster will come to your home.
[11]He has put his angels in charge of you
   to watch over you wherever you go.
[12]They will catch you in their hands
   so that you will not hit your foot on a
      rock.
[13]You will walk on lions and cobras;
   you will step on strong lions and snakes.

PROVERBS 22:13–14

[13]The lazy person says, "There's a lion
      outside!
   I might get killed out in the street!"

[14]The words of an unfaithful wife are like a
      deep trap.
   Those who make the LORD angry will
      get caught by them.

ROMANS 7:1–25

An Example from Marriage

7 Brothers and sisters, all of you understand the law of Moses. So surely you know that the law rules over people only while they are alive. [2]For example, a woman must stay married to her husband as long as he is alive. But if her husband dies, she is free from the law of marriage. [3]But if she marries another man while her husband is still alive, the law says she is guilty of adultery. But if her husband dies, she is free from the law of marriage. Then if she marries another man, she is not guilty of adultery.

[4]In the same way, my brothers and sisters, your old selves died, and you became free from the law through the body of Christ. This happened so that you might belong to someone else—the One who was raised from the dead—and so that we might be used in service to God. [5]In the past, we were ruled by our sinful selves. The law made us want to do sinful things that controlled our bodies, so the things we did were bringing us death. [6]In the past, the law held us like prisoners, but our old selves died, and we were made free from the law. So now we serve God in a new way with the Spirit, and not in the old way with written rules.

Our Fight Against Sin

[7]You might think I am saying that sin and the law are the same thing. That is not true. But the law was the only way I could learn what sin meant. I would never have known what it means to want to take something belonging to someone else if the law had not said, "You must not want to take your neighbor's things."[n] [8]And sin found a way to use that command and cause me to want all kinds of things I should not want. But without the law, sin has no power. [9]I was alive before I knew the law. But when the law's command came to me, then sin began to live, [10]and I died. The command was meant to bring life, but for me it brought death. [11]Sin found a way to fool me by using the command to make me die.

[12]So the law is holy, and the command is holy and right and good. [13]Does this mean that something that is good brought death to me? No! Sin used something that is good to bring death to me. This happened so that I could see what sin is really like; the command was used to show that sin is very evil.

7:7 "You . . . things." Quotation from Exodus 20:17.

The War Within Us

¹⁴We know that the law is spiritual, but I am not spiritual since sin rules me as if I were its slave. ¹⁵I do not understand the things I do. I do not do what I want to do, and I do the things I hate. ¹⁶And if I do not want to do the hated things I do, that means I agree that the law is good. ¹⁷But I am not really the one who is doing these hated things; it is sin living in me that does them. ¹⁸Yes, I know that nothing good lives in me—I mean nothing good lives in the part of me that is earthly and sinful. I want to do the things that are good, but I do not do them. ¹⁹I do not do the good things I want to do, but I do the bad things I do not want to do. ²⁰So if I do things I do not want to do, then I am not the one doing them. It is sin living in me that does those things.

²¹So I have learned this rule: When I want to do good, evil is there with me. ²²In my mind, I am happy with God's law. ²³But I see another law working in my body, which makes war against the law that my mind accepts. That other law working in my body is the law of sin, and it makes me its prisoner. ²⁴What a miserable man I am! Who will save me from this body that brings me death? ²⁵I thank God for saving me through Jesus Christ our Lord!

So in my mind I am a slave to God's law, but in my sinful self I am a slave to the law of sin.

AUGUST 6

JOB 3:1—4:21

Job Curses His Birth

3 After seven days Job cried out and cursed the day he had been born, ²saying:

³"Let the day I was born be destroyed,
and the night it was said, 'A boy is born!'
⁴Let that day turn to darkness.
Don't let God care about it.
Don't let light shine on it.
⁵Let darkness and gloom have that day.
Let a cloud hide it.
Let thick darkness cover its light.
⁶Let thick darkness capture that night.
Don't count it among the days of the year
or put it in any of the months.
⁷Let that night be empty,
with no shout of joy to be heard.
⁸Let those who curse days curse that day.
Let them prepare to wake up the sea
monster Leviathan.
⁹Let that day's morning stars never appear;
let it wait for daylight that never comes.
Don't let it see the first light of dawn,
¹⁰because it allowed me to be born
and did not hide trouble from my eyes.

¹¹"Why didn't I die as soon as I was born?
Why didn't I die when I came out of the
womb?
¹²Why did my mother's knees receive me,
and my mother's breasts feed me?
¹³If they had not been there,
I would be lying dead in peace;
I would be asleep and at rest
¹⁴with kings and wise men of the earth
who built places for themselves that are
now ruined.
¹⁵I would be asleep with rulers
who filled their houses with gold and
silver.
¹⁶Why was I not buried like a child born
dead,
like a baby who never saw the light of
day?
¹⁷In the grave the wicked stop making
trouble,
and the weary workers are at rest.
¹⁸In the grave there is rest for the
captives
who no longer hear the shout of the
slave driver.
¹⁹People great and small are in the grave,
and the slave is freed from his master.

²⁰"Why is light given to those in misery?
Why is life given to those who are so
unhappy?
²¹They want to die, but death does not
come.

They search for death more than for
hidden treasure.
²²They are very happy
when they get to the grave.
²³They cannot see where they are going.
God has hidden the road ahead.
²⁴I make sad sounds as I eat;
my groans pour out like water.
²⁵Everything I feared and dreaded
has happened to me.
²⁶I have no peace or quietness.
I have no rest, only trouble."

Eliphaz Speaks

4 Then Eliphaz the Temanite answered:
²"If someone tried to speak with you,
would you be upset?
I cannot keep from speaking.
³Think about the many people you have
taught
and the weak hands you have made
strong.
⁴Your words have comforted those who
fell,
and you have strengthened those who
could not stand.
⁵But now trouble comes to you, and you
are discouraged;
trouble hits you, and you are terrified.
⁶You should have confidence because you
respect God;
you should have hope because you are
innocent.

⁷"Remember that the innocent will not die;
honest people will never be destroyed.
⁸I have noticed that people who plow evil
and plant trouble, harvest it.
⁹God's breath destroys them,
and a blast of his anger kills them.
¹⁰Lions may roar and growl,
but when the teeth of a strong lion are
broken,
¹¹that lion dies of hunger.
The cubs of the mother lion are
scattered.

¹²"A word was brought to me in secret,
and my ears heard a whisper of it.

¹³It was during a nightmare
when people are in deep sleep.
¹⁴I was trembling with fear;
all my bones were shaking.
¹⁵A spirit glided past my face,
and the hair on my body stood on end.
¹⁶The spirit stopped,
but I could not see what it was.
A shape stood before my eyes,
and I heard a quiet voice.
¹⁷It said, 'Can a human be more right than
God?
Can a person be pure before his maker?
¹⁸God does not trust his angels;
he blames them for mistakes.
¹⁹So he puts even more blame on people
who live in clay houses,ⁿ
whose foundations are made of dust,
who can be crushed like a moth.
²⁰Between dawn and sunset many people
are broken to pieces;
without being noticed, they die and are
gone forever.
²¹The ropes of their tents are pulled up,
and they die without wisdom.'

PSALM 91:14–16

¹⁴The LORD says, "Whoever loves me, I will
save.
I will protect those who know me.
¹⁵They will call to me, and I will answer
them.
I will be with them in trouble;
I will rescue them and honor them.
¹⁶I will give them a long, full life,
and they will see how I can save."

PROVERBS 22:15

¹⁵Every child is full of foolishness,
but punishment can get rid of it.

ROMANS 8:1–17

Be Ruled by the Spirit

8 So now, those who are in Christ Jesus are
not judged guilty.ⁿ ²Through Christ Jesus
the law of the Spirit that brings life made

4:19 clay houses This is probably talking about people's bodies. • **8:1 guilty** Some Greek copies continue, "those who
do not live in the power of their sinful selves, but in the power of the Spirit."

you[n] free from the law that brings sin and death. [3]The law was without power, because the law was made weak by our sinful selves. But God did what the law could not do. He sent his own Son to earth with the same human life that others use for sin. By sending his Son to be an offering for sin, God used a human life to destroy sin. [4]He did this so that we could be the kind of people the law correctly wants us to be. Now we do not live following our sinful selves, but we live following the Spirit.

[5]Those who live following their sinful selves think only about things that their sinful selves want. But those who live following the Spirit are thinking about the things the Spirit wants them to do. [6]If people's thinking is controlled by the sinful self, there is death. But if their thinking is controlled by the Spirit, there is life and peace. [7]When people's thinking is controlled by the sinful self, they are against God, because they refuse to obey God's law and really are not even able to obey God's law. [8]Those people who are ruled by their sinful selves cannot please God.

[9]But you are not ruled by your sinful selves. You are ruled by the Spirit, if that Spirit of God really lives in you. But the person who does not have the Spirit of Christ does not belong to Christ. [10]Your body will always be dead because of sin. But if Christ is in you, then the Spirit gives you life, because Christ made you right with God. [11]God raised Jesus from the dead, and if God's Spirit is living in you, he will also give life to your bodies that die. God is the One who raised Christ from the dead, and he will give life through[n] his Spirit that lives in you.

[12]So, my brothers and sisters, we must not be ruled by our sinful selves or live the way our sinful selves want. [13]If you use your lives to do the wrong things your sinful selves want, you will die spiritually. But if you use the Spirit's help to stop doing the wrong things you do with your body, you will have true life.

[14]The true children of God are those who let God's Spirit lead them. [15]The Spirit we received does not make us slaves again to fear; it makes us children of God. With that Spirit we cry out, "Father."[n] [16]And the Spirit himself joins with our spirits to say we are God's children. [17]If we are God's children, we will receive blessings from God together with Christ. But we must suffer as Christ suffered so that we will have glory as Christ has glory.

AUGUST 7

JOB 5:1—6:30

5 "Call if you want to, Job, but no one will answer you.
You can't turn to any of the holy ones.
[2]Anger kills the fool,
and jealousy slays the stupid.
[3]I have seen a fool succeed,
but I cursed his home immediately.
[4]His children are far from safety
and are crushed in court with no defense.
[5]The hungry eat his harvest,
even taking what grew among the thorns,

and thirsty people want his wealth.
[6]Hard times do not come up from the ground,
and trouble does not grow from the earth.
[7]People produce trouble
as surely as sparks fly upward.

[8]"But if I were you, I would call on God
and bring my problem before him.
[9]God does wonders that cannot be understood;
he does so many miracles they cannot be counted.

[10]He gives rain to the earth
and sends water on the fields.
[11]He makes the humble person important
and lifts the sad to places of safety.
[12]He ruins the plans of those who trick
others
so they have no success.
[13]He catches the wise in their own clever
traps
and sweeps away the plans of those
who try to trick others.
[14]Darkness covers them up in the daytime;
even at noon they feel around in the dark.
[15]God saves the needy from their lies
and from the harm done by powerful
people.
[16]So the poor have hope,
while those who are unfair are silenced.

[17]"The one whom God corrects is happy,
so do not hate being corrected by the
Almighty.
[18]God hurts, but he also bandages up;
he injures, but his hands also heal.
[19]He will save you from six troubles;
even seven troubles will not harm you.
[20]God will buy you back from death in
times of hunger,
and in battle he will save you from the
sword.
[21]You will be protected from the tongue
that strikes like a whip,
and you will not be afraid when
destruction comes.
[22]You will laugh at destruction and hunger,
and you will not fear the wild animals,
[23]because you will have an agreement with
the stones in the field,
and the wild animals will be at peace
with you.
[24]You will know that your tent is safe,
because you will check the things you
own and find nothing missing.
[25]You will know that you will have many
children,
and your descendants will be like the
grass on the earth.
[26]You will come to the grave with all your
strength,
like bundles of grain gathered at the
right time.

[27]"We have checked this, and it is true,
so hear it and decide what it means to
you."

Job Answers Eliphaz

6 Then Job answered:
[2]"I wish my suffering could be weighed
and my misery put on scales.
[3]My sadness would be heavier than the
sand of the seas.
No wonder my words seem careless.
[4]The arrows of the Almighty are in me;
my spirit drinks in their poison;
God's terrors are gathered against me.
[5]A wild donkey does not bray when it has
grass to eat,
and an ox is quiet when it has feed.
[6]Tasteless food is not eaten without salt,
and there is no flavor in the white of an
egg.
[7]I refuse to touch it;
such food makes me sick.

[8]"How I wish that I might have what I ask
for
and that God would give me what I
hope for.
[9]How I wish God would crush me
and reach out his hand to destroy me.
[10]Then I would have this comfort
and be glad even in this unending pain,
because I would know I did not reject
the words of the Holy One.

[11]"I do not have the strength to wait.
There is nothing to hope for,
so why should I be patient?
[12]I do not have the strength of stone;
my flesh is not bronze.
[13]I have no power to help myself,
because success has been taken away
from me.

[14]"They say, 'A person's friends should be
kind to him when he is in trouble,
even if he stops fearing the Almighty.'
[15]But my brothers cannot be counted on.
They are like streams that do not
always flow,
streams that sometimes run over.
[16]They are made dark by melting ice
and rise with melting snow.
[17]But they stop flowing in the dry season;

they disappear when it is hot.
¹⁸Travelers turn away from their paths
and go into the desert and die.
¹⁹The groups of travelers from Tema look
for water,
and the traders of Sheba look hopefully.
²⁰They are upset because they had been
sure;
when they arrive, they are disappointed.
²¹You also have been no help.
You see something terrible, and you are
afraid.
²²I have never said, 'Give me a gift.
Use your wealth to pay my debt.
²³Save me from the enemy's power.
Buy me back from the clutches of cruel
people.'

²⁴"Teach me, and I will be quiet.
Show me where I have been wrong.
²⁵Honest words are painful,
but your arguments prove nothing.
²⁶Do you mean to correct what I say?
Will you treat the words of a troubled
man as if they were only wind?
²⁷You would even gamble for orphans
and would trade away your friend.

²⁸"But now please look at me.
I would not lie to your face.
²⁹Change your mind; do not be unfair;
think again, because my innocence is
being questioned.
³⁰What I am saying is not wicked;
I can tell the difference between right
and wrong.

PSALM 92:1–8

Thanksgiving for God's Goodness

A psalm. A song for the Sabbath day.

92 It is good to praise you, LORD,
to sing praises to God Most High.
²It is good to tell of your love in the
morning
and of your loyalty at night.
³It is good to praise you with the
ten-stringed lyre
and with the soft-sounding harp.

⁴LORD, you have made me happy by what
you have done;

I will sing for joy about what your
hands have done.
⁵LORD, you have done such great things!
How deep are your thoughts!
⁶Stupid people don't know these things,
and fools don't understand.
⁷Wicked people grow like the grass.
Evil people seem to do well,
but they will be destroyed forever.
⁸But, LORD, you will be honored forever.

PROVERBS 22:16

¹⁶Whoever gets rich by mistreating the
poor,
and gives presents to the wealthy, will
become poor.

ROMANS 8:18–39

Our Future Glory

¹⁸The sufferings we have now are nothing compared to the great glory that will be shown to us. ¹⁹Everything God made is waiting with excitement for God to show his children's glory completely. ²⁰Everything God made was changed to become useless, not by its own wish but because God wanted it and because all along there was this hope: ²¹that everything God made would be set free from ruin to have the freedom and glory that belong to God's children.

²²We know that everything God made has been waiting until now in pain, like a woman ready to give birth. ²³Not only the world, but we also have been waiting with pain inside us. We have the Spirit as the first part of God's promise. So we are waiting for God to finish making us his own children, which means our bodies will be made free. ²⁴We were saved, and we have this hope. If we see what we are waiting for, that is not really hope. People do not hope for something they already have. ²⁵But we are hoping for something we do not have yet, and we are waiting for it patiently.

²⁶Also, the Spirit helps us with our weakness. We do not know how to pray as we should. But the Spirit himself speaks to God for us, even begs God for us with deep feelings that words cannot explain. ²⁷God can see what is in people's hearts. And he knows

what is in the mind of the Spirit, because the Spirit speaks to God for his people in the way God wants.

[28]We know that in everything God works for the good of those who love him.[n] They are the people he called, because that was his plan. [29]God knew them before he made the world, and he chose them to be like his Son so that Jesus would be the firstborn[n] of many brothers and sisters. [30]God planned for them to be like his Son; and those he planned to be like his Son, he also called; and those he called, he also made right with him; and those he made right, he also glorified.

God's Love in Christ Jesus

[31]So what should we say about this? If God is for us, no one can defeat us. [32]He did not spare his own Son but gave him for us all. So with Jesus, God will surely give us all things. [33]Who can accuse the people God has chosen? No one, because God is the One who makes them right. [34]Who can say God's people are guilty? No one, because Christ Jesus died, but he was also raised from the dead, and now he is on God's right side, appealing to God for us. [35]Can anything separate us from the love Christ has for us? Can troubles or problems or sufferings or hunger or nakedness or danger or violent death? [36]As it is written in the Scriptures:

"For you we are in danger of death all
the time.
People think we are worth no more
than sheep to be killed." *Psalm 44:22*

[37]But in all these things we are completely victorious through God who showed his love for us. [38]Yes, I am sure that neither death, nor life, nor angels, nor ruling spirits, nothing now, nothing in the future, no powers, [39]nothing above us, nothing below us, nor anything else in the whole world will ever be able to separate us from the love of God that is in Christ Jesus our Lord.

AUGUST 8

JOB 7:1—8:22

7 "People have a hard task on earth,
and their days are like those of a
laborer.
[2]They are like a slave wishing for the
evening shadows,
like a laborer waiting to be paid.
[3]But I am given months that are empty,
and nights of misery have been given
to me.
[4]When I lie down, I think, 'How long until
I get up?'
The night is long, and I toss until dawn.
[5]My body is covered with worms and
scabs,
and my skin is broken and full of sores.

[6]"My days go by faster than a weaver's
tool,
and they come to an end without hope.

[7]Remember, God, that my life is only a
breath.
My eyes will never see happy times
again.
[8]Those who see me now will see me no
more;
you will look for me, but I will be gone.
[9]As a cloud disappears and is gone,
people go to the grave and never return.
[10]They will never come back to their
houses again,
and their places will not know them
anymore.

[11]"So I will not stay quiet;
I will speak out in the suffering of my
spirit.
I will complain because I am so
unhappy.
[12]I am not the sea or the sea monster.
So why have you set a guard over me?

8:28 We . . . him. Some Greek copies read "We know that everything works together for good for those who love God."
8:29 firstborn Here this probably means that Christ was the first in God's family to share God's glory.

¹³Sometimes I think my bed will comfort me
    or that my couch will stop my complaint.
¹⁴Then you frighten me with dreams
    and terrify me with visions.
¹⁵My throat prefers to be choked;
    my bones welcome death.
¹⁶I hate my life; I don't want to live forever.
    Leave me alone, because my days have no meaning.

¹⁷"Why do you make people so important
    and give them so much attention?
¹⁸You examine them every morning
    and test them every moment.
¹⁹Will you never look away from me
    or leave me alone even long enough to swallow?
²⁰If I have sinned, what have I done to you,
    you watcher of humans?
    Why have you made me your target?
    Have I become a heavy load for you?
²¹Why don't you pardon my wrongs
    and forgive my sins?
    I will soon lie down in the dust of death.
    Then you will search for me, but I will be no more."

Bildad Speaks to Job

8 Then Bildad the Shuhite answered:
²"How long will you say such things?
    Your words are no more than wind.
³God does not twist justice;
    the Almighty does not make wrong what is right.
⁴Your children sinned against God,
    and he punished them for their sins.
⁵But you should ask God for help
    and pray to the Almighty for mercy.
⁶If you are good and honest,
    he will stand up for you
    and bring you back where you belong.
⁷Where you began will seem unimportant,
    because your future will be so successful.

⁸"Ask old people;
    find out what their ancestors learned,
⁹because we were only born yesterday and know nothing.
    Our days on earth are only a shadow.

¹⁰Those people will teach you and tell you
    and speak about what they know.
¹¹Papyrus plants cannot grow where there is no swamp,
    and reeds cannot grow tall without water.
¹²While they are still growing and not yet cut,
    they will dry up quicker than grass.
¹³That is what will happen to those who forget God;
    the hope of the wicked will be gone.
¹⁴What they hope in is easily broken;
    what they trust is like a spider's web.
¹⁵They lean on the spider's web, but it breaks.
    They grab it, but it does not hold up.
¹⁶They are like well-watered plants in the sunshine
    that spread their roots all through the garden.
¹⁷They wrap their roots around a pile of rocks
    and look for a place among the stones.
¹⁸But if a plant is torn from its place,
    then that place rejects it and says, 'I never saw you.'
¹⁹Now joy has gone away;
    other plants grow up from the same dirt.

²⁰"Surely God does not reject the innocent
    or give strength to those who do evil.
²¹God will yet fill your mouth with laughter
    and your lips with shouts of joy.
²²Your enemies will be covered with shame,
    and the tents of the wicked will be gone."

PSALM 92:9–15

⁹LORD, surely your enemies,
    surely your enemies will be destroyed,
    and all who do evil will be scattered.
¹⁰But you have made me as strong as an ox.
    You have poured fine oils on me.
¹¹When I looked, I saw my enemies;

I heard the cries of those who are
against me.

^{12}But good people will grow like palm trees;
they will be tall like the cedars of
Lebanon.
^{13}Like trees planted in the Temple of the
LORD,
they will grow strong in the courtyards
of our God.
^{14}When they are old, they will still produce
fruit;
they will be healthy and fresh.
^{15}They will say that the LORD is good.
He is my Rock, and there is no wrong
in him.

PROVERBS 22:17–21

Other Wise Sayings

^{17}Listen carefully to what wise people say;
pay attention to what I am teaching you.
^{18}It will be good to keep these things in
mind
so that you are ready to repeat them.
^{19}I am teaching them to you now
so that you will put your trust in the
LORD.
^{20}I have written thirty sayings for you,
which give knowledge and good advice.
^{21}I am teaching you true and reliable words
so that you can give true answers to
anyone who asks.

ROMANS 9:1–18

God and the Jewish People

9 I am in Christ, and I am telling you the
truth; I do not lie. My conscience is ruled
by the Holy Spirit, and it tells me I am not lying. ^{2}I have great sorrow and always feel much
sadness. ^{3}I wish I could help my Jewish brothers and sisters, my people. I would even wish
that I were cursed and cut off from Christ if
that would help them. ^{4}They are the people of
Israel, God's chosen children. They have seen
the glory of God, and they have the agree-

ments that God made between himself and
his people. God gave them the law of Moses
and the right way of worship and his promises. ^{5}They are the descendants of our great
ancestors, and they are the earthly family into
which Christ was born, who is God over all.
Praise him forever!^{n} Amen.

^{6}It is not that God failed to keep his promise to them. But only some of the people of Israel are truly God's people,^{n} ^{7}and only some of
Abraham's^n descendants are true children of
Abraham. But God said to Abraham: "The descendants I promised you will be from
Isaac."^{n} ^{8}This means that not all of Abraham's
descendants are God's true children. Abraham's true children are those who become
God's children because of the promise God
made to Abraham. ^{9}God's promise to Abraham was this: "At the right time I will return,
and Sarah will have a son."^{n} ^{10}And that is not
all. Rebekah's sons had the same father, our
father Isaac. $^{11-12}$But before the two boys were
born, God told Rebekah, "The older will serve
the younger."^{n} This was before the boys had
done anything good or bad. God said this so
that the one chosen would be chosen because
of God's own plan. He was chosen because he
was the one God wanted to call, not because
of anything he did. ^{13}As the Scripture says, "I
loved Jacob, but I hated Esau."^{n}

^{14}So what should we say about this? Is
God unfair? In no way. ^{15}God said to Moses,
"I will show kindness to anyone to whom I
want to show kindness, and I will show
mercy to anyone to whom I want to show
mercy."^{n} ^{16}So God will choose the one to
whom he decides to show mercy; his choice
does not depend on what people want or try
to do. ^{17}The Scripture says to the king of
Egypt: "I made you king for this reason: to
show my power in you so that my name will
be talked about in all the earth."^{n} ^{18}So God
shows mercy where he wants to show mercy,
and he makes stubborn the people he wants
to make stubborn.

9:5 born . . . forever This can also mean "born. May God, who rules over all things, be praised forever!" **9:6 God's people** Literally, "Israel," the people God chose to bring his blessings to the world. **9:7 Abraham** Most respected ancestor of the Jews.
Every Jew hoped to see Abraham. **9:7 "The descendants . . . Isaac."** Quotation from Genesis 21:12. **9:9 "At . . . son."** Quotation from Genesis 18:10, 14. **9:11–12 "The older . . . younger."** Quotation from Genesis 25:23. **9:13 "I . . . Esau."** Quotation from Malachi 1:2–3. **9:15 "I . . . mercy."** Quotation from Exodus 33:19. **9:17 "I . . . earth."** Quotation from Exodus 9:16.

AUGUST 9

JOB 9:1—10:22

Job Answers Bildad

9 Then Job answered:
²"Yes, I know that this is true,
but how can anyone be right in the
presence of God?
³Someone might want to argue with God,
but no one could answer God,
not one time out of a thousand.
⁴God's wisdom is deep, and his power is
great;
no one can fight him without getting
hurt.
⁵God moves mountains without anyone
knowing it
and turns them over when he is angry.
⁶He shakes the earth out of its place
and makes its foundations tremble.
⁷He commands the sun not to shine
and shuts off the light of the stars.
⁸He alone stretches out the skies
and walks on the waves of the sea.
⁹It is God who made the Bear, Orion, and
the Pleiades[n]
and the groups of stars in the southern
sky.
¹⁰He does wonders that cannot be
understood;
he does so many miracles they cannot
be counted.
¹¹When he passes me, I cannot see him;
when he goes by me, I do not recognize
him.
¹²If he snatches something away, no one
can stop him
or say to him, 'What are you doing?'
¹³God will not hold back his anger.
Even the helpers of the monster Rahab
lie at his feet in fear.
¹⁴So how can I argue with God,
or even find words to argue with him?
¹⁵Even if I were right, I could not answer
him;
I could only beg God, my Judge, for
mercy.

¹⁶If I called to him and he answered,
I still don't believe he would listen to me.
¹⁷He would crush me with a storm
and multiply my wounds for no reason.
¹⁸He would not let me catch my breath
but would overwhelm me with misery.
¹⁹When it comes to strength, God is
stronger than I;
when it comes to justice, no one can
accuse him.
²⁰Even if I were right, my own mouth
would say I was wrong;
if I were innocent, my mouth would say
I was guilty.

²¹"I am innocent,
but I don't care about myself.
I hate my own life.
²²It is all the same. That is why I say,
'God destroys both the innocent and
the guilty.'
²³If the whip brings sudden death,
God will laugh at the suffering of the
innocent.
²⁴When the land falls into the hands of evil
people,
he covers the judges' faces so they can't
see it.
If it is not God who does this, then who
is it?

²⁵"My days go by faster than a runner;
they fly away without my seeing any
joy.
²⁶They glide past like paper boats.
They attack like eagles swooping down
to feed.
²⁷Even though I say, 'I will forget my
complaint;
I will change the look on my face and
smile,'
²⁸I still dread all my suffering.
I know you will hold me guilty.
²⁹I have already been found guilty,
so why should I struggle for no reason?
³⁰I might wash myself with soap
and scrub my hands with strong soap,

9:9 Bear . . . Pleiades Names of well-known groups of stars.

³¹but you would push me into a dirty pit,
and even my clothes would hate me.

³²"God is not human like me, so I cannot
answer him.
We cannot meet each other in court.
³³I wish there were someone to make
peace between us,
someone to decide our case.
³⁴Maybe he could remove God's
punishment
so his terror would no longer frighten
me.
³⁵Then I could speak without being afraid,
but I am not able to do that.

10 "I hate my life,
so I will complain without holding
back;
I will speak because I am so unhappy.
²I will say to God: Do not hold me guilty,
but tell me what you have against me.
³Does it make you happy to trouble me?
Don't you care about me, the work of
your hands?
Are you happy with the plans of evil
people?
⁴Do you have human eyes
that see as we see?
⁵Are your days like the days of humans,
and your years like our years?
⁶You look for the evil I have done
and search for my sin.
⁷You know I am not guilty,
but no one can save me from your
power.

⁸"Your hands shaped and made me.
Do you now turn around and destroy
me?
⁹Remember that you molded me like a
piece of clay.
Will you now turn me back into dust?
¹⁰You formed me inside my mother
like cheese formed from milk.
¹¹You dressed me with skin and flesh;
you sewed me together with bones and
muscles.
¹²You gave me life and showed me
kindness,
and in your care you watched over my
life.

¹³"But in your heart you hid other plans.
I know this was in your mind.
¹⁴If I sinned, you would watch me
and would not let my sin go
unpunished.
¹⁵How terrible it will be for me if I am
guilty!
Even if I am right, I cannot lift my head.
I am full of shame
and experience only pain.
¹⁶If I hold up my head, you hunt me like a
lion
and again show your terrible power
against me.
¹⁷You bring new witnesses against me
and increase your anger against me.
Your armies come against me.

¹⁸"So why did you allow me to be born?
I wish I had died before anyone saw
me.
¹⁹I wish I had never lived,
but had been carried straight from
birth to the grave.
²⁰The few days of my life are almost over.
Leave me alone so I can have a moment
of joy.
²¹Soon I will leave; I will not return
from the land of darkness and gloom,
²²the land of darkest night,
from the land of gloom and confusion,
where even the light is darkness."

PSALM 93:1–5

The Majesty of the Lord

93 The LORD is king. He is clothed in
majesty.
The LORD is clothed in majesty
and armed with strength.
The world is set,
and it cannot be moved.
²LORD, your kingdom was set up long ago;
you are everlasting.

³LORD, the seas raise,
the seas raise their voice.
The seas raise up their pounding
waves.
⁴The sound of the water is loud;
the ocean waves are powerful,
but the LORD above is much greater.

⁵LORD, your laws will stand forever.
Your Temple will be holy forevermore.

PROVERBS 22:22–23

²²Do not abuse poor people because they
are poor,
and do not take away the rights of the
needy in court.
²³The LORD will defend them in court
and will take the life of those who take
away their rights.

ROMANS 9:19–33

¹⁹So one of you will ask me: "Then why
does God blame us for our sins? Who can
fight his will?" ²⁰You are only human, and
human beings have no right to question
God. An object should not ask the person
who made it, "Why did you make me like
this?" ²¹The potter can make anything he
wants to make. He can use the same clay to
make one thing for special use and another
thing for daily use.

²²It is the same way with God. He wanted
to show his anger and to let people see his
power. But he patiently stayed with those
people he was angry with—people who
were made ready to be destroyed. ²³He
waited with patience so that he could make
known his rich glory to the people who receive his mercy. He has prepared these people to have his glory, ²⁴and we are those
people whom God called. He called us not
from the Jews only but also from those who
are not Jews. ²⁵As the Scripture says in
Hosea:

"I will say, 'You are my people'

to those I had called 'not my people.'
And I will show my love
to those people I did not love." *Hosea 2:1, 23*
²⁶"They were called,
'You are not my people,'
but later they will be called
'children of the living God.'" *Hosea 1:10*
²⁷And Isaiah cries out about Israel:
"The people of Israel are many,
like the grains of sand by the sea.
But only a few of them will be saved,
²⁸ because the Lord will quickly and
completely punish the
people on the earth." *Isaiah 10:22–23*
²⁹It is as Isaiah said:
"The Lord All-Powerful
allowed a few of our descendants to
live.
Otherwise we would have been
completely destroyed
like the cities of Sodom and
Gomorrah."ⁿ *Isaiah 1:9*
³⁰So what does all this mean? Those who
are not Jews were not trying to make themselves right with God, but they were made
right with God because of their faith. ³¹The
people of Israel tried to follow a law to make
themselves right with God. But they did not
succeed, ³²because they tried to make themselves right by the things they did instead of
trusting in God to make them right. They
stumbled over the stone that causes people
to stumble. ³³As it is written in the Scripture:
"I will put in Jerusalem a stone that
causes people to stumble,
a rock that makes them fall.
Anyone who trusts in him will never be
disappointed." *Isaiah 8:14; 28:16*

AUGUST 10

JOB 11:1—12:25

Zophar Speaks to Job

11 Then Zophar the Naamathite answered:

²"Should these words go unanswered?
Is this talker in the right?
³Your lies do not make people quiet;
people should correct you when you
make fun of God.

9:29 Sodom and Gomorrah Two cities that God destroyed because the people were so evil.

[4]You say, 'My teachings are right,
and I am clean in God's sight.'
[5]I wish God would speak
and open his lips against you
[6]and tell you the secrets of wisdom,
because wisdom has two sides.
Know this: God has even forgotten some
of your sin.

[7]"Can you understand the secrets of God?
Can you search the limits of the
Almighty?
[8]His limits are higher than the heavens;
you cannot reach them!
They are deeper than the grave; you
cannot understand them!
[9]His limits are longer than the earth
and wider than the sea.

[10]"If God comes along and puts you in
prison
or calls you into court, no one can stop
him.
[11]God knows who is evil,
and when he sees evil, he takes note of
it.
[12]A fool cannot become wise
any more than a wild donkey can be
born tame.

[13]"You must give your whole heart to him
and hold out your hands to him for
help.
[14]Put away the sin that is in your hand;
let no evil remain in your tent.
[15]Then you can lift up your face without
shame,
and you can stand strong without fear.
[16]You will forget your trouble
and remember it only as water gone by.
[17]Your life will be as bright as the noonday
sun,
and darkness will seem like morning.
[18]You will feel safe because there is hope;
you will look around and rest in safety.
[19]You will lie down, and no one will scare
you.
Many people will want favors from you.
[20]But the wicked will not be able to see,
so they will not escape.
Their only hope will be to die."

Job Answers Zophar

12Then Job answered:
[2]"You really think you are the only
wise people
and that when you die, wisdom will die
with you!
[3]But my mind is as good as yours;
you are not better than I am.
Everyone knows all these things.
[4]My friends all laugh at me
when I call on God and expect him to
answer me;
they laugh at me even though I am
right and innocent!
[5]Those who are comfortable don't care
that others have trouble;
they think it right that those people
should have troubles.
[6]The tents of robbers are not bothered,
and those who make God angry are
safe.
They have their god in their pocket.

[7]"But ask the animals, and they will teach
you,
or ask the birds of the air, and they will
tell you.
[8]Speak to the earth, and it will teach you,
or let the fish of the sea tell you.
[9]Every one of these knows
that the hand of the LORD has done this.
[10]The life of every creature
and the breath of all people are in God's
hand.
[11]The ear tests words
as the tongue tastes food.
[12]Older people are wise,
and long life brings understanding.

[13]"But only God has wisdom and power,
good advice and understanding.
[14]What he tears down cannot be rebuilt;
anyone he puts in prison cannot be let
out.
[15]If God holds back the waters, there is no
rain;
if he lets the waters go, they flood the
land.
[16]He is strong and victorious;
both the one who fools others and the
one who is fooled belong to him.

17God leads the wise away as captives
  and turns judges into fools.
18He takes off chains that kings put on
  and puts a garment on their bodies.
19He leads priests away naked
  and destroys the powerful.
20He makes trusted people be silent
  and takes away the wisdom of elders.
21He brings disgrace on important people
  and takes away the weapons of the
  strong.
22He uncovers the deep things of
  darkness
  and brings dark shadows into the light.
23He makes nations great and then
  destroys them;
  he makes nations large and then
  scatters them.
24He takes understanding away from the
  leaders of the earth
  and makes them wander through a
  pathless desert.
25They feel around in darkness with no
  light;
  he makes them stumble like drunks.

PSALM 94:1–11

God Will Pay Back His Enemies

94 The LORD is a God who punishes.
  God, show your greatness and
  punish!
2Rise up, Judge of the earth,
  and give the proud what they deserve.
3How long will the wicked be happy?
  How long, LORD?

4They are full of proud words;
  those who do evil brag about what they
  have done.
5LORD, they crush your people
  and make your children suffer.
6They kill widows and foreigners
  and murder orphans.
7They say, "The LORD doesn't see;
  the God of Jacob doesn't notice."

8You stupid ones among the people, pay
  attention.
  You fools, when will you understand?

9Can't the creator of ears hear?
  Can't the maker of eyes see?
10Won't the one who corrects nations
  punish you?
  Doesn't the teacher of people know
  everything?
11The LORD knows what people think.
  He knows their thoughts are just a puff
  of wind.

PROVERBS 22:24–25

24Don't make friends with quick-tempered
  people
  or spend time with those who have bad
  tempers.
25If you do, you will be like them.
  Then you will be in real danger.

ROMANS 10:1–21

10 Brothers and sisters, the thing I want
most is for all the Jews to be saved.
That is my prayer to God. 2I can say this
about them: They really try to follow God,
but they do not know the right way. 3Because
they did not know the way that God makes
people right with him, they tried to make
themselves right in their own way. So they
did not accept God's way of making people
right. 4Christ ended the law so that everyone
who believes in him may be right with God.

5Moses writes about being made right by
following the law. He says, "A person who
obeys these things will live because of
them."n 6But this is what the Scripture says
about being made right through faith: "Don't
say to yourself, 'Who will go up into heaven?'"
(That means, "Who will go up to heaven and
bring Christ down to earth?") 7"And do not
say, 'Who will go down into the world below?'" (That means, "Who will go down and
bring Christ up from the dead?") 8This is
what the Scripture says: "The word is near
you; it is in your mouth and in your heart."n
That is the teaching of faith that we are
telling. 9If you declare with your mouth, "Jesus is Lord," and if you believe in your heart
that God raised Jesus from the dead, you will
be saved. 10We believe with our hearts, and

10:5 "A person . . . them." Quotation from Leviticus 18:5. **10:6–8 But . . . heart."** Quotations from Deuteronomy 9:4; 30:12–14; Psalm 107:26.

so we are made right with God. And we declare with our mouths that we believe, and so we are saved. [11]As the Scripture says, "Anyone who trusts in him will never be disappointed."[n] [12]That Scripture says "anyone" because there is no difference between those who are Jews and those who are not. The same Lord is the Lord of all and gives many blessings to all who trust in him, [13]as the Scripture says, "Anyone who calls on the Lord will be saved."[n]

[14]But before people can ask the Lord for help, they must believe in him; and before they can believe in him, they must hear about him; and for them to hear about the Lord, someone must tell them; [15]and before someone can go and tell them, that person must be sent. It is written, "How beautiful is the person who comes to bring good news."[n] [16]But not all the Jews accepted the good news. Isaiah said, "Lord, who believed what we told them?"[n] [17]So faith comes from hearing the Good News, and people hear the Good News when someone tells them about Christ.

[18]But I ask: Didn't people hear the Good News? Yes, they heard—as the Scripture says:

"Their message went out through all the
    world;
their words go everywhere on earth."

Psalm 19:4

[19]Again I ask: Didn't the people of Israel understand? Yes, they did understand. First, Moses says:

"I will use those who are not a nation to
    make you jealous.
I will use a nation that does not
    understand to make you angry."

Deuteronomy 32:21

[20]Then Isaiah is bold enough to say:

"I was found by those who were not
    asking me for help.
I made myself known to people who
    were not looking for me." *Isaiah 65:1*

[21]But about Israel God says,

"All day long I stood ready to accept
people who disobey and are stubborn."

Isaiah 65:2

AUGUST 11

JOB 13:1—14:22

13 "Now my eyes have seen all this;
    my ears have heard and understood it.
[2]What you know, I also know.
    You are not better than I am.
[3]But I want to speak to the Almighty
    and to argue my case with God.
[4]But you smear me with lies.
    You are worthless doctors, all of you!
[5]I wish you would just stop talking;
    then you would really be wise!
[6]Listen to my argument,
    and hear the pleading of my lips.
[7]You should not speak evil in the name of
    God;
    you cannot speak God's truth by telling
    lies.

[8]You should not unfairly choose his side
    against mine;
    you should not argue the case for God.
[9]You will not do well if he examines you;
    you cannot fool God as you might fool
    humans.
[10]God would surely scold you
    if you unfairly took one person's side.
[11]His bright glory would scare you,
    and you would be very much afraid of
    him.
[12]Your wise sayings are worth no more
    than ashes,
    and your arguments are as weak as
    clay.

[13]"Be quiet and let me speak.
    Let things happen to me as they will.

¹⁴Why should I put myself in danger
and take my life in my own hands?
¹⁵Even if God kills me, I have hope in him;
I will still defend my ways to his face.
¹⁶This is my salvation.
The wicked cannot come before him.
¹⁷Listen carefully to my words;
let your ears hear what I say.
¹⁸See, I have prepared my case,
and I know I will be proved right.
¹⁹No one can accuse me of doing wrong.
If someone can, I will be quiet and die.

²⁰"God, please just give me these two
things,
and then I will not hide from you:
²¹Take your punishment away from me,
and stop frightening me with your
terrors.
²²Then call me, and I will answer,
or let me speak, and you answer.
²³How many evil things and sins have I
done?
Show me my wrong and my sin.
²⁴Don't hide your face from me;
don't think of me as your enemy.
²⁵Don't punish a leaf that is blown by the
wind;
don't chase after straw.
²⁶You write down cruel things against me
and make me suffer for my boyhood
sins.
²⁷You put my feet in chains
and keep close watch wherever I go.
You even mark the soles of my feet.

²⁸"Everyone wears out like something
rotten,
like clothing eaten by moths.

14 "All of us born to women
live only a few days and have lots of
trouble.
²We grow up like flowers and then dry up
and die.
We are like a passing shadow that does
not last.
³Lord, do you need to watch me like this?
Must you bring me before you to be
judged?
⁴No one can bring something clean from
something dirty.

⁵Our time is limited.
You have given us only so many months
to live
and have set limits we cannot go beyond.
⁶So look away from us and leave us alone
until we put in our time like a laborer.

⁷"If a tree is cut down,
there is hope that it will grow again
and will send out new branches.
⁸Even if its roots grow old in the ground,
and its stump dies in the dirt,
⁹at the smell of water it will bud
and put out new shoots like a plant.
¹⁰But we die, and our bodies are laid in the
ground;
we take our last breath and are gone.
¹¹Water disappears from a lake,
and a river loses its water and dries up.
¹²In the same way, we lie down and do not
rise again;
we will not get up or be awakened
until the heavens disappear.

¹³"I wish you would hide me in the grave;
hide me until your anger is gone.
I wish you would set a time
and then remember me!
¹⁴Will the dead live again?
All my days are a struggle;
I will wait until my change comes.
¹⁵You will call, and I will answer you;
you will desire the creature your hands
have made.
¹⁶Then you will count my steps,
but you will not keep track of my sin.
¹⁷My wrongs will be closed up in a bag,
and you will cover up my sin.

¹⁸"A mountain washes away and crumbles;
and a rock can be moved from its place.
¹⁹Water washes over stones and wears
them down,
and rushing waters wash away the dirt.
In the same way, you destroy hope.
²⁰You defeat people forever, and they are
gone;
you change their appearance and send
them away.
²¹Their children are honored, but they do
not know it;

their children are disgraced, but they
do not see it.
[22]They only feel the pain of their body
and feel sorry for themselves."

PSALM 94:12–19

[12]LORD, those you correct are happy;
you teach them from your law.
[13]You give them rest from times of trouble
until a pit is dug for the wicked.
[14]The LORD won't leave his people
nor give up his children.
[15]Judgment will again be fair,
and all who are honest will follow it.

[16]Who will help me fight against the wicked?
Who will stand with me against those
who do evil?
[17]If the LORD had not helped me,
I would have died in a minute.
[18]I said, "I am about to fall,"
but, LORD, your love kept me safe.
[19]I was very worried,
but you comforted me and made me
happy.

PROVERBS 22:26–27

[26]Don't promise to pay what someone else
owes,
and don't guarantee anyone's loan.
[27]If you cannot pay the loan,
your own bed may be taken right out
from under you.

ROMANS 11:1–21

God Shows Mercy to All People

11 So I ask: Did God throw out his people? No! I myself am an Israelite from the family of Abraham, from the tribe of Benjamin. [2]God chose the Israelites to be his people before they were born, and he has not thrown his people out. Surely you know what the Scripture says about Elijah, how he prayed to God against the people of Israel. [3]"Lord," he said, "they have killed your prophets, and they have destroyed your altars. I am the only prophet left, and now they are trying to kill me, too."[n] [4]But what answer

did God give Elijah? He said, "But I have left seven thousand people in Israel who have never bowed down before Baal."[n] [5]It is the same now. There are a few people that God has chosen by his grace. [6]And if he chose them by grace, it is not for the things they have done. If they could be made God's people by what they did, God's gift of grace would not really be a gift.

[7]So this is what has happened: Although the Israelites tried to be right with God, they did not succeed, but the ones God chose did become right with him. The others were made stubborn and refused to listen to God. [8]As it is written in the Scriptures:

"God gave the people a dull mind so they
could not understand." *Isaiah 29:10*
"He closed their eyes so they could not
see
and their ears so they could not hear.
This continues until today." *Deuteronomy 29:4*
[9]And David says:
"Let their own feasts trap them and
cause their ruin;
let their feasts cause them to stumble
and be paid back.
[10]Let their eyes be closed so they cannot
see
and their backs be forever weak from
troubles." *Psalm 69:22–23*
[11]So I ask: When the Jews fell, did that fall destroy them? No! But their failure brought salvation to those who are not Jews, in order to make the Jews jealous. [12]The Jews' failure brought rich blessings for the world, and the Jews' loss brought rich blessings for the non-Jewish people. So surely the world will receive much richer blessings when enough Jews become the kind of people God wants.

[13]Now I am speaking to you who are not Jews. I am an apostle to those who are not Jews, and since I have that work, I will make the most of it. [14]I hope I can make my own people jealous and, in that way, help some of them to be saved. [15]When God turned away from the Jews, he became friends with other people in the world. So when God accepts the Jews, surely that will bring them life after death.

11:3 **"they . . . too"** Quotation from 1 Kings 19:10, 14.   11:4 **"But . . . Baal."** Quotation from 1 Kings 19:18.

¹⁶If the first piece of bread is offered to God, then the whole loaf is made holy. If the roots of a tree are holy, then the tree's branches are holy too.

¹⁷It is as if some of the branches from an olive tree have been broken off. You non-Jewish people are like the branch of a wild olive tree that has been joined to that first tree. You now share the strength and life of the first tree, the Jews. ¹⁸So do not brag about those branches that were broken off. If you brag, remember that you do not support the root, but the root supports you. ¹⁹You will say, "Branches were broken off so that I could be joined to their tree." ²⁰That is true. But those branches were broken off because they did not believe, and you continue to be part of the tree only because you believe. Do not be proud, but be afraid. ²¹If God did not let the natural branches of that tree stay, then he will not let you stay if you don't believe.

AUGUST 12

JOB 15:1—17:2

Eliphaz Answers Job

15 Then Eliphaz the Temanite answered:
²"A wise person would not answer
   with empty words
   or fill his stomach with the hot east
      wind.
³He would not argue with useless words
   or make speeches that have no value.
⁴But you even destroy respect for God
   and limit the worship of him.
⁵Your sin teaches your mouth what to say;
   you use words to trick others.
⁶It is your own mouth, not mine, that
      shows you are wicked;
   your own lips testify against you.

⁷"You are not the first man ever born;
   you are not older than the hills.
⁸You did not listen in on God's secret
      council.
   But you limit wisdom to yourself.
⁹You don't know any more than we
      know.
   You don't understand any more than we
      understand.
¹⁰Old people with gray hair are on our
      side;
   they are even older than your father.
¹¹Is the comfort God gives you not enough
      for you,
   even when words are spoken gently to
      you?

¹²Has your heart carried you away from
      God?
   Why do your eyes flash with anger?
¹³Why do you speak out your anger against
      God?
   Why do these words pour out of your
      mouth?

¹⁴"How can anyone be pure?
   How can someone born to a woman be
      good?
¹⁵God places no trust in his holy ones,
   and even the heavens are not pure in
      his eyes.
¹⁶How much less pure is one who is
      terrible and rotten
   and drinks up evil as if it were water!

¹⁷"Listen to me, and I will tell you about it;
   I will tell you what I have seen.
¹⁸These are things wise men have told;
   their ancestors told them, and they
      have hidden nothing.
¹⁹(The land was given to their fathers only,
   and no foreigner lived among them.)
²⁰The wicked suffer pain all their lives;
   the cruel suffer during all the years
      saved up for them.
²¹Terrible sounds fill their ears,
   and when things seem to be going well,
      robbers attack them.
²²Evil people give up trying to escape from
      the darkness;
   it has been decided that they will die by
      the sword.

²³They wander around and will become
food for vultures.
They know darkness will soon come.
²⁴Worry and suffering terrify them;
they overwhelm them, like a king ready
to attack,
²⁵because they shake their fists at God
and try to get their own way against the
Almighty.
²⁶They stubbornly charge at God
with thick, strong shields.

²⁷"Although the faces of the wicked are
thick with fat,
and their bellies are fat with flesh,
²⁸they will live in towns that are ruined,
in houses where no one lives,
which are crumbling into ruins.
²⁹The wicked will no longer get rich,
and the riches they have will not last;
the things they own will no longer
spread over the land.
³⁰They will not escape the darkness.
A flame will dry up their branches;
God's breath will carry the wicked
away.
³¹The wicked should not fool themselves
by trusting what is useless.
If they do, they will get nothing in
return.
³²Their branches will dry up before they
finish growing
and will never turn green.
³³They will be like a vine whose grapes are
pulled off before they are ripe,
like an olive tree that loses its
blossoms.
³⁴People without God can produce
nothing.
Fire will destroy the tents of those who
take money to do evil,
³⁵who plan trouble and give birth to evil,
whose hearts plan ways to trick others."

Job Answers Eliphaz

16 Then Job answered:
²"I have heard many things like these.
You are all painful comforters!
³Will your long-winded speeches never
end?
What makes you keep on arguing?

⁴I also could speak as you do
if you were in my place.
I could make great speeches against you
and shake my head at you.
⁵But, instead, I would encourage you,
and my words would bring you relief.

⁶"Even if I speak, my pain is not less,
and if I don't speak, it still does not go
away.
⁷God, you have surely taken away my
strength
and destroyed my whole family.
⁸You have made me thin and weak,
and this shows I have done wrong.
⁹God attacks me and tears me with anger;
he grinds his teeth at me;
my enemy stares at me with his angry
eyes.
¹⁰People open their mouths to make fun of
me
and hit my cheeks to insult me.
They join together against me.
¹¹God has turned me over to evil people
and has handed me over to the wicked.
¹²Everything was fine with me,
but God broke me into pieces;
he held me by the neck and crushed me.
He has made me his target;
¹³ his archers surround me.
He stabs my kidneys without mercy;
he spills my blood on the ground.
¹⁴Again and again God attacks me;
he runs at me like a soldier.

¹⁵"I have sewed rough cloth over my skin
to show my sadness
and have buried my face in the dust.
¹⁶My face is red from crying;
I have dark circles around my eyes.
¹⁷Yet my hands have never done anything
cruel,
and my prayer is pure.

¹⁸"Earth, please do not cover up my blood.
Don't let my cry ever stop being heard!
¹⁹Even now I have one who speaks for me
in heaven;
the one who is on my side is high
above.
²⁰The one who speaks for me is my friend.
My eyes pour out tears to God.

21He begs God on behalf of a human
as a person begs for his friend.

22"Only a few years will pass
before I go on the journey of no return.

17 My spirit is broken;
the days of my life are almost gone.
The grave is waiting for me.
2Those who laugh at me surround me;
I watch them insult me.

PSALM 94:20-23

20Crooked leaders cannot be your
friends.
They use the law to cause suffering.
21They join forces against people who do
right
and sentence to death the innocent.
22But the LORD is my defender;
my God is the rock of my protection.
23God will pay them back for their sins
and will destroy them for their evil.
The LORD our God will destroy them.

PROVERBS 22:28-29

28Don't move an old stone that marks a
border,
because those stones were set up by
your ancestors.

29Do you see people skilled in their work?
They will work for kings, not for
ordinary people.

ROMANS 11:22-36

22So you see that God is kind and also
very strict. He punishes those who stop following him. But God is kind to you, if you
continue following in his kindness. If you do
not, you will be cut off from the tree. 23And if
the Jews will believe in God again, he will accept them back. God is able to put them back
where they were. 24It is not natural for a wild
branch to be part of a good tree. And you
who are not Jews are like a branch cut from a
wild olive tree and joined to a good olive
tree. But since those Jews are like a branch

that grew from the good tree, surely they can
be joined to their own tree again.

25I want you to understand this secret,
brothers and sisters, so you will understand that you do not know everything:
Part of Israel has been made stubborn, but
that will change when many who are not
Jews have come to God. 26And that is how
all Israel will be saved. It is written in the
Scriptures:

"The Savior will come from Jerusalem;
he will take away all evil from the
family of Jacob.n
27And I will make this agreement with
those people
when I take away their sins."
Isaiah 59:20-21; 27:9

28The Jews refuse to accept the Good
News, so they are God's enemies. This has
happened to help you who are not Jews. But
the Jews are still God's chosen people, and he
loves them very much because of the promises he made to their ancestors. 29God never
changes his mind about the people he calls
and the things he gives them. 30At one time
you refused to obey God. But now you have
received mercy, because those people refused to obey. 31And now the Jews refuse to
obey, because God showed mercy to you. But
this happened so that they also cann receive
mercy from him. 32God has given all people
over to their stubborn ways so that he can
show mercy to all.

Praise to God
33Yes, God's riches are very great, and his
wisdom and knowledge have no end! No
one can explain the things God decides
or understand his ways. 34As the Scripture
says,

"Who has known the mind of the Lord,
or who has been able to give him
advice?" *Isaiah 40:13*
35"No one has ever given God anything
that he must pay back." *Job 41:11*
36Yes, God made all things, and everything continues through him and for him. To
him be the glory forever! Amen.

11:26 Jacob Father of the twelve family groups of Israel, the people God chose to be his people. **11:31 can** Some Greek copies read "can now."

AUGUST 13

JOB 17:3—18:21

³"God, make me a promise.
No one will make a pledge for me.
⁴You have closed their minds to understanding.
Do not let them win over me.
⁵People might speak against their friends for money,
but if they do, the eyes of their children go blind.

⁶"God has made my name a curse word;
people spit in my face.
⁷My sight has grown weak because of my sadness,
and my body is as thin as a shadow.
⁸Honest people are upset about this;
innocent people are upset with those who do wrong.
⁹But those who do right will continue to do right,
and those whose hands are not dirty with sin will grow stronger.

¹⁰"But, all of you, come and try again!
I do not find a wise person among you.
¹¹My days are gone, and my plans have been destroyed,
along with the desires of my heart.
¹²These men think night is day;
when it is dark, they say, 'Light is near.'
¹³If the only home I hope for is the grave,
if I spread out my bed in darkness,
¹⁴if I say to the grave, 'You are my father,'
and to the worm, 'You are my mother'
or 'You are my sister,'
¹⁵where, then, is my hope?
Who can see any hope for me?
¹⁶Will hope go down to the gates of death?
Will we go down together into the dust?"

Bildad Answers Job

18 Then Bildad the Shuhite answered:
²"When will you stop these speeches?
Be sensible, and then we can talk.
³You think of us as cattle,
as if we are stupid.
⁴You tear yourself to pieces in your anger.

Should the earth be vacant just for you?
Should the rocks move from their places?

⁵"The lamp of the wicked will be put out,
and the flame in their lamps will stop burning.
⁶The light in their tents will grow dark,
and the lamps by their sides will go out.
⁷Their strong steps will grow weak;
they will fall into their own evil traps.
⁸Their feet will be caught in a net
when they walk into its web.
⁹A trap will catch them by the heel
and hold them tight.
¹⁰A trap for them is hidden on the ground,
right in their path.
¹¹Terrible things startle them from every side
and chase them at every step.
¹²Hunger takes away their strength,
and disaster is at their side.
¹³Disease eats away parts of their skin;
death gnaws at their arms and legs.
¹⁴They are torn from the safety of their tents
and dragged off to Death, the King of Terrors.
¹⁵Their tents are set on fire,
and sulfur is scattered over their homes.
¹⁶Their roots dry up below ground,
and their branches die above ground.
¹⁷People on earth will not remember them;
their names will be forgotten in the land.
¹⁸They will be driven from light into darkness
and chased out of the world.
¹⁹They have no children or descendants among their people,
and no one will be left alive where they once lived.
²⁰People of the west will be shocked at what has happened to them,
and people of the east will be very frightened.

²¹Surely this is what will happen to the
wicked;
such is the place of one who does not
know God."

PSALM 95:1–5

A Call to Praise and Obedience

95 Come, let's sing for joy to the LORD.
Let's shout praises to the Rock who
saves us.
²Let's come to him with thanksgiving.
Let's sing songs to him,
³because the LORD is the great God,
the great King over all gods.
⁴The deepest places on earth are his,
and the highest mountains belong to
him.
⁵The sea is his because he made it,
and he created the land with his own
hands.

PROVERBS 23:1–3

23 If you sit down to eat with a ruler,
notice the food that is in front of you.
²Control yourself
if you have a big appetite.
³Don't be greedy for his fine foods,
because that food might be a trick.

ROMANS 12:1–21

Give Your Lives to God

12 So brothers and sisters, since God has
shown us great mercy, I beg you to offer your lives as a living sacrifice to him.
Your offering must be only for God and
pleasing to him, which is the spiritual way
for you to worship. ²Do not be shaped by
this world; instead be changed within by a
new way of thinking. Then you will be able
to decide what God wants for you; you will
know what is good and pleasing to him and
what is perfect. ³Because God has given me
a special gift, I have something to say to
everyone among you. Do not think you are
better than you are. You must decide what
you really are by the amount of faith God
has given you. ⁴Each one of us has a body
with many parts, and these parts all have

different uses. ⁵In the same way, we are
many, but in Christ we are all one body.
Each one is a part of that body, and each
part belongs to all the other parts. ⁶We all
have different gifts, each of which came because of the grace God gave us. The person
who has the gift of prophecy should use
that gift in agreement with the faith. ⁷Anyone who has the gift of serving should
serve. Anyone who has the gift of teaching
should teach. ⁸Whoever has the gift of encouraging others should encourage. Whoever has the gift of giving to others should
give freely. Anyone who has the gift of being
a leader should try hard when he leads.
Whoever has the gift of showing mercy to
others should do so with joy.

⁹Your love must be real. Hate what is evil,
and hold on to what is good. ¹⁰Love each
other like brothers and sisters. Give each
other more honor than you want for yourselves. ¹¹Do not be lazy but work hard, serving the Lord with all your heart. ¹²Be joyful
because you have hope. Be patient when
trouble comes, and pray at all times. ¹³Share
with God's people who need help. Bring
strangers in need into your homes.

¹⁴Wish good for those who harm you;
wish them well and do not curse them. ¹⁵Be
happy with those who are happy, and be sad
with those who are sad. ¹⁶Live in peace with
each other. Do not be proud, but make
friends with those who seem unimportant.
Do not think how smart you are.

¹⁷If someone does wrong to you, do not
pay him back by doing wrong to him. Try to
do what everyone thinks is right. ¹⁸Do your
best to live in peace with everyone. ¹⁹My
friends, do not try to punish others when
they wrong you, but wait for God to punish
them with his anger. It is written: "I will punish those who do wrong; I will repay them,"ⁿ
says the Lord. ²⁰But you should do this:

"If your enemy is hungry, feed him;
if he is thirsty, give him a drink.
Doing this will be like pouring burning
coals on his head."   *Proverbs 25:21–22*
²¹Do not let evil defeat you, but defeat evil by
doing good.

12:19 "I . . . them." Quotation from Deuteronomy 32:35.

AUGUST 14

JOB 19:1—20:29

Job Answers Bildad

19 Then Job answered:
² "How long will you hurt me
and crush me with your words?
³ You have insulted me ten times now
and attacked me without shame.
⁴ Even if I have sinned,
it is my worry alone.
⁵ If you want to make yourselves look
better than I,
you can blame me for my suffering.
⁶ Then know that God has wronged me
and pulled his net around me.

⁷ "I shout, 'I have been wronged!'
But I get no answer.
I scream for help
but I get no justice.
⁸ God has blocked my way so I cannot
pass;
he has covered my paths with
darkness.
⁹ He has taken away my honor
and removed the crown from my head.
¹⁰ He beats me down on every side until I
am gone;
he destroys my hope like a fallen tree.
¹¹ His anger burns against me,
and he treats me like an enemy.
¹² His armies gather;
they prepare to attack me.
They camp around my tent.

¹³ "God has made my brothers my enemies,
and my friends have become strangers.
¹⁴ My relatives have gone away,
and my friends have forgotten me.
¹⁵ My guests and my female servants treat
me like a stranger;
they look at me as if I were a foreigner.
¹⁶ I call for my servant, but he does not
answer,
even when I beg him with my own
mouth.
¹⁷ My wife can't stand my breath,
and my own family dislikes me.
¹⁸ Even the little boys hate me
and talk about me when I leave.
¹⁹ All my close friends hate me;
even those I love have turned against
me.
²⁰ I am nothing but skin and bones;
I have escaped by the skin of my teeth.
²¹ Pity me, my friends, pity me,
because the hand of God has hit me.
²² Why do you chase me as God does?
Haven't you hurt me enough?

²³ "How I wish my words were written down,
written on a scroll.
²⁴ I wish they were carved with an iron pen
into lead,
or carved into stone forever.
²⁵ I know that my Defender lives,
and in the end he will stand upon the
earth.
²⁶ Even after my skin has been destroyed,
in my flesh I will see God.
²⁷ I will see him myself;
I will see him with my very own eyes.
How my heart wants that to happen!

²⁸ "If you say, 'We will continue to trouble
Job,
because the problem lies with him,'
²⁹ you should be afraid of the sword
yourselves.
God's anger will bring punishment by
the sword.
Then you will know there is judgment."

Zophar Answers

20 Then Zophar the Naamathite answered:
² "My troubled thoughts cause me to
answer,
because I am very upset.
³ You correct me and I am insulted,
but I understand how to answer you.
⁴ "You know how it has been for a long
time,
ever since people were first put on the
earth.
⁵ The happiness of evil people is brief,
and the joy of the wicked lasts only a
moment.

6Their pride may be as high as the heavens,
   and their heads may touch the clouds,
7but they will be gone forever, like their
      own dung.
   People who knew them will say, 'Where
      are they?'
8They will fly away like a dream
   and not be found again;
   they will be chased away like a vision in
      the night.
9Those who saw them will not see them
      again;
   the places where they lived will see
      them no more.
10Their children will have to pay back the
      poor,
   and they will have to give up their wealth.
11They had the strength of their youth in
      their bones,
   but it will lie with them in the dust of
      death.

12"Evil may taste sweet in their mouths,
   and they may hide it under their
      tongues.
13They cannot stand to let go of it;
   they keep it in their mouths.
14But their food will turn sour in their
      stomachs,
   like the poison of a snake inside them.
15They have swallowed riches, but they will
      spit them out;
   God will make them vomit their riches
      up.
16They will suck the poison of snakes,
   and the snake's fangs will kill them.
17They will not admire the sparkling
      streams
   or the rivers flowing with honey and
      cream.
18They must give back what they worked
      for without eating it;
   they will not enjoy the money they
      made from their trading,
19because they troubled the poor and left
      them with nothing.
   They have taken houses they did not
      build.

20"Evil people never lack an appetite,
   and nothing escapes their selfishness.
21But nothing will be left for them to eat;
   their riches will not continue.
22When they still have plenty, trouble will
      catch up to them,
   and great misery will come down on
      them.
23When the wicked fill their stomachs,
   God will send his burning anger
      against them,
   and blows of punishment will fall on
      them like rain.
24The wicked may run away from an iron
      weapon,
   but a bronze arrow will stab them.
25They will pull the arrows out of their
      backs
   and pull the points out of their livers.
   Terrors will come over them;
26   total darkness waits for their treasure.
   A fire not fanned by people will destroy
      them
   and burn up what is left of their tents.
27The heavens will show their guilt,
   and the earth will rise up against them.
28A flood will carry their houses away,
   swept away on the day of God's anger.
29This is what God plans for evil people;
   this is what he has decided they will
      receive."

PSALM 95:6–11

6Come, let's worship him and bow down.
   Let's kneel before the LORD who made us,
7because he is our God
   and we are the people he takes care of,
   the sheep that he tends.

Today listen to what he says:
8   "Do not be stubborn, as your ancestors
      were at Meribah,
   as they were that day at Massah in the
      desert.
9There your ancestors tested me
   and tried me even though they saw
      what I did.
10I was angry with those people for forty
      years.
   I said, 'They are not loyal to me
   and have not understood my ways.'
11I was angry and made a promise,
   'They will never enter my rest.'"

PROVERBS 23:4–5

⁴Don't wear yourself out trying to get rich;
  be wise enough to control yourself.
⁵Wealth can vanish in the wink of an eye.
  It can seem to grow wings
  and fly away like an eagle.

ROMANS 13:1–14

Christians Should Obey the Law

13 All of you must yield to the government rulers. No one rules unless God has given him the power to rule, and no one rules now without that power from God. ²So those who are against the government are really against what God has commanded. And they will bring punishment on themselves. ³Those who do right do not have to fear the rulers; only those who do wrong fear them. Do you want to be unafraid of the rulers? Then do what is right, and they will praise you. ⁴The ruler is God's servant to help you. But if you do wrong, then be afraid. He has the power to punish; he is God's servant to punish those who do wrong. ⁵So you must yield to the government, not only because you might be punished, but because you know it is right.

⁶This is also why you pay taxes. Rulers are working for God and give their time to their work. ⁷Pay everyone, then, what you owe. If you owe any kind of tax, pay it. Show respect and honor to them all.

Loving Others

⁸Do not owe people anything, except always owe love to each other, because the person who loves others has obeyed all the law. ⁹The law says, "You must not be guilty of adultery. You must not murder anyone. You must not steal. You must not want to take your neighbor's things."[n] All these commands and all others are really only one rule: "Love your neighbor as you love yourself."[n] ¹⁰Love never hurts a neighbor, so loving is obeying all the law.

¹¹Do this because we live in an important time. It is now time for you to wake up from your sleep, because our salvation is nearer now than when we first believed. ¹²The "night"[n] is almost finished, and the "day"[n] is almost here. So we should stop doing things that belong to darkness and take up the weapons used for fighting in the light. ¹³Let us live in a right way, like people who belong to the day. We should not have wild parties or get drunk. There should be no sexual sins of any kind, no fighting or jealousy. ¹⁴But clothe yourselves with the Lord Jesus Christ and forget about satisfying your sinful self.

AUGUST 15

JOB 21:1—22:30

Job Answers Zophar

21 Then Job answered:
  ²"Listen carefully to my words,
    and let this be the way you comfort me.
³Be patient while I speak.
  After I have finished, you may continue to make fun of me.

⁴"My complaint is not just against people;
  I have reason to be impatient.
⁵Look at me and be shocked;
  put your hand over your mouth in shock.
⁶When I think about this, I am terribly afraid
  and my body shakes.
⁷Why do evil people live a long time?
  They grow old and become more powerful.
⁸They see their children around them;
  they watch them grow up.

13:9 "You . . . things." Quotation from Exodus 20:13–15, 17. **13:9 "Love . . . yourself."** Quotation from Leviticus 19:18.
13:12 "night" This is used as a symbol of the sinful world we live in. This world will soon end. **13:12 "day"** This is used as a symbol of the good time that is coming, when we will be with God.

who is weak, believes it is right to eat only vegetables. ³The one who knows that it is right to eat any kind of food must not reject the one who eats only vegetables. And the person who eats only vegetables must not think that the one who eats all foods is wrong, because God has accepted that person. ⁴You cannot judge another person's servant. The master decides if the servant is doing well or not. And the Lord's servant will do well because the Lord helps him do well.

⁵Some think that one day is more important than another, and others think that every day is the same. Let all be sure in their own mind. ⁶Those who think one day is more important than other days are doing that for the Lord. And those who eat all kinds of food are doing that for the Lord, and they give thanks to God. Others who refuse to eat some foods do that for the Lord, and they give thanks to God. ⁷We do not live or die for ourselves. ⁸If we live, we are living for the Lord, and if we die, we are dying for the Lord. So living or dying, we belong to the Lord.

⁹The reason Christ died and rose from the dead to live again was so he would be Lord over both the dead and the living. ¹⁰So why do you judge your brothers or sisters in Christ? And why do you think you are better than they are? We will all stand before God to be judged, ¹¹because it is written in the Scriptures:

" 'As surely as I live,' says the Lord,
'Everyone will bow before me;
everyone will say that I am God.' "

Isaiah 45:23

¹²So each of us will have to answer to God.

Do Not Cause Others to Sin

¹³For that reason we should stop judging each other. We must make up our minds not to do anything that will make another Christian sin. ¹⁴I am in the Lord Jesus, and I know that there is no food that is wrong to eat. But if a person believes something is wrong, that thing is wrong for him. ¹⁵If you hurt your brother's or sister's faith because of something you eat, you are not really following the way of love. Do not destroy someone's faith by eating food he thinks is wrong, because Christ died for him. ¹⁶Do not allow what you think is good to become what others say is evil. ¹⁷In the kingdom of God, eating and drinking are not important. The important things are living right with God, peace, and joy in the Holy Spirit. ¹⁸Anyone who serves Christ by living this way is pleasing God and will be accepted by other people.

¹⁹So let us try to do what makes peace and helps one another. ²⁰Do not let the eating of food destroy the work of God. All foods are all right to eat, but it is wrong to eat food that causes someone else to sin. ²¹It is better not to eat meat or drink wine or do anything that will cause your brother or sister to sin.

²²Your beliefs about these things should be kept secret between you and God. People are happy if they can do what they think is right without feeling guilty. ²³But those who eat something without being sure it is right are wrong because they did not believe it was right. Anything that is done without believing it is right is a sin.

AUGUST 16

JOB 23:1—25:6

Job Answers

23 Then Job answered:
²"My complaint is still bitter today.
    I groan because God's heavy hand is on me.
³I wish I knew where to find God
    so I could go to where he lives.
⁴I would present my case before him
    and fill my mouth with arguments.
⁵I would learn how he would answer me
    and would think about what he would say.
⁶Would he not argue strongly against me?
    No, he would really listen to me.
⁷Then an honest person could present his case to God,

and I would be saved forever by my
judge.

8"If I go to the east, God is not there;
if I go to the west, I do not see him.
9When he is at work in the north, I catch
no sight of him;
when he turns to the south, I cannot
see him.
10But God knows the way that I take,
and when he has tested me, I will come
out like gold.
11My feet have closely followed his steps;
I have stayed in his way;
I did not turn aside.
12I have never left the commands he has
spoken;
I have treasured his words more than
my own.

13"But he is the only God.
Who can come against him?
He does anything he wants.
14He will do to me what he said he would do,
and he has many plans like this.
15That is why I am frightened of him;
when I think of this, I am afraid of
him.
16God has made me afraid;
the Almighty terrifies me.
17But I am not hidden by the darkness,
by the thick darkness that covers my
face.

24 "I wish the Almighty would set a time
for judging.
Those who know God do not see such a
day.
2Wicked people take other people's land;
they steal flocks and take them to new
pastures.
3They chase away the orphan's donkey
and take the widow's ox when she has
no money.
4They push needy people off the path;
all the poor of the land hide from them.
5The poor become like wild donkeys in
the desert
who go about their job of finding food.
The desert gives them food for their
children.

6They gather hay and straw in the fields
and pick up leftover grapes from the
vineyard of the wicked.
7They spend the night naked, because
they have no clothes,
nothing to cover themselves in the cold.
8They are soaked from mountain rains
and stay near the large rocks because
they have no shelter.
9The fatherless child is grabbed from its
mother's breast;
they take a poor mother's baby to pay
for what she owes.
10So the poor go around naked without
any clothes;
they carry bundles of grain but still go
hungry;
11they crush olives to get oil
and grapes to get wine, but they still go
thirsty.
12Dying people groan in the city,
and the injured cry out for help,
but God accuses no one of doing wrong.

13"Those who fight against the light
do not know God's ways
or stay in his paths.
14When the day is over, the murderers get up
to kill the poor and needy.
At night they go about like thieves.
15Those who are guilty of adultery watch
for the night,
thinking, 'No one will see us,'
and they keep their faces covered.
16In the dark, evil people break into
houses.
In the daytime they shut themselves up
in their own houses,
because they want nothing to do with
the light.
17Darkness is like morning to all these evil
people
who make friends with the terrors of
darkness.

18"They are like foam floating on the water.
Their part of the land is cursed;
no one uses the road that goes by their
vineyards.
19As heat and dryness quickly melt the
snow,

so the grave quickly takes away the
sinners.
20Their mothers forget them,
and worms will eat their bodies.
They will not be remembered,
so wickedness is broken in pieces like a
stick.
21These evil people abuse women who
cannot have children
and show no kindness to widows.
22But God drags away the strong by his
power.
Even though they seem strong, they do
not know how long they will live.
23God may let these evil people feel safe,
but he is watching their ways.
24For a little while they are important, and
then they die;
they are laid low and buried like
everyone else;
they are cut off like the heads of grain.
25If this is not true, who can prove I am
wrong?
Who can show that my words are worth
nothing?"

Bildad Answers

25 Then Bildad the Shuhite answered:
2"God rules and he must be honored;
he set up order in his high heaven.
3No one can count God's armies.
His light shines on all people.
4So no one can be good in the presence of
God,
and no one born to a woman can be
pure.
5Even the moon is not bright
and the stars are not pure in his eyes.
6People are much less! They are like insects.
They are only worms!"

PSALM 96:7–10

7Praise the LORD, all nations on earth;
praise the LORD's glory and power.
8Praise the glory of the LORD's name.
Bring an offering and come into his
Temple courtyards.
9Worship the LORD because he is holy.

Tremble before him, everyone on earth.
10Tell the nations, "The LORD is king."
The earth is set, and it cannot be
moved.
He will judge the people fairly.

PROVERBS 23:9

9Don't speak to fools;
they will only ignore your wise words.

ROMANS 15:1–13

15 We who are strong in faith should help
the weak with their weaknesses, and not
please only ourselves. 2Let each of us please
our neighbors for their good, to help them be
stronger in faith. 3Even Christ did not live to
please himself. It was as the Scriptures said:
"When people insult you, it hurts me."n
4Everything that was written in the past was
written to teach us. The Scriptures give us patience and encouragement so that we can have
hope. 5May the patience and encouragement
that come from God allow you to live in harmony with each other the way Christ Jesus
wants. 6Then you will all be joined together,
and you will give glory to God the Father of
our Lord Jesus Christ. 7Christ accepted you, so
you should accept each other, which will bring
glory to God. 8I tell you that Christ became a
servant of the Jews to show that God's promises to the Jewish ancestors are true. 9And he
also did this so that those who are not Jews
could give glory to God for the mercy he gives
to them. It is written in the Scriptures:
"So I will praise you among the
non-Jewish people.
I will sing praises to your name."
Psalm 18:49
10The Scripture also says,
"Be happy, you who are not Jews, together
with his people." *Deuteronomy 32:43*
11Again the Scripture says,
"All you who are not Jews, praise the Lord.
All you people, sing praises to him."
Psalm 117:1
12And Isaiah says,
"A new king will come from the family of
Jesse."n

He will come to rule over the
non-Jewish people,
and they will have hope because of him."

Isaiah 11:10

AUGUST 17

JOB 26:1–14

Job Answers Bildad

26 Then Job answered:
2"You are no help to the helpless!
You have not aided the weak!
3Your advice lacks wisdom!
You have shown little understanding!
4Who has helped you say these words?
And where did you get these ideas?

5"The spirits of the dead tremble,
those who are beneath and in the
waters.
6Death is naked before God;
destruction is uncovered before him.
7God stretches the northern sky out over
empty space
and hangs the earth on nothing.
8He wraps up the waters in his thick
clouds,
but the clouds do not break under their
weight.
9He covers the face of the moon,
spreading his clouds over it.
10He draws the horizon like a circle on the
water
at the place where light and darkness
meet.
11Heaven's foundations shake
when he thunders at them.
12With his power he quiets the sea;
by his wisdom he destroys Rahab, the
sea monster.
13He breathes, and the sky clears.
His hand stabs the fleeing snake.
14And these are only a small part of God's
works.
We only hear a small whisper of him.
Who could understand God's
thundering power?"

13I pray that the God who gives hope will
fill you with much joy and peace while you
trust in him. Then your hope will overflow
by the power of the Holy Spirit.

PSALM 96:11–13

11Let the skies rejoice and the earth be
glad;
let the sea and everything in it shout.
12 Let the fields and everything in them
rejoice.
Then all the trees of the forest will sing
for joy
13 before the LORD, because he is coming.
He is coming to judge the world;
he will judge the world with fairness
and the peoples with truth.

PROVERBS 23:10–12

10Don't move an old stone that marks a
border,
and don't take fields that belong to
orphans.
11God, their defender, is strong;
he will take their side against you.

12Remember what you are taught,
and listen carefully to words of
knowledge.

ROMANS 15:14–33

Paul Talks About His Work

14My brothers and sisters, I am sure that
you are full of goodness. I know that you
have all the knowledge you need and that
you are able to teach each other. 15But I have
written to you very openly about some
things I wanted you to remember. I did this
because God gave me this special gift: 16to be
a minister of Christ Jesus to those who are
not Jews. I served God by teaching his Good
News, so that the non-Jewish people could
be an offering that God would accept—an
offering made holy by the Holy Spirit.

¹⁷So I am proud of what I have done for God in Christ Jesus. ¹⁸I will not talk about anything except what Christ has done through me in leading those who are not Jews to obey God. They have obeyed God because of what I have said and done, ¹⁹because of the power of miracles and the great things they saw, and because of the power of the Holy Spirit. I preached the Good News from Jerusalem all the way around to Illyricum, and so I have finished that part of my work. ²⁰I always want to preach the Good News in places where people have never heard of Christ, because I do not want to build on the work someone else has already started. ²¹But it is written in the Scriptures:

"Those who were not told about him will
    see,
and those who have not heard about
    him will understand."   *Isaiah 52:15*

Paul's Plan to Visit Rome

²²This is the reason I was stopped many times from coming to you. ²³Now I have finished my work here. Since for many years I have wanted to come to you, ²⁴I hope to visit you on my way to Spain. After I enjoy being with you for a while, I hope you can help me on my trip. ²⁵Now I am going to Jerusalem to help God's people. ²⁶The believers in Macedonia and Southern Greece were happy to give their money to help the poor among God's people at Jerusalem. ²⁷They were happy to do this, and really they owe it to them. These who are not Jews have shared in the Jews' spiritual blessings, so they should use their material possessions to help the Jews. ²⁸After I am sure the poor in Jerusalem get the money that has been given for them, I will leave for Spain and stop and visit you. ²⁹I know that when I come to you I will bring Christ's full blessing.

³⁰Brothers and sisters, I beg you to help me in my work by praying to God for me. Do this because of our Lord Jesus and the love that the Holy Spirit gives us. ³¹Pray that I will be saved from the nonbelievers in Judea and that this help I bring to Jerusalem will please God's people there. ³²Then, if God wants me to, I will come to you with joy, and together you and I will have a time of rest. ³³The God who gives peace be with you all. Amen.

AUGUST 18

JOB 27:1—28:28

27 And Job continued speaking:
²"As surely as God lives, who has
        taken away my rights,
    the Almighty, who has made me
        unhappy,
³as long as I am alive
    and God's breath of life is in my nose,
⁴my lips will not speak evil,
    and my tongue will not tell a lie.
⁵I will never agree you are right;
    until I die, I will never stop saying I am
        innocent.
⁶I will insist that I am right; I will not
        back down.
    My conscience will never bother me.

⁷"Let my enemies be like evil people,
    my foes like those who are wrong.

⁸What hope do the wicked have when
        they die,
    when God takes their life away?
⁹God will not listen to their cries
    when trouble comes to them.
¹⁰They will not find joy in the Almighty,
    even though they call out to God all the
        time.

¹¹"I will teach you about the power of God
    and will not hide the ways of the
        Almighty.
¹²You have all seen this yourselves.
    So why are we having all this talk that
        means nothing?

¹³"Here is what God has planned for evil
        people,
    and what the Almighty will give to
        cruel people:

[14]They may have many children, but the sword will kill them.

Their children who are left will never have enough to eat.

[15]Then they will die of disease and be buried,

and the widows will not even cry for them.

[16]The wicked may heap up silver like piles of dirt

and have so many clothes they are like piles of clay.

[17]But good people will wear what evil people have gathered,

and the innocent will divide up their silver.

[18]The houses the wicked build are like a spider's web,

like a hut that a guard builds.

[19]The wicked are rich when they go to bed, but they are rich for the last time;

when they open their eyes, everything is gone.

[20]Fears come over them like a flood,

and a storm snatches them away in the night.

[21]The east wind will carry them away, and then they are gone,

because it sweeps them out of their place.

[22]The wind will hit them without mercy as they try to run away from its power.

[23]It will be as if the wind is clapping its hands;

it will whistle at them as they run from their place.

28 "There are mines where people dig silver

and places where gold is made pure.

[2]Iron is taken from the ground,

and copper is melted out of rocks.

[3]Miners bring lights

and search deep into the mines

for ore in thick darkness.

[4]Miners dig a tunnel far from where people live,

where no one has ever walked;

they work far from people, swinging and swaying from ropes.

[5]Food grows on top of the earth,

but below ground things are changed as if by fire.

[6]Sapphires are found in rocks,

and gold dust is also found there.

[7]No hawk knows that path;

the falcon has not seen it.

[8]Proud animals have not walked there,

and no lions cross over it.

[9]Miners hit the rocks of flint

and dig away at the bottom of the mountains.

[10]They cut tunnels through the rock

and see all the treasures there.

[11]They search for places where rivers begin

and bring things hidden out into the light.

[12]"But where can wisdom be found,

and where does understanding live?

[13]People do not understand the value of wisdom;

it cannot be found among those who are alive.

[14]The deep ocean says, 'It's not in me;'

the sea says, 'It's not in me.'

[15]Wisdom cannot be bought with gold,

and its cost cannot be weighed in silver.

[16]Wisdom cannot be bought with fine gold

or with valuable onyx or sapphire gems.

[17]Gold and crystal are not as valuable as wisdom,

and you cannot buy it with jewels of gold.

[18]Coral and jasper are not worth talking about,

and the price of wisdom is much greater than rubies.

[19]The topaz from Cush cannot compare to wisdom;

it cannot be bought with the purest gold.

[20]"So where does wisdom come from,

and where does understanding live?

[21]It is hidden from the eyes of every living thing,

even from the birds of the air.

[22]The places of destruction and death say, 'We have heard reports about it.'

[23]Only God understands the way to wisdom,

and he alone knows where it lives,
24because he looks to the farthest parts of
the earth
and sees everything under the sky.
25When God gave power to the wind
and measured the water,
26when he made rules for the rain
and set a path for a thunderstorm to
follow,
27then he looked at wisdom and decided
its worth;
he set wisdom up and tested it.
28Then he said to humans,
'The fear of the Lord is wisdom;
to stay away from evil is understanding.'"

PSALM 97:1–6

A Hymn About the Lord's Power

97 The LORD is king. Let the earth
rejoice;
faraway lands should be glad.
2Thick, dark clouds surround him.
His kingdom is built on what is right
and fair.
3A fire goes before him
and burns up his enemies all around.
4His lightning lights up the world;
when the people see it, they tremble.
5The mountains melt like wax before the
LORD,
before the Lord of all the earth.
6The heavens tell about his goodness,
and all the people see his glory.

PROVERBS 23:13–14

13Don't fail to punish children.
If you spank them, they won't die.
14If you spank them,
you will save them from death.

ROMANS 16:1–27

Greetings to the Christians

16 I recommend to you our sister Phoebe,
who is a helper" in the church in
Cenchrea. 2I ask you to accept her in the Lord
in the way God's people should. Help her
with anything she needs, because she has
helped me and many other people also.

3Give my greetings to Priscilla and Aquila,
who work together with me in Christ Jesus
4and who risked their own lives to save my life.
I am thankful to them, and all the non-Jewish
churches are thankful as well. 5Also, greet for
me the church that meets at their house.

Greetings to my dear friend Epenetus,
who was the first person in Asia to follow
Christ. 6Greetings to Mary, who worked very
hard for you. 7Greetings to Andronicus and
Junia, my relatives, who were in prison with
me. They are very important apostles. They
were believers in Christ before I was. 8Greet-
ings to Ampliatus, my dear friend in the
Lord. 9Greetings to Urbanus, a worker together with me for Christ. And greetings to
my dear friend Stachys. 10Greetings to
Apelles, who was tested and proved that he
truly loves Christ. Greetings to all those who
are in the family of Aristobulus. 11Greetings
to Herodion, my fellow citizen. Greetings to
all those in the family of Narcissus who belong to the Lord. 12Greetings to Tryphena
and Tryphosa, women who work very hard
for the Lord. Greetings to my dear friend
Persis, who also has worked very hard for the
Lord. 13Greetings to Rufus, who is a special
person in the Lord, and to his mother, who
has been like a mother to me also. 14Greet-
ings to Asyncritus, Phlegon, Hermes, Pat-
robas, Hermas, and all the brothers and
sisters who are with them. 15Greetings to
Philologus and Julia, Nereus and his sister,
and Olympas, and to all God's people with
them. 16Greet each other with a holy kiss. All
of Christ's churches send greetings to you.

17Brothers and sisters, I ask you to look
out for those who cause people to be against
each other and who upset other people's
faith. They are against the true teaching you
learned, so stay away from them. 18Such people are not serving our Lord Christ but are
only doing what pleases themselves. They
use fancy talk and fine words to fool the
minds of those who do not know about evil.
19All the believers have heard that you obey,
so I am very happy because of you. But I
want you to be wise in what is good and innocent in what is evil.

16:1 helper Literally, "deaconess." This might mean the same as one of the special women helpers in 1 Timothy 3:11.

[20]The God who brings peace will soon defeat Satan and give you power over him.

The grace of our Lord Jesus be with you.

[21]Timothy, a worker together with me, sends greetings, as well as Lucius, Jason, and Sosipater, my relatives.

[22]I am Tertius, and I am writing this letter from Paul. I send greetings to you in the Lord.

[23]Gaius is letting me and the whole church here use his home. He also sends greetings to you, as do Erastus, the city treasurer, and our brother Quartus. [[24]The grace of our Lord Jesus Christ be with all of you. Amen.][n]

[25]Glory to God who can make you strong in faith by the Good News that I tell people and by the message about Jesus Christ. The message about Christ is the secret that was hidden for long ages past but is now made known. [26]It has been made clear through the writings of the prophets. And by the command of the eternal God it is made known to all nations that they might believe and obey.

[27]To the only wise God be glory forever through Jesus Christ! Amen.

AUGUST 19

JOB 29:1—30:31

Job Continues

29 Job continued to speak:
[2]"How I wish for the months that have passed
and the days when God watched over me.
[3]God's lamp shined on my head,
and I walked through darkness by his light.
[4]I wish for the days when I was strong,
when God's close friendship blessed my house.
[5]The Almighty was still with me,
and my children were all around me.
[6]It was as if my path were covered with cream
and the rocks poured out olive oil for me.
[7]I would go to the city gate
and sit in the public square.
[8]When the young men saw me, they would step aside,
and the old men would stand up in respect.
[9]The leading men stopped speaking
and covered their mouths with their hands.
[10]The voices of the important men were quiet,

as if their tongues stuck to the roof of their mouths.
[11]Anyone who heard me spoke well of me,
and those who saw me praised me,
[12]because I saved the poor who called out
and the orphan who had no one to help.
[13]The dying person blessed me,
and I made the widow's heart sing.
[14]I put on right living as if it were clothing;
I wore fairness like a robe and a turban.
[15]I was eyes for the blind
and feet for the lame.
[16]I was like a father to needy people,
and I took the side of strangers who were in trouble.
[17]I broke the fangs of evil people
and snatched the captives from their teeth.
[18]"I thought, 'I will live for as many days as there are grains of sand,
and I will die in my own house.
[19]My roots will reach down to the water.
The dew will lie on the branches all night.[n]
[20]New honors will come to me continually,
and I will always have great strength.'
[21]"People listened to me carefully
and waited quietly for my advice.

16:24 The . . . Amen. Some Greek copies do not contain the bracketed text.

22After I finished speaking, they spoke no
  more.
  My words fell very gently on their ears.
23They waited for me as they would for
  rain
  and drank in my words like spring rain.
24I smiled at them when they doubted,
  and my approval was important to
  them.
25I chose the way for them and was their
  leader.
  I lived like a king among his army,
  like a person who comforts sad people.

30 "But now those who are younger
    than I
  make fun of me.
  I would not have even let their fathers
  sit with my sheep dogs.
2What use did I have for their strength
  since they had lost their strength to
  work?
3They were thin from hunger
  and wandered the dry and ruined land
  at night.
4They gathered desert plants among the
  brush
  and ate the root of the broom tree.
5They were forced to live away from
  people;
  people shouted at them as if they were
  thieves.
6They lived in dried-up streambeds,
  in caves, and among the rocks.
7They howled like animals among the
  bushes
  and huddled together in the brush.
8They are worthless people without
  names
  and were forced to leave the land.

9"Now they make fun of me with songs;
  my name is a joke among them.
10They hate me and stay far away from me,
  but they do not mind spitting in my
  face.
11God has taken away my strength and
  made me suffer,
  so they attack me with all their anger.
12On my right side they rise up like a mob.
  They lay traps for my feet
  and prepare to attack me.

13They break up my road
  and work to destroy me,
  and no one helps me.
14They come at me as if through a hole in
  the wall,
  and they roll in among the ruins.
15Great fears overwhelm me.
  They blow my honor away as if by a
  great wind,
  and my safety disappears like a cloud.

16"Now my life is almost over;
  my days are full of suffering.
17At night my bones ache;
  gnawing pains never stop.
18In his great power God grabs hold of my
  clothing
  and chokes me with the collar of my
  coat.
19He throws me into the mud,
  and I become like dirt and ashes.

20"I cry out to you, God, but you do not
  answer;
  I stand up, but you just look at me.
21You have turned on me without mercy;
  with your powerful hand you attacked
  me.
22You snatched me up and threw me into
  the wind
  and tossed me about in the storm.
23I know you will bring me down to death,
  to the place where all living people
  must go.

24"Surely no one would hurt those who are
  ruined
  when they cry for help in their time of
  trouble.
25I cried for those who were in trouble;
  I have been very sad for poor people.
26But when I hoped for good, only evil
  came to me;
  when I looked for light, darkness came.
27I never stop being upset;
  days of suffering are ahead of me.
28I have turned black, but not by the sun.
  I stand up in public and cry for help.
29I have become a brother to wild dogs
  and a friend to ostriches.
30My skin has become black and peels off,
  as my body burns with fever.

[31]My harp is tuned to sing a sad song,
and my flute is tuned to moaning.

PSALM 97:7–12

[7]Those who worship idols should be
ashamed;
they brag about their gods.
All the gods should worship the LORD.
[8]When Jerusalem hears this, she is glad,
and the towns of Judah rejoice.
They are happy because of your
judgments, LORD.
[9]You are the LORD Most High over all the
earth;
you are supreme over all gods.

[10]People who love the LORD hate evil.
The LORD watches over those who
follow him
and frees them from the power of the
wicked.
[11]Light shines on those who do right;
joy belongs to those who are honest.
[12]Rejoice in the LORD, you who do right.
Praise his holy name.

PROVERBS 23:15–16

[15]My child, if you are wise,
then I will be happy.
[16]I will be so pleased
if you speak what is right.

1 CORINTHIANS 1:1–31

1 From Paul. God called me to be an apostle of Christ Jesus because that is what God wanted. Also from Sosthenes, our brother in Christ.
[2]To the church of God in Corinth, to you who have been made holy in Christ Jesus. You were called to be God's holy people with all people everywhere who pray in the name of the Lord Jesus Christ—their Lord and ours:
[3]Grace and peace to you from God our Father and the Lord Jesus Christ.

Paul Gives Thanks to God
[4]I always thank my God for you because of the grace God has given you in Christ Jesus.

[5]I thank God because in Christ you have been made rich in every way, in all your speaking and in all your knowledge. [6]Just as our witness about Christ has been guaranteed to you, [7]so you have every gift from God while you wait for our Lord Jesus Christ to come again. [8]Jesus will keep you strong until the end so that there will be no wrong in you on the day our Lord Jesus Christ comes again. [9]God, who has called you into fellowship with his Son, Jesus Christ our Lord, is faithful.

Problems in the Church
[10]I beg you, brothers and sisters, by the name of our Lord Jesus Christ that all of you agree with each other and not be split into groups. I beg that you be completely joined together by having the same kind of thinking and the same purpose. [11]My brothers and sisters, some people from Chloe's family have told me quite plainly that there are quarrels among you. [12]This is what I mean: One of you says, "I follow Paul"; another says, "I follow Apollos"; another says, "I follow Peter"; and another says, "I follow Christ." [13]Christ has been divided up into different groups! Did Paul die on the cross for you? No! Were you baptized in the name of Paul? No! [14]I thank God I did not baptize any of you except Crispus and Gaius [15]so that now no one can say you were baptized in my name. [16](I also baptized the family of Stephanas, but I do not remember that I baptized anyone else.) [17]Christ did not send me to baptize people but to preach the Good News. And he sent me to preach the Good News without using words of human wisdom so that the cross[n] of Christ would not lose its power.

Christ Is God's Power and Wisdom
[18]The teaching about the cross is foolishness to those who are being lost, but to us who are being saved it is the power of God. [19]It is written in the Scriptures:
"I will cause the wise to lose their
wisdom;
I will make the wise unable to
understand."   *Isaiah 29:14*

1:17 cross Paul uses the cross as a picture of the Good News, the story of Christ's death and rising from the dead for people's sins. The cross, or Christ's death, was God's way to save people.

²⁰Where is the wise person? Where is the educated person? Where is the skilled talker of this world? God has made the wisdom of the world foolish. ²¹In the wisdom of God the world did not know God through its own wisdom. So God chose to use the message that sounds foolish to save those who believe. ²²The Jews ask for miracles, and the Greeks want wisdom. ²³But we preach a crucified Christ. This causes the Jews to stumble and is foolishness to non-Jews. ²⁴But Christ is the power of God and the wisdom of God to those people God has called—Jews and Greeks. ²⁵Even the foolishness of God is wiser than human wisdom, and the weakness of God is stronger than human strength.

²⁶Brothers and sisters, look at what you were when God called you. Not many of you were wise in the way the world judges wisdom. Not many of you had great influence. Not many of you came from important families. ²⁷But God chose the foolish things of the world to shame the wise, and he chose the weak things of the world to shame the strong. ²⁸He chose what the world thinks is unimportant and what the world looks down on and thinks is nothing in order to destroy what the world thinks is important. ²⁹God did this so that no one can brag in his presence. ³⁰Because of God you are in Christ Jesus, who has become for us wisdom from God. In Christ we are put right with God, and have been made holy, and have been set free from sin. ³¹So, as the Scripture says, "If people want to brag, they should brag only about the Lord."ⁿ

AUGUST 20

JOB 31:1—32:22

31 "But I made an agreement with my eyes not to look with desire at a girl.
²What has God above promised for people?
What has the Almighty planned from on high?
³It is ruin for evil people
and disaster for those who do wrong.
⁴God sees my ways
and counts every step I take.

⁵"If I have been dishonest
or lied to others,
⁶then let God weigh me on honest scales.
Then he will know I have done nothing wrong.
⁷If I have turned away from doing what is right,
or my heart has been led by my eyes to do wrong,
or my hands have been made unclean,
⁸then let other people eat what I have planted,
and let my crops be plowed up.

⁹"If I have desired another woman
or have waited at my neighbor's door for his wife,
¹⁰then let my wife grind another man's grain,
and let other men have sexual relations with her.
¹¹That would be shameful,
a sin to be punished.
¹²It is like a fire that burns and destroys;
all I have done would be plowed up.

¹³"If I have been unfair to my male and female slaves
when they had a complaint against me,
¹⁴how could I tell God what I did?
What will I answer when he asks me to explain what I've done?
¹⁵God made me in my mother's womb, and he also made them;
the same God formed both of us in our mothers' wombs.

¹⁶"I have never refused the appeals of the poor
or let widows give up hope while looking for help.

1:31 "If . . . Lord." Quotation from Jeremiah 9:24.

¹⁷I have not kept my food to myself
  but have given it to the orphans.
¹⁸Since I was young, I have been like a
    father to the orphans.
  From my birth I guided the widows.
¹⁹I have not let anyone die for lack of clothes
  or let a needy person go without a coat.
²⁰That person's heart blessed me,
    because I warmed him with the wool of
      my sheep.
²¹I have never hurt an orphan
  even when I knew I could win in court.
²²If I have, then let my arm fall off my
      shoulder
    and be broken at the joint.
²³I fear destruction from God,
    and I fear his majesty, so I could not do
      such things.

²⁴"I have not put my trust in gold
  or said to pure gold, 'You are my
    security.'
²⁵I have not celebrated my great wealth
  or the riches my hands had gained.
²⁶I have not thought about worshiping the
    sun in its brightness
  nor admired the moon moving in glory
²⁷so that my heart was pulled away from
    God.
  My hand has never offered the sun and
    moon a kiss of worship.
²⁸If I had, these also would have been sins
    to be punished,
  because I would have been unfaithful to
    God.

²⁹"I have not been happy when my enemies
    fell
  or laughed when they had trouble.
³⁰I have not let my mouth sin
  by cursing my enemies' life.
³¹The servants of my house have always
    said,
  'All have eaten what they want of Job's
    food.'
³²No stranger ever had to spend the night in
    the street,
  because I always let travelers stay in my
    home.
³³I have not hidden my sin as others do,
  secretly keeping my guilt to myself.
³⁴I was not so afraid of the crowd

that I kept quiet and stayed inside
    because I feared being hated by other
      families.

³⁵("How I wish a court would hear my case!
    Here I sign my name to show I have told
      the truth.
  Now let the Almighty answer me;
    let the one who accuses me write it
      down.
³⁶I would wear the writing on my shoulder;
    I would put it on like a crown.
³⁷I would explain to God every step I took,
    and I would come near to him like a
      prince.)
³⁸"If my land cries out against me
    and its plowed rows are not wet with
      tears,
³⁹if I have taken the land's harvest without
      paying
    or have broken the spirit of those who
      worked the land,
⁴⁰then let thorns come up instead of wheat,
    and let weeds come up instead of barley."
  The words of Job are finished.

Elihu Speaks

32 These three men stopped trying to answer Job, because he was so sure he was right. ²But Elihu son of Barakel the Buzite, from the family of Ram, became very angry with Job, because Job claimed he was right instead of God. ³Elihu was also angry with Job's three friends who had no answer to show that Job was wrong, yet continued to blame him. ⁴Elihu had waited before speaking to Job, because the three friends were older than he was. ⁵But when Elihu saw that the three men had nothing more to say, he became very angry.

⁶So Elihu son of Barakel the Buzite said this:
"I am young,
    and you are old.
That is why I was afraid
    to tell you what I know.
⁷I thought, 'Older people should speak,
    and those who have lived many years
      should teach wisdom.'
⁸But it is the spirit in a person,
    the breath of the Almighty, that gives
      understanding.

⁹It is not just older people who are wise;
they are not the only ones who
understand what is right.
¹⁰So I say, listen to me.
I too will tell you what I know.
¹¹I waited while you three spoke,
and listened to your explanations.
While you looked for words to use,
¹² I paid close attention to you.
But not one of you has proved Job wrong;
none of you has answered his
arguments.
¹³Don't say, 'We have found wisdom;
only God will show Job to be wrong, not
people.'
¹⁴Job has not spoken his words against me,
so I will not use your arguments to
answer Job.

¹⁵"These three friends are defeated and
have no more to say;
words have failed them.
¹⁶Now they are standing there with no
answers for Job.
Now that they are quiet, must I wait to
speak?
¹⁷No, I too will speak
and tell what I know.
¹⁸I am full of words,
and the spirit in me causes me to speak.
¹⁹I am like wine that has been bottled up;
I am ready to burst like a new leather
wine bag.
²⁰I must speak so I will feel relief;
I must open my mouth and answer.
²¹I will be fair to everyone
and not flatter anyone.
²²I don't know how to flatter,
and if I did, my Maker would quickly
take me away.

PSALM 98:1–3

The Lord of Power and Justice

A psalm.

98 Sing to the LORD a new song,
because he has done miracles.
By his right hand and holy arm
he has won the victory.

²The LORD has made known his power to
save;
he has shown the other nations his
victory for his people.
³He has remembered his love
and his loyalty to the people of Israel.
All the ends of the earth have seen
God's power to save.

PROVERBS 23:17–18

¹⁷Don't envy sinners,
but always respect the LORD.
¹⁸Then you will have hope for the future,
and your wishes will come true.

1 CORINTHIANS 2:1–16

The Message of Christ's Death

2 Dear brothers and sisters, when I came to
you, I did not come preaching God's secret[n]
with fancy words or a show of human wisdom. ²I decided that while I was with you I
would forget about everything except Jesus
Christ and his death on the cross. ³So when I
came to you, I was weak and fearful and trembling. ⁴My teaching and preaching were not
with words of human wisdom that persuade
people but with proof of the power that the
Spirit gives. ⁵This was so that your faith would
be in God's power and not in human wisdom.

God's Wisdom

⁶However, I speak a wisdom to those who
are mature. But this wisdom is not from this
world or from the rulers of this world, who
are losing their power. ⁷I speak God's secret
wisdom, which he has kept hidden. Before
the world began, God planned this wisdom
for our glory. ⁸None of the rulers of this
world understood it. If they had, they would
not have crucified the Lord of glory. ⁹But as
it is written in the Scriptures:

"No one has ever seen this,
and no one has ever heard about it.
No one has ever imagined
what God has prepared for those who
love him."   *Isaiah 64:4*

¹⁰But God has shown us these things
through the Spirit.

2:1 God's secret Some Greek copies read "God's message."

The Spirit searches out all things, even the deep secrets of God. [11]Who knows the thoughts that another person has? Only a person's spirit that lives within him knows his thoughts. It is the same with God. No one knows the thoughts of God except the Spirit of God. [12]Now we did not receive the spirit of the world, but we received the Spirit that is from God so that we can know all that God has given us. [13]And we speak about these things, not with words taught us by human wisdom but with words taught us by the Spirit. And so we explain spiritual truths to spiritual people. [14]A person who does not have the Spirit does not accept the truths that come from the Spirit of God. That person thinks they are foolish and cannot understand them, because they can only be judged to be true by the Spirit. [15]The spiritual person is able to judge all things, but no one can judge him. The Scripture says:

[16]"Who has known the mind of the
    Lord?
Who has been able to teach him?"

Isaiah 40:13

But we have the mind of Christ.

AUGUST 21

JOB 33:1—34:37

33 "Now, Job, listen to my words.
    Pay attention to everything I say.
[2]I open my mouth
    and am ready to speak.
[3]My words come from an honest heart,
    and I am sincere in saying what I know.
[4]The Spirit of God created me,
    and the breath of the Almighty gave me
    life.
[5]Answer me if you can;
    get yourself ready and stand before me.
[6]I am just like you before God;
    I too am made out of clay.
[7]Don't be afraid of me;
    I will not be hard on you.

[8]"But I heard what you have said;
    I heard every word.
[9]You said, 'I am pure and without sin;
    I am innocent and free from guilt.
[10]But God has found fault with me;
    he considers me his enemy.
[11]He locks my feet in chains
    and closely watches everywhere I go.'

[12]"But I tell you, you are not right in saying
    this,
    because God is greater than we are.
[13]Why do you accuse God
    of not answering anyone?

[14]God does speak—sometimes one way
    and sometimes another—
    even though people may not
    understand it.
[15]He speaks in a dream or a vision of the
    night
    when people are in a deep sleep,
    lying on their beds.
[16]He speaks in their ears
    and frightens them with warnings
[17]to turn them away from doing wrong
    and to keep them from being proud.
[18]God does this to save people from death,
    to keep them from dying.
[19]People may be corrected while in bed in
    great pain;
    they may have continual pain in their
    very bones.
[20]They may be in such pain that they even
    hate food,
    even the very best meal.
[21]Their body becomes so thin there is
    almost nothing left of it,
    and their bones that were hidden now
    stick out.
[22]They are near death,
    and their life is almost over.
[23]"But there may be an angel to speak for
    him,
    one out of a thousand, who will tell
    him what to do.

²⁴The angel will beg for mercy and say:
'Save him from death.
I have found a way to pay for his life.'
²⁵Then his body is made new like a child's.
It will return to the way it was when he
was young.
²⁶That person will pray to God, and God
will listen to him.
He will see God's face and will shout
with happiness.
And God will set things right for him
again.
²⁷Then he will say to others,
'I sinned and twisted what was right,
but I did not receive the punishment I
should have received.
²⁸God bought my life back from death,
and I will continue to enjoy life.'

²⁹"God does all these things to a person
two or even three times
³⁰so he won't die as punishment for his sins
and so he may still enjoy life.

³¹"Job, pay attention and listen to me;
be quiet, and I will speak.
³²If you have anything to say, answer me;
speak up, because I want to prove you
right.
³³But if you have nothing to say, then listen
to me;
be quiet, and I will teach you wisdom."

34 Then Elihu said:
²"Hear my words, you wise men;
listen to me, you who know a lot.
³The ear tests words
as the tongue tastes food.
⁴Let's decide for ourselves what is right,
and let's learn together what is good.

⁵"Job says, 'I am not guilty,
and God has refused me a fair trial.
⁶Instead of getting a fair trial,
I am called a liar.
I have been seriously hurt,
even though I have not sinned.'
⁷There is no other man like Job;
he takes insults as if he were drinking
water.
⁸He keeps company with those who do evil
and spends time with wicked men,

⁹because he says, 'It is no use
to try to please God.'

¹⁰"So listen to me, you who can
understand.
God can never do wrong!
It is impossible for the Almighty to do
evil.
¹¹God pays people back for what they have
done
and gives them what their actions
deserve.
¹²Truly God will never do wrong;
the Almighty will never twist what is
right.
¹³No one chose God to rule over the earth
or put him in charge of the whole
world.
¹⁴If God should decide
to take away life and breath,
¹⁵then everyone would die together
and turn back into dust.

¹⁶"If you can understand, hear this;
listen to what I have to say.
¹⁷Can anyone govern who hates what is
right?
How can you blame God who is both
fair and powerful?
¹⁸God is the one who says to kings, 'You are
worthless,'
or to important people, 'You are evil.'
¹⁹He is not nicer to princes than other
people,
nor kinder to rich people than poor
people,
because he made them all with his own
hands.
²⁰They can die in a moment, in the middle
of the night.
They are struck down, and then they
pass away;
powerful people die without help.

²¹"God watches where people go;
he sees every step they take.
²²There is no dark place or deep shadow
where those who do evil can hide from
him.
²³He does not set a time
for people to come before him for
judging.

²⁴Without asking questions, God breaks
powerful people into pieces
and puts others in their place.
²⁵Because God knows what people do,
he defeats them in the night, and they
are crushed.
²⁶He punishes them for the evil they do
so that everyone else can watch,
²⁷because they stopped following God
and did not care about any of his ways.
²⁸The cry of the poor comes to God;
he hears the cry of the needy.
²⁹But if God keeps quiet, who can blame
him?
If he hides his face, who can see him?
God still rules over both nations and
persons alike.
³⁰ He keeps the wicked from ruling
and from trapping others.

³¹"But suppose someone says to God,
'I am guilty, but I will not sin anymore.'
³²Teach me what I cannot see.
If I have done wrong, I will not do it
again.'
³³So, Job, should God reward you as you
want
when you refuse to change?
You must decide, not I,
so tell me what you know.

³⁴"Those who understand speak,
and the wise who hear me say,
³⁵'Job speaks without knowing what is
true;
his words show he does not
understand.'
³⁶I wish Job would be tested completely,
because he answered like an evil man!
³⁷Job now adds to his sin by turning
against God.
He claps his hands in protest,
speaking more and more against God."

PSALM 98:4–9

⁴Shout with joy to the LORD, all the earth;
burst into songs and make music.
⁵Make music to the LORD with harps,
with harps and the sound of singing.
⁶Blow the trumpets and the sheep's horns;
shout for joy to the LORD the King.

⁷Let the sea and everything in it shout;
let the world and everyone in it sing.
⁸Let the rivers clap their hands;
let the mountains sing together for joy.
⁹Let them sing before the LORD,
because he is coming to judge the
world.
He will judge the world fairly;
he will judge the peoples with fairness.

PROVERBS 23:19–21

¹⁹Listen, my child, and be wise.
Keep your mind on what is right.
²⁰Don't drink too much wine
or eat too much food.
²¹Those who drink and eat too much
become poor.
They sleep too much and end up
wearing rags.

1 CORINTHIANS 3:1–23

Following People Is Wrong

3 Brothers and sisters, in the past I could
not talk to you as I talk to spiritual people. I had to talk to you as I would to people
without the Spirit—babies in Christ. ²The
teaching I gave you was like milk, not solid
food, because you were not able to take solid
food. And even now you are not ready. ³You
are still not spiritual, because there is jealousy and quarreling among you, and this
shows that you are not spiritual. You are acting like people of the world. ⁴One of you says,
"I belong to Paul," and another says, "I belong to Apollos." When you say things like
this, you are acting like people of the world.
⁵Is Apollos important? No! Is Paul important? No! We are only servants of God who
helped you believe. Each one of us did the
work God gave us to do. ⁶I planted the seed,
and Apollos watered it. But God is the One
who made it grow. ⁷So the one who plants is
not important, and the one who waters is not
important. Only God, who makes things
grow, is important. ⁸The one who plants and
the one who waters have the same purpose,
and each will be rewarded for his own work.
⁹We are God's workers, working together;
you are like God's farm, God's house.
¹⁰Using the gift God gave me, I laid the

foundation of that house like an expert builder. Others are building on that foundation, but all people should be careful how they build on it. [11]The foundation that has already been laid is Jesus Christ, and no one can lay down any other foundation. [12]But if people build on that foundation, using gold, silver, jewels, wood, grass, or straw, [13]their work will be clearly seen, because the Day of Judgment[n] will make it visible. That Day will appear with fire, and the fire will test everyone's work to show what sort of work it was. [14]If the building that has been put on the foundation still stands, the builder will get a reward. [15]But if the building is burned up, the builder will suffer loss. The builder will be saved, but it will be as one who escaped from a fire.

[16]Don't you know that you are God's temple and that God's Spirit lives in you? [17]If anyone destroys God's temple, God will destroy that person, because God's temple is holy and you are that temple.

[18]Do not fool yourselves. If you think you are wise in this world, you should become a fool so that you can become truly wise, [19]because the wisdom of this world is foolishness with God. It is written in the Scriptures, "He catches those who are wise in their own clever traps."[n] [20]It is also written in the Scriptures, "The Lord knows what wise people think. He knows their thoughts are just a puff of wind."[n] [21]So you should not brag about human leaders. All things belong to you: [22]Paul, Apollos, and Peter; the world, life, death, the present, and the future—all these belong to you. [23]And you belong to Christ, and Christ belongs to God.

AUGUST 22

JOB 35:1—36:33

35 Then Elihu said:
  [2]"Do you think this is fair?
    You say, 'God will show that I am right,'
  [3]but you also ask, 'What's the use?
    I don't gain anything by not sinning.'

[4]"I will answer you
    and your friends who are with you.
[5]Look up at the sky
    and see the clouds so high above you.
[6]If you sin, it does nothing to God;
    even if your sins are many, they do
      nothing to him.
[7]If you are good, you give nothing to God;
    he receives nothing from your hand.
[8]Your evil ways only hurt others like
      yourself,
    and the good you do only helps other
      human beings.

[9]"People cry out when they are in trouble;
    they beg for relief from powerful
      people.

[10]But no one asks, 'Where is God, my
      Maker,
    who gives us songs in the night,
[11]who makes us smarter than the animals
      of the earth
    and wiser than the birds of the air?'
[12]God does not answer evil people when
      they cry out,
    because the wicked are proud.
[13]God does not listen to their useless
      begging;
    the Almighty pays no attention to
      them.
[14]He will listen to you even less
    when you say that you do not see him,
    that your case is before him,
    that you must wait for him,
[15] that his anger never punishes,
    and that he doesn't notice evil.
[16]So Job is only speaking nonsense,
    saying many words without knowing
      what is true."

3:13 Day of Judgment The day Christ will come to judge all people and take his people home to live with him.   **3:19 "He . . . traps."** Quotation from Job 5:13.   **3:20 "The Lord . . . wind."** Quotation from Psalm 94:11.

Elihu's Speech Continues

36

Elihu continued:

2"Listen to me a little longer, and I
will show you
    that there is more to be said for God.
3What I know comes from far away.
    I will show that my Maker is right.
4You can be sure that my words are not
false;
    one who really knows is with you.

5"God is powerful, but he does not hate
people;
    he is powerful and sure of what he
    wants to do.
6He will not keep evil people alive,
    but he gives the poor their rights.
7He always watches over those who do
right;
    he sets them on thrones with kings
    and they are honored forever.
8If people are bound in chains,
    or if trouble, like ropes, ties them up,
9God tells them what they have done,
    that they have sinned in their pride.
10God makes them listen to his warning
    and commands them to change from
    doing evil.
11If they obey and serve him,
    the rest of their lives will be successful,
    and the rest of their years will be
    happy.
12But if they do not listen,
    they will die by the sword,
    and they will die without knowing why.

13"Those who have wicked hearts hold on
to anger.
    Even when God punishes them, they do
    not cry for help.
14They die while they are still young,
    and their lives end in disgrace.
15But God saves those who suffer through
    their suffering;
    he gets them to listen through their
    pain.

16"God is gently calling you from the jaws
of trouble
    to an open place of freedom
    where he has set your table full of the
    best food.

17But now you are being punished like the
wicked;
    you are getting justice.
18Be careful! Don't be led away from God
    by riches;
    don't let much money turn you away.
19Neither your wealth nor all your great
    strength
    will keep you out of trouble.
20Don't wish for the night
    when people are taken from their
    homes.
21Be careful not to turn to evil,
    which you seem to want more than
    suffering.

22"God is great and powerful;
    no other teacher is like him.
23No one has planned his ways for him;
    no one can say to God, 'You have done
    wrong.'
24Remember to praise his work,
    about which people have sung.
25Everybody has seen it;
    people look at it from far off.
26God is so great, greater than we can
    understand!
    No one knows how old he is.

27"He evaporates the drops of water from
the earth
    and turns them into rain.
28The rain then pours down from the
    clouds,
    and showers fall on people.
29No one understands how God spreads
    out the clouds
    or how he sends thunder from where
    he lives.
30Watch how God scatters his lightning
    around him,
    lighting up the deepest parts of the
    sea.
31This is the way God governs the
    nations;
    this is how he gives us enough food.
32God fills his hands with lightning
    and commands it to strike its target.
33His thunder announces the coming
    storm,
    and even the cattle know it is near.

PSALM 99:1–9

The Lord, the Fair and Holy King

99 The LORD is king.
Let the peoples shake with fear.
He sits between the gold creatures with
wings.
Let the earth shake.
²The LORD in Jerusalem is great;
he is supreme over all the peoples.
³Let them praise your name;
it is great, holy and to be feared.

⁴The King is powerful and loves justice.
LORD, you made things fair;
you have done what is fair and right
for the people of Jacob.
⁵Praise the LORD our God,
and worship at the Temple, his footstool.
He is holy.

⁶Moses and Aaron were among his
priests,
and Samuel was among his worshipers.
They called to the LORD,
and he answered them.
⁷He spoke to them from the pillar of
cloud.
They kept the rules and laws he gave
them.

⁸LORD our God, you answered them.
You showed them that you are a
forgiving God,
but you punished them for their
wrongs.
⁹Praise the LORD our God,
and worship at his holy mountain,
because the LORD our God is holy.

PROVERBS 23:22–25

²²Listen to your father, who gave you life,
and do not forget your mother when
she is old.
²³Learn the truth and never reject it.
Get wisdom, self-control, and
understanding.
²⁴The father of a good child is very happy;
parents who have wise children are
glad because of them.
²⁵Make your father and mother happy;
give your mother a reason to be glad.

1 CORINTHIANS 4:1–21

Apostles Are Servants of Christ

4 People should think of us as servants of
Christ, the ones God has trusted with his
secrets. ²Now in this way those who are
trusted with something valuable must show
they are worthy of that trust. ³As for myself, I
do not care if I am judged by you or by any
human court. I do not even judge myself. ⁴I
know of no wrong I have done, but this does
not make me right before the Lord. The Lord
is the One who judges me. ⁵So do not judge
before the right time; wait until the Lord
comes. He will bring to light things that are
now hidden in darkness, and will make
known the secret purposes of people's hearts.
Then God will praise each one of them.

⁶Brothers and sisters, I have used Apollos
and myself as examples so you could learn
through us the meaning of the saying, "Follow
only what is written in the Scriptures." Then
you will not be more proud of one person
than another. ⁷Who says you are better than
others? What do you have that was not given
to you? And if it was given to you, why do you
brag as if you did not receive it as a gift?

⁸You think you already have everything
you need. You think you are rich. You think
you have become kings without us. I wish you
really were kings so we could be kings together with you. ⁹But it seems to me that God
has put us apostles in last place, like those
sentenced to die. We are like a show for the
whole world to see—angels and people. ¹⁰We
are fools for Christ's sake, but you are very
wise in Christ. We are weak, but you are
strong. You receive honor, but we are shamed.
¹¹Even to this very hour we do not have
enough to eat or drink or to wear. We are often beaten, and we have no homes in which to
live. ¹²We work hard with our own hands for
our food. When people curse us, we bless
them. When they hurt us, we put up with it.
¹³When they tell evil lies about us, we speak
nice words about them. Even today, we are
treated as though we were the garbage of the
world—the filth of the earth.

¹⁴I am not trying to make you feel ashamed.
I am writing this to give you a warning as my
own dear children. ¹⁵For though you may

have ten thousand teachers in Christ, you do not have many fathers. Through the Good News I became your father in Christ Jesus, [16]so I beg you, please follow my example. [17]That is why I am sending to you Timothy, my son in the Lord. I love Timothy, and he is faithful. He will help you remember my way of life in Christ Jesus, just as I teach it in all the churches everywhere.

[18]Some of you have become proud, thinking that I will not come to you again. [19]But I will come to you very soon if the Lord wishes. Then I will know what the proud ones do, not what they say, [20]because the kingdom of God is present not in talk but in power. [21]Which do you want: that I come to you with punishment or with love and gentleness?

AUGUST 23

JOB 37:1—38:41

37[1]"At the sound of his thunder, my heart pounds
as if it will jump out of my chest.
[2]Listen! Listen to the thunder of God's voice
and to the rumbling that comes from his mouth.
[3]He turns his lightning loose under the whole sky
and sends it to the farthest parts of the earth.
[4]After that you can hear the roar
when he thunders with a great sound.
He does not hold back the flashing
when his voice is heard.
[5]God's voice thunders in wonderful ways;
he does great things we cannot understand.
[6]He says to the snow, 'Fall on the earth,'
and to the shower, 'Be a heavy rain.'
[7]With it, he stops everyone from working
so everyone knows it is the work of God.
[8]The animals take cover from the rain
and stay in their dens.
[9]The storm comes from where it was stored;
the cold comes with the strong winds.
[10]The breath of God makes ice,
and the wide waters become frozen.
[11]He fills the clouds with water
and scatters his lightning through them.
[12]At his command they swirl around
over the whole earth,
doing whatever he commands.
[13]He uses the clouds to punish people
or to water his earth and show his love.

[14]"Job, listen to this:
Stop and notice God's miracles.
[15]Do you know how God controls the clouds
and makes his lightning flash?
[16]Do you know how the clouds hang in the sky?
Do you know the miracles of God, who knows everything?
[17]You suffer in your clothes
when the land is silenced by the hot, south wind.
[18]You cannot stretch out the sky like God
and make it look as hard as polished bronze.
[19]Tell us what we should say to him;
we cannot get our arguments ready
because we do not have enough understanding.
[20]Should God be told that I want to speak?
Would a person ask to be swallowed up?
[21]No one can look at the sun
when it is bright in the sky
after the wind has blown all the clouds away.
[22]God comes out of the north in golden light,
in overwhelming greatness.
[23]The Almighty is too high for us to reach.
He has great strength;

he is always right and never punishes
  unfairly.
²⁴That is why people honor him;
  he does not respect those who say they
    are wise."

The Lord Questions Job

38 Then the LORD answered Job from the
  storm. He said:
²"Who is this that makes my purpose
    unclear
  by saying things that are not true?
³Be strong like a man!
  I will ask you questions,
  and you must answer me.
⁴Where were you when I made the earth's
    foundation?
  Tell me, if you understand.
⁵Who marked off how big it should be?
    Surely you know!
  Who stretched a ruler across it?
⁶What were the earth's foundations set on,
  or who put its cornerstone in place
⁷while the morning stars sang together
  and all the angels shouted with joy?

⁸"Who shut the doors to keep the sea in
  when it broke through and was born,
⁹when I made the clouds like a coat for the
    sea
  and wrapped it in dark clouds,
¹⁰when I put limits on the sea
  and put its doors and bars in place,
¹¹when I said to the sea, 'You may come this
    far, but no farther;
  this is where your proud waves must
    stop'?

¹²"Have you ever ordered the morning to
    begin,
  or shown the dawn where its place was
¹³in order to take hold of the earth by its
    edges
  and shake evil people out of it?
¹⁴At dawn the earth changes like clay being
    pressed by a seal;
  the hills and valleys stand out like folds
    in a coat.
¹⁵Light is not given to evil people;
  their arm is raised to do harm, but it is
    broken.

¹⁶"Have you ever gone to where the sea
    begins
  or walked in the valleys under the sea?
¹⁷Have the gates of death been opened to
    you?
  Have you seen the gates of the deep
    darkness?
¹⁸Do you understand how wide the earth is?
  Tell me, if you know all these things.

¹⁹"What is the path to light's home,
  and where does darkness live?
²⁰Can you take them to their places?
  Do you know the way to their homes?
²¹Surely you know, if you were already born
    when all this happened!
  Have you lived that many years?

²²"Have you ever gone into the storehouse
    of the snow
  or seen the storehouses for hail,
²³which I save for times of trouble,
  for days of war and battle?
²⁴Where is the place from which light
    comes?
  Where is the place from which the east
    winds blow over the earth?
²⁵Who cuts a waterway for the heavy rains
  and sets a path for the thunderstorm?
²⁶Who waters the land where no one lives,
  the desert that has no one in it?
²⁷Who sends rain to satisfy the empty land
  so the grass begins to grow?
²⁸Does the rain have a father?
  Who is father to the drops of dew?
²⁹Who is the mother of the ice?
  Who gives birth to the frost from the sky
³⁰when the water becomes hard as stone,
  and even the surface of the ocean is
    frozen?

³¹"Can you tie up the stars of the Pleiades
  or loosen the ropes of the stars in Orion?
³²Can you bring out the stars on time
  or lead out the stars of the Bear with its
    cubs?
³³Do you know the laws of the sky
  and understand their rule over the
    earth?
³⁴"Can you shout an order to the clouds
  and cover yourself with a flood of water?

³⁵Can you send lightning bolts on their way?
  Do they come to you and say, 'Here we
  are'?
³⁶Who put wisdom inside the mind
  or understanding in the heart?
³⁷Who has the wisdom to count the
  clouds?
  Who can pour water from the jars of
  the sky
³⁸when the dust becomes hard
  and the clumps of dirt stick together?

³⁹"Do you hunt food for the female lion
  to satisfy the hunger of the young lions
⁴⁰while they lie in their dens
  or hide in the bushes waiting to attack?
⁴¹Who gives food to the birds
  when their young cry out to God
  and wander about without food?

PSALM 100:1–5

A Call to Praise the Lord

A psalm of thanks.

100 Shout to the LORD, all the earth.
  ² Serve the LORD with joy;
  come before him with singing.
³Know that the LORD is God.
  He made us, and we belong to him;
  we are his people, the sheep he tends.

⁴Come into his city with songs of
  thanksgiving
  and into his courtyards with songs of
  praise.
  Thank him and praise his name.
⁵The LORD is good. His love is forever,
  and his loyalty goes on and on.

PROVERBS 23:26–28

²⁶My son, pay attention to me,
  and watch closely what I do.
²⁷A prostitute is as dangerous as a deep
  pit,
  and an unfaithful wife is like a narrow
  well.
²⁸They ambush you like robbers
  and cause many men to be unfaithful
  to their wives.

1 CORINTHIANS 5:1–13

Wickedness in the Church

5 It is actually being said that there is sexual sin among you. And it is a kind that does not happen even among people who do not know God. A man there has his father's wife. ²And you are proud! You should have been filled with sadness so that the man who did this should be put out of your group. ³I am not there with you in person, but I am with you in spirit. And I have already judged the man who did that sin as if I were really there. ⁴When you meet together in the name of our Lord Jesus, and I meet with you in spirit with the power of our Lord Jesus, ⁵then hand this man over to Satan. So his sinful self[n] will be destroyed, and his spirit will be saved on the day of the Lord.

⁶Your bragging is not good. You know the saying, "Just a little yeast makes the whole batch of dough rise." ⁷Take out all the old yeast so that you will be a new batch of dough without yeast, which you really are. For Christ, our Passover lamb, has been sacrificed. ⁸So let us celebrate this feast, but not with the bread that has the old yeast—the yeast of sin and wickedness. Let us celebrate this feast with the bread that has no yeast—the bread of goodness and truth.

⁹I wrote you in my earlier letter not to associate with those who sin sexually. ¹⁰But I did not mean you should not associate with those of this world who sin sexually, or with the greedy, or robbers, or those who worship idols. To get away from them you would have to leave this world. ¹¹I am writing to tell you that you must not associate with those who call themselves believers in Christ but who sin sexually, or are greedy, or worship idols, or abuse others with words, or get drunk, or cheat people. Do not even eat with people like that.

¹²⁻¹³It is not my business to judge those who are not part of the church. God will judge them. But you must judge the people who are part of the church. The Scripture says, "You must get rid of the evil person among you."[n]

5:5 sinful self Literally, "flesh." This could also mean his body. **5:12–13 "You . . . you."** Quotation from Deuteronomy 17:7; 19:19; 22:21, 24; 24:7.

AUGUST 24

JOB 39:1—40:24

39 "Do you know when the mountain goats give birth?
Do you watch when the deer gives birth to her fawn?
²Do you count the months until they give birth
and know the right time for them to give birth?
³They lie down, their young are born,
and then the pain of giving birth is over.
⁴Their young ones grow big and strong in the wild country.
Then they leave their homes and do not return.

⁵"Who let the wild donkey go free?
Who untied its ropes?
⁶I am the one who gave the donkey the desert as its home;
I gave it the desert lands as a place to live.
⁷The wild donkey laughs at the confusion in the city,
and it does not hear the drivers shout.
⁸It roams the hills looking for pasture,
looking for anything green to eat.

⁹"Will the wild ox agree to serve you
and stay by your feeding box at night?
¹⁰Can you hold it to the plowed row with a harness
so it will plow the valleys for you?
¹¹Will you depend on the wild ox for its great strength
and leave your heavy work for it to do?
¹²Can you trust the ox to bring in your grain
and gather it to your threshing floor?

¹³"The wings of the ostrich flap happily,
but they are not like the feathers of the stork.
¹⁴The ostrich lays its eggs on the ground
and lets them warm in the sand.
¹⁵It does not stop to think that a foot might step on them and crush them;
it does not care that some animal might walk on them.

¹⁶The ostrich is cruel to its young, as if they were not even its own.
It does not care that its work is for nothing,
¹⁷because God did not give the ostrich wisdom;
God did not give it a share of good sense.
¹⁸But when the ostrich gets up to run, it is so fast
that it laughs at the horse and its rider.

¹⁹"Job, are you the one who gives the horse its strength
or puts a flowing mane on its neck?
²⁰Do you make the horse jump like a locust?
It scares people with its proud snorting.
²¹It paws wildly, enjoying its strength,
and charges into battle.
²²It laughs at fear and is afraid of nothing;
it does not run away from the sword.
²³The bag of arrows rattles against the horse's side,
along with the flashing spears and swords.
²⁴With great excitement, the horse races over the ground;
and it cannot stand still when it hears the trumpet.
²⁵When the trumpet blows, the horse snorts, 'Aha!'
It smells the battle from far away;
it hears the shouts of commanders and the battle cry.

²⁶"Is it through your wisdom that the hawk flies
and spreads its wings toward the south?
²⁷Are you the one that commands the eagle to fly
and build its nest so high?
²⁸It lives on a high cliff and stays there at night;
the rocky peak is its protected place.
²⁹From there it looks for its food;
its eyes can see it from far away.

[30]Its young eat blood,
and where there is something dead, the
eagle is there."

40The LORD said to Job:
[2]"Will the person who argues with the
Almighty correct him?
Let the person who accuses God
answer him."

[3]Then Job answered the LORD:
[4]"I am not worthy; I cannot answer you
anything,
so I will put my hand over my mouth.
[5]I spoke one time, but I will not answer
again;
I even spoke two times, but I will say
nothing more."

[6]Then the LORD spoke to Job from the storm:
[7]"Be strong, like a man!
I will ask you questions,
and you must answer me.
[8]Would you say that I am unfair?
Would you blame me to make yourself
look right?
[9]Are you as strong as God?
Can your voice thunder like his?
[10]If so, then decorate yourself with glory
and beauty;
dress in honor and greatness as if they
were clothing.
[11]Let your great anger punish;
look at the proud and bring them
down.
[12]Look at the proud and make them
humble.
Crush the wicked wherever they are.
[13]Bury them all in the dirt together;
cover their faces in the grave.
[14]If you can do that, then I myself will
praise you,
because you are strong enough to save
yourself.

[15]"Look at Behemoth,[n]
which I made just as I made you.
It eats grass like an ox.
[16]Look at the strength it has in its body;
the muscles of its stomach are powerful.
[17]Its tail is like a cedar tree;

the muscles of its thighs are woven
together.
[18]Its bones are like tubes of bronze;
its legs are like bars of iron.
[19]It is one of the first of God's works,
but its Maker can destroy it.
[20]The hills, where the wild animals play,
provide food for it.
[21]It lies under the lotus plants,
hidden by the tall grass in the swamp.
[22]The lotus plants hide it in their shadow;
the poplar trees by the streams
surround it.
[23]If the river floods, it will not be afraid;
it is safe even if the Jordan River rushes
to its mouth.
[24]Can anyone blind its eyes and capture it?
Can anyone put hooks in its nose?

PSALM 101:1–4

A Promise to Rule Well

A psalm of David.

101I will sing of your love and fairness;
LORD, I will sing praises to you.
[2]I will be careful to live an innocent life.
When will you come to me?

I will live an innocent life in my house.
[3] I will not look at anything wicked.
I hate those who turn against you;
they will not be found near me.
[4]Let those who want to do wrong stay
away from me;
I will have nothing to do with evil.

PROVERBS 23:29–30

[29]Who has trouble? Who has pain?
Who fights? Who complains?
Who has unnecessary bruises?
Who has bloodshot eyes?
[30]It is people who drink too much wine,
who try out all different kinds of strong
drinks.

1 CORINTHIANS 6:1–20

Judging Problems Among Christians

6When you have something against another Christian, how can you bring your-

---

40:15 Behemoth A large land animal, exact identity unknown.

self to go before judges who are not right with God? Why do you not let God's people decide who is right? ²Surely you know that God's people will judge the world. So if you are to judge the world, are you not able to judge small cases as well? ³You know that in the future we will judge angels, so surely we can judge the ordinary things of this life. ⁴If you have ordinary cases that must be judged, are you going to appoint people as judges who mean nothing to the church? ⁵I say this to shame you. Surely there is someone among you wise enough to judge a complaint between believers. ⁶But now one believer goes to court against another believer—and you do this in front of unbelievers!

⁷The fact that you have lawsuits against each other shows that you are already defeated. Why not let yourselves be wronged? Why not let yourselves be cheated? ⁸But you yourselves do wrong and cheat, and you do this to other believers!

⁹⁻¹⁰Surely you know that the people who do wrong will not inherit God's kingdom. Do not be fooled. Those who sin sexually, worship idols, take part in adultery, those who are male prostitutes, or men who have sexual relations with other men, those who steal, are greedy, get drunk, lie about others, or rob—these people will not inherit God's kingdom. ¹¹In the past, some of you were like that, but you were washed clean. You were made holy, and you were made right with God in the name of the Lord Jesus Christ and in the Spirit of our God.

Use Your Bodies for God's Glory

¹²"I am allowed to do all things," but not all things are good for me to do. "I am allowed to do all things," but I will not let anything make me its slave. ¹³"Food is for the stomach, and the stomach for food," but God will destroy them both. The body is not for sexual sin but for the Lord, and the Lord is for the body. ¹⁴By his power God has raised the Lord from the dead and will also raise us from the dead. ¹⁵Surely you know that your bodies are parts of Christ himself. So I must never take the parts of Christ and join them to a prostitute! ¹⁶It is written in the Scriptures, "The two will become one body."ⁿ So you should know that anyone who joins with a prostitute becomes one body with the prostitute. ¹⁷But the one who joins with the Lord is one spirit with the Lord.

¹⁸So run away from sexual sin. Every other sin people do is outside their bodies, but those who sin sexually sin against their own bodies. ¹⁹You should know that your body is a temple for the Holy Spirit who is in you. You have received the Holy Spirit from God. So you do not belong to yourselves, ²⁰because you were bought by God for a price. So honor God with your bodies.

AUGUST 25

JOB 41:1—42:17

41 "Can you catch Leviathanⁿ on a fishhook
　or tie its tongue down with a rope?
²Can you put a cord through its nose
　or a hook in its jaw?
³Will it keep begging you for mercy
　and speak to you with gentle words?
⁴Will it make an agreement with you
　and let you take it as your slave for life?

⁵Can you make a pet of Leviathan as you
　would a bird
　or put it on a leash for your girls?
⁶Will traders try to bargain with you for it?
　Will they divide it up among the
　merchants?
⁷Can you stick darts all over its skin
　or fill its head with fishing spears?
⁸If you put one hand on it,
　you will never forget the battle,
　and you will never do it again!

6:16 "The two . . . body." Quotation from Genesis 2:24. • **41:1 Leviathan** A sea creature, exact identity unknown.

⁹There is no hope of defeating it;
just seeing it overwhelms people.
¹⁰No one is brave enough to make it angry,
so who would be able to stand up
against me?
¹¹No one has ever given me anything that I
must pay back,
because everything under the sky
belongs to me.

¹²"I will speak about Leviathan's arms and
legs,
its great strength and well-formed
body.
¹³No one can tear off its outer hide
or poke through its double armor.
¹⁴No one can force open its great jaws;
they are filled with frightening teeth.
¹⁵It has rows of shields on its back
that are tightly sealed together.
¹⁶Each shield is so close to the next one
that no air can go between them.
¹⁷They are joined strongly to one
another;
they hold on to each other and cannot
be separated.
¹⁸When it snorts, flashes of light are
thrown out,
and its eyes look like the light at dawn.
¹⁹Flames blaze from its mouth;
sparks of fire shoot out.
²⁰Smoke pours out of its nose,
as if coming from a large pot over a hot
fire.
²¹Its breath sets coals on fire,
and flames come out of its mouth.
²²There is great strength in its neck.
People are afraid and run away.
²³The folds of its skin are tightly joined;
they are set and cannot be moved.
²⁴Its chest is as hard as a rock,
even as hard as a grinding stone.
²⁵The powerful fear its terrible looks
and draw back in fear as it moves.
²⁶The sword that hits it does not hurt it,
nor the arrows, darts, and spears.
²⁷It treats iron as if it were straw
and bronze metal as if it were rotten
wood.
²⁸It does not run away from arrows;
stones from slings are like chaff to it.

²⁹Clubs feel like pieces of straw to it,
and it laughs when they shake a spear
at it.
³⁰The underside of its body is like broken
pieces of pottery.
It leaves a trail in the mud like a
threshing board.
³¹It makes the deep sea bubble like a
boiling pot;
it stirs up the sea like a pot of oil.
³²When it swims, it leaves a shining path in
the water
that makes the sea look as if it had
white hair.
³³Nothing else on earth is equal to it;
it is a creature without fear.
³⁴It looks down on all those who are too
proud;
it is king over all proud creatures."

Job Answers the Lord

42 Then Job answered the LORD:
²"I know that you can do all things
and that no plan of yours can be
ruined.
³You asked, 'Who is this that made my
purpose unclear by saying things
that are not true?'
Surely I spoke of things I did not
understand;
I talked of things too wonderful for me
to know.
⁴You said, 'Listen now, and I will speak.
I will ask you questions,
and you must answer me.'
⁵My ears had heard of you before,
but now my eyes have seen you.
⁶So now I hate myself;
I will change my heart and life.
I will sit in the dust and ashes."

End of the Story

⁷After the LORD had said these things to
Job, he said to Eliphaz the Temanite, "I am
angry with you and your two friends, because you have not said what is right about
me, as my servant Job did. ⁸Now take seven
bulls and seven male sheep, and go to my
servant Job, and offer a burnt offering for
yourselves. My servant Job will pray for you,
and I will listen to his prayer. Then I will not
punish you for being foolish. You have not

said what is right about me, as my servant Job did." ⁹So Eliphaz the Temanite, Bildad the Shuhite, and Zophar the Naamathite did as the LORD said, and the LORD listened to Job's prayer.

¹⁰After Job had prayed for his friends, the LORD gave him success again. The LORD gave Job twice as much as he had owned before. ¹¹Job's brothers and sisters came to his house, along with everyone who had known him before, and they all ate with him there. They comforted him and made him feel better about the trouble the LORD had brought on him, and each one gave Job a piece of silver and a gold ring.

¹²The LORD blessed the last part of Job's life even more than the first part. Job had fourteen thousand sheep, six thousand camels, a thousand teams of oxen, and a thousand female donkeys. ¹³Job also had seven sons and three daughters. ¹⁴He named the first daughter Jemimah, the second daughter Keziah, and the third daughter Keren-Happuch. ¹⁵There were no other women in all the land as beautiful as Job's daughters. And their father Job gave them land to own along with their brothers.

¹⁶After this, Job lived one hundred forty years. He lived to see his children, grandchildren, great-grandchildren, and great-great-grandchildren. ¹⁷Then Job died; he was old and had lived many years.

PSALM 101:5–8

⁵If anyone secretly says things against his neighbor,
I will stop him.
I will not allow people
to be proud and look down on others.
⁶I will look for trustworthy people
so I can live with them in the land.
Only those who live innocent lives
will be my servants.
⁷No one who is dishonest will live in my house;
no liars will stay around me.
⁸Every morning I will destroy the wicked in the land.
I will rid the LORD's city of people who do evil.

PROVERBS 23:31–35

³¹Don't stare at the wine when it is red,
when it sparkles in the cup,
when it goes down smoothly.
³²Later it bites like a snake
with poison in its fangs.
³³Your eyes will see strange sights,
and your mind will be confused.
³⁴You will feel dizzy as if you're in a storm on the ocean,
as if you're on top of a ship's sails.
³⁵You will think, "They hit me, but I'm not hurt.
They beat me up, but I don't remember it.
I wish I could wake up.
Then I would get another drink."

1 CORINTHIANS 7:1–16

About Marriage

7Now I will discuss the things you wrote me about. It is good for a man not to have sexual relations with a woman. ²But because sexual sin is a danger, each man should have his own wife, and each woman should have her own husband. ³The husband should give his wife all that he owes her as his wife. And the wife should give her husband all that she owes him as her husband. ⁴The wife does not have full rights over her own body; her husband shares them. And the husband does not have full rights over his own body; his wife shares them. ⁵Do not refuse to give your bodies to each other, unless you both agree to stay away from sexual relations for a time so you can give your time to prayer. Then come together again so Satan cannot tempt you because of a lack of self-control. ⁶I say this to give you permission to stay away from sexual relations for a time. It is not a command to do so. ⁷I wish that everyone were like me, but each person has his own gift from God. One has one gift, another has another gift.

⁸Now for those who are not married and for the widows I say this: It is good for them to stay unmarried as I am. ⁹But if they cannot control themselves, they should marry. It is better to marry than to burn with sexual desire.

¹⁰Now I give this command for the married

people. (The command is not from me; it is from the Lord.) A wife should not leave her husband. [11]But if she does leave, she must not marry again, or she should make up with her husband. Also the husband should not divorce his wife.

[12]For all the others I say this (I am saying this, not the Lord): If a Christian man has a wife who is not a believer, and she is happy to live with him, he must not divorce her. [13]And if a Christian woman has a husband who is not a believer, and he is happy to live with her, she must not divorce him. [14]The husband who is not a believer is made holy through his believing wife. And the wife who is not a believer is made holy through her believing husband. If this were not true, your children would not be clean, but now your children are holy.

[15]But if those who are not believers decide to leave, let them leave. When this happens, the Christian man or woman is free. But God called us[n] to live in peace. [16]Wife, you don't know; maybe you will save your husband. And husband, you don't know; maybe you will save your wife.

AUGUST 26

ECCLESIASTES 1:1—2:26

1 These are the words of the Teacher, a son of David, king in Jerusalem.
[2]The Teacher says,
"Useless! Useless!
Completely useless!
Everything is useless."

[3]What do people really gain
    from all the hard work they do here on
        earth?

Things Never Change

[4]People live, and people die,
    but the earth continues forever.
[5]The sun rises, the sun sets,
    and then it hurries back to where it
        rises again.
[6]The wind blows to the south;
    it blows to the north.
It blows from one direction and then
        another.
Then it turns around and repeats the
        same pattern, going nowhere.
[7]All the rivers flow to the sea,
    but the sea never becomes full.
[8]Everything is boring,
    so boring that you don't even want to
        talk about it.
Words come again and again to our ears,
    but we never hear enough,

nor can we ever really see all we want to
        see.
[9]All things continue the way they have
        been since the beginning.
What has happened will happen again;
    there is nothing new here on earth.
[10]Someone might say,
    "Look, this is new,"
but really it has always been here.
    It was here before we were.
[11]People don't remember what happened
        long ago,
    and in the future people will not
        remember what happens now.
Even later, other people will not
    remember what was done before
        them.

Does Wisdom Bring Happiness?

[12]I, the Teacher, was king over Israel in Jerusalem. [13]I decided to use my wisdom to learn about everything that happens on earth. I learned that God has given us terrible things to face. [14]I looked at everything done on earth and saw that it is all useless, like chasing the wind.

[15]If something is crooked,
    you can't make it straight.
If something is missing,
    you can't say it is there.

[16]I said to myself, "I have become very wise and am now wiser than anyone who ruled Jerusalem before me. I know what wisdom and knowledge really are." [17]So I decided to find out about wisdom and knowledge and also about foolish thinking, but this turned out to be like chasing the wind.

[18]With much wisdom comes much
disappointment;
the person who gains more knowledge
also gains more sorrow.

Does "Having Fun" Bring Happiness?

2 I said to myself, "I will try having fun. I will enjoy myself." But I found that this is also useless. [2]It is foolish to laugh all the time, and having fun doesn't accomplish anything. [3]I decided to cheer myself up with wine while my mind was still thinking wisely. I wanted to find a way to enjoy myself and see what was good for people to do during their few days of life.

Does Hard Work Bring Happiness?

[4]Then I did great things: I built houses and planted vineyards for myself. [5]I made gardens and parks, and I planted all kinds of fruit trees in them. [6]I made pools of water for myself and used them to water my growing trees. [7]I bought male and female slaves, and slaves were also born in my house. I had large herds and flocks, more than anyone in Jerusalem had ever had before. [8]I also gathered silver and gold for myself, treasures from kings and other areas. I had male and female singers and all the women a man could ever want. [9]I became very famous, even greater than anyone who had lived in Jerusalem before me. My wisdom helped me in all this.

[10]Anything I saw and wanted, I got for
myself;
I did not miss any pleasure I desired.
I was pleased with everything I did,
and this pleasure was the reward for all
my hard work.

[11]But then I looked at what I had done,
and I thought about all the hard work.
Suddenly I realized it was useless, like
chasing the wind.
There is nothing to gain from anything
we do here on earth.

Maybe Wisdom Is the Answer

[12]Then I began to think again about being
wise,
and also about being foolish and doing
crazy things.
But after all, what more can anyone do?
He can't do more than what the other
king has already done.

[13]I saw that being wise is certainly better
than being foolish,
just as light is better than darkness.

[14]Wise people see where they are going,
but fools walk around in the dark.
Yet I saw that
both wise and foolish people end the
same way.

[15]I thought to myself,
"What happens to a fool will happen to
me, too,
so what is the reward for being wise?"
I said to myself,
"Being wise is also useless."

[16]The wise person and the fool
will both die,
and no one will remember either one for
long.
In the future, both will be forgotten.

Is There Real Happiness in Life?

[17]So I hated life. It made me sad to think that everything here on earth is useless, like chasing the wind. [18]I hated all the things I had worked for here on earth, because I must leave them to someone who will live after me. [19]Someone else will control everything for which I worked so hard here on earth, and I don't know if he will be wise or foolish. This is also useless. [20]So I became sad about all the hard work I had done here on earth. [21]People can work hard using all their wisdom, knowledge, and skill, but they will die, and other people will get the things for which they worked. They did not do the work, but they will get everything. This is also unfair and useless. [22]What do people get for all their work and struggling here on earth? [23]All of their lives their work is full of pain and sorrow, and even at night their minds don't rest. This is also useless.

[24]The best that people can do is eat, drink, and enjoy their work. I saw that even this

comes from God, [25]because no one can eat or enjoy life without him. [26]If people please God, God will give them wisdom, knowledge, and joy. But sinners will get only the work of gathering and storing wealth that they will have to give to the ones who please God. So all their work is useless, like chasing the wind.

PSALM 102:1–11

A Cry for Help

A prayer of a person who is suffering when he is discouraged and tells the LORD his complaints.

102 LORD, listen to my prayer;
let my cry for help come to you.
[2]Do not hide from me
in my time of trouble.
Pay attention to me.
When I cry for help, answer me quickly.

[3]My life is passing away like smoke,
and my bones are burned up with fire.
[4]My heart is like grass
that has been cut and dried.
I forget to eat.
[5]Because of my grief,
my skin hangs on my bones.
[6]I am like a desert owl,
like an owl living among the ruins.
[7]I lie awake.
I am like a lonely bird on a housetop.
[8]All day long enemies insult me;
those who make fun of me use my
name as a curse.
[9]I eat ashes for food,
and my tears fall into my drinks.
[10]Because of your great anger,
you have picked me up and thrown me
away.
[11]My days are like a passing shadow;
I am like dried grass.

PROVERBS 24:1–2

24 Don't envy evil people
or try to be friends with them.
[2]Their minds are always planning
violence,
and they always talk about making
trouble.

1 CORINTHIANS 7:17–40

Live as God Called You

[17]But in any case each one of you should continue to live the way God has given you to live—the way you were when God called you. This is a rule I make in all the churches. [18]If a man was already circumcised when he was called, he should not undo his circumcision. If a man was without circumcision when he was called, he should not be circumcised. [19]It is not important if a man is circumcised or not. The important thing is obeying God's commands. [20]Each one of you should stay the way you were when God called you. [21]If you were a slave when God called you, do not let that bother you. But if you can be free, then make good use of your freedom. [22]Those who were slaves when the Lord called them are free persons who belong to the Lord. In the same way, those who were free when they were called are now Christ's slaves. [23]You all were bought at a great price, so do not become slaves of people. [24]Brothers and sisters, each of you should stay as you were when you were called, and stay there with God.

Questions About Getting Married

[25]Now I write about people who are not married. I have no command from the Lord about this; I give my opinion. But I can be trusted, because the Lord has shown me mercy. [26]The present time is a time of trouble, so I think it is good for you to stay the way you are. [27]If you have a wife, do not try to become free from her. If you are not married, do not try to find a wife. [28]But if you decide to marry, you have not sinned. And if a girl who has never married decides to marry, she has not sinned. But those who marry will have trouble in this life, and I want you to be free from trouble.

[29]Brothers and sisters, this is what I mean: We do not have much time left. So starting now, those who have wives should live as if they had no wives. [30]Those who are crying should live as if they were not crying. Those who are happy should live as if they were not happy. Those who buy things should live as if they own nothing. [31]Those who use the things of the world should live

as if they were not using them, because this world in its present form will soon be gone.

³²I want you to be free from worry. A man who is not married is busy with the Lord's work, trying to please the Lord. ³³But a man who is married is busy with things of the world, trying to please his wife. ³⁴He must think about two things—pleasing his wife and pleasing the Lord. A woman who is not married or a girl who has never married is busy with the Lord's work. She wants to be holy in body and spirit. But a married woman is busy with things of the world, as to how she can please her husband. ³⁵I am saying this to help you, not to limit you. But I want you to live in the right way, to give yourselves fully to the Lord without concern for other things.

³⁶If a man thinks he is not doing the right thing with the girl he is engaged to, if she is almost past the best age to marry and he feels he should marry her, he should do what he wants. They should get married. It is no sin. ³⁷But if a man is sure in his mind that there is no need for marriage, and has his own desires under control, and has decided not to marry the one to whom he is engaged, he is doing the right thing. ³⁸So the man who marries his girl does right, but the man who does not marry will do better.

³⁹A woman must stay with her husband as long as he lives. But if her husband dies, she is free to marry any man she wants, but she must marry another believer. ⁴⁰The woman is happier if she does not marry again. This is my opinion, but I believe I also have God's Spirit.

AUGUST 27

ECCLESIASTES 3:1–22

There Is a Time for Everything

3 There is a time for everything,
   and everything on earth has its special
      season.
²There is a time to be born
   and a time to die.
There is a time to plant
   and a time to pull up plants.
³There is a time to kill
   and a time to heal.
There is a time to destroy
   and a time to build.
⁴There is a time to cry
   and a time to laugh.
There is a time to be sad
   and a time to dance.
⁵There is a time to throw away stones
   and a time to gather them.
There is a time to hug
   and a time not to hug.
⁶There is a time to look for something
   and a time to stop looking for it.
There is a time to keep things
   and a time to throw things away.
⁷There is a time to tear apart
   and a time to sew together.
There is a time to be silent
   and a time to speak.
⁸There is a time to love
   and a time to hate.
There is a time for war
   and a time for peace.

God Controls His World

⁹Do people really gain anything from their work? ¹⁰I saw the hard work God has given people to do. ¹¹God has given them a desire to know the future. He does everything just right and on time, but people can never completely understand what he is doing. ¹²So I realize that the best thing for them is to be happy and enjoy themselves as long as they live. ¹³God wants all people to eat and drink and be happy in their work, which are gifts from God. ¹⁴I know that everything God does will continue forever. People cannot add anything to what God has done, and they cannot take anything away from it. God does it this way to make people respect him.

[15]What happens now has happened in the past,
and what will happen in the future has happened before.
God makes the same things happen again and again.

Unfairness on Earth

[16]I also saw this here on earth:
Where there should have been justice, there was evil;
where there should have been right, there was wrong.
[17]I said to myself,
God has planned a time for every thing and every action,
so he will judge both good people and bad.
[18]I decided that God leaves it the way it is to test people and to show them they are just like animals. [19]The same thing happens to animals and to people; they both have the same breath, so they both die. People are no better off than the animals, because everything is useless. [20]Both end up the same way; both came from dust and both will go back to dust. [21]Who can be sure that the human spirit goes up to God and that the spirit of an animal goes down into the ground? [22]So I saw that the best thing people can do is to enjoy their work, because that is all they have. No one can help another person see what will happen in the future.

PSALM 102:12–17

[12]But, LORD, you rule forever,
and your fame goes on and on.
[13]You will come and have mercy on Jerusalem,
because the time has now come to be kind to her;
the right time has come.
[14]Your servants love even her stones;
they even care about her dust.
[15]Nations will fear the name of the LORD,
and all the kings on earth will honor you.
[16]The LORD will rebuild Jerusalem;
there his glory will be seen.

[17]He will answer the prayers of the needy;
he will not reject their prayers.

PROVERBS 24:3–4

[3]It takes wisdom to have a good family,
and it takes understanding to make it strong.
[4]It takes knowledge to fill a home
with rare and beautiful treasures.

1 CORINTHIANS 8:1–13

About Food Offered to Idols

8 Now I will write about meat that is sacrificed to idols. We know that "we all have knowledge." Knowledge puffs you up with pride, but love builds up. [2]If you think you know something, you do not yet know anything as you should. [3]But if any person loves God, that person is known by God.

[4]So this is what I say about eating meat sacrificed to idols: We know that an idol is really nothing in the world, and we know there is only one God. [5]Even though there are things called gods, in heaven or on earth (and there are many "gods" and "lords"), [6]for us there is only one God—our Father. All things came from him, and we live for him. And there is only one Lord—Jesus Christ. All things were made through him, and we also were made through him.

[7]But not all people know this. Some people are still so used to idols that when they eat meat, they still think of it as being sacrificed to an idol. Because their conscience is weak, when they eat it, they feel guilty. [8]But food will not bring us closer to God. Refusing to eat does not make us less pleasing to God, and eating does not make us better in God's sight.

[9]But be careful that your freedom does not cause those who are weak in faith to fall into sin. [10]Suppose one of you who has knowledge eats in an idol's temple.[n] Someone who is weak in faith might see you eating there and be encouraged to eat meat sacrificed to idols while thinking it is wrong to do so. [11]This weak believer for whom Christ died is ruined because of your "knowledge." [12]When you sin against your

---

8:10 idol's temple Building where a god is worshiped.

brothers and sisters in Christ like this and cause them to do what they feel is wrong, you are also sinning against Christ. [13]So if the food I eat causes them to fall into sin, I will never eat meat again so that I will not cause any of them to sin.

AUGUST 28

ECCLESIASTES 4:1—6:12

Is It Better to Be Dead?

4 Again I saw all the people who were mistreated here on earth.
I saw their tears
and that they had no one to comfort them.
Cruel people had all the power,
and there was no one to comfort those they hurt.
[2]I decided that the dead
are better off than the living.
[3]But those who have never been born
are better off still;
they have not seen the evil
that is done here on earth.

Why Work So Hard?

[4]I realized the reason people work hard and try to succeed: They are jealous of each other. This, too, is useless, like chasing the wind.
[5]Some say it is foolish to fold your hands and do nothing,
because you will starve to death.
[6]Maybe so, but I say it is better to be content
with what little you have.
Otherwise, you will always be struggling for more,
and that is like chasing the wind.
[7]Again I saw something here on earth that was useless:
[8]I saw a man who had no family,
no son or brother.
He always worked hard
but was never satisfied with what he had.
He never asked himself, "For whom am I working so hard?
Why don't I let myself enjoy life?"
This also is very sad and useless.

Friends and Family Give Strength

[9]Two people are better than one,
because they get more done by working together.
[10]If one falls down,
the other can help him up.
But it is bad for the person who is alone and falls,
because no one is there to help.
[11]If two lie down together, they will be warm,
but a person alone will not be warm.
[12]An enemy might defeat one person,
but two people together can defend themselves;
a rope that is woven of three strings is hard to break.

Fame and Power Are Useless

[13]A poor but wise boy is better than a foolish but old king who doesn't listen to advice. [14]A boy became king. He had been born poor in the kingdom and had even gone to prison before becoming king. [15]I watched all the people who live on earth follow him and make him their king. [16]Many followed him at first, but later, they did not like him, either. So fame and power are useless, like chasing the wind.

Be Careful About Making Promises

5 Be careful when you go to worship at the Temple. It is better to listen than to offer foolish sacrifices without even knowing you are doing wrong.
[2]Think before you speak,
and be careful about what you say to God.
God is in heaven,
and you are on the earth,
so say only a few words to God.
[3]The saying is true: Bad dreams come from too much worrying,

and too many words come from foolish people.

[4]If you make a promise to God, don't be slow to keep it. God is not happy with fools, so give God what you promised. [5]It is better not to promise anything than to promise something and not do it. [6]Don't let your words cause you to sin, and don't say to the priest at the Temple, "I didn't mean what I promised." If you do, God will become angry with your words and will destroy everything you have worked for. [7]Many useless promises are like so many dreams; they mean nothing. You should respect God.

Officers Cheat Each Other

[8]In some places you will see poor people mistreated. Don't be surprised when they are not treated fairly or given their rights. One officer is cheated by a higher officer who in turn is cheated by even higher officers. [9]The wealth of the country is divided up among them all. Even the king makes sure he gets his share of the profits.

Wealth Cannot Buy Happiness

[10]Whoever loves money
will never have enough money;
Whoever loves wealth
will not be satisfied with it.
This is also useless.
[11]The more wealth people have,
the more friends they have to help
spend it.
So what do people really gain?
They gain nothing except to look at
their riches.
[12]Those who work hard sleep in peace;
it is not important if they eat little or
much.
But rich people worry about their wealth
and cannot sleep.

[13]I have seen real misery here on earth:
Money saved is a curse to its owners.
[14] They lose it all in a bad deal
and have nothing to give to their
children.
[15]People come into this world with
nothing,
and when they die they leave with
nothing.

In spite of all their hard work,
they leave just as they came.
[16]This, too, is real misery:
They leave just as they came.
So what do they gain from chasing the
wind?
[17]All they get are days full of sadness and
sorrow,
and they end up sick, defeated, and
angry.

Enjoy Your Life's Work

[18]I have seen what is best for people here on earth. They should eat and drink and enjoy their work, because the life God has given them on earth is short. [19]God gives some people the ability to enjoy the wealth and property he gives them, as well as the ability to accept their state in life and enjoy their work. [20]They do not worry about how short life is, because God keeps them busy with what they love to do.

6 I have seen something else wrong here on earth that causes serious problems for people. [2]God gives great wealth, riches, and honor to some people; they have everything they want. But God does not let them enjoy such things; a stranger enjoys them instead. This is useless and very wrong. [3]A man might have a hundred children and live a long time, but what good is it if he can't enjoy the good God gives him or have a proper burial? I say a baby born dead is better off than he is. [4]A baby born dead is useless. It returns to darkness without even a name. [5]That baby never saw the sun and never knew anything, but it finds more rest than that man. [6]Even if he lives two thousand years, he doesn't enjoy the good God gives him. Everyone is going to the same place.
[7]People work just to feed themselves,
but they never seem to get enough to eat.
[8]In this way a wise person
is no better off than a fool.
Then, too, it does a poor person little
good
to know how to get along in life.
[9]It is better to see what you have
than to want more.
Wanting more is useless—
like chasing the wind.

Who Can Understand God's Plan?

[10]Whatever happens was planned long ago.
    Everyone knows what people are like.
No one can argue with God,
    who is stronger than anyone.
[11]The more you say,
    the more useless it is.
    What good does it do?
[12]People have only a few useless days of life on the earth; their short life passes like a shadow. Who knows what is best for them while they live? Who can tell them what the future will bring?

PSALM 102:18–28

[18]Write these things for the future
    so that people who are not yet born will
        praise the LORD.
[19]The LORD looked down from his holy
        place above;
    from heaven he looked down at the earth.
[20]He heard the moans of the prisoners,
    and he freed those sentenced to die.
[21]The name of the LORD will be heard in
        Jerusalem;
    his praise will be heard there.
[22]People will come together,
    and kingdoms will serve the LORD.

[23]God has made me tired of living;
    he has cut short my life.
[24]So I said, "My God, do not take me in the
        middle of my life.
    Your years go on and on.
[25]In the beginning you made the earth,
    and your hands made the skies.
[26]They will be destroyed, but you will
        remain.
    They will all wear out like clothes.
    And, like clothes, you will change them
        and throw them away.
[27]But you never change,
    and your life will never end.
[28]Our children will live in your presence,
    and their children will remain with you."

PROVERBS 24:5–6

[5]Wise people have great power,
    and those with knowledge have great
        strength.

[6]So you need advice when you go to war.
    If you have lots of good advice, you will
        win.

1 CORINTHIANS 9:1–27

Paul Is like the Other Apostles

9 I am a free man. I am an apostle. I have seen Jesus our Lord. You people are all an example of my work in the Lord. [2]If others do not accept me as an apostle, surely you do, because you are proof that I am an apostle in the Lord.

[3]This is the answer I give people who want to judge me: [4]Do we not have the right to eat and drink? [5]Do we not have the right to bring a believing wife with us when we travel as do the other apostles and the Lord's brothers and Peter? [6]Are Barnabas and I the only ones who must work to earn our living? [7]No soldier ever serves in the army and pays his own salary. No one ever plants a vineyard without eating some of the grapes. No person takes care of a flock without drinking some of the milk.

[8]I do not say this by human authority; God's law also says the same thing. [9]It is written in the law of Moses: "When an ox is working in the grain, do not cover its mouth to keep it from eating."[n] When God said this, was he thinking only about oxen? No. [10]He was really talking about us. Yes, that Scripture was written for us, because it goes on to say: "The one who plows and the one who works in the grain should hope to get some of the grain for their work." [11]Since we planted spiritual seed among you, is it too much if we should harvest material things? [12]If others have the right to get something from you, surely we have this right, too. But we do not use it. No, we put up with everything ourselves so that we will not keep anyone from believing the Good News of Christ. [13]Surely you know that those who work at the Temple get their food from the Temple, and those who serve at the altar get part of what is offered at the altar. [14]In the same way, the Lord has commanded that those who tell the Good News should get their living from this work.

9:9 "When an ox . . . eating." Quotation from Deuteronomy 25:4.

¹⁵But I have not used any of these rights. And I am not writing this now to get anything from you. I would rather die than to have my reason for bragging taken away. ¹⁶Telling the Good News does not give me any reason for bragging. Telling the Good News is my duty—something I must do. And how terrible it will be for me if I do not tell the Good News. ¹⁷If I preach because it is my own choice, I have a reward. But if I preach and it is not my choice to do so, I am only doing the duty that was given to me. ¹⁸So what reward do I get? This is my reward: that when I tell the Good News I can offer it freely. I do not use my full rights in my work of preaching the Good News.

¹⁹I am free and belong to no one. But I make myself a slave to all people to win as many as I can. ²⁰To the Jews I became like a Jew to win the Jews. I myself am not ruled by the law. But to those who are ruled by the law I became like a person who is ruled by the law. I did this to win those who are ruled by the law. ²¹To those who are without the law I became like a person who is without the law. I did this to win those people who are without the law. (But really, I am not without God's law—I am ruled by Christ's law.) ²²To those who are weak, I became weak so I could win the weak. I have become all things to all people so I could save some of them in any way possible. ²³I do all this because of the Good News and so I can share in its blessings.

²⁴You know that in a race all the runners run, but only one gets the prize. So run to win! ²⁵All those who compete in the games use self-control so they can win a crown. That crown is an earthly thing that lasts only a short time, but our crown will never be destroyed. ²⁶So I do not run without a goal. I fight like a boxer who is hitting something—not just the air. ²⁷I treat my body hard and make it my slave so that I myself will not be disqualified after I have preached to others.

AUGUST 29

ECCLESIASTES 7:1–29

Some Benefits of Serious Thinking

7 It is better to have respect than good perfume.
The day of death is better than the day of birth.
²It is better to go to a funeral
than to a party.
We all must die,
and everyone living should think about this.
³Sorrow is better than laughter,
and sadness has a good influence on you.
⁴A wise person thinks about death,
but a fool thinks only about having a good time.
⁵It is better to be criticized by a wise person
than to be praised by a fool.
⁶The laughter of fools

is like the crackling of thorns in a cooking fire.
Both are useless.

⁷Even wise people are fools
if they let money change their thinking.

⁸It is better to finish something
than to start it.
It is better to be patient
than to be proud.
⁹Don't become angry quickly,
because getting angry is foolish.

¹⁰Don't ask, "Why was life better in the 'good old days'?"
It is not wise to ask such questions.

¹¹Wisdom is better when it comes with money.
They both help those who are alive.
¹²Wisdom is like money:
they both help.

But wisdom is better,
because it can save whoever has it.

¹³Look at what God has done:
No one can straighten what he has
bent.
¹⁴When life is good, enjoy it.
But when life is hard, remember:
God gives good times and hard times,
and no one knows what tomorrow will
bring.

It Is Impossible to Be Truly Good

¹⁵In my useless life I have seen both of
these:
I have seen good people die in spite of
their goodness
and evil people live a long time in
spite of their evil.
¹⁶Don't be too right,
and don't be too wise.
Why destroy yourself?
¹⁷Don't be too wicked,
and don't be too foolish.
Why die before your time?
¹⁸It is good to grab the one and not let go
of the other;
those who honor God will hold them
both.

¹⁹Wisdom makes a person stronger
than ten leaders in a city.

²⁰Surely there is not a good person on
earth
who always does good and never
sins.

²¹Don't listen to everything people say,
or you might hear your servant
insulting you.
²²You know that many times
you have insulted others.

²³I used wisdom to test all these things.
I wanted to be wise,
but it was too hard for me.
²⁴I cannot understand why things are as
they are.
It is too hard for anyone to
understand.
²⁵I studied and tried very hard to find
wisdom,
to find some meaning for everything.

I learned that it is foolish to be evil,
and it is crazy to act like a fool.

²⁶I found that some women are worse than
death
and are as dangerous as traps.
Their love is like a net,
and their arms hold men like chains.
A man who pleases God will be saved
from them,
but a sinner will be caught by them.

²⁷The Teacher says, "This is what I
learned:
I added all these things together
to find some meaning for everything.
²⁸While I was searching,
I did not find one man among the
thousands I found.
Nor did I find a woman among all these.
²⁹One thing I have learned:
God made people good,
but they have found all kinds of ways
to be bad."

PSALM 103:1–5

Praise to the Lord of Love

Of David.

103 All that I am, praise the LORD;
everything in me, praise his holy
name.
²My whole being, praise the LORD
and do not forget all his kindnesses.
³He forgives all my sins
and heals all my diseases.
⁴He saves my life from the grave
and loads me with love and mercy.
⁵He satisfies me with good things
and makes me young again, like the
eagle.

PROVERBS 24:7–9

⁷Foolish people cannot understand
wisdom.
They have nothing to say in a
discussion.

⁸Whoever makes evil plans
will be known as a troublemaker.
⁹Making foolish plans is sinful,
and making fun of wisdom is hateful.

1 CORINTHIANS 10:1–22

Warnings from Israel's Past

10Brothers and sisters, I want you to know what happened to our ancestors who followed Moses. They were all under the cloud and all went through the sea. [2]They were all baptized as followers of Moses in the cloud and in the sea. [3]They all ate the same spiritual food, [4]and all drank the same spiritual drink. They drank from that spiritual rock that followed them, and that rock was Christ. [5]But God was not pleased with most of them, so they died in the desert.

[6]And these things happened as examples for us, to stop us from wanting evil things as those people did. [7]Do not worship idols, as some of them did. Just as it is written in the Scriptures: "They sat down to eat and drink, and then they got up and sinned sexually."[n] [8]We must not take part in sexual sins, as some of them did. In one day twenty-three thousand of them died because of their sins. [9]We must not test Christ as some of them did; they were killed by snakes. [10]Do not complain as some of them did; they were killed by the angel that destroys.

[11]The things that happened to those people are examples. They were written down to teach us, because we live in a time when all these things of the past have reached their goal. [12]If you think you are strong, you should be careful not to fall. [13]The only temptation that has come to you is that which everyone has. But you can trust God, who will not permit you to be tempted more than you can stand. But when you are tempted, he will also give you a way to escape so that you will be able to stand it.

[14]So, my dear friends, run away from the worship of idols. [15]I am speaking to you as to reasonable people; judge for yourselves what I say. [16]We give thanks for the cup of blessing,[n] which is a sharing in the blood of Christ. And the bread that we break is a sharing in the body of Christ. [17]Because there is one loaf of bread, we who are many are one body, because we all share that one loaf.

[18]Think about the Israelites: Do not those who eat the sacrifices share in the altar? [19]I do not mean that the food sacrificed to an idol is important. I do not mean that an idol is anything at all. [20]But I say that what is sacrificed to idols is offered to demons, not to God. And I do not want you to share anything with demons. [21]You cannot drink the cup of the Lord and the cup of demons also. You cannot share in the Lord's table and the table of demons. [22]Are we trying to make the Lord jealous? We are not stronger than he is, are we?

AUGUST 30

ECCLESIASTES 8:1—10:20

Obey the King

8No one is like the wise person
who can understand what things mean.
Wisdom brings happiness;
it makes sad faces happy.
[2]Obey the king's command, because you made a promise to God. [3]Don't be too quick to leave the king. Don't support something that is wrong, because the king does whatever he pleases. [4]What the king says is law; no one tells him what to do.

[5]Whoever obeys the king's command will
be safe.
A wise person does the right thing at
the right time.
[6]There is a right time and a right way for
everything,
yet people often have many troubles.
[7]They do not know what the future
holds,

10:7 "They . . . sexually." Quotation from Exodus 32:6.   **10:16 cup of blessing** The cup of the fruit of the vine that Christians thank God for and drink at the Lord's Supper.

and no one can tell them what will
  happen.
[8]No one can control the wind
  or stop his own death.
No soldier is released in times of war,
  and evil does not set free those who do
  evil.

Justice, Rewards, and Punishment

[9]I saw all of this as I considered all that is
done here on earth. Sometimes people
harm those they control. [10]I saw the funerals
of evil people who used to go in and out of
the holy place. They were honored in the
same towns where they had done evil. This
is useless, too.

[11]When evil people are not punished right
away, it makes others want to do evil, too.
[12]Though a sinner might do a hundred evil
things and might live a long time, I know it
will be better for those who honor God. [13]I
also know it will not go well for evil people,
because they do not honor God. Like a
shadow, they will not last. [14]Sometimes something useless happens on earth. Bad things
happen to good people, and good things happen to bad people. I say that this is also useless. [15]So I decided it was more important to
enjoy life. The best that people can do here on
earth is to eat, drink, and enjoy life, because
these joys will help them do the hard work
God gives them here on earth.

We Cannot Understand All God Does

[16]I tried to understand all that happens
on earth. I saw how busy people are, working
day and night and hardly ever sleeping. [17]I
also saw all that God has done. Nobody can
understand what God does here on earth. No
matter how hard people try to understand it,
they cannot. Even if wise people say they understand, they cannot; no one can really understand it.

Is Death Fair?

9 I thought about all this and tried to understand it. I saw that God controls good people and wise people and what they do, but no
one knows if they will experience love or hate.
[2]Good and bad people end up the same—
  those who are right and those who are
  wrong,

those who are good and those who are
  evil,
those who are clean and those who are
  unclean,
those who sacrifice and those who do
  not.
The same things happen to a good person
  as happen to a sinner,
to a person who makes promises to God
  and to one who does not.

[3]This is something wrong that happens
here on earth: What happens to one happens
to all. So people's minds are full of evil and
foolish thoughts while they live. After that,
they join the dead. [4]But anyone still alive has
hope; even a live dog is better off than a dead
lion!

[5]The living know they will die,
  but the dead know nothing.
Dead people have no more reward,
  and people forget them.
[6]After people are dead,
  they can no longer love or hate or envy.
They will never again share
  in what happens here on earth.

Enjoy Life While You Can

[7]So go eat your food and enjoy it;
  drink your wine and be happy,
  because that is what God wants you to
    do.
[8]Put on nice clothes
  and make yourself look good.
[9]Enjoy life with the wife you love. Enjoy all
the useless days of this useless life God has
given you here on earth, because it is all you
have. So enjoy the work you do here on
earth. [10]Whatever work you do, do your best,
because you are going to the grave, where
there is no working, no planning, no knowledge, and no wisdom.

Time and Chance

[11]I also saw something else here on earth:
The fastest runner does not always win
  the race,
  the strongest soldier does not always
    win the battle,
the wisest does not always have food,
  the smartest does not always become
    wealthy,

and the talented one does not always
  receive praise.
Time and chance happen to everyone.
¹²No one knows what will happen next.
Like a fish caught in a net,
  or a bird caught in a trap,
people are trapped by evil
  when it suddenly falls on them.

Wisdom Does Not Always Win

¹³I also saw something wise here on earth
that impressed me. ¹⁴There was a small town
with only a few people in it. A great king
fought against it and put his armies all
around it. ¹⁵Now there was a poor but wise
man in the town who used his wisdom to
save his town. But later on, everyone forgot
about him. ¹⁶I still think wisdom is better
than strength. But those people forgot about
the poor man's wisdom and stopped listening to what he said.
¹⁷The quiet words of a wise person are
  better
    than the shouts of a foolish ruler.
¹⁸Wisdom is better than weapons of war,
  but one sinner can destroy much good.

10 Dead flies can make even perfume
      stink.
    In the same way, a little foolishness can
      spoil wisdom.
²The heart of the wise leads to right,
  but the heart of a fool leads to wrong.
³Even in the way fools walk along the
  road,
    they show they are not wise;
    they show everyone how stupid they
      are.
⁴Don't leave your job
  just because your boss is angry with
    you.
    Remaining calm solves great problems.

⁵There is something else wrong that
  happens here on earth.
    It is the kind of mistake rulers make:
⁶Fools are given important positions
  while gifted people are given lower
    ones;
⁷I have seen servants ride horses
  while princes walk like servants on
    foot.

⁸Anyone who digs a pit might fall into it;
  anyone who knocks down a wall might
    be bitten by a snake;
⁹anyone who moves boulders might be
  hurt by them;
    and anyone who cuts logs might be
      harmed by them.
¹⁰A dull ax means
  harder work.
    Being wise will make it easier.
¹¹If a snake bites the tamer before it is
  tamed,
    what good is the tamer?
¹²The words of the wise bring them praise,
  but the words of a fool will destroy
    them.
¹³A fool begins by saying foolish things
  and ends by saying crazy and wicked
    things.
¹⁴A fool talks too much.
  No one knows the future,
    and no one can tell what will happen
      after death.
¹⁵Work wears fools out;
  they don't even know how to get home.

The Value of Work

¹⁶How terrible it is for a country whose
  king is a child
    and whose leaders eat all morning.
¹⁷How lucky a country is whose king
  comes from a good family,
    whose leaders eat only at mealtime
    and for strength, not to get drunk.

¹⁸If someone is lazy, the roof will begin to
  fall.
    If he doesn't fix it, the house will leak.
¹⁹A party makes you feel good,
  wine makes you feel happy,
    and money buys anything.
²⁰Don't make fun of the king,
  and don't make fun of rich people, even
    in your bedroom.
    A little bird might carry your words;
    a bird might fly and tell what you said.

PSALM 103:6-14

⁶The LORD does what is right and fair
  for all who are wronged by others.

[7]He showed his ways to Moses
and his deeds to the people of Israel.
[8]The LORD shows mercy and is kind.
He does not become angry quickly, and
he has great love.
[9]He will not always accuse us,
and he will not be angry forever.
[10]He has not punished us as our sins
should be punished;
he has not repaid us for the evil we
have done.
[11]As high as the sky is above the earth,
so great is his love for those who
respect him.
[12]He has taken our sins away from us
as far as the east is from west.
[13]The LORD has mercy on those who
respect him,
as a father has mercy on his children.
[14]He knows how we were made;
he remembers that we are dust.

PROVERBS 24:10–12

[10]If you give up when trouble comes,
it shows that you are weak.
[11]Save those who are being led to their death;
rescue those who are about to be killed.
[12]If you say, "We don't know anything
about this,"
God, who knows what's in your mind,
will notice.
He is watching you, and he will know.
He will reward each person for what he
has done.

1 CORINTHIANS 10:23—11:1

How to Use Christian Freedom

[23]"We are allowed to do all things," but not
all things are good for us to do. "We are allowed to do all things," but not all things help
others grow stronger. [24]Do not look out only
for yourselves. Look out for the good of others also.
[25]Eat any meat that is sold in the meat
market. Do not ask questions about it. [26]You
may eat it, "because the earth belongs to the
Lord, and everything in it."[n]
[27]Those who are not believers may invite
you to eat with them. If you want to go, eat
anything that is put before you. Do not ask
questions about it. [28]But if anyone says to you,
"That food was offered to idols," do not eat it.
Do not eat it because of that person who told
you and because eating it might be thought to
be wrong. [29]I don't mean you think it is
wrong, but the other person might. But why,
you ask, should my freedom be judged by
someone else's conscience? [30]If I eat the meal
with thankfulness, why am I criticized because of something for which I thank God?
[31]The answer is, if you eat or drink, or if
you do anything, do it all for the glory of
God. [32]Never do anything that might hurt
others—Jews, Greeks, or God's church—
[33]just as I, also, try to please everybody in
every way. I am not trying to do what is good
for me but what is good for most people so
they can be saved.

11 Follow my example, as I follow the example of Christ.

AUGUST 31

ECCLESIASTES 11:1—12:14

Boldly Face the Future

11 Invest what you have,
because after a while you will get a
return.
[2]Invest what you have in several different
businesses,
because you don't know what disasters
might happen.
[3]If clouds are full of rain,
they will shower on the earth.
A tree can fall to the north or south,
but it will stay where it falls.
[4]Those who wait for perfect weather

10:26 "because . . . it" Quotation from Psalms 24:1; 50:12; 89:11.

will never plant seeds;
those who look at every cloud
will never harvest crops.

[5]You don't know where the wind will blow,
and you don't know how a baby grows
inside the mother.
In the same way, you don't know what
God is doing,
or how he created everything.
[6]Plant early in the morning,
and work until evening,
because you don't know if this or that
will succeed.
They might both do well.

Serve God While You Are Young

[7]Sunshine is sweet;
it is good to see the light of day.
[8]People ought to enjoy every day of their
lives,
no matter how long they live.
But they should also remember this:
You will be dead a long time.
Everything that happens then is useless.
[9]Young people, enjoy yourselves while you
are young;
be happy while you are young.
Do whatever your heart desires,
whatever you want to do.
But remember that God will judge you
for everything you do.
[10]Don't worry,
and forget the troubles of your body,
because youth and childhood are
useless.

The Problems of Old Age

12 Remember your Creator
while you are young,
before the days of trouble come
and the years when you say,
"I find no pleasure in them."
[2]When you get old,
the light from the sun, moon, and stars
will grow dark;
the rain clouds will never seem to go
away.
[3]At that time your arms will shake
and your legs will become weak.
Your teeth will fall out so you cannot
chew,

and your eyes will not see clearly.
[4]Your ears will be deaf to the noise in the
streets,
and you will barely hear the millstone
grinding grain.
You'll wake up when a bird starts
singing,
but you will barely hear singing.
[5]You will fear high places
and will be afraid to go for a walk.
Your hair will become white like the
flowers on an almond tree.
You will limp along like a grasshopper
when you walk.
Your appetite will be gone.
Then you will go to your everlasting
home,
and people will go to your funeral.

[6]Soon your life will snap like a silver chain
or break like a golden bowl.
You will be like a broken pitcher at a
spring,
or a broken wheel at a well.
[7]You will turn back into the dust of the
earth again,
but your spirit will return to God who
gave it.

[8]Everything is useless!
The Teacher says that everything is
useless.

Conclusion: Honor God

[9]The Teacher was very wise and taught
the people what he knew. He very carefully
thought about, studied, and set in order
many wise teachings. [10]The Teacher looked
for just the right words to write what is dependable and true.

[11]Words from wise people are like sharp
sticks used to guide animals. They are like
nails that have been driven in firmly. Altogether they are wise teachings that come
from one Shepherd. [12]So be careful, my son,
about other teachings. People are always
writing books, and too much study will
make you tired.

[13]Now, everything has been heard,
so I give my final advice:
Honor God and obey his commands,
because this is all people must do.

14God will judge everything,
    even what is done in secret,
    the good and the evil.

PSALM 103:15–22

15Human life is like grass;
    we grow like a flower in the field.
16After the wind blows, the flower is gone,
    and there is no sign of where it was.
17But the LORD's love for those who respect
        him
    continues forever and ever,
    and his goodness continues to their
        grandchildren
18and to those who keep his agreement
    and who remember to obey his orders.

19The LORD has set his throne in heaven,
    and his kingdom rules over everything.
20You who are his angels, praise the LORD.
    You are the mighty warriors who do
        what he says
    and who obey his voice.
21You, his armies, praise the LORD;
    you are his servants who do what he
        wants.
22Everything the LORD has made
    should praise him in all the places he
        rules.
    My whole being, praise the LORD.

PROVERBS 24:13–14

13My child, eat honey because it is good.
    Honey from the honeycomb tastes
        sweet.
14In the same way, wisdom is pleasing to
        you.
    If you find it, you have hope for the
        future,
    and your wishes will come true.

1 CORINTHIANS 11:2–16

Being Under Authority

2I praise you because you remember me in everything, and you follow closely the teachings just as I gave them to you. 3But I want you to understand this: The head of every man is Christ, the head of a woman is the man,[n] and the head of Christ is God. 4Every man who prays or prophesies with his head covered brings shame to his head. 5But every woman who prays or prophesies with her head uncovered brings shame to her head. She is the same as a woman who has her head shaved. 6If a woman does not cover her head, she should have her hair cut off. But since it is shameful for a woman to cut off her hair or to shave her head, she should cover her head. 7But a man should not cover his head, because he is the likeness and glory of God. But woman is man's glory. 8Man did not come from woman, but woman came from man. 9And man was not made for woman, but woman was made for man. 10So that is why a woman should have a symbol of authority on her head, because of the angels.

11But in the Lord women are not independent of men, and men are not independent of women. 12This is true because woman came from man, but also man is born from woman. But everything comes from God. 13Decide this for yourselves: Is it right for a woman to pray to God with her head uncovered? 14Even nature itself teaches you that wearing long hair is shameful for a man. 15But long hair is a woman's glory. Long hair is given to her as a covering. 16Some people may still want to argue about this, but I would add that neither we nor the churches of God have any other practice.

11:3 the man This could also mean "her husband."

SEPTEMBER 1

SONG OF SONGS 1:1—2:17

1 Solomon's Song of Songs.

The Woman Speaks to the Man She Loves

[2] Kiss me with the kisses of your mouth,
because your love is better than wine.
[3] The smell of your perfume is pleasant,
and your name is pleasant like
expensive perfume.
That's why the young women love you.
[4] Take me with you; let's run together.
The king takes me into his rooms.

Friends Speak to the Man

We will rejoice and be happy with you;
we praise your love more than wine.
With good reason, the young women
love you.

The Woman Speaks

[5] I'm dark but lovely,
women of Jerusalem,
dark like the tents of Kedar,
like the curtains of Solomon.
[6] Don't look at how dark I am,
at how dark the sun has made me.
My brothers were angry with me
and made me tend the vineyards,
so I haven't tended my own vineyard!
[7] Tell me, you whom I love,
where do you feed your sheep?
Where do you let them rest at noon?
Why should I look for you near your
friend's sheep,
like a woman who wears a veil?[n]

The Man Speaks to the Woman

[8] You are the most beautiful of women.
Surely you know to follow the sheep
and feed your young goats
near the shepherds' tents.
[9] My darling, you are like a mare
among the king's stallions.
[10] Your cheeks are beautiful with
ornaments,
and your neck with jewels.
[11] We will make for you gold earrings
with silver hooks.

The Woman Speaks

[12] The smell of my perfume spreads out
to the king on his couch.
[13] My lover is like a bag of myrrh
that lies all night between my breasts.
[14] My lover is like a bunch of flowers
from the vineyards at En Gedi.

The Man Speaks

[15] My darling, you are beautiful!
Oh, you are beautiful,
and your eyes are like doves.

The Woman Answers the Man

[16] You are so handsome, my lover,
and so pleasant!
Our bed is the grass.
[17] Cedar trees form our roof;
our ceiling is made of juniper wood.

The Woman Speaks Again

2 I am a rose in the Plain of Sharon,
a lily in the valleys.

The Man Speaks Again

[2] Among the young women, my darling
is like a lily among thorns!

The Woman Answers

[3] Among the young men, my lover
is like an apple tree in the woods!
I enjoy sitting in his shadow;
his fruit is sweet to my taste.
[4] He brought me to the banquet room,
and his banner over me is love.
[5] Strengthen me with raisins,
and refresh me with apples,
because I am weak with love.
[6] My lover's left hand is under my head,
and his right arm holds me tight.

The Woman Speaks to the Friends

[7] Women of Jerusalem, promise me
by the gazelles and the deer
not to awaken
or excite my feelings of love
until it is ready.

1:7 veil This was the way a prostitute usually dressed.

The Woman Speaks Again

[8]I hear my lover's voice.
Here he comes jumping across the
mountains,
skipping over the hills.
[9]My lover is like a gazelle or a young deer.
Look, he stands behind our wall
peeking through the windows,
looking through the blinds.
[10]My lover spoke and said to me,
"Get up, my darling;
let's go away, my beautiful one.
[11]Look, the winter is past;
the rains are over and gone.
[12]Blossoms appear through all the land.
The time has come to sing;
the cooing of doves is heard in our
land.
[13]There are young figs on the fig trees,
and the blossoms on the vines smell
sweet.
Get up, my darling;
let's go away, my beautiful one."

The Man Speaks

[14]My beloved is like a dove hiding in the
cracks of the rock,
in the secret places of the cliff.
Show me your face,
and let me hear your voice.
Your voice is sweet,
and your face is lovely.
[15]Catch the foxes for us—
the little foxes that ruin the vineyards
while they are in blossom.

The Woman Speaks

[16]My lover is mine, and I am his.
He feeds among the lilies
[17]until the day dawns
and the shadows disappear.
Turn, my lover.
Be like a gazelle or a young deer
on the mountain valleys.

PSALM 104:1–9

Praise to God Who Made the World

104 My whole being, praise the LORD.
LORD my God, you are very great.

You are clothed with glory and majesty;
[2] you wear light like a robe.
You stretch out the skies like a tent.
[3] You build your room above the clouds.
You make the clouds your chariot,
and you ride on the wings of the wind.
[4]You make the winds your messengers,
and flames of fire are your servants.

[5]You built the earth on its foundations
so it can never be moved.
[6]You covered the earth with oceans;
the water was above the mountains.
[7]But at your command, the water rushed
away.
When you thundered your orders, it
hurried away.
[8]The mountains rose; the valleys sank.
The water went to the places you made
for it.
[9]You set borders for the seas that they
cannot cross,
so water will never cover the earth
again.

PROVERBS 24:15–16

[15]Don't be wicked and attack a good
family's house;
don't rob the place where they live.
[16]Even though good people may be
bothered by trouble seven times,
they are never defeated,
but the wicked are overwhelmed by
trouble.

1 CORINTHIANS 11:17–34

The Lord's Supper

[17]In the things I tell you now I do not
praise you, because when you come together
you do more harm than good. [18]First, I hear
that when you meet together as a church you
are divided, and I believe some of this. [19](It is
necessary to have differences among you so
that it may be clear which of you really have
God's approval.) [20]When you come together,
you are not really eating the Lord's Supper.[n]
[21]This is because when you eat, each person
eats without waiting for the others. Some

11:20 Lord's Supper The meal Jesus told his followers to eat to remember him (Luke 22:14–20).

people do not get enough to eat, while others have too much to drink. [22]You can eat and drink in your own homes! You seem to think God's church is not important, and you embarrass those who are poor. What should I tell you? Should I praise you? I do not praise you for doing this.

[23]The teaching I gave you is the same teaching I received from the Lord: On the night when the Lord Jesus was handed over to be killed, he took bread [24]and gave thanks for it. Then he broke the bread and said, "This is my body; it is[n] for you. Do this to remember me." [25]In the same way, after they ate, Jesus took the cup. He said, "This cup is the new agreement that is sealed with the blood of my death. When you drink this, do it to remember me." [26]Every time you eat this bread and drink this cup you are telling others about the Lord's death until he comes.

[27]So a person who eats the bread or drinks the cup of the Lord in a way that is not worthy of it will be guilty of sinning against the body and the blood of the Lord. [28]Look into your own hearts before you eat the bread and drink the cup, [29]because all who eat the bread and drink the cup without recognizing the body eat and drink judgment against themselves. [30]That is why many in your group are sick and weak, and some of you have died. [31]But if we judged ourselves in the right way, God would not judge us. [32]But when the Lord judges us, he disciplines us so that we will not be destroyed along with the world.

[33]So my brothers and sisters, when you come together to eat, wait for each other. [34]Anyone who is too hungry should eat at home so that in meeting together you will not bring God's judgment on yourselves. I will tell you what to do about the other things when I come.

SEPTEMBER 2

SONG OF SONGS 3:1—4:16

The Woman Dreams

3 At night on my bed,
  I looked for the one I love;
  I looked for him, but I could not find him.
[2]I got up and went around the city,
  in the streets and squares,
looking for the one I love.
  I looked for him, but I could not find him.
[3]The watchmen found me as they
  patrolled the city,
  so I asked, "Have you seen the one I love?"
[4]As soon as I had left them,
  I found the one I love.
  I held him and would not let him go
  until I brought him to my mother's house,
  to the room where I was born.

The Woman Speaks to the Friends
[5]Women of Jerusalem, promise me
  by the gazelles and the deer
not to awaken
  or excite my feelings of love
  until it is ready.
[6]Who is this coming out of the desert
  like a cloud of smoke?
Who is this that smells like myrrh,
  incense,
  and other spices?
[7]Look, it's Solomon's couch[n]
  with sixty soldiers around it,
  the finest soldiers of Israel.
[8]These soldiers all carry swords
  and have been trained in war.
  Every man wears a sword at his side
  and is ready for the dangers of the night.
[9]King Solomon had a couch made for himself
  of wood from Lebanon.

11:24 it is Some Greek copies read "it is broken." • **3:7 couch** Something like a bed carried by slaves on which the king lay or sat while traveling.

[10]He made its posts of silver
and its braces of gold.
The seat was covered with purple cloth
that the women of Jerusalem wove with
love.
[11]Women of Jerusalem, go out and see
King Solomon.
He is wearing the crown his mother put
on his head
on his wedding day,
when his heart was happy!

The Man Speaks to the Woman

4 How beautiful you are, my darling!
Oh, you are beautiful!
Your eyes behind your veil are like doves.
Your hair is like a flock of goats
streaming down Mount Gilead.
[2]Your teeth are white like newly sheared
sheep
just coming from their bath.
Each one has a twin,
and none of them is missing.
[3]Your lips are like red silk thread,
and your mouth is lovely.
Your cheeks behind your veil
are like slices of a pomegranate.
[4]Your neck is like David's tower,
built with rows of stones.
A thousand shields hang on its walls;
each shield belongs to a strong soldier.
[5]Your breasts are like two fawns,
like twins of a gazelle,
feeding among the lilies.
[6]Until the day dawns
and the shadows disappear,
I will go to that mountain of myrrh
and to that hill of incense.
[7]My darling, everything about you is
beautiful,
and there is nothing at all wrong with
you.
[8]Come with me from Lebanon, my bride.
Come with me from Lebanon,
from the top of Mount Amana,
from the tops of Mount Senir and
Mount Hermon.
Come from the lions' dens
and from the leopards' hills.
[9]My sister, my bride,
you have thrilled my heart;

you have thrilled my heart
with a glance of your eyes,
with one sparkle from your necklace.
[10]Your love is so sweet, my sister, my bride.
Your love is better than wine,
and your perfume smells better than
any spice.
[11]My bride, your lips drip honey;
honey and milk are under your tongue.
Your clothes smell like the cedars of
Lebanon.
[12]My sister, my bride, you are like a garden
locked up,
like a walled-in spring, a closed-up
fountain.
[13]Your limbs are like an orchard
of pomegranates with all the best fruit,
filled with flowers and nard,
[14]nard and saffron, calamus, and
cinnamon,
with trees of incense, myrrh, and
aloes—
all the best spices.
[15]You are like a garden fountain—
a well of fresh water
flowing down from the mountains of
Lebanon.

The Woman Speaks

[16]Awake, north wind.
Come, south wind.
Blow on my garden,
and let its sweet smells flow out.
Let my lover enter the garden
and eat its best fruits.

PSALM 104:10–23

[10]You make springs pour into the ravines;
they flow between the mountains.
[11]They water all the wild animals;
the wild donkeys come there to drink.
[12]Wild birds make nests by the water;
they sing among the tree branches.
[13]You water the mountains from above.
The earth is full of the things you
made.
[14]You make the grass for cattle
and vegetables for the people.
You make food grow from the earth.
[15]You give us wine that makes happy
hearts

and olive oil that makes our faces
    shine.
You give us bread that gives us
    strength.
16The LORD's trees have plenty of water;
    they are the cedars of Lebanon, which
    he planted.
17The birds make their nests there;
    the stork's home is in the fir trees.
18The high mountains belong to the wild
    goats.
    The rocks are hiding places for the
    badgers.

19You made the moon to mark the seasons,
    and the sun always knows when to set.
20You make it dark, and it becomes night.
    Then all the wild animals creep
    around.
21The lions roar as they attack.
    They look to God for food.
22When the sun rises, they leave
    and go back to their dens to lie down.
23Then people go to work
    and work until evening.

PROVERBS 24:17–18

17Don't be happy when your enemy is
    defeated;
    don't be glad when he is overwhelmed.
18The LORD will notice and be displeased.
    He may not be angry with them
    anymore.

1 CORINTHIANS 12:1–31a

Gifts from the Holy Spirit

12Now, brothers and sisters, I want you
    to understand about spiritual gifts.
2You know the way you lived before you were
believers. You let yourselves be influenced
and led away to worship idols—things that
could not speak. 3So I want you to understand that no one who is speaking with the
help of God's Spirit says, "Jesus be cursed."
And no one can say, "Jesus is Lord," without
the help of the Holy Spirit.

4There are different kinds of gifts, but
they are all from the same Spirit. 5There are

different ways to serve but the same Lord to
serve. 6And there are different ways that God
works through people but the same God.
God works in all of us in everything we do.
7Something from the Spirit can be seen in
each person, for the common good. 8The
Spirit gives one person the ability to speak
with wisdom, and the same Spirit gives another the ability to speak with knowledge.
9The same Spirit gives faith to one person.
And, to another, that one Spirit gives gifts of
healing. 10The Spirit gives to another person
the power to do miracles, to another the ability to prophesy. And he gives to another the
ability to know the difference between good
and evil spirits. The Spirit gives one person
the ability to speak in different kinds of languages[n] and to another the ability to interpret those languages. 11One Spirit, the same
Spirit, does all these things, and the Spirit
decides what to give each person.

The Body of Christ Works Together

12A person's body is one thing, but it has
many parts. Though there are many parts to
a body, all those parts make only one body.
Christ is like that also. 13Some of us are Jews,
and some are Greeks. Some of us are slaves,
and some are free. But we were all baptized
into one body through one Spirit. And we
were all made to share in the one Spirit.

14The human body has many parts. 15The
foot might say, "Because I am not a hand, I am
not part of the body." But saying this would
not stop the foot from being a part of the
body. 16The ear might say, "Because I am not
an eye, I am not part of the body." But saying
this would not stop the ear from being a part
of the body. 17If the whole body were an eye, it
would not be able to hear. If the whole body
were an ear, it would not be able to smell.
18-19If each part of the body were the same
part, there would be no body. But truly God
put all the parts, each one of them, in the
body as he wanted them. 20So then there are
many parts, but only one body.

21The eye cannot say to the hand, "I don't
need you!" And the head cannot say to the
foot, "I don't need you!" 22No! Those parts of

12:10 languages This can also be translated "tongues."

the body that seem to be the weaker are really necessary. [23]And the parts of the body we think are less deserving are the parts to which we give the most honor. We give special respect to the parts we want to hide. [24]The more respectable parts of our body need no special care. But God put the body together and gave more honor to the parts that need it [25]so our body would not be divided. God wanted the different parts to care the same for each other. [26]If one part of the body suffers, all the other parts suffer with it. Or if one part of our body is honored, all the other parts share its honor.

[27]Together you are the body of Christ, and each one of you is a part of that body. [28]In the church God has given a place first to apostles, second to prophets, and third to teachers. Then God has given a place to those who do miracles, those who have gifts of healing, those who can help others, those who are able to govern, and those who can speak in different languages.[n] [29]Not all are apostles. Not all are prophets. Not all are teachers. Not all do miracles. [30]Not all have gifts of healing. Not all speak in different languages. Not all interpret those languages. [31]But you should truly want to have the greater gifts.

SEPTEMBER 3

SONG OF SONGS 5:1—6:13

The Man Speaks

5 I have entered my garden, my sister, my bride.
  I have gathered my myrrh with my spice.
  I have eaten my honeycomb and my honey.
  I have drunk my wine and my milk.

The Friends Speak

  Eat, friends, and drink;
    yes, drink deeply, lovers.

The Woman Dreams

[2]I sleep, but my heart is awake.
  I hear my lover knocking.
  "Open to me, my sister, my darling,
    my dove, my perfect one.
  My head is wet with dew,
    and my hair with the dampness of the night."
[3]I have taken off my garment
    and don't want to put it on again.
  I have washed my feet
    and don't want to get them dirty again.
[4]My lover put his hand through the opening,
    and I felt excited inside.

[5]I got up to open the door for my lover.
  Myrrh was dripping from my hands
    and flowing from my fingers,
    onto the handles of the lock.
[6]I opened the door for my lover,
    but my lover had left and was gone.
  When he spoke, he took my breath away.
  I looked for him, but I could not find him;
    I called for him, but he did not answer.
[7]The watchmen found me
    as they patrolled the city.
  They hit me and hurt me;
    the guards on the wall took away my veil.
[8]Promise me, women of Jerusalem,
    if you find my lover,
    tell him I am weak with love.

The Friends Answer the Woman

[9]How is your lover better than other lovers,
    most beautiful of women?
  How is your lover better than other lovers?
    Why do you want us to promise this?

The Woman Answers the Friends

[10]My lover is healthy and tan,
    the best of ten thousand men.

[11]His head is like the finest gold;
  his hair is wavy and black like a raven.
[12]His eyes are like doves
  by springs of water.
They seem to be bathed in cream
  and are set like jewels.
[13]His cheeks are like beds of spices;
  they smell like mounds of perfume.
His lips are like lilies
  flowing with myrrh.
[14]His hands are like gold hinges,
  filled with jewels.
His body is like shiny ivory
  covered with sapphires.
[15]His legs are like large marble posts,
  standing on bases of fine gold.
He is like a cedar of Lebanon,
  like the finest of the trees.
[16]His mouth is sweet to kiss,
  and I desire him very much.
Yes, daughters of Jerusalem,
  this is my lover
  and my friend.

The Friends Speak to the Woman

6 Where has your lover gone,
  most beautiful of women?
Which way did your lover turn?
We will look for him with you.

The Woman Answers the Friends

[2]My lover has gone down to his garden,
  to the beds of spices,
to feed in the gardens
  and to gather lilies.
[3]I belong to my lover,
  and my lover belongs to me.
He feeds among the lilies.

The Man Speaks to the Woman

[4]My darling, you are as beautiful as the
  city of Tirzah,
as lovely as the city of Jerusalem,
  like an army flying flags.
[5]Turn your eyes from me,
  because they excite me too much.
Your hair is like a flock of goats
  streaming down Mount Gilead.
[6]Your teeth are white like sheep
  just coming from their bath;
each one has a twin,
  and none of them is missing.

[7]Your cheeks behind your veil
  are like slices of a pomegranate.
[8]There may be sixty queens and eighty
  slave women
and so many girls you cannot count
  them,
[9]but there is only one like my dove, my
  perfect one.
She is her mother's only daughter,
  the brightest of the one who gave her
  birth.
The young women saw her and called
  her happy;
  the queens and the slave women also
  praised her.

The Young Women Praise the Woman

[10]Who is that young woman
  that shines out like the dawn?
She is as pretty as the moon,
  as bright as the sun,
  as wonderful as an army flying flags.

The Man Speaks

[11]I went down into the orchard of nut trees
  to see the blossoms of the valley,
to look for buds on the vines,
  to see if the pomegranate trees had
  bloomed.
[12]Before I realized it, my desire for you
  made me feel
  like a prince in a chariot.

The Friends Call to the Woman

[13]Come back, come back, woman of
  Shulam.
Come back, come back,
  so we may look at you!

The Woman Answers the Friends

Why do you want to look at the woman
  of Shulam
as you would at the dance of two
  armies?

PSALM 104:24–30

[24]LORD, you have made many things;
  with your wisdom you made them all.
The earth is full of your riches.
[25]Look at the sea, so big and wide,
  with creatures large and small that
  cannot be counted.
[26]Ships travel over the ocean,

and there is the sea monster Leviathan,
which you made to play there.

27All these things depend on you
    to give them their food at the right
    time.
28When you give it to them,
    they gather it up.
When you open your hand,
    they are filled with good food.
29When you turn away from them,
    they become frightened.
When you take away their breath,
    they die and turn to dust.
30When you breathe on them,
    they are created,
    and you make the land new again.

PROVERBS 24:19–20

19Don't envy evil people,
    and don't be jealous of the wicked.
20An evil person has nothing to hope for;
    the wicked will die like a flame that is
    put out.

1 CORINTHIANS 12:31b–13:13

Love Is the Greatest Gift

And now I will show you the best way of
all.

13 I may speak in different languages[n] of
people or even angels. But if I do not
have love, I am only a noisy bell or a crashing
cymbal. 2I may have the gift of prophecy. I
may understand all the secret things of God
and have all knowledge, and I may have faith
so great I can move mountains. But even
with all these things, if I do not have love,
then I am nothing. 3I may give away everything I have, and I may even give my body as
an offering to be burned.[n] But I gain nothing
if I do not have love.

4Love is patient and kind. Love is not jealous, it does not brag, and it is not proud.
5Love is not rude, is not selfish, and does not
get upset with others. Love does not count up
wrongs that have been done. 6Love takes no
pleasure in evil but rejoices over the truth.
7Love patiently accepts all things. It always
trusts, always hopes, and always endures.

8Love never ends. There are gifts of
prophecy, but they will be ended. There are
gifts of speaking in different languages, but
those gifts will stop. There is the gift of knowledge, but it will come to an end. 9The reason is
that our knowledge and our ability to prophesy are not perfect. 10But when perfection
comes, the things that are not perfect will end.
11When I was a child, I talked like a child, I
thought like a child, I reasoned like a child.
When I became a man, I stopped those
childish ways. 12It is the same with us. Now
we see a dim reflection, as if we were looking
into a mirror, but then we shall see clearly.
Now I know only a part, but then I will know
fully, as God has known me. 13So these three
things continue forever: faith, hope, and
love. And the greatest of these is love.

SEPTEMBER 4

SONG OF SONGS 7:1–8:14

The Man Speaks to the Woman

7 Your feet are beautiful in sandals,
    you daughter of a prince.
Your round thighs are like jewels
    shaped by an artist.

2Your navel is like a round drinking cup
    always filled with wine.
Your stomach is like a pile of wheat
    surrounded with lilies.
3Your breasts are like two fawns,
    like twins of a gazelle.
4Your neck is like an ivory tower.

13:1 languages This can also be translated "tongues."   **13:3 give . . . burned** Other Greek copies read "hand over my body
in order that I may brag."

Your eyes are like the pools in Heshbon
near the gate of Bath Rabbim.
Your nose is like the mountain of
Lebanon
that looks down on Damascus.
⁵Your head is like Mount Carmel,
and your hair is like purple cloth;
the king is captured in its folds.
⁶You are beautiful and pleasant;
my love, you are full of delights.
⁷You are tall like a palm tree,
and your breasts are like its bunches of
fruit.
⁸I said, "I will climb up the palm tree
and take hold of its fruit."
Let your breasts be like bunches of
grapes,
the smell of your breath like apples,
⁹ and your mouth like the best wine.

The Woman Speaks to the Man

Let this wine go down sweetly for my
lover;
may it flow gently past the lips and
teeth.
¹⁰I belong to my lover,
and he desires only me.
¹¹Come, my lover,
let's go out into the country
and spend the night in the fields.
¹²Let's go early to the vineyards
and see if the buds are on the vines.
Let's see if the blossoms have already
opened
and if the pomegranates have bloomed.
There I will give you my love.
¹³The mandrake flowers give their sweet
smell,
and all the best fruits are at our gates.
I have saved them for you, my lover,
the old delights and the new.

8 I wish you were like my brother
who fed at my mother's breasts.
If I found you outside,
I would kiss you,
and no one would look down on me.
²I would lead you and bring you
to my mother's house;
she is the one who taught me.
I would give you a drink of spiced wine
from my pomegranates.

The Woman Speaks to the Friends
³My lover's left hand is under my head,
and his right arm holds me tight.
⁴Women of Jerusalem,
promise not to awaken
or excite my feelings of love
until it is ready.

The Friends Speak
⁵Who is this coming out of the desert,
leaning on her lover?

The Man Speaks to the Woman
I woke you under the apple tree
where you were born;
there your mother gave birth to you.
⁶Put me like a seal on your heart,
like a seal on your arm.
Love is as strong as death;
jealousy is as strong as the grave.
Love bursts into flames
and burns like a hot fire.
⁷Even much water cannot put out the
flame of love;
floods cannot drown love.
If a man offered everything in his house
for love,
people would totally reject it.

The Woman's Brothers Speak
⁸We have a little sister,
and her breasts are not yet grown.
What should we do for our sister
on the day she becomes engaged?
⁹If she is a wall,
we will put silver towers on her.
If she is a door,
we will protect her with cedar boards.

The Woman Speaks
¹⁰I am a wall,
and my breasts are like towers.
So I was to him,
as one who brings happiness.
¹¹Solomon had a vineyard at Baal Hamon.
He rented the vineyards for others to
tend,
and everyone who rented had to pay
twenty-five pounds of silver for the
fruit.
¹²But my own vineyard is mine to give.
Solomon, the twenty-five pounds of
silver are for you,

and five pounds are for those who tend the fruit.

The Man Speaks to the Woman

[13]You who live in the gardens,
my friends are listening for your voice;
let me hear it.

The Woman Speaks to the Man

[14]Hurry, my lover,
be like a gazelle
or a young deer
on the mountains where spices grow.

PSALM 104:31–35

[31]May the glory of the LORD be forever.
May the LORD enjoy what he has made.
[32]He just looks at the earth, and it shakes.
He touches the mountains, and they
smoke.

[33]I will sing to the LORD all my life;
I will sing praises to my God as long as
I live.
[34]May my thoughts please him;
I am happy in the LORD.
[35]Let sinners be destroyed from the earth,
and let the wicked live no longer.

My whole being, praise the LORD.
Praise the LORD.

PROVERBS 24:21–22

[21]My child, respect the LORD and the king.
Don't join those people who refuse to
obey them.
[22]The LORD and the king will quickly
destroy such people.
Those two can cause great disaster!

1 CORINTHIANS 14:1–25

Desire Spiritual Gifts

14You should seek after love, and you should truly want to have the spiritual gifts, especially the gift of prophecy. [2]I will explain why. Those who have the gift of speaking in different languages[n] are not speaking to people; they are speaking to God. No one understands them; they are speaking secret

things through the Spirit. [3]But those who prophesy are speaking to people to give them strength, encouragement, and comfort. [4]The ones who speak in different languages are helping only themselves, but those who prophesy are helping the whole church. [5]I wish all of you had the gift of speaking in different kinds of languages, but more, I wish you would prophesy. Those who prophesy are greater than those who can only speak in different languages—unless someone is there who can explain what is said so that the whole church can be helped.

[6]Brothers and sisters, will it help you if I come to you speaking in different languages? No! It will help you only if I bring you a new truth or some new knowledge, or prophecy, or teaching. [7]It is the same as with lifeless things that make sounds—like a flute or a harp. If they do not make clear musical notes, you will not know what is being played. [8]And in a war, if the trumpet does not give a clear sound, who will prepare for battle? [9]It is the same with you. Unless you speak clearly with your tongue, no one can understand what you are saying. You will be talking into the air! [10]It may be true that there are all kinds of sounds in the world, and none is without meaning. [11]But unless I understand the meaning of what someone says to me, we will be like foreigners to each other. [12]It is the same with you. Since you want spiritual gifts very much, seek most of all to have the gifts that help the church grow stronger.

[13]The one who has the gift of speaking in a different language should pray for the gift to interpret what is spoken. [14]If I pray in a different language, my spirit is praying, but my mind does nothing. [15]So what should I do? I will pray with my spirit, but I will also pray with my mind. I will sing with my spirit, but I will also sing with my mind. [16]If you praise God with your spirit, those persons there without understanding cannot say amen[n] to your prayer of thanks, because they do not know what you are saying. [17]You may be thanking God in a good way, but the other person is not helped.

[18]I thank God that I speak in different kinds of languages more than all of you. [19]But in the church meetings I would rather speak five words I understand in order to teach others than thousands of words in a different language.

[20]Brothers and sisters, do not think like children. In evil things be like babies, but in your thinking you should be like adults. [21]It is written in the Scriptures:

"With people who use strange words and
    foreign languages
I will speak to these people.
But even then they will not listen to me,"

Isaiah 28:11–12

says the Lord.

[22]So the gift of speaking in different kinds of languages is a sign for those who do not believe, not for those who do believe. And prophecy is for people who believe, not for those who do not believe. [23]Suppose the whole church meets together and everyone speaks in different languages. If some people come in who do not understand or do not believe, they will say you are crazy. [24]But suppose everyone is prophesying and some people come in who do not believe or do not understand. If everyone is prophesying, their sin will be shown to them, and they will be judged by all that they hear. [25]The secret things in their hearts will be made known. So they will bow down and worship God saying, "Truly, God is with you."

SEPTEMBER 5

ISAIAH 1:1—2:22

1 This is the vision Isaiah son of Amoz saw about what would happen to Judah and Jerusalem. Isaiah saw these things while Uzziah, Jotham, Ahaz, and Hezekiah were kings of Judah.

God's Case Against His Children

[2]Heaven and earth, listen,
    because the LORD is speaking:
"I raised my children and helped them
    grow up,
but they have turned against me.
[3]An ox knows its master,
    and a donkey knows where its owner
        feeds it,
but the people of Israel do not know
    me;
my people do not understand."

[4]How terrible! Israel is a nation of sin,
    a people loaded down with guilt,
a group of children doing evil,
    children who are full of evil.
They have left the LORD;
    they hate God, the Holy One of Israel,
and have turned away from him as if
    he were a stranger.

[5]Why should you continue to be punished?
    Why do you continue to turn against
        him?
Your whole head is hurt,
    and your whole heart is sick.
[6]There is no healthy spot
    from the bottom of your foot to the top
        of your head;
you are covered with wounds, hurts,
    and open sores
that are not cleaned and covered,
    and no medicine takes away the pain.

[7]Your land is ruined;
    your cities have been burned with fire.
While you watch,
    your enemies are stealing everything
        from your land;
it is ruined like a country destroyed by
    enemies.
[8]Jerusalem is left alone
    like an empty shelter in a vineyard,
like a hut left in a field of melons,
    like a city surrounded by enemies.
[9]The LORD All-Powerful
    allowed a few of our people to live.
Otherwise we would have been
        completely destroyed
like the cities of Sodom and Gomorrah.

¹⁰Jerusalem, your rulers are like those of
  Sodom,
  and your people are like those of
  Gomorrah.
  Hear the word of the LORD;
  listen to the teaching of our God!
¹¹The LORD says,
  "I do not want all these sacrifices.
  I have had enough of your burnt sacrifices
  of male sheep and fat from fine animals.
  I am not pleased
  by the blood of bulls, lambs, and goats.
¹²You come to meet with me,
  but who asked you to do
  all this running in and out of my
  Temple's rooms?
¹³Don't continue bringing me worthless
  sacrifices!
  I hate the incense you burn.
  I can't stand your New Moons, Sabbaths,
  and other feast days;
  I can't stand the evil you do in your holy
  meetings.
¹⁴I hate your New Moon feasts
  and your other yearly feasts.
  They have become a heavy weight on me,
  and I am tired of carrying it.
¹⁵When you raise your arms to me in prayer,
  I will refuse to look at you.
  Even if you say many prayers,
  I will not listen to you,
  because your hands are full of blood.
¹⁶Wash yourselves and make yourselves
  clean.
  Stop doing the evil things I see you do.
  Stop doing wrong.
¹⁷ Learn to do good.
  Seek justice.
  Punish those who hurt others.
  Help the orphans.
  Stand up for the rights of widows."

¹⁸The LORD says,
  "Come, let us talk about these things.
  Though your sins are like scarlet,
  they can be as white as snow.
  Though your sins are deep red,
  they can be white like wool.
¹⁹If you become willing and obey me,
  you will eat good crops from the land.
²⁰But if you refuse to obey and if you turn
  against me,

  you will be destroyed by your enemies'
  swords."
  The LORD himself said these things.

Jerusalem Is Not Loyal to God
²¹The city of Jerusalem once followed the
  LORD,
  but she is no longer loyal to him.
  She used to be filled with fairness;
  people there lived the way God wanted.
  But now, murderers live there.
²²Jerusalem, you have become like the scum
  left when silver is purified;
  you are like wine mixed with water.
²³Your rulers are rebels
  and friends of thieves.
  They all accept money for doing wrong,
  and they are paid to cheat people.
  They don't seek justice for the orphans
  or listen to the widows' needs.
²⁴So the Lord GOD All-Powerful,
  the Mighty One of Israel, says:
  "You, my enemies, will not cause me any
  more trouble.
  I will pay you back for what you did.
²⁵I will turn against you
  and clean away all your wrongs as if with
  soap;
  I will take all the worthless things out of
  you.
²⁶I will bring back judges as you had long
  ago;
  your counselors will be like those you
  had in the beginning.
  Then you will be called the City That Is
  Right with God,
  the Loyal City."

²⁷By doing what is fair,
  Jerusalem will be free again.
  By doing what is right,
  her people who come back to the LORD
  will have freedom.
²⁸But sinners and those who turn against
  him will be destroyed;
  those who have left the LORD will die.

²⁹"You will be ashamed,
  because you have worshiped gods under
  the oak trees.
  You will be disgraced,
  because you have worshiped idols in
  your gardens.

³⁰You will be like an oak whose leaves are
dying
or like a garden without water.
³¹Powerful people will be like small, dry
pieces of wood,
and their works will be like sparks.
They will burn together,
and no one will be able to put out that
fire."

The Message About Jerusalem

2 Isaiah son of Amoz saw this message about
Judah and Jerusalem:
² In the last days
the mountain on which the LORD's
Temple stands
will become the most important of all
mountains.
It will be raised above the hills,
and people from all nations will come
streaming to it.
³Many nations will come and say,
"Come, let us go up to the mountain of
the LORD,
to the Temple of the God of Jacob.
Then God will teach us his ways,
and we will obey his teachings."
His teachings will go out from
Jerusalem;
the message of the LORD will go out
from Jerusalem.
⁴He will settle arguments among the
nations
and will make decisions for many
nations.
Then they will make their swords into
plows
and their spears into hooks for
trimming trees.
Nations will no longer fight other nations,
nor will they train for war anymore.
⁵Come, family of Jacob,
and let us follow the way of the LORD.

A Terrible Day Is Coming

⁶LORD, you have left your people,
the family of Jacob,
because they have become filled with
wrong ideas from people in the East.
They try to tell the future like the
Philistines,

and they have completely accepted
those foreign ideas.
⁷Their land has been filled with silver and
gold;
there are a great many treasures there.
Their land has been filled with horses;
there are many chariots there.
⁸Their land is full of idols.
The people worship these idols they
made with their own hands
and shaped with their own fingers.
⁹People will not be proud any longer
but will bow low with shame.
God, do not forgive them.

¹⁰Go into the caves of the cliffs;
dig holes and hide in the ground
from the anger of the LORD
and from his great power!
¹¹Proud people will be made humble,
and they will bow low with shame.
At that time only the LORD will still be
praised.

¹²The LORD All-Powerful has a certain day
planned
when he will punish the proud and
those who brag,
and they will no longer be important.
¹³He will bring down the tall cedar trees
from Lebanon
and the great oak trees of Bashan,
¹⁴all the tall mountains
and the high hills,
¹⁵every tall tower
and every high, strong wall,
¹⁶all the trading ships
and the beautiful ships.
¹⁷At that time proud people will be made
humble,
and they will bow low with shame.
At that time only the LORD will be
praised,
¹⁸ but all the idols will be gone.

¹⁹People will run to caves in the rocky
cliffs
and will dig holes and hide in the
ground
from the anger of the LORD
and his great power,
when he stands to shake the earth.

²⁰At that time people will throw away
their gold and silver idols,
which they made for themselves to
worship;
they will throw them away to the bats
and moles.
²¹Then the people will hide in caves
and cracks in the rocks
from the anger of the LORD
and his great power,
when he stands to shake the earth.

²²You should stop trusting in people to save
you,
because people are only human;
they aren't able to help you.

PSALM 105:1–7

God's Love for Israel

10 5 Give thanks to the LORD and pray
to him.
Tell the nations what he has done.
²Sing to him; sing praises to him.
Tell about all his miracles.
³Be glad that you are his;
let those who seek the LORD be happy.
⁴Depend on the LORD and his strength;
always go to him for help.
⁵Remember the miracles he has done;
remember his wonders and his
decisions.
⁶You are descendants of his servant
Abraham,
the children of Jacob, his chosen people.
⁷He is the LORD our God.
His laws are for all the world.

PROVERBS 24:23–25

More Words of Wisdom

²³These are also sayings of the wise:
It is not good to take sides when you are
the judge.
²⁴Don't tell the wicked that they are
innocent;
people will curse you, and nations will
hate you.
²⁵But things will go well if you punish the
guilty,
and you will receive rich blessings.

1 CORINTHIANS 14:26–40

Meetings Should Help the Church

²⁶So, brothers and sisters, what should you do? When you meet together, one person has a song, and another has a teaching. Another has a new truth from God. Another speaks in a different language,ⁿ and another person interprets that language. The purpose of all these things should be to help the church grow strong. ²⁷When you meet together, if anyone speaks in a different language, it should be only two, or not more than three, who speak. They should speak one after the other, and someone should interpret. ²⁸But if there is no interpreter, then those who speak in a different language should be quiet in the church meeting. They should speak only to themselves and to God.

²⁹Only two or three prophets should speak, and the others should judge what they say. ³⁰If a message from God comes to another person who is sitting, the first speaker should stop. ³¹You can all prophesy one after the other. In this way all the people can be taught and encouraged. ³²The spirits of prophets are under the control of the prophets themselves. ³³God is not a God of confusion but a God of peace.

As is true in all the churches of God's people, ³⁴women should keep quiet in the church meetings. They are not allowed to speak, but they must yield to this rule as the law says. ³⁵If they want to learn something, they should ask their own husbands at home. It is shameful for a woman to speak in the church meeting. ³⁶Did God's teaching come from you? Or are you the only ones to whom it has come?

³⁷Those who think they are prophets or spiritual persons should understand that what I am writing to you is the Lord's command. ³⁸Those who ignore this will be ignored by God.ⁿ

³⁹So my brothers and sisters, you should truly want to prophesy. But do not stop people from using the gift of speaking in different kinds of languages. ⁴⁰But let everything be done in a right and orderly way.

14:26 language This can also be translated "tongue." **14:38 Those . . . God.** Some Greek copies read "Those who are ignorant of this will stay ignorant."

SEPTEMBER 6

ISAIAH 3:1—4:6

God Will Punish Judah and Jerusalem

3 Understand this:
The Lord GOD All-Powerful
will take away everything Judah and
Jerusalem need—
all the food and water,
²the heroes and great soldiers,
the judges and prophets,
people who do magic and elders,
³the military leaders and government
leaders,
the counselors, the skilled craftsmen,
and those who try to tell the future.
⁴The LORD says, "I will cause young boys
to be your leaders,
and foolish children will rule over you.
⁵People will be against each other;
everyone will be against his
neighbor.
Young people will not respect older
people,
and common people will not respect
important people."
⁶At that time a man will grab one of his
brothers
from his own family and say,
"You have a coat, so you will be our
leader.
These ruins will be under your
control."
⁷But that brother will stand up and say,
"I cannot help you,
because I do not have food or clothes in
my house.
You will not make me your leader."
⁸This will happen because Jerusalem has
stumbled,
and Judah has fallen.
The things they say and do are against
the LORD;
they turn against him.
⁹The look on their faces shows they are
guilty;
like the people of Sodom, they are
proud of their sin.
They don't care who sees it.

How terrible it will be for them,
because they have brought much
trouble on themselves.

¹⁰Tell those who do what is right that
things will go well for them,
because they will receive a reward for
what they do.
¹¹But how terrible it will be for the wicked!
They will be punished for all the wrong
they have done.
¹²Children treat my people cruelly,
and women rule over them.
My people, your guides lead you in the
wrong way
and turn you away from what is right.

¹³The LORD takes his place in court
and stands to judge the people.
¹⁴The LORD presents his case
against the elders and other leaders of
his people:
"You have burned the vineyard.
Your houses are full of what you took
from the poor.
¹⁵What gives you the right to crush my
people
and grind the faces of the poor into the
dirt?"
The Lord GOD All-Powerful says this.

A Warning to Women of Jerusalem

¹⁶The LORD says,
"The women of Jerusalem are proud.
They walk around with their heads held
high,
and they flirt with their eyes.
They take quick, short steps,
making noise with their ankle
bracelets."
¹⁷So the Lord will put sores on the heads of
those women in Jerusalem,
and he will make them lose their hair.
¹⁸At that time the Lord will take away
everything that makes them proud: their
beautiful ankle bracelets, their headbands,
their necklaces shaped like the moon, ¹⁹their
earrings, bracelets, and veils, ²⁰their scarves,

ankle chains, the cloth belts worn around their waists, their bottles of perfume, and charms, ²¹their signet rings, nose rings, ²²their fine robes, capes, shawls, and purses, ²³their mirrors, linen dresses, turbans, and long shawls.

²⁴Instead of wearing sweet-smelling
  perfume, they will stink.
Instead of fine cloth belts, they will
  wear the ropes of captives.
Instead of having their hair fixed in
  fancy ways, they will be bald.
Instead of fine clothes, they will wear
  clothes of sadness.
Instead of being beautiful, they will
  wear the brand of a captive.
²⁵At that time your men will be killed with
  swords,
and your heroes will die in war.
²⁶There will be crying and sadness near
  the city gates.
Jerusalem will be like a woman who
  has lost everything and sits on the
  ground.

4 At that time seven women will grab one
  man
and say, "We will eat our own bread
  and make our own clothes,
but please marry us!
  Please, take away our shame."

The Branch of the Lord
²At that time the LORD's branch will be very beautiful and great. The people still living in Israel will be proud of what the land grows. ³Those who are still living in Jerusalem will be called holy; their names are recorded among the living in Jerusalem. ⁴The Lord will wash away the filth from the women of Jerusalem. He will wash the bloodstains out of Jerusalem and clean the city with the spirit of fairness and the spirit of fire. ⁵Then the LORD will cover Mount Zion and the people who meet there with a cloud of smoke during the day and with a bright, flaming fire at night. There will be a covering over every person. ⁶This covering will protect the people from the heat of the sun and will provide a safe place to hide from the storm and rain.

PSALM 105:8–15

⁸He will keep his agreement forever;
  he will keep his promises always.
⁹He will keep the agreement he made with
  Abraham
  and the promise he made to Isaac.
¹⁰He made it a law for the people of
  Jacob;
  he made it an agreement with Israel to
  last forever.
¹¹The LORD said, "I will give you the land of
  Canaan,
  and it will belong to you."

¹²Then God's people were few in number.
  They were strangers in the land.
¹³They went from one nation to another,
  from one kingdom to another.
¹⁴But the LORD did not let anyone hurt
  them;
  he warned kings not to harm them.
¹⁵He said, "Don't touch my chosen people,
  and don't harm my prophets."

PROVERBS 24:26–27

²⁶An honest answer is as pleasing
  as a kiss on the lips.

²⁷First, finish your outside work
  and prepare your fields.
After that, you can build your house.

1 CORINTHIANS 15:1–34

The Good News About Christ
15 Now, brothers and sisters, I want you to remember the Good News I brought to you. You received this Good News and continue strong in it. ²And you are being saved by it if you continue believing what I told you. If you do not, then you believed for nothing.

³I passed on to you what I received, of which this was most important: that Christ died for our sins, as the Scriptures say; ⁴that he was buried and was raised to life on the third day as the Scriptures say; ⁵and that he was seen by Peter and then by the twelve apostles. ⁶After that, Jesus was seen by more than five hundred of the believers at the same time. Most of them are still living today, but some have died. ⁷Then he was seen by James and

later by all the apostles. [8]Last of all he was seen by me—as by a person not born at the normal time. [9]All the other apostles are greater than I am. I am not even good enough to be called an apostle, because I persecuted the church of God. [10]But God's grace has made me what I am, and his grace to me was not wasted. I worked harder than all the other apostles. (But it was not I really; it was God's grace that was with me.) [11]So if I preached to you or the other apostles preached to you, we all preach the same thing, and this is what you believed.

We Will Be Raised from the Dead

[12]Now since we preached that Christ was raised from the dead, why do some of you say that people will not be raised from the dead? [13]If no one is ever raised from the dead, then Christ has not been raised. [14]And if Christ has not been raised, then our preaching is worth nothing, and your faith is worth nothing. [15]And also, we are guilty of lying about God, because we testified of him that he raised Christ from the dead. But if people are not raised from the dead, then God never raised Christ. [16]If the dead are not raised, Christ has not been raised either. [17]And if Christ has not been raised, then your faith has nothing to it; you are still guilty of your sins. [18]And those in Christ who have already died are lost. [19]If our hope in Christ is for this life only, we should be pitied more than anyone else in the world.

[20]But Christ has truly been raised from the dead—the first one and proof that those who sleep in death will also be raised. [21]Death has come because of what one man did, but the rising from death also comes because of one

man. [22]In Adam all of us die. In the same way, in Christ all of us will be made alive again. [23]But everyone will be raised to life in the right order. Christ was first to be raised. When Christ comes again, those who belong to him will be raised to life, [24]and then the end will come. At that time Christ will destroy all rulers, authorities, and powers, and he will hand over the kingdom to God the Father. [25]Christ must rule until he puts all enemies under his control. [26]The last enemy to be destroyed will be death. [27]The Scripture says that God put all things under his control.[n] When it says "all things" are under him, it is clear this does not include God himself. God is the One who put everything under his control. [28]After everything has been put under the Son, then he will put himself under God, who had put all things under him. Then God will be the complete ruler over everything.

[29]If the dead are never raised, what will people do who are being baptized for the dead? If the dead are not raised at all, why are people being baptized for them?

[30]And what about us? Why do we put ourselves in danger every hour? [31]I die every day. That is true, brothers and sisters, just as it is true that I brag about you in Christ Jesus our Lord. [32]If I fought wild animals in Ephesus only with human hopes, I have gained nothing. If the dead are not raised, "Let us eat and drink, because tomorrow we will die."[n]

[33]Do not be fooled: "Bad friends will ruin good habits." [34]Come back to your right way of thinking and stop sinning. Some of you do not know God—I say this to shame you.

SEPTEMBER 7

Israel, the Lord's Vineyard

5 Now I will sing for my friend a song about his vineyard.

My friend had a vineyard
 on a hill with very rich soil.
[2]He dug and cleared the field of stones
 and planted the best grapevines there.
He built a tower in the middle of it

and cut out a winepress as well.
He hoped good grapes would grow there,
but only bad ones grew.

³My friend says, "You people living in
Jerusalem,
and you people of Judah,
judge between me and my vineyard.
⁴What more could I have done for my
vineyard
than I have already done?
Although I expected good grapes to grow,
why were there only bad ones?
⁵Now I will tell you
what I will do to my vineyard:
I will remove the hedge,
and it will be burned.
I will break down the stone wall,
and it will be walked on.
⁶I will ruin my field.
It will not be trimmed or hoed,
and weeds and thorns will grow there.
I will command the clouds
not to rain on it."

⁷The vineyard belonging to the LORD
All-Powerful
is the nation of Israel;
the garden that he loves
is the people of Judah.
He looked for justice, but there was only
killing.
He hoped for right living, but there
were only cries of pain.

⁸How terrible it will be for you who add
more houses to your houses
and more fields to your fields
until there is no room left for other
people.
Then you are left alone in the land.
⁹The LORD All-Powerful said this to me:
"The fine houses will be destroyed;
the large and beautiful houses will be
left empty.
¹⁰At that time a ten-acre vineyard will
make only six gallons of wine,
and ten bushels of seed will grow only
half a bushel of grain."

¹¹How terrible it will be for people who
rise early in the morning
to look for strong drink,
who stay awake late at night,
becoming drunk with wine.
¹²At their parties they have lyres, harps,
tambourines, flutes, and wine.
They don't see what the LORD has done
or notice the work of his hands.
¹³So my people will be captured and taken
away,
because they don't really know me.
All the great people will die of hunger,
and the common people will die of
thirst.
¹⁴So the place of the dead wants more and
more people,
and it opens wide its mouth.
Jerusalem's important people and
common people will go down into it,
with their happy and noisy ones.
¹⁵So the common people and the great
people will be brought down;
those who are proud will be humbled.
¹⁶The LORD All-Powerful will receive glory
by judging fairly;
the holy God will show himself holy by
doing what is right.
¹⁷Then the sheep will go anywhere they
want,
and lambs will feed on the land that
rich people once owned.

¹⁸How terrible it will be for those people!
They pull their guilt and sins behind
them
as people pull wagons with ropes.
¹⁹They say, "Let God hurry;
let him do his work soon
so we may see it.
Let the plan of the Holy One of Israel
happen soon
so that we will know what it is."

²⁰How terrible it will be for people who call
good things bad
and bad things good,
who think darkness is light
and light is darkness,
who think sour is sweet
and sweet is sour.

²¹How terrible it will be for people who
think they are wise
and believe they are clever.

²²How terrible it will be for people who are
famous for drinking wine
and are champions at mixing drinks.
²³They take money to set the guilty free
and don't allow good people to be
judged fairly.
²⁴They will be destroyed
just as fire burns straw or dry grass.
They will be destroyed
like a plant whose roots rot
and whose flower dies and blows away
like dust.
They have refused to obey the teachings
of the LORD All-Powerful
and have hated the message from the
Holy God of Israel.
²⁵So the LORD has become very angry with
his people,
and he has raised his hand to punish
them.
Even the mountains are frightened.
Dead bodies lie in the streets like
garbage.

But the LORD is still angry;
his hand is still raised to strike down
the people.

²⁶He raises a banner for the nations far
away.
He whistles to call those people from
the ends of the earth.
Look! The enemy comes quickly!
²⁷Not one of them becomes tired or falls
down.
Not one of them gets sleepy and falls
asleep.
Their weapons are close at hand,
and their sandal straps are not broken.
²⁸Their arrows are sharp,
and all of their bows are ready to shoot.
The horses' hoofs are hard as rocks,
and their chariot wheels move like a
whirlwind.
²⁹Their shout is like the roar of a lion;
it is loud like a young lion.
They growl as they grab their captives.
There is no one to stop them from
taking their captives away.
³⁰On that day they will roar
like the waves of the sea.

And when people look at the land,
they will see only darkness and pain;
all light will become dark in this thick
cloud.

Isaiah Becomes a Prophet

6 In the year that King Uzziah died, I saw
the Lord sitting on a very high throne. His
long robe filled the Temple. ²Heavenly creatures of fire stood above him. Each creature
had six wings: It used two wings to cover its
face, two wings to cover its feet, and two
wings for flying. ³Each creature was calling
to the others:

"Holy, holy, holy is the LORD All-Powerful.
His glory fills the whole earth."

⁴Their calling caused the frame around the
door to shake, as the Temple filled with smoke.

⁵I said, "Oh, no! I will be destroyed. I am
not pure, and I live among people who are
not pure, but I have seen the King, the LORD
All-Powerful."

⁶One of the heavenly creatures used a pair
of tongs to take a hot coal from the altar.
Then he flew to me with the hot coal in his
hand. ⁷The creature touched my mouth with
the hot coal and said, "Look, your guilt is
taken away, because this hot coal has
touched your lips. Your sin is taken away."

⁸Then I heard the Lord's voice, saying,
"Whom can I send? Who will go for us?"

So I said, "Here I am. Send me!"

⁹Then the Lord said, "Go and tell this to
the people:

'You will listen and listen, but you will
not understand.
You will look and look, but you will not
learn.'

¹⁰Make the minds of these people dumb.
Shut their ears. Cover their eyes.
Otherwise, they might really understand
what they see with their eyes
and hear with their ears.
They might really understand in their
minds
and come back to me and be healed."

¹¹Then I asked, "Lord, how long should I
do this?"

He answered,

"Until the cities are destroyed
and the people are gone,

until there are no people left in the
houses,
until the land is destroyed and left
empty.
¹²The LORD will send the people far away,
and the land will be left empty.
¹³One-tenth of the people will be left in the
land,
but it will be destroyed again.
These people will be like an oak tree
whose stump is left when the tree is
chopped down.
The people who remain will be like a
stump that will sprout again."

PSALM 105:16–36

¹⁶God ordered a time of hunger in the
land,
and he destroyed all the food.
¹⁷Then he sent a man ahead of them—
Joseph, who was sold as a slave.
¹⁸They put chains around his feet
and an iron ring around his neck.
¹⁹Then the time he had spoken of came,
and the LORD's words proved that
Joseph was right.
²⁰The king of Egypt sent for Joseph and
freed him;
the ruler of the people set him free.
²¹He made him the master of his house;
Joseph was in charge of his riches.
²²He could order the princes as he wished.
He taught the older men to be wise.
²³Then his father Israel came to Egypt;
Jacob[n] lived in Egypt.[n]
²⁴The LORD made his people grow in
number,
and he made them stronger than their
enemies.
²⁵He caused the Egyptians to hate his
people
and to make plans against his servants.
²⁶Then he sent his servant Moses,
and Aaron, whom he had chosen.
²⁷They did many signs among the Egyptians
and worked wonders in Egypt.
²⁸The LORD sent darkness and made the
land dark,

but the Egyptians turned against what
he said.
²⁹So he changed their water into blood
and made their fish die.
³⁰Then their country was filled with frogs,
even in the bedrooms of their rulers.
³¹The LORD spoke and flies came,
and gnats were everywhere in the
country.
³²He made hail fall like rain
and sent lightning through their land.
³³He struck down their grapevines and fig
trees,
and he destroyed every tree in the
country.
³⁴He spoke and grasshoppers came;
the locusts were too many to count.
³⁵They ate all the plants in the land
and everything the earth produced.
³⁶The LORD also killed all the firstborn
sons in the land,
the oldest son of each family.

PROVERBS 24:28–29

²⁸Don't testify against your neighbor for no
good reason.
Don't say things that are false.
²⁹Don't say, "I'll get even;
I'll do to him what he did to me."

1 CORINTHIANS 15:35–58

What Kind of Body Will We Have?

³⁵But someone may ask, "How are the
dead raised? What kind of body will they
have?" ³⁶Foolish person! When you sow a
seed, it must die in the ground before it can
live and grow. ³⁷And when you sow it, it does
not have the same "body" it will have later.
What you sow is only a bare seed, maybe
wheat or something else. ³⁸But God gives it a
body that he has planned for it, and God
gives each kind of seed its own body. ³⁹All
things made of flesh are not the same: People have one kind of flesh, animals have another, birds have another, and fish have
another. ⁴⁰Also there are heavenly bodies
and earthly bodies. But the beauty of the
heavenly bodies is one kind, and the beauty

105:23 Jacob Also called Israel. **105:23 Egypt** Literally, "the land of Ham." Also in verse 27. The people in Egypt were descendants of Ham, one of Noah's sons. See Genesis 10:6.

of the earthly bodies is another. [41]The sun has one kind of beauty, the moon has another beauty, and the stars have another. And each star is different in its beauty.

[42]It is the same with the dead who are raised to life. The body that is "planted" will ruin and decay, but it is raised to a life that cannot be destroyed. [43]When the body is "planted," it is without honor, but it is raised in glory. When the body is "planted," it is weak, but when it is raised, it is powerful. [44]The body that is "planted" is a physical body. When it is raised, it is a spiritual body.

There is a physical body, and there is also a spiritual body. [45]It is written in the Scriptures: "The first man, Adam, became a living person."[n] But the last Adam became a spirit that gives life. [46]The spiritual did not come first, but the physical and then the spiritual. [47]The first man came from the dust of the earth. The second man came from heaven. [48]People who belong to the earth are like the first man of earth. But those people who belong to heaven are like the man of heaven. [49]Just as we were made like the man of earth, so we will[n] also be made like the man of heaven.

[50]I tell you this, brothers and sisters: Flesh and blood cannot have a part in the kingdom of God. Something that will ruin can-not have a part in something that never ruins. [51]But look! I tell you this secret: We will not all sleep in death, but we will all be changed. [52]It will take only a second—as quickly as an eye blinks—when the last trumpet sounds. The trumpet will sound, and those who have died will be raised to live forever, and we will all be changed. [53]This body that can be destroyed must clothe itself with something that can never be destroyed. And this body that dies must clothe itself with something that can never die. [54]So this body that can be destroyed will clothe itself with that which can never be destroyed, and this body that dies will clothe itself with that which can never die. When this happens, this Scripture will be made true:

"Death is destroyed forever in victory."

Isaiah 25:8

[55]"Death, where is your victory?

Death, where is your pain?" *Hosea 13:14*

[56]Death's power to hurt is sin, and the power of sin is the law. [57]But we thank God! He gives us the victory through our Lord Jesus Christ.

[58]So my dear brothers and sisters, stand strong. Do not let anything move you. Always give yourselves fully to the work of the Lord, because you know that your work in the Lord is never wasted.

SEPTEMBER 8

ISAIAH 7:1—8:22

Trouble with Aram

7 Now Ahaz was the son of Jotham, who was the son of Uzziah. When Ahaz was king of Judah, Rezin king of Aram and Pekah son of Remaliah, the king of Israel, went up to Jerusalem to fight against it. But they were not able to defeat the city.

[2]Ahaz king of Judah received a message saying, "The armies of Aram and Israel[n] have joined together."

When Ahaz heard this, he and the people were frightened. They shook with fear like trees of the forest blown by the wind.

[3]Then the LORD told Isaiah, "You and your son Shear-Jashub[n] should go and meet Ahaz at the place where the water flows into the upper pool, on the road where people do their laundry. [4]Tell Ahaz, 'Be careful. Be calm and don't worry. Don't let those two men, Rezin and Pekah son of Remaliah, scare you. Don't be afraid of their anger or Aram's anger, because they are like two barely burn-

15:45 "The first . . . person." Quotation from Genesis 2:7.   **15:49 so we will** Some Greek copies read "so let us."
•   **7:2 Israel** Literally, "Ephraim." Isaiah often uses "Ephraim" to mean all of Israel.   **7:3 Shear-Jashub** This name means "a part of the people will come back."

ing sticks that are ready to go out. ⁵They have made plans against you, saying, ⁶"Let's fight against Judah and tear it apart. We will divide the land for ourselves and make the son of Tabeel the new king of Judah." ⁷But I, the Lord God, say,

" 'Their plan will not succeed;
it will not happen,
⁸because Aram is led by the city of Damascus,
and Damascus is led by its weak king, Rezin.
Within sixty-five years Israel will no longer be a nation.
⁹Israel is led by the city of Samaria,
and Samaria is led by its weak king, the son of Remaliah.
If your faith is not strong,
you will not have strength enough to last.' "

Immanuel—God Is with Us

¹⁰Then the Lord spoke to Ahaz again, saying, ¹¹"Ask for a sign from the Lord your God to prove to yourself that these things are true. It may be a sign from as deep as the place of the dead or as high as the heavens."

¹²But Ahaz said, "I will not ask for a sign or test the Lord."

¹³Then Isaiah said, "Ahaz, descendant of David, listen carefully! Isn't it bad enough that you wear out the patience of people? Do you also have to wear out the patience of my God? ¹⁴The Lord himself will give you a sign: The virgin[n] will be pregnant. She will have a son, and she will name him Immanuel.[n] ¹⁵He will be eating milk curds and honey when he learns to reject what is evil and to choose what is good. ¹⁶You are afraid of the kings of Israel and Aram now. But before the child learns to choose good and reject evil, the lands of Israel and Aram will be empty. ¹⁷The Lord will bring troubled times to you, your people, and to the people of your father's family. They will be worse than anything that has happened since Israel separated from Judah. The Lord will bring the king of Assyria to fight against you.

¹⁸"At that time the Lord will whistle for the Egyptians, and they will come like flies from Egypt's faraway streams. He will call for the Assyrians, and they will come like bees. ¹⁹These enemies will camp in the deep ravines and in the cliffs, by the thornbushes and watering holes. ²⁰The Lord will hire Assyria and use it like a razor to punish Judah. It will be as if the Lord is shaving the hair from Judah's head and legs and removing Judah's beard.

²¹"At that time a person will be able to keep only one young cow and two sheep alive. ²²There will be only enough milk for that person to eat milk curds. All who remain in the land will go back to eating just milk curds and honey. ²³In this land there are now vineyards that have a thousand grapevines, which are worth about twenty-five pounds of silver. But these fields will become full of weeds and thorns. ²⁴The land will become wild and useful only as a hunting ground. ²⁵People once worked and grew food on these hills, but at that time people will not go there, because the land will be filled with weeds and thorns. Only sheep and cattle will go to those places."

Assyria Will Come Soon

8 The Lord told me, "Take a large scroll and write on it with an ordinary pen: 'Maher-Shalal-Hash-Baz.' ²I will gather some men to be reliable witnesses: Uriah the priest and Zechariah son of Jeberekiah."

³Then I went to the prophetess, and she became pregnant and had a son. The Lord told me, "Name the boy Maher-Shalal-Hash-Baz,[n] ⁴because the king of Assyria will take away all the wealth and possessions of Damascus and Samaria before the boy learns to say 'my father' or 'my mother.' "

⁵Again the Lord spoke to me, saying,
⁶"These people refuse to accept
the slow-moving waters of the pool of Shiloah
and are terrified of Rezin
and Pekah son of Remaliah.
⁷So I, the Lord, will bring

7:14 virgin The Hebrew word means "a young woman." Often this meant a girl who was not married and had not yet had sexual relations with anyone. **7:14 Immanuel** This name means "God is with us." **8:3 Maher-Shalal-Hash-Baz** This name means "there will soon be looting and stealing."

the king of Assyria and all his power
against them,
like a powerful flood of water from the
Euphrates River.
The Assyrians will be like water rising
over the banks of the river,
flowing over the land.
⁸That water will flow into Judah and pass
through it,
rising to Judah's throat.
Immanuel, this army will spread its
wings like a bird
until it covers your whole country."

⁹Be broken, all you nations,
and be smashed to pieces.
Listen, all you faraway countries.
Prepare for battle and be smashed to
pieces!
Prepare for battle and be smashed to
pieces!
¹⁰Make your plans for the fight,
but they will be defeated.
Give orders to your armies,
but they will be useless,
because God is with us.

Warnings to Isaiah
¹¹The LORD spoke to me with his great
power and warned me not to follow the lead
of the rest of the people. He said,
¹²"People are saying that others make
plans against them,
but you should not believe them.
Don't be afraid of what they fear;
do not dread those things.
¹³But remember that the LORD
All-Powerful is holy.
He is the one you should fear;
he is the one you should dread.
¹⁴Then he will be a place of safety for you.
But for the two families of Israel,
he will be like a stone that causes
people to stumble,
like a rock that makes them fall.
He will be like a trap for the people of
Jerusalem,
and he will catch them in his trap.
¹⁵Many people will fall over this rock.
They will fall and be broken;
they will be trapped and caught."

¹⁶Make an agreement.
Seal up the teaching while my
followers are watching.
¹⁷I will wait for the LORD to help us,
the LORD who is ashamed of the family
of Israel.
I will wait for him.
¹⁸I am here, and with me are the children
the LORD has given me. We are signs and
proofs for the people of Israel from the
LORD All-Powerful, who lives on Mount
Zion.

¹⁹Some people say, "Ask the mediums
and fortune-tellers, who whisper and mut-
ter, what to do." But I tell you that people
should ask their God for help. Why should
people who are still alive ask something
from the dead? ²⁰You should follow the
teachings and the agreement with the LORD.
The mediums and fortune-tellers do not
speak the word of the LORD, so their words
are worth nothing.

²¹People will wander through the land
troubled and hungry. When they become
hungry, they will become angry and will
look up and curse their king and their God.
²²They will look around them at their land
and see only trouble, darkness, and awful
gloom. And they will be forced into the
darkness.

PSALM 105:37–45

³⁷Then he brought his people out,
and they carried with them silver and
gold.
Not one of his people stumbled.
³⁸The Egyptians were glad when they left,
because the Egyptians were afraid of
them.
³⁹The LORD covered them with a cloud
and lit up the night with fire.
⁴⁰When they asked, he brought them quail
and filled them with bread from
heaven.
⁴¹God split the rock, and water flowed out;
it ran like a river through the desert.
⁴²He remembered his holy promise
to his servant Abraham.

⁴³So God brought his people out with joy,
his chosen ones with singing.

[44]He gave them lands of other nations,
so they received what others had
worked for.
[45]This was so they would keep his orders
and obey his teachings.

Praise the LORD!

PROVERBS 24:30–34

[30]I passed by a lazy person's field
and by the vineyard of someone with
no sense.
[31]Thorns had grown up everywhere.
The ground was covered with weeds,
and the stone walls had fallen down.
[32]I thought about what I had seen;
I learned this lesson from what I saw.
[33]You sleep a little; you take a nap.
You fold your hands and lie down to
rest.
[34]Soon you will be as poor as if you had
been robbed;
you will have as little as if you had
been held up.

1 CORINTHIANS 16:1–24

The Gift for Other Believers

16Now I will write about the collection of
money for God's people. Do the same
thing I told the Galatian churches to do: [2]On
the first day of every week, each one of you
should put aside money as you have been
blessed. Save it up so you will not have to collect money after I come. [3]When I arrive, I
will send whomever you approve to take
your gift to Jerusalem. I will send them with
letters of introduction, [4]and if it seems good
for me to go also, they will go along with me.

Paul's Plans

[5]I plan to go through Macedonia, so I
will come to you after I go through there.
[6]Perhaps I will stay with you for a time or
even all winter. Then you can help me on
my trip, wherever I go. [7]I do not want to see
you now just in passing. I hope to stay a
longer time with you if the Lord allows it.
[8]But I will stay at Ephesus until Pentecost,

[9]because a good opportunity for a great and
growing work has been given to me now.
And there are many people working against
me.
[10]If Timothy comes to you, see to it that
he has nothing to fear with you, because he
is working for the Lord just as I am. [11]So
none of you should treat Timothy as unimportant, but help him on his trip in peace so
that he can come back to me. I am expecting him to come with the brothers.
[12]Now about our brother Apollos: I
strongly encouraged him to visit you with
the other brothers. He did not at all want to
come now; he will come when he has the
opportunity.

Paul Ends His Letter

[13]Be alert. Continue strong in the faith.
Have courage, and be strong. [14]Do everything in love.
[15]You know that the family of Stephanas
were the first believers in Southern Greece
and that they have given themselves to the
service of God's people. I ask you, brothers
and sisters, [16]to follow the leading of people
like these and anyone else who works and
serves with them.
[17]I am happy that Stephanas, Fortuna-
tus, and Achaicus have come. You are not
here, but they have filled your place. [18]They
have refreshed my spirit and yours. You
should recognize the value of people like
these.
[19]The churches in Asia send greetings to
you. Aquila and Priscilla greet you in the
Lord, as does the church that meets in their
house. [20]All the brothers and sisters here
send greetings. Give each other a holy kiss
when you meet.
[21]I, Paul, am writing this greeting with
my own hand.
[22]If anyone does not love the Lord, let
him be separated from God—lost forever!
Come, O Lord!
[23]The grace of the Lord Jesus be with
you.
[24]My love be with all of you in Christ Jesus.[n]

16:24 My . . . Jesus. Some Greek copies add "Amen."

SEPTEMBER 9

ISAIAH 9:1—10:34

A New Day Is Coming

9 But suddenly there will be no more gloom for the land that suffered. In the past God made the lands of Zebulun and Naphtali hang their heads in shame, but in the future those lands will be made great. They will stretch from the road along the Mediterranean Sea to the land beyond the Jordan River and north to Galilee, the land of people who are not Israelites.

²Before those people lived in darkness,
but now they have seen a great light.
They lived in a dark land,
but a light has shined on them.
³God, you have caused the nation to grow
and made the people happy.
And they have shown their happiness to
you,
like the joy during harvest time,
like the joy of people
taking what they have won in war.
⁴Like the time you defeated Midian,
you have taken away their heavy load
and the heavy pole from their backs
and the rod the enemy used to punish
them.
⁵Every boot that marched in battle
and every uniform stained with blood
has been thrown into the fire.
⁶A child has been born to us;
God has given a son to us.
He will be responsible for leading the
people.
His name will be Wonderful Counselor,
Powerful God,
Father Who Lives Forever, Prince of
Peace.
⁷Power and peace will be in his kingdom
and will continue to grow forever.
He will rule as king on David's throne
and over David's kingdom.
He will make it strong
by ruling with justice and goodness
from now on and forever.
The LORD All-Powerful will do this
because of his strong love for his
people.

God Will Punish Israel

⁸The Lord sent a message against the
people of Jacob;
it says that God will judge Israel.
⁹Then everyone in Israel, even the leaders
in Samaria,
will know that God has sent it.
Those people are proud and brag by
saying,
¹⁰"These bricks have fallen,
but we will build again with cut stones.
These small trees have been chopped
down,
but we will put great cedars there."
¹¹But the LORD has brought the enemies of
Rezin against them;
he has stirred up their enemies against
them.
¹²The Arameans came from the east
and the Philistines from the west,
and they ate up Israel with their armies.
But the LORD was still angry;
his hand was still raised to punish the
people.
¹³But the people did not return to the one
who had struck them;
they did not follow the LORD
All-Powerful.
¹⁴So the LORD cut off Israel's head and
tail,
taking away both the branch and stalk
in one day.
¹⁵The elders and important men were the
head,
and the prophets who speak lies were
the tail.
¹⁶Those who led the people led them in the
wrong direction,
and those who followed them were
destroyed.
¹⁷So the Lord is not happy with the young
people,
nor will he show mercy to the orphans
and widows.
All the people are separated from God
and are very evil;
they all speak lies.

But the LORD is still angry;
his hand is still raised to strike down
the people.

¹⁸Evil is like a small fire.
First, it burns weeds and thorns.
Next, it burns the larger bushes in the
forest,
and they all go up in a column of smoke.
¹⁹The LORD All-Powerful is angry,
so the land will be burned.
The people are like fuel for the fire;
no one will try to save his brother or
sister.
²⁰People will grab something on the right,
but they will still be hungry.
They will eat something on the left,
but they will not be filled.
Then they will each turn and eat their
own children.
²¹The people of Manasseh will fight
against the people of Ephraim,
and Ephraim will fight against
Manasseh.
Then both of them will turn against
Judah.

But the LORD is still angry;
his hand is still raised to strike down
the people.

10 How terrible it will be for those who
make unfair laws,
and those who write laws that make life
hard for people.
²They are not fair to the poor,
and they rob my people of their rights.
They allow people to steal from widows
and to take from orphans what really
belongs to them.
³How will you explain the things you have
done?
What will you do when your
destruction comes from far away?
Where will you run for help?
Where will you hide your riches then?
⁴You will have to bow down among the
captives
or fall down among the dead bodies.
But the LORD is still angry;
his hand is still raised to strike down
the people.

God Will Punish Assyria

⁵God says, "How terrible it will be for
the king of Assyria.
I use him like a rod to show my anger;
in anger I use Assyria like a club.
⁶I send it to fight against a nation that is
separated from God.
I am angry with those people,
so I command Assyria to fight against
them,
to take their wealth from them,
to trample them down like dirt in the
streets.
⁷But Assyria's king doesn't understand
that I am using him;
he doesn't know he is a tool for me.
He only wants to destroy other people
and to defeat many nations.
⁸The king of Assyria says to himself,
'All of my commanders are like kings.
⁹The city Calno is like the city
Carchemish.
The city Hamath is like the city Arpad.
The city Samaria is like the city
Damascus.
¹⁰I defeated those kingdoms that worship
idols,
and those idols were more than the
idols of Jerusalem and Samaria.
¹¹As I defeated Samaria and her idols,
I will also defeat Jerusalem and her
idols.'"

¹²When the Lord finishes doing what he
planned to Mount Zion and Jerusalem, he
will punish Assyria. The king of Assyria is
very proud, and his pride has made him do
these evil things, so God will punish him.
¹³The king of Assyria says this:
"By my own power I have done these
things;
by my wisdom I have defeated many
nations.
I have taken their wealth,
and, like a mighty one, I have taken
their people.
¹⁴I have taken the riches of all these people,
like a person reaching into a bird's nest.
I have taken these nations,
like a person taking eggs.
Not one raised a hand
or opened its mouth to stop me."

15An ax is not better than the person who
  swings it.
A saw is not better than the one who
  uses it.
A stick cannot control the person who
  picks it up.
A club cannot pick up the person!
16So the Lord GOD All-Powerful
  will send a terrible disease upon
    Assyria's soldiers.
The strength of Assyria will be burned
  up
  like a fire burning until everything is
    gone.
17God, the Light of Israel, will be like a fire;
  the Holy One will be like a flame.
He will be like a fire
  that suddenly burns the weeds and
    thorns.
18The fire burns away the great trees and
    rich farmlands,
  destroying everything.
  It will be like a sick person who wastes
    away.
19The trees left standing will be so few
  that even a child could count them.

20At that time some people will be left alive
    in Israel
  from the family of Jacob.
They will not continue to depend
  on the person who defeated them.
They will learn truly to depend on the
    LORD,
  the Holy One of Israel.
21Those who are left alive in Jacob's family
  will again follow the powerful God.
22Israel, your people are many,
  like the grains of sand by the sea.
But only a few of them will be left alive
  to return to the LORD.
God has announced that he will destroy
    the land
  completely and fairly.
23The Lord GOD All-Powerful will certainly
    destroy this land,
  as he has announced.
  24This is what the Lord GOD All-Powerful
says:
  "My people living in Jerusalem,
    don't be afraid of the Assyrians,

who beat you with a rod
  and raise a stick against you, as Egypt
    did.
25After a short time my anger against you
    will stop,
  and then I will turn my anger to
    destroying them."

26Then the LORD All-Powerful will beat the
    Assyrians with a whip
  as he defeated Midian at the rock of
    Oreb.
He will raise his stick over the waters
  as he did in Egypt.
27Then the troubles that Assyria puts on
    you
  will be removed,
and the load they make you carry
  will be taken away.

Assyria Invades Israel

28The army of Assyria will enter near
    Aiath.
  Its soldiers will walk through Migron.
  They will store their food in Micmash.
29The army will go over the pass.
  The soldiers will sleep at Geba.
  The people of Ramah will be afraid,
    and the people at Gibeah of Saul will
      run away.
30Cry out, Bath Gallim!
  Laishah, listen!
  Poor Anathoth!
31The people of Madmenah are running
    away;
  the people of Gebim are hiding.
32This day the army will stop at Nob.
  They will shake their fist at Mount
    Zion,
  at the hill of Jerusalem.

33Watch! The Lord GOD All-Powerful
  with his great power will chop them
    down like a great tree.
Those who are great will be cut down;
  those who are important will fall to the
    ground.
34He will cut them down
  as a forest is cut down with an ax.
And the great trees of Lebanon
  will fall by the power of the Mighty
    One.

PSALM 106:1–5

Israel's Failure to Trust God

106 Praise the LORD!

Thank the LORD because he is good.
His love continues forever.
[2]No one can tell all the mighty things the
LORD has done;
no one can speak all his praise.
[3]Happy are those who do right,
who do what is fair at all times.

[4]LORD, remember me when you are kind
to your people;
help me when you save them.
[5]Let me see the good things you do for
your chosen people.
Let me be happy along with your happy
nation;
let me join your own people in praising
you.

PROVERBS 25:1–2

More Wise Sayings of Solomon

25 These are more wise sayings of Solomon, copied by the men of Hezekiah
king of Judah.
[2]God is honored for what he keeps secret.
Kings are honored for what they can
discover.

2 CORINTHIANS 1:1—2:4

1 From Paul, an apostle of Christ Jesus. I am
an apostle because that is what God
wanted. Also from Timothy our brother in
Christ.
To the church of God in Corinth, and to all
of God's people everywhere in Southern
Greece:
[2]Grace and peace to you from God our Father and the Lord Jesus Christ.

Paul Gives Thanks to God

[3]Praise be to the God and Father of our
Lord Jesus Christ. God is the Father who is
full of mercy and all comfort. [4]He comforts
us every time we have trouble, so when others have trouble, we can comfort them with
the same comfort God gives us. [5]We share in
the many sufferings of Christ. In the same
way, much comfort comes to us through
Christ. [6]If we have troubles, it is for your
comfort and salvation, and if we have comfort, you also have comfort. This helps you to
accept patiently the same sufferings we have.
[7]Our hope for you is strong, knowing that
you share in our sufferings and also in the
comfort we receive.

[8]Brothers and sisters, we want you to
know about the trouble we suffered in Asia.
We had great burdens there that were beyond our own strength. We even gave up
hope of living. [9]Truly, in our own hearts we
believed we would die. But this happened so
we would not trust in ourselves but in God,
who raises people from the dead. [10]God
saved us from these great dangers of death,
and he will continue to save us. We have put
our hope in him, and he will save us again.
[11]And you can help us with your prayers.
Then many people will give thanks for us—
that God blessed us because of their many
prayers.

The Change in Paul's Plans

[12]This is what we are proud of, and I can
say it with a clear conscience: In everything
we have done in the world, and especially
with you, we have had an honest[n] and sincere heart from God. We did this by God's
grace, not by the kind of wisdom the world
has. [13-14]We write to you only what you can
read and understand. And I hope that as you
have understood some things about us, you
may come to know everything about us.
Then you can be proud of us, as we will be
proud of you on the day our Lord Jesus
Christ comes again.

[15]I was so sure of all this that I made plans
to visit you first so you could be blessed
twice. [16]I planned to visit you on my way to
Macedonia and again on my way back. I
wanted to get help from you for my trip to
Judea. [17]Do you think that I made these plans
without really meaning it? Or maybe you
think I make plans as the world does, so that
I say yes, yes and at the same time no, no.

1:12 honest Some Greek copies read "holy."

[18]But since you can believe God, you can believe that what we tell you is never both yes and no. [19]The Son of God, Jesus Christ, that Silas and Timothy and I preached to you, was not yes and no. In Christ it has always been yes. [20]The yes to all of God's promises is in Christ, and through Christ we say yes to the glory of God. [21]Remember, God is the One who makes you and us strong in Christ. God made us his chosen people. [22]He put his mark on us to show that we are his, and he put his Spirit in our hearts to be a guarantee for all he has promised.

[23]I tell you this, and I ask God to be my witness that this is true: The reason I did not come back to Corinth was to keep you from being punished or hurt. [24]We are not trying to control your faith. You are strong in faith. But we are workers with you for your own joy.

2 So I decided that my next visit to you would not be another one to make you sad. [2]If I make you sad, who will make me glad? Only you can make me glad—particularly the person whom I made sad. [3]I wrote you a letter for this reason: that when I came to you I would not be made sad by the people who should make me happy. I felt sure of all of you, that you would share my joy. [4]When I wrote to you before, I was very troubled and unhappy in my heart, and I wrote with many tears. I did not write to make you sad, but to let you know how much I love you.

SEPTEMBER 10

ISAIAH 11:1—12:6

The King of Peace Is Coming

11 A new branch will grow
   from a stump of a tree;
so a new king will come
   from the family of Jesse.[n]
[2]The Spirit of the LORD will rest upon that
      king.
   The Spirit will give him wisdom and
      understanding, guidance and power.
   The Spirit will teach him to know and
      respect the LORD.
[3]This king will be glad to obey the LORD.
   He will not judge by the way things look
   or decide by what he hears.
[4]But he will judge the poor honestly;
   he will be fair in his decisions for the
      poor people of the land.
   At his command evil people will be
      punished,
   and by his words the wicked will be put
      to death.
[5]Goodness and fairness will give him
      strength,
   like a belt around his waist.

[6]Then wolves will live in peace with
      lambs,
   and leopards will lie down to rest with
      goats.
   Calves, lions, and young bulls will eat
      together,
   and a little child will lead them.
[7]Cows and bears will eat together in
      peace.
   Their young will lie down to rest
      together.
   Lions will eat hay as oxen do.
[8]A baby will be able to play near a cobra's
      hole,
   and a child will be able to put his hand
      into the nest of a poisonous snake.
[9]They will not hurt or destroy each other
   on all my holy mountain,
   because the earth will be full of the
      knowledge of the LORD,
   as the sea is full of water.
[10]At that time the new king from the family of Jesse will stand as a banner for all peoples. The nations will come together around him, and the place where he lives will be filled with glory. [11]At that time the Lord will

---

11:1 Jesse King David's father.

again reach out and take his people who are
left alive in Assyria, North Egypt, South
Egypt, Cush, Elam, Babylonia, Hamath, and
all the islands of the sea.

¹²God will raise a banner as a sign for all
    nations,
  and he will gather the people of Israel
      who were forced from their country.
  He will gather the scattered people of
      Judah
    from all parts of the earth.
¹³At that time Israel will not be jealous
    anymore,
  and Judah will have no more enemies.
  Israel will not be jealous of Judah,
    and Judah will not hate Israel.
¹⁴But Israel and Judah will attack the
    Philistines on the west.
  Together they will take the riches from
      the people of the east.
  They will conquer Edom and Moab,
    and the people of Ammon will be
        under their control.
¹⁵The LORD will dry up
    the Red Sea of Egypt.
  He will wave his arm over the Euphrates
      River
    and dry it up with a scorching wind.
  He will divide it into seven small rivers
    so that people can walk across them
        with their sandals on.
¹⁶So God's people who are left alive
    will have a way to leave Assyria,
  just like the time the Israelites
    came out of Egypt.

A Song of Praise to God

12 At that time you will say:
  "I praise you, LORD!
  You were angry with me,
    but you are not angry with me now!
    You have comforted me.
²God is the one who saves me;
  I will trust him and not be afraid.
  The LORD, the LORD gives me strength
      and makes me sing.
  He has saved me."
³You will receive your salvation with joy
    as you would draw water from a well.
⁴At that time you will say,
  "Praise the LORD and worship him.

  Tell everyone what he has done
    and how great he is.
⁵Sing praise to the LORD, because he has
    done great things.
  Let all the world know what he has
      done.
⁶Shout and sing for joy, you people of
    Jerusalem,
  because the Holy One of Israel does
      great things before your eyes."

PSALM 106:6–18

⁶We have sinned just as our ancestors did.
  We have done wrong; we have done evil.
⁷Our ancestors in Egypt
    did not learn from your miracles.
  They did not remember all your
      kindnesses,
    so they turned against you at the Red
        Sea.
⁸But the LORD saved them for his own
    sake,
  to show his great power.
⁹He commanded the Red Sea, and it dried
    up.
  He led them through the deep sea as if
      it were a desert.
¹⁰He saved them from those who hated
    them.
  He saved them from their enemies,
¹¹and the water covered their foes.
  Not one of them escaped.
¹²Then the people believed what the LORD
    said,
  and they sang praises to him.

¹³But they quickly forgot what he had
    done;
  they did not wait for his advice.
¹⁴They became greedy for food in the
    desert,
  and they tested God there.
¹⁵So he gave them what they wanted,
  but he also sent a terrible disease
      among them.

¹⁶The people in the camp were jealous of
    Moses
  and of Aaron, the holy priest of the LORD.
¹⁷Then the ground opened up and
    swallowed Dathan

and closed over Abiram's group.
[18]A fire burned among their followers,
and flames burned up the wicked.

PROVERBS 25:3–5

[3]No one can measure the height of the
skies or the depth of the earth.
So also no one can understand the
mind of a king.

[4]Remove the scum from the silver,
so the silver can be used by the
silversmith.
[5]Remove wicked people from the king's
presence;
then his government will be honest and
last a long time.

2 CORINTHIANS 2:5–17

Forgive the Sinner

[5]Someone there among you has caused
sadness, not to me, but to all of you. I mean
he caused sadness to all in some way. (I do
not want to make it sound worse than it really is.) [6]The punishment that most of you
gave him is enough for him. [7]But now you
should forgive him and comfort him to keep
him from having too much sadness and giving up completely. [8]So I beg you to show that
you love him. [9]I wrote you to test you and to
see if you obey in everything. [10]If you forgive
someone, I also forgive him. And what I have
forgiven—if I had anything to forgive—I
forgave it for you, as if Christ were with me.
[11]I did this so that Satan would not win anything from us, because we know very well
what Satan's plans are.

Paul's Concern in Troas

[12]When I came to Troas to preach the
Good News of Christ, the Lord gave me a
good opportunity there. [13]But I had no
peace, because I did not find my brother Titus. So I said good-bye to them at Troas and
went to Macedonia.

Victory Through Christ

[14]But thanks be to God, who always leads
us as captives in Christ's victory parade. God
uses us to spread his knowledge everywhere
like a sweet-smelling perfume. [15]Our offering to God is this: We are the sweet smell of
Christ among those who are being saved and
among those who are being lost. [16]To those
who are lost, we are the smell of death that
brings death, but to those who are being
saved, we are the smell of life that brings life.
So who is able to do this work? [17]We do not
sell the word of God for a profit as many
other people do. But in Christ we speak the
truth before God, as messengers of God.

SEPTEMBER 11

ISAIAH 13:1—14:32

God's Message to Babylon

13 God showed Isaiah son of Amoz this
message about Babylon:
[2]Raise a flag on the bare mountain.
Call out to the men.
Raise your hand to signal them
to enter through the gates for
important people.
[3]I myself have commanded those people
whom I have separated as mine.
I have called those warriors to carry out
my anger.
They rejoice and are glad to do my
will.

[4]Listen to the loud noise in the
mountains,
the sound of many people.
Listen to the noise among the kingdoms,
the sound of nations gathering
together.
The LORD All-Powerful is calling
his army together for battle.
[5]This army is coming from a faraway
land,
from the edge of the horizon.

In anger the LORD is using this army like
a weapon
to destroy the whole country.

⁶Cry, because the LORD's day of judging is
near;
the Almighty is sending destruction.
⁷People will be weak with fear,
and their courage will melt away.
⁸Everyone will be afraid.
Pain and hurt will grab them;
they will hurt like a woman giving birth
to a baby.
They will look at each other in fear,
with their faces red like fire.

God's Judgment Against Babylon
⁹Look, the LORD's day of judging is
coming—
a terrible day, a day of God's anger.
He will destroy the land
and the sinners who live in it.
¹⁰The stars will not show their light;
the skies will be dark.
The sun will grow dark as it rises,
and the moon will not give its light.
¹¹The LORD says, "I will punish the world
for its evil
and wicked people for their sins.
I will cause proud people to lose their
pride,
and I will destroy the pride of those
who are cruel to others.
¹²People will be harder to find than pure
gold;
there will be fewer people than there is
fine gold in Ophir.
¹³I will make the sky shake,
and the earth will be moved from its
place
by the anger of the LORD All-Powerful
at the time of his burning anger.
¹⁴"Then the people from Babylon will run
away like hunted deer
or like sheep who have no shepherd.
Everyone will turn back to his own
people;
each will run back to his own land.
¹⁵Everyone who is captured will be killed;
everyone who is caught will be killed
with a sword.

¹⁶Their little children will be beaten to
death in front of them.
Their houses will be robbed
and their wives raped.
¹⁷"Look, I will cause the armies of Media
to attack Babylon.
They do not care about silver
or delight in gold.
¹⁸Their soldiers will shoot the young men
with arrows;
they will show no mercy on children,
nor will they feel sorry for little ones.
¹⁹Babylon is the most beautiful of all
kingdoms,
and the Babylonians are very proud of
it.
But God will destroy it
like Sodom and Gomorrah.
²⁰No one will ever live there
or settle there again.
No Arab will put a tent there;
no shepherd will bring sheep there.
²¹Only desert animals will live there,
and their houses will be full of wild
dogs.
Owls will live there,
and wild goats will leap about in the
houses.
²²Wolves will howl within the strong walls,
and wild dogs will bark in the beautiful
buildings.
The end of Babylon is near;
its time is almost over."

Israel Will Return Home
14The LORD will show mercy to the people of Jacob, and he will again choose
the people of Israel. He will settle them in
their own land. Then non-Israelite people
will join the Israelites and will become a part
of the family of Jacob. ²Nations will take the
Israelites back to their land. Then those men
and women from the other nations will become slaves to Israel in the LORD's land. In
the past the Israelites were their slaves, but
now the Israelites will defeat those nations
and rule over them.

The King of Babylon Will Fall
³The LORD will take away the Israelites'
hard work and will comfort them. They will

no longer have to work hard as slaves. ⁴On that day Israel will sing this song about the king of Babylon:

> The cruel king who ruled us is finished;
>   his angry rule is finished!

⁵The LORD has broken the scepter of evil rulers
    and taken away their power.
⁶The king of Babylon struck people in anger
    again and again.
He ruled nations in anger
    and continued to hurt them.
⁷But now, the whole world rests and is quiet.
    Now the people begin to sing.
⁸Even the pine trees are happy,
    and the cedar trees of Lebanon rejoice.
They say, "The king has fallen,
    so no one will ever cut us down again."

⁹The place of the dead is excited
    to meet you when you come.
It wakes the spirits of the dead,
    the leaders of the world.
It makes kings of all nations
    stand up from their thrones to greet you.
¹⁰All these leaders will make fun of you
    and will say,
"Now you are weak, as we are.
    Now you are just like us."
¹¹Your pride has been sent down to the place of the dead.
    The music from your harps goes with it.
Flies are spread out like your bed beneath you,
    and worms cover your body like a blanket.
¹²King of Babylon, morning star, you have fallen from heaven,
    even though you were as bright as the rising sun!
In the past all the nations on earth bowed down before you,
    but now you have been cut down.
¹³You told yourself,
    "I will go up to heaven.
I will put my throne
    above God's stars.

I will sit on the mountain of the gods,
    on the slopes of the sacred mountain.
¹⁴I will go up above the tops of the clouds.
    I will be like God Most High."
¹⁵But you were brought down to the grave,
    to the deep places where the dead are.

¹⁶Those who see you stare at you.
    They think about what has happened to you
and say, "Is this the same man who caused great fear on earth,
    who shook the kingdoms,
¹⁷who turned the world into a desert,
    who destroyed its cities,
who captured people in war
    and would not let them go home?"

¹⁸Every king of the earth has been buried with honor,
    each in his own grave.
¹⁹But you are thrown out of your grave,
    like an unwanted branch.
You are covered by bodies
    that died in battle,
by bodies to be buried in a rocky pit.
    You are like a dead body other soldiers walk on.
²⁰ You will not be buried with those bodies,
because you ruined your own country
    and killed your own people.
The children of evil people
    will never be mentioned again.

²¹Prepare to kill his children,
    because their father is guilty.
They will never again take control of the earth;
    they will never again fill the world with their cities.

²²The LORD All-Powerful says this:
    "I will fight against those people;
I will destroy Babylon and its people,
    its children and their descendants," says the LORD.
²³"I will make Babylon fit only for owls
    and for swamps.
I will sweep Babylon as with a broom of destruction,"
    says the LORD All-Powerful.

God Will Punish Assyria

24The LORD All-Powerful has made this promise:

"These things will happen exactly as I planned them;
they will happen exactly as I set them up.
25I will destroy the king of Assyria in my country;
I will trample him on my mountains.
He placed a heavy load on my people,
but that weight will be removed.

26"This is what I plan to do for all the earth.
And this is the hand that I have raised over all nations."

27When the LORD All-Powerful makes a plan,
no one can stop it.
When the LORD raises his hand to punish people,
no one can stop it.

God's Message to Philistia

28This message was given in the year that King Ahaz died:

29Country of Philistia, don't be happy
that the king who struck you is now dead.
He is like a snake that will give birth to another dangerous snake.
The new king will be like a quick, dangerous snake to bite you.
30Even the poorest of my people will be able to eat safely,
and people in need will be able to lie down in safety.
But I will kill your family with hunger,
and all your people who are left will die.

31People near the city gates, cry out!
Philistines, be frightened,
because a cloud of dust comes from the north.
It is an army, full of men ready to fight.
32What shall we tell the messengers from Philistia?

Say that the LORD has made Jerusalem strong
and that his poor people will go there for safety.

PSALM 106:19-23

19The people made a gold calf at Mount Sinai
and worshiped a metal statue.
20They exchanged their glorious God
for a statue of a bull that eats grass.
21They forgot the God who saved them,
who had done great things in Egypt,
22who had done miracles in Egypt[n]
and amazing things by the Red Sea.
23So God said he would destroy them.
But Moses, his chosen one, stood before him
and stopped God's anger from destroying them.

PROVERBS 25:6-8

6Don't brag to the king
and act as if you are great.
7It is better for him to give you a higher position
than to bring you down in front of the prince.

Because of something you have seen,
8 do not quickly take someone to court.
What will you do later
when your neighbor proves you wrong?

2 CORINTHIANS 3:1-18

Servants of the New Agreement

3 Are we starting to brag about ourselves again? Do we need letters of introduction to you or from you, like some other people? 2You yourselves are our letter, written on our hearts, known and read by everyone. 3You show that you are a letter from Christ sent through us. This letter is not written with ink but with the Spirit of the living God. It is not written on stone tablets[n] but on human hearts.

4We can say this, because through Christ

106:22 Egypt Literally, "the land of Ham." The people in Egypt were descendants of Ham, one of Noah's sons. See Genesis 10:6. • **3:3 stone tablets** Meaning the Law of Moses that was written on stone tablets (Exodus 24:12; 25:16).

we feel certain before God. [5]We are not saying that we can do this work ourselves. It is God who makes us able to do all that we do. [6]He made us able to be servants of a new agreement from himself to his people. This new agreement is not a written law, but it is of the Spirit. The written law brings death, but the Spirit gives life.

[7]The law that brought death was written in words on stone. It came with God's glory, which made Moses' face so bright that the Israelites could not continue to look at it. But that glory later disappeared. [8]So surely the new way that brings the Spirit has even more glory. [9]If the law that judged people guilty of sin had glory, surely the new way that makes people right with God has much greater glory. [10]That old law had glory, but it really loses its glory when it is compared to the much greater glory of this new way. [11]If that law which disappeared came with glory, then this new way which continues forever has much greater glory.

[12]We have this hope, so we are very bold. [13]We are not like Moses, who put a covering over his face so the Israelites would not see it. The glory was disappearing, and Moses did not want them to see it end. [14]But their minds were closed, and even today that same covering hides the meaning when they read the old agreement. That covering is taken away only through Christ. [15]Even today, when they read the law of Moses, there is a covering over their minds. [16]But when a person changes and follows the Lord, that covering is taken away. [17]The Lord is the Spirit, and where the Spirit of the Lord is, there is freedom. [18]Our faces, then, are not covered. We all show the Lord's glory, and we are being changed to be like him. This change in us brings ever greater glory, which comes from the Lord, who is the Spirit.

SEPTEMBER 12

ISAIAH 15:1—16:14

God's Message to Moab

15This is a message about Moab:
In one night armies took the wealth
    from Ar in Moab,
  and it was destroyed.
In one night armies took the wealth from
    Kir in Moab,
  and it was destroyed.
[2]The people of Dibon go to the places of
    worship to cry.
  The people of Moab cry for the cities of
    Nebo and Medeba.
  Every head and beard has been shaved
    to show how sad Moab is.
[3]In the streets they wear rough cloth to
    show their sadness.
  On the roofs[n] and in the public
    squares,
  they are crying loudly.

[4]People in the cities Heshbon and Elealeh
    cry out loud.
  You can hear their voices far away in
    the city Jahaz.
  Even the soldiers are frightened;
    they are shaking with fear.

[5]My heart cries with sorrow for Moab.
  Its people run away to Zoar for
    safety;
  they run to Eglath Shelishiyah.
  People are going up the mountain road
    to Luhith,
    crying as they go.
  People are going on the road to
    Horonaim,
    crying over their destruction.
[6]But the water of Nimrim has dried up.
  The grass has dried up,
  and all the plants are dead;
    nothing green is left.

15:3 roofs In Bible times houses were built with flat roofs. The roof was used for drying things such as flax and fruit. And it was used as an extra room, as a place for worship, and as a cool place to sleep in the summer.

⁷So the people gather up what they have
  saved
  and carry it across the Ravine of the
  Poplars.
⁸Crying is heard everywhere in Moab.
  Their crying is heard as far away as the
  city Eglaim;
  it is heard as far away as Beer Elim.
⁹The water of the city Dibon is full of blood,
  and I, the LORD, will bring even more
  troubles to Dibon.
A few people living in Moab have
  escaped the enemy,
  but I will send lions to kill them.

16 Send the king of the land
  the payment he demands.
Send a lamb from Sela through the desert
  to the mountain of Jerusalem.
²The women of Moab
  try to cross the river Arnon
like little birds
  that have fallen from their nest.

³They say: "Help us.
  Tell us what to do.
Protect us from our enemies
  as shade protects us from the noon
  sun.
Hide us, because we are running for
  safety!
Don't give us to our enemies.
⁴Let those of us who were forced out of
  Moab live in your land.
Hide us from our enemies."

The robbing of Moab will stop.
  The enemy will be defeated;
  those who hurt others will disappear
  from the land.
⁵Then a new loyal king will come;
  this faithful king will be from the
  family of David.
He will judge fairly
  and do what is right.

⁶We have heard that the people of Moab
  are proud
  and very conceited.
They are very proud and angry,
  but their bragging means nothing.
⁷So the people of Moab will cry;
  they will all be sad.

They will moan and groan
  for the raisin cakes they had in Kir
  Hareseth.
⁸But the fields of Heshbon and the vines
  of Sibmah cannot grow grapes;
  foreign rulers have destroyed the
  grapevines.
The grapevines once spread as far as the
  city of Jazer and into the desert;
  they had spread as far as the sea.
⁹I cry with the people of Jazer
  for the grapevines of Sibmah.
I will cry with the people of Heshbon
  and Elealeh.
There will be no shouts of joy,
  because there will be no harvest or ripe
  fruit.
¹⁰There will be no joy and happiness in the
  orchards
  and no songs or shouts of joy in the
  vineyards.
No one makes wine in the winepresses,
  because I have put an end to shouts of
  joy.
¹¹My heart cries for Moab like a harp
  playing a funeral song;
  I am very sad for Kir Hareseth.
¹²The people of Moab will go to their
  places of worship
  and will try to pray.
But when they go to their temple to pray,
  they will not be able.
¹³Earlier the LORD said these things about
Moab. ¹⁴Now the LORD says, "In three years
all those people and what they take pride in
will be hated. (This is three years as a hired
helper would count time.) There will be a
few people left, but they will be weak."

PSALM 106:24–31

²⁴Then they refused to go into the
  beautiful land of Canaan;
  they did not believe what God promised.
²⁵They grumbled in their tents
  and did not obey the LORD.
²⁶So he swore to them
  that they would die in the desert.
²⁷He said their children would be killed by
  other nations
  and that they would be scattered
  among other countries.

[28]They joined in worshiping Baal at Peor
and ate meat that had been sacrificed
to lifeless statues.
[29]They made the LORD angry by what they
did,
so many people became sick with a
terrible disease.
[30]But Phinehas prayed to the LORD,
and the disease stopped.
[31]Phinehas did what was right,
and it will be remembered from now on.

PROVERBS 25:9–10

[9]If you have an argument with your
neighbor,
don't tell other people what was said.
[10]Whoever hears it might shame you,
and you might not ever be respected
again.

2 CORINTHIANS 4:1–15

Preaching the Good News

4 God, with his mercy, gave us this work to do,
so we don't give up. [2]But we have turned
away from secret and shameful ways. We use
no trickery, and we do not change the teaching
of God. We teach the truth plainly, showing
everyone who we are. Then they can know in
their hearts what kind of people we are in
God's sight. [3]If the Good News that we preach
is hidden, it is hidden only to those who are
lost. [4]The devil who rules this world has
blinded the minds of those who do not believe.

They cannot see the light of the Good News—
the Good News about the glory of Christ, who
is exactly like God. [5]We do not preach about
ourselves, but we preach that Jesus Christ is
Lord and that we are your servants for Jesus.
[6]God once said, "Let the light shine out of the
darkness!" This is the same God who made his
light shine in our hearts by letting us know the
glory of God that is in the face of Christ.

Spiritual Treasure in Clay Jars

[7]We have this treasure from God, but we are
like clay jars that hold the treasure. This shows
that the great power is from God, not from us.
[8]We have troubles all around us, but we are not
defeated. We do not know what to do, but we
do not give up the hope of living. [9]We are persecuted, but God does not leave us. We are hurt
sometimes, but we are not destroyed. [10]We
carry the death of Jesus in our own bodies so
that the life of Jesus can also be seen in our
bodies. [11]We are alive, but for Jesus we are always in danger of death so that the life of Jesus
can be seen in our bodies that die. [12]So death
is working in us, but life is working in you.

[13]It is written in the Scriptures, "I believed, so I spoke."[n] Our faith is like this, too.
We believe, and so we speak. [14]God raised
the Lord Jesus from the dead, and we know
that God will also raise us with Jesus. God
will bring us together with you, and we will
stand before him. [15]All these things are for
you. And so the grace of God that is being
given to more and more people will bring increasing thanks to God for his glory.

SEPTEMBER 13

ISAIAH 17:1—18:7

God's Message to Aram

17 This is a message about Damascus:
"The city of Damascus will be
destroyed;
only ruins will remain.
[2]People will leave the cities of Aroer.
Flocks will wander freely in those
empty towns,

and there will be no one to bother them.
[3]The strong, walled cities of Israel will be
destroyed.
The government in Damascus will end.
Those left alive of Aram will be
like the glory of Israel," says the LORD
All-Powerful.

[4]"At that time Israel's wealth will all be
gone.

4:13 "I . . . spoke." Quotation from Psalm 116:10.

Israel will be like someone who has lost
much weight from sickness.
⁵That time will be like the grain harvest in
the Valley of Rephaim.
The workers cut the wheat.
Then they cut the heads of grain from
the plants
and collect the grain.
⁶That time will also be like the olive
harvest,
when a few olives are left.
Two or three olives are left in the top
branches.
Four or five olives are left on full
branches," says the LORD, the God of
Israel.

⁷At that time people will look to God,
their Maker;
their eyes will see the Holy One of
Israel.
⁸They will not trust the altars they have
made,
nor will they trust what their hands
have made,
not even the Asherah idols and altars.
⁹In that day all their strong cities will be
empty. They will be like the cities the Hivites
and the Amorites left when the Israelites came
to take the land. Everything will be ruined.
¹⁰You have forgotten the God who saves you;
you have not remembered that God is
your place of safety.
You plant the finest grapevines
and grapevines from faraway places.
¹¹You plant your grapevines one day and
try to make them grow,
and the next day you make them
blossom.
But at harvest time everything will be
dead;
a sickness will kill all the plants.

¹²Listen to the many people!
Their crying is like the noise from the
sea.
Listen to the nations!
Their crying is like the crashing of
great waves.
¹³The people roar like the waves,
but when God speaks harshly to them,
they will run away.

They will be like chaff on the hills being
blown by the wind,
or like tumbleweeds blown away by a
storm.
¹⁴At night the people will be very frightened.
Before morning, no one will be left.
So our enemies will come to our land,
but they will become nothing.

God's Message to Cush

18 How terrible it will be for the land
beyond the rivers of Cush.
It is filled with the sound of wings.
²That land sends messengers across the
sea;
they go on the water in boats made of
reeds.

Go, quick messengers,
to a people who are tall and
smooth-skinned,
who are feared everywhere.
They are a powerful nation that defeats
other nations.
Their land is divided by rivers.

³All you people of the world, look!
Everyone who lives in the world, look!
You will see a banner raised on a
mountain.
You will hear a trumpet sound.
⁴The LORD said to me,
"I will quietly watch from where I live,
like heat in the sunshine,
like the dew in the heat of harvest time."
⁵The time will come, after the flowers
have bloomed and before the
harvest,
when new grapes will be budding and
growing.
The enemy will cut the plants with knives;
he will cut down the vines and take
them away.
⁶They will be left for the birds of the
mountains
and for the wild animals.
Birds will feed on them all summer,
and wild animals will eat them that
winter."

⁷At that time a gift will be brought to the
LORD All-Powerful
from the people who are tall and
smooth-skinned,

who are feared everywhere.
They are a powerful nation that defeats
other nations.
Their land is divided by rivers.
These gifts will be brought to the place of
the LORD All-Powerful,
to Mount Zion.

PSALM 106:32–39

[32]The people also made the LORD angry at
Meribah,
and Moses was in trouble because of
them.
[33]The people turned against the Spirit of
God,
so Moses spoke without stopping to
think.

[34]The people did not destroy the other
nations
as the LORD had told them to do.
[35]Instead, they mixed with the other nations
and learned their customs.
[36]They worshiped other nations' idols
and were trapped by them.
[37]They even killed their sons and daughters
as sacrifices to demons.
[38]They killed innocent people,
their own sons and daughters,
as sacrifices to the idols of Canaan.
So the land was made unholy by their
blood.
[39]The people became unholy by their sins;
they were unfaithful to God in what
they did.

PROVERBS 25:11–12

[11]The right word spoken at the right time
is as beautiful as gold apples in a silver
bowl.

[12]A wise warning to someone who will
listen
is as valuable as gold earrings or fine
gold jewelry.

2 CORINTHIANS 4:16—5:21

Living by Faith

[16]So we do not give up. Our physical body
is becoming older and weaker, but our spirit

inside us is made new every day. [17]We have
small troubles for a while now, but they are
helping us gain an eternal glory that is much
greater than the troubles. [18]We set our eyes
not on what we see but on what we cannot
see. What we see will last only a short time,
but what we cannot see will last forever.

5 We know that our body—the tent we live
in here on earth—will be destroyed. But
when that happens, God will have a house for
us. It will not be a house made by human
hands; instead, it will be a home in heaven
that will last forever. [2]But now we groan in
this tent. We want God to give us our heavenly
home, [3]because it will clothe us so we will not
be naked. [4]While we live in this body, we have
burdens, and we groan. We do not want to be
naked, but we want to be clothed with our
heavenly home. Then this body that dies will
be fully covered with life. [5]This is what God
made us for, and he has given us the Spirit to
be a guarantee for this new life.

[6]So we always have courage. We know that
while we live in this body, we are away from
the Lord. [7]We live by what we believe, not by
what we can see. [8]So I say that we have
courage. We really want to be away from this
body and be at home with the Lord. [9]Our
only goal is to please God whether we live
here or there, [10]because we must all stand
before Christ to be judged. Each of us will receive what we should get—good or bad—
for the things we did in the earthly body.

Becoming Friends with God

[11]Since we know what it means to fear the
Lord, we try to help people accept the truth
about us. God knows what we really are, and
I hope that in your hearts you know, too.
[12]We are not trying to prove ourselves to you
again, but we are telling you about ourselves
so you will be proud of us. Then you will
have an answer for those who are proud
about things that can be seen rather than
what is in the heart. [13]If we are out of our
minds, it is for God. If we have our right
minds, it is for you. [14]The love of Christ controls us, because we know that One died for
all, so all have died. [15]Christ died for all so
that those who live would not continue to
live for themselves. He died for them and

was raised from the dead so that they would live for him.

¹⁶From this time on we do not think of anyone as the world does. In the past we thought of Christ as the world thinks, but we no longer think of him in that way. ¹⁷If anyone belongs to Christ, there is a new creation. The old things have gone; everything is made new! ¹⁸All this is from God. Through Christ, God made peace between us and himself, and God gave us the work of telling everyone about the peace we can have with him. ¹⁹God was in Christ, making peace between the world and himself. In Christ, God did not hold the world guilty of its sins. And he gave us this message of peace. ²⁰So we have been sent to speak for Christ. It is as if God is calling to you through us. We speak for Christ when we beg you to be at peace with God. ²¹Christ had no sin, but God made him become sin so that in Christ we could become right with God.

SEPTEMBER 14

ISAIAH 19:1—20:6

God's Message to Egypt

19This is a message about Egypt:
Look, the LORD is coming on a fast cloud
   to enter Egypt.
The idols of Egypt will tremble before him,
   and Egypt's courage will melt away.

²The LORD says, "I will cause the Egyptians to fight against themselves.
   People will fight with their relatives;
   neighbors will fight neighbors;
   cities will fight cities;
   kingdoms will fight kingdoms.
³The Egyptians will be afraid,
   and I will ruin their plans.
They will ask advice from their idols and spirits of the dead,
   from their mediums and fortune-tellers."
⁴The Lord GOD All-Powerful says,
   "I will hand Egypt over to a hard master,
   and a powerful king will rule over them."

⁵The sea will become dry,
   and the water will disappear from the Nile River.
⁶The canals will stink;
   the streams of Egypt will decrease and dry up.
All the water plants will rot;

⁷ all the plants along the banks of the Nile will die.
Even the planted fields by the Nile
   will dry up, blow away, and disappear.
⁸The fishermen, all those who catch fish from the Nile,
   will groan and cry;
   those who fish in the Nile will be sad.
⁹All the people who make cloth from flax will be sad,
   and those who weave linen will lose hope.
¹⁰Those who weave cloth will be broken.
   All those who work for money will be sad.

¹¹The officers of the city of Zoan are fools;
   the wise men who advise the king of Egypt give wrong advice.
How can you say to him, 'I am wise'?
   How can you say, 'I am from the old family of the kings'?
¹²Egypt, where are your wise men?
   Let them show you
   what the LORD All-Powerful has planned for Egypt.
¹³The officers of Zoan have been fooled;
   the leaders of Memphis have believed false things.
So the leaders of Egypt
   lead that nation the wrong way.
¹⁴The LORD has made the leaders confused.
   They have led Egypt to wander in the wrong ways,

like drunk people stumbling in their own vomit.

¹⁵There is nothing Egypt can do;
no one there can help.

¹⁶In that day the Egyptians will be like women. They will be afraid of the LORD All-Powerful, because he will raise his hand to strike them down. ¹⁷The land of Judah will bring fear to Egypt. Anyone there who hears the name Judah will be afraid, because the LORD All-Powerful has planned terrible things for them. ¹⁸At that time five cities in Egypt will speak Hebrew, the language of Canaan, and they will promise to be loyal to the LORD All-Powerful. One of these cities will be named the City of Destruction. ¹⁹At that time there will be an altar for the LORD in the middle of Egypt and a monument to the LORD at the border of Egypt. ²⁰This will be a sign and a witness to the LORD All-Powerful in the land of Egypt. When the people cry to the LORD for help, he will send someone to save and defend them. He will rescue them from those who hurt them.

²¹So the LORD will show himself to the Egyptians, and then they will know he is the LORD. They will worship God and offer many sacrifices. They will make promises to the LORD and will keep them. ²²The LORD will punish the Egyptians, but then he will heal them. They will come back to the LORD, and he will listen to their prayers and heal them.

²³At that time there will be a highway from Egypt to Assyria, and the Assyrians will go to Egypt, and the Egyptians will go to Assyria. The Egyptians and Assyrians will worship God together. ²⁴At that time Israel, Assyria, and Egypt will join together, which will be a blessing for the earth. ²⁵The LORD All-Powerful will bless them, saying, "Egypt, you are my people. Assyria, I made you. Israel, I own you. You are all blessed!"

Assyria Will Defeat Egypt and Cush

20 Sargon king of Assyria sent a military commander to Ashdod to attack that city. So the commander attacked and captured it. ²Then the LORD spoke through Isaiah son of Amoz, saying, "Take the rough cloth off your body, and take your sandals off your feet." So Isaiah obeyed and walked around naked and barefoot.

³Then the LORD said, "Isaiah my servant has walked around naked and barefoot for three years as a sign against Egypt and Cush. ⁴The king of Assyria will carry away prisoners from Egypt and Cush. Old people and young people will be led away naked and barefoot, with their buttocks bare. So the Egyptians will be shamed. ⁵People who looked to Cush for help will be afraid, and those who were amazed by Egypt's glory will be shamed. ⁶People who live near the sea will say, 'Look at those countries. We trusted them to help us. We ran to them so they would save us from the king of Assyria. So how will we be able to escape?'"

PSALM 106:40–48

⁴⁰So the LORD became angry with his people
and hated his own children.
⁴¹He handed them over to other nations
and let their enemies rule over them.
⁴²Their enemies were cruel to them
and kept them under their power.
⁴³The LORD saved his people many times,
but they continued to turn against him.
So they became even more wicked.

⁴⁴But God saw their misery
when he heard their cry.
⁴⁵He remembered his agreement with them,
and he felt sorry for them because of
his great love.
⁴⁶He caused them to be pitied
by those who held them captive.

⁴⁷LORD our God, save us
and bring us back from other nations.
Then we will thank you
and will gladly praise you.

⁴⁸Praise the LORD, the God of Israel.
He always was and always will be.
Let all the people say, "Amen!"

Praise the LORD!

PROVERBS 25:13

¹³Trustworthy messengers refresh those
who send them,
like the coolness of snow in the
summertime.

2 CORINTHIANS 6:1—7:1

6 We are workers together with God, so we beg you: Do not let the grace that you received from God be for nothing. [2]God says,

"At the right time I heard your prayers.
On the day of salvation I helped you."

Isaiah 49:8

I tell you that the "right time" is now, and the "day of salvation" is now.

[3]We do not want anyone to find fault with our work, so nothing we do will be a problem for anyone. [4]But in every way we show we are servants of God: in accepting many hard things, in troubles, in difficulties, and in great problems. [5]We are beaten and thrown into prison. We meet those who become upset with us and start riots. We work hard, and sometimes we get no sleep or food. [6]We show we are servants of God by our pure lives, our understanding, patience, and kindness, by the Holy Spirit, by true love, [7]by speaking the truth, and by God's power. We use our right living to defend ourselves against everything. [8]Some people honor us, but others blame us. Some people say evil things about us, but others say good things. Some people say we are liars, but we speak the truth. [9]We are not known, but we are well known. We seem to be dying, but we continue to live. We are punished, but we are not killed. [10]We have much sadness, but we are always rejoicing. We are poor, but we are making many people rich in faith. We have nothing, but really we have everything.

[11]We have spoken freely to you in Corinth and have opened our hearts to you. [12]Our feelings of love for you have not stopped, but you have stopped your feelings of love for us. [13]I speak to you as if you were my children. Do to us as we have done—open your hearts to us.

Warning About Non-Christians

[14]You are not the same as those who do not believe. So do not join yourselves to them. Good and bad do not belong together. Light and darkness cannot share together. [15]How can Christ and Belial, the devil, have any agreement? What can a believer have together with a nonbeliever? [16]The temple of God cannot have any agreement with idols, and we are the temple of the living God. As God said: "I will live with them and walk with them. And I will be their God, and they will be my people."[n]

[17]"Leave those people,
    and be separate, says the Lord.
Touch nothing that is unclean,
    and I will accept you."

Isaiah 52:11; Ezekiel 20:34, 41

[18]"I will be your father,
    and you will be my sons and daughters,
says the Lord Almighty."   *2 Samuel 7:14*

7 Dear friends, we have these promises from God, so we should make ourselves pure—free from anything that makes body or soul unclean. We should try to become holy in the way we live, because we respect God.

SEPTEMBER 15

ISAIAH 21:1—22:25

God's Message to Babylon

21 This is a message about the Desert by the Sea:[n]

Disaster is coming from the desert
    like wind blowing in the south.
It is coming from a terrible country.

[2]I have seen a terrible vision.
    I see traitors turning against you
    and people taking your wealth.

Elam, attack the people!
    Media, surround the city and attack it!
    I will bring an end to the pain the city
        causes.

6:16 "I . . . people." Quotation from Leviticus 26:11–12; Jeremiah 32:38; Ezekiel 37:27. • **21:1 Desert by the Sea** Probably Babylon.

³I saw those terrible things, and now I am
in pain;
my pains are like the pains of giving
birth.
What I hear makes me very afraid;
what I see causes me to shake with fear.
⁴I am worried,
and I am shaking with fear.
My pleasant evening
has become a night of fear.

⁵They set the table;
they spread the rugs;
they eat and drink.
Leaders, stand up.
Prepare the shields for battle!

⁶The Lord said to me,
"Go, place a lookout for the city
and have him report what he sees.
⁷If he sees chariots and teams of horses,
donkeys, or camels,
he should pay very close attention."

⁸Then the lookout called out,
"My master, each day I stand in the
watchtower watching;
every night I have been on guard.
⁹Look, I see a man coming in a chariot
with a team of horses."
The man gives back the answer,
"Babylon has fallen. It has fallen!
All the statues of her gods
lie broken on the ground."
¹⁰My people are crushed like grain on the
threshing floor.
My people, I tell you what I have heard
from the LORD All-Powerful,
from the God of Israel.

God's Message to Edom

¹¹This is a message about Dumah:ⁿ
Someone calls to me from Edom,
"Watchman, how much of the night is
left?
Watchman, how much longer will it be
night?"
¹²The watchman answers,
"Morning is coming, but then night will
come again.

If you have something to ask,
then come back and ask."

God's Message to Arabia

¹³This is a message about Arabia:
A group of traders from Dedan
spent the night near some trees in
Arabia.
¹⁴ They gave water to thirsty travelers;
the people of Tema gave food
to those who were escaping.
¹⁵They were running from swords,
from swords ready to kill,
from bows ready to shoot,
from a hard battle.

¹⁶This is what the Lord said to me: "In one
year all the glory of the country of Kedar will
be gone. (This is a year as a hired helper
counts time.) ¹⁷At that time only a few of the
archers, the soldiers of Kedar, will be left
alive." The LORD, the God of Israel, has spoken.

God's Message to Jerusalem

22 This is a message about the Valley of
Vision:ⁿ
What is wrong with you people?
Why are you on your roofs?ⁿ
²This city was a very busy city,
full of noise and wild parties.
Now your people have been killed,
but not with swords,
nor did they die in battle.
³All your leaders ran away together,
but they have been captured without
using a bow.
All you who were captured
tried to run away before the enemy came.
⁴So I say, "Don't look at me.
Let me cry loudly.
Don't hurry to comfort me
about the destruction of Jerusalem."
⁵The Lord GOD All-Powerful has chosen a
special day
of riots and confusion.
People will trample each other in the
Valley of Vision.
The city walls will be knocked down,
and the people will cry out to the
mountain.

21:11 **Dumah** Another name for Edom.   22:1 **Valley of Vision** This probably means a valley near Jerusalem.   22:1 **roofs**
In Bible times houses were built with flat roofs. The roof was used for drying things such as flax and fruit. And it was used
as an extra room, as a place for worship, and as a cool place to sleep in the summer.

⁶The soldiers from Elam will gather their
arrows
and their chariots and men on horses.
Kir will prepare their shields.
⁷Your nicest valleys will be filled with
chariots.
Horsemen will be ordered to guard the
gates of the city.
⁸ The walls protecting Judah will fall.

At that time the people of Jerusalem
depended on
the weapons kept at the Palace of the
Forest.
⁹You saw that the walls of Jerusalem
had many cracks that needed repairing.
You stored up water in the lower pool.
¹⁰You counted the houses of Jerusalem,
and you tore down houses to repair the
walls with their stones.
¹¹You made a pool between the two walls
to save water from the old pool,
but you did not trust the God who made
these things;
you did not respect the One who
planned them long ago.

¹²The Lord GOD All-Powerful told the
people
to cry and be sad,
to shave their heads and wear rough
cloth.
¹³But look, the people are happy
and are having wild parties.
They kill the cattle and the sheep;
they eat the food and drink the wine.
They say, "Let us eat and drink,
because tomorrow we will die."
¹⁴The LORD All-Powerful said to me: "You
people will die before this guilt is forgiven."
The Lord GOD All-Powerful said this.

God's Message to Shebna

¹⁵This is what the Lord GOD All-Powerful
says:
"Go to this servant Shebna,
the manager of the palace.
¹⁶Say to him, 'What are you doing here?
Who said you could cut out a tomb for
yourself here?
Why are you preparing your tomb in a
high place?

Why are you carving out a tomb from
the rock?
¹⁷Look, mighty one! The LORD will throw
you away.
He will take firm hold of you
¹⁸and roll you tightly into a ball
and throw you into another country.
There you will die,
and there your fine chariots will remain.
You are a disgrace to your master's house.
¹⁹I will force you out of your important job,
and you will be thrown down from your
important place.'

²⁰"At that time I will call for my servant
Eliakim son of Hilkiah. ²¹I will take your robe
and put it on him and give him your belt. I
will hand over to him the important job you
have, and he will be like a father to the people
of Jerusalem and the family of Judah. ²²I will
put the key to the house of David around his
neck. If he opens a door, no one will be able
to close it; if he closes a door, no one will be
able to open it. ²³He will be like an honored
chair in his father's house. I will make him
strong like a peg that is hammered into a
strong board. ²⁴All the honored and important things of his family will depend on him;
all the adults and little children will depend
on him. They will be like bowls and jars
hanging on him.
²⁵"At that time," says the LORD All-Powerful, "the peg hammered into the strong board
will weaken. It will break and fall, and everything hanging on it will be destroyed." The
LORD says this.

PSALM 107:1–9

God Saves from Many Dangers

107 ¹Thank the LORD because he is good.
His love continues forever.
²That is what those whom the LORD has
saved should say.
He has saved them from the enemy
³and has gathered them from other lands,
from east and west, north and south.

⁴Some people had wandered in the desert
lands.
They found no city in which to live.
⁵They were hungry and thirsty,
and they were discouraged.

⁶In their misery they cried out to the
LORD,
and he saved them from their troubles.
⁷He led them on a straight road
to a city where they could live.
⁸Let them give thanks to the LORD for his
love
and for the miracles he does for people.
⁹He satisfies the thirsty
and fills up the hungry.

PROVERBS 25:14–15

¹⁴People who brag about gifts they never give
are like clouds and wind that give no
rain.

¹⁵With patience you can convince a ruler,
and a gentle word can get through to
the hard-headed.

2 CORINTHIANS 7:2–16

Paul's Joy

²Open your hearts to us. We have not done
wrong to anyone, we have not ruined the faith
of anyone, and we have not cheated anyone. ³I
do not say this to blame you. I told you before
that we love you so much we would live or die
with you. ⁴I feel very sure of you and am very
proud of you. You give me much comfort, and
in all of our troubles I have great joy.

⁵When we came into Macedonia, we had
no rest. We found trouble all around us. We
had fighting on the outside and fear on the
inside. ⁶But God, who comforts those who are
troubled, comforted us when Titus came. ⁷We
were comforted, not only by his coming but
also by the comfort you gave him. Titus told
us about your wish to see me and that you are
very sorry for what you did. He also told me
about your great care for me, and when I
heard this, I was much happier.

⁸Even if my letter made you sad, I am not
sorry I wrote it. At first I was sorry, because it
made you sad, but you were sad only for a
short time. ⁹Now I am happy, not because you
were made sad, but because your sorrow
made you change your lives. You became sad
in the way God wanted you to, so you were
not hurt by us in any way. ¹⁰The kind of sorrow God wants makes people change their
hearts and lives. This leads to salvation, and
you cannot be sorry for that. But the kind of
sorrow the world has brings death. ¹¹See
what this sorrow—the sorrow God wanted
you to have—has done to you: It has made
you very serious. It made you want to restore
yourselves. It made you angry and afraid. It
made you want to see me. It made you care. It
made you want to do the right thing. In every
way you have regained your innocence. ¹²I
wrote that letter, not because of the one who
did the wrong or because of the person who
was hurt. I wrote the letter so you could see,
before God, the great care you have for us.
¹³That is why we were comforted.

Not only were we very comforted, we were
even happier to see that Titus was so happy.
All of you made him feel much better. ¹⁴I
bragged to Titus about you, and you showed
that I was right. Everything we said to you
was true, and you have proved that what we
bragged about to Titus is true. ¹⁵And his love
for you is stronger when he remembers that
you were all ready to obey. You welcomed him
with respect and fear. ¹⁶I am very happy that
I can trust you fully.

SEPTEMBER 16

ISAIAH 23:1—24:23

God's Message to Lebanon

23 This is a message about Tyre:
You trading ships, cry!
The houses and harbor of Tyre are
destroyed.
This news came to the ships
from the land of Cyprus.
²Be silent, you who live on the island of Tyre;
you merchants of Sidon, be silent.
Sailors have made you rich.
³They traveled the sea to bring grain from
Egypt;

the sailors of Tyre brought grain from
the Nile Valley
and sold it to other nations.

⁴Sidon, be ashamed.
Strong city of the sea, be ashamed,
because the sea says:
"I have not felt the pain of giving birth;
I have not reared young men or
women."

⁵Egypt will hear the news about Tyre,
and it will make Egypt hurt with
sorrow.

⁶You ships should return to Tarshish.
You people living near the sea should
be sad.

⁷Look at your once happy city!
Look at your old, old city!
People from that city have traveled
far away to live.

⁸Who planned Tyre's destruction?
Tyre made others rich.
Its merchants were treated like princes,
and its traders were greatly respected.

⁹It was the LORD All-Powerful who
planned this.
He decided to make these proud people
unimportant;
he decided to disgrace those who were
greatly respected.

¹⁰Go through your land, people of Tarshish,
like the Nile goes through Egypt.
There is no harbor for you now!

¹¹The LORD has stretched his hand over the
sea
and made its kingdoms tremble.
He commands that Canaan's
strong, walled cities be destroyed.

¹²He said, "Sidon, you will not rejoice any
longer,
because you are destroyed.
Even if you cross the sea to Cyprus,
you will not find a place to rest."

¹³Look at the land of the Babylonians;
it is not a country now.
Assyria has made it a place for wild
animals.
Assyria built towers to attack it;
the soldiers took all the treasures from
its cities,
and they turned it into ruins.

¹⁴So be sad, you trading ships,
because your strong city is destroyed.

¹⁵At that time people will forget about
Tyre for seventy years, which is the length of
a king's life. After seventy years, Tyre will be
like the prostitute in this song:

¹⁶"Oh woman, you are forgotten.
Take your harp and walk through the
city.
Play your harp well. Sing your song
often.
Then people will remember you."

¹⁷After seventy years the LORD will deal
with Tyre, and it will again have trade. It will
be like a prostitute for all the nations of the
earth. ¹⁸The profits will be saved for the
LORD. Tyre will not keep the money she earns
but will give them to the people who serve
the LORD, so they will have plenty of food
and nice clothes.

The Lord Will Punish the World

24Look! The LORD will destroy the earth
and leave it empty;
he will ruin the surface of the land and
scatter its people.

²At that time the same thing will happen
to everyone:
to common people and priests,
to slaves and masters,
to women slaves and their women
masters,
to buyers and sellers,
to those who borrow and those who
lend,
to bankers and those who owe the bank.

³The earth will be completely empty.
The wealth will all be taken,
because the LORD has commanded it.

⁴The earth will dry up and die;
the world will grow weak and die;
the great leaders in this land will
become weak.

⁵The people of the earth have ruined it,
because they do not follow God's
teachings
or obey God's laws
or keep their agreement with God that
was to last forever.

⁶So a curse will destroy the earth.
The people of the world are guilty,

so they will be burned up;
only a few will be left.
⁷The new wine will be bad, and the
grapevines will die.
People who were happy will be sad.
⁸The happy music of the tambourines will
end.
The happy sounds of wild parties will
stop.
The joyful music from the harps will
end.
⁹People will no longer sing while they
drink their wine.
The beer will taste bitter to those who
drink it.
¹⁰The ruined city will be empty,
and people will hide behind closed
doors.
¹¹People in the streets will ask for wine,
but joy will have turned to sadness;
all the happiness will have left.
¹²The city will be left in ruins,
and its gates will be smashed to pieces.
¹³This is what will happen all over the
earth
and to all the nations.
The earth will be like an olive tree after
the harvest
or like the few grapes left on a vine
after harvest.

¹⁴The people shout for joy.
From the west they praise the greatness
of the LORD.
¹⁵People in the east, praise the LORD.
People in the islands of the sea,
praise the name of the LORD, the God of
Israel.
¹⁶We hear songs from every part of the
earth
praising God, the Righteous One.
But I said, "I am dying! I am dying!
How terrible it will be for me!
Traitors turn against people;
with their dishonesty, they turn against
people."
¹⁷There are terrors, holes, and traps
for the people of the earth.
¹⁸Anyone who tries to escape from the
sound of terror
will fall into a hole.

Anyone who climbs out of the hole
will be caught in a trap.
The clouds in the sky will pour out rain,
and the foundations of the earth will
shake.
¹⁹The earth will be broken up;
the earth will split open;
the earth will shake violently.
²⁰The earth will stumble around like
someone who is drunk;
it will shake like a hut in a storm.
Its sin is like a heavy weight on its back;
it will fall and never rise again.

²¹At that time the LORD will punish
the powers in the sky above
and the rulers on earth below.
²²They will be gathered together
like prisoners thrown into a dungeon;
they will be shut up in prison.
After much time they will be punished.
²³The moon will be embarrassed,
and the sun will be ashamed,
because the LORD All-Powerful will rule
as king
on Mount Zion in Jerusalem.
Jerusalem's leaders will see his
greatness.

PSALM 107:10–22

¹⁰Some sat in gloom and darkness;
they were prisoners suffering in chains.
¹¹They had turned against the words of God
and had refused the advice of God
Most High.
¹²So he broke their pride by hard work.
They stumbled, and no one helped.
¹³In their misery they cried out to the
LORD,
and he saved them from their troubles.
¹⁴He brought them out of their gloom and
darkness
and broke their chains.
¹⁵Let them give thanks to the LORD for his
love
and for the miracles he does for people.
¹⁶He breaks down bronze gates
and cuts apart iron bars.

¹⁷Some fools turned against God
and suffered for the evil they did.

¹⁸They refused to eat anything,
    so they almost died.
¹⁹In their misery they cried out to the
    LORD,
    and he saved them from their troubles.
²⁰God gave the command and healed
    them,
    so they were saved from dying.
²¹Let them give thanks to the LORD for his
    love
    and for the miracles he does for people.
²²Let them offer sacrifices to thank him.
    With joy they should tell what he has
    done.

PROVERBS 25:16–17

¹⁶If you find honey, don't eat too much,
    or it will make you throw up.
¹⁷Don't go to your neighbor's house too
    often;
    too much of you will make him hate you.

2 CORINTHIANS 8:1–24

Christian Giving

8 And now, brothers and sisters, we want you to know about the grace God gave the churches in Macedonia. ²They have been tested by great troubles, and they are very poor. But they gave much because of their great joy. ³I can tell you that they gave as much as they were able and even more than they could afford. No one told them to do it. ⁴But they begged and pleaded with us to let them share in this service for God's people. ⁵And they gave in a way we did not expect: They first gave themselves to the Lord and to us. This is what God wants. ⁶So we asked Titus to help you finish this special work of grace since he is the one who started it. ⁷You are rich in everything—in faith, in speaking, in knowledge, in truly wanting to help, and in the love you learned from us.ⁿ In the same way, be strong also in the grace of giving.

⁸I am not commanding you to give. But I want to see if your love is true by comparing you with others that really want to help. ⁹You know the grace of our Lord Jesus Christ. You know that Christ was rich, but for you he be-

came poor so that by his becoming poor you might become rich. ¹⁰This is what I think you should do: Last year you were the first to want to give, and you were the first who gave. ¹¹So now finish the work you started. Then your "doing" will be equal to your "wanting to do." Give from what you have. ¹²If you want to give, your gift will be accepted. It will be judged by what you have, not by what you do not have. ¹³We do not want you to have troubles while other people are at ease, but we want everything to be equal. ¹⁴At this time you have plenty. What you have can help others who are in need. Then later, when they have plenty, they can help you when you are in need, and all will be equal. ¹⁵As it is written in the Scriptures, "The person who gathered more did not have too much, nor did the person who gathered less have too little."ⁿ

Titus and His Companions Help

¹⁶I thank God because he gave Titus the same love for you that I have. ¹⁷Titus accepted what we asked him to do. He wanted very much to go to you, and this was his own idea. ¹⁸We are sending with him the brother who is praised by all the churches because of his service in preaching the Good News. ¹⁹Also, this brother was chosen by the churches to go with us when we deliver this gift of money. We are doing this service to bring glory to the Lord and to show that we really want to help. ²⁰We are being careful so that no one will criticize us for the way we are handling this large gift. ²¹We are trying hard to do what the Lord accepts as right and also what people think is right.

²²Also, we are sending with them our brother, who is always ready to help. He has proved this to us in many ways, and he wants to help even more now, because he has much faith in you. ²³Now about Titus—he is my partner who is working with me to help you. And about the other brothers—they are sent from the churches, and they bring glory to Christ. ²⁴So show these men the proof of your love and the reason we are proud of you. Then all the churches can see it.

8:7 in . . . us Some Greek copies read "in your love for us." **8:15 "The person . . . little."** Quotation from Exodus 16:18.

SEPTEMBER 17

ISAIAH 25:1—26:21

A Song of Praise to God

25 LORD, you are my God.
I honor you and praise you,
because you have done amazing things.
    You have always done what you said
        you would do;
    you have done what you planned long
        ago.
²You have made the city a pile of rocks
    and have destroyed her walls.
The city our enemies built with strong
        walls is gone;
    it will never be built again.
³People from powerful nations will honor
        you;
    cruel people from strong cities will fear
        you.
⁴You protect the poor;
    you protect the helpless when they are
        in danger.
You are like a shelter from storms,
    like shade that protects them from the
        heat.
The cruel people attack
    like a rainstorm beating against the wall,
5   like the heat in the desert.
But you, God, stop their violent attack.
    As a cloud cools a hot day,
    you silence the songs of those who have
        no mercy.

God's Banquet for His Servants

⁶The LORD All-Powerful will prepare a
        feast
    on this mountain for all people.
It will be a feast with all the best food
        and wine,
    the finest meat and wine.
⁷On this mountain God will destroy
    the veil that covers all nations,
    the veil that stretches over all peoples;
8   he will destroy death forever.
The Lord GOD will wipe away every tear
        from every face.
He will take away the shame of his
        people from the earth.
The LORD has spoken.

⁹At that time people will say,
    "Our God is doing this!
We have waited for him, and he has
        come to save us.
This is the LORD. We waited for him,
    so we will rejoice and be happy when he
        saves us."
¹⁰The LORD will protect Jerusalem,
    but he will crush our enemy Moab
like straw that is trampled down in the
        manure.
¹¹They will spread their arms in it
    like a person who is swimming.
But God will bring down their pride,
    and all the clever things they have
        made will mean nothing.
¹²Moab's high walls protect them,
    but God will destroy these walls.
He will throw them down to the
        ground,
    even to the dust.

A Song of Praise to God

26 At that time people will sing this song
in Judah:
We have a strong city.
    God protects us with its strong walls
        and defenses.
²Open the gates,
    and the good people will enter,
    those who follow God.
³You, LORD, give true peace
    to those who depend on you,
    because they trust you.
⁴So, trust the LORD always,
    because he is our Rock forever.
⁵He will destroy the proud city,
    and he will punish the people living
        there.
He will bring that high city down to the
        ground
    and throw it down into the dust.
⁶Then those who were hurt by the city
    will walk on its ruins;
    those who were made poor by the city
        will trample it under their feet.
⁷The path of life is level for those who are
    right with God;

LORD, you make the way of life smooth
for those people.
⁸But, LORD, we are waiting
for your way of justice.
Our souls want to remember
you and your name.
⁹My soul wants to be with you at night,
and my spirit wants to be with you at
the dawn of every day.
When your way of justice comes to the
land,
people of the world will learn the right
way of living.
¹⁰Evil people will not learn to do good
even if you show them kindness.
They will continue doing evil, even if
they live in a good world;
they never see the LORD's greatness.
¹¹LORD, you are ready to punish those
people,
but they do not see that.
Show them your strong love for your
people.
Then those who are evil will be
ashamed.
Burn them in the fire
you have prepared for your enemies.
¹²LORD, all our success is because of what
you have done,
so give us peace.
¹³LORD, our God, other masters besides you
have ruled us,
but we honor only you.
¹⁴Those masters are now dead;
their ghosts will not rise from death.
You punished and destroyed them
and erased any memory of them.
¹⁵LORD, you multiplied the number of your
people;
you multiplied them and brought
honor to yourself.
You made the borders of the land wide.
¹⁶LORD, people remember you when they
are in trouble;
they say quiet prayers to you when you
punish them.
¹⁷LORD, when we are with you,
we are like a woman giving birth to a
baby;
she cries and has pain from the birth.
¹⁸In the same way, we had pain.
We gave birth, but only to wind.

We don't bring salvation to the land
or make new people for the world.
¹⁹Your people have died, but they will live
again;
their bodies will rise from death.
You who lie in the ground,
wake up and be happy!
The dew covering you is like the dew of a
new day;
the ground will give birth to the dead.

Judgment: Reward or Punishment
²⁰My people, go into your rooms
and shut your doors behind you.
Hide in your rooms for a short time
until God's anger is finished.
²¹The LORD will leave his place
to punish the people of the world for
their sins.
The earth will show the blood of the
people who have been killed;
it will not cover the dead any longer.

PSALM 107:23–32
²³Others went out to sea in ships
and did business on the great oceans.
²⁴They saw what the LORD could do,
the miracles he did in the deep oceans.
²⁵He spoke, and a storm came up,
which blew up high waves.
²⁶The ships were tossed as high as the sky
and fell low to the depths.
The storm was so bad that they lost
their courage.
²⁷They stumbled and fell like people who
were drunk.
They did not know what to do.
²⁸In their misery they cried out to the
LORD,
and he saved them from their troubles.
²⁹He stilled the storm
and calmed the waves.
³⁰They were happy that it was quiet,
and God guided them to the port they
wanted.
³¹Let them give thanks to the LORD for his
love
and for the miracles he does for people.
³²Let them praise his greatness in the
meeting of the people;
let them praise him in the meeting of
the elders.

PROVERBS 25:18–19

¹⁸When you lie about your neighbors,
  it hurts them as much as a club, a
  sword, or a sharp arrow.

¹⁹Trusting unfaithful people when you are
  in trouble
  is like eating with a broken tooth or
  walking with a crippled foot.

2 CORINTHIANS 9:1–15

Help for Fellow Christians

9 I really do not need to write you about
  this help for God's people. ²I know you
want to help. I have been bragging about this
to the people in Macedonia, telling them that
you in Southern Greece have been ready to
give since last year. And your desire to give
has made most of them ready to give also.
³But I am sending the brothers to you so that
our bragging about you in this will not be
empty words. I want you to be ready, as I said
you would be. ⁴If any of the people from
Macedonia come with me and find that you
are not ready, we will be ashamed that we
were so sure of you. (And you will be
ashamed, too!) ⁵So I thought I should ask
these brothers to go to you before we do.
They will finish getting in order the generous gift you promised so it will be ready
when we come. And it will be a generous
gift—not one that you did not want to give.

⁶Remember this: The person who plants a
little will have a small harvest, but the person
who plants a lot will have a big harvest. ⁷Each
of you should give as you have decided in your
heart to give. You should not be sad when you
give, and you should not give because you feel
forced to give. God loves the person who gives
happily. ⁸And God can give you more blessings
than you need. Then you will always have
plenty of everything—enough to give to every
good work. ⁹It is written in the Scriptures:

  "He gives freely to the poor.
  The things he does are right and will
    continue forever."   *Psalm 112:9*

¹⁰God is the One who gives seed to the farmer
and bread for food. He will give you all the
seed you need and make it grow so there will
be a great harvest from your goodness. ¹¹He
will make you rich in every way so that you
can always give freely. And your giving
through us will cause many to give thanks to
God. ¹²This service you do not only helps the
needs of God's people, it also brings many
more thanks to God. ¹³It is a proof of your
faith. Many people will praise God because
you obey the Good News of Christ—the
gospel you say you believe—and because you
freely share with them and with all others.
¹⁴And when they pray, they will wish they
could be with you because of the great grace
that God has given you. ¹⁵Thanks be to God
for his gift that is too wonderful for words.

SEPTEMBER 18

ISAIAH 27:1—28:29

27 At that time the LORD will punish
    Leviathan, the gliding snake.
  He will punish Leviathan, the coiled
    snake,
    with his great and hard and powerful
      sword.
  He will kill the monster in the sea.

²At that time
  people will sing about the pleasant
    vineyard.

³"I, the LORD, will care for that vineyard;
  I will water it at the right time.
No one will hurt it,
  because I will guard it day and night.
⁴I am not angry.
  If anyone builds a wall of thornbushes in
    war,
  I will march to it and burn it.
⁵But if anyone comes to me for safety
  and wants to make peace with me,
  he should come and make peace with
    me."

⁶In the days to come, the people of Jacob
    will be like a plant with good roots;
  Israel will grow like a plant beginning
    to bloom.
  Then the world will be filled with their
    children.

The Lord Will Send Israel Away
⁷The LORD has not hurt his people as he
    hurt their enemies;
  his people have not been killed like
    those who tried to kill them.
⁸He will settle his argument with Israel by
    sending it far away.
  Like a hot desert wind, he will drive it
    away.
⁹This is how Israel's guilt will be
    forgiven;
  this is how its sins will be taken
    away:
  Israel will crush the rocks of the altar to
    dust,
    and no statues or altars will be left
    standing for the Asherah idols.
¹⁰At that time the strong, walled city will
    be empty
    like a desert.
  Calves will eat grass there.
  They will lie down there
    and eat leaves from the branches.
¹¹The limbs will become dry and break
    off,
  so women will use them for firewood.
  The people refuse to understand,
    so God will not comfort them;
    their Maker will not be kind to them.
¹²At that time the LORD will begin gathering his people one by one from the Euphrates River to the brook of Egypt. He will
separate them from others as grain is separated from chaff. ¹³Many of my people are
now lost in Assyria. Some have run away to
Egypt. But at that time a great trumpet will
be blown, and all those people will come and
worship the LORD on that holy mountain in
Jerusalem.

Warnings to Israel
28 How terrible it will be for Samaria,
    the pride of Israel's drunken
    people!
  That beautiful crown of flowers is just a
    dying plant
  set on a hill above a rich valley where
    drunkards live.
²Look, the Lord has someone who is
    strong and powerful.
  Like a storm of hail and strong wind,
  like a sudden flood of water pouring over
    the country,
  he will throw Samaria down to the
    ground.
³That city, the pride of Israel's drunken
    people,
  will be trampled underfoot.
⁴That beautiful crown of flowers is just a
    dying plant
  set on a hill above a rich valley.
  That city will be like the first fig of
    summer.
  Anyone who sees it
  quickly picks it and eats it.

⁵At that time the LORD All-Powerful
  will be like a beautiful crown,
  like a wonderful crown of flowers
  for his people who are left alive.
⁶Then he will give wisdom to the judges
    who must decide cases
  and strength to those who battle at the
    city gate.
⁷But now those leaders are drunk with
    wine;
  they stumble from drinking too much
    beer.
  The priests and prophets are drunk with
    beer
  and are filled with wine.
  They stumble from too much beer.
  The prophets are drunk when they see
    their visions;
  the judges stumble when they make
    their decisions.
⁸Every table is covered with vomit,
  so there is not a clean place anywhere.

⁹The LORD is trying to teach the people a
    lesson;
  he is trying to make them understand
    his teachings.
  But the people are like babies too old for
    breast milk,
  like those who no longer nurse at their
    mother's breast.

[10]So they make fun of the LORD's prophet
and say:
"A command here, a command there.
A rule here, a rule there.
A little lesson here, a little lesson there."
[11]So the LORD will use strange words and
foreign languages
to speak to these people.
[12]God said to them,
"Here is a place of rest;
let the tired people come and rest.
This is the place of peace."
But the people would not listen.
[13]So the words of the LORD will be,
"A command here, a command there.
A rule here, a rule there.
A little lesson here, a little lesson there."
They will fall back and be defeated;
they will be trapped and captured.

[14]So listen to the LORD's message, you who
brag,
you leaders in Jerusalem.
[15]You say, "We have made an agreement
with death;
we have a contract with death.
When terrible punishment passes by,
it won't hurt us.
Our lies will keep us safe,
and our tricks will hide us."
[16]Because of these things, this is what the
Lord GOD says:
"I will put a stone in the ground in
Jerusalem,
a tested stone.
Everything will be built on this
important and precious rock.
Anyone who trusts in it will never be
disappointed.
[17]I will use justice as a measuring line
and goodness as the standard.
The lies you hide behind will be
destroyed as if by hail.
They will be washed away as if in a
flood.
[18]Your agreement with death will be
erased;
your contract with death will not help
you.
When terrible punishment comes,
you will be crushed by it.

[19]Whenever punishment comes, it will take
you away.
It will come morning after morning;
it will defeat you by day and by night.
Those who understand this punishment
will be terrified."
[20]You will be like the person who tried to
sleep
on a bed that was too short
and with a blanket that was too narrow
to wrap around himself.
[21]The LORD will fight as he did at Mount
Perazim.
He will be angry as he was in the Valley
of Gibeon.
He will do his work, his strange work.
He will finish his job, his strange job.
[22]Now, you must not make fun of these
things,
or the ropes around you will become
tighter.
The Lord GOD All-Powerful has told me
how the whole earth will be destroyed.

The Lord Punishes Fairly

[23]Listen closely to what I tell you;
listen carefully to what I say.
[24]A farmer does not plow his field all the
time;
he does not go on working the soil.
[25]He makes the ground flat and smooth.
Then he plants the dill and scatters the
cumin.
He plants the wheat in rows,
the barley in its special place,
and other wheat as a border around the
field.
[26]His God teaches him
and shows him the right way.
[27]A farmer doesn't use heavy boards to
crush dill;
he doesn't use a wagon wheel to crush
cumin.
He uses a small stick to break open the dill,
and with a stick he opens the cumin.
[28]The grain is ground to make bread.
People do not ruin it by crushing it
forever.
The farmer separates the wheat from the
chaff with his cart,
but he does not let his horses grind it.

[29]This lesson also comes from the LORD All-Powerful,
  who gives wonderful advice, who is very wise.

PSALM 107:33–43

[33]He changed rivers into a desert
  and springs of water into dry ground.
[34]He made fertile land salty,
  because the people there did evil.
[35]He changed the desert into pools of water
  and dry ground into springs of water.
[36]He had the hungry settle there
  so they could build a city in which to live.
[37]They planted seeds in the fields and vineyards,
  and they had a good harvest.
[38]God blessed them, and they grew in number.
  Their cattle did not become fewer.

[39]Because of disaster, troubles, and sadness,
  their families grew smaller and weaker.
[40]He showed he was displeased with their leaders
  and made them wander in a pathless desert.
[41]But he lifted the poor out of their suffering
  and made their families grow like flocks of sheep.
[42]Good people see this and are happy,
  but the wicked say nothing.

[43]Whoever is wise will remember these things
  and will think about the love of the LORD.

PROVERBS 25:20

[20]Singing songs to someone who is sad
  is like taking away his coat on a cold day
  or pouring vinegar on soda.

2 CORINTHIANS 10:1–18

Paul Defends His Ministry

10 I, Paul, am begging you with the gentleness and the kindness of Christ. Some people say that I am easy on you when I am with you and bold when I am away. [2]They think we live in a worldly way, and I plan to be very bold with them when I come. I beg you that when I come I will not need to use that same boldness with you. [3]We do live in the world, but we do not fight in the same way the world fights. [4]We fight with weapons that are different from those the world uses. Our weapons have power from God that can destroy the enemy's strong places. We destroy people's arguments [5]and every proud thing that raises itself against the knowledge of God. We capture every thought and make it give up and obey Christ. [6]We are ready to punish anyone there who does not obey, but first we want you to obey fully.

[7]You must look at the facts before you. If you feel sure that you belong to Christ, you must remember that we belong to Christ just as you do. [8]It is true that we brag freely about the authority the Lord gave us. But this authority is to build you up, not to tear you down. So I will not be ashamed. [9]I do not want you to think I am trying to scare you with my letters. [10]Some people say, "Paul's letters are powerful and sound important, but when he is with us, he is weak. And his speaking is nothing." [11]They should know this: We are not there with you now, so we say these things in letters. But when we are there with you, we will show the same authority that we show in our letters.

[12]We do not dare to compare ourselves with those who think they are very important. They use themselves to measure themselves, and they judge themselves by what they themselves are. This shows that they know nothing. [13]But we will not brag about things outside the work that was given us to do. We will limit our bragging to the work that God gave us, and this includes our work with you. [14]We are not bragging too much, as we would be if we had not already come to you. But we have come to you with the Good News of Christ. [15]We limit our bragging to the work that is ours, not what others have done. We hope that as your faith continues to grow, you will help our work to grow much larger. [16]We want to tell the Good News in the areas beyond your city. We do not want to

brag about work that has already been done in another person's area. [17]But, "If people want to brag, they should brag only about the Lord."[n] [18]It is not those who say they are good who are accepted but those the Lord thinks are good.

SEPTEMBER 19

ISAIAH 29:1–24

Warnings to Jerusalem

29[1]How terrible it will be for you,
Jerusalem,
the city where David camped.
Your festivals have continued
year after year.
[2]I will attack Jerusalem,
and that city will be filled with sadness
and crying.
It will be like an altar to me.
[3]I will put armies all around you,
Jerusalem;
I will surround you with towers
and with devices to attack you.
[4]You will be pulled down and will speak
from the ground;
I will hear your voice rising from the
ground.
It will sound like the voice of a ghost;
your words will come like a whisper
from the dirt.

[5]Your many enemies will become like fine
dust;
the many cruel people will be like chaff
that is blown away.
Everything will happen very quickly.
[6] The LORD All-Powerful will come
with thunder, earthquakes, and great
noises,
with storms, strong winds, and a fire
that destroys.
[7]Then all the nations that fight against
Jerusalem
will be like a dream;
all the nations that attack her
will be like a vision in the night.
[8]They will be like a hungry man who
dreams he is eating,

but when he awakens, he is still hungry.
They will be like a thirsty man who
dreams he is drinking,
but when he awakens, he is still weak
and thirsty.
It will be the same way with all the
nations
who fight against Mount Zion.

[9]Be surprised and amazed.
Blind yourselves so that you cannot see.
Become drunk, but not from wine.
Trip and fall, but not from beer.
[10]The LORD has made you go into a deep
sleep.
He has closed your eyes. (The prophets
are your eyes.)
He has covered your heads. (The seers
are your heads.)
[11]This vision is like the words of a book that is closed and sealed. You may give the book to someone who can read and tell that person to read it. But he will say, "I can't read the book, because it is sealed." [12]Or you may give the book to someone who cannot read and tell him to read it. But he will say, "I don't know how to read."
[13]The Lord says:

"These people worship me with their
mouths,
and honor me with their lips,
but their hearts are far from me.
Their worship is based on
nothing but human rules.
[14]So I will continue to amaze these
people
by doing more and more miracles.
Their wise men will lose their wisdom;
their wise men will not be able to
understand."

10:17 "**If . . . Lord.**" Quotation from Jeremiah 9:24.

Warnings About Other Nations

¹⁵How terrible it will be for those who try
to hide things from the LORD
and who do their work in darkness.
They think no one will see them or
know what they do.
¹⁶You are confused.
You think the clay is equal to the potter.
You think that an object can tell the one
who made it,
"You didn't make me."
This is like a pot telling its maker,
"You don't know anything."

A Better Time Is Coming

¹⁷In a very short time, Lebanon will
become rich farmland,
and the rich farmland will seem like a
forest.
¹⁸At that time the deaf will hear the words
in a book.
Instead of having darkness and gloom,
the blind will see.
¹⁹The LORD will make the poor people
happy;
they will rejoice in the Holy One of
Israel.
²⁰Then the people without mercy will
come to an end;
those who do not respect God will
disappear.
Those who enjoy doing evil will be gone:
²¹those who lie about others in court,
those who trap people in court,
those who lie and take justice from
innocent people in court.
²²This is what the LORD who set Abraham
free says to the family of Jacob:
"Now the people of Jacob will not be
ashamed
or disgraced any longer.
²³When they see all their children,
the children I made with my hands,
they will say my name is holy.
They will agree that the Holy One of
Jacob is holy,
and they will respect the God of Israel.
²⁴People who do wrong will now
understand.
Those who complain will accept being
taught."

PSALM 108:1-5

A Prayer for Victory

A song. A psalm of David.

108 God, my heart is steady.
I will sing and praise you with all
my being.
²Wake up, harp and lyre!
I will wake up the dawn.
³LORD, I will praise you among the
nations;
I will sing songs of praise about you to
all the nations.
⁴Your great love reaches to the skies,
your truth to the heavens.
⁵God, you are supreme above the skies.
Let your glory be over all the earth.

PROVERBS 25:21-22

²¹If your enemy is hungry, feed him.
If he is thirsty, give him a drink.
²²Doing this will be like pouring burning
coals on his head,
and the LORD will reward you.

2 CORINTHIANS 11:1-15

Paul and the False Apostles

11 I wish you would be patient with me
even when I am a little foolish, but you
are already doing that. ²I am jealous over you
with a jealousy that comes from God. I
promised to give you to Christ, as your only
husband. I want to give you as his pure
bride. ³But I am afraid that your minds will
be led away from your true and pure following of Christ just as Eve was tricked by the
snake with his evil ways. ⁴You are very patient with anyone who comes to you and
preaches a different Jesus from the one we
preached. You are very willing to accept a
spirit or gospel that is different from the
Spirit and Good News you received from us.

⁵I do not think that those "great apostles"
are any better than I am. ⁶I may not be a
trained speaker, but I do have knowledge. We
have shown this to you clearly in every way.

⁷I preached God's Good News to you without pay. I made myself unimportant to make
you important. Do you think that was

wrong? [8]I accepted pay from other churches, taking their money so I could serve you. [9]If I needed something when I was with you, I did not trouble any of you. The brothers who came from Macedonia gave me all that I needed. I did not allow myself to depend on you in any way, and I will never depend on you. [10]No one in Southern Greece will stop me from bragging about that. I say this with the truth of Christ in me. [11]And why do I not depend on you? Do you think it is because I do not love you? God knows that I love you.

[12]And I will continue doing what I am doing now, because I want to stop those people from having a reason to brag. They would like to say that the work they brag about is the same as ours. [13]Such men are not true apostles but are workers who lie. They change themselves to look like apostles of Christ. [14]This does not surprise us. Even Satan changes himself to look like an angel of light.[n] [15]So it does not surprise us if Satan's servants also make themselves look like servants who work for what is right. But in the end they will be punished for what they do.

SEPTEMBER 20

ISAIAH 30:1—32:20

Warnings to the Stubborn Nation

30 The LORD said,
"How terrible it will be for these stubborn children.
They make plans, but they don't ask me to help them.
They make agreements with other nations, without asking my Spirit.
They are adding more and more sins to themselves.
[2]They go down to Egypt for help without asking me about it first.
They hope they will be saved by the king of Egypt;
they want Egypt to protect them.
[3]But hiding in Egypt will bring you only shame;
Egypt's protection will only disappoint you.
[4]Your officers have gone to Zoan,
and your messengers have gone to Hanes,
[5]but they will be put to shame,
because Egypt is useless to them.
It will give no help and will be of no use;
it will cause them only shame and embarrassment."

God's Message to Judah

[6]This is a message about the animals in southern Judah:
Southern Judah is a dangerous place full of lions and lionesses,
poisonous snakes and darting snakes.
The messengers travel through there with their wealth on the backs of donkeys
and their treasure on the backs of camels.
They carry them to a nation that cannot help them,
[7] to Egypt whose help is useless.
So I call that country Rahab the Do-Nothing.

[8]Now write this on a sign for the people,
write this on a scroll,
so that for the days to come
this will be a witness forever.
[9]These people are like children who lie and refuse to obey;
they refuse to listen to the LORD's teachings.
[10]They tell the seers,
"Don't see any more visions!"
They say to the prophets,
"Don't tell us the truth!

11:14 angel of light Messenger from God. The devil fools people so that they think he is from God.

Say things that will make us feel good;
see only good things for us.
¹¹Stop blocking our path.
Get out of our way.
Stop telling us
about God, the Holy One of Israel."
¹²So this is what the Holy One of Israel
says:
"You people have refused to accept this
message
and have depended on cruelty and lies
to help you.
¹³You are guilty of these things.
So you will be like a high wall with
cracks in it
that falls suddenly and breaks into
small pieces.
¹⁴You will be like a clay jar that breaks,
smashed into many pieces.
Those pieces will be too small
to take coals from the fire
or to get water from a well."
¹⁵This is what the Lord GOD, the Holy One
of Israel, says:
"If you come back to me and trust me,
you will be saved.
If you will be calm and trust me, you
will be strong."
But you don't want to do that.
¹⁶You say, "No, we need horses to run away
on."
So you will run away on horses.
You say, "We will ride away on fast horses."
So those who chase you will be fast.
¹⁷One enemy will make threats,
and a thousand of your men will run
away.
Five enemies will make threats,
and all of you will run from them.
You will be left alone like a flagpole on a
hilltop,
like a banner on a hill.
¹⁸The LORD wants to show his mercy to you.
He wants to rise and comfort you.
The LORD is a fair God,
and everyone who waits for his help
will be happy.

The Lord Will Help His People
¹⁹You people who live on Mount Zion in
Jerusalem will not cry anymore. The LORD

will hear your crying, and he will comfort
you. When he hears you, he will help you.
²⁰The Lord has given you sorrow and hurt
like the bread and water you ate every day.
He is your teacher; he will not continue to
hide from you, but you will see your teacher
with your own eyes. ²¹If you go the wrong
way—to the right or to the left—you will
hear a voice behind you saying, "This is the
right way. You should go this way." ²²You have
statues covered with silver and gold, but you
will ruin them for further use. You will throw
them away like filthy rags and say, "Go
away!"
²³At that time the LORD will send rain for
the seeds you plant in the ground, and the
ground will grow food for you. The harvest
will be rich and great, and you will have
plenty of food in the fields for your animals.
²⁴Your oxen and donkeys that work the soil
will have all the food they need. You will have
to use shovels and pitchforks to spread all
their food. ²⁵Every mountain and hill will
have streams filled with water. These things
will happen after many people are killed and
the towers are pulled down. ²⁶At that time the
light from the moon will be bright like the
sun, and the light from the sun will be seven
times brighter than now, like the light of
seven days. These things will happen when
the LORD bandages his broken people and
heals the hurts he gave them.
²⁷Look! The LORD comes from far away.
His anger is like a fire with thick clouds
of smoke.
His mouth is filled with anger,
and his tongue is like a burning fire.
²⁸His breath is like a rushing river,
which rises to the throat.
He will judge the nations as if he is
sifting them through the strainer of
destruction.
He will place in their mouths a bit that
will lead them the wrong way.
²⁹You will sing happy songs
as on the nights you begin a festival.
You will be happy like people listening to
flutes
as they come to the mountain of the
LORD,
to the Rock of Israel.

[30]The LORD will cause all people to hear his
  great voice
and to see his powerful arm come
  down with anger,
like a great fire that burns everything,
like a great storm with much rain and
  hail.
[31]Assyria will be afraid when it hears the
  voice of the LORD,
because he will strike Assyria with a
  rod.
[32]When the LORD punishes Assyria with a
  rod,
he will beat them to the music of
  tambourines and harps;
he will fight against them with his
  mighty weapons.
[33]Topheth[n] has been made ready for a long
  time;
it is ready for the king.
It was made deep and wide
  with much wood and fire.
And the LORD's breath will come
like a stream of burning sulfur and set
  it on fire.

Warnings About Relying on Egypt

31 How terrible it will be for those people
  who go down to Egypt for help.
They think horses will save them.
They think their many chariots
  and strong horsemen will save them.
But they don't trust God, the Holy One of
  Israel,
or ask the LORD for help.
[2]But he is wise and can bring them
  disaster.
He does not change his warnings.
He will rise up and fight against the evil
  people
and against those who try to help evil
  people.
[3]The Egyptians are only people and are
  not God.
Their horses are only animals and are
  not spirit.
The LORD will stretch out his arm,
and the one who helps will stumble,
and the people who wanted help will
  fall.

All of them will be destroyed together.
[4]The LORD says this to me:
"When a lion or a lion's cub kills an
  animal to eat,
it stands over the dead animal and
  roars.
A band of shepherds
  may be assembled against it,
but the lion will not be afraid of their
  yelling
or upset by their noise.
So the LORD All-Powerful will come
  down
to fight on Mount Zion and on its hill.
[5]The LORD All-Powerful will defend
  Jerusalem
like birds flying over their nests.
He will defend and save it;
he will 'pass over' and save Jerusalem."
[6]You children of Israel, come back to the
God you fought against. [7]The time is coming
when each of you will stop worshiping idols
of gold and silver, which you sinned by making.
[8]"Assyria will be defeated by a sword, but
  not the sword of a person;
Assyria will be destroyed, but not by a
  person's sword.
Assyria will run away from the sword of
  God,
but its young men will be caught and
  made slaves.
[9]They will panic, and their protection will
  be destroyed.
Their commanders will be terrified
  when they see God's battle flag,"
says the LORD,
whose fire is in Jerusalem
and whose furnace is in Jerusalem.

A Good Kingdom Is Coming

32 A king will rule in a way that brings
  justice,
and leaders will make fair decisions.
[2]Then each ruler will be like a shelter
  from the wind,
like a safe place in a storm,
like streams of water in a dry land,
like a cool shadow from a large rock in
  a hot land.

30:33 Topheth Gehenna; the Valley of Hinnom. Here people burned the bodies of criminals and animals, along with garbage.

³People will look to the king for help,
and they will truly listen to what he
says.
⁴People who are now worried will be able
to understand.
Those who cannot speak clearly now
will then be able to speak clearly and
quickly.
⁵Fools will not be called great,
and people will not respect the wicked.
⁶A fool says foolish things,
and in his mind he plans evil.
A fool does things that are wicked,
and he says wrong things about the
LORD.
A fool does not feed the hungry
or let thirsty people drink water.
⁷The wicked person uses evil like a tool.
He plans ways to take everything from
the poor.
He destroys the poor with lies,
even when the poor person is in the
right.
⁸But a good leader plans to do good,
and those good things make him a
good leader.

Hard Times Are Coming

⁹You women who are calm now,
stand up and listen to me.
You women who feel safe now,
hear what I say.
¹⁰You women feel safe now,
but after one year you will be afraid.
There will be no grape harvest
and no summer fruit to gather.
¹¹Women, you are calm now, but you
should shake with fear.
Women, you feel safe now, but you
should tremble.
Take off your nice clothes
and put rough cloth around your waist
to show your sadness.
¹²Beat your breasts in grief, because the
fields that were pleasant are now
empty.
Cry, because the vines that once had
fruit now have no more grapes.
¹³Cry for the land of my people,
in which only thorns and weeds now
grow.

Cry for the city that once was happy
and for all the houses that once were
filled with joy.
¹⁴The palace will be empty;
people will leave the noisy city.
Strong cities and towers will be empty.
Wild donkeys will love to live there, and
sheep will go there to eat.

Things Will Get Better

¹⁵This will continue until God pours his
Spirit from above upon us.
Then the desert will be like a fertile
field
and the fertile field like a forest.
¹⁶Justice will be found even in the desert,
and fairness will be found in the fertile
fields.
¹⁷That fairness will bring peace,
and it will bring calm and safety forever.
¹⁸My people will live in peaceful places
and in safe homes
and in calm places of rest.
¹⁹Hail will destroy the forest,
and the city will be completely
destroyed.
²⁰But you will be happy as you plant seeds
near every stream
and as you let your cattle and donkeys
wander freely.

PSALM 108:6–13

⁶Answer us and save us by your power
so the people you love will be rescued.
⁷God has said from his Temple,
"When I win, I will divide Shechem
and measure off the Valley of Succoth.
⁸Gilead and Manasseh are mine.
Ephraim is like my helmet.
Judah holds my royal scepter.
⁹Moab is like my washbowl.
I throw my sandals at Edom.
I shout at Philistia."

¹⁰Who will bring me to the strong, walled
city?
Who will lead me to Edom?
¹¹God, surely you have rejected us;
you do not go out with our armies.
¹²Help us fight the enemy.
Human help is useless,

13but we can win with God's help.
He will defeat our enemies.

PROVERBS 25:23–24

23As the north wind brings rain,
telling gossip brings angry looks.

24It is better to live in a corner on the roof[n]
than inside the house with a quarreling
wife.

2 CORINTHIANS 11:16–33

Paul Tells About His Sufferings

16I tell you again: No one should think I
am a fool. But if you think so, accept me as
you would accept a fool. Then I can brag a
little, too. 17When I brag because I feel sure of
myself, I am not talking as the Lord would
talk but as a fool. 18Many people are bragging about their lives in the world. So I will
brag too. 19You are wise, so you will gladly be
patient with fools! 20You are even patient
with those who order you around, or use
you, or trick you, or think they are better
than you, or hit you in the face. 21It is shameful to me to say this, but we were too "weak"
to do those things to you!

But if anyone else is brave enough to brag,
then I also will be brave and brag. (I am talking as a fool.) 22Are they Hebrews?[n] So am I.
Are they Israelites? So am I. Are they from
Abraham's family? So am I. 23Are they serving Christ? I am serving him more. (I am
crazy to talk like this.) I have worked much

harder than they. I have been in prison more
often. I have been hurt more in beatings. I
have been near death many times. 24Five
times the Jews have given me their punishment of thirty-nine lashes with a whip.
25Three different times I was beaten with
rods. One time I was almost stoned to death.
Three times I was in ships that wrecked, and
one of those times I spent a night and a day
in the sea. 26I have gone on many travels and
have been in danger from rivers, thieves, my
own people, the Jews, and those who are not
Jews. I have been in danger in cities, in
places where no one lives, and on the sea.
And I have been in danger with false Christians. 27I have done hard and tiring work,
and many times I did not sleep. I have been
hungry and thirsty, and many times I have
been without food. I have been cold and
without clothes. 28Besides all this, there is on
me every day the load of my concern for all
the churches. 29I feel weak every time someone is weak, and I feel upset every time
someone is led into sin.

30If I must brag, I will brag about the
things that show I am weak. 31God knows I
am not lying. He is the God and Father of the
Lord Jesus Christ, and he is to be praised forever. 32When I was in Damascus, the governor under King Aretas wanted to arrest me,
so he put guards around the city. 33But my
friends lowered me in a basket through a
hole in the city wall. So I escaped from the
governor.

SEPTEMBER 21

ISAIAH 33:1—34:17

Warnings to Assyria and Promises to God's People

33 How terrible it will be for you who
destroy others
but have not been destroyed yet.

How terrible it will be for you, traitor,
whom no one has turned against yet.
When you stop destroying,
others will destroy you.
When you stop turning against
others,
they will turn against you.

25:24 roof In Bible times houses were built with flat roofs. The roof was used for drying things such as flax and fruit. And it
was used as an extra room, as a place for worship, and as a cool place to sleep in the summer.   •   11:22 Hebrews A name
for the Jews that some Jews were very proud of.

²LORD, be kind to us.
We have waited for your help.
Give us strength every morning.
Save us when we are in trouble.
³Your powerful voice makes people run
away in fear;
your greatness causes the nations to
run away.
⁴Like locusts, your enemies will take away
the things you stole in war.
Like locusts rushing about, they will
take your wealth.
⁵The LORD is very great, and he lives in a
high place.
He fills Jerusalem with fairness and
justice.
⁶He will be your safety.
He is full of salvation, wisdom, and
knowledge.
Respect for the LORD is the greatest
treasure.
⁷See, brave people are crying out in the
streets;
those who tried to bring peace are
weeping loudly.
⁸There is no one on the roads,
no one walking in the paths.
People have broken the agreements they
made.
They refuse to believe the proof from
witnesses.
No one respects other people.
⁹The land is sick and dying;
Lebanon is ashamed and dying.
The Plain of Sharon is dry like the
desert,
and the trees of Bashan and Carmel are
dying.
¹⁰The LORD says, "Now, I will stand up
and show my greatness.
Now, I will become important to the
people.
¹¹You people do useless things
that are like hay and straw.
A destructive wind will burn you like
fire.
¹²People will be burned until their bones
become like lime;
they will burn quickly like dry
thornbushes."

¹³You people in faraway lands, hear what I
have done.
You people who are near me, learn
about my power.
¹⁴The sinners in Jerusalem are afraid;
those who are separated from God
shake with fear.
They say, "Can any of us live through this
fire that destroys?
Who can live near this fire that burns
on and on?"
¹⁵A person who does what is right
and speaks what is right,
who refuses to take money unfairly,
who refuses to take money to hurt
others,
who does not listen to plans of murder,
who refuses to think about evil—
¹⁶this is the kind of person who will be
safe.
He will be protected as he would be in a
high, walled city.
He will always have bread,
and he will not run out of water.
¹⁷Your eyes will see the king in his beauty.
You will see the land that stretches far
away.
¹⁸You will think about the terror of the
past:
"Where is that officer?
Where is the one who collected the
taxes?
Where is the officer in charge of our
defense towers?"
¹⁹No longer will you see those proud
people from other countries,
whose strange language you couldn't
understand.

God Will Protect Jerusalem

²⁰Look at Jerusalem, the city of our
festivals.
Look at Jerusalem, that beautiful place
of rest.
It is like a tent that will never be moved;
the pegs that hold her in place will
never be pulled up,
and her ropes will never be broken.
²¹There the LORD will be our Mighty One.
That land is a place with streams and
wide rivers,

but there will be no enemy boats on
those rivers;
no powerful ship will sail on them.
²²This is because the LORD is our judge.
The LORD makes our laws.
The LORD is our king.
He will save us.
²³You sailors from other lands, hear:
The ropes on your boats hang loose.
The mast is not held firm.
The sails are not spread open.
Then your great wealth will be divided.
There will be so much wealth that even
the crippled people will carry off a
share.
²⁴No one living in Jerusalem will say, "I am
sick."
The people who live there will have
their sins forgiven.

God Will Punish His Enemies

34 All you nations, come near and listen.
Pay attention, you peoples!
The earth and all the people in it should
listen,
the world and everything in it.
²The LORD is angry with all the nations;
he is angry with their armies.
He will destroy them and kill them all.
³Their bodies will be thrown outside.
The stink will rise from the bodies,
and the blood will flow down the
mountains.
⁴The sun, moon, and stars will dissolve,
and the sky will be rolled up like a scroll.
The stars will fall
like dead leaves from a vine
or dried-up figs from a fig tree.
⁵The LORD's sword in the sky is covered
with blood.
It will cut through Edom
and destroy those people as an offering
to the LORD.
⁶The LORD's sword will be covered with
blood;
it will be covered with fat,
with the blood from lambs and goats,
with the fat from the kidneys of sheep.
This is because the LORD decided there
will be a sacrifice in Bozrah
and much killing in Edom.

⁷The oxen will be killed,
and the cattle and the strong bulls.
The land will be filled with their blood,
and the dirt will be covered with their
fat.
⁸The LORD has chosen a time for
punishment.
He has chosen a year when people must
pay for the wrongs they did to
Jerusalem.
⁹Edom's rivers will be like hot tar.
Its dirt will be like burning sulfur.
Its land will be like burning tar.
¹⁰The fires will burn night and day;
the smoke will rise from Edom forever.
Year after year that land will be empty;
no one will ever travel through that
land again.
¹¹Birds and small animals will own that
land,
and owls and ravens will live there.
God will make it an empty wasteland;
it will have nothing left in it.
¹²The important people will have no one
left to rule them;
the leaders will all be gone.
¹³Thorns will take over the strong towers,
and wild bushes will grow in the walled
cities.
It will be a home for wild dogs
and a place for owls to live.
¹⁴Desert animals will live with the hyenas,
and wild goats will call to their friends.
Night animals will live there
and find a place of rest.
¹⁵Owls will nest there and lay eggs.
When they hatch open, the owls will
gather their young under their
wings.
Hawks will gather
with their own kind.
¹⁶Look at the LORD's scroll and read what
is written there:
None of these will be missing;
none will be without its mate.
God has given the command,
so his Spirit will gather them together.
¹⁷God has divided the land among them,
and he has given them each their
portion.

So they will own that land forever
and will live there year after year.

PSALM 109:1–5

A Prayer Against an Enemy

For the director of music. A psalm of David.

109 God, I praise you.
Do not be silent.
[2] Wicked people and liars have spoken
against me;
they have told lies about me.
[3] They have said hateful things about me
and attack me for no reason.
[4] They attacked me, even though I loved
them
and prayed for them.
[5] I was good to them, but they repay me
with evil.
I loved them, but they hate me in
return.

PROVERBS 25:25–26

[25] Good news from a faraway place
is like a cool drink when you are tired.

[26] A good person who gives in to evil
is like a muddy spring or a dirty well.

2 CORINTHIANS 12:1–21

A Special Blessing in Paul's Life

12 I must continue to brag. It will do no
good, but I will talk now about visions
and revelations[n] from the Lord. [2] I know a
man in Christ who was taken up to the third
heaven fourteen years ago. I do not know
whether the man was in his body or out of
his body, but God knows. [3-4] And I know that
this man was taken up to paradise.[n] I don't
know if he was in his body or away from his
body, but God knows. He heard things he is
not able to explain, things that no human is
allowed to tell. [5] I will brag about a man like
that, but I will not brag about myself, except
about my weaknesses. [6] But if I wanted to
brag about myself, I would not be a fool, because I would be telling the truth. But I will

not brag about myself. I do not want people
to think more of me than what they see me
do or hear me say.
[7] So that I would not become too proud of
the wonderful things that were shown to me,
a painful physical problem[n] was given to me.
This problem was a messenger from Satan,
sent to beat me and keep me from being too
proud. [8] I begged the Lord three times to take
this problem away from me. [9] But he said to
me, "My grace is enough for you. When you
are weak, my power is made perfect in you."
So I am very happy to brag about my weaknesses. Then Christ's power can live in me.
[10] For this reason I am happy when I have
weaknesses, insults, hard times, sufferings,
and all kinds of troubles for Christ. Because
when I am weak, then I am truly strong.

Paul's Love for the Christians

[11] I have been talking like a fool, but you
made me do it. You are the ones who should
say good things about me. I am worth nothing, but those "great apostles" are not worth
any more than I am!
[12] When I was with you, I patiently did the
things that prove I am an apostle—signs,
wonders, and miracles. [13] So you received
everything that the other churches have received. Only one thing was different: I was
not a burden to you. Forgive me for this!
[14] I am now ready to visit you the third
time, and I will not be a burden to you. I
want nothing from you, except you. Children
should not have to save up to give to their
parents. Parents should save to give to their
children. [15] So I am happy to give everything
I have for you, even myself. If I love you
more, will you love me less?
[16] It is clear I was not a burden to you, but
you think I was tricky and lied to catch you.
[17] Did I cheat you by using any of the messengers I sent to you? No, you know I did not.
[18] I asked Titus to go to you, and I sent our
brother with him. Titus did not cheat you,
did he? No, you know that Titus and I did the
same thing and with the same spirit.
[19] Do you think we have been defending
ourselves to you all this time? We have been

12:1 revelations Revelation is making known a truth that was hidden.   **12:3–4 paradise** Another word for heaven.
12:7 painful physical problem Literally, "thorn in the flesh."

speaking in Christ and before God. You are our dear friends, and everything we do is to make you stronger. [20]I am afraid that when I come, you will not be what I want you to be, and I will not be what you want me to be. I am afraid that among you there may be arguing, jealousy, anger, selfish fighting, evil talk, gossip, pride, and confusion. [21]I am afraid that when I come to you again, my God will make me ashamed before you. I may be saddened by many of those who have sinned because they have not changed their hearts or turned from their sexual sins and the shameful things they have done.

SEPTEMBER 22

ISAIAH 35:1—36:22

God Will Comfort His People

35The desert and dry land will become happy;
   the desert will be glad and will produce flowers.
Like a flower, [2]it will have many blooms.
   It will show its happiness, as if it were shouting with joy.
It will be beautiful like the forest of Lebanon,
   as beautiful as the hill of Carmel and the Plain of Sharon.
Everyone will see the glory of the LORD
   and the splendor of our God.
[3]Make the weak hands strong
   and the weak knees steady.
[4]Say to people who are frightened,
   "Be strong. Don't be afraid.
Look, your God will come,
   and he will punish your enemies.
He will make them pay for the wrongs they did,
   but he will save you."

[5]Then the blind people will see again,
   and the deaf will hear.
[6]Crippled people will jump like deer,
   and those who can't talk now will shout with joy.
Water will flow in the desert,
   and streams will flow in the dry land.
[7]The burning desert will have pools of water,
   and the dry ground will have springs.
Where wild dogs once lived,
   grass and water plants will grow.

[8]A road will be there;
   this highway will be called "The Road to Being Holy."
Evil people will not be allowed to walk on that road;
   only good people will walk on it.
No fools will go on it.
[9]No lions will be there,
   nor will dangerous animals be on that road.
They will not be found there.
That road will be for the people God saves;
[10]the people the LORD has freed will return there.
They will enter Jerusalem with joy,
   and their happiness will last forever.
Their gladness and joy will fill them completely,
   and sorrow and sadness will go far away.

The Assyrians Invade Judah

36During Hezekiah's fourteenth year as king, Sennacherib king of Assyria attacked all the strong, walled cities of Judah and captured them. [2]The king of Assyria sent out his field commander with a large army from Lachish to King Hezekiah in Jerusalem. When the commander came near the waterway from the upper pool on the road where people do their laundry, he stopped. [3]Eliakim, Shebna, and Joah went out to meet him. Eliakim son of Hilkiah was the palace manager, Shebna was the royal secretary, and Joah son of Asaph was the recorder.
[4]The field commander said to them, "Tell Hezekiah this:

"'The great king, the king of Assyria, says: What can you trust in now? ⁵You say you have battle plans and power for war, but your words mean nothing. Whom are you trusting for help so that you turn against me? ⁶Look, you are depending on Egypt to help you, but Egypt is like a splintered walking stick. If you lean on it for help, it will stab your hand and hurt you. The king of Egypt will hurt all those who depend on him. ⁷You might say, "We are depending on the LORD our God," but Hezekiah destroyed the LORD's altars and the places of worship. Hezekiah told Judah and Jerusalem, "You must worship only at this one altar."

⁸"'Now make an agreement with my master, the king of Assyria: I will give you two thousand horses if you can find enough men to ride them. ⁹You cannot defeat one of my master's least important officers, so why do you depend on Egypt to give you chariots and horsemen? ¹⁰I have not come to attack and destroy this country without an order from the LORD. The LORD himself told me to come to this country and destroy it.'"

¹¹Then Eliakim, Shebna, and Joah said to the field commander, "Please speak to us in the Aramaic language. We understand it. Don't speak to us in Hebrew, because the people on the city wall can hear you."

¹²But the commander said, "My master did not send me to tell these things only to you and your king. He sent me to speak also to those people sitting on the wall who will have to eat their own dung and drink their own urine like you."

¹³Then the commander stood and shouted loudly in the Hebrew language, "Listen to what the great king, the king of Assyria says, ¹⁴The king says you should not let Hezekiah fool you, because he can't save you. ¹⁵Don't let Hezekiah talk you into trusting the LORD by saying, 'The LORD will surely save us. This city won't be handed over to the king of Assyria.'

¹⁶"Don't listen to Hezekiah. The king of Assyria says, 'Make peace with me, and come out of the city to me. Then everyone will be free to eat the fruit from his own grapevine and fig tree and to drink water from his own well. ¹⁷After that I will come and take you to a land like your own—a land with grain and new wine, bread and vineyards.'

¹⁸"Don't let Hezekiah fool you, saying, 'The LORD will save us.' Has a god of any other nation saved his people from the power of the king of Assyria? ¹⁹Where are the gods of Hamath and Arpad? Where are the gods of Sepharvaim? They did not save Samaria from my power. ²⁰Not one of all the gods of these countries has saved his people from me. Neither can the LORD save Jerusalem from my power."

²¹The people were silent. They didn't answer the commander at all, because King Hezekiah had ordered, "Don't answer him."

²²Then Eliakim, Shebna, and Joah tore their clothes to show how upset they were. (Eliakim son of Hilkiah was the palace manager, Shebna was the royal secretary, and Joah son of Asaph was the recorder.) The three men went to Hezekiah and told him what the field commander had said.

PSALM 109:6–15

⁶They say about me, "Have an evil person
    work against him,
  and let an accuser stand against him.
⁷When he is judged, let him be found
    guilty,
  and let even his prayers show his guilt.
⁸Let his life be cut short,
  and let another man replace him as
    leader.
⁹Let his children become orphans
  and his wife a widow.
¹⁰Make his children wander around,
    begging for food.
  Let them be forced out of the ruins in
    which they live.
¹¹Let the people to whom he owes money
    take everything he owns,
  and let strangers steal everything he
    has worked for.
¹²Let no one show him love
  or have mercy on his orphaned children.
¹³Let all his descendants die
  and be forgotten by those who live after
    him.
¹⁴LORD, remember how wicked his
    ancestors were,

and don't let the sins of his mother be
wiped out.
[15]LORD, always remember their sins.
    Then make people forget about them
    completely.

PROVERBS 25:27–28

[27]It is not good to eat too much honey,
    nor does it bring you honor to brag
    about yourself.

[28]Those who do not control themselves
    are like a city whose walls are broken
    down.

2 CORINTHIANS 13:1–14

Final Warnings and Greetings

13I will come to you for the third time.
"Every case must be proved by two or
three witnesses."[n] [2]When I was with you the
second time, I gave a warning to those who
had sinned. Now I am away from you, and I
give a warning to all the others. When I come
to you again, I will not be easy with them.
[3]You want proof that Christ is speaking
through me. My proof is that he is not weak
among you, but he is powerful. [4]It is true that
he was weak when he was killed on the
cross, but he lives now by God's power. It is
true that we are weak in Christ, but for you
we will be alive in Christ by God's power.

[5]Look closely at yourselves. Test yourselves to see if you are living in the faith. You
know that Jesus Christ is in you—unless you
fail the test. [6]But I hope you will see that we
ourselves have not failed the test. [7]We pray to
God that you will not do anything wrong. It
is not important to see that we have passed
the test, but it is important that you do what
is right, even if it seems we have failed. [8]We
cannot do anything against the truth, but
only for the truth. [9]We are happy to be weak,
if you are strong, and we pray that you will
become complete. [10]I am writing this while I
am away from you so that when I come I will
not have to be harsh in my use of authority.
The Lord gave me this authority to build you
up, not to tear you down.

[11]Now, brothers and sisters, I say good-
bye. Live in harmony. Do what I have asked
you to do. Agree with each other, and live in
peace. Then the God of love and peace will
be with you.

[12]Greet each other with a holy kiss. [13]All of
God's holy people send greetings to you.

[14]The grace of the Lord Jesus Christ, the
love of God, and the fellowship of the Holy
Spirit be with you all.

SEPTEMBER 23

ISAIAH 37:1—38:22

Hezekiah Asks God to Help

37When King Hezekiah heard the message, he tore his clothes and put on
rough cloth to show how sad he was. Then he
went into the Temple of the LORD. [2]Hezekiah
sent Eliakim, the palace manager, and
Shebna, the royal secretary, and the older
priests to Isaiah. They were all wearing
rough cloth when they came to Isaiah the
prophet, the son of Amoz. [3]They told Isaiah,
"This is what Hezekiah says: Today is a day
of sorrow and punishment and disgrace, as
when a child should be born, but the mother
is not strong enough to give birth to it. [4]The
king of Assyria sent his field commander to
make fun of the living God. Maybe the LORD
your God will hear what the commander
said and will punish him for it. So pray for
the few of us who are left alive."

[5]When Hezekiah's officers came to Isaiah,
[6]he said to them, "Tell your master this: The
LORD says, 'Don't be afraid of what you have
heard. Don't be frightened by the words the
servants of the king of Assyria have spoken
against me. [7]Listen! I am going to put a spirit
in the king of Assyria. He will hear a report

that will make him return to his own country, and I will cause him to die by the sword there.'"

⁸The field commander heard that the king of Assyria had left Lachish. When he went back, he found the king fighting against the city of Libnah.

⁹The king received a report that Tirhakah, the Cushite king of Egypt, was coming to attack him. When the king of Assyria heard this, he sent messengers to Hezekiah, saying, ¹⁰"Tell Hezekiah king of Judah: Don't be fooled by the god you trust. Don't believe him when he says Jerusalem will not be handed over to the king of Assyria. ¹¹You have heard what the kings of Assyria have done. They have completely defeated every country, so do not think you will be saved. ¹²Did the gods of those people save them? My ancestors destroyed them, defeating the cities of Gozan, Haran, and Rezeph, and the people of Eden living in Tel Assar. ¹³Where are the kings of Hamath and Arpad? Where are the kings of Sepharvaim, Hena, and Ivvah?"

Hezekiah Prays to the Lord

¹⁴When Hezekiah received the letter from the messengers and read it, he went up to the Temple of the LORD. He spread the letter out before the LORD ¹⁵and prayed to the LORD: ¹⁶"LORD All-Powerful, you are the God of Israel, whose throne is between the gold creatures with wings, only you are God of all the kingdoms of the earth. You made the heavens and the earth. ¹⁷Hear, LORD, and listen. Open your eyes, LORD, and see. Listen to all the words Sennacherib has said to insult the living God. ¹⁸It is true, LORD, that the kings of Assyria have destroyed all these countries and their lands. ¹⁹They have thrown the gods of these nations into the fire, but they were only wood and rock statues that people made. So the kings have destroyed them. ²⁰Now, LORD our God, save us from the king's power so that all the kingdoms of the earth will know that you, LORD, are the only God."

The Lord Answers Hezekiah

²¹Then Isaiah son of Amoz sent a message to Hezekiah that said, "This is what the LORD, the God of Israel, says: 'You prayed to me about Sennacherib king of Assyria. ²²So this is what the LORD has said against Sennacherib:

The people of Jerusalem
hate you and make fun of you;
the people of Jerusalem
laugh at you as you run away.
²³You have insulted me and spoken against
me;
you have raised your voice against me.
You have a proud look on your face,
which is against me, the Holy One of
Israel!
²⁴You have sent your messengers to insult
the Lord.
You have said, "With my many chariots
I have gone to the tops of the mountains,
to the highest mountains of Lebanon.
I have cut down its tallest cedars
and its best pine trees.
I have gone to its greatest heights
and its best forests.
²⁵I have dug wells in foreign countries
and drunk water there.
By the soles of my feet,
I have dried up all the rivers of Egypt."

²⁶" 'King of Assyria, surely you have heard.
Long ago I, the LORD, planned these
things.
Long ago I designed them,
and now I have made them happen.
I allowed you to turn those strong,
walled cities
into piles of rocks.
²⁷The people in those cities were weak;
they were frightened and put to shame.
They were like grass in the field,
like tender, young grass,
like grass on the housetop
that is burned by the wind before it can
grow.

²⁸" 'I know when you rest,
when you come and go,
and how you rage against me.
²⁹Because you rage against me,
and because I have heard your proud
words,
I will put my hook in your nose
and my bit in your mouth.

Then I will force you to leave my country the same way you came.'

³⁰"Then the LORD said, 'Hezekiah, I will give you this sign:

This year you will eat the grain that
grows wild,
and the second year you will eat what
grows wild from that.
But in the third year, plant grain and
harvest it.
Plant vineyards and eat their fruit.
³¹Some of the people in the family of Judah
will escape.
Like plants that take root,
they will grow strong and have many
children.
³²A few people will come out of Jerusalem
alive;
a few from Mount Zion will live.
The strong love of the LORD All-Powerful
will make this happen.'

³³"So this is what the LORD says about the king of Assyria:

'He will not enter this city
or even shoot an arrow here.
He will not fight against it with shields
or build a ramp to attack the city walls.
³⁴He will return to his country the same
way he came,
and he will not enter this city,'
says the LORD.
³⁵'I will defend and save this city
for my sake and for David, my servant.'"

³⁶Then the angel of the LORD went out and killed one hundred eighty-five thousand men in the Assyrian camp. When the people got up early the next morning, they saw all the dead bodies. ³⁷So Sennacherib king of Assyria left and went back to Nineveh and stayed there.

³⁸One day as Sennacherib was worshiping in the temple of his god Nisroch, his sons Adrammelech and Sharezer killed him with a sword. Then they escaped to the land of Ararat. So Sennacherib's son Esarhaddon became king of Assyria.

Hezekiah's Illness

38 At that time Hezekiah became very sick; he was almost dead. The prophet Isaiah son of Amoz went to see him and told him, "This is what the LORD says: Make arrangements, because you are not going to live, but die."

²Hezekiah turned toward the wall and prayed to the LORD, ³"LORD, please remember that I have always obeyed you. I have given myself completely to you and have done what you said was right." Then Hezekiah cried loudly.

⁴Then the LORD spoke his word to Isaiah: ⁵"Go to Hezekiah and tell him: 'This is what the LORD, the God of your ancestor David, says: I have heard your prayer and seen your tears. So I will add fifteen years to your life. ⁶I will save you and this city from the king of Assyria; I will defend this city.

⁷"'The LORD will do what he says. This is the sign from the LORD to show you: ⁸The sun has made a shadow go down the stairway of Ahaz, but I will make it go back ten steps.'" So the shadow made by the sun went back up the ten steps it had gone down.

⁹After Hezekiah king of Judah got well, he wrote this song:

¹⁰I said, "I am in the middle of my life.
Do I have to go through the gates of
death?
Will I have the rest of my life taken
away from me?"
¹¹I said, "I will not see the LORD
in the land of the living again.
I will not again see the people
who live on the earth.
¹²Like a shepherd's tent,
my home has been pulled down and
taken from me.
I am finished
like the cloth a weaver rolls up and cuts
from the loom.ⁿ
In one day you brought me to this end.
¹³All night I cried loudly.
Like a lion, he crushed all my bones.
In one day you brought me to this end.
¹⁴I cried like a bird
and moaned like a dove.
My eyes became tired as I looked to the
heavens.
Lord, I have troubles. Please help me."

¹⁵What can I say?
The Lord told me what would happen
and then made it happen.

38:12 **loom** A machine for making cloth from thread.

I have had these troubles in my soul,
so now I will be humble all my life.
¹⁶Lord, because of you, people live.
Because of you, my spirit also lives;
you made me well and let me live.
¹⁷It was for my own good
that I had such troubles.
Because you love me very much,
you did not let me die
but threw my sins
far away.
¹⁸People in the place of the dead cannot
praise you;
those who have died cannot sing
praises to you;
those who die don't trust you
to help them.
¹⁹The people who are alive are the ones
who praise you.
They praise you as I praise you today.
A father should tell his children
that you provide help.
²⁰The LORD saved me,
so we will play songs on stringed
instruments
in the Temple of the LORD
all the days of our lives.
²¹Then Isaiah said, "Make a paste from
figs and put it on Hezekiah's boil. Then he
will get well." ²²Hezekiah then asked Isaiah,
"What will be the sign? What will show that
I will go up to the Temple of the LORD?"

PSALM 109:16–20

¹⁶"He did not remember to be loving.
He hurt the poor, the needy, and those
who were sad
until they were nearly dead.
¹⁷He loved to put curses on others,
so let those same curses fall on him.
He did not like to bless others,
so do not let good things happen to
him.
¹⁸He cursed others as often as he wore
clothes.
Cursing others filled his body and his
life,
like drinking water and using olive oil.

¹⁹So let curses cover him like clothes
and wrap around him like a belt."
²⁰May the LORD do these things to those
who accuse me,
to those who speak evil against me.

PROVERBS 26:1

26 It shouldn't snow in summer or rain
at harvest.
Neither should a foolish person ever be
honored.

GALATIANS 1:1–24

1 From Paul, an apostle. I was not chosen to
be an apostle by human beings, nor was I
sent from human beings. I was made an
apostle through Jesus Christ and God the Father who raised Jesus from the dead. ²This
letter is also from all those of God's family[n]
who are with me.
To the churches in Galatia:[n]
³Grace and peace to you from God our Father and the Lord Jesus Christ. ⁴Jesus gave
himself for our sins to free us from this evil
world we live in, as God the Father planned.
⁵The glory belongs to God forever and ever.
Amen.

The Only Good News

⁶God, by his grace through Christ, called
you to become his people. So I am amazed
that you are turning away so quickly and believing something different than the Good
News. ⁷Really, there is no other Good News.
But some people are confusing you; they
want to change the Good News of Christ. ⁸We
preached to you the Good News. So if we
ourselves, or even an angel from heaven,
should preach to you something different,
we should be judged guilty! ⁹I said this before, and now I say it again: You have already
accepted the Good News. If anyone is
preaching something different to you, let
that person be judged guilty!
¹⁰Do you think I am trying to make people accept me? No, God is the One I am trying to please. Am I trying to please people? If
I still wanted to please people, I would not be
a servant of Christ.

1:2 those . . . family The Greek text says "brothers." **1:2 Galatia** Probably the same country where Paul preached and began churches on his first missionary trip. Read the Book of Acts, chapters 13 and 14.

Paul's Authority Is from God

¹¹Brothers and sisters, I want you to know that the Good News I preached to you was not made up by human beings. ¹²I did not get it from humans, nor did anyone teach it to me, but Jesus Christ showed it to me.

¹³You have heard about my past life in the Jewish religion. I attacked the church of God and tried to destroy it. ¹⁴I was becoming a leader in the Jewish religion, doing better than most other Jews of my age. I tried harder than anyone else to follow the teachings handed down by our ancestors.

¹⁵But God had special plans for me and set me apart for his work even before I was born. He called me through his grace ¹⁶and showed his son to me so that I might tell the Good News about him to those who are not Jewish. When God called me, I did not get advice or help from any person. ¹⁷I did not go to Jerusalem to see those who were apostles before I was. But, without waiting, I went away to Arabia and later went back to Damascus.

¹⁸After three years I went to Jerusalem to meet Peter and stayed with him for fifteen days. ¹⁹I met no other apostles, except James, the brother of the Lord. ²⁰God knows that these things I write are not lies. ²¹Later, I went to the areas of Syria and Cilicia.

²²In Judea the churches in Christ had never met me. ²³They had only heard it said, "This man who was attacking us is now preaching the same faith that he once tried to destroy." ²⁴And these believers praised God because of me.

SEPTEMBER 24

ISAIAH 39:1—40:31

Messengers from Babylon

39At that time Merodach-Baladan son of Baladan was king of Babylon. He sent letters and a gift to Hezekiah, because he had heard that Hezekiah had been sick and was now well. ²Hezekiah was pleased and showed the messengers what was in his storehouses: the silver, gold, spices, expensive perfumes, his swords and shields, and all his wealth. He showed them everything in his palace and in his kingdom.

³Then Isaiah the prophet went to King Hezekiah and asked him, "What did these men say? Where did they come from?"

Hezekiah said, "They came from a faraway country—from Babylon."

⁴So Isaiah asked him, "What did they see in your palace?"

Hezekiah said, "They saw everything in my palace. I showed them all my wealth."

⁵Then Isaiah said to Hezekiah: "Listen to the words of the LORD All-Powerful: ⁶'In the future everything in your palace and everything your ancestors have stored up until this day will be taken away to Babylon. Nothing will be left,' says the LORD. ⁷Some of your own children, those who will be born to you, will be taken away, and they will become servants in the palace of the king of Babylon."

⁸Hezekiah told Isaiah, "These words from the LORD are good." He said this because he thought, "There will be peace and security in my lifetime."

Israel's Punishment Will End

40Your God says,
"Comfort, comfort my people.
²Speak kindly to the people of Jerusalem
    and tell them
that their time of service is finished,
    that they have paid for their sins,
that the LORD has punished Jerusalem
    twice for every sin they did."
³This is the voice of one who calls out:
"Prepare in the desert
    the way for the LORD.
Make a straight road in the dry lands
    for our God.
⁴Every valley should be raised up,
    and every mountain and hill should be
        made flat.
The rough ground should be made level,

and the rugged ground should be made
   smooth.
⁵Then the glory of the Lᴏʀᴅ will be shown,
   and all people together will see it.
The Lᴏʀᴅ himself said these things."

⁶A voice says, "Cry out!"
   Then I said, "What shall I cry out?"
"Say all people are like the grass,
   and all their glory is like the flowers of
      the field.
⁷The grass dies and the flowers fall
   when the breath of the Lᴏʀᴅ blows on
      them.
Surely the people are like grass.
⁸The grass dies and the flowers fall,
   but the word of our God will live
      forever."
⁹Jerusalem, you have good news to tell.
   Go up on a high mountain.
Jerusalem, you have good news to tell.
   Shout out loud the good news.
Shout it out and don't be afraid.
   Say to the towns of Judah,
   "Here is your God."
¹⁰Look, the Lord Gᴏᴅ is coming with power
   to rule all the people.
Look, he will bring reward for his people;
   he will have their payment with him.
¹¹He takes care of his people like a
      shepherd.
He gathers them like lambs in his arms
   and carries them close to him.
He gently leads the mothers of the
      lambs.

God Is Supreme

¹²Who has measured the oceans in the
   palm of his hand?
Who has used his hand to measure the
      sky?
Who has used a bowl to measure all the
   dust of the earth
   and scales to weigh the mountains and
      hills?
¹³Who has known the mind of the Lᴏʀᴅ
   or been able to give him advice?
¹⁴Whom did he ask for help?
   Who taught him the right way?
Who taught him knowledge
   and showed him the way to
      understanding?

¹⁵The nations are like one small drop in a
      bucket;
   they are no more than the dust on his
      measuring scales.
To him the islands are no more than
   fine dust on his scales.
¹⁶All the trees in Lebanon are not enough
   for the altar fires,
   and all the animals in Lebanon are not
      enough for burnt offerings.
¹⁷Compared to the Lᴏʀᴅ all the nations are
   worth nothing;
   to him they are less than nothing.
¹⁸Can you compare God to anything?
   Can you compare him to an image of
      anything?
¹⁹An idol is formed by a craftsman,
   and a goldsmith covers it with gold
   and makes silver chains for it.
²⁰A poor person cannot buy those
      expensive statues,
   so he finds a tree that will not rot.
Then he finds a skilled craftsman
   to make it into an idol that will not fall
      over.

²¹Surely you know. Surely you have heard.
   Surely from the beginning someone
      told you.
Surely you understand how the earth
      was created.
²²God sits on his throne above the circle of
   the earth,
   and compared to him, people are like
      grasshoppers.
He stretches out the skies like a piece of
   cloth
   and spreads them out like a tent to sit
      under.
²³He makes rulers unimportant
   and the judges of this world worth
      nothing.
²⁴They are like plants that are placed in the
      ground,
   like seeds that are planted.
As soon as they begin to grow strong,
   he blows on them and they die,
   and the wind blows them away like chaff.

²⁵God, the Holy One, says, "Can you
      compare me to anyone?
   Is anyone equal to me?"

26Look up to the skies.
Who created all these stars?
He leads out the army of heaven one by
one
and calls all the stars by name.
Because he is strong and powerful,
not one of them is missing.

27People of Jacob, why do you complain?
People of Israel, why do you say,
"The LORD does not see what happens to
me;
he does not care if I am treated fairly"?
28Surely you know.
Surely you have heard.
The LORD is the God who lives forever,
who created all the world.
He does not become tired or need to rest.
No one can understand how great his
wisdom is.
29He gives strength to those who are tired
and more power to those who are weak.
30Even children become tired and need to
rest,
and young people trip and fall.
31But the people who trust the LORD will
become strong again.
They will rise up as an eagle in the sky;
they will run and not need rest;
they will walk and not become tired.

PSALM 109:21-25

21But you, Lord GOD,
be kind to me so others will know you
are good.
Because your love is good, save me.
22I am poor and helpless
and very sad.
23I am dying like an evening shadow;
I am shaken off like a locust.
24My knees are weak from fasting,
and I have grown thin.
25My enemies insult me;
they look at me and shake their heads.

PROVERBS 26:2

2Curses will not harm someone who is
innocent;
they are like sparrows or swallows that
fly around and never land.

GALATIANS 2:1-21

Other Apostles Accepted Paul

2After fourteen years I went to Jerusalem
again, this time with Barnabas. I also took
Titus with me. 2I went because God showed
me I should go. I met with the believers there,
and in private I told their leaders the Good
News that I preach to the non-Jewish people.
I did not want my past work and the work I
am now doing to be wasted. 3Titus was with
me, but he was not forced to be circumcised,
even though he was a Greek. 4We talked about
this problem because some false believers
had come into our group secretly. They came
in like spies to overturn the freedom we have
in Christ Jesus. They wanted to make us
slaves. 5But we did not give in to those false
believers for a minute. We wanted the truth of
the Good News to continue for you.

6Those leaders who seemed to be important did not change the Good News that I
preach. (It doesn't matter to me if they were
"important" or not. To God everyone is the
same.) 7But these leaders saw that I had
been given the work of telling the Good
News to those who are not Jewish, just as Peter had the work of telling the Jews. 8God
gave Peter the power to work as an apostle
for the Jewish people. But he also gave me
the power to work as an apostle for those
who are not Jews. 9James, Peter, and John,
who seemed to be the leaders, understood
that God had given me this special grace, so
they accepted Barnabas and me. They
agreed that they would go to the Jewish people and that we should go to those who are
not Jewish. 10The only thing they asked us
was to remember to help the poor—something I really wanted to do.

Paul Shows that Peter Was Wrong

11When Peter came to Antioch, I challenged him to his face, because he was wrong.
12Peter ate with the non-Jewish people until
some Jewish people sent from James came to
Antioch. When they arrived, Peter stopped
eating with those who weren't Jewish, and he
separated himself from them. He was afraid
of the Jews. 13So Peter was a hypocrite, as were
the other Jewish believers who joined with
him. Even Barnabas was influenced by what

these Jewish believers did. [14]When I saw they were not following the truth of the Good News, I spoke to Peter in front of them all. I said, "Peter, you are a Jew, but you are not living like a Jew. You are living like those who are not Jewish. So why do you now try to force those who are not Jewish to live like Jews?"

[15]We were not born as non-Jewish "sinners," but as Jews. [16]Yet we know that a person is made right with God not by following the law, but by trusting in Jesus Christ. So we, too, have put our faith in Christ Jesus, that we might be made right with God because we trusted in Christ. It is not because we followed the law, because no one can be made right with God by following the law.

[17]We Jews came to Christ, trying to be made right with God, and it became clear that we are sinners, too. Does this mean that Christ encourages sin? No! [18]But I would really be wrong to begin teaching again those things that I gave up. [19]It was the law that put me to death, and I died to the law so that I can now live for God. [20]I was put to death on the cross with Christ, and I do not live anymore—it is Christ who lives in me. I still live in my body, but I live by faith in the Son of God who loved me and gave himself to save me. [21]By saying these things I am not going against God's grace. Just the opposite, if the law could make us right with God, then Christ's death would be useless.

SEPTEMBER 25

ISAIAH 41:1—42:25

The Lord Will Help Israel

41 The LORD says, "Faraway countries,
        listen to me.
    Let the nations become strong.
    Come to me and speak;
        we will meet together to decide who is
        right.

[2]"Who caused the one to come from the
        east?
    Who gives him victories everywhere he
        goes?
    The one who brought him gives nations
        over to him
        and defeats kings.
    He uses his sword, and kings become
        like dust.
    He uses his bow, and they are blown
        away like chaff.
[3]He chases them and is never hurt,
    going places he has never been before.
[4]Who caused this to happen?
    Who has controlled history since the
        beginning?
    I, the LORD, am the one. I was here at the
        beginning,
    and I will be here when all things are
        finished."

[5]All you faraway places, look and be afraid;
    all you places far away on the earth,
        shake with fear.
    Come close and listen to me.
[6] The workers help each other
    and say to each other, "Be strong!"
[7]The craftsman encourages the
        goldsmith,
    and the workman who smooths the
        metal with a hammer encourages
        the one who shapes the metal.
    He says, "This metal work is good."
    He nails the statue to a base so it can't
        fall over.

Only the Lord Can Save Us

[8]The LORD says, "People of Israel, you are
        my servants.
    People of Jacob, I chose you.
    You are from the family of my friend
        Abraham.
[9]I took you from places far away on the
        earth
    and called you from a faraway country.
    I said, 'You are my servants.'
    I have chosen you and have not turned
        against you.
[10]So don't worry, because I am with you.
    Don't be afraid, because I am your God.

I will make you strong and will help you;
I will support you with my right hand
that saves you.

11"All those people who are angry with you
will be ashamed and disgraced.
Those who are against you
will disappear and be lost.
12You will look for your enemies,
but you will not find them.
Those who fought against you
will vanish completely.
13I am the LORD your God,
who holds your right hand,
and I tell you, 'Don't be afraid.
I will help you.'
14You few people of Israel who are left,
do not be afraid even though you are
weak as a worm.
I myself will help you," says the LORD.
"The one who saves you is the Holy
One of Israel.
15Look, I have made you like a new
threshing board
with many sharp teeth.
So you will walk on mountains and
crush them;
you will make the hills like chaff.
16You will throw them into the air, and the
wind will carry them away;
a windstorm will scatter them.
Then you will be happy in the LORD;
you will be proud of the Holy One of
Israel.
17"The poor and needy people look for
water,
but they can't find any.
Their tongues are dry with thirst.
But I, the LORD, will answer their prayers;
I, the God of Israel, will not leave them
to die.
18I will make rivers flow on the dry hills
and springs flow through the valleys.
I will change the desert into a lake of
water
and the dry land into fountains of
water.
19I will make trees grow in the desert—
cedars, acacia, myrtle, and olive trees.

I will put pine, fir, and cypress trees
growing together in the desert.
20People will see these things and
understand;
they will think carefully about these
things and learn
that the LORD's power did this,
that the Holy One of Israel made these
things."

The Lord Challenges False Gods

21The LORD says, "Present your case."
The King of Jacob says, "Tell me your
arguments.
22Bring in your idols to tell us
what is going to happen.
Have them tell us what happened in the
beginning.
Then we will think about these things,
and we will know how they will turn
out.
Or tell us what will happen in the future.
23 Tell us what is coming next
so we will believe that you are gods.
Do something, whether it is good or bad,
and make us afraid.
24You gods are less than nothing;
you can't do anything.
Those who worship you should be hated.

25"I have brought someone to come out of
the north[n]
I have called by name a man from the
east, and he knows me.
He walks on kings as if they were mud,
just as a potter walks on the clay.
26Who told us about this before it
happened?
Who told us ahead of time so we could
say, 'He was right'?
None of you told us anything;
none of you told us before it happened;
no one heard you tell about it.
27I, the LORD, was the first one to tell
Jerusalem that the people were
coming home.
I sent a messenger to Jerusalem with
the good news.
28I look at the idols, but there is not one
that can answer.

41:25 someone . . . north This probably means Cyrus, a king of Persia.

None of them can give advice;
none of them can answer my questions.
²⁹Look, all these idols are false.
They cannot do anything;
they are worth nothing.

The Lord's Special Servant

42 "Here is my servant, the one I support.
He is the one I chose, and I am
pleased with him.
I have put my Spirit upon him,
and he will bring justice to all nations.
²He will not cry out or yell
or speak loudly in the streets.
³He will not break a crushed blade of
grass
or put out even a weak flame.
He will truly bring justice;
⁴ he will not lose hope or give up
until he brings justice to the world.
And people far away will trust his
teachings."

⁵God, the LORD, said these things.
He created the skies and stretched them
out.
He spread out the earth and everything
on it.
He gives life to all people on earth,
to everyone who walks on the earth.
⁶The LORD says, "I, the LORD, called you to
do right,
and I will hold your hand
and protect you.
You will be the sign of my agreement
with the people,
a light to shine for all people.
⁷You will help the blind to see.
You will free those who are in prison,
and you will lead those who live in
darkness out of their prison.

⁸"I am the LORD. That is my name.
I will not give my glory to another;
I will not let idols take the praise that
should be mine.
⁹The things I said would happen have
happened,
and now I tell you about new things.
Before those things happen,
I tell you about them."

A Song of Praise to the Lord

¹⁰Sing a new song to the LORD;
sing his praise everywhere on the
earth.
Praise him, you people who sail on the
seas and you animals who live in
them.
Praise him, you people living in faraway
places.
¹¹The deserts and their cities should praise
him.
The settlements of Kedar should praise
him.
The people living in Sela should sing for
joy;
they should shout from the
mountaintops.
¹²They should give glory to the LORD.
People in faraway lands should praise
him.
¹³The LORD will march out like a strong
soldier;
he will be excited like a man ready to
fight a war.
He will shout out the battle cry
and defeat his enemies.

¹⁴The LORD says, "For a long time I have
said nothing;
I have been quiet and held myself back.
But now I will cry out
and strain like a woman giving birth to
a child.
¹⁵I will destroy the hills and mountains
and dry up all their plants.
I will make the rivers become dry land
and dry up the pools of water.
¹⁶Then I will lead the blind along a way
they never knew;
I will guide them along paths they have
not known.
I will make the darkness become light
for them,
and the rough ground smooth.
These are the things I will do;
I will not leave my people.
¹⁷But those who trust in idols,
who say to their statues,
'You are our gods'
will be rejected in disgrace.

Israel Refused to Listen to the Lord

18"You who are deaf, hear me.
   You who are blind, look and see.
19No one is more blind than my servant
      Israel
   or more deaf than the messenger I send.
   No one is more blind than the person I
      own
   or more blind than the servant of the
      LORD.
20Israel, you have seen much, but you have
      not obeyed.
   You hear, but you refuse to listen."
21The LORD made his teachings wonderful,
      because he is good.
22These people have been defeated and
      robbed.
   They are trapped in pits
      or locked up in prison.
   Like robbers, enemies have taken them
      away,
   and there is no one to save them.
   Enemies carried them off,
      and no one said, "Bring them back."

23Will any of you listen to this?
   Will you listen carefully in the future?
24Who let the people of Jacob be carried
      off?
   Who let robbers take Israel away?
   The LORD allowed this to happen,
      because we sinned against him.
   We did not live the way he wanted us to
      live
   and did not obey his teaching.
25So he became very angry with us
      and brought terrible wars against us.
   It was as if the people of Israel had fire
      all around them,
   but they didn't know what was
      happening.
   It was as if they were burning,
      but they didn't pay any attention.

PSALM 109:26–31

26LORD my God, help me;
      because you are loving, save me.
27Then they will know that your power has
      done this;

they will know that you have done it,
   LORD.
28They may curse me, but you bless me.
   They may attack me, but they will be
      disgraced.
   Then I, your servant, will be glad.
29Let those who accuse me be disgraced
      and covered with shame like a coat.

30I will thank the LORD very much;
   I will praise him in front of many
      people.
31He defends the helpless
      and saves them from those who accuse
      them.

PROVERBS 26:3–4

3Whips are for horses, and harnesses are
      for donkeys,
   so paddles are good for fools.

4Don't answer fools when they speak
      foolishly,
   or you will be just like them.

GALATIANS 3:1—4:7

Blessing Comes Through Faith

3 You people in Galatia were told very clearly about the death of Jesus Christ on the cross. But you were foolish; you let someone trick you. 2Tell me this one thing: How did you receive the Holy Spirit? Did you receive the Spirit by following the law? No, you received the Spirit because you heard the Good News and believed it. 3You began your life in Christ by the Spirit. Now are you trying to make it complete by your own power? That is foolish. 4Were all your experiences wasted? I hope not! 5Does God give you the Spirit and work miracles among you because you follow the law? No, he does these things because you heard the Good News and believed it.

6The Scriptures say the same thing about Abraham: "Abraham believed God, and God accepted Abraham's faith, and that faith made him right with God."n 7So you should know that the true children of Abraham are those who have faith. 8The Scriptures, telling

3:6 "Abraham . . . God." Quotation from Genesis 15:6.

what would happen in the future, said that God would make the non-Jewish people right through their faith. This Good News was told to Abraham beforehand, as the Scripture says: "All nations will be blessed through you."[n] [9]So all who believe as Abraham believed are blessed just as Abraham was. [10]But those who depend on following the law to make them right are under a curse, because the Scriptures say, "Anyone will be cursed who does not always obey what is written in the Book of the Law."[n] [11]Now it is clear that no one can be made right with God by the law, because the Scriptures say, "Those who are right with God will live by faith."[n] [12]The law is not based on faith. It says, "A person who obeys these things will live because of them."[n] [13]Christ took away the curse the law put on us. He changed places with us and put himself under that curse. It is written in the Scriptures, "Anyone whose body is displayed on a tree[n] is cursed." [14]Christ did this so that God's blessing promised to Abraham might come through Jesus Christ to those who are not Jews. Jesus died so that by our believing we could receive the Spirit that God promised.

The Law and the Promise

[15]Brothers and sisters, let us think in human terms: Even an agreement made between two persons is firm. After that agreement is accepted by both people, no one can stop it or add anything to it. [16]God made promises both to Abraham and to his descendant. God did not say, "and to your descendants." That would mean many people. But God said, "and to your descendant." That means only one person; that person is Christ. [17]This is what I mean: God had an agreement with Abraham and promised to keep it. The law, which came four hundred thirty years later, cannot change that agreement and so destroy God's promise to Abraham. [18]If the law could give us Abraham's blessing, then the promise would not be necessary. But that is not possible, because God

freely gave his blessings to Abraham through the promise he had made.

[19]So what was the law for? It was given to show that the wrong things people do are against God's will. And it continued until the special descendant, who had been promised, came. The law was given through angels who used Moses for a mediator[n] to give the law to people. [20]But a mediator is not needed when there is only one side, and God is only one.

The Purpose of the Law of Moses

[21]Does this mean that the law is against God's promises? Never! That would be true only if the law could make us right with God. But God did not give a law that can bring life. [22]Instead, the Scriptures showed that the whole world is bound by sin. This was so the promise would be given through faith to people who believe in Jesus Christ.

[23]Before this faith came, we were all held prisoners by the law. We had no freedom until God showed us the way of faith that was coming. [24]In other words, the law was our guardian leading us to Christ so that we could be made right with God through faith. [25]Now the way of faith has come, and we no longer live under a guardian.

[26-27]You were all baptized into Christ, and so you were all clothed with Christ. This means that you are all children of God through faith in Christ Jesus. [28]In Christ, there is no difference between Jew and Greek, slave and free person, male and female. You are all the same in Christ Jesus. [29]You belong to Christ, so you are Abraham's descendants. You will inherit all of God's blessings because of the promise God made to Abraham.

4 I want to tell you this: While those who will inherit their fathers' property are still children, they are no different from slaves. It does not matter that the children own everything. [2]While they are children, they must obey those who are chosen to care for them. But when the children reach the age set by their fathers, they are free. [3]It is the same for us. We were once like children, slaves to the

---

3:8 "All . . . you." Quotation from Genesis 12:3 and 18:18.   **3:10 "Anyone . . . Law."** Quotation from Deuteronomy 27:26.
3:11 "Those . . . faith." Quotation from Habakkuk 2:4.   **3:12 "A person . . . them."** Quotation from Leviticus 18:5.
3:13 displayed on a tree Deuteronomy 21:22–23 says that when a person was killed for doing wrong, the body was hung on a tree to show shame. Paul means that the cross of Jesus was like that.   **3:19 mediator** A person who helps one person talk to or give something to another person.

useless rules of this world. [4]But when the right time came, God sent his Son who was born of a woman and lived under the law. [5]God did this so he could buy freedom for those who were under the law and so we could become his children.

[6]Since you are God's children, God sent the Spirit of his Son into your hearts, and the Spirit cries out, "Father."[n] [7]So now you are not a slave; you are God's child, and God will give you the blessing he promised, because you are his child.

SEPTEMBER 26

ISAIAH 43:1—44:28

God Is Always with His People

43 [1]Now this is what the LORD says.
He created you, people of Jacob;
he formed you, people of Israel.
He says, "Don't be afraid, because I have
saved you.
I have called you by name, and you are
mine.
[2]When you pass through the waters, I will
be with you.
When you cross rivers, you will not
drown.
When you walk through fire, you will not
be burned,
nor will the flames hurt you.
[3]This is because I, the LORD, am your God,
the Holy One of Israel, your Savior.
I gave Egypt to pay for you,
and I gave Cush and Seba to make you
mine.
[4]Because you are precious to me,
because I give you honor and love you,
I will give other people in your place;
I will give other nations to save your
life.
[5]Don't be afraid, because I am with you.
I will bring your children from the east
and gather you from the west.
[6]I will tell the north: Give my people to
me.
I will tell the south: Don't keep my
people in prison.
Bring my sons from far away
and my daughters from faraway places.
[7]Bring to me all the people who are mine,

whom I made for my glory,
whom I formed and made."

Judah Is God's Witness

[8]Bring out the people who have eyes but
don't see
and those who have ears but don't hear.
[9]All the nations gather together,
and all the people come together.
Which of their gods said this would
happen?
Which of their gods can tell what
happened in the beginning?
Let them bring their witnesses to prove
they were right.
Then others will say, "It is true."
[10]The LORD says, "You are my witnesses
and the servant I chose.
I chose you so you would know and
believe me,
so you would understand that I am the
true God.
There was no God before me,
and there will be no God after me.
[11]I myself am the LORD;
I am the only Savior.
[12]I myself have spoken to you, saved you,
and told you these things.
It was not some foreign god among you.
You are my witnesses, and I am God,"
says the LORD.
[13] "I have always been God.
No one can save people from my power;
when I do something, no one can
change it."
[14]This is what the LORD, who saves you,
the Holy One of Israel, says:

4:6 "Father" Literally, "Abba, Father." Jewish children called their fathers "Abba."

"I will send armies to Babylon for you,
    and I will knock down all its locked
      gates.
  The Babylonians will shout their cries of
    sorrow.
¹⁵I am the LORD, your Holy One,
    the Creator of Israel, your King."

God Will Save His People Again

¹⁶This is what the LORD says.
  He is the one who made a road through
    the sea
  and a path through rough waters.
¹⁷He is the one who defeated the chariots
    and horses
    and the mighty armies.
  They fell together and will never rise
    again.
  They were destroyed as a flame is put
    out.
¹⁸The LORD says, "Forget what happened
    before,
  and do not think about the past.
¹⁹Look at the new thing I am going to do.
  It is already happening. Don't you see
    it?
  I will make a road in the desert
    and rivers in the dry land.
²⁰Even the wild animals will be thankful to
    me—
      the wild dogs and owls.
  They will honor me when I put water in
    the desert
  and rivers in the dry land
  to give water to my people, the ones I
    chose.
²¹The people I made
  will sing songs to praise me.

²²"People of Jacob, you have not called to
    me;
  people of Israel, you have become tired
    of me.
²³You have not brought me your sacrifices
    of sheep
  nor honored me with your sacrifices.
  I did not weigh you down with sacrifices
    to offer
  or make you tired with incense to
    burn.
²⁴So you did not buy incense for me;

  you did not freely bring me fat from
    your sacrifices.
  Instead you have weighed me down with
    your many sins;
  you have made me tired of your many
    wrongs.

²⁵"I, I am the One who erases all your sins,
    for my sake;
  I will not remember your sins.
²⁶But you should remind me.
  Let's meet and decide what is right.
  Tell what you have done and show you
    are right.
²⁷Your first father sinned,
  and your leaders have turned against
    me.
²⁸So I will make your holy rulers unholy.
  I will bring destruction on the people
    of Jacob,
  and I will let Israel be insulted."

The Lord Is the Only God

44 The LORD says, "People of Jacob, you
    are my servants. Listen to me!
  People of Israel, I chose you."
²This is what the LORD says, who made
    you,
  who formed you in your mother's body,
  who will help you:
  "People of Jacob, my servants, don't be
    afraid.
  Israel, I chose you.
³I will pour out water for the thirsty land
  and make streams flow on dry land.
  I will pour out my Spirit into your children
  and my blessing on your descendants.
⁴Your children will grow like a tree in the
    grass,
  like poplar trees growing beside
    streams of water.
⁵One person will say, 'I belong to the
    LORD,'
  and another will use the name Jacob.
  Another will sign his name 'I am the
    LORD's,'
  and another will use the name Israel."

⁶The LORD, the king of Israel,
  is the LORD All-Powerful, who saves
    Israel.

This is what he says: "I am the beginning and the end.

I am the only God.

[7]Who is a god like me?

That god should come and prove it.

Let him tell and explain all that has happened since I set up my ancient people.

He should also tell what will happen in the future.

[8]Don't be afraid! Don't worry!

I have always told you what will happen.

You are my witnesses.

There is no other God but me.

I know of no other Rock; I am the only One."

Idols Are Useless

[9]Some people make idols, but they are worth nothing.

People treasure them, but they are useless.

Those people are witnesses for the statues, but those people cannot see.

They know nothing, so they will be ashamed.

[10]Who made these gods?

Who made these useless idols?

[11]The workmen who made them will be ashamed,

because they are only human.

If they all would come together,

they would all be ashamed and afraid.

[12]One workman uses tools to heat iron,

and he works over hot coals.

With his hammer he beats the metal and makes a statue,

using his powerful arms.

But when he becomes hungry, he loses his power.

If he does not drink water, he becomes tired.

[13]Another workman uses a line and a compass

to draw on the wood.

Then he uses his chisels to cut a statue

and his calipers to measure the statue.

In this way, the workman makes the wood look exactly like a person,

and this statue of a person sits in the house.

[14]He cuts down cedars

or cypress or oak trees.

Those trees grew by their own power in the forest.

Or he plants a pine tree, and the rain makes it grow.

[15]Then he burns the tree.

He uses some of the wood for a fire to keep himself warm.

He also starts a fire to bake his bread.

But he uses part of the wood to make a god, and then he worships it!

He makes the idol and bows down to it!

[16]The man burns half of the wood in the fire.

He uses the fire to cook his meat,

and he eats the meat until he is full.

He also burns the wood to keep himself warm. He says,

"Good! Now I am warm. I can see because of the fire's light."

[17]But he makes a statue from the wood that is left and calls it his god.

He bows down to it and worships it.

He prays to it and says,

"You are my god. Save me!"

[18]Those people don't know what they are doing. They don't understand!

It is as if their eyes are covered so they can't see.

Their minds don't understand.

[19]They have not thought about these things;

they don't understand.

They have never thought to themselves,

"I burned half of the wood in the fire

and used the hot coals to bake my bread.

I cooked and ate my meat.

And I used the wood that was left to make this hateful thing.

I am worshiping a block of wood!"

[20]He doesn't know what he is doing;

his confused mind leads him the wrong way.

He cannot save himself

or say, "This statue I am holding is a false god."

The Lord Is the True God

21"People of Jacob, remember these things!
  People of Israel, remember you are my
    servants.
  I made you, and you are my servants.
  So Israel, I will not forget you.
22I have swept away your sins like a big
    cloud;
  I have removed your sins like a cloud
    that disappears into the air.
  Come back to me because I saved you."

23Skies, sing for joy because the LORD did
    great things!
  Earth, shout for joy, even in your
    deepest parts!
  Sing, you mountains, with thanks to
    God.
  Sing, too, you trees in the forest!
  The LORD saved the people of Jacob!
  He showed his glory when he saved
    Israel.
24This is what the LORD says, who saved
    you,
  who formed you in your mother's
    body:
  "I, the LORD, made everything,
  stretching out the skies by myself
  and spreading out the earth all alone.
25I show that the signs of the lying
    prophets are false;
  I make fools of those who do magic.
  I confuse even the wise;
  they think they know much, but I make
    them look foolish.
26I make the messages of my servants
    come true;
  I make the advice of my messengers
    come true.
  I say to Jerusalem,
    'People will live in you again!'
  I say to the towns of Judah,
    'You will be built again!'
  I say to Jerusalem's ruins,
    'I will repair you.'
27I tell the deep waters, 'Become dry!
  I will make your streams become dry!'
28I say of Cyrus,n 'He is my shepherd

and will do all that I want him to do.
  He will say to Jerusalem, "You will be
    built again!"
  He will tell the Temple, "Your
    foundations will be rebuilt."'"

PSALM 110:1–7

The Lord Appoints a King

A psalm of David.

110 The LORD said to my Lord,
  "Sit by me at my right side
  until I put your enemies under your
    control."
2The LORD will enlarge your kingdom
    beyond Jerusalem,
  and you will rule over your enemies.
3Your people will join you on your day of
    battle.
  You have been dressed in holiness from
    birth;
  you have the freshness of a child.
4The LORD has made a promise
  and will not change his mind.
  He said, "You are a priest forever,
  a priest like Melchizedek."

5The Lord is beside you to help you.
  When he becomes angry, he will crush
    kings.
6He will judge those nations, filling them
    with dead bodies;
  he will defeat rulers all over the world.
7The king will drink from the brook on
    the way.
  Then he will be strengthened.

PROVERBS 26:5–9

5Answer fools when they speak foolishly,
  or they will think they are really wise.

6Sending a message by a foolish person
  is like cutting off your feet or drinking
    poison.

7A wise saying spoken by a fool
  is as useless as the legs of a crippled
    person.

⁸Giving honor to a foolish person
    is like tying a stone in a slingshot.

⁹A wise saying spoken by a fool
    is like a thorn stuck in the hand of a
    drunk.

GALATIANS 4:8–31

Paul's Love for the Christians

⁸In the past you did not know God. You were slaves to gods that were not real. ⁹But now you know the true God. Really, it is God who knows you. So why do you turn back to those weak and useless rules you followed before? Do you want to be slaves to those things again? ¹⁰You still follow teachings about special days, months, seasons, and years. ¹¹I am afraid for you, that my work for you has been wasted.

¹²Brothers and sisters, I became like you, so I beg you to become like me. You were very good to me before. ¹³You remember that it was because of an illness that I came to you the first time, preaching the Good News. ¹⁴Though my sickness was a trouble for you, you did not hate me or make me leave. But you welcomed me as an angel from God, as if I were Jesus Christ himself! ¹⁵You were very happy then, but where is that joy now? I am ready to testify that you would have taken out your eyes and given them to me if that were possible. ¹⁶Now am I your enemy because I tell you the truth?

¹⁷Those people[n] are working hard to persuade you, but this is not good for you. They want to persuade you to turn against us and follow only them. ¹⁸It is good for people to show interest in you, but only if their purpose is good. This is always true, not just when I am with you. ¹⁹My little children, again I feel the pain of childbirth for you until you truly become like Christ. ²⁰I wish I could be with you now and could change the way I am talking to you, because I do not know what to think about you.

The Example of Hagar and Sarah

²¹Some of you still want to be under the law. Tell me, do you know what the law says? ²²The Scriptures say that Abraham had two sons. The mother of one son was a slave woman, and the mother of the other son was a free woman. ²³Abraham's son from the slave woman was born in the normal human way. But the son from the free woman was born because of the promise God made to Abraham.

²⁴This story teaches something else: The two women are like the two agreements between God and his people. One agreement is the law that God made on Mount Sinai,[n] and the people who are under this agreement are like slaves. The mother named Hagar is like that agreement. ²⁵She is like Mount Sinai in Arabia and is a picture of the earthly city of Jerusalem. This city and its people are slaves to the law. ²⁶But the heavenly Jerusalem, which is above, is like the free woman. She is our mother. ²⁷It is written in the Scriptures:
"Be happy, Jerusalem.
    You are like a woman who never gave
        birth to children.
Start singing and shout for joy.
    You never felt the pain of giving
        birth,
but you will have more children
    than the woman who has a husband."

Isaiah 54:1

²⁸My brothers and sisters, you are God's children because of his promise, as Isaac was then. ²⁹The son who was born in the normal way treated the other son badly. It is the same today. ³⁰But what does the Scripture say? "Throw out the slave woman and her son. The son of the slave woman should not inherit anything. The son of the free woman should receive it all."[n] ³¹So, my brothers and sisters, we are not children of the slave woman, but of the free woman.

4:17 Those people They are the false teachers who were bothering the believers in Galatia (Galatians 1:7).
4:24 Mount Sinai Mountain in Arabia where God gave his Law to Moses (Exodus 19 and 20).
4:30 "Throw . . . all." Quotation from Genesis 21:10.

SEPTEMBER 27

ISAIAH 45:1—46:13

God Chooses Cyrus to Free Israel

45 This is what the LORD says to Cyrus, his appointed king:
"I hold your right hand
and will help you defeat nations
and take away other kings' power.
I will open doors for you
so city gates will not stop you.
2I will go before you
and make the mountains flat.
I will break down the bronze gates of the cities
and cut through their iron bars.
3I will give you the wealth that is stored away
and the hidden riches
so you will know I am the LORD,
the God of Israel, who calls you by name.
4I do these things for my servants, the people of Jacob,
and for my chosen people, the Israelites.
Cyrus, I call you by name,
and I give you a title of honor even though you don't know me.
5I am the LORD. There is no other God;
I am the only God.
I will make you strong,
even though you don't know me,
6so that everyone will know
there is no other God.
From the east to the west they will know
I alone am the LORD.
7I made the light and the darkness.
I bring peace, and I cause troubles.
I, the LORD, do all these things.

8"Sky above, make victory fall like rain;
clouds, pour down victory.
Let the earth receive it,
and let salvation grow,
and let victory grow with it.
I, the LORD, have created it.

9"How terrible it will be for those who
argue with the God who made them.
They are like a piece of broken pottery
among many pieces.
The clay does not ask the potter,
'What are you doing?'
The thing that is made doesn't say to its maker,
'You have no hands.'
10How terrible it will be for the child who
says to his father,
'Why are you giving me life?'
How terrible it will be for the child who
says to his mother,
'Why are you giving birth to me?'"

11This is what the LORD,
the Holy One of Israel, and its Maker, says:
"You ask me about what will happen.
You question me about my children.
You give me orders about what I have made.
12I made the earth
and all the people living on it.
With my own hands I stretched out the skies,
and I commanded all the armies in the sky.
13I will bring Cyrus to do good things,
and I will make his work easy.
He will rebuild my city
and set my people free
without any payment or reward.
The LORD All-Powerful says this."

14The LORD says,
"The goods made in Egypt and Cush
and the tall people of Seba
will come to you
and will become yours.
The Sabeans will walk behind you,
coming along in chains.
They will bow down before you
and pray to you, saying,
'God is with you,
and there is no other God.'"

15God and Savior of Israel,
you are a God that people cannot see.
16All the people who make idols will be put
to great shame;

they will go off together in disgrace.
[17]But Israel will be saved by the LORD,
and that salvation will continue forever.
Never again will Israel be put to shame.

[18]The LORD created the heavens.
He is the God who formed the earth
and made it.
He did not want it to be empty,
but he wanted life on the earth.
This is what the LORD says:
"I am the LORD. There is no other God.
[19]I did not speak in secret
or hide my words in some dark place.
I did not tell the family of Jacob
to look for me in empty places.
I am the LORD, and I speak the truth;
I say what is right.

[20]"You people who have escaped from
other nations,
gather together and come before me;
come near together.
People who carry idols of wood don't
know what they are doing.
They pray to a god who cannot save
them.
[21]Tell these people to come to me.
Let them talk about these things
together.
Who told you long ago that this would
happen?
Who told about it long ago?
I, the LORD, said these things.
There is no other God besides me.
I am the only good God. I am the Savior.
There is no other God.

[22]"All people everywhere,
follow me and be saved.
I am God. There is no other God.
[23]I will make a promise by my own power,
and my promise is true;
what I say will not be changed.
I promise that everyone will bow before
me
and will promise to follow me.
[24]People will say about me, 'Goodness and
power
come only from the LORD.'"
Everyone who has been angry with him
will come to him and be ashamed.

[25]But with the LORD's help, the people of
Israel
will be found to be good,
and they will praise him.

False Gods Are Useless

46 Bel and Nebo bow down.
Their idols are carried by animals.
The statues are only heavy loads that
must be carried;
they only make people tired.
[2]These gods will all bow down.
They cannot save themselves
but will all be carried away like
prisoners.

[3]"Family of Jacob, listen to me!
All you people from Israel who are still
alive, listen!
I have carried you since you were born;
I have taken care of you from your
birth.
[4]Even when you are old, I will be the
same.
Even when your hair has turned gray, I
will take care of you.
I made you and will take care of you.
I will carry you and save you.

[5]"Can you compare me to anyone?
No one is equal to me or like me.
[6]Some people are rich with gold
and weigh their silver on the scales.
They hire a goldsmith, and he makes it
into a god.
Then they bow down and worship it.
[7]They put it on their shoulders and carry
it.
They set it in its place, and there it
stands;
it cannot move from its place.
People may yell at it, but it cannot
answer.
It cannot save them from their
troubles.

[8]"Remember this, and do not forget it!
Think about these things, you who turn
against God.
[9]Remember what happened long ago.
Remember that I am God, and there is
no other God.
I am God, and there is no one like me.

[10]From the beginning I told you what
would happen in the end.
A long time ago I told you things that
have not yet happened.
When I plan something, it happens.
What I want to do, I will do.
[11]I am calling a man from the east to carry
out my plan;
he will come like a hawk from a
country far away.
I will make what I have said come true;
I will do what I have planned.
[12]Listen to me, you stubborn people,
who are far from what is right.
[13]I will soon do the things that are right.
I will bring salvation soon.
I will save Jerusalem
and bring glory to Israel."

PSALM 111:1–6

Praise the Lord's Goodness

111 Praise the LORD!
I will thank the LORD with all my
heart
in the meeting of his good people.
[2]The LORD does great things;
those who enjoy them seek them.
[3]What he does is glorious and splendid,
and his goodness continues forever.
[4]His miracles are unforgettable.
The LORD is kind and merciful.
[5]He gives food to those who fear him.
He remembers his agreement forever.
[6]He has shown his people his power
when he gave them the lands of other
nations.

PROVERBS 26:10

[10]Hiring a foolish person or anyone just
passing by
is like an archer shooting at just
anything.

GALATIANS 5:1–26

Keep Your Freedom

5 We have freedom now, because Christ
made us free. So stand strong. Do not
change and go back into the slavery of the
law. [2]Listen, I Paul tell you that if you go back
to the law by being circumcised, Christ does
you no good. [3]Again, I warn every man: If
you allow yourselves to be circumcised, you
must follow all the law. [4]If you try to be made
right with God through the law, your life
with Christ is over—you have left God's
grace. [5]But we have the true hope that comes
from being made right with God, and by the
Spirit we wait eagerly for this hope. [6]When
we are in Christ Jesus, it is not important if
we are circumcised or not. The important
thing is faith—the kind of faith that works
through love.

[7]You were running a good race. Who
stopped you from following the true way?
[8]This change did not come from the One
who chose you. [9]Be careful! "Just a little yeast
makes the whole batch of dough rise." [10]But I
trust in the Lord that you will not believe
those different ideas. Whoever is confusing
you with such ideas will be punished.

[11]My brothers and sisters, I do not teach
that a man must be circumcised. If I teach
circumcision, why am I still being attacked?
If I still taught circumcision, my preaching
about the cross would not be a problem. [12]I
wish the people who are bothering you
would castrate[n] themselves!

[13]My brothers and sisters, God called you
to be free, but do not use your freedom as an
excuse to do what pleases your sinful self.
Serve each other with love. [14]The whole law
is made complete in this one command:
"Love your neighbor as you love yourself."[n]
[15]If you go on hurting each other and tearing
each other apart, be careful, or you will completely destroy each other.

The Spirit and Human Nature

[16]So I tell you: Live by following the Spirit.
Then you will not do what your sinful selves
want. [17]Our sinful selves want what is against
the Spirit, and the Spirit wants what is
against our sinful selves. The two are against
each other, so you cannot do just what you
please. [18]But if the Spirit is leading you, you
are not under the law.

5:12 castrate To cut off part of the male sex organ. Paul uses this word because it is similar to "circumcision." Paul wanted
to show that he is very upset with the false teachers.   **5:14 "Love . . . yourself."** Quotation from Leviticus 19:18.

[19]The wrong things the sinful self does are clear: being sexually unfaithful, not being pure, taking part in sexual sins, [20]worshiping gods, doing witchcraft, hating, making trouble, being jealous, being angry, being selfish, making people angry with each other, causing divisions among people, [21]feeling envy, being drunk, having wild and wasteful parties, and doing other things like these. I warn you now as I warned you before: Those who do these things will not inherit God's kingdom. [22]But the Spirit produces the fruit of love, joy, peace, patience, kindness, goodness, faithfulness, [23]gentleness, self-control. There is no law that says these things are wrong. [24]Those who belong to Christ Jesus have crucified their own sinful selves. They have given up their old selfish feelings and the evil things they wanted to do. [25]We get our new life from the Spirit, so we should follow the Spirit. [26]We must not be proud or make trouble with each other or be jealous of each other.

SEPTEMBER 28

ISAIAH 47:1—48:22

God Will Destroy Babylon

47 The LORD says, "City of Babylon, go
down and sit in the dirt.
People of Babylon, sit on the ground.
  You are no longer the ruler.
You will no longer be called
  tender or beautiful.
[2] You must use large stones to grind
    grain into flour.
  Remove your veil and your nice skirts.
  Uncover your legs and cross the rivers.
[3]People will see your nakedness;
  they will see your shame.
I will punish you;
  I will punish every one of you."

[4]Our Savior is named the LORD
    All-Powerful;
  he is the Holy One of Israel.

[5]"Babylon, sit in darkness and say
    nothing.
  You will no longer be called the queen
    of kingdoms.
[6]I was angry with my people,
  so I rejected those who belonged to me.
I gave them to you,
  but you showed them no mercy.
You even made the old people
  work very hard.
[7]You said, 'I will live forever
  as the queen.'

But you did not think about these things
  or consider what would happen.

[8]"Now, listen, you lover of pleasure.
  You think you are safe.
You tell yourself,
  'I am the only important person.
I will never be a widow
  or lose my children.'
[9]Two things will happen to you suddenly,
  in a single day.
  You will lose your children and your
    husband.
These things will truly happen to you,
  in spite of all your magic,
  in spite of your powerful tricks.
[10]You do evil things, but you feel safe
  and say, 'No one sees what I do.'
Your wisdom and knowledge
  have fooled you.
You say to yourself,
  'I am God, and no one is equal to me.'
[11]But troubles will come to you,
  and you will not know how to stop
    them.
Disaster will fall on you,
  and you will not be able to keep it away.
You will be destroyed quickly;
  you will not even see it coming.

[12]"Keep on using your tricks
  and doing all your magic
  that you have used since you were
    young.

Maybe they will help you;
  maybe you will be able to scare
    someone.
[13]You are tired of the advice you have
    received.
  So let those who study the sky—
  those who tell the future by looking at
    the stars and the new moons—
  let them save you from what is about to
    happen to you.
[14]But they are like straw;
  fire will quickly burn them up.
  They cannot save themselves
  from the power of the fire.
  They are not like coals that give warmth
  nor like a fire that you may sit beside.
[15]You have worked with these people,
  and they have been with you since you
    were young,
  but they will not be able to help you.
  Everyone will go his own way,
  and there will be no one left to save
    you."

God Controls the Future

48 The LORD says, "Family of Jacob, listen
    to me.
  You are called Israel,
  and you come from the family of Judah.
  You swear by the LORD's name
  and praise the God of Israel,
  but you are not honest or sincere.
[2]You call yourselves people of the holy
    city,
  and you depend on the God of Israel,
  who is named the LORD All-Powerful.
[3]Long ago I told you what would happen.
  I said these things and made them
    known;
  suddenly I acted, and these things
    happened.
[4]I knew you were stubborn;
  your neck was like an iron muscle,
  and your head was like bronze.
[5]So a long time ago I told you about these
    things;
  I told you about them before they
    happened
  so you couldn't say, 'My idols did this,
  and my wooden and metal statues
    made these things happen.'

[6]"You heard and saw everything that
    happened,
  so you should tell this news to others.
  Now I will tell you about new things,
  hidden things that you don't know yet.
[7]These things are happening now, not
    long ago;
  you have not heard about them before
    today.
  So you cannot say, 'We already knew
    about that.'
[8]But you have not heard me; you have not
    understood.
  Even long ago you did not listen to me.
  I knew you would surely turn against
    me;
  you have fought against me since you
    were born.
[9]But for my own sake I will be patient.
  People will praise me for not becoming
    angry
  and destroying you.
[10]I have made you pure, but not by fire, as
    silver is made pure.
  I have purified you by giving you
    troubles.
[11]I do this for myself, for my own sake.
  I will not let people speak evil against
    me,
  and I will not let some god take my
    glory.

Israel Will Be Free

[12]"People of Jacob, listen to me.
  People of Israel, I have called you to be
    my people.
  I am God;
  I am the beginning and the end.
[13]I made the earth with my own hands.
  With my right hand I spread out the
    skies.
  When I call them,
  they come together before me."

[14]All of you, come together and listen.
  None of the gods said these things
    would happen.
  The LORD has chosen someone
  to attack the Babylonians;
  he will carry out his wishes against
    Babylon.

15"I have spoken; I have called him.[n]
I have brought him, and I will make
him successful.
16Come to me and listen to this.
From the beginning I have spoken
openly.
From the time it began, I was there."

Now, the Lord GOD
has sent me with his Spirit.

17This is what the LORD, who saves you,
the Holy One of Israel, says:
"I am the LORD your God,
who teaches you to do what is good,
who leads you in the way you should go.
18If you had obeyed me,
you would have had peace like a
full-flowing river.
Good things would have flowed to you
like the waves of the sea.
19You would have had many children,
as many as the grains of sand.
They would never have died out
nor been destroyed."

20My people, leave Babylon!
Run from the Babylonians!
Tell this news with shouts of joy to the
people;
spread it everywhere on earth.
Say, "The LORD has saved his servants,
the people of Jacob."
21They did not become thirsty when he led
them through the deserts.
He made water flow from a rock for
them.
He split the rock,
and water flowed out.
22"There is no peace for evil people," says
the LORD.

PSALM 111:7–10

7Everything he does is good and fair;
all his orders can be trusted.
8They will continue forever.
They were made true and right.
9He sets his people free.
He made his agreement everlasting.
He is holy and wonderful.

10Wisdom begins with respect for the LORD;
those who obey his orders have good
understanding.
He should be praised forever.

PROVERBS 26:11–12

11A fool who repeats his foolishness
is like a dog that goes back to what it
has thrown up.

12There is more hope for a foolish person
than for those who think they are wise.

GALATIANS 6:1–18

Help Each Other

6Brothers and sisters, if someone in your
group does something wrong, you who
are spiritual should go to that person and
gently help make him right again. But be
careful, because you might be tempted to sin,
too. 2By helping each other with your troubles, you truly obey the law of Christ. 3If anyone thinks he is important when he really is
not, he is only fooling himself. 4Each person
should judge his own actions and not compare himself with others. Then he can be
proud for what he himself has done. 5Each
person must be responsible for himself.
6Anyone who is learning the teaching of
God should share all the good things he has
with his teacher.

Life Is like Planting a Field

7Do not be fooled: You cannot cheat God.
People harvest only what they plant. 8If they
plant to satisfy their sinful selves, their sinful
selves will bring them ruin. But if they plant
to please the Spirit, they will receive eternal
life from the Spirit. 9We must not become
tired of doing good. We will receive our harvest of eternal life at the right time if we do
not give up. 10When we have the opportunity
to help anyone, we should do it. But we
should give special attention to those who
are in the family of believers.

Paul Ends His Letter

11See what large letters I use to write this
myself. 12Some people are trying to force you
to be circumcised so the Jews will accept

them. They are afraid they will be attacked if they follow only the cross of Christ.[n] [13]Those who are circumcised do not obey the law themselves, but they want you to be circumcised so they can brag about what they forced you to do. [14]I hope I will never brag about things like that. The cross of our Lord Jesus Christ is my only reason for bragging. Through the cross of Jesus my world was crucified, and I died to the world. [15]It is not important if a man is circumcised or uncircumcised. The important thing is being the new people God has made. [16]Peace and mercy to those who follow this rule—and to all of God's people.

[17]So do not give me any more trouble. I have scars on my body that show[n] I belong to Christ Jesus.

[18]My brothers and sisters, the grace of our Lord Jesus Christ be with your spirit. Amen.

SEPTEMBER 29

ISAIAH 49:1—50:11

God Calls His Special Servant

49 All of you people in faraway places,
   listen to me.
Listen, all you nations far away.
Before I was born, the LORD called me to
   serve him.
The LORD named me while I was still
   in my mother's womb.
[2]He made my tongue like a sharp sword.
He hid me in the shadow of his hand.
He made me like a sharp arrow.
   He hid me in the holder for his arrows.
[3]He told me, "Israel, you are my servant.
   I will show my glory through you."
[4]But I said, "I have worked hard for
      nothing;
   I have used all my power, but I did
      nothing useful.
But the LORD will decide what my work
      is worth;
   God will decide my reward."
[5]The LORD made me in the body of my
      mother
   to be his servant,
to lead the people of Jacob back to him
so that Israel might be gathered to
      him.
The LORD will honor me,
   and I will get my strength from my
      God.

[6]Now he told me,
   "You are an important servant to me
      to bring back the tribes of Jacob,
      to bring back the people of Israel who
         are left alive.
But, more importantly, I will make you a
      light for all nations
   to show people all over the world the
      way to be saved."
[7]The LORD who saves you
   is the Holy One of Israel.
He speaks to the one who is hated by the
      people,
   to the servant of rulers.
This is what he says: "Kings will see you
      and stand to honor you;
   great leaders will bow down before
      you,
because the LORD can be trusted.
   He is the Holy One of Israel, who has
      chosen you."

The Day of Salvation

[8]This is what the LORD says:
   "At the right time I will hear your
      prayers.
   On the day of salvation I will help you.
I will protect you,
   and you will be the sign of my
      agreement with the people.
You will bring back the people to the
      land

6:12 cross of Christ Paul uses the cross as a picture of the Good News, the story of Christ's death and rising from the dead to pay for our sins. The cross, or Christ's death, was God's way to save us. **6:17 that show** Many times Paul was beaten and whipped by people who were against him because he was teaching about Christ. The scars were from these beatings.

and give the land that is now ruined
back to its owners.
⁹You will tell the prisoners, 'Come out of
your prison.'
You will tell those in darkness, 'Come
into the light.'
The people will eat beside the roads,
and they will find food even on bare
hills.
¹⁰They will not be hungry or thirsty.
Neither the hot sun nor the desert
wind will hurt them.
The God who comforts them will lead
them
and guide them by springs of water.
¹¹I will make my mountains into roads,
and the roads will be raised up.
¹²Look, people are coming to me from far
away,
from the north and from the west,
from Aswan in southern Egypt."

¹³Heavens and earth, be happy.
Mountains, shout with joy,
because the LORD comforts his people
and will have pity on those who suffer.

Jerusalem and Her Children
¹⁴But Jerusalem said, "The LORD has left
me;
the Lord has forgotten me."

¹⁵The LORD answers, "Can a woman forget
the baby she nurses?
Can she feel no kindness for the child
to which she gave birth?
Even if she could forget her children,
I will not forget you.
¹⁶See, I have written your name on my
hand.
Jerusalem, I always think about your
walls.
¹⁷Your children will soon return to you,
and the people who defeated you and
destroyed you will leave.
¹⁸Look up and look around you.
All your children are gathering to
return to you."
The LORD says, "As surely as I live,
your children will be like jewels
that a bride wears proudly.

¹⁹"You were destroyed and defeated,
and your land was made useless.
But now you will have more people than
the land can hold,
and those people who destroyed you
will be far away.
²⁰Children were born to you while you
were sad,
but they will say to you,
'This place is too small for us.
Give us a bigger place to live.'
²¹Then you will say to yourself,
'Who gave me all these children?
I was sad and lonely,
defeated and separated from my people.
So who reared these children?
I was left all alone.
Where did all these children come
from?'"

²²This is what the Lord GOD says:
"See, I will lift my hand to signal the
nations;
I will raise my banner for all the
people to see.
Then they will bring your sons back to
you in their arms,
and they will carry your daughters on
their shoulders.
²³Kings will teach your children,
and daughters of kings will take care of
them.
They will bow down before you
and kiss the dirt at your feet.
Then you will know I am the LORD.
Anyone who trusts in me will not be
disappointed."

²⁴Can the wealth a soldier wins in war be
taken away from him?
Can a prisoner be freed from a
powerful soldier?
²⁵This is what the LORD says:
"The prisoners will be taken from the
strong soldiers.
What the soldiers have taken will be
saved.
I will fight your enemies,
and I will save your children.

²⁶I will force those who trouble you to eat
their own flesh.
Their own blood will be the wine that
makes them drunk.
Then everyone will know
I, the LORD, am the One who saves you;
I am the Powerful One of Jacob who
saves you."

Israel Was Punished for Its Sin

50 This is what the LORD says:
"People of Israel, you say I divorced
your mother.
Then where is the paper that proves it?
Or do you think I sold you
to pay a debt?
Because of the evil things you did, I sold
you.
Because of the times she turned
against me, your mother was sent
away.
²I came home and found no one there;
I called, but no one answered.
Do you think I am not able to save you?
Do I not have the power to save you?
Look, I need only to shout and the sea
becomes dry.
I change rivers into a desert,
and their fish rot because there is no
water;
they die of thirst.
³I can make the skies dark;
I can make them black like clothes of
sadness."

God's Servant Obeys

⁴The Lord GOD gave me the ability to
teach
so that I know what to say to make the
weak strong.
Every morning he wakes me.
He teaches me to listen like a student.
⁵The Lord GOD helps me learn,
and I have not turned against him
nor stopped following him.
⁶I offered my back to those who beat me.
I offered my cheeks to those who
pulled my beard.
I won't hide my face from them
when they make fun of me and spit at
me.

⁷The Lord GOD helps me,
so I will not be ashamed.
I will be determined,
and I know I will not be disgraced.
⁸He shows that I am innocent, and he is
close to me.
So who can accuse me?
If there is someone, let us go to court
together.
If someone wants to prove I have done
wrong,
he should come and tell me.
⁹Look! It is the Lord GOD who helps me.
So who can prove me guilty?
Look! All those who try will become
useless like old clothes;
moths will eat them.

¹⁰Who among you fears the LORD
and obeys his servant?
That person may walk in the dark
and have no light.
Then let him trust in the LORD
and yet depend on his God.
¹¹But instead, some of you want to light
your own fires
and make your own light.
So, go, walk in the light of your fires,
and trust your own light to guide
you.
But this is what you will receive from
me:
You will lie down in a place of pain.

PSALM 112:1-4

Honest People Are Blessed

112 Praise the LORD!
Happy are those who respect the
LORD,
who want what he commands.
²Their descendants will be powerful in
the land;
the children of honest people will be
blessed.
³Their houses will be full of wealth and
riches,
and their goodness will continue
forever.
⁴A light shines in the dark for honest
people,

for those who are merciful and kind
and good.

PROVERBS 26:13–15

[13]The lazy person says, "There's a lion in
the road!
There's a lion in the streets!"

[14]Like a door turning back and forth on its
hinges,
the lazy person turns over and over in
bed.

[15]Lazy people may put their hands in the
dish,
but they are too tired to lift the food to
their mouths.

EPHESIANS 1:1–23

1 From Paul, an apostle of Christ Jesus. I
am an apostle because that is what God
wanted.
To God's holy people living in Ephesus,[n]
believers in Christ Jesus:
[2]Grace and peace to you from God our
Father and the Lord Jesus Christ.

Spiritual Blessings in Christ

[3]Praise be to the God and Father of our
Lord Jesus Christ. In Christ, God has given
us every spiritual blessing in the heavenly
world. [4]That is, in Christ, he chose us before
the world was made so that we would be his
holy people—people without blame before
him. [5]Because of his love, God had already
decided to make us his own children
through Jesus Christ. That was what he
wanted and what pleased him, [6]and it
brings praise to God because of his wonderful grace. God gave that grace to us freely, in
Christ, the One he loves. [7]In Christ we are set
free by the blood of his death, and so we
have forgiveness of sins. How rich is God's
grace, [8]which he has given to us so fully and
freely. God, with full wisdom and understanding, [9]let us know his secret purpose.
This was what God wanted, and he planned
to do it through Christ. [10]His goal was to
carry out his plan, when the right time

came, that all things in heaven and on earth
would be joined together in Christ as the
head.
[11]In Christ we were chosen to be God's
people, because from the very beginning
God had decided this in keeping with his
plan. And he is the One who makes everything agree with what he decides and
wants. [12]We are the first people who hoped
in Christ, and we were chosen so that we
would bring praise to God's glory. [13]So it is
with you. When you heard the true teaching—the Good News about your salvation—you believed in Christ. And in Christ,
God put his special mark of ownership on
you by giving you the Holy Spirit that he
had promised. [14]That Holy Spirit is the
guarantee that we will receive what God
promised for his people until God gives full
freedom to those who are his—to bring
praise to God's glory.

Paul's Prayer

[15]That is why since I heard about your
faith in the Lord Jesus and your love for all
God's people, [16]I have not stopped giving
thanks to God for you. I always remember
you in my prayers, [17]asking the God of our
Lord Jesus Christ, the glorious Father, to
give you a spirit of wisdom and revelation
so that you will know him better. [18]I pray
also that you will have greater understanding in your heart so you will know the hope
to which he has called us and that you will
know how rich and glorious are the blessings God has promised his holy people.
[19]And you will know that God's power is
very great for us who believe. That power is
the same as the great strength [20]God used to
raise Christ from the dead and put him at
his right side in the heavenly world. [21]God
has put Christ over all rulers, authorities,
powers, and kings, not only in this world but
also in the next. [22]God put everything under
his power and made him the head over
everything for the church, [23]which is Christ's
body. The church is filled with Christ, and
Christ fills everything in every way.

1:1 in Ephesus Some Greek copies do not have this phrase.

SEPTEMBER 30

ISAIAH 51:1—52:15

Jerusalem Will Be Saved

51 The Lord says, "Listen to me,
those of you who try to live right
and follow the Lord.
Look at the rock from which you were cut;
look at the stone quarry from which
you were dug.
²Look at Abraham, your ancestor,
and Sarah, who gave birth to your
ancestors.
Abraham had no children when I called
him,
but I blessed him and gave him many
descendants.
³So the Lord will comfort Jerusalem;
he will show mercy to those who live in
her ruins.
He will change her deserts into a garden
like Eden;
he will make her empty lands like the
garden of the Lord.
People there will be very happy;
they will give thanks and sing songs.

⁴"My people, listen to me;
my nation, pay attention to me.
I will give the people my teachings,
and my decisions will be like a light to
all people.
⁵I will soon show that I do what is right.
I will soon save you.
I will use my power and judge all
nations.
All the faraway places are waiting for me;
they wait for my power to help them.
⁶Look up to the heavens.
Look around you at the earth below.
The skies will disappear like clouds of
smoke.
The earth will become useless like old
clothes,
and its people will die like flies.
But my salvation will continue forever,
and my goodness will never end.

⁷"You people who know what is right
should listen to me;

you people who follow my teachings
should hear what I say.
Don't be afraid of the evil things people
say,
and don't be upset by their insults.
⁸Moths will eat those people as if they
were clothes,
and worms will eat them as if they
were wool.
But my goodness will continue forever,
and my salvation will continue from
now on."

⁹Wake up, wake up, and use your strength,
powerful Lord.
Wake up as you did in the old times,
as you did a long time ago.
With your own power, you cut Rahab
into pieces
and killed that sea monster.
¹⁰You dried up the sea
and the waters of the deep ocean.
You made the deepest parts of the sea
into a road
for your people to cross over and be
saved.
¹¹The people the Lord has freed will return
and enter Jerusalem with joy.
Their happiness will last forever.
They will have joy and gladness,
and all sadness and sorrow will be
gone far away.

¹²The Lord says, "I am the one who
comforts you.
So why should you be afraid of people,
who die?
Why should you fear people who die
like the grass?
¹³Have you forgotten the Lord who made
you,
who stretched out the skies
and made the earth?
Why are you always afraid
of those angry people who trouble you
and who want to destroy?
But where are those angry people now?
¹⁴ People in prison will soon be set free;
they will not die in prison,

and they will have enough food.

[15]I am the LORD your God,
who stirs the sea and makes the waves
roar.
My name is the LORD All-Powerful.
[16]I will give you the words I want you to
say.
I will cover you with my hands and
protect you.
I made the heavens and the earth,
and I say to Jerusalem, 'You are my
people.'"

God Punished Israel

[17]Awake! Awake!
Get up, Jerusalem.
The LORD was very angry with you;
your punishment was like wine in a
cup.
The LORD made you drink that wine;
you drank the whole cup until you
stumbled.
[18]Jerusalem had many people,
but there was not one to lead her.
Of all the people who grew up there,
no one was there to guide her.
[19]Troubles came to you two by two,
but no one will feel sorry for you.
There was ruin and disaster, great
hunger and fighting.
No one can comfort you.
[20]Your people have become weak.
They fall down and lie on every street
corner,
like animals caught in a net.
They have felt the full anger of the LORD
and have heard God's angry shout.
[21]So listen to me, poor Jerusalem,
you who are drunk but not from wine.
[22]Your God will defend his people.
This is what the LORD your God says:
"The punishment I gave you is like a cup
of wine.
You drank it and could not walk
straight.
But I am taking that cup of my anger
away from you,
and you will never be punished by my
anger again.
[23]I will now give that cup of punishment to
those who gave you pain,

who told you,
'Bow down so we can walk over you.'
They made your back like dirt for them
to walk on;
you were like a street for them to travel
on."

Jerusalem Will Be Saved

52Wake up, wake up, Jerusalem! Become
strong!
Be beautiful again,
holy city of Jerusalem.
The people who do not worship God and
who are not pure
will not enter you again.
[2]Jerusalem, you once were a prisoner.
Now shake off the dust and stand up.
Jerusalem, you once were a prisoner.
Now free yourself from the chains
around your neck.
[3]This is what the LORD says:
"You were not sold for a price,
so you will be saved without cost."
[4]This is what the Lord GOD says:
"First my people went down to Egypt to
live.
Later Assyria made them slaves.
[5]"Now see what has happened," says the
LORD.
"Another nation has taken away my
people for nothing.
This nation who rules them makes fun
of me," says the LORD.
"All day long they speak against me.
[6]This has happened so my people will
know who I am,
and so, on that future day, they will
know
that I am the one speaking to them.
It will really be me."

[7]How beautiful is the person
who comes over the mountains to bring
good news,
who announces peace
and brings good news,
who announces salvation
and says to Jerusalem,
"Your God is King."
[8]Listen! Your guards are shouting.
They are all shouting for joy!

They all will see with their own eyes
   when the LORD returns to Jerusalem.
[9]Jerusalem, your buildings are destroyed
   now,
   but shout and rejoice together,
because the LORD has comforted his
   people.
   He has saved Jerusalem.
[10]The LORD will show his holy power
   to all the nations.
   Then everyone on earth
   will see the salvation of our God.
[11]You people, leave, leave; get out of
   Babylon!
   Touch nothing that is unclean.
You men who carry the LORD's things
   used in worship,
   leave there and make yourselves pure.
[12]You will not be forced to leave Babylon
   quickly;
   you will not be forced to run away,
because the LORD will go before you,
   and the God of Israel will guard you
   from behind.

The Lord's Suffering Servant

[13]The LORD says, "See, my servant will act
   wisely.
   People will greatly honor and respect
   him.
[14]Many people were shocked when they
   saw him.
   His appearance was so damaged he did
   not look like a man;
   his form was so changed they could
   barely tell he was human.
[15]But now he will surprise many nations.
   Kings will be amazed and shut their
   mouths.
   They will see things they had not been
   told about him,
   and they will understand things they
   had not heard."

PSALM 112:5–10

[5]It is good to be merciful and generous.
   Those who are fair in their business
[6]will never be defeated.
   Good people will always be
   remembered.
[7]They won't be afraid of bad news;

their hearts are steady because they
   trust the LORD.
[8]They are confident and will not be afraid;
   they will look down on their enemies.
[9]They give freely to the poor.
   The things they do are right and will
   continue forever.
   They will be given great honor.

[10]The wicked will see this and become
   angry;
   they will grind their teeth in anger and
   then disappear.
   The wishes of the wicked will come to
   nothing.

PROVERBS 26:16

[16]The lazy person thinks he is wiser
   than seven people who give sensible
   answers.

EPHESIANS 2:1–22

We Now Have Life

2 In the past you were spiritually dead because of your sins and the things you did against God. [2]Yes, in the past you lived the way the world lives, following the ruler of the evil powers that are above the earth. That same spirit is now working in those who refuse to obey God. [3]In the past all of us lived like them, trying to please our sinful selves and doing all the things our bodies and minds wanted. We should have suffered God's anger because we were sinful by nature. We were the same as all other people.

[4]But God's mercy is great, and he loved us very much. [5]Though we were spiritually dead because of the things we did against God, he gave us new life with Christ. You have been saved by God's grace. [6]And he raised us up with Christ and gave us a seat with him in the heavens. He did this for those in Christ Jesus [7]so that for all future time he could show the very great riches of his grace by being kind to us in Christ Jesus. [8]I mean that you have been saved by grace through believing. You did not save yourselves; it was a gift from God. [9]It was not the result of your own efforts, so you cannot brag about it. [10]God has made us what we

are. In Christ Jesus, God made us to do good works, which God planned in advance for us to live our lives doing.

One in Christ

[11]You were not born Jewish. You are the people the Jews call "uncircumcised."[n] Those who call you "uncircumcised" call themselves "circumcised." (Their circumcision is only something they themselves do on their bodies.) [12]Remember that in the past you were without Christ. You were not citizens of Israel, and you had no part in the agreements[n] with the promise that God made to his people. You had no hope, and you did not know God. [13]But now in Christ Jesus, you who were far away from God are brought near through the blood of Christ's death. [14]Christ himself is our peace. He made both Jewish people and those who are not Jews one people. They were separated as if there were a wall between them, but Christ broke down that wall of hate by giving his own body. [15]The Jewish law had many commands and rules, but Christ ended that law. His pur-

pose was to make the two groups of people become one new people in him and in this way make peace. [16]It was also Christ's purpose to end the hatred between the two groups, to make them into one body, and to bring them back to God. Christ did all this with his death on the cross. [17]Christ came and preached peace to you who were far away from God, and to those who were near to God. [18]Yes, it is through Christ we all have the right to come to the Father in one Spirit.

[19]Now you who are not Jewish are not foreigners or strangers any longer, but are citizens together with God's holy people. You belong to God's family. [20]You are like a building that was built on the foundation of the apostles and prophets. Christ Jesus himself is the most important stone[n] in that building, [21]and that whole building is joined together in Christ. He makes it grow and become a holy temple in the Lord. [22]And in Christ you, too, are being built together with the Jews into a place where God lives through the Spirit.

2:11 "uncircumcised" People not having the mark of circumcision as the Jews had. **2:12 agreements** The agreements that God gave to his people in the Old Testament. **2:20 most important stone** Literally, "cornerstone." The first and most important stone in a building.

OCTOBER 1

ISAIAH 53:1—54:17

53 Who would have believed what we heard?
Who saw the LORD's power in this?
[2]He grew up like a small plant before the LORD,
like a root growing in a dry land.
He had no special beauty or form to make us notice him;
there was nothing in his appearance to make us desire him.
[3]He was hated and rejected by people.
He had much pain and suffering.
People would not even look at him.
He was hated, and we didn't even notice him.

[4]But he took our suffering on him
and felt our pain for us.
We saw his suffering
and thought God was punishing him.
[5]But he was wounded for the wrong we did;
he was crushed for the evil we did.
The punishment, which made us well,
was given to him,
and we are healed because of his wounds.
[6]We all have wandered away like sheep;
each of us has gone his own way.
But the LORD has put on him the punishment
for all the evil we have done.

[7]He was beaten down and punished,
but he didn't say a word.
He was like a lamb being led to be killed.
He was quiet, as a sheep is quiet while its wool is being cut;
he never opened his mouth.
[8]Men took him away roughly and unfairly.
He died without children to continue his family.
He was put to death;
he was punished for the sins of my people.
[9]He was buried with wicked men,
and he died with the rich.

He had done nothing wrong,
and he had never lied.
[10]But it was the LORD who decided
to crush him and make him suffer.
The LORD made his life a penalty offering,
but he will still see his descendants and live a long life.
He will complete the things the LORD wants him to do.
[11]"After his soul suffers many things,
he will see life and be satisfied.
My good servant will make many people right with God;
he will carry away their sins.
[12]For this reason I will make him a great man among people,
and he will share in all things with those who are strong.
He willingly gave his life
and was treated like a criminal.
But he carried away the sins of many people
and asked forgiveness for those who sinned."

People Will Return to Jerusalem

54 The LORD says, "Sing, Jerusalem.
You are like a woman who never gave birth to children.
Start singing and shout for joy.
You never felt the pain of giving birth,
but you will have more children
than the woman who has a husband.
[2]Make your tent bigger;
stretch it out and make it wider.
Do not hold back.
Make the ropes longer
and its stakes stronger,
[3]because you will spread out to the right and to the left.
Your children will take over other nations,
and they will again live in cities that once were destroyed.
[4]"Don't be afraid, because you will not be ashamed.

Don't be embarrassed, because you will
    not be disgraced.
You will forget the shame you felt earlier;
    you will not remember the shame you
    felt when you lost your husband.
[5]The God who made you is like your
    husband.
    His name is the Lord All-Powerful.
The Holy One of Israel is the one who
    saves you.
    He is called the God of all the earth.
[6]You were like a woman whose husband
    left her,
    and you were very sad.
You were like a wife who married young
    and then her husband left her.
But the Lord called you to be his,"
    says your God.
[7]God says, "I left you for a short time,
    but with great kindness I will bring you
    back again.
[8]I became very angry
    and hid from you for a time,
but I will show you mercy with kindness
    forever,"
    says the Lord who saves you.

[9]The Lord says, "This day is like the time
    of Noah to me.
I promised then that I would never
    flood the world again.
In the same way, I promise I will not be
    angry with you
    or punish you again.
[10]The mountains may disappear,
    and the hills may come to an end,
but my love will never disappear;
    my promise of peace will not come to
    an end,"
    says the Lord who shows mercy to you.

[11]"You poor city. Storms have hurt you,
    and you have not been comforted.
But I will rebuild you with turquoise
    stones,
    and I will build your foundations with
    sapphires.
[12]I will use rubies to build your walls
    and shining jewels for the gates
    and precious jewels for all your outer
    walls.

[13]All your children will be taught by the
    Lord,
    and they will have much peace.
[14]I will build you using fairness.
You will be safe from those who would
    hurt you,
    so you will have nothing to fear.
Nothing will come to make you afraid.
[15]I will not send anyone to attack you,
    and you will defeat those who do attack
    you.

[16]"See, I made the blacksmith.
    He fans the fire to make it hotter,
    and he makes the kind of tool he wants.
In the same way I have made the
    destroyer to destroy.
[17] So no weapon that is used against you
    will defeat you.
You will show that those who speak
    against you are wrong.
These are the good things my servants
    receive.
    Their victory comes from me," says the
    Lord.

PSALM 113:1–4

Praise for the Lord's Kindness

113 [1]Praise the Lord!
    Praise him, you servants of the
    Lord;
    praise the name of the Lord.
[2]The Lord's name should be praised
    now and forever.
[3]The Lord's name should be praised
    from where the sun rises to where it
    sets.
[4]The Lord is supreme over all the nations;
    his glory reaches to the skies.

PROVERBS 26:17–19

[17]Interfering in someone else's quarrel as
    you pass by
    is like grabbing a dog by the ears.

[18]Like a madman shooting
    deadly, burning arrows
[19]is the one who tricks a neighbor
    and then says, "I was just joking."

EPHESIANS 3:1–21

Paul's Work in Telling the Good News

3 So I, Paul, am a prisoner of Christ Jesus for you who are not Jews. ²Surely you have heard that God gave me this work to tell you about his grace. ³He let me know his secret by showing it to me. I have already written a little about this. ⁴If you read what I wrote then, you can see that I truly understand the secret about the Christ. ⁵People who lived in other times were not told that secret. But now, through the Spirit, God has shown that secret to his holy apostles and prophets. ⁶This is that secret: that through the Good News those who are not Jews will share with the Jews in God's blessing. They belong to the same body, and they share together in the promise that God made in Christ Jesus.

⁷By God's special gift of grace given to me through his power, I became a servant to tell that Good News. ⁸I am the least important of all God's people, but God gave me this gift— to tell those who are not Jews the Good News about the riches of Christ, which are too great to understand fully. ⁹And God gave me the work of telling all people about the plan for his secret, which has been hidden in him since the beginning of time. He is the One who created everything. ¹⁰His purpose was that through the church all the rulers and powers in the heavenly world will now know God's wisdom, which has so many forms. ¹¹This agrees with the purpose God had since the beginning of time, and he carried out his plan through Christ Jesus our Lord. ¹²In Christ we can come before God with freedom and without fear. We can do this through faith in Christ. ¹³So I ask you not to become discouraged because of the sufferings I am having for you. My sufferings are for your glory.

The Love of Christ

¹⁴So I bow in prayer before the Father ¹⁵from whom every family in heaven and on earth gets its true name. ¹⁶I ask the Father in his great glory to give you the power to be strong inwardly through his Spirit. ¹⁷I pray that Christ will live in your hearts by faith and that your life will be strong in love and be built on love. ¹⁸And I pray that you and all God's holy people will have the power to understand the greatness of Christ's love—how wide and how long and how high and how deep that love is. ¹⁹Christ's love is greater than anyone can ever know, but I pray that you will be able to know that love. Then you can be filled with the fullness of God.

²⁰With God's power working in us, God can do much, much more than anything we can ask or imagine. ²¹To him be glory in the church and in Christ Jesus for all time, forever and ever. Amen.

OCTOBER 2

ISAIAH 55:1—56:12

God Gives What Is Good

55 The LORD says, "All you who are thirsty,
come and drink.
Those of you who do not have money,
come, buy and eat!
Come buy wine and milk
without money and without cost.
²Why spend your money on something
that is not real food?
Why work for something that doesn't
really satisfy you?
Listen closely to me, and you will eat
what is good;
your soul will enjoy the rich food that
satisfies.
³Come to me and listen;
listen to me so you may live.
I will make an agreement with you that
will last forever.
I will give you the blessings I promised
to David.
⁴I made David a witness of my power for
all nations,
a ruler and commander of many
nations.

[5]You will call for nations that you don't yet
know.
And these nations that do not know
you will run to you
because of the LORD your God,
because of the Holy One of Israel who
honors you."

[6]So you should look for the LORD before it
is too late;
you should call to him while he is near.
[7]The wicked should stop doing wrong,
and they should stop their evil
thoughts.
They should return to the LORD so he
may have mercy on them.
They should come to our God, because
he will freely forgive them.

[8]The LORD says, "My thoughts are not like
your thoughts.
Your ways are not like my ways.
[9]Just as the heavens are higher than the
earth,
so are my ways higher than your ways
and my thoughts higher than your
thoughts.
[10]Rain and snow fall from the sky
and don't return without watering the
ground.
They cause the plants to sprout and
grow,
making seeds for the farmer
and bread for the people.
[11]The same thing is true of the words I
speak.
They will not return to me empty.
They make the things happen that I want
to happen,
and they succeed in doing what I send
them to do.

[12]"So you will go out with joy
and be led out in peace.
The mountains and hills will burst into
song before you,
and all the trees in the fields will clap
their hands.
[13]Large cypress trees will grow where
thornbushes were.
Myrtle trees will grow where weeds
were.

These things will be a reminder of the
LORD's promise,
and this reminder will never be
destroyed."

All Nations Will Obey the Lord

56 This is what the LORD says:
"Give justice to all people,
and do what is right,
because my salvation will come to you
soon.
Soon everyone will know that I do what
is right.
[2]The person who obeys the law about the
Sabbath
will be blessed,
and the person who does no evil
will be blessed."

[3]Foreigners who have joined the LORD
should not say,
"The LORD will not accept me with his
people."
The eunuch should not say,
"Because I cannot have children, the
LORD will not accept me."
[4]This is what the LORD says:
"The eunuchs should obey the law about
the Sabbath
and do what I want
and keep my agreement.
[5]If they do, I will make their names
remembered
within my Temple and its walls.
It will be better for them than children.
I will give them a name that will last
forever,
that will never be forgotten.
[6]Foreigners will join the LORD
to worship him and love him,
to serve him,
to obey the law about the Sabbath,
and to keep my agreement.
[7]I will bring these people to my holy
mountain
and give them joy in my house of
prayer.
The offerings and sacrifices
they place on my altar will please me,
because my Temple will be called
a house for prayer for people from all
nations."

8The Lord God says—
he who gathers the Israelites that were
forced to leave their country:
"I will bring together other people
to join those who are already gathered."

Israel's Leaders Are Evil

9All you animals of the field,
all you animals of the forest, come to eat.
10The leaders who are to guard the people
are blind;
they don't know what they are doing.
All of them are like quiet dogs
that don't know how to bark.
They lie down and dream
and love to sleep.
11They are like hungry dogs
that are never satisfied.
They are like shepherds
who don't know what they are doing.
They all have gone their own way;
all they want to do is satisfy
themselves.
12They say, "Come, let's drink some wine;
let's drink all the beer we want.
And tomorrow we will do this again,
or, maybe we will have an even better
time."

PSALM 113:5–9

5No one is like the Lord our God,
who rules from heaven,
6who bends down to look
at the skies and the earth.
7The Lord lifts the poor from the dirt
and takes the helpless from the ashes.
8He seats them with princes,
the princes of his people.
9He gives children to the woman who has
none
and makes her a happy mother.

Praise the Lord!

PROVERBS 26:20–21

20Without wood, a fire will go out,
and without gossip, quarreling will
stop.
21Just as charcoal and wood keep a fire
going,

a quarrelsome person keeps an
argument going.

EPHESIANS 4:1–32

The Unity of the Body

4I am in prison because I belong to the
Lord. Therefore I urge you who have been
chosen by God to live up to the life to which
God called you. 2Always be humble, gentle,
and patient, accepting each other in love.
3You are joined together with peace through
the Spirit, so make every effort to continue
together in this way. 4There is one body and
one Spirit, and God called you to have one
hope. 5There is one Lord, one faith, and one
baptism. 6There is one God and Father of
everything. He rules everything and is
everywhere and is in everything.

7Christ gave each one of us the special gift
of grace, showing how generous he is. 8That
is why it says in the Scriptures,

"When he went up to the heights,
he led a parade of captives,
and he gave gifts to people."   *Psalm 68:18*

9When it says, "He went up," what does it
mean? It means that he first came down to the
earth. 10So Jesus came down, and he is the
same One who went up above all the heaven.
Christ did that to fill everything with his presence. 11And Christ gave gifts to people—he
made some to be apostles, some to be
prophets, some to go and tell the Good News,
and some to have the work of caring for and
teaching God's people. 12Christ gave those gifts
to prepare God's holy people for the work of
serving, to make the body of Christ stronger.
13This work must continue until we are all
joined together in the same faith and in the
same knowledge of the Son of God. We must
become like a mature person, growing until
we become like Christ and have his perfection.

14Then we will no longer be babies. We
will not be tossed about like a ship that the
waves carry one way and then another. We
will not be influenced by every new teaching
we hear from people who are trying to fool
us. They make plans and try any kind of
trick to fool people into following the wrong
path. 15No! Speaking the truth with love, we
will grow up in every way into Christ, who is

the head. [16]The whole body depends on Christ, and all the parts of the body are joined and held together. Each part does its own work to make the whole body grow and be strong with love.

The Way You Should Live

[17]In the Lord's name, I tell you this. Do not continue living like those who do not believe. Their thoughts are worth nothing. [18]They do not understand, and they know nothing, because they refuse to listen. So they cannot have the life that God gives. [19]They have lost all feeling of shame, and they use their lives for doing evil. They continually want to do all kinds of evil. [20]But what you learned in Christ was not like this. [21]I know that you heard about him, and you are in him, so you were taught the truth that is in Jesus. [22]You were taught to leave your old self—to stop living the evil way you lived before. That old self becomes worse, because people are fooled by the evil things they want to do. [23]But you were taught to be made new in your hearts, [24]to become a new person. That new person is made to be like God—made to be truly good and holy.

[25]So you must stop telling lies. Tell each other the truth, because we all belong to each other in the same body.[n] [26]When you are angry, do not sin, and be sure to stop being angry before the end of the day. [27]Do not give the devil a way to defeat you. [28]Those who are stealing must stop stealing and start working. They should earn an honest living for themselves. Then they will have something to share with those who are poor.

[29]When you talk, do not say harmful things, but say what people need—words that will help others become stronger. Then what you say will do good to those who listen to you. [30]And do not make the Holy Spirit sad. The Spirit is God's proof that you belong to him. God gave you the Spirit to show that God will make you free when the final day comes. [31]Do not be bitter or angry or mad. Never shout angrily or say things to hurt others. Never do anything evil. [32]Be kind and loving to each other, and forgive each other just as God forgave you in Christ.

OCTOBER 3

ISAIAH 57:1—58:14

Israel Does Not Follow God

57 Those who are right with God may die,
   but no one pays attention.
Good people are taken away,
   but no one understands.
Those who do right are being taken away
      from evil
[2]   and are given peace.
   Those who live as God wants
   find rest in death.

[3]"Come here, you magicians!
   Come here, you children of prostitutes
      and those who take part in adultery!
[4]Of whom are you making fun?
   Whom are you insulting?
   At whom do you stick out your tongue?

You turn against God,
      and you are liars.
[5]You have sexual relations under every
      green tree
   to worship your gods.
You kill children in the ravines
   and sacrifice them in the rocky
      places.
[6]You take the smooth rocks from the
      ravines
   as your portion.
You pour drink offerings on them to
      worship them,
   and you give grain offerings to them.
   Do you think this makes me want to
      show you mercy?
[7]You make your bed on every hill and
      mountain,
   and there you offer sacrifices.

4:25 Tell . . . body. Quotation from Zechariah 8:16.

[8]You have hidden your idols
  behind your doors and doorposts.
You have left me, and you have
  uncovered yourself.
You have pulled back the covers and
  climbed into bed.
You have made an agreement with those
  whose beds you love,
  and you have looked at their
  nakedness.
[9]You use your oils and perfumes
  to look nice for Molech.
You have sent your messengers to
  faraway lands;
  you even tried to send them to the
  place of the dead.
[10]You were tired from doing these things,
  but you never gave up.
You found new strength,
  so you did not quit.

[11]"Whom were you so afraid of
  that you lied to me?
You have not remembered me
  or even thought about me.
I have been quiet for a long time.
  Is that why you are not afraid of me?
[12]I will tell about your 'goodness' and what
  you do,
  and those things will do you no good.
[13]When you cry out for help,
  let the gods you have gathered help you.
The wind will blow them all away;
  just a puff of wind will take them away.
But the person who depends on me will
  receive the land
  and own my holy mountain."

The Lord Will Save His People

[14]Someone will say, "Build a road! Build a
  road! Prepare the way!
  Make the way clear for my people."
[15]And this is the reason: God lives forever
  and is holy.
He is high and lifted up.
He says, "I live in a high and holy place,
  but I also live with people who are sad
  and humble.
I give new life to those who are humble
  and to those whose hearts are broken.
[16]I will not accuse forever,
  nor will I always be angry,

because then human life would grow
  weak.
Human beings, whom I created, would
  die.
[17]I was angry because they were dishonest
  in order to make money.
I punished them and turned away from
  them in anger,
  but they continued to do evil.
[18]I have seen what they have done, but I
  will heal them.
I will guide them and comfort them
  and those who felt sad for them.
They will all praise me.
[19]I will give peace, real peace, to those far
  and near,
  and I will heal them," says the LORD.
[20]But evil people are like the angry sea,
  which cannot rest,
  whose waves toss up waste and mud.
[21]"There is no peace for evil people," says
  my God.

How to Honor God

58 The LORD says, "Shout out loud. Don't
  hold back.
Shout out loud like a trumpet.
Tell my people what they have done
  against their God;
  tell the family of Jacob about their sins.
[2]They still come every day looking for me
  and want to learn my ways.
They act just like a nation that does what
  is right,
  that obeys the commands of its God.
They ask me to judge them fairly.
They want God to be near them.
[3]They say, 'To honor you we had special
  days when we fasted,
  but you didn't see.
We humbled ourselves to honor you,
  but you didn't notice.'"

But the LORD says, "You do what pleases
  yourselves on these special days,
  and you are unfair to your workers.
[4]On these special days when you fast, you
  argue and fight
  and hit each other with your fists.
You cannot do these things as you do now
  and believe your prayers are heard in
  heaven.

⁵This kind of special day is not what I want.
　This is not the way I want people to be
　　sorry for what they have done.
I don't want people just to bow their
　heads like a plant
　and wear rough cloth and lie in ashes
　　to show their sadness.
This is what you do on your special days
　when you fast,
　but do you think this is what the LORD
　　wants?

⁶"I will tell you the kind of fast I want:
Free the people you have put in prison
　unfairly
　and undo their chains.
Free those to whom you are unfair
　and stop their hard labor.
⁷Share your food with the hungry
　and bring poor, homeless people into
　　your own homes.
When you see someone who has no
　clothes, give him yours,
　and don't refuse to help your own
　　relatives.
⁸Then your light will shine like the dawn,
　and your wounds will quickly heal.
Your God will walk before you,
　and the glory of the LORD will protect
　　you from behind.
⁹Then you will call out, and the LORD will
　answer.
You will cry out, and he will say, 'Here I
　am.'

"If you stop making trouble for others,
　if you stop using cruel words and
　　pointing your finger at others,
¹⁰if you feed those who are hungry
　and take care of the needs of those who
　　are troubled,
then your light will shine in the darkness,
　and you will be bright like sunshine at
　　noon.
¹¹The LORD will always lead you.
He will satisfy your needs in dry lands
　and give strength to your bones.
You will be like a garden that has much
　water,
　like a spring that never runs dry.
¹²Your people will rebuild the old cities
　that are now in ruins;

you will rebuild their foundations.
You will be known for repairing the
　broken places
　and for rebuilding the roads and houses.

¹³"You must obey God's law about the
　Sabbath
　and not do what pleases yourselves on
　　that holy day.
You should call the Sabbath a joyful day
　and honor it as the LORD's holy day.
You should honor it by not doing
　whatever you please
　nor saying whatever you please on that
　　day.
¹⁴Then you will find joy in the LORD,
　and I will carry you to the high places
　　above the earth.
I will let you eat the crops of the land
　your ancestor Jacob had."
The LORD has said these things.

PSALM 114:1–8

God Brought Israel from Egypt

114 When the Israelites went out of
　　　　Egypt,
　the people of Jacob left that foreign
　　country.
²Then Judah became God's holy place;
　Israel became the land he ruled.

³The Red Sea looked and ran away;
　the Jordan River turned back.
⁴The mountains danced like sheep
　and the hills like little lambs.
⁵Sea, why did you run away?
　Jordan, why did you turn back?
⁶Mountains, why did you dance like
　sheep?
　Hills, why did you dance like little
　　lambs?

⁷Earth, shake with fear before the Lord,
　before the God of Jacob.
⁸He turned a rock into a pool of water,
　a hard rock into a spring of water.

PROVERBS 26:22

²²The words of a gossip are like tasty bits
　of food;
　people like to gobble them up.

EPHESIANS 5:1–20

Living in the Light

5 You are God's children whom he loves, so try to be like him. [2]Live a life of love just as Christ loved us and gave himself for us as a sweet-smelling offering and sacrifice to God.

[3]But there must be no sexual sin among you, or any kind of evil or greed. Those things are not right for God's holy people. [4]Also, there must be no evil talk among you, and you must not speak foolishly or tell evil jokes. These things are not right for you. Instead, you should be giving thanks to God. [5]You can be sure of this: No one will have a place in the kingdom of Christ and of God who sins sexually, or does evil things, or is greedy. Anyone who is greedy is serving a false god.

[6]Do not let anyone fool you by telling you things that are not true, because these things will bring God's anger on those who do not obey him. [7]So have nothing to do with them. [8]In the past you were full of darkness, but now you are full of light in the Lord. So live like children who belong to the light. [9]Light brings every kind of goodness, right living, and truth. [10]Try to learn what pleases the Lord. [11]Have nothing to do with the things done in darkness, which are not worth anything. But show that they are wrong. [12]It is shameful even to talk about what those people do in secret. [13]But the light makes all things easy to see, [14]and everything that is made easy to see can become light. This is why it is said:

"Wake up, sleeper!
    Rise from death,
and Christ will shine on you."

[15]So be very careful how you live. Do not live like those who are not wise, but live wisely. [16]Use every chance you have for doing good, because these are evil times. [17]So do not be foolish but learn what the Lord wants you to do. [18]Do not be drunk with wine, which will ruin you, but be filled with the Spirit. [19]Speak to each other with psalms, hymns, and spiritual songs, singing and making music in your hearts to the Lord. [20]Always give thanks to God the Father for everything, in the name of our Lord Jesus Christ.

OCTOBER 4

ISAIAH 59:1—60:22

The Evil That People Do

59 Surely the Lord's power is enough to save you.
    He can hear you when you ask him for help.
[2]It is your evil that has separated you from your God.
    Your sins cause him to turn away from you,
    so he does not hear you.
[3]With your hands you have killed others,
    and with your fingers you have done wrong.
With your lips you have lied,
    and with your tongue you say evil things.
[4]People take each other to court unfairly,
    and no one tells the truth in arguing his case.
They accuse each other falsely and tell lies.
    They cause trouble and create more evil.
[5]They hatch evil like eggs from poisonous snakes.
    If you eat one of those eggs, you will die,
    and if you break one open, a poisonous snake comes out.
People tell lies as they would spin a spider's web.
[6] The webs they make cannot be used for clothes;

you can't cover yourself with those
webs.
The things they do are evil,
and they use their hands to hurt others.
[7]They eagerly run to do evil,
and they are always ready to kill
innocent people.
They think evil thoughts.
Everywhere they go they cause ruin
and destruction.
[8]They don't know how to live in peace,
and there is no fairness in their lives.
They are dishonest.
Anyone who lives as they live will never
have peace.

Israel's Sin Brings Trouble

[9]Fairness has gone far away;
goodness is nowhere to be found.
We wait for the light, but there is only
darkness now.
We hope for a bright light, but all we
have is darkness.
[10]We are like the blind feeling our way
along a wall.
We feel our way as if we had no eyes.
In the brightness of day we trip as if it
were night.
We are like dead men among the
strong.
[11]All of us growl like the bears.
We call out sadly like the doves.
We look for justice, but there isn't any.
We want to be saved, but salvation is far
away.
[12]We have done many wrong things against
our God;
our sins show we are wrong.
We know we have turned against God;
we know the evil things we have done:
[13]sinning and rejecting the LORD,
turning away from our God,
planning to hurt others and to disobey
God,
planning and speaking lies.
[14]So we have driven away justice,
and we have kept away from what is
right.
Truth is not spoken in the streets;
what is honest is not allowed to enter
the city.

[15]Truth cannot be found anywhere,
and people who refuse to do evil are
attacked.

The LORD looked and could not find any
justice,
and he was displeased.
[16]He could not find anyone to help the
people,
and he was surprised that there was no
one to help.
So he used his own power to save the
people;
his own goodness gave him strength.
[17]He covered himself with goodness like
armor.
He put the helmet of salvation on his
head.
He put on his clothes for punishing
and wrapped himself in the coat of his
strong love.
[18]The LORD will pay back his enemies for
what they have done.
He will show his anger to those who
were against him;
he will punish the people in faraway
places as they deserve.
[19]Then people from the west will fear the
LORD,
and people from the east will fear his
glory.
The LORD will come quickly like a
fast-flowing river,
driven by the breath of the LORD.

[20]"Then a Savior will come to Jerusalem
and to the people of Jacob who have
turned from sin,"
says the LORD.
[21]The LORD says, "This is my agreement
with these people: My Spirit and my words
that I give you will never leave you or your
children or your grandchildren, now and
forever."

Jerusalem Will Be Great

60 "Jerusalem, get up and shine, because
your light has come,
and the glory of the LORD shines on you.
[2]Darkness now covers the earth;
deep darkness covers her people.
But the LORD shines on you,
and people see his glory around you.

³Nations will come to your light;
  kings will come to the brightness of
    your sunrise.
⁴"Look around you.
  People are gathering and coming to
    you.
  Your sons are coming from far away,
    and your daughters are coming with
      them.
⁵When you see them, you will shine with
      happiness;
  you will be excited and full of joy,
  because the wealth of the nations across
    the seas will be given to you;
  the riches of the nations will come to
    you.
⁶Herds of camels will cover your land,
  young camels from Midian and Ephah.
  People will come from Sheba
    bringing gold and incense,
    and they will sing praises to the LORD.
⁷All the sheep from Kedar will be given to
    you;
  the sheep from Nebaioth will be
    brought to you.
  They will be pleasing sacrifices on my
    altar,
    and I will make my beautiful Temple
      more beautiful.

⁸"The people are returning to you like
      clouds,
  like doves flying to their nests.
⁹People in faraway lands are waiting for
      me.
  The great trading ships will come first,
  bringing your children from faraway
      lands,
    and with them silver and gold.
  This will honor the LORD your God,
    the Holy One of Israel,
    who does wonderful things for you.

¹⁰"Jerusalem, foreigners will rebuild your
      walls,
    and their kings will serve you.
  When I was angry, I hurt you,
    but now I want to be kind to you and
      comfort you.
¹¹Your gates will always be open;
  they will not be closed day or night

so the nations can bring their wealth to
      you,
    and their kings will be led to you.
¹²The nation or kingdom that doesn't serve
      you will be destroyed;
    it will be completely ruined.

¹³"The great trees of Lebanon will be given
      to you:
    its pine, fir, and cypress trees together.
  You will use them to make my Temple
      beautiful,
    and I will give much honor to this place
      where I rest my feet.
¹⁴The people who have hurt you will bow
      down to you;
    those who hated you will bow down at
      your feet.
  They will call you The City of the LORD,
    Jerusalem, city of the Holy One of Israel.

¹⁵"You have been hated and left empty
    with no one passing through.
  But I will make you great from now on;
    you will be a place of happiness forever
      and ever.
¹⁶You will be given what you need from the
      nations,
    like a child drinking milk from its
      mother.
  Then you will know that it is I, the LORD,
    who saves you.
  You will know that the Powerful One of
    Jacob protects you.
¹⁷I will bring you gold in place of bronze,
    silver in place of iron,
  bronze in place of wood,
    iron in place of rocks.
  I will change your punishment into
      peace,
    and you will be ruled by what is right.
¹⁸There will be no more violence in your
      country;
    it will not be ruined or destroyed.
  You will name your walls Salvation
    and your gates Praise.
¹⁹The sun will no longer be your light
      during the day
    nor will the brightness from the moon
      be your light,
  because the LORD will be your light
      forever,

and your God will be your glory.
20Your sun will never set again,
and your moon will never be dark,
because the LORD will be your light forever,
and your time of sadness will end.
21All of your people will do what is right.
They will receive the earth forever.
They are the plant I have planted,
the work of my own hands
to show my greatness.
22The smallest family will grow to a
thousand.
The least important of you will become
a powerful nation.
I am the LORD,
and when it is time, I will make these
things happen quickly."

PSALM 115:1–8

The One True God

115 It does not belong to us, LORD.
The glory belongs to you
because of your love and loyalty.

2Why do the nations ask,
"Where is their God?"
3Our God is in heaven.
He does what he pleases.
4Their idols are made of silver and gold,
the work of human hands.
5They have mouths, but they cannot speak.
They have eyes, but they cannot see.
6They have ears, but they cannot hear.
They have noses, but they cannot smell.
7They have hands, but they cannot feel.
They have feet, but they cannot walk.
No sounds come from their throats.
8People who make idols will be like them,
and so will those who trust them.

PROVERBS 26:23

23Kind words from a wicked mind
are like a shiny coating on a clay pot.

EPHESIANS 5:21–33

Wives and Husbands

21Yield to obey each other as you would to
Christ.
22Wives, yield to your husbands, as you do
to the Lord, 23because the husband is the
head of the wife, as Christ is the head of the
church. And he is the Savior of the body,
which is the church. 24As the church yields to
Christ, so you wives should yield to your
husbands in everything.

25Husbands, love your wives as Christ
loved the church and gave himself for it 26to
make it belong to God. Christ used the word
to make the church clean by washing it with
water. 27He died so that he could give the
church to himself like a bride in all her
beauty. He died so that the church could be
pure and without fault, with no evil or sin or
any other wrong thing in it. 28In the same
way, husbands should love their wives as
they love their own bodies. The man who
loves his wife loves himself. 29No one ever
hates his own body, but feeds and takes care
of it. And that is what Christ does for the
church, 30because we are parts of his body.
31The Scripture says, "So a man will leave his
father and mother and be united with his
wife, and the two will become one body."^{n}
32That secret is very important—I am talking about Christ and the church. 33But each
one of you must love his wife as he loves
himself, and a wife must respect her husband.

OCTOBER 5

ISAIAH 61:1—62:12

The Lord's Message of Freedom

61 The Lord GOD has put his Spirit in
me,

because the LORD has appointed me to
tell the good news to the poor.
He has sent me to comfort those whose
hearts are broken,
to tell the captives they are free,

5:31 "So . . . body." Quotation from Genesis 2:24.

and to tell the prisoners they are
released.
²He has sent me to announce the time
when the Lord will show his
kindness
and the time when our God will punish
evil people.
He has sent me to comfort all those who
are sad
³ and to help the sorrowing people of
Jerusalem.
I will give them a crown to replace their
ashes,
and the oil of gladness to replace their
sorrow,
and clothes of praise to replace their
spirit of sadness.
Then they will be called Trees of
Goodness,
trees planted by the Lord to show his
greatness.

⁴They will rebuild the old ruins
and restore the places destroyed long
ago.
They will repair the ruined cities
that were destroyed for so long.

⁵My people, foreigners will come to tend
your sheep.
People from other countries will tend
your fields and vineyards.
⁶You will be called priests of the Lord;
you will be named the servants of our
God.
You will have riches from all the nations
on earth,
and you will take pride in them.
⁷Instead of being ashamed, my people will
receive twice as much wealth.
Instead of being disgraced, they will be
happy because of what they receive.
They will receive a double share of the
land,
so their happiness will continue forever.
⁸"I, the Lord, love justice.
I hate stealing and everything that is
wrong.
I will be fair and give my people what
they should have,
and I will make an agreement with
them that will continue forever.

⁹Everyone in all nations will know the
children of my people,
and their children will be known
among the nations.
Anyone who sees them will know
that they are people the Lord has
blessed."

¹⁰The Lord makes me very happy;
all that I am rejoices in my God.
He has covered me with clothes of
salvation
and wrapped me with a coat of
goodness,
like a bridegroom dressed for his
wedding,
like a bride dressed in jewels.
¹¹The earth causes plants to grow,
and a garden causes the seeds planted
in it to grow.
In the same way the Lord God will make
goodness and praise
come from all the nations.

New Jerusalem

62 Because I love Jerusalem, I will
continue to speak for her;
for Jerusalem's sake I will not stop
speaking
until her goodness shines like a bright
light,
until her salvation burns bright like a
flame.
²Jerusalem, the nations will see your
goodness,
and all kings will see your glory.
Then you will have a new name,
which the Lord himself will give you.
³You will be like a beautiful crown in the
Lord's hand,
like a king's crown in your God's hand.
⁴You will never again be called the People
that God Left,
nor your land the Land that God
Destroyed.
You will be called the People God Loves,
and your land will be called the Bride
of God,
because the Lord loves you.
And your land will belong to him as a
bride belongs to her husband.
⁵As a young man marries a woman,

so your children will marry your land.
As a man rejoices over his new wife,
so your God will rejoice over you.

6Jerusalem, I have put guards on the walls
to watch.
They must not be silent day or night.
You people who remind the LORD of your
needs in prayer
should never be quiet.
7You should not stop praying to him until
he builds up Jerusalem
and makes it a city all people will praise.

8The LORD has made a promise,
and by his power he will keep his
promise.
He said, "I will never again give your grain
as food to your enemies.
I will not let your enemies drink the new
wine
that you have worked to make.
9Those who gather food will eat it,
and they will praise the LORD.
Those who gather the grapes will drink
the wine
in the courts of my Temple."

10Go through, go through the gates!
Make the way ready for the people.
Build up, build up the road!
Move all the stones off the road.
Raise the banner as a sign for the people.

11The LORD is speaking
to all the faraway lands:
"Tell the people of Jerusalem,
'Look, your Savior is coming.
He is bringing your reward to you;
he is bringing his payment with him.'"
12His people will be called the Holy People,
the Saved People of the LORD,
and Jerusalem will be called the City
God Wants,
the City God Has Not Rejected.

PSALM 115:9–13

9Family of Israel, trust the LORD;
he is your helper and your protection.

10Family of Aaron, trust the LORD;
he is your helper and your protection.
11You who respect the LORD should trust
him;
he is your helper and your protection.
12The LORD remembers us and will bless
us.
He will bless the family of Israel;
he will bless the family of Aaron.
13The LORD will bless those who respect
him,
from the smallest to the greatest.

PROVERBS 26:24–26

24Those who hate you may try to fool you
with their words,
but in their minds they are planning
evil.
25People's words may be kind, but don't
believe them,
because their minds are full of evil
thoughts.
26Lies can hide hate,
but the evil will be plain to everyone.

EPHESIANS 6:1–24

Children and Parents

6Children, obey your parents as the Lord
wants, because this is the right thing to
do. 2The command says, "Honor your father
and mother."[n] This is the first command that
has a promise with it— 3"Then everything
will be well with you, and you will have a
long life on the earth."[n]
4Fathers, do not make your children angry, but raise them with the training and
teaching of the Lord.

Slaves and Masters

5Slaves, obey your masters here on earth
with fear and respect and from a sincere
heart, just as you obey Christ. 6You must do
this not only while they are watching you, to
please them. With all your heart you must do
what God wants as people who are obeying
Christ. 7Do your work with enthusiasm.
Work as if you were serving the Lord, not as

6:2 "Honor . . . mother." Quotation from Exodus 20:12; Deuteronomy 5:16.   **6:3 "Then . . . earth."** Quotation from Exodus 20:12; Deuteronomy 5:16.

if you were serving only men and women. [8]Remember that the Lord will give a reward to everyone, slave or free, for doing good.

[9]Masters, in the same way, be good to your slaves. Do not threaten them. Remember that the One who is your Master and their Master is in heaven, and he treats everyone alike.

Wear the Full Armor of God

[10]Finally, be strong in the Lord and in his great power. [11]Put on the full armor of God so that you can fight against the devil's evil tricks. [12]Our fight is not against people on earth but against the rulers and authorities and the powers of this world's darkness, against the spiritual powers of evil in the heavenly world. [13]That is why you need to put on God's full armor. Then on the day of evil you will be able to stand strong. And when you have finished the whole fight, you will still be standing. [14]So stand strong, with the belt of truth tied around your waist and the protection of right living on your chest. [15]On your feet wear the Good News of peace to help you stand strong. [16]And also use the shield of faith with which you can stop all the burning arrows of the Evil One. [17]Accept God's salvation as your helmet, and take the sword of the Spirit, which is the word of God. [18]Pray in the Spirit at all times with all kinds of prayers, asking for everything you need. To do this you must always be ready and never give up. Always pray for all God's people.

[19]Also pray for me that when I speak, God will give me words so that I can tell the secret of the Good News without fear. [20]I have been sent to preach this Good News, and I am doing that now, here in prison. Pray that when I preach the Good News I will speak without fear, as I should.

Final Greetings

[21]I am sending to you Tychicus, our brother whom we love and a faithful servant of the Lord's work. He will tell you everything that is happening with me. Then you will know how I am and what I am doing. [22]I am sending him to you for this reason—so that you will know how we are, and he can encourage you.

[23]Peace and love with faith to you brothers and sisters from God the Father and the Lord Jesus Christ. [24]Grace to all of you who love our Lord Jesus Christ with love that never ends.

OCTOBER 6

ISAIAH 63:1—64:12

The Lord Judges His People

63 Who is this coming from Edom, from the city of Bozrah, dressed in red?
Who is this dressed in fine clothes
  and marching forward with his great power?

He says, "I, the LORD, speak what is right.
  I have the power to save you."

[2]Someone asks, "Why are your clothes bright red
  as if you had walked on the grapes to make wine?"

[3]The LORD answers, "I have walked in the winepress alone,
and no one among the nations helped
  me.
I was angry and walked on the nations
  and crushed them because of my anger.
Blood splashed on my clothes,
  and I stained all my clothing.
[4]I chose a time to punish people,
  and the time has come for me to save.
[5]I looked around, but I saw no one to help
  me.
I was surprised that no one supported
  me.
So I used my own power to save my
  people;
  my own anger supported me.
[6]While I was angry, I walked on the
  nations.

In my anger I punished them
and poured their blood on the
ground."

The Lord's Kindness to His People

⁷I will tell about the LORD's kindness
and praise him for everything he has
done.
I will praise the LORD for the many
good things he has given us
and for his goodness to the people of
Israel.
He has shown great mercy to us
and has been very kind to us.
⁸He said, "These are my people;
my children will not lie to me."
So he saved them.
⁹When they suffered, he suffered also.
He sent his own angel to save them.
Because of his love and kindness, he
saved them.
Since long ago he has picked them up
and carried them.
¹⁰But they turned against him
and made his Holy Spirit very sad.
So he became their enemy,
and he fought against them.

¹¹But then his people remembered what
happened long ago,
in the days of Moses and the Israelites
with him.
Where is the LORD who brought the
people through the sea,
with the leaders of his people?
Where is the one
who put his Holy Spirit among them,
¹²who led Moses by the right hand
with his wonderful power,
who divided the water before them
to make his name famous forever,
¹³who led the people through the deep
waters?
Like a horse walking through a desert,
the people did not stumble.
¹⁴Like cattle that go down to the valley,
the Spirit of the LORD gave the people
a place to rest.
LORD, that is the way you led your
people,
and by this you won for yourself
wonderful fame.

A Prayer for Help

¹⁵LORD, look down from the heavens and
see;
look at us from your wonderful and
holy home in heaven.
Where is your strong love and power?
Why are you keeping your love and
mercy from us?
¹⁶You are our father.
Abraham doesn't know we are his
children,
and Israel doesn't recognize us.
LORD, you are our father.
You are called "the one who has always
saved us."
¹⁷LORD, why are you making us wander
from your ways?
Why do you make us stubborn so that
we don't honor you?
For our sake come back to us,
your servants, who belong to you.
¹⁸Your people had your Temple for a while,
but now our enemies have walked on
your holy place and crushed it.
¹⁹We have become like people you never
ruled over,
like those who have never worn your
name.

64 Tear open the skies and come down to
earth
so that the mountains will tremble
before you.
²Like a fire that burns twigs,
like a fire that makes water boil,
let your enemies know who you are.
Then all nations will shake with fear
when they see you.
³You have done amazing things we did not
expect.
You came down, and the mountains
trembled before you.
⁴From long ago no one has ever heard of a
God like you.
No one has ever seen a God besides
you,
who helps the people who trust you.
⁵You help those who enjoy doing good,
who remember how you want them to
live.
But you were angry because we sinned.
For a long time we disobeyed,

so how can we be saved?
⁶All of us are dirty with sin.
   All the right things we have done are
      like filthy pieces of cloth.
   All of us are like dead leaves,
      and our sins, like the wind, have
         carried us away.
⁷No one worships you
      or even asks you to help us.
   That is because you have turned away
      from us
      and have let our sins destroy us.

⁸But LORD, you are our father.
   We are like clay, and you are the potter;
      your hands made us all.
⁹LORD, don't continue to be angry with us;
      don't remember our sins forever.
   Please, look at us,
      because we are your people.
¹⁰Your holy cities are empty like the desert.
   Jerusalem is like a desert;
      it is destroyed.
¹¹Our ancestors worshiped you
      in our holy and wonderful Temple,
   but now it has been burned with fire,
      and all our precious things have been
         destroyed.
¹²When you see these things, will you hold
      yourself back from helping us, LORD?
   Will you be silent and punish us
      beyond what we can stand?

PSALM 115:14–18

¹⁴May the LORD give you success,
      and may he give you and your children
         success.
¹⁵May you be blessed by the LORD,
      who made heaven and earth.

¹⁶Heaven belongs to the LORD,
      but he gave the earth to people.
¹⁷Dead people do not praise the LORD;
      those in the grave are silent.
¹⁸But we will praise the LORD
      now and forever.

   Praise the LORD!

PROVERBS 26:27

²⁷Whoever digs a pit for others will fall
      into it.

   Whoever tries to roll a boulder down
      on others will be crushed by it.

PHILIPPIANS 1:1—2:4

1 From Paul and Timothy, servants of
   Christ Jesus.
   To all of God's holy people in Christ Jesus
who live in Philippi, including your overseers and deacons:
   ²Grace and peace to you from God our Father and the Lord Jesus Christ.

Paul's Prayer

³I thank my God every time I remember
you, ⁴always praying with joy for all of you. ⁵I
thank God for the help you gave me while I
preached the Good News—help you gave
from the first day you believed until now.
⁶God began doing a good work in you, and I
am sure he will continue it until it is finished
when Jesus Christ comes again.
   ⁷And I know that I am right to think like
this about all of you, because I have you in
my heart. All of you share in God's grace
with me while I am in prison and while I am
defending and proving the truth of the Good
News. ⁸God knows that I want to see you
very much, because I love all of you with the
love of Christ Jesus.
   ⁹This is my prayer for you: that your love
will grow more and more; that you will have
knowledge and understanding with your
love; ¹⁰that you will see the difference between
good and bad and will choose the good; that
you will be pure and without wrong for the
coming of Christ; ¹¹that you will be filled with
the good things produced in your life by
Christ to bring glory and praise to God.

Paul's Troubles Help the Work

¹²I want you brothers and sisters to know
that what has happened to me has helped to
spread the Good News. ¹³All the palace
guards and everyone else knows that I am in
prison because I am a believer in Christ.
¹⁴Because I am in prison, most of the believers have become more bold in Christ and are
not afraid to speak the word of God.
   ¹⁵It is true that some preach about Christ
because they are jealous and ambitious, but
others preach about Christ because they

want to help. [16]They preach because they have love, and they know that God gave me the work of defending the Good News. [17]But the others preach about Christ for selfish and wrong reasons, wanting to make trouble for me in prison.

[18]But it doesn't matter. The important thing is that in every way, whether for right or wrong reasons, they are preaching about Christ. So I am happy, and I will continue to be happy. [19]Because you are praying for me and the Spirit of Jesus Christ is helping me, I know this trouble will bring my freedom. [20]I expect and hope that I will not fail Christ in anything but that I will have the courage now, as always, to show the greatness of Christ in my life here on earth, whether I live or die. [21]To me the only important thing about living is Christ, and dying would be profit for me. [22]If I continue living in my body, I will be able to work for the Lord. I do not know what to choose—living or dying. [23]It is hard to choose between the two. I want to leave this life and be with Christ, which is much better, [24]but you need me here in my body. [25]Since I am sure of this, I know I will stay with you to help you grow and have joy in your faith. [26]You will be very happy in Christ Jesus when I am with you again.

[27]Only one thing concerns me: Be sure that you live in a way that brings honor to the Good News of Christ. Then whether I come and visit you or am away from you, I will hear that you are standing strong with one purpose, that you work together as one for the faith of the Good News, [28]and that you are not afraid of those who are against you. All of this is proof that your enemies will be destroyed but that you will be saved by God. [29]God gave you the honor not only of believing in Christ but also of suffering for him, both of which bring glory to Christ. [30]When I was with you, you saw the struggles I had, and you hear about the struggles I am having now. You yourselves are having the same kind of struggles.

2 Does your life in Christ give you strength? Does his love comfort you? Do we share together in the spirit? Do you have mercy and kindness? [2]If so, make me very happy by having the same thoughts, sharing the same love, and having one mind and purpose. [3]When you do things, do not let selfishness or pride be your guide. Instead, be humble and give more honor to others than to yourselves. [4]Do not be interested only in your own life, but be interested in the lives of others.

OCTOBER 7

ISAIAH 65:1—66:24

All People Will Learn About God

65 The LORD says, "I made myself known to people who were not looking for me.
I was found by those who were not asking me for help.
I said, 'Here I am. Here I am,'
to a nation that was not praying to me.
[2]All day long I stood ready to accept people who turned against me,
but the way they continue to live is not good;
they do anything they want to do.
[3]Right in front of me

they continue to do things that make me angry.
They offer sacrifices to their gods in their gardens,
and they burn incense on altars of brick.
[4]They sit among the graves
and spend their nights waiting to get messages from the dead.
They eat the meat of pigs,
and their pots are full of soup made from meat that is wrong to eat.
[5]But they tell others, 'Stay away, and don't come near me.
I am too holy for you.'
These people are like smoke in my nose.

Like a fire that burns all the time, they
continue to make me angry.

⁶"Look, it is written here before me.
I will not be quiet; instead, I will repay
you in full.
I will punish you for what you have
done.
⁷I will punish you for your sins and your
ancestors' sins,"
says the LORD.
"They burned incense to gods on the
mountains
and shamed me on those hills.
So I will punish them as they should be
punished
for what they did."

⁸This is what the LORD says:
"When there is juice left in the grapes,
people do not destroy them,
because they know there is good left in
them.
So I will do the same thing to my
servants—
I will not completely destroy them.
⁹I will leave some of the children of Jacob,
and some of the people of Judah will
receive my mountain.
I will choose the people who will live
there;
my servants will live there.
¹⁰Then the Plain of Sharon will be a field
for flocks,
and the Valley of Achor will be a place
for herds to rest.
They will be for the people who want to
follow me.

¹¹"But as for you who left the LORD,
who forgot about my holy mountain,
who worship the god Luck,
who hold religious feasts for the god
Fate,
¹²I decide your fate, and I will punish you
with my sword.
You will all be killed,
because I called you, but you refused to
answer.
I spoke to you, but you wouldn't listen.
You did the things I said were evil

and chose to do things that displease
me."
¹³So this is what the Lord GOD says:
"My servants will eat,
but you evil people will be hungry.
My servants will drink,
but you evil people will be thirsty.
My servants will be happy,
but you evil people will be shamed.
¹⁴My servants will shout for joy
because of the goodness of their hearts,
but you evil people will cry,
because you will be sad.
You will cry loudly, because your spirits
will be broken.
¹⁵Your names will be like curses to my
servants,
and the Lord GOD will put you to death.
But he will call his servants by another
name.
¹⁶People in the land who ask for blessings
will ask for them from the faithful God.
And people in the land who make a
promise
will promise in the name of the faithful
God,
because the troubles of the past will be
forgotten.
I will make those troubles go away.

A New Time Is Coming
¹⁷"Look, I will make new heavens and a
new earth,
and people will not remember the past
or think about those things.
¹⁸My people will be happy forever
because of the things I will make.
I will make a Jerusalem that is full of joy,
and I will make her people a delight.
¹⁹Then I will rejoice over Jerusalem
and be delighted with my people.
There will never again be heard in that
city
the sounds of crying and sadness.
²⁰There will never be a baby from that
city
who lives only a few days.
And there will never be an older person
who doesn't have a long life.
A person who lives a hundred years will
be called young,

and a person who dies before he is a
hundred will be thought of as a
sinner.

[21]In that city those who build houses will
live there.
Those who plant vineyards will get to
eat their grapes.

[22]No more will one person build a house
and someone else live there.
One person will not plant a garden and
someone else eat its fruit.
My people will live a long time,
as trees live long.
My chosen people will live there
and enjoy the things they make.

[23]They will never again work for nothing.
They will never again give birth to
children who die young.
All my people will be blessed by the LORD;
they and their children will be blessed.

[24]I will provide for their needs before they
ask,
and I will help them while they are still
asking for help.

[25]Wolves and lambs will eat together in
peace.
Lions will eat hay like oxen,
and a snake on the ground will not hurt
anyone.
They will not hurt or destroy each other
on all my holy mountain,"
says the LORD.

The Lord Will Judge All Nations

66 This is what the LORD says:
"Heaven is my throne,
and the earth is my footstool.
So do you think you can build a house for
me?
Do I need a place to rest?

[2]My hand made all things.
All things are here because I made
them,"
says the LORD.

"These are the people I am pleased with:
those who are not proud or stubborn
and who fear my word.

[3]But those people who kill bulls as a
sacrifice to me

are like those who kill people.
Those who kill sheep as a sacrifice
are like those who break the necks of
dogs.
Those who give me grain offerings
are like those who offer me the blood of
pigs.[n]
Those who burn incense
are like those who worship idols.
These people choose their own ways, not
mine,
and they love the terrible things they do.

[4]So I will choose their punishments,
and I will punish them with what they
fear most.
This is because I called to them, but they
did not listen.
I spoke to them, but they did not hear
me.
They did things I said were evil;
they chose to do things I did not like."

[5]You people who obey the words of the
LORD,
listen to what he says:
"Your brothers hated you
and turned against you because you
followed me.
Your brothers said, 'Let the LORD be
honored
so we may see you rejoice,'
but they will be punished.

[6]Listen to the loud noise coming from the
city;
hear the noise from the Temple.
It is the LORD punishing his enemies,
giving them the punishment they
should have.

[7]"A woman does not give birth before she
feels the pain;
she does not give birth to a son before
the pain starts.

[8]No one has ever heard of that happening;
no one has ever seen that happen.
In the same way no one ever saw a
country begin in one day;
no one has ever heard of a new nation
beginning in one moment.
But Jerusalem will give birth to her
children

66:3 dogs . . . pigs God did not want his people to offer dogs and pigs as sacrifices because they were unclean animals.

just as soon as she feels the birth
  pains.
⁹In the same way I will not cause pain
  without allowing something new to be
  born," says the LORD.
"If I cause you the pain,
  I will not stop you from giving birth to
    your new nation," says your God.
¹⁰"Jerusalem, rejoice.
  All you people who love Jerusalem, be
    happy.
  Those of you who felt sad for Jerusalem
    should now feel happy with her.
¹¹You will take comfort from her and be
    satisfied,
  as a child is nursed by its mother.
You will receive her good things
  and enjoy her wealth."
¹²This is what the LORD says:
"I will give her peace that will flow to her
  like a river.
The wealth of the nations will come to
  her like a river overflowing its banks.
Like babies you will be nursed and held in
  my arms
  and bounced on my knees.
¹³I will comfort you
  as a mother comforts her child.
  You will be comforted in Jerusalem."
¹⁴When you see these things, you will be
    happy,
  and you will grow like the grass.
The LORD's servants will see his power,
  but his enemies will see his anger.
¹⁵Look, the LORD is coming with fire
  and his armies with clouds of dust.
He will punish those people with his
    anger;
  he will punish them with flames of
    fire.
¹⁶The LORD will judge the people with fire,
  and he will destroy many people with
    his sword;
  he will kill many people.
¹⁷"These people make themselves holy and
  pure to go to worship their gods in their gardens. Following each other into their special
  gardens, they eat the meat of pigs and rats
  and other hateful things. But they will all be
  destroyed together," says the LORD.

¹⁸"I know they have evil thoughts and do
evil things, so I am coming to punish them. I
will gather all nations and all people, and they
will come together and see my glory.
¹⁹"I will put a mark on some of the people,
and I will send some of these saved people to
the nations: to Tarshish, Libya, Lud (the land
of archers), Tubal, Greece, and all the faraway
lands. These people have never heard about
what I have done nor seen my glory. So the
saved people will tell the nations about my
glory. ²⁰And they will bring all your fellow Israelites from all nations to my holy mountain
in Jerusalem. Your fellow Israelites will come
on horses, donkeys, and camels and in chariots and wagons. They will be like the grain
offerings that the people bring in clean containers to the Temple," says the LORD. ²¹"And I
will choose even some of these people to be
priests and Levites," says the LORD.
²²"I will make new heavens and the new
earth, which will last forever," says the LORD.
"In the same way, your names and your children will always be with me. ²³All people will
come to worship me every Sabbath and every
New Moon," says the LORD. ²⁴"They will go out
and see the dead bodies of the people who
sinned against me. The worms that eat them
will never die, and the fires that burn them
will never stop, and everyone will hate to see
those bodies."

PSALM 116:1–4

Thanksgiving for Escaping Death

116 I love the LORD,
  because he listens to my prayers
    for help.
²He paid attention to me,
  so I will call to him for help as long as I
    live.
³The ropes of death bound me,
  and the fear of the grave took hold of
    me.
  I was troubled and sad.
⁴Then I called out the name of the LORD.
  I said, "Please, LORD, save me!"

PROVERBS 26:28

²⁸Liars hate the people they hurt,
  and false praise can ruin others.

PHILIPPIANS 2:5–30

Be Unselfish Like Christ

5In your lives you must think and act like Christ Jesus.

6Christ himself was like God in everything.
But he did not think that being equal
with God was something to be used
for his own benefit.

7But he gave up his place with God and
made himself nothing.
He was born as a man
and became like a servant.

8And when he was living as a man,
he humbled himself and was fully
obedient to God,
even when that caused his death—
death on a cross.

9So God raised him to the highest place.
God made his name greater than every
other name

10so that every knee will bow to the name
of Jesus—
everyone in heaven, on earth, and
under the earth.

11And everyone will confess that Jesus
Christ is Lord
and bring glory to God the Father.

Be the People God Wants You to Be

12My dear friends, you have always obeyed God when I was with you. It is even more important that you obey now while I am away from you. Keep on working to complete your salvation with fear and trembling, 13because God is working in you to help you want to do and be able to do what pleases him.

14Do everything without complaining or arguing. 15Then you will be innocent and without any wrong. You will be God's children without fault. But you are living with crooked and mean people all around you, among whom you shine like stars in the dark world. 16You offer the teaching that gives life. So when Christ comes again, I can be happy because my work was not wasted. I ran the race and won.

17Your faith makes you offer your lives as a sacrifice in serving God. If I have to offer my own blood with your sacrifice, I will be happy and full of joy with all of you. 18You also should be happy and full of joy with me.

Timothy and Epaphroditus

19I hope in the Lord Jesus to send Timothy to you soon. I will be happy to learn how you are. 20I have no one else like Timothy, who truly cares for you. 21Other people are interested only in their own lives, not in the work of Jesus Christ. 22You know the kind of person Timothy is. You know he has served with me in telling the Good News, as a son serves his father. 23I plan to send him to you quickly when I know what will happen to me. 24I am sure that the Lord will help me to come to you soon.

25Epaphroditus, my brother in Christ, works and serves with me in the army of Christ. When I needed help, you sent him to me. I think now that I must send him back to you, 26because he wants very much to see all of you. He is worried because you heard that he was sick. 27Yes, he was sick, and nearly died, but God had mercy on him and me too so that I would not have more sadness. 28I want very much to send him to you so that when you see him you can be happy, and I can stop worrying about you. 29Welcome him in the Lord with much joy. Give honor to people like him, 30because he almost died for the work of Christ. He risked his life to give me the help you could not give in your service to me.

OCTOBER 8

JEREMIAH 1:1—2:37

1These are the words of Jeremiah son of Hilkiah. He belonged to the family of priests who lived in the town of Anathoth in the land of Benjamin. 2The LORD spoke his word to Jeremiah during the thirteenth year that Josiah son of Amon was king of Judah. 3The LORD also spoke to Jeremiah while Jehoiakim son of Josiah was king of Judah and during the eleven years that Zedekiah son of Josiah was king of Judah. In the fifth month of his last year, the people of Jerusalem were taken away as captives.

The Lord Calls Jeremiah

⁴The LORD spoke his word to me, saying:
⁵"Before I made you in your mother's
     womb, I chose you.
   Before you were born, I set you apart
     for a special work.
   I appointed you as a prophet to the
     nations."

⁶Then I said, "But Lord GOD, I don't know how to speak. I am only a boy."

⁷But the LORD said to me, "Don't say, 'I am only a boy.' You must go everywhere I send you, and you must say everything I tell you to say. ⁸Don't be afraid of anyone, because I am with you to protect you," says the LORD.

⁹Then the LORD reached out his hand and touched my mouth. He said to me, "See, I am putting my words in your mouth. ¹⁰Today I have put you in charge of nations and kingdoms. You will pull up and tear down, destroy and overthrow, build up and plant."

Jeremiah Sees Two Visions

¹¹The LORD spoke his word to me, saying: "Jeremiah, what do you see?"

I answered, "I see a stick of almond wood."

¹²The LORD said to me, "You have seen correctly, because I am watching to make sure my words come true."

¹³The LORD spoke his word to me again: "What do you see?"

I answered, "I see a pot of boiling water, tipping over from the north."

¹⁴The LORD said to me, "Disaster will come from the north and strike all the people who live in this country. ¹⁵In a short time I will call all of the people in the northern kingdoms," said the LORD.
   "Those kings will come and set up their
     thrones
   near the entrance of the gates of
     Jerusalem.
   They will attack all the city walls around
     Jerusalem
   and all the cities in Judah.
¹⁶And I will announce my judgments
     against my people

because of their evil in turning away
     from me.
   They offered sacrifices to other gods
   and worshiped idols they had made
     with their own hands.

¹⁷"Jeremiah, get ready. Stand up and tell them everything I command you to say. Don't be afraid of the people, or I will give you good reason to be afraid of them. ¹⁸Today I am going to make you a strong city, an iron pillar, a bronze wall. You will be able to stand against everyone in the land: Judah's kings, officers, priests, and the people of the land. ¹⁹They will fight against you, but they will not defeat you, because I am with you to protect you!" says the LORD.

Israel Turns from God

2 The LORD spoke his word to me, saying: ²"Go and speak to the people of Jerusalem, saying: This is what the LORD says:
   'I remember how faithful you were to me
     when you were a young nation.
   You loved me like a young bride.
   You followed me through the desert,
     a land that had never been planted.
³The people of Israel were holy to the
     LORD,
   like the firstfruits from his harvest.
   Those who tried to hurt Israel were
     judged guilty.
   Disasters struck them,'" says the LORD.

⁴Hear the word of the LORD, family of
     Jacob,
   all you family groups of Israel.
⁵This is what the LORD says:
   "I was fair to your ancestors,
     so why did they turn away from me?
   Your ancestors worshiped useless idols
   and became useless themselves.
⁶Your ancestors didn't say,
   'Where is the LORD who brought us out
     of Egypt?
   He led us through the desert,
     through a dry and rocky land,
   through a dark and dangerous land.
   He led us where no one travels or lives.'
⁷I brought you into a fertile land
     so you could eat its fruit and produce.
   But you came and made my land unclean;
   you made it a hateful place.

[8]The priests didn't ask,
'Where is the LORD?'
The people who know the teachings
didn't know me.
The leaders turned against me.
The prophets prophesied in the name of
Baal
and worshiped useless idols.

[9]"So now I will again tell what I have
against you," says the LORD.
"And I will tell what I have against your
grandchildren.
[10]Go across the sea to the island of Cyprus
and see.
Send someone to the land of Kedar to
look closely.
See if there has ever been anything like
this.
[11]Has a nation ever exchanged its gods?
(Of course, its gods are not really gods
at all.)
But my people have exchanged their
glorious God
for idols worth nothing.
[12]Skies, be shocked at the things that have
happened
and shake with great fear!" says the
LORD.
[13]"My people have done two evils:
They have turned away from me,
the spring of living water.
And they have dug their own wells,
which are broken wells that cannot
hold water.
[14]Have the people of Israel become slaves?
Have they become like someone who
was born a slave?
Why were they taken captive?
[15]Enemies have roared like lions at Israel;
they have growled at Israel.
They have destroyed the land of Israel.
The cities of Israel lie in ruins,
and all the people have left.
[16]The men from the cities of Memphis and
Tahpanhes
have disgraced you by shaving the top
of your head.
[17]Haven't you brought this on yourselves
by turning away from the LORD your God
when he was leading you in the right
way?

[18]It did not help to go to Egypt
and drink from the Shihor River.
It did not help to go to Assyria
and drink from the Euphrates River.
[19]Your evil will bring punishment to you,
and the wrong you have done will teach
you a lesson.
Think about it and understand
that it is a terrible evil to turn away from
the LORD your God.
It is wrong not to fear me,"
says the Lord GOD All-Powerful.

[20]"Long ago you refused to obey me as an
ox breaks its yoke.
You broke the ropes I used to hold you
and said, 'I will not serve you!'
In fact, on every high hill
and under every green tree
you lay down as a prostitute.
[21]But I planted you as a special vine,
as a very good seed.
How then did you turn
into a wild vine that grows bad fruit?
[22]Although you wash yourself with
cleanser
and use much soap,
I can still see the stain of your guilt,"
says the Lord GOD.
[23]"How can you say to me, 'I am not guilty.
I have not worshiped the Baal idols'?
Look at the things you did in the valley.
Think about what you have done.
You are like a she-camel in mating
season
that runs from place to place.
[24]You are like a wild donkey that lives in
the desert
and sniffs the wind at mating time.
At that time who can hold her back?
Any male who chases her will easily
catch her;
at mating time, it is easy to find her.
[25]Don't run until your feet are bare
or until your throat is dry.
But you say, 'It's no use!
I love those other gods,
and I must chase them!'

[26]"A thief is ashamed when someone
catches him stealing.

In the same way, the family of Israel is
ashamed—
they, their kings, their officers,
their priests, and their prophets.
27They say to things of wood, 'You are my
father,'
and to idols of stone, 'You gave birth to
me.'
Those people won't look at me;
they have turned their backs to me.
But when they get into trouble, they say,
'Come and save us!'
28Where are the idols you made for
yourselves?
Let them come and save you
when you are in trouble!
People of Judah, you have as many idols
as you have towns!

29"Why do you complain to me?
All of you have turned against me," says
the LORD.
30"I punished your people, but it did not
help.
They didn't come back when they were
punished.
With your swords you killed your
prophets
like a hungry lion.

31"People of Judah, pay attention to the
word of the LORD:
Have I been like a desert to the people of
Israel
or like a dark and dangerous land?
Why do my people say, 'We are free to
wander.
We won't come to you anymore'?
32A young woman does not forget her
jewelry,
and a bride does not forget the
decorations for her dress.
But my people have forgotten me
for more days than can be counted.
33You really know how to chase after love.
Even the worst women can learn evil
ways from you.
34Even on your clothes you have the blood
of poor and innocent people,
but they weren't thieves you caught
breaking in.
You do all these things,

35 but you say, 'I am innocent.
God is not angry with me.'
But I will judge you guilty of lying,
because you say, 'I have not sinned.'
36It is so easy for you to change your mind.
Even Egypt will let you down,
as Assyria let you down.
37You will eventually leave that place
with your hands on your head, like
captives.
You trusted those countries,
but you will not be helped by them,
because the LORD has rejected them.

PSALM 116:5–14

5The LORD is kind and does what is right;
our God is merciful.
6The LORD watches over the foolish;
when I was helpless, he saved me.
7I said to myself, "Relax,
because the LORD takes care of you."
8LORD, you saved me from death.
You stopped my eyes from crying;
you kept me from being defeated.
9So I will walk with the LORD
in the land of the living.
10I believed, so I said,
"I am completely ruined."
11In my distress I said,
"All people are liars."

12What can I give the LORD
for all the good things he has given to
me?
13I will lift up the cup of salvation,
and I will pray to the LORD.
14I will give the LORD what I promised
in front of all his people.

PROVERBS 27:1

27Don't brag about tomorrow;
you don't know what may happen
then.

PHILIPPIANS 3:1–21

The Importance of Christ

3My brothers and sisters, be full of joy in
the Lord. It is no trouble for me to write
the same things to you again, and it will help
you to be more ready. 2Watch out for those

who do evil, who are like dogs, who demand to cut[n] the body. [3]We are the ones who are truly circumcised. We worship God through his Spirit, and our pride is in Christ Jesus. We do not put trust in ourselves or anything we can do, [4]although I might be able to put trust in myself. If anyone thinks he has a reason to trust in himself, he should know that I have greater reason for trusting in myself. [5]I was circumcised eight days after my birth. I am from the people of Israel and the tribe of Benjamin. I am a Hebrew, and my parents were Hebrews. I had a strict view of the law, which is why I became a Pharisee. [6]I was so enthusiastic I tried to hurt the church. No one could find fault with the way I obeyed the law of Moses. [7]Those things were important to me, but now I think they are worth nothing because of Christ. [8]Not only those things, but I think that all things are worth nothing compared with the greatness of knowing Christ Jesus my Lord. Because of him, I have lost all those things, and now I know they are worthless trash. This allows me to have Christ [9]and to belong to him. Now I am right with God, not because I followed the law, but because I believed in Christ. God uses my faith to make me right with him. [10]I want to know Christ and the power that raised him from the dead. I want to share in his sufferings and become like him in his death. [11]Then I have hope that I myself will be raised from the dead.

Continuing Toward Our Goal

[12]I do not mean that I am already as God wants me to be. I have not yet reached that goal, but I continue trying to reach it and to make it mine. Christ wants me to do that, which is the reason he made me his. [13]Brothers and sisters, I know that I have not yet reached that goal, but there is one thing I always do. Forgetting the past and straining toward what is ahead, [14]I keep trying to reach the goal and get the prize for which God called me through Christ to the life above.

[15]All of us who are spiritually mature should think this way, too. And if there are things you do not agree with, God will make them clear to you. [16]But we should continue following the truth we already have.

[17]Brothers and sisters, all of you should try to follow my example and to copy those who live the way we showed you. [18]Many people live like enemies of the cross of Christ. I have often told you about them, and it makes me cry to tell you about them now. [19]In the end, they will be destroyed. They do whatever their bodies want, they are proud of their shameful acts, and they think only about earthly things. [20]But our homeland is in heaven, and we are waiting for our Savior, the Lord Jesus Christ, to come from heaven. [21]By his power to rule all things, he will change our humble bodies and make them like his own glorious body.

OCTOBER 9

JEREMIAH 3:1—4:31

Judah Is Unfaithful

3 "If a man divorces his wife
　　and she leaves him and marries
　　　　another man,
　　should her first husband come back to
　　　　her again?
　　If he went back to her, wouldn't the
　　　　land become completely unclean?

But you have acted like a prostitute with
　　many lovers,
　　and now you want to come back to
　　　　me?" says the LORD.
[2]"Look up to the bare hilltops, Judah.
　　Is there any place where you have not
　　　　been a prostitute?
You have sat by the road waiting for
　　lovers,
　　like an Arab in the desert.

3:2 cut The word in Greek is like the word "circumcise," but it means "to cut completely off."

You made the land unclean,
  because you did evil and were like a
    prostitute.
³So the rain has not come,
  and there have not been any spring rains.
But your face still looks like the face of a
    prostitute.
You refuse even to be ashamed of what
    you did.
⁴Now you are calling to me,
  'My father, you have been my friend
    since I was young.
⁵Will you always be angry at me?
  Will your anger last forever?'
Judah, you said this,
  but you did as much evil as you could!"

Judah and Israel Are like Sisters

⁶When King Josiah was ruling Judah, the LORD said to me, "Did you see what unfaithful Israel did? She was like a prostitute with her idols on every hill and under every green tree. ⁷I said to myself, 'Israel will come back to me after she does this evil,' but she didn't come back. And Israel's wicked sister Judah saw what she did. ⁸Judah saw that I divorced unfaithful Israel because of her adultery, but that didn't make Israel's wicked sister Judah afraid. She also went out and acted like a prostitute! ⁹And she didn't care that she was acting like a prostitute. So she made her country unclean and was guilty of adultery, because she worshiped idols made of stone and wood. ¹⁰Israel's wicked sister didn't even come back to me with her whole heart, but only pretended," says the Lord.

¹¹The LORD said to me, "Unfaithful Israel had a better excuse than wicked Judah. ¹²Go and speak this message toward the north:
  'Come back, unfaithful people of Israel,'
    says the LORD.
  'I will stop being angry at you,
    because I am full of mercy,' says the
      LORD.
  'I will not be angry with you forever.
¹³All you have to do is admit your sin—
    that you turned against the LORD your
      God
  and worshiped gods under every green
    tree
  and didn't obey me,'" says the LORD.

¹⁴"Come back to me, you unfaithful children," says the LORD, "because I am your master. I will take one person from every city and two from every family group, and I will bring you to Jerusalem. ¹⁵Then I will give you new rulers who will be faithful to me, who will lead you with knowledge and understanding. ¹⁶In those days there will be many of you in the land," says the LORD. "At that time people will no longer say, 'I remember the Ark of the Agreement.' They won't think about it anymore or remember it or miss it or make another one. ¹⁷At that time people will call Jerusalem The Throne of the LORD, and all nations will come together in Jerusalem to show respect to the LORD. They will not follow their stubborn, evil hearts anymore. ¹⁸In those days the family of Judah will join the family of Israel. They will come together from a land in the north to the land I gave their ancestors.

¹⁹"I, the LORD, said,
  'How happy I would be to treat you as
    my own children
  and give you a pleasant land,
  a land more beautiful than that of any
    other nation.'
I thought you would call me 'My Father'
  and not turn away from me.
²⁰But like a woman who is unfaithful to
    her husband,
  family of Israel, you have been
    unfaithful to me," says the LORD.

²¹You can hear crying on the bare hilltops.
  It is the people of Israel crying and
    praying for mercy.
They have become very evil
  and have forgotten the LORD their God.

²²"Come back to me, you unfaithful
    children,
  and I will forgive you for being
    unfaithful."

"Yes, we will come to you,
  because you are the LORD our God.
²³It was foolish to worship idols on the hills
  and on the mountains.
Surely the salvation of Israel
  comes from the LORD our God.
²⁴Since our youth, shameful gods have
  eaten up in sacrifice

everything our ancestors worked for—
their flocks and herds,
their sons and daughters.
²⁵Let us lie down in our shame,
and let our disgrace cover us like a
blanket.
We have sinned against the LORD our God,
both we and our ancestors.
From our youth until now,
we have not obeyed the LORD our God."

4 "If you will return, Israel,
then return to me," says the LORD.
"If you will throw away your idols that I
hate,
then don't wander away from me.
²If you say when you make a promise,
'As surely as the LORD lives,'
and you can say it in a truthful, honest,
and right way,
then the nations will be blessed by him,
and they will praise him for what he
has done."

³This is what the LORD says to the people
of Judah and to Jerusalem:
"Plow your unplowed fields,
and don't plant seeds among thorns.
⁴Give yourselves to the service of the
LORD,
and decide to obey him,
people of Judah and people of
Jerusalem.
If you don't, my anger will spread among
you like a fire,
and no one will be able to put it out,
because of the evil you have done.

Trouble from the North

⁵"Announce this message in Judah and say
it in Jerusalem:
'Blow the trumpet throughout the
country!'
Shout out loud and say,
'Come together!
Let's all escape to the strong, walled
cities!'
⁶Raise the signal flag toward Jerusalem!
Run for your lives, and don't wait,
because I am bringing disaster from the
north
There will be terrible destruction."

⁷A lion has come out of his den;
a destroyer of nations has begun to
march.
He has left his home
to destroy your land.
Your towns will be destroyed
with no one left to live in them.
⁸So put on rough cloth,
show how sad you are, and cry loudly.
The terrible anger of the LORD
has not turned away from us.

⁹"When this happens," says the LORD,
"the king and officers will lose their
courage.
The priests will be terribly afraid,
and the prophets will be shocked!"

¹⁰Then I said, "Lord GOD, you have tricked
the people of Judah and Jerusalem. You said,
'You will have peace,' but now the sword is
pointing at our throats!"

¹¹At that time this message will be given
to Judah and Jerusalem: "A hot wind blows
from the bare hilltops of the desert toward
the LORD's people. It is not a gentle wind to
separate grain from chaff. ¹²I feel a stronger
wind than that. Now even I will announce
judgments against the people of Judah."

¹³Look! The enemy rises up like a cloud,
and his chariots come like a tornado.
His horses are faster than eagles.
How terrible it will be for us! We are
ruined!
¹⁴People of Jerusalem, clean the evil from
your hearts so that you can be saved.
Don't continue making evil plans.
¹⁵A voice from Dan makes an
announcement
and brings bad news from the
mountains of Ephraim.
¹⁶"Report this to the nations.
Spread this news in Jerusalem:
'Invaders are coming from a faraway
country,
shouting words of war against the cities
of Judah.
¹⁷The enemy has surrounded Jerusalem as
men guard a field,
because Judah turned against me,'"
says the LORD.
¹⁸"The way you have lived and acted

has brought this trouble to you.
This is your punishment.
How terrible it is!
The pain stabs your heart!"

Jeremiah's Cry

¹⁹Oh, how I hurt! How I hurt!
I am bent over in pain.
Oh, the torture in my heart!
My heart is pounding inside me.
I cannot keep quiet,
because I have heard the sound of the
trumpet.
I have heard the shouts of war.
²⁰Disaster follows disaster;
the whole country has been destroyed.
My tents are destroyed in only a moment.
My curtains are torn down quickly.
²¹How long must I look at the war flag?
How long must I listen to the war
trumpet?

²²The Lord says, "My people are foolish.
They do not know me.
They are stupid children;
they don't understand.
They are skillful at doing evil,
but they don't know how to do good."

Disaster Is Coming

²³I looked at the earth,
and it was empty and had no shape.
I looked at the sky,
and its light was gone.
²⁴I looked at the mountains,
and they were shaking.
All the hills were trembling.
²⁵I looked, and there were no people.
Every bird in the sky had flown away.
²⁶I looked, and the good, rich land had
become a desert.
All its towns had been destroyed
by the Lord and his great anger.
²⁷This is what the Lord says:
"All the land will be ruined,
but I will not completely destroy it.
²⁸So the people in the land will cry loudly,
and the sky will grow dark,
because I have spoken and will not
change my mind.
I have made a decision, and I will not
change it."

²⁹At the sound of the horsemen and the
archers,
all the people in the towns run away.
They hide in the thick bushes
and climb up into the rocks.
All of the cities of Judah are empty;
no one lives in them.
³⁰Judah, you destroyed nation, what are
you doing?
Why do you put on your finest dress
and decorate yourself with gold
jewelry?
Why do you put color around your eyes?
You make yourself beautiful, but it is all
useless.
Your lovers hate you;
they want to kill you.
³¹I hear a cry like a woman having a baby,
distress like a woman having her first
child.
It is the sound of Jerusalem gasping for
breath.
She lifts her hands in prayer and says,
"Oh! I am about to faint
before my murderers!"

PSALM 116:15–19

¹⁵The death of one that belongs to the
Lord
is precious in his sight.
¹⁶Lord, I am your servant;
I am your servant and the son of your
female servant.
You have freed me from my chains.
¹⁷I will give you an offering to show thanks
to you,
and I will pray to the Lord.
¹⁸I will give the Lord what I promised
in front of all his people,
¹⁹in the Temple courtyards
in Jerusalem.

Praise the Lord!

PROVERBS 27:2

²Don't praise yourself. Let someone else
do it.
Let the praise come from a stranger
and not from your own mouth.

PHILIPPIANS 4:1–23

What the Christians Are to Do

4 My dear brothers and sisters, I love you and want to see you. You bring me joy and make me proud of you, so stand strong in the Lord as I have told you.

²I ask Euodia and Syntyche to agree in the Lord. ³And I ask you, my faithful friend, to help these women. They served with me in telling the Good News, together with Clement and others who worked with me, whose names are written in the book of life.ⁿ

⁴Be full of joy in the Lord always. I will say again, be full of joy.

⁵Let everyone see that you are gentle and kind. The Lord is coming soon. ⁶Do not worry about anything, but pray and ask God for everything you need, always giving thanks. ⁷And God's peace, which is so great we cannot understand it, will keep your hearts and minds in Christ Jesus.

⁸Brothers and sisters, think about the things that are good and worthy of praise. Think about the things that are true and honorable and right and pure and beautiful and respected. ⁹Do what you learned and received from me, what I told you, and what you saw me do. And the God who gives peace will be with you.

Paul Thanks the Christians

¹⁰I am very happy in the Lord that you have shown your care for me again. You continued to care about me, but there was no way for you to show it. ¹¹I am not telling you

this because I need anything. I have learned to be satisfied with the things I have and with everything that happens. ¹²I know how to live when I am poor, and I know how to live when I have plenty. I have learned the secret of being happy at any time in everything that happens, when I have enough to eat and when I go hungry, when I have more than I need and when I do not have enough. ¹³I can do all things through Christ, because he gives me strength.

¹⁴But it was good that you helped me when I needed it. ¹⁵You Philippians remember when I first preached the Good News there. When I left Macedonia, you were the only church that gave me help. ¹⁶Several times you sent me things I needed when I was in Thessalonica. ¹⁷Really, it is not that I want to receive gifts from you, but I want you to have the good that comes from giving. ¹⁸And now I have everything, and more. I have all I need, because Epaphroditus brought your gift to me. It is like a sweet-smelling sacrifice offered to God, who accepts that sacrifice and is pleased with it. ¹⁹My God will use his wonderful riches in Christ Jesus to give you everything you need. ²⁰Glory to our God and Father forever and ever! Amen.

²¹Greet each of God's people in Christ Jesus. Those who are with me send greetings to you. ²²All of God's people greet you, particularly those from the palace of Caesar.

²³The grace of the Lord Jesus Christ be with you all.

OCTOBER 10

JEREMIAH 5:1—6:30

No One Is Right

5 The LORD says, "Walk up and down the streets of Jerusalem.
Look around and discover these things.
Search the public squares of the city.

If you can find one person who does
honest things,
who searches for the truth,
I will forgive this city.
²Although the people say, 'As surely as the
LORD lives!'
they don't really mean it."

4:3 book of life God's book that has the names of all God's chosen people (Revelation 3:5; 21:27).

³L ᴏʀᴅ, don't you look for truth in people?
You struck the people of Judah,
  but they didn't feel any pain.
You crushed them,
  but they refused to learn what is right.
They became more stubborn than a
    rock;
  they refused to turn back to God.
⁴But I thought,
  "These are only the poor, foolish
    people.
They have not learned the way of the
    L ᴏʀᴅ
  and what their God wants them to do.
⁵So I will go to the leaders of Judah
  and talk to them.
Surely they understand the way of the
    L ᴏʀᴅ
  and know what God wants them to do."
But even the leaders had all joined
    together to break away from the
    L ᴏʀᴅ;
  they had broken their ties with him.
⁶So a lion from the forest will attack them.
A wolf from the desert will kill them.
A leopard is waiting for them near their
    towns.
It will tear to pieces anyone who comes
    out of the city,
because the people of Judah have sinned
    greatly.
They have wandered away from the
    L ᴏʀᴅ many times.
⁷The L ᴏʀᴅ said, "Tell me why I should
    forgive you.
Your children have left me
  and have made promises to idols that
    are not gods at all.
I gave your children everything they
    needed,
  but they still were like an unfaithful
    wife to me.
They spent much time in houses of
    prostitutes.
⁸They are like well-fed horses filled with
    sexual desire;
  each one wants another man's wife.
⁹Shouldn't I punish the people of Judah
    for doing these things?" says the
    L ᴏʀᴅ.

"Shouldn't I give a nation such as this
    the punishment it deserves?

¹⁰"Go along and cut down Judah's
    vineyards,
  but do not completely destroy them.
Cut off all her people as if they were
    branches,
  because they do not belong to the L ᴏʀᴅ.
¹¹The families of Israel and Judah
  have been completely unfaithful to me,"
    says the L ᴏʀᴅ.

¹²Those people have lied about the L ᴏʀᴅ
  and said, "He will not do anything to us!
Nothing bad will happen to us!
  We will never see war or hunger!
¹³The prophets are like an empty wind;
  the word of God is not in them.
Let the bad things they say happen to
    them."

¹⁴So this is what the L ᴏʀᴅ God All-Powerful says:
  "The people said I would not punish
    them.
So, the words I give you will be like fire,
  and these people will be like wood that
    it burns up.
¹⁵Listen, family of Israel," says the L ᴏʀᴅ,
  "I will soon bring a nation from far
    away to attack you.
It is an old nation that has lasted a long
    time.
The people there speak a language you
    do not know;
  you cannot understand what they say.
¹⁶Their arrows bring death.
  All their people are strong warriors.
¹⁷They will eat your crops and your food.
  They will eat your sons and daughters.
They will eat your flocks and herds.
  They will eat your grapes and figs.
They will destroy with their swords
  the strong, walled cities you trust.
¹⁸"Yet even then," says the L ᴏʀᴅ, "I will not
destroy you completely. ¹⁹When the people of
Judah ask, 'Why has the L ᴏʀᴅ our God done
all these terrible things to us?' then give
them this answer: 'You have left the L ᴏʀᴅ and
served foreign idols in your own land. So
now you will serve foreigners in a land that
does not belong to you.'

20"Announce this message to the family of Jacob,
  and tell it to the nation of Judah:
21Hear this message, you foolish people
    who have no sense.
  They have eyes, but they don't really see.
  They have ears, but they don't really listen.
22Surely you are afraid of me," says the LORD.
  "You should shake with fear in my presence.
  I am the one who made the beaches to be a border for the sea,
  a border the water can never go past.
  The waves may pound the beach, but they can't win over it.
  They may roar, but they cannot go beyond it.
23But the people of Judah are stubborn and have turned against me.
  They have turned aside and gone away from me.
24They do not say to themselves,
  'We should fear the LORD our God,
  who gives us autumn and spring rains in their seasons,
  who makes sure we have the harvest at the right time.'
25But your evil has kept away both rain and harvest.
  Your sins have kept you from enjoying good things.
26There are wicked men among my people.
  Like those who make nets for catching birds,
  they set their traps to catch people.
27Like cages full of birds,
  their houses are full of lies.
  They have become rich and powerful.
28 They have grown big and fat.
  There is no end to the evil things they do.
  They won't plead the case of the orphan or help the poor be judged fairly.
29Shouldn't I punish the people of Judah for doing these things?" says the LORD.
  "Shouldn't I give a nation such as this the punishment it deserves?

30"A terrible and shocking thing
  has happened in the land of Judah:
31The prophets speak lies,
  and the priests take power into their own hands,
  and my people love it this way.
  But what will you do when the end comes?

Jerusalem Is Surrounded

6 "Run for your lives, people of Benjamin!
  Run away from Jerusalem!
  Blow the war trumpet in the town of Tekoa!
  Raise the warning flag over the town of Beth Hakkerem!
  Disaster is coming from the north;
  terrible destruction is coming to you.
2Jerusalem, I will destroy you,
  you who are fragile and gentle.
3Shepherds with their flocks will come against Jerusalem.
  They will set up their tents all around her,
  each shepherd taking care of his own section."
4They say, "Get ready to fight against Jerusalem!
  Get up! We will attack at noon!
  But it is already getting late;
  the evening shadows are growing long.
5So get up! We will attack at night.
  We will destroy the strong towers of Jerusalem!"
6This is what the LORD All-Powerful says:
  "Cut down the trees around Jerusalem,
  and build an attack ramp to the top of its walls.
  This city must be punished.
  Inside it is nothing but slavery.
7Jerusalem pours out her evil
  as a well pours out its water.
  The sounds of violence and destruction are heard within her.
  I can see the sickness and hurts of Jerusalem.
8Listen to this warning, Jerusalem,
  or I will turn my back on you
  and make your land an empty desert
  where no one can live."
9This is what the LORD All-Powerful says:

"Gather the few people of Israel who are
  left alive,
  as you would gather the last grapes on
    a grapevine.
Check each vine again,
  like someone who gathers grapes."

¹⁰To whom can I speak? Whom can I warn?
  Who will listen to me?
The people of Israel have closed ears,
  so they cannot hear my warnings.
They don't like the word of the LORD;
  they don't want to listen to it!
¹¹But I am full of the anger of the LORD,
  and I am tired of holding it in.

"Pour out my anger on the children who
  play in the street
  and on the young men gathered
    together.
A husband and his wife will both be
  caught in his anger,
  as will the very old.
¹²Their houses will be turned over to others,
  along with their fields and wives,
  because I will raise my hand
    and punish the people of Judah," says
      the LORD.
¹³"Everyone, from the least important to
    the greatest,
  is greedy for money.
Even the prophets and priests
  all tell lies.
¹⁴They tried to heal my people's serious
    injuries
  as if they were small wounds.
They said, 'It's all right, it's all right.'
  But really, it is not all right.
¹⁵They should be ashamed of the terrible
    way they act,
  but they are not ashamed at all.
They don't even know how to blush
  about their sins.
So they will fall, along with everyone
  else.
They will be thrown to the ground
  when I punish them," says the LORD.
¹⁶This is what the LORD says:
"Stand where the roads cross and look.
  Ask where the old way is,
  where the good way is, and walk on it.

If you do, you will find rest for
  yourselves.
But they have said, 'We will not walk on
  the good way.'
¹⁷I set watchmen over you
  and told you, 'Listen for the sound of
    the war trumpet!'
But they said, 'We will not listen.'
¹⁸So listen, all you nations,
  and pay attention, you witnesses.
Watch what I will do to the people of
  Judah.
¹⁹Hear this, people of the earth:
  I am going to bring disaster to the
    people of Judah
  because of the evil they plan.
They have not listened to my messages
  and have rejected my teachings.
²⁰Why do you bring me offerings of
    incense from the land of Sheba?
  Why do you bring me sweet-smelling
    cane from a faraway land?
Your burnt offerings will not be
  accepted;
  your sacrifices do not please me."
²¹So this is what the LORD says:
"I will put problems in front of Judah.
  Fathers and sons will stumble over
    them together.
  Neighbors and friends will die."
²²This is what the LORD says:
"Look, an army is coming
  from the land of the north;
a great nation is coming
  from the far sides of the earth.
²³The soldiers carry bows and spears.
  They are cruel and show no mercy.
They sound like the roaring ocean
  when they ride their horses.
That army is coming lined up for battle,
  ready to attack you, Jerusalem."

²⁴We have heard the news about that army
  and are helpless from fear.
We are gripped by our pain,
  like a woman having a baby.
²⁵Don't go out into the fields
  or walk down the roads,
  because the enemy has swords.
  There is terror on every side.
²⁶My people, put on rough cloth

and roll in the ashes to show how sad
you are.
Cry loudly for those who are dead,
as if your only son were dead,
because the destroyer
will soon come against us.

27"Jeremiah, I have made you like a worker
who tests metal,
and my people are like the ore.
You must observe their ways
and test them.
28All my people have turned against me
and are stubborn.
They go around telling lies about others.
They are like bronze and iron
that became covered with rust.
They all act dishonestly.
29The fire is fanned to make it hotter,
but the lead does not melt.
The pure metal does not come out;
the evil is not removed from my people.
30My people will be called rejected silver,
because the LORD has rejected them."

PSALM 117:1–2

A Hymn of Praise

117 All you nations, praise the LORD.
All you people, praise him
2because the LORD loves us very much,
and his truth is everlasting.

Praise the LORD!

PROVERBS 27:3–4

3Stone is heavy, and sand is weighty,
but a complaining fool is worse than
either.

4Anger is cruel and destroys like a flood,
but no one can put up with jealousy!

COLOSSIANS 1:1—2:5

1 From Paul, an apostle of Christ Jesus. I am
an apostle because that is what God
wanted. Also from Timothy, our brother.

2To the holy and faithful brothers and sisters in Christ that live in Colossae:

Grace and peace to you from God our Father.[n]

3In our prayers for you we always thank
God, the Father of our Lord Jesus Christ, 4be-
cause we have heard about the faith you have
in Christ Jesus and the love you have for all
of God's people. 5You have this faith and love
because of your hope, and what you hope for
is kept safe for you in heaven. You learned
about this hope when you heard the message
about the truth, the Good News 6that was
told to you. Everywhere in the world that
Good News is bringing blessings and is
growing. This has happened with you, too,
since you heard the Good News and understood the truth about the grace of God. 7You
learned about God's grace from Epaphras,
whom we love. He works together with us
and is a faithful servant of Christ for us.[n] 8He
also told us about the love you have from the
Holy Spirit.

9Because of this, since the day we heard
about you, we have continued praying for you,
asking God that you will know fully what he
wants. We pray that you will also have great
wisdom and understanding in spiritual
things 10so that you will live the kind of life
that honors and pleases the Lord in every
way. You will produce fruit in every good work
and grow in the knowledge of God. 11God will
strengthen you with his own great power so
that you will not give up when troubles come,
but you will be patient. 12And you will joyfully
give thanks to the Father who has made you[n]
able to have a share in all that he has prepared
for his people in the kingdom of light. 13God
has freed us from the power of darkness, and
he brought us into the kingdom of his dear
Son. 14The Son paid for our sins,[n] and in him
we have forgiveness.

The Importance of Christ

15No one can see God, but Jesus Christ is
exactly like him. He ranks higher than
everything that has been made. 16Through
his power all things were made—things in
heaven and on earth, things seen and unseen, all powers, authorities, lords, and
rulers. All things were made through Christ

and for Christ. ¹⁷He was there before anything was made, and all things continue because of him. ¹⁸He is the head of the body, which is the church. Everything comes from him. He is the first one who was raised from the dead. So in all things Jesus has first place. ¹⁹God was pleased for all of himself to live in Christ. ²⁰And through Christ, God has brought all things back to himself again— things on earth and things in heaven. God made peace through the blood of Christ's death on the cross.

²¹At one time you were separated from God. You were his enemies in your minds, and the evil things you did were against God. ²²But now God has made you his friends again. He did this through Christ's death in the body so that he might bring you into God's presence as people who are holy, with no wrong, and with nothing of which God can judge you guilty. ²³This will happen if you continue strong and sure in your faith. You must not be moved away from the hope brought to you by the Good News that you heard. That same Good News has been told to everyone in the world, and I, Paul, help in preaching that Good News.

Paul's Work for the Church

²⁴I am happy in my sufferings for you. There are things that Christ must still suffer through his body, the church. I am accepting, in my body, my part of these things that must be suffered. ²⁵I became a servant of the church because God gave me a special work to do that helps you, and that work is to tell fully the message of God. ²⁶This message is the secret that was hidden from everyone since the beginning of time, but now it is made known to God's holy people. ²⁷God decided to let his people know this rich and glorious secret which he has for all people. This secret is Christ himself, who is in you. He is our only hope for glory. ²⁸So we continue to preach Christ to each person, using all wisdom to warn and to teach everyone, in order to bring each one into God's presence as a mature person in Christ. ²⁹To do this, I work and struggle, using Christ's great strength that works so powerfully in me.

2 I want you to know how hard I work for you, those in Laodicea, and others who have never seen me. ²I want them to be strengthened and joined together with love so that they may be rich in their understanding. This leads to their knowing fully God's secret, that is, Christ himself. ³In him all the treasures of wisdom and knowledge are safely kept.

⁴I say this so that no one can fool you by arguments that seem good, but are false. ⁵Though I am absent from you in my body, my heart is with you, and I am happy to see your good lives and your strong faith in Christ.

OCTOBER 11

JEREMIAH 7:1—8:22

Jeremiah's Temple Message

7 This is the word that the LORD spoke to Jeremiah: ²"Stand at the gate of the Temple and preach this message there:

" 'Hear the word of the LORD, all you people of the nation of Judah! All you who come through these gates to worship the LORD, listen to this message! ³This is what the LORD All-Powerful, the God of Israel, says: Change your lives and do what is right! Then I will let you live in this place. ⁴Don't trust the lies of people who say, "This is the Temple of the LORD. This is the Temple of the LORD. This is the Temple of the LORD!" ⁵You must change your lives and do what is right. Be fair to each other. ⁶You must not be hard on strangers, orphans, and widows. Don't kill innocent people in this place! Don't follow other gods, or they will ruin your lives. ⁷If you do these things, I will let you live in this land that I gave to your ancestors to keep forever.

⁸" 'But look, you are trusting lies, which is useless. ⁹Will you steal and murder and be guilty of adultery? Will you falsely accuse other people? Will you burn incense to the god Baal and follow other gods you have not known? ¹⁰If you do that, do you think you can come before me and stand in this place where I have chosen to be worshiped? Do you think you can say, "We are safe!" when you do all these hateful things? ¹¹This place where I have chosen to be worshiped is nothing more to you than a hideout for robbers. I have been watching you, says the LORD.

¹²" 'You people of Judah, go now to the town of Shiloh, where I first made a place to be worshiped. See what I did to it because of the evil things the people of Israel had done. ¹³You people of Judah have done all these evil things too, says the LORD. I spoke to you again and again, but you did not listen to me. I called you, but you did not answer. ¹⁴So I will destroy the place where I have chosen to be worshiped in Jerusalem. You trust in that place, which I gave to you and your ancestors, but I will destroy it just as I destroyed Shiloh. ¹⁵I will push you away from me just as I pushed away your relatives, the people of Israel!'

¹⁶"As for you, Jeremiah, don't pray for these people. Don't cry out for them or ask anything for them or beg me to help them, because I will not listen to you. ¹⁷Don't you see what they are doing in the towns of Judah and in the streets of Jerusalem? ¹⁸The children gather wood, and the fathers use the wood to make a fire. The women make the dough for cakes of bread, and they offer them to the Queen Goddess. They pour out drink offerings to other gods to make me angry. ¹⁹But I am not the one the people of Judah are really hurting, says the LORD. They are only hurting themselves and bringing shame upon themselves.

²⁰" 'So this is what the Lord GOD says: I will pour out my anger on this place, on people and animals, on the trees in the field and the crops in the ground. My anger will be like a hot fire that no one can put out.

Obedience Is More than Sacrifice

²¹" 'This is what the LORD All-Powerful, the God of Israel, says: Offer burnt offerings along with your other sacrifices, and eat the meat yourselves! ²²When I brought your ancestors out of Egypt, I did not speak to them and give them commands only about burnt offerings and sacrifices. ²³I also gave them this command: Obey me, and I will be your God and you will be my people. Do all that I command so that good things will happen to you. ²⁴But your ancestors did not listen or pay attention to me. They were stubborn and did whatever their evil hearts wanted. They went backward, not forward. ²⁵Since the day your ancestors left Egypt, I have sent my servants, the prophets, again and again to you. ²⁶But your ancestors did not listen or pay attention to me. They were very stubborn and did more evil than their ancestors.'

²⁷"Jeremiah, you will tell all these things to the people of Judah, but they will not listen to you. You will call to them, but they will not answer you. ²⁸So say to them, 'This is the nation that has not obeyed the LORD its God. These people do nothing when I correct them. They do not tell the truth; it has disappeared from their lips.

The Valley of Killing

²⁹" 'Cut off your hair and throw it away. Go up to the bare hilltop and cry out, because the LORD has rejected these people. He has turned his back on them, and in his anger will punish them. ³⁰The people of Judah have done what I said was evil, says the LORD. They have set up their hateful idols in the place where I have chosen to be worshiped and have made it unclean. ³¹The people of Judah have built places of worship at Topheth in the Valley of Ben Hinnom. There they burned their own sons and daughters as sacrifices, something I never commanded. It never even entered my mind. ³²So, I warn you. The days are coming, says the LORD, when people will not call this place Topheth or the Valley of Ben Hinnom anymore. They will call it the Valley of Killing. They will bury the dead in Topheth until there is no room to bury anyone else. ³³Then the bodies of the dead will become food for the birds of the sky and for the wild animals. There will be no one left alive to chase them away. ³⁴I will end the happy sounds of the

bride and bridegroom. There will be no happy sounds in the cities of Judah or in the streets of Jerusalem, because the land will become an empty desert!

8 "The LORD says: At that time they will remove from their tombs the bones of Judah's kings and officers, priests and prophets, and the people of Jerusalem. ²The bones will be spread on the ground under the sun, moon, and stars that the people loved and served and went after and searched for and worshiped. No one will gather up the bones and bury them. So they will be like dung thrown on the ground. ³I will force the people of Judah to leave their homes and their land. Those of this evil family who are not dead will wish they were, says the LORD All-Powerful.'

Sin and Punishment

⁴"Say to the people of Judah: 'This is what the LORD says:

When people fall down, don't they get up
    again?
And when someone goes the wrong
    way, doesn't he turn back?
⁵Why, then, have the people of Jerusalem
    gone the wrong way
and not turned back?
They believe their own lies
and refuse to turn around and come
    back.
⁶I have listened to them very carefully,
    but they do not say what is right.
They do not feel sorry about their
    wicked ways,
    saying, "What have I done?"
Each person goes his own way,
    like a horse charging into a battle.
⁷Even the birds in the sky
    know the right times to do things.
The storks, doves, swifts, and thrushes
    know when it is time to migrate.
But my people don't know
    what the LORD wants them to do.

⁸"You keep saying, "We are wise,
    because we have the teachings of the
    LORD."
But actually, those who explain the
    Scriptures
    have written lies with their pens.

⁹These wise teachers refused to listen to
    the word of the LORD,
    so they are not really wise at all.
They will be ashamed.
They will be shocked and trapped.
¹⁰So I will give their wives to other men
    and their fields to new owners.
Everyone, from the least important to the
    greatest,
    is greedy for money.
Even the prophets and priests
    all tell lies.
¹¹They tried to heal my people's serious
    injuries
    as if they were small wounds.
They said, "It's all right, it's all right."
    But really, it is not all right.
¹²They should be ashamed of the terrible
    way they act,
    but they are not ashamed at all.
They don't even know how to blush
    about their sins.
So they will fall, along with everyone
    else.
They will be thrown to the ground
    when I punish them, says the LORD.

¹³" 'I will take away their crops, says the
    LORD.
There will be no grapes on the vine
and no figs on the fig tree.
Even the leaves will dry up and die.
I will take away what I gave them.'"

¹⁴"Why are we just sitting here?
    Let's get together!
We have sinned against the LORD,
    so he has given us poisoned water to
    drink.
Come, let's run to the strong, walled
    cities.
The LORD our God has decided that we
    must die,
    so let's die there.
¹⁵We hoped to have peace,
    but nothing good has come.
We hoped for a time when he would heal
    us,
    but only terror has come.
¹⁶From the land of Dan,
    the snorting of the enemy's horses is
    heard.

The ground shakes from the neighing
 of their large horses.
They have come and destroyed
 the land and everything in it,
 the city and all who live there."

¹⁷"Look! I am sending poisonous snakes to
 attack you.
 These snakes cannot be charmed,
 and they will bite you," says the LORD.

Jeremiah's Sadness

¹⁸God, you are my comfort when I am very
 sad
 and when I am afraid.
¹⁹Listen to the sound of my people.
 They cry from a faraway land:
 "Isn't the LORD still in Jerusalem?
 Isn't Jerusalem's king still there?"

But God says, "Why did the people make
 me angry by worshiping idols,
 useless foreign idols?"

²⁰And the people say, "Harvest time is over;
 summer has ended,
 and we have not been saved."

²¹Because my people are crushed, I am
 crushed.
 I cry loudly and am afraid for them.
²²Isn't there balm in the land of Gilead?
 Isn't there a doctor there?
 So why aren't the hurts of my people
 healed?

PSALM 118:1–4

Thanksgiving for Victory

118 Thank the LORD because he is
 good.
 His love continues forever.
²Let the people of Israel say,
 "His love continues forever."
³Let the family of Aaron say,
 "His love continues forever."
⁴Let those who respect the LORD say,
 "His love continues forever."

PROVERBS 27:5–6

⁵It is better to correct someone openly
 than to have love and not show it.

⁶The slap of a friend can be trusted to
 help you,
 but the kisses of an enemy are nothing
 but lies.

COLOSSIANS 2:6–23

Continue to Live in Christ

⁶As you received Christ Jesus the Lord, so
continue to live in him. ⁷Keep your roots
deep in him and have your lives built on
him. Be strong in the faith, just as you were
taught, and always be thankful.

⁸Be sure that no one leads you away with
false and empty teaching that is only human, which comes from the ruling spirits of
this world, and not from Christ. ⁹All of God
lives fully in Christ (even when Christ was
on earth), ¹⁰and you have a full and true life
in Christ, who is ruler over all rulers and
powers.

¹¹Also in Christ you had a different kind
of circumcision, a circumcision not done by
hands. It was through Christ's circumcision,
that is, his death, that you were made free
from the power of your sinful self. ¹²When
you were baptized, you were buried with
Christ, and you were raised up with him
through your faith in God's power that was
shown when he raised Christ from the dead.
¹³When you were spiritually dead because of
your sins and because you were not free
from the power of your sinful self, God made
you alive with Christ, and he forgave all our
sins. ¹⁴He canceled the debt, which listed all
the rules we failed to follow. He took away
that record with its rules and nailed it to the
cross. ¹⁵God stripped the spiritual rulers and
powers of their authority. With the cross, he
won the victory and showed the world that
they were powerless.

Don't Follow People's Rules

¹⁶So do not let anyone make rules for you
about eating and drinking or about a religious feast, a New Moon Festival, or a Sabbath day. ¹⁷These things were like a shadow
of what was to come. But what is true and
real has come and is found in Christ. ¹⁸Do
not let anyone disqualify you by making you
humiliate yourself and worship angels. Such
people enter into visions, which fill them

with foolish pride because of their human way of thinking. [19]They do not hold tightly to Christ, the head. It is from him that all the parts of the body are cared for and held together. So it grows in the way God wants it to grow.

[20]Since you died with Christ and were made free from the ruling spirits of the world, why do you act as if you still belong to this world by following rules like these: [21]"Don't handle this," "Don't taste that," "Don't even touch that thing"? [22]These rules refer to earthly things that are gone as soon as they are used. They are only human commands and teachings. [23]They seem to be wise, but they are only part of a human religion. They make people pretend not to be proud and make them punish their bodies, but they do not really control the evil desires of the sinful self.

OCTOBER 12

JEREMIAH 9:1—10:25

9 [1]I wish my head were like a spring of water
and my eyes like a fountain of tears!
Then I could cry day and night
for my people who have been killed.
[2]I wish I had a place in the desert—
a house where travelers spend the
night—
so I could leave my people.
I could go away from them,
because they are all unfaithful to God;
they are all turning against him.

Judah's Failures
[3]"They use their tongues like a bow,
shooting lies from their mouths like
arrows.
Lies, not truth,
have grown strong in the land.
They go from one evil thing to another.
They do not know who I am," says the
LORD.
[4]"Watch out for your friends,
and don't trust your own relatives,
because every relative is a cheater,
and every friend tells lies about you.
[5]Everyone lies to his friend,
and no one speaks the truth.
The people of Judah have taught their
tongues to lie.
They have become tired from sinning.
[6]Jeremiah, you live in the middle of lies.
With their lies the people refuse to
know me," says the LORD.

[7]So this is what the LORD All-Powerful says:
"I will test the people of Judah as a
person tests metal in a fire.
I have no other choice,
because my people have sinned.
[8]Their tongues are like sharp arrows.
Their mouths speak lies.
Everyone speaks nicely to his neighbor,
but he is secretly planning to attack
him.
[9]Shouldn't I punish the people for doing
this?" says the LORD.
"Shouldn't I give a nation like this the
punishment it deserves?"

[10]I, Jeremiah, will cry loudly for the
mountains
and sing a funeral song for the empty
fields.
They are empty, and no one passes
through.
The mooing of cattle cannot be heard.
The birds have flown away,
and the animals are gone.

[11]"I, the LORD, will make the city of
Jerusalem a heap of ruins,
a home for wild dogs.
I will destroy the cities of Judah
so no one can live there."
[12]What person is wise enough to understand these things? Is there someone who has been taught by the LORD who can explain them? Why was the land ruined? Why has it .

been made like an empty desert where no one goes?

¹³The LORD answered, "It is because Judah quit following my teachings that I gave them. They have not obeyed me or done what I told them to do. ¹⁴Instead, they were stubborn and followed the Baals, as their ancestors taught them to do. ¹⁵So this is what the LORD All-Powerful, the God of Israel, says: "I will soon make the people of Judah eat bitter food and drink poisoned water. ¹⁶I will scatter them through other nations that they and their ancestors never knew about. I will chase the people of Judah with the sword until they are all killed."

¹⁷This is what the LORD All-Powerful says:
"Now, think about these things!
    Call for the women who cry at funerals
        to come.
    Send for those women who are good at
        that job.
¹⁸Let them come quickly
    and cry loudly for us.
Then our eyes will fill with tears,
    and streams of water will flow from our
        eyelids.
¹⁹The sound of loud crying is heard from
        Jerusalem:
    'We are truly ruined!
    We are truly ashamed!
We must leave our land,
    because our houses are in ruins.'"

²⁰Now, women of Judah, listen to the word
        of the LORD;
    open your ears to hear the words of his
        mouth.
Teach your daughters how to cry loudly.
    Teach one another a funeral song.
²¹Death has climbed in through our
        windows
    and has entered our strong cities.
Death has taken away our children who
        play in the streets
    and the young men who meet in the
        city squares.
²²Say, "This is what the LORD says:
'The dead bodies of people will lie
    in the open field like dung.
They will lie like grain a farmer has cut,
    but there will be no one to gather them.'"

²³This is what the LORD says:
"The wise must not brag about their
        wisdom.
    The strong must not brag about their
        strength.
    The rich must not brag about their
        money.
²⁴But if people want to brag, let them brag
        that they understand and know me.
    Let them brag that I am the LORD,
        and that I am kind and fair,
        and that I do things that are right on
            earth.
    This kind of bragging pleases me," says
        the LORD.

²⁵The LORD says, "The time is coming when I will punish all those who are circumcised only in the flesh: ²⁶the people of Egypt, Judah, Edom, Ammon, Moab, and the desert people who cut their hair short. The men in all those countries are not circumcised. And the whole family of Israel does not give itself to serving me."

The Lord and the Idols

10 Family of Israel, listen to what the LORD says to you. ²This is what he says:
"Don't live like the people from other
        nations,
    and don't be afraid of special signs in
        the sky,
    even though the other nations are
        afraid of them.
³The customs of other people are worth
        nothing.
    Their idols are just wood cut from the
        forest,
    shaped by a worker with his chisel.
⁴They decorate their idols with silver and
        gold.
    With hammers and nails they fasten
        them down
    so they won't fall over.
⁵Their idols are like scarecrows in melon
        fields;
    they cannot talk.
Since they cannot walk,
    they must be carried.
Do not be afraid of those idols,
    because they can't hurt you,
    and they can't help you either."

⁶LORD, there is no one like you.
You are great,
and your name is great and powerful.
⁷Everyone should respect you, King of the
nations;
you deserve respect.
Of all the wise people among the nations
and in all the kingdoms,
none of them is as wise as you.
⁸Those wise people are stupid and
foolish.
Their teachings come from worthless
wooden idols.
⁹Hammered silver is brought from
Tarshish
and gold from Uphaz,
so the idols are made by craftsmen and
goldsmiths.
They put blue and purple clothes on
the idols.
All these things are made by skilled
workers.
¹⁰But the LORD is the only true God.
He is the only living God, the King
forever.
The earth shakes when he is angry,
and the nations cannot stand up to his
anger.
¹¹"Tell them this message: 'These gods
did not make heaven and earth; they will be
destroyed and disappear from heaven and
earth.'"
¹²God made the earth by his power.
He used his wisdom to build the world
and his understanding to stretch out
the skies.
¹³When he thunders, the waters in the
skies roar.
He makes clouds rise in the sky all over
the earth.
He sends lightning with the rain
and brings out the wind from his
storehouses.

¹⁴People are so stupid and know so little.
Goldsmiths are made ashamed by their
idols,
because those statues are only false gods.
They have no breath in them.
¹⁵They are worth nothing; people make fun
of them.

When they are judged, they will be
destroyed.
¹⁶But God, who is Jacob's Portion, is not
like the idols.
He made everything,
and he chose Israel to be his special
people.
The LORD All-Powerful is his name.

Destruction Is Coming

¹⁷Get everything you own and prepare to
leave,
you people who are trapped by your
enemies.
¹⁸This is what the LORD says:
"At this time I will throw out the people
who live in this land.
I will bring trouble to them
so that they may be captured."
¹⁹How terrible it will be for me because of
my injury.
My wound cannot be healed.
Yet I told myself,
"This is my sickness; I must suffer
through it."
²⁰My tent is ruined,
and all its ropes are broken.
My children have gone away and left me.
No one is left to put up my tent again
or to set up a shelter for me.
²¹The shepherds are stupid
and don't ask the LORD for advice.
So they do not have success,
and all their flocks are scattered and
lost.
²²Listen! The news is coming.
A loud noise comes from the north
to make the towns of Judah an empty
desert
and a home for wild dogs!

Jeremiah's Prayer

²³LORD, I know that our lives don't really
belong to us.
We can't control our own lives.
²⁴LORD, correct me, but be fair.
Don't punish me in your anger,
or you will destroy me.
²⁵Pour out your anger on other nations
that do not know you
and do not pray to you.

Those nations have destroyed the people
of Jacob.
They have eaten them up completely
and destroyed their homeland.

PSALM 118:5–9

[5]I was in trouble, so I called to the LORD.
The LORD answered me and set me free.
[6]I will not be afraid, because the LORD is
with me.
People can't do anything to me.
[7]The LORD is with me to help me,
so I will see my enemies defeated.
[8]It is better to trust the LORD
than to trust people.
[9]It is better to trust the LORD
than to trust princes.

PROVERBS 27:7

[7]When you are full, not even honey tastes
good,
but when you are hungry, even
something bitter tastes sweet.

COLOSSIANS 3:1–4:1

Your New Life in Christ

3 Since you were raised from the dead with
Christ, aim at what is in heaven, where
Christ is sitting at the right hand of God.
[2]Think only about the things in heaven, not
the things on earth. [3]Your old sinful self has
died, and your new life is kept with Christ in
God. [4]Christ is your[n] life, and when he comes
again, you will share in his glory.

[5]So put all evil things out of your life: sexual sinning, doing evil, letting evil thoughts
control you, wanting things that are evil, and
greed. This is really serving a false god.
[6]These things make God angry.[n] [7]In your
past, evil life you also did these things.

[8]But now also put these things out of your
life: anger, bad temper, doing or saying
things to hurt others, and using evil words
when you talk. [9]Do not lie to each other. You
have left your old sinful life and the things
you did before. [10]You have begun to live the
new life, in which you are being made new
and are becoming like the One who made
you. This new life brings you the true knowledge of God. [11]In the new life there is no difference between Greeks and Jews, those who
are circumcised and those who are not circumcised, or people who are foreigners, or
Scythians.[n] There is no difference between
slaves and free people. But Christ is in all believers, and Christ is all that is important.

[12]God has chosen you and made you his
holy people. He loves you. So you should always clothe yourselves with mercy, kindness, humility, gentleness, and patience.
[13]Bear with each other, and forgive each
other. If someone does wrong to you, forgive
that person because the Lord forgave you.
[14]Even more than all this, clothe yourself in
love. Love is what holds you all together in
perfect unity. [15]Let the peace that Christ
gives control your thinking, because you
were all called together in one body[n] to have
peace. Always be thankful. [16]Let the teaching
of Christ live in you richly. Use all wisdom to
teach and instruct each other by singing
psalms, hymns, and spiritual songs with
thankfulness in your hearts to God. [17]Every-
thing you do or say should be done to obey
Jesus your Lord. And in all you do, give
thanks to God the Father through Jesus.

Your New Life with Other People

[18]Wives, yield to the authority of your
husbands, because this is the right thing to
do in the Lord.

[19]Husbands, love your wives and be gentle
with them.

[20]Children, obey your parents in all
things, because this pleases the Lord.

[21]Fathers, do not nag your children. If you
are too hard to please, they may want to stop
trying.

[22]Slaves, obey your masters in all things.
Do not obey just when they are watching
you, to gain their favor, but serve them honestly, because you respect the Lord. [23]In all
the work you are doing, work the best you
can. Work as if you were doing it for the

3:4 your Some Greek copies read "our." **3:6 These . . . angry** Some Greek copies continue, "against the people who do not
obey God." **3:11 Scythians** The Scythians were known as very wild and cruel people. **3:15 body** The spiritual body of
Christ, meaning the church or his people.

Lord, not for people. [24]Remember that you will receive your reward from the Lord, which he promised to his people. You are serving the Lord Christ. [25]But remember that anyone who does wrong will be pun-ished for that wrong, and the Lord treats everyone the same.

4 Masters, give what is good and fair to your slaves. Remember that you have a Master in heaven.

OCTOBER 13

JEREMIAH 11:1—12:17

The Agreement Is Broken

11 These are the words that the LORD spoke to Jeremiah: [2]"Listen to the words of this agreement and tell them to the people of Judah and those living in Jerusalem. [3]Tell them this is what the LORD, the God of Israel, says: 'Cursed is the person who does not obey the words of this agreement [4]that I made with your ancestors when I brought them out of Egypt. Egypt was like a furnace for melting iron!' I told them, 'Obey me and do everything I command you. Then you will be my people, and I will be your God. [5]Then I will keep the promise I made to your ancestors to give them a fertile land.' And you are living in that country today."

I answered, "Amen, LORD."

[6]The LORD said to me, "Announce this message in the towns of Judah and in the streets of Jerusalem: 'Listen to the words of this agreement and obey them. [7]I warned your ancestors to obey me when I brought them out of Egypt. I have warned them again and again to this very day: "Obey me!" [8]But your ancestors did not listen to me. They were stubborn and did what their own evil hearts wanted. So I made all the curses of this agreement come upon them. I commanded them to obey the agreement, but they did not.'"

[9]Then the LORD said to me, "I know the people of Judah and those living in Jerusalem have made secret plans. [10]They have gone back to the same sins their ancestors did. Their ancestors refused to listen to my message and followed and worshiped other gods instead. The families of Israel and Judah have broken the agreement I made with their ancestors. [11]So this is what the LORD says: 'I will soon bring a disaster on the people of Judah which they will not be able to escape. They will cry to me for help, but I will not listen to them. [12]The people living in the towns of Judah and the city of Jerusalem will pray to their idols to whom they burn incense. But those idols will not be able to help when disaster comes. [13]Look, people of Judah, you have as many idols as there are towns in Judah. You have built as many altars to burn incense to that shameful god Baal as there are streets in Jerusalem.'

[14]"As for you, Jeremiah, don't pray for these people or cry out for them or ask anything for them. I will not listen when they call to me in the time of their trouble.

[15]"What is my beloved Judah doing in my
      Temple
   when she makes many evil plans?
   Do you think animal sacrifices will stop
      your punishment?
When you do your evil, then you are
      happy."
[16]The LORD called you "a leafy olive tree,
   with beautiful fruit and shape."
But with the roar of a strong storm
   he will set that tree on fire,
   and its branches will be burned up.

[17]The LORD All-Powerful, who planted you, has announced that disaster will come to you. This is because the families of Israel and Judah have done evil and have made him angry by burning incense to Baal.

Evil Plans Against Jeremiah

[18]The LORD showed me that people were making plans against me. Because he showed me what they were doing, I knew they were against me. [19]Before this, I was like a gentle

lamb waiting to be butchered. I did not know they had made plans against me, saying:

"Let us destroy the tree and its fruit.
Let's kill him so people will forget him."

²⁰But, Lord All-Powerful, you are a fair judge.

You know how to test peoples' hearts and minds.

I have told you what I have against them.
So let me see you give them the punishment they deserve.

²¹So the Lord speaks about the people from Anathoth who plan to kill Jeremiah and say, "Don't prophesy in the name of the Lord, or we will kill you!" ²²So this is what the Lord All-Powerful says: "I will soon punish the men from Anathoth. Their young men will die in war. Their sons and daughters will die from hunger. ²³No one from the city of Anathoth will be left alive, because I will cause a disaster to happen to them that year."

Jeremiah's First Complaint

12 Lord, when I bring my case to you,
you are always right.

But I want to ask you about the justice you give.

Why are evil people successful?
Why do dishonest people have such easy lives?

²You have put the evil people here
like plants with strong roots.

They grow and produce fruit.

With their mouths they speak well of you,

but their hearts are really far away from you.

³But you know my heart, Lord.

You see me and test my thoughts about you.

Drag the evil people away like sheep to be butchered.

Set them aside for the day of killing.

⁴How much longer will the land stay dried up

and the grass in every field be dead?

The animals and birds in the land have died,

because the people are evil.

Yes, they are even saying,

"God does not see what happens to us."

The Lord's Answer to Jeremiah

⁵"If you get tired while racing against people,

how can you race against horses?

If you stumble in a country that is safe,

what will you do in the thick thornbushes along the Jordan River?

⁶Even your own brothers and members of your own family

are making plans against you.

They are crying out against you.

Don't trust them,

even when they say nice things to you!

⁷"I have left Israel;

I have left my people.

I have given the people I love
over to their enemies.

⁸My people have become to me
like a lion in the forest.

They roar at me,
so I hate them.

⁹My people have become to me
like a speckled bird attacked on all sides by hawks.

Go, gather the wild animals.
Bring them to get something to eat.

¹⁰Many shepherds have ruined my vineyards

and trampled the plants in my field.

They have turned my beautiful field
into an empty desert.

¹¹They have turned my field into a desert
that is wilted and dead.

The whole country is an empty desert,
because no one who lives there cares.

¹²Many soldiers have marched over those barren hills.

The Lord is using the armies to punish that land

from one end to the other.
No one is safe.

¹³The people have planted wheat,
but they have harvested only thorns.

They have worked hard until they were very tired,

but they have nothing for all their work.

They are ashamed of their poor harvest,

because the LORD's terrible anger has caused this."

¹⁴This is what the LORD said to me: "Here is what I will do to all my wicked neighbors who take the land I gave my people Israel. I will pull them up and throw them out of their land. And I will pull up the people of Judah from among them. ¹⁵But after I pull them up, I will feel sorry for them again. I will bring each person back to his own property and to his own land. ¹⁶I want them to learn their lessons well. In the past they taught my people to swear by Baal's name. But if they will now learn to swear by my name, saying, 'As surely as the LORD lives . . . ' I will allow them to rebuild among my people. ¹⁷But if a nation will not listen to my message, I will pull it up completely and destroy it," says the LORD.

PSALM 118:10–14

¹⁰All the nations surrounded me,
    but I defeated them in the name of the
    LORD.
¹¹They surrounded me on every side,
    but with the LORD's power I defeated
    them.
¹²They surrounded me like a swarm of
    bees,
    but they died as quickly as thorns
    burn.
    By the LORD's power, I defeated them.
¹³They chased me until I was almost
    defeated,
    but the LORD helped me.
¹⁴The LORD gives me strength and a
    song.
    He has saved me.

PROVERBS 27:8

⁸A person who leaves his home
    is like a bird that leaves its nest.

COLOSSIANS 4:2–18

What the Christians Are to Do

²Continue praying, keeping alert, and always thanking God. ³Also pray for us that God will give us an opportunity to tell peo-

ple his message. Pray that we can preach the secret that God has made known about Christ. This is why I am in prison. ⁴Pray that I can speak in a way that will make it clear, as I should.

⁵Be wise in the way you act with people who are not believers, making the most of every opportunity. ⁶When you talk, you should always be kind and pleasant so you will be able to answer everyone in the way you should.

News About the People with Paul

⁷Tychicus is my dear brother in Christ and a faithful minister and servant with me in the Lord. He will tell you all the things that are happening to me. ⁸This is why I am sending him: so you may know how we are[n] and he may encourage you. ⁹I send him with Onesimus, a faithful and dear brother in Christ, and one of your group. They will tell you all that has happened here.

¹⁰Aristarchus, a prisoner with me, and Mark, the cousin of Barnabas, greet you. (I have already told you what to do about Mark. If he comes, welcome him.) ¹¹Jesus, who is called Justus, also greets you. These are the only Jewish believers who work with me for the kingdom of God, and they have been a comfort to me.

¹²Epaphras, a servant of Jesus Christ, from your group, also greets you. He always prays for you that you will grow to be spiritually mature and have everything God wants for you. ¹³I know he has worked hard for you and the people in Laodicea and in Hierapolis. ¹⁴Demas and our dear friend Luke, the doctor, greet you.

¹⁵Greet the brothers and sisters in Laodicea. And greet Nympha and the church that meets in her house. ¹⁶After this letter is read to you, be sure it is also read to the church in Laodicea. And you read the letter that I wrote to Laodicea. ¹⁷Tell Archippus, "Be sure to finish the work the Lord gave you."

¹⁸I, Paul, greet you and write this with my own hand. Remember me in prison. Grace be with you.

4:8 so . . . are Some Greek copies read "so he may know how you are."

OCTOBER 14

Jeremiah's Linen Belt

13 This is what the LORD said to me: "Go and buy a linen belt and put it around your waist. Don't let the belt get wet."

²So I bought a linen belt, just as the LORD told me, and put it around my waist. ³Then the LORD spoke his word to me a second time: ⁴"Take the belt you bought and are wearing, and go to Perath. Hide the belt there in a crack in the rocks." ⁵So I went to Perath and hid the belt there, just as the LORD told me.

⁶Many days later the LORD said to me, "Now go to Perath and get the belt I told you to hide there." ⁷So I went to Perath and dug up the belt and took it from where I had hidden it. But now it was ruined; it was good for nothing.

⁸Then the LORD spoke his word to me. ⁹This is what the LORD said: "In the same way I will ruin the pride of the people of Judah and the great pride of Jerusalem. ¹⁰These evil people refuse to listen to my warnings. They stubbornly do only what they want to do, and they follow other gods to serve and worship them. So they will become like this linen belt—good for nothing. ¹¹As a belt is wrapped tightly around a person's waist, I wrapped the families of Israel and Judah around me," says the LORD. "I did that so they would be my people and bring fame, praise, and honor to me. But my people would not listen.

Warnings About Leather Wine Bags

¹²"Say to them: 'This is what the LORD, the God of Israel, says: All leather bags for holding wine should be filled with wine.' People will say to you: 'Of course, we know all wine bags should be filled with wine.' ¹³Then you will say to them, 'This is what the LORD says: I will make everyone in this land like a drunken person—the kings who sit on David's throne, the priests and the prophets, and all the people who live in Jerusalem. ¹⁴I will make them smash against one another, fathers and sons alike, says the LORD. I will

not feel sorry or have pity on them or show mercy that would stop me from destroying them.'"

Threat of Slavery

¹⁵Listen and pay attention.
  Don't be too proud,
  because the LORD has spoken to you.
¹⁶Give glory to the LORD your God
  before he brings darkness
and before you slip and fall
  on the dark hills.
You hope for light,
  but he will turn it into thick darkness;
  he will change it into deep gloom.
¹⁷If you don't listen to him,
  I will cry secretly
  because of your pride.
I will cry painfully,
  and my eyes will overflow with tears,
  because the LORD's people will be
    captured.

¹⁸Tell this to the king and the queen
    mother:
  "Come down from your thrones,
  because your beautiful crowns
  have fallen from your heads."
¹⁹The cities of southern Judah are locked
    up,
  and no one can open them.
All Judah will be taken as captives to a
    foreign land;
  they will be carried away completely.

²⁰Jerusalem, look up and see
  the people coming from the north.
Where is the flock God gave you to care
    for,
  the flock you bragged about?
²¹What will you say when they appoint as
    your heads
  those you had thought were your
    friends?
Won't you have much pain and trouble,
  like a woman giving birth to a baby?
²²You might ask yourself,
  "Why has this happened to me?"
It happened because of your many sins.

Because of your sins, your skirt was
torn off
and your body has been treated badly.
²³Can a person from Cush change the color
of his skin?
Can a leopard change his spots?
In the same way, Jerusalem, you cannot
change and do good,
because you are accustomed to doing
evil.
²⁴"I will scatter you like chaff that is blown
away by the desert wind.
²⁵This is what will happen to you;
this is your part in my plans," says the
LORD.
"Because you forgot me
and trusted in false gods,
²⁶I will pull your skirts up over your face
so everyone will see your shame.
²⁷I have seen the terrible things you have
done:
your acts of adultery and your
snorting,
your prostitution,
your hateful acts
on the hills and in the fields.
How terrible it will be for you, Jerusalem.
How long will you continue being
unclean?"

A Time Without Rain

14 These are the words that the LORD spoke
to Jeremiah about the time when there
was no rain:
²"The nation of Judah cries as if someone
has died,
and her cities are very sad.
They are distressed over the land.
A cry goes up to God from Jerusalem.
³The important men send their servants
to get water.
They go to the wells,
but they find no water.
So they return with empty jars.
They are ashamed and embarrassed
and cover their heads in shame.
⁴The ground is dry and cracked open,
because no rain falls on the land.
The farmers are upset and sad,
so they cover their heads in shame.
⁵Even the mother deer in the field

leaves her newborn fawn to die,
because there is no grass.
⁶Wild donkeys stand on the bare hills
and sniff the wind like wild dogs.
But their eyes go blind,
because there is no food."

⁷We know that we suffer because of our
sins.
LORD, do something to help us for the
good of your name.
We have left you many times;
we have sinned against you.
⁸God, the Hope of Israel,
you have saved Israel in times of
trouble.
Why are you like a stranger in the land,
or like a traveler who only stays one
night?
⁹Why are you like someone who has been
attacked by surprise,
like a warrior who is not able to save
anyone?
But you are among us, LORD,
and we are called by your name
so don't leave us without help!

¹⁰This is what the LORD says about the
people of Judah:
"They really love to wander from me;
they don't stop themselves from leaving
me.
So now the LORD will not accept them.
He will now remember the evil they do
and will punish them for their sins."

¹¹Then the LORD said, "Don't pray for good
things to happen to the people of Judah.
¹²Even if they fast, I will not listen to their
prayers. Even if they offer burnt offerings
and grain offerings to me, I will not accept
them. Instead, I will destroy the people of Judah with war, hunger, and terrible diseases."

¹³But I said, "Oh, Lord GOD, the prophets
keep telling the people, 'You will not suffer
from an enemy's sword or from hunger. I, the
LORD, will give you peace in this land.'"

¹⁴Then the LORD said to me, "Those
prophets are prophesying lies in my name. I
did not send them or appoint them or speak
to them. They have been prophesying false
visions, idolatries, worthless magic, and
their own wishful thinking. ¹⁵So this is what

I say about the prophets who are prophesying in my name. I did not send them. They say, 'No enemy will attack this country with swords. There will never be hunger in this land.' So those prophets will die from hunger and from an enemy's sword. [16]And the people to whom the prophets speak will be thrown into the streets of Jerusalem. There they will die from hunger and from an enemy's sword. And no one will be there to bury them, or their wives, or their sons, or their daughters. I will punish them.

[17]"Jeremiah, speak this message to the people of Judah:

'Let my eyes be filled with tears
    night and day, without stopping.
My people have received a terrible blow;
    they have been hurt badly.
[18]If I go into the country,
    I see people killed by swords.
If I go into the city,
    I see much sickness, because the people
        have no food.
Both the priests and the prophets
    have been taken to a foreign land.'"

[19]LORD, have you completely rejected the
        nation of Judah?
    Do you hate Jerusalem?
Why have you hurt us so badly
    that we cannot be made well again?
We hoped for peace,
    but nothing good has come.
We looked for a time of healing,
    but only terror came.
[20]LORD, we admit that we are wicked
    and that our ancestors did evil things.
    We have sinned against you.
[21]For your sake, do not hate us.
    Do not take away the honor from your
        glorious throne.
    Remember your agreement with us,
        and do not break it.
[22]Do foreign idols have the power to bring
        rain?
    Does the sky itself have the power to
        send down showers?
No, it is you, LORD our God.
    You are our only hope,
        because you are the one who made all
            these things.

PSALM 118:15–21

[15]Shouts of joy and victory
    come from the tents of those who do
        right:
    "The LORD has done powerful things."
[16]The power of the LORD has won the victory;
    with his power the LORD has done
        mighty things.

[17]I will not die, but live,
    and I will tell what the LORD has done.
[18]The LORD has taught me a hard lesson,
    but he did not let me die.

[19]Open for me the Temple gates.
    Then I will come in and thank the LORD.
[20]This is the LORD's gate;
    only those who are good may enter
        through it.
[21]LORD, I thank you for answering me.
    You have saved me.

PROVERBS 27:9

[9]The sweet smell of perfume and oils is
        pleasant,
    and so is good advice from a friend.

1 THESSALONIANS 1:1–10

1 From Paul, Silas, and Timothy.
    To the church in Thessalonica, the church in God the Father and the Lord Jesus Christ:
    Grace and peace to you.

The Faith of the Thessalonians

[2]We always thank God for all of you and mention you when we pray. [3]We continually recall before God our Father the things you have done because of your faith and the work you have done because of your love. And we thank him that you continue to be strong because of your hope in our Lord Jesus Christ.

[4]Brothers and sisters, God loves you, and we know he has chosen you, [5]because the Good News we brought to you came not only with words, but with power, with the Holy Spirit, and with sure knowledge that it is true. Also you know how we lived when we were with you in order to help you. [6]And you

became like us and like the Lord. You suffered much, but still you accepted the teaching with the joy that comes from the Holy Spirit. [7]So you became an example to all the believers in Macedonia and Southern Greece. [8]And the Lord's teaching spread from you not only into Macedonia and Southern Greece, but now your faith in God has become known everywhere. So we do not need to say anything about it. [9]People everywhere are telling about the way you accepted us when we were there with you. They tell how you stopped worshiping idols and began serving the living and true God. [10]And you wait for God's Son, whom God raised from the dead, to come from heaven. He is Jesus, who saves us from God's angry judgment that is sure to come.

OCTOBER 15

JEREMIAH 15:1—16:21

15 Then the LORD said to me: "I would not feel sorry for the people of Judah even if Moses and Samuel prayed for them. Send them away from me! Tell them to go! [2]When they ask you, 'Where will we go?' tell them: 'This is what the LORD says:
Those who are meant to die
  will die.
Those who are meant to die in war
  will die in war.
Those who are meant to die from hunger
  will die from hunger.
Those who are meant to be taken captive
  will be taken captive.'
[3]"I will send four kinds of destroyers against them," says the LORD. "I will send war to kill, dogs to drag the bodies away, and the birds of the air and wild animals to eat and destroy the bodies. [4]I will make the people of Judah hated by everyone on earth because of what Manasseh did in Jerusalem. (Manasseh son of Hezekiah was king of the nation of Judah.)
[5]"Who will feel sorry for you, Jerusalem?
  Who will be sad and cry for you?
  Who will go out of his way to ask how
    you are?
[6]Jerusalem, you have left me," says the LORD.
  "You keep going farther and farther away,
  so I have taken hold of you and
    destroyed you.
  I was tired of holding back my anger.
[7]I have separated the people of Judah with
    my pitchfork
  and scattered them at the city gates of
    the land.

My people haven't changed their ways.
  So I have destroyed them
  and taken away their children.
[8]There are more widows than grains of
    sand in the sea.
  I brought a destroyer at noontime
  against the mothers of the young men
    of Judah.
  I suddenly brought pain and fear
  on the people of Judah.
[9]When the enemy attacked, a woman with
    seven sons felt faint because they
    would all die.
  She became weak and unable to
    breathe.
  Her bright day became dark from
    sadness.
  She felt shame and disgrace.
And everyone else left alive in Judah
  I will hand over to the enemies, too!"
    says the LORD.

Jeremiah's Second Complaint
[10]Mother, I am sorry that you gave birth to
    me
  since I must accuse and criticize the
    whole land.
  I have not loaned or borrowed
    anything,
  but everyone curses me.
[11]The LORD said,
  "I have saved you for a good reason.
  I have made your enemies beg you
  in times of disaster and trouble.
[12]No one can smash a piece of iron or
    bronze
  that comes from the north.

¹³Your wealth and treasures
  I will give to others free of charge,
because the people of Judah have sinned
  throughout the country.
¹⁴I will make you slaves to your enemies
  in a land you have never known.
My anger is like a hot fire,
  and it will burn against you."

¹⁵LORD, you understand.
  Remember me and take care of me.
  Punish for me those who are hurting me.
Don't destroy me while you remain
  patient with them.
Think about the shame I suffer for you.
¹⁶Your words came to me, and I listened
  carefully to them.
Your words made me very happy,
because I am called by your name,
  LORD God All-Powerful.
¹⁷I never sat with the crowd
  as they laughed and had fun.
I sat by myself, because you were there,
  and you filled me with anger at the evil
  around me.
¹⁸I don't understand why my pain has no
  end.
  I don't understand why my injury is not
  cured or healed.
Will you be like a brook that goes dry?
Will you be like a spring that stops
  flowing?
¹⁹So this is what the LORD says:
"If you change your heart and return to
  me, I will take you back.
  Then you may serve me.
And if you speak things that have worth,
  not useless words,
  then you may speak for me.
Let the people of Judah turn to you,
  but you must not change and be like
  them.
²⁰I will make you as strong as a wall to this
  people,
  as strong as a wall of bronze.
They will fight against you,
  but they will not defeat you,
because I am with you.
  I will rescue you and save you," says the
  LORD.
²¹"I will save you from these wicked people

and rescue you from these cruel
  people."

The Day of Disaster

16²Then the LORD spoke his word to me:
"You must not get married or have
sons or daughters in this place."

³The LORD says this about the sons and
daughters born in this land and their mothers and fathers: ⁴"They will die of terrible
diseases, and no one will cry for them or
bury them. Their bodies will lie on the
ground like dung. They will die in war, or
they will starve to death. Their bodies will be
food for the birds of the sky and for the wild
animals."

⁵So this is what the LORD says: "Jeremiah,
do not go into a house where there is a funeral meal. Do not go there to cry for the
dead or to show your sorrow for them, because I have taken back my blessing, my
love, and my pity from these people," says the
LORD. ⁶"Important people and common people will die in the land of Judah. No one will
bury them or cry for them or cut himself or
shave his head to show sorrow for them. ⁷No
one will bring food to comfort those who are
crying for the dead. No one will offer a drink
to comfort someone whose mother or father
has died.

⁸"Do not go into a house where the people
are having a feast to sit down to eat and drink,
⁹because this is what the LORD All-Powerful,
the God of Israel, says: I will soon stop the
sounds of joy and gladness and the happy
sounds of brides and bridegrooms in this
place. This will happen during your lifetime.

¹⁰"When you tell the people of Judah
these things, they will ask you, 'Why has the
LORD said these terrible things to us? What
have we done wrong? What sin have we done
against the LORD our God?'

¹¹"Then say to them: 'This is because your
ancestors quit following me,' says the LORD.
'And they followed other gods and served
and worshiped them. Your ancestors left me
and quit obeying my teaching. ¹²But you
have done even more evil than your ancestors. You are very stubborn and do only what
you want to do; you have not obeyed me. ¹³So
I will throw you out of this country and send

you into a land that you and your ancestors never knew. There you can serve other gods day and night, because I will not help you or show you any favors.'

14"People say, 'As surely as the LORD lives, who brought the people of Israel out of Egypt . . . ' But the time is coming," says the LORD, "when people will not say this anymore. 15They will say instead, 'As surely as the LORD lives, who brought the Israelites from the northern land and from all the countries where he had sent them . . . ' And I will bring them back to the land I gave to their ancestors.

16"I will soon send for many fishermen to come to this land," says the LORD. "And they will catch the people of Judah. After that, I will send for many hunters to come to this land. And they will hunt the people of Judah on every mountain and hill and in the cracks of the rocks. 17I see everything they do. They cannot hide from me the things they do; their sin is not hidden from my eyes. 18I will pay back the people of Judah twice for every one of their sins, because they have made my land unclean. They have filled my country with their hateful idols."

19LORD, you are my strength and my
     protection,
   my safe place in times of trouble.
The nations will come to you from all
     over the world
   and say, "Our ancestors had only false
     gods,
   useless idols that didn't help them.
20Can people make gods for themselves?
   They will not really be gods!"
21The LORD says, "So I will teach those who
     make idols.
   This time I will teach them
   about my power and my strength.
   Then they will know
   that my name is the LORD.

PSALM 118:22–24

22The stone that the builders rejected
   became the cornerstone.
23The LORD did this,

and it is wonderful to us.
24This is the day that the LORD has made.
   Let us rejoice and be glad today!

PROVERBS 27:10

10Don't forget your friend or your parent's
   friend.
Don't always go to your family for help
   when trouble comes.
A neighbor close by is better than a
   family far away.

1 THESSALONIANS 2:1–16

Paul's Work in Thessalonica

2Brothers and sisters, you know our visit to you was not a failure. 2Before we came to you, we suffered in Philippi. People there insulted us, as you know, and many people were against us. But our God helped us to be brave and to tell you his Good News. 3Our appeal does not come from lies or wrong reasons, nor were we trying to trick you. 4But we speak the Good News because God tested us and trusted us to do it. When we speak, we are not trying to please people, but God, who tests our hearts. 5You know that we never tried to influence you by saying nice things about you. We were not trying to get your money; we had no selfishness to hide from you. God knows that this is true. 6We were not looking for human praise, from you or anyone else, 7even though as apostles of Christ we could have used our authority over you.

But we were very gentle with you,[n] like a mother caring for her little children. 8Because we loved you, we were happy to share not only God's Good News with you, but even our own lives. You had become so dear to us! 9Brothers and sisters, I know you remember our hard work and difficulties. We worked night and day so we would not burden any of you while we preached God's Good News to you.

10When we were with you, we lived in a holy and honest way, without fault. You know this is true, and so does God. 11You know that we treated each of you as a father treats his own children. ¹²We encouraged you, we urged you, and we insisted that you live good lives for God, who calls you to his glorious kingdom.

¹³Also, we always thank God because when you heard his message from us, you accepted it as the word of God, not the words of humans. And it really is God's message which works in you who believe. ¹⁴Brothers and sisters, your experiences have been like those of God's churches in Christ that are in Judea.ⁿ You suffered from the people of your own country, as they suffered from the Jews ¹⁵who killed both the Lord Jesus and the prophets and forced us to leave that country. They do not please God and are against all people. ¹⁶They try to stop us from teaching those who are not Jews so they may be saved. By doing this, they are increasing their sins to the limit. The anger of God has come to them at last.

OCTOBER 16

JEREMIAH 17:1—18:23

Judah's Guilty Heart

17 "The sin of the people of Judah is written with an iron tool.
Their sins were cut with a hard point into the stone that is their hearts.
Their sins were cut into the corners of their altars.
²Even their children remember their altars to idols and their Asherah idols
beside the green trees
and on the high hills.
³My mountain in the open country
and your wealth and treasures
I will give away to other people.
I will give away the places of worship in your country,
because you sinned by worshiping there.
⁴You will lose the land I gave you,
and it is your own fault.
I will let your enemies take you as their slaves
to a land you have never known.
This is because you have made my anger burn like a hot fire,
and it will burn forever."

Trusting in Humans or God

⁵This is what the LORD says:
"A curse is placed on those who trust other people,
who depend on humans for strength,
who have stopped trusting the LORD.
⁶They are like a bush in a desert
that grows in a land where no one lives,
a hot and dry land with bad soil.
They don't know about the good things God can give.

⁷"But the person who trusts in the LORD will be blessed.
The LORD will show him that he can be trusted.
⁸He will be strong, like a tree planted near water
that sends its roots by a stream.
It is not afraid when the days are hot;
its leaves are always green.
It does not worry in a year when no rain comes;
it always produces fruit.

⁹"More than anything else, a person's mind is evil
and cannot be healed.
Who can understand it?
¹⁰But I, the LORD, look into a person's heart and test the mind.
So I can decide what each one deserves;
I can give each one the right payment for what he does."

¹¹Like a bird hatching an egg it did not lay,
so are the people who get rich by cheating.
When their lives are half finished, they will lose their riches.

2:14 Judea The Jewish land where Jesus lived and taught and where the church first began.

At the end of their lives, it will be clear
they were fools.

¹²From the beginning, our Temple has
been honored
as a glorious throne for God.
¹³LORD, hope of Israel,
those who leave you will be shamed.
People who quit following the LORD will
be like a name written in the dust,
because they have left the LORD, the
spring of living water.

Jeremiah's Third Complaint

¹⁴LORD, heal me, and I will truly be healed.
Save me, and I will truly be saved.
You are the one I praise.
¹⁵The people of Judah keep asking me,
"Where is the word from the LORD?
Let's see that message come true!"

¹⁶LORD, I didn't run away from being the
shepherd you wanted.
I didn't want the terrible day to come.
You know everything I have said;
you see all that is happening.
¹⁷Don't be a terror to me.
I run to you for safety in times of
trouble.
¹⁸Make those who are hurting me be
ashamed,
but don't bring shame to me.
Let them be terrified,
but keep me from terror.
Bring the day of disaster on my enemies.
Destroy them, and destroy them again.

Keeping the Sabbath Holy

¹⁹This is what the LORD said to me: "Go
and stand at the People's Gate of Jerusalem,
where the kings of Judah go in and out. And
then go to all the other gates of Jerusalem.
²⁰Say to them there: 'Hear the word of the
LORD, kings of Judah, all you people of Judah,
and all who live in Jerusalem, who come
through these gates into the city. ²¹This is
what the LORD says: Be careful not to carry a
load on the Sabbath day or bring it through
the gates of Jerusalem. ²²Don't take a load
out of your houses on the Sabbath or do any
work on that day. But keep the Sabbath as a
holy day, as I commanded your ancestors.

²³But your ancestors did not listen or pay attention to me. They were very stubborn and
did not listen. I punished them, but it didn't
do any good. ²⁴But you must be careful to
obey me, says the LORD. You must not bring a
load through the gates of Jerusalem on the
Sabbath, but you must keep the Sabbath as a
holy day and not do any work on that day.

²⁵" 'If you obey this command, kings who
sit on David's throne will come through the
gates of Jerusalem with their officers. They
will come riding in chariots and on horses,
along with the people of Judah and Jerusalem. And the city of Jerusalem will have people living in it forever. ²⁶People will come to
Jerusalem from the villages around it, from
the towns of Judah, from the land of Benjamin, from the western hills, from the mountains, and from southern Judah. They will all
bring to the Temple of the LORD burnt offerings, sacrifices, grain offerings, incense, and
offerings to show thanks to God. ²⁷But you
must obey me and keep the Sabbath day as a
holy day. You must not carry any loads into
Jerusalem on the Sabbath. If you don't obey
me, I will start a fire at the gates of Jerusalem,
and it will burn until it burns even the strong
towers. And it will not be put out.' "

The Potter and the Clay

18 This is the word the LORD spoke to Jeremiah: ²"Go down to the potter's
house, and I will give you my message there."
³So I went down to the potter's house and
saw him working at the potter's wheel. ⁴He
was using his hands to make a pot from clay,
but something went wrong with it. So he
used that clay to make another pot the way
he wanted it to be.

⁵Then the LORD spoke his word to me:
⁶"Family of Israel, can't I do the same thing
with you?" says the LORD. "You are in my
hands like the clay in the potter's hands.
⁷There may come a time when I will speak
about a nation or a kingdom that I will pull
up by its roots or that I will pull down to destroy it. ⁸But if the people of that nation stop
doing the evil they have done, I will change
my mind and not carry out my plans to
bring disaster to them. ⁹There may come another time when I will speak about a nation

that I will build up and plant. [10]But if I see it doing evil by not obeying me, I will change my mind and not carry out my plans to do good for them.

[11]"So, say this to the people of Judah and those who live in Jerusalem: 'This is what the LORD says: I am preparing disaster for you and making plans against you. So stop doing evil. Change your ways and do what is right.' [12]But the people of Judah will answer, 'It won't do any good to try! We will continue to do what we want. Each of us will do what his stubborn, evil heart wants!'"

[13]So this is what the LORD says:
"Ask the people in other nations this
    question:
'Have you ever heard anything like this?'
The people of Israel have done a
    horrible thing.
[14]The snow on the mountains of Lebanon
    never melts from the rocks.
Its cool, flowing streams
    do not dry up.
[15]But my people have forgotten me.
    They burn incense to worthless idols
and have stumbled in what they do
    and in the old ways of their ancestors.
They walk along back roads
    and on poor highways.
[16]So Judah's country will become an empty
    desert.
    People will not stop making fun of it.
They will shake their heads as they pass
    by;
    they will be shocked at how the country
        was destroyed.
[17]Like a strong east wind,
    I will scatter them before their
        enemies.
At that awful time they will not see me
    coming to help them;
    they will see me leaving."

Jeremiah's Fourth Complaint

[18]Then the people said, "Come, let's make plans against Jeremiah. Surely the teaching of the law by the priest will not be lost. We will still have the advice from the wise teachers and the words of the prophets. So let's ruin him by telling lies about him. We won't pay attention to anything he says."

[19]LORD, listen to me.
    Listen to what my accusers are saying!
[20]Good should not be paid back with evil,
    but they have dug a pit in order to kill
        me.
Remember that I stood before you
    and asked you to do good things for
        these people
    and to turn your anger away from
        them.
[21]So now, let their children starve,
    and let their enemies kill them with
        swords.
Let their wives lose their children and
    husbands.
Let the men from Judah be put to death
    and the young men be killed with
        swords in battle.
[22]Let them cry out in their houses
    when you bring an enemy against them
        suddenly.
Let all this happen, because my enemies
    have dug
    a pit to capture me and have hidden
        traps for my feet.
[23]LORD, you know
    about all their plans to kill me.
Don't forgive their crimes
    or erase their sins from your mind.
Make them fall from their places;
    punish them while you are angry.

PSALM 118:25-29

[25]Please, LORD, save us;
    please, LORD, give us success.
[26]God bless the one who comes in the
    name of the LORD.
We bless all of you from the Temple of
    the LORD.
[27]The LORD is God,
    and he has shown kindness to us.
With branches in your hands, join the
    feast.
Come to the corners of the altar.

[28]You are my God, and I will thank you;
    you are my God, and I will praise your
        greatness.

[29]Thank the LORD because he is good.
    His love continues forever.

PROVERBS 27:11–12

¹¹Be wise, my child, and make me happy.
Then I can respond to any insult.

¹²The wise see danger ahead and avoid it,
but fools keep going and get into
trouble.

1 THESSALONIANS 2:17—3:13

Paul Wants to Visit Them Again

¹⁷Brothers and sisters, though we were separated from you for a short time, our thoughts were still with you. We wanted very much to see you and tried hard to do so. ¹⁸We wanted to come to you. I, Paul, tried to come more than once, but Satan stopped us. ¹⁹You are our hope, our joy, and the crown we will take pride in when our Lord Jesus Christ comes. ²⁰Truly you are our glory and our joy. 3When we could not wait any longer, we decided it was best to stay in Athens alone ²and send Timothy to you. Timothy, our brother, works with us for God and helps us tell people the Good News about Christ. We sent him to strengthen and encourage you in your faith ³so none of you would be upset by these troubles. You yourselves know that we must face these troubles. ⁴Even when we were with you, we told you we all would have

to suffer, and you know it has happened. ⁵Because of this, when I could wait no longer, I sent Timothy to you so I could learn about your faith. I was afraid the devil had tempted you, and perhaps our hard work would have been wasted.

⁶But Timothy now has come back to us from you and has brought us good news about your faith and love. He told us that you always remember us in a good way and that you want to see us just as much as we want to see you. ⁷So, brothers and sisters, while we have much trouble and suffering, we are encouraged about you because of your faith. ⁸Our life is really full if you stand strong in the Lord. ⁹We have so much joy before our God because of you. We cannot thank him enough for all the joy we feel. ¹⁰Night and day we continue praying with all our heart that we can see you again and give you all the things you need to make your faith strong. ¹¹Now may our God and Father himself and our Lord Jesus prepare the way for us to come to you. ¹²May the Lord make your love grow more and multiply for each other and for all people so that you will love others as we love you. ¹³May your hearts be made strong so that you will be holy and without fault before our God and Father when our Lord Jesus comes with all his holy ones.

OCTOBER 17

JEREMIAH 19:1—20:18

Judah Is like a Broken Jar

19This is what the Lᴏʀᴅ said to me: "Go and buy a clay jar from a potter. ²Take some of the elders of the people and the priests, and go out to the Valley of Ben Hinnom, near the front of the Potsherd Gate. There speak the words I tell you. ³Say, 'Kings of Judah and people of Jerusalem, listen to this message from the Lᴏʀᴅ. This is what the Lᴏʀᴅ All-Powerful, the God of Israel, says: I will soon bring a disaster on this place that will amaze and frighten everyone who hears about it. ⁴The people of Judah have quit fol-

lowing me. They have made this a place for foreign gods. They have burned sacrifices to other gods that neither they, nor their ancestors, nor the kings of Judah had ever known before. They filled this place with the blood of innocent people. ⁵They have built places on hilltops to worship Baal, where they burn their children in the fire to Baal. That is something I did not command or speak about; it never even entered my mind. ⁶Now people call this place the Valley of Ben Hinnom or Topheth, but the days are coming, says the Lᴏʀᴅ, when people will call it the Valley of Killing.

⁷"'At this place I will ruin the plans of the

people of Judah and Jerusalem. The enemy will chase them, and I will have them killed with swords. I will make their dead bodies food for the birds and wild animals. ⁸I will completely destroy this city. People will make fun of it and shake their heads when they pass by. They will be shocked when they see how the city was destroyed. ⁹An enemy army will surround the city and will not let anyone go out to get food. I will make the people so hungry that they will eat the bodies of their own sons and daughters, and then they will begin to eat each other.'

¹⁰"While the people with you are watching, break that jar. ¹¹Then say this: 'The LORD All-Powerful says: I will break this nation and this city just as someone breaks a clay jar that cannot be put back together again. The dead people will be buried here in Topheth, because there is no other place for them. ¹²This is what I will do to these people and to this place, says the LORD. I will make this city like Topheth. ¹³The houses in Jerusalem and the king's palaces will become as unclean as this place, Topheth, because the people worshiped gods on the roofs*ⁿ* of their houses. They worshiped the stars and burned incense to honor them and gave drink offerings to gods.'"

¹⁴When Jeremiah left Topheth where the LORD had sent him to prophesy, he went to the LORD's Temple, stood in the courtyard, and said to all the people: ¹⁵"This is what the LORD All-Powerful, the God of Israel, says: 'I will soon bring disaster to Jerusalem and the villages around it, as I said I would. This will happen because the people are very stubborn and do not listen at all to what I say.'"

Pashhur Will Be Captured

20 Pashhur son of Immer was a priest and the highest officer in the Temple of the LORD. When he heard Jeremiah prophesying in the Temple courtyard, ²he had Jeremiah the prophet beaten. And he locked Jeremiah's hands and feet between large blocks of wood at the Upper Gate of Benjamin of the LORD's Temple. ³The next day when Pashhur took Jeremiah out of the blocks of wood, Jeremiah

said to him, "The LORD's name for you is not Pashhur. Now his name for you is Terror on Every Side. ⁴This is what the LORD says: 'I will soon make you a terror to yourself and to all your friends. You will watch enemies killing your friends with swords. And I will give all the people of Judah to the king of Babylon, who will take them away as captives to Babylon and then will kill them with swords. ⁵I will give all the wealth of this city to its enemies—its goods, its valuables, and the treasures of the kings of Judah. The enemies will carry all those valuables off to Babylon. ⁶And Pashhur, you and everyone in your house will be taken captive. You will be forced to go to Babylon, where you will die and be buried, you and your friends to whom you have prophesied lies.'"

Jeremiah's Fifth Complaint

⁷LORD, you tricked me, and I was fooled.
　You are stronger than I am, so you won.
I have become a joke;
　everyone makes fun of me all day long.
⁸Every time I speak, I shout.
　I am always shouting about violence
　　and destruction.
I tell the people about the message I
　　received from the LORD,
　but this only brings me insults.
The people make fun of me all day long.
⁹Sometimes I say to myself,
　"I will forget about the LORD.
I will not speak anymore in his name."
But then his message becomes like a
　　burning fire inside me,
　deep within my bones.
I get tired of trying to hold it inside of me,
　and finally, I cannot hold it in.
¹⁰I hear many people whispering about me:
　"Terror on every side!
Tell on him! Let's tell the rulers about
　　him."
My friends are all just waiting for me to
　　make some mistake.
They are saying,
　"Maybe we can trick him
so we can defeat him
　and pay him back."

[11]But the LORD is with me like a strong
warrior,
so those who are chasing me will trip
and fall;
they will not defeat me.
They will be ashamed because they have
failed,
and their shame will never be forgotten.

[12]LORD All-Powerful, you test good people;
you look deeply into the heart and
mind of a person.
I have told you my arguments against
these people,
so let me see you give them the
punishment they deserve.

[13]Sing to the LORD!
Praise the LORD!
He saves the life of the poor
from the power of the wicked.

Jeremiah's Sixth Complaint

[14]Let there be a curse on the day I was
born;
let there be no blessing on the day
when my mother gave birth to me.
[15]Let there be a curse on the man
who brought my father the news:
"You have a son!"
This made my father very glad.
[16]Let that man be like the towns
the LORD destroyed without pity.
Let him hear loud crying in the morning
and battle cries at noon,
[17]because he did not kill me before I was
born.
Then my mother would have been my
grave;
she would have stayed pregnant forever.
[18]Why did I have to come out of my
mother's body?
All I have known is trouble and sorrow,
and my life will end in shame.

PSALM 119:1–8

The Word of God

119 [1]Happy are those who live pure lives,
who follow the LORD's teachings.
[2]Happy are those who keep his rules,

who try to obey him with their whole
heart.
[3]They don't do what is wrong;
they follow his ways.
[4]LORD, you gave your orders
to be obeyed completely.
[5]I wish I were more loyal
in obeying your demands.
[6]Then I would not be ashamed
when I study your commands.
[7]When I learned that your laws are fair,
I praised you with an honest heart.
[8]I will obey your demands,
so please don't ever leave me.

PROVERBS 27:13

[13]Take the coat of someone who promises
to pay a stranger's loan,
and keep it until he pays what the
stranger owes.

1 THESSALONIANS 4:1–18

A Life that Pleases God

4 Brothers and sisters, we taught you how
to live in a way that will please God, and
you are living that way. Now we ask and encourage you in the Lord Jesus to live that way
even more. [2]You know what we told you to do
by the authority of the Lord Jesus. [3]God
wants you to be holy and to stay away from
sexual sins. [4]He wants each of you to learn to
control your own body[n] in a way that is holy
and honorable. [5]Don't use your body for sexual sin like the people who do not know God.
[6]Also, do not wrong or cheat another Christian in this way. The Lord will punish people
who do those things as we have already told
you and warned you. [7]God called us to be
holy and does not want us to live in sin. [8]So
the person who refuses to obey this teaching
is disobeying God, not simply a human
teaching. And God is the One who gives us
his Holy Spirit.
[9]We do not need to write you about having love for your Christian family, because
God has already taught you to love each
other. [10]And truly you do love the Christians
in all of Macedonia. Brothers and sisters,

4:4 **learn . . . body** This might also mean "learn to live with your own wife."

now we encourage you to love them even more. [11]Do all you can to live a peaceful life. Take care of your own business, and do your own work as we have already told you. [12]If you do, then people who are not believers will respect you, and you will not have to depend on others for what you need.

The Lord's Coming

[13]Brothers and sisters, we want you to know about those Christians who have died so you will not be sad, as others who have no hope. [14]We believe that Jesus died and that he rose again. So, because of him, God will raise with Jesus those who have died. [15]What we tell you now is the Lord's own message. We who are living when the Lord comes again will not go before those who have already died. [16]The Lord himself will come down from heaven with a loud command, with the voice of the archangel,[n] and with the trumpet call of God. And those who have died believing in Christ will rise first. [17]After that, we who are still alive will be gathered up with them in the clouds to meet the Lord in the air. And we will be with the Lord forever. [18]So encourage each other with these words.

OCTOBER 18

JEREMIAH 21:1—22:30

God Rejects King Zedekiah's Request

21 This is the word that the LORD spoke to Jeremiah. It came when Zedekiah king of Judah sent Pashhur son of Malkijah and the priest Zephaniah son of Maaseiah to Jeremiah. [2]They said, "Ask the LORD for us what will happen, because Nebuchadnezzar king of Babylon is attacking us. Maybe the LORD will do miracles for us as he did in the past so Nebuchadnezzar will stop attacking us and leave."

[3]But Jeremiah answered them, "Tell King Zedekiah this: [4]Here is what the LORD, the God of Israel, says: You have weapons of war in your hands to defend yourselves against the king of Babylon and the Babylonians, who are all around the city wall. But I will make those weapons useless. Soon I will bring them into the center of this city. [5]In my anger, my very great anger, I myself will fight against you with my great power and strength. [6]I will kill everything living in Jerusalem—both people and animals. They will die from terrible diseases. [7]Then, says the LORD, I'll hand over Zedekiah king of Judah, his officers, and the people in Jerusalem who do not die from the terrible diseases or

battle or hunger, to Nebuchadnezzar king of Babylon. I will let those win who want to kill the people of Judah, so the people of Judah and Jerusalem will be killed in war. Nebuchadnezzar will not show any mercy or pity or feel sorry for them!'

[8]"Also tell this to the people of Jerusalem: 'This is what the LORD says: I will let you choose to live or die. [9]Anyone who stays in Jerusalem will die in war or from hunger or from a terrible disease. But anyone who goes out of Jerusalem and surrenders to the Babylonians who are attacking you will live. Anyone who leaves the city will save his life as if it were a prize won in war. [10]I have decided to make trouble for this city and not to help it, says the LORD. I will give it to the king of Babylon, and he will burn it with fire.'

[11]"Say to Judah's royal family: 'Hear the word of the LORD. [12]Family of David, this is what the LORD says:

You must judge people fairly every
  morning.
Save the person who has been robbed
  from the power of his attacker.
If you don't, I will become very angry.
  My anger will be like a fire that no one
    can put out,
  because you have done evil things.

4:16 archangel The leader among God's angels or messengers.

¹³" 'Jerusalem, I am against you,
you who live on top of the mountain
over this valley, says the LORD.
You say, "No one can attack us
or come into our strong city."
¹⁴But I will give you the punishment you
deserve, says the LORD.
I will start a fire in your forests
that will burn up everything around
you!' "

Judgment Against Evil Kings

22 This is what the LORD says: "Go down to
the palace of the king of Judah and
prophesy this message there: ²'Hear the word
of the LORD, king of Judah, who rules from
David's throne. You and your officers, and
your people who come through these gates,
listen! ³This is what the LORD says: Do what is
fair and right. Save the one who has been
robbed from the power of his attacker. Don't
mistreat or hurt the foreigners, orphans, or
widows. Don't kill innocent people here. ⁴If
you carefully obey these commands, kings
who sit on David's throne will come through
the gates of this palace with their officers and
people, riding in chariots and on horses. ⁵But
if you don't obey these commands, says the
LORD, I swear by my own name that this
king's palace will become a ruin.' "

⁶This is what the LORD says about the
palace where the king of Judah lives:
"You are tall like the forests of Gilead,
like the mountaintops of Lebanon.
But I will truly make you into a desert,
into towns where no one lives.
⁷I will send men to destroy the palace,
each with his weapons.
They will cut up your strong, beautiful
cedar beams
and throw them into the fire.

⁸"People from many nations will pass by
this city and ask each other, 'Why has the
LORD done such a terrible thing to Jerusalem,
this great city?' ⁹And the answer will be: 'Because the people of Judah quit following the
agreement with the LORD their God. They
worshiped and served other gods.' "

Judgment Against Jehoahaz

¹⁰Don't cry for the dead king or be sad
about him.

But cry painfully for the king who is
being taken away,
because he will never return
or see his homeland again.
¹¹This is what the LORD says about Jehoa-
haz son of Josiah who became king of Judah
after his father died and who has left this
place: "He will never return. ¹²He will die
where he has been taken captive, and he will
not see this land again."

Judgment Against Jehoiakim

¹³"How terrible it will be for one who
builds his palace by doing evil,
who cheats people so he can build its
upper rooms.
He makes his own people work for
nothing
and does not pay them.
¹⁴He says, 'I will build a great palace for
myself
with large upper rooms.'
So he builds it with large windows
and uses cedar wood for the walls,
which he paints red.

¹⁵"Does having a lot of cedar in your house
make you a great king?
Your father was satisfied to have food
and drink.
He did what was right and fair,
so everything went well for him.
¹⁶He helped those who were poor and
needy,
so everything went well for him.
That is what it means to know God,"
says the LORD.
¹⁷"But you only look for and think about
what you can get dishonestly.
You are even willing to kill innocent
people to get it.
You feel free to hurt people and to steal
from them."

¹⁸So this is what the LORD says to Jehoiakim
son of Josiah king of Judah:
"The people of Judah will not cry when
Jehoiakim dies,
saying: 'Oh, my brother,' or 'Oh, my
sister.'
They will not cry for him, saying:
'Oh, master,' or 'Oh, my king.'
¹⁹They will bury him like a donkey,

dragging his body away
and throwing it outside the gates of
Jerusalem.

²⁰"Judah, go up to Lebanon and cry out.
Let your voice be heard in Bashan.
Cry out from Abarim,
because all your friends are destroyed!
²¹Judah, when you were successful, I
warned you,
but you said, 'I won't listen.'
You have acted like this since you were
young;
you have not obeyed me.
²²Like a storm, my punishment will blow
all your shepherds away
and send your friends into captivity.
Then you will really be ashamed and
disgraced
because of all the wicked things you
did.
²³King, you live in your palace,
cozy in your rooms of cedar.
But when your punishment comes, how
you will groan
like a woman giving birth to a baby!

Judgment upon Jehoiachin

²⁴"As surely as I live," says the LORD, "Jehoiachin son of Jehoiakim king of Judah, even if you were a signet ring on my right hand, I would still pull you off. ²⁵I will hand you over to Nebuchadnezzar king of Babylon and to the Babylonians—those people you fear because they want to kill you. ²⁶I will throw you and your mother into another country. Neither of you was born there, but both of you will die there. ²⁷They will want to come back, but they will never be able to return."

²⁸Jehoiachin is like a broken pot someone
threw away;
he is like something no one wants.
Why will Jehoiachin and his children be
thrown out
and sent into a foreign land?
²⁹Land, land, land of Judah,
hear the word of the LORD!
³⁰This is what the LORD says:
"Write this down in the record about
Jehoiachin:
He is a man without children,

a man who will not be successful in his
lifetime.
And none of his descendants will be
successful;
none will sit on the throne of David
or rule in Judah."

PSALM 119:9–16

⁹How can a young person live a pure life?
By obeying your word.
¹⁰With all my heart I try to obey you.
Don't let me break your commands.
¹¹I have taken your words to heart
so I would not sin against you.
¹²LORD, you should be praised.
Teach me your demands.
¹³My lips will tell about
all the laws you have spoken.
¹⁴I enjoy living by your rules
as people enjoy great riches.
¹⁵I think about your orders
and study your ways.
¹⁶I enjoy obeying your demands,
and I will not forget your word.

PROVERBS 27:14

¹⁴If you loudly greet your neighbor early in
the morning,
he will think of it as a curse.

1 THESSALONIANS 5:1–28

Be Ready for the Lord's Coming

5 Now, brothers and sisters, we do not need to write you about times and dates. ²You know very well that the day the Lord comes again will be a surprise, like a thief that comes in the night. ³While people are saying, "We have peace and we are safe," they will be destroyed quickly. It is like pains that come quickly to a woman having a baby. Those people will not escape. ⁴But you, brothers and sisters, are not living in darkness, and so that day will not surprise you like a thief. ⁵You are all people who belong to the light and to the day. We do not belong to the night or to darkness. ⁶So we should not be like other people who are sleeping, but we should be alert and have self-control. ⁷Those who sleep, sleep at night. Those who get drunk, get drunk at

night. [8]But we belong to the day, so we should control ourselves. We should wear faith and love to protect us, and the hope of salvation should be our helmet. [9]God did not choose us to suffer his anger but to have salvation through our Lord Jesus Christ. [10]Jesus died for us so that we can live together with him, whether we are alive or dead when he comes. [11]So encourage each other and give each other strength, just as you are doing now.

Final Instructions and Greetings

[12]Now, brothers and sisters, we ask you to appreciate those who work hard among you, who lead you in the Lord and teach you. [13]Respect them with a very special love because of the work they do.

Live in peace with each other. [14]We ask you, brothers and sisters, to warn those who do not work. Encourage the people who are afraid. Help those who are weak. Be patient with everyone. [15]Be sure that no one pays back wrong for wrong, but always try to do what is good for each other and for all people.

[16]Always be joyful. [17]Pray continually, [18]and give thanks whatever happens. That is what God wants for you in Christ Jesus.

[19]Do not hold back the work of the Holy Spirit. [20]Do not treat prophecy as if it were unimportant. [21]But test everything. Keep what is good, [22]and stay away from everything that is evil.

[23]Now may God himself, the God of peace, make you pure, belonging only to him. May your whole self—spirit, soul, and body—be kept safe and without fault when our Lord Jesus Christ comes. [24]You can trust the One who calls you to do that for you.

[25]Brothers and sisters, pray for us.

[26]Give each other a holy kiss when you meet. [27]I tell you by the authority of the Lord to read this letter to all the believers.

[28]The grace of our Lord Jesus Christ be with you.

OCTOBER 19

JEREMIAH 23:1—24:10

The Evil Leaders of Judah

23 "How terrible it will be for the leaders of Judah, who are scattering and destroying my people," says the LORD.

[2]They are responsible for the people, so the LORD, the God of Israel, says to them: "You have scattered my people and forced them away and not taken care of them. So I will punish you for the evil things you have done," says the LORD. [3]"I sent my people to other countries, but I will gather those who are left alive and bring them back to their own country. Then they will have many children and grow in number. [4]I will place new leaders over my people, who will take care of them. And my people will not be afraid or terrified again, and none of them will be lost," says the LORD.

The Good Branch Will Come

[5]"The days are coming," says the LORD,
   "when I will raise up a good branch in
      David's family.

He will be a king who will rule in a wise
      way;
   he will do what is fair and right in the
      land.
[6]In his time Judah will be saved,
   and Israel will live in safety.
This will be his name:
   The LORD Does What Is Right.

[7]"So the days are coming," says the LORD, "when people will not say again: 'As surely as the LORD lives, who brought Israel out of Egypt . . . ' [8]But people will say something new: 'As surely as the LORD lives, who brought the descendants of Israel from the land of the north and from all the countries where he had sent them away . . . ' Then the people of Israel will live in their own land."

False Prophets Will Be Punished

[9]A message to the prophets:
   My heart is broken.
   All my bones shake.

I'm like someone who is drunk,
like someone who has been overcome
with wine.
This is because of the LORD
and his holy words.
[10]The land of Judah is full of people who
are guilty of adultery.
Because of this, the LORD cursed the
land.
It has become a very sad place,
and the pastures have dried up.
The people are evil
and use their power in the wrong way.

[11]"Both the prophets and the priests live as
if there were no God.
I have found them doing evil things
even in my own Temple," says the
LORD.
[12]"So they will be in danger.
They will be forced into darkness
where they will be defeated.
I will bring disaster on them
in the year I punish them," says the LORD.

[13]"I saw the prophets of Samaria
do something wrong.
Those prophets prophesied by Baal
and led my people Israel away.
[14]And I have seen the prophets of
Jerusalem
do terrible things.
They are guilty of adultery
and live by lies.
They encourage evil people to keep on
doing evil,
so the people don't stop sinning.
All of those people are like the city of
Sodom.
The people of Jerusalem are like the
city of Gomorrah to me!"
[15]So this is what the LORD All-Powerful
says about the prophets:
"I will make those prophets eat bitter
food
and drink poisoned water,
because the prophets of Jerusalem
spread wickedness
through the whole country."
[16]This is what the LORD All-Powerful says:
"Don't pay attention to what those
prophets are saying to you.

They are trying to fool you.
They talk about visions their own minds
made up,
not about visions from me.
[17]They say to those who hate me:
'The LORD says: You will have peace.'
They say to all those who are stubborn
and do as they please:
'Nothing bad will happen to you.'
[18]But none of these prophets has stood in
the meeting of angels
to see or hear the message of the LORD.
None of them has paid close attention
to his message.
[19]Look, the punishment from the LORD
will come like a storm.
His anger will be like a hurricane.
It will come swirling down on the
heads of those wicked people.
[20]The LORD's anger will not stop
until he finishes what he plans to do.
When that day is over,
you will understand this clearly.
[21]I did not send those prophets,
but they ran to tell their message.
I did not speak to them,
but they prophesied anyway.
[22]But if they had stood in the meeting of
angels,
they would have told my message to my
people.
They would have turned the people from
their evil ways
and from doing evil.

[23]"I am a God who is near," says the LORD.
"I am also a God who is far away.
[24]No one can hide
where I cannot see him," says the LORD.
"I fill all of heaven and earth," says the
LORD.

[25]"I have heard the prophets who prophesy lies in my name. They say, 'I have had a
dream! I have had a dream!' [26]How long will
this continue in the minds of these lying
prophets? They prophesy from their own
wishful thinking. [27]They are trying to make
the people of Judah forget me by telling each
other these dreams. In the same way, their
ancestors forgot me and worshiped Baal. [28]Is
straw the same thing as wheat?" says the

LORD. "If a prophet wants to tell about his dreams, let him! But let the person who hears my message speak it truthfully! 29Isn't my message like a fire?" says the LORD. "Isn't it like a hammer that smashes a rock?

30"So I am against the false prophets," says the LORD. "They keep stealing words from each other and say they are from me. 31I am against the false prophets," says the LORD. "They use their own words and pretend it is a message from me. 32I am against the prophets who prophesy false dreams," says the LORD. "They mislead my people with their lies and false teachings! I did not send them or command them to do anything for me. They can't help the people of Judah at all," says the LORD.

The Sad Message from the Lord

33"Suppose the people of Judah, a prophet, or a priest asks you: 'Jeremiah, what is the message from the LORD?' You will answer them and say, 'You are a heavy load to the LORD, and I will throw you down, says the LORD.' 34A prophet or a priest or one of the people might say, 'This is a message from the LORD.' That person has lied, so I will punish him and his whole family. 35This is what you will say to each other: 'What did the LORD answer?' or 'What did the LORD say?' 36But you will never again say, 'The message of the LORD,' because the only message you speak is your own words. You have changed the words of our God, the living God, the LORD All-Powerful. 37This is how you should speak to the prophets: 'What answer did the LORD give you?' or 'What did the LORD say?' 38But don't say, 'The message from the LORD.' If you use these words, this is what the LORD says: Because you called it a 'message from the LORD,' though I told you not to use those words, 39I will pick you up and throw you away from me, along with Jerusalem, which I gave to your ancestors and to you. 40And I will make a disgrace of you forever; your shame will never be forgotten."

The Good and Bad Figs

24 Nebuchadnezzar king of Babylon captured Jehoiachin son of Jehoiakim and king of Judah, his officers, and all the craftsmen and metalworkers of Judah. He took them away from Jerusalem and brought them to Babylon. It was then that the LORD showed me two baskets of figs arranged in front of the Temple of the LORD. 2One of the baskets had very good figs in it, like figs that ripen early in the season. But the other basket had figs too rotten to eat.

3The LORD said to me, "What do you see, Jeremiah?"

I answered, "I see figs. The good figs are very good, but the rotten figs are too rotten to eat."

4Then the LORD spoke his word to me: 5"This is what the LORD, the God of Israel, says: 'I sent the people of Judah out of their country to live in the country of Babylon. I think of those people as good, like these good figs. 6I will look after them and bring them back to the land of Judah. I will not tear them down, but I will build them up. I will not pull them up, but I will plant them so they can grow. 7I will make them want to know me, that I am the LORD. They will be my people, and I will be their God, because they will return to me with their whole hearts.

8"'But the bad figs are too rotten to eat.' So this is what the LORD says: 'Zedekiah king of Judah, his officers, and all the people from Jerusalem who are left alive, even those who live in Egypt, will be like those rotten figs. 9I will make those people hated as an evil people by all the kingdoms of the earth. People will make fun of them and tell jokes about them and point fingers at them and curse them everywhere I scatter them. 10I will send war, hunger, and disease against them. I will attack them until they have all been killed. Then they will no longer be in the land I gave to them and their ancestors.'"

PSALM 119:17–24

17Do good to me, your servant, so I can
    live,
    so I can obey your word.
18Open my eyes to see
    the miracles in your teachings.
19I am a stranger on earth.
    Do not hide your commands from me.
20I wear myself out with desire
    for your laws all the time.

²¹You scold proud people;
  those who ignore your commands are
  cursed.
²²Don't let me be insulted and hated
  because I keep your rules.
²³Even if princes speak against me,
  I, your servant, will think about your
  demands.
²⁴Your rules give me pleasure;
  they give me good advice.

PROVERBS 27:15–16

¹⁵A quarreling wife is as bothersome
  as a continual dripping on a rainy day.
¹⁶Stopping her is like stopping the wind
  or trying to grab oil in your hand.

2 THESSALONIANS 1:1–12

1 From Paul, Silas, and Timothy.
  To the church in Thessalonica in God
our Father and the Lord Jesus Christ:
²Grace and peace to you from God the Father and the Lord Jesus Christ.

Paul Talks About God's Judgment
³We must always thank God for you, brothers and sisters. This is only right, because
your faith is growing more and more, and the
love that every one of you has for each other is
increasing. ⁴So we brag about you to the other
churches of God. We tell them about the way

you continue to be strong and have faith even
though you are being treated badly and are
suffering many troubles.
⁵This is proof that God is right in his judgment. He wants you to be counted worthy of
his kingdom for which you are suffering. ⁶God
will do what is right. He will give trouble to
those who trouble you. ⁷And he will give rest
to you who are troubled and to us also when
the Lord Jesus appears with burning fire from
heaven with his powerful angels. ⁸Then he
will punish those who do not know God and
who do not obey the Good News about our
Lord Jesus Christ. ⁹Those people will be punished with a destruction that continues forever. They will be kept away from the Lord
and from his great power. ¹⁰This will happen
on the day when the Lord Jesus comes to receive glory because of his holy people. And all
the people who have believed will be amazed
at Jesus. You will be in that group, because you
believed what we told you.
¹¹That is why we always pray for you, asking our God to help you live the kind of life
he called you to live. We pray that with his
power God will help you do the good things
you want and perform the works that come
from your faith. ¹²We pray all this so that the
name of our Lord Jesus Christ will have
glory in you, and you will have glory in him.
That glory comes from the grace of our God
and the Lord Jesus Christ.

OCTOBER 20

JEREMIAH 25:1—26:24

A Summary of Jeremiah's Preaching
25 This is the message that came to Jeremiah concerning all the people of
Judah. It came in the fourth year that Jehoiakim son of Josiah was king of Judah and the
first year Nebuchadnezzar was king of Babylon. ²This is the message Jeremiah the
prophet spoke to all the people of Judah and
Jerusalem:
³The LORD has spoken his word to me
again and again for these past twenty-three

years. I have been a prophet since the thirteenth year of Josiah son of Amon king of Judah. I have spoken messages from the LORD
to you from that time until today, but you
have not listened.
⁴The LORD has sent all his servants the
prophets to you over and over again, but you
have not listened or paid any attention to
them. ⁵Those prophets have said, "Stop your
evil ways. Stop doing what is wrong so you
can stay in the land that the LORD gave to you
and your ancestors to live in forever. ⁶Don't
follow other gods to serve them or to wor-

ship them. Don't make me, the LORD, angry by worshiping idols that are the work of your own hands, or I will punish you."

⁷"But you people of Judah did not listen to me," says the LORD. "You made me angry by worshiping idols that were the work of your own hands, so I punished you."

⁸So this is what the LORD All-Powerful says: "Since you have not listened to my messages, ⁹I will send for all the peoples of the north," says the LORD, "along with my servant Nebuchadnezzar king of Babylon. I will bring them all against Judah, those who live there, and all the nations around you, too. I will completely destroy all those countries and leave them in ruins forever. People will be shocked when they see how badly I have destroyed those countries. ¹⁰I will bring an end to the sounds of joy and happiness, the sounds of brides and bridegrooms, and the sound of people grinding meal. And I will take away the light of the lamp. ¹¹That whole area will be an empty desert, and these nations will be slaves of the king of Babylon for seventy years.

¹²"But when the seventy years have passed, I will punish the king of Babylon and his entire nation for their evil," says the LORD. "I will make that land a desert forever. ¹³I will make happen all the terrible things I said about Babylonia—everything Jeremiah prophesied about all those foreign nations, the warnings written in this book. ¹⁴Even the Babylonians will have to serve many nations and many great kings. I will give them the punishment they deserve for all their own hands have done."

Judgment on the Nations

¹⁵The LORD, the God of Israel, said this to me: "My anger is like the wine in a cup. Take it from my hand and make all the nations, to whom I am sending you, drink all of my anger from this cup. ¹⁶They will drink my anger and stumble about and act like madmen because of the war I am going to send among them."

¹⁷So I took the cup from the LORD's hand and went to those nations and made them drink from it. ¹⁸I served this wine to the people of Jerusalem and the towns of Judah, and

the kings and officers of Judah, so they would become a ruin. Then people would be shocked and would insult them and speak evil of them. And so it has been to this day. ¹⁹I also made these people drink of the LORD's anger: the king of Egypt, his servants, his officers, all his people, ²⁰and all the foreigners there; all the kings of the land of Uz; all the kings of the Philistines (the kings of the cities of Ashkelon, Gaza, Ekron, and the people left at Ashdod); ²¹the people of Edom, Moab, and Ammon; ²²all the kings of Tyre and Sidon; all the kings of the coastal countries to the west; ²³the people of Dedan and Tema and Buz; all who cut their hair short; ²⁴all the kings of Arabia; and the kings of the people who live in the desert; ²⁵all the kings of Zimri, Elam, and Media; ²⁶and all the kings of the north, near and far, one after the other. I made all the kingdoms on earth drink from the cup of the LORD's anger, but the king of Babylon will drink from this cup after all the others.

²⁷"Then say to them, 'This is what the LORD All-Powerful, the God of Israel, says: Drink this cup of my anger. Get drunk from it and vomit. Fall down and don't get up because of the war I am sending among you!'

²⁸"If they refuse to take the cup from your hand and drink, say to them, 'The LORD All-Powerful says this: You must drink from this cup. ²⁹Look! I am already bringing disaster on Jerusalem, the city that is called by my name. Do you think you will not be punished? You will be punished! I am sending war on all the people of the earth, says the LORD All-Powerful.'

³⁰"You, Jeremiah, will prophesy against them with all these words. Say to them:

'The LORD will roar from heaven
    and will shout from his Holy Temple.
He will roar loudly against his land.
He will shout like people who walk on
        grapes to make wine;
    he will shout against all who live on the
        earth.
³¹The noise will spread all over the earth,
    because the LORD will accuse all the
        nations.
He will judge and tell what is wrong with
    all people,

and he will kill the evil people with a
sword,'" says the LORD.

³²This is what the LORD All-Powerful says:

"Disasters will soon spread
from nation to nation.

They will come like a powerful storm
from the faraway places on earth."

³³At that time those killed by the LORD will
reach from one end of the earth to the other.
No one will cry for them or gather up their
bodies and bury them. They will be left lying
on the ground like dung.

³⁴Cry, you leaders! Cry out loud!
Roll around in the dust, leaders of the
people!

It is now time for you to be killed.

You will fall and be scattered,
like pieces of a broken jar.

³⁵There will be no place for the leaders to
hide;
they will not escape.

³⁶I hear the sound of the leaders shouting.
I hear the leaders of the people crying
loudly,
because the LORD is destroying their
land.

³⁷Those peaceful pastures will be like an
empty desert,
because the LORD is very angry.

³⁸Like a lion, he has left his den.

Their land has been destroyed
because of the terrible war he brought,
because of his fierce anger.

Jeremiah's Lesson at the Temple

26 This message came from the LORD soon
after Jehoiakim son of Josiah became
king of Judah. ²This is what the LORD said: "Jeremiah, stand in the courtyard of the Temple
of the LORD. Give this message to all the people of the towns of Judah who are coming to
worship at the Temple of the LORD. Tell them
everything I tell you to say; don't leave out a
word. ³Maybe they will listen and stop their
evil ways. If they will, I will change my mind
about bringing on them the disaster that I am
planning because of the evil they have done.
⁴Say to them: 'This is what the LORD says: You
must obey me and follow my teachings that I
gave you. ⁵You must listen to what my servants the prophets say to you. I have sent

them to you again and again, but you did not
listen. ⁶If you don't obey me, I will destroy my
Temple in Jerusalem as I destroyed my Holy
Tent at Shiloh. When I do, people all over the
world will curse Jerusalem.'"

⁷The priests, the prophets, and all the people heard Jeremiah speaking these words in
the Temple of the LORD. ⁸When Jeremiah finished speaking everything the LORD had commanded him to say, the priests, prophets, and
all the people grabbed Jeremiah. They said,
"You must die! ⁹How dare you prophesy in the
name of the LORD that this Temple will be destroyed like the one at Shiloh! How dare you
say that Jerusalem will become a desert without anyone to live in it!" And all the people
crowded around Jeremiah in the Temple of the
LORD.

¹⁰Now when the officers of Judah heard
about what was happening, they came out of
the king's palace and went up to the Temple
of the LORD and took their places at the entrance of the New Gate. ¹¹Then the priests
and prophets said to the officers and all the
other people, "Jeremiah should be killed. He
prophesied against Jerusalem, and you
heard him yourselves."

¹²Then Jeremiah spoke these words to all
the officers of Judah and all the other people:
"The LORD sent me to say everything you have
heard about this Temple and this city. ¹³Now
change your lives and start doing good and
obey the LORD your God. Then he will change
his mind and not bring on you the disaster he
has told you about. ¹⁴As for me, I am in your
power. Do to me what you think is good and
right. ¹⁵But be sure of one thing. If you kill me,
you will be guilty of killing an innocent person. You will make this city and everyone who
lives in it guilty, too! The LORD truly sent me
to you to give you this message."

¹⁶Then the officers and all the people said
to the priests and the prophets, "Jeremiah
must not be killed. What he told us comes
from the LORD our God."

¹⁷Then some of the elders of Judah stood
up and said to all the people, ¹⁸"Micah, from
the city of Moresheth, was a prophet during
the time Hezekiah was king of Judah. Micah
said to all the people of Judah, 'This is what
the LORD All-Powerful says:

Jerusalem will be plowed like a field.
It will become a pile of rocks,
and the hill where the Temple stands
will be covered with bushes.'

¹⁹"Hezekiah king of Judah and the people of Judah did not kill Micah. You know that Hezekiah feared the Lord and tried to please the Lord. So the Lord changed his mind and did not bring on Judah the disaster he had promised. If we hurt Jeremiah, we will bring a terrible disaster on ourselves!"

²⁰(Now there was another man who prophesied in the name of the Lord. His name was Uriah son of Shemaiah from the city of Kiriath Jearim. He preached the same things against Jerusalem and the land of Judah that Jeremiah did. ²¹When King Jehoiakim, all his army officers, and all the leaders of Judah heard Uriah preach, King Jehoiakim wanted to kill Uriah. But Uriah heard about it and was afraid. So he escaped to Egypt. ²²Then King Jehoiakim sent Elnathan son of Acbor and some other men to Egypt, ²³and they brought Uriah back from Egypt. Then they took him to King Jehoiakim, who had Uriah killed with a sword. His body was thrown into the burial place where poor people are buried.)

²⁴Ahikam son of Shaphan supported Jeremiah. So Ahikam did not hand Jeremiah over to be killed by the people.

PSALM 119:25–32

²⁵I am about to die.
Give me life, as you have promised.
²⁶I told you about my life, and you
answered me.
Teach me your demands.
²⁷Help me understand your orders.
Then I will think about your miracles.
²⁸I am sad and tired.
Make me strong again as you have
promised.
²⁹Don't let me be dishonest;
have mercy on me by helping me obey
your teachings.
³⁰I have chosen the way of truth;
I have obeyed your laws.
³¹I hold on to your rules.
Lord, do not let me be disgraced.
³²I will quickly obey your commands,
because you have made me happy.

PROVERBS 27:17

¹⁷As iron sharpens iron,
so people can improve each other.

2 THESSALONIANS 2:1–17

Evil Things Will Happen

2 Brothers and sisters, we have something to say about the coming of our Lord Jesus Christ and the time when we will meet together with him. ²Do not become easily upset in your thinking or afraid if you hear that the day of the Lord has already come. Someone may have said this in a prophecy or in a message or in a letter as if it came from us. ³Do not let anyone fool you in any way. That day of the Lord will not come until the turning away[n] from God happens and the Man of Evil,[n] who is on his way to hell, appears. ⁴He will be against and put himself above any so-called god or anything that people worship. And that Man of Evil will even go into God's Temple and sit there and say that he is God.

⁵I told you when I was with you that all this would happen. Do you not remember? ⁶And now you know what is stopping that Man of Evil so he will appear at the right time. ⁷The secret power of evil is already working in the world, but there is one who is stopping that power. And he will continue to stop it until he is taken out of the way. ⁸Then that Man of Evil will appear, and the Lord Jesus will kill him with the breath that comes from his mouth and will destroy him with the glory of his coming. ⁹The Man of Evil will come by the power of Satan. He will have great power, and he will do many different false miracles, signs, and wonders. ¹⁰He will use every kind of evil to trick those who are lost. They will die, because they refused to love the truth. (If they loved the truth, they would be saved.) ¹¹For this reason God sends them something powerful that leads them away from the truth so they

---

2:3 turning away Or "the rebellion." **2:3 Man of Evil** Some Greek copies read "Man of Sin."

will believe a lie. [12]So all those will be judged guilty who did not believe the truth, but enjoyed doing evil.

You Are Chosen for Salvation

[13]Brothers and sisters, whom the Lord loves, God chose you from the beginning[n] to be saved. So we must always thank God for you. You are saved by the Spirit that makes you holy and by your faith in the truth. [14]God used the Good News that we preached to call you to be saved so you can share in the glory of our Lord Jesus Christ. [15]So, brothers and sisters, stand strong and continue to believe the teachings we gave you in our speaking and in our letter.

[16-17]May our Lord Jesus Christ himself and God our Father encourage you and strengthen you in every good thing you do and say. God loved us, and through his grace he gave us a good hope and encouragement that continues forever.

OCTOBER 21

JEREMIAH 27:1—28:17

Nebuchadnezzar Is Made Ruler

27 The LORD spoke his word to Jeremiah soon after Zedekiah son of Josiah was made king of Judah. [2]This is what the LORD said to me: "Make a yoke out of straps and poles, and put it on the back of your neck. [3]Then send messages to the kings of Edom, Moab, Ammon, Tyre, and Sidon by their messengers who have come to Jerusalem to see Zedekiah king of Judah. [4]Tell them to give this message to their masters: 'The LORD All-Powerful, the God of Israel, says: "Tell your masters: [5]I made the earth, its people, and all its animals with my great power and strength. I can give the earth to anyone I want. [6]Now I have given all these lands to Nebuchadnezzar king of Babylon, my servant. I will make even the wild animals obey him. [7]All nations will serve Nebuchadnezzar and his son and grandson. Then the time will come for Babylon to be defeated, and many nations and great kings will make Babylon their servant.

[8]"'"But if some nations or kingdoms refuse to serve Nebuchadnezzar king of Babylon and refuse to be under his control, I will punish them with war, hunger, and terrible diseases, says the LORD. I will use Nebuchadnezzar to destroy them. [9]So don't listen to your false prophets, those who use magic to tell the future, those who explain dreams, the mediums, or magicians. They all tell you, 'You will not be slaves to the king of Babylon.' [10]They are telling you lies that will cause you to be taken far from your homeland. I will force you to leave your homes, and you will die in another land. [11]But the nations who put themselves under the control of the king of Babylon and serve him I will let stay in their own country, says the LORD. The people from those nations will live in their own land and farm it."'"

[12]I gave the same message to Zedekiah king of Judah. I said, "Put yourself under the control of the king of Babylon and serve him, and you will live. [13]Why should you and your people die from war, hunger, or disease, as the LORD said would happen to those who do not serve the king of Babylon? [14]But the false prophets are saying, 'You will never be slaves to the king of Babylon.' Don't listen to them because they are prophesying lies to you! [15]I did not send them,' says the LORD. 'They are prophesying lies and saying the message is from me. So I will send you away, Judah. And you and those prophets who prophesy to you will die.'"

[16]Then I, Jeremiah, said to the priests and all the people, "This is what the LORD says: Those false prophets are saying, 'The Babylonians will soon return what they took from the Temple of the LORD.' Don't listen to

them! They are prophesying lies to you. [17]Don't listen to those prophets. But serve the king of Babylon, and you will live. There is no reason for you to cause Jerusalem to become a ruin. [18]If they are prophets and have the message from the LORD, let them pray to the LORD All-Powerful. Let them ask that the items which are still in the Temple of the LORD and in the king's palace and in Jerusalem not be taken away to Babylon.

[19]"This is what the LORD All-Powerful says about those items left in Jerusalem: the pillars, the large bronze bowl, which is called the Sea, the stands that can be moved, and other things. [20]Nebuchadnezzar king of Babylon did not take these away when he took as captives Jehoiachin son of Jehoiakim king of Judah and all the other important people from Judah and Jerusalem to Babylon. [21]This is what the LORD All-Powerful, the God of Israel, says about the items left in the Temple of the LORD and in the king's palace and in Jerusalem: [22]'All of them will also be taken to Babylon. And they will stay there until the day I go to get them,' says the LORD. 'Then I will bring them back and return them to this place.'"

The False Prophet Hananiah

28It was in that same year, in the fifth month of Zedekiah's fourth year as king of Judah, soon after he began to rule. The prophet Hananiah son of Azzur, from the town of Gibeon, spoke to me in the Temple of the LORD in front of the priests and all the people. He said: [2]"The LORD All-Powerful, the God of Israel, says: 'I have broken the yoke the king of Babylon has put on Judah. [3]Before two years are over, I will bring back everything that Nebuchadnezzar king of Babylon took to Babylon from the LORD's Temple. [4]I will also bring back Jehoiachin son of Jehoiakim king of Judah and all the other captives from Judah who went to Babylon,' says the LORD. 'So I will break the yoke the king of Babylon put on Judah.'"

[5]Then the prophet Jeremiah spoke to the prophet Hananiah in front of the priests and all the people who were standing in the Temple of the LORD. [6]He said, "Amen! Let the LORD really do that! May the LORD make the

message you prophesy come true. May he bring back here everything from the LORD's Temple and all the people who were taken as captives to Babylon.

[7]"But listen to what I am going to say to you and all the people. [8]There were prophets long before we became prophets, Hananiah. They prophesied that war, hunger, and terrible diseases would come to many countries and great kingdoms. [9]But if a prophet prophesies that we will have peace and that message comes true, he can be recognized as one truly sent by the LORD."

[10]Then the prophet Hananiah took the yoke off Jeremiah's neck and broke it. [11]Hananiah said in front of all the people, "This is what the LORD says: 'In the same way I will break the yoke of Nebuchadnezzar king of Babylon. He put that yoke on all the nations of the world, but I will break it before two years are over.'" After Hananiah had said that, Jeremiah left the Temple.

[12]The LORD spoke his word to Jeremiah after the prophet Hananiah had broken the yoke off of the prophet Jeremiah's neck. [13]The LORD said, "Go and tell Hananiah, 'This is what the LORD says: You have broken a wooden yoke, but I will make a yoke of iron in its place! [14]The LORD All-Powerful, the God of Israel, says: I will put a yoke of iron on the necks of all these nations to make them serve Nebuchadnezzar king of Babylon, and they will be slaves to him. I will even give Nebuchadnezzar control over the wild animals.'"

[15]Then the prophet Jeremiah said to the prophet Hananiah, "Listen, Hananiah! The LORD did not send you, and you have made the people of Judah trust in lies. [16]So this is what the LORD says: 'Soon I will remove you from the earth. You will die this year, because you taught the people to turn against the LORD.'"

[17]Hananiah died in the seventh month of that same year.

PSALM 119:33–40

[33]LORD, teach me your demands,
  and I will keep them until the end.
[34]Help me understand, so I can keep your
    teachings,
  obeying them with all my heart.

35Lead me in the path of your commands,
  because that makes me happy.
36Make me want to keep your rules
  instead of wishing for riches.
37Keep me from looking at worthless
  things.
  Let me live by your word.
38Keep your promise to me, your servant,
  so you will be respected.
39Take away the shame I fear,
  because your laws are good.
40How I want to follow your orders.
  Give me life because of your
  goodness.

PROVERBS 27:18

18Whoever tends a fig tree gets to eat its
  fruit,
  and whoever takes care of his master
  will receive honor.

2 THESSALONIANS 3:1–18

Pray for Us

3And now, brothers and sisters, pray for us
that the Lord's teaching will continue to
spread quickly and that people will give
honor to that teaching, just as happened
with you. 2And pray that we will be protected
from stubborn and evil people, because not
all people believe.

3But the Lord is faithful and will give you
strength and will protect you from the Evil
One. 4The Lord makes us feel sure that you
are doing and will continue to do the things
we told you. 5May the Lord lead your hearts
into God's love and Christ's patience.

The Duty to Work

6Brothers and sisters, by the authority of
our Lord Jesus Christ we command you to
stay away from any believer who refuses to
work and does not follow the teaching we
gave you. 7You yourselves know that you
should live as we live. We were not lazy when
we were with you. 8And when we ate another
person's food, we always paid for it. We
worked very hard night and day so we would
not be an expense to any of you. 9We had the
right to ask you to help us, but we worked to
take care of ourselves so we would be an example for you to follow. 10When we were with
you, we gave you this rule: "Anyone who refuses to work should not eat."

11We hear that some people in your group
refuse to work. They do nothing but busy
themselves in other people's lives. 12We command those people and beg them in the Lord
Jesus Christ to work quietly and earn their
own food. 13But you, brothers and sisters,
never become tired of doing good.

14If some people do not obey what we tell
you in this letter, then take note of them.
Have nothing to do with them so they will
feel ashamed. 15But do not treat them as enemies. Warn them as fellow believers.

Final Words

16Now may the Lord of peace give you
peace at all times and in every way. The Lord
be with all of you.

17I, Paul, end this letter now in my own
handwriting. All my letters have this to show
they are from me. This is the way I write.

18The grace of our Lord Jesus Christ be
with you all.

OCTOBER 22

JEREMIAH 29:1–30:24

A Letter to the Captives in Babylon

29This is the letter that Jeremiah the
prophet sent from Jerusalem to the elders who were among the captives, the priests,
and the prophets. He sent it to all the other
people Nebuchadnezzar had taken as captives
from Jerusalem to Babylon. 2(This letter was
sent after all these people were taken away:
Jehoiachin the king and the queen mother;
the officers and leaders of Judah and Jerusalem; and the craftsmen and metalworkers
from Jerusalem.) 3Zedekiah king of Judah

sent Elasah son of Shaphan and Gemariah son of Hilkiah to Babylon to Nebuchadnezzar king of Babylon. So Jeremiah gave them this letter to carry to Babylon:

⁴This is what the LORD All-Powerful, the God of Israel, says to all those people I sent away from Jerusalem as captives to Babylon: ⁵"Build houses and settle in the land. Plant gardens and eat the food they grow. ⁶Get married and have sons and daughters. Find wives for your sons, and let your daughters be married so they also may have sons and daughters. Have many children in Babylon; don't become fewer in number. ⁷Also do good things for the city where I sent you as captives. Pray to the LORD for the city where you are living, because if good things happen in the city, good things will happen to you also." ⁸The LORD All-Powerful, the God of Israel, says: "Don't let the prophets among you and the people who do magic fool you. Don't listen to their dreams. ⁹They are prophesying lies to you, saying that their message is from me. But I did not send them," says the LORD.

¹⁰This is what the LORD says: "Babylon will be powerful for seventy years. After that time I will come to you, and I will keep my promise to bring you back to Jerusalem. ¹¹I say this because I know what I am planning for you," says the LORD. "I have good plans for you, not plans to hurt you. I will give you hope and a good future. ¹²Then you will call my name. You will come to me and pray to me, and I will listen to you. ¹³You will search for me. And when you search for me with all your heart, you will find me! ¹⁴I will let you find me," says the LORD. "And I will bring you back from your captivity. I forced you to leave this place, but I will gather you from all the nations, from the places I have sent you as captives," says the LORD. "And I will bring you back to this place."

¹⁵You might say, "The LORD has given us prophets here in Babylon."

¹⁶But the LORD says this about the king who is sitting on David's throne now and all the other people still in Jerusalem, your relatives who did not go as captives to Babylon with you. ¹⁷The LORD All-Powerful says: "I will soon send war, hunger, and terrible dis-

eases against those still in Jerusalem. I will make them like bad figs that are too rotten to eat. ¹⁸I will chase them with war, hunger, and terrible diseases. I will make them hated by all the kingdoms of the earth. People will curse them and be shocked and will use them as a shameful example wherever I make them go. ¹⁹This is because they have not listened to my message," says the LORD. "I sent my message to them again and again through my servants, the prophets, but they did not listen," says the LORD.

²⁰You captives, whom I forced to leave Jerusalem and go to Babylon, listen to the message from the LORD. ²¹The LORD All-Powerful, the God of Israel, says this about Ahab son of Kolaiah and Zedekiah son of Maaseiah: "These two men have been prophesying lies to you, saying that their message is from me. But soon I will hand over those two prophets to Nebuchadnezzar king of Babylon, and he will kill them in front of you. ²²Because of them, all the captives from Judah in Babylon will use this curse: 'May the LORD treat you like Zedekiah and Ahab, whom the king of Babylon burned in the fire.' ²³They have done evil things among the people of Israel. They are guilty of adultery with their neighbors' wives. They have also spoken lies and said those lies were a message from me. I did not tell them to do that. I know what they have done; I am a witness to it," says the LORD.

²⁴Also give a message to Shemaiah from the Nehelamite family. ²⁵The LORD All-Powerful, the God of Israel, says: "Shemaiah, you sent letters in your name to all the people in Jerusalem, to the priest Zephaniah son of Maaseiah, and to all the priests. ²⁶You said to Zephaniah, 'The LORD has made you priest in place of Jehoiada. You are to be in charge of the Temple of the LORD. You should arrest any madman who acts like a prophet. Lock his hands and feet between wooden blocks, and put iron rings around his neck. ²⁷Now Jeremiah from Anathoth is acting like a prophet. So why haven't you arrested him? ²⁸Jeremiah has sent this message to us in Babylon: You will be there for a long time, so build houses and settle down. Plant gardens and eat what they grow.'"

²⁹Zephaniah the priest read the letter to

Jeremiah the prophet. ³⁰Then the LORD spoke his word to Jeremiah: ³¹"Send this message to all the captives in Babylon: 'This is what the LORD says about Shemaiah the Nehelamite: Shemaiah has prophesied to you, but I did not send him. He has made you believe a lie. ³²So the LORD says, I will soon punish Shemaiah the Nehelamite and his family. He will not see the good things I will do for my people, says the LORD. None of his family will be left alive among the people, because he has taught the people to turn against me.'"

Promises of Hope

30These are the words that the LORD spoke to Jeremiah. ²The LORD, the God of Israel, said: "Jeremiah, write in a book all the words I have spoken to you. ³The days will come when I will bring Israel and Judah back from captivity," says the LORD. "I will return them to the land I gave their ancestors, and they will own it!" says the LORD.

⁴The LORD spoke this message about the people of Israel and Judah: ⁵This is what the LORD said:
"We hear people crying from fear.
 They are afraid; there is no peace.
⁶Ask this question, and consider it:
 A man cannot have a baby.
So why do I see every strong man
 holding his stomach in pain like a
  woman having a baby?
Why is everyone's face turning white
 like a dead man's face?
⁷This will be a terrible day!
 There will never be another time like
  this.
This is a time of great trouble for the
 people of Jacob,
 but they will be saved from it."

⁸The LORD All-Powerful says, "At that time I will break the yoke from their necks and tear off the ropes that hold them. Foreign people will never again make my people slaves. ⁹They will serve the LORD their God and David their king, whom I will send to them.

¹⁰"So people of Jacob, my servants, don't be afraid.

Israel, don't be frightened," says the LORD.
"I will soon save you from that faraway
 place where you are captives.
I will save your family from that land.
The people of Jacob will be safe and have
 peace again;
 there will be no enemy to frighten
  them.
¹¹I am with you and will save you,"
 says the LORD.
"I will completely destroy all those
 nations
 where I scattered you,
 but I will not completely destroy you.
I will punish you fairly,
 but I will still punish you."
¹²This is what the LORD said:
"You people have a wound that cannot be
 cured;
 your injury will not heal.
¹³There is no one to argue your case
 and no cure for your sores.
 So you will not be healed.
¹⁴All those nations who were your friends
 have forgotten you.
 They don't care about you.
I have hurt you as an enemy would.
 I punished you very hard,
because your guilt was so great
 and your sins were so many.
¹⁵Why are you crying out about your
 injury?
 There is no cure for your pain.
I did these things to you because of your
 great guilt,
 because of your many sins.
¹⁶But all those nations that destroyed you
 will now be destroyed.
All your enemies will become captives
 in other lands.
Those who stole from you will have their
 own things stolen.
Those who took things from you in war
 will have their own things taken.
¹⁷I will bring back your health
 and heal your injuries," says the LORD,
"because other people forced you away.
 They said about you, 'No one cares
  about Jerusalem!'"
¹⁸This is what the LORD said:

"I will soon make the tents of Jacob's
   people as they used to be,
   and I will have pity on Israel's houses.
The city will be rebuilt on its hill of ruins,
   and the king's palace will stand in its
      proper place.
¹⁹People in those places will sing songs of
   praise.
   There will be the sound of laughter.
I will give them many children
   so their number will not be small.
I will bring honor to them
   so no one will look down on them.
²⁰Their descendants will be as they were in
   the old days.
   I will set them up as a strong people
      before me,
   and I will punish the nations who have
      hurt them.
²¹One of their own people will lead them;
   their ruler will come from among
      them.
He will come near to me when I invite
   him.
Who would dare to come to me
   uninvited?" says the LORD.
²²"So you will be my people,
   and I will be your God."

²³Look! It is a storm from the LORD!
   He is angry and has gone out to punish
      the people.
Punishment will come like a storm
   crashing down on the evil people.
²⁴The LORD will stay angry
   until he finishes punishing the people.
He will stay angry
   until he finishes the punishment he
      planned.
When that day comes,
   you will understand this.

PSALM 119:41–48

⁴¹LORD, show me your love,
   and save me as you have promised.
⁴²I have an answer for people who insult
   me,
   because I trust what you say.
⁴³Never keep me from speaking your truth,
   because I depend on your fair laws.
⁴⁴I will obey your teachings
   forever and ever.
⁴⁵So I will live in freedom,
   because I want to follow your orders.
⁴⁶I will discuss your rules with kings
   and will not be ashamed.
⁴⁷I enjoy obeying your commands,
   which I love.
⁴⁸I praise your commands, which I love,
   and I think about your demands.

PROVERBS 27:19

¹⁹As water reflects your face,
   so your mind shows what kind of
      person you are.

1 TIMOTHY 1:1–20

1 From Paul, an apostle of Christ Jesus, by
   the command of God our Savior and
Christ Jesus our hope.
   ²To Timothy, a true child to me because
you believe:
   Grace, mercy, and peace from God the Father and Christ Jesus our Lord.

Warning Against False Teaching

³I asked you to stay longer in Ephesus when I went into Macedonia so you could command some people there to stop teaching false things. ⁴Tell them not to spend their time on stories that are not true and on long lists of names in family histories. These things only bring arguments; they do not help God's work, which is done in faith. ⁵The purpose of this command is for people to have love, a love that comes from a pure heart and a good conscience and a true faith. ⁶Some people have missed these things and turned to useless talk. ⁷They want to be teachers of the law, but they do not understand either what they are talking about or what they are sure about.
   ⁸But we know that the law is good if someone uses it lawfully. ⁹We also know that the law is not made for good people but for those who are against the law and for those who refuse to follow it. It is for people who are against God and are sinful, who are unholy and ungodly, who kill their fathers and mothers, who murder, ¹⁰who take part in sexual sins, who have sexual relations with

people of the same sex, who sell slaves, who tell lies, who speak falsely, and who do anything against the true teaching of God. [11]That teaching is part of the Good News of the blessed God that he gave me to tell.

Thanks for God's Mercy

[12]I thank Christ Jesus our Lord, who gave me strength, because he trusted me and gave me this work of serving him. [13]In the past I spoke against Christ and persecuted him and did all kinds of things to hurt him. But God showed me mercy, because I did not know what I was doing. I did not believe. [14]But the grace of our Lord was fully given to me, and with that grace came the faith and love that are in Christ Jesus.

[15]What I say is true, and you should fully accept it: Christ Jesus came into the world to save sinners, of whom I am the worst. [16]But I was given mercy so that in me, the worst of all sinners, Christ Jesus could show that he has patience without limit. His patience with me made me an example for those who would believe in him and have life forever. [17]To the King that rules forever, who will never die, who cannot be seen, the only God, be honor and glory forever and ever. Amen.

[18]Timothy, my child, I am giving you a command that agrees with the prophecies that were given about you in the past. I tell you this so you can follow them and fight the good fight. [19]Continue to have faith and do what you know is right. Some people have rejected this, and their faith has been shipwrecked. [20]Hymenaeus and Alexander have done that, and I have given them to Satan so they will learn not to speak against God.

OCTOBER 23

JEREMIAH 31:1—32:44

The New Israel

31 The LORD says, "At that time I will be God of all Israel's family groups, and they will be my people."

[2]This is what the LORD says:
"The people who were not killed by the enemy's sword
    found help in the desert.
I came to give rest to Israel."
[3]And from far away the LORD appeared to his people and said,
"I love you people
    with a love that will last forever.
That is why I have continued
    showing you kindness.
[4]People of Israel, I will build you up again,
    and you will be rebuilt.
You will pick up your tambourines again
    and dance with those who are joyful.
[5]You will plant vineyards again
    on the hills around Samaria.
The farmers will plant them
    and enjoy their fruit.
[6]There will be a time when watchmen in the mountains of Ephraim shout
    this message:
'Come, let's go up to Jerusalem to
    worship the LORD our God!'"
[7]This is what the LORD says:
"Be happy and sing for the people of
    Jacob.
Shout for Israel, the greatest of the
    nations.
Sing your praises and shout this:
'LORD, save your people,
    those who are left alive from the nation
    of Israel!'
[8]Look, I will soon bring Israel from the
    country in the north,
    and I will gather them from the
    faraway places on earth.
Some of the people are blind and
    crippled.
Some of the women are pregnant, and
    some are ready to give birth.
A great many people will come back.
[9]They will be crying as they come,
    but they will pray as I bring them back.
I will lead those people by streams of
    water

on an even road where they will not
stumble.
I am Israel's father,
and Israel is my firstborn son.

¹⁰"Nations, listen to the message from the
LORD.
Tell this message in the faraway lands
by the sea:
'The one who scattered the people of
Israel will bring them back,
and he will watch over his people like a
shepherd.'
¹¹The LORD will pay for the people of Jacob
and will buy them back from people
stronger than they were.
¹²The people of Israel will come to the high
points of Jerusalem
and shout for joy.
Their faces will shine with happiness
about all the good things from the
LORD:
the grain, new wine, oil, young sheep,
and young cows.
They will be like a garden that has plenty
of water,
and they will not be troubled anymore.
¹³Then young women of Israel will be
happy and dance,
the young men and old men also.
I will change their sadness into
happiness;
I will give them comfort and joy
instead of sadness.
¹⁴The priests will have more than enough
sacrifices,
and my people will be filled with the
good things I give them!" says the
LORD.

¹⁵This is what the LORD says:
"A voice was heard in Ramah
of painful crying and deep sadness:
Rachel crying for her children.
She refused to be comforted,
because her children are dead!"
¹⁶But this is what the LORD says:
"Stop crying;
don't let your eyes fill with tears.
You will be rewarded for your work!"
says the LORD.
"The people will return from their
enemy's land.

¹⁷So there is hope for you in the future,"
says the LORD.
"Your children will return to their own
land.

¹⁸"I have heard Israel moaning:
'LORD, you punished me, and I have
learned my lesson.
I was like a calf that had never been
trained.
Take me back so that I may come back.
You truly are the LORD my God.
¹⁹LORD, after I wandered away from you,
I changed my heart and life.
After I understood,
I beat my breast with sorrow.
I was ashamed and disgraced,
because I suffered for the foolish things
I did when I was young.'
²⁰"You know that Israel is my dear son,
The child I love.
Yes, I often speak against Israel,
but I still remember him.
I love him very much,
and I want to comfort him," says the
LORD.

²¹"People of Israel, fix the road signs.
Put up signs to show you the way home.
Watch the road.
Pay attention to the road on which you
travel.
People of Israel, come home,
come back to your towns.
²²You are an unfaithful daughter.
How long will you wander before you
come home?
The LORD has made something new
happen in the land:
A woman will go seeking a man."

²³The LORD All-Powerful, the God of Is-
rael, says: "I will again do good things for the
people of Judah. At that time the people in
the land of Judah and its towns will again
use these words: 'May the LORD bless you,
home of what is good, holy mountain.' ²⁴Peo-
ple in all the towns of Judah will live together
in peace. Farmers and those who move
around with their flocks will live together in
peace. ²⁵I will give rest and strength to those
who are weak and tired."

²⁶After hearing that, I, Jeremiah, woke up and looked around. My sleep had been very pleasant.

²⁷The LORD says, "The time is coming when I will help the families of Israel and Judah and their children and animals to grow. ²⁸In the past I watched over Israel and Judah, to pull them up and tear them down, to destroy them and bring them disaster. But now I will watch over them to build them up and make them strong," says the LORD.

²⁹"At that time people will no longer say:
'The parents have eaten sour grapes,
  and that caused the children to grind
    their teeth from the sour taste.'
³⁰Instead, each person will die for his own sin; the person who eats sour grapes will grind his own teeth.

The New Agreement

³¹"Look, the time is coming," says the LORD,
  "when I will make a new agreement
with the people of Israel
  and the people of Judah.
³²It will not be like the agreement
  I made with their ancestors
when I took them by the hand
  to bring them out of Egypt.
I was a husband to them,
  but they broke that agreement," says the
    LORD.
³³"This is the agreement I will make
  with the people of Israel at that time,"
    says the LORD:
"I will put my teachings in their minds
  and write them on their hearts.
I will be their God,
  and they will be my people.
³⁴People will no longer have to teach their
    neighbors and relatives
  to know the LORD,
because all people will know me,
  from the least to the most important,"
    says the LORD.
"I will forgive them for the wicked things
    they did,
  and I will not remember their sins
    anymore."

The Lord Will Never Leave Israel

³⁵The LORD makes the sun shine in the day
  and the moon and stars to shine at
    night.

He stirs up the sea so that its waves
  crash on the shore.
The LORD All-Powerful is his name.
This is what the LORD says:
³⁶"Only if these laws should ever fail,"
  says the LORD,
  "will Israel's descendants ever stop
    being a nation before me."
³⁷This is what the LORD says:
"Only if people can measure the sky
    above
  and learn the secrets of the earth
    below,
will I reject all the descendants of Israel
  because of what they have done," says
    the LORD.

The New Jerusalem

³⁸The LORD says, "The time is coming when Jerusalem will be rebuilt for me—everything from the Tower of Hananel to the Corner Gate. ³⁹The measuring line will stretch from the Corner Gate straight to the hill of Gareb. Then it will turn to the place named Goah. ⁴⁰The whole valley where dead bodies and ashes are thrown, and all the terraces out to the Kidron Valley on the east as far as the corner of the Horse Gate—all that area will be holy to the LORD. The city of Jerusalem will never again be torn down or destroyed."

Jeremiah Buys a Field

32 This is the word the LORD spoke to Jeremiah in the tenth year Zedekiah was king of Judah, which was the eighteenth year of Nebuchadnezzar. ²At that time the army of the king of Babylon was surrounding Jerusalem. Jeremiah the prophet was under arrest in the courtyard of the guard, which was at the palace of the king of Judah.

³Zedekiah king of Judah had put Jeremiah in prison there. Zedekiah had asked, "Why have you prophesied the things you have?" (Jeremiah had said, "This is what the LORD says: 'I will soon hand the city of Jerusalem over to the king of Babylon, and he will capture it. ⁴Zedekiah king of Judah will not escape from the Babylonian army, but he will surely be handed over to the king of Babylon. And he will speak to the king of Babylon face to face and see him with his own eyes.

⁵The king will take Zedekiah to Babylon, where he will stay until I have punished him,' says the LORD. 'If you fight against the Babylonians, you will not succeed.'")

⁶While Jeremiah was in prison, he said, "The LORD spoke this word to me: ⁷Your cousin Hanamel, son of your uncle Shallum, will come to you soon. Hanamel will say to you, 'Jeremiah, you are my nearest relative, so buy my field near the town of Anathoth. It is your right and your duty to buy that field.'

⁸"Then it happened just as the LORD had said. My cousin Hanamel came to me in the courtyard of the guard and said to me, 'Buy for yourself my field near Anathoth in the land of Benjamin. It is your right and duty to buy it and own it.' So I knew this was a message from the LORD.

⁹"I bought the field at Anathoth from my cousin Hanamel, weighing out seven ounces of silver for him. ¹⁰I signed the record and sealed it and had some people witness it. I also weighed out the silver on the scales. ¹¹Then I took both copies of the record of ownership—the one that was sealed that had the demands and limits of ownership, and the one that was not sealed. ¹²And I gave them to Baruch son of Neriah, the son of Mahseiah. My cousin Hanamel, the other witnesses who signed the record of ownership, and many Jews sitting in the courtyard of the guard saw me give the record of ownership to Baruch.

¹³"With all the people watching, I told Baruch, ¹⁴'This is what the LORD All-Powerful, the God of Israel, says: Take both copies of the record of ownership—the sealed copy and the copy that was not sealed—and put them in a clay jar so they will last a long time. ¹⁵This is what the LORD All-Powerful, the God of Israel, says: In the future my people will once again buy houses and fields for grain and vineyards in the land of Israel.'

¹⁶"After I gave the record of ownership to Baruch son of Neriah, I prayed to the LORD, ¹⁷Oh, Lord GOD, you made the skies and the earth with your very great power. There is nothing too hard for you to do. ¹⁸You show

love and kindness to thousands of people, but you also bring punishment to children for their parents' sins. Great and powerful God, your name is the LORD All-Powerful. ¹⁹You plan and do great things. You see everything that people do, and you reward people for the way they live and for what they do. ²⁰You did miracles and wonderful things in the land of Egypt. You have continued doing them in Israel and among the other nations even until today. So you have become well known. ²¹You brought your people, the Israelites, out of Egypt using signs and miracles and your great power and strength. You brought great terror on everyone. ²²You gave them this land that you promised to their ancestors long ago, a fertile land. ²³They came into this land and took it for their own, but they did not obey you or follow your teachings. They did not do everything you commanded. So you made all these terrible things happen to them.

²⁴"Look! The enemy has surrounded the city and has built roads to the top of the walls to capture it. Because of war, hunger, and terrible diseases, the city will be handed over to the Babylonians who are attacking it. You said this would happen, and now you see it is happening. ²⁵But now, Lord GOD, you tell me, 'Buy the field with silver and call in witnesses.' You tell me this while the Babylonian army is ready to capture the city.'"

²⁶Then the LORD spoke this word to Jeremiah: ²⁷"I am the LORD, the God of every person on the earth. Nothing is impossible for me. ²⁸So this is what the LORD says: I will soon hand over the city of Jerusalem to the Babylonian army and to Nebuchadnezzar king of Babylon, who will capture it. ²⁹The Babylonian army is already attacking the city of Jerusalem. They will soon enter it and start a fire to burn down the city and its houses. The people of Jerusalem offered sacrifices to Baal on the roofs[n] of those same houses and poured out drink offerings to other idols to make me angry. ³⁰From their youth, the people of Israel and Judah have done only the things I said were wrong. They

---

32:29 roofs In Bible times houses were built with flat roofs. The roof was used for drying things such as flax and fruit. And it was used as an extra room, as a place for worship, and as a cool place to sleep in the summer.

have made me angry by worshiping idols made with their own hands," says the LORD. ³¹"From the day Jerusalem was built until now, this city has made me angry, so angry that I must remove it from my sight. ³²I will destroy it, because of all the evil the people of Israel and Judah have done. The people, their kings and officers, their priests and prophets, all the people of Judah, and the people of Jerusalem have made me angry. ³³They turned their backs to me, not their faces. I tried to teach them again and again, but they wouldn't listen or learn. ³⁴They put their hateful idols in the place where I have chosen to be worshiped, so they made it unclean. ³⁵In the Valley of Ben Hinnom they built places to worship Baal so they could burn their sons and daughters as sacrifices to Molech. But I never commanded them to do such a hateful thing. It never entered my mind that they would do such a thing and cause Judah to sin.

³⁶"You are saying, 'Because of war, hunger, and terrible diseases, the city will be handed over to the king of Babylon.' But the LORD, the God of Israel, says about Jerusalem: ³⁷I forced the people of Israel and Judah to leave their land, because I was furious and very angry with them. But soon I will gather them from all the lands where I forced them to go, and I will bring them back to this place, where they may live in safety. ³⁸The people of Israel and Judah will be my people, and I will be their God. ³⁹I will make them truly want to be one people with one goal. They will truly want to worship me all their lives, for their own good and for the good of their children after them.

⁴⁰"I will make an agreement with them that will last forever. I will never turn away from them; I will always do good to them. I will make them want to respect me so they will never turn away from me. ⁴¹I will enjoy doing good to them. And with my whole being I will surely plant them in this land and make them grow."

⁴²This is what the LORD says: "I have brought this great disaster to the people of Israel and Judah. In the same way I will bring the good things that I promise to do for them. ⁴³You are saying, 'This land is an empty desert, without people or animals. It has been handed over to the Babylonians.' But in the future, people will again buy fields in this land. ⁴⁴They will use their money to buy fields. They will sign and seal their agreements and call in witnesses. They will again buy fields in the land of Benjamin, in the area around Jerusalem, in the towns of Judah and in the mountains, in the western hills, and in southern Judah. I will make everything as good for them as it once was," says the LORD.

PSALM 119:49–56

⁴⁹Remember your promise to me, your
    servant;
  it gives me hope.
⁵⁰When I suffer, this comforts me:
  Your promise gives me life.
⁵¹Proud people always make fun of me,
  but I do not reject your teachings.
⁵²I remember your laws from long ago,
  and they comfort me, LORD.
⁵³I become angry with wicked people
  who do not keep your teachings.
⁵⁴I sing about your demands
    wherever I live.
⁵⁵LORD, I remember you at night,
  and I will obey your teachings.
⁵⁶This is what I do:
  I follow your orders.

PROVERBS 27:20

²⁰People will never stop dying and being
    destroyed,
  and they will never stop wanting more
    than they have.

1 TIMOTHY 2:1–15

Some Rules for Men and Women

2 First, I tell you to pray for all people, asking God for what they need and being thankful to him. ²Pray for rulers and for all who have authority so that we can have quiet and peaceful lives full of worship and respect for God. ³This is good, and it pleases God our Savior, ⁴who wants all people to be saved and to know the truth. ⁵There is one God and one mediator so that human beings

can reach God. That way is through Christ Jesus, who is himself human. ⁶He gave himself as a payment to free all people. He is proof that came at the right time. ⁷That is why I was chosen to tell the Good News and to be an apostle. (I am telling the truth; I am not lying.) I was chosen to teach those who are not Jews to believe and to know the truth.

⁸So, I want the men everywhere to pray, lifting up their hands in a holy manner, without anger and arguments.

⁹Also, women should wear proper clothes that show respect and self-control, not using braided hair or gold or pearls or expensive clothes. ¹⁰Instead, they should do good deeds, which is right for women who say they worship God.

¹¹Let a woman learn by listening quietly and being ready to cooperate in everything. ¹²But I do not allow a woman to teach or to have authority over a man, but to listen quietly, ¹³because Adam was formed first and then Eve. ¹⁴And Adam was not tricked, but the woman was tricked and became a sinner. ¹⁵But she will be saved through having children if she continues in faith, love, and holiness, with self-control.

OCTOBER 24

JEREMIAH 33:1—34:22

The Promise of the Lord

33 While Jeremiah was still locked up in the courtyard of the guards, the LORD spoke his word to him a second time: ²"These are the words of the LORD, who made the earth, shaped it, and gave it order, whose name is the LORD: ³Judah, pray to me, and I will answer you. I will tell you important secrets you have never heard before.' ⁴This is what the LORD, the God of Israel, says about the houses in Jerusalem and the royal palaces of Judah that have been torn down to be used in defense of the attack by the Babylonian army: ⁵'Some people will come to fight against the Babylonians. They will fill these houses with the bodies of people I killed in my hot anger. I have turned away from this city because of all the evil its people have done.

⁶" 'But then I will bring health and healing to the people there. I will heal them and let them enjoy great peace and safety. ⁷I will bring Judah and Israel back from captivity and make them strong countries as in the past. ⁸They sinned against me, but I will wash away that sin. They did evil and turned away from me, but I will forgive them. ⁹Then "Jerusalem" will be to me a name that brings joy! And people from all nations of the earth will praise it when they hear about the good things I am doing there. They will be surprised and shocked at all the good things and the peace I will bring to Jerusalem.'

¹⁰"You are saying, 'Our country is an empty desert, without people or animals.' But this is what the LORD says: It is now quiet in the streets of Jerusalem and in the towns of Judah, without people or animals, but it will be noisy there soon! ¹¹There will be sounds of joy and gladness and the happy sounds of brides and bridegrooms. There will be the sounds of people bringing to the Temple of the LORD their offerings of thanks to the LORD. They will say,

'Praise the LORD All-Powerful,
  because the LORD is good!
  His love continues forever!'
They will say this because I will again do good things for Judah, as I did in the beginning," says the LORD.

¹²This is what the LORD All-Powerful says: "This place is empty now, without people or animals. But there will be shepherds in all the towns of Judah and pastures where they let their flocks rest. ¹³Shepherds will again count their sheep as the sheep walk in front of them. They will count them in the mountains and in the western hills, in southern Judah and the land of Benjamin, and around Jerusalem and the other towns of Judah!" says the LORD.

The Good Branch

[14]The LORD says, "The time is coming when I will do the good thing I promised to the people of Israel and Judah.

[15]In those days and at that time,
   I will make a good branch sprout from
      David's family.
   He will do what is fair and right in the
      land.
[16]At that time Judah will be saved,
   and the people of Jerusalem will live in
      safety.
   The branch will be named:
      The LORD Does What Is Right."

[17]This is what the LORD says: "Someone from David's family will always sit on the throne of the family of Israel. [18]And there will always be priests from the family of Levi. They will always stand before me to offer burnt offerings and grain offerings and sacrifices to me."

[19]The LORD spoke his word to Jeremiah, saying: [20]"This is what the LORD says: I have an agreement with day and night that they will always come at the right times. If you could change that agreement, [21]only then could you change my agreement with David and Levi. Only then would my servant David not have a descendant ruling as king on David's throne. And only then would the family of Levi not be priests serving me in the Temple. [22]But I will give many descendants to my servant David and to the family group of Levi who serve me in the Temple. They will be as many as the stars in the sky that no one can count. They will be as many as the grains of sand on the seashore that no one can measure."

[23]The LORD spoke his word to Jeremiah, saying: [24]"Jeremiah, have you heard what the people are saying? They say: 'The LORD turned away from the two families of Israel and Judah that he chose.' Now they don't think of my people as a nation anymore!"

[25]This is what the LORD says: "If I had not made my agreement with day and night, and if I had not made the laws for the sky and earth, [26]only then would I turn away from Jacob's descendants. And only then would I not let the descendants of David my servant rule over the descendants of Abraham, Isaac, and Jacob. But I will be kind to them and cause good things to happen to them again."

A Warning to Zedekiah

34 The LORD spoke his word to Jeremiah when Nebuchadnezzar king of Babylon was fighting against Jerusalem and all the towns around it. Nebuchadnezzar had with him all his army and the armies of all the kingdoms and peoples he ruled. [2]This is what the LORD, the God of Israel, said: "Jeremiah, go to Zedekiah king of Judah and tell him: 'This is what the LORD says: I will soon hand the city of Jerusalem over to the king of Babylon, and he will burn it down! [3]You will not escape from the king of Babylon; you will surely be captured and handed over to him. You will see the king of Babylon with your own eyes, and he will talk to you face to face. And you will go to Babylon. [4]But, Zedekiah king of Judah, listen to the promise of the LORD. This is what the LORD says about you: You will not be killed with a sword. [5]You will die in a peaceful way. As people made funeral fires to honor your ancestors, the kings who ruled before you, so people will make a funeral fire to honor you. They will cry for you and sadly say, "Ah, master!" I myself make this promise to you, says the LORD.' "

[6]So Jeremiah the prophet gave this message to Zedekiah in Jerusalem. [7]This was while the army of the king of Babylon was fighting against Jerusalem and the cities of Judah that had not yet been taken—Lachish and Azekah. These were the only strong, walled cities left in the land of Judah.

Slaves Are Mistreated

[8]The LORD spoke his word to Jeremiah. This was after King Zedekiah had made an agreement with all the people in Jerusalem to free all the Hebrew slaves. [9]Everyone was supposed to free his Hebrew slaves, both male and female. No one was to keep a fellow Jew as a slave. [10]All the officers and all the people accepted this agreement; they agreed to free their male and female slaves and no longer keep them as slaves. So all the slaves were set free. [11]But after that, the people who had slaves changed their minds. So they took back the people they had set free and made them slaves again.

[12]Then the LORD spoke his word to Jere-

miah: [13]"This is what the LORD, the God of Israel, says: I brought your ancestors out of Egypt where they were slaves and made an agreement with them. [14]I said to your ancestors: 'At the end of every seven years, each one of you must set his Hebrew slaves free. If a fellow Hebrew has sold himself to you, you must let him go free after he has served you for six years.' But your ancestors did not listen or pay attention to me. [15]A short time ago you changed your hearts and did what I say is right. Each of you gave freedom to his fellow Hebrews who were slaves. And you even made an agreement before me in the place where I have chosen to be worshiped. [16]But now you have changed your minds. You have shown you do not honor me. Each of you has taken back the male and female slaves you had set free, and you have forced them to become your slaves again.

[17]"So this is what the LORD says: You have not obeyed me. You have not given freedom to your fellow Hebrews, neither relatives nor friends. But now I will give freedom, says the LORD, to war, to terrible diseases, and to hunger. I will make you hated by all the kingdoms of the earth. [18]I will hand over the men who broke my agreement, who have not kept the promises they made before me. They cut a calf into two pieces before me and walked between the pieces.[n] [19]These people made the agreement before me by walking between the pieces of the calf: the leaders of Judah and Jerusalem, the officers of the court, the priests, and all the people of the land. [20]So I will hand them over to their enemies and to everyone who wants to kill them. Their bodies will become food for the birds of the air and for the wild animals of the earth. [21]I will hand Zedekiah king of Judah and his officers over to their enemies, and to everyone who wants to kill them, and to the army of the king of Babylon, even though they have left Jerusalem. [22]I will give the order, says the LORD, to bring the Babylonian army back to Jerusalem. It will fight against Jerusalem, capture it, set it on fire, and burn it down. I will destroy the towns in Judah so that they become ruins where no one lives!"

PSALM 119:57–64

[57]LORD, you are my share in life;
    I have promised to obey your words.
[58]I prayed to you with all my heart.
    Have mercy on me as you have
        promised.
[59]I thought about my life,
    and I decided to follow your rules.
[60]I hurried and did not wait
    to obey your commands.
[61]Wicked people have tied me up,
    but I have not forgotten your teachings.
[62]In the middle of the night, I get up to
        thank you
    because your laws are right.
[63]I am a friend to everyone who fears you,
    to anyone who obeys your orders.
[64]LORD, your love fills the earth.
    Teach me your demands.

PROVERBS 27:21

[21]A hot furnace tests silver and gold,
    and people are tested by the praise they
        receive.

1 TIMOTHY 3:1–16

Elders in the Church

3 What I say is true: Anyone wanting to become an overseer desires a good work. [2]An overseer must not give people a reason to criticize him, and he must have only one wife. He must be self-controlled, wise, respected by others, ready to welcome guests, and able to teach. [3]He must not drink too much wine or like to fight, but rather be gentle and peaceable, not loving money. [4]He must be a good family leader, having children who cooperate with full respect. [5](If someone does not know how to lead the family, how can that person take care of God's church?) [6]But an elder must not be a new believer, or he might be too proud of himself and be judged guilty just as the devil was. [7]An elder must also have the respect of people who are not in the church so he will not be criticized by others and caught in the devil's trap.

34:18 They . . . pieces. This showed that the men were willing to be killed, like this animal, if they did not keep their agreement.

Deacons in the Church

[8]In the same way, deacons must be respected by others, not saying things they do not mean. They must not drink too much wine or try to get rich by cheating others. [9]With a clear conscience they must follow the secret of the faith that God made known to us. [10]Test them first. Then let them serve as deacons if you find nothing wrong in them. [11]In the same way, women[n] must be respected by others. They must not speak evil of others. They must be self-controlled and trustworthy in everything. [12]Deacons must have only one wife and be good leaders of their children and their own families. [13]Those who serve well as deacons are making an honorable place for themselves, and they will be very bold in their faith in Christ Jesus.

The Secret of Our Life

[14]Although I hope I can come to you soon, I am writing these things to you now. [15]Then, even if I am delayed, you will know how to live in the family of God. That family is the church of the living God, the support and foundation of the truth. [16]Without doubt, the secret of our life of worship is great:

He[n] was shown to us in a human body,
    proved right in spirit,
    and seen by angels.
He was proclaimed to the nations,
    believed in by the world,
    and taken up in glory.

OCTOBER 25

JEREMIAH 35:1—36:32

The Recabite Family Obeys God

35When Jehoiakim son of Josiah was king of Judah, the LORD spoke his word to Jeremiah, saying: [2]"Go to the family of Recab. Invite them to come to one of the side rooms of the Temple of the LORD, and offer them wine to drink."

[3]So I went to get Jaazaniah son of Jeremiah,[n] the son of Habazziniah. And I gathered all of Jaazaniah's brothers and sons and the whole family of the Recabites together. [4]Then I brought them into the Temple of the LORD. We went into the room of the sons of Hanan son of Igdaliah, who was a man of God. The room was next to the one where the officers stay and above the room of Maaseiah son of Shallum, the doorkeeper in the Temple. [5]Then I put some bowls full of wine and some cups before the men of the Recabite family. And I said to them, "Drink some wine."

[6]But the Recabite men answered, "We never drink wine. Our ancestor Jonadab son of Recab gave us this command: 'You and your descendants must never drink wine. [7]Also you must never build houses, plant seeds, or plant vineyards, or do any of those things. You must live only in tents. Then you will live a long time in the land where you are wanderers.' [8]So we Recabites have obeyed everything Jonadab our ancestor commanded us. Neither we nor our wives, sons, or daughters ever drink wine. [9]We never build houses in which to live, or own fields or vineyards, or plant crops. [10]We have lived in tents and have obeyed everything our ancestor Jonadab commanded us. [11]But when Nebuchadnezzar king of Babylon attacked Judah, we said to each other, 'Come, we must enter Jerusalem so we can escape the Babylonian army and the Aramean army.' So we have stayed in Jerusalem."

[12]Then the LORD spoke his word to Jeremiah: [13]"This is what the LORD All-Powerful, the God of Israel, says: Jeremiah, go and tell the men of Judah and the people of Jerusalem: 'You should learn a lesson and obey my message,' says the LORD. [14]Jonadab

---

3:11 women This might mean the wives of the deacons, or it might mean women who serve in the same way as deacons.
3:16 He Some Greek copies read "God." • **35:3 Jeremiah** Not the prophet Jeremiah, but a different man with the same name.

son of Recab ordered his descendants not to drink wine, and that command has been obeyed. Until today they have obeyed their ancestor's command; they do not drink wine. But I, the LORD, have given you messages again and again, but you did not obey me. ¹⁵I sent all my servants the prophets to you again and again, saying, "Each of you must stop doing evil. You must change and be good. Do not follow other gods to serve them. If you obey me, you will live in the land I have given to you and your ancestors." But you have not listened to me or paid attention to my message. ¹⁶The descendants of Jonadab son of Recab obeyed the commands their ancestor gave them, but the people of Judah have not obeyed me.'

¹⁷"So the LORD God All-Powerful, the God of Israel, says: 'I will soon bring every disaster I said would come to Judah and to everyone living in Jerusalem. I spoke to those people, but they refused to listen. I called out to them, but they did not answer me.'"

¹⁸Then Jeremiah said to the Recabites, "This is what the LORD All-Powerful, the God of Israel, says: 'You have obeyed the commands of your ancestor Jonadab and have followed all of his teachings; you have done everything he commanded.' ¹⁹So this is what the LORD All-Powerful, the God of Israel, says: 'There will always be a descendant of Jonadab son of Recab to serve me.'"

Jehoiakim Burns Jeremiah's Scroll

36 The LORD spoke this word to Jeremiah during the fourth year that Jehoiakim son of Josiah was king of Judah: ²"Get a scroll. Write on it all the words I have spoken to you about Israel and Judah and all the nations. Write everything from when I first spoke to you, when Josiah was king, until now. ³Maybe the family of Judah will hear what disasters I am planning to bring on them and will stop doing wicked things. Then I would forgive them for the sins and the evil things they have done."

⁴So Jeremiah called for Baruch son of Neriah. Jeremiah spoke the messages the LORD had given him, and Baruch wrote those messages on the scroll. ⁵Then Jeremiah commanded Baruch, "I cannot go to the Temple of the LORD. I must stay here. ⁶So I want you to go to the Temple of the LORD on a day when the people are fasting. Read from the scroll to all the people of Judah who come into Jerusalem from their towns. Read the messages from the LORD, which are the words you wrote on the scroll as I spoke them to you. ⁷Perhaps they will ask the LORD to help them. Perhaps each one will stop doing wicked things, because the LORD has announced that he is very angry with them."

⁸So Baruch son of Neriah did everything Jeremiah the prophet told him to do. In the LORD's Temple he read aloud the scroll that had the LORD's messages written on it.

⁹In the ninth month of the fifth year that Jehoiakim son of Josiah was king, a fast was announced. All the people of Jerusalem and everyone who had come into Jerusalem from the towns of Judah were supposed to give up eating to honor the LORD. ¹⁰At that time Baruch read to all the people there the scroll containing Jeremiah's words. He read the scroll in the Temple of the LORD in the room of Gemariah son of Shaphan, a royal secretary. That room was in the upper courtyard at the entrance of the New Gate of the Temple.

¹¹Micaiah son of Gemariah, the son of Shaphan, heard all the messages from the LORD that were on the scroll. ¹²Micaiah went down to the royal secretary's room in the king's palace where all of the officers were sitting: Elishama the royal secretary; Delaiah son of Shemaiah; Elnathan son of Acbor; Gemariah son of Shaphan; Zedekiah son of Hananiah; and all the other officers. ¹³Micaiah told those officers everything he had heard Baruch read to the people from the scroll.

¹⁴Then the officers sent a man named Jehudi son of Nethaniah to Baruch. (Nethaniah was the son of Shelemiah, who was the son of Cushi.) Jehudi said to Baruch, "Bring the scroll that you read to the people and come with me."

So Baruch son of Neriah took the scroll and went with Jehudi to the officers. ¹⁵Then the officers said to Baruch, "Please sit down and read the scroll to us."

So Baruch read the scroll to them. ¹⁶When the officers heard all the words, they became afraid and looked at each other. They said to Baruch, "We must certainly tell the king about these words." 17Then the officers asked Baruch, "Tell us, please, where did you get all these words you wrote on the scroll? Did you write down what Jeremiah said to you?"

18"Yes," Baruch answered. "Jeremiah spoke them all to me, and I wrote them down with ink on this scroll."

19Then the officers said to Baruch, "You and Jeremiah must go and hide, and don't tell anyone where you are."

20The officers put the scroll in the room of Elishama the royal secretary. Then they went to the king in the courtyard and told him all about the scroll. 21So King Jehoiakim sent Jehudi to get the scroll. Jehudi brought the scroll from the room of Elishama the royal secretary and read it to the king and to all the officers who stood around the king. 22It was the ninth month of the year, so King Jehoiakim was sitting in the winter apartment. There was a fire burning in a small firepot in front of him. 23After Jehudi had read three or four columns, the king cut those columns off of the scroll with a penknife and threw them into the firepot. Finally, the whole scroll was burned in the fire. 24King Jehoiakim and his servants heard everything that was said, but they were not frightened! They did not tear their clothes to show their sorrow. 25Elnathan, Delaiah, and Gemariah even tried to talk King Jehoiakim out of burning the scroll, but he would not listen to them. 26Instead, the king ordered Jerahmeel son of the king, Seraiah son of Azriel, and Shelemiah son of Abdeel to arrest Baruch the secretary and Jeremiah the prophet. But the LORD had hidden them.

27So King Jehoiakim burned the scroll where Baruch had written all the words Jeremiah had spoken to him. Then the LORD spoke his word to Jeremiah: 28"Get another scroll. Write all the words on it that were on the first scroll that Jehoiakim king of Judah burned up. 29Also say this to Jehoiakim king of Judah: 'This is what the LORD says: You burned up that scroll and said, "Why, Jeremiah, did you write on it 'the king of Babylon will surely come and destroy this land and the people and animals in it'?" 30So this is what the LORD says about Jehoiakim king of

Judah: Jehoiakim's descendants will not sit on David's throne. When Jehoiakim dies, his body will be thrown out on the ground. It will be left out in the heat of the day and in the cold frost of the night. 31I will punish Jehoiakim and his children and his servants, because they have done evil things. I will bring disasters upon them and upon all the people in Jerusalem and Judah—everything I promised but which they refused to hear.'"

32So Jeremiah took another scroll and gave it to Baruch son of Neriah, his secretary. As Jeremiah spoke, Baruch wrote on the scroll the same words that were on the scroll Jehoiakim king of Judah had burned in the fire. And many similar words were added to the second scroll.

PSALM 119:65-72

65You have done good things for your
  servant,
  as you have promised, LORD.
66Teach me wisdom and knowledge
  because I trust your commands.
67Before I suffered, I did wrong,
  but now I obey your word.
68You are good, and you do what is good.
  Teach me your demands.
69Proud people have made up lies about me,
  but I will follow your orders with all my
  heart.
70Those people have no feelings,
  but I love your teachings.
71It was good for me to suffer
  so I would learn your demands.
72Your teachings are worth more to me
  than thousands of pieces of gold and
  silver.

PROVERBS 27:22

22Even if you ground up a foolish person
  like grain in a bowl,
  you couldn't remove the foolishness.

1 TIMOTHY 4:1-16

A Warning About False Teachers

4 Now the Holy Spirit clearly says that in the later times some people will stop believing the faith. They will follow spirits that

lie and teachings of demons. [2]Such teachings come from the false words of liars whose consciences are destroyed as if by a hot iron. [3]They forbid people to marry and tell them not to eat certain foods which God created to be eaten with thanks by people who believe and know the truth. [4]Everything God made is good, and nothing should be refused if it is accepted with thanks, [5]because it is made holy by what God has said and by prayer.

Be a Good Servant of Christ

[6]By telling these things to the brothers and sisters, you will be a good servant of Christ Jesus. You will be made strong by the words of the faith and the good teaching which you have been following. [7]But do not follow foolish stories that disagree with God's truth, but train yourself to serve God. [8]Training your body helps you in some ways, but serving God helps you in every way by bringing you blessings in this life and in the future life, too. [9]What I say is true, and you should fully accept it. [10]This is why we work and struggle:[n] We hope in the living God who is the Savior of all people, especially of those who believe.

[11]Command and teach these things. [12]Do not let anyone treat you as if you are unimportant because you are young. Instead, be an example to the believers with your words, your actions, your love, your faith, and your pure life. [13]Until I come, continue to read the Scriptures to the people, strengthen them, and teach them. [14]Use the gift you have, which was given to you through prophecy when the group of elders laid their hands on[n] you. [15]Continue to do those things; give your life to doing them so your progress may be seen by everyone. [16]Be careful in your life and in your teaching. If you continue to live and teach rightly, you will save both yourself and those who listen to you.

OCTOBER 26

JEREMIAH 37:1—38:28

Jeremiah in Prison

37 Nebuchadnezzar king of Babylon had appointed Zedekiah son of Josiah to be king of Judah. Zedekiah took the place of Jehoiachin son of Jehoiakim. [2]But Zedekiah, his servants, and the people of Judah did not listen to the words the LORD had spoken through Jeremiah the prophet.

[3]Now King Zedekiah sent Jehucal son of Shelemiah and the priest Zephaniah son of Maaseiah with a message to Jeremiah the prophet. This was the message: "Jeremiah, please pray to the LORD our God for us."

[4]At that time Jeremiah had not yet been put into prison. So he was free to go anywhere he wanted. [5]The army of the king of Egypt had marched from Egypt toward Judah. Now the Babylonian army had surrounded the city of Jerusalem. When they heard about the Egyptian army marching toward them, the Babylonian army left Jerusalem.

[6]The LORD spoke his word to Jeremiah the prophet: [7]"This is what the LORD, the God of Israel, says: Jehucal and Zephaniah, I know Zedekiah king of Judah sent you to seek my help. Tell this to King Zedekiah: 'The army of the king of Egypt came here to help you, but they will go back to Egypt. [8]After that, the Babylonian army will return and attack Jerusalem and capture it and burn it down.'

[9]"This is what the LORD says: People of Jerusalem, do not fool yourselves. Don't say, 'The Babylonian army will surely leave us alone.' They will not! [10]Even if you defeated all of the Babylonian army that is attacking you and there were only a few injured men left in their tents, they would come from their tents and burn down Jerusalem!"

[11]So the Babylonian army left Jerusalem

4:10 struggle Some Greek copies read "suffer." **4:14 laid their hands on** The laying on of hands had many purposes, including the giving of a blessing, power, or authority.

to fight the army of the king of Egypt. ¹²Now Jeremiah tried to travel from Jerusalem to the land of Benjamin to get his share of the property that belonged to his family. ¹³When Jeremiah got to the Benjamin Gate of Jerusalem, the captain in charge of the guards arrested him. The captain's name was Irijah son of Shelemiah son of Hananiah. Irijah said, "You are leaving us to join the Babylonians!"

¹⁴But Jeremiah said to Irijah, "That's not true! I am not leaving to join the Babylonians." Irijah refused to listen to Jeremiah, so he arrested Jeremiah and took him to the officers of Jerusalem. ¹⁵Those rulers were very angry with Jeremiah and beat him. Then they put him in jail in the house of Jonathan the royal secretary, which had been made into a prison. ¹⁶So those people put Jeremiah into a cell in a dungeon, and Jeremiah was there for a long time.

¹⁷Then King Zedekiah sent for Jeremiah and had him brought to the palace. Zedekiah asked him in private, "Is there any message from the LORD?"

Jeremiah answered, "Yes, there is. Zedekiah, you will be handed over to the king of Babylon." ¹⁸Then Jeremiah said to King Zedekiah, "What crime have I done against you or your officers or the people of Jerusalem? Why have you thrown me into prison? ¹⁹Where are your prophets that prophesied this message to you: 'The king of Babylon will not attack you or this land of Judah'? ²⁰But now, my master, king of Judah, please listen to me, and please do what I ask of you. Do not send me back to the house of Jonathan the royal secretary, or I will die there!"

²¹So King Zedekiah gave orders for Jeremiah to be put under guard in the courtyard of the guard and to be given bread each day from the street of the bakers until there was no more bread in the city. So he stayed under guard in the courtyard of the guard.

Jeremiah Is Thrown into a Well

38 Shephatiah son of Mattan, Gedaliah son of Pashhur, Jehucal son of Shelemiah, and Pashhur son of Malkijah heard what Jeremiah was telling all the people. He

said: ²"This is what the LORD says: 'Everyone who stays in Jerusalem will die from war, or hunger, or terrible diseases. But everyone who surrenders to the Babylonian army will live; they will escape with their lives and live.' ³And this is what the LORD says: 'This city of Jerusalem will surely be handed over to the army of the king of Babylon. He will capture this city!' "

⁴Then the officers said to the king, "Jeremiah must be put to death! He is discouraging the soldiers who are still in the city, and all the people, by what he is saying to them. He does not want good to happen to us; he wants to ruin us."

⁵King Zedekiah said to them, "Jeremiah is in your control. I cannot do anything to stop you."

⁶So the officers took Jeremiah and put him into the well of Malkijah, the king's son, which was in the courtyard of the guards. The officers used ropes to lower Jeremiah into the well, which did not have any water in it, only mud. And Jeremiah sank down into the mud.

⁷But Ebed-Melech, a Cushite and a servant in the palace, heard that the officers had put Jeremiah into the well. As King Zedekiah was sitting at the Benjamin Gate, ⁸Ebed-Melech left the palace and went to the king. Ebed-Melech said to him, ⁹"My master and king, these rulers have acted in an evil way. They have treated Jeremiah the prophet badly. They have thrown him into a well and left him there to die! When there is no more bread in the city, he will starve to death."

¹⁰Then King Zedekiah commanded Ebed-Melech the Cushite, "Take thirty men from the palace and lift Jeremiah the prophet out of the well before he dies."

¹¹So Ebed-Melech took the men with him and went to a room under the storeroom in the palace. He took some old rags and worn-out clothes from that room. Then he let those rags down with some ropes to Jeremiah in the well. ¹²Ebed-Melech the Cushite said to Jeremiah, "Put these old rags and worn-out clothes under your arms to be pads for the ropes." So Jeremiah did as Ebed-Melech said. ¹³The men pulled Jeremiah up with the ropes and lifted him out of the well.

And Jeremiah stayed under guard in the courtyard of the guard.

Zedekiah Questions Jeremiah

¹⁴Then King Zedekiah sent someone to get Jeremiah the prophet and bring him to the third entrance to the Temple of the LORD. The king said to Jeremiah, "I am going to ask you something. Do not hide anything from me, but tell me everything honestly."

¹⁵Jeremiah said to Zedekiah, "If I give you an answer, you will surely kill me. And even if I give you advice, you will not listen to me."

¹⁶But King Zedekiah made a secret promise to Jeremiah, "As surely as the LORD lives who has given us breath and life, I will not kill you. And I promise not to hand you over to the officers who want to kill you."

¹⁷Then Jeremiah said to Zedekiah, "This is what the LORD God All-Powerful, the God of Israel, says: 'If you surrender to the officers of the king of Babylon, your life will be saved. Jerusalem will not be burned down, and you and your family will live. ¹⁸But if you refuse to surrender to the officers of the king of Babylon, Jerusalem will be handed over to the Babylonian army, and they will burn it down. And you yourself will not escape from them.'"

¹⁹Then King Zedekiah said to Jeremiah, "I'm afraid of some Jews who have already gone over to the side of the Babylonian army. If the Babylonians hand me over to them, they will treat me badly."

²⁰But Jeremiah answered, "The Babylonians will not hand you over to the Jews. Obey the LORD by doing what I tell you. Then things will go well for you, and your life will be saved. ²¹But if you refuse to surrender to the Babylonians, the LORD has shown me what will happen. ²²All the women left in the palace of the king of Judah will be brought out and taken to the important officers of the king of Babylon. Your women will make fun of you with this song:

'Your good friends misled you
    and were stronger than you.
While your feet were stuck in the mud,
    they left you.'

²³"All your wives and children will be brought out and given to the Babylonian army. You yourself will not even escape from them.

You will be taken prisoner by the king of Babylon, and Jerusalem will be burned down."

²⁴Then Zedekiah said to Jeremiah, "Do not tell anyone that I have been talking to you, or you will die. ²⁵If the officers find out I talked to you, they will come to you and say, 'Tell us what you said to King Zedekiah and what he said to you. Don't keep any secrets from us. If you don't tell us everything, we will kill you.' ²⁶If they ask you, tell them, 'I was begging the king not to send me back to Jonathan's house to die.'"

²⁷All the officers did come to question Jeremiah. So he told them everything the king had ordered him to say. Then the officers said no more to Jeremiah, because no one had heard what Jeremiah and the king had discussed.

²⁸So Jeremiah stayed under guard in the courtyard of the guard until the day Jerusalem was captured.

PSALM 119:73–80

⁷³You made me and formed me with your
        hands.
    Give me understanding so I can learn
        your commands.
⁷⁴Let those who respect you rejoice when
        they see me,
    because I put my hope in your word.
⁷⁵LORD, I know that your laws are right
    and that it was right for you to punish
        me.
⁷⁶Comfort me with your love,
    as you promised me, your servant.
⁷⁷Have mercy on me so that I may live.
    I love your teachings.
⁷⁸Make proud people ashamed because
        they lied about me.
    But I will think about your orders.
⁷⁹Let those who respect you return to me,
    those who know your rules.
⁸⁰Let me obey your demands perfectly
    so I will not be ashamed.

PROVERBS 27:23–27

²³Be sure you know how your sheep are
        doing,
    and pay attention to the condition of
        your cattle.

²⁴Riches will not go on forever,
nor do governments go on forever.
²⁵Bring in the hay, and let the new grass
appear.
Gather the grass from the hills.
²⁶Make clothes from the lambs' wool,
and sell some goats to buy a field.
²⁷There will be plenty of goat's milk
to feed you and your family
and to make your servant girls healthy.

1 TIMOTHY 5:1—6:2

Rules for Living with Others

5 Do not speak angrily to an older man, but plead with him as if he were your father. Treat younger men like brothers, ²older women like mothers, and younger women like sisters. Always treat them in a pure way.

³Take care of widows who are truly widows. ⁴But if a widow has children or grandchildren, let them first learn to do their duty to their own family and to repay their parents or grandparents. That pleases God. ⁵The true widow, who is all alone, puts her hope in God and continues to pray night and day for God's help. ⁶But the widow who uses her life to please herself is really dead while she is alive. ⁷Tell the believers to do these things so that no one can criticize them. ⁸Whoever does not care for his own relatives, especially his own family members, has turned against the faith and is worse than someone who does not believe in God.

⁹To be on the list of widows, a woman must be at least sixty years old. She must have been faithful to her husband. ¹⁰She must be known for her good works—works such as raising her children, welcoming strangers, washing the feet of God's people, helping those in trouble, and giving her life to do all kinds of good deeds.

¹¹But do not put younger widows on that list. After they give themselves to Christ, they are pulled away from him by their physical desires, and then they want to marry again. ¹²They will be judged for not doing what they first promised to do. ¹³Besides that, they learn to waste their time, going from house to house. And they not only waste their time but also begin to gossip and busy themselves with other people's lives, saying things they should not say. ¹⁴So I want the younger widows to marry, have children, and manage their homes. Then no enemy will have any reason to criticize them. ¹⁵But some have already turned away to follow Satan.

¹⁶If any woman who is a believer has widows in her family, she should care for them herself. The church should not have to care for them. Then it will be able to take care of those who are truly widows.

¹⁷The elders who lead the church well should receive double honor, especially those who work hard by speaking and teaching, ¹⁸because the Scripture says: "When an ox is working in the grain, do not cover its mouth to keep it from eating,"ⁿ and "A worker should be given his pay."ⁿ

¹⁹Do not listen to someone who accuses an elder, without two or three witnesses. ²⁰Tell those who continue sinning that they are wrong. Do this in front of the whole church so that the others will have a warning.

²¹Before God and Christ Jesus and the chosen angels, I command you to do these things without showing favor of any kind to anyone.

²²Think carefully before you lay your hands onⁿ anyone, and don't share in the sins of others. Keep yourself pure.

²³Stop drinking only water, but drink a little wine to help your stomach and your frequent sicknesses.

²⁴The sins of some people are easy to see even before they are judged, but the sins of others are seen only later. ²⁵So also good deeds are easy to see, but even those that are not easily seen cannot stay hidden.

6 All who are slaves under a yoke should show full respect to their masters so no one will speak against God's name and our teaching. ²The slaves whose masters are believers should not show their masters any less respect because they are believers. They should serve their masters even better, because they are helping believers they love.

You must teach and preach these things.

5:18 "When . . . eating." Quotation from Deuteronomy 25:4. **5:18 "A worker . . . pay."** Quotation from Luke 10:7.
5:22 lay your hands on The laying on of hands had many purposes, including the giving of a blessing, power, or authority.

OCTOBER 27

JEREMIAH 39:1—40:16

The Fall of Jerusalem

39 This is how Jerusalem was captured: Nebuchadnezzar king of Babylon marched against Jerusalem with his whole army and surrounded the city to attack it. This was during the tenth month of the ninth year Zedekiah was king of Judah. ²This lasted until the ninth day of the fourth month in Zedekiah's eleventh year. Then the city wall was broken through. ³And all these officers of the king of Babylon came into Jerusalem and sat down at the Middle Gate: Nergal-Sharezer of the district of Samgar; Nebo-Sarsekim, a chief officer; Nergal-Sharezer, an important leader; and all the other important officers.

⁴When Zedekiah king of Judah and all his soldiers saw them, they ran away. They left Jerusalem at night and went out from the king's garden. They went through the gate that was between the two walls and then headed toward the Jordan Valley. ⁵But the Babylonian army chased them and caught up with Zedekiah in the plains of Jericho. They captured him and took him to Nebuchadnezzar king of Babylon, who was at the town of Riblah in the land of Hamath. There Nebuchadnezzar passed his sentence on Zedekiah. ⁶At Riblah the king of Babylon killed Zedekiah's sons and all the important officers of Judah as Zedekiah watched. ⁷Then he put out Zedekiah's eyes. He put bronze chains on Zedekiah and took him to Babylon.

⁸The Babylonians set fire to the palace and to the houses of the people, and they broke down the walls around Jerusalem. ⁹Nebuzaradan, commander of the king's special guards, took the people left in Jerusalem, those captives who had surrendered to him earlier, and the rest of the people of Jerusalem, and he took them all away to Babylon. ¹⁰But Nebuzaradan, commander of the guard, left some of the poorest people of Judah behind. They owned nothing, but that day he gave them vineyards and fields.

¹¹Nebuchadnezzar king of Babylon had given these orders about Jeremiah through Nebuzaradan, commander of the guard: ¹²"Find Jeremiah and take care of him. Do not hurt him, but do for him whatever he asks you." ¹³So Nebuchadnezzar sent these men for Jeremiah: Nebuzaradan, commander of the guards; Nebushazban, a chief officer; Nergal-Sharezer, an important leader; and all the other officers of the king of Babylon. ¹⁴They had Jeremiah taken out of the courtyard of the guard. Then they turned him over to Gedaliah son of Ahikam son of Shaphan, who had orders to take Jeremiah back home. So they took him home, and he stayed among the people left in Judah.

¹⁵While Jeremiah was guarded in the courtyard, the LORD spoke his word to him: ¹⁶"Jeremiah, go and tell Ebed-Melech the Cushite this message: 'This is what the LORD All-Powerful, the God of Israel, says: Very soon I will make my words about Jerusalem come true through disaster, not through good times. You will see everything come true with your own eyes. ¹⁷But I will save you on that day, Ebed-Melech, says the LORD. You will not be handed over to the people you fear. ¹⁸I will surely save you, Ebed-Melech. You will not die from a sword, but you will escape and live. This will happen because you have trusted in me, says the LORD.'"

Jeremiah Is Set Free

40 The LORD spoke his word to Jeremiah after Nebuzaradan, commander of the guards, had set Jeremiah free at the city of Ramah. He had found Jeremiah in Ramah bound in chains with all the captives from Jerusalem and Judah who were being taken away to Babylon. ²When commander Nebuzaradan found Jeremiah, Nebuzaradan said to him, "The LORD your God announced this disaster would come to this place. ³And now the LORD has done everything he said he would do. This disaster happened because the people of Judah sinned against the LORD and did not obey him. ⁴But today I am freeing you from the chains on your wrists. If you want to, come with me to Babylon, and I will take good care of you. But if you don't want to come, then don't. Look, the whole country is open to you. Go wherever you wish." ⁵Before Jeremiah turned to leave, Nebuzaradan said, "Or go back to Gedaliah son of Ahikam, the son of Shaphan. The king of Babylon has chosen him to be governor over the towns of Judah. Go and live with Gedaliah among the people, or go anywhere you want."

Then Nebuzaradan gave Jeremiah some food and a present and let him go. ⁶So Jeremiah went to Gedaliah son of Ahikam at Mizpah and stayed with him there. He lived among the people who were left behind in Judah.

The Short Rule of Gedaliah

⁷Some officers and their men from the army of Judah were still out in the open country. They heard that the king of Babylon had put Gedaliah son of Ahikam in charge of the people who were left in the land: the men, women, and children who were the poorest. They were the ones who were not taken to Babylon as captives. ⁸So these soldiers came to Gedaliah at Mizpah: Ishmael son of Nethaniah, Johanan and Jonathan sons of Kareah, Seraiah son of Tanhumeth, the sons of Ephai the Netophathite, Jaazaniah son of the Maacathite, and their men.

⁹Gedaliah son of Ahikam, the son of Shaphan, made a promise to them, saying, "Do not be afraid to serve the Babylonians. Stay in the land and serve the king of Babylon. Then everything will go well for you. ¹⁰I myself will live in Mizpah and will speak for you before the Babylonians who come to us here. Harvest the wine, the summer fruit, and the oil, and put what you harvest in your storage jars. Live in the towns you control."

¹¹The Jews in Moab, Ammon, Edom, and other countries also heard that the king of Babylon had left a few Jews alive in the land. And they heard the king of Babylon had chosen Gedaliah as governor over them.

(Gedaliah was the son of Ahikam, the son of Shaphan.) ¹²When the people of Judah heard this news, they came back to Judah from all the countries where they had been scattered. They came to Gedaliah at Mizpah and gathered a large harvest of wine and summer fruit.

¹³Johanan son of Kareah and all the army officers of Judah still in the open country came to Gedaliah at Mizpah. ¹⁴They said to him, "Don't you know that Baalis king of the Ammonite people wants you dead? He has sent Ishmael son of Nethaniah to kill you." But Gedaliah son of Ahikam did not believe them.

¹⁵Then Johanan son of Kareah spoke to Gedaliah in private at Mizpah. He said, "Let me go and kill Ishmael son of Nethaniah. No one will know anything about it. We should not let Ishmael kill you. Then all the Jews gathered around you would be scattered to different countries again, and the few people of Judah who are left alive would be lost."

¹⁶But Gedaliah son of Ahikam said to Johanan son of Kareah, "Do not kill Ishmael! The things you are saying about Ishmael are not true."

PSALM 119:81–88

⁸¹I am weak from waiting for you to save me,
 but I hope in your word.
⁸²My eyes are tired from looking for your promise.
 When will you comfort me?
⁸³Even though I am like a wine bag going up in smoke,
 I do not forget your demands.
⁸⁴How long will I live?
 When will you judge those who are hurting me?
⁸⁵Proud people have dug pits to trap me.
 They have nothing to do with your teachings.
⁸⁶All of your commands can be trusted.
 Liars are hurting me. Help me!
⁸⁷They have almost put me in the grave,
 but I have not rejected your orders.
⁸⁸Give me life by your love
 so I can obey your rules.

PROVERBS 28:1

28 Evil people run even though no one is
chasing them,
but good people are as brave as a lion.

1 TIMOTHY 6:3–21

False Teaching and True Riches

³Anyone who has a different teaching does not agree with the true teaching of our Lord Jesus Christ and the teaching that shows the true way to serve God. ⁴This person is full of pride and understands nothing, but is sick with a love for arguing and fighting about words. This brings jealousy, fighting, speaking against others, evil mistrust, ⁵and constant quarrels from those who have evil minds and have lost the truth. They think that serving God is a way to get rich.

⁶Serving God does make us very rich, if we are satisfied with what we have. ⁷We brought nothing into the world, so we can take nothing out. ⁸But, if we have food and clothes, we will be satisfied with that. ⁹Those who want to become rich bring temptation to themselves and are caught in a trap. They want many foolish and harmful things that ruin and destroy people. ¹⁰The love of money causes all kinds of evil. Some people have left the faith, because they wanted to get more money, but they have caused themselves much sorrow.

Some Things to Remember

¹¹But you, man of God, run away from all those things. Instead, live in the right way,

serve God, have faith, love, patience, and gentleness. ¹²Fight the good fight of faith, grabbing hold of the life that continues forever. You were called to have that life when you confessed the good confession before many witnesses. ¹³In the sight of God, who gives life to everything, and of Christ Jesus, I give you a command. Christ Jesus made the good confession when he stood before Pontius Pilate. ¹⁴Do what you were commanded to do without wrong or blame until our Lord Jesus Christ comes again. ¹⁵God will make that happen at the right time. He is the blessed and only Ruler, the King of all kings and the Lord of all lords. ¹⁶He is the only One who never dies. He lives in light so bright no one can go near it. No one has ever seen God, or can see him. May honor and power belong to God forever. Amen.

¹⁷Command those who are rich with things of this world not to be proud. Tell them to hope in God, not in their uncertain riches. God richly gives us everything to enjoy. ¹⁸Tell the rich people to do good, to be rich in doing good deeds, to be generous and ready to share. ¹⁹By doing that, they will be saving a treasure for themselves as a strong foundation for the future. Then they will be able to have the life that is true life.

²⁰Timothy, guard what God has trusted to you. Stay away from foolish, useless talk and from the arguments of what is falsely called "knowledge." ²¹By saying they have that "knowledge," some have missed the true faith.

Grace be with you.

OCTOBER 28

JEREMIAH 41:1—42:22

41 In the seventh month Ishmael son of Nethaniah and ten of his men came to Gedaliah son of Ahikam at Mizpah. (Nethaniah was the son of Elishama.) Now Ishmael was a member of the king's family and had been one of the officers of the king of Judah. While they were eating a meal with Gedaliah

at Mizpah, ²Ishmael and his ten men got up and killed Gedaliah son of Ahikam, the son of Shaphan, with a sword. (Gedaliah was the man the king of Babylon had chosen as governor over Judah.) ³Ishmael also killed all the Jews and the Babylonian soldiers who were there with Gedaliah at Mizpah.

⁴The day after Gedaliah was murdered, before anyone knew about it, ⁵eighty men

came to Mizpah bringing grain offerings and incense to the Temple of the LORD. Those men from Shechem, Shiloh, and Samaria had shaved off their beards, torn their clothes, and cut themselves." [6]Ishmael son of Nethaniah went out from Mizpah to meet them, crying as he walked. When he met them, he said, "Come with me to meet Gedaliah son of Ahikam." [7]So they went into Mizpah. Then Ishmael son of Nethaniah and his men killed seventy of them and threw the bodies into a deep well. [8]But the ten men who were left alive said to Ishmael, "Don't kill us! We have wheat and barley and oil and honey that we have hidden in a field." So Ishmael let them live and did not kill them with the others. [9]Now the well where he had thrown all the bodies had been made by King Asa as a part of his defenses against Baasha king of Israel. But Ishmael son of Nethaniah put dead bodies in it until it was full.

[10]Ishmael captured all the other people in Mizpah: the king's daughters and all the other people who were left there. They were the ones whom Nebuzaradan commander of the guard had chosen Gedaliah son of Ahikam to take care of. So Ishmael son of Nethaniah captured those people, and he started to cross over to the country of the Ammonites.

[11]Johanan son of Kareah and all his army officers with him heard about all the evil things Ishmael son of Nethaniah had done. [12]So they took their men and went to fight Ishmael son of Nethaniah and caught him near the big pool of water at Gibeon. [13]When the captives Ishmael had taken saw Johanan and the army officers, they were glad. [14]So all the people Ishmael had taken captive from Mizpah turned around and ran to Johanan son of Kareah. [15]But Ishmael son of Nethaniah and eight of his men escaped from Johanan and ran away to the Ammonites.

[16]So Johanan son of Kareah and all his army officers saved the captives that Ishmael son of Nethaniah had taken from Mizpah after he murdered Gedaliah son of Ahikam. Among those left alive were sol-

diers, women, children, and palace officers. And Johanan brought them back from the town of Gibeon.

The Escape to Egypt

[17-18]Johanan and the other army officers were afraid of the Babylonians. Since the king of Babylon had chosen Gedaliah son of Ahikam to be governor of Judah but Ishmael son of Nethaniah had murdered him, Johanan was afraid that the Babylonians would be angry. So they decided to run away to Egypt. On the way they stayed at Geruth Kimham, near the town of Bethlehem.

42 While there, Johanan son of Kareah and Jezaniah son of Hoshaiah went to Jeremiah the prophet. All the army officers and all the people, from the least important to the greatest, went along, too. [2]They said to him, "Jeremiah, please listen to what we ask. Pray to the LORD your God for all the people left alive from the family of Judah. At one time there were many of us, but you can see that there are few of us now. [3]So pray that the LORD your God will tell us where we should go and what we should do."

[4]Then Jeremiah the prophet answered, "I understand what you want me to do. I will pray to the LORD your God as you have asked. I will tell you everything he says and not hide anything from you."

[5]Then the people said to Jeremiah, "May the LORD be a true and loyal witness against us if we don't do everything the LORD your God sends you to tell us. [6]It does not matter if we like the message or not. We will obey the LORD our God, to whom we are sending you. We will obey what he says so good things will happen to us."

[7]Ten days later the LORD spoke his word to Jeremiah. [8]Then Jeremiah called for Johanan son of Kareah, the army officers with him, and all the other people, from the least important to the greatest. [9]Jeremiah said to them, "You sent me to ask the LORD for what you wanted. This is what the God of Israel says: [10]If you will stay in Judah, I will build you up and not tear you down. I will plant you and not pull you up, because

I am sad about the disaster I brought on you. ¹¹Now you fear the king of Babylon, but don't be afraid of him. Don't be afraid of him,' says the LORD, 'because I am with you. I will save you and rescue you from his power. ¹²I will be kind to you, and he will also treat you with mercy and let you stay in your land.'

¹³"But if you say, 'We will not stay in Judah,' you will disobey the LORD your God. ¹⁴Or you might say, 'No, we will go and live in Egypt. There we will not see war, or hear the trumpets of war, or be hungry.' ¹⁵If you say that, listen to the message of the LORD, you who are left alive from Judah. This is what the LORD All-Powerful, the God of Israel, says: 'If you make up your mind to go and live in Egypt, these things will happen: ¹⁶You are afraid of war, but it will find you in the land of Egypt. And you are worried about hunger, but it will follow you into Egypt, and you will die there. ¹⁷Everyone who goes to live in Egypt will die in war or from hunger or terrible disease. No one who goes to Egypt will live; no one will escape the terrible things I will bring to them.'

¹⁸"This is what the LORD All-Powerful, the God of Israel, says: 'I showed my anger against the people of Jerusalem. In the same way I will show my anger against you when you go to Egypt. Other nations will speak evil of you. People will be shocked by what will happen to you. You will become a curse word, and people will insult you. And you will never see Judah again.'

¹⁹"You who are left alive in Judah, the LORD has told you, 'Don't go to Egypt.' Be sure you understand this; I warn you today ²⁰that you are making a mistake that will cause your deaths. You sent me to the LORD your God, saying, 'Pray to the LORD our God for us. Tell us everything the LORD our God says, and we will do it.' ²¹So today I have told you, but you have not obeyed the LORD your God in all that he sent me to tell you. ²²So now be sure you understand this: You want to go to live in Egypt, but you will die there by war, hunger, or terrible diseases."

PSALM 119:89–96

⁸⁹LORD, your word is everlasting;
  it continues forever in heaven.
⁹⁰Your loyalty will go on and on;
  you made the earth, and it still stands.
⁹¹All things continue to this day because of your laws,
  because all things serve you.
⁹²If I had not loved your teachings,
  I would have died from my sufferings.
⁹³I will never forget your orders,
  because you have given me life by them.
⁹⁴I am yours. Save me.
  I want to obey your orders.
⁹⁵Wicked people are waiting to destroy me,
  but I will think about your rules.
⁹⁶Everything I see has its limits,
  but your commands have none.

PROVERBS 28:2

²When a country is lawless, it has one ruler after another;
  but when it is led by a leader with understanding and knowledge, it continues strong.

2 TIMOTHY 1:1–18

1 From Paul, an apostle of Christ Jesus by the will of God. God sent me to tell about the promise of life that is in Christ Jesus.

²To Timothy, a dear child to me:

Grace, mercy, and peace to you from God the Father and Christ Jesus our Lord.

Encouragement for Timothy

³I thank God as I always mention you in my prayers, day and night. I serve him, doing what I know is right as my ancestors did. ⁴Remembering that you cried for me, I want very much to see you so I can be filled with joy. ⁵I remember your true faith. That faith first lived in your grandmother Lois and in your mother Eunice, and I know you now have that same faith. ⁶This is why I remind you to keep using the gift God gave you when I laid my hands on[n] you. Now let it grow, as a

---

1:6 laid my hands on The laying on of hands had many purposes, including the giving of a blessing, power, or authority.

small flame grows into a fire. [7]God did not give us a spirit that makes us afraid but a spirit of power and love and self-control.

[8]So do not be ashamed to tell people about our Lord Jesus, and do not be ashamed of me, in prison for the Lord. But suffer with me for the Good News. God, who gives us the strength to do that, [9]saved us and made us his holy people. That was not because of anything we did ourselves but because of God's purpose and grace. That grace was given to us through Christ Jesus before time began, [10]but it is now shown to us by the coming of our Savior Christ Jesus. He destroyed death, and through the Good News he showed us the way to have life that cannot be destroyed. [11]I was chosen to tell that Good News and to be an apostle and a teacher. [12]I am suffering now because I tell

the Good News, but I am not ashamed, because I know Jesus, the One in whom I have believed. And I am sure he is able to protect what he has trusted me with until that day." [13]Follow the pattern of true teachings that you heard from me in faith and love, which are in Christ Jesus. [14]Protect the truth that you were given; protect it with the help of the Holy Spirit who lives in us.

[15]You know that everyone in Asia has left me, even Phygelus and Hermogenes. [16]May the Lord show mercy to the family of Onesiphorus, who has often helped me and was not ashamed that I was in prison. [17]When he came to Rome, he looked eagerly for me until he found me. [18]May the Lord allow him to find mercy from the Lord on that day. You know how many ways he helped me in Ephesus.

OCTOBER 29

JEREMIAH 43:1—44:30

43 So Jeremiah finished telling the people the message from the LORD their God; he told them everything the LORD their God had sent him to tell them.

[2]Azariah son of Hoshaiah, Johanan son of Kareah, and some other men were too proud. They said to Jeremiah, "You are lying! The LORD our God did not send you to say, 'You must not go to Egypt to live there.' [3]Baruch son of Neriah is causing you to be against us. He wants you to hand us over to the Babylonians so they can kill us or capture us and take us to Babylon."

[4]So Johanan, the army officers, and all the people disobeyed the LORD's command to stay in Judah. [5]But Johanan son of Kareah and the army officers led away those who were left alive from Judah. They were the people who had run away from the Babylonians to other countries but then had come back to live in Judah. [6]They led away the men, women, and children, and the king's

daughters. Nebuzaradan commander of the guard had put Gedaliah son of Ahikam son of Shaphan in charge of those people. Johanan also took Jeremiah the prophet and Baruch son of Neriah. [7]These people did not listen to the LORD. So they all went to Egypt to the city of Tahpanhes.

[8]In Tahpanhes the LORD spoke his word to Jeremiah: [9]"Take some large stones. Bury them in the clay in the brick pavement in front of the king of Egypt's palace in Tahpanhes. Do this while the Jews are watching you. [10]Then say to them, 'This is what the LORD All-Powerful, the God of Israel, says: I will soon send for my servant, Nebuchadnezzar king of Babylon. I will set his throne over these stones I have buried, and he will spread his covering for shade above them. [11]He will come here and attack Egypt. He will bring death to those who are supposed to die. He will make prisoners of those who are to be taken captive, and he will bring war to those who are to be killed with a sword. [12]Nebuchadnezzar will set fire to the temples

1:12 day The day Christ will come to judge all people and take his people to live with him.

of the gods of Egypt and burn them. And he will take the idols away as captives. As a shepherd wraps himself in his clothes, so Nebuchadnezzar will wrap Egypt around him. Then he will safely leave Egypt. [13]He will destroy the stone pillars in the temple of the sun god in Egypt, and he will burn down the temples of the gods of Egypt.'"

Disaster in Egypt

44 Jeremiah received a message from the LORD for all the Jews living in Egypt—in the cities of Migdol, Tahpanhes, Memphis, and in southern Egypt. This was the message: [2]"The LORD All-Powerful, the God of Israel, says: You saw all the terrible things I brought on Jerusalem and the towns of Judah, which are ruins today with no one living in them. [3]It is because the people who lived there did evil. They made me angry by burning incense and worshiping other gods that neither they nor you nor your ancestors ever knew. [4]I sent all my servants, the prophets, to you again and again. By them I said to you, 'Don't do this terrible thing that I hate.' [5]But they did not listen or pay attention. They did not stop doing evil things and burning incense to other gods. [6]So I showed my great anger against them. I poured out my anger in the towns of Judah and the streets of Jerusalem so they are only ruins and piles of stones today.

[7]"Now the LORD All-Powerful, the God of Israel, says: Why are you doing such great harm to yourselves? You are cutting off the men and women, children and babies from the family of Judah, leaving yourselves without anyone from the family of Judah. [8]Why do you want to make me angry by making idols? Why do you burn incense to the gods of Egypt, where you have come to live? You will destroy yourselves. Other nations will speak evil of you and make fun of you. [9]Have you forgotten about the evil things your ancestors did? And have you forgotten the evil the kings and queens of Judah did? Have you forgotten about the evil you and your wives did? These things were done in the country of Judah and in the streets of Jerusalem. [10]Even to this day the people of Judah are still too proud. They have not learned to respect me or to follow

my teachings. They have not obeyed the laws I gave you and your ancestors.

[11]"So this is what the LORD All-Powerful, the God of Israel, says: I am determined to bring disasters on you. I will destroy the whole family of Judah. [12]The few who were left alive from Judah were determined to go to Egypt and settle there, but they will all die in Egypt. They will be killed in war or die from hunger. From the least important to the greatest, they will be killed in war or die from hunger. Other nations will speak evil about them. People will be shocked by what has happened to them. They will become a curse word, and people will insult them. [13]I will punish those people who have gone to live in Egypt, just as I punished Jerusalem, using swords, hunger, and terrible diseases. [14]Of the people of Judah who were left alive and have gone to live in Egypt, none will escape my punishment. They want to return to Judah and live there, but none of them will live to return to Judah, except a few people who will escape."

[15]A large group of the people of Judah who lived in southern Egypt were meeting together. Among them were many women of Judah who were burning incense to other gods, and their husbands knew it. All these people said to Jeremiah, [16]"We will not listen to the message from the LORD that you spoke to us. [17]We promised to make sacrifices to the Queen Goddess, and we will certainly do everything we promised. We will burn incense and pour out drink offerings to worship her, just as we, our ancestors, kings, and officers did in the past. All of us did these things in the towns of Judah and in the streets of Jerusalem. At that time we had plenty of food and were successful, and nothing bad happened to us. [18]But since we stopped making sacrifices to the Queen Goddess and stopped pouring out drink offerings to her, we have had great problems. Our people have also been killed in war and by hunger."

[19]The women said, "Our husbands knew what we were doing. We had their permission to burn incense to the Queen Goddess and to pour out drink offerings to her. Our husbands knew we were making cakes that

looked like her and were pouring out drink offerings to her."

²⁰Then Jeremiah spoke to all the people—men and women—who answered him. ²¹He said to them, "The LORD remembered that you and your ancestors, kings and officers, and the people of the land burned incense in the towns of Judah and in the streets of Jerusalem. He remembered and thought about it. ²²Then he could not be patient with you any longer. He hated the terrible things you did. So he made your country an empty desert, where no one lives. Other people curse that country. And so it is today. ²³All this happened because you burned incense to other gods. You sinned against the LORD. You did not obey him or follow his teachings or the laws he gave you. You did not keep your part of the agreement with him. So this disaster has happened to you. It is there for you to see."

²⁴Then Jeremiah said to all those men and women, "People of Judah who are now in Egypt, hear the word of the LORD: ²⁵The LORD All-Powerful, the God of Israel, says: You and your wives did what you said you would do. You said, 'We will certainly keep the promises we made. We promised to make sacrifices to the Queen Goddess and to pour out drink offerings to her.' So, go ahead. Do the things you promised, and keep your promises. ²⁶But hear the word of the LORD. Listen, all you Jews living in Egypt. The LORD says, 'I have sworn by my great name: The people of Judah now living in Egypt will never again use my name to make promises. They will never again say in Egypt, "As surely as the Lord GOD lives . . . " ²⁷I am watching over them, not to take care of them, but to hurt them. The Jews who live in Egypt will die from swords or hunger until they are all destroyed. ²⁸A few will escape being killed by the sword and will come back to Judah from Egypt. Then, of the people of Judah who came to live in Egypt, those who are left alive will know if my word or their word came true. ²⁹I will give you a sign that I will punish you here in Egypt,' says the LORD. 'When you see it happen, you will know that my promises to hurt you will really happen.' ³⁰This is what the LORD says: 'Hophra king of Egypt

has enemies who want to kill him. Soon I will hand him over to his enemies just as I handed Zedekiah king of Judah over to Nebuchadnezzar king of Babylon, who wanted to kill him.'"

PSALM 119:97–104

⁹⁷How I love your teachings!
  I think about them all day long.
⁹⁸Your commands make me wiser than my
    enemies,
  because they are mine forever.
⁹⁹I am wiser than all my teachers,
  because I think about your rules.
¹⁰⁰I have more understanding than the
    elders,
  because I follow your orders.
¹⁰¹I have avoided every evil way
  so I could obey your word.
¹⁰²I haven't walked away from your laws,
  because you yourself are my teacher.
¹⁰³Your promises are sweet to me,
  sweeter than honey in my mouth!
¹⁰⁴Your orders give me understanding,
  so I hate lying ways.

PROVERBS 28:3

³Rulers who mistreat the poor
  are like a hard rain that destroys the
    crops.

2 TIMOTHY 2:1–26

A Loyal Soldier of Christ Jesus

2 You then, Timothy, my child, be strong in the grace we have in Christ Jesus. ²You should teach people whom you can trust the things you and many others have heard me say. Then they will be able to teach others. ³Share in the troubles we have like a good soldier of Christ Jesus. ⁴A soldier wants to please the enlisting officer, so no one serving in the army wastes time with everyday matters. ⁵Also an athlete who takes part in a contest must obey all the rules in order to win. ⁶The farmer who works hard should be the first person to get some of the food that was grown. ⁷Think about what I am saying, because the Lord will give you the ability to understand everything.

[8]Remember Jesus Christ, who was raised from the dead, who is from the family of David. This is the Good News I preach, [9]and I am suffering because of it to the point of being bound with chains like a criminal. But God's teaching is not in chains. [10]So I patiently accept all these troubles so that those whom God has chosen can have the salvation that is in Christ Jesus. With that salvation comes glory that never ends.

[11]This teaching is true:
If we died with him, we will also live with him.
[12]If we accept suffering, we will also rule with him.
If we say we don't know him, he will say he doesn't know us.
[13]If we are not faithful, he will still be faithful,
because he must be true to who he is.

A Worker Pleasing to God

[14]Continue teaching these things, warning people in God's presence not to argue about words. It does not help anyone, and it ruins those who listen. [15]Make every effort to give yourself to God as the kind of person he will approve. Be a worker who is not ashamed and who uses the true teaching in the right way. [16]Stay away from foolish, useless talk, because that will lead people further away from God. [17]Their evil teaching will spread like a sickness inside the body. Hymenaeus and Philetus are

like that. [18]They have left the true teaching, saying that the rising from the dead has already taken place, and so they are destroying the faith of some people. [19]But God's strong foundation continues to stand. These words are written on the seal: "The Lord knows those who belong to him,"[n] and "Everyone who wants to belong to the Lord must stop doing wrong."

[20]In a large house there are not only things made of gold and silver, but also things made of wood and clay. Some things are used for special purposes, and others are made for ordinary jobs. [21]All who make themselves clean from evil will be used for special purposes. They will be made holy, useful to the Master, ready to do any good work.

[22]But run away from the evil desires of youth. Try hard to live right and to have faith, love, and peace, together with those who trust in the Lord from pure hearts. [23]Stay away from foolish and stupid arguments, because you know they grow into quarrels. [24]And a servant of the Lord must not quarrel but must be kind to everyone, a good teacher, and patient. [25]The Lord's servant must gently teach those who disagree. Then maybe God will let them change their minds so they can accept the truth. [26]And they may wake up and escape from the trap of the devil, who catches them to do what he wants.

OCTOBER 30

JEREMIAH 45:1—46:28

A Message to Baruch

45 It was the fourth year that Jehoiakim son of Josiah was king of Judah. Jeremiah the prophet told these things to Baruch son of Neriah, and Baruch wrote them on a scroll: [2]"This is what the LORD, the God of Israel, says to you, Baruch: [3]You have said, 'How terrible it is for me! The

LORD has given me sorrow along with my pain. I am tired because of my suffering and cannot rest.'"

[4]The LORD said, "Say this to Baruch: 'This is what the LORD says: I will soon tear down what I have built, and I will pull up what I have planted everywhere in Judah. [5]Baruch, you are looking for great things for yourself. Don't look for them, because I will bring disaster on all the people, says the LORD. You

will have to go many places, but I will let you escape alive wherever you go.'"

Messages to the Nations

46 The LORD spoke this word to Jeremiah the prophet about the nations:

²This message is to Egypt. It is about the army of Neco king of Egypt, which was defeated at the city of Carchemish on the Euphrates River by Nebuchadnezzar king of Babylon. This was in the fourth year that Jehoiakim son of Josiah was king of Judah. This is the LORD's message to Egypt:

³"Prepare your shields, large and small,
  and march out for battle!
⁴Harness the horses
  and get on them!
Go to your places for battle
  and put on your helmets!
Polish your spears.
Put on your armor!
⁵What do I see?
  That army is terrified,
and the soldiers are running away.
  Their warriors are defeated.
They run away quickly
  without looking back.
There is terror on every side!" says the
  LORD.
⁶"The fast runners cannot run away;
  the strong soldiers cannot escape.
They stumble and fall
  in the north, by the Euphrates River.
⁷Who is this, rising up like the Nile River,
  like strong, fast rivers?
⁸Egypt rises up like the Nile River,
  like strong, fast rivers.
Egypt says, 'I will rise up and cover the
  earth.
I will destroy cities and the people in
  them!'
⁹Horsemen, charge into battle!
  Chariot drivers, drive hard!
March on, brave soldiers—
  soldiers from the countries of Cush and
  Put who carry shields,
  soldiers from Lydia who use bows.
¹⁰"But that day belongs to the Lord GOD
  All-Powerful.
At that time he will give those people
  the punishment they deserve.

The sword will kill until it is finished,
  until it satisfies its thirst for their
  blood.
The Lord GOD All-Powerful will offer a
  sacrifice
in the land of the north, by the
  Euphrates River.

¹¹"Go up to Gilead and get some balm,
  people of Egypt!
You have prepared many medicines,
  but they will not work;
  you will not be healed.
¹²The nations have heard of your shame,
  and your cries fill all the earth.
One warrior has run into another;
  both of them have fallen down
  together!"

¹³This is the message the LORD spoke to Jeremiah the prophet about Nebuchadnezzar king of Babylon's coming to attack Egypt:

¹⁴"Announce this message in Egypt, and
  preach it in Migdol.
Preach it also in the cities of Memphis
  and Tahpanhes:
'Get ready for war,
  because the battle is all around you.'
¹⁵Egypt, why were your warriors killed?
  They could not stand because the LORD
  pushed them down.
¹⁶They stumbled again and again
  and fell over each other.
They said, 'Get up. Let's go back
  to our own people and our homeland.
We must get away from our enemy's
  sword!'
¹⁷In their homelands those soldiers called
  out,
'The king of Egypt is only a lot of noise.
  He missed his chance for glory!'"

¹⁸The King's name is the LORD
  All-Powerful.
He says, "As surely as I live,
a powerful leader will come.
He will be like Mount Tabor among the
  mountains,
  like Mount Carmel by the sea.
¹⁹People of Egypt, pack your things
  to be taken away as captives,
because Memphis will be destroyed.

It will be a ruin, and no one will live there.

20"Egypt is like a beautiful young cow,
but a horsefly is coming
from the north to attack her.
21The hired soldiers in Egypt's army
are like fat calves,
because even they all turn and run away together;
they do not stand strong against the attack.
Their time of destruction is coming;
they will soon be punished.
22Egypt is like a hissing snake that is trying to escape.
The enemy comes closer and closer.
They come against Egypt with axes
like men who cut down trees.
23They will chop down Egypt's army
as if it were a great forest," says the LORD.
"There are more enemy soldiers than locusts;
there are too many to count.
24The people of Egypt will be ashamed.
They will be handed over to the enemy
from the north."

25The LORD All-Powerful, the God of Israel, says: "Very soon I will punish Amon, the god of the city of Thebes. And I will punish Egypt, her kings, her gods, and the people who depend on the king. 26I will hand those people over to their enemies, who want to kill them. I will give them to Nebuchadnezzar king of Babylon and his officers. But in the future, Egypt will live in peace as it once did," says the LORD.

A Message to Israel

27"People of Jacob, my servants, don't be afraid;
don't be frightened, Israel.
I will surely save you from those faraway places
and your children from the lands where they are captives.
The people of Jacob will have peace and safety again,
and no one will make them afraid.
28People of Jacob, my servants, do not be afraid,

because I am with you," says the LORD.
"I will completely destroy the many different nations
where I scattered you.
But I will not completely destroy you.
I will punish you fairly,
but I will not let you escape your punishment."

PSALM 119:105–112

105Your word is like a lamp for my feet
and a light for my path.
106I will do what I have promised
and obey your fair laws.
107I have suffered for a long time.
LORD, give me life by your word.
108LORD, accept my willing praise
and teach me your laws.
109My life is always in danger,
but I haven't forgotten your teachings.
110Wicked people have set a trap for me,
but I haven't strayed from your orders.
111I will follow your rules forever,
because they make me happy.
112I will try to do what you demand
forever, until the end.

PROVERBS 28:4

4Those who disobey what they have been taught praise the wicked,
but those who obey what they have been taught are against them.

2 TIMOTHY 3:1—4:8

The Last Days

3 Remember this! In the last days there will be many troubles, 2because people will love themselves, love money, brag, and be proud. They will say evil things against others and will not obey their parents or be thankful or be the kind of people God wants. 3They will not love others, will refuse to forgive, will gossip, and will not control themselves. They will be cruel, will hate what is good, 4will turn against their friends, and will do foolish things without thinking. They will be conceited, will love pleasure instead of God, 5and will act as if they serve God but will not have his power. Stay away from those

people. ⁶Some of them go into homes and get control of silly women who are full of sin and are led by many evil desires. ⁷These women are always learning new teachings, but they are never able to understand the truth fully. ⁸Just as Jannes and Jambres were against Moses, these people are against the truth. Their thinking has been ruined, and they have failed in trying to follow the faith. ⁹But they will not be successful in what they do, because as with Jannes and Jambres, everyone will see that they are foolish.

Obey the Teachings

¹⁰But you have followed what I teach, the way I live, my goal, faith, patience, and love. You know I never give up. ¹¹You know how I have been hurt and have suffered, as in Antioch, Iconium, and Lystra. I have suffered, but the Lord saved me from all those troubles. ¹²Everyone who wants to live as God desires, in Christ Jesus, will be persecuted. ¹³But people who are evil and cheat others will go from bad to worse. They will fool others, but they will also be fooling themselves.

¹⁴But you should continue following the teachings you learned. You know they are true, because you trust those who taught you. ¹⁵Since you were a child you have known the Holy Scriptures which are able to make you wise. And that wisdom leads to salvation through faith in Christ Jesus. ¹⁶All Scripture is inspired by God and is useful for teaching, for showing people what is wrong in their lives, for correcting faults, and for teaching how to live right. ¹⁷Using the Scriptures, the person who serves God will be capable, having all that is needed to do every good work.

4 I give you a command in the presence of God and Christ Jesus, the One who will judge the living and the dead, and by his coming and his kingdom: ²Preach the Good News. Be ready at all times, and tell people what they need to do. Tell them when they are wrong. Encourage them with great patience and careful teaching, ³because the time will come when people will not listen to the true teaching but will find many more teachers who please them by saying the things they want to hear. ⁴They will stop listening to the truth and will begin to follow false stories. ⁵But you should control yourself at all times, accept troubles, do the work of telling the Good News, and complete all the duties of a servant of God.

⁶My life is being given as an offering to God, and the time has come for me to leave this life. ⁷I have fought the good fight, I have finished the race, I have kept the faith. ⁸Now, a crown is being held for me—a crown for being right with God. The Lord, the judge who judges rightly, will give the crown to me on that dayⁿ—not only to me but to all those who have waited with love for him to come again.

OCTOBER 31

JEREMIAH 47:1—48:47

A Message to the Philistines

47 Before the king of Egypt attacked the city of Gaza, the LORD spoke his word to Jeremiah the prophet. This message is to the Philistine people.

²This is what the LORD says:
"See, the enemy is gathering in the north like rising waters.
They will become like an overflowing stream

and will cover the whole country like a flood,
   even the towns and the people living in them.
Everyone living in that country
   will cry for help;
   the people will cry painfully.
³They will hear the sound of the running horses
   and the noisy chariots
   and the rumbling chariot wheels.

4:8 day The day Christ will come to judge all people and take his people to live with him.

Parents will not help their children to
safety,
because they will be too weak to help.
[4]The time has come
to destroy all the Philistines.
It is time to destroy all who are left alive
who could help the cities of Tyre and
Sidon.
The LORD will soon destroy the Philistines,
those left alive from the island of Crete.
[5]The people from the city of Gaza will be
sad and shave their heads.
The people from the city of Ashkelon
will be made silent.
Those left alive from the valley,
how long will you cut yourselves?[n]

[6]"You cry, 'Sword of the LORD,
how long will you keep fighting?
Return to your holder.
Stop and be still.'
[7]But how can his sword rest
when the LORD has given it a
command?
He has ordered it
to attack Ashkelon and the seacoast."

A Message to Moab

48 This message is to the country of
Moab.

This is what the LORD All-Powerful, the
God of Israel, says:
"How terrible it will be for the city of
Nebo,
because it will be ruined.
The town of Kiriathaim will be disgraced
and captured;
the strong city will be disgraced and
shattered.
[2]Moab will not be praised again.
Men in the town of Heshbon plan
Moab's defeat.
They say, 'Come, let us put an end to
that nation!'
Town of Madmen,[n] you will also be
silenced.
The sword will chase you.
[3]Listen to the cries from the town of
Horonaim,

cries of much confusion and
destruction.
[4]Moab will be broken up.
Her little children will cry for help.
[5]Moab's people go up the path to the town
of Luhith,
crying loudly as they go.
On the road down to Horonaim,
cries of pain and suffering can be
heard.
[6]Run! Run for your lives!
Go like a bush being blown through the
desert.
[7]You trust in the things you do and in
your wealth,
so you also will be captured.
The god Chemosh will go into captivity
and his priests and officers with him.
[8]The destroyer will come against every
town;
not one town will escape.
The valley will be ruined,
and the high plain will be destroyed,
as the LORD has said.
[9]Give wings to Moab,
because she will surely leave her land.
Moab's towns will become empty,
with no one to live in them.
[10]A curse will be on anyone who doesn't do
what the LORD says,
and a curse will be on anyone who
holds back his sword from killing.

[11]"The people of Moab have never known
trouble.
They are like wine left to settle;
they have never been poured from one
jar to another.
They have not been taken into
captivity.
So they taste as they did before,
and their smell has not changed.
[12]A time is coming," says the LORD,
"When I will send people to pour you
from your jars.
They will empty Moab's jars
and smash her jugs.
[13]The people of Israel trusted that god in
the town of Bethel,

---

and they were ashamed when there was
no help.
In the same way Moab will be ashamed
of their god Chemosh.

¹⁴"You cannot say, 'We are warriors!
We are brave men in battle!'
¹⁵The destroyer of Moab and her towns
has arrived.
Her best young men will be killed!"
says the King,
whose name is the LORD All-Powerful.
¹⁶"The end of Moab is near,
and she will soon be destroyed.
¹⁷All you who live around Moab,
all you who know her, cry for her.
Say, 'The ruler's power is broken;
Moab's power and glory are gone.'

¹⁸"You people living in the town of Dibon,
come down from your place of
honor
and sit on the dry ground,
because the destroyer of Moab has come
against you.
And he has destroyed your strong,
walled cities.
¹⁹You people living in the town of Aroer,
stand next to the road and watch.
See the man running away and the
woman escaping.
Ask them, 'What happened?'
²⁰Moab is filled with shame, because she is
ruined.
Cry, Moab, cry out!
Announce at the Arnon River
that Moab is destroyed.
²¹People on the high plain have been
punished.
Judgment has come to these towns:
Holon, Jahzah, and Mephaath;
²² Dibon, Nebo, and Beth Diblathaim;
²³ Kiriathaim, Beth Gamul, and Beth
Meon;
²⁴ Kerioth and Bozrah.
Judgment has come to all the towns of
Moab, far and near.
²⁵Moab's strength has been cut off,
and its arm broken!" says the LORD.

²⁶"The people of Moab thought they were
greater than the LORD,

so punish them until they act as if they
are drunk.
Moab will fall and roll around in its own
vomit,
and people will even make fun of it.
²⁷Moab, you made fun of Israel.
Israel was caught in the middle of a
gang of thieves.
When you spoke about Israel,
you shook your head and acted as if
you were better than it.
²⁸People in Moab, leave your towns empty
and go live among the rocks.
Be like a dove that makes its nest
at the entrance of a cave.

²⁹"We have heard that the people of Moab
are proud,
very proud.
They are proud, very proud,
and in their hearts they think they are
important."
³⁰The LORD says,
"I know Moab's great pride, but it is
useless.
Moab's bragging accomplishes nothing.
³¹So I cry sadly for Moab,
for everyone in Moab.
I moan for the people from the town of
Kir Hareseth.
³²I cry with the people of the town of Jazer
for you, the grapevines of the town of
Sibmah.
In the past your vines spread all the way
to the sea,
as far as the sea of Jazer.
But the destroyer has taken over
your fruit and grapes.
³³Joy and happiness are gone
from the large, rich fields of Moab.
I have stopped the flow of wine from the
winepresses.
No one walks on the grapes with shouts
of joy.
There are shouts,
but not shouts of joy.

³⁴"Their crying can be heard from Moabite
towns,
from Heshbon to Elealeh and Jahaz.
It can be heard from Zoar as far away as
Horonaim and Eglath Shelishiyah.

Even the waters of Nimrim are dried
up.
[35]I will stop Moab
from making burnt offerings at the
places of worship
and from burning incense to their
gods," says the LORD.

[36]"My heart cries sadly for Moab like a
flute playing a funeral song.
It cries like a flute for the people from
Kir Haseth.
The money they made has all been
taken away.
[37]Every head has been shaved
and every beard cut off.
Everyone's hands are cut,
and everyone wears rough cloth around
his waist.[n]
[38]People are crying on every roof[n] in
Moab
and in every public square.
There is nothing but sadness,
because I have broken Moab
like a jar no one wants," says the
LORD.
[39]"Moab is shattered! The people are
crying!
Moab turns away in shame!
People all around her make fun of her.
The things that happened fill them
with great fear."

[40]This is what the LORD says:
"Look! Someone is coming, like an eagle
diving down from the sky
and spreading its wings over Moab.
[41]The towns of Moab will be captured,
and the strong, walled cities will be
defeated.
At that time Moab's warriors will be
frightened,
like a woman who is having a baby.
[42]The nation of Moab will be destroyed,
because they thought they were greater
than the LORD.
[43]Fear, deep pits, and traps wait for you,
people of Moab," says the LORD.

[44]"People will run from fear,
but they will fall into the pits.
Anyone who climbs out of the pits
will be caught in the traps.
I will bring the year of punishment to
Moab," says the LORD.

[45]"People have run from the powerful
enemy
and have gone to Heshbon for safety.
But fire started in Heshbon;
a blaze has spread from the hometown
of Sihon king of Moab.
It burned up the leaders of Moab
and destroyed those proud people.
[46]How terrible it is for you, Moab!
The people who worship Chemosh have
been destroyed.
Your sons have been taken captive,
and your daughters have been taken
away.

[47]"But in days to come,
I will make good things happen again
to Moab," says the LORD.
This ends the judgment on Moab.

PSALM 119:113–120

[113]I hate disloyal people,
but I love your teachings.
[114]You are my hiding place and my shield;
I hope in your word.
[115]Get away from me, you who do evil,
so I can keep my God's commands.
[116]Support me as you promised so I can
live.
Don't let me be embarrassed because of
my hopes.
[117]Help me, and I will be saved.
I will always respect your demands.
[118]You reject those who ignore your
demands,
because their lies mislead them.
[119]You throw away the wicked of the world
like trash.
So I will love your rules.
[120]I shake in fear of you;
I respect your laws.

48:37 Every head . . . waist. The people did these things to show their sadness for those who had died.   **48:38 roof** In Bible
times houses were built with flat roofs. The roof was used for drying things such as flax and fruit. And it was used as an extra room, as a place for worship, and as a cool place to sleep in the summer.

PROVERBS 28:5

5Evil people do not understand justice,
   but those who follow the LORD
   understand it completely.

2 TIMOTHY 4:9-22

Personal Words

9Do your best to come to me as soon as
you can, 10because Demas, who loved this
world, left me and went to Thessalonica.
Crescens went to Galatia, and Titus went to
Dalmatia. 11Luke is the only one still with
me. Get Mark and bring him with you when
you come, because he can help me in my
work here. 12I sent Tychicus to Ephesus.
13When I was in Troas, I left my coat there
with Carpus. So when you come, bring it to
me, along with my books, particularly the
ones written on parchment.[n]

14Alexander the metalworker did many
harmful things against me. The Lord will
punish him for what he did. 15You also
should be careful that he does not hurt you,
because he fought strongly against our
teaching.

16The first time I defended myself, no one
helped me; everyone left me. May they be
forgiven. 17But the Lord stayed with me and
gave me strength so I could fully tell the
Good News to all those who are not Jews. So
I was saved from the lion's mouth. 18The
Lord will save me when anyone tries to hurt
me, and he will bring me safely to his heavenly kingdom. Glory forever and ever be the
Lord's. Amen.

Final Greetings

19Greet Priscilla and Aquila and the family of Onesiphorus. 20Erastus stayed in
Corinth, and I left Trophimus sick in Miletus. 21Try as hard as you can to come to me
before winter.

Eubulus sends greetings to you. Also Pu-
dens, Linus, Claudia, and all the brothers
and sisters in Christ greet you.

22The Lord be with your spirit. Grace be
with you.

4:13 parchment A writing paper made from the skins of sheep.

NOVEMBER 1

JEREMIAH 49:1—50:46

A Message to Ammon

49 This message is to the Ammonite people.

This is what the Lord says:
"Do you think that Israel has no children?
Do you think there is no one to take the
land when the parents die?
If that were true, why did Molech take
Gad's land
and why did Molech's people settle in
Gad's towns?"
²The Lord says,
"The time will come when I will make
Rabbah,
the capital city of the Ammonites, hear
the battle cry.
It will become a hill covered with ruins,
and the towns around it will be burned.
Those people forced Israel out of that land,
but now Israel will force them out!"
says the Lord.
³"People in the town of Heshbon, cry
sadly because the town of Ai is
destroyed!
Those who live in Rabbah, cry out!
Put on your rough cloth to show your
sadness, and cry loudly.
Run here and there for safety inside the
walls,
because Molech will be taken captive
and his priests and officers with him.
⁴You brag about your valleys
and about the fruit in your valleys.
You are like an unfaithful child
who believes his treasures will save him.
You think, 'Who would attack me?'
⁵I will soon bring terror on you
from everyone around you,"
says the Lord God All-Powerful.
"You will all be forced to run away,
and no one will be able to gather you.

⁶"But the time will come
when I will make good things happen
to the Ammonites again,"
says the Lord.

A Message to Edom

⁷This message is to Edom. This is what
the Lord All-Powerful says:
"Is there no more wisdom in the town of
Teman?
Can the wise men of Edom no longer
give good advice?
Have they lost their wisdom?
⁸You people living in the town of Dedan,
run away and hide in deep caves,
because I will bring disaster on the
people of Esau.
It is time for me to punish them.
⁹If workers came and picked the grapes
from your vines,
they would leave a few grapes behind.
If robbers came at night,
they would steal only enough for
themselves.
¹⁰But I will strip Edom bare.
I will find all their hiding places,
so they will not be able to hide from
me.
The children, relatives, and neighbors
will die,
and Edom will be no more.
¹¹Leave the orphans, and I will take care of
them.
Your widows also can trust in me."
¹²This is what the Lord says: "Some people did not deserve to be punished, but they
had to drink from the cup of suffering anyway. People of Edom, you deserve to be
punished, so you will not escape punishment. You must certainly drink from the
cup of suffering." ¹³The Lord says, "I swear
by my own name that the city of Bozrah
will become a pile of ruins! People will be
shocked by what happened there. They will
insult that city and speak evil of it. And all
the towns around it will become ruins forever."
¹⁴I have heard a message from the Lord.
A messenger has been sent among the
nations, saying,
"Gather your armies to attack it!
Get ready for battle!"

¹⁵"Soon I will make you the smallest of
  nations,
  and you will be greatly hated by
    everyone.
¹⁶Edom, you frightened other nations,
  but your pride has fooled you.
You live in the hollow places of the cliff
  and control the high places of the hills.
Even if you build your home as high as
    an eagle's nest,
  I will bring you down from there," says
    the LORD.

¹⁷"Edom will be destroyed.
  People who pass by will be shocked to
    see the destroyed cities,
  and they will be amazed at all her
    injuries.
¹⁸Edom will be destroyed like the cities of
    Sodom and Gomorrah
  and the towns around them," says the
    LORD.
  "No one will live there!
  No one will stay in Edom.

¹⁹"Like a lion coming up from the thick
    bushes near the Jordan River
  to attack a strong pen for sheep,
I will suddenly chase Edom from its
    land.
  Who is the one I have chosen to do
    this?
There is no one like me,
  no one who can take me to court.
  None of their leaders can stand up
    against me."

²⁰So listen to what the LORD has planned to
  do against Edom.
  Listen to what he has decided to do to
    the people in the town of Teman.
He will surely drag away the young ones
    of Edom.
  Their hometowns will surely be
    shocked at what happens to them.
²¹At the sound of Edom's fall, the earth will
    shake.
  Their cry will be heard all the way to
    the Red Sea.
²²The LORD is like an eagle swooping down
  and spreading its wings over the city of
    Bozrah.

At that time Edom's soldiers will become
    very frightened,
  like a woman having a baby.

A Message to Damascus

²³This message is to the city of Damascus:
  "The towns of Hamath and Arpad are
    put to shame,
  because they have heard bad news.
They are discouraged.
  They are troubled like the tossing sea.
²⁴The city of Damascus has become weak.
  The people want to run away;
  they are ready to panic.
The people feel pain and suffering,
  like a woman giving birth to a baby.
²⁵Damascus was a city of my joy.
  Why have the people not left that
    famous city yet?
²⁶Surely the young men will die in the city
    squares,
  and all her soldiers will be killed at that
    time," says the LORD All-Powerful.
²⁷"I will set fire to the walls of Damascus,
  and it will completely burn the strong
    cities of King Ben-Hadad."

A Message to Kedar and Hazor

²⁸This message is to the tribe of Kedar
and the kingdoms of Hazor, which Nebuchadnezzar king of Babylon defeated. This
is what the LORD says:
  "Go and attack the people of Kedar,
  and destroy the people of the East.
²⁹Their tents and flocks will be taken
    away.
  Their belongings will be carried off—
    their tents, all their goods, and their
      camels.
Men will shout to them,
  'Terror on every side!'

³⁰"Run away quickly!
  People in Hazor, find a good place to
    hide!" says the LORD.
  "Nebuchadnezzar king of Babylon has
    made plans against you
  and wants to defeat you.

³¹"Get up! Attack the nation that is
    comfortable,
  that is sure no one will defeat it," says
    the LORD.

"It does not have gates or fences to
    protect it.
Its people live alone.
32The enemy will steal their camels
    and their large herds of cattle as war
        prizes.
I will scatter the people who cut their
        hair short to every part of the earth,
    and I will bring disaster on them from
        everywhere," says the LORD.
33"The city of Hazor will become a home
    for wild dogs;
it will be an empty desert forever.
No one will live there,
    and no one will stay in it."

A Message to Elam

34Soon after Zedekiah became king of Judah, the LORD spoke this word to Jeremiah
the prophet. This message is to the nation of
Elam.

35This is what the LORD All-Powerful says:
"I will soon break Elam's bow,
    its greatest strength.
36I will bring the four winds against Elam
    from the four corners of the skies.
I will scatter its people everywhere the
        four winds blow;
    its captives will go to every nation.
37I will terrify Elam in front of their
        enemies,
    who want to destroy them.
I will bring disaster to Elam
    and show them how angry I am!" says
        the LORD.
"I will send a sword to chase Elam
    until I have killed them all.
38I will set up my throne in Elam to show
        that I am king,
    and I will destroy its king and its
        officers!" says the LORD.

39"But I will make good things happen to
        Elam again
    in the future," says the LORD.

A Message to Babylon

50 This is the message the LORD spoke to
Babylon and the Babylonian people
through Jeremiah the prophet.
2"Announce this to the nations.
Lift up a banner and tell them.

Speak the whole message and say:
'Babylon will be captured.
The god Bel will be put to shame,
    and the god Marduk will be afraid.
Babylon's gods will be put to shame,
    and her idols will be afraid!'
3A nation from the north will attack
        Babylon
    and make it like an empty desert.
No one will live there;
    both people and animals will run
        away."

4The LORD says, "At that time
    the people of Israel and Judah will
        come together.
They will cry and look for the LORD
    their God.
5Those people will ask how to go to
        Jerusalem
    and will start in that direction.
They will come and join themselves to
    the LORD.
They will make an agreement with him
    that will last forever,
an agreement that will never be
    forgotten.

6"My people have been like lost sheep.
    Their leaders have led them in the
        wrong way
and made them wander around in the
    mountains and hills.
They forgot where their resting place
    was.
7Whoever saw my people hurt them.
    And those enemies said, 'We did
        nothing wrong.
Those people sinned against the LORD,
    their true resting place,
the God their fathers trusted.'

8"Run away from Babylon,
    and leave the land of the Babylonians.
Be like the goats that lead the flock.
9I will soon bring against Babylon
    many great nations from the north.
They will take their places for war
        against it,
    and it will be captured by people from
        the north.
Their arrows are like trained soldiers

who do not return from war with
empty hands.

¹⁰The enemy will take all the wealth from
the Babylonians.

Those enemy soldiers will get all they
want," says the LORD.

¹¹"Babylon, you are excited and happy,
because you took my land.

You dance around like a young cow in
the grain.

Your laughter is like the neighing of
male horses.

¹²Your mother will be very ashamed;
the woman who gave birth to you will
be disgraced.

Soon Babylonia will be the least
important of all the nations.

She will be an empty, dry desert.

¹³Because of the LORD's anger,
no one will live there.

She will be completely empty.

Everyone who passes by Babylon will be
shocked.

They will shake their heads when they
see all her injuries.

¹⁴"Take your positions for war against
Babylon,
all you soldiers with bows.

Shoot your arrows at Babylon! Do not
save any of them,

because Babylon has sinned against the
LORD.

¹⁵Soldiers around Babylon, shout the war
cry!

Babylon has surrendered, her towers
have fallen,
and her walls have been torn down.

The LORD is giving her people the
punishment they deserve.

You nations should give her what she
deserves;
do to her what she has done to others.

¹⁶Don't let the people from Babylon plant
their crops
or gather the harvest.

The soldiers treated their captives
cruelly.

Now, let everyone go back home.

Let everyone run to his own country.

¹⁷"The people of Israel are like a flock of
sheep that are scattered
from being chased by lions.

The first lion to eat them up
was the king of Assyria.

The last lion to crush their bones
was Nebuchadnezzar king of Babylon."

¹⁸So this is what the LORD All-Powerful,
the God of Israel, says:

"I will punish the king of Babylon and
his country
as I punished the king of Assyria.

¹⁹But I will bring the people of Israel back
to their own pasture.

They will eat on Mount Carmel and in
Bashan.

They will eat and be full
on the hills of Ephraim and Gilead."

²⁰The LORD says,
"At that time people will try to find
Israel's guilt,
but there will be no guilt.

People will try to find Judah's sins,
but no sins will be found,

because I will leave a few people alive
from Israel and Judah,
and I will forgive their sins.

²¹"Attack the land of Merathaim.
Attack the people who live in Pekod.

Chase them, kill them, and completely
destroy them.

Do everything I commanded you!" says
the LORD.

²²"The noise of battle can be heard all over
the country;
it is the noise of much destruction.

²³Babylon was the hammer of the whole
earth,
but how broken and shattered that
hammer is now.

It is truly the most ruined
of all the nations.

²⁴Babylon, I set a trap for you,
and you were caught before you knew
it.

You fought against the LORD,
so you were found and taken prisoner.

²⁵The LORD has opened up his storeroom
and brought out the weapons of his
anger,

because the Lord God All-Powerful has
work to do
in the land of the Babylonians.
²⁶Come against Babylon from far away.
Break open her storehouses of grain.
Pile up her dead bodies like heaps of
grain.
Completely destroy Babylon
and do not leave anyone alive.
²⁷Kill all the young men in Babylon;
let them be killed like animals.
How terrible it will be for them, because
the time has come for their defeat;
it is time for them to be punished.
²⁸Listen to the people running to escape
the country of Babylon!
They are telling Jerusalem
how the Lord our God is punishing
Babylon as it deserves
for destroying his Temple.

²⁹"Call for the archers
to come against Babylon.
Tell them to surround the city,
and let no one escape.
Pay her back for what she has done;
do to her what she has done to other
nations.
Babylon acted with pride against the Lord,
the Holy One of Israel.
³⁰So her young men will be killed in her
streets.
All her soldiers will die on that day,"
says the Lord.
³¹"Babylon, you are too proud, and I am
against you,"
says the Lord God All-Powerful.
"The time has come
for you to be punished.
³²Proud Babylon will stumble and fall,
and no one will help her get up.
I will start a fire in her towns,
and it will burn up everything around
her."
³³This is what the Lord All-Powerful says:
"The people of Israel
and Judah are slaves.
The enemy took them as prisoners
and won't let them go.
³⁴But God is strong and will buy them back.
His name is the Lord All-Powerful.

He will surely defend them with power
so he can give rest to their land.
But he will not give rest to those living
in Babylon."
³⁵The Lord says,
"Let a sword kill the people living in
Babylon
and her officers and wise men!
³⁶Let a sword kill her false prophets,
and they will become fools.
Let a sword kill her warriors,
and they will be full of terror.
³⁷Let a sword kill her horses and chariots
and all the soldiers hired from other
countries!
Then they will be like frightened
women.
Let a sword attack her treasures,
so they will be taken away.
³⁸Let a sword attack her waters
so they will be dried up.
She is a land of idols,
and the people go crazy with fear over
them.

³⁹"Desert animals and hyenas will live
there,
and owls will live there,
but no people will ever live there again.
She will never be filled with people
again.
⁴⁰God completely destroyed the cities of
Sodom and Gomorrah
and the towns around them," says the
Lord.
"In the same way no people will live in
Babylon,
and no human being will stay there.

⁴¹"Look! An army is coming from the
north.
A powerful nation and many kings
are coming together from all around
the world.
⁴²Their armies have bows and spears.
The soldiers are cruel and have no
mercy.
As the soldiers come riding on their
horses,
the sound is loud like the roaring sea.
They stand in their places, ready for
battle.

They are ready to attack you, city of
Babylon.
⁴³The king of Babylon heard about those
armies,
and he became helpless with fear.
Distress has gripped him.
His pain is like that of a woman giving
birth to a baby.

⁴⁴"Like a lion coming up from the thick
bushes near the Jordan River
to attack a strong pen for sheep,
I will suddenly chase the people of
Babylon from their land.
Who is the one I have chosen to do this?
There is no one like me,
no one who can take me to court.
None of their leaders can stand up
against me."

⁴⁵So listen to what the LORD has planned to
do against Babylon.
Listen to what he has decided to do to
the people in the city of Babylon.
He will surely drag away the young ones
of Babylon.
Their hometowns will surely be
shocked at what happens to them.
⁴⁶At the sound of Babylon's capture, the
earth will shake.
People in all nations will hear Babylon's
cry of distress.

PSALM 119:121–128

¹²¹I have done what is fair and right.
Don't leave me to those who wrong me.
¹²²Promise that you will help me, your
servant.
Don't let proud people wrong me.
¹²³My eyes are tired from looking for your
salvation
and for your good promise.
¹²⁴Show your love to me, your servant,
and teach me your demands.
¹²⁵I am your servant. Give me wisdom
so I can understand your rules.
¹²⁶LORD, it is time for you to do something,
because people have disobeyed your
teachings.
¹²⁷I love your commands
more than the purest gold.

¹²⁸I respect all your orders,
so I hate lying ways.

PROVERBS 28:6

⁶It is better to be poor and innocent
than to be rich and wicked.

TITUS 1:1–16

1 From Paul, a servant of God and an apostle of Jesus Christ. I was sent to help the
faith of God's chosen people and to help
them know the truth that shows people how
to serve God. ²That faith and that knowledge
come from the hope for life forever, which
God promised to us before time began. And
God cannot lie. ³At the right time God let the
world know about that life through preaching. He trusted me with that work, and I
preached by the command of God our Savior.
⁴To Titus, my true child in the faith we
share:
Grace and peace from God the Father and
Christ Jesus our Savior.

Titus' Work in Crete

⁵I left you in Crete so you could finish doing the things that still needed to be done
and so you could appoint elders in every
town, as I directed you. ⁶An elder must not be
guilty of doing wrong, must have only one
wife, and must have believing children. They
must not be known as children who are wild
and do not cooperate. ⁷As God's managers,
overseers must not be guilty of doing wrong,
being selfish, or becoming angry quickly.
They must not drink too much wine, like to
fight, or try to get rich by cheating others.
⁸Overseers must be ready to welcome guests,
love what is good, be wise, live right, and be
holy and self-controlled. ⁹By holding on to
the trustworthy word just as we teach it, overseers can help people by using true teaching,
and they can show those who are against the
true teaching that they are wrong.
¹⁰There are many people who refuse to
cooperate, who talk about worthless things
and lead others into the wrong way—
mainly those who insist on circumcision to
be saved. ¹¹These people must be stopped,
because they are upsetting whole families by

teaching things they should not teach, which they do to get rich by cheating people. ¹²Even one of their own prophets said, "Cretans are always liars, evil animals, and lazy people who do nothing but eat." ¹³The words that prophet said are true. So firmly tell those people they are wrong so they may become strong in the faith, ¹⁴not accepting Jewish false stories and the commands of people who reject the truth. ¹⁵To those who are pure, all things are pure, but to those who are full of sin and do not believe, nothing is pure. Both their minds and their consciences have been ruined. ¹⁶They say they know God, but their actions show they do not accept him. They are hateful people, they refuse to obey, and they are useless for doing anything good.

NOVEMBER 2

JEREMIAH 51:1—52:34

51 This is what the LORD says:
"I will soon cause a destroying wind to blow
    against Babylon and the Babylonian people.
²I will send foreign people to destroy Babylon
    like a wind that blows chaff away.
They will destroy the land.
Armies will surround the city
    when the day of disaster comes upon her.
³Don't let the Babylonian soldiers prepare their bows to shoot.
    Don't even let them put on their armor.
Don't feel sorry for the young men of Babylon,
    but completely destroy her army.
⁴They will be killed in the land of the Babylonians
    and will die in her streets.
⁵The Lord GOD All-Powerful
    did not leave Israel and Judah,
even though they were completely guilty
    in the presence of the Holy One of Israel.
⁶"Run away from Babylon
    and save your lives!
Don't stay and be killed because of Babylon's sins.
It is time for the LORD to punish Babylon;
    he will give Babylon the punishment she deserves.
⁷Babylon was like a gold cup in the LORD's hand
    that made the whole earth drunk.

The nations drank Babylon's wine,
    so they went crazy.
⁸Babylon has suddenly fallen and been broken.
    Cry for her!
Get balm for her pain,
    and maybe she can be healed.
⁹"Foreigners in Babylon say, 'We tried to heal Babylon,
    but she cannot be healed.
So let us leave her and each go to his own country.
    Babylon's punishment is as high as the sky;
    it reaches to the clouds.'
¹⁰"The people of Judah say, 'The LORD has shown us to be right.
    Come, let us tell in Jerusalem
    what the LORD our God has done.'
¹¹"Sharpen the arrows!
    Pick up your shields!
The LORD has stirred up the kings of the Medes,
    because he wants to destroy Babylon.
The LORD will punish them as they deserve
    for destroying his Temple.
¹²Lift up a banner against the walls of Babylon!
    Bring more guards.
Put the watchmen in their places,
    and get ready for a secret attack!
The LORD will certainly do what he has planned

and what he said he would do against
the people of Babylon.
¹³People of Babylon, you live near much
water
and are rich with many treasures,
but your end as a nation has come.
It is time to stop you from robbing
other nations.
¹⁴The LORD All-Powerful has promised in
his own name:
'Babylon, I will surely fill you with so
many enemy soldiers they will be
like a swarm of locusts.
They will stand over you and shout
their victory.'

¹⁵"The LORD made the earth by his power.
He used his wisdom to build the world
and his understanding to stretch out
the skies.
¹⁶When he thunders, the waters in the
skies roar.
He makes clouds rise in the sky all over
the earth.
He sends lightning with the rain
and brings out the wind from his
storehouses.

¹⁷"People are so stupid and know so little.
Goldsmiths are made ashamed by their
idols,
because those statues are only false gods.
They have no breath in them.
¹⁸They are worth nothing; people make fun
of them.
When they are judged, they will be
destroyed.
¹⁹But God, who is Jacob's Portion, is not
like the idols.
He made everything,
and he chose Israel to be his special
people.
The LORD All-Powerful is his name.

²⁰"You are my war club,
my battle weapon.
I use you to smash nations.
I use you to destroy kingdoms.
²¹I use you to smash horses and riders.
I use you to smash chariots and
drivers.
²²I use you to smash men and women.

I use you to smash old people and
young people.
I use you to smash young men and
young women.
²³I use you to smash shepherds and flocks.
I use you to smash farmers and oxen.
I use you to smash governors and
officers.
²⁴"But I will pay back Babylon and all the
Babylonians for all the evil things they did to
Jerusalem in your sight," says the LORD.
²⁵The LORD says,
"Babylon, you are a destroying
mountain,
and I am against you.
You have destroyed the whole land.
I will put my hand out against you.
I will roll you off the cliffs,
and I will make you a burned-out
mountain.
²⁶People will not find any rocks in Babylon
big enough for cornerstones.
People will not take any rocks from
Babylon to use for the foundation of
a building,
because your city will be just a pile of
ruins forever," says the LORD.

²⁷"Lift up a banner in the land!
Blow the trumpet among the nations!
Get the nations ready for battle against
Babylon.
Call these kingdoms of Ararat, Minni,
and Ashkenaz to fight against her.
Choose a commander to lead the army
against Babylon.
Send so many horses that they are like
a swarm of locusts.
²⁸Get the nations ready for battle against
Babylon—
the kings of the Medes,
their governors and all their officers,
and all the countries they rule.
²⁹The land shakes and moves in pain,
because the LORD will do what he has
planned to Babylon.
He will make Babylon an empty desert,
where no one will live.
³⁰Babylon's warriors have stopped fighting.
They stay in their protected cities.
Their strength is gone,

and they have become like frightened women.
Babylon's houses are burning.
The bars of her gates are broken.
³¹One messenger follows another;
messenger follows messenger.
They announce to the king of Babylon
that his whole city has been captured.
³²The river crossings have been captured,
and the swamplands are burning.
All of Babylon's soldiers are terribly afraid."

³³This is what the LORD All-Powerful, the God of Israel, says:
"The city of Babylon is like a threshing floor,
where people crush the grain at harvest time.
The time to harvest Babylon is coming soon."

³⁴"Nebuchadnezzar king of Babylon has defeated and destroyed us.
In the past he took our people away,
and we became like an empty jar.
He was like a giant snake that swallowed us.
He filled his stomach with our best things.
Then he spit us out.
³⁵Babylon did terrible things to hurt us.
Now let those things happen to Babylon,"
say the people of Jerusalem.
"The people of Babylon killed our people.
Now let them be punished for what they did," says Jerusalem.
³⁶So this is what the LORD says:
"I will soon defend you, Judah,
and make sure that Babylon is punished.
I will dry up Babylon's sea
and make her springs become dry.
³⁷Babylon will become a pile of ruins,
a home for wild dogs.
People will be shocked by what happened there.
No one will live there anymore.
³⁸Babylon's people roar like young lions;
they growl like baby lions.

³⁹While they are stirred up,
I will give a feast for them
and make them drunk.
They will shout and laugh.
And they will sleep forever and never wake up!" says the LORD.
⁴⁰"I will take the people of Babylon to be killed.
They will be like lambs,
like sheep and goats waiting to be killed.

⁴¹"How Babylon has been defeated!
The pride of the whole earth has been taken captive.
People from other nations are shocked at what happened to Babylon,
and the things they see make them afraid.
⁴²The sea has risen over Babylon;
its roaring waves cover her.
⁴³Babylon's towns are ruined and empty.
It has become a dry, desert land,
a land where no one lives.
People do not even travel through Babylon.
⁴⁴I will punish the god Bel in Babylon.
I will make him spit out what he has swallowed.
Nations will no longer come to Babylon;
even the wall around the city will fall.

⁴⁵"Come out of Babylon, my people!
Run for your lives!
Run from the LORD's great anger.
⁴⁶Don't lose courage;
rumors will spread through the land,
but don't be afraid.
One rumor comes this year, and another comes the next year.
There will be rumors of terrible fighting in the country,
of rulers fighting against rulers.
⁴⁷The time will surely come
when I will punish the idols of Babylon,
and the whole land will be disgraced.
There will be many dead people lying all around.
⁴⁸Then heaven and earth and all that is in them
will shout for joy about Babylon.

They will shout because the army comes
from the north
to destroy Babylon," says the LORD.

⁴⁹"Babylon must fall, because she killed
people from Israel.
She killed people from everywhere on
earth.
⁵⁰You who have escaped being killed with
swords,
leave Babylon! Don't wait!
Remember the LORD in the faraway
land
and think about Jerusalem."

⁵¹"We people of Judah are disgraced,
because we have been insulted.
We have been shamed,
because strangers have gone into
the holy places of the LORD's Temple!"

⁵²So the LORD says, "The time is coming
soon
when I will punish the idols of Babylon.
Wounded people will cry with pain
all over that land.
⁵³Even if Babylon grows until she touches
the sky,
and even if she makes her highest cities
strong,
I will send people to destroy her," says
the LORD.

⁵⁴"Sounds of people crying are heard in
Babylon.
Sounds of people destroying things
are heard in the land of the
Babylonians.
⁵⁵The LORD is destroying Babylon
and making the loud sounds of the city
become silent.
Enemies come roaring in like ocean
waves.
The roar of their voices is heard all
around.
⁵⁶The army has come to destroy Babylon.
Her soldiers have been captured,
and their bows are broken,
because the LORD is a God who punishes
people for the evil they do.
He gives them the full punishment they
deserve.

⁵⁷I will make Babylon's rulers and wise
men drunk,
and her governors, officers, and
soldiers, too.
Then they will sleep forever and never
wake up," says the King,
whose name is the LORD All-Powerful.
⁵⁸This is what the LORD All-Powerful says:
"Babylon's thick wall will be completely
pulled down
and her high gates burned.
The people will work hard, but it won't
help;
their work will only become fuel for the
flames!"

A Message to Babylon

⁵⁹This is the message that Jeremiah the
prophet gave to the officer Seraiah son of Neriah, who was the son of Mahseiah. Seraiah
went to Babylon with Zedekiah king of Judah in the fourth year Zedekiah was king of
Judah. His duty was to arrange the king's
food and housing on the trip. ⁶⁰Jeremiah had
written on a scroll all the terrible things that
would happen to Babylon, all these words
about Babylon. ⁶¹Jeremiah said to Seraiah,
"As soon as you come to Babylon, be sure to
read this message so all the people can hear
you. ⁶²Then say, 'LORD, you have said that you
will destroy this place so that no people or
animals will live in it. It will be an empty
ruin forever.' ⁶³After you finish reading this
scroll, tie a stone to it and throw it into the
Euphrates River. ⁶⁴Then say, 'In the same way
Babylon will sink and will not rise again because of the terrible things I will make happen here. Her people will fall.'"

The words of Jeremiah end here.

The Fall of Jerusalem

52 Zedekiah was twenty-one years old
when he became king, and he was king
in Jerusalem for eleven years. His mother's
name was Hamutal daughter of Jeremiah,ⁿ
and she was from Libnah. ²Zedekiah did what
the LORD said was wrong, just as Jehoiakim
had done. ³All this happened in Jerusalem and
Judah because the LORD was angry with them.
Finally, he threw them out of his presence.

52:1 Jeremiah This is not the prophet Jeremiah but a different man with the same name.

Zedekiah turned against the king of Babylon. [4]Then Nebuchadnezzar king of Babylon marched against Jerusalem with his whole army. They made a camp around the city and built devices all around the city walls to attack it. This happened on Zedekiah's ninth year, tenth month, and tenth day as king. [5]And the city was under attack until Zedekiah's eleventh year as king.

[6]By the ninth day of the fourth month, the hunger was terrible in the city; there was no food for the people to eat. [7]Then the city wall was broken through, and the whole army of Judah ran away at night. They left the city through the gate between the two walls by the king's garden. Even though the Babylonians were surrounding the city, Zedekiah and his men headed toward the Jordan Valley.

[8]But the Babylonian army chased King Zedekiah and caught him in the plains of Jericho. All of his army was scattered from him. [9]So the Babylonians captured Zedekiah and took him to the king of Babylon at the town of Riblah in the land of Hamath. There he passed sentence on Zedekiah. [10]At Riblah the king of Babylon killed Zedekiah's sons as he watched. The king also killed all the officers of Judah. [11]Then he put out Zedekiah's eyes, and put bronze chains on him, and took him to Babylon. And the king kept Zedekiah in prison there until the day he died.

[12]Nebuzaradan, commander of the king's special guards and servant of the king of Babylon, came to Jerusalem on the tenth day of the fifth month. This was in Nebuchadnezzar's nineteenth year as king of Babylon. [13]Nebuzaradan set fire to the Temple of the LORD, the palace, and all the houses of Jerusalem; every important building was burned. [14]The whole Babylonian army, led by the commander of the king's special guards, broke down all the walls around Jerusalem. [15]Nebuzaradan, the commander of the king's special guards, took captive some of the poorest people, those who were left in Jerusalem, those who had surrendered to the king of Babylon, and the skilled craftsmen who were left in Jerusalem. [16]But Nebuzaradan left behind some of the poorest people of the land to take care of the vineyards and fields.

[17]The Babylonians broke into pieces the bronze pillars, the bronze stands, and the large bronze bowl, called the Sea, which were in the Temple of the LORD. Then they carried all the bronze pieces to Babylon. [18]They also took the pots, shovels, wick trimmers, bowls, dishes, and all the bronze objects used to serve in the Temple. [19]The commander of the king's special guards took away bowls, pans for carrying hot coals, large bowls, pots, lampstands, pans, and bowls used for drink offerings. He took everything that was made of pure gold or silver.

[20]There was so much bronze that it could not be weighed: two pillars, the large bronze bowl called the Sea with the twelve bronze bulls under it, and the movable stands, which King Solomon had made for the Temple of the LORD. [21]Each of the pillars was about twenty-seven feet high, eighteen feet around, and hollow inside. The wall of each pillar was three inches thick. [22]The bronze capital on top of the one pillar was about seven and one-half feet high. It was decorated with a net design and bronze pomegranates all around it. The other pillar also had pomegranates and was like the first pillar. [23]There were ninety-six pomegranates on the sides of the pillars. There was a total of a hundred pomegranates above the net design.

[24]The commander of the king's special guards took as prisoners Seraiah the chief priest, Zephaniah the priest next in rank, and the three doorkeepers. [25]He also took from the city the officer in charge of the soldiers, seven people who advised the king, the royal secretary who selected people for the army, and sixty other men from Judah who were in the city when it fell. [26]Nebuzaradan, the commander, took these people and brought them to the king of Babylon at the town of Riblah. [27]There at Riblah, in the land of Hamath, the king had them killed.

So the people of Judah were led away from their country as captives. [28]This is the number of the people Nebuchadnezzar took away as captives: in the seventh year, 3,023 Jews; [29]in Nebuchadnezzar's eighteenth year,

832 people from Jerusalem; ³⁰in Nebuchadnezzar's twenty-third year, Nebuzaradan, commander of the king's special guards, took 745 Jews as captives.

In all 4,600 people were taken captive.

Jehoiachin Is Set Free

³¹Jehoiachin king of Judah was in prison in Babylon for thirty-seven years. The year Evil-Merodach became king of Babylon he let Jehoiachin king of Judah out of prison. He set Jehoiachin free on the twenty-fifth day of the twelfth month. ³²Evil-Merodach spoke kindly to Jehoiachin and gave him a seat of honor above the seats of the other kings who were with him in Babylon. ³³So Jehoiachin put away his prison clothes, and for the rest of his life, he ate at the king's table. ³⁴Every day the king of Babylon gave Jehoiachin an allowance. This lasted as long as he lived, until the day Jehoiachin died.

PSALM 119:129–136

¹²⁹Your rules are wonderful.
That is why I keep them.
¹³⁰Learning your words gives wisdom
and understanding for the foolish.
¹³¹I am nearly out of breath.
I really want to learn your commands.
¹³²Look at me and have mercy on me
as you do for those who love you.
¹³³Guide my steps as you promised;
don't let any sin control me.
¹³⁴Save me from harmful people
so I can obey your orders.
¹³⁵Show your kindness to me, your
servant.
Teach me your demands.
¹³⁶Tears stream from my eyes,
because people do not obey your
teachings.

PROVERBS 28:7–8

⁷Children who obey what they have been
taught are wise,
but friends of troublemakers disgrace
their parents.
⁸Some people get rich by overcharging
others,
but their wealth will be given to those
who are kind to the poor.

TITUS 2:1–15

Following the True Teaching

2But you must tell everyone what to do to follow the true teaching. ²Teach older men to be self-controlled, serious, wise, strong in faith, in love, and in patience.

³In the same way, teach older women to be holy in their behavior, not speaking against others or enslaved to too much wine, but teaching what is good. ⁴Then they can teach the young women to love their husbands, to love their children, ⁵to be wise and pure, to be good workers at home, to be kind, and to yield to their husbands. Then no one will be able to criticize the teaching God gave us.

⁶In the same way, encourage young men to be wise. ⁷In every way be an example of doing good deeds. When you teach, do it with honesty and seriousness. ⁸Speak the truth so that you cannot be criticized. Then those who are against you will be ashamed because there is nothing bad to say about us.

⁹Slaves should yield to their own masters at all times, trying to please them and not arguing with them. ¹⁰They should not steal from them but should show their masters they can be fully trusted so that in everything they do they will make the teaching of God our Savior attractive.

¹¹That is the way we should live, because God's grace that can save everyone has come. ¹²It teaches us not to live against God nor to do the evil things the world wants to do. Instead, that grace teaches us to live in the present age in a wise and right way and in a way that shows we serve God. ¹³We should live like that while we wait for our great hope and the coming of the glory of our great God and Savior Jesus Christ. ¹⁴He gave himself for us so he might pay the price to free us from all evil and to make us pure people who belong only to him—people who are always wanting to do good deeds.

¹⁵Say these things and encourage the people and tell them what is wrong in their lives, with all authority. Do not let anyone treat you as if you were unimportant.

NOVEMBER 3

LAMENTATIONS 1:1—2:22

Jerusalem Cries over Her Loss

1 Jerusalem once was full of people,
but now the city is empty.
Jerusalem once was a great city among
the nations,
but now she[n] is like a widow.
She was like a queen of all the other cities,
but now she is a slave.

[2]She cries loudly at night,
and tears are on her cheeks.
There is no one to comfort her;
all who loved her are gone.
All her friends have turned against her
and are now her enemies.

[3]Judah has gone into captivity
where she suffers and works hard.
She lives among other nations,
but she has found no rest.
Those who chased her caught her
when she was in trouble.

[4]The roads to Jerusalem are sad,
because no one comes for the feasts.
No one passes through her gates.
Her priests groan,
her young women are suffering,
and Jerusalem suffers terribly.

[5]Her foes are now her masters.
Her enemies enjoy the wealth they have
taken.
The LORD is punishing her
for her many sins.
Her children have gone away
as captives of the enemy.

[6]The beauty of Jerusalem
has gone away.
Her rulers are like deer
that cannot find food.
They are weak
and run from the hunters.

[7]Jerusalem is suffering and homeless.
She remembers all the good things
from the past.
But her people were defeated by the
enemy,
and there was no one to help her.
When her enemies saw her,
they laughed to see her ruined.

[8]Jerusalem sinned terribly,
so she has become unclean.
Those who honored her now hate her,
because they have seen her nakedness.
She groans
and turns away.

[9]She made herself dirty by her sins
and did not think about what would
happen to her.
Her defeat was surprising,
and no one could comfort her.
She says, "LORD, see how I suffer,
because the enemy has won."

[10]The enemy reached out and took
all her precious things.
She even saw foreigners
enter her Temple.
The LORD had commanded foreigners
never to enter the meeting place of his
people.

[11]All of Jerusalem's people groan,
looking for bread.
They are trading their precious things
for food
so they can stay alive.
The city says, "Look, LORD, and see.
I am hated."

[12]Jerusalem says, "You who pass by on the
road don't seem to care.
Come, look at me and see:
Is there any pain like mine?
Is there any pain like that he has
caused me?
The LORD has punished me
on the day of his great anger.

[13]"He sent fire from above
that went down into my bones.

1:1 she In this poem the city of Jerusalem is described as a woman.

He stretched out a net for my feet
and turned me back.
He made me so sad and lonely
that I am weak all day.

14"He has noticed my sins;
they are tied together by his hands;
they hang around my neck.
He has turned my strength into
weakness.
The Lord has handed me over
to those who are stronger than I.

15"The Lord has rejected
all my mighty men inside my walls.
He brought an army against me
to destroy my young men.
As if in a winepress, the Lord has
crushed
the capital city of Judah.

16"I cry about these things;
my eyes overflow with tears.
There is no one near to comfort me,
no one who can give me strength again.
My children are left sad and lonely,
because the enemy has won."

17Jerusalem reaches out her hands,
but there is no one to comfort her.
The LORD commanded the people of
Jacob
to be surrounded by their enemies.
Jerusalem is now unclean
like those around her.

18Jerusalem says, "The LORD is right,
but I refused to obey him.
Listen, all you people,
and look at my pain.
My young women and men
have gone into captivity.

19"I called out to my friends,
but they turned against me.
My priests and my elders
have died in the city
while looking for food
to stay alive.

20"Look at me, LORD. I am upset
and greatly troubled.
My heart is troubled,
because I have been so stubborn.

Out in the streets, the sword kills;
inside the houses, death destroys.

21"People have heard my groaning,
and there is no one to comfort me.
All my enemies have heard of my
trouble,
and they are happy you have done this
to me.
Now bring that day you have announced
so that my enemies will be like me.

22"Look at all their evil.
Do to them what you have done to me
because of all my sins.
I groan over and over again,
and I am afraid."

The Lord Destroyed Jerusalem

2 Look how the Lord in his anger
has brought Jerusalem to shame.
He has thrown down the greatness of
Israel
from the sky to the earth;
he did not remember the Temple, his
footstool,
on the day of his anger.

2The Lord swallowed up without mercy
all the houses of the people of Jacob;
in his anger he pulled down
the strong places of Judah.
He threw her kingdom and its rulers
down to the ground in dishonor.

3In his anger he has removed
all the strength of Israel;
he took away his power from Israel
when the enemy came.
He burned against the people of Jacob
like a flaming fire
that burns up everything around it.

4Like an enemy, he prepared to shoot his
bow,
and his hand was against us.
Like an enemy, he killed
all the good-looking people;
he poured out his anger like fire
on the tents of Jerusalem.

5The Lord was like an enemy;
he swallowed up Israel.
He swallowed up all her palaces

and destroyed all her strongholds.
He has caused more moaning and
groaning
for Judah.

⁶He cut down his Temple like a garden;
he destroyed the meeting place.
The LORD has made Jerusalem forget
the set feasts and Sabbath days.
He has rejected the king and the priest
in his great anger.

⁷The Lord has rejected his altar
and abandoned his Temple.
He has handed over to the enemy
the walls of Jerusalem's palaces.
Their uproar in the LORD's Temple
was like that of a feast day.

⁸The LORD planned to destroy
the wall around Jerusalem.
He measured the wall
and did not stop himself from
destroying it.
He made the walls and defenses sad;
together they have fallen.

⁹Jerusalem's gates have fallen to the
ground;
he destroyed and smashed the bars of
the gates.
Her king and her princes are among the
nations.
The teaching of the LORD has
stopped,
and the prophets do not have
visions from the LORD.

¹⁰The elders of Jerusalem
sit on the ground in silence.
They throw dust on their heads
and put on rough cloth to show their
sadness.
The young women of Jerusalem
bow their heads to the ground in
sorrow.

¹¹My eyes have no more tears,
and I am sick to my stomach.
I feel empty inside,
because my people have been
destroyed.
Children and babies are fainting
in the streets of the city.

¹²They ask their mothers,
"Where is the grain and wine?"
They faint like wounded soldiers
in the streets of the city
and die in their mothers' arms.

¹³What can I say about you, Jerusalem?
What can I compare you to?
What can I say you are like?
How can I comfort you, Jerusalem?
Your ruin is as deep as the sea.
No one can heal you.

¹⁴Your prophets saw visions,
but they were false and worth nothing.
They did not point out your sins
to keep you from being captured.
They preached what was false
and led you wrongly.

¹⁵All who pass by on the road
clap their hands at you;
they make fun of Jerusalem
and shake their heads.
They ask, "Is this the city that people
called
the most beautiful city,
the happiest place on earth?"

¹⁶All your enemies open their mouths
to speak against you.
They make fun and grind their teeth in
anger.
They say, "We have swallowed you up.
This is the day we were waiting for!
We have finally seen it happen."

¹⁷The LORD has done what he planned;
he has kept his word
that he commanded long ago.
He has destroyed without mercy,
and he has let your enemies laugh at
you.
He has strengthened your enemies.

¹⁸The people cry out to the Lord.
Wall of Jerusalem,
let your tears flow
like a river day and night.
Do not stop
or let your eyes rest.

¹⁹Get up, cry out in the night,
even as the night begins.

Pour out your heart like water
in prayer to the Lord.
Lift up your hands in prayer to him
for the life of your children
who are fainting with hunger
on every street corner.

²⁰Jerusalem says: "Look, LORD, and see
to whom you have done this.
Women eat their own babies,
the children they have cared for.
Priests and prophets are killed
in the Temple of the Lord.

²¹"People young and old
lie outside on the ground.
My young women and young men
have been killed by the sword.
You killed them on the day of your anger;
you killed them without mercy.

²²"You invited terrors to come against me
on every side,
as if you were inviting them to a feast.
No one escaped or remained alive
on the day of the LORD's anger.
My enemy has killed
those I cared for and brought up."

PSALM 119:137–144

¹³⁷LORD, you do what is right,
and your laws are fair.
¹³⁸The rules you commanded are right
and completely trustworthy.
¹³⁹I am so upset I am worn out,
because my enemies have forgotten
your words.
¹⁴⁰Your promises are proven,
so I, your servant, love them.
¹⁴¹I am unimportant and hated,
but I have not forgotten your orders.
¹⁴²Your goodness continues forever,
and your teachings are true.
¹⁴³I have had troubles and misery,
but I love your commands.
¹⁴⁴Your rules are always good.
Help me understand so I can live.

PROVERBS 28:9–10

⁹If you refuse to obey what you have been
taught,
your prayers will not be heard.

¹⁰Those who lead good people to do wrong
will be ruined by their own evil,
but the innocent will be rewarded with
good things.

TITUS 3:1–15

The Right Way to Live

3 Remind the believers to yield to the authority of rulers and government leaders, to obey them, to be ready to do good, ²to speak no evil about anyone, to live in peace, and to be gentle and polite to all people.

³In the past we also were foolish. We did not obey, we were wrong, and we were slaves to many things our bodies wanted and enjoyed. We spent our lives doing evil and being jealous. People hated us, and we hated each other. ⁴But when the kindness and love of God our Savior was shown, ⁵he saved us because of his mercy. It was not because of good deeds we did to be right with him. He saved us through the washing that made us new people through the Holy Spirit. ⁶God poured out richly upon us that Holy Spirit through Jesus Christ our Savior. ⁷Being made right with God by his grace, we could have the hope of receiving the life that never ends.

⁸This teaching is true, and I want you to be sure the people understand these things. Then those who believe in God will be careful to use their lives for doing good. These things are good and will help everyone.

⁹But stay away from those who have foolish arguments and talk about useless family histories and argue and quarrel about the law. Those things are worth nothing and will not help anyone. ¹⁰After a first and second warning, avoid someone who causes arguments. ¹¹You can know that such people are evil and sinful; their own sins prove them wrong.

Some Things to Remember

¹²When I send Artemas or Tychicus to you, make every effort to come to me at Nicopolis, because I have decided to stay there this winter. ¹³Do all you can to help Zenas the lawyer and Apollos on their journey so that they have everything they need.

¹⁴Our people must learn to use their lives for doing good deeds to provide what is necessary so that their lives will not be useless.

¹⁵All who are with me greet you. Greet those who love us in the faith.

Grace be with you all.

NOVEMBER 4

LAMENTATIONS 3:1—5:22

The Meaning of Suffering

3 I am a man who has seen the suffering that comes from the rod of the LORD's anger.

²He led me
into darkness, not light.

³He turned his hand against me
again and again, all day long.

⁴He wore out my flesh and skin
and broke my bones.

⁵He surrounded me with sadness
and attacked me with grief.

⁶He made me sit in the dark,
like those who have been dead a long
time.

⁷He shut me in so I could not get out;
he put heavy chains on me.

⁸I cry out and beg for help,
but he ignores my prayer.

⁹He blocked my way with a stone wall
and led me in the wrong direction.

¹⁰He is like a bear ready to attack me,
like a lion in hiding.

¹¹He led me the wrong way and let me
stray
and left me without help.

¹²He prepared to shoot his bow
and made me the target for his arrows.

¹³He shot me in the kidneys
with the arrows from his bag.

¹⁴I was a joke to all my people,
who make fun of me with songs all day
long.

¹⁵The LORD filled me with misery;
he made me drunk with suffering.

¹⁶He broke my teeth with gravel
and trampled me into the dirt.

¹⁷I have no more peace.
I have forgotten what happiness is.

¹⁸I said, "My strength is gone,
and I have no hope in the LORD."

¹⁹LORD, remember my suffering and my
misery,
my sorrow and trouble.

²⁰Please remember me
and think about me.

²¹But I have hope
when I think of this:

²²The LORD's love never ends;
his mercies never stop.

²³They are new every morning;
LORD, your loyalty is great.

²⁴I say to myself, "The LORD is mine,
so I hope in him."

²⁵The LORD is good to those who hope in
him,
to those who seek him.

²⁶It is good to wait quietly
for the LORD to save.

²⁷It is good for someone to work hard
while he is young.

²⁸He should sit alone and be quiet;
the LORD has given him hard work to do.

²⁹He should bow down to the ground;
maybe there is still hope.

³⁰He should let anyone slap his cheek;
he should be filled with shame.

³¹The Lord will not reject
his people forever.

³²Although he brings sorrow,
he also has mercy and great love.

³³He does not like to punish people
or make them sad.

³⁴He sees if any prisoner of the earth
is crushed under his feet;

³⁵he sees if someone is treated unfairly
  before the Most High God;
³⁶the Lord sees
  if someone is cheated in his case in
    court.

³⁷Nobody can speak and have it happen
  unless the Lord commands it.
³⁸Both bad and good things
  come by the command of the Most
    High God.
³⁹No one should complain
  when he is punished for his sins.

⁴⁰Let us examine and see what we have done
  and then return to the LORD.
⁴¹Let us lift up our hands and pray from
    our hearts
  to God in heaven:
⁴²"We have sinned and turned against you,
  and you have not forgiven us.

⁴³"You wrapped yourself in anger and
    chased us;
  you killed us without mercy.
⁴⁴You wrapped yourself in a cloud,
  and no prayer could get through.
⁴⁵You made us like scum and trash
  among the other nations.

⁴⁶"All of our enemies
  open their mouths and speak against
    us.
⁴⁷We have been frightened and fearful,
  ruined and destroyed."
⁴⁸Streams of tears flow from my eyes,
  because my people are destroyed.

⁴⁹My tears flow continually,
  without stopping,
⁵⁰until the LORD looks down
  and sees from heaven.
⁵¹I am sad when I see
  what has happened to all the women of
    my city.

⁵²Those who are my enemies for no reason
  hunted me like a bird.
⁵³They tried to kill me in a pit;
  they threw stones at me.
⁵⁴Water came up over my head,
  and I said, "I am going to die."
⁵⁵I called out to you, LORD,
  from the bottom of the pit.

⁵⁶You heard me calling, "Do not close your
    ears
  and ignore my gasps and shouts."
⁵⁷You came near when I called to you;
  you said, "Don't be afraid."

⁵⁸Lord, you have taken my case
  and given me back my life.
⁵⁹LORD, you have seen how I have been
    wronged.
  Now judge my case for me.
⁶⁰You have seen how my enemies took
    revenge on me
  and made evil plans against me.

⁶¹LORD, you have heard their insults
  and all their evil plans against me.
⁶²The words and thoughts of my
    enemies
  are against me all the time.
⁶³Look! In everything they do
  they make fun of me with songs.

⁶⁴Pay them back, LORD,
  for what they have done.
⁶⁵Make them stubborn,
  and put your curse on them.
⁶⁶Chase them in anger, LORD,
  and destroy them from under your
    heavens.

The Attack on Jerusalem

4 See how the gold has lost its shine,
  how the pure gold has dulled!
  The stones of the Temple are scattered
    at every street corner.

²The precious people of Jerusalem
  were more valuable than gold,
  but now they are thought of as clay jars
    made by the hands of a potter.

³Even wild dogs give their milk
  to feed their young,
  but my people are cruel
    like ostriches in the desert.

⁴The babies are so thirsty
  their tongues stick to the roofs of their
    mouths.
  Children beg for bread,
    but no one gives them any.

⁵Those who once ate fine foods
  are now starving in the streets.

People who grew up wearing nice clothes
now pick through trash piles.

⁶My people have been punished
more than Sodom was.
Sodom was destroyed suddenly,
and no hands reached out to help her.

⁷Our princes were purer than snow,
and whiter than milk.
Their bodies were redder than rubies;
they looked like sapphires.

⁸But now they are blacker than coal,
and no one recognizes them in the
streets.
Their skin hangs on their bones;
it is as dry as wood.

⁹Those who were killed in the war were
better off
than those killed by hunger.
They starve in pain and die,
because there is no food from the field.

¹⁰With their own hands kind women
cook their own children.
They became food
when my people were destroyed.

¹¹The LORD turned loose all of his anger;
he poured out his strong anger.
He set fire to Jerusalem,
burning it down to the foundations.

¹²Kings of the earth and people of the world
could not believe
that enemies and foes
could enter the gates of Jerusalem.

¹³It happened because her prophets sinned
and her priests did evil.
They killed in the city
those who did what was right.

¹⁴They wandered in the streets
as if they were blind.
They were dirty with blood,
so no one would touch their clothes.

¹⁵"Go away! You are unclean," people
shouted at them.
"Get away! Get away! Don't touch us!"
So they ran away and wandered.
Even the other nations said, "Don't stay
here."

¹⁶The LORD himself scattered them
and did not look after them anymore.
No one respects the priests
or honors the elders.

¹⁷Also, our eyes grew tired,
looking for help that never came.
We kept watch from our towers
for a nation to save us.

¹⁸Our enemies hunted us,
so we could not even walk in the
streets.
Our end is near. Our time is up.
Our end has come.

¹⁹Those who chased us
were faster than eagles in the sky.
They ran us into the mountains
and ambushed us in the desert.

²⁰The LORD's appointed king, who was our
very breath,
was caught in their traps.
We had said about him, "We will be
protected by him
among the nations."

²¹Be happy and glad, people of Edom,
you who live in the land of Uz.
The cup of God's anger will come to you;
then you will get drunk and go naked.

²²Your punishment is complete, Jerusalem.
He will not send you into captivity
again.
But the LORD will punish the sins of
Edom;
he will uncover your evil.

A Prayer to the Lord

5 Remember, LORD, what happened to us.
Look and see our disgrace.
²Our land has been turned over to
strangers;
our houses have been given to
foreigners.
³We are like orphans with no father;
our mothers are like widows.
⁴We have to buy the water we drink;
we must pay for the firewood.
⁵Those who chase after us want to catch
us by the neck.

We are tired and find no rest.
⁶We made an agreement with Egypt
  and with Assyria to get enough food.
⁷Our ancestors sinned against you, but
    they are gone;
  now we suffer because of their sins.
⁸Slaves have become our rulers,
  and no one can save us from them.
⁹We risk our lives to get our food;
  we face death in the desert.
¹⁰Our skin is hot like an oven;
  we burn with starvation.
¹¹The enemy abused the women of
    Jerusalem
  and the girls in the cities of Judah.
¹²Princes were hung by the hands;
  they did not respect our elders.
¹³The young men ground grain at the mill,
  and boys stumbled under loads of
    wood.
¹⁴The elders no longer sit at the city gates;
  the young men no longer sing.
¹⁵We have no more joy in our hearts;
  our dancing has turned to sadness.
¹⁶The crown has fallen from our head.
  How terrible it is because we sinned.
¹⁷Because of this we are afraid,
  and now our eyes are dim.
¹⁸Mount Zion is empty,
  and wild dogs wander around it.
¹⁹But you rule forever, LORD.
  You will be King from now on.
²⁰Why have you forgotten us for so long?
  Have you left us forever?
²¹Bring us back to you, LORD, and we will
    return.
  Make our days as they were before,
²²or have you completely rejected us?
  Are you so angry with us?

PSALM 119:145–152

¹⁴⁵LORD, I call to you with all my heart.
  Answer me, and I will keep your
    demands.
¹⁴⁶I call to you.
  Save me so I can obey your rules.
¹⁴⁷I wake up early in the morning and cry
    out.

I hope in your word.
¹⁴⁸I stay awake all night
  so I can think about your promises.
¹⁴⁹Listen to me because of your love;
  LORD, give me life by your laws.
¹⁵⁰Those who love evil are near,
  but they are far from your teachings.
¹⁵¹But, LORD, you are also near,
  and all your commands are true.
¹⁵²Long ago I learned from your rules
  that you made them to continue
    forever.

PROVERBS 28:11

¹¹Rich people may think they are wise,
  but the poor with understanding will
    prove them wrong.

PHILEMON 1–25

¹From Paul, a prisoner of Christ Jesus, and from Timothy, our brother.

To Philemon, our dear friend and worker with us; ²to Apphia, our sister; to Archippus, a worker with us; and to the church that meets in your home:

³Grace and peace to you from God our Father and the Lord Jesus Christ.

Philemon's Love and Faith

⁴I always thank my God when I mention you in my prayers, ⁵because I hear about the love you have for all God's holy people and the faith you have in the Lord Jesus. ⁶I pray that the faith you share may make you understand every blessing we have in Christ. ⁷I have great joy and comfort, my brother, because the love you have shown to God's people has refreshed them.

Accept Onesimus as a Brother

⁸So, in Christ, I could be bold and order you to do what is right. ⁹But because I love you, I am pleading with you instead. I, Paul, an old man now and also a prisoner for Christ Jesus, ¹⁰am pleading with you for my child Onesimus, who became my child while I was in prison. ¹¹In the past he was useless to you, but now he has become useful for both you and me.

¹²I am sending him back to you, and with him I am sending my own heart. ¹³I wanted

to keep him with me so that in your place he might help me while I am in prison for the Good News. [14]But I did not want to do anything without asking you first so that any good you do for me will be because you want to do it, not because I forced you. [15]Maybe Onesimus was separated from you for a short time so you could have him back forever— [16]no longer as a slave, but better than a slave, as a loved brother. I love him very much, but you will love him even more, both as a person and as a believer in the Lord.

[17]So if you consider me your partner, welcome Onesimus as you would welcome me. [18]If he has done anything wrong to you or if he owes you anything, charge that to me. [19]I, Paul, am writing this with my own hand. I will pay it back, and I will say nothing about what you owe me for your own life. [20]So, my brother, I ask that you do this for me in the Lord: Refresh my heart in Christ. [21]I write this letter, knowing that you will do what I ask you and even more.

[22]One more thing—prepare a room for me in which to stay, because I hope God will answer your prayers and I will be able to come to you.

Final Greetings

[23]Epaphras, a prisoner with me for Christ Jesus, sends greetings to you. [24]And also Mark, Aristarchus, Demas, and Luke, workers together with me, send greetings.

[25]The grace of our Lord Jesus Christ be with your spirit.

NOVEMBER 5

EZEKIEL 1:1—2:10

Ezekiel's Vision of Living Creatures

1 It was the thirtieth year, on the fifth day of the fourth month of our captivity. I was by the Kebar River among the people who had been carried away as captives. The sky opened, and I saw visions of God.

[2]It was the fifth day of the month of the fifth year that King Jehoiachin had been a prisoner. [3]The LORD spoke his word to Ezekiel son of Buzi in the land of the Babylonians by the Kebar River. There he felt the power of the LORD.

[4]When I looked, I saw a stormy wind coming from the north. There was a great cloud with a bright light around it and fire flashing out of it. Something that looked like glowing metal was in the center of the fire. [5]Inside the cloud was what looked like four living creatures, who were shaped like humans, [6]but each of them had four faces and four wings. [7]Their legs were straight. Their feet were like a calf's hoofs and sparkled like polished bronze. [8]The living creatures had human hands under their wings on their four sides. All four of them had faces and wings, [9]and their wings touched each other. The living creatures did not turn when they moved, but each went straight ahead.

[10]Their faces looked like this: Each living creature had a human face and the face of a lion on the right side and the face of an ox on the left side. And each one also had the face of an eagle. [11]That was what their faces looked like. Their wings were spread out above. Each had two wings that touched one of the other living creatures and two wings that covered its body. [12]Each went straight ahead. Wherever the spirit would go, the living creatures would also go, without turning. [13]The living creatures looked like burning coals of fire or like torches. Fire went back and forth among the living creatures. It was bright, and lightning flashed from it. [14]The living creatures ran back and forth like bolts of lightning.

[15]Now as I looked at the living creatures, I saw a wheel on the ground by each of the living creatures with its four faces. [16]The wheels and the way they were made were like this: They looked like sparkling chrysolite. All four of them looked the same, like one wheel crossways inside another wheel. [17]When they moved, they went in any one of

the four directions, without turning as they went. [18]The rims of the wheels were high and frightening and were full of eyes all around.

[19]When the living creatures moved, the wheels moved beside them. When the living creatures were lifted up from the ground, the wheels also were lifted up. [20]Wherever the spirit would go, the living creatures would go. And the wheels were lifted up beside them, because the spirit of the living creatures was in the wheels. [21]When the living creatures moved, the wheels moved. When the living creatures stopped, the wheels stopped. And when the living creatures were lifted from the ground, the wheels were lifted beside them, because the spirit of the living creatures was in the wheels.

[22]Now, over the heads of the living creatures was something like a dome that sparkled like ice and was frightening. [23]And under the dome the wings of the living creatures were stretched out straight toward one another. Each living creature also had two wings covering its body. [24]I heard the sound of their wings, like the roaring sound of the sea, as they moved. It was like the voice of God Almighty, a roaring sound like a noisy army. When the living creatures stopped, they lowered their wings.

[25]A voice came from above the dome over the heads of the living creatures. When the living creatures stopped, they lowered their wings. [26]Now above the dome there was something that looked like a throne. It looked like a sapphire gem. And on the throne was a shape like a human. [27]Then I noticed that from the waist up the shape looked like glowing metal with fire inside. From the waist down it looked like fire, and a bright light was all around. [28]The surrounding glow looked like the rainbow in the clouds on a rainy day. It seemed to look like the glory of the LORD. So when I saw it, I bowed facedown on the ground and heard a voice speaking.

The Lord Speaks to Ezekiel

2 He said to me, "Human, stand up on your feet so I may speak with you." [2]While he spoke to me, the Spirit entered me and put me on my feet. Then I heard the LORD speaking to me.

[3]He said, "Human, I am sending you to the people of Israel. That nation has turned against me and broken away from me. They and their ancestors have sinned against me until this very day. [4]I am sending you to people who are stubborn and who do not obey. You will say to them, 'This is what the Lord GOD says.' [5]They may listen, or they may not, since they are a people who have turned against me. But they will know that a prophet has been among them. [6]You, human, don't be afraid of the people or their words. Even though they may be like thorny branches and stickers all around you, and though you may feel like you live with poisonous insects, don't be afraid. Don't be afraid of their words or their looks, because they are a people who turn against me. [7]But speak my words to them. They may listen, or they may not, because they turn against me. [8]But you, human, listen to what I say to you. Don't turn against me as those people do. Open your mouth and eat what I am giving you."

[9]Then I looked and saw a hand stretched out to me, and a scroll was in it. [10]He opened the scroll in front of me. Funeral songs, sad writings, and words about troubles were written on the front and back.

PSALM 119:153–160

[153]See my suffering and rescue me,
  because I have not forgotten your
    teachings.
[154]Argue my case and save me.
  Let me live by your promises.
[155]Wicked people are far from being saved,
  because they do not want your
    demands.
[156]LORD, you are very kind;
  give me life by your laws.
[157]Many enemies are after me,
  but I have not rejected your rules.
[158]I see those traitors, and I hate them,
  because they do not obey what you
    say.
[159]See how I love your orders.
  LORD, give me life by your love.
[160]Your words are true from the start,
  and all your laws will be fair forever.

PROVERBS 28:12

[12]When good people triumph, there is
   great happiness,
   but when the wicked get control,
   everybody hides.

HEBREWS 1:1–14

God Spoke Through His Son

[1] In the past God spoke to our ancestors
through the prophets many times and in
many different ways. [2]But now in these last
days God has spoken to us through his Son.
God has chosen his Son to own all things,
and through him he made the world. [3]The
Son reflects the glory of God and shows exactly what God is like. He holds everything
together with his powerful word. When the
Son made people clean from their sins, he
sat down at the right side of God, the Great
One in heaven. [4]The Son became much
greater than the angels, and God gave him a
name that is much greater than theirs.

[5]This is because God never said to any of
the angels,

"You are my Son.
Today I have become your Father."
                                    Psalm 2:7

Nor did God say of any angel,

"I will be his Father,
and he will be my Son."   *2 Samuel 7:14*

[6]And when God brings his firstborn Son into
the world, he says,

"Let all God's angels worship him."[n]
                                    Psalm 97:7

[7]This is what God said about the angels:

"God makes his angels become like
   winds.
He makes his servants become like
   flames of fire."   *Psalm 104:4*

[8]But God said this about his Son:

"God, your throne will last forever and
   ever.
You will rule your kingdom with
   fairness.
[9]You love right and hate evil,
so God has chosen you from among
   your friends;
he has set you apart with much joy."
                                  Psalm 45:6–7

[10]God also says,

"Lord, in the beginning you made the
   earth,
and your hands made the skies.
[11]They will be destroyed, but you will
   remain.
They will all wear out like clothes.
[12]You will fold them like a coat.
And, like clothes, you will change them.
But you never change,
and your life will never end."
                                Psalm 102:25–27

[13]And God never said this to an angel:

"Sit by me at my right side
until I put your enemies under your
   control."[n]   *Psalm 110:1*

[14]All the angels are spirits who serve God
and are sent to help those who will receive
salvation.

NOVEMBER 6

EZEKIEL 3:1—4:17

[3] Then the LORD said to me, "Human, eat
what you find; eat this scroll. Then go and
speak to the people of Israel." [2]So I opened
my mouth, and he gave me the scroll to eat.
[3]He said to me, "Human, eat this scroll

which I am giving you, and fill your stomach
with it." Then I ate it, and it was as sweet as
honey in my mouth.

[4]Then he said to me, "Human, go to the
people of Israel, and speak my words to
them. [5]You are not being sent to people
whose speech you can't understand, whose

1:6 "Let . . . him." These words are found in Deuteronomy 32:43 in the Septuagint, the Greek version of the Old Testament,
and in a Hebrew copy among the Dead Sea Scrolls.   **1:13 until . . . control** Literally, "until I make your enemies a footstool
for your feet."

language is difficult. You are being sent to Israel. [6]You are not being sent to many nations whose speech you can't understand, whose language is difficult, whose words you cannot understand. If I had sent you to them, they would have listened to you. [7]But the people of Israel will not be willing to listen to you, because they are not willing to listen to me. Yes, all the people of Israel are stubborn and will not obey. [8]See, I now make you as stubborn and as hard as they are. [9]I am making you as hard as a diamond, harder than stone. Don't be afraid of them or be frightened by them, though they are a people who turn against me."

[10]Also, he said to me, "Human, believe all the words I will speak to you, and listen carefully to them. [11]Then go to the captives, your own people, and say to them, 'The Lord GOD says this.' Tell them this whether they listen or not."

[12]Then the Spirit lifted me up, and I heard a loud rumbling sound behind me, saying, "Praise the glory of the LORD in heaven." [13]I heard the wings of the living creatures touching each other and the sound of the wheels by them. It was a loud rumbling sound. [14]So the Spirit lifted me up and took me away. I was unhappy and angry, and I felt the great power of the LORD. [15]I came to the captives from Judah, who lived by the Kebar River at Tel Abib. I sat there seven days where these people lived, feeling shocked.

Israel's Warning

[16]After seven days the LORD spoke his word to me again. He said, [17]"Human, I now make you a watchman for Israel. Any time you hear a word from my mouth, warn them for me. [18]When I say to the wicked, 'You will surely die,' you must warn them so they may live. If you do not speak out to warn the wicked to stop their evil ways, they will die in their sin. But I will hold you responsible for their death. [19]If you warn the wicked and they do not turn from their wickedness or their evil ways, they will die because of their sin. But you will have saved your life.

[20]"Again, those who do right may turn away from doing good and do evil. If I make something bad happen to them, they will die. Because you have not warned them, they will die because of their sin, and the good they did will not be remembered. But I will hold you responsible for their deaths. [21]But if you have warned those good people not to sin, and they do not sin, they will surely live, because they believed the warning. And you will have saved your life."

[22]Then I felt the power of the LORD there. He said to me, "Get up and go out to the plain. There I will speak to you." [23]So I got up and went out to the plain. I saw the glory of the LORD standing there, like the glory I saw by the Kebar River, and I bowed facedown on the ground.

[24]Then the Spirit entered me and made me stand on my feet. He spoke to me and said, "Go, shut yourself up in your house. [25]As for you, human, the people will tie you up with ropes so that you will not be able to go out among them. [26]Also, I will make your tongue stick to the roof of your mouth so you will be silent. You will not be able to argue with the people, even though they turn against me. [27]But when I speak to you, I will open your mouth, and you will say to them, 'The Lord GOD says this.' Those who will listen, let them listen. Those who refuse, let them refuse, because they are a people who turn against me.

The Map of Jerusalem

4 "Now, human, get yourself a brick, put it in front of you, and draw a map of Jerusalem on it. [2]Then surround it with an army. Build battle works against the city and a dirt road to the top of the city walls. Set up camps around it, and put heavy logs in place to break down the walls. [3]Then get yourself an iron plate and set it up like an iron wall between you and the city. Turn your face toward the city as if to attack it and then attack. This is a sign to Israel.

[4]"Then lie down on your left side, and take the guilt of Israel on yourself. Their guilt will be on you for the number of days you lie on your left side. [5]I have given you the same number of days as the years of the people's sin. So you will have the guilt of Israel's sin on you for three hundred ninety days. [6]"After you have finished these three hun-

dred ninety days, lie down a second time, on your right side. You will then have the guilt of Judah on you. I will give it to you for forty days, a day for each year of their sin. [7]Then you will look toward Jerusalem, which is being attacked. With your arm bare, you will prophesy against Jerusalem. [8]I will put ropes on you so you cannot turn from one side to the other until you have finished the days of your attack on Jerusalem.

[9]"Take wheat, barley, beans, small peas, and millet seeds, and put them in one bowl, and make them into bread for yourself. You will eat it the three hundred ninety days you lie on your side. [10]You will eat eight ounces of food every day at set times. [11]You will drink about two-thirds of a quart of water every day at set times. [12]Eat your food as you would eat a barley cake, baking it over human dung where the people can see." [13]Then the LORD said, "In the same way Israel will eat unclean food among the nations where I force them to go."

[14]But I said, "No, Lord GOD! I have never been made unclean. From the time I was young until now I've never eaten anything that died by itself or was torn by animals. Unclean meat has never entered my mouth."

[15]"Very well," he said. "Then I will give you cow's dung instead of human dung to use for your fire to bake your bread."

[16]He also said to me, "Human, I am going to cut off the supply of bread to Jerusalem. They will eat the bread that is measured out to them, and they will worry as they eat. They will drink water that is measured out to them, and they will be in shock as they drink it. [17]This is because bread and water will be hard to find. The people will be shocked at the sight of each other, and they will become weak because of their sin.

PSALM 119:161–168

[161]Leaders attack me for no reason,
　　but I fear your law in my heart.
[162]I am as happy over your promises
　　as if I had found a great treasure.
[163]I hate and despise lies,
　　but I love your teachings.

[164]Seven times a day I praise you
　　for your fair laws.
[165]Those who love your teachings will find
　　true peace,
　　and nothing will defeat them.
[166]I am waiting for you to save me, LORD.
　　I will obey your commands.
[167]I obey your rules,
　　and I love them very much.
[168]I obey your orders and rules,
　　because you know everything I do.

PROVERBS 28:13

[13]If you hide your sins, you will not
　　succeed.
　　If you confess and reject them, you will
　　receive mercy.

HEBREWS 2:1–18

Our Salvation Is Great

2 So we must be more careful to follow what we were taught. Then we will not stray away from the truth. [2]The teaching God spoke through angels was shown to be true, and anyone who did not follow it or obey it received the punishment that was earned. [3]So surely we also will be punished if we ignore this great salvation. The Lord himself first told about this salvation, and those who heard him testified it was true. [4]God also testified to the truth of the message by using wonders, great signs, many kinds of miracles, and by giving people gifts through the Holy Spirit, just as he wanted.

Christ Became like Humans

[5]God did not choose angels to be the rulers of the new world that was coming, which is what we have been talking about. [6]It is written in the Scriptures,

"Why are people even important to you?
　　Why do you take care of human beings?
[7]You made them a little lower than the
　　angels
　　and crowned them with glory and
　　honor."
[8]You put all things under their control."

　　　　　　　　　　　　　　　　Psalm 8:4–6

2:7 **You . . . honor.** Some Greek copies continue, "You put them in charge of everything you made." See Psalm 8:6.

When God put everything under their control, there was nothing left that they did not rule. Still, we do not yet see them ruling over everything. 9But we see Jesus, who for a short time was made lower than the angels. And now he is wearing a crown of glory and honor because he suffered and died. And by God's grace, he died for everyone.

10God is the One who made all things, and all things are for his glory. He wanted to have many children share his glory, so he made the One who leads people to salvation perfect through suffering.

11Jesus, who makes people holy, and those who are made holy are from the same family. So he is not ashamed to call them his brothers and sisters. 12He says,

"Then, I will tell my brothers and sisters
  about you;
I will praise you in the public meeting."
Psalm 22:22

13He also says,

"I will trust in God."
Isaiah 8:17
And he also says,

"I am here, and with me are the children
  God has given me."
Isaiah 8:18
14Since these children are people with physical bodies, Jesus himself became like them. He did this so that, by dying, he could destroy the one who has the power of death—the devil— 15and free those who were like slaves all their lives because of their fear of death. 16Clearly, it is not angels that Jesus helps, but the people who are from Abraham.*n* 17For this reason Jesus had to be made like his brothers and sisters in every way so he could be their merciful and faithful high priest in service to God. Then Jesus could die in their place to take away their sins. 18And now he can help those who are tempted, because he himself suffered and was tempted.

NOVEMBER 7

EZEKIEL 5:1—6:14

Ezekiel Cuts His Hair

5 "Now, human, take a sharp sword, and use it like a barber's razor to shave your head and beard. Then take scales and weigh and divide the hair. 2Burn one-third with fire in the middle of the city when the days of the attack on Jerusalem are over. Then take one-third and cut it up with the knife all around the city. And scatter one-third to the wind. This is how I will chase them with a sword. 3Also take a few of these hairs and tie them in the folds of your clothes. 4Take a few more and throw them into the fire and burn them up. From there a fire will spread to all the people of Israel.

5"This is what the Lord GOD says: This is Jerusalem. I have put her at the center of the nations with countries all around her. 6But she has refused to obey my laws and has been more evil than the nations. She has refused to obey my rules, even more than nations around her. The people of Jerusalem have rejected my laws and have not lived by my rules.

7"So this is what the Lord GOD says: You have caused more trouble than the nations around you. You have not followed my rules or obeyed my laws. You have not even obeyed the laws of the nations around you.

8"So this is what the Lord GOD says: I myself am against you, and I will punish you as the nations watch. 9I will do things among you that I have not done before and that I will never do anything like again, because you do the things I hate. 10So parents among you will eat their children, and children will eat their parents. I will punish you and will scatter to the winds all who are left alive. 11So the Lord GOD says: You have made my Temple unclean with all your evil idols and the hateful things you do. Because of this, as surely as I live, I will cut you off. I will have no pity, and I will show no mercy. [12]A third of you will die by disease or be destroyed by hunger inside your walls. A third will fall dead by the sword outside your walls. And a third I will scatter in every direction as I chase them with a sword. [13]Then my anger will come to an end. I will use it up against them, and then I will be satisfied. Then they will know that I, the LORD, have spoken. After I have carried out my anger against them, they will know how strongly I felt.

[14]"I will make you a ruin and a shame among the nations around you, to be seen by all who pass by. [15]Then the nations around you will shame you and make fun of you. You will be a warning and a terror to them. This will happen when I punish you in my great anger. I, the LORD, have spoken. [16]I will send a time of hunger to destroy you, and then I will make your hunger get even worse, and I will cut off your supply of food. [17]I will send a time of hunger and wild animals against you, and they will kill your children. Disease and death will sweep through your people, and I will bring the sword against you to kill you. I, the LORD, have spoken."

Prophecies Against the Mountains

6 Again the LORD spoke his word to me, saying: [2]"Human, look toward the mountains of Israel, and prophesy against them. [3]Say, 'Mountains of Israel, listen to the word of the Lord GOD. The Lord GOD says this to the mountains, the hills, the ravines, and the valleys: I will bring a sword against you, and I will destroy your places of idol worship. [4]Your altars will be destroyed and your incense altars broken down. Your people will be killed in front of your idols. [5]I will lay the dead bodies of the Israelites in front of their idols, and I will scatter your bones around your altars. [6]In all the places you live, cities will become empty. The places of idol worship will be ruined; your altars will become lonely ruins. Your idols will be broken and brought to an end. Your incense altars will be cut down, and the things you made will be wiped out. [7]Your people will be killed and fall among you. Then you will know that I am the LORD.

[8]" 'But I will leave some people alive; some will not be killed by the nations when you are scattered among the foreign lands. [9]Then those who have escaped will remember me, as they live among the nations where they have been taken as captives. They will remember how I was hurt because they were unfaithful to me and turned away from me and desired to worship their idols. They will hate themselves because of the evil things they did that I hate. [10]Then they will know that I am the LORD. I did not bring this terrible thing on them for no reason.

[11]" 'This is what the Lord GOD says: Clap your hands, stamp your feet, and groan because of all the hateful, evil things the people of Israel have done. They will die by war, hunger, and disease. [12]The person who is far away will die by disease. The one who is nearby will die in war. The person who is still alive and has escaped these will die from hunger. So I will carry out my anger on them. [13]Their people will lie dead among their idols around the altars, on every high hill, on all the mountain tops, and under every green tree and leafy oak—all the places where they offered sweet-smelling incense to their idols. Then you will know that I am the LORD. [14]I will use my power against them to make the land empty and wasted from the desert to Diblah, wherever they live. Then they will know that I am the LORD.' "

PSALM 119:169–176

[169]Hear my cry to you, LORD.
    Let your word help me understand.
[170]Listen to my prayer;
    save me as you promised.
[171]Let me speak your praise,
    because you have taught me your
      demands.
[172]Let me sing about your promises,
    because all your commands are fair.
[173]Give me your helping hand,
    because I have chosen your commands.
[174]I want you to save me, LORD.
    I love your teachings.
[175]Let me live so I can praise you,
    and let your laws help me.
[176]I have wandered like a lost sheep.
    Look for your servant, because I have
      not forgotten your commands.

PROVERBS 28:14

[14]Those who are always respectful will be happy,
but those who are stubborn will get into trouble.

HEBREWS 3:1–19

Jesus Is Greater than Moses

3 So all of you holy brothers and sisters, who were called by God, think about Jesus, who was sent to us and is the high priest of our faith. [2]Jesus was faithful to God as Moses was in God's family. [3]Jesus has more honor than Moses, just as the builder of a house has more honor than the house itself. [4]Every house is built by someone, but the builder of everything is God himself. [5]Moses was faithful in God's family as a servant, and he told what God would say in the future. [6]But Christ is faithful as a Son over God's house. And we are God's house if we confidently maintain our hope.

We Must Continue to Follow God

[7]So it is as the Holy Spirit says:
"Today listen to what he says.
[8]Do not be stubborn as in the past
when you turned against God,
when you tested God in the desert.
[9]There your ancestors tried me and tested me

and saw the things I did for forty years.
[10]I was angry with them.
I said, 'They are not loyal to me
and have not understood my ways.'
[11]I was angry and made a promise,
'They will never enter my rest.'"[n]

Psalm 95:7–11

[12]So brothers and sisters, be careful that none of you has an evil, unbelieving heart that will turn you away from the living God. [13]But encourage each other every day while it is "today."[n] Help each other so none of you will become hardened because sin has tricked you. [14]We all share in Christ if we keep till the end the sure faith we had in the beginning. [15]This is what the Scripture says:
"Today listen to what he says.
Do not be stubborn as in the past
when you turned against God."

Psalm 95:7–8

[16]Who heard God's voice and was against him? It was all those people Moses led out of Egypt. [17]And with whom was God angry for forty years? He was angry with those who sinned, who died in the desert. [18]And to whom was God talking when he promised that they would never enter his rest? He was talking to those who did not obey him. [19]So we see they were not allowed to enter and have God's rest, because they did not believe.

NOVEMBER 8

EZEKIEL 7:1—8:18

Ezekiel Tells of the End

7 Again the LORD spoke his word to me, saying: [2]"Human, the Lord GOD says this to the land of Israel: An end! The end has come on the four corners of the land. [3]Now the end has come for you, and I will send my anger against you. I will judge you for the way you have lived, and I will make you pay for all your actions that I hate. [4]I will have no

pity on you; I will not hold back punishment from you. Instead, I will make you pay for the way you have lived and for your actions that I hate. Then you will know that I am the LORD.

[5]"This is what the Lord GOD says: Disaster on top of disaster is coming. [6]The end has come! The end has come! It has stirred itself up against you! Look! It has come! [7]Disaster has come for you who live in the land! The time has come; the day of confusion is near.

3:11 rest A place of rest God promised to give his people.   **3:13 "today"** This word is taken from verse 7. It means that it is important to do these things now.

There will be no happy shouting on the mountains. [8]Soon I will pour out my anger against you; I will carry out my anger against you. I will judge you for the way you have lived and will make you pay for everything you have done that I hate. [9]I will show no pity, and I will not hold back punishment. I will pay you back for the way you have lived and the things you have done that I hate. Then you will know that I am the LORD who punishes.

[10]"Look, the day is here. It has come. Disaster has come, violence has grown, and there is more pride than ever. [11]Violence has grown into a weapon for punishing wickedness. None of the people will be left—none of that crowd, none of their wealth, and nothing of value. [12]The time has come; the day has arrived. Don't let the buyer be happy or the seller be sad, because my burning anger is against the whole crowd. [13]Sellers will not return to the land they have sold as long as they live, because the vision against all that crowd will not be changed. Because of their sins, they will not save their lives. [14]They have blown the trumpet, and everything is ready. But no one is going to the battle, because my anger is against all that crowd.

[15]"The sword is outside, and disease and hunger are inside. Whoever is in the field will die by the sword. Hunger and disease will destroy those in the city. [16]Those who are left alive and who escape will be on the mountains, moaning like doves of the valleys about their own sin. [17]All hands will hang weakly with fear, and all knees will become weak as water. [18]They will put on rough cloth to show how sad they are. They will tremble all over with fear. Their faces will show their shame, and all their heads will be shaved. [19]The people will throw their silver into the streets, and their gold will be like trash. Their silver and gold will not save them from the LORD's anger. It will not satisfy their hunger or fill their stomachs, because it caused them to fall into sin. [20]They were proud of their beautiful jewelry and used it to make their idols and their evil statues, which I hate. So I will turn their wealth into trash. [21]I will give it to foreigners as loot from war and to the most evil people in the world as treasure, and they will dishonor it. [22]I will also turn away from the people of Israel, and they will dishonor my treasured place. Then robbers will enter and dishonor it.

[23]"Make chains for captives, because the land is full of bloody crimes and the city is full of violence. [24]So I will bring the worst of the nations to take over the people's houses. I will also end the pride of the strong, and their holy places will be dishonored. [25]When the people are suffering greatly, they will look for peace, but there will be none. [26]Disaster will come on top of disaster, and rumor will be added to rumor. Then they will try to get a vision from a prophet; the teachings of God from the priest and the advice from the elders will be lost. [27]The king will cry greatly, the prince will give up hope, and the hands of the people who own land will shake with fear. I will punish them for the way they have lived. The way they have judged others is the way I will judge them. Then they will know that I am the LORD."

Ezekiel's Vision of Jerusalem

8 It was the sixth year, on the fifth day of the sixth month of our captivity. I was sitting in my house with the elders of Judah in front of me. There I felt the power of the Lord GOD. [2]I looked and saw something that looked like a human. From the waist down it looked like fire, and from the waist up it looked like bright glowing metal. [3]It stretched out the shape of a hand and caught me by the hair on my head. The Spirit lifted me up between the earth and the sky. He took me in visions of God to Jerusalem, to the entrance to the north gate of the inner courtyard of the Temple. In the courtyard was the idol that caused God to be jealous. [4]I saw the glory of the God of Israel there, as I had seen on the plain.

[5]Then he said to me, "Human, now look toward the north." So I looked up toward the north, and in the entrance north of the gate of the altar was the idol that caused God to be jealous.

[6]He said to me, "Human, do you see what they are doing? Do you see how many

hateful things the people of Israel are doing here that drive me far away from my Temple? But you will see things more hateful than these."

⁷Then he brought me to the entry of the courtyard. When I looked, I saw a hole in the wall. ⁸He said to me, "Human, dig through the wall." So I dug through the wall and saw an entrance.

⁹Then he said to me, "Go in and see the hateful, evil things they are doing here." ¹⁰So I entered and looked, and I saw every kind of crawling thing and hateful beast and all the idols of the people of Israel, carved on the wall all around. ¹¹Standing in front of these carvings and idols were seventy of the elders of Israel and Jaazaniah son of Shaphan. Each man had his pan for burning incense in his hand, and a sweet-smelling cloud of incense was rising.

¹²Then he said to me, "Human, have you seen what the elders of Israel are doing in the dark? Have you seen each man in the room of his own idol? They say, 'The Lord doesn't see us. The Lord has left the land.' " ¹³He also said to me, "You will see even more hateful things that they are doing."

¹⁴Then he brought me to the entrance of the north gate of the Temple of the Lord, where I saw women sitting and crying for Tammuz.[n] ¹⁵He said to me, "Do you see, human? You will see things even more hateful than these."

¹⁶Then he brought me into the inner courtyard of the Temple. There I saw about twenty-five men at the entrance to the Temple of the Lord, between the porch and the altar. With their backs turned to the Temple of the Lord, they faced east and were worshiping the sun in the east.

¹⁷He said to me, "Do you see, human? Is it unimportant that the people of Judah are doing the hateful things they have done here? They have filled the land with violence and made me continually angry. Look, they are insulting me every way they can. ¹⁸So I will act in anger. I will have no pity, nor will

I show mercy. Even if they shout in my ears, I won't listen to them."

PSALM 120:1–7

A Prayer of Someone Far from Home

A psalm for going up to worship.

120 When I was in trouble, I called to the Lord,
  and he answered me.
²Lord, save me from liars
  and from those who plan evil.

³You who plan evil, what will God do to you?
  How will he punish you?
⁴He will punish you with the sharp arrows of a warrior
  and with burning coals of wood.

⁵How terrible it is for me to live in the land of Meshech,
  to live among the people of Kedar.
⁶I have lived too long
  with people who hate peace.
⁷When I talk peace,
  they want war.

PROVERBS 28:15

¹⁵A wicked ruler is as dangerous to poor people
  as a roaring lion or a charging bear.

HEBREWS 4:1–13

4Now, since God has left us the promise that we may enter his rest, let us be very careful so none of you will fail to enter. ²The Good News was preached to us just as it was to them. But the teaching they heard did not help them, because they heard it but did not accept it with faith.[n] ³We who have believed are able to enter and have God's rest. As God has said,

"I was angry and made a promise,
  'They will never enter my rest.' "

Psalm 95:11

But God's work was finished from the time

8:14 Tammuz Tammuz was a god in Babylon. Every year people thought this god died when the plants died. After they cried for him, they believed he came back to life, and the plants lived again. • **4:2 because . . . faith** Some Greek copies read "because they did not share the faith of those who heard it."

he made the world. [4]In the Scriptures he talked about the seventh day of the week: "And on the seventh day God rested from all his works."[n] [5]And again in the Scripture God said, "They will never enter my rest."

[6]It is still true that some people will enter God's rest, but those who first heard the way to be saved did not enter, because they did not obey. [7]So God planned another day, called "today." He spoke about that day through David a long time later in the same Scripture used before:

"Today listen to what he says.

Do not be stubborn."   *Psalm 95:7–8*

[8]We know that Joshua[n] did not lead the people into that rest, because God spoke later about another day. [9]This shows that the rest[n] for God's people is still coming. [10]Anyone who enters God's rest will rest from his work as God did. [11]Let us try as hard as we can to enter God's rest so that no one will fail by following the example of those who refused to obey.

[12]God's word is alive and working and is sharper than a double-edged sword. It cuts all the way into us, where the soul and the spirit are joined, to the center of our joints and bones. And it judges the thoughts and feelings in our hearts. [13]Nothing in all the world can be hidden from God. Everything is clear and lies open before him, and to him we must explain the way we have lived.

NOVEMBER 9

EZEKIEL 9:1—10:22

Vision of the Angels

9 Then he shouted with a loud voice in my ears, "You who are chosen to punish this city, come near with your weapon in your hand." [2]Then six men came from the direction of the upper gate, which faces north, each with his powerful weapon in his hand. Among them was a man dressed in linen with a writing case at his side. The men went in and stood by the bronze altar.

[3]Then the glory of the God of Israel went up from above the creatures with wings, where it had been, to the place in the Temple where the door opened. He called to the man dressed in linen who had the writing case at his side. [4]He said to the man, "Go through Jerusalem and put a mark on the foreheads of the people who groan and cry about all the hateful things being done among them."

[5]As I listened, he said to the other men, "Go through the city behind the man dressed in linen and kill. Don't pity anyone, and don't show mercy. [6]Kill and destroy old men, young men and women, little children, and older women, but don't touch any who have the mark on them. Start at my Temple." So they started with the elders who were in front of the Temple.

[7]Then he said to the men, "Make the Temple unclean, and fill the courtyards with those who have been killed. Go out!" So the men went out and killed the people in the city. [8]While the men were killing the people, I was left alone. I bowed facedown on the ground and I cried out, "Oh, Lord GOD! Will you destroy everyone left alive in Israel when you turn loose your anger on Jerusalem?"

[9]Then he said to me, "The sin of the people of Israel and Judah is very great. The land is filled with people who murder, and the city is full of people who are not fair. The people say, 'The LORD has left the land, and the LORD does not see.' [10]But I will have no pity, nor will I show mercy. I will bring their evil back on their heads."

[11]Then the man dressed in linen with the writing case at his side reported, "I have done just as you commanded me."

4:4 "And . . . works." Quotation from Genesis 2:2.   **4:8 Joshua** After Moses died, Joshua became leader of the Jewish people and led them into the land that God promised to give them.   **4:9 rest** Literally, "sabbath rest," meaning a sharing in the rest that God began after he created the world.

The Coals of Fire

10 Then I looked and saw in the dome above the heads of the living creatures something like a sapphire gem which looked like a throne. [2]The LORD said to the man dressed in linen, "Go in between the wheels under the living creatures, fill your hands with coals of fire from between the living creatures, and scatter the coals over the city."

As I watched, the man with linen clothes went in. [3]Now the living creatures were standing on the south side of the Temple when the man went in. And a cloud filled the inner courtyard. [4]Then the glory of the LORD went up from the living creatures and stood over the door of the Temple. The Temple was filled with the cloud, and the courtyard was full of the brightness from the glory of the LORD. [5]The sound of the wings of the living creatures was heard all the way to the outer courtyard. It was like the voice of God Almighty when he speaks.

[6]When the LORD commanded the man dressed in linen, "Take fire from between the wheels, from between the living creatures," the man went in and stood by a wheel. [7]One living creature put out his hand to the fire that was among them, took some of the fire, and put it in the hands of the man dressed in linen. Then the man took the fire and went out.

The Wheels and the Creatures

[8]Something that looked like a human hand could be seen under the wings of the living creatures. [9]I saw the four wheels by the living creatures, one wheel by each living creature. The wheels looked like shining chrysolite. [10]All four wheels looked alike: Each looked like a wheel crossways inside another wheel. [11]When the wheels moved, they went in any of the directions that the four living creatures faced. The wheels did not turn about, and the living creatures did not turn their bodies as they went. [12]All their bodies, their backs, their hands, their wings, and the wheels were full of eyes all over. Each of the four living creatures had a wheel. [13]I heard the wheels being called "whirling wheels." [14]Each living creature had four faces. The first face was the face of a creature with wings. The second face was a human face, the third was the face of a lion, and the fourth was the face of an eagle.

[15]Then the living creatures flew up. They were the same living creatures I had seen by the Kebar River. [16]When the living creatures moved, the wheels moved beside them. When the living creatures lifted their wings to fly up from the ground, the wheels did not leave their place beside them. [17]When the living creatures stopped, the wheels stopped. When the creatures went up, the wheels went up also, because the spirit of the living creatures was in the wheels.

[18]Then the glory of the LORD left the door of the Temple and stood over the living creatures. [19]As I watched, the living creatures spread their wings and flew up from the ground, with the wheels beside them. They stood where the east gate of the Temple of the LORD opened, and the glory of the God of Israel was over them.

[20]These were the living creatures I had seen under the God of Israel by the Kebar River. I knew they were called cherubim. [21]Each one had four faces and four wings, and under their wings were things that looked like human hands. [22]Their faces looked the same as the ones I had seen by the Kebar River. They each went straight ahead.

PSALM 121:1–8

The Lord Guards His People

A song for going up to worship.

121 I look up to the hills,
but where does my help come from?
[2]My help comes from the LORD,
who made heaven and earth.

[3]He will not let you be defeated.
He who guards you never sleeps.
[4]He who guards Israel
never rests or sleeps.
[5]The LORD guards you.
The LORD is the shade that protects you
from the sun.
[6]The sun cannot hurt you during the day,
and the moon cannot hurt you at night.

[7]The LORD will protect you from all
dangers;
he will guard your life.
[8]The LORD will guard you as you come
and go,
both now and forever.

PROVERBS 28:16

[16]A ruler without wisdom will be cruel,
but the one who refuses to take dishonest
money will rule a long time.

HEBREWS 4:14—5:10

Jesus Is Our High Priest

[14]Since we have a great high priest, Jesus
the Son of God, who has gone into heaven, let
us hold on to the faith we have. [15]For our high
priest is able to understand our weaknesses.
He was tempted in every way that we are, but
he did not sin. [16]Let us, then, feel very sure
that we can come before God's throne where
there is grace. There we can receive mercy
and grace to help us when we need it.

5 Every high priest is chosen from among
other people. He is given the work of going before God for them to offer gifts and
sacrifices for sins. [2]Since he himself is weak,
he is able to be gentle with those who do not
understand and who are doing wrong
things. [3]Because he is weak, the high priest
must offer sacrifices for his own sins and
also for the sins of the people.

[4]To be a high priest is an honor, but no
one chooses himself for this work. He must
be called by God as Aaron[n] was. [5]So also
Christ did not choose himself to have the
honor of being a high priest, but God chose
him. God said to him,

"You are my Son.
Today I have become your Father."
Psalm 2:7

[6]And in another Scripture God says,

"You are a priest forever,
a priest like Melchizedek."[n]   *Psalm 110:4*

[7]While Jesus lived on earth, he prayed to
God and asked God for help. He prayed with
loud cries and tears to the One who could
save him from death, and his prayer was
heard because he trusted God. [8]Even though
Jesus was the Son of God, he learned obedience by what he suffered. [9]And because his
obedience was perfect, he was able to give
eternal salvation to all who obey him. [10]In
this way God made Jesus a high priest, a
priest like Melchizedek.

NOVEMBER 10

EZEKIEL 11:1—12:28

Prophecies Against Evil Leaders

11 The Spirit lifted me up and brought
me to the front gate of the Temple of
the LORD, which faces east. I saw twenty-five
men where the gate opens, among them
Jaazaniah son of Azzur and Pelatiah son of
Benaiah, who were leaders of the people.
[2]Then the LORD said to me, "Human, these
are the men who plan evil and give wicked
advice in this city of Jerusalem. [3]They say, 'It
is almost time for us to build houses. This
city is like a cooking pot, and we are like the

best meat.' [4]So prophesy against them,
prophesy, human."

[5]Then the Spirit of the LORD entered me
and told me to say: "This is what the LORD
says: You have said these things, people of Israel, and I know what you are thinking. [6]You
have killed many people in this city, filling
its streets with their bodies.

[7]"So this is what the Lord GOD says: Those
people you have killed and left in the middle
of the city are like the best meat, and this
city is like the cooking pot. But I will force
you out of the city. [8]You have feared the
sword, but I will bring a sword against you,

5:4 Aaron Moses' brother and the first Jewish high priest.
(Read Genesis 14:17–24.)

5:6 Melchizedek A priest and king who lived in the time of
Abraham.

says the Lord GOD. [9]I will force you out of the city and hand you over to strangers and punish you. [10]You will die by the sword. I will punish you at the border of Israel so you will know that I am the LORD. [11]This city will not be your cooking pot, and you will not be the best meat in the middle of it. I will punish you at the border of Israel. [12]Then you will know that I am the LORD. You did not live by my rules or obey my laws. Instead, you did the same things as the nations around you."

[13]As I prophesied, Pelatiah son of Benaiah died. Then I bowed facedown on the ground and shouted with a loud voice, "Oh no, Lord GOD! Will you completely destroy the Israelites who are left alive?"

Promise to Those Remaining

[14]The LORD spoke his word to me, saying, [15]"Human, the people still in Jerusalem have spoken about your own relatives and all the people of Israel who are captives with you, saying, 'They are far from the LORD. This land has been given to us as our property.'

[16]"So say, 'This is what the Lord GOD says: I sent the people far away among the nations and scattered them among the countries. But for a little while I have become a Temple to them in the countries where they have gone.'

[17]"So say: 'This is what the Lord GOD says: I will gather you from the nations and bring you together from the countries where you have been scattered. Then I will give you back the land of Israel.'

[18]"When they come to this land, they will remove all the evil idols and all the hateful images. [19]I will give them a desire to respect me completely, and I will put inside them a new way of thinking. I will take out the stubborn heart of stone from their bodies, and I will give them an obedient heart of flesh. [20]Then they will live by my rules and obey my laws and keep them. They will be my people, and I will be their God. [21]But those who want to serve their evil statues and hateful idols, I will pay back for their evil ways, says the Lord GOD."

Ezekiel's Vision Ends

[22]Then the living creatures lifted their wings with the wheels beside them, and the glory of the God of Israel was above them. [23]The glory of the LORD went up from inside Jerusalem and stopped on the mountain on the east side of the city. [24]The Spirit lifted me up and brought me to the captives who had been taken from Judah to Babylonia. This happened in a vision given by the Spirit of God, and then the vision I had seen ended. [25]And I told the captives from Judah all the things the LORD had shown me.

Ezekiel Moves Out

[12]Again the LORD spoke his word to me, saying: [2]"Human, you are living among a people who refuse to obey. They have eyes to see, but they do not see, and they have ears to hear, but they do not hear, because they are a people who refuse to obey.

[3]"So, human, pack your things as if you will be taken away captive, and walk away like a captive in the daytime with the people watching. Move from your place to another with the people watching. Maybe they will understand, even though they are a people who refuse to obey. [4]During the day when the people are watching, bring out the things you would pack as captive. At evening, with the people watching, leave your place like those who are taken away as captives from their country. [5]Dig a hole through the wall while they watch, and bring your things out through it. [6]Lift them onto your shoulders with the people watching, and carry them out in the dark. Cover your face so you cannot see the ground, because I have made you a sign to the people of Israel."

[7]I did these things as I was commanded. In the daytime I brought what I had packed as if I were being taken away captive. Then in the evening I dug through the wall with my hands. I brought my things out in the dark and carried them on my shoulders as the people watched.

[8]Then in the morning the LORD spoke his word to me, saying: [9]"Human, didn't Israel, who refuses to obey, ask you, 'What are you doing?'

[10]"Say to them, 'This is what the Lord GOD says: This message is about the king in Jerusalem and all the people of Israel who live there.' [11]Say, 'I am a sign to you.'

"The same things I have done will be done to the people in Jerusalem. They will be taken away from their country as captives. ¹²The king among them will put his things on his shoulder in the dark and will leave. The people will dig a hole through the wall to bring him out. He will cover his face so he cannot see the ground. ¹³But I will spread my net over him, and he will be caught in my trap. Then I will bring him to Babylon in the land of the Babylonians. He will not see that land, but he will die there. ¹⁴All who are around the king—his helpers and all his army—I will scatter in every direction, and I will chase them with a sword.

¹⁵"They will know that I am the LORD when I scatter them among the nations and spread them among the countries. ¹⁶But I will save a few of them from the sword and from hunger and disease. Then they can tell about their hateful actions among the nations where they go. Then they will know that I am the LORD."

The Lesson of Ezekiel's Shaking

¹⁷The LORD spoke his word to me, saying: ¹⁸"Human, tremble as you eat your food, and shake with fear as you drink your water. ¹⁹Then say to the people of the land: 'This is what the Lord GOD says about the people who live in Jerusalem in the land of Israel: They will eat their food with fear and drink their water in shock, because their land will be stripped bare because of the violence of the people who live in it. ²⁰The cities where people live will become ruins, and the land will become empty. Then you will know that I am the LORD.'"

The Visions Will Come True

²¹The LORD spoke his word to me, saying: ²²"Human, what is this saying you have in the land of Israel: 'The days go by and every vision comes to nothing'? ²³So say to them, 'This is what the Lord GOD says: I will make them stop saying this, and nobody in Israel will use this saying anymore.' But tell them, 'The time is near when every vision will come true. ²⁴There will be no more false visions or pleasing prophecies inside the nation of Israel, ²⁵but I, the LORD, will speak. What I say will be done, and it will not be de-

layed. You refuse to obey, but in your time I will say the word and do it, says the Lord GOD.'"

²⁶The LORD spoke his word to me, saying: ²⁷"Human, the people of Israel are saying, 'The vision that Ezekiel sees is for a time many years from now. He is prophesying about times far away.' ²⁸So say to them: 'The Lord GOD says this: None of my words will be delayed anymore. What I have said will be done, says the Lord GOD.'"

PSALM 122:1–5

Happy People in Jerusalem

A song for going up to worship. Of David.

122 I was happy when they said to me,
"Let's go to the Temple of the LORD."
²Jerusalem, we are standing
at your gates.

³Jerusalem is built as a city
with the buildings close together.
⁴The tribes go up there,
the tribes who belong to the LORD.
It is the rule in Israel
to praise the LORD at Jerusalem.
⁵There the descendants of David
set their thrones to judge the people.

PROVERBS 28:17–18

¹⁷Don't help those who are guilty of
murder;
let them run until they die.

¹⁸Innocent people will be kept safe,
but those who are dishonest will
suddenly be ruined.

HEBREWS 5:11—6:20

Warning Against Falling Away

¹¹We have much to say about this, but it is hard to explain because you are so slow to understand. ¹²By now you should be teachers, but you need someone to teach you again the first lessons of God's message. You still need the teaching that is like milk. You are not ready for solid food. ¹³Anyone who lives on milk is still a baby and knows nothing about right teaching. ¹⁴But solid food is

for those who are grown up. They are mature enough to know the difference between good and evil.

6 So let us go on to grown-up teaching. Let us not go back over the beginning lessons we learned about Christ. We should not again start teaching about faith in God and about turning away from those acts that lead to death. ²We should not return to the teaching about baptisms,ⁿ about laying on of hands,ⁿ about the raising of the dead and eternal judgment. ³And we will go on to grown-up teaching if God allows.

⁴Some people cannot be brought back again to a changed life. They were once in God's light, and enjoyed heaven's gift, and shared in the Holy Spirit. ⁵They found out how good God's word is, and they received the powers of his new world. ⁶But they fell away from Christ. It is impossible to bring them back to a changed life again, because they are nailing the Son of God to a cross again and are shaming him in front of others.

⁷Some people are like land that gets plenty of rain. The land produces a good crop for those who work it, and it receives God's blessings. ⁸Other people are like land that grows thorns and weeds and is worthless. It is about to be cursed by God and will be destroyed by fire.

⁹Dear friends, we are saying this to you, but we really expect better things from you that will lead to your salvation. ¹⁰God is fair; he will not forget the work you did and the love you showed for him by helping his people. And he will remember that you are still helping them. ¹¹We want each of you to go on with the same hard work all your lives so you will surely get what you hope for. ¹²We do not want you to become lazy. Be like those who through faith and patience will receive what God has promised.

¹³God made a promise to Abraham. And as there is no one greater than God, he used himself when he swore to Abraham, ¹⁴saying, "I will surely bless you and give you many descendants."ⁿ ¹⁵Abraham waited patiently for this to happen, and he received what God promised.

¹⁶People always use the name of someone greater than themselves when they swear. The oath proves that what they say is true, and this ends all arguing. ¹⁷God wanted to prove that his promise was true to those who would get what he promised. And he wanted them to understand clearly that his purposes never change, so he made an oath. ¹⁸These two things cannot change: God cannot lie when he makes a promise, and he cannot lie when he makes an oath. These things encourage us who came to God for safety. They give us strength to hold on to the hope we have been given. ¹⁹We have this hope as an anchor for the soul, sure and strong. It enters behind the curtain in the Most Holy Place in heaven, ²⁰where Jesus has gone ahead of us and for us. He has become the high priest forever, a priest like Melchizedek.ⁿ

NOVEMBER 11

Ezekiel Speaks Against False Prophets

13 The LORD spoke his word to me, saying: ²"Human, prophesy against the prophets of Israel. Say to those who make up their own prophecies: 'Listen to the word of the LORD. ³This is what the Lord GOD says: How terrible it will be for the foolish prophets who follow their own ideas and have not seen a vision from me! ⁴People of Israel, your prophets have been like wild

---

6:2 baptisms The word here may refer to Christian baptism, or it may refer to the Jewish ceremonial washings.
6:2 laying on of hands The laying on of hands had many purposes, including the giving of a blessing, power, or authority.
6:14 "I . . . descendants." Quotation from Genesis 22:17.   **6:20 Melchizedek** A priest and king who lived in the time of Abraham. (Read Genesis 14:17–24.)

dogs hunting to kill and eat among ruins. [5]Israel is like a house in ruins, but you have not gone up into the broken places or repaired the wall. So how can Israel hold back the enemy in the battle on the LORD's day of judging? [6]Your prophets see false visions and prophesy lies. They say, "This is the message of the LORD," when the LORD has not sent them. But they still hope their words will come true. [7]You said, "This is the message of the LORD," but that is a false vision. Your prophecies are lies, because I have not spoken.

[8]" 'So this is what the Lord GOD says: Because you prophets spoke things that are false and saw visions that do not come true, I am against you, says the Lord GOD. [9]I will punish the prophets who see false visions and prophesy lies. They will have no place among my people. Their names will not be written on the list of the people of Israel, and they will not enter the land of Israel. Then you will know that I am the Lord GOD.

[10]" 'It is because they lead my people the wrong way by saying, "Peace!" when there is no peace. When the people build a weak wall, the prophets cover it with whitewash to make it look strong. [11]So tell those who cover a weak wall with whitewash that it will fall down. Rain will pour down, hailstones will fall, and a stormy wind will break the wall down. [12]When the wall has fallen, people will ask you, "Where is the whitewash you used on the wall?"

[13]" 'So this is what the Lord GOD says: I will break the wall with a stormy wind. In my anger rain will pour down, and hailstones will destroy the wall. [14]I will tear down the wall on which you put whitewash. I will level it to the ground so that people will see the wall's foundation. And when the wall falls, you will be destroyed under it. Then you will know that I am the LORD. [15]So I will carry out my anger on the wall and against those who covered it with whitewash. Then I will tell you, "The wall is gone, and those who covered it with whitewash are gone. [16]The prophets of Israel who prophesy to Jerusalem and who see visions of peace for the city, when there is no peace, will be gone, says the Lord GOD." '

False Women Prophets

[17]"Now, human, look toward the women among your people who make up their own prophecies. Prophesy against them. [18]Say, 'This is what the Lord GOD says: How terrible it will be for women who sew magic charms on their wrists and make veils of every length to trap people! You ruin the lives of my people but try to save your own lives. [19]For handfuls of barley and pieces of bread, you have dishonored me among my people. By lying to my people, who listen to lies, you have killed people who should not die, and you have kept alive those who should not live.

[20]" 'So this is what the Lord GOD says: I am against your magic charms, by which you trap people as if they were birds. I will tear those charms off your arms, and I will free those people you have trapped like birds. [21]I will also tear off your veils and save my people from your hands. They will no longer be trapped by your power. Then you will know that I am the LORD. [22]By your lies you have caused those who did right to be sad, when I did not make them sad. And you have encouraged the wicked not to stop being wicked, which would have saved their lives. [23]So you will not see false visions or prophesy anymore, and I will save my people from your power so you will know that I am the LORD.' "

Stop Worshiping Idols

14 Some of the elders of Israel came to me and sat down in front of me. [2]Then the LORD spoke his word to me, saying: [3]"Human, these people want to worship idols. They put up evil things that cause people to sin. Should I allow them to ask me for help? [4]So speak to them and tell them, 'This is what the Lord GOD says: When any of the people of Israel want to worship idols and put up evil things that cause people to sin and then come to the prophet, I, the LORD, will answer them myself for worshiping idols. [5]Then I will win back my people Israel, who have left me because of all their idols.'

[6]"So say to the people of Israel, 'This is what the Lord GOD says: Change your hearts and lives, and stop worshiping idols. Stop

doing all the things I hate. [7]Any of the Israelites or foreigners in Israel can separate themselves from me by wanting to worship idols or by putting up the things that cause people to sin. Then if they come to the prophet to ask me questions, I, the LORD, will answer them myself. [8]I will reject them. I will make them a sign and an example, and I will separate them from my people. Then you will know that I am the LORD.

[9]"'But if the prophet is tricked into giving a prophecy, it is because I, the LORD, have tricked that prophet to speak. Then I will use my power against him and destroy him from among my people Israel. [10]The prophet will be as guilty as the one who asks him for help; both will be responsible for their guilt. [11]Then the nation of Israel will not leave me anymore or make themselves unclean anymore with all their sins. They will be my people, and I will be their God, says the Lord GOD.'"

Jerusalem Will Not Be Spared

[12]The LORD spoke his word to me, saying: [13]"Human, if the people of a country sin against me by not being loyal, I will use my power against them. I will cut off their supply of food and send a time of hunger, destroying both people and animals. [14]Even if three great men like Noah, Daniel, and Job were in that country, their goodness could save only themselves, says the Lord GOD.

[15]"Or I might send wild animals into that land, leaving the land empty and without children. Then no one would pass through it because of the animals. [16]As surely as I live, says the Lord GOD, even if Noah, Daniel, and Job were in the land, they could not save their own sons or daughters. They could save only themselves, but that country would become empty.

[17]"Or I might bring a war against that country. I might say, 'Let a war be fought in that land,' in this way destroying its people and its animals. [18]As surely as I live, says the Lord GOD, even if those three men were in the land, they could not save their sons or daughters. They could save only themselves.

[19]"Or I might cause a disease to spread in that country. I might pour out my anger against it, destroying and killing people and animals. [20]As surely as I live, says the Lord GOD, even if Noah, Daniel, and Job were in the land, they could not save their son or daughter. They could save only themselves because they did what was right.

[21]"This is what the Lord GOD says: My plans for Jerusalem are much worse! I will send my four terrible punishments against it—war, hunger, wild animals, and disease—to destroy its people and animals. [22]But some people will escape; some sons and daughters will be led out. They will come out to you, and you will see what happens to people who live as they did. Then you will be comforted after the disasters I have brought against Jerusalem, after all the things I have brought against it. [23]You will be comforted when you see what happens to them for living as they did, because you will know there was a good reason for what I did to Jerusalem, says the Lord GOD."

PSALM 122:6–9

[6]Pray for peace in Jerusalem:
   "May those who love her be safe.
[7]May there be peace within her walls
   and safety within her strong towers."
[8]To help my relatives and friends,
   I say, "Let Jerusalem have peace."
[9]For the sake of the Temple of the LORD
      our God,
   I wish good for her.

PROVERBS 28:19

[19]Those who work their land will have
      plenty of food,
   but the ones who chase empty dreams
      instead will end up poor.

HEBREWS 7:1–28

The Priest Melchizedek

7 Melchizedek[n] was the king of Salem and a priest for God Most High. He met Abra-

---

7:1 **Melchizedek** A priest and king who lived in the time of Abraham. (Read Genesis 14:17–24.)

ham when Abraham was coming back after defeating the kings. When they met, Melchizedek blessed Abraham, [2]and Abraham gave him a tenth of everything he had brought back from the battle. First, Melchizedek's name means "king of goodness," and he is king of Salem, which means "king of peace." [3]No one knows who Melchizedek's father or mother was,[n] where he came from, when he was born, or when he died. Melchizedek is like the Son of God; he continues being a priest forever.

[4]You can see how great Melchizedek was. Abraham, the great father, gave him a tenth of everything that he won in battle. [5]Now the law says that those in the tribe of Levi who become priests must collect a tenth from the people—their own people—even though the priests and the people are from the family of Abraham. [6]Melchizedek was not from the tribe of Levi, but he collected a tenth from Abraham. And he blessed Abraham, the man who had God's promises. [7]Now everyone knows that the more important person blesses the less important person. [8]Priests receive a tenth, even though they are only men who live and then die. But Melchizedek, who received a tenth from Abraham, continues living, as the Scripture says. [9]We might even say that Levi, who receives a tenth, also paid it when Abraham paid Melchizedek a tenth. [10]Levi was not yet born, but he was in the body of his ancestor when Melchizedek met Abraham.

[11]The people were given the law[n] concerning the system of priests from the tribe of Levi, but they could not be made perfect through that system. So there was a need for another priest to come, a priest like Melchizedek, not Aaron. [12]And when a different kind of priest comes, the law must be changed, too. [13]We are saying these things about Christ, who belonged to a different tribe. No one from that tribe ever served as a priest at the altar. [14]It is clear that our Lord

came from the tribe of Judah, and Moses said nothing about priests belonging to that tribe.

Jesus Is like Melchizedek

[15]And this becomes even more clear when we see that another priest comes who is like Melchizedek.[n] [16]He was not made a priest by human rules and laws but through the power of his life, which continues forever. [17]It is said about him,

"You are a priest forever,
    a priest like Melchizedek." *Psalm 110:4*

[18]The old rule is now set aside, because it was weak and useless. [19]The law of Moses could not make anything perfect. But now a better hope has been given to us, and with this hope we can come near to God. [20]It is important that God did this with an oath. Others became priests without an oath, [21]but Christ became a priest with God's oath. God said:

"The Lord has made a promise
    and will not change his mind.
'You are a priest forever.'" *Psalm 110:4*

[22]This means that Jesus is the guarantee of a better agreement[n] from God to his people.

[23]When one of the other priests died, he could not continue being a priest. So there were many priests. [24]But because Jesus lives forever, he will never stop serving as priest. [25]So he is able always to save those who come to God through him because he always lives, asking God to help them.

[26]Jesus is the kind of high priest we need. He is holy, sinless, pure, not influenced by sinners, and he is raised above the heavens. [27]He is not like the other priests who had to offer sacrifices every day, first for their own sins, and then for the sins of the people. Christ offered his sacrifice only once and for all time when he offered himself. [28]The law chooses high priests who are people with weaknesses, but the word of God's oath came later than the law. It made God's Son to be the high priest, and that Son has been made perfect forever.

7:3 No . . . was Literally, "Melchizedek was without father, without mother, without genealogy." **7:11 The . . . law** This refers to the people of Israel who were given the Law of Moses. **7:15 Melchizedek** A priest and king who lived in the time of Abraham. (Read Genesis 14:17–24.) **7:22 agreement** God gives a contract or agreement to his people. For the Jews, this agreement was the Law of Moses. But now God has given a better agreement to his people through Christ.

NOVEMBER 12

EZEKIEL 15:1—16:63

Story of the Vine

15 The LORD spoke his word to me, saying: ²"Human, is the wood of the vine better than the wood of any tree in the forest? ³Can wood be taken from the vine to make anything? Can you use it to make a peg on which to hang something? ⁴If the vine is thrown into the fire for fuel, and the fire burns up both ends and starts to burn the middle, is it useful for anything? ⁵When the vine was whole, it couldn't be made into anything. When the fire has burned it completely, it certainly cannot be made into anything."

⁶So this is what the Lord GOD says: "Out of all the trees in the forest, I have given the wood of the vine as fuel for fire. In the same way I have given up the people who live in Jerusalem ⁷and will turn against them. Although they came through one fire, fire will still destroy them. When I turn against them, you will know that I am the LORD. ⁸So I will make the land empty, because the people have not been loyal, says the Lord GOD."

The Lord's Kindness to Jerusalem

16 The LORD spoke his word to me, saying: ²"Human, tell Jerusalem about her hateful actions. ³Say, 'This is what the Lord GOD says to Jerusalem: Your beginnings and your ancestors were in the land of the Canaanites. Your father was an Amorite, and your mother was a Hittite. ⁴On the day you were born, your cord[n] was not cut. You were not washed with water to clean you. You were not rubbed with salt or wrapped in cloths. ⁵No one felt sorry enough for you to do any of these things for you. No, you were thrown out into the open field, because you were hated on the day you were born.

⁶"'When I passed by and saw you kicking about in your blood, I said to you, "Live!" ⁷I made you grow like a plant in the field. You grew up and became tall and became like a beautiful jewel. Your breasts formed, and

your hair grew, but you were naked and without clothes.

⁸"'Later when I passed by and looked at you, I saw that you were old enough for love. So I spread my robe over you and covered your nakedness. I also made a promise to you and entered into an agreement with you so that you became mine, says the Lord GOD.

⁹"'Then I bathed you with water, washed all the blood off of you, and put oil on you. ¹⁰I put beautiful clothes made with needlework on you and put sandals of fine leather on your feet. I wrapped you in fine linen and covered you with silk. ¹¹I put jewelry on you: bracelets on your arms, a necklace around your neck, ¹²a ring in your nose, earrings in your ears, and a beautiful crown on your head. ¹³So you wore gold and silver. Your clothes were made of fine linen, silk, and beautiful needlework. You ate fine flour, honey, and olive oil. You were very beautiful and became a queen. ¹⁴Then you became famous among the nations, because you were so beautiful. Your beauty was perfect, because of the glory I gave you, says the Lord GOD.

Jerusalem Becomes a Prostitute

¹⁵"'But you trusted in your beauty. You became a prostitute, because you were so famous. You had sexual relations with anyone who passed by. ¹⁶You took some of your clothes and made your places of worship colorful. There you carried on your prostitution. These things should not happen; they should never occur. ¹⁷You also took your beautiful jewelry, made from my gold and silver I had given you, and you made for yourselves male idols so you could be a prostitute with them. ¹⁸Then you took your clothes with beautiful needlework and covered the idols. You gave my oil and incense as an offering to them. ¹⁹Also, you took the bread I gave you, the fine flour, oil, and honey I gave you to eat, and you offered

---

16:4 cord The umbilical cord that gives the unborn baby food and air from its mother.

them before the gods as a pleasing smell. This is what happened, says the Lord GOD.

20"'But your sexual sins were not enough for you. You also took your sons and daughters who were my children, and you sacrificed them to the idols as food. 21You killed my children and offered them up in fire to the idols. 22While you did all your hateful acts and sexual sins, you did not remember when you were young, when you were naked and had no clothes and were left in your blood.

23"'How terrible! How terrible it will be for you, says the Lord GOD. After you did all these evil things, 24you built yourself a place to worship gods. You made for yourself a place of worship in every city square. 25You built a place of worship at the beginning of every street. You made your beauty hateful, offering your body for sex to anyone who passed by, so your sexual sins became worse and worse. 26You also had sexual relations with the Egyptians, who were your neighbors and partners in sexual sin. Your sexual sins became even worse, and they caused me to be angry. 27So then, I used my power against you and took away some of your land. I let you be defeated by those who hate you, the Philistine women, who were ashamed of your evil ways. 28Also, you had sexual relations with the Assyrians, because you could not be satisfied. Even though you had sexual relations with them, you still were not satisfied. 29You did many more sexual sins in Babylonia, the land of traders, but even this did not satisfy you.

30"'Truly your will is weak, says the Lord GOD. You do all the things a stubborn prostitute does. 31You built your place to worship gods at the beginning of every street, and you made places of worship in every city square. But you were not like a prostitute when you refused to accept payment.

32"'You are a wife who is guilty of adultery. You desire strangers instead of your husband. 33Men pay prostitutes, but you pay all your lovers to come to you. And they come from all around for sexual relations. 34So you are different from other prostitutes. No man asks you to be a prostitute, and you pay money instead of having money paid to you. Yes, you are different.

The Prostitute Is Judged

35"'So, prostitute, hear the word of the LORD. 36This is what the Lord GOD says: You showed your nakedness to other countries. You uncovered your body in your sexual sins with them as your lovers and with all your hateful idols. You killed your children and offered their blood to your idols. 37So I will gather all your lovers with whom you found pleasure. Yes, I will gather all those you loved and those you hated. I will gather them against you from all around, and I will strip you naked in front of them so they can see your nakedness. 38I will punish you as women guilty of adultery or as murderers are punished. I will put you to death because I am angry and jealous. 39I will also hand you over to your lovers. They will tear down your places of worship and destroy other places where you worship gods. They will tear off your clothes and take away your jewelry, leaving you naked and bare. 40They will bring a crowd against you to throw stones at you and to cut you into pieces with their swords. 41They will burn down your houses and will punish you in front of many women. I will put an end to your sexual sins, and you will no longer pay your lovers. 42Then I will rest from my anger against you, and I will stop being jealous. I will be quiet and not angry anymore.

43"'Because you didn't remember when you were young, but have made me angry in all these ways, I will repay you for what you have done, says the Lord GOD. Didn't you add sexual sins to all your other acts which I hate?

44"'Everyone who uses wise sayings will say this about you: "The daughter is like her mother." 45You are like your mother, who hated her husband and children. You are also like your sisters, who hated their husbands and children. Your mother was a Hittite, and your father was an Amorite. 46Your older sister is Samaria, who lived north of you with her daughters; your younger sister is Sodom, who lived south of you with her daughters. 47You not only followed their ways and did the hateful things they did, but you were soon worse than they were in all your ways. 48As surely as I live, says the Lord GOD, this is true. Your sister Sodom and her daughters never did what you and your daughters have done.

⁴⁹" 'This was the sin of your sister Sodom: She and her daughters were proud and had plenty of food and lived in great comfort, but she did not help the poor and needy. ⁵⁰So Sodom and her daughters were proud and did things I hate in front of me. So I got rid of them when I saw what they did. ⁵¹Also, Samaria did not do half the sins you do; you have done more hateful things than they did. So you make your sisters look good because of all the hateful things you have done. ⁵²You will suffer disgrace, because you have provided an excuse for your sisters. They are better than you are. Your sins were even more terrible than theirs. Feel ashamed and suffer disgrace, because you made your sisters look good.

⁵³" 'But I will give back to Sodom and her daughters the good things they once had. I will give back to Samaria and her daughters the good things they once had. And with them I will also give back the good things you once had ⁵⁴so you may suffer disgrace and feel ashamed for all the things you have done. You even gave comfort to your sisters in their sins. ⁵⁵Your sisters, Sodom with her daughters and Samaria with her daughters, will return to what they were before. You and your daughters will also return to what you were before. ⁵⁶You humiliated your sister Sodom when you were proud, ⁵⁷before your evil was uncovered. And now the Edomite women and their neighbors humiliate you. Even the Philistine women humiliate you. Those around you hate you. ⁵⁸This is your punishment for your terrible sins and for actions that I hate, says the LORD.

God Keeps His Promises

⁵⁹" 'This is what the Lord GOD says: I will do to you what you have done. You hated and broke the agreement you promised to keep. ⁶⁰But I will remember my agreement I made with you when you were young, and I will make an agreement that will continue forever with you. ⁶¹Then you will remember what you have done and feel ashamed when you receive your sisters—both your older

and your younger sisters. I will give them to you like daughters, but not because they share in my agreement with you. ⁶²I will set up my agreement with you, and you will know that I am the LORD. ⁶³You will remember what you did and feel ashamed. You will not open your mouth again because of your shame, when I forgive you for all the things you have done, says the Lord GOD.' "

PSALM 123:1–4

A Prayer for Mercy

A song for going up to worship.

123 LORD, I look upward to you,
you who live in heaven.
²Slaves depend on their masters,
and a female servant depends on her mistress.
In the same way, we depend on the LORD our God;
we wait for him to show us mercy.

³Have mercy on us, LORD. Have mercy on us,
because we have been insulted.
⁴We have suffered many insults from lazy people
and much cruelty from the proud.

PROVERBS 28:20

²⁰A truthful person will have many blessings,
but those eager to get rich will be punished.

HEBREWS 8:1–13

Jesus Is Our High Priest

8 Here is the point of what we are saying: We have a high priest who sits on the right side of God's throne in heaven. ²Our high priest serves in the Most Holy Place, the true place of worship that was made by God, not by humans.

³Every high priest has the work of offering gifts and sacrifices to God. So our high priest must also offer something to God. ⁴If our high priest were now living on earth, he would not be a priest, because there are al-

ready priests here who follow the law by offering gifts to God. [5]The work they do as priests is only a copy and a shadow of what is in heaven. This is why God warned Moses when he was ready to build the Holy Tent: "Be very careful to make everything by the plan I showed you on the mountain."[n] [6]But the priestly work that has been given to Jesus is much greater than the work that was given to the other priests. In the same way, the new agreement that Jesus brought from God to his people is much greater than the old one. And the new agreement is based on promises of better things.

[7]If there had been nothing wrong with the first agreement,[n] there would have been no need for a second agreement. [8]But God found something wrong with his people. He says:[n]

"Look, the time is coming, says the Lord,
when I will make a new agreement
with the people of Israel
and the people of Judah.
[9]It will not be like the agreement
I made with their ancestors
when I took them by the hand
to bring them out of Egypt.
But they broke that agreement,
and I turned away from them, says the Lord.
[10]This is the agreement I will make
with the people of Israel at that time,
says the Lord.
I will put my teachings in their minds
and write them on their hearts.
I will be their God,
and they will be my people.
[11]People will no longer have to teach their neighbors and relatives
to know the Lord,
because all people will know me,
from the least to the most important.
[12]I will forgive them for the wicked things they did,
and I will not remember their sins anymore." *Jeremiah 31:31–34*

[13]God called this a new agreement, so he has made the first agreement old. And anything that is old and worn out is ready to disappear.

NOVEMBER 13

EZEKIEL 17:1—18:32

The Eagle and the Vine

17 The LORD spoke his word to me, saying: [2]"Human, give a riddle and tell a story to the people of Israel. [3]Say, 'This is what the Lord GOD says: A giant eagle with big wings and long feathers of many different colors came to Lebanon and took hold of the top of a cedar tree. [4]He pulled off the top branch and brought it to a land of traders, where he planted it in a city of traders.

[5]"'The eagle took some seed from the land and planted it in a good field near plenty of water. He planted it to grow like a willow tree. [6]It sprouted and became a low vine that spread over the ground. The branches turned toward the eagle, but the roots were under the eagle. So the seed became a vine, and its branches grew, sending out leaves.

[7]"'But there was another giant eagle with big wings and many feathers. The vine then bent its roots toward this eagle. It sent out its branches from the area where it was planted toward the eagle so he could water it. [8]It had been planted in a good field by plenty of water so it could grow branches and give fruit. It could have become a fine vine.'

[9]"Say to them, 'This is what the Lord GOD says: The vine will not continue to grow. The first eagle will pull up the vine's roots and

---

strip off its fruit. Then the vine and all its new leaves will dry up and die. It will not take a strong arm or many people to pull the vine up by its roots. [10]Even if it is planted again, it will not continue to grow. It will completely dry up and die when the east wind hits it in the area where it grew.'"

Zedekiah Against Nebuchadnezzar

[11]Then the LORD spoke his word to me, saying: [12]"Say now to the people who refuse to obey: 'Do you know what these things mean?' Say: 'The king of Babylon came to Jerusalem and took the king and important men of Jerusalem and brought them to Babylon. [13]Then he took a member of the family of the king of Judah and made an agreement with him, forcing him to take an oath. The king also took away the leaders of Judah [14]to make the kingdom weak so it would not be strong again. Then the kingdom of Judah could continue only by keeping its agreement with the king of Babylon. [15]But the king of Judah turned against the king of Babylon by sending his messengers to Egypt and asking them for horses and many soldiers. Will the king of Judah succeed? Will the one who does such things escape? He cannot break the agreement and escape.

[16]"'As surely as I live, says the Lord GOD, he will die in Babylon, in the land of the king who made him king of Judah. The king of Judah hated his promise to the king of Babylon and broke his agreement with him. [17]The king of Egypt with his mighty army and many people will not help the king of Judah in the war. The Babylonians will build devices to attack the cities and to kill many people. [18]The king of Judah showed that he hated the promise by breaking the agreement. He promised to support Babylon, but he did all these things. So he will not escape.

[19]"'So this is what the Lord GOD says: As surely as I live, this is true: I will pay back the king of Judah for hating my promise and breaking my agreement. [20]I will spread my net over him, and he will be caught in my trap. Then I will bring him to Babylon, where I will punish him for the unfaithful acts he did against me. [21]All the best of his soldiers who escape will die by the sword, and those

who live will be scattered to every wind. Then you will know that I, the LORD, have spoken.

[22]"'This is what the Lord GOD says: I myself will also take a young branch from the top of a cedar tree, and I will plant it. I will cut off a small twig from the top of the tree's young branches, and I will plant it on a very high mountain. [23]I will plant it on the high mountain of Israel. Then it will grow branches and give fruit and become a great cedar tree. Birds of every kind will build nests in it and live in the shelter of the tree's branches. [24]Then all the trees in the countryside will know that I am the LORD. I bring down the high tree and make the low tree tall. I dry up the green tree and make the dry tree grow. I am the LORD. I have spoken, and I will do it.'"

God Is Fair

18 The LORD spoke his word to me, saying: [2]"What do you mean by using this saying about the land of Israel:

'The parents have eaten sour grapes,
    and that caused the children to grind
        their teeth from the sour taste'?

[3]"As surely as I live, says the Lord GOD, this is true: You will not use this saying in Israel anymore. [4]Every living thing belongs to me. The life of the parent is mine, and the life of the child is mine. The person who sins is the one who will die.

[5]"Suppose a person is good and does what is fair and right. [6]He does not eat at the mountain places of worship. He does not look to the idols of Israel for help. He does not have sexual relations with his neighbor's wife or with a woman during her time of monthly bleeding. [7]He does not mistreat anyone but returns what was given as a promise for a loan. He does not rob other people. He gives bread to the hungry and clothes to those who have none. [8]He does not lend money to get too much interest or profit. He keeps his hand from doing wrong. He judges fairly between one person and another. [9]He lives by my rules and obeys my laws faithfully. Whoever does these things is good and will surely live, says the Lord GOD.

[10]"But suppose this person has a wild son who murders people and who does any of

these other things. ¹¹(But the father himself has not done any of these things.) This son eats at the mountain places of worship. He has sexual relations with his neighbor's wife. ¹²He mistreats the poor and needy. He steals and refuses to return what was promised for a loan. He looks to idols for help. He does things which I hate. ¹³He lends money for too much interest and profit. Will this son live? No, he will not live! He has done all these hateful things, so he will surely be put to death. He will be responsible for his own death.

¹⁴"Now suppose this son has a son who has seen all his father's sins, but after seeing them does not do those things. ¹⁵He does not eat at the mountain places of worship. He does not look to the idols of Israel for help. He does not have sexual relations with his neighbor's wife. ¹⁶He does not mistreat anyone or keep something promised for a loan or steal. He gives bread to the hungry and clothes to those who have none. ¹⁷He keeps his hand from doing wrong. He does not take too much interest or profit when he lends money. He obeys my laws and lives by my rules. He will not die for his father's sin; he will surely live. ¹⁸But his father took other people's money unfairly and robbed his brother and did what was wrong among his people. So he will die for his own sin.

¹⁹"But you ask, 'Why is the son not punished for the father's sin?' The son has done what is fair and right. He obeys all my rules, so he will surely live. ²⁰The person who sins is the one who will die. A child will not be punished for a parent's sin, and a parent will not be punished for a child's sin. Those who do right will enjoy the results of their own goodness; evil people will suffer the results of their own evil.

²¹"But suppose the wicked stop doing all the sins they have done and obey all my rules and do what is fair and right. Then they will surely live; they will not die. ²²Their sins will be forgotten. Because they have done what is right, they will live. ²³I do not really want the wicked to die, says the Lord GOD. I want them to stop their bad ways and live.

²⁴"But suppose good people stop doing good and do wrong and do the same hateful things the wicked do. Will they live? All their

good acts will be forgotten, because they became unfaithful. They have sinned, so they will die because of their sins.

²⁵"But you say, 'What the Lord does isn't fair.' Listen, people of Israel. I am fair. It is what you do that is not fair! ²⁶When good people stop doing good and do wrong, they will die because of it. They will die, because they did wrong. ²⁷When the wicked stop being wicked and do what is fair and right, they will save their lives. ²⁸Because they thought about it and stopped doing all the sins they had done, they will surely live; they will not die. ²⁹But the people of Israel still say, 'What the Lord does isn't fair.' People of Israel, I am fair. It is what you do that is not fair.

³⁰"So I will judge you, people of Israel; I will judge each of you by what you do, says the Lord GOD. Change your hearts and stop all your sinning so sin will not bring your ruin. ³¹Get rid of all the sins you have done, and get for yourselves a new heart and a new way of thinking. Why do you want to die, people of Israel? ³²I do not want anyone to die, says the Lord GOD, so change your hearts and lives so you may live.

PSALM 124:1-8

The Lord Saves His People

A song for going up to worship. Of David.

124 What if the LORD had not been on our side?
(Let Israel repeat this.)
²What if the LORD had not been on our side when we were attacked?
³When they were angry with us, they would have swallowed us alive.
⁴They would have been like a flood drowning us;
they would have poured over us like a river.
⁵ They would have swept us away like a mighty stream.

⁶Praise the LORD, who did not let them chew us up.
⁷We escaped like a bird from the hunter's trap.
The trap broke, and we escaped.

[8]Our help comes from the LORD,
who made heaven and earth.

PROVERBS 28:21

[21]It is not good for a judge to take sides,
but some will sin for only a piece of
bread.

HEBREWS 9:1–22

The Old Agreement

9 The first agreement[n] had rules for worship and a place on earth for worship.
[2]The Holy Tent was set up for this. The first
area in the Tent was called the Holy Place. In
it were the lamp and the table with the bread
that was made holy for God. [3]Behind the second curtain was a room called the Most Holy
Place. [4]In it was a golden altar for burning
incense and the Ark covered with gold that
held the old agreement. Inside this Ark was a
golden jar of manna, Aaron's rod that once
grew leaves, and the stone tablets of the old
agreement. [5]Above the Ark were the creatures that showed God's glory, whose wings
reached over the lid. But we cannot tell
everything about these things now.

[6]When everything in the Tent was made
ready in this way, the priests went into the
first room every day to worship. [7]But only
the high priest could go into the second
room, and he did that only once a year. He
could never enter the inner room without
taking blood with him, which he offered to
God for himself and for sins the people did
without knowing they did them. [8]The Holy
Spirit uses this to show that the way into the
Most Holy Place was not open while the system of the old Holy Tent was still being used.
[9]This is an example for the present time. It
shows that the gifts and sacrifices offered
cannot make the conscience of the wor-
shiper perfect. [10]These gifts and sacrifices
were only about food and drink and special
washings. They were rules for the body, to be
followed until the time of God's new way.

The New Agreement

[11]But when Christ came as the high priest
of the good things we now have,[n] he entered
the greater and more perfect tent. It is not
made by humans and does not belong to this
world. [12]Christ entered the Most Holy Place
only once—and for all time. He did not take
with him the blood of goats and calves. His
sacrifice was his own blood, and by it he set
us free from sin forever. [13]The blood of goats
and bulls and the ashes of a cow are sprinkled on the people who are unclean, and this
makes their bodies clean again. [14]How much
more is done by the blood of Christ. He offered himself through the eternal Spirit[n] as a
perfect sacrifice to God. His blood will make
our consciences pure from useless acts so we
may serve the living God.

[15]For this reason Christ brings a new
agreement from God to his people. Those
who are called by God can now receive the
blessings he has promised, blessings that
will last forever. They can have those things
because Christ died so that the people who
lived under the first agreement could be set
free from sin.

[16]When there is a will,[n] it must be proven
that the one who wrote that will is dead. [17]A
will means nothing while the person is
alive; it can be used only after the person
dies. [18]This is why even the first agreement
could not begin without blood to show
death. [19]First, Moses told all the people
every command in the law. Next he took the
blood of calves and mixed it with water.
Then he used red wool and a branch of the
hyssop plant to sprinkle it on the book of
the law and on all the people. [20]He said,
"This is the blood that begins the Agreement that God commanded you to obey."[n]
[21]In the same way, Moses sprinkled the
blood on the Holy Tent and over all the
things used in worship. [22]The law says that
almost everything must be made clean by
blood, and sins cannot be forgiven without
blood to show death.

9:1 first agreement The contract God gave the Jewish people when he gave them the Law of Moses. **9:11 good . . . have**
Some Greek copies read "good things that are to come." **9:14 Spirit** This refers to the Holy Spirit, to Christ's own spirit, or
to the spiritual and eternal nature of his sacrifice. **9:16 will** A legal document that shows how a person's money and
property are to be distributed at the time of death. This is the same word in Greek as "agreement" in verse 15.
9:20 "This . . . obey." Quotation from Exodus 24:8.

NOVEMBER 14

EZEKIEL 19:1—20:49

A Sad Song for Israel

19 "Sing a funeral song for the leaders of Israel. ²Say:

'Your mother was like a female lion.
   She lay down among the young lions.
   She had many cubs.
³When she brought up one of her cubs,
   he became a strong lion.
He learned to tear the animals he
      hunted,
   and he ate people.
⁴The nations heard about him.
   He was trapped in their pit,
and they brought him with hooks
   to the land of Egypt.

⁵" 'The mother lion waited and saw
   that there was no hope for her cub.
So she took another one of her cubs
   and made him a strong lion.
⁶This cub roamed among the lions.
   He was now a strong lion.
He learned to tear the animals he
      hunted,
   and he ate people.
⁷He tore down their strong places
   and destroyed their cities.
The land and everything in it
   were terrified by the sound of his roar.
⁸Then the nations came against him
   from areas all around,
and they spread their net over him.
   He was trapped in their pit.
⁹Then they put him into a cage with
      chains
   and brought him to the king of
      Babylon.
They put him into prison
   so his roar could not be heard again
   on the mountains of Israel.

¹⁰" 'Your mother was like a vine in your
      vineyard,
   planted beside the water.
The vine had many branches and gave
      much fruit,
   because there was plenty of water.
¹¹The vine had strong branches,
   good enough for a king's scepter.
The vine became tall
   among the thick branches.
And it was seen, because it was tall
   with many branches.
¹²But it was pulled up by its roots in anger
   and thrown down to the ground.
The east wind dried it up.
   Its fruit was torn off.
Its strong branches were broken off
   and burned up.
¹³Now the vine is planted in the desert,
   in a dry and thirsty land.
¹⁴Fire spread from the vine's main branch,
   destroying its fruit.
There is not a strong branch left on it
   that could become a scepter for a king.'
This is a funeral song; it is to be used as a funeral song."

Israel Has Refused God

20 It was the seventh year of our captivity, in the fifth month, on the tenth day of the month. Some of the elders of Israel came to ask about the LORD and sat down in front of me.

²The LORD spoke his word to me, saying: ³"Human, speak to the elders of Israel and say to them: 'This is what the Lord GOD says: Did you come to ask me questions? As surely as I live, I will not let you ask me questions.'

⁴"Will you judge them? Will you judge them, human? Let them know the hateful things their ancestors did. ⁵Say to them: 'This is what the Lord GOD says: When I chose Israel, I made a promise to the descendants of Jacob. I made myself known to them in Egypt, and I promised them, "I am the LORD your God." ⁶At that time I promised them I would bring them out of Egypt into a land I had found for them, a fertile land, the best land in the world. ⁷I said to them, "Each one of you must throw away the hateful idols you have seen and liked. Don't make yourselves unclean with the idols of Egypt. I am the LORD your God."

⁸"But they turned against me and refused

to listen to me. They did not throw away the hateful idols which they saw and liked; they did not give up the idols of Egypt. Then I decided to pour out my anger against them while they were still in Egypt. ⁹But I acted for the sake of my name so it would not be dishonored in full view of the nations where the Israelites lived. I made myself known to the Israelites with a promise to bring them out of Egypt while the nations were watching. ¹⁰So I took them out of Egypt and brought them into the desert. ¹¹I gave them my rules and told them about my laws, by which people will live if they obey them. ¹²I also gave them my Sabbaths to be a sign between us so they would know that I am the LORD who made them holy.

¹³" 'But in the desert Israel turned against me. They did not follow my rules, and they rejected my laws, by which people will live if they obey them. They dishonored my Sabbaths. Then I decided to pour out my anger against them and destroy them in the desert. ¹⁴But I acted for the sake of my name so it would not be dishonored in full view of the nations who watched as I had brought the Israelites out of Egypt. ¹⁵And in the desert I swore to the Israelites that I would not bring them into the land I had given them. It is a fertile land, the best land in the world. ¹⁶This was because they rejected my laws and did not follow my rules. They dishonored my Sabbaths and wanted to worship their idols. ¹⁷But I had pity on them. I did not destroy them or put an end to them in the desert. ¹⁸I said to their children in the desert, "Don't live by the rules of your parents, or obey their laws. Don't make yourselves unclean with their idols. ¹⁹I am the LORD your God. Live by my rules, obey my laws, and follow them. ²⁰Keep my Sabbaths holy, and they will be a sign between me and you. Then you will know that I am the LORD your God."

²¹" 'But the children turned against me. They did not live by my rules, nor were they careful to obey my laws, by which people will live if they obey them. They dishonored my Sabbaths. So I decided to pour out my anger against them in the desert. ²²But I held back my anger. I acted for the sake of my name so it would not be dishonored in full view of the

nations who watched as I brought the Israelites out. ²³And in the desert I swore to the Israelites that I would scatter them among the nations and spread them among the countries, ²⁴because they had not obeyed my laws. They had rejected my rules and dishonored my Sabbaths and worshiped the idols of their parents. ²⁵I also allowed them to follow rules that were not good and laws by which they could not live. ²⁶I let the Israelites make themselves unclean by the gifts they brought to their gods when they sacrificed their first children in the fire. I wanted to terrify them so they would know that I am the LORD.'

²⁷"So, human, speak to the people of Israel. Say to them, 'This is what the Lord GOD says: Your ancestors spoke against me by being unfaithful to me in another way. ²⁸When I had brought them into the land I promised to give them, they saw every high hill and every leafy tree. There they offered their sacrifices to gods. They brought offerings that made me angry and burned their incense and poured out their drink offerings. ²⁹Then I said to them: What is this high place where you go to worship?' " (It is still called High Place today.)

³⁰"So say to the people of Israel: 'This is what the Lord GOD says: Are you going to make yourselves unclean as your ancestors did? Are you going to be unfaithful and desire their hateful idols? ³¹When you offer your children as gifts and sacrifice them in the fire, you are making yourselves unclean with all your idols even today. So, people of Israel, should I let you ask me questions? As surely as I live, says the Lord GOD, I will not accept questions from you.

³²" 'What you want will not come true. You say, "We want to be like the other nations, like the people in other lands. We want to worship idols made of wood and stone." ³³As surely as I live, says the Lord GOD, I will use my great power and strength and anger to rule over you. ³⁴I will bring you out from the foreign nations. With my great power and strength and anger I will gather you from the lands where you are scattered. ³⁵I will bring you among the nations as I brought your ancestors into the desert with Moses. There I

will judge you face to face. ³⁶I will judge you the same way I judged your ancestors in the desert of the land of Egypt, says the Lord GOD. ³⁷I will count you like sheep and will bring you into line with my agreement. ³⁸I will get rid of those who refuse to obey me and who turn against me. I will bring them out of the land where they are now living, but they will never enter the land of Israel. Then you will know that I am the LORD.

³⁹"'This is what the Lord GOD says: People of Israel, go serve your idols for now. But later you will listen to me; you will not continue to dishonor my holy name with your gifts and gods. ⁴⁰On my holy mountain, the high mountain of Israel, all Israel will serve me in the land, says the Lord GOD. There I will accept you. There I will expect your offerings, the first harvest of your offerings, and all your holy gifts. ⁴¹I will accept you like the pleasing smell of sacrifices when I bring you out from the foreign nations and gather you from the lands where you are scattered. Then through you I will show how holy I am so the nations will see. ⁴²When I bring you into the land of Israel, the land I promised your ancestors, you will know that I am the LORD. ⁴³There you will remember everything you did that made you unclean, and then you will hate yourselves for all the evil things you have done. ⁴⁴I will deal with you for the sake of my name, not because of your evil ways or unclean actions. Then you will know I am the LORD, people of Israel, says the Lord GOD.'"

Babylon, the Lord's Sword

⁴⁵Now the LORD spoke his word to me, saying: ⁴⁶"Human, look toward the south. Prophesy against the south and against the forest of the southern area. ⁴⁷Say to that forest: 'Hear the word of the LORD. This is what the Lord GOD says: I am ready to start a fire in you that will destroy all your green trees and all your dry trees. The flames that burn will not be put out. Every face from south to north will feel their heat. ⁴⁸Then all the people will see that I, the LORD, have started the fire. It will not be put out.'"

⁴⁹Then I said, "Ah, Lord GOD! The people are saying about me, 'He is only telling stories.'"

PSALM 125:1–5

God Protects Those Who Trust Him

A song for going up to worship.

125 ¹Those who trust the LORD are like Mount Zion,
which sits unmoved forever.
²As the mountains surround Jerusalem,
the LORD surrounds his people
now and forever.

³The wicked will not rule
over those who do right.
If they did, the people who do right
might use their power to do evil.

⁴LORD, be good to those who are good,
whose hearts are honest.
⁵But, LORD, when you remove those who do evil,
also remove those who stop following you.

Let there be peace in Israel.

PROVERBS 28:22

²²Selfish people are in a hurry to get rich
and do not realize they soon will be poor.

HEBREWS 9:23—10:18

Christ's Death Takes Away Sins

²³So the copies of the real things in heaven had to be made clean by animal sacrifices. But the real things in heaven need much better sacrifices. ²⁴Christ did not go into the Most Holy Place made by humans, which is only a copy of the real one. He went into heaven itself and is there now before God to help us. ²⁵The high priest enters the Most Holy Place once every year with blood that is not his own. But Christ did not offer himself many times. ²⁶Then he would have had to suffer many times since the world was made. But Christ came only once and for all time at just the right time to take away all sin by sacrificing himself. ²⁷Just as everyone must die once and then be judged, ²⁸so Christ was offered as a sacrifice one time to take away the sins of many people. And he will come a second time, not to offer himself

for sin, but to bring salvation to those who are waiting for him.

10The law is only an unclear picture of the good things coming in the future; it is not the real thing. The people under the law offer the same sacrifices every year, but these sacrifices can never make perfect those who come near to worship God. ²If the law could make them perfect, the sacrifices would have already stopped. The worshipers would be made clean, and they would no longer have a sense of sin. ³But these sacrifices remind them of their sins every year, ⁴because it is impossible for the blood of bulls and goats to take away sins.

⁵So when Christ came into the world, he said:

"You do not want sacrifices and
  offerings,
but you have prepared a body for me.
⁶You do not ask for burnt offerings
and offerings to take away sins.
⁷Then I said, 'Look, I have come.
It is written about me in the book.
God, I have come to do what you
  want.'" *Psalm 40:6–8*

⁸In this Scripture he first said, "You do not want sacrifices and offerings. You do not ask for burnt offerings and offerings to take away sins." (These are all sacrifices that the law commands.) ⁹Then he said, "Look, I have come to do what you want." God ends the first system of sacrifices so he can set up the new system. ¹⁰And because of this, we are made holy through the sacrifice Christ made in his body once and for all time.

¹¹Every day the priests stand and do their religious service, often offering the same sacrifices. Those sacrifices can never take away sins. ¹²But after Christ offered one sacrifice for sins, forever, he sat down at the right side of God. ¹³And now Christ waits there for his enemies to be put under his power. ¹⁴With one sacrifice he made perfect forever those who are being made holy.

¹⁵The Holy Spirit also tells us about this. First he says:

¹⁶"This is the agreement[n] I will make
  with them at that time, says the Lord.
I will put my teachings in their hearts
  and write them on their minds."
                              Jeremiah 31:33

¹⁷Then he says:

"Their sins and the evil things they do—
  I will not remember anymore."
                              Jeremiah 31:34

¹⁸Now when these have been forgiven, there is no more need for a sacrifice for sins.

NOVEMBER 15

EZEKIEL 21:1—22:31

21Then the LORD spoke his word to me, saying: ²"Human, look toward Jerusalem and speak against the holy place. Prophesy against the land of Israel. ³Say to Israel: 'This is what the LORD says: I am against you. I will pull my sword out of its holder, and I will cut off from you both the wicked and those who do right. ⁴Because I am going to cut off the wicked and those who do right, my sword will come out from its holder and attack all people from south to north. ⁵Then all people will know that I, the LORD, have pulled my sword out from its holder. My sword will not go back in again.'

⁶"So, human, groan with breaking heart and great sadness. Groan in front of the people. ⁷When they ask you, 'Why are you groaning?' you will say, 'Because of what I have heard is going to happen. When it happens, every heart will melt with fear, and all hands will become weak. Everyone will be afraid; all knees will become weak as water. Look, it is coming, and it will happen, says the Lord GOD.'"

10:16 agreement God gives a contract or agreement to his people. For the Jews, this agreement was the Law of Moses. But now God has given a better agreement to his people through Christ.

[8]The LORD spoke his word to me, saying: [9]"Human, prophesy and say, 'This is what the Lord says:

A sword, a sword,
　made sharp and polished.
[10]It is made sharp for the killing.
　It is polished to flash like lightning.
" 'You are not happy about this horrible punishment by the sword. But my son Judah, you did not change when you were only beaten with a rod.
[11]The sword should be polished.
　It is meant to be held in the hand.
　It is made sharp and polished,
　ready for the hand of a killer.
[12]Shout and yell, human,
　because the sword is meant for my
　　people,
　for all the rulers of Israel.
They will be killed by the sword,
　along with my people.
So beat your chest in sadness.
[13]" 'The test will come. And Judah, who is hated by the armies of Babylon, will not last, says the Lord GOD.'
[14]"So, human, prophesy
　and clap your hands.
Let the sword strike
　two or three times.
It is a sword meant for killing,
　a sword meant for much killing.
This sword surrounds the people to be
　killed.
[15]Their hearts will melt with fear,
　and many people will die.
I have placed the killing sword
　at all their city gates.
Oh! The sword is made to flash like
　lightning.
　It is held, ready for killing.
[16]Sword, cut on the right side;
　then cut on the left side.
　Cut anywhere your blade is turned.
[17]I will also clap my hands
　and use up my anger.
I, the LORD, have spoken."

Jerusalem to Be Destroyed

[18]The LORD spoke his word to me, saying: [19]"Human, mark two roads that the king of Babylon and his sword can follow. Both of these roads will start from the same country. And make signs where the road divides and one way goes toward the city. [20]Mark one sign to show the road he can take with his sword to Rabbah in the land of the Ammonites. Mark the other sign to show the road to Judah and Jerusalem, which is protected with strong walls. [21]The king of Babylon has come to where the road divides, and he is using magic. He throws lots with arrows and asks questions of his family idols. He looks at the liver of a sacrificed animal to learn where he should go. [22]The lot in his right hand tells him to go to Jerusalem. It tells him to use logs to break down the city gates, to shout the battle cry and give the order to kill, and to build a dirt road to the top of the walls and devices to attack the walls. [23]The people of Jerusalem have made agreements with other nations to help them fight Babylon. So they will think this prediction is wrong, but it is really proof of their sin, and they will be captured.

[24]"So this is what the Lord GOD says: 'You have shown how sinful you are by turning against the LORD. Your sins are seen in all the things you do. Because of this proof against you, you will be taken captive by the enemy.

[25]" 'You unclean and evil leader of Israel, you will be killed! The time of your final punishment has come. [26]This is what the Lord GOD says: Take off the royal turban, and remove the crown. Things will change. Those who are important now will be made unimportant, and those who are unimportant now will be made important. [27]A ruin! A ruin! I will make it a ruin! This place will not be rebuilt until the one comes who has a right to be king. Then I will give him that right.'

The Punishment of Ammon

[28]"And you, human, prophesy and say: 'This is what the Lord GOD says about the people of Ammon and their insults:

A sword, a sword
　is pulled out of its holder.
It is polished to kill and destroy,
　to flash like lightning!
[29]Prophets see false visions about you
　and prophesy lies about you.

The sword will be put on the necks
  of these unclean and evil people.
Their day of judging has come;
  the time of final punishment has come.
30Put the sword back in its holder.
  I will judge you
in the place where you were created,
  in the land where you were born.
31I will pour out my anger against you
  and blast you with the fire of my anger.
I will hand you over to cruel men,
  experts in destruction.
32You will be like fuel for the fire;
  you will die in the land.
You will not be remembered,
  because I, the LORD, have spoken.'"

The Sins of Jerusalem

22 The LORD spoke his word to me, saying: 2"And you, human, will you judge? Will you judge the city of murderers? Then tell her about all her hateful acts. 3You are to say: 'This is what the Lord GOD says: You are a city that kills those who come to live there. You make yourself unclean by making idols. 4You have become guilty of murder and have become unclean by your idols which you have made. So you have brought your time of punishment near; you have come to the end of your years. That is why I have made you a shame to the nations and why all lands laugh at you. 5Those near and those far away laugh at you with your bad name, you city full of confusion.

6" 'Jerusalem, see how each ruler of Israel in you has been trying to kill people. 7The people in you hate their fathers and mothers. They mistreat the foreigners in you and wrong the orphans and widows in you. 8You hate my holy things and dishonor my Sabbaths. 9The men in you tell lies to cause the death of others. The people in you eat food offered to idols at the mountain places of worship, and they take part in sexual sins. 10The men in you have sexual relations with their fathers' wives and with women who are unclean, during their time of monthly bleeding. 11One man in you does a hateful act with his neighbor's wife, while another has shamefully made his daughter-in-law unclean sexually. And another forces his half

sister to have sexual relations with him. 12The people in you take money to kill others. You take unfair interest and profits and make profits by mistreating your neighbor. And you have forgotten me, says the Lord GOD.

13" 'So, Jerusalem, I will shake my fist at you for stealing money and for murdering people. 14Will you still be brave and strong when I punish you? I, the LORD, have spoken, and I will act. 15I will scatter you among the nations and spread you through the countries. That is how I will get rid of your uncleanness. 16But you, yourself, will be dishonored in the sight of the nations. Then you will know that I am the LORD.'"

Israel Is Worthless

17The LORD spoke his word to me, saying: 18"Human, the people of Israel have become useless like scum to me. They are like the copper, tin, iron, and lead left in the furnace when silver is purified. 19So this is what the Lord GOD says: 'Because you have become useless like scum, I am going to put you together inside Jerusalem. 20People put silver, copper, iron, lead, and tin together inside a furnace to melt them down in a blazing fire. In the same way I will gather you in my hot anger and put you together in Jerusalem and melt you down. 21I will put you together and make you feel the heat of my anger. You will be melted down inside Jerusalem. 22As silver is melted in a furnace, you will be melted inside the city. Then you will know that I, the LORD, have poured out my anger on you.'"

Sins of the People

23The LORD spoke his word to me, saying: 24"Human, say to the land, 'You are a land that has not had rain or showers when God is angry.' 25Like a roaring lion that tears the animal it has caught, Israel's rulers make evil plans. They have destroyed lives and have taken treasure and valuable things. They have caused many women to become widows. 26Israel's priests do cruel things to my teachings and do not honor my holy things. They make no difference between holy and unholy things, and they teach there is no difference between clean and unclean things. They do not remember my Sabbaths, so I am dishonored by them. [27]Like wolves tearing a dead animal, Jerusalem's leaders have killed people for profit. [28]And the prophets try to cover this up by false visions and by lying messages. They say, 'This is what the Lord GOD says' when the LORD has not spoken. [29]The people cheat others and steal. They hurt people who are poor and needy. They cheat foreigners and do not treat them fairly.

[30]"I looked for someone to build up the walls and to stand before me where the walls are broken to defend these people so I would not have to destroy them. But I could not find anyone. [31]So I let them see my anger. I destroyed them with an anger that was like fire because of all the things they have done, says the Lord GOD."

PSALM 126:1–6

Lord, Bring Your People Back

A song for going up to worship.

126 When the LORD brought the prisoners back to Jerusalem, it seemed as if we were dreaming.
[2]Then we were filled with laughter, and we sang happy songs.
Then the other nations said,
"The LORD has done great things for them."
[3]The LORD has done great things for us, and we are very glad.

[4]LORD, return our prisoners again, as you bring streams to the desert.
[5]Those who cry as they plant crops will sing at harvest time.
[6]Those who cry as they carry out the seeds will return singing and carrying bundles of grain.

PROVERBS 28:23

[23]Those who correct others will later be liked more than those who give false praise.

HEBREWS 10:19–39

Continue to Trust God

[19]So, brothers and sisters, we are completely free to enter the Most Holy Place without fear because of the blood of Jesus' death. [20]We can enter through a new and living way that Jesus opened for us. It leads through the curtain—Christ's body. [21]And since we have a great priest over God's house, [22]let us come near to God with a sincere heart and a sure faith, because we have been made free from a guilty conscience, and our bodies have been washed with pure water. [23]Let us hold firmly to the hope that we have confessed, because we can trust God to do what he promised.

[24]Let us think about each other and help each other to show love and do good deeds. [25]You should not stay away from the church meetings, as some are doing, but you should meet together and encourage each other. Do this even more as you see the day[n] coming.

[26]If we decide to go on sinning after we have learned the truth, there is no longer any sacrifice for sins. [27]There is nothing but fear in waiting for the judgment and the terrible fire that will destroy all those who live against God. [28]Anyone who refused to obey the law of Moses was found guilty from the proof given by two or three witnesses. He was put to death without mercy. [29]So what do you think should be done to those who do not respect the Son of God, who look at the blood of the agreement that made them holy as no different from others' blood, who insult the Spirit of God's grace? Surely they should have a much worse punishment. [30]We know that God said, "I will punish those who do wrong; I will repay them."[n] And he also said, "The Lord will judge his people."[n] [31]It is a terrible thing to fall into the hands of the living God.

[32]Remember those days in the past when you first learned the truth. You had a hard struggle with many sufferings, but you continued strong. [33]Sometimes you were hurt and attacked before crowds of people, and sometimes you shared with those who were

being treated that way. [34]You helped the prisoners. You even had joy when all that you owned was taken from you, because you knew you had something better and more lasting.

[35]So do not lose the courage you had in the past, which has a great reward. [36]You must hold on, so you can do what God wants and receive what he has promised. [37]For in a very short time,

"The One who is coming will come
and will not be delayed.
[38]Those who are right with me
will live by faith.
But if they turn back with fear,
I will not be pleased with them."

Habakkuk 2:3–4

[39]But we are not those who turn back and are lost. We are people who have faith and are saved.

NOVEMBER 16

EZEKIEL 23:1—24:27

Samaria and Jerusalem

23 The LORD spoke his word to me, saying: [2]"Human, a woman had two daughters. [3]While they were young, they went to Egypt and became prostitutes. They let men touch and hold their breasts. [4]The older girl was named Oholah, and her sister was named Oholibah. They became my wives and had sons and daughters. Oholah is Samaria, and Oholibah is Jerusalem."

[5]"While still my wife, Samaria had sexual relations with other men. She had great sexual desire for her lovers, men from Assyria. The Assyrians were warriors and [6]wore blue uniforms. They were all handsome young captains and lieutenants riding on horseback. [7]Samaria became a prostitute for all the important men in Assyria and made herself unclean with all the idols of everyone she desired. [8]She continued the prostitution she began in Egypt. When she was young, she had slept with men, and they touched her breasts and had sexual relations with her.

[9]"So I handed her over to her lovers, the Assyrians, that she wanted so badly. [10]They stripped her naked and took away her sons and daughters. Then they killed her with a sword. Women everywhere began talking about how she had been punished.

[11]"Her sister Jerusalem saw what happened, but she became worse than her sister in her sexual desire and prostitution. [12]She also desired the Assyrians, who were all soldiers in beautiful uniforms—handsome young captains and lieutenants riding horses. [13]I saw that both girls were alike; both were prostitutes.

[14]"But Jerusalem went even further. She saw carvings of Babylonian men on a wall. They wore red [15]and had belts around their waists and turbans on their heads. They all looked like chariot officers born in Babylonia. [16]When she saw them, she wanted to have sexual relations with them and sent messengers to them in Babylonia. [17]So these Babylonian men came and had sexual relations with her and made her unclean. After that, she became sick of them. [18]But she continued her prostitution so openly that everyone knew about it. And I finally became sick of her, as I had her sister. [19]But she remembered how she was a young prostitute in Egypt, so she took part in even more prostitution. [20]She wanted men who behaved like animals in their sexual desire. [21]In the same way you desired to do the sinful things you had done in Egypt. There men touched and held your young breasts.

God's Judgment on Jerusalem

[22]"So, Jerusalem, this is what the Lord GOD says: You are tired of your lovers. So now I will

---

23:4 Oholah . . . Jerusalem Throughout this chapter Samaria is used in place of Oholah, and Jerusalem is used in place of Oholibah.

make them angry with you and have them attack you from all sides. ²³Men from Babylon and all Babylonia and men from Pekod, Shoa, and Koa will attack you. All the Assyrians will attack you: handsome young captains and lieutenants, all of them important men and all riding horses. ²⁴Those men will attack with great armies and with their weapons, chariots, and wagons. They will surround you with large and small shields and with helmets. And I will give them the right to punish you, and they will give you their own kind of punishment. ²⁵Then you will see how strong my anger can be when they punish you in their anger. They will cut off your noses and ears. They will take away your sons and daughters, and those who are left will be burned. ²⁶They will take off your clothes and steal your jewelry. ²⁷I will put a stop to the sinful life you began when you were in Egypt so that you will not desire it or remember Egypt anymore.

²⁸"This is what the Lord GOD says: You became tired of your lovers, but I am going to hand you over to those men you now hate. ²⁹They will treat you with hate and take away everything you worked for, leaving you empty and naked. Everyone will know about the sinful things you did. Your sexual sins ³⁰have brought this on you. You have had sexual relations with the nations and made yourselves unclean by worshiping their idols. ³¹You did the same things your sister did, so you will get the same punishment, like a bitter cup to drink.

³²"This is what the Lord GOD says:
You will drink the same cup your sister did,
    and that cup is deep and wide.
Everyone will make fun of you,
    because the cup is full.
³³It will make you miserable and drunk.
    It is the cup of fear and ruin.
    It is the cup of your sister Samaria.
³⁴You will drink everything in it,
    and then you will smash it
    and tear at your breasts.
I have spoken, says the Lord GOD.

³⁵"So this is what the Lord GOD says: You have forgotten me and turned your back on me. So you will be punished for your sexual sins."

Judgment on Samaria and Jerusalem

³⁶The LORD said to me: "Human, will you judge Samaria and Jerusalem, showing them their hateful acts? ³⁷They are guilty of adultery and murder. They have taken part in adultery with their idols. They even offered our children as sacrifices in the fire to be food for these idols. ³⁸They have also done this to me: They made my Temple unclean at the same time they dishonored my Sabbaths. ³⁹They sacrificed their children to their idols. Then they entered my Temple at that very time to dishonor it. That is what they did inside my Temple!

⁴⁰"They even sent for men from far away, who came after a messenger was sent to them. The two sisters bathed themselves for them, painted their eyes, and put on jewelry. ⁴¹They sat on a fine bed with a table set before it, on which they put my incense and my oil.

⁴²"There was the noise of a reckless crowd in the city. Common people gathered, and drunkards were brought from the desert. They put bracelets on the wrists of the two sisters and beautiful crowns on their heads. ⁴³Then I said about the one who was worn out by her acts of adultery, 'Let them continue their sexual sins with her. She is nothing but a prostitute.' ⁴⁴They kept going to her as they would go to a prostitute. So they continued to go to Samaria and Jerusalem, these shameful women. ⁴⁵But men who do right will punish them as they punish women who take part in adultery and who murder people, because they are guilty of adultery and murder.

⁴⁶"This is what the Lord GOD says: Bring together a mob against Samaria and Jerusalem, and hand them over to be frightened and robbed. ⁴⁷Let the mob kill them by throwing stones at them, and let them cut them down with their swords. Let them kill their sons and daughters and burn their houses down.

⁴⁸"So I will put an end to sexual sins in the land. Then all women will be warned, and they will not do the sexual sins you have done. ⁴⁹You will be punished for your sexual sins and the sin of worshiping idols. Then you will know that I am the Lord GOD."

The Pot and the Meat

24 The LORD spoke his word to me in the ninth year of our captivity, in the tenth month, on the tenth day of the month. He said: [2]"Human, write down today's date, this very date. The king of Babylon has surrounded Jerusalem this very day. [3]And tell a story to the people who refuse to obey me. Say to them: 'This is what the Lord GOD says:

Put on the pot; put it on
 and pour water in it.
[4]Put in the pieces of meat,
 the best pieces—the legs and the
  shoulders.
Fill it with the best bones.
[5] Take the best of the flock,
 and pile wood under the pot.
Boil the pieces of meat
 until even the bones are cooked.
[6]" 'This is what the Lord GOD says:
How terrible it will be for the city of
  murderers!
How terrible it will be for the rusty pot
 whose rust will not come off!
Take the meat out of it, piece by piece.
 Don't choose any special piece.

[7]" 'The blood from her killings is still in
  the city.
She poured the blood on the bare rock.
She did not pour it on the ground
 where dust would cover it.
[8]To stir up my anger and revenge,
 I put the blood she spilled on the bare
  rock
 so it will not be covered.
[9]" 'So this is what the Lord GOD says:
How terrible it will be for the city of
  murderers!
I myself will pile the wood high for
  burning.
[10]Pile up the wood
 and light the fire.
Finish cooking the meat.
Mix in the spices,
 and let the bones burn.
[11]Then set the empty pot on the coals
 so it may become hot and its copper
  sides glow.
The dirty scum stuck inside it may then
  melt
 and its rust burn away.

[12]But efforts to clean the pot have failed.
Its heavy rust cannot be removed,
 even in the fire.
[13]" 'By your sinful action you have become unclean. I wanted to cleanse you, but you are still unclean. You will never be cleansed from your sin until my anger against you is carried out.
[14]" 'I, the LORD, have spoken. The time has come for me to act. I will not hold back punishment or feel pity or change my mind. I will judge you by your ways and actions, says the Lord GOD.' "

The Death of Ezekiel's Wife

[15]Then the LORD spoke his word to me, saying: [16]"Human, I am going to take your wife from you, the woman you look at with love. She will die suddenly, but you must not be sad or cry loudly for her or shed any tears. [17]Groan silently; do not cry loudly for the dead. Tie on your turban, and put your sandals on your feet. Do not cover your face, and do not eat the food people eat when they are sad about a death."

[18]So I spoke to the people in the morning, and my wife died in the evening. The next morning I did as I had been commanded. [19]Then the people asked me, "Tell us, what do the things you are doing mean for us?"

[20]Then I said to them, "The LORD spoke his word to me. He said, [21]Say to the people of Israel, This is what the Lord GOD says: I am going to dishonor my Temple. You think it gives you strength. You are proud of it, and you look at it with love and tenderness. But your sons and daughters that you left behind in Jerusalem will fall dead by the sword. [22]When that happens, you are to act as I have: you are not to cover your face, and you are not to eat the food people eat when they are sad about a death. [23]Your turbans must stay on your heads, and your sandals on your feet. You must not cry loudly, but you must rot away in your sins and groan to each other. [24]So Ezekiel is to be an example for you. You must do all the same things he did. When all this happens, you will know that I am the Lord GOD.'

[25]"And as for you, human, this is how it will be. I will take away the Temple that gives

them strength and joy, that makes them proud. They look at it with love, and it makes them happy. And I will take away their sons and daughters also. [26]At that time a person who escapes will come to you with information for you to hear. [27]At that very time your mouth will be opened. You will speak and be silent no more. So you will be a sign for them, and they will know that I am the LORD."

PSALM 127:1–5

All Good Things Come from God

A song for going up to worship. Of Solomon.

127 If the LORD doesn't build the house,
the builders are working for
nothing.
If the LORD doesn't guard the city,
the guards are watching for nothing.
[2]It is no use for you to get up early
and stay up late,
working for a living.
The LORD gives sleep to those he loves.
[3]Children are a gift from the LORD;
babies are a reward.
[4]Children who are born to a young man
are like arrows in the hand of a warrior.
[5]Happy is the man
who has his bag full of arrows.
They will not be defeated
when they fight their enemies at the
city gate.

PROVERBS 28:24

[24]Whoever robs father or mother
and says, "It's not wrong,"
is just like someone who destroys
things.

HEBREWS 11:1–16

What Is Faith?

11 Faith means being sure of the things we hope for and knowing that something is real even if we do not see it. [2]Faith is the reason we remember great people who lived in the past.

[3]It is by faith we understand that the whole world was made by God's command so what we see was made by something that cannot be seen.

[4]It was by faith that Abel offered God a better sacrifice than Cain did. God said he was pleased with the gifts Abel offered and called Abel a good man because of his faith. Abel died, but through his faith he is still speaking.

[5]It was by faith that Enoch was taken to heaven so he would not die. He could not be found, because God had taken him away. Before he was taken, the Scripture says that he was a man who truly pleased God. [6]Without faith no one can please God. Anyone who comes to God must believe that he is real and that he rewards those who truly want to find him.

[7]It was by faith that Noah heard God's warnings about things he could not yet see. He obeyed God and built a large boat to save his family. By his faith, Noah showed that the world was wrong, and he became one of those who are made right with God through faith.

[8]It was by faith Abraham obeyed God's call to go to another place God promised to give him. He left his own country, not knowing where he was to go. [9]It was by faith that he lived like a foreigner in the country God promised to give him. He lived in tents with Isaac and Jacob, who had received that same promise from God. [10]Abraham was waiting for the city[n] that has real foundations—the city planned and built by God.

[11]He was too old to have children, and Sarah could not have children. It was by faith that Abraham was made able to become a father, because he trusted God to do what he had promised.[n] [12]This man was so old he was almost dead, but from him came as many descendants as there are stars in the sky. Like the sand on the seashore, they could not be counted.

[13]All these great people died in faith. They did not get the things that God promised his people, but they saw them coming far in the

---

11:10 city The spiritual "city" where God's people live with him. Also called "the heavenly Jerusalem." (See Hebrews 12:22.)
11:11 It . . . promised. Some Greek copies refer to Sarah's faith, rather than Abraham's.

future and were glad. They said they were like visitors and strangers on earth. [14]When people say such things, they show they are looking for a country that will be their own. [15]If they had been thinking about the country they had left, they could have gone back. [16]But they were waiting for a better country—a heavenly country. So God is not ashamed to be called their God, because he has prepared a city for them.

NOVEMBER 17

Prophecy Against Ammon

25 The LORD spoke his word to me, saying: [2]"Human, look toward the people of Ammon and prophesy against them. [3]Say to them, 'Hear the word of the Lord GOD. This is what the Lord GOD says: You were glad when my Temple was dishonored, when the land of Israel was ruined, and when the people of Judah were taken away as captives. [4]So I am going to give you to the people of the East to be theirs. They will set up their camps among you and make their homes among you. They will eat your fruit and drink your milk. [5]I will make the city of Rabbah a pasture for camels and the land of Ammon a resting place for sheep. Then you will know that I am the LORD. [6]This is what the Lord GOD says: You have clapped your hands and stamped your feet; you have laughed about all the insults you made against the land of Israel. [7]So I will use my power against you. I will give you to the nations as if you were treasures taken in war. I will wipe you out of the lands so you will no longer be a nation, and I will destroy you. Then you will know that I am the LORD.'

Prophecy Against Moab and Edom

[8]"This is what the Lord GOD says: 'Moab and Edom say, "The people of Judah are like all the other nations." [9]So I am going to take away the cities that protect Moab's borders, the best cities in that land: Beth Jeshimoth, Baal Meon, and Kiriathaim. [10]Then I will give Moab, along with the Ammonites, to the people of the East as their possession. Then, along with the Ammonites, Moab will not be a nation anymore. [11]So I will punish the people of Moab, and they will know that I am the LORD.'

Prophecy Against Edom

[12]"This is what the Lord GOD says: 'Edom took revenge on the people of Judah, and the Edomites became guilty because of it. [13]So this is what the Lord GOD says: I will use my power against Edom, killing every human and animal in it. And I will destroy Edom all the way from Teman to Dedan as they die in battle. [14]I will use my people Israel to take revenge on Edom. So the Israelites will do to Edom what my hot anger demands. Then the Edomites will know what my revenge feels like, says the Lord GOD.'

Prophecy Against Philistia

[15]"This is what the Lord GOD says: 'The Philistines have taken revenge with hateful hearts. Because of their strong hatred, they have tried to destroy Judah. [16]So this is what the Lord GOD says: I will use my power against the Philistines. I will kill the Kerethites, and I will destroy those people still alive on the coast of the Mediterranean Sea. [17]I will punish them in my anger and do great acts of revenge to them. They will know that I am the LORD when I take revenge on them.'"

Prophecy Against Tyre

26 It was the eleventh year of our captivity, on the first day of the month. The LORD spoke his word to me, saying: [2]"Human, the city of Tyre has spoken against Jerusalem: 'The city that traded with the nations is destroyed. Now we can be the trading center. Since the city of Jerusalem is

ruined, we can make money.' ³So this is what the Lord GOD says: I am against you, Tyre. I will bring many nations against you, like the sea beating its waves on your island shores. ⁴They will destroy the walls of Tyre and pull down her towers. I will also scrape away her ruins and make her a bare rock. ⁵Tyre will be an island where fishermen dry their nets. I have spoken, says the Lord GOD. The nations will steal treasures from Tyre. ⁶Also, her villages on the shore across from the island will be destroyed by war. Then they will know that I am the LORD.

Nebuchadnezzar to Attack Tyre

⁷"This is what the Lord GOD says: I will bring a king from the north against Tyre. He is Nebuchadnezzar king of Babylon, the greatest king, with his horses, chariots, horsemen, and a great army. ⁸He will fight a battle and destroy your villages on the shore across from the island. He will set up devices to attack you. He will build a road of earth to the top of the walls. He will raise his shields against you. ⁹He will bring logs to pound through your city walls, and he will break down your towers with his iron bars. ¹⁰His horses will be so many that they will cover you with their dust. Your walls will shake at the noise of horsemen, wagons, and chariots. The king of Babylon will enter your city gates as men enter a city where the walls are broken through. ¹¹The hoofs of his horses will run over your streets. He will kill your army with the sword, and your strong pillars will fall down to the ground. ¹²Also, his men will take away your riches and will steal the things you sell. They will break down your walls and destroy your nice houses. They will throw your stones, wood, and trash into the sea. ¹³So I will stop your songs; the music of your harps will not be heard anymore. ¹⁴I will make you a bare rock, and you will be a place for drying fishing nets. You will not be built again, because I, the LORD, have spoken, says the Lord GOD.

¹⁵"This is what the Lord GOD says to Tyre: The people who live along the seacoast will shake with fear when they hear about your defeat. Those of you who are in-

jured and dying will groan. ¹⁶Then all the leaders of the seacoast will get down from their thrones, take off their beautiful needlework clothes, and show how afraid they are. They will sit on the ground and tremble all the time. When they see you, they will be shocked. ¹⁷They will begin singing a funeral song about you and will say to you:

'Tyre, you famous city, you have been destroyed!
You have lost your sea power!
You and your people
had great power on the seas.
You made everyone around you afraid of you.
¹⁸Now the people who live by the coast tremble,
now that you have fallen.
The islands of the sea
are afraid because you have been defeated.'

¹⁹"This is what the Lord GOD says: I will make you an empty city, like cities that have no people living in them. I will bring the deep ocean waters over you, and the Mediterranean Sea will cover you. ²⁰At that time I will send you down to the place of the dead to join those who died long ago. I will make you live with the dead below the earth in places that are like old ruins. You will not come back from there or have any place in the world of the living again. ²¹Other people will be afraid of what happened to you, and it will be the end of you. People will look for you, but they will never find you again, says the Lord GOD."

PSALM 128:1–6

The Happy Home

A song for going up to worship.

128 Happy are those who respect the LORD and obey him.
²You will enjoy what you work for,
and you will be blessed with good things.
³Your wife will give you many children,
like a vine that produces much fruit.
Your children will bring you much good,

like olive branches that produce many
olives.
⁴This is how the man who respects the
LORD
will be blessed.
⁵May the LORD bless you from Mount
Zion;
may you enjoy the good things of
Jerusalem all your life.
⁶May you see your grandchildren.

Let there be peace in Israel.

PROVERBS 28:25

²⁵A greedy person causes trouble,
but the one who trusts the LORD will
succeed.

HEBREWS 11:17–40

¹⁷It was by faith that Abraham, when
God tested him, offered his son Isaac as a
sacrifice. God made the promises to Abraham, but Abraham was ready to offer his
own son as a sacrifice. ¹⁸God had said, "The
descendants I promised you will be from
Isaac."ⁿ ¹⁹Abraham believed that God could
raise the dead, and really, it was as if Abraham got Isaac back from death.

²⁰It was by faith that Isaac blessed the future of Jacob and Esau. ²¹It was by faith that
Jacob, as he was dying, blessed each one of
Joseph's sons. Then he worshiped as he
leaned on the top of his walking stick.

²²It was by faith that Joseph, while he was
dying, spoke about the Israelites leaving
Egypt and gave instructions about what to
do with his body.

²³It was by faith that Moses' parents hid
him for three months after he was born.
They saw that Moses was a beautiful baby,
and they were not afraid to disobey the
king's order.

²⁴It was by faith that Moses, when he
grew up, refused to be called the son of the
king of Egypt's daughter. ²⁵He chose to suffer with God's people instead of enjoying
sin for a short time. ²⁶He thought it was bet-

ter to suffer for the Christ than to have all
the treasures of Egypt, because he was
looking for God's reward. ²⁷It was by faith
that Moses left Egypt and was not afraid of
the king's anger. Moses continued strong as
if he could see the God that no one can see.
²⁸It was by faith that Moses prepared the
Passover and spread the blood on the doors
so the one who brings death would not kill
the firstborn sons of Israel.

²⁹It was by faith that the people crossed
the Red Sea as if it were dry land. But when
the Egyptians tried it, they were drowned.

³⁰It was by faith that the walls of Jericho
fell after the people had marched around
them for seven days.

³¹It was by faith that Rahab, the prostitute, welcomed the spies and was not killed
with those who refused to obey God.

³²Do I need to give more examples? I do
not have time to tell you about Gideon,
Barak, Samson, Jephthah, David, Samuel,
and the prophets. ³³Through their faith they
defeated kingdoms. They did what was
right, received God's promises, and shut the
mouths of lions. ³⁴They stopped great fires
and were saved from being killed with
swords. They were weak, and yet were made
strong. They were powerful in battle and
defeated other armies. ³⁵Women received
their dead relatives raised back to life. Others were tortured and refused to accept
their freedom so they could be raised from
the dead to a better life. ³⁶Some were
laughed at and beaten. Others were put in
chains and thrown into prison. ³⁷They were
stoned to death, they were cut in half,ⁿ and
they were killed with swords. Some wore
the skins of sheep and goats. They were
poor, abused, and treated badly. ³⁸The world
was not good enough for them! They wandered in deserts and mountains, living in
caves and holes in the earth.

³⁹All these people are known for their
faith, but none of them received what God
had promised. ⁴⁰God planned to give us
something better so that they would be
made perfect, but only together with us.

11:18 "The descendants . . . Isaac." Quotation from Genesis 21:12.   **11:37 they were cut in half** Some Greek copies also
include, "they were tested."

NOVEMBER 18

EZEKIEL 27:1—28:26

A Funeral Song for Tyre

27 The LORD spoke his word to me, saying: 2"Human, sing a funeral song for the city of Tyre. 3Speak to Tyre, which has ports for the Mediterranean Sea and is a place for trade for the people of many lands along the seacoast. This is what the Lord GOD says:

Tyre, you have said,
"I am like a beautiful ship."
4You were at home on the high seas.
Your builders made your beauty
   perfect.
5They made all your boards
   of fir trees from Mount Hermon.
They took a cedar tree from Lebanon
   to make a ship's mast for you.
6They made your oars
   from oak trees from Bashan.
They made your deck
   from cypress trees from the coast of
   Cyprus
   and set ivory into it.
7Your sail of linen with designs sewed on
   it came from Egypt
   and became like a flag for you.
Your cloth shades over the deck were
   blue and purple
   and came from the island of Cyprus.
8Men from Sidon and Arvad used oars to
   row you.
Tyre, your skilled men were the sailors
   on your deck.
9Workers of Byblos were with you,
   putting caulk*n* in your ship's seams.
All the ships of the sea and their sailors
   came alongside to trade with you.

10"Men of Persia, Lydia, and Put
   were warriors in your navy
   and hung their shields and helmets on
   your sides.
They made you look beautiful.
11Men of Arvad and Cilicia
   guarded your city walls all around.

Men of Gammad
   were in your watchtowers
   and hung their shields around your
   walls.
They made your beauty perfect.

12" 'People of Tarshish became traders for you because of your great wealth. They traded your goods for silver, iron, tin, and lead.

13" 'People of Greece, Tubal, and Meshech became merchants for you. They traded your goods for slaves and items of bronze.

14" 'People of Beth Togarmah traded your goods for work horses, war horses, and mules.

15" 'People of Rhodes became merchants for you, selling your goods on many coastlands. They brought back ivory tusks and valuable black wood as your payment.

16" 'People of Aram became traders for you, because you had so many good things to sell. They traded your goods for turquoise, purple cloth, cloth with designs sewed on, fine linen, coral, and rubies.

17" 'People of Judah and Israel became merchants for you. They traded your goods for wheat from Minnith, and for honey, olive oil, and balm.

18-19" 'People of Damascus became traders for you because you have many good things and great wealth. They traded your goods for wine from Helbon, wool from Zahar, and barrels of wine from Izal. They received wrought iron, cassia, and sugar cane in payment for your good things.

20" 'People of Dedan became merchants for you, trading saddle blankets for riding.

21" 'People of Arabia and all the rulers of Kedar became traders for you. They received lambs, male sheep, and goats in payment for you.

22" 'The merchants of Sheba and Raamah became merchants for you. They traded your goods for all the best spices, valuable gems, and gold.

23" 'People of Haran, Canneh, Eden, and

27:9 caulk Something like tar put between the boards of a ship to make it waterproof.

the traders of Sheba, Asshur, and Kilmad became merchants for you. 24They were paid with the best clothes, blue cloth, cloth with designs sewed on, carpets of many colors, and tightly wound ropes.

25" 'Trading ships
carried the things you sold.
You were like a ship full of heavy cargo
in the middle of the sea.
26The men who rowed you
brought you out into the high seas,
but the east wind broke you to pieces
in the middle of the sea.
27Your wealth, your trade, your goods,
your seamen, your sailors, your
workers,
your traders, your warriors,
and everyone else on board
sank into the sea
on the day your ship was wrecked.
28The people on the shore shake with fear
when your sailors cry out.
29All the men who row
leave their ships;
the seamen and the sailors of other ships
stand on the shore.
30They cry loudly about you;
they cry very much.
They throw dust on their heads
and roll in ashes to show they are sad.
31They shave their heads for you,
and they put on rough cloth to show
they are upset.
They cry and sob for you;
they cry loudly.
32And in their loud crying
they sing a funeral song for you:
"No one was ever destroyed like Tyre,
surrounded by the sea."
33When the goods you traded went out
over the seas,
you met the needs of many nations.
With your great wealth and goods,
you made kings of the earth rich.
34But now you are broken by the sea
and have sunk to the bottom.
Your goods and all the people on board
have gone down with you.
35All those who live along the shore
are shocked by what happened to you.
Their kings are terribly afraid,

and their faces show their fear.
36The traders among the nations hiss at
you.
You have come to a terrible end,
and you are gone forever.' "

Prophecy Against the King of Tyre

28The LORD spoke his word to me, saying: 2"Human, say to the ruler of Tyre: 'This is what the Lord GOD says:
Because you are proud,
you say, "I am a god.
I sit on the throne of a god
in the middle of the seas."
You think you are as wise as a god,
but you are a human, not a god.
3You think you are wiser than Daniel.
You think you can find out all secrets.
4Through your wisdom and
understanding
you have made yourself rich.
You have gained gold and silver
and have saved it in your storerooms.
5Through your great skill in trading,
you have made your riches grow.
You are too proud
because of your riches.
6" 'So this is what the Lord GOD says:
You think you are wise
like a god,
7but I will bring foreign people against
you,
the cruelest nation.
They will pull out their swords
and destroy all that your wisdom has
built,
and they will dishonor your greatness.
8They will kill you;
you will die a terrible death
like those who are killed at sea.
9While they are killing you,
you will not be able to say anymore, "I
am a god."
You will be only a human, not a god,
when your murderers kill you.
10You will die like an unclean person;
foreigners will kill you.
I have spoken, says the Lord GOD.' "
11The LORD spoke his word to me, saying:
12"Human, sing a funeral song for the king of Tyre. Say to him: 'This is what the Lord GOD says:

You were an example of what was perfect,
full of wisdom and perfect in beauty.
[13]You had a wonderful life,
as if you were in Eden, the garden of
God.
Every valuable gem was on you:
ruby, topaz, and emerald,
yellow quartz, onyx, and jasper,
sapphire, turquoise, and chrysolite.
Your jewelry was made of gold.
It was prepared on the day you were
created.
[14]I appointed a living creature to guard
you.
I put you on the holy mountain of God.
You walked among the gems that
shined like fire.
[15]Your life was right and good
from the day you were created,
until evil was found in you.
[16]Because you traded with countries far
away,
you learned to be cruel, and you
sinned.
So I threw you down in disgrace from
the mountain of God.
And the living creature who guarded you
forced you out from among the gems
that shined like fire.
[17]You became too proud
because of your beauty.
You ruined your wisdom
because of your greatness.
I threw you down to the ground.
Your example taught a lesson to other
kings.
[18]You dishonored your places of worship
through your many sins and dishonest
trade.
So I set on fire the place where you lived,
and the fire burned you up.
I turned you into ashes on the ground
for all those watching to see.
[19]All the nations who knew you
are shocked about you.
Your punishment was so terrible,
and you are gone forever.'"

Prophecy Against Sidon

[20]The LORD spoke his word to me, saying:
[21]"Human, look toward the city of Sidon and
prophesy against her. [22]Say: 'This is what the
Lord GOD says:
I am against you, Sidon,
and I will show my glory among you.
People will know that I am the LORD
when I have punished Sidon;
I will show my holiness by defeating her.
[23]I will send diseases to Sidon,
and blood will flow in her streets.
Those who are wounded in Sidon will
fall dead,
attacked from all sides.
Then they will know that I am the LORD.

God Will Help Israel

[24]"'No more will neighboring nations be
like thorny branches or sharp stickers to
hurt Israel. Then they will know that I am
the Lord GOD.
[25]"'This is what the Lord GOD says: I will
gather the people of Israel from the nations
where they are scattered. I will show my holiness when the nations see what I do for my
people. Then they will live in their own
land—the land I gave to my servant Jacob.
[26]They will live safely in the land and will
build houses and plant vineyards. They will
live in safety after I have punished all the nations around who hate them. Then they will
know that I am the LORD their God.'"

PSALM 129:1–4

A Prayer Against the Enemies

A song for going up to worship.

129 They have treated me badly all my
life.
(Let Israel repeat this.)
[2]They have treated me badly all my life,
but they have not defeated me.
[3]Like farmers plowing, they plowed over
my back,
making long wounds.
[4]But the LORD does what is right;
he has set me free from those wicked
people.

PROVERBS 28:26

[26]Those who trust in themselves are
foolish,

but those who live wisely will be kept safe.

HEBREWS 12:1–29

Follow Jesus' Example

12 We are surrounded by a great cloud of people whose lives tell us what faith means. So let us run the race that is before us and never give up. We should remove from our lives anything that would get in the way and the sin that so easily holds us back. ²Let us look only to Jesus, the One who began our faith and who makes it perfect. He suffered death on the cross. But he accepted the shame as if it were nothing because of the joy that God put before him. And now he is sitting at the right side of God's throne. ³Think about Jesus' example. He held on while wicked people were doing evil things to him. So do not get tired and stop trying.

God Is like a Father

⁴You are struggling against sin, but your struggles have not yet caused you to be killed. ⁵You have forgotten the encouraging words that call you his children:

"My child, don't think the Lord's
    discipline is worth nothing,
and don't stop trying when he corrects
    you.
⁶The Lord disciplines those he loves,
and he punishes everyone he accepts as
    his child." *Proverbs 3:11–12*

⁷So hold on through your sufferings, because they are like a father's discipline. God is treating you as children. All children are disciplined by their fathers. ⁸If you are never disciplined (and every child must be disciplined), you are not true children. ⁹We have all had fathers here on earth who disciplined us, and we respected them. So it is even more important that we accept discipline from the Father of our spirits so we will have life. ¹⁰Our fathers on earth disciplined us for a short time in the way they thought was best. But God disciplines us to help us, so we can become holy as he is. ¹¹We do not enjoy be-

ing disciplined. It is painful at the time, but later, after we have learned from it, we have peace, because we start living in the right way.

Be Careful How You Live

¹²You have become weak, so make yourselves strong again. ¹³Keep on the right path, so the weak will not stumble but rather be strengthened.

¹⁴Try to live in peace with all people, and try to live free from sin. Anyone whose life is not holy will never see the Lord. ¹⁵Be careful that no one fails to receive God's grace and begins to cause trouble among you. A person like that can ruin many of you. ¹⁶Be careful that no one takes part in sexual sin or is like Esau and never thinks about God. As the oldest son, Esau would have received everything from his father, but he sold all that for a single meal. ¹⁷You remember that after Esau did this, he wanted to get his father's blessing, but his father refused. Esau could find no way to change what he had done, even though he wanted the blessing so much that he cried.

¹⁸You have not come to a mountain that can be touched and that is burning with fire. You have not come to darkness, sadness, and storms. ¹⁹You have not come to the noise of a trumpet or to the sound of a voice like the one the people of Israel heard and begged not to hear another word. ²⁰They did not want to hear the command: "If anything, even an animal, touches the mountain, it must be put to death with stones."ⁿ ²¹What they saw was so terrible that Moses said, "I am shaking with fear."ⁿ

²²But you have come to Mount Zion,ⁿ to the city of the living God, the heavenly Jerusalem. You have come to thousands of angels gathered together with joy. ²³You have come to the meeting of God's firstbornⁿ children whose names are written in heaven. You have come to God, the judge of all people, and to the spirits of good people who have been made perfect. ²⁴You have come to Jesus,

---

12:20 "If . . . stones." Quotation from Exodus 19:12–13. **12:21 "I . . . fear."** Quotation from Deuteronomy 9:19. **12:22 Mount Zion** Another name for Jerusalem, here meaning the spiritual city of God's people. **12:23 firstborn** The first son born in a Jewish family was given the most important place in the family and received special blessings. All of God's children are like that.

the One who brought the new agreement from God to his people, and you have come to the sprinkled blood[n] that has a better message than the blood of Abel.[n]

[25]So be careful and do not refuse to listen when God speaks. Others refused to listen to him when he warned them on earth, and they did not escape. So it will be worse for us if we refuse to listen to God who warns us from heaven. [26]When he spoke before, his voice shook the earth, but now he has prom-

ised, "Once again I will shake not only the earth but also the heavens."[n] [27]The words "once again" clearly show us that everything that was made—things that can be shaken—will be destroyed. Only the things that cannot be shaken will remain.

[28]So let us be thankful, because we have a kingdom that cannot be shaken. We should worship God in a way that pleases him with respect and fear, [29]because our God is like a fire that burns things up.

NOVEMBER 19

EZEKIEL 29:1—30:26

Prophecy Against Egypt

29 It was the tenth year of our captivity, in the tenth month, on the twelfth day of the month. The LORD spoke his word to me, saying: [2]"Human, look toward the king of Egypt, and prophesy against him and all Egypt. [3]Say: 'This is what the Lord GOD says:

I am against you, king of Egypt.
You are like a great crocodile that lies in
the Nile River.
You say, "The Nile is mine;
I made it for myself."
[4]But I will put hooks in your jaws,
and I will make the fish of the Nile
stick to your sides.
I will pull you up out of your rivers,
with all the fish sticking to your sides.
[5]I will leave you in the desert,
you and all the fish from your rivers.
You will fall onto the ground;
you will not be picked up or buried.
I have given you to the wild animals
and to the birds of the sky for food.
[6]Then all the people who live in Egypt will know that I am the LORD.

" 'Israel tried to lean on you for help, but you were like a crutch made out of a weak stalk of grass. [7]When their hands grabbed you, you splintered and tore open their

shoulders. When they leaned on you, you broke and made all their backs twist.

[8]" 'So this is what the Lord GOD says: I will cause an enemy to attack you and kill your people and animals. [9]Egypt will become an empty desert. Then they will know that I am the LORD.

" 'Because you said, "The Nile River is mine, and I have made it," [10]I am against you and your rivers. I will destroy the land of Egypt and make it an empty desert from Migdol in the north to Aswan in the south, all the way to the border of Cush. [11]No person or animal will walk through it, and no one will live in Egypt for forty years. [12]I will make the land of Egypt the most deserted country of all. Her cities will be the most deserted of all ruined cities for forty years. I will scatter the Egyptians among the nations, spreading them among the countries.

[13]" 'This is what the Lord GOD says: After forty years I will gather Egypt from the nations where they have been scattered. [14]I will bring back the Egyptian captives and make them return to southern Egypt, to the land they came from. They will become a weak kingdom there. [15]It will be the weakest kingdom, and it will never again rule other nations. I will make it so weak it will never again rule over the nations. [16]The Israelites will never again depend on Egypt. Instead,

Egypt's punishment will remind the Israelites of their sin in turning to Egypt for help. Then they will know that I am the Lord GOD.'"

Egypt Is Given to Babylon

[17] It was the twenty-seventh year of our captivity, in the first month, on the first day of the month. The LORD spoke his word to me, saying: [18] "Human, Nebuchadnezzar king of Babylon made his army fight hard against Tyre. Every soldier's head was rubbed bare, and every shoulder was rubbed raw. But Nebuchadnezzar and his army gained nothing from fighting Tyre. [19] So this is what the Lord GOD says: I will give the land of Egypt to Nebuchadnezzar king of Babylon. He will take away Egypt's people and its wealth and its treasures as pay for his army. [20] I am giving Nebuchadnezzar the land of Egypt as a reward for working hard for me, says the Lord GOD.

[21] "At that time I will make Israel grow strong again, and I will let you, Ezekiel, speak to them. Then they will know that I am the LORD."

Egypt Will Be Punished

30 The LORD spoke his word to me, saying: [2] "Human, prophesy and say, 'This is what the Lord GOD says:
Cry and say,
"The terrible day is coming."
[3] The day is near;
the LORD's day of judging is near.
It is a cloudy day
and a time when the nations will be judged.
[4] An enemy will attack Egypt,
and Cush will tremble with fear.
When the killing begins in Egypt,
her wealth will be taken away,
and her foundations will be torn down.
[5] Cush, Put, Lydia, Arabia, Libya, and some of my people who had made an agreement with Egypt will fall dead in war.
[6] "This is what the LORD says:
Those who fight on Egypt's side will fall.
The power she is proud of will be lost.
The people in Egypt will fall dead in war
from Migdol in the north to Aswan in the south,
says the Lord GOD.

[7] They will be the most deserted lands.
Egypt's cities will be the worst of cities
that lie in ruins.
[8] Then they will know that I am the LORD
when I set fire to Egypt
and when all those nations on her side
are crushed.
[9] "At that time I will send messengers in ships to frighten Cush, which now feels safe. The people of Cush will tremble with fear when Egypt is punished. And that time is sure to come.

[10] "This is what the Lord GOD says:
I will destroy great numbers of people in Egypt
through the power of Nebuchadnezzar
king of Babylon.
[11] Nebuchadnezzar and his army,
the cruelest army of any nation,
will be brought in to destroy the land.
They will pull out their swords against Egypt
and will fill the land with those they kill.
[12] I will make the streams of the Nile River
become dry land,
and then I will sell the land to evil people.
I will destroy the land and everything in it
through the power of foreigners.
I, the LORD, have spoken.

Egypt's Idols Are Destroyed

[13] "This is what the Lord GOD says:
I will destroy the idols
and take away the statues of gods from
the city of Memphis.
There will no longer be a leader in Egypt,
and I will spread fear through the land
of Egypt.
[14] I will make southern Egypt empty
and start a fire in Zoan
and punish Thebes.
[15] And I will pour out my anger against Pelusium,
the strong place of Egypt.
I will destroy great numbers of people
in Thebes.
[16] I will set fire to Egypt.
Pelusium will be in great pain.

The walls of Thebes will be broken open,
and Memphis will have troubles every
day.
¹⁷The young men of Heliopolis and
Bubastis
will fall dead in war,
and the people will be taken away as
captives.
¹⁸In Tahpanhes the day will be dark
when I break Egypt's power.
Then she will no longer be proud of her
power.
A cloud will cover Egypt,
and her villages will be captured and
taken away.
¹⁹So I will punish Egypt,
and they will know I am the LORD.'"

Egypt Becomes Weak

²⁰It was in the eleventh year of our captivity, in the first month, on the seventh day of the month. The LORD spoke his word to me, saying: ²¹"Human, I have broken the powerful arm of the king of Egypt. It has not been tied up, so it will not get well. It has not been wrapped with a bandage, so it will not be strong enough to hold a sword in war. ²²So this is what the Lord GOD says: I am against the king of Egypt. I will break his arms, both the strong arm and the broken arm, and I will make the sword fall from his hand. ²³I will scatter the Egyptians among the nations, spreading them among the countries. ²⁴I will make the arms of the king of Babylon strong and put my sword in his hand. But I will break the arms of the king of Egypt. Then when he faces the king of Babylon, he will cry out in pain like a dying person. ²⁵So I will make the arms of the king of Babylon strong, but the arms of the king of Egypt will fall. Then people will know that I am the LORD when I put my sword into the hand of the king of Babylon and he uses it in war against Egypt. ²⁶Then I will scatter the Egyptians among the nations, spreading them among the countries. Then they will know that I am the LORD."

PSALM 129:5-8

⁵Let those who hate Jerusalem
be turned back in shame.
⁶Let them be like the grass on the roof
that dries up before it has grown.
⁷There is not enough of it to fill a hand
or to make into a bundle to fill one's
arms.
⁸Let those who pass by them not say,
"May the LORD bless you.
We bless you by the power of the LORD."

PROVERBS 28:27

²⁷Whoever gives to the poor will have
everything he needs,
but the one who ignores the poor will
receive many curses.

HEBREWS 13:1-25

13 Keep on loving each other as brothers and sisters. ²Remember to welcome strangers, because some who have done this have welcomed angels without knowing it. ³Remember those who are in prison as if you were in prison with them. Remember those who are suffering as if you were suffering with them.

⁴Marriage should be honored by everyone, and husband and wife should keep their marriage pure. God will judge as guilty those who take part in sexual sins. ⁵Keep your lives free from the love of money, and be satisfied with what you have. God has said,
"I will never leave you;
I will never abandon you." *Deuteronomy 31:6*
⁶So we can be sure when we say,
"I will not be afraid, because the Lord is
my helper.
People can't do anything to me."
Psalm 118:6
⁷Remember your leaders who taught God's message to you. Remember how they lived and died, and copy their faith. ⁸Jesus Christ is the same yesterday, today, and forever.

⁹Do not let all kinds of strange teachings lead you into the wrong way. Your hearts should be strengthened by God's grace, not by obeying rules about foods, which do not help those who obey them.

¹⁰We have a sacrifice, but the priests who serve in the Holy Tent cannot eat from it. ¹¹The high priest carries the blood of animals into the Most Holy Place where he

offers this blood for sins. But the bodies of the animals are burned outside the camp. ¹²So Jesus also suffered outside the city to make his people holy with his own blood. ¹³So let us go to Jesus outside the camp, holding on as he did when we are abused.

¹⁴Here on earth we do not have a city that lasts forever, but we are looking for the city that we will have in the future. ¹⁵So through Jesus let us always offer to God our sacrifice of praise, coming from lips that speak his name. ¹⁶Do not forget to do good to others, and share with them, because such sacrifices please God.

¹⁷Obey your leaders and act under their authority. They are watching over you, because they are responsible for your souls. Obey them so that they will do this work with joy, not sadness. It will not help you to make their work hard.

¹⁸Pray for us. We are sure that we have a clear conscience, because we always want to do the right thing. ¹⁹I especially beg you to pray so that God will send me back to you soon.

²⁰⁻²¹I pray that the God of peace will give you every good thing you need so you can do what he wants. God raised from the dead our Lord Jesus, the Great Shepherd of the sheep, because of the blood of his death. His blood began the eternal agreement that God made with his people. I pray that God will do in us what pleases him, through Jesus Christ, and to him be glory forever and ever. Amen.

²²My brothers and sisters, I beg you to listen patiently to this message I have written to encourage you, because it is not very long. ²³I want you to know that our brother Timothy has been let out of prison. If he arrives soon, we will both come to see you.

²⁴Greet all your leaders and all of God's people. Those from Italy send greetings to you.

²⁵Grace be with you all.

NOVEMBER 20

EZEKIEL 31:1—32:32

A Cedar Tree

31 It was in the eleventh year of our captivity, in the third month, on the first day of the month. The LORD spoke his word to me, saying: ²"Human, say to the king of Egypt and his people:

'No one is like you in your greatness.
³Assyria was once like a cedar tree in
    Lebanon
with beautiful branches that shaded the
    forest.
It was very tall;
    its top was among the clouds.
⁴Much water made the tree grow;
    the deep springs made it tall.
Rivers flowed
    around the bottom of the tree
and sent their streams
    to all other trees in the countryside.
⁵So the tree was taller

than all the other trees in the
    countryside.
Its limbs became long and big
    because of so much water.
⁶All the birds of the sky
    made their nests in the tree's limbs.
And all the wild animals
    gave birth under its branches.
All great nations
    lived in the tree's shade.
⁷So the tree was great and beautiful,
    with its long branches,
because its roots reached down to
    much water.
⁸The cedar trees in the garden of God
    were not as great as it was.
The pine trees
    did not have such great limbs.
The plane trees
    did not have such branches.
No tree in the garden of God
    was as beautiful as this tree.

⁹I made it beautiful
  with many branches,
  and all the trees of Eden in the garden of
     God
  wanted to be like it.
¹⁰"So this is what the Lord GOD says: The
tree grew tall. Its top reached the clouds, and
it became proud of its height. ¹¹So I handed
it over to a mighty ruler of the nations for
him to punish it. Because it was evil, I got rid
of it. ¹²The cruelest foreign nation cut it
down and left it. The tree's branches fell on
the mountains and in all the valleys, and its
broken limbs were in all the ravines of the
land. All the nations of the earth left the
shade of that tree. ¹³The birds of the sky live
on the fallen tree. The wild animals live
among the tree's fallen branches. ¹⁴So the
trees that grow by the water will not be
proud to be tall; they will not put their tops
among the clouds. None of the trees that are
watered well will grow that tall, because they
all are meant to die and go under the
ground. They will be with people who have
died and have gone down to the place of the
dead.

¹⁵"This is what the Lord GOD says: On the
day when the tree went down to the place of
the dead, I made the deep springs cry loudly.
I covered them and held back their rivers,
and the great waters stopped flowing. I
dressed Lebanon in black to show her sadness about the great tree, and all the trees in
the countryside were sad about it. ¹⁶I made
the nations shake with fear at the sound of
the tree falling when I brought it down to the
place of the dead. It went to join those who
have gone down to the grave. Then all the
trees of Eden and the best trees of Lebanon,
all the well-watered trees, were comforted in
the place of the dead below the earth.
¹⁷These trees had also gone down with the
great tree to the place of the dead. They
joined those who were killed in war and
those among the nations who had lived under the great tree's shade.

¹⁸"So no tree in Eden is equal to you,
Egypt, in greatness and honor, but you will
go down to join the trees of Eden in the place
below the earth. You will lie among unclean
people, with those who were killed in war.

"This is about the king of Egypt and all
his people, says the Lord GOD.'"

A Funeral Song

32 It was in the twelfth year of our captivity, in the twelfth month, on the first
day of the month. The LORD spoke his word
to me, saying: ²"Human, sing a funeral song
about the king of Egypt. Say to him:

'You are like a young lion among the
     nations.
  You are like a crocodile in the seas.
  You splash around in your streams
     and stir up the water with your feet,
     making the rivers muddy.
³"This is what the Lord GOD says:
  I will spread my net over you,
     and I will use a large group of people
     to pull you up in my net.
⁴Then I will throw you on the land
     dropping you onto the ground.
  I will let the birds of the sky rest on you
     and all the animals of the earth eat you
     until they are full.
⁵I will scatter your flesh on the mountains
     and fill the valleys with what is left of
     you.
⁶I will drench the land with your flowing
     blood
  as far as the mountains,
     and the ravines will be full of your
     flesh.
⁷When I make you disappear,
  I will cover the sky and make the stars
     dark.
  I will cover the sun with a cloud,
     and the moon will not shine.
⁸I will make all the shining lights in the
     sky
  become dark over you;
  I will bring darkness over your land,
     says the Lord GOD.
⁹I will cause many people to be afraid
  when I bring you as a captive into other
     nations,
  to lands you have not known.
¹⁰I will cause many people to be shocked
     about you.
  Their kings will tremble with fear
     because of you
  when I swing my sword in front of
     them.

They will shake every moment
    on the day you fall;
    each king will be afraid for his own life.
[11] " 'So this is what the Lord GOD says:
The sword of the king of Babylon
    will attack you.
[12]I will cause your people to fall
    by the swords of mighty soldiers,
    the most terrible in the world.
They will destroy the pride of Egypt
    and all its people.
[13]I will also destroy all Egypt's cattle
    which live alongside much water.
The foot of a human will not stir the
    water,
    and the hoofs of cattle will not muddy
    it anymore.
[14]So I will let the Egyptians' water become
    clear.
    I will cause their rivers to run as
    smoothly as olive oil,
    says the Lord GOD.
[15]When I make the land of Egypt empty
    and take everything that is in the land,
    when I destroy all those who live in
      Egypt,
    then they will know that I am the LORD.'
[16]"This is the funeral song people will
sing for Egypt. The women of the nations
will sing it; they will sing a funeral song for
Egypt and all its people, says the Lord GOD."

Egypt to Be Destroyed

[17]It was in the twelfth year of our captivity, on the fifteenth day of the month. The LORD spoke his word to me, saying: [18]"Human, cry for the people of Egypt. Bring down Egypt, together with the women of the powerful nations; bring them down to the place of the dead below the earth to join those who go to the place of the dead. [19]Say to them: 'Are you more beautiful than others? Go lie down in death with those who are unclean.' [20]The Egyptians will fall among those killed in war. The sword is ready; the enemy will drag Egypt and all her people away. [21]From the place of the dead the leaders of the mighty ones will speak about the king of Egypt and the nations which help him: 'The unclean, those killed in war, have come down here and lie dead.'

[22]"Assyria and all its army lie dead there. The graves of their soldiers are all around. All were killed in war, [23]and their graves were put in the deepest parts of the place of the dead. Assyria's army lies around its grave. When they lived on earth, they frightened people, but now all of them have been killed in war.

[24]"The nation of Elam is there with all its army around its grave. All of them were killed in war. They had frightened people on earth and were unclean, so they went down to the lowest parts of the place of the dead. They must carry their shame with those who have gone down to the place of the dead. [25]A bed has been made for Elam with all those killed in war. The graves of her soldiers are all around her. All Elam's people are unclean, killed in war. They frightened people when they lived on earth, but now they must carry their shame with those who have gone down to the place of the dead. Their graves are with the rest who were killed.

[26]"Meshech and Tubal are there with the graves of all their soldiers around them. All of them are unclean and have been killed in war. They also frightened people when they lived on earth. [27]But they are not buried with the other soldiers who were killed in battle long ago, those who went with their weapons of war to the place of the dead. These soldiers had their swords laid under their heads and their shields on their bodies. These mighty soldiers used to frighten people when they lived on earth.

[28]"You, king of Egypt, will be broken and lie among those who are unclean, who were killed in war.

[29]"Edom is there also, with its kings and all its leaders. They were mighty, but now they lie in death with those killed in war, with those who are unclean, with those who have gone down to the place of the dead.

[30]"All the rulers of the north and all the Sidonians are there. Their strength frightened people, but they have gone down in shame with those who were killed. They are unclean, lying with those killed in war. They carry their shame with those who have gone down to the place of the dead.

[31]"The king of Egypt and his army will

see these who have been killed in war. Then he will be comforted for all his soldiers killed in war, says the Lord God. ³²I made people afraid of the king of Egypt while he lived on earth. But he and all his people will lie among those who are unclean, who were killed in war, says the Lord God."

PSALM 130:1–4

A Prayer for Mercy

A song for going up to worship.

130 Lord, I am in great trouble,
so I call out to you.
²Lord, hear my voice;
listen to my prayer for help.
³Lord, if you punished people for all their sins,
no one would be left, Lord.
⁴But you forgive us,
so you are respected.

PROVERBS 28:28

²⁸When the wicked get control, everybody hides,
but when they die, good people do well.

JAMES 1:1–27

1 From James, a servant of God and of the Lord Jesus Christ.

To all of God's people who are scattered everywhere in the world:

Greetings.

Faith and Wisdom

²My brothers and sisters, when you have many kinds of troubles, you should be full of joy, ³because you know that these troubles test your faith, and this will give you patience. ⁴Let your patience show itself perfectly in what you do. Then you will be perfect and complete and will have everything you need. ⁵But if any of you needs wisdom, you should ask God for it. He is generous to everyone and will give you wisdom without criticizing you. ⁶But when you ask God, you must believe and not doubt. Anyone who doubts is like a wave in the sea,

blown up and down by the wind. ⁷⁻⁸Such doubters are thinking two different things at the same time, and they cannot decide about anything they do. They should not think they will receive anything from the Lord.

True Riches

⁹Believers who are poor should take pride that God has made them spiritually rich. ¹⁰Those who are rich should take pride that God has shown them that they are spiritually poor. The rich will die like a wild flower in the grass. ¹¹The sun rises with burning heat and dries up the plants. The flower falls off, and its beauty is gone. In the same way the rich will die while they are still taking care of business.

Temptation Is Not from God

¹²When people are tempted and still continue strong, they should be happy. After they have proved their faith, God will reward them with life forever. God promised this to all those who love him. ¹³When people are tempted, they should not say, "God is tempting me." Evil cannot tempt God, and God himself does not tempt anyone. ¹⁴But people are tempted when their own evil desire leads them away and traps them. ¹⁵This desire leads to sin, and then the sin grows and brings death.

¹⁶My dear brothers and sisters, do not be fooled about this. ¹⁷Every good action and every perfect gift is from God. These good gifts come down from the Creator of the sun, moon, and stars, who does not change like their shifting shadows. ¹⁸God decided to give us life through the word of truth so we might be the most important of all the things he made.

Listening and Obeying

¹⁹My dear brothers and sisters, always be willing to listen and slow to speak. Do not become angry easily, ²⁰because anger will not help you live the right kind of life God wants. ²¹So put out of your life every evil thing and every kind of wrong. Then in gentleness accept God's teaching that is planted in your hearts, which can save you.

²²Do what God's teaching says; when you only listen and do nothing, you are fooling yourselves. ²³Those who hear God's teaching and do nothing are like people who look at themselves in a mirror. ²⁴They see their faces and then go away and quickly forget what they looked like. ²⁵But the truly happy people are those who carefully study God's perfect law that makes people free, and they continue to study it. They do not forget what they heard, but they obey what God's teaching says. Those who do this will be made happy.

The True Way to Worship God

²⁶People who think they are religious but say things they should not say are just fooling themselves. Their "religion" is worth nothing. ²⁷Religion that God accepts as pure and without fault is this: caring for orphans or widows who need help, and keeping yourself free from the world's evil influence.

NOVEMBER 21

EZEKIEL 33:1—34:31

Ezekiel Is Watchman for Israel

33 The LORD spoke his word to me, saying: ²"Human, speak to your people and say to them: 'Suppose I bring a war against a land. The people of the land may choose one of their men and make him their watchman. ³When he sees the enemy coming to attack the land, he will blow the trumpet and warn the people. ⁴If they hear the sound of the trumpet but do nothing, the enemy will come and kill them. They will be responsible for their own deaths. ⁵They heard the sound of the trumpet but didn't do anything. So they are to blame for their own deaths. If they had done something, they would have saved their own lives. ⁶But if the watchman sees the enemy coming to attack and does not blow the trumpet, the people will not be warned. Then if the enemy comes and kills any of them, they have died because of their own sin. But I will punish the watchman for their deaths.'

⁷"You, human, are the one I have made a watchman for Israel. If you hear a word from my mouth, you must warn them for me. ⁸Suppose I say to the wicked: 'Wicked people, you will surely die,' but you don't speak to warn the wicked to stop doing evil. Then they will die because they were sinners, but I will punish you for their deaths. ⁹But if you warn the wicked to stop doing evil and they do not stop, they will die because they were sinners. But you have saved your life.

¹⁰"So you, human, say to Israel: 'You have said: Surely our law-breaking and sins are hurting us. They will kill us. What can we do so we will live?' ¹¹Say to them: 'The Lord GOD says: As surely as I live, I do not want any who are wicked to die. I want them to stop doing evil and live. Stop! Stop your wicked ways! You don't want to die, do you, people of Israel?'

¹²"Human, say to your people: 'The goodness of those who do right will not save them when they sin. The evil of wicked people will not cause them to be punished if they stop doing it. If good people sin, they will not be able to live by the good they did earlier.' ¹³If I tell good people, 'You will surely live,' they might think they have done enough good and then do evil. Then none of the good things they did will be remembered. They will die because of the evil they have done. ¹⁴Or, if I say to the wicked people, 'You will surely die,' they may stop sinning and do what is right and honest. ¹⁵For example, they may return what somebody gave them as a promise to repay a loan, or pay back what they stole. If they live by the rules that give life and do not sin, then they will surely live, and they will not die. ¹⁶They will not be punished for any of their sins. They now do what is right and fair, so they will surely live.

¹⁷"Your people say: 'The way of the Lord is not fair.' But it is their own ways that are not fair. ¹⁸When the good people stop doing good and do evil, they will die for their evil. ¹⁹But when the wicked stop doing evil and do what is right and fair, they will live. ²⁰You still say: 'The way of the Lord is not fair.' Israel, I will judge all of you by your own ways."

The Fall of Jerusalem Explained

²¹It was in the twelfth year of our captivity, on the fifth day of the tenth month. A person who had escaped from Jerusalem came to me and said, "Jerusalem has been captured." ²²Now I had felt the power of the LORD on me the evening before. He had made me able to talk again before this person came to me. I could speak; I was not without speech anymore.

²³Then the LORD spoke his word to me, saying: ²⁴"Human, people who live in the ruins in the land of Israel are saying: 'Abraham was only one person, yet he was given the land as his own. Surely the land has been given to us, who are many, as our very own.' ²⁵So say to them: 'This is what the Lord GOD says: You eat meat with the blood still in it, you ask your idols for help, and you murder people. Should you then have the land as your very own? ²⁶You depend on your sword and do terrible things which I hate. Each of you has sexual relations with his neighbor's wife. So should you have the land?'

²⁷"Say to them: 'This is what the Lord GOD says: As surely as I live, those who are among the city ruins in Israel will be killed in war. I will cause those who live in the country to be eaten by wild animals. People hiding in the strongholds and caves will die of disease. ²⁸I will make the land an empty desert. The people's pride in the land's power will end. The mountains of Israel will become empty so that no one will pass through them. ²⁹They will know that I am the LORD when I make the land an empty desert because of the things they have done that I hate.'

³⁰"But as for you, human, your people are talking about you by the walls and in the doorways of houses. They say to each other: 'Come now, and hear the message from the LORD.' ³¹So they come to you in crowds as if they were really ready to listen. They sit in front of you as if they were my people and hear your words, but they will not obey them. With their mouths they tell me they love me, but their hearts desire their selfish profits. ³²To your people you are nothing more than a singer who sings love songs and has a beautiful voice and plays a musical instrument well. They hear your words, but they will not obey them.

³³"When this comes true, and it surely will happen, then the people will know that a prophet has been among them."

The Leaders Are like Shepherds

34 The LORD spoke his word to me, saying: ²"Human, prophesy against the leaders of Israel, who are like shepherds. Prophesy and say to them: 'This is what the Lord GOD says: How terrible it will be for the shepherds of Israel who feed only themselves! Why don't the shepherds feed the flock? ³You eat the milk curds, and you clothe yourselves with the wool. You kill the fat sheep, but you do not feed the flock. ⁴You have not made the weak strong. You have not healed the sick or put bandages on those that were hurt. You have not brought back those who strayed away or searched for the lost. But you have ruled the sheep with cruel force. ⁵The sheep were scattered, because there was no shepherd, and they became food for every wild animal. ⁶My flock wandered over all the mountains and on every high hill. They were scattered all over the face of the earth, and no one searched or looked for them.

⁷" 'So, you shepherds, hear the word of the LORD. This is what the Lord GOD says: ⁸As surely as I live, my flock has been caught and eaten by all the wild animals, because the flock has no shepherd. The shepherds did not search for my flock. No, they fed themselves instead of my flock. ⁹So, you shepherds, hear the word of the LORD. ¹⁰This is what the Lord GOD says: I am against the shepherds. I will blame them for what has happened to my sheep and will

not let them tend the flock anymore. Then the shepherds will stop feeding themselves, and I will take my flock from their mouths so they will no longer be their food. [11]"'This is what the Lord GOD says: I, myself, will search for my sheep and take care of them. [12]As a shepherd takes care of his scattered flock when it is found, I will take care of my sheep. I will save them from all the places where they were scattered on a cloudy and dark day. [13]I will bring them out from the nations and gather them from the countries. I will bring them to their own land and pasture them on the mountains of Israel, in the ravines, and in all the places where people live in the land. [14]I will feed them in a good pasture, and they will eat grass on the high mountains of Israel. They will lie down on good ground where they eat grass, and they will eat in rich grassland on the mountains of Israel. [15]I will feed my flock and lead them to rest, says the Lord GOD. [16]I will search for the lost, bring back those that strayed away, put bandages on those that were hurt, and make the weak strong. But I will destroy those sheep that are fat and strong. I will tend the sheep with fairness.

[17]"'This is what the Lord GOD says: As for you, my flock, I will judge between one sheep and another, between the male sheep and the male goats. [18]Is it not enough for you to eat grass in the good land? Must you crush the rest of the grass with your feet? Is it not enough for you to drink clear water? Must you make the rest of the water muddy with your feet? [19]Must my flock eat what you crush, and must they drink what you make muddy with your feet?

[20]"'So this is what the Lord GOD says to them: I, myself, will judge between the fat sheep and the thin sheep. [21]You push with your side and with your shoulder, and you knock down all the weak sheep with your horns until you have forced them away. [22]So I will save my flock; they will not be hurt anymore. I will judge between one sheep and another. [23]Then I will put over them one shepherd, my servant David. He will feed them and tend them and be their shepherd. [24]Then I, the LORD, will be their

God, and my servant David will be a ruler among them. I, the LORD, have spoken.

[25]"'I will make an agreement of peace with my sheep and will remove harmful animals from the land. Then the sheep will live safely in the desert and sleep in the woods. [26]I will bless them and let them live around my hill. I will cause the rains to come when it is time; there will be showers to bless them. [27]Also the trees in the countryside will give their fruit, and the land will give its harvest. And the sheep will be safe on their land. Then they will know that I am the LORD when I break the bars of their captivity and save them from the power of those who made them slaves. [28]They will not be led captive by the nations again. The wild animals will not eat them, but they will live safely, and no one will make them afraid. [29]I will give them a place famous for its good crops, so they will no longer suffer from hunger in the land. They will not suffer the insults of other nations anymore. [30]Then they will know that I, the LORD their God, am with them. The nation of Israel will know that they are my people, says the Lord GOD. [31]You, my human sheep, are the sheep I care for, and I am your God, says the Lord GOD.'"

PSALM 130:5-8

[5]I wait for the LORD to help me,
 and I trust his word.
[6]I wait for the Lord to help me
 more than night watchmen wait for
  the dawn,
 more than night watchmen wait for
  the dawn.

[7]People of Israel, put your hope in the
 LORD
 because he is loving
 and able to save.
[8]He will save Israel
 from all their sins.

PROVERBS 29:1

29 Whoever is stubborn after being
 corrected many times
 will suddenly be hurt beyond cure.

JAMES 2:1–26

Love All People

2 My dear brothers and sisters, as believers in our glorious Lord Jesus Christ, never think some people are more important than others. ²Suppose someone comes into your church meeting wearing nice clothes and a gold ring. At the same time a poor person comes in wearing old, dirty clothes. ³You show special attention to the one wearing nice clothes and say, "Please, sit here in this good seat." But you say to the poor person, "Stand over there," or, "Sit on the floor by my feet." ⁴What are you doing? You are making some people more important than others, and with evil thoughts you are deciding that one person is better.

⁵Listen, my dear brothers and sisters! God chose the poor in the world to be rich with faith and to receive the kingdom God promised to those who love him. ⁶But you show no respect to the poor. The rich are always trying to control your lives. They are the ones who take you to court. ⁷And they are the ones who speak against Jesus, who owns you.

⁸This royal law is found in the Scriptures: "Love your neighbor as you love yourself."ⁿ If you obey this law, you are doing right. ⁹But if you treat one person as being more important than another, you are sinning. You are guilty of breaking God's law. ¹⁰A person who follows all of God's law but fails to obey even one command is guilty of breaking all the commands in that law. ¹¹The same God who said, "You must not be guilty of adultery,"ⁿ also said, "You must not murder anyone."ⁿ So if you do not take part in adultery but you murder someone, you are guilty of breaking all of God's law. ¹²In everything you say and do, remember that you will be judged by the law that makes people free. ¹³So you must show mercy to others, or God will not show

mercy to you when he judges you. But the person who shows mercy can stand without fear at the judgment.

Faith and Good Works

¹⁴My brothers and sisters, if people say they have faith, but do nothing, their faith is worth nothing. Can faith like that save them? ¹⁵A brother or sister in Christ might need clothes or food. ¹⁶If you say to that person, "God be with you! I hope you stay warm and get plenty to eat," but you do not give what that person needs, your words are worth nothing. ¹⁷In the same way, faith by itself—that does nothing—is dead.

¹⁸Someone might say, "You have faith, but I have deeds." Show me your faith without doing anything, and I will show you my faith by what I do. ¹⁹You believe there is one God. Good! But the demons believe that, too, and they tremble with fear.

²⁰You foolish person! Must you be shown that faith that does nothing is worth nothing? ²¹Abraham, our ancestor, was made right with God by what he did when he offered his son Isaac on the altar. ²²So you see that Abraham's faith and the things he did worked together. His faith was made perfect by what he did. ²³This shows the full meaning of the Scripture that says: "Abraham believed God, and God accepted Abraham's faith, and that faith made him right with God."ⁿ And Abraham was called God's friend.ⁿ ²⁴So you see that people are made right with God by what they do, not by faith only.

²⁵Another example is Rahab, a prostitute, who was made right with God by something she did. She welcomed the spies into her home and helped them escape by a different road.

²⁶Just as a person's body that does not have a spirit is dead, so faith that does nothing is dead!

2:8 **"Love . . . yourself."** Quotation from Leviticus 19:18.   2:11 **"You . . . adultery."** Quotation from Exodus 20:14 and Deuteronomy 5:18.   2:11 **"You . . . anyone."** Quotation from Exodus 20:13 and Deuteronomy 5:17.   2:23 **"Abraham . . . God."** Quotation from Genesis 15:6.   2:23 **God's friend** These words about Abraham are found in 2 Chronicles 20:7 and Isaiah 41:8.

NOVEMBER 22

Prophecy Against Edom

35 The LORD spoke his word to me, saying: ²"Human, look toward Edom and prophesy against it. ³Say to it: 'This is what the Lord GOD says: I am against you, Edom. I will stretch out my hand against you and make you an empty desert. ⁴I will destroy your cities, and you will become empty. Then you will know that I am the LORD.

⁵"'You have always been an enemy of Israel. You let them be defeated in war when they were in trouble at the time of their final punishment. ⁶So the Lord GOD says, as surely as I live, I will let you be murdered. Murder will chase you. Since you did not hate murdering people, murder will chase you. ⁷I will make Edom an empty ruin and destroy everyone who goes in or comes out of it. ⁸I will fill its mountains with those who are killed. Those killed in war will fall on your hills, in your valleys, and in all your ravines. ⁹I will make you a ruin forever; no one will live in your cities. Then you will know that I am the LORD.

¹⁰"'You said, "These two nations, Israel and Judah, and these two lands will be ours. We will take them for our own." But the LORD was there. ¹¹So this is what the Lord GOD says: As surely as I live, I will treat you just as you treated them. You were angry and jealous because you hated them. So I will punish you and show the Israelites who I am. ¹²Then you will know that I, the LORD, have heard all your insults against the mountains of Israel. You said, "They have been ruined. They have been given to us to eat." ¹³You have not stopped your proud talk against me. I have heard you. ¹⁴This is what the Lord GOD says: All the earth will be happy when I make you an empty ruin. ¹⁵You were happy when the land of Israel was ruined, but I will do the same thing to you. Mount Seir and all Edom, you will become an empty ruin. Then you will know that I am the LORD.'

Israel to Come Home

36 "Human, prophesy to the mountains of Israel and say: 'Mountains of Israel, hear the word of the LORD. ²This is what the Lord GOD says: The enemy has said about you, "Now the old places to worship gods have become ours." ' ³So prophesy and say: 'This is what the Lord GOD says: They have made you an empty ruin and have crushed you from all around. So you became a possession of the other nations. People have talked and whispered against you. ⁴So, mountains of Israel, hear the word of the Lord GOD. The Lord GOD speaks to the mountains, hills, ravines, and valleys, to the empty ruins and abandoned cities that have been robbed and laughed at by the other nations. ⁵This is what the Lord GOD says: I speak in hot anger against the other nations. I speak against the people of Edom, who took my land for themselves with joy and with hate in their hearts. They forced out the people and took their pastureland.' ⁶So prophesy about the land of Israel and say to the mountains, hills, ravines, and valleys: 'This is what the Lord GOD says: I speak in my jealous anger, because you have suffered the insults of the nations. ⁷So this is what the Lord GOD says: I promise that the nations around you will also have to suffer insults.

⁸"'But you, mountains of Israel, will grow branches and fruit for my people, who will soon come home. ⁹I am concerned about you; I am on your side. You will be plowed, and seed will be planted in you. ¹⁰I will increase the number of people who live on you, all the people of Israel. The cities will have people living in them, and the ruins will be rebuilt. ¹¹I will increase the number of people and animals living on you. They will grow and have many young. You will have people living on you as you did before, and I will make you better off than at the beginning. Then you will know that I am the LORD. ¹²I will cause my people Israel to walk on you and own you, and you will belong to them. You will never again take their children away from them.

¹³"'This is what the Lord GOD says: People say about you, "You eat people and take children from your nation." ¹⁴But you will not eat

people anymore or take away the children, says the Lord GOD. [15]I will not make you listen to insults from the nations anymore; you will not suffer shame from them anymore. You will not cause your nation to fall anymore, says the Lord GOD.'"

The Lord Acts for Himself

[16]The LORD spoke his word to me again, saying: [17]"Human, when the nation of Israel was living in their own land, they made it unclean by their ways and the things they did. Their ways were like a woman's uncleanness in her time of monthly bleeding. [18]So I poured out my anger against them, because they murdered in the land and because they made the land unclean with their idols. [19]I scattered them among the nations, and they were spread through the countries. I punished them for how they lived and what they did. [20]They dishonored my holy name in the nations where they went. The nations said about them, 'These are the people of the LORD, but they had to leave the land which he gave them.' [21]But I had concern for my holy name, which the nation of Israel had dishonored among the nations where they went.

[22]"So say to the people of Israel, 'This is what the Lord GOD says: Israel, I am going to act, but not for your sake. I will do something to help my holy name, which you have dishonored among the nations where you went. [23]I will prove the holiness of my great name, which has been dishonored among the nations. You have dishonored it among these nations, but the nations will know that I am the LORD when I prove myself holy before their eyes, says the Lord GOD.

[24]" 'I will take you from the nations and gather you out of all the lands and bring you back into your own land. [25]Then I will sprinkle clean water on you, and you will be clean. I will cleanse you from all your uncleanness and your idols. [26]Also, I will teach you to respect me completely, and I will put a new way of thinking inside you. I will take out the stubborn hearts of stone from your bodies, and I will give you obedient hearts of flesh. [27]I will put my Spirit inside you and help you live by my rules and carefully obey my laws. [28]You will live in the land I gave to your an-

cestors, and you will be my people, and I will be your God. [29]So I will save you from all your uncleanness. I will command the grain to come and grow; I will not allow a time of hunger to hurt you. [30]I will increase the harvest of the field so you will never again suffer shame among the nations because of hunger. [31]Then you will remember your evil ways and actions that were not good, and you will hate yourselves because of your sins and your terrible acts that I hate. [32]I want you to know that I am not going to do this for your sake, says the Lord GOD. Be ashamed and embarrassed about your ways, Israel.

[33]" 'This is what the Lord GOD says: This is what will happen on the day I cleanse you from all your sins: I will cause the cities to have people living in them again, and the destroyed places will be rebuilt. [34]The empty land will be plowed so it will no longer be a ruin for everyone who passes by to see. [35]They will say, "This land was ruined, but now it has become like the garden of Eden. The cities were destroyed, empty, and ruined, but now they are protected and have people living in them." [36]Then those nations still around you will know that I, the LORD, have rebuilt what was destroyed and have planted what was empty. I, the LORD, have spoken, and I will do it.'

[37]"This is what the Lord GOD says: I will let myself be asked by the people of Israel to do this for them again: I will make their people grow in number like a flock. [38]They will be as many as the flocks brought to Jerusalem during her holy feasts. Her ruined cities will be filled with flocks of people. Then they will know that I am the LORD."

PSALM 131:1–3

Childlike Trust in the Lord

A song for going up to worship. Of David.

131
LORD, my heart is not proud;
  I don't look down on others.
I don't do great things,
  and I can't do miracles.
[2]But I am calm and quiet,
  like a baby with its mother.
I am at peace, like a baby with its
  mother.

³People of Israel, put your hope in the
LORD
now and forever.

PROVERBS 29:2–3

²When good people do well, everyone is
happy,
but when evil people rule, everyone
groans.

³Those who love wisdom make their
parents happy,
but friends of prostitutes waste their
money.

JAMES 3:1–18

Controlling the Things We Say

3 My brothers and sisters, not many of you
should become teachers, because you
know that we who teach will be judged more
strictly. ²We all make many mistakes. If people never said anything wrong, they would
be perfect and able to control their entire
selves, too. ³When we put bits into the
mouths of horses to make them obey us, we
can control their whole bodies. ⁴Also a ship
is very big, and it is pushed by strong winds.
But a very small rudder controls that big
ship, making it go wherever the pilot wants.
⁵It is the same with the tongue. It is a small
part of the body, but it brags about great
things.

A big forest fire can be started with only a
little flame. ⁶And the tongue is like a fire. It is
a whole world of evil among the parts of our
bodies. The tongue spreads its evil through
the whole body. The tongue is set on fire by
hell, and it starts a fire that influences all of
life. ⁷People can tame every kind of wild animal, bird, reptile, and fish, and they have
tamed them, ⁸but no one can tame the
tongue. It is wild and evil and full of deadly
poison. ⁹We use our tongues to praise our
Lord and Father, but then we curse people,
whom God made like himself. ¹⁰Praises and
curses come from the same mouth! My
brothers and sisters, this should not happen.
¹¹Do good and bad water flow from the same
spring? ¹²My brothers and sisters, can a fig
tree make olives, or can a grapevine make
figs? No! And a well full of salty water cannot
give good water.

True Wisdom

¹³Are there those among you who are
truly wise and understanding? Then they
should show it by living right and doing
good things with a gentleness that comes
from wisdom. ¹⁴But if you are selfish and
have bitter jealousy in your hearts, do not
brag. Your bragging is a lie that hides the
truth. ¹⁵That kind of "wisdom" does not
come from God but from the world. It is not
spiritual; it is from the devil. ¹⁶Where jealousy and selfishness are, there will be confusion and every kind of evil. ¹⁷But the wisdom
that comes from God is first of all pure, then
peaceful, gentle, and easy to please. This wisdom is always ready to help those who are
troubled and to do good for others. It is always fair and honest. ¹⁸People who work for
peace in a peaceful way plant a good crop of
right-living.

NOVEMBER 23

EZEKIEL 37:1—38:23

The Vision of Dry Bones

37 I felt the power of the LORD on me, and
he brought me out by the Spirit of the
LORD and put me down in the middle of a
valley. It was full of bones. ²He led me
around among the bones, and I saw that
there were many bones in the valley and that
they were very dry. ³Then he asked me, "Human, can these bones live?"

I answered, "Lord GOD, only you know."

⁴He said to me, "Prophesy to these bones
and say to them, 'Dry bones, hear the word of
the LORD. ⁵This is what the Lord GOD says to
the bones: I will cause breath to enter you so

you will come to life. [6]I will put muscles on you and flesh on you and cover you with skin. Then I will put breath in you so you will come to life. Then you will know that I am the LORD.'"

[7]So I prophesied as I was commanded. While I prophesied, there was a noise and a rattling. The bones came together, bone to bone. [8]I looked and saw muscles come on the bones, and flesh grew, and skin covered the bones. But there was no breath in them.

[9]Then he said to me, "Prophesy to the wind.[n] Prophesy, human, and say to the wind, 'This is what the Lord GOD says: Wind, come from the four winds, and breathe on these people who were killed so they can come back to life.'" [10]So I prophesied as the LORD commanded me. And the breath came into them, and they came to life and stood on their feet, a very large army.

[11]Then he said to me, "Human, these bones are like all the people of Israel. They say, 'Our bones are dried up, and our hope has gone. We are destroyed.' [12]So, prophesy and say to them, 'This is what the Lord GOD says: My people, I will open your graves and cause you to come up out of your graves. Then I will bring you into the land of Israel. [13]My people, you will know that I am the LORD when I open your graves and cause you to come up from them. [14]And I will put my Spirit inside you, and you will come to life. Then I will put you in your own land. And you will know that I, the LORD, have spoken and done it, says the LORD.'"

Judah and Israel Back Together

[15]The LORD spoke his word to me, saying, [16]"Human, take a stick and write on it, 'For Judah and all the Israelites with him.' Then take another stick and write on it, 'The stick of Ephraim, for Joseph and all the Israelites with him.' [17]Then join them together into one stick so they will be one in your hand.

[18]"When your people say to you, 'Explain to us what you mean by this,' [19]say to them, 'This is what the Lord GOD says: I will take the stick for Joseph and the tribes of Israel with him, which is in the hand of Ephraim, and I will put it with the stick of Judah. I will

make them into one stick, and they will be one in my hand.' [20]Hold the sticks on which you wrote these names in your hand so the people can see them. [21]Say to the people, 'This is what the Lord GOD says: I am going to take the people of Israel from among the nations where they have gone. I will gather them from all around and bring them into their own land. [22]I will make them one nation in the land, on the mountains of Israel. One king will rule all of them. They will never again be two nations; they will not be divided into two kingdoms anymore. [23]They will not continue to make themselves unclean by their idols, their statues of gods which I hate, or by their sins. I will save them from all the ways they sin and turn against me, and I will make them clean. Then they will be my people, and I will be their God.

[24]" 'My servant David will be their king, and they will all have one shepherd. They will live by my rules and obey my laws. [25]They will live on the land I gave to my servant Jacob, the land in which your ancestors lived. They will all live on the land forever: they, their children, and their grandchildren. David my servant will be their king forever. [26]I will make an agreement of peace with them, an agreement that continues forever. I will put them in their land and make them grow in number. Then I will put my Temple among them forever. [27]The place where I live will be with them. I will be their God, and they will be my people. [28]When my Temple is among them forever, the nations will know that I, the LORD, make Israel holy.'"

Prophecy Against Gog

38 The LORD spoke his word to me, saying, [2]"Human, look toward Gog of the land of Magog, the chief ruler of the nations of Meshech and Tubal. Prophesy against him [3]and say, 'The Lord GOD says this: I am against you, Gog, chief ruler of Meshech and Tubal. [4]I will turn you around and put hooks in your jaws. And I will bring you out with all your army, horses, and horsemen, all of whom will be dressed in beautiful uniforms. They will be a large army with large and small shields and all having swords. [5]Persia,

---

37:9 wind This Hebrew word could also mean "breath" or "spirit."

Cush, and Put will be with them, all of them having shields and helmets. [6]There will also be Gomer with all its troops and the nation of Togarmah from the far north with all its troops—many nations with you.

[7]" 'Be prepared. Be prepared, you and all the armies that have come together to make you their commander. [8]After a long time you will be called for service. After those years you will come into a land that has been rebuilt from war. The people in the land will have been gathered from many nations to the mountains of Israel, which were empty for a long time. These people were brought out from the nations, and they will all be living in safety. [9]You will come like a storm. You, all your troops, and the many nations with you will be like a cloud covering the land.

[10]" 'This is what the Lord GOD says: At that time ideas will come into your mind, and you will think up an evil plan. [11]You will say, "I will march against a land of towns without walls. I will attack those who are at rest and live in safety. All of them live without city walls or gate bars or gates. [12]I will capture treasures and take loot. I will turn my power against the rebuilt ruins that now have people living in them. I will attack these people who have been gathered from the nations, who have become rich with farm animals and property, who live at the center of the world." [13]Sheba, Dedan, and the traders of Tarshish, with all its villages, will say to you, "Did you come to capture treasure? Did you bring your troops together to take loot? Did you bring them to carry away silver and gold and to take away farm animals and property?" '

[14]"So prophesy, human, and say to Gog, 'This is what the Lord GOD says: Now that my people Israel are living in safety, you will know about it. [15]You will come with many people from your place in the far north. You will have a large group with you, a mighty army, all riding on horses. [16]You will attack my people Israel like a cloud that covers the land. This will happen in the days to come when I bring you against my land. Gog, then the nations will know me when they see me prove how holy I am in what I do through you.

[17]" 'This is what the Lord GOD says: You are the one about whom I spoke in past days. I spoke through my servants, the prophets of Israel, who prophesied for many years that I would bring you against them. [18]This is what will happen: On the day Gog attacks the land of Israel, I will become very angry, says the Lord GOD. [19]With jealousy and great anger I tell you that at that time there will surely be a great earthquake in Israel. [20]The fish of the sea, the birds of the sky, the wild animals, everything that crawls on the ground, and all the people on the earth will shake with fear before me. Also the mountains will be thrown down, the cliffs will fall, and every wall will fall to the ground. [21]Then I will call for a war against Gog on all my mountains, says the Lord GOD. Everyone's sword will attack the soldier next to him. [22]I will punish Gog with disease and death. I will send a heavy rain with hailstones and burning sulfur on Gog, his army, and the many nations with him. [23]Then I will show how great I am. I will show my holiness, and I will make myself known to the many nations that watch. Then they will know that I am the LORD.'

PSALM 132:1–9

In Praise of the Temple

A song for going up to worship.

132 LORD, remember David
and all his suffering.
[2]He made an oath to the LORD,
a promise to the Mighty God of Jacob.
[3]He said, "I will not go home to my house,
or lie down on my bed,
[4]or close my eyes,
or let myself sleep
[5]until I find a place for the LORD.
I want to provide a home for the
Mighty God of Jacob."

[6]We heard about the Ark in Bethlehem.
We found it at Kiriath Jearim.
[7]Let's go to the LORD's house.
Let's worship at his footstool.
[8]Rise, LORD, and come to your resting
place;
come with the Ark that shows your
strength.

[9]May your priests do what is right.
May your people sing for joy.

PROVERBS 29:4

[4]If a king is fair, he makes his country
strong,
but if he takes gifts dishonestly, he tears
his country down.

JAMES 4:1—17

Give Yourselves to God

4 Do you know where your fights and arguments come from? They come from the
selfish desires that war within you. [2]You
want things, but you do not have them. So
you are ready to kill and are jealous of other
people, but you still cannot get what you
want. So you argue and fight. You do not get
what you want, because you do not ask God.
[3]Or when you ask, you do not receive because the reason you ask is wrong. You want
things so you can use them for your own
pleasures.

[4]So, you are not loyal to God! You should
know that loving the world is the same as
hating God. Anyone who wants to be a friend
of the world becomes God's enemy. [5]Do you
think the Scripture means nothing that says,
"The Spirit that God made to live in us wants
us for himself alone"?[n] [6]But God gives us
even more grace, as the Scripture says,

"God is against the proud,
but he gives grace to the humble."

Proverbs 3:34

[7]So give yourselves completely to God.
Stand against the devil, and the devil will
run from you. [8]Come near to God, and God
will come near to you. You sinners, clean
sin out of your lives. You who are trying to
follow God and the world at the same time,
make your thinking pure. [9]Be sad, cry, and
weep! Change your laughter into crying
and your joy into sadness. [10]Humble yourself in the Lord's presence, and he will
honor you.

You Are Not the Judge

[11]Brothers and sisters, do not tell evil lies
about each other. If you speak against your
fellow believers or judge them, you are judging and speaking against the law they follow.
And when you are judging the law, you are
no longer a follower of the law. You have become a judge. [12]God is the only Lawmaker
and Judge. He is the only One who can save
and destroy. So it is not right for you to judge
your neighbor.

Let God Plan Your Life

[13]Some of you say, "Today or tomorrow we
will go to some city. We will stay there a year,
do business, and make money." [14]But you do
not know what will happen tomorrow! Your
life is like a mist. You can see it for a short
time, but then it goes away. [15]So you should
say, "If the Lord wants, we will live and do
this or that." [16]But now you are proud and
you brag. All of this bragging is wrong.
[17]Anyone who knows the right thing to do,
but does not do it, is sinning.

NOVEMBER 24

EZEKIEL 39:1—40:49

The Death of Gog and His Army

39 "Human, prophesy against Gog and
say, 'This is what the Lord God says: I
am against you, Gog, chief ruler of Meshech
and Tubal. [2]I will turn you around and lead
you. I will bring you from the far north and

send you to attack the mountains of Israel. [3]I
will knock your bow out of your left hand
and throw down your arrows from your
right hand. [4]You, all your troops, and the
nations with you will fall dead on the mountains of Israel. I will let you be food for every
bird that eats meat and for every wild animal. [5]You will lie fallen on the ground,

because I have spoken, says the Lord GOD. ⁶I will send fire on Magog and those who live in safety on the coastlands. Then they will know that I am the LORD.

⁷" 'I will make myself known among my people Israel, and I will not let myself be dishonored anymore. Then the nations will know that I am the LORD, the Holy One in Israel. ⁸It is coming! It will happen, says the Lord GOD. The time I talked about is coming.

⁹" 'Then those who live in the cities of Israel will come out and make fires with the enemy's weapons. They will burn them, both large and small shields, bows and arrows, war clubs, and spears. They will use the weapons to burn in their fires for seven years. ¹⁰They will not need to take wood from the field or chop firewood from the forests, because they will make fires with the weapons. In this way they will take the treasures of those who took their treasures; they will take the loot of those who took their loot, says the Lord GOD.

¹¹" 'At that time I will give Gog a burial place in Israel, in the Valley of the Travelers, east of the Dead Sea. It will block the road for travelers. Gog and all his army will be buried there, so people will call it The Valley of Gog's Army.

¹²" 'The people of Israel will be burying them for seven months to make the land clean again. ¹³All the people in the land will bury them, and they will be honored on the day of my victory, says the Lord GOD.

¹⁴" 'The people of Israel will choose men to work through the land to make it clean. Along with others, they will bury Gog's soldiers still lying dead on the ground. After the seven months are finished, they will still search. ¹⁵As they go through the land, anyone who sees a human bone is to put a marker by it. The sign will stay there until the gravediggers bury the bone in The Valley of Gog's Army. ¹⁶A city will be there named Hamonah. So they will make the land clean again.'

¹⁷"Human, this is what the Lord GOD says: Speak to every kind of bird and wild animal: 'Come together, come! Come together from all around to my sacrifice, a great sacrifice which I will prepare for you on the moun-

tains of Israel. Eat flesh and drink blood! ¹⁸You are to eat the flesh of the mighty and drink the blood of the rulers of the earth as if they were fat animals from Bashan: male sheep, lambs, goats, and bulls. ¹⁹You are to eat and drink from my sacrifice which I have prepared for you, eating fat until you are full and drinking blood until you are drunk. ²⁰At my table you are to eat until you are full of horses and riders, mighty men and all kinds of soldiers,' says the Lord GOD.

²¹"I will show my glory among the nations. All the nations will see my power when I punish them. ²²From that time onward the people of Israel will know that I am the LORD their God. ²³The nations will know Israel was taken away captive because they turned against me. So I turned away from them and handed them over to their enemies until all of them died in war. ²⁴Because of their uncleanness and their sins, I punished them and turned away from them.

²⁵"So this is what the Lord GOD says: Now I will bring the people of Jacob back from captivity, and I will have mercy on the whole nation of Israel. I will not let them dishonor me. ²⁶The people will forget their shame and how they rejected me when they live again in safety on their own land with no one to make them afraid. ²⁷I will bring the people back from other lands and gather them from the lands of their enemies. So I will use my people to show many nations that I am holy. ²⁸Then my people will know that I am the LORD their God, because I sent them into captivity among the nations, but then I brought them back to their own land, leaving no one behind. ²⁹I will not turn away from them anymore, because I will put my Spirit into the people of Israel, says the Lord GOD."

The New Temple

40 It was the twenty-fifth year of our captivity, at the beginning of the year, on the tenth day of the month. It was in the fourteenth year after Jerusalem was captured. On that same day I felt the power of the LORD, and he brought me to Jerusalem. ²In the visions of God he brought me to the land of Israel and put me down on a very high mountain. On the south of the mountain there were some buildings that looked like a city. ³He took me closer to the buildings, and I saw a man who looked as if he were made of bronze, standing in the gateway. He had a cord made of linen and a stick in his hand, both for measuring. ⁴The man said to me, "Human, look with your eyes and hear with your ears. Pay attention to all that I will show you, because that's why you have been brought here. Tell the people of Israel all that you see."

The East Gateway

⁵I saw a wall that surrounded the Temple area. The measuring stick in the man's hand was ten and one-half feet long. So the man measured the wall, which was ten and one-half feet thick and ten and one-half feet high.

⁶Then the man went to the east gateway. He went up its steps and measured the opening of the gateway. It was ten and one-half feet deep. ⁷The rooms for the guards were ten and one-half feet long and ten and one-half feet wide. The walls that came out between the guards' rooms were about nine feet thick. The opening of the gateway next to the porch that faced the Temple was ten and one-half feet deep.

⁸Then the man measured the porch of the gateway. ⁹It was about fourteen feet deep, and its side walls were three and one-half feet thick. The porch of the gateway faced the Temple.

¹⁰On each side of the east gateway were three rooms, which measured the same on each side. The walls between each room were the same thickness. ¹¹The man measured the width of the entrance to the gateway, which was seventeen and one-half feet wide. The width of the gate was about twenty-three feet. ¹²And there was a low wall about twenty-one inches high in front of each room. The rooms were ten and one-half feet on each side. ¹³The man measured the gateway from the roof of one room to the roof of the opposite room. It was about forty-four feet from one door to the opposite door. ¹⁴The man also measured the porch, which was about thirty-five feet wide. The

courtyard was around the porch. ¹⁵From the front of the outer side of the gateway to the front of the porch of the inner side of the gateway was eighty-seven and one-half feet. ¹⁶The rooms and porch had small windows on both sides. The windows were narrower on the side facing the gateway. Carvings of palm trees were on each side wall of the rooms.

The Outer Courtyard

¹⁷Then the man brought me into the outer courtyard where I saw rooms and a pavement of stones all around the court. Thirty rooms were along the edge of the paved walkway. ¹⁸The pavement ran alongside the gates and was as deep as the gates were wide. This was the lower pavement. ¹⁹Then the man measured from the outer wall to the inner wall. The outer court between these two walls was one hundred seventy-five feet on the east and on the north.

The North Gateway

²⁰The man measured the length and width of the north gateway leading to the outer courtyard. ²¹Its three rooms on each side, its inner walls, and its porch measured the same as the first gateway. It was eighty-seven and one-half feet long and forty-four feet wide. ²²Its windows, porch, and carvings of palm trees measured the same as the east gateway. Seven steps went up to the gateway, and the gateway's porch was at the inner end. ²³The inner courtyard had a gateway across from the northern gateway like the one on the east. The man measured it and found it was one hundred seventy-five feet from inner gateway to outer gateway.

The South Gateway

²⁴Then the man led me south where I saw a gateway facing south. He measured its inner walls and its porch, and they measured the same as the other gateways. ²⁵The gateway and its porch had windows all around like the other gateways. It was eighty-seven and one-half feet long and forty-four feet wide. ²⁶Seven steps went up to this gateway. Its porch was at the inner end, and it had carvings of palm trees on its inner walls. ²⁷The inner courtyard had a gateway on its

south side. The man measured from gate to gate on the south side, which was one hundred seventy-five feet.

The Inner Courtyard

28Then the man brought me through the south gateway into the inner courtyard. The inner south gateway measured the same as the gateways in the outer wall. 29The inner south gateway's rooms, inner walls, and porch measured the same as the gateways in the outer wall. There were windows all around the gateway and its porch. The gateway was eighty-seven and one-half feet long and forty-four feet wide. 30Each porch of each inner gateway was about forty-four feet long and about nine feet wide. 31The inner south gateway's porch faced the outer courtyard. Carvings of palm trees were on its side walls, and its stairway had eight steps.

32The man brought me into the inner courtyard on the east side. He measured the inner east gateway, and it was the same as the other gateways. 33The inner east gateway's rooms, inside walls, and porch measured the same as the other gateways. Windows were all around the gateway and its porch. The inner east gateway was eighty-seven and one-half feet long and forty-four feet wide. 34Its porch faced the outer courtyard. Carvings of palm trees were on its inner walls on each side, and its stairway had eight steps.

35Then the man brought me to the inner north gateway. He measured it, and it was the same as the other gateways. 36Its rooms, inner walls, and porch measured the same as the other gateways. There were windows all around the gateway, which was eighty-seven and one-half feet long and forty-four feet wide. 37Its porch faced the outer courtyard. Carvings of palm trees were on its inner walls on each side, and its stairway had eight steps.

Rooms for Preparing Sacrifices

38There was a room with a door that opened onto the porch of the inner north gateway. In this room the priests washed animals for the burnt offerings. 39There were two tables on each side of the porch, on which animals for burnt offerings, sin offer-

ings, and penalty offerings were killed. 40Outside, by each side wall of the porch, at the entrance to the north gateway, were two more tables. 41So there were four tables inside the gateway, and four tables outside. In all there were eight tables on which the priests killed animals for sacrifices. 42There were four tables made of cut stone for the burnt offering. These tables were about three feet long, three feet wide, and about two feet high. On these tables the priests put their tools which they used to kill animals for burnt offerings and the other sacrifices. 43Double shelves three inches wide were put up on all the walls. The flesh for the offering was put on the tables.

The Priests' Rooms

44There were two rooms in the inner courtyard. One was beside the north gateway and faced south. The other room was beside the south gateway and faced north. 45The man said to me, "The room which faces south is for the priests who serve in the Temple area, 46while the room that faces north is for the priests who serve at the altar. This second group of priests are descendants of Zadok, the only descendants of Levi who can come near the LORD to serve him."

47The man measured the inner courtyard. It was a square—one hundred seventy-five feet long and one hundred seventy-five feet wide. The altar was in front of the Temple.

The Temple Porch

48The man brought me to the porch of the Temple and measured each side wall of the porch. Each was about nine feet thick. The doorway was twenty-four and one-half feet wide. The side walls of the doorway were each about five feet wide. 49The porch was thirty-five feet long and twenty-one feet wide, with ten steps leading up to it. Pillars were by the side walls, one on each side of the entrance.

PSALM 132:10–18

10For the sake of your servant David,
    do not reject your appointed king.
11The LORD made a promise to David,
    a sure promise that he will not take back.

He promised, "I will make one of your descendants
rule as king after you.
¹²If your sons keep my agreement
and the rules that I teach them,
then their sons after them will rule
on your throne forever and ever."

¹³The LORD has chosen Jerusalem;
he wants it for his home.
¹⁴He says, "This is my resting place
forever.
Here is where I want to stay.
¹⁵I will bless her with plenty;
I will fill her poor with food.
¹⁶I will cover her priests with salvation,
and those who worship me will really
sing for joy.

¹⁷"I will make a king come from the family
of David.
I will provide my appointed one
descendants to rule after him.
¹⁸I will cover his enemies with shame,
but his crown will shine."

PROVERBS 29:5

⁵Those who give false praise to their
neighbors
are setting a trap for them.

JAMES 5:1–20

A Warning to the Rich

5 You rich people, listen! Cry and be very
sad because of the troubles that are coming to you. ²Your riches have rotted, and your
clothes have been eaten by moths. ³Your gold
and silver have rusted, and that rust will be a
proof that you were wrong. It will eat your
bodies like fire. You saved your treasure for
the last days. ⁴The pay you did not give the
workers who mowed your fields cries out
against you, and the cries of the workers
have been heard by the Lord All-Powerful.
⁵Your life on earth was full of rich living and
pleasing yourselves with everything you
wanted. You made yourselves fat, like an animal ready to be killed. ⁶You have judged

guilty and then murdered innocent people,
who were not against you.

Be Patient

⁷Brothers and sisters, be patient until the
Lord comes again. A farmer patiently waits
for his valuable crop to grow from the earth
and for it to receive the autumn and spring
rains. ⁸You, too, must be patient. Do not give
up hope, because the Lord is coming soon.
⁹Brothers and sisters, do not complain
against each other or you will be judged
guilty. And the Judge is ready to come!
¹⁰Brothers and sisters, follow the example of
the prophets who spoke for the Lord. They
suffered many hard things, but they were patient. ¹¹We say they are happy because they
did not give up. You have heard about Job's
patience, and you know the Lord's purpose
for him in the end. You know the Lord is full
of mercy and is kind.

Be Careful What You Say

¹²My brothers and sisters, above all, do
not use an oath when you make a promise.
Don't use the name of heaven, earth, or anything else to prove what you say. When you
mean yes, say only yes, and when you mean
no, say only no so you will not be judged
guilty.

The Power of Prayer

¹³Anyone who is having troubles should
pray. Anyone who is happy should sing
praises. ¹⁴Anyone who is sick should call the
church's elders. They should pray for and pour
oil on the person" in the name of the Lord.
¹⁵And the prayer that is said with faith will
make the sick person well; the Lord will heal
that person. And if the person has sinned, the
sins will be forgiven. ¹⁶Confess your sins to
each other and pray for each other so God can
heal you. When a believing person prays, great
things happen. ¹⁷Elijah was a human being
just like us. He prayed that it would not rain,
and it did not rain on the land for three and a
half years! ¹⁸Then Elijah prayed again, and the
rain came down from the sky, and the land
produced crops again.

5:14 pour oil on the person Oil was used in the name of the Lord as a sign that the person was now set apart for God's special attention and care.

Saving a Soul

[19]My brothers and sisters, if one of you wanders away from the truth, and someone helps that person come back, [20]remember this: Anyone who brings a sinner back from the wrong way will save that sinner's soul from death and will cause many sins to be forgiven.

NOVEMBER 25

EZEKIEL 41:1—42:20

The Holy Place of the Temple

41 The man brought me to the Holy Place and measured its side walls, which were each ten and one-half feet thick. [2]The entrance was seventeen and one-half feet wide. The walls alongside the entrance were each about nine feet wide. The man measured the Holy Place, which was seventy feet long and thirty-five feet wide.

[3]Then the man went inside and measured the side walls of the next doorway. Each was three and one-half feet thick. The doorway was ten and one-half feet wide, and the walls next to it were each more than twelve feet thick. [4]Then the man measured the room at the end of the Holy Place. It was thirty-five feet long and thirty-five feet wide. The man said to me, "This is the Most Holy Place."

[5]Then the man measured the wall of the Temple, which was ten and one-half feet thick. There were side rooms seven feet wide all around the Temple. [6]The side rooms were on three different stories, each above the other, with thirty rooms on each story. All around the Temple walls there were ledges for the side rooms. The upper rooms rested on the ledges but were not attached to the Temple walls. [7]The side rooms around the Temple were wider on each higher story, so rooms were wider on the top story. A stairway went up from the lowest story to the highest through the middle story.

[8]I also saw that the Temple had a raised base all around. Its edge was the foundation for the side rooms, and it was ten and one-half feet thick. [9]The outer wall of the side rooms was about nine feet thick. There was an open area between the side rooms of the Temple [10]and some other rooms. It was thirty-five feet wide and went all around the Temple. [11]The side rooms had doors which led to the open area around the outside of the Temple. One door faced north, and the other faced south. The open area was about nine feet wide all around.

[12]The building facing the private area at the west side was one hundred twenty-two and one-half feet wide. The wall around the building was about nine feet thick and one hundred fifty-seven and one-half feet long.

[13]Then the man measured the Temple. It was one hundred seventy-five feet long. The private area, including the building and its walls, was in all one hundred seventy-five feet long. [14]Also the front of the Temple and the private area on its east side were one hundred seventy-five feet wide.

[15]The man measured the length of the building facing the private area on the west side, and it was one hundred seventy-five feet from one wall to the other.

The Holy Place, the Most Holy Place, and the outer porch [16]had wood panels on the walls. By the doorway, the Temple had wood panels on the walls. The wood covered all the walls from the floor up to the windows, [17]up to the part of the wall above the entrance.

All the walls inside the Most Holy Place and the Holy Place, and on the outside, in the porch, [18]had carvings of creatures with wings and palm trees. A palm tree was between each carved creature, and every creature had two faces. [19]One was a human face looking toward the palm tree on one side. The other was a lion's face looking toward the palm tree on the other side. They were carved all around the Temple walls. [20]From the floor to above the entrance, palm trees and creatures with wings were carved. The walls of the Holy Place [21]had square doorposts. In front of the Most Holy Place was something that looked like ²²an altar of wood. It was more than five feet high and three feet wide. Its corners, base, and sides were wood. The man said to me, "This is the table that is in the presence of the LORD." ²³Both the Holy Place and the Most Holy Place had double doors. ²⁴Each of the doors had two pieces that would swing open. ²⁵Carved on the doors of the Holy Place were palm trees and creatures with wings, like those carved on the walls. And there was a wood roof over the front Temple porch. ²⁶There were windows and palm trees on both side walls of the porch. The side rooms of the Temple were also covered by a roof over the stairway.

The Priests' Rooms

42 Then the man led me north out into the outer courtyard and to the rooms across from the private area and the building. ²These rooms on the north side were one hundred seventy-five feet long and eighty-seven and one-half feet wide. ³There was thirty-five feet of the inner courtyard between them and the Temple. On the other side, they faced the stone pavement of the outer courtyard. The rooms were built in three stories like steps and had balconies. ⁴There was a path on the north side of the rooms, which was seventeen and one-half feet wide and one hundred seventy-five feet long. Doors led into the rooms from this path. ⁵The top rooms were narrower, because the balconies took more space from them. The rooms on the first and second stories of the building were wider. ⁶The rooms were on three stories. They did not have pillars like the pillars of the courtyards. So the top rooms were farther back than those on the first and second stories. ⁷There was a wall outside parallel to the rooms and to the outer courtyard. It ran in front of the rooms for eighty-seven and one-half feet. ⁸The row of rooms along the outer courtyard was eighty-seven and one-half feet long, and the rooms that faced the Temple were about one hundred seventy-five feet long. ⁹The lower rooms had an entrance on the east side so a person could enter them from the outer courtyard, ¹⁰at the start of the wall beside the courtyard.

There were rooms on the south side, which were across from the private area and the building. ¹¹These rooms had a path in front of them. They were like the rooms on the north with the same length and width and the same doors. ¹²The doors of the south rooms were like the doors of the north rooms. There was an entrance at the open end of a path beside the wall, so a person could enter at the east end.

¹³The man said to me, "The north and south rooms across from the private area are holy rooms. There the priests who go near the LORD will eat the most holy offerings. There they will put the most holy offerings: the grain offerings, sin offerings, and the penalty offerings, because the place is holy. ¹⁴The priests who enter the Holy Place must leave their serving clothes there before they go into the outer courtyard, because these clothes are holy. After they put on other clothes, they may go to the part of the Temple area which is for the people."

Outside the Temple Area

¹⁵When the man finished measuring inside the Temple area, he brought me out through the east gateway. He measured the area all around. ¹⁶The man measured the east side with the measuring stick; it was eight hundred seventy-five feet by the measuring stick. ¹⁷He measured the north side; it was eight hundred seventy-five feet by the measuring stick. ¹⁸He measured the south side; it was eight hundred seventy-five feet by the measuring stick. ¹⁹He went around to the west side; it measured eight hundred seventy-five feet by the measuring stick. ²⁰So he measured the Temple area on all four sides. The Temple area had a wall all around it that was eight hundred seventy-five feet long and eight hundred seventy-five feet wide. It separated what was holy from that which was not holy.

PSALM 133:1–3

The Love of God's People

A song for going up to worship. Of David.

133 It is good and pleasant
when God's people live together
in peace!

²It is like perfumed oil poured on the
  priest's head
and running down his beard.
It ran down Aaron's beard
  and on to the collar of his robes.
³It is like the dew of Mount Hermon
  falling on the hills of Jerusalem.
There the LORD gives his blessing
  of life forever.

PROVERBS 29:6

⁶Evil people are trapped by their own
  sin,
but good people can sing and be happy.

1 PETER 1:1–25

1 From Peter, an apostle of Jesus Christ.
    To God's chosen people who are away
from their homes and are scattered all
around Pontus, Galatia, Cappadocia, Asia,
and Bithynia. ²God planned long ago to
choose you by making you his holy people,
which is the Spirit's work. God wanted you to
obey him and to be made clean by the blood
of the death of Jesus Christ.
    Grace and peace be yours more and more.

We Have a Living Hope

³Praise be to the God and Father of our
Lord Jesus Christ. In God's great mercy he
has caused us to be born again into a living
hope, because Jesus Christ rose from the
dead. ⁴Now we hope for the blessings God
has for his children. These blessings, which
cannot be destroyed or be spoiled or lose
their beauty, are kept in heaven for you.
⁵God's power protects you through your
faith until salvation is shown to you at the
end of time. ⁶This makes you very happy,
even though now for a short time different
kinds of troubles may make you sad. ⁷These
troubles come to prove that your faith is
pure. This purity of faith is worth more than
gold, which can be proved to be pure by fire
but will ruin. But the purity of your faith will
bring you praise and glory and honor when
Jesus Christ is shown to you. ⁸You have not
seen Christ, but still you love him. You can-

not see him now, but you believe in him. So
you are filled with a joy that cannot be explained, a joy full of glory. ⁹And you are receiving the goal of your faith—the salvation
of your souls.

¹⁰The prophets searched carefully and
tried to learn about this salvation. They
prophesied about the grace that was coming
to you. ¹¹The Spirit of Christ was in the
prophets, telling in advance about the sufferings of Christ and about the glory that would
follow those sufferings. The prophets tried to
learn about what the Spirit was showing
them, when those things would happen, and
what the world would be like at that time. ¹²It
was shown them that their service was not
for themselves but for you, when they told
about the truths you have now heard. Those
who preached the Good News to you told
you those things with the help of the Holy
Spirit who was sent from heaven—things
into which angels desire to look.

A Call to Holy Living

¹³So prepare your minds for service and
have self-control. All your hope should be for
the gift of grace that will be yours when Jesus Christ is shown to you. ¹⁴Now that you
are obedient children of God do not live as
you did in the past. You did not understand,
so you did the evil things you wanted. ¹⁵But
be holy in all you do, just as God, the One
who called you, is holy. ¹⁶It is written in the
Scriptures: "You must be holy, because I am
holy."ⁿ

¹⁷You pray to God and call him Father,
and he judges each person's work equally. So
while you are here on earth, you should live
with respect for God. ¹⁸You know that in the
past you were living in a worthless way, a
way passed down from the people who lived
before you. But you were saved from that
useless life. You were bought, not with something that ruins like gold or silver, ¹⁹but with
the precious blood of Christ, who was like a
pure and perfect lamb. ²⁰Christ was chosen
before the world was made, but he was
shown to the world in these last times for
your sake. ²¹Through Christ you believe in
God, who raised Christ from the dead and

1:16 **"You must be . . . holy."** Quotation from Leviticus 11:45; 19:2; 20:7.

gave him glory. So your faith and your hope are in God.

[22] Now that your obedience to the truth has purified your souls, you can have true love for your Christian brothers and sisters. So love each other deeply with all your heart.[n] [23] You have been born again, and this new life did not come from something that dies, but from something that cannot die. You were born again through God's living message that continues forever. [24] The Scripture says,

"All people are like the grass,
  and all their glory is like the flowers of
    the field.
The grass dies and the flowers fall,
[25] but the word of the Lord will live
    forever."   *Isaiah 40:6–8*

And this is the word that was preached to you.

NOVEMBER 26

EZEKIEL 43:1—44:31

The Lord Among His People

43 Then the man led me to the outer east gateway, [2] and I saw the glory of the God of Israel coming from the east. It sounded like the roar of rushing water, and its brightness made the earth shine. [3] The vision I saw was like the vision I had seen when the LORD came to destroy the city and also like the vision I had seen by the Kebar River. I bowed facedown on the ground. [4] The glory of the LORD came into the Temple area through the east gateway.

[5] Then the Spirit picked me up and brought me into the inner courtyard. There I saw the LORD's glory filling the Temple. [6] As the man stood at my side, I heard someone speaking to me from inside the Temple. [7] The voice from the Temple said to me, "Human, this is my throne and the place where my feet rest. I will live here among the Israelites forever. The people of Israel will not make my holy name unclean again. Neither the people nor their kings will make it unclean with their sexual sins or with the dead bodies of their kings. [8] The kings made my name unclean by putting their doorway next to my doorway, and their doorpost next to my doorpost so only a wall separated me from them. When they did their acts that I hate, they made my holy name unclean, and so I destroyed them in my anger. [9] Now let them stop their sexual sins and take the dead bodies of their kings far away from me. Then I will live among them forever.

[10] "Human, tell the people of Israel about the Temple so they will be ashamed of their sins. Let them think about the plan of the Temple. [11] If they are ashamed of all they have done, let them know the design of the Temple and how it is built. Show them its exits and entrances, all its designs, and also all its rules and teachings. Write the rules as they watch so they will obey all the teachings and rules about the Temple. [12] This is the teaching about the Temple: All the area around the top of the mountain is most holy. This is the teaching about the Temple.

The Altar

[13] "These are the measurements of the altar, using the measuring stick. The altar's gutter is twenty-one inches high and twenty-one inches wide, and its rim is about nine inches around its edge. And the altar is this tall: [14] From the ground up to the lower ledge, it measures three and one-half feet. It is twenty-one inches wide. It measures seven feet from the smaller ledge to the larger ledge and is twenty-one inches wide. [15] The place where the sacrifice is burned on the altar is seven feet high, with its four corners shaped like horns and reaching up above it. [16] It is square, twenty-one feet long and twenty-one feet wide. [17] The upper ledge is also square,

---

1:22 with all your heart Some Greek copies read "with a pure heart."

twenty-four and one-half feet long and twenty-four and one-half feet wide. The rim around the altar is ten and one-half inches wide, and its gutter is twenty-one inches wide all around. Its steps are on the east side."

¹⁸Then the man said to me, "Human, this is what the Lord GOD says: These are the rules for the altar. When it is built, use these rules to offer burnt offerings and to sprinkle blood on it. ¹⁹You must give a young bull as a sin offering to the priests, the Levites who are from the family of Zadok and who come near me to serve me, says the Lord GOD. ²⁰Take some of the bull's blood and put it on the four corners of the altar, on the four corners of the ledge, and all around the rim. This is how you will make the altar pure and ready for God's service. ²¹Then take the bull for the sin offering and burn it in the proper place in the Temple area, outside the Temple building.

²²"On the second day offer a male goat that has nothing wrong with it for a sin offering. The priests will make the altar pure and ready for God's service as they did with the young bull. ²³When you finish making the altar pure and ready, offer a young bull and a male sheep from the flock, which have nothing wrong with them. ²⁴You must offer them in the presence of the LORD, and the priests are to throw salt on them and offer them as a burnt offering to the LORD.

²⁵"You must prepare a goat every day for seven days as a sin offering. Also, the priests must prepare a young bull and male sheep from the flock, which have nothing wrong with them. ²⁶For seven days the priests are to make the altar pure and ready for God's service. Then they will give the altar to God. ²⁷After these seven days, on the eighth day, the priests must offer your burnt offerings and your fellowship offerings on the altar. Then I will accept you, says the Lord GOD."

The Outer East Gate

44 Then the man brought me back to the outer east gateway of the Temple area, but the gate was shut. ²The LORD said to me, "This gate will stay shut; it will not be opened. No one may enter through it, because the LORD God of Israel has entered through it. So it must stay shut. ³Only the ruler himself may sit in the gateway to eat a meal in the presence of the LORD. He must enter through the porch of the gateway and go out the same way."

⁴Then the man brought me through the outer north gate to the front of the Temple. As I looked, I saw the glory of the LORD filling the Temple of the LORD, and I bowed facedown on the ground.

⁵The LORD said to me, "Human, pay attention. Use your eyes to see, and your ears to hear. See and hear everything I tell you about all the rules and teachings of the Temple of the LORD. Pay attention to the entrance to the Temple and to all the exits from the Temple area. ⁶Then speak to those who refuse to obey. Say to the people of Israel, 'This is what the Lord GOD says: Stop doing all your acts that I hate, Israel! ⁷You brought foreigners into my Holy Place who were not circumcised in the flesh and had not given themselves to serving me. You dishonored my Temple when you offered me food, fat, and blood. You broke my agreement by all the things you did that I hate. ⁸You did not take care of my holy things yourselves but put foreigners in charge of my Temple. ⁹This is what the Lord GOD says: Foreigners who are not circumcised in flesh and who do not give themselves to serving me may not enter my Temple. Not even a foreigner living among the people of Israel may enter.

¹⁰" 'But the Levites who stopped obeying me when Israel left me and who followed their idols must be punished for their sin. ¹¹These Levites are to be servants in my Holy Place. They may guard the gates of the Temple and serve in the Temple area. They may kill the animals for the burnt offering and the sacrifices for the people. They may stand before the people to serve them. ¹²But these Levites helped the people worship their idols and caused the people of Israel to fall, so I make this promise: They will be punished for their sin, says the Lord GOD. ¹³They will not come near me to serve as priests, nor will they come near any of my holy things or the most holy offerings. But they will be made ashamed of the things they did that I hate. ¹⁴I will put them in charge of taking care of the Temple area, all the work that must be done in it.

¹⁵" 'But the priests who are Levites and descendants of Zadok took care of my Holy Place when Israel left me, so they may come near to serve me. They may stand in my presence to offer me the fat and blood of the animals they sacrifice, says the Lord GOD. ¹⁶They are the only ones who may enter my Holy Place. Only they may come near my table to serve me and take care of the things I gave them to do.

¹⁷" 'When they enter the gates of the inner courtyard, they must wear linen robes. They must not wear wool to serve at the gates of the inner courtyard or in the Temple. ¹⁸They will wear linen turbans on their heads and linen underclothes. They will not wear anything that makes them perspire. ¹⁹When they go out into the outer courtyard to the people, they must take off their serving clothes before they go. They must leave these clothes in the holy rooms and put on other clothes. Then they will not let their holy clothes hurt the people.

²⁰" 'They must not shave their heads or let their hair grow long but must keep the hair of their heads trimmed. ²¹None of the priests may drink wine when they enter the inner courtyard. ²²The priests must not marry widows or divorced women. They may marry only virgins from the people of Israel or widows of priests. ²³They must teach my people the difference between what is holy and what is not holy. They must help my people know what is unclean and what is clean.

²⁴" 'In court they will act as judges. When they judge, they will follow my teachings. They must obey my laws and my rules at all my special feasts and keep my Sabbaths holy.

²⁵" 'They must not go near a dead person, making themselves unclean. But they are allowed to make themselves unclean if the dead person is their father, mother, son, daughter, brother, or a sister who has not married. ²⁶After a priest has been made clean again, he must wait seven days. ²⁷Then he may go into the inner courtyard to serve in the Temple, but he must offer a sin offering for himself, says the Lord GOD.

²⁸" 'These are the rules about the priests and their property: They will have me instead of property. You will not give them any land to own in Israel; I am what they will own. ²⁹They will eat the grain offerings, sin offerings, and penalty offerings. Everything Israel gives to me will be theirs. ³⁰The best fruits of all the first harvests and all the special gifts offered to me will belong to the priests. You will also give to the priests the first part of your grain that you grind and so bring a blessing on your family. ³¹The priests must not eat any bird or animal that died a natural death or one that has been torn by wild animals.

PSALM 134:1–3

Temple Guards, Praise the Lord

A song for going up to worship.

134 Praise the LORD, all you servants of
the LORD,
you who serve at night in the Temple of
the LORD.
²Raise your hands in the Temple
and praise the LORD.

³May the LORD bless you from Mount
Zion,
he who made heaven and earth.

PROVERBS 29:7

⁷Good people care about justice for the
poor,
but the wicked are not concerned.

1 PETER 2:1–25

Jesus Is the Living Stone

2 So then, rid yourselves of all evil, all lying, hypocrisy, jealousy, and evil speech. ²As newborn babies want milk, you should want the pure and simple teaching. By it you can mature in your salvation, ³because you have already examined and seen how good the Lord is.

⁴Come to the Lord Jesus, the "stone"ⁿ that lives. The people of the world did not want this stone, but he was the stone God chose, and he was precious. ⁵You also are like living stones, so let yourselves be used to build a

2:4 "stone" The most important stone in God's spiritual temple or house (his people).

spiritual temple—to be holy priests who offer spiritual sacrifices to God. He will accept those sacrifices through Jesus Christ. [6]The Scripture says:

"I will put a stone in the ground in
Jerusalem.
Everything will be built on this
important and precious rock.
Anyone who trusts in him
will never be disappointed." *Isaiah 28:16*

[7]This stone is worth much to you who believe. But to the people who do not believe,

"the stone that the builders rejected
has become the cornerstone." *Psalm 118:22*

[8]Also, he is

"a stone that causes people to stumble,
a rock that makes them fall." *Isaiah 8:14*

They stumble because they do not obey what God says, which is what God planned to happen to them.

[9]But you are a chosen people, royal priests, a holy nation, a people for God's own possession. You were chosen to tell about the wonderful acts of God, who called you out of darkness into his wonderful light. [10]At one time you were not a people, but now you are God's people. In the past you had never received mercy, but now you have received God's mercy.

Live for God

[11]Dear friends, you are like foreigners and strangers in this world. I beg you to avoid the evil things your bodies want to do that fight against your soul. [12]People who do not believe are living all around you and might say that you are doing wrong. Live such good lives that they will see the good things you do and will give glory to God on the day when Christ comes again.

Yield to Every Human Authority

[13]For the Lord's sake, yield to the people who have authority in this world: the king, who is the highest authority, [14]and the leaders who are sent by him to punish those who do wrong and to praise those who do right. [15]It is God's desire that by doing good you should stop foolish people from saying stupid things about you. [16]Live as free people, but do not use your freedom as an excuse to do evil. Live as servants of God. [17]Show respect for all people: Love the brothers and sisters of God's family, respect God, honor the king.

Follow Christ's Example

[18]Slaves, yield to the authority of your masters with all respect, not only those who are good and kind, but also those who are dishonest. [19]A person might have to suffer even when it is unfair, but if he thinks of God and can stand the pain, God is pleased. [20]If you are beaten for doing wrong, there is no reason to praise you for being patient in your punishment. But if you suffer for doing good, and you are patient, then God is pleased. [21]This is what you were called to do, because Christ suffered for you and gave you an example to follow. So you should do as he did.

[22]"He had never sinned,
and he had never lied." *Isaiah 53:9*

[23]People insulted Christ, but he did not insult them in return. Christ suffered, but he did not threaten. He let God, the One who judges rightly, take care of him. [24]Christ carried our sins in his body on the cross so we would stop living for sin and start living for what is right. And you are healed because of his wounds. [25]You were like sheep that wandered away, but now you have come back to the Shepherd and Overseer of your souls.

NOVEMBER 27

The Land Is Divided

45 "'When you divide the land for the Israelite tribes by throwing lots, you must give a part of the land to belong to the LORD. It will be about seven miles long and about six miles wide; all of this land will be holy. [2]From this land, an area eight hundred seventy-five feet square will be for the Tem-

ple. There will be an open space around the Temple that is eighty-seven and one-half feet wide. [3]In the holy area you will measure a part about seven miles long and three miles wide, and in it will be the Most Holy Place. [4]This holy part of the land will be for the priests who serve in the Temple, who come near to the LORD to serve him. It will be a place for the priests' houses and for the Temple. [5]Another area about seven miles long and more than three miles wide will be for the Levites, who serve in the Temple area. It will belong to them so they will have cities in which to live.

[6]" 'You must give the city an area that is about one and one-half miles wide and about seven miles long, along the side of the holy area. It will belong to all the people of Israel.

[7]" 'The ruler will have land on both sides of the holy area and the city. On the west of the holy area, his land will reach to the Mediterranean Sea. On the east of the holy area, his land will reach to the eastern border. It will be as long as the land given to each tribe. [8]Only this land will be the ruler's property in Israel. So my rulers will not be cruel to my people anymore, but they will let each tribe in the nation of Israel have its share of the land.

[9]" 'This is what the Lord GOD says: You have gone far enough, you rulers of Israel! Stop being cruel and hurting people, and do what is right and fair. Stop forcing my people out of their homes, says the Lord GOD. [10]You must have honest scales, an honest dry measurement and an honest liquid measurement. [11]The dry measure and the liquid measure will be the same: The liquid measure will always be a tenth of a homer,[n] and the ephah will always be a tenth of a homer. The measurement they follow will be the homer. [12]The shekel[n] will be worth twenty gerahs, and a mina will be worth sixty shekels.

Offerings and Holy Days
[13]" 'This is the gift you should offer: a sixth of an ephah from every homer of wheat, and a sixth of an ephah from every homer of barley. [14]The amount of oil you are to offer is a tenth of a bath from each cor. (Ten baths make a homer and also make a cor.) [15]You should give one sheep from each flock of two hundred from the watering places of Israel. All these are to be offered for the grain offerings, burnt offerings, and fellowship offerings to remove sins so you will belong to God, says the Lord GOD. [16]All people in the land will give this special offering to the ruler of Israel. [17]It will be the ruler's responsibility to supply the burnt offerings, grain offerings, and drink offerings. These offerings will be given at the feasts, at the New Moons, on the Sabbaths, and at all the other feasts of Israel. The ruler will supply the sin offerings, grain offerings, and fellowship offerings to pay for the sins of Israel.

[18]" 'This is what the Lord GOD says: On the first day of the first month take a young bull that has nothing wrong with it. Use it to make the Temple pure and ready for God's service. [19]The priest will take some of the blood from this sin offering and put it on the doorposts of the Temple, on the four corners of the ledge of the altar, and on the posts of the gate to the inner courtyard. [20]You will do the same thing on the seventh day of the month for anyone who has sinned by accident or without knowing it. This is how you make the Temple pure and ready for God's service.

Passover Feast Offerings
[21]" 'On the fourteenth day of the first month you will celebrate the Feast of Passover. It will be a feast of seven days when you eat bread made without yeast. [22]On that day the ruler must offer a bull for himself and for all the people of the land as a sin offering. [23]During the seven days of the feast he must offer seven bulls and seven male sheep that have nothing wrong with them. They will be burnt offerings to the LORD, which the ruler will offer every day of the seven days of the feast. He must also offer a male goat every day as a sin offering. [24]The

---

45:11 homer The Hebrew word means "donkey-load." It measured about five dry bushels or one hundred seventy-five liquid quarts. So an ephah was about one-half bushel, and a bath was about eighteen quarts.   **45:12 shekel** In Ezekiel's time a shekel weighed about two-fifths of an ounce.

ruler must give as a grain offering one-half bushel for each bull and one-half bushel for each sheep. He must give a gallon of olive oil for each half bushel.

²⁵"Beginning on the fifteenth day of the seventh month, when you celebrate the Feast of Shelters, the ruler will supply the same things for seven days: the sin offerings, burnt offerings, grain offerings, and the olive oil.

Rules for Worship

46"This is what the Lord GOD says: The east gate of the inner courtyard will stay shut on the six working days, but it will be opened on the Sabbath day and on the day of the New Moon. ²The ruler will enter from outside through the porch of the gateway and stand by the gatepost, while the priests offer the ruler's burnt offering and fellowship offering. The ruler will worship at the entrance of the gateway, and then he will go out. But the gate will not be shut until evening. ³The people of the land will worship at the entrance of that gateway in the presence of the LORD on the Sabbaths and New Moons. ⁴This is the burnt offering the ruler will offer to the LORD on the Sabbath day: six male lambs that have nothing wrong with them and a male sheep that has nothing wrong with it. ⁵He must give a half-bushel grain offering with the male sheep, but he may give as much grain offering with the lambs as he pleases. He must also give a gallon of olive oil for each half bushel of grain. ⁶On the day of the New Moon he must offer a young bull that has nothing wrong with it. He must also offer six lambs and a male sheep that have nothing wrong with them. ⁷The ruler must give a half-bushel grain offering with the bull and one-half bushel with the male sheep. With the lambs, he may give as much grain as he pleases. But he must give a gallon of olive oil for each half bushel of grain. ⁸When the ruler enters, he must go in through the porch of the gateway, and he must go out the same way.

⁹"When the people of the land come into the LORD's presence at the special feasts, those who enter through the north gate to worship must go out through the south gate.

Those who enter through the south gate must go out through the north gate. They must not return the same way they entered; everyone must go out the opposite way. ¹⁰The ruler will go in with the people when they go in and go out with them when they go out.

¹¹"At the feasts and regular times of worship one-half bushel of grain must be offered with a young bull, and one-half bushel of grain must be offered with a male sheep. But with an offering of lambs, the ruler may give as much grain as he pleases. He should give a gallon of olive oil for each half bushel of grain. ¹²The ruler may give an offering as a special gift to the LORD; it may be a burnt offering or fellowship offering. When he gives it to the LORD, the inner east gate is to be opened for him. He must offer his burnt offering or his fellowship offering as he does on the Sabbath day. Then he will go out, and the gate will be shut after he has left.

¹³"'Every day you will give a year-old lamb that has nothing wrong with it for a burnt offering to the LORD. Do it every morning. ¹⁴Also, you must offer a grain offering with the lamb every morning. For this you will give three and one-third quarts of grain and one and one-third quarts of olive oil, to make the fine flour moist, as a grain offering to the LORD. This is a rule that must be kept from now on. ¹⁵So you must always give the lamb, together with the grain offering and the olive oil, every morning as a burnt offering.

Rules for the Ruler

¹⁶"'This is what the Lord GOD says: If the ruler gives a gift from his land to any of his sons, that land will belong to the son and then to the son's children. It is their property passed down from their family. ¹⁷But if the ruler gives a gift from his land to any of his servants, that land will belong to the servant only until the year of freedom. Then the land will go back to the ruler. Only the ruler's sons may keep a gift of land from the ruler. ¹⁸The ruler must not take any of the people's land, forcing them out of their land. He must give his sons some of his own land so my people will not be scattered out of their own land.'"

The Special Kitchens

¹⁹The man led me through the entrance at the side of the gateway to the priests' holy rooms that face north. There I saw a place at the west end. ²⁰The man said to me, "This is where the priests will boil the meat of the penalty offering and sin offering and bake the grain offering. Then they will not need to bring these holy offerings into the outer courtyard, because that would hurt the people."

²¹Then the man brought me out into the outer courtyard and led me to its four corners. In each corner of the courtyard was a smaller courtyard. ²²Small courtyards were in the four corners of the courtyard. Each small courtyard was the same size, seventy feet long and fifty-two and one-half feet wide. ²³A stone wall was around each of the four small courtyards, and places for cooking were built in each of the stone walls. ²⁴The man said to me, "These are the kitchens where those who work in the Temple will boil the sacrifices offered by the people."

PSALM 135:1–7

The Lord Saves, Idols Do Not

135 Praise the LORD!
Praise the name of the LORD;
praise him, you servants of the LORD,
²you who stand in the LORD's Temple
and in the Temple courtyards.
³Praise the LORD, because he is good;
sing praises to him, because it is
pleasant.

⁴The LORD has chosen the people of Jacob
for himself;
he has chosen the people of Israel for
his very own.
⁵I know that the LORD is great.
Our Lord is greater than all the gods.
⁶The LORD does what he pleases,
in heaven and on earth,
in the seas and the deep oceans.
⁷He brings the clouds from the ends of the
earth.
He sends the lightning with the rain.
He brings out the wind from his
storehouses.

PROVERBS 29:8

⁸People who make fun of wisdom cause
trouble in a city,
but wise people calm anger down.

1 PETER 3:1–22

Wives and Husbands

3In the same way, you wives should yield to your husbands. Then, if some husbands do not obey God's teaching, they will be persuaded to believe without anyone's saying a word to them. They will be persuaded by the way their wives live. ²Your husbands will see the pure lives you live with your respect for God. ³It is not fancy hair, gold jewelry, or fine clothes that should make you beautiful. ⁴No, your beauty should come from within you—the beauty of a gentle and quiet spirit that will never be destroyed and is very precious to God. ⁵In this same way, the holy women who lived long ago and followed God made themselves beautiful, yielding to their own husbands. ⁶Sarah obeyed Abraham, her husband, and called him her master. And you women are true children of Sarah if you always do what is right and are not afraid.

⁷In the same way, you husbands should live with your wives in an understanding way, since they are weaker than you. But show them respect, because God gives them the same blessing he gives you—the grace that gives true life. Do this so that nothing will stop your prayers.

Suffering for Doing Right

⁸Finally, all of you should be in agreement, understanding each other, loving each other as family, being kind and humble. ⁹Do not do wrong to repay a wrong, and do not insult to repay an insult. But repay with a blessing, because you yourselves were called to do this so that you might receive a blessing. ¹⁰The Scripture says,

"A person must do these things
to enjoy life and have many happy days.
He must not say evil things,
and he must not tell lies.
¹¹He must stop doing evil and do good.
He must look for peace and work for it.
¹²The Lord sees the good people
and listens to their prayers.

But the Lord is against
those who do evil."   *Psalm 34:12–16*
¹³If you are trying hard to do good, no one
can really hurt you. ¹⁴But even if you suffer
for doing right, you are blessed.

"Don't be afraid of what they fear;
do not dread those things."   *Isaiah 8:12–13*
¹⁵But respect Christ as the holy Lord in your
hearts. Always be ready to answer everyone
who asks you to explain about the hope you
have, ¹⁶but answer in a gentle way and with
respect. Keep a clear conscience so that those
who speak evil of your good life in Christ will
be made ashamed. ¹⁷It is better to suffer for
doing good than for doing wrong if that is
what God wants. ¹⁸Christ himself suffered for
sins once. He was not guilty, but he suffered
for those who are guilty to bring you to God.
His body was killed, but he was made alive in
the spirit. ¹⁹And in the spirit he went and
preached to the spirits in prison ²⁰who refused to obey God long ago in the time of
Noah. God was waiting patiently for them
while Noah was building the boat. Only a few
people—eight in all—were saved by water.
²¹And that water is like baptism that now
saves you—not the washing of dirt from the
body, but the promise made to God from a
good conscience. And this is because Jesus
Christ was raised from the dead. ²²Now Jesus
has gone into heaven and is at God's right side
ruling over angels, authorities, and powers.

NOVEMBER 28

EZEKIEL 47:1—48:35

The River from the Temple

47 The man led me back to the door of
the Temple, and I saw water coming
out from under the doorway and flowing
east. (The Temple faced east.) The water
flowed down from the south side wall of the
Temple and then south of the altar. ²The man
brought me out through the outer north gate
and led me around outside to the outer east
gate. I found the water coming out on the
south side of the gate.

³The man went toward the east with a line
in his hand and measured about one-third
of a mile. Then he led me through water that
came up to my ankles. ⁴The man measured
about one-third of a mile again and led me
through water that came up to my knees.
Then he measured about one-third of a mile
again and led me through water up to my
waist. ⁵The man measured about one-third
of a mile again, but it was now a river that I
could not cross. The water had risen too
high; it was deep enough for swimming; it
was a river that no one could cross. ⁶The
man asked me, "Human, do you see this?"

Then the man led me back to the bank of
the river. ⁷As I went back, I saw many trees
on both sides of the river. ⁸The man said to
me, "This water will flow toward the eastern areas and go down into the Jordan Valley. When it enters the Dead Sea, it will
become fresh. ⁹Everywhere the river goes,
there will be many fish. Wherever this water goes the Dead Sea will become fresh,
and so where the river goes there will be
many living things. ¹⁰Fishermen will stand
by the Dead Sea. From En Gedi all the way
to En Eglaim there will be places to spread
fishing nets. There will be many kinds of
fish in the Dead Sea, as many as in the
Mediterranean Sea. ¹¹But its swamps and
marshes will not become fresh; they will be
left for salt. ¹²All kinds of fruit trees will
grow on both banks of the river, and their
leaves will not dry and die. The trees will
have fruit every month, because the water
for them comes from the Temple. The fruit
from the trees will be used for food, and
their leaves for medicine."

Borders of the Land

¹³This is what the Lord GOD says: "These
are the borders of the land to be divided
among the twelve tribes of Israel. Joseph will
have two parts of land. ¹⁴You will divide the
land equally. I promised to give it to your an-

cestors, so this land will belong to you as family property.

cestors, so this land will belong to you as family property.

¹⁵"This will be the border line of the land: "On the north side it will start at the Mediterranean Sea. It will go through Hethlon, toward Lebo Hamath and on to the towns of Zedad, ¹⁶Berothah, and Sibraim on the border between Damascus and Hamath. Then it will go on to the town of Hazer Hatticon on the border of the country of Hauran. ¹⁷So the border line will go from the Mediterranean Sea east to the town of Hazar Enan, where the land belonging to Damascus and Hamath lies on the north side. This will be the north side of the land.

¹⁸"On the east side the border runs south from a point between Hauran and Damascus. It will go along the Jordan between Gilead and the land of Israel and will continue to the town of Tamar on the Dead Sea. This will be the east side of the land.

¹⁹"On the south side the border line will go west from Tamar all the way to the waters of Meribah Kadesh. Then it will run along the brook of Egypt to the Mediterranean Sea. This will be the south side of the land.

²⁰"On the west side the Mediterranean Sea will be the border line up to a place across from Lebo Hamath. This will be the west side of your land.

²¹"You will divide this land among the tribes of Israel. ²²You will divide it as family property for yourselves and for the foreigners who live and have children among you. You are to treat these foreigners the same as people born in Israel; they are to share the land with the tribes of Israel. ²³In whatever tribe the foreigner lives, you will give him some land," says the Lord GOD.

Dividing the Land

48 "These are the areas of the tribes named here: Dan will have one share at the northern border. It will go from the sea through Hethlon to Lebo Hamath, all the way to Hazar Enan, where Damascus lies to the north. It will stop there next to Hamath. This will be Dan's northern border from the east side to the Mediterranean Sea on the west side.

²"South of Dan's border, Asher will have one share. It will go from the east side to the west side.

³"South of Asher's border, Naphtali will have one share. It will go from the east side to the west side.

⁴"South of Naphtali's border, Manasseh will have one share. It will go from the east side to the west side.

⁵"South of Manasseh's border, Ephraim will have one share. It will go from the east side to the west side.

⁶"South of Ephraim's border, Reuben will have one share. It will go from the east side to the west side.

⁷"South of Reuben's border, Judah will have one share. It will go from the east side to the west side.

⁸"South of Judah's border will be the holy area which you are to give. It will be about seven miles wide and as long and wide as one of the tribes' shares. It will run from the east side to the west side. The Temple will be in the middle of this area.

⁹"The share which you will give the LORD will be about seven miles long and three miles wide. ¹⁰The holy area will be divided among these people. The priests will have land about seven miles long on the north and south sides, and three miles wide on the west and east sides. The Temple of the LORD will be in the middle of it. ¹¹This land is for the priests who are given the holy duty of serving the LORD. They are the descendants of Zadok who did my work and did not leave me when Israel and the Levites left me. ¹²They will have as their share a very holy part of the holy portion of the land. It will be next to the land of the Levites.

¹³"Alongside the land for the priests, the Levites will have a share about seven miles long and three miles wide; its full length will be about seven miles and its full width about three miles. ¹⁴The Levites are not to sell or trade any of this land. They are not to let anyone else own any of this best part of the land, because it belongs to the LORD.

City Property

¹⁵"The rest of the area will be about one and one-half miles wide and seven miles long. It will not be holy but will belong to the city

and be used for homes and pastures. The city will be in the middle of it. ¹⁶These are the city's measurements: the north side will be about one mile, the south side about one mile, the east side about one mile, and the west side about one mile. ¹⁷The city's land for pastures will be about four hundred thirty-seven feet on the north, four hundred thirty-seven feet on the south, four hundred thirty-seven feet on the east, and four hundred thirty-seven feet on the west. ¹⁸Along the long side of the holy area there will be left three miles on the east and three miles on the west. It will be used to grow food for the city workers. ¹⁹The city workers from all the tribes of Israel will farm this land. ²⁰This whole area will be square, seven miles by seven miles. You shall give to the LORD the holy share along with the city property.

²¹"Land that is left over on both sides of the holy area and city property will belong to the ruler. That land will extend east of the holy area to the eastern border and west of it to the Mediterranean Sea. Both of these areas run the length of the lands of the tribes, and they belong to the ruler. The holy area with the Holy Place of the Temple will be in the middle. ²²The Levites' land and the city property will be in the middle of the lands belonging to the ruler. Those lands will be between Judah's border and Benjamin's border.

The Other Tribes' Land

²³"Here is what the rest of the tribes will receive: Benjamin will have one share. It will go from the east side to the Mediterranean Sea on the west side.

²⁴"South of Benjamin's land, Simeon will have one share. It will go from the east side to the west side.

²⁵"South of Simeon's land, Issachar will have one share. It will go from the east side to the west side.

²⁶"South of Issachar's land, Zebulun will have one share. It will go from the east side to the west side.

²⁷"South of Zebulun's land, Gad will have one share. It will go from the east side to the west side.

²⁸"The southern border of Gad's land will go east from Tamar on the Dead Sea to the waters of Meribah Kadesh. Then it will run along the brook of Egypt to the Mediterranean Sea.

²⁹"This is the land you will divide among the tribes of Israel to be their shares," says the Lord GOD.

The Gates of the City

³⁰"These will be the outside borders of the city: The north side will measure more than one mile. ³¹There will be three gates facing north: Reuben's Gate, Judah's Gate, and Levi's Gate, named for the tribes of Israel.

³²"The east side will measure more than one mile. There will be three gates facing east: Joseph's Gate, Benjamin's Gate, and Dan's Gate.

³³"The south side will measure more than one mile. There will be three gates facing south: Simeon's Gate, Issachar's Gate, and Zebulun's Gate.

³⁴"The west side will measure more than one mile. There will be three gates facing west: Gad's Gate, Asher's Gate, and Naphtali's Gate.

³⁵"The city will measure about six miles around. From then on the name of the city will be The LORD Is There."

PSALM 135:8–14

⁸He destroyed the firstborn sons in Egypt
    the firstborn of both people and
        animals.
⁹He did many signs and miracles in Egypt
    against the king and his servants.
¹⁰He defeated many nations
    and killed powerful kings:
¹¹Sihon king of the Amorites,
    Og king of Bashan,
    and all the kings of Canaan.
¹²Then he gave their land as a gift,
    a gift to his people, the Israelites.

¹³LORD, your name is everlasting;
    LORD, you will be remembered forever.
¹⁴The LORD defends his people
    and has mercy on his servants.

PROVERBS 29:9

⁹When a wise person takes a foolish
    person to court,

the fool only shouts or laughs, and there is no peace.

1 PETER 4:1-19

Change Your Lives

4 Since Christ suffered while he was in his body, strengthen yourselves with the same way of thinking Christ had. The person who has suffered in the body is finished with sin. [2]Strengthen yourselves so that you will live here on earth doing what God wants, not the evil things people want. [3]In the past you wasted too much time doing what nonbelievers enjoy. You were guilty of sexual sins, evil desires, drunkenness, wild and drunken parties, and hateful idol worship. [4]Nonbelievers think it is strange that you do not do the many wild and wasteful things they do, so they insult you. [5]But they will have to explain this to God, who is ready to judge the living and the dead. [6]For this reason the Good News was preached to those who are now dead. Even though they were judged like all people, the Good News was preached to them so they could live in the spirit as God lives.

Use God's Gifts Wisely

[7]The time is near when all things will end. So think clearly and control yourselves so you will be able to pray. [8]Most importantly, love each other deeply, because love will cause people to forgive each other for many sins. [9]Open your homes to each other, without complain-ing. [10]Each of you has received a gift to use to serve others. Be good servants of God's various gifts of grace. [11]Anyone who speaks should speak words from God. Anyone who serves should serve with the strength God gives so that in everything God will be praised through Jesus Christ. Power and glory belong to him forever and ever. Amen.

Suffering as a Christian

[12]My friends, do not be surprised at the terrible trouble which now comes to test you. Do not think that something strange is happening to you. [13]But be happy that you are sharing in Christ's sufferings so that you will be happy and full of joy when Christ comes again in glory. [14]When people insult you because you follow Christ, you are blessed, because the glorious Spirit, the Spirit of God, is with you. [15]Do not suffer for murder, theft, or any other crime, nor because you trouble other people. [16]But if you suffer because you are a Christian, do not be ashamed. Praise God because you wear that name. [17]It is time for judgment to begin with God's family. And if that judging begins with us, what will happen to those people who do not obey the Good News of God?

[18]"If it is very hard for a good person to be saved,
the wicked person and the sinner will surely be lost!"[n]

[19]So those who suffer as God wants should trust their souls to the faithful Creator as they continue to do what is right.

NOVEMBER 29

DANIEL 1:1—2:49

Daniel Taken to Babylon

1 During the third year that Jehoiakim was king of Judah, Nebuchadnezzar king of Babylon came to Jerusalem and surrounded it with his army. [2]The Lord allowed Nebuchadnezzar to capture Jehoiakim king of Judah. Nebuchadnezzar also took some of the things from the Temple of God, which he carried to Babylonia and put in the temple of his gods.

[3]Then King Nebuchadnezzar ordered Ashpenaz, his chief officer, to bring some of the men of Judah into his palace. He wanted them to be from important families, including the

4:18 "If . . . lost!" Quotation from Proverbs 11:31 in the Septuagint, the Greek version of the Old Testament.

family of the king of Judah. ⁴King Nebuchadnezzar wanted only young Israelite men who had nothing wrong with them. They were to be handsome and well educated, capable of learning and understanding, and able to serve in his palace. Ashpenaz was to teach them the language and writings of the Babylonians. ⁵The king gave the young men a certain amount of food and wine every day, just like the food he ate. The young men were to be trained for three years, and then they would become servants of the king of Babylon. ⁶Among those young men were Daniel, Hananiah, Mishael, and Azariah from the people of Judah.

⁷Ashpenaz, the chief officer, gave them Babylonian names. Daniel's new name was Belteshazzar, Hananiah's was Shadrach, Mishael's was Meshach, and Azariah's was Abednego.

⁸Daniel decided not to eat the king's food or drink his wine because that would make him unclean. So he asked Ashpenaz for permission not to make himself unclean in this way.

⁹God made Ashpenaz, the chief officer, want to be kind and merciful to Daniel, ¹⁰but Ashpenaz said to Daniel, "I am afraid of my master, the king. He ordered me to give you this food and drink. If you begin to look worse than other young men your age, the king will see this. Then he will cut off my head because of you."

¹¹Ashpenaz had ordered a guard to watch Daniel, Hananiah, Mishael, and Azariah. ¹²Daniel said to the guard, "Please give us this test for ten days: Don't give us anything but vegetables to eat and water to drink. ¹³After ten days compare how we look with how the other young men look who eat the king's food. See for yourself and then decide how you want to treat us, your servants."

¹⁴So the guard agreed to test them for ten days. ¹⁵After ten days they looked healthier and better fed than all the young men who ate the king's food. ¹⁶So the guard took away the king's special food and wine, feeding them vegetables instead.

¹⁷God gave these four young men wisdom and the ability to learn many things that people had written and studied. Daniel could also understand visions and dreams.

¹⁸At the end of the time set for them by the king, Ashpenaz brought all the young men to King Nebuchadnezzar. ¹⁹The king talked to them and found that none of the young men were as good as Daniel, Hananiah, Mishael, and Azariah. So those four young men became the king's servants. ²⁰Every time the king asked them about something important, they showed much wisdom and understanding. They were ten times better than all the fortune-tellers and magicians in his kingdom! ²¹So Daniel continued to be the king's servant until the first year Cyrus was king.

Nebuchadnezzar's Dream

2 During Nebuchadnezzar's second year as king, he had dreams that bothered him and kept him awake at night. ²So the king called for his fortune-tellers, magicians, wizards, and wise men, because he wanted them to tell him what he had dreamed. They came in and stood in front of the king.

³Then the king said to them, "I had a dream that bothers me, and I want to know what it means."

⁴The wise men answered the king in the Aramaic language, "O king, live forever! Please tell us, your servants, your dream. Then we will tell you what it means."

⁵King Nebuchadnezzar said to them, "I meant what I said. You must tell me the dream and what it means. If you don't, I will have you torn apart, and I will turn your houses into piles of stones. ⁶But if you tell me my dream and its meaning, I will reward you with gifts and great honor. So tell me the dream and what it means."

⁷Again the wise men said to the king, "Tell us, your servants, the dream, and we will tell you what it means."

⁸King Nebuchadnezzar answered, "I know you are trying to get more time, because you know that I meant what I said. ⁹If you don't tell me my dream, you will be punished. You have all agreed to tell me lies and wicked things, hoping things will change. Now, tell me the dream so that I will know you can tell me what it really means!"

¹⁰The wise men answered the king, saying, "No one on earth can do what the king

asks! No great and powerful king has ever asked the fortune-tellers, magicians, or wise men to do this; [11]the king is asking something that is too hard. Only the gods could tell the king this, but the gods do not live among people."

[12]When the king heard their answer, he became very angry. He ordered that all the wise men of Babylon be killed. [13]So King Nebuchadnezzar's order to kill the wise men was announced, and men were sent to look for Daniel and his friends to kill them.

[14]Arioch, the commander of the king's guards, was going to kill the wise men of Babylon. But Daniel spoke to him with wisdom and skill, [15]saying, "Why did the king order such a terrible punishment?" Then Arioch explained everything to Daniel. [16]So Daniel went to King Nebuchadnezzar and asked for an appointment so that he could tell the king what his dream meant.

[17]Then Daniel went to his house and explained the whole story to his friends Hananiah, Mishael, and Azariah. [18]Daniel asked his friends to pray that the God of heaven would show them mercy and help them understand this secret so he and his friends would not be killed with the other wise men of Babylon.

[19]During the night God explained the secret to Daniel in a vision. Then Daniel praised the God of heaven. [20]Daniel said:

"Praise God forever and ever,
   because he has wisdom and power.
[21]He changes the times and seasons of
      the year.
   He takes away the power of kings
      and gives their power to new kings.
   He gives wisdom to those who are wise
      and knowledge to those who
         understand.
[22]He makes known secrets that are deep
         and hidden;
   he knows what is hidden in darkness,
      and light is all around him.
[23]I thank you and praise you, God of my
         ancestors,
   because you have given me wisdom
         and power.
   You told me what we asked of you;
      you told us about the king's dream."

The Meaning of the Dream

[24]Then Daniel went to Arioch, the man King Nebuchadnezzar had chosen to kill the wise men of Babylon. Daniel said to him, "Don't put the wise men of Babylon to death. Take me to the king, and I will tell him what his dream means."

[25]Very quickly Arioch took Daniel to the king and said, "I have found a man among the captives from Judah who can tell the king what his dream means."

[26]The king asked Daniel, who was also called Belteshazzar, "Are you able to tell me what I dreamed and what it means?"

[27]Daniel answered, "No wise man, magician, or fortune-teller can explain to the king the secret he has asked about. [28]But there is a God in heaven who explains secret things, and he has shown King Nebuchadnezzar what will happen at a later time. This is your dream, the vision you saw while lying on your bed: [29]O king, as you were lying there, you thought about things to come. God, who can tell people about secret things, showed you what is going to happen. [30]God also told this secret to me, not because I have greater wisdom than any other living person, but so that you may know what it means. In that way you will understand what went through your mind.

[31]"O king, in your dream you saw a huge, shiny, and frightening statue in front of you. [32]The head of the statue was made of pure gold. Its chest and arms were made of silver. Its stomach and the upper part of its legs were made of bronze. [33]The lower part of the legs were made of iron, while its feet were made partly of iron and partly of baked clay. [34]While you were looking at the statue, you saw a rock cut free, but no human being touched the rock. It hit the statue on its feet of iron and clay and smashed them. [35]Then the iron, clay, bronze, silver, and gold broke to pieces at the same time. They became like chaff on a threshing floor in the summertime; the wind blew them away, and there was nothing left. Then the rock that hit the statue became a very large mountain that filled the whole earth.

[36]"That was your dream. Now we will tell the king what it means. [37]O king, you are the

greatest king. God of heaven has given you a kingdom, power, strength, and glory. ³⁸Wherever people, wild animals, and birds live, God made you ruler over them. King Nebuchadnezzar, you are the head of gold on that statue.

³⁹"Another kingdom will come after you, but it will not be as great as yours. Next a third kingdom, the bronze part, will rule over the earth. ⁴⁰Then there will be a fourth kingdom, strong as iron. In the same way that iron crushes and smashes things to pieces, the fourth kingdom will smash and crush all the other kingdoms.

⁴¹"You saw that the statue's feet and toes were partly baked clay and partly iron. That means the fourth kingdom will be a divided kingdom. It will have some of the strength of iron in it, just as you saw iron was mixed with clay. ⁴²The toes of the statue were partly iron and partly clay. So the fourth kingdom will be partly strong like iron and partly breakable like clay. ⁴³You saw the iron mixed with clay, but iron and clay do not hold together. In the same way the people of the fourth kingdom will be a mixture, but they will not be united as one people.

⁴⁴"During the time of those kings, the God of heaven will set up another kingdom that will never be destroyed or given to another group of people. This kingdom will crush all the other kingdoms and bring them to an end, but it will continue forever.

⁴⁵"King Nebuchadnezzar, you saw a rock cut from a mountain, but no human being touched it. The rock broke the iron, bronze, clay, silver, and gold to pieces. In this way the great God showed you what will happen. The dream is true, and you can trust this explanation."

⁴⁶Then King Nebuchadnezzar fell facedown on the ground in front of Daniel. The king honored him and commanded that an offering and incense be presented to him. ⁴⁷Then the king said to Daniel, "Truly I know your God is the greatest of all gods, the Lord of all the kings. He tells people about things they cannot know. I know this is true, because you were able to tell these secret things to me."

⁴⁸Then the king gave Daniel many gifts plus an important position in his kingdom.

Nebuchadnezzar made him ruler over the whole area of Babylon and put him in charge of all the wise men of Babylon. ⁴⁹Daniel asked the king to make Shadrach, Meshach, and Abednego leaders over the area of Babylon, so the king did as Daniel asked. Daniel himself became one of the people who stayed at the royal court.

PSALM 135:15–21

¹⁵The idols of other nations are made of
silver and gold,
the work of human hands.
¹⁶They have mouths, but they cannot speak.
They have eyes, but they cannot see.
¹⁷They have ears, but they cannot hear.
They have no breath in their mouths.
¹⁸People who make idols will be like them,
and so will those who trust them.

¹⁹Family of Israel, praise the LORD.
Family of Aaron, praise the LORD.
²⁰Family of Levi, praise the LORD.
You who respect the LORD should praise
him.
²¹You people of Jerusalem, praise the LORD
on Mount Zion.
Praise the LORD!

PROVERBS 29:10

¹⁰Murderers hate an honest person
and try to kill those who do right.

1 PETER 5:1–14

The Flock of God

5 Now I have something to say to the elders in your group. I also am an elder. I have seen Christ's sufferings, and I will share in the glory that will be shown to us. I beg you to ²shepherd God's flock, for whom you are responsible. Watch over them because you want to, not because you are forced. That is how God wants it. Do it because you are happy to serve, not because you want money. ³Do not be like a ruler over people you are responsible for, but be good examples to them. ⁴Then when Christ, the Chief Shepherd, comes, you will get a glorious crown that will never lose its beauty.

[5]In the same way, younger people should be willing to be under older people. And all of you should be very humble with each other.

"God is against the proud,
but he gives grace to the humble."

Proverbs 3:34

[6]Be humble under God's powerful hand so he will lift you up when the right time comes. [7]Give all your worries to him, because he cares about you.

[8]Control yourselves and be careful! The devil, your enemy, goes around like a roaring lion looking for someone to eat. [9]Refuse to give in to him, by standing strong in your faith. You know that your Christian family all over the world is having the same kinds of suffering.

[10]And after you suffer for a short time, God, who gives all grace, will make everything right. He will make you strong and support you and keep you from falling. He called you to share in his glory in Christ, a glory that will continue forever. [11]All power is his forever and ever. Amen.

Final Greetings

[12]I wrote this short letter with the help of Silas, who I know is a faithful brother in Christ. I wrote to encourage you and to tell you that this is the true grace of God. Stand strong in that grace.

[13]The church in Babylon, who was chosen like you, sends you greetings. Mark, my son in Christ, also greets you. [14]Give each other a kiss of Christian love when you meet.

Peace to all of you who are in Christ.

NOVEMBER 30

DANIEL 3:1—4:37

The Gold Idol and Blazing Furnace

3 King Nebuchadnezzar made a gold statue ninety feet high and nine feet wide and set it up on the plain of Dura in the area of Babylon. [2]Then he called for the leaders: the governors, assistant governors, captains of the soldiers, people who advised the king, keepers of the treasury, judges, rulers, and all other officers in his kingdom. He wanted them to come to the special service for the statue he had set up. [3]So they all came for the special service and stood in front of the statue that King Nebuchadnezzar had set up. [4]Then the man who made announcements for the king said in a loud voice, "People, nations, and those of every language, this is what you are commanded to do: [5]When you hear the sound of the horns, flutes, lyres, zithers,[n] harps, pipes, and all the other musical instruments, you must bow down and worship the gold statue that King Nebuchadnezzar has set up. [6]Anyone who doesn't bow down and worship will immediately be thrown into a blazing furnace."

[7]Now people, nations, and those who spoke every language were there. When they heard the sound of the horns, flutes, lyres, zithers, pipes, and all the other musical instruments, they bowed down and worshiped the gold statue King Nebuchadnezzar had set up.

[8]Then some Babylonians came up to the king and began speaking against the men of Judah. [9]They said to King Nebuchadnezzar, "O king, live forever! [10]O king, you gave a command that everyone who heard the horns, lyres, zithers, harps, pipes, and all the other musical instruments would have to bow down and worship the gold statue. [11]Anyone who wouldn't do this was to be thrown into a blazing furnace. [12]O king, there are some men of Judah whom you made officers in the area of Babylon that did not pay attention to your order. Their names

---

3:5 zithers Musical instruments with thirty to forty strings.

are Shadrach, Meshach, and Abednego. They do not serve your gods and do not worship the gold statue you have set up."

13Nebuchadnezzar became very angry and called for Shadrach, Meshach, and Abednego. When they were brought to the king, 14Nebuchadnezzar said, "Shadrach, Meshach, and Abednego, is it true that you do not serve my gods nor worship the gold statue I have set up? 15In a moment you will again hear the sound of the horns, flutes, lyres, zithers, harps, pipes, and all the other musical instruments. If you bow down and worship the statue I made, that will be good. But if you do not worship it, you will immediately be thrown into the blazing furnace. What god will be able to save you from my power then?"

16Shadrach, Meshach, and Abednego answered the king, saying, "Nebuchadnezzar, we do not need to defend ourselves to you. 17If you throw us into the blazing furnace, the God we serve is able to save us from the furnace. He will save us from your power, O king. 18But even if God does not save us, we want you, O king, to know this: We will not serve your gods or worship the gold statue you have set up."

19Then Nebuchadnezzar was furious with Shadrach, Meshach, and Abednego, and he changed his mind. He ordered the furnace to be heated seven times hotter than usual. 20Then he commanded some of the strongest soldiers in his army to tie up Shadrach, Meshach, and Abednego and throw them into the blazing furnace.

21So Shadrach, Meshach, and Abednego were tied up and thrown into the blazing furnace while still wearing their robes, trousers, turbans, and other clothes. 22The king's command was very strict, and the furnace was made so hot that the flames killed the strong soldiers who threw Shadrach, Meshach, and Abednego into the furnace. 23Firmly tied, Shadrach, Meshach, and Abednego fell into the blazing furnace.

24Then King Nebuchadnezzar was so surprised that he jumped to his feet. He asked the men who advised him, "Didn't we tie up only three men and throw them into the fire?"

They answered, "Yes, O king."

25The king said, "Look! I see four men walking around in the fire. They are not tied up, and they are not burned. The fourth man looks like a son of the gods."

26Then Nebuchadnezzar went to the opening of the blazing furnace and shouted, "Shadrach, Meshach, and Abednego, come out! Servants of the Most High God, come here!"

So Shadrach, Meshach, and Abednego came out of the fire. 27When they came out, the governors, assistant governors, captains of the soldiers, and royal advisers crowded around them and saw that the fire had not harmed their bodies. Their hair was not burned, their robes were not burned, and they didn't even smell like smoke!

28Then Nebuchadnezzar said, "Praise the God of Shadrach, Meshach, and Abednego. Their God has sent his angel and saved his servants from the fire! These three men trusted their God and refused to obey my command. They were willing to die rather than serve or worship any god other than their own. 29So I now give this command: Anyone from any nation or language who says anything against the God of Shadrach, Meshach, and Abednego will be torn apart and have his house turned into a pile of stones. No other god can save his people like this." 30Then the king promoted Shadrach, Meshach, and Abednego in the area of Babylon.

Nebuchadnezzar's Dream of a Tree

4 King Nebuchadnezzar sent this letter to the people, nations, and those who speak every language in all the world:

I wish you peace and great wealth!

2The Most High God has done miracles and wonderful things for me that I am happy to tell you about.
3His wonderful acts are great,
and his miracles are mighty.
His kingdom goes on forever,
and his rule continues from now on.
4I, Nebuchadnezzar, was happy and successful at my palace, 5but I had a

dream that made me afraid. As I was lying on my bed, I saw pictures and visions in my mind that alarmed me. [6]So I ordered all the wise men of Babylon to come to me and tell me what my dream meant. [7]The fortune-tellers, magicians, and wise men came, and I told them about the dream. But they could not tell me what it meant.

[8]Finally, Daniel came to me. (I called him Belteshazzar to honor my god, because the spirit of the holy gods is in him.) I told my dream to him. [9]I said, "Belteshazzar, you are the most important of all the fortune-tellers. I know that the spirit of the holy gods is in you, so there is no secret that is too hard for you to understand. This was what I dreamed; tell me what it means. [10]These are the visions I saw while I was lying in my bed: I looked, and there in front of me was a tree standing in the middle of the earth. And it was very tall. [11]The tree grew large and strong. The top of the tree touched the sky and could be seen from anywhere on earth. [12]The leaves of the tree were beautiful. It had plenty of good fruit on it, enough food for everyone. The wild animals found shelter under the tree, and the birds lived in its branches. Every animal ate from it.

[13]"As I was looking at those things in the vision while lying on my bed, I saw an observer, a holy angel coming down from heaven. [14]He spoke very loudly and said, 'Cut down the tree and cut off its branches. Strip off its leaves and scatter its fruit. Let the animals under the tree run away, and let the birds in its branches fly away. [15]But leave the stump and its roots in the ground with a band of iron and bronze around it; let it stay in the field with the grass around it.

" 'Let the man become wet with dew, and let him live among the animals and plants of the earth. [16]Let him not think like a human any longer, but let him

have the mind of an animal for seven years.

[17]" 'The observers gave this command; the holy ones declared the sentence. This is so all people may know that the Most High God rules over every kingdom on earth. God gives those kingdoms to anyone he wants, and he chooses people to rule them who are not proud.'

[18]"That is what I, King Nebuchadnezzar, dreamed. Now Belteshazzar,[n] tell me what the dream means. None of the wise men in my kingdom can explain it to me, but you can, because the spirit of the holy gods is in you."

Daniel Explains the Dream

[19]Then Daniel, who was called Belteshazzar, was very quiet for a while, because his understanding of the dream frightened him. So the king said, "Belteshazzar, do not let the dream or its meaning make you afraid."

Then Belteshazzar answered, "My master, I wish the dream were about your enemies, and I wish its meaning were for those who are against you! [20]You saw a tree in your dream that grew large and strong. Its top touched the sky, and it could be seen from all over the earth. [21]Its leaves were beautiful, and it had plenty of fruit for everyone to eat. It was a home for the wild animals, and its branches were nesting places for the birds. [22]O king, you are that tree! You have become great and powerful, like the tall tree that touched the sky. Your power reaches to the far parts of the earth.

[23]"O king, you saw an observer, a holy angel, coming down from heaven who said, 'Cut down the tree and destroy it. But leave the stump and its roots in the ground with a band of iron and bronze around it; leave it in the field with the grass. Let him become wet with dew and live like a wild animal for seven years.'

4:18 Belteshazzar Another name for Daniel.

[24]"This is the meaning of the dream, O king. The Most High God has commanded these things to happen to my master the king: [25]You will be forced away from people to live among the wild animals. People will feed you grass like an ox, and dew from the sky will make you wet. Seven years will pass, and then you will learn this lesson: The Most High God is ruler over every kingdom on earth, and he gives those kingdoms to anyone he chooses.

[26]"Since the stump of the tree and its roots were left in the ground, your kingdom will be given back to you when you learn that one in heaven rules your kingdom. [27]So, O king, please accept my advice. Stop sinning and do what is right. Stop doing wicked things and be kind to the poor. Then you might continue to be successful."

The King's Dream Comes True

[28]All these things happened to King Nebuchadnezzar. [29]Twelve months later as he was walking on the roof[n] of his palace in Babylon, [30]he said, "I have built this great Babylon as my royal home. I built it by my power to show my glory and my majesty."

[31]The words were still in his mouth when a voice from heaven said, "King Nebuchadnezzar, these things will happen to you: Your royal power has been taken away from you. [32]You will be forced away from people. You will live with the wild animals and will be fed grass like an ox. Seven years will pass before you learn this lesson: The Most High God rules over every kingdom on earth and gives those kingdoms to anyone he chooses."

[33]Immediately the words came true. Nebuchadnezzar was forced to go away from people, and he began eating grass like an ox. He became wet from dew. His hair grew long like the feathers of an eagle, and his nails grew like the claws of a bird.

[34]At the end of that time, I, Nebuchadnezzar, looked up toward heaven, and I could think normally again! Then I gave praise to the Most High God; I gave honor and glory to him who lives forever.

God's rule is forever,
and his kingdom continues for all
time.
[35]People on earth
are not truly important.
God does what he wants
with the powers of heaven
and the people on earth.
No one can stop his powerful hand
or question what he does.

[36]At that time I could think normally again, and God gave back my great honor and power and returned the glory to my kingdom. The people who advised me and the royal family came to me for help again. I became king again and was even greater and more powerful than before. [37]Now I, Nebuchadnezzar, give praise and honor and glory to the King of heaven. Everything he does is right and fair, and he is able to make proud people humble.

PSALM 136:1-9

God's Love Continues Forever

136 Give thanks to the LORD because he
is good.
His love continues forever.
[2]Give thanks to the God of gods.
His love continues forever.
[3]Give thanks to the Lord of lords.
His love continues forever.

[4]Only he can do great miracles.
His love continues forever.
[5]With his wisdom he made the skies.
His love continues forever.
[6]He spread out the earth on the seas.
His love continues forever.
[7]He made the sun and the moon.
His love continues forever.
[8]He made the sun to rule the day.
His love continues forever.

4:29 roof In Bible times houses were built with flat roofs. The roof was used for drying things such as flax and fruit. And it was used as an extra room, as a place for worship, and as a cool place to sleep in the summer.

[9]He made the moon and stars to rule the night.
His love continues forever.

PROVERBS 29:11

[11]Foolish people lose their tempers,
but wise people control theirs.

2 PETER 1:1–21

1 From Simon Peter, a servant and apostle of Jesus Christ.

To you who have received a faith as valuable as ours, because our God and Savior Jesus Christ does what is right. [2]Grace and peace be given to you more and more, because you truly know God and Jesus our Lord.

God Has Given Us Blessings

[3]Jesus has the power of God, by which he has given us everything we need to live and to serve God. We have these things because we know him. Jesus called us by his glory and goodness. [4]Through these he gave us the very great and precious promises. With these gifts you can share in God's nature, and the world will not ruin you with its evil desires.

[5]Because you have these blessings, do your best to add these things to your lives: to your faith, add goodness; and to your goodness, add knowledge; [6]and to your knowledge, add self-control; and to your self-control, add patience; and to your patience, add service for God; [7]and to your service for God, add kindness for your brothers and sisters in Christ; and to this kindness, add love. [8]If all these things are in you and are growing, they will help you to be useful and productive in your knowledge of our Lord Jesus Christ. [9]But any-one who does not have these things cannot see clearly. He is blind and has forgotten that he was made clean from his past sins.

[10]My brothers and sisters, try hard to be certain that you really are called and chosen by God. If you do all these things, you will never fall. [11]And you will be given a very great welcome into the eternal kingdom of our Lord and Savior Jesus Christ.

[12]You know these things, and you are very strong in the truth, but I will always help you remember them. [13]I think it is right for me to help you remember as long as I am in this body. [14]I know I must soon leave this body, as our Lord Jesus Christ has shown me. [15]I will try my best so that you may be able to remember these things even after I am gone.

We Saw Christ's Glory

[16]When we told you about the powerful coming of our Lord Jesus Christ, we were not telling just clever stories that someone invented. But we saw the greatness of Jesus with our own eyes. [17]Jesus heard the voice of God, the Greatest Glory, when he received honor and glory from God the Father. The voice said, "This is my Son, whom I love, and I am very pleased with him." [18]We heard that voice from heaven while we were with Jesus on the holy mountain.

[19]This makes us more sure about the message the prophets gave. It is good for you to follow closely what they said as you would follow a light shining in a dark place, until the day begins and the morning star rises in your hearts. [20]Most of all, you must understand this: No prophecy in the Scriptures ever comes from the prophet's own interpretation. [21]No prophecy ever came from what a person wanted to say, but people led by the Holy Spirit spoke words from God.

DECEMBER 1

DANIEL 5:1—6:28

The Writing on the Wall

5 King Belshazzar gave a big banquet for a thousand royal guests and drank wine with them. ²As Belshazzar was drinking his wine, he gave orders to bring the gold and silver cups that his ancestor Nebuchadnezzar had taken from the Temple in Jerusalem. This was so the king, his royal guests, his wives, and his slave women could drink from those cups. ³So they brought the gold cups that had been taken from the Temple of God in Jerusalem. And the king and his royal guests, his wives, and his slave women drank from them. ⁴As they were drinking, they praised their gods, which were made from gold, silver, bronze, iron, wood, and stone.

⁵Suddenly the fingers of a person's hand appeared and began writing on the plaster of the wall, near the lampstand in the royal palace. The king watched the hand as it wrote.

⁶King Belshazzar was very frightened. His face turned white, his knees knocked together, and he could not stand up because his legs were too weak. ⁷The king called for the magicians, wise men, and wizards of Babylon and said to them, "Anyone who can read this writing and explain it will receive purple clothes fit for a king and a gold chain around his neck. And I will make that person the third highest ruler in the kingdom."

⁸Then all the king's wise men came in, but they could not read the writing or tell the king what it meant. ⁹King Belshazzar became even more afraid, and his face became even whiter. His royal guests were confused.

¹⁰Then the king's mother, who had heard the voices of the king and his royal guests, came into the banquet room. She said, "O king, live forever! Don't be afraid or let your face be white with fear! ¹¹There is a man in your kingdom who has the spirit of the holy gods. In the days of your father, this man showed understanding, knowledge, and wisdom like the gods. Your father, King Nebuchadnezzar, put this man in charge of all

the wise men, fortune-tellers, magicians, and wizards. ¹²The man I am talking about is named Daniel, whom the king named Belteshazzar. He was very wise and had knowledge and understanding. He could explain dreams and secrets and could answer very hard problems. Call for Daniel. He will tell you what the writing on the wall means."

¹³So they brought Daniel to the king, and the king asked, "Is your name Daniel? Are you one of the captives my father the king brought from Judah? ¹⁴I have heard that the spirit of the gods is in you, and that you are very wise and have knowledge and extraordinary understanding. ¹⁵The wise men and magicians were brought to me to read this writing and to explain what it means, but they could not explain it. ¹⁶I have heard that you are able to explain what things mean and can find the answers to hard problems. Read this writing on the wall and explain it to me. If you can, I will give you purple clothes fit for a king and a gold chain to wear around your neck. And you will become the third highest ruler in the kingdom."

¹⁷Then Daniel answered the king, "You may keep your gifts for yourself, or you may give those rewards to someone else. But I will read the writing on the wall for you and will explain to you what it means.

¹⁸"O king, the Most High God made your father Nebuchadnezzar a great, important, and powerful king. ¹⁹Because God made him important, all the people, nations, and those who spoke every language were very frightened of Nebuchadnezzar. If he wanted someone to die, he killed that person. If he wanted someone to live, he let that person live. Those he wanted to promote, he promoted. Those he wanted to be less important, he made less important.

²⁰"But Nebuchadnezzar became too proud and stubborn, so he was taken off his royal throne. His glory was taken away. ²¹He was forced away from people, and his mind became like the mind of an animal. He lived with the wild donkeys and was fed grass like an ox and became wet with dew. These

things happened to him until he learned his lesson: The Most High God rules over every kingdom on earth, and he sets anyone he chooses over those kingdoms.

²²"Belshazzar, you already knew these things, because you are a descendant of Nebuchadnezzar. Still you have not been sorry for what you have done. ²³Instead, you have set yourself against the Lord of heaven. You ordered the drinking cups from the Temple of the Lord to be brought to you. Then you and your royal guests, your wives, and your slave women drank wine from them. You praised the gods of silver, gold, bronze, iron, wood, and stone that are not really gods; they cannot see or hear or understand anything. You did not honor God, who has power over your life and everything you do. ²⁴So God sent the hand that wrote on the wall.

²⁵"These are the words that were written on the wall: 'Mene, mene, tekel, and parsin.'

²⁶"This is what the words mean: Mene: God has counted the days until your kingdom will end. ²⁷Tekel: You have been weighed on the scales and found not good enough. ²⁸Parsin: Your kingdom is being divided and will be given to the Medes and the Persians."

²⁹Then Belshazzar gave an order for Daniel to be dressed in purple clothes and to have a gold chain put around his neck. And it was announced that Daniel was the third highest ruler in the kingdom. ³⁰That very same night Belshazzar, king of the Babylonian people, was killed. ³¹So Darius the Mede became the new king when he was sixty-two years old.

Daniel and the Lions

6 Darius thought it would be a good idea to choose one hundred twenty governors who would rule his kingdom. ²He chose three men as supervisors over those governors, and Daniel was one of the supervisors. The supervisors were to ensure that the governors did not try to cheat the king. ³Daniel showed that he could do the work better than the other supervisors and governors, so the king planned to put Daniel in charge of the whole kingdom. ⁴Because of this, the other supervisors and governors tried to find reasons to accuse Daniel about his work in the government. But they could not find anything wrong with him or any reason to accuse him, because he was trustworthy and not lazy or dishonest. ⁵Finally these men said, "We will never find any reason to accuse Daniel unless it is about the law of his God."

⁶So the supervisors and governors went as a group to the king and said: "King Darius, live forever! ⁷The supervisors, assistant governors, governors, the people who advise you, and the captains of the soldiers have all agreed that you should make a new law for everyone to obey: For the next thirty days no one should pray to any god or human except to you, O king. Anyone who doesn't obey will be thrown into the lions' den. ⁸Now, O king, make the law and sign your name to it so that it cannot be changed, because then it will be a law of the Medes and Persians and cannot be canceled." ⁹So King Darius signed the law.

¹⁰Even though Daniel knew that the new law had been written, he went to pray in an upstairs room in his house, which had windows that opened toward Jerusalem. Three times each day Daniel would kneel down to pray and thank God, just as he always had done.

¹¹Then those men went as a group and found Daniel praying and asking God for help. ¹²So they went to the king and talked to him about the law he had made. They said, "Didn't you sign a law that says no one may pray to any god or human except you, O king? Doesn't it say that anyone who disobeys during the next thirty days will be thrown into the lions' den?"

The king answered, "Yes, that is the law, and the laws of the Medes and Persians cannot be canceled."

¹³Then they said to the king, "Daniel, one of the captives from Judah, is not paying attention to you, O king, or to the law you signed. Daniel still prays to his God three times every day." ¹⁴The king became very upset when he heard this. He wanted to save Daniel, and he worked hard until sunset trying to think of a way to save him.

¹⁵Then those men went as a group to the king. They said, "Remember, O king, the law of the Medes and Persians says that no law or command given by the king can be changed."

¹⁶So King Darius gave the order, and Daniel was brought in and thrown into the lions' den. The king said to Daniel, "May the God you serve all the time save you!" ¹⁷A big stone was brought and placed over the opening of the lions' den. Then the king used his signet ring and the rings of his royal officers to put special seals on the rock. This ensured that no one would move the rock and bring Daniel out. ¹⁸Then King Darius went back to his palace. He did not eat that night, he did not have any entertainment brought to him, and he could not sleep.

¹⁹The next morning King Darius got up at dawn and hurried to the lions' den. ²⁰As he came near the den, he was worried. He called out to Daniel, "Daniel, servant of the living God! Has your God that you always worship been able to save you from the lions?"

²¹Daniel answered, "O king, live forever! ²²My God sent his angel to close the lions' mouths. They have not hurt me, because my God knows I am innocent. I never did anything wrong to you, O king."

²³King Darius was very happy and told his servants to lift Daniel out of the lions' den. So they lifted him out and did not find any injury on him, because Daniel had trusted in his God.

²⁴Then the king commanded that the men who had accused Daniel be brought to the lions' den. They, their wives, and their children were thrown into the den. The lions grabbed them before they hit the floor of the den and crushed their bones.

²⁵Then King Darius wrote a letter to all people and all nations, to those who spoke every language in the world:

I wish you great peace and wealth.

²⁶I am making a new law for people in every part of my kingdom. All of you must fear and respect the God of Daniel.

Daniel's God is the living God;
 he lives forever.

His kingdom will never be
 destroyed,
 and his rule will never end.
²⁷God rescues and saves people
 and does mighty miracles
 in heaven and on earth.
 He is the one who saved Daniel
 from the power of the lions.

²⁸So Daniel was successful during the time Darius was king and when Cyrus the Persian was king.

PSALM 136:10–26

¹⁰He killed the firstborn sons of the
 Egyptians.
 His love continues forever.
¹¹He brought the people of Israel out of
 Egypt.
 His love continues forever.
¹²He did it with his great power and
 strength.
 His love continues forever.
¹³He parted the water of the Red Sea.
 His love continues forever.
¹⁴He brought the Israelites through the
 middle of it.
 His love continues forever.
¹⁵But the king of Egypt and his army
 drowned in the Red Sea.
 His love continues forever.

¹⁶He led his people through the desert.
 His love continues forever.
¹⁷He defeated great kings.
 His love continues forever.
¹⁸He killed powerful kings.
 His love continues forever.
¹⁹He defeated Sihon king of the Amorites.
 His love continues forever.
²⁰He defeated Og king of Bashan.
 His love continues forever.
²¹He gave their land as a gift.
 His love continues forever.
²²It was a gift to his servants, the Israelites.
 His love continues forever.

²³He remembered us when we were in
 trouble.
 His love continues forever.
²⁴He freed us from our enemies.
 His love continues forever.

²⁵He gives food to every living creature.
His love continues forever.

²⁶Give thanks to the God of heaven.
His love continues forever.

PROVERBS 29:12–13

¹²If a ruler pays attention to lies,
all his officers will become wicked.

¹³The poor person and the cruel person
are alike
in that the LORD gave eyes to both of
them.

2 PETER 2:1–22

False Teachers

2There used to be false prophets among
God's people, just as you will have some
false teachers in your group. They will secretly teach things that are wrong—teachings that will cause people to be lost. They
will even refuse to accept the Master, Jesus,
who bought their freedom. So they will bring
quick ruin on themselves. ²Many will follow
their evil ways and say evil things about the
way of truth. ³Those false teachers only want
your money, so they will use you by telling
you lies. Their judgment spoken against
them long ago is still coming, and their ruin
is certain.

⁴When angels sinned, God did not let
them go free without punishment. He sent
them to hell and put them in caves*ⁿ* of darkness where they are being held for judgment.
⁵And God punished the world long ago when
he brought a flood to the world that was full
of people who were against him. But God
saved Noah, who preached about being right
with God, and seven other people with him.
⁶And God also destroyed the evil cities of
Sodom and Gomorrah*ⁿ* by burning them
until they were ashes. He made those cities
an example of what will happen to those
who are against God. ⁷But he saved Lot from
those cities. Lot, a good man, was troubled
because of the filthy lives of evil people.
⁸(Lot was a good man, but because he lived

with evil people every day, his good heart
was hurt by the evil things he saw and
heard.) ⁹So the Lord knows how to save
those who serve him when troubles come.
He will hold evil people and punish them,
while waiting for the Judgment Day. ¹⁰That
punishment is especially for those who live
by doing the evil things their sinful selves
want and who hate authority.

These false teachers are bold and do anything they want. They are not afraid to speak
against the angels. ¹¹But even the angels,
who are much stronger and more powerful
than false teachers, do not accuse them with
insults before*ⁿ* the Lord. ¹²But these people
speak against things they do not understand. They are like animals that act without
thinking, animals born to be caught and
killed. And, like animals, these false teachers
will be destroyed. ¹³They have caused many
people to suffer, so they themselves will suffer. That is their pay for what they have done.
They take pleasure in openly doing evil, so
they are like dirty spots and stains among
you. They delight in deceiving you while eating meals with you. ¹⁴Every time they look at
a woman they want her, and their desire for
sin is never satisfied. They lead weak people
into the trap of sin, and they have taught
their hearts to be greedy. God will punish
them! ¹⁵These false teachers left the right
road and lost their way, following the way
Balaam went. Balaam was the son of Beor,
who loved being paid for doing wrong. ¹⁶But
a donkey, which cannot talk, told Balaam he
was sinning. It spoke with a man's voice and
stopped the prophet's crazy thinking.

¹⁷Those false teachers are like springs
without water and clouds blown by a storm.
A place in the blackest darkness has been
kept for them. ¹⁸They brag with words that
mean nothing. By their evil desires they lead
people into the trap of sin—people who are
just beginning to escape from others who
live in error. ¹⁹They promise you freedom,
but they themselves are not free. They are
slaves of things that will be destroyed. For
people are slaves of anything that controls

2:4 caves Some Greek copies read "chains." **2:6 Sodom and Gomorrah** Two cities God destroyed because the people were
so evil. **2:11 before** Some Greek copies read "from."

them. [20]They were made free from the evil in the world by knowing our Lord and Savior Jesus Christ. But if they return to evil things and those things control them, then it is worse for them than it was before. [21]Yes, it would be better for them to have never known the right way than to know it and to turn away from the holy teaching that was given to them. [22]What they did is like this true saying: "A dog goes back to what it has thrown up,"[n] and, "After a pig is washed, it goes back and rolls in the mud."

DECEMBER 2

DANIEL 7:1—8:27

Daniel's Dream About Four Animals

7 In Belshazzar's first year as king of Babylon, Daniel had a dream. He saw visions as he was lying on his bed, and he wrote down what he had dreamed.

[2]Daniel said: "I saw my vision at night. In the vision the wind was blowing from all four directions, which made the sea very rough. [3]I saw four huge animals come up from the sea, and each animal was different from the others.

[4]"The first animal looked like a lion, but had wings like an eagle. I watched this animal until its wings were torn off. It was lifted from the ground so that it stood up on two feet like a human, and it was given the mind of a human.

[5]"Then I saw a second animal before me that looked like a bear. It was raised up on one of its sides and had three ribs in its mouth between its teeth. It was told, 'Get up and eat all the meat you want!'

[6]"After that, I looked, and there before me was another animal. This animal looked like a leopard with four wings on its back that looked like a bird's wings. This animal had four heads and was given power to rule.

[7]"After that, in my vision at night I saw in front of me a fourth animal that was cruel, terrible, and very strong. It had large iron teeth. It crushed and ate what it killed, and then it walked on whatever was left. This fourth animal was different from any animal I had seen before, and it had ten horns.

[8]"While I was thinking about the horns, another horn grew up among them. It was a little horn with eyes like a human's eyes. It also had a mouth, and the mouth was bragging. The little horn pulled out three of the other horns.

[9]"As I looked,
  thrones were put in their places,
    and God, the Eternal One, sat on his
      throne.
His clothes were white like snow,
  and the hair on his head was white like
    wool.
His throne was made from fire,
  and the wheels of his throne were
    blazing with fire.
[10]A river of fire was flowing
  from in front of him.
Many thousands of angels were serving
  him,
  and millions of angels stood before
    him.
Court was ready to begin,
  and the books were opened.

[11]"I kept on looking because the little horn was bragging. I kept watching until finally the fourth animal was killed. Its body was destroyed, and it was thrown into the burning fire. [12](The power and rule of the other animals had been taken from them, but they were permitted to live for a certain period of time.)

[13]"In my vision at night I saw in front of me someone who looked like a human being coming on the clouds in the sky. He came near God, who has been alive forever, and he was led to God. [14]He was given authority, glory, and the strength of a king. People of

every tribe, nation, and language will serve him. His rule will last forever, and his kingdom will never be destroyed.

The Meaning of the Dream

[15]"I, Daniel, was worried. The visions that went through my mind frightened me. [16]I came near one of those standing there and asked what all this meant.

"So he told me and explained to me what these things meant: [17]'The four great animals are four kingdoms that will come from the earth. [18]But the holy people who belong to the Most High God will receive the power to rule and will have the power to rule forever, from now on.'

[19]"Then I wanted to know what the fourth animal meant, because it was different from all the others. It was very terrible and had iron teeth and bronze claws. It was the animal that crushed and ate what it killed and then walked on whatever was left. [20]I also wanted to know about the ten horns on its head and about the little horn that grew there. It had pulled out three of the other ten horns and looked greater than the others. It had eyes and a mouth that kept bragging. [21]As I watched, the little horn began making war against God's holy people and was defeating them [22]until God, who has been alive forever, came. He judged in favor of the holy people who belong to the Most High God; then the time came for them to receive the power to rule.

[23]"And he explained this to me: 'The fourth animal is a fourth kingdom that will come on the earth. It will be different from all the other kingdoms and will destroy people all over the world. It will walk on and crush the whole earth. [24]The ten horns are ten kings who will come from this fourth kingdom. After those ten kings are gone, another king will come. He will be different from the kings who ruled before him, and he will defeat three of the other kings. [25]This king will speak against the Most High God, and he will hurt and kill God's holy people. He will try to change times and laws that have already been set. The holy people that belong to God will be in that king's power for three and one-half years.

[26]"'But the court will decide what should happen. The power of the king will be taken away, and his kingdom will be completely destroyed. [27]Then the holy people who belong to the Most High God will have the power to rule. They will rule over all the kingdoms under heaven with power and greatness, and their power to rule will last forever. People from all the other kingdoms will respect and serve them.'

[28]"That was the end of the dream. I, Daniel, was very afraid. My face became white from fear, but I kept everything to myself."

Daniel's Vision

8 During the third year of King Belshazzar's rule, I, Daniel, saw another vision, which was like the first one. [2]In this vision I saw myself in the capital city of Susa, in the area of Elam. I was standing by the Ulai Canal [3]when I looked up and saw a male sheep standing beside the canal. It had two long horns, but one horn was longer and newer than the other. [4]I watched the sheep charge to the west, the north, and the south. No animal could stand before him, and none could save another animal from his power. He did whatever he wanted and became very powerful.

[5]While I was watching this, I saw a male goat come from the west. This goat had one large horn between his eyes that was easy to see. He crossed over the whole earth so fast that his feet hardly touched the ground. [6]In his anger the goat charged the sheep with the two horns that I had seen standing by the canal. [7]I watched the angry goat attack the sheep and break the sheep's two horns. The sheep was not strong enough to stop it. The goat knocked the sheep to the ground and then walked all over him. No one was able to save the sheep from the goat, [8]so the male goat became very great. But when he was strong, his big horn broke off and four horns grew in place of the one big horn. Those four horns pointed in four different directions and were easy to see.

[9]Then a little horn grew from one of those four horns, and it became very big. It grew to the south, the east, and toward the beautiful

land of Judah. [10]That little horn grew until it reached to the sky. It even threw some of the army of heaven to the ground and walked on them! [11]That little horn set itself up as equal to God, the Commander of heaven's armies. It stopped the daily sacrifices that were offered to him, and the Temple, the place where people worshiped him, was pulled down. [12]Because there was a turning away from God, the people stopped the daily sacrifices. Truth was thrown down to the ground, and the horn was successful in everything it did.

[13]Then I heard a holy angel speaking. Another holy angel asked the first one, "How long will the things in this vision last—the daily sacrifices, the turning away from God that brings destruction, the Temple being pulled down, and the army of heaven being walked on?"

[14]The angel said to me, "This will happen for twenty-three hundred evenings and mornings. Then the holy place will be repaired."

[15]I, Daniel, saw this vision and tried to understand what it meant. In it I saw someone who looked like a man standing near me. [16]And I heard a man's voice calling from the Ulai Canal: "Gabriel, explain the vision to this man."

[17]Gabriel came to where I was standing. When he came close to me, I was very afraid and bowed facedown on the ground. But Gabriel said to me, "Human being, understand that this vision is about the time of the end."

[18]While Gabriel was speaking, I fell into a deep sleep with my face on the ground. Then he touched me and lifted me to my feet. [19]He said, "Now, I will explain to you what will happen in the time of God's anger. Your vision was about the set time of the end.

[20]"You saw a male sheep with two horns, which are the kings of Media and Persia. [21]The male goat is the king of Greece, and the big horn between its eyes is the first king. [22]The four horns that grew in the place of the broken horn are four kingdoms. Those four kingdoms will come from the nation of the first king, but they will not be as strong as the first king.

[23]"When the end comes near for those kingdoms, a bold and cruel king who tells lies will come. This will happen when many people have turned against God. [24]This king will be very powerful, but his power will not come from himself. He will cause terrible destruction and will be successful in everything he does. He will destroy powerful people and even God's holy people. [25]This king will succeed by using lies and force. He will think that he is very important. He will destroy many people without warning; he will try to fight even the Prince of princes! But that cruel king will be destroyed, and not by human power.

[26]"The vision that has been shown to you about these evenings and mornings is true. But seal up the vision, because those things won't happen for a long time."

[27]I, Daniel, became very weak and was sick for several days after that vision. Then I got up and went back to work for the king, but I was very upset about the vision. I didn't understand what it meant.

PSALM 137:1-6

Israelites in Captivity

137 By the rivers in Babylon we sat and cried
when we remembered Jerusalem.
[2]On the poplar trees nearby
we hung our harps.
[3]Those who captured us asked us to sing;
our enemies wanted happy songs.
They said, "Sing us a song about Jerusalem!"

[4]But we cannot sing songs about the LORD
while we are in this foreign country!
[5]Jerusalem, if I forget you,
let my right hand lose its skill.
[6]Let my tongue stick to the roof of my mouth
if I do not remember you,
if I do not think about Jerusalem
as my greatest joy.

PROVERBS 29:14

[14]If a king judges poor people fairly,
his government will continue forever.

2 PETER 3:1–18

Jesus Will Come Again

3 My friends, this is the second letter I have written you to help your honest minds remember. ²I want you to think about the words the holy prophets spoke in the past, and remember the command our Lord and Savior gave us through your apostles. ³It is most important for you to understand what will happen in the last days. People will laugh at you. They will live doing the evil things they want to do. ⁴They will say, "Jesus promised to come again. Where is he? Our fathers have died, but the world continues the way it has been since it was made." ⁵But they do not want to remember what happened long ago. By the word of God heaven was made, and the earth was made from water and with water. ⁶Then the world was flooded and destroyed with water. ⁷And that same word of God is keeping heaven and earth that we now have in order to be destroyed by fire. They are being kept for the Judgment Day and the destruction of all who are against God.

⁸But do not forget this one thing, dear friends: To the Lord one day is as a thousand years, and a thousand years is as one day. ⁹The Lord is not slow in doing what he promised—the way some people understand slowness. But God is being patient with you. He does not want anyone to be lost, but he wants all people to change their hearts and lives.

¹⁰But the day of the Lord will come like a thief. The skies will disappear with a loud noise. Everything in them will be destroyed by fire, and the earth and everything in it will be exposed.ⁿ ¹¹In that way everything will be destroyed. So what kind of people should you be? You should live holy lives and serve God, ¹²as you wait for and look forward to the coming of the day of God. When that day comes, the skies will be destroyed with fire, and everything in them will melt with heat. ¹³But God made a promise to us, and we are waiting for a new heaven and a new earth where goodness lives.

¹⁴Dear friends, since you are waiting for this to happen, do your best to be without sin and without fault. Try to be at peace with God. ¹⁵Remember that we are saved because our Lord is patient. Our dear brother Paul told you the same thing when he wrote to you with the wisdom that God gave him. ¹⁶He writes about this in all his letters. Some things in Paul's letters are hard to understand, and people who are ignorant and weak in faith explain these things falsely. They also falsely explain the other Scriptures, but they are destroying themselves by doing this.

¹⁷Dear friends, since you already know about this, be careful. Do not let those evil people lead you away by the wrong they do. Be careful so you will not fall from your strong faith. ¹⁸But grow in the grace and knowledge of our Lord and Savior Jesus Christ. Glory be to him now and forever! Amen.

DECEMBER 3

DANIEL 9:1–11:1

Daniel's Prayer

9 These things happened during the first year Darius son of Xerxes was king over Babylon. He was a descendant of the Medes. ²During Darius' first year as king, I, Daniel, was reading the Scriptures. I saw that the

Lord told Jeremiah that Jerusalem would be empty ruins for seventy years.

³Then I turned to the Lord God and prayed and asked him for help. To show my sadness, I fasted, put on rough cloth, and sat in ashes. ⁴I prayed to the Lord my God and told him about all of our sins. I said, "Lord, you are a great God who causes fear and

wonder. You keep your agreement of love with all who love you and obey your commands.

⁵"But we have sinned and done wrong. We have been wicked and turned against you, your commands, and your laws. ⁶We did not listen to your servants, the prophets, who spoke for you to our kings, our leaders, our ancestors, and all the people of the land.

⁷"Lord, you are good and right, but we are full of shame today—the people of Judah and Jerusalem, all the people of Israel, those near and far whom you scattered among many nations because they were not loyal to you. ⁸LORD, we are all ashamed. Our kings and leaders and our fathers are ashamed, because we have sinned against you.

⁹"But, Lord our God, you show us mercy and forgive us even though we have turned against you. ¹⁰We have not obeyed the LORD our God or the teachings he gave us through his servants, the prophets. ¹¹All the people of Israel have disobeyed your teachings and have turned away, refusing to obey you. So you brought on us the curses and promises of punishment written in the Teachings of Moses, the servant of God, because we sinned against you.

¹²"You said these things would happen to us and our leaders, and you made them happen; you brought on us a great disaster. Nothing has ever been done on earth like what was done to Jerusalem. ¹³All this disaster came to us just as it is written in the Teachings of Moses. But we have not pleaded with the LORD our God. We have not stopped sinning. We have not paid attention to your truth. ¹⁴The LORD was ready to bring the disaster on us, and he did it because the LORD our God is right in everything he does. But we still did not obey him.

¹⁵"Lord our God, you used your power and brought us out of Egypt. Because of that, your name is known even today. But we have sinned and have done wrong. ¹⁶Lord, you do what is right, but please do not be angry with Jerusalem, your city on your holy hill. Because of our sins and the evil things done by our ancestors, people all around insult and make fun of Jerusalem and your people.

¹⁷"Now, our God, hear the prayers of your servant. Listen to my prayer for help, and for your sake do good things for your holy place that is in ruins. ¹⁸My God, pay attention and hear me. Open your eyes and see all the terrible things that have happened to us. See how our lives have been ruined and what has happened to the city that is called by your name. We do not ask these things because we are good; instead, we ask because of your mercy. ¹⁹Lord, listen! Lord, forgive! Lord, hear us and do something! For your sake, don't wait, because your city and your people are called by your name."

Gabriel's Explanation

²⁰While I was saying these things in my prayer to the LORD, my God, confessing my sins and the sins of the people of Israel and praying for God's holy hill, ²¹Gabriel came to me. (I had seen him in my last vision.) He came flying quickly to me about the time of the evening sacrifice, while I was still praying. ²²He taught me and said to me, "Daniel, I have come to give you wisdom and to help you understand. ²³When you first started praying, an answer was given, and I came to tell you, because God loves you very much. So think about the message and understand the vision.

²⁴"God has ordered four hundred ninety years for your people and your holy city for these reasons: to stop people from turning against God; to put an end to sin; to take away evil; to bring in goodness that continues forever; to bring about the vision and prophecy; and to appoint a most holy place.

²⁵"Learn and understand these things. A command will come to rebuild Jerusalem. The time from this command until the appointed leader comes will be forty-nine years and four hundred thirty-four years. Jerusalem will be rebuilt with streets and a trench filled with water around it, but it will be built in times of trouble. ²⁶After the four hundred thirty-four years the appointed leader will be killed; he will have nothing. The people of the leader who is to come will destroy the city and the holy place. The end of the city will come like a flood, and war will continue until the end. God has ordered that place to be completely destroyed. ²⁷That

leader will make firm an agreement with many people for seven years. He will stop the offerings and sacrifices after three and one-half years. A destroyer will do blasphemous things until the ordered end comes to the destroyed city."

Daniel's Vision of a Man

10 During Cyrus' third year as king of Persia, Daniel, whose name was Belteshazzar, received a vision about a great war. It was a true message that Daniel understood.

2At that time I, Daniel, had been very sad for three weeks. 3I did not eat any fancy food or meat, or drink any wine, or use any perfumed oil for three weeks.

4On the twenty-fourth day of the first month, I was standing beside the great Tigris River. 5While standing there, I looked up and saw a man dressed in linen clothes with a belt of fine gold wrapped around his waist. 6His body was like shiny yellow quartz. His face was bright like lightning, and his eyes were like fire. His arms and legs were shiny like polished bronze, and his voice sounded like the roar of a crowd.

7I, Daniel, was the only person who saw the vision. The men with me did not see it, because they were so frightened that they ran away and hid. 8So I was left alone, watching this great vision. I lost my strength, my face turned white like a dead person, and I was helpless. 9Then I heard the man in the vision speaking. As I listened, I fell into a deep sleep with my face on the ground.

10Then a hand touched me and set me on my hands and knees. I was so afraid that I was shaking. 11The man in the vision said to me, "Daniel, God loves you very much. Think carefully about the words I will speak to you, and stand up, because I have been sent to you." When he said this, I stood up, but I was still shaking.

12Then the man said to me, "Daniel, do not be afraid. Some time ago you decided to get understanding and to humble yourself before your God. Since that time God has listened to you, and I have come because of your prayers. 13But the prince of Persia has been fighting against me for twenty-one

days. Then Michael, one of the most important angels, came to help me, because I had been left there with the king of Persia. 14Now I have come to explain to you what will happen to your people, because the vision is about a time in the future."

15While he was speaking to me, I bowed facedown and could not speak. 16Then one who looked like a man touched my lips, so I opened my mouth and started to speak. I said to the one standing in front of me, "Master, I am upset and afraid because of what I saw in the vision. I feel helpless. 17Master, how can I, your servant, talk with you? My strength is gone, and it is hard for me to breathe."

18The one who looked like a man touched me again and gave me strength. 19He said, "Daniel, don't be afraid. God loves you very much. Peace be with you. Be strong now; be courageous."

When he spoke to me, I became stronger and said, "Master, speak, since you have given me strength."

20Then he said, "Daniel, do you know why I have come to you? Soon I must go back to fight against the prince of Persia. When I go, the prince of Greece will come, 21but I must first tell you what is written in the Book of Truth. No one stands with me against these enemies except Michael, the angel ruling over your people.

11 In the first year that Darius the Mede was king, I stood up to support Michael in his fight against the prince of Persia.

PSALM 137:7–9

7Lord, remember what the Edomites did
    on the day Jerusalem fell.
They said, "Tear it down!
    Tear it down to its foundations!"

8People of Babylon, you will be destroyed.
    The people who pay you back for what
        you did to us will be happy.
9They will grab your babies
    and throw them against the rocks.

PROVERBS 29:15

15Correction and punishment make
    children wise,

but those left alone will disgrace their mother.

1 JOHN 1:1–10

1 We write you now about what has always existed, which we have heard, we have seen with our own eyes, we have looked at, and we have touched with our hands. We write to you about the Word[n] that gives life. [2]He who gives life was shown to us. We saw him and can give proof about it. And now we announce to you that he has life that continues forever. He was with God the Father and was shown to us. [3]We announce to you what we have seen and heard, because we want you also to have fellowship with us. Our fellowship is with God the Father and with his Son, Jesus Christ. [4]We write this to you so we may be full of joy.[n]

God Forgives Our Sins

[5]Here is the message we have heard from Christ and now announce to you: God is light,[n] and in him there is no darkness at all. [6]So if we say we have fellowship with God, but we continue living in darkness, we are liars and do not follow the truth. [7]But if we live in the light, as God is in the light, we can share fellowship with each other. Then the blood of Jesus, God's Son, cleanses us from every sin.

[8]If we say we have no sin, we are fooling ourselves, and the truth is not in us. [9]But if we confess our sins, he will forgive our sins, because we can trust God to do what is right. He will cleanse us from all the wrongs we have done. [10]If we say we have not sinned, we make God a liar, and we do not accept God's teaching.

DECEMBER 4

DANIEL 11:2—12:13

Kingdoms of the South and North

[2]"Now then, Daniel, I tell you the truth: Three more kings will rule in Persia, and then a fourth king will come. He will be much richer than all the kings of Persia before him and will use his riches to get power. He will stir up everyone against the kingdom of Greece. [3]Then a mighty king will come, who will rule with great power and will do anything he wants. [4]After that king has come, his kingdom will be broken up and divided out toward the four parts of the world. His kingdom will not go to his descendants, and it will not have the power that he had, because his kingdom will be pulled up and given to other people.

[5]"The king of the South will become strong, but one of his commanders will become even stronger. He will begin to rule his own kingdom with great power. [6]Then after a few years, a new friendship will develop. The daughter of the king of the South will marry the king of the North in order to bring peace. But she will not keep her power, and his family will not last. She, her husband, her child, and those who brought her to that country will be killed.

[7]"But a person from her family will become king of the South and will attack the armies of the king of the North. He will go into that king's strong, walled city and will fight and win. [8]He will take their gods, their metal idols, and their valuable things made of silver and gold back to Egypt. Then he will not bother the king of the North for a few years. [9]Next, the king of the North will attack the king of the South, but he will be beaten back to his own country.

[10]"The sons of the king of the North will prepare for war. They will get a large army together that will move through the land very quickly, like a powerful flood. Later, that army will come back and fight all the way to

---

1:1 Word The Greek word is "logos," meaning any kind of communication. Here, it means Christ, who was the way God told people about himself. **1:4 so . . . joy** Some Greek copies read "so you may be full of joy." **1:5 light** Here, it is used as a symbol of God's goodness or truth.

the strong, walled city of the king of the South. ¹¹Then the king of the South will become very angry and will march out to fight against the king of the North. The king of the North will have a large army, but he will lose the battle, ¹²and the soldiers will be carried away. The king of the South will then be very proud and will kill thousands of soldiers from the northern army, but he will not continue to be successful. ¹³The king of the North will gather another army, larger than the first one. After several years he will attack with a large army and many weapons.

¹⁴"In those times many people will be against the king of the South. Some of your own people who love to fight will turn against the king of the South, thinking it is time for God's promises to come true. But they will fail. ¹⁵Then the king of the North will come. He will build ramps to the tops of the city walls and will capture a strong, walled city. The southern army will not have the power to fight back; even their best soldiers will not be strong enough to stop the northern army. ¹⁶So the king of the North will do whatever he wants; no one will be able to stand against him. He will gain power and control in the beautiful land of Israel and will have the power to destroy it. ¹⁷The king of the North will decide to use all his power to fight against the king of the South, but he will make a peace agreement with the king of the South. The king of the North will give one of his daughters as a wife to the king of the South so that he can defeat him. But those plans will not succeed or help him. ¹⁸Then the king of the North will turn his attention to cities along the coast of the Mediterranean Sea and will capture them. But a commander will put an end to the pride of the king of the North, turning his pride back on him. ¹⁹After that happens the king of the North will go back to the strong, walled cities of his own country, but he will lose his power. That will be the end of him.

²⁰"The next king of the North will send out a tax collector so he will have plenty of money. In a few years that ruler will be killed, although he will not die in anger or in a battle.

²¹"That ruler will be followed by a very cruel and hated man, who will not have the honor of being from a king's family. He will attack the kingdom when the people feel safe, and he will take power by lying to the people. ²²He will sweep away in defeat large and powerful armies and even a prince who made an agreement. ²³Many nations will make agreements with that cruel and hated ruler, but he will lie to them. He will gain much power, but only a few people will support him. ²⁴The richest areas will feel safe, but that cruel and hated ruler will attack them. He will succeed where his ancestors did not. He will rob the countries he defeats and will give those things to his followers. He will plan to defeat and destroy strong cities, but he will be successful for only a short time.

²⁵"That very cruel and hated ruler will have a large army that he will use to stir up his strength and courage. He will attack the king of the South. The king of the South will gather a large and very powerful army and prepare for war. But the people who are against him will make secret plans, and the king of the South will be defeated. ²⁶People who were supposed to be his good friends will try to destroy him. His army will be swept away in defeat; many of his soldiers will be killed in battle. ²⁷Those two kings will want to hurt each other. They will sit at the same table and lie to each other, but it will not do either one any good, because God has set a time for their end to come. ²⁸The king of the North will go back to his own country with much wealth. Then he will decide to go against the holy agreement. He will take action and then return to his own country.

²⁹"At the right time the king of the North will attack the king of the South again, but this time he will not be successful as he was before. ³⁰Ships from the west will come and fight against the king of the North, so he will be afraid. Then he will return and show his anger against the holy agreement. He will be good to those who have stopped obeying the holy agreement.

³¹"The king of the North will send his army to make the Temple in Jerusalem unclean. They will stop the people from offering the daily sacrifice, and then they will set

up a blasphemous object that brings destruction. ³²The king of the North will tell lies and cause those who have not obeyed God to be ruined. But those who know God and obey him will be strong and fight back.

³³"Those who are wise will help the others understand what is happening. But they will be killed with swords, or burned, or taken captive, or robbed of their homes and possessions. These things will continue for many days. ³⁴When the wise ones are suffering, they will get a little help, but many who join the wise ones will not help them in their time of need. ³⁵Some of the wise ones will be killed. But the hard times must come so they can be made stronger and purer and without faults until the time of the end comes. Then, at the right time, the end will come.

The King Who Praises Himself

³⁶"The king of the North will do whatever he wants. He will brag about himself and praise himself and think he is even better than a god. He will say things against the God of gods that no one has ever heard. And he will be successful until all the bad things have happened. Then what God has planned to happen will happen. ³⁷The king of the North will not care about the gods his ancestors worshiped or the god that women worship. He won't care about any god. Instead, he will make himself more important than any god. ³⁸The king of the North will worship power and strength, which his ancestors did not worship. He will honor the god of power with gold and silver, expensive jewels and gifts. ³⁹That king will attack strong, walled cities with the help of a foreign god. He will give much honor to the people who join him, making them rulers in charge of many other people. And he will make them pay him for the land they rule.

⁴⁰"At the time of the end, the king of the South will fight a battle against the king of the North. The king of the North will attack with chariots, soldiers on horses, and many large ships. He will invade many countries and sweep through their lands like a flood. ⁴¹The king of the North will attack the beautiful land of Judah. He will defeat many countries, but Edom, Moab, and the leaders of Ammon will be saved from him. ⁴²The king of the North will show his power in many countries; Egypt will not escape. ⁴³The king will get treasures of gold and silver and all the riches of Egypt. The Libyan and Nubian people will obey him. ⁴⁴But the king of the North will hear news from the east and the north that will make him afraid and angry. He will go to destroy completely many nations. ⁴⁵He will set up his royal tents between the sea and the beautiful mountain where the holy Temple is built. But, finally, his end will come, and no one will help him.

The Time of the End

12 "At that time Michael, the great prince who protects your people, will stand up. There will be a time of much trouble, the worst time since nations have been on earth, but your people will be saved. Everyone whose name is written in God's book will be saved. ²Many people who have already died will live again. Some of them will wake up to have life forever, but some will wake up to find shame and disgrace forever. ³The wise people will shine like the brightness of the sky. Those who teach others to live right will shine like stars forever and ever.

⁴"But you, Daniel, close up the book and seal it. These things will happen at the time of the end. Many people will go here and there to find true knowledge."

⁵Then I, Daniel, looked, and saw two other men. One was standing on my side of the river, and the other was standing on the far side. ⁶The man who was dressed in linen was standing over the water in the river. One of the two men spoke to him and asked, "How long will it be before these amazing things come true?"

⁷The man dressed in linen, who stood over the water, raised his hands toward heaven. And I heard him swear by the name of God who lives forever, "It will be for three and one-half years. The power of the holy people will finally be broken, and then all these things will come true."

⁸I heard the answer, but I did not really understand, so I asked, "Master, what will happen after all these things come true?"

⁹He answered, "Go your way, Daniel. The

message is closed up and sealed until the time of the end. [10]Many people will be made clean, pure, and spotless, but the wicked will continue to be wicked. Those wicked people will not understand these things, but the wise will understand them.

[11]"The daily sacrifice will be stopped. Then, after 1,290 days from that time, a blasphemous object that brings destruction will be set up. [12]Those who wait for the end of the 1,335 days will be happy.

[13]"As for you, Daniel, go your way until the end. You will get your rest, and at the end you will rise to receive your reward."

PSALM 138:1–3

A Hymn of Thanksgiving

A psalm of David.

138LORD, I will thank you with all my heart;
I will sing to you before the gods.
[2]I will bow down facing your holy Temple,
and I will thank you for your love and loyalty.
You have made your name and your word
greater than anything.
[3]On the day I called to you, you answered me.
You made me strong and brave.

PROVERBS 29:16

[16]When there are many wicked people,
there is much sin,
but those who do right will see them destroyed.

1 JOHN 2:1–29

Jesus Is Our Helper

2My dear children, I write this letter to you so you will not sin. But if anyone does sin, we have a helper in the presence of the Father—Jesus Christ, the One who does what is right. [2]He died in our place to take away our sins, and not only our sins but the sins of all people.

[3]We can be sure that we know God if we

obey his commands. [4]Anyone who says, "I know God," but does not obey God's commands is a liar, and the truth is not in that person. [5]But if someone obeys God's teaching, then in that person God's love has truly reached its goal. This is how we can be sure we are living in God: [6]Whoever says that he lives in God must live as Jesus lived.

The Command to Love Others

[7]My dear friends, I am not writing a new command to you but an old command you have had from the beginning. It is the teaching you have already heard. [8]But also I am writing a new command to you, and you can see its truth in Jesus and in you, because the darkness is passing away, and the true light is already shining.

[9]Anyone who says, "I am in the light,"[n] but hates a brother or sister, is still in the darkness. [10]Whoever loves a brother or sister lives in the light and will not cause anyone to stumble in his faith. [11]But whoever hates a brother or sister is in darkness, lives in darkness, and does not know where to go, because the darkness has made that person blind.

[12]I write to you, dear children,
because your sins are forgiven through Christ.
[13]I write to you, fathers,
because you know the One who existed from the beginning.
I write to you, young people,
because you have defeated the Evil One.
[14]I write to you, children,
because you know the Father.
I write to you, fathers,
because you know the One who existed from the beginning.
I write to you, young people,
because you are strong;
the teaching of God lives in you,
and you have defeated the Evil One.

[15]Do not love the world or the things in the world. If you love the world, the love of the Father is not in you. [16]These are the ways of the world: wanting to please our sinful selves, wanting the sinful things we see, and being too proud of what we have. None of

2:9 light Here, it is used as a symbol of God's goodness or truth.

these come from the Father, but all of them come from the world. [17]The world and everything that people want in it are passing away, but the person who does what God wants lives forever.

Reject the Enemies of Christ

[18]My dear children, these are the last days. You have heard that the enemy of Christ is coming, and now many enemies of Christ are already here. This is how we know that these are the last days. [19]These enemies of Christ were in our fellowship, but they left us. They never really belonged to us; if they had been a part of us, they would have stayed with us. But they left, and this shows that none of them really belonged to us. [20]You have the gift[n] that the Holy One gave you, so you all know the truth.[n] [21]I do not write to you because you do not know the truth but because you do know the truth. And you know that no lie comes from the truth.

[22]Who is the liar? It is the person who does not accept Jesus as the Christ. This is the enemy of Christ: the person who does not accept the Father and his Son. [23]Whoever does not accept the Son does not have the Father. But whoever confesses the Son has the Father, too.

[24]Be sure you continue to follow the teaching you heard from the beginning. If you continue to follow what you heard from the beginning, you will stay in the Son and in the Father. [25]And this is what the Son promised to us—life forever.

[26]I am writing this letter about those people who are trying to lead you the wrong way. [27]Christ gave you a special gift that is still in you, so you do not need any other teacher. His gift teaches you about everything, and it is true, not false. So continue to live in Christ, as his gift taught you.

[28]Yes, my dear children, live in him so that when Christ comes back, we can be without fear and not be ashamed in his presence. [29]Since you know that Christ is righteous, you know that all who do right are God's children.

DECEMBER 5

HOSEA 1:1—2:23

1The LORD spoke his word to Hosea son of Beeri during the time that Uzziah, Jotham, Ahaz, and Hezekiah were kings of Judah and Jeroboam son of Jehoash was king of Israel.

Hosea's Wife and Children

[2]When the LORD began speaking through Hosea, the LORD said to him, "Go, and marry an unfaithful woman and have unfaithful children, because the people in this country have been completely unfaithful to the LORD." [3]So Hosea married Gomer daughter of Diblaim, and she became pregnant and gave birth to Hosea's son.

[4]The LORD said to Hosea, "Name him Jezreel, because soon I will punish the family of Jehu for the people they killed at Jezreel. In the future I will put an end to the kingdom of Israel [5]and break the power of Israel's army in the Valley of Jezreel."

[6]Gomer became pregnant again and gave birth to a daughter. The LORD said to Hosea, "Name her Lo-Ruhamah,[n] because I will not pity Israel anymore, nor will I forgive them. [7]But I will show pity to the people of Judah. I will save them, but not by using bows or swords, horses or horsemen, or weapons of war. I, the LORD their God, will save them."

[8]After Gomer had stopped nursing Lo-Ruhamah, she became pregnant again and gave birth to another son. [9]The LORD said,

---

2:20 gift This might mean the Holy Spirit, or it might mean teaching or truth as in verse 24.   **2:20 you . . . truth** Some Greek copies read "so you know all things."   •   **1:6 Lo-Ruhamah** This name in Hebrew means "not pitied."

"Name him Lo-Ammi,ⁿ because you are not my people, and I am not your God.

God's Promise to Israel

¹⁰"But the number of the Israelites will become like the grains of sand of the sea, which no one can measure or count. They were called, 'You are not my people,' but later they will be called 'children of the living God.' ¹¹The people of Judah and Israel will join together again and will choose one leader for themselves. They will come up from the land, because the day of Jezreelⁿ will be truly great.

2 "You are to call your brothers, 'my people,' and your sisters, 'you have been shown pity.'

God Speaks About Israel

²"Plead with your mother.ⁿ
    Accuse her, because she is no longer my wife,
        and I am no longer her husband.
    Tell her to stop acting like a prostitute,
        to stop behaving like an unfaithful wife.
³If she refuses, I will strip her naked
        and leave her bare like the day she was born.
    I will make her dry like a desert,
        like a land without water,
        and I will kill her with thirst.
⁴I will not take pity on her children,
        because they are the children of a prostitute.
⁵Their mother has acted like a prostitute;
        the one who became pregnant with them has acted disgracefully.
    She said, 'I will chase after my lovers,ⁿ
        who give me my food and water,
        wool and flax, wine and olive oil.'
⁶So I will block her road with thornbushes;
    I will build a wall around her
        so she cannot find her way.
⁷She will run after her lovers,
        but she won't catch them.
    She will look for them,
        but she won't find them.

Then she will say, 'I will go back to my first husband,ⁿ
        because life was better then for me than it is now.'
⁸But she does not know that I was the one
        who gave her grain, new wine, and oil.
    I gave her much silver and gold,
        but she used it for Baal.

⁹"So I will come back and take away my grain at harvest time
        and my new wine when it is ready.
    I will take back my wool and linen
        that covered her nakedness.
¹⁰So I will show her nakedness to her lovers,
        and no one will save her from me.
¹¹I will put an end to all her celebrations:
        her yearly festivals, her New Moon festivals, and her Sabbaths.
    I will stop all of her special feasts.
¹²I will destroy her vines and fig trees,
        which she said were her pay from her lovers.
    I will turn them into a forest,
        and wild animals will eat them.
¹³I will punish her for all the times
        she burned incense to the Baals.
    She put on her rings and jewelry
        and went chasing after her lovers,
    but she forgot me!"
        says the LORD.

¹⁴"So I am going to attract her;
        I will lead her into the desert
        and speak tenderly to her.
¹⁵There I will give her back her vineyards,
        and I will make the Valley of Trouble a door of hope.
    There she will respond as when she was young,
        as when she came out of Egypt."
¹⁶The LORD says, "In the future she will call me 'my husband';
        no longer will she call me 'my baal.'ⁿ
¹⁷I will never let her say the names of Baal again;
        people won't use their names anymore.

1:9 Lo-Ammi This name in Hebrew means "not my people." **1:11 Jezreel** This name in Hebrew means "God plants." **2:2 mother** Refers to the nation of Israel here. **2:5 lovers** Refers to the nations surrounding Israel, who led Israel to worship false gods. **2:7 husband** Refers to God here. **2:16 baal** Another Hebrew word for husband, but it was the same word as the false god Baal.

[18]At that time I will make an agreement for
them
with the wild animals, the birds, and
the crawling things.
I will smash from the land
the bow and the sword and the
weapons of war,
so my people will live in safety.
[19]And I will make you my promised bride
forever.
I will be good and fair;
I will show you my love and mercy.
[20]I will be true to you as my promised bride,
and you will know the LORD.

[21]"At that time I will speak to you," says the
LORD.
"I will speak to the skies,
and they will give rain to the earth.
[22]The earth will produce grain, new wine,
and oil;
much will grow because my people are
called Jezreel.[n]
[23]I will plant my people in the land,
and I will show pity to the one I had
called 'not shown pity.'
I will say, 'You are my people'
to those I had called 'not my people.'
And they will say to me, 'You are our
God.'"

PSALM 138:4–5

[4]LORD, let all the kings of the earth praise
you
when they hear the words you speak.
[5]They will sing about what the LORD has
done,
because the LORD's glory is great.

PROVERBS 29:17

[17]Correct your children, and you will be
proud;
they will give you satisfaction.

1 JOHN 3:1–24

We Are God's Children

3 The Father has loved us so much that we
are called children of God. And we really

are his children. The reason the people in the
world do not know us is that they have not
known him. [2]Dear friends, now we are children of God, and we have not yet been
shown what we will be in the future. But we
know that when Christ comes again, we will
be like him, because we will see him as he really is. [3]Christ is pure, and all who have this
hope in Christ keep themselves pure like
Christ.
[4]The person who sins breaks God's law.
Yes, sin is living against God's law. [5]You know
that Christ came to take away sins and that
there is no sin in Christ. [6]So anyone who
lives in Christ does not go on sinning. Anyone who goes on sinning has never really
understood Christ and has never known
him.
[7]Dear children, do not let anyone lead you
the wrong way. Christ is righteous. So to be
like Christ a person must do what is right.
[8]The devil has been sinning since the beginning, so anyone who continues to sin belongs to the devil. The Son of God came for
this purpose: to destroy the devil's work.
[9]Those who are God's children do not
continue sinning, because the new life from
God remains in them. They are not able to go
on sinning, because they have become children of God. [10]So we can see who God's children are and who the devil's children are:
Those who do not do what is right are not
God's children, and those who do not love
their brothers and sisters are not God's children.

We Must Love Each Other

[11]This is the teaching you have heard
from the beginning: We must love each
other. [12]Do not be like Cain who belonged to
the Evil One and killed his brother. And why
did he kill him? Because the things Cain did
were evil, and the things his brother did were
good.
[13]Brothers and sisters, do not be surprised when the people of the world hate
you. [14]We know we have left death and have
come into life because we love each other.
Whoever does not love is still dead. [15]Every-

2:22 Jezreel This name in Hebrew means "God plants."

one who hates a brother or sister is a murderer,[n] and you know that no murderers have eternal life in them. [16]This is how we know what real love is: Jesus gave his life for us. So we should give our lives for our brothers and sisters. [17]Suppose someone has enough to live and sees a brother or sister in need, but does not help. Then God's love is not living in that person. [18]My children, we should love people not only with words and talk, but by our actions and true caring. [19-20]This is the way we know that we belong to the way of truth. When our hearts make us feel guilty, we can still have peace before God. God is greater than our hearts, and he knows everything. [21]My dear friends, if our hearts do not make us feel guilty, we can come without fear into God's presence. [22]And God gives us what we ask for because we obey God's commands and do what pleases him. [23]This is what God commands: that we believe in his Son, Jesus Christ, and that we love each other, just as he commanded. [24]The people who obey God's commands live in God, and God lives in them. We know that God lives in us because of the Spirit God gave us.

DECEMBER 6

HOSEA 3:1—4:19

Hosea Buys a Wife

3 The LORD said to me again, "Go, show your love to a woman loved by someone else, who has been unfaithful to you. In the same way the LORD loves the people of Israel, even though they worship other gods and love to eat the raisin cakes."[n]

[2]So I bought her for six ounces of silver and ten bushels of barley. [3]Then I told her, "You must wait for me for many days. You must not be a prostitute, and you must not have sexual relations with any other man. I will act the same way toward you."

[4]In the same way Israel will live many days without a king or leader, without sacrifices or holy stone pillars, and without the holy vest or an idol. [5]After this, the people of Israel will return to the LORD their God and follow him and the king from David's family. In the last days they will turn in fear to the LORD, and he will bless them.

The Lord's Word Against Israel

4 People of Israel, listen to the LORD's message.
The LORD has this
against you who live in the land:

"The people are not true, not loyal to God,
nor do those who live in the land even
know him.
[2]Cursing, lying, killing, stealing and
adultery are everywhere.
One murder follows another.
[3]Because of this the land dries up,
and all its people are dying.
Even the wild animals and the birds of
the air
and the fish of the sea are dying.

God's Case Against the Priests

[4]"No one should accuse
or blame another person.
Don't blame the people, you priests,
when they quarrel with you.
[5]You will be ruined in the day,
and your prophets will be ruined with
you in the night.
I will also destroy your mother.[n]
[6]My people will be destroyed,
because they have no knowledge.
You have refused to learn,
so I will refuse to let you be priests to me.
You have forgotten the teachings of your
God,
so I will forget your children.

3:15 Everyone . . . murderer If one person hates a brother or sister, then in the heart that person has killed that brother or sister. Jesus taught about this sin to his followers (Matthew 5:21–26). • **3:1 raisin cakes** This food was eaten in the feasts that honored false gods. **4:5 mother** Refers to the nation of Israel here.

[7]The more priests there are,
the more they sin against me.
I will take away their honor
and give them shame.
[8]Since the priests live off the sin offerings
of the people,
they want the people to sin more and
more.
[9]The priests are as wrong as the people,
and I will punish them both for what
they have done.
I will repay them for the wrong they
have done.

[10]"They will eat
but not have enough;
they will have sexual relations with the
prostitutes,
but they will not have children,
because they have left the LORD
to give themselves to [11]prostitution,
to old and new wine,
which take away their ability to
understand.

God's Case Against the People

[12]"My people ask wooden idols for advice;
they ask those sticks of wood to advise
them!
Like prostitutes, they have chased after
other gods
and have left their own God.
[13]They make sacrifices on the tops of the
mountains.
They burn offerings on the hills,
under oaks, poplars, and other trees,
because their shade is nice.
So your daughters become prostitutes,
and your daughters-in-law are guilty of
adultery.

[14]"But I will not punish your daughters
for becoming prostitutes,
nor your daughters-in-law
for their sins of adultery.
I will not punish them,
because the men have sexual relations
with prostitutes
and offer sacrifices with the temple
prostitutes.
A foolish people will be ruined.

[15]"Israel, you act like a prostitute,
but do not be guilty toward the LORD.
Don't go to Gilgal
or go up to Beth Aven.[n]
Don't make promises,
saying, 'As surely as the LORD lives ...'
[16]The people of Israel are stubborn
like a stubborn young cow.
Now the LORD will feed them
like lambs in the open country.
[17]The Israelites have chosen to worship
idols,
so leave them alone.
[18]When they finish their drinking,
they completely give themselves to
being prostitutes;
they love these disgraceful ways.
[19]They will be swept away as if by a
whirlwind,
and their sacrifices will bring them
only shame.

PSALM 138:6-8

[6]Though the LORD is supreme,
he takes care of those who are humble,
but he stays away from the proud.
[7]LORD, even when I have trouble all
around me,
you will keep me alive.
When my enemies are angry,
you will reach down and save me by
your power.
[8]LORD, you do everything for me.
LORD, your love continues forever.
Do not leave us, whom you made.

PROVERBS 29:18

[18]Where there is no word from God, people
are uncontrolled,
but those who obey what they have
been taught are happy.

1 JOHN 4:1-21

Warning Against False Teachers

4 My dear friends, many false prophets
have gone out into the world. So do not
believe every spirit, but test the spirits to
see if they are from God. [2]This is how you

---

can know God's Spirit: Every spirit who confesses that Jesus Christ came to earth as a human is from God. ³And every spirit who refuses to say this about Jesus is not from God. It is the spirit of the enemy of Christ, which you have heard is coming, and now he is already in the world.

⁴My dear children, you belong to God and have defeated them; because God's Spirit, who is in you, is greater than the devil, who is in the world. ⁵And they belong to the world, so what they say is from the world, and the world listens to them. ⁶But we belong to God, and those who know God listen to us. But those who are not from God do not listen to us. That is how we know the Spirit that is true and the spirit that is false.

Love Comes from God

⁷Dear friends, we should love each other, because love comes from God. Everyone who loves has become God's child and knows God. ⁸Whoever does not love does not know God, because God is love. ⁹This is how God showed his love to us: He sent his one and only Son into the world so that we could have life through him. ¹⁰This is what real love is: It is not our love for God; it is God's love for us. He sent his Son to die in our place to take away our sins. ¹¹Dear friends, if God loved us that much

we also should love each other. ¹²No one has ever seen God, but if we love each other, God lives in us, and his love is made perfect in us.

¹³We know that we live in God and he lives in us, because he gave us his Spirit. ¹⁴We have seen and can testify that the Father sent his Son to be the Savior of the world. ¹⁵Whoever confesses that Jesus is the Son of God has God living inside, and that person lives in God. ¹⁶And so we know the love that God has for us, and we trust that love.

God is love. Those who live in love live in God, and God lives in them. ¹⁷This is how love is made perfect in us: that we can be without fear on the day God judges us, because in this world we are like him. ¹⁸Where God's love is, there is no fear, because God's perfect love drives out fear. It is punishment that makes a person fear, so love is not made perfect in the person who fears.

¹⁹We love because God first loved us. ²⁰If people say, "I love God," but hate their brothers or sisters, they are liars. Those who do not love their brothers and sisters, whom they have seen, cannot love God, whom they have never seen. ²¹And God gave us this command: Those who love God must also love their brothers and sisters.

DECEMBER 7

HOSEA 5:1—7:2

God's Word Against the Leaders

5 "Listen, you priests.
  Pay attention, people of Israel.
Listen, royal family,
  because you will all be judged.
You have been like a trap at Mizpah
  and like a net spread out at Mount Tabor.
²You have done many evil things,
  so I will punish you all.
³I know all about the people of Israel;
  what they have done is not hidden from me.

Now that Israel acts like a prostitute,
  it has made itself unclean.

⁴"They will not give up their deeds
  and return to their God.
They are determined to be unfaithful to me;
  they do not know the LORD.
⁵Israel's pride testifies against them.
  The people of Israel will stumble
  because of their sin,
  and the people of Judah will stumble with them.
⁶They will come to worship the LORD,
  bringing their flocks and herds,

but they will not be able to find him,
    because he has left them.
[7]They have not been true to the LORD;
    they are children who do not belong to
        him.
So their false worship
    will destroy them and their land.

[8]"Blow the horn in Gibeah
    and the trumpet in Ramah.
Give the warning at Beth Aven,
    and be first into battle, people of
        Benjamin.
[9]Israel will be ruined
    on the day of punishment.
To the tribes of Israel
    I tell the truth.
[10]The leaders of Judah are like those
    who steal other people's land.
I will pour my punishment over them
    like a flood of water.
[11]Israel is crushed by the punishment,
    because it decided to follow idols.
[12]I am like a moth to Israel,
    like a rot to the people of Judah.

[13]"When Israel saw its illness
    and Judah saw its wounds,
Israel went to Assyria for help
    and sent to the great king of Assyria.
But he cannot heal you
    or cure your wounds.
[14]I will be like a lion to Israel,
    like a young lion to Judah.
I will attack them
    and tear them to pieces.
I will drag them off,
    and no one will be able to save them.
[15]Then I will go back to my place
    until they suffer for their guilt and turn
        back to me.
In their trouble they will look for me."

The People Are Not Faithful

6 "Come, let's go back to the LORD.
    He has hurt us, but he will heal us.
He has wounded us, but he will
    bandage our wounds.
[2]In two days he will put new life in us;
    on the third day he will raise us up

so that we may live in his presence [3]and
    know him.
Let's try to learn about the LORD;
    he will come to us as surely as the
        dawn comes.
He will come to us like rain,
    like the spring rain that waters the
        ground."

[4]The LORD says, "Israel, what should I do
    with you?
Judah, what should I do with you?
Your faithfulness is like a morning mist,
    like the dew that goes away early in the
        day.
[5]I have warned you by my prophets
    that I will kill you and destroy you.
My justice comes out like bright light.
[6]I want faithful love
    more than I want animal sacrifices.
I want people to know me
    more than I want burnt offerings.
[7]But they have broken the agreement as
        Adam did;
    they have been unfaithful to me.
[8]Gilead is a city of people who do evil;
    their footprints are bloody.
[9]The priests are like robbers waiting to
        attack people;
    they murder people on the road to
        Shechem[n]
    and do wicked things.
[10]I have seen horrible things in Israel.
    Look at Israel's prostitution;
    Israel has become unclean.

[11]"Judah, I have set a harvest time for you
    when I will make the lives of my people
        good again.

7 When I heal Israel,
    Israel's sin will go away,
    and so will Samaria's evil.

"They cheat a lot!
    Thieves break into houses,
    and robbers are in the streets.
[2]It never enters their minds
    that I remember all their evil deeds.
The bad things they do are all around
        them;
    they are right in front of me.

6:9 Shechem A city of safety where people could go for protection.

PSALM 139:1–6

God Knows Everything

For the director of music. A psalm of David.

139 LORD, you have examined me
and know all about me.
²You know when I sit down and when I
get up.
You know my thoughts before I think
them.
³You know where I go and where I lie
down.
You know everything I do.
⁴LORD, even before I say a word,
you already know it.
⁵You are all around me—in front and in
back—
and have put your hand on me.
⁶Your knowledge is amazing to me;
it is more than I can understand.

PROVERBS 29:19

¹⁹Words alone cannot correct a servant,
because even if they understand, they
won't respond.

1 JOHN 5:1–21

Faith in the Son of God

5 Everyone who believes that Jesus is the
Christ is God's child, and whoever loves
the Father also loves the Father's children.
²This is how we know we love God's children: when we love God and obey his commands. ³Loving God means obeying his
commands. And God's commands are not
too hard for us, ⁴because everyone who is a
child of God conquers the world. And this is
the victory that conquers the world—our
faith. ⁵So the one who conquers the world is
the person who believes that Jesus is the
Son of God.

⁶Jesus Christ is the One who came by water*ⁿ* and blood.*ⁿ* He did not come by water
only, but by water and blood. And the Spirit
says that this is true, because the Spirit is the
truth. ⁷So there are three witnesses:*ⁿ* ⁸the

Spirit, the water, and the blood; and these
three witnesses agree. ⁹We believe people
when they say something is true. But what
God says is more important, and he has told
us the truth about his own Son. ¹⁰Anyone
who believes in the Son of God has the truth
that God told us. Anyone who does not believe makes God a liar, because that person
does not believe what God told us about his
Son. ¹¹This is what God told us: God has
given us eternal life, and this life is in his
Son. ¹²Whoever has the Son has life, but
whoever does not have the Son of God does
not have life.

We Have Eternal Life Now

¹³I write this letter to you who believe in
the Son of God so you will know you have
eternal life. ¹⁴And this is the boldness we
have in God's presence: that if we ask God for
anything that agrees with what he wants, he
hears us. ¹⁵If we know he hears us every time
we ask him, we know we have what we ask
from him.

¹⁶If anyone sees a brother or sister sinning (sin that does not lead to eternal
death), that person should pray, and God
will give the sinner life. I am talking about
people whose sin does not lead to eternal
death. There is sin that leads to death. I do
not mean that a person should pray about
that sin. ¹⁷Doing wrong is always sin, but
there is sin that does not lead to eternal
death.

¹⁸We know that those who are God's children do not continue to sin. The Son of God
keeps them safe, and the Evil One cannot
touch them. ¹⁹We know that we belong to
God, but the Evil One controls the whole
world. ²⁰We also know that the Son of God
has come and has given us understanding so
that we can know the True One. And our
lives are in the True One and in his Son, Jesus Christ. He is the true God and the eternal
life.

²¹So, dear children, keep yourselves away
from false gods.

5:6 water This probably means the water of Jesus' baptism. **5:6 blood** This probably means the blood of Jesus' death.
5:7–8 So . . . witnesses A few very late Greek copies and the Latin Vulgate continue, "in heaven: the Father, the Word, and
the Holy Spirit, and these three witnesses agree. ⁸And there are three witnesses on earth:"

DECEMBER 8

HOSEA 7:3—8:14

Israel's Evil Kings

3"They make the king happy with their
    wickedness;
  their rulers are glad with their lies.
4But all of them are traitors.
  They are like an oven heated by a baker.
  While he mixes the dough,
    he does not need to stir up the fire.
5The kings get so drunk they get sick every
    day.
  The rulers become crazy with wine;
    they make agreements with those who
      do not know the true God.
6They burn like an oven;
    their hearts burn inside them.
  All night long their anger is low,
    but when morning comes, it becomes a
      roaring fire.
7All these people are as hot as an oven;
    they burn up their rulers.
  All their kings fall,
    and no one calls on me.

Israel and the Other Nations

8"Israel mixes with other nations;
  he is like a pancake cooked only on one
    side.
9Foreign nations have eaten up his
    strength,
  but he doesn't know it.
  Israel is weak and feeble, like an old man,
    but he doesn't know it.
10Israel's pride will cause their defeat;
  they will not turn back to the LORD their
    God
  or look to him for help in all this.
11Israel has become like a pigeon—
  easy to fool and stupid.
  First they call to Egypt for help.
  Then they run to Assyria.
12When they go, I will catch them in a net,
  I will bring them down like birds from
    the sky;
  I will punish them countless times for
    their evil.
13How terrible for them because they left
  me!

They will be destroyed, because they
    turned against me.
  I want to save them,
    but they have spoken lies against me.
14They do not call to me from their hearts.
  They just lie on their beds and cry.
  They come together to ask for grain and
    new wine,
    but they really turn away from me.
15Though I trained them and gave them
    strength,
  they have made evil plans against me.
16They did not turn to the Most High God.
  They are like a loose bow that can't
    shoot.
  Because their leaders brag about their
    strength,
    they will be killed with swords,
  and the people in Egypt
    will laugh at them.

Israel Has Trusted Wrong Things

8"Put the trumpet to your lips and give
    the warning!
  The enemy swoops down on the LORD's
    people like an eagle.
  The Israelites have broken my agreement
    and have turned against my teachings.
2They cry out to me,
  'Our God, we in Israel know you!'
3But Israel has rejected what is good,
  so the enemy will chase them.
4They chose their own kings
    without asking my permission.
  They chose their own leaders,
    people I did not know.
  They made their silver and gold into idols,
    and for all this they will be destroyed.
5I hate the calf-shaped idol of Israel!
  I am very angry with the people.
  How long will they remain unclean?
6The idol is something a craftsman made;
    it is not God.
  Israel's calf-shaped idol
    will surely be smashed to pieces.

7"Israel's foolish plans are like planting the
    wind,
  but they will harvest a storm.

Like a stalk with no head of grain,
it produces nothing.
Even if it produced something,
other nations would eat it.
[8]Israel is eaten up;
the people are mixed among the other
nations
and have become useless to me.
[9]Israel is like a wild donkey all by itself.
They have run to Assyria;
They have hired other nations to protect
them.
[10]Although Israel is mixed among the
nations,
I will gather them together.
They will become weaker and weaker
as they suffer under the great king of
Assyria.
[11]"Although Israel built more altars to
remove sin,
they have become altars for sinning.
[12]I have written many teachings for them,
but they think the teachings are strange
and foreign.
[13]The Israelites offer sacrifices to me as gifts
and eat the meat,
but the LORD is not pleased with them.
He remembers the evil they have done,
and he will punish them for their sins.
They will be slaves again as they were in
Egypt.
[14]Israel has forgotten their Maker and has
built palaces;
Judah has built many strong, walled
cities.
But I will send fire on their cities
and destroy their strong buildings."

PSALM 139:7–12

[7]Where can I go to get away from your
Spirit?
Where can I run from you?
[8]If I go up to the heavens, you are there.
If I lie down in the grave, you are
there.
[9]If I rise with the sun in the east

and settle in the west beyond the sea,
[10]even there you would guide me.
With your right hand you would hold
me.
[11]I could say, "The darkness will hide me.
Let the light around me turn into night."
[12]But even the darkness is not dark to you.
The night is as light as the day;
darkness and light are the same to you.

PROVERBS 29:20

[20]Do you see people who speak too quickly?
There is more hope for a foolish person
than for them.

2 JOHN 1–13

[1]From the Elder.[n]
To the chosen lady[n] and her children:
I love all of you in the truth,[n] and all those
who know the truth love you. [2]We love you because of the truth that lives in us and will be
with us forever.
[3]Grace, mercy, and peace from God the Father and his Son, Jesus Christ, will be with us
in truth and love.
[4]I was very happy to learn that some of
your children are following the way of truth, as
the Father commanded us. [5]And now, dear
lady, this is not a new command but is the
same command we have had from the beginning. I ask you that we all love each other. [6]And
love means living the way God commanded us
to live. As you have heard from the beginning,
his command is this: Live a life of love.
[7]Many false teachers are in the world now
who do not confess that Jesus Christ came to
earth as a human. Anyone who does not confess this is a false teacher and an enemy of
Christ. [8]Be careful yourselves that you do not
lose everything you[n] have worked for, but that
you receive your full reward.
[9]Anyone who goes beyond Christ's teaching and does not continue to follow only his
teaching does not have God. But whoever
continues to follow the teaching of Christ

has both the Father and the Son. [10]If someone comes to you and does not bring this teaching, do not welcome or accept that person into your house. [11]If you welcome such a person, you share in the evil work.

[12]I have many things to write to you, but I do not want to use paper and ink. Instead, I hope to come to you and talk face to face so we can be full of joy. [13]The children of your chosen sister[n] greet you.

DECEMBER 9

HOSEA 9:1—10:15

Israel's Punishment

9 Israel, do not rejoice;
 don't shout for joy as the other nations do.
  You have been like a prostitute against your God.
  You love the pay of prostitutes on every threshing floor.
 [2]But the threshing floor and the winepress will not feed the people,
  and there won't be enough new wine.
[3]The people will not stay in the LORD's land.
  Israel will return to being captives as they were in Egypt,
  and in Assyria they will eat food that they are not allowed to eat.
[4]The Israelites will not give offerings of wine to the LORD;
  they will not give him sacrifices.
  Their sacrifices will be like food that is eaten at a funeral;
  it is unclean, and everyone who eats it becomes unclean.
  Their food will only satisfy their hunger;
  they cannot sacrifice it in the Temple.
[5]What will you do then on the day of feasts
  and on the day of the LORD's festival?
[6]Even if the people are not destroyed,
  Egypt will capture them;
  Memphis[n] will bury them.
  Weeds will grow over their silver treasures,
  and thorns will drive them out of their tents.

[7]The time of punishment has come,
  the time to pay for sins.
  Let Israel know this:
  You think the prophet is a fool,
  and you say the spiritual person is crazy.
  You have sinned very much,
  and your hatred is great.
[8]Is Israel a watchman?
  Are God's people prophets?
  Everywhere Israel goes, traps are set for him.
  He is an enemy in God's house.
[9]The people of Israel have gone deep into sin
  as the people of Gibeah[n] did.
  The Lord will remember the evil things they have done,
  and he will punish their sins.

[10]"When I found Israel,
  it was like finding grapes in the desert.
  Your ancestors were like
  finding the first figs on the fig tree.
  But when they came to Baal Peor,
  they began worshiping an idol,
  and they became as hateful as the thing they worshiped.
[11]Israel's glory will fly away like a bird;
  there will be no more pregnancy, no more births, no more getting pregnant.
[12]But even if the Israelites bring up children,
  I will take them all away.
  How terrible it will be for them
  when I go away from them!
[13]I have seen Israel, like Tyre,
  given a pleasant place.

---

13 sister Sister of the "lady" in verse 1. This might be another woman or another church. • **9:6 Memphis** A city in Egypt famous for its tombs. **9:9 Gibeah** The sins of the people of Gibeah caused a civil war. See Judges 19–21.

But the people of Israel will soon bring out
their children to be killed."
[14]LORD, give them what they should have.
What will you give them?
Make their women unable to have
children;
give them dried-up breasts that cannot
feed their babies.

[15]"The Israelites were very wicked in Gilgal,
so I have hated them there.
Because of the sinful things they have
done,
I will force them to leave my land.
I will no longer love them;
their leaders have turned against me.
[16]Israel is beaten down;
its root is dying, and it has no fruit.
If they have more children,
I will kill the children they love."

[17]God will reject them,
because they have not obeyed him;
they will wander among the nations.

Israel Will Pay for Sin

10 Israel is like a large vine
that produced plenty of fruit.
As the people became richer,
they built more altars for idols.
As their land became better,
they put up better stone pillars to
honor gods.
[2]Their heart was false,
and now they must pay for their guilt.
The LORD will break down their altars;
he will destroy their holy stone pillars.

[3]Then they will say, "We have no king,
because we didn't honor the LORD.
As for the king,
he couldn't do anything for us."
[4]They make many false promises
and agreements which they don't keep.
So people sue each other in court;
they are like poisonous weeds growing
in a plowed field.
[5]The people from Israel are worried about
the calf-shaped idol at Beth Aven.
The people will cry about it,
and the priests will cry about it.

They used to shout for joy about its glory,
[6]but it will be carried off to Assyria
as a gift to the great king.
Israel will be disgraced,
and the people will be ashamed for not
obeying.
[7]Israel will be destroyed;
its king will be like a chip of wood
floating on the water.
[8]The places of false worship will be
destroyed,
the places where Israel sins.
Thorns and weeds will grow up
and cover their altars.
Then they will say to the mountains,
"Cover us!"
and to the hills, "Fall on us!"

[9]"Israel, you have sinned since the time of
Gibeah,[n]
and the people there have continued
sinning.
But war will surely overwhelm them in
Gibeah,
because of the evil they have done there.
[10]When I am ready,
I will come to punish them.
Nations will come together against them,
and they will be punished for their
double sins.
[11]Israel is like a well-trained young cow
that likes to thresh grain.
I will put a yoke on her neck
and make her work hard in the field.
Israel will plow,
and Judah will break up the ground.
[12]I said, 'Plant goodness,
harvest the fruit of loyalty,
plow the new ground of knowledge.
Look for the LORD until he comes
and pours goodness on you like water.'
[13]But you have plowed evil
and harvested trouble;
you have eaten the fruit of your lies.
Because you have trusted in your own
power
and your many soldiers,
[14]your people will hear the noise of battle,
and all your strong, walled cities will be
destroyed.

10:9 Gibeah The sins of the people of Gibeah caused a civil war. See Judges 19–21.

It will be like the time King Shalman
destroyed Beth Arbel in battle,
when mothers and their children were
bashed to death.
[15]The same will happen to you, people of
Bethel,
because you did so much evil.
When the sun comes up,
the king of Israel will die.

PSALM 139:13–16

[13]You made my whole being;
you formed me in my mother's body.
[14]I praise you because you made me in an
amazing and wonderful way.
What you have done is wonderful.
I know this very well.
[15]You saw my bones being formed
as I took shape in my mother's body.
When I was put together there,
[16] you saw my body as it was formed.
All the days planned for me
were written in your book
before I was one day old.

PROVERBS 29:21

[21]If you spoil your servants when they are
young,
they will bring you grief later on.

3 JOHN 1–15

[1]From the Elder.[n]
To my dear friend Gaius, whom I love in
the truth:[n]
[2]My dear friend, I know your soul is doing
fine, and I pray that you are doing well in every

way and that your health is good. [3]I was very
happy when some brothers and sisters came
and told me about the truth in your life and
how you are following the way of truth. [4]Nothing gives me greater joy than to hear that my
children are following the way of truth.

[5]My dear friend, it is good that you help
the brothers and sisters, even those you do
not know. [6]They told the church about your
love. Please help them to continue their trip
in a way worthy of God. [7]They started out in
service to Christ, and they have been accepting nothing from nonbelievers. [8]So we
should help such people; when we do, we
share in their work for the truth.

[9]I wrote something to the church, but
Diotrephes, who loves to be their leader, will
not listen to us. [10]So if I come, I will talk
about what Diotrephes is doing, about how
he lies and says evil things about us. But
more than that, he refuses to accept the
other brothers and sisters; he even stops
those who do want to accept them and puts
them out of the church.

[11]My dear friend, do not follow what is
bad; follow what is good. The one who does
good belongs to God. But the one who does
evil has never known God.

[12]Everyone says good things about
Demetrius, and the truth agrees with what
they say. We also speak well of him, and you
know what we say is true.

[13]I have many things I want to write you,
but I do not want to use pen and ink. [14]I hope
to see you soon and talk face to face. [15]Peace
to you. The friends here greet you. Please
greet each friend there by name.

DECEMBER 10

HOSEA 11:1—12:14

God's Love for Israel

11 "When Israel was a child, I loved him,
and I called my son out of Egypt.

[2]But when I called the people of Israel,
they went away from me.
They offered sacrifices to the Baals
and burned incense to the idols.
[3]It was I who taught Israel to walk,

---

1 Elder "Elder" means an older person. It can also mean a special leader in the church (as in Titus 1:5).   **1 truth** The truth or "Good News" about Jesus Christ that joins all believers together.

and I took them by the arms,
but they did not understand
that I had healed them.
[4]I led them with cords of human kindness,
with ropes of love.
I lifted the yoke from their neck
and bent down and fed them.

[5]"The Israelites will become captives again,
as they were in Egypt,
and Assyria will become their king,
because they refuse to turn back to God.
[6]War will sweep through their cities
and will destroy them
and kill them because of their wicked
plans.
[7]My people have made up their minds
to turn away from me.
The prophets call them to turn to me,
but none of them honors me at all.

[8]"Israel, how can I give you up?
How can I give you away, Israel?
I don't want to make you like Admah
or treat you like Zeboiim."[n]
My heart beats for you,
and my love for you stirs up my pity.
[9]I won't punish you in my anger,
and I won't destroy Israel again.
I am God and not a human;
I am the Holy One, and I am among you.
I will not come against you in anger.
[10]They will go after the LORD,
and he will roar like a lion.
When he roars,
his children will hurry to him from the
west.
[11]They will come swiftly
like birds from Egypt
and like doves from Assyria.
I will settle them again in their homes,"
says the LORD.

The Lord Is Against Israel

[12]Israel has surrounded me with lies;
the people have made evil plans.
And Judah turns against God,
the faithful Holy One.

12 What Israel does is as useless as
chasing the wind;
he chases the east wind all day.

They tell more and more lies
and do more and more violence.
They make agreements with Assyria,
and they send a gift of olive oil to Egypt.
[2]The LORD also has some things against
Judah.
He will punish Israel for what they have
done;
he will give them what they deserve.
[3]Their ancestor Jacob held on to his
brother's heel
while the two of them were being born.
When he grew to be a man,
he wrestled with God.
[4]When Jacob wrestled with the angel and
won,
he cried and asked for his blessing.
Later, God met with him at Bethel
and spoke with him there.
[5]It was the LORD God All-Powerful;
the LORD is his great name.
[6]You must return to your God;
love him, do what is just,
and always trust in him as your God.

[7]The merchants use dishonest scales;
they like to cheat people.
[8]Israel said, "I am rich! I am someone
with power!"
All their money will do them no good
because of the sins they have done.

[9]"But I am the LORD your God,
who brought you out of Egypt.
I will make you live in tents again
as you used to do on worship days.
[10]I spoke to the prophets
and gave them many visions;
through them, I taught my lessons to
you."

[11]The people of Gilead are evil,
worth nothing.
Though people sacrifice bulls at Gilgal,
their altars will become like piles of
stone
in a plowed field.
[12]Your ancestor Jacob fled to Northwest
Mesopotamia
where he worked to get a wife;
he tended sheep to pay for her.

11:8 Admah . . . Zeboiim Two other cities destroyed when God destroyed Sodom and Gomorrah.

¹³Later the LORD used a prophet
    to bring Jacob's descendants out of
    Egypt;
he used a prophet
    to take care of the Israelites.
¹⁴But the Israelites made the Lord angry
    when they killed other people,
    and they deserve to die for their crimes.
The Lord will make them pay
    for the disgraceful things they have done.

PSALM 139:17–24

¹⁷God, your thoughts are precious to me.
    They are so many!
¹⁸If I could count them,
    they would be more than all the grains
        of sand.
    When I wake up,
    I am still with you.

¹⁹God, I wish you would kill the wicked!
    Get away from me, you murderers!
²⁰They say evil things about you.
    Your enemies use your name
        thoughtlessly.
²¹LORD, I hate those who hate you;
    I hate those who rise up against you.
²²I feel only hate for them;
    they are my enemies.

²³God, examine me and know my heart;
    test me and know my anxious
        thoughts.
²⁴See if there is any bad thing in me.
    Lead me on the road to everlasting life.

PROVERBS 29:22

²²An angry person causes trouble;
    a person with a quick temper sins a lot.

JUDE 1–25

¹From Jude, a servant of Jesus Christ and
a brother of James.

To all who have been called by God. God
the Father loves you, and you have been kept
safe in Jesus Christ:

²Mercy, peace, and love be yours richly.

God Will Punish Sinners

³Dear friends, I wanted very much to
write you about the salvation we all share.
But I felt the need to write you about something else: I want to encourage you to fight
hard for the faith that was given the holy
people of God once and for all time. ⁴Some
people have secretly entered your group.
Long ago the prophets wrote about these
people who will be judged guilty. They are
against God and have changed the grace of
our God into a reason for sexual sin. They
also refuse to accept Jesus Christ, our only
Master and Lord.

⁵I want to remind you of some things you
already know: Remember that the Lordⁿ
saved his people by bringing them out of
the land of Egypt. But later he destroyed all those
who did not believe. ⁶And remember the angels who did not keep their place of power but
left their proper home. The Lord has kept
these angels in darkness, bound with everlasting chains, to be judged on the great day.
⁷Also remember the cities of Sodom and Go-
morrahⁿ and the other towns around them. In
the same way they were full of sexual sin and
people who desired sexual relations that God
does not allow. They suffer the punishment of
eternal fire, as an example for all to see.

⁸It is the same with these people who have
entered your group. They are guided by
dreams and make themselves filthy with sin.
They reject God's authority and speak against
the angels. ⁹Not even the archangelⁿ Michael,
when he argued with the devil about who
would have the body of Moses, dared to judge
the devil guilty. Instead, he said, "The Lord
punish you." ¹⁰But these people speak against
things they do not understand. And what they
do know, by feeling, as dumb animals know
things, are the very things that destroy them.
¹¹It will be terrible for them. They have fol-
lowed the way of Cain, and for money they
have given themselves to doing the wrong that
Balaam did. They have fought against God as
Korah did, and like Korah, they surely will be
destroyed. ¹²They are like dirty spots in your
special Christian meals you share. They eat

---

5 the Lord Some Greek copies read "Jesus." **7 Sodom and Gomorrah** Two cities God destroyed because they were so evil.
9 archangel The leader among God's angels or messengers.

with you and have no fear, caring only for themselves. They are clouds without rain, which the wind blows around. They are autumn trees without fruit that are pulled out of the ground. So they are twice dead. [13]They are like wild waves of the sea, tossing up their own shameful actions like foam. They are like stars that wander in the sky. A place in the blackest darkness has been kept for them forever.

[14]Enoch, the seventh descendant from Adam, said about these people: "Look, the Lord is coming with many thousands of his holy angels to [15]judge every person. He is coming to punish all who are against God for all the evil they have done against him. And he will punish the sinners who are against God for all the evil they have said against him."

[16]These people complain and blame others, doing the evil things they want to do. They brag about themselves, and they flatter others to get what they want.

A Warning and Things to Do

[17]Dear friends, remember what the apostles of our Lord Jesus Christ said before. [18]They said to you, "In the last times there will be people who laugh about God, following their own evil desires which are against God." [19]These are the people who divide you, people whose thoughts are only of this world, who do not have the Spirit.

[20]But dear friends, use your most holy faith to build yourselves up, praying in the Holy Spirit. [21]Keep yourselves in God's love as you wait for the Lord Jesus Christ with his mercy to give you life forever. [22]Show mercy to some people who have doubts. [23]Take others out of the fire, and save them. Show mercy mixed with fear to others, hating even their clothes which are dirty from sin.

Praise God

[24]God is strong and can help you not to fall. He can bring you before his glory without any wrong in you and can give you great joy. [25]He is the only God, the One who saves us. To him be glory, greatness, power, and authority through Jesus Christ our Lord for all time past, now, and forever. Amen.

DECEMBER 11

HOSEA 13:1—14:9

The Final Word Against Israel

13 People used to fear the tribe of Ephraim;
they were important people in Israel.
But they sinned by worshiping Baal,
so they must die.
[2]But they still keep on sinning more and more.
They make idols of their silver,
idols that are cleverly made,
the work of a craftsman.
Yet the people of Israel say to each other,
"Kiss those calf idols and sacrifice to them."
[3]So those people will be like the morning mist;
they will disappear like the morning dew.

They will be like chaff blown from the threshing floor,
like smoke going out a window.

[4]"I, the LORD, have been your God since you were in the land of Egypt.
You should have known no other God except me.
I am the only one who saves.
[5]I cared for them in the desert where it was hot and dry.
[6]I gave them food, and they became full and satisfied.
But then they became too proud and forgot me.
[7]That is why I will be like a lion to them,
like a leopard waiting by the road.
[8]I will attack like a bear robbed of her cubs,
ripping their bodies open.
I will devour them like a lion

and tear them apart like a wild
animal.

9"Israel, I will destroy you.
Who will be your helper then?
10What good is your king?
Can he save you in any of your towns?
What good are your leaders?
You said, 'Give us a king and leaders.'
11So I gave you a king, but only in anger,
and I took him away in my great anger.
12The sins of Israel are on record,
stored away, waiting for punishment.
13The pain of birth will come for him,
but he is like a foolish baby
who won't come out of its mother's
womb.
14Will I save them from the place of the
dead?
Will I rescue them from death?
Where is your sickness, death?
Where is your pain, place of death?
I will show them no mercy.
15Israel is doing well among the nations,
but the LORD will send a wind from the
east,
coming from the desert,
that will dry up his springs and wells of
water.
He will destroy from their treasure
houses everything of value.
16The nation of Israel will be ruined,
because it fought against God.
The people of Israel will die in war;
their children will be torn to pieces,
and their pregnant women will be
ripped open."

Israel Returns to God

14 Israel, return to the LORD your God,
because your sins have made you fall.
2Come back to the LORD
and say these words to him:
"Take away all our sin
and kindly receive us,
and we will keep the promises we made
to you.
3Assyria cannot save us,
nor will we trust in our horses.
We will not say again, 'Our gods,'
to the things our hands have made.
You show mercy to orphans."

4The LORD says,
"I will forgive them for leaving me
and will love them freely,
because I am not angry with them
anymore.
5I will be like the dew to Israel,
and they will blossom like a lily.
Like the cedar trees in Lebanon,
their roots will be firm.
6They will be like spreading branches,
like the beautiful olive trees
and the sweet-smelling cedars in
Lebanon.
7The people of Israel will again live under
my protection.
They will grow like the grain,
they will bloom like a vine,
and they will be as famous as the wine
of Lebanon.
8Israel, have nothing to do with idols.
I, the LORD, am the one who answers
your prayers and watches over you.
I am like a green pine tree;
your blessings come from me."

9A wise person will know these things,
and an understanding person will take
them to heart.
The LORD's ways are right.
Good people live by following them,
but those who turn against God die
because of them.

PSALM 140:1–5

A Prayer for Protection

For the director of music. A psalm of David.

140 LORD, rescue me from evil people;
protect me from cruel people
2who make evil plans,
who always start fights.
3They make their tongues sharp as a
snake's;
their words are like snake poison. *Selah*

4LORD, guard me from the power of
wicked people;
protect me from cruel people
who plan to trip me up.
5The proud hid a trap for me.
They spread out a net beside the road;
they set traps for me. *Selah*

PROVERBS 29:23

²³Pride will ruin people,
but those who are humble will be
honored.

REVELATION 1:1–20

John Tells About This Book

1 This is the revelation[n] of Jesus Christ, which God gave to him, to show his servants what must soon happen. And Jesus sent his angel to show it to his servant John, ²who has told everything he has seen. It is the word of God; it is the message from Jesus Christ. ³Blessed is the one who reads the words of God's message, and blessed are the people who hear this message and do what is written in it. The time is near when all of this will happen.

Jesus' Message to the Churches

⁴From John.

To the seven churches in Asia:

Grace and peace to you from the One who is and was and is coming, and from the seven spirits before his throne, ⁵and from Jesus Christ. Jesus is the faithful witness, the first among those raised from the dead. He is the ruler of the kings of the earth.

He is the One who loves us, who made us free from our sins with the blood of his death. ⁶He made us to be a kingdom of priests who serve God his Father. To Jesus Christ be glory and power forever and ever! Amen.

⁷Look, Jesus is coming with the clouds, and everyone will see him, even those who stabbed him. And all peoples of the earth will cry loudly because of him. Yes, this will happen! Amen.

⁸The Lord God says, "I am the Alpha and the Omega.[n] I am the One who is and was and is coming. I am the Almighty."

⁹I, John, am your brother. All of us share with Christ in suffering, in the kingdom, and in patience to continue. I was on the island of Patmos,[n] because I had preached the word of God and the message about Jesus. ¹⁰On the Lord's day I was in the Spirit, and I heard a loud voice behind me that sounded like a trumpet. ¹¹The voice said, "Write what you see in a book and send it to the seven churches: to Ephesus, Smyrna, Pergamum, Thyatira, Sardis, Philadelphia, and Laodicea."

¹²I turned to see who was talking to me. When I turned, I saw seven golden lampstands ¹³and someone among the lampstands who was "like a Son of Man."[n] He was dressed in a long robe and had a gold band around his chest. ¹⁴His head and hair were white like wool, as white as snow, and his eyes were like flames of fire. ¹⁵His feet were like bronze that glows hot in a furnace, and his voice was like the noise of flooding water. ¹⁶He held seven stars in his right hand, and a sharp double-edged sword came out of his mouth. He looked like the sun shining at its brightest time.

¹⁷When I saw him, I fell down at his feet like a dead man. He put his right hand on me and said, "Do not be afraid. I am the First and the Last. ¹⁸I am the One who lives; I was dead, but look, I am alive forever and ever! And I hold the keys to death and to the place of the dead. ¹⁹So write the things you see, what is now and what will happen later. ²⁰Here is the secret of the seven stars that you saw in my right hand and the seven golden lampstands: The seven lampstands are the seven churches, and the seven stars are the angels of the seven churches.

DECEMBER 12

JOEL 1:1—3:21

Locusts Destroy the Crops

1 The LORD spoke his word to Joel son of Pethuel:

²Elders, listen to this message.
Listen to me, all you who live in the land.
Nothing like this has ever happened
during your lifetime
or during your ancestors' lifetimes.

1:1 revelation Making known truth that has been hidden. **1:8 Alpha and the Omega** The first and last letters of the Greek alphabet. This means "the beginning and the end." **1:9 Patmos** A small island in the Aegean Sea, near the coast of Asia Minor (modern Turkey). **1:13 "like ... Man"** "Son of Man" is a name Jesus called himself.

[3]Tell your children about these things,
let your children tell their children,
and let your grandchildren tell their
children.

[4]What the cutting locusts have left,
the swarming locusts have eaten;
what the swarming locusts have left,
the hopping locusts have eaten,
and what the hopping locusts have left,
the destroying locusts[n] have eaten.

[5]Drunks, wake up and cry!
All you people who drink wine, cry!
Cry because your wine
has been taken away from your
mouths.

[6]A powerful nation has come into my
land
with too many soldiers to count.
It has teeth like a lion,
jaws like a female lion.

[7]It has made my grapevine a waste
and made my fig tree a stump.
It has stripped all the bark off my trees
and left the branches white.

[8]Cry as a young woman cries
when the man she was going to marry
has died.

[9]There will be no more grain or drink
offerings
to offer in the Temple of the LORD.
Because of this, the priests,
the servants of the LORD, are sad.

[10]The fields are ruined;
the ground is dried up.
The grain is destroyed,
the new wine is dried up,
and the olive oil runs out.

[11]Be sad, farmers.
Cry loudly, you who grow grapes.
Cry for the wheat and the barley.
Cry because the harvest of the field is
lost.

[12]The vines have become dry,
and the fig trees are dried up.
The pomegranate trees, the date palm
trees, the apple trees—
all the trees in the field have died.

And the happiness of the people has
died, too.

[13]Priests, put on your rough cloth and cry
to show your sadness.
Servants of the altar, cry out loud.
Servants of my God,
keep your rough cloth on all night to
show your sadness.
Cry because there will be no more grain
or drink offerings
to offer in the Temple of your God.

[14]Call for a day when everyone fasts!
Tell everyone to stop work!
Bring the elders
and everyone who lives in the land
to the Temple of the LORD your God,
and cry out to the LORD.

[15]What a terrible day it will be!
The LORD's day of judging is near,
when punishment will come
like a destroying attack from the
Almighty.

[16]Our food is taken away
while we watch.
Joy and happiness are gone
from the Temple of our God.

[17]Though we planted fig seeds,
they lie dry and dead in the dirt.
The barns are empty and falling
down.
The storerooms for grain have been
broken down,
because the grain has dried up.

[18]The animals are groaning!
The herds of cattle wander around
confused,
because they have no grass to eat;
even the flocks of sheep suffer.

[19]LORD, I am calling to you for help,
because fire has burned up the open
pastures,
and flames have burned all the trees in
the field.

[20]Wild animals also need your help.
The streams of water have dried up,
and fire has burned up the open
pastures.

1:4 cutting ... locusts These are different names for an insect like a large grasshopper. The locust can quickly destroy trees, plants, and crops, and in this destruction, Joel sees a warning. God will cause this type of destruction when he punishes his people.

The Coming Day of Judgment

2 Blow the trumpet in Jerusalem;
  shout a warning on my holy mountain.
  Let all the people who live in the land
      shake with fear,
    because the LORD's day of judging is
      coming;
    it is near.
²It will be a dark, gloomy day,
    cloudy and black.
  Like the light at sunrise,
    a great and powerful army will spread
      over the mountains.
  There has never been anything like it
      before,
    and there will never be anything like it
      again.
³In front of them a fire destroys;
    in back of them a flame burns.
  The land in front of them is like the
      garden of Eden;
    the land behind them is like an empty
      desert.
  Nothing will escape from them.
⁴They look like horses,
    and they run like war horses.
⁵It is like the noise of chariots
      rumbling over the tops of the
      mountains,
    like the noise of a roaring fire
      burning dry stalks.
  They are like a powerful army lined up
      for battle.
⁶When they see them, nations shake with
      fear,
    and everyone's face becomes pale.

⁷They charge like soldiers;
    they climb over the wall like warriors.
  They all march straight ahead
    and do not move off their path.
⁸They do not run into each other,
    because each walks in line.
  They break through all efforts to stop
      them
    and keep coming.
⁹They run into the city.
  They run at the wall
  and climb into the houses,
    entering through windows like
      thieves.

¹⁰Before them, earth and sky shake.
  The sun and the moon become dark,
    and the stars stop shining.
¹¹The LORD shouts out orders
    to his army.
  His army is very large!
  Those who obey him are very strong!
  The LORD's day of judging
    is an overwhelming and terrible day.
  No one can stand up against it!

Change Your Hearts

¹²The LORD says, "Even now, come back to
      me with all your heart.
    Fast, cry, and be sad."

¹³Tearing your clothes is not enough to
      show you are sad;
    let your heart be broken.
  Come back to the LORD your God,
    because he is kind and shows mercy.
  He doesn't become angry quickly,
    and he has great love.
  He can change his mind about doing
      harm.
¹⁴Who knows? Maybe he will turn back to
      you
    and leave behind a blessing for you.
  Grain and drink offerings belong to the
      LORD your God.

¹⁵Blow the trumpet in Jerusalem;
    call for a day when everyone fasts.
  Tell everyone to stop work.
¹⁶Bring the people together
    and make the meeting holy for the LORD.
  Bring together the elders,
    as well as the children,
    and even babies that still feed at their
      mothers' breasts.
  The bridegroom should come from his
      room,
    the bride from her bedroom.
¹⁷The priests, the LORD's servants, should
      cry
    between the altar and the entrance to
      the Temple.
  They should say, "LORD, have mercy on
      your people.
  Don't let them be put to shame;
    don't let other nations make fun of
      them.

Don't let people in other nations ask,
'Where is their God?'"

The Lord Restores the Land

¹⁸Then the LORD became concerned about
his land
and felt sorry for his people.
¹⁹He said to them:
"I will send you grain, new wine, and
olive oil,
so that you will have plenty.
No more will I shame you
among the nations.
²⁰I will force the army from the north to
leave your land
and go into a dry, empty land.
Their soldiers in front will be forced into
the Dead Sea,
and those in the rear into the
Mediterranean Sea.
Their bodies will rot and stink.
The LORD has surely done a wonderful
thing!"

²¹Land, don't be afraid;
be happy and full of joy,
because the LORD has done a wonderful
thing.
²²Wild animals, don't be afraid,
because the open pastures have grown
grass.
The trees have given fruit;
the fig trees and the grapevines have
grown much fruit.
²³So be happy, people of Jerusalem;
be joyful in the LORD your God.
Because he does what is right,
he has brought you rain;
he has sent the fall rain
and the spring rain for you, as before.
²⁴And the threshing floors will be full of
grain;
the barrels will overflow with new wine
and olive oil.

The Lord Speaks

²⁵"Though I sent my great army against
you—

those swarming locusts and hopping
locusts,
the destroying locusts and the cutting
locusts*ⁿ* that ate your crops—
I will pay you back
for those years of trouble.
²⁶Then you will have plenty to eat
and be full.
You will praise the name of the LORD
your God,
who has done miracles for you.
My people will never again be shamed.
²⁷Then you will know that I am among the
people of Israel,
that I am the LORD your God,
and there is no other God.
My people will never be shamed again.

²⁸"After this,
I will pour out my Spirit on all kinds of
people.
Your sons and daughters will prophesy,
your old men will dream dreams,
and your young men will see visions.
²⁹At that time I will pour out my Spirit
also on male slaves and female slaves.
³⁰I will show miracles
in the sky and on the earth:
blood, fire, and thick smoke.
³¹The sun will become dark,
the moon red as blood,
before the overwhelming and terrible
day of the LORD comes.
³²Then anyone who calls on the LORD
will be saved,
because on Mount Zion and in Jerusalem
there will be people who will be saved,
just as the LORD has said.
Those left alive after the day of punishment
are the people whom the LORD called.

Punishment for Judah's Enemies

3 "In those days and at that time,
when I will make things better for
Judah and Jerusalem,
²I will gather all the nations together
and bring them down into the Valley
Where the LORD Judges.

2:25 swarming ... locusts These are different names for an insect like a large grasshopper. The locust can quickly destroy
trees, plants, and crops, and in this destruction, Joel sees a warning. God will cause this type of destruction when he punishes his people.

There I will judge them,
because those nations scattered my own
   people Israel
and forced them to live in other nations.
They divided up my land
3and threw lots for my people.
They traded boys for prostitutes,
   and they sold girls to buy wine to drink.
4"Tyre and Sidon and all of you regions of
Philistia! What did you have against me?
Were you punishing me for something I did,
or were you doing something to hurt me? I
will very quickly do to you what you have
done to me. 5You took my silver and gold,
and you put my precious treasures in your
temples. 6You sold the people of Judah and
Jerusalem to the Greeks so that you could
send them far from their land.

7"You sent my people to that faraway place,
but I will get them and bring them back, and
I will do to you what you have done to them.
8I will sell your sons and daughters to the
people of Judah, and they will sell them to the
Sabean people far away." The LORD said this.

God Judges the Nations

9Announce this among the nations:
   Prepare for war!
   Wake up the soldiers!
   Let all the men of war come near and
      attack.
10Make swords from your plows,
   and make spears from your hooks for
      trimming trees.
   Let even the weak person say,
   "I am a soldier."
11All of you nations, hurry,
   and come together in that place.
LORD, send your soldiers
   to gather the nations.

12"Wake up, nations,
   and come to attack in the Valley Where
      the LORD Judges.
   There I will sit to judge
   all the nations on every side.
13Swing the cutting tool,
   because the harvest is ripe.
   Come, walk on them as you would walk
      on grapes to get their juice,

because the winepress is full
   and the barrels are spilling over,
because these people are so evil!"

14There are huge numbers of people
   in the Valley of Decision,n
because the LORD's day of judging is near
   in the Valley of Decision.
15The sun and the moon will become dark,
   and the stars will stop shining.
16The LORD will roar like a lion from
      Jerusalem;
   his loud voice will thunder from that
      city,
   and the sky and the earth will shake.
But the LORD will be a safe place for his
      people,
   a strong place of safety for the people of
      Israel.

17"Then you will know that I, the LORD
      your God,
   live on my holy Mount Zion.
Jerusalem will be a holy place,
   and strangers will never even go
      through it again.

A New Life Promised for Judah

18"On that day wine will drip from the
      mountains,
   milk will flow from the hills,
   and water will run through all the
      ravines of Judah.
A fountain will flow from the Temple of
      the LORD
   and give water to the valley of acacia
      trees.
19But Egypt will become empty,
   and Edom an empty desert,
because they were cruel to the people of
      Judah.
   They killed innocent people in that
      land.
20But there will always be people living in
      Judah,
   and people will live in Jerusalem from
      now on.
21Egypt and Edom killed my people,
   so I will definitely punish them."

The LORD lives in Jerusalem!

3:14 Valley of Decision This is like the name "Valley Where the LORD Judges" in 3:2 and 3:12.

PSALM 140:6–13

[6] I said to the LORD, "You are my God."
   LORD, listen to my prayer for help.
[7] LORD God, my mighty savior,
   you protect me in battle.
[8] LORD, do not give the wicked what they
      want.
   Don't let their plans succeed,
   or they will become proud.   *Selah*

[9] Those around me have planned trouble.
   Now let it come to them.
[10] Let burning coals fall on them.
   Throw them into the fire
   or into pits from which they cannot
      escape.
[11] Don't let liars settle in the land.
   Let evil quickly hunt down cruel
      people.

[12] I know the LORD will get justice for the
      poor
   and will defend the needy in court.
[13] Good people will praise his name;
   honest people will live in his presence.

PROVERBS 29:24

[24] Partners of thieves are their own worst
      enemies.
   If they have to testify in court, they are
      afraid to say anything.

REVELATION 2:1–29

To the Church in Ephesus

2 "Write this to the angel of the church in
  Ephesus:

"The One who holds the seven stars in his
right hand and walks among the seven
golden lampstands says this: [2] I know what
you do, how you work hard and never give
up. I know you do not put up with the false
teachings of evil people. You have tested
those who say they are apostles but really are
not, and you found they are liars. [3] You have
patience and have suffered troubles for my
name and have not given up.

[4] "But I have this against you: You have left
the love you had in the beginning. [5] So remember where you were before you fell. Change
your hearts and do what you did at first. If you
do not change, I will come to you and will take
away your lampstand from its place. [6] But there
is something you do that is right: You hate
what the Nicolaitans[n] do, as much as I.

[7] "Every person who has ears should listen
to what the Spirit says to the churches. To
those who win the victory I will give the
right to eat the fruit from the tree of life,
which is in the garden of God.

To the Church in Smyrna

[8] "Write this to the angel of the church in
Smyrna:

"The One who is the First and the Last,
who died and came to life again, says this: [9] I
know your troubles and that you are poor,
but really you are rich! I know the bad things
some people say about you. They say they
are Jews, but they are not true Jews. They are
a synagogue that belongs to Satan. [10] Do not
be afraid of what you are about to suffer. I tell
you, the devil will put some of you in prison
to test you, and you will suffer for ten days.
But be faithful, even if you have to die, and I
will give you the crown of life.

[11] "Everyone who has ears should listen to
what the Spirit says to the churches. Those
who win the victory will not be hurt by the
second death.

To the Church in Pergamum

[12] "Write this to the angel of the church in
Pergamum:

"The One who has the sharp, double-
edged sword says this: [13] I know where you
live. It is where Satan has his throne. But you
are true to me. You did not refuse to tell
about your faith in me even during the time
of Antipas, my faithful witness who was
killed in your city, where Satan lives.

[14] "But I have a few things against you: You
have some there who follow the teaching of
Balaam. He taught Balak how to cause the
people of Israel to sin by eating food offered
to idols and by taking part in sexual sins.
[15] You also have some who follow the teaching of the Nicolaitans.[n] [16] So change your

---

2:6, 15 Nicolaitans This is the name of a religious group that followed false beliefs and ideas.

hearts and lives. If you do not, I will come to you quickly and fight against them with the sword that comes out of my mouth.

¹⁷"Everyone who has ears should listen to what the Spirit says to the churches.

"I will give some of the hidden manna to everyone who wins the victory. I will also give to each one who wins the victory a white stone with a new name written on it. No one knows this new name except the one who receives it.

To the Church in Thyatira

¹⁸"Write this to the angel of the church in Thyatira:

"The Son of God, who has eyes that blaze like fire and feet like shining bronze, says this: ¹⁹I know what you do. I know about your love, your faith, your service, and your patience. I know that you are doing more now than you did at first.

²⁰"But I have this against you: You let that woman Jezebel spread false teachings. She says she is a prophetess, but by her teaching she leads my people to take part in sexual sins and to eat food that is offered to idols.

²¹I have given her time to change her heart and turn away from her sin, but she does not want to change. ²²So I will throw her on a bed of suffering. And all those who take part in adultery with her will suffer greatly if they do not turn away from the wrongs she does. ²³I will also kill her followers. Then all the churches will know I am the One who searches hearts and minds, and I will repay each of you for what you have done.

²⁴"But others of you in Thyatira have not followed her teaching and have not learned what some call Satan's deep secrets. I say to you that I will not put any other load on you. ²⁵Only continue in your loyalty until I come.

²⁶"I will give power over the nations to everyone who wins the victory and continues to be obedient to me until the end.

²⁷'You will rule over them with an iron rod, as when pottery is broken into pieces.'

Psalm 2:9

²⁸This is the same power I received from my Father. I will also give him the morning star. ²⁹Everyone who has ears should listen to what the Spirit says to the churches.

DECEMBER 13

AMOS 1:1—3:15

1 These are the words of Amos, one of the shepherds from the town of Tekoa. He saw this vision about Israel two years before the earthquake. It was at the time Uzziah was king of Judah and Jeroboam son of Jehoash was king of Israel.

²Amos said,

"The LORD will roar from Jerusalem;
 he will send his voice from Jerusalem.
The pastures of the shepherds will
  become dry,
 and even the top of Mount Carmel will
  dry up."

Israel's Neighbors Are Punished

The People of Aram

³This is what the LORD says:
"For the many crimes of Damascus,

I will punish them.
They drove over the people of Gilead
 with threshing boards that had iron
  teeth.
⁴So I will send fire upon the house of
  Hazael
 that will destroy the strong towers of
  Ben-Hadad.
⁵I will break down the bar of the gate to
  Damascus
 and destroy the king who is in the
  Valley of Aven,
 as well as the leader of Beth Eden.
The people of Aram will be taken
  captive to the country of Kir," says
  the LORD.

The People of Philistia

⁶This is what the LORD says:
"For the many crimes of Gaza,

I will punish them.
They sold all the people of one area
  as slaves to Edom.
[7]So I will send a fire on the walls of Gaza
  that will destroy the city's strong
    buildings.
[8]I will destroy the king of the city of
    Ashdod,
  as well as the leader of Ashkelon.
Then I will turn against the people of the
    city of Ekron,
  and the last of the Philistines will die,"
  says the Lord God.

The People of Phoenicia

[9]This is what the Lord says:
"For the many crimes of Tyre,
  I will punish them.
They sold all the people of one area
  as slaves to Edom,
  and they forgot the agreement among
    relatives they had made with Israel.
[10]So I will send fire on the walls of Tyre
  that will destroy the city's strong
    buildings."

The People of Edom

[11]This is what the Lord says:
"For the many crimes of Edom,
  I will punish them.
They hunted down their relatives, the
    Israelites, with the sword,
  showing them no mercy.
They were angry all the time
  and kept on being very angry.
[12]So I will send fire on the city of Teman
  that will even destroy the strong
    buildings of Bozrah."[n]

The People of Ammon

[13]This is what the Lord says:
"For the many crimes of Ammon,
  I will punish them.
They ripped open the pregnant women
    in Gilead
  so they could take over that land
  and make their own country larger.
[14]So I will send fire on the city wall of
    Rabbah
  that will destroy its strong buildings.

It will come during a day of battle,
  during a stormy day with strong winds.
[15]Then their king and leaders will be taken
    captive;
  they will all be taken away together,"
  says the Lord.

The People of Moab

2 This is what the Lord says:
"For the many crimes of Moab,
  I will punish them.
They burned the bones of the king of
    Edom into lime.
[2]So I will send fire on Moab
  that will destroy the strong buildings of
    the city of Kerioth.
The people of Moab will die in a great
    noise,
  in the middle of the sounds of war and
    trumpets.
[3]So I will bring an end to the king of Moab,
  and I will kill all its leaders with him,"
  says the Lord.

The People of Judah

[4]This is what the Lord says:
"For the many crimes of Judah,
  I will punish them.
They rejected the teachings of the Lord
  and did not keep his commands;
they followed the same gods
  as their ancestors had followed.
[5]So I will send fire on Judah,
  and it will destroy the strong buildings
    of Jerusalem."

Israel Is Punished

[6]This is what the Lord says:
"For the many crimes of Israel,
  I will punish them.
For silver, they sell people who have done
    nothing wrong;
  they sell the poor to buy a pair of
    sandals.
[7]They walk on poor people as if they were
    dirt,
  and they refuse to be fair to those who
    are suffering.
Fathers and sons have sexual relations
    with the same woman,

1:12 Teman . . . Bozrah Since Teman was in northern Edom and Bozrah was in southern Edom, this means the whole country will be destroyed.

and so they ruin my holy name.
⁸As they worship at their altars,
  they lie down on clothes taken from the
    poor.
They fine people,
  and with that money they buy wine to
    drink in the house of their god.

⁹"But it was I who destroyed the Amorites
    before them,
  who were tall like cedar trees and as
    strong as oaks—
I destroyed them completely.
¹⁰It was I who brought you from the land
    of Egypt
  and led you for forty years through the
    desert
  so I could give you the land of the
    Amorites.
¹¹I made some of your children to be
    prophets
  and some of your young people to be
    Nazirites.
People of Israel, isn't this true?" says the
    Lord.
¹²"But you made the Nazirites drink wine
  and told the prophets not to prophesy.
¹³Now I will make you get stuck,
  as a wagon loaded with grain gets
    stuck.
¹⁴No one will escape, not even the fastest
    runner.
  Strong people will not be strong
    enough;
  warriors will not be able to save
    themselves.
¹⁵Soldiers with bows and arrows will not
    stand and fight,
  and even fast runners will not get away;
  soldiers on horses will not escape alive.
¹⁶At that time even the bravest warriors
  will run away without their armor," says
    the Lord.

Warning to Israel

3 Listen to this word that the Lord has spoken against you, people of Israel, against
the whole family he brought out of Egypt.
²"I have chosen only you
  out of all the families of the earth,
  so I will punish you
    for all your sins."

³Two people will not walk together
  unless they have agreed to do so.
⁴A lion in the forest does not roar
  unless it has caught an animal;
  it does not growl in its den
    when it has caught nothing.
⁵A bird will not fall into a trap
  where there is no bait;
  the trap will not spring shut
    if there is nothing to catch.
⁶When a trumpet blows a warning in a
    city,
  the people tremble.
When trouble comes to a city,
  the Lord has caused it.
⁷Before the Lord God does anything,
  he tells his plans to his servants the
    prophets.
⁸The lion has roared!
  Who wouldn't be afraid?
The Lord God has spoken.
  Who will not prophesy?

⁹Announce this to the strong buildings of
    Ashdod
  and to the strong buildings of Egypt:
"Come to the mountains of Samaria,
  where you will see great confusion
  and people hurting others."

¹⁰"The people don't know how to do what
    is right," says the Lord.
  "Their strong buildings are filled with
    treasures they took by force from
    others."
¹¹So this is what the Lord God says:
"An enemy will take over the land
  and pull down your strongholds;
  he will take the treasures out of your
    strong buildings."
¹²This is what the Lord says:
"A shepherd might save from a lion's
    mouth
  only two leg bones or a scrap of an ear
    of his sheep.
In the same way only a few Israelites in
    Samaria will be saved—
  people who now sit on their beds
  and on their couches."

¹³"Listen and be witnesses against the
family of Jacob," says the Lord God, the God
All-Powerful.

[14]"When I punish Israel for their sins,
I will also destroy the altars at Bethel.
The corners of the altar will be cut off,
and they will fall to the ground.
[15]I will tear down the winter house,
together with the summer house.
The houses decorated with ivory will be
destroyed,
and the great houses will come to an
end," says the LORD.

PSALM 141:1–4

A Prayer Not to Sin

A psalm of David.

141 LORD, I call to you. Come quickly.
Listen to me when I call to you.
[2]Let my prayer be like incense placed
before you,
and my praise like the evening
sacrifice.

[3]LORD, help me control my tongue;
help me be careful about what I say.
[4]Take away my desire to do evil
or to join others in doing wrong.
Don't let me eat tasty food
with those who do evil.

PROVERBS 29:25

[25]Being afraid of people can get you into
trouble,
but if you trust the LORD, you will be safe.

REVELATION 3:1–22

To the Church in Sardis

3 "Write this to the angel of the church in
Sardis:

"The One who has the seven spirits and
the seven stars says this: I know what you do.
People say that you are alive, but really you
are dead. [2]Wake up! Strengthen what you
have left before it dies completely. I have
found that what you are doing is less than
what my God wants. [3]So do not forget what
you have received and heard. Obey it, and
change your hearts and lives. So you must
wake up, or I will come like a thief, and you
will not know when I will come to you. [4]But
you have a few there in Sardis who have kept
their clothes unstained, so they will walk
with me and will wear white clothes, because
they are worthy. [5]Those who win the victory
will be dressed in white clothes like them.
And I will not erase their names from the
book of life, but I will say they belong to me
before my Father and before his angels.
[6]Everyone who has ears should listen to
what the Spirit says to the churches.

To the Church in Philadelphia

[7]"Write this to the angel of the church in
Philadelphia:

"This is what the One who is holy and
true, who holds the key of David, says. When
he opens a door, no one can close it. And
when he closes it, no one can open it. [8]I know
what you do. I have put an open door before
you, which no one can close. I know you have
little strength, but you have obeyed my
teaching and were not afraid to speak my
name. [9]Those in the synagogue that belongs
to Satan say they are Jews, but they are not
true Jews; they are liars. I will make them
come before you and bow at your feet, and
they will know that I have loved you. [10]You
have obeyed my teaching about not giving
up your faith. So I will keep you from the
time of trouble that will come to the whole
world to test those who live on earth.

[11]"I am coming soon. Continue strong in
your faith so no one will take away your
crown. [12]I will make those who win the victory pillars in the temple of my God, and
they will never have to leave it. I will write on
them the name of my God and the name of
the city of my God, the new Jerusalem,[n] that
comes down out of heaven from my God. I
will also write on them my new name.
[13]Everyone who has ears should listen to
what the Spirit says to the churches.

To the Church in Laodicea

[14]"Write this to the angel of the church in
Laodicea:

"The Amen,[n] the faithful and true witness,
the ruler of all God has made, says this: [15]I
know what you do, that you are not hot or cold.

3:12 Jerusalem This name is used to mean the spiritual city God built for his people. See Revelation 21–22. **3:14 Amen**
Used here as a name for Jesus; it means to agree fully that something is true.

I wish that you were hot or cold! [16]But because you are lukewarm—neither hot, nor cold—I am ready to spit you out of my mouth. [17]You say, 'I am rich, and I have become wealthy and do not need anything.' But you do not know that you are really miserable, pitiful, poor, blind, and naked. [18]I advise you to buy from me gold made pure in fire so you can be truly rich. Buy from me white clothes so you can be clothed and so you can cover your shameful nakedness. Buy from me medicine to put on your eyes so you can truly see.

[19]"I correct and punish those whom I love. So be eager to do right, and change your hearts and lives. [20]Here I am! I stand at the door and knock. If you hear my voice and open the door, I will come in and eat with you, and you will eat with me.

[21]"Those who win the victory will sit with me on my throne in the same way that I won the victory and sat down with my Father on his throne. [22]Everyone who has ears should listen to what the Spirit says to the churches."

DECEMBER 14

AMOS 4:1—5:27

Israel Will Not Return

4 Listen to this message, you cows of Bashan[n]
  on the Mountain of Samaria.
  You take things from the poor
    and crush people who are in need.
  Then you command your husbands,
    "Bring us something to drink!"
[2]The Lord God has promised this:
  "Just as surely as I am a holy God,
  the time will come
    when you will be taken away by
      hooks,
    and what is left of you with fishhooks.
[3]You will go straight out of the city
    through holes in the walls,
  and you will be thrown on the garbage
    dump," says the LORD.

[4]"Come to the city of Bethel and sin;
    come to Gilgal and sin even more.
  Offer your sacrifices every morning,
    and bring one-tenth of your crops
      every three days.
[5]Offer bread made with yeast as a
      sacrifice to show your thanks,
    and brag about the special offerings
      you bring,
  because this is what you love to do,
    Israelites," says the Lord God.

[6]"I did not give you any food in your cities,
    and there was not enough to eat in any
      of your towns,
  but you did not come back to me," says
    the LORD.
[7]"I held back the rain from you
    three months before harvest time.
  Then I let it rain on one city
    but not on another.
  Rain fell on one field,
    but another field got none and dried up.
[8]People weak from thirst went from town
      to town for water,
    but they could not get enough to
      drink.
  Still you did not come back to me," says
    the LORD.
[9]"I made your crops die from disease and
      mildew.
  When your gardens and your vineyards
      got larger,
  locusts ate your fig and olive trees.
    But still you did not come back to me,"
      says the LORD.
[10]"I sent disasters against you,
    as I did to Egypt.
  I killed your young men with swords,
    and your horses were taken from you.
  I made you smell the stink from all the
    dead bodies,

4:1 Bashan Amos compares the rich, lazy women of Samaria to well-fed cows from Bashan, a place known for its rich animal pastures.

but still you did not come back to me,"
says the LORD.

¹¹"I destroyed some of you
as I destroyed Sodom and Gomorrah.
You were like a burning stick pulled from
a fire,
but still you did not come back to me,"
says the LORD.

¹²"So this is what I will do to you, Israel;
because I will do this to you,
get ready to meet your God, Israel."

¹³He is the one who makes the
mountains
and creates the wind
and makes his thoughts known to
people.
He changes the dawn into darkness
and walks over the mountains of the
earth.
His name is the LORD God All-Powerful.

Israel Needs to Repent

5 Listen to this funeral song that I sing about
you, people of Israel.
²"The young girl Israel has fallen,
and she will not rise up again.
She was left alone in her own land,
and there is no one to help her up."

³This is what the Lord GOD says:
"If a thousand soldiers leave a city,
only a hundred will return;
if a hundred soldiers leave a city,
only ten will return."

⁴This is what the LORD says to the nation
of Israel:
"Come to me and live.
⁵ But do not look in Bethel
or go to Gilgal,
and do not go down to Beersheba.
The people of Gilgal will be taken away
as captives,
and Bethel will become nothing."
⁶Come to the LORD and live,
or he will move like fire against the
descendants of Joseph.
The fire will burn Bethel,
and there will be no one to put it out.
⁷You turn justice upside down,
and you throw on the ground what is
right.

⁸God is the one who made the star groups
Pleiades and Orion;
he changes darkness into the morning
light,
and the day into dark night.
He calls for the waters of the sea
to pour out on the earth.
The LORD is his name.
⁹He destroys the protected city;
he ruins the strong, walled city.

¹⁰You hate those who speak in court
against evil,
and you can't stand those who tell the
truth.
¹¹You walk on poor people,
forcing them to give you grain.
You have built fancy houses of cut stone,
but you will not live in them.
You have planted beautiful vineyards,
but you will not drink the wine from
them.
¹²I know your many crimes,
your terrible sins.
You hurt people who do right,
you take money to do wrong,
and you keep the poor from getting
justice in court.
¹³In such times the wise person will keep
quiet,
because it is a bad time.

¹⁴Try to do good, not evil,
so that you will live,
and the LORD God All-Powerful will be
with you
just as you say he is.
¹⁵Hate evil and love good;
be fair in the courts.
Maybe the LORD God All-Powerful will be
kind
to the people of Joseph who are left
alive.
¹⁶This is what the Lord, the LORD God All-
Powerful, says:
"People will be crying in all the streets;
they will be saying, 'Oh, no!' in the
public places.
They will call the farmers to come and
weep
and will pay people to cry out loud for
them.

17People will be crying in all the vineyards,
because I will pass among you to
punish you," says the LORD.

The Lord's Day of Judging
18How terrible it will be for you who want
the LORD's day of judging to come.
Why do you want that day to come?
It will bring darkness for you, not light.
19It will be like someone who runs from a
lion
and meets a bear,
or like someone who goes into his house
and puts his hand on the wall,
and then is bitten by a snake.
20So the LORD's day of judging will bring
darkness, not light;
it will be very dark, not light at all.

21The LORD says, "I hate and reject your
feasts;
I cannot stand your religious meetings.
22If you offer me burnt offerings and grain
offerings,
I won't accept them.
You bring your best fellowship offerings
of fattened cattle,
but I will ignore them.
23Take the noise of your songs away from
me!
I won't listen to the music of your
harps.
24But let justice flow like a river,
and let goodness flow like a
never-ending stream.

25"People of Israel, you did not bring me
sacrifices and offerings
while you traveled in the desert for
forty years.
26You have carried with you
your king, the god Sakkuth,
and Kaiwan your idol,
and the star gods you have made.
27So I will send you away as captives
beyond Damascus,"
says the LORD, whose name is the God
All-Powerful.

PSALM 141:5–10

5If a good person punished me, that
would be kind.

If he corrected me, that would be like
perfumed oil on my head.
I shouldn't refuse it.
But I pray against those who do evil.
6 Let their leaders be thrown down the
cliffs.
Then people will know that I have
spoken correctly:
7"The ground is plowed and broken up.
In the same way, our bones have been
scattered at the grave."

8GOD, I look to you for help.
I trust in you, LORD. Don't let me die.
9Protect me from the traps they set for me
and from the net that evil people have
spread.
10Let the wicked fall into their own nets,
but let me pass by safely.

PROVERBS 29:26

26Many people want to speak to a ruler,
but justice comes only from the LORD.

REVELATION 4:1–11

John Sees Heaven
4After the vision of these things I looked,
and there before me was an open door in
heaven. And the same voice that spoke to me
before, that sounded like a trumpet, said,
"Come up here, and I will show you what
must happen after this." 2Immediately I was
in the Spirit, and before me was a throne in
heaven, and someone was sitting on it. 3The
One who sat on the throne looked like precious stones, like jasper and carnelian. All
around the throne was a rainbow the color of
an emerald. 4Around the throne there were
twenty-four other thrones with twenty-four
elders sitting on them. They were dressed in
white and had golden crowns on their heads.
5Lightning flashes and noises and thunder
came from the throne. Before the throne
seven lamps were burning, which are the
seven spirits of God. 6Also before the throne
there was something that looked like a sea of
glass, clear like crystal.
   In the center and around the throne were
four living creatures with eyes all over
them, in front and in back. 7The first living

creature was like a lion. The second was like a calf. The third had a face like a man. The fourth was like a flying eagle. [8]Each of these four living creatures had six wings and was covered all over with eyes, inside and out. Day and night they never stop saying:

"Holy, holy, holy is the Lord God
Almighty.
He was, he is, and he is coming."

[9]These living creatures give glory, honor, and thanks to the One who sits on the throne, who lives forever and ever. [10]Then the twenty-four elders bow down before the One who sits on the throne, and they worship him who lives forever and ever. They put their crowns down before the throne and say:

[11]"You are worthy, our Lord and God,
to receive glory and honor and power,
because you made all things.
Everything existed and was made,
because you wanted it."

DECEMBER 15

AMOS 6:1—7:17

Israel Will Be Destroyed

6 How terrible it will be for those who
have an easy life in Jerusalem,
for those who feel safe living on Mount
Samaria.
You think you are the important people
of the best nation in the world;
the Israelites come to you for help.
[2]Go look at the city of Calneh,
and from there go to the great city
Hamath;
then go down to Gath of the Philistines.
You are no better than these kingdoms.
Your land is no larger than theirs.
[3]You put off the day of punishment,
but you bring near the day when you
can do evil to others.
[4]You lie on beds decorated with ivory
and stretch out on your couches.
You eat tender lambs
and fattened calves.
[5]You make up songs on your harps,
and, like David, you compose songs on
musical instruments.
[6]You drink wine by the bowlful
and use the best perfumed lotions.
But you are not sad over the ruin of
Israel,
[7]so you will be some of the first ones
taken as slaves.

Your feasting and lying around will
come to an end.
[8]The Lord GOD made this promise; the
LORD God All-Powerful says:
"I hate the pride of the Israelites,
and I hate their strong buildings,
so I will let the enemy take the city
and everything in it."

[9]At that time there might be only ten people left alive in just one house, but they will also die. [10]When the relatives come to get the bodies to take them outside, one of them will call to the other and ask, "Are there any other dead bodies with you?"

That person will answer, "No."

Then the one who asked will say, "Hush! We must not say the name of the LORD."

[11]The LORD has given the command;
the large house will be broken into
pieces,
and the small house into bits.
[12]Horses do not run on rocks,
and people do not plow rocks with
oxen.
But you have changed fairness into
poison;
you have changed what is right into a
bitter taste.
[13]You are happy that the town of Lo Debar
was captured,
and you say, "We have taken Karnaim[n]
by our own strength."

6:13 **Lo Debar . . . Karnaim** These were two not especially significant cities that the Israelites had captured in war.

14The LORD God All-Powerful says,
"Israel, I will bring a nation against you
that will make your people suffer from
Lebo Hamath in the north
to the valley south of the Dead Sea."

The Vision of Locusts

7This is what the Lord GOD showed me: He
was forming a swarm of locusts, after the
king had taken his share of the first crop and
the second crop had just begun growing.
2When the locusts ate all the crops in the
country, I said, "Lord GOD, forgive us. How
could Israel live through this? It is too small
already!"

3So the LORD changed his mind about
this. "It will not happen," said the LORD.

The Vision of Fire

4This is what the Lord GOD showed me:
The Lord GOD was calling for fire to come
down like rain. It burned up the deep water
and was going to burn up the land. 5Then I
cried out, "Lord GOD, stop! How could Israel
live through this? It is too small already."

6So the LORD changed his mind about this
too. "It will not happen," said the Lord GOD.

The Vision of the Plumb Line

7This is what he showed me: The Lord
stood by a straight wall, with a plumb line in
his hand. 8The LORD said to me, "Amos, what
do you see?"

I said, "A plumb line."

Then the Lord said, "See, I will put a
plumb line among my people Israel to show
how crooked they are. I will not look the
other way any longer.

9"The places where Isaac's descendants
worship will be destroyed,
Israel's holy places will be turned into
ruins,
and I will attack King Jeroboam's
family with the sword."

Amaziah Speaks Against Amos

10Amaziah, a priest at Bethel, sent this
message to Jeroboam king of Israel: "Amos is
making evil plans against you with the people of Israel. He has been speaking so much
that this land can't hold all his words. 11This
is what Amos has said:

'Jeroboam will die by the sword,
and the people of Israel will be taken as
captives
out of their own country.'"

12Then Amaziah said to Amos, "Seer, go
back right now to Judah. Do your prophesying and earn your living there, 13but don't
prophesy anymore here at Bethel. This is the
king's holy place, and it is the nation's temple."

14Then Amos answered Amaziah, "I do not
make my living as a prophet, nor am I a member of a group of prophets. I make my living as
a shepherd, and I take care of sycamore trees.
15But the LORD took me away from tending the
flock and said to me, 'Go, prophesy to my people Israel.' 16So listen to the LORD's word. You
tell me,

'Don't prophesy against Israel,
and stop prophesying against the
descendants of Isaac.'

17"Because you have said this, the LORD says:
'Your wife will become a prostitute in the
city,
and your sons and daughters will be
killed with swords.
Other people will measure your land and
divide it among themselves,
and you will die in a foreign country.
The people of Israel will definitely be
taken
from their own land as captives.'"

PSALM 142:1–7

A Prayer for Safety

A maskil of David when he was in the cave. A prayer.

142 I cry out to the LORD;
I pray to the LORD for mercy.
2I pour out my problems to him;
I tell him my troubles.
3When I am afraid,
you, LORD, know the way out.
In the path where I walk,
a trap is hidden for me.
4Look around me and see.
No one cares about me.
I have no place of safety;
no one cares if I live.

5LORD, I cry out to you.
I say, "You are my protection.
You are all I want in this life."

⁶Listen to my cry,
because I am helpless.
Save me from those who are chasing me,
because they are too strong for me.
⁷Free me from my prison,
and then I will praise your name.
Then good people will surround me,
because you have taken care of me.

PROVERBS 29:27

²⁷Good people hate those who are dishonest,
and the wicked hate those who are
honest.

REVELATION 5:1–14

5Then I saw a scroll in the right hand of
the One sitting on the throne. The scroll
had writing on both sides and was kept
closed with seven seals. ²And I saw a powerful angel calling in a loud voice, "Who is worthy to break the seals and open the scroll?"
³But there was no one in heaven or on earth
or under the earth who could open the scroll
or look inside it. ⁴I cried bitterly because
there was no one who was worthy to open
the scroll or look inside. ⁵But one of the elders said to me, "Do not cry! The Lion[n] from
the tribe of Judah, David's descendant, has
won the victory so that he is able to open the
scroll and its seven seals."

⁶Then I saw a Lamb standing in the center of the throne and in the middle of the
four living creatures and the elders. The
Lamb looked as if he had been killed. He had
seven horns and seven eyes, which are the
seven spirits of God that were sent into all

the world. ⁷The Lamb came and took the
scroll from the right hand of the One sitting
on the throne. ⁸When he took the scroll, the
four living creatures and the twenty-four
elders bowed down before the Lamb. Each
one of them had a harp and golden bowls
full of incense, which are the prayers of
God's holy people. ⁹And they all sang a new
song to the Lamb:
"You are worthy to take the scroll
and to open its seals,
because you were killed,
and with the blood of your death you
bought people for God
from every tribe, language, people, and
nation.
¹⁰You made them to be a kingdom of
priests for our God,
and they will rule on the earth."
¹¹Then I looked, and I heard the voices of
many angels around the throne, and the four
living creatures, and the elders. There were
thousands and thousands of angels, ¹²saying
in a loud voice:
"The Lamb who was killed is worthy
to receive power, wealth, wisdom, and
strength,
honor, glory, and praise!"
¹³Then I heard all creatures in heaven and
on earth and under the earth and in the sea
saying:
"To the One who sits on the throne
and to the Lamb
be praise and honor and glory and power
forever and ever."
¹⁴The four living creatures said, "Amen,"
and the elders bowed down and worshiped.

DECEMBER 16

AMOS 8:1—9:15

The Vision of Ripe Fruit

8This is what the Lord GOD showed me: a
basket of summer fruit. ²He said to me,
"Amos, what do you see?"

I said, "A basket of summer fruit."
Then the LORD said to me, "An end[n] has
come for my people Israel, because I will not
overlook their sins anymore.
³"On that day the palace songs will become funeral songs," says the Lord GOD.

"There will be dead bodies thrown everywhere! Silence!"

⁴Listen to me, you who walk on helpless people,
  you who are trying to destroy the poor people of this country, saying,

⁵"When will the New Moon festival be over so we can sell grain?
  When will the Sabbath be over so we can bring out wheat to sell?
  We can charge them more and give them less,
  and we can change the scales to cheat the people.
⁶We will buy poor people for silver,
  and needy people for the price of a pair of sandals.
  We will even sell the wheat that was swept up from the floor."

⁷The LORD has sworn by his name, the Pride of Jacob, "I will never forget everything that these people did.

⁸The whole land will shake because of it, and everyone who lives in the land will cry for those who died.
  The whole land will rise like the Nile; it will be shaken, and then it will fall like the Nile River in Egypt."

⁹The Lord GOD says:
"At that time I will cause the sun to go down at noon
  and make the earth dark on a bright day.
¹⁰I will change your festivals into days of crying for the dead,
  and all your songs will become songs of sadness.
  I will make all of you wear rough cloth to show your sadness;
  I will make you shave your heads as well.
  I will make it like a time of crying for the death of an only son,
  and its end like the end of an awful day."

¹¹The Lord GOD says: "The days are coming when I will cause a time of hunger in the land.
  The people will not be hungry for bread or thirsty for water,
  but they will be hungry for words from the LORD.

¹²They will wander from the Mediterranean Sea to the Dead Sea,
  from the north to the east.
  They will search for the word of the LORD, but they won't find it.
¹³At that time the beautiful young women and the young men
  will become weak from thirst.
¹⁴They make promises by the idol in Samaria
  and say, 'As surely as the god of Dan lives ...'
  and, 'As surely as the god of Beersheba^n lives, we promise ...'
  So they will fall
  and never get up again."

Israel Will Be Destroyed

9 I saw the Lord standing by the altar, and he said:
"Smash the top of the pillars
  so that even the bottom of the doors will shake.
  Make the pillars fall on the people's heads; anyone left alive I will kill with a sword.
  Not one person will get away; no one will escape.
²If they dig down as deep as the place of the dead,
  I will pull them up from there.
  If they climb up into heaven,
  I will bring them down from there.
³If they hide at the top of Mount Carmel,
  I will find them and take them away.
  If they try to hide from me at the bottom of the sea,
  I will command a snake to bite them.
⁴If they are captured and taken away by their enemies,
  I will command the sword to kill them.
  I will keep watch over them,
  but I will keep watch to give them trouble, not to do them good."

⁵The Lord GOD All-Powerful touches the land,
  and the land shakes.
  Then everyone who lives in the land cries for the dead.
  The whole land rises like the Nile River and falls like the river of Egypt.

8:14 Dan ... Beersheba Dan was the city farthest north in Israel, and Beersheba was the city farthest south.

⁶The LORD builds his upper rooms above
the skies;
he sets their foundations on the earth.
He calls for the waters of the sea
and pours them out on the land.
The LORD is his name.
⁷The LORD says,
"Israel, you are no different to me than
the people of Cush.
I brought Israel out of the land of Egypt,
and the Philistines from Crete,
and the Arameans from Kir.
⁸I, the Lord GOD, am watching the sinful
kingdom Israel.
I will destroy it
from off the earth,
but I will not completely destroy
Jacob's descendants," says the LORD.
⁹"I am giving the command
to scatter the nation of Israel among all
nations.
It will be like someone shaking grain
through a strainer,
but not even a tiny stone falls through.
¹⁰All the sinners among my people
will die by the sword—
those who say,
'Nothing bad will happen to us.'

The Lord Promises to Restore Israel

¹¹"The kingdom of David is like a fallen
tent,
but in that day I will set it up again
and mend its broken places.
I will rebuild its ruins
as it was before.
¹²Then Israel will take over what is left of
Edom
and the other nations that belong to
me,"
says the LORD,
who will make it happen.

¹³The LORD says, "The time is coming when
there will be all kinds of food.
People will still be harvesting crops
when it's time to plow again.
People will still be taking the juice from
grapes
when it's time to plant again.
Wine will drip from the mountains
and pour from the hills.

¹⁴I will bring my people Israel back from
captivity;
they will build the ruined cities again,
and they will live in them.
They will plant vineyards and drink the
wine from them;
they will plant gardens and eat their
fruit.
¹⁵I will plant my people on their land,
and they will not be pulled out again
from the land which I have given them,"
says the LORD your God.

PSALM 143:1–6

A Prayer Not to Be Killed

A psalm of David.

143 LORD, hear my prayer;
listen to my cry for mercy.
Answer me
because you are loyal and good.
²Don't judge me, your servant,
because no one alive is right before you.
³My enemies are chasing me;
they crushed me to the ground.
They made me live in darkness
like those long dead.
⁴I am afraid;
my courage is gone.

⁵I remember what happened long ago;
I consider everything you have done.
I think about all you have made.
⁶I lift my hands to you in prayer.
As a dry land needs rain, I thirst for you.
Selah

PROVERBS 30:1–4

Wise Words from Agur

30 These are the words of Agur son of
Jakeh.
This is his message to Ithiel and Ucal:
²"I am the most stupid person there is,
and I have no understanding.
³I have not learned to be wise,
and I don't know much about God, the
Holy One.
⁴Who has gone up to heaven and come
back down?
Who can hold the wind in his hand?

Who can gather up the waters in his coat?
Who has set in place the ends of the
earth?
What is his name or his son's name?
Tell me, if you know!

REVELATION 6:1–17

6Then I watched while the Lamb opened
the first of the seven seals. I heard one of
the four living creatures say with a voice like
thunder, "Come!" ²I looked, and there before
me was a white horse. The rider on the horse
held a bow, and he was given a crown, and he
rode out, determined to win the victory.

³When the Lamb opened the second seal, I
heard the second living creature say, "Come!"
⁴Then another horse came out, a red one. Its
rider was given power to take away peace
from the earth and to make people kill each
other, and he was given a big sword.

⁵When the Lamb opened the third seal, I
heard the third living creature say, "Come!" I
looked, and there before me was a black
horse, and its rider held a pair of scales in his
hand. ⁶Then I heard something that sounded
like a voice coming from the middle of the
four living creatures. The voice said, "A quart
of wheat for a day's pay, and three quarts of
barley for a day's pay, and do not damage the
olive oil and wine!"

⁷When the Lamb opened the fourth seal, I
heard the voice of the fourth living creature
say, "Come!" ⁸I looked, and there before me
was a pale horse. Its rider was named death,
and Hades[n] was following close behind him.

They were given power over a fourth of the
earth to kill people by war, by starvation, by
disease, and by the wild animals of the earth.

⁹When the Lamb opened the fifth seal, I
saw under the altar the souls of those who
had been killed because they were faithful to
the word of God and to the message they had
received. ¹⁰These souls shouted in a loud
voice, "Holy and true Lord, how long until you
judge the people of the earth and punish
them for killing us?" ¹¹Then each one of them
was given a white robe and was told to wait a
short time longer. There were still some of
their fellow servants and brothers and sisters
in the service of Christ who must be killed as
they were. They had to wait until all of this
was finished.

¹²Then I watched while the Lamb opened
the sixth seal, and there was a great earthquake. The sun became black like rough black
cloth, and the whole moon became red like
blood. ¹³And the stars in the sky fell to the
earth like figs falling from a fig tree when the
wind blows. ¹⁴The sky disappeared as a scroll
when it is rolled up, and every mountain and
island was moved from its place.

¹⁵Then the kings of the earth, the rulers,
the generals, the rich people, the powerful
people, the slaves, and the free people hid
themselves in caves and in the rocks on the
mountains. ¹⁶They called to the mountains
and the rocks, "Fall on us. Hide us from the
face of the One who sits on the throne and
from the anger of the Lamb! ¹⁷The great day
for their anger has come, and who can stand
against it?"

DECEMBER 17

OBADIAH 1–21

The Lord Will Punish the Edomites
¹This is the vision of Obadiah.

This is what the Lord GOD says about
Edom:[n]
We have heard a message from the LORD.

A messenger has been sent among the
nations, saying,
"Attack! Let's go attack Edom!"

The Lord Speaks to the Edomites
²"Soon I will make you the smallest of
nations.

6:8 Hades The unseen world of the dead. • **1 Edom** The Edomites were the people who came from Esau, Jacob's twin
brother. They were enemies of the Israelites.

You will be greatly hated by everyone.
3Your pride has fooled you,
you who live in the hollow places of the
cliff.
Your home is up high,
you who say to yourself,
'No one can bring me down to the
ground.'
4Even if you fly high like the eagle
and make your nest among the stars,
I will bring you down from there," says
the LORD.
5"You will really be ruined!
If thieves came to you,
if robbers came by night,
they would steal only enough for
themselves.
If workers came and picked the grapes
from your vines,
they would leave a few behind.
6But you, Edom, will really lose
everything!
People will find all your hidden
treasures!
7All the people who are your friends
will force you out of the land.
The people who are at peace with you
will trick you and defeat you.
Those who eat your bread with you now
are planning a trap for you,
and you will not notice it."

8The LORD says, "On that day
I will surely destroy the wise people
from Edom,
and those with understanding from the
mountains of Edom.
9Then, city of Teman, your best warriors
will be afraid,
and everyone from the mountains of
Edom will be killed.
10You did violence to your relatives, the
Israelites,
so you will be covered with shame
and destroyed forever.
11You stood aside without helping
while strangers carried Israel's
treasures away.
When foreigners entered Israel's city gate

and threw lots to decide what part of
Jerusalem they would take,
you were like one of them.

Commands That Edom Broke
12"Edom, do not laugh at your brother
Israel in his time of trouble
or be happy about the people of Judah
when they are destroyed.
Do not brag when cruel things are done
to them.
13Do not enter the city gate of my people
in their time of trouble
or laugh at their problems
in their time of trouble.
Do not take their treasures
in their time of trouble.
14Do not stand at the crossroads
to destroy those who are trying to
escape.
Do not capture those who escape alive
and turn them over to their enemy
in their time of trouble.

The Nations Will Be Judged
15"The LORD's day of judging is coming
soon
to all the nations.
The same evil things you did to other
people
will happen to you;
they will come back upon your own
head.
16Because you drank in my Temple,
all the nations will drink on and on.
They will drink and drink
until they disappear.
17But on Mount Zion some will escape the
judgment,
and it will be a holy place.
The people of Jacob will take back their
land
from those who took it from them.
18The people of Jacob will be like a fire
and the people of Joseph[n] like a flame.
But the people of Esau[n] will be like dry
stalks.
The people of Jacob will set them on
fire and burn them up.

18 people of Jacob . . . Joseph The people who came from Jacob and Joseph, or the Israelites.
18 people of Esau The people who came from Esau, or the Edomites.

There will be no one left of the people of
Esau."
This will happen because the LORD has
said it.

¹⁹Then God's people will regain southern
Judah from Edom;
they will take back the mountains of
Edom.
They will take back the western hills
from the Philistines.
They will regain the lands of Ephraim
and Samaria,
and Benjamin will take over Gilead.
²⁰People from Israel who once were forced
to leave their homes
will take the land of the Canaanites,
all the way to Zarephath.
People from Judah who once were forced
to leave Jerusalem and live in
Sepharad
will take back the cities of southern
Judah.
²¹Powerful warriors will go up on Mount
Zion,
where they will rule the people living
on Edom's mountains.
And the kingdom will belong to the
LORD.

PSALM 143:7–12

⁷LORD, answer me quickly,
because I am getting weak.
Don't turn away from me,
or I will be like those who are dead.
⁸Tell me in the morning about your love,
because I trust you.
Show me what I should do,
because my prayers go up to you.
⁹LORD, save me from my enemies;
I hide in you.
¹⁰Teach me to do what you want,
because you are my God.
Let your good Spirit
lead me on level ground.

¹¹LORD, let me live
so people will praise you.
In your goodness
save me from my troubles.
¹²In your love defeat my enemies.

Destroy all those who trouble me,
because I am your servant.

PROVERBS 30:5–6

⁵"Every word of God is true.
He guards those who come to him for
safety.
⁶Do not add to his words,
or he will correct you and prove you are
a liar.

REVELATION 7:1–17

The 144,000 People of Israel

7 After the vision of these things I saw four
angels standing at the four corners of the
earth. The angels were holding the four
winds of the earth to keep them from blowing on the land or on the sea or on any tree.
²Then I saw another angel coming up from
the east who had the seal of the living God.
And he called out in a loud voice to the four
angels to whom God had given power to
harm the earth and the sea. ³He said to
them, "Do not harm the land or the sea or
the trees until we mark with a sign the foreheads of the people who serve our God."
⁴Then I heard how many people were
marked with the sign. There were one hundred forty-four thousand from every tribe of
the people of Israel.
⁵From the tribe of Judah twelve thousand
were marked with the sign,
from the tribe of Reuben twelve
thousand,
from the tribe of Gad twelve thousand,
⁶from the tribe of Asher twelve thousand,
from the tribe of Naphtali twelve
thousand,
from the tribe of Manasseh twelve
thousand,
⁷from the tribe of Simeon twelve thousand,
from the tribe of Levi twelve thousand,
from the tribe of Issachar twelve
thousand,
⁸from the tribe of Zebulun twelve
thousand,
from the tribe of Joseph twelve thousand,
and from the tribe of Benjamin twelve
thousand were marked with the sign.

The Great Crowd Worships God

⁹After the vision of these things I looked, and there was a great number of people, so many that no one could count them. They were from every nation, tribe, people, and language of the earth. They were all standing before the throne and before the Lamb, wearing white robes and holding palm branches in their hands. ¹⁰They were shouting in a loud voice, "Salvation belongs to our God, who sits on the throne, and to the Lamb." ¹¹All the angels were standing around the throne and the elders and the four living creatures. They all bowed down on their faces before the throne and worshiped God, ¹²saying, "Amen! Praise, glory, wisdom, thanks, honor, power, and strength belong to our God forever and ever. Amen!"

¹³Then one of the elders asked me, "Who are these people dressed in white robes? Where did they come from?"

¹⁴I answered, "You know, sir."

And the elder said to me, "These are the people who have come out of the great distress. They have washed their robes*ⁿ* and made them white in the blood of the Lamb. ¹⁵Because of this, they are before the throne of God. They worship him day and night in his temple. And the One who sits on the throne will be present with them. ¹⁶Those people will never be hungry again, and they will never be thirsty again. The sun will not hurt them, and no heat will burn them, ¹⁷because the Lamb at the center of the throne will be their shepherd. He will lead them to springs of water that give life. And God will wipe away every tear from their eyes."

DECEMBER 18

JONAH 1:1—4:11

God Calls and Jonah Runs

1 The LORD spoke his word to Jonah son of Amittai: ²"Get up, go to the great city of Nineveh, and preach against it, because I see the evil things they do."

³But Jonah got up to run away from the LORD by going to Tarshish. He went to the city of Joppa, where he found a ship that was going to the city of Tarshish. Jonah paid for the trip and went aboard, planning to go to Tarshish to run away from the LORD.

⁴But the LORD sent a great wind on the sea, which made the sea so stormy that the ship was in danger of breaking apart. ⁵The sailors were afraid, and each man cried to his own god. They began throwing the cargo from the ship into the sea to make the ship lighter.

But Jonah had gone down far inside the ship to lie down, and he fell fast asleep. ⁶The captain of the ship came and said, "Why are you sleeping? Get up and pray to your god!

Maybe your god will pay attention to us, and we won't die!"

⁷Then the men said to each other, "Let's throw lots to see who caused these troubles to happen to us."

When they threw lots, the lot showed that the trouble had happened because of Jonah. ⁸Then they said to him, "Tell us, who caused our trouble? What is your job? Where do you come from? What is your country? Who are your people?"

⁹Then Jonah said to them, "I am a Hebrew. I fear the LORD, the God of heaven, who made the sea and the land."

¹⁰The men were very afraid, and they asked Jonah, "What terrible thing did you do?" (They knew he was running away from the LORD because he had told them.)

¹¹Since the wind and the waves of the sea were becoming much stronger, they said to him, "What should we do to you to make the sea calm down for us?"

¹²Jonah said to them, "Pick me up, and throw me into the sea, and then it will calm

---

7:14 washed their robes This means they believed in Jesus so that their sins could be forgiven by Christ's blood.

down. I know it is my fault that this great storm has come on you."

13Instead, the men tried to row the ship back to the land, but they could not, because the sea was becoming more stormy.

Jonah's Punishment

14So the men cried to the LORD, "LORD, please don't let us die because of this man's life; please don't think we are guilty of killing an innocent person. LORD, you have caused all this to happen; you wanted it this way." 15So they picked up Jonah and threw him into the sea, and the sea became calm. 16Then they began to fear the LORD very much; they offered a sacrifice to the LORD and made promises to him.

17The LORD caused a big fish to swallow Jonah, and Jonah was inside the fish three days and three nights.

2 While Jonah was inside the fish, he prayed to the LORD his God and said,

2"When I was in danger,
  I called to the LORD,
  and he answered me.
I was about to die,
  so I cried to you,
  and you heard my voice.
3You threw me into the sea,
  down, down into the deep sea.
The water was all around me,
  and your powerful waves flowed over
  me.
4I said, 'I was driven out of your presence,
  but I hope to see your Holy Temple
  again.'
5The waters of the sea closed around my
  throat.
The deep sea was all around me;
  seaweed was wrapped around my head.
6When I went down to where the
  mountains of the sea start to rise,
  I thought I was locked in this prison
  forever,
but you saved me from the pit of death,
  LORD my God.

7"When my life had almost gone,
  I remembered the LORD.
I prayed to you,
  and you heard my prayers in your Holy
  Temple.

8"People who worship useless idols
  give up their loyalty to you.
9But I will praise and thank you
  while I give sacrifices to you,
  and I will keep my promises to you.
  Salvation comes from the LORD!"

10Then the LORD spoke to the fish, and the fish threw up Jonah onto the dry land.

God Calls and Jonah Obeys

3 The LORD spoke his word to Jonah again and said, 2"Get up, go to the great city Nineveh, and preach to it what I tell you to say."

3So Jonah obeyed the LORD and got up and went to Nineveh. It was a very large city; just to walk across it took a person three days. 4After Jonah had entered the city and walked for one day, he preached to the people, saying, "After forty days, Nineveh will be destroyed!"

5The people of Nineveh believed God. They announced that they would fast for a while, and they put on rough cloth to show their sadness. All the people in the city did this, from the most important to the least important.

6When the king of Nineveh heard this news, he got up from his throne, took off his robe, and covered himself with rough cloth and sat in ashes to show how upset he was.

7He sent this announcement through Nineveh:

By command of the king and his important men: No person or animal, herd or flock, will be allowed to taste anything. Do not let them eat food or drink water. 8But every person and animal should be covered with rough cloth, and people should cry loudly to God. Everyone must turn away from evil living and stop doing harm all the time. 9Who knows? Maybe God will change his mind. Maybe he will stop being angry, and then we will not die.

10When God saw what the people did, that they stopped doing evil, he changed his mind and did not do what he had warned. He did not punish them.

God's Mercy Makes Jonah Angry

4 But this made Jonah very unhappy, and he became angry. 2He prayed to the LORD,

"When I was still in my own country this is what I said would happen, and that is why I quickly ran away to Tarshish. I knew that you are a God who is kind and shows mercy. You don't become angry quickly, and you have great love. I knew you would choose not to cause harm. ³So now I ask you, LORD, please kill me. It is better for me to die than to live."

⁴Then the LORD said, "Do you think it is right for you to be angry?"

⁵Jonah went out and sat down east of the city. There he made a shelter for himself and sat in the shade, waiting to see what would happen to the city. ⁶The LORD made a plant grow quickly up over Jonah, which gave him shade and helped him to be more comfortable. Jonah was very pleased to have the plant. ⁷But the next day when the sun rose, God sent a worm to attack the plant so that it died.

⁸As the sun rose higher in the sky, God sent a very hot east wind to blow, and the sun became so hot on Jonah's head that he became very weak and wished he were dead. He said, "It is better for me to die than to live."

⁹But God said to Jonah, "Do you think it is right for you to be angry about the plant?"

Jonah answered, "It is right for me to be angry! I am so angry I could die!"

¹⁰And the LORD said, "You are so concerned for that plant even though you did nothing to make it grow. It appeared one day, and the next day it died. ¹¹Then shouldn't I show concern for the great city Nineveh, which has more than one hundred twenty thousand people who do not know right from wrong, and many animals, too?"

PSALM 144:1-8

A Prayer for Victory

Of David.

144 Praise the LORD, my Rock,
who trains me for war,
who trains me for battle.
²He protects me like a strong, walled city,
and he loves me.
He is my defender and my Savior,
my shield and my protection.

He helps me keep my people under
control.

³LORD, why are people important to you?
Why do you even think about human
beings?
⁴People are like a breath;
their lives are like passing shadows.

⁵LORD, tear open the sky and come down.
Touch the mountains so they will
smoke.
⁶Send the lightning and scatter my
enemies.
Shoot your arrows and force them
away.
⁷Reach down from above.
Save me and rescue me out of this sea
of enemies,
from these foreigners.
⁸They are liars;
they are dishonest.

PROVERBS 30:7-9

⁷"I ask two things from you, LORD.
Don't refuse me before I die.
⁸Keep me from lying and being dishonest.
And don't make me either rich or poor;
just give me enough food for each day.
⁹If I have too much, I might reject you
and say, 'I don't know the LORD.'
If I am poor, I might steal
and disgrace the name of my God.

REVELATION 8:1-13

The Seventh Seal

8 When the Lamb opened the seventh seal, there was silence in heaven for about half an hour. ²And I saw the seven angels who stand before God and to whom were given seven trumpets.

³Another angel came and stood at the altar, holding a golden pan for incense. He was given much incense to offer with the prayers of all God's holy people. The angel put this offering on the golden altar before the throne. ⁴The smoke from the incense went up from the angel's hand to God with the prayers of God's people. ⁵Then the angel filled the incense pan with fire from the altar and threw it on the earth, and there were

flashes of lightning, thunder and loud noises, and an earthquake.

The Seven Angels and Trumpets

⁶Then the seven angels who had the seven trumpets prepared to blow them.

⁷The first angel blew his trumpet, and hail and fire mixed with blood were poured down on the earth. And a third of the earth, and all the green grass, and a third of the trees were burned up.

⁸Then the second angel blew his trumpet, and something that looked like a big mountain, burning with fire, was thrown into the sea. And a third of the sea became blood, ⁹a third of the living things in the sea died, and a third of the ships were destroyed.

¹⁰Then the third angel blew his trumpet, and a large star, burning like a torch, fell from the sky. It fell on a third of the rivers and on the springs of water. ¹¹The name of the star is Wormwood.ⁿ And a third of all the water became bitter, and many people died from drinking the water that was bitter.

¹²Then the fourth angel blew his trumpet, and a third of the sun, and a third of the moon, and a third of the stars were struck. So a third of them became dark, and a third of the day was without light, and also the night.

¹³While I watched, I heard an eagle that was flying high in the air cry out in a loud voice, "Trouble! Trouble! Trouble for those who live on the earth because of the remaining sounds of the trumpets that the other three angels are about to blow!"

DECEMBER 19

MICAH 1:1—3:12

Samaria and Israel to Be Punished

1 During the time that Jotham, Ahaz, and Hezekiah were kings of Judah, the word of the LORD came to Micah, who was from Moresheth. He saw these visions about Samaria and Jerusalem.

²Hear this, all you nations;
  listen, earth and all you who live on it.
The Lord GOD will be a witness against you,
  the Lord from his Holy Temple.
³See, the LORD is coming out of his place;
  he is coming down to walk on the tops of the mountains.
⁴The mountains will melt under him,
  and the valleys will crack open,
like wax near a fire,
  like water running down a hillside.
⁵All this is because of Jacob's sin,
  because of the sins of the nation of Israel.
What is the place of Jacob's sin?
  Isn't it Samaria?

What is Judah's place of idol worship?
  Isn't it Jerusalem?

The Lord Speaks

⁶"So I will make Samaria a pile of ruins in the open country,
  a place for planting vineyards.
I will pour her stones down into the valley
  and strip her down to her foundations.
⁷All her idols will be broken into pieces;
  all the gifts to her idols will be burned with fire.
I will destroy all her idols,
  and because Samaria earned her money by being unfaithful to me,
  this money will be carried off by others who are not faithful to me."

Micah's Great Sadness

⁸I will moan and cry because of this evil,
  going around barefoot and naked.
I will cry loudly like the wild dogs
  and make sad sounds like the owls do,
⁹because Samaria's wound cannot be healed.

8:11 Wormwood Name of a very bitter plant; used here to give the idea of bitter sorrow.

It will spread to Judah;
it will reach the city gate of my people,
all the way to Jerusalem.
[10]Don't tell it in Gath.[n]
Don't cry in Acco.[n]
Roll in the dust
at Beth Ophrah.[n]
[11]Pass on your way, naked and ashamed,
you who live in Shaphir.[n]
Those who live in Zaanan[n]
won't come out.
The people in Beth Ezel[n] will cry,
but they will not give you any support.
[12]Those who live in Maroth[n]
will be anxious for good news to come,
because trouble will come from the
LORD,
all the way to the gate of Jerusalem.
[13]You people living in Lachish,[n]
harness the fastest horse to the chariot.
Jerusalem's sins started in you;
yes, Israel's sins were found in you.
[14]So you must give farewell gifts
to Moresheth[n] in Gath.
The houses in Aczib[n] will be false help
to the kings of Israel.
[15]I will bring against you people who will
take your land,
you who live in Mareshah.[n]
The glory of Israel
will go in to Adullam.
[16]Cut off your hair to show you are sad
for the children you love.
Make yourself bald like the eagle,
because your children will be taken
away to a foreign land.

The Evil Plans of People

2 How terrible it will be for people who
plan wickedness,
who lie on their beds and make evil
plans.
When the morning light comes, they do
what they planned,
because they have the power to do so.

[2]They want fields, so they take them;
they want houses, so they take them
away.
They cheat people to get their houses;
they rob them even of their property.
[3]That is why the LORD says:
"Look, I am planning trouble against
such people,
and you won't be able to save
yourselves.
You will no longer walk proudly,
because it will be a terrible time.
[4]At that time people will make fun of you
and sing this sad song about you:
'We are completely ruined;
the LORD has taken away my people's
land.
Yes, he has taken it away from me
and divided our fields among our
enemies!'"
[5]So you will have no one from the LORD's
people
to throw lots to divide the land.

Micah Is Asked Not to Prophesy

[6]The prophets say, "Don't prophesy to us!
Don't prophesy about these things!
Nothing to make us feel bad will
happen!"
[7]But I must say this, people of Jacob:
The LORD is becoming angry about
what you have done.
My words are welcome
to the person who does what is right.
[8]But you are fighting against my people
like an enemy.
You take the coats from people who
pass by;
you rob them of their safety;
you plan war.
[9]You've forced the women of my people
from their nice houses;
you've taken my glory
from their children forever.
[10]Get up and leave.

1:10 Gath This name sounds like the Hebrew word for "tell." **1:10 Acco** This name sounds like the Hebrew word for "cry." **1:10 Beth Ophrah** This name means "house of dust." **1:11 Shaphir** This name means "beautiful." **1:11 Zaanan** This name sounds like the Hebrew word for "come out." **1:11 Beth Ezel** This name means "house by the side of another," suggesting help or support. **1:12 Maroth** This name sounds like the Hebrew word for "sad" or "miserable." **1:13 Lachish** This name sounds like the Hebrew word for "horses." **1:14 Moresheth** This may be a play on the word "engaged," referring to a farewell gift to a bride. **1:14 Aczib** This name means "lie" or "trick." **1:15 Mareshah** This name sounds like the Hebrew word for a person who captures other cities and lands.

This is not your place of rest anymore.
You have made this place unclean,
and it is doomed to destruction.
¹¹But you people want a false prophet
who will tell you nothing but lies.
You want one who promises to prophesy
good things for you
if you give him wine and beer.
He's just the prophet for you.

The Lord Promises to Rescue His People

¹²"Yes, people of Jacob, I will bring all of
you together;
I will bring together all those left alive
in Israel.
I will put them together like sheep in a
pen,
like a flock in its pasture;
the place will be filled with many
people.
¹³Someone will open the way and lead the
people out.
The people will break through the gate
and leave the city where they were
held captive.
Their king will go out in front of them,
and the LORD will lead them."

The Leaders of Israel Are Guilty of Evil

3 Then I said,
"Listen, leaders of the people of Jacob;
listen, you rulers of the nation of Israel.
You should know how to decide cases
fairly,
2 but you hate good and love evil.
You skin my people alive
and tear the flesh off their bones.
³You eat my people's flesh
and skin them and break their bones;
you chop them up like meat for the pot,
like meat in a cooking pan.
⁴They will cry to the LORD,
but he won't answer them.
At that time he will hide his face from
them,
because what they have done is evil."
⁵The LORD says this about the prophets
who teach his people the wrong way of living:
"If these prophets are given food to eat,
they shout, 'Peace!'

But if someone doesn't give them what
they ask for,
they call for a holy war against that
person.
⁶So it will become like night for them,
without visions.
It will become dark for them, without
any way to tell the future.
The sun is about to set for the prophets;
their day will become dark.
⁷The seers will be ashamed;
the people who see the future will be
embarrassed.
Yes, all of them will cover their mouths,
because there will be no answer from
God."

Micah Is an Honest Prophet of God

⁸But I am filled with power,
with the Spirit of the LORD,
and with justice and strength,
to tell the people of Jacob how they have
turned against God,
and the people of Israel how they have
sinned.
⁹Leaders of Jacob and rulers of Israel,
listen to me,
you who hate fairness
and twist what is right.
¹⁰You build Jerusalem by murdering
people;
you build it with evil.
¹¹Its judges take money
to decide who wins in court.
Its priests only teach for pay,
and its prophets only look into the
future when they get paid.
But they lean on the LORD and say,
"The LORD is here with us,
so nothing bad will happen to us."
¹²Because of you,
Jerusalem will be plowed like a field.
The city will become a pile of rocks,
and the hill on which the Temple
stands will be covered with bushes.

PSALM 144:9–15

⁹God, I will sing a new song to you;
I will play to you on the ten-stringed
harp.

[10]You give victory to kings.
     You save your servant David from cruel
       swords.
[11]Save me, rescue me from these
       foreigners.
     They are liars; they are dishonest.

[12]Let our sons in their youth
       grow like plants.
     Let our daughters be
       like the decorated stones in the Temple.
[13]Let our barns be filled
       with crops of all kinds.
     Let our sheep in the fields have
       thousands and tens of thousands of
         lambs.
[14] Let our cattle be strong.
     Let no one break in.
     Let there be no war,
       no screams in our streets.

[15]Happy are those who are like this;
     happy are the people whose God is the
       LORD.

PROVERBS 30:10

[10]"Do not say bad things about servants to
       their masters,
     or they will curse you, and you will
       suffer for it.

REVELATION 9:1–21

9 Then the fifth angel blew his trumpet, and
I saw a star fall from the sky to the earth.
The star was given the key to the deep hole
that leads to the bottomless pit. [2]Then it
opened up the hole that leads to the bottomless pit, and smoke came up from the hole
like smoke from a big furnace. Then the sun
and sky became dark because of the smoke
from the hole. [3]Then locusts came down to
the earth out of the smoke, and they were
given the power to sting like scorpions.[n]
[4]They were told not to harm the grass on the
earth or any plant or tree. They could harm
only the people who did not have the sign of
God on their foreheads. [5]These locusts were
not given the power to kill anyone, but to
cause pain to the people for five months. And
the pain they felt was like the pain a scorpion
gives when it stings someone. [6]During those
days people will look for a way to die, but
they will not find it. They will want to die, but
death will run away from them.

[7]The locusts looked like horses prepared
for battle. On their heads they wore what
looked like crowns of gold, and their faces
looked like human faces. [8]Their hair was like
women's hair, and their teeth were like lions'
teeth. [9]Their chests looked like iron breastplates, and the sound of their wings was like
the noise of many horses and chariots hurrying into battle. [10]The locusts had tails with
stingers like scorpions, and in their tails was
their power to hurt people for five months.
[11]The locusts had a king who was the angel
of the bottomless pit. His name in the Hebrew language is Abaddon and in the Greek
language is Apollyon.[n]

[12]The first trouble is past; there are still
two other troubles that will come.

[13]Then the sixth angel blew his trumpet,
and I heard a voice coming from the horns
on the golden altar that is before God. [14]The
voice said to the sixth angel who had the
trumpet, "Free the four angels who are tied
at the great river Euphrates." [15]And they let
loose the four angels who had been kept
ready for this hour and day and month and
year so they could kill a third of all people on
the earth. [16]I heard how many troops on
horses were in their army—two hundred
million.

[17]The horses and their riders I saw in the
vision looked like this: They had breastplates
that were fiery red, dark blue, and yellow like
sulfur. The heads of the horses looked like
heads of lions, with fire, smoke, and sulfur
coming out of their mouths. [18]A third of all
the people on earth were killed by these
three terrible disasters coming out of the
horses' mouths: the fire, the smoke, and the
sulfur. [19]The horses' power was in their
mouths and in their tails; their tails were like
snakes with heads, and with them they hurt
people.

9:3 scorpions A scorpion is an insect that stings with a bad poison.   **9:11 Abaddon, Apollyon** Both names mean "Destroyer."

²⁰The other people who were not killed by these terrible disasters still did not change their hearts and turn away from what they had made with their own hands. They did not stop worshiping demons and idols made of gold, silver, bronze, stone, and wood—things that cannot see or hear or walk. ²¹These people did not change their hearts and turn away from murder or evil magic, from their sexual sins or stealing.

DECEMBER 20

MICAH 4:1—5:15

The Mountain of the Lord

4 In the last days
 the mountain on which the LORD's
   Temple stands
 will become the most important of all
   mountains.
It will be raised above the hills,
 and people from other nations will
   come streaming to it.
²Many nations will come and say,
 "Come, let us go up to the mountain of
   the LORD,
 to the Temple of the God of Jacob,
 so that he can teach us his ways,
 and we can obey his teachings."
His teachings will go out from Jerusalem,
 the word of the LORD from that city.
³The Lord will judge many nations;
 he will make decisions about strong
   nations that are far away.
They will hammer their swords into
   plow blades
 and their spears into hooks for
   trimming trees.
Nations will no longer raise swords
   against other nations;
 they will not train for war anymore.
⁴Everyone will sit under his own vine and
   fig tree,
 and no one will make him afraid,
 because the LORD All-Powerful has said
   it.
⁵All other nations may follow their own
   gods,
 but we will follow the LORD our God
   forever and ever.

⁶The LORD says, "At that time,
 I will gather the crippled;
 I will bring together those who were
   sent away,
 those whom I caused to have trouble.
⁷I will keep alive those who were crippled,
 and I will make a strong nation of
   those who were sent away.
The LORD will be their king in Mount
   Zion from now on and forever.
⁸And you, watchtower of the flocks,ⁿ hill
   of Jerusalem,
 to you will come the kingdom as in the
   past.
 Jerusalem, the right to rule will come
   again to you."

Why the Israelites Must Go to Babylon

⁹Now, why do you cry so loudly?
 Is your king gone?
Have you lost your helper,
 so that you are in pain, like a woman
   trying to give birth?
¹⁰People of Jerusalem, strain and be in
   pain.
 Be like a woman trying to give birth,
because now you must leave the city
 and live in the field.
You will go to Babylon,
 but you will be saved from that place.
The LORD will go there
 and buy you back from your enemies.

¹¹But now many nations
 have come to fight against you,
 saying, "Let's destroy Jerusalem.
 We will look at her and be glad we have
   defeated her."

4:8 watchtower . . . flocks This probably means a part of Jerusalem. The leaders would be like shepherds in a tower watching their sheep.

¹²But they don't know
    what the LORD is thinking;
they don't understand his plan.
He has gathered them like bundles of
    grain to the threshing floor.

¹³"Get up and beat them, people of
    Jerusalem.
I will make you strong as if you had
    horns of iron
and hoofs of bronze.
    You will beat many nations into small
        pieces
and give their wealth to the LORD,
    their treasure to the Lord of all the
        earth."

5 So, strong city, gather your soldiers
    together,
because we are surrounded and
    attacked.
They will hit the leader of Israel
    in the face with a club.

The Ruler to Be Born in Bethlehem

²"But you, Bethlehem Ephrathah,
    though you are too small to be among
        the army groups from Judah,
from you will come one who will rule
    Israel for me.
He comes from very old times,
    from days long ago."

³The LORD will give up his people
    until the one who is having a baby
        gives birth;
then the rest of his relatives will return
    to the people of Israel.
⁴At that time the ruler of Israel will stand
    and take care of his people
with the LORD's strength
    and with the power of the name of the
        LORD his God.
The Israelites will live in safety,
    because his greatness will reach all over
        the earth.
⁵ He will bring peace.

Rescue and Punishment

Assyria will surely come into our country
    and walk over our large buildings.
We will set up seven shepherds,
    eight leaders of the people.

⁶They will destroy the Assyrians with
    their swords;
they will conquer the land of Assyria
    with their swords drawn.
They will rescue us from the Assyrians
    when they come into our land,
    when they walk over our borders.

⁷Then the people of Jacob who are left alive
    will be to other people
like dew from the LORD
    or rain on the grass—
it does not wait for human beings;
    it does not pause for any person.
⁸Those of Jacob's people who are left alive
    will be scattered among many nations
        and peoples.
They will be like a lion among the
    animals of the forest,
    like a young lion in a flock of sheep:
As it goes, it jumps on them
    and tears them to pieces,
    and no one can save them.
⁹So you will raise your fist in victory over
    your enemies,
    and all your enemies will be destroyed.

¹⁰The LORD says, "At that time,
    I will take your horses from you
    and destroy your chariots.
¹¹I will destroy the cities in your country
    and tear down all your defenses.
¹²I will take away the magic charms you use
    so you will have no more fortune-tellers.
¹³I will destroy your statues of gods
    and the stone pillars you worship
so that you will no longer worship
    what your hands have made.
¹⁴I will tear down Asherah idols from you
    and destroy your cities.
¹⁵In my anger and rage,
    I will pay back the nations that have
        not listened."

PSALM 145:1–7

Praise to God the King

A psalm of praise. Of David.

145 I praise your greatness, my God
        the King;
I will praise you forever and ever.

²I will praise you every day;
I will praise you forever and ever.
³The LORD is great and worthy of our
praise;
no one can understand how great he is.

⁴Parents will tell their children what you
have done.
They will retell your mighty acts,
⁵wonderful majesty, and glory.
And I will think about your miracles.
⁶They will tell about the amazing things
you do,
and I will tell how great you are.
⁷They will remember your great goodness
and will sing about your fairness.

PROVERBS 30:11–14

¹¹"Some people curse their fathers
and do not bless their mothers.
¹²Some people think they are pure,
but they are not really free from evil.
¹³Some people have such a proud look!
They look down on others.
¹⁴Some people have teeth like swords;
their jaws seem full of knives.
They want to remove the poor from the
earth
and the needy from the land.

REVELATION 10:1–11

The Angel and the Small Scroll

10 Then I saw another powerful angel
coming down from heaven dressed in a
cloud with a rainbow over his head. His face
was like the sun, and his legs were like pillars
of fire. ²The angel was holding a small scroll
open in his hand. He put his right foot on the
sea and his left foot on the land. ³Then he
shouted loudly like the roaring of a lion. And
when he shouted, the voices of seven thunders spoke. ⁴When the seven thunders spoke,
I started to write. But I heard a voice from
heaven say, "Keep hidden what the seven
thunders said, and do not write them down."

⁵Then the angel I saw standing on the sea
and on the land raised his right hand to
heaven, ⁶and he made a promise by the
power of the One who lives forever and ever.
He is the One who made the skies and all
that is in them, the earth and all that is in it,
and the sea and all that is in it. The angel
promised, "There will be no more waiting!
⁷In the days when the seventh angel is ready
to blow his trumpet, God's secret will be finished. This secret is the Good News God told
to his servants, the prophets."

⁸Then I heard the same voice from heaven
again, saying to me: "Go and take the open
scroll that is in the hand of the angel that is
standing on the sea and on the land."

⁹So I went to the angel and told him to
give me the small scroll. And he said to me,
"Take the scroll and eat it. It will be sour in
your stomach, but in your mouth it will be
sweet as honey." ¹⁰So I took the small scroll
from the angel's hand and ate it. In my
mouth it tasted sweet as honey, but after I ate
it, it was sour in my stomach. ¹¹Then I was
told, "You must prophesy again about many
peoples, nations, languages, and kings."

DECEMBER 21

MICAH 6:1—7:20

The Lord's Case

6 Now hear what the LORD says:
"Get up; plead your case in front of the
mountains;
let the hills hear your story.
²Mountains, listen to the LORD's legal case.
Foundations of the earth, listen.

The LORD has a legal case against his
people,
and he will accuse Israel."

³He says, "My people, what did I do to
you?
How did I make you tired of me?
Tell me.
⁴I brought you from the land of Egypt

and freed you from slavery;
I sent Moses, Aaron, and Miriam to
you.
⁵My people, remember
the evil plans of Balak king of Moab
and what Balaam son of Beor told
Balak.
Remember what happened from Acacia
to Gilgal
so that you will know the LORD does
what is right!"

⁶You say, "What can I bring with me
when I come before the LORD,
when I bow before God on high?
Should I come before him with burnt
offerings,
with year-old calves?
⁷Will the LORD be pleased with a thousand
male sheep?
Will he be pleased with ten thousand
rivers of oil?
Should I give my first child for the evil I
have done?
Should I give my very own child for my
sin?"
⁸The LORD has told you, human, what is
good;
he has told you what he wants from
you:
to do what is right to other people,
love being kind to others,
and live humbly, obeying your God.

⁹The voice of the LORD calls to the city,
and the wise person honors him.
So pay attention to the rod of
punishment;
pay attention to the One who threatens
to punish.
¹⁰Are there still in the wicked house
wicked treasures
and the cursed false measure?
¹¹Can I forgive people who cheat others
with wrong weights and scales?
¹²The rich people of the city
do cruel things.
Its people tell lies;
they do not tell the truth.

¹³As for me, I will make you sick.
I will attack you, ruining you because of
your sins.
¹⁴You will eat, but you won't become full;
you will still be hungry and empty.
You will store up, but save nothing,
and what you store up, the sword will
destroy.
¹⁵You will plant,
but you won't harvest.
You will step on your olives,
but you won't get any oil from them.
You will crush the grapes,
but you will not drink the new wine.
¹⁶This is because you obey the laws of King
Omri
and do all the things that Ahab's family
does;
you follow their advice.
So I will let you be destroyed.
The people in your city will be laughed
at,
and other nations will make fun of you.

The Evil That People Do

7 Poor me! I am like a hungry man,
and all the summer fruit has been
picked—
there are no grapes left to eat,
none of the early figs I love.
²All of the faithful people are gone;
there is not one good person left in this
country.
Everyone is waiting to kill someone;
everyone is trying to trap someone
else.
³With both hands they are doing evil.
Rulers ask for money,
and judges' decisions are bought for a
price.
Rich people tell what they want,
and they get it.
⁴Even the best of them is like a
thornbush;
the most honest of them is worse than
a prickly plant.
The day that your watchmenⁿ warned
you about has come.
Now they will be confused.

7:4 watchmen Another name for prophets. The prophets were like guards who stood on a city's wall and watched for trouble coming from far away.

⁵Don't believe your neighbor
    or trust a friend.
Don't say anything,
    even to your wife.
⁶A son will not honor his father,
    a daughter will turn against her mother,
and a daughter-in-law will be against her
    mother-in-law;
a person's enemies will be members of
    his own family.

The Lord's Kindness

⁷Israel says, "I will look to the LORD for help.
    I will wait for God to save me;
    my God will hear me.
⁸Enemy, don't laugh at me.
    I have fallen, but I will get up again.
I sit in the shadow of trouble now,
    but the LORD will be a light for me.
⁹I sinned against the LORD,
    so he was angry with me,
but he will defend my case in court.
    He will bring about what is right for me.
Then he will bring me out into the light,
    and I will see him set things right.
¹⁰Then my enemies will see this,
    and they will be ashamed,
those who said to me,
    'Where is the LORD your God?'
I will look down on them.
    They will get walked on, like mud in the
    street."

Israel Will Return

¹¹The time will come when your walls will
    be built again,
when your country will grow.
¹²At that time your people will come back to
    you
    from Assyria and the cities of Egypt,
    and from Egypt to the Euphrates River,
    and from sea to sea and mountain to
    mountain.
¹³The earth will be ruined for the people
    who live in it
    because of their deeds.

A Prayer to God

¹⁴So shepherd your people with your stick;
    tend the flock of people who belong to
    you.

That flock now lives alone in the forest
    in the middle of a garden land.
Let them feed in Bashan and Gilead
    as in days long ago.
¹⁵"As in the days when I brought you out of
    Egypt,
    I will show them miracles."
¹⁶When the nations see those miracles,
    they will no longer brag about their
    power.
They will put their hands over their
    mouths,
    refusing to listen.
¹⁷They will crawl in the dust like a snake,
    like insects crawling on the ground.
They will come trembling from their
    holes to the LORD our God
    and will turn in fear before you.
¹⁸There is no God like you.
    You forgive those who are guilty of sin;
    you don't look at the sins of your people
    who are left alive.
You will not stay angry forever,
    because you enjoy being kind.
¹⁹You will have mercy on us again;
    you will conquer our sins.
You will throw away all our sins
    into the deepest part of the sea.
²⁰You will be true to the people of Jacob,
    and you will be kind to the people of
    Abraham
as you promised to our ancestors long ago.

PSALM 145:8–16

⁸The LORD is kind and shows mercy.
    He does not become angry quickly but
    is full of love.
⁹The LORD is good to everyone;
    he is merciful to all he has made.
¹⁰LORD, everything you have made will
    praise you;
    those who belong to you will bless you.
¹¹They will tell about the glory of your
    kingdom
    and will speak about your power.
¹²Then everyone will know the mighty
    things you do
    and the glory and majesty of your
    kingdom.

[13]Your kingdom will go on and on,
and you will rule forever.

The LORD will keep all his promises;
he is loyal to all he has made.
[14]The LORD helps those who have been
defeated
and takes care of those who are in
trouble.
[15]All living things look to you for food,
and you give it to them at the right
time.
[16]You open your hand,
and you satisfy all living things.

PROVERBS 30:15a

[15]"Greed has two daughters
named 'Give' and 'Give.'

REVELATION 11:1-19

The Two Witnesses

11 I was given a measuring stick like a
rod, and I was told, "Go and measure
the temple of God and the altar, and count
the people worshiping there. [2]But do not
measure the yard outside the temple. Leave
it alone, because it has been given to those
who are not God's people. And they will
trample on the holy city for forty-two
months. [3]And I will give power to my two
witnesses to prophesy for one thousand two
hundred sixty days, and they will be dressed
in rough cloth to show their sadness."

[4]These two witnesses are the two olive
trees and the two lampstands that stand before the Lord of the earth. [5]And if anyone
tries to hurt them, fire comes from their
mouths and kills their enemies. And if anyone tries to hurt them in whatever way, in
that same way that person will die. [6]These
witnesses have the power to stop the sky
from raining during the time they are
prophesying. And they have power to make
the waters become blood, and they have
power to send every kind of trouble to the
earth as many times as they want.

[7]When the two witnesses have finished
telling their message, the beast that comes
up from the bottomless pit will fight a war
against them. He will defeat them and kill
them. [8]The bodies of the two witnesses will
lie in the street of the great city where the
Lord was killed. This city is named Sodom[n]
and Egypt, which has a spiritual meaning.
[9]Those from every race of people, tribe, language, and nation will look at the bodies of
the two witnesses for three and one-half
days, and they will refuse to bury them.
[10]People who live on the earth will rejoice
and be happy because these two are dead.
They will send each other gifts, because
these two prophets brought much suffering
to those who live on the earth.

[11]But after three and one-half days, God
put the breath of life into the two prophets
again. They stood on their feet, and everyone
who saw them became very afraid. [12]Then
the two prophets heard a loud voice from
heaven saying, "Come up here!" And they
went up into heaven in a cloud as their enemies watched.

[13]In the same hour there was a great
earthquake, and a tenth of the city was destroyed. Seven thousand people were killed
in the earthquake, and those who did not die
were very afraid and gave glory to the God of
heaven.

[14]The second trouble is finished. Pay attention: The third trouble is coming soon.

The Seventh Trumpet

[15]Then the seventh angel blew his trumpet. And there were loud voices in heaven,
saying:

"The power to rule the world now
belongs to our Lord and his Christ,
and he will rule forever and ever."

[16]Then the twenty-four elders, who sit on
their thrones before God, bowed down on
their faces and worshiped God. [17]They said:

"We give thanks to you, Lord God
Almighty,
who is and who was,
because you have used your great power
and have begun to rule!
[18]The people of the world were angry,
but your anger has come.

11:8 Sodom City that God destroyed because the people were so evil.

The time has come to judge the dead,
and to reward your servants the prophets
and your holy people,
all who respect you, great and small.
The time has come to destroy those who
destroy the earth!"

[19]Then God's temple in heaven was opened. The Ark that holds the agreement God gave to his people could be seen in his temple. Then there were flashes of lightning, noises, thunder, an earthquake, and a great hailstorm.

DECEMBER 22

NAHUM 1:1—3:19

1 This is the message for the city of Nineveh.[n] This is the book of the vision of Nahum, who was from the town of Elkosh.

The Lord Is Angry with Nineveh

[2]The LORD is a jealous God who
punishes;
the LORD punishes and is filled with
anger.
The LORD punishes those who are
against him,
and he stays angry with his enemies.
[3]The LORD does not become angry
quickly,
and his power is great.
The LORD will not let the guilty go
unpunished.
Where the LORD goes, there are
whirlwinds and storms,
and the clouds are the dust beneath
his feet.
[4]He speaks to the sea and makes it dry;
he dries up all the rivers.
The areas of Bashan and Carmel dry up,
and the flowers of Lebanon dry up.
[5]The mountains shake in front of him,
and the hills melt.
The earth trembles when he comes;
the world and all who live in it shake
with fear.
[6]No one can stay alive when he is angry;
no one can survive his strong anger.
His anger is poured out like fire;
the rocks are smashed by him.
[7]The LORD is good,
giving protection in times of trouble.

He knows who trusts in him.
[8]But like a rushing flood,
he will completely destroy Nineveh;
he will chase his enemies until he kills
them.

[9]The LORD will completely destroy
anyone making plans against him.
Trouble will not come a second time.
[10]Those people will be like tangled thorns
or like people drunk from their wine;
they will be burned up quickly like
dry weeds.
[11]Someone has come from Nineveh
who makes evil plans against the LORD
and gives wicked advice.
[12]This is what the LORD says:
"Although Assyria is strong and has
many people,
it will be defeated and brought to an
end.
Although I have made you suffer, Judah,
I will make you suffer no more.
[13]Now I will free you from their control
and tear away your chains."

[14]The LORD has given you this command,
Nineveh:
"You will not have descendants to
carry on your name.
I will destroy the idols and metal
images
that are in the temple of your gods.
I will make a grave for you,
because you are wicked."

[15]Look, there on the hills,
someone is bringing good news!

1:1 Nineveh The capital city of the country of Assyria. Nahum uses Nineveh to stand for all of Assyria.

He is announcing peace!
Celebrate your feasts, people of Judah,
and give your promised sacrifices to
God.
The wicked will not come to attack you
again;
they have been completely destroyed.

Nineveh Will Be Defeated

2 The destroyer[n] is coming to attack you,
Nineveh.
Guard the defenses.
Watch the road.
Get ready.
Gather all your strength!
[2] Destroyers have destroyed God's people
and ruined their vines,
but the LORD will bring back Jacob's
greatness
like Israel's greatness.

[3] The shields of his soldiers are red;
the army is dressed in red.
The metal on the chariots flashes like
fire
when they are ready to attack;
their horses are excited.
[4] The chariots race through the streets
and rush back and forth through the
city squares.
They look like torches;
they run like lightning.

[5] He[n] calls his officers,
but they stumble on the way.
They hurry to the city wall,
and the shield is put into place.
[6] The river gates are thrown open,
and the palace is destroyed.
[7] It has been announced that the people
of Nineveh
will be captured and carried away.
The slave girls moan like doves
and beat their breasts, because they
are sad.
[8] Nineveh is like a pool,
and now its water is draining away.
"Stop! Stop!" the people yell,
but no one turns back.
[9] Take the silver!

Take the gold!
There is no end to the treasure—
piles of wealth of every kind.
[10] Nineveh is robbed, ruined, and
destroyed.
The people lose their courage, and
their knees knock.
Stomachs ache, and everyone's face
grows pale.
[11] Where is the lions'[n] den
and the place where they feed their
young?
Where did the lion, lioness, and cubs go
without being afraid?
[12] The lion killed enough for his cubs,
enough for his mate.
He filled his cave with the animals he
caught;
he filled his den with meat he had
killed.

[13] "I am against you, Nineveh,"
says the LORD All-Powerful.
"I will burn up your chariots in smoke,
and the sword will kill your young
lions.
I will stop you from hunting down
others on the earth,
and your messengers' voices
will no longer be heard."

It Will Be Terrible for Nineveh

3 How terrible it will be for the city that
has killed so many.
It is full of lies
and goods stolen from other countries.
It is always killing somebody.
[2] Hear the sound of whips
and the noise of the wheels.
Hear horses galloping
and chariots bouncing along!
[3] Horses are charging,
swords are shining,
spears are gleaming!
Many are dead;
their bodies are piled up—
too many to count.
People stumble over the dead bodies.
[4] The city was like a prostitute;

2:1 destroyer The Babylonians, the Scythians, and the Medes destroyed Nineveh. **2:5 He** This probably means the king of Assyria. **2:11 lions'** The symbol of Assyria was the lion.

she was charming and a lover of
   magic.
She made nations slaves with her
      prostitution
and her witchcraft.

[5]"I am against you, Nineveh," says the
   Lord All-Powerful.
   "I will pull your dress up over your
      face
and show the nations your nakedness
and the kingdoms your shame.
[6]I will throw filthy garbage on you
and make a fool of you.
I will make people stare at you.
[7]Everyone who sees you will run away
      and say,
   'Nineveh is in ruins. Who will cry for
      her?'
   Nineveh, where will I find anyone to
      comfort you?"

[8]You are no better than Thebes,[n]
who sits by the Nile River
with water all around her.
The river was her defense;
   the waters were like a wall around her.
[9]Cush and Egypt gave her endless
      strength;
   Put and Libya supported her.
[10]But Thebes was captured
and went into captivity.
Her small children were beaten to death
   at every street corner.
Lots were thrown for her important
      men,
   and all of her leaders were put in
      chains.

[11]Nineveh, you will be drunk, too.
   You will hide;
   you will look for a place safe from the
      enemy.
[12]All your defenses are like fig trees with
      ripe fruit.
   When the tree is shaken, the figs fall
      into the mouth of the eater.
[13]Look at your soldiers.
   They are all women!
   The gates of your land

are wide open for your enemies;
fire has burned the bars of your gates.

[14]Get enough water before the long war
      begins.
   Make your defenses strong!
Get mud,
   mix clay,
   make bricks!
[15]There the fire will burn you up.
   The sword will kill you;
   like grasshoppers eating crops, the
      battle will completely destroy you.
   Grow in number like hopping locusts;
      grow in number like swarming
      locusts!
[16]Your traders are more than the stars in
      the sky,
   but like locusts, they strip the land
      and then fly away.
[17]Your guards are like locusts.
   Your officers are like swarms of locusts
      that hang on the walls on a cold day.
   When the sun comes up, they fly away,
      and no one knows where they have
      gone.
[18]King of Assyria, your rulers are asleep;
   your important men lie down to rest.
   Your people have been scattered on the
      mountains,
      and there is no one to bring them
      back.
[19]Nothing can heal your wound;
   your injury will not heal.
   Everyone who hears about you applauds,
      because everyone has felt your endless
      cruelty.

PSALM 145:17–21

[17]Everything the Lord does is right.
   He is loyal to all he has made.
[18]The Lord is close to everyone who prays
      to him,
   to all who truly pray to him.
[19]He gives those who respect him what
      they want.
   He listens when they cry, and he saves
      them.

3:8 Thebes A great city in Egypt.

[20]The LORD protects everyone who loves
him,
but he will destroy the wicked.

[21]I will praise the LORD.
Let everyone praise his holy name
forever.

PROVERBS 30:15b–16

There are three things that are never
satisfied,
really four that never say, 'I've had
enough!':
[16]the cemetery, the childless mother,
the land that never gets enough rain,
and fire that never says, 'I've had
enough!'

REVELATION 12:1–18

The Woman and the Dragon

12 And then a great wonder appeared in
heaven: A woman was clothed with
the sun, and the moon was under her feet,
and a crown of twelve stars was on her
head. [2]She was pregnant and cried out with
pain, because she was about to give birth.
[3]Then another wonder appeared in heaven:
There was a giant red dragon with seven
heads and seven crowns on each head. He
also had ten horns. [4]His tail swept a third of
the stars out of the sky and threw them
down to the earth. He stood in front of the
woman who was ready to give birth so he
could eat her baby as soon as it was born.
[5]Then the woman gave birth to a son who
will rule all the nations with an iron rod.
And her child was taken up to God and to
his throne. [6]The woman ran away into the
desert to a place God prepared for her
where she would be taken care of for one
thousand two hundred sixty days.

[7]Then there was a war in heaven.
Michael[n] and his angels fought against the
dragon, and the dragon and his angels
fought back. [8]But the dragon was not strong
enough, and he and his angels lost their
place in heaven. [9]The giant dragon was

thrown down out of heaven. (He is that old
snake called the devil or Satan, who tricks
the whole world.) The dragon with his angels was thrown down to the earth.
[10]Then I heard a loud voice in heaven
saying:
"The salvation and the power and the
kingdom of our God
and the authority of his Christ have
now come.
The accuser of our brothers and sisters,
who accused them day and night
before our God,
has been thrown down.
[11]And our brothers and sisters defeated
him
by the blood of the Lamb's death
and by the message they preached.
They did not love their lives so much
that they were afraid of death.
[12]So rejoice, you heavens
and all who live there!
But it will be terrible for the earth and
the sea,
because the devil has come down to
you!
He is filled with anger,
because he knows he does not have
much time."

[13]When the dragon saw he had been
thrown down to the earth, he hunted for the
woman who had given birth to the son.
[14]But the woman was given the two wings
of a great eagle so she could fly to the place
prepared for her in the desert. There she
would be taken care of for three and one-
half years, away from the snake. [15]Then the
snake poured water out of its mouth like a
river toward the woman so the flood would
carry her away. [16]But the earth helped the
woman by opening its mouth and swallow-
ing the river that came from the mouth of
the dragon. [17]Then the dragon was very angry at the woman, and he went off to make
war against all her other children—those
who obey God's commands and who have
the message Jesus taught.
[18]And the dragon[n] stood on the seashore.

12:7 Michael The archangel—leader among God's angels or messengers (Jude 9). **12:18 the dragon** Some Greek copies
read "I."

DECEMBER 23

HABAKKUK 1:1—3:19

1 This is the message Habakkuk the prophet received.

Habakkuk Complains

2 LORD, how long must I ask for help
  and you ignore me?
I cry out to you about violence,
  but you do not save us!
3 Why do you make me see wrong things
  and make me look at trouble?
People are destroying things and hurting
  others in front of me;
  they are arguing and fighting.
4 So the teachings are weak,
  and justice never comes.
Evil people gain while good people lose;
  the judges no longer make fair decisions.

The Lord Answers

5 "Look at the nations!
  Watch them and be amazed and
    shocked.
I will do something in your lifetime
  that you won't believe even when you
    are told about it.
6 I will use the Babylonians,
  those cruel and wild people
who march across the earth
  and take lands that don't belong to them.
7 They scare and frighten people.
  They do what they want to do
  and are good only to themselves.
8 Their horses are faster than leopards
  and quicker than wolves at sunset.
Their horse soldiers attack quickly;
  they come from places far away.
They attack quickly, like an eagle
  swooping down for food.
9 They all come to fight.
Nothing can stop them.
  Their prisoners are as many as the
    grains of sand.
10 They laugh at kings
  and make fun of rulers.
They laugh at all the strong, walled cities
  and build dirt piles to the top of the
    walls to capture them.

11 Then they leave like the wind and move
    on.
They are guilty of worshiping their own
    strength."

Habakkuk Complains Again

12 LORD, you live forever,
  my God, my holy God.
We will not die.
LORD, you have chosen the Babylonians
    to punish people;
  our Rock, you picked them to punish.
13 Your eyes are too good to look at evil;
  you cannot stand to see those who do
    wrong.
So how can you put up with those evil
    people?
How can you be quiet when the wicked
    swallow up people who are better
    than they are?
14 You treat people like fish in the sea,
  like sea animals without a leader.
15 The enemy brings them in with hooks.
  He catches them in his net
  and drags them in his fishnet.
So he rejoices and sings for joy.
16 The enemy offers sacrifices to his net
  and burns incense to worship it,
because it lets him live like the rich
  and enjoy the best food.
17 Will he keep on taking riches with his
    net?
  Will he go on destroying people
    without showing mercy?

2 I will stand like a guard to watch
  and place myself at the tower.
I will wait to see what he will say to me;
  I will wait to learn how God will answer
    my complaint.

The Lord Answers

2 The LORD answered me:
  "Write down the vision;
  write it clearly on clay tablets
  so whoever reads it can run to tell
    others.
3 It is not yet time for the message to come
    true,

but that time is coming soon;
the message will come true.
It may seem like a long time,
but be patient and wait for it,
because it will surely come;
it will not be delayed.
⁴The evil nation is very proud of itself;
it is not living as it should.
But those who are right with God will
live by faith.

⁵"Just as wine can trick a person,
those who are too proud will not last,
because their desire is like a grave's
desire for death,
and like death they always want more.
They gather other nations for themselves
and collect for themselves all the
countries.
⁶But all the nations the Babylonians have
hurt will laugh at them.
They will make fun of the Babylonians
and say, 'How terrible it will be for the
one that steals many things.
How long will that nation get rich by
forcing others to pay them?'

⁷"One day the people from whom you
have taken money will turn against
you.
They will realize what is happening and
make you shake with fear.
Then they will take everything you
have.
⁸Because you have stolen from many
nations,
those who are left will take much from
you.
This is because you have killed many
people,
destroying countries and cities and
everyone in them.

⁹"How terrible it will be for the nation
that becomes rich by doing wrong,
thinking they will live in a safe place
and escape harm.
¹⁰Because you have made plans to destroy
many people,
you have made your own houses
ashamed of you.
Because of it, you will lose your lives.

¹¹The stones of the walls will cry out
against you,
and the boards that support the roof
will agree that you are wrong.
¹²"How terrible it will be for the nation
that kills people to build a city,
that wrongs others to start a town.
¹³The LORD All-Powerful will send fire
to destroy what those people have built;
all the nations' work will be for nothing.
¹⁴Then, just as water covers the sea,
people everywhere will know the
LORD's glory.

¹⁵"How terrible for the nation that makes
its neighbors drink,
pouring from the jug of wine until they
are drunk
so that it can look at their naked
bodies.
¹⁶You Babylonians will be filled with
disgrace, not respect.
It's your turn to drink and fall to the
ground like a drunk person.
The cup of anger from the LORD's right
hand is coming around to you.
You will receive disgrace, not respect.
¹⁷You hurt many people in Lebanon,
but now you will be hurt.
You killed many animals there,
and now you must be afraid
because of what you did
to that land, those cities, and the people
who lived in them.

The Message About Idols

¹⁸"An idol does no good, because a human
made it;
it is only a statue that teaches lies.
The one who made it expects his own
work to help him,
but he makes idols that can't even
speak!
¹⁹How terrible it will be for the one who says
to a wooden statue, 'Come to life!'
How terrible it will be for the one who
says to a silent stone, 'Get up!'
It cannot tell you what to do.
It is only a statue covered with gold and
silver;
there is no life in it.

20The LORD is in his Holy Temple;
 all the earth should be silent in his
 presence."

Habakkuk's Prayer

3 This is the prayer of Habakkuk the
 prophet, on shigionoth.
2LORD, I have heard the news about you;
 I am amazed at what you have done.
 LORD, do great things once again in our
 time;
 make those things happen again in our
 own days.
 Even when you are angry,
 remember to be kind.

3God is coming from Teman;
 the Holy One comes from Mount
 Paran.[n]   Selah
 His glory covers the skies,
 and his praise fills the earth.
4He is like a bright light.
 Rays of light shine from his hand,
 and there he hides his power.
5Sickness goes before him,
 and disease follows behind him.
6He stands and shakes the earth.
 He looks, and the nations shake with
 fear.
 The mountains, which stood for ages,
 break into pieces;
 the old hills fall down.
 God has always done this.

7I saw that the tents of Cushan were in
 trouble
 and that the tents of Midian trembled.
8LORD, were you angry at the rivers,
 or were you angry at the streams?
 Were you angry with the sea
 when you rode your horses and
 chariots of victory?[n]
9You uncovered your bow
 and commanded many arrows to be
 brought to you.   Selah
 You split the earth with rivers.
10 The mountains saw you and shook with
 fear.
 The rushing water flowed.
 The sea made a loud noise,

and its waves rose high.
11The sun and moon stood still in the sky;
 they stopped when they saw the flash of
 your flying arrows
 and the gleam of your shining spear.
12In anger you marched on the earth;
 in anger you punished the nations.
13You came out to save your people,
 to save your chosen one.
 You crushed the leader of the wicked
 ones
 and took everything he had, from head
 to toe.   Selah
14With the enemy's own spear you stabbed
 the leader of his army.
 His soldiers rushed out like a storm to
 scatter us.
 They were happy
 as they were robbing the poor people in
 secret.
15But you marched through the sea with
 your horses,
 stirring the great waters.

16I hear these things, and my body
 trembles;
 my lips tremble when I hear the sound.
 My bones feel weak,
 and my legs shake.
 But I will wait patiently for the day of
 disaster
 that will come to the people who attack
 us.
17Fig trees may not grow figs,
 and there may be no grapes on the
 vines.
 There may be no olives growing
 and no food growing in the fields.
 There may be no sheep in the pens
 and no cattle in the barns.
18But I will still be glad in the LORD;
 I will rejoice in God my Savior.
19The Lord GOD is my strength.
 He makes me like a deer that does not
 stumble
 so I can walk on the steep mountains.
 For the director of music. On my stringed
instruments.

3:3 Teman . . . Paran God is seen as again coming from the direction of Mount Sinai. He came from Sinai when he rescued his people from Egypt.   **3:8 sea . . . victory** This is probably talking about the Israelites crossing the Red Sea.

PSALM 146:1–10

Praise God Who Helps the Weak

146 Praise the LORD!
My whole being, praise the LORD.
[2] I will praise the LORD all my life;
I will sing praises to my God as long as
I live.

[3] Do not put your trust in princes
or other people, who cannot save you.
[4] When people die, they are buried.
Then all of their plans come to an end.
[5] Happy are those who are helped by the
God of Jacob.
Their hope is in the LORD their God.
[6] He made heaven and earth,
the sea and everything in it.
He remains loyal forever.
[7] He does what is fair for those who have
been wronged.
He gives food to the hungry.
The LORD sets the prisoners free.
[8] The LORD gives sight to the blind.
The LORD lifts up people who are in
trouble.
The LORD loves those who do right.
[9] The LORD protects the foreigners.
He defends the orphans and widows,
but he blocks the way of the wicked.

[10] The LORD will be King forever.
Jerusalem, your God is everlasting.

Praise the LORD!

PROVERBS 30:17

[17] "If you make fun of your father
and refuse to obey your mother,
the birds of the valley will peck out your
eyes,
and the vultures will eat them.

REVELATION 13:1–18

The Two Beasts

13 Then I saw a beast coming up out of
the sea. It had ten horns and seven
heads, and there was a crown on each horn. A
name against God was written on each head.
[2] This beast looked like a leopard, with feet
like a bear's feet and a mouth like a lion's

mouth. And the dragon gave the beast all of
his power and his throne and great authority.
[3] One of the heads of the beast looked as if it
had been killed by a wound, but this death
wound was healed. Then the whole world
was amazed and followed the beast. [4] People
worshiped the dragon because he had given
his power to the beast. And they also worshiped the beast, asking, "Who is like the
beast? Who can make war against it?"

[5] The beast was allowed to say proud
words and words against God, and it was allowed to use its power for forty-two months.
[6] It used its mouth to speak against God,
against God's name, against the place where
God lives, and against all those who live in
heaven. [7] It was given power to make war
against God's holy people and to defeat
them. It was given power over every tribe,
people, language, and nation. [8] And all who
live on earth will worship the beast—all the
people since the beginning of the world
whose names are not written in the Lamb's
book of life. The Lamb is the One who was
killed.

[9] Anyone who has ears should listen:
[10] If you are to be a prisoner,
then you will be a prisoner.
If you are to be killed with the sword,
then you will be killed with the sword.
This means that God's holy people must
have patience and faith.

[11] Then I saw another beast coming up out
of the earth. It had two horns like a lamb, but
it spoke like a dragon. [12] This beast stands
before the first beast and uses the same
power the first beast has. By this power it
makes everyone living on earth worship the
first beast, who had the death wound that
was healed. [13] And the second beast does
great miracles so that it even makes fire
come down from heaven to earth while people are watching. [14] It fools those who live on
earth by the miracles it has been given the
power to do. It does these miracles to serve
the first beast. The second beast orders people to make an idol to honor the first beast,
the one that was wounded by the deadly
sword but sprang to life again. [15] The second
beast was given power to give life to the idol
of the first one so that the idol could speak.

And the second beast was given power to command all who will not worship the image of the beast to be killed. [16]The second beast also forced all people, small and great, rich and poor, free and slave, to have a mark on their right hand or on their forehead. [17]No one could buy or sell without this mark, which is the name of the beast or the number of its name. [18]This takes wisdom. Let the one who has understanding find the meaning of the number, which is the number of a person. Its number is 666.[n]

DECEMBER 24

ZEPHANIAH 1:1—3:20

1 This is the word of the LORD that came through Zephaniah while Josiah son of Amon was king of Judah. Zephaniah was the son of Cushi, who was the son of Gedaliah. Gedaliah was the son of Amariah, who was the son of Hezekiah.

The Lord's Judgment
[2]"I will sweep away everything
  from the earth," says the LORD.
[3]"I will sweep away the people and
    animals;
  I will destroy the birds in the air
  and the fish of the sea.
  I will ruin the evil people,
  and I will remove human beings from
    the earth," says the LORD.

The Future of Judah
[4]"I will punish Judah
  and all the people living in Jerusalem.
  I will remove from this place
  all signs of Baal, the false priests, and
    the other priests.
[5]I will destroy those who worship
  the stars from the roofs,[n]
  and those who worship and make
    promises
  by both the LORD and the god Molech,
[6]and those who turned away from the
    LORD,
  and those who quit following the LORD
    and praying to him for direction.
[7]Be silent before the Lord GOD,

because the LORD's day for judging
    people is coming soon.
The LORD has prepared a sacrifice;
  he has made holy his invited guests.
[8]On the day of the LORD's sacrifice,
  I, the LORD, will punish the princes and
    the king's sons
  and all those who wear foreign clothes.
[9]On that day I will punish those who
    worship Dagon,
  those who hurt others and tell lies in
    the temples of their gods.

[10]"On that day," says the LORD,
  "a cry will be heard at the Fish Gate.
  A wail will come from the new area of
    the city,
  and a loud crash will echo from the hills.
[11]Cry, you people living in the market area,
  because all the merchants will be
    dead;
  all the silver traders will be gone.
[12]At that time I, the LORD, will search
    Jerusalem with lamps.
  I will punish those who are satisfied
    with themselves,
  who think, 'The LORD won't help us or
    punish us.'
[13]Their wealth will be stolen
  and their houses destroyed.
  They may build houses,
  but they will not live in them.
  They may plant vineyards,
  but they will not drink any wine from
    them.

13:18 666 Some Greek copies read "616." • **1:5 roofs** In Bible times houses were built with flat roofs. The roof was used for drying things such as flax and fruit. And it was used as an extra room, as a place for worship, and as a cool place to sleep in the summer.

The Lord's Day of Judging

[14]"The LORD's day of judging is coming
    soon;
  it is near and coming fast.
  The cry will be very sad on the day of
    the LORD;
  even soldiers will cry.
[15]That day will be a day of anger,
  a day of terror and trouble,
  a day of destruction and ruin,
  a day of darkness and gloom,
  a day of clouds and blackness,
[16]a day of alarms and battle cries.
  'Attack the strong, walled cities!
  Attack the corner towers!'
[17]I will make life hard on the people;
  they will walk around like the blind,
  because they have sinned against the
    LORD.
  Their blood will be poured out like dust,
  and their insides will be dumped like
    trash.
[18]On the day that God will show his anger,
  neither their silver nor gold will save
    them.
  The LORD's anger will be like a fire
  that will burn up the whole world;
  suddenly he will bring an end, yes, an end
    to everyone on earth."

The Lord Asks People to Change

2 Gather together, gather,
  you unwanted people.
[2]Do it before it's too late,
  before you are blown away like chaff,
  before the LORD's terrible anger reaches
    you,
  before the day of the LORD's anger
    comes to you.
[3]Come to the LORD, all you who are not
    proud,
  who obey his laws.
  Do what is right. Learn to be humble.
  Maybe you will escape
  on the day the LORD shows his anger.

Philistia Will Be Punished

[4]No one will be left in the city of Gaza,
  and the city of Ashkelon will be
    destroyed.

Ashdod will be empty by noon,
  and the people of Ekron will be chased
    away.
[5]How terrible it will be for you who live by
    the Mediterranean Sea,
  you Philistines!
  The word of the LORD is against you,
  Canaan, land of the Philistines.

"I will destroy you
  so that no one will be left."
[6]The land by the Mediterranean Sea, in
    which you live,
  will become pastures, fields for
    shepherds, and pens for sheep.
[7]It will belong to the descendants of Judah
    who are left alive.
  There they will let their sheep eat grass.
  At night they will sleep
  in the houses of Ashkelon.
  The LORD their God will pay attention to
    them
  and will make their life good again.

Moab and Ammon Will Be Punished

[8]"I have heard the insults of the country
    of Moab
  and the threats of the people of Ammon.
  They have insulted my people
  and have taken their land."
[9]So the LORD All-Powerful, the God of
    Israel, says,
  "As surely as I live,
  Moab will be destroyed like Sodom,
  and Ammon will be destroyed like
    Gomorrah[n]—
  a heap of weeds, a pit of salt,
  and a ruin forever.
  Those of my people who are left alive
    will take whatever they want from
    them;
  those who are left from my nation will
    take their land."

[10]This is what Moab and Ammon get for
    being proud,
  because they insulted and made fun of
    the people of the LORD All-Powerful.
[11]The LORD will frighten them,
  because he will destroy all the gods of
    the earth.

2:9 Sodom . . . Gomorrah Two cities God destroyed because the people were so evil.

Then everyone in faraway places
will worship him wherever they are.

Cush and Assyria Will Be Destroyed

¹²"You Cushites also
will be killed by my sword."

¹³Then the LORD will turn against the
north
and destroy Assyria.
He will make Nineveh
a ruin as dry as a desert.

¹⁴Flocks and herds will lie down there,
and all wild animals.
The owls and crows will sit
on the stone pillars.
The owl will hoot through the windows,
trash will be in the doorways,
and the wooden boards of the
buildings will be gone.

¹⁵This is the happy and safe city
that thinks there is no one else as
strong as it is.
But what a ruin it will be,
a place where wild animals live.
All those who pass by will make fun
and shake their fists.

Jerusalem Will Be Punished

3 How terrible for the wicked, stubborn
city of Jerusalem,
which hurts its own people.

²It obeys no voice;
it can't be taught to do right.
It doesn't trust the LORD;
it doesn't worship its God.

³Its officers are like roaring lions.
Its rulers are like hungry wolves that
attack in the evening,
and in the mornng nothing is left of
those they attacked.

⁴Its prophets are proud;
they are people who cannot be trusted.
Its priests don't respect holy things;
they break God's teachings.

⁵But the LORD is good, and he is there in
that city.
He does no wrong.
Every morning he governs the people
fairly;
every day he can be trusted.
But evil people are not ashamed of
what they do.

⁶"I have destroyed nations;
their towers were ruined.
I made their streets empty
so no one goes there anymore.
Their cities are ruined;
no one lives there at all.

⁷I said, 'Surely now Jerusalem will respect
me
and will accept my teaching.'
Then the place where they lived would
not be destroyed,
and I would not have to punish them.
But they were still eager
to do evil in everything they did.

⁸Just wait," says the LORD.
"Someday I will stand up as a witness.
I have decided that I will gather
nations
and assemble kingdoms.
I will pour out my anger on them,
all my strong anger.
My anger will be like fire
that will burn up the whole world.

A New Day for God's People

⁹"Then I will give the people of all nations
pure speech
so that all of them will speak the name
of the LORD
and worship me together.

¹⁰People will come from where the Nile
River begins;
my scattered people will come with
gifts for me.

¹¹Then Jerusalem will not be ashamed
of the wrongs done against me,
because I will remove from this city
those who like to brag;
there will never be any more proud
people
on my holy mountain in Jerusalem.

¹²But I will leave in the city
the humble and those who are not
proud,
and they will trust in the LORD.

¹³Those who are left alive in Israel won't do
wrong or tell lies;
they won't trick people with their
words.
They will eat and lie down
with no one to make them afraid."

A Happy Song

¹⁴Sing, Jerusalem.
  Israel, shout for joy!
  Jerusalem, be happy
  and rejoice with all your heart.
¹⁵The LORD has stopped punishing you;
  he has sent your enemies away.
  The King of Israel, the LORD, is with you;
  you will never again be afraid of being
    harmed.
¹⁶On that day Jerusalem will be told,
  "Don't be afraid, city of Jerusalem.
  Don't give up.
¹⁷The LORD your God is with you;
  the mighty One will save you.
  He will rejoice over you.
  You will rest in his love;
  he will sing and be joyful about you."

¹⁸"I will take away the sadness planned for
    you,
  which would have made you very
    ashamed.
¹⁹At that time I will punish
  all those who harmed you.
  I will save my people who cannot walk
  and gather my people who have been
    thrown out.
  I will give them praise and honor
  in every place where they were shamed.
²⁰At that time I will gather you;
  at that time I will bring you back home.
  I will give you honor and praise
  from people everywhere
  when I make things go well again for
    you,
  as you will see with your own eyes,"
  says the LORD.

PSALM 147:1–6

Praise God Who Helps His People

147¹Praise the LORD!

It is good to sing praises to our
    God;
  it is good and pleasant to praise him.
²The LORD rebuilds Jerusalem;
  he brings back the captured Israelites.
³He heals the brokenhearted
  and bandages their wounds.

⁴He counts the stars
  and names each one.
⁵Our Lord is great and very powerful.
  There is no limit to what he knows.
⁶The LORD defends the humble,
  but he throws the wicked to the
    ground.

PROVERBS 30:18–19

¹⁸"There are three things that are too hard
    for me,
  really four I don't understand:
¹⁹the way an eagle flies in the sky,
  the way a snake slides over a rock,
  the way a ship sails on the sea,
  and the way a man and a woman fall in
    love.

REVELATION 14:1–20

The Song of the Saved

14Then I looked, and there before me
  was the Lamb standing on Mount
Zion.ⁿ With him were one hundred forty-
four thousand people who had his name and
his Father's name written on their foreheads.
²And I heard a sound from heaven like the
noise of flooding water and like the sound of
loud thunder. The sound I heard was like
people playing harps. ³And they sang a new
song before the throne and before the four
living creatures and the elders. No one could
learn the new song except the one hundred
forty-four thousand who had been bought
from the earth. ⁴These are the ones who did
not do sinful things with women, because
they kept themselves pure. They follow the
Lamb every place he goes. These one hundred forty-four thousand were bought from
among the people of the earth as people to
be offered to God and the Lamb. ⁵They were
not guilty of telling lies; they are without
fault.

The Three Angels

⁶Then I saw another angel flying high in
the air. He had the eternal Good News to
preach to those who live on earth—to every
nation, tribe, language, and people. ⁷He
preached in a loud voice, "Fear God and give

14:1 Mount Zion Another name for Jerusalem; here meaning the spiritual city of God's people.

him praise, because the time has come for God to judge all people. So worship God who made the heavens, and the earth, and the sea, and the springs of water."

⁸Then the second angel followed the first angel and said, "Ruined, ruined is the great city of Babylon! She made all the nations drink the wine of the anger of her adultery."

⁹Then a third angel followed the first two angels, saying in a loud voice: "If anyone worships the beast and his idol and gets the beast's mark on the forehead or on the hand, ¹⁰that one also will drink the wine of God's anger, which is prepared with all its strength in the cup of his anger. And that person will be put in pain with burning sulfur before the holy angels and the Lamb. ¹¹And the smoke from their burning pain will rise forever and ever. There will be no rest, day or night, for those who worship the beast and his idol or who get the mark of his name." ¹²This means God's holy people must be patient. They must obey God's commands and keep their faith in Jesus.

¹³Then I heard a voice from heaven saying, "Write this: Blessed are the dead who die from now on in the Lord."

The Spirit says, "Yes, they will rest from their hard work, and the reward of all they have done stays with them."

The Earth Is Harvested

¹⁴Then I looked, and there before me was a white cloud, and sitting on the white cloud was One who looked like a Son of Man.ⁿ He had a gold crown on his head and a sharp sickleⁿ in his hand. ¹⁵Then another angel came out of the temple and called out in a loud voice to the One who was sitting on the cloud, "Take your sickle and harvest from the earth, because the time to harvest has come, and the fruit of the earth is ripe." ¹⁶So the One who was sitting on the cloud swung his sickle over the earth, and the earth was harvested.

¹⁷Then another angel came out of the temple in heaven, and he also had a sharp sickle. ¹⁸And then another angel, who has power over the fire, came from the altar. This angel called to the angel with the sharp sickle, saying, "Take your sharp sickle and gather the bunches of grapes from the earth's vine, because its grapes are ripe." ¹⁹Then the angel swung his sickle over the earth. He gathered the earth's grapes and threw them into the great winepress of God's anger. ²⁰They were trampled in the winepress outside the city, and blood flowed out of the winepress as high as horses' bridles for a distance of about one hundred eighty miles.

DECEMBER 25

HAGGAI 1:1—2:23

It Is Time to Build the Temple

1 The prophet Haggai spoke the word of the LORD to Zerubbabel son of Shealtiel, the governor of Judah, and to Joshua son of Jehozadak, the high priest. This message came in the second year that Darius was king, on the first day of the sixth month: ²"This is what the LORD All-Powerful says: 'The people say the right time has not come to rebuild the Temple of the LORD.'"

³Then Haggai the prophet spoke the word of the LORD: ⁴"Is it right for you to be living in fancy houses while the Temple is still in ruins?"

⁵This is what the LORD All-Powerful says: "Think about what you have done. ⁶You have planted much, but you harvest little. You eat, but you do not become full. You drink, but you are still thirsty. You put on clothes, but you are not warm enough. You earn money, but then you lose it all as if you had put it into a purse full of holes."

14:14 Son of Man "Son of Man" is a name Jesus called himself.   **14:14 sickle** A farming tool with a curved blade. It was used to harvest grain.

[7]This is what the LORD All-Powerful says: "Think about what you have done. [8]Go up to the mountains, bring back wood, and build the Temple. Then I will be pleased with it and be honored," says the LORD. [9]"You look for much, but you find little. When you bring it home, I destroy it. Why?" asks the LORD All-Powerful. "Because you all work hard for your own houses while my house is still in ruins! [10]Because of what you have done, the sky holds back its rain and the ground holds back its crops. [11]I have called for a time without rain on the land, and on the mountains, and on the grain, the new wine, the olive oil, the plants which the earth produces, the people, the farm animals, and all the work of your hands."

[12]Zerubbabel son of Shealtiel and Joshua son of Jehozadak, the high priest, and all the rest of the people who were left alive obeyed the LORD their God and the message from Haggai the prophet, because the LORD their God had sent him. And the people feared the LORD.

[13]Haggai, the LORD's messenger, gave the LORD's message to the people, saying, "The LORD says, 'I am with you.'" [14]The LORD stirred up Zerubbabel son of Shealtiel, the governor of Judah, and Joshua son of Jehozadak, the high priest, and all the rest of the people who were left alive. So they came and worked on the Temple of their God, the LORD All-Powerful. [15]They began on the twenty-fourth day of the sixth month in the second year Darius was king.

The Beauty of the Temple

2 On the twenty-first day of the seventh month, the LORD spoke his word through Haggai the prophet, saying, [2]"Speak to Zerubbabel son of Shealtiel, governor of Judah, and to Joshua son of Jehozadak, the high priest, and to the rest of the people who are left alive. Say, [3]'Do any of you remember how great the Temple was before it was destroyed? What does it look like now? Doesn't it seem like nothing to you?' [4]But the LORD says, 'Zerubbabel, be brave. Also, Joshua son of Jehozadak, the high priest, be brave. And all you people who live in the

land, be brave,' says the LORD. 'Work, because I am with you,' says the LORD All-Powerful. [5]'I made a promise to you when you came out of Egypt, and my Spirit is still with you. So don't be afraid.'

[6]"This is what the LORD All-Powerful says: 'In a short time I will once again shake the heavens and the earth, the sea and the dry land. [7]I will shake all the nations, and they will bring their wealth. Then I will fill this Temple with glory,' says the LORD All-Powerful. [8]'The silver is mine, and the gold is mine,' says the LORD All-Powerful. [9]'The new Temple will be greater than the one before,' says the LORD All-Powerful. 'And in this place I will give peace,' says the LORD All-Powerful."

[10]On the twenty-fourth day of the ninth month in the second year Darius was king, the LORD spoke his word to Haggai the prophet, saying, [11]"This is what the LORD All-Powerful says: 'Ask the priests for a teaching. [12]Suppose a person carries in the fold of his clothes some meat made holy for the LORD. If that fold touches bread, cooked food, wine, olive oil, or some other food, will that be made holy?'"

The priests answered, "No."

[13]Then Haggai said, "A person who touches a dead body will become unclean. If he touches any of these foods, will it become unclean, too?"

The priests answered, "Yes, it would become unclean."

[14]Then Haggai answered, "The LORD says, 'This is also true for the people of this nation. They are unclean, and everything they do with their hands is unclean to me. Whatever they offer at the altar is also unclean.

[15]"'Think about this from now on! Think about how it was before you started laying stones on top of stones to build the Temple of the LORD. [16]A person used to come to a pile of grain expecting to find twenty basketfuls, but there were only ten. And a person used to come to the wine vat to take out fifty jarfuls, but only twenty were there. [17]I destroyed your work with diseases, mildew, and hail, but you still did not come back to me,' says the LORD. [18]'It is the twenty-fourth

day of the ninth month, the day in which the people finished working on the foundation of the Temple of the LORD. From now on, think about these things: [19]Do you have seeds for crops still in the barn? Your vines, fig trees, pomegranates, and olive trees have not given fruit yet. But from now on I will bless you!'"

The Lord Makes a Promise to Zerubbabel

[20]Then the LORD spoke his word a second time to Haggai on the twenty-fourth day of the month. He said, [21]"Tell Zerubbabel, the governor of Judah, 'I am going to shake the heavens and the earth. [22]I will destroy the foreign kingdoms and take away the power of the kingdoms of the nations. I will destroy the chariots and their riders. The horses will fall with their riders, as people kill each other with swords.' [23]The LORD All-Powerful says, 'On that day I will take you, Zerubbabel son of Shealtiel, my servant,' says the LORD, 'and I will make you important like my signet ring, because I have chosen you!' says the LORD All-Powerful."

PSALM 147:7–11

[7]Sing praises to the LORD;
  praise our God with harps.
[8]He fills the sky with clouds
  and sends rain to the earth
  and makes grass grow on the hills.
[9]He gives food to cattle
  and to the little birds that call.

[10]He is not impressed with the strength of
    a horse
  or with human might.
[11]The LORD is pleased with those who
    respect him,
  with those who trust his love.

PROVERBS 30:20

[20]"This is the way of a woman who takes
    part in adultery:
  She acts as if she had eaten and
    washed her face;

she says, 'I haven't done anything wrong.'

REVELATION 15:1–8

The Last Troubles

15 Then I saw another wonder in heaven that was great and amazing. There were seven angels bringing seven disasters. These are the last disasters, because after them, God's anger is finished.

[2]I saw what looked like a sea of glass mixed with fire. All of those who had won the victory over the beast and his idol and over the number of his name were standing by the sea of glass. They had harps that God had given them. [3]They sang the song of Moses, the servant of God, and the song of the Lamb:

"You do great and wonderful things,
                                          Psalm 111:2
  Lord God Almighty.   *Amos 3:13*
Everything the Lord does is right and
    true,   *Psalm 145:17*
  King of the nations."[n]
[4]Everyone will respect you, Lord,
                                      Jeremiah 10:7
  and will honor you.
Only you are holy.
All the nations will come
    and worship you,   *Psalm 86:9–10*
because the right things you have
    done
are now made known."   *Deuteronomy 32:4*
[5]After this I saw that the temple (the Tent of the Agreement) in heaven was opened. [6]And the seven angels bringing the seven disasters came out of the temple. They were dressed in clean, shining linen and wore golden bands tied around their chests. [7]Then one of the four living creatures gave to the seven angels seven golden bowls filled with the anger of God, who lives forever and ever. [8]The temple was filled with smoke from the glory and the power of God, and no one could enter the temple until the seven disasters of the seven angels were finished.

15:3 King . . . nations Some Greek copies read "King of the ages."

DECEMBER 26

ZECHARIAH 1:1—3:10

The Lord Calls His People Back

1 In the eighth month of the second year Darius was king, the LORD spoke his word to the prophet Zechariah son of Berekiah, who was the son of Iddo. The LORD said, ²"The LORD was very angry with your ancestors. ³So tell the people: This is what the LORD All-Powerful says: 'Return to me, and I will return to you,' says the LORD All-Powerful. ⁴Don't be like your ancestors. In the past the prophets said to them: This is what the LORD All-Powerful says: 'Stop your evil ways and evil actions.' But they wouldn't listen or pay attention to me, says the LORD. ⁵Your ancestors are dead, and those prophets didn't live forever. ⁶I commanded my words and laws to my servants the prophets, and they preached to your ancestors, who returned to me. They said, 'The LORD All-Powerful did as he said he would. He punished us for the way we lived and for what we did.'"

The Vision of the Horses

⁷It was on the twenty-fourth day of the eleventh month, which is the month of Shebat, in Darius's second year as king. The LORD spoke his word to the prophet Zechariah son of Berekiah, who was the son of Iddo.

⁸During the night I had a vision. I saw a man riding a red horse. He was standing among some myrtle trees in a ravine, with red, brown, and white horses behind him.

⁹I asked, "What are these, sir?"

The angel who was talking with me answered, "I'll show you what they are."

¹⁰Then the man standing among the myrtle trees explained, "They are the ones the LORD sent through all the earth."

¹¹Then they spoke to the LORD's angel, who was standing among the myrtle trees. They said, "We have gone through all the earth, and everything is calm and quiet."

¹²Then the LORD's angel asked, "LORD All-Powerful, how long will it be before you show mercy to Jerusalem and the cities of Judah? You have been angry with them for seventy years now." ¹³So the LORD answered the angel who was talking with me, and his words were comforting and good.

¹⁴Then the angel who was talking to me said to me, "Announce this: This is what the LORD All-Powerful says: 'I have a strong love for Jerusalem. ¹⁵And I am very angry with the nations that feel so safe. I was only a little angry at them, but they made things worse.'

¹⁶"So this is what the LORD says: 'I will return to Jerusalem with mercy. My Temple will be rebuilt,' says the LORD All-Powerful, 'and the measuring line will be used to rebuild Jerusalem.'

¹⁷"Also announce: This is what the LORD All-Powerful says: 'My towns will be rich again. The LORD will comfort Jerusalem again, and I will again choose Jerusalem.'"

The Vision of the Horns

¹⁸Then I looked up and saw four animal horns. ¹⁹I asked the angel who was talking with me, "What are these?"

He said, "These are the horns that scattered the people of Judah, Israel, and Jerusalem."

²⁰Then the LORD showed me four craftsmen. ²¹I asked, "What are they coming to do?"

He answered, "They have come to scare and throw down the horns. These horns scattered the people of Judah so that no one could even lift up his head. These horns stand for the nations that attacked the people of Judah and scattered them."

The Vision of the Measuring Line

2 Then I looked up and saw a man holding a line for measuring things. ²I asked him, "Where are you going?"

He said to me, "I am going to measure Jerusalem, to see how wide and how long it is."

³Then the angel who was talking with me left, and another angel came out to meet him. ⁴The second angel said to him, "Run and tell that young man, 'Jerusalem will become a city without walls, because there will be so many people and cattle in it. ⁵I will be a wall of fire around it,' says the LORD. 'And I will be the glory within it.'

6"Oh no! Oh no! Run away from Babylon, because I have scattered you like the four winds of heaven," says the LORD.

7"Oh no, Jerusalem! Escape, you who live right in Babylon." 8This is what the LORD All-Powerful says: "After he has honored me and sent me against the nations who took your possessions—because whoever touches you hurts what is precious to me—9I will shake my hand against them so that their slaves will rob them."

Then you will know that the LORD All-Powerful sent me.

10"Shout and be glad, Jerusalem. I am coming, and I will live among you," says the LORD. 11"At that time people from many nations will join with the LORD and will become my people. Then I will live among you, and you will know that the LORD All-Powerful has sent me to you. 12The LORD will take Judah as his own part of the holy land, and Jerusalem will be his chosen city again. 13Be silent, everyone, in the presence of the LORD. He is coming out of the holy place where he lives."

The Vision of the High Priest

3 Then he showed me Joshua, the high priest, standing in front of the LORD's angel. And Satan was standing by Joshua's right side to accuse him. 2The LORD said to Satan, "The LORD says no to you, Satan! The LORD who has chosen Jerusalem says no to you! This man was like a burning stick pulled from the fire."

3Joshua was wearing dirty clothes and was standing in front of the angel. 4The angel said to those standing in front of him, "Take off those dirty clothes."

Then the angel said to Joshua, "Look, I have taken away your sin from you, and I am giving you beautiful, fine clothes."

5Then I said, "Put a clean turban on his head." So they put a clean turban on his head and dressed him while the LORD's angel stood there.

6Then the LORD's angel said to Joshua, 7"This is what the LORD All-Powerful says: 'If you do as I tell you and serve me, you will be in charge of my Temple and my courtyards. And I will let you be with these angels who are standing here.

8"'Listen, Joshua, the high priest, and your

friends who are sitting in front of you. They are symbols of what will happen. I am going to bring my servant called the Branch. 9Look, I put this stone in front of Joshua, a stone with seven sides. I will carve a message on it,' says the LORD All-Powerful. 'And in one day I will take away the sin of this land.'

10"The LORD All-Powerful says, 'In that day, each of you will invite your neighbor to sit under your own grapevine and under your own fig tree.'"

PSALM 147:12-20

12Jerusalem, praise the LORD;
    Jerusalem, praise your God.
13He makes your city gates strong
    and blesses your children inside.
14He brings peace to your country
    and fills you with the finest grain.
15He gives a command to the earth,
    and it quickly obeys him.
16He spreads the snow like wool
    and scatters the frost like ashes.
17He throws down hail like rocks.
    No one can stand the cold he sends.
18Then he gives a command, and it
    melts.
    He sends the breezes, and the waters
    flow.
19He gave his word to Jacob,
    his laws and demands to Israel.
20He didn't do this for any other nation.
    They don't know his laws.

Praise the LORD!

PROVERBS 30:21-23

21"There are three things that make the
    earth tremble,
    really four it cannot stand:
22a servant who becomes a king,
    a foolish person who has plenty to eat,
23a hated woman who gets married,
    and a maid who replaces her mistress.

REVELATION 16:1-21

The Bowls of God's Anger

16 Then I heard a loud voice from the temple saying to the seven angels, "Go and

pour out the seven bowls of God's anger on the earth."

²The first angel left and poured out his bowl on the land. Then ugly and painful sores came upon all those who had the mark of the beast and who worshiped his idol.

³The second angel poured out his bowl on the sea, and it became blood like that of a dead man, and every living thing in the sea died.

⁴The third angel poured out his bowl on the rivers and the springs of water, and they became blood. ⁵Then I heard the angel of the waters saying:

"Holy One, you are the One who is and
     who was.
You are right to decide to punish these
     evil people.
⁶They have poured out the blood of your
     holy people and your prophets.
So now you have given them blood to
     drink as they deserve."

⁷And I heard a voice coming from the altar saying:

"Yes, Lord God Almighty,
the way you punish evil people is right
     and fair."

⁸The fourth angel poured out his bowl on the sun, and he was given power to burn the people with fire. ⁹They were burned by the great heat, and they cursed the name of God, who had control over these disasters. But the people refused to change their hearts and lives and give glory to God.

¹⁰The fifth angel poured out his bowl on the throne of the beast, and darkness covered its kingdom. People gnawed their tongues because of the pain. ¹¹They also cursed the God of heaven because of their pain and the sores they had, but they refused to change their

hearts and turn away from the evil things they did.

¹²The sixth angel poured out his bowl on the great river Euphrates so that the water in the river was dried up to prepare the way for the kings from the east to come. ¹³Then I saw three evil spirits that looked like frogs coming out of the mouth of the dragon, out of the mouth of the beast, and out of the mouth of the false prophet. ¹⁴These evil spirits are the spirits of demons, which have power to do miracles. They go out to the kings of the whole world to gather them together for the battle on the great day of God Almighty.

¹⁵"Listen! I will come as a thief comes! Blessed are those who stay awake and keep their clothes on so that they will not walk around naked and have people see their shame."

¹⁶Then the evil spirits gathered the kings together to the place that is called Armageddon in the Hebrew language.

¹⁷The seventh angel poured out his bowl into the air. Then a loud voice came out of the temple from the throne, saying, "It is finished!" ¹⁸Then there were flashes of lightning, noises, thunder, and a big earthquake—the worst earthquake that has ever happened since people have been on earth. ¹⁹The great city split into three parts, and the cities of the nations were destroyed. And God remembered the sins of Babylon the Great, so he gave that city the cup filled with the wine of his terrible anger. ²⁰Then every island ran away, and mountains disappeared. ²¹Giant hailstones, each weighing about a hundred pounds, fell from the sky upon people. People cursed God for the disaster of the hail, because this disaster was so terrible.

DECEMBER 27

ZECHARIAH 4:1—6:15

The Vision of the Lampstand

4 Then the angel who was talking with me returned and woke me up as if I had

been asleep. ²He asked me, "What do you see?"

I said, "I see a solid gold lampstand with a bowl at the top. And there are seven lamps and also seven places for wicks. ³There are two olive trees by it, one on the right of the bowl and the other on the left."

⁴I asked the angel who talked with me, "Sir, what are these?"

⁵The angel said, "Don't you know what they are?"

"No, sir," I said.

⁶Then he told me, "This is the word of the LORD to Zerubbabel: 'You will not succeed by your own strength or by your own power, but by my Spirit,' says the LORD All-Powerful.

⁷"Who are you, big mountain? In front of Zerubbabel you will become flat land, and he will bring out the topmost stone, shouting, 'It's beautiful! It's beautiful!'"

⁸Then the LORD spoke his word to me again, saying, ⁹"Zerubbabel has laid the foundation of this Temple, and he will complete it. Then you will know that the LORD All-Powerful has sent me to you.

¹⁰"The people should not think that small beginnings are unimportant. They will be happy when they see Zerubbabel with tools, building the Temple.

"(These are the seven eyes of the LORD, which look back and forth across the earth.)"

¹¹Then I asked the angel, "What are the two olive trees on the right and left of the lampstand?"

¹²I also asked him, "What are the two olive branches beside the two gold pipes, from which the olive oil flows to the lamps?"

¹³He answered, "Don't you know what they are?"

"No, sir," I said.

¹⁴So he said, "They are symbols of the two who have been appointed to serve the Lord of all the earth."

The Vision of the Flying Scroll

5 I looked up again and saw a flying scroll. ²The angel asked me, "What do you see?"

I answered, "I see a flying scroll, thirty feet long and fifteen feet wide."

³And he said to me, "This is the curse that will go all over the land. One side says every thief will be taken away. The other side says everyone who makes false promises will be taken away. ⁴The LORD All-Powerful says, 'I will send it to the houses of thieves and to those who use my name to make false promises. The scroll will stay in that person's house and destroy it with its wood and stones.'"

The Vision of the Woman

⁵Then the angel who was talking with me came forward and said to me, "Look up and see what is going out."

⁶"What is it?" I asked.

He answered, "It is a measuring basket going out." He also said, "It is a symbol of the people's sins in all the land."

⁷Then the lid made of lead was raised, and there was a woman sitting inside the basket. ⁸The angel said, "The woman stands for wickedness." Then he pushed her back into the basket and put the lid back down.

⁹Then I looked up and saw two women going out with the wind in their wings. Their wings were like those of a stork, and they lifted up the basket between earth and the sky.

¹⁰I asked the angel who was talking with me, "Where are they taking the basket?"

¹¹"They are going to Babylonia to build a temple for it," he answered. "When the temple is ready, they will set the basket there in its place."

The Vision of the Four Chariots

6 I looked up again and saw four chariots going out between two mountains, mountains of bronze. ²Red horses pulled the first chariot. Black horses pulled the second chariot. ³White horses pulled the third chariot, and strong, spotted horses pulled the fourth chariot. ⁴I asked the angel who was talking with me, "What are these, sir?"

⁵He said, "These are the four spirits of heaven. They have just come from the presence of the Lord of the whole world. ⁶The chariot pulled by the black horses will go to the land of the north. The white horses will go to the land of the west, and the spotted horses will go to the land of the south."

⁷When the powerful horses went out, they were eager to go through all the earth. So he said, "Go through all the earth," and they did.

⁸Then he called to me, "Look, the horses that went north have caused my spirit to rest in the land of the north."

A Crown for Joshua

⁹The LORD spoke his word to me, saying, ¹⁰"Take silver and gold from Heldai, Tobijah, and Jedaiah, who were captives in Babylon. Go that same day to the house of Josiah son of Zephaniah, who came from Babylon. ¹¹Make the silver and gold into a crown, and put it on the head of Joshua son of Jehozadak, the high priest. ¹²Tell him this is what the LORD All-Powerful says: 'A man whose name is the Branch will branch out from where he is, and he will build the Temple of the LORD. ¹³One manⁿ will build the Temple of the LORD, and the otherⁿ will receive honor. One man will sit on his throne and rule, and the other will be a priest on his throne. And these two men will work together in peace.' ¹⁴The crown will be kept in the Temple of the LORD to remind Heldai, Tobijah, Jedaiah, and Josiah son of Zephaniah. ¹⁵People living far away will come and build the Temple of the LORD. Then you will know the LORD All-Powerful has sent me to you. This will happen if you completely obey the LORD your God."

PSALM 148:1–6

The World Should Praise the Lord

148 Praise the LORD!
Praise the LORD from the skies.
Praise him high above the earth.
²Praise him, all you angels.
Praise him, all you armies of heaven.
³Praise him, sun and moon.
Praise him, all you shining stars.
⁴Praise him, highest heavens
and you waters above the sky.
⁵Let them praise the LORD,
because they were created by his
command.
⁶He put them in place forever and ever;
he made a law that will never change.

PROVERBS 30:24–28

²⁴"There are four things on earth that are
small,
but they are very wise:
²⁵Ants are not very strong,
but they store up food in the summer.

²⁶Rock badgers are not very powerful,
but they can live among the rocks.
²⁷Locusts have no king,
but they all go forward in formation.
²⁸Lizards can be caught in the hand,
but they are found even in kings'
palaces.

REVELATION 17:1–18

The Woman on the Animal

17Then one of the seven angels who had the seven bowls came and spoke to me. He said, "Come, and I will show you the punishment that will be given to the great prostitute, the one sitting over many waters. ²The kings of the earth sinned sexually with her, and the people of the earth became drunk from the wine of her sexual sin."

³Then the angel carried me away by the Spirit to the desert. There I saw a woman sitting on a red beast. It was covered with names against God written on it, and it had seven heads and ten horns. ⁴The woman was dressed in purple and red and was shining with the gold, precious jewels, and pearls she was wearing. She had a golden cup in her hand, a cup filled with evil things and the uncleanness of her sexual sin. ⁵On her forehead a title was written that was secret. This is what was written:

THE GREAT BABYLON

MOTHER OF PROSTITUTES

AND OF THE EVIL THINGS OF THE EARTH

⁶Then I saw that the woman was drunk with the blood of God's holy people and with the blood of those who were killed because of their faith in Jesus.

When I saw the woman, I was very amazed. ⁷Then the angel said to me, "Why are you amazed? I will tell you the secret of this woman and the beast she rides—the one with seven heads and ten horns. ⁸The beast you saw was once alive but is not alive now. But soon it will come up out of the bottomless pit and go away to be destroyed. There are people who live on earth whose names have not been written in the book of life since the beginning of the world. They will be amazed when they see the beast, because he was once alive, is not alive now, but will come again.

9"You need a wise mind to understand this. The seven heads on the beast are seven mountains where the woman sits. 10And they are seven kings. Five of the kings have already been destroyed, one of the kings lives now, and another has not yet come. When he comes, he must stay a short time. 11The beast that was once alive, but is not alive now, is also an eighth king. He belongs to the first seven kings, and he will go away to be destroyed.

12"The ten horns you saw are ten kings who have not yet begun to rule, but they will receive power to rule with the beast for one hour. 13All ten of these kings have the same purpose, and they will give their power and

authority to the beast. 14They will make war against the Lamb, but the Lamb will defeat them, because he is Lord of lords and King of kings. He will defeat them with his called, chosen, and faithful followers."

15Then the angel said to me, "The waters that you saw, where the prostitute sits, are peoples, races, nations, and languages. 16The ten horns and the beast you saw will hate the prostitute. They will take everything she has and leave her naked. They will eat her body and burn her with fire. 17God made the ten horns want to carry out his purpose by agreeing to give the beast their power to rule, until what God has said comes about. 18The woman you saw is the great city that rules over the kings of the earth."

DECEMBER 28

ZECHARIAH 7:1—9:17

The People Should Show Mercy

7 In the fourth year Darius was king, on the fourth day of the ninth month, which is called Kislev, the LORD spoke his word to Zechariah. 2The city of Bethel sent Sharezer, Regem-Melech, and their men to ask the LORD a question. 3They went to the prophets and priests who were at the Temple of the LORD All-Powerful. The men said, "For years in the fifth month of each year we have shown our sadness and fasted. Should we continue to do this?"

4The LORD All-Powerful spoke his word to me, saying, 5"Tell the priests and the people in the land: 'For seventy years you fasted and cried in the fifth and seventh months, but that was not really for me. 6And when you ate and drank, it was really for yourselves. 7The LORD used the earlier prophets to say the same thing, when Jerusalem and the surrounding towns were at peace and wealthy, and people lived in the southern area and the western hills.'"

8And the LORD spoke his word to Zechariah again, saying, 9"This is what the LORD All-Powerful says: 'Do what is right and

true. Be kind and merciful to each other. 10Don't hurt widows and orphans, foreigners or the poor; don't even think of doing evil to somebody else.'

11"But they refused to pay attention; they were stubborn and did not want to listen anymore. 12They made their hearts as hard as rock and would not listen to the teachings of the LORD All-Powerful. And they would not hear the words he sent by his Spirit through the earlier prophets. So the LORD All-Powerful became very angry.

13"When I called to them, they would not listen. So when they called to me, I would not listen,' says the LORD All-Powerful. 14'I scattered them like a hurricane to other countries they did not know. This good land was left so ruined behind them that no one could live there. They had made the desired land a ruin.'"

The Lord Will Bless Jerusalem

8 The LORD All-Powerful spoke his word, saying, 2This is what the LORD All-Powerful says: "I have a very strong love for Jerusalem. My strong love for her is like a fire burning in me."

3This is what the LORD says: "I will return

to Jerusalem and live in it. Then it will be called the City of Truth, and the mountain of the LORD All-Powerful will be called the Holy Mountain."

⁴This is what the LORD All-Powerful says: "Old men and old women will again sit along Jerusalem's streets, each carrying a cane because of age. ⁵And the streets will be filled with boys and girls playing."

⁶This is what the LORD All-Powerful says: "Those who are left alive then may think it is too difficult to happen, but it is not too difficult for me," says the LORD All-Powerful. ⁷This is what the LORD All-Powerful says: "I will save my people from countries in the east and west. ⁸I will bring them back, and they will live in Jerusalem. They will be my people, and I will be their good and loyal God."

⁹This is what the LORD All-Powerful says: "Work hard, you who are hearing these words today. The prophets spoke these words when the foundation was laid for the house of the LORD All-Powerful, for the building of the Temple. ¹⁰Before that time there was no money to hire people or animals. People could not safely come and go because of the enemies; I had turned everyone against his neighbor. ¹¹But I will not do to these people who are left what I did in the past," says the LORD All-Powerful.

¹²"They will plant their seeds in peace, their grapevines will have fruit, the ground will give good crops, and the sky will send rain. I will give all this to the people who are left alive. ¹³Judah and Israel, your names have been used as curses in other nations. But I will save you, and you will become a blessing. So don't be afraid; work hard."

¹⁴This is what the LORD All-Powerful says: "When your ancestors made me angry, I planned to punish you. I did not change my mind," says the LORD All-Powerful. ¹⁵"But now I will do something different. I am planning to do good to Jerusalem and Judah. So don't be afraid. ¹⁶These are the things you should do: Tell each other the truth. In the courts judge with truth and complete fairness. ¹⁷Do not make plans to hurt your neighbors, and don't love false promises. I hate all these things," says the LORD.

¹⁸The LORD All-Powerful spoke his word to me again. ¹⁹This is what the LORD All-Powerful says: "The special days when you fast in the fourth, fifth, seventh, and tenth months will become good, joyful, happy feasts in Judah. But you must love truth and peace."

²⁰This is what the LORD All-Powerful says: "Many people from many cities will still come to Jerusalem. ²¹People from one city will go and say to those from another city, 'We are going to pray to the LORD and to ask the LORD All-Powerful for help. Come and go with us.' ²²Many people and powerful nations will come to worship the LORD All-Powerful in Jerusalem and to pray to the LORD for help."

²³This is what the LORD All-Powerful says: "At that time, ten men from different countries will come and take hold of a Judean by his coat. They will say to him, 'Let us go with you, because we have heard that God is with you.'"

Punishment on Israel's Enemies

9 This message is the word of the LORD. The message is against the land of Hadrach
and the city of Damascus.
The tribes of Israel and all people
belong to the LORD.
²The message is also against the city of
Hamath, on the border,
and against Tyre and Sidon, with their
skill.
³Tyre has built a strong wall for herself.
She has piled up silver like dust
and gold like the mud in the streets.
⁴But the Lord will take away all she has
and destroy her power on the sea.
That city will be destroyed by fire.
⁵The city of Ashkelon will see it and be
afraid.
The people of Gaza will shake with fear,
and the people of Ekron will lose hope.
No king will be left in Gaza,
and no one will live in Ashkelon
anymore.
⁶Foreigners will live in Ashdod,
and I will destroy the pride of the
Philistines.

⁷I will stop them from drinking blood
  and from eating forbidden food.
Those left alive will belong to God.
  They will be leaders in Judah,
  and Ekron will become like the
    Jebusites.
⁸I will protect my Temple
  from armies who would come or go.
No one will hurt my people again,
  because now I am watching them.

The King Is Coming

⁹Rejoice greatly, people of Jerusalem!
Shout for joy, people of Jerusalem!
  Your king is coming to you.
  He does what is right, and he saves.
  He is gentle and riding on a donkey,
    on the colt of a donkey.
¹⁰I will take away the chariots from
    Ephraim
  and the horses from Jerusalem.
The bows used in war will be broken.
  The king will talk to the nations about
    peace.
  His kingdom will go from sea to sea,
  and from the Euphrates River to the
    ends of the earth.

¹¹As for you, because of the blood of the
    agreement with you
  I will set your prisoners free from the
    waterless pit.
¹²You prisoners who have hope,
  return to your place of safety.
Today I am telling you
  that I will give you back twice as much
    as before.
¹³I will use Judah like a bow
  and Ephraim like the arrows.
Jerusalem, I will use your men
  to fight the men of Greece.
  I will use you like a warrior's sword.

¹⁴Then the LORD will appear above them,
  and his arrows will shoot like lightning.
The Lord GOD will blow the trumpet,
  and he will march in the storms of the
    south.
¹⁵The LORD All-Powerful will protect them;
  they will destroy the enemy with
    slingshots.
They will drink and shout like drunks.

They will be filled like a bowl
  used for sprinkling blood at the corners
    of the altar.
¹⁶On that day the LORD their God will save
    them
  as if his people were sheep.
They will shine in his land
  like jewels in a crown.
¹⁷They will be so pretty and beautiful.
  The young men will grow strong on the
    grain
  and the young women on new wine.

PSALM 148:7-14

⁷Praise the LORD from the earth,
  you large sea animals and all the
    oceans,
⁸lightning and hail, snow and mist,
  and stormy winds that obey him,
⁹mountains and all hills,
  fruit trees and all cedars,
¹⁰wild animals and all cattle,
  crawling animals and birds,
¹¹kings of the earth and all nations,
  princes and all rulers of the earth,
¹²young men and women,
  old people and children.

¹³Praise the LORD,
  because he alone is great.
He is more wonderful than heaven and
    earth.
¹⁴God has given his people a king.
  He should be praised by all who belong
    to him;
  he should be praised by the Israelites,
    the people closest to his heart.

Praise the LORD!

PROVERBS 30:29-31

²⁹"There are three things that strut
    proudly,
  really four that walk as if they were
    important:
³⁰a lion, the proudest animal,
  which is strong and runs from nothing,
³¹a rooster, a male goat,
  and a king when his army is around
    him.

REVELATION 18:1–24

Babylon Is Destroyed

18After the vision of these things, I saw another angel coming down from heaven. This angel had great power, and his glory made the earth bright. [2]He shouted in a powerful voice:

"Ruined, ruined is the great city of
    Babylon!
She has become a home for demons
and a prison for every evil spirit,
    and a prison for every unclean bird and
        unclean beast.
[3]She has been ruined, because all the
        peoples of the earth
    have drunk the wine of the desire of
        her sexual sin.
She has been ruined also because the
        kings of the earth
    have sinned sexually with her,
and the merchants of the earth
    have grown rich from the great wealth
        of her luxury."

[4]Then I heard another voice from heaven saying:

"Come out of that city, my people,
    so that you will not share in her sins,
    so that you will not receive the disasters
        that will come to her.
[5]Her sins have piled up as high as the sky,
    and God has not forgotten the wrongs
        she has done.
[6]Give that city the same as she gave to
        others.
    Pay her back twice as much as she did.
    Prepare wine for her that is twice as strong
        as the wine she prepared for others.
[7]She gave herself much glory and rich
        living.
    Give her that much suffering and
        sadness.
    She says to herself, 'I am a queen sitting
        on my throne.
    I am not a widow; I will never be sad.'
[8]So these disasters will come to her in one
        day:
    death, and crying, and great hunger,
    and she will be destroyed by fire,
        because the Lord God who judges her is
            powerful."

[9]The kings of the earth who sinned sexually with her and shared her wealth will see the smoke from her burning. Then they will cry and be sad because of her death. [10]They will be afraid of her suffering and stand far away and say:

"Terrible! How terrible for you, great city,
        powerful city of Babylon,
    because your punishment has come in
        one hour!"

[11]And the merchants of the earth will cry and be sad about her, because now there is no one to buy their cargoes— [12]cargoes of gold, silver, jewels, pearls, fine linen, purple cloth, silk, red cloth; all kinds of citron wood and all kinds of things made from ivory, expensive wood, bronze, iron, and marble; [13]cinnamon, spice, incense, myrrh, frankincense, wine, olive oil, fine flour, wheat, cattle, sheep, horses, carriages, slaves, and human lives.

[14]The merchants will say,

"Babylon, the good things you wanted
        are gone from you.
All your rich and fancy things have
        disappeared.
You will never have them again."

[15]The merchants who became rich from selling to her will be afraid of her suffering and will stand far away. They will cry and be sad [16]and say:

"Terrible! How terrible for the great city!
    She was dressed in fine linen, purple
        and red cloth,
    and she was shining with gold, precious
        jewels, and pearls!
[17]All these riches have been destroyed in
        one hour!"

Every sea captain, every passenger, the sailors, and all those who earn their living from the sea stood far away from Babylon. [18]As they saw the smoke from her burning, they cried out loudly, "There was never a city like this great city!" [19]And they threw dust on their heads and cried out, weeping and being sad. They said:

"Terrible! How terrible for the great city!
All the people who had ships on the sea
        became rich because of her wealth!
But she has been destroyed in one hour!
[20]Be happy because of this, heaven!

Be happy, God's holy people and
apostles and prophets!
God has punished her because of what
she did to you."
²¹Then a powerful angel picked up a large
stone, like one used for grinding grain, and
threw it into the sea. He said:
"In the same way, the great city of
Babylon will be thrown down,
and it will never be found again.
²²The music of people playing harps and
other instruments, flutes, and
trumpets,
will never be heard in you again.
No workman doing any job

will ever be found in you again.
The sound of grinding grain
will never be heard in you again.
²³The light of a lamp
will never shine in you again,
and the voices of a bridegroom and
bride
will never be heard in you again.
Your merchants were the world's great
people,
and all the nations were tricked by your
magic.
²⁴You are guilty of the death of the
prophets and God's holy people
and all who have been killed on earth."

DECEMBER 29

ZECHARIAH 10:1—12:9

The Lord's Promises

10 Ask the Lord for rain during the
springtime rains.
The Lord is the one who makes the
clouds.
He sends the showers
and gives everyone green fields.
²Idols tell lies;
fortune-tellers see false visions
and tell about false dreams.
The comfort they give is worth nothing.
So the people are like lost sheep.
They are abused, because there is no
shepherd.

³The Lord says, "I am angry at my
shepherds,
and I will punish the leaders.
I, the Lord All-Powerful, care
for my flock, the people of Judah.
I will make them like my proud war
horses.
⁴From Judah will come the cornerstone,
and the tent peg,
the battle bow,
and every ruler.
⁵Together they will be like soldiers
marching to battle through muddy
streets.

The Lord is with them,
so they will fight and defeat the
horsemen.
⁶"I will strengthen the people of Judah
and save the people of Joseph.
I will bring them back,
because I care about them.
It will be as though
I had never left them,
because I am the Lord their God,
and I will answer them.
⁷The people of Ephraim will be strong like
soldiers;
they will be glad as when they have
drunk wine.
Their children will see it and rejoice;
they will be happy in the Lord.
⁸I will call my people
and gather them together.
I will save them,
and they will grow in number as they
grew in number before.
⁹I have scattered them among the nations,
but in those faraway places, they will
remember me.
They and their children will live and
return.
¹⁰I will bring them back from the land of
Egypt

and gather them from Assyria.
I will bring them to Gilead and Lebanon
until there isn't enough room for them
all.
[11]They will come through the sea of
trouble.
The waves of the sea will be calm,
and the Nile River will dry up.
I will defeat Assyria's pride
and destroy Egypt's power over other
countries.
[12]I will make my people strong,
and they will live as I say," says the
Lord.

11 Lebanon, open your gates
so fire may burn your cedar trees.[n]
[2]Cry, pine trees, because the cedar has
fallen,
because the tall trees are ruined.
Cry, oaks in Bashan,
because the mighty forest has been cut
down.
[3]Listen to the shepherds crying
because their rich pastures are
destroyed.
Listen to the lions roaring
because the lovely land of the Jordan
River is ruined.

The Two Shepherds
[4]This is what the Lord my God says: "Feed
the flock that are about to be killed. [5]Their
buyers kill them and are not punished.
Those who sell them say, 'Praise the Lord, I
am rich.' Even the shepherds don't feel sorry
for their sheep. [6]I don't feel sorry anymore
for the people of this country," says the Lord.
"I will let everyone be under the power of his
neighbor and king. They will bring trouble
to the country, and I will not save anyone
from them."

[7]So I fed the flock about to be killed, particularly the weakest ones. Then I took two
sticks; I called one Pleasant and the other
Union, and I fed the flock. [8]In one month I got
rid of three shepherds. The flock did not pay
attention to me, and I got impatient with
them. [9]I said, "I will no longer take care of you

like a shepherd. Let those that are dying die,
and let those that are to be destroyed be destroyed. Let those that are left eat each other."
[10]Then I broke the stick named Pleasant
to break the agreement God made with all
the nations. [11]That day it was broken. The
weak ones in the flock who were watching
me knew this message was from the Lord.
[12]Then I said, "If you want to pay me, pay
me. If not, then don't." So they paid me thirty
pieces of silver.
[13]The Lord said to me, "Throw the money
to the potter." That is how little they thought
I was worth.[n] So I took the thirty pieces of
silver and threw them to the potter in the
Temple of the Lord.
[14]Then I broke the second stick, named
Union, to break the brotherhood between Judah and Israel.
[15]Then the Lord said to me, "Get the
things used by a foolish shepherd again,
[16]because I am going to get a new shepherd
for the country. He will not care for the dying
sheep, or look for the young ones, or heal the
injured ones, or feed the healthy. But he will
eat the best sheep and tear off their hoofs.
[17]"How terrible it will be for the useless
shepherd
who abandoned the flock.
A sword will strike his arm and his right
eye.
His arm will lose all its strength,
and his right eye will go blind."

Jerusalem Will Be Saved
12 This message is the word of the Lord
to Israel. This is what the Lord says,
who stretched out the skies, and laid the
foundations of the earth, and put the human
spirit within: [2]"I will make Jerusalem like a
cup of poison to the nations around her.
They will come and attack Jerusalem and Judah. [3]One day all the nations on earth will
come together to attack Jerusalem, but I will
make it like a heavy rock; anyone who tries
to move it will get hurt. [4]At that time I will
confuse every horse and cause its rider to go
crazy," says the Lord. "I will watch over Ju-

11:1 trees In this poem, trees, bushes, and animals stand for leaders of countries around Judah. **11:13 worth** This was
a small amount. It was about the price paid for a slave.

dah, but I will blind all the horses of the enemies. ⁵Then the leaders of Judah will say to themselves, 'The people of Jerusalem are strong, because the LORD All-Powerful is their God.'

⁶"At that time I will make the leaders of Judah like a fire burning a stack of wood or like a fire burning straw. They will destroy all the people around them left and right. But the people of Jerusalem will remain safe.

⁷"The LORD will save the homes of Judah first so that the honor given to David's family and to the people of Jerusalem won't be greater than the honor given to Judah. ⁸At that time the LORD will protect the people in Jerusalem. Then even the weakest of them will be strong like David. And the family of David will be like God, like an angel of the LORD in front of them. ⁹At that time I will go to destroy all the nations that attack Jerusalem.

PSALM 149:1–5

Praise the God of Israel

149 Praise the LORD!
Sing a new song to the LORD;
  sing his praise in the meeting of his
    people.

²Let the Israelites be happy because of
    God, their Maker.
  Let the people of Jerusalem rejoice
    because of their King.
³They should praise him with dancing.
  They should sing praises to him with
    tambourines and harps.
⁴The LORD is pleased with his people;
  he saves the humble.
⁵Let those who worship him rejoice in his
    glory.
  Let them sing for joy even in bed!

PROVERBS 30:32–33

³²"If you have been foolish and proud,
  or if you have planned evil, shut your
    mouth.
³³Just as stirring milk makes butter,
  and twisting noses makes them bleed,
  so stirring up anger causes trouble."

REVELATION 19:1–21

People in Heaven Praise God

19After this vision and announcement I
heard what sounded like a great many people in heaven saying:
  "Hallelujah!ⁿ
  Salvation, glory, and power belong to our
    God,
² because his judgments are true and
    right.
  He has punished the prostitute
    who made the earth evil with her
      sexual sin.
  He has paid her back for the death of his
    servants."
³Again they said:
  "Hallelujah!
  She is burning, and her smoke will rise
    forever and ever."
⁴Then the twenty-four elders and the four living creatures bowed down and worshiped God, who sits on the throne. They said:
  "Amen, Hallelujah!"
⁵Then a voice came from the throne, saying:
  "Praise our God, all you who serve him
    and all you who honor him, both small
      and great!"
⁶Then I heard what sounded like a great many people, like the noise of flooding water, and like the noise of loud thunder. The people were saying:
  "Hallelujah!
  Our Lord God, the Almighty, rules.
⁷Let us rejoice and be happy
    and give God glory,
  because the wedding of the Lamb has
    come,
    and the Lamb's bride has made herself
      ready.
⁸Fine linen, bright and clean, was given to
    her to wear."
(The fine linen means the good things done by God's holy people.)

⁹And the angel said to me, "Write this: Blessed are those who have been invited to the wedding meal of the Lamb!" And the angel said, "These are the true words of God." ¹⁰Then I bowed down at the angel's feet to

---

19:1 Hallelujah This means "praise God!"

worship him, but he said to me, "Do not worship me! I am a servant like you and your brothers and sisters who have the message of Jesus. Worship God, because the message about Jesus is the spirit that gives all prophecy."

The Rider on the White Horse

[11]Then I saw heaven opened, and there before me was a white horse. The rider on the horse is called Faithful and True, and he is right when he judges and makes war. [12]His eyes are like burning fire, and on his head are many crowns. He has a name written on him, which no one but himself knows. [13]He is dressed in a robe dipped in blood, and his name is the Word of God. [14]The armies of heaven, dressed in fine linen, white and clean, were following him on white horses. [15]Out of the rider's mouth comes a sharp sword that he will use to defeat the nations, and he will rule them with a rod of iron. He will crush out the wine in the winepress of the terrible anger of God the Almighty. [16]On his robe and on his upper leg was written this name: KING OF KINGS AND LORD OF LORDS.

[17]Then I saw an angel standing in the sun, and he called with a loud voice to all the birds flying in the sky: "Come and gather together for the great feast of God [18]so that you can eat the bodies of kings, generals, mighty people, horses and their riders, and the bodies of all people—free, slave, small, and great."

[19]Then I saw the beast and the kings of the earth. Their armies were gathered together to make war against the rider on the horse and his army. [20]But the beast was captured and with him the false prophet who did the miracles for the beast. The false prophet had used these miracles to trick those who had the mark of the beast and worshiped his idol. The false prophet and the beast were thrown alive into the lake of fire that burns with sulfur. [21]And their armies were killed with the sword that came out of the mouth of the rider on the horse, and all the birds ate the bodies until they were full.

DECEMBER 30

ZECHARIAH 12:10—14:21

Crying for the One They Stabbed

[10]"I will pour out on David's family and the people in Jerusalem a spirit of kindness and mercy. They will look at me, the one they have stabbed, and they will cry like someone crying over the death of an only child. They will be as sad as someone who has lost a firstborn son. [11]At that time there will be much crying in Jerusalem, like the crying for Hadad Rimmon in the plain of Megiddo. [12]The land will cry, each family by itself: the family of David by itself and their wives by themselves, the family of Nathan by itself and their wives by themselves, [13]the family of Levi by itself and their wives by themselves, the family of Shimei by itself and their wives by themselves, [14]and all the rest of the families by themselves and their wives by themselves.

13 "At that time a fountain will be open for David's descendants and for the people of Jerusalem to cleanse them of their sin and uncleanness."

[2]The LORD All-Powerful says, "At that time I will get rid of the names of the idols from the land; no one will remember them anymore. I will also remove the prophets and unclean spirits from the land. [3]If a person continues to prophesy, his own father and mother, the ones who gave birth to him, will tell him, 'You have told lies using the LORD's name, so you must die.' When he prophesies, his own father and mother who gave birth to him will stab him.

[4]"At that time the prophets will be ashamed of their visions and prophecies. They won't wear the prophet's clothes made of hair to trick people. [5]Each of them will say, 'I am not a prophet. I am a farmer and

have been a farmer since I was young.' ⁶But someone will ask, 'What are the deep cuts on your body?' And each will answer, 'I was hurt at my friend's house.'

The Shepherd Is Killed

⁷"Sword, hit the shepherd.
Attack the man who is my friend,"
says the LORD All-Powerful.
"Kill the shepherd,
and the sheep will scatter,
and I will punish the little ones."

⁸The LORD says, "Two-thirds of the people
through all the land will die. They will
be gone,
and one-third will be left.
⁹The third that is left I will test with fire,
purifying them like silver,
testing them like gold.
Then they will call on me,
and I will answer them.
I will say, 'You are my people,'
and they will say, 'The LORD is our God.'"

The Day of Punishment

14 The LORD's day of judging is coming
when the wealth you have taken will be
divided among you.

²I will bring all the nations together to fight Jerusalem. They will capture the city and rob the houses and attack the women. Half the people will be taken away as captives, but the rest of the people won't be taken from the city.

³Then the LORD will go to war against those nations; he will fight as in a day of battle. ⁴On that day he will stand on the Mount of Olives, east of Jerusalem. The Mount of Olives will split in two, forming a deep valley that runs east and west. Half the mountain will move toward the north, and half will move toward the south. ⁵You will run through this mountain valley to the other side, just as you ran from the earthquake when Uzziah was king of Judah. Then the LORD my God will come and all the holy ones with him.

⁶On that day there will be no light, cold, or frost. ⁷There will be no other day like it, and the LORD knows when it will come. There will be no day or night; even at evening it will still be light.

⁸At that time fresh water will flow from Jerusalem. Half of it will flow east to the Dead Sea, and half will flow west to the Mediterranean Sea. It will flow summer and winter.

⁹Then the LORD will be king over the whole world. At that time there will be only one LORD, and his name will be the only name.

¹⁰All the land south of Jerusalem from Geba to Rimmon will be turned into a plain. Jerusalem will be raised up, but it will stay in the same place. The city will reach from the Benjamin Gate and to the First Gate to the Corner Gate, and from the Tower of Hananel to the king's winepresses. ¹¹People will live there, and it will never be destroyed again. Jerusalem will be safe.

¹²But the LORD will bring a terrible disease on the nations that fought against Jerusalem. Their flesh will rot away while they are still standing up. Their eyes will rot in their sockets, and their tongues will rot in their mouths. ¹³At that time the LORD will cause panic. Everybody will grab his neighbor, and they will attack each other. ¹⁴The people of Judah will fight in Jerusalem. And the wealth of the nations around them will be collected—much gold, silver, and clothes. ¹⁵A similar disease will strike the horses, mules, camels, donkeys, and all the animals in the camps.

¹⁶All of those left alive of the people who came to fight Jerusalem will come back to Jerusalem year after year to worship the King, the LORD All-Powerful, and to celebrate the Feast of Shelters. ¹⁷Anyone from the nations who does not go to Jerusalem to worship the King, the LORD All-Powerful, will not have rain fall on his land. ¹⁸If the Egyptians do not go to Jerusalem, they will not have rain. Then the LORD will send them the same terrible disease he sent the other nations that did not celebrate the Feast of Shelters. ¹⁹This will be the punishment for Egypt and any nation which does not go to celebrate the Feast of Shelters.

²⁰At that time the horses' bells will have written on them: HOLY TO THE LORD. The cooking pots in the Temple of the Lord will be like the holy altar bowls. ²¹Every pot in Jerusalem and Judah will be holy to the LORD All-Powerful, and everyone who offers sacrifices will be able to take food from them and cook

in them. At that time there will not be any buyers or sellers in the Temple of the LORD All-Powerful.

PSALM 149:6–9

⁶Let them shout his praise
  with their two-edged swords in their
  hands.
⁷They will punish the nations
  and defeat the people.
⁸They will put those kings in chains
  and those important men in iron
  bands.
⁹They will punish them as God has
  written.
  God is honored by all who worship him.

  Praise the LORD!

PROVERBS 31:1–9

Wise Words of King Lemuel

31 These are the words of King Lemuel, the message his mother taught him:
²"My son, I gave birth to you.
  You are the son I prayed for.
³Don't waste your strength on women
  or your time on those who ruin kings.

⁴"Kings should not drink wine, Lemuel,
  and rulers should not desire beer.
⁵If they drink, they might forget the law
  and keep the needy from getting their
  rights.
⁶Give beer to people who are dying
  and wine to those who are sad.
⁷Let them drink and forget their need
  and remember their misery no more.

⁸"Speak up for those who cannot speak
  for themselves;
  defend the rights of all those who have
  nothing.
⁹Speak up and judge fairly,
  and defend the rights of the poor and
  needy."

REVELATION 20:1–15

The Thousand Years

20 I saw an angel coming down from heaven. He had the key to the bottom-less pit and a large chain in his hand. ²The angel grabbed the dragon, that old snake who is the devil and Satan, and tied him up for a thousand years. ³Then he threw him into the bottomless pit, closed it, and locked it over him. The angel did this so he could not trick the people of the earth anymore until the thousand years were ended. After a thousand years he must be set free for a short time.

⁴Then I saw some thrones and people sitting on them who had been given the power to judge. And I saw the souls of those who had been killed because they were faithful to the message of Jesus and the message from God. They had not worshiped the beast or his idol, and they had not received the mark of the beast on their foreheads or on their hands. They came back to life and ruled with Christ for a thousand years. ⁵(The others that were dead did not live again until the thousand years were ended.) This is the first raising of the dead. ⁶Blessed and holy are those who share in this first raising of the dead. The second death has no power over them. They will be priests for God and for Christ and will rule with him for a thousand years.

⁷When the thousand years are over, Satan will be set free from his prison. ⁸Then he will go out to trick the nations in all the earth—Gog and Magog—to gather them for battle. There are so many people they will be like sand on the seashore. ⁹And Satan's army marched across the earth and gathered around the camp of God's people and the city God loves. But fire came down from heaven and burned them up. ¹⁰And Satan, who tricked them, was thrown into the lake of burning sulfur with the beast and the false prophet. There they will be punished day and night forever and ever.

People of the World Are Judged

¹¹Then I saw a great white throne and the One who was sitting on it. Earth and sky ran away from him and disappeared. ¹²And I saw the dead, great and small, standing before the throne. Then books were opened, and the book of life was opened. The dead were judged by what they had done, which was written in the books. ¹³The sea gave up the

dead who were in it, and Death and Hades[n] gave up the dead who were in them. Each person was judged by what he had done. [14]And Death and Hades were thrown into the lake of fire. The lake of fire is the second death. [15]And anyone whose name was not found written in the book of life was thrown into the lake of fire.

DECEMBER 31

MALACHI 1:1—4:6

1 This message is the word of the LORD given to Israel through Malachi.

God Loves Israel

[2]The LORD said, "I have loved you."

But you ask, "How have you loved us?"

The LORD said, "Esau and Jacob were brothers. I loved Jacob, [3]but I hated Esau. I destroyed his mountain country and left his land to the wild dogs of the desert."

[4]The people of Edom might say, "We were destroyed, but we will go back and rebuild the ruins."

But the LORD All-Powerful says, "If they rebuild them, I will destroy them. People will say, 'Edom is a wicked country. The LORD is always angry with the Edomites.' [5]You will see these things with your own eyes. And you will say, 'The LORD is great, even outside the borders of Israel!'"

The Priests Don't Respect God

[6]The LORD All-Powerful says, "A son honors his father, and a servant honors his master." I am a father, so why don't you honor me? I am a master, so why don't you respect me? You priests do not respect me.

"But you ask, 'How have we shown you disrespect?'

[7]"You have shown it by bringing unclean food to my altar.

"But you ask, 'What makes it unclean?'

"It is unclean because you don't respect the altar of the LORD. [8]When you bring blind animals as sacrifices, that is wrong. When you bring crippled and sick animals, that is wrong. Try giving them to your governor. Would he be pleased with you? He wouldn't accept you," says the LORD All-Powerful.

[9]"Now ask God to be kind to you, but he won't accept you with such offerings," says the LORD All-Powerful.

[10]"I wish one of you would close the Temple doors so that you would not light useless fires on my altar! I am not pleased with you and will not accept your gifts," says the LORD All-Powerful. [11]"From the east to the west I will be honored among the nations. Everywhere they will bring incense and clean offerings to me, because I will be honored among the nations," says the LORD All-Powerful.

[12]"But you don't honor me. You say about the Lord's altar, 'It is unclean, and the food has no worth.' [13]You say, 'We are tired of doing this,' and you sniff at it in disgust," says the LORD All-Powerful.

"And you bring hurt, crippled, and sick animals as gifts. You bring them as gifts, but I won't accept them from you," says the LORD. [14]"The person who cheats will be cursed. He has a male animal in his flock and promises to offer it, but then he offers to the Lord an animal that has something wrong with it. I am a great king," says the LORD All-Powerful, "and I am feared by all the nations.

Rules for Priests

2 "Priests, this command is for you. [2]Listen to me. Pay attention to what I say. Honor my name," says the LORD All-Powerful. "If you don't, I will send a curse on you and on your blessings. I have already cursed them, because you don't pay attention to what I say.

[3]"I will punish your descendants. I will smear your faces with the animal insides left from your feasts, and you will be thrown away with it. [4]Then you will know that I am giving you this command so my agreement

with Levi will continue," says the LORD All-Powerful. 5"My agreement for priests was with the tribe of Levi. I promised them life and peace so they would honor me. And they did honor me and fear me. 6They taught the true teachings and spoke no lies. With peace and honesty they did what I said they should do, and they kept many people from sinning.

7"A priest should teach what he knows, and people should learn the teachings from him, because he is the messenger of the LORD All-Powerful. 8But you priests have stopped obeying me. With your teachings you have caused many people to do wrong. You have broken the agreement with the tribe of Levi!" says the LORD All-Powerful. 9"You have not been careful to do what I say, but instead you take sides in court cases. So I have caused you to be hated and disgraced in front of everybody."

Judah Was Not Loyal to God

10We all have the same father; the same God made us. So why do people break their promises to each other and show no respect for the agreement our ancestors made with God? 11The people of Judah have broken their promises. They have done something God hates in Israel and Jerusalem: The people of Judah did not respect the Temple that the LORD loves, and the men of Judah married women who worship foreign gods. 12Whoever does this might bring offerings to the LORD All-Powerful, but the LORD will still cut that person off from the community of Israel.

13This is another thing you do. You cover the LORD's altar with your tears. You cry and moan, because he does not accept your offerings and is not pleased with what you bring. 14You ask, "Why?" It is because the LORD sees how you treated the wife you married when you were young. You broke your promise to her, even though she was your partner and you had an agreement with her. 15God made husbands and wives to become one body and one spirit for his purpose—so they would have children who are true to God.

So be careful, and do not break your promise to the wife you married when you were young.

16The LORD God of Israel says, "I hate divorce. And I hate people who do cruel things as easily as they put on clothes," says the LORD All-Powerful.

So be careful. And do not break your trust.

The Special Day of Judging

17You have tired the LORD with your words.

You ask, "How have we tired him?"

You did it by saying, "The LORD thinks anyone who does evil is good, and he is pleased with them." Or you asked, "Where is the God who is fair?"

3 The LORD All-Powerful says, "I will send my messenger, who will prepare the way for me. Suddenly, the Lord you are looking for will come to his Temple; the messenger of the agreement, whom you want, will come." 2No one can live through that time; no one can survive when he comes. He will be like a purifying fire and like laundry soap. 3Like someone who heats and purifies silver, he will purify the Levites and make them pure like gold and silver. Then they will bring offerings to the LORD in the right way. 4And the LORD will accept the offerings from Judah and Jerusalem, as it was in the past. 5The LORD All-Powerful says, "Then I will come to you and judge you. I will be quick to testify against those who take part in evil magic, adultery, and lying under oath, those who cheat workers of their pay and who cheat widows and orphans, those who are unfair to foreigners, and those who do not respect me.

Stealing from God

6"I the LORD do not change. So you descendants of Jacob have not been destroyed. 7Since the time of your ancestors, you have disobeyed my rules and have not kept them. Return to me, and I will return to you," says the LORD All-Powerful.

"But you ask, 'How can we return?'

8"Should a person rob God? But you are robbing me.

"You ask, 'How have we robbed you?'

"You have robbed me in your offerings and the tenth of your crops. 9So a curse is on you, because the whole nation has robbed me.

[10]Bring to the storehouse a full tenth of what you earn so there will be food in my house. Test me in this," says the LORD All-Powerful. "I will open the windows of heaven for you and pour out all the blessings you need. [11]I will stop the insects so they won't eat your crops. The grapes won't fall from your vines before they are ready to pick," says the LORD All-Powerful. [12]"All the nations will call you blessed, because you will have a pleasant country," says the LORD All-Powerful.

The Lord's Promise of Mercy

[13]The LORD says, "You have said terrible things about me.

"But you ask, 'What have we said about you?'

[14]"You have said, 'It is useless to serve God. It did no good to obey his laws and to show the LORD All-Powerful that we were sorry for what we did. [15]So we say that proud people are happy. Evil people succeed. They challenge God and get away with it.'"

[16]Then those who honored the LORD spoke with each other, and the LORD listened and heard them. The names of those who honored the LORD and respected him were written in his presence in a book to be remembered.

[17]The LORD All-Powerful says, "They belong to me; on that day they will be my very own. As a parent shows mercy to his child who serves him, I will show mercy to my people. [18]You will again see the difference between good and evil people, between those who serve God and those who don't.

The Day of the Lord's Judging

4 "There is a day coming that will burn like a hot furnace, and all the proud and evil people will be like straw. On that day they will be completely burned up so that not a root or branch will be left," says the LORD All-Powerful. [2]"But for you who honor me, goodness will shine on you like the sun, with healing in its rays. You will jump around, like well-fed calves. [3]Then you will crush the wicked like ashes under your feet on the day I will do this," says the LORD All-Powerful.

[4]"Remember the teaching of Moses my servant, those laws and rules I gave to him on Mount Sinai for all the Israelites.

[5]"But I will send you Elijah the prophet before that great and terrifying day of the LORD's judging. [6]Elijah will help parents love their children and children love their parents. Otherwise, I will come and put a curse on the land."

PSALM 150:1–6

Praise the Lord with Music

150 Praise the LORD!
Praise God in his Temple;
    praise him in his mighty heaven.
[2]Praise him for his strength;
    praise him for his greatness.
[3]Praise him with trumpet blasts;
    praise him with harps and lyres.
[4]Praise him with tambourines and
        dancing;
    praise him with stringed instruments
        and flutes.
[5]Praise him with loud cymbals;
    praise him with crashing cymbals.
[6]Let everything that breathes praise the
    LORD.

Praise the LORD!

PROVERBS 31:10–31

The Good Wife

[10]It is hard to find a good wife,
        because she is worth more than
        rubies.
[11]Her husband trusts her completely.
    With her, he has everything he needs.
[12]She does him good and not harm
    for as long as she lives.
[13]She looks for wool and flax
    and likes to work with her hands.
[14]She is like a trader's ship,
    bringing food from far away.
[15]She gets up while it is still dark
    and prepares food for her family
    and feeds her servant girls.
[16]She inspects a field and buys it.
    With money she earned, she plants a
        vineyard.
[17]She does her work with energy,
    and her arms are strong.
[18]She knows that what she makes is good.
    Her lamp burns late into the night.

[19]She makes thread with her hands
and weaves her own cloth.
[20]She welcomes the poor
and helps the needy.
[21]She does not worry about her family
when it snows,
because they all have fine clothes to
keep them warm.
[22]She makes coverings for herself;
her clothes are made of linen and other
expensive material.
[23]Her husband is known at the city
meetings,
where he makes decisions as one of the
leaders of the land.
[24]She makes linen clothes and sells them
and provides belts to the merchants.
[25]She is strong and is respected by the
people.
She looks forward to the future with
joy.
[26]She speaks wise words
and teaches others to be kind.
[27]She watches over her family
and never wastes her time.
[28]Her children speak well of her.
Her husband also praises her,
[29]saying, "There are many fine women,
but you are better than all of them."
[30]Charm can fool you, and beauty can trick
you,
but a woman who respects the LORD
should be praised.
[31]Give her the reward she has earned;
she should be praised in public for
what she has done.

REVELATION 21:1—22:21

The New Jerusalem

21 Then I saw a new heaven and a new
earth. The first heaven and the first
earth had disappeared, and there was no sea
anymore. [2]And I saw the holy city, the new
Jerusalem,[n] coming down out of heaven
from God. It was prepared like a bride
dressed for her husband. [3]And I heard a loud
voice from the throne, saying, "Now God's
presence is with people, and he will live with
them, and they will be his people. God himself will be with them and will be their God.[n]
[4]He will wipe away every tear from their
eyes, and there will be no more death, sadness, crying, or pain, because all the old ways
are gone."

[5]The One who was sitting on the throne
said, "Look! I am making everything new!"
Then he said, "Write this, because these
words are true and can be trusted."

[6]The One on the throne said to me, "It is
finished. I am the Alpha and the Omega,[n] the
Beginning and the End. I will give free water
from the spring of the water of life to anyone
who is thirsty. [7]Those who win the victory
will receive this, and I will be their God, and
they will be my children. [8]But cowards, those
who refuse to believe, who do evil things,
who kill, who sin sexually, who do evil
magic, who worship idols, and who tell
lies—all these will have a place in the lake of
burning sulfur. This is the second death."

[9]Then one of the seven angels who had
the seven bowls full of the seven last troubles
came to me, saying, "Come with me, and I
will show you the bride, the wife of the
Lamb." [10]And the angel carried me away by
the Spirit to a very large and high mountain.
He showed me the holy city, Jerusalem, coming down out of heaven from God. [11]It was
shining with the glory of God and was bright
like a very expensive jewel, like a jasper, clear
as crystal. [12]The city had a great high wall
with twelve gates with twelve angels at the
gates, and on each gate was written the name
of one of the twelve tribes of Israel. [13]There
were three gates on the east, three on the
north, three on the south, and three on the
west. [14]The walls of the city were built on
twelve foundation stones, and on the stones
were written the names of the twelve apostles of the Lamb.

[15]The angel who talked with me had a
measuring rod made of gold to measure the
city, its gates, and its wall. [16]The city was
built in a square, and its length was equal to

its width. The angel measured the city with the rod. The city was 1,500 miles long, 1,500 miles wide, and 1,500 miles high. [17]The angel also measured the wall. It was 216 feet high, by human measurements, which the angel was using. [18]The wall was made of jasper, and the city was made of pure gold, as pure as glass. [19]The foundation stones of the city walls were decorated with every kind of jewel. The first foundation was jasper, the second was sapphire, the third was chalcedony, the fourth was emerald, [20]the fifth was onyx, the sixth was carnelian, the seventh was chrysolite, the eighth was beryl, the ninth was topaz, the tenth was chrysoprase, the eleventh was jacinth, and the twelfth was amethyst. [21]The twelve gates were twelve pearls, each gate having been made from a single pearl. And the street of the city was made of pure gold as clear as glass.

[22]I did not see a temple in the city, because the Lord God Almighty and the Lamb are the city's temple. [23]The city does not need the sun or the moon to shine on it, because the glory of God is its light, and the Lamb is the city's lamp. [24]By its light the people of the world will walk, and the kings of the earth will bring their glory into it. [25]The city's gates will never be shut on any day, because there is no night there. [26]The glory and the honor of the nations will be brought into it. [27]Nothing unclean and no one who does shameful things or tells lies will ever go into it. Only those whose names are written in the Lamb's book of life will enter the city.

22 Then the angel showed me the river of the water of life. It was shining like crystal and was flowing from the throne of God and of the Lamb [2]down the middle of the street of the city. The tree of life was on each side of the river. It produces fruit twelve times a year, once each month. The leaves of the tree are for the healing of all the nations. [3]Nothing that God judges guilty will be in that city. The throne of God and of the Lamb will be there, and God's servants will worship him. [4]They will see his face, and his name will be written

on their foreheads. [5]There will never be night again. They will not need the light of a lamp or the light of the sun, because the Lord God will give them light. And they will rule as kings forever and ever.

[6]The angel said to me, "These words can be trusted and are true." The Lord, the God of the spirits of the prophets, sent his angel to show his servants the things that must happen soon.

[7]"Listen! I am coming soon! Blessed is the one who obeys the words of prophecy in this book."

[8]I, John, am the one who heard and saw these things. When I heard and saw them, I bowed down to worship at the feet of the angel who showed these things to me. [9]But the angel said to me, "Do not worship me! I am a servant like you, your brothers the prophets, and all those who obey the words in this book. Worship God!"

[10]Then the angel told me, "Do not keep secret the words of prophecy in this book, because the time is near for all this to happen. [11]Let whoever is doing evil continue to do evil. Let whoever is unclean continue to be unclean. Let whoever is doing right continue to do right. Let whoever is holy continue to be holy."

[12]"Listen! I am coming soon! I will bring my reward with me, and I will repay each one of you for what you have done. [13]I am the Alpha and the Omega,[n] the First and the Last, the Beginning and the End.

[14]"Blessed are those who wash their robes[n] so that they will receive the right to eat the fruit from the tree of life and may go through the gates into the city. [15]Outside the city are the evil people, those who do evil magic, who sin sexually, who murder, who worship idols, and who love lies and tell lies.

[16]"I, Jesus, have sent my angel to tell you these things for the churches. I am the descendant from the family of David, and I am the bright morning star."

[17]The Spirit and the bride say, "Come!" Let the one who hears this say, "Come!" Let

---

22:13 Alpha and the Omega The first and last letters of the Greek alphabet. This means "the beginning and the end."
22:14 wash their robes This means they believed and obeyed Jesus so that their sins could be forgiven by Christ's blood. The "washing" may refer to baptism (Acts 22:16).

whoever is thirsty come; whoever wishes may have the water of life as a free gift.

[18]I warn everyone who hears the words of the prophecy of this book: If anyone adds anything to these words, God will add to that person the disasters written about in this book. [19]And if anyone takes away from the words of this book of prophecy, God will take away that one's share of the tree of life and of the holy city, which are written about in this book.

[20]Jesus, the One who says these things are true, says, "Yes, I am coming soon."

Amen. Come, Lord Jesus!

[21]The grace of the Lord Jesus be with all. Amen.

January Notes

JANUARY NOTES

FEBRUARY NOTES

FEBRUARY NOTES

MARCH NOTES

MARCH NOTES

APRIL NOTES

April notes

MAY NOTES

MAY NOTES

JUNE NOTES

JUNE NOTES

JULY NOTES

JULY NOTES

AUGUST NOTES

AUGUST NOTES

SEPTEMBER NOTES

SEPTEMBER NOTES

OCTOBER NOTES

OCTOBER NOTES

NOVEMBER NOTES

NOVEMBER NOTES

DECEMBER NOTES

December notes